CONTENTS

KU-022-802

*NOTE: the explanations of abbreviations are repeated inside
the front and back covers.

© CBD Research Ltd · Beckenham · BR3 5JS · Tel 020 8650 7745 · Fax 020 8650 0768 · E-mail cbd@cbdresearch.com · www.cbdresearch.com

Councils
Committees
& Boards

a handbook of advisory, consultative, executive, regulatory & similar bodies in British public life including government agencies & authorities

giving their:

- address
- telephone
- fax
- e-mail
- web site
- names of chairman & other senior officials
- date of formation
- authority for establishment
- constitution
- terms of reference

- geographical area of competence
- responsibilities, duties & activities
- publications

- index of officials
- abbreviated names index
- index of activities & interests fields

We welcome your enquiries

CBD Research Ltd
15 Wickham Road, Beckenham, Kent, BR3 5JS
Tel: 020 8650 7745 **Fax:** 020 8650 0768
E-mail: cbd@cbdresearch.com
www.cbdresearch.com

Directory of British Associations
& Associations in Ireland

Edition 19

CBD Research Ltd

15 Wickham Rd, Beckenham, Kent BR3 5JS, England
Tel: 020 8650 7745   Fax: 020 8650 0768
Email: cbd@cbdresearch.com www.cbdresearch.com

First Published   1965

Edition 19   2009

Copyright ©   2009 CBD Research Ltd

Published by   CBD Research Ltd
15 Wickham Road, Beckenham, Kent, BR3 5JS, England

Telephone: 020 8650 7745   E-mail: cbd@cbdresearch.com
Fax: 020 8650 0768   Internet: www.cbdresearch.com
UK Registered Company No. 700855

ISBN   978-0-955451-43-0

Price   £234.00   US$468.00

No payment is either solicited or accepted for the inclusion of entries in this publication. Every possible precaution has been taken to ensure that the information it contains is accurate at the time of going to press and the publishers cannot accept any liability for errors or omissions however caused.

All rights reserved   No part of this publication may be reproduced in any form or by any means, graphic, electronic or mechanical; including photocopying, recording, taping or information storage and retrieval systems, without the written permission of CBD Research Ltd. The publication in whole or part may not be used to prepare or compile other directories or mailing lists, without the written permission of CBD Research Ltd.

The publisher's permission will usually be granted for limited use of data for mailing purposes if applications are made in writing stating the quantity to be mailed, timing and including a copy of the intended mailing piece. Measures have been adopted during the preparation of this publication which will assist the publishers to protect their copyright. Any unauthorised use of the data will result in immediate legal proceedings.

CBD Research Ltd   founder members of the Data Publishers Association (DPA) and the European Association of Directory Publishers, and are pledged to a strict code of professional practice designed to protect against fraudulent directory publishing and dubious selling methods.

Printing and binding: Polestar Wheatons Ltd.

Directory of British Associations

& Associations in Ireland

Edition 19

CBD Research Ltd

15 Wickham Rd, Beckenham, Kent BR3 5JS, England
Tel: 020 8650 7745   Fax: 020 8650 0768
Email: cbd@cbdresearch.com www.cbdresearch.com

First Published   1965

Edition 19   2009

Copyright ©   2009 CBD Research Ltd

Published by   CBD Research Ltd
                        15 Wickham Road, Beckenham, Kent, BR3 5JS, England

                        Telephone: 020 8650 7745   E-mail: cbd@cbdresearch.com
                        Fax: 020 8650 0768   Internet: www.cbdresearch.com
                        UK Registered Company No. 700855

ISBN   978-0-955451-43-0

Price   £234.00   US$468.00

LIVERPOOL LIBRARY AND
INFORMATION SERVICE

HJ	13-Apr-2009
062.058 CBD	£234.00

No payment is either solicited or accepted for the inclusion of entries in this publication. Every possible precaution has been taken to ensure that the information it contains is accurate at the time of going to press and the publishers cannot accept any liability for errors or omissions however caused.

All rights reserved   No part of this publication may be reproduced in any form or by any means, graphic, electronic or mechanical; including photocopying, recording, taping or information storage and retrieval systems, without the written permission of CBD Research Ltd. The publication in whole or part may not be used to prepare or compile other directories or mailing lists, without the written permission of CBD Research Ltd.

The publisher's permission will usually be granted for limited use of data for mailing purposes if applications are made in writing stating the quantity to be mailed, timing and including a copy of the intended mailing piece. Measures have been adopted during the preparation of this publication which will assist the publishers to protect their copyright. Any unauthorised use of the data will result in immediate legal proceedings.

CBD Research Ltd   founder members of the Data Publishers Association (DPA) and the European Association of Directory Publishers, and are pledged to a strict code of professional practice designed to protect against fraudulent directory publishing and dubious selling methods.

Printing and binding: Polestar Wheatons Ltd.

INTRODUCTION

1.   This book provides information on national associations, societies, institutes, and similar organisations – in all fields of activity – which have a voluntary membership. Regional and local organisations concerned with important industries and trades (e.g. Birmingham Metallurgical Association) are included, as are local chambers of commerce and county agricultural, archaeological, historical, natural history, and similar organisations which are the principal sources of information and contacts in their areas.

Particular attention has been given to the inclusion in DBA of national federations of local organisations and of 'controlling bodies' of various sports and interest which can usually provide a means of contact with local or specialised units. A complete listing of voluntary organisations in the British Isles, including all social, political, sports, young people's clubs and all specialised societies with major hobbies and interests would require a library of volumes the size of DBA.

Excluded are friendly societies, building societies, benevolent societies in aid of specific trades or professions, advice centres, trusts, and certain other categories; but a number of organisations strictly outside our definition of 'associations' are listed because the user of DBA might, from the wording of their names, expect to find them listed (e.g. British Malignant Hyperthermia Association) – such entries are marked § and generally contain an explanation of their status.

All entries are FREE, no payment is sought or accepted for entries in the Directory, nor are entries made conditional on the purchase of the book. The publishers reserve the right to edit information supplied, and to exclude any organisation considered to be outside the scope of the Directory, for any reason.

2. AREA

'British' in the title has been used in the sense of relating to the British Isles: England, Wales, Scotland, Northern Ireland, the Irish Republic, the Isle of Man and the Channel Islands. Some British organisations overseas (e.g. British Chamber of Commerce in Mexico) are also included.

3. BASIS OF COMPILATION

(a)   Questionnaires or revision documents were sent to all of the organisations listed and the courtesy of those who responded is acknowledged by the symbol ■ preceding their addresses. The abbreviation NR shows that the organisation failed to return our questionnaire, but that its validity has been checked by telephone or e-mail.

(b)   Entries for associations in the Republic of Ireland are distinguished by the letters IRL and are limited to name, abbreviation, date of formation and contact details. Most of them are included in DBA by courtesy of the Institute of Public Administration, Dublin, whose publication 'Administration Yearbook and Diary' contains extensive information about most associations and many other organisations in Ireland. Copies of the Yearbook are available from the Institute at 57–61 Lansdowne Road, Dublin 4; telephone (from UK) 00 353 (1) 240 3600, fax 00 353 (1) 668 9135, e-mail information@ipa.ie.

(c)   Associations which we believe to exist, but for which we have not been able to find or validate the address, or from whose last known address our questionnaires have been returned marked 'Gone Away' are listed by name only, prefixed by two ** in the main directory. Any information regarding the existence and whereabouts of these organisations will be welcomed by the editors.

4. ARRANGEMENT AND ALPHABETISATION

DBA is arranged in four parts:

(a)   The main directory, in the alphabetisation of which prepositions, articles and conjunctions are ignored, thus:

Society of Antiquaries of London
Society for Applied Philosophy
Society of the Irish Motor Industry
Society for the Promotion of New Music

(b)   abbreviations index – an index to the initials, acronyms or other forms of abbreviation by which organisations are generally known.

(c)   publications index – an index to the titles of publications notified by associations

(d)   subject index – an index to the activities, professions, groups or interests served by associations

SPECIAL NOTE

In the indexes names of associations are shortened to the words which govern their arrangement in the main directory, abbreviated as shown on page xiii and inside the back cover.

5. FORM OF ENTRY

Each entry in the main directory consists of:

Name of organisation – the full name as stated in Articles, Constitution or Rules

Abbreviation (in parentheses) by which the organisation is known

Date of formation (not necessarily the date of incorporation, which in many cases is later)

Validity indicator (see paragraph 3(a) above)

Address of headquarters, secretary or person to contact

Telephone number

Fax number

E-mail address

Website address

Letters (in parentheses) indicating whether the address is that of the organisation's permanent headquarters (hq), the honorary secretary's business or private address (hsb) or (hsp), registered office (regd off), official secretariat (asa) or other

Name of the organisation's secretary or other officer, with designation of office held

© CBD Research Ltd · Beckenham · BR3 5JS · Tel 020 8650 7745 · Fax 020 8650 0768 · E-mail cbd@cbdresearch.com · www.cbdresearch.com

Legal Status of Organisation (prefixed ▲)

Branches: number of branches in UK, number or location of branches elsewhere

Type of organisation and sphere of interest (prefixed ○): the symbol followed by a code letter (see Abbreviations 1) indicate the type of organisation, a brief note amplifying or explaining the purpose of the organisation may follow

Groups: details of specialist groups, sections, divisions, committees etc.

Activities (prefixed ●): a series of abbreviations – in a set order – indicating the types of activity within the organisation, followed by notes of any special activities

Affiliations (prefixed <): especially international; in most cases this information is printed exactly as received – often in the form of abbreviations or acronyms

Affiliations (prefixed >): bodies affiliated to the organisation

Membership data (prefixed M): indicating whether individuals (i), firms (f) or other organisations (org) form the membership. "Firms" is used in the colloquial sense, to denote all forms of commercial enterprise. Wherever received for publication, the number of members in each category in the UK and overseas is shown (e.g. 250 i, 32 org UK/17 org o'seas) but in many cases, a total has been received without analysis; thus 2,250 i, f & org = total membership 2,250 made up of unspecified numbers of individuals, firms and other organisations.

Publications (prefixed ¶): title, frequency (number of issues a year) and supply data. Titles such as "Journal of the Society of Fireback Collectors" containing the whole name of the issuing body are abbreviated to Jnl, Proceedings, etc. Other abbreviations used in this heading are shown on page xi and inside front cover

Thus: Backfire – 4; ftm, £9.50 yr nm. NL – 12; ftm only

indicates that the society publishes a quarterly periodical called "Backfire" distributed free to members and on sale to non-members at £9.50 per annum; and a free monthly newsletter distributed to members only.

Previous names (prefixed ✕): if the name of the organisation has been changed within the last 5 years the former name or names and the date of the change are given. Names of organisations which have been absorbed are also entered here

6. OTHER SOURCES

Users of DBA are reminded of standard sources for certain categories excluded from this book. Advisory, consultative, executive and similar bodies, including Government agencies and authorities, in Great Britain and Northern Ireland are listed, described and indexed in COUNCILS, COMMITTEES AND BOARDS (CBD Research Ltd – see advert). Certain organisations which used to appear in DBA have been transferred to our publication CENTRES, BUREAUX AND RESEARCH INSTITUTES (see advert). Full details of building societies are given in the Building Societies Yearbook (Building Societies Association) and of charitable organisations in the Charities Digest (Waterlow Publishing). Friendly societies are to be found in the lists available from the Registrar of Friendly Societies (Financial Services Authority).

A complete list of livery companies in the City of London is contained in the City of London Directory (City Press Ltd, Colchester) and in Whitaker's Almanack. For full particulars of these directories and many others that include local and specialised lists of associations, refer to CURRENT BRITISH DIRECTORIES (see advert).

Multi-national European associations (many of which are based in Great Britain) can be found in PAN-EUROPEAN ASSOCIATIONS (see advert).

For national associations in Europe we recommend our other publications: DIRECTORY OF EUROPEAN INDUSTRIAL & TRADE ASSOCIATIONS and DIRECTORY OF EUROPEAN PROFESSIONAL & LEARNED SOCIETIES (see adverts).

7. ENQUIRIES AND SUGGESTIONS

The greatest care is taken in the compilation of DBA and every effort is made to ensure the inclusion of all organisations which purchasers may reasonably expect to find listed; some associations have been omitted because the editors have doubts about their bona fides; certain others have been left out at the specific and reasonable request of their secretaries. The publishers have records of several thousand associations which, for various reasons, are not listed in DBA – these records are constantly under review and we are always glad to assist enquirers seeking to trace organisations not listed.

Secretaries of unlisted associations or of those marked "unverified and lost" are invited to use the questionnaire reproduced in this volume (or to write or telephone for another) so that their organisations can be recorded in readiness for the next edition.

8. ACKNOWLEDGEMENTS

We have benefited, as usual, from the helpful response of countless secretaries, and the advice of many users of the Directory who tell us of associations newly formed or recently defunct. Editors' names are not shown on the title page; the reason is simple: everyone in the 'CBD' team has been involved in all the tasks of mailing, verification, preparation of entries. . .
To all who have helped in any way we express our thanks.

© CBD Research Ltd · Beckenham · BR3 5JS · Tel 020 8650 7745 · Fax 020 8650 0768 · E-mail cbd@cbdresearch.com · www.cbdresearch.com

ABBREVIATIONS: 1 – IN MAIN ALPHABETICAL DIRECTORY

Validity indicators:

■   entry based on questionnaire, or other document, returned by organisation
NR   No reply received for this edition
IRL   Irish entry - see introduction 3(b)
§   Organisation outside normal scope of DBA but included for convenience of users
**   Organisation unverified or lost

Address:

asa	official secretariat	hsp	honorary secretary's private address
hq	organisation's permanent headquarters	sb/p	secretary's business or private address
hsb	honorary secretary's business address	regd off	registered office

Name of secretary or chief executive, with designation of office held:

Chmn	Chairman	Sec	Secretary	Org Sec	Organising Secretary
Dir	Director	Gen Sec	General Secretary	Pres	President
Exec	Executive	Hon Sec	Honorary Secretary	Hon Treas	Honorary Treasurer
Mgr	Manager	Mem Sec	Membership Secretary	PRO	Public Relations Officer

▲   Legal Status of Organisation

Br   Branches

○   Type of organisation & sphere of interest: indicated by one or more of the following letters, with an amplification or explanation only where necessary; if an organisation's interests are obvious from its name, only the starred letter is given

*A	Art & Literature		*N	Co-ordinating bodies
*B	Breed Societies		*P	Professional
*C	Chambers of Commerce		*Q	Research Organisations
	Industry or Trade		*R	Religious Organisations
*D	Dance, Music & Theatre		*S	Sports
*E	Educational		*T	Trade
*F	Farming & Agriculture		*U	Trade Unions
*G	General Interest & Hobbies		*V	Veterinary & Animal Welfare
*H	Horticultural		*W	Welfare Organisations
*K	Campaigns & Pressure Groups		*X	International Friendship
*L	Learned, Scientific & Technical Socs		*Y	Youth Organisations
*M	Medical Interest		*Z	Political Organisations

Gp(s)   Groups

●   Activities:

Comp	Competitions		LG	Liaison with Government
Conf	Conference(s)		Lib	Library
Empl	Negotiations of pay & conditions of employment		Mtgs	Regular Meetings
ET	Education &/or training for professional or other qualifications		PL	Picture Library
Exam	Examinations for professional or other qualifications		Res	Scientific or other systematic research
Exhib	Exhibitions & Shows		SG	Study Groups
Expt	Export promotion		Stat	Collection of Statistics
Inf	Information service available		VE	Visits & Excursions

<   Affiliations to international & other organisations
>   Bodies affiliated to the organisation

M   Membership Data

    i=individuals   f=firms   org=organisations

¶   Publications

AR	Annual Report		m	members
ftm	free to members		NL	Newsletter
hbk	Handbook		nm	non-members
Jnl	Journal		Ybk	Year book
LM	List of members		yr	per annum

X   Former name or names of organisation if changed during past five years (preceded by date of change, if known)

the "CBD" of CBD

Current British Directories

a guide to directories published in the British Isles

Over 4,100 titles listed A-Z and including:

- **Publisher**
- **year first published**
- **frequency**
- **latest known edition**
- **price in £ and US$**
- **number of pages**
- **international standards serial number**
- **description of contents**
- **geographic area covered**
- **availability in other formats, e.g. CD-ROM**
- **index of publishers with full addresses and titles**
- **detailed subject index**

We welcome your enquiries

CBD Research Ltd
15 Wickham Road, Beckenham, Kent, BR3 5JS
Tel: 020 8650 7745 **Fax:** 020 8650 0768
E-mail: cbd@cbdresearch.com
www.cbdresearch.com

ABBREVIATIONS 2 – IN INDEXES

Advy	Advisory	Gp	Group
Agricl	Agricultural	H'capped	Handicapped
Amal	Amalgamated	Hist	History
Amat	Amateur	Histl	Historical
Amer	American	Hortl	Horticultural
Archaeol	Archaeological	Inc	Incorporated
Assd	Associated	Ind	Industry
Assn	Association	Indep	Independent
Bd(s)	Board(s)	Indl	Industrial
Bldg	Building	Inf	Information
Brit	British	Inst	Institute
C'ee	Committee	Instn	Institution
Cent	Central	Intl	International
Cham	Chamber	Ir	Irish
Chart	Chartered	(IRL)	Republic of Ireland
Co	Company	Jt	Joint
Coll	College	Lond	London
Comm	Commerce	Manch	Manchester
Comml	Commercial	Mchts	Merchants
Conf	Conference	Med	Medical
Confedn	Confederation	Mfrg	Manufacturing
Consvn	Conservation	Mfrs	Manufacturers
Contrs	Contractors	Mgrs	Managers
Corpn	Corporation	Mgt	Management
Coun	Council	Mid	Midland
C'wealth	Commonwealth	Mult	Multiple
Dept	Department	N	North
Devt	Development	Nat	National
Distbn	Distribution	NI	Northern Ireland
Distbrs	Distributors	Nthn	Northern
E	East	Org	Organisation
Eastn	Eastern	Presvn	Preservation
Educ	Education	Profl	Professional
Educl	Educational	Pubr	Publisher
Emplr	Employer	R	Royal
Engg	Engineering	Res	Research
Engl	English	Rly	Railway
Engr	Engineer	S	South
Envt	Environment	Scot	Scottish
Envtl	Environmental	Soc	Society
Eqpt	Equipment	Sthn	Southern
Eur	European	Tr(s)	Trade(s)
Expt	Export	TV	Television
Fac	Faculty	U	Union
Fed	Federated	UK	United Kingdom
Fedn	Federation	Utd	United
GB	Great Britain	W	West
Gen	General	Whls	Wholesale
Gld	Guild	Wld	World
Govt	Government	Wstn	Western

© CBD Research Ltd · Beckenham · BR3 5JS · Tel 020 8650 7745 · Fax 020 8650 0768 · E-mail cbd@cbdresearch.com · www.cbdresearch.com

Directory of European Professional & Learned Societies

Répertoire des Sociétés Professionnelles et Savantes en Europe

Handbuch der beruflichen und gelehrten Gesellschaften Europas

Over 6,000 important national organisations in Europe arranged under 900 different subject headings and giving their:

- *address*
- *telephone, fax and telex numbers*
- *abbreviation*
- *year of formation*
- *subject area*
- *membership statistics*
- *affiliations*
- *publications*
- *translated names*

- *index to subjects*
- *index of abbreviations or acronyms*
- *full A-Z index of main & translated titles*

We welcome your enquiries

CBD Research Ltd

15 Wickham Road, Beckenham, Kent, BR3 5JS

Tel: 020 8650 7745 **Fax:** 020 8650 0768

E-mail: cbd@cbdresearch.com

www.cbdresearch.com

A1 Motor Stores Ltd (AIMS) 1983
NR A1 House / 3 Peckleton Business Park, PECKLETON COMMON,
Leics, LE9 7RN. (hq)
01455 822000   fax 01455 824444
email admin@a1motorstores.co.uk
http://www.a1motorstores.co.uk
Chief Exec: Derrick Lawton
▲ Company Limited by Guarantee
○ *T; voluntary group of independent automotive accessory &
spare parts retailers. The association offers marketing &
purchasing support
● Conf - Mtgs - ET - Exhib - Comp - Stat - Inf - Lib - VE - Empl -
LG
M 115 f
¶ Newstime - 24; ftm only.

A-T Society
see **Ataxia-Telangiectasia Society**

AAA - Action against Allergy (AAA) 1978
■ PO Box 278, TWICKENHAM, Middx, TW1 4QQ. (hq)
020 8892 2711 + 4949   fax 020 8892 4950
email aaa@actionagainstallergy.freeserve.co.uk
http://www.actionagainstallergy.co.uk
Exec Dir: Patricia Schooling
▲ Company Limited by Guarantee; Registered Charity
○ *G, *K, *W; to provide information & advice to all those who
have allergies or allergy-related illness & those who care for
them; to campaign for the improvement of NHS resources
for treatment of these conditions
● Conf - Inf - Workshops for parents of allergic children
< The Allergy Alliance
M 1,000 i
(Sub: £15)
¶ Allergy (NL) - 3; ftm, £15 yr nm.

Abbeyfield Society 1956
§ Abbeyfield House, 53 Victoria St, ST ALBANS, Herts, AL1 3UW.
01727 857536   fax 01727 846168
email post@abbeyfield.com
http://www.abbeyfield.com
Volunteers work tirelessly to provide housing, support and
companionship to older people in their local communities.

Aberdeen-Angus Cattle Society 1879
■ 6 King's Place, PERTH, PH2 8AD. (regd/office)
01738 622477   fax 01738 636436
email info@aberdeen-angus.co.uk
http://www.aberdeen-angus.com
Chief Exec: R McHattie
▲ Company Limited by Guarantee
○ *B
● Mtgs - Res - Exhib - Stat - Expt - Inf
M 1,100 i, f & org
¶ Aberdeen Angus Review - 1; ftm, £6 nm.
Aberdeen-Angus Herdbook - 1; £30.   AR; free.

Aberdeen Fish Curers' & Merchants' Association Ltd
(AFCMA) 1944
NR South Esplanade West, ABERDEEN, AB11 9FJ. (hq)
01224 897744   fax 01224 871405
▲ Company Limited by Guarantee
○ *T; to promote & protect the interests of fish merchants in
Aberdeen & district
● Conf - Mtgs - ET - Inf - Empl
M 60 f
¶ Ybk & Diary; free.
LM - 1;   Information circulars - 52;   AR; all ftm only.

Aberdeen and Grampian Chamber of Commerce (Inc) 1877
■ Greenhole Place, Bridge of Don, ABERDEEN, AB23 8EU. (hq)
01224 343900   fax 01224 343943
email info@agcc.co.uk   http://www.agcc.co.uk
Chief Exec: Geoff Runcie
▲ Company Limited by Guarantee
○ *C
Gp UK West Africa Action Group; Aberdeen Freight Agents'
Association; Business Gateway International Trade
● Conf - Mtgs - ET - Stat - Expt - Inf - VE - LG
< Scot Chams Comm; Brit Chams Comm
> Chambers of Commerce in: Moray, Cairngorms, Caithness,
Sutherland, Inverness, Orkney, Western Isles
M 1,200 f
¶ Business Bulletin - 10; ftm, £30 yr nm.   AR; ftm.
Scottish National Directory - 1; ftm, £50 nm.
Members Listing (LM) - as required; £150.

Abertay Historical Society 1947
■ c/o Matthew Jarron, Museum Services, University of Dundee,
DUNDEE, DD1 4HN. (hsb)
email museum@dundee.ac.uk
Sec: Matthew Jarron
○ *L; to promote the study & discussion of local history in
Dundee, Angus, Tayside & Fife
● Conf - Workshops - VE - Lectures
M i
¶ NL.
Annual publication on specific aspects of the area.

Abortion Rights 1936
NR 18 Ashwin St, LONDON, E8 3DL. (hq)
020 7923 9792
▲ Un-incorporated Society
○ *K; to realise, in law & in practice, a woman's right to choose
on abortion
M i

Absorbent Hygiene Products Manufacturers Association
(AHPMA) 1995
■ 46 Bridge St, GODALMING, Surrey, GU7 1HL. (hq)
01483 418221
Dir Gen: Tracy Stewart
▲ Company Limited by Guarantee
○ *T; to represent the non-competitive interests of UK companies
involved in the manufacture of tampons, feminine hygiene
products, disposable nappies & adult continence care
products
● Mtgs
M 9 f

ACADEMI - Welsh National Literature Promotion Agency
(ACADEMI) 1959
■ Mount Stuart House, Mount Stuart Square, CARDIFF,
Glamorgan, CF10 5FQ. (hq)
029 2047 2266   fax 019 2049 2930
email post@academi.org   http://www.academi.org
Chief Exec: Peter Finch
○ *L; to promote the literature of Wales & its authors
● Conf - Mtgs - ET - Comp - Lib
M 516 i
¶ Taliesin (Jnl) - 4; £7 m, £3.50 each nm.
New Welsh Review.   A470 - 6; free.

Academic Paediatrics Association of Great Britain & Ireland (APA(GBI)) 1976
- ■ c/o Prof N J Bishop, Academic Unit of Child Health, Sheffield Children's NHS Foundation Trust, SHEFFIELD, S Yorks, S10 2TH.   (hsb)
  0114-271 7228   fax 0114-275 5364
  email n.j.bishop@sheffield.ac.uk
  Hon Sec: Prof N J Bishop
- ▲ Un-incorporated Society
- ○ *M, *P
- ● Mtgs - ET
- < Fedn Clinical Professors
- M 93 i
- × 2007 Association of Clinical Professors of Paediatrics

Academic & Professional Publishers
  a group of the **Publishers Association**

Academy of Culinary Arts
- NR 53 Cavendish Rd, London, SW12 0BL.
  020 8673 6300   fax 020 8673 6543
  email info@academyofculinaryarts.org.uk
  http://www.academyofculinaryarts.org.uk
  Dir: Sara Jayne-Stanes
- ○ *P

Academy of Curative Hypnotherapists (ACH)
- NR Central Buildings, 15 Station Rd, CHEADLE HULME, Cheshire, SK8 5AE.
  0161-485 4009   fax 0161-485 4009
  email admin@ach.co.uk   http://www.ach.co.uk
- ○ *M

Academy of Executives & Administrators (AEA) 2002
- ■ Warwick Corner, 42 Warwick Rd, KENILWORTH, Warks, CV8 1HE.   (hsb)
  01926 855498   fax 01926 513100
  email info@group-ims.com   http://www.group-ims.com
  Pres: Prof H J Manners
- ○ *P
- ● ET - Exam
- < Academy of Multi-Skills, Inst of Mgt Specialists, Inst of Manufacturing, Profl Business & Technical Mgt
- ¶ Jnl - 2; ftm, £7 nm.

Academy of Experts 1987
- ■ 3 Gray's Inn Square, LONDON, WC1R 5AH.   (hq)
  020 7430 0333   fax 020 7430 0666
  email ara@atlas.co.uk
  http://www.academy-experts.org/
  Sec Gen: Nicola Cohen
- ○ *P; to promote a more effective use of experts in all professions & trades; to maintain & develop the excellence already achieved; to provide a cost efficient service to facilitate the quick resolution of disputes
- Gp Register of experts; Register of mediators
- ● Conf - Mtgs - ET - Exam - Exhib - SG - Inf - VE
- M [not for publication]
- ¶ The Expert (Jnl) - 4; ftm, £55 nm.
  NL - 12;   Hbk; both ftm only.

Academy of Learned Societies in/for the Social Sciences
  see **Academy for the Social Sciences**

Academy of Medical Sciences (AMS) 1998
- ■ 10 Carlton House Terrace, LONDON, SW1Y 5AH.   (hq)
  020 7969 5288   fax 020 7969 5298
  email info@acmedsci.ac.uk
  http://www.acmedsci.ac.uk
  Chief Exec: Mrs Mary E Manning
- ▲ Company Limited by Guarantee; Registered Charity
- ○ *P; to promote advance in medical science & campaign to ensure these are converted as quickly as possible into healthcare benefits for society
- Gp specialist working groups created for specific studies & publications
- ● Conf - SG - LG
- M c 850 i
- ¶ Fellows' Directory - 1; ftm only.   Review - 2 yrly. Miscellaneous Reports - see on website.

Academy of Multi-Skills (AMS) 1995
- ■ Academy House, Warwick Corner, 42 Warwick Rd, KENILWORTH, Warks, CV8 1HE.   (hsb)
  01926 855498   fax 01926 513100
  email info@group-ims.com   http://www.group-ims.com
  Founder/Pres: Prof H J Manners
- ○ *P; to bring together 'those who have multi-skilled potential, those who wish to lift themselves to higher positions in life by perfecting & securing recognition for their skills. . .'
- ● ET - Exam
- M 3 org:
    Institute of Management Specialists
    Institute of Manufacturing
    Professional Business & Technical Management

Academy of Pharmaceutical Sciences (APSGB) 2001
- ■ 840 Melton Rd, Thurmaston, LEICESTER, LE4 8BN.   (asa)
  0116-269 2299   fax 0116-264 0141
  email aps@associationhq.org.uk
  http://www.apsgb.org
  Sec: Robert Seager
- ▲ Company Limited by Guarantee
- ○ *L, *M, *Q
- ● ET - Res - SG
- M 310 i
- ¶ NL - 4; ftm only.

Academy of Social Sciences (AcSS) 1982
- ■ 30 Tabernacle St, LONDON, EC2A 4UE.   (hq)
  020 7330 0898
  email administrator@acss.org.uk   http://www.acss.org.uk
  Exec Sec: Stephen Anderson
- ▲ Company Limited by Guarantee; Registered Charity
- ○ *L, *N; the voice of the social sciences in the UK
- ● Conf - Mtgs - Res - SG - Inf - LG
- M 469 i, 35 org
    (Sub: £180/90 i, £0.63 (per mem) org)
- ¶ 21 Century Society (Jnl) - 3.
- × 2007 (5 July) Academy of Learned Societies for the Social Sciences

access CINEMA 1977
- IRL The Studio Building, Meeting House Sq, DUBLIN 2, Republic of Ireland.
  353 (1) 679 4420   fax 353 (1) 679 4166
  email info@accesscinema.ie
  Director: Maretta Dillon
- ○ *N

© CBD Research Ltd · Beckenham · BR3 5JS · Tel 020 8650 7745 · Fax 020 8650 0768 · E-mail cbd@cbdresearch.com · www.cbdresearch.com

Accident Management Association   (AMA)   2001
NR   105 St Peter's St, ST ALBANS, Herts, AL1 3EJ.   (asa)
    01727 896086   fax 020 7689 6329
    email general@amassociation.co.uk
    http://www.amassociation.co.uk
    Dir Gen: Tony Baker
▲   Company Limited by Guarantee
○   *T; for companies providing services to motorists involved in
    accidents that are not their fault - replacement vehicle hire,
    vehicle repair & legal insurance; supply of services to
    accident management companies - legal services & fleet car
    hire
●   Mtgs - Inf - LG
M   23 f
¶   Members' Bulletin - 12;   AR - 1.

Account Planning Group   (APG)   1978
■   16 Creighton Ave, LONDON, N10 1NU.   (hq)
    020 8444 3692
    email mail@apg.org.uk   http://www.apg.org.uk
    Gen Sec: Steve Martin
▲   Un-incorporated Society
○   *P; to promote excellence in creative thinking in account
    planning & communications strategy in the advertising
    industry & business
●   Conf - Mtgs - ET
M   700 i, UK / 100 i, o'seas

Ace Credit Union Services   1999
NR   2 Chirton Wynd, Byker, NEWCASTLE upon TYNE, NE6 2PW.
    (hq)
    0191-224 4061   fax 0191-224 4061
    email rosalieperry@acecus.org   http://www.acecus.org
    Gen Mgr: Barbara S Hann
▲   Un-incorporated Society
○   *N; training & support for credit unions
●   Conf - ET - Inf - LG - Provision of credit union stationery -
    Model rules for credit unions - Advice & support: computer
    specialist software, insurance, banking
M   44 credit unions

ACFO Ltd   (ACFO)   1970
■   Rivendell House, Winton Rd, PETERSFIELD, Hants, GU32 3LL.
    (dir/mem/sp)
    01730 260162   fax 01730 263937
    Chmn: Tony Leigh,   Dir & Mem Sec: Stewart Whyte
▲   Company Limited by Guarantee
Br   9 regions
○   *T; to represent all fleet operators to all levels of government,
    motor manufacturers, suppliers & insurance companies; to
    improve the professionalism of fleet managers
Gp   Motor cars & light vans up to 7.5 tonnes GVW; Fleet
    consultancy; Defect reporting
●   Conf - Mtgs - LG
M   12 i, 750 f
¶   Fleet Operator - 6;   NewsFax - 52; both ftm only.

Acne Support Group
    Reported as closed 2008

ACT TravelWise   2008
NR   1 Vernon Mews, Vernon St, LONDON, W14 0RL.   (regd/off)
    020 7348 1970
    http://www.acttravelwise.org
○   *K; 'to drop the level of pollution caused by traffic; to reduce
    the use of cars for inappropriate journeys'
×   2008 (Association for Commuter Transport
    (National TravelWise Association

Action against Allergy
    styles itself **AAA - Action against Allergy**

Action with Communities in Rural England   (ACRE)   1987
■   Somerford Court, Somerford Rd, CIRENCESTER, Glos,
    GL7 1TW.   (hq)
    01285 653477   fax 01285 654537
    email acre@acre.org.uk   http://www.acre.org.uk
    Chief Exec: Sylvia Brown
▲   Company Limited by Guarantee; Registered Charity
○   *N, *W; to support sustainable rural community development
●   Conf - Mtgs - ET - Res - Inf - Lib - LG
M   38 rural community councils
¶   Publications list available on website:
    acre.org.uk/DOCUMENTS/resources/publicationlist/pdf

Action on Dementia
    alternative name of **Alzheimer Scotland**

Action for ME   1987
■   Canningford House (3rd floor), 38 Victoria St, BRISTOL,
    BS1 6BY.   (mail/address)
    0117-927 9551   fax 0117-927 9552
    email admin@afme.org.uk   http://www.afme.org.uk
▲   Registered Charity
○   *K; working to improve the lives of people with ME (Myalgic
    Encephalomyelitis), CFS (Chronic Fatigue Syndrome) &
    PVFS (Post Viral Fatigue Syndrome)
●   Inf - Fundraising - Provision of services for people with ME -
    Campaigning
    lo-call 0845 123 2380
M   8,000 i
¶   Interaction - 4; ftm only.
×   2002 (September) Westcare UK (merged)

Action against Medical Accidents   (AvMA)   1982
NR   44 High St, CROYDON, Surrey, CR0 1YB.   (hq)
    fax 020 8667 9065
    email admin@avma.org.uk   http://www.avma.org.uk
    Chief Exec: Peter Walsh
▲   Registered Charity
○   *K, *W; to offer advice & information to anyone who has been
    the victim of a medical accident; this can include referral to a
    specialist medical negligence solicitor
●   Mtgs - Inf - Co-ordination of the Support Network
    Helpline: 0845 123 2352
M   [not stated]

Action on Pre-Eclampsia   (APEC)   1991
NR   2C The Halfcroft, SYSTON, Leics, LE7 1LD.   (hq)
    0116-260 8088 (admin only)   fax 020 8424 0653
    email info@apec.org.uk   http://www.apec.org.uk
    Chief Exec: Mike Rich
▲   Company Limited by Guarantee; Registered Charity
Br   Australia, New Zealand
○   *W; to inform & educate parents & health professionals about
    pre-eclampsia; to support sufferers; to campaign for better
    care & promote research into all aspects of the condition
●   Conf - ET - Inf
    Helpline: 020 8863 3271 (Mon-Fri 0900-1700)
<   Australian Action on Pre-Eclampsia (AAPEC); Stichting Hellp
    Syndroom
M   800 i, UK / 40 i, o'seas
¶   NL - 3;   AR - 1; both free.
    Information pack; ftm, £5 nm.

Action for Prisoners' Families   1990
■ Unit 21 Carlson Court, 116 Putney Bridge Rd, LONDON, SW15 2NQ.   (hq)
020 8812 3600   fax 020 8871 0473
email info@actionpf.org.uk
http://www.prisonersfamilies.org.uk
Dir: Lucy Gampell
▲ Company Limited by Guarantee; Registered Charity
Br 2
○ *K; to promote the development of a nationwide network of support groups for prisoners' families
● Conf - Mtgs - ET - Res - Inf - LG
M 122 org
¶ NL - 4;   AR - 1.
Danny's Mum - 1;   Tommy's Dad - 1; both £2 m, £3 nm.
Finding Dad - 1; £3.50 m, £4.50 nm.
✕ 2002 Federation of Prisoners' Families Support Groups

Action for the Proper Regulation of Private Hospitals
'we have achieved our aims & now we're winding down.''

Action on Rights for Children   (ARCH)
NR 62 Wallwood Road, LONDON, E11 1AZ.
020 8558 9317
○ *K

Action for Sick Children   (ASC/NAWCH)   1961
NR 36 Jackson's Edge Rd, Disley, STOCKPORT, Cheshire, SK12 2JL.   (hq)
0800 074 4519
▲ Registered Charity
○ *W; to raise awareness of the psychosocial & emotional needs of sick children at home & in hospital
● Conf - Mtgs - Res - Stat - Inf - Lib - LG - Parents advice service (free)
M 800 i, 150 f, UK / 10 i, o'seas
¶ Cascade (Jnl) - 4; ftm.
Leaflets & other publications.

Action on Smoking & Health   (ASH)   1971
NR 144-145 Shoreditch High St (1st floor), LONDON, E1 6JE. (hq)
020 7739 5902   fax 020 7729 4732
email enquiries@ash.org.uk   http://www.ash.org.uk
Dir: Deborah Arnott
▲ Company Limited by Guarantee; Registered Charity
Br 14
○ *K; 'to work for a comprehensive societal response to tobacco aimed at achieving a sharp reduction & eventual elimination of the health problems caused by tobacco'
● ET - Stat - Inf - LG - Campaigning

Acupuncture Society   (AS)   1992
NR 27 Cavendish Drive, EDGWARE, Middx, HA8 7NR.   (hsp)
0773 466 8402
email acusoc@yahoo.co.uk
http://www.acupuncturesociety.org.uk
Chmn: Paul Robin
▲ Company Limited by Guarantee
○ *P; for professional acupuncturists & chinese herbal practitioners
Gp Acupuncture; Chinese herbal medicine
● Mtgs - ET - Exam - Res - SG - LG
< College of Chinese Medicine
M 50 i, UK / 10 i, o'seas

Additional Curates Society   (ACS)   1837
§ Gordon Browning House, 8 Spitfire Rd, BIRMINGHAM, B24 9PB.   (hq)
0121-382 5533   fax 0121-382 6999
email info@additionalcurates.co.uk
http://www.additionalcurates.co.uk
Gen Sec: Fr Darren Smith
To ensure that the Christian faith is proclaimed to poor and populous parishes, by funding assistant priests and encouraging vocations to the priesthood.

ADFAM   (ADFAM)   1986
§ 25 Corsham St, LONDON, N1 6DR.   (hq)
020 7553 7640   fax 020 7253 7991
http://www.adfam.org.uk
Chief Exec: Vivienne Evans
National organisation working with and for families affected by drug and alcohol misuse.

Adhesive Tape Manufacturers' Association   (ATMA)   1950
■ Sussex House, 8-10 Homesdale Rd, BROMLEY, Kent, BR2 9LZ.   (asa)
020 8464 0131   fax 020 8464 6018
email tradeassn@craneandpartners.com
Secs: Crane & Partners
▲ Un-incorporated Society
○ *T; to promote the sale of all types of pressure sensitive tape; to promote & undertake research into all forms of technical development in pressure sensitive adhesive tape
● Conf - Mtgs - LG
< Assn des Fabricants Européens de Rubans Auto-adhesifs (AFERA)
M 2 f
¶ LM - irreg; free.

ADI Federation   1996
NR Kingsmith House, 63a Marshalls Rd, RAUNDS, Northants, NN9 6EY.   (hq)
01933 461821
email info@theadifederation.org.uk
○ *P; for approved driving instructors

Adlerian Society (UK) & the Institute for Individual Psychology (ASIIP)   1952
■ 73 South Ealing Rd, LONDON, W5 4QR.   (admin/p)
020 8567 8360   fax 020 8567 8360
email a.hariades@sky.com
http://www.adleriansociety.co.uk
Admin: Ann Rosemary Hariades
▲ Registered Charity
Br 5; Latvia
○ *L; to promote the work & teachings of Alfred Adler (1870-1937), psychologist
● Conf - Mtgs - ET - Inf - Lib - Training counsellors in private practice - Parent education
< Intl Assn of Individual Psychology (IAIP); Brit Assn of Counselling & Psychotherapy (BASP); Parenting Educ & Support Forum
M 220 i, UK / 7 i, o'seas
(Sub: £35 UK / £45 o'seas)
¶ NL - 4;   AER - 1; both ftm only.   Ybk - 1; £10.

© CBD Research Ltd · Beckenham · BR3 5JS · Tel 020 8650 7745 · Fax 020 8650 0768 · E-mail cbd@cbdresearch.com · www.cbdresearch.com

Adoption UK   1971

- ■ 46 The Green, South Bar St, BANBURY, Oxon, OX16 9AB. (hq)
   01295 752240
   email admin@adoptionuk.org.uk
   http://www.adoptionuk.org.uk
   Dir: Jonathan Pearce
- ▲ Registered Charity; Adopotion Support Agency
- Br coordinators in most counties
- ○ *W; self-help group for prospective & existing adoptive families giving information, advice & support through all stages of adoption
- ● Conf - Mtgs - ET - Inf - Lib
- < Brit Assn for Adoption & Fostering; Nat Foster Care Assn; Natural Parents Support Gp; Nat Org for Counselling Adoptees & their Parents
- M 4,500 i, adoption agencies
- ¶ Adoption Today - 6; ftm only.
   Publications list available.

** Adrenoleukodystrophy Family Support Trust   (ALD Family Support Trust)

Organisation lost: see Introduction paragraph 3.

Adrian Bell Society   1996

- ■ 3 The Maltings, Church Close, COLTISHALL, Norfolk, NR12 7DZ. (hsp)
   01603 737168
   Hon Sec: Moya Leighton
- ▲ Un-incorporated Society
- ○ *A; for those interested in the writing of Adrian Bell (1901-1980), who was born in London but lived & wrote mainly in Suffolk
- ● Mtgs - Inf - VE
- M c 250 i, 2 org, UK / 3 i, o'seas
- ¶ Jnl - 2; ftm only.

ADSET   (ADSET)   1990

- ■ 23 The Business Exchange, Rockingham Rd, KETTERING, Northants, NN16 8JX.   (hq)
   01536 526424   fax 0845 833 2615
   email info@adset.org.uk   http://www.adset.org.uk
   Chief Exec: Mrs Hazel Edmunds
- ▲ Limited Company
- ○ *E, *T; organisations using or providing information on education, training guidance & the local economy; to ensure individuals have access to appropriate information for decision making about careers & lifetime learning
- ● Conf - Res - Inf - Lib - Seminars
- < Nat Assn for Educl Guidance for Adults; Assn of Careers Educ & Guidance
- M [not stated]
- ¶ Careers Software News - 3 (termly); £31 m.
   Directory of Guidance Provision for Adults in the UK - 2 yrly; £45 m.
   Opportunity: a directory of sources of careers & life-time learning information - 2 yrly; £40 m.
   Price to nm add 10% p&p.

Adult Education Officers' Association

- IRL Adult Education Officer, Mayo VEC Adult Education Service, Cavendish House, CASTLEBAR, Co Mayo, Republic of Ireland.
   353 (94) 902 3159
   Hon Sec: Pat Higgins
- ○ *P
- × 2005 Adult Education Organisers' Assn

Adult Industry Trade Association   (AITA)   2003

- NR 77 Beak St (suite 14), LONDON, W1F 9DB.   (hq)
   0845 500 ITA (2482)
   email aita.co.uk/
- ○ *T; for all in the trade - video & magazine producers, advertising, artists, bondage, condoms, cosmetic surgery, entertainers, fetish, furniture, models, piercing, sex shops etc
- ● Inf (on regulation & legislation) - LG
- M i, f

Adult Residential Colleges Association   (ARCA)   1983

- NR Alston Lane, Longridge, PRESTON, Lancs, PR3 3BP.   (hsp)
   01772 784661   fax 01772 785835
- ▲ Un-incorporated Society
- ○ *E; to promote & disseminate knowledge of the opportunities for adult learning, in short-term residential situations, to central & local government, other institutions & the general public
- ● Conf - ET - SG - Inf - Lib
- M 32 colleges
- ¶ ARCA Short breaks - 1.   Leaflets.

Adults Affected by Adoption - NORCAP   (AAA-NORCAP)   1982

- NR 112 Church Rd, WHEATLEY, Oxon, OX33 1LU.   (hq)
   01865 875000   fax 01865 875656
   email enquiries@norcap.org   http://www.norcap.org.uk
- ▲ Registered Charity
- ○ *W; to support adults affected by adoption who want to find out more about their families
- M i & org
- × 2008(?) Supporting Adults affected by Adoption
   2004-05 National Organisation for Counselling Adoptees & their Parents

Advantage   1978

- NR 21 Provost St, LONDON, N1 7NH.   (hq)
   020 7324 3930   fax 020 7324 3999
   http://www.advantagemembers.com
   Contact: Colin O'Neill
- ▲ Company Limited by Guarantee
- ○ *T; for independent travel agents
- M 400 f
- × 2005 (May) National Association of Independent Travel Agents

Advertising Association   (AA)   1926

- NR North Artillery House (7th floor), 11-19 Artillery Row, LONDON, SW1P 1RT.   (hq)
   020 7340 1100   fax 020 7222 1504
   email aa@adassoc.org.uk   http://www.adassoc.org.uk
   Dir-Gen: Peta Buscombe
- ○ *N, *T; to represent the common interests of all sides of the UK advertising business
- ● Conf - Mtgs - Res - Stat - Inf - Lib - LG - Educational material
- < Intl Advertising Assn; Intl Cham Comm; Advertising Inf Gp
- M 6 f, 24 org
- ¶ Quarterly Survey of Advertising Expenditure - 4; £590 yr m, £715 yr nm.
   Advertising Statistics Ybk - 1; £170 (2005).
   Long Term Advertising Expenditure Forecast - 1; £535 m, £995 nm.
   The European Advertising & Media Forecast; £730 yr m, £1,365 yr nm.
   The Marketing Pocket Book (2006); £34.95.   AR; free.
   List of constituent organisations on website.
   publications list available from the Information Centre or website.

Advertising Producers Association (APA) 1978

NR 47 Beak St, LONDON, W1F 9SE. (hq)
    020 7434 2651 fax 020 7434 9002
    Chief Exec: Stephen Davies
▲ Un-incorporated Society
○ *T; to represent the interests of commercial film production
    companies
● Mtgs - ET - Inf
< Comml Film Producers of Europe (CFP/E)
M 110 f

Advice NI (AIAC) 1995

NR 1 Rushfield Avenue, BELFAST, BT7 3FP. (hq)
    028 9064 5919 fax 028 9049 2313
    email info@adviceni.net http://www.adviceni.net
    Dir: Bob Stronge
▲ Registered Charity
○ *N; to develop an independent advice sector that provides the
    best possible advice to those that need it most
● Conf - Mtgs - ET - Res - Exhib - Stat - Inf - LG
< Fedn of Indep Advice Centres; AdviceUK
M 4 i, 74 f, 8 org
¶ NL - 4; AR - 1; both free.
✕ Association of Independent Advice Centres

Advice Services Alliance (ASA) 1980

NR 63 St Mary Axe (6th floor), LONDON, EC3A 8AA. (hq)
    020 7398 1470 fax 020 7398 1471
    email info@asauk.org.uk http://www.asauk.org.uk
    Dir: Richard Jenner
▲ Company Limited by Guarantee
○ *N; brings together Citizens Advice Bureaux, Law Centres & a
    wide range of local & national independent advice agencies
● Conf - Mtgs - ET - Res - Inf - LG
M 10 org (& 16 associate members):
    Advice UK
    Age Concern England
    Citizens Advice
    Citizens Advice Scotland
    Dial UK
    Law Centres Federation
    Scottish Association of Law Centres
    Shelter
    Shelter Cymru
    Youth Access
¶ 'We produce regular briefings for our members & occasional
    policy reports'

AdviceUK 1979

■ 63 St Mary Axe (6th floor), LONDON, EC3A 8AA. (hq)
    020 7469 5700 fax 020 7469 5701
    email general@adviceuk.org.uk
    http://www.adviceuk.org.uk
    Chief Exec: Steve Johnson
▲ Company Limited by Guarantee; Registered Charity
○ *N; to promote the provision of independent advice centres
    across the UK; to provide services to support centres
    delivering independent advice to the public
Gp East Midlands, Eastern, London, Scotland, Wales; BME (Black &
    Ethnic Minority); Money & Debt
● Conf - Mtgs - ET - Exhib - Stat - Inf - LG - Case management
    software - Consultancy - Insurance - Recruitment advertising
< Advice Services Alliance
M 900 org
    (Sub: £100-£460)
¶ Independent Adviser - 4; ftm, £20-£30 nm.
    Jobs in Advice email - 52; free.
    Members E-Bulletin - 52; ftm only.
    Money Advice E-Bulletin - 26; ftm only.
    Note: AdviceUK is the operating name of the Federation of
    Information & Advice Centres Ltd.

Advisory Committee for the Marketing of Infant Formula
    a group of **Food & Drink Industry Ireland**

Advocates for Animals (AFA) 1912

■ 10 Queensferry St, EDINBURGH, EH2 4PG. (hq)
    0131-225 6039 fax 0131-220 6377
    email info@advocatesforanimals.org
    http://www.advocatesforanimals.org
    Chief Exec Officer: Fiona Ogg
▲ Company Limited by Guarantee
○ *K, *V; campaigns against all animal cruelty; promotes the
    protection of all animals through investigation, high profile
    campaigns, public education & political lobbying
● Campaigning
M 2,000 i, UK / 1,000 i, o'seas
¶ Campaign Updates - 2; free.

The Aeroplane Collection Ltd (TAC) 1972

■ 7 Mayfield Avenue, Stretford, MANCHESTER, M32 9HL. (hsp)
    0161-866 8255
    email aeroplanecol@aol.com
    Chmn: Edward Sherratt
▲ Company Limited by Guarantee; Registered Charity
○ *G; preservation, restoration & display of aircraft & associated
    artifacts
● Mtgs - ET - Res
< Brit Aviation Presvn Coun
M 24 i
¶ TAC NL - 12.

Aerosol Society 1986

■ PO Box 34, Portishead, BRISTOL, BS20 7FE. (hq)
    01275 849019 (Tues-Thurs 0930-1430)
    fax 01275 844877
    email admin@aerosol-soc.org.uk
    http://www.aerosol-soc.org.uk
    Admin: Shelia Coates
○ *P; to promote: all scientific branches of aerosol research (the
    study of particles suspended in a gas); the spread of
    information on an interdisciplinary basis; to make available a
    pool of expert knowledge; to assist in training; to encourage
    investment in aerosol research
● Conf - Mtgs - ET - Res - Exhib

Aerosopace Composites Group
    a group of **Composites UK Ltd**

Aetherius Society 1955

■ 757 Fulham Rd, LONDON, SW6 5UU. (hq)
    020 7736 4187 fax 020 7731 1067
    email info@aetherius.co.uk http://www.aetherius.org
    European HQ Exec Sec: Dr Richard Lawrence
▲ Un-incorporated Society
Br 2; Ghana, New Zealand, Nigeria
○ *R; a metaphysical organisation dedicated to the service of
    mankind in numerous ways - world & individual healing,
    service to God through humankind, cooperation with higher
    intelligences on earth & from other planets
Gp The Inner Potential Centre - an educational centre run by the
    Society in the UK
● Mtgs - ET - Exhib - SG - Divine services - Cosmic missions -
    Pilgrimages - Spiritual healing
M i
    (Sub: £8-£50, £45 full associate membership)
¶ Cosmic Voice - 4; NL - 12.

© CBD Research Ltd · Beckenham · BR3 5JS · Tel 020 8650 7745 · Fax 020 8650 0768 · E-mail cbd@cbdresearch.com · www.cbdresearch.com

Afasic (Afasic) 1968
- ■ 20 Bowling Green Lane, LONDON, EC1R 0BD.   (hq)
  020 7490 9410   fax 020 7251 2834
  email info@afasic.org.uk   http://www.afasic.org.uk
  Chief Exec: Mrs Linda Lascelles
- ▲ Registered Charity
- ○ *E, *W; to represent children & young adults with speech,
  language & communication impairments; to work for their
  inclusion in society; to support their parents & carers
- ● Conf - ET - Res - Inf
  Helpline: 0845 355 5577
- M 2,000 i, 65 org, UK / 20 i, o'seas
  (Sub: £15 family, £20 profl, £35 instns, £5 benefits/pension)
- ¶ NL - 3; on website.   AR.
  Publications list available.

African Studies Association of the United Kingdom   (ASAUK) 1963
- NR Royal African Society, 36 Gordon Square, LONDON,
  WC1H 0PD.   (hq)
  020 3073 8335   fax 020 3073 8340
  email secretary@asauk.net   http://www.asauk.net
  Hon Sec: Gemma Haxby
- ○ *L, *Q; advancement of African studies in the UK
- ● Conf - Symposia - Inf
- < R African Soc
- M 278 i, 6 libraries, UK / 304 i, 9 libraries, o'seas
- ¶ African Affairs (Jnl of Royal African Society) - 4; ftm.
  AR; free.

Against Legalised Euthanasia - Research & Teaching
alternative name of **ALERT**

Agents' Association (Great Britain)   1927
- NR 54 Keyes House, Dolphin Sq, LONDON, SW1V 3NA.   (hq)
  020 7834 0515   fax 020 7821 0261
- ○ *P; to maintain the standard of ethics among members,
  performers & the entertainment industry in general
- M c 430 f

Agents & Organisers Association
this is an internal Lib-Dem organisation

Agricultural Economics Society (AES)   1926
- ■ The Mount Lodge, Church St, WHITCHURCH, Hants,
  RG28 7AR.   (hsb)
  01256 892705   fax 01256 893090
  email aes@cingnet.org.uk   http://www.aes.ac.uk
  Hon Sec: Mr Wilfrid Legg
- ▲ Company Limited by Guarantee
- ○ *L; study & teaching of all disciplines relevant to agricultural
  economics as they apply to the agricultural, food & related
  industries & rural communities
- ● Conf - Comp
- < Intl / Eur / Amer Assn[s] of Agricl Economics
- M 300 i, 50 org, UK / 100 i, 600 org, o'seas
- ¶ Jnl of Agricultural Economics - 3; ftm, £250 yr nm.
  EuroChoices - 3; £12 m, £80 yr nm.

Agricultural Engineers' Association   (AEA)   1875
- ■ Samuelson House, Forder Way, Hampton, PETERBOROUGH,
  Cambs, PE7 8JB.   (hq)
  0845 6448748   fax 01733 314767
  email dg@aea.uk.com   http://www.aea.uk.com
  Dir Gen: Roger Lane-Nott
- ▲ Company Limited by Guarantee
- ○ *F, *H, *T; for manufacturers of tractors & equipment used in
  agriculture, horticulture, forestry, professional turf & lawn &
  garden
- Gp Forestry; Grain & cereals; Lawn & garden; Livestock & grass;
  Professional turf; Root crops
  Councils, Overseas, Technical
- ● Conf - Mtgs - ET - Exhib - Stat - Expt - Inf - LG
- M 157 f, UK / 3 f, o'seas
- ¶ OPE Price Guide - 2; £30 (for 2 editions).   AR - 1.

Agricultural Industries Confederation   (AIC)   2003
- ■ Confederation House, East of England Showground,
  PETERBOROUGH, Cambs, PE2 6XE.   (hq)
  01733 385230   fax 01733 385270
  email enquiries@agindustries.org.uk
  http://www.agindustries.org.uk
  Co Sec: David Caffall
- ▲ Company Limited by Guarantee
- ○ *F, *T; to promote the benefits of modern, commercial,
  sustainable agriculture in the UK; to develop collaboration
  throughout the food chain
- Gp UK Association of the FIS
- ● Conf - ET - Stat - LG
- < Intl Seed Fedn
- M 300 f
- ¶ AIC Jnl - 4; ftm only.

Agricultural Law Association   (ALA)   1975
- NR Kimblewick Cottage, Prince Albert Rd, WEST MERSEA, Essex,
  CO5 8AZ.   (hsp)
  01206 383521   fax 01206 385943
  email enquiries@ala.org.uk   http://www.ala.org.uk
  Consultant & Adviser: Geoff Whittaker
- ▲ Un-incorporated Society
- ○ *F, *P; 'to promote the study, knowledge & understanding of the
  law & practice relating to agriculture, the environment,
  farming, forestry & the rural community . . . in the United
  Kingdom of Great Britain & Northern Ireland & the European
  Union'
- Gp C'ees: European affairs, Land & property, Litigation & dispute
  resolution, Planning & environment, Taxation, Tenancies
- ● Conf - Mtgs - ET - Res - LG
- < Comité Européen Droit de Rural (CEDR)
- M 881 i, UK / 6 i, o'seas
- ¶ The Bulletin - 4; ftm only.

Agricultural Lime Association   (ALA)
- NR c/o AIC, Confederation House, East of England Showground,
  PETERBOROUGH, PE2 6XE.   (hq)
  01733 385240   fax 01733 385270
  email eileen.pullinger@agindustries.org.uk
  http://www.aglime.org.uk
- ○ *T; to represent the interests of the agricultural lime industry
- < Quarry Products Assn
- M 9 f

Agricultural Manpower Society   (AMS)   1969
- NR c/o Farm Management Unit, Dept of Agriculture, Earley Gate,
  PO Box 236, READING, Berks, RG6 2AT.
  01235 851515
- ○ *F; the systematic study or applications of principles & practices
  in agriculture, which promote a satisfied & healthy workforce
- M i
- ¶ Jnl of Agricultural Manpower - 2.

Agricultural Science Association

IRL Irish Farm Centre, Bluebell, DUBLIN 12, Republic of Ireland.
   353 (1) 460 3682   fax 353 (1) 456 5415
   email msasa@gofree.indigo.ie
   http://www.asaireland.ie
   Pres: James Fitzgerald
○ *F, *P

Aid for Children with Tracheostomies   (ACT)   1983

■ Lammas Cottage, Stathe, BRIDGWATER, Somerset, TA7 0JL.
   (sp)
   01823 698398
   email support@actfortrachykids.com
   http://www.actfortrachykids.com
   Sec: Amanda Saunders
▲ Registered Charity
○ *W; a self-help group run by parents to give support & help to
   other parents with children with a tracheostomy; to promote
   knowledge nationally about the needs involved in the care of
   a child with a tracheostomy
● Conf - Mtgs - Stat - Inf - Hire of medical equipment - Holiday
   caravan - Seminars for professionals in the medical field
< Contact a Family
M 250 i
¶ NL - 4; ftm only.

Air-Britain (Historians) Ltd   1948

■ 74 High Ridge Rd, Apsley, HEMEL HEMPSTEAD, Herts,
   HP3 0AU.   (hsp)
   01442 267883
   http://www.air-britain.com
   Sec: Ronald A Webb
▲ Company Limited by Guarantee
Br 17; Holland & France
○ *G; for those interested in all aspects of current & historical
   aviation
Gp Specialists & groups cover the whole spectrum of aviation
   worldwide
● Res - Inf - Lib - PL - VE
< Amer Aviation Histl Soc
M 3,500 i, 10 f, UK / 120 i, 7 f, o'seas
¶ Subscription rates apply to (a) UK+NI+CI+BFPO, (b)
   Europe,   (c) outside Europe:
   (1) News - 12; £43(a) £52(b) £58(c).
   (2) Aeromilitaria - 4; £25(a) £28(b) £31(c).
   (3) Archive - 4; £25(a) £28(b) £31(c).
      (1)+(2); £53(a) £62(b) £69(c).
      (2)+(3); £33(a) £38(b) £41(c).
      (1)+(3); £53(a) £62(b) £69(c).
      (1)+(2)+(3); £62(a) £72(b) £79(c).
      Membership only; £18(a) £20(b) £22(c).

Air Cleaner Manufacturers' Association

   'please delete'

Air Conditioning & Refrigeration Industry Board   (ACRIB)   1994

NR 76 Mill Lane, CARSHALTON, Surrey, SM5 2JR.   (hq)
   020 8254 7842   fax 020 8773 0165
   email acrib@acrib.org.uk
   Chief Exec: M J Horlick
▲ Company Limited by Guarantee
○ *N; for representative organisations with a direct interest in the
   provision or use of air conditioning, refrigeration &
   mechanical ventilation
Gp Working groups: Environment (incl energy efficiency); Education
   & training (incl implementation of NVQs); Food safety (incl
   de-regulation); Building regulations
M 3 org (Full members):
   Federation of Environmental Trade Associations
   Heating & Ventilating Contractors Association
   Institute of Refrigeration
   6 org (Associate members):
   Associated Air Conditioning & Refrigeration Contractors
   Association of Manufacturers of Domestic Electrical
      Appliances
   British Frozen Food Federation
   Cambridge Refrigeration Technology
   Chartered Institution of Building Services Engineers
   Cold Storage & Distribution Federation

Air League   1909

■ Broadway House, Tothill St, LONDON, SW1H 9NS.   (hq)
   020 7222 8463   fax 020 7222 8462
   email exec@airleague.co.uk
   http://www.airleague.co.uk
   Dir: Edward Cox
▲ Company Limited by Guarantee
○ *P; to promote the cause of British aviation
Gp The Air League Educational Trust (air education - awards flying
   scholarships & bursaries & engineering scholarships);
   Associate Parliamentary Aerospace Group
● Mtgs - ET - Comp - Inf - VE - LG
< Flight Safety Foundation
M 950 i, 115 f, 95 org, UK / 1 org, o'seas
¶ NL - 6; ftm only.

Air Safety Group   (ASG)   1964

NR 51 Wellington Way, HORLEY, Surrey, RH6 8JL.   (hsp)
   email secretary@airsafetygroup.org
   Hon Sec: Robin Boning
▲ Un-incorporated Society
○ *K; 'a voluntary effort to promote greater safety for air
   travellers'
Gp Accident investigation; Certification requirements; Engineering;
   Medical; Operations
● Mtgs - Res - SG - Inf - LG
M 30 i

Air Transport Auxiliary Association   (ATA Assn)   1946

■ 40 Goldcrest Rd, CHIPPING SODBURY, S Glos, BS37 6XG.
   (hsp)
   01454 319175   fax 01454 319175
   Hon Sec: Mrs M Viles
○ *G; for retired war-time ferry pilots
● Social gatherings only
< RAFA
M i
¶ NL - 1.

© CBD Research Ltd · Beckenham · BR3 5JS · Tel 020 8650 7745 · Fax 020 8650 0768 · E-mail cbd@cbdresearch.com · www.cbdresearch.com

Aircraft Owners & Pilots Association   (AOPA)   1965
NR 50a Cambridge St, LONDON, SW1V 4QQ.   (hq)
    020 7834 5631   fax 020 7834 8623
▲ Company Limited by Guarantee
○ *P, *T; 'to further the cause of pilots, instructors & flying training
    organisations; fighting for legislation etc to protect the rights
    of individuals in general aviation, keeping costs to a
    minimum'
● Conf - ET - Exhib - Inf
< Intl Coun of Aircraft Owner & Pilot Assns (IAOPA)
M i
¶ Light Aviation - 4; ftm only.

Aircraft Owners & Pilots Association of Ireland   (AOPA Ireland)
IRL The Old Cottage, Rathdown Rd, GREYSTONES, Co Wicklow,
    Republic of Ireland.
    353 (87) 787 5000
    email platformfirst@eircom.net
    Hon Sec: Paul Chamberlain
○ *P, *T
< Intl Coun of Aircraft Owner & Pilot Assns (IAOPA)

Aircraft Research Association Ltd   (ARA)   1952
■ Manton Lane, BEDFORD, Beds, MK41 7PF.   (hq)
    01234 350681   fax 01234 328584
    email ara.co.uk   http://www.ara.co.uk
    Chief Exec: D Hunter,   Sec: K J Rentle
▲ Company Limited by Guarantee
○ *Q; aerodynamic wind-tunnel testing & ancillary services
Gp Research
● Conf - Res - Inf - Lib
< AIRTO
M 4 f
¶ Research Reports.

Aircrete Products Association
    an affiliated association of the **British Precast Concrete Federation**

Aircrew Association   (ACA)   1975
■ 22 Victoria St, Billingborough, SLEAFORD, Lincs, NG34 0NX.
    (hsp)
    07811 488269
    email secretary@aircrew.org.uk
    http://www.aircrew.org.uk
▲ Un-incorporated Society
Br 90; 15 o'seas
○ *P; to foster comradeship amongst those who have been
    awarded an official flying badge, have qualified to operate
    military aircraft & are serving, or who have served, as
    military aircrew in the armed forces of nations allied to the
    UK & the Commonwealth
● Conf - Mtgs - Inf - VE
M 7,000 i, UK / 1,500 i, o'seas
¶ Intercom - 4; £3.00.

Aircrewman's Association   (ACA)   1977
■ 18 Stathern Walk, Bestwood Park, NOTTINGHAM, NG5 6RR.
    (hsp)
    0115-849 9372
    http://www.aircrewman.org.uk
    Sec: Ian Williams
○ *P; membership is restricted to non-commissioned rating
    aircrew gaining flying wings whilst serving in the Royal Navy;
    all members fly, or have flown, in all types of naval
    helicopters; honorary membership is offered to widows of
    members, & associate membership to interested parties
M i

Airport Operators Association   (AOA)   1934
NR 3 Birdcage Walk, LONDON, SW1H 9JJ.   (hq)
    020 7222 2249   fax 020 7976 7405
    http://www.aoa.org.uk
    Chief Exec: Keith Jowett
▲ Company Limited by Guarantee
○ *T; the trade association that speaks for British airports -
    representing all of the nation's international hub & major
    regional airports as well as many of those serving
    community, business & leisure aviation
Gp Operations & safety; Environment & planning; Security;
    Government & industry affairs; General aviation; Finance
● Conf - Mtgs - ET - Res - Inf - LG
< Airports Coun Intl (ACI)
M 71 airports, 150 f (associates)
¶ Airport Operator (Jnl) - 5; free.

Airship Association   1971
NR 6 Kings Rd, Cheriton, FOLKESTONE, Kent, CT20 3LG.
    (h/treas/p)
    01303 277650
    email treas@airship-association.org
    http://www.airship-association.org
▲ Company Limited by Guarantee
○ *G, *K, *L; a forum for those interested in the technology of
    airships
● Conf - ET - Res - Exhib - Inf - LG
M 336 i, UK / 313 i, o'seas
¶ Airship (Jnl) - 4.
    Airships Today & Tomorrow, by Oliver Netherclift; £8.90.

AIRTO Ltd: Association of Independent Research & Technology Organisations   (AIRTO)   1986
NR c/o CCFRA, Station Rd, CHIPPING CAMPDEN, Glos,
    GL55 6LD.   (hq)
    01386 842247
    email airto@campden.co.uk   http://www.airto.co.uk
    Pres: Prof Richard Brook,
    Hon Sec: John Wilkinson
▲ Company Limited by Guarantee
○ N; to represent the contract research & knowledge transfer
    sector
Gp Finance & contracts; Marketing; Personnel; Secretaries; Health
    & safety; Testing & accreditation; Environment
● Conf - Res - LG
M 34 f
¶ AIRTO Review - 2;   Policy Papers - 2/3; both free.

Al-Anon Family Groups UK & Eire   (Al-Anon)   1960
§ 61 Great Dover St, LONDON, SE1 4YF.   (hq)
    020 7403 0888   fax 020 7378 9910
    email enquiries@al-anonuk.org.uk
    http://www.al-anonuk.org.uk
    Provides understanding, strength and hope to anyone whose
    life is, or has been, affected by someone else's drinking.

Al Bowlly Circle   1968
■ Memory Lane, PO Box 1939, LEIGH-on-SEA, Essex,
    SS9 3UH.   (hsb)
    email ray@memorylane.org.uk
    http://www.memorylane.org.uk
    Sec: Ray Pallett
▲ Un-incorporated Society
○ *D, *G; to promote interest in the life & works of 1930s crooner
    Al Bowlly (1899-1941) & interest in the popular music of that
    time
● Mtgs - Res - Inf - PL
M 1,700 i, UK / 300 i, o'seas
¶ Memory Lane - 4; ftm, £4 nm UK (£5 o'seas).

ALARM: the National Forum for Risk Management in the Public Sector   (ALARM)
NR   Ladysmith House, High Street, SIDMOUTH, Devon,
        EX10 8LN.   (hq)
        01395 519083   fax 01395 517990
        email admin@alarm-uk.com
        http://www.alarm-uk.com
        Chief Exec: Dr Lynn Drennan
▲   Company Limited by Guarantee
○   *P; 'to advise, encourage & represent public sector
        organisations in the development of risk management
        strategies to address the risks which might threaten the
        successful achievement of their objectives'
●   Conf - Mtgs - ET - Res - Exhib - Lib
M   1,635 i, 117 f, UK / 13 i, o'seas

Albinism Fellowship   (AF)   1979
■   PO Box 77, BURNLEY, Lancs, BB11 5GN.   (mail/address)
        01282 771900
        email info@albinism.org.uk   http://www.albinism.org.uk
        Pres: Mark Sanderson
▲   Registered Charity
○   *W; to provide advice & support for people with Albinism, their
        family & those with a professional insterest in Albinism
●   Conf - Mtgs
M   350 i
        (Sub: £15)
¶   Albinism Life - 2.
        Real Lives; by Archie Roy & Robin Spinks (2005).
        (ISBN 0955 0344 0 X).

Alcohol Concern   1984
■   64 Leman St, LONDON, E1 8EU.   (hq)
        020 7264 0510   fax 020 7488 9213
        email contact@alcoholconcern.org.uk
        http://www.alcoholconcern.org.uk
        Chief Exec: Don Shenker
▲   Company Limited by Guarantee; Registered Charity
○   *K; to reduce the incidence & costs of alcohol abuse; to
        develop the range & quality of services to people with alcohol
        related problems; to support specialist & non-specialist
        service providers tackling alcohol problems at local level
●   Conf - Stat - Inf - Bookshop
        Drinkline: 0800 917 8262 (for those concerned with their own
        or another's drink problems)
M   c 1,000 i
¶   Straight Talk - 4;   Leaflets & Reports; prices on application.
        A series of books on aspects of alcohol; c £2.75-£16 (available
        from the online bookshop, pre-paid)

Alcoholics Anonymous   (AA)   1947
■   PO Box 1, 10 Toft Green, YORK, YO1 7NJ.
        01904 644026   fax 01904 629091
        http://www.alcoholics-anonymous.org.uk
▲   Registered Charity
Br   2,800; Worldwide
○   *K; 'primary purpose is to stay sober & help other alcoholics
        achieve sobriety'
●   Mtgs - Inf
M   40-45,000 i, UK / c 1,750,000 i, o'seas
¶   AA News.
        List of publications.

Alcuin Club   1897
■   Ty Nant, 6 Parc Bach, TREFNANT, Denbighshire, LL16 4YE.
        (hsp)
        01745 730585
        email alcuinclub@gmail.com
        http://www.alcuinclub.org.uk
        Sec: J Ryding
▲   Registered Charity
○   *L; to promote study of Christian liturgy & worship - especially
        the Anglican Communion
●   Conf - Res - Inf - Lib
M   350 i, 50 org, UK / 130 i, 50 org, o'seas
¶   Liturgical Studies - 2.
        Collections - 1; ftm, prices vary nm.   AR; ftm.

ALERT   (ALERT)   1991
■   27 Walpole St, LONDON, SW3 4QS.   (hsp)
        020 7730 2800   fax 020 7730 0818
        email info@alertuk.org   http://www.alertuk.org
        Hon Sec: Mrs Elspeth Chowdharay-Best
▲   Company Limited by Guarantee
○   *K; to defend vulnerable people's right to live; is against
        legalised euthanasia
Gp   Carers
●   Mtgs - Exhib - Inf
<   Care not Killing
M   600 subscribers
¶   Various pamphlets; 3/4.   Mailings to supporters; irreg.
        [subscription to mailings £5 yr (£1 un-waged)]
        Note: Also known as ALERT Against Euthanasia, the
        organisation takes its name from 'Against Legalised
        Euthanasia - Research & Teaching'

Alexander Thomson Society   1991
NR   7 Walmer Crescent, GLASGOW, G51 1AT.
        email info@greekthomson.org.uk
        http://www.greekthomson.org.uk
○   *A, *G; to promote the life & work of the Glasgow architect
        Alexander 'Greek' Thomson (1817-1875)
M   i & f
¶   NL - 3/4.

** Alexandra Palace Television Society
        Organisation lost: see Introduction paragraph 3

Alkan Society   1977
■   42 St Albans Hill, HEMEL HEMPSTEAD, Herts, HP3 9NG.   (hsp)
        01442 262895
        email secretary@alkansociety.org
        http://www.alkansociety.org
        Hon Sec: Nicholas King
▲   Un-incorporated Society
○   *D; to encourage the knowledge, understanding & appreciation
        of the life & works of the French pianist & composer Charles-
        Valentine Alkan (1813-1888)
●   Mtgs - Inf - Lib - 1-day lectures & recitals
M   90 i, UK / 50 i, o'seas
¶   Bulletin - 3.   Discography & Library Catalogue - irreg;
        both ftm.

** All British Martial Arts Council
        Organisation lost; see Introduction paragraph 3

All England Netball Association Ltd   1926
NR   9 Paynes Park, HITCHIN, Herts, SG5 1EH.   (hq)
        01462 442344   fax 01462 442343
        email info@englandnetball.co.uk
        http://www.englandnetball.co.uk
        Co Sec: Paul Smith
○   *S; to promote the game of netball in England for women of all
        ages
M   i, clubs
        Note: the association is known as England Netball

All Terrain Boarding Association   (ATBA-UK)   1997
NR   PO Box 107, OSSETT, W Yorks, WF5 8WA.
        0870 765 8240
        email info@atbauk.org   http://www.atbauk.org
○   *S; the enjoyment & promotion of the sport of boarding

All Year Round Chrysanthemum Growers' Association Ltd
      since 2005 **UK Chrysanthemum Growers Association**

Allergy UK   1991
NR   3 White Oak Square, London Rd, SWANLEY, Kent, BR8 7AG.
        (hq)
        01322 619898   fax 01322 663480
        http://www.allergyuk.org
        Chief Exec: Mrs Muriel Simmons
▲   Registered Charity
○   *W; to provide information, support & advice for all people with
        allergies, their families & carers
●   Conf - ET - Inf - National allergy masterclasses
        Helpline: -1322 619898
<   Brit Soc for Allergy & Clinical Immunology (BSACI)
M   6,000 i, 42 f, 135 org, UK / 35 i, 4 f, o'seas
¶   Publications list available.
        Note: Allergy UK is the operational name of the British Allergy
        Foundation.

Alliance for Better Food & Farming
      alternative name of **Sustain**

**Alliance for Beverage Cartons & the Environment   (ACE)
1986**
NR   c/o Tetra Pak Ltd, Bedwell Road, Cross Lanes, WREXHAM,
        Clwyd, LL13 0UT.   (hq)
        0870 442 6623
        Chmn: Richard Hands
▲   Un-incorporated Society
○   *T; to represent manufacturers of liquid food/beverage cartons;
        to address environmental issues (recovery, re-cycling,
        renewability)
<   Alliance for Beverage Cartons & the Envt (Brussels) [this is the
        umbrella organisation for marketing activities]
M   3 f
¶   Alliance NL - 4; free.
        The Alliance for Beverage Cartons & the Environment
        (brochure); free.
×   2007 Liquid Food Carton Manufacturers' Association

Alliance of Business Consultants
NR   24 The Street, Lydiard Millicent, SWINDON, Wilts, SN5 3NU.
        (mem/sec/b)
        01793 772920
        email pete@anaconn.com
        Mem Sec: Peter Jones
○   *P

Alliance against Counterfeiting & Piracy
      since 2005 **Alliance against Intellectual Property Theft**

Alliance of Healing Associations   (AHA)   1977
■   7 Ashcombe Drive, EDENBRIDGE, Kent, TN8 6JY.   (hsp)
        01732 862478
        Chmn: Ken Baker
▲   Registered Charity
○   *N; an umbrella organisation for independent healing groups
        & centres throughout the UK; to promote spiritual healing &
        healer training
●   Conf - Mtgs - ET - Res - Exhib - Inf
<   Eur Confedn of Healing Orgs; Confedn of Healing
        Orgs (CHO); UK Healers
M   15,000 i in 60 orgs
¶   Alliance Review - 2.
×   British Alliance of Healing Associations

Alliance for Health Professionals   1998
NR   14 Bedford Row, LONDON, WC1R 4ED.   (hq)
        020 7306 6683
        Dir of Empt Relations: Lesley Mercer
▲   Un-incorporated Society
○   *N, *U; operating mainly in the health care sector
●   Conf - Mtgs - ET - Empl - LG
M   i in 7 org:
        British Dietetic Association
        British & Irish Orthoptic Society
        Chartered Society of Physiotherapy
        Community & District Nursing Association
        Federation of Clinical Scientists
        Society of Chiropodists & Podiatrists
        Society of Radiographers

** **Alliance of Independent Retailers**
        Organisation lost: see Introduction paragraph 3.

Alliance against Intellectual Property Theft
NR   Riverside Building, County Hall, Westminster Bridge Rd,
        LONDON, SE1 7JA.   (hq)
        020 7803 1324   fax 020 7803 1310
        email info@allianceagainstiptheft.co.uk
        http://www.allianceagainstiptheft.co.uk
        Dir Gen: Susie Winter
○   *N; trade enforcement organisations concerned to prevent
        intellectual property theft
×   2005 Alliance against Counterfeiting & Piracy

Alliance of Literary Societies   (ALS)   1973
NR   22 Belmont Grove, Bedhampton, HAVANT, Hants, PO9 3PU.
        (hsp)
        023 9247 5855   fax 0870 056 0330
        email rosemary@sndc.demon.co.uk
        http://www.sndc.demon.co.uk
        Hon Sec: Rosemary Culley,   Chmn: Nicholas Reed
▲   Un-incorporated Society
○   *N; to act as a liaison / spokesman for literary societies; to
        assist in any way with advice on anything concerning the
        societies; to promote interest in their work
●   Conf - Mtgs - Res - Comp
>   over 100 societies
M   c 100 org UK / 3 org, o'seas
¶   NL - 2;   Open Book - 1; both ftm.

Alliance for Natural Health   (ANH)   2002
■   The Atrium, Curtis Rd, DORKING, Surrey, RH4 1XA.   (hq)
        01306 646600   fax 01306 646552
        email info@anhcampaign.org
        http://www.anhcampaign.org
        Exec Dir: Dr Robert Verkerk
▲   Company Limited by Guarantee
○   *K, *W; to support the development of natural & sustainable
        healthcare; to positively shape EU & international legislation
        affecting natural health
Gp   Complementary healthcare practitioners; Health food
        manufacturers; Health food retailers; Organic food
        producers/retailers; Health-conscious consumers
●   Conf - Mtgs - ET - Res - Stat - Inf - LG
<   Amer Assn for Health Freedom; Nat Health Fedn (USA): New
        Zealand Health Trust; Fritt Helsevalg (Norway)
M   i & f
¶   Information by email to subscribers - irreg.

Alliance of Private Sector Chiropody & Podiatry Practitioners
NR   3 Pendorlan Ave, COLWYN BAY, Conwy, LL29 8EA.
        (regd/office)
        01492 535795
        http://www.thealliancepsp.com
        Admin: Janet Taylor
○   *M, *P

Alliance of Registered Homeopaths (ARH) 2001
- ■ Millbrook, Millbrook Hill, NUTLEY, E Sussex, TN22 3PJ. (hq)
  01825 714506 fax 01825 712242
  email info@a-r-h.org http://www.a-r-h.org
  Co Sec: June Sayer, Dir: Karin Mont
- ▲ Company Limited by Guarantee
- ○ *P; to provide a register of practitioners competent to practice
  safely & effectively; to ensure homeopathy is available to all;
  to raise public awareness of the potential of homeopathy
- Gp Homeopathy; Healthcare; Complementary medicine
- ● Conf - ET - Res - SG - Inf - LG
- < Eur Coun for Classical Homeopathy
- M 700 i, UK / 60 i, o'seas
- ¶ Homeopathy in Practice -4; ftm, £32 yr UK , £40 yr o'seas.

Alliance of Religions & Conservation (ARC) 1995
- NR The House, Kelston Park, BATH, BA1 9LE.
  01225 758004
  http://www.arcworld.org
  Sec Gen: Martin Palmer
- ▲ Company Limited by Guarantee
- ○ *K; to promote for the public benefit the protection and
  preservation of the natural environment throughout the
  world, in accordance with the religious teachings and beliefs
  which encourage respect for nature

Alliance of UK Virtual Assistants (AUKVA) 2000
- NR Walnut Trees, 4 Southwall Rd, DEAL, Kent, CT14 9QA.
  01304 389338
  email enquiries@v-sec.co.uk
  http://www.allianceofukvirtualassistants.org.uk
  Founder: Jo Johnston
- ▲ Un-incorporated Society
- ○ *P; to link to clients, freelance workers with office skills who
  work from their own premises

Alliance against Urban 4x4s 2004
- NR The Hub, 5 Torrens St, LONDON, EC1V 1NQ. (hq)
  email info@stopurban4x4s.org.uk
  http://www.stopurban4x4s.org.uk
- ▲ a non-profit organisation
- ○ *K; a campaign for the increase of taxes & congestion charges
  on big 4-wheel drive vehicles & a ban on advertising in the
  mainstream media
- ● Mtgs - Res - LG - Lobbying - Promotion
- M [a non-membership body]
- ¶ [website only]

ALLMI Ltd (ALLMI) 1978
- ■ Prince Maurice House (Unit 7b), Cavalier Court, Bumpers
  Farm, CHIPPENHAM, Wilts, SN14 6LH. (hq)
  01249 659150 fax 01249 464675
  email enquiries@allmi.com http://www.allmi.com
  Chmn: Mark Rigby, Dir: Tom Wakefield
- ▲ Company Limited by Guarantee
- ○ *T; is the only association devoted exclusively to the lorry loader
  industry; to promote the safe use of lorry loaders; to ensure it
  is involved in the formulation of any legislation which affects
  the industry's interests; to promote compliance with training
  requirements embodied in current legislation
- ● Conf - Mtgs - ET - Exhib - Stat - Inf - Lib - PL - Work with BSI for
  development of standards - Produce technical &/or training
  literature
- M 40 mfrs & service companies, 40 fleet owners
  (Sub: £350-£1,350)
- ¶ ALLMI Code of Practice; £15 m, £33 nm.
  ALLMI Lorry Loader Operator's Manual; £32.50 ftm only.
  ALLMI Slinger/Signaller Manual; £32.50 ftm only.
  ALLMI Thorough Examinations Manual; £32.50 ftm only.
  ALLMI Guidance Notes; ALLMI Membership Book;
  both ftm only.
- × 2008 (Association of Lorry Loader Manufacturers & Importers
  (ALLMI Training Ltd (merged 1 February)

Almshouse Association
  alternative name of the **National Association of Almshouses**

Alopecia Patients' Society
  alternative name of **Hairline International**

Alpine Club (AC) 1857
- NR 55-56 Charlotte Rd, LONDON, EC2A 3QT. (hq)
  020 7613 0755
  Hon Sec: Martin Scott
- ▲ Un-incorporated Society
- ○ *S; mountaineering in alpine & greater ranges (including ski
  mountaineering)
- ¶ Alpine Jnl.

Alpine Garden Society (AGS) 1929
- ■ AGS Centre, Avon Bank, PERSHORE, Worcs, WR10 3JP. (hq)
  01386 554790 fax 01386 554801
  email ags@alpinegardensociety.net
  http://www.alpinegardensociety.net
  Dir: Chris McGregor
- ▲ Registered Charity
- Br 60
- ○ *H; promotion of knowledge & cultivation of all plants suitable
  for rock gardens, frame or alpine house
- Gp Androsace; Frit
- ● Conf - Mtgs - ET - Comp - SG - Inf - Lib - PL - VE - Seed
  distribution scheme
- < R Horticl Soc
- M 11,500 i, 15 f, 5 org, UK / 2,500 i, 3 f, 3 org, o'seas
- ¶ Bulletin - 4; NL - 4; both ftm.
  Gardens Open Directory - 1; Show Hbk - 1; both free.
  Monographs & alpine titles.
  Publications list available on request.

Alternative Operators in the Communications Sector
  styles itself **ALTO - Alternative Operators in the
  Communications Sector**

**ALTO - Alternative Operators in the Communications Sector
(ALTO)**
- IRL Clifton House, Lower Fitzwilliam St, DUBLIN 2, Republic of
  Ireland.
  353 (01) 661 3788
  email info@alto.ie http://www.alto.ie
  Chmn: Liam O'Halloran
- ○ *T
- × 2004 Association of Licensed Telecommunications Operators

Altrincham & Sale Chamber of Commerce 1909
- NR 1 Kingsway, ALTRINCHAM, Cheshire, WA14 1PN. (hq)
  0161-941 3250 fax 0161-941 1909
  email info@altrinchamchamber.co.uk
  http://www.altrinchamchamber.co.uk
  Chief Exec: Ian Stuart
- ▲ Un-incorporated Society
- ○ *C; for the business community within South Trafford
- ● Mtgs - ET - Inf - LG & local & regional bodies - Advice service -
  Networking
- < Chams Comm NE; also local societies etc
- M 15 i, 405 f, 10 org
- ¶ Altruism - 6; ftm, £18 nm. Diary (incl LM) - 1.
  Annual Accounts - 1.
- × 2004 (March) Greater Altrincham Chamber of Commerce,
  Trade & Industry
  2005 (September) Greater Altrincham Chamber of Commerce

© CBD Research Ltd · Beckenham · BR3 5JS · Tel 020 8650 7745 · Fax 020 8650 0768 · E-mail cbd@cbdresearch.com · www.cbdresearch.com

Aluminium Alloy Manufacturing and Recycling Association (AAMRA) 1958
■ National Metalforming Centre, 47 Birmingham Rd,
WEST BROMWICH, W Midlands, B70 6PY.   (hq)
0121-601 6363   fax 0870 138 9714
email alfed@alfed.org.uk   http://www.alfed.org.uk
Sec: Will Savage
○ *T; an independent organisation promoting the production of
unwrought light alloys (aluminium) made in general from
secondary light metals; the extension of the trade in products
manufactured from the alloys
● Mtgs - Stat - Inf
< a member association of the Aluminium Federation
M 24 f

Aluminium Extruders Association   (AEA)
■ National Metalforming Centre, 47 Birmingham Rd,
WEST BROMWICH, W Midlands, B70 6PY.
0121-601 6363   fax 0870 138 9714
email alfed@alfed.org.uk   http://www.alfed.org.uk
Sec: Will Savage
○ *T
< a member association of the Aluminium Federation
M 11 f

Aluminium Federation Ltd   (ALFED) 1962
■ National Metalforming Centre, 47 Birmingham Rd,
WEST BROMWICH, W Midlands, B70 6PY.   (hq)
0121-601 6363   fax 0870 138 9714
email alfed@alfed.org.uk   http://www.alfed.org.uk
Sec Gen: Will Savage
○ *T; interests of those engaged in reduction, smelting, rolling,
extrusion, drawing, casting, forging & flaking of aluminium &
aluminium alloys
● Conf - Mtgs - ET - Exhib - Stat - Inf - Lib (technical enquiries &
other queries) - LG
< Eur Aluminium Assn
M 200+ f
¶ AR.

Aluminium Finishing Association   (AFA)
■ National Metalforming Centre, 47 Birmingham Rd,
WEST BROMWICH, W Midlands, B70 6PY.   (hq)
0121-601 6363   fax 0870 138 9714
email alfed@alfed.org.uk   http://www.alfed.org.uk
Sec: T Siddle
○ *T; aluminium coatings & anodising
< a member association of the Aluminium Federation
M 28 f

Aluminium Powder & Paste Association
■ National Metalforming Centre, 47 Birmingham Rd,
WEST BROMWICH, W Midlands, B70 6PY.   (hq)
0121-601 6363   fax 0870 138 9714
email alfed@alfed.org.uk   http://www.alfed.org.uk
Sec: T Siddle
○ *T
< a member association of the Aluminium Federation
M f

Aluminium Primary Producers Association   (APPA)
■ National Metalforming Centre, 47 Birmingham Rd,
WEST BROMWICH, W Midlands, B70 9PY.   (hq)
0121-601 6363   fax 0870 138 9714
email alfed@alfed.org.uk   http://www.alfed.org.uk
Sec: Will Savage
○ *T
< a member association of the Aluminium Federation
M f

Aluminium Rolled Products Manufacturers Association (ARPMA)
■ National Metalforming Centre, 47 Birmingham Rd,
WEST BROMWICH, W Midlands, B70 9PY.   (hq)
0121-601 6363   fax 0870 138 9714
email alfed@alfed.org.uk   http://www.alfed.org.uk
Sec: Will Savage
○ *T
● Stat - Inf - Lib
< a member association of the Aluminium Federation
M 4 f
¶ Various booklets.

Aluminium Stockholders Association   (ASA) 1962
■ National Metalforming Centre, 47 Birmingham Rd,
WEST BROMWICH, W Midlands, B70 9PY.   (hq)
0121-601 6363   fax 0870 138 9714
email asa@alfed.org.uk
Sec: Will Savage
▲ Un-incorporated Society
○ *T; representative body for UK aluminium, stainless steel & non-
ferrous stockholders & distributors
● Conf - Mtgs - ET - Inf - VE
< Aluminium Fedn
M 19 f, 12 associates
¶ Review - 2;   NL - 6; free.

Alzheimer Scotland - Action on Dementia   1994
NR 22 Drumsheugh Gardens, EDINBURGH, EH3 7RN.   (hq)
0131-243 1453   fax 0131-243 1450
email alzheimer@alzscot.org   http://www.alzscot.org
Chief Exec: Henry Simmons
▲ Company Limited by Guarantee
○ *K, *W; to be the national & local voice in Scotland, for people
with dementia & their carers; to improve public policies &
secure provision of high quality services; to provide high
quality services
● Conf - ET - Res - Care service provision - Campaigning
Helpline: 0808 808 3000
< Alzheimer's Disease Intl; Alzheimer's Europe
M 2,541 i, 35 f, 59 org
¶ Dementia in Scotland (NL) - 4; ftm, £1 nm.   AR; ftm.

Alzheimer's Society   (AS)   1979
NR Devon House, 58 St Katherine's Way, LONDON, E1W 1JX.
(hq)
020 7423 3500   fax 020-7423 35018
email enquiries@alzheimers.org.uk
http://www.alzheimers.org.uk
Dir: Neil Hunt
▲ Company Limited by Guarantee; Registered Charity
Br c 200
○ *W; the leading care & research charity for people with
dementia; to provide information, education & support for
carers as well as day & home care
● Conf - Res - Inf - Lib
Helpline: 0845 300 0336 (Mon-Fri 0830-1830); charged at
local rates
M c 24,000 i
¶ NL - 12.
Publications list available.

Amateur Athletic Association of England Ltd   (AAAofE)   1880
NR PO Box 557, CHICHESTER, W Sussex, PO19 9DS.   (hq)
01928 733067
http://www.aaa-athletics.org
Hon Sec: Walter Nicholls
○ *S; governing body for athletics in England; to control, promote
& provide athletic competitions, coaching & training
M clubs

Amateur Boxing Association of England Ltd   (ABAE)   1880
NR   English Institute of Sport, Coleridge Rd, SHEFFIELD, S Yorks,
       S9 5DA.   (hq)
       0114-223 5654
       http://www.abae.co.uk
       Chief Exec: Paul King
▲   Company Limited by Guarantee
Br   10 regions
○   *S; to further the sport of amateur boxing in England
Gp   Commissions: Coaching & performance, Development, Ethics,
       Medical, Referees & judges, Technical & rules
●   Mtgs - ET - Exam - Comp - Inf
<   Intl Amat Boxing Assns (IABA); Eur Amat Boxing Assns (AEBA
M   10,330 i, 638 clubs

Amateur Boxing Scotland   (ABS)   1908
NR   14 South College St, ELGIN, Morayshire, IV30 1EP.
       fax 0870 135 2257
       email info@scottishboxing.co.uk
       http://www.scottishboxing.co.uk
       Admin: Donald Campbell
▲   Company Limited by Guarantee
○   *S; the governing body of amateur boxing in Scotland
<   Amat Intl Boxing Assn (AIBA); Eur Amat Boxing Assn (EABA)

Amateur Entomologists' Society   (AES)   1935
NR   PO Box 8774, LONDON, SW7 5ZG.   (mail address)
       email enquiries@amentsoc.org   http://www.amentsoc.org
       Registrar: Nick Holford
▲   Registered Charity
○   *L; to promote the study of entomology (insects) particularly
       amongst amateurs & young people
Gp   AES Bug Club (for those aged 13 & under)
●   Exhib - SG - Inf
<   R Entomological Soc London (RES)
>   R Entomological Soc London (RES)
M   1,200 i, 20 org, UK / 100 i, 6 org, o'seas
¶   Bulletin - 6; free.
       Various handbooks & pamphlets.

Amateur Football Alliance   (AFA)   1907
NR   55 Islington Park St, LONDON, N1 1QB.   (hq)
       020 7359 3493
○   *S; administration of Association Football clubs, referees &
       competitions (primarily in the Greater London area)

Amateur Jockeys Association of Great Britain Ltd   (AJA)   1995
■   Crews Hill House, Alfrick, WORCESTER, WR6 5HF.   (hq)
       01886 884488   fax 01886 884068
       email sph.oliver@btinternet.com
       http://www.amateurjockeys.org.uk
       Chief Exec: Mrs Sarah Oliver
▲   Company Limited by Guarantee
○   *S; to protect & promote the role of amateur jockey
●   Conf - Mtgs - ET - Stat - Inf
<   Intl Fedn of Gentlemen Riders & Lady Riders (FEGENTRI)
M   500 i, UK / 25 i, o'seas
       (Sub: £75)
¶   NL - 4; ftm only.

Amateur Martial Association   (AMA)   1972
NR   66 Chaddesden Lane, DERBY, DE21 6LP.   (hq)
       01332 663086   fax 01332 280286
       email tom@amauk.co.uk   http://www.amauk.co.uk
       Chief Exec: Tom Hibbert
▲   Un-incorporated Society
○   *S; martial arts
●   ET - Res - Comp

Amateur Motor Cycle Association Ltd   (AMCA)   1932
■   28 Navigation Way, Mill Park, CANNOCK, Staffs,
       WS11 7XU.   (hq)
       01543 466282   fax 01543 466283
       email office@amca.uk.com   http://www.amca.uk.com
       Sec: Carol Davis
▲   Company Limited by Guarantee
○   *S; to promote off road motor cycle sporting events
●   Conf - Mtgs - Res - Inf - LG
<   Intl Motor Sport Band for Amateurs (IMBA); Land Access &
       Recreation Assn (LARA)
M   5,000 i
¶   Off Road Rider - 8; ftm, 2 nm.

Amateur Rose Breeders Association   (ARBA)   1975
■   48 Shrewsbury Fields, SHIFNAL, Shropshire, TF11 8AN.   (hsp)
       01952 461333
       Hon Sec: Derrick Everitt
▲   Un-incorporated Society
○   *H; to protect & further the interests, knowledge & status of
       amateur rosebreeders by the best, honest means including a
       willingness by members to share their expertise & to
       cooperate with other organisations (amateur or professional),
       & a common interest in the rose
●   Mtgs - Res - Exhib - Comp - VE
<   R Nat Rose Soc (a specialist interest gp)
M   125 i, UK / 20 i, o'seas
¶   NL - 2/4.   ARBA Annual - 1.
       Specialist publications - irreg.

Amateur Rowing Association Ltd   (ARA)   1882
NR   6 Lower Mall, Hammersmith, LONDON, W6 9DJ.   (hq)
       020 8237 6700   fax 020 8237 6749
       email info@ara-rowing.org   http://www.ara-rowing.org
       Sec: Liz O'Flaherty
▲   Company Limited by Guarantee
○   *S; the governing body for the sport of rowing
<   Boating Alliance
M   i & clubs

Amateur Swimming Association   (ASA)   1869
■   Harold Fern House, Derby Square, LOUGHBOROUGH, Leics,
       LE11 5AL.   (hq)
       01509 618700   fax 01509 618701
       email chiefexecutive@swimming.org
       Chief Exec: David Sparkes
Br   8 regions
○   *S; to promote the teaching & practice of swimming, diving,
       synchronised swimming & water polo; to stimulate public
       opinion in favour of provision of facilities for them; to enforce
       laws for the control of the four disciplines in England
Gp   Swimming; Diving; Water polo; Synchronised swimming;
       Education
●   Conf - Mtgs - ET - Exam - Comp
<   Fédn Intle de Natation Amateur (FINA); Ligue Eur de
       Natation (LEN)
M   194,443 i, 1,584 clubs, 30 org
¶   Hbk - 1; £6.   AR; free.

Amateur Swimming Federation of Great Britain Ltd
       since 2008 **British Swimming**

Amateur Yacht Research Society Ltd   (AYRS)   1955
NR   BCM AYRS, LONDON, WC1N 3XX.   (hs)
       01727 862268   fax 0870 052 6657
       email office@ayrs.org   http://www.ayrs.org
       Hon Sec: Sheila Fishwick
▲   Company Limited by Guarantee; Registered Charity
○   *G, *Q; to improve yachts & equipment through research &
       development
●   Conf - Mtgs - Exhib
M   352 i, 29 org, UK / 281 i, 10 org, o'seas
¶   NL - 4; ftm.

© CBD Research Ltd · Beckenham · BR3 5JS · Tel 020 8650 7745 · Fax 020 8650 0768 · E-mail cbd@cbdresearch.com · www.cbdresearch.com

Ambulance Service Association
    on 14 January 2008 merged with the NHS Confederation to form the
    Ambulance Service Network

Ambulance Service Institute   (ASI)   1976
NR   c/o tmc.events, Acorn House, 74-94 Cherry Orchard Rd,
        CROYDON, Surrey, CR0 4HP.   (hsp)
        http://www.asi-international.com
        Nat Admin & Sec: Graham Sleight
▲   Company Limited by Guarantee; Registered Charity
Br   20; Hong Kong, Canada
○   *P; to promote, advance & encourage the education & training
        of ambulance service employees & to extend the training to
        the general public
●   Conf - Mtgs - ET - Exam - Comp - SG - LG
<   Inst of Ambulance Officers Australia (& N Zealand); Ambulance
        Service Assn
M   i
¶   NL - 4.

Ambulance Service Network   1997
NR   29 Bressenden Place (3rd floor), LONDON, SW1E 5DD.   (hq)
        020 7074 3200
▲   Registered Charity
○   *N; to represent the interests of all NHS bodies across the UK;
        includes over 95% of NHS trusts, health authorities & boards
✕   2008 (Ambulance Service Association
        (NHS Confederation

American Civil War Round Table (UK)   (ACWRT(UK))   1953
■   34 Linden Rd, Muswell Hill, LONDON, N10 3DH.   (msp)
        020 8883 3552
        email tonybrown@americancivilwar.org.uk
        http://www.americancivilwar.org.uk
        Mem Sec: Tony Brown
▲   Un-incorporated Society
○   *L; serious & impartial study of the War Between The States
        1861-1865
●   Mtgs - SG - Inf - Lib - Historical research
<   Civil War Round Table Associates (USA)
M   c 170 i, UK / 10 i, o'seas
¶   Crossfire - 3; free.

American Quarter Horse Association UK Ltd   (AQHA-UK)
1974
■   63 Laughton Rd, Lubenham, MARKET HARBOROUGH, Leics,
        LE16 9TE.
        0870 609 1654
        http://www.aqha.uk.com
▲   Registered Charity
○   *B; to promote, record & preserve the Quarter horse breed in
        the UK
●   ET - Exhib - Comp
<   Fedn of Eur Quarter Horses; American Quarter Horse Assn; Brit
        Horse Soc (BHS)
M   650 i
¶   Jnl - 4; ftm only.
        Stud Book Vols I-III.

American Saddlebred Association of GB   (ASAoGB)   1985
NR   Uplands, ALFRISTON, E Sussex, BN26 5XE.   (founder/pres/p)
        01323 870977   fax 01323 871375
▲   Un-incorporated Society
○   *B; to promote the breed in Great Britain
M   i

Amicus
    in May 2007 merged with the Transport & General Workers' Union to
    form **Unite the Union**

Amusement & Gaming Industry Forum   (AGIF)   1985
NR   Alders House, 133 Aldersgate St, LONDON, EC1A 4JA.   (hq)
        020 7726 9826
▲   Un-incorporated Society
○   *T; to bring together the experience of users of amusement
        machines
●   Mtgs
M   f

Anaesthetic Research Society   (ARS)   1958
NR   c/o Dr R P Mahajan, University Division of Anaesthesia &
        Intensive Care, Queen's Medical Centre, NOTTINGHAM,
        NG7 2UH.   (hsb)
        0115-823 1002
        Hon Sec: Dr R P Mahajan
▲   Registered Charity
○   *L; forum for discussion of current research in anaesthesia
●   Conf
M   650 i, UK / 75 i, o'seas
¶   Proceedings of Conferences - 3. (in British Jnl of Anaesthesia).

Anaphylaxis Campaign   1994
NR   PO Box 275, FARNBOROUGH, Hants, GU14 6SX.   (hq)
        01252 542029   fax 01252 377140
        http://www.anaphylaxis.org.uk
        Dir: David Reading
▲   Registered Charity
Br   21 regions
○   *K; to offer support & guidance to those affected by potentially
        fatal food allergies; it is dedicated to raising awareness in the
        food industry; it is seeking to ensure that the medical
        profession at every level offers the best possible advice &
        treatment
●   Inf - LG
M   c 7,500 i
¶   Anaphylaxis Campaign (NL) - 4.

Anatomical Society of Great Britain & Ireland   (ASGBI)   1887
■   School of Biomedical & Health Sciences, King's College
        London, Guy's Hospital Campus, Henriette Raphael Bldg
        (room 3.8), London Bridge, LONDON, SE1 1UL.   (sb)
        020 7848 8234   fax 020 7848 8234
        email maryanne.piggott@kcl.ac.uk
        http://www.anatsoc.org.uk
        Exec Admin: Mary-Anne Piggott
▲   Registered Charity
○   *L, *Q; the promotion, study, development & advancement of
        research & education in the anatomical & related sciences
●   Conf - Mtgs - ET - Res
<   Eur Fedn for Experimental Morphology; Intl Fedn Assns
        Anatomists
M   c 700 i
        Subs: £35 (without Jnl), £65 (with Jnl)
¶   Jnl of Anatomy - 12;   Aging Cell;
        Anastomosis (NL) - 4; prices on application.

Ancient Cattle of Wales
    English name of **Gwartheg Hynafol Cymru**

Ancient Egypt & Middle East Society   (AEMES)   1987
■   2 Seathorne Crescent, SKEGNESS, Lincs, PE25 1RP.   (hsp)
        01754 765341   fax 01754 765341
        email sue.kirk12@btinternet.com
        http://www.aemes.co.uk
        Hon Sec: Mrs Sue Kirk
▲   Un-incorporated Society
○   *G; the history, archaeology & cultures of the ancient Near East
●   Conf - Mtgs - ET - Res - Exhib - SG - Inf - Lib (members only) -
        VE
M   90 i, UK / 2 i, o'seas
        (Sub: £14.50 i, £20,50 family, UK / on request o'seas)
¶   AEMES Jnl - 3; ftm, on application nm.

Ancient & Honourable Guild of Town Criers (AHGTC) 1978

- ■ 10 Weston Rd, GUILDFORD, Surrey, GU2 8AS. (hsp)
  01483 532796 fax 01483 833489
  email secretary@ahgtc.org.uk   http://www.ahgtc.org.uk
  Sec: D Peters
- ▲ Company Limited by Guarantee
- Br Australia, Bahamas, Belgium, Canada, Germany, Netherlands, New Zealand, Poland, USA
- ○ *P; promotion & regulation of town-crying; preservation of ancient art of town-crying
- ● Conf - Mtgs - Comp - LG
- > Gld of Eur Town Criers; Gld of Australian Town Criers
- M c 120 i, UK / c 25 i, o'seas
- ¶ The Crier - 4; ftm only.

Ancient Monuments Society (AMS) 1924

- ■ St Ann's Vestry Hall, 2 Church Entry, LONDON, EC4V 5HB. (hq)
  020 7236 3934
  email office@ancientmonumentssociety.org.uk
  http://www.ancientmonumentssociety.org.uk
  Chmn: Giles Quarme,   Sec: Matthew Saunders
- ▲ Registered Charity
- ○ *K; study & conservation of historic buildings of all types
- Gp a working partnership with Friends of Friendless Churches
- ● Conf - Res - Inf - VE - Comments to local authorities on the demolition of listed buildings - Dissemination of methods & techniques of preservation - Advice to planning authorities on listed buildings
- M 2,000 i, 200 libraries, UK / c 100 i, 50 libraries, o'seas
- ¶ Transactions - 1; ftm.   NL - 3.

Ancient Tree Forum

- ■ c/o Woodland Trust, Autumn Park, Dysart Rd, GRANTHAM, Lincs, NG31 6LL.
  01476 581135
  http://www.woodland-trust.org.uk/ancient-tree-forum
- ○ *K; conservation of ancient trees

Androgen Insensitivity Syndrome Support Group (AISSG)

- ○ *W
  Note: Address changes frequently - check website for contact

Angela Thirkell Society 1980

- ■ 54 Belmont Park, LONDON, SE13 5BN. (hsp)
  020 8244 9339
  email penny.aldred@ntlworld.com
  http://www.angelathirkellsociety.com
  Hon Sec: Mrs Penny Aldred
- Br Eire, USA
- ○ *A, *G; to honour the memory of Angela Thirkell (1890-1961) as a writer & to make her works available to new generations
- ● Mtgs - VE
- < Alliance Literary Socs
- M 150 i, UK / 500 i, o'seas
- ¶ Jnl - 1; ftm, £5 nm.

Anglers' Conservation Association (ACA) 1948

- ■ 6 Rainbow St, LEOMINSTER, Herefords, HR6 8DQ. (hq)
  01568 620447
  email admin@a-c-a.org   http://www.a-c-a.org
  Exec Dir: Mark Lloyd
- ▲ Un-incorporated Society
- ○ *G, *K, *S; a pollution fighting body set up in order to protect anglers' interest & fisheries in general, by pursuing any legal claim from members which arises from a pollution incident
- ● LG - Legal advice to members
- M 8,000 i, 1,000 org
- ¶ AR - 1; ftm only.

Anglesey Agricultural Society 1886

- ■ Ty Glyn Williams, Anglesey Showground, Gwalchmai, HOLYHEAD, Anglesey, LL65 4RW. (hq)
  01407 720072
  Show Admin: Aled W Hughes
- ▲ Company Limited by Guarantee; Registered Charity
- ○ *F; to promote agriculture, horticulture & forestry
- Gp Poultry; Rabbits; Goats; Pigs; Sheep; Dairy & beef cattle; Shire & heavy horses; Light horses; Show jumping; Cookery; Produce; Horticultural; Shearing; Dry stone walling
- ● Mtgs - ET - Exhib - Comp - Expt - Inf - LG
- < Assn of Shows & Agricl Orgs
- M 1,100 i
- ¶ Show Catalogue - 1.   AR - 1.
  Winter Show Catalogue - 1.
  Schedules of Events & Classes; - 1.

Anglesey Antiquarian Society & Field Club (AAS) 1911

- ■ 1 Fronheulog, Sling, TREGARTH, Caernarfonshire, LL57 4RD. (hsp)
  01248 600083
  http://www.hanesmon.btinternet.co.uk
  Hon Sec: Siôn C G Caffell
- ▲ Registered Charity
- ○ *L; archaeology, natural science, art & literature of Anglesey
- ● Mtgs - Inf - Lib - VE
- M 900 i, 118 org
- ¶ Transactions - 1; £6 m, £10 nm.   NL - 2; ftm.
  Studies in Anglesey History - irreg.

Angling Trades Association Ltd (ATA)

- ■ Federation House, STONELEIGH PARK, Warks, CV8 2RF. (hq)
  024 7641 4999   fax 024 7641 4990
  email ata@sportsandplay.com
  http://www.anglingtradesassociation.com
  Chief Exec: David Pomfret
- ○ *T; to represent manufacturers, wholesalers & distributors; to defend angling
- ● Mtgs - Exhib - Stat - Expt - Inf - LG
- < a group of the Fedn of Sports & Play Assns (FSPA)
- M c 50 f

Angling Trust

Anglo-Argentine Society 1948

- ■ Canning House, 2 Belgrave Sq, LONDON, SW1X 8PJ. (hq)
  020 7235 9505   fax 020 7235 9505
  email angloargentinesociety@hotmail.co.uk
  http://www.angloargentinesociety.org.uk
  Chmn: Mrs Alexandra Daniell,   Hon Sec: J Wilson
- ▲ Registered Charity
- ○ *X; to advance the education of the people of GB about Argentinian people, history, language, institutions & culture (& vice-versa)
- ● Conf - Mtgs - Exhib - Social gatherings
- M i & f
- ¶ AR.

Anglo-Austrian Society 1954

- NR 60 Brimmers Hill, Widmer End, HIGH WYCOMBE, Bucks, HP15 6NP. (hq)
  01494 711116
  email info@angloaustrian.demon.co.uk
  http://www.angloaustrian.org.uk
  Sec: Peter Gieler
- ○ *X; promotion of friendship & understanding between peoples of GB & Austria
- M 2,500 i

© CBD Research Ltd · Beckenham · BR3 5JS · Tel 020 8650 7745 · Fax 020 8650 0768 · E-mail cbd@cbdresearch.com · www.cbdresearch.com

Anglo-Belgian Society (ABS) 1918
■ 5 Hartley Close, BICKLEY, Kent, BR1 2TP. (hsp)
  020 8467 8442   fax 020 8467 8442
  Hon Sec: Patrick Bresnan
▲ Un-incorporated Society
Br Belgium
○ *X; maintain & develop friendship between the British & Belgian
  peoples through cultural & social relations
● Conf - Mtgs - VE - Cultural & social activities
M 480 i, 17 f, UK / 40 i, 5 f, o'seas
¶ LM - 5 yrly.   AR - 1.

Anglo-Brazilian Society 1943
NR 32 Green St, LONDON, W1K 7AU. (hq)
  020 7493 8493
○ *X; to promote friendly relations between Brazil & the UK
● Mtgs - VE - Concerts, social functions
M c 400 i & f
¶ AR; free.

Anglo Catalan Society (ACS) 1954
■ Dept of Hispanic Studies, University of Birmingham, Edgbaston,
  BIRMINGHAM, B15 2TT. (hsb)
  0121-414 3820   fax 0121-414 3184
  email h.b.f.buffery@bham.ac.uk
  http://www.anglo-catalan.org
  Hon Sec: Dr Helena Buffery
▲ Un-incorporated Society
○ *L, *X; the promotion of Catalan language & culture, Catalan
  studies & Anglo-Catalan relations
● Conf - Mtgs - ET - Res - Inf
< Institut Ramon Llull; Fundació Congrés de Cultura Catalana
> NACS
M 200 i, 4 f, UK / 80 i, 5 f, o'seas
¶ NL - 2; free.   Annual Lecture - 1.
  Publications available at www.kent.ac.uk/acsop/

Anglo-Chilean Society 1944
NR 12 Devonshire St, LONDON, W1G 7DS. (hq)
○ *X

Anglo-Danish Society (A-DS) 1924
NR 6 Keats Ave, Littleover, DERBY, DE23 4ED. (sp)
  01332 517160
  Sec: Mrs Margit Staehr
▲ Registered Charity
○ *X; to promote understanding between the two countries
● Mtgs - VE - Award of scholarships to post-graduates for Danes
  to study in the UK & for British students to study in Denmark
  for a maximum of 6 months & worth £200 per month
< Confedn of Scandinavian Socs of GB & Ireland (CoSCAN)
M 380 i, 40 f, UK / 10 i, Denmark
¶ News & Views Magazine - 4; ftm only.
  NL with visits & meetings programme - 4; ftm only.

Anglo-Ecuadorian Society
NR 29 Chantry Hurst, EPSOM, Surrey, KT19 7BW. (treas/p)
  Contact: Mr Simpson
▲ Un-incorporated Society
○ *X; to encourage & promote friendly relations between Ecuador
  & the UK; proceeds from cultural & social events provide
  funds for children-in-need charities in Ecuador
● Mtgs - Annual dinner (Autumn) - Fiesta Latina (May in London)
M [not stated]
¶ NL - 4; ftm only.

Anglo-German Family History Society 1987
NR 5 Oldbury Grove, BEACONSFIELD, Bucks, HP9 2AJ. (hsp)
  01494 676812
  email gwendoline.davis@aol.com
  http://www.agfhs.org.uk
  Hon Sec: Gwen Davis
▲ Un-incorporated Society
○ *G; family history for those wishing to research their German
  ancestors
● Mtgs - Res - Inf - Lib - VE
< Fedn of Family History Socs
M 1,500 i, UK / 150 i, o'seas
¶ Mitteilungsblatt - 4.

Anglo-Hellenic League 1913
■ The Hellenic Centre, 16-18 Paddington St, LONDON,
  W1U 5AS. (hq)
  020 7486 9410
  email info@anglohellenicleague.org
  http://www.anglohellenicleague.org
  Chmn: Sir David Dain, KCVO, CMG
  Admin: Dr Sophia B Economides
▲ Registered Charity
○ *X; to strengthen ties between GB & Greece; to spread
  information & encourage travel, social & cultural relations
  between the peoples of the two countries
● Mtgs - VE - Administers the Runciman Literary Award, the Katie
  Lentakis Award (for students)
M 320 i, 29 f, 2 org, UK / 50 i, o'seas
  (Sub: £25 i, £150 f, UK / £25 i, o'seas)
¶ The Anglo-Hellenic Review - 2; ftm, £6 (£7.50 o'seas) nm.
  AR.

Anglo-Indonesian Society (AIS) 1956
■ Church Cottage, Pedlinge, HYTHE, Kent, CT21 4JL. (hsp)
  01303 260541   fax 01303 238058
  email info@angloindonesiansociety.org
  http://www.angloindonesiansociety.org
  Chmn & Hon Sec: Christopher Scarlett
▲ Un-incorporated Society
○ *X; a non-political society fostering friendship & understanding
  between the people in Britain interested in Indonesia &
  people of Indonesian nationality resident in Britain; to
  encourage cultural, literary & social relations between the two
  countries
● Mtgs - VE
M 250 i, 20 f
¶ NL - 26;   AR & Accounts - 1; both ftm only.

Anglo-Israel Association (AIA) 1949
NR PO Box 47819, LONDON, NW11 7WD. (hq)
  020 8458 1284
▲ Registered Charity
○ *X; to foster understanding between GB & Israel
M i & f

Anglo-Jewish Association (AJA) 1871
NR 107 Gloucester Place (suite 4), LONDON, W1U 6BY. (hq)
  020 7486 5055
  email info@anglojewish.co.uk
  http://www.anglojewish.co.uk
  Pres: Michael Hilsenrath
▲ Registered Charity
○ *W; administration of charitable educational funds for Jewish
  students in financial need in higher education in the UK
● Mtgs - ET - Arrangement of lectures
< Conf on Jewish Material Claims
> CCJO
M 500 i

Anglo-Jordanian Society   (AJS)   1981
■   PO Box 32663, LONDON, W14 9YZ.   (hsb)
      020 7603 8663
      email ajs@manara.com
      Hon Sec: Majed Najjar
▲   Registered Charity
○   *X
●   Mtgs - Exhib - Expt - VE
<   Jordan British Society
M   677 i, 39 f, UK / 53 i, o'seas
¶   Jordaniana - 3/4.

Anglo-Malagasy Society   1961
■   1 Golding Crescent, STANFORD le HOPE, Essex, SS17 7AZ.
      (hsp)
      01375 677138
      http://www.anglo-malagasysociety.co.uk
      Hon Sec: Stuart Edgill
▲   Un-incorporated Society
○   *X; to further friendship between GB & Madagascar; to
      promote business with & visits to the Republic
●   Conf - Mtgs - Exhib
M   300 i, 20 f
      (Sub: £20 i, £100 f, UK)
¶   NL - 4.   AR; both ftm only.

** Anglo-Mongolian Society
      Organisation lost: see Introduction paragraph 3

Anglo-Netherlands Society   1920
NR   PO Box 68, Unilever House, LONDON, EC4P 4BQ.   (hq)
      020 7767 6959
○   *X; to promote friendship between British & Dutch subjects by
      organising events (in Britain) at which they can meet

Anglo-Norman Text Society   (ANTS)   1938
■   c/o French Dept, Birkbeck College, Malet St, LONDON,
      WC1E 7HX.   (hsb)
      020 7631 6170 & 020 8239 9424
      email ishort@bbk.ac.uk
      Hon Sec: Prof Ian Short
▲   Registered Charity
○   *L; the publication of Anglo-Norman texts of literary, linguistic,
      historical & legal value & interest
●   Publication - Compilation of an Anglo-Norman Dictionary
M   74 i, 48 f, universities, UK / 114 i, 96 f, o'seas
¶   1 volume of Anglo-Norman text - 1.
      Prospectus (incl LM).   Occasional volumes.

Anglo-Norse Society   1918
■   25 Belgrave Sq, LONDON, SW1X 8QD.   (hq)
      020 7235 9529   fax 020 7235 9529
      http://www.secretariat@anglonorse.org.uk
      Sec: Irene Garland
▲   Registered Charity
Br   Norway
○   *X; promotion of better understanding/knowledge of Norway in
      the UK
Gp   Bursaries for study of a 'Norwegian' subject
●   Mtgs - Selling books for language study, & Norwegian literature
M   c 400 i
¶   Anglo Norse Review - 2; ftm.

**Anglo North Irish Fish Producers Organisation   (ANIFPO)
      1984**
NR   The Harbour, KILKEEL, Co Down, BT34 4AX.
      028 4176 2855   fax 028 4176 4904
      email info@anifpo.com   http://www.anifpo.com
○   *T

Anglo-Nubian Breed Society   1972
NR   3 Wadehouse Lane, Draxhales, Drax, SELBY, N Yorks, YO8 8PN.
      01757 618756
      http://www.anglo-nubian.org.uk
      Sec: Mrs Margaret Edginton
○   *B; Nubian goats

Anglo-Omani Society   1976
NR   29 Chipperfield Rd, BOVINGDON, Herts, HP3 0JN.
      01442 833589
      Sec: Richard R Owens
▲   Registered Charity; Un-incorporated Society
○   *X
●   Mtgs - VE - LG
M   600 i, 12 f

Anglo-Peruvian Society   1961
NR   PO Box 494, WEMBLEY, Middx, HA9 8ZB.   (hq)
      020 8908 1916
▲   Registered Charity
○   *X; to advance the education of the people of Great Britain
      about Peru, its people, history, language & literature,
      institutions, folklore & artistic & economic life
●   Conf - Mtgs - ET - Lectures - Concerts - Seminars - Fundraising
      - Cultural events
M   i & f

Anglo-Polish Society   1832
NR   c/o The Polish Institute, 20 Princes Gate, LONDON,
      SW7 1PT.   (mail/address)
○   *X; to promote friendship & understanding between British &
      Polish people; to protect the interests of the Poles in Britain
M   i

Anglo-Portuguese Society   1938
NR   Canning House, 2 Belgrave Sq, LONDON, SW1X 8PJ.   (hq)
      020 7245 5331
      Sec: Miss Ann Waterfall
○   *X; the education of the people of the United Kingdom about
      Portugal, its people & its culture

Anglo-Spanish Society   1958
■   102 Eaton Square, LONDON, SW1W 9AN.   (hsp)
      07903 801576
      email anglospanish@clara.co.uk
      http://www.anglospanishsociety.org
      Hon Sec: Dorothy H McLean
▲   Registered Charity
○   *X; to promote friendship between the peoples of Britain &
      Spain through a knowledge of each other's customs,
      institutions, history & way of life
●   Mtgs - VE
M   300 i, 11 f, UK / 40 i, 1 f, o'seas
¶   Anglo-Spanish Quarterly Review - 4.

Anglo-Swedish Society of Great Britain & Ireland   1919
NR   6a Oakfield St, LONDON, SW10 9JB.
      020 7352 0599   fax 020 7352 0599
      email info@angloswedishsociety.org.uk
      http://www.angloswedishsociety.org.uk
      Hon Sec: Kari Hedly
▲   Registered Charity
○   *X; to promote good relations & awareness between the
      peoples of GB & Sweden in the fields of culture, science, art,
      literature, music, history, economics & philosophy
●   VE - Scholarship scheme
M   283 i, 11 f
¶   NL - 3;   AR; both ftm only.

© CBD Research Ltd · Beckenham · BR3 5JS · Tel 020 8650 7745 · Fax 020 8650 0768 · E-mail cbd@cbdresearch.com · www.cbdresearch.com

Anglo-Thai Society   1962
- ■ Southwood, 62a Dore Rd, SHEFFIELD, S Yorks, S17 3NE. (hsp)
   0114-236 8129
   email info@anglothaisociety.org
   http://www.anglothaisociety.org
   Hon Sec: T J Knox
- ▲ Un-incorporated Society
- ○ *X
- ● Mtgs
- M 250 i, 10 f, UK / 20 i, o'seas

Anglo-Turkish Society   1953
- ■ c/o High Beeches, Boyneswood Rd, Four Marks, ALTON, Hants, GU34 5DY.   (hsp)
   01420 562506   http://www.anglo-turkish-society.co.uk
   Mem Sec: Mrs B A McKernan
- ▲ Company Limited by Guarantee; Registered Charity
- ○ *X; a social & cultural society
- ● Lectures, social gatherings & outings
- M 400 i, 2 f, UK / 10 i, o'seas

Anglo-Venezuelan Society   1976
- NR PO Box 930, ST ALBANS, Herts, AL1 9GE.   (sp)
   email secretary@angloven.org   http://www.angloven.org
   Sec: Valerie Lucien
- ▲ Un-incorporated Society
- ○ *X; to promote informed discussion on Venezuelan issues, particularly those relating to British investment & trade
- ● Conf - Mtgs - Lectures - Concerts - Annual dinner
- M 90 i, 38 f, UK / 5 i, 1 f, o'seas

Animal Concern Ltd   1988
- ■ PO Box 5178, DUMBARTON, G82 5YJ.   (mail address)
   01389 841639   fax 0870 706 0327
   email animals@jrobins.force9.co.uk
   http://www.animalconcern.org
   Sec: John F Robins
- ▲ Company Limited by Guarantee
- ○ *K; for animal rights
- ● ET - Inf - Lobbying
- M 290 i, UK / 4 i, o'seas
- ¶ Animal Concern News - 2/3; free.

Animal Consultants & Trainers Association   (ACTA)   1989
- ■ 147 Coppermill Rd, WRAYSBURY, Berks, TW19 5NX.
   01753 683773
   http://www.acta4animals.com
   Sec: Jill Clark
- ○ *V; training & provision of animals for the film, television & advertising industries; provision of expert & professional advice; members must hold a valid licence under the Performing Animals (Regulation) Act 1925 & hold an adequate public liability insurance policy
- M 30 i, 24 f, UK / 1 i, o'seas

Animal Health Distributors Association (UK) Ltd   (AHDA)   1985
- ■ Belmesthorpe Grange, Newstead Lane, STAMFORD, Lincs, PE9 4JJ.   (sp)
   01780 767757   fax 01780 767221
   email ian@ahda.org.uk   http://www.ahda.org.uk
   Sec Gen: Ian Scott
- ▲ Company Limited by Guarantee
- ○ *T; 'interests of distributors of animal health products - particularly those who distribute animal medicines to farmers (in order to try to prevent EU legislating members out of business)'
- ● Conf - Mtgs - Exhib - LG
- M 148 f, UK / 2 f, o'seas
- ¶ NL - 12.   Animal Medicines Record Book.

Animal Medicines Training Regulatory Authority   (AMTRA)   1983
- ■ 8 Parsons Hill, Hollesley, WOODBRIDGE, Suffolk, IP12 3RB. (hsb/p)
   01394 411010   fax 01394 410455
   email info@amtra.org   http://www.amtra.org.uk
   Co Sec: Dr Roger R Dawson
- ▲ Company Limited by Guarantee
- ○ *N; independent regulatory body ensuring that the distribution of animal medicines in the UK is undertaken in a responsible manner by qualified persons
- ● ET - Exam (for the staff of manufacturers) - LG - Register of those licensed to hold medicines & those qualified to distribute them
- M c 3,500 i
- ¶ AMTRA News - c 2-yrly.   AR.
   Syllabus & examination course leaflet.

Animal & Plant Health Association   (APHA)
- IRL 8 Woodbine Park, BLACKROCK, Co Dublin, Republic of Ireland.
   353 (1) 260 3050   fax 353 (1) 260 3021
   email info@apha.ie   http://www.apha.ie
   Dir: Brendan Barnes
- ○ *F, *T, *V; manufacturers & sole distributors of veterinary medicines & plant protection products/agrochemicals
- M c 30 f

Animal Welfare Filming Federation   (AWFF)   1998
- § 19 Greaves Rd, HIGH WYCOMBE, Bucks, HP13 7JU.   (hsp)
   01494 442750   fax 01494 441385
   email animalwork1@yahoo.co.uk
   http://www.animalworld.org.uk
   for those concerned with the welfare of animals used in film & TV

** Animal Welfare Science, Ethics & Law Veterinary Association
   Organisation lost: see Introduction paragraph 3

** Anomalous Phenomena Research Agency
   Organisation lost: see Introduction paragraph 3.

Anorchidism Support Group   (ASG)
- ■ PO Box 3025, ROMFORD, Essex, RM3 8GX.
   01708 372597
   email contact.asg@virgin.net
   Contact: Mrs Lorraine Bookless
- ○ *W; to support men & boys with anorchidism (congenital or acquired absence of the testes) & their families

Anrhydeddus Gymdeithas y Cymmrodorion
   Welsh name of the **Honourable Society of Cymmrodorion**

Anthroposophical Medical Association   (AMA)
- NR c/o St Luke's Medical Centre, 53 Cainscross Rd, STROUD, Glos, GL5 4EX.   (hq)
   01453 762151
   email medical.section@yahoo.co.uk
   Hon Sec: Dr Frank A Mulder
- ▲ Un-incorporated Society
- ○ *M; for doctors practising anthroposophical medicine in the UK
- ● Conf - Mtgs - ET - Res - SG - Inf - LG
- < Intl Fedn of Anthroposophical Medical Assns (IVAA); Anthroposophical Health Professions Coun (AHPC)
- M 60 i
- ¶ Anthroposophical Medical NL - 6;
   Worldwide NL - 6 (published in English in association with the medical section at the Goetheanum, Switzerland); both ftm. £30 yr for both publications, or £20 yr for 1, to nm.

Anthroposophical Society in Great Britain   (ASinGB)   1923
- ■ Rudolf Steiner House, 35 Park Rd, LONDON, NW1 6XT.   (hq)
  020 7723 4400   fax 020 7724 4364
  email rsh-office@anth.org.uk
  http://www.anthroposophy.org.uk
- ▲ Registered Charity
- ○ *L; philosophy, art & education, based on the work of Rudolf Steiner - 'a union of human beings who desire to further the life of the soul, both in the individual & in society at large, based on a true knowledge of the spiritual world'
- < General Anthroposophical Soc (Switzerland)

Anti Common Market League   (ACML)   1961
- ■ 28 Highdown, WORCESTER PARK, Surrey, KT4 7HZ.   (hsp)
  Mem Sec: Mrs J Phillips,   Chmn: Peter Dul
- ▲ Un-incorporated Society
- ○ *K; to campaign for British withdrawal from the European Union
- ● Mtgs - Campaigning
- < Campaign for an Indep Britain (CIB); Anti Maastricht Alliance (AMA)
- M c 400 i, UK / c 50 i, o'seas
- ¶ Britain (NL) - 3/4;   £10 yr.   Bound to Fail; £3.
  No Pound: No Independence by Brian Burkitt; £4.

Anti Copying in Design Ltd   (ACID)   1996
- NR Adelaide House, London Bridge, LONDON, EC4R 9HA.   (hq)
  0845 644 3617   fax 0845 644 3618
  email help@acid.uk.com   http://www.acid.uk.com
  Chief Exec: Dids Macdonald
- ▲ a not-for-profit organisation
- ○ *K; for all designers & manufacturers; to fight copyright theft
- Gp Exhibitions & shows; Information service
- ● Conf - Exhib - Inf

Anti Counterfeiting Group   (ACG)   1980
- NR PO Box 578, HIGH WYCOMBE, Bucks, HP11 1YD.   (hq)
  01494 449165   fax 01494 465052
  email admin@a-cg.com   http://www.a-cg.com
  Dir Gen: Ruth Orchard
- ▲ Company Limited by Guarantee
- ○ *T; to combat counterfeiting of branded products
- Gp Affiliates; Clothing & footwear; International; Public policy; Watches
- ● Conf - Mtgs - ET - Res - Exhib - Comp - Stat - Inf - LG
- < Assn des Inds Marques (AIM); Alliance against Counterfeiting & Piracy (AACP)
- M 130 f, UK / 44 f, o'seas
- ¶ NL - 5/6;   Enforcement Guides;
  Hbk;   AR - 1; all ftm only.

Anti-Graffiti Association
- NR Kemp House, 152-160 City Road, LONDON, EC1V 2NX.
  email info@theaga.org.uk   http://www.theaga.org.uk
- ○ *K, *T; 'to promote best practice in the management of graffiti, vandalism & related crime'

Antiquarian Booksellers Association (International)   (ABA)   1906
- ■ Sackville House, 40 Piccadilly, LONDON, W1J 0DR.   (hq)
  020 7439 3118   fax 020 7439 3119
  email admin@aba.org.uk   http://www.aba.org.uk
  Sec: John Critchley,   Pres: Robert Frew
- ▲ Company Limited by Guarantee (without a share capital)
- ○ *T; for dealers of rare books, manuscripts, maps, prints & ephemera in the British Isles
- ● Lib - Books fairs - Benevolent fund
- < Intl League Antiquarian Booksellers
- M 230 f, UK / 40 f, o'seas
- ¶ NL - 8;   AR - 1; both ftm only.
  LM (with geographical index & list of specialities); on request & on website.
  Book Fair Guide.

Antiquarian Horological Society   (AHS)   1953
- ■ New House, High St, Ticehurst, WADHURST, E Sussex, TN5 7AL.   (hq)
  01580 200155   fax 01580 201323
  email secretary@ahsoc.demon.co.uk
  http://www.ahsoc.demon.co.uk
  Sec: Mrs Wendy B Barr
- ▲ Registered Charity
- Br 6; Canada, USA
- ○ *L; to promote the study & conservation of timepieces
- Gp Electrical horology; Turret clock
- ● Conf - Mtgs - ET - Res - Exhib - SG - Lib - VE
- M 2,000 i, 100 f, 100 org
  (Sub: £40)
- ¶ Antiquarian Horology - 4; ftm, £40 nm.

Antique Metalware Society   (AMS)   1991
- ■ The Secretary AMS, Metalwork Section, Victoria & Albert Museum, Cromwell Rd, LONDON, SW7 2RL.   (hsb)
  020 7942 2079
  email s.seavers@vam.ac.uk
  http://www.oldcopper.org.uk/ams.htm
  Chmn: Tony North,   Sec: Stephanie Seavers
- ▲ Un-incorporated Society
- ○ *G; to study artifacts, mainly domestic, made of non-precious metals & their alloys, their manufacture & history
- ● Mtgs - Res - VE
- M 146 i, UK / 35 i, o'seas
  (Sub: £20 single, £28 joint)
- ¶ Jnl - 1 - 1;   Base Thoughts (NL) - 1; both ftm only.

Antiquities Dealers Association   (ADA)   1982
- NR Faustus Ancient Art & Jewellery, 41 Dover St, LONDON, W1S 4NS.   (hsb)
  020 7930 1864
  Sec: Mrs Susan Hadida
- ○ *T; for dealers, professionals & collectors of antiquities
- Gp Dealers; Collectors (associates)
- ● ET - Exhib - Inf - LG - International fairs
- < Museums Association; Brit Art Market Fedn (BAMF)
- M 61 i, UK / 38 i (dealers) o'seas, 35 i associates (collectors)
- ¶ LM.

Apostrophe Protection Society
- NR 23 Vauxhall Rd, BOSTON, Lincs, PE21 0JB.
  01205 350056
  http://www.apostrophe.fsnet.co.uk
  Founder: John Richards
- ○ *K; to preserve the correct usage of the apostrophe in written English

Applied Arts Scotland
- in June 2007 restructured, left the Edinburgh College of Art & set up a website for contact for interested parties: http://groups.google.co.uk/group/Applied-Arts-Scotland

Approved Driving Instructors National Joint Council   (ADINJC)   1974
- NR 47 Sweetman's Road, SHAFTESBURY, Dorset, SP7 8EH.   (pres/p)
  01747 855091
- ○ *N; a consortium of driving instructors associations representing the members in negotiations with official bodies likely to influence the sphere of their activities
- ● Conf - Mtgs - ET - SG - VE - LG
- M 6,500 i, 3 f
- ¶ Report of Annual Conference - 1; free.

Arab-British Chamber of Commerce   1975
- NR 43 Upper Grosvenor St, LONDON, W1K 2NJ.   (hq)
- ○ *C

© CBD Research Ltd · Beckenham · BR3 5JS · Tel 020 8650 7745 · Fax 020 8650 0768 · E-mail cbd@cbdresearch.com · www.cbdresearch.com

Arab Horse Society   1918

NR   Windsor House, The Square, Ramsbury, MARLBOROUGH,
       Wilts, SN8 2PE.   (hq)
       01672 521411   fax 01672 520880
       http://www.arabhorsesociety.com
       The Registrar
▲   Company Limited by Guarantee; Registered Charity
Br   17 regional groups
○   *B, *S; breeding & importation of Arabian horses; encouraging
       the wider use of Arab blood in light horse breeding; welfare
       of horses; education of equestrian skills
Gp   C'ees: Stud Book; Registration activities; Marketing; Public
       relations
●   Conf - Mtgs - ET - Comp - Lib - LG
<   Wld Arabian Horse Org (WAHO); Eur Conf of Arab Horse
       Orgs (ECAHO)
M   3,013 i, UK / 171 i, o'seas
¶   Arab Horse Society News - 5.   NL - 3; ftm only.
       Ybk - 1 (December).
       Anglo Arab Stud Book.
       Directory of Pure Arabian Studs in GB & Ireland - 2 yrly.
       Arabian Type & Standard.   AR.

Arboricultural Association   (AA)   1964

■   Ampfield House, Ampfield, ROMSEY, Hants, SO51 9PA.   (hq)
       01794 368717   fax 01794 368978
       email admin@trees.org.uk   http://www.trees.org.uk
       Dir: Nick Eden
▲   Company Limited by Guarantee; Registered Charity
Br   9
○   *H, *P; to promote excellence in tree care to government,
       professionals & society
Gp   Registered consultants; Approved contractors
●   Conf - ET - Exhib - LG - Publishing information - Promotion of
       competent consultants & specialists
M   1,600 i, 200 f, UK / 60 i, 25 f, o'seas
¶   Jnl - 4.   NL - 4.
       Directory of Approved Contractors; free.
       Directory of Registered Consultants; free.
       Guidance Note(s); all £12.50:
          1. Trees & Bats;
          3. Planting & Managing Amenity Woodlands;
          4. Amenity Valuation of Trees & Woodland;
       12 leaflets on maintenance of trees & hedges; £3 a set.
       publications list available.

Archaeology Abroad   1972

■   31-34 Gordon Sq, LONDON, WC1H 0PY.   (mail/address)
       020 8537 0849
       email arch.abroad@ucl.ac.uk   http://www.britarch.ac.uk/
       archabroad
       Hon Sec & Editor: Wendy Rix Morton
▲   Un-incorporated Society
○   *G; to list opportunities for volunteers & staff to work on
       archaeological excavations outside the UK
●   Inf
M   427 i, 90 f, UK / 100 i, 10 f, o'seas
¶   Archaeology Abroad - 2; £20-£24 i, £30-£34 instns.
       Factsheets; free for large sae, (general guidance & information
       for those interested in fieldwork in countries from which few
       entries are received).

** Archaeology Cymru

       Organisation lost; see Introduction paragraph 3

Archaeology Scotland   1944

NR   Causewayside House, 160 Causewayside, EDINBURGH,
       EH9 1PR.   (hq)
       0131-668 4189   fax 0131-668 4275
       email info@scottisharchaeology.org.uk
       http://www.scottisharchaeology.org.uk
       Dir: Eila McQueen
▲   Registered Charity
○   *E, *G, *N; to secure Scotland's past for the future by
       promoting public education & appreciation of Scotland's
       archaeology
✕   2008 Council for Scottish Archaeology

Architectural & Archaeological Society for the County of Buckinghamshire   1847

■   County Museum, Church St, AYLESBURY, Bucks, HP20 2QP.
       (hq)
       01296 387341 (Wed: 1000-1600 only)
       email bucksas@buckscc.gov.uk
       http://www.bucksas.org.uk
       Hon Sec: Maureen Brown
▲   Registered Charity
○   *L
Gp   Natural history section
●   Mtgs - Res - Lib - VE
<   Coun Brit Archaeol
M   500 i, 14 org, UK / 6 i, o'seas
¶   Records of Buckinghamshire - 1; ftm, £16 nm.
       NL - 2; ftm.

Architectural & Archaeological Society of Durham & Northumberland   (AASDN)   1861

■   Broom Cottage, 29 Foundry Fields, CROOK, Co Durham,
       DL15 9JY.   (hsp)
       01388 762620
       email belindalburke@aol.com
       http://www.communigate.co.uk/ne/aasdn
       Hon Sec: Mrs Belinda Burke
▲   Registered Charity
○   *G, *L; to stimulate interest in all aspects of the archaeology &
       architecture of North East England
●   Mtgs - ET - Inf - VE
M   124 i, 27 f
       (Sub: £15 i, £19 f)
¶   Durham Archaeological Jnl - 1; ftm, £19 nm.

Architectural Association

NR   34-36 Bedford Sq, LONDON, WC1B 3EG.
       020 7887 4000
○   *P

Architectural Cladding Association
       a product association of the **British Precast Concrete Federation**

Architectural Heritage Society of Scotland   (AHSS)   1956

■   33 Barony St, EDINBURGH, EH3 6NX.   (hq)
       0131-557 0019   fax 0131-557 0049
       email headoffice@ahss.org.uk   http://www.ahss.org.uk
       Dirs: Dr Susan Buckham, Audrey Dakin
▲   Registered Charity
Br   7
○   *A, *G, *L; to promote the study, protection & conservation of
       Scotland's built heritage
●   Conf - Mtgs - Inf - VE - LG - Representations on applications for
       listed building consent
<   Soc Protection Ancient Bldgs; Georgian Gp; Victorian Soc; Nat
       Trust for Scotland; Scot Civic Trust; Twentieth Century Soc
M   1,400 i, 50 f, 40 org, UK / 10 i, o'seas
¶   Architectural Heritage Jnl - 1.
       Magazine - 2.

Architectural & Specialist Door Manufacturers Association (ASDMA) 1989
- ■ 3 Coates Lane, HIGH WYCOMBE, Bucks, HP13 5EY. (hsb)
  01494 447370   fax 01494 462094
  email enquiries@asdma.com   http://www.asdma.com
  Sec: Mrs L A Parry
- ○ *T; for specialists in timber doors & doorsets; to promote quality assured doors which meet all British & European standards of fire resistance & safety
- Gp Full membership open to manufacturers, fabricators & suppliers of doorsets;
  Associate membership open to companies providing associated components & services;
  Sponsor membership open to providers of relevant testing &/or certification services
- ● Mtgs - Inf - LG
- M 15 f (full), 11 f (associate), 1 sponsor
- ¶ The Facts on the Performance of Timber Doors & Doorsets.
  LM - 2;   Leaflet on ASDMA - 1; both free.
  Best Practice Guide to Timber Fire Doors (free download from website).

Argentine-British Chamber of Commerce
English name of **Cámara de Comercio Argentino Británica**

Aristotelian Society for the systematic study of philosophy 1870
- NR Stewart House (room 281), Russell Square, LONDON, WC1E 6BT. (execsec/b)
  020 7862 8685
  email mail@aristoteliansociety.org.uk
  http://www.aristoteliansociety.org.uk
  Exec Sec: Rachel Carter
- ▲ Registered Charity
- ○ *L; to advance systematic study of philosophy
- ● Conf - Mtgs - Res
- < Brit Philosophical Assn
- M 500 i, UK / 150 i, o'seas
- ¶ Proceedings - 3 pts a yr (or 1 vol bound).
  Supplementary volume - 1;   Various other publications.

Arkwright Society 1971
- NR Cromford Mill, Mill Lane, Cromford, MATLOCK, Derbys, DE4 3RQ. (hq)
  01629 823256
  Chmn: Bob Faithorn,   Sec: Dr Christopher Charlton
- ▲ Company Limited by Guarantee; Registered Charity
- ○ *L; the restoration of Sir Richard Arkwright's Cromford Mill; to preserve & promote conservation of buildings, monuments & machinery of industrial archaeological & historical interest
- ● Conf - Mtgs - ET - Res - Exhib - Inf - VE
- < Regeneration through Heritage; Nat Coun Civic Trust Socs
- M 250 i, 2 f
- ¶ NL - 4.   Cromford Venture Centre - 1.
  Lecture Programmes - 2.   AR & Accounts - 1.
  Cromford Venture Centre Prospectus - 1.

ARLIS/UK & Ireland: the Art Libraries Society (ARLIS) 1969
- NR Word & Image Dept, Victoria & Albert Museum, Cromwell Rd, LONDON, SW7 2RL.
  020 7942 2317
  email arlis@vam.ac.uk   http://www.arlis.org.uk
  Business Mgr: Natasha Held
- ▲ Registered Charity
- ○ *A, *L; for people & organisations with an interest in the documentation of art & design and the promotion of library & information services to artists, designers & architects
- ● Conf - Mtgs - ET - SG - Stat - VE
- < Library Assn; IFLA section of art libraries
- ¶ Art Libraries Jnl - 4.

Arms & Armour Society 1950
- NR PO Box 10232, LONDON, SW19 2ZD. (hsb)
  01323 844278
  Hon Sec: Anthony Dove
- ○ *L, *Q; the study of arms & armour from the earliest times to the present day; to conserve specimens of arms & armour for the future
- ● Mtgs - Res - Inf - VE
- M i, f & org
- ¶ Jnl - 2 (Mar & Sep).   NL - 4.

Army Cadet Force Association (ACFA) 1930
- ■ Holderness House, 51-61 Clifton St, LONDON, EC2A 4OW. (hq)
  020 7426 8377   fax 020 7426 8378
  email acfa@armycadets.com
  http://www.armycadets.com
  Gen Sec: Brig M Wharmby
- ▲ Company Limited by Guarantee; Registered Charity
- Br 1,754
- ○ *Y; a voluntary youth organisation for 12-18 year old young men & women; to provide a challenging & stimulating environment & develop self respect & confidence through citizenship & service
- ● Conf - Mtgs - ET - Exhib - Comp - Inf - LG
- < St John Ambulance; Heartstart; Duke of Edinburgh Award
- > Nat Coun Voluntary Youth Orgs
- M 50,000 i, 80 f, 20 orgs
- ¶ Jnl - 4; ftm, £20 nm.   AR - 1; ftm only.

Army Parachute Association (APA) 1963
- NR Airfield Camp, Netheravon, SALISBURY, Wilts, SP4 9SF. (hq)
- Br Cyprus, Germany
- ○ *S; runs courses of basic sports parachuting for members of all three services
- Gp AFF (Accelerated Free Fall to gain competency in a quicker time); Tandem (the method of introducing non parachutists to sky diving with the minimum of instruction - approximately 3 / 4 hour)
- ● ET - Res - Comp
- < Brit Parachute Assn

Army Records Society 1983
- NR School of ESPaCH, Crescent House, SALFORD, Greater Manchester, M5 4WT. (hsb)
  email j.m.beach@salford.ac.uk
  http://www.armyrecordssociety.org.uk
  Hon Sec: Dr Jim Beach
- ▲ Registered Charity
- ○ *L; publication of original records concerning the history of the British Army
- ● Res - Annual lecture
- M 350 i, 30 org UK / 100 i, 30 org, o'seas
- ¶ Annual Volume - 1; ftm only.

Arnold Bennett Society 1955
- ■ 4 Field End Close, Trentham, STOKE-on-TRENT, Staffs, ST4 8DA. (hsp)
  01782 641337
  http://www.arnoldbennettsociety.org.uk
  Hon Sec: Carol Gorton
- ▲ Un-incorporated Society
- ○ *A; to promote the study & appreciation of the life, works & times of Arnold Bennett (1867-1931) & other provincial writers with particular reference to North Staffordshire
- ● Mtgs
- < Alliance of Literary Socs
- M 250 i, UK / 25 i, o'seas
- ¶ NL - 3; ftm, £1 nm.

Aromatherapy & Allied Practitioners Association
NR PO Box 36248, LONDON, SE19 3YD.
    020 8653 9152 (Mon-Fri 1300-1600)   fax 020 8653 9152
    http://www.aromatherapyuk.net
○ *P

Aromatherapy Trade Council (ATC) 1993
■ PO Box 387, IPSWICH, Suffolk, IP2 9AN.   (mail/address)
    01473 603630   fax 01473 603630
    email info@a-t-c.org.uk   http://www.a-t-c.org.uk
    Admin: Sylvia Baker,   Chmn: Geoff Lyth
▲ Company Limited by Guarantee
○ *T; to act as the authoritative body for the specialist aromatherapy essential oil industry; to promote consumer safety through safe usage of essential oils; to offer advice on the responsible marketing of aromatherapy products
● Conf - Mtgs - Res - Exhib - Expt - Inf - LG
< Eur Fedn of Essential Oils (EFEO); Parliamentary Gp for Alternative & Complementary Medicine
M 58 f
¶ Guidelines on the Regulation, Labelling, Advertising & Promotion of Aromatherapy Products - irreg; £50 m, £100 nm.
    General Information Booklet.   LM.

Arrhythmia Alliance (A-A)
■ PO Box 3697, STRATFORD-upon-AVON, Warks, CV37 8YL. (hq)
    01789 450787
    email info@heartrhythmcharity.org.uk
    http://www.heartrhythmcharity.org.uk
    Chief Exec: Mrs Trudi Lobban
▲ Registered Charity
○ *W; a patient support group for those with heart rhythm disorders; aims to promote better understanding, diagnosis, treatment & quality of life for individuals with cardiac arrhythmia. Members include medical professionals, industry, patients, carers & parent groups
● Conf - Mtgs - ET - Exhib - Inf - LG - Parent support helpline
< Brit Cardiovascular Soc
> Arrythmia Alliance Portugal; APPCC (Italy): Brit Cardiovascular Soc;
M [not stated]

Art & Architecture (A&A) 1972
NR 70 Cowcross St, LONDON, EC1M 6EJ.   (mail/address)
▲ Un-incorporated Society
○ *A, *K; promotes collaboration between artists, crafts people & architects in the interests of a better environment; campaigns for the Percent for Art scheme & for the employment of art & artists in architecture & construction; acts as a network for all concerned with public art
M i, f & org

The Art Fund
    alternative name of the **National Art Collections Fund**

Art Libraries Society
    alternative name of **ARLIS/UK & Ireland**

Art Metalware Manufacturers' Association (AMMA) 1965
■ Federation House, 10 Vyse St, BIRMINGHAM, B18 6LT.   (hq)
    0121-237 1149
○ *T
● Mtgs - Inf
< Brit Jewellery, Giftware & Finishing Fedn
M 6 f

Art Workers Guild (AWG) 1884
NR 6 Queen Sq, LONDON, WC1N 3AT.   (hq)
    020 7713 0966   fax 020 7713 0967
    email monica@artworkersguild.org
    http://www.artworkersguild.org
    Sec: Monica Grose-Hodge
○ *A; to advance education & to foster & maintain high standards of design & craftsmanship in all the visual arts & crafts

Arthritic Association (AA) 1942
■ 1 Upperton Gardens, EASTBOURNE, E Sussex, BN21 2AA.
    01323 416550   fax 01323 639793
    email info@arthriticassociation.org.uk
    http://www.arthriticassociation.org.uk
    Mgr: Bruce Hester
▲ Company Limited by Guarantee; Registered Charity
○ *M; to relieve symptoms of arthritis by natural methods
● Res - Inf
M 3,900 i, UK / 100 i, o'seas
¶ Rheumatic Review - Jnl.   Treating Arthritis Naturally. A Balanced View: Practical Tips for a Healthy Diet. Recipes Compiled for the Arthritic Association. [subscription £6].

Arthritis Care 1947
NR 18 Stephenson Way, LONDON, NW1 2HD.   (hq)
    020 7380 6500
    email info@arthritiscare.org.uk
    http://www.arthritiscare.org.uk
    Chief Exec: Neil Betteridge
▲ Company Limited by Guarantee; Registered Charity
Br 6
○ *W; a national voluntary organisation working with & for people with arthritis
● ET - Publishing - Campaigning
    Helpline: 0808 800 4050
M i
¶ Arthritis News - 6;   Information & advisory leaflets. Publications list available.

Arthritis & Musculoskeletal Alliance (ARMA) 1972
NR Bride House, 18-20 Bride Lane, LONDON, EC4Y 8EE.   (hq)
    020 7842 0910   fax 020 7842 0901
▲ Registered Charity
○ *N; an umbrella organisation of professional & user groups working together to ensure high quality services are maintained for people with arthritis
● Mtgs
< EULAR; LMCA
M 23 org

Arthrogryposis Group (TAG) 1984
■ Beak Cottage, Dunley, STOURPORT-on-SEVERN, Worcs, DY13 0TZ.   (hq)
    01299 825781 (Mon-Thurs 1000-1500)
    Chmn: Peter Lacey
▲ Registered Charity
○ *W; to offer support, contact & information for the families, children & adults affected with arthrogryposis, & those involved in their care; also known as Arthrogryposis Multiplex Congenita, is congenital disorder that causes joint contractures, muscle weakness & fibrosis
● Conf - Mtgs - Res - Inf - VE - Activity camps for young people aged 10-15
M 800 i, 12 org, UK / 40 i, o'seas
¶ Tag Talk - 4; ftm.

Arthur Ransome Society Ltd (TARS) 1990

- ■ Abbot Hall, Kirkland, KENDAL, Cumbria, LA9 5AL. (regd/office)
  01539 722464
  email tarsinfo@arthur-ransome.org
  http://www.arthur-ransome.org
  Co Sec: Peter Hyland
- ▲ Company Limited by Guarantee
- Br 5; Australia, Canada, Japan, New Zealand, USA
- ○ *A; to promote the works of Arthur Ransome (1884-1967) & support research into his life & writings; to encourage children in the reading of his books & to participate in outdoor activities
- ● Conf - Mtgs - Res - Lib - VE
- < Alliance of Literary Socs
- M 1,200 i, UK / 260 i, o'seas
- ¶ Mixed Moss (Jnl) - 1; Outlaw (junior magazine) - 2; Signals (NL) - 3; all ftm only.

Arts & Business 1976

- NR Nutmeg House, 60 Gainsford St, LONDON, SE1 2NY. (hq)
  020 7378 8143
  http://www.aandb.org.uk
- ▲ Company Limited by Guarantee; Registered Charity
- Br 13
- ○ *A, *T; to promote & encourage partnership between business & the arts
- Gp Development forum
- ● Conf - Mtgs - ET - Res - Stat - Inf - Lib - LG
- < Coun for Business & the Arts in Canada; CEREC; Foundation for Business in Support of the Arts (Hong Kong); Assn for Corporate Support of the Arts (Japan)
- M c 350 f, 700 org
- ¶ Re-creating Communities: business, the arts & regeneration. AR (incl LM) - 1.

Arts Centre Group (ACG) 1971

- ■ The Menier Chocolate Factory (1st floor), 51-53 Southwark St, LONDON, SE1 1BU. (hq)
  0845 458 1881; 020 7407 1881
  email info@artscentregroup.org.uk
  http://www.artscentregroup.org.uk
  Sec: Susanne Scott
- ▲ Company Limited by Guarantee; Registered Charity
- ○ *A; to provide a network & support for Christians professionally involved in the arts, media & entertainment business
- Gp Actors, Dancers, Photographers, Architects, Graphics, Teachers, Writers, Musicians, Arts admin, Designers, Entertainers, Fashion & textiles, Media, Visual artists
- ● Mtgs - ET - Exhib - Comp
- M 500 i, 15 f, 20 org, UK / 30 i, 5 f, 10 org, o'seas
- ¶ E-info - 12; ftm only.

Arts Marketing Association (AMA) 1993

- ■ 7A Clifton Court, CAMBRIDGE, CB1 7BN. (hq)
  01223 578078
  email info@a-m-a.co.uk http://www.a-m-a.org.uk
  Dir: Julie Aldridge
- ▲ Company Limited by Guarantee
- ○ *P; professional development in arts marketing
- Gp Freelancers
- ● Conf - ET - Inf
- M c 1,800 i
- ¶ Jnl of Arts Marketing - 4. Ybk. Books.

ArtWatch UK

- NR 15 Capel Rd, EAST BARNET, Herts, EN4 8JD.
  020 8216 3492
  Dir: Michael Daley
- ○ *A, *K; to preserve the integrity of works of art
- M c 150 i
- ¶ NL - 4.

ASBCI - the Forum for Clothing & Textiles (ASBCI) 1974

- ■ Unit 5, 25 Square Rd, HALIFAX, W Yorks, HX1 1QG. (hq)
  01422 354666 fax 01422 381184
  email info@asbci.co.uk http://www.asbci.co.uk
  Co Sec: Stephanie Ingham, Chmn: Malcolm Ball
- ▲ Company Limited by Guarantee
- ○ *T; 'a recognised centre of excellence where companies at the forefront of their specific sectors can discuss, share & develop practices, processes & initiatives that will benefit their organisations & the UK clothes & textile supply chain as a whole'
- Gp C'ees: Ball, Conference, Marketing, Student membership, Technical
- ● Conf - Mtgs - ET - Comp - Inf - VE
- < Soc of Dyers & Colourists (SDC); Textile Inst
- > Soc of Dyers & Colourists; Textile Inst
- M 10 i, 80 f, 3 org
- ¶ Technical booklets available - details on website; £10 m, £15 nm.
  Conference Proceedings booklets; £30.
- × 2005 Association of Suppliers to the British Clothing Industry

Asbestos Removal Contractors Association (ARCA) 1980

- ■ ARCA House, 237 Branston Rd, BURTON upon TRENT, Staffs, DE14 3BT. (hq)
  01283 531126 fax 01283 568228
  email info@arca.org.uk http://www.arca.org.uk
  Chief Exec: Stephen Sadley
- ▲ Company Limited by Guarantee
- ○ *T; for HSE licensed contractors & UKAS accredited asbestos testing & inspection laboratories
- ● Conf - Mtgs - ET - Exam - Inf - LG
- M 30 i, 320 f
- ¶ ARCA News - 4; ftm, £20 yr nm. AR - 1.

ASET, the Work-Based & Placement Learning Association (ASET) 1982

- NR DIUS, W11, 1 Moorfoot, SHEFFIELD, N Yorks, S1 4PQ. (hq)
  0114-221 2902 fax 0114-221 2903
  email aset@asetonline.org http://www.asetonline.org
  Admin: Keith Fildes
- ▲ Company Limited by Guarantee; Registered Charity
- ○ *E; to develop, promote & implement the concept of higher education courses that integrate periods of relevant work in an employing organisation
- ● Conf - Mtgs - Res - Exhib - Comp - Stat - LG
- M 47 i, 110 f & universities, UK / 2 i, 2 f, o'seas
- ¶ ASET Directory of Sandwich Courses - 1.
- × 2008 Association for Sandwich Education & Training

Ashford (Kent) Chamber of Commerce, Industry & Enterprise
since 2005 **Kent Invicta Chamber of Commerce**

Ashmolean Natural History Society of Oxfordshire (ANHSO) 1828

- NR Oxford Univ Museum of Natural History, Parks Rd, OXFORD, OX1 3PW. (mtgs)
  http://www.anhso.org.uk
- ▲ Un-incorporated Society
- ○ *L; natural science
- Gp Education; Rare plants; Verges
- ● Mtgs - Comp - Lib - VE - Survey of rare plants
- M 100 i
- ¶ Fritillary (Jnl) - 4; (produced in conjunction with the Berks, Bucks & Oxon Naturalists' Trust).

Aslib: The Association for Information Management (aslib) 1924

- NR Holywell Centre, 1 Phipp St, LONDON, EC2A 4PS. (hq)
  020 7613 3031 fax 020 7613 5080
  email aslib@aslib.com http://www.aslib.com
- ▲ Registered Charity
- ○ *L, *P, *Q; to promote better management & provision of information in information centres & libraries
- M i, f & org

© CBD Research Ltd · Beckenham · BR3 5JS · Tel 020 8650 7745 · Fax 020 8650 0768 · E-mail cbd@cbdresearch.com · www.cbdresearch.com

Asparagus Growers' Association (AGA)
■ 133 Eastgate, LOUTH, Lincs, LN11 9QG. (asa)
  01507 602427 fax 01507 607165
  email crop.association@pvga.co.uk
  http://www.british-asparagus.co.uk
  Sec: Mrs Jayne Dyas
○ *T; to provide technical, commercial & marketing information
  for growers
● Conf - Mtgs - Res - Exhib - Stat - Inf - LG
M 120 f

Asphalt Industry Alliance 2000
NR 14a Eccleston St, LONDON, SW1W 9LT. (hq)
  020 7730 1100 fax 020 7730 2213
  email asphalt@hmpr.co.uk
  http://www.asphaltindustryalliance.com
▲ Un-incorporated Society
○ *T; to promote adequate funding of road maintenance
● Conf - Mtgs - Res - Stat - Inf - LG
M 2 org:
  Quarry Products Association
  Refined Bitumen Association
¶ Asphalt Now - 2;
  Annual Local Authority Road Maintenance Survey - 1; both free.

Asset Based Finance Association (ABFA) 1996
NR Boston House (2nd floor), The Little Green, RICHMOND,
  Surrey, TW9 1QE. (hq)
  020 8332 9955 fax 020 8332 2585
  http://www.factors.org.uk
  Chief Exec: Kate Sharp
▲ Company Limited by Guarantee; Registered Charity
○ *P; an association of British & Irish companies in business to
  business financial services
● Conf - Mtgs - ET - Exam - Stat - Inf - LG
M 42 f
¶ NL - 4; ftm & limited associated companies
✕ 2007 Factors & Discounters Association

** Associated Chiropodists & Podiatrists Union
  Organisation lost: see Introduction paragraph 3

Associated National Electrical Wholesalers Ltd (ANEW Ltd) 1993
NR Titmore Court (suite 3), Titmore Green, HITCHIN, Herts,
  SG4 7JT. (hq)
  01438 750075
  Chief Exec: Neal Wilcox
▲ Company Limited by Guarantee
○ *T; an alliance of electrical wholesalers
● Mtgs
< FEGIME Ltd
M 37 f
¶ LM - irreg; ftm only.

Associated Train Crew Union (ATCU) 2005
NR PO Box 647, BARNSLEY, S Yorks, S72 8XU.
  01226 16417
  email admin@atcu.org.uk http://www.atcu.org.uk
  Chmn of Formation C'ee: Steven Trumm
▲ Un-incorporated Society
Br 9
○ *U; non-affiliated, non-political
Gp Crew section; Driver section
● Representation - Legal cover
M 50 i

Association for Accountancy & Business Affairs (AABA)
NR PO Box 5874, BASILDON, Essex, SS16 5FR.
○ *K; to broaden public choices & to advance public policy
  reform

Association of Accounting Technicians (AAT) 1980
NR 140 Aldersgate St, LONDON, EC1A 4HY.
  020 7397 3009
  http://www.aat.org.uk
  Chief Exec: Miss Jane Scott Paul
▲ Registered Charity
○ *E, *P; a vocational training body awarding NVs/SVQs levels 2,
  3 & 4 in accounting

Association of Advertisers in Ireland Ltd (AAI) 1951
IRL Unit 3013, Lake Drive, Citywest Business Campus, DUBLIN 24,
  Republic of Ireland.
  353 (1) 469 7370 fax 353 (1) 469 3350
  email info@aai.ie http://www.aai.ie
  Hon Sec: Catherine Bent
○ *T

Association of Air Ambulance Charities (AAAC)
NR Unit 14 Wheelbarrow Park Estate, Pattenden Lane, MARDEN,
  Kent, TN12 9QJ. (chmn/b)
  01622 833833
  Chmn: David Philpott
○ *N

Association of Alabaster Importers & Wholesalers (AAI) 1977
■ 423 Upper Elmers End Rd, BECKENHAM, Kent, BR3 3DA.
  (hsp)
○ *T; interests of importers of unworked alabaster & articles made
  of alabaster
● Mtgs - Inf - Lib - Stat - VE
M 7 f

Association of American Dancing (AAD) 1936
■ Aspenshaw Hall, THORNSETT, High Peak, Derbys,
  SK22 1AU. (hq)
  01663 744986
  Dir: Miss Anna Scott
▲ Un-incorporated Society
○ *D; an examining body promoting all forms of dance
  movement amongst professionals, teachers & the public
Gp Modern art group (for younger people)
● ET - Exam - Inf - Scholarships & awards
< Coun for Dance Educ & Training
M i (through examination qualification)
¶ Text books covering the five disciplines of dance within the
  syllabus.

Association of Anaesthetists of Great Britain & Ireland (AAGBI) 1932
NR 21 Portland Place, LONDON, W1B 1PY. (hq)
  020 7631 1650
▲ Company Limited by Guarantee
○ *L, *Q; to promote & support the speciality of anaesthesia
● Conf - ET - Exhib - Inf - Lib - Seminars
< R Coll Anaesthetists
M c 5,200 i
¶ Publications list available.

Association of Applied Biologists (AAB) 1904
- ■ Warwick HRI, Wellesbourne, WARWICK, CV35 9EF. (hq)
  01789 472020   fax 01789 470234
  email carol@aab.org.uk   http://www.aab.org.uk
  Hon Gen Sec: A J Keys
- ▲ Registered Charity
- ○ *L, *Q; 'to promote the study & advancement of all branches of biology & in particular (but without prejudice to the generality of the foregoing) to foster the practice, growth & development of applied biology, incl the application of biological sciences for the production & preservation of food, fibre & other materials for the maintenance & improvement of the environment'
- Gp Applied micrology & bacteriology; Biological control; Cropping & the environment; Food systems; Nematology; Pesticide application; Plant physiology & crop improvement; Post harvest biology; Virology
- ● Conf - Mtgs - ET - Publication of scientific research
- < Assn of Learned & Profl Soc Publishers; Inst Biology
- M 800 i, UK / 100 i, o'seas
- ¶ Annals of Applied Biology (Jnl) - 6.   NL - 3; ftm only.
  Aspects of Applied Biology (proceedings of conferences) - irreg.
  Descriptions of Plant Viruses (CD-ROM) - irreg.

Association of Archaeological Illustrators & Surveyors (AAI&S) 1978
- ■ SHES, University of Reading, Whiteknights, PO Box 227, READING, Berks RG6 6AB. (mail/address)
  email admin@aais.org.uk   http://www.aais.org.uk
  Hon Sec: Lesley Collett
- ○ *P; to set standards & promote best practice within the profession
- ● Conf - Production of special technical reports on special material or technique
- M c 254 i, UK & o'seas
- ¶ Graphic Archaeology (Jnl) - 2.   AAI&S NL - 4.
  Technical Papers (1-13) - irreg.

Association of Art & Antique Dealers Ltd   (LAPADA)   1974
- NR 535 Kings Rd, LONDON, SW10 0SZ. (hq)
  020 7823 3511   fax 020 7823 3522
  email lapada@lapada.co.uk   http://www.lapada.co.uk
  Chief Exec: John Newgas
- ▲ Company Limited by Guarantee
- ○ *T; for professional art & antiques dealers
- Gp Antiques dealers; Art dealers; Specialist shippers; Art & antiques valuers & restorers
- ● Conf - Stat - Expt - Inf - LG - Fairs
- < Confédn Intle des Négociants en Oeuvres d'Art (CINOA); other local associations
- M 700 f, UK / 25 f, o'seas
- ¶ LAPADA Views (NL) - 2; ftm.   LM - 1; free.

Association of Art Historians   (AAH)   1974
- NR 70 Cowcross St, LONDON, EC1M 6EJ. (hq)
  020 7490 3211   fax 020 7490 3277
  email admin@aah.org.uk   http://www.aah.org.uk
  Chmn: Colin Cruise
- ▲ Registered Charity
- ○ *P; to promote the study of art history & visual culture; to ensure a wider public recognition of the field. The national organisation for professional art historians & researchers (incuding academics, teachers, students & museum & gallery professionals)
- Gp Students; Museum & gallery professionals; University & college academics; School teachers; Independent freelance art historians
- ● Conf - Mtgs - Res - Comp - VE - Empl - LG
- < Comité Intl d'Histoire de l'Art (CIHA); College Art Assn (CAA)(USA); Intl Assn of Art Critics (AICA)
- M c 1,200 i
- ¶ Art History (Jnl) - 5;   The Art Book (Jnl) - 4;
  Bulletin (NL) - 3; details on application.

Association of Arts Fundraisers
  2008, in the process of merging with **Institute of Fundraising**

Association for Astronomy Education   (AAE)   1980
- NR c/o Royal Astronomical Society, Burlington House, Piccadilly, LONDON, W1J 0BQ. (mail/address)
  http://www.aae.org.uk
  Sec: Dr Anne Urquhart-Potts
- ▲ Registered Charity
- ○ *E; to promote & advance public education in the science of astronomy; to support the teaching of astronomy at all levels of education
- ● Conf - Mtgs - ET
- M i & org
- ¶ Gnomon (NL) - 4; ftm.

Association of ATOL Companies   (AAC)   1995
- ■ Regal House (5th floor), 70 London Rd, TWICKENHAM, Middx, TW1 3QS. (secretariat)
  020 8607 9539   fax 020 8944 2993
  email secretariat@aac-uk.org   http://www.aac-uk.org
  Contact: Ian Hawkes
- ○ *T
- ● Mtgs - LG
- M 65 f

Association of Authorised Public Accountants Ltd   (AAPA) 1978
- ■ 10 Lincoln's Inn Fields, LONDON, WC2A 3BP. (hq)
  020 7059 5916
  http://www.aapa.co.uk
  Contact: Ros Leah
- ▲ Company Limited by Guarantee
- ○ *P; 'a recognised Supervisory Body under the provisions of the Companies Act 1989.   No student membership or examinations are held as all members must already be fully qualified under the provisions of the Companies Act 1985 section 389(1)(b) or section 389(2)'
- ● Conf - LG
- < is part of the Association of Chartered Certified Accountants
- M c 200 f, UK / 50 f, o'seas
- ¶ Accounting Business (Jnl) - 10.   NL   LM.   AR.

Association of Authors' Agents   (AAA)   1974
- NR c/o Caroline Sheldon Literary Agency Ltd, 70-75 Cowcross St, LONDON, EC1M 6EJ. (hsb)
  020 7336 6550
  email aaa@carolinesheldon.co.uk
  http://www.agentsassoc.co.uk
- ▲ Un-incorporated Society
- ○ *T; to act as a forum for authors' agents
- M f

Association of Auto Theft Investigators
  see **International Association of Auto Theft Investigators (UK branch)**

Association for Automatic Identification & Mobile Data Capture (AIMUK) 1984
- ■ The Old Vicarage, All Souls Rd, HALIFAX, W Yorks, HX3 6DR. (hq)
  01422 368368
  http://www.aimuk.org
  Business Devt Mgr: Neil G Smith
- ○ *T; for automatic data capture industry - bar codes, radio frequency identification & communication, optical character recognition, magnetic strip cards, voice recognition
- × Automatic Identification Manufacturers & Suppliers Association

© CBD Research Ltd · Beckenham · BR3 5JS · Tel 020 8650 7745 · Fax 020 8650 0768 · E-mail cbd@cbdresearch.com · www.cbdresearch.com

Association of Average Adjusters (AAA) 1869
NR   c/o The Baltic Exchange, St Mary Axe, LONDON, EC3A 8BH.
    (sb)
    020 7623 5501   fax 020 7369 1623
    email AAA@balticexchange.com
    http://www.Average-Adjusters.com
    Chmn: Nigel Rogers
▲   Un-incorporated Society
○   *P
●   ET - Exam
M   450 i
¶   AR; ftm.

Association of Aviation Medical Examiners   (AAME)
NR   The Tollgate, Staverton Rd, DAVENTRY, Northants, NN11 4NN.
    email enquiries@aame.org.uk
    Hon Sec: Dr Kevin Herbert
○   *P

**Association of Bakery Ingredient Manufacturers   (ABIM)
1917**
■   4a Torphichen St, EDINBURGH, EH3 8JQ.   (hq)
    0131-229 9415   fax 0131-229 9407
    email steven.birrell@sfdf.org.uk
    http://www.abim.org.uk
    Exec Sec: Geraldine Smith
▲   Company Limited by Guarantee
○   *T; interests of manufacturers & suppliers of ingredients to the
    bakery trade
●   Mtgs - Inf
<   EEC Assn of Suppliers of Raw Materials to the Baking Ind
    (FEDIMA); Food & Drink Fedn; UK Baking Ind Consultative
    C'ee (UKBICC)
M   23 f

**Association of Basic Science Teachers in Dentistry   (ABSTD)
1978**
■   c/o Genes & Proteins Laboratory, Jarrett Building, University of
    Glasgow, Garscube Estate, GLASGOW, G61 1QH.   (hsb)
    07860 149079   fax 0141-330 2483
    email j.beeley@dental.gla.ac.uk   http://www.abstd.org
    Hon Sec: Dr Josie A Beeley
▲   Registered Charity
○   *E, *P; university lecturers concerned with education in dentistry
●   Conf - Mtgs
M   110 i
¶   NL - 2/3; free.

**Association of Bee Appliance Manufacturers of Great Brtain
1960**
NR   Beehive Works, WRAGBY, Lincs, LN8 5LA.   (hsb)
    01673 858555
○   *T; to represent the trade at exhibitions, shows & in meetings
    with Defra & BBKA

Association of Biomedical Andrologists   (ABA)
NR   Fertility Unit, Queen's Medical Centre, NOTTINGHAM,
    NG7 2UH.   (redg/add)
    0114-226 8290
    http://www.aba.uk.net
○   *P

Association of Blind Piano Tuners   (ABPT) 1953
■   31 Wyre Crescent, Lynwood, DARWEN, Lancs, BB3 0JG.   (hsp)
    01254 776148   fax 01254 773158
    email abpt@uk-piano.org   http://www.uk-piano.org/
    abpt
    Sec: Barrie Heaton
▲   Registered Charity
Br   4; 9 o'seas
○   *P; to give all possible assistance to blind piano tuners in
    carrying out their work
●   Conf - ET
M   80 i
¶   ABPT NL - 4 (on cassette).

Association of Block Paving Contractors
    alternative name of Interlay, an affiliated association of the **British
Precast Concrete Federation**

Association for Boarding School Survivors   1990
NR   6 Chester Court, Lissenden Gardens, LONDON, NW5 1LY.
    020 7267 7098
    http://www.boardingschoolsurvivors.co.uk
○   *K, *W; to raise public consciousness about the psychological
    effects of sending children to boarding school

Association of Boat Safety Examiners   (ABSE)
NR   23 Keswick Drive, FRODSHAM, Cheshire, WA6 7LT.   (chmn/p)
    01928 732444   fax 01928 732444
    http://www.abse.org.uk
    Chmn: Brian Hayes
▲   Un-incorporated Society
○   *P
●   Mtgs - Inf - Lib
M   132 i
¶   The Examiner - 4; ftm only.

Association of Bonded Sailing Companies
    in September 2005 merged with the National Federation of Sea
    Schools & the Yacht Charter Association to form the **Marine Leisure
Association**

Association of Breast Surgery at BASO
    a specialist group of **BASO ~ the Association for Cancer
Surgery**

Association of Breastfeeding Mothers   (ABM)   1980
■   PO Box 207, BRIDGWATER, Somerset, TA6 7YT.   (mail/add)
    0844 412 2948
    email info@abm.me.uk   http://www.abm.me.uk
▲   Registered Charity
○   *W; to provide education in the techniques & benefits of
    breastfeeding; to train breastfeeding counsellors
●   Conf - ET - Inf
M   600 i, UK / 50 i, o'seas
    (Sub: £18)
¶   ABM Magazine - 3; ftm.
    Breastfeeding Leaflets.   AR.
    List of publications available.

Association of Brickwork Contractors Ltd   (ABC)   2004
■   Woodside House, Winkfield, WINDSOR, Berks, SL4 2DX.   (hq)
    01344 882607   fax 01344 890129
    email info@brickworkcontractors.info
    http://www.brickworkcontractors.info
    Chief Exec: Michael Driver
▲   Company Limited by Guarantee
○   *T; to promote quality brickwork by training of operatives &
    health & safety of site workers
●   Mtgs - Inf - LG
M   24 f, 10 associates
¶   [NL - 2; free. To come]

Association of British Bookmakers   2002
NR   Regency House, 1-4 Warwick St, LONDON, W1B 5LT.   (hq)
        020 7434 2111
        http://www.abb.uk.com
▲   Company Limited by Guarantee
○   *T; for off course bookmakers
Gp   Racing security; Technical
M   f

Association for British Brewery Collectables   (ABBC)   1983
■   28 Parklands, Kidsgrove, STOKE-ON-TRENT, Staffs, ST7 4US.
        (ed/p)
        01782 761048
        email mike.breweriana@gmail.com
        http://www.abbclist.info
        Newsletter Editor: Mike Peterson
▲   Un-incorporated Society
○   *G; to promote the hobby of collecting brewery memorabilia
●   Mtgs - Res - Inf
M   150 i
¶   What's Bottling - 6; £7 m only.

Association of British Certification Bodies   (ABCB)   1984
NR   Sandover Centre, 129a White Horse Hill, CHISLEHURST, Kent,
        BR7 6DQ.   (hq)
        020 8295 1128
        http://www.acbc.org.uk
▲   Company Limited by Guarantee
○   *T; the UK's centre of excellence for product, quality
        management & environmental certification
●   Mtgs - SG - Inf - LG
M   f

Association of British Choral Directors   (ABCD)   1986
■   15 Granville Way, SHERBORNE, Dorset, DT9 4AS.   (sp)
        01935 389482
        email rachel.greaves@abcd.org.uk
        http://www.abcd.org.uk
        Gen Sec: Rachel Greaves
▲   Registered Charity
Br   11; 1
○   *P; to promote the education, training & development of choral
        directors from all choral sectors; to encourage the
        composition of choral music
●   Conf - Mtgs - ET - SG - Inf - VE - Workshops
<   Intl Fedn for Choral Music (IFCM); Inc Soc of Musicians; Music
        Educ Coun
M   700 i, 50 f
        (Sub: £45 i)
¶   Mastersinger - 4; ftm.   Membership Annual - 1; m only.

**Association of British Civilian Internees Far East Region
(ABCIFER)   1994**
NR   c/o Guillaume & Sons, 2 St Martin's Ct, 37 Queens Rd,
        WEYBRIDGE, Surrey, KT13 9UQ.   (chmn/b)
        020 8398 1387   fax 01892 655888
        Chmn: R W Bridge, AFC
▲   Un-incorporated Society
Br   Australia, Canada, New Zealand, USA
○   *G, *K; to campaign for justice from the Japanese government
        in respect of losses & suffering endured during World War II
        at the hands of Japanese Imperial Forces; to maintain
        friendships formed during internment by the Japanese
●   Mtgs - President's Memorial Library at the School of Oriental &
        African Studies
M   480 i, UK / 380 i, o'seas
¶   Bamboo Wireless (NL) - 3; ftm only.

Association of British Climatologists
        This association is no longer active. Previous members usually
        attend meetings organised by the Royal Meteorological
        Society,

Association of British Climbing Walls   (ABC)   1994
NR   c/o Foundry Climbing Centre (Unit 2), 45 Mowbray St,
        SHEFFIELD, S3 3EN.
        0114-279 6331
        Mem Sec: Jenny Clinging
▲   Company Limited by Guarantee
○   *S, *T; for owners of climbing walls in centres, leisure centres &
        schools
M   c 45 walls

Association of British Concert Promoters   (ABCP)   1989
■   St David's Hall, The Hayes, CARDIFF, Glamorgan,
        CF10 1SH.   (hsb)
        029 2087 8512   fax 029 2087 8517
        email s.king2@cardiff.gov.uk
        Hon Sec: Susan King
○   *T; a forum for discussion between concert promoters
●   Conf - Mtgs - SG - Inf
M   38 f

Association of British Conifer Growers
        a group of the **Horticultural Trades Association**

Association of British Correspondence Colleges   (ABCC)   1956
■   PO Box 17926, LONDON, SW19 3WB.   (hq)
        020 8544 9559
        email info@homestudy.org.uk
        http://www.homestudy.org.uk
        Sec: Heather Owen
▲   Company Limited by Guarantee
○   *E, *P; to represent the major private correspondence colleges
        in the UK
●   ET - Inf - LG - Advice on correspondence education in Britain
M   21 f

Association of British Counties   (ABC)   1989
■   28 Alfreda Rd, Whitchurch, CARDIFF, Glamorgan,
        CF14 2EH.   (chmn/p)
        029 2033 3728
        email peterboyce@ntlworld.com
        http://www.abcounties.co.uk
        Hon Sec: J M Bradford
▲   Un-incorporated Society
○   *K; to promote an awareness of the continuing existence of all
        the historic, traditional counties of Britain, as distinct from
        administrative counties
Gp   Campaign for True Identity; County of Middlesex Trust; Friends
        of Real Lancashire; Historic Counties Trust; Huntingdonshire
        Society; North Riding Society; Saddleworth White Rose
        Society; Staffordshire Society
●   Mtgs - Inf
<   Historic Counties Trust
M   1,000 i
¶   The Counties (Jnl) - 2; ftm only.
        Gazetteer - showing traditional counties & local government
        areas; on website: gazetteer.co.uk

Association of British Credit Unions Ltd   (ABCUL)   1979
■   Holyoake House, Hanover St, MANCHESTER, M60 0AS.   (hq)
        0161-832 3694   fax 0161-832 3706
        email info@abcul.org   http://www.abcul.coop
        Chief Exec: Mark Lyonette
▲   Industrial & Provident Society
Br   3
○   *N; the principal trade association for credit unions in Britain
        with members in England, Scotland & Wales
Gp   35 study groups
●   Conf - Mtgs - ET - Res - SG - Inf - LG
<   Wld Coun of Credit Us (WOCCU); Co-operatives UK
M   385 credit unions
¶   Credit Union News - 4;   AR - 1; both ftm.

Association of British Cycling Coaches   (ABCC)
NR   19 Forbes Avenue, Beverley High Rd, HULL, HU6 7AJ.
        Contact: Jim Sampson
○   *P

Association of British Designer Silversmiths   (ABDS)   1996
■   PO Box 42034, LONDON, E5 9WG.
        0794 478 6011
        email info   http://www.theabds.co.uk   (admin)
        http://www.theabds.co.uk
        Chmn: Julie Chamberlain
○   *P, *T; to act as forum for silversmiths throughout the country; to
        promote the highest standards in design & craftsmanship
Gp
        Full: full-time silversmith (by selection);
        Graduate: all graduates up to 3 years from leaving a course;
        Student; Friend - anyone interested in the field
●   Mtgs - Exhib
M   81 i, 12 f, 30 org
¶   NL - 4; ftm.

Association of British Dispensing Opticians   (ABDO)   1986
■   199 Gloucester Terrace, LONDON, W2 6LD.   (hq)
        020 7298 5100   fax 020 7298 5111
        email general@abdo.org.uk   http://www.abdo.org.uk
        Gen Sec: Sir Anthony Garrett
▲   Company Limited by Guarantee
○   *P
●   Conf - ET - Exam
M   7,396 i, UK / 909 i, o'seas
¶   Dispensing Optics - 9; ftm, £'10 m   AR - 1; free.
        Bifocals without Tears (L E Swift).
        Practical Ophthalmic Lenses (M Jalie/Ray).
        Principles of Ophthalmic Lenses (M Jalie).
        Optics (A H Tunnicliffe & J G Hurst).
        Other publications available.

Association of British Drivers   (ABD)   1992
NR   PO Box 2228, KENLEY, Surrey, CR8 5ZT.   (hsp)
        0700 078 1544
        email enquiries@abd.org.uk   http://www.abd.org.uk
        Mem Sec: Susan Newby-Robson
▲   Company Limited by Guarantee
○   *G, *K; to provide an active, reasonable voice & lobby for the
        British driver
●   Mtgs - Exhib
<   Amer Auto Enthusiast Club; Fiat Motor Club; Nat Assn of Street
        Clubs
M   1,600 i, 3,775 affiliates, UK / 5 i, o'seas
¶   On the Road (NL) - 6; ftm, £2 nm.
        The Association of British Drivers is the operating name of Pro-
        Motor (a Company Limited by Guarantee).

Association of British Fire Trades Ltd
        2007 merged with the British Fire Protection Systems Association, the
        Fire Extinguishing Trades Association & the Fire Industry
        Confederation to form the **Fire Industry Association**

Association of British Fungus Groups   (ABFG)   1996
NR   Harveys, Alston, AXMINSTER, Devon, EX13 7LG.
        01460 221788   fax 01460 221788
        email inquiries@abfg-adsl.demon.co.uk
        http://www.abfg.org
        Contacts: Michael Jordan & Hazel Malcolm
○   *G; for those interested in mushrooms & toadstools
M   i

Association of British Hammer Throwers   (The Hammer Circle)
        see **Hammer Circle: the Association of British Hammer**
        Throwers

Association of British Healthcare Industries   (ABHI)   1988
■   111 Westminster Bridge Rd, LONDON, SE1 7HR.   (hq)
        020 7960 4360   fax 020 7960 4361
        email enquiries@abhi.org.uk   http://www.abhi.org.uk
        Dir Gen: John Wilkinson
▲   Company Limited by Guarantee
○   *T; for the medical technology industry - manufacturers &
        distributors of products ranging from plasters to pacemakers
●   Mtgs - Expt - LG
<   Eucomed
M   226 f, 5 trade assns
¶   Health-Care Focus - 6.   In Focus - 6.   Primed - 24.   AR.

Association of British Independent Oil Exploration Companies
(BRINDEX)   1974
■   55 Riddlesdown Rd, PURLEY, Surrey, CR8 1DJ.   (hsp)
        020 8668 3359   fax 020 8668 3359
        http://www.brindex.co.uk
        Admin: Jackie Steer
○   *T; to develop & promote the British independent oil industry
Gp   North Sea taxation
●   Conf - Mtgs - SG
M   12 f

Association of British Insurers   (ABI)   1985
NR   51 Gresham St, LONDON, EC2V 7HQ.   (hq)
        020 7600 3333
○   *T; for insurers authorised to transact any class of insurance
        business in the UK
M   f

Association of British Introduction Agencies   (ABIA)   1981
NR   315 Chiswick High Rd (suite 109), LONDON, W4 4HH.
        (chmn/b)
        020 8742 0386
        email hhepercy@aol.com   http://www.abia.org.uk
        Chmn: Heather Heber-Percy
▲   Un-incorporated Society
○   *T; 'assisting consumer & agency with advice; monitoring
        industry & trying to persuade agencies to a set minimum
        standard of service'
●   Conf - Mtgs - ET - Res - Stat - Inf - LG
M   35 f
¶   LM - (updated); free.

Association of British Investigators   (ABI)   1913
■   295-297 Church St, BLACKPOOL, Lancs, FY1 3PJ.   (hsb)
        0871 474 0006; 01253 297502   fax 0871 474
        0007; 01253 752185
        email info@theabi.org.uk   http://www.theabi.org.uk
        Gen Sec: Eric Shelmerdine
▲   Company Limited by Guarantee
Br   4
○   *P; for private investigators & process servers (many members
        are certified bailiffs)
●   Conf - Mtgs - ET - Exam - Inf - LG
<   Intle Kommission der Detektiv-Verbände (IKD)
M   369 i, UK / 61 i, o'seas
¶   Investigate - 4.   LM - 1.

Association of British & Irish Showcaves   (ABIS)
NR   c/o Peak Cavern, Castleton, HOPE VALLEY, Derbys, S33 8WS.
        01433 620285
        email info@visitcaves.com   http://www.visitcaves.com
        Chmn: John Harrison
○   *T; underground tourist attractions across the British Isles
M   12 f

Association of British & Irish Wild Animal Keepers   (ABWAK)
1974
- ■ Twycross Zoo, Burton Rd, ATHERSTONE, Warks, CV9 3PX.
  (hsb)
  01827 883126   fax 01827 881049
  email amy.hulse@twycrosszoo.org
  http://www.abwak.co.uk
  Hon Sec: Amy Hulse
- ▲ Un-incorporated Society
- ○ *P, *V; captive husbandry of exotic animals in zoos & private
  collections
- ● Conf - Mtgs
- < Intl Congress of Zoo Keepers (ICZ)
- M 298 i, UK / 16 i, o'seas
  (Sub: £22 i, UK / £40 i, o'seas)
- ¶ RATEL (Jnl) - 4; £20 yr UK, £30 yr o'seas.
  Conference Proceedings (CD) - 1; £5 m, £7 nm.
- ✕ 2007 Association of British Wild Animal Keepers

Association of British Jazz Musicians   (ABJM)   1987
NR c/o Jazz Services Ltd, 132 Southwark St (1st floor), LONDON,
  SE1 0SW.   (hsb)
  020 7928 9089   fax 020 7401 6870
  email touring@jazzservices.org.uk
  http://www.jazzservices.org.uk
  Hon Sec: Chris Hodgkins
- ▲ Un-incorporated Society
- ○ *D; interests of jazz musicians in the UK
- ● Conf - Mtgs - Inf - LG
- M i
- ¶ ABJM News - 4.

Association of British Kart Clubs   (ABKC)   1990
- ■ Stoneycroft, Godsons Lane, Napton, SOUTHAM, Warks,
  CV47 8LX.   (sp)
  01926 812177   fax 01926 812177
  email secretary@abkc.org.uk   http://www.abkc.org.uk
  Sec: Graham Smith
- ▲ Un-incorporated Society
- ○ *N, *S; provision of technical & procedural regulations for
  competition kart racing in the UK
- ● Conf - Mtgs - Comp - Stat - Inf - Organisation of national
  championships - Setting technical regulations for kart racing
- < Motor Sports Assn
- M 31 clubs
- ¶ ABKC News - 4; free.

Association of British Language Schools   (ABLS)   1993
- ■ PO Box 3382, NORWICH, Norfolk, NR7 7HS.
  01493 393471
  email info@abls.co.uk   http://www.abls.co.uk
  Sec: Joanne Adcock
- ▲ Un-incorporated Society
- ○ *E, *P; accreditation body for establishments teaching English
  as a foreign language (TEFL)
- ● Conf - Mtgs - ET - Expt - Inf - LG - Lobbying embassies abroad
  - Networking for members
- M c 30 f
- ¶ LM - 1; free.

Association of British Mining Equipment Companies
(ABMEC)   1967
NR Unit 1 Thornes Office Park, Monckton Rd, WAKEFIELD, W Yorks,
  WF2 7AN.   (hq)
  01924 360200   fax 01924 380553
  email deakin@abmec.org.uk
  http://www.abmec.org.uk
  Dir Gen: Philip Deakin
- ▲ Un-incorporated Society
- ○ *T; to promote the UK mining equipment manufacturers
- ● Conf - Mtgs - ET - Exhib - Expt - Inf - LG
- M 33 f
- ¶ Buyers' Guide - 1. free.

Association of British Neurologists   (ABN)   1933
- ■ Ormond House, 27 Boswell St, LONDON, WC1N 3JZ.   (hq)
  020 7405 4060   fax 020 7405 4070
  email info@theabn.org   http://www.abn.org.uk
  Admin: Karen Reeves
- ▲ Registered Charity
- ○ *P; to promote education in, & the advancement of, the
  neurological sciences including the practice of neurology in
  the UK & Ireland
- ● Conf - ET - Res - Stat - LG
- M 1,000 i

Association of British Offshore Industries   (ABOI)   1983
NR 28-29 Threadneedle St, LONDON, EC2R 8AY.   (hq)
  020 7628 2555   fax 020 7638 4376
  email info@maritimeindustries.org
  http://www.maritimeindustries.org
  Dir: Ken Gibbons
- ○ *T; 'companies who develop specialist offshore systems &
  provide worldwide services & facilities for oil & gas
  exploration, production, transportation & conversion'
- ● Conf - Mtgs - Exhib - SG - Expt - LG
- < Soc of Maritime Inds
- M f

Association of British Orchestras   (ABO)   1947
- ■ 20 Rupert St, LONDON, W1D 6DF.   (hq)
  020 7287 0333   fax 020 7287 0444
  email info@abo.org.uk   http://www.abo.org.uk
  Dir: Mark Pemberton
- ▲ Company Limited by Guarantee
- ○ *N, *T; to support, develop & advance the interests & activities
  of orchestras in the UK
- ● Conf - Mtgs - ET - Res - Stat - Inf - Lib - Empl - LG - Seminars -
  Public symposia
- < Intl Alliance of Orchestral Assns (IAOA); Performing Arts
  Employers Assns League Europe (PEARLE); American
  Symphony Orchestra League (ASOL); Inc Soc of
  Musicians (ISM); Nat Campaign for the Arts (NCA); Sound
  Sense
- M 11 i, 47 f, 89 org, UK / 4 f, 5 org, o'seas
  (Sub: £260 f, UK)
- ¶ ABO Update (email NL) - 12; ftm.
  A Sound Ear; A Wright Reid (2001); £10.
  Knowing the Score 2; A Lewis-Crosby & R Moon (2002); £20.
  Review of the Year.
  Publications list available.

Association of British Paediatric Nurses   (ABPN)   1938
- ■ Faculty of Health, Birmingham City University, Westbourne Rd,
  Edgbaston, BIRMINGHAM, B15 3TN.   (chmn/b)
  http://www.abpn.org.uk
  Chmn: Duncan Randall
- ▲ Registered Charity
- ○ *P; to promote the development of children's nursing through
  evidence based information about practice & education
- Gp Children Nurse Education
- ● Conf - Mtgs - Exhib - LG - Policy influence - Scholarships
- M 1,000 i, UK / 20 i, o'seas
  (Sub: c £35).
- ¶ Jnl of Child Health Care - 4.   NL - 4;   AR - 1; all free.

Association of British Pewter Craftsmen   (ABPC)   1971
NR Unit 10 Edmund Road Business Centre, 135 Edmund Rd,
  SHEFFIELD, S Yorks, S2 4ED.   (asa)
  0114-252 7550   fax 0114-252 7555
  email enquiries@abpcltd.co.uk
  http://www.britishpewter.com
  Co Sec: Mrs C T Steele
- ▲ Company Limited by Guarantee
- ○ *T; the promotion of pewter
- ● Mtgs - Exhib - Inf
- < Worshipful Company of Pewterers
- M 35 f

© CBD Research Ltd · Beckenham · BR3 5JS · Tel 020 8650 7745 · Fax 020 8650 0768 · E-mail cbd@cbdresearch.com · www.cbdresearch.com

Association of the British Pharmaceutical Industry   (ABPI)   1930

NR   12 Whitehall, LONDON, SW1A 2DY.   (hq)
020 7930 3477   fax 020 7747 1411
http://www.abpi.org.uk
▲   Un-incorporated Society
Br   3
○   *T
●   Conf - Mtgs - ET - Exam - Stat - Inf - LG
M   [not stated]

Association of British Philatelic Societies Ltd   (ABPS)   1994

NR   4 Sunderland Place, Wellesbourne, WARWICK, CV35 9LE.
07879 665658
email searle@gmail.com   http://www.ukphilately.org.uk/abps
Sec: Colin Searle
▲   Company Limited by Guarantee
○   *N; to promote philately in the UK; to represent philatelic societies
●   Conf - Comp - SG - Inf
<   Fédn Intle de Philatélie; FEPA
M   c 400 org
¶   ABPS News (NL) - 4; ftm, £10 yr nm.
National & Specialists Society Hbk - 1.
ABPS Directory - 2 yrly; ftm, £15 nm.

Association of British Physiotherapists
alternative name of the **SMAE Fellowship**

Association of British Professional Conference Organisers   (ABPCO)   1981

NR   Charles House (6th floor), 148-149 Great Charles St,
BIRMINGHAM, B3 3HT.   (hq)
0121-212 1400   fax 0121-212 3131
email info@abpco.org   http://www.abpco.org
Exec Dir: Tony Rogers
▲   Company Limited by Guarantee
○   *P; to develop & enhance the professional status of conference & event organisers
●   Conf - Mtgs - ET - Exhib - Inf
<   Business Tourism Partnership
M   72 i

Association of British Riding Schools   (ABRS)   1954

■   Queen's Chambers, 38-40 Queen St, PENZANCE, Cornwall,
TR18 4BH.   (hq)
01736 369440   fax 01736 351390
email office@abrs-info.org   http://www.abrs-info.org
Chmn: Julian Marczak
▲   Company Limited by Guarantee
○   *P, *S; to raise the standards of riding instruction & horsemanship
●   Conf - ET - Exam - Exhib - LG
<   Cent Coun for Physical Recreation (CCPR); Brit Equestrian Fedn (BEF); Lantra; Brit Equestrian Tr Assn (BETA); Nat Equine Forum
M   450 i, 350 f, UK / 20 i, 16 f, o'seas
¶   NL - 3/4; ftm only.
Locations leaflet - 1; free.

Association of British Roofing Felt Manufacturers
was, after 1997 merger with the Flat Roofing Contractors' Advisory Board, a separate entity within the **Flat Roofing Alliance**

Association of British Sailmakers   (ABS)   1984

NR   2 Orchard Rd, Locks Heath, SOUTHAMPTON, Hants,
SO31 6PR.   (hsp/b)
01489 601517 (0900-1700)   fax 01489 601518
○   *T; to provide technical support for sailmakers

Association of British Salted Fish Curers & Exporters

This organisation has effectively closed

Association of British Science Writers   (ABSW)   1947

NR   Wellcome Wolfson Building, 165 Queen's Gate, LONDON,
SW7 5HD.   (hsb)
0870 770 3361
Admin: Barbara Drillsma
○   *P; to encourage & improve science writing in the UK
●   Mtgs - VE
<   Eur U of Science Journalists' Assns (EUSJA)
M   900 i
¶   NL - 12; ftm only.

Association of British Scrabble Players   (ABSP)   1986

NR   206 Cleveland Rd High Barnes, SUNDERLAND, Tyne & Wear,
SR4 7QR.   (hsp)
email secretary@absp.org.uk   http://www.absp.org.uk
Sec: Laura Finley
○   *G; to promote matchplay scrabble tournaments
●   Comp
<   Wld Engl Speaking Scrabble Players Asn
M   c 700 i
¶   The Last Word - 6; £15 yr m.

Association of British Tennis Officials   (ABTO)   2000

NR   Officiating Dept, The Lawn Tennis Association, The National
Tennis Centre, 100 Priory Lane, Roehampton, LONDON,
SW15 5JQ.   (hq)
020 8487 7000   fax 420 8487 7301
Hon Sec: B L J Maddock,
Officiating Mgr: W J Perkins
○   *P; to officiate at tennis events & apply & uphold rules & regulations in force; to promote advancement of high standards for tennis officials
Gp   Referees; Umpires
●   Mtgs - ET - Exam - Inf - Empl
<   Lawn Tennis Assn
M   920 i, UK / 40 i, o'seas
¶   Officiating News (NL) - 4;   ABTO Members' Hbk - 1;
ABTO Constitution & Procedures - 1;   AR - 1; all free.

Association of British Theatre Technicians   (ABTT)   1961

NR   55 Farringdon Rd, LONDON, EC1M 3JB.   (hq)
020 7242 9200
email office@abtt.org.uk   http://www.abtt.org.uk
▲   Registered Charity
○   *A, *P; 'to act as a forum for theatre technicians & express their corporate view on matters affecting the industry; to collect & disseminate technical information; to advise on the planning of new theatres & the conversion of existing buildings'
M   i

Association of British Theological & Philosophical Libraries   (ABTAPL)   1956

NR   c/o Alan Linfield, London Sch of Theology, Green Lane,
NORTHWOOD, Middx, HA6 2UW.   (chmn/b)
01923 456192
http://www.abtapl.org.uk
Chmn: Alan Linfield
○   *P; to promote bibliographical work & common interests among librarians specialising in theology, religious studies & philosophy
●   Conf - ET - inf
<   Bibliothèques Européenes de Théologie
M   97 i, 75 f, 5 org, UK / 29 i, 44 f, o'seas
¶   Bulletin - 3; ftm.

Association of British Tour Operators to France Ltd (ABTOF) 1993

NR Ravensbourne, Westerham Road, KESTON, Kent, BR2 6HE. (hq)
01689 868112   fax 01689 868115
email info@abtof.org.uk
Chief Exec: Richard Brierly
▲ Company Limited by Guarantee
○ *T
Gp French & UK affiliate members who are suppliers of services to ABTOF members
● Conf - Mtgs - ET - Exhib - SG - Stat - Inf - VE - LG - PR Service
M 220 f, UK / 70 f, o'seas
¶ ABTOF News Update - 12; ftm only.

Association of British Transport & Engineering Museums (ABTEM) 1962

■ c/o Tim Bryan, Heritage Motor Centre, Banbury Rd, GAYDON, Warks, CV35 0BJ.   (hsb)
01926 645105   fax 01926 645111
email tbryan9@landrover.com   http://www.abtem.co.uk
Hon Sec: Tim Bryan
▲ Un-incorporated Society
○ *N; to act as a forum for the discussion of matters of common interest to transport & engineering museums; to provids a means of representing their views on matters of inportance
● Conf - VE
M c 20 i, c 50 org
(Sub £10 i, £22 f)
¶ NL - 4.

Association of British Travel Agents Ltd (ABTA) 1950

NR 68-71 Newman St, LONDON, W1T 3AH.   (hq)
020 7637 2444   fax 020 7637 0713
email abta@abta.co.uk   http://www.abta.com
Sec: Riccardo Nardi
▲ Company Limited by Guarantee
○ *T; interests of travel agents and tour operators in GB and Ireland; administration of codes of conduct; administration of tour operators' bonds & their utilisation as public protection in the event of financial failure; administration of fund for compensation of holidaymakers in case of financial failure by retail travel agent
Gp Airways; Railways; Roadways; Shipping; UK tourism; Technology; Insurance; Finance; Codes of conduct; ABTA National Training Board, Woking, Surrey
● Conf - Mtgs - ET - Res - Inf - LG
< Confedn of Brit Ind (CBI), Assn of Travel Agents & Tour Operators in the EU (ECTAA)
M 2,700 f
¶ ABTA Magazine - 12; ftm only.

Association of British Veterinary Acupuncture
a group of the **British Small Animal Veterinary Association**

Association of British Wild Animal Keepers
since 2007 **Association of British & Irish Wild Animal Keepers**

Association of Broadcasting Doctors (ABD) 1988

■ 1 Lark Bank, Prickwillow, ELY, Cambs, CB7 4SW.   (hq)
01353 687966
email jackiepetts@mac.com
http://www.broadcasting-doctor.org
Dir: Jacqueline Petts
▲ Un-incorporated Society
○ *P; to represent practising clinicians who also broadcast on radio & TV
Gp Dentists' media
● Conf - Mtgs - ET - Inf - Lib - LG
< GP Writers Assn
M 760 i
¶ NL - 12.

Association of Brokers & Yacht Agents (ABYA)

■ The Glass Works, Penns Rd, PETERSFIELD, Hants, GU32 2EW. (hq)
01730 266430   fax 01730 710423
email info@ybdsa.co.uk   http://www.abya.co.uk
Chief Exec: Jane Gentry
▲ Company Limited by Guarantee
Br Spain
○ *P; for yacht brokers, agents & dealers
● Conf - Mtgs
M 85 i, UK / 15 f, o'seas
¶ NL - 4; ftm only.
Note: The Yacht Brokers, Designers & Surveyors Association is the management company for the ABYA & the Yacht Designers & Surveyors Association

Association of Building Cleaning Direct Service Providers (ABCD) 1989

■ PO Box 137, NORTHAMPTON, NN3 6AD.   (hsp)
01604 705934   fax 01604 705934
email abcd@wherton.freeserve.co.uk
http://www.abcdsp.org.uk
Exec Gen Sec: Patricia Wherton
▲ Un-incorporated Society
Br 3
○ *T; to support managers of direct service cleaning provision in local authorities throughout the UK
● Conf - Mtgs - Exhib - Stat - LG
< Asset Skills; Brit Cleaning Coun; Assn of Public Service Excellence; Brit Brit Inst of Cleaning Science
M 75 local authorities, 20 suppliers
(Sub: £205)

Association of Building Component Manufacturers Ltd (ABCM) 1965

NR Clark House, 3 Brassey Drive, AYLESFORD, Kent, ME20 7QL. (hq)
01622 715577   fax 0870 054 3915
email abcm@building-components.org
http://www.building-components.org
Dir: Peter B Caplin
▲ Company Limited by Guarantee
○ *T; to provide commercial & technical intelligence to members
Gp Technical; Commercial c'ee
● Conf - Mtgs - LG
< BSI; Roofing Ind Alliance
M 24 f
¶ NL - 8; ftm only.

Association of Building Engineers (ABE) 1925

■ Lutyens House, Billing Brook Rd, Weston Favell, NORTHAMPTON, NN3 8NW.   (hq)
01604 404121   fax 01604 784220
email building.engineers@abe.org.uk
http://www.abe.org.uk
Chief Exec: David R Gibson
▲ Company Limited by Guarantee
○ *P; to promote & advance the study & practice of the arts & sciences concerned with building technology, planning, design, construction, maintenance & repair of the built environment
Gp Fire safety engineering; ABE Assess - home inspector training
● Conf - ET - Exam - Inf - Lib - LG
< Assn d'Experts Eur du Bâtiment et de la Construction (AEEBC); Construction Ind Coun
M 5,000 i, 200 f, UK / 400 i, o'seas
(Sub: from £45 for students to £200 for fellows)
2008 (April) Institute of Maintenance & Building Management (merged)
¶ Building Engineer - 12; ftm, £40 yr nm.
AR; free.

Association of Building Hardware Manufacturers
2005 merged with the Door & Shutter Manufacturers' Association to form the **Door & Hardware Federation**

© CBD Research Ltd · Beckenham · BR3 5JS · Tel 020 8650 7745 · Fax 020 8650 0768 · E-mail cbd@cbdresearch.com · www.cbdresearch.com

Association of Burial Authorities Ltd (ABA) 1993

- ■ Waterloo House, 155 Upper St, LONDON, N1 1RA. (hq)
  020 7288 2522 fax 020 7288 2533
  email aba@burials.org.uk http://www.burials.org.uk
  Chief Exec & Hon Sec: Deborah Powton
  Dir: John Clark
- ▲ Company Limited by Guarantee
- ○ *T; to promote & protect the interests of organisations engaged in the management & operation of burial grounds
- ● Conf - Res - Comp - Inf - Lib - VE - LG - Advice on planning, designing & layout of burial grounds & extensions, & on acquisitions of burial grounds (incl churchyards, municipal & private cemeteries) - Legal advice
- < Fédn Intle des Assns Thanatologues FIAT/IFTA); Assn Significant Cemeteries Europe (ASCE); Eur Fedn of Funeral Services (EFFS); Coun Brit Funeral Services
- M 9 i, 23 f, 315 local authorities
  (Sub: £24 i, £175 f, £90-£335 local authorities
- ¶ ABA Info (NL) - 4.
  ABA Informatives - factsheets. .
  Cemetery & Churchyard Regulations.
  Planning for Memorials.
  Planning for Memorials after Cremation.
  Guide to Funerals & Bereavement.
  ABA/ZM Guide to Safety in Burial Grounds.

Association of Business Administration (ABA) 1984

- ■ PO Box 70, LONDON, E13 0UU. (hq)
  0870 042 2062
  email info@business-administration.org.uk
  http://www.business-administration.org.uk
  Dir: C Oham
- ○ *P; to encourage professional business administration especially in education, training & professional practice
- ● ET - Exam - SG
- M [not stated]
- ¶ ABA Jnl - 4; ftm, £25 nm. Membership Hbk; ftm, £5 nm.
  Dictionary of Business Administration; [to come 2009].
  Directory of Business Administration - 1.

Association of Business-to-Business Agencies (ABBA) 1985

- ■ Clarence Mill, Clarence Rd, Bollington, MACCLESFIELD, Cheshire, SK10 5JZ. (hq)
  01625 578511 fax 01625 578579
  email info@abba.co.uk http://www.abba.co.uk
  Chmn: John Stanton
- ▲ Un-incorporated Society
- ○ *P; to establish professional standards of service & competence in business to business marketing; to encourage a strategic, business-focussed, integrated approach
- Gp Business to business marketing & communications
- ● Conf - Mtgs - ET - Res - Exhib - Stat
- M 26 f
  (Sub: £1,250)

Association of Business Executives (ABE) 1973

- ■ CI Tower (5th floor), St Georges Sq, NEW MALDEN, Surrey, KT3 4TE. (hq)
  020 8329 2930 fax 020 8329 2945
  email info@abeuk.com http://www.abeuk.com
  Founder/Chmn: Lyndon Jones
- ▲ Company Limited by Guarantee
- Br 11 countries
- ○ *P; examination board setting professional qualifications & advanced diplomas in business nominations, business information systems, travel, tourism & hospitality resource management
- ● Conf - ET - Exam
- M 4,000 i, UK / 18,000 i, o'seas
- ¶ Business Executives - 2; ftm, £20 nm.

Association of Business Managers & Administrators (ABMA) 1975

- ■ Wembley Point (18th floor), 1 Harrow Rd, WEMBLEY, Middx, HA9 6DE. (hq)
  020 8733 7000 fax 020 8733 7033
  email info@abma.uk.com http://www.abma.uk.com
  Senior Exec: Alan Hodson
- ▲ Company Limited by Guarantee
- ○ *T; a non-profit making, independent examinations board, recognised worldwide for providing a unique solution in terms of British qualifications; offers customised courses to suit the needs of both institutions & students as direct entry requirements for bachelor courses in the UK & USA
- ● ET - Exam
- M c 12,000 i, 89 f, affiliated universities in UK & USA

Association of Business Psychologists (ABP) 2000

- ■ 211-212 Piccadilly, LONDON, W1J 9HG. (hsb)
  020 7917 1733
  email admin@theabp.org http://www.theabp.org
  Gen Administrator: Richard Taylor
- ▲ Company Limited by Guarantee
- ○ *P; for practitioners in business psychology
- ● Conf - Mtgs - ET - Res - Inf - LG
- M 900 i, UK / 10 i, o'seas
- ¶ NL - 3 [email].

Association of Business Recovery Professionals (R3) 1990

- NR 120 Aldersgate St (8th floor), LONDON, EC1A 4JQ. (hq)
  020 7566 4200 fax 020 7566 4224
  http://www.r3.org.uk
- ▲ Company Limited by Guarantee
- ○ *P; for all those who deal with Britain's underperforming businesses & individuals in financial trouble
- Gp Insolvency practitioners; Turnaround specialists
- ● Conf - Mtgs - ET - SG - Lib - LG
- < Insol Intl
- M 3,400 i
- ¶ Recovery - 4; ftm only.

Association of Business Schools (ABS) 1992

- NR 137 Euston Rd, LONDON, NW1 2AA. (hq)
  020 7388 0007
  Chief Exec: Jonathan Slack
- ○ *P; to promote business & management education, training & development so as to improve the quality & effectiveness of the practice of management in the UK
- ● Conf - Mtgs - Res - Inf - LG
- M 100 f, 6 org
- ¶ The ABS Directory of Business Schools - 1.

Association of Button Merchants 1928

- ■ Southernhay (suite 7), 207 Hook Rd, CHESSINGTON, Surrey, KT9 1HJ. (asa)
  020 8391 2266 fax 020 8391 4466
  email abm@sleat.co.uk
  Sec: David M Hart
- ▲ Company Limited by Guarantee
- ○ *T; interests of button merchants in the UK
- ● Mtgs - Inf
- < Brit Button Coun
- M 15 f
- ¶ NL - irreg; AR; both m only.

Association for Cancer Surgery
      styles itself **BASO ~ the Association for Cancer Surgery**

Association of Cannibals' Equipment Suppliers (ACES) 2000
■ 15 Wickham Road, BECKENHAM, Kent, BR3 5JS. (hq)
○ *T
Gp Vegetarian
● Conf - Mtgs - Exhib - Expt - Lib - Stat - VE - LG
M f
¶ Eat You - 4; ftm only.
   Note: this is a control entry

Association of Canoe Trades (ACT) 1970
NR Kenn Business Park, Kenn Rd, CLEVEDON, Somerset,
    BS21 6TH. (hsb)
    01275 796100   fax 01275 796110
    email act@britishmarine.co.uk
    Sec: Bob Slee
▲ Un-incorporated Society
○ *T; the manufacture, retailing, design & safety of canoes,
    kayaks & their accessories
● Mtgs - ET - Res - Exhib - Stat - Expt - Inf - PL - LG
< Brit Marine Fedn
M 22 f

**Association of Caravan & Camping Exempted Organisations
(ACCEO) 1985**
■ PO Box 5191, RUGELEY, Staffs, WS15 9BS. (hq)
    0845 419 1520
    http://www.acceo.org.uk
○ *N, *T; for camping & caravanning clubs holding meetings of
    not more than 5 days; site licences are not required if the site
    is under the supervision of an organisation holding the
    Certificate of Exemption from the Dept for Environment, Food
    & Rural Affairs; ACCEO is one of 5 organisations permitted,
    in conjunction with member clubs, to hold meetings of up to
    28 days
M i in c 200 clubs

Association of Cardiothoracic Anaesthetists (ACTA) 1985
NR Dept of Anaesthesia, Golden Jubilee National Hospital,
    Beardmore St, CLYDEBANK, G81 4HX. (hsb)
    0141-951 5600
    http://www.acta.org.uk
    Sec: Dr Alistair Macfie
▲ Company Limited by Guarantee
○ *M, *P; promotion education, training, taching & research in
    the field of cardiothoracic anaesthesia & intensive care
● Conf - Mtgs - ET - Exam - Res - Stat - Inf
< Eur Assn of Cardiothoracic Anaesthesia
M 470 i
¶ ACTA News - 2; ftm only.

Association for Careers Education & Guidance (ACEG) 1969
■ 9 Lawrence Leys, Bloxham, BANBURY, Oxon, OX15 4NU.
    (hsp)
    01295 720809   fax 01295 720809
    email info@aceg.org.uk   http://www.aceg.org.uk
    Sec: Alan Vincent
▲ Company Limited by Guarantee
○ *E, *P; to promote excellence & innovation in careers education
    & guidance for all young people
● Conf - ET - Res - Inf - LG
< Intl Assn Educl & Vocational Guidance; Fedn of Profl Assns in
    Guidance; Guidance Coun; Profl Assns Res Network
M 1,750 i
¶ Careers Education & Guidance (Jnl) - 4; ftm, £10.50 nm.
× 2006 (January) National Association of Careers & Guidance
    Teachers

Association of Catering Excellence (ACE) 1937
■ Bourne House, Horsell Park, WOKING, Surrey, GU21 4LY.
    (hq)
    01483 765111   fax 01483 751991
    email admin@acegb.org   http://www.acegb.org
    Admin: Vic Laws
▲ Company Limited by Guarantee
Br 8
○ *P; provision of catering services - comprising managers,
    executives, contract caterers, etc
● Conf - Mtgs - ET - Exhib - Comp - Inf - Lib - VE - Book service
< Eur Catering Assn
M 200 i, 30 f
× 2006 European Catering Association (GB)

Association of Celebrity Assistants (UK) (ACA (UK)) 2003
NR 206 Canalot Studios, 222 Kensal Rd, LONDON, W10 5BN.
    (hq)
    email hello@aca-uk.com   http://www.aca-uk.com
    Sec: Carlene Findlay
○ *P; personal assistants who work for high profile individuals in
    the worlds of film, TV, theatre, music, fashion & beauty,
    charity, business and politics
× United Kingdom Association of Celebrity Assistants

Association of Cereal Food Manufacturers (ACFM) 1955
NR 6 Catherine St, LONDON, WC2B 5JJ. (hq)
    020 7420 7113   fax 020 7836 0580
    email geraldine.smith@fdf.org.uk
    http://www.fdf.org.uk
    Exec Sec: Geraldine Smith
▲ Un-incorporated Society
○ *T; manufacturers of breakfast cereal products
● Mtgs - Inf
< Eur Breakfast Cereal Assn (CEEREAL); Food & Drink Fedn
M 8 f

Association of Certified Commercial Diplomats (ACCD) 2006
■ PO Box 50561, Docklands, LONDON, E16 3WY. (hq)
    0870 321 9481   fax 0870 321 9437
    email enquiries@chartereddiplomats.org
    http://www.chartereddiplomats.org
    Mem Sec: Miss Debbie Bailey
▲ Company Limited by Guarantee
Br Brunei, Cambodia, North Borneo, Saudi Arabia, UAE
○ *P; an independent, global institution providing training &
    accreditation for commercial & economic diplomats in
    government ministries, parastatals, corporations, diplomatic
    missions, educational institutions & intergovernmental
    organisations
● Conf - Mtgs - ET - Exam - Res - SG - Lib - VE - LG -
    Accreditation
< United Nations Global Compact; OECD; UN Office on Drugs
    & Crime; Inst for Tr & Comml Diplomacy; UN Principles for
    Responsible Mgt Educ
> Eur Diplomatic Acad; Eur Inst Campus Stellae; Instn of Comml
    Diplomats
M [not stated]

Association of Certified IT Professionals
NR Wolverton Park, WOLVERTON, Hants, RG26 5RU. (hq)
    0845 060 3456   fax 01494 483581
    http://www.acitp.com
    Chief Exec: Garry Carter
▲ Company Limited by Guarantee
M 10,000 i
    no further information supplied

© CBD Research Ltd · Beckenham · BR3 5JS · Tel 020 8650 7745 · Fax 020 8650 0768 · E-mail cbd@cbdresearch.com · www.cbdresearch.com

Association of Charitable Foundations (ACF) 1989

NR   Central House, 14 Upper Woburn Place, LONDON,
WC1H 0AE.   (hq)
020 7255 4499   fax 020 7255 4496
email acf@acf.org.uk   http://www.acf.org.uk
Chief Exec: David Emerson

▲   Company Limited by Guarantee; Registered Charity
○   *N; to promote & support the work of charitable grant-making
trusts & foundations
Gp   Alcohol & drugs; Arts; Children & young people; Disability;
Education; Environment; Health; Housing; Individuals in
need; International; Neighbourhood issues; Northern
Ireland; Penal affairs; Race equality; Rural issues; Scotland;
Strategic issues in the voluntary sector; Wales; Women's
issues
●   Conf - Mtgs - Inf - LG
M   300 org
¶   Trust & Foundation News - 4; ftm.   NL.   AR.
A Guide to Giving (2nd ed); £20.
Monitoring & Evaluation; a practical guide for grant-making
trusts; £10.
SORP Made Simple: a guidance for grant-making
charities (2006).
Why Rich People Give; £15.
Various other publications.

Association for Charities (AfC) 1999

NR   83 Priory Gardens, LONDON, N6 5QU.   (hsb/p)
020 8348 9114
http://www.association4charities.org
Coordinator: Belinda McKenzie
▲   Un-incorporated Society
○   *K; to support & protect charities, trustees & beneficiaries
affected by the actions of Charity Commission for England &
Wales; to campaign for a fairer system of charity regulation
& a more accountable Commission
●   Conf - Mtgs - Lib (video) - Public seminars
M   50 i, 30 charities
¶   New Help for Charities (2001): a leaflet.

Association of Charity Independent Examiners (ACIE) 1999

■   Bentley Resource Centre, High St, Bentley, DONCASTER,
S Yorks, DN5 0AA.   (asa)
01302 828338   fax 01302 872973
email info@acie.org.uk   http://www.acie.org.uk
Dir: Fiona Gordon
▲   Registered Charity; Un-incorporated Society
○   *P; to promote the greater effectiveness of UK charities by
providing support & encouraging professional standards for
all persons acting as independent examiners of charity
accounts
●   Conf - ET - Exam - Inf - LG
M   570 i
¶   Independent Examiner (NL) - 3; ftm, £40 yr nm.
ACIE Hbk - 1; ftm, £10 nm.
AR & Financial Statement - 1; free.

Association of Charity Officers (ACO) 1946

■   Five Ways, 57-59 Hatfield Rd, POTTERS BAR, Herts,
EN6 1HS.   (hq)
01707 651777   fax 01707 660477
email info@aco.uk.net   http://www.aco.uk.net
Dir: Mrs Valerie J Barrow
Chmn: Mike Carter
▲   Registered Charity
○   *N, *W; to promote efficiency & encourage liaison &
cooperation between charities
Gp   Forums: Residential care - dealing with all matters relating to
residential & nursing home care; Grant making - dealing
with all matters relating to grant aid for individuals /
benevolence & the interface with Social Security; special work
on occupational benevolent funds; Under 5's group for very
small charities
●   Mtgs - Res - LG
<   Age Concern; NCVO; HELPLINES for members
M   250 charities (giving non-contributory relief)
¶   NL - 4/5.   AR.
Various other publications - irreg.

Association of Charity Shops (ACS) 1999

■   Central House, 14 Upper Woburn Place, LONDON,
WC1H 0AE.   (hq)
020 7255 4470   fax 020 7255 4475
email mail@charityshops.org.uk
http://www.charityshops.org.uk
Exec Sec: Lekha Klouda
▲   Company Limited by Guarantee
○   *N; to promote & support charities, that run shops as part of
their fund-raising activities, by pooling expertise to enable
them to run their shops as effectively as possible
●   Conf - Mtgs - ET - Res - Exhib - Stat - LG
<   Brit Retail Consortium
M   c 250 charities, c 30 associate m (commercial interests)
¶   Bulletin - 10;   AR - 1; both free.

Association of Charter Trustee Towns & Charter Town Councils (ACTCTC) 1975

■   Barratts Court, Rectory Lane, Rock, KIDDERMINSTER, Worcs,
DY14 9RR.   (hsb/hsp)
01299 832797
email charles@talbotkidder.demon.co.uk
Hon Sec: Charles Ellis Talbot
▲   Un-incorporated Society
○   *N; to preserve & enhance the status & traditions of charter
trustee cities, towns & charter town councils
●   Conf - Mtgs - Inf - LG
M   16 towns

Association of Chartered Certified Accountants (ACCA) 1904

■   29 Lincoln's Inn Fields, LONDON, WC2A 3EE.   (hq)
020 7059 5000   fax 020 7059 5959
email info@accaglobal.com
http://www.accaglobal.com
Sec: Michael Sleigh
▲   Incorporated by Royal Charter
Br   3; Botswana, China, Ethiopia, Ghana, Ireland, Malaysia,
Mauritius, Pakistan, Singapore, UAE, Vietnam
○   *P
●   Mtgs - ET - Exam - Inf - LG
<   Intl Fedn of Accountants; Intl Accounting Standings Bd
M   58,000 i, UK / 68,000 i, o'seas
(Sub: £175 UK & o'seas)
¶   Jnl - 12; ftm, £10 nm.
Rulebook - 1; £20 (+available online).   AR - 1; ftm.

** Association of Chief Archivists in Local Government

Organisation lost: see Introduction paragraph 3.

Association of Chief Estates Surveyors & Property Managers in the Public Sector   (ACES)   1908
- ■ 23 Athol Rd, BRAMHALL, Cheshire, SK7 1BR.   (sb)
  0161-439 9589
  email secretary@aces.org.uk   http://www.aces.org.uk
  Consultant Sec: Tim Foster
- ▲ Un-incorporated Society
- Br 10
- ○ *P; to provide a forum for debate about public property; sharing of best practice in property asset management
- Gp Housing; Town centre management; Best value; PFI; Regeneration; Rural affairs; Compensation
- ● Conf - Mtgs - Res - LG
- < Fedn of Property Socs
- M 390 i
- ¶ The Terrier - 4; free,   Per Annum (Ybk) - 1; ftm only.
- × Association of Chief Estates Officers & Property Managers in Local Government.

Association of Chief Executives of Voluntary Organisations (ACEVO)   1988
- NR 1 New Oxford St, LONDON, WC1A 1NU.   (hq)
  0845 345 8481   fax 0845 345 8482
  email info@acevo.org.uk   http://www.acevo.org.uk
  Chief Exec: Stephen Bubb
- ▲ Company Limited by Guarantee
- ○ *P; for chief executives of voluntary organisations in England & Wales
- ● Conf - Mtgs - ET - Res - Exhib - LG
- M 1,500 i, 125 f, 40 org
- ¶ NoticeBoard (NL) - 9;   Hbk - 1;   Annual Review; all ftm only.
  Basic Guides to Good Practice [20 published]; £5 each.
  Replacing the State?; £12.50.
  Publications list available.
- × 2000 (February) Association of Chief Executives of National Voluntary Organisations

Association of Chief Officers of Scottish Voluntary Organisations (ACOSVO)
- ■ Thorn House, 5 Rose St, EDINBURGH, EH2 2PR.
  0131-243 2755
  email office@acosvo.org.uk   http://www.acosvo.org.uk
  Exec Dir: Pat Armstrong
- ○ *P: to promote excellence in leadership & management in the voluntary sector
  No further information supplied

Association of Chief Police Officers of England, Wales & Northern Ireland   (ACPO)   1948
- NR 10 Victoria St (1st floor), LONDON, SW1H 0NN.   (hq)
- ○ *P
- M i

Association of Chief Police Officers in Scotland   (ACPOS)   1870
- ■ 26 Holland St, GLASGOW, G2 4NH.   (hsb)
  0141-435 1230
  email secretariat@acpos.pnn.police.uk
  http://www.acpos.police.uk
  Hon Sec: Sir William Rae
- ○ *N; to oversee the direction & development of the Scottish Police Service
- Gp Crime; Finance; General policing; Road policing; Information management; Personnel & training; Professional standards; Diversity; Criminal justice; Performance; Management
- ● Conf - Mtgs - Empl - LG
- M i
- ¶ AR - 1.

Association of Child Abuse Lawyers   (ACAL)
- NR Claremont House (suite 5), 22-24 Claremont Rd, SURBITON, Surrey, KT6 4QU.   (asa)
  020 8390 4701   fax 020 8399 1152
  http://www.childabuselawyers.com
- ○ *P

Association for Child & Adolescent Mental Health   (ACAMH)   1956
- NR St Saviour's House, 39-41 Union St, LONDON, SE1 1SD.   (hq)
  020 7403 7458   fax 020 7403 7081
  email acamh@acamh.org.uk
  http://www.acamh.org.uk
  Exec Dir: Ingrid King
- ▲ Registered Charity
- Br 2
- ○ *L; to further the study of the mental health of children, young people & their families, through the media of meetings & publications
- ● Mtgs - ET - Res - SG - Inf
- M 2,410 i, UK / 300 i, o'seas
- ¶ Jnl of Child Psychology & Psychiatry - 8.
  Child & Adolescent Mental Health - 4.
- × 2006 (March) Association for Child Psychology & Psychiatry

Association for Child Psychology & Psychiatry
  since March 2006 **Association for Child & Adolescent Mental Health**

Association of Child Psychotherapists   (ACP)   1949
- NR 120 West Heath Rd, LONDON, NW3 7TU.   (hq)
  020 8458 1609   fax 020 8458 1482
  email admin@acp-uk.eu   http://www.acp.uk.net
- ○ *P
- ● Mtgs - Lectures
- M 693 i

Association for Children with Hand or Arm Deficiency
  alternative name of **REACH**

Association for Children with Heart Disorders
  since 2005 **Children's Heart Association**

Association of Children's Hospices
- NR Canningford House (1st floor), 38 Victoria St, BRISTOL, BS1 6BY.
  0117-989 7820
  http://www.childhospice.org.uk
- ○ *M

Association for Children with Life-Threatening or Terminal Conditions & their Families
  since June 2006 **Association for Children's Palliative Care**

Association for Children's Palliative Care   (ACT)   1993
- ■ Orchard House, Orchard Lane, BRISTOL, BS1 5DT.
  0117-922 1556 (admin)   fax 0117-930 4707
  email info@act.org.uk   http://www.act.org.uk
  Chief Exec Officer: Lizzie Chambers
- ▲ Company Limited by Guarantee
- ○ *K, *M, *W; campaigns for the provision of locally coordinated palliative care services for terminally ill children; to provide information on services available to families caring for a child with a life-threatening or terminal condition
- Gp ACT Council (Chmn: Heather Wood),
  Children's palliative care (Chmn: Dr Angela Thompson)
- ● Conf - Mtgs - ET - Inf - Lib - LG
  Helpline: 0845 108 2201
- < Inst of Child Health (Bristol)
- M [not stated]
  (Sub: £50 i, £60-£150 f UK / £70 i, £80-170 f o'seas)
- ¶ Act Now (NL) - 5; ftm, £20 yr nm.
  Act for Families - 5; ftm, £20 yr nm.
  Transition Care Pathway; ftm, £10 nm.
  Voice for Change (2003).
  Other publications.
- × 2006 (June) Association for Children with Life-Threatening or Terminal Conditions & their Families

© CBD Research Ltd · Beckenham · BR3 5JS · Tel 020 8650 7745 · Fax 020 8650 0768 · E-mail cbd@cbdresearch.com · www.cbdresearch.com

Association of Christian Teachers   (ACT)   1971
NR   94A London Rd, ST ALBANS, Herts, AL1 1NX.   (hq)
       01727 840298
       http://www.christian-teachers.org
▲   Company Limited by Guarantee; Registered Charity
○   *E, *R; to support Christians employed in education
M   i

Association for Church Editors
NR   Carousel, 1 Barrow Slade, Keyworth, NOTTINGHAM,
       NG12 5JQ.   (mem/office)
       0115-914 2930   fax 0115-914 2960
       http://www.ac-editors.co.uk
       Sec: Margaret Wood
○   *P; for all editors of church magazines
M   i

Association of Circulation Executives   (ACE)   1951
NR   5 Willesborough Court, Willesborough Lees, ASHFORD, Kent,
       TN24 0SW.
       01233 662369
       http://www.acecirculation.com
       Contact: Trevor Collier
▲   Un-incorporated Society
○   *P, *T; for senior executives responsible for circulation,
       marketing & distribution of newspapers, magazines,
       periodicals (national & regional); for the dissemination of
       information & promotion of goodwill between publishers
       (members) & the wholesalers & retailers who handle their
       publications
●   Conf - Mtgs - ET - Exhib - SG
M   420 i, UK / 6 i, o'seas
¶   Sisyphus (NL) - 4; free.

Association of Circus Proprietors of Great Britain   (ACP)   1932
■   PO Box 131, BLACKBURN, Lancs, BB1 9GA.   (hsp)
       01254 814789   fax 01254 814789
       email malcolmclay@talk21.com
       http://www.circus-uk.co.uk
       Sec: Malcolm S Clay
▲   Un-incorporated Society
○   *T; the conduct of the circus industry in GB; the welfare of
       animals in circuses
●   Conf - Mtgs - Inf - LG
M   20 f

Association of Civic Hosts
       in 2006 merged with the **Association for Public Service
       Excellence**

Association of Civil Enforcement Agencies   (ACEA)   1996
NR   513 Bradford Rd, BATLEY, W Yorks, WF17 8LL.   (regd/office)
       01924 350090   fax 01924 474441
       email dir-gen@acea.org.uk   http://www.acea.org.uk
       Dir Gen: Dr Steven Everson
▲   Company Limited by Guarantee
○   *P; to promote higher standards in the civil enforcement
       industry
●   Mtgs - Res - Empl - LG
M   26 i, 31 f

Association of Classic Trials Clubs Ltd   (ACTC)   1979
■   Dumbleton Brook, TENBURY WELLS, Worcs, WR15 8JR.   (hsp)
       01584 881348
       http://www.actc.org.uk
▲   Company Limited by Guarantee
Br   22
○   *K, *S; to promote grass-roots motorsport through national
       classic reliability trials championships for cars & motorcycles
Gp   Technical panel; Public relations; Rights of way; Championships
●   Mtgs - Exhib - Comp - PL - LG
<   Motor Sports Assn UK; Byways & Bridleways Trust Coun
M   c 3,000 i, 22 org
¶   Restart - 4.

Association for Clinical Biochemistry   (ACB)   1953
NR   130-132 Tooley St, LONDON, SE1 2TU.   (hq)
       020 7403 8001   fax 020 7403 8006
       email admin@acb.org.uk   http://www.acb.org.uk
       Chmn: Dr I D Watson,   Hon Sec: Dr G McCreanor
▲   Company Limited by Guarantee
○   *L; advancement of clinical biochemistry in the UK
Gp   C'ees: Scientific, Education, Publications, Workforce advisory
●   Conf - Mtgs - ET - Res - Exhib - Empl - LG
<   Intl Fedn of Clinical Chemistry (IFCC)
M   1,835 i, 56 f, UK / 306 i, o'seas
¶   Annals of Clinical Biochemistry - 6; ftm, £136 yr nm.
×   2005 Association of Clinical Biochemists

Association for Clinical Cytogenetics
       a group of the **British Society for Human Genetics**

Association for Clinical Data Management   (ACDM)
NR   105 St Peter's St, ST ALBANS, Herts, AL1 3EJ.   (hq)
       01727 896080
       http://www.acdm.org.uk
       Sec: Angela Ison
▲   Company Limited by Guarantee
○   *P; data management in the pharmaceutical industry
<   Conf - Mtgs - ET - Exam - Exhib
M   1,438 i, UK / 259 i, o'seas

Association of Clinical Pathologists   (ACP)   1927
NR   189 Dyke Rd, HOVE, E Sussex, BN3 1TL.   (hq)
       01273 775700   fax 01273 773303
       email info@pathologists.org.uk
       http://www.pathologists.org.uk
       Gen Admin: Alison Martin
▲   Company Limited by Guarantee; Registered Charity
Br   12
○   *L, *P; the study & practice of clinical pathology
●   Conf - Mtgs - ET
M   2,200 i, UK & o'seas
¶   ACP News - 3;   ACP Ybk - 1.

Association of Clinical Professors of Paediatrics
       since 2007 **Academic Paediatrics Association of Great Britain
       & Ireland**

Association for Coaching   (AC)
NR   66 Church Rd, LONDON, W7 1LB.
       http://www.associationforcoaching.com
       Chmn: Katherine Tulpa
○   *P; lifestyle coaching

Association for Cognitive Analytic Therapy   (ACAT)
NR   PO Box 6793, DORCHESTER, Dorset, DT1 9DL.
       0844 800 9496
       http://www.acat.me.uk
       Admin: Susan van Baars
○   *P

Association of Collaborative Family Lawyers
       a group of the **Law Society of Northern Ireland**

Association for College Management   (ACM)   1987
NR   35 The Point, MARKET HARBOROUGH, Leics, LE16 7QU.
      (admin)
      01858 461110   fax 01858 461366
      email administration@acm.uk.com
      http://www.acm.uk.com
      Chief Exec & Gen Sec: Peter Pendle
Br   110
○   *P, *U; a trade union for college managers (principals, vice-
      principals & other senior college managers)
Gp   Many connected with vocational education & training
●   Conf - Mtgs - ET - SG - Empl - LG
M   3,500 i, UK / 10 i, o'seas
¶   NL - 10;   Information & Briefing Sheet - irreg; both ftm only.

Association of Colleges   (AoC)   1893
■   2-5 Stedham Place, LONDON, WC1A 1HU.   (hq)
      020 7034 9900   fax 020 7034 9950
      email debra-stych@aoc.co.uk   http://www.aoc.co.uk
      Chief Exec: Martin Doel,   Co Sec: Debra Stych
▲   Company Limited by Guarantee
○   *E, *N; 'leading body in the UK on further education'
●   Conf - Mtgs - ET - Empl - LG
M   332 colleges
      (Sub: varies, £4,000,000 in total)

Association of Coloproctology of Great Britain & Ireland   1990
■   at the Royal College of Surgeons, 35-43 Lincoln's Inn Fields,
      LONDON, WC2A 3PE.   (hq)
      020 7973 0307   fax 020 7430 9235
      email acpgbi@asgbi.org.uk   http://www.acpgbi.org.uk
      Hon Sec: Karen Nugent
▲   Company Limited by Guarantee; Registered Charity
○   *P; the advancement of the science & practice of
      coloproctology; to promote high standards in training &
      research
●   Conf - Mtgs - ET - Res - Exhib
M   1,200 i, UK / 100 i, o'seas
¶   Colorectal Disease - 9; prices vary (published by Blackwell
      Publishing).

Association of Commonwealth Universities   (ACU)   1913
NR   Woburn House, 20-24 Tavistock Sq, LONDON, WC1H 9NF.
      (hq)
      020 7380 6700
      http://www.acu.ac.uk
▲   Registered Charity
○   *E; a Commonwealth body, governed & financed by the
      membership throughout the Commonwealth which promotes
      contact & cooperation between universities

Association of Community & Comprehensive Schools   1982
IRL   10H Centrepoint Business Park, Oak Drive, DUBLIN 12,
      Republic of Ireland.
      353 (1) 460 1150   fax 353 (1) 460 1203
      email office@accs.ie   http://www.accs.ie
      Hon Sec: Ciarán Flynn
○   *E
M   92 schools

**Association for Community-based Maternity Care   (ACBMC)
1989**
NR   Newby End Farm, Newby, PENRITH, Cumbria, CA10 3EX.
      (admin/p)
      01931 714338
      email jennyatnewbyend@ukonline.co.uk
      Membership & Database Admin: Jenny Jones,
      Chmn: Richard Porter
▲   Un-incorporated Society
○   *P; to support & develop appropriate care, based in the
      community, for women during pregnancy, birth & the
      puerperium; to support those currently involved in promoting
      such care
●   Mtgs - ET - Inf

Association of Community Rail Partnerships   (ACoRP)   1999
■   Rail & River Centre, Canal Side, Civic Hall, 15a New St,
      Slaithwaite, HUDDERSFIELD, W Yorks, HD7 5AB.   (hq)
      01484 847790   fax 01484 847877
      http://www.acorp.uk.com
      Sec: Philip Jenkinson
▲   Company Limited by Guarantee
○   *K; to encourage local communities to become actively involved
      with their local railway station/train service, predominantly in
      the rural sector
Gp   Station design; Rolling stock
●   Conf - Res - Exhib - SG - Inf - Lib - VE - LG
<   Community Transport Assn
>   Community Transport Assn; Heritage Rly Assn; Sustrans
M   7 i, 7 f, 57 org
¶   Train Times - 4; ftm, £70 nm (includes discounts at
      conferences, specialist advice; email NL - ftm only).
      Research/consultancy Reports - 2/3; ftm.   AR.
×   2004 Transport Research & Information Network (merged)

Association of Community Television Operators   (ACTO)   1989
NR   Institute of Local Television, 13 Bellevue Place, EDINBURGH,
      EH7 4BS.   (hq)
      0131-466 3021
      Co-ordinator: Dave Rushton

*Association for Commuter Transport
      since 2008* **ACT TravelWise**

**Association of Company Registration Agents Ltd   (ACRA)
1978**
NR   Temple House, 20 Holywell Row, LONDON, EC2A 4XH.   (hsb)
      020 7377 0381   fax 020 7377 6646
      Hon Sec: M R Chettleburgh
▲   Company Limited by Guarantee
○   *P; 'to promote the interests of those using the facilities of the
      Companies Registration Office; to maintain a high standard
      among members'
●   LG
<   Law Services Assn
M   13 f

Association of Computer Cable Manufacturers   (ACCM)   1993
■   Kingsway House, Wrotham Rd, GRAVESEND, Kent,
      DA13 0AU.   (asa)
○   *T
●   Conf - Mtgs - LG - Lib
M   f

Association of Computer Engineers & Technicians   (ACET)
NR   Wellington House, East Rd, CAMBRIDGE, CB1 1BH.
      01223 451027   fax 01223 451100
      http://www.acet-uk.org
○   *P

Association of Computer Professionals   (ACP)   1984
■   Chilverbridge House, ARLINGTON, E Sussex, BN26 6SB.   (hq)
      01323 871874   fax 01323 871875
      email admin@acpexamboard.com
      http://www.acpexamboard.com
      Sec Gen: Mrs N Keats
○   *P; to provide high standards of efficiency throughout the
      industry; to prepare candidates, through examinations, for a
      successful career in computing
●   Exam (for: Certificate in information technology &
      programming; Diploma in information systems analysis &
      design; Advanced diploma in computer science
M   i

© CBD Research Ltd · Beckenham · BR3 5JS · Tel 020 8650 7745 · Fax 020 8650 0768 · E-mail cbd@cbdresearch.com · www.cbdresearch.com

Association of Concrete Industrial Flooring Contractors (ACIFC) 1994
■ 22-25 Finsbury Square, LONDON, EC2A 1DX.   (asa)
    0844 249 9176   fax 0844 249 9177
    email acifc@nscc.org   http://www.acifc.org
    Secretariat: S Doshi,   Chmn: David Harvey
▲ Un-incorporated Society
○ *T; interests of specialist contractors & the development of
    concrete floors
Gp Technical - all aspects of slab construction
● Conf - Mtgs - Inf - Liaison with technical & trade bodies
< ACIFC (France)
M 40 f, UK / 10 f, o'seas
¶ Technical publications, published through the Concrete Society:
    Concrete Mix Design
    Steel Fibre Reinforcement
    Admixtures
    Dry Shake Topping.

Association for Conferences & Events   (ACE)   1971
■ Riverside House, High St, HUNTINGDON, Cambs,
    PE29 3SG.   (hq)
    01480 457595   fax 01480 412863
    email ace@aceinternational.org
    http://www.aceinternational.org
    Mem Mgr: John Thompson
▲ Company Limited by Guarantee
○ *N, *P, *T; information centre & forum for member
    organisations involved in the organising, marketing,
    accommodating & servicing of events
● ET - Inf - VE - LG
> Business Visits & Events Partnership (BVEP)
M 150 f, UK / 2 f, o'seas
¶ NL - 12; ftm only.
    Conference & Exhibition Fact Finder - 12; ftm, £36 nm.
    ACE Ybk - Who's Who in the Meetings Industry - 1; ftm,
    £14.99 nm.
    ACE Guide to a Career in Conferences (Hbk); ftm, £2.50 nm.
    AR; ftm only.

Association for the Conservation of Energy   (ACE)   1981
NR Westgate House, 2a Prebend St, LONDON, N1 8PT.   (hq)
    020 7359 8000
    http://www.ukace.org
    Dir: Andrew Warren
▲ Company Limited by Guarantee
○ *K, *T; to encourage a positive national awareness of the
    benefits & need for energy conservation
● Res
< EUROACE
M 16 f
¶ The Fifth Fuel (NL) - 2; free.
    Publications list available on website.

Association for Consultancy & Engineering   (ACE)   1913
NR Alliance House, 12 Caxton St, LONDON, SW1H 0QL.   (hq)
    020 7222 6557   fax 020 7222 0750
    email consult@acenet.co.uk   http://www.acenet.co.uk
    Chief Exec: Nelson Ogunshakin
▲ Company Limited by Guarantee
○ *T
Gp Civil; Structural; Electrical; Mechanical; Chemical; Mining &
    metallurgy; Building services; Telecommunications; Gas;
    Marine & naval; Aeronautical; Production; Computer &
    control engineering; Civil engineering (incl road, rail,
    airports, docks & harbours)
● Conf - Exhib - SG - Stat - Expt - Inf - LG
< Fédn Intle des Ingénieurs Conseils; Eur Fedn of Consultancy
    Assns
M 750 f, UK / 10 f, o'seas
¶ Consult - 10; ftm only.
    ACE Directory - 1; ftm, £35 nm.
    Many other publications.

Association of Consultant Approved Inspectors   (ACAI)   1996
NR c/o 14 Berkeley St, LONDON, W1J 8DX.
    http://www.acai.org.uk
    Hon Sec: Paul Timmins
▲ Un-incorporated Society
○ *P; to promote the role & development of private sector
    building control by approved inspectors instead of the use of
    local authorities in England & Wales.   Approved Inspectors
    are statutory appointees under Part II of the Building
    Act 1984, such appointees being made by the Secretary of
    State for Local Government & the Regions, or the
    Construction Industry Council
● Mtgs - SG - LG
M 14 i, 12 f, 7 affiliates
¶ LM.

Association of Consultant Architects   (ACA)   1973
■ 98 Hayes Rd, BROMLEY, Kent, BR2 9AB.   (hq)
    020 8325 1402   fax 020 8466 9079
    email office@acarchitects.co.uk
    http://www.acarchitects.co.uk
    Sec Gen: Mrs Fiona Griffiths
▲ Company Limited by Guarantee
○ *T; for architects in private practice
Gp Planning advisory; Conservation; Small business
● Conf - Mtgs - Res - Exhib - Comp - SG - VE - LG
M 250 f
¶ NL - 4; ftm only.
    ACA Specialist Services Directory - 1; ftm, £10 nm.
    ACA Form of Building Agreement (Contract
    document); £7.87 m, £10.50 nm.

Association of Consulting Actuaries   (ACA)   1951
■ Warnford Court, 29 Throgmorton St, LONDON, EC2N 2AT.
    (hq)
    020 7382 4594   fax 020 7374 6220
    http://www.aca.org.uk
    Hon Sec: Andrew Vaughan
○ *P; to advise individuals, institutions, the government &
    corporate bodies on pensions, life & general insurance &
    other financial issues

Association of Consulting Engineers of Ireland
IRL 46 Merrion Sq, DUBLIN 2, Republic of Ireland.
    353 (1) 642 5588   fax 353 (1) 642 5590
    http://www.acei.ie
    Exec Dir: Anne Potter
○ *P

Association of Consulting Scientists   (ACS)   1958
■ 5 Willow Heights, CRADLEY HEATH, W Midlands, B64 7PL.
    (hsb)
    0121-602 3515
    http://www.consultingscientists.co.uk
    Hon Sec: Dr Stuart Guy
▲ Company Limited by Guarantee
○ *P; to make known the services of consulting scientists; to
    promote scientific & technical research through contracts with
    member firms; to ascertain & make known the views of
    independent scientists on matters of wider interest
Gp Forensic & expert witness; Testing laboratories
● Conf - Mtgs - Res - Inf - LG
M 42 f
¶ NL - 4; free.
    Directory of Members & Services - on website.

Association of Contact Lens Manufacturers Ltd (ACLM) 1962
NR PO Box 735, DEVIZES, Wilts, SN10 3TQ. (sec-gen/b)
 01380 860418 fax 01380 860863
 email info@aclm.org.uk http://www.aclm.org.uk
 Sec Gen: Simon Rodwell
▲ Company Limited by Guarantee
○ *T; to promote the wearing of contact lenses
Gp Technical working; Labelling; Ethics; EDI; PR; Packaging waste;
 Hygienic management
● Conf - Mtgs - ET - Exhib - Stat - LG - Regulatory [activities] in
 connection with CE marking
< Eur Fedn Nat Assns Contact Lens Mfrs (Euromcontact);
 Eyecare UK (E-UK)
M 3 i, 30 f
¶ ACLM Contact Lens Ybk - 1; £17.

Association for Contemporary Iberian Studies (ACIS) 1968
■ c/o Dr Mark Gant, Languages Dept, University of Chester,
 CHESTER, CH1 4BJ. (hsb)
 01244 513049 fax 01244 511311
 email m.gant@chester.ac.uk
 http://www.iberianstudies.net
 Sec: Dr Mark Gant
▲ Un-incorporated Society
○ *L; the study of social, economic & political affairs of the
 Iberian area, together with its languages
● Conf - ET - Res
M 180 i, 30 f, UK / 20 i, o'seas
 (Sub: £40 UK / £54 o'seas)
¶ International Jnl of Iberian Studies - 3; ftm, £33 i, £90 instns.
 [see: www.intellectbooks.co.uk]

Association for Contemporary Jewellery (ACJ) 1997
■ PO Box 37807, LONDON, SE23 1XJ (admin/p)
 020 8291 4201 fax 020 8291 4452
 email enquiries@acj.org.uk http://www.acj.org.uk
 Admin: Sue Hyams, Chmn: Frances Julie Whitelaw
○ *G, *P, *T
● Conf - ET - Exhib - Inf - VE
¶ Findings - 4.

Association for Continence Advice (ACA) 1981
■ c/o Fitwise Management Ltd, Drumcross Hall, BATHGATE,
 W Lothian, EH48 4JT. (asa)
 01506 811077 fax 01506 811477
 http://www.aca.uk.com
▲ Company Limited by Guarantee; Registered Charity
Br 10
○ *P; a multi-professional membership organisation, open to all
 interested in the promotion of continence & who have a
 concern for the better management of incontinence
Gp Special interest: Bowel, Pelvic floor
● Conf - Mtgs - ET - Res - Exhib - SG
< Works closely with: Incontact; PromoCon
M c 600 i, 35 f, UK / 29 i, o'seas
 (Sub: £45 i, £450 f, UK / £60 o'seas)
¶ NL - 4; ftm, £22 yr nm.
 Notes for Good Practice; on-line (annual updates).
 Resource Pack for Care Homes; ftm, £15 nm.
 Directory of members - 2 yrly; ftm, £587.50 nm.

Association of Convenience Stores (ACS) 1994
■ Federation House, 17 Farnborough St, FARNBOROUGH,
 Hants, GU14 8AG. (hq)
 01252 515001
 http://www.acs.org.uk
 Chief Exec: James Lowman
▲ Company Limited by Guarantee
○ *T; to represent convenience stores across the UK; to foster the
 development of the whole of the professional convenience
 store sector, for the benefit of retailers, wholesalers &
 suppliers; to optimise the benefit to the sector of legislation
 emanating from UK & EU parliaments & by anticipating
 demand for information & training required by the sector
Gp Association of News Retailing
● Conf - Mtgs - Res - Inf - VE - LG
< Intl Fedn of Grocers' Assns
M 33,000 stores
¶ ACS News - 12; ftm.

Association of Copyright Infringement Investigators (ASCII) 2000
■ 15 Wickham Rd, BECKENHAM, Kent, BR3 5JS. (hq)
○ *P
● Mtgs - Stat - LG
M i & f
✕ 2007 Association of Copyright Investigators

Association of Corporate Treasurers (ACT) 1979
NR 51 Moorgate, LONDON, EC2R 6BH. (hq)
 020 7847 2540 fax 020 7374 8744
 http://www.treasurers.org
 Chief Exec: Richard Raeburn
Br 16; Belgium, Eire, Hong Kong
○ *P; the management of financial risk, liquidity, corporate
 finance, the balance sheet
● Conf - Mtgs - ET - Exam - Res - Exhib - SG - Lib - LG
M c 4,000 i
¶ The Treasurer - 12; The Treasurers Hbk - 1; both ftm.

Association of Corporate Trustees (TACT) 1974
NR 3 Brackerne Close, Cooden, BEXHILL-on-SEA, E Sussex,
 TN39 3BT. (hsb)
 01424 844144 fax 01424 844144
 http://www.trustees.org.uk
 Sec: W J Stephenson
▲ Un-incorporated Society
○ *P; to consider & act on items of mutual interest in the fields of
 law, taxation, investment & related technical & practical
 subjects
Gp Pensions; Loan capital; Private trusts; Charities
● Mtgs - ET
M 70 f, UK / 1 f, o'seas
¶ TACT Review - 2; free.

Association of Cost Engineers Ltd (ACostE) 1962
NR Lea House, 5 Middlewich Rd, SANDBACH, Cheshire,
 CW11 1XL. (hq)
 01270 764798 fax 01270 766180
 email enquiries@acoste.org.uk
 http://www.acoste.org.uk
▲ Company Limited by Guarantee
○ *P; to represent the professional interests of those with
 responsibility for the prediction, planning & control of
 resources & cost for activities that involve engineering,
 manufacturing & construction
M i

© CBD Research Ltd · Beckenham · BR3 5JS · Tel 020 8650 7745 · Fax 020 8650 0768 · E-mail cbd@cbdresearch.com · www.cbdresearch.com

Association of Cost Management Consultants   (ACMC)   1999
NR   Blays House, Churchfield Rd, CHALFONT ST PETER, Bucks,
       SL9 9EW.   (hsb)
       01753 891313
       http://www.theacmc.co.uk
       Hon Sec: Tony Gibson
▲   Un-incorporated Society
○   *P; business cost reduction specialists
M   7 f

Association of Council Secretaries & Solicitors   (ACSeS)   1974
NR   4 Sutton Court Lawns, Sutton Poyntz, WEYMOUTH, Dorset,
       DT3 6LH.   (hq)
       01305 836328
       http://www.acses.org.uk
○   *P; local government administration, law & management

Association for Counselling at Work
       a group of the **British Association for Counselling &
       Psychotherapy**

Association of Countryside Voluntary Wardens   (ACVW)   1967
NR   60 Defoe Drive, Parkhall, STOKE-on-TRENT, STaffs, ST3 5RS.
       (hsb)
       01782 316046
▲   Un-incorporated Society
○   *P; to promote effective wardening by volunteers throughout the
       countryside
●   Conf - SG - LG
<   Coun for Nat Parks; LANTRA NTO
M   380 i
¶   NL - 2;   Newssheet - 2; both ftm only.

Association of County Chief Executives   (ACCE)   1974
■   Office of the Chief Executive, County Hall, TROWBRIDGE,
       Wilts, BA14 8JF.   (hsb)
       01225 713101   fax 01225 713092
       email jeanpotter@wiltshire.gov.uk
       Hon Sec: M Lloyd
▲   Un-incorporated Society
○   *P
●   Conf - Mtgs - LG
<   County section of the Society of Local Authority Chief Executives
M   38 i
¶   ACCE Members' Hbk; ftm.

Association of County & City Councils   (ACCC)   1899
IRL   Office Unit 10 Manor Mills, MAYNOOTH, Co Kildare, Republic
       of Ireland.
       353 (1) 610 6100   fax 353 (1) 610 6640
       email councillors@gmail.com   http://www.councillors.ie
       Dir: Liam Kenny
○   *N
×   2007 General Council of County Councils

Association of County Cricket Scorers   (ACCS)   1993
■   14 Briery Avenue, BOLTON, Lancs, BL2 4AJ.   (hsp)
       Hon Sec: Alan West
○   *P; to improve the standards of cricket scoring; 'to cooperate &
       cultivate good relations with all bodies associated with cricket
       for the betterment of the game'
●   AGM; Annual lunch
M   47 i
¶   The Scorer (NL) - 4; ftm only.

** **Association of County Public Health Officers**
       Organisation lost: see Introduction paragraph 3.

Association of Cricket Statisticians & Historians   (ACS)   1973
NR   Archives Dept, Glamorgan Cricket, Sophia Gardens, CARDIFF,
       CF11 9XR.   (hsb)
       029 2041 9383
       email office@acscricket.com   http://www.acscricket.com
       Hon Sec: Andrew Hignell
▲   Un-incorporated Society
Br   Victoria (Australia)
○   *S; cricket history & statistics
●   Mtgs - Res - SG - Stat - Inf - Compilation of records of feats &
       matches worldwide
M   1,000 i, UK / 250 i, o'seas
¶   The Cricket Statistician - 4; ftm. 4.
       ACS International Cricket Ybk - 1.
       Various other annual publications.

Association of Cricket Umpires & Scorers
       on 1 January 2008 merged with the ECB Officials Association to form
       the **England & Wales Cricket Board Association of Cricket
       Officials**

Association of Cruise Experts   (ACE)   1958
NR   41-42 Eastcastle St (1st floor), London, W1W 8DU.   (hq)
       020 7436 2449   fax 020 7636 9206
       http://www.cruiseexperts.org
▲   Company Limited by Guarantee
○   *T; for cruise lines & ferry operators
●   Mtgs - ET - Inf - VE
M   54 f
¶   Get Cruisewise - 4; ftm only.
×   2007 Passenger Shipping Association

**Association for Cultural Advancement through Visual Art
(ACAVA)   1983**
NR   54 Blechynden St, LONDON, W10 6RJ.   (hq)
       020 8960 5015
       http://www.acava.org
       Artistic Dir: Duncan Smith
▲   Company Limited by Guarantee; Registered Charity
Br   6
○   *A; promotion of the visual arts by provision of facilities
       (including studios & galleries) & organisation of programmes
       for their production & access as well as education
●   ET - Exhib
M   300 i
¶   NL - 4; free.

Association for Cushing's Treatment & Help   (ACTH)   1993
NR   54 Powney Rd, MAIDENHEAD, Berks, SL6 6EQ.
       (coordinator/p)
       01628 670389   fax 01628 415603
       email cushingsacth@btinternet.com
       http://www.cushingsacth.co.uk
       Coordinator: Mrs Elaine Eldridge
Br   Regional coordinators
○   *W; a self-help group of offering experience, help & advice to
       sufferers of Cushing's Sydrome (over production of
       cortocisterid hormones) & their carers
●   Mtgs (small & informal)
M   C 170 i
¶   Cushy (NL) - 3; ftm only.
       Directory of member contacts.
       Information booklet for newly diagnosed patients.
       Information booklet for post surgery.

Association of Cycle Traders   (ACT)   1982
NR   PO Box 5110, HOVE, E Sussex, BN52 9EB.   (hq)
      0870 428 8404   fax 0870 428 8403
      email act@cyclesource.co.uk
      http://www.act-bicycles.com
      Nat Sec: Anne Killick
▲   Company Limited by Guarantee
Br   30
○   *T; to promote the interests of the independent cycle trader
●   Conf - Mtgs - ET - Exam - Exhib - Inf - LG - Operation of a
      national cycle technicians accreditation programme
<   Eur Twowheel Retailers Assn; Bicycle Assn GB; Indep Retailers
      Consortium
M   30 i, 800 f
¶   The Independent - 4; ftm only.

** Association of Dance & Freestyle Professionals
      Organisation lost: see Introduction paragraph 3

Association for Dance Movement Therapy UK Ltd   (ADMT UK)   1982
■   32 Meadfoot Lane, TORQUAY, Devon, TQ1 2BW.
      (mail address)
      email queries@admt.org.uk   http://www.admt.org.uk
      Co Sec & Administrator: Andrew Clements
▲   Company Limited by Guarantee
○   *P; to promote mental & physical health by the use of dance
      movement therapy; to ensure that proper standards of
      professional competence & ethics are maintained
●   Conf - Mtgs - ET - Inf - LG - Courses & accreditation of
      practitioners
<   Eur Dance Movement Assn
M   200 i
¶   E-Motion (NL) - 4; ftm, £16 nm.   AR.

Association of Deer Management Groups   (ADMG)   1992
■   c/o Finlay Clark, Bidwells, 33 High St, FORT WILLIAM,
      Inverness-shire, PH33 6DJ.   (asa)
      01397 707641   fax 01397 702010
      email finlay.clark@bidwells.co.uk
      http://www.deer-management.co.uk
      Sec: Finlay Clark
▲   Un-incorporated Society
○   *N, *T, *V; coordination & representation of deer management
      groups in Scotland; also representation of the Scottish wild
      venison industry
●   Conf - Mtgs - LG
M   30 groups
¶   NL - 2; free.

Association of Denominational Historical Societies & Cognate Libraries   1993
NR   33 Addison Rd, CATERHAM, Surrey, CR3 5LU.   (sp)
      email secretary@adhscl.org.uk
      Sec: Mrs Pauline Jones
▲   Un-incorporated Society
○   *P, *R; to encourage research into the traditions of the various
      Christian denominations
●   Conf - Mtgs - Res - Inf
M   21 soc & libraries
¶   NL - 1; ftm.

Association of Dental Anaesthetists   (ADA)   1977
■   21 Portland Place, LONDON, W1B 1PY.   (hq)
      020 7631 1650   fax 020 7631 4352
      email info@aagbi.org
      http://www.dentalanaesthesia.org.uk
      Pres: Dr Ken Ruiz,   Hon Sec: Diana Terry
▲   Registered Charity
○   *P; to promote management of highest standards in the
      conduct of sedation & anaesthesia for dentistry
●   Conf - Mtgs - ET
<   Assn of Anaesthetists of GB & Ireland
M   350 i
      (Sub: £10)
¶   Proceedings - 1;   NL - 2/3; both ftm.

Association of Dental Hospitals of the United Kingdom   (ADH)   1948
NR   Birmingham Dental Hospital, St Chad's Queensway,
      BIRMINGHAM, B4 6NN.
      0121-237 2722
      Sec: Mrs P Harrington
Br   14
○   *N; for dental teaching hospitals
●   Mtgs
M   28 i

Association of Dental Implantology UK   (ADI)   1986
■   98 South Worple Way, LONDON, SW14 8ND.   (hq)
      020 8487 5555   fax 020 8487 5566
      email office@adi.org.uk   http://www.adi.org.uk
      Hon Sec: Dr Steve Byfield,   Chief Exec: Cherry Wilson
▲   Company Limited by Guarantee; Registered Charity
○   *P; to provide post graduate education in dental implantology
      profession
Gp   Dentists; Dental technicians; Hygienists; Nurses; Restorative
      consultants; Max-Fax surgeons
●   Conf - Mtgs - ET - Res - Exhib - SG - Inf
M   1,500 i, 30 f, UK / 25 i, o'seas
      (Sub: £210)
¶   Dental Implant Summaries - 6;
      European Jnl for Dental Implantologists - 4; both ftm.

Association of Directors of Adult Social Services   (ADASS)   2007
NR   ADASS Business Unit, Local Government House, Smith Sq,
      LONDON, SW1P 3HZ.   (hsb)
      020 7072 7433
      http://www.adass.org.uk
      Admin: Marinda Oosthuizen
▲   Registered Charity
Br   11
○   *P; promotion of a comprehensive social service for families,
      individuals & communities
●   Conf - Mtgs - Res - Stat - Inf - LG
M   135 i
¶   ADSS News - 4/5.   AR - 1.   Hbk (incl LM).
      Directory of Contracting Officers.
      Abuse of Older People.   Towards Community Care.
      Training for the Caring Business.
×   2007 Association of Directors of Social Services - adult element

Association of Directors of Children's Services   (ADCS)   2007
■   Ellen Wilkinson Bldg, University of Manchester, Oxford Rd,
      MANCHESTER, M13 9PL.   (hq)
      0161-275 8810   fax 0161-275 8811
      http://www.adcs.org.uk
      Sec: Sarah Caton
○   *P
●   Conf - Mtgs - Res - LG - Representation to government & other
      bodies on educational matters
M   950 i
×   2007 (Confederation of Children's Services Managers   (
      pre-2005 Confederation of Education Service
      Managers   (Association of Directors of Social
      Services   (- childrens' element

© CBD Research Ltd · Beckenham · BR3 5JS · Tel 020 8650 7745 · Fax 020 8650 0768 · E-mail cbd@cbdresearch.com · www.cbdresearch.com

Association of Directors of Education in Scotland (ADES) 1920
NR   Lochan House, Birse, ABOYNE, AB34 5FP.   (hsb)
    01339 887160
    email jstodter@freeserve.co.uk
    http://www.adescotland.org.uk
    Sec Gen: John Stodter
○   *E, *P
M   ['not applicable']

Association of Directors of Public Health (ADPH)
■   Nightingale Court, Ida Darwin, Fulbourn, CAMBRIDGE,
    CB21 5EE.   (hq)
    01223 884800   fax 01223 884801
    email enquiries@adph.nhs.uk   http://www.adph.org.uk
    Chief Exec: Nicola Close
○   *M, *P; 'public health advocacy & policy work supporting DPH
    role'
M   i
    No further information supplied

Association of Directors of Social Services
    since 2007 **Association of Directors of Adult Social Services**
    and **Association of Directors of Children's Services**

Association of Directors of Social Work (ADSW) 1969
NR   Rosebery House, 9 Haymarket Terrace, EDINBURGH,
    EH12 5ZX.   (hq)
    0131-474 9220   fax 0131-474 9292
    email sophie.mills@adsw.org.uk
    http://www.adsw.org.uk
    Sec: Jim Dean, Admin: Sophie Mills
○   *P; for senior social workers working in Scottish local
    government
<   Conf - Mtgs
M   140 i

Association of Disabled Professionals (ADP) 1971
■   BCM ADP, LONDON, WC1N 3XX.   (mail/address)
    01204 431638   fax 01204 431638
    email adp.admin@ntlworld.com
    http://www.adp.org.uk
    Chmn: Jane Hunt
▲   Registered Charity
○   *W; improvement of rehabilitation, education, training &
    employment opportunities of the disabled
●   Conf - Res - Inf - LG
M   c 240 i, 3 f, UK / 3 i, o'seas
¶   Quarterly - 4.

Association of Distributors, Coaters & Converters of Adhesive Tapes (ADCCAT) 2000
NR   PO Box 704, AYLESBURY, Bucks, HP22 9WQ.
    01296 747451
    http://www.adccat.com
○   *T; for companies and individuals involved in manufacture,
    supply & conversion of adhesive tapes
●   Mtgs - Exhib - Expt
M   40 f

Association of Dogs & Cats Homes (ADCH) 1985
■   c/o MGFT Animal Sanctuary, Church Knowle, WAREHAM,
    Dorset, BH20 5NQ.   (hsb)
    01929 480474
    email mgft.trustees@btopenworld.com
    http://www.adch.org.uk
    Sec: Matt Devereux
▲   Un-incorporated Society
○   *N; to provide a forum for people in dog & cat rescue
    organisations to discuss common issues
●   Conf - Mtgs
M   51 org, UK / 3 org, o'seas
¶   Code of Practice - 1; ftm, on website.

Association of Domestic Management
    since 2007 the **Association of Healthcare Cleaning Professionals**

Association of Drainage Authorities (ADA) 1937
■   12 Cranes Drive, SURBITON, Surrey, KT5 8AL.   (hsb)
    020 8399 7350   fax 020 8390 9368
    email admin@ada.org.uk   http://www.ada.org.uk
    Chief Exec: Dr Jean Venables
▲   Un-incorporated Society
Br 9
○   *N, *T; for those involved in water level management, including
    Internal Drainage Boards, RFDSs, local authorities &
    suppliers
Gp Finance & administration; Publicity; Technical & environmental
●   Conf - Mtgs - Exhib - Stat - Inf - VE - Demonstration of land
    drainage eqpt & products (3 yrly)
<   Eur U of Water Managers Assn (EUWMA)
M   157 f, 90 associates
    (Sub: IDBds varies according to size, £209.15 Associates)
¶   ADA Gazette - 3; ftm.

Association of Drum Manufacturers
    in 2004 merged with the Federation of Drum Reconditioners & the
    Rigid Intermediate Bulk Container Association to form the **Industrial Packaging Association**

Association of Ductwork Contractors & Allied Services (ADCAS)
■   2 Waltham Court, Milley Lane, Hare Hatch, READING, Berks,
    RG10 9TH.
    0118-940 3416   fax 0118-940 6258
    email adcas@feta.co.uk   http://www.feta.co.uk
    Pres: Malcolm Moss
○   *T; dedicated to ductwork contractors, allied suppliers &
    manufacturers of equipment for ventilation & air conditioning
    systems
M   68 f

Association of Dunkirk Little Ships (ADLS) 1966
■   35 Finians Close, UXBRIDGE, Middx, UB10 9NW.   (hsp)
    01895 254193   fax 01895 813788
    email info@adls.org.uk   http://www.adls.org.uk
    Hon Sec: M Cormack
○   *G; to commemorate the Little Ships' rescue mission to Dunkirk
    in 1940, & to keep them afloat
●   Mtgs:
    Afloat: Trip from Dover/Ramsgate to Dunkirk every 5 yrs -
    Annual commemorative cruise
    Ashore: AGM - Annual Fitting-out & Laying-up Supper
M   130 privately owned boats (not people)
¶   NL - 2; ftm only, appropriate advertising accepted

Association for Education & Ageing (AEA) 1985
■   132 Dawes Rd, LONDON, SW6 7EF.   (hsp)
    020 7385 4641
    email carol@carolallen.wanadoo.co.uk
    http://www.aeaonline.org.uk/
    Hon Sec: Carol Allen
▲   Registered Charity
Br 1
○   *E, *P; promotion of education in later life
●   Conf - Mtgs - ET - Res
M   c 50 i, c 10 org
¶   AEA Digest (NL) - 4; ftm & to potential members only.
    Educational Gerontology (Jnl); £50 m, £200+ nm.

Association for Education & Guardianship of International Students   (AEGIS)   1994
- ■   66 Humphreys Close, Randwick, STROUD, Glos, GL5 4NY. (chmn/p)
      01453 755160   fax 01453 755160
      email secretary@aegisuk.net   http://www.aegisuk.net
- ▲   Registered Charity
- ○   *W; to promote best & legal practice in all areas of guardianship in order to safeguard the welfare & happiness of overseas students at school in Britain
- ●   Conf - Mtgs - ET
- M   17 org, 65 schools
- ¶   NL - 2;   LM - continuous; both free.

Association for Education Welfare Management   (AEWM)   1917
- NR   Education Welfare Service, Chantry House, 123 Kirkgate, WAKEFIELD, W Yorks, WF1 2ZS.   (vice-pres/b)
      01924 305519
      email jenny.price@aewm.co.uk   http://www.aewm.co.uk
      Vice-Pres: Jennifer A Price
- ▲   Un-incorporated Society
- ○   *P; managers of education welfare & social work services; to help children & young people maximise their educational opportunities through regular attendance at school
- ●   Conf - Mtgs - ET
- M   150 i

Association of Educational Psychologists   (AEP)   1962
- ■   4 The Riverside Centre, Frankland Lane, DURHAM, DH1 5TA.   (hsp)
      0191-384 9512   fax 0191-386 5287
      email enquiries@sao.org.uk
      Gen Sec: Charles Ward
- ▲   Un-incorporated Society
- ○   *E, *P, *U; to promote educational psychology as a profession; to liaise with government, local authorities & others concerned with the development of children & young people
- ●   Conf - Mtgs - ET - Res - Stat - Empl - LG
- <   TUC; GFTU; IPSA; Nat Children's Bureau
- M   3,067 i
- ¶   Educational Psychology in Practice - 4; ftm, £67 i, £200 instns, £190 online, nm.

Association of Electoral Administrators   (AEA)
- NR   PO Box 201, South Eastern, LIVERPOOL, L16 5HH.   (hsb)
      0151-281 8246
      http://www.aea-elections.co.uk
- ○   *P; for the consistent & efficient administration of electoral registration & the conduct of elections
- M   i
- ¶   Arena (NL) - 4.

Association of Electrical Contractors, Ireland   (AECI)
- IRL   16 Main St, BLACKROCK, Co Dublin, Republic of Ireland.
      353 (1) 288 6499   fax 353 (1) 288 5870
      Hon Sec: Michael Mangan
- ○   *T
- M   360 f

Association of Electrical & Mechanical Trades   (AEMT)   1945
- NR   St Saviour's House, St Saviour's Place, YORK, N Yorks, YO1 7PJ.
      01904 674899
      http://www.aemt.org.uk
- ▲   Company Limited by Guarantee
- ○   *T; interests of electrical motor apparatus repairers & manufacturers (electric motors, pumps & rotating plant, controls & electronic equipment)
- M   f

Association of Electricity Producers   (AEP)   1987
- NR   17 Waterloo Place (1st floor), LONDON, SW1Y 4AR.   (hq)
      020 7930 9390   fax 020 7930 9391
      email enquiries@aepuk.com   http://www.aepuk.com
      Chief Exec: David Porter
- ▲   Company Limited by Guarantee
- ○   *T; to promote & protect the interests of privately owned companies producing electricity
- Gp   C'ees: Electricity & gas, Electricity trading, Environment, European, Health & safety, Renewable energy, Scottish
- ●   Conf - Mtgs - Res - SG - Expt - Inf - Lib - VE - LG
- M   6 i, 97 f, 3 org

Association of Endoscopic Surgeons of Great Britain & Ireland
a group of the **Association of Surgeons of Great Britain & Ireland**

Association of English Singers & Speakers   (AESS)   1913
- ■   Melin-y-Grogue, Llanfair Waterdine, KNIGHTON, Powys, LD7 1TU.   (chmn/p)
      01547 510327   fax 01547 510327
      email graham.trew@virgin.net
      http://www.aofess.org.uk
      Chmn: Graham Trew
- ▲   Registered Charity
- ○   *D, *P; to encourage the communication of English words in singing & speech, with clarity, understanding & imagination
- ●   Mtgs - ET - Comp - Master classes - Concerts
- <   Inc Soc of Musicians
- M   170 i
- ¶   NL - 3; ftm only.

Association for Environment Conscious Building   (AECB)   1989
- ■   PO Box 32, LLANDYSUL, Cardiganshire, SA44 5ZA.   (hq)
      0845 456 9773
      email info@aecb.net   http://www.aecb.net
      Sec: Peter Wilkinson
- ▲   Company Limited by Guarantee
- ○   *K, *T; to promote & encourage sustainable building within the construction industry
- Gp   Energy efficiency; Tropical rain forests; Pollution; Native fauna & flora; Health & safety; Chemicals; Environment conscious housing
- ●   Mtgs - ET - Res - Exhib - Inf - Lib - VE - LG
- M   c 1,500 f & org
- ¶   Green Building Magazine - 4; ftm, prices vary nm.

Association for Environmental Archaeology   (AEA)   1979
- NR   8 Kirby Place (room 211), Drake Circus, PLYMOUTH, Devon, PL4 8AA.   (memsec/b)
      01752 233129
      email membership@envarch.net   http://www.envarch.net
      Mem Officer: Dr Ralph Fyfe
- ▲   Un-incorporated Society
- ○   *L, *Q; to study the human use of & effects on the environment in the past
- ●   Conf - Mtgs - Res
- M   c 400 i
- ¶   Environmental Archaeology: Jnl of Human Palaeoecology - 2; £38 m.

© CBD Research Ltd · Beckenham · BR3 5JS · Tel 020 8650 7745 · Fax 020 8650 0768 · E-mail cbd@cbdresearch.com · www.cbdresearch.com

Association of Erotic Artists (AEA) 2003
- ■ Flat 3 / 50 Britannia St, LONDON, WC1X 9JH.
  (co-founder/sp)
  020 7837 7049
  email admin@associationoferoticartists.co.uk
  http://www.associationoferoticartists.co.uk
  Co-Founders: Christopher J Ball,   Paul Woods
- ○ *A; to promote positive interest within the public & media with
  regard to the erotic arts; to generate debate & fight
  censorship of the production & display of erotic arts made by
  consenting adults
- Gp Body painting/painters; Comic book artists; Dancers; Erotic art:
  galleries, collectors, publications; Film makers; Illustrators;
  Models (as muse); Multi-media artists; Musicians; Painters;
  Photographers; Pin-up artists; Poets; Printmakers; Sculptors;
  Videographers; Writers
- ● Mtgs - Res - Exhib - Comp - SG - Inf - VE - Awards
- M 58 i, 3 f, UK / 9 i, o'seas
- ¶ [membership £35 i, £60 org]
  Note: membership is available by invitation, after submission of
  a panel of work which is viewed by all the members, & on its
  receiving a simple majority in favour
- ✕ Association of British, Commonwealth & European Erotic Artists

Association of European Trade Mark Owners
  alternative name of **MARQUES**

Association of Event Organisers (AEO) 1921
- ■ 119 High St, BERKHAMSTED, Herts, HP4 2DJ.   (hq)
  01442 285810   fax 01442 875551
  email info@aeo.org.uk
  Chief Exec: Trevor Foley
- ▲ Company Limited by Guarantee
- ○ *T; exhibition organisers working in partnership with contractors
  & venues to raise the profile of exhibitions as a medium
- ● Conf - Mtgs - ET - Res - Inf - LG
- < Events Ind Alliance
- M 184 f, UK / 20 f, o'seas
- ¶ Exhibition Standard - 6; ftm.
- ✕ 2008 Association of Exhibition Organisers Ltd

Association of Event Venues (AEV) 2004
- ■ 119 High St, BERKHAMSTED, Herts, HP4 2DJ.   (hq)
  01442 285811   fax 01442 875551
  email info@aev.org.uk   http://www.aev.org.uk
  Sec: Trevor Foley
- ▲ Company Limited by Guarantee
- ○ *T; venues working in partnership with organisers & contractors
  to promote quality & value for exhibitors, thus raising the
  profile of exhibitions as a medium
- ● Conf - Mtgs - ET - Res - Inf - LG
- M 24 f, UK / 15 f, o'seas
- ¶ Exhibition Standard - 6; ftm.
- ✕ 2006 (merged) Exhibition Venues Association

Association for Events Management Education (AEME) 2004
- NR F1006 UK Centre for Events Management, Leeds Metropolitan
  University, Civic Quarter, LEEDS, W Yorks, LS1 3HE.
  0113-812 3494
  http://www.aeme.org
  Chmn: Glenn Bowdin
- ○ *P

Association of Exhibition Contractors
  in January 2008 merged with the British Exhibition Contractors'
  Association to form the **Event Supplier and Services Association**

Association of Exhibition Organisers Ltd
  since 2008 the **Association of Event Organisers**

Association of External Verifiers (AEV) 1999
- NR PO Box 97, WIRRAL, Cheshire, CH63 0QX.
  0151-327 5007
  http://www.ava.org.uk
- ○ *P; 'to provide professional services for people working in
  quality assurance in learning & development & for those
  working as external verifiers for awarding or regulator
  bodies'

**Association for Families who have Adopted from Abroad
(AFAA) 1987**
- ■ 30 Bradgate, CUFFLEY, Herts, EN6 4RL.   (hsp)
  01707 872129   fax 01707 872129
  email information.afaa@ntlworld.com
  http://www.afaa.org.uk
  Gen Sec: Patricia Wordley
- ▲ Registered Charity
- ○ *W; to help adopted children to grow up happy & well
  adjusted, proud of their birth country and well integrated into
  their country of adoption
- ● Conf - Mtgs - ET - Inf - VE - LG
- M 400 i, 20 org, UK / 6 i, o'seas
- ¶ NL - 2/3;   LM - 1;   AR - 1; all free.

**Association of Family History Societies of Wales (AFHSW)
1981**
- ■ 3 Cagebrook Avenue, Hunderton, HEREFORD, HR2 7AS.
  (hsp)
  email philbufton@hotmail.com   http://www.fhswales.info
  Hon Sec: Phil Bufton
- ▲ Un-incorporated Society
- ○ *G, *N; to coordinate the activities of Welsh family history
  societies
- ● Mtgs - Inf
- M 'not applicable'
  Note: When writing to the Association, please enclose an SAE
  or 2 International Reply Coupons if a reply is required.

Association for Family Therapy (AFT) 1976
- NR 7 Executive Suite, St James Court, Wilderspool Causeway,
  WARRINGTON, WA4 6PS.   (hq)
  01925 444414
  email s.kennedy@aft.org.uk   http://www.aft.org.uk
  Exec Officer: Sue Kennedy
- ▲ Company Limited by Guarantee
- ○ *N, *P; to promote & bring together professional disciplines
  involved in family therapy, training, research, family law &
  practice
- M i & org
- ¶ Jnl of Family Therapy - 4; ftm.   NL - 4.

Association of Festival Organisers (AFO) 1987
- NR PO Box 296, MATLOCK, Derbys, DE4 3XU.   (hq)
  01629 827014   fax 01629 821874
  email info@folkarts-england.org
  http://www.folkarts-england.org
  Dir: Steve Heap
- ▲ Registered Charity
- ○ *D; to act as a channel of communication bewtween festivals &
  events in the folk, roots, traditional & acoustic music world,
  or community events
- ● Conf - Mtgs - ET - Res - Inf - LG
- > Folk Arts England; Folk Arts Network; Shooting Roots Youth
  Project
- M 4 i, 30 f, 150 org
- ¶ Folk Arts England News - 4; free.   LM - continuous.

Association of Financial Controllers & Administrators (AFCA) 1991
- ■ Akhtar House, 2 Shepherd's Bush Rd, LONDON, W6 7PJ.   (hq)
  020 8749 7126   fax 020 8749 7127
  email icea@enta.net   http://www.icea.enta.net
  Chief Exec & Sec: Dr Sushil K das Gupta
- ▲ Company Limited by Guarantee
- ○ *P
- ● Conf - Mtgs - ET - Exam - Res - Exhib - SG - LG
- M c 300 i, UK / c 500 i, o'seas
- ¶ Financial Controller - 2; ftm only.

Association of Fire Consultants
- NR 20 Park St, PRINCES RISBOROUGH, Bucks, HP27 9AH.
  0870 011 4514
  http://www.afc.eu.com
- ○ *P, *T; for fire safety professional consultants, independent of any commercial interests, offering advice on the prevention of fire in buildings or any other structure
- M i

Association of First Aiders (AoFA)
- NR 24 Thomas Drive, NEWPORT PAGNELL, Bucks, MK16 8TH.
  01908 610093   fax 01908 610808
  email admin@aofa.org   http://www.aofa.org
  Contact: David Arnold
- ○ *P; to be the independent authoritative body representing & supporting a membership of all persons & organisations involved in the training, provision & practice of first aid
- M 2,000 i

Association of First Division Civil Servants
  former name of the **First Division Association**

Association of Football Statisticians (AFS) 1978
- ■ 53a St Philip St, LONDON, SW8 3SR.   (regd/office)
  020 7720 5079
  email enquiries@11v11.com   http://www.11v11.com
  Chief Exec: Mark Baker
- ○ *S; research & publishing of football statistics from 1860
- ● Mtgs - Res - Stat - Inf - Lib
- M 1,100 i, UK / 400 i, o'seas

Association of Foreign Banks (AFB) 1947
- ■ 1 Bengal Court, LONDON, EC3V 9DD.   (hq)
  020 7283 8300
  http://www.foreignbanks.org.uk
  Managing Dir: John Treadwell
- ○ *T; foreign banks operating in the UK
- ● Mtgs - ET - SG - Inf
- M f

Association of Franchised Distributors of Electronic Components Ltd (AFDEC) 1970
- ■ The Manor House, High St, BUNTINGFORD, Herts, SG9 9AB.   (hq)
  01763 274748   fax 01763 273255
  email enquiries@afdec.org.uk   http://www.afdec.org.uk
  Sec: Jill Waite
- ○ *T
- M 100 f

Association of Freelance Editors, Proofreaders & Indexers
- IRL 11 Clonard Rd, Sandyford, DUBLIN 16, Republic of Ireland.
  353 (1) 295 2194   http://www.afepi.ie
  Contact: Brenda O'Hanlon
- ○ *P; to act as a point of contact between members & publishers

Association of Freelance Writers
- NR Sevendale House, 7 Dale St, MANCHESTER, M1 1JB.
  0161-228 2362   fax 0161-228 3533
  http://www.freelancemarketnews.com
  Contact: Angela Cox

Association for French Language Studies (AFLS) 1981
- NR c/o Dr Emmanuelle Labeau, School of Languages & Social Sciences, Aston University, Aston Triangle, BIRMINGHAM, B4 7ET.   (sb)
  0121-204 3773
  http://www.afls.net
  Sec: Dr Emmanuelle Labeau
- ▲ Registered Charity
- ○ *L
- ● Conf - Mtgs - ET - Res - SG - Inf - LG - Workshops
- M 50 i, UK / 50 i, o'seas
- ¶ Journal of French Language Studies - 3.
  Cahiers (NL) - 2.

Association of Friendly Societies (AFS) 1995
- NR PO Box 21, ALTRINCHAM, Cheshire, WA14 4PD.   (hq)
  0161-952 5051   fax 0161-929 5163
  email info@afs.org.uk   http://www.afs.org.uk
- ▲ Company Limited by Guarantee
- ○ *T; for the Friendly Society movement
- ● Conf - Mtgs - ET - Exhib - Stat - Inf - LG
- M 57 friendly societies, 2 friendly society councils
- ¶ Ybk - 1; ftm, £25 nm.   Friends for Life (leaflet); free.

Association of Friends of the Waterloo Committee 1972
- NR Hillcrest, 23A Wylde Green Rd, SUTTON COLDFIELD, B72 1HD.
  0121-240 9030
  http://www.waterloocommittee.org.uk
  Hon Sec: John S White
- ▲ Registered Charity
- ○ *L; to promote study & research into the events of the Napoleonic Wars, during 1789-1815, & the Battle of Waterloo & the campaigns of the Duke of Wellington
- ● Conf - Mtgs - Res - SG - Inf - VE
- < Waterloo C'ee in Belgium; The Wellington Museum at Waterloo
- M 500+ i, 10 f, 15+ org, UK / 150+ i, o'seas
- ¶ The Waterloo Jnl - 3; ftm only.

Association of Fundraising Consultants (AFC)
- NR Linen Hall (suite 316), 162-168 Regent St, LONDON, W1B 4JN.
  01582 762446   fax 01582 461489
  http://www.afc.org.uk
- ○ *P

Association of Garage Door Specialists (AGDS) 1993
- ■ PO Box 560, SOUTH PRESTON, Lancs, PR5 6FF.
  (mail/address)
  01772 334828
  http://www.agds.co.uk
  Chmn: Julie Chester
- ▲ Company Limited by Guarantee
- ○ *T; to develop & maintain standards within the garage door industry in relation to products, installation & service
- ● Conf - Mtgs - ET
- < Intl Door Assn
- M 80 f
- ¶ Jnl - 3;   Update - 6; both ftm only.

Association of Gardens Trusts (AGT) 1992
- ■ 70 Cowcross St, LONDON, EC1M 6EJ.   (hq)
  020 7251 2610   fax 020 7251 2610
  email agt@gardens-trusts.org.uk
  http://www.gardenstrusts.org.uk
  Admin: Mary Cruickshank
- ▲ Registered Charity
- ○ *N; a national organisation representing gardens trusts in counties of England & Wales, which are actively engaged in researching, documenting, protecting & caring for designed landscapes
- ● Conf - ET - Res - SG - Inf - Lib - LG
- M 34 county gardens trusts
- ¶ NL - 2; ftm only.

© CBD Research Ltd · Beckenham · BR3 5JS · Tel 020 8650 7745 · Fax 020 8650 0768 · E-mail cbd@cbdresearch.com · www.cbdresearch.com

Association of Gastroenterological Research Charities
believed to have closed; we should appreciate confirmation

Association of GB Athletics Clubs   (ABAC)   2005
- ■ 19 Sheephouse Green, Wotton, DORKING, Surrey,
  RH5 6QW.   (hsp)
  01306 888886
  email mandy@white1966.freeserve.co.uk
  http://www.britishathleticsclubs.com
  Sec: Michael White
- ▲ Company Limited by Guarantee
- ○ *S; to protect & advance the interests of Britain's athletic clubs
- M 97 clubs
  (Sub: £25)

**Association of Genealogists & Researchers in Archives
(AGRA)   1968**
- ■ 29 Badgers Close, HORSHAM, W Sussex, RH12 5RU.   (sp)
  email agra@agra.org.uk   http://www.agra.org.uk
  Joint & Co Sec: David Young
- ▲ Company Limited by Guarantee
- ○ *P; to promote high standards of research amongst members
- ● Conf - Res
- < Fedn of Family History Socs
- M 100 i, 2 f
- ¶ NL - 2.   LM - 1.
- ✕ 2001 (July) Association of Genealogists & Record Agents

Association of Genetic Nurses & Counsellors
a group of the **British Society for Human Genetics**

Association for Geographic Information   (AGI)   1989
- ■ 5 St Helen's Place, Bishopsgate, LONDON, EC3A 6AU.   (hq)
  020 7036 0430   fax 020 7036 0301
  email info@agi.org.uk   http://www.agi.org.uk
  Chief Operating Officer: Angel Baker
- ▲ Company Limited by Guarantee
- Br 3
- ○ *L, *P; to maximise the use of geographic information for the
  benefit of the citizen, good governance & commerce
- Gp Address geography; Crime & disorder; Environment; European;
  Emergency planning; Health; Local government; Marine &
  coastal zone; Technical; Utilities; Public policy
- ● Conf - Mtgs - ET - Exhib - Inf - Lib
- M 1,788 i, 322 f
- ¶ enewsletter - 26;   AR - 1; both free online.

**Association of Geotechnical & Geoenvironmental Specialists
(AGS)   1988**
- ■ 83 Copers Cope Rd, BECKENHAM, Kent, BR3 1NR.   (asa)
  020 8658 8212   fax 020 8663 0949
  email ags@ags.org.uk   http://www.ags.org.uk
  Admin: Dianne Jennings
- ▲ Company Limited by Guarantee
- ○ *T; site investigation, geotechnics, engineering geology &
  related disciplines of environmental engineering &
  contaminated land assessment & remediation
- ● Conf - Mtgs - LG
- < Ground Forum
- M 24 i, 85 f
- ¶ Geoenvironmental Site Assessment: guide to the model report.
  Electronic Transfer of Geotechnical Data from Ground
  Investigations; available as download from Internet.
  Collateral Warranties (2nd ed).
  Guide to Laboratory Testing.
  Guidelines for Combined Geoenvironmental & Geotechnical
  Investigation.

**Association for Glycogen Storage Disease (UK)   (AGSD(UK))
1984**
- ■ 9 Lindop Rd, Hale, ALTRINCHAM, Cheshire, WA15 9DZ.   (sp)
  0161-980 7303
  email agsduk@googlemail.com   http://www.agsd.org.uk
  Gen Sec: Mrs Ann Phillips
- ▲ Registered Charity
- Br 6 countries o'seas
- ○ *W; to provide support for all persons affected with some form
  of glycogen storage disease (which occurs when there is an
  absence or deficiency of the enzymes needed to produce or
  break down glycogen in the body).   It primarily affects the
  liver & muscles
- Gp Project II - to establish centres for collating treatment of children
  & adults; Pompe's Research Fund; McArdles Clinic (Oswestry)
- ● Conf - ET - Res - Exhib - SG - Inf - Lib - VE
- < Assn Glycogen Storage Disease (USA) & other countries o'seas
- M 200 families, 100 professionals, libraries & health centres, UK /
  8 i, o'seas
- ¶ NL - 2; ftm, £1.50 nm (incl all back numbers).
  Special Reports & AR.   Workshop Reports; on website.

Association of Golf Club Secretaries
since 2007 the **Golf Club Managers' Association**

Association of Golf Writers   (AGW)   1938
- ■ 1 Pilgrim's Bungalow, Mulberry Hill, CHILHAM, Kent,
  CT4 8AH.   (hsp)
  01227 732496   fax 01227 732496
  email andyfarrell292@btinternet.com
  Hon Sec: Andy Farrell
- ▲ Un-incorporated Society
- ○ *P, *S; to liaise with governing bodies of golf for improved
  working conditions
- ● Liaison with golfing bodies
- M 109 i, UK / 48 i, o'seas
- ¶ NL - 10; ftm only.   Members' Hbk - 1; free.

**Association of Governing Bodies of Independent Schools
(AGBIS)   1941**
- ■ Renshaw Barns, Upper Woodford, SALISBURY, Wilts,
  SP4 6FA.   (hq)
  01722 782900
  email gensec@agbis.org.uk   http://www.agbis.org.uk
  Gen Sec: Shane Rutter-Jerome
- ▲ Registered Charity
- ○ *E; to support governing bodies of independent schools; to
  promote good school governance in the independent sector
- ● Conf - Mtgs - ET - Inf - LG
- < Indep Schools Coun
- M independent day & boarding schools
- ¶ NL - 2;   AR; both ftm.

Association of Government Veterinarians
a group of the **British Veterinary Association**

**Association of Graduate Careers Advisory Services   (AGCAS)
1967**
- NR Millennium House, 30 Junction Rd, SHEFFIELD, S Yorks,
  S11 8XB.   (hq)
  0114-251 5750
  http://www.agcas.org.uk
- ▲ Company Limited by Guarantee; Registered Charity
- ○ *E, *P; to support the work of careers services in higher
  education
- M i

Association of Graduate Recruiters   (AGR)   1968

NR   Innovation Centre, Warwick Technology Park, Gallows Hill,
     WARWICK, CV34 6UW.   (hq)
     01926 623236
     http://www.agr.org.uk
     Chief Exec: Carl Gilleard
▲   Company Limited by Guarantee
○   *T; to provide a forum for the discussion of issues relevant to
     graduate recruitment

Association for Group & Individual Psychotherapy   (AGIP)   1974

NR   1 Fairbridge Rd, LONDON, N19 3EW.   (hq)
     020 7272 7013
     http://www.agip.org.uk
▲   Registered Charity
○   *P; to promote education in psychotherapy; to make
     psychotherapy more widely available
M   i

Association of Guernsey Banks   (AGB)

■   c/o Bank Sarasin (CI) Ltd, PO Box 348, Park Court, Park St,
     ST PETER PORT, Guernsey, GY1 3UY.   (chmn/b)
     email ken.gibbs@sarasin.com   http://www.agb.org.gg
     Chmn: Ken Gibbs
▲   Un-incorporated Society
○   *T; to represent all licensed Guernsey banks
●   Mtgs - LG
<   Guernsey Intl Bankers Assn
M   48 f

Association of Guilds of Weavers, Spinners & Dyers   1955

■   17 Shearer Rd, Fratton, PORTSMOUTH, Hants, PO1 5LL.
     (hsp)
     023 9285 1429
     email v.thorne@ntlworld.com   http://www.wsd.org.uk
     Correspondence Sec: Valerie Thorne
▲   Registered Charity
Br   102; France, Japan, New Zealand, Serbia, South Africa, USA
○   *A, *G; to preserve & improve craftsmanship in handweaving,
     spinning & dyeing; to promote public awareness & education
     in such craftsmanship
●   Conf - Mtgs - ET - Exam - Exhib - Inf
M   4,500 i, 102 org, UK / i, 9 org, o'seas
     (Sub: £3.75)
¶   The Jnl for Weavers, Spinners & Dyers - 4; ftm, £5 nm.

Association of Head Teachers in Scotland
     since March 2006 the **Association of Headteachers & Deputes in Scotland**

Association of Heads of Independent Schools   (AHIS)   1924

NR   The Ancient Forresters, Bush End, Takeley,
     BISHOP'S STORTFORD Herts, CM22 6NN.
     01279 871865
     Contact: F V Morgan
○   *E; to further interests of education on independent lines

Association of Heads of Outdoor Education Centres   (AHOEC)   1963

NR   Woodlands OEC, Glasbury-on-Wye, via HEREFORD,
     HR3 5LP.   (chmn/b)
     01497 847272
     http://www.ahoec.org
     Chmn: Kevin Jackson
▲   Un-incorporated Society
○   *S; to encourage all-round personal development through
     residential experience & the use of the outdoors; to develop,
     establish & maintain safe practice in outdoor activities
●   Conf - Mtgs - ET
<   Engl Outdoor Coun
M   120 i, UK / 1 i, o'seas

Association of Headteachers & Deputes in Scotland   (AHDS)   1975

■   PO Box 18532, INVERURIE, Aberdeenshire, AB51 0WS.
     (mail/address)
     0845 260 7560
     email info@ahds.org.uk   http://www.ahds.org.uk
     Gen Sec: Greg Dempster
▲   Un-incorporated Society
○   *U; to represent the interests & perspectives of Scotland's
     headteachers & deputes from nursery, primary & special
     schools
Gp   Headteachers; Depute headteachers
●   Conf - Mtgs - ET - Empl - LG
<   Eur School Heads Assn
M   1,400 i
¶   Head to Head - 4; ftm only.
×   2006 (March) Association of Head Teachers in Scotland

Association of Healthcare Cleaning Professionals   (AHCP)

■   c/o Watson Associates, A6 Kingfisher House, Kingsway TVTE,
     GATESHEAD, Tyne & Wear, NE11 0JQ.
     07946 772620
     Business Mgr: Mrs Penny Harrison
▲   Company Limited by Guarantee
Br   10
○   *P; for managers in the cleaning & support services, suppliers
     of goods for these services, & students & lecturers in colleges
     & universities
Gp   Cleaning
●   Conf - Mtgs - ET - Exhib - SG - Inf - VE
<   Brit Cleaning Coun
M   c 300 i, c 50 f
¶   Excel (NL) - 4; ftm.   Annual Programme.
     Conference Report.   Guidance Booklets.   AR.
     Standards of Environmental Cleanliness in Hospitals.
×   2007 Association of Domestic Management

Association of Healthcare Communicators   (AHC)   1997

■   PO Box 4277, DUNSTABLE, Beds, LU6 2WU.   (admin/p)
     01525 222155   fax 01525 222155
     email katherine.baldwin@virgin.net
     http://www.assochealth.org.uk
     Chmn: Nick Samuels,   Admin: Kate Baldwin
Br   2
○   *P; for healthcare communications professionals working in, or
     mainly with, the NHS
●   Conf - ET - Inf
M   350 i
     (Sub: £50)
¶   ARC News (NL) - 4; ftm only.

Association of Healthcare Human Resource Management
     since 2005 the **Healthcare People Management Association**

Association for Heritage Interpretation   (AHI)   1975

NR   37 Cholmeley RD, READING, Berks, RG1 3NQ.   (hq)
     0118-966 4894
     email mail@ahi.org.uk   http://www.ahi.org.uk
     Contact: The Administrator
▲   Registered Charity
○   *L; to encourage excellence in the presentation & management
     of our natural & cultural environments
●   Conf - ET - Res - Inf - Lib - VE
M   300 i, 250 f & org
¶   Jnl - 3;   NL - 6; both ftm only.

** Association for High Speed Photography & Photonics

     Organisation lost: see introduction paragraph 3

© CBD Research Ltd · Beckenham · BR3 5JS · Tel 020 8650 7745 · Fax 020 8650 0768 · E-mail cbd@cbdresearch.com · www.cbdresearch.com

Association of Higher Civil & Public Servants

IRL Fleming's Hall, 12 Fleming's Place, DUBLIN 4, Republic of Ireland.
 353 (1) 668 6077 fax 353 (1) 668 6380
 email info@ahcps.ie http://www.ahcps.ie
 Gen Sec: Séan Ó Ríordáin
○ *P

Association of Hispanists of Great Britain and Ireland (AHGBI)

NR School of Modern Languages & Cultures, Room B 34 1 Trent, University Park, NOTTINGHAM, NG7 2RD.
 http://www.hispanists.org.uk
 Sec: Dr Jean Andrews

Association of History & Computing UK (AHC-UK) 1997

NR c/o Derek Harding, Centre for Learning & Quality Enhancement, University of Teesside, MIDDLESBROUGH, Tees Valley, TS1 3BA. (hsb)
 email derek.harding@tees.ac.uk http://www.ahc.ac.uk
 Sec: Derek Harding
▲ Un-incorporated Society
○ *L; to promote the use of computers in historical research & training

Association for the History of Glass (1977) (AHG) 1977

■ c/o Society of Antiquaries, Burlington House, Piccadilly, LONDON, W1J 0BE. (regd/office)
 http://www.historyofglass.org.uk
 Hon Sec: Sandra Davidson
▲ Company Limited by Guarantee; Registered Charity
○ *L; to advance the education of the public in the historical, archaeological, aesthetic & technological study of glass, for all periods of history & all parts of the world; the problems of conservation & presentation
● Conf - Mtgs
< Assn Intle pour l'Histoire du Verre
M 154 i, instns
 (Sub: £5)
¶ Glass News (NL) - 2; ftm, £5 nm.

Association of Home Information Pack Providers (AHIPP)

■ The Old Rectory, Church Lane, Thornby, NORTHAMPTON, NN6 8SN. (hq)
 0870 950 7739 fax 01604 743249
 email info@hipassociation.co.uk
 http://www.hipassociation.co.uk
 Dir Gen: Mike Ockenden
▲ Company Limited by Guarantee
○ *T; for HIP providers to act as a consultative body to government & other organisations with a stake in HIPs; to promote standards & benefits to consumers, industry & politicians alike
● Conf - Mtgs - Res - Stat - Inf - LG
M 105 f
 (Sub: £12,000 execs, £6,000 associates, £2,400 affiliates)
¶ e-NL - 52; HIP Handling Guide - up-dated; both ftm only.

Association of Hot Foil Printers (AssHFP) 1991

NR 15 Hunt St, Atherton, MANCHESTER, M46 9JF. (hq)
 01942 873574 fax 0845 166 8396
 email association@hotfoilprinting.org
 http://www.hotfoilprinting.org
 Sec: Paul Forshaw
▲ Un-incorporated Society
○ *T; to promote the benefits of hot foil printed products
● ET - Inf
M [not available]
¶ Monthly Magazine - 12; £25 yr m only.
 Hot Foil Printing: a guide to the whole business; £25.
× 1998-2005 National Association of Hot Foil Printers

Association for Humanistic Psychology in Britain (AHP(B)) 1968

NR BM Box 3582, LONDON, WC1N 3XX. (mail/address)
 0845 707 8506
 email admin@ahpb.org.uk http://www.ahpb.org.uk
▲ Registered Charity
○ *L; to encourage interest in humanistic psychology
● Conf - Mtgs - ET - SG - Inf
M 1,000 i, 30 f
¶ Self & Society - 6.

Association of Illustrators (AoI) 1973

■ Back Building (2nd floor), 150 Curtain Rd, LONDON, EC2A 3AT. (hq)
 020 7613 4328 fax 020 7613 4417
 email info@theaoi.com http://www.theaoi.com
 Chmn: Russell Cobb
▲ Company Limited by Guarantee
○ *P; to advance & protect illustrators' rights; to raise the profile of illustration & the standard of practice within the industry
● Conf - ET - Exhib - Comp - Inf - Empl - LG
< Eur Illustrators Forum (EIF); Brit Copyright Coun
> Soc of Artists Agents
M 1,300 i, 20 f, 50 colleges, UK / 20 i, o'seas
 (Sub: £120 i, £185 f, £100 colleges)
¶ Varoom [Jnl] - 3; ftm, £30 nm.
 Survive; £17.50 m, £27.50 nm. Pricing; £7.50 m, £10 nm.
 Illustrators Guide to Law & Business Practice; £19.95, £24.95 nm.
 Publishing Directory; Editorial Directory; Advertising Directory; all £25 m, £33 nm.
 Images;£29.95 m, £39.95 nm.

Association for Improvements in the Maternity Services (AIMS) 1960

■ 5 Ann's Court, Grove Rd, SURBITON, Surrey, KT6 4BE. (chmn/p)
 0870 765 1433
 http://www.aims.org.uk
 Chmn: Beverley Beech
▲ Un-incorporated Society
○ *K; a pressure group providing information to new parents on rights & choices in the maternity services; supports midwives as practitioners in their own right
Gp VBAC (Vaginal birth after Caesarean Section) support; Home birth support
● Conf - Inf
M 1,000 i
¶ AIMS Quarterly Jnl - 4.
 Wide range of books & leaflets.

** Association of Incorporated Managers & Administrators

 Organisation lost: see Introduction paragraph 3

Association of Independent Advice Centres
 see **Advice NI**

Association of Independent Care Advisers (AICA) 1994

NR Orchard House, Albury, GUILDFORD, Surrey, GU5 9AG. (hq)
 01483 203066 fax 01483 202535
 email info@aica.org.uk http://www.aica.org.uk
 Chmn: Christopher Cain
▲ Un-incorporated Society
○ *P; to represent private organisations who offer independent advice to older people, their families & carers, to help find appropriate care at home or in residential care or nursing homes
● Conf - Mtgs - LG
M 250 i, 12 f

Association of Independent Clinical Research Contractors
 ceased trading in March 2004 & was replaced by the **Clinical Contract Research Association**

**Association of Independent Computer Specialists   (AICS)
1972**
- ■ Honeyhill, Bismore, Eastcombe, STROUD, Glos, GL6 7DG.
  (hsp)
  0845 123 5399   fax 0845 130 5812
  email honsec@aics.org.uk   http://www.aics.org.uk
  Hon Sec: R K Brooks
- ▲ Company Limited by Guarantee
- ○ *T; the provision of specialist computer related services by
  individual practitioners & owner-directed firms
- ● Conf - Networking
- M 40 i, 30 f
- ¶ NL - 4; ftm, £10 yr nm.

Association of Independent Construction Adjudicators   (AICA)
- NR Royal London House, 22-25 Finsbury Square, LONDON,
  EC2A 1DX.
  0844 249 5353   fax 0844 249 5354
  email enquiries@aica-adjudication.co.uk
  http://www.aica.bbsnet.co.uk
  Chmn: Peter Shiells
- ▲ Company Limited by Guarantee
- ○ *P; nomination body for appointment of adjudicators to resolve
  construction disputes
- ● Conf - Mtgs - ET - Inf
- M 136 i

Association of Independent Crop Consultants   (AICC)   1980
- ■ Agriculture Place, Drayton Farm, East Meon, PETERSFIELD,
  Hants, GU32 1PN.   (hq)
  01730 823881   fax 01730 823882
  email aicc@farmline.com   http://www.aicc.org.uk
  Chief Exec: Sarah Cowlrick
- ▲ Company Limited by Guarantee
- ○ *F, *P; for independent crop consultants
- ● Conf - Mtgs - ET - Inf - LG
- M 180 i, 1 f
- ¶ NL - 4; ftm only.   LM - 1; free.

Association of Independent Financial Advisers   (AIFA)   1999
- NR 2-6 Austin Friars House, Austin Friars, LONDON,
  EC2N 2HD.   (hq)
  020 7628 1287
  http://www.aifa.net
- ▲ Company Limited by Guarantee
- ○ *P
- ● Conf - Mtgs - ET - Res - Stat - Inf - Lib - LG
- M 13,364 i, 5,069 f, 1 org (CBI)

**Association of Independent First Aid at Work Training
Organisations**
- NR PO Box 8810, ASHBY de la ZOUCH, Leics, LE65 9BG.
  07952 361 158
  email aifawto@btconnect.com   http://www.aifawto.co.uk

Association of Independent Inventory Clerks   (AIIC)   1996
- ■ PO Box 1288, West End, WOKING, Surrey, GU24 9WE.
  01276 855388   fax 01276 855388
  email centraloffice@theaiic.co.uk
  http://www.theaiic.co.uk
  Hon Sec: Holly Doole
- ▲ Un-incorporated Society
- ○ *P
- ● ET - Inf
- M 220 i
- ¶ The Declaration.

Association of Independent Libraries   (AIL)   1989
- NR The Leeds Library, 18 Commercial St, LEEDS, W Yorks,
  LS1 6AL.   (chmn/b)
  0113-245 3071
  http://www.independentlibraries.co.uk
  Chmn: Geoffrey Forster
- ○ *A; subscription libraries founded between c 1690 & 1841
  before the creation of the public library service; to care for
  their historic collections & buildings; to supply the latest
  books, periodicals & a personal service to their members
- M 28 libraries

Association of Independent Management & Maritime Services
  is no longer in business

Association of Independent Meat Suppliers   (AIMS)   2001
- NR PO Box 125, NORTHALLERTON, N Yorks, DL6 2YG.
  01609 761547   fax 01609 761548
  http://www.aims2001.co.uk
- ○ *T; small & medium-sized abattoirs

Association of Independent Museums   (AIM)   1977
- NR 4 Clayhall Rd, GOSPORT, Hants, PO12 2BY.   (admin/p)
  email admin@aim-museums.co.uk
  http://www.aim-museums.co.uk
  Administrator: Roger Hornsham
- ▲ Company Limited by Guarantee
- ○ *L, *N; to comnnect, support & represent independent
  museums (those not supported by government)
- ● Conf - Mtgs - ET - Stat - Inf - VE - LG
- M 100 i, 100 f, 500 org
- ¶ AIM Bulletin - 5; free.

Association of Independent Music   (AIM)   1999
- NR Lamb House, Church Street, LONDON, W4 2PD.   (hq)
  020 8994 5599
  http://www.musicindie.org
- ▲ Company Limited by Guarantee
- ○ *D, *T; independent record companies
- ● LG - Negotiating - Advising - Networking
- < IMPALA
- M 700 f
- ¶ AR; free.

Association of Independent Organ Advisers   (AIOA)   1996
  [witheld]
- ▲ Un-incorporated Society
- ○ *P; to offer independent, professional advice on new pipe
  organs & pipe organ restoration
- ● Mtgs - Accreditation of advisers
- M 8 i

Association of Independent Practitioners
  a group of the **British Association for Counselling &
Psychotherapy**

** **Association of Independent Psychotherapists**

Association of Independent Research & Technology Organisations
  alternative name of **AIRTO Ltd**

© CBD Research Ltd · Beckenham · BR3 5JS · Tel 020 8650 7745 · Fax 020 8650 0768 · E-mail cbd@cbdresearch.com · www.cbdresearch.com

Association of Independent Specialist Medical Accountants (AISMA)   1995

- ■ 48 St Leonards Rd, BEXHILL-on-SEA, E Sussex, TN40 1JB.
  01424 730345   fax 01424 730330
  email aisma@honeybarrett.co.uk
  http://www.aisma.org.uk
  Sec: Liz Densley
- ▲ Un-incorporated Society
- ○ *P
- ● Conf - Mtgs - Stat
- M 75 f
- ¶ NL - 4; ftm only.
  Medical Practitioners' Financial Hbk - 3 yrly.

Association of Independent Tobacco Specialists   (AITS)   1976

- ■ 14 Wyndham Arcade, CARDIFF, Glamorgan, CF10 1FJ.   (hsp)
  029 2066 4114
  Sec: Donald C Higgins
- Br 103
- ○ *T; to keep the tobacconist in the high street
- ● Conf - Mtgs - Exhib - SG - Inf - VE
- M 73 i, 103 f
- ¶ NL - 12.   Tobacco Index - 1.
  National Tobacconists Trade Exhibition Catalogue.

Association of Independent Tour Operators   (AITO)   1976

- ■ 133a St Margaret's Rd, TWICKENHAM, Middx, TW1 1RG.
  (hq)
  020 8744 9280   fax 020 8744 3187
  email info@aito.co.uk   http://www.aito.co.uk
  Chmn: Derek Moore
- ○ *T; includes small & specialist tour operators
- M c 150 f

Association for Industrial Archaeology   (AIA)   1973

- NR AIA Liaison Office, The Ironbridge Institute, Ironbridge Gorge
  Museum, Coalbrookdale, TELFORD, Shropshire, TF8 7DX.
  (regd/office)
  01325 3598467
  email aia-enquiries@contacts.bham.ac.uk
  http://www.industrial-archaeology.org.uk
  Liaison Officer: Anne Lowes
- ▲ Registered Charity
- ○ *L; to promote the study, preservation & presentation of Britain's
  industrial heritage; a national organisation for people who
  share an interest in Britain's industrial past
- ● Conf - ET - Res - Inf - VE
- M 900 i, 71 org
- ¶ Industrial Archaeology Review - 2;
  Industrial Archaeology News - 4; both ftm.

Association of Industrial Laser Users
   since 14 April 2007 the **Association of Laser Users**

Association of Industrial Road Safety Officers   (AIRSO)   1965

- ■ 68 The Boulevard, WORTHING, W Sussex, BN13 1LA.   (hsb)
  01903 506095   fax 01903 506095
  email airso@talk21.com   http://www.airso.org.uk
  Sec: Graham Feest
- ▲ Registered Charity
- ○ *P; to promote road safety within vehicle fleet undertakings;
  exchange of information on accident prevention schemes,
  driver training techniques & vehicle construction & usage
- ● Conf - Mtgs - ET - LG
- M 500 i, UK / 10 i, o'seas
- ¶ Directory of Members - 1; ftm only.

Association of Industrial Truck Trainers   (AITT)   1985

- NR Unit 20 The Springboard Centre, Mantle Lane, COALVILLE,
  Leics, LE67 3DW.   (hsb)
  01530 277857   fax 01530 810231
  email sueaitt@aol.com   http://www.aitt.co.uk
  Sec: Mrs Susan Finney
- ▲ Un-incorporated Society
- ○ *P; research into methods of training, operation & maintenance
  of equipment
- Gp Independent Training Scheme & Register Ltd (ITSSAR Ltd):
  provides standards & monitoring of training of fork lift truck
  operators & maintains a register of tutors, trainers &
  operators of fork lift trucks
- ● Conf - Mtgs - ET - Exam - Res - Exhib - Inf - LG
- < Brit Indl Truck Assn (BITA)
- M i & f
- ¶ NL - 2;   LM - 1;   AR; all ftm only.

Association for Infant Mental Health UK   (AIMH UK)

- NR Knowle Clinic, Broadfield Rd, BRISTOL, BS4 2UH.
  020 8144 2386   fax 0117-370 1011
  email info@aimh.org.uk   http://www.aimh.org.uk
  Chmn: Catherine Lowenhoff
- ▲ Company Limited by Guarantee
- ○ *P; to bring together professionals to promote the mental health
  of infants

Association of Inflatable Manufacturers, Operators, Designers & Suppliers
   a group of the **Performance Textiles Association**

Association for Information Management
   alternative name of **Aslib**

Association of Information Officers in the Pharmaceutical Industry
   since 2005 the **Pharmaceutical Information &
   Pharmacovigilance Association**

Association of Inland Navigation Authorities   (AINA)   1996

- NR Fearns Wharf, Neptune St, LEEDS, W Yorks, LS9 8PB.   (hq)
  0113-243 3125   fax 0113-245 8394
  email info@aina.org.uk   http://www.aina.org.uk
  Contact: The Executive Director
- ▲ Un-incorporated Society
- ○ *T; to develop, share & promote good practice in the
  management & use of the UK's inland waterways; to
  represent the views of owners & operators of the waterways
  to government & its agencies, local authorities, policy
  makers, funders & stakeholders
- ● Conf - Mtgs - LG
- M 30 org
- ¶ [Publications on website].

Association of Inner Wheel Clubs in Great Britain & Ireland   1934

- NR 51 Warwick Sq, LONDON, SW1V 2AT.   (hq)
  020 7834 4600 (Mon-Fri 0930-1630)
  Sec/Admin: Ann Koh
- Br 1,057
- ○ *W; 'friendship & service', membership is limited to the
  womenfolk of Rotarians
- ● Conf - Mtgs
- < Intl Inner Wheel; Women's Nat Commission
- M 29,500 i
- ¶ Inner Wheel - 3; m only.

*Association of Installers of Unvented Hot Water Systems (Scotland &
   N Ireland)*
   a group of the **Scottish & Northern Ireland Plumbing
   Employers' Federation**

** **Association for Institutional Multi-Manager Investing**
   Organisation lost: see Introduction paragraph 3.

Association for Instrumentation, Control, Automation & Laboratory Technology   GAMBICA   1981
- ■ Broadwall House, 21 Broadwall, LONDON, SE1 9PL.   (hq)
     020 7642 8080   fax 020 7642 8096
     email assoc@gambica.org.uk
     http://www.gambica.org.uk
     Chief Exec: Geoff C Young
- ○ *T; 'for instrumentation, control, automation'
- Gp Product areas: Industrial control & power electronics
     components & systems; Process measurement & control
     equipment & systems; Environmental analysis & monitoring
     equipment; Test & measurement equipment; Laboratory
     based analytical & measuring equipment; Laboratory
     technology
- ● Conf - Mtgs - ET - Exhib - Stat - Expt - Inf
- M   150 f
- ¶   Product Guide - 1;   AR;   Brochure; all free.

Association of Insurance & Risk Managers   (AIRMIC)   1963
- NR   6 Lloyd's Ave, LONDON, EC3N 3AX.   (hq)
     020 7480 7610   fax 020 7702 3752
     http://www.airmic.com
     Exec Dir: David Gamble
- ▲ Company Limited by Guarantee
- ○ *P; to provide a forum for the exchange of data & opinion
     concerning risk management in industry, commerce & local
     government
- M   i

Association of Insurance Surveyors Ltd   (AIS)
- NR   PO Box 454, FAREHAM, Hants, PO14 4UW.   (mail/address)
     http://www.insurancesurveyors.org
- ○ *P; research into methods of burglary protection; cooperation
     with security organisations
     No further information supplied
- ✕ 2004 Association of Burglary Insurance Surveyors

Association of Inter-Varsity Clubs   (AIVC)   1946
- NR   c/o Manchester IVC, 94-96 Grosvenor St, MANCHESTER,
     M1 7HL.   (forwarding/add)
     0870 321 0482
     http://www.ivc.org.uk
- ▲ Un-incorporated Society
- Br   46; Bermuda
- ○ *N; coordinating body for member clubs; to provide cultural,
     social & sporting activities within the British Isles, for
     graduates & others of like interests
- ● Conf - Mtgs - ET - Inf - VE
- M   c 6,000 i, 46 clubs, UK / 20 i, 1 club, o'seas
- ¶   Newslines - 12;   LM - 2; both ftm only.
     (Each club publishes a monthly bulletin with a list of social
     events).

Association of Interchurch Families   (AIF)   1968
- ■ Bastille Court, 2 Paris Garden, LONDON, SE1 8ND.   (hq)
     020 7654 7251   fax 020 7654 7222
     email info@interchurchfamilies.org.uk
     http://www.interchurchfamilies.org.uk
     Chief Exec: Keith Lander
- ▲ Registered Charity
- ○ *E, *R; offers a support network for interchurch families (usually
     a Roman Catholic married to a Christian of another
     communion) & a voice for such families as they seek to
     contribute to the growing together of their churches
- ● Conf - Mtgs - Res - Inf - VE
- <   Interchurch Families Intl Network; (sister assns in Australia,
     Austria, Canada, France, Germany, Italy, N Zealand,
     N Ireland, Switzerland, USA)
- M   940 i (mostly couples/families)
- ¶   AIF News - 3; ftm only.
     Issues, Reflections, News [internet bulletin]; 1/3; free.
     Annual Review - 1; free.

Association of Interior Specialists   (AIS)   1998
- ■ Olton Bridge, 245 Warwick Rd, SOLIHULL, W Midlands,
     B92 7AH.   (hq)
     0121-707 0077   fax 0121-706 1949
     email info@ais-interiors.org.uk
     http://www.ais-interiors.org.uk
     Chief Exec: Simon Forrester
- ▲ Company Limited by Guarantee
- ○ *T; to represent companies involved in the manufacture, supply
     & installation of all aspects of interior fit-outs &
     refurbishment; members operate in retail & commercial
     offices, the public sector, banks, hotels, hospitals, schools
     factories etc (including access floors, ceilings, lighting,
     movablewalls, partitioning)
- ● Conf - Mtgs - ET - Res - Exhib - Stat - Inf - LG - website features
     an interactive directory search
- <   Nat Specialist Contrs Coun; Construction Products Assn
- M   430 f, UK / 4 f, o'seas
- ¶   Interiors Focus - 2; ftm, free to specifiers nm.
     Interior Insight (NL) - 4; ftm only.
     LM - 2; ftm & specifiers.

Association of International Accountants Ltd   (AIA)   1928
- ■ Staithes 3, The Watermark, Metro Riverside,
     NEWCASTLE upon TYNE, NE11 9SN.   (hq)
     0191-493 0277   fax 0191-493 0278
     email aia@aiaworldwide.com
     http://www.aiaworldwide.com
     Chief Exec: Philip J J Turnbull
- ▲ Company Limited by Guarantee
- Br   9; China, Cyprus, Ghana, Greece, Hong Kong, Ireland,
     Malaysia, Singapore
- ○ *P; to offer a recognised professional accountancy qualification
- ● Conf - Mtgs - ET - Exam - Exhib - Comp - Expt - Inf - Lib
- M   i
- ¶   International Accountant - 6; ftm, £40 yr nm.
     Student Focus - 2;   AR - 1; both ftm.

Association for International Cancer Research   (AICR)   1979
- NR   Madras House, South St, ST ANDREWS, Fife, KY16 9EH.   (hq)
     01334 477910   fax 01334 478667
     http://www.airc.org.uk
     Chief Exec: Norman Barrett
- ▲ Company Limited by Guarantee; Registered Charity
- ○ *Q; a charity which endeavours to support & fund basic (as
     opposed to clinical) research into the basic mechanisms
     which are involved in the development of those diseases
     commonly known as cancer
- Gp   Scientific advy c'ee (determines research direction)

**Association of International Courier & Express Services
(AICES)   1977**
- NR   Global House, Poyle Rd, Colnbrook, SLOUGH, Berks,
     SL3 0AY.   (hq)
     01753 680550
     http://www.aices.org
- ○ *T
- M   45 f

Association of International Marketing
     since 2008 the **Institute of International Marketing**

Association of International Property Professionals   (AIPP)
- NR   94 New Bond St, LONDON, W1S 1SJ.   (hq)
     020 7409 7061
     email enquiries@aipp.org.uk   http://www.aipp.org.uk
- ○ *P; to protect the interests of UK citizens buying property abroad
- M   c 380 i

© CBD Research Ltd · Beckenham · BR3 5JS · Tel 020 8650 7745 · Fax 020 8650 0768 · E-mail cbd@cbdresearch.com · www.cbdresearch.com

Association of Investment Companies (AIC) 1932

NR 24 Chiswell St (9th floor), LONDON, EC1Y 4YY. (hq)
020 7282 5555 fax 020 7282 5556
email info@theaic.co.uk http://www.theaic.co.uk
Dir Gen: Daniel Godfrey
▲ Company Limited by Guarantee
○ *T; to work with member investment trust companies to add value to their shareholders over the long-term; to provide a coordinated response to any new developments in regulation or tax & initiate favourable legislative changes
● Conf - Mtgs - ET - Exhib - Stat - Inf - LG
Information line: 0800 085 8520
M 246 f
¶ Monthly Information Service - 12.
IT Hbk - 1.
Information packs & Factsheets.
✕ 2006 Association of Investment Trust Companies

Association of Investment Trust Companies
since 2006 the **Association of Investment Companies**

Association of Irish Choirs 1980

IRL Drinan St, CORK, Co Cork, Republic of Ireland.
353 (21) 431 2296 fax 353 (21) 496 2457
email info@cnc.ie http://www.cnc.ie
Chmn: Kevin O'Callaghan
○ *D; to promote choral music and singing in Ireland

Association of the Irish Dental Industry Ltd

IRL PO Box 59, DROGHEDA, Co Louth, Republic of Ireland.
353 (41) 983 8210 fax 353 (41) 983 8210
http://www.aidi.ie
Gen Sec: Anne Flaherty
○ *T

Association of Irish Humanists
since 2004 the **Humanist Association of Ireland**

Association of Irish Racecourses

IRL 63 Fitzwilliam Square, Dublin 2, Republic of Ireland
353 (1) 676 0911
email air@iol.ie http://www.air.ie
Chief Exec: Paddy Walsh

Association of Jewish Ex-Servicemen & Women (AJEX) 1930

NR Shield House, Harmony Way, LONDON, NW4 2BZ. (hq)
020 8202 2323 fax 020 8202 9900
email headoffice@ajexuk.org.uk
http://www.ajex.org.uk
Gen Sec: S J Weisser
▲ Registered Charity
Br 60
○ *W; to assist ex-service men & women & their dependents; to observe remembrance of the fallen; to combat religious & racial intolerance
Gp Public relations; Welfare & social services; Remembrance Jewish military museum
● Conf - Mtgs - Res - Exhib - SG - Inf - Lib & museum - VE
< Intl Congress of Jewish War Veterans
M c 5,000 i

Association of Jungian Analysts 1977

NR 7 Eton Ave, LONDON, NW3 3EL.
020 7794 8711 fax 020 7794 8711
http://www.jungiananalysts.org.uk
○ *P

Association of Labour Providers (ALP) 2004

■ 102 Frimley House, 5 The Parade, High Street, FRIMLEY, Surrey, GU16 7JQ. (mail/address)
01276 5093066 fax 01276 7610769
email info@labourproviders.org.uk
http://www.labourproviders.org.uk
Chmn: Mark Boleat
▲ Un-incorporated Society
○ *T; to represent the interests of, & provide services to, labour providers
● Res - LG
M 120 f
¶ NL - 12; ftm only. AR - 1; free.

Association for Land Based Colleges (Napaeo)
since 2008 **Landex**

Association of Land Rover Clubs Ltd (ALRC) 1983

NR 1a Duncan Ave, Huncote, LEICESTER, LE9 3AN. (regd/off)
email tonybirch@btopenworld.com http://www.alrc.co.uk
Hon Sec: Simone Birch
○ *G, *S; renovation & restoration of all Rover vehicles; Rover marque enthusiasts clubs
M org
✕ 2005 Association of Rover Clubs

Association of Landscape Contractors of Ireland (Northern Ireland) (ALCI) 1971

NR 22 Summerhill Park, BANGOR, Co Down, BT20 5QQ. (hsp)
028 9127 2823 fax 028 9127 2823
http://www.alci.org.uk
Admin Coordinator: Lyn Sherriff
▲ Un-incorporated Society
○ *T; to represent the landscape industry in Northern Ireland
Gp Sportsground construction; Grounds maintenance; Tree surgery; General landscaping
● Conf - Mtgs - ET - Exhib - Comp - Inf - Lib - VE - LG
< Brit Assn Landscape Inds
M 10 i, 50 f, 4 org
¶ ALCI Directory - 2 yrly; free.

Association for Language Learning (ALL) 1990

■ University of Leicester, University Road, LEICESTER, LE1 7RH. (hq)
0116-229 7453 fax 0116-229 7454
email yvonneh@all-languages.org.uk
http://www.all-languages.org.uk
Office Mgr: Yvonne Hogben
▲ Registered Charity
Br 21
○ *N, *P; 'the major professional organisation for language teachers in the UK; the teaching, learning & use of languages in education & society as a whole'
Gp C'ees: Dutch, French, German, Italian, Russian, Spanish & Portuguese, Asian languages, Publications, Policy
● Conf - Mtgs - ET - Exhib - Inf - LG
¶ Language Learning Jnl - 2; £78 (£95 EU) (£107 o'seas).
Language World (NL) - 4; free.
Francophonie - 2; £60 (£72 EU) (£82 o'seas).
Deutsch: Lehren und Lernen (the German Jnl) - 2; £60 (£72 EU) (£82 o'seas).
Vida Hispánica (the Spanish & Portuguese Jnl) - 2; £60 (£72 EU) (£82 o'seas).
Tuttitalia (the Italian Jnl) - 2; £60 (£72 EU) (£82 o'seas).
Russistika (the Russian Jnl) - 1; £32 (£37 EU) (£42 o'seas).
All seven titles; £203 (£253 EU) (£300 o'seas).
Onze Taal - 10; ftm only.

** Association of Larger Local Councils (ALLC) 1981

Organisation lost: see Introduction paragraph 3

Association of Laser Users (AILU) 1995
- ■ Oxford House, 100 Ock St, ABINGDON, Oxon, OX14 5DH. (hq)
   01235 539595   fax 01235 550499
   email info@ailu.org.uk   http://www.ailu.org.uk
   Sec: Dr J M Green
- ▲ Company Limited by Guarantee
- ○ *T; to foster cooperation & collaboration on non-competitive technical matters relating to the commercial use of lasers & laser-related research
- Gp Medical Lasers Group; Design for Laser Manufacturer Group; Laser job shop
- ● Mtgs - ET - Res - Inf
- < Eur Laser Applications Network (ELAN); Laser Inst of America (LIA)
- M 50 i, 198 f, UK / 12 i, 12 f, o'seas
   (Sub: £70 i, £290 f, £25 students)
- ¶ The Laser User - 4; ftm only.
- × 2007 (14 April) Association of Industrial Laser Users

Association for Latin Liturgy (ALL) 1969
- ■ 47 Western Park Rd, LEICESTER, LE3 6HQ.   (hsp)
   0116-285 6158
   email enquiries@latin-liturgy.org.uk
   http://www.latin-liturgy.org
   Chmn: Bernard Marriott
- ▲ Registered Charity
- ○ *R; to promote understanding of the theological, pastoral & spiritual quality of the liturgy in Latin; to preserve the sacredness & dignity of the Roman rite; to secure, for the present & future generations, the Church's unique inheritance of liturgical music
- ● Mtgs - ET - Res - Inf - Liturgical celebrations - Talks by scholars
- < Latin Liturgy Assn (USA); Vereniging voor Latijnse Liturgie (Netherlands); Association pro Liturgia (France)
- M 340 i, UK / 30 i, o'seas
- ¶ NL - 3; ftm only.
   New Approach to Latin for the Mass; £12.
   New Latin-English Sunday Missal; £12 (paperback).
   Latin CD; £12.   A Voice for all Time; £6.
   Various musical publications.

Association for Latin Teaching (ARLT) 1911
- ■ 45 Thorpe Rd, Thornton, BRADFORD, W Yorks, BD13 3AT. (hsp)
   01274 818098
   http://www.arlt.co.uk
   Hon Treas & Mem Sec: Robert West
- ▲ Registered Charity
- ○ *E; to promote by discussion, cooperation & experiment, the teaching of classics in schools
- ● Conf - ET - Inf - Resources service to members
- < Jt Assn Classical Teachers (JACT)
- M 2,000 i
- ¶ The Jnl of Latin Teaching (published jointly with JACT) - 3; NL [email] - 6; both ftm only.

Association of Law Costs Draftsmen (ALCD) 1977
- ■ Williams & Associates, T109 Titan House,
   Cardiff Bay Business Centre, Ocean Park, CARDIFF, CF24 5BS.
   029 2045 0772
   email enquiries@alcd.org.uk   http://www.alcd.org.uk
   Hon Sec: Joe Locke
- ▲ Voluntary Professional Association
- ○ *P; 'specialists in the law who operate by advising upon & applying laws & directions which relate to the evaluation & recovery of solicitors' fees'
   Members are based throughout England & Wales
- ● Conf - Mtgs - ET - Exam - Lib
- M 900 i, UK / 2 i, o'seas
- ¶ ALCD NL - 6; ftm only.

Association of Law Teachers (ALT) 1965
- NR Sch of Law & Social Science, University of Plymouth, Drake Circus, PLYMOUTH, Devon, PL4 8AA.   (chmn/b)
   http://www.lawteacher.ac.uk
   Chmn: Hugo de Rijke
- ▲ Un-incorporated Society
- ○ *E, *L; to study understanding & reform of the educational aspects of law & the teaching of law; to research into legal education systems & methods
- ● Conf - ET - Res - SG - LG
- < UK Assn for Eur Law
- M 800 i, UK / 50 i, o'seas
- ¶ The Law Teacher (Jnl) - 3.
   The Bulletin - 3.   LM - 1.

Association of Lawyers for Children (ALC) 1993
- ■ PO Box 283, EAST MOLESEY, Surrey, KT8 0WH.   (hsp)
   020 8224 7071
   email admin@alc.org.uk   http://www.alc.org.uk
   Admin: Julia Higgins
- ○ *P; to promote justice for children & young people within the justice system; for lawyers involved in work relating to children
- ● Conf - Mtgs - ET - SG - LG
- M 1,200 i
- ¶ ALC NL - 4; ftm only.

Association of Lawyers & Legal Advisors 1995
- NR 40 Bowling Green Lane, LONDON, EC1R 0NE.
   01745 582006
   http://www.lawyersassoc.org
- ▲ Company Limited by Guarantee
- Br 2
- ○ *P; accreditation of persons or organisations who provide specialised legal services & advice & who are relied upon for legal information or opinions (conveyancers, willwriters, company formation agents, claims specialists, as well as lecturers in law, forensic scientists, expert witnesses & law costs draftsmen
   Note: The Association of Lawyers is a trading name owned & operated by the Association of Lawyers & Legal Advisers.

Association of Leading Visitor Attractions (ALVA) 1990
- ■ 4 Westminster Palace Gardens, LONDON, SW1P 1RL.   (hq)
   020 7222 1728   fax 020 7222 1729
   email email@alva.org.uk   http://www.alva.org.uk
   Dir: Robin Broke
- ▲ Company Limited by Guarantee
- ○ *T; to represent the country's major visitor attractions on matters which concern the effectiveness of the tourism industry
- Gp Museums & galleries; Cathedrals; Heritage organisations; Large leisure attractions; Gardens & conservation sites
- ● Conf - Mtgs - ET - Stat - VE - LG
- M 29 org
- ¶ LM.   AR.

© CBD Research Ltd · Beckenham · BR3 5JS · Tel 020 8650 7745 · Fax 020 8650 0768 · E-mail cbd@cbdresearch.com · www.cbdresearch.com

Association of Learned & Professional Society Publishers (ALPSP) 1972
■ Bluebell Lodge, 8 Rickford Road, Nailsea, BRISTOL, BS48 4PY. (hsp)
01275 856444
http://www.alpsp.org
Chief Exec: Ian Russell
▲ Company Limited by Guarantee
Br Australia, N America, New Zealand
○ *N; to represent not-for-profit publishers & those who work with them
Gp C'ees: Copyright, Professional development
● Conf - Mtgs - ET - Res - Exhib - Stat - Inf - VE - LG - Professional development
< Intl Fedn of Scholarly Publishers
M 216 f, UK / 124 f, o'seas
¶ Learned Publishing - 4; ftm (extra copies £60 yr), £75 (i), £145 (instns), £115/60 email only.
ALPSP Alert - 12; ftm only.

Association for Learning Languages en Famille (ALLEF UK)
■ 225 Carmel Rd, NORTH DARLINGTON, Co Durham, DL3 9TF.
http://www.allef.org.uk
○ *X; arranges mutual exchanges between children in the UK, France & Germany
no further information supplied

Association of Learning Providers (ALP)
NR Colenso House, 46 Bath Hill, Keynsham, BRISTOL, BS31 1HG. (hq)
0117-986 5389
email enquiries@learningproviders.org
http://www.learningproviders.org.uk
Chief Exec: Graham Hoyle
▲ Company Limited by Guarantee
○ *E, *T; providers of work-based learning
● ET
M 400 f

Association for Learning Technology (ALT) 1993
NR Gipsy Lane, Headington, OXFORD, OX3 0BP. (hq)
01865 484125   fax 01865 484165
email alt@brookes.ac.uk   http://www.alt.ac.uk
Dir: Rhonda Riachi
▲ Registered Charity
○ *P; promotion of good practice in the use of learning technology in education & industry
● Conf - ET - Res - Inf
M 426 i, 38 f, 104 universities, 52 colleges, UK / 38 i, o'seas
¶ Alt-J (Jnl) - 3; £10/£15.   Alt-N (NL) - 4; free.
Conference Abstracts - 1; £5.   AR; free.

Association of Leasehold Enfranchisement Practitioners (ALEP) 2003
■ Southbridge House, Southbridge Place, CROYDON, Surrey, CR0 4HA. (hsp)
0845 225 2277   fax 0870 225 2287
email info@alep.org.uk   http://www.alep.org.uk
Hon Sec: Alex Greenslade
○ *P; to foster best practice & integrity & maintain professional standards in leasehold enfranchisement
M 2 i, 1 f

Association of Leisure Industry Professionals (ALIP) 2001
NR 2A The Drove Estate, Avis Way, NEWHAVEN, E Sussex, BN9 0EB. (hq)
01273 612300   fax 01273 612812
email info@alip.org.uk   http://www.alip.org.uk
Dir: Dr Michael Pinchbeck
▲ Un-incorporated Society
○ *P; tourism industry
● Conf - ET - SG - Inf
> Intl Work Experience Program
¶ Lipservice (NL) - 4; ftm only.

Association of Library Equipment Suppliers (TALES) 1980
■ Forge Cottage, 3 Church End, Sandridge, ST ALBANS, Herts, AL4 9DL. (hsb)
01727 837507
email john@newtondavies.plus.com
http://www.tales.org.uk
Mem Sec/Hon Treas: John Newton-Davies
▲ Un-incorporated Society
○ *T; 'providing representation for suppliers into the library & information marketplace'
Gp Shelving, furniture & associated equipment; Books, journals & other print material; Automation, ICT & security; Conservation, large print, AV & other media supply; Human resources & other professional services
● Mtgs - Exhib - Inf - LG
< The British Library
M 1 i, 46 f

Association of Licensed Aircraft Engineers (1981) (ALAE) 1981
NR Bourn House, 8 Park St, BAGSHOT, Surrey, GU19 5AQ. (hq)
01276 474888
http://www.alae.org
▲ Un-incorporated Society
○ *U; for licensed aircraft maintenance engineers & flight engineers
M i

Association of Licensed Deep Sea Pilots
alternative name of **Europilots**

** Association of Licensed Mortgage Advisors
Organisation lost: see Introduction paragraph 3

Association of Licensed Multiple Retailers (ALMR) 1992
■ 9b Walpole Court, Ealing Studios, LONDON, W5 5ED. (hq)
020 8579 2080   fax 020 8579 7579
email info@almr.org.uk   http://www.almr.org.uk
Chief Exec: Nick Bish
▲ Un-incorporated Society
○ *T; to promote members' interests; to be a positive influence for the future of licensed retailing
Gp Operator members: pub companies or other licensed retailers having at least 2 units
Supplier members: suppliers of foods & services to the licensed trade
● Conf - Mtgs - Exhib - SG - Stat - Inf - VE - LG
M 205 f
¶ NL - 12;   Political Digest - 12;
On Trade Media Review - 1; all ftm only.

Association of Licensed Telecommunications Operators
since 2004 **ALTO - Alternative Operators in the Communications Sector**

Association of Light Touch Therapists (ALTT) 1988
■ 22 Baldock St, WARE, Herts, SG12 9DZ. (hsb)
01920 485265
email info@altt.org   http://www.altt.org
Sec: Geraldine V Jones
▲ Un-incorporated Society
○ *P; to assist in the establishment of light touch therapies within the normal health-care provision of the nation
Gp Body mechanics; Biomobility; Bowen technique; Cranio-sacral therapy; Emotional freedom technique; Health kinesiology; Light touch healing; Lymph drainage; Metamorphic technique; Muscle release therapy; Orthobionomy; Polarity therapy; Pulsing; Rejuvanessence; Reflexology; Reharmonisation; Reiki; Spontaneous muscle release; Spinal touch therapy; Touch for health; Therapeutic touch
● Conf - Mtgs - Inf
< Brit Complementary Medicine Assn (BCMA)
M 73 i, UK / 1 i, o'seas
¶ NL - 4;   Register of Members - 1; both free.

Association of Lighthouse Keepers (ALK) 1988

■ 116 Abbeyfield Drive, FAREHAM, Hants, PO15 5PQ. (hsp)
   01329 843883   fax 01329 843883 (on request)
   email secretary@alk.org.uk   http://www.alk.org.uk
   Hon Sec: Keith W Morton
▲ Registered Charity
○ *G; the advancement of education of the public in pharology -
   the history & current practice of coastal & inland aids to
   navigation
● ET - Res - Exhib - Inf - Lib - PL - VE - Archive of artifacts
< Wld Lighthouse Soc (WLS)
M 550 i, UK / 20 i, o'seas
   (Sub: £16 UK / 30, $50 o'seas)
¶ Lamp (Jnl) - 4.

Association of Lighting Designers (ALD)

NR PO Box 680, OXFORD, OX1 9DG.   (sb)
   07817 060189
   email office@ald.org.uk   http://www.ald.org.uk
   Admin Sec: Geoff Spain
▲ Un-incorporated Society
○ *P; for lighting designers in the entertainment field
● Conf - Mtgs - ET - Exhib - SG - Stat - Inf - Lib - VE - Empl
M 486 i, 24 f, 29 org, UK / 45 i, 3 f, o'seas
¶ Focus (Jnl) - 6; ftm only.   Ybk - 1; ftm, £7.50 nm.

** Association of Lightweight Aggregate Manufacturers
   Organisation lost: see Introduction paragraph 3

Association of Lightweight Campers
   a group of the **Camping & Caravanning Club**

Association of Liner Producers
   a group of **Horticultural Trades Association**

Association of Lipspeakers (ALS) 1992

NR 5 Furlong Close, Upper Tean, STOKE-on-TRENT, Staffs,
   ST10 4LB.   (inf offr/p)
   01538 722482
   http://www.lipspeaking.co.uk
   Inf Officer: Dilys Palin
▲ Un-incorporated Society
Br regional gps
○ *P; for lipspeakers (providers of communication services for
   deaf & hard of hearing people who lipread)
● Conf - Mtgs - ET - Exhib - Inf - Workshops
< R Nat Inst for Deaf People (RNID); Coun for the Advancement
   of Communication with Deaf People (CACDD); UK Coun on
   Deafness (UKCOD)
M 115 i
¶ ALS News - 2.
   Leaflets: General, Legal, For Users, For Agencies.
   NOTE: please enclose SAE if an answer is required

Association of Lloyd's Members (ALM) 1983

NR 100 Fenchurch St, LONDON, EC3M 5LG.   (admin/dir)
   020 7488 0033   fax 020 7488 7555
   email mail@alm.ltd.uk
   http://www.association-lloyds-members.co.uk
   Snr Admin: Linda Evans
○ *P, *T; 'trade association for Names' - the underwriting
   members of Lloyd's of London (insurance market)
M c 6,750 i, UK / c 2,250 i, o'seas
¶ ALM News (NL) - 6.
   Members' Agents' Profiles - 1.

Association of Load Restraint Equipment Manufacturers
   is a group of the **Performance Textiles Association**

Association of Loading & Elevating Equipment Manufacturers (ALEM) 1973

■ Airport House, Purley Way, CROYDON, Surrey, CR0 0XZ.
   (asa)
   020 8253 4501   fax 020 8253 4510
   email alem@admin.co.uk   http://www.alem.org.uk
▲ Un-incorporated Society
○ *T; safety & good design of lift tables, dock levellers, platform
   lifts, tailboard lifts
● Mtgs - Exhib - SG - Inf - LG
< Brit Materials Handling Fedn; Fédn Eur de la Manutention
M 29 f
¶ LM & Product Guide; free.

Association of Local Authority Chief Executives (ALACE) 1974

■ c/o Watford Borough Council, Town Hall, WATFORD, Herts,
   WD17 3EX.   (hsb)
   01923 278186
   email alastair.robertson@watford.gov.uk
   http://www.alace.org.uk
   Hon Sec: Alastair Robertson
Br 2
○ *U; to represent the chief executives of local authorities in
   England, Wales, Scotland & Northern Ireland. The Council of
   ALACE forms the 'staff side' of the Joint Negotiating
   Committee for Chief Executives (the body responsible for the
   salary & terms/conditions of employment & regulations which
   affect the role of the 'head of the paid service' together with
   issues such as reorganisation of local government)
● Mtgs - LG
M 330 i
¶ NL - 4.

Association of Local Bus Company Managers (ALBUM) 1984

NR c/o Plymouth CityBus Ltd, 1 Milehouse Rd, Milehouse,
   PLYMOUTH, Devon, PL3 4AA.   (hsb)
   Hon Sec: Stephen Burd
▲ Un-incorporated Society
○ *P, *T
● Conf - Mtgs - LG
¶ NL - irreg; ftm only.

Association of Local Government Archaeological Officers (ALGAO) 1996

NR Cornerstone, ALFORD, Aberdeenshire, AB33 8QH.
   01975 564071
   email admin@algao.org.uk   http://www.algao.org.uk
   Contact: Caroline Ingle
▲ Un-incorporated Society
○ *P; to represent archaeologists working in local government
   throughout the UK
Gp Maritime; Historic environment records; Historic buildings;
   Urban; European; Planning & legislation; Countryside
● Mtgs - ET - Res - Exhib - Stat - LG
< Eur Assn Archaeologists
M 115 local authorities

Association of Local Government Communications (LGcommunications) 1971

NR Communications Unit, City Hall (17th floor), 64 Victoria St,
   LONDON, SW1E 6QP.   (v/chmn/b)
   020 7641 2575
   email lgcommunications@westminster.gov.uk
   http://www.lgcomms.org.uk
   Sec: Alex Aitken
▲ Un-incorporated Society
○ *P; to enhance the reputation of local government; to provide a
   united voice to public relations & communications functions
   in all UK principal local authorities
● Conf - Mtgs - Res - Comp - Stat - VE - LG
M 158 local authorities
¶ NL - 12 (email based distribution); ftm only.

Association of Local History Tutors
   in 2008 merged with **British Association for Local History**

© CBD Research Ltd · Beckenham · BR3 5JS · Tel 020 8650 7745 · Fax 020 8650 0768 · E-mail cbd@cbdresearch.com · www.cbdresearch.com

Association of London Clubs   (ALC)

■ c/o Oriental Club, Stratford House, Stratford Place, LONDON, W1C 1ES.   (sb)
020 7629 5126   fax 020 7629 0494
email sec@orientalclub.org.uk
http://www.alclubs.org.uk
Sec: Mrs June M Aitken
○ *N; to provide a forum for matters of common interest to member clubs
● Mtgs - ET - Comp - Empl - LG
M 55 London clubs

Association of London Government
since October 2006 **London Councils**

Association of Lorry Loader Manufacturers & Importers of Great Britain
since 1 February 2008 **ALLMI Ltd**

Association for Low Countries Studies in Great Britain & Ireland (ALCS)

■ Dept of Germanic Studies, University of Sheffield, SHEFFIELD, S Yorks, S10 2TN.   (pres/b)
0114-222 4396   fax 0114-222 2160
email alcs@sheffield.ac.uk
http://www.alcs.group.shef.ac.uk
Pres: Dr Nicola McLelland
▲ Un-incorporated Society
○ *L, *X; 'to promote the scholarly study of the language, culture, history & society of the Low Countries; to increase public awareness of the Low Countries, especially the Dutch language & Dutch & Flemish culture, history & society
● Conf - Mtgs - ET - Res - Inf - LG - Postgraduate training days - Undergraduate days
< Intle Vereniging voor Neerlandistiek
M 65 i, UK / 40 i, o'seas
¶ Dutch Crossing: a jnl of Low Countries studies - 2; £15 yr m, £25 yr nm.
Crossways: a series of books & collections of papers - irreg.

Association of Lurcher Clubs

NR 171 Wash Lane, BURY, Lancs, BL9 7DP.   (chmn/p)
Chmn: Alan Tyer
○ *B, *N; to promote the lurcher, a working farm dog

Association of Magisterial Officers
2005 merged with the **Public & Commercial Services Union**

Association of Mainframe Operators & Network Administrators (AMONO)   1992

■ 1 Caryl House, Windlesham Grove, LONDON, SW19 6AH.   (hsp)
○ *T; operation & maintenance of large computer systems
M 879 i, 53 f, UK / 38 i, 4 f, o'seas

Association of Makers of Soft Tissue Papers
since 2004 the Tissue Sector of the **Confederation of Paper Industries**

Association for Management Education & Development (AMED)   1960

NR 7 & 8 Roman Way, Godmanchester, HUNTINGDON, Cambs, PE29 2LN.   (hq)
01480 459575   fax 01480 450721
email office@amed.org.uk   http://www.amed.org.uk
Co-Chmn: David Shepherd,   Helen Roome
▲ Company Limited by Guarantee; Registered Charity
○ *E, *P; a professional network for people in individual & organisational development (trainers, HR directors, management consultants & business school lecturers)
Gp Sustainable development; Leadership; Learning organisation
● Conf - Mtgs
< Eur Foundation for Mgt Devt
M 1,300 i, UK / 100 i, o'seas
¶ Organisation & People Jnl - 4; ftm, £50 nm, (£65 instns).
AMED News - 10; ftm only.
Report & Accounts (Review) - 1.

Association of Management & Professional Staffs   (AMPS)   1984

NR AEEU House, Borough Rd, WAKEFIELD, W Yorks, WF1 3AZ.   (hq)
01924 371765
http://www.amps.demon.co.uk
Exec Sec: Ian Waddell
○ *U; non-certificated, non-political managerial union for professional employees in science-based industries
< Amicus
M c 4,000 i

Association of Manufacturers of Domestic Appliances (AMDEA)   1969

■ Rapier House, 40-46 Lamb's Conduit St, LONDON, WC1N 3NW.   (hq)
020 7405 0666   fax 020 7405 6609
email info@amdea.org.uk   http://www.amdea.org.uk
Chief Exec: Douglas Herbison
▲ Company Limited by Guarantee
○ *T; interests of manufacturers of electric domestic appliances, and/or their components
● Mtgs - Stat - LG
< Eur C'ee of Domestic Appliance Mfrs (CECED)
M [depending on annual turnover]
¶ NL - 12;   AR - 1; both free.   LM - printout on request.
AMDEA Technical News - 12; ftm only.

Association of Manufacturers of Power generating Systems (AMPS)   1977

■ Samuelson House, Forder Way, Hampton, PETERBOROUGH, Cambs, PE7 8JB.   (hq)
0845 644 8748   fax 01733 314767
email dg@amps.org.uk   http://www.amps.org.uk
Dir-Gen: Roger Lane-Nott
▲ Company Limited by Guarantee
○ *T; for manufacturers & importers of generating systems, component & control systems
Gp Statistics; Technical
● Conf - Mtgs - Exhib - Stat - Expt - Inf - VE - LG
< Eur Generating Set Assn (EUROPGEN); Electrical Generating Systems Assn (EGSA)(USA)
M 57 f, UK / 3 f, o'seas
¶ Brochure (incl LM).   Technical Guidelines.
AMPS Guide to ISO 8528 (BS 7698) Reciprocating Internal Combustion Engine driven Alternating Current Generating Sets:
Pt 1: Application rating & performance.
Pt 2: Specification for engines.
Pt 3: Specification for AC generators.
Pt 4: Control & switchgear.
Pt 5: Specification for generating sets.
Pt 6: Test methods.

Association of Marine Scientific Industries   (AMSI)
NR   28-29 Threadneedle St, LONDON, EC2R 8AY.
        020 7628 2555   fax 020 7638 4376
        email info@maritimeindustries.org
        http://www.maritimeindustries.org
        Chmn: Richard Burt
○   *T; to support companies in the marine science & technology
        sector
<   Soc of Maritime Inds

**Association for Marketing & Development in Independent
    Schools   (AMDIS)   1993**
■   2 St Michael's St, MALTON, N Yorks, YO17 7LJ.   (hq)
        0700 062 3347
        http://www.amdis.co.uk
        Admin: Victoria Gillingham
▲   Un-incorporated Society
○   *P; 'to promote good marketing practice in independent
        education'
●   Conf - Mtgs - ET - Stat
<   ADAPA (Australia)
M   430 schools

Association for Marriage Enrichment
    has closed

**Association of Master Upholsterers & Soft Furnishers Ltd
    (AMUSF)   1947**
■   Francis Vaughan House, Q1 Capital Point, Capital Business
        Park, Parkway, CARDIFF, CF3 2PU.   (hq)
        029 2077 8918
        http://www.upholsterers.co.uk
        Chief Exec: Michael B Spencer
▲   Company Limited by Guarantee
Br   11
○   *T
●   Conf - Mtgs - Exhib - Inf - Li - PL - LG
<   Fedn of Small Businesses; Assn of Soft Furnishers Ltd
M   c 550 f
¶   Upholsterer & Soft Furnisher - 12; ftm, £35 yr nm.
        CFC Contract Furnishing Concepts - 6; ftm, £21.50 yr nm.
        Note: incorporates the Chair Frame Manufacturers'
        Association.

Association of Masters of Harriers & Beagles   1891
NR   Langley House, Winchcombe, CHELTENHAM, Glos, GL54 5AB.
        01242 602564
        email director@amhb.org.uk   http://www.amhb.org.uk
        Dir: Elizabeth Salmon
○   *F

Association of MBAs Ltd   1967
NR   25 Hosier Lane, LONDON, EC1A 9LQ.   (hq)
        020 7246 2686
        http://www.mbaworld.com
▲   Company Limited by Guarantee; Registered Charity
○   *E; for holders of the MBA degree; to promote management
        education in order to maximise its contribution to British
        industry
M   i, f & org

**Association for Measurement & Evaluation of Communication
    (AMEC)**
NR   Communications House, 26 York St, LONDON, W1U 6PZ.
        (hsp)
        020 8675 4442
        email jacquelinemilton@amecorg.com
        http://www.amecorg.com
        Admin: Jacqueline Milton
▲   Un-incorporated Society
○   *T; to represent the interest of media evaluation companies
●   Mtgs - Promotion of media evaluation
M   11 f, UK / 4 f, o'seas
×   2006 Association of Media Evaluation Companies

Association of Meat Inspectors GB Ltd   (AMI)   1960
■   25 Down Field Rd, STROUD, Glos, GL5 4HQ.   (hsb)
        01453 756487
        email idrobinsonmani@yahoo.com
        http://www.meatinspectors.co.uk
        Gen Sec: Ian D Robinson
▲   Un-incorporated Society
Br   7 divisions
○   *P; meat inspection & hygiene in abattoirs, meat curing
        premises & cold stores; to promote research & publish the
        results; to promote high standards of meat inspection &
        hygiene
Gp   Technical, Legislative; Educational trust
●   Conf - Mtgs - ET - Lib - LG
M   1,200-1,400 i
        (Sub: £70)
¶   Meat Hygienist - 4; ftm; £75 nm.

Association of Media Evaluation Companies
        since 2006 the **Association for Measurement & Evaluation of
        Communication**

Association of Media Practice Educators
        see **Media, Communication & Cultural Studies Association**

**Association of Medical Advisers to British Orchestras
    (AMABO)   1990**
NR   Totara Park House (4th floor), 34-36 Gray's Inn Rd, LONDON,
        WC1X 8HR.   (hq)
        020 7404 5888   fax 020 7404 3222
        email amabo@bapam.org.uk
        http://www.bapam.org.uk/amabo
        Sec: Dr Penny Wright
▲   Registered Charity
Br   19
○   *M, *P; for doctors attached to major British orchestras;
        research & training in performing arts medicine
●   Mtgs - ET - Res - SG
<   Brit Assn for Performing Arts Medicine
M   21 i

Association of Medical Insurance Intermediaries   (amii)   1998
■   c/o Premier Choice Healthcare Ltd, The Old Coach House,
        1a Brackley Rd, TOWCESTER, Northants, NN12 6DH.   (hsb)
        01327 353911   fax 01327 352416
        http://www.amii.org.uk
        Chmn: Mike Izzard,   Treas: Wayne Pontin
○   *T; to offer specialist independent advice on health issues
●   Conf - Mtgs - ET - Exhib
M   c 98 f

Association of Medical Microbiologists   (AMM)   1983
■   c/o Dr Steve Barrett, Microbiology Dept, Charing Cross
        Hospital, LONDON, W6 8RF.   (hsb)
        email honsec@amm.co.uk   http://www.amm.co.uk
        Hon Sec: Dr Steve Barrett
○   *L, *P; to further the science & practice of medical microbiology
●   Conf - Mtgs - ET - Inf - LG
M   510 i, UK / 15 i, o'seas
¶   Medical Microbiologists (Jnl) - 4; ftm only.

Association of Medical Research Charities   (AMRC)   1987
NR   61 Gray's Inn Rd, LONDON, WC1X 8TL.   (hq)
        020 7269 8820   fax 020 7269 8821
        email info@amrc.org.uk   http://www.amrc.org.uk
        Chief Exec: Simon Denegri
▲   Company Limited by Guarantee; Registered Charity
○   *K, *M, *Q; to further medical interests in the UK generally & in
        particular the advancement of the effectiveness of those
        charities of which a principal activity is medical research
●   ET - LG
M   112 charities
¶   NL - 6/8; ftm only.   AR - 1; free.

© CBD Research Ltd · Beckenham · BR3 5JS · Tel 020 8650 7745 · Fax 020 8650 0768 · E-mail cbd@cbdresearch.com · www.cbdresearch.com

Association of Medical Secretaries, Practice Managers, Administrators & Receptionists (AMSPAR) 1964
NR Tavistock House North, Tavistock Sq, LONDON, WC1H 9LN.
(hq)
020 7387 6005
http://www.amspar.co.uk
Chief Exec: Tom Brownlie
▲ Company Limited by Guarantee; Registered Charity
○ *P
● Conf - Mtgs - ET - Exam - Inf
< Eur Fedn of Med Secretary Assns
M 5,500 i, UK / 90 i, o'seas
¶ AMSPAR Magazine - 4. NL - 4.
Professional Guidelines. Careers leaflets.

Association of Member-Directed Pension Schemes (AMPS) 1979
■ c/o Barnett Waddingham LLP, Port of Liverpool Building,
Pier Head, LIVERPOOL, L3 1BW. (hsb)
0151-235 6600 fax 0151-235 6640
http://www.ampsonline.co.uk
Hon Sec: Andrew Roberts
▲ Un-incorporated Society
○ *P; to represent small self-administered pension schemes &
self-invested personal pensions
● Conf - Mtgs - ET - Inf - LG
M 193 f
(Sub: £200)
¶ NL - 12; ftm only.
× 2005 (Association of Pensioneer Trustees
(Sipp Provider Group

Association of Members of Independent Monitoring Boards (AMIMB) 1981
■ 3 Forsham Cottages, Forsham Lane, Sutton Valence,
MAIDSTONE, Kent, ME17 3WQ. (chmn/p)
01622 844481
email info@amimb.co.uk http://www.amimb.co.uk
Sec: Helen Boothman, Chmn: Mrs Angela Clay
▲ Registered Charity
○ *W; independent monitoring of every prison & immigration
removal in the UK
● Conf - Mtgs - ET - Res - SG - Stat - Inf - VE - LG
< Criminal Justice Alliance
M 400 i
(Sub: £20 i, c £300 org)
¶ The Independent Monitor - 3; free.

Association of Men of Kent & Kentish Men (MKKM) 1897
NR Cantium Lodge, Terrace Rd, MAIDSTONE, Kent, ME16 8HU.
(hq)
01622 758722
Sec: Mrs T M Robinson
Br 19
○ *G, *K; to foster a sense of pride in the County of Kent; to
protect the county's heritage & the beauty of the countryside
● Conf - Mtgs - Inf - Lib - VE
M 3,000 i
¶ Kent - 3.

Association of Meter Operators (AMO) 1996
NR Power Data Associates Ltd, Wrest House, Wrest Park, SILSOE,
Beds, MK45 4HR. (contact/b)
01525 862870
http://www.meteroperators.org.uk
Contact: Tom Chevalier
▲ Un-incorporated Society
○ *T; for meter operators in the UK electricity & gas markets
● Mtgs - Inf (to members only)
M 14 f
¶ LM on website.

Association of Miniature Engine Manufacturers (AMEM) 1975
■ 423 Upper Elmers End Rd, BECKENHAM, Kent, BR3 3DA.
(mail address)
○ *T; includes petrol, diesel & bio fuel, battery & solar powered
units
● Conf - Mtgs - SG - Inf - LG
¶ Mini-motion - 3/4; ftm only.

Association of Mining Analysts (AMA)
NR c/o Bankside plc, 1 Frederick's Place, LONDON, EC2R 8AE.
(mail add)
020 8878 2308
http://www.ama.org.uk
Sec: Carl Noack
▲ Un-incorporated Society
○ *P; for fund managers, bankers & analysts
● Mtgs - VE
M 251 i, UK / 24 i, o'seas

Association of Model Agents (AMA) 1974
■ 11-19 Fashion St, LONDON, E1 6PX. (hq)
020 7422 0699 fax 020 7247 9230
email amainfo@btinternet.com
○ *T; to protect the reputation of models & model agents
● Mtgs - Inf
M 22 f

Association of Model Railway Societies in Scotland (AMRSS) 1966
NR Model Rail Scotland, PO Box 19564, JOHNSTONE, PA6 7YP.
(mail/address)
0845 226 3061
▲ Un-incorporated Society
○ *G; to promote 'Modelrail Scotland', the national model
railway exhibition held at the SECC Glasgow, on the last
weekend in February
● Exhib
M 34 clubs

Association of Mortgage Intermediaries (AMI)
NR 2-6 Austin Friars House, Austin Friars, LONDON,
EC2N 2HD. (hq)
020 7628 1288
http://www.a-m-i.org.uk
Dir Gen: Chris Cummings
○ *P

Association of Motion Picture Sound (AMPS) 1989
NR 28 Knox St, LONDON, W1H 1FS. (hq)
020 7723 6727 fax 020 7723 6727
email admin@amps.net http://www.amps.net
Hon Sec: Brian Hickin
▲ Un-incorporated Society
○ *P; to promote & encourage the science, technology & creative
application of all aspects of motion picture sound recording
& reproduction
Gp Sound for film & television
● Mtgs - Private film screenings
M 340 i, 35 f, UK / 23 i, 1 f, o'seas
¶ AMPS Jnl - 4.

Association of Motor Racing Circuit Owners Ltd   (AMRCO) 1962
- ■ c/o BARC Ltd, Thruxton Circuit, ANDOVER, Hants, SP11 8PN. (sb)
  01264 882200   fax 01264 882233
  email amrco@barc.net
  http://www.motorsportsuk.co.uk
  Sec: Mrs A J Curley
- ▲ Company Limited by Guarantee
- ○ *T; to represent the interests of motor racing licensed circuit owners
- ● Mtgs
- M 17 f, UK / 1 f, o'seas

Association of Municipal Authorities of Ireland
- IRL c/o Tom Ryan, AMAI House, 63 Ormond St, NENAGH, Co Tipperary, Republic of Ireland.
  353 (67) 42222
  email director@amai.ie
  Dir: Tom Ryan
- ○ *N

Association of Muslim Lawyers
a group of the **Law Society of England & Wales**

Association of National Driver Improvement Scheme Providers (ANDISP)   1998
- NR c/o Professional Driver Services Ltd, 159 Holton Rd, BARRY, Glamorgan, CF63 4HP.
  01446 722229   fax 01446 722401
  http://www.driver-improvement.co.uk
  Sec: Stephen Davies
- ▲ Un-incorporated Society
- ○ *T; organisation & practice of driver improvement courses on behalf of police constabularies.   The association manages these courses on behalf of the Dept of Transport (DFT) & Association of Chief Police Officers (ACPO)
- ● Mtgs - ET - LG
- M 42 f & local authorities

Association of National Park Authorities   (ANPA)   1992
- NR 126 Bute St, CARDIFF, Glamorgan, CF10 5LE.   (hq)
  029 2049 9966
  email info@anpa.gov.uk
  http://www.nationalparks.gov.uk
  Co-ordinator: Cathryn Marcus
- ▲ Un-incorporated Society
- ○ *N; for the national park authorities of England & Wales
- ● Conf - Mtgs - Res - Comp - SG - LG - Public relations of NPA's at national level
- M 14 National Park Authorities
- ¶ Annual Review - 1;   Technical papers - irreg.

Association of National Tourist Office Representatives (ANTOR)   1953
- ■ 39 Pennington Close, Colden Common, WINCHESTER, Hants, SO21 1UR.   (mail/address)
  0870 241 9084
  http://www.antor.com
  Exec Sec: Esther C Smith
- ▲ Company Limited bu Guarantee
- ○ *T; 'the principal lobbying organisaton for the world's tourist offices'
- ● Mtgs - Exhib - Inf - LG
- M 60 overseas tourist offices represented in the UK
- ¶ LM - 1; free.

Association of Natural Burial Grounds   (ANBG)   1994
- NR 12a Blackstock Mews, Blackstock Rd, LONDON, N4 2BT.   (hq)
  0871 288 2098
  email office@anbg.co.uk   http://www.anbg.co.uk
  Administrator: Michael Jarvis
- ▲ Registered Charity
- ○ *K; 'to promote 'natural' burial, where trees or flowers are planted on the grave instead of having headstones'
- ● Conf - ET - Res - Exhib - Stat - Inf - LG
- < Natural Death Centre
- M 50 f
- ¶ The Natural Death Hbk - 3 yrly; £14.99. Living Will + Forms; £7.

Association of Natural Medicine   (ANM)   1983
- ■ 27 Braintree Rd, WITHAM, Essex, CM8 2DD.   (hq)
  01376 502762   fax 01376 502762
  email a-nm@hotmail.co.uk
  http://www.associationnaturalmedicine.co.uk
  Chief Exec: Martin Duncombe
- ▲ Registered Charity
- ○ *P; training courses for professional practice of natural medicine & therapies
- ● Mtgs - ET - Exam - Res - Exhib - SG - Inf
- < Parliamentary Gp for Integrated & Complementary Medicine
- M c 300 i
- ¶ Natural Medicine (Jnl) - 4.

Association for Neuro-Linguistic Programming (UK) Ltd (ANLP)   1985
- NR 41 The Marlowes, HEMEL HEMPSTEAD, Herts, HP1 1LD. (admin/p)
  0845 053 1162
  http://www.anlp.org
  Admin Mgr: C Coughlan,   Chmn: Carol Harris
- ▲ Company Limited by Guarantee; Registered Charity
- ○ *E
- ● Conf - Mtgs - ET - SG - Inf
- M 750 i, 40 f, UK / 50 i, o'seas
- ¶ Rapport (Jnl) - 4.   Information booklet - 1. Directory of Members.   AR; free.

Association of New Age Industries   (ANAIS)   1995
- ■ c/o Honeybees, Milkhouse Water, PEWSEY, Wilts, SN9 5JX.
- ▲ Un-incorporated Society
- ○ *T
- Gp Water power; Wind power
- M i, f & org

Association of News Retailing
a group of the **Association of Convenience Stores**

Association of Newspaper & Magazine Wholesalers (ANMW)   1917
- NR PO Box 40, 4 Acre Rd, READING, Berks, RG2 0XZ.   (hq)
  0845 121 3210
  email enquiries@anmw.co.uk
  Chmn: Adrian Smith
- ▲ Un-incorporated Society
- ○ *T
- ● Mtgs - ET - Inf - LG
- M 29 f

Association of Noise Consultants   (ANC)   1964
- ■ 105 St Peter's St, ST ALBANS, Herts, AL1 3EJ.   (asa)
  01727 896092   fax 01727 896026
  email anc@kingstonsmith.co.uk
  http://www.theanc.co.uk
  Manager: Robert Osborne
- ▲ Company Limited by Guarantee
- ○ *P; to represent & support noise & consultancy companies
- ● Conf - Mtgs - Res
- M 100 f

© CBD Research Ltd · Beckenham · BR3 5JS · Tel 020 8650 7745 · Fax 020 8650 0768 · E-mail cbd@cbdresearch.com · www.cbdresearch.com

Association of North East Councils (ANEC) 1986
NR   The Guildhall, Quayside, NEWCASTLE upon TYNE, NE1 3AF.
(hq)
0191-261 7388   fax 0191-232 4558
http://www.northeastcouncils.gov.uk
Dir: Melanie Laws
▲   Un-incorporated Society
○   *N; an association of the local councils (county councils, district
councils & metropolitan district councils) in the counties
forming the North East Region of England - Durham,
Northumberland, Tyne & Wear & Tees Valley; to promote the
economic & social wellbeing of the people of the region.
Is the Joint Directorate for the North East Assembly
●   Conf - Mtgs - Res - Stat - LG
M   24 local authorities
¶   NL - 6;   Corporate Plan - 1;
State of the Region Profile Report - 2;
State of the Region Fact Card - 2; all free.

Association of Northern Ireland Colleges (ANIC)
NR   Millennium Community Outreach Centre, Springfield
Educational Village, 400 Springfield Rd, BELFAST, BT12 7DU.
028 9090 0060
http://www.anic.ac.uk
Chief Exec: John D'Arcy
○   *E; further education in Northern Ireland

**Association of Northern Ireland Education & Library Boards
(ANIELB) 1973**
■   Belfast Education & Library Board, 40 Academy St, BELFAST,
BT1 2NQ.   (hsb)
028 9056 4030   fax 028 9043 3861
email johnm@belb.co.uk   http://www.anielb.org
Pres: Bill Reilly,   Hon Sec: John McCullough
▲   Un-incorporated Society
○   *E, *N; to seek to achieve the highest standards in education &
library services for all the people of Northern Ireland
●   Conf - Mtgs
M   202 i

**Association of Northumberland Local History Societies
(ANLHS) 1966**
■   c/o The Black Gate, Castle Garth, NEWCASTLE upon TYNE,
NE1 1RQ.   (hsb)
0191-284 0555
email mark@anlhs.org.uk   http://www.anlhs.org.uk
Hon Sec: Mrs Patricia Hix
▲   Registered Charity
○   *L; to stimulate interest & research in the local history of the
ancient county of Northumberland
Gp Projects (incl research)
●   Conf - Mtgs - ET - Res - Exhib - SG - Inf - VE
<   Brit Assn for Local History
M   82 i, 15 instns, 53 org, UK / 4 i, o'seas
(Sub: £9 i & instns, £12.50-£22.50 org, UK / £10 i, o'seas)
¶   Tyne & Tweed (Jnl) - 1; £3.50 yr m, £4.50 yr nm.   AR; free.

Association of Nursery Training Colleges Ltd (ANTC) 1934
NR   Chiltern College, 16 Peppard Rd, Caversham, READING,
Berks, RG4 8JZ.   (regd/off)
▲   Registered Charity
○   *E; promotion of nursery nurse training
●   Mtgs - ET - LG

Association of Nurses in Substance Abuse (ANSA) 1983
NR   37 Star St, WARE, Herts, SG12 7AA.
0870 241 3503   fax 01920 462730
http://www.ansauk.org

Association of Nursing Religious (ANR) 1952
NR   Pield Heath House School, Pield Heath Rd, UXBRIDGE, Middx,
UB8 3NW.
01895 233092
Contact: Sr Catherine P Lehane
▲   Registered Charity
○   *P; to promote the professional & pastoral service of its
members to the sick
●   Conf - Mtgs - ET
<   Conf of Religious (COR); Nat Board of Catholic
Women (NBCW); CAFOD
M   75 i

**Association of Occupational Health Nurse Practitioners (UK)
(AOHNP (UK)) 1992**
■   PO Box 11785, PETERHEAD, Aberdeenshire, AB42 5YG.
(mail/address)
0845 225 5937   fax 0845 255 5937
email admin@aohnp.co.uk   http://www.aohnp.co.uk
Admin: Linda Riseborough
▲   Un-incorporated Association
○   *P; to increase representation & raise the profile of
occupational health nurses
●   Conf - Mtgs - SG - LG (DoH, NMC) - Networking - Job
introduction scheme
M   350 i, UK / 6 i, o'seas
¶   OH Today (NL) - 6; ftm.

Association of Occupational Therapists of Ireland (AOTI)
IRL Ground floor office, Bow Bridge House, Bow Lane, Kilmainham,
DUBLIN 8, Republic of Ireland.
353 (1) 633 7222
email aoti@eircom.net   http://www.aoti.ie
Chmn: Yvonne Finn-Orde
○   *P

Association of Occupational Therapists in Mental Health
a specialist section of the **British Association of Occupational
Therapists**

**Association of Old Vehicle Clubs in Northern Ireland (AOVC)
1973**
■   38 Ballymaconnell Rd, BANGOR, Co Down, BT20 5PS.   (hsb)
028 9146 7886   fax 028 9146 3211
email secretary@aovc.co.uk   http://www.aovc.co.uk
Dir & Co Sec: Trevor Mitchell
▲   Company Limited by Guarantee
○   *G; the restoration & use of all types of historic vehicles in
Northern Ireland
Gp Car clubs; Vintage clubs
●   Mtgs - Exhib - VE
<   Fedn of Brit Historic Vehicle Clubs
M   i, 28 clubs
¶   Ybk - 1; free to affiliated clubs.

Association of On-Track Labour Suppliers
since January 2006 **Rail Industry Contractors Association**

Association of Online Publishers (AOP) 2002
NR   Queen's House, 55/56 Lincoln's Inn Fields, LONDON,
WC2A 3LJ.   (hq)
020 7404 4166   fax 020 7404 4167
○   *T; for interactive (online) publishers from all sectors of media,
whether from newspaper, magazine or broadcasting
industries, or solely online. The primary purpose of AOP is to
raise standards & revenue across all sectors of online
publishing, & to raise the credibility & profile of the industry

Association of Operating Department Practitioners
is incorporated into the **College of Operating Department
Practitioners**

Association of Optometrists (AOP) 1946
- ■ 61 Southwark St, LONDON, SE1 0HL. (hq)
  020 7261 9661
  http://www.assoc-optometrists.org
  Chief Exec: Bob Hughes
- ▲ Company Limited by Guarantee
- ○ *P; to represent the interests of optometrists
- Gp Hospital optometrists
- ● Conf - Mtgs - ET - Inf - Empl - LG - Professional indemnity insurance - Provision of representation of individual members in legal & disciplinary cases
- < Eur Coun of Optometry & Optics; Jt Optical C'ee on the EU
- M 11,000 i, UK / 100 i, o'seas
- ¶ OT (Optometry Today/OpticsToday) - 26;   Blink (NL) - 4; both ftm.

Association of Optometrists: Ireland
- IRL 18 Greenmount House, Harold's Cross Rd, DUBLIN 6W, Republic of Ireland.
  353 (1) 453 8850   fax 353 (1) 453 8867
  email info@optometrists.ie
  Sec: Peter Coleman
- ○ *P

Association of Organics Recycling (AOR) 1995
- ■ 3 Burystead Place, WELLINGBOROUGH, Northants, NN8 1AH. (hq)
  0870 160 3270   fax 0870 160 3280
  email enquiries@organics-recycling.org.uk
  http://www.organics-recycling.org.uk
  Acting Chief Exec: Jeremy Jacobs
- ▲ Company Limited by Guarantee
- ○ *Q; to promote the sustainable management of biodegradable resources & the use of biological treatment techniques
- ● Conf - Mtgs - ET - Stat - Inf - Lib - VE - LG
- M 20 i, 550 f, 10 org, UK / 2 i, o'seas
- ¶ Composting News (Jnl) - 4; ftm only.
  Technical Manuals:
  A Guide to Anerobic Digestion + a Directory of Suppliers; £25 m, £50 nm.
  A Guide to In-Vessel Composting + a Directory of Suppliers; £45 m, £65 nm.
  Health & Safety at Composting Sites - a guide for managers; £45 m, £65 nm.
  Standardised Protocol for the Sampling & Enumeration of Airborne Microorganisms at Composting Facilities (1999); £5 m, £25 nm.
  Hazard Analysis & Critical Control Point for Composting; £35 m, £55 nm.
- × 2008 Composting Association

Association of Paediatric Anaesthetists (Great Britain & Ireland) (APAGBI) 1973
- ■ Churchill House, 35 Red Lion Sq, LONDON. WC1R 4SG. (hsb)
  020 7092 1739
  Hon Sec: Dr Kathleen Wilkinson
- ▲ Un-incorporated Society
- ○ *L, *P; education & research in paediatric anaesthesia
- Gp Clinical trials; Guidelines; Peer review
- ● Conf - ET - Res - SG - LG - Liaison with medical royal colleges
- < Fedn of Eur Assns in Paediatric Anaesthesia; Assn of Anaesthetists
- M 450 i, UK / 180 i, o'seas
- ¶ NL - 12; free.

Association of Painting Craft Teachers (APCT) 1921
- ■ 17 Belgrave Rd, Leyton, LONDON, E10 6LD. (hsp)
  020 8539 7027
  email stephendaws@talk21.com   http://www.apct.co.uk
  Nat Sec: Steve Daws
- ○ *E; 'craft skills throughout the painting & decorating industry'
- ● Mtgs - ET - Exhib - Comp
- M 265 i, 5 f, UK / 2 i, o'seas

Association for Palliative Medicine of Great Britain & Ireland (APM) 1985
- NR Peterkin House, 76 Botley Rd, SOUTHAMPTON, Hants, SO31 1BA. (hq)
  01489 565665
  http://www.palliative-medicine.org
  Chmn: Dr Bill Noble,   Admin: Miss Sabine Tuck
- ▲ Registered Charity
- ○ *P
- ● Conf - Mtgs - ET - Res - SG
- < Eur Assn for Palliative Care
- M 500 i, UK / 10 i, o'seas
- ¶ NL - 2; ftm only.

Association of Past Rotarians 1960
- ■ 11 Highgate Place, West Park, LYTHAM ST ANNES, Lancs, FY8 4QJ. (hsp)
  01253 732342   fax 01253 732342
  email jonandkateha8852@aol.com
  http://www.past-rotarians.org.uk
  Hon Sec: John Harrop
- ▲ Un-incorporated Society
- Br 24
- ○ *G; a fellowship of member clubs of former Rotarians
- ● Conf - Mtgs - VE
- M 374 i
- ¶ Proclaim - 4;   AR; both free.
  Pioneers & Pathfinders (1948) [&] Forty Years On (2000) by W R Braide, (histories of the Past Rotarian movement).

Association for Pastoral Care in Mental Health (APCMH) 1986
- NR c/o Marylebone Parish Church, Marylebone Rd, LONDON, NW1 5LT. (postal/address)
  020 7383 0167   fax 020 8395 9022
  email john.rawson@blueyonder.co.uk
  http://www.pastoral.org.uk
  Co Sec: John Vallat
- ▲ Registered Charity
- Br 4
- ○ *W; to support & facilitate groups who wish to seek advice on setting up projects for people with mental health problems - mainly in the churches
- ● Conf - Mtgs - ET - Drop in centres - Befriending schemes - Awareness raising conferences
  Helpline: 01483 538936
- < Gld of Health; Nat Schizophrenia Fellowship
- M 200 i, 20 org
- ¶ NL - 6; ftm only.

Association for Pastoral & Spiritual Care & Counselling
  a group of the **British Association for Counselling & Psychotherapy**

Association for Payment Clearing Services (APACS) 1985
- NR Mercury House, Triton Court, 14 Finsbury Sq, LONDON, EC2A 1LQ. (hq)
  020 7711 6200
- ○ *T; to oversee & coordinate the operation, planning & development of money transmission & payment clearing services in the UK
- M f
  Note: in 2004 took over the functions of the Credit Card Research Group

© CBD Research Ltd · Beckenham · BR3 5JS · Tel 020 8650 7745 · Fax 020 8650 0768 · E-mail cbd@cbdresearch.com · www.cbdresearch.com

Association of Pension Lawyers   (APL)   1984
NR   PMI House (room 10), 4-10 Artillery Lane, LONDON,
         E1 7LS.   (mail add)
         Hon Sec: Jill Clucas
○   *P; to promote awareness of the importance of the role of law
         in the provision of pensions; to afford opportunities for
         discussion & consideration of matters of interest as well as
         education
Gp   Education & seminars; International; Investment; Leigislative &
         parliamentary; Litigation Investment
●   Conf - Mtgs - LG
M   c 950 i
¶   Pension Lawyer - 4.

Association of Pensioneer Trustees
         2005 merged with the Sipp Provider Group to form the **Association
         of Member-Directed Pension Schemes**

Association for Perioperative Practice   (NATN)   1964
■   Daisy Ayris House, 6 Grove Park Court, HARROGATE, N Yorks,
         HG1 4DP.   (hq)
         01423 508079   fax 01423 531613
         email hq@afpp.org.uk   http://www.afpp.org.uk
         Chief Exec: Alison Tait
▲   Company Limited by Guarantee; Registered Charity
Br   15
○   *P; for those working in & around operating theatres
●   Conf - Mtgs - ET - Res - Exhib - SG - Inf - Lib - VE
M   8,500 i, 10 f, UK / 250 i, o'seas
¶   Jnl of Perioperative Practice - 12; ftm, £65 yr nm.
✕   2005 (April) National Association of Theatre Nurses

Association of Personal Injury Lawyers   (APIL)   1989
NR   11 Castle Quay, NOTTINGHAM, NG7 1FW.   (hq)
         0115-958 0585   fax 0115-958 0885
         http://www.apil.org.uk
         Sec: Frances Swaine,   Chief Exec: Denise Kitchener
▲   Company Limited by Guarantee
○   *P; to promote full & prompt compensation for all types of
         personal injury; to promote wider redress for personal injury
         in the legal system; to campaign for improvements in
         personal injury law for the public good
Gp   Special interest: Procedure, Brain injury, Child abuse, Child
         injury, Clinical negligence, Costs & funding, Damages,
         Environment, International, Military, Multi party actions,
         Occupational health, Product liability, Spinal cord injury,
         Transport
●   Conf - Mtgs - ET - Exam - Res - Exhib - Stat - Inf - LG
M   5,213 i, UK / 62 i, o'seas + 150 f
¶   Jnl - 4.
         Focus (NL) - 6; Agenda - 12; both ftm only.
         Rehab Directory - 1; ftm, £20 nm.
         Membership Directory - 1; ftm, £100 nm.   AR; free.

Association of Pet Behaviour Counsellors   (APBC)   1989
NR   PO Box 46, WORCESTER, WR8 9YS.   (mail address)
         01386 751151   fax 01386 750743
         http://www.apbc.org.uk
○   *P; for practising pet behaviour therapists who work exclusively
         on referral from veterinary practitioners, to treat behaviour
         problems in dogs & cats primarily, but also horses, rabbits,
         parrots & occasional exotic species
M   practices

Association of Pet Dog Trainers   (APDT)   1995
■   PO Box 17, KEMPSFORD, Glos, GL7 4WZ.   (hq)
         01285 810811
         email apdtoffice@aol.com   http://www.apdt.co.uk
         Chmn: Val Harvey
▲   Un-incorporated Society
○   *P; to promote kind, fair & effective dog training
●   ET - Inf - Lib
M   500 i
         (Sub: £45)
¶   Dog Trainer - 3; free.

**Association for Petroleum & Explosives Administration
(APEA)   1958**
■   PO Box 106, SAFFRON WALDEN, Essex, CB11 3XT.   (hq)
         0845 603 5507   fax 0845 603 5507
         email admin@apea.org.uk   http://www.apea.org.uk
         Business Mgr: Jane Mardell
▲   Company Limited by Guarantee
○   *P; to represent all sides of the petroleum industry (incl:
         national & local government, oil companies, equipment
         manufacturers & suppliers, service & installation
         organisations & training establishments)
●   Conf - Mtgs - ET - Exhib - Inf - VE - LG - Publication
M   630 i, 321 f, UK / 32 i, 24 f, o'seas
¶   Guidance for the Design, Construction & Maintenance of Petrol
         Filling Stations - 1; £30 m, £90 nm.

Association of Pharmacy Technicians   1952
NR   1 Mabledon Place (4th floor), LONDON, WC1H 9AJ.
         020 7551 1551
○   *P; dispensing prescriptions for doctors at doctors' surgeries

Association of Photographers Ltd   1968
■   81 Leonard St, LONDON, EC2A 4QS.   (hq)
         020 7739 6669
         Managing Dir: Kingsley Martin
▲   Company Limited by Guarantee
Br   3
○   *P, *T; for professional photographers working in fashion,
         advertising & editorial fields
●   Conf - Mtgs - ET - Exhib - Comp - Inf - Lib - Copyright advice
         service
<   Pyramide Europe; Pyramide GB
M   1,000 i, 10 f, 18 org, UK / 21 i, o'seas
¶   Image - 12;   The Annual Awards - 1;
         Business Info Beyond the Lens; all ftm.

Association for Physical Education   (AfPE)   1899
NR   Building 25 London Rd, READING, Berks, RG1 5AQ.   (hq)
         0118-378 6240
         email enquiries@afpe.org.uk   http://www.afpe.org.uk
         Sec: John Matthews
▲   Company Limited by Guarantee; Registered Charity
Br   2
○   *E, *P; to promote & maintain high standards & safe practice in
         all aspects of physical education
●   Conf - Mtgs - ET - Res - SG
<   Intl Coun of Sport Science & Physical Educ (ICSSPE); Eur
         Physical Educ Assn EUPEA)
M   2,000 i, 50 f, UK / 50 i, 10 f, o'seas
¶   Physical Education Matters - 4;
         Physical Education & Sports Pedagogy - 3;
         Members Ybk - 1; all ftm.
✕   2006 (British Association of Advisers & Lecturers in Physical
         Education
         (Physical Education Association (March)

Association of Physical & Natural Therapists   (APNT)
NR   27 Old Gloucester St, LONDON, WC1N 3XX.
         0845 345 2345
         email info@apnt.org   http://www.apnt.org
         Chmn: Albie McMahon
○   *P; to represent practitioners of complementary medicine in
         educational, professional & political matters

Association of Pioneer Motor Cyclists (APMC) 1928
NR   Heather Bank, May Close, Headley, BORDON, Hants,
       GU35 8LR.   (hsp)
       01428 712666
       Hon Sec: Mrs J McBeath
Br   Counties; Belgium, Holland, USA
O   *G; for all who contributed to the establishment of the sport,
       pastime & industry of motorcycling. 'Companion'
       membership available to those having held a licence for 40+
       years, 'Pioneer' membership for those licensed for 50+ years
●   Mtgs - Comp - VE - Social activities
M   550 i, UK / 20 i, o'seas
¶   NL - 4;   Rules & register of members - 2; ftm only.

Association of Planning Supervisors
       since 2004 the **Association for Project Safety**

Association of Play Industries   (API)
■   Federation House, STONELEIGH PARK, Warks, CV8 2RF.   (hq)
       024 7641 4999   fax 024 7641 4990
       http://www.api-play.org
       Co Sec: Deborah Holt
▲   Company Limited by Guarantee
O   *T; manufacturers & suppliers of play equipment & impact
       absorbing surfaces (incl inflatable structures)
●   Mtgs - Exhib - Inf - LG
<   a group of the Fedn of Sports & Play Assns (FSPA)
M   c 60 f

Association of Pleasure Craft Operators   (APCO)   1954
■   Marine House, Thorpe Lea Rd, EGHAM, Surrey, TW20 8BF.
       (hq)
       0844 800 9575   fax 01327 349468
       email info@apco.org.uk   http://www.apco.org.uk
       Sec: Samantha Clarke
▲   Un-incorporated Society
O   *T; interests of members who are all in business connected with
       inland waterways in the UK
Gp   Sections: Hotel boat, Passenger boat
●   Conf - Mtgs - ET - Res - Stat - Inf - LG
<   Brit Marine Fedn
M   120 f
¶   NL - 4; ftm.
       LM - 1;   Members Directory - 1; both free.

Association of Plumbing & Heating Contractors   (APHC)   1925
NR   14 Ensign House, Ensign Business Centre, Westwood Way,
       COVENTRY, Warks, CV4 8JA.   (hq)
       024 7647 2503   fax 024 7647 0942
       email info@aphc.co.uk   http://www.aphc.co.uk
       Chief Exec: Clive Dickin
▲   Company Limited by Guarantee
O   *T; for employers in the plumbing & heating industry in England
       & Wales
●   Conf - Mtgs - ET - Exam - Exhib - Empl - LG
M   1,200 f
¶   Hot & Cold - 6; free.

Association of Police Authorities   (APA)   1997
■   15 Greycoat Place, LONDON, SW1P 1BN.
       020 7664 3096
O   *N
       no further information supplied

Association of Police & Court Interpreters   (APCI)   1974
■   The Octagon, Exchange Tower, 2 Harbour Exchange Square,
       LONDON, E14 9GE.   (hq)
       email secretary@apciinterpreters.org.uk
       http://www.apciinterpreters.org.uk
       Sec: Alan P M Thompson
▲   Un-incorporated Society
O   *P; for independent, freelance interpreters working within the
       Criminal Justice System
●   Mtgs - ET - Empl - LG
M   100 i
¶   The Interpreter - 2;   Membership Directory - irreg; both free.

**Association of Police & Public Security Suppliers   (APPSS)
1993**
■   Marlborough House, Headley Rd, GRAYSHOTT, Surrey,
       GU26 6LG.   (hq)
       01428 602627   fax 01428 602628
       email inform@appss.org.uk   http://www.appss.org.uk
       Dir: Bob Rose
▲   Company Limited by Guarantee
O   *T; to support the UK public security industry;   to promote UK
       products to police, prisons and other public security agencies
       worldwide
Gp   UK security export focus group; Olympic group
●   Conf - Res - Expt - Inf - Lib - VE - LG
<   a division of the Defence Mfrs Assn
M   250 f
¶   Public Security - 4; free.
       Directory of Police & Public Security Suppliers - 1.

Association of Policy Market Makers   (APMM)   1992
■   PO Box 6717, STURMINSTER NEWTON, Dorset, DT10 9AR.
       (hq)
       0845 833 0088   fax 0845 833 0089
       email enquiries@apmm.org   http://www.apmm.org
       Dir: Tim Villiers
▲   Company Limited by Guarantee
O   *T; 'to promote the business of policy market makers in the
       acquisition & disposal of traded (second-hand) endowment
       policies'
●   Mtgs - Stat - Inf - LG
M   f [not given]
¶   AR - 1; ftm only.

Association of Port Health Authorities   (APHA)   1899
■   2-02 Suffolk Enterprise Centre, Felaw Maltings, Felaw St,
       IPSWICH, Suffolk, IP2 8SJ.   (hq)
       01473 407040
       Exec Sec: Mike Young
▲   Company Limited by Guarantee
O   *T; health control of ships & aircraft & the people & cargo
       landed from them on arrival in the UK
Gp   C'ees: Imported food; Environmental health & hygiene; Border
       inspection post
●   Conf - Mtgs - Inf - LG
M   70 port health & local authorities
¶   Port Health Hbk - 1;   AR; both free.

Association for Postnatal Illness   (APNI)   1979
NR   145 Dawes Rd, LONDON, SW6 7EB.   (hq)
       020 7386 0868   fax 020 7386 8885
       email info@apni.org   http://www.apni.org
       Hon Sec: Mrs Diane Nehmé
▲   Registered Charity
O   *W; to offer advice & support to women suffering from
       postnatal depression; support is offered by volunteers who
       are all ex-sufferers
●   Inf
M   4,455 i
¶   Puerperal Psychosis;   Post Natal Depression;   Baby Blues &
       Post Natal Depression; all free.

© CBD Research Ltd · Beckenham · BR3 5JS · Tel 020 8650 7745 · Fax 020 8650 0768 · E-mail cbd@cbdresearch.com · www.cbdresearch.com

Association of Practising Accountants   (APA)   1987
- ■ 105 St Peter's St, ST ALBANS, Herts, AL1 3EJ.   (hq)
    01727 896000   fax 01727 8960262
    email ksam@kingstonsmith.co.uk
    http://www.kingstonsmith.co.uk
    Chmn: Michael J Snyder
- ▲ Un-incorporated Society
- ○ *P; for medium sized firms of chartered accountants
- ● Mtgs - Inf
- M 16 f
- ¶ Becoming a Chartered Accountant - training with a medium
    sized firm.
    Medium sized firms of Chartered Accountants - the vital link
    between businesses & the City.
    Research document: challenge & opportunity for medium sized
    accountancy firms; ftm, £70 nm.

Association of Primary Care Groups & Trusts
    since 2006 the **NHS Trusts Association**

Association of Print Specialists & Manufacturers
    alternative name of **Prism**

Association of Printing Machinery Importers
    in 2007-08 merged with **Picon Ltd**

**Association of Private Client Investment Managers &
Stockbrokers   (APCIMS)   1990**
- NR 22 City Rd, Finsbury Square, LONDON, EC1Y 2AJ.   (hq)
    020 7448 7100
    email info@apcims.co.uk   http://www.apcims.co.uk
    Chief Exec: David Bennett
- ▲ Company Limited by Guarantee
- ○ *T; for wealth management & banking firms which provide
    services to private investors
- Gp UK & European financial regulation; Corporate governance;
    Clearing & settlement; Indices
- ● Conf - Mtgs - Res - Stat - Inf - LG
- M 200 f, UK / 20 f, o'seas
- ¶ APCIMS Update - 12;   Q Review - 4;   LM - 1;
    AR - 1; all free.

Association of Private Crematoria & Cemeteries   (APCC)   1944
- NR 129 Bloomsbury Lane, Timperley, ALTRINCHAM, Cheshire,
    WA15 6NS.   (sp)
    0161-291 8547
    email info@apcrem.org   http://www.apcrem.org
    Sec: Andrew P Helsby
- ▲ Un-incorporated Society
- ○ *T; interests of proprietary cemeteries & crematoria
- ● Mtgs - Stat - Inf - LG
- < Fedn Brit Cremation Authorities; Cremation Soc; Inst of Burial &
    Cremation Administration
- M 15 crematoria, 7 cemeteries

Association of Private Market Operators   (APMO)   1990
- NR 4 Worrygoose Lane, Whiston, ROTHERHAM, S Yorks,
    S60 4AD.   (sb)
    01709 700072   fax 01709 703648
    Gen Sec: David J Glasby
- ▲ Company Limited by Guarantee
- ○ *T; interests of private market operators in the UK; to foster
    professionalism in the UK retail markets
- ● Mtgs - Inf - LG
- < Brit Chams Comm
- M 20 f
- ¶ Hbk - 2/3 yrly; free.

**Association of Private Pet Cemeteries & Crematoria   (APPCC)
1993**
- NR Paws to Rest, Nunclose, Armathwaite, CARLISLE, CA4 9TJ.
    01697 472232   fax 01697 472260
    email contact@appcc.org.uk   http://www.appcc.org.uk
    Chmn: N J Ricketts
- ▲ Company Limited by Guarantee
- ○ *T; to provide a post death pet care service; to educate pet
    owners, vets & others in the pet world, to the advantages of
    giving pet animals a decent, dignified departure
- ● Conf - Mtgs - Res - LG - Keeping abreast of the deluge of EU
    legislation which threatens the livelihood of members
    Helpline 01252 844478
- < Coun of Brit Funeral Services
- M 41 f
- ¶ Chairman's Update - irreg; free.

Association of Private Railway Wagon Owners   (APRO)
- NR Homelea, Westland Green, Little Hadham, WARE, Herts,
    SG11 2AG.   (hsp)
    01279 843487
    email geoffrey.pratt@btconnect.com
    Sec Gen: Geoffrey Pratt
- ○ *T

**Association of Professional Ambulance Personnel   (APAP)
1981**
- NR 6 The Old Brewery, The Charlton Estate, SHEPTON MALLET,
    Somerset, BA4 5QE.   (hq)
    0870 167 0999
- ○ *U; for ambulance services personnel
- M i

Association of Professional Astrologers   (APA)   1990
- NR 8 Queen Close, HENLEY-on-THAMES, Oxon, RG9 1BP.
    (chmn/p)
    0800 074 6113
    Sec: Sharon Knight,   Chmn: Maureen Randall
- ○ *P; to provide a forum for professional discussion of astrology
    on all levels; to promote astrology as a serious subject,
    counter the star-sign image of the astrologer & take active
    steps to correct misinterpretation in the press
- M 69 i, UK / 5 i, o'seas
- ¶ NL - 4;   Consultants list - updated;
    Minutes of AGM & all meetings; all free.

**Association of Professional Genealogists in Ireland   (APGI)
1987**
- IRL 30 Harlech Crescent, Clonskeagh, DUBLIN 14, Republic of
    Ireland.   (hsb)   http://www.apgi.ie
    Hon Sec: Robert C Davison
- ○ *G; the promotion of genealogical research by members using
    records for the whole of Ireland
- M i (NI), i (Republic of Ireland)
- ¶ LM - 1; free.

Association of Professional Landscapers
    a specialist group of the **Horticultural Trades Association**

Association of Professional Music Therapists   (APMT)   1976
- NR 24-27 White Lion St, LONDON, N1 9PD.   (hq)
    020 8440 4153   fax 020 8440 4153
    email apmtoffice@aol.com   http://www.apmt.org.uk
    Admin: Louise Karena
- ▲ Un-incorporated Society
- ○ *P
- Gp Courses liaison; Jobs; Grading; Parliamentary; Employment
- ● Conf - Mtgs - Res - SG - Inf - Clearing house for jobs - Register
    of members
- < Brit Soc for Music Therapy (BSMT); Links with overseas
    associations
- M 540 i, UK / 25 i, o'seas

Association of Professional Political Consultants   (APPC)   1995
■   c/o Precise Public Affairs, The Registry, Royal Mint Court,
    LONDON, EC3N 4QN.   (chmn/b)
    020 7866 7871   fax 0871 247 2304
    email mail@appc.org.uk   http://www.appc.org.uk
    Chmn: Robbie McDuff
▲   Company Limited by Guarantee
○   *P; the representative & regulatory body for professional
    political consultants
●   Mtgs - ET - LG
M   58 f
¶   Register of Members' Interests; on request.

**Association of Professional Recording Services Ltd   (APRS)
1947**
■   PO Box 22, TOTNES, Devon, TQ9 7YZ.   (hq)
    01803 868600   fax 01803 868444
    email info@aprs.co.uk   http://www.aprs.co.uk
    Chief Exec: Peter Filleul
▲   Company Limited by Guarantee
○   *T; for all commercially involved in professional sound
    recording & associated fields
Gp Sound recording studios & post-production facilities;
    Manufacturers & distributors; Consultancies, education &
    hire; Mastering & music services; Individuals - freelance &
    industry professionals; Students
●   ET - Expt - Inf - LG
M   250 i, 200 f, 8 educational org, UK / 10 i, o'seas
¶   NL.   LM.   Hbk.   AR; all ftm.

**Association of Professional Sales Agents (Sports & Leisure
Industries)   (APSA)**
■   Federation House, STONELEIGH PARK, Warks, CV8 2RF.   (hq)
    024 7641 4999   fax 024 7641 4990
    email apsa@sportsandplay.com
    http://www.sportsandplay.com
    Assn Mgr: Mrs Jane Montgomery
▲   Company Limited by Guarantee
○   *T
●   Mtgs - Exhib - Inf
<   a group of the Fedn of Sports & Play Assns (FSPA)
M   55 i

Association of Professional Shooting Instructors   (APSI)   1997
NR 24 Nobles Close, Grove, WANTAGE, Oxon, OX12 0NR.
    01235 768280
    email apsi@totalshooting.com
    http://www.apsishooting.co.uk
    Sec: Paul Bentley

**Association of Professional Staffs in Colleges of Education &
Humanities   (APSCEH)**
IRL c/o Irish Federation of University Teachers, 11 Merrion Sq,
    DUBLIN 2, Republic of Ireland.
    353 (1) 661 0910   fax 353 (1) 661 0909
    email ifut@eircom.net   http://www.ifut.ie
○   *E, *P

Association of Professional Stress Managers & Life Support Managers
    see **Society of Stress Managers (the Association of
    Professional Stress Managers & Life Support Managers)**

Association of Professional Tourist Guides   (APTG)   1987
NR 33-37 Moreland St, LONDON, EC1V 8HA.   (hq)
    020 7780 4060   fax 020 7780 4142
    email aptg@aptg.org.uk
    http://www.touristguides.org.uk
    Admin: Annie Simpson,   Chmn: Robina Brown
○   *P; for London registered blue badge tourist guides
●   Conf - SG - VE - Walking tours - Tours with private car & guide
    - General sightseeing tours
<   ICOMOS; Wld Fedn of Tourist Guides Assns; Fedn of Eur
    Tourist Guides Assns
    is part of Amicus U
M   465 i
¶   Tourist Guides' Directory - 1.

Association of Professional Videomakers   (APV)   1994
NR 7 Nether Grove, Shenley Brook End, MILTON KEYNES, Bucks,
    MK5 7BQ.   (hq)
    01908 522145   fax 01908 524699
    http://www.apv.org.uk
    Sec: Jan Parry
▲   Company Limited by Guarantee
○   *P, *T; to provide help & support to the small independent video
    provider in the wedding & event video industry
●   Conf - Mtgs - ET - Exhib - Comp
M   500 i, UK / 10 i, o'seas
¶   Videoprofessional - 6; ftm, £2 nm.

**Association of Professionals in Education & Children's Trusts
(ASPECT)   1919**
NR Woolley Hall, Woolley, WAKEFIELD, W Yorks, WF4 2JR.   (hq)
    01226 383428   fax 01226 383427
    email info@aspect.org.uk   http://www.aspect.org.uk
○   *P, *U
M   i
×   2005 (November) National Association of Educational
    Inspectors, Advisors & Consultants

**Association for Professionals in Services for Adolescents
(APSA)   1969**
■   Holtwood, Red Lion St, Cropredy, BANBURY, Oxon,
    OX17 1PD.   (admin)
    01295 750182   fax 01295 750182
    email apsa@cingnet.org.uk   http://www.apsa-web.info
▲   Company Limited by Guarantee; Registered Charity
○   *P; to promote the study, understanding & care of adolescents;
    to generate new thinking about adolescent care, both
    residential & community based
●   Conf - ET
<   Young Minds; Nat Children's Bureau
M   360 i, UK / 25 i, o'seas
¶   The Jnl of Adolescence - 6; ftm, £607 nm.
    APSA Rapport - 4; ftm, £16 nm.

Association for Project Management   (APM)   1972
■   150 West Wycombe Rd, HIGH WYCOMBE, Bucks,
    HP12 3AE.   (hq)
    0845 458 1944   fax 01494 528937
    email info@apm.org.uk   http://www.apm.org.uk
    Hon Sec: David Roper,   Co Sec: John Salisbury
▲   Company Limited by Guarantee; Registered Charity
Br 12; Hong Kong
○   *P; run by project managers for project managers
Gp Contracts & procurement; Earned value; Governance of project
    management; Programme management; Project &
    programme excellence; People; Value management; Women
    in project management
●   Conf - Mtgs - ET - Exam - Res - Exhib - Comp - Stat - Inf - LG
<   Intl Project Mgt Assn (IPMA); Engg Coun UK
M   13,630 i, 355 f, UK / 673 i, 8 f, o'seas
¶   Project (Jnl) - 10.   Network (NL) - 10; Ybk - 1;   AR - 1;
    all ftm only.
    International Jnl of Project Management - 8; £35 m, 217 nm.

Association for Project Safety   (APS)   1995
■   Stanhope House, 12 Stanhope Place, EDINBURGH,
    EH12 5HH.   (hq)
    0845 612 1290   fax 0845 612 1291
    email info@aps.org.uk   http://www.aps.org.uk
    Chief Exec: Brian B Law
▲   Company Limited by Guarantee
Br   16
○   *P; to provide support, guidance & development for all those
    involved in construction health & safety & risk management
    in terms of the Construction (Design & Management)
    Regulations 2007
Gp   CDM co-ordinators
●   Conf - Mtgs - ET - Exam - Stat - Inf - LG
<   Intl Safety & Health Construction Coordinators Org;
    Cosntruction Ind Coun (CIC)
M   5,000 i, 600 f, UK / 31 i, o'seas
    (Sub: £129 i, £240 f, UK / £129 i, o'seas)
¶   NL - 6.   Practice Notes - 6.   AR; all ftm.
    Design Risk Management Guide (book+CD-ROM); £35 m,
    £45 nm.
    Management of CDM Coordination (book+CD-ROM); £76 m,
    £95 nm.
    Pre-construction Information (guide+CD-ROM); £80 m,
    £140 nm.
    H+S File (CD-ROM); £95 m, £155 nm.
    Form of Appointment; £8.50.
×   2004 Association of Planning Supervisors

Association for Promoting Retreats   (APR)   1913
■   The Central Hall, 256 Bermondsey St, LONDON, SE1 3UJ.
    (hq)
    020 7357 7736   fax 0871 715 1917
    email apr@retreats.org.uk
    Admin: Alison MacTier
▲   Registered Charity
○   *R; promoting retreats; to provide a national network of those
    able to advise on the subject
●   Conf - ET - Exhib - Inf
M   1,700 i, 300 org
¶   Retreats - 1.

Association for the Promotion of Preconceptual Care
    alternative name of **Foresight**

**Association for the Promotion of Quality in TESOL Education
(QuiTE)**
NR   c/o Institute of Education, University of London, 20 Bedford
    Way, LONDON, WC1H 0AL.   (chmn/b)
    http://www.quality-tesol-ed.org.uk
    Chmn: John Norrish
○   *E; for teacher educators, course providers & all working in
    areas relating to the training, education & development of
    teachers of English to speakers of other languages
●   Seminars

Association of Property Bankers   (APB)   1991
NR   c/o Eurohypo AG, 90 Long Acre (9th floor), LONDON,
    WC2E 9RA.
    http://www.theapb.co.uk
    Mem Sec: Bill Lindsay

Association of Property & Fixed Charge Receivers
    alternative name of **NARA**

Association for the Protection of Rural Scotland   (APRS)   1926
NR   Gladstone's Land (3rd floor), 483 Lawnmarket, EDINBURGH,
    EH1 2NT.   (hq)
    0131-225 7012
    email info@ruralscotland.org
    http://www.ruralscotland.org
    Contact: Walter Simpson
▲   Charitable Company; Limited by Guarantee
○   *G; to improve, protect & preserve the rural scenery &
    amenities of country districts, towns & villages in Scotland for
    the benefit of the public
M   i, f & org

**Association for Psychoanalytic Psychotherapy in the NHS
(APP)   1981**
NR   5 Windsor Rd, LONDON, N3 3SN.   (hq)
    020 8349 9873   fax 020 8343 3197
    email joycepiper@compuserve.com
    http://www.app-nhs.org.uk
    Admin Sec: Mrs Joyce Piper
▲   Registered Charity
○   *M; to promote psychoanalytic psychotherapy in the NHS
Gp   Adult psychiatry; Child & adolescent; Group section; Nursing;
    Older adults; Primary care
●   Conf - Mtgs - Res
<   Eur Fedn for Psychoanalytic Psychotherapy (EFPP); Brit
    Psychoanalytic Coun; Assn Child Psychotherapists (ACP)
M   800 i, UK / 20 i, o'seas
¶   Psychoanalytic Psychotherapy (Jnl) - 4; ftm, £71 yr nm.
    APP NL - 2.   AR.

Association for Psychological Therapies   (APT)
NR   1 Saxby St, LEICESTER, LE2 0ND.   (mail/address)
    0116-255 5963
○   *P
<   Mtgs

Association of Psychosexual Nursing   1998
NR   PO Box 2762, LONDON, W1A 5HQ.
○   *M

Association of Public Analysts   (APA)   1953
NR   Burlington House, Piccadilly, LONDON, W1J 0BG.   (regd/off)
○   *P; to coordinate the activities of public analysts in the provision
    of scientific advice to local authorities on matters concerning
    food, water, animal feeds, consumer safety & the
    environment

Association of Public Analysts of Scotland   (APAS)   1897
■   c/o Analytical & Scientific Services, 4 Marine Esplanade,
    EDINBURGH, EH6 7LV.   (hsb)
    0131-555 7980   fax 0131-555 7987
    Hon Sec: Dr Andrew Mackie
▲   Un-incorporated Society
○   *P; analysis of food, waters, environmental materials, consumer
    products, & agricultural products for public protection;
    interpretation of public protection legislation
Gp   Sub-gps: Chemistry, Microbiology, Quality & IT
●   Mtgs - ET - LG
<   Assn Public Analysts
M   9 i

Association for Public Service Excellence   (APSE)   1981
NR   Washbrook House (2nd floor), Lancastrian Office Centre,
       32 Talbot Rd, Old Trafford, MANCHESTER, M32 0FP.   (hq)
       0161-772 1810   fax 0161-772 1811
       email enquiries@apse.org.uk   http://www.apse.org.uk
▲   Un-incorporated Society
Br   2
○   *N, *T; the networking organisation which consults, develops,
       promotes & advises on best practice in the delivery of local
       authority services
Gp   Advisory groups for local authority service areas; Performance
       networks; Best value consultancy: Life long learning
●   Conf - Mtgs - ET - Res - Exhib - SG - Stat - Inf - Lib - LG
M   3 f, 244 local authorities
¶   Direct News - 6;   Briefing Notes - 1; both ftm only.
       AR (incl LM) - 1; ftm.   Publications - 2; at cost.
×   2006 Association of Civic Hosts (merged)

Association of Publishing Agencies   (APA)   1993
NR   Queen's House(3rd floor), 55-56 Lincoln's Inn Fields,
       LONDON, WC2A 3LJ.   (hq)
       020 7404 4166   fax 020 7404 4167
       email info@apa.co.uk   http://www.apa.co.uk
       Chief Exec: Patrick Fuller
○   *T; to promote the customer magazine publishing industry; to
       promote awareness of the effectiveness of such magazines as
       a marketing tool
●   Mtgs - Res - Inf - Marketing - Awards
<   Periodical Publishers Assn (PPA)
M   29 f, UK / 5 f, o'seas
¶   NL - 4;   A Guide to Customer Publishing - 1;
       Case Studies - 2; all free.
       The Case for Customer Magazines;   Info Pack;
       Membership pack; all on request.

Association for Punjab Studies (UK)   (APS (UK))   1994
NR   c/o Shinder Thandi, Dept of Economics, Finance & Accounting,
       Coventry University Business School, Priory St, COVENTRY,
       CV1 5FB.   (hsp)
       Hon Sec: S S Thandi
▲   Company Limited by Guarantee
○   *L; promotion of punjab studies in the UK
●   Conf - ET - Res - SG
M   6 i, 25 org
¶   International Journal of Punjab Studies - 2.

Association of Qualified Curative Hypnotherapists
       has closed

Association for Qualitative Research   (AQR)   1980
■   Davey House, 31 St Neots Rd, Eaton Ford, ST NEOTS, Cambs,
       PE19 7BA.   (hq)
       01480 407227   fax 01480 211267
       email info@aqr.org.uk   http://www.aqr.org.uk
       Sec: Rose Molloy
▲   Company Limited by Guarantee
○   *P, *T; for qualitative research
●   Conf - ET
M   1,000 i, UK / 100 i, o'seas
¶   In Brief (Jnl) - 6; ftm, subject to availability nm.
       Directory - 1; free.

Association of Racing Kart Schools Ltd   (ARKS)   1994
■   Stoneycroft, Godsons Lane, Napton, SOUTHAM, Warks,
       CV47 8LX.   (sp)
       01926 812177   fax 01926 812177
       email secretary@arks.co.uk   http://www.arks.co.uk
       Sec: Graham Smith
▲   Company Limited by Guarantee
Br   13; Dubai
○   *T
●   Conf - ET - Exam - Stat - Inf
<   Motor Activities Training Coun (MATC)
M   13 f, UK / 1 f, o;seas

Association for Radiation Research   (ARR)   1958
NR   c/o Dr Tracy Robson, Reader in Molecular Pharmacology,
       Experimental Therapeutics, School of Pharmacy,
       Queen's University Belfast, Medical Biology Centre,
       97 Lisburn Rd, BELFAST, BT9 7BL.
       028 9097 2360   fax 028 9024 7794
       http://www.graylab.ac.uk/usr/arr/home.html
       Hon Sec: Dr Tracy Robson
○   *L; promotion of learning & education in the field of radiation
       research
M   i

Association of Radical Midwives   (ARM)   1976
■   16 Wytham St, OXFORD, OX1 4SU.   (sp)
       01865 248159
       email sarahmontagu@gmail.com
       Admin Sec: Sarah Montagu
▲   Registered Charity
Br   50 local contacts
○   *K, *P; to preserve & increase the choices in childbirth for
       women; to restore & strengthen the role of midwife
●   Conf - Mtgs - LG
<   Intl Confedn of Midwives; Eur Midwives Liaison C'ee
M   1,200 i, 140 orgs & colleges, UK / 80 i, o'seas
¶   Midwifery Matters - 4; ftm, £2 each nm.

Association of Railway Training Providers   (ARTP)   1997
■   22 Headfort Place, LONDON, SW1X 7RY.   (asa)
       020 7201 0778   fax 020 7235 5777
       email info@artp.co.uk   http://www.artp.co.uk
       Secretariat: Peter Loosley
▲   Company Limited by Guarantee
○   *T; for training providers competence assessors to the railway
       industry
Gp   Audit protocols (Achilles); Communications; Competence
       management; Rule book / standards / documentation; Track
       safety assessment; Track safety plans
●   Conf - Mtgs - ET - Res - Wxhib - Inf
<   Rly Ind Assn
M   100 f
¶   E-NL - 4; ftm only.

**Association for Rational Emotive Behaviour Therapy   (AREBT)
1973**
■   Englewood, Farningham Hill Rd, FARNINGHAM, Kent,
       DA4 0JR.   (hsp)
       01322 862158
       http://www.arebt.org
       Hon Sec: Irene Tubbs
▲   Company Limited by Guarantee
Br   New Zealand, USA
○   *P, *W; for those offering behavioural therapy to clients; to
       counsel clients on how their belief systems largely determine
       how they feel about & act towards situations & life events
●   Conf - ET - Res- LG - Continuing professional development
       programmes
<   UK Coun of Psychotherapists (UKCP); Brit Assn of Behavioural &
       Cognitive Psychotherapists (BABCP)
M   167 i, 2 org, UK / 10 i, o'seas
       (Sub:£40 i, £60 org)
¶   Jnl - 1;   NL - 3; both ftm only.

© CBD Research Ltd · Beckenham · BR3 5JS · Tel 020 8650 7745 · Fax 020 8650 0768 · E-mail cbd@cbdresearch.com · www.cbdresearch.com

Association for Real Change (ARC) 1976
- ■ ARC House, Marsden St, CHESTERFIELD, Derbys, S40 1JY. (hq)
  01246 555043 fax 01246 555045
  email contact.us@arcuk.org.uk
  http://www.arcuk.org.uk
  Chief Exec: James Churchill
- ▲ Company Limited by Guarantee; Registered Charity
- Br 8
- ○ *T, *W; to support providers of services for people with a learning disability
- ● Conf - Mtgs - ET - Inf - Lib - LG
- < Eur Assn for Service Providers for Persons with a Disability (EASPD); Nat Coun for Voluntary Orgs (NCVO); Assn Chief Execs of Voluntary Orgs (ACEVO); Brit Inst of Learning Disabilities (BILD); Indep Care Orgs Network (IVCON); Learning Disability Coalition
- M 350 f
- ¶ Basic Steps; £55 m, £75 nm.
  Getting Started: the common induction standards in adult social care; £45 m, £80 nm.
  Banking Matters to Me; £10 m, £15 nm.
  Moving on Up: a short guide for professionals; £10.
  Moving on Up: young people & families guide; £20 m, £25 nm.

Association of Real Estate Funds (AREF) 1970
- ■ c/o ING Real Estate, 25 Copthall Ave, LONDON, EC2R 7BP. (hq)
  email info@aref.org.uk http://www.aref.org.uk
  Chief Exec: Rachel McIsaac
- ○ *T; to develop the interests of property unit trusts
- M 64 f
- × 2005 Association of Property Unit Trusts

Association of Recognised English Language Services
  since 12 May 2004 **English UK**

Association of Reflexologists (AoR) 1984
- ■ 5 Fore St, TAUNTON, Somerset, TA1 1HX. (hq)
  01823 351010 fax 01823 336646
  email info@aor.org.uk http://www.aor.org.uk
  Chief Exec: Doreen Baker
- ▲ Company Limited by Guarantee
- Br 62
- ○ *P; to promote the knowledge & understanding of reflexology; to set standards for qualifications
- ● Conf - Mtgs - ET - Res - Inf - LG
- < Reflexology in Europe Network; Reflexology Forum
- > Intl Inst of Reflexologists
- M 6,674 i, UK / 171 i, o'seas
  (Sub: £71)
- ¶ Reflexions (Jnl) - 4; ftm only.

Association of Regional City Editors 1969
- NR 1 Fern Dene, Templewood, LONDON, W13 8AN. (hsp)
  020 8997 6868
  email john.heffernan@virgin.net
  Hon Sec: John Heffernan
- ○ *P; interests of those concerned with economic & financial news (incl London-based wire service correspondents, & radio)
- M 22 i

Association of Registrars of Scotland (AROS) 1865
- ■ Area/Registration Office, Municipal Buildings, College St, DUMBARTON, G82 1NR. (hsb)
  01389 738350 fax 01389 738352
  email tony.gallagher@west-dunbarton.gov.uk
  Hon Sec: A (Tony) P P Gallagher
- ▲ Un-incorporated Society
- ○ *P; to promote the registration service in Scotland on behalf of registrars & the legislation which may affect them
- ● Conf - Mtgs - ET - Exam
- M 250 i
- ¶ Informant (NL) - 2; ftm only.

Association of Registration & Celebratory Services
  Association has been inactive since November 2007

Association for Rehabilitation of Communication & Oral Skills (ARCOS) 1992
- NR Whitbourne Lodge, 137 Church St, MALVERN, Worcs, WR14 2AN. (hq)
  01684 576795 fax 01684 576895
  email arcos@globalnet.co.uk http://www.arcos.org.uk
- ▲ Registered Charity
- ○ *W; provision of specialist help for children & adults with voice, speech, language & eating (swallowing) problems, & for their families & those working with them
- ● ET - Lib
- ¶ AR - 1.

Association of Relocation Agents
  since 2005-06 the **Association of Relocation Professionals**

Association of Relocation Professionals (ARP) 1986
- ■ PO Box 189, DISS, Norfolk, IP22 1PE. (hq)
  0870 073 7475 fax 0870 071 8719
  email info@relocationagents.com
  http://www.relocationagents.com
  Chief Exec: Tad Zurlinden
- ▲ Company Limited by Guarantee
- ○ *P; to promote the services & benefits of using relocation agents
- ● Conf - Mtgs - ET - Res - Exhib - Stat - Inf - LG
- < US Employee Relocation Coun; Eur Relocation Assn; CBI; Relocation Network (Australia)
- M 140 f, UK / 15 f, o'seas
- ¶ Directory of Members - 1; free.
  Guide to the United Kingdom - 2 yrly; £5 m, £9.95 nm.
  Guide to Homesearch (for those starting a business) - 1; ftm, £75 nm.
- × 2005-06 Association of Relocation Agents

Association of Research Centres in the Social Sciences (ARCISS) 1997
- NR PREST, Manchester University, Harold Hankins Building, Booth West St, MANCHESTER, M13 9PL. (hsb)
  020 7222 7665
  http://www.arciss.ac.uk
  Hon Sec: Deborah Cox
- ▲ Registered Charity
- ○ *Q; promotion, management & dissemination of independent social science research
- ● Conf - Res
- M c 45 non-profit independent university-based centres

Association for Research in the Voluntary & Community Sector (ARVAC) 1978
- NR c/o School of Business & Social Sciences, Roehampton University, Southlands College, 80 Roehampton Lane, LONDON, SW15 5SL. (hq)
  http://www.arvac.org.uk
  Dir: Lesley Symes
- ▲ Company Limited by Guarantee; Registered Charity
- ○ *P, *N; to promote effective community action through research; to help community groups carry out their own research
- ● Conf - Inf - Training workshops
- M 200 i, 150 org
- ¶ ARVAC Bulletin - 4; £30 i, £75 org.

Association of Researchers in Medicine & Science Ltd (ARMS) 1979
- NR Thomas Guy House (5th floor), Guy's Hospital, LONDON, SE1 9RT.
  http://www.hop.man.ac.uk/arms/arms.html
  Hon Sec: Dr A Unger
- ▲ Company Limited by Guarantee
- ○ *P; the interests of scientists engaged in research in medical & allied fields; to promote public awareness of that research
- M i

** Association of Resettlement & Employment Advisors
    Organisation lost: see Introduction paragraph 3.

Association of Residential Letting Agents   (ARLA)   1981
■ Arbon House, 6 Tournament Court, Edgehill Drive, WARWICK,
    CV34 6LG.   (hq)
    01926 496800   fax 01926 417788
    email info@arla.co.uk   http://www.arla.co.uk
    Operations Mgr: Ian Potter
▲ Company Limited by Guarantee
○ *P; for agents letting residential property
● Conf - Mtgs - ET - Exam - Stat - LG
< a division of the National Federation of Property Professionals
M 1,500 i, 2,250 f
    (Sub: £155 i, varies f)
¶ Agreement (NL) - 6; ftm, £54 nm.

Association of Residential Managing Agents Ltd   (ARMA)
1991
■ 178 Battersea Park Rd, LONDON, SW11 4ND.   (hq)
    020 7978 2607   fax 020 7498 6153
    email info@arma.org.uk   http://www.arma.org.uk
    Contact: The Executive Secretary
▲ Company Limited by Guarantee
○ *P; members focus exclusively on matters relating to block
    management of leasehold property (at least 60% of the flats
    are lessee-owned properties)
● Conf - Mtgs - ET - LG
M 200+ f
¶ [publications available to nm are on website]

Association of Respiratory Technology & Physiology   (ARTP)
1972
■ Sovereign House (Suite 4), 22 Gate Lane,
    SUTTON COLDFIELD, W Midlands, B73 5TT.   (hq)
    0121-354 8200
    Admin: Mrs Jackie Hutchinson
▲ Registered Charity
○ *P
Gp Education; Manufacturers liaison
● Conf - Mtgs - ET - Exam - Res - Inf - Empl - LG
< Brit Thoracic Soc; Assn of Clinical Scientists; Registration Coun
    for Clinical Physiology
M 530 i, 25 f (affiliated), UK / 5 i, 5 f (affiliated), o'seas
¶ Inspire - 3; ftm only.

Association of Retired & Persons over 50
    has been replaced by **Heyday**

Association of Retirement Housing Managers   (ARHM)   1991
NR Southbank House, Black Prince Rd, LONDON, SE1 7SJ.   (hq)
    020 7463 0660
▲ Company Limited by Guarantee
○ *P; to represent managers of private sheltered housing
M f

Association of Revenue and Customs   (ARC)   2005
NR 8 Leake St, LONDON, SE1 7NN.   (hq)
    020 7401 5555
    email info@arc-union.org.uk
    http://www.arc-union.org.uk
    Sec Gen: Jonathan Baume
○ *P, *U; the union of choice for senior managers & professionals
    in HM Revenue & Customs
● Conf - Mtgs - Empl - LG
< FDA
M 2,200 i
× 2005 Union of Senior Revenue Officials

** Association of Risk Management
    Organisation lost: see Introduction paragraph 3.

Association of Rivers Trusts   2004
■ 10 Exeter St, LAUNCESTON, Cornwall, PL15 9EQ.   (hq)
    0870 774 0689
    email arlin@associationofriverstrusts.org.uk
    http://www.associationofriverstrusts.org.uk
    Dir: Arlin Rickard,   Sec: Alan Hawken
▲ Company Limited by Guarantee; Registered Charity
○ *K; to improve the rivers of England & Wales; to advance the
    education of the public in the management of water &
    environmental protection, conservation, rehabilitation &
    improvement, & the understanding of rivers & their basins,
    fauna & flora
● Conf - ET - Res - LG
M 6 i, 6 org
¶ e-newsletters; free.

Association for Road Traffic Safety & Management   (ARTSM)
1933
NR Epic House (Office 8), 128 Fulwell Rd, TEDDINGTON, Middx,
    TW11 0RQ.   (hq)
    020 8977 6952
    http://www.artsm.org.uk
▲ Un-incorporated Society
○ *T; interests of makers & suppliers of road traffic signs, portable
    traffic signals, variable message signs, vehicle & pedestrian
    detectors, sign luminaires, fittings, fixings & components, sign
    design software & related products & services
M f

Association for Roman Archaeology   (ARA)   1966
NR 75 York Rd, SWINDON, Wilts, SN1 2JU.   (hsp)
    01793 534008   fax 01793 534008
    Dir: Bryn Walters
▲ Company Limited by Guarantee
○ *K, *L; free access to Roman archaeology events & venues
● Conf - Mtgs - Inf - VE
< Coun Brit Archaeology (CBA)
M 2,500 i
¶ ARA News Bulletin - 2.

Association of Rover Clubs Ltd
    since 2005 **Association of Land Rover Clubs**

Association of Royal Navy Officers   (ARNO)   1925
NR 70 Porchester Terrace, LONDON, W2 3TP.   (hq)
    020 7402 5231
▲ Registered Charity
○ *W; to give general & financial assistance to members, their
    widows & families (membership is open to serving & retired
    officers of the RN, RM, WRNS, QARNNS & their Reserves)
● Inf - VE
< Officers' Assn
M 8,500 i, UK / 300 i, o'seas
¶ Ybk - 1; ftm only.

Association of Running Clubs   (ARC)   2007
■ 19 Sheephouse Green, Wotton, DORKING, Surrey,
    RH5 6QW.   (hsp)
    01306 888886
    email mandy@white1966.freeserve.co.uk
    http://www.runningclubs.org.uk
    Hon Sec: Michael White
▲ Company Limited by Guarantee
○ *S; the governing body for road running, cross country running,
    trail running & fell running
M 135 org
    (Sub: varies)

Association of Safety Fencing Contractors
    a group of the **Fencing Contractors' Association**

© CBD Research Ltd · Beckenham · BR3 5JS · Tel 020 8650 7745 · Fax 020 8650 0768 · E-mail cbd@cbdresearch.com · www.cbdresearch.com

Association of Salmon Fishery Boards   (ASFB)   1932
- ■ CBC House, 24 Canning St, EDINBURGH, EH3 8EG.   (hsb)
  0131-272 2797   fax 0131-272 2800
  Dir: Andrew Wallace
- ▲ Un-incorporated Society
- ○ *F, *N; to protect, preserve & develop salmon fisheries in Scotland; to coordinate the work of district salmon fishery boards
- ● Mtgs - LG
- M 44 district salmon fishery boards

Association for Sandwich Education & Training
  since 2008 **ASET, the Work-Based & Placement Learning Association**

Association of School & College Leaders   (ASCL)   1975
- ■ 130 Regent Rd, LEICESTER, LE1 7PG.   (hq)
  0116-299 1122   fax 0116-299 1123
  email info@ascl.org.uk
  Gen Sec: Dr John Dunford
- Br c150
- ○ *E, *P, *U; for leaders of schools & colleges
- ● Conf - Mtgs - ET - Res - Exhib - Empl - LG - Legal support - Provision of professional publications
- M 14,000 i
- × 2006 Secondary Heads Association

Association for Science Education   (ASE)   1963
- ■ College Lane, HATFIELD, Herts, AL10 9AA.   (hq)
  01707 283000
  http://www.ase.org.uk
  Chief Exec: Prof Derek Bell
- ▲ Registered Charity
- ○ *E; improvement of the teaching of science in schools
- ● Conf - Mtgs - ET - Res - Exhib - SG - Stat - Inf
- M 14,000 i
- ¶ School Science Review - 4;   Education in Science - 5. Primary Science Review - 5;   all ftm.

Association for the Scientific Study of Anomalous Phenomena (ASSAP)   1981
- ■ 27 Old Gloucester St, LONDON, WC1N 3XX.   (hsb)
  0845 652 1648
  email enquiries@assap.org   http://www.assap.org
  Hon Sec: Nicky Sewell
- ▲ Company Limited by Guarantee; Registered Charity
- ○ *G, *Q; to obtain & store information & to encourage research & investigation on all aspects of the paranormal & observed phenomena for which, as yet, there is no generally accepted explanation; to educate & promote an informed public attitude
- Gp Altered states of consciousness; Dowsing; Hauntings; Leylines; Mental mediumship; Metal-bending; Physical mediumship; Poltergeists; Regressive hypnosis & survival of bodily death; UFOs; Fortean events; Earth mysteries
- ● Conf - Mtgs - Lib
- M 350 i
- ¶ Anomaly (Jnl) - 2.   ASSAP News (NL) - 12.

Association of Scintigraphers   1994
- NR Beau Lodge, Kelsey Lane, BECKENHAM, Kent, BR3 3NF.   (hsp)
- ▲ Un-incorporated Society
- ○ *P; veterinary radiology
- ● Conf - Mtgs - ET - LG
- M i

Association of Scotland's Colleges   (ASC)
- NR Argyll Court, The Castle Business Park, STIRLING, FK9 4TY. (hq)
  01786 892100
  http://www.ascol.org.uk
  Co Sec: Shena Mitchell
- ▲ Company Limited by Guarantee; Registered Charity
- ○ *E; to support Scottish further education, advance its interests & represent the views of colleges
- M org
- × 2006 Association of Scottish Colleges

Association in Scotland to Research into Astronautics Ltd (ASTRA)   1953
- NR 96 Bloomfield Rd, AIRDRIE, Lanarkshire, ML6 9LX.   (pres/p)
  01236 602076
  email info@astra.org.uk   http://www.astra.org.uk
  Pres: George McCue
- ▲ Company Limited by Guarantee
- Br 2
- ○ *L; all aspects of space research & related subjects; to stimulate public interest
- Gp Waverider aerodynamic study programme; Aidrie public observatory; Exhibitions; Publications; Amateur rocketry
- ● Conf - Mtgs - ET - Res - Exhib - PL - VE - Amateur astronomy & rocketry
- < Scot Astronomers Gp; Fedn of Astronomical Socs; Scot Coun for Voluntary Orgs
- M 65 i, UK / 5 i, o'seas
- ¶ Spacereport - 4;   ASGARD - irreg; both ftm only.

Association of Scotland's Self-Caterers   (ASSC)   1978
- ■ PO Box 23, TAYNUILT, Argyll, PA35 1WX.   (hsb)
  01866 822122
  Sec: Jenifer Moffat
- ▲ Un-incorporated Society
- ○ *T; representation, services & marketing for owners of holiday properties; 'the only trade association to represent the self-catering industry in Scotland'
- ● Conf - Mtgs - Res - Inf - LG
- < Fedn of Nat Self-Catering Assns (FONSCA); Scot Tourism Forum (STF)
- M 560 f
- ¶ The Standard (NL) - 2.

Association of Scottish Colleges
  since 2006 the **Association of Scotland's Colleges**

Association of Scottish Community Councils   (ASCC)   1993
- NR PO Box 5099, GLASGOW, G79 9AL.   (hq)
  0845 644 5153
  email info@ascc.org.uk   http://www.ascc.org.uk
  Sec: Douglas Murray
- ▲ Un-incorporated Society
- ○ *N; to provide advice & information to Community Councils in Scotland; to promote their role, effectiveness & status through liaison with local & national governments
- ● Conf - Mtgs - Res - SG - Stat - Inf - Lib - LG
- M 625 community councils
- ¶ ASCC NL - 4; ftm.

Association of Scottish Genealogists & Researchers in Archives (ASGRA)   1981
- NR 259 Braod St, COWDENBEATH, Fife, KY4 8LG.   (hsp)
  01383 515485
  http://www.asgra.co.uk
- ▲ Un-incorporated Society
- ○ *G; genealogical & family history research in Scotland
- ● Res
- < Scot Assn of Family History Socs
- M 25 i
- × 2005 Association of Scottish Genealogists & Record Agents

Association for Scottish Literary Studies (ASLS) 1970
- ■ Dept of Scottish Literature, 7 University Gardens, GLASGOW, G12 8QH.   (hq)
  0141-330 5309   fax 0141-330 5309
  email office@asls.org.uk   http://www.asls.org.uk
  Gen Mgr: Duncan Jones
- ▲ Registered Charity
- ○ *A, *L; to promote the study, teaching & writing of Scottish language & literature
- ● Conf - Comp
- < Scot Arts Coun
- M 343 i, 91 f, UK / 121 i, 55 f, o'seas
- ¶ Scottish Studies Review (Jnl) - 2;   Scotlit - 2;
  Scottish Language (Jnl) - 1; all ftm only.
  New Writing Scotland (Anthology) - 1; ftm, £6.95 nm.
  Scotnotes (study guides); £3.60 m, £4.50 nm.
  ScotLit (NM); ftm.
  Annual Volume (book); ftm, £25 nm.

Association of Scottish Philatelic Societies (ASPS) 1924
- ■ 44 Rennie St, FALKIRK, Stirlingshire, FK1 5AL.   (hsp)
  01324 415558
  email scottishphilately.co.uk
  http://www.scottishphilately.co.uk
  Hon Sec: Alan Watson
- ▲ Un-incorporated Society
- ○ *N; to promote philately & allied areas within Scotland
- ● Conf - Exhib - Comp
- < Assn of Brit Philatelic Socs
- M 41 societies
- ¶ Scottish Philately (NL) -6; ftm, postage nm.

Association of Scottish Police Superintendents (ASPS) 1924
- NR Strathclyde Police HQ, 173 Pitt St, GLASGOW, G2 4JS.   (asa)
  0141-221 5796
- ○ *P
- < Intl Assn Chiefs Police (IACP)
- M i
- ¶ NL - 4;   AR; both free.

Association of Scottish Schools of Architecture (ASSA) 1983
- NR c/o Murray + Dunlop, Breckenridge House, 274 Sauchiehall St, GLASGOW, G2 3EH.   (chmn/b)
  0141-331 2926
  Hon Chmn: Gordon Murray
- ▲ Un-incorporated Society
- ○ *N; to maintain & improve the education provision for architecture in Scotland; to foster areas of collaboration between the schools
- Gp Professional practice; Environmental design
- ● Mtgs - ET - Exhib - Comp - SG
- < R Incorporation of Architects in Scotland
- M 6 schools

Association of Scottish Shellfish Growers (ASSG) 1983
- NR Mountview, ARDVASAR, Isle of Skye, IV45 8RU.   (chmn/p)
  01471 844324
  email douglasmcleod@aol.com
  Chmn: Douglas A McLeod
- ▲ Company Limited by Guarantee
- ○ *T; interests of Scottish shellfish farmers
- Gp Mussels; Scallops; Oysters
- ● Conf - Mtgs - ET - Res - Exhib - Inf - LG
- < Shellfish Assn of GB
- M 200 f, 25 org
- ¶ The Grower - 4; ftm, £2 nm.   Ybk - 1; £5 m.

Association of Scottish Visitor Attractions (ASVA) 1989
- NR Argyll's Lodging, Castle Wynd, STIRLING, FK8 1EG.   (hq)
  01786 475152   fax 01786 474288
  email info@asva.co.uk   http://www.asva.co.uk
  Devt Mgr: Eva McDiarmid
- ▲ Company Limited by Guarantee
- ○ *T; concerned with the improvements at, & marketing of, visitor attractions in Scotland
- Gp covering each of the first 9 activities below
- ● Conf - Mtgs - ET - Exhib - SG - Stat - Inf - VE - LG - Consultancy
- M 500 org
- ¶ Scotland's Finest Visitor Attractions - 1.

Association of Scottish Yacht Charterers (ASYC) 1980
- NR Arduaine Farmhouse, ARDUAINE, Argyll, PA34 4XQ.   (sp)
  01852 200258
  email info@asyc.co.uk   http://www.asyc.co.uk
  Sec: Robert Fleck
- ▲ Un-incorporated Society
- ○ *T; to represent the major yacht charter companies operating in the west of Scotland
- ● Conf - Mtgs - Exhib - Inf - LG
- < Sail Scotland Ltd
- M 18 f
- ¶ LM - irreg; free.

Association of Sea Fisheries Committees of England & Wales (ASFCEW) 1919
- ■ 6 Ashmeadow Rd, Arnside, CARNFORTH, Lancs, LA5 0AE.   (hsp)
  01524 761616
  Chief Exec: Peter Winterbottom
- ○ *N; regulation & development of inshore fisheries (within territorial limits)
- ● Mtgs
- M 15 sea fisheries' committees

Association of Sea Training Organisations (ASTO) 1971
- NR Unit 10 North Meadow, Royal Clarence Yard, GOSPORT, Hants, PO12 1PB.   (hq)
  023 9250 3222
  http://www.asto.org.uk
- ○ *Y; to further personal development of young people & adults by seamanship training under sail
- ● Mtgs - ET - Exhib - Comp - Inf
- M 18 org
- ¶ Sail to Adventure - 1; free.

Association of Sealant Applicators Ltd (ASA) 1986
- NR Grovedell House, 15 Knightswick Rd, CANVEY ISLAND, Essex, SS8 9PA.   (asa)
  01268 696878   fax 01268 511247
  email arichardson@rowlandhall.co.uk
  http://www.associationofsealantapplicators.org
  Sec: A E Richardson
- ▲ Company Limited by Guarantee
- ○ *T; for sealant applicators & manufacturers
- ● Mtgs - ET
- < Nat Specialist Contrs Coun
- M 51 f

Association of Second Home Owners
  has closed.

Association of Secondary Teachers, Ireland (ASTI) 1909
- IRL Thomas MacDonagh House, Winetavern St, DUBLIN 8, Republic of Ireland.
  353 (1) 604 0160   fax 353 (1) 671 9287
  email info@asti.ie   http://www.asti.ie
  Gen Sec: John White
- ○ *E, *P

© CBD Research Ltd · Beckenham · BR3 5JS · Tel 020 8650 7745 · Fax 020 8650 0768 · E-mail cbd@cbdresearch.com · www.cbdresearch.com

Association of Security Consultants   (ASC)   1990
NR   42 Amis Avenue, New Haw, ADDLESTONE, Surrey,
       KT15 3ET.   (sb)
       07071 224865   fax 01923 345033
       email info@securityconsultants.org.uk
       http://www.securityconsultants.org.uk
       Sec: Maurice Parsons
▲   Company Limited by Guarantee
○   *P; for independent security consultants having no allegiance to
     specific suppliers of goods or services; to stay in the forefront
     of work on security methods, technology & applications; to
     contribute to the development of national & international
     standards
●   Conf - Mtgs - ET - Exhib - LG
<   Jt Security Ind Coun
M   59 i
¶   NL.   Consultancy Resources Directory - 1; free.
     Your Introduction to the ASC - 1; free.

Association of Senior Children's & Education Librarians
     Please remove this entry in its entirety

Association of Separated & Divorced Catholics   (ASDC)   1981
■   c/o 250 Chapel St, SALFORD, M3 5LL.   (hq)
       http://www.asdcengland.org.uk
▲   Registered Charity
Br   19
○   *W; to provide mutual help and spiritual support to those who
     have experienced the pain of marriage failure
●   Conf - Mtgs
     Helpline: 0113-264 0638
M   c 200 i
¶   New Vision - 6; £6 yr.

Association of Service Providers   (ASP)   1985
NR   Edgcott House, Lawn Hill, Edgcott, AYLESBURY, Bucks,
       HP18 0QW.   (sb)
       01296 770458   fax 01296 770423
       email bc@aspfm.cc
       Sec: Brian Copsey
○   *T; the agency for radio licensing outside of the UK
●   Inf - LG
M   i & f
¶   NL - irreg.

Association of Sewing Machine Distributors   (ASMD)   1992
■   Sheaf House, Holland Fen, LINCOLN, LN4 4QH.   (secretariat)
       01205 280094
       Sec: Mike Houldershaw
▲   Un-incorporated Society
○   *T; importers & suppliers of domestic sewing machines &
     overlockers
●   Mtgs - Stat - LG
M   6 f

Association for Shared Parenting   1993
■   Spring Cottage, Binton Hill, Binton, STRATFORD-upon-AVON,
       Warks, CV37 9TN.   (mail/address)
       01789 751157 (helpline message only)
       Hon Sec: Jim Rowan
▲   Registered Charity
Br   5
○   *K; to promote the right of children to continue to receive love
     & nurture from both their parents after separation or divorce
●   Conf - Mtgs - ET - Advice & support sessions open to the public
     - Telephone helpline - Child contact centre (where children
     can meet the parent they no longer live with)
M   100 i

**Association of Show & Agricultural Organisations   (ASAO)
1923**
■   Oakley Farm, Bletchingley Rd, MERSTHAM, Surrey,
       RH1 3QN.   (mem/sec/p)
       01737 645857   fax 01737 645121
       email jackie@asao.co.uk   http://www.asao.co.uk
       Sec: Paul J Hooper
       Mem Sec: Mrs J Shearman
▲   Company Limited by Guarantee
○   *F; to promote improvement of agriculture, kindred shows &
     allied industries
●   Conf - Stat - LG - Agricultural shows
M   180 org
¶   Official List of Shows & Events - 1; ftm, £5 nm.

**Association of Signals, Lighting & other Highway Electrical
Connections   (ASLEC)   1952**
■   Bowden House, 1 Church St, HENFIELD, W Sussex, BN5 9NS.
       (hq)
       01273 491145   fax 01273 491147
       email aslec@bowden-house.co.uk
       http://www.highwayelectrical.org.uk/aslec
       Chief Exec: Gareth Pritchard
▲   Company Limited by Guarantee
○   *T; contractors operating in the highway electrical industry, in
     particular street lighting
●   Conf - Mtgs - ET - Res - Exhib - Inf - LG
M   c 70 f
×   2007 Association of Street Lighting Electrical Contractors

**Association of Small Historic Towns & Villages of the United
Kingdom   (ASHTAV)   1988**
■   2 Warwick Court, Abbey Rd, GREAT MALVERN, Worcs,
       WR14 3HU.   (sp)
       01684 566543   fax 0870 136 0926
       email mail@ashtav.org.uk   http://www.ashtav.org.uk
       Hon Sec: Dan Wild
       Vice-Chmn: Ed Grimsdale
▲   Registered Charity
○   *K, *N; uniting amenity societies & groups, parish & town
     councils in small historic towns & villages in a common effort
     for the preservation, protection & where appropriate,
     sensitive adaptation of their features of historic & public
     interest; to encourage high standards of architecture &
     planning; to stimulate the public interest & care for the
     beauty, character & fabric of small historic towns & villages in
     the context of an understanding of the social & economic
     changes which affect them
●   Conf - Mtgs - ET - Res - SG - Inf - VE
<   Coun for the Protection of Rural England
M   35 i, 2 f, 85 amenity org & parish / town councils
¶   ASHTAV News - 4; ftm.

Association of Social Alarms Providers
     since 2005 the **Telecare Services Association**

**Association of Social Anthropologists of the UK & the
Commonwealth   (ASA)   1946**
NR   PO Box 5230, HOVE, E Sussex, BN52 9NB.   (hq)
       email admin@theasa.org
       Admin: Rohan Jackson,   Hon Sec: Dr Simone Abram
▲   Un-incorporated Society
○   *L; to promote the study & teaching of social anthropology
●   Conf - ET
<   Academy of the Learned Socs in the Social Sciences (ALSISS)
M   452 i, UK / 134 i, o'seas
¶   Annals - 1;   LM - 2-yearly; both ftm, £50 together nm.

Association of Soft Furnishers (ASF) 2007
NR Francis Vaughan House, Q1 Capital Point, Capital Business
     Park, Parkway, CARDIFF, CF3 2PU.
     029 2077 8918   fax 029 2079 3508
     email susan.spencer@the furnishinggroup.co.uk
     http://www.associationofsoftfurnishiers.org
     Mgr: Sue Spencer
○ *T; for curtain makers, drapery specialists, track fitters, loose
     cover makers, quilters & others associated with the craft of
     soft furnishing

**Association of Solicitor Notaries in Greater London   (ASN)
1996**
■ 15 William Mews, LONDON, SW1X 9HF.   (asa)
     020 7235 7216   fax 020 8681 8183
     Dir: Hans J Hartwig
○ *P; representation of notaries in the Greater London region who
     are also qualified solicitors &/or foreign lawyers
● Conf - Mtgs - ET - Res - SG - LG - Devt of 'best standards' for
     international documentation & translations
M 30 i
¶ Membership Register - 1; ftm.

**Association of Solicitors & Investment Managers   (ASIM)
1993**
■ Riverside House, River Lawn Rd, TONBRIDGE, Kent, TN9 1EP.
     (hq)
     01732 783548   fax 01732 362626
     email admin@asim.org.uk
     Sec: Elaine Reilly
▲ Company Limited by Guarantee
○ *P, *T; to encourage the wider provision of portfolio investment
     services by solicitor's firms
● Conf - Mtgs - ET - Stat - VE - LG
M 51 f
¶ NL - 4.   LM - 1.   AR.
✕ 2004 Association of Solicitor Investment Managers

**Association of South-East Asian Studies in the United Kingdom
(ASEASUK)**
■ Centre for South-East Asian Studies, SOAS, Thornhaugh St,
     LONDON, WC1H 0XG.   (hsb)
     020 7352 9890
     email sc66@soas.ac.uk   http://www.aseauk.org
     Sec: Dr Susan Conway
○ *L; 'to facilitate cooperation & coordination between individual
     scholars & institutions in the development of South-East Asian
     studies & research programmes... the circulation of
     professional information amongst scholars with South East
     Asian interests & the projection of South East Asia as an
     important field of study within the UK generally'
● Conf - Res
< Eur South-East Asian Studies (ASEASUK-EUROSEAS); UK
     Coordinating Coun of Area Studies Assns (UKCCASA)
M 180 i, UK / 20 i, o'seas
     (Sub: £12 (full mems), £5 students)
¶ Aseasuk News - 2; ftm only.

Association of Speakers Clubs   (ASC)   1972
NR 36 Pemberton Rd, Winstanley, WIGAN, Lancs, WN3 6DA.
     (nat/sp)
     email nationalsecretary@the-asc.org.uk
     http://www.the-asc.org.uk
     Nat Sec: Mrs Gwyneth Millard
▲ Un-incorporated Society
Br 141
○ *G; promotion of the art of public speaking, chairmanship &
     the proper conduct of meetings
● Conf - Mtgs - ET - Comp - SG
M 2,000 i, 141 clubs
¶ The Speaker - 3.

Association for Specialist Fire Protection   (ASFP)   1975
■ Tournai Hall, Evelyn Woods Rd, ALDERSHOT, Hants,
     GU11 2LL.   (asa)
     01252 357832   fax 01252 357831
     email info@associationhouse.org.uk
     http://www.asfp.org.uk
     Sec: John G Fairley
▲ Company Limited by Guarantee
○ *T; all questions affecting the fire protection of structural
     steelwork & buildings
Gp Fire testing & standards; Spray applied materials; Health &
     safety; Contracting conditions; Intumescent materials;
     European harmonisation; Assessment of fire tests; BSI
     representation; Technical matters
● Conf - Mtgs - ET - Res - Exhib - Inf
< Eur Assn for Structural Fire Protection; BSI
M 54 f, UK / 4 f, o'seas
¶ Fire Protection for Structural Steel in Buildings, 2nd ed; £30.
     Supplement to 2nd ed; £5.
     Ybk & Directory of Members - 1; free.
     Other publications & guidance notes; list available.
✕ Association of Specialist Fire Protection Contractors &
     Manufacturers Ltd.

**Association of Specialist Technical Organisations for Space
(ASTOS)   1988**
■ c/o Mr J Barrington-Brown, Nohmia Ltd, 79 Larksway,
     BISHOP'S STORTFORD, Herts, CM23 4DG.   (chmn/b)
     01279 505047
     Chmn: James Barrington-Brown
▲ Company Limited by Guarantee
○ *T; aims to promote & support the interests of UK small &
     medium enterprises in the space industry
● Mtgs - Res - Inf - VE - LG - Guest Speaker programme
M 20 f

**Association of Speech & Language Therapists in Independent
Practice   (ASLTIP)   1989**
■ Coleheath Bottom, Speen, PRINCES RISBOROUGH, Bucks,
     HP27 0SZ.   (asa)
     http://www.helpwithtalking.com
     Chmn: Robyn Johnson,   Sec: Julie Andrews
▲ Un-incorporated Society
○ *P; the only database of speech & language therapists working
     independently
Gp Medico legal; Sendist Tribunal (Special Educational Needs &
     Disability Tribunal)
● Conf - Mtgs - ET - Exhib - SG - Inf
< R Coll of Speech & Language Therapists (RCSLT)
M 700 i
     (Sub: £109)
¶ Independent Talking Pages - 4; ftm only.

** **Association of Speedway Referees**
     Organisation lost: see Introductiom paragraph 3.

Association for Spina Bifida & Hydrocephalus   (ASBAH)   1966
NR 42 Park Rd, PETERBOROUGH, Cambs, PE1 2UQ.   (hq)
     01733 555988   fax 01733 555985
     email info@asbah.org   http://www.asbah.org
     Exec Dir: Andrew Russell
▲ Registered Charity
Br 5 regional
○ *W; provides information & advice to people with spina bifida
     &/or hydrocephalus & their carers.   Team of area advisers
     is backed by specialist advisers in education, continence,
     hydrocephalus etc
● LG - Study days
     Helpline: 0845 450 7755
< Nat Coun for Voluntary Orgs (NCVO); Assn Med Res Charities;
     R Assn for Disability & Rehabilitation (RADAR); Disabled Living
     Foundation; Neurological Alliance
M 14,000 i
¶ Link (Jnl) - 6.
     AR.   Various booklets (list available).

Association for Spinal Injury Research, Rehabilitation & Reintegration   (ASPIRE)   1983

■ Wood Lane, STANMORE, Middx, HA7 4AP.   (hq)
  020 8420 6700   fax 020 8420 6352
  email info@aspire.org.uk   http://www.aspire.org.uk
  Chief Exec: Brian Carlin
▲ Registered Charity
○ *Q; works with the 40,000 people with spinal cord injury, & offers practical support to them hroughout the UK, so that they can lead fulfilled & independent lives
● Res - Specialist IT facilities - Integrated leisure centre
M [not given]
¶ Aspirations! (NL) - 2; free.

Association of Stainless Fastener Distributors
  a specialist group of the **British Association of Fastener Distributors**

Association for Standards & Practices in Electronic Trade - EAN UK Ltd
  since February 2005 **GS1 UK**

Association of Stillwater Game Fishery Managers   (ASGFM)   1983

NR Avington Trout Fisheries, Avington, WINCHESTER, Hants, SO21 1BZ   (hq)
  01962 779312
  Sec: Mrs Penny Wigley
○ *T; for owners &/or managers of stillwater fishery businesses
● Conf - Mtgs - ET - Exhib - LG
< Country Landowners Assn
M 100 i & f
¶ Newsline - 2/3; ftm only.

Association of Street Lighting Electrical Contractors
  since 2007 the **Association of Signals, Lighting & other Highway Electrical Connections**

Association of Stress Therapists   (AST)   1991

■ 14 Sycamore Close, MARGATE, Kent, CT9 4NL.   (founder/p)
  01843 291255
  email ssnashfold@hotmail.com
  Founder: Nita M Yeoman,
  Business Admin: Sandra L Snashfold
▲ Un-incorporated Society
○ *M, *P; to establish a network of therapists to alleviate the physical & mental symptoms caused by stress
● ET - Exam - SG
< Crystal Healing Fedn (CHF)
M 50 i, UK / 3 i, o'seas
¶ NL; ftm.

Association for Student Residential Accommodation   (ASRA)   1997

■ Accommodation Office, King's College, Strand, LONDON, WC2R 2LS.   (sb)
  020 7848 2332
  email secretary@asra.ac.uk   http://www.asra.ac.uk
  Sec: Susannah Stringer
▲ Un-incorporated Society
○ *P; concerned with student housing - institutionally owned, managed or private sector
● Conf - Mtgs - ET - EXhib - LG
< Assn for College & University Housing Officers (ACUHOI)
M 580 i, 12 f
¶ NL (website); m only.

Association for Studies in the Conservation of Historic Buildings (ASCHB)   1968

■ c/o 77 Cowcross St, LONDON, EC1M 6EJ.   (mail/address)
  020 7720 4764   fax 020 7720 4764
  email info@aschb.org.uk   http://www.aschb.org.uk
  Hon Sec: John Adams
▲ Registered Charity
○ *L; to provide a forum to keep members informed on all aspects of building conservation
● Conf - Mtgs - VE
< ICCROM; ICOMOS UK; COTAC; UPKEEP; IHBC
M 350 i, UK / 4 i, o'seas
  (Sub:£35)
¶ Transactions - 1; ftm, £25 nm.   NL - 6; ftm only.

Association of Studio & Production Equipment Companies Ltd (ASPEC)   1993

■ 17 Ember Farm Way, EAST MOLESEY, Surrey, KT8 0BH.   (sb)
  email contact@aspec-uk.com   http://www.aspec-uk.com
▲ Company Limited by Guarantee
○ *T; to represent the interests of all film facility companies providing their services to the film & television production industry
Gp Lighting; Studio; Camera
● Mtgs - ET - Empl
< Production Eqpt Rental Assn (PERA) (USA)
M 25 f

Association for the Study of Ethnicity & Nationalism   (ASEN)   1990

NR London School of Economics, Houghton St, LONDON, WC2A 2AE.   (hq)
  020 7955 6801   fax 020 7955 6218
  email ASEN@lse.ac.uk   http://www.lse.ac.uk/ASEN
  Chief Exec: Mitchell Young
▲ Un-incorporated Society
○ *Q; an academic association fostering research into the areas of ethnicity & nationalism
● Conf - Res - SG
< London School of Economics
M 180 i, 3 university research centres, UK / 120 i, o'seas
¶ Nations & Nationalism (Jnl) - 4.
  Studies in Ethnicity & Nationalism [SEN] - 2.

Association for the Study of German Politics   (ASGP)   1974

NR c/o Dr Dan Hough, Dept of Politics & Contemporary European Studies, University of Sussex, Falmer, BRIGHTON, E Sussex, BN1 9SN.   (hsb)
  01273 877648
  email c.s.j.lees@sheffield.ac.uk   http://www.bham.ac.uk/asgp/
  Sec: Dr Dan Hough
▲ Registered Charity
○ *L; to promote the study & teaching of German politics & society in the widest possible context
● Conf - Mtgs - ET - Res - Comp - Inf - VE
< German Studies Assn
> German Studies Assn
¶ German Politics - 4.   ASGP NL - 2.   Books.

Association for the Study of Medical Education   (ASME)   1957
- ■ 12 Queen St, EDINBURGH, EH2 1JE.   (hq)
  0131-225 9111   fax 0131-225 9444
  email info@asme.org.uk   http://www.asme.org.uk
  Chief Exec: Prof David Blaney
- ▲ Registered Charity
- ○ *E, *P, *Q; to bring together doctors, behavioural scientists & educationalists with interests & responsibilities in medical education
- Gp Research c'ee
- ● Conf - Mtgs - ET - Res - Exhib - Inf
- M c 850 i, UK / c 350 i, o'seas, 90 corporate
  (Sub: £120 i, £420 corporate)
- ¶ Bulletin - 6;   AR - 1; both free.
  Understanding Medical Education - a series of extended papers designed to meet the needs of all newcomers, whether under- or post-graduate.
  Books on various aspects of medical education; £5.99 m, £9.99 nm.
  List of publications available.

Association for the Study of Modern & Contemporary France (ASMCF)   1979
- NR Park Bldg, King Henry I St, University of Portsmouth, PORTSMOUTH, Hants, PO1 2DZ.   (hsb)
  023 9284 8484
  email secretary@asmcf.org   http://www.asmcf.org
  Hon Sec: Emmanuel Godin
- ▲ Registered Charity
- Br Oxford, S Wales & W of England
- ○ *L; to promote research & scholarship into all aspects of modern French history, politics, society & culture, as well as relations between France & other countries, including those in the French-speaking world
- ● Conf - Mtgs - ET - Res - SG
- M [not stated]
  (Sub: £44)
- ¶ Modern & Contemporary France - 4; ftm, £78 nm.
  Annual Conference Proceedings.

Association for the Study of Modern Italy   (ASMI)   1982
- ■ c/o Paola Filippucci, New Hall, CAMBRIDGE, CB3 0DF.   (hsb)
  email pf107@cam.ac.uk   http://www.asmi.org.uk
  Hon Sec: Paola Filippucci
- ▲ Registered Charity
- ○ *L; the study of modern & contemporary Italian history, society, politics, culture & economy in the period between 1780 & the present
- ● Conf - Mtgs - Comp
- M 61 i, UK / 2 i, o'seas
  (Sub: £33 (waged) £18 (unwaged), Online £333, Print & online £351)
- ¶ Jnl of Modern Italy - 4.
  (Taylor & Francis/Routledge: www.informaworld.com)

Association for the Study of Obesity   (ASO)   1967
- ■ 20 Brook Meadow Close, WOODFORD GREEN, Essex, IG8 9NR.   (hsb)
  020 8503 2042   fax 020 8503 2042
  email chris@aso.ndo.co.uk   http://www.aso.org.uk
  Admin Officer: Christine Hawkins
- ▲ Registered Charity
- ○ *L, *Q; study of causes, treatment & prevention of human obesity
- ● Conf - Res - Stat - Inf
- < Intl Assn for the Study of Obesity; Eur Assn for the Study of Obesity
- M 520 i, UK / 24 i, o'seas

Association for the Study & Preservation of Roman Mosaics (ASPROM)   1978
- NR 38 Oaklea, Ash Vale, ALDERSHOT, Hants, GU12 5HP   (hsp)
  01252 316018
- ▲ Registered Charity
- ○ *G, *L; study & preservation of Roman mosaics, principally from Britain
- M i & f

Association for the Study of Primary Education   (ASPE)   1987
- ■ The Swallow Barn, Brandon Court, Station Rd, LONG MARSTON, Herts, HP23 4RA.   (hsb)
  email mary@swallowbarn.fsnet.co.uk
  http://www.aspe.org.uk
  Hon Sec: Mary Woodcock
- ▲ Registered Charity
- ○ *P; dedicated to the belief that good primary school practice should be based on best scholarship & research evidence available
- ● Conf - Mtgs - Res - SG
- < Brit Educl Res Assn (BERA)
- M 135 i
- ¶ Education 3-13 (Jnl) - 3.

Association of Subscription Agents & Intermediaries   (ASA)   1934
- NR Field Cottage, School Lane, BENHALL, Suffolk, IP17 1HE.   (sp)
  01728 633196
  Sec Gen: Sarah Durrant
- ▲ Un-incorporated Society
- ○ *T; interests of periodical subscription agents & intermediaries worldwide
- ● Conf - Mtgs - Discussion groups
- M 4 f, UK / 36 f, o'seas
- ¶ NL - irreg; ftm.   LM - irreg; free.
  The Work of Subscription Agents - irreg; free.

Association of Supervisors of Midwives   (ASM)   1912
- NR 31 Cotmer Rd, Oulton Broad, LOWESTOFT, Suffolk, NR33 9PN.   (hsp)
  01502 564805
  email elayne.guest@jpaget.nhs.uk
  Hon Sec: Mrs Elayne Guest,   Pres: Sandra Arthur
- ▲ Un-incorporated Society
- ○ *P; to promote a high standard of supervision of midwives in the practice & teaching of midwifery
- ● Conf - Mtgs
- < Intl Confedn of Midwives
- M 350 i

Association of Suppliers to the British Clothing Industry
  since 2005 **ASBCI - the Forum for Clothing & Textiles**

Association of Suppliers to the Furniture Industry   (ASFI)   1978
- NR The Counting House, Mill Rd, Cromford, MATLOCK, Derbys, DE4 3RQ.   (hq)
  01629 827039   fax 01629 826997
  email info@asfi.co.uk   http://www.asfi.co.uk
  Gen Mgr: Graham Holdsworth
- ▲ Company Limited by Guarantee
- ○ *T; to promote component suppliers to the furniture industry
- ● Conf - Mtgs - Res - Exhib - Expt - Inf - LG
- M 176 f, UK / 5 f, o'seas
- ¶ Trade Talk (NL) - 4; ftm.
  Members Directory & Product Guide - 2 yrly.
  Export Directory & Product Guide - 2 yrly.

Association for Supported Employment
  in 2006 merged with the National Association of Supported Employment to form the **British Association for Supported Employment**

© CBD Research Ltd · Beckenham · BR3 5JS · Tel 020 8650 7745 · Fax 020 8650 0768 · E-mail cbd@cbdresearch.com · www.cbdresearch.com

Association of Surgeons of Great Britain & Ireland   (ASGBI)   1920
- ◼ at the Royal College of Surgeons, 35-43 Lincoln's Inn Fields, LONDON, WC2A 3PE.   (hq)
  020 7973 0300
- ▲ Company Limited by Guarantee; Registered Charity
- ○ *P; advancement of science & art of surgery - general surgery to include GI, vascular, endocrine, breast, transplant, endoscopic
- Gp Association of Endoscopic Surgeons GB&I; Association of Upper Gastro Intestinal Surgeons; Vascular Surgical Society. Association of Coloproctology GB&I; Association of Surgeons in Training; & British Association of Endocrine Surgeons - see separate entries
- ● Conf - ET - Exhib - LG
- M i
- ¶ LM - 1; ftm only.

Association of Surgeons in Training   (ASiT)   1976
- NR at the Royal College of Surgeons, 35-43 Lincoln's Inn Fields, LONDON, WC2A 3PE.   (hq)
  020 7973 0300   fax 020 7430 9235
  email asit@asgbi.org.uk   http://www.asit.org
- ▲ Registered Charity
- ○ *M, *P; surgical training
- ● Conf - Mtgs - ET
- M 768 i
- ¶ Ybk; ftm.

Association for Survey Computing   1971
- ◼ PO Box 76, BERKELEY, Glos, GL13 9WU.
  01453 511511   fax 01453 511512
  email admin@asc.org.uk   http://www.asc.org.uk
  Admin: Christine Jenkins
- ○ *T; the application of computing & software technology to market research & government surveys
- ● Conf
- M 450 i & f
- ¶ Survey Computing - NL.

Association of Systematic Kinesiology   (ASK)   1988
- NR 104A Sedlescombe Rd North, ST LEONARDS-on-SEA, E Sussex, TN37 7EN.   (hq)
  0845 020 0383
  http://www.systematic-kinesiology.co.uk
  Chief Exec: Mrs Marie Cheshire
- ▲ Registered Charity
- ○ *M, *P; applied systematic kinesiology (muscle testing) enables holistic functional analysis of nutritional sensitivities/needs & structural imbalances; helps resolve emotional problems
- ● Mtgs - ET - Exam - Exhib
- M 160 i

Association of Tank & Cistern Manufacturers   (ATCM)   1965
- ◼ 22 Grange Park, St Arvans, CHEPSTOW, Monmouthshire, NP16 6EA.   (hsp)
  01291 623634   fax 01291 623634
  email imce@atcmtanks.org.uk
  http://www.atcmtanks.org.uk
  Chmn & Sec: Ian McCrone
- ○ *T; for manufacturers of vessels for storing drinking water, waste water & other liquids (incl domestic heating oil & chemicals); to promote good practice in the manufacture of tank & cistern products
- Gp Thermoplastics tanks & cisterns; GRP tanks & cisterns; Plastic oil tanks; Plastic chemical tanks; Steel tanks & cisterns
- ● Mtgs - Inf
- < Inst of Plumbing (as industrial associate)
- M 11 f
- ¶ ATCM News Update - 12; free.

Association of Taxation Technicians   (ATT)   1989
- NR 12 Upper Belgrave St, LONDON, SW1X 8BB.   (hq)
  020 7235 2544   fax 020 7235 4571
  email info@att.org.uk   http://www.att.org.uk
  Sec: Andrew R Pickering
- ▲ Company Limited by Guarantee; Registered Charity
- Br 27; Europe, Hong Kong, Singapore
- ○ *P; to provide an appropriate qualification for individuals working in taxation on a day-to-day basis
- ● Conf - Mtgs - ET - Exam - Lib
- < Chart Inst of Taxation
- M 5,406 i
- ¶ Tax Adviser - 12.   LM - 2 yrly.
  Annotated Finance Act - 1.
  Tax Advisers Practice Hbk.   AR.
  Professional Rules & Practice Guidelines.
  Note: the association is sponsored by the Chartered Institute of Taxation

Association of Teachers & Lecturers   (ATL)   1884
- NR 7 Northumberland St, LONDON, WC2N 5RD.   (hq)
  020 7930 6441
  http://www.atl.org.uk
- ○ *P, *U; to promote & protect (in Englnad, Wales, Northern Ireland & the Channel Islands) the interests of education professionals from early years through further education
- M i

Association of Teachers of Lipreading to Adults   (ATLA)   1976
- ◼ Westwood Park, London Rd, Little Horkesley, COLCHESTER, Essex, CO6 4BS.   (mail/address)
  email atla@lipreading.org.uk
  http://www.lipreading.org.uk
  Chmn: Bert Smale,   Sec: Mary Baynton
- ▲ Registered Charity
- ○ *P; to maintain & develop standards of lipreading teaching to adults; to promote understanding of the needs of adults with any level of acquired hearing loss
- Gp Deaf; Deafened; Hard of hearing
- ● Conf - Mtgs - ET - Exhib - LG
- < UK Coun on Deafness (UKCOD)
- M 300+ i, 4 org, UK / 6+ i, o'seas
- ¶ Catchword - 2;   NL - 2; both ftm only.

Association of Teachers of Mathematics   (ATM)   1952
- NR Unit 7 Prime Industrial Park, Shaftesbury St, DERBY, DE23 8YB.   (hq)
  01332 346599
  http://www.atm.org.uk
- ▲ Company Limited by Guarantee; Registered Charity
- ○ *E, *P; to support the teaching & learning of mathematics teaching by encouraging increased understanding & enjoyment of maths, understanding how people learn maths, the exploration of new ideas & practices
- M i & instns

Association of Teachers of Singing   (AOTOS)   1975
- ◼ Weir House, 108 Newton Rd, BURTON upon TRENT, Staffs, DE15 0TT.   (hsp/b)
  01283 542198
  email coralgould7@aol.com   http://www.aotos.co.uk
  Hon Sec: Coral Gould
- ▲ Registered Charity
- ○ *E, *P; to promote the understanding of aspects of the teaching of singing
- ● Conf - ET (teacher training course) - Inf
- < Eur Voice Teachers Assn; Inc Soc Musicians
- > Assn of English Singers & Speakers; Vocal Faculty Birmingham Conservatoire; R Coll of Music; Napier University
- M 435 i, 5 f, UK / 18 i, o'seas
  (Sub: £40 i, £80 f)
- ¶ Voice - 2; ftm, £4 nm.

Association for Teaching Psychology (ATP) 1971

NR Sch of Health & Social Sciences, Napier University,
    EDINBURGH, EH9 2TB.   (hsb)
    0131-455 6010
       email m.williamson@napier.ac.uk   http://www.theatp.org
    Hon Sec: Morag Williamson
○ *E, *L, *P; to further the study & teaching of psychology
● Conf - Mtgs - ET - Exam - LG
< Brit Psychological Soc
M 38,485 i, UK / 3,705 i, o'seas
¶ Psychology Teaching (Jnl) - 1; ftm, £5 nm.
    ATP NL - 3; ftm only.
    Various other publications.

Association for the Teaching of the Social Sciences (ATSS) 1965

NR Old Hall Lane, MANCHESTER, M13 0XT.   (regd/office)
    0116-248 9375
       email atss@btconnect.com   http://www.atss.org.uk
    Chmn: Andy Pilkington
▲ Company Limited by Guarantee; Registered Charity
○ *P; dissemination of good teaching practices in the field of
    social science
● Conf - ET - LG
< Brit Sociological Assn (BSA)
> General Teaching Coun
M c 500 i
¶ Social Science Teacher (Jnl) - 3; ftm only.

Association of Technical Lighting & Access Specialists (ATLAS) 1946

■ 4c St Mary's Place, The Lace Market, NOTTINGHAM,
    NG1 1PH.   (hq)
    0115-955 8818   fax 0115-941 2238
       email info@atlas-1.org.uk   http://www.atlas-1.org.uk
    Contact; The Secretary
○ *T; interests of steeplejacks & firms involved in the erection &
    maintenance of lightning conductors
Gp Chimney steeplejacks; Lightning conductor engineers; Training
● Mtgs - ET - Inf - Empl
M 59 f
¶ LM - 1; free.   Codes of Practice.

Association of Technology Staffing Companies (ATSCO) 1999

NR 109 Regent House, 291 Kirkdale, LONDON, SE26 4QD.   (hq)
    020 8676 9888   fax 020 8676 9933
       email info@atsco.org   http://www.atsco.org
    Chief Exec: Ann Swain
▲ Company Limited by Guarantee
○ *T; IT, telecomms & professional level engineering; to inform on
    industry changes & knowledge
● Conf - Mtgs - Res - Stat - Inf - LG - Industry awards
M 80 f, 2 org, UK / 2 f, o'seas
¶ NL - 4;   LM - 12;   Ybk - 1;   AR - 1; all ftm only.

Association of Thallophyte Treatment Plants (ATTP) 1997

■ 1 Caryl House, Windlesham Grove, LONDON, SW19 6AH.
    (sb)
○ *T;
● Conf - Mtgs - LG - VE
M 6 f

Association of Therapeutic Communities (ATC) 1972

NR Barns Centre, Church Lane, Toddington, CHELTENHAM, Glos,
    GL54 5DQ.   (mail/add)
    01242 620077   fax 01242 620077
       email post@therapeuticcommunities.org
    http://www.therapeuticcommunities.org
▲ Registered Charity
○ *W; to further implementation of the therapeutic community
    approach & ideology in the psychiatric hospital & social
    services for the psychiatric patient & appropriate related
    fields
● Conf - ET - Res
M 87 i, 49 f, UK / 37 i, 3 f, o'seas
¶ Therapeutic Communities Jnl - 4.
    NL - 4.

Association for Therapeutic Healers (ATH) 1983

NR 23 Chiswick Court, Moss Lane, PINNER, Middx, HA5 3AP.
    (hsp)
    07074 222284
       email enquiries@ath.org.uk   http://www.ath.org.uk
    Sec: Helen Spark
▲ Un-incorporated Society
○ *P; for professional healers who combine healing with other
    therapies; to promote health, wellbeing & self wisdom
● Mtgs - Clinic (at above address) - Professional liability service
    for members
< Confedn of Healing Orgs; UK Healers
M 70 i, UK / 2 i, o'seas
¶ NL - 3.

Association for Therapeutic Philosophy (ATP) 1983

■ 33 Marlborough Rd, SWINDON, Wilts, SN3 1PH.   (hq)
    07939 460013   fax 07939 460013
       email sofroniou@gmail.com
    Sec: Dr Andreas Sofroniou
▲ Un-incorporated Society
Br 2
○ *P
Gp Therapeutic philosophy; Psychotherapy; Hypnotherapy;
    Development of people, management & systems; Political
    philosophy
● Conf - Mtgs - ET - Exam - Res - SG - Inf - Lib - VE
> Assn for Psychological Counselling & Training (USA)
M 270 i, 2 f, 3 org, UK / 130 i, 2 f, o'seas
¶ Books:
    Therapeutic Philosophy; £29.95 m, £32.50 nm.
    Philosophic Counselling; £19.95 m, £22.50 nm.
    Moral Philosophy; £55.50 m, £58.95 nm.
    Other publications, list available; £9.95-£23.50.

Association of Therapy Lecturers (ATL) 1963

NR 18 Shakespeare Business Centre, Hathaway Close, EASTLEIGH,
    Hants, SO50 4SR.   (hq)
    0870 420 2022   fax 023 8062 4398
       email info@fht.org.uk   http://www.fht.org.uk
▲ Company Limited by Guarantee
○ *P; to promote & maintain the highest standard of
    professionalism within the following industries: beauty,
    holistic & sports therapies
● Conf - Mtgs - ET - Exhib - Comp - Inf - LG
< is part of the Fedn of Holistic Therapists
M [not stated]
¶ International Therapist - 6; ftm only.

Association of Timber Growers & Forestry Professionals
since 2006 the **Confederation of Forest Industries**

Association of Tourism Teachers & Trainers
a specialist section of the **Tourism Society**

Association of Town Centre Management   (ATCM)   1991
NR   1 Queen Anne's Gate, LONDON, SW1H 9BT.   (hq)
           020 7222 0120
           email info@atcm.org   http://www.atcm.org
           Chief Exec: Simon Quin
▲   Company Limited by Guarantee
○   *T; to promote the long term survival of the town centre as a
           place to live, work, shop & find entertainment
M   f

Association of Town Clerks of Ireland
IRL   c/o Town Clerk, A/a/ras Chaiseal Mumhan, Friar St, CASHEL,
           Co Tipperary, Republic of Ireland.
           353 (62) 64700   fax 353 (62) 64797
           email seamus.maher@casheltc.ie
           Hon Sec: Seamus Maher
○   *P

Association for Toy Importers
           since 2006 **Equitoy: the association for toy importers**

Association of Traditional Chinese Medicine   (ATCM)   1994
NR   5A Grosvenor House, 1 High St, EDGWARE, Midddx,
           HA8 7TA.   (hq)
           020 8951 3030   fax 020 8951 3030
           email atcm.co.uk
           Gen Sec: Jidong Wu (020 8411 2647)
○   *P; for practitioners of Chinese medicine - herbal, cupping,
           therapeutic massage & Qi Gong; promotes proper
           professional qualifications
M   i

Association of Train Operating Companies   (ATOC)   1994
NR   40 Bernard St (3rd floor), LONDON, WC1N 1BY.   (hq)
           020 7841 8000
           http://www.atoc.org
○   *T; for the passenger rail industry
●   Conf - Mtgs - Res - Inf - LG
M   27 f
¶   [In-house only]

Association of Translation Companies   (ATC)   1976
■   Unit 28 Level 6 North, New England House, New England St,
           BRIGHTON, E Sussex, BN1 4GH.   (hq)
           01273 676777   fax 0845 058 2590
           email info@atc.org.uk   http://www.atc.org.uk
           Gen Sec: Geoffrey Bowden
▲   Company Limited by Guarantee
○   *T; to encourage use of professionally produced translations by
           industry, commerce, public sector organisations &
           government depts
●   Conf - Mtgs - ET - Res - LG
<   Eur U of Assns of Translation Companies (EUATC)
M   178 f, UK / 22 f, o'seas
¶   Communicate - 4; online.

Association of Transport Co-ordinating Officers   (ATCO)   1974
■   3 Pine Way, GLOUCESTER, G14 4AE.   (hsp)
           01452 411491
           http://www.atco.org.uk
           Sec: Janet Taplin
▲   Un-incorporated Society
Br   8
○   *P; to secure nationwide a better transport service for
           passengers
Gp   Sub-c'ees: Performing management; Best value; Bus;
           Community health & social transport; Education transport;
           Information & ticketing; Rail
●   Conf - Mtgs - ET - Res - Exhib - Stat - LG
<   Assn County Councils; Convention Scot Local Authorities;
           County Surveyors Soc
M   600 i
¶   ATCO News - 4;   Membership Directory - 1; both ftm only.

Association of Transport Photographers & Historians
           is winding down

Association of Tutors   (AoT)   1958
■   Sunnycroft, 63 King Edward Rd, NORTHAMPTON, NN1 5LY.
           (hsp)
           01604 624171   fax 01604 624718
           http://www.tutor.co.uk
           Hon Sec: Dr D J Cornelius
▲   Un-incorporated Society
○   *E; *P; for independent private tutors; the Association is
           registered with the Criminal Records Bureau & has stringent
           vetting procedures
●   Conf - Mtgs - Inf
M   i
¶   NL - 2;   LM - 1; both ftm only.
           Information Leaflets; free.

Association of UK Media Librarians   (AUKML)   1986
NR   PO Box 14254, LONDON, SE1 9WL.   (mail address)
           email chair@aukml.org.uk   http://www.aukml.org.uk
▲   Un-incorporated Society
○   *P; for librarians & information specialists in the media industry
●   Conf - Mtgs - ET - VE
M   70 i, UK / 30 i, o'seas
¶   Deadline (NL) - 4; ftm only.

Association of UK RIGS Groups
           a variant title for the **National UK Association of UK Regionally
           Important Geological Sites**

**Association of United Kingdom Oil Independents   (AUKOI)
1976**
NR   Cutlers Cottage, Carbrooke Lane, Shipdham, THETFORD,
           Norfolk, IP25 7RP.   (hsb)
           01362 820739   fax 01362 820124
           email secretariat@aukoi.co.uk
           Sec: M I Annesley
▲   Un-incorporated Society
○   *T; to represent & protect within the UK & the EEC the common
           interests of independent oil importers &/or distributors
Gp   Oil: distribution, importation, wholesaling, retailing
●   Mtgs - LG - Liaison in EU
<   Union Pétrolière Européenne Indépendante (UPEI)
M   11 f

Association of United Recording Artists
           in 2007 merged with **Phonographic Performance Ltd**

Association of University Administrators   (AUA)   1993
NR   The University of Manchester, Oxford Rd, MANCHESTER,
           M13 9PL.   (hq)
           0161-275 2063
           Exec Sec: Lynn Rawlinson
▲   Registered Charity
Br   180
○   *E, *P; for all with administrative & managerial responsibilities
           in higher education incl the Republic of Ireland
Gp   Equal opportunities working gp; Quality assurance network;
           Corporate planning forum; S/NVQ national support & focus
●   Conf - Mtgs - ET - Exhib - SG - VE - LG
M   4,000 i, UK / 52 i, o'seas
¶   Perspectives (Jnl) - 4; ftm, £120 nm.
           Newslink (NL) - 4;   AR - 1; both ftm only.

Association for University & College Counselling
           a group of the **British Association for Counselling &
           Psychotherapy**

Association of University Radiation Protection Officers (AURPO) 1961

NR   Corporate Assurance Team, National Physical Laboratory, TEDDINGTON, Middx, TW11 0LW.   (hsb)
        020 8943 6480   fax 020 8614 0487
        email john.makepeace@npl.co.uk
        http://www.aurpo.org
        Sec: John Makepeace
▲   Un-incorporated Society
○   *P; radiation protection from ionizing & non-ionizing radiations
●   Conf - Mtgs - ET - Res - LG
<   Intl Radiation Protection Assn
M   208 i, 13 f, UK / 3 i, o'seas
¶   NL - 4; ftm only.

Association of University Research & Industry Links   (AURIL) 1994

NR   c/o Queen's University, Lanyon North, University Rd, BELFAST, BT7 1NN.   (hq)
        028 9097 2589   fax 028 9097 2570
        email auril@qub.ac.uk
        10 Fleet Place (3rd floor), Limeburner Lane, LONDON, EC4M 7SB.   (regd office)
        Exec Dir: Dr Philip Graham
▲   Company Limited by Guarantee
○   *N, *P; to support universities in the UK & Eire in the development of mutually beneficial partnerships with industry & other sectors, in the field of research, technology & knowledge transfer, consultancy & related activities

Association of University Teachers
        in 2006 merged with NATFHE to form the **University & College Union**

Association of Unpasteurised Milk Producers & Consumers (AUMPC) 1989

NR   Hardwick Estate Office, Whitchurch-on-Thames, READING, RG8 7RE.
        0118-984 2955
        Founders: Sir Julian Rose,   Marwood Yeatman
▲   Un-incorporated Society
○   *F, *K, *T; for producers & consumers of unpasteurised milk; to keep small producers in business & allow consumers freedom of choice
●   Inf - LG
¶   The Case for Untreated Milk.
        Note: The association was first formed to fight a 1989 attempt to ban the sale of unpasteurised milk. It was reactivated, to mobilise public opinion again, to fight another move to ban the milk in 1997.

Association of Upper Gastro Intestinal Surgeons
        a group of the **Association of Surgeons of Great Britain & Ireland**

Association of Users of Research Agencies   (AURA)   1965

NR   51 Dalkeith Rd, HARPENDEN, Herts, AL5 5PP.   (admin/p)
        01582 620331
        http://www.aura.org.uk
        Admin: Peter Goudge
▲   Company Limited by Guarantee
○   *P; forum for clientside researchers to exchange information
Gp   General Insurance Market Research Association; Advertising; Database marketing; International research
●   Mtgs - Res - Networking
M   240 i, UK / 135 i, o'seas

Association of Valuers of Licensed Property   (AVLP)   1894

■   c/o Fleurets, Wellesley House, 96 East St, SUDBURY, Suffolk, CO10 2TP.   (hsb)
        01787 378050   fax 01787 880292
        email bob.whittle@fleurets.com
        Hon Sec: R Whittle
○   *P; for auctioneers, surveyors & valuers whose sole or main business is concerned with the sale & valuation of hotels, public houses & licensed property generally
M   c 120 i

Association of Vehicle Recovery Operators Ltd   (AVRO)   1977

■   1 Bath St, RUGBY, Warks, CV21 3JF.   (hq)
        01788 572850   fax 01788 572850
        email info@avrouk.com   http://www.avrouk.com
        Chief Exec: Gary Satchwell
▲   Company Limited by Guarantee
○   *T
Gp   AVRO show; Finance; Insurance; Legal; Magazine, Directory, Website; Membership; Motoring organisations; Police schemes; Standards & safety
●   Mtgs - Inf - LG
<   Intl Fedn Recovery Services
M   500 f
¶   Recovery Operator Magazine - 6; ftm, £2.40 nm.
        Members NL - 6; ftm only.   AR; free.
        Members Directory - 1; ftm, £15 nm.

Association of Veterinarians in Industry
        a group of the **British Veterinary Association**

Association of Veterinary Anaesthetists
        a group of the **British Small Animal Veterinary Association**

Association of Veterinary Clinical Pharmacology & Therapeutics
        a group of the **British Small Animal Veterinary Association**

Association of Veterinary Soft Tissue Surgery
        a group of the **British Small Animal Veterinary Association**

Association of Veterinary Students
        a group of the **British Veterinary Association**

Association of Veterinary Teaching & Research Work
        a group of the **British Veterinary Association**

Association of Visitors to Immigration Detainees   (AVID) 1997

NR   PO Box 1496, OXFORD, OX4 9DY.   (mail/address)
        01865 250690
        email coordinator@aviddetention.org.uk
        http://www.aviddetention.org.uk
▲   Registered Charity
○   *N, *W; an umbrella organisation supporting visiting groups, individual visitors & immigration detainees held in removal, reception & holding centres by the Immigration Service; to advocate for improved conditions in detention
●   Conf - ET - Res - Stat - Inf - LG
M   350 i, 25 gps
¶   Hbk - ftm, £5 nm.   AR.

© CBD Research Ltd · Beckenham · BR3 5JS · Tel 020 8650 7745 · Fax 020 8650 0768 · E-mail cbd@cbdresearch.com · www.cbdresearch.com

Association of Welding Distributors   (AWD)   1973
NR   Unit 42 Business Development Centre, Stafford Park 4,
       TELFORD, Shropshire, TF3 3BA.   (hq)
       01952 290036   fax 01952 290037
       email info@awd.org.uk   http://www.awd.org.uk
       Chmn: Dave Ellwood
▲   Un-incorporated Society
○   *T; for the welding supply industry - distributors, manufacturers,
       wholesalers & importers with a UK operational base
●   Conf - Mtgs - ET - Exhib - Stat - Inf - Lib - VE - LG (through
       METCOM)
<   Mechanical & Metal Trades Confedn (METCOM)
M   161 f
¶   NL - 12; m only.
       AWD Business Bulletin - 4; free.

Association of Well Head Equipment Manufacturers
(AWHEM)   1961
NR   c/o Dril-Quip (Europe) Ltd, Stoneywood Park, Dyce,
       ABERDEEN, AB21 7DZ.   (chmn/b)
       North Sea Committee Chmn: H Ubhi
▲   Un-incorporated Society
○   *T; repair & manufacture of well control equipment used within
       the Continental shelf

Association of Wheelchair Children
NR   6 Woodman Parade, North Woolwich, LONDON, E16 2LL.
       (hq)
       0870 121 0050
▲   Registered Charity
       no further information supplied

Association of Wholesale Electrical Bulk Buyers Ltd   (AWEBB)
1975
NR   AWEBB House, 2 Kensington Works, Hallamfields Rd,
       ILKESTON, Derbys, DE7 4BR.   (hq)
       0115-944 3334
       Chief Exec: John Horton
○   *T
M   59 f

Association of Wine Educators   (AWE)
■   Scots Firs, 70 Joiners Lane, CHALFONT ST PETER, Bucks,
       SL9 0AU.   (admin/p)
       01753 882320   fax 01753 882320
       email admin@wineeducators.com
       http://www.wineeducators.com
       Admin: Andrea Warren;   Hon Sec: Richard Bampfield
▲   Un-incorporated Society
○   *P; to inform, educate & inspire the general public on the
       subject of wines
M   60 i
¶   AWE Inspiring News

Association of Women Solicitors
   a group of the **Law Society of England & Wales**

** Association of Woodwind Teachers
   Organisation lost: see introduction paragraph 3.

Association of X-ray Equipment Manufacturers   (AXrEM)
1974
■   Broadwall House, 21 Broadwall, LONDON, SE1 9PL.   (hq)
       020 7642 8083   fax 020 7642 8096
       email axrem@gambica.org.uk
       Dir: Peter J Lawson
▲   Un-incorporated Society
○   *T; medical X-ray diagnostic & radiotherapy equipment
●   Mtgs - Stat - LG
<   Eur Coordination C'ee of the Radiological & Electromedical
       Ind (COCIR)
M   7 f

Association of Young Medical Scientists
   a group of the **Medical Research Society**

Association of Young People with ME   (AYME)   1996
■   9a Vermont Place, Tongwell, MILTON KEYNES, Bucks,
       MK15 8JA.   (hq)
       0845 123 2389
       email info@ayme.org.uk   http://www.ayme.org.uk
       Chair of Trustees: Jill Moss
▲   Company Limited by Guarantee; Registered Charity
○   *M, *W, *Y; 'cheerful support, friendship & information to
       children & young people aged 0 to 25 with ME. Free
       membership to eligible applicants living in the UK'
●   Inf - Lib - Peer support
       Helpline: 0845 123 2389
M   2,000 i
¶   NL - 6.
       Books:
         A Ray of Hope; £10.99.   Three Villains?; £6.50.
         My Daughter & ME; £7.50.
       Videos:
         Education DVD; £9.00.
       Numerous other publications for sufferers, schools & doctors.

Assurance Medical Society   (AMS)   1893
■   Lettsom House, 11 Chandos St, LONDON, W1G 9EB.   (hq)
       020 7636 6308
       Exec Sec: Col Richard Kinsella-Bevan
○   *L; life assurance medicine
●   Mtgs
<   Intl Congress Life Assurance Medicine
M   450 i, 70 f
¶   Transactions - 2; ftm only.

ASTA BEAB Certification Services
   The service has been bought by Intertec Group plc who hold
   the records for ASTA/BEAB certification marks

Asthma Society of Ireland
IRL   26 Mountjoy Square, DUBLIN 1, Republic of Ireland.
       353 (1) 878 8511   fax 353 (1) 878 8128
       email office@asthmasociety
       http://www.asthmasociety.ie
       Chmn: Angela Edghill
○   *W

Asthma UK   1927
■   Summit House, 70 Wilson St, LONDON, EC2A 2DB.   (hq)
       020 7786 4900   fax 020 7256 6075
       email info@asthma.org.uk   http://www.asthma.org.uk
       Chief Exec: Neil Churchill
▲   Registered Charity
Br   Scotland, Wales, Northern Ireland
○   *K, *W; to research into asthma & related allergy; to give
       information & advice for people with asthma, their relatives,
       carers & health professionals
Gp   People with asthma; Parents of children with asthma; Carers;
       Healthcare professionals; Researchers & scientists
●   ET - Res - Stat - Inf
       Helpline: 0845 710 0203
<   Assn Medical Res Charities
M   20,000 i
¶   all publications on website
✕   2004 National Asthma Campaign

Astrological Association of Great Britain   (AAGB)   1958
■   BCM 450, LONDON, WC1N 3XX.   (hq)
     020 8625 0098
     email office@astrologicalassociation.com
     http://www.astrologicalassociation.com
     Chmn: Wendy Stacey
▲   Un-incorporated Society
○   *G; for people interested in western & Vedic astrology
●   Conf - Inf - Lib - VE
M   1,200 i, UK / 500 i, o'seas
¶   Astrological Jnl - 6.   Transit Magazine - 6.
     Correlation (research jnl) - 2.   Cosmos & Culture - 4.
     Astrology & Medicine - 3.

Astrological Lodge of London   (ALL)   1915
NR   50 Gloucester Place, LONDON, W1U 8HQ.   (mail/address)
○   *P; the study of astrology in all its branches
●   Mtgs - ET - Comp - SG - Lib
M   400 i, UK / 90 i, o'seas
¶   Astrology - 4.

Astronomical Society of Edinburgh   (ASE)   1924
NR   105/19 Causewayside, EDINBURGH, EH9 1QG.   (hq)
     0131-556 4365
▲   Registered Charity
○   *L; to promote interest in astronomy in Edinburgh
M   i

ASUCplus   (ASUCplus)   1991
■   Tournai Hall, Evelyn Woods Rd, ALDERSHOT, Hants,
     GU11 2LL.   (asa)
     01252 357833   fax 01252 357831
     email asuc@associationhouse.org.uk
     http://www.asuc.org.uk
     Sec: John Fairley
○   *T; 'specialists in subsidence repair techniques & engineered
     foundation solutions, including new build foundations &
     basement development'
●   Conf - Mtgs - ET - Exhib
M   20 f

Ataxia-Telangiectasia Society   (A-T Society)   (ATS)   1989
■   c/o IACR, Rothamsted, HARPENDEN, Herts, AL5 2JQ.   (hq)
     01582 760733   fax 01582 760162
     email atsociety@btconnect.com
     http://www.atsociety.org.uk
     Hon Sec: Mrs Maureen Poupard
▲   Company Limited by Guarantee; Registered Charity
○   *M, *W; the relief of suffering caused by A-T
●   Mtgs - Inf - 2 specialist clinics - Support for families
<   Assn Med Res Charities; Genetic Interest Gp; Contact a Family
M   120 families, UK / 30 families, o'seas
¶   NL - 2; free.
     What is A-T?   A-T: an overview.
     Ataxia-Telangiectasia [guides for/to]: Therapies; Parents;
     Teachers.

Ataxia UK   (ATAXIA)   1964
NR   Lincoln House, 1-3 Brixton Rd, LONDON, SW9 6DE.   (hq)
     020 7582 1444   fax 020 7582 9444
     email office@ataxia.org.uk   http://www.ataxia.org.uk
     Chief Exec: Alastair MacDougall
▲   Registered Charity
Br   8
○   *W; to provide advice, support & information to sufferers & their
     families; to finance research into Friedreich's, cerebellar &
     other ataxias; to offer information for health-care & social
     service professionals
●   Conf - Inf
     Helpline: 0845 644 0606
<   Neurological Alliance; Genetic Interest Gp
M   1,854 i, f & org, UK / 51 i, o'seas
¶   The Ataxia - 4;   AR - 1; both ftm only.
     Freidreichs Ataxia / Cerebellar (leaflets); free.

Æthelflæd
■   1a Auckland Rd, LONDON, SW11 1EW.
     020 7924 5868
     email c.maddern@gold.ac.uk
     Hon Sec: Dr Carole Maddern
○   *L; research & scholarly activities relating to Alfred the Great's
     daughter Æthelflæd, the Lady of the Mercians; and to studies
     of manuscripts in Old English
●   Conf - Res
M   12 i

Athletics Association of Wales
     since 2005 **Welsh Athletics**

Atlantic Council of the United Kingdom
NR   130 City Rd, LONDON, EC1V 2NW.   (hq)
     020 7251 6111
     http://www.atlanticcounciluk.org
▲   Registered Charity
○   *K; 'to explain, in simple & lucid terms to schools, universities &
     public opinion generally, the implications of the momentous
     changes that have taken place in Europe since the end of the
     Cold War'
M   i

Attend   1949
NR   11-13 Cavendish Square, LONDON, W1G 0AN.   (hq)
     0845 450 0285
     email info@attend.org.uk   http://www.attend.org.uk
     Chief Exec: David Wood
▲   Registered Charity
○   *N, *W; supporting volunteering to enhance health & social
     care for local communities
M   750 org
¶   Friends Connect - 4.
     AR.   Training publications.
✕   2006 (April) National Association of Hospital & Community
     Friends

Aubrac Cattle Society of the UK Ltd   1990
NR   Gore Farm, Ashmore, SALISBURY, Wilts, SP5 5AR.   (hsp)
     01747 811157   fax 01747 811157
     Sec: Mrs Jennifer Biles,   Pres: Sir John Eliot Gardiner
○   *B; promotion, registration & import of registered Aubrac beef
     cattle
M   2 i

Audio Engineering Society (British Section)   (AES)   1970
NR   PO Box 645, SLOUGH, Berks, SL1 8BJ.   (hq)
     01628 663725   fax 0870 7626137
     email uk@aes.org   http://www.aes.org
     Sec: Mrs Heather Lane
○   *L, *P
M   i & f
¶   Jnl - 10.

Audio Visual Association
     is a specialist group within the **British Institute of Professional
     Photography**

Audiobook Publishing Association   (APA)   1994
■   18 Green Lanes, HATFIELD, Herts, AL10 9JT.   (hsp)
     0797 128 0788
     email info@theapa.net   http://www.theapa.net
     Admin: Charlotte McCandlish
○   *P
●   Mtgs - Comp - Stat - Inf - Social events
M   c200 i, c100 f
¶   APA Resources Directory - 1; ftm.
✕   2004 Spoken Word Publishing Association

© CBD Research Ltd · Beckenham · BR3 5JS · Tel 020 8650 7745 · Fax 020 8650 0768 · E-mail cbd@cbdresearch.com · www.cbdresearch.com

Audiovisual Federation   (AF)
IRL Confederation House, 84-86 Lower Baggot St, DUBLIN 2, Republic of Ireland.
     353 (1) 660 1011   fax 353 (1) 660 1717
     http://www.ibec.ie/avf
     Dir: Tommy McCabe
○   *T
<   IBEC

Australia & New Zealand Chamber of Commerce
    since 2006 **Australian Business**

Australian Business   1910
NR Dudley House, 34-35 Southampton St, LONDON, WC2E 7HE.   (hq)
     0870 890 0720   fax 0870 890 0721
     email enquiries@australianbusiness.co.uk
     http://www.australianbusiness.co.uk
     Dir: Melissa Brown
▲   Non-profit organisation
○   *C; to promote & facilitate bilateral trade between Australia/ New Zealand & the UK
Gp UK, Australia/New Zealand Business
●   Inf - Lib - Events & functions relevant to business involving Australasia & the UK
<   Australian Brit Cham Comm
M   500 i, 2300 f, 3,000 org UK / 10 i, 10 f, 1,000 org, o'seas
¶   Up & Under Updates - 6; ftm.
×   2006 Australia & New Zealand Chamber of Commerce

Austro-British Chamber   (ABC)   1963
NR Ebendorferstrasse 3, A-1010 WIEN, Austria.
     43 (1) 404 43 255   fax 43 (1) 404 43 9255
     email info@abchamber.org   http://www.abchamber.org
○   *C
×   2004 British Trade Council in Austria

Authors' Licensing & Collecting Society   (ALCS)   1977
NR The Writers' House, 13 Haydon St, LONDON, EC3N 1DB.   (hq)
     020 7264 5700
     Chief Exec: Owen Atkinson
▲   Company Limited by Guarantee
○   *T; the British rights management society for all writers; to distribute fees to writers whose work has been copied, broadcast or recorded
●   Inf
<   Intl Confedn of Socs for Authors & Composers (CISAC); Intl Forum for Reprographic Rights (IFRRO); Soc of Authors; Writers Gld of GB
M   15,000 i, UK / 1,000 i, o'seas
¶   ALCS News - 3; ftm only.
    Information leaflet; on request.

Autism Independent UK (Society for the Autistically Handicapped)   (SFTAH)   1987
■   199-203 Blandford Avenue, KETTERING, Northants, NN16 9AT.   (hq)
     01536 523274   fax 01536 523274
     email autism@autismuk.com
     http://www.autismuk.com
     Dir: Keith Lovett
▲   Registered Charity
○   *W; to promote the understanding & awareness of autism; to provide support for families and carers; training for professionals
●   Conf - ET - Res - Lib - LG
<   TEACCH (USA)
M   209 i, 850 org, UK / 20 i, o'seas
¶   Autism News - 4.   AR.   (both on web).

Auto-Cycle Union Ltd   (ACU)   1903
NR ACU House, Wood St, RUGBY, Warks, CV21 2YX.   (hq)
     01788 566400   fax 01788 573585
     email admin@acu.org.uk   http://www.acu.org.uk
     Gen Sec: Gary Thompson
▲   Company Limited by Guarantee
○   *S; governing body of British motorcycle sport & leisure
●   Conf - Mtgs - ET - Exhib - Comp - Inf
<   Fédn Intle Motocyclisme (FIM)
M   29,415 i, 650 clubs
¶   Motorcycling GB - 4.   ACU Hbk - 1.

Auto Locksmiths Association   (ALA)   1997
NR PO Box 66, SAXMUNDHAM, Suffolk, IP17 3WA.   (sb)
○   *T; to enhance & develop the auto locksmith industry
●   Conf - Mtgs - ET - Res - Exhib - Inf - Lib - VE - LG
M   50 i
¶   NL - 6; ftm only.

Autoclaved Aerated Concrete Products Association
    the former name in 2005-6 of the Aircrete Products Association, an affiliated association of the **British Precast Concrete Federation**

Autograph Club of Great Britain   (ACOGB)   1996
■   12 Duxmore Way, Dawley, TELFORD, Shropshire, TF4 2RD.   (hsp)
     01952 410332
     email contactacogb@blueyonder.co.uk
     http://www.acogb.co.uk
     Chmn: Robert Gregson
▲   Un-incorporated Society
○   *G; to keep autograph collectors in touch with each other; to raise money for charities
●   Mtgs - Exhib - Inf - Help & advice - Collections bought & sold
M   c 200 i
     Free membership)
¶   [website forum only].

Automated Material Handling Systems Association Ltd   (AMHSA)   1986
NR PO Box 7113, LEICESTER, LE7 9XX.   (hq)
     0116-259 8518
▲   Company Limited by Guarantee
○   *T; to promote the use of automated material handling & unit load conveyor systems in the UK
M   f

Automatic Door Suppliers Association   (ADSA)   1985
■   411 Limpsfield Rd, The Green, WARLINGHAM, Surrey, CR6 9HA.   (hq)
     01883 624961
     Contact: Anne Saxby
○   *T; safety standards for automatic door installations
●   Mtgs - Exam - Stat - Inf - LG
M   13 f

Automatic Identification Manufacturers & Suppliers Association
    see **Association for Automatic Identification and Mobile Data Capture**

Automatic Vending Association (AVA) 1929
■ 1 Villiers Court, 40 Upper Mulgrave Rd, CHEAM, Surrey, SM2 7AJ. (hq)
   020 8661 1112   fax 020 8661 2224
   http://www.ava-vending.co.uk
   Dir: Janette Gledhill
▲ Company Limited by Guarantee
Br 5
○ *T; for the automatic refreshment industry
Gp Coinage; Commodities; Technical
● Conf - Mtgs - Res - Exhib - Stat - Inf - Lib - LG - Preparation of
   technical standards - Sales promotion & publicity
< Eur Vending Assn; Brit Retail Consortium; CBI
M 29 i, 264 f, UK / 6 f, o'seas
¶ VENDinform - 6.   LM - 1.   Census - 1.
   Explaining Vending;   Vending Quality Standards.
× Automatic Vending Association of Britain

Automobile Association (AA) 1905
NR Contact Centre, Lambert House, Stockport Rd, CHEADLE,
   Cheshire, SK8 2DY.   (hq)
   0161-488 7544
   email customer.services@theaa.com
   http://www.theaa.com
▲ Un-incorporated Society
○ *G
● Insurance services - Motoring services - Publishing
M c 12,000,000 i
¶ AR.

** **Automotive Aftermarket Association**
   Organisation lost: see Introduction paragraph 3.

Automotive Distribution Federation (ADF) 1930
■ 5 Marlin Office Village, 1250 Chester Rd, Castle Bromwich,
   BIRMINGHAM, B35 7AZ.   (hq)
   0845 313 1506   fax 0845 313 1508
   email admin@adf.org.uk   http://www.adf.org.uk
   Chief Exec: Brian Spratt
▲ Company Limited by Guarantee
○ *T; interests of manufacturers, importers & wholesale
   distributors of vehicle components operating in the
   independent automotive aftermarket (the section of the motor
   trade independent of the vehicle manufacturers & their
   dealers)
Gp Commercial vehicle section (specialists in components for
   trucks & buses);
   Bodyshop supply section (specialists in supplying the body
   repair industry)
● Conf - Mtgs - ET - Exhib - Comp - SG - Stat - Expt - Inf - Lib -
   LG - Provision of business services (insurance, pensions,
   credit management & information, stationery)
< Intl Fedn of Automotive Aftermarket Parts &
   Wholesalers (FIGIEFA); Eur Liaison C'ee for Automotive Parts
   Wholesalers (CLEDIPA)
M 320 f
¶ Eyes & Ears - 6; ftm, £2 each nm.   AR - 1; ftm only.

Automotive Manufacturers' Racing Association (AMRA) 1952
NR The Nook 27 Top Side, Grenoside, SHEFFIELD, S Yorks,
   S35 8RD.   (hsp)
   0114-246 4878   fax 0114-246 4858
   email info@amrauk.com   http://www.amrauk.com
   Coordinator: Stuart Barnes
▲ Company Limited by Guarantee
○ *T; to raise standards & efficiency of service to competitors
   throughout motor sport
● Conf - Mtgs - ET - Exhib - Expt - LG
M 4 i, 112 f, 3 org
¶ AMRA News - irreg.

Aviation Environment Federation (AEF) 1975
NR Broken Wharf House, 2 Broken Wharf, LONDON, EC4V 3DT.
   (hq)
   020 7248 2223   fax 020 7329 8160
   email info@aef.org.uk   http://www.aef.org.uk
   Chief Exec: Tim Johnson
▲ Company Limited by Guarantee
○ *K; 'UK-based association concerned exclusively with the
   environmental impacts of aviation'
● Conf - ET - Res - SG - Stat - Inf - Lib - LG
< Intl Coalition for Sustainable Aviation (ICSA); Eur Fedn for
   Transport & Envt (T&E)
M 120 i, f & org
¶ NL - 4.

Aviation Society (TAS) 1973
NR The Airport Tour Centre, MANCHESTER AIRPORT, M90 1SZ.
   (hq)
   0161-489 2443   fax 0161-436 3030
   email admin@tasmanchester.com
   http://www.tasmanchester.com
   Chmn: Peter Hampson
▲ Un-incorporated Society
○ *G; all aspects of aviation for enthusiasts
Gp Civil & military; Aviation; Manchester airport
● Mtgs - Res - Exhib - Comp - SG - Stat - Inf - VE - Coach tours &
   flights to airports in the UK & o'seas
M 2,000 i
¶ Winged Words (NL) - 12; ftm.

Avicultural Society (AS) 1894
■ Arcadia, The Mounts, East Allington, TOTNES, Devon,
   TQ9 7QJ.   (hsb)
   Sec: Paul Boulden
▲ Un-incorporated Society
○ *L; study of British & foreign birds in freedom & captivity
● VE
< Nat Coun Aviculture
M 200 i, 10 instns, UK / 50 i, 66 instns, o'seas
¶ The Avicultural Magazine - 4.

Ayrshire Agricultural Association (AAA) 1836
NR Oswald Hall, Auchincruive, AYR, KA6 5HW.   (hsp)
   0845 201 1460   fax 01292 525939
   email lorrainem@ayrcountyshow.co.uk
▲ Registered Charity
○ *F; to promote agriculture in Ayrshire
● Exhib
< Assn of Agricl Shows
M i

Ayrshire Cattle Society of Great Britain & Ireland 1887
NR 17 Barns St, AYR, KA7 1XB.   (hq)
   01292 267123
   http://www.ayrshirescs.org
   Gen Mgr: Irene Kirkpatrick
▲ Registered Charity
○ *B; to promote & register Ayrshire dairy cows
● Conf - Mtgs - Promotion of breed - Register cattle
M 1,100 i, UK / 30 i, o'seas
¶ Ayrshire Jnl - 2.
   Ayrshire Dairyman (NL) - 2.   AR.

© CBD Research Ltd · Beckenham · BR3 5JS · Tel 020 8650 7745 · Fax 020 8650 0768 · E-mail cbd@cbdresearch.com · www.cbdresearch.com

Ayrshire Chamber of Commerce & Industry   (ACCI)   1992

NR   Suite 1005, Glasgow Prestwick International Airport,
     PRESTWICK, Ayrshire, KA9 2PL.   (hq)
     01292 678666   fax 01292 678667
     email enquiries@ayrshire-chamber.org
     http://www.ayrshire-chamber.org
     Chief Exec: Bob Leitch
▲   Company Limited by Guarantee
○   *C
M   f

Ayurvedic Medical Association UK   1995

NR   59 Dulverton Rd, SELSDON, Surrey, CR2 8PJ.   (hsp)
     020 8682 3876   fax 020 8333 7904
     email dr-nsmoorthy@hotmail.com
     Gen Sec: Dr N Sathiya Moorthy
▲   Company Limited by Guarantee
Br   3; India, Sri Lanka
○   *M, *P; to promote the Ayurvedic medical system (which aims to
     boost the immune system in order to return the body to true
     health)
Gp   Qualified Ayurvedic physicians from India, Sri Lanka & Pakistan
●   Conf - Mtgs - ET - Exam - Res - Exhib - SG - Inf - Lib
<   Inst of Complementary Medicine
M   60 i, UK / 25 i, o'seas
¶   [to come].

Baby Equipment Hirers Association (BEHA) 2000

■ 8 Anselm Rd, HATCH END, Middx, HA5 4LJ.
020 8621 4378
http://www.beha.co.uk
Contact: Juliette Morrison
○ *T; to supply members with insurance & equipment through
buyers
● Conf - Res
M 10 i
¶ BEHA News - 6; AR; both ftm only.

Baby Milk Action 1979

■ 34 Trumpington St, CAMBRIDGE, CB2 1QY. (hq)
01223 464420 fax 01223 464417
email info@babymilkaction.org
http://www.babymilkaction.org
Office Mgr: Sarah Hansen
▲ Company Limited by Guarantee
○ *K; 'to save infant lives & to end the avoidable suffering caused
by inappropriate infant feeding by working within a global
network (IBFAN); to strengthen independent, transparent &
effective controls on the marketing of the baby feeding
industry worldwide; the Independent Baby Food Action
Network is a coalition of more than 200 citizen & health
worker groups in more than 100 countries working for better
child health & nutrition through the promotion of
breastfeeding & the elimination of irresponsible marketing of
infant foods, bottles & teats
● Conf - ET - Exhib - LG
< Intl Baby Food Action Network (IBFAN)
M 2,000 i
¶ Update NL - 2; ftm, £15 nm.

Baby Products Association (BPA) 1945

■ 2 Carrera House, Merlin Court, Gatehouse Close, AYLESBURY,
Bucks, HP19 8DP. (hq)
0845 456 9570 fax 0845 456 9573
email info@b-p-a.org http://www.b-p-a.org
Chief Exec: Peter White
▲ Company Limited by Guarantee
○ *T; for manufacturers & importers of baby & nursery goods,
including wheeled goods, nursery furniture, baby walkers,
soft goods, child restraints, toys & early learning
● Conf - Mtgs - Exhib - Comp - Inf - Lib - LG - Organises BPA
Baby & Child Trade Fair
< Eur C'ee for Standardization (CEN); Brit Standards Instn (BSI);
Tr Assn Forum (TAF)
M 80 f, UK / 10 f, o'seas
¶ NL - 4; LM - 4; both ftm only.
BPA Ybk - 1; ftm, £35 nm. AR - 1.
BPA Baby & Child Exhibition Catalogue - 1; free to exhibitors &
visitors, £6 non-exhibitors.

BackCare
alternative name of the **National Backpain Association**

Backpackers Club (BPC) 1972

NR 56 The Leys, CHIPPING NORTON, Oxon, OX7 5HH.
(memsec/p)
http://www.backpackersclub.co.uk
Mem Sec: Geoff Gafford
▲ Un-incorporated Society
Br County groups; Canada, Holland
○ *G; lightweight camping travelling on foot, by bicycle, canoe or
ski
● Mtgs - Inf - Lib - Informal weekends
M 1,150 i, UK / 24 i, o'seas
¶ Backpack (Jnl) - 4; ftm only.

Badge Collectors Circle (BCC) 1980

NR 57 Middleton Place, LOUGHBOROUGH, Leics, LE11 2BY. (sp)
01509 569270
email f.setchfield@ntlworld.com
Editor: Frank Setchfield
○ *G; collecting non-military, enamel & tin lapel badges as a
hobby
Gp Badges: Button, Enamel
● Mtgs - Res - SG - Inf - Swapping badges
M 450 i, 2 f, UK / 6 i, o'seas
¶ The Badger (NL) - 6; £15 yr (£2.50 each).

Badger Face Welsh Mountain Sheep Society (Cymdeithas Defaid Torddu Cymreig Torwen) (BFWMSS) 1976

NR Stall House, Vowchurch, HEREFORD, HR2 0QE. (hsp)
01981 550685
email lucy.levinge@fwi.co.uk
http://www.badgerfacesheep.co.uk
Gen Sec: Miss L K Levinge
▲ Un-incorporated Society
○ *B
● Mtgs - Exhib - Comp
M 250 i, UK / 2 i, o'seas
¶ NL - 4; ftm only. Flockbook - 1; ftm, £5 nm.

Badger Trust 1986

NR PO Box 708, EAST GRINSTEAD, W Sussex, RH19 2WN. (hq)
0845 828 7878
email enquiries@badgertrust.org.uk
http://www.badgertrust.org.uk
▲ Registered Charity
○ *K, *V; to develop & support a network of badger protection
groups in the UK; to campaign for the protection of badgers
& against persecution, including snares
Gp Badgers & TB; Badgers & roads; Badgers' rehabilitation &
welfare
● Conf - Mtgs - Inf
M 80 groups
¶ NL - 2. AR.
Report of Annual Conference - 1.
Occasional papers & guidance notes - irreg; ftm.
✕ 2005 National Federation of Badger Groups

Badminton Association of England
since 2006 **Badminton England**

Badminton England 1893

NR National Badminton Centre, MILTON KEYNES, Bucks,
MK8 9LA. (hq)
01908 268400
http://www.badmintonengland.co.uk
Chief Exec: Adrian Christy
▲ Company Limited by Guarantee
Br 41 assns
○ *S; the governing body for the game of Badminton in England,
the Channel Islands and the Isle of Man
Gp Badminton Umpires Association; English Schools' Badminton
Association; Regional coaching scheme
● Conf - Mtgs - ET - Exam - Exhib - Comp - Stat - Inf - VE - LG
< Intl Badminton Fedn; Eur Badminton U
M 45,000 i, 2,000 clubs
¶ Badminton Magazine - 4. Coaches Register - 4.
ESBA Post - 10. Ybk. AR & Accounts.
✕ 2006 Badminton Association of England

Badminton Umpires Association
a group of **Badminton England**

Bagot Goat Society 1988
NR   Pen-Twyn, Llangenny, CRICKHOWELL, Brecknockshire,
        NP8 1HD.
        01873 810547   fax 01873 810547
        email info@bagotgoats.co.uk
        http://www.bagotgoats.co.uk
        Sec: Rose Kent
○   *B

Bagpipe Society 1985
NR   11 Queens Place, OTLEY, W Yorks, LS21 3HY.   (mem/sp)
        email bagpipes@snozz.com
        http://www.bagpipesociety.org.uk
        Mem Sec: Michael Ross
▲   Un-incorporated Society
○   *D; to promote the playing & music of bagpipes, including
        English, Scottish, French, Spanish & Balkan bagpipes
●   Workshops
M   250 i, UK / 100 i, o'seas
¶   Chanter - 4; ftm, £3 on request nm.

Bakers', Food & Allied Workers' Union   (BFAWU) 1849
NR   Stanborough House, Great North Rd, Stanborough,
        WELWYN GARDEN CITY, Herts, AL8 7TA.   (hq)
        01707 260150
○   *U
M   i

Balint Society 1969
■   Tollgate Medical Centre, 220 Tollgate Rd, LONDON, E6 5JS.
        (hsb)
        020 7473 9399   fax 020 7473 9388
        email david.watt@gp-f84093.nhs.uk
        http://www.balint.co.uk
        Hon Sec: Dr David E Watt
▲   Registered Charity
○   *L; an organisation of general practitioners seeking to promote
        the study of the healer-patient relationship, particularly in
        general practice, as first investigated by the psychoanalyst
        Dr Michael Balint
●   Conf - Mtgs - ET - Res - Comp - SG
<   Intl Balint Fedn
>   Assn Psychosexual Nursing
M   140 i, UK / 50 i, o'seas
¶   Jnl - 1; ftm, £8 nm.

Ball & Roller Bearing Manufacturers Association   (BRBMA)
■   Heathcote House, 136 Hagley Rd, Edgbaston, BIRMINGHAM,
        B16 9PN.   (asa)
        0121-454 4141   fax 0121-454 4949
        email info@brbma.org   http://www.brbma.org
        Sec: Victor Lyttle
▲   Un-incorporated Society
○   *T
Gp   Standards
●   Conf - Mtgs - Stat - Standards
<   Fedn of Eur Bearing Mfrs Assn (FEBMA)
M   6 f

Balloon Association
        alternative name of **NABAS Ltd**

Ballroom Dancers Federation   (BDF) 1956
NR   12 Warren Lodge Drive, KINGSWOOD, Surrey, KT20 6QN.
        (sp)
        Sec: David Sycamore
▲   Un-incorporated Society
○   *D; competitive ballroom & Latin American dancing

Ballymena Borough Chamber of Commerce & Industry
NR   4 Wellington Court, Wellington St, BALLYMENA, BT43 6EQ.
        (hq)
        Pres: Raymond Ruckan
○   *C
×   2006 Ballymena Chamber of Commerce & Industry

Baltic Air Charter Association   (BACA) 1949
NR   c/o The Baltic Exchange, St Mary Axe, LONDON, EC3A 8BH.
        (hsb)
        020 7623 5501   fax 020 7369 1623
        http://www.baca.org.uk
        Contact: W van der Pol
▲   Un-incorporated Society
○   *T; chartering, sale, purchase & lease of aircraft
●   Conf - Mtgs - Inf
M   86 f, UK / 14 f, o'seas
¶   LM - 1;   AR; both ftm only.   Diaries - 1; £7.50.

**Balwen Welsh Mountain Sheep Society (Cymdeithas Defaid
        Mynydd Cymreig Balwen) 1985**
NR   Swffryd Farm, Harodyrynys, CRUMLIN, Gwent, NP11 5HY.
        (hsp)
        01495 247869
        http://www.balwensheepsociety.com
        Sec: Mrs Anne Groucott
○   *B
●   Mtgs - Exhib - Comp
<   Nat Sheep Assn
M   150 i

Bamboo Society 1985
NR   St Paulinus, Brough Park, RICHMOND, N Yorks, DL10 7PJ.
        (hsp)
        01748 812127
        email secretary@bamboo-society.org.uk
        http://www.bamboo-society.org.uk
        Sec: Greville Worthington
▲   Un-incorporated Society
○   *H; to study the distribution of bamboo plants & seeds grown in
        the UK
●   Mtgs - ET - VE
<   Eur Bamboo Soc (EBS)
M   163 i, 6 org, UK / 4 i, o'seas
¶   NL - 4; ftm only.

Banbury & District Chamber of Commerce 1947
NR   Colin Sanders Innovation Centre, Mewburn Rd, BANBURY,
        Oxon, OX16 9PA.   (hq)
        01295 817642 (Mon-Fri: 1000-1330)
        fax 01295 8177601
        email bcoc@banburychamber.com
        http://www.banburychamber.com
▲   Company Limited by Guarantee
○   *C; business interests of Banbury & the surrounding area
Gp   Business & professional; Industrial; Retail
●   Mtgs
M   3 i, 150 f, 1 org
¶   NL - 6.   AR.

Bankruptcy Association 1983
NR   FREEPOST LA1118, 4 Johnson Close, LANCASTER, LA1 5BR.
        (hq)
        01524 782713 (Mon-Fri: 1000-1230)
        email johnmcqueen@theba.org.uk
        http://www.theba.org.uk
        Chief Exec: John McQueen
▲   Un-incorporated Society
○   *K, *W; to provide help & advice to bankrupts & debtors; to
        campaign for reform of insolvency legislation
●   Mtgs - Res - Inf - LG
M   c 1,500 i
¶   NL - 3; free.
        Bankruptcy Explained.
        List of books available.

Baptist Historical Society   1908
NR   PO Box 44, 129 Broadway, DIDCOT, Oxon, OX11 8RT.
    (regd/office)
    01235 517700
    email stephen.bhs@dial.pipex.com
    http://www.baptisthistory.org.uk
    Sec: Revd Stephen Copson
▲   Registered Charity
○   *L, *Q; study of Baptist history in the UK
●   Conf - Mtgs - Res - Inf - Lib
M   600 including 150 libraries, churches & colleges
¶   Baptist Quarterly - 4.

Baptist Union of Great Britain   (BU)   1812
NR   PO Box 44, 129 Broadway, DIDCOT, Oxon, OX11 8RT.   (hq)
    01235 517700   fax 01235 517715
    http://www.baptist.org.uk
    Gen Sec: Rev Jonathan Edwards
○   *R
Gp Theological; Sociological; Current affairs; Christian education;
    Women; Young people; Trusts & property; Pensions; Christian
    ministry
●   Conf - Mtgs - Exhib - SG - Stat - Inf - Lib - VE
<   Baptist Wld Alliance; Free Church Federal Coun; Conf of Eur
    Churches; Eur Baptist Fedn; Coun of Churches for Britain &
    Ireland; Churches Together in England
M   c 140,000 i in 2,000 churches, 6 theological colleges
¶   Baptist Times - 52.
    Baptist Union Directory - 1.   AR - 1.

**Bar Association for Commerce, Finance & Industry   (BACFI)
1965**
NR   PO Box 4352, Edlesborough, DUNSTABLE, Beds, LU6 9EF.
    (mail address)
    01525 222244
○   *L, *P; to represent the interests of members of The Bar who are
    employed in commerce, finance & industry
M   i
×   2004 Employed & Non-Practising Bar Association (merged)

**Bar Association for Local Government & the Public Service
(BALGPS)   1945**
■   Chief Legal Officer, Birmingham City Council, Ingleby House,
    11-14 Cannon St, BIRMINGHAM, B2 5EN.   (chmn/treas/b)
    0121-303 9991
    email chairman@balgps.org.uk
    http://www.balgps.org.uk
    Chmn/Treas: M F N Ahmad
▲   Un-incorporated Society
○   *P; for barristers employed in local government & the public
    sector
●   Conf - ET - Inf - LG - Representation on Bar Council
M   c 110 i
¶   NL;   (publications on website).

Bar Entertainment & Dance Association
    in February 2008 merged with the British Entertainment &
    Discotheque Association to form **Noctis**

Barbirolli Society   1972
■   2 Cedar Close, UTTOXETER, Staffs, ST14 7NP.   (chmn p)
    01889 564562   fax 01889 564562
    Hon Chmn: Miss R P Pickering
▲   Registered Charity
○   *D; to advance knowledge, understanding & appreciation of
    music in general & of the work of Sir John Barbirolli in
    particular
M   400 i, UK / 50 i, o'seas
¶   Jnl - 2;   NL - irreg; both ftm only.

Barema   (BAREMA)   1977
■   The Stables, Sugworth Lane, RADLEY, Oxon, OX14 2HX.   (hq)
    01865 736393   fax 01865 736393
    email barema@btinternet.com
    http://www.barema.org.uk
    Chmn: M F Freeman,   Sec: Harrie Cooke
▲   Company Limited by Guarantee
○   *T: to promote the interests of suppliers to the NHS/private
    sector for anaesthetic & respiratory products
●   Mtgs - Inf - LG
<   Eur Med Device Tr Assn (EUROM VI); Assn of Brit Health Care
    Inds (ABHI)
M   31 f
¶   Barema Hbk - updated; ftm, £10 nm.

Barge Association
    alternative name of **DBA - The Barge Association**

Barking & Dagenham Chamber of Commerce   1995
NR   Roycraft House (ground floor), 15 Linton Rd, BARKING, Essex,
    IG11 8HE.   (hq)
    020 8591 6966
    Admin: John Tame
▲   Company Limited by Guarantee
○   *C
●   Mtgs - ET - Inf - VE - LG
<   London Cham Comm & Ind
M   180 f
¶   NL - 12;   Ybk - 1; both free.

Barn Owl Conservation Network
    a group of the **Hawk & Owl Trust**

Barnsley Chamber of Commerce & Industry
▲   Company Limited by Guarantee
    on 1 August 2006 merged with the Rotherham Chamber of
    Commerce to form the **Chamber of Commerce (Barnsley
    & Rotherham) Ltd**

BaseballSoftballUK   (BSUK)   1890
NR   Ariel House (5th floor), 74A Charlotte St, LONDON,
    W1T 4QJ.   (hq)
    020 7453 7055   fax 020 7453 7007
    email info@baseballsoftballuk.com
    http://www.baseballsoftballuk.com
    Chief Operations Dir: John Boyd
▲   Un-incorporated Society
○   *S; to promote the games of Baseball & Softball in Britain
Gp Scorers; Umpires; Coaching; Old Timers; Players
●   Conf - Mtgs - ET - Comp - Stat - Inf - PL
<   Brit Olympic Assn (BOA); Intl Baseball Assn (IBA); Confedn of
    Eur Amat Baseball; CCPR
M   c 1,500 i, 50 teams (baseball); c 3,000 i, 240 teams (softball)
¶   Baseball & Softball Bulletins - 12;
    Information booklets; all free.

Basketball Association of Wales   (BAW)   1956
NR   c/o 30 Eileen Place, TREHERBERT, Glamorgan, CF42 5BU.
    (hsp)
    Sec: Will Jones
○   *S; governing body for basketball in Wales

Basketball Ireland   1945
IRL   National Basketball Arena, Tymon Park, Tallaght, DUBLIN 24,
    Republic of Ireland.
    353 (1) 459 0211   fax 353 (1) 459 0212
    email info@basketballireland.ie
    http://www.basketballireland.ie
    Chief Exec: Debbie Massey
○   *S
×   2003 Irish Basketball Association

Basketball Scotland Ltd   1947
NR   Caledonia House, South Gyle, EDINBURGH, EH12 9DQ.   (hq)
      0131-317 7260   fax 0191-317 7489
      email enquiries@basketball-scotland.com
      http://www.basketball-scotland.com
      Chief Exec: Kevin Pringle
▲   Company Limited by Guarantee
○   *S; to develop, promote & facilitate the playing of basketball; to
      encourage interest in the sport in Scotland
<   Intl Fedn Basketball (FIBA)
✕   Scottish Basketball Association

Basketmaker's Association   (BA)   1975
■   Glenwayth, Hervines Rd, AMERSHAM, Bucks, HP6 5HS.   (hsp)
      0845 201 1936
      email rae@glenwayth.wanadoo.co.uk
      http://www.basketassoc.org
      Hon Sec: Rae Gillott
○   *T; to promote the design, practice & teaching of basket
      making, chair seating & allied crafts
●   ET - Exam - Exhib - Inf - PL
M   800 i, UK / 100 i, o'seas
¶   NL - 4; ftm, £20 nm.

Basking Shark Society   1995
■   Cronk Mooar, Curragh Rd, ST JOHN'S, Isle of Man,
      IM4 3LN.   (hq)
      01624 801207
      email kenwatterson@iom.com
      http://www.isle-of-man.com/interests/shark/index.htm
▲   Registered Charity
○   *G, *K; research into & preservation of basking sharks
●   ET - Res
¶   NL - 2.   Basking Shark & Whale Report - 1.

**BASO ~ the Association for Cancer Surgery   (BASO-ACS)
1973**
■   at the Royal College of Surgeons, 35-43 Lincoln's Inn Fields,
      LONDON, WC2A 3PE.   (hq)
      020 7405 5612   fax 020 7404 6574
      email lucydavies@baso.org.uk   http://www.baso.org.uk
      Hon Sec: Zenon Rayter
▲   Registered Charity
○   *P; to advance the practice of surgical oncology for surgeons
      involved with cancer
Gp Association of Breast Surgery at BASO; British Stomach Cancer
      Gp
●   Conf - Mtgs - ET
M   740 i, UK / 20 i, o'seas
¶   European Jnl of Surgical Oncology - 6; ftm.
      Note: this organisation deals with enquiries from professional
      members ONLY & does not answer queries from the general
      public.

BASP UK Ltd (British Association of Ski Patrollers)   1978
■   20 Lorn Drive, GLENCOE, Argyllshire, PH49 4HR.   (hsp)
      01855 811443
      email skipatrol@basp.org.uk   http://www.basp.org.uk
      Sec: Fiona Gunn
▲   Company Limited by Guarantee
○   *P; ski patrol & rescue; exchange of knowledge & information
      internationally with other patrollers
Gp First aid training in the outdoors; Training & grading of ski
      patrollers
●   ET - Stat
<   Fédn Intl Patrouilles de Ski (FIPS); Brit Assn of Snowsport
      Instructors (BASI)
M   125 i, UK / 5 i, o'seas
¶   NL - 4.   BASP Outdoor First Aid & Safety Manual; £10.

Bat Conservation Trust   (BCT)   1990
NR   Unit 2 / 15 Cloisters House, 8 Battersea Park Rd, LONDON,
      SW8 4BG.   (hq)
      020 7627 2629
      email enquiries@bats.org.uk   http://www.bats.org.uk
      Chief Exec: Amy Coyte
▲   Company Limited by Guarantee; Registered Charity
○   *K; the conservation of bats & their habitats; to stop further
      declines in populations & aid the recovery of threatened
      species
●   Conf - ET - Res - Exhib
      Helpline: 0845 130 0228
M   c 4,000 i in 90 gps
¶   Bat News - 4;   Young Batworker - 4;
      Bat Monitoring Post - 4; all ftm.
      Books & educational leaflets.

Bates Association for Vision Education   (BAVE)   1989
■   12 Luath St - 3/1, GLASGOW, G51 3ED.   (hsp)
      0800 055 6130
      email info@seeing.org   http://www.seeing.org
      Hon Sec: Anna Bambridge
▲   Un-incorporated Society
○   *P; to advance the knowledge & practice of the methods of
      visual re-education developed by William H Bates
●   Mtgs - ET
M   20 i
      (Sub: £100)

Bath Chamber of Commerce Inc   1902
■   Trimbridge House, Trim St, BATH, Somerset, BA1 1PB.   (hq)
      01225 460655
▲   Company Limited by Guarantee
○   *C
<   is part of GWE Business West the trading name of the Bristol
      Chamber of Commerce & Industry
M   i, f & org

Bath & West
      familiar name of the **Royal Bath & West of England Society**

Bathroom Manufacturers' Association   (BMA)   2001
NR   Federation House, Station Rd, STOKE-ON-TRENT, Staffs,
      ST4 2RT.   (hq)
      01782 747123
▲   Un-incorporated Society
○   *T; interests of bathroom manufacturers trading in the UK
M   f

Batten Disease Family Association   (BDFA)   1998
■   c/o Heather House, Heather Drive, TADLEY, Hants,
      RG26 4QR.   (mail/address)
      0115-965 4815
      http://www.bdfa-uk.org.uk
      Sec: Sarah Kenrick
▲   Registered Charity
○   *M, *W; a supportive, informative national networking
      organisation for the families, carers & professionals, giving
      care to children & adults with Batten Disease; to promote
      awareness of, & research into, the disease
●   Conf - ET - Res - Direct family liaison
<   Batten Disease Support & Res Assn (BDSRA); GOLD; GIG;
      CLIMB
M   c 200 i, associates
¶   NL - 2; ftm.   AR.

Battery Vehicle Society (BVS) 1973
■ Coasters Cottage, Hermitage, DORCHESTER, Dorset,
   DT2 7BB.   (chmn/p)
   01963 210449
   http://www.bvs.org.uk
   Chmn: Alan Ward,   Sec: John Lilly
▲ Un-incorporated Society
Br 3
○ *K; the exchange of information on battery-powered vehicles
● Mtgs - Exhib - Comp - Inf - Lib - VE
   01874 730320 (for road vehicle coordinator & competitions)
< Transport Trust
M 361 i, UK / 20 i, o'seas
¶ Battery Vehicle Review - 6; ftm, £12 yr nm (subscription).

Battle of Britain Historical Society
NR Greenfields, Gunthorpe, MELTON CONSTABLE, Norfolk,
   NR24 2NS.
   0845 130 0588   fax 01263 861483
   email billatBOBHS@aol.com
   http://www.battleofbritain.net
   Chief Exec: Bill Bond
▲ Registered Charity
○ *L; 'education of the young regarding the Battle of Britain'
● Conf - Mtgs - ET
M c 1,500 i
¶ Scramble (NL) - 6.
   Battle of Britain Remembered - 1.

Battlefields Trust   1993
NR 60 Seymour Rd, ST ALBANS, Herts, AL3 5HW.   (coor/p)
   01727 831413
   email nationalcoordinator@battlefieldtrust.com
   http://www.battlefieldstrust.com
   Coordinator: Peter Burley
▲ Company Limited by Guarantee; Registered Charity
○ *K; preservation, interpretation & presentation of battlefields
   worldwide
● Conf - ET - Res - Inf - VE
M 380 i, 5 f, 15 org, UK / 10 i, o'seas
¶ NL - 4; ftm only.

Bead Society of Great Britain   (BSGB)   1989
■ 1 Casburn Lane, Burwell, CAMBRIDGE, CB25 0ED.   (hsp)
   01638 742024   fax 01638 742024
   email bead.society@ntlworld.com
   http://www.beadsociety.freeserve.co.uk
   Hon Sec: Dr Carole Morris
▲ Un-incorporated Society
○ *G; for all interested, either privately or professionally, in beads
   ancient & modern, of all shapes, sizes, materials & colours,
   their techniques of manufacture & their application
● Mtgs - Exhib - Workshops - Annual fair
M 800 i, UK / 50 i, o'seas
¶ NL - 4; ftm only.

BEAMA Capacitor Manufacturers' Association
   an association in **BEAMA Ltd**

BEAMA Energy
   section of **BEAMA Ltd**

BEAMA Installation
   section of **BEAMA Ltd**

BEAMA Ltd   (BEAMA)   1905
■ Westminster Tower, 3 Albert Embankment, LONDON,
   SE1 7SL.   (hq)
   020 7793 3000   fax 020 7793 3003
   email info@beama.org.uk   http://www.beama.org.uk
   Chief Exec: David Dossett
○ *N, *T; the national grouping of trade associations serving the
   electrical installation & cable management equipment
   industries of Great Britain
Gp BEAMAinstallation (Dir: Dr Howard Porter)
      for manufacturers of electrical installation & cable
         management equipment
      Industrial & Single Phase Product Group
      Engineered Systems Product Group
      Cable Management Product Group
      Cutout & Feeder Pillar Group
      European Association of Copper Clad Laminate
         Manufacturers (ELAM)
   BEAMAenergy (Dir: Dr Howard Porter)
      BEAMA Metering & Communication Association (BEMCA)
      Controls Manufacturers Association incorporating the
         Domestic Heating Controls Group (TACMA)
      Domestic Water Treatment Association (DWTA)
      Electric Heating & Ventilation Association (TEHVA)
      Electroheat Manufacturers' Association (EMAB)
      Thermostatic Mixing Valves Association (TMVA)
   BEAMA Power (Dir: Nigel Grant)
      BEAMA Power Ltd
      Rotating Electrical Machines Association (REMA)
      Welding Manufacturers' Association (WMA)
   BEAMA Capacitor Manufacturers' Association
   European Smart Metering Alliance (ESMA)
● Conf - Exhib - Stat - LG
M [see groups above]
¶ BEAMA Bulletin - 4; ftm only.   AR; free.
✕ British Electrotechnical & Allied Manufacturers' Association

BEAMA Metering & Communication Association
   association in Energy section of **BEAMA Ltd**

BEAMA Power
   a section of **BEAMA Ltd**

Bean Curd & Tofu Canners & Preservers Group   1976
■ 32 Coombe End, CROWBOROUGH, E Sussex, TN6 1NH.
   (mail address)
○ *T
Gp Freeze drying
● Conf - Mtgs - Stat - LG
M 17 f
¶ NL; ftm only.

beat
   working name of the **Eating Disorders Association**

Beatrix Potter Society   1980
NR The Lodge, Salisbury Avenue, HARPENDEN, Herts, AL5 2PS.
   (admin/p)
   01582 769755
▲ Registered Charity
○ *L; to promote the study & appreciation of the life & works of
   Beatrix Potter (1866-1943) author, artist, diarist, farmer &
   conservationist
M i
¶ NL - 4.   LM - 1.   Books.

© CBD Research Ltd · Beckenham · BR3 5JS · Tel 020 8650 7745 · Fax 020 8650 0768 · E-mail cbd@cbdresearch.com · www.cbdresearch.com

Beaumont Society   (BS)   1966
- ■ 27 Old Gloucester St, LONDON, WC1N 3XX.   (mail address)
  01582 412220
  email enquiries@beaumontsociety.org.uk
  http://www.beaumontsociety.org.uk
  Pres: Shirley Keel
- ○ *W; self-help group for those that cross-dress, or who are transsexual; support for partners & families
- Gp Transvestite; Transsexual
- ● Conf - Mtgs - ET - Res - Lib - VE
- < Beaumont Trust
- M 852 i, UK / 22 i, o'seas
- ¶ Beaumont Magazine - 4; ftm.

Beckford Society   1995
- ■ The Timber Cottage, Crockerton, WARMINSTER, Wilts, BA12 8AX.   (hsp)
  01985 213195
  email sidney.blackmore@btinternet.com
  Hon Sec: Sidney Blackmore
- ▲ Un-incorporated Society
- ○ *A; to promote interest in the life & work of William Beckford, writer & art collector (1760-1844)
- ● Conf - Mtgs - SG - VE
- M 151 i, 5 f, UK / 101 i, o'seas
- ¶ The Beckford Jnl - 1; ftm, £10 nm.   NL - 2; ftm only.

Bedfordshire Historical Record Society   (BHRS)   1912
- ■ 48 St Augustine's Rd, BEDFORD, MK40 2ND.   (hsp)
  01234 309548
  email rsmart@ntlworld.com
  http://www.bedfordshirehrs.org.uk
  Hon Sec: Dr Richard Smart
- ▲ Company Limited by Guarantee; Registered Charity
- ○ *L; the publication of sources & monographs relating to the history of Bedfordshire
- ● Res
- M 150 i, 50 org, UK / 50 i, 50 org, o'seas
- ¶ Vauxhall Motors & the Luton Economy 1900-2002 - 1; £12 m, £25 nm.
  The Bousfield Diaries; £12 m, £25 nm.

Bee Farmers Association of the United Kingdom   (BFA)
- NR 8 Olivers Close, West Totton, SOUTHAMPTON, Hants, SO40 8FH.   (hsp/b)
  023 8090 7850
  http://www.beefarmers.co.uk
  Gen Sec: John Howat
- ○ *P, *T
- M i

Bee Improvement & Bee Breeders Association   (BIBBA)   1964
- NR 26 Coldharbour Lane, Hildenborough, TONBRIDGE, Kent, TN11 8JT.   (sec/p)
  01732 833984
  http://www.bibba.com
- ▲ Registered Charity
- ○ *B, *G; conservation, restoration, study, selection & improvement of our native honeybees of GB & Ireland
- M i

Beef Shorthorn Cattle Society   1936
- ■ 4th Street, Stoneleigh Park, KENILWORTH, Warks, CV8 2LG.   (hq)
  024 7669 6549   fax 024 7669 6729
  email shorthorn@shorthorn.co.uk
  http://www.shorthorn.co.uk
  Sec: Frank Milnes
- ▲ Registered Charity
- ○ *B
- ● Conf - Mtgs - Res - Exhib - Comp - SG - Stat - Expt - Inf - PL - VE - Empl
- M 330 i, UK / 30 i, o'seas
- ¶ Shorthorn Jnl - 1.   Coates Herd Book - 1.

Behçet's Syndrome Society   1983
- ■ 8 Abbey Gardens, EVESHAM, Worcs, WR11 4SP.   (dir/p)
  01386 47920
  email info@behcetsdisease.org.uk
  http://www.behcets.org.uk
  Dir: Chris Phillips
- ▲ Registered Charity
- ○ *M, *W; a charity providing a contact support network, information & financial aid for sufferers of the disease (a vasculitic disorder with orogenital ulceration, uveitis & arthritis)
- ● Inf
- < Longterm Medical Conditions Alliance (LMCA); UK Rare Diseases Assn; Nat Coun for Voluntary Orgs
- M 1,200 i, UK / 100 i, o'seas
- ¶ NL - 2; ftm, £2.50 nm.

Belgian-Luxembourg Chamber of Commerce in Great Britain (BLCC)
- ■ 105 Ferriby Rd, HESSLE, E Yorks, HU13 0HX.
  0870 246 1610   fax 0870 429 2148
  email info@blcc.co.uk   http://www.blcc.co.uk
  Chief Exec: Michel Van Hoonacker
- ▲ Company Limited by Guarantee
- ○ *C; to help Belgian & Luxembourg companies exporting to the UK, & British companies wishing to do business with Belgian & Luxembourg exporters
- ● Conf - Mtgs - ET - Res - Exhib - Comp - SG - Expt - Inf - VE - Empl - LG
- < Coun of Foreign Chams Comm; Belgian Fedn of Chams Comm
- M 12 i, 68 f, UK / 49 f, o'seas
- ¶ BELUX (NL) - 3; ftm.

Belted Galloway Cattle Society   1922
- NR Parklea, Tongland, KIRKCUDBRIGHT, DG6 4ND.   (hsp)
  http://www.belties.com
- ○ *B
- M i

Beltex Sheep Society   1989
- ■ Shepherd's View, Barras, KIRKBY STEPHEN, Cumbria, CA17 4ES.   (hq)
  017683 41124   fax 017683 41124
  email beltexsheep@btconnect.com
  http://www.beltex.co.uk
  Sec: Rachel Buckle
- ▲ Company Limited by Guarantee; Registered Charity
- ○ *B; to promote the Beltex breed of sheep
- ● Mtgs - ET - Res
- < Nat Sheep Assn
- M 465 i
- ¶ Ybk - 1;   NL - 4; both free.

Benesh Institute
  a group of the **Royal Academy of Dance**

Berkshire Archaeological Society   1871
- ■ 19 Challenor Close, WOKINGHAM, Berks, RG40 4UJ.   (hsp)
  0118-973 2882
  email andrew_hutt@talktalk.net
  http://www.berksarch.co.uk
  Hon Sec: Dr Andrew Hutt
- ▲ Registered Charity
- ○ *L; to advance the education of the public in the fields of archaeology & history in the past & present County of Berkshire
- ● Conf - Mtgs - Res - Lib - VE
- M 100 i, 15 f
  (Sub: £10 i, £15 f)
- ¶ Berkshire Archaeological Jnl - irreg; ftm, £15 nm.
  NL - 4.

Berkshire Archaeology Research Group (BARG) 1958
- ■ 48 Hawkesbury Drive, Calcot, READING, Berks, RG31 7ZR.
  (chmn/p)
  0118-942 9712
  email mail@barg-online.org
  http://www.berkshire-archaeology.info
  Chmn: G C Johnson
- ▲ Un-incorporated Society
- ○ *L; to provide an opportunity for people to partake in the
  practical investigation, understanding & publication of
  archaeology in Berkshire
- Gp Archive research; Excavation; Fieldworking; Geophysical
  surveying; Hedgerow dating; Post-excavation analysis; Site
  monitoring
- ● Mtgs - ET - Res - Exhib - Inf - Lib - VE
- M 65 i, UK / 1 i, o'seas
- ¶ In the Field (NL) - 4.

Berlioz Society 1952
- NR 450b Lea Bridge Rd, LONDON, E10 7DY.   (hsp)
  020 8359 9122
  email sqing@btinternet.com
  http://www.theberliozsociety.org.uk
  Sec: Simon Jones
- ▲ Un-incorporated Society
- ○ *D; to bring together & provide a focal point for all enthusiasts
  of the music & writing of Hector Berlioz
- ● Mtgs - Lib
- M 46 i, UK / 66 i, 20 libraries, o'seas
- ¶ The Bulletin - 3;   NL - 4; both ftm only.

Berwickshire Agricultural Association 1885
- ■ The Cottage, Nabdean Farm, PAXTON, Berwickshire,
  TD15 1SZ.   (hsb)
  01289 386412   fax 01289 386852
  email dunsshow@btopenworld.com
  Sec: Natalie Cormack
- ▲ Registered Charity
- ○ *F; to promote the interests of agriculture primarily through the
  organisation of the Berwickshire County Show
- ● Exhib - Comp
- M 250 i, 75 f
- ¶ Show Schedule & Catalogue.   AR.

Berwickshire Naturalists' Club (BNC) 1831
- ■ c/o The Borough Museum, The Barracks, BERWICK-upon-
  TWEED, TD15 1DQ.   (hq)
  01289 330933
- ▲ Registered Charity
- ○ *L; all matters connected with the natural history & antiquities of
  Berwickshire & North Northumberland
- ● Mtgs - Res - Exhib - Stat - Inf - Lib - VE
- < Coun Brit Archaeology
- M 360 i, 39 org
- ¶ History of the Berwickshire Naturalists' Club - 1; ftm, £10 nm.

BESA New Educational Technologies Group
  a group of the **British Educational Suppliers Association**

BESA Special Needs Group
  a group of the **British Educational Suppliers Association**

BESO (British Executive Service Overseas)
  in April 2005 merged with **Voluntary Service Overseas**

Betjeman Society 1988
- NR 386 Hurst Rd, BEXLEY, Kent, DA5 3JY.   (hsp)
  email colin@colin-wright.freeserve.co.uk
  Mem Sec: Martin H Revill
- ▲ Un-incorporated Society
- Br 7
- ○ *A; 'to advance the education of the public in the works of Sir
  John Betjeman by promoting the knowledge, appreciation &
  study of his life & works'
- ● Mtgs - ET - Res - Exhib - VE
- M 878 i, 4 f, UK / 17 i, 2 f, o'seas
- ¶ The Betjemanian (Jnl) - 1.

Better Brickwork Alliance (BBA) 1999
- ■ c/o BDA, Woodside House, Winkfield, WINDSOR, Berks,
  SL4 2DX.   (hsb)
  01344 885651   fax 01344 890129
  email brick@brick.org.uk
  Sec: Michael Driver
- ▲ Un-incorporated Society
- ○ *N, *T; an alliance of organisations interested in the
  development of all aspects of masonry, with special interest
  in the training / recruitment of craftspeople
- ● Mtgs - ET
- M 15 f

Beverage Council of Ireland
- IRL Unit 19a Naas Road Business Park, DUBLIN 12, Republic of
  Ireland.
  353 (1) 460 0811   fax 353 (1) 460 0814
  email bci@esatlink.com
  Dir: Bernard J Murphy
- ○ *T

Beverage Service Association (BSA)
- ■ Hartfield House, 40-44 High St, NORTHWOOD, Middx,
  HA6 1BN.
  01923 848392
  http://www.beverageserviceassociation.com
  Chmn: David Veal
- ○ *T
  no further information supplied

Bewick Society 1985
- ■ c/o The Hancock Museum, NEWCASTLE upon TYNE,
  NE2 4PT.   (hsb)
  http://www.bewicksociety.org
  Hon Mem Sec: Mrs J Holmes
- ▲ Un-incorporated Society
- ○ *L; to study the life & work of Thomas Bewick (naturalist &
  wood engraver, 1753-1828); to encourage wood engraving
- ● Mtgs - VE
- M 140 i, UK / 10 i, o'seas
- ¶ Cherryburn Times - 2; ftm only.

BFM Ltd (British Furniture Manufacturers) (BFM) 1943
- NR Wycombe House, 9 Amersham Hill, HIGH WYCOMBE, Bucks,
  HP13 6NR.   (hq)
  01494 523021   fax 01494 474270
  email info@bfm.org.uk   http://www.bfm.org.uk
  Managing Dir: Roger Mason
- ▲ Company Limited by Guarantee
- ○ *T; the manufacture, sale & export of furniture
- ● ET - Res - Exhib - Stat - Expt - Inf - Empl - LG
- M 378 f
- ¶ Export Directory - 1;   UK Directory of Members - 1; both free.

BIA Scotland
  Roslin branch of the **BioIndustry Association**

© CBD Research Ltd · Beckenham · BR3 5JS · Tel 020 8650 7745 · Fax 020 8650 0768 · E-mail cbd@cbdresearch.com · www.cbdresearch.com

Biblical Creation Society (BCS) 1976

■ PO Box 22, RUGBY, Warks, CV22 7SY. (mail address)
01788 810633
http://www.biblicalcreation.org.uk
Sec: Dr David J Tyler
▲ Registered Charity (Scotland)
○ *L, *R; a Christian society that advances & defends biblical teaching on creation; to think through issues related to origins from a biblical & scientific standpoint; to challenge Christians who have accepted the evolutionary theory
● Mtgs - ET - Lectures
M c 500 i
¶ Origins (Jnl) - 2.
The Creation Manifesto (a systematic overview of the implications of the Genesis account of the Creation).

Bibliographical Society 1892

■ c/o Institute of English Studies, University of London, Senate House, Malet St, LONDON, WC1E 7HU. (hsb)
020 7862 8679
email admin@bibsoc.org.uk   http://www.bibsoc.org.uk
Sec: Margaret Ford
▲ Registered Charity
○ *L; promotion of study & research of historical, analytical, descriptive & textual bibliography; the history of the book (printing, publishing, collecting & bookbinding)
● Mtgs - Res - Lib - Awards grants to support bibliographical research
M 400 i, 100 f, UK / 400 i, 100 f, o'seas
¶ The Library - 4; £33 m.   AR; ftm.
Monographs - irreg; prices vary.

Bicycle Association of Great Britain Ltd 1973

NR 3 The Quadrant, COVENTRY, Warks, CV1 2DY. (hq)
247 655 3838
email office@ba-gb.com
Sec: Mrs Patricia Morris
○ *T
Gp Mfrs: Bicycles, components & accessories; Concessionaires (bicycles); Ancillary members
● Mtgs - Exhib - Stat - LG
< Comité de Liaison des Fabricants de Pièces et Equipements de Deux-Roues (COLIPED)
M 50 f
¶ AR.   LM.

Bingo Association (BAGB) 1998

NR Lexham House, 75 High St North, DUNSTABLE, Beds, LU6 1JF. (hq)
01582 860921
email info@bingo-association.co.uk
http://www.bingo-association.co.uk
▲ Un-incorporated Society
○ *T; to promote & develop the interests of the licensed bingo industry; to represent members' interests in contact with third parties
M f

Biochemical Society 1911

NR Eagle House (3rd floor), 16 Procter St, LONDON, WC1V 6NX. (hq)
020 7280 4110   fax 020 7280 4170
email genadim@biochemistry.org
http://www.biochemistry.org
Chief Exec: Dr Chris Kirk
▲ Registered Charity
Br 2
○ *L; to advance the science of biochemistry in the context of cellular & molecular life sciences as a seamless continuum
Gp Theme panels: Genes, Molecular structure, Bioenergetics & metabolism, Cell biology, Biotechnology & bioinformatics, Development & disease & disease
● Conf - Mtgs - ET - Res - Exhib - Stat - Inf
< Fedn Eur Biochemical Socs; Intl U Biochemistry
M 6,000 i
¶ Biochemical Jnl - 24.   Clinical Science - 12.
Transactions - 6.   Symposia - 1.
Biotechnology & Applied Biochemistry - 6.
Essays in Biochemistry - 2.

Biodynamic Agricultural Association (BDAA) 1928

■ Painswick Inn Project, Gloucester St, STROUD, Glos, GL5 1QG. (hq)
01453 759501   fax 01453 759501
email office@biodynamic.org.uk
http://www.biodynamic.org.uk
Exec Dir: Bernard Jarman
▲ Registered Charity
○ *F, *H, *Q; to support, promote & develop biodynamic farming, gardening & forestry; part of a worldwide movement inspired by the insights of Rudolf Steiner (1861-1925) Austrian philosopher, scientist & social reformer
Gp Training; Demeter (organic certification UK6) scheme; Biodynamic seed gp
● Conf - ET - Exhib - Inf - Lib - LG - Training apprenticeships - Res & devt of seeds suited to organic & biodynamic systems
< Intl Fedn of Organic Agricl Movements (IFOAM); Anthroposophical Soc (GB); GM Freeze; Sustain; Agricl Dept of the School of Spiritual Science
M 800 i, UK / 50 i, o'seas
¶ Star & Furrow - 2; £4.50.   Newssheet - 4; free.

BioIndustry Association (BIA) 1985

NR 14-15 Belgrave Sq, LONDON, SW1X 8PS. (hq)
020 7565 7190   fax 020 7565 7191
email admin@bioindustry.org
http://www.bioindustry.org
Chief Exec: Aisling Burnand
Br BIA Scotland
○ *T; to promote the commercial interests of companies actively involved in biotechnology in the UK; interests include: biotechnology, genetic engineering, monoclonal antibodies, fermentation, pharmaceuticals, recombinant DNA; all aspects of industrial biotechnology
M f & org

Biological Recording in Scotland (BRISC)

■ 140 Pitcorthie Drive, DUNFERMLINE, Fife, KY11 8BJ. (mem/sp)
http://www.brisc.org.uk
Mem Sec: Duncan Davidson
▲ Registered Charity
○ *P; to promote best practise in biological recording methods; to provide liaison between local records centres
● Conf - ET - Inf
M 100 i, 30 f
¶ Recorder News - 4.

Biosciences Federation (BSF) 2002
- ■ PO Box 502, CAMBRIDGE, CB1 0AL.   (sb)
  - 01223 400189   fax 01223 246858
  - email info@bsf.ac.uk   http://www.bsf.ac.uk
  - Chief Exec: Dr Richard Dyer
- ▲ Registered Charity
- ○ *L; to promote the advancement of the biosciences; to influence policy & strategy in biology-based research & in school & university teaching
- Gp Animal science; International liaison; Science policy; Education C'ee
- ● Conf - Inf - LG
- M 40 i
- ¶ NL - 4;   Science Policy Report - 12;   E.U.News - 12. Science Policy Priorities 2005-2009. Building on Success.   Enthusing the Next Generation. [all online at:
  - www.bsf.ac.uk/elg/default.htm   &
  - www.bsf.ac.uk/newsletters.htm.]

BiPolar Organisation
  alternative name of **MDF**

Birdcare Standards Association
- NR Market Link, 30 St George's Square, WORCESTER, WR1 1HX.
  - 01905 726575
  - email enquiries@birdcare.org.uk
- ○ *T; suppliers of bird care products
- M 10 f

Birmingham Chamber of Commerce & Industry (BCCI) 1813
- NR 75 Harborne Rd, Edgbaston, BIRMINGHAM, B15 3DH.   (hq)
  - 0121-607 0809   fax 0121-455 8670
  - email info@birminghamchamber.org.uk
  - http://www.birmingham-chamber.com
- ▲ Company Limited by Guarantee
- ○ *C
- ● Conf - Mtgs - ET - Expt - Inf - LG
- M 4,000 f

Birmingham Metallurgical Association (B MET A) 1903
- NR c/o School of Metallurgy & Materials, University of Birmingham, Edgbaston, BIRMINGHAM, B15 2TT.   (hsb)
  - Hon Sec: Prof Rex Harris
- ▲ Company Limited by Guarantee
- ○ *L; to promote the science & application of engineering materials
- ● Conf - Mtgs - ET - Comp - VE
- < Inst of Materials (IOM)
- M c 120 i
- ¶ AR & Accounts; ftm only.

Birmingham & Midland Institute (BMI) 1854
- ■ 9 Margaret St, BIRMINGHAM, B3 3BS.   (hq)
  - 0121-236 3591   fax 0121-212 4577
  - email admin@bmi.org.uk   http://www.bmi.org.uk
  - Admin & Gen Sec: Philip A Fisher
- ▲ Registered Charity
- ○ *A, *L; the diffusion & advancement of science, art & literature
- Gp Birmingham & Midland Society for Genealogy & History; Society for the History of Astronomy
- ● Conf - Mtgs - ET - Res - SG - Lib
- < Assn of Indep Libs
- M 300 i
- ¶ BMI Insight - 1; ftm, £3.50 nm.   AR; free.

Birmingham & Midland Society for Genealogy & History
  is a group of the **Birmingham & Midland Institute**

Birmingham Natural History Society (BNHS) 1858
- ■ 23 Crosbie Rd, Harborne, BIRMINGHAM, B17 9BG.   (hsp)
  - 0121-427 1010
  - http://www.freespace.virgin.net/clare.h/bnhs.htm
  - Hon Sec: Dr Peter Jarvis
- ▲ Registered Charity
- ○ *L; all aspects of natural history
- Gp Entomology; Mycology [with the Warwickshire Fungus Survey - http://freespace.virgin.net/william.moodie/wfs.htm]
- ● Mtgs - Res - Inf - Lib - Supervision of Edgbaston Nature Reserve (SSSI)
- M 120 i, 4 org
- ¶ Proceedings - 2 yrly; ftm, £5 nm.   NL - 3; ftm. Programmes - 2; ftm.

Birmingham Transport Historical Group (BTHG) 1963
- ■ 21 The Oaklands, DROITWICH SPA, Worcs, WR9 8AD.   (hsp)
  - 01905 778243
  - Hon Sec: Peter Jaques
- ▲ Un-incorporated Society
- ○ *G; research into public passenger transport in Birmingham & the West Midlands from its commencement to the present day
- ● Mtgs - Res - Inf
- M 21 i, 1 org
- ¶ A Comprehensive History - vol 1.   Various booklets.

Birmingham & Warwickshire Archaeological Society (BWAS) 1870
- NR c/o Birmingham & Midland Institute, Margaret St, BIRMINGHAM, B3 3BS.   (hq)
  - http://www.birminghamandwarwickshirearchaeological society.co.uk
  - Hon Sec: Miss S Middleton
- ▲ Registered Charity
- ○ *L; study of archaeology in Birmingham, Warwickshire & West Midlands
- Gp Field
- ● Mtgs - VE - Field study - Publishing
- < Birmingham & Midland Inst
- M c 150 i, c 75 org
- ¶ Transactions - 1; price varies nm.   NL;   AR; all ftm only.

Birth Trauma Association (BTA) 2004
- ■ PO Box 671, IPSWICH, Suffolk, IP1 9AT.   (mail/address)
  - http://www.birthtraumaassociation.org.uk
  - Sec: Maureen Treadwell,   Chmn: Julie Orford
- ▲ Company Limited by Guarantee; Registered Charity
- ○ *W; a non-professional organisation (of mothers) supporting women suffering Post Natal Post Traumatic Stress Disorder, or birth trauma; the only organisation in the UK which deals solely & specifically with this issue
- ● Conf - ET - Res - Inf - LG
- M 800 i
- ¶ BTA NL - 2/3 (available on web: www.birthtraumaassociation.org.uk/publications.htm

Birthmark Support Group (BSG) 1998
- ■ BM The Birthmark Support Group, LONDON, WC1N 3XX.   (mail/address)
  - 0845 045 4700
  - email info@birthmarksupportgroup.org.uk
  - http://www.birthmarksupportgroup.org.uk
  - Sec: Alana Smith
- ▲ Registered Charity
- ○ *G; to provide information & advice to people affected by birthmarks
- Gp Sub-Groups:
  - Teenagers (teentalk@birthmarksupportgroup.org.uk)
  - Adults (faceittogether@birthmarksupportgroup.org.uk)
- ● Conf - Res - Fun-days - Support network available to all
- M voluntary membership
- ¶ NL - 3; free.

© CBD Research Ltd · Beckenham · BR3 5JS · Tel 020 8650 7745 · Fax 020 8650 0768 · E-mail cbd@cbdresearch.com · www.cbdresearch.com

Biscuit, Cake, Chocolate & Confectionery Association
have merged with a sector group of the **Food & Drink Federation**

Biscuit Industry Council
a group of **Food & Drink Industry Ireland**

BKSTS - the Moving Image Society   (BKSTS)   1933
NR   Pinewood Studios, IVER HEATH, Bucks, SL0 0NH.   (hq)
       01753 656656
       http://www.bksts.com
▲   Company Limited by Guarantee
○   *L; to support those who creatively or technologically are
       involved in the production of moving images & associated
       sound
M   i, f & org

Black & Asian Studies Association   (BASA)   1992
NR   18 Ridge Rd, MITCHAM, Surrey, CR4 2ET.   (hsp)
       020 8640 2014
       email sean.creighton@btinternet.com
       http://www.blackandasianstudies.org/
       Sec: Sean Creighton
▲   Un-incorporated Society
○   *L; to encourage study, publishing, teaching & research into the
       history of African, Asian & Caribbean peoples in Britain; to
       foster the collection & preservation of archives & artifacts
Gp   Newsletter editorial board
●   Conf - Mtgs - EDiscussion forum - Lobbying
M   i, f & org
¶   NL - 3; ftm, £1.25 nm.

Black Country Chamber of Commerce   2001
NR   Dudley Court South, Waterfront East, BRIERLEY HILL,
       W Midlands, DY5 1XN.   (hq)
       0845 002 1234
       email info@blackcountrychamber.co.uk
       http://www.blackcountrychamber.co.uk
       Chief Exec: John Reader
▲   Company Limited by Guarantee
Br   3
○   *C; covers Dudley, Sandwell, Walsall & Wolverhampton
●   Mtgs - Expt - Inf - Lib - VE - LG
M   3,380 f
¶   Prosper - 4.   Chamber Directory - 1; ftm, £90 nm.

Black Country Society   (BCS)   1967
■   PO Box 71, KINGSWINFORD, W Midlands, DY6 9YN.   (hsb)
       http://www.blackcountrysociety.co.uk
       Hon Sec: Judith Watkin
▲   Un-incorporated Society
Br   4
○   *G; to promote interest in the past, present & future of the Black
       Country
Gp   Indl Archaeology Branch
●   Mtgs - Res - Exhib - Inf - VE
<   Civic Trust; Assn Indl Archaeology; Family Hist Soc
M   c 2,000 i, f & org, UK / 32 i, o'seas
¶   The Blackcountryman - 4; ftm, £2.75 each nm.
       Publications list available.

Black Simmental Society   1997
■   Grove Farm, Felbrigg, NORWICH, Norfolk, NR11 8PL.   (hsb)
       01263 512028   fax 01263 515617
       Sec: Mrs Zoe Hall,   Chmn: Brian Filby
▲   Un-incorporated Society
○   *B; British Black Simmental cattle
●   Mtgs - Res - Expt
M   (Sub: £20)

Black Solicitors Network
a group of the **Law Society of England & Wales**

Black Welsh Mountain Sheep Breeders' Association   1798
■   Lake Villa, Bradworthy, HOLSWORTHY, Devon, EX22 7SQ.
       01409 241579
       email lesley-lewin@blackwelshmountain.org.uk
       http://www.blackwelshmountain.org.uk
       Sec: Lesley Lewin
▲   Company Limited by Guarantee; Registered Charity
○   *B
●   Mtgs - ET - Exhib - Comp - SG - Stat - Inf - LG
<   Nat Sheep Assn
M   250 i, UK / 15 i, o'seas
¶   NL - 2/3; ftm only.   LM - 1; free.
       Ybk (Flock Book); ftm, £5 nm.

Blackface Sheep Breeders' Association   1920
NR   Woodhead of Mailer, PERTH, PH2 0QA.
       01738 634018
       http://www.scottish-blackface.co.uk
       Sec: Aileen McFadzean
○   *B; incl matters relevant to hill & upland farming
●   Mtgs - Exhib - Inf
<   Nat Sheep Assn
M   1,600 i
¶   Jnl - 1; free.

Blair Bell Research Society   (BBRS)   1986
■   Institute for Women's Health (UCL), 86-96 Chenies Mews,
       LONDON, WC1E 6HX.   (hsb)
       020 7679 6651   fax 020 7383 7429
       email a.david@ucl.ac.uk   http://www.rcog.org.uk/
       index.asp?page10=1793
       Hon Sec: Dr Anna David
▲   Registered Charity
○   *P, *Q; to ptomote research byb clinicians & scientists into
       women's health & obstetrics & gynaecology
●   Conf - Mtgs - ET - Res - Comp
<   R Coll of Obstetricians & Gynaecologists
M   335 i
       [Sub: £20]
¶   Abstracts (of papers presented at meetings) are published in the
       British Jnl of Obstetrics & Gynaecology - 1; free.

Blake Society at St James's   1986
NR   St James's Church, 197 Piccadilly, LONDON, W1J 9LL.
       (mail/address)
       020 7495 5654
       email secretary@blakesociety.org.uk
       http://www.blakesociety.org.uk
       Hon Sec: Dr Keri Davies
▲   Registered Charity
○   *A; to celebrate the life work of William Blake (1757-1827)
       poet, printer, visionary
Gp   250th anniversary celebration
●   Conf - Mtgs - VE
M   300 i, UK / 40 i, o'seas
¶   Blake Jnl - 1; ftm.

BLC, Leather Technology Centre Ltd   (BLC)   1984
NR   Leather Trade House, King's Park Rd, Moulton Park,
       NORTHAMPTON, NN3 6JD.   (hq)
       01604 679999
▲   Limited Company
○   *Q, *T; servicing leather manufacturing & related industries
<   a subsidiary of BLC Research
M   f & org

BLISS (BLISS) 1979
NR 9 Holyrood St, London Bridge, LONDON, SE1 2EL.   (hq)
    020 7378 1122   fax 020 7403 0673
    email information@bliss.org.uk   http://www.bliss.org.uk
    Chief Exec: Andy Cole
▲ Company Limited by Guarantee; Registered Charity
Br 40
○ *K, *W; to campaign for improved neonatal services; to support
    nurse training; to support families
Gp Befriending service for parents of babies born too soon, too
    small, too sick
● Conf - Mtgs - ET - Exhib - SG - Stat - Inf - Lib - PL - Provision of
    specialist equipment - Funds research
M 1,000 i
¶ Little Bliss - 4; free.   AR - 1.
    BLISS (formerly Baby Life Support Systems) prefers to be known
    as BLISS - the special care baby charity

Blood Pressure Association   2000
NR 60 Cranmer Terrace, LONDON, SW17 0QS.
    020 8772 4994   fax 020 8772 4999
    http://www.bpassoc.org.uk
    Exec Dir: Nickie Roberts
▲ Registered Charity
○ *M, *W; for people whose lives are affected by their blood
    pressure

Blue Albion Cattle Society
NR Cronkstone Grange, Hurdlow, BUXTON, Derbys, SK17 9QL.
    01298 832246
    Sec: Tonia Fox
○ *B

Blue Badge Network (BBN) 1991
NR 198 Wolverhampton St, DUDLEY, W Midlands, DY1 1DZ.   (hq)
    01384 257001
    http://www.bluebadgenetwork.org
    Chmn: Mrs Mary Grace
▲ Registered Charity
Br 44
○ *W; 'to help disabled people integrate more effectively with
    people in the community at large'
● Exhib - Inf - LG - Advocacy
M c 10,500 i
¶ Blue Badge Network NL - 4; ftm.

Bluebell Railway Preservation Society (BRPS) 1960
NR Sheffield Park Station, UCKFIELD, E Sussex, TN22 3QL.   (hq)
    01825 720800   fax 01825 720804
    Hon Sec: Gavin Bennett
▲ Un-incorporated Society
○ *G; railway preservation & running 'The Bluebell Line' (part of
    the Lewes & E Grinstead Railway)
● Conf - Mtgs - ET - Exhib - Lib - VE
< Heritage Rly Assn
M c 10,000 i
¶ Bluebell News - 4; ftm, £2 nm.

Bluefaced Leicester Sheep Breeders Association (BLSBA)
    1962
■ Furmiston, Carsphairn, CASTLE DOUGLAS, Kirkcudbrightshire,
    DG7 3TE.   (hq)
    01644 460647
    email info@blueleicester.co.uk
    http://www.blueleicester.co.uk
    Sec: Jean Gibbon
▲ Registered Charity
○ *B
● Mtgs - Exhib - Inf - VE
M c 1,400 i
¶ Looking Ahead - 1; November News - 1; both ftm.
    Flock Book - 1; ftm.

BMF Sailmakers Association
    a group of the **British Marine Federation**

Boarding Schools Association (BSA) 1966
■ Grosvenor Gardens House, 35-37 Grosvenor Gdns,
    LONDON, SW1W 0BS.   (hq)
    020 7798 1580   fax 020 7798 1581
    email bsa@boarding.org.uk
    http://www.boarding.org.uk
    Nat Dir: Mrs Hilary Moriarty
▲ Company Limited by Guarantee
○ *E; to promote the qualities of boarding education; to
    encourage the highest standards of welfare in boarding
    schools
● Conf - Mtgs - ET - Res - Inf - LG
M 500 schools, UK / 50 schools, o'seas
¶ Good Practice in Boarding Schools: a resource handbook for
    all those working in boarding.
    Parents' Guide to Maintained Boarding Schools.
    Choosing a Boarding School: a guide for parents.
    Briefing Paper(s) 1-23.
        Other publications available.

Boat Jumble Association (BJA) 1987
NR Compass Marine, Compass Cottage, DARTMOUTH, Devon,
    TQ6 0JN.   (sb/p)
    01803 835915
    Sec: Tim Mear
▲ Un-incorporated Society
○ *G, *T; organisation & regulation of boat jumbles
Gp Stallholders; Event organisers
● Exhib
M 1,350 i, 650 f
¶ Boat Jumble Fixtures List - 1.

Boat Retailers & Brokers Association
    a group of the **British Marine Federation**

Body Control Pilates Association   1997
■ 35 Little Russell St, LONDON, WC1A 2HH.
    020 7636 8900   fax 020 7636 8898
    http://www.bodycontrol.co.uk
    Dir: Lynne Robinson
○ *S; exercise similar to the Alexander technique
    Note: send sae for details

Bodyshop Services Division
    a division of the **Retail Motor Industry Federation**

Boiler & Radiator Manufacturers Association Ltd   (BARMA)
    1941
NR Earls Gate, Falkirk Rd, GRANGEMOUTH, FK3 8XZ.   (hq)
    email fcruickshanks@metcom.org.uk
    Sec: Fiona Cruickshanks
▲ Company Limited by Guarantee
○ *T
Gp Commercial boiler; Technical c'ee
● Mtgs - Stat - LG
< Eur Heating Ind (EHI); Eur Radiator Assn (EURORAD)
M 8 f
¶ LM; free.

© CBD Research Ltd · Beckenham · BR3 5JS · Tel 020 8650 7745 · Fax 020 8650 0768 · E-mail cbd@cbdresearch.com · www.cbdresearch.com

Bonded Warehousekeepers' Association (BWA) 1885
■ PO Box 29089, DUNFERMLINE, Fife, KY11 9WB. (hsb)
   07736 633162
   Hon Sec: John Tripp
▲ Un-incorporated Society
○ *T; (incl implementation of UK & EC legislation as it effects HM
   Customs & Excise & related documentation issues)
Gp Health & safety; HM Customs & Excise
● Conf - Mtgs - ET - Inf - VE - LG
< Scotch Whisky Assn; Road Haulage Assn; Freight Transport
   Assn; Wine & Spirit Assn; Gin & Vodka Assn
M 65 i, 45 f
¶ NL - 4. LM - 1.   Minutes of meetings.

Bone Research Society (BRS) 1950
■ The Roslin Institute, University of Edinburgh, EDINBURGH,
   EH25 9PS. (sb)
   0131-527 4399   fax 0131-440 0434
   email colin.farquharson@roslin.ed.ac.uk
   http://www.brsoc.org.uk
   Sec: Dr Colin Farquharson
▲ Registered Charity
○ *L, *Q; to advance basic & clinical research into the calcified
   tissues
● Conf - Mtgs - ET - Res - Inf - PL - LG
< Intl Osteoporosis Foundation; Brit Endocrine Socs
M c 250 i, UK / 10 i, o'seas
   (Sub: £40)
¶ Meeting abstracts published in Calcified Tissue International - 1.
× 2005 Bone & Tooth Society

Bone & Tooth Society
   since 2005 **Bone Research Society**

Bookmark Society 1991
NR 53 Victoria Rd, Horwich, BOLTON, Lancs, BL6 5ND. (hsp)
   01204 692458
   Hon Sec: Joe Stephenson
○ *G; collecting & research into bookmarks
● Mtgs - Res - Inf - VE
M i
¶ Bookmark - 4; ftm.
   Note: please enclose an SAE with any enquiries requiring a
   reply.

Bookplate Society 1983
■ Yarkhill, Upper Bucklebury, READING, Berks, RG7 6QH. (hsp)
   01635 862226
   email geoffreyvevers2@tiscali.co.uk
   http://www.bookplatesociety.org
   Hon Sec: Geoffrey Vevers
▲ Registered Charity
○ *A, *G; to promote the study & collecting of bookplates; to
   publish material & arrange exhibitions
● Mtgs - Res - Exhib - VE
< Fédn Intle des Sociétés d'Amateurs d'Exlibris
M 250 i
   (Sub: £30 UK / £50 o'seas)
¶ The Bookplate Jnl - 2; ftm.NL - 2; ftm only.   Book - 2 yrly;
   ftm, prices vary nm.

**Booksellers Association of the United Kingdom & Ireland
(BA) 1895**
NR Minster House, 272 Vauxhall Bridge Rd, LONDON,
   SW1V 1BA. (hq)
   020 7802 0802   fax 020 7802 0803
   email mail@booksellers.org.uk
   http://www.booksellers.org.uk
   Chief Exec: T E Godfray
▲ Company Limited by Guarantee
Br 15
○ *T
Gp Academic bookselling; Children's bookselling; Christian
   bookselling; Internet bookselling; Library supply; School
   supply; Small business forum
● Conf - Mtgs - Exhib - Stat - Inf - LG
M 1,282 f, UK / 165 i, o'seas
¶ Bookselling Essentials - 4/5;   AR; both free.
   Directory of Booksellers - 1; ftm, £34 nm.
   Directory of Book Publishers - 1; £58.75 m, £76.38 nm.
   The Complete Guide to Starting & Running a Bookshop; £28.

Booktrust 2004
§ Book House, 45 East Hill, LONDON, SW18 2QZ. (hq)
   020 8516 2977   fax 020 8516 2978
   email query@booktrust.org.uk
   http://www.booktrust.org.uk
   Dir: Viv Bird
   An independent national charity that encourages people of all
   ages and cultures to discover and enjoy reading.

Boot & Shoe Manufacturers' Association (BASMA) 1882
NR 24-25 Bloomsbury Sq, LONDON, WC1A 2PL. (hq)
   020 7612 7757
   Chief Exec: Michael Gilbert
▲ Company Limited by Guarantee
○ *T; to provide credit management services (including debt
   recovery, credit reporting & credit insurance) to the footwear
   manufacturing sector in the UK & overseas
● Inf - Credit management
M c 380 f
¶ BASMA News - 4; free.

Border Union Agricultural Society 1813
NR Showground Office, Springwood Park, KELSO, Roxburghshire,
   TD5 8LS. (hq)
   01573 224188
▲ Registered Charity
○ *F; organisation of events & competitions; to promote interest in
   agriculture
< Assn of Show & Agricl Orgs
M i

BOSS Federation
   alternative name of the **British Office Supplies & Services
   Federation**

Boston Chamber of Commerce & Industry (BCC) 1930
NR Boston Business Centre, Norfolk St, BOSTON, Lincs,
   PE21 9HH. (hq)
   01205 358800
▲ Company Limited by Guarantee
○ *C
M f

Botanical Society of the British Isles (BSBI) 1836
- ■ c/o Dept of Botany, Natural History Museum, Cromwell Rd,
    LONDON, SW7 5BD.
    020 7942 5002 (answerphone)
    http://www.bsbi.org.uk
    Hon Gen Sec: D Pearman
- ▲ Registered Charity
- ○ *L; study of flowering plants, cryptogams & charophyta of the
    British Isles & of the problems of their conservation
- Gp Records; Meetings; Publications; Science & research; Training &
    education
- ● Conf - Mtgs - Res - Exhib - SG - Inf - Surveys
- M 2,800 i, 60 libraries, UK / 150 i, o'seas
- ¶ BSBI News - 3; ftm only.
    Watsonia - 2;   Abstracts - 1; both ftm, prices on
    application nm.
    (to Mr R G Ellis, 41 Marlborough Rd, Roath, CARDIFF,
    CF23 5BU)

Botanical Society of Scotland (BSS) 1836
- ■ c/o Royal Botanic Garden Edinburgh, 20A Inverleith Row,
    EDINBURGH, EH3 5LR.   (hsb)
    http://www.botsocscot.org.uk
    Hon Sec: Dr M P Cochrane
- ▲ Registered Scottish Charity
- ○ *L; all branches of botanical science
- Gp Cryptogamic; Alpine plants; Conservation
- ● Conf - Mtgs - Exhib - Conf - VE
- M 280 i, 1 school, UK / 16 i, o'seas
- ¶ BSS News - 2; ftm only.
    Plant Ecology & Diversity - 2, ftm.

Bottled Water Cooler Association
    since 2005 the **British Water Cooler Association**

Bournemouth Chamber of Trade & Commerce (bctc) 1916
- ■ Top Table House, 15 Alum Chine Rd, Westbourne,
    BOURNEMOUTH, Dorset, BH4 8DT.   (hq)
    01202 540870   fax 01202 751997
    email info@bournemouthchamber.org.uk
    http://www.bournemouthchamber.org.uk
    Chief Exec: Peter J Goodson
- ▲ Un-incorporated Society
- ○ *C
- Gp C'ees: Local government affairs; Executive
- ● Mtgs - Inf - VE - LG
- < Dorset Cham Comm & Ind
- M 180 f
- ¶ [emails to members]

Bowls England 1903
- ■ Lyndhurst Rd, WORTHING, W Sussex, BN11 2AZ.   (hq)
    01903 820222   fax 01903 820444
    email enquiries@bowlsengland.com
    http://www.bowlsengland.com
    Chief Exec: Anthony Allcock
- ▲ Company Limited by Guarantee
- ○ *S; governing body of outdoor bowls in England
- Gp Greens maintenance; Coaching scheme; Child protection
    panel; Youth development
- ● Mtgs - ET - Comp
- < World Bowls; Brit Isles Bowling Coun; Brit Isles Womens
    Bowling;
- M 135,000 i, 4,201 clubs
    (Sub: £4.50)
- ¶ Ybk - 1; £3.50,
- × 2007 (English Bowling Association
    (English Women's Bowling Association

Bowls Group
    since 2006 the **Sporting Goods Industry Association**

Box Culvert Association
    a product association of the **British Precast Concrete Federation**

Boys' Brigade (BB) 1883
- NR Felden Lodge, HEMEL HEMPSTEAD, Herts, HP3 0BL.   (hq)
    01442 231681   fax 01442 235391
    email enquiries@boys-brigade.org.uk
    http://www.boys-brigade.org.uk
    Brigade Sec: Steven Dickinson
- ▲ Company Limited by Guarantee; Registered Charity
- Br 1,650; 70 o'seas
- ○ *Y; Christian youth work with boys & young people aged 4-18
- < Global Fellowship of Christian Youth
- M 75,000 i, UK / 600,000 i, o'seas
- ¶ The Boys' Brigade Gazette - 4.

Boys' & Girls' Clubs of Northern Ireland
    since 2007 **Clubs for Young People (NI)**

Boys' & Girls' Clubs of Scotland
    since 2007 **CYP Scotland**

BPI (British Recorded Music Industry) Ltd   (BPI) 1973
- ■ Riverside Building, County Hall, Westminster Bridge Rd,
    LONDON, SE1 7JA.   (hq)
    020 7803 1300   fax 020 7803 1310
    email general@bpi.co.uk   http://www.bpi.co.uk
    Chief Exec: Geoff Taylor
- ▲ Company Limited by Guarantee
- ○ *T; for British record companies
- ● Mtgs - Res - Stat - Inf - Lib - LG
- < Intl Fedn of the Phonographic Ind (IFPI)
- M c 370 f
- ¶ BPI Statistical Hbk - 1.   LM - website.
- × 2007 British Phonographic Industry Ltd

Bradford Chamber of Commerce & Industry   (BCofC) 1851
- NR Devere House, Vicar Lane, Little Germany, BRADFORD,
    W Yorks, BD1 5AH.   (hq)
    01274 772777   fax 01274 771081
    email info@bradfordchamber.co.uk
    http://www.bradfordchamber.co.uk
    Chief Exec: Sandy Needham
- ▲ Company Limited by Guarantee
- ○ *C
- ● Conf - Mtgs - ET - Res - Exhib - Stat - Expt - Inf - Lib - VE - LG
- < Brit Chams Comm
- M 1,000 f
- ¶ Business Plus - 6; ftm, £2.50 nm.   M Dir - 1; ftm, £125 nm.

Braid Society 1993
- ■ Thyrnegate, The Street, Gasthorpe, DISS, Norfolk, IP22 2TL.
    (hsp)
    01953 681779
    email inkles@tiscali.co.uk   http://www.braidsociety.org
    Hon Sec: Anne Dixon
- ▲ Un-incorporated Society
- ○ *G; education & practice in the art & craft of making
    constructed or embellished braids & narrow bands
- ● Mtgs - Exhib - Comp - SG - VE
- M 138 i, UK / 32 i, o'seas
- ¶ Strands (Jnl) - 1; ftm, £3.75 nm.
    NL - 4;   LM - 1;   Booklist - 2 yrly;
    Suppliers' List - 2 yrly;   all ftm only.
    Tutors' List - 1; free.

Brain Injury Association
    alternative name of **HEADWAY**

© CBD Research Ltd · Beckenham · BR3 5JS · Tel 020 8650 7745 · Fax 020 8650 0768 · E-mail cbd@cbdresearch.com · www.cbdresearch.com

Brain Tumour UK   1997
- ■ PO Box 27108, EDINBURGH, EH10 7WS.   (hq)
  0845 450 0386   fax 0845 450 0386
  email enquiries@braintumouruk.org.uk
  http://www.braintumouruk.org.uk
  Inf & Support Services Mgr: Jane Stephens
- ▲ Registered Charity
- ○ *M; all aspects of brain tumours, their treatment & effects of treatment
- ● Conf - Res
- < NCVO; Assn of Chief Execs for Voluntary Orgs
- M 2,800 i
- ¶ Magazine - 4; free.
- × 2004 United Kingdom Brain Tumour Society

Brainwave, the Irish Epilepsy Association   1967
- IRL 249 Crumlin Rd, DUBLIN 12, Republic of Ireland.
  353 (1) 455 7500   fax 353 (1) 455 7013
  email info@epilepsy.ie
  Chief Exec: Mike Glynn
- ○ *W

Branch Line Society   (BLS)   1955
- ■ 73 Norfolk Park Avenue, SHEFFIELD, S Yorks, S2 2RB.   (hsp)
  0114-275 2303   fax 0114-275 2303
  email BLS.Sales@tesco.net
  http://www.branchline.org.uk
  Hon Gen Sec: N J Hill
- ▲ Un-incorporated Society
- ○ *G; study of branch & minor railway lines, principally in the British Isles, but also throughout the world
- ● Mtgs (annual) - Inf - VE
- M 1,000 i, 4 org, UK / 20 i, o'seas
- ¶ Branch Line News - 24;   AR; both ftm only.

Brassica Growers Association   (BGA)
- ■ 133 Eastgate, LOUTH, Lincs, LN11 9QG.   (hq)
  01507 602427   fax 01507 607165
  email crop.association@pvga.co.uk
  http://www.brassicas.org
  Co Sec: Mrs Jayne Dyas
- ▲ Company Limited by Guarantee
- ○ *T; marketing information, research & development
- Gp British Sprout Growers Association
- ● Conf - Mtgs
- M 25 f

Brazilian Chamber of Commerce in Great Britain
- NR 32 Green St, LONDON, W1K 7AT.
  020 7399 9281   fax 020 7499 0186
  email pavlova@brazilianchamber.org.uk
  http://www.brazilianchamber.org.uk
  Chmn: Sir Peter Heap
- ▲ Company Limited by Guarantee
- ○ *C; bilateral trade between Brazil & the UK
- Gp Brazilian exporters to the UK; British investors in Brazil
- ● Conf - Mtgs - Expt - Inf - LG
- M i, f & org
- ¶ Brazil Business Brief - 3; ftm only.

BRE Trust   (BRE)   1946
- NR Bucknalls Lane, WATFORD, Herts, WD25 9XX.   (regd off)
  01923 664000
  email secretary@bretrust.org.uk
  http://www.bretrust.org.uk
- ▲ Company Limited by Guarantee; Registered Charity
- ○ *L, *P; to advance knowledge, innovation & communication in all matters concerning the built environment for public benefit
- × 2005 Foundation for the Built Environment, or Faculty of Building

Breast Implant Information Society   (BIIS)   1998
- ■ Highway Farm, Horsley Rd, Downside, COBHAM, Surrey, KT11 3JZ.   (founder/p)
  0704 147 1225   fax 0704 147 1225
  email info@biis.org   http://www.biis.org
  Founder: Maxine Heasman
- ▲ Un-incorporated Society
- ○ *G; to provide comprehensive information & advice &/or guidance to women who have, or are considering, breast implant surgery
- ● ET - Res - Stat - Inf - Lib - LG
  Helpline: 0704 147 1255 (weekdays 1800-2000 hours, not Bank Holidays)
- M c 350 i, UK / 20 i, o'seas
- ¶ B-Plus - 1; m only.
  The Ultimate Cleavage: a complete practical guide to cosmetic breast enlargement surgery.

Brecknock Hill Cheviot Sheep Society
- NR 13 Lion St, BRECON, Brecknockshire, LD3 7HY.
  01874 622488
  Contact: Peter Francis
- ○ *B

Brecknockshire Agricultural Society   (Brecon County Show)   1755
- NR Parclands House, Raglan, USK, Monmouthshire, NP15 2BX.   (hq)
  01291 691134
  Admin: Vicki Spencer
- ▲ Registered Charity
- ○ *F; interests of farming & breed societies
- ● Mtgs - ET - Exhib - Comp - Brecknock Show
- M 500 i, 15 f, 10 org
- ¶ LM;   AR.

Brewery History Society   1972
- ■ Manor Side East, Mill Lane, Byfleet, WEST BYFLEET, Surrey, KT14 7RS.   (chmn/p)
  01932 341084
  email chairman@breweryhistory.com
  http://www.breweryhistory.com
  Chmn: Jeff Sechiari
- ○ *L; research into the history of the British brewing & related industries
- ● Conf - Mtgs - Res - Exhib - Lib - PL - VE
- > Engl Heritage; Assn for Indl Archaeology
- M 400 i, 32 f, 40 org, UK / 12 i, 6 f, o'seas
  (Sub: £18 i, £60 f, £27 org, UK / £25 i, £60 f, o'seas)
- ¶ Jnl - 4; ftm, £4.50 each nm.   NL - 4; ftm only.
  County Directories -1; c £12.

Brewing, Food & Beverage Industry Suppliers Association   (BFBi)   1907
- ■ 3 Brewery Rd, WOLVERHAMPTON, W Midlands, WV1 4JT.   (hq)
  01902 422303   fax 01902 795744
  email info@bfbi.org.uk   http://www.bfbi.org.uk
  Chief Exec: Ruth Evans
- ▲ Un-incorporated Society
- Br 5
- ○ *T; companies supplying raw materials, engineering components, process control & consultancy to the brewing, food & beverage industries
- ● Conf - Mtgs - ET - Res - Exhib - SG - Inf - VE - LG
- M 156 i, 350 f, UK / 8 f, o'seas
- ¶ Directory - 1; ftm, £95 nm.

Briar Pipe Trade Association
  This organisation has closed

Brick Development Association Ltd (BDA) 1954
- ■ Woodside House, Winkfield, WINDSOR, Berks, SL4 2DX. (hq)
  01344 885651   fax 01344 890129
  email brick@brick.org.uk   http://www.brick.org.uk
  Chief Exec: Michael Driver
- ▲ Company Limited by Guarantee
- ○ *T; interests of clay brick industry
- ● Mtgs - ET - Exhib - Comp - Stat - Inf - Lectures - Symposia
- < Fédn Européenne des Fabricants de Tuiles et de Briques;
  Construction Products Assn; Brit Ceramic Res Ltd; Brit
  Ceramic Fedn
- M 24 f (representing 95% of UK clay & calcium silicate & 100% of
  Republic of Ireland clay & brickmaking interests)
- ¶ Brick Bulletin - 2; £10 yr.   Technical literature.
- ✕ 2006-07 (amalgamated) National Brickmakers Federation

Bridge Deck Waterproofing Association (BWA) 1990
- NR 4 Meadows Business Park, Station Approach, Blackwater,
  CAMBERLEY, Surrey, GU17 9AB. (hsb)
  01276 608700   fax 01276 608701
- ▲ Company Limited by Guarantee
- ○ *T; for those concerned with the waterproofing of bridges
  (highway, railway & waterway)
- M i & f

Bridlington Chamber of Trade
  a local chamber of the **Hull & Humber Chamber of Commerce,
  Industry & Shipping**

Bristol Chamber of Commerce & Industry 1823
- NR Leigh Court Business Centre, Abbots Leigh, BRISTOL,
  BS8 3RA. (hq)
  01275 373373
  email info@businesswest.co.uk
  http://www.businesswest.co.uk
  Jt Managing Dirs: John Savage, Phil Smith
- ▲ Company Limited by Guarantee
- ○ *C
- Gp Information services; Export services
- ● Expt - Inf - Lib
- < Business Link West; Euro Info Centre Network; Brit Chams
  Comm
- M 2,500 f
- ¶ Business Update - 10; ftm only.
  Members Directory - 1; ftm, £62.50 nm
  Note: uses the trading name of GWE Business West

Bristol & Gloucestershire Archaeological Society (BGAS) 1876
- ■ Stonehatch, Oakridge Lynch, STROUD, Glos, GL6 7NR. (hsp)
  01285 760460
  email john@loosleyj.freeserve.co.uk
  http://www.bgas.org.uk
  Hon Gen Sec: John Loosley
- ▲ Registered Charity
- ○ *L; to promote the study of the history, archaeology &
  antiquities of Bristol & Gloucestershire; to encourage
  conservation
- Gp Sections: Bristol, Gloucester
- ● Mtgs - Lib - VE - Publications of historical records of
  Gloucestershire
- M 700 i, 70 org, UK / 10 i, 60 org, o'seas
- ¶ NL - 2; ftm only.   Transactions - 1; ftm, £12 nm.
  Record Series - 1; £12 m, £30 nm.

Bristol Industrial Archaeological Society (BIAS) 1967
- NR 8 Northfield Rd, Portishead, BRISTOL, BS20 8LE. (sec/p)
  01225 847522
  Sec: Roger Davis,   Chmn: Stuart Burroughs
- ○ *L; research into industrial archaeology of the Bristol region
- < Assn for Indl Archaeol
- M i, f & org

Britain-Australia Society (B-AS) 1937
- NR Swire House, 59 Buckingham Gate, LONDON, SW1E 6AJ.
  (hq)
  020 7630 1075   fax 020 7828 2260
  email britaus@britain-australia.org.uk
  http://www.britain-australia.org.uk
  Nat Dir: Kim Hemmingway
- ▲ Un-incorporated Society
- Br 10
- ○ *X
- ● Mtgs - VE
- M 1,200 i, 30 f
- ¶ Brit Oz Bulletin - 3; ftm only.

**Britain & Ireland Association of Aquatic Science Libraries &
Information Centres**
  This organisation is dormant

Britain-Nepal Chamber of Commerce (BNCC) 1995
- ■ Tamesis House, 33 St Philip's Avenue, WORCESTER PARK,
  Surrey, KT4 8JS. (asa)
  020 8330 6446   fax 020 8330 7447
  email bncc@tamgroup.co.uk
  http://www.nepal-trade.org.uk
  Sec: N Barry Jaynes
- ▲ Un-incorporated Society
- ○ *C; to encourage import & export trade between UK & Nepal
- ● Mtgs - Exhib - LG
- M f

Britain Nepal Society (BNS) 1960
- ■ Greensand Cottage, Seale, FARNHAM, Surrey, GU10 1HP.
  (hsp)
  01252 783265
  email secretary@britain-nepal-society.org.uk
  http://www.britain-nepal-society.org.uk
  Hon Sec: Dr Neil Weir
- ▲ Un-incorporated Society
- ○ *X; to promote good relations between the peoples of the UK &
  Nepal; & in particular between UK citizens with an interest in
  Nepal & Nepalese citizens resident in the UK
- ● Mtgs - VE
- > Britain Nepal Cham Comm; R Nepalese Embassy in UK; Britain
  Nepal Otology Service
- M 450 i, 20 f, UK / 50 i, o'seas
- ¶ BNS Jnl - 1; ftm only.
  Note: also at the same address is the Britain Nepal Otology
  Service - a charity dedicated to the prevention & treatment of
  deafness in Nepal.

Britain Nigeria Business Council (BNBC) 1977
- ■ 2 Vincent St, LONDON, SW1P 4LD. (hq)
  020 7828 5544   fax 020 7828 5251
  email info@waba.co.uk   http://www.bnbc.uk.com
  Exec Vice Chmn: Clive Carpenter
- ▲ Company Limited by Guarantee
- ○ *C; to promote trade & investment between Britain & Nigeria
- ● Conf - Mtgs - Inf - LG
- < West Africa Business Assn
- > West Africa Business Assn
- M c 80 f
  (Sub: £355)
- ¶ Nigeria News Report - 12;   AR - 1; both ftm only.

© CBD Research Ltd · Beckenham · BR3 5JS · Tel 020 8650 7745 · Fax 020 8650 0768 · E-mail cbd@cbdresearch.com · www.cbdresearch.com

Britain-Nigeria Educational Trust   (BNA)   1961
- ■ 2 Vincent St, LONDON, SW1P 4LD.   (hq)
    020 7828 5588   fax 020 7828 5251
    http://www.britain-nigeria.org
    Hon Sec: G Clark
- ▲ Registered Charity
- ○ *X
- ● Mtgs - LG - Social gatherings & receptions
- < Nigeria-Britain Assn, Nigeria
- M c 850 i & f
- ¶ BNA NL - 3; ftm only.
- × Britain-Nigeria Association

Britain-Tanzania Society   (BTS)   1975
- NR 24 Oakfield Drive, REIGATE, Surrey, RH2 9NR.   (memsec/p)
    01737 349437   fax 01737 210532
    http://www.btsociety.org
    Exec Sec: Judy Tice;   Mem Sec: Ann Brumfit
- ▲ Un-incorporated Society
- Br 2; Tanzania
- ○ *X; to increase mutual knowledge, understanding & respect
    between the peoples of the two countries
- ● Conf - Mtgs - Exhib - Inf - VE - LG
- < BOND
- M 750 i, UK / 100 i, o'seas, & 20 org
- ¶ Tanzanian Affairs - 3; ftm, £7.50 nm.
    NL;   AR; ftm only.

Britain Zimbabwe Society   (BZS)   1981
- ■ 5A Crick Rd, OXFORD, OX2 6QJ.   (mem/sp)
    01865 557807
    email mariekefclarke@pop3.poptel.org.uk
    http://www.britain-zimbabwe.org.uk
    Mem Sec: Marieke Clarke
- ▲ Un-incorporated Society
- ○ *X; to foster friendship & understanding between the peoples of
    Zimbabwe & Britain; to encourage open discussion about
    Zimbabwean affairs; to inform the British & Zimbabwe public
    about Zimbabwean culture & economy
- ● Annual research day - email network - Networking support -
    AGM
- M 260 i, 2 f, 8 org, UK / 13 i, 1 embassy, o'seas
    (Sub: £18 i, £40 instns)
- ¶ Zimbabwe Review [with NL] - 4; prices vary.

British Abrasives Federation   (The BAF)   1968
- ■ Toad Hall, Hinton Rd, HURST, Berks, RG10 0BS.   (hsp)
    0845 612 1380   fax 0845 612 1380
    email info@thebaf.org.uk   http://www.thebaf.org.uk
    Sec: Stuart Lane
- ▲ Un-incorporated Society
- ○ *N, *T; to represent manufacturers & producers of abrasives in
    the UK
- Gp Technical standards; Training; Safe use of abrasive
- ● ET - Stat - Inf - Safety codes - Standards
- < Fedn of Eur Producers of Abrasives (FEPA) (Paris)
- M 22 f

British Academy   1902
- ■ 10 Carlton House Terrace, LONDON, SW1Y 5AH.   (hq)
    020 7969 5200   fax 020 7969 5300
    email secretary@britac.ac.uk   http://www.britac.ac.uk
    Sec: Robin Jackson
- ▲ Registered Charity
- ○ *L; is the Uk's national academy for the humanities & social
    sciences.   Scholars are elected for distinction in their area
    of study
- Gp Classical antiquity; Theology & religious studies; African &
    oriental studies; Linguistics & philology; Early modern
    languages & literature; Modern languages, literature & other
    media; Archaeology; Medieval studies: history & literature;
    Early modern history to c 1800; Modern history from c 1800;
    History of art & music; Philosophy; Law; Economics &
    economic history; Social anthropology & geography;
    Sociology, demography & social statistics; Political studies:
    political theory, government & international relations;
    Psychology
- ● Conf - Mtgs - Res - Comp - LG - Awards to support
    fundamental research - Symposia
- M c 800 i
- ¶ Proceedings;   Review (monographs) - irreg; ftm, prices
    vary nm.
    Directory - 1; ftm only.   AR - 1; free.
- × 2005-06 British Academy for the Promotion of Historial,
    Philosophical & Philological Studies

British Academy of Audiology   (BAA)   1985
- ■ Association House, South Park Rd, MACCLESFIELD, Cheshire,
    SK11 6SH.   (hq)
    01625 504066
    email admin@baaudiology.org
    http://www.baaudiology.org
    Pres: Mark Lutman
- ▲ Company Limited by Guarantee
- ○ *P; the professional body for audiologists in the UK
- ● Conf - ET - Exam - Exhib - Inf - LG
- × 2004 (British Association of Audiologists
        (British Association of Audiological Scientists
        (British Society of Hearing Therapists

British Academy of Composers + Songwriters   (BAC+S)   1999
- NR British Music House, 26 Berners St, LONDON, W1T 3LR.   (hq)
    020 7636 2929   fax 020 7636 2212
    email info@britishacademy.com
    http://www.britishacademy.com
    Chief Exec: Chris Green
- ▲ Company Limited by Guarantee
- ○ *P; the interests of composers & songwriters across all genres
- ● Mtgs - Comp - Inf - LG - Administration of the Ivor Novello &
    the Gold Badge Awards
- < Creators' Rights Assn; Brit Music Rights; MCPS; PRS
- M 2,500 i
- ¶ The Works - 2;   Four Four - 4; both ftm only.

British Academy of Dramatic Combat   (BADC)   1969
- ○ *D, *P; to advance the art of stage combat in all forms of
    performance media
- M 91 i

British Academy of Film & Television Arts   (BAFTA)   1963
- NR 195 Piccadilly, LONDON, W1J 9LN.   (hq)
    020 7734 0022   fax 020 7734 1792
    email reception@bafta.org.   http://www.bafta.org
    Chief Exec: Amanda Berry
- ▲ Registered Charity
- ○ *A; to support, develop & promote the art forms of the moving
    image
- Gp Film; Games; Television
- ● Awards - Events - Archive
- M c 5,000 i, UK / 1,500 i, o'seas

British Academy of Forensic Sciences   (BAFS)   1959
- ■   104 Barnsbury Rd, LONDON, N1 0ES.   (hsb)
  020 7837 0069
  Admin: Mrs Sandra Dawson
- ○   *L; to encourage the study, improve the practice & advance the knowledge of legal medicine & forensic science
- M   i
- ¶   Medicine, Science & the Law (Jnl) - 4.

British Accounting Association   (BAA)   1984
- NR   c/o The Management School, University of Sheffield, 9 Mappin St, SHEFFIELD, S Yorks, S1 4DT.   (admin/b)
  0114-222 3462
  Admin: Kathryn Hewitt
- ▲   Registered Charity
- ○   *E; *Q; advancement of education & encouragement of research in accounting
- M   i

British Acoustic Neuroma Association   (BANA)   1992
- NR   Oak House, Ransom Wood Business Park, Southwell Road West, MANSFIELD, Notts, NG21 0HJ.   (hq)
  01623 632143
- ▲   Registered Charity
- ○   *W; for people with acoustic neuromas (brain tumours), their families & interested medical personnel
- M   i

British Activity Holiday Association   (BAHA)   1986
- ■   The Hollies, Oak Bank Lane, Hoole Village, CHESTER, CH2 4ER.   (hq)
  01244 301342
  email info@baha.org.uk   http://www.baha.org.uk
  Sec: Jane Tomlin
- ▲   Company Limited by Guarantee
- ○   *T; for providers of activity & special-interest holidays & courses
- ●   Conf - Mtgs - ET - Inf - LG
- <   English Outdoor Coun; Skills Active
- M   32 f
  (Sub: £81-£970)
- ¶   Publications; m only.

British Actors' Equity Association   (Equity)   1930
- NR   Guild House, Upper St Martin's Lane, LONDON, WC2H 9EG.   (hq)
  020 7379 6000   fax 020 7379 7001
  email info@equity.org.uk   http://www.equity.org.uk
- ▲   Un-incorporated Society
- Br   7
- ○   *U; for performers, stage managers, choreographers, directors, stunt arrangers & professional broadcasters in theatre, television, radio, film & variety
- M   i

British Acupuncture Council   (BAcC)   1995
- ■   63 Jeddo Rd, LONDON, W12 9HQ.   (hq)
  020 8735 0400   fax 020 8735 0404
  email info@acupuncture.org.uk
  http://www.acupuncture.org.uk
- ○   *P; to represent acupuncturists; to maintain standards of education, methods & practice in the acupuncture profession in the UK
- Gp   Finance; Code of Practice, ethics & disciplinary procedures; Education; Conference; Admissions; Research; Safe practice; PR & marketing; Regulation
- ●   Mtgs - ET - Res - Inf - LG
- <   Wld Fedn of Acupuncture Socs; Brit Acupuncture Accreditation Bd
- M   2,600 i
- ¶   LM - 1.   AR.
  List of Local Practitioner Members - daily.

British Adhesives & Sealants Association   (BASA)   1983
- ■   5 Alderson Rd, WORKSOP, Notts, S80 1UZ.   (sb)
  01909 480888   fax 01909 473834
  email secretary@basaonline.org
  http://www.basaonline.org
  Sec: John Murdoch
- ▲   Un-incorporated Society
- ○   *T; interests of British manufacturers of sealants & adhesives
- ●   Conf - ET - SG - Stat - Inf - LG
- <   Assn of Eur Adhesives Mfrs (FEICA); Alliance of Ind Assns
- M   82 f
- ¶   BASA Bulletin - 3; ftm only.   AR; free.
  BASA Members Hbk - 1; ftm, £50 nm.
  Manuals:
  Guide to Reach; free.
  Manual of Sealant Practice; ftm, POA nm.

British Aerobatic Association   (BAeA)   1974
- NR   Mayfield House, Wrens Warren, Chuck Hatch, HARTFIELD, E Sussex, TN7 4WW.   (hq)
  01892 771310
  email info@aerobatics.org.uk
  http://www.aerobatics.org.uk
  Sec: David Cowden
- ▲   Company Limited by Guarantee
- ○   *S; for all interested in aerobatic flying
- ●   ET - Comp - Arranging contests
- <   R Aero Club
- M   200 i, 5 f, UK / 10 i, o'seas
- ¶   Aerobatics News Review - 6; ftm only.

British Aerobiology Federation   (BAF)   1990
- NR   c/o NPARU, University of Worcester, Henwick Grove, WORCESTER, WR2 6AJ.   (hsb)
  01905 855200   fax 01905 855234
  email j.emberlin@worc.ac.uk
  http://www.pollenuk.co.uk
  Pres: Prof J Emberlin
- ▲   Registered Charity
- ○   *P; aerobiology, pollen counts, pollen spores, hayfever, asthma
- ●   Conf - Mtgs - ET
- <   Intl Assn for Aerobiology
- M   15 i, 30 f
- ¶   NL - 2; ftm only.

British Aerophilatelic Federation
  since May 2007 **British Air Mail Society**

British Aerosol Manufacturers Association   (BAMA)   1961
- ■   Kings Buildings, Smith Sq, LONDON, SW1P 3JJ.   (hq)
  020 7828 5111
  Dir: Sue Rogers
- ▲   Company Limited by Guarantee
- ○   *T; to promote & protect the aerosol industry & its products
- ●   Mtgs - Stat - Inf - LG
- <   Chemical Inds Assn
- M   c 75 f
- ¶   Volatile Substance Abuse - be aware.
  BAMA Code of Practice.
  BAMA Electrostatic Guidelines.
  BAMA Guide to Safety in the Laboratory.
  Aerosol Product Recall Guide.
  Other similar publications.

British African Business Association   (BABA)
- NR   2 Vincent St, LONDON, SW1P 4LD.
  020 7828 5544   fax 020 7828 5251
  http://www.waba.co.uk
- ○   *N
- M   3 org:
  Eastern Africa Association
  Southern Africa Business Association
  West Africa Committee

© CBD Research Ltd · Beckenham · BR3 5JS · Tel 020 8650 7745 · Fax 020 8650 0768 · E-mail cbd@cbdresearch.com · www.cbdresearch.com

British Aggregates Association (BAA) 1999
- ■ 10 Brookfields, Calver, HOPE VALLEY, Derbys, S32 3XB. (hsp)
  01206 274051
  email phuxtable@british-aggregates.com
  http://www.british-aggregates.com
  Sec: Peter Huxtable
  Dir: Robert Durward, Exec Officer: Richard Bird
- ▲ Company Limited by Guarantee
- ○ *T; to represent the independent, privately owned SME quarry operator in the UK minerals industry in consultation with government, EU regulators, officials & politicians
- ● Conf - Mtgs - ET - Inf - LG
- < Confedn of Brit Ind (CBI); Construction Product Assn (CPA); Mineral Ind Res Org (MIRO)
- M 52 f (indep), 24 associates

British Agricultural & Garden Machinery Association (BAGMA) 1917
- ■ Salamander Quay West (entrance B/level 1), Park Lane, HAREFIELD, Middx, UB9 6NZ. (hq)
  0870 205 2834 fax 0870 205 2824
  email info@bagma.com http://www.bagma.com
  Dir: Keith Christian
- ▲ Un-incorporated Society
- ○ *F, *H, *T; farming & agriculture
- ● Mtgs - ET - Inf - Empl - LG
- < Brit Hardware Fedn
- M c 900 f
- ¶ BAGMA Bulletin - 6; free.

British Agricultural History Society (BAHS) 1952
- NR Dept of Humanities, Arts & Languages, London Metropolitan University, 166-220 Holloway Rd, LONDON, N7 8DB. (hsb)
  020 7133 2781
  Hon Sec: Dr John Broad
- ▲ Registered Charity
- ○ *L; to encourage the study of all aspects of the history of the countryside
- ● Conf - Mtgs - Res
- M c 500 i, 450 f, UK & o'seas
- ¶ Agricultural History Review - 2.
  Rural History Today - 2.

British Air Line Pilots Association (BALPA) 1937
- NR BALPA House 5 Heathrow Blvd, 278 Bath Rd, WEST DRAYTON, UB7 0DQ. (hq)
  020 8476 4000
  email balpa@balpa.org http://www.balpa.org
  Gen Sec: Jim McAusnan
- ▲ Un-incorporated Society
- ○ *U; the representation of British commercial airline pilots & flight engineers to their employers & aviation authorities
- ● Mtgs - SG - Empl - LG
- < Intl Fedn of Airline Pilots Assns; Eur Cockpit Assn
- M 9,000 i, UK / 300 i, o'seas
- ¶ The Log - 6.

British Air Mail Society (BAMS) 1985
- ■ 97 Albany Park Avenue, ENFIELD HIGHWAY, Middx, EN3 5NX. (hsp)
  http://www.britishairmailsociety.co.uk
  Hon Sec: Keith D Hanman
- ▲ Un-incorporated Society
- ○ *G; to encourage & contribute to the advancement & study of all material relating to the carriage of mail by air
- ● Conf - Mtgs - Res - Exhib - Comp - SG - Lib - VE
- < Assn of Brit Philatelic Socs
- M 280 i, UK / 50 i, o'seas
- ¶ Airmail News - 4; free.
- × 2007 (May) British Aerophilatelic Federation

British Air Transport Association (BATA) 1976
- ■ Artillery House, 11-19 Artillery Row, LONDON, SW1P 1RT. (hq)
  020 7222 9494 fax 020 7222 9595
  email info@bata.uk.com http://www.bata.uk.com
  Sec Gen: Roger Wiltshire
- ▲ Company LImited by Guarantee
- Br 1
- ○ *T; to be the voice of UK airlines
- Gp Aviation security; Flight operators; Security; Technical
- ● Mtgs - ET - LG
- M 12 f

British Airgun Shooters' Association (BASA)
- NR 3 The Courtyard, Denmark St, WOKINGHAM, Berks, RG40 2AZ.
  0118-977 1677
  Sec: Nigel Allen
- ○ *G
- M c 4,500 i

British Airport Services & Equipment Association (BASEA) 1988
- NR Homelife House, 26-32 Oxford Rd, BOURNEMOUTH, Dorset, BH8 8EZ. (hq)
  01202 508234
- ▲ Un-incorporated Society
- ○ *T; to promote the British suppliers to the airport industry & their products in the UK & overseas; to serve as a bureau for purchasers of airport equipment & services worldwide; to offer members a wide range of marketing support services
- M i, f, 2 org (Airport Owners Assn & Jt Security Ind Coun)

British Allergy Foundation
operates under the name **Allergy UK**

British Alliance of Healing Associations
renamed **Alliance of Healing Associations**

British Alpaca Society (BAS) 1997
- ■ PO Box 251, EXETER, Devon, EX2 8WX. (hq)
  01382 437788 fax 01392 270421
  email info@bas-uk.com http://www.bas-uk.com
  Admin: Elizabeth Henson
- ▲ Company Limited by Guarantee
- ○ *B; for owners & breeders of alpacas
- Gp Fibre production; Welfare; Shows; Education
- ● Conf - Mtgs - ET - Res - Exhib - Comp - SG - Stat - Expt - Inf - PL - VE - LG
- M 1,000 i, UK / 30 i, o'seas
  (Sub: £70)
- ¶ Alpaca - 4; Members Handbook - 1; both ftm only.

British Amateur Gymnastics Association (British Gymnastics)
see **British Gymnastics**

British Amateur Rugby League Association (BARLA) 1973
- NR 4 New North Parade, HUDDERSFIELD, W Yorks, HD1 5JP. (hq)
  01484 544131 fax 01484 519985
  email info@barla.org.uk http://www.barla.org.uk
  Sec: Nigel Hollingsworth
- ▲ Un-incorporated Society
- ○ *S; the governing body of amateur Rugby League football in Great Britain
- ● Conf - Mtgs - ET - Exam - Res - Exhib - Comp - Stat - Inf - PL - VE - LG
- < BARLA is the amateur section of the Rugby Football League
- M 1,400 teams, 900 youth & junior sides
- ¶ BARLA Bulletin - 6. Hbk - 1.

British Ambulance Association
NR   PO Box 100, PAIGNTON, Devon, TQ3 1YE.
        01803 843966
            email info@baa999.com
○   *T; for private ambulance providers

British Ambulance Society   (BAS)   1977
NR   21 Victoria Rd, HORLEY, Surrey, RH6 9BN.   (sp)
            http://www.britishambulancesociety.co.uk
        Chmn: Roger Leonard,   Gen Sec: Graham Andrews
▲   Un-incorporated Society
○   *G; compilation & storage of ambulance history: vehicles,
            uniforms, badges, equipment & photographs & any other
            artifacts concerning ambulance manufacture, services etc
M   i, f & org

British American Business Council   (BABC)   1954
NR   235 Montgomery Street (suite 907), SAN FRANCISCO, CA
            94104, USA.   (hq)
        1 (415) 296 8645   fax 1 (415) 296 9649
        email info@babcsf.org   http://www.babcsf.org
        Exec Dir: Mostyn T Lloyd
▲   Company Limited by Guarantee
○   *C; to provide a forum for information, networking &
            identification of business opportunities, trade & investment in
            Northern California & the UK
●   Conf - Mtgs - Expt - Inf - Lib - LG
<   Brit Amer Business Coun
M   85 i, 165 f, o'seas
¶   Membership Directory - 1; ftm only.
✕   2005-6 British American Chamber of Commerce Northern
            California

British-American Business Inc   (BABi)   1920
■   75 Brook St, LONDON, W1K 4AD.   (hq)
        020 7290 9888   fax 020 7491 9172
        http://www.babinc.org
        Dir: Peter Hunt
▲   Company Limited by Guarantee
○   *C; to promote the growth & development of trade between
            British & American companies in both Britain & USA
●   Conf - Mtgs - Stat - Expt - Inf - Lib - LG
<   Eur Coun of Amer Chams Comm; Brit-Amer Cham Comm
M   700 f
¶   Network London - 4;   Network New York - 4; both free.
        British American Business, the UK Hbk - 1; ftm; £60 nm.
        American British Business - 1; ftm, £60 nm.
        Membership Directory - 1; ftm only.

British American Chamber of Commerce Northern California
    since 2005-06 the **British American Business Council**

British American Football Association   (BAFA)   1987
NR   West House, Hedley-on-the-Hill, STOCKSFIELD,
            Northumberland, NE43 7SW.   (chmn/p)
        01661 843179
        Chmn: Gary Marshall
▲   Company Limited by Guarantee
○   *S; to act as the governing body for amateur American football
            in GB
M   c 4,500 i

**British Amusement Catering Trades Association   (BACTA)
1974**
NR   Alders House, 133 Aldersgate St, LONDON, EC1A 4JA.   (hq)
        020 7726 9826
        http://www.bacta.org.uk
        Chief Exec: Leslie Macleod-Miller
Br   10
○   *T; to represent the pay-to-play leisure machine industry
            including manufacturers, suppliers & amusement centre
            owners
Gp   Seaside amusement arcades; Inland amusement centres;
            Manufacturers, importers, distributors of amusement
            machines; Operators of amusement machines
●   Conf - Mtgs - ET - Exhib - SG - Stat - Expt - Inf - Lib - VE - LG
<   Fedn of Coin Machine Trade Assns of Europe (EUROMAT);
            Music Users' Coun of Europe; Nat Amusements Coun; Music
            Users' Coun
M   1,205 i, 800 f, UK / 10 i, 8 f, o'seas
¶   NL - 10 ftm only.   AR; free.
        Hbk (LM) - 1; ftm.

British Andrology Society   (BAS)   1975
NR   Academic Unit of Reproductive & Developmental Medicine,
            University of Sheffield, Level 4, Jessop Wing, Tree Root Walk,
            SHEFFIELD, S Yorks, S10 2SF.   (hsb)
        0114-226 8195
        Sec: Dr Alizera Fazeli
○   *Q; promotion of research & professional training in male
            infertility & reproduction research
M   i

British Angora Goat Society   1981
NR   5 The Langlands, HAMPTON LUCY, Warks, CV35 8BN.   (hq)
        01789 841930
        email secretary@angoragoat.fsnet.co.uk
        http://www.britishangoragoats.org.uk
○   *B
M   i & groups
¶   NL - 3.   Ybk - 1.

British Anti-Vivisection Association   (BAVA)
NR   PO Box 73, CHESTERFIELD, Derbys, S41 0YZ.
            http://www.london77truth.com/BAVA.htm
        Pat Rattigan

British Antique Dealers' Association   (BADA)   1918
■   20 Rutland Gate, LONDON, SW7 1BD.   (hq)
        020 7589 4128   fax 020 7581 9083
        email info@bada.org   http://www.bada.org
        Sec Gen: Mrs Elaine J Dean
▲   Company Limited by Guarantee
○   *T; for the leading antique dealers in the UK - the association
            was incorporated in 1951
●   ET - Exhib - Stat - Inf - LG
<   Confédn Intle des Négociants en Oeuvres d'Art (CINOA)
M   400 f
¶   LM - 2; free.

© CBD Research Ltd · Beckenham · BR3 5JS · Tel 020 8650 7745 · Fax 020 8650 0768 · E-mail cbd@cbdresearch.com · www.cbdresearch.com

British Antique Furniture Restorers' Association   (BAFRA) 1979
■   The Old Rectory, Warmwell, DORCHESTER, Dorset,
DT2 8HQ.   (hq)
01305 854822   fax 01305 854822
email headoffice@bafra.org.uk
http://www.bafra.org.uk
Chief Exec: Michael Barrington
▲   Company Limited by Guarantee
○   *P; to promote study & research in furniture conservation & restoration; to maintain high professional standards among members
Gp Carving & gilding; Marble & stone; Metalware; Oriental lacquerwork & japanning; Persian carpets; Upholstery
●   Conf - ET - Res - Exhib - Inf - Workshop seminars
M   101 i, 1 f, UK / 10 i, o£seas
(Sub: £265 i, £500 f, £50 BAFRA Friends, UK / £95 i o'seas)
¶   BAFRA Jnl - 2; ftm, £16-£21 nm.
The BAFRA Directory - 1; ftm, £8-£20 nm.

British Aphasiology Society   (BAS)   1987
NR Dept of Human Communication Sciences, University of Sheffield, 31 Claremont Crescent, SHEFFIELD, S Yorks, S10 2TA.   (chmn/b)
0114-222 2403
Chmn: Ruth Herbert
▲   Un-incorporated Society
○   *L; to foster the study of aphasia (language disorder following brain injury); to promote professional & scientific work on aphasia
M   i

British Appaloosa Society   (BApS)   1976
NR Crook Farm, Roadhead, CARLISLE, Cumbria, CA6 6PJ.
(chmn/p)
01697 748347
http://www.appaloosa.org.uk
Chmn: Brian Entwistle,
Sec: Suzanne Entwistle
▲   Registered Charity
○   *B; to provide a registry for Appaloosa horses; to preserve & improve the breed
●   Conf - Mtgs - Comp - Expt
<   Brit Horse Soc
M   750 i
¶   NL - 4; ftm only.   Register of Horses - 1.
Stallion Directory - 2.

British Apparel & Textile Confederation   (BATC)   1992
NR 5 Portland Place, LONDON, W1B 1PW.   (hq)
020 7636 7788   fax 020 7636 7515
email batc@dial.pipex.com
http://www.apparel-textiles.co.uk
Dir Gen: John Wilson
▲   Company Limited by Guarantee
○   *T; representation of the apparel & textile industry in the UK to government, the press & others
●   Mtgs - Stat - Inf - LG
<   Eur Apparel & Textile Org (EURATEX)
M   7 f, 2 org, 13 trade org

British Approvals for Fire Equipment   (BAFE)   1984
NR 31 Thames St, KINGSTON upon THAMES, Surrey, KT1 1PH.
(hq)
020 8541 1950   fax 020 8547 1564
email info@bafe.org.uk   http://www.bafe.org.uk
▲   Company Limited by Guarantee
○   *P; registration & certification of providers of active fire protection equipment & services
●   Mtgs - LG - Certification & registration
M   c 100 f, UK / 4 f, o'seas
¶   BAFE Brochure;   BAFE Supplement;
BAFE List of Approved Registered Organisations; all free.

British Arachnological Society   (BAS)   1963
NR 19 Duxford Close, REDDITCH, Worcs, B97 5BY.   (hsp)
01527 544952
http://www.britishspiders.org.uk
Hon Sec: John Partridge
▲   Registered Charity
○   *L, *Q; distribution, behaviour, taxonomy etc of spiders (araneae), harvestmen (opilionidae), & pseudoscorpions (pseudoscorpionidae)
●   Conf - Mtgs - ET - Res - SG - Stat - Inf - Lib - PL
M   c 300 i, 20 libraries & universities, UK / 275 i, 100 libraries & universities, o'seas
¶   Bulletin - 3.   NL - 3.   Hbk.

British Archaeological Association   (BAA)   1843
NR 18 Stanley Rd, OXFORD, OX4 1QZ.   (hsp)
01865 724378
http://www.britarch.ac.uk/baa   (hsb)
Hon Sec: John McNeill
○   *L; study of archaeology & the preservation of national antiquities

British Argentine Chamber of Commerce   (BACC)   1995
NR 65 Brook St, LONDON, W1K 4AH.   (hq)
020 7495 8730
http://www.britargcham.co.uk
Chmn: Peter Edbrooke
▲   Company Limited by Guarantee
○   *C; trade & investment promotion
●   Conf - Exhib - Stat - Expt - VE - LG
¶   Bulletin.

British Armwrestling Federation   (BAF)
NR 13 Westland Avenue, DARWEN, Lancs, BB3 2ST.   (memsec)
http://www.armwrestling.co.uk
Pres: Neil Pickup
○   *S

British Art Market Federation   (BAMF)   1996
NR 10 Bury St, LONDON, SW1Y 6AA.   (hq)
020 7389 2148
Chmn: Anthony Browne,   Sec: Christopher Battiscombe
▲   Un-incorporated Society
○   *T; to represent the various elements of the British art trade
M   3 f, 8 org

British Art Medal Society   (BAMS)   1982
■   Dept of Coins & Medals, British Museum, Great Russell St, LONDON, WC1B 3DG.   (hsb)
020 7323 8568   fax 020 7323 8171
http://www.bams.org.uk
Sec: Miss Janet Larkin
○   *A; study of the history of the medal
●   Conf - Mtgs - Exhib - Comp
M   c 370 i, f & org
¶   The Medal - 2

British Artist Blacksmiths Association   (BABA)   1978
■   Anwick Forge, 62 Main Rd, Anwick, SLEAFORD, Lincs, NG34 9SU.   (hsb)
01526 830303
email babasecretary@baba.org.uk
http://www.baba.org.uk
Hon Sec: Tim Mackereth
▲   Un-incorporated Society
○   *P, *T; to encourage a greater awareness of the blacksmiths' art amongst architects, interior designers & the general public
●   Conf - Mtgs - ET - Exhib - Comp - SG - Inf - PL
M   638 i, UK / 30 i, o'seas
¶   Artist Blacksmith - 4;
Members' Address Book - 1; both ftm only.

British Arts Festivals Association   (BAFA)   1970
NR   28 Charing Cross Rd (2nd floor), LONDON, WC2H 0DD.
      (hq)
      020 7240 4532
      email info@artsfestivals.co.uk
      Admin: Kim Hart
▲   Registered Charity; Un-incorporated Society
○   *A, *N; the meeting point of arts festivals in the UK. It aims to
      strengthen the arts festivals; to raise their profit & status; to
      provide a centre for information
●   Conf - Mtgs - ET - Res - Inf
<   Eur Festivals Assn
M   c 100 festivals
¶   Arts Festivals Calendar & Directory - 1; free.

British Association of Academic Phoneticians   (BAAP)   1982
■   Dept of English Language, The University, GLASGOW,
      G12 8QQ.   (archivist b)
      0141-330 4596   fax 0141-330 3531
      email m.macmahon@englang.arts.gla.ac.uk
      Hon Sec & Archivist: Prof M K C MacMahon
▲   Un-incorporated Society
○   *P; for people with a teaching or research post in phonetics in
      an institute of higher education in the UK or the Republic of
      Ireland
●   Conf
M   150 i, UK / c 50 i, o'seas
      Note: The Convenorship changes every 2 years.

British Association for Adoption & Fostering   (BAAF)   1980
NR   Saffron House, 6-10 Kirby St, LONDON, EC1N 8TS.   (hq)
      020 7421 2600
      email mail@baaf.org.uk   http://www.baaf.org.uk
      Dir: Felicity Collier
▲   Registered Charity
Br   6
○   *N, *W; to promote the interests of children separated from
      their parents
●   Conf - Mtgs - ET - Inf - Lib - LG (Dept of Health)
M   1,250 i, 210 agencies, 80 associate members
¶   Adoption & Fostering (Jnl) - 4.
      Adoption & Fostering News - 8.
      List of Agency Members.   Legal Member Directory.
      Medical Member Directory.
      Be My Parent Newspaper - 6.
      Focus on Fives NL - 26.   AR - 1.

**British Association for the Advancement of Science   (The BA)
1831**
NR   Wellcome Wolfson Building, 165 Queen's Gate, LONDON,
      SW7 5HD.   (hq)
      0870 770 7101   fax 0870 770 7102
      email help@the-ba.net   http://www.the-ba.net
      Chief Exec: Dr Roland Jackson
▲   Registered Charity
○   *L; 'to connect science with people, making science itself & the
      ways in which it is applied accessible to all'
Gp   16 sections covering the main areas of science, social science,
      engineering, mathematics & medicine
●   Conf - Mtgs
M   3,000 i, 100 f, 200 org, UK / 100 i, o'seas
¶   Science & Public Affairs.

British Association of Advisers & Lecturers in Physical Education
      in 2006 merged with the Physical Education Association to form the
      Association for Physical Education

**British Association of Aesthetic Plastic Surgeons   (BAAPS)
1985**
■   at the Royal College of Surgeons, 35-43 Lincoln's Inn Fields,
      LONDON, WC2A 3PE.   (hq)
      020 7405 2234 (advice line)   fax 020 7242 4922
      email secretariat@baaps.org.uk
      http://www.baaps.org.uk
      Pres: Adam Searle
▲   Company Limited by Guarantee; Registered Charity
○   *P; teaching & research of aesthetic plastic surgery
●   Conf - Mtgs - ET - Res - Exhib - Stat - Inf - PL
<   Intl Soc of Aesthetic Plastic Surgeons (ISAPS); Brit Assn of Plastic
      Surgeons (BAPS); Intl Confedn of Plastic & Reconstructive
      Surgery
M   170 i, UK / 5 i, o'seas
¶   Factsheets on Aesthetic Surgery.
      Syllabus for Surgeons.   LM; all free.

**British Association of American Square Dance Clubs
(BAASDC)   1953**
NR   87 Brabazon Rd, HESTON, Middx, TW5 9LL.   (hsp)
      020 8897 0723
      http://www.uksquaredancing.com
      Sec: Mrs Patricia Connett-Woodcock
▲   Un-incorporated Society
Br   230
○   *D; promotion of modern American square dancing for fun &
      friendship
Gp   Square Dance Clubs; Round Dance Clubs
●   Mtgs
M   c 5,000 i
¶   Let's Square Dance - 10.

British Association for American Studies   (BAAS)   1955
■   c/o Dr Catherine Morley, Dept of English, University of
      Leicester, University Rd, LEICESTER, LE1 7RH.   (hsb)
      07841 288478
      email cm260@le.ac.uk   http://www.baas.ac.uk
      Hon Sec: Dr Catherine Morley
▲   Registered Charity
Br   2
○   *L; to promote serious study of the United States of America
●   Conf - Mtgs - ET - Res - Comp - Inf
<   Eur Assn for Amer Studies; Amer Studies Assn; Canadian Assn
      for Amer Studies; Ir Assn for Amer Studies
M   500 i, UK / 30 i, o'seas
      (Sub: £41-£28)
¶   Jnl of American Studies - 3.   NL - 2.
      American Studies (book series) - 3.

British Association of Anger Management   (BAAM)   2001
■   4 The Bothy, Plawhatch Hall, Plawhatch Lane, Sharpthorne,
      EAST GRINSTEAD, W Sussex, RH19 4JL.   (hq)
      0845 130 0286   fax 01342 811513
      email info@angermanage.co.uk
      http://www.angermanage.co.uk
      Dir: Mike Fisher
▲   Un-incorporated Society
○   *G, *P; all issues concerning anger, conflict & stress
      management for people, education, organisations &
      government bodies; training for those wishing to move into
      anger management
●   Conf - ET - SG - Inf - Programmes in anger management &
      conflict management - One-to-one therapy - Bespoke anger
      management courses
<   Codes & practices of the British Association for Counselling &
      Psychotherapy & the UK Council for Psychotherapy
M   i, f, org
¶   NL - 4.
      Beating Anger (published by Rider Book); £7.99 m, £7.55 nm.

© CBD Research Ltd · Beckenham · BR3 5JS · Tel 020 8650 7745 · Fax 020 8650 0768 · E-mail cbd@cbdresearch.com · www.cbdresearch.com

British Association for Applied Linguistics   (BAAL)   1967
- ■ PO Box 6688, LONDON, SE15 3WB.   (asa)
  020 7639 0090   fax 020 7635 6014
  email admin@baal.org.uk   http://www.baal.org.uk
  Chmn: Prof Susan Hunston,   Hon Sec: Dr Paul Thompson
- ▲ Registered Charity
- ○ *L; to promote the study of language in use; to foster
  interdisciplinary collaboration; to provide a common forum
  for those engaged in the theoretical study of language & for
  those whose interest is in the practical applications of such
  work
- ● Conf - Mtgs - ET - Res
- < Assn Intl de Linguistique Appliquée (AILA)
- M 737 i, 20 f, UK / 201 i, o'seas
- ¶ NL - 3;   LM - 1;   Annual Proceedings - 1; all ftm only.
  Publications of the International Association:
  AILA News - 2/3;   AILA Review - 1; both ftm.

British Association of Art Therapists Ltd   (BAAT)   1991
- ■ 24-27 White Lion St, LONDON, N1 9PD.   (hq)
  020 7686 4216   fax 020 7837 7945
  email info@baat.org   http://www.baat.org
  Chief Exec: Val Hvet
- ▲ Company Limited by Guarantee
- ○ *U; to promote art therapy in hospitals, clinics & special
  schools; to support therapists
- Gp Art therapy &: Autism & spectrum disorder, Education,
  Forensics, Learning disabilities, Neurology, Older people
- ● Conf - Mtgs - ET - SG - Inf - Empl - LG
- M i & org
- ¶ Inscape - International Jnl of Art Therapy - 2; ftm, £25 nm.
  Newsbriefing Magazine (NL) - 4;
  Newsbulletin (jobs & news) - 12; both ftm only.

British Association of Audiological Scientists
in 2004 merged with the British Association of Audiologists & the
British Society of Hearing Therapists to form the**British Academy of
Audiology**

British Association of Audiologists
2004 merged with the British Association of Audiological Scientists &
the British Society of Hearing Therapists to form the **British
Academy of Audiology**

**British Association of Audiovestibular Physicians   (BAAP)
1977**
- Admin Sec: Carol Bishop
- ○ *M, *P; for consultant & trainee physicians & paediatricians
  practising audiovestibular medicine
- × British Association of Audiological Physicians

British Association of Aviation Consultants   (BAAC)   1972
- NR c/o Jacobs Consultancy, 16 Connaught Place, LONDON,
  W2 2ES.   (asa)
  email committee@baac.org.uk   http://www.baac.org.uk
  Co Sec: Peter Mackenzie-Williams
- ▲ Company Limited by Guarantee
- Br Australia, New Zealand
- ○ *P, *T; to ensure that all services provided by its registered
  Aviation Consultants are subjected to definite standards of
  professional competence with the interests of the customer
  paramount
- ● Consultancy services - Training - Personnel selection - Social
  events
- < Academy of Experts; Farnborough Aerospace Consortium
- M c 80 i
- ¶ NL - 2/3; ftm only.   Register (LM) - 1; free.

British Association of Balloon Operators   (BABO)   1993
- NR Buckshot Barn, Rignall Rd, GREAT MISSENDEN, Bucks,
  HP16 9PE.   (chmn/p)
  01494 866128   fax 01494 868677
  email chairman@babo.org.uk   http://www.babo.org.uk
  Chmn: Ted Moore
- ▲ Company Limited by Guarantee
- ○ *T; to represent UK Balloon Air Operators Certificate holders
  (passenger carrying hot air balloons)
- ● Mtgs - ET - Inf
- < Brit Balloon & Airship Club
- M c 70 f
- ¶ NL - 12; ftm only.

British Association of Barbershop Singers   (BABS)   1974
- ■ Druids Lea, Upper Stanton Drew, BRISTOL, BS39 4EG.   (hsp)
  01275 332778   fax 01275 332778
  email babs@crbennett.co.uk
  http://www.singbarbershop.com
  Admin Dir & Co Sec: Colin Bennett
- ▲ Company Limited by Guarantee; Registered Charity
- Br 50+
- ○ *D; to encourage barbershop singing in the UK
- Gp Guild of Judges; Directorate of music services (education);
  Convention; Harmony Foundation;
  Colleges: Harmony, Directors
- ● Conf - ET - Comp - Inf
- < Barbershop Harmony Soc (USA); Making Music (UK)
- M 2,000 i
  (Sub: £37)
- ¶ Harmony Express - 6; ftm.   AR - 1.

**British Association of Beauty Therapy & Cosmetology Ltd
(BABTAC)   1977**
- NR Meteor Court, Barnett Way, Barnwood, GLOUCESTER,
  GL4 3GG.   (hq)
  0845 065 9000
  email enquiries@babtac.com   http://www.babtac.com
- ○ *P

**British Association for Behavioural & Cognitive
Psychotherapies   (BABCP)   1972**
- NR Victoria Buildings, 9-13 Silver St, BURY, Lancs, BL9 0EU.   (hq)
  0161-797 4484   fax 0161-797 2670
  email babcp@babcp.com   http://www.babcp.com
  Hon Sec: Helen Macdonald
- ▲ Registered Charity
- Br 12
- ○ *K; to advance the theory & practice of the psychotherapies; in
  particular the application of experimental methodology &
  learning techniques to the assessment & modification of
  behaviour in a wide variety of settings
- ● Conf - Mtgs - ET - SG - Inf - Accreditation & registration of
  psychotherapists
- < Eur Assn for Behaviour & Cognitive Therapy (EABCT); Ir Assn for
  Behaviour & Cognitive Therapies (IABCP); UK Coun
  Psychotherapy (UKCP)
- M 6,000 i
- ¶ Behavioural & Cognitive Psychotherapy - 4.
  BABCP News - 4.
  Directory of Accredited Behavioural / Cognitive & REBT
  Psychotherapists - 1.

British Association for Biofuels & Oils
in 2006 merged with **Renewable Energy Association**

British Association for Canadian Studies (BACS) 1975

- 31 Tavistock Square, LONDON, WC1H 9HA. (hq)
  020 7117 1875   fax 020 7117 1875
  email jodie.robson@canadian-studies.net
  http://www.canadian-studies.net
  Admin Sec: Jodie Robson
- ▲ Registered Charity
- ○ *L; to encourage & support research & teaching concerning Canada across the whole of the educational community in the UK; the dissemination of knowledge & understanding of Canada to the public of the UK
- Gp Groups: Canada/UK cities research; Library & resources; Legal studies
  Aboriginal studies circle; Business & economic studies; History & politics; International studies; Literature; Groupe de Récherches et d'études sur le Canada francophone
- ● Conf - ET - SG - Inf
- < Intl Coun for Canadian Studies; Eur Canadian Studies Network; UK Coun forArea Studies Assns
- M 280 i, 120 org, UK / 50 i, o'seas
  (Sub: £30 i, £45 org)
- ¶ British Jnl of Canadian Studies - 2;   NL - 2.
  BACS E-news (electronic bulletin - 12.

British Association for Cancer Research (BACR) 1960

- c/o Institute of Cancer Research, 15 Cotswold Rd, SUTTON, Surrey, SM2 5NG. (hq)
  020 8722 4208
  email bacr@icr.ac.uk   http://www.bacr.org.uk
  Hon Sec: Dr Sue Bailey
- ▲ Registered Charity
- ○ *P, *Q; clinical & basic researchers interested in cancer
- ● Conf - Mtgs - ET
- M 1,589 i

British Association for Cemeteries in South Asia (BACSA) 1977

- 135 Burntwood Lane, LONDON, SW17 0AJ. (hsp)
  email rosieljai@clara.co.uk
  Hon Sec: Dr Rosie Llewellyn-Jones
- ▲ Registered Charity
- Br India
- ○ *K; preservation of historical cemeteries; conversion of those dilapidated beyond repair to social use; recording & publishing information relating to Europeans in Asia
- ● Mtgs - Res - Exhib - SG - Inf - VE - Collecting monumental inscriptions from UK churches, or churchyards, with references to S Asia
- < Fedn Family History Socs; Indian Nat Trust of Art & Cultural Heritage (INTACH); Assn for Presvn of Histl Cemeteries in India (APHCI)
- M c 1,900 i, f & org
- ¶ Chowkidar (Jnl) - 2.
  Publications list available.

British Association for Central & Eastern Europe

no longer in existence

British Association for Chemical Specialities (BACS) 1983

- Simpson House, Windsor Court, Clarence Drive, HARROGATE, N Yorks, HG1 2PE. (hq)
  01423 700249   fax 01423 520297
  email enquiries@bacsnet.org   http://www.bacsnet.org
  Sec: John Reid
- ▲ Company Limited by Guarantee
- ○ *T; manufacturers & formulators of speciality chemicals & intermediates (incl maintenance products for consumer & industrial use), disinfectants & industrial biocides (incl water treatment chemicals & services) & speciality surfactants
- Gp Biocides forum; Speciality surfactants; Water treatment; COSRAM
- ● Conf - Mtgs - LG
- < Confedn Brit Ind; Brit Business Bureau
- M 135 f
- ¶ AR - 1; free.

British Association for Chinese Studies (BACS) 1976

- NR Sch of E Asian Studies, University of Sheffield, Western Bank, SHEFFIELD, S Yorks, S10 2TN. (pres/b)
  0114-222 8400
  http://www.bacsuk.org.uk
  Pres: Prof Tim Wright
- ▲ Registered Charity
- ○ *L; to promote & support Chinese studies in the UK
- ● Conf - Mtgs - Inf - VE - LG
- < Eur Assn of Chinese Studies; Coordinating Coun Area Studies Assns; Jt E Asian Studies Conf/C'ee
- M c 200 i & org
- ¶ Bulletin - 1; ftm only.

British Association of Clinical Anatomists (BACA) 1977

- School of Medicine, Health Policy & Practice, University of East Anglia, NORWICH, NR4 7TJ. (hsb)
  01603 591104
  email d.heylings@uea.ac.uk
  Hon Sec: Dr David Heylings
- ▲ Registered Charity
- ○ *E, *M, *P
- ● Mtgs - Res
- < Amer Assn of Clinical Anatomists (AACA); Australian & New Zealand Assn of Clinical Anatomists (ANZACA)
- > Amer Assn of Clinical Anatomists (AACA); Australian & New Zealand Assn of Clinical Anatomists (ANZACA)
- M 171 i, UK / 69 i, o'seas
- ¶ Clinical Anatomy - 8.

British Association of Colliery Management, Technical Energy Administrative Management (BACM-TEAM) 1947

- 6A South Parade, DONCASTER, S Yorks, DN1 2DY. (hq)
  01302 815551
  Gen Sec: P M Carragher
- Br 7
- ○ *U; for energy management, technical & administrative management employees
- ● Lib - Empl - LG
- < EC Steel & Coal; Fédn Eur des Cadres de l'Energie et de la Recherche; Trades U Congress
- M 4,065 i, c 30 f, UK / 5 i, o'seas
- ¶ Focus NL - 4;   AR - 1; both ftm only.

British Association of Communicators in Business Ltd (BACB)

- Oak House (GA2), Woodlands Business Park, Linford Wood, MILTON KEYNES, Bucks, MK14 6EY. (hq)
  01908 313755   fax 01908 313661
  email enquiries@cib.co.uk   http://www.cib.co.uk
- ▲ Company Limited by Guarantee
- ○ *P; 'aims to be the market leader for those involved in corporate media management & practice by providing professional, authoritative, dynamic, supportive & innovative services'
- ● Conf - Mtgs - ET - Exhib - Comp - SG - Lib
- < Fedn Eur Indl Editors Assns (FEIEA)
- M 1,050 i, UK / 30 i, o'seas
- ¶ Communicators - 10; ftm.

British Association for Community Child Health
  a group of the **Royal College of Paediatrics & Child Health**

© CBD Research Ltd · Beckenham · BR3 5JS · Tel 020 8650 7745 · Fax 020 8650 0768 · E-mail cbd@cbdresearch.com · www.cbdresearch.com

British Association of Community Doctors in Audiology (BACDA)   1985

- ■ c/o 23 Stokesay Rd, SALE, Cheshire, M33 6QN.   (sb)
   0161-962 8915   fax 0161-291 9398
   email pamelawilliams@onetel.com
   http://www.bacda.org.uk
   Sec: Pam Williams
- ▲ Registered Charity
- ○ *M, *P; the study of audiology & the prevention, diagnosis & management of hearing impairment in children; the promotion of standards in training, & of regular exchange of views between medical staff & professional colleagues
- Gp Research group; Training group
- ● Conf - Mtgs - ET
- M c 270 f
- ¶ Audiens - 2; ftm only.

British Association of Conference Destinations
   merged on 1 January 2009 with **Eventia**

British Association of Cosmetic Doctors

- NR 30b Wimpole St, LONDON, W1U 2RW.
   01474 823900
   email info@cosmeticdoctors.co.uk
   http://www.cosmeticdoctors.co.uk
- ○ *P

** British Association of Cosmetic Surgeons

   Organisation lost: see Introduction paragraph 3

British Association for Counselling & Psychotherapy   (BACP)   1977

- ■ BACP House, 15 St John's Business Park, LUTTERWORTH, Leics, LE17 4HB.   (hq)
   01455 883300   fax 01455 550243
   email bacp@bacp.co.uk   http://www.bacp.co.uk
   Chief Exec: Laurie Clarke
- ▲ Company Limited by Guarantee; Registered Charity
- ○ *P; to lead the effort to make counselling & psychotherapy widely recognised as a profession whose purpose & activity is understood by the general public; to be the professional body for counselling & psychotherapy
- Gp Association for Counselling at Work; Association of Independent Practitioners (AIP); Association for Pastoral & Spiritual Care & Counselling (APSCC); Association for University & College Counselling; Counselling Children & Young People (CCYP); Faculty of Healthcare Counsellors & Psychotherapists Ltd (FHCP)
- ● Conf - Mtgs - ET - Res - Exhib - Inf - Lib - LG
- M 24,500 i, 1,000 f, UK / 326 i, 12 f, o'seas
- ¶ Therapy Today - 10; ftm, £69 nm.
   Counselling & Psychotherapy Research (CPR) - 4; ftm, £54 nm.
   Healthcare Counselling & Psychotherapy Jnl - 4; ftm, £30 nm.
   Counselling at Work (Jnl of the Assn for Counselling at Work) - 4; free to ACW members, £30 nm.
   AUCC (Jnl of the Assn for University & College Counselling) - 4; free to AUCC members, £30 nm.

British Association of Crystal Growth   (BACG)   1969

- ■ c/o Dr Mike Quayle, AstraZeneca R&D, Avalon Works - Hallen, BRISTOL, BS10 7ZE.   (hsb)
   0117-938 5157
   email mike.quayle@astrazeneca.com
   http://www.bacg.org.uk
   Hon Sec: Dr Mike Quayle
- ▲ Registered Charity
- ○ *L; to encourage discussion of the theory & practice of crystal growth in industry, government laboratories & universities in the UK including all types of inorganic & organic crystalline materials including metals, ceramics, polymers & electronic device materials
- Gp Semiconductor materials; Biological / chemical materials; Optical materials; Oxide materials
- ● Conf - Mtgs - ET - Exhib - Comp
- < Intl Org Crystal Growth (IOCG)
- M 400 i, UK / 50 i, o'seas
- ¶ NL - 2; ftm only.

British Association for Day Surgery   (BADS)   1989

- NR at the Royal College of Surgeons, 35-43 Lincoln's Inn Fields, LONDON, WC2A 3PE.   (hq)
   020 7973 0308   fax 020 7973 0314
   email bads@bads.co.uk   http://www.bads.co.uk
   Admin: Mrs V Hall   Hon Sec: Douglas McWhinnie
- ▲ Registered Charity
- ○ *P; to promote good practice in day surgery
- ● Conf - Mtgs - ET - Res - Exhib - VE - LG
- < Intl Assn of Ambulatory Surgery
- M c 750 i
- ¶ Jnl of One-Day Surgery - 4.

British Association of Dental Nurses   (BADN)   1940

- ■ Room 200, Hillhouse International Business Centre, THORNTON-CLEVELEYS, Lancs, FY5 4QD.   (hq)
   01253 338360
   email admin@badn.org.uk   http://www.badn.org.uk
   Chief Exec: Pamela Swain
- ○ *P
- Gp National gps for Dental nurses in: Conscious sedation; Special care; Armed forces; Education; Practice management; Reception; Orthodontics Special care (for dental nurses working with patients with special needs); Orthodontic (for dental nurses working in ortho conscious sedation / anaesthesia) [in process of formation]
- ● Conf - SG - Empl - LG
- M c 5,600 i
   (Sub: £70 (rates vary for students, retired etc)
- ¶ British Dental Nurses' Jnl - 4; ftm.

British Association of Dental Therapists   (BADT)   1961

- ■ 24 Boundary St, BRYNMAWR, Gwent, NP23 4EX.   (sp)
   email secretary@badt.org.uk   http://www.badt.org.uk
   Sec: Kate Oakes
- Br c 8
- ○ *P
- ● Conf - Mtgs - ET - SG - Inf - Empl - LG
- M 300 i
- ¶ Dental Therapy Update - 4.   Contact Point (NL) - 2.

British Association of Dermatologists   (BAD)   1921
- ■ 4 Fitzroy Sq, LONDON, W1T 5HQ.   (hq)
  020 7383 0266   fax 020 7388 5263
  email admin@bad.org.uk   http://www.bad.org.uk
  Chief Exec: Miss Marilyn Benham
- ▲ Registered Charity
- ○ *P; study & teaching of dermatology (diseases of the skin); to
  promote high quality care for sufferers
- Gp British Contact Dermatitis Group; British Dermatological
  Nursing Group; British Epidermo-Epidemiology Society;
  British Photodermatology Group; British Society for
  Dermatological Surgery; British Society for
  Dermatopathology; British Society for Investigative
  Dermatology; British Society for Paediatric Dermatology;
  British Teledermatology Society; Dowling Club
- ● Conf - Mtgs - Exhib
- M 741 i, UK / 202 i, o'seas
- ¶ British Jnl of Dermatology - 12.   NL - 4.
  Clinical & Experimental Dermatology - 6.

British Association of Domiciliary Care
    since 2004 **Ceretas**

British Association of Dramatherapists   (BADth)   1976
- ■ Waverley, Battledown Approach, CHELTENHAM, Glos,
  GL52 6RE.   (postal/address)
  01242 235515
  email enquiries@badth.org.uk   http://www.badth.org.uk
  Chmn: Madeline Andersen-Warren
- ▲ Company Limited by Guarantee
- ○ *P; to promote, maintain, improve & advance the education of
  the public about the benefits, theory & practice of
  dramatherapy
- ● Conf - ET - Res - Inf
- M 'varies'
- ¶ The Prompt - 4;   The Dramatherapy Jnl - 3; both ftm.

**British Association for Early Childhood Education   (Early
Education)   1923**
- ■ 136 Cavell St, LONDON, E1 2JA.   (hq)
  020 7539 5400   fax 020 7539 5409
  email office@early-education.org.uk
  http://www.early-education.org.uk
  Operations Mgr: Jenny Rabin
- ▲ Company Limited by Guarantee; Registered Charity
- Br 52
- ○ *E, *K, *W; to promote the right of all children to education of
  the highest quality; to provide a multi-disciplinary network of
  support & advice for everyone concerned with the care &
  education of children from birth to eight
- ● Conf - Mtgs - ET - Res - Exhib - Inf
- M 6,000 i, UK / 25 i, o'seas
- ¶ Early Education (Jnl) - 3;   NL - 3;   AR - 1; all ftm only.

British Association of Electrolysists Ltd
    2004 merged with the Institute of Electrolysis to form the **British
Institute & Association of Electrolysis**

British Association for Emergency Medicine
    in 2008 merged with the **College of Emergency Medicine**

**British Association of Endocrine & Thyroid Surgeons   (BAETS)
1980**
- NR Royal Victoria Infirmary, Queen Victoria Rd,
  NEWCASTLE upon TYNE, NE1 4LP.   (hsb)
  http://www.baes.info
  Hon Sec: Richard D Bliss
- ▲ Registered Charity
- ○ *M, *P; to promote the dissemination of education &
  information about endocrine & thyroid diseases particularly
  insofar as they may be treated by surgeons; to promote
  research
- < Assn Surgeons GB & I
- M i
- × 2007 British Association of Endocrine Surgeons

**British Association of European Pharmaceutical Distributors
(BAEPD)   1984**
- NR 4 Connaught Rd, Chingford, LONDON, E4 7DL.   (sb)
  020 8529 3646
  Sec: Catherine Evans
- ▲ Company Limited by Guarantee
- ○ *T; the importation of licensed pharmaceutical products from
  within the EU & their distribution into the supply chain in the
  UK
- M 20 i, 6 f, UK / 1 i, 1 f, o'seas

British Association for Fair Trade Shops   (BAFTS)   1996
- NR 9 Thames St, CHARLBURY, Oxon, OX7 3QL.   (hq)
  0786 675 9201
  email info@bafts.org.uk   http://www.bafts.org.uk
  Contact: Chris Davis
- ▲ Company Limited by Guarantee
- ○ *K, *T; to develop fair trade retailing; to raise profile of fair
  trade shops; to campaign on fair trade issues
- ● Conf - Inf
- < Intl Fedn for Alternative Trade (IFAT); Network of Eur Wld Shops
  (NEWS)
- M c 80 org
- ¶ NL;   AR; both ftm only.

British Association of Fastener Distributors   (BAFD)
- ■ Heathcote House, 136 Hagley Rd, Edgbaston, BIRMINGHAM,
  B16 9PN.   (hq)
  0121-521 0100   fax 0121-521 0101
  email callum@bafd.org   http://www.bafd.org
  Sec: Callum Pye
- ▲ Un-incorporated Society
- ○ *T; interests of all fastener distributors
- Gp Association of Stainless Fastener Distributors
- ● Conf - Mtgs - ET - Exhib - Stat - Lib
- < Eur Fastener Distribr Assn
- M 75 f
- ¶ News from BAFD - 2;   LM - 1; both ftm.

**British Association of Feed Supplement & Additives
Manufacturers   (BAFSAM)   1968**
- NR 238 Chester Rd, Hartford, NORTHWICH, Cheshire,
  CW8 1LW.   (hsb)
  01606 783314   fax 01606 783314
  email hwebafsam@onetel.com
  Sec Gen: Harry Evans
- ▲ Company Limited by Guarantee
- ○ *T; manufacturers of animal feed
- ● Mtgs - Consultees to FSA, DEFRA, VMD in all legislative matters
  in relation to animal nutrition
- < EU Food Additives & Premixtures Assn (FEFANA)
- M 20 f

© CBD Research Ltd · Beckenham · BR3 5JS · Tel 020 8650 7745 · Fax 020 8650 0768 · E-mail cbd@cbdresearch.com · www.cbdresearch.com

**British Association of Flower Essence Producers   (BAFEP)
2000**
- ■ PO Box 100, Exminster, EXETER, Devon, EX6 8YT.   (hsp)
  01392 832005   fax 01392 832005
  email info@bafep.com   http://www.bafep.com
  Hon Sec: Sue Lilly
- ▲ Un-incorporated Society
- Br 60; Brazil, Eire
- ○ *T; for producers of flower & all types of essences
- M 55 i, 5 f, UK / 2 f, o'seas
  (Sub: £25 i, £250+ f, UK / £50+ i. o'seas)
- ¶ The Bioneer (NL) - 4; ftm only.
  Guidelines on Essence Production; free.
  Note: formed by practitional members of the British Flower &
  Vibrational Essences Association to fight the political issues
  that have arisen

British Association in Forensic Medicine   (BAFM)   1951
- NR Dept of Forensic Medicine & Science, University College of
  Glasgow, GLASGOW, G12 8QQ.   (hsb)
  0141-330 4145
  http://www.bafm.org
  Hon Sec: Dr J Clark
- ▲ Un-incorporated Society
- ○ *P; to advance the study & practice of forensic pathology; to act
  as a negotiating & advisory body when required
- ● Conf
- M 135 i, UK / 35 i, o'seas

British Association of Forensic Odontology
- NR Morialta, Palmerston Rd, NEWHAVEN, E Sussex, BN9 0NS.
  01539 720923   fax 01539 737589
  http://www.bafo.org.uk
  Sec: Dr S Sampson

**British Association of Former United Nations Civil Servants
(BAFUNCS)   1977**
- NR Rydal House, 36 Manor Park Ave, PRINCES RISBOROUGH,
  Bucks, HP27 9AS.   (ed/p)
  01844 343652
  email tony.loftas@btinternet.com
  Newsletter Editor: Tony Loftas
- ▲ Un-incorporated Society
- Br 10 regions
- ○ *W; comradeship, fellowship and associated social activities
- ● Mtgs - VE
- < Fedn of Assns of Former UN Civil Servants (FAFICS)
- M 769 i, UK /c 76 i, o'seas
- ¶ NL - 2;   LM; both ftm.

British Association of Friends of Museums   (BAFM)   1973
- ■ West Lodge, Cotherstone, BARNARD CASTLE, Co Durham,
  DL12 9PF.   (hq)
  email admin@bafm.org.uk   http://www.bafm.org.uk
  Sec: Carol Lynn
- ▲ Registered Charity
- Br 330
- ○ *A, *N; 'the only national independent organisation for friends,
  volunteers & supporters of museums, galleries, archives,
  libraries, historic house gardens & parks, churches & other
  institutions preserving the UK's cultural heritage'
- ● Conf - Mtgs - SG - Inf - Lib - VE - LG
  Central source of inf: 'about Friends for Friends'
- < Wld Fedn of Friends of Museums
- M 97 i, 30 museums etc, 330 Friends gps (representing
  200,000 i)
- ¶ NL - 3.   Hbk for Friends.   Information Sheets 1-15 - irreg.
  Charter & Hbk for Volunteer Managers & Administrators.

**British Association of Golf Course Constructors   (BAGCC)
1981**
- ■ Savannah, 32 New Rd, RINGWOOD, Hants, BH24 3AU.
  (chmn/p)
  01425 475584   fax 01425 475643
  email brian.pierson@137openworld.com
  http://www.bagcc.org.uk
  Chmn: Brian D Pierson
- ▲ Un-incorporated Society
- ○ *T; golf course construction, remodelling & renovation
- Gp Golf course constructors (full members); Suppliers (associate
  members)
- ● Conf - Mtgs - Exhib - Inf
- M 18 members
- ¶ Folder of brochures of BAGCC members; free.

British Association of Green Crop Driers Ltd   (BAGCD)   1950
- ■ March Hares, Montagu Rd, Canwick, LINCOLN, LN4 2RW.
  (asa)
  01522 523322   fax 01522 568539
  email info@bagcd.org   http://www.bagcd.org
  Sec: Mrs Elizabeth Harding
- ▲ Company Limited by Guarantee
- ○ *T; to promote use of dried green crops for animal feed
- ● Conf - Mtgs - Inf - VE - LG
- < Commission Intersyndicale des Déshydrateurs Européens
- M [not stated]

**British Association of Head & Neck Oncologists   (BAHNO)
1968**
- NR Dept of Maxillofacial Surgery, Sunderland Royal Hospital,
  Kayll Rd, SUNDERLAND, SR4 7TP.   (hsb)
  0191-569 9132
  Hon Sec: Ian Martin
- ▲ Registered Charity
- ○ *P; to advance the understanding & treatment of head & neck
  cancer. Members are surgeons, oncologists, pathologists &
  other interested medical staff involved in the care &
  management of patients with head & neck cancer
- ● Conf - Mtgs - Res - SG
- M c 450 i, UK / 50 i, o'seas
- ¶ Abstracts of meetings incl in Clinical Oncology - 1.

**British Association of Health Services in Higher Education
(BAHSHE)   1947**
- ■ 35 Hazelwood Rd, Bush Hill Park, ENFIELD, Middx, EN1 1JG.
  (hq)
  020 8482 2412   fax 010 8482 2412
  email s.furmston@middx.ac.uk
  http://www.bahshe.demon.co.uk
  Admin Officer: Sandra Furmston
- ▲ Registered Charity
- ○ *W; health of students studying in universities & colleges in UK
- ● Conf

British Association of Homoeopathic Manufacturers   (BAHM)
- ■ 65 Church St, Langham, OAKHAM, Leics, LE15 7JE.
  (secretariat)
  01572 771115
  Sec: Penny Viner
- ▲ Un-incorporated Society
- ○ *T; to advance the knowledge & practice of homoeopathy; to
  maintain standards, research, quality control & development
  of homoeopathic medicines
- < Homoeopathic Devt Foundation
- M 6 f
  NOTE: is active only in a crisis; eg with a change of the
  licensing law

British Association of Homoeopathic Veterinary Surgeons (BAHVS) 1981

NR   103 Golf Drive, NUNEATON, Warks, CV11 6ND.   (hsp/b)
        07768 322075
        http://www.bahvs.com
        Hon Sec: Stuart Fritton
○   *L, *P, *V; to promote veterinary homoeopathy amongst the
        veterinary profession
●   Conf - ET - Res (clinical only) - SG - Inf
<   Intl Assn for Veterinary Homoeopathy
M   c 140 i
¶   NL - 2; ftm only.

British Association of Hospitality Accountants   (BAHA)   1969

■   Merley House Business Centre (suite 6), Merley House Lane,
        WIMBORNE, Dorset, BH21 3AA.   (hq)
        01202 889430   fax 01202 887969
        http://www.baha-uk.org
        Admin: Phillipa Graham
○   *P; interests of financial managers in the hotel, catering &
        leisure industry
●   Conf - Mtgs - ET - Exam - Advice
<   Chart Inst Mgt Accountants (CIMA) - for BAHA's training
        programme
M   550 i, UK / 150 i, o'seas
¶   BAHA Times (NL) - 10;   AR - 1; both ftm only.

British Association of Hotel Representatives   (BAHREP)

NR   127 New House Park, ST ALBANS, Herts, AL1 1UT.   (hsb)
        01727 812722
        Sec: Diana Hall
▲   Un-incorporated Society
○   *P
●   Mtgs - ET - Exhib - Inf - LG
M   60 i, 60 f

British Association for Human Identification   (BAHID)   2001

NR   2 Market Square, STONEHAVEN, Kincardineshire, AB39 2BT.
        (asa)
        01569 760022
        email info@bahid.org   http://www.bahid.org
        Treas: Mr Black
▲   Un-incorporated Society
○   *P; to bring together forensic practitioners & academics
        involved in the field of human identification & address
        common problems & develop research & communication
Gp   Forensic: Anthropology, Archaeology, Entomology, Pathology,
        Podiatry, Radiology;
        Facial analysis; Molecular genetics; Police; Anatomy
●   Conf - ET - Res - Current information on up-dated website
M   c 300 i, UK / c 60 i, o'seas
¶   [Textbook on Human ID; in preparation]

British Association for Immediate Care   (BASICS)   1977

■   Turret House, 2 Turret Lane, IPSWICH, Suffolk, IP4 1DL.   (hq)
        01473 218407   fax 01473 280585
        email admin@basics.org.uk   http://www.basics.org.uk
        Hon Sec: Anthony Kemp,   Chief Exec: Mrs Ruth Lloyd
▲   Registered Charity
Br   41 affiliated schemes
○   *W; to promote & improve all aspects of immediate care
        (provision of skilled medical help at the site of accidents,
        major incidents & other emergencies)
Gp   BASICS Education Ltd (provides courses on pre-hospital
        emergency care, Extricaton, Paediatic & others); International
        directorate
●   Conf - Mtgs - ET - Exam - Exhib - Stat - Inf - Lib - LG
M   c 1,300 i   (Sub: £88)
¶   NL - 3;   AR - 1; both ftm only.   Monographs; £10.

British Association for Information & Library Education & Research   (BAILER)   1962

■   Dept of Information Studies, University of Sheffield, Regent
        Court (room 230), 211 Portobello St, SHEFFIELD, S Yorks,
        S1 4DP.   (chmn/b)
        0114-222 2632
        http://www.bailer.org.uk
        Chmn: Prof Sheila Corrall
○   *E, *P; information & library studies education & research in the
        UK
Gp   Information policy; Information management; Records
        management
●   Conf - Mtgs - ET - Res
M   220 i
¶   Directory of Courses in Library & Information Studies in the
        UK - 1; free.

British Association for Irish Studies   (BAIS)   1985

NR   School of English, Communication & Philosophy, Humanities
        Building, Cardiff University, CARDIFF, CF10 3EU.   (sb)
        email connolly@cardiff.ac.uk
        Sec: Dr Claire Connolly
▲   Registered Charity
○   *E; promotion & support for Irish studies in the UK
●   Conf - ET - LG - Organisation of public lectures
M   c 300 i & f, UK / 30 i, o'seas
¶   Irish Studies Review - 3.   NL - 4.

British Association of Japanese Studies   (BAJS)   1974

NR   BAJS Secretariat, University of Essex, COLCHESTER, Essex,
        CO4 3SQ.
        01206 872543 (answerphone)   fax 01206 873408
        Exec Sec: Mrs Lynn Baird
○   *L
¶   NL -3;   Japan Forum - 3.

British Association of Journalists

■   89 Fleet St, LONDON, EC4Y 1DH.   (hq)
        020 7353 3003   fax 020 7353 2310
        email office@bajunion.org.uk
        Gen Sec: Steve Turner
○   *P, *U; raising the status & rewards of journalists: seeks to
        protect & improve fees for freelance members & pay,
        conditions & pensions for staff members
M   1,000 i, UK / 25 i, o'seas
¶   BAJ News (NL) - 4.

British Association of Korean Studies   (BAKS)   1983

■   c/o Dr J Grayson, School of East Asian Studies, University of
        Sheffield, SHEFFIELD, S Yorks, S10 2TN.
        http://www.baks.org.uk
        Pres; Dr J Grayson
▲   Un-incorporated Society
○   *L, *X; to promote, in the UK, the study & understanding of
        Korea
●   Conf
<   UK Area Studies Assn
M   59 i, UK / 8 i, o'seas
¶   Papers - 1-2 yrly; prices vary.

© CBD Research Ltd · Beckenham · BR3 5JS · Tel 020 8650 7745 · Fax 020 8650 0768 · E-mail cbd@cbdresearch.com · www.cbdresearch.com

British Association of Landscape Industries (BALI) 1972

■ Landscape House, STONELEIGH PARK, Warks, CV8 2LG. (hq)
0870 770 4971 fax 0870 779 4972
email contact@bali.org.uk http://www.bali.org.uk
Chief Exec Officer: Sandra Loton-Jones
▲ Company Limited by Guarantee
Br 9
○ *T; to represent UK firms undertaking landscaping, both interior
& exterior, & a wide range of associated suppliers
Gp Affiliates; Designers; Domestic; Grounds; Interiors;
Maintenance; Students
● Mtgs - ET - Exhib - Comp - Inf - VE - LG - Annual awards
ceremony
< Eur Landscape Contrs Assn (ELCA)
> Assn of Landscape Contrs Ireland (Northern & Southern) (ALCI)
M 54 i, 687 f, UK / 9 f, o'seas
¶ Landscape News - 4. Business News - 4;
Awards Brochure - 1; all ftm only.
Who's Who Directory - 1; ftm, £40 nm.

British Association of Leisure Parks, Piers & Attractions (BALPPA) 1936

NR 37 Tanner St (suite 12), LONDON, SE1 3LF. (hq)
020 7403 4455
http://www.balppa.org
▲ Company Limited by Guarantee
○ *T; for British private sector leisure parks, piers, attractions &
suppliers to the industry
M f

British Association for Literacy in Development (BALID)

NR 36 Causton St, LONDON, SW1P 4AU. (hq)
email admin@balid.org.uk http://www.balid.org.uk
Sec: Juliet McCaffery
▲ Un-incorporated Society
○ *E, *K, to promote literacy & numeracy for adults as an integral
part of human development; to increase awareness of the
relationship between literacy & numeracy & economic
development & social change
● Conf - Mtgs - Res
< UNESCO; Universities of: Pennsylvania, Brighton, London, East
Anglia & Sussex
> Education Action Intl; Nat Res & Devt Centre; Nottingham
University
M [not stated]
¶ Reports [on website].

British Association for Local History (BALH) 1982

NR PO Box 6549, Somersal Herbert, ASHBOURNE, Derbys,
DE6 5WH. (hq)
01283 585947
http://www.balh.co.uk
Business Mgr: A Jones
▲ Registered Charity; Un-incorporated Society
○ *L, *P; to promote the advancement of public education thrugh
the study & teaching of local history
● Conf - SG - Inf - VE
M c 2,300 i
¶ The Local Historian - 4. Local History News - 4.

British Association for Lung Research (BALR) 1982

NR c/o Dr N K Harrison, Respiratory Unit, Morriston Hospital,
SWANSEA, SA6 6NL. (hsb)
01792 7032131 fax 01792 703845
Chmn: Dr Kim Harrison
▲ Registered Charity
○ *P
● Conf - Mtgs
M c 350 i
¶ NL - 3; ftm only. LM.

British Association of Medical Hypnosis 2001

NR 28 Old Brompton Rd (suite 296), LONDON, SW7 3SS.
020 8998 4436
email rnp@medicalhypnotherapy.co.uk
Organising Sec: Dr Rumi Peynovska
○ *P
¶ European Journal of Clinical Hypnosis.

British Association of Medical Managers (BAMM) 1992

NR Petersgate House (3rd floor), 64 St Petersgate, STOCKPORT,
Cheshire, SK1 1HE. (hq)
0161-474 1141
email bamm@bamm.co.uk
Chief Exec: Dr Jenny Simpson
▲ Company Limited by Guarantee
○ *P; for clinicians in management who are part of the medical
profession
Gp Medical; Clinical governance
● Conf - Mtgs - ET - Res
M i

British Association of Mountain Guides (BMG) 1975

■ Siabod Cottage, CAPEL CURIG, Conwy, LL24 0ES.
(regd/office)
01690 720386 fax 01690 720248
email guiding@bmg.org.uk http://www.bmg.org.uk
Hon Sec: Libby Peter
▲ Company Limited by Guarantee
○ *P, *S; professional mountaineering services, mountain guiding,
rock climbing, ice climbing, alpine guiding, ski
mountaineering
● Mtgs - ET - Exam
< Intl Fedn of Mountain Guide Assns (IFMGA)
M 125 i, UK / 52 i, o'seas
¶ NL - 3; AR; both ftm.
Members' Directory; free (also available on website).

British Association of Nature Conservationists (BANC) 1997

NR Denton Wood Farm. Bedford Rd, NORTHAMPTON,
NN7 2EA. (memsec/b)
email banc@dentonwood.co.uk http://www.banc.org.uk
Mem Sec: Karen Cropper
▲ Company Limited by Guarantee, Registered Charity
○ *K; to advance nature conservation in the UK; to act as a
network for conservationists & people who care about the
natural world
M i & org
¶ Ecos: a review of conservation - 3; ftm.

British Association of Numismatic Societies (BANS) 1953

■ Dept of Numismatics, Manchester Museum, Oxford Rd,
MANCHESTER, M13 9PL. (hsb)
0161-275 2643
email phyllis.stoddart@manchester.ac.uk
http://www.coinclubs.freeserve.co.uk
Hon Sec: Phyllis Stoddart
▲ Un-incorporated Society
Br 60
○ *N; to promote & coordinate interest & research by local &
regional societies
● Conf - Res - SG - Inf - PL - VE
M c 2,000 i
¶ Doris Stockwell Memorial Papers - irreg; price varies.

British Association for Nutritional Therapy (BANT) 1997
NR 27 Old Gloucester St, LONDON, WC1N 3XX. (mail address)
0870 606 1284 fax 0870 606 1284
email theadministrator@bant.org.uk
http://www.bant.org.uk
Sec: Susan McGinty
▲ Company Limited by Guarantee
○ *P; the application of nutrition science in the promotion of
optimum health & peak performance, disease prevention &
patient care
● Conf - ET
M c 1,500 i
¶ The BANT Membership NL - 4.

British Association of Occupational Therapists Ltd (BAOT/ COT) 1932
NR 106-114 Borough High St, LONDON, SE1 1LB. (hq)
020 7357 6480 fax 020 7450 2299
http://www.cot.org.uk
Sec: Julia Scott
▲ Company Limited by Guarantee; Registered Charity
○ *P, *U; for all occupational therapy staff & students in the UK
Gp College of Occupational Therapists; Association of
Occupational Therapists in Mental Health; Housing; HIV/
AIDS oncology, palliative care & education; Neurology; Rapid
intervention; Paediatric; Rheumatology; Work practice &
productivity; Working with people with learning disabilities;
Independent practice; Older people; Trauma & orthopaedics
● Conf - Mtgs - ET - Comp - Res - Exhib - SG - Lib - Empl - LG
< Wld Fedn of Occupational Therapists (WFOT); Coun of
Occupational Therapists for the Eur Countries (COTEC)
M 27,000 i, UK / 500 i, o'seas
¶ British Journal of Occupational Therapy - 12; ftm, £153 nm.
Occupational Therapy News - 12; ftm. AR; free.
Publications list on website.

British Association of Oral & Maxillofacial Surgeons (BAOMS) 1962
NR at the Royal College of Surgeons, 35-43 Lincoln's Inn Fields,
LONDON, WC2A 3PE. (hq)
020 7405 8074 fax 020 7430 9997
○ *L, *P; mouth, jaws, face & neck surgery
● Conf - Mtgs - ET - Res - SG
M 797 i, UK / 303 i, o'seas
¶ British Journal of Oral & Maxillofacial Surgery - 6; ftm.

British Association of Otorhinolaryngologists - Head & Neck Surgeons (ENT.UK (BAO-HNS)) 1943
■ at the Royal College of Surgeons, 35-43 Lincoln's Inn Fields,
LONDON, WC2A 3PE. (hq)
020 7404 8373 fax 020 7404 4200
email entuk@entuk.org http://www.entuk.org
Hon Sec: Prof Janet A Wilson,
Admin Mgr: Nechama Lewis
▲ Registered Charity
○ *L, *M, *P; to promote education research & audit & works to
achieve the highest standards of medical & surgical practice
in otology, laryngology, rhinology & head & neck surgery
● Conf - Mtgs - ET - Exhib - Inf - LG
> Brit Otology, Hearing & Balance Gp
M 1,404 i, UK / 26 i, o'seas
¶ NL - 6; AR; LM & Constitution - irreg; all ftm only.
Note: in Autumn 2003 adopted the working name of ENT.UK

British Association for Paediatric Nephrology
a group of the **Royal College of Paediatrics & Child Health**

British Association of Paediatric Surgeons (BAPS) 1954
NR at the Royal College of Surgeons, 35-43 Lincoln's Inn Fields,
LONDON, WC2A 3PE. (hq)
020 7312 6638
Sec: Richard Stewart
○ *P
● Conf - Mtgs - Exhib - Inf
M 140 i, UK / 460 i, o'seas
¶ Jnl of Paediatric Surgery - 6; NL - 4; LM - 1; all ftm.

British Association of Paintings Conservator-Restorers (BAPCR) 1943
■ PO Box 258, NORWICH, Norfolk, NR13 4WY. (sb)
01603 516237 fax 01603 510985
email secretary@bapcr.org.uk http://www.bapcr.org.uk
Sec: Lucy Tetlow
▲ Un-incorporated Society
○ *A, *P; conservation & restoration of paintings
● Conf - Mtgs - ET - Exam - Exhib - Comp - VE
< Intl Inst for Consvn (IIC); Scot Soc for Consvn &
Restoration (SSCR); Inst of Paper Consvn (IPC)
M 400 i, UK / 30 i, o'seas
(Sub: £45)
¶ The Picture Restorer (Jnl) - 2; ftm, £3.50 each nm.
Conference preprints.

British Association of Paper Historians (BAPH) 1989
■ 27 North End, Longhaughton, ALNWICK, Northumberland,
NE66 3JG. (memsec/p)
01665 577988
http://www.baph.org.uk
Littlefield, Christmas Common, WATLINGTON, Oxon,
OX45 5HR. (chmn/p)
Sec: Ian Hendry
▲ Un-incorporated Society
○ *L; to promote all aspects of the study of paper & papermaking
history
● Conf - Mtgs - VE
M 170 i, 37 f, UK / 40 i, 18 f, o'seas
¶ The Quarterly (Jnl) - 4. LM - 1.
BAPH News (NL) - 4. Conference Report - 1.

British Association for Performing Arts Medicine (BAPAM) 1984
NR Totara Park House (4th floor), 34-36 Gray's Inn Rd, LONDON,
WC1X 8HR. (hq)
020 7404 5888 fax 020 7404 3222
email admin@bapam.org.uk
http://www.bapam.org.uk
Chief Exec: Naomi Wayne
▲ Registered Charity
○ *K, *P; to ensure the highest standards of medical care for
those involved in the performing arts; to monitor the
incidence of performing arts injuries & to record the way in
which they are treated
● Conf - ET - Res
M 350 i, 5 f, UK / 5 i, o'seas
¶ Jnl - 2; NL - 4; both ftm only.

British Association of Perinatal Medicine (BAPM) 1976
■ 5-11 Theobalds Rd, LONDON, WC1X 8SH. (hq)
020 7092 6085 fax 020 7092 6001
email bapm@rcpch.ac.uk http://www.bapm.org
Hon Sec: Dr Alan Bryan Gill
▲ Registered Charity
○ *M, *P; to support newborn babies & their families by providing
services that help all those involved in perinatal practice; to
improve the standards of perinatal care in the British Isles
Gp Neonatologists; Obstetricians; Nurses; Midwives; Dietitians
● Conf - Mtgs - ET - SG - LG
< R Coll Paediatrics & Child Health; R Coll Obstetricians &
Gynaecologists
M 850 i, UK / 50 i, o'seas
(Sub: £100 medical, £50 non-medical)
¶ NL - 3; AR - 1; both ftm.

© CBD Research Ltd · Beckenham · BR3 5JS · Tel 020 8650 7745 · Fax 020 8650 0768 · E-mail cbd@cbdresearch.com · www.cbdresearch.com

British Association for the Person-Centred Approach (BAPCA) 1989
NR PO Box 143, ROSS-on-WYE, Herefs, HR9 9AH.
    01989 763863
    email enquiries@bapca.org.uk   http://www.bapca.org.uk

British Association of Pharmaceutical Physicians (BrAPP)
NR Royal Station Court, Station Rd, Twyford, READING, Berks,
    RG10 9NF.
    0118-934 1943
    Assn Mgr: Elizabeth Langley
○ *P
¶ Jnl - 6.

British Association of Pharmaceutical Wholesalers (BAPW) 1966
■ 90 Long Acre, LONDON, WC2E 9RA.   (hq)
    020 7031 0590   fax 020 7031 0591
    email mail@bapw.net   http://www.bapw.net
    Sec: Kayleigh Ross
▲ Company Limited by Guarantee
○ *T; to secure the safest & most cost effective distribution of a
    comprehensive range of healthcare products & related
    services; to advance efficient healthcare management
● Conf - SG - Inf - LG
< Intl Fedn of Pharmaceutical Wholesalers; Groupement Intl de la
    Réparation Pharmaceutique des Pays de la CE; Assn of the
    Brit Pharmaceutical Ind
M 11 f (full), 43 f (associate), 3 f (affiliate)

British Association for Physical Training (BAPT) 1919
NR 14 Moorside Close, WEYMOUTH, Dorset, DT4 7RQ.
    (jt/chmn/p)
    01305 784637
    email patgordon@dt47rq.freeserve.co.uk
    Jt Chmn: Gordon Knowles
▲ Registered Charity
○ *P; promotion of physical education
M i
¶ Bulletin - 3; ftm only.

British Association of Picture Libraries & Agencies (BAPLA) 1975
NR 18 Vine Hill, LONDON, EC1R 5DZ.   (hq)
    020 7713 1780
▲ Company Limited by Guarantee
○ *T, *P; issues relevant to the picture library industry: copyright
    laws & rights, technology, standards, digital imagery,
    archiving
Gp Collective management; Copyright; Technology - digital images
● Conf - Mtgs - ET - Res - Exhib - SG - PL - VE - LG
M 4 i, 450 f, UK / 2 f, o'seas
¶ Lightbox - 4.   Weekly NL - 52.
    BAPLA Directory of Picture Libraries & Agencies - 1.

British Association of Plastic, Reconstructive & Aesthetic Surgeons (BAPRAS) 1946
■ at the Royal College of Surgeons, 35-43 Lincoln's Inn Fields,
    LONDON, WC2A 3PE.   (hq)
    020 7831 5161   fax 020 7831 4041
    email secretariat@bapras.co.uk
    http://www.bapras.co.uk
    Hon Sec: D J Coleman
▲ Company Limited by Guarantee, Registered Charity
○ *L, *M, *P, *Q; promotion & development of plastic surgery; to
    advance education in the field
Gp Breast special interest; Head & neck; Overseas service of
    training
● Conf - Mtgs - ET - Res
< Brit Assn of Aesthetic Plastic Surgeons (BAAPS)
M 570 i, UK / 160 i, o'seas
¶ Jnl of Plastic, Reconstructive & Aesthetic Surgery - 12; ftm.
✕ 2006 British Association of Plastic Surgeons

British Association of Play Therapists (BAPT) 1992
■ 1 Beacon Mews, South Rd, WEYBRIDGE, Surrey, KT13 9DZ.
    (admin/asst/p)
    01932 828638
    email info@bapt.uk.com   http://www.bapt.uk.com
    Chmn: Mary Carden
○ *P; to promote & develop standards of training in play therapy
● Conf - Mtgs - Res - SG - Inf
M c 350 i
¶ NL - 4; ftm only.   Jnl for Play Therapy - 1.
    What is Play Therapy? (leaflet for parents & carers).
    What is Play Therapy? (booklet for children).
    A Guide to Play Therapy.

British Association of Pool Table Operators (BAPTO) 1975
NR Silverdale, Oakfield Close, SHREWSBURY, Shropshire,
    SY3 8AB.   (chmn/p)
    01743 464232
    http://www.bapto.org.uk
    Chmn: Alan Boswell
▲ Company Limited by Guarantee
○ *T; to promote the game of pool
● Conf - Mtgs - ET - Exam - Comp - Stat - Inf
M 43 f, UK / 3 f, o'seas

British Association for Print & Communication (BAPC) 1979
■ Catalyst House / 720 Centennial Court, Centennial Park,
    ELSTREE, Herts, WD6 3SY.   (hq)
    020 8736 5862   fax 020 8224 9090
    email info@bapc.org.uk   http://www.bapc.co.uk
    Dir: Tony Honnor,   Chmn & CEO: Sidney Bobb
▲ Company Limited by Guarantee
○ *T; for the creative industry, including graphic arts, print &
    communication sectors
● Conf - Mtgs - ET - Res - Exhib - Stat
M 3,800 f
¶ Bulletin [NL] - 6; free.

British Association of Prosthetists & Orthotists (BAPO) 1994
■ Sir James Clark Building, Abbeymill Business Centre, PAISLEY,
    Renfrewshire, PA1 1TJ.   (hq)
    0141-561 7217   fax 0141-561 7218
    email enquiries@bapo.com   http://www.bapo.org
    Chmn: Steve Mottram
▲ Un-incorporated Society
○ *M, *P; Prosthetics: healthcare involved in fitting prostheses
    (artificial limbs); Orthotics: healthcare in fitting orthoses
    (braces, splints & other devices externally / to the human
    body)
● Conf - Mtgs - ET - Exhib - SG - Inf - LG
< Health Professions Coun - Regulatory Body
M 734 i, UK / 22 i, o'seas
¶ BAPOMAG - 4; ftm, £20 yr nm.

British Association for Psychological Type (BAPT) 1989
■ 17 Royal Crescent, CHELTENHAM, Glos, GL50 3DA.   (sp)
    01242 282990
    email office@bapt.org.uk   http://www.bapt.org.uk
    Sec: Bill Davies
▲ Registered Charity
○ *L; Jungian psychological type theory
    no further information supplied

British Association for Psychopharmacology (BAP) 1974
■ 36 Cambridge Place, Hills Rd, CAMBRIDGE, CB2 1NS.   (hq)
    01223 358395   fax 01223 321268
    email susan@bap.org.uk   http://www.bap.org.uk
    Exec Officer: Mrs Susan Chandler (01223 358428)
▲ Registered Charity
○ *L; to advance education & research in the science of
    psychopharmacology both clinical & experimental
● Conf - Mtgs - ET
M 850 i, UK / 150 i, o'seas
¶ Jnl of Psychopharmacology - 4.   NL - 4; ftm.

British Association of Psychotherapists   (BAP)   1951
NR   37 Mapesbury Rd, LONDON, NW2 4HJ.   (hq)
          020 8452 9823   fax 020 8452 0310
          email mail@bap-psychotherapy.org
          http://www.bap-psychotherapy.org
          Chief Exec: Mrs Elise Ormerod
          Publicity Officer: Dr Tim Fox
▲   Registered Charity
○   *E, *P; a training organisation for adult, child & adolescent
          psychoanalytic & Jungian analytic psychotherapy; to offer
          assessment & where appropriate, treatment for people
          seeking individual psychotherapy.
          The BAP aims to provide information to the public & to the
          caring professions, to make psychotherapy more widely
          available; to maintain standards in training & clinical practice
          & professional conduct
Gp   Jungian analytic; Psychoanalytic (adult); Psychoanalytic (child &
          adolescent)
●   Conf - Mtgs - ET - Res - SG - Lib - Assessment for, & provision
          of, psychotherapy
<   Assn Child Psychotherapists (ACP); Brit Confedn of
          Psychotherapists (BCP); Intl Assn of Analytical
          Psychology (IAAP)
M   500 i, UK / 12 i, o'seas
¶   Jnl - 2; ftm, £27 i, £55 instns, nm.

**British Association of Public Safety Communications Officers
(BAPCO)   1994**
NR   PO Box 374, LINCOLN, LN1 1FY.
          01522 575542
          http://www.bapco.org.uk
          Chief Exec: Ken Mott
○   *P; the development of communications & supporting
          information technologies to enhance delivery of public safety
          & civil contingency services
M   i, f & org

**British Association for the Purebred Spanish Horse   (BAPSH)
1982**
NR   Wrancarr Mill, Wrancarr Lane, Moss, DONCASTER, S Yorks,
          DN6 0DP.   (hsp)
          01302 888986
          http://www.bapsh.co.uk
          Chmn: Amanda Tomlinson
○   *B
●   Exhib
<   Jefatura de Cria Caballar; FICCE
M   c 400 i
¶   Pura Raza Española - 4; ftm.

British Association of Record Dealers
          since July 2006 the **Entertainment Retailers Association**

**British Association of Remote Sensing Companies   (BARSC)
1985**
NR   c/o Vega Group plc, 2 Falcon Way, Shire Park,
          WELWYN GARDEN CITY, Herts, AL7 1TW.   (hsb)
          01707 391999
          http://www.barsc.org.uk
          Exec Sec: Gareth Davies
▲   Un-incorporated Society
○   *T; companies undertaking activities directly connected with
          remote sensing (the collection of information about physical
          objects & the environment from remote platforms - aircraft &
          satellites)
Gp   Applications working gp - focus on commercial opportunities to
          exploit earth observation data
●   Conf - Mtgs - Exhib - Expt - LG - Liaison European agencies
M   18 f

British Association of Removers   (BAR)   1900
NR   Tangent House, 62 Exchange Rd, WATFORD, Herts,
          WD18 0TG.   (hq)
          01923 699480   fax 01923 699481
          email info@bar.co.uk   http://www.bar.co.uk
          Gen Sec: Robert D Syers
▲   Company Limited by Guarantee
○   *T; for the professional moving industry; to maintain standards
          for the benefit of members & their customers
Gp   National & European domestic moves; Overseas; Commercial
●   Conf - Mtgs - ET - Exam - Exhib - Comp - SG - Inf - VE - LG
<   Fedn Eur Moving Assns (FEDEMAC); Fedn Intl Movers (FIDI)
M   650 f, UK / 250 f, o'seas
¶   Removals & Storage - 12.

British Association Representing Breeders
          since 2006 **British Association of Rose Breeders**

**British Association for Research Quality Assurance   (BARQA)
1977**
NR   3 Wherry Lane, IPSWICH, Suffolk, IP4 1LG.   (hq)
          01473 221411
          Assn Mgr: David Weller
▲   Company Limited by Guarantee
○   *P; to evaluate & appraise the quality assurance aspects of
          regulations, guidelines & principles, both national &
          international, related to studies conducted on chemicals,
          biologicals & devices which affect humans, animals & the
          environment known as good laboratory practice (GLP), good
          clinical practice (GCP) & good manufacturing practice (GMP)
Gp   C'ees: Meetings; Education & training; Good clinical practice;
          Good manufacturing practice; Animal health; Field studies;
          Computing; Good laboratory practice; Publications
●   Conf - Mtgs - ET - Exam - Comp - SG - Inf
<   Eur Quality Assurance Soc (EQAS); US Soc of Quality
          Assurance (SQA); Japan Soc of Quality Assurance (JSQA)
M   1,100 i, UK / 500 i, o'seas
¶   Quasar Magazine - 4;   AR - 1;
          Members' Directory - 1;   all ftm only.

British Association of Rose Breeders   (BARB)   1973
■   17 Wren Centre, Westbourne Rd, EMSWORTH, Hants,
          PO10 7SU.   (hq)
          01243 389532   fax 01243 389509
          email info@barbuk.org.uk   http://www.rosesuk.com/
          barb/
          Pres: Colin Dickson,   Gen Mgr: Ian Kennedy
▲   Un-incorporated Society
○   *H, *T; to encourage, improve & extend the introduction &
          growing of roses & other ornamental plants under Plant-
          Breeders' Rights
Gp   Plant breeders; Roses, Rose growers
●   Mtgs - Exhib - Stat - Inf - Rose trials - International liaison
M   17 f
¶   Ybk (listing protected plants available through BARB) - 1; free.
×   2006 British Association Representing Breeders

British Association of Seating Equipment Suppliers   (BASES)
■   Federation House, STONELEIGH PARK, Warks, CV8 2RF.   (hq)
          024 7641 4999   fax 024 7641 4990
          email bases@sportsandplay.com
          http://www.basesuk.com
▲   Company Limited by Guarantee
○   *T; manufacturers & suppliers of various types of audience
          seating
●   Mtgs - Inf - LG
<   a group of the Fedn of Sports & Play Assns (FSPA)
M   6 f

© CBD Research Ltd · Beckenham · BR3 5JS · Tel 020 8650 7745 · Fax 020 8650 0768 · E-mail cbd@cbdresearch.com · www.cbdresearch.com

British Association of Seed Analysts   (BASA)   1925
- ■   Confederation House, East of England Showground, PETERBOROUGH, PE2 6XE.   (hq)
  01733 385271   fax 01733 385270
  email paul.rooke@agindustries.org.uk
  Sec: Paul Rooke
- ○   *T; advancement of seed testing & seed testing stations
- ●   Conf - Mtgs - Inf - VE
- <   UK Agricl Supply Tr Assn
- M   80 i
- ¶   e-newsletters

British Association of Seed Producers
- NR   Unit 3, Burcot Farm, East Stratton, WINCHESTER, Hants, SO21 3DZ.
  01962 774432
  Contact: W Welling
- ○   *T

British Association for Service to the Elderly   (BASE)   1974
- NR   c/o James Lewis, Community Sciences Centre, Northern General Hospital NHS Trust, Herries Rd, SHEFFIELD, S Yorks, S5 7AU.   (hq)
  0845 130 0675
  email enquiries@base.org.uk   http://www.base.org.uk
- ▲   Registered Charity
- Br   4
- ○   *W; to provide education & training for all those working with older people, vulnerable adults & their carers in health & social care
- ●   ET
- M   720 i, 100 f
- ¶   Quality in Agency - 4; £55 m.

British Association of Settlements & Social Action Centres (BASSAC)   1920
- NR   33 Corsham St, LONDON, N1 6DR.   (hq)
  0845 241 0375
  Contact: Carole McQueen
- ▲   Company Limited by Guarantee; Registered Charity
- ○   *W; 'is a national organisation of multi-purpose urban centres committed to helping local communities to bring about social change'
- M   c100 centres
- ¶   Monthly ENews - 10; ftm.   BASSAC Directory - 1.

British Association for Sexual Health & HIV   (BASHH)   1922
- ■   c/o Royal Society of Medicine, 1 Wimpole St, LONDON, W1G 0AE.   (hq)
  020 7290 2968   fax 020 7290 2989
  email bashh@rsm.ac.uk   http://www.bashh.org
  Hon Sec: Dr Janette Clarke
- ▲   Registered Charity
- Br   17
- ○   *L, *M; to promote the study of the art & science of diagnosing & treating sexually transmitted infections, including HIV & other sexual health problems
- Gp   British Co-operative Clinical Group; Genito-Urinary Physicians Colposcopy Group
  Special interest: Adolescence, Bacterial, Herpes simplex virus, HIV, HPV, Sexual dysfunction
- ●   Conf - Mtgs - ET - Res - Lib - LG
- M   900 i, UK / 72 i, o'seas
- ¶   NL -3/5.
  Guidelines - irreg;   AR;   both free.

British Association for Sexual & Relationship Therapy (BASRT)   1972
- ■   PO Box 13686, LONDON, SW20 9ZH.   (mail address)
  020 8543 2707   fax 020 8543 2707
  email info@basrt.org.uk   http://www.basrt.org.uk
  Chief Exec Officer: Corinna Furse
- ▲   Company Limited by Guarantee; Registered Charity
- ○   *P; for clinicians & therapists who treat sexual & relationship problems
- ●   Conf - ET - Res - Approves training courses in sex therapy - Provides list of local therapists
- M   700 i, UK / 30 i, o'seas
- ¶   Sexual & Relationship Therapy - 3; ftm.

British Association of Ship Suppliers   (BASS)   1906
- NR   The Moorings, Heron Lakes, Routh, BEVERLEY, E Yorks, HU17 9SL.   (sp)
  01964 544554
  email britship@gmx.co.uk   http://www.bassweb.co.uk
  Sec: Mrs E A Marchant
- ○   *T
- ●   Mtgs - SG - Inf - VE
- <   Intl Ship Suppliers Assn
- M   55 f
- ¶   LM - 1; ftm, £5 nm.

British Association for Shooting & Conservation   (BASC)   1908
- ■   Marford Mill, Rossett, WREXHAM, Denbighshire, LL12 0HL. (hq)
  01244 573000   fax 01244 573013
  email enq@basc.org.uk   http://www.basc.org.uk
  Chief Exec: John Swift
- ▲   Industrial & Provident Society
- Br   8
- ○   *S; national representative body for sporting & shooting
- Gp   Firearms; Gamekeeping & gameshooting; Land management & conservation; Research; Shooting standards; Stalking; Wildfowling
- ●   Conf - Et - Exam - Res - Exhib - Inf - Lib - PL - LG
- <   F Assn des Chasseurs Eur (FACE)
- M   127,000 i
  (Sub: £62)
- ¶   Shooting & Conservation (Jnl) - 6; ftm, £4.25 nm.
  The Custodian (for Gamekeepers) - 4, ftm, £3 nm.
  Wildfowling - 2; ftm, £2 nm.

British Association of Ski Patrollers
alternative name of **BASP UK Ltd**

British Association of Skin Camouflage   (BASC)   1986
- ■   PO Box 202, MACCLESFIELD, Cheshire, SK11 6FP.   (asa)
  01625 871129
  email basc9@hotmail.com
  http://www.skin-camouflage.net
  Chmn: Liz Hawkins
- ▲   Registered Charity
- ○   *P; to promote, support & further the remedial technique of skin camouflage, for the relief of those who need to be restored to confidence in a normal appearance, by means of prescribable camouflage creams
- ●   Conf - Mtgs - ET - Inf
- M   c 60 i, UK
- ¶   NL - 4; free.

British Association for Slavonic & East European Studies (BASEES)   1953
- NR   Wadham College, OXFORD, OX1 3BN.   (infoffr/b)
  Inf Officer: Dr Philip Bullock
- ▲   Registered Charity
- ○   *L; study of language & literature, history, politics, economics & society of the former USSR & Eastern Europe
- M   c 650 i
- ¶   NL - 3; ftm only.

British Association of Snowsport Instructors (BASI) 1913
■ Glenmore, AVIEMORE, Inverness-shire, PH22 1QU. (hq)
  01479 861717 fax 01479 861718
  email basi@basi.org.uk http://www.basi.org.uk
  Chief Exec: Peter Kuwall
▲ Company Limited by Guarantee
○ *P, *S; the UK authority for training & grading professional
  snowsport instructors
Gp Skiing: Alpine, Nordic, Telemark, Adaptive (disabled);
  Snowboarding
● ET - Exam
M c 4,000 i
¶ BASI News (Jnl) - 2; BASI Manual - 1;
  BASI Alpine Manual - 2 yrly; all ftm only.

British Association of Social Workers (BASW) 1970
■ 16 Kent St, BIRMINGHAM, B5 6RD. (hq)
  0121-622 3911 fax 0121-622 4860
  email info@basw.co.uk http://www.basw.co.uk
  Chief Exec: Ian Johnston
▲ Company Limited by Guarantee; Registered Charity
○ *P; to promote an active involvement of members who share a
  commitment to good social work practice & uphold the code
  of ethics of the association
● Conf - Mtgs - ET - Exhib - SG - Policy reports - Professional
  publications
< Intl Fedn of Social Work
M 11,200 i
¶ British Jnl of Social Work - 8. Practice (Jnl) - 4.
  Professional Social Work - 12; ftm, corporate subscription
  only nm.

British Association for South Asian Studies (BASAS) 1972
NR 14 Stephenson Way, LONDON, NW1 2HD. (hq)
  email ssas@btconnect.com http://www.basas.ac.uk
  Asst Sec: Brenda McGregor
▲ Registered Charity
○ *L; to promote & support South Asian studies in Britain
● Conf - Mtgs - Res
< British Academy
¶ BASAS Bulletin (NL) - 1
× 2007 (1 October) Society for South Asian Studies (merged)

British Association of Spinal Surgeons
  a specialist society of the **British Orthopaedic Association**

**British Association of Sport & Exercise Medicine (BASEM)
1952**
NR Hutton Business Centre (suite 1C), Bentley Rd, DONCASTER,
  S Yorks, DN5 9QP. (hq)
  01302 822300 fax 01302 822300
  email basemcentral@basem.co.uk
  http://www.basem.co.uk
  Mgr: Katy Jones
▲ Company Limited by Guarantee; Registered Charity
Br 9 regions in England; Scotland, Wales
○ *S; for sports orientated consultants & dental surgeons, GPs,
  chartered physiotherapists, educationalists, osteopaths,
  podiatrists (sports medics & paramedics), veterinary
  surgeons, chiropodists, pure & applied scientists
● Conf - ET
< Intl Fedn of Sports Medicine; Eur Fedn of Sports Medicine
M 1,000 i, UK / 100 i, o'seas
¶ British Jnl of Sports Medicine - 6.

**British Association of Sport & Exercise Sciences (BASES)
1985**
■ BASES - GO7-GO8 Leeds Metropolitan University, Carnegie
  Faculty of Sport & Education, Fairfax Hall, Headingley
  Campus Beckett Park, LEEDS, LS6 3QS. (hq)
  0113-283 6162 fax 0113-283 6162 (tel first)
  email info@bases.org.uk http://www.bases.org.uk
  Chmn: Prof Craig Mahoney
  Hon Sec: Prof Edward Winter
▲ Company Limited by Guarantee
○ *P, *S; to promote excellence in sport & exercise sciences
  through evidence-based practice
Gp Psychology; Physiology; Bio-mechanics; Interdisciplinary
● Conf - Mtgs - ET - Res - Exhib - Stat
M 3,300 i
¶ The Sport & Exercise Scientist - 4; m only [various rates].

British Association for Sports & Law Ltd (NASL) 1992
■ c/o The School of Law, King's College London, Strand,
  LONDON, WC2R 2LS. (admin/b)
  020 7848 2278 fax 020 7848 2788
  email basl@kcl.co.uk http://www.britishsportslaw.org
  Admin: Lorraine Stylianou
▲ Company Limited by Guarantee
○ *P
● Conf
M i & f
  (Sub: £164.50 i, £822.50 f)
¶ Sport & the Law Jnl - 3; ftm only.

British Association of State English Language Teaching
  since 12 May 2004 **English UK**

British Association of Steelbands (BAS) 1995
■ 20 Queensbury Road, WEMBLEY, Middx, HA0 1LR. (hsp)
  07956 546724
  email debi@panpodium.com
  http://www.panpodium.com
  Hon Sec: Debi Gardner
▲ Company Limited by Guarantee
○ *D
● Conf - Mtgs - ET - Comp - Acts as booking agency
M 10 i, 43 org, UK / 2 org, o'seas
¶ Panpodium (Jnl) - 2; ftm, £3 yr nm.

**British Association for the Study of Community Dentistry
(BASCD) 1974**
■ KCL Dental Institute, Denmark Hill, LONDON, SE5 9RDS
  (hsb)
  020 3299 3840 fax 020 2399 3267
  email liana.zoitopoulos@kch.nhs.uk
  http://www.bascd.org
  Hon Sec: Dr Liana Zoitopoulos
○ *L, *M; study, research & teaching of all aspects of dentistry in
  the community
Gp Community clinical practice; Education; Epidemiology
● Conf - ET - Res
< Eur Assn Dental Public Health
M 500 i
¶ Community Dental Health - 4; £50 m, £88 nm (EU).

British Association for the Study of Headache (BASH) 1992
■ Dept of Neurology, Hull Royal Infirmary, Anlaby Rd, HULL,
  E Yorks, HU3 2JZ. (regd off)
  http://www.bash.org.uk
  Vice Chmn: Dr Fayyaz Ahmed
▲ Company Limited by Guarantee; Registered Charity
○ *M; to relieve persons suffering from headache by the
  advancement of scientific study into that condition
Gp Management guidelines writing c'ee;
  Working gps: Organisation of headache services; Education
● Conf - ET - Res - LG
< Intl Headache Soc; Eur Headache Fedn

© CBD Research Ltd · Beckenham · BR3 5JS · Tel 020 8650 7745 · Fax 020 8650 0768 · E-mail cbd@cbdresearch.com · www.cbdresearch.com

British Association for the Study & Prevention of Child Abuse & Neglect   (BASPCAN)   1975
- ■   17 Priory St, YORK, YO1 6ET.   (hq)
    01904 613605   fax 01904 642239
    email baspcan@baspcan.org.uk
    http://www.baspcan.org.uk
    Chmn: Jonathan Picken
    Nat Office Mgr: Judy Sanderson
- ▲   Registered Charity
- Br   10
- ○   *P
- ●   Conf - ET - Res - SG - Inf - LG
- <   Intl Soc for the Study & Prevention of Child Abuse & Neglect
- M   1,590 i, 50 f, UK / 38 i, 3 f, o'seas
- ¶   Child Abuse Review - 6; ftm.
    BASPCAN News - 4; ftm.

British Association for the Study of Religions   (BASR)   1954
- NR   Dept of Religious Studies, Arts Faculty, The Open University,
    Walton Hall, MILTON KEYNES, Bucks, MK7 6AA.   (hsb)
    01908 654033   fax 01908 653750
    email g.harvey@open.ac.uk
    http://www.basr.open.ac.uk
    Hon Sec: Dr Graham Harvey
- ▲   Registered Charity
- ○   *L; to promote the academic study of religions
- ●   Conf
- <   Intl Assn for the History of Religions; Eur Assn for the Study of Religions
- M   200 i, UK / 10 i, o'seas
- ¶   Bulletin - 3; ftm only.

British Association for Supported Employment   (BASE)   2006
- ■   Unit 26 Sudmeadow Rd, Hempsted, GLOUCESTER, Glos, GL2 5HS.   (regd/office)
    0844 561 7445   fax 0844 561 7441
    email admin@base-uk.org   http://www.base-uk.org
    Org Sec: Christopher Wise
- ▲   Company Limited by Guarantee; Registered Charity
- ○   *K; promotion & development of supported employment in order to enable people with a disability to be able to succeed in employment
- Gp   Supported business interest group
- ●   Conf - Mtgs - ET - SG - Inf
- <   Eur U of Supported Employment
- M   200 f
    (Sub: £250)
- ×   2006 (Association for Supported Employment
    (National Association of Supported Employment

British Association for Surgery of the Knee
    a specialist society of the **British Orthopaedic Association**

British Association of Symphonic Bands & Wind Ensembles (BASBWE)   1981
- ■   Fron, LLANSADWRN, Anglesey, LL59 5SL.   (mem/sec)
    01248 811285
    http://www.basbwe.org
    Editor: Richard Edwards
- ▲   Un-incorporated Society
- ○   *D; to support wind band music in the UK by helping the formation of new bands
- M   i, f & org
- ¶   Winds - 4; ftm.   LM - 1; ftm only.
    Leaflets Series - 1; ftm.

British Association of Teachers of Conservative Dentistry
- NR   University of Dundee Dental School, Park Place, DUNDEE, DD1 4HN.
    01382 635984
    Sec: Dr D Ricketts
- ○   *P

British Association of Teachers of Dancing   (BATD)   1892
- ■   23 Marywood Sq, GLASGOW, G41 2BP.   (hq)
    0141-423 4029   fax 0141-423 0677
    email enquiries@batd.co.uk   http://www.batd.co.uk
    Gen Sec: Mrs Katrina Allan
- ▲   Registered Friendly Society
- Br   8; Canada, USA.
- ○   *D, *P; all forms of dancing
- ●   Conf - Mtgs - ET - Exam - Exhib - Comp - Stat - Inf - VE
- <   Stage Dance Council Intl; Brit Dance Council; Scot Official Bd of Highland Dancing; Cent Coun Physical Recreation (CCPR)
- M   2,000 i, UK / 1,500 i, o'seas
- ¶   Conference Guide - 1;   Conference Report - 1;
    December Bulletin - 1; all ftm only.

British Association of Teachers of the Deaf   (BATOD)   1976
- ■   175 Dashwood Ave, HIGH WYCOMBE, Bucks, HP12 3DB.
    01494 464190   fax 01494 464190
    email secretary@batod.org.uk
    http://www.batod.org.uk
    Sec: Paul A Simpson
- ▲   Un-incorporated Society
- Br   7 regions
- ○   *P; to promote the interests of all hearing impaired children & young people; to safeguard the interests of their teachers
- Gp   Audiology; Education & research; Teacher training for teachers of the deaf; Pre-school; GCSE; Transition & post-16; Conference; Publications
- ●   Conf - Mtgs - ET - Res - Exhib - Stat - Inf - LG
- M   1,750 i, UK / c 25 i, o'seas
- ¶   Deafness & Education (Jnl) - 4; ftm, £50 yr nm.
    Association Magazine - 5; ftm only.

British Association of Therapeutical Hypnotists   (BAThH)   1951
- NR   Even Keel, 25 Shepherds Hill, Wick Hill, BRACKNELL, Berks, RG12 2LS.
    http://www.bathh.co.uk
    Sec: Ann Bruce

British Association for Tissue Banking   (BATB)
- NR   c/o Institute of Biology, 9 Red Lion Court, LONDON, EC4A 3EF.
    http://www.batb.org.uk
- ○   *M

British Association of Toy Retailers
    since 2004 **Toy Retailers Association**

British Association of Urological Surgeons   (BAUS)   1945
- NR   at the Royal College of Surgeons, 35-43 Lincoln's Inn Fields, LONDON, WC2A 3PE.   (hq)
    020 7869 6950   fax 020 7404 5048
    email admin@baus.org.uk   http://www.baus.org.uk
    Hon Sec: John Anderson
- ▲   Registered Charity
- ○   *P; to promote high standards in practice of urology
- ●   Conf - Mtgs - ET - Exhib
- M   900 i, UK / 300 i, o'seas
- ¶   Members Hbk - 1; ftm only.

British Association for Vedic Astrology
- NR   121 Campden Houses, Peel St, LONDON, W8 7PJ.
    01256 486523
    http://www.bava.org
    Sec: Geoffrey Pearce

British Association of Veterinary Emergency Care
    a group of the **British Small Animal Veterinary Association**

British Association of Veterinary Ophthalmologists
    a group of the **British Small Animal Veterinary Association**

British Association of Women Entrepreneurs (BAWE) 1953

■   112 John Player Building, STIRLING, FK7 7RP.   (pres/b)
    01786 446044
    http://www.bawe-uk.org
    Nat Pres: Tatjana Hine
▲   Company Limited by Guarantee
Br 4; 50
○   *P; to bring together all women who are qualified to be called
    'Heads of Business', whether they operate alone, with co-
    directors, or with members of their families; to confine
    activities to economic matters; to explore & advise on the
    means by which the rights & duties of women in business,
    industry & domestic spheres may be reconciled & improved
●   Conf - Mtgs - ET - Exhib - Comp - SG - Expt - Inf - VE - Empl -
    LG
<   Les Femmes Chefs d'Entreprises Mondiales (FCEM); Amer
    Cham Comm; CBI; IoD; London Cham Comm
M   150 i
¶   BAWE National NL - 4;   BAWE West NL - 4; FCEM News
    International - 4; all ftm only.

British Astrological & Psychic Society   (BAPS)   1976

■   PO Box 5687, Springfield, MILTON KEYNES, Bucks,
    MK6 3WZ.   (mail/address)
    01908 201368
    email info@baps.ws   http://www.baps.ws
    Sec& Co Sec: Mrs Eve Bingham
▲   Company Limited by Guarantee
Br 3
○   *G, *P; astrology & all esoteric/psychic disciplines - tarot, runes,
    palmistry, astrology, numerology, psy cards, crystal
    divination, psychic perception, mediumship, clairvoyance,
    aura readings etc
Gp BAPS School of: Astrology (1995) / Palmistry, runes, tarot
    (1996) / Numerology (correspondence courses)
●   ET - Exhib - Workshops
M   257 i, 100 vetted counsellors, UK / 10 i, o'seas
¶   Mercury (Jnl) - 4; ftm, £3.50 each nm.
    National Register of Consultants; ftm, cover price nm.

British Astronomical Association   (BAA)   1890

NR Burlington House, Piccadilly, LONDON, W1J 0DU.   (hq)
    http://www.britastro.org
▲   Company Limited by Guarantee; Registered Charity
Br Australia (New South Wales)
○   *L; organisation of observers in the work of astronomical
    observation, encouragement of popular interests in
    astronomy
Gp Solar; Lunar; Mercury & Venus; Mars; Asteroids & remote
    planets; Jupiter; Saturn; Comet; Variable star; Meteor;
    Aurora; Deep sky; Computing; Instruments & imaging
●   Mtgs - ET - Res - Exhib - Comp - SG - Inf - Lib - VE
M   c 3,500 i, c 100 org
¶   Jnl - 6.   Hbk - 1.

British Audio Dealers Association   (BADA)   1982

NR 248 Lee High Rd, LONDON, SE13 5PL.   (hq)
    020 8150 6741   fax 020 8318 0909
    email info@bada.co.uk   http://www.bada.co.uk
    Operations & Marketing Mgr: Phil Hansen
▲   Company Limited by Guarantee
○   *T; to promote, raise & monitor the standards of retail practice
    in the UK Hi Fi industry
●   Mtgs - ET - Stat
M   75 f

British Autogenic Society   (BAS)   1984

NR c/o Royal London Homoeopathic Hospital, Gt Ormond Street,
    LONDON, WC1N 3HR.   (hq)
    020 7391 8908
    email admin@autogenic-therapy.org.uk
    http://www.autogenic-therapy.org.uk
    Sec: Mrs Jane Bird,   Chmn: Mrs Sonia Saunders
▲   Company Limited by Guarantee; Registered Charity
○   *P; 'the professional & regulatory body for autogenic therapists
    & psychotherapists in the UK; sets training standards, runs
    training courses & provides information for the public.
    Autogenic therapy is self-help for mind & body. Therapists
    teach easy mental exercises over 8-10 weeks; allows switch-
    off of stress response, helps many problems & also helps
    realise potential in many areas'
●   Mtgs - ET - SG
<   Intl C'ee for Autogenic Therapy (ICAT); Eur Assn for
    Psychotherapy (EAP)
M   94 i, UK / 12 i, o'seas
¶   NL - 2; ftm only.

**British Automatic Fire Sprinkler Association Ltd   (BAFSA)
1974**

NR Richmond House, Broad St, ELY, Cambs, CB7 4AH.   (hq)
    01353 659187   fax 01353 666619
    email info@bafsa.org.uk   http://www.bafsa.org.uk
    Sec Gen: Stewart Kidd
▲   Company Limited by Guarantee
○   *T; to promote the use of automatic sprinkler & other systems
    using water as a means of controlling & extinguishing fires in
    all types of premises
Gp Technical; Contractual; Marketing & promotion
●   Conf - Exhib - LG
<   Fire Ind Confedn; Fire Ind Coun (Trade Enterprises) Ltd;
M   96 f, 3 org
¶   LM & affiliates;   Sprinkler Systems: the facts; both free.
    Sprinklers for Safety; ftm, £25 nm.
    Sprinklers in:
        Schools; Heritage Buildings; Retail Premises; Warehouses.
    Sprinkler Facts (CD-ROM).   Domestic Sprinkler Systems.
    Joint Code of Practice for Sprinklers in Schools; £5.
×   2005 British Automatic Sprinkler Association Ltd

British Automatic Sprinkler Association Ltd
    since 2005 **British Automatic Fire Sprinkler Association**

British Automation & Robot Association Ltd   (BARA)   1977

■   IMC, University of Warwick, COVENTRY, Warks, CV4 7AL.
    (hq)
    024 7657 3742   fax 024 7657 3743
    email bara@wmgmail.wmg.warwick.ac.uk
    http://www.bara.org.uk
    Pres: Mike Wilson,   Chmn: Ken Young
▲   Company Limited by Guarantee
○   *T; the development & application of automation in British
    industry; suppliers of robotics & automation
Gp Advanced robotics; Safety; Aerospace, control system security
●   Conf - Mtgs - Res - Exhib - Stat - Inf - LG
<   Intl Fedn of Robotics (IFR); EAMA
M   30 f
¶   Quartermation (email NL) - 4; free.

British Automobile Racing Club   (BARC Ltd)   1912

■   Thruxton Circuit, ANDOVER, Hants, SP11 8PN.   (hq)
    01264 882200   fax 01264 882233
    email info@barc.net   http://www.barc.net
    Chief Exec: Dennis Carter
▲   Company Limited by Guarantee
Br 7; Canada
○   *S; organisation of circuit motor racing, hill climbs & sprints
●   Mtgs - Social events
M   4,000 i, UK / 100 i, o'seas
¶   Startline - 6; ftm, £2.75 nm.
    Programme of events - 1; free.

© CBD Research Ltd · Beckenham · BR3 5JS · Tel 020 8650 7745 · Fax 020 8650 0768 · E-mail cbd@cbdresearch.com · www.cbdresearch.com

British Aviation Enthusiasts Society   (BAES)   2001
- ■ 28a Frogmore Lane, Lovedean, WATERLOOVILLE, Hants,
      PO8 9QL.   (hsp)
      023 9242 1903   fax 023 9242 1903
      email mail@baes.org.uk   http://www.baes.org.uk
      Sec: Deryn Hawkins
- ▲ Un-incorporated Society
- ○ *G; to visit aviation facilities worldwide (airports, airfields, air
      forces, museum collections); to experience, photograph &
      record details of aircraft & historic aviation buildings
- ● Mtgs - VE (an experienced tour escort is provided)
- M 180 i, UK / 23 i, o'seas
- ¶ NL - 4; ftm only.

British Aviation Preservation Council   (BAPC)   1967
- ■ 19 Acton Place, High Heaton, NEWCASTLE upon TYNE,
      NE7 7RL.   (sec/p)
      0191-266 2049   fax 0191-266 2049
      email secretarybapc@btconnect.com
      http://www.bapc.org.uk
      Chmn: Steve Hague, Sec: Brian Dixon
- ▲ Un-incorporated Society
- ○ *N; coordinating body for all aviation museums & collections
      working for the advancement of aviation preservation &
      promotion of aviation heritage
- Gp National Aviation Heritage Registers; Stopping the Rot
      conferences
- ● Conf - Mtgs - ET - Res - Inf
- < Eur Aviation Presvn Coun
- M 135 org, UK / 10 org, o'seas
- ¶ Update (NL) - 4; ftm only.

British Badge Collectors Association   1980
- ■ PO Box 1362, LICHFIELD, Staffs, WS13 7YD.   (mem/sp)
      01543 256486
      email bbca1980@hotmail.com
      Mem Sec: Peter Duffen
- ▲ Un-incorporated Society
- ○ *G; for collectors of any type & every description of badge
- ● Mtgs - Exhib
- M i
      (Sub: £5 i, UK / £7 i, o'seas)
- ¶ NL - 6.   The Badge Mag - 1.

British Ballet Organization Ltd   (BBO)   1930
- ■ Woolborough House, 39 Lonsdale Rd, Barnes, LONDON,
      SW13 9JP.   (hq)
      020 8748 1241
      http://www.bbo.org.uk
      Dir: John Travis
- ▲ Company Limited by Guarantee
- Br Australia, New Zealand
- ○ *D, *G; ballet, tap, jazz & modern dancing examinations; ballet
      & tap teaching qualifications
- ● Conf - Mtgs - ET - Exam - Lib
- < Regd by Coun for Dance Education & Training (UK) (CDET)
- M c 300 teachers, UK / 135 teachers, o'seas
- ¶ The Dancer - 1.

British Balloon & Airship Club   (BBAC)   1965
- ■ c/o Cameron Balloons, St John St, Bedminster, BRISTOL,
      BS3 4NH.   (pro/b)
      email information@bbac.org   http://www.bbac.org
      Inf Officer: Hannah Cameron,   Chmn: Crispin Williams
- ▲ Company Limited by Guarantee
- Br regional clubs
- ○ *S; to promote all aspects of lighter than air flight, including hot
      airballooning, gas ballooning & airship flying; to serve
      sporting & commercial interests equally
- Gp Clubs: Regional in UK, Competitions
- ● Conf - Mtgs - ET - Exam - Comp - Inf - LG
      BBAC carries delegated authority from the CAA for
      airworthiness & pilot training
- < UK Civil Aviation Authority
- > British Balloon Museum & Library
- M c 2,300 i, 20 f, UK / 100 i, o'seas
- ¶ Aerostat - 6.

British Bamboo Society
      see **Bamboo Society**

British Bankers' Association   (BBA)   1919
- NR Pinners Hall, 105-108 Old Broad St, LONDON, EC2N 1EX.
      (hq)
      020 7216 8800   fax 020 7216 8811
      http://www.bba.org.uk
      Chief Exec: Angela Knight
- ○ *T; for banks carrying out business in the UK
- Gp Press Office (020 7216 8989)
- ● Conf - Stat - LG
- M 300 f
- ¶ NL; ftm.

British Banking History Society   (BHSS)   1980
- ■ 71 Mile Lane, Cheylesmore, COVENTRY, CV3 5GB.   (hsp)
      024 7650 3245
      email info@banking-history.co.uk
      http://www.banking-history.co.uk
      Hon Sec: John Purser
- ▲ Un-incorporated Society
- ○ *G; to encourage & popularise the collection of cheques,
      banknotes & memorabilia relating to banking; to promote
      the study of the history of banking
- ● Mtgs - Res - Inf
- M 110 i, 10 f, UK / 30 i, o'seas
- ¶ Counterfoil - 4; subscription only.

British Barometer Makers Association   (BBMA)   2006
- ■ c/o Barometer World Ltd, Quicksilver Barn, Merton,
      OKEHAMPTON, Devon, EX20 3DS.   (hsb)
      01805 603443   fax 01805 603344
      email prc@barometerworld.co.uk
      Sec: Phillip Collins
- ▲ Un-incorporated Society
- ○ *G, *K; to lobby support for mercury barometers
- ● Stat - Inf - Lobbying in the EU
- < Eur Barometer Makers Assn
- M 3 i

British Basketball Federation   (BBF)   2005
- NR PO Box 3971, SHEFFIELD, S Yorks, S9 9AZ.
      email info@british-basketball.co.uk
      http://www.british-basketball.co.uk
- ○ *N, *S; represents the national basketball associations of
      England, Scotland & Wales on the national Olympic
      Committee
- < Brit Olympic Assn
- M 3 org

British Battery Manufacturers Association   (BBMA)   1986
NR   3 London Wall Buildings, London Wall, LONDON,
        EC2M 5SY.   (hq)
        020 7826 2690   fax 020 7826 2601
        email info@bbma.co.uk   http://www.bbma.co.uk
        Gen Sec: Jonathan Roberts
▲   Company Limited by Guarantee
○   *T; manufacturers of primary (non-rechargeable) & secondary
        (re-chargeable) portable consumer batteries - NOT
        automotive lead-acid
●   Mtgs - Stat - Inf - LG
<   Eur Portable Battery Assn (EPBA)
M   7 f
¶   LM.
        Guidelines on: Battery Safety; Battery Compartment; Battery
            Insertion; Battery Ingestion.
        The Future for Dead Batteries: disposal & recycling of portable
            batteries.
        Organisation lost: see Introduction paragraph 3.

** British Battery Manufacturers Association
        Organisation lost: see Introduction paragraph 3.

British Bazadaise Cattle Society   1989
■   6 Town Close, HOLT, Norfolk, NR25 6JN.   (hsp)
        01263 713507   fax 01263 713507
        email cmatthews@bazadaise.org.uk
        http://www.bazadaise.org.uk
        Co Sec: Corinne Matthews
▲   Company Limited by Guarantee; Registered Charity
○   *B; a beef breed originating in South West France
M   44 i
        (Sub: £30)

British Bedding & Pot Plant Association
        since 2007 **British Protected Ornamentals Association**

British Bee-Keepers' Association   (BBKA)   1874
■   National Beekeeping Centre, NAC, Stoneleigh Park,
        KENILWORTH, Warks, CV8 2LG.   (hq)
        024 7669 6679
        Gen Sec: Mike Harris
▲   Registered Charity
Br   61
○   *G, *T; to further the craft of keeping bees
Gp   Appliance trade; Bee health; Bee disease; Insurance; Research;
        Education; Bee breeding; Protection against spray &
        pesticides
●   Conf - ET - Exam - Res - Exhib - LG
<   Cent Assn of Beekeepers; Bee Improvement & Bee Breeders
        Assn; Assn of Beekeeping Appliance Mfrs
M   9,824 i, 5 org
¶   BBKA News - 5; ftm.

British Beer & Pub Association   1904
■   Market Towers, 1 Nine Elms Lane, LONDON, SW8 5NQ.   (hq)
        020 7627 9191   fax 020 7627 9123
        email enquiries@beerandpub.com
        http://www.beerandpub.com
        Chief Exec: Robert Hayward
▲   Company Limited by Guarantee
Br   Scottish Beer & Pub Association
○   *T; to represent the beer & pub industry when dealing with
        government & government bodies in the UK & EU; to
        enhance the reputation of the brewing & pub sector
●   Conf - Mtgs - ET - Res - Comp - Stat - Expt - LG
<   Hotels, Restaurants & Cafés in Europe (HOTREC); The Brewers
        of Europe (BoE); Confedn of Brit Ind (CBI)
M   72 f
¶   Digest - 11; ftm only.
        Statistical Hbk - 1; £27.75 m, £47.50 nm.   AR; ftm.
        Publications list available from: Brewing Publications Ltd, at
        above address.

British Beermat Collectors' Society   (BBCS)   1960
■   69 Dunnington Avenue, KIDDERMINSTER, Worcs, DY10 2YT.
        (hsp)
        http://www.britishbeermats.org.uk
        Hon Sec: Tony Matthews
▲   Un-incorporated Society
○   *G; to encourage the hobby of beermat collecting (tegestology)
●   Mtgs
M   260 i, UK / 41 i, o'seas
¶   Beermat NL - 12; ftm only.

British Belgian Blue Cattle Society
        since 2008 **British Blue Cattle Society**

British Berrichon du Cher Sheep Society   1986
NR   Tregwynt, Three Ashes, HEREFORD, HR2 8LY.   (sp)
        01989 770071
        http://www.berrichonsociety.com
        Sec: Emma Hillhouse
▲   Company Limited by Guarantee
○   *B
●   Exhib - Inf
<   Nat Sheep Assn
M   150 i, UK / 2 i, Republic of Ireland
¶   NL - 4;   Magazine - 1;   Flock Book - 1;   all free.

British Big Cats Society   (BBCS)   2001
NR   PO Box 28, PLYMOUTH, Devon, PL1 1AA.
        01752 226535   fax 01752 664547
        email sightings@britishbigcats.org
        http://www.britishbigcats.org
        Founder: Danny Bamping
○   *G, *V; to scientifically identify, quantify, catalogue & protect the
        big cats that freely roam the British countryside
M   c 500 i

British Binders & Finishers Association
        since 2005 a special interest group (BPIF Finishers) of the **British
        Printing Industries Federation**

British BioGen
        in 2005 merged with the Renewable Power Association to form the
        Renewable Energy Association

British Biomagnetic Association   (BBA)
NR   The Williams Clinic, 31 St Marychurch Rd, TORQUAY, Devon,
        TQ1 3JF.   (hq)
        01803 293346
        Exec Vice-Chmn: Graham Gardener
▲   Un-incorporated Society
○   *E, *M; post graduate training & research in the use of magnet
        application to acupuncture points for the correction of
        skeletal mis-alignments

British Biophysical Society   (BBS)   1966
NR   c/o Dr R M Cooke, GlaxoSmithKline, New Frontiers Science
        Park, Third Avenue, HARLOW, Essex, CM19 5AW.   (hq)
        01279 627981
        Hon Sec: Dr R M Cooke
▲   Registered Charity
○   *L; advancement of science of biophysics - 'the study of the
        functioning & structure of living organisms viewed from a
        physical standpoint, & the application of physical & physio-
        chemical techniques to biological problems'

British Bird Council
        a group of the **National Council for Aviculture**

© CBD Research Ltd · Beckenham · BR3 5JS · Tel 020 8650 7745 · Fax 020 8650 0768 · E-mail cbd@cbdresearch.com · www.cbdresearch.com

British Bison Association (BBA) 1991
■ Bush Farm, West Knoyle, WARMINSTER, Wilts, BA12 6AE. (hsp/b)
01747 830263
email info@bisonfarm.co.uk   http://www.bisonfarm.co.uk
Hon Sec: Lord Seaford
▲ Un-incorporated Society
○ *B; to promote the interests of bison & bison farmers & meat producers
● Conf - Mtgs - Inf - VE - LG
< Nat Bison Assn (USA)
M 40 i, UK / 4 i, o'seas
(Sub: £25)
¶ NL - 2;   Bison Hbk; £12 nm.   AR.

British Bleu du Maine Sheep Society   1982
NR Long Wood Farm, Trostrey, USK, Monmouthshire, NP15 1LA. (sp)
01291 673816
Breed Sec: Mrs Jane Smith
▲ Registered Charity
○ *B
● Mtgs - Res - Exhib - SG
M 250 i, 10 f
¶ NL - 4;   Flock Book - 1; ftm only.
Breeder's Directory [LM] - 2/3 years; free.

British Blind & Shutter Association (BBSA) 1919
NR 36 Broadway, LONDON, SW1H 0BH.   (hq)
020 7799 4050   fax 020 7340 6261
email info@bbsa.org.uk   http://www.bbsa.org.uk
Sec: A D Skelding
▲ Company Limited by Guarantee
○ *T; represents leading UK manufacturers of interior & exterior window blinds, security shutters & grilles
● Mtgs - Exhib - ET - Inf - VE
M 350 f, UK / 8 f, o'seas
¶ Blinds & Shutters - 4.

British Blonde Cattle Society   2002
■ 4th Street, NAC, Stoneleigh Park, KENILWORTH, Warks, CV8 2LG.   (hq)
024 7641 9058   fax 024 7641 9082
email secretary@britishblondesociety.co.uk
http://www.britishblondesociety.co.uk
Breed Sec: Caroline Jackson
▲ Registered Charity
Br 9
○ *B
Gp Farmers; Abattoirs; Agricultural
● Mtgs - Exhib - Comp - Stat - Expt - VE
M 530 i
¶ Blonde (Jnl) [incl LM] - 1;   Blonde News {NL} - 1; both free.
Note: Also uses title British Blonde Society

British Blood Transfusion Society (BBTS) 1983
NR Enterprise House, Manchester Science Park, Lloyd Street North, MANCHESTER, M15 6JJ.   (hq)
0161-232 7999   fax 0161-232 7979
email bbts@bbts.org.uk   http://www.bbts.org.uk
Hon Sec: Dr Sheila MacLennan
▲ Registered Charity
○ *M, *P; for those engaged in transfusion medicine & transfusion science in hospitals & blood centres
● Conf - Mtgs - ET - Exam - Res - SG
M 1,400 i & f, UK / 300 i, o'seas
¶ Transfusion Medicine (Jnl) - 6.
NL - 4; ftm only.

British Blue Cattle Society
NR Fell View, Blencarn, PENRITH, Cumbria, CA10 1TX.
01768 88775   fax 01768 88779
email info@belgianblue.co.uk
http://www.britishbluecattle.org
○ *B
✕ 2008 British Belgian Blue Cattle Society

British Bluegrass Music Association (BBMA) 1990
NR Park Farm, Buckland Down, FROME, Somerset, BA11 2RG. (chmn/p)
01373 813590
email john.wirtz@hipposound.co.uk
http://www.britishbluegrass.co.uk
Chmn: John Wirtz
▲ Un-incorporated Society
○ *D; promotion of bluegrass music & associated traditions in UK
● Mtgs - Inf - Organising tours - Producing CDs - Sponsoring events - Teaching / tuition - Publicising concerts & tours
< Intl Bluegrass Music Assn
M c 600 i, UK / c 20 i, o'seas
¶ British Bluegrass News - 4; ftm, £2 yr nm.

British Bob Skeleton Association
NR Norwood House (level 9), University of Bath, Claverton Down, BATH, BA2 7AY.
01225 323696
http://www.bobskeleton.org.uk
Gen Sec: Phil Searle
○ *S

British Bobsleigh Association Ltd   (BBA) 1956
■ 4-10 Barttelot Rd, HORSHAM, W Sussex, RH12 1DQ.   (hq)
01403 221844   fax 01403 219079
http://www.bobteamgb.org
Admin: Jane Clark
▲ Company Limited by Guarantee
○ *S; to promote British bobsleighing; to attain world prominence in championships
M i
¶ The British Bobsleigh Annual - 1; ftm.

British Body Piercing Association   (BBPA)
NR Dalton House, 60 Windsor Rd, LONDON, SW19 2RR.
http://www.bbpa.org.uk
○ *P

British Bodyboard Club   (BBC) 1993
NR 3 Quintet Close, EXETER, Devon, EX1 3HZ.   (hsb)
07594 705475
email matt@britishbodyboardclub.co.uk
http://www.britishbodyboardclub.co.uk
Hon Sec: Matt Hawken
○ *S; a form of surfing
M i

British Boomerang Society   (BBS) 1980
■ 36 Fox Dene, GODALMING, Surrey, GU7 1YG.   (chmn/p)
01483 417236
email mckennaslade@inbox.com
http://www.boomerangs.org.uk
Chmn: Seán McKenna-Slade
▲ Un-incorporated Society
○ *S; to promote boomerang throwing as a sport; to provide designs of boomerangs & the materials to make boomerangs from; to research the history of boomerangs & the physics of their flight
● Mtgs - Res - Comp - Talks on various aspects of boomerangs
< Fedn of Intl Boomerang Assns
M 50 i, 3 f, UK / 5 i, c 20 org, o'seas
(Sub: £15 i, free reciprocal exchange org)
¶ Jnl - irreg; ftm only.

British Bottlers' Institute   (BBI)   1953
- ■   PO Box 374, SOUTHAMPTON, Hants, SO31 4WZ.   (hsp)
     0776 100 5276   fax 023 8056 1646
     email secretary@bbi.org.uk   http://www.bbi.org.uk
     Gen Sec: John Yates
- ▲   Un-incorporated Society
- ○   *T; a forum for those concerned with the bottling, canning &
     packaging of beverages, food & other products, enabling
     them to share their experience & problems
- ●   Conf - Mtgs - Exhib - Comp - VE
- M   40 i, 70 f, UK / 2 i, 2 f, o'seas

British Brands Group   (BBG)
- ■   8 Henrietta Place, LONDON, W1G 0NB.   (hq)
     0702 093 4250   fax 0702 093 4252
     email info@britishbrandsgroup.org.uk
     http://www.britishbrandsgroup.org.uk
     Dir: John Noble
- ▲   Company Limited by Guarantee
- ○   *K, *N; 'to represent brand manufacturers with a mission to
     create a deeper understanding of brands & their benefits; to
     help create an environment of fair competition'
- ●   Mtgs - ET - Res - Exhib - Inf - PL - VE - LG
- <   AIM (Brussels)
- M   25 f
- ¶   NL - 4.

British Brick Society   (BBS)   1972
- ■   19 Woodcroft Avenue, STANMORE, Middx, HA7 3PT.   (hsp)
     email micksheila67@hotmail.com
     http://www.britishbricksoc.free-online.co.uk
     Hon Sec: Mick Oliver
- ▲   Un-incorporated Society
- ○   *G, *L; to study & record all aspects of the archaeology &
     history of brick, brickmaking & brick building
- ●   Inf - VE - Coordinating records of brickmaking sites &
     manufacturers' names in the British Isles
- <   Brit Archaeological Assn (Brick section)
- M   c 300 i, c 20 f, UK / c 20 i, o'seas
- ¶   BBS Information (NL) - 3; ftm, back issue prices on
     application nm.

British Bridalwear Association   (BBA)   1995
- NR   11 Boldmere Road, SUTTON COLDFIELD, W Midlands,
     B73 5UY.
     0121-321 3121
     http://www.bbabridalwear.com
- ○   *P, *T;

British Brush Manufacturers Association   (BBMA)   1908
- ■   Brooke House, 4 The Lakes, Bedford Rd, NORTHAMPTON,
     NN4 7YD.   (hq)
     01604 622023   fax 01604 631252
     email bbma@bheta.co.uk   http://www.bheta.co.uk
     Sec: Andy Vaughan
- ○   *T
- Gp   Brushes: Artists, Household, Pet, Clothes, Industrial, Personal;
     Brush machinery; Brush raw materials; Paint applicators
- ●   Conf - Mtgs - Exhib - Expt - Inf - Empl - LG
- <   Eur Brush Fedn (FEIBP); CBI
- M   32 f
- ¶   NL - 12;   Membership Directory - 1; ftm, £75 nm.
     Note: incorporated within the British Hardware & Housewares
     Manufacturers' Association 1 January 1995 as a sub-product
     sector

British Bryological Society   (BBS)   1896
- NR   6 Darnford Close, Parkside, STAFFORD, Staffs, ST1 1LR.
     (mem/sp)
     Mem Sec: M F Godfrey
- ▲   Registered Charity
- ○   *L, *Q; study & conservation of mosses & liverworts, especially
     those in the British Isles
- Gp   Reading circle; Tropical bryology
- ●   Conf - Mtgs - ET - Res - Exhib - SG - Stat - Inf - Lib - VE
- <   N Western Naturalist U
- M   382 i, UK / 215 i, o'seas
- ¶   Jnl of Bryology - 4; ftm.
     Bulletin - 2; ftm.

British Buddhist Association   (BBA)   1974
- ■   11 Biddulph Rd, LONDON, W9 1JA.   (hq)
     020 7286 5575
     Dir: A Haviland-Nye
- ▲   Registered Charity
- ○   *R
- ●   Conf - Mtgs - ET (courses & weekends) - SG - VE - Courses for
     teachers of religious education in schools
- M   'confidential'

British Bulgarian Chamber of Commerce   (BBCC)   1993
- ■   PO Box 123, BROMLEY, Kent, BR1 4ZX.   (hq)
     020 8464 5007
     email info@bbcc.bg   http://www.bbcc.bg
     Exec Dir: Mrs Christine Booth
- ▲   Company Limited by Guarantee
- Br   Bulgaria
- ○   *C; promotion of business between Britain & Bulgaria
- ●   Conf - Mtgs - Expt - Inf - LG - Business missions
- M   80 f, UK / 70 f, o'seas
- ¶   NL - 52 [email only]; ftm only.

British Bulgarian Friendship Society   (BBFS)   1952
- NR   22 Modena Rd, HOVE, E Sussex, BN3 5QG.   (hsb)
     01273 726433   fax 01273 726433
     email bbfs@care4free.net   http://www.bbfs.org.uk
     Hon Sec: K Barker
- ▲   Un-incorporated Society
- ○   *X; to promote friendship between British & Bulgarian peoples
- ●   Mtgs - Exhib - Inf - Lib - VE
- M   c 300 i,
- ¶   NL - 3/4; ftm.

British Burn Association   (BBA)   1967
- ■   Burns & Plastics, University Hospital Birmingham,
     Selly Oak Hospital, BIRMINGHAM, B29 6JD.   (hsb)
     0121-627 8793
     email bba@smuht.nwest.nhs.uk
     http://www.britishburnassociation.co.uk
     Hon Sec/Treas: N S M Moiemen
- ▲   Registered Charity
- ○   *P; to promote burn prevention, treatment, care & rehabilitation
- ●   Conf - Mtgs - Exhib
- <   Intl Soc for Burn Injuries
- M   c 400 i

© CBD Research Ltd · Beckenham · BR3 5JS · Tel 020 8650 7745 · Fax 020 8650 0768 · E-mail cbd@cbdresearch.com · www.cbdresearch.com

British Business Angels Association (BBAA) 2005
■ New City Court, 20 St Thomas Street, LONDON, SE1 9RS.
     (hq)
     020 7089 2305   fax 020 7089 2301
     email info@bbaa.org.uk   http://www.bbaa.org.uk
     Sec: A Clarke
▲ Company Limited by Guarantee
○ *T; the national trade body for the Uk's Business Angels
     Networks & its associates
Gp Business Angel Networks; Early stage funds; Business support
     services; Lawyers; Accountants; Banks; Regional
     Development Agencies
● Conf - ET - Res - Stat - Inf - LG
< Eur Business Angels Network (EBAN)
M 500-750 f
¶ NL - 12;   Directory - 1;   Research - 1.

British Business Awards Association (BBAA) 1993
§ Highfield Park, Creaton, NORTHAMPTON, NN6 8NT.
     01604 505480   fax 01604 505861
     email info@bbaa.co.uk   http://www.bbaa.co.uk
     Chief Exec: David Wright
     Designs and organises awards programmes for leading
     publishing groups throughout the UK.

**British Business & General Aviation Association (BBGA)
1975**
■ 19 Church St, Brill, AYLESBURY, Bucks, HP18 9RT.   (hq)
     01844 238020   fax 01844 238087
     email info@bbga.aero   http://www.bbga.aero
     Chief Exec: Guy Lachlan
▲ Company Limited by Guarantee
○ *T; to represent companies operating & trading in the industry -
     including manufacturers, business aviation operators,
     organisations in repair & overhaul, training & aircraft &
     helicopter sales, also spares stockists & supporting
     organisations in finance, insurance & publishing
Gp Sales & support; Air transport; Engineering; Flying training;
     Airport working
● Conf - Mtgs - Res - Exhib - SG - Stat - Inf - LG
M 180 f
¶ BBGA Industry Directory - 18 months; free.
× 2004 (Business Aircraft Users Association
          (General Aviation Manufacturers & Traders Association

British Button Society (BBS) 1976
■ 32 Chichester Rd, TONBRIDGE, Kent, TN9 2TL.   (hsp)
     01732 364309
     email angelaclarkbuttons@btinternet.com
     http://www.britishbuttonsociety.org
     Hon Sec: Mrs A Clark
▲ Un-incorporated Society
○ *G; the collection & preservation of antique & modern buttons
● Mtgs - Res - Lib - VE - Publication of articles on, & photographs
     of, buttons
M 300 i, 10 f, UK / 50 i, o'seas
¶ Button Lines - 4; ftm only.

British Cables Association (BCA) 1965
NR Flat 7, 11 The Grange, LONDON, SW19 4PT.   (hq)
     020 8946 6978
     email admin@bcauk.org   http://www.bcauk.org
     Sec Gen: Peter Smeeth
▲ Un-incorporated Society
○ *T; manufacturers of metallic & optical fibre cables & wires for
     transmission & distribution of electric power for
     communications (telephones, electronic data control &
     broadcasting)
Gp Accessories; Communications cables; Covered Conductors
     Association; Energy cables; Supertension cables
● Conf - Mtgs - Res - SG - Stat - Expt - LG
< Eur Confedn Assns Mfrs Insulated Wires & Cables
     (EUROPACABLE); CBI; BEAMA
M 18 f

British Cactus & Succulent Society (BCSS) 1945
■ 49 Chestnut Glen, HORNCHURCH, Essex, RM12 4HL.   (hsp)
     01708 447778   fax 01444 454061
     email bcss@cactus-mall.com   http://www.bcss.org.uk
     Hon Sec: E A Harris
▲ Registered Charity
Br 94; Republic of Ireland
○ *H; study & conservation of cacti & succulent plants
Gp Robins
● Conf - Mtgs - Res - Exhib - Comp - LG
< Cactus & Succulent Soc of America, German Cactus &
     Succulent Soc; Succulent Soc S Australia; R Horticl Soc
M 3,500 i, UK / 500 i, o'seas
¶ Cactus World (Jnl) - 4; £15 m (£20 or 38 o'seas).
     Bradleya (Ybk) - 1; £16 m, (£20 o'seas)

British Calcium Carbonates Federation (BCCF) 1943
NR Omya UK Ltd, Omya House, Stephensons Way, Wyvern
     Business Park, Chaddesden, DERBY, DE21 6LY.   (hsb)
     01332 887435
     Sec: Mike Nocivelli
▲ Un-incorporated Society
○ *T; to foster & develop the manufacture & sale of calcium
     carbonates
● Mtgs - Stat - Inf
M 5 f
¶ LM; ftm only.

British Camargue Horse Society (BCHS) 1991
■ The Cottage - Valley Rd, Wickham Market, WOODBRIDGE,
     Suffolk, IP13 0ND.   (hq)
     01728 746916
     http://www.valleyfarmonline.co.uk
     Sec: Sarah Ling
○ *B; to promote the Camargue horse & educate children
● ET - VE
M 40 i

British Camelids Association (BCA) 1987
■ Puckpitts Farm, Tredington, SHIPSTON on STOUR, Warks,
     CV36 4NH.   (hsp)
     01608 661893
     email camelids@btinternet.com
     http://www.britishcamelids.co.uk
     Sec: Jane Brown
▲ Company Limited by Guarantee; Registered Charity
○ *B; breeding & farming of Camelids - Vicunas, Lamas, Alpacas,
     Guanacoes
Gp Lama Glama; Lama Pacos (Alpacas); Lama Guanacos;
     Vicugna Vicugna (Vicunas); Bactrian & dromedary camels
M i & f
     Note: is the trading name of British Camelids Ltd.
× 2005 British Camelids Owners & Breeders Association

British Canadian Chamber of Trade & Commerce 1951
■ PO Box 1358, Station K, TORONTO, Ontario, Canada,
     M4P 3J4.   (hq)
     1 (416) 502 0847   fax 1 (416) 502 9319
     Contact: The National Secretary
○ *C; to foster bi-lateral trade between Britain & Canada
M i & f

British Candlemakers Federation 1995
NR c/o Tallow Chandlers Hall, 4 Dowgate Hill, LONDON,
     EC4R 2SH.
     020 7248 4726
▲ Un-incorporated Society
○ *T; to ensure that the skills & arts of candlemaking in Britain are
     continued along with modern methods & future development
● Mtgs - Exhib - Stat
< Eur Candlemakers Fedn
M 33 f, UK / 1 f, o'seas

British Canoe Union (BCU) 1936
NR 18 Market Place, Bingham, NOTTINGHAM, NG2 5AS. (hq)
0845 370 9500 fax 0845 370 9501
email info@bcu.org.uk http://www.bcu.org.uk
Sec: Paul Owen
▲ Company Limited by Guarantee
Br 10 regions
○ *S; the national body governing the sport of canoeing
Gp Sprint racing; Marathon; Slalom; Canoe sailing; Wild water
racing; Surf; Canoe polo; Sea canoeing; Freestyle;
Coaching; Lifeguards; Touring
● ET - Exhib - Comp - SG - Stat - Inf - Lib - VE
< Intl Canoe Fedn; Eur Canoe Assn; Brit Olympic Assn; C'wealth
Games Coun for England; Cent Coun for Physical
Recreation (CCPR); Boating Alliance
M 21,430 i, 420 org
¶ Canoe Focus - 6; ftm, £2 each nm.
Canoeing Hbk - 1; £15.95.

British Caravanners' Club
a group of the **Camping & Caravanning Club Ltd**

**British Cardiac Patients Association (Zipper Club) (BCPA)
1982**
■ Unit D1, 2 Station Rd, SWAVESEY, Cambs, CB24 5QJ. (hq)
01954 202022
email admin@bcpa.co.uk http://www.bcpa.co.uk
Chmn: Keith Jackson
▲ Registered Charity
Br 20
○ *W; to offer practical advice, support & reassurance to all heart
patients & families, particularly those awaiting or who have
undergone investigations, procedures or heart surgery
● Mtgs
M 4,000 i, UK / 20 i, o'seas
¶ Zipper News - 6; ftm, £1.00 each nm.

British Cardiac Society
since 2006 **British Cardiovascular Society**

British Cardiovascular Society (BCS) 1922
NR 9 Fitzroy Sq, LONDON, W1T 5HW. (hq)
020 7383 3887 fax 020 7388 0903
email enquiries@bcs.com http://www.bcs.com
Chief Exec: Steven Yeats
▲ Company Limited by Guarantee; Registered Charity
○ *L; advancement of knowledge of diseases of the heart &
circulation
M 1,400 i
× 2006 (April) British Cardiac Society

British Carillon Society (BCS) 1976
Hon Sec: Michael Boyd
▲ Un-incorporated Society
○ *D; to promote the art of the carillon in the British Isles (a
musical instrument of 23 or more cast bronze bells played
from a baton keyboard & pedal-board); to propagate music
for the same
● Mts - Exhib - Lib - VE
< Wld Carillon Fedn
M 2 org, 1 f, UK / 19 i, 1 f, 1 org, o'seas
¶ NL - 3.
Music Albums (anthologies) for Carillon of 2 or 3 octaves; irreg.

British Carrot Growers' Association
NR Beech House, Kingerby, MARKET RASEN, Lincs, LN8 3PF. (hsp)
020 8892 5033
email info@mustardcommunications.co.uk
http://www.britishcarrots.co.uk
SeC: John Birkenshaw
○ *T; for commercial carrot & parsnip growers

British Cartographic Society (BCS) 1963
■ at the Royal Geographical Society, 1 Kensington Gore,
LONDON, SW7 2AR. (mail/address)
01823 665775 fax 01823 665775
email admin@cartography.org.uk
http://www.cartography.org.uk
Hon Sec: Dr Tim Rideout
▲ Registered Charity
○ *E, *L, *P, *Q; to promote all aspects of cartography &
geographical information science; its structure & members
reflect maps in all their forms & the art & science of
cartography as a whole
Gp Map Curators; Map Design; Historical Military Mapping;
Corporate members forum
● Conf - ET - Exhib - SG - Lib - VE
< Intl Cartographic Assn (ICA); Intl Map Trade Assn (IMTA); UK
Geoforum: Assn for Geographic Inf (AGI)
M 466 i, 53 f, UK / 86 i, 4 f, o'seas
(Sub: £35 i, £75-£180 f)
¶ The Cartographic Jnl - 4; ftm, £61 i UK+EU ($144 USA),
£232 instns UK+EU ($415 USA).
Maplines (NL) - 3; ftm only.
Cartographiti (NL) - 3; ftm, £10 UK (£15 airmail).
Maps & Surveys (NL) - 2; ftm, £10 UK (£15 airmail).

British Cartoonists' Association 1966
■ Mead Cottage, 77 Woodfield Rd, Hadleigh, BENFLEET, Essex,
SS7 2ES. (hsp)
01702 557205
email collinscartoons@aol.com
Hon Sec: Clive Collins
○ *P; to aid cartoonists & young cartoonists
Gp Animators; Caricaturists; Cartoonists; Designers; Editors;
Illustrators; Painters; Writers for cartoons
● Conf - Exhib - Comp - Inf - VE
< Cartoon Arts Trust & Museum
M 100 i
(Sub: £20)
¶ NL - irreg. Ybk; AR - 1; all ftm.

British Casino Association Ltd (BCA) 1973
■ 38 Grosvenor Gardens, LONDON, SW1W 0EB. (hq)
020 7730 1055 fax 020 7730 1050
email enquiries@britishcasinoassociation.org.uk
http://www.britishcasinoassociation.org.uk
Dir of Policy: K Watling
▲ Company Limited by Guarantee
○ *T; representing the interests of the land-based casino industry
in GB
● Mtgs - LG
< Eur Casino Assn
M 12 f
¶ NL - irreg; ftm only.

British Cattle Breeders' Club (BCBC) 1947
■ Lake Villa, Bradworthy, HOLWORTHY, Devon, EX22 7SQ.
01409 241579
email lesley.lewin@cattlebreeders.org.uk
http://www.cattlebreeders.org.uk
Sec: Mrs Lesley Lewin
▲ Company Limited by Guarantee; Registered Charity
○ *B; improvements in sphere of cattle breeding; dissemination of
information & new ideas
● Conf - Publication of proceedings
M 238 i
¶ Digest - 1; ftm, £25 nm. NL - irreg; ftm only.

British Cattle Veterinary Association
a group of the **British Veterinary Association**

© CBD Research Ltd · Beckenham · BR3 5JS · Tel 020 8650 7745 · Fax 020 8650 0768 · E-mail cbd@cbdresearch.com · www.cbdresearch.com

British Cave Rescue Council (BCRC) 1967
- ■ Pearl Hill, Dent, SEDBERGH, Cumbria, LA10 5TG.   (hsp)
  01539 625412; 07803 028830 (mobile)
  email secretary@caverescue.org.uk
  http://www.caverescue.org.uk
  Hon Sec: Pete Allwright
- ▲ Un-incorporated Society
- ○ *G, *W; representation & coordination of voluntary cave rescue throughout the UK
- ● Conf - Mtgs - ET - Stat - Inf - LG
- < UK Search & Rescue (UKSAR); Mountain Rescue England & Wales; Brit Caving Assn
- > Mountain Rescue England & Wales
- M 16 member teams
- ¶ Information & Briefing CD; ftm only.
  Incident Report - 1 [on website, donation appreciated].

British Cave Research Association (BCRA) 1973
- ■ The Old Methodist Chapel, Great Hucklow, BUXTON, Derbys, SK17 8RG.   (hq)
  01298 873810
  email enquiries@bcra.org.uk   http://www.bcra.org.uk
  Chmn: Steve Whitlock
- ▲ Registered Charity
- ○ *L; all aspects of sciences & technology associated with caves, caving & karst: geology, hydrology, archaeology, biology, surveying, photography, cave exploration, etc
- Gp Cave radio & electronics; Cave surveying; Hydrology; Speleohistory; Explosives users
- ● Conf - Mtgs - ET - Res - SG - Lib
- < U Intl de Speleologie (UIS); Brit Caving Assn (BCA)
- M 212 i, 53 org
  (Sub: £18)
- ¶ Cave & Karst Science - 3; ftm, price on application nm.

British Caving Association (BCA) 2004
- NR Old Methodist Chapel, Great Hucklow, BUXTON, Derbys, SK17 8RG.
  01298 873810   fax 01298 873801
  email enquiries@british-caving.org.uk
  http://www.british-caving.org.uk
  Insurance Mgr: Nick Williams
- ▲ Un-incorporated Society
- ○ *N, *S; to act as the governing body of the sport in the UK; to act as the umbrella organisation on behalf of 9 constituent bodies in respect of Sports Council aid
- Gp British Cave Rescue Council; British Cave Research Association; National Association of Mining History Organisations; William Pengelly Cave Studies Trust Ltd & 5 regional Caving Councils (Southern, Northern, Cambrian, Derbyshire, Devon & Cornwall)
- ● Mtgs - ET - Inf - LG
- < Intl Speleological U (UIS)
- M 4,000 i, 10 f, 250 org, UK / 500 i, 10 org, o'seas
- ¶ NL;   Hbk;   Speleology; all ftm only.
- ✕ 2004 (1 January) National Caving Association

British Cement Association (BCA) 1935
- NR 4 Meadows Business Park, Station Approach, Blackwater, CAMBERLEY, Surrey, GU17 9AB. (hq)
  01276 608700   fax 01276 608701
  email library@bca.org.uk   http://www.bca.org.uk
- ○ *Q, T; to research into: concrete, the greater & better use of concrete, the British Portland Cement industry
- Gp Centre for Concrete Information; Cement Industry Suppliers' Forum
- ● Conf - ET - Res - Exhib - Inf - Lib - PL - LG - Production of technical publications - Development of standards
- < Cembureau; Concrete Industry Alliance
- M 4 f
- ¶ Concrete Quarterly (Jnl) - 4.   Industry Update - 4.
  Concrete Current Awareness - 12.

British Ceramic Confederation (BCC) 1986
- ■ Federation House, Station Rd, STOKE-ON-TRENT, Staffs, ST4 2SA. (hq)
  01782 744631   fax 01782 744102
  email bcc@ceramfed.co.uk
  Dir: K C Farrell
- ▲ Un-incorporated Society
- ○ *T
- Gp Gift & tableware; Sanitaryware; Tiles; Bricks; Roofing tiles; Pipes & land drains; Industrial ceramics; Refractories; Material supplies; Plant & machinery
- ● Conf - Mtgs - Comp - SG - Stat - Expt - Inf - VE - Empl - LG
- < Cerame Unie; CBI
- M 120 f
- ¶ Bulletin - 6;   Briefing Documents - irreg; both ftm only.

British Ceramic Gift & Tableware Manufacturers' Association (BCGTMA)
- ■ Federation House, Station Rd, STOKE-ON-TRENT, Staffs, ST4 2SA. (hq)
  01782 744631   fax 01782 744102
  email bcc@ceramfed.co.uk
  Sec: C P Hall
- ▲ Un-incorporated Society
- ○ *T
- ● Mtgs - SG - Stat - Expt - Inf - LG
- < Brit Ceramic Confedn (BCC); Fédn Eur des Inds de Porcelaine et de Faïence de Table et d'Ornementation (FEPF)
- M 26 f

British Ceramic Research Ltd
  see subsidiary **CERAM Research Ltd**

British Cervical Spine Society
  a specialist society of the **British Orthopaedic Association**

British Chamber of Business in Southern Africa   (SABRITA) 1965
- NR P O Box 66, Parklands, JOHANNESBURG 2121, South Africa. (hq)
  27 (11) 482 8833   fax 27 (11) 726 1871
  email info@britishchamber.co.za
  PRO: Adam Ginster
- ○ *C; promotion of trade & investment between UK & South Africa
- < SABA (UK)
- M i, f & org

British Chamber of Commerce for Belgium (BCCB) 1898
- ■ Boulevard Saint-Michel 47, 1040 BRUXELLES, Belgium. (hq)
  32 (02) 540 9030   fax 32 (02) 512 8263
  email britcham@britcham.be   http://www.britcham.be
  Exec Dir: Glenn Vaughan
- ▲ Company Limited by Guarantee
- Br Belgium
- ○ *C; to encourage business contacts between Belgium & the UK; to influence the development of public policy & facilitate networking
- Gp C'ees: Business development, EU, ICT
- ● Conf - Mtgs - ET - Inf - LG (EU institutions)
- < Coun Brit Chams Comm Continental Europe (COBCOE)
- M 20 i, 260 f, Belgium
- ¶ BCC NL - 10.   Trade & Membership Directory - 1.

British Chamber of Commerce in China - Beijing   (BCCC) 1993

NR   The British Centre (Room 1001), China Life Tower,
No 16 Chaoyangmenwai Avenue, BEIJING 100020,
China.   (hq)
86 (10) 8525 1111   fax 86 (10) 8525 1100
email information@pek.britcham.org
http://www.britcham.org
Exec Dir: Christopher Baron
○   *C
¶   British Business in China (Jnl) - 4.

British Chamber of Commerce in China - Shanghai   1995

NR   Westgate Tower (suite 1703), 1038 Nanjing Xi Lu, SHANGHAI
200041, China.   (hq)
86 (21) 6218 5022   fax 86 (21) 6218 5066
email admin@sha.britcham.org
http://www.sha.britcham.org
Exec Dir: Ian Crawford
○   *C; to promote & deepen the relationship between China & the
UK; to support the increasing number of business interests in
Shanghai & the East China region; to act as a central source
of information, including a contract data-base, on issues
facing foreign companies operating in China
●   Conf - Mtgs - Inf - LG
M   86 i, 535 f
¶   The Beat - 12; free.
British Business in China Directory.
✕   British Chamber of Commerce Shanghai (Britcham Shanghai)

British Chamber of Commerce in the Czech Republic   (BCC CR)

■   Pobezní 3, 186 00 PRAGUE 8, Czech Republic.
420 2 2483 5161   fax 420 2 2483 5862
http://www.britishchamber.cz
Exec Dir: Simon Rawlence
○   *C

British Chamber of Commerce in Germany e.V.   (BCCG)   1960

■   Französischestrasse 48, D-10117 BERLIN, Germany.   (hq)
49 (30) 20 67 080   fax 49 (30) 20 67 08 29
email info@bccg.de   http://www.bccg.de
Exec Dir: Andreas Meyer-Schwickerath
▲   Eingetragener Verein
Br   London; 8 in Germany
○   *C; to further British-German trade, business contacts &
cooperation
M   900 i, f & org, UK & Germany
¶   NL - 3-4; E-NL - 52; both ftm.
LM - 1; Ybk; both ftm, 200 nm.

British Chamber of Commerce in Hong Kong   1987

NR   Emperor Group Centre (room 1201), 288 Hennessy Rd,
WAN CHAI, Hong Kong.   (hq)
(852) 2824 2211   fax (852) 2824 1333
email info@britcham.com   http://www.britcham.com
Exec Dir: Christopher Hammerbeck
▲   Company Limited by Guarantee
○   *C
Gp   C'ees: General, China, Education, Environment, IT, Marketing
& communications, Real estate; Gps: Construction industry,
Financial services focus, Logistics, Scottish business, Small &
medium enterprise, YNetwork (Young executives); Business
policy unit: Women in business
●   Conf - Mtgs - ET - Inf - VE - LG
M   500 f
¶   British Business in China (LM) - 1.
The British Directory (LM) - 1.

British Chamber of Commerce in Hungary   (BCCH)   1991

■   Szt István krt 24 IV/3, H-1137 BUDAPEST, Hungary.   (hq)
36 (1) 302 5200   fax 36 (1) 302 3069
email bcch@bcch.com   http://www.bcch.com
▲   Un-incorporated Society
○   *C; 'to represent British business values & promote trade &
investment flows between the UK & Hungary
Gp   Communications; CSR (Corporate Social Responsibility);
Education; Government relations; Hospitality & tourism; HR
(Human resources); IT; Membership; SME (Small & Medium
Enterprises); Tax & Legal
●   Conf - Mtgs - Res - SG - Inf - LG
M   c 170 f
¶   Business News (NL) - 4; free.
BCCH Trade & Membership Directory - 1; ftm.
CSR brochure - occasional;
Electronic NL - 12; both free.

British Chamber of Commerce & Industry in Brazil   (BCCIB) 1916

NR   Rua Ferreira de Araújo, 741-1° andar Pinheiros, São Paulo SP,
SÃO PAULO SP 05428-002, Brazil.   (hq)
55 (11) 3819 0265
http://www.britcham.com.br
Exec Dir: Philip Hamer
▲   Registered Charity
Br   Rio de Janeiro
○   *C; to encourage the growth of trade & commercial
relationships between Great Britain & Brazil
Gp   Legal; Tax; Foreign trade; Foreign investment; Events; Seminar
●   Conf - Mtgs - ET - Expt - Inf - Lib
<   Eurochambres; Brit Cham Comm in Latin-America; London
Cham Comm & Ind
M   2 f, UK / 5 f, o'seas
¶   Britain Brasil - 6.   Doing Business in Brazil - 1.   Ybk - 1.

British Chamber of Commerce for Italy, Inc   (BCCI)   1904

■   via Dante 12, I-20121 MILANO, Italy.   (hq)
39 (02) 877 798   fax 39 (02) 8646 1855
email bcci@britchamitaly.com
http://www.britchamitaly.com
Chief Exec: Kelly Ben Frech
▲   Incorporated Society
Br   London: 020 7222 7040
○   *C
Gp   Commercial services; English language consultancy service;
Business examinations; Events (seminars, cultural events);
English courses in UK
●   Conf - Mtgs - ET - Exam - Res - Inf - Debt & VAT recovery -
Company searches
<   Maintains ties with UK Dept for Business, Enterprise &
Regulatory Reform; Coun of Brit Chams Comm in
Continental Europe (COBCOE), U of Foreign Chams Comm
& Italo-Foreign Chams Comm (UNIONESTERE)
M   i, f
¶   Britaly (NL online) - 12;   Focus on Italy - 1;
Speak to the World - 1; all free.
Trade Directory - 2 yrly; ftm, 25.

British Chamber of Commerce in Japan   (BCCJ)   1948

■   3F Kenkyusha Eigo Centre Building, 1-2 Kagurazaka, Shinjuku-
ku, TOKYO 162-0825, Japan.   (hq)
81 (3) 3267 1901   fax 81 (3) 3267 1903
email info@bccjapan.com   http://www.bccjapan.com
Chief Exec: Ian de Stains
○   *C; to promote Anglo-Japanese commercial relations
Gp   C'ees: Membership, Finance, Technology; Property forum;
British Industry Centre
●   Conf - Mtgs - Stat - Expt - Inf - LG

© CBD Research Ltd · Beckenham · BR3 5JS · Tel 020 8650 7745 · Fax 020 8650 0768 · E-mail cbd@cbdresearch.com · www.cbdresearch.com

British Chamber of Commerce in Korea   1981
NR   Regus Business Centre (20th floor), Korea First Bank Bldg, 100
        Gongpyong-dong, Jongro-gu, SEOUL 110 702,
        South Korea.   (hq)
        82 (2) 720 9407
        Dir Gen: Ms Jeongmi Seo
○   *C
●   Mtgs - Stat - Inf
M   c 200 f
¶   NL - 12; free.

British Chamber of Commerce in Latvia   (BCCL)   1996
■   Kr Valdemara 33 (office 33), LV-1010 RIGA, Latvia.   (hq)
        371 6724 9043   fax 371 6721 8045
        email info@bccl.lv   http://www.bccl.lv
        Exec Dir: Juris Benkis
▲   Un-incorporated Society
○   *C; promoting trade & partnership in British-Latvian business
●   Conf - Mtgs - Expt - Inf - VE - LG
<   Foreign Investors' Coun in Latvia
M   17 i, 99 f, 3 org
¶   British Latvian Trade (Jnl) - 6; free.

British Chamber of Commerce for Luxembourg   (BCC)   1992
■   6 rue Antoine de Saint Exupéry, L-1432 LUXEMBOURG.   (hq)
        00 352 (-) 465466   fax 00 352 (-) 220384
        email mail@bcc.lu   http://www.bcc.lu
        Mgr: Sophie Kerschen
○   *C
●   Conf - Mtgs - LG
¶   LM - 2 yrly; free.

British Chamber of Commerce for Morocco   (BCCM)   1923
■   65 avenue Hassan Seghir, 20000 CASABLANCA, Morocco.
        (hq)
        212 (22) 44 88 60/61/65   fax 212 (22) 44 88 68
        email britcham@casanet.net.ma
        http://www.bccm.co.ma
        Pres: Barry Marsh
○   *C; to promote bi-lateral trade between the UK & Morocco
●   Conf - Mtgs - Exhib - Expt - Inf - Lib - VE
<   Moroccan Brit Business Coun (MBBC); Assn des Chambres de
        Commerce et d'Industrie Européenne au Maroc (ACCIEM)
M   10 f, UK / 400 f, Morocco
¶   Business Link - 4;   Annual Review - 1; both ftm only.

British Chamber of Commerce Singapore   (BritCham)   1954
■   138 Cecil St, 11-01 Cecil Court, SINGAPORE 069538.   (hq)
        00 (65) 6222 3552   fax 00 (65) 6222 3556
        email info@britcham.org.sg
        http://www.britcham.org.sg
        Exec Dir: Brigitte Holtschneider
○   *C
Gp   Consumer; Education; Energy & utilities; Financial services;
        Hospitality, tourism & entertainment; Media & marketing;
        Professional services; Science & technology; Shipping; SME
●   Conf - Mtgs - Inf
M   750 i, 300 f
¶   Orient - 6.
        Membership Directory - 1.

British Chamber of Commerce in the Slovak Republic
■   Sedlárska 5 (3rd floor), 811 01 BRATISLAVA, Slovakia.   (hq)
        421 (2) 5292 0371   fax 421 (2) 5292 0371
        email director@britcham.sk   http://www.britcham.sk
        Exec Dir: Lívia Eperjesiová
▲   Un-incorporated Society
○   *C; to support its members & their business relations between
        Slovakia & the UK
Gp   Action groups: EU funds, Events, Government relations, Small /
        medium enterprises
●   Conf - Mtgs - Res - Expt - Inf - LG
<   Brit Chams Comm; COBCOE
M   1 i, 3 f, UK / 6 i, 107 f, o'seas
¶   E-Digest - 12; free.
        Bridges (Jnl).
        UK-Slovakia Trade Guide.
        Membership Directory.   AR.

**British Chamber of Commerce in Spain   (Cámara de Comercio
Británica en España)   1908**
NR   c/ Bruc 21 - 1° 4a, E-08010 BARCELONA, Spain.
        34 933 173 220
        email britchamber@britchamber.com
        http://www.britishchambersspain.com
        Dir: Charlotte Fraser-Prynne
○   *C

British Chamber of Commerce in Taipei   (BCCT)
■   207 Dun Hwa N Rd (suite 805-8th floor), TAIPEI 10595,
        Taiwan.   (hq)
        00 (02) 2547 1199   fax 00 (02) 2547 2378
        http://www.bcctaipei.com
        Chmn: Paul Burke,   Exec Dir: Lee Ting
▲   Company Limited by Guarantee
○   *C; to promote & develop trade & investment between Britain &
        Taiwan; to provide members in both countries with a forum
        to express their views on commercial & trade related issues
        affecting the two countries
●   Mtgs - Res - Inf - VE - LG
<   Britain in Asia Pacific (BIAP)
M   10 i, 100 f, (Taiwan)
¶   Effective Business in Taiwan - 1; ftm, £30 nm.
        LM - 1; ftm, £120 nm.

British Chamber of Commerce Thailand   (BCCT)   1946
■   208 Wireless Rd (7th floor), Lumphini, Pathumwan,
        BANGKOK 10330, Thailand.   (hq)
        66 (2) 651 5350-3   fax 66 (2) 651 5354
        email greg@bccthai.com   http://www.bccthai.com
        Exec Dir: Greg Watkins
○   *C
●   Conf - Mtgs - ET - Exam - Exhib - SG - Stat - Expt - Inf - Lib - VE
        - LG
M   c 620 f
¶   The Brief - 6;   The Digest - 12;
        Annual Hbk: Partners in Progress;
        Monthly Industry Sector Reports;
        Annual Expatriate Cost of Living Survey (online);
        Annual Compensation & Benefits Survey (online);
        LM (online);   all ftm only.

British Chamber of Commerce of Turkey (Association)   (BCCT)
NR   Mešrutiyet Caddesi 18, Asli Han Kat 6, Galatasaray, TR-
          80050 ISTANBUL, Turkey.   (hq)
          90 (212) 249 0420   fax 90 (212) 252 5551
          email buscenter@bcct.org.tr   http://www.bcct.org.tr
          Sec Gen: Mr İlter Koral
○   *C; to promote Anglo-Turkish trade
●   Conf - Mtgs - Exhib - Expt - Inf - Lib - VE
<   Assn Brit Cham Comm
M   51 i, UK / 410 i, Turkey – under Turkish law, only individuals
          can be members
¶   Trade Journal [in English] - 4; ftm.
          Trade Journal [in Turkish] - 6; ftm.
          Trade Fairs & Exhibitions in Turkey - 1; free.
          Hints to Businessmen: Turkey - 1; ftm.

British Chambers of Commerce   (BCC)   1890
NR   65 Petty France, LONDON, SW1H 9EU.   (hq)
          020 7654 5800   fax 020 7654 5819
          email info@britishchambers.org.uk
▲   Company Limited by Guarantee
○   *C; business representation, international, national & local
M   i, f & org

British Charolais Cattle Society Ltd   1962
■   Avenue M, NAC - Stoneleigh, KENILWORTH, Warks,
          CV8 2RG.   (hq)
          024 7669 7222   fax 024 7669 0270
          email charolais@charolais.co.uk
          http://www.charolais.co.uk
          Sec: David Benson
▲   Company Limited by Guarantee; Registered Charity
○   *B
●   Conf - Mtgs - Exhib - Comp - Expt - Inf - VE - Empl - LG
M   3,000 i, UK / 100 i, o'seas
¶   Charolais News - 3; free.

British Charollais Sheep Society Ltd   (BCSS)   1977
NR   Crogham Farm, Youngmans Rd, WYMONDHAM, Norfolk,
          NR18 0RR.   (hq)
          01953 603335   fax 01953 607626
          Jt Secs: Jonathan & Carroll Barber
○   *B
Gp   Trials: Ram, Halfbred ewe, Crossbred lamb; Charollais lamb
          marketing org
●   Conf - Mtgs - ET - Res - Exhib - SG - Stat - Expt - Inf - VE
<   UPRA Mouton Charollais (France); Nat Sheep Assn
M   1,100 i
¶   Flock Book - 1.   LM.   NL - 3.   AR.

British Chauffeurs Guild
NR   13 Stonecot Hill, SUTTON, Surrey, SM3 9HB.
          020 8641 1740   fax 020 8644 1945
○   *P

British Cheerleading Association   (BCA)   1984
NR   54c High St, NORTHWOOD, Middx, HA6 1BL.   (chmn)
          01923 825527
          http://www.cheerleading.org.uk
▲   Un-incorporated Society
○   *G; to act as the governing body for cheerleading in Britain
M   i in clubs

British Chelonia Group   (BCG)   1976
NR   PO Box 1176, CHIPPENHAM, Wilts, SN15 1XB.   (mail address)
          http://www.britishcheloniagroup.org.uk
▲   Registered Charity
○   *G, *L; the study, conservation & welfare of tortoises, terrapins
          & turtles worldwide
M   i

British Chemical Distributors & Traders Association Ltd
     since September 2006 **Chemical Business Association**

**British Chemical Engineering Contractors Association
(BCECA)   1966**
■   1 Regent St, LONDON, SW1Y 4NR.   (hq)
          020 7839 6514
          Dir: Don Latimer
▲   Un-incorporated Society
○   *T; interests of the principal companies in the UK which provide
          engineering, procurement, construction & project
          management services to the process industries
M   22 f

British Cheque Cashers Association   (BCCA)   1994
■   PO Box 3414, CHESTER, CH1 9BF.   (hq)
          01244 505904   fax 01244 505909
          email info@bcca.co.uk   http://www.bcca.co.uk
          Chief Exec: Geoff Holland
▲   Company Limited by Share
○   *T; for companies in the UK offering third party cheque
          encashment services & pay day advances (consumer credit)
●   Conf - Mtgs - ET - Res - Inf - LG - Liaison with orgs in the
          finance sector
<   Tr Assn Forum; Confedn Brit Ind (CBI); MALG
M   1,250 f
¶   Cheque This Out (NL) - 2;   AR - 1;
          Money Laundering Guidelines - irreg; all ftm only.
          Code of Practice; free.

British Chess Federation
     since 2005 **English Chess Federation**

British Chilean Chamber of Commerce   (BCCC)   1989
NR   12 Devonshire St, LONDON, W1G 7DS.   (hq)
          020 7323 3053   fax 020 7580 5901
          email info@bcc.org.uk   http://www.bccc.org.uk
          Gen Mgr: Christián León
▲   Company Limited by Guarantee
○   *C; to promote bi-lateral trade between Chile & the UK
Gp   Mining; Extractive industries; Exhibitions
●   Conf - Exhib - Inf - LG
<   Santiago Cham Comm; Chilean Brit Cham Comm
M   68 f
¶   Chile News (NL) - 6.

British Chilean Chamber of Commerce
     English name of **Cámara Chileno Británica de Comercio**

British Chiropody & Podiatry Association   (BChA)   1959
NR   New Hall, 149 Bath Rd, MAIDENHEAD, Berks, SL6 4LA.
          (pres/b)
          01628 632440   fax 01628 674483
          http://www.bcha-uk.org
          Hon Pres: Michael J Batt
▲   Un-incorporated Society
○   *P; for fully trained chiropodists & podiatrists
M   i

British Chiropractic Association   (BCA)   1925
■   59 Castle St, READING, Berks, RG1 7SN.   (hq)
          0118-950 5950   fax 0118-958 8946
          email enquiries@chiropractic-uk.co.uk
          http://www.chiropractic-uk.co.uk
          Exec Dir: Susan Wakefield
▲   Company Limited by Guarantee
○   *P; the registration body for chiropractors; an independent
          branch of medicine which specialises in mechanical disorders
          of the joints (particularly those of the spine) & their effect on
          the nervous system
●   Conf - Mtgs - ET - Res - Exhib - Stat - Inf - LG
<   Eur Chiropractic U; Wld Fedn of Chiropractic
M   1,073 i, UK / 36 i, o'seas
¶   Contact (NL) - 4;   In Touch - 12; both ftm only.

© CBD Research Ltd · Beckenham · BR3 5JS · Tel 020 8650 7745 · Fax 020 8650 0768 · E-mail cbd@cbdresearch.com · www.cbdresearch.com

British Christmas Tree Growers Association   (BCTGA)   1980
- ■ 13 Wolrige Rd, EDINBURGH, EH16 6HX.   (hq)
    0131-664 1100   fax 0131-664 2669
    http://www.christmastree.org.uk
    Sec: Roger Hay
- ▲ Un-incorporated Society
- ○ *T; to provide marketing assistance & technical advice to
    growers of live Christmas trees
- ● Conf - Mtgs - Stat - Inf
- < Timber Growers Assn; Christmas Tree Growers Assn of Western
    Europe; Amer Nat Christmas Tree Assn
- M 300 i, 50 f, 1 org, UK / 1 i, o'seas
- ¶ NL - 2; ftm.   LM.   AR; ftm.

**British Civil Engineering Test Equipment Manufacturers
Association   (CTMA)   1968**
- NR 28 Wing Rd, Linslade, LEIGHTON BUZZARD, Beds, LU7 2NJ.
    (chmn/b)
    01525 854819   fax 01525 854819
    email jtc@jtconsult.co.uk
    Chmn: John Turner
- ▲ Un-incorporated Society
- ○ *T; for manufacturers & suppliers of test equipment for the
    construction industry (civil engineering & building)
- ● Mtgs - BSI Standards Development (Test Methods) C'ees
- M 8 f

British Classification Society   (BCS)   1986
- ■ c/o Dr J Padmore, University of Sheffield Management Sch,
    9 Mappin St, SHEFFIELD, S Yorks, S1 4DT.   (sb)
    0114-222 3439   fax 0114-222 3348
    email j.padmore@sheffield.ac.uk
    http://www.thames.cs.rhul.ac.uk/~bcs
    Sec: Dr Jo Padmore
- ▲ Un-incorporated Society
- ○ *L; to encourage the cooperation & exchange of views &
    information among those interested in the principles &
    practice of classification in any discipline where they are used
- ● Conf - Mtgs - Res - Stat
- < Intl Fedn of Classification Socs (ICFS)
- M c 50 i

British Cleaning Council (BCC Ltd)   (BCC)   1982
- ■ PO Box 1328, KIDDERMINSTER, Worcs, DY11 5ZJ.   (hsb)
    01562 851129   fax 01562 851129
    email info@britishcleaningcouncil.org
    http://www.britishcleaningcouncil.org
    Co Sec: John Stinton
- ▲ Company Limited by Guarantee
- ○ *N, *T; interests of the cleaning industry in general
- ● Conf - Mtgs - ET - Exhib - LG - Voice of Industry - Council of
    Associations
- M 18 org
- ¶ The Voice - 4; free.

British Clematis Society   1991
- ■ 12 Oakwood Drive, FRIMLEY, Surrey, GU16 8LF.   (chmn)
    01276 28630
    http://www.britishclematis.org.uk
    Hon Sec: William Davies
- ▲ Registered Charity
- ○ *H; to promote the cultivation & preservation of clematis
- ● Mtgs - Exhib - Inf - Slide library - VE - Seed exchange - Plant
    sales
- < R Horticl Soc
- M 750 i
- ¶ The Clematis (Jnl) - 1.

British Clothing Industry Association   (BCIA)   1981
- NR 5 Portland Place, LONDON, W1B 1PW.   (hq)
    020 7636 7788   fax 020 7636 7515
    email bcia@dial.pipex.com
    http://www.5portlandplace.org.uk
    Dir: John R Wilson,   Asst Dir: Elizabeth P Fox
- ○ *T; to encourage, promote, develop & protect the clothing
    industry of the UK
- Gp Sectors: Shirt, Workwear, Women's & girls' outerwear, Men's &
    boys' outerwear, Foundation & swimwear; Tailoring
    Guild of British Tie Makers; Knitting Industries Federation
- ● Mtgs - Stat - Inf - Empl - LG
- < Intl Apparel Fedn; CBI; Apparel, Knitting & Textiles Alliance; Brit
    Apparel & Textile Confedn
- M f (membership covers 70% of UK production)
- ¶ News Sheet - 12;   Fact Card - 1;   AR; all ftm.

**British Coalition of Heritable Disorders of Connective Tissue
1990**
- ■ Rochester House, 5 Aldershot Rd, FLEET, Hants, GU51 3NG.
    Founder/Coordinator: Mrs Diane L Rust
- ○ *M, *W; to promote contact & cooperation between voluntary
    organisations working with connective tissue disorder
- M Independent support groups representing patients with
    rheumatological & orthopaedic symptoms
- ¶ Leaflet.

British Coatings Federation Ltd   (BCF)   1993
- NR James House, Bridge St, LEATHERHEAD, Surrey, KT22 7EP.
    (hq)
    01372 360660   fax 01372 376069
    email enquiry@bcf.co.uk   http://www.bcf.co.uk
    Chief Exec: Mrs Moira McMillan
- ▲ Company Limited by Guarantee
- ○ *T; interests of UK manufacturers of surface coatings, printing
    inks, wallcoverings & solvents
- Gp Sector councils:
    Decorative coatings
    Industrial coatings
    Powder coatings
    Printing ink
    Wallcoverings
- M 130 f
- ✕ 2005 Wallcoverings Manufacturers' Association of GB (merged)

British Coffee Association   2001
- NR PO Box 5, CHIPPING NORTON, Oxon, OX7 5UD.   (hq)
    01608 644995   fax 01608 644996
    http://www.britishcoffeeassociation.org
    Communications Mgr: Zoë Wheeldon
- ▲ Un-incorporated Society
- ○ *T
- ● Mtgs - Inf
- < Assn EEC Soluble Coffee Mfrs (AFCASOLE); Food & Drink Fedn
- M 2 f

British & Colombian Chamber of Commerce   (B&CCC)   1996
- NR 2 Belgrave Sq, LONDON, SW1X 8PJ.   (hq)
    020 7235 2106   fax 020 7235 0933
    email director@britishandcolombianchamber.com
    http://www.britishandcolombianchamber.com
    Chmn: Alexander Kennedy,   Exec Dir: Tania Hoxos
- ▲ Company Limited by Guarantee
- Br Colombia
- ○ *C; to promote commercial links between Colombia & the
    United Kingdom
- ● Conf - Mtgs - ET - Expt - Inf - VE - LG
- M 20 i, 60 f, UK / 15 f, o'seas
- ¶ Colombian Correspondent (NL) - 52; ftm, £30 nm.

British Colour Makers Association (BCMA) 1932
■   19 Wyatville Avenue, BUXTON, Derbys, SK17 6WJ.   (sp)
    01298 27028
    email info@bcma.org.uk   http://www.bcma.org.uk
    Sec: P D Johnson
▲   Un-incorporated Society
○   *T; represents manufacturers & suppliers of pigments in the UK
Gp Standing technical c'ee
●   Mtgs - ET - Inf - LG
<   Eurocolour; Colour Pigment Makers of America; Ecological &
    Toxicological Assn of Dyes & Organic Pigments Mfrs (ETAD);
    Alliance of Ind Assns (AIA)
M   12 f

British Coloured Sheep Breeders Association   1985
NR Daren Uchaf, Cwmyoy, ABERGAVENNY, Monmouthshire,
    NP7 7NR.   (sp)
    01873 890712
    Mem Sec: Sarah Stacey
○   *B; to promote coloured sheep & use of their fleece & by -
    products
●   Inf - Demonstrations
M   120 i
¶   Coloured Sheep News - 4.

British Combustion Equipment Manufacturers Association
    since May 2004 **ICOM Energy Association**

British Comedy Society (BCS) 1991
■   37 Langbourne Ave, LONDON, N6 6PS.   (regd/office)
    020 8347 0115   fax 020 8347 0115
    email johngatenby@yahoo.com
    Treas: John Gatenby
▲   Company Limited by Guarantee
○   *G; to preserve & foster the tradition of British Comedy
●   Plaque unveilings - Charity fundraising - Celebrity luncheons -
    Pinewood Studio Hall of Fame - Elstree Wall of Fame
M   150 i
¶   NL - irreg.

British Commercial Boatbuilders Association
    a group of the **British Marine Federation**

British Committee for Standards in Haematology
    a group of the **British Society for Haematology**

British Compact Collectors' Society (BCCS) 1994
■   PO Box 131, WOKING, Surrey, GU24 9YR.   (hsp)
    http://www.compactcollectors.co.uk
    Pres: Juliette Edwards
○   *G; for collectors of ladies' powder compacts & related vintage
    glamour items
●   Conf - Res - Exhib
M   c 400 i
¶   Face Facts - 3; ftm only.
    Note: Please enclose sae on initial contact

British Comparative Literature Association (BCLA) 1975
NR Dept of French Studies, University of Manchester, Oxford Rd,
    MANCHESTER, M13 9PL.   (hsb)
    Sec: Mrs Penny Brown
○   *A; to promote the scholarly study of literature without
    confinement to national or linguistic boundaries
●   Conf - Mtgs - Comp
<   Intl Comparative Literature Assn
M   150 i
¶   New Comparison - 2; ftm.
    Comparative Criticism - 3.

British Complementary Medicine Association (BCMA) 1992
NR PO Box 5122, BOURNEMOUTH, Dorset, BH8 0WG.   (hq)
    0845 345 5977
    email info@bcma.co.uk   http://www.bcma.co.uk
    Admin: Tracy Smith
▲   Un-incorporated Society
○   *M, *P; complementary medicine & healthcare; to make
    available public efficacious & safe complementary medicine
Gp Professional organisations; Practitioners register
●   Mtgs - ET - Res - Exhib - SG - Inf - LG - Maintaining the register
    of practitioners
<   Indep Care Org Coun
M   20,000 i, 40 assns, 30 colleges/schools
¶   NL;   AR; both ftm only.

British Composites Society
    a group of the **Institute of Materials, Minerals & Mining**

British Compressed Air Society (BCAS) 1930
NR 33-34 Devonshire St, LONDON, W1G 6PY.   (hq)
    020 7935 2464   fax 020 7935 3307
    email info@britishcompressedairsociety.co.uk
    http://www.britishcompressedairsociety.co.uk
    Exec Dir & Co Sec: C P Dee
▲   Company Limited by Guarantee
○   *T; manufacturers & distributors of compressed air products &
    services in the UK; to represent members to UK government
    & European institutions; to provide a forum for the
    manufacturers & the broad distribution, supply & installation
    interests in the compressed air, vacuum & pneumatics
    industry
Gp Industrial process compressors; Portable compressors &
    contractors' tools; Industrial tools; Pneumatic control & air
    treatment; Service industries equipment;
    C'ees: Air treatment & pneumatic control, Compressor &
    vacuum, Distributors, Tools
●   Mtgs - ET - Stat - Inf - LG
<   Eur C'ee of Mfrs of Compressors, Vacuum Pumps & Pneumatic
    Tools PNEUROP
M   5 i, 105 f, UK / 7 f, o'seas
¶   NL - 12; ftm [email].
    Air treatment & general services:
        Installation Guide.   Pipe Joint Guide.
        Compressed Air Condensate.
        Air Treatment Contamination & Purity Classes &
        Measurement Methods.   AR - 1; free.

British Compressed Gases Association (BCGA) 1971
NR 1 Gleneagles House, Vernongate, DERBY, DE1 1UP.   (hq)
    01332 225120   fax 01332 225101
    http://www.bcga.co.uk
    Dir: Doug Thornton
▲   Company Limited by Guarantee
○   *T; interests of companies engaged in the manufacture,
    distribution & safe use of gases, cylinders & equipment
●   Conf - Mtgs - Exhib - Inf - LG - Representation on BSI, CEN &
    ISO C'ees - Advice on use & application of gases
<   Eur Indl Gases Assn (EIGA); Engg Eqpt & Materials Users Assn;
    CBI; BSI; Tr Assn Forum; Instn Mechanical Engrs
M   57 i, 3 associate members
¶   Codes of Practice & Guidance Notes;   Technical Reports;
    Leaflets - all 3-yrly; prices vary.

British Computer Association of the Blind
NR 58-72 John Bright St, BIRMINGHAM, B1 1BN.
    0845 430 8627
    http://www.bcab.org.uk
    Chmn: Derek Naysmith
○   *G; visually impaired computer professionals & users

© CBD Research Ltd · Beckenham · BR3 5JS · Tel 020 8650 7745 · Fax 020 8650 0768 · E-mail cbd@cbdresearch.com · www.cbdresearch.com

British Computer Society (BCS) 1957
NR North Star House (Block D 1st floor), North Star Avenue, SWINDON, Wilts, SN2 1FA. (hq)
01793 417417
Chief Exec: David Clarke
▲ Registered Charity
○ *P; 'the authoritative voice of those seeking excellence in computing; a national source of advice to government & industry on all issues affected by computing; maintaining both technical & ethical standards in the profession'
M i

British Concrete Pumping Group
a special interest group of the **Construction Plant-hire Association**

British Confectioners Association (BCA) 1905
NR Unit 4 Home Farm Business Centre, BRIGHTON, E Sussex, BN1 9HU. (hsb)
01273 601404
Hon Sec: Tim Cutress
▲ Un-incorporated Society
○ *T; to promote craftsmanship & good training in the flour confectionery trade (not sugar confectionery sweets)
● Mtgs - ET - Exhib - Comp - SG - VE
M i
¶ LM - 1; ftm only.

British Confederation of Psychotherapists
since 2005-06 **British Psychoanalytic Council**

British Conifer Society (BCS) 2003
NR Bedgebury National Pinetum, GOUDHURST, Kent, TN17 2SL.
01580 211044 fax 01580 212423
http://www.britishconifersociety.org.uk
Sec: Daniel Luscombe
○ *H
M i

British Connemara Pony Society (BCPS) 1947
■ 2 East Green, Bowsden, BERWICK-upon-TWEED, Northumberland, TD15 2TJ. (sb)
01289 388800
email secretary@britishconnemaras.co.uk
http://www.britishconnemaras.co.uk
Sec: Mrs S Mansell
○ *B
< Connemara Pony Breeders Soc (Republic of Ireland)
✕ 2003-04 English Connemara Pony Society

British Constructional Steelwork Association Ltd (BCSA) 1906
NR 4 Whitehall Court, LONDON, SW1A 2ES. (hq)
020 7839 8566
http://www.steelconstruction.org
Chief Exec: Dr Derek Tordoff
▲ Company Limited by Guarantee
○ *T; fabricators of constructional steelwork & suppliers of components & services to the steel construction industry
Gp Steel construction certification scheme; Register of Qualified Steelwork Contractors Scheme
● Conf - Mtgs - ET - Res - Comp - SG - Stat - Expt - Inf - VE - LG
< Eur Convention for Constructional Steelwork (ECCS)
M 150 f
¶ Directory for Specifiers & Buyers - 1;
Steel Construction News [incl LM] - 3;
New Steel Construction [incl LM] - 6; Annual Review; all free.
Various technical publications: list available.

British Contact Dermatitis Group
a group of the **British Association of Dermatologists**

British Contact Lens Association (BCLA)
NR Walmar House, 288-292 Regent St, LONDON, W1B 3AL.
020 7580 6661 fax 020 7580 6669
http://www.bcla.org.uk
▲ Registered Charity
○ *T
Gp Dispensing; Medical; Optometric; Technical; Student membership; Overseas
M i
¶ Jnl.

British Contract Furnishing Association Ltd (BCFA) 1970
NR Project House, 25 West Wycombe Rd, HIGH WYCOMBE, Bucks, HP11 2LQ. (hq)
01494 896790 fax 01494 896799
email enquiries@bcfa.org.uk http://www.thebcfa.com
Contact: Trudy Pearce
▲ Company Limited by Guarantee
○ *T
● Mtgs - ET - Exhib - Stat - Inf
M 300 f
¶ UK Contract Furnishing Directory - 1; ftm, £85 nm.

British Contract Manufacturers & Packers Association (BCMPA)
NR St Mary's Court, The Broadway, OLD AMERSHAM, Bucks, HP7 0UT.
01494 582013 fax 01494 778147
email info@bcmpa.org.uk http://www.bcmpa.org.uk
Chief Exec: Rodney Steel
○ *T

British Cooperative Clinical Group
a group of the **British Association for Sexual Health & HIV**

British Cooperative Clinical Group
a specialist group of the **British Association for Sexual Health & HIV**

British Correspondence Chess Association (BCCA) 1906
NR 61 Swanswell Rd, SOLIHULL, W Midlands, B92 7ET.
0121-707 3850
http://www.bcca.info
Sec: Stan Grayland
○ *G;

British Correspondence Chess Society
has folded.

British Costume Association (BCA) 1986
NR PO Box 136, ASHINGTON, Northumberland, NE62 5ZX. (chmn/p)
0845 230 0515
http://www.incostume.co.uk
Chmn: Peter Denton
▲ Un-incorporated Society
○ *T; costume & fancy dress suppliers
● ET - Exhib - Inf - LG
M 300 f
¶ In Costume - 4; ftm.

BRITISH COUNCIL ...
For details of British Councils, other than those below, see the companion volume **'Councils, Committees & Boards'**

British Council for Chinese Martial Arts (BCCMA) 1973
■ c/o 110 Fensham Drive, NUNEATON, Warks, CV10 9QL.
024 7639 4642
email bob@bccma.com info@bccma.com
○ *N, *S;; the governing body for Chinese martial arts in the UK recognised by the Sports Council since 1980
M 10,000 i in 75 org/assns

British Council for Offices (BCO) 1990
- 78-79 Leadenhall St, LONDON, EC3A 3DH. (hq)
  020 7283 0125   fax 020 7626 1553
  email mail@bco.org.uk   http://www.bco.org.uk
  Chief Exec: Richard Kauntze
▲ Company Limited by Guarantee
○ *N, *T; to research, develop & communicate best practice in all
  aspects of the office sector; to provide a forum for discussion
  & debate of relevant issues; members are organisations
  involved in creating, acquiring & occupying office space
● Conf - Mtgs - Res - Awards programme
M c 1,500 i & f, UK & o'seas
¶ Publications list available.

British Council of Shopping Centres (BCSC) 1983
NR 1 Queen Anne's Gate, LONDON, SW1H 9BT. (hq & regd
  office)
  020 7222 1122
▲ Company Limited by Guarantee
○ *T; for those engaged in the development, design &
  management of shopping centres & the retailing & other
  functions therein
M i & f

British Country Music Association (BCMA) 1969
- PO Box 240, HARROW, Middx, HA3 7PH. (mail address)
  01273 559750   fax 01273 559750
  email theBCMA@yahoo.com   http://www.cmib.co.uk/
  bcma
○ *A; promotion of country music in GB
● Comp - Inf - VE
M 3,000 i, UK / 80 i, o'seas
¶ Bulletin - 6;   Ybk - 1; both ftm only.

British Crossbow Society
  see **National Crossbow Federation of Great Britain**

British Crown Green Bowling Association (BCGBA) 1907
NR 94 Fishers Lane, Pensby, WIRRAL, Merseyside, CH61 8SB.
  (chief/exec/p)
  0151-648 5740
  http://www.crowngreenbowls.org
  Chief Exec: John Crowther
○ *S; the governing body of crown green bowling

British Cryoengineering Society
  in 2006 reverted to its pre-1998 name: **British Cryogenics Council**

British Cryogenics Council (BCC) 1997
NR PO Box 41, LEATHERHEAD, Surrey, KT22 9YY. (hsp)
  01372 376544   fax 01372 376544
  http://www.bcryo.org.uk
  Hon Sec: P Cook
▲ Registered Charity
○ *P; to promote knowledge & interest in cryogenics (low
  temperature science & technology); to foster development &
  application of cryogenics for public benefit
● Conf - Mtgs - ET
M 70 i
¶ Low Temperature News - 4; ftm only.
✕ 2006 British Cryoengineering Society

British Crystallographic Association (BCA) 1982
NR Dr Georgina Rosair, School of EPS & Chemistry,
  Perking Building, Heriot-Watt University, EDINBURGH,
  EH14 4AS. (sb)
  0131-451 8036
  email g.m.rosair@ed.ac.uk
  http://www.bca.chem.ucl.ac.uk
  Sec: Dr Georgina Rosair
▲ Registered Charity
○ *L; for those interested in study & research into crystallography
  - of biological structures, chemical, industrial & physical
  applications
Gp Biological structure; Chemical crystallography; Industrial;
  Physical crystallography
● Conf - Mtgs - ET - Awarding bursaries for students
< Intl U of Crystallography (IUCr)
M c 875 i
¶ Crystallography News - 4.

British Culinary Federation 2005
NR PO Box 10532, ALCESTER, Warks, B50 4ZY.
  01789 491218
  http://www.britishculinaryfederation.co.uk
  Admin: Jayne Mottram
○ *P

British Cutlery & Silverware Association (BCSA)
NR Unit 10 1st floor, Edmund Road Business Centre, SHEFFIELD,
  S Yorks, S2 4ED. (hq)
  0114-252 7550   fax 0114-252 7555
  Chief Exec: Mrs C T Steele
○ *T; promotion of cutlery & silverware
● Conf - Mtgs - Inf
M f

British Cycling Federation (BCF) 1959
NR National Cycling Centre, Stuart St, MANCHESTER,
  M11 4DQ. (hq)
  0161-274 2000   fax 0161-274 2001
  email info@britishcycling.org.uk
  http://www.britishcycling.org.uk
  Chief Exec: Peter King
▲ Un-incorporated Society
○ *S; to act as the governing body of UK cycle sport
M i & clubs
  Note: British Cycling is the trading name of the BCF

British Dam Society (BDS) 1950
NR Institution of Civil Engineers, One Great George St, LONDON,
  SW1P 3AA. (hq)
  020 7665 2234
  email bds@ice.org.uk
  Sec: Tim Fuller,   Chmn: Dr Andy Hughes
▲ Registered Charity
○ *P; to stimulate interest & encourage improvements in the
  design, construction, maintenance, operation & safety of
  dams & reservoirs
● Conf - Mtgs - ET - Res - Exhib - Comp - Inf - LG
< Intl Commission Large Dams (ICOLD)
M i & f
¶ Dams & Reservoirs (NL) - 4.

British Damage Management Association (BDMA) 1999
- Willow Business Centre, Connect House, 21 Willow Lane,
  MITCHAM, Surrey, CR4 4NA. (hq)
  0700 0843 2362   fax 0700 0236 2329
  email info@bdma.org.uk   http://www.bdma.org.uk
  Chmn: Emma Dadson
▲ Company Limited by Guarantee
○ *P, *T
Gp Damage management; Fire & flood restoration
● Conf - Mtgs - Exam
M 1,110 i, 600 f
¶ Recovery - 4; free.

© CBD Research Ltd · Beckenham · BR3 5JS · Tel 020 8650 7745 · Fax 020 8650 0768 · E-mail cbd@cbdresearch.com · www.cbdresearch.com

British Darts Organisation Ltd   (BDO)   1973
- ■ 2 Pages Lane, Muswell Hill, LONDON, N10 1PS.   (hq)
  020 8883 5544
  Hon Sec: O A Croft
- ▲ Company Limited by Guarantee
- Br 66
- ○ *S; promoting the sport of darts
- ● Comp
- < Wld Darts Fedn
- M 25,000 i in 66 member counties, 60 affiliated national darts bodies
- ¶ Ybk.

British Deaf Association   (BDA)   1890
- ■ Coventry Point (10th floor), Market Way, COVENTRY, W Midlands, CV1 1EA.   (hq)
  024 7655 0936
  http://www.signcommunity.org.uk
  Chief Exec: Simon Wilkinson-Blake
- ▲ Registered Charity
- Br 5
- ○ *W; a democratic, membership-led body campaigning on behalf of deaf sign language users in the UK; to increase deaf people's access to lifestyles that most hearing people take for granted
- ● Conf - ET - Inf
  Textphone: 024 7655 0393
- M 3,500 i, UK / 15-20 i, o'seas
- ¶ Sign Matters; £25 yr (annual sub).
  BDN British Deaf News - 12.

British Deaf Sports Council   (BDSC)   1930
- NR 49 Fonnerau Rd, IPSWICH, IP1 3JN.   (hq)
  fax 01268 510621
  email bdsc_mikewebster@yahoo.co.uk
  http://www.britishdeafsportscouncil.org.uk
  Sec: Mike Webster
- ▲ Company Limited by Guarantee; Registered Charity
- Br 115
- ○ *S; national governing body for sport for deaf people locally, regionally, nationally (England, Scotland, Wales) & internationally
- ● Mtgs - Comp
- < Comité Intl de Sport de Sourds (CISS); Eur Deaf Sports Org EDSO)
- M 3,000 i, 115 clubs

British Decoy Wildfowl Carvers Association   (BDWCA)   1990
- ■ 26 Shendish Edge, HEMEL HEMPSTEAD, Herts, HP3 9SZ. (hsp)
  01442 247610
  http://www.bdwca.org.uk
  Sec: Janet Nash
- ▲ Un-incorporated Society
- Br 8
- ○ *A; for decoy (bird) & wildfowl carvers & collectors
- ● Mtgs - ET - Res - Exhib - Comp - SG - Inf - VE
- M 174 i, 4 f, UK / 8 i, o'seas
- ¶ NL - 4; free.

British Deer Farmers Association   (BDFA)   1978
- NR PO Box 7522, MATLOCK, Derbys, DE4 9BR.   (hq)
  0845 634 4758   fax 0845 634 4759
  email info@bdfa.co.uk   http://www.bdfa.co.uk
  Sec: Claire Parkinson
- ▲ Un-incorporated Society
- ○ *F, *T; to promote deer farming & the interests of deer farmers & venison producers
- ● Conf - ET - Inf - VE - LG
- M f
- ¶ Deer Farming (Jnl) - 4.   Deer News (NL) - 6.

British Deer Society   (BDS)   1963
- ■ The Walled Garden, Burgate Manor, FORDINGBRIDGE, Hants, SP6 1EF.   (hq)
  01425 655434   fax 01425 655433
  email h.q@bds.org.uk   http://www.bds.org.uk
  Gen Mgr: Sarah Stride
- ▲ Company Limited by Guarantee; Registered Charity
- ○ *L, *V; to promote & conserve the 6 species of wild deer within the UK
- ● Mtgs - ET - Res - Exhib - Comp - Stat - Inf - VE - LG
- M c 6,000 i, UK & o'seas
- ¶ Deer (Jnl) - 4; ftm, £5 nm.   Annual Review; ftm, postage nm.

** British Dendrobatid Group
  Organisation lost: see Introduction paragraph 3

British Dental Association   (BDA)   1880
- ■ 64 Wimpole St, LONDON, W1G 8YS.   (hq)
  020 7935 0875   fax 020 7487 5232
  email enquiries@bda.org   http://www.bda.org
  Sec: Peter Ward
- ▲ Company Limited by Guarantee
- Br 21
- ○ *P, *U; to represent dentists in the UK
- Gp Dental services: Community, Hospital; University dental teachers & research workers; Armed forces dentists
- ● Conf - Mtgs - SG - Stat - Inf - Lib - Empl - LG
- < Fédn Dentaire Intl; C'wealth Dental Assn
- M 20,500 i, UK / 600 i, o'seas
- ¶ British Dental Jnl - 24.   BDA News (NL) - 12.
  Hbk - 1;   AR.

British Dental Hygienists Association
   since 2008 **British Society of Dental Hygiene & Therapy**

British Dental Practice Managers Association   (BDPMA)   1993
- NR 3 Kestrel Court, Waterwells Drive, Waterwells Business Park, GLOUCESTER, GL2 2AT.   (hq)
  01452 886364   fax 01452 886468
  email info@bdpma.org.uk   http://www.bdpma.org.uk
  Chmn: Miss Bridget M Crump
- ▲ Un-incorporated Society
- Br 7
- ○ *P; to promote a payscale & job description; to offer job opportunities
- ● Conf - Mtgs - ET - Res - Exhib - Inf - Empl
- M 460 i
- ¶ Networking (NL) - 4; ftm only.

British Dental Trade Association   (BDTA)   1923
- ■ Mineral Lane, CHESHAM, Bucks, HP5 1NL.   (hq)
  01494 782873   fax 01494 786659
  email admin@bdta.org.uk   http://www.bdta.org.uk
  Exec Dir: A H Reed
- ▲ Company Limited by Guarantee
- ○ *T; to promote the dental industry & trade
- Gp Manufacturers; Importers/Exporters; Dental dealers; Financial services; Computer services; Wholesalers; Publishers
- ● Conf - ET - Exam - Exhib - Stat - Inf - LG
- < Fedn of the Eur Dental Ind (FIDE); Assn of Dental Dealers in Europe (ADDE); Assn Brit Health Care Inds (ABHCI)
- M 123 f, UK / 4 f, o'seas
- ¶ The Dental Trader (Jnl) - 4;   NL;   LM;
  Exhibition Catalogue - 1;   AR; all ftm.

British Dermatological Nursing Group
   a group of the **British Association of Dermatologists**

British Dietetic Association (BDA) 1936
- ■ Charles House (5th floor), 148-9 Great Charles St, Queensway, BIRMINGHAM, B3 3HT.   (hq)
  0121-200 8080
  email info@bda.uk.com   http://www.bda.uk.com
  Chief Exec: Andy Burman
- ▲ Company Limited by Guarantee; Registered Charity
- ○ *P; for qualified dieticians; to advance the science & practice of dietetics & associated subjects
- Gp Renal dialysis; Paediatric; Mental health; Parenteral & enteral nutrition; Metabolic & research; Nutrition advice for the elderly; Community nutrition; National dietetic managers; Diabetes management & education; Dieticians in HIV/AIDS.
- ● Conf - Mtgs - ET - Res - Empl
- M 7,500 i, UK / 180 i, o'seas
- ¶ Jnl of Human Nutrition & Dietetics - 6; Dietetics Today (NL) - 12;   all ftm.   AR - 1.

British Disabled Flying Association   (BDFA)
- NR c/o Lasham Gliding Society, Lasham Airfield, ALTON, Hants, GU34 5SS.
  01256 346424
  email info@bdfa.net   http://www.bdfa.net

British Disc Golf Association   (BDGA)
- ■ 5 Railway Terrace, SHREWSBURY, Shropshire, SY2 7AG.
  (dir/p)
  01743 243190
  email secretary@bdga.org.uk   http://www.bdga.org.uk
  Communications Dir: Nigel Williams
- ▲ Un-incorporated Society
- ○ *S; the national governing body for the sport of disc golf; to be responsible for coordination of competitive disc golf; to promote disc golf
- ● Comp - Inf
- < Wld Flying Disc Fedn; Profl Disc Golf Assn
- M 80 i
- ¶ In Flight Magazine - 4; ftm only.

British Display Society Ltd   (BDS)   1943
- ■ 12 Cliff Avenue, Chalkwell, LEIGH-on-SEA, Essex, SS9 1HF.
  (regd/office)
  020 8856 2030   fax 0870 421 5589
  http://www.britishdisplaysociety.co.uk
  Sec: Rebecca Carson
- ▲ Registered Charity
- ○ *P; for visual merchandising, display, point-of-sale, exhibition design & training
- ● ET - Exam - Comp
- M [not disclosed]
- ¶ BDS NL - 11; free.   AR; ftm only.

British Domesticated Ostrich Association   (BDOA)   1992
- ■ 33 Eden Grange, Little Corby, CARLISLE, Cumbria, CA4 8QW.   (asa)
  01228 562532   fax 01228 562187
  email craig@bdoa.info   http://www.ostrich.org.uk
  Sec: F C Culley
- ▲ Un-incorporated Society
- ○ *B, *F; promotion of ostrich farming in the UK
- M i, f

British Double Reed Society   (BDRS)   1988
- ■ 5 North Avenue, Stoke Park, COVENTRY, Warks, CV2 4DH.
  (hsp)
  024 7665 0322
  email secretary@bdrs.org.uk   http://www.bdrs.org.uk
  Hon Sec: Mrs Maxine Moody
- ▲ Registered Charity
- ○ *D; for practitioners & enthusiasts of the bassoon, oboe & other double reed instruments; to improve the standards of teaching; to encourage research into design & to encourage the writing of new music
- ● Conf - ET - Comp - Inf - Annual convention to promote all double reed players & activities
- < Intl Double Reed Soc (IDRS)
- M c 1,000, UK & o'seas
  (Sub: £25)
- ¶ Double Reed News (Jnl) - 4; ftm, £3.95 nm.

British Doula Association   (BDA)   1998
- NR 49 Harrington Gdns, LONDON, SW7 4JU.   (hsb)
  020 7244 6053   fax 020 7244 9035
  email info@britishdoulas.co.uk
  http://www.britishdoulas.co.uk
  Sec: Mrs Jean Birtles
- ▲ Un-incorporated Society
- ○ *W; to promote Doula care for pregnant, birthing & postpartum mothers; care is that traditionally offered by mothers or experienced sisters & concentrates on helping the mother rather than caring only for the child
- ● Conf
- M 150 i, UK / 20 i, o'seas
- ¶ Doula News - 1.

British Dragon Boat Racing Association   (BDA)   1987
- ■ 13 The Prebend, Northend, ROYAL LEAMINGTON SPA, Warks, CV47 2TR.   (hsp)
  01295 770734
  Co Sec: David A Cogswell
- ▲ Company Limited by Guarantee
- ○ *S; governing body for Chinese Dragon Boat racing in the UK
- ● Conf - Mtgs - Comp
- < Intl Dragon Boat Fedn (IDBF); Eur Dragon Boat Fedn (EDBF); C'wealth Dragon Boat Fedn (CDBF)
- M 800 i, 35 clubs, UK / 50 i, o'seas
- ¶ Dragon Line NL - 12; ftm only.

British Dragonfly Society   (BDS)   1983
- NR 23 Bowker Way, Whittlesey, PETERBOROUGH, Cambs, PE7 1PY.   (hsp)
  01733 204286
  email bdssecretary@dragonflysoc.org.uk
  http://www.dragonflysoc.org.uk
  Hon Sec: Henry Curry
- ▲ Registered Charity
- ○ *L; to promote & encourage the study & conservation of dragonflies & their natural habitats
- Gp Conservation
- ● Mtgs - ET - Inf - Lib - PL - VE - LG
- < Soc Intle Odontologica; Wld Dragonfly Assn
- M 1,400 i, 15 f, UK / 75 i, o'seas
- ¶ Jnl - 2;   Dragonfly News - 2; both ftm only.

British Dressage
   a discipline member of the **British Equestrian Federation**

© CBD Research Ltd · Beckenham · BR3 5JS · Tel 020 8650 7745 · Fax 020 8650 0768 · E-mail cbd@cbdresearch.com · www.cbdresearch.com

British Dried Flowers Association **(BDFA)** **1988**
NR   Chalkpit Farm, School Lane, Bekesbourne, CANTERBURY, Kent,
     CT4 5EU.   (chmn/b)
     01227 830964
     http://www.flowergrowers.co.uk
     Sec: Amanda Barker
▲   Un-incorporated Society
○   *H, *T; for producers & suppliers of British dried flowers &
     grasses
●   ET - Exhib - Inf - VE
M   10 f
¶   Members' Directory; free.

British Drilling Association Ltd **(BDA)** **1975**
NR   Wayside, London End, Upper Boddington, DAVENTRY,
     Northants, NN11 6DP.   (hsb)
     01327 264622   fax 01327 264623
     email office@britishdrillingassociation.co.uk
     http://www.britishdrillingassociation.co.uk
     Nat Sec: Brian Stringer
▲   Company Limited by Guarantee
○   *T; to group together companies engaged in all aspects of
     ground drilling
●   Conf - Mtgs - ET - Exhib - SG - Stat - Inf
M   600 i, 130 f
¶   BDA NL - 6.   LM - 1.

British Driving Society **(BDS)** **1957**
NR   83 New Rd, Helmingham, STOWMARKET, Suffolk, IP14 6EA.
     (hsp)
     01473 892001   fax 01473 892005
     email email@britishdrivingsociety.co.uk
     http://www.britishdrivingsociety.co.uk
     Co Sec: Mrs T K Styles
▲   Company Limited by Guarantee
○   *S; to encourage & assist those interested in the driving of
     horses & ponies
Gp   Carriage Foundation
●   Conf - Mtgs - ET - Exam - Exhib - Comp - Inf - VE
M   75 driving clubs
¶   NL - 4.   Ybk.

British Drug Free Powerlifting Association **(BDFPA)** **1989**
■   49 Hackthorn Rd, Woodseats, SHEFFIELD, S Yorks, S8 8TB.
     (sp)
     0114-225 8443
     http://www.bdfpa.co.uk
     Gen Sec: Sharron Clegg
○   *S
●   Mtgs
M   i
¶   Raw Power - 4; ftm, £24 nm.

British Durum Association
     this company has ceased to trade.

British Dyslexia Association **(BDA)** **1972**
■   Unit 8 Bracknell Beeches, Old Bracknell Lane, BRACKNELL,
     Berks, RG12 7BW.   (hq)
     0845 251 9003   fax 0845 251 9005
     http://www.bdadyslexia.org.uk
     Chief Exec: Judi Stewart
▲   Registered Charity
○   *N; to represent all with dyslexia; to work towards early
     identification & appropriate remediation, teacher training &
     support
●   Helpline: 0845 251 9002
M   i

British Earth Sheltering Association **(BESA)** **1983**
■   15 Maes-y-fron, ABERCRAVE, Glam, SA9 1XE.   (hsp)
     01639 730006
     email undergroundwoods@hotmail.co.uk
     http://www.besa-uk.org
     Hon Sec: David Woods
▲   Un-incorporated Society
○   *P; to promote the development of earth sheltered building
     design in the UK for the environmental & energy saving
     benefits to be accrued
●   Mtgs - Inf - Lib
M   150 i, 10 f, 5 org, UK / 15 i, o'seas
¶   NL - 4; ftm, £2.50 nm.

British Ecological Society **(BES)** **1913**
NR   26 Blades Court, Deodar Rd, LONDON, SW15 2NU.   (hq)
     020 8871 9797   fax 020 8871 9779
     Exec Sec: Dr Hazel J Norman
▲   Registered Charity
○   *L; promotion of the study of ecology through research
M   i

British Edible Pulse Association **(BEPA)** **1935**
■   c/o Stuart Cree, Ebbage Seeds, The Stable Yard, Ryston Hall,
     DOWNHAM MARKET, Norfolk, PE38 0AA.   (mail/address)
     01366 387877   fax 01366 384285
     email stuartcree@ebbageseeds.co.uk
     http://www.bepa.co.uk
     Pres: Howard Jackson
▲   Registered Charity
○   *T; 'to promote the uses of edible pulses from the farmer to the
     housewife'
●   Conf - Mtgs - Exhib - Comp - Stat - Expt - Inf - LG
M   48 f
¶   Monthly Member Report - 12; free.

British Educational Furniture Manufacturers Group
     a group of the **British Educational Suppliers Association**

British Educational Leadership, Management & Administration
Society **(BELMAS)** **1971**
NR   Victoria Hall (room 50), Norfolk St, SHEFFIELD, S Yorks,
     S1 2JB.   (hq)
     0114-279 9926   fax 0114-279 6868
     email info@belmas.org.uk   http://www.belmas.org.uk
     Hon Sec: Nigel Bennett
▲   Registered Charity
○   *E; development of practice, teaching, training & research in
     educational administration
Gp   Teachers of education management; Research in education
     management
●   Conf - Mtgs - Res
<   Eur Forum on Educ Admin (EFEA); C'wealth Coun for Educl
     Admin & Mgt (CCEAM)
M   c 550 i, c 50 org UK / c 30 i, o'seas
¶   Education Management & Administration - 4.
     Management in Education - 5.
     Books on related subjects.

British Educational Research Association (BERA) 1974

- ■ Association House, South Park Rd, MACCLESFIELD, Cheshire, SK11 6SH. (asa)
  01625 504062   fax 01625 267879
  email admin@bera.ac.uk   http://www.bera.ac.uk
  Chief Exec: Jeremy Hoad
  Assn Mgr: Dan Hollingshurst
- ▲ Registered Charity
- ○ *E, *L, *Q; to further education research & in particular, the link between education policy & practice of teachers, lecturers, teachers' assistants & researchers
- Gp Assessment; Comparative & international education; Creativity in education; Early childhood; Educational research & policy-making; Educational effectiveness & improvement; Higher education; Inclusive education; Leading & managing schools & colleges; Learning in the professions; Literacy & languages; Mathematics education; Mentoring & Coaching; Neuroscience & education; New researchers; New technologies in education; Philosophy of education; Physical education & sports pedagogy; Post-compulsory & lifelong learning; Practitioner research; Primary school teachers' work; Race, ethnicity & education; Religious & moral education; Research methodology in education; Science education; Sexualities; Social justice; Social theory & education; Social-cultural history activity theory; Teacher education & development
- ● Conf - Mtgs - ET - Res - Comp - SG - Inf - Lib - LG
- < Eur Educl Res Assn
- M 1,700 i, UK / 400 i, o'seas
  (Sub: £65)
- ¶ British Educational Research Jnl - 6; ftm.
  Research Intelligence (NL) - 4; free.
  Occasional Publications - see website.

British Educational Suppliers Association (BESA) 1933

- ■ 20 Beaufort Court, Admirals Way, LONDON, E14 9XL. (hq)
  020 7537 4997   fax 020 7537 4846
  email besa@besa.org.uk   http://www.besa.org.uk
  Dir Gen: Dominic Savage
- ▲ Company Limited by Guarantee
- ○ *T; for the British educational supply industry; to represent manufacturers & distributors of educational equipment, materials, consumables, books, furniture, technology, ICT hardware & software related services in the UK & to international markets
- Gp BESA New Educational Technologies Group (BNETG)
  BESA Special Needs Group (BSNG)
  British Educational Furniture Manufacturers Group (BEFMG)
  Educational Software Publishers Association (ESPA)
  Engineering Training Equipment Manufacturers
     Association (ETEMA)
- ● Conf - Mtgs - Res - Expt - Inf - LG
- M 260 f
- ¶ BESAbook - 1; free.   ICT in State Schools - 1; ftm, £350 nm.
  UK Schools Survey on Budget & Resource Provision - 1; ftm, £350 nm.

British Educational Travel Association (BETA) 2003

- ■ PO Box 182, CARSHALTON, Surrey, SM5 2XW. (hq)
  020 8669 1444
  email info@betauk.com   http://www.betauk.com
  Exec Dir: Emma English
- ▲ Company Limited by Guarantee
- ○ *T; to promote youth, student & educational travel to, from & within the UK
- ● Conf - Mtgs - ET - Res - Exhib - SG - Stat - Inf - VE - LG
- < Intl Student Travel Confedn; Fedn of Intl Youth Travel Orgs; English UK
- M 120 f, UK / 20 f, o'seas
- ¶ NL - free.

British Egg Association (BEA) 1961

- NR 89 Charterhouse St (2nd floor), LONDON, EC1M 6HR. (hq)
  020 7608 3760   fax 020 7608 3860
  email Louisa.Platt@brittisheggindustrycouncil.com
  http://www.britegg.co.uk
  Sec: Louisa Platt
- ▲ Company Limited by Guarantee
- ○ *F, *T
- ● Mtgs - ET - Res - Stat - Inf - VE - LG
- < Eur U of Whlsrs with Eggs, Egg Products, Poultry & Game (EUWEP); Brit Egg Ind Coun
- M 26 i, 30 f
- ¶ Quarterly Report;   LM;   AR; all ftm only.

British Egg Products Association (BEPA) 1971

- ■ 89 Charterhouse St (2nd floor), LONDON, EC1M 6HR. (hq)
  020 7608 3760   fax 020 7608 3860
  email Louisa.Platt@brittisheggindustrycouncil.com
  http://www.britegg.co.uk
  Sec: Louisa Platt
- ▲ Company Limited by Guarantee
- ○ *T; to maintain & improve the high quality of egg products
- ● Mtgs - Res - Stat - Inf - LG
- < Intl Egg Commission (IEC); Brit Egg Ind Coun (BEIC)
- M 10 f
- ¶ Import & Export Statistics - 10;
  Breaking & Production - 10; both ftm only.

British Elastic Rope Sports Association (BERSA) 1989

- ■ 33a Canal St, OXFORD, OX2 6BQ. (hq)
  01865 311179   fax 01865 426007
  email info@bersa.org
  Chmn: David Boston
- ▲ Company Limited by Guarantee
- Br 10; Eire, Greece, Spain
- ○ *S; promotion & safety regulation of bungee jumping & other elastic rope sport
- ● Mtgs - Exam - Res - Comp - Stat - Inf - Lib - PL - LG
- < RoSPA; Brit Standards Inst
- M i, f & org
- ¶ Code of Safe Practice.
  Guidelines for Local Safety Officers.

British Elbow & Shoulder Society
   a specialist society of the **British Orthopaedic Association**

British Electroless Nickel Society
   a division of the Metal Finishing Association which is a group of the
   Surface Engineering Association

British Electrophoresis Society
   since 2004 **British Society for Proteome Research**

British Electrostatic Control Association (BECA)

- ■ Heathcote House, 136 Hagley Rd, Edgbaston, BIRMINGHAM, B16 9PN.
  0121-454 4141   fax 0121-454 4949
  email sp@heathcote-coleman.co.uk
  http://www.becaonline.co.uk
  Contact: Sharon Parker
- ○ *T; suppliers, manufacturers and users of equipment, materials and services for the UK electrostatic control industry
- M 8 f

British Electrotechnical & Allied Manufacturers Association Ltd
   former name of **BEAMA Ltd**

British Electrotechnical Approvals Board

   in 2004 nerged with ASTA Certification Services to become
   ASTA BEAB Certification Services, in 2007, was taken over by
   Intertec Group plc who hold the certification records

British Endodontic Society   (BES)   1963
NR   PO Box 707, GERRARDS CROSS, Bucks, SL9 0DR.   (admin/p)
        01494 581542   fax 01494 581542
        Hon Sec: Annabel Thomas
▲   Registered Charity
○   *L; to promote and advance the study of all endodontic
        procedures; to improve dental services to the public
●   Conf - Mtgs - ET - Res - SG - LG
<   Amer Assn Endodontics; Eur Soc Endodontology
M   760 i, UK / 40 i, o'seas
¶   International Endodontic Jnl - 6; ftm, £60 yr nm.

**British Energy Association of the World Energy Council
        (BEAWec)   1924**
■   12 St Hildas Close, College Gardens, LONDON, SW17 7UL.
        (mem/sp)
        020 8768 9744   fax 020 8767 9744
        email BEAwec@aol.com   http://www.worldenergy.org/
        uk
        Mem Sec: Di Hammet
▲   Registered Charity; Un-incorporated Society
○   *N; to promote the sustainable supply & use of energy for the
        greatest benefit of all people
●   Conf - Mtgs - Inf - LG
<   Utd Nations (cat 3); Wld Coal Inst; Wld Nuclear Assn; Wld
        Renewable Energy Congress
>   Energy Inst; Westminster Energy Policy Forum
M   15 i, 19 f, 6 org
        (Sub: £100 i, £2,900 f, £475 org)
¶   BEA Chronicle - 1; free (by e-mail).

**British Engineering Manufacturers' Association Ltd   (BEMA)
        1936**
NR   BEMA House, Unit 1 Millers Court, Windmill Rd, Kenn,
        CLEVEDON, Somerset, BS21 6UL.   (hq)
        0870 998 0268   fax 0870 998 0269
        email enquiries@bema.co.uk   http://www.bema.co.uk
        Dir: J M Whitlow
▲   Company Limited by Guarantee
○   *T; for engineering companies operating nationally
●   Mtgs - ET - Exhib - Expt - Inf - Lib - VE - LG
M   150 f
¶   Handbook - 12; ftm, on request nm.

British Engineers' Cutting Tools Association
        In February 2004 merged with the British Hardmetal Association to
        form the **British Hardmetal & Engineers' Cutting Tools
        Association**

British Engraved Stationery Association
        since 2005 a special interest group (BPIF Engraved Stationery) of the
        British Printing Industries Federation

British Entertainment & Discotheque Association
        in February 2008 merged with the Bar Entertainment & Dance
        Association to form **Noctis**

**British Entomological & Natural History Society   (BENHS)
        1872**
NR   The Pelham-Clinton Building, Dinton Pastures Country Park,
        Davis St, Hurst, READING, Berks, RG10 0TH.   (hq)
▲   Registered Charity
○   *L; study of natural history, particularly entomology & insect
        conservation; principally in the British Isles but extends into
        Europe as a whole
M   i

British Epidermo-Epidemiology Society
        a group of the **British Association of Dermatologists**

British Epigraphy Society   1996
■   19 Purcell Rd, Marston, OXFORD, OX3 0EZ.   (hsp)
        http://www.csad.ox.ac.uk/BES/
        Sec: Dr Peter Haarer
▲   Registered Charity
○   *L; the study of Greek, Roman & other inscriptions, texts &
        historical documents
Gp   Conf - ET
<   l'Assn Intle d'Epigraphie grecque et latine (AIEGL)
M   125 i, UK / 22 i, o'seas
        (Sub: £6)
¶   NL - 2; ftm only.

British Epilepsy Association   (BEA)   1950
NR   New Anstey House, Gate Way Drive, Yeadon, LEEDS, W Yorks,
        LS19 7XY.   (hq)
        0113-210 8800
        email epilepsy@epilepsy.org.uk
        http://www.epilepsy.org.uk
▲   Registered Charity
○   *W; to provide care in the community for those with epilepsy
●
        Helpline: freephone 0808 800 5050 (Mon-Thurs 0900-1630,
        Fri 0900-1600)
M   21,000 i
¶   Epilepsy Today - 4.   AR.
        Various publications.
        Note: the working title of this body is Epilepsy Action.

British Equestrian Federation   (BEF)   1972
NR   Stoneleigh Park, KENILWORTH, Warks, CV8 2RH.   (hq)
        024 7669 8871   fax 024 7669 6484
        email info@bef.co.uk   http://www.bef.co.uk
        Chmn: Keith Taylor
▲   Company Limited by Guarantee
○   *N, *S; acts as the international secretariat on behalf of
        member disciplines & represents their interests in all matters
        concerned with the Fédération Equestre Internationale (FEI)
Gp   Discipline members: Association of British Riding Schools;
        British Dressage; British Equestrian Trade Association; British
        Equestrian Vaulting Association; British Eventing Association;
        British Horse Driving Trials Association; British Reining; British
        Show Jumping Association; Endurance GB; Riding for the
        Disabled; Scottish Equestrian Association
●   Mtgs - Comp - SG - Stat - Inf - LG
<   Fédn Equestre Intle; a member of the Brit Horse Ind Confedn
M   6 org (discipline members),
        affiliates: British Horse Society, Pony Club

British Equestrian Trade Association   (BETA)   1979
■   East Wing, Stockeld Park, WETHERBY, W Yorks, LS22 4AW.
        (hsb)
        01937 587062   fax 01937 582728
        email info@beta-uk.org   http://www.beta-uk.org
        Chief Exec: Claire Williams
▲   Company Limited by Guarantee
○   *T; to promote the British equestrian industry from retailers to
        manufacturers, associated services & dealers; to promote
        riding as a sport
Gp   Feed merchants; Mobile retailers; Saddlers; Pharmaceutical,
        Equestrian organisations; Dealers; Safety equipment
●   Mtgs - ET - Exam - Res - Exhib - Stat - Expt - Inf - LG -
        Administration of VAT second hand scheme for horses &
        ponies on behalf of HM Customs & Excise - BETA Body
        Protector Standard
<   Brit Equestrian Fedn; Brit Horse Soc; Countryside Alliance; Soc
        of Master Saddlers; Horse & Pony Taxation C'ee
M   700 f, 5 org, UK / 5 org, o'seas
¶   Equestrian Trade News - 12; free to retailers
        (£59 manufacturers).
        British Equestrian Directory - 1; £9.95 m.
        Trade Suppliers Directory - 1; £16 m.
        What to Wear - 2 yrly; £5.50.

British Equestrian Vaulting Association
a discipline member of the **British Equestrian Federation**

British Equine Veterinary Association
a group of the **British Veterinary Association**

British Essence Manufacturers' Association   (BEMA)   1917
■   PO Box 172, CRANLEIGH, Surrey, GU6 8WU.   (hq)
01483 275411   fax 01483 275411
email secretariat@bemaorg.org
http://www.bemaorg.org
Sec: Julie Young
▲   Un-incorporated Society
○   *T; interests of makers of essences & flavours for food & drink
●   Mtgs - Inf
<   Intl Org Flavour Ind (IOFI); Eur Flavours & Fragrances
Assn (EFFA)
M   32 f

British Essential Oils Association Ltd   (BEOA)   1978
NR   15 Exeter Mansions, Exeter Rd, LONDON, NW2 3UG.   (sec/p)
020 8450 3713
email secretariat@beoa.co.uk   http://www.beoa.co.uk
Sec: Malcolm Irvine
▲   Company Limited by Guarantee
○   *T; to promote the essential oil, oleoresin & aromatic chemical
trade
Gp   Technical c'ee
●   Conf - Mtgs - ET - Res - SG - Inf - Lib - LG
<   Eur Fedn for Essential Oils (EFEO); Eur Flavour & Fragrance
Org (EFFA)
M   53 f, UK / 3 f, o'seas
¶   NL - 3; free.   Hbk & LM - 1; ftm only.

British Ethical Jewellers Association   2008
NR   Glasgow,
0141-339 8943
email admin@fifibijoux.com
Chmn: Vivien Johnston
○   *T; for jewellers who source ethically produced metals &
minerals for making their designs
M   f

British & European Geranium Society
since 2008 **Pelargonium & Geranium Society**

British Eventing Association
a discipline member of the **British Equestrian Federation**

British Exhibition Contractors' Association
in January 2008 merged with the Association of Exhibition
Contractors to form the **Event Supplier and Services Association**

British Exporters Association   (BExA)   1940
■   Broadway House, Tothill St, LONDON, SW1H 9NQ.   (hq)
020 7222 5419   fax 020 7799 2468
email hughbailey@bexa.co.uk   http://www.bexa.co.uk
Dir: Hugh W Bailey
▲   Un-incorporated Society
○   *T; to lobby on behalf of members on export, export credit
insurance & trade finance issues
●   Mtgs - VE - LG
M   70 f
¶   AR.

British Falconers' Club   (BFC)   1924
■   Westfield, Meeting Hill, Worstead, NORTH WALSHAM, Norfolk,
NR28 9LS.   (hsb)
http://www.britishfalconersclub.co.uk
Sec: Jacqui Morris
▲   Un-incorporated Society
Br   9 regions
○   *G; the promotion of practical falconry in the British Isles; to
promote the captive breeding of birds of prey
●   Mtgs - Lib
<   Intl Assn for Falconry & Consvn of Birds of Prey (IAF); Fedn of
Field Sports Assns of the EEC (FACE); Countryside Alliance
M   1,270 i, UK / 79 i, o'seas
(Sub: £42)
¶   Falconer (Jnl) - 1; ftm.   NL - 2; ftm.

British False Memory Society   (BFMS)   1993
■   Newtown, BRADFORD-on-AVON, Wilts, BA15 1NF.
01225 868682   fax 01225 862251
Dir: Madeline Greenhalgh
▲   Registered Charity
○   *K; a support group for accused parents
●   Conf - Mtgs - Res - Stat - Inf - Lib
Helpline: 01225 868682

British Fantasy Society   (BFS)   1971
■   23 Mayne St, Hanford, STOKE-on-TRENT, Staffs, ST4 4RF.   (sp)
email secretary@britishfantasysociety.org
http://www.britishfantasysociety.org
Sec: Helen Hopley
▲   Un-incorporated Society
○   *A, *G; to promote interest in the fields of horror & fantasy
literature, media & art
●   Conf - Mtgs
M   350 i, UK / 50 i, o'seas
(Sub: £30 UK / £45-60 o'seas)
¶   Prism NL - 4;   Dark Horizons - 6;   New Horizons;
all ftm only.

British Federation of Audio Ltd   (BFA)   1994
NR   PO Box 365, FARNHAM, Surrey, GU10 2BD.   (hq)
01428 714616
Sec: C I C Cowan,   Chmn: S N Harris
▲   Company Limited by Guarantee
○   *T; to promote the use of domestic audio equipment & the
interests of the UK audio manufacturers & the British high
fidelity audio industry
Gp   BTI sponsorship to overseas exhibitions
●   Mtgs - Exhib - Stat - LG
<   Intellect
M   c 45 f

British Federation of Brass Bands   (BFBB)   1997
■   Unit 12 Maple Estate, Stocks Lane, BARNSLEY, S Yorks,
S75 2BL.   (hq)
01226 771015   fax 01226 732630
http://www.bfbb.co.uk
Gen Sec: Carol Tattersfield
▲   Registered Charity
○   *D; to promote brass bands; to develop bands & youth bands
●   Conf - Mtgs - ET - Lib
<   Eur Brass Band Assn (EBBA)
M   500 bands
(Sub: £100)
¶   Forum - 1; ftm only.

British Federation of Film Societies (BFFS) 1945
NR   Unit 315 The Workstation, 15 Paternoster Row, SHEFFIELD,
     S Yorks, S1 2BX.   (hq)
     0845 603 7278
     email info@bffs.org.uk
     Chief Exec: David Phillips
○   *A, *N; a national body which promotes voluntary film
     exhibition & represents the interests of film societies
●   Technical & legal advice
M   171 societies

British Federation for Historical Swordplay (BFHS) 1998
■   213 Queenspark Rd, BRIGHTON, E Sussex, BN2 2ZA.   (dir/p)
     01273 685664
     http://www.bfhs.org
     Pres: Andrew Feest
▲   Un-incorporated Society
Br   16
○   *G, *N; for individual groups & societies studying & practising
     fencing & European martial arts
●   Conf - Mtgs - ET -Exam - Res - Inf
M   16 org

**British Federation of Sand & Land Yacht Clubs (British
Landsailing) 1962**
■   Y Bwthyn, Druidston Cross, BROAD HAVEN, Pembrokeshire,
     SA62 3ND.   (hsp)
     01437 781458   fax 01437 767151
     email secretary@bfslyc.org.uk   http://www.bfslyc.org.uk
     Sec: Andy Parr
▲   Un-incorporated Society
Br   18
○   *S; to regulate, administer & promote land yachting in the UK
Gp   Landsailing; Landyachting; Sandyachting; Parakarting; Kite
     buggying
●   Mtgs - ET - Res - Comp - Inf - LG
<   Fedn Intl of Sand & Land Yachting
M   800 i, 18 org
¶   Land Sailor (Jnl) - 4; ftm.

**British Federation against Sexually Transmitted Diseases
(BFSTD) 1948**
■   The Milne Centre, Bristol Royal Infirmary, Marlborough St,
     BRISTOL, BS2 3HW.   (hsb)
     0117-928 3093
     Hon Sec: Peter Greenhouse
▲   Registered Charity
○   *L, *M; issues relating to sexually transmitted infections
     including HIV/AIDS
Gp   representatives from main UK organisations working in the field
     of sexual & reproductive health
●   Mtgs - ET - Inf - LG
<   EUROPAP
M   21 org
¶   AR; free.

British Federation of Women Graduates (BFWG) 1907
NR   4 Mandeville Courtyard, 142 Battersea Park Rd, LONDON,
     SW11 4NB.   (hq/regd office)
     020 7498 8037   fax 020 7498 5213
     email bfwg@bfwg.demon.co.uk
     http://www.bfwg.org.uk
     Exec Sec: Mrs A B Stein
▲   Company Limited by Guarantee; Registered Educational
     Charity
Br   35
○   *E, *P, *X
●   Conf - Mtgs - Comp - SG - Stat - Lib - VE - LG
<   Intl Fedn of University Women (Geneva)
M   180,000 i, UK & o'seas
¶   NL;   LM;   AR; all ftm.

British Federation of Young Choirs (youngchoirs)
     This organisation closed in 2007

British Fencing Association 1902
NR   1 Baron's Gate, 33-35 Rothschild Rd, LONDON, W4 5HT.
     (hq)
     020 8742 3032   fax 020 8742 3033
     email headoffice@britishfencing.com
     http://www.britishfencing.com
     Chief Exec: Piers Martin
▲   Company Limited by Guarantee
○   *S; governing body for the sport of fencing in the UK
M   i & clubs

British Fertility Society (BFS) 1974
■   22 Apex Court, Woodlands, Bradley Stoke, BRISTOL,
     BS32 4JT.   (asa)
     01454 642217
     http://www.fertility.org.uk
▲   Company Limited by Guarantee
○   *M; to promote the knowledge & study of fertility & infertility
Gp   Doctors; Scientists; Counsellors; Nurses
●   Conf - Mtgs - ET
<   Intl Fedn of Fertility Socs
M   760 i, 12 f
¶   Human Fertility (Jnl) - 3.   NL - 3.

British FIB (Flying Inflatable Boat) Association
     is no longer in existence.

British Film Institute (BFI) 1933
NR   21 Stephen St, LONDON, W1T 1LN.   (hq)
     020 7255 1444
     http://www.bfi.org.uk
     Dir: Amanda Nevill
▲   Registered Charity
○   *A, *Q; to promote understanding & appreciation of Britain's
     rich film & television & culture
M   i, f & org
¶   Sight & Sound - 12.

British Fire Consortium (BFC) 1983
NR   47 Poplar Avenue, HOVE, E Sussex, BN3 8PT.   (hsb)
     01273 297274   fax 01273 297275
     email secretariat@tbfc.co.uk
     http://www.britishfireconsortium.org.uk
     Gen Sec: Roger Chamberlain
▲   Company Limited by Guarantee
○   *T; for nationally based independent fire protection companies
Gp   Fire: Extinguisher mfrs, Extinguisher suppliers, Protection service
     companies, Alarms
     Training; Consultants; Signs; Intumescent materials; Health &
     safety
●   Conf - Mtgs - ET - Exam - Res - Exhib - Lib
<   BSI
M   200 f
¶   NL - 4; ftm only.

British Fire Protection Systems Association Ltd
     in 2007 merged with the Association of British Fire Trades, the Fire
     Extinguishing Trades Association & the Fire Industry Confederation to
     form the **Fire Industry Association**

British Fire Services Association (BFSA) 1950
NR   8 Clover House, Boston Rd, SLEAFORD, Lincs, NG34 7HD.
     (hq)
     01526 830255
     Gen Sec: Derrick Crouch
▲   Registered Charity
○   *T; for fire fighters
M   i, f & org

British Fireworks Association

NR c/o Cosmic Fireworks Ltd, Fauld Industrial Estate, BURTON on
    TRENT, Staffs, DE13 9HS.
    01283 520771   fax 01283 520351
    http://www.b-f-a.org
    Chmn: John Woodhead
○   *T; firework manufacturers
M   16 f

British Flat Roofing Council   (BFRC)   1982

NR Newstead House, Pelham Rd, NOTTINGHAM, NG5 1AP.   (hq)
▲   Company Limited by Guarantee
○   *M, *T; to represent both manufacturers & contractors in the flat
    & low pitched roof industry; to act as an independent
    advisory body to the construction sector & the consumer
●   Conf - Mtgs - ET - Res - Exhib - Comp - Inf
<   Bitumen Waterproofing Assn (BWA); Construction Ind Coun
    (CIC)
M   2 trade associations:
    Association of British Roofing Felt Manufacturers
    Single Ply Roofing Association
¶   Flat Roofing: design & good practice; £56.25 m, £75 nm.
    Householders Guide to Flat Roofing; free.

British Florist Association Ltd   (BFA)   1979

■   PO Box 5161, DUDLEY, W Midlands, DY1 9FX.   (mail/address)
    0844 800 7299
    email info@britishfloristassociation.org
    http://www.britishfloristassociation.org
    Co Sec: Victoria Willsone
▲   Company Limited by Guarantee
○   *N, *T; to represent professional retail florists
●   Conf - Mtgs - ET - Exhib - Comp - Inf - LG
<   Fédn Européenne Unions Professionelles de Fleuristes
>   Teleflorist; Flowergram; Masterflorist
M   180 i, 5 f, UK / 1 f, o'seas
    (Sub: £10,500 i, £53,000 f, UK / £500 f o'seas)
¶   NL - 12; ftm only.

British Flower Bulbs Association   1945

■   Springfield Gardens, Camelgate, SPALDING, Lincs,
    PE12 6ET.   (hq)
    01775 724843   fax 01775 711209
    Sec: David Norton
▲   Un-incorporated Society
○   *T; all connected in the sale & distribution of flower bulbs,
    corms etc in the UK
●   Mtgs - Inf
M   40 f
✕   2006 Bulb Distributors' Association

**British Flower & Vibrational Essences Association   (BFVEA)
1997**

■   BM BFVEA, LONDON, WC1N 3XX.   (mail/address)
    01209 218984
    email info@bfvea.com   http://www.bfvea.com
    Chmn: Jan Stewart,   Sec: Emma le Monnier
▲   Un-incorporated Society
○   *T; to stimulate interest in & standards for training in flower &
    vibrational essences
●   Conf - Mtgs - ET - Res - Inf - LG
<   Brit Assn of Flower Essence Producers
M   120 i, UK / 40 i, o'seas
    (Sub: £35 UK / £40 o'seas)
¶   Essence - 3/4; ftm, £20 yr nm.   E-NL - 4; free.

**British Flue & Chimney Manufacturers' Association   (BFCMA)
1977**

■   2 Waltham Court, Milley Lane, Hare Hatch, READING, Berks,
    RG10 9TH.   (hq)
    0118-940 3416   fax 0118-940 6258
    email info@feta.co.uk   http://www.feta.co.uk/
    Dir Gen: C Sloan
○   *T; natural draught flues & chimneys
●   Mtgs - SG - Representation on standards c'ees
<   Fedn Envtl Tr Assns (FETA)
M   11 f, 6 associates

**British Fluid Power Association (incorporating AHEM)   (BFPA)
1959**

■   Cheriton House, Cromwell Park, CHIPPING NORTON, Oxon,
    OX7 5SR.   (hq)
    01608 647900   fax 01608 647919
    email enquiries@bfpa.co.uk   http://www.bfpa.co.uk
    Chief Exec: Ian Morris
▲   Company Limited by Guarantee
○   *T; engineering, hydraulic & pneumatic fluid power equipment
    systems
Gp Commercial & promotions; Component performance;
    Connectors; Contamination control; Control components;
    Cylinders; Education & training; Electrohydraulic control
    systems; Fluids; Market forecasting & statistics; Pneumatic
    equipment; Quality assurance; Research; Seals
●   Conf - Mtgs - ET - Exhib - SG - Stat - Expt - Inf - Lib
<   Comité Eur des Transmissions Oléohydraulique et
    Pneumatique (CETOP); CBI; BSI; METCOM
M   100 f
¶   NL - 10; ftm only.   Directory - irreg;   Product list - 1;
    LM;   AR; all free.
    Publications lists BFPA/CETOP.

British Fluid Power Distributors' Association   (BFPDA)   1989

■   Cheriton House, Cromwell Park, CHIPPING NORTON, Oxon,
    OX7 5SR.   (hq)
    01608 647900   fax 01608 647919
    email bfpda@bfpa.org.uk   http://www.bfpa.co.uk
    Chief Exec: Ian Morris
▲   Company Limited by Guarantee
○   *T; for British distributors of oil-hydraulic & pneumatic
    equipment
●   Conf - Mtgs - ET - Exhib - SG - Stat - Expt - Inf - Lib
<   Brit Fluid Power Assn
M   100 f
¶   NL - 4; ftm only.   Directory - irreg;   Product list;   LM;
    AR; all free.
    Publications lists BFPA.

British Fluoridation Society   1969

NR c/o Sheila Jones (Ward 4), Booth Hall Children's Hospital,
    Charlestown Rd, MANCHESTER, Lancs, M4 7AA.   (hq)
    0161-220 5223   fax 0161-220 5223
    http://www.bfsweb.org
    Inf & Res Officer: Sheila Jones
▲   Company Limited by Guarantee
○   *K; 'to promote fluoridation of the public water supplies for the
    benefit of dental health'
●   Conf - ET - Res - Inf - Lib - LG
¶   Briefings on various aspects of fluoridation & dental health
    statistics - irreg.

British Flute Society   (BFS)   1983

NR 27 Eskdale Gardens, PURLEY, Surrey, CR8 1ET.   (hsp)
    020 8668 3360
    email secretary@bfs.org.uk
    Hon Sec: Anna Munks
▲   Registered Charity
○   *D; furtherance & enjoyment of playing the flute
Gp Junior Section
●   Mtgs - ET - Comp - SG - Inf - Concerts - Flute Festivals
M   c 1,800 i
¶   Pan - 4.

© CBD Research Ltd · Beckenham · BR3 5JS · Tel 020 8650 7745 · Fax 020 8650 0768 · E-mail cbd@cbdresearch.com · www.cbdresearch.com

British Flyball Association   (BFA)   1993
■   PO Box 990, DONCASTER, S Yorks, DN1 9FY.   (sp)
        01628 829623
        email secretary@flyball.org.uk   http://www.flyball.org.uk
    Sec: Penny Charlton
▲   Un-incorporated Society
○   *G, *S; to promote flyball - a team sport for dogs & dog owners
●   Conf - ET - Exam - Exhib - Comp - Internet information
<   Australian / Dutch / North American / South African [Assns];
        Belgian Flyball Fedn
M   1,500 i
¶   Flyball Record - 4; ftm only.

**British Food Importers & Distributors Association   (BFIDA)
1997**
■   Crescent House, 34 Eastbury Way, SWINDON, Wilts,
        SN25 2EN.   (asa)
        01793 727387   fax 01793 726486
        email foodimporters@aol.com
    Sec: Walter J Anzer
○   *T; to represent the interests of food importers in the UK
●   LG
<   FRUCOM
M   22 f

British Foosball Association
NR   BCM 1731, LONDON, WC1N 3XX.
        http://www.britfoos.com
    Sec: Jude Fitzgerald
○   *S; table football

British Footwear Association   (BFA)   1996
■   3 Burystead Place, WELLINGBOROUGH, Northants,
        NN8 1AH.   (hq)
        01933 229005   fax 01933 225009
        email info@britfoot.com   http://www.britfoot.com
    Chief Exec: Richard Kottler
▲   Company Limited by Guarantee
○   *T; to promote & protect the interests of the UK footwear
        industry
●   Conf - Mtgs - Stat - Empl
<   Eur Footwear Mfrs Confedn (CEC)
M   80 f
¶   NL; ftm only.

British Fragrance Association   (BFA)   1941
■   PO Box 173, CRANLEIGH, Surrey, GU6 8WU.
        01483 275411   fax 01483 275411
        email secretariat@bfaorg.org   http://www.bfaorg.org
    Sec: Julie Young
▲   Un-incorporated Society
○   *T; for makers of fragrances for cosmetics, toiletries & perfumes
●   Mtgs - Distribution of code of practice
<   Intl Fragrance Assn (IFRA); Eur Flavours & Fragrances
        Assn (EFFA)
M   31 f
¶   NL.

British Franchise Association Ltd   (BFA)   1977
NR   A2 Danebrook Court, Oxford Office Village, Langford Lane,
        OXFORD, OX5 1LQ.   (hq)
        01865 379892
        email mailroom@british-franchise.org.uk
        http://www.british-franchise.org.uk
    Dir-Gen: Brian Smart
▲   Company Limited by Guarantee
○   *T; promoting ethical franchising, voluntary self-regulatory body
        for franchisors, providing advice to potential franchisees /
        franchisors, education in franchising, lobbying on behalf of
        franchise community
●   Conf - Mtgs - ET - Res - Exhib - Stat - Inf - LG
<   Wld Franchise Coun; Eur Franchise Assn
M   250 f
¶   Members Newsline (NL) - 12; ftm only.
    Franchise Link - 2; ftm, part of infopacks for nm.
    Franchisee Guide.   Franchisor Guide.

**British Free Range Egg Producers Association   (BFREPA)
1991**
■   PO Box 3425, Ashton Keynes, SWINDON, Wilts, SN6 6WR.
        (admin)
        01285 869913
        email admin@bfrepa.co.uk   http://www.bfrepa.co.uk
    Admin: Alison Bone
▲   Un-incorporated Society
○   *F, *T
●   Conf - Mtgs - ET - Res - Exhib - Stat - Inf - PL - VE - LG
<   Brit Egg Assn; Nat Farmers U
M   271 i, 41 f
¶   The Ranger - 12; ftm, £35 (+VAT) yr nm.

British Freediving Association
        has asked to be removed from the directory.

British Friction Materials Council   (BFMC)   1957
NR   Brazennose House, Lincoln Sq, MANCHESTER, M2 5BL.   (asa)
        0161-834 5777
○   *T
<   Fedn of Eur Mfrs of Friction Materials (FEMFM)
M   4 f
    no further information supplied

British Friesland Sheep Society   1980
■   Weir Park Farm, Waterwell Lane, Christow, EXETER, Devon,
        EX6 7PB.   (hsp)
        01647 252549
    Hon Sec: Peter Baber
▲   Un-incorporated Society
○   *B; to promote the use of British Friesland sheep as a supreme
        dairy animal & as a crossing sire to produce profitable cross-
        bred ewes for prime lamb production
●   Mtgs (AGM)
<   Nat Sheep Assn
M   48 i
¶   NL - irreg.   Hbk;   LM - updated.

British Frozen Food Federation   (BFFF)   1951
NR   Springfield House (3rd floor), Springfield Rd, GRANTHAM,
        Lincs, NG31 7BG.   (hq)
        01476 515300
    Contact: Emma Holberry
○   *T
M   f

British Fruit Juice Association   (BFJA)   1947
■   Shoelands House, Seale, FARNHAM, Surrey, GU10 1HL.   (hsp)
   01483 811433   fax 01483 811433
   email clive@clivewebster.co.uk   http://www.bfja.co.uk
   Exec Sec/Treas: Clive Webster
▲   Un-incorporated Society
○   *T; interests of companies & organisations which have dealings
   in fruit juices
Gp   Importers; Manufacturers/packers; Laboratories; Handlers
●   Conf - Mtgs - Inf - LG
<   Brit Soft Drinks Assn
>   Brit Soft Drinks Assn
M   52 f
   (Sub: £130)

British Fuchsia Society   (BFS)   1938
■   PO Box 178, EVESHAM, Worcs, WR11 3WY.   (hsp)
   01386 45158
   http://www.thebfs.org.uk
   Hon Sec: Geoffrey Oke
▲   Registered Charity
○   *H; to further interest in the cultivation & understanding of
   Fuchsias
Gp   Special Interest: Hybridising, Species, Pre-1914 cultivars;
   Show organisation & exhibiting; Photography; Fuchsia
   (collecting fuschsia memorabilia)
●   Conf - ET - Exam - Exhib - Comp - Inf
<   Fuchsia Res Intl; Eurofuchsia; R Horticl Soc
>   Fuchsia Res Intl
M   3,800 i, 280 org, UK / 325 i, 20 org, o'seas
¶   Spring [& Autumn] Bulletin(s) - 1; ftm, £3 nm.
   Annual publication - 1; ftm, £4 nm.

British Fur Trade Association Inc   (BFTA)   1964
■   Brookstone House, 6 Elthorne Rd, LONDON, N19 4AG.   (hq)
   020 7281 9299   fax 020 7281 1374
   email info@britishfur.co.uk   http://www.britishfur.co.uk
   Contact: The Executive Officer
▲   Company Limited by Guarantee
○   *T
●   Mtgs - Exhib - Comp - Expt - Inf - Empl
M   50 f

British Furniture Confederation
NR   c/o FIRA International Ltd, Maxwell Rd, STEVENAGE, Herts,
   SG1 2EW.   (hq)
   01438 777700   fax 01438 777800
   http://www.britishfurnitureconfederation.org.uk
   Chmn: Martin Jourdan

British Furniture Manufacturers
   alternative name of **BFM Ltd**

British Gear Association   (BGA)   1986
■   Suite 43 Imex Business Park, Shobnall Rd, BURTON upon
   TRENT, Staffs, DE14 2AU.   (hq)
   01283 515521   fax 01283 515841
   email admin@bga.org.uk   http://www.bga.org.uk
   Technical Exec: Andrew Harry
▲   Company Limited by Guarantee
○   *E, *Q, *T; to promote technical, economic, educational,
   training & research activities in the interest of the mechanical
   power transmission sector
Gp   C'ees: Technical, Education & training; Marketing; Research
   Foundation
●   Conf - Mtgs - ET - Res - Exhib - SG - Stat - Expt - Inf - Lib - VE -
   LG
<   Eur C'ee of Assns of Mfrs of Gears & Transmission
   Parts (EUROTRANS); Mechanical & Metal Trs
   Confedn (METCOM)
M   6 i, 82 f, 8 org
¶   BGA NL - 4; free.
   Technical Bulletin - 12;   Technical Literature Survey - 12;
   AR - 1; all ftm only.
   Buyers Guide - 2 yrly; ftm, £10 nm.

British Gelbvieh Cattle Society   1972
NR   Castlefield, Graig Llwyn Rd, Lisvane, CARDIFF, CF14 0RP.
   (hsp)
   Hon Sec: Mandy Hawkins
▲   Registered Charity
○   *B
●   Conf - Exhib - Comp - VE - Shows
M   c 20 i
¶   NL - 4;   AR - 1; both ftm.   LM - 1; free.

British Generic Manufacturers' Association   (BGMA)   1989
NR   The Registry, Royal Mint Court, LONDON, EC3N 4QN.   (hq)
   020 7457 2018   fax 020 7866 7900
   email info@britishgenerics.co.uk
   http://www.britishgenerics.co.uk
   Sec: Alex Harris
▲   Company Limited by Guarantee
○   *T; for UK manufacturers & suppliers of generic medicines; to
   promote the industry
●   Mtgs - LG
<   Eur Generic Medicines Assn (EGA)
M   14 f

British Geomembrane Association   (BGA)   1999
NR   c/o Naue Geosynthetics Ltd, The Genesis Centre, Birchwood,
   WARRINGTON, Cheshire, WA3 7BH.   (hsb)
   01925 810280   fax 01925 810284
   email info@bga.uk/net   http://www.bga.uk.net
   Sec: Chris Quirk
▲   Un-incorporated Society
○   *T
●   Conf- Mtgs - ET - Exam
M   1 i, 20 f

British Geophysical Association
   a group of the **Geological Society**

British Geotechnical Association   (BGA)   1949
NR   c/o Institution of Civil Engineers, 1-7 Great George St,
   LONDON, SW1P 3AA.   (hq)
▲   Registered Charity
○   *P; promotion of cooperation among engineers & scientists for
   the advancement of knowledge in the fields of soil & rock
   mechanics & engineering geology & their application to
   engineering
M   i

British Geriatrics Society   (BGS)   1947
NR   Marjory Warren House, 31 St John's Square, LONDON,
   EC1M 4DN.   (hq)
   020 7608 1369   fax 020 7608 1041
   email info@bgs.org.uk   http://www.bgs.org.uk
   Hon Sec: Dr David Beaumont
▲   Registered Charity
○   *P; to improve standards of health; to put the case for a well-
   funded health & community care service for elderly people
Gp   Bladder & bowel; Cardiovascular; Cerebral ageing & mental
   health; Diabetes; Drugs & prescribing; Falls & bone health;
   Gastroenterology & nutrition; Health services research;
   Medical ethics; New technology in elderly care; Parkinson's
   disease; Primary & continuing care; Respiratory
●   Conf - Mtgs - ET - Res
<   Intl Assn of Gerontology
M   c 2,000 i, UK / 500 i, o'seas
¶   Age & Ageing (Jnl) - 6; ftm.

© CBD Research Ltd · Beckenham · BR3 5JS · Tel 020 8650 7745 · Fax 020 8650 0768 · E-mail cbd@cbdresearch.com · www.cbdresearch.com

British-German Association (BGA) 1951
NR　34 Belgrave Square, LONDON, SW1X 8QD.　(hq)
　　　020 7235 1922　　fax 020 7235 1902
　　　email info@britishgermanassociation.org
　　　http://www.britishgermanassociation.org
　　　Exec Sec: Martina Schmidt
▲　Company Limited by Guarantee; Registered Charity
○　*X; promotion of understanding between British & German
　　　peoples, their culture & history
●　Conf - Mtgs - Annual Nutcracker Ball
<　Deutsch-Englische Gesellschaft (Berlin)
M　c 700 i
¶　British-German Review - 4; ftm.

British-German Jurists' Association (BGJA) 1970
NR　14 New St, LONDON, EC2M 4HE.　(chmn/b)
　　　020 7972 9727　　fax 020 7972 9721
　　　http://www.bgja.org.uk
　　　Hon Chmn: Dr Sybille Steiner,
　　　Hon Sec: Peter Stevens
○　*P
●　Conf - Mtgs
<　Deutsch-Britische Juristenvereinigung eV (Hamburg)
M　350 i
¶　NL.

British Gestalt Society (BGS)
NR　J413 Ducane Court, Balham High Rd, LONDON, SW17 7JX.
　　　(admin/p)
　　　020 8772 3202
　　　email info@britishgestaltsociety.co.uk
　　　http://www.britishgestaltsociety.co.uk
　　　Admin: Gareth Walker
○　*P; promotes gestalt therapy
×　Gestalt Association UK

British Gladiolus Society (BGS) 1926
■　197 Aston Clinton Rd, AYLESBURY, Bucks, HP22 5AD.　(hsp)
　　　01296 630360
　　　email duckglads@aol.com　　http://www.britglad.com
　　　Hon Sec: Mrs Susan Fawcett
▲　Un-incorporated Society
○　*H; the cultivation, breeding & exhibition of all types of
　　　gladiolus
Gp　3 test grounds for cultivars supplied for trial from UK & o'seas,
　　　in South of England, Midlands & Scotland
●　Conf - Mtgs - Res - Exhib - Stat - Inf - Lib - PL - Regional
　　　annual show
<　N Amer Gladiolus Coun (NAGC)
M　275 i, 55 affiliated socs, UK / 22 i, o'seas
¶　NL - 3.　Ybk.

**British Glass Manufacturers' Confederation　(British Glass)
1988**
■　9 Churchill Way, SHEFFIELD, S Yorks, S35 2PY.　(hq)
　　　0114-290 1850
　　　email info@britglass.co.uk　　http://www.britglass.org.uk
　　　Dir Gen: David Workman,　Inf Officer: Theresa Green
▲　Company Limited by Guarantee
○　*T; to represent the interests of members to government at EU,
　　　national & local level; to provide technical & consultancy
　　　services to members & non members
Gp　Glass Technology Services (the technical arm of British Glass
　　　offering specialist services in consultancy, project
　　　management, environmental monitoring & all types of glass
　　　analysis)
●　Conf - Mtgs - ET - Res - Stat - Inf - Lib - LG
<　FGUE; CPIV; EDGA; EDG; CBI; CETUE; CEN; Packaging Fedn
M　95 f, UK / 2 f, o'seas
¶　NL - 2;　Legislative Update;　Digest of Information - 4;
　　　Various NL;　AR - 1; all ftm.

British Gliding Association Ltd (BGA) 1929
■　Kimberley House, Vaughan Way, LEICESTER, LE1 4SE.　(hq)
　　　0116-253 1051　　fax 0116-251 5939
　　　email office@gliding.co.uk　　http://www.gliding.co.uk
　　　Chief Exec: Peter Stratten
▲　Company Limited by Guarantee
○　*S; promotion of every aspect of gliding & soaring
M　c 11,000 i

British Glove Association (BGA) 1998
■　32 Park Hill Rd, Harborne, BIRMINGHAM, W Midlands,
　　　B17 9SL.　(asa)
　　　0121-242 2602　　fax 0121-427 5358
　　　email info@gloveassociation.org
　　　http://www.gloveassociation.org
○　*T; to promote glove sales; to encourage designers; to bring
　　　together manufacturers & retailers
M　30 f

British Go Association (BGA) 1953
■　30 Market St, ST ANDREWS, Fife, KY16 9NS.　(hsp)
　　　01334 470585
　　　email bga@britgo.org　　http://www.britgo.org
　　　Sec: Edwin Brady
▲　Un-incorporated Society
Br　68 clubs
○　*G, *S; to promote the playing of the ancient oriental board
　　　game of Go
●　Conf Mtgs - ET - Comp - SG
<　Intl Go Fedn; Eur Go Fedn
M　c 600 i, UK; 50 i, o'seas
¶　British Go Jnl - 4; ftm, £3.50 nm.
　　　BGA NL - 6; ftm only.

British Goat Society (BGS) 1879
■　34-36 Fore St, Bovey Tracey, NEWTON ABBOT, Devon,
　　　TQ13 9AD.　(hq)
　　　01626 833168
　　　Sec: Ms Susan Knowles
▲　Registered Charity
○　*B; to increase supply & consumption of goats' milk; to improve
　　　the various breeds of goats; to safeguard against cruelty;
　　　production of cashmere & cashgora fibre, hides & leather
Gp　Working party on the composition & utilisation of goats milk;
　　　Caprine & Ovine Breeding Services Ltd (artificial
　　　insemination)
●　Conf - Mtgs - ET - Res - Exhib - SG - Stat - Expt - Inf - Sales of
　　　products allied to goat keeping & dairy work, production of
　　　butter, cheeses & yoghurt
<　Breed Societies: Saanen, Brit Saanen, Toggenburg, Brit
　　　Toggenburg, Anglo-Nubian, Brit Alpine, Golden Guernsey;
　　　Harness Goat Soc; Regional Goat Socs
M　3,000 i, 15 f, 100 org, UK / 50 i, o'seas
¶　Jnl - 11.　Ybk.　Herdbook - 1.　AR.

British Goldpanning Association 1988
■　2 Spout Cottages, The Spout, ELLESMERE, Shropshire,
　　　SY12 0NE.　(sp)
　　　01691 623954
　　　http://www.britishgoldpanningassociation.com
　　　Sec: Barbara Copley
○　*G; for British goldpanners
<　Wld Goldpanning Assn
M　c 45 i

British Golf Industry Association (BGIA) 1919
- ■ Federation House, STONELEIGH PARK, Warks, CV8 2RF.   (hq)
      024 7641 7141   fax 024 7641 4990
      email bgia@sportsandplay.com
      http://www.bgia.org.uk
      Sec: Mrs Jacqui Baldwin
- ▲ Company Limited by Guarantee
- ○ *T; manufacturers & distributors of golf equipment
- ● Conf - Mtgs - Res - Stat - Expt - Inf - LG
- < Eur Golf Ind Assn; Fedn of Sports & Play Assns (FSPA)
- M 70 f

British Gotland Sheep Society (BGSS) 1990
- ■ Whitehall Farm, Luppitt, HONITON, Devon, EX14 4TR.   (hsp)
      01404 42141
      http://www.gotlandsheep.com
      davidbarlo@aol.com   (chmn)
      Sec: Mrs Lyn Barlow
- ▲ Un-incorporated Society
- ○ *B
- ● Mtgs - ET - Exhib - LG - Promotion & breed registration of
      British Gotland Sheep
- < Nat Sheep Assn
- M 26 i
- ¶ NL - 4;   Flock Book - 1; both ftm only.
      Breed Hbk - 2 yrly; ftm, £2 nm.

British Grassland Society (BGS) 1945
- ■ Trent Lodge, Stroud Rd, CIRENCESTER, Glos, GL7 6JN.   (hq)
      01285 885166
      email office@britishgrassland.com
      http://www.britishgrassland.com
      Dir: Jessica Buss
- ▲ Registered Charity
- ○ *A, *L; grass & forage production, study & research
- ● Conf - Mtgs - ET - EXhib - SG - Inf - VE - LG - Networking -
      Knowledge transfer
- M 600 i, 69 org, UK / 100 i, o'seas
      (Sub: £40 i, £45 org)
- ¶ Grass & Forage Science - 4.   Grass & Forage Farmer- 4.

British Grooms Association (BGA) 2007
- ■ PO Box 248, CHIPPING NORTON, Oxon, OX7 9BN.
      0845 331 6039
      email info@britishgrooms.org.uk
      http://www.britishgrooms.org.uk
      Chief Executive: Lucy Katan
- ▲ Company Limited by Guarantee
- ○ *P; representation and support for grooms working in the
      equine industry
- ● ET - Res - Inf
- M 150 i, UK / 2 i, o'seas
- ¶ British Grooms - 4, ftm, £2.50 nm.

British Group of Altimeter Specialists
      a group of the **Challenger Society for Marine Science**

British Guild of Beer Writers 1988
- ■ Woodcote, 2 Jury Rd, DULVERTON, Somerset, TA22 9DU.
      (hsp)
      01398 324314
      email tierneyjones@btinternet.com
      http://www.beerwriters.co.uk
      Hon Sec: Adrian Tierney-Jones
- ▲ Un-incorporated Society
- ○ *P; to improve the standards of beer writing; to extend public
      knowledge of beers & brewing
- ● Conf - Mtgs - Res - Comp - Inf
- < Intl Fedn of Beer Writers
- M 132 i, 21 f, UK / 10 i, o'seas
- ¶ BGBW NL - 10; ftm.

British Guild of Travel Writers (BGTW) 1960
- NR 5 Berwick Courtyard, Berwick St Leonard, SALISBURY, Wilts,
      SP3 5UA.   (hsb)
      01747 820455
- ○ *P; for specialist travel writers, broadcasters, producers, editors
      & photographers
- ● Mtgs - Res - Inf - VE
- < all members are also members of Eur Fedn of Tourism
      Journalists (FEDAJT)
- M 220 i
- ¶ Globe Trotter - 12; ftm only.

British Gymnastics (BG) 1888
- NR Ford Hall, Lilleshall National Sports Centre, NEWPORT,
      Shropshire, TF10 9NB.   (hq)
      0845 129 7129
      http://www.british-gymnastics.org
- ▲ Company Limited by Guarantee
- ○ *S; governing body for gymnastics in GB
- × British Amateur Gymnastics Association

British Haiku Society (BHS) 1990
- ■ 38 Wayside Ave, HORNCHURCH, Essex, RM12 4LL.   (hsp)
      01708 475774
      http://www.britishhaikusociety.org
      Gen Sec: Doreen King
- ▲ Registered Charity
- ○ *A; to promote the appreciation & writing of haiku & related
      forms (Japanese poetry & prose)
- ● Conf - Mtgs - Comp - SG - Inf - Lib - VE
- M c 200-500 i
- ¶ Blithe Spirit (Jnl) - 4; ftm.

British Hamster Association (BHA) 1954
- ■ 42 Stonebridge Drive, FROME, Somerset, BA11 2TN.   (hsp)
      01373 300766
      email info@southernhamsterclub.co.uk
      http://www.southernhamsterclub.co.uk
      Sec: Mrs Wendy Barry
- ▲ Un-incorporated Society
- ○ *B; to promote the care welfare & keeping of hamsters
- ● Mtgs - ET - Exhib (hamster shows) - Comp - Inf - Maintains a
      breeders' register
- < Nat Hamster Coun
- M c 150 i
- ¶ National Hamster Council Jnl - 12; ftm only.
      Information leaflets on various types of hamster.

British Hand Knitting Confederation
      since January 2007 the **United Kingdom Hand Knitting
      Association**

British Handball Association
      registered name of the **England Handball Association**

British Hang Gliding & Paragliding Association (BHPA) 1974
- ■ The Old Schoolroom, Loughborough Rd, LEICESTER, LE4 5PJ.
      (hq)
      0116-261 1322   fax 0116-261 1323
      email office@bhpa.co.uk   http://www.bhpa.co.uk
- ▲ Company Limited by Guarantee
- Br 120
- ○ *S; control & development of the sport of hang gliding &
      paragliding
- Gp Over land towed ascent; Self launched (unassisted) flight
- ● Conf - ET - Exhib - Comp - Stat
- < R Aero Club; CCPR; Fédn Aéronautique Intle
- M 8,000 i, 120 clubs
- ¶ Skywings (Jnl) - 12; ftm, £2.50 nm.

© CBD Research Ltd · Beckenham · BR3 5JS · Tel 020 8650 7745 · Fax 020 8650 0768 · E-mail cbd@cbdresearch.com · www.cbdresearch.com

British Hanoverian Horse Society   (BHHS)   1992
- ■ Ecton Field Plantation, Ecton Lane, SYWELL, Northants, NN6 0BP.   (hsp)
  01604 492750   fax 01604 492750
  email info@hanoverian-gb.org.uk
  http://www.hanoverian-gb.org.uk
  Hon Sec: John Shenfield
- ▲ Company Limited by Guarantee
- ○ *B; breeding the Hanoverian horse for competition
- ● Licensing of stallions - Maintaining UK studbook
- < Verband Hannoverscher Warmblützüchter eV
- M 120 i
- ¶ NL - 3; ftm only.

British Hardmetal Association
  in February 2004 merged with the British Engineers' Cutting Tools Association to form the **British Hardmetal & Engineers' Cutting Tool Association**

British Hardmetal & Engineers' Cutting Tool Association   (BHECTA)   2004
- ■ c/o 62 Bayswater Rd, LONDON, W2 3PS.   (MTA/hq)
  020 7298 6400   fax 020 7298 6430
  email bhecta@mta.org.uk
  Dir Gen (MTA): Graham Dewhurst
- ▲ Un-incorporated Society
- ○ *T; to act as the national organisation representing the interests of manufacturers within the hardmetal & cutting tool industry
- Gp Research & development (hardmetal)
- ● Conf - Mtgs - ET - Res - Exhib - SG - Stat - Expt - Inf - VE - LG -
- < World Cutting Tool Conf; Eur Cutting Tool Assn
- M 30 f
  Note: in April 2006 was incorporated into the Manufacturing Technologies Association
- × 2004 (British Engineers' Cutting Tools Association
     (British Hardmetal Association

British Hardware Federation   (BHF)   1899
- NR 225 Bristol Rd, Edgbaston, BIRMINGHAM, B5 7UB.   (hq)
  0121-446 6688   fax 0121-446 5215
  email information@bhfgroup.co.uk
  http://www.bhfgroup.co.uk
  Managing Dir: Alan Hawkins
- Br 9 regional groups; 29 local branches
- ○ *T; retailers of kitchenware, housewares, hardware, DIY, home decor, tools, garden products, pet products, building supplies, outdoor power equipment & agricultural machinery
- Gp British Agricultural & Garden Machinery Association
  Cookshop & Housewares Association
  Home Decoration Retailers Association
  Independent Builders Merchants Services
  Pet Product Retailers Association
- ● Conf - Mtgs - ET - Res - Exhib - SG - Stat - Inf - Lib - VE - Empl - LG - Business services for retailers
- < Intl Fedn Ironmongers; Assn Brit Chams Comm; Brit Retail Consortium
- M 4,463 f
- ¶ Hardware Today - 12.
  Hbk & LM - 1.

British Hardware & Housewares Manufacturers' Association
  since 2007 **British Home Enhancement Trade Association**

British Harness Racing Club   (BHRC)   1963
- NR Burlington Crescent, GOOLE, E Yorks, DN14 5EG.
  (regd/office)
  01405 766877   fax 01405 766878
  email harnessgb@aol.com   http://www.bhrc.org.uk
  Sec: Miss Geraldine Berry
- ▲ Company Limited by Guarantee
- ○ *S; governing body for harness racing in GB
- ● Mtgs - Comp - Inf - Race meetings - Issuing of licences
- < Wld Trotting Assn
- M 1,500 i (licence holders)
- ¶ Calendar - 6; £12.   Fixtures List (Jan).
  Record Book - 1; £14.

British Hat Guild   (BHG)   1978
- NR c/o Baxter Hart & Abrahams, 141 New Bedford Road, LUTON, Beds, LU3 1LF.
  01582 721381
  email info@britishhatguild.co.uk
  http://www.britishhatguild.co.uk
- ▲ Un-incorporated Society
- ○ *T; to encourage & promote hat making & millinery in the UK
- ● ET - Exhib - Receptions
- M 25 i, 25 f

British Hawking Association   (BHA)   1967
- NR 43 Amherst Crescent, HOVE, E Sussex, BN3 7EP.   (chmn/p)
  0870 755 0211
  Chmn: Jose Souto
- ▲ Un-incorporated Society
- Br 6
- ○ *G
- ● Mtgs - ET - Apprenticeship scheme - campaign to licence raptor keepers in the UK
- < 3 Spanish falconry clubs
- M 'Unable to disclose due to constitution'
- ¶ Yarak Jnl - 1;   Yarak NL - 4; both ftm.

British Hay & Straw Merchants' Association   (BHSMA)   1917
- ■ Top Farm, Coppingford, HUNTINGDON, Cambs, PE28 5XX.
  (sb)
  01487 830980   fax 01487 830980
  email janelawman@btinternet.com
  http://www.hay-straw-merchants.co.uk
  Sec: Mrs Jane Lawman
- ○ *T; interests of members incl new uses of straw
- Gp Technical
- ● Mtgs - ET - EXhib - SG - Inf - VE - LG
- < Eur Hay & Straw Merchants (CIPF)
- M 50 f
  (Sub: £150)
- ¶ LM.

British Health Care Association   (BHCA)   1931
- NR Unit 8 Cherry Hall Rd, North Kettering Business Park, KETTERING, Northants, NN14 1UE.   (hq)
  01536 519960   fax 01536 519379
  email steve.fritz@bhcaservices.co.uk
  http://www.bhca.org.uk
- ▲ Un-incorporated Society
- ○ *W; to encourage the extension of hospital contributory schemes; to assist in the establishing of new schemes; to encourage voluntary effort for the benefit of hospital patients, others in need & medical charities, including research
- ● Conf - Mtgs - SG - Stat - Inf - Lib - LG
- M 30 f
- ¶ NL - 4; ftm only.   AR (incl LM) - 1; free.
  Caring for the Nation's Health (brochure) - 1; free.

British Health Professionals in Rheumatology   (BHPR)   1985
NR   Bride House, 18-20 Bride Lane, LONDON, EC4Y 8EE.   (hq)
        020 7842 0900   fax 020 7842 0901
        email bhpr@rheumatology.org.uk
        http://www.rheumatology.org.uk
        Chief Exec: Samantha Peters
▲   Registered Charity
○   *P; to encourage & emphasise the multi-disciplinary approach
        to the management of people with rheumatic diseases; to
        provide a forum for health professionals to exchange
        knowledge, skills & experience
●   Conf - Mtgs - ET - Res - Annual clinical prize - Annual Spring
        meeting
<   Brit Soc for Rheumatology (BSR); Arthritis & Musculoskeletal
        Alliance (ARMA)
M   600 i, UK / 3 i, o'seas
¶   BHPR NL - 2;   BHPR Hbk - 2 yrly, both ftm only.

British Healthcare Business Intelligence Association   (BHBIA)
NR   105 St Peter's St, ST ALBANS, Herts, AL1 3EJ.
        01727 896085   fax 01727 896026
        email admin@bhbia.org.uk   http://www.bhbia.org.uk
○   *P

British Healthcare Trades Association   (BHTA)   1917
■   New Loom House, 101 Backchurch Lane, LONDON, E1 1LU.
        (hq)
        020 7702 2141
        email bhta@bhta.com   http://www.bhta.com
        Dir Gen: Ray Hodgkinson
▲   Company Limited by Guarantee
○   *T; to represent companies providing healthcare & assistive
        technology products & services
Gp   Beds & support services; Dispensing appliance contractors; First
        aid medical equipment; Health & safety training
        organisations; Infection control; Mobility access & stairlifts;
        Mobility vehicles (manufacturers, distributors); Orthotics;
        Postural control; Prosthetics; Rehabilitation products; Seating
        & positioning; Stoma & continence; Visual impairment
        products & services
●   Conf - Mtgs - ET - Stat - Inf - LG
M   350 f
¶   Friday Morning at BHTA (NL) - 52;   Bulletin; both ftm only.

British Heather Growers
        a specialist group of the **Horticultural Trades Association**

British Hedgehog Preservation Society   (BHPS)   1982
■   Hedgehog House, Dhustone, LUDLOW, Shropshire, SY8 3PL.
        (hq)
        01584 890801   fax 01584 891313
        email info@britshhedgehogs.org.uk
        http://www.britishhedgehogs.org.uk
        Chief Exec: Fay Vass
▲   Registered Charity
○   *K, *V; to encourage & give advice to the public on the care of
        hedgehogs, particularly when injured, sick, orphaned or in
        any other danger; to fund research into behavioural habits in
        order to assist their survival; to encourage the younger
        generation to value and respect our natural wildlife & to
        foster their interest in hedgehogs
●   Conf - ET - Res - Exhib - Inf - Lib
M   11,000 i, UK & o'seas
        (Sub: £7.50 i, UK / £10 i o'seas)
¶   NL - 2; ftm, 60p nm.   Catalogue - 1; free.

British Helicopter Advisory Board Ltd   (BHAB)   1969
NR   Graham Suite West Entrance, Fairoaks Airport, Chobham,
        WOKING, Surrey, GU24 8HX.   (hq)
        01276 856100   fax 01276 856126
        email info@bhab.org   http://www.bhab.org
        Chief Exec: Peter Norton
○   *T; 'to promote the use of helicopters in the UK; to help
        helicopter operations to be conducted safely & responsibly'
Gp   Onshore operations; Offshore operations; Heliport &
        environmental matters; Technical matters
●   Mtgs - Inf - Lib - LG
<   Eur Helicopter Assn (EHA)
M   i, f & org
¶   The Rotorhead - 4; ftm only.   Leaflets.
        BHAB Information Hbk - 1; ftm.

British Hellenic Chamber of Commerce   (BHCC)   1945
■   25 Vas Sophias Avenue, GR-106 74 ATHENS, Greece.   (hq)
        30 (210) 72 10 361   fax 30 (210) 72 12 119
        email info@bhcc.gr   http://www.bhcc.gr
        Jt Pres: Harilaos Goritsas & Irene Watson
▲   Un-incorporated Society
○   *C; to serve the business world in Greece & Britain
●   Conf - Mtgs - Exhib - Inf - Social events
M   2 i, 21 f, UK / 85 i, 307 f, o'seas
¶   BH Magazine - 4; free.
        Business Directory of Members - 1; ftm, £50 nm.

British Herb Trade Association   (BHTA)   1976
■   133 Eastgate, LOUTH, Lincs, LN11 9QG.   (hq)
        01507 602427   fax 01507 600689
        email tim.mudge@pvga.co.uk   http://www.bhta.org.uk
        Chmn: M H Prestwich
▲   Un-incorporated Society
○   *T; for herb growers, processors & retailers in the UK
●   Conf - Mtgs - Res - LG
<   Nat Farmers U
M   80 f
¶   Herbnews - 4; ftm only.

British Herbal Medicine Association   (BHMA)   1964
■   PO Box 583, EXETER, Devon, EX1 9GX.   (sb)
        0845 680 1134   fax 0845 680 1136
        email secretary@bhma.info   http://www.bhma.info
        Sec: Roberta Hutchins
▲   Company Limited by Guarantee
○   *K, *T; to advance & protect the status of herbal medicine & the
        right to choose herbal remedies; to foster research into
        phytotherapy; to continue to revise & publish the British
        Herbal Pharmacopoeia
Gp   Advertising; Scientific; Database; Pharmacopoeia; Code of
        advertising practice
●   Conf - Mtgs - Res - Inf
<   Nat Inst of Med Herbalists; Natural Medicine Gp
M   c 300 i, f & org
¶   BHMA Post - 4.
        The British Herbal Pharmacopoeia; 1996.
        British Herbal Compendium, Vol 1 & 2.
        A Guide to Traditional Herbal Medicines.

British Herpetological Society   (BHS)   1948
NR   11 Strathmore Place, MONTROSE, Angus, DD10 8LQ.   (hsp)
        email info@thebhs.org
        Sec: Trevor Rose
▲   Registered Charity
○   *L; to promote the study, protection, captive breeding, research
        & conservation of amphibians & reptiles
Gp   Captive breeding; Conservation
●   Mtgs - Res - Inf - Lib
M   c 450 i, UK / 350 i, o'seas
¶   Jnl - 4;   Natterjack (NL) - 3;   Bulletin - 4.

British Hip Society
        a specialist society of the **British Orthopaedic Association**

© CBD Research Ltd · Beckenham · BR3 5JS · Tel 020 8650 7745 · Fax 020 8650 0768 · E-mail cbd@cbdresearch.com · www.cbdresearch.com

British Hire Cruiser Federation   (BHCF)
NR   10 Marina Drive, MARCH, Cambs, PE15 0AU.   (hsp)
    01354 652770   fax 01354 650369
    email paula@zoxboats.co.uk
    Sec: Paula Syred
○   *T; represents hire cruiser operators in the UK
<   Brit Marine Fedn

British Historical Games Society   (BHGS)   1996
■   8 West Hill Avenue, EPSOM, Surrey, KT19 8LE.
    01372 812132   fax 01372 800005
    email bhgs@slitherine.co.uk   http://www.bhgs.co.uk
    Chmn: J D McNeil
▲   Un-incorporated Society
○   *G; to organise & run table top wargaming with miniature
    figurines on a tournament basis; to liaise with other national
    bodies to organise tournaments internationally
●   Exhib - Comp
<   Intl Wargames Fedn
M   500 i

British HIV Association   (BHIVA)
■   c/o Mediscript Ltd, 1 Mountview Court, 310 Friern Barnet Lane,
    LONDON, N20 0LD.   (hq)
    020 8369 5380   fax 020 8446 9194
    email bhiva@bhiva.org   http://www.bhiva.org
▲   Registered Charity
○   *M; for the relief of sickness, protection & preservation of health
    through the development & promotion of good practice in
    the treatment of HIV & related illnesses; to act as a national
    advisory body to the profession & other organisations on all
    aspects of HIV care
●   Conf - ET - Res - Promotion of graduate & continuing medical
    education within HIV care
<   Intl Aids Soc
M   566 i, UK / 8 i, o'seas
¶   HIV Medicine - 4; ftm.

British Holiday & Home Parks Association   (BH&HPA)   1952
■   6 Pullman Court, Great Western Rd, GLOUCESTER,
    GL1 3ND.   (hq)
    01452 526911   fax 01452 508508
    email enquiries@bhhpa.org.uk
    http://www.ukparks.com
    Dir-Gen: Mrs Ros Pritchard
Br   22
○   *T; for owners of caravan holiday parks, touring parks, mobile
    home parks, chalets & all types of self-service holiday
    accommodation
●   Conf - Mtgs - ET - Exhib - SG - PL - LG
<   Eur Fedn of Camping/Caravanning Orgs
M   2,500 i, 3,000 f
¶   Jnl - 6;   Ybk - 1;   NL - irreg; all ftm only.

British Holistic Medical Association   (BHMA)   1983
NR   PO Box 371, BRIDGWATER, Somerset, TA6 9BG.   (hq)
    01278 722000
    Admin: Diana Brown
▲   Registered Charity
○   *L; education of doctors & medical students to the principles &
    practice of holistic medicine & dissemination of information
    to the public
M   i

British Home Enhancement Trade Association   (BHETA)   1958
■   Brooke House, 4 The Lakes, Bedford Rd, NORTHAMPTON,
    NN4 7YD.   (hq)
    01604 622023   fax 01604 631252
    email info@bheta.co.uk   http://www.bheta.co.uk
    Chief Exec: David French
▲   Company Limited by Guarantee
○   *T
Gp   Housewares; Cookware; Hardware; DIY; Brush
●   Conf - Mtgs - Exhib - Stat - Expt - Inf - LG
<   Intl Housewares Assn (USA); Fedn of Eur DIY Mfrs (FEDIYMA)
M   300 f, 10 affiliate org
¶   NL - 12; free.   Membership Directory - 1; ftm, £75 nm.
×   2007 British Hardware & Housewares Manufacturers'
    Association

British Homeopathic Dental Association   1991
■   Menehey, Shawbury Lane, Shustoke, Coleshill, BIRMINGHAM,
    B46 2LA.
    01675 481535
    email brianteall@bhda.co.uk   http://www.bhda.co.uk
    Hon Sec: Brian Teall
▲   Registered Charity
○   *P; to encourage dentists & ancillaries to use homoeopathic
    remedies in their work
●   Conf - ET - Exam - Res - SG - Inf
M   143 i
    (Sub: £40)
¶   NL.

British Homoeopathic Association   (BHA)   1902
NR   Hahnemann House, 29 Park Street West, LUTON, Beds,
    LU1 3BE.   (hq)
    0870 444 3950   fax 0870 444 3960
    email info@trusthomeopathy.org
    http://www.trusthomeopathy.org
    Chief Exec: Sally Penrose
▲   Registered Charity
○   *P, *Q; to provide an information service to the public; to
    campaign for more homeopathy in the NHS; to fund
    research & training in homeopathy
Gp   Supporters' scheme - Friends of the BHA
●   Inf - LG - Provides list of homeopathic doctors, dentists,
    pharmacists, vets & podiatrists
M   3,000 i
¶   Health & Homeopathy - 4.

British Horn Society   (BHS)   1980
NR   The Cottage, Ramsdell Rd, Monk Sherborne, TADLEY, Hants,
    RG26 5HS.   (chmn/p)
    01256 855066
▲   Registered Charity
○   *D; promotion & knowledge of the art, craft & fun of horn &
    horn playing - the French Horn & Wagner Tuba
M   i

British Horological Federation   (BHF)   1935
■   11 Drayton Close, BIDFORD-on-AVON, Warks, B50 4QD.
    (hq)
    01789 490725
    http://www.b-h-f.org
    Sec Gen: Sidney Child
▲   Company Limited by Guarantee
○   *T; for the watch & clock industry
●   Mtgs - Exhib - Expt - Inf - LG
M   50 f, UK / 1 org, o'seas
¶   Horological Jnl - 12; ftm.

British Horological Institute (BHI) 1858
- ■ Upton Hall, Upton, NEWARK, Notts, NG23 5TE.   (hq)
   01636 813795   fax 01636 812258
   email clocks@bhi.co.uk   http://www.bhi.co.uk
   The Secretary
- ▲ Company Limited by Guarantee
- Br 20; 6 area representatives o'seas
- ○ *P; promotion of the art & science of horology to cover both the
   professional & the amateur member
- ● Conf - Mtgs - ET - Exam - Exhib - Inf - Lib - LG
- M c 3,000 i, UK / 500 i, o'seas
- ¶ Horological Journal - 12; ftm only.

British Horse Driving Trials Association (BHDTA) 1925
- NR East Overhill, Stewarton, KILMARNOCK, Ayrshire, KA3 5JT.
   0845 643 2116   fax 0845 643 9474
   email bhdta@horsedrivingtrials.co.uk
   http://www.horsedrivingtrials.co.uk
   Co Sec: Peter Bridson
- ○ *S; carriage driving
- ¶ Carriage Driving Magazine - 12.   Ybk - 1.

British Horse Society (BHS) 1947
- NR Stoneleigh Deer Park, KENILWORTH, Warks, CV8 2XZ.   (hq)
   0844 848 1666   fax 01926 707800
   email enquiry@bhs.org.uk   http://www.bhs.org.uk
   Chief Exec: Graham Cory
- ▲ Registered Charity
- ○ *B, *V; to promote the welfare, care & use of the horse & pony;
   to encourage horsemanship & the improvement of horse
   management & breeding
- Gp Access & rights of way; Welfare; Riding & road safety; Training
   & education; Riding clubs
- ● Conf - ET - Exam - Exhib - Comp - Inf - LG
- M c 100,000 (with those in affiliated riding clubs)
- ¶ British Horse - 6;   Ybk - 1; both ftm only.   AR; free.

British Horseball Association (BHA) 1991
- ■ Arkenfield Stables, Lowdham Rd, Gunthorpe, NOTTINGHAM,
   NG14 7ER.   (hsp)
   0115-966 4574
   email mary.pettifor@lstrillium.com
   http://www.horseball.org.uk
   Intl Sec: Mary Pettifor
- ▲ Company Limited by Guarantee
- Br 10
- ○ *S; to promote & regulate the sport of horseball
- ● Mtgs - ET - Exam - Comp
- < Fedn Intl Horseball (FIHB)
- M 200 i, 10 org, UK / 7,000 i, o'seas
- ¶ BHA NL - 4; free (on website).   BHA Ybk - 1; ftm, £2.50 nm.

British Hospitality Association (BHA) 1910
- ■ Queen's House, 55-56 Lincoln's Inn Fields, LONDON,
   WC2A 3BH.   (hq)
   020 7404 7744   fax 020 7404 7799
   email bha@bha.org.uk   http://www.bha.org.uk
   Chief Exec: Bob Cotton
- ▲ Company Limited by Guarantee
- ○ *T; to be 'the effective voice of the national hotel & food service
   industry'
- ● Conf - Mtgs - ET - Stat - Inf - LG
- < Intl Hotel & Restaurants Assn (IH&RA); Eur Hotel, Restaurant &
   Catering Assn (HOTREC); Eur Fedn of Contract Caterers
   (FERCO)
- M 25,000 f
- ¶ Hospitality Matters (Jnl) 3-6; ftm, £40 yr nm.
   Contract Catering Survey - 1; ftm, £60 nm.
   Trends & Statistics - 1; ftm, £195 nm.

British Hosta & Hemerocallis Society (BHHS) 1980
- ■ Cherry Trees, 37 St John's Rd, STANSTED, Essex, CM24 8JS.
   (hsp)
   01279 813887
   email margaret.loynds@tesco.net
   http://www.hostahem.org.uk
   Hon Gen Sec: Margaret Loynds
- ▲ Registered Charity
- Br 2
- ○ *H; to promote the breeding & growing of hosta & hemerocallis
- Gp Hosta; Hemerocallis
- ● Mtgs - Res - Exhib - SG - Inf - Lib - VE - Lectures
- < R Horticl Soc; Hardy Plant Soc
- M 360 i, 18 f, UK / 28 i, 8 f, 2 org, o'seas
- ¶ British Hosta & Hemerocallis Society Bulletin - 1; ftm, £5 nm.
   NL - 3; ftm, £1 nm.

British Housewives League (BHL) 1945
- ■ Alderley, Meadowfield Rd, STOCKSFIELD, Northumberland,
   NE43 7PZ.   (hsp)
   01661 843226
   Hon Sec: Mrs Lynn Riley
- ▲ Un-incorporated Society
- ○ *K; to provide housewives with an effective non-party political
   voice in all matters concerning the welfare of themselves &
   their families; mainly pro-British independence, family &
   farming matters
- Gp Medical ethics; Nutrition
- ● Conf - Mtgs - Res - Inf - LG
- M i
- ¶ The Lantern (Jnl) - 4; £15 m (includes free entry to Lantern
   lectures), £10 nm.

British Humanist Association (BHA) 1963
- ■ 1 Gower St, LONDON, WC1E 6HD.   (hq)
   020 7079 3580   fax 020 7079 3588
   email info@humanism.org.uk
   http://www.humanism.org.uk
   Exec Dir: Hanne Stinson
- ▲ Company Limited by Guarantee; Registered Charity
- Br 50
- ○ *K; 'to promote humanism & campaign against religious
   privilege & discrimination on grounds of religion or belief'
- Gp Education; ceremonies
- ● Conf - Mtgs - ET - Res - Inf - Lib
- < Intl Humanist & Ethical U
- M 7,000 i, UK / 100 i, o'seas
   (Sub: £35)
- ¶ BHA News - 6.
   Books on non-religious ceremonies:
   Funerals without God; £4.50.
   New Arrivals; £4.
   Sharing the Future; £5.
   Booklets & leaflets on humanism & ethical issues.

British Hydrological Society (BHS) 1983
- NR Institution of Civil Engineers, One Great George St, LONDON,
   SW1P 3AA.   (hq)
   020 7222 7722   fax 020 7222 7500
   email bhs@ice.org.uk   http://www.hydrology.org.uk
   Sec: Tim Fuller,   Hon Sec: Dr Tim Jolley
- ▲ Registered Charity
- Br 6
- ○ *L; to promote interest & scholarships in both scientific &
   applied aspects of hydrology
- ● Conf - Mtgs - VE - LG
- < Instn of Civil Engrs; Inst of Hydrology
- M 736 i, UK / 68 i, o'seas
- ¶ Circulation (NL) - 4.

© CBD Research Ltd · Beckenham · BR3 5JS · Tel 020 8650 7745 · Fax 020 8650 0768 · E-mail cbd@cbdresearch.com · www.cbdresearch.com

British Hydropower Association   (BHA)   1975
■   12 Riverside Park, Station Rd, WIMBORNE, Dorset,
      BH21 1QU.   (hq)
      01202 880333   fax 01202 886609
      email info@british-hydro.org
      http://www.british-hydro.org
      Chief Exec: David Williams
▲   Company Limited by Guarantee
○   *G, *K; to represent the interests of the UK Hydropower industry
      & its associated stakeholders
Gp   Exporters
●   Conf - Mtgs - ET - Res - Exhib - Stat - Expt - Inf - VE - LG
<   Intl Hydropower Assn; Eur Small Hydro Assn (ESHA); Scot
      Renewables Forum
M   20 i, 80 f, 5 org
¶   NL - 4.

British Hypertension Society   (BHS)   1981
■   Hampton Medical Conferences Ltd, 113-119 High St,
      HAMPTON HILL, Middx, TW12 1NJ.   (meetingssec/b)
      020 8979 8300   fax 020 8979 6700
      email hmc@hamptonmedical.com
      http://www.bhsoc.org
      BHS Information Service, c/o Jackie Howarth:
      Clinical Sciences Bldg (Level 5), Leicester Royal Infirmary,
      PO Box 65, LEICESTER, LE2 7LX.   0771 746 7973.
      email bhs@le.ac.uk
      Meetings Sec: Mrs Gerry McCarthy
      Pres: Prof Gordon McInnes
▲   Registered Charity
○   *L, *M, *P; the pathophysiology, epidemiology, detection,
      investigation & treatment of arterial hypertension & related
      vascular diseases
●   Conf - ET - Res - Inf - LG
>   Nurses' Hypertension Assn
M   226 i, UK / 20 i, o'seas

British Hypnotherapy Association   (BHA)   1958
■   30 Cotsford Ave, NEW MALDEN, Surrey, KT3 5EU.   (hq)
      020 8942 3988
      http://www.british-hypnotherapy-association.org
▲   Un-incorporated Society
○   *P; for psychotherapists using hypnotherapy (when appropriate)
      in the treatment of nervous disorders, relationship difficulties,
      emotional problems
●   Mtgs - ET - Exam - Res - SG - Inf - Lib - LG - Provision of
      speakers for seminars & lectures
M   368 i, UK / 16 i, o'seas
¶   Publications list available (prices £1 - £20).

British Icelandic Sheep Breeders Group   (BISGBG)   1994
■   Cefn Maen Isaf, Saron, DENBIGH, LL16 4TH.   (hsp)
      01745 550515
      email jill@britishicelandicsheepbreedersgroup.co.uk
      http://icelandicsheepbreedersofbritain.co.uk
      Hon Sec: Mrs Jill Tyrer
▲   Un-incorporated Society
○   *B; promotion of the Icelandic sheep in Britain & of the
      products from the fleece
●   ET - Exhib - Inf - LG - eGroup - Maintaining a register of
      pedigree Icelandic sheep born in Britain
<   Nat Sheep Soc
M   34 i, UK / 2 i, o'seas
      (Sub: £10 UK / £15 o'seas)
¶   Icenews & Ramblings - 2;   Flock Book - 1; both ftm only.
      also known as Icelandic Sheep Breeders of Britain

British Île de France Sheep Society
■   6 Fort Rd, Kilroot, CARRICKFERGUS, Co Antrim, BT38 9BS.
      (hsp)
      07711 071209
      Sec: Edward Adamson
▲   Un-incorporated Society
○   *B
●   Mtgs - Exhib - Comp - VE
<   Nat Sheep Assn
M   50 i

**British In Vitro Diagnostics Association Ltd   (BIVDA Ltd)
1992**
■   1 Queen Anne's Gate, LONDON, SW1H 9BT.   (hq)
      020 7957 4633   fax 020 7957 4644
      email enquiries@bivda.co.uk
      http://www.bivda.co.uk   or www.medicallab.org.uk
      Dir Gen: Doris-Ann Williams
▲   Company Limited by Guarantee
○   *T; for UK manufacturers & suppliers of in-vitro diagnostic
      products
Gp   Procurement; Public affairs; Regulatory affairs; Point of care
      testing; Diabetes; Market audit; Interest groups
●   Mtgs - ET - Exhib - Stat - Expt - Inf - LG
<   Eur Diagnostic Mfrs Assn (EDMA)
M   130 f
¶   Diagnostics in Healthcare - 3;   Annual Review - 1; both free.

British Incoming Tour Operators Association
   since November 2004 **UKinbound**

British Independent Fruit Growers Association   (BIFGA)
■   Aylsham, Broad Oak, Brenchley, TONBRIDGE, Kent,
      TN12 7NN.   (contact/p)
      01892 722080
      Contact: Mrs Perry
○   *T

British Independent Motor Trade Association   (BIMTA)   1998
NR   14B Chapel Place (1st floor), TUNBRIDGE WELLS, Kent,
      TN1 1YG.   (hq)
      01892 515425   fax 01892 515495
      email queries@bimta.org   http://www.bimta.org
      Gen Sec: Richard Moore
▲   Un-incorporated Society
○   *T; for all sectors of the independent motor trade
Gp   Importers of European & Japanese vehicles; Parts suppliers &
      servicing agents; Professional PR & lobbying
●   Conf - Mtgs - Inf - LG
<   Eur Assn of Indep Vehicle Traders (EAIVT); Eur Parallel Import
      Coalition (EPIC)
M   c 140 fUK / 4 f, o'seas
¶   LM; free for sae.

British Independent Plastic Extruders Association
   has ceased all activities

British Indoor Cricket Association
▲   Company Limited by Guarantee
      see **England Indoor Cricket Association**

**British Industrial Furnace Construction Association   (BIFCA)
1946**
NR   National Metalforming Centre, 47 Birmingham Rd,
      WEST BROMWICH, W Midlands, B70 6PY.   (hq)
      0121-601 6350   fax 0121-601 6387
      email enquiry@bifca.org.uk   http://www.bifca.org.uk
      Sec: David B Corns
▲   Company Limited by Guarantee
○   *T; to represent the interests of leading manufacturers of
      industrial furnaces & component suppliers
●   Mtgs - Exhib - LG - Seminars - Tech course
<   METCOM; Eur C'ee Indl Furnace & Heating Eqpt Mfrs (CECOF)
M   17 f

British Industrial Truck Association Ltd   (BITA)   1942
NR   5-7 High St, Sunninghill, ASCOT, Berks, SL5 9NQ.   (hq)
       01344 623800   fax 01244 291197
       http://www.bita.org.uk
       Sec Gen: James Clark
○   *T; industrial fork lift trucks industry
Gp   Major mfrs; Smaller mfrs; Suppliers; Importers; Finance houses
●   Conf - Mtgs - ET - Exhib - SG - Inf - LG
M   c 70 f
¶   LM & their products; free.   AR; ftm.
       Operators Safety Code for Powered Industrial Trucks.
       List of publications available.

British Industry Offset Group
       a group of the **Defence Manufacturers Association**

British Infection Society   1974
NR   Hartley Taylor Medical Communications,
       Naphill House Cottage, Hunts Hill Lane, NAPHILL, Bucks,
       HP14 4RL.   (hsb)
       01494 563804   fax 01494 583804
       http://www.britishinfectionsociety.org
       Sec: Dr Peter Moss
▲   Registered Charity
○   *V, *P, *Q; to relieve sickness by the study of all aspects of
       infection; to promote the wide dissemination of relevant
       knowledge
●   Conf - Mtgs - ET - Res
<   Fedn of Infection Socs
M   c 600 i, UK / 100 i, o'seas
¶   Jnl of Infection - 6.

British Infertility Counselling Association   (BICA)   1988
NR   111 Harley St, LONDON, W1G 6AW.   (mail/address)
       01744 750660
       email info@bica.net   http://www.bica.net
       Chmn: Mollie Graneek
▲   Registered Charity
○   *P, *W; to promote highest standards of counselling for those
       considering, or undergoing, fertility investigations & treatment
●   Conf - Mtgs - ET - SG - Inf - LG
M   c 170 i
¶   Jnl of Infertility Counselling - 3; ftm.

British Inflatable Boat Owners Association   (BIBOA)   1990
NR   Mewstone Cottage, Back Lane, Sway, LYMINGTON, Hants,
       SO41 6BU.
       http://www.biboa.com
○   *B; for owners of rigid inflatable boats
¶   Riblines - 5

British Inline Puck Hockey Association   (BIPHA)
NR   PO Box 641, ROTHERHAM, S Yorks, S60 9BU
       http://www.bipha.co.uk

British Inline Skater Hockey Association   (BiSHA)   1984
NR   17 Queen's Rd, BRIXHAM, Devon, TQ5 8BG.   (hq)
       01803 850644
▲   Company Limited by Guarantee
Br   12; Denmark, France, Germany, Holland, Switzerland
○   *S; governing body for (roller) skater hockey in Britain (formerly
       known as street hockey)

British Institute of Agricultural Consultants   (BIAC)   1957
NR   The Estate Office, Torry Hill, Milstead, SITTINGBOURNE, Kent,
       ME9 0SP.   (hq)
       01795 830100   fax 01795 830243
       email info@biac.co.uk   http://www.biac.co.uk
       Chief Exec: C Anthony Hyde
Br   1
○   *F, *H, *P; independent qualified specialists in agriculture,
       horticulture, forestry & related sciences which have
       application in the countryside; members work in the UK &
       overseas
Gp   Business management; Engineering; Environmnet; Expert
       opinion; International; Livestock; Rural planning
●   Conf - Mtgs - ET - Exhib
<   Brit Consultants Bureau
M   c 300 i
¶   NL - 12;   LM - 1; both free.

British Institute for Allergy & Environmental Therapy   1987
■   Ffynnonwen, Llangwyryfon, ABERYSTWYTH, Ceredigion,
       SY23 4EY.   (hq)
       01974 241376   fax 01974 241795
       email allergy@onetel.com   http://www.allergy.org.uk
       Dir: Donald M Harrison
▲   Un-incorporated Society
○   *M, *P; is concerned with the development of techniques &
       dissemination of information to & from health professionals
       in the diagnosis & treatment of food, chemical &
       environmental allergy; to maintain a register of therapists
       working in this field
●   SG - Inf
M   308 i, UK / 6 i, o'seas

British Institute of Architectural Technologists
       since 2005 **Chartered Institute of Architectural Technologists**

British Institute & Association of Electrolysis Ltd   1956
NR   40 Parkfield Rd, ICKENHAM, Middx, UB10 8LW.   (sb)
       0844 544 1373
       email sec@electrolysis.co.uk
       Sec: Nicky Wilsher
▲   Company Limited by Guarantee
○   *P
Gp   some members offer specialised treatment of broken veins,
       removal of warts, moles & skin tags
●   Conf - Mtgs - ET - Exam - Exhib - Comp - Inf
M   c 320 i
¶   The BIAE Probe - 6;   AR; both ftm only.
       LM - up-dated; free.
×   2004 (British Association of Electrolysists
              (Institute of Electrolysis

British Institute of Cleaning Science   (BICSc)   1960
NR   9 Premier Court, Boarden Close, Moulton Park,
       NORTHAMPTON, NN3 6LF.   (hq)
       01604 678710   fax 01604 645988
       email info@bics.org.uk   http://www.bics.org.uk
○   *P; training, education, qualification & certification for the
       cleaning industry

**British Institute of Dental & Surgical Technologists   (BIDST)
1935**
■   4 Thompson Green, SHIPLEY, W Yorks, BD17 7PR.   (sp)
       0845 644 3726
       http://www.bidst.org
       Sec: Beryl Dawe
▲   Company Limited by Guarantee
○   *P
●   Conf - ET - SG

© CBD Research Ltd · Beckenham · BR3 5JS · Tel 020 8650 7745 · Fax 020 8650 0768 · E-mail cbd@cbdresearch.com · www.cbdresearch.com

British Institute of Embalmers (BIE) 1927
■ 21c Station Rd, Knowle, SOLIHULL, W Midlands, B93 0HL. (hq)
  01564 778991 fax 01564 770812
  email info@bioe.co.uk http://www.bioe.co.uk
  Admin Sec: I Grainger
○ *P; to encourage & promote the practice of embalming
M i
¶ The Embalmer - 4; ftm.

British Institute of Energy Economics (BIEE) 1976
■ Stars Cottage, Stars Lane, DINTON, Bucks, HP17 8UL. (hq)
  01296 747916
  http://www.biee.org
  Admin: Debbie Heywood
▲ Registered Charity
○ *L, *P; the study & exchange of information about energy economics

British Institute of Facilities Management Ltd (BIFM) 1993
NR Number One Building, The Causeway, BISHOP'S STORTFORD, Herts, CM23 2ER. (hq)
  0845 058 1356 fax 01279 712669
  Sec: Philip Margesson, Chief Exec: Ian Fielder
▲ Company Limited by Guarantee
Br 10
○ *P; to promote & develop the science & understanding of facilities management (planning & designing office premises, buying office equipment & furniture); the institute provides a national qualification & continuing professional development (CPD) through presentations, meetings & visits
Gp C'ees: Communications, Executive, Health & safety, Membership, Professional development, Research
  Special interest groups: Building services, Information management
● Conf - Mtgs - ET - Exam - Res - Exhib - Inf - Lib - VE - LG
< EURO FM
M c 10,000 i, 375 fK / 117 i, o'seas
¶ FM World - 26; ftm only.

British Institute of Funeral Directors (BIFD) 1981
NR 1 Gleneagles House, Vernongate, DERBY, DE1 1UP. (sp)
  0800 032 2733 fax 01332 225101
  email admin@bifd.org.uk http://www.bifd.org.uk
  Chief Exec: John M G Payne
▲ Un-incorporated Society
○ *P; a professional organisation for individual qualified funeral directors
● Conf - Mtgs - ET - Exhib - LG - Diploma in funeral directing
< Coun of Brit Funeral Services
M 1,657 i, UK / 10 i, o'seas
¶ Jnl - 4; ftm, £12.50 yr nm.
  LM - 1; Membership Hbk - 1; both ftm only

British Institute of Graphologists (BIG) 1983
■ PO Box 3060, GERRARDS CROSS, Bucks, SL9 9XP. (admin/p)
  01753 891241 fax 01753 886412
  email elaine.quigley@britishgraphology.org
  http://www.britishgraphology.org
  Chmn: John Beck, Admin: Mrs Elaine Quigley
▲ Registered Charity
○ *P; to promote the use of graphology as a scientific tool in understanding the behavioural patterns & potential of people
Gp Counselling; Recruitment; Team building; Career advice
● Conf - Mtgs - ET - Exam - Res - SG
M 109 i, UK / 30 i, o'seas
¶ The Graphologist - 4; ftm, £4 nm.

British Institute of Innkeeping (BII) 1981
NR Wessex House, 80 Park St, CAMBERLEY, Surrey, GU15 3PT. (hq)
  01276 684449
  Chief Exec: John McNamara
▲ Company Limited by Guarantee; Registered Charity
○ *P; the education & training of persons concerned with the day-to-day running of premises having a Justice's full licence for the sale of intoxicating liquor
● Conf - Mtgs - ET - Exam - Res - Exhib - Comp - SG - LG
M c 17,500 i
¶ biiBUSINESS - 10. AR.

British Institute of International & Comparative Law (BIICL) 1958
NR Charles Clore House, 17 Russell Square, LONDON, WC1B 5JP. (hq)
  020 7862 5151
  http://www.biicl.org
  Dir: Prof Robert McCorquodale
▲ Registered Charity
○ *L, *Q; an established independent centre with unique focus on linking academics & legal practitioners in the understanding & development of international law including the law of Human Rights, the Commonwealth & the European Union
  Our mission is to understand & influence the development of law as this applies to an increasingly international community.
  This mission is fulfilled by serving as: a research organisation; the publisher of academic volumes; a training & advice centre
M i

British Institute for Learning & Development (BILD)
NR Trym Lodge, 1 Henbury Rd, Westbury on Trym, BRISTOL, B9 3HQ.
  0117-959 6517 fax 0117-959 6518
  email info@thebild.org http://www.thebild.org
  Manager: Sarah Wills
▲ Company Limited by Guarantee; Registered Charity
○ *E; a dynamic community, with a global reach, committed to innovation, best practice & excellence in innovative & well established techniques & technologies for learning
Gp '
● Conf - Mtgs - Res - Exhib - Inf - LG
M 314 i & org (a network of 600 i)
¶ Connect (Jnl) - 4;
  Learning Blitz (NL) [online] - 26; both ftm only.

British Institute of Learning Disabilities (BILD) 1972
NR Campion House, Green St, KIDDERMINSTER, Worcs, DY10 1JL. (hq)
  01562 723010 fax 01562 723029
  email enquiries@bild.org.uk http://www.bild.org.uk
  Chief Exec: Keith Smith
▲ Registered Charity
○ *W; to contribute towards quality lifestyles for people with learning disabilities
Gp People with learning disabilities; People with profound & multiple disabilities
● Conf - ET - Res - Inf - Lib - Publishing
< University of Birmingham
M c 1,300 i, f & org
¶ British Jnl of Learning Disabilities - 4;
  Learning Disability Bulletin - 4;
  Journal of Applied Research in Intellectual Disabilities - 4;
  Current Awareness Service - 12; all ftm.

British Institute of Musculoskeletal Medicine (BIMM) 1992
NR   PO Box 1116, BUSHEY, Herts, WD23 9BY.   (hsp)
     020 8421 9910
     email info@bimm.org.uk   http://www.bimm.org.uk
     Chief Exec: Deena Harris
▲   Registered Charity
○   *E, *M, *P; dissemination of knowledge & increase of expertise
     in musculoskeletal medicine within the medical profession
●   Conf - Mtgs - ET - Res
<   Brit League against Rheumatism (BLAR); Intl Fedn Manual
     Medicine (FIMM)
M   300 i, UK / 60 i, o'seas
¶   Jnl of Orthopaedic Medicine - 4; ftm.

British Institute of Non-Destructive Testing (BInstNDT) 1954
NR   1 Spencer Parade, NORTHAMPTON, NN1 5AA.   (hq)
     01604 630124
     email info@bindt.org   http://www.bindt.org
▲   Company Limited by Guarantee; Registered Charity
○   *L; 'to promote the advancement of the science & practice of
     non-destructive testing & all other associated materials
     testing disciplines'
M   i

British Institute of Organ Studies (BIOS) 1976
■   Lime Tree Cottage, 39 Church St, Haslingfield, CAMBRIDGE,
     CB23 1JE.   (hsp)
     01223 872190   fax 01223 872190
     http://www.bios.org.uk
     Hon Sec: Mrs José Hopkins
▲   Registered Charity
○   *L; promotion of scholarly research into the history of organs
     (particularly British organs); preservation & conservation of
     historic organs; information sources & materials
Gp   Brit Organ Archive; National Pipe Organ Register; Historic
     organs certificate scheme
●   Conf - Mtgs - Res - SG - VE - LG
M   671 i
¶   Jnl - 1;   Reporter - 4; both ftm.

British Institute of Persian Studies (BIPS) 1961
NR   c/o The British Academy, 10 Carlton House Terrace, LONDON,
     SW1Y 5AH.   (hq)
     020 7969 5203
▲   Registered Charity
○   *L; promotion of Iranian studies incl language, history, art
     history & archaeology
M   i

British Institute of Professional Dog Trainers (BIPDT) 1974
■   PO Box 5894, MILTON KEYNES, Bucks, MK10 1FJ.   (gensec/p)
     01908 526856   fax 01908 526856
     email info@bipdt.org.uk   http://www.bipdt.org.uk
     Gen Sec: John McNeil,   Co Sec: Ann Fisher
▲   Company Limited by Guarantee
○   *P; to compile a register of qualified trainers of working dogs;
     to raise the standard of training, management, welfare &
     usage of working dogs
Gp   Security
●   ET - Exam - Inf - Seminars
M   750 i, 27 f, 37 org, UK / 40 i, o'seas
¶   Training & Education Jnl - 3.

British Institute of Professional Photography (BIPP) 1901
■   Fox Talbot House, 2 Amwell End, WARE, Herts, SG12 9HN.
     (hq)
     01920 464011   fax 01920 487056
     email info@bipp.com   http://www.bipp.com
     Exec Officer: M Berry
▲   Company Limited by Guarantee
○   *P
Gp   Advertising; Architectural; Audio Visual Association; Cine;
     Commercial/Industrial; Education; Medical; Photo-science;
     Portraiture; Theatre; Wedding
●   Conf - Mtgs - ET - Exam - Exhib - Comp - SG - Inf - LG
<   Wld Coun Profl Photographers; Fedn Eur Photographers; Profl
     Photographers of America; Brit Copyright Coun; BSI; Photo
     Imaging Coun
M   3,673 i, UK / 260 i, o'seas
¶   The Photographer - 12; ftm, £4,25 nm.   AR; ftm only.

British Institute of Radiology (BIR) 1897
NR   36 Portland Place, LONDON, W1B 1AT.   (hq)
     020 7307 1400
▲   Registered Charity
○   *L; an independent forum to bring together all the professions
     in radiology; to share medical & scientific knowledge to
     detect & treat disease
M   i

** **British Institute of Securities Laws**
     Organisation lost: see Introduction paragraph 3

British Institute of Verbatim Reporters (BIVR) 1887
NR   73 Alicia Gardens, Kenton, HARROW, Middx, HA3 8JD.   (regd
     off)
     fax 020 8907 5820
     email sec@bivr.org   http://www.bivr.org.uk
     Sec: Mary Sorene
▲   Company Limited by Guarantee
○   *P; to promote the more efficient practice of the art of machine
     & pen shorthand in connection with legal & other
     proceedings
M   179 i
¶   NL - 3; free.

British Insurance Brokers' Association (BIBA) 1977
■   BIBA House, 14 Bevis Marks, LONDON, EC3A 7NT.   (hq)
     0844 770 0266   fax 020 7626 9676
     email enquiries@biba.org.uk   http://www.biba.org.uk
     Chief Exec: Eric Galbraith
▲   Company Limited by Guarantee
○   *T; representing insurance brokers & independent
     intermediaries
●   Conf - Mtgs - ET - Inf - LG
M   2,100 f
¶   The Broker (Jnl) - 4;
     BIBA Membership Directory - 1; both ftm only.

British Insurance Law Association (BILA) 1964
■   47 Bury St, STOWMARKET, Suffolk, IP14 1HD.   (hsb)
     07776 115795   fax 01449 770941
     email secretariat@bila.org.uk   http://www.bila.org.uk
     Secretariat: Doug Jordan
▲   Un-incorporated Society
○   *P; to consider & discuss matters of general interest arising out
     of the law, (both statutory & common, including tax law &
     regulations & current revenue practice) in so far as it affects
     any branch of insurance
●   Conf - Mtgs - Res - SG
<   Assn Intle de Droit des Assurances (AIDA)
M   225 i, 485 f, UK / 20 i, 23 f, o'seas
¶   BILA Jnl - 3; ftm.

British Interactive Group

NR c/o Inspire Discovery Centre, St Michael's Church, Oak St, NORWICH, NR3 3AE.   (sb)
    01603 612612
    http://www.big.uk.com
    Vice-Chmn: James Piercy
○   'for individuals involved in all aspects of hands-on exhibitions & activities; hands-on approach beyond physical science into other areas of science & technology & non-science subjects, artists, archaeologists, educators, students, front-of-house staff, evaluators'

British Interactive Media Association   (BIMA)   1984

NR Briarlea House, Southend Rd, BILLERICAY, Essex, CM11 2PR.   (hsp)
    01277 658107   fax 0870 051 7842
    email info@bima.co.uk   http://www.bima.co.uk
    Principal Admin: Janice Cable
○   *T; to promote the use of interactive media in commerce & industry
●   Conf - Mtgs - ET - Exhib - Comp - SG - Expt - Inf - LG - BIMA Awards
M   i & f
¶   E-Newsletter - 12; m only.

British Interior Design Association   (BIDA)   1966

NR Units 109-111 The Chambers, Chelsea Harbour, LONDON, SW10 0XF.   (hq)
    020 7349 0800   fax 020 7349 0500
    email enquiries@bida.org
    Sec: Karin Velzario
▲   Company Limited by Guarantee
○   *P, *T; to support the interior decorator/designer member & the corporate member
●   Mtgs - ET - Exhib - PL - VE
<   Intl Fedn of Interior Architects (IFI)
M   c 1,100 i & f
¶   Review - 4; ftm, £117.50 nm.
    Directory of Members & Associates - 1; ftm.

British Interior Textiles Association   (BITA)   1987

NR 5 Portland Place, LONDON, W1B 1PW.   (hq)
    020 7636 7788   fax 020 7636 7515
    email bita@dial.pipex.com
    http://www.interiortextiles.co.uk
    Sec: Adam Mansell
○   *T
●   Mtgs - Exhib - Comp - Stat - Expt - LG
<   Brit Apparel & Textile Confedn
M   f

** **British Interlingua Society**

    Organisation lost, see Introduction paragraph 3

British & International Federation of Festivals for Music, Dance & Speech   1921

NR Festivals House, 198 Park Lane, MACCLESFIELD, Cheshire, SK11 6UD.   (hq)
    0870 774 4290
▲   Company Limited by Guarantee
○   *G; headquarters of the amateur competitive festival movement
M   i & f

British International Freight Association   (BIFA)   1944

■   Redfern House, Browells Lane, FELTHAM, Middx, TW13 7EP.   (hq)
    020 8844 2266   fax 020 8890 5546
    email bifa@bifa.org   http://www.bifa.org
    Dir Gen: Peter Quantrill
▲   Company Limited by Guarantee
○   *T; for the international transport sector
Gp Freight forwarders; Logistics services supplies; Supply chain management; International traders; General sales agents; Transit shed operators; Export packers
●   Conf - Mtgs - ET - Exhib - LG - Political lobbying - Promotion & advice
<   Intl Fedn of Freight Forwarders Assns (FIATA); Intl Air Transport Assn (IATA); Eur Org for Forwarding & Logistics (CLECAT)
M   1,203 f
¶   Bifalink (NL) - 12; ftm.   AR - 1; both ftm.
    Freight Services Directory - 1; ftm, £95 nm.
    in 2004 the individual members of BIFA became the Freight Forwarding Forum of the **Chartered Institute of Logistics & Transport**

British & International Golf Greenkeepers' Association   (BIGGA)   1987

NR BIGGA House, Aldwark, Alne, YORK, YO61 1UF.   (hq)
    01347 833800
    Chief Exec Dir: John Pemberton
▲   Un-incorporated Society
○   *P; to represent golf greenkeepers throughout the UK
M   i

British International Studies Association   (BISA)   1975

NR International Politics Bldg, Aberystwyth University, Penglais, ABERYSTWYTH, SY23 3FE.   (admin/b)
    01970 628672
    http://www.bisa.ac.uk
    Admin:
▲   Registered Charity
○   *P; to promote the study of international relations & related subjects through teaching, research & facilitating contact between scholars
M   c 900 i
¶   Review of International Studies.   NL.

British Internet Publishers Alliance   (BIPA)   1997

■   49 Park Town, OXFORD, OX2 6SL.   (hsb)
    01865 310732
    http://www.bipa.co.uk
    Hon Sec: Angela Mills Wade
▲   Un-incorporated Society
○   *T
●   Mtgs - ET - Res - Inf - LG
<   Digital Content Forum
M   8 f, 2 org

British Interplanetary Society   (BIS)   1933

NR 27-29 South Lambeth Rd, LONDON, SW8 1SZ.   (hq)
    020 7735 3160
○   *L; promotion of the science, engineering & technology of astronautics
M   i

British Iris Society (BIS) 1922

- ■ 15 Parkwood Drive, RAWTENSTALL, Lancs, BB4 6RP.
    (memsec/p)
    email ehf.bis@btinternet.com
    http://www.britishirissociety.org.uk
    Mem Sec: E H Furnival
- ▲ Registered Charity
- ○ *H; irises, in the wild & in cultivation & other members of the Iridaceae
- Gp Remontant; Species; Siberian; Spuria & Japanese; Crocus
- ● Conf - Mtgs - Exhib - Comp - SG - Inf - Lib - PL (& slides) - Registration & trials for new cultivars
- < R Horticl Soc; American Iris Soc
- M 300 i, UK / 100 i, 20 org, o'seas
    (Sub: £12, $70/60 for 3 years)
- ¶ NL - 2;   Ybk - 1; both ftm only.

British & Irish Association of Law Librarians (BIALL) 1969

- ■ The Boots Library, Nottingham Trent University, Goldsmith St, NOTTINGHAM, NG1 5LS.   (hsb)
    0115-848 2893
    email admin@biall.org.uk   http://www.biall.org.uk
    Hon Sec: Angela Donaldson
- ▲ Un-incorporated Society
- ○ *P; to promote the better administration & exploitation of law libraries & legal information units; to encourage bibliographical study & research in law & librarianship, & cooperation with other organisations & societies
- Gp Marketing; Academic; Law libraries
- ● Conf - ET - Exhib
- < Amer Assn of Law Libs (AALL); Canadian Assn of Law Libs (CALL)
- M 680 i, 162 f
- ¶ Legal Information Management - 4; ftm, £98 nm.
    BIALL NL - 6; ftm only.

British & Irish Association of Zoos & Aquariums (BIAZA) 1966

- NR Regent's Park, LONDON, NW1 4RY.   (hq)
    020 7449 6351   fax 020 7449 6359
    http://www.biaza.org.uk
    Dir: Dr Miranda Stevenson,   Admin: Gwen Manning
- ▲ Registered Charity
- ○ *P, *V; to represent the zoo community in Britain & Ireland; to maintain the world's biodiversity, the welfare of animals in zoos & the advancement of scientific knowledge
- ● Conf - Mtgs - ET - Inf - LG
- < Wld Assn Zoos & Aquaria (WAZA); Wld Consvn U (IUCN); Eur Assn Zoos & Aquaria (EAZA)
- > Wld Assn of Zoos & Aquariums (WAZA); Eur Assn of Zoos & Aquaria (EAZA)
- M 66 i, 69 zoos
- ¶ Zoo Federation News - 3;   LM; both ftm only.
- × 2004 Federation of Zoological Gardens of GB & I

British & Irish Legal Education Technology Association (BILETA) 1986

- NR c/o UK Centre for Legal Education, University of Warwick, COVENTRY, Warks, CV4 7AL.   (hq)
    024 7652 3117   fax 024 7652 3290
- ○ *P; promoting technology in legal education & improving contacts between academics & practising professionals in UK & Ireland
- M i

British & Irish Ombudsman Association (BIOA) 1993

- ■ PO Box 308, TWICKENHAM, Middx, TW1 9BE.   (hq)
    020 8894 9272
    email secretary@bioa.org.uk   http://www.bioa.org.uk
    Sec: Ian Pattison
- ○ *P; the role of ombudsmen in both public & private sectors
- ● Conf - Mtgs - SG - Inf - LG
- M 112 i, 45 org, UK / 11 i, 6 org, o'seas
- ¶ NL - 3/4;   Reports of Conferences - 2 yrly; both ftm only.
    Directory of Ombudsmen - up-dated; on Internet.

British & Irish Orthoptic Society (BIOS) 1937

- ■ Tavistock House North, Tavistock Sq, LONDON, WC1H 9HX.
    (hq)
    020 7387 7992   fax 020 7383 2584
    email bos@orthoptics.org.uk
    http://www.orthoptics.org.uk
    Hon Sec: Mrs Shelagh Baynham
- ▲ Company Limited by Guarantee; Registered Charity
- Br 6
- ○ *M, *P, *U; to encourage, study & improve practice of orthoptics
- Gp Glaucoma; Low vision; Special learning difficulties; Stroke & rehabilitation
- ● Conf - Mtgs - ET - Stat - Inf - Empl - LG
- < Intl Orthoptic Assn (IOA); Orthoptistes de la Communauté Européenne (OCE)
- M 1,450 i, UK / 72 i, o'seas
- ¶ British Orthoptic Jnl; ftm, £50 nm.
    Parallel Vision - 12; ftm only.
- × 2004 (January) British Orthoptic Society

British & Irish Spa & Hot Tub Association
    a part of **Swimming Pool & Allied Trades Association**

British Isles Backgammon Association (BIBA) 1989

- NR 2 Redbourne Drive, LINCOLN, LN2 2HG.   (hq)
    01522 888676   fax (telephone first)
    Dir: Michael Crane
- ▲ Un-incorporated Society
- ○ *S; to promote the game of backgammon
- ● Conf - Mtgs - ET - Comp - Stat - Inf
- M 1,200 i, clubs
- ¶ Bibafax (NL) - 6; free.

British Isles Baton Twirling Association (BIBTA)

- NR 208 Horninglow Rd, Firth Park, SHEFFIELD, S Yorks, S5 6SG.
    (hq)
    0114-220 4010
    Sec: D Lucas
- ▲ Registered Charity
- ○ *G
- ● Mtgs - ET - Exhib - Comp - Inf - VE

British Isles Bowls Council (BIBC) 1903

- ■ 23 Leysland Avenue, Countesthorpe, LEICESTER, LE8 5XX.
    (hsp)
    0116-277 3234
    email michaelswatland@btinternet.com
    http://www.britishislesbowls.com
    Hon Sec: Michael W G Swatland
- ▲ Un-incorporated Society
- ○ *S; the game of flat green bowls
- ● Comp - Organisation of British Isles championships; & the Senior & Junior International series
- < World Bowls Ltd
- > English / Scottish / Irish / Welsh / Jersey / Guernsey Bowling Assns
- M 265,000 i

British Isles Indoor Bowls Council (BIIBC)

- NR 16 Hendre Avenue, Ogmore Vale, BRIDGEND, Glamorgan, CF32 7HD.   (hsp)
    01656 841361   fax 01656 849160
    email briandaviesbowls@btinternet.com
    http://www.biibc.org.uk
    Hon Sec & Treas: Brian Davies
- ▲ Un-incorporated Society
- Br 5
- ○ *S; to promote the game of indoor bowls & to be responsible for the promotion of all British Isles run championships
- ● Mtgs - Comp - Inf
- < Wld Indoor Bowls Coun
- > English / Welsh / Scot / Guernsey Indoor Bowling Assn[s]; Assn of Irish Indoor Bowls; Brit Wheelchair Bowling Assn
- M 13,781 i, 6 f, 435 org

© CBD Research Ltd · Beckenham · BR3 5JS · Tel 020 8650 7745 · Fax 020 8650 0768 · E-mail cbd@cbdresearch.com · www.cbdresearch.com

British Italian Society   (BIS)   1941
NR   c/o The Venice in Peril Fund, Hurlingham Studios (Unit 4),
      Ranelagh Gardens, LONDON, SW6 3PA.   (mail/address)
      020 7924 6883
      email info@british-italian.org
      http://www.british-italian.org
      Hon Dir: Mrs susan Kikoler,   Treas: Mrs Gillian Wettern
▲   Registered Charity
○   *X; to increase knowledge & understanding in the UK of Italian
      culture in terms of history, institutions, way of life, language &
      contribution to civilisation; to promote the traditional
      friendship between UK & Italy
●   Mtgs - Exhib - Inf - VE - Archive
<   Associazione Cultivale Italia-Inghilterra (Sardinia); St Peter's
      Italian Church (London)
M   445 i, 9 f, 1 org, UK / 17 i, 1 org, o'seas
¶   Rivista - 3/4; free.

British Jazz Society
      This organisation is dormant

British Jewellers' Association   (BJA)   1887
■   Federation House, 10 Vyse St, BIRMINGHAM, B18 6LT.   (hq)
      0121-237 1110   fax 0121-237 1113
      http://www.bja.org.uk
○   *T; representing manufacturing jewellers, silversmiths, fashion
      jewellers, & dealers in bullion, precious stones, & horology
<   Brit Jewellery, Giftware & Finishing Fedn
M   f

**British Jewellery, Giftware & Finishing Federation Ltd   (BJGF)
1970**
■   Federation House, 10 Vyse St, BIRMINGHAM, B18 6LT.   (hq)
      0121-236 2657   fax 0121-236 3921
      http://www.bjgf.org.uk
      Chief Exec: Krys Zalewska
▲   Company Limited by Guarantee
○   *N, *T; to support 6 trade associations in the jewellery, giftware,
      leathergoods & metal finishing industries
Gp   Giftware; Jewellery; Surface engineering; Travel goods &
      accessories
●   Conf - Mtgs - Exhib - SG - Expt - Inf - Lib - LG available
<   Art Metalware Mfrs' Assn (AMMA); Brit Jewellers' Assn (BJA); Brit
      Travelgoods & Accessories Assn (BTAA); Giftware Assn (GA);
      JewelleryDistributors' Assn (JDA); Surface Engg Assn (SEA)
M   1,800 f, UK / 50 f, o'seas, 721 others
¶   Export News - 4.
×   2004 British Jewellery & Giftware Federation

British Jigsaw Puzzle Library   (BJPL)   1933
■   Clarendon, Parsonage Rd, HERNE BAY, Kent, CT6 5TA.   (hsp)
      01227 742222
      http://www.britishjigsawpuzzlelibrary.co.uk
      Owner: Dave Cooper
○   *G; lending library of wooden jigsaws operated on a postal
      basis to private individuals who join by subscription;
      (personal callers by appointment only)
●   Lib
M   c 350 i, UK / 10 i, o'seas

British Judo Association Ltd   (BJA)   1948
NR   Loughborough Technology Park (suite B), Epinal Way,
      LOUGHBOROUGH, Leics, LE11 3GE.   (hq)
      01509 631693   fax 01509 631681
      Commercial Manager: Emma Davies
▲   Company Limited by Guarantee
○   *S; the governing body to control, foster & develop the practice
      & spirit of judo
●   Conf - Mtgs - ET - Exam - Res - Comp - Stat - Inf
<   Intl Judo Fedn; Eur Judo U; Brit Olympic Assn; Sports Coun;
      Central Coun for Physical Recreation (CCPR)
M   30,000 i
¶   British Judo (club NL) - 6.   AR; both ftm only.
      List of Clubs per Area; on request.

British Kerry Cattle Society
NR   Windle Hill Farm, Sutton on the Hill, ASHBOURNE, Derbys,
      DE6 5JH.   (hsp)
      01283 732377
      Hon Sec: Mrs Joan Lennard
▲   Registered Charity
○   *B
●   Inf
M   c 40 i
¶   NL - irreg.

British Kidney Patient Association   (BKPA)   1975
NR   Oakhanger Place, BORDON, Hants, GU35 9JZ.   (hq)
      01420 472021
      Pres: Mrs Elizabeth Ward
▲   Company Limited by Guarantee; Registered Charity
○   *W; benefit & welfare of kidney patients & their families; to
      lobby for more & improved facilities & increased government
      funding so that all patients may benefit from improvements
      in technology & pharmaceutical achievements
●   Inf
M   i
¶   Silver Lining Appeal Brochure - 1; free.

British Kite Surfing Association   (BKSA)   1999
NR   Manor Barn, Stottingway St, Uppway, WEYMOUTH, Dorset,
      DT3 5QA.   (hq)
      01305 8135552; 07980 553057 (mob)
      email info@bksaonline.org
      http://www.britishkitesurfingassociation.co.uk
      Chmn: Richard Gowers
○   *S

British Kodály Academy   (BKA)   1981
■   13 Midmoor Rd, LONDON, SW19 4JD.   (treas/p)
      020 8971 2062   fax 020 8946 6528
      email enquiries@britishkodalyacademy.org
      http://www.britishkodalyacademy.org
      Hon Treas: Celia Cviić,   Hon Sec: Judy Hildesley
▲   Registered Charity
○   *E; a music education charity, using the voice as the main
      instrument; to improve British music education through
      courses for anyone wanting to develop their own, or others,
      musical skills, using Kodály's principles
Gp   Courses: Certificate in early years music education; Certificate
      in primary education; Intermediate & advanced diplomas in
      Kodály's musicianship; Elementary & foundation courses,
      early years & SEN
●   Conf - ET - Exam - Res - Exhib - Inf - Lib
<   Intl Kodály Soc (IKS)
M   210 i
¶   NL - 3; ftm.
      How Can I Keep from Singing (songbook for ages 8-11);
      £20 including double CD.

British Korfball Association   (BKA)   1946
NR   37 Fontenoy Rd, LONDON, SW12 9LX.   (gensec/p)
      07814 004135
      email secretary@korfball.co.uk   http://www.korfball.co.uk
      Gen Sec: Jackie Hoare
▲   Un-incorporated Society
○   *S; governing body of the sport of Korfball in the UK
Gp   Area associations; Competitions; Exams
●   Mtgs - ET - Exam - Comp
<   Intl Korfball Fedn (IKF)
M   51 clubs
¶   Korfball - 3; ftm, £1.50 each nm.

British Kune Kune Pig Society   (BKKPS)   1993
NR   Hall Cottage, 11 Radwinter Rd, Seawards End,
     SAFFRON WALDEN, Essex, CB10 2XT.   (registrar/p)
     email kune.kune@tesco.net
     http://www.britishkunekunepigsociety.co.uk
     Registrar: David Lacon
▲   Un-incorporated Society
○   *B
●   Mtgs - ET - Expt - Inf - PL
<   New Zealand Kune Kune Pig Soc
M   c 300 i

British Lace Federation   (BLF)   1914
NR   c/o Lemans, 29 Arboretum St, NOTTINGHAM, NG1 4JA.
     (asa)
     0115-978 7291
     email davidm@lemans.co.uk
     Gen Sec: Jane Whitfield,   Contact: David Marshall
○   *T; all aspects of lace manufacture
M   f

British Ladder Manufacturers Association   (BLMA)   1947
■   PO Box 183, LEEDS, W Yorks, LS11 1AG.   (hsb)
     0845 260 1048   fax 0845 260 1049
     Sec: Cameron Clow
○   *T; for manufacturers of access equipment in the UK
●   Conf - Mtgs - LG
M   37 f
¶   Leaning Ladder & Stepladder User Guide.

British Laminate Fabricators Association
■   PO Box 8841, NOTTINGHAM, NG11 1AJ.
     0115-921 3889   fax 0115-921 3889
     http://www.blfa.co.uk
     Contact: Christopher D Thomas
○   *T

British Land Speedsail Association   (BLSA)   1989
■   103 Mead Vale, Worle, WESTON-super-MARE, Somerset,
     BS22 8XE.   (chmn/p)
     01934 511780
     email chris@theblsa.com   http://www.theblsa.com
     Chmn: Chris Moore
○   *S; to promote blokarting & land speedsailing in the UK; to
     organise racing in the UK
Gp   Land speedsailing; Blokarting
●   Comp - Provision of 3rd party liability insurance
<   Land Yachting Assn
M   180 i
     (Sub: £40)

British Landsailing
     alternative name of the **British Federation of Sand & Land Yacht
     Clubs**

British Lawn Mower Racing Association   (BLMRA)   1973
■   Hunt Cottage, Wisborough Green, BILLINGSHURST, W Sussex,
     RH14 0HN.   (hsp)
     email info@blmra.co.uk   http://www.blmra.co.uk
     Pres & Hon Sec: Jim Gavin
▲   Company Limited by Guarantee
○   *G; organisation of lawn mower races
●   Mtgs - ET - Comp - Inf - VE - Film shows
<   R Automobile Club
M   c 300 i, UK & o'seas
¶   Cuttings (NL) - 12; ftm.

British Leafy Salad Association   (BLSA)
■   133 Eastgate, LOUTH, Lincs, LN11 9QG.   (asa)
     01507 602427   fax 01507 607165
     http://www.britishleafysalads.co.uk
     Sec: Mrs Jayne Dyas
○   *T; to provide technical, commercial & marketing information
     for growers of all lettuces
●   Conf - Mtgs - Res - Exhib - Stat - Inf - LG
M   120 f

British Learning Association
     since 2007 **British Institute for Learning & Development**

British Lebanese Association
NR   1 Hyde Park Gate, LONDON, SW7 5EW.
     020 7370 2572
     Dir: Lenia Tannous
○   *X

British Legal Association   (BLA)   1964
NR   2 Princess Way, SWANSEA, Glam, SA1 3LW.   (hq)
     01792 648096
     Contact: Liz McGlynn
○   *P; to look after the interests of solicitors in general
M   1,700 i

British Legion
     see **Royal British Legion**

British Lichen Society   (BLS)   1958
NR   c/o Botany Dept, Natural History Museum, Cromwell Rd,
     LONDON, SW7 5BD.   (hsb)
     020 7942 5250
▲   Registered Charity
○   *L; to promote the study of lichens
●   Mtgs - ET - Res - Exhib - Inf - Lib
M   c 600 i, 160 institutions
¶   The Lichenologist - 6.   Bulletin - 2.

British Limb Reconstruction Society
     a specialist society of the **British Orthopaedic Association**

**British Limbless Ex-Service Men's Association   (BLESMA)
1932**
■   Frankland Moore House 185-187 High Rd, Chadwell Heath,
     ROMFORD, Essex, RM6 6NA.   (hq)
     020 8590 1124   fax 020 8599 2932
     email headquarters@blesma.org
     http://www.blesma.org
     Gen Sec: J W Church
▲   Company Limited by Guarantee; Registered Charity
Br   36
○   *W; to promote the welfare of all those, of either sex, who have
     lost limb(s) or eye(s), or the use of limb(s) or sight, after or as
     a result of service in any branch of HM Forces (incl their
     needy dependents)
Gp   Amputee counselling; Residential homes
●   Conf - Mtgs - Res - Inf - VE - LG - Counselling service for
     amputees - Welfare visiting service - Residential homes -
     Grants
<   Wld Veterans Fedn; Intl Soc of Prosthetics & Orthotics; Confedn
     of British Service & Ex-service Orgs; NCVO; RADAR
M   4,720 i, UK / 95 i, o'seas
¶   BLESMAG - 3; ftm, £1 each nm.
     Out on a Limb [history of association] (1982); £2 m, £5 nm.
     Making the Best of Amputation (2003); ftm, 20p + postage nm.
     Driving after Amputation (1991); postage.
     Amputees Guide; £1.   AR; free.

British Lime Association (BLA) 1989
NR   Gillingham House, 38-44 Gillingham St, LONDON,
     SW1V 1HU.   (hq)
     020 7963 8000
     email lime@gpa.org   http://www.britishlime.org
○   *T; to represent the interests of the UK lime industry
M   6 f

British Limousin Cattle Society Ltd (BLCS) 1970
■   NAC, Stoneleigh Park, KENILWORTH, Warks, CV8 2LG.   (hq)
     024 7669 6500
     Chief Exec: Iain Kerr
▲   Registered Charity
○   *B; pedigree beef cattle society
●   Mtgs - Expt - VE
<   Intl Limousin Coun; Eurolim; Nat Beef Assn
M   2,500 i, 10 f, 10 org
¶   News Magazine - 3.   Studbook - 1.   AR.
     Herdbook - 1.   Sire & Dam Summary - 1.

British Lingual Orthodontic Society (BLOS)
NR   BLOS Office, British Orthodontic Society, 12 Bridewell Place,
     LONDON, EC4V 6AP.
     020 7353 8680   fax 020 7353 8682
     http://www.blos.co.uk
M
     (Sub: £150 i, £75 (postgraduate))

British Livestock Genetics Consortium Ltd
NR   Narracombe, Ilsington, NEWTON ABBOT, Devon, TQ13 9RD.
     01364 661506
     Contact: Rob Wills
○   *T; the development & maintenance of profitable long-term
     business generated by exports of British livestock & genetics;
     to create a positive, favourable image in international
     markets & promote Britain as a supplier of high quality
     animals & germplasm

British Llama Society 2005
NR   Lower Braundsworthy, Shebbear, BEAWORTHY, Devon,
     EX21 5TB.
     01409 231704
     email secretary@britishllamasociety.org
     http://www.britishllamasociety.org
     Sec: Brenda Birmingham
○   *B

British Locksmiths & Keycutters Association (BLKA)
NR   3 Murrow Lane, Parson Drove, WISBECH, Cambs, PE13 4JH.
     (hq)
     0845 644 5397   fax 01945 701552
     email enquire@blka.co.uk   http://www.blka.co.uk
     Mem Sec: Denise Mace (Adenash@aol.com)
○   *P

British Long-Bow Society
     The society has asked not to be listed in this directory:
     'This society is NOT concerned with modern target archery.
     Please contact the **Grand National Archery Society**'

British Long Distance Swimming Association (BLDSA) 1956
■   521 London Rd, Stretton, WARRINGTON, Cheshire,
     WA4 5PH.   (hsp)
     01925 730652
     email secretary_bldsa@tiscali.co.uk
     http://www.bldsa.org.uk
     Hon Sec: Maurice Ferguson
▲   Un-incorporated Society
○   *S; to further & promote the sport of open water, long distance
     (below 25km) & marathon (25km & above) swimming
●   Mtgs - ET - Exam - Comp - Stat
M   c 450 i, c 20 org
¶   Hbk - 1.

British Longevity Society (BLS) 1993
NR   PO Box 4202, DUNSTABLE, Beds, LU5 5WU.
     07092 350063
     http://www.thebls.org
○   to further public education on issues connected with the means
     of counteracting the processes, causes and effects of ageing

British Lop Pig Society (BLPS) 1920
■   Farm Five, The Moss, WHIXALL, Shropshire, SY13 2PF.   (hsp)
     01948 880243; 07759 487469
     email secretary@britishloppig.org.uk
     http://www.britishloppig.org.uk
     Hon Sec: Frank Miller
▲   Un-incorporated Society
○   *B
●   Mtgs
<   Rare Breeds Survival Trust
M   c 40 i
¶   Herd Book - 1; £3.

British Lubricants Federation Ltd
     since 1 January 2005 **United Kingdom Lubricants Association
     Ltd**

British Luggage & Leathergoods Association
     since 2005-06 **British Travelgoods & Accessories Association**

British Lymphology Society (BLS) 1985
■   9-11 Oldbury Rd, CHELTENHAM, Glos, GL51 0HH.   (hq)
     01242 699980
     email info@thebls.com   http://www.thebls.co.uk
     Chmn: Rebecca Billingham
▲   Registered Charity
○   *P; for health care professionals & other interested parties
     involved in the management of lymphoedema; to raise
     awareness of oedema amongst all health professionals
●   Conf - Mtgs - ET - Res - Exhib - Sg - Inf - LG - Writing protocols
<   Intl Soc of Lymphologists (ISL); Eur Soc of Lymphologists (ESL);
     Intl Lymphoedema Framework (ILF); Lymphoedema Support
     Network
M   350 i, 8 f, UK / 10 i, o'seas
     (Sub £48 i, £1,280 f, UK / £15 o'seas
¶   BLS News & Views - 6; ftm, £5 nm.   AR - 1; free.

**British Machine Vision Association & Society for Pattern
Recognition (BMVA) 1990**
■   c/o Dr Andrew Fitzgibbon, Microsoft Research Ltd,
     7 JJ Thomson Avenue, CAMBRIDGE, CB3 0FB.   (hsb)
     01223 479899
     http://www.bmva.ac.uk
     Hon Sec: Dr Andrew Fitzgibbon
▲   Company Limited by Guarantee; Registered Charity
Br   3
○   *L; to promote knowledge & application of machine vision &
     pattern recognition
Gp   Computer vision, image analysis; Machine vision education &
     training
●   Conf - Mtgs - ET - Res - Exhib - SG - Stat - Inf - PL - VE - LG
<   Intl Assn for Pattern Recognition (IAPR); Mammographic Image
     Analysis Soc
M   c 400 i, UK / c 50 i, o'seas
¶   BMVA News - 4; free.
     Proceedings of the British Machine Vision Conference - 1; free
     to delegates, £25 (sales).

British Magical Society   (BMS)   1905
NR   20 Nortune Close, Kings Norton, BIRMINGHAM, B38 8AJ.
        (hsp)
        0121-451 3944
        Hon Sec: Paul Cadley
▲   Un-incorporated Society
○   *G, *P; the furtherance of the art of magic
Gp   Junior section (ages 10-16)
●   Mtgs - Comp - Lib
M   107 i, UK / 4 i, o'seas
¶   BMS News - 6; ftm only.

British Malaysian Society   (BMS)   1983
NR   Asia House, 63 New Cavendish St, LONDON, W1G 7LP.
        (asa)
        020 7307 5454
▲   Un-incorporated Society
○   *X; bi-lateral friendship society
M   i & f

British Malignant Hyperthermia Association   (BMHA)   1983
§   MH Investigation Unit, St James Hospital, Beckett St, LEEDS,
        W Yorks, LS9 7TF.
        01773 717901
        email helpline@bmha.co.uk   http://www.bmha.co.uk
        Sec: Mrs Alison Winks
        To provide medical and medico-social support for individuals
        affected by malignant hyperthermia (progressive raising of
        body temperature during general anaesthesia).

British Manual Lymph Drainage Association   (BMLDA)   2000
■   PO Box 309, SUTTON, Surrey, SM1 9DE.   (hsp)
        020 8133 5686
        http://www.bmlda.org.uk
        Contact: Nina Pearson
▲   Company Limited by Guarantee
Br   Regional
○   *M, *P; to advance education & knowledge & develop the
        standards of practice of therapists in the treatment of manual
        lymph drainage; membership is open to those who have
        qualified
●   Conf - Mtgs - ET - Exam - Res - Exhib - Inf
<   Inst of Complementary Medicine; Brit Lymphology Soc
M   c 50 i & f
¶   Networks (NL) - 6; ftm only.

**British Marine Aggregate Producers' Association   (BMAPA)
1993**
■   Gillingham House, 38-44 Gillingham St, LONDON,
        SW1V 1HU.   (hq)
        020 7963 8000
○   *T; interests of the producers of marine aggregates (those
        dredged from the sea bed)
<   Quarry Products Association
M   f

British Marine Electronics Association   (BMEA)
NR   7 Eton Close, WEEDON, Northants, NN7 4PJ.   (hsp)
        01327 341729   fax 01327 341004
        http://www.bmea.org
        Sec: Tony Johns
○   *T; manufacturers & waterside dealers who provide advice,
        sales, installation & service of marine electronic & electrical
        equipment
M   86 f

British Marine Equipment Association   (BMEA)   1966
NR   28-29 Threadneedle St, LONDON, EC2R 8AY.   (hq)
        020 7628 2555   fax 020 7638 4376
        email bmea@maritimeindustries.org
        http://www.maritimeindustries.org
        Dir: John Southerden
▲   Company Limited by Guarantee
○   *T; 'representing the interests of suppliers of marine equipment
        & associated services for every type of merchant vessel, from
        low tonnage work-boats through every class of cargo-
        carrying ship, including container carriers & tankers,
        specialist ships, passenger-car ferries, Ro-Ro's, up to the
        largest cruise liners'
●   Conf - Mtgs - Exhib - Expt - Inf - LG - Trade missions
<   Soc of Maritime Inds
>   Soc of Maritime Inds
M   200 f
¶   Directory 2005-2006 - 1.

British Marine Federation   (BMF)   1913
NR   Marine House, Thorpe Lea Rd, EGHAM, Surrey, TW20 8BF.
        (hq)
        01784 473377   fax 01784 439678
        email info@britishmarine.co.uk
        http://www.britishmarine.co.uk
        Chief Exec: Rob Stevens
▲   Company Limited by Guarantee
Br   12 regions
○   *T; for the leisure marine industry
Gp   Association of Canoe Trades (ACT); Association of Pleasure
        Craft Operators (APCO); BMF Sailmakers Association; Boat
        Retailers & Brokers Association (BRBA); British Commercial
        Boatbuilders Association (BCBA); British Hire Cruiser
        Federation (BHCF); British Marine Electronics
        Association (BMEA); British Sailing (BS); British Small
        Boatbuilders Association (BSBA); Broads Hire Boat
        Federation (BHBF); Canal Boatbuilders Association (CBA);
        Insurance Financial & Legal Services Association (ILFSA);
        Leisure Boat Builders Association (LBBA); Marine Engine &
        Equipment Manufacturers Association (MEEMA); Marine
        Leisure Association (MLA); Marine Trades Association (MTA);
        Superyacht UK; Thames Hire Cruiser Association (THCA);
        Yacht Harbour Association (TYHA)
●   Conf - Mtgs - ET - Res - Exhib - Stat - Expt - Inf - Lib - PL - Empl
        - LG
<   Boating Alliance
M   c 1,500 f
¶   BM News - 12; ftm only.
        Membership Hbk & Classified Buyers' Guide - 1; ftm.
        Industry Statistics - 1; ftm.
        Publications list available.

British Marine Federation Scotland   1920
■   Westgate, Toward, DUNOON, Argyllshire, PA23 7UA.   (hsp)
        01369 870251
        Sec: Michael B Balmforth
▲   Un-incorporated Society
○   *T; to service & further the interests of the marine leisure &
        small commercial boating industry in Scotland
●   Conf - Mtgs - ET - Expt - Inf - VE
<   Intl Congress of Marine Inds Assns (ICOMIA); Brit Marine
        Fedn (BMF)
M   c 60 f
        Note: is a branch of the British Marine Federation

© CBD Research Ltd · Beckenham · BR3 5JS · Tel 020 8650 7745 · Fax 020 8650 0768 · E-mail cbd@cbdresearch.com · www.cbdresearch.com

British Marine Finfish Association   (BMFA)   1987
NR   15 Shielhill Park, STANLEY, Perthshire, PH1 4QT.   (hsp)
 01738 828170
 http://www.bmfa.uk.com
 Sec/Admin: Richard Slaski
▲ Company Limited by Guarantee
○ *T; to investigate marketing & technical issues concerning the
 farming of Atlantic halibut in Britain; to provide
 representation for farmers of other marine fish eg cod, turbot
 & lemon sole
Gp Hatchery operators; Ongrowers; Feed companies
● Conf - Res - LG
M 22 f
¶ Jnl - 4; ftm only.

British Marine Life Study Society   (BMLSS)   1990
NR   Glaucus House, 14 Corbyn Crescent, SHOREHAM-BY-SEA,
 W Sussex, BN43 6PQ.   (hsb)
 01273 465433
 email glaucus@hotmail.com   http://www.glaucus.org.uk
 Chief Exec: Andy Horton
▲ Un-incorporated Society
○ *G, *L; the study of the wildlife & ecology of the marine
 environment of the British Isles; for the layman, amateur &
 professional naturalist
Gp Aquariology (aquaria); Scuba diving; Rockpooling (seashore
 study); Marine biology; Biological recording
● Exhib - SG - Inf - Lib - PL
< Inst of Biology; Nat Fedn of Biological Recording
M 349 i
¶ Glaucus (Jnl) - irreg; m only.
 Shorewatch (NL) - irreg.
 Torpedo (electronic NL) - 12.

British Maritime Law Association   (BMLA)   1908
■ c/o ReedSmith Richards Buler, Beaufort House, 15 St Botolph St,
 LONDON, EC3A 7EE.   (asa)
 020 7247 6555   fax 020 7247 5091
 email adt@richardsbutler.com   http://www.bmla.org.uk
 Sec & Treas: Andrew Taylor
▲ Un-incorporated Society
○ *P; to coordinate the contributions of members, who operate
 within the shipping & support industries, to national &
 international shipping related legislation
● Conf - Mtgs - ET - Res - SG - Inf - Lib - LG
< Comité Maritime Intl (CMI)
M 260 i, 52 f
¶ AR & Accounts; ftm.

British Market Research Association
 in 2006 merged with the **Market Research Society**

British Masonry Society
 since 1 January 2008 **International Masonry Society**

British Matchbox, Label & Booklet Society   (BML&BS)   1945
■ 122 High St, MELBOURN, Cambs, SG8 6AL.   (hsp)
 01763 260399
 email secretary@phillumeny.com
 http://www.phillumeny.com
 Hon Sec: Arthur Alderton
▲ Un-incorporated Society
○ *G; for collectors of match-boxes, labels, bookmatch covers,
 containers, strikers & associated ephemera
● Mtgs - Res - Exhib - Inf - Lib
M 480 i, UK / 110 i, o'seas
¶ Match Label News (Jnl) - 6; ftm, £3.50 nm.

British Materials Handling Federation   (BMHF)   1964
NR   National Metalforming Centre, 47 Birmingham Rd,
 WEST BROMWICH, W Midlands, B70 6PY.   (hq)
 0121-601 6350   fax 0121-601 6387
 email enquiry@bmhf.org.uk   http://www.bmhf.org.uk
▲ Company Limited by Guarantee
○ *N; 'constitutes the British national c'ee of FEM & is the UK's
 voice in Europe on materials handling matters'
● Mtgs - Exhib - Stat - Inf - LG - Intl Handling & Storage
 Exhibition (3 yrly)
< Fédération Européenne de la Manutention
M 5 associations:
 Association of Loading & Elevating Equipment Manufacturers
 Automated Material Handling Systems Association
 British Industrial Truck Association
 International Powered Access Federation
 Storage Equipment Manufacturers' Association
¶ Ybk & Dir - 1; ftm.

British Maternal & Fetal Medicine Society   (BMFMS)
NR   c/o RCOG, 27 Sussex Place, LONDON, NW1 4RG.
 email bmfms@rcog.org.uk   http://www.bmfms.org.uk
 Coordinator: Sabi Proctor

British Measurement & Testing Association   (BMTA)   1990
▣ East Malling Enterprise Centre, New Rd, EAST MALLING, Kent,
 ME19 6BJ.   (hq)
 0845 644 4603   fax 01732 897453
 email enquiries@bmta.co.uk   http://www.bmta.co.uk
 Sec: Peter Russell
▲ Company Limited by Guarantee
○ *T; interests of the measurement & testing laboratory
 community to government, UK Accreditation Service, BSI &
 other official bodies & UK laboratories in Europe through
 EUROLAB
Gp Accredited laboratories
● Conf - Mtgs - Exhib - Inf - LG
< EUROLAS
M 5 i, 75 f
¶ Electronic NL - 4; free.

British Meat Processors Association   (BMPA)   2003
NR   12 Cock Lane, LONDON, EC1A 9BU.   (hq)
 020 7329 0776   fax 020 7329 0653
 email info@bmpa.uk.com   http://www.bmpa.uk.com
 Dir: Stuart Roberts
▲ Company Limited by Guarantee
○ *T; slaughtering, processing, manufacturing, wholesale
 distribution & packaging sectors of the meat industry
● Conf - Mtgs - Inf - LG
M f

British Medical Acupuncture Society   (BMAS)   1980
■ BMAS House, 3 Winnington Court, NORTHWICH, Cheshire,
 CW8 1AQ.   (hq)
 01606 786782   fax 01606 786783
 email admin@medical-acupuncture.org.uk
 http://www.medical-acupuncture.org.uk
 c/o Royal London Homoeopathic Hospital, 60
 Great Ormond St, LONDON, WC1N 3HR.
 020 7713 9437.
 Gen Mgr: Jane Llewellyn
▲ Registered Charity
Br London: 020 7713 9437
○ *L; training for doctors, dentists, vets & registered health
 professionals in medical acupuncture
● Conf - Mtgs - ET - Exam - Res - SG - LG
< Intl Coun of Med Acupuncture & Related Techniques (ICMART)
> Acupuncture Assn of Chart Physiotherapists (AACP); Brit
 Academy of Wstn Acupuncture (BAWA)
M 2,100 i, UK / 120 i, o'seas
¶ Acupuncture in Medicine - 4; ftm, £11 each nm.

British Medical Association   (BMA)   1832
- ■ BMA House, Tavistock Square, LONDON, WC1H 9JP.   (hq)
  020 7387 4499
  http://www.bma.org.uk
  Chief Exec/Sec: Tony Bourne
- ▲ Company Limited by Guarantee
- Br Offices in the 3 national capitals, a regional network
- ○ *E, *P, *U; to promote the medical & allied sciences, to maintain the honour & interests of the medical profession; to promote the achievement of high quality health care
- Gp C'ees on: Equal opportunities, Medical ethics, Medical education, Science, International affairs
  Practice c'ees: Central consultants & specialists, General practitioners, Junior doctors, Medical academic staff, Medical students, Public health medicine & community health, Staff & associate specialists
- ● Conf - Mtgs - ET - Res - Stat - Inf - Lib - Empl - LG
- M 115,512 i, 19.053 students, UK / 3.060 i, o'seas
- ¶ British Medical Jnl.   Specialist Jnls.   AR.
  Branch of Practice Committees ARs.
  Various other reports on health & health policy.

British Medical Laser Association   (BMLA)   1983
- ■ Photobiology Unit, University of Dundee, Ninewells Hospital & Medical School, DUNDEE, DD1 9SY.   (hq)
  01382 636722   fax 01382 646047
  email h.moseley@dundee.ac.uk
  http://www.bmla.co.uk
  Pres: Dr Harry Moseley
- ▲ Registered Charity
- ○ *L, *M, *P; medical uses of lasers & associated technology
- ● Conf - Mtgs - ET - LG
- < Eur Laser Assn
- M 120 i, UK / 20 i, o'seas
- ¶ Lasers in Medical Science (Jnl) - 4; ftm.

British Medical Ultrasound Society   (BMUS)   1984
- ■ 36 Portland Place, LONDON, W1B 1LS.   (hq)
  020 7636 3714   fax 020 7323 2175
  email secretariat@bmus.org   http://www.bmus.org
  Gen Sec: Mrs Ann Tailor
- ▲ Company Limited by Guarantee
- ○ *L; the advancement of the science & technology of ultrasonics as applied in medicine; the maintenance of the highest standards
- ● Conf - Mtgs - ET - Exhib - Comp - SG - Lib
- < Eur Fedn Socs for Ultrasound in Medicine & Biology
- M c 2,500 i
- ¶ Jnl of Ultrasound - 4.

British Menopause Society   (BMS)   1989
- NR 4-6 Eton Place, MARLOW, Bucks, SL7 2QA.   (hq)
  01628 890199
- ▲ Company Limited by Guarantee; Registered Charity
- ○ *L; the advancement of knowledge, interest & study of all matters connected with the menopause; to promote high standards of training for those involved in advising women
- M i

British Menswear Guild Ltd   (BMG)   1959
- NR 5 Portland Place, LONDON, W1B 1PW.   (hq)
  020 7580 8783   fax 020 7436 8833
  http://www.british-menswear-guild.co.uk
  Dir: David Challinor
- ○ *T; for manufacturers of high quality men's clothing & accessories, luggage, leathergoods & umbrellas; to promote & increase export worldwide
- M 16 f

British Metallurgical Plant Constructors' Association (BMPCA)   1963
- ■ c/o EEF, Broadway House, Tothill St, London, SW1H 9NQ.   (hq)
  01709 362288   fax 01709 724999
  email enquiries@bmpca.org.uk
  Dir: R W Welburn
- ○ *T; the design & manufacture of systems, plant & equipment for the metals industry worldwide
- ● Mtgs - Exhib - Stat - Expt - Inf - VE - LG
- < EEF; UK Steel
- M 30 f
- ¶ List of Member Companies & Product Range; free.

British Metals Recycling Association   (BMRA)   1919
- ■ 16 High St, Brampton, HUNTINGDON, Cambs, PE28 4TU.   (hq)
  01480 455249   fax 01480 453680
  email admin@recyclemetals.org
  http://www.recyclemetals.org
  Dir Gen: Lindsay Millington
- ▲ Company Limited by Guarantee
- ○ *T; to represent metal recyclers
- Gp Exporters; Shredders division
- ● Conf - Mtgs - ET - Exhib - SG - Stat - Expt - Inf - LG
- < Bureau Intl de la Récupération (BIR); Eur Ferrous Recovery & Recycling Fedn (EFR); Freight Transport Assn (FTA); CBI
- M 350 f, UK / 30 f, o'seas
- ¶ Recycling Health & Safety Manual - 4; ftm only.

British Mexican Society   (BMS)   1942
- NR Cameo House, 11 Bear St, Leicester Square, LONDON, WC2H 7AS.
  0870 922 0679
- ▲ Registered Charity
- ○ *X
- M i & f

British Microcirculation Society   (BMS)   1963
- NR Microvascular Research Laboratory, Dept of Physiology, Preclinical Veterinary School, University of Bristol, Southwell St, BRISTOL, BS2 8EJ.   (hsb)
  0117-928 9818
- ▲ Registered Charity
- ○ *L; study of microvascular structure, function & disease & related vascular phenomena
- M i

British Microlight Aircraft Association   (BMAA)   1979
- NR The Bullring, Deddington, BANBURY, Oxon, OX15 0TT.   (hq)
  01869 338888   fax 01869 337116
  email general@bmaa.org   http://www.bmaa.org
- ▲ Company Limited by Guarantee
- Br 100; France, Gambia, Portugal, Spain
- ○ *S; to foster & safeguard the interests of microlight flying in the UK
- Gp Flying schools (training of students up to PPL(A) microlights standard)
- ● ET - Exam - Exhib - Comp - Inf
- < Fédn Aéronautique Intle; R Aero Club of GB
- M 4,300 i, 100 clubs & schools
- ¶ Microlight Flying - 6; ftm only.

British Milksheep Society   1983
- NR St Kenelms, Broad Lane, Tanworth-in-Arden, SOLIHULL, W Midlands, B94 5HX.   (sp)
  01564 742398
  Sec: W J Hopkins
- ▲ Un-incorporated Society
- Br France, Hungary
- ○ *B; registration, promotion & export of British milksheep
- ● Mtgs - Exhib - Expt
- < Nat Sheep Assn
- M 26 i, 4 f, UK / 1 i, 2 f, o'seas

© CBD Research Ltd · Beckenham · BR3 5JS · Tel 020 8650 7745 · Fax 020 8650 0768 · E-mail cbd@cbdresearch.com · www.cbdresearch.com

British Miniature Horse Society
  'We do not want our details to be included'

British Model Flying Association   (BMFA)   1922
■ Chacksfield House, 31 St Andrews Rd, LEICESTER, LE2 8RE.
  (hq)
  0116-244 0028   fax 0116-244 0645
  email admin@bmfa.org   http://www.bmfa.org
  Chief Exec: David Phipps
▲ Company Limited by Guarantee (as Society of Model
  Aeronautical Engineers Ltd)
○ *G, *S; the promotion, protection, organisation &
  encouragement of model aircraft building, flying &
  development in all its aspects in the UK
Gp Control line; Free flight; Gas turbines; Indoor; Model rocketry;
  Radio control power (fixed wing & rotary wing); Radio control
  silent flight (thermal, slope soaring, electric)
● Conf - Mtgs - ET - Exam - Res - Exhib - Comp - Stat - Inf - VE -
  LG
< Fédn Aéronautique Intle (FAI); R Aero Club (RAC); Cent Coun of
  Physical Recreation (CCPR)
M 37,000 i, 740 clubs
¶ BMFA News - 6; ftm, £1.50 nm.   AR - 1; ftm only.
  Members Hbk - 3 yrly; ftm, £3 nm.

British Model Soldier Society   (BMSS)   1935
■ 12 Savay Lane, Denham Green, DENHAM, Bucks, UB9 5NH.
  (hsp)
  01895 832757   fax 01895 832757
  Hon Sec: Julie Newman
▲ Un-incorporated Society
Br 22
○ *E, *G, *Q; to promote research & scholarship in all aspects of
  military history, weaponry, uniforms etc, through the media of
  military models & the portraying of historical events
Gp American civil war; Artillery; Military bands; Britain's figures;
  Conversions; Indian army; Military aircraft; Military vehicles;
  Yeomanry
● Mtgs - ET - Res - Exhib - Comp - SG - Inf
M 425 i, UK / 50 i, o'seas
¶ Bulletin - 4;   Bulletin Extra - 4;   Hbk - irreg; all ftm only.

British Morgan Horse Society   (BMHS)   1975
■ 9 First Avenue, Astley, Tyldesley, MANCHESTER, M29 7JH.
  (hq)
  01942 886141
  email admin@morganhorse.org.uk
  http://www.morganhorse.org.uk
  Exec Officer: Dawn Sharif
○ *B; to promote the Morgan horse in Britain
● Conf - Exhib - Comp - Inf
< Amer Morgan Horse Assn (AMHA)
M 85 i (adult), 33 i (youth)
¶ NL - 6.
  European Morgan Horse Magazine - 1.

British Moroccan Society   (BMS)   1976
NR Dartmouth House, Dartmouth Place, LONDON, W4 2RH.
  (v-chmn/b)
  0783 126 1830
  email admin@british-moroccansoc.org
  http://www.british-moroccansoc.org
  Hon Sec: Benedicte Clarkson
▲ Un-incorporated Society
○ *X; to foster links between the Kingdoms of Great Britain &
  Morocco through commercial, cultural & social contacts; to
  promote events to raise money for Moroccan charitable
  institutions
● Mtgs - VE - Social events - Dinner (November) to raise money
  for the most needy in Morocco
M 400 i, UK / 2 i, o'seas
¶ NL - 8; free.

British Motor Cycle Racing Club Ltd   (BMCRC)   1909
■ Unit 85 Seedbed Centre, Davidson Way, ROMFORD, Essex,
  RM7 0AZ.   (hq)
  01708 720305   fax 01708 720235
  email mikedommett@hotmail.com
  http://www.bemsee.net
  Sec: Eddie Bellas   Chief Exec: Mike Dommett
▲ Company Limited by Guarantee
○ *S; organising motor cycle racing events
● Comp
< Auto-Cycle U
> Brit Motorcycle Club Marshals Assn
M 1,000 i
    (Sub: £30)

British Motorcyclists' Federation   (BMF)   1960
NR Jack Wiley House, 25 Warren Park Way, Enderby, LEICESTER,
  LE19 4SA.   (hq)
  0116-284 5380
  Press & PR Mgr: Jeff Stone
  Chief Exec Officer: Simon Wilkinson-Blake
▲ Company Limited by Guarantee
○ *K, *S; to pursue, protect & promote the interests of
  motorcyclists
● Mtgs - ET - Res - Exhib - SG - Stat - Inf - VE - LG - Attendance
  at exhibitions & rallies - Legal & insurance advice - European
  lobbying - Preservation of green lanes
< Eur Motorcyclists U (EMU); CCPR; RAC; Motorcycle Inds Assn
  (MCIA); Nat Motorcycle Coun (NMC); Fedn Eur Motorcyclists
  (FEM)
M 25,000 i, 115,000 i (affiliates), 100 f, 330 clubs, UK / 40 i,
  o'seas
¶ Motorcycle Rider - 6.

British Motorsport Marshals Club   (BMMC)   1957
NR 25 Bowlish, SHEPTON MALLET, Somerset, BA4 5JA.   (hsp)
  01749 345633 mobile: 07793 485166
  email secretary@bmmc.org.uk
  http://www.marshals.co.uk
  Sec: Andy Baker
▲ Company Limited by Guarantee
Br 7
○ *S; to bring together, train & organise marshals for all types of
  motor sport events
● Mtgs - ET - Exhib - Comp
< RAC Motor Sport Assn (RACMSA)
> Brit Rally Marshals Club
M 1,500 i
¶ Trackside - 4; ftm, £2 nm.
× 2002 British Motor Racing Marshals Club

British Mountaineering Council   (BMC)   1944
NR The Old Church, 177-179 Burton Rd, West Didsbury,
  MANCHESTER, M20 2BB.   (hq)
  0870 010 4878
  email office@thebmc.co.uk
▲ Company Limited by Guarantee
○ *S; to help, protect & promote the interests of British climbers,
  hill walkers & mountaineers
M i & clubs

British Mule Society   (BMS)   1978
■ 2 Boscombe Rd, SWINDON, Wilts, SN25 3EY.   (hsp)
  01793 615478
  email anndyer57@aol.com
  http://www.britishmulesociety.org.uk
  Hon Sec: Mrs Ann Hunter
▲ Company Limited by Guarantee; Registered Charity
○ *B; to encourage the breeding of good quality mules
● Conf - Mtgs - ET - Res - Exhib - Comp - Stat - Inf - Lib - VE
< Brit Driving Soc; Amer Donkey & Mule Soc
M 150 i, 2 org, UK / 19 i, 5 org, o'seas
¶ The Mule - 4; ftm only.

British Museum Friends (BMS) 1968
■   c/o The British Museum, Great Russell St, LONDON,
     WC1B 3BR.   (hq)
     020 7323 8605; 8195   fax 020 7323 8985
     email friends@britishmuseum.org
     Chmn: Prof Sir Barry Cunliffe
     Head of Friends: Carolyn Young
▲   Registered Charity
○   *G; to support the British Museum
●   Exhib - Inf
M   17,500 i
¶   British Museum Magazine - 3.

British Music Hall Society (BMHS) 1963
■   Meander, 361 Watford Rd, Chiswell Green, ST ALBANS,
     AL2 3DB.   (hsb)
     01727 768878
     http://www.music-hall-society.com
     Hon Sec: Mrs Daphne Masterton
○   *D; to preserve the history of music hall & variety; to recall the
     artistes who were part of the scene; to support the
     entertainers of the present
●   Conf - Mtgs - Res - Exhib - SG - Inf - VE - 5 shows a year at the
     Concert Artistes Association, 20 Bedford St, London,
     WC2E 9HP
M   900 i, UK / 50 i, o'seas
¶   The Call Boy - 4; ftm, £3 each nm.

British Music Rights 1996
NR British Music House, 26 Berners St, LONDON, W1T 3LR.   (hq)
     020 7306 4446   fax 020 7306 4449
     email britishmusic@bmr.org   http://www.bmr.org
     Dir Gen: Frances Lowe
○   *N, *P, *T; an umbrella organisation representing the interests of
     composers, songwriters & music publishers

British Music Society (BMS) 1978
■   7 Tudor Gardens, UPMINSTER, Essex, RM14 3DE.   (treas/p)
     01708 224795
     http://www.britishmusicsociety.co.uk
     Hon Treas: Stephen Trowell
▲   Registered Charity
○   *D; to promote the music of neglected British composers who
     do not have a society, or trust, to champion their cause
●   Mtgs - Res - Exhib - Comp - Inf - Lib - VE - Concert promotion -
     Recordings - Publications
M   525 i, 5 f, 15 org, UK / 77 i, 7 org, o'seas
¶   Jnl - 1; ftm, £5 nm.   NL - 4; ftm only.

British Music Writers' Council
     a group of the **Musicians' Union**

British Mycological Society (BMS) 1896
■   The Wolfson Wing, Jodrell Laboratory, Royal Botanic Gardens,
     KEW, Surrey, TW9 3AB.
     020 8332 5720   fax 020 8332 5768
     email info@britmycolsoc.org.uk
     http://www.britmycolsoc.org.uk
▲   Registered Charity
○   *L, *Q; to promote all aspects of mycology (fungi, ecology,
     molecular biology, biodiversity, conservation, pathogens,
     biocontrol, systematics, physiology, secondary metabolites)
M   c 2,000 i

British Myriapod & Isopod Group (BMIG)
■   2 Egypt Wood Cottages, Egypt Lane, FARNHAM COMMON,
     Bucks, SL2 3LE.   (hsp)
     01753 646699   fax 01753 646699
     email helen.read@dsl.pipex.com
     Sec: Helen Read
▲   Un-incorporated Society
○   *L; the study of myriapods (millipedes, centipedes) & isopods
     (woodlice, water-slaters)
●   Conf - Res - SG - Lib - VE
<   Brit Entomological & Natural History Soc
M   240 i, UK / 36 i, o'seas
¶   Bulletin - 1; £10.   NL - 2; free.

British Narrow Fabrics Association   (BNFA)
NR 12 Beaumanor Rd, LEICESTER, LE4 5QA.
     0116-266 3332   fax 0116-266 3335
     email directorate@knitfed.co.uk
     Sec: Mrs Anne Carvell
▲   Un-incorporated Society
○   *T; to promote the narrow fabrics industry in the UK - is a non-
     profit making organisation (manufacturers of ribbon, tapes,
     woven labels & webbing etc)
●   Mtgs - ET (of technical textiles technicians) - Inf - Empl
<   Knitting Inds Fedn
M   f
¶   NL - 12;   AR - 1; both ftm only.

British National Carnation Society (BNCS) 1948
■   Linfield, Duncote, TOWCESTER, Northants, NN12 8AH.   (hsp)
     01327 351594
     email dianthusinduncote@tiscali.co.uk
     Hon Sec: Mrs B M Linnell
▲   Un-incorporated Society
○   *H; cultivation, breeding & exhibition of the Dianthus family of
     carnations & pinks
●   Competitive shows & displays
<   R Horticl Soc
M   c 370 i
¶   NL - 2; ftm only.   Carnation Ybk - 1; ftm.

British National Martial Arts Associations (BNMAA) 1992
■   12 Princes Avenue, Corringham, STANFORD le HOPE, Essex,
     SS17 7PU.   (hq)
     0871 990 3203   fax 01375 411953
     http://www.bnmaa.co.uk
     Chief Exec Officer: Paul Griffin,   Sec: Iris Balding
▲   Un-incorporated Society
Br 4; Malta, Spain, USA
○   *N, *S; the safe development of traditional & freestyle martial
     arts
Gp Competitions - the S factor (skill no contact); Training provider -
     Mastarr; Grade register - official grade
●   Conf - Mtgs - ET - Exam - Res - Exhib - Comp - SG - Stat - Expt
     - Inf - PL - VE - LG
<   Wld Black Belt; Sports Coach; Mastarr; Chart Inst of Envtl
     Health; Office of Fair Trading; Sports Devt Initiative
>   Wld Black Belt; Profl Unification of Martial Arts (PUMA)
M   270,000 i, 1,040 f, 5 org, UK / 200,000 i, 150 f, 2 org, o'seas
¶   NL - 12;ftm only.   Online magazine - updated; free.

British National Temperance League (BNTL) 1834
■   30 Keswick Rd, WORKSOP, Notts, S81 7PT.   (hq)
     01909 477882
     email bntl@btconnect.com   http://www.bntl.org
     Chief Exec & Co Sec: Mrs Barbara Briggs
▲   Company Limited by Guarantee; Registered Charity
○   *E, *K, *Y; an initiative of the League that offers children &
     young people the options to not drink alcohol, or take illegal
     drugs, solvents or other addictive substances, through
     educational resources & training
●   ET
M   35 i, 1,000 i (associates)
¶   Freeway (NL) - 4.   AR - 1; both free.
     Note: uses the abbreviated title of BNTL Freeway

© CBD Research Ltd · Beckenham · BR3 5JS · Tel 020 8650 7745 · Fax 020 8650 0768 · E-mail cbd@cbdresearch.com · www.cbdresearch.com

British Natural Bodybuilding Federation
NR c/o The Body Academy, 40 South William St, PERTH, PH2 8LS.
    email info@bnbf.co.uk   http://www.bnbf.co.uk

British Natural Hygiene Society (BNHS) 1956
■ Shalimar 14 The Weavers, Farndon Rd, NEWARK, Notts,
    NG24 4RY.   (hsp)
    01636 682941
    Pres & Hon Sec: Dr K R Sidhwa
▲ Un-incorporated Society
○ *K; to propagate the message of natural healthy living in
    accordance with natural law
Gp Nutrition; Diet; Fasting for health
● Conf - Inf
< Intl Assn of Profl Natural Hygienists; Amer Natural Hygiene Soc
M c 400 i
¶ The Hygienist - 4.

British Naturalists' Association (BNA) 1905
NR PO Box 5682, CORBY, Northants, NN17 2ZW.
    01536 262977
    http://www.bna-naturalists.org
▲ Company Limited by Guarantee; Registered Charity
○ *K; the education of the public in natural history areas &
    sanctuaries

British Naturism
    is the trading name of the **Central Council for British Naturism**

British Naturopathic Association (BNA) 1992
■ Goswell House, 2 Goswell Rd, STREET, Somerset, BA16 0JG.
    (hsb)
    0870 745 6984
    Sec: M W F Szewiel
▲ Company Limited by Guarantee
○ *P; for qualified & registered naturopaths
● Conf - Mtgs - Res - Inf
M 310 i, UK / 19 i, o'seas
¶ British Naturopathic Jnl - 4.

British Naval Equipment Association (BNEA) 1973
NR 28-29 Threadneedle St, LONDON, EC2R 8AY.   (hq)
    020 7628 2555   fax 020 7638 4376
    email info@maritimeindustries.org
    http://www.maritimeindustries.org
    Dir: Christopher McHugh
○ *T; 'dedicated to the needs of companies in the British naval
    industrial sector which build, refit & modernise warships,
    supply operations & weapons systems & other equipment;
    also dedicated to the needs of the companies providing
    related services in design, consultancy & finance'
● Conf - Mtgs - ET - Exhib - SG - Expt - LG
< Soc of Maritime Inds
M f

British Neuropathological Society (BNS) 1950
NR c/o Dr D Hilton, Dept of Histopathology, Derriford Hospital,
    Derriford Rd, PLYMOUTH, Devon, PL6 8DH.   (hsb)
    01752 763599   fax 01752 763590
    Hon Sec: Dr David Hilton
▲ Registered Charity
○ *L; to promote research, education & clinical practice relating
    to neuropathy (study of brain, nerve & muscle disorders)
● Conf - Mtgs - ET - Res
< Intl Soc Neuropathology
M c 200 i
¶ Neuropathology & Applied Neurobiology - 10.

British Neuropsychiatry Association (BNPA) 1987
■ Unit 3E Hampton Works, 117-119 Sheen Lane (back of),
    LONDON, SW14 8AE.   (admin/p)
    0560 114 1307   fax 020 8878 0573
    email admin@bnpa.org.uk   http://www.bnpa.org.uk
    Admin: Jackie Ashmenall,   Hon Sec: Dr Hugh Rickards
○ *M, *P; to provide a forum for cross-disciplinary discussion
    among psychiatrists, neurologists, neuropsychologists &
    workers in the related sciences, as well as qualified persons
    with an interest in brain function in relation to behaviour
● Mtgs
M c 400 i

British Neuropsychological Society (BNS) 1989
NR R3 Neurosciences, Box 83, Addenbrookes Hospital,
    CAMBRIDGE, CB2 0QQ.   (pres/b)
    http://www.the-bns.org
    Pres: Dr Narinder Kapur
○ *M

British Neuroscience Association (BNA) 1965
NR The Sherrington Buildings, Ashton St, LIVERPOOL, L69 3GE.
    0151-794 4943
    Exec Dir: Yvonne Allen
▲ Registered Charity
○ *L, *P; to promote an understanding of the structure, function &
    development of the nervous system in health & disease
● Conf - Mtgs - ET - Res
< Intl Brain Res Org (IBRO); Fedn of Eur Neuroscience
    Socs (FENS)
M c 1,900 i, 9 f, UK / c 1,000 i, o'seas
¶ BNA NL - 4; free.
    National Meeting Book of Abstracts - 2 yrly; ftm.

**British/New Zealand Trade Council (Incorporated) (BNZTC)
1917**
■ PO Box 37162, Parnell, AUCKLAND, New Zealand.   (hq)
    64 (9) 578 1312   fax 64 (9) 578 1326
    email info@bnztc.co.nz   http://www.bnztc.co.nz
    Nat Dir: David J Catty
▲ Incorporated society
Br 2 o'seas
○ *C; to foster trade & investment between UK & New Zealand
● Conf - Mtgs - Expt - Inf - VE - LG - Promotion of investment in
    UK
< NZ Europe Business Council (NZEUBC)
M 20 i, 50 f

British Non-Ferrous Metals Federation   (BNFMF)
■ c/o Copper Development Association, 5 Grovelands Business
    Centre, Boundary Way, HEMEL HEMPSTEAD, Herts,
    HP2 7TE.   (hq)
    fax 01442 275716
    email bnfmf@copperuk.org.uk
    Exec Sec: Carol Godfrey
▲ Un-incorporated Society
○ *T; fabricators of copper & copper-based alloy wire, tube, sheet
    & strip, & rods & profiles
● Mtgs
M 14 f
¶ LM.

British North American Research Association   (BNARA)
NR Warnford Court, 29 Throgmorton St, LONDON, EC2N 2AT.
    (hq)
    email bnara@underlinegroup.com
    Secretariat: David Robertson,   Chmn: Sir Paul Judge
▲ Registered Charity
Br Canada; USA
○ *X; promotion of Anglo-North American trade, commercial &
    political relations
● Conf - Mtgs - ET - Res - SG
M 45 i, UK / 30 i, o'seas

British Nuclear Energy Society
on 1 January 2009 merged with the Institution of Nuclear Engineers
to form the **Nuclear Institute**

British Nuclear Medicine Society (BNMS) 1969
■   Regent House, 291 Kirkdale, LONDON, SE26 4QD.   (hq)
    020 8676 7864   fax 020 8676 8417
    email suehatchard@bnms.org.uk
    http://www.bnms.org.uk
    Pres: Dr Gillian Vivian
    Chief Exec: Mrs Susan Hatchard
▲   Registered Charity
○   *P; to advance the science & public education in nuclear
    medicine
●   Conf - ET - Exhib
M   c 700 i
¶   Nuclear Medicine Communications - 12.

British Number Plate Manufacturers Association   (BNMA)
■   PO Box 23, BLACKPOOL, Lancs, FY4 3DA.   (chmn/b)
    01253 345287   fax 01253 344595
    email tmc@bestplate.com
    Chmn: Tony McNamee
▲   Un-incorporated Society
○   *T
●   Mtgs - Res - LG
M   9 f

British Numismatic Society   (BNS)   1903
■   c/o Warburg Institute, Woburn Sq, LONDON, WC1H 0AB.
    (hsb)
    01223 332915
    email secretary@britnumsoc.org
    http://www.britnumsoc.org
    Hon Sec: Richard Kelleher
▲   Registered Charity
○   *L; promotion of numismatic science with regard to the coins,
    tokens & medals of Great Britain, our Empire &
    Commonwealth, & the English speaking world
●   Mtgs - Inf - Lib
<   Brit Assn of Numismatics Socs
M   393 i, 50 org, UK / 112 i, 62 org, o'seas
¶   British Numismatic Jnl - 1; ftm only.
    Specialist numismatic publications; at cost m.

British Numismatic Trade Association Ltd   (BNTA)   1973
■   PO Box 2, RYE, E Sussex, TN31 7WE.   (hq)
    01797 229988   fax 01797 229988
    email bnta@lineone.net   http://www.bnta.net
    Gen Sec: Mrs R Cooke
▲   Company Limited by Guarantee
○   *T; to ensure a high standard of ethical conduct within the
    numismatic trade
●   Coin fairs
<   Fedn of Eur Numismatic Trade Assns (FENAP)
M   73 i & f

British Nutrition Foundation (BNF) 1967
■   High Holborn House, 52-54 High Holborn, LONDON,
    WC1V 6RQ.   (hq)
    020 7404 6504   fax 020 7404 6747
    email postbox@nutrition.org.uk
    http://www.nutrition.org.uk
    Co Sec: T Barclay,   Admin Officer: Nicholas Baldwin
▲   Company Limited by Guarantee; Registered Charity
○   *L; to provide unbiased information; to encourage education;
    to foster research concerned with human nutrition
Gp School education; Publishing
●   Conf - Mtgs - ET - Inf
M   42 f
¶   BNF Bulletin - 4; £67 yr.   AR - 1; £10.

British Oat & Barley Millers' Association   (BOBMA)   1978
■   6 Catherine St, LONDON, WC2B 5JJ.   (hq)
    020 7420 7109   fax 020 7836 0580
    email grace.foyle@fdf.org.uk
    Exec: Grace Foyle
▲   Un-incorporated Society
○   *T; interests of UK millers of oat & barley for human
    consumption
●   Mtgs
<   Eur Breakfast Cereal Assn (CEEREAL); Food & Drink Fedn (FDF)
M   8 f

British Obesity Surgery Patient Association   (BOSPA)   2003
NR PO Box 805, TAUNTON, Somerset, TA4 9DU.
    0845 602 0446
    email enquiries@bospa.org   http://www.bospa.org
▲   Registered Charity
○   *K, *M; to provide support & information to patients for whom
    obesity surgery can provide an enormous benefit

British Obesity Surgery Society   (BOSS)   2000
■   c/o Prof J N Baxter, Dept Surgery, Morriston Hospital,
    SWANSEA, SA6 6NL.   (asa)
    01792 703573   fax 01792 703574
    email j.n.baxter@swan.ac.uk
    Hon Pres: Prof J N Baxter
▲   Un-incorporated Society
○   *L, *P; to promote awareness of obesity surgery; to advise on
    training & accreditation
●   Conf - ET
<   Intl Fedn for the Surgery of Obesity (IFSO); Assn for the Study of
    Obesity (ASO); Assn of Upper GI Surgeons (AUGIS)
M   70 i
¶   NL - 2/3; free.

British Occupational Hygiene Society   (BOHS)   1953
NR 5-6 Melbourne Business Court, Millennium Way, Pride Park,
    DERBY, DE24 8LZ.   (hq)
    01332 298101
    email admin@bohs.org
    Hon Sec: Heather Jackson
▲   Company Limited by Guarantee; Registered Charity
Br 8 regions
○   *L; to promote the good practice of occupational hygiene; to
    prevent workplace conditions affecting the health & wellbeing
    of workers
Gp Technology; Standards; Chemical hazard & risk;
    Environmental; Management; Microbiology; NHS; Offshore;
    Radiation; Sampling & analytical methods
●   Conf - Mtgs - ET - Res - SG
<   Intl Occupational Hygiene Assn
M   c 1,200 i
¶   Annals of Occupational Hygiene - 8.   NL - 4.
    Abstracts of Conference Papers - 1.   AR.

British Off Road Driving Association   (BORDA)   1995
NR Leisure House, Salisbury Rd, ANDOVER, Hants, SP11 7DN.
    (hq)
    01264 712093
    email info@borda.org.uk   http://www.borda.org.uk
    Sec: David Heaton
▲   Un-incorporated Society
○   *T; to encourage best practice in the organisation of events
    among member operators; to develop technical guidance for
    off road driving

© CBD Research Ltd · Beckenham · BR3 5JS · Tel 020 8650 7745 · Fax 020 8650 0768 · E-mail cbd@cbdresearch.com · www.cbdresearch.com

British Office Supplies & Services Federation   (BOSS Federation)   1987
- ■ Farringdon Point, 29-35 Farringdon Rd, LONDON, EC1M 3JF.   (hq)
  0845 450 1565   fax 020 7405 7784
  http://www.bossfederation.com
  Chief Exec: Michael Gardner
- ▲ Company Limited by Guarantee
- Br 13
- ○ *T; to represent manufacturers, importers, wholesalers, distributors, mail order, resellers, retailers, dealers, superstores & commercial contract dealers
- Gp Letter File Manufacturers' Association; Office Products & Stationery Association; Rubber Stamp Manufacturers' Guild; Writing Instruments Association
- ● Conf - Mtgs - ET - Exam - Exhib - Comp - SG - Stat - Expt - Inf - LG
- < Eur Stationery & Office Products Trade Assn
- M f

British Oil Spill Control Association
    since 2004 **UK Spill Association**

British Olive Oil Buyer's Association   (BOOBA)
- ■ Kingsway House, Wrotham Rd, Meopham, GRAVESEND, Kent, DA13 0AU.   (asa)
- ○ *T
- ● Conf - Mtgs - Stat - LG
- M 7 f

British Olympic Association   (BOA)   1905
- NR 1 Wandsworth Plain, LONDON, SW18 1EH.   (hq)
  020 8871 2677   fax 020 8871 9104
  email boa@boa.org.uk   http://www.olympics.org.uk
  Chief Exec: Simon Clegg
- ○ *S; to provide services to elite sport in the UK; to promote the Olympic movement in the UK; to prepare & manage the Great Britain Olympic team for the games
- ● Conf - ET - Res - Inf - Lib - LG
- < Intl Olympic C'ee
- M 2,289 i
- ¶ Cutting Edge (NL) - 4;   Inside Track (NL) - 4.   AR - 1.

British Oncological Association   (BOA)   1985
- NR Royal Marsden Hospital, Orchard House, Downs Rd, SUTTON, Surrey, SM2 5PT.   (sb)
  020 8661 3063   fax 020 8661 3470
  http://www.boanet.org
  Sec: Romayne McMahon
- ▲ Registered Charity
- ○ *L, *P, *Q; for clinicians & scientists working in oncology specialities
- ● Conf - Mtgs - ET - Comp
- M c 400 i
- ¶ BOA News - 4; ftm only.

British Oncology Data Managers Association
    closed 1 April 2008. For information about courses contact Sharon Forsyth on 020 7679 9264.

British Onion Producers' Association   (British Onions)
- ■ 133 Eastgate, LOUTH, Lincs, LN11 9QG.
  01507 602427   fax 01507 607165
  email crop-association@pvga.co.uk
  http://www.britishonions.org.uk
- ○ *F, *T

British Ophthalmic Anaesthesia Society   (BOAS)   1998
- ■ Dept of Anaesthesia, City Hospital, Dudley Rd, BIRMINGHAM, B18 7QH.   (hsb)
  0121-507 4343   fax 0121-507 4349
  http://www.boas.org
  Sec: Dr K-L Kong
- ○ *P; for anaesthetists, ophthalmologists & other clinicians who are committed to sharing information & education that will enable them to provide the highest level of anaesthetic management during ophthalmic surgery
- ● Conf - Mtgs - ET - Comp - Inf
- < Wld Congress of Ophthalmic Anaestheia; Ophthalmic Anesthesia Soc
- M c 200 i
  (Sub: £25)
- ¶ BOAS NL - 2; free.

British Orchid Council   (BOC)   1971
- ■ Hall Farm House, Shelton, NEWARK, Notts, NG23 5JG.   (hsp)
  email bocsecretary@tiscali.co.uk
  http://www.british-orchid-council.info
  Hon Sec: Richard Baxter
- ▲ Registered Charity
- ○ *H; to provide a single forum for amateur & commercial orchid growers & orchid scientists; to broaden the knowledge of orchids; to promote & encourage excellence in their culture
- Gp Judging scheme; Lecturers panel; Slide library
  C'ees: Conservation, Congress, Communications
- ● Conf - Mtgs - Exhib - SG - Inf - PL
- < Eur Orchid Coun
- M 47 org
- ¶ A Grower's & Buyer's Guide - 1; ftm, £1 nm.

British Orchid Growers Association   (BOGA)   1949
- ■ Burnham Nurseries, Forches Cross, NEWTON ABBOT, Devon, TQ12 6PZ.   (hsb)
  01626 352233   fax 01276 32947
  email mail@orchids.uk.com   http://www.boga.org.uk
  Hon Sec: Brian Rittershausen
- ○ *H, *T; 'for orchid growers & sundries traders to promote & maintain the highest standards of our trade'
- ● Conf - Mtgs - Exhib - Inf - LG re CITES (Convention for International Trade of Endangered Species)
- < Brit Orchid Coun
- M 17 f
- ¶ Grower's & Buyer's Guide (LM) - 1; ftm, 50p or 2 1st class stamps nm.

British Organ Archive
    a group of the **British Institute of Organ Studies**

British Organ Donor Society   (BODY)   1984
- § Balsham, CAMBRIDGE, CB1 6DL.
  01223 893636
  email body@argonet.co.uk
  http://www.body.orpheusweb.co.uk
  Promotes the carrying of Donor Cards, and acts as a help and support group for donor and recipient families.

British Oriental Rug Dealers Association   (BORDA)   1993
- ■ c/o RuGallery Ltd, 42 Verulam Rd, ST ALBANS, Herts, AL3 4DQ.   (hsb)
  01727 841046
  Sec: Richard H Mathias
- ▲ Un-incorporated Society
- ○ *T
- Gp Exhibitions; Information
- ● Mtgs - Inf - PL
- M 20 f

British Orienteering Federation Ltd (BOF) 1967

■ 8A Stancliffe House, Whitworth Rd, Darley Dale, MATLOCK, Derbys, DE4 2HJ. (hq)
01629 734042 fax 01629 733769
email info@britishorienteering.org.uk
http://www.britishorienteering.org.uk
Chief Exec: Mike Hamilton
▲ Company Limited by Guarantee
○ *S; national governing body for the sport of orienteering
Gp Federated regional & home national associations & affiliated clubs
● Conf - Mtgs - ET - Comp - LG
< Intl Orienteering Fedn (IOF)
M 8,500 i, 140 clubs
¶ Focus Magazine (NL) - 4; Fixtures List - 4; both ftm only. Leaflets & posters.

British Origami Society (BOS) 1967

■ 2a The Chestnuts, COUNTESTHORPE, Leics, LE8 5TL. (mem/sp)
Mem Sec: Mrs P A Groom
▲ Registered Charity
○ *A; the development of Origami (folding paper) & related techniques of manipulation of paper as a form of art, education, therapy & recreation
● Conf - Mtgs - ET - Exhib
< Origami associations worldwide
M 350 i, UK / 350 i, o'seas
¶ British Origami - 6; ftm only.

British Ornithologists' Club (BOC) 1892

NR PO Box 417, PETERBOROUGH, Cambs, PE7 3FX. (mail)
01733 844820
○ *L; to promote scientific discussion & facilitate publication & dissemination of scientific information connected with ornithology; to maintain a special interest in avian systematics, taxonomy & distribution
M i

British Ornithologists' Union (BOU) 1858

■ PO Box 417, PETERBOROUGH, Cambs, PE7 3FX. (mail)
01733 844820
email bou@bou.org.uk http://www.bou.org.uk
Admin: Steve P Dudley
▲ Registered Charity
○ *L; promoting the understanding of avian biology & conservation
Gp BOU Records C'ee (BOURC)
● Conf - Res - Publishing - Grants
M c 1,000 i
(Sub: £35)
¶ Ibis (Jnl) - 4; ftm (ibis.ac.uk)
BOU Checklist Series - irreg: prices vary.

British Orthodontic Society (BOS) 1994

■ 12 Bridewell Place, LONDON, EC4V 6AP. (hq)
020 7353 8680 fax 020 7353 8682
email ann.wright@bos.org.uk http://www.bos.org.uk
Sec: Ann Wright
▲ Company Limited by Guarantee; Registered Charity
○ *P; a branch of dentistry concerned with developmental abnormalities of the teeth & face
Gp Consultant orthodontists; Community; Practitioners; Specialist practitioners; Training grades; University teachers
● Conf - Mtgs - Res - LG
< Orthodontic Technicians Assn; Orthodontic Nat Gp for Dental Burses; Brit Lingual Orthodontic Soc
M 1,700 i, UK / 150 i, o'seas
¶ British Jnl of Orthodontics - 4. BOS NL - 4.

British Orthopaedic Association (BOA) 1918

■ 35-43 Lincoln's Inn Fields, LONDON, WC2A 3PE. (hq)
020 7405 6507 fax 020 7831 2676
email secretary@boa.ac.uk http://www.boa.ac.uk
Chief Exec: D C Adams, Hon Sec: Joseph Dias
▲ Company Limited by Guarantee; Registered Charity
○ *P; science, art & practice of orthopaedic surgery
Gp Specialist societies:
British Association of Spinal Surgeons
British Association for Surgery of the Knee
British Cervical Spine Society
British Elbow & Shoulder Society
British Hip Society
British Limb Reconstruction Society
British Orthopaedic Foot & Ankle Surgery Society
British Orthopaedic Oncology Society
British Orthopaedic Research Society
British Orthopaedic Specialists Association
British Orthopaedic Sports Trauma Association
British Orthopaedic Trainees Association
British Scoliosis Society
British Society for Children's Orthopaedic Surgery
British Trauma Society
Rheumatoid Arthritis Surgical Society
Society for Back Pain Research
World Orthopaedic Concern
● Conf - ET - Exhib - Stat - Inf - LG
M c 4,220 i
¶ Jnl of Bone & Joint Surgery - 24.
British Orthopaedic News - 3.
Hbk & LM - 1; ftm only. AR - 1; free.

British Orthopaedic Foot & Ankle Surgery Society
a specialist society of the **British Orthopaedic Association**

British Orthopaedic Oncology Society
a specialist society of the **British Orthopaedic Association**

British Orthopaedic Research Society
a specialist society of the **British Orthopaedic Association**

British Orthopaedic Specialists Association
a specialist society of the **British Orthopaedic Association**

British Orthopaedic Sports Trauma Association
a specialist society of the **British Orthopaedic Association**

British Orthopaedic Trainees Association
a specialist society of the **British Orthopaedic Association**

British Orthoptic Society
since January 2004 **British & Irish Orthoptic Society**

British Osteopathic Association (BOA) 1998

■ 3 Park Terrace, Manor Rd, LUTON, Beds, LU1 3HN. (hq)
01582 488455 fax 01582 481533
email boa@osteopathy.org http://www.osteopathy.org
Chief Exec: Michael Watson
▲ Company Limited by Guarantee
○ *M, *P; to provide independent representation, care & support for osteopaths
● Conf - Res - Inf
M c 2,600 i
¶ Osteopathy Today - 10.

© CBD Research Ltd · Beckenham · BR3 5JS · Tel 020 8650 7745 · Fax 020 8650 0768 · E-mail cbd@cbdresearch.com · www.cbdresearch.com

British Othello Federation (BOF) 1984
■ 1 Beaconsfield Terrace, Victoria Rd, CAMBRIDGE, CB4 3BP.
(chmn/p)
01223 366197
email atc12@mole.bio.cam.ac.uk
http://www.britishothello.org.uk
Chmn: Geoff Hubbard, Mem Sec: Adelaide Carpenter
○ *S; to promote the playing & understanding of the game of
Othello - a board game of pure skill sometimes known as
'Reversi'
● Comp
< US Othello Assn; Fédn Française d'Othello; Japan Othello
Assn
M 50 i, UK / 50 i, o'seas
¶ NL - 2; ftm, £3 nm.

British Outdoor Professionals Association (BOPA) 1993
NR The Roast Ox Inn, Painscastle, BUILTH WELLS, Powys,
LD2 3JL. (hq)
07071 225853 fax 01479 851279
email info@the-bopa.co.uk http://www.the-bopa.co.uk
Gen Sec: Chris Charters
○ *P; to encourage professionalism in providing the best training
in outdoor activities (incl abseiling, archery, ballooning,
caving, gliding, golf, horse-riding, orienteering, sailing, etc)
● ET - Database providing activities available, instructors & their
qualifications - Workshops & seminars
M 1,200 i (associate membership for trainees)
¶ NL - 12; free.

British Packaging Association (BPA) 1908
NR 24 Grange St, KILMARNOCK, Ayrshire, KA1 2AR. (hq)
01563 570518 fax 01563 572728
email npc@natpack.org.uk
http://www.british-packaging.co.uk
Exec Dir: Allan Glen
▲ Un-incorporated Society
○ *T; (members are mainly small to medium sized owner-run
boxmakers)
● Conf - Mtgs - Comp - Inf - Empl
< CITPA
M 70 f, UK / 3 f, o'seas

British Paediatric Cardiac Association
a group of the **Royal College of Paediatrics & Child Health**

British Paediatric Neurology Association
a group of the **Royal College of Paediatrics & Child Health**

British Paediatric Pathology Association
a group of the **Royal College of Paediatrics & Child Health**

British Paediatric Respiratory Society
a group of the **Royal College of Paediatrics & Child Health**

British Pain Society (the British Chapter of IASP) 1968
NR Churchill House (3rd floor), 35 Red Lion Square, LONDON,
WC1R 4SG. (hq)
Secretariat: Jenny Duncan (020 7296 7844)
▲ Registered Charity
Br 14 regional
○ *P; to relieve the suffering of pain by promotion of education,
research & training; to increase professional & public
awareness of the prevalence of pain & the facilities available
for its management
Gp (deal with specific aspects of pain - acute, in children, etc)
● Conf - ET - Res - Exhib - Inf - LG
< Intl Assn for the Study of Pain (IASP)
M 1,387 i, 5 f
¶ NL; ftm only. Information for Patients; free.
Desirable Criteria for Pain Management Programmes.

British Palomino Society (BPS)
■ Penrhiwllan, LLANDYSUL, Cardiganshire, SA44 5NZ. (hq)
01239 851387 fax 01239 851040
email britpal@lineone.net
http://www.britishpalominosociety.co.uk
Hon Sec: Mrs Peter Howell
▲ Company Limited by Guarantee
○ *B
● Annual show
M i
¶ Palomino - 3; ftm, £3 nm.

British Paper Machinery Makers Association
a divisionof **Picon Ltd**

British Parachute Association (BPA) 1962
■ 5 Wharf Way, Glen Parva, LEICESTER, LE2 9TF. (hq)
0116-278 5271 fax 0116-247 7662
email skydive@bpa.org.uk http://www.bpa.org.uk
Sec-Gen: Martin Shuttleworth, Chmn: John Smyth
▲ Company Limited by Guarantee
Br 25; Cyprus, Germany
○ *S; governing body of sport parachuting in the UK
Gp Safety & training; Development; Competitions (international &
national)
● Mtgs - ET - Exam - Exhib - Comp
< Fédn Aéronautique Intle; Sports Coun; CCPR; R Aero Club; UK
Sport
M 5,100 i, 33,000 i (students)
¶ Skydive, the British Mag - 6; ftm, £22 nm.

British Paralympic Association (BPA) 1989
NR 40 Bernard St, LONDON, WC1N 1ST. (hq)
020 7211 5222 fax 020 7211 5233
email info@paralympics.org.uk
http://www.paralympics.org.uk
▲ Registered Charity
○ *S; to support & manage British Paralympic team
● Mtgs - Comp - Organisation of teams for the winter & summer
Paralympic Games
< Intl Paralympic C'ee
M 78 org

British Parking Association (BPA) 1970
NR Stuart House, 41-43 Perrymount Rd, HAYWARDS HEATH,
W Sussex, RH16 3BN. (hq)
01444 447300 fax 01444 454105
email info@britishparking.co.uk
http://www.britishparking.co.uk
Managing Dir: Keith Banbury
▲ Company Limited by Guarantee
○ *T; to promote the advancement of knowledge & standards in
the management, planning, design, improvement, regulation
& maintenance of all types of parking facilities on & off-street
● Conf - Mtgs - ET - Exhib - Inf - Lib - LG
M c 600 i, f & local authorities
¶ Parking News (Jnl) - 10; ftm only.

British Parthenais Cattle Society 1988
NR Willow Creek Farm, Mill Race, Tetney, GRIMSBY, Lincs,
DN36 5JZ. (hsp)
01472 814736
http://www.parthenais.co.uk
▲ Company Limited by Guarantee
○ *B; to promote the Parthenais breed for pedigree & beef
production
● Agricultural shows - Beef events
< Nat Beef Assn
M 30 i, UK / 1 i, o'seas
¶ NL - 5/6; Promotional leaflets; both free.

British Peanut Council   (BPC)   1967
- ■   20 St Dunstan's Hill, LONDON, EC3R 8NQ.   (hq)
  020 7283 2707   fax 020 7623 1310
  http://www.peanuts.org.uk
  Sec: Stuart Logan
- ▲   Company Limited by Guarantee
- ○   *T; to protect & promote the interests of the British peanut industry
- Gp   Manufacturers; Packers; Importers & distributors; Traders
- ●   Mtgs - Inf - LG
- M   34 f, 1 org, UK / 5 f, o'seas
- ¶   BPC NL - 4; ftm only.   BPC Hbk - 1.

British Pelargonium & Geranium Society
  since 2008 **Pelargonium & Geranium Society**

British Pensioners & Trade Union Action Association (BP&TUAA)   1972
- ■   22 Auburn House, Aikman Ave, LEICESTER, LE3 9JN.   (hsp)
  0116-232 2125
  Gen Sec: Ann Green
- ▲   Un-incorporated Society
- Br   150
- ○   *K; active campaigning over pensions, health & social services, transport & other issues affecting OAPs
- ●   Conf - Mtgs - Res - VE - LG
- M   c 5,000 i
- ¶   British Pensioner Jnl - 4; 35p each.

British Percheron Horse Society   (BPHS)   1919
- NR   3 Field Barn Cottages, North Charford, Breamore, FORDINGBRIDGE, Hants, SP6 2DW.   (hsp)
  01725 511047
  email secretary@percheron.org.uk
  http://www.percheron.org.uk
  Sec: Mrs Rowena McDermott
- ▲   Company Limited by Guarantee
- ○   *B
- ●   Mtgs - Res - VE - Progress Days - Open Days - Marathons - Trials
- M   c 270 i
- ¶   NL - 4; ftm only.   Studbook, Vol XIV.

British-Peruvian Chamber   1988
- ■   Torre Parque Mar (piso 22), Av José Larco 1301, LIMA 18, Peru.   (hq)
  51 (1) 617 3090   fax 51 (1) 617 3095
  email bpcc@bpcc.org.pe   http://www.bpcc.org.pe
  Pres: Charles Fyfe
- ▲   Registered Charity
- Br   Peru
- ○   *C; a bilateral chamber which seeks to promote investment & commerce between Peru & the UK as well as corporate social responsibility amongst its members
- ●   Conf - Mtgs - Comp - Stat - Expt - Inf - VE - LG
- <   Assn Bilateral Brit Chams Latin America (BRITLAN)
- M   10 i, 92 f
- ¶   Opportunities (Jnl) - 4; free.
  Members Directory - 2; free.
  Online bulletin - 12; ftm only.

British Pest Control Association   (BPCA)   1942
- ■   1 Gleneagles House, Vernongate, DERBY, DE1 1UP.   (hq)
  01332 294288   fax 01332 295904
  email enquiry@bpca.org.uk   http://www.bpca.org.uk
  Exec Dir: O Madge
- ▲   Company Limited by Guarantee
- ○   *T; for servicing companies & others engaged in the control of food, hygiene or nuisance pests, or having a close interest in industrial pest control; it includes control of pests in food storage & preparation areas in domestic premises, factories, hospitals, hotels, restaurants, shops & transport; BPCA also represents manufacturers & distributors of the pesticides & equipment used by the servicing companies & responsible & safe use of pesticides in the interests of the general public
- ●   Mtgs - ET - Exam - Exhib - Inf - LG
- M   22 i, 229 f, UK / 38 f, o'seas
- ¶   Professional Pest Controller (Jnl) - 4; free.

British Pétanque Federation
  has been dissolved.

British Pharmacological Society   (BPS)   1931
- NR   16 Angel Gate, City Rd, LONDON, EC1V 2SG.   (hq)
  020 7239 0171   fax 020 7417 0114
  email ml@bps.ac.uk   http://www.bps.ac.uk
  Exec Officer: Sarah-Jane Stagg
- ▲   Company Limited by Guarantee; Registered Charity
- ○   *L; to promote & advance the science of pharmacology; to research into drugs & the way in which they work
- Gp   Clinical pharmacology; Pharmacology
- ●   Conf - Mtgs - ET - Exam - Res - Exhib
- <   Intl U of Pharmacology; Fedn of Eur Pharmacological Socs; Eur Assn for Clinical Pharmacology & Therapeutics
- M   1,700 i, UK / 8060i, o'seas
- ¶   British Jnl of Pharmacology - 12; £103 m.
  British Jnl of Clinical Pharmacology - 12; £55 m.
  PA2 (NL) - 4; ftm only.   AR; free.

British Phonographic Industry Ltd
  since 2007 **BPI (British Recorded Music Industry) Ltd**

British Photodermatology Group   (BPG)   1988
- ■   c/o Mr David Taylor (Clinical Scientist), Gloucester Royal Hospital, Great Western Rd, GLOUCESTER, GL1 3NN.   (sb)
  0845 422 5976   fax 0845 422 6489
  email david.taylor@glos.nhs.uk   http://www.BPG.org.uk
  Hon Sec: David Taylor
- ○   *L, *N, *Q; the study & effects of optical radiations, in health & disease, on human skin
- ●   Conf - Mtgs - ET - Res - Inf
- <   Brit Assn of Dermatologists; Photomedicine Soc (USA)
- M   c 110 i, UK / c 10 i, o'seas

British Photovoltaic Association
  on 1 April 2006 merged with the **Renewable Energy Associaton**

British Phycological Society   1952
- NR   c/o Dr Jackie Parry, Dept of Biological Sciences, Lancaster University, LANCASTER, LA1 4YQ.   (hsb)
  01524 593489
  Hon Sec: Dr Jackie Parry
- ▲   Registered Charity
- ○   *L; study of algae (seaweed and related forms)
- ●   Conf - Res - SG - VE
- <   Biosciences Fedn
- M   613 i, UK & o'seas
- ¶   European Jnl of Phycology - 4.   NL - 3.

© CBD Research Ltd · Beckenham · BR3 5JS · Tel 020 8650 7745 · Fax 020 8650 0768 · E-mail cbd@cbdresearch.com · www.cbdresearch.com

British Piemontese Cattle Society Ltd   1988
■   33 Eden Grange, Little Corby, CARLISLE, Cumbria, CA4 8QW.
      01228 562946   fax 01228 562187
      email craig@piemontese.info
      http://www.piemontese.org.uk
      Sec: F C Culley
▲   Company Limited by Guarantee; Registered Charity
○   *B
M   i & f

British Pig Association   (BPA)   1884
NR   Trumpington Mews, 40b High St, Trumpington, CAMBRIDGE,
      CB2 2LS.   (hq)
      01223 845100
      email bpa@britishpigs.org   http://www.britishpigs.org
▲   Company Limited by Guarantee; Registered Charity
○   *B, *V; to represent the pig industry
M   i, f & org

British Plant Gall Society   (BPGS)   1986
NR   2 The Dene, NETTLEHAM, Lincs, LN2 2LS.   (hsp)
      01522 875939
      http://www.britishgalls.org.uk
      Hon Sec: Graeme Clayton
○   *L; to encourage & co-ordinate the study of cecidology (plant
      galls - an abnormal growth produced by a plant or other
      host under the influence of another organism) with particular
      reference to the British Isles
Gp   Checklist; Insect & invertebrate; Recording
●   Conf - Mtgs - PL
M   147 i
¶   Cecidology (Jnl) - 2.   NL.   Occasional papers.

British Plastics Federation   (BPF)   1933
NR   6 Bath Place, Rivington St, LONDON, EC2A 3JE.   (hq)
      020 7457 5000   fax 020 7457 5045
      email bpf@bpf.co.uk
      Dir Gen: Peter Davis
○   *T; for all sectors of the plastics industry; to carry out
      commercial studies & provide commercial trade &
      information services
●   Plastics & Rubber Advisory Service: 0906 190 8070
M   f

British Plumbing Fittings Manufacturers' Association
      no longer exists

British Polarological Research Society   (BPRS)   1970
■   6 Beechvale, Hillview Rd, WOKING, Surrey, GU22 7NS.   (hq)
      Pres & Res Dir: Emeritus Research Prof W J Parker
▲   Un-incorporated Society
○   *L, *Q; 'scientific & statistical operational research studies of
      polarological phenomena; development of polarological
      operational-research theory & sciences for forecasting,
      optimisation, problem solving & decision making in non-
      orthodox OR scenarios in all disciplines'
Gp   Medical OR polarology; Environmental OR polarology
●   Mtgs - SG - Inf - Research into: polarological fog dispersal,
      CO-poisoning, p-prevention (by chimneying of gas-heater
      wall-vents), cardiovascular p-therapy instrumentation,
      hospital 'bed-blocker' p-rehabilitation; Water aid (drinking
      water p-production)
<   Brit Polarographic Res Inst; Nat Inst of Polarology;
      Polarodynamics Res Inst; Polarographic Soc; UK Instn of
      Polarological Sciences
M   i (Post-doctoral research fellows, polarological OR intelligence
      officers & scientists)
¶   (Research papers are published in journals).

British Polio Fellowship   (BPF)   1939
NR   Unit A (ground floor), Eagle Office Centre, The Runway,
      SOUTH RUISLIP, Middx, HA4 6SE.   (hq)
      0800 018 0586
      email info@britishpolio.org.uk
▲   Registered Charity
○   *W; welfare of people in the UK & Ireland who are disabled by
      poliomyelitis
M   i

British-Polish Chamber of Commerce   (BPCC)
■   240 King St, LONDON, W6 0RF.   (hq)
      020 8563 0044   fax 020 8563 0026
      email manageruk@bpcc.org.pl   http://www.bpcc.org.pl
      London Mgr: Anna Maria McKeever
Br   3
○   *C; to develop British business links with Poland
●   Conf - Res - Expt - Inf
<   the British office of BPCC in Warsaw
M   2 i, 30 f, UK / 10 i, 350 f, o'seas
¶   Contact - 6; free.   Membership Directory - 1; ftm, £45 nm.

British-Polish Chamber of Commerce   (BPCC)
NR   ul Fabryczna 16-22, PL-00-446 WARSAW, Poland.   (hq)
      48 (22) 320 01 00   fax 48 (22) 621 19 37
      Exec Dir: Barbara Stachowiak
▲   Company Limited by Guarantee
Br   London
○   *C
Gp   C'ees: Banking, Energy, Environment, Human resources &
      management training, Privatisation, Tax
●   Conf - Mtgs - ET - Res - Inf - Lib - LG
<   Confedn Brit Chams Comm Continental Europe (COBCOE);
      Assn Brit Chams Comm
M   5 i, 24 f, UK / 16 i, 301 f, Poland
¶   Contact (NL) - 6.
      Membership Directory - 1.

British Polling Council   (BPC)   2004
■   c/o ICM Research, Berkshire House, 168-173 High Holborn,
      LONDON, WC1V 7AA.   (hsb)
      020 7845 8300
      email nick.sparrow@icmresearch.co.uk
      http://www.britishpollingcouncil.org
      Hon Sec: Nick Sparrow
▲   Un-incorporated Society
○   *T; to ensure the highest standards of disclosure; designed to
      ensure that consumers of survey results which enter the
      public domain have an adequate basis for judging the
      reliability & validity of the results
●   Conf - Mtgs - Res - Inf - LG - Apply rules of disclosure to
      published polls & investigate alleged breaches
M   12 f

British Polyolefin Textiles Association   (BPTA)   1971
NR   c/o Scott & Fyfe Ltd, Nelson St, TAYPORT, Fife, DD6 9DQ.
      (hsb)
      01382 553502   fax 01382 552170
      Sec: Thomas Hill
○   *T; interests of UK producers of polyolefin tapes, yarns, fibres &
      fabrics
●   Mtgs - Stat - Inf - LG
M   5 f

British Porphyria Association   (BPA)   1998
- ■   136 Devonshire Rd, DURHAM, DH1 2BL.   (regd/address)
       01474 369231
       email helpline@porphyria.org.uk
       http://www.porphyria.org.uk
       Chmn: John Chamberlayne,   Admin: Sarah Pepperdine
- ▲   Registered Charity
- ○   *W; to encourage research & improve understanding of
       Porphyria; to offer help & advice to sufferers & their families
- ●   Mtgs - ET - Res - Inf
- <   Eur Porphyria Initiative; Amer (& Canadian) Porphyria Assn(s)
- >   Porphyria Interest Gp; Genetic Interest Gp (GIG)
- M   c 300 families
- ¶   NL - 2.
       Patients booklets & drugs list.

British Ports Association   (BPA)   1992
- ■   Carthusian Court (4th floor), 12 Carthusian St, LONDON,
       EC1M 6EZ.   (hq)
       020 7260 1780   fax 020 7260 1784
       email info@britishports.org.uk
       http://www.britishports.org.uk
       Dir: David Whitehead,   Sec: Richard Ballantyne
- ▲   Un-incorporated Society
- ○   *T; to represent the interests of member ports in the UK &
       Europe
- ●   Conf - Mtgs
- M   110 f & org
- ¶   Monthly Update - 12; m only.

British-Portuguese Chamber of Commerce (Câmara de Comércio Luso-Británica)   (BPCC)   1911
- ■   Rua da Estrela 8, 1200-669 LISBOA, Portugal.   (hq)
       351 213 942 020   fax 351 213 942 029
       email info@bpcc.pt   http://www.bpcc.pt
       Chief Exec: Christopher Barton
- ▲   Un-incorporated Society
- ○   *C; to promote Anglo-Portuguese trade relations; to provide
       services for members
- ●   Conf - ET - Res - Expt - Inf
- <   Coun Brit Cham Comm Continental Europe (COBCOE)
- M   23 f, UK / 469 f, Portugal
- ¶   Members Directory - 1; ftm, 56 nm.

British Postmark Society   (BPS)   1958
- ■   12 Dunavon Park, STRATHAVEN, Lanarks, ML10 6LP.   (hsp)
       01357 522430
       email johlen@stracml10.freeserve.co.uk
       http://www.britishpostmarksociety.org.uk
       Hon Sec: John A Strachan
- ▲   Registered Charity
- ○   *G; 'to promote & to co-ordinate the study & collection of
       British postal markings, particularly of the 20th century &
       subsequently, & the means & & methods by which they are
       applied; to publish & disseminate the results of such study for
       the education of the public'
- Gp   Printed Postage Impression Study Circle
- ●   Mtgs - Res - Comp - SG - Lib - Yearly auction - Yearly sale -
       Circulating exchange packets
- M   219 i, UK / 19 i, o'seas
       (Sub: £12 UK / £17 o'seas)
- ¶   Jnl - 4; ftm, £12 yr nm.
       PPI News & Junk Mail (NL) - irreg; ftm, £3 yr nm.
       LM - 3 yrly; ftm only.   Library List; on website.

British Potato Trade Association   (NASPM)   1940
- NR   12 Buckstone Hill, EDINBURGH, EH10 6TH.   (regd off)
       0131-623 0183
       http://www.bpta.org.uk
       Sec: Charlie Greenslade
- ▲   Un-incorporated Society
- ○   *T
- ●   Mtgs - ET - SG - Inf - VE - LG
- <   Brit Eur Potato Assn; Jt Potato Trade Coun; Nat Inst Agricl
       Botany
- ×   2006 (National Association of Seed Potato Merchants
       (Scottish Potato Trades Association

British Poultry Council   (BPC)   2002
- NR   Europoint House, 5 Lavington St, LONDON, SE1 0NZ.   (hq)
       020 7202 4760   fax 020 7928 6366
       email bpc@poultry.uk.com   http://www.poultry.uk.com
       Chief Exec: Peter Bradnock
- ▲   Company Limited by Guarantee
- ○   *T; to promote the interest of the British poultry meat production
       (all species - chicken, turkeys, ducks & geese are
       represented)
- ●   LG
- <   avec (Association of Poultry Processors & Poultry Import &
       Export Trade in the EU)
- M   95% of the sector

British Power Kitesports Association   (BPKA)   1994
- NR   PO Box 4015, SMETHWICK, W Midlands, B67 6HJ.
       email admin@bpka.co.uk   http://www.bpka.co.uk
- ○   *S; Kite buggying, kite surfing, kite landboarding, snow kiting &
       power kiting
- ×   2006 British Buggy Club

British Precast Concrete Federation Ltd   (BPCF)   1964
- ■   60 Charles St, LEICESTER, LE1 1FB.   (hq)
       0116-253 6161   fax 0116-251 4568
       email info@britishprecast.org
       http://www.britishprecast.org
       Sec: David J Zanker
- ▲   Company Limited by Guarantee
- ○   *T; promoting the interests of the precast concrete industry;
       provision of central services; (is structured on product
       associations, see below)
- Gp   9 product associations:
       Architectural Cladding Association
       Box Culvert Association
       Concrete Pipeline Systems Association
       Concrete Sleeper Manufacturers' Association
       Construction Packed Products Association
       Interpave, the Precast Concrete Paving & Kerb Association
       Precast Flooring Federation
       Prestressed Concrete Association
       Structural Precast Association
       & 6 affiliated associations:
       Aircrete Products Association
       Concrete Block Association
       Concrete Tile Manufacturers Association
       Interlay, the Association of Block Paving Contractors
       Modern Masonry Alliance
       Traditional Housing Bureau
- ●   Mtgs - Inf - Empl - LG
- <   Bureau Intl du Beton Manufacture
- M   106 f, UK / 5 f, o'seas

© CBD Research Ltd · Beckenham · BR3 5JS · Tel 020 8650 7745 · Fax 020 8650 0768 · E-mail cbd@cbdresearch.com · www.cbdresearch.com

British Precision Pilots Association   (BPPA)   1975
■   1 Lavender Way, BOURNE, Lincs, PE10 9TT.
01778 421346
email chairman@rallyflyingclub.org
http://www.rallyflyingclub.org
Chmn: Martin Reynolds
▲   Company Limited by Guarantee
○   *P, *S; to promote the sport of precision & rally flying; to
represent GB in international competitions
●   Comp
<   R Aero Club
M   30 i
(Sub: £50)

British Printing Industries Federation   (BPIF)   1900
NR   Farringdon Point, 29-35 Farringdon Rd, LONDON,
EC1M 3JF.   (hq)
0870 240 4085   fax 020 7405 7784
http://www.britishprint.com
Chief Exec: Michael Johnson
▲   Company Limited by Guarantee
Br   6
○   *T; to encourage efficiency & profitability in the printing industry
Gp   Book production, Cartons, Digital, Direct marketing special
products, Engraved stationery, Finishers, In-house &
corporate print services, Labels, Operational print suppliers,
Promotional finishers, Web offset
M   f

British Printing Society   (BPS)   1944
■   19 Hillbrow Rd, BOURNEMOUTH, Dorset, BH6 5NT.   (hsp)
email enquiries@bpsnet.org.uk
Sec: Teresa St Clair
▲   Un-incorporated Society
Br   20; Germany, Italy, Japan, N Zealand, South Africa, Spain,
USA
○   *G; to unite full-time, part-time & hobby printers in friendly
association; to improve the standards of craftsmanship of its
members; to encourage printing as a hobby
Gp   Publishing; Blockmaking; Letterpress; Bookbinding; Printing (25
specialist printers)
●   Conf - Mtgs - Exhib - Inf - Lib - VE
M   400 i, UK / 30 i, o'seas
(Sub: £20 UK / £30 o'seas)
¶   Small Printer - 12.   Small Printing - 1.
Basic Letterpress for Beginners (Jubilee issue).
1: History of Printing Ink.
2: Glossary of Printing Terms.
3: Index to ISPA News & Small Printer (Pt 1) 1954-82.
4: The Adana Collection: a history of the Adana Company &
its machines.

British Private Equity & Venture Capital Association
alternative name of **BVCA (British Private Equity & Venture
Capital Association)**

British Professional Pool Players Association
NR   23 Kendal Rd, Stretford Marina, MANCHESTER, M32 0DZ.
http://www.bpppa.org
○   *S

British Professional Toastmasters Authority   1995
■   12 Little Bornes, Dulwich, LONDON, SE21 8SE.   (chmn/b)
020 8670 5585   fax 020 8670 0055
http://www.ivorspencer.com
○   *P; to monitor all aspects of the profession & to provide
comprehensive advice (for which there is a charge) to
companies regarding the profession
●   Conf - Exam
<   Gld of Intl Profl Toastmasters
M   20 affiliated toastmasters

British Promotional Merchandise Association   (BPMA)   1965
■   Arena House, 66-68 Pentonville Rd, LONDON, N1 9HS.   (hq)
020 7689 5555   fax 020 7837 5326
email enquiries@bpma.co.uk   http://www.bpma.co.uk
Co Sec: Colin Levine
▲   Company Limited by Guarantee
○   *T; to bring together buyers & sellers within the promotional
merchandise industry
●   ET - Res - Exhib - Inf - LG
<   Marketing Assn Alliance
M   700 f
(Sub: £375-£750)
¶   Promotions Buyer - 12; free.
bpma Directory: the authoritative guide for buyers of
promotional merchandise (2007-2008).
Promotions Buyer [Ybk] - 1; free.

British Property Federation   (BPF)   1974
NR   1 Warwick Row (7th floor), LONDON, SW1E 5ER.   (hq)
020 7828 0111   fax 020 7834 3442
email info@bpf.org.uk   http://www.bpf.org.uk
Chief Exec: Liz Peace,   Co Sec: Alice McMahon
▲   Company Limited by Guarantee
○   *T; to represent the views of the property industry, both
commercial & residential
Gp   Ad hoc working parties & standing c'ees on different aspects of
Taxation, Planning, the Environment
●   Conf - Mtgs - Res - Inf - LG
<   Eur Property Fedn
M   430 i, f & org
¶   AR; free.

British Protected Ornamentals Association   (BPOA)   1980
NR   PO Box 475, HUNTINGDON, Cambs, PE28 3YP.   (hq)
0870 241 6526
http://www.thebbpa.org.uk
Sec: Dawn Smith
○   *H, *T; 'to represent bedding & pot plant growers in aspects of
promotion, political & technical issues relating to their
business'
●   Conf - Mtgs - ET - Res - Exhib - SG - Stat - Inf - PL - VE - Empl -
LG - Social events
<   Nat Farmers U
M   180+ i, 100 f, 25 org
¶   NL - 12;   News & Views - 4; both ftm only.
✕   2007 British Bedding & Pot Plant Association

British Psychoanalytic Council   (BPC)   1993
■   West Hill House, 6 Swains Lane, LONDON, N6 6QS.   (hq)
020 7267 3626   fax 020 7267 4772
email mail@psychoanalytic-council.org
http://www.psychoanalytic-council.org
Chief Exec: Malcolm Allen
▲   Company Limited by Guarantee
○   *N; an association of training institutions & professional
associations of psychoanalysts, Jungian analysts,
psychoanalytic psychotherapists & child psychotherapists
●   Conf - Mtgs - ET - Res - LG
<   Eur Fedn of Psychoanalytic Psychotherapists (EFPP)
>   Soc of Analytical Psychology; Brit Psychoanalytical Soc; Brit Assn
of Psychotherapists; Scot Assn of Psychoanalytic
Psychotherapists; NI Assn for the Study of Psychoanalysis
M   1,700 i
(Sub: £98)
¶   Register of Psychotherapists - 1; ftm, £35 nm.
NL - 2;   AR - 1; both ftm only.
Brochures:
What is Psychoanalytic Psychotherapy? free.
Making sense of Psychotherapy and Psychoanalysis; £1.50.
✕   2005-06 British Confederation of Psychotherapists

British Psychoanalytical Society   1913
NR   Byron House, 112A Shirland Rd, LONDON, W9 2EQ.
    020 7563 5000   fax 020 7563 5001
    http://www.psychoanalysis.org.uk
    Hon Sec: M Mercer
▲   Registered Charity
○   *L, *P; promotion & dissemination of the theory & practice of
    Freudian psychoanalysis
●   Conf - Mtgs - ET - Inf - Lib - VE
<   Intl Psychoanalytical Assn; Eur Psychoanalytical Fedn
M   352 i, UK / 97 i, o'seas
¶   International Jnl of Psychoanalysis - 6.

British Psychodrama Association   (BPA)   1984
NR   Flat 1/1, 105 Hyndland Rd, GLASGOW, G12 9JD.   (hq)
    0141-339 0141
▲   Company Limited by Guarantee
○   *L, *P; to promote & encourage the use of psychodrama
M   i & org

British Psychological Society   (BPS)   1901
■   St Andrews House, 48 Princess Rd East, LEICESTER, LE1 7DR.
    (hq)
    0116-254 9568   fax 0116-247 0787
    email mail@bps.org.uk   http://www.bps.org.uk
    Hon Sec: A Sabbadini
▲   Registered Charity
Br   7
○   *L, *P; advancement of knowledge of psychology both pure &
    applied
Gp   Sections: Cognitive, Consciousness, Developmental, Education,
    History & philosophy, Lesbian & gay, Mathematical,
    Psychobiology, Psychotherapy, Social, Sports & exercise,
    Statistical & computing, Transpersonal, Women
    Divisions: Clinical, Counselling, Educational, Forensic, Health,
    Neuropsychology, Occupational, Teachers & researchers;
    Special groups: Social services
●   Conf - Mtgs - ET - Exam - LG
<   Eur Fedn of Psychological Assns
M   38, 485 i, UK / 3,705 i, o'seas
¶   The Psychologist - 12; ftm, £66 yr nm.
    British Jnl of Psychology - 4; £17 m.
    British Jnl of Clinical Psychology - 4.
    British Jnl of Developmental Psychology - 4.
    British Jnl of Educational Psychology - 4.
    British Jnl of Health Psychology - 4.
    British Jnl of Mathematical & Statistical Psychology - 2.
    Jnl of Occupational & Organisational Psychology - 4.
    Psychology & Psychotherapy - 4.
    Legal & Criminological Psychotherapy - 2.

British Pteridological Society   (BPS)   1891
NR   c/o Dept of Botany, Natural History Museum, Cromwell Rd,
    LONDON, SW7 5BD.   (mail/address)
    020 8850 3218   fax 010 8850 3218
    email secretary@ebps.org.uk   http://www.ebps.org.uk
    Gen Sec: Dr Yvonne C Golding
▲   Registered Society
○   *H, *L, *Q; study, growing & conservation of ferns & other
    pteridophytes
Gp   Tree-ferns
●   Conf - Mtgs - ET - SG - Inf - VE - Spore & plant exchange
<   Nat Coun Consvn Plants & Gardens; Plantlife; R Horticl Society
M   478 i, UK / 248 i, o'seas
¶   Fern Gazette - 1;   Pteridologist - 1;   Bulletin - 1; all ftm only.
    Special publications series - irreg.

British Pugwash Group   1959
■   Ground floor flat, 63A Great Russell St, LONDON,
    WC1B 3BJ.   (hq)
    020 7405 6661
    email pugwash@mac.com   http://www.pugwash.org/uk
    Sec: Dr Christopher Watson
▲   Un-incorporated Society
○   *L; social implications of development of science & technology,
    especially in military area (international relations, nuclear
    weapons, peace research, science policy); education &
    dissemination of information
●   Conf - Mtgs - ET - Res
<   Pugwash Conferences on Science & World Affairs
M   240 i, UK / 10 i, o'seas
¶   Pugwash NL - 2.   BPG Reports - irreg;   Occasional Reports.

British Pump Manufacturers' Association   (BPMA)   1941
NR   National Metalforming Centre, 47 Birmingham Rd,
    WEST BROMWICH, W Midlands, B70 6PY.   (hq)
    0121-601 6350   fax 0121-601 6373
    email admin@bpma.org.uk   http://www.bpma.org.uk
    Dir: Brian Huxley
○   *T; liquid pumps
Gp   C'ees: Marketing/commercial; Marketing data; Small firms;
    Technical; Training
●   Conf - Mtgs - ET - Res - Expt - Inf - LG
<   C'ee Eur Pump Assns (EUROPUMP); Mechanical & Metal Trs
    Confedn (METCOM)
M   c 80 f
¶   Pumps from Britain - 2 yrly.

British Puppet & Model Theatre Guild   (BPMTG)   1925
■   65 Kingsley Ave, LONDON, W13 0EH.   (chmn/p)
    020 8997 8236   fax 020 8997 8236
    email peter@peterpuppet.co.uk
    http://www.puppetguild.org.uk
    Hon Chmn: Peter Charlton
○   *D; to advocate the use of puppets & model theatres; to
    encourage the art & practice of puppetry
●   Mtgs - Inf - Shows
M   c 270 i & org
¶   Puppet Master - 1;   NL - 12; both ftm.

British Pyrotechnists Association   (BPA)   1980
■   8 Aragon Place, Kimbolton, HUNTINGDON, Cambs,
    PE28 0JD.   (hsb)
    01480 861975   fax 01480 861108
    email enquiries@bpa-fmg.org.uk
    http://www.pyro.org.uk
    Sec: Dr Tom Smith
▲   Registered Charity
○   *T; a non-commercial organisation promoting the safe
    manufacture, handling & use of pyrotechnics
●   Mtgs - Exam - Stat - Inf - LG
<   Eur Fireworks Assn (EUFIAS)
M   36 f
    (Sub: £450)

British Quadrathlon Association   (BQA)   1995
■   105A Sedbergh Rd, KENDAL, Cumbria, LA9 6BE.   (hsp)
    01539 727350   fax 01539 741512
    email claire@acorncoaching.com
    http://www.britishquadrathlon.org.uk
    Sec: Claire Longney
▲   Un-incorporated Society
○   *S; to promote & suport the sport of quadrathlon (swimming,
    cycling, kayaking & running)
●   Comp
<   Wld Quadrathalon Fedn
M   50 i
    (Sub: 15)

© CBD Research Ltd · Beckenham · BR3 5JS · Tel 020 8650 7745 · Fax 020 8650 0768 · E-mail cbd@cbdresearch.com · www.cbdresearch.com

British Quality Foundation   (BQF)   1993
NR   32-34 Great Peter St, LONDON, SW1P 2QX.   (hq)
　　 020 7654 5000
▲   Company Limited by Guarantee
○   *T; 'total quality management & business excellence'
Gp　Automotive; Construction; Education & training; Engineering,
　　 projects & operations; Financial services; Food & drink;
　　 Founder members; Health; IT & telecommunications;
　　 Insurance; Local authorities; Printing, paper, packaging &
　　 media; Social care; T Q professionals; Tourism & hospitality
●   Conf - Mtgs - ET - Res - SG - Inf - Lib
M　 f
¶   UK Excellence - 6.

British Quilt Study Group
　　 a group of the **Quilters' Guild of the British Isles**

British Rabbit Council   (BRC)   1918
■   Purefoy House, 7 Kirkgate, NEWARK, Notts, NG24 1AD.   (hq)
　　 01636 676042   fax 01636 611683
　　 email info@thebrc.org   http://www.thebrc.org
　　 Co Sec: Mrs Susan Mason,   Hon Treas: J F Fletcher
▲   Un-incorporated Society
○   *B; for breeders of pure-bred & show rabbits
●   Conf - Mtgs - Exhib - Comp - Inf - Lib
M　 2,436 i, 220 org
　　 (Sub: varies)
¶   Fur & Feather (inc Rabbits) - 12; £3.50 m only.

British Racing & Sports Car Club   (BRSCC)   1946
NR   Homesdale Business Centre, Platt Industrial Estate,
　　 Maidstone Rd, BOROUGH GREEN, Kent, TN15 8JL.   (hq)
　　 01732 780100
○   *S; organisation of motor racing
M　 i

British Radio Car Association   (BRCA)   1972
■   Park View, Uffculme, CULLOMPTON, Devon, EX15 3DN.
　　 (mem/sp)
　　 01884 840158   fax 01884 840158
　　 email membership@brca.org   http://www.brca.org
　　 Mem Sec: Jacquie Rowcliffe
○   *G; to organise all aspects of radio controlled model car racing
　　 in Britain
●   Organising races
<   RAC
M　 9,500 i, 230 clubs
¶   Circuit Chatter (NL) - 4;   BRCA Hbk - 1; both ftm only.

British Rally Marshals Club
　　 see **British Motorsport Marshals Club**

British Ready Mixed Concrete Association   (BRMCA)   2005
■   4 Meadows Business Park, Station Approach, Blackwater,
　　 CAMBERLEY, Surrey, GU17 9AB.   (hq)
　　 01276 606800   fax 01276 606801
　　 http://www.brmca.org
○   *T; re-launched with new branding the BRMCA represents the
　　 interests of ready-mixed concrete producers within the
　　 Quarry Products Association; to promote building systems
　　 using ready-mixed concrete; its remit covers generic
　　 technical, environmental & health & safety issues
<   Quarry Products Assn
M　 f

British Record Society Ltd   1888
NR   Richmond Herald, College of Arms, Queen Victoria St,
　　 LONDON, EC4V 4BT.   (hsb)
　　 Hon Sec: P L Dickinson
○   *L
●   Compilation & publication of indexes to historical records,
　　 particularly testamentary records

British Recorded Music Industry Ltd
　　 alternative name of **BPI (British Recorded Music Industry) Ltd**

British Records Association   (BRA)   1932
■   c/o Finsbury Library, 245 St John Street, LONDON,
　　 EC1V 4NB.   (hq)
　　 020 7833 0428   fax 020 7833 0416
　　 email britrecassoc@hotmail.com
　　 http://www.britishrecordsassociation.org.uk
　　 Hon Sec: Catherine Taylor
▲   Registered Charity
○   *L; to encourage & assist the preservation, care, study &
　　 publication of records; acts as a clearing-house & rescue
　　 body for historic documents
Gp　Records preservation
●   Conf - Mtgs - ET - Exhib - SG - Inf - Storage - Preservation
M　 551 i, 416 f (incl museums, galleries, libraries, universities)
　　 (Sub: £25 i, £55 f, £20 org, UK / £35 i, £65 f,
　　 £30 org, o'seas)
¶   Archives (Jnl) - 2; ftm, £55 yr nm.   NL - 2; ftm only.
　　 Archives & User Series (guides to source material for research).
　　 Guidelines 1-5; on website.

British Recovered Paper Association
　　 since 2004 the Recovered Paper Sector of the **Confederation of
　　 Paper Industries**

British Red Cross Society   (BRCS)   1870
NR   44 Moorfields, LONDON, EC2Y 9AL.   (hq)
　　 020 7877 7000   fax 020 7562 2000
　　 email information@redcross.org.uk
　　 http://www.redcross.org.uk
　　 Chief Exec: Sir Nicholas Young
▲   Registered Charity
Br　 70; 8 o'seas
○   *W; an officially recognised organisation for humanitarian aid;
　　 disaster preparedness & response; refugees & asylum
　　 seekers; overseas development; first aid training & health
　　 activities; supporting statutory authorities in UK; community
　　 services, education / youth & schools
●   Conf - Mtgs - ET - Res - Exhib - SG - Stat - Inf - Lib - PL - LG
<   Intl Red Cross; Red Crescent Movement
M　 40,000 i
¶   Lifeline (Jnl).   Information pack.
　　 Annual Review.   Trustees' Report & Accounts.

British Reed Growers' Association   (BRGA)   1967
NR   c/o Brown & Co, Old Bank of England Court, Queen St,
　　 NORWICH, Norfolk, NR2 4TA.   (hsb)
　　 01603 629871   fax 01603 760756
　　 email ilonsdale@brown-co.com
　　 http://www.mhp-ltd.co.uk (associate's site)
　　 Sec: I D Lonsdale,   Chmn: R Buxton
▲   Un-incorporated Society
○   *T; promotion of reed & sedge growing; coordination of supply
　　 to thatchers, monitoring supply & demand; promotion of
　　 research into improved production
●   Mtgs - Res - Stat - Inf - LG
M　 16 i, 5 f, 15 org
¶   Reedbed Management for Commercial & Wildlife
　　 Interests; £14.95 (published by RSPB).
　　 Norfolk Reed Roofing Today;   Buying & Selling Reed;
　　 Reedbed Management for Bitterns;
　　 New Wetland Harvests - New Life for the Broads Fens; all free.

British Reflexology Association   (BRA)   1985
- Monks Orchard, Whitbourne, WORCESTER, WR6 5RB.   (hq)
  - 01886 821207   fax 01886 822017
  - email bra@britreflex.co.uk   http://www.britreflex.co.uk
  - Chmn: Miss Nicola Hall
- ▲ Company Limited by Guarantee
- ○ *P; to promote the practice of reflexology
- ● Conf - Mtgs - Res - Inf
- < Reflexology in Europe Network (RIEN)
- M 700 i
- ¶ Footprints (NL) - 4; £10 yr (UK) (£13 Europe).

British Refractories & Industrial Ceramics   (BRIC)   1918
- NR Federation House, Station Rd, STOKE-ON-TRENT, Staffs,
  - ST4 2SA.   (hq)
  - 01782 744631   fax 01782 744102
  - email bcc@ceramfed.co.uk   http://www.ceramfed.co.uk
  - Sec: Pauline Neate
- ○ *T
- ● Conf - Mtgs - ET - Stat - Inf
- < Eur Refractories Fedn; Brit Ceramic Confedn
- M 35 f

British Refrigeration Association   (BRA)   1940
- 2 Waltham Court, Milley Lane, Hare Hatch, READING, Berks,
  - RG10 9TH.   (hq)
  - 0118-940 3416   fax 0118-940 6258
  - email info@feta.co.uk   http://www.feta.co.uk/
  - Dir Gen: C Sloan
- ○ *T; the interests of the refrigeration & air conditioning plant &
  equipment industry
- Gp Refrigeration machinery & air conditioning machinery; Cabinet
  & cold store; Contractors; Components; Education &
  training; Statistics; Users & specifiers
- ● Conf - Mtgs - ET - Exhib - SG - Stat - Inf - Lib - VE - Empl
- < Fedn Envtl Tr Assns (FETA)
- M 84 f
- ¶ NL - 4; ftm.   LM - 1;   AR; both free.

**British Register of Complementary Practitioners   (ICM-BRCP)
1989**
- NR 25 Tavern Quay Business Centre, Sweden Gate, LONDON,
  - SE16 7TX.   (hq)
  - 020 7231 5855
  - Chief Exec: Michael Endacott
- ▲ Registered Charity
- ○ *P; to provide a register for referral of practitioners
  professionally trained, subject where appropriate to clinical
  supervision - insured for professional indemnity & public
  liability - governed by a code of practice & ethics
- Gp Divisions: Aromatherapy, Chinese medicine, Colour therapy,
  Counselling, Energy medicine, Healer counselling,
  Homoeopathy, Hypnotherapy, Massage, Nutrition,
  Osteopathy, Reflexology
- ● Registration
- M i

British Reining
  a discipline member of the **British Equestrian Federation**

British Resorts & Destinations Association   (BRADA)   1921
- Crown Buildings, 9-11 Eastbank St, SOUTHPORT, Merseyside,
  - PR8 1DL.   (hsb)
  - 0151-934 2286   fax 0151-934 2287
  - email bresorts@sefton.u-net.com
  - http://www.britishresorts.co.uk
  - Hon Sec: Mr G Haywood   Dir: Peter Hampson
- ○ *T; interests of UK inland & seaside resorts & tourist regions
- ● Conf - Mtgs
- M 60 local authorities, 8 tourist boards
- ¶ AR; m only.
- × 2006 (1 April) British Resorts Association

British Retail Consortium   (BRC)   1992
- 21 Dartmouth St (2nd floor), LONDON, SW1H 9BP.   (hq)
  - 020 7854 8900   fax 020 7854 8901
  - email info@brc.org.uk   http://www.brc.org.uk
  - Dir Gen: Stephen Robertson
- ▲ Company Limited by Guarantee
- Br Edinburgh; Belgium
- ○ *T; 'represents over 90% of the retail industry'
- < EUROCOMMERCE (retail, wholesale & international trade
  representation to the European Community)
- M f

British Retinitis Pigmentosa Society   (BRPS)   1975
- PO Box 350, BUCKINGHAM, MK18 1GZ.   (hsp)
  - 01280 821334 (office)   fax 01280 815900
  - email info@brps.org.uk   http://www.brps.org.uk +
  - fightingblindness.org.uk
  - Chief Exec: David Head
- ▲ Registered Charity
- Br 30 & o'seas
- ○ *W; to raise funds for scientific research; to provide treatments
  leading to a cure for RP; to provide a welfare support &
  guidance service to members & their families
- ● Res - Inf - Provision of a welfare & guidance service to
  members
  - Helpline: 0845 123 2354 - helpline@brps.org.uk
- < Retina Intl; Assn Med Res Charities (AMRC); Genetic Interest
  Gp (GIG)
- M c 3,000 i
  - (Sub: £15)
- ¶ NL - 4.   e-bulletin - 12.
  Publications list available.

British Rig Owners' Association   (BROA)   1983
- Carthusian Court, 12 Carthusian St, LONDON, EC1M 6EZ.
  - (hq)
  - 020 7417 2827   fax 020 7726 2080
  - email edmund.brookes@broa.org
  - Gen Mgr: E J N Brookes
- ○ *T; promote & protect the interests of British oil rig owners &
  managers
- ● Mtgs - SG - Inf - LG
- M 9 f

**British Rigid Urethane Foam Manufacturers' Association Ltd
(BRUFMA)   1967**
- 12A High St East, GLOSSOP, Derbys, SK13 8DA.   (hq)
  - 01457 855884
- ▲ Company Limited by Guarantee
- ○ *T; interests of manufacturers, raw materials & chemicals
  suppliers & machinery manufacturers of rigid urethane foam
- Gp Technical; Building applications; Environmental health & safety
- ● Conf - Mtgs - LG
- < Fedn of Eur Rigid Polyurethane Foam Assns (BING); Brit Plastics
  Fedn
- M 18 f
- ¶ LM - on change of details.   AR.
  Information Documents - irreg.

British Roll Label Association
  since 2005 a special interest group (BPIF Labels) of the **British
  Printing Industries Federation**

British Rootzone & Top Dressing Manufacturers Association (BRTMA) 2000
NR Federation House, STONELEIGH PARK, Warks, CV8 2RF. (hq)
024 7641 4999 fax 024 7641 4990
email brtma@sportsandplay.com
http://www.brtma.com
Sec: Jacqui Baldwin
▲ Un-incorporated Society
○ *T; 'manufacture of quality construction mixes & top dressings'
● Mtgs - ET - Res - Stat - Inf
< a group of the Fedn of Sports & Play Assns (FSPA)
M 11 f
¶ Ybk - 1; free.

British Rope Skipping Association (BRSA)
NR 39 Riverside, STUDLEY, Warks, B80 7SD.
01527 854194
http://www.brsa.org.uk
Sec: Sue Dale
○ *G, *S

British Rose Group (formerly the British Rose Growers Association)
a specialist group of the **Horticultural Trades Association**

British Rouge de l'Ouest Sheep Society (Rouge Society)
NR Marstonmill Farm, Wolston, COVENTRY, Warks, CV8 3FX.
0845 600 1503
http://www.rouge-society.co.uk
Sec: Mrs Sue Archer
▲ Company Limited by Guarantee; Registered Charity
○ *B
< Nat Sheep Assn
M c 120 i

British Rubber Manufacturers' Association Ltd
since 2005 **British Tyre Manufacturers Association**

British Rubber & Polyurethane Products Association (BRPPA) 2006
NR 6 Bath Place, Rivington St, LONDON, EC2A 3JE.
020 7457 5040 fax 020 7972 9008
http://www.brppa.co.uk

British Saddleback Breeders Club 1995
■ Freepost (GL442), CIRENCESTER, Glos, GL7 5BR. (hsp)
01285 860229 fax 01285 860229
email mail@saddlebacks.org.uk
http://www.saddlebacks.org.uk
Hon Sec: Richard Lutwyche
▲ Un-incorporated Society
○ *B
● Mtgs - Comp - Workshops
M 120 i, 5 f, UK / 2 i, o'seas
¶ NL.
✕ 2007 British Saddleback Pig Breeders Club

British Safety Industry Federation (BSIF) 1994
■ 93 Bowen Court, St Asaph Business Park, ST ASAPH, Denbighs, LL17 0JE. (asa)
01745 585600 fax 01745 585800
email b.s.i.f@virgin.net http://www.bsif.co.uk
Dec Gen: Geoff Hooke
▲ Company Limited by Guarantee
○ *T
Gp Personal Safety Manufacturers Association;
Pipe manufacturers; Safety distributors; Safety products manufacturers; Testing & certification organisations; Safety professionals
● Conf - Mtgs - Exam - Res - Exhib - Expt - Inf - Lib - LG
< Eur Safety Fedn
M 162 f
¶ BSIF Guide - 1; Health & Safety Matters - 6; both free.

British Sailing
a group of the **British Marine Federation**

British Sandwich Association (BSA) 1990
NR Association House, 18c Moor St, CHEPSTOW, Monmouthshire, NP16 5DB. (hq)
01291 636331 fax 01291 630402
email admin@sandwich.org.uk
http://www.sandwich.org.uk
Dir: Jim Winship
○ *T; to raise standards in the UK sandwich industry
● Conf - Mtgs - Res - Comp - Inf - VE - LG
M 1,450 i & f, UK / 87 i & f, o'seas
¶ Sandwich & Snack News - 8; ftm, £55 yr nm.

British Sausage Appreciation Society (BSAS) 1992
■ PO Box 44 Winterhill House, Snowdon Drive, MILTON KEYNES, Bucks, MK6 1AX. (hq)
01908 844194 fax 01908 671722
email theresa.bignall@ahdbms.org.uk
http://www.meatmatters.com
Sec: Alison Cook
▲ Un-incorporated Society
○ *G; to promote interest in British sausage eating & the range of sausages available in Britain
● ET - Comp - Inf - Promotional roadshow
¶ The Missing Link - 1.

British Science Fiction Association Ltd (BSFA) 1958
NR 39 Glyn Ave, NEW BARNET, Herts, EN4 9PJ. (msp)
http://www.bsfa.co.uk
Mem Sec: Peter Wilkinson
▲ Company Limited by Guarantee
○ *A, *G; promotion of science fiction & related genre in all media
Gp Orbiter: postal writers' workshops
● Inf - Publishing
M 550 i, UK / 50 i, o'seas
¶ Vector (Jnl) - 6; Matrix (NL) - 6; Focus (Writers' Jnl) - 2; all ftm.

British Scoliosis Society
a specialist society of the **British Orthopaedic Association**

British Scooter Sport Organisation (BSSO) 1969
NR 219 Elmers End Rd, BECKENHAM, Kent, BR3 4EL. (sp)
020 8658 4378 fax 020 8249 3510
email sylvia.caldecutt@ntlworld.com
http://www.scooterracing.org.uk
Gen Sec: Sylvia Caldecutt
○ *S; to promote scooter road racing
Gp Road racing: Scooter cross (off road, on grass)
● Mtgs - Comp
< Auto-Cycle U
> Lambretta Club of GB; Vespa Club of GB
M 100 i, 500 org
¶ NL - 12; ftm only.

British Security Industry Association Ltd (BSIA) 1967
■ Kirkham House, John Comyn Drive, WORCESTER, WR3 7NS. (hq)
  0845 389 3889   fax 0845 389 0761
  email info@bsia.co.uk   http://www.bsia.co.uk
  Chief Exec: David Dickinson
▲ Company Limited by Guarantee
○ *T; to represent the security sector; members have to adhere to British standards & codes of practice
Gp Security Manufacturers' Export Council
  Cash & property marking; Cash & valuables in transit; Closed circuit television; Information destruction; Physical security; Security guarding; Security systems
● Conf - Mtgs - Res - Exhib - Comp - Stat - Expt - Inf - LG - Formation of technical standards & codes of practice
< Eurosafe; Euralarm; CoESS
M 450 f, UK / 10 f, o'seas
¶ Spectrum (NL) - 2;   Security Direct (directory) - 1; both free. LM - 6; free (& on website). Publications list on website.

British Sedimentological Research Group
  a group of the **Geological Society**

British Shakespeare Association (BSA) 2003
NR 79 Marsham St, Suite 6.17, LONDON, SW1P 4SB.
  http://www.britishshakespeare.ws
  Co & Mem Sec: Susan Ronald
○ *A

British Sheep Dairying Association (BSDA) 1983
NR The Estate Office, Torry Hill, Milstead, SITTINGBOURNE, Kent, ME9 0SP. (hsp)
  email anthony.hyde@farmline.com
  http://www.sheepdairying.co.uk
○ *T; to sponsor the improvement of dairy sheep in the UK; to promote the marketing of sheep milk
Gp Sheep milk marketing; Milk products
● Conf - Comp - SG - Expt - Inf - VE - LG
< Schweiz Milchschafzucht-Genossenschaft; N Amer Sheep Dairying Soc
M c 300 i
¶ Sheep Dairy News (Jnl) - 3; ftm.

British Shell Collectors Club (BSCC) 1972
■ 38 Redlands Rd, READING, Berks, RG1 5HD.   (hsp)
  0118-987 4294
  email tom@tmwalker.co.uk
  http://www.britishshellclub.org.uk
  Hon Sec: Tom Walker
○ *G, *L; to promote the study of all aspects of shells, both land & marine, British & foreign, & of the molluscs which produce them
● Exhib - Comp
M c 230 i
¶ Pallidula (NL) - 2; ftm only.

British Shippers Council
  a group of the **Freight Transport Association**

British Shogi Federation (BSF)
NR 29 Lavender Close, CORBY, Northants, NN18 8NX.   (hsp)
  Sec/Treas: Stuart Patterson
Br 3
○ *S; the play & study of Shogi (Japanese chess) & its variants
● Comp - British Shogi championship
< Fedn of Eur Shogi Assns (FESA); Nihon Shogi Renmai (Japanese Shogi Assn)
M c 60 i

British Shooting 1988
■ Edmonton House, Bisley Camp, BROOKWOOD, Surrey, GU24 0NP.   (hq)
  01483 486948   fax 01483 486940
  http://www.britishshooting.org.uk
  Hon Sec: Keith Murray
▲ Un-incorporated Society
○ *N, *S; a coordinating body for services & international events undertaken by target shooting associations
M 4 org & 4 national bodies (England, Scotland, Wales & N Ireland)
✕ 2007 Great Britain Target Shooting Federation

British Shooting Sports Council (BSSC) 1978
■ PO Box 53608, LONDON, SE24 9YN.   (hsb)
  020 7095 8181
  email djpbssc@btconnect.com   http://www.bssc.org.uk
  Sec: David Penn
▲ Un-incorporated Society
○ *S; to promote shooting sports & firearms legislation
● Conf - Mtgs - Res - Inf - LG
< Wld Forum on the Future of Sports Shooting Activities (WFSA)
M 12 affiliated org:
  Association of Professional Clay Target Shooting Grounds
  Association of Professional Shooting Instructors
  British Association for Shooting & Conservation
  Countryside Alliance
  Clay Pigeon Shooting Association
  Gun Trade Association
  Institute of Clay Shooting Instructors
  Muzzle Loaders Association of GB
  National Rifle Association
  National Smallbore Rifle Association
  Sportsman's Association of GB & NI
  UK Practical Shooting Association
¶ AR; ftm, £5 nm (free from website).

British Shops & Stores Association (bssa) 1989
■ Middleton House, 2 Main Rd, Middleton Cheney, BANBURY, Oxon, OX17 2TN.   (hq)
  01295 712277   fax 01295 711665
  email info@british-shops.co.uk   http://www.bssa.co.uk
  Chief Exec: John Dean
▲ Company Limited by Shares
○ *T; a non-food trade association for independent small retail businesses
● Conf - Mtgs - ET - VE - LG
M 4,000 f
¶ Retail Alert - 12 (online).

British Shorinji Kempo Federation (BSKF) 1974
NR 864 Harrow Rd, WEMBLEY, Middx, HA0 2PX.
  020 8908 6265   fax 020 8385 1821
  email skmizuno@freeuk.com   http://www.bskf.org
  Chief Instructor: Sensei Tameo Mizuno
▲ Un-incorporated Society
○ *S; Shorinji Kempo (a Japanese martial art incorporating punching, kicking & blocking techniques with releases, pins & throws, combined with meditation, therapeutic massage & basic philosophy)

British Show Horse Association (BSHA) 1936
NR 2 High St, HITCHIN, Herts, SG5 1BH.   (hq)
  01462 437770   fax 01462 437776
  http://www.britishshowhorse.org
  Sec: Tracy Hullat
▲ Company Limited by Guarantee
○ *S; to promote the showing & breeding of the ridden hack, cob & riding horse; to promote equine welfare
● Conf - Mtgs - ET - Comp
M c 1,500 i
¶ NL - 4.
✕ 2008 British Show Hack, Cob & Riding Horse Association

© CBD Research Ltd · Beckenham · BR3 5JS · Tel 020 8650 7745 · Fax 020 8650 0768 · E-mail cbd@cbdresearch.com · www.cbdresearch.com

British Show Jumping Association
is a discipline member of the **British Equestrian Federation**

British Show Pony Society (BSPS) 1949
- ■ 124 Green End Rd, Sawtry, HUNTINGDON, Cambs,
  PE28 5XS. (hq)
  01487 831376   fax 01487 832779
  Chief Exec/Sec: Mrs P J Hall
- ▲ Limited Company
- ○ *S; to promote & encourage the showing of children's ponies
  via classes & competitions for show ponies, show hunter
  ponies, working hunter ponies, & mountain & moorland, for
  riders between the ages of 3 and 25 & ponies up to 15.2hh
- ● Mtgs
- M 4,601 i, 20 f
- ¶ News Review - 10; £20.   Ybk - 1; £25.   Rule Book; free.

British Sign & Graphics Association Ltd (BSGA) 1977
- ■ 5 Orton Enterprise Centre, Bakewell Rd, Orton Southgate,
  PETERBOROUGH, Cambs, PE2 6XU.   (hq)
  01733 230033   fax 01733 230993
  email info@bsga.co.uk   http://www.bsga.co.uk
  Dir/Co Sec: Albert W Baxter
- ▲ Company Limited by Guarantee
- Br 1
- ○ *T; interests of sign manufacturers & traders in the UK
- Gp Sign manufacture - illuminated & non-illuminated; Sign writing;
  Publicity items - banners, buntings, flags, plaques etc
- ● Mtgs - ET - Exhib - LG
- < Eur Sign Fedn; Inst of Assn Mgt
- M 240 f, UK / 14 f, o'seas
- ¶ BSGA News - 4; ftm.

British Simmental Cattle Society Ltd (BSCS) 1971
- ■ NAC, Stoneleigh Park, KENILWORTH, Warks, CV8 2LG. (hq)
  024 7669 6513   fax 024 7669 6724
  email information@britishsimmental.co.uk
  http://www.britishsimmental.co.uk
- ▲ Registered Charity
- ○ *B
- M 1,400 i, UK / 200 i, o'seas
- ¶ Review - 1; ftm, £12 nm.

British Sjogren's Syndrome Association (BSSA) 1987
- NR PO Box 10867, BIRMINGHAM, B16 0ZW. (hq)
  0121-455 6532
  email kate@bssa.uk.net   http://www.bssa.uk.net
  Office Mgr: Kate Endacott
- ▲ Company Limited by Guarantee; Registered Charity
- Br 15 regional groups
- ○ *W; to provide information on Sjogren's Syndrome (an auto-
  immune disorder in which the body's immune system turns
  against itself, destroying the mucous-secreting glands as
  though they were foreign bodies); to spread information on
  alleviation of the symptoms; to support medical research
- ● Mtgs - Res - Inf
- M c 2,500 i, UK & o'seas
- ¶ Sjogren's Today - 4; ftm, £2.50 per back issue nm.
  New Sjogren's Hbk (3rd ed 2005); £17.50 m, £18.50 nm.
  Advisory Guide for Patients & Doctors; ftm, £2.50 nm
  (£3.50 o'seas).

British Skeet Shooting Association (BSSA) 1985
- NR c/o Lakenheath Clay Target Centre, Brandon Rd, Eriswell,
  BRANDON, Suffolk, IP27 9FB.   (sb)
  01638 533353   fax 01638 532037
  email info@mynssa.co.uk   http://www.mynssa.co.uk
  Custodian Sec: Peter Usher
- ○ *S

British Skewbald & Piebald Association (BSPA) 1989
- NR Stanley House, Silt Drove, Tipps End, Welney, WISBECH,
  Cambs, PE14 9SL.
  01354 638226
  http://www.bspaonline.com
  Sec: Mrs Alice Neaves
- ▲ Un-incorporated Society
- ○ *B
- ● Mtgs - Comp - Inf - Registration - Stallion licensing - Shows
- < Brit Horse Database; Brit Cent Prefix Register
- M c 1,800 i, f & org
- ¶ NL - 3;   Hbk; both ftm only.
  Stallion List - 1; on application.

British Ski Club for the Disabled
is part of Disability Snowsport UK & is therefore outside the
scope of this directory.

British Ski & Snowboard Federation
registered name of **Snowsport GB**

British Slate Association
a group of **Stone Federation Great Britain**

British Sleep Society (BSS) 1989
- ■ PO Box 247, Colne, HUNTINGDON, Cambs, PE28 3UZ. (hq)
  fax 01480 840618
  email bssoffice@btopenworld.com
  http://www.sleeping.org.uk
  Hon Sec: Paul Reading
- ▲ Registered Charity
- ○ *L, *Q; to promote knowledge & research in sleep & its
  disorders & treatment
- ● Conf - Mtgs - ET - Res - SG
- < Wld Fedn of Sleep Res Socs; Eur Sleep Res Soc
- M 500 i, 10 f, UK / 30 i, o'seas
- ¶ NL - 2; ftm, £5 nm.   Conference Papers Abstracts - 1.

British Slot Car Racing Association (BSCRA) 1964
- ■ 48 Wiltshire Gardens, Bransgore, CHRISTCHURCH, Dorset,
  BH23 8BJ.   (hsp)
  01425 672060
  email info@bscra.co.uk   http://www.bscra.co.uk
  Hon Sec: C M Frost
- ▲ Un-incorporated Society
- Br 64; 13 countries o'seas
- ○ *G, *S; controlling body for slot car racing in the UK; the cars
  are controlled by a guide running in a slot in the track, (NOT
  radio-controlled)
- ● Conf - Mtgs - Exhib - Comp - Inf - Promotion of national &
  international championships
- < Intl Slot Racing Assn (ISRA)
- M 300 i, 64 org, UK / 13 org, o'seas
- ¶ Slot Car Racing News - 4; ftm, £20 yr nm.
  Members Handbook - 2 yrly; ftm, £3 nm.
  [subscription, £20 yr].

British Small Animal Veterinary Association   (BSAVA)   1956
- ■ Woodrow House, 1 Telford Way, Waterwells Business Park, Quedgeley, GLOUCESTER, GL2 2AB.   (hq)
  01452 726700   fax 01452 726701
  email customerservices@bsava.com
  http://www.bsava.com
  Hon Sec: Alison Speakman
- ▲ Registered Charity
- Br 13 regions; 1
- ○ *P; to foster & promote high scientific & educational standards in small animal medicine & surgery
- Gp Association of British Veterinary Acupuncture
  Association of Veterinary Anaesthetists
  Association of Veterinary Clinical Pharmacology & Therapeutics
  Association of Veterinary Soft Tissue Surgery
  British Association of Veterinary Emergency Care
  British Association of Veterinary Ophthalmologists
  British Veterinary Dental Association
  British Veterinary Dermatology Study Group
  British Veterinary Neurology Study Group
  Companion Animal Behaviour Therapy Study Group
  Veterinary Cardiovascular Society
  Veterinary Orthopaedic Association
  European Society for Feline Medicine
- ● Conf - Mtgs - ET - Res - Exhib - SG - Stat - Inf - LG
- < Wld Small Animal Veterinary Assn (WSAVA); Fedn of Eur Companion Animal Veterinary Assns (FECAVA); Brit Veterinary Assn (BVA)
- M c 5,600 i
- ¶ Jnl of Small Animal Practice - 12; ftm.
  Manuals & CD-ROMs:
    Practice Resource Manual.
    Client Information leaflets.

British Small Boatbuilders Association
  a group of the **British Marine Federation**

British Snoring & Sleep Apnoea Association   (BSSAA)   1991
- § Castle Court, 41 London Rd, REIGATE, Surrey, RH2 9RJ.   (hq)
  01737 245638   fax 0870 052 9212
  email info@britishsnoring.co.uk
  http://www.britishsnoring.co.uk
  Dir: Marianne Davey
  A not-for-profit organisation dedicated to helping snorers and their bed partners improve their sleep, returning them again to peaceful nights together.

British Society of Aesthetics   (BSA)   1963
- NR Dept of Philosophy, Open University, MILTON KEYNES, Bucks, MK7 6AA.   (hsb)
  http://www.british-aesthetics.org
  Contact: Derek Matravers
- ▲ Company Limited by Guarantee; Registered Charity
- ○ *A, *L; to promote study, research & discussion of the fine arts & related types of experience from a philosophical, sociological, historical, critical & educational standpoint
- ● Conf
- < Intl Assn of Aesthetics; Amer Soc for Aesthetics
- M 170 i
- ¶ British Jnl of Aesthetics - 4.   NL - 2.

British Society for Allergy & Clinical Immunology   (BSACI)   1947
- ■ Queen Anne's Business Centre (Suite 268 / 269), 28 Broadway, LONDON, SW1H 9JX.   (hq)
  020 7340 9614   fax 020 7340 9617
  email info@bsaci.org   http://www.bsaci.org
  Co Sec: Mrs Fiona Rayner
- ▲ Registered Charity
- ○ *L; to advance & encourage the study of allergy & clinical immunology & their recognition as specialised branches of medicine
- Gp Occupational allergy; ENT allergy; Ophthalmology; Primary Health Care; Gastroenterology; Paediatrics; Anaphylaxis; Dermatology
- ● Conf - Mtgs - Res
- < Intl Union Immunological Socs; Intl Assn Allergy & Clinical Immunology; Eur Academy Allergology & Clinical Immunology; Allergy UK; Brit Soc Immunology
- M 400 i, UK / 80 i, o'seas
- ¶ Clinical & Experimental Allergy (Jnl) - 12;
  Allergy Update (NL)- 3;   both ftm only.
  UK Allergy Clinic Database available on website.

British Society for Allergy, Environmental & Nutritional Medicine
  since 2005 **British Society for Ecological Medicine**

British Society of Animal Science   (BSAS)   1943
- NR PO Box 3, PENICUIK, Midlothian, EH26 0RZ.   (hq)
  0131-445 4508   fax 0131-535 3120
  email bsas@sac.ac.uk   http://www.bsas.org.uk
  Chief Exec: Mike Steele
- ▲ Registered Charity
- ○ *E, *L; an educational charity for those interested in animal production, animal products & related sciences
- ● Conf - Mtgs - ET - Res - SG - LG
- < Eur Assn Animal Production; Biosciences Fedn; Genesis Faraday; Assn of Learned & Profl Soc Publishers
- M 600 i, UK / 200 i, o'seas
- ¶ Animal Science - 6.   BSAS Annual Proceedings; ftm, £50 nm.

British Society for Antimicrobial Chemotherapy   (BSAC)   1972
- NR 11 The Wharf, 16 Bridge St, BIRMINGHAM, B1 2JS.   (hq)
  0121-633 0410
  http://www.bsac.org.uk
- ▲ Registered Charity
- ○ *L, *Q; to facilitate the acquisition & dissemination of knowledge in the field of antimicrobial chemotherapy
- Gp Microbiology; Mycology; Virology
- M i

British Society of Audiology   (BSA)   1967
- ■ 80 Brighton Rd, READING, Berks, RG6 1PS.   (hq)
  0118-966 0622   fax 0118-935 1915
  email bsa@thebsa.org.uk   http://www.thebsa.org.uk
  Admin Sec: Jan Deevey,   Hon Sec: Dr Sally Hind
- ▲ Registered Charity
- ○ *P; for professionals working in hearing & balance
- Gp Hearing
  Interest groups: Auditory process, Balance, Paediatric
- ● Conf - Mtgs - ET - SG - Inf
- M 1,169 i, 24 f, UK / 226 i, o'seas
- ¶ International Jnl of Audiology - 12.
  BSA News - 3.

British Society for Cell Biology   (BSCB)   1959
- NR Dept of Biological Science, Firth Court, University of Sheffield, SHEFFIELD, S10 2TN.   (hsb)
  0114-222 4635
  Hon Sec: Prof Elizabeth Smythe
- ○ *L; cell biology including: cell membranes, cell secretions, cytoskeleton, nuclei, growth factors, cell differentiation, cell matrix & cell motility etc

© CBD Research Ltd · Beckenham · BR3 5JS · Tel 020 8650 7745 · Fax 020 8650 0768 · E-mail cbd@cbdresearch.com · www.cbdresearch.com

British Society for Children's Orthopaedic Surgery
a specialist society of the **British Orthopaedic Association**

British Society of Cinematographers Ltd   (BSC)   1949
■   PO Box 2587, GERRARDS CROSS, Bucks, SL9 7WZ.
    (4egd office)
    01753 888052   fax 01753 891486
    email bscine@btconnect.com   http://www.bscine.com
    Sec Treas: Mrs Frances K Russell
▲   Company Limited by Guarantee
○   *P; motion picture cinematography
Gp Full members: Directors of photography;
    Honorary members: Retired DoPs & camera operators;
    Associate members: Top [film] camera operators;
    Patron members: Companies closely associated with motion
      picture photography
●   Mtgs - ET - Exhib - Awards
<   Eur Fedn of Cinematographers (IMAGO); Cine Guilds of Great
      Britain (CGGB)
M   260 i, UK / 41 i, o'seas
¶   BSC NL - 4; ftm only.
    British Cinematographer Magazine - 6; £16.80 yr
      (£3.50 each).

British Society of Clinical & Academic Hypnosis
    styles itself **BSCAH - British Society of Clinical & Academic
    Hypnosis**

British Society for Clinical Cytology   (BSCC)   1962
NR 12 Coldbath Square, LONDON, EC1R 5HL.   (hsb)
    020 7278 6907
    http://www.clinicalcytology.co.uk
▲   Registered Charity
○   *L, *P; promotion of the growth & practice of cytopathology
<   Eur Fedn Cytology Socs
M   i

British Society of Clinical Hypnosis   (BSCH)   1987
■   125 Queensgate, BRIDLINGTON, E Yorks, YO16 7JQ.   (hq)
    01262 403103
    email sec@bsch.org.uk   http://www.bsch.org.uk
    Sec: Tom Connelly
▲   Un-incorporated Society
Br 2
○   *P; to maintain a register of properly trained therapists; to set &
      maintain the standard for hypnotherapy in the UK
●   Inf - Liaison between the public & the body of therapists
M   1,435 i

British Society of Clinical Neurophysiology   (BSCN)   1942
NR c/o Dr Robin Kennett, Radcliffe Infirmary, OXFORD,
    OX2 6HE.   (sb)
    01865 224589   fax 01865 228541
    email bscn@secretariat.freeserve.co.uk
    http://www.bscn.org.uk
    Sec: Dr Robin Kennett
▲   Registered Charity
○   *M, *P; 'education & scientific advancement in the field of
      electrodiagnostic medicine & physiological investigation of
      the human nervous system'
Gp Electroencephalography; Infra-operative monitoring
●   Conf - Mtgs - ET
<   Intl Fedn for Clinical Neurophysiology (IFCN)
M   c 400 i
¶   Abstracts of presentations to society scientific meetings - 3;
    NL - 1; both free.

British Society of Comedy Writers   (BSCW)   1999
■   61 Parry Rd, WOLVERHAMPTON, W Midlands, WV11 2PS.
    (pres/p)
    01902 722729
    email info@bscw.co.uk   http://www.bscw.co.uk
    Pres: Kenneth Rock
Br 5
○   *P; to develop & promote the work of comedy writers & the art
      of comedy writing
Gp Situation comedy; Sketch shows; Soap operas; quiz shows;
      Speeches; Corporate videos; Radio; Stage; Films;
      Publications
●   Conf - Mtgs
M   c 100 i
¶   NL - 4; ftm only.

British Society of Criminology   (BSC)
NR 2-6 Cannon St, LONDON, EC4M 6YH.   (hq)
    07908 966543
    http://www.britsoccrim.org
    Exec Sec: Dr Kate Williams
▲   Company Limited by Guarantee, Registered Charity
Br 7
○   *L, *P; promotion of criminological knowledge
●   Conf - Mtgs - ET - Comp - Inf - LG
M   850 i, UK / 80 i, o'seas
¶   NL - 4; ftm only.

British Society of Dental Hygiene & Therapy   (BSDHT)   1949
NR 3 Kestrel Court, Waterwells Drive, Waterwells Business Park,
    GLOUCESTER, GL2 2AT.   (admin/b)
    0870 243 0752
    http://www.bsdht.org.uk
    Admin: Mrs Ann Craddock
○   *L, *P; study & practice of oral hygiene
M   i
×   2008 British Dental Hygienists' Association

**British Society of Dental & Maxillofacial Radiology   (BSDMFR)
1958**
NR Dept of Dental Radiological Imaging, Guy's Tower (floor 23),
    LONDON, SE1 9RT.   (s/b)
    http://www.liv.ac.uk/~ppnixon/
    Hon Sec: Dr Suk Ng
▲   Registered Charity
○   *L; to promote study & research into all aspects of dental &
      maxillofacial radiology & radiography
●   Conf - Mtgs - Comp - SG - LG
M   110 i, UK / 20 i, o'seas
¶   NL - 2; ftm only.

British Society for Dental Research   (BSDR)   1950
NR Dental School, Framlington Place, NEWCASTLE upon TYNE,
    NE2 4BW.   (sb)
    fax 0191-222 8191
    email a.w.g.walls@newcastle.ac.uk
    http://www.bsdr.org.uk
    Sec: Prof Angus Wells
▲   Registered Charity
Br 2
○   *L, *Q; to advance research & increase knowledge for the
      improvement of oral health worldwide
Gp Mineralised tissue research; Oral biology; Oral microbiology &
      immunology; Dental materials; Implant research;
      Behavioural sciences & health services
●   Conf - Res - Exhib - SG - LG
<   Intl Assn of Dental Res (USA)
M   898 i, 3 org, UK / 14 i, o'seas
¶   Jnl of Dental Research - 12.   NL - 1.

British Society for Dermatological Surgery
    a group of the **British Association of Dermatologists**

British Society for Dermatopathology
a group of the **British Association of Dermatologists**

British Society for Developmental Biology (BSDB) 1964
NR   Cardiff School of Biosciences, Cardiff University Main Building,
     Park Place, CARDIFF, CF10 3TL.   (hsb)
     029 2087 5881
     email taylor@cardiff.ac.uk
     http://www.bms.ed.ac.uk/services/webspace/bsdb/
     people/taylor.htm
     Sec: Mike Taylor
▲   Registered Charity
○   *L; research in developmental biology (concerned with the
     mechanisms of embryonic development, growth &
     regeneration in animals & plants)
●   Conf - ET - Res
<   Eur Developmental Biology Org; Biological Sciences Fedn;
     Company of Biologists
M   c 900 i, UK / c 300 i, o'seas
¶   NL - 2; ftm only.

British Society for Disability & Oral Health (BSDH) 1976
NR   138 Woodstock Rd, OXFORD, OX2 7NG.   (hsb)
     http://www.bsdh.org.uk
     Hon Sec: Pauline Watt-Smith
▲   Registered Charity
○   *P; to improve, preserve & protect the oral health of peoples of
     all ages with disabilities
M   i

British Society of Dowsers (BSD) 1933
■   2 St Ann's Rd, MALVERN, Worcs, WR14 4RG.   (hq)
     01684 576969   fax 01684 576969
     email info@britishdowsers.org
     http://www.britishdowsers.org
     Dir: John Moss
▲   Company Limited by Guarantee; Registered Charity
○   *L; to promote a greater understanding of dowsing & its use in
     all its forms
Gp   Archaeological dowsing; Earth energies; Health; Water divining
●   Conf - Mtgs - ET - Res - Exhib - SG - Lib - VE - LG
     Office hours: Mon-Fri 1030-1500
M   1,200 i, UK / 200 i, o'seas
¶   Dowsing Today (Jnl) - 4; ftm, £6 nm.

British Society of Echocardiography (BSE) 1990
■   Dockland Business Centre, 10-19 Tiller Rd, Docklands,
     LONDON, E14 8PX.
     email info@bsecho.org   http://www.bsecho.org
     Sec: Jane Allen

British Society for Ecological Medicine (BSEM) 1981
NR   PO Box 7, KNIGHTON, Powys, LD7 1WT.   (hq)
     01547 550378
▲   Registered Charity
○   *P; to promote the study of allergy, environmental & nutritional
     medicine
M   i
✕   2005 British Society for Allergy, Environmental & Nutritional
     Medicine

British Society of Enamellers (BSOE) 1985
NR   16 West End, BRASTED, Kent, TN16 1HT.   (memsec/p)
     01959 569721
     http://www.enamellers.org
     Contact: Penny Davis
▲   Un-incorporated Society
○   *P; to promote excellence in British enamelling & professional
     enamellers worldwide
●   Conf - ET - Exhib - Lib - PL
<   societies in: Australia, France, Germany, Holland, Spain, USA
M   49 i, 51 i (associates)
¶   NL - 4; ftm only.

British Society of Experimental & Clinical Hypnosis
in May 2007 merged with the British Society of Medical & Dental
Hypnosis to form **BSCAH - British Society of Clinical &
Academic Hypnosis**

British Society of Flavourists (BSF) 1960
■   1 Wansford Close, BRENTFORD, Essex, CM14 4PU.   (hsp)
     01277 224587
     email christogoddard@aol.com   http://www.bsf.org.uk
     Sec: Christopher A Goddard
▲   Un-incorporated Society
○   *L, *P, *Q; the technology & application of flavours
●   Conf - Mtgs - ET - Exhib - VE
<   American Flavour Soc; Brit Soc Perfumers
M   c 500 i, UK / c 150 i, o'seas
¶   News & Views - 4;   LM;   AR; all ftm.

British Society of Gastroenterology (BSG) 1937
■   3 St Andrew's Place, LONDON, NW1 4LB.   (hq)
     020 7387 3534   fax 020 7487 3734
     email bsg@mailbox.ucc.ac.uk   http://www.bsg.org.uk
     Hon Secs: Dr A Harris, Dr S Kapadia
▲   Registered Charity
○   *L; advancement of gastroenterology (incl endoscopy,
     pathology, radiology, basic science, liver disease, colorectal
     disease)
Gp   Pathology; Radiology; Basic science; Endoscopy; Pancreas;
     Paediatrics; Oesophagus; Surgery; Liver; Small bowel;
     Nutrition
●   Conf - ET - Exhib
M   1,500 i, UK / 300 i, o'seas
¶   Gut - 12; ftm, £260 nm.

British Society for Gene Therapy (BSGT)
NR   Dept of Clinical Pharmacology, Old Rd Campus Research Bldg,
     Roosevelt Drive, Headington, OXFORD, OX3 7DQ.
     01865 220555
     email info@bsgt.org   http://www.bsgt.org
     Secretariat: Rachel Mager
○   *M; *Q; to accelerate scientific progress & promote ethical &
     efficient transfer gene- & cell-based technologies from the
     laboratory to the clinic

British Society for General Dental Surgery (BSGDS) 1981
NR   c/o Centre for Excellence in Dentistry, 10 Priory Queensway,
     BIRMINGHAM, B4 6BS.   (hsb)
     0121-236 2277   fax 0121-236 3149
     email birmingham@jameshull.co.uk
     http://www.bsgds.com
     Hon Sec: Roy Dixon
▲   Registered Charity
○   *P; quality of care in general dental practice; training of dentists
     in primary care
●   Conf - ET - Res
M   359 i, UK / 15 i, o'seas
¶   NL - 4; free.

British Society for Geomorphology
a group of the **Geological Society**

British Society of Gerodontology
NR   Dental Dept, Ringland Health Centre, NEWPORT, Gwent,
     NP19 9PS.   (hsb)
     01633 283190
     http://www.gerodontology.com
     Hon Sec: Vicki Jones
○   to protect, maintain and improve the oral health of older
     people

© CBD Research Ltd · Beckenham · BR3 5JS · Tel 020 8650 7745 · Fax 020 8650 0768 · E-mail cbd@cbdresearch.com · www.cbdresearch.com

British Society of Gerontology (BSG) 1973
NR PO Box 607, YORK, YO26 0EQ.   (hsb)
   http://www.britishgerontology.org
▲ Registered Charity
○ *L, *Q; to promote research & study of human ageing & later
   life
● Conf - Mtgs - Res
< Intl Assn of Gerontology (Eur Region); Academy of Learned
   Socs for the Social Sciences
M 441 i, 19 org, UK / 34 i, o'seas
¶ Generations Review - 4; ftm.   Ageing & Society - 6; £29 m.
   Directory of Members' Research - 2 yrly; ftm only.

** **British Society of Graphoanalysts**
   reported to us as having closed

British Society of Gynaecological Endoscopy (BSGE) 1989
■ Castle Hill Hospital, COTTINGHAM, E Yorks, HU16 5JQ.
   (hsb)
   01482 875875   fax 01482 624051
   Sec: Kevin Phillips
▲ Registered Charity
○ *M, *P, *Q; to promote endoscopic gynaecological surgery &
   research; to coordinate training & teaching programmes; to
   advise on safety in diagnostic & operative hysteroscopy &
   laparoscopic surgery
Gp Gynaecologists; Laparoscopic surgeons
● Conf - Mtgs - ET - Res - SG
< Eur Soc of Gynaecological Endoscopy; Amer Assn of
   Gynaecological Laparoscopists
M c 450 i

British Society of Habromaniacs
NR 81 Park View, Collins Rd, LONDON, N5 2UD.
○ *G; 'for mutual appreciation of morbid gaiety'
● Exhib - Mtgs - PL - VE
M ['confidential']
¶ Happy Talk (NL) - irreg.

British Society for Haematology (BSH) 1960
■ 100 White Lion St, LONDON, N1 9PF.   (hq)
   020 7713 0990   fax 020 7837 1931
   email info@b-s-h.org.uk   http://www.b-s-h.org.uk
   Sec: Dr Patrick Carrington
▲ Company Limited by Guarantee; Registered Charity
○ *L; to advance the practice & study of haematology
Gp Brit C'ee for Standards in Haematology (BCSH);
   Sub-c'ees: Paediatric (PHF); Clinical science (CSHF)
● Conf - Mtgs - ET - Res - Exhib
< Intl Soc for Haematology; Intl Coun for Standardisation in
   Haematology
M 993 i, 28 f, UK / 113 i, o'seas
¶ British Jnl of Haematology - 16; (price on application).
   [www.bloodmed.com]
   BSH Bulletin - 3; ftm only.
   Guidelines Documents - irreg; ftm only. (Published in
   haematology jnls). [www.bcshguidelines.com].

**British Society of Hearing Aid Audiologists Ltd   (BSHAA)
1954**
■ 9 Lukins Drive, GREAT DUNMOW, Essex, CM6 1XQ.   (sp)
   01371 876623   fax 01371 876623
   email secretary@bshaa.com   http://www.bshaa.com
   Sec: Jill Humphreys,
   Pres: M Georgevic
▲ Company Limited by Guarantee
○ *P; to represent the interests of the private hearing aid
   dispenser; to provide ongoing education
● Conf - Mtgs - ET - Exhib
M 1,100 i, UK / 50 i, o'seas
¶ BSHAA News - 4; ftm.

British Society of Hearing Therapists
   2004 merged with the British Association of Audiological Scientists &
   the British Association of Audiologists to form the **British Academy
   of Audiology**

British Society for the History of Mathematics (BSHM) 1971
NR School of Computing & Mathematical Sciences, University of
   Greenwich, Maritime Greenwich Campus, Old Royal Naval
   College, Park Row, Greenwich, LONDON, SE10 9LS.   (hsb)
   http://www.bshm.org
   Hon Sec: Tony Mann
▲ Registered Charity
○ *L; to provide a forum for all interested in the history &
   development of mathematics & related disciplines
● Conf - Mtgs - SG - VE
M 282 i, 3 org, UK / 142 i, o'seas
¶ NL - 2/3;   AR - 1; both ftm only.

British Society for the History of Medicine (BSHM) 1965
■ 24 Foxes Dale, LONDON, SE3 9BQ.   (sp)
   020 8852 6245
   email drfdavidson@yahoo.co.uk
   http://www.bshm.org.uk
   Sec: Dr Fiona Davidson
▲ Un-incorporated Society
Br 17
○ *N; to foster interest & research in the history of medicine &
   bring together various smaller societies
● Conf - Mtgs
< Intl Soc for the History of Medicine
M 24 org
¶ NL - 1; free on website.

British Society for the History of Pharmacy (BSHP) 1967
NR 840 Melton Rd, Thurmaston, LEICESTER, LE4 8BN.   (asa)
   0116-264 0083   fax 0116-264 0141
   email bshp@associationhq.org.uk
   http://www.bshp.org
   Hon Sec: Peter G Homan
▲ Registered Charity
○ *L; to act as a focus for the development of all areas of the
   history of pharmacy, from the works of the ancient
   apothecary to today's ever changing role of the community,
   hospital, wholesale or industrial chemist
● Conf - Mtgs - Res - VE
< Intl Soc for the History of Pharmacy; R Pharmaceutical
   Soc of GB
M 250 i, 4 org, UK / 24 i, 4 org, o'seas
¶ The Pharmaceutical Historian (NL) - 4; ftm, £1.50 each nm.

British Society for the History of Philosophy (BSHP) 1984
NR Dept of Philosophy, University of York, YORK, YO10 5DD.
   (hsb)
   01904 433254
   email jac505@york.ac.uk
   Sec: Dr James Clarke
▲ Registered Charity
○ *P; to promote & foster all aspects of the study of the history of
   philosophy
● Conf - Mtgs
M 100 i
¶ British Jnl for the History of Philosophy - 4.

British Society for the History of Science   (BSHS)   1947
- ■ PO Box 3401, NORWICH, Norfolk, NR7 3JF.   (exec/s)
  01603 516236
  Exec Sec: Lucy Tetlow
- ▲ Registered Charity
- ○ *L; to further the study of history & philosophy of science
- Gp Education (to promote the wider use of the history of science in the teaching of both science & history in schools)
- ● Conf - Mtgs - Publication
- M 850 i
- ¶ British Jnl for the History of Science - 4.   NL - 3.
  List of theses in history of science in British universities in progress, or recently catalogued.
  Guide to History of Science Courses in Britain.

British Society for Human Genetics   (BSHG)   1996
- ■ Clinical Genetics Unit, Birmingham Women's Hospital, Edgbaston, BIRMINGHAM, B15 2TG.   (hq)
  0121-627 2634   fax 0121-623 6971
  email bshg@bshg.org.uk   http://www.bshg.org.uk
  Gen Sec: Prof Diana Eccles
- ▲ Registered Charity
- ○ *P; to advance the science of human genetics; to promote research relating to health & disease; to promote public awareness of human genetics
- Gp Association for Clinical Cytogenetics; Association of Genetic Nurses & Counsellors; Cancer Genetics Group; Clinical Genetics Society; Clinical Molecular Genetics Society
- ● Conf - Mtgs - ET - Res - SG - Inf - LG
- < Intl Fedn of Human Genetics Socs
- M i
- ¶ BSHG NL - 3.

British Society of Hypnotherapists (1950)   (BSH)   1950
- ■ 37 Orbain Rd, LONDON, SW6 7JZ.   (hsp/b)
  020 7385 1166   fax 020 7385 1166
  email enquiries@britishhypnotherapists.org.uk
  http://www.britishhypnotherapists.org.uk
  Hon Sec: S C Young
- ▲ Un-incorporated Society
- ○ *P; the application of hypnosis for therapeutic purposes - phobias, anxiety & other emotional problems - behaviour change public
- ● Mtgs - Inf
- < Hypnotherapy Training Inst of Britain
- M [not stated]
- ¶ AR / AGM Minutes - 1; ftm only.

British Society for Immunology   (BSI)   1956
- NR Vintage House, 37 Albert Embankment, LONDON, SE1 7TL.   (hq)
  020 3031 9800   fax 020 7582 2882
  http://www.immunology.org
  Gen Sec: Prof Adrian Hayday
- ▲ Registered Charity
- Br 18
- ○ *P; to advance the science of immunology
- Gp Autoimmunity; Biochemistry; Cellular signalling; Clinical immunology; Comparative & veterinary immunology; Developmental immunology; Histocompatibility & immunogenetics; Infection & immunity; Lymphocyte Immunosenescence & differentiation; Mucosal; Neuroimmunology; Nutritional immunology; Parasitology; Reproductive immunology; Tumour immunology; Vaccines
- ● Conf - Mtgs - ET - Exhib - Inf - LG
- < Intl U Immunological Socs; Eur Fedn Immunological Socs; UK Life Sciences C'ee
- M c 3,500 i, UK / 500 i, o'seas
- ¶ Immunology - 12.   Immunology News - 6.
  Clinical & Experimental Immunology - 12.
  Directory - 1; ftm only.   AR - 1; ftm.

British Society for Investigative Dermatology
  a group of the **British Association of Dermatologists**

British Society of Magazine Editors   (BSME)   1960
- ■ c/o Gill Branston Associates, 137 Hale Lane, EDGWARE, Middx, HA8 9QP.   (hq/admin)
  020 8906 4664   fax 020 8959 2137
  email admin@gillbranston.com   http://www.bsme.com
  Admin: Gill Branston
- ○ *P; for magazine editors in the UK
  no further information supplied

British Society of Master Glass Painters   (BSMGP)   1921
- NR PO Box 15, MINEHEAD, Somerset, TA24 8ZX.   (hsp)
  01643 862807
  email secretary@bsmgp.org.uk
  http://www.bsmgp.org.uk
  Hon Sec: Chris Wyard
- ▲ Company Limited by Guarantee
- ○ *P; to promote contemporary stained glass & the appreciation & scholarly study of historic glass
- ● Conf - Mtgs - ET - Res - Exhib - Inf - Lib - VE
- M c 600 (incl 50 instns, libraries etc)
- ¶ The Jnl of Stained Glass - 1.
  Stained Glass (NL) - 4; ftm.

British Society of Medical & Dental Hypnosis
  in May 2007 merged with the British Society of Experimental & Clinical Hypnosis to form **BSCAH - British Society of Clinical & Academic Hypnosis**

British Society for Medical Mycology   (BSMM)   1965
- ■ Mycology - St John's Institute of Dermatology, St Thomas' Hospital, LONDON, SE1 7EH.   (hsb)
  020 7188 6400
  http://www.bsmm.org
  Hon Sec: Sue Howell
- ▲ Registered Charity
- ○ *P; to advance research into fungal infections in humans & animals, the pathogenesis & virulence of fungal infections, diagnosis & treatment, agents & mechanics of resistance
- Gp Diploma working party; Standards of care working party
- ● Conf - ET - Grant funding (travel grants)
- < Intl Soc for Human & Animal Mycology; Biosciences Fedn; Inst Biology
- M 212 i, UK / 75 i, o'seas
- ¶ BSNN News (NL) - 2;   LM; both ftm only.

British Society for Mercury Free Dentistry   (BSMFD)   1984
- NR The Weathervane, 22A Moorend Park Rd, CHELTENHAM, Glos, GL53 0JY.   (hq)
  01242 226918
  http://www.mercuryfreedentistry.org.uk
  Contact: Dr Gareth Rhidian
- ▲ Registered Charity
- ○ *P; the investigation of potential side-effects of dental materials, particularly mercury; to identify patients affected
- ● Conf - Mtgs - ET - Res - SG - Inf

British Society for Microbial Technology   (BSMT)
- NR Microbiology Dept (F Floor), Royal Hallamshire Hospital, Glossop Rd, SHEFFIELD, S Yorks, S10 2JF.   (chmn/b)
  0114-271 3121   fax 0114-278 9376
  email lgwinstanley@hotmail.com
  http://www.bsmt.org.uk
  Chmn: Trevor Winstanley

© CBD Research Ltd · Beckenham · BR3 5JS · Tel 020 8650 7745 · Fax 020 8650 0768 · E-mail cbd@cbdresearch.com · www.cbdresearch.com

British Society for Middle Eastern Studies   (BRISMES)   1973
NR   Institute for Middle Eastern & Islamic Studies, University of
     Durham, Elvet Hill Rd, DURHAM, DH1 3TU.   (admin)
     0191-334 5179   fax 0191-334 5661
     email a.l.haysey@durham.ac.uk
     http://www.brismes.ac.uk
     Admin: Louise Haysey
▲   Registered Charity
○   *L; to promote the study of the Middle Eastern region, its
     culture, languages, literature, history & politics
●   Conf - ET
<   Middle East Studies Assn of America (MESA); Eur Assn of
     Middle Eastern Studies (EURAMES)
M   400 i, 2 f, 18 org, UK / 200 i, o'seas
¶   British Jnl of Middle Eastern Studies - 2; ftm, £64 nm.
     Business NL - 3; ftm, £20 nm

British Society for Music Therapy   (BSMT)   1958
■   61 Church Hill Rd, EAST BARNET, Herts, EN4 8SY.   (hq)
     020 8441 6226   fax 020 8441 4118
     email info@bsmt.org   http://www.bsmt.org
▲   Registered Charity
○   *D; to promote the use of music therapy in the treatment,
     education, rehabilitation & training of children & adults
     suffering from physical, emotional or mental handicap
●   Conf - Mtgs - ET - Res - Exhib - Inf
M   600 i, 50 f, UK / 50 i, 150 f, o'seas
¶   British Jnl of Music Therapy - 2.
     BSMT Bulletin - 3.

British Society of Neuroradiologists   (BSNR)   1970
NR   c/o Dr M Gawne-Cain, Southampton General Hospital,
     SOUTHAMPTON, Hants, SO16 6YD.   (sb)
     023 8079 6641
     email bsnr.sec@googlemail.com   http://www.bsnr.co.uk
     Sec: Dr M Gawne-Cain
▲   Un-incorporated Society
○   *P; all matters relating to neuroradiology
●   Conf - LG
<   Wld Fedn of Neuroradiological Socs
M   190 i, UK / 10 i, o'seas

British Society for Oral & Maxillofacial Pathology   (BSOP)   1967
NR   Diagnostic Services / Level 6, Medical & Dental School,
     University of Leeds, LEEDS, W Yorks, LS2 9LU.   (hsb)
     0113-343 6115   fax 0113-343 6264
     email a.s.high@leeds.ac.uk
     Hon Sec: Dr Alec S High
▲   Un-incorporated Society
○   *L, *M, *P; to promote & encourage the study & practice of
     head & neck histopathology; to facilitate communication
     between pathologists with an interest in head, neck, oral &
     dental disease
Gp   Council; Members; Overseas members; Teachers
●   Conf - ET - Res
M   110 i, UK / 20 i, o'seas

British Society for Oral Medicine   (BSOM)   1976
NR   c/o Prof F Fortune, Institute of Dentistry, 4 Newark St, LONDON,
     E1 2AT.   (pres/b)
     020 7882 7158
     http://www.bsom.org.uk
     Pres: Prof F Fortune
○   *L; oral soft tissue disease
●   Conf - ET - Comp - Inf - Devt of higher training programmes
M   c 180 i
¶   NL - 1; free.

British Society of Paediatric Dentistry
■   c/o Dr Ben Cole, Dept of Child Dental Health,
     Newcastle Dental Hospital, Richardson Rd,
     NEWCASTLE upon TYNE, NE2 4AX.
     http://www.bspd.co.uk
     Hon Sec: Dr Ben Cole
▲   Registered Charity
Br   13
○   *P; dental care of children
Gp   Consultants; Teachers
●   Conf - Mtgs - ET - Res - LG
<   Intl Assn of Paediatric Dentistry
M   c 800 i
¶   Intl Jnl of Paediatric Dentistry - 4.

British Society for Paediatric Dermatology
     a group of the **British Association of Dermatologists** & of the
     Royal College of Paediatrics & Child Health

British Society of Paediatric Endocrinology & Diabetes
     a group of the **Royal College of Paediatrics & Child Health**

British Society for Paediatric Gastroenterology & Nutrition
     a group of the **Royal College of Paediatrics & Child Health**

British Society of Painters (in Oil, Pastels & Acrylic)
NR   13 Manor Orchards, KNARESBOROUGH, N Yorks,
     HG5 0BW.   (dir b/p)
     01423 540603
     email info@britpaint.co.uk   http://www.britpaint.co.uk
     Dir: Leslie Simpson
○   *A; to promote excellence in the field of painting
●   Exhib - Comp - Free entry to exhibitions
M   50 i, UK / 3 i, o'seas
¶   Catalogue; £1.

British Society for Parasitology   (BSP)   1962
NR   87 Gladstone St, BEDFORD, MK41 7RS.   (asa)
     01234 211015   fax 01234 211015
     http://www.bsp.uk.net
     Secretariat: Cathy Fuller
▲   Registered Charity
Br   2
○   *L; to advance the study of parasitology; to promote wider
     dissemination of advances in the subject
M   i

British Society of Perfumers   (BSP)   1963
NR   15 Underwood Close, CANTERBURY, Kent, CT4 7BS.   (gen/sp)
     http://www.bsp.org.uk
     Gen Sec: Roger Duprey
▲   Un-incorporated Society
○   *P; the art, craft & science of creative perfumery
●   Mtgs - Occasional workshops
<   La Société Technique des Parfumeurs de France
M   c 200 i
¶   NL; m only.

British Society of Periodontology   (BSP)   1949
■   Green Hayes, Malvern Rd, Hill Brow, LISS, Hants, GU33 7PZ.
     (conf/mgr)
     01252 843598   fax 01252 607800
     email bspadmin@btinternet.com
     http://www.bsperio.org.uk
     Admin Mgr: Mrs A Hallows,   Conf Mgr: Mrs G Owen
▲   Registered Charity
○   *P; to promote the art & science of dentistry & in particular the
     art & science of periodontology
Gp   Teachers; General practitioners
●   Conf - Mtgs - ET - Comp
<   Eur Fedn of Periodontology
M   775 i, UK / 125 i, o'seasas
     (Sub: £85-140)
¶   The Jnl of Clinical Periodontology - 12; ftm.   NL - 1; ftm.

British Society for the Philosophy of Science   (BSPS)   1959
- ■ c/o Dr Rachel Cooper, Institute for Philosophy & Public Policy, Furness College, Lancaster University, LANCASTER, LA1 4YG.   (hsb)
  http://www.thebsps.org
  Hon Sec: Dr Rachel Cooper
- ▲ Registered Charity
- ○ *L; to study the logic, methods & the philosophy of science, as well as those of the various special sciences, incl the social sciences
- ● Conf - Mtgs - Res - Inf
- M i
- ¶ British Jnl for the Philosophy of Science - 4.

British Society of Plant Breeders Ltd   (BSPB Ltd)   1966
- NR Woolpack Chambers, Market St, ELY, Cambs, CB7 4ND.   (hq)
  01353 653200   fax 01353 661156
  email enquiries@bsbp.co.uk   http://www.bspb.co.uk
  Chief Exec: Dr Penny Maplestone
- ▲ Company Limited by Guarantee
- ○ *T; to license and collect royalties on plant varieties; to promote the interests of plant breeders
- Gp British Sugar Beet Seed Producers Association
- ● LG
- < Intl Seed Fedn; Eur Seed Assn
- M 50 f, UK / 1 i, 2 f, o'seas

British Society for Plant Pathology   (BSPP)   1981
- NR 1 St Fillans Grove, ABERDOUR, Fife, KY3 0XG.   (hsp)
  01383 860695
  email secretary@bspp.org.uk   http://www.bspp.org.uk
  Sec: Bill Rennie
- ▲ Company Limited by Guarantee; Registered Charity
- ○ *L; advancement of plant pathology (study & control of plant disease)

British Society for Population Studies   (BSPS)   1973
- NR PS201, London School of Economics, Houghton St, LONDON, WC2A 2AE.   (hq)
  020 7955 7666   fax 020 7955 6831
  email pic@lse.ac.uk   http://www.bsps.org.uk
- ▲ Registered Charity
- ○ *L, *P; to further the study of biological, economic, historical, medical, social & other disciplines connected with human populations; to contribute to public awareness of these problems; to provide facilities for study & research
- ● Conf - Mtgs - Inf
- M 250 i, 10 f, UK / 50 i, o'seas
- ¶ BSPS News - 4; free.

British Society for Proteome Research   (BSPR)   1984
- NR c/o Dr Kathryn Lilley, Dept Biochemistry, Bldg O, Downing Site, CAMBRIDGE, CB2 3DZ.   (hsb)
  01223 765255   fax 01223 333345
  email k.s.lilley@bioc.cam.ac.uk   http://www.bspr.org
  Hon Sec: Dr Kathryn Lilley
- ▲ Registered Charity
- ○ *L; to promote the study of proteomics - the study of proteins as a system group
- ● Conf - ET - Res - Exhib - SG - Inf - LG
- < Biosciences Fedn
- M 165 i
- ¶ NL - 2/3; ftm only.
- × 2004 British Electrophoresis Society

British Society of Psychosomatic Obstetrics, Gynaecology & Andrology   (BSPOGA)   1988
- NR c/o Dr Mira Lal, Dept of Obstetrics & Gynaecology, Russells Hall Hospital, DUDLEY, DY1 2QH.   (chmn/b)
  http://www.bspoga.org
  Chmn: Dr Mira Lal
- ▲ Registered Charity
- ○ *L, *M; to promote & increase knowledge & research into psychological problems related to all aspects of reproductive medicine incl pre & post menopause
- ● Conf - ET
- < Intl Soc of Psychosomatic Obstetrics & Gynaecology
- M 100 i
- ¶ NL - 2.

British Society of Rehabilitation Medicine   (BSRM)   1984
- NR c/o Royal College of Physicians, 11 St Andrew's Place, LONDON, NW1 4LE.   (mail/address)
  01992 638865
  Exec Sec: Sandy Weatherhead
- ▲ Registered Charity
- ○ *M, *P; to promote the development, understanding & management of acute & chronic disabling diseases & injuries
- M i

British Society for Research on Ageing   (BSRA)   1947
- NR c/o Dr Sian Henson,
  Dept of Immunology & Molecular Pathology,
  University College London, 46 Cleveland St,
  LONDON, W1T 4JF.   (hsb)
  Hon Sec: Dr Sian Henson
- ▲ Registered Charity
- ○ *L, *Q; promotion of teaching & research on the biology of ageing
- M i

British Society for Restorative Dentistry   (BSRD)   1968
- NR Restorative Dentistry (Room 6,24), Leeds Dental Institute, Worsley Building, University of Leeds, LEEDS, LS2 9LU.   (admin/s)
  0113-343 7829   fax 0113-343 6165
  http://www.bsrd.org
  Hon Sec: Prof Paul A Brunton
- ▲ Registered Charity
- ○ *M, *P; to promote study & high standards of restorative dentistry
- ● Conf - ET
- < Brit Prosthodontic Conference
- M 704 i
- ¶ European Jnl of Prosthodontics & Restorative Dentistry - 4; ftm, £60 nm.
  NL - 1; ftm only.

British Society of Rheology   (BSR)   1940
- ■ c/o Dr Helen Wilson, Mathematics Dept, University College London, Gower St, LONDON, WC1E 6BT.   (hsb)
  020 7679 1302   fax 020 7383 5519
  email helen.wilson@ucl.ac.uk   http://www.bsr.org.uk
  Hon Sec: Dr Helen Wilson
- ▲ Registered Charity
- ○ *L, *Q; to promote science & disseminate knowledge in pure & applied rheology - defined as the science of the flow & deformation of matter.   Rheology finds application in engineering, materials processing, physics, chemistry, applied maths & biological / medical systems
- ● Conf - Mtgs - Lib - Awards - Student sponsorships
- < Intl C'ee of Rheology; Eur Soc of Rheology
- M 400 i, UK / 200 i, o'seas
  (Sub: £25)
- ¶ Rheology Reviews (Jnl) - 1; £20 m, £35 nm.
  Rheology Bulletin - 3.   Rheology Abstracts - 4; both ftm only.

© CBD Research Ltd · Beckenham · BR3 5JS · Tel 020 8650 7745 · Fax 020 8650 0768 · E-mail cbd@cbdresearch.com · www.cbdresearch.com

British Society for Rheumatology (BSR) 1984

- ■ Bride House, 18 Bride Lane, LONDON, EC4Y 8EE. (hq)
  020 7842 0900   fax 020 7842 0901
  email bsr@rheumatology.org.uk
  http://www.rheumatology.org.uk
  Chief Exec: Samantha Peters
- ▲ Registered Charity
- ○ *L, *P; to advance the knowledge & practice in the field of rheumatology; to work for high standards of care for patients with rheumatic disorders
- ● Conf - Mtgs - ET - Res - Stat - Lib
- < Arthritis & Musculoskeletal Alliance (ARMA); Brit Health Profls in Rheumatology (BHPR)
- M 950 i, UK / 450 i, o'seas
- ¶ Rheumatology (Jnl) - 12; ftm, prices vary nm.
  BSR News - 3;   Hbk - 2 yrly;   AR; all ftm only.

British Society of Scientific Glassblowers (BSSG) 1960

- ■ Glendale, Sinclair St, THURSO, Caithness, KW14 7AQ. (hq)
  01847 895637   fax 01847 802971
  email ian.pearson@ukaea.org.uk
  http://www.bssg.co.uk
  Chmn: Ian Pearson
- ▲ Un-incorporated Society
- ○ *P
- ● Conf - Mtgs - Exam - Comp - Inf - Lib
- < Amer Soc Scientific Glassblowers; Soc Glass Technology; Glass Mfrs Confedn
- M 200 i, 5 f, UK / 40 i, 1 f, o'seas
- ¶ Jnl - 4; £5 m, £6 nm.

British Society for Sexual Medicine (BSSM) 1997

- NR Holly Cottage, Fisherwick, LICHFIELD, Staffs, WS14 9JL.
  01543 432757   fax 01543 433303
  http://www.bssm.org.uk
  Sec: Mrs Sally Hackett
- ○ *M; 'for the purpose of promoting research & exchange of knowledge of impotence & other aspects of sexual function & dysfunction'

British Society of Soil Science (BSSS) 1947

- ■ School of Biological Sciences, University of Plymouth, Drake Circus, PLYMOUTH, Devon, PL4 8AA. (sb)
  http://www.soils.org.uk
  Sec: Dr Rob Parkinson
- ▲ Un-incorporated Society
- ○ *L; to promote the study of soils & increase awareness of the importance of soils in many aspects of life
- ● Conf - ET - Exhib
- < Intl Soc of Soil Science
- M 750 i, UK / 250 i, o'seas
- ¶ European Jnl of Soil Science.
  Soil Use & Management - 4.

British Society of Sports History

- NR Dingle Barn, Bradley, FRODSHAM, Cheshire, WA6 7EP.
  email richard.cox@zen.co.uk
  http://www.bssh.mcs-creations.com
  Web Services Mgr: Richard Cox
- ○ *G, *P; to stimulate, promote & coordinate interest in the historical study of sport, physical education, recreation & leisure; to encourage & assist in the preservation & cataloguing of historical records

British Society for Strain Measurement (BSSM) 1965

- ■ TechniMeasure, Alexandra Buildings, 59 Alcester Rd, STUDLEY, Warks, B80 7NU. (hq)
  01525 712779   fax 01525 712779
  email info@bssm.org   http://www.bssm.org
  Hon Sec: Ian Ramage
- ▲ Company Limited by Guarantee
- Br 11
- ○ *L; engineering strain measurement & associated measurement
- Gp C'ees: Technical, Centrification
- ● Conf - Mtgs - ET - Exam - Exhib - Comp - Inf
- < Soc of Experimental Mechanics (USA)
- M 100 i, 100 f, UK / 20 i, o'seas
- ¶ Strain (Jnl) - 4; ftm, £50 yr nm.

British Society for the Study of Prosthetic Dentistry (BSSPD) 1953

- NR Restorative Dentistry / School of Dental Sciences, Newcastle University, Framlington Place, NEWCASTLE upon TYNE, NE2 4BW. (hsb)
  0191-222 8198
- ▲ Registered Charity
- ○ *L; the study & development of prosthetic dentistry (the artificial replacement of teeth)
- M c 500 i
- ¶ NL - 2;   Proceedings of the Annual Conference - 1; ftm.

British Society for the Study of Religions (BASR) 1954

- ■ The Open University - Faculty of Arts, Dept of Religious Studies, Walton Hall, MILTON KEYNES, MK7 6AA. (hsb)
  01908 654033
  Sec: Dr Graham Harvey
- ▲ Registered Charity
- ○ *L; to promote the academic study of religions
- ● Conf
- < Intl Assn for the History of Religions; Eur Assn for the Study of Religions
- M 230 i, UK / 7 i, o'seas
- ¶ Bulletin - 2; ftm only.
  DISKUS [online Jnl] - 1; free.

British Society for the Study of Vulval Diseases (BSSVD)

- NR c/o Dr D Mandal, GUM Dept, Kendrick Wing, Warrington Hospital, Lovely Lane, WARRINGTON, Cheshire, WA5 1QG. (hsb)
  01925 662476   fax 01925 275217
  http://www.bssvd.org
  Sec: Dr D Mandal
- ○ *M

British Society for Surgery of the Hand (BSSH) 1968

- ■ at the Royal College of Surgeons, 35-43 Lincoln's Inn Fields, LONDON, WC2A 3PE. (hq)
  020 7831 5162   fax 020 7831 4041
  email secretariat@bssh.ac.uk   http://www.bssh.ac.uk
  Hon Sec: R Eckersley
- ▲ Company Limited by Guarantee, Registered Charity
- ○ *M, *P; to promote & direct development of hand surgery; to foster & co-ordinate education, study & research
- ● Conf - Mtgs - ET - Res
- < Intl Fedn of Socs for the Surgery of the Hand
- M 520 i, UK / 150 i, o'seas
- ¶ Jnl of Hand Surgery (European volume) - 6; ftm only.

British Society of Toxicological Pathologists (BSTP) 1985

- ■ PO Box 6356, ISLE of SKYE, IV41 8WZ. (admin)
  07894 123533
  email bstpostoffice@aol.com   http://www.bstp.org.uk
  Secretariat
- ▲ Registered Charity
- ○ *P; to advance education in toxicological pathology for the public benefit
- ● Conf - Mtgs - ET
- M 105 i, UK / 67 i, o'seas
- ¶ BSTP NL - 1; ftm only.

British Society of Underwater Photographers (BSoUP) 1967
NR 12 Coningsby Rd, SOUTH CROYDON, Surrey, CR2 6QP. (hsp)
     020 8668 8168
     http://www.bsoup.org
     Pres: Brian Pitkin
▲ Un-incorporated Society
○ *P; underwater photography, cinematography & video
● Mtgs - Exhib - Comp
M c 300 i
¶ In Focus (NL) - 6.

British Sociological Association (BSA) 1951
■ Palatine House (Bailey suite), Belmont Business Park, DURHAM,
    DH1 1TW. (hq)
    0191-383 0839   fax 0191-383 0782
    email enquiries@britsoc.org.uk
    http://www.britsoc.co.uk
    Chief Exec: Judith Mudd
▲ Company Limited by Guarantee; Registered Charity
○ *P; promotion of interest in sociology & advancement of its
    study & application in the UK
Gp over 30 specialist study groups
● Conf - Mtgs - ET - Res - Exhib - Comp - SG - Stat - Inf - LG
< Intl Sociological Assn; Foundation for Science & Technology;
    Standing Conf of Arts & Social Sciences; Amer/ Australian /
    Indian Sociological Assn(s); Canadian Sociological &
    Anthropological Assn
M 2,127 i, UK / 180 i, o'seas
¶ Sociology (Jnl) - 6; ftm, £82 yr nm.
    Work, Employment & Society (Jnl) - 4; ftm, £66 yr nm.
    [1st copy to m, free; 2nd copy, £35].
    Network (NL) - 3; AR; both ftm only.

British Soft Drinks Association (BSDA) 1987
■ 20-22 Stukeley St, LONDON, WC2B 5LR. (hq)
    020 7430 0356   fax 020 7831 6014
    email bsda@britishsoftdrinks.com
    http://www.britishsoftdrinks.com
    Dir Gen: Jill Ardagh
▲ Company Limited by Guarantee
○ *T; for all manufacturers of soft drinks, fruit juices & bottled
    waters; cover packaging, dispensing & vending machines &
    environmental concerns
Gp Various specialist c'ees
● Conf - ET - Inf - PL - LG
< UNESDA; EFBW; AIJN
M 47 f, 47 f (associates)
¶ Publications list available.

**British Soluble Coffee Packers & Importers Association
(BSCPIA) 1994**
■ Crescent House, 34 Eastbury Way, SWINDON, Wilts,
    SN25 2EN. (sb)
    01793 723387   fax 01793 726486
    email bscpia@aol.com
    Sec: Walter J Anzer
▲ Company Limited by Guarantee
○ *T; to represent the needs of the soluble coffee packers &
    importers on an international basis supplying the British & EU
    markets
● LG
M 10 f
¶ Code of Practice for the Soluble Coffee Industry in the UK; ftm,
    £5 nm.

British Sound Recording Association (BSRA) 1958
■ 42 Lewis Rd, CHIPPING NORTON, Oxon, OX7 5JS. (hsp)
    email bsra@soundhunters.com
    http://www.soundhunters.com/bsra/
    Hon Sec: Peta Simmons
○ *G; all aspects of amateur sound recording, including video
    with creative sound
● Conf - Mtgs - Comp - VE
< Fédn Intle des Chasseurs de Sons (Intl Fedn Soundhunters)
M 65 i, 2 f, 4 org
¶ Recording News - 4;
    Sound Track Audio Magazine - 4; both ftm only.

British Spas Federation
    since 2004 **Spa Business Association**

British Speedway Promoters' Association (BSPA) 1965
NR ACU House, Wood St, RUGBY, Warks, CV21 2YX. (hq)
    01788 560648   fax 01788 546785
    email office@britishspeedway.plus.com
    http://www.british-speedway.co.uk
○ *S; organisation of British speedway racing
M 25 f

British Spotted Pony Society (BSpPS) 1946
■ Heiffers Farm, Rackenford, TIVERTON, Devon, EX16 8EW.
    (hsp)
    01884 881258   fax 01757 288087
    email marlyn@heiffers.orangehome.co.uk
    http://www.britishspottedponysociety.co.uk
    Chmn & Sec: Miss Marlyn Pollard
▲ Company Limited by Guarantee; Registered Charity
○ *B
● Mtgs - Exhib - Comp - Inf - PL - LG - Breed show
M i
¶ NL - 2; AR - 1; both ftm only.

British Sprouts Growers Association
    a group of the **Brassica Growers Association**

British Stainless Steel Association (BSSA) 1992
■ Broomgrove, 59 Clarkehouse Rd, SHEFFIELD, S Yorks,
    S10 2LE. (hq)
    0114-267 1260   fax 0114-266 1252
    email enquiry@bssa.org.uk   http://www.bssa.org.uk
    Dir: Nigel Ward
▲ Un-incorporated Society
○ *T; to promote & develop the use of stainless steel in all regions
    of the UK
Gp Industry forum; Rebar; Architecture & building construction;
    Finishing section
● Conf - Mtgs - ET - Exhib - Stat - Inf - LG
< Intl Stainless Steel Forum; Euro-Inox
> Nickel Inst
M 100 f
¶ Stainless Steel Industry (Jnl) - 6; ftm, £105 nm (UK & Europe)
    NL (email).

© CBD Research Ltd · Beckenham · BR3 5JS · Tel 020 8650 7745 · Fax 020 8650 0768 · E-mail cbd@cbdresearch.com · www.cbdresearch.com

British Stammering Association (BSA) 1978
■ 15 Old Ford Rd, LONDON, E2 9PJ.   (hq)
020 8983 1003
email mail@stammering.org   http://www.stammering.org
Chief Exec Officer: Norbert Lieckfeldt
▲ Registered Charity
○ *W; to promote awareness of stammering; to offer support for
all whose lives are affected by stammering; to identify &
promote effective therapies; to initiate & support research
into stammering
Gp Helping stammering pupils project
● Conf - ET - Inf - Lib - Counselling & information service on
speech therapy
Counselling & information service on speech therapy provision
& self-help groups for the whole of the UK
Helpline: 0845 603 2001
< Intl Fluency Assn; Intl Stuttering Assn
M 1,600 i
¶ Speaking Out - 4; ftm only.

British Standards Institution
styles itself as **BSI**

British Standards Society (BSS) 1960
NR c/o BSI, 389 Chiswick High Rd, LONDON, W4 4AL.   (hq)
○ *K; to promote techniques & benefits of standardisation; to help
standards users in their understanding & use of standards
M i
Note: is a part of BSI

British Starch Industry Association (BSIA) 1989
NR 6 Catherine St, LONDON, WC2B 5JJ.   (hq)
▲ Un-incorporated Society
○ *T
● Mtgs - LG
< Eur Starch Assn; Food & Drink Fedn
M 6 f

British Stickmakers Guild (BSG) 1984
■ Ebbisham, 19 Woodmancote Rd, WORTHING, W Sussex,
BN14 7HT.   (hsp)
01903 205015
http://www.thebsg.org.uk
Hon Sec: Charles Hutcheon
▲ Un-incorporated Society
○ *G; for all interested in the history, making, collection,
stickdressing & uses of walking sticks, canes & crooks
● Exhib - Comp
M 1,940 i, UK / 41 i, o'seas
¶ The Stickmaker - 4.

British Stock Car Drivers Association (BSCDA) 1956
NR PO Box 662, HALIFAX, W Yorks, HX3 0WZ.   (hsp)
Hon Sec: Barry Tempest
▲ Un-incorporated Society
○ *P

British Stomach Cancer Group
a specialist group of **BASO ~ the Association for Cancer
Surgery**

British Streptocarpus Society 1999
NR 9 Wharf Lane, Chasetown, BURNTWOOD, Staffs, WS7 8QY.
01543 672938   http://www.streptocarpussociety.org.uk
Sec: Frank Davies
○ *H; for those interested in the flower species

British Structural Waterproofing Association (BSWA) 1992
NR Westcott House, Catlins Lane, PINNER, Middx, HA5 2EZ.
020 8866 8339   fax 0871 522 7442
email enquiries@bswa.org.uk   http://www.bswa.org.uk
○ *T; waterproofing contractors, consultants, manufacturers &
distributors
M 58 f

British Sub-Aqua Club (BSAC) 1953
NR Telford's Quay, South Pier Rd, ELLESMERE PORT, Cheshire,
CH65 4FL.   (hq)
0151-350 6200
email info@basc.com   http://www.basc.com
▲ Company Limited by Guarantee
○ *S; the governing body for the sport of sub-aqua in the UK
M i

British Sugar Beet Seed Producers Association
is a specialist group within the **British Society of Plant Breeders**

British Sugarcraft Guild (BSG) 1983
■ Wellington House, Messeter Place, LONDON, SE9 5DP.   (hq)
020 8859 6943   fax 020 8859 6117
email nationaloffice@bsguk.org   http://www.bsguk.org
Sec: Nicky Fuller
▲ Un-incorporated Society
Br 225; Japan
○ *G; to promote & stimulate interest in sugarcraft as an art form
● Conf - Mtgs - ET - Exam - Res - Exhib - Comp - SG - Expt - Inf
M 6,700 i, UK / 1,500 i, o'seas
¶ The British Sugarcraft News - 4; ftm only.

British Summer Fruits
NR Sputnik Communications, 31 Great Malborough St, LONDON,
W1F 7JA.
020 7439 2780   fax 020 7439 2781
http://www.britishsummerfruits.co.uk
Vicky Cotton or Bridget Bottomley
○ *T; the growers of British-grown soft & stone fruits

British Sundial Society (BSS) 1989
■ 4 New Wokingham Rd, CROWTHORNE, Berks, RG45 7NR.
(hsp)
01344 772303
email douglas.bateman@btinternet.com
http://www.sundialsoc.org.uk
Hon Sec: Douglas Bateman
▲ Registered Charity
○ *G, *L; to promote the science of gnomonics & knowledge of
all types of sundial; research & advice on the restoration &
preservation of old sundials in the British Isles & the
construction of new ones
Gp Restoration; Education; Recording; Mass dials
● Conf - Mtgs - ET - Res - SG - Inf - Lib - PL - VE - Cataloguing
the dials which still exist in the British Isles
< N Amer Sundial Soc; R Astronomical Soc
M 400 i, 12 f, 25 org, UK / 150 i, o'seas
¶ The Bulletin (Jnl) - 4; ftm, £6.50 nm.
Make a Sundial (book for schools); £7.
Sets of Slides for lectures (6 sets); £5.50 each.
Listing of Dials in UK - 3 yrly; m only.
Sundial Makers.

British Superkart Association 1998
NR 6 Mansfield Avenue, Quorn, LOUGHBOROUGH, Leics,
LE12 8BD.
01509 620702   fax 01509 414117
http://www.superkart.org.uk
Competion Sec: Ian Rushforth
○ *S

British Surface Treatment Suppliers Association
a group of the **Surface Engineering Association**

British Surfing Association (BSA) 1966
NR International Surfing Centre, Fistral Beach, NEWQUAY,
Cornwall, TR7 1HY. (hq)
01637 876474   fax 01637 878608
email info@britsurf.co.uk   http://www.britsurf.co.uk
Admin: Karen Walton
▲ Company Limited by Guarantee
○ *S; the national governing body for surfing
Gp Boarding: Long, Body, Short, Knee
● Mtgs - ET - Exam - Comp - Stat - Inf - LG
< Intl Surfing Assn
> Surfing Assns: English, Welsh, Scottish, Channel Islands
M c 10,000 i & org
¶ Groundswell (NL) - 12.

British Suzuki Institute (BSI) 1980
NR Charles House (4th floor), 375 Kensington High St, LONDON,
W14 8QH. (hq)
020 7471 6780   fax 020 7471 6778
email info@britishsuzuki.com
http://www.britishsuzuki.com
Admin: Minette Joyce
▲ Registered Charity
○ *D; to advance education in the Suzuki method of teaching for
violin, cello, flute, piano & recorder
Gp Music education
● Conf - Mtgs - ET - Exam - Inf - Teacher training - Concerts
< Eur Suzuki Assn
M 2,000 i, UK / 100 i, o'seas
¶ Ability - 4; ftm, £3 nm.

British Swedish Chamber of Commerce in Sweden (BSCC) 1954
NR Jakobs Torg 3 (4th floor), Box 16050, SE-103 21
STOCKHOLM, Sweden. (hq)
46 (8) 555 100 00
Sec Gen: Martin Dworén
▲ Company Limited by Guarantee
○ *C
M c 120 f

British Swimming
■ Harold Fern House, Derby Square, LOUGHBOROUGH, Leics,
LE11 5AL. (hq)
01509 618700   fax 01509 618701
email chiefexecutive@swimming.org
Chief Exec: David Sparkes
○ *N, *S; determination of policies for participation in world
events
Gp Swimming; Diving; Water polo; Synchronised swimming
● Comp - Determination of policies for participation in world
championships
< Fédn Intle de Natation Amateur (FINA); Ligue Eur de Natation
(LEN)
M [not stated]
¶ AR - 1; ftm.
✕ 2008 Amateur Swimming Federation

British Swimming Pool Federation (BSPFA) 1961
■ 4 Eastgate House, East St, ANDOVER, Hants, SP10 1EP. (hq)
01264 356210   fax 01264 332628
email admin@bspf.org.uk   http://www.bspf.org.uk
Managing Dir: Chris Hayes
○ *N; umbrella organisation for the Swimming Pool & Allied
Trades Association, the British & Irish Spa & Hot Tub
Association, the Swimming Teachers' Association, & SPATEX
(the annual trade exhibition for the industry)
M 4 org
no further information supplied

British-Swiss Chamber of Commerce (BSCC) 1920
■ Bellerivestrasse 209, CH-8008 ZRICH, Switzerland. (hq)
41 44 422 31 31   fax 41 44 422 32 44
email info@bscc.co.uk   http://www.bscc.co.uk
London Office: 14 New St, London, EC2M 4HE.
020 7650 3802
Mgr: Carolyn Helbling
Br 8 regional chapters
○ *C; to support the development of Anglo Swiss business
relations; to assist individual entrepreneurs & businesses in
advancing their own commercial interests
Gp Legal & tax chapter; Public affairs commission; Business
technology
● Conf - Business luncheons - Seminars
< Coun of Brit Chams Comm in Continental Europe (COBCOE)
M f
¶ NL (email) - 6;   Perspectives (NL) - 1; both free.

British Syrian Society
NR Bury House, 33 Bury St, LONDON, SW1Y 6AX.
020 7839 1637   fax 020 7839 1638
http://www.britishsyriansociety.org
○ *X

British Tarantula Society (BTS) 1984
NR 3 Shepham Lane, POLEGATE, E Sussex, BN26 6LZ. (hsp)
Hon Sec: Angela Hale
▲ Un-incorporated Society
○ *B, *G; to educate & provide information on captive husbandry
of theraphosid spiders & associated fauna (scorpions etc)
Gp Captive breeding directory
● Mtgs - Res - Exhib - SG - Inf - Lib
M c 700 i
¶ Jnl - 4.

British Tattoo Artists Federation (BTAF) 1975
NR 389 Cowley Rd, OXFORD, OX4 2BS. (hq)
01865 716877   fax 01865 775610
email btaf@tattoo.co.uk   http://www.tattoo.co.uk
Sec: Lionel Titchener
○ *P; to improve & encourage high standards of hygiene in
professional tattoo studios
Gp Tattoo history museum, archives & library
● LG
< Tattoo Club of GB
M 500 i
¶ Tattoo International - 6.
Note: is part of the Tattoo Club of Great Britain

British Technical Council of the Motor & Petroleum Industries
since 1 July 2005 **BTC Testing Advisory Group**

British Technion Society (BTS) 1951
NR 62 Grosvenor St, LONDON, W1K 3JF. (hq)
020 7495 6824
http://www.britishtechnionsociety.org
▲ Registered Charity
○ *K; to promote the Technion (Israel Institute of Technology); to
ensure research by introducing active partners; to fundraise
for various projects
M i

British Teledermatology Society
a group of the **British Association of Dermatologists**

British Temperance Society
Please delete from your directory, May 2008.

British Tennis Coaches Association   (BTCA)
NR   c/o Wolverhampton LT & SC, Neville Lodge,
    Newbridge Crescent, WOLVERHAMPTON, WV6 0LH.
    01902 758500
    Admin: Amanda Yates
○   *P, *S
¶   Coachline - 6.

British Tenpin Bowling Association   (BTBA)   1961
NR   114 Balfour Rd, ILFORD, Essex, IG1 4JD.   (hq)
    020 8478 1745   fax 020 8514 3665
    email admin@btba.org.uk   http://www.btba.org.uk
○   *S; to act as the governing body for tenpin bowling in the UK;
    to promote the sport
M   c 30,000 i

British Tensional Strapping Association   (BTSA)   1950
NR   5 Church Mews, Barlby, SELBY, N Yorks, YO8 5LL.   (hq)
    01757 708555
    Sec: Graham Cooper
▲   Un-incorporated Society
○   *T; strapping equipment & materials
●   Mtgs - SG - Stat
M   7 f
¶   An Introduction to Tensional Strapping.
    Health & Safety guides:
       Steel strapping.   Non-metallic strapping.
       Strapping machines.
    Hazard Data Sheets.

British Tersk Society
NR   Drummond, Dores, INVERNESS, IV2 6TX.
    01463 751251   fax 01463 751240
    email candy@dores.demon.co.uk
    Contact: Candy Cameron

British Texel Sheep Society Ltd   (BTSS)   1972
NR   4th Avenue NAC, Stoneleigh Park, KENILWORTH, Warks,
    CV8 2LG.   (hq)
    024 7669 6629   fax 024 7669 6472
    email office@texel.co.uk   http://www.texel.co.uk
    Chief Exec & Co Sec: Steven J McLean
▲   Company Limited by Guarantee; Registered Charity
○   *B
●   Exhib - Comp - Expt - Inf
<   Nat Sheep Assn
M   2,500 i, 1 f, 19 breeders' clubs
¶   Jnl - 1;   Texel Bulletin - 4; both free.

British Textile Machinery Association   (BTMA)   1940
■   Mount Pleasant, Glazebrook Lane, Glazebrook,
    WARRINGTON, Lancs, WA3 5BN.   (hq)
    0161-775 5710   fax 0161-775 5485
    email btma@btma.org.uk   http://www.btma.org.uk
    Dir: Alan Little
▲   Company Limited by Guarantee
○   *T
Gp   Sub-c'ees: Exhibitions, Technical, Executive
●   Mtgs - Exhib - Stat - Expt - Inf - LG
<   Eur C'ee Textile Machinery Mfrs (CEMATEX)
M   100 f
¶   Monthly Circular - 12;   Export Financing & Insurance;
    Outfitter conditions;   AR; all ftm only.
    BTMA Directory - 1; free.

British Textile Technology Group   (BTTG)   1988
NR   Wira House, West Park Ring Rd, LEEDS, W Yorks, LS16 6QL.
    (hq)
    0113-259 1999
    Chmn: William Laidlaw
▲   Company Limited by Guarantee
Br   4
○   *Q; a centre of excellence in textile & materials related testing,
    investigation & evaluation
Gp   Spinning & nonwovens; Shirley technologies; Certification;
    Wiratec; CASE (Coatings, adhesives, sealant & encapsulate
    testing); Fire technology services; BCTC (British Carpet
    Technical Centre)
●   Conf - ET - Res - Inf - Exhib
M   143 f, UK / 19 f, o'seas
¶   Independent - 4.

British Theatre Dance Association   (BTDA)   1973
■   Garden St, LEICESTER, LE1 3UA.   (hq)
    0845 166 2179   fax 0845 166 2189
    Gen Sec: Helen Mence
▲   Company Limited by Guarantee
○   *P; to provide dance syllabi for teachers throughout the UK &
    overseas
●   Mtgs - ET - Exam - Comp
M   1,800 i, UK / 100 i, o'seas
¶   Danceworld - 2.

British Throwsters Association
NR   5 Portland Place, LONDON, W1B 1PW.   (hq)
    020 7636 7788   fax 020 7636 7515
    email bta@dial.pipex.com
    Dir: Adam Mansell
○   *P; to promote & protect the UK throwing & texturising industry
    (both stages in yarn production)
●   Mtgs - LG
<   Brit Apparel & Textile Confedn

British Thyroid Association   (BTA)
NR   Grampian Diabetes Centre, Aberdeen Royal Infirmary,
    Foresterhill, ABERDEEN, AB25 2ZN.
    0870 770 7933
    http://www.british-thyroid-association.org
    Sec: Dr Prakash Abraham
○   *W

British Tinnitus Association   (BTA)   1979
■   Unit 5 Acorn Business Park, Woodseats Close, SHEFFIELD,
    S Yorks, S8 0TB.   (hq)
    0114-250 9922 freephone: 0800 018 0527   fax 0114-
    258 2279
    email info@tinnitus.org.uk   http://www.tinnitus.org.uk
    Operations Mgr: Mrs Val Rose
▲   Company Limited by Guarantee; Registered Charity
Br   80 self-help groups
○   *M, *W; to support people with information & advice; to fund
    tinnitus research projects in order to find a cure; to promote
    awareness & understanding of the condition
●   Conf - Mtgs - ET - Res - Pen pal register
M   c 10,000 i, UK / c 300 i, o'seas
¶   Quiet (Jnl) - 4.
    Leaflets;   Audio cassette relaxation tapes.

British Titanic Society   (BTS)   1986
NR   PO Box 401, Hope Carr Way, LEIGH, Lancs, WN7 3WW.
    Sec: Steve Rigby
▲   Un-incorporated Society
○   *G; to research & preserve the memory of RMS Titanic & her
    passengers & crew
●   Conf - Res - Exhib - Comp - SG - VE
M   1,000 i, UK / 200 i, o'seas
¶   Atlantic Daily Bulletin (NL) - 4.

British Toilet Association (BTA) 1999
- ■ PO Box 847, HORSHAM, W Sussex, RH12 5AL.   (hq)
  01403 258779
  email enquiries@britloos.co.uk   http://www.britloos.co.uk
  Managing Dir: Mike Bone
- ▲ Company Limited by Guarantee
- ○ *K; pressure group campaigning for more & better public lavatories
- ● Conf - Mtgs - Res - Stat - Inf - Lib - LG - Awards: Loo of the Year & Attendant of the Year
- M   i, f, org

British Tomato Growers Association (TGA) 1997
- ■ Pollards Nursery, Lake Lane, BARNHAM, W Sussex, PO22 0AD.
  01243 554859   fax 01243 554645
  email tga@britishtomatoes.co.uk
  http://www.britishtomatoes.co.uk
  Sec: Mrs Julie Woolley
- ▲ Company Limited by Guarantee
- ○ *H, *T; represents British growers; marketing information, research & development
- ● Conf - Mtgs - ET - Res - Exhib - LG
- M   45 f

British Town Criers Authority
- ■ 12 Little Bornes, Dulwich, LONDON, SE21 8SE.
  020 8670 5585
  http://www.ivorspencer.com
- ○ *P
- < Gld of Intl Profl Toastmasters
- M   20 affiliated town criers

British Toxicology Society (BTS) 1979
- ■ PO Box 249, MACCLESFIELD, Cheshire, SK11 6FT.   (hq)
  01625 267881
  email secretariat@thebts.org
  Sec: Dr H Wallace,   Meetings Sec: Dr S Price
- ▲ Registered Charity
- ○ *L; to advance the science & education of toxicology & the safety of chemicals for people & the environment
- Gp Biotechnology; Human toxicology; Immunotoxicology; Neurotoxicology; Occupational toxicology; Regulatory toxicology; Risk Assessment
- ● Conf - Mtgs - Specialist working parties on scientific topics
- < Intl U of Toxicology; Fedn of Eur Socs of Toxicology; Biological Coun
- M   692 i, UK / 158 i, o'seas

British Toy & Hobby Association Ltd (BTHA) 1944
- ■ 80 Camberwell Rd, LONDON, SE5 0EG.   (hq)
  020 7701 7271   fax 020 7708 2437
  email admin@btha.co.uk   http://www.btha.co.uk
  Dir Gen & Sec: David L Hawtin
- ○ *T
- ● Mtgs - Res - Exhib - Stat - Expt - Inf
- M   180 i & f
- ¶ Buyers Guide - 1; ftm, £15 nm.
  NTC leaflets; free.

British Toy Importers Association
  since 2006 **Equitoy: the association for toy importers**

British Toymakers Guild (BTG) 1955
- ■ PO Box 240, UCKFIELD, E Sussex, TN22 9AS.   (hq)
  01225 442440
  email info@toymakersguild.co.uk
  http://www.toymakersguild.co.uk
  Mgr: Robert Nathan
- ▲ Un-incorporated Society
- ○ *T; to promote excellence in toy design & manufacture
- Gp Craft toy making
- ● Mtgs - Exhib - Stat - Inf - LG
- M   35 i, 140 f
- ¶ The Toymaker - 4.   Directory - 1.

British Trade Council in Austria
  since 2004 **Austro-British Chamber**

British Transplantation Society (BTS) 1971
- NR Association House, South Park Rd, MACCLESFIELD, Cheshire, SK11 6SH.   (hsb)
  01625 504060   fax 01625 267879
  http://www.bts.org.uk
  Sec: J Forsythe
- ▲ Company Limited by Guarantee; Registered Charity
- ○ *L; to advance the study of the biological & clinical problems of tissue & organ donation; to facilitate contact between persons interested in transplantation; to make new knowledge available for the general good of the community
- Gp Clinical trials; Standards; Training
- ● Mtgs - ET - Res
- M   c 650 i
- ¶ NL - 2.

British Transport Officers' Guild (BTOG) 1944
- NR Hayes Court, West Common Rd, HAYES, Kent, BR2 7AU.   (hq)
  020 8462 7755
- ▲ Un-incorporated Society
- ○ *U; a section of Amicus-AEEU
- M   i

British Trauma Society
  a specialist society of the **British Orthopaedic Association**

British Travel Health Association (BTHA) 1999
- NR PO Box 336, SALE, M33 3UU.   (hq)
  0845 003 9197   fax 0870 005 3521
  email info@byha.org   http://www.btha.org
  Hon Sec: Dr George Kassianos
- ▲ Registered Charity
- ○ *K, *M; to promote a multi-disciplinary approach to travel health; to increase public awareness of travel health hazards
- ● Conf - Mtgs - ET - Res - SG - Inf
- M   c 530 i
- ¶ Jnl - 2;   Travelwise - 4; both ftm only.

British Travelgoods & Accessories Association (BTAA) 1918
- NR Federation House, 10 Vyse St, BIRMINGHAM, B18 6LT.   (hq)
  0121-237 1107
  http://www.btaa.org.uk
  Sec: Diana Fiveash
- ▲ Company Limited by Guarantee
- ○ *T; representing manufacturers, distributors & importers of luggage, handbags & small leathergoods
- ● Conf - Mtgs - Exhib - Expt - Inf - LG
- < Brit Jewellery, Giftware & Finishing Fedn
- M   90 f
- ¶ Buyer's Guide - amended as necessary.
- × 2005-06 British Luggage & Leathergoods Association

British Trials & Rally Drivers Association (BTRDA)
- NR Woodlands, Anthony's Cross, NEWENT, Glos, GL18 1JF.   (hsp)
  01531 820761
  http://www.btrda.com
  Contact: Simon Harris

British Triathlon Federation 1984
- NR PO Box 25, LOUGHBOROUGH, Leics, LE11 3WX.   (hq)
  01509 226161   fax 01509 226165
  email info@britishtriathlon.org
  http://www.britishtriathlon.org
  Chief Exec: Zara Hyde Peters
- ▲ Company Limited by Guarantee
- ○ *S; to govern, administer & develop the sport of triathlon by providing opportunities for athletes of all ages & abilities to compete at the highest level
- M   3 org
- × 2007 British Triathlon Association Ltd

© CBD Research Ltd · Beckenham · BR3 5JS · Tel 020 8650 7745 · Fax 020 8650 0768 · E-mail cbd@cbdresearch.com · www.cbdresearch.com

British Trolleybus Society (BTS) 1961
- ■ 2 Josephine Court, Southcote Rd, READING, Berks, RG30 2DG.   (hsp)
  0118-958 3974
  Hon Sec: A J Barton
- ▲ Registered Charity
- ○ *G; to study the history & development of the trolley bus & trolley bus networks
- ● Mtgs - VE
- M 320 i, UK / 10 i, o'seas
- ¶ Trolleybus - 12.   Bus Fare - 12.   Wheels - 12.

British Trombone Society (BTS) 1983
- ■ 1-3 Church St, Hutton, DRIFFIELD, E Yorks, YO25 9PR.   (hsp)
  01377 202209
  email secretary@britishtrombonesociety.org
  http://www.britishtrombonesociety.org
  Sec: Geoff Wolmark
- ▲ Un-incorporated Society
- ○ *D; to promote the trombone & trombone-related issues in the UK
- ● Conf - ET - Comp - Inf - Commissioning of compositions
- < Intl Trombone Assn
- M 700 i, UK / 300 i, o'seas
  (Sub: £22, UK / £25, o'seas)
- ¶ The Trombonist - 4.

British Trout Association Ltd (BTA) 1982
- ■ The Rural Centre, West Mains, INGLISTON, Midlothian, EH28 8NZ.   (hq)
  0131-472 4080   fax 0131-472 4083
  email mail@britishtrout.co.uk
  http://www.britishtrout.co.uk
  Chief Exec: David Bassett
- ▲ Company Limited by Guarantee
- ○ *T; to represent the UK trout aquaculture industry; research relating to trout health & welfare
- Gp British Trout Farmers Restocking Association
- ● Conf - Mtgs - Res - Stat - Inf - VE - LG - Marketing - PR - Technical advice - QA scheme
- < Fedn of Eur Aquaculture Producers (FEAP); Fedn of Scot Aquaculture Producers (FSAP)
- M 100 f
- ¶ NL - 4;   AR - 1; both ftm.
  Code of Practice;   QTUK Standards;   Technical Briefing Notes; all ftm only.

British Trout Farmers Restocking Association
    a group of the **British Trout Association**

British Truck Racing Association (BTRA) 1985
- NR Roughwood, Thibet Rd, SANDHURST, Berks, GU47 9AR.
  (sec/p)
  01344 762774
  http://www.britishtruckracing.co.uk
  Sec: Terry Cox
- ○ *S; to further interest in motoring & motor sport with trucks

British Trust for Conservation Volunteers (BTCV) 1959
- NR Sedum House, Mallard Way, Potteric Carr, DONCASTER, S Yorks, DN4 8DB.   (hq)
  01302 388883
  email information@btcv.org.uk   http://www.btcv.org
- ▲ Registered Charity
- ○ *K; to ensure that the potential for voluntary action for the environment is fully realised; to ensure that people of the world value their environment & take practical action to improve it
- M i

British Trust for Ornithology (BTO) 1933
- ■ The Nunnery, THETFORD, Norfolk, IP24 2PU.   (hq)
  01842 750050   fax 01842 750030
  email general@bto.org   http://www.bto.org
  Dir: Dr Andy Clements,   Sec: Andrew T Scott
- ▲ Company Limited by Guarantee; Registered Charity
- Br BTO Scotland, Stirling
- ○ *L; 'to promote & encourage wider understanding, appreciation & conservation of birds through scientific studies. . . by members, other birdwatchers & staff'
- Gp Habitats research: Coastal & wetlands, Terrestrial
  Populations research: Ringing, Censuses, Nest records
  Membership & development; Administration
- ● Conf - Mtgs - ET - Res - SG - Stat - Inf - Lib - LG - Research & monitoring consultancy
- M 9,000 i, 300 org, UK / 500 i, 20 org, o'seas
- ¶ Bird Table - 4.
  Bird Study - 3.   BTO News (NL) - 6.
  Ringing Migration - 2.   AR,

British Tugowners Association (BTA) 1934
- ■ Carthusian Court, 12 Carthusian St, LONDON, EC1M 6EZ.
  (hq)
  020 7417 2875   fax 020 7600 1534
  email info@britishtug.org   http://www.britishtug.org
  Sec: David Asprey
- ▲ Un-incorporated Society
- ○ *T; 'members own/operate tugs for shiptowage services in ports of the UK, coastal & ocean towage & salvage'
- ● Conf - Mtgs - ET - Stat - Inf - LG
- < Eur Tugowners Assn
- M 18 f, UK / 1 f, o'seas

British Tunnelling Society (BTS) 1971
- ■ Institution of Civil Engineers, One Great George St, LONDON, SW1P 3AA.   (hq)
  http://www.britishtunnelling.org.uk
- ▲ Registered Charity
- ○ *L, *Q; to develop the art, science & techniques of tunnelling
- ● Conf - Mtgs - Comp - Inf
- < Intl Tunnelling Assn
- M 780 i, 40 f, UK / 165 i, o'seas
- ¶ Tunnels & Tunnelling International - 12.
  NL - 3.   AR.

British Turf & Landscape Irrigation Association (BTLIA) 1978
- NR 41 Pennine Way, Great Eccleston, PRESTON, Lancs, PR3 0YS.
  (sp)
  01995 670675   fax 01995 670675
  email info@btlia.org.uk   http://www.btlia.org.uk
  Sec: Martyn T Jones
- ▲ Company Limited by Guarantee
- ○ *T; to promote the proper & responsible installation of turf & landscape irrigation schemes; to provide eduational opportunities to fulfil these criteria
- Gp Irrigation: Equipment manufacturers, Consultants, Installation contractors
- ● Conf - Mtgs - ET - Exam - Exhib - Inf
- < Irrigation Assn (USA); Eur Irrigation Assn; UK Irrigation Assn
- M c 50 f
- ¶ LM - 1; ftm, on request nm.

British Turned-Parts Manufacturers Association   (BTMA) 1920
- ■ Pear Tree Cottage, Snitterfield Lane, Norton Lindsey, WARWICK, CV35 8JQ.   (dir/p)
  01789 730877   fax 01789 730899
  email iangold@btma.org   http://www.btma.org
  Dir: Ian Gold
- ○ *T; for precision turned parts & machined component manufacturers
- ● Conf - Mtgs - ET - Exhib - SG - Stat - Inf - VE - LG
- M 75 f
- ¶ BTMA Buyer's Guide (LM) - 1; free.

British Tyre Manufacturers' Association Ltd (BTMA) 1968
NR 6 Bath Place, Rivington St, LONDON, EC2A 3JE. (hq)
     020 7457 5040   fax 020 7972 9008
     http://www.btmauk.com
     Dir: A J Dorken,   Admin: Christine Joyce
▲ Company Limited by Guarantee
○ *T; to promote & protect the interests of the rubber
     manufacturing industry in the UK
Gp Tyre management c'ee (TNC); General rubber goods (GRG)
● Conf - Mtgs - ET - Stat - Inf - LG
< Eur Rubber Assn (BLIC); Tyre Ind Coun (TIC)
M 61 f
✕ 2005 British Rubber Manufacturers Association

British UFO Research Association (BUFORA) 1963
§ 41 Castlebar Rd, Ealing, LONDON, W5 2DJ. (hsp)
     email enquiries@bufora.org.uk
     http://www.bufora.org.uk
     Hon Sec: Mrs Judith M Jaafar
▲ Company Limited by Guarantee
¶ [all publications on website].
     Originally named the British Unidentified Flying Object
     Research Association, BUFORA Ltd assumed dormancy status
     in 2007 and now exists solely as a non-membership
     organisation researching unidentified flying phenomena
     throughout the UK; disseminating & collating evidence &
     cooperating with others doing similar research throughout
     the world.

British Union for the Abolition of Vivisection (BUAV) 1898
■ 16a Crane Grove, LONDON, N7 8NN. (hq)
     020 7700 4888   fax 020 7700 0252
     email info@buav.org   http://www.buav.org
     Chief Exec: Michelle Thew
▲ Company Limited by Guarantee
○ *K; campaigning to end all animal experiments
● Conf - Res - Exhib - Comp - Stat - Inf - Lib - PL - LG - Lobbying
     UK/EU legislation - Undercover investigations
< Intl Coun for Animal Protection in OECD Programmes; Eur
     Coalition to End Animal Experiments
¶ BUAV Action (NL) - 3 (email - 6);   BUAV Update (NL) - 4; AR -
     1; all free.

British Union of Social Work Employees
     in 2008 merged with **Community**

British Universities Film & Video Council (BUFVC) 1948
NR 77 Wells St, LONDON, W1T 3QJ. (hq)
     020 7393 1500
     email ask@bufvc.ac.uk   http://www.bufvc.ac.uk
     Chief Exec: Murray Weston
▲ Company Limited by Guarantee; Registered Charity
○ *E; to foster the production, study & use of film & related audio-
     visual media (incl TV, video & computer-based multi media)
     for higher education & research
M c 220 universities, insts etc
✕ 2004 (April) Learning on Screen (merged)

British Universities Industrial Relations Association (BUIRA) 1950
NR c/o MMU Business School, Aytoun Building, Aytoun St,
     MANCHESTER, M1 3GH. (sb)
     0161-247 6160
     Contact: Ann Marie McDonald
○ *P; the academic study of industrial relations & allied areas in
     Britain & internationally
● Conf - Res - SG - Specialist bibliographies research register
< Intl Indl Relations Assn; Academy of Learned Socs for the Social
     Sciences
M i

British Universities Sports Association (BUSA) 1994
NR 20-24 King's Bench St, LONDON, SE1 0QX. (hq)
     020 7633 5080   fax 020 3268 2120
     http://www.busa.org.uk
▲ Registered Charity
○ *S, *K; organisation & promotion of sport to students in higher
     education through organisation of championships
     representing fixtures & British teams for international events
● Conf - Mtgs - ET - Comp - Sporting championships
     Fixtures & results: www.busaresults.org.uk
M 150 universities
¶ Hbk - 1;   AR - 1; both free.

British Urban Regeneration Association (BURA) 1990
■ 63-66 Hatton Garden (4th floor), LONDON, EC1N 8LE. (hq)
     020 7539 4030   fax 020 7404 9614
     email info@bura.org.uk   http://www.bura.org.uk
     Chief Exec: Jon Ladd
▲ Company Limited by Guarantee
○ *K, *P; to provide a forum for the exchange of ideas on
     regeneration issues; to identify examples of best practice
Gp Steering & development forum
● Conf - Mtgs - Res - Exhib - SG - Inf - VE - LG - Award schemes
M 1,500 i, 550 f, UK / 50 i, 10 f, o'seas
¶ Urban Regeneration - a handbook; £18.99.
     Learning from Experience; £10.
     Guide to Best Practice in Sport & Regeneration; £10.
     Breaking old Ground - a guide to contaminated land; £10.

British Urethane Foam Contractors Association (BUFCA Ltd) 1980
■ PO Box 12, HASLEMERE, Surrey, GU27 3AH. (hq)
     01428 654011   fax 01428 651401
     email info@bufca.co.uk   http://www.bufca.co.uk
     Co Sec: Leonie Onslow
▲ Company Limited by Guarantee
○ *T; contractors & suppliers in the sprayed urethane foam
     industry for thermal insulation of buildings & plant
Gp Health & safety; Fire hazards; Coatings; Foam specification
● Conf - Mtgs - Exhib - SG - Stat - Inf
M f
¶ NL;   Technical Bulletin;   Technical Guidelines; all ftm only.

British-Uruguayan Chamber of Commerce
     English name of **Cámara de Comercio Uruguayo Británica**

British Uruguayan Society 1945
NR 222 Brooklands Rd, WEYBRIDGE, Surrey, KT13 0RJ. (sp)
     01932 847455
     Sec: Jill Quaife
▲ Registered Charity
○ *X; to advance the knowledge of Britons about Uruguay &
     Uruguayans about the UK
● Mtgs - Exhib - Inf - Lib (at Hispanic Council, Canning House) -
     VE
M c 250 i, UK / c 30 i, o'seas
¶ El Hornero - 2.
     Tales of Uruguay (members' reminiscences of Uruguay),
     (1988);
     A History of the Society 1945-1985, (1997);
     The Uruguayan Short Story, (2007); all £5.

British Used Printing Machinery Suppliers Association (BUPMSA) 1993
■ 20 Spencer Bridge Rd, NORTHAMPTON, NN5 5EZ. (hq)
     01604 756100   fax 01604 750910
     email info@bupmsa.org.uk   http://www.bupmsa.org.uk
     Chmn: Michael Steele
▲ Company Limited by Guarantee
○ *T; for dealers of used print related equipment who buy & sell
     worldwide
● Exhib - Expt - Inf

© CBD Research Ltd · Beckenham · BR3 5JS · Tel 020 8650 7745 · Fax 020 8650 0768 · E-mail cbd@cbdresearch.com · www.cbdresearch.com

British Vacuum Council   (BVC)   1965
NR   76 Portland Place, LONDON, W1B 1NT.   (hq)
    020 7470 4838   fax 020 7470 4848
    http://www.british-vacuum-council.org.uk
    Sec: Dr Mark Bowden
▲   Registered Charity
○   *L; to promote & advance the understanding & teaching of
    vacuum science, technology & its applications
●   Sponsorship of conferences & training courses organised by its
    affiliated bodies
<   Intl U of Vacuum Science, Technique & its Applications
M   2 org:
    Institute of Physics
    Royal Society of Chemistry
¶   Vacuum Technology, Applications & Ion Physics - 12.

British Valve & Actuator Association Ltd   (BVAA)   1939
■   9 Manor Park, BANBURY, Oxon, OX16 3TB.   (hq)
    01295 221270   fax 01295 268965
    email enquiry@bvaa.org.uk   http://www.bvaa.org.uk
    Dir: Rob Bartlett
▲   Company Limited by Guarantee
○   *T; to represent interests of British manufacturers, distributors &
    repairers of industrial valves & actuators
Gp   Technical; Marketing; Actuator; Executive; Manufacturing &
    quality; Training
●   Conf - Mtgs - ET - Exhib - Stat - Expt - Inf - VE - Journal
<   CBI Trade Assn Forum
M   100 f (annual)
¶   NL - 4;   Buyers Guide - 1 yrly;   AR; all free.
    Valve Users Manual (Technical Handbook); £10.

**British Vehicle Rental & Leasing Association Ltd   (BVRLA)
1967**
NR   River Lodge, Badminton Court, AMERSHAM, Bucks,
    HP7 0DD.   (hq)
    01494 434747   fax 01494 434499
    email info@bvrla.co.uk   http://www.bvrla.co.uk
    Dir Gen: John Lewis
▲   Company Limited by Guarantee
○   *T; to represent the interests of operators of daily rental,
    leasing, contract hire & fleet management for cars, minibuses
    & light & heavy commercial vehicles
Gp   Vehicle rental; Vehicle leasing & contract hire
●   Conf - Mtgs - ET - Exam - Exhib - SG - Stat - Inf - VE - LG
<   Eur Car & Truck Rental Assn (ECATRA)
M   c 800 f
¶   BVRLA News (NL) - 12;   BVLRA Directory - 1; both ftm only.
    Fair Wear & Tear Guides; prices vary.
    Various other publications - list available.

British Vehicle Salvage Federation   (BVSF)   1998
■   Bates Business Centre, Church Rd, Harold Wood, ROMFORD,
    Essex, RM3 0JF.   (hq)
    01708 381046   fax 01708 340485
    email email@bvsf.org.uk   http://www.bvsf.org.uk
    Chmn & Sec Gen: Alan W Greenouff
▲   Un-Incorporated Society
○   *T; representative body for the UK vehicle salvage industry
Gp   Management c'ee
●   Conf - Mtgs - LG
<   Assn of Brit Insurers; Motor Repair Res Centre (Thatcham)
M   98 f
¶   Vehicle Salvage Professional - 4; free.   AR.

British Vendeen Sheep Society   1984
■   Darkes House, Conderton, TEWKESBURY, Glos, GL20 7PP.
    (hsp)
    01386 725229
    email info@vendeen.co.uk
    Sec: Andrew John
▲   Registered Charity
○   *B; the promotion & improvement of British Vendeen sheep
Gp   Sire reference scheme
●   Comp - Inf
M   80 i
¶   Flock Book - 1; £10.

British Venture Capital Association
    since 2001 **BVCA (British Private Equity & Venture Capital
Association**

British Veterinary Association   (BVA)   1881
NR   7 Mansfield St, LONDON, W1G 9NQ.   (hq)
    020 7636 6541
    email bvahq@bva.co.uk   http://www.bva.co.uk
▲   Company Limited by Guarantee
○   *P, *V; standards of animal health; veterinary surgeons' working
    practices; profl standards of quality of service; relations with
    external bodies; policy development; service provision
M   i

British Veterinary Camelid Society   (BVCS)   1994
NR   Foxes Grove - Spring Hill, Punnetts Town, HEATHFIELD,
    E Sussex, TN21 9PE.   (hsp)
    01435 864422
    email secretary@camelidvets.org
    http://www.camelidvets.org
    Sec: Janet Nuttall
▲   Un-incorporated Society
○   *V; to stimulate knowledge of diseases & management of South
    American camelids (alpaca, llama, guanaco & vicuña); to
    promote interest in these fascinating animals with respect to
    their management, breeding, feeding, health & disease
●   Conf - Mtgs - ET - Inf - LG
M   c 110 i, f & org
¶   Proceedings of Conference - 1.

British Veterinary Dental Association
    a group of the **British Small Animal Veterinary Association**

British Veterinary Dermatology Study Group
    a group of the **British Small Animal Veterinary Association**

British Veterinary Hospitals Association   (BVHA)   1960
■   c/o Station Bungalow, Main Rd, STOCKSFIELD,
    Northumberland, NE43 7HJ.   (office/mgr/p)
    0796 690 1619   fax 0781 391 5954
    email office@bvha.org.uk   http://www.bvha.org.uk
    Office Manager: Christine Shield,   Hon Sec: Ian Harris
▲   Un-incorporated Society
○   *P, *V; to promote the highest standards of excellence in animal
    treatment through the design, construction & equipping of
    veterinary hospitals
●   Conf - ET - Exhib - Comp - Inf - VE
<   a division of the Brit Veterinary Assn
M   108 i, 116 f
¶   Bulletin - 4; ftm only.

British Veterinary Neurology Study Group
    a group of the **British Small Animal Veterinary Association**

British Veterinary Nursing Association Ltd   (BVNA)   1965
NR   82 Greenway Business Centre, Harlow Business Park,
        HARLOW, Essex, CM19 5QE.   (hq)
        01279 408644   fax 01279 408645
        email bvna@bvna.co.uk   http://www.bvna.co.uk
▲   Company Limited by Guarantee
○   *P, *V; for veterinary nurses
●   Conf - ET - Exam - Exhib - Inf
<   Intl Veterinary Nurses & Technicians Assn (IVNTA)
M   4,020 i, UK / 59 i, o'seas
¶   Veterinary Nursing Jnl - 12; free.

British Veterinary Poultry Association
        a group of the **British Veterinary Association**

British Veterinary Zoological Society
        a group of the **British Veterinary Association**

British Video Association   (BVA)   1980
NR   167 Great Portland St, LONDON, W1W 5PE.   (hq)
        020 7436 0041   fax 020 7436 0043
        email general@bva.org.uk   http://www.bva.org.uk
        Dir Gen: Mrs Lavinia Carey
▲   Company Limited by Guarantee
○   *T; to represent the interests of publishers and rights owners of
        pre-recorded video home entertainment
●   Conf - Mtgs - Res - Exhib - Stat - Inf - LG
M   46 f (26 full, 20 associate)
¶   NL - 12.   LM - 12.   Ybk - 1.

British Vintage Wireless Society   (BVWS)   1976
NR   AOPP, Clarendon Laboratory, Parks Rd, OXFORD, OX1 3PU.
        (hq)
        01865 247971
        http://www.bvws.org.uk
        Sec: Dr Guy Peskett
▲   Un-incorporated Society
○   *G; the history & preservation of vintage wireless & television
        equipment
●   Mtgs - Res - Exhib - Comp - Inf - Lib - PL
M   1,400 i, 55 org, UK / 200 i, 16 org, o'seas
¶   Bulletin (incorporating 405 Alive) - 4; ftm only.

British Violin Making Association   (BVMA)   1995
NR   7 Widcombe Parade, BATH, BA2 4JT.
        01225 337734
        email secretary@bvms.org.uk   http://www.bvma.org.uk
        Sec: Corrie Schrijver
▲   Un-incorporated Society
○   *P, *T; to raise the standards & skills of violin & bow makers &
        restorers; to encourage dissemination of information
        amongst them
●   Conf - ET - Exhib - Comp
M   479 i, 20 org
¶   [Jnl] - 4

British Voice Association   (BVA)   1991
■   330 Gray's Inn Rd, LONDON, WC1X 8EE.   (hq)
        020 7713 0064   fax 020 7915 1388
        email bva@dircon.co.uk
        http://www.british-voice-association.com
        Co Sec: Kristine Carroll-Porczynski
▲   Company Limited by Guarantee
○   *P; for all professionals interested in the human voice
Gp   Laryngology; Singing; Speech therapy; Phonetics; Voice
        teaching; Singing teaching
●   Conf - Mtgs - ET - Res - Comp - Inf - Professional standards in
        related medical groups
<   Intl Assn of Logopedics & Phoniatrics
M   470 i, UK / 30 i, o'seas
        (Sub: £55 UK / £65 o'seas)
¶   Logopedics, Phoniatrics & Vocology - 4;
        NL - 3;   LM - 1; all ftm only.

British Volleyball Federation   (BVF)   1981
NR   English Institute of Sport, Coleridge Rd, SHEFFIELD, S Yorks,
        S9 5DA.   (hq)
        0114-223 5731   fax 0114-223 5660
        http://www.britishperformancevolleyball.org
        Programme Mgr: Kenny Barton
▲   Un-incorporated Society
○   *N, *S; umbrella organisation to coordinate activities of the
        English, Northern Ireland, Scottish & Welsh Volleyball
        Associations
Gp   Volleyball Association(s): English / Northern Ireland / Scottish /
        Welsh;
        Great Britain National Volleyball Teams
M   4 org

British Walking Federation   (BWF)   1983
NR   4a Clandon Terrace, Kingston Rd, Raynes Park, LONDON,
        SW20 8SE.   (hq)
        020 8543 1283
        email info@bwf-ivv.org.uk   http://www.bwf-ivv.org.uk
        Sec: Jim Nelson
▲   Un-incorporated Society
○   *G, *S; walking for health
●   Conf - Mtgs - LG - Monitoring of non-competitive walks
<   Intl Fedn of Popular Sports (IVV)
M   i & org
¶   Footprint - 6.

British Warm Air Hand Drier Association   (BWAHDA)   1981
■   Technology House, Oakfield Industrial Estate, EYNSHAM,
        Oxon, OX29 4AQ.   (regd off)
        01865 882330   fax 01865 881647
        Sec: Graham Davies
▲   Company Limited by Guarantee
○   *T; promotion of warm air hand driers
●   Mtgs - Inf - LG
M   5 f, UK / 1 f, o'seas

British Warm-Blood Society
        since January 2008 the **Warmblood Breeders' Studbook - UK**

British Watch & Clock Makers' Guild   (BWCMG)   1907
■   PO Box 2368, ROMFORD, Essex, RM1 2YZ.   (hsp)
        01708 750616   fax 01708 750616
        email sec@bwcmg.org   http://www.bwcmg.org
        Hon Sec: P Craddock
▲   Company Limited by Guarantee
○   *P, *T; for those professionally engaged in the manufacture,
        restoration or repair of watches & clocks
●   Inf
M   1,000 i, UK / 15 i, o'seas
¶   NL - 2; ftm only.

© CBD Research Ltd · Beckenham · BR3 5JS · Tel 020 8650 7745 · Fax 020 8650 0768 · E-mail cbd@cbdresearch.com · www.cbdresearch.com

British Water 1993

- 1 Queen Anne's Gate, LONDON, SW1H 9BT. (hq)
020 7957 4554 fax 020 7957 4565
email info@britishwater.co.uk
http://www.britishwater.co.uk
Chief Exec: David Neil-Gallacher
- ▲ Company Limited by Guarantee
- ○ *N, *T; to represent the collective interests of the supply chain of the UK water & waste water industry in relation to government, regulators, trade promotion, industry standards, legislative & regulatory affairs. Membership includes civil & process contractors, management, engineering & IT consultants, equipment manufacturers & suppliers, law firms, financial institutions & specialist research & training organisations
- Gp UK Forum, International Forum
Technical Forum and specialist focus groups
Overseas (Asia-Pacific, Europe, Middle East)
- ● Conf - Mtgs - ET - Exhib - Expt - Inf - LG
- < Intl Water Assn (IWA); Aqua Europa; Mechanical & Metal Trs Confedn (METCOM)
- M 175 f
- ¶ Codes of Practice; prices vary. AR; both free.

British Water Cooler Association (BWCA) 1991

- Hartfield House, 40-44 High St, NORTHWOOD, Middx, HA6 1BN. (asa)
01923 825355
email info@bwca.org.uk http://www.bwca.org.uk
Secretariat: Phillipa Atkinson-Clow
- ○ *T; all aspects of chain of supply from water source to satisfaction & health of consumers
- ● Mtgs - ET - Res - SG - Stat - Inf - LG
- M f
- ¶ Handbooks.
- × 2005 Bottled Water Cooler Association

British Water Ski 1951

- NR The Tower, Thorpe Rd, CHERTSEY, Surrey, KT16 8PH. (hq)
01932 570885 fax 01932 566719
email info@bwsf.co.uk http://www.britishwaterski.co.uk
Exec Officer: Patrick Donovan
- ▲ Company Limited by Guarantee
- Br 2
- ○ *S; the governing body for water skiing in the UK
- ● ET - Exam - Comp - Inf
- < Intl Water Ski Fedn (IWSF); Boating Alliance
- M c 11,000 i, 150 clubs
- ¶ British Water Ski & Wakeboard - 5; free.
- × 1999 British Water Ski Federation Ltd

British Waterbed Association (BWA) 1984

- Manchester Waterbed Centre, 7a Victoria Lane, Whitefield, MANCHESTER, M45 6BL. (sb)
0870 603 0202 fax 0870 603 0202
http://www.waterbed.org
Sec: Michael Hand
- ▲ Un-incorporated Society
- Br 35; Belgium, Denmark, Netherlands
- ○ *T; to promote quality waterbed products; to advance sleep research; to increase consumer awareness & advise waterbed users
- Gp Manufacturers, Wholesalers, Retailers
- ● Exhib - Annual trade show
- < Speciality Sleep Assn (USA)
- M 35 f, UK / 4 f, o'seas
- ¶ Waterbeds - the facts. Fact & Fiction.
Backaches & Waterbeds. Arthritis & Waterbeds.
Waterbed Owners Manual.

British Watercolour Society (BWS) 1985

- NR 13 Manor Orchards, KNARESBOROUGH, N Yorks, HG5 0BW. (hq)
01423 540603
email info@britpaint.co.uk http://www.britpaint.co.uk
Dir: Leslie Simpson
- ○ *A; to promote excellence in the field of watercolours, both in the UK & internationally
- M i
- ¶ Catalogue - 2.

British Waterfowl Association (BWA) 1887

- PO Box 163, OXTED, Surrey, RH8 0WP. (mail/add)
01892 740212
email info@waterfowl.org.uk
http://www.waterfowl.org.uk
Sec/Treas: Mrs Sue Schubert
- ▲ Registered Charity
- ○ *B, *G; to promote the conservation, education & preservation of wildfowl & domestic waterfowl; to assist breeders
- ● Mtgs - Exhib - Inf - LG - Open days
- < Nat Coun for Aviculture
- > Call Duck Assn; Indian Runner Duck Assn
- M 750 i, 6 f, UK / 30 i, o'seas
- ¶ Waterfowl - 3; ftm, £3.50 nm.
The Breeders Directory - 1. Ybk - 1.

British Wave Ski Association

- NR Trevellian, Ham Lane South, LLANTWIT MAJOR, Glamorgan, CF61 1RP.
http://www.waveski.co.uk
Mem Sec: Neil Sutch

British Web Design & Marketing Association

has closed.

British Weight Lifters Association (BWLA) 1904

- NR Lilleshall National Sports Centre, NEWPORT, Shropshire, TF10 9AT. (hq)
01952 604201
http://www.bwla.co.uk
Admin: Lorraine Fleming
- ▲ Company Limited by Guarantee
- ○ *S; promotes & controls all aspects of weight lifting, power lifting & weight training
- M i & clubs
- ¶ The British Weightlifter - 6.

British Weights & Measures Association (BWMA) 1995

- 11 Greensleeves Avenue, BROADSTONE, Dorset, BH18 8BJ. (hsb)
email bwma@email.com http://www.bwmaonline.com
Pres: Vivian Thornton Linacre, Dir: John Gardner
- ▲ Un-incorporated Society
- ○ *K; preservation & promotion of imperial weights & measures; to oppose compulsory metrication & the repeal of EEC/EU directives as enforced by UK government
- Gp Technical research; Historical & cultural; Educational; International
- ● Conf - Mtgs - ET - Res - LG - Political representation
- M [not given]
(Sub: £12)
- ¶ The Yardstick - 4; ftm.

British Western Dance Association (BWDA2000) 1989

- NR 13 Coltsfoot Drive, WATERLOOVILLE, Hants, PO7 8DF. (hq)
023 9226 6205 fax 023 9226 6205
email bwda.2000@ntlworld.com
http://www.bwda2000.com
- ▲ Un-incorporated Society
- ○ *D, *K; to promote Country Western Line & Partner dancing
- ● Mtgs - ET - Exam - Inf
- M 400 i, UK / 6 i, o'seas
- ¶ The Western Dancer Magazine - 6; ftm only.

British Westerners Association (BWA) 1973
NR   6 Renoir Close, Blackdam, BASINGSTOKE, Hants,
        RG21 3EW.   (chmn/p)
        01256 331337
     Chmn: Mark Gaden
▲   Un-incorporated Society
○   *G; for anyone interested in all aspects of the American West
●   Conf - Mtgs - Res - Exhib - Comp - Inf - VE
<   Westerners Intl (USA)
M   1,200 i, 30 f, 40 org, UK / 20 i, o'seas
¶   Round-Up - 4; ftm.

British Wheel of Yoga (BWY) 1965
NR   25 Jermyn St, SLEAFORD, Lincs, NG34 7RU.   (hq)
        01529 306851   fax 01529 303233
        email office@bwy.org.uk   http://www.bwy.org.uk
▲   Registered Charity
Br   11
○   *G; to further the practice & teaching of yoga
●   Conf - Mtgs - ET - Exam - Exhib - SG - Inf
<   Eur U of Fedns of Yoga
M   c 8,500 i
¶   Spectrum - 4;   Yoga the World Over - 4; both ftm only.

British Wheelchair Bowls Association (BWBA) 1984
NR   Kerria, Station Rd, EAST PRESTON, W Sussex, BN16 3AJ.
        (chmn/b)
        http://www.bwba.org.uk
     Chmn: Ian Blackmore
▲   Registered Charity
○   *S
●   ET - Comp - Inf
<   Brit Wheelchair Sports Foundation, Brit Isles Indoor Bowls Assn,
        Brit Paralympic Assn, English Bowling Assn, English Indoor
        Bowls Assn
M   150 i, 20 bowls clubs
¶   The Shot - 4; ftm only.

British Wheelchair Pool Players' Association
NR   23 Kendal Rd, Stretford Marina, MANCHESTER, M32 0DZ.
        http://www.bwppa.org
○   *S

British Wheelchair Sports Foundation
        since 2004-05 **Wheelpower: British Wheelchair Sport**

British Whippet Racing Association (BWRA) 1967
NR   186 Byerley Rd, SHILDON, Co Durham, DL4 1HW.   (sp)
        01388 776307
        http://www.thebwra.co.uk
     Sec: Mrs Alison Armstrong
▲   Un-incorporated Society
Br   8
○   *S; to promote & control all issues to do with non-pedigree
        whippet racing, breeding, registering & welfare
●   Race mtgs
M   c300 i, 23 clubs
¶   [pages in Whippet News - 12].

British White Cattle Society (BWCS) 1918
NR   Southfield Rd, Woodbastwick, NORWICH, Norfolk,
        NR13 6AL.   (breed/sec/p)
        01603 722288
        http://www.britishwhitecattle.co.uk
     Breed Sec: Angela Hamilton
▲   Un-incorporated Society
○   *B
●   Mtgs - Expt - Inf - Lib (archive) - VE
<   Nat Cattle Assn; Rare Breeds Survival Trust
M   291 i
¶   Ybk (incl Herdbook) - 1; ftm.
     NL - 4; ftm.   Leaflet.

British Wild Boar Association
     no longer exists

British Wind Energy Association (BWEA) 1979
NR   1 Aztec Row, Berners Rd, LONDON, N1 0PN.   (hq)
        020 7689 1960   fax 020 7689 1969
        email info@bwea.com   http://www.bwea.com
     Chief Exec: Marcus Rand
▲   Company Limited by Guarantee
○   *T; to represent companies in the UK wind & marine
        renewables industries
Gp   Wind energy development; Onshore & offshore; Small scale
        wind systems; Wave & tidal stream; Associated services from
        manufacturing through planning & consultancy
●   Conf - ET - Res - Exhib - Stat - PL - LG
<   Eur Wind Energy Assn (EWEA); Scot Renewables Forum (SRF)
M   320 f
¶   Real Power (Jnl) - 4;   Annual Review - 1.
     Specialist topic conference & seminar briefing sheets.

British Women Pilots Association (BWPA) 1955
■   Brooklands Museum, Brooklands Rd, WEYBRIDGE, Surrey,
        KT13 0QN.   (mail/address)
        http://www.bwpa.co.uk
     Hon Sec: Lesley Roff,   Chmn: Tricia Nelmes
▲   Un-incorporated Society
○   *G, *P; to encourage & help women who have an interest in
        aviation, either as a private pilot or commercially
●   Mtgs - ET - Comp - VE - LG
<   Fedn of Eur Women Pilots; R Aero Club; Aircraft Owners &
        Pilots Assn; Air League
M   c 300 i
¶   NL - 5; free.   Careers Book - irreg; ftm.

British Wood Preserving & Damp-proofing Association
        in 2003 formed divisions the **Property Care Association** *and the*
        Wood Protection Association; *BWPDA incorporated into the*
        former in 2006 when its divisions became independent associations

British Wood Pulp Association (BWPA) 1896
■   Penrallt, Copthill Lane, KINGSWOOD, Surrey, KT20 6HL.
        (hsp)
        01737 358444   fax 01737 363069
        email bwpasec@tiscali.co.uk   http://www.bwpa.org.uk
     Sec: Michael D Hobday
▲   Un-incorporated Society
○   *T; to further the interest of the pulp selling industries to the UK
●   Conf - Mtgs - Stat
<   Europulp
M   34 i, 17 f, UK / 20 i, 7 f, o'seas
        (Sub: £75 i, £225 f)
¶   AR - 1; £50.

British Wood Turners Association (BWTA) 1946
■   c/o The Old Sawmills, Wetmore Rd, BURTON-on-TRENT, Staffs,
        DE14 1QN.   (hsb)
        01283 563445   fax 01283 511526
        email secretary@britishwoodturners.co.uk
        http://www.britishwoodturners.co.uk
     Hon Sec: Mike Cherry
▲   Un-incorporated Society
○   *T; to promote British wood turners & their production
        capabilities
●   Mtgs - LG
<   Brit Woodworking Fedn
>   Brit Woodworking Fedn
M   35 f
¶   Members Directory - 2/3 yrly.

British Woodcarvers Association (BWA) 1987
- ■ 25 Summerfield Drive, Nottage, PORTHCAWL, Glamorgan, CF36 3PB. (hsp)
  01656 786937   fax 01656 786937
  email johnb@sullivanjb.freeserve.co.uk
  http://www.bwa-woodcarving.fsnet.co.uk
  Nat Sec: John Sullivan
- ▲ Un-incorporated Society
- Br Australia, Canada, France, Netherlands, Russia, S Africa, USA
- ○ *A, *P
- Gp Chainsaw; Lovespoons; Netsuke; Sticks (walking)
- ● Conf - Mtgs - ET - Exhib - Comp - Inf - VE
- M c 600 i, UK / c 20 i, o'seas
- ¶ Woodcarver Gazette; ftm only.

British Woodworking Federation (BWF) 1976
- NR 55 Tufton St, LONDON, SW1P 3QL.   (hq)
  0870 458 6939   fax 0870 458 6949
  email bwf@bwf.org.uk   http://www.bwf.org.uk
  Chief Exec: Richard Lambert
- ○ *T; joinery & woodworking incl timber frame construction & timber engineering, architectural & general joinery, windows, doors & kitchen furniture
- M i, f & org

British Wool Textile Export Corporation
  alternative name of the **National Wool Trade Export Corporation**

British Wrestling Association (BWA) 2001
- NR 12 Westwood Lane, Brimington, CHESTERFIELD, Derbys, S43 1PA.   (admin/p)
  01246 236443
  email admin@britishwrestling.org
  http://www.britishwrestling.org
  Admin: Yvonne Ball
- ▲ Company Limited by Guarantee
- ○ *S; to develop Olympic freestyle wrestling in the UK
- ● Comp - Sporting activities
- < Fédn Intle des Lottes Associées (Switzerland)
- M c 2,500 i, 40 clubs
- ¶ Takedown - 4.

British Youth Band Association (BYBA) 1974
- NR 12 Hunter Ave, BURNTWOOD, Staffs, WS7 9AF.   (chmn/p)
  http://www.byba.org.uk
  Chmn: T Patrick; Sec: Mrs P Ingram
- ▲ Registered Charity
- Br regions
- ○ *D, *G; to raise the profile of bands nationally; to encourage the playing of all forms of wind & percussion instruments
- ● Mtgs - ET - Comp - Marching bands
- M 1,500 i

** British Zen Aiki Association
  Organisation lost: see Introduction paragraph 3

British Zeolite Association (BZA) 1977
- ■ c/o Dr Michael Stockenhuber, Catalysis Research Laboratory, School of Biomedical & Natural Sciences, Nottingham Trent University, Clifton Lane, NOTTINGHAM, NG11 8NS.   (sec/b)
  0115-848 6694   fax 0115-848 6694
  email michael.stockenhuber@ntu.ac.uk
  http://www.bza.org
  Sec: Dr Michael Stockenhuber
- ▲ Registered Charity
- ○ *L; the study & research into the technology & applications in the fields of chemistry, geology, chemical engineering & other branches of science & engineering of zeolites (aluminosilicate minerals)
- ● Conf - Mtgs - ET
- < Intl Zeolite Assn; Fedn of Eur Zeolite Assns
- M 117 i, UK / 88 i, o'seas
- ¶ Template - 1; free.

Britpave (British In-situ Concrete Paving Association) (Britpave) 1991
- NR 4 Meadows Business Park, Station Approach, Blackwater, CAMBERLEY, Surrey, GU17 9AB.   (hq)
  01276 33160
  email djones@britpave.org.uk
  http://www.britpave.org.uk
  Dir & Co Sec: D P Jones
- ▲ Company Limited by Guarantee
- ○ *T; the authoritative voice of the in-situ concrete paving industry
- Gp Airfields; Environment; Rail; Roads; Specialist applications
- ● Conf - Mtgs - ET - Res - Exhib - VE - LG
- M 50 f, UK / 2 f, o'seas
- ¶ NL - 3; free.   Technical Guidance Sheets - 12; ftm only. Videos & CD-ROMs.

Brittle Bone Society (BBS) 1972
- ■ 30 Guthrie St, DUNDEE, DD1 5BS.   (hq)
  0800 028 2459   fax 01382 206771
  email bbs@brittlebone.org   http://www.brittlebone.org
  Chief Exec: Raymond Lawrie
- ▲ Registered Charity
- Br 6
- ○ *K; to promote research into the causes, inheritance & treatment of osteogenesis imperfecta & similar disorders; to provide advice, encouragement & practical help for patients & their families
- ● Conf - Mtgs - Inf
- M 1,000 i, UK / 300 i, o'seas
- ¶ NL - 4; free.   Factsheets.

Broadcasting Entertainment Cinematograph & Theatre Union (BECTU) 1991
- NR 373-377 Clapham Rd, LONDON, SW9 9BT.   (hq)
  020 7346 0900   fax 020 7346 0901
  email rbolton@bectu.org.uk   http://www.bectu.org.uk
  Gen Sec: Roger Bolton
- ▲ Un-incorporated Society
- Br 300; Channel Islands, Ireland, Isle of Man
- ○ *U; for workers (not performers) in broadcasting, film, theatre & other areas of the entertainment & media industry
- ● Conf - Mtgs - Inf - Empl - LG
- < Media Entertainment Intl; Fedn of Entertainment Us; TUC; STUC; Labour Party
- M c 27,000 i
- ¶ Stage Screen & Radio (Jnl) - 10. Directories of Members (freelance) - irreg; prices vary. AR - 1; ftm.

Broads Hire Boat Federation   (BHBF)
- NR Lamorna, 55 Coltishall Lane, NORWICH, Norfolk, NR10 3HU.
  01603 897326   fax 01603 897326
  email tony@thowes.wanadoo.co.uk
  Sec: Tony Howes
- ○ *T

Brontë Society 1893
- NR Brontë Parsonage Museum, Haworth, KEIGHLEY, W Yorks, BD22 8DR.   (hq)
  01535 642323   fax 01535 647131
  http://www.bronte.info
  Hon Council Sec: Lyn C Glading
  Mem Sec: Hedley Hickling
- ▲ Registered Charity
- Br 1; 7 countries
- ○ *L; preservation of the history, home & literature of the Brontë family
- ● Conf - Mtgs - ET - Res - Exhib - SG - Inf - Lib - VE
- M 2,000 i, UK / 900 i, o'seas
- ¶ Transactions - 2;   Gazette - 2; both ftm.

Brooklands Society Ltd   1967
- ■ Culverden, Azalea Drive, HASLEMERE, Surrey, GU27 1JR. (hsp)
   01428 645724   fax 01428 645724
   http://www.brooklands.org.uk
   Hon Sec: Len Battyll
- ▲ Company Limited by Guarantee
- ○ *G; to perpetuate the story, history & preservation of the Brooklands Motor course & site
- ● Disseminating Brooklands motor course history
- < Fedn Brit Historic Vehicle Clubs; Motor Sports Assn
- M 1,150 i
- ¶ Gazette - 4; with NL - 4; £30.

Brown Swiss Cattle Society (UK)   1973
- NR Shawcroft Farm, Wootton, ASHBOURNE, Derbys, DE6 2GW. (asa)
   01335 324009
   Sec: Angus Dalton
- ▲ Registered Charity
- ○ *B; Brown Swiss dairy cattle
- ● Mtgs - SG - VE - Open farm days
- M 110 i, 5 f, UK / 5 i, 1 f, o'seas
- ¶ Swiss Chimes Jnl - 4; ftm only.

Browning Society   1970
- ■ 38B Victoria Rd, LONDON, NW6 6PX.   (hsp)
   020 7604 4257
   email v.l.greenaway@btinternet.com
   http://www.browningsociety.org
   Hon Sec: Dr Vicky Greenaway
- ▲ Registered Charity
- ○ *A; to promote appreciation of the poetry of Robert & Elizabeth Barrett Browning
- ● Mtgs
- < Browning Institute Inc (New York); Friends of Casa Guidi; Assn of Literary Socs
- M 65 i, UK / 30 i, o'seas
   (Sub: £15 UK / $38.50 o'seas)
- ¶ Browning Society Notes - 1; ftm only.

BSCAH - British Society of Cinical & Academic Hypnosis (BSCAH)   2007
- ■ 28 Dale Park Gardens, Cookridge, LEEDS, W Yorks, LS16 7PT.   (nat/sp)
   0844 884 3116   fax 0844 884 3116
   email natoffice@bscah.co.uk   http://www.bscah.com
   Nat Sec: Mrs Jacky Owens
- ▲ Company Limited by Guarantee; Registered Charity
- Br 7
- ○ *L; to promote the study, teaching & use of hypnosis in the fields of medicine, dentistry, psychology & other clinical applications; to support the academic research into hypnosis
- Gp Doctors; Dentists; Psychologists; Nurses; Physios; Counsellors & other health professionals; Academic professionals involved in research
- ● Conf - Mtgs - ET - Res - Inf
- < Intl Soc of Hypnosis (ISH); Eur Soc of Hypnosis & Psychosomatic Medicine (ESH)
- M 490 i, UK / 6 i, o'seas
   (Sub: £60)
- ¶ NL - 3;   Membership Directory - 1; both ftm only.
   Contemporary Hypnosis - 4; ftm, (price nm via Wiley, publishers).
- ✕ 2007 (British Society of Medical & Dental Hypnosis (British Society of Experimental & Clinical Hypnosis

BSES Expeditions   (BSES)   1932
- NR at the Royal Geographical Society, 1 Kensington Gore, LONDON, SW7 2AR.   (hq)
   020 7591 3141
   Exec Dir: William Taunton-Bornet
- ▲ Company Limited by Guarantee; Registered Charity
- ○ *E; to foster the spirit of exploration & self-reliance in young people, through expeditions with a scientific purpose
- M c 4,000 i, 120 schools
- ¶ NL - 3; ftm.   AR; ftm.

BSI   1901
- NR 389 Chiswick High Rd, LONDON, W4 4AL.   (hq)
   020 8996 9000
   http://www.bsigroup.com
- ▲ Royal Charter
- ○ *G, *T; the development & promulgation of standards
- M f

BSRIA Ltd   (BSRIA)   1955
- NR Old Bracknell Lane West, BRACKNELL, Berks, RG12 7AH.   (hq)
   01344 465600
   http://www.bsria.co.uk
   Dir: Andrew Eastwell
- ○ *T, *Q; 'provision of collaborative research programmes; supply of information & expertise'
- Gp Information centre; Market intelligence centre; Building energy management systems; Test; Instrument Hire; Ventilation & air movement; Energy utilisation; Quality; Systems design; Operations & management
- ● Mtgs - ET - Res - SG - Inf - Lib
- M c 1,000 f
- ¶ 'too numerous'.

BTC Testing & Advisory Group   (BTC)   1963
- ■ Lynk House, 17 Peckleton Lane, DESFORD, Leics, LE9 9JU. (regd/address)
   01455 821921   fax 01455 821921
   email btc@interlynk.co.uk   http://www.btctag.org
   Co Sec: Mrs Lyn Dearling
- ▲ Company Limited by Guarantee
- ○ *Q; for technical & procedural consultation between organisations conducting vehicle &/or engine dynamometer based testing & research
- Gp Engine coolants; Laboratory managers; Technician training; Vehicle & engine emissions
- ● Mtgs - ET - Res - SG - VE - Training for technicians engaged in testing activities in motor, petroleum & chemical industries
- M 20 f
   (Sub: £2,500)
- ✕ 2005 (1 July) British Technical Council of the Motor & Petroleum Industries

Bucks County Agricultural Association   (Bucks County Show) 1840
- ■ The Old Barn, Wingbury Courtyard, Business Village, Leighton Rd, WINGRAVE, Bucks, HP22 4LW.   (hq)
   01296 680400   fax 01296 680445
   email alison@buckscountyshow.co.uk
   http://www.buckscountyshow.co.uk
   Sec: Mrs Alison Baylis
- ▲ Company Limited by Guarantee, Registered Charity
- ○ *F, *H; agricultural county show promoting agriculture, farming & country life
- ● Comp - County show
- < Brit Show Jumping Assn; Nat Show Pony Soc; all: horse breed socs, cattle socs & sheep socs
- M 800 i

© CBD Research Ltd · Beckenham · BR3 5JS · Tel 020 8650 7745 · Fax 020 8650 0768 · E-mail cbd@cbdresearch.com · www.cbdresearch.com

Buddhist Society   1924
- ■ 58 Eccleston Sq, LONDON, SW1V 1PH.   (hq)
   020 7834 5858   fax 020 7976 5238
   email info@thebuddhistsociety.org
   http://www.thebuddhistsociety.org
   Registrar: Louise Marchant
- ▲ Registered Charity
- ○ *R; to publish & make known the principles of Buddhism; to encourage the study & practice of Buddhism
- Gp Pure Hand; Theravada; Tibetan; Zen
- ● Mtgs - ET - SG - Inf - Lib - Lectures - Summer schools
- < Wld Fellowship of Buddhists
- M 2,000 i, UK / 500 i, o'seas
- ¶ The Middle Way (Jnl) - 4; ftm, £4.50 each nm.
   The Buddhist Directory; 2004-06; £12 m, £14 nm. [subscription; £18].

Budgerigar Society   (BS)   1925
- ■ Davies House, Spring Gardens, NORTHAMPTON, NN1 1DR.
   01604 624549   fax 01604 627108
   http://www.budgerigarsociety.com
   Sec: David Whittaker
- ▲ Un-incorporated Society
- ○ *B, *G; to promote the breeding & development of the budgerigar in all parts of the world
- ● Conf - Exhib - Comp
- < Wld Budgerigar Org
   is a group of the National Council for Aviculture
- M 4,500 i
- ¶ The Budgerigar - 6; ftm only.

Buglife - The Invertebrate Conservation Trust   2000
- NR 90 Bridge St (1st floor), PETERBOROUGH, Cambs, PE1 1DY.
   01733 201210
   email info@buglife.org.uk   http://www.buglife.org.uk
   Sec: Helen Boothman
- ▲ Registered Charity
- ○ *G; devoted to the conservation of all invertebrates (slugs, snails, bees, wasps, ants, spiders, beetles & many more)

Builders' Conference   1935
- ■ Crest House, 19 Lewis Rd, SUTTON, Surrey, SM1 4BR.   (hq)
   020 8770 0111
   email info@buildersconf.co.uk
   http://www.buildersconference.co.uk
   Chief Exec: Neil Edwards
- ▲ Registered Charity; Un-incorporated Society
- Br 3
- ○ *T; to reduce industry insufficiencies in construction industry; to provide market analysis of construction industry at tender & contract stage
- ● Conf - Mtgs - ET - Stat - Inf - LG
- M professionals, main contractors, sub-contractors
   (Sub: as above categories - on application, up to £2,000 yr, £1,185 yr)
- ¶ List of Contractors - 1; ftm.   AR; ftm only.

Builders Merchants Federation   (BMF)   1901
- ■ 15 Soho Sq, LONDON, W1D 3HL.   (hq)
   020 7439 1753
   Dir: C Pateman,   Sec: P D Matthews
- ○ *T
- ● Mtgs - ET - Inf - LG
- < Eur Assn Nat Builders' Merchants Assns (UFEMAT); Eur Fedn Heating & Sanitary Wholesalers (FEST)
- M 300 f (with 3,000 outlets)
- ¶ Internal NL - 12;   LM - 1;   Ybk - 1; all ftm only.

Building Controls Industry Association   (BCIA)   2004
- ■ 2 Waltham Court, Milley Lane, Hare Hatch, READING, Berks, RG10 9TH.
   0118-940 3416   fax 0118-940 6258
   email bcia@feta.co.uk   http://www.feta.co.uk
- ○ *T; to establish & maintain the highest standards in proiduct & system development, application & customer service
- M 34 f, 4 associates

Building Cost Information Service   (BCIS)   1962
- NR 12 Great George St, LONDON, SW1P 3AD.   (hq)
   020 7695 1500   fax 020 7695 1501
   email bcis@bcis.co.uk   http://www.bcis.co.uk
   Gen Mgr: Andrew Thompson
- ▲ Company Limited by Guarantee
- ○ *T; to publish information services relating to cost of construction & occupancy & maintenance of buildings
- Gp Building Maintenance Information (BMI)
- ● Conf - ET - Res - Stat - Inf
- < is a trading division of RBS Ltd (Royal Institution of Chartered Surveyors Building Services Ltd)
- M 2,000 f, UK / 50 f, o'seas
- ¶ BCIS Bulletin (online) - constant; £355-£1,315.
   BMI Bulletin - 12; £365 m, £465 nm.
   Review of Building Prices - constant; £225-£765.
   Rebuilding Cost Guides for Houses & Flats - 1; £65.
   Guide to Daywork Rates - 1; £37.50.
   BMI Price Book - 1; £75.
- × 2004 (January) Building Maintenance Information

Building Maintenance Information
   a service of the **Building Cost Information Service**

Building Materials Federation
- IRL Confederation House, 84/86 Lower Baggot St, DUBLIN 2, Republic of Ireland.
   353 (1) 605 1621   fax 353 (1) 638 1621
   http://www.ibec.ie/bmf
   Contact: Mark McCauley
- ○ *T; manufacturers of adhesives, bricks, cement, chimney systems, cladding products, concrete products, insulation products, plasterboard, plastic pipes & roofing products
- < IBEC

Building Societies Association   (BSA)   1869
- ■ York House, 23 Kingsway, LONDON, WC2B 6UJ.   (hq)
   020 7520 5900   fax 020 7240 5290
   email information@bsa.org.uk   http://www.bsa.org.uk
   Dir Gen: Adrian Coles
- ▲ Un-incorporated Society
- ○ *T; for the building industry sector
- ● Conf - Mtgs - ET - Res - Stat - Inf - Lib - LG
- M 59 org
- ¶ Society Matters - 4;   AR - 1; both free.
   Building Societies Ybk - 1; ftm, £20 nm.

Building Societies Members Association   (BSMA)   1982
- NR 49 Clifford Ave, TAUNTON, Somerset, TA2 6DL.   (hsp)
   01823 321304
   Hon Sec: Mrs Edith M Davis
- ▲ Un-incorporated Society
- ○ *K; 'our field of interest is the maintenance of the principles of mutuality in building societies; we campaign against them in converting to PLCs;... to advocate that building societies' rules are framed to allow & encourage the maximum participation by members in their societies' affairs...'
- ● Mtgs
- M 200 i
- ¶ BSMA NL - 4; free.

Buildings Archaeology Group
   a group of the **Institute of Field Archaeologists**

Buildings Energy Efficiency Federation (BEEF) 1997
NR   Westgate House, 2a Prebend St, LONDON, N1 8PT.   (chmn/b)
      020 7359 8000
      Chmn: Andrew Warren
▲   Un-incorporated Society
○   *N, *T; to act as a coordination body for the energy efficiency
      industry & for liaison purposes between the industry & the
      Energy Efficiency Office; to stimulate the market for products
      & processes used in buildings (predominantly domestic)
●   Mtgs - LG
M   17 org

Bulb Distributors' Association
      since 2006 **British Flower Bulbs Association**

Bumblebee Conservation Trust (BBCT)
■   School of Biological & Environmental Sciences, University of
      Stirling, STIRLING, FK9 4LA.
      http://www.bumblebeeconservationtrust.co.uk
      Dirs: Prof David Goulson,   Dr Ben Darvill
○   *K

Bureau of Engineer Surveyors
      a sector of the **Society of Operations Engineers**

Burney Society   1990
■   36 Henty Gardens, CHICHESTER, W Sussex, PO19 3DL.   (hsp)
      01243 533928
      email tregear.david@virgin.net
      http://www.dc37.dawsoncollege.qc.ca/burney
      Hon Secs: David & Janet Tregear
▲   Un-incorporated Society
○   *A, *G; life & times of Fanny Burney (Madame D'Arblay)
●   Conf
M   75 i, UK / 90 i, o'seas
¶   Burney Letter - 2; ftm, £5 nm.   Burney Jnl - 1; ftm, £10 nm.

Burton & District Chamber of Commerce & Industry
      since 2007 a division of the **Southern Staffordshire Chamber of
      Commerce & Industry**

Bury St Edmunds Chamber of Commerce & Industry   1938
NR   90 Guildhall St (2nd floor), BURY ST EDMUNDS, Suffolk,
      IP33 1PR.   (hq)
      01284 700800
      http://www.burystedmundschamber.co.uk
      Sec: Robert Bourne
▲   Company Limited by Guarantee
○   *C
●   Mtgs - Inf - VE - Lobbying
M   200 f
¶   NL - 12; free.

Bus Users UK   (BUUK)   1985
■   PO Box 2950, STOKE-on-TRENT, Staffs, ST4 9EW.   (hq)
      01782 442855   fax 01782 442856
      email enquiries@bususers.org   http://www.bususers.org
      Chmn: Gavin Booth,   Pres: Dr Caroline Cahm
Br   18
○   *K; to campaign for better services for bus users; to increase
      the influence of bus users in public transport issues; to
      improve communication between bus users & providers
●   Conf - Mtgs - Comp - Bus appeals body
<   Campaign for Better Transport; Pedestrians' Assn
M   725 i, 110 f, 82 org
¶   Bus User (NL) - 4; £10 yr m, £1 each nm.
      Welcome Aboard: good practice - 2; free (send sae).
×   2005 National Federation of Bus Users

Business Aircraft Users Association Ltd
      in 2004 merged with the General Aviation Manufacturers & Traders
      Association to form the **British Business & General Aviation
      Association**

**Business Application Software Developers Association
(BASDA)   1993**
■   92 High St, GREAT MISSENDEN, Bucks, HP16 0AN.   (chmn/b)
      01494 868030   fax 01494 868031
      email info@basda.org   http://www.basda.org
      Chief Exec: Dennis Keeling
▲   Company Limited by Guarantee
○   *T; to bring together people & organisations with an interest in
      the accreditation, development & marketing of business &
      accounting software products
Gp   EMU - the introduction of the Eurp; VAT-specification;
      eCommerce-business-to-business (eBIS); VAT-specification
●   Conf - Mtgs - Exhib - SG - Stat - Inf - LG
¶   BASDA News (NL) - 3. ftm only.
      eBusiness Booklet;   IFRS White Paper;
      Sarbanes Oxley White Paper;
      Selecting a Business System & Selecting a Reseller - 1; all free.
×   2003-04 Business & Accounting Software Developers
      Association

Business Archives Council   (BAC)   1934
■   c/o Lloyds TSB Group Archives, Princess House (5th floor),
      1 Suffolk Lane, LONDON, EC4R 0AX.   (hq)
      020 7489 3945
      email karen.sampson@lloydstsb.co.uk
      Hon Sec: Karen Sampson
▲   Registered Charity
○   *L; promoting the efficient management, preservation & use of
      business records
M   i, f & org
¶   Jnl - 2;   NL - 4;   Ybk - 1; all ftm.

Business Centre Association   (bca)   1988
■   ECC London City, 3 Bunhill Row, LONDON, EC1Y 8YZ.   (hq)
      020 7847 4018   fax 020 7847 4081
      email info@bca.uk.com   http://www.bca.uk.com
      Exec Dir: Jennifer Brooke
▲   Company Limited by Guarantee
○   *T; for owners & operators of business centres & managed
      workspaces
●   Conf (& exhibition showcase) - Inf - LG - Annual industry
      awards gala dinner
M   700+ business centres / managed workspaces
¶   bca News (NL) - 4; ftm only.

Business Continuity Institute   (BCI)   1994
NR   10 Southview Park, Marsack St, Caversham. READING, Berks,
      RG4 5AF.   (hq)
      0118-947 8215   fax 0118-947 6237
▲   Company Limited by Guarantee
○   *P; promotion of the art & science of business continuity
      management
M   i

Business English UK
      a group of **English UK**

Business Management Association   1981
■   North House, 5 Parkins Close, Colliers End, WARE, Herts,
      SG11 1ED.   (hq)
      01920 823261
      email info@businessmanagement.org.uk
      http://www.businessmanagement.org.uk
○   *P; with specific reference to small business to improve the
      performance of business management at every level in terms
      of management skills, education & planning
      no further information supplied

© CBD Research Ltd · Beckenham · BR3 5JS · Tel 020 8650 7745 · Fax 020 8650 0768 · E-mail cbd@cbdresearch.com · www.cbdresearch.com

Business for New Europe   (BNE)   2006
NR   PO Box 57054, LONDON, EC2P 2YS.
    020 7256 6575   fax 020 7256 6582
    email info@bnegroup.org   http://www.bnegroup.org
    Dir: Zaki Cooper
○   independent coalition of business leaders articulating a possible
    case for reform in Europe

Business & Professional Women UK Ltd   (BPW UK Ltd)   1938
■   74 Fairfield Rise, BILLERICAY, Essex, CM12 9NU.   (hq)
    01225 837251
    email hq@bpwuk.co.uk   http://www.bpwuk.co.uk
▲   Company Limited by Guarantee
Br   45
○   *K, *P; 'for all working women to discuss, develop, network,
    influence & participate in issues affecting women'
Gp   Carers; Computers; Finance; Lawyers; Health; Property;
    Science; Training; Criminal justice; Marketing & media;
    Women in business
●   Conf - Mtgs - ET - LG
<   Intl Fedn Business & Profl Women; Eur Fedn of Business & Profl
    Women
¶   BPW News - 4;   Annual Review; both ftm only.

Business Services Association Ltd   (BSA)   1993
■   Warnford Court, 29 Throgmorton St, LONDON, EC2N 2AT.
    (hq)
    020 7786 6300   fax 020 7786 6309
    email mark.fox@bsa-org.com   http://www.bsa-org.com
    Chief Exec: Mark Fox
▲   Company Limited by Guarantee
○   *T; represents companies providing business & outsourced
    services in the public & private sectors - driving innovation,
    training, efficiency & raising professional standards &
    improving productivity
●   Res - Events - Publications
<   Confedn Brit Ind
M   15 f, 14 associates
    (Sub: £2,500 associates)
¶   NL - 12; on website.

Business Software Alliance   (BSA)   1988
■   2 Queen Anne's Gate Buildings, Dartmouth St, LONDON,
    SW1H 9BP.   (European hq)
    020 7340 6080   fax 020 7340 6090
    email europe@bsa.org   http://www.bsa.org
Br   Singapore, USA
○   *K, *T; to eradicate software piracy
Gp   Computer software publishers
●   Mtgs - ET - Res - Stat - Inf - LG
M   f

Business in Sport & Leisure   (BISL)   1985
NR   17A Chartfield Ave, LONDON, SW15 6DX.
    020 8780 2377   fax 020 8780 2277
    email brigid.simmonds@bisl.org   http://www.bisl.org
    Chief Exec: Brigid Simmonds
○   the hospitality, sport and leisure industry

Business Tourism Scotland
    no longer active

Business Volunteer Mentors Association
    run by the **National Federation of Enterprise Agencies**

Business West
    trading name of the **Bristol Chamber of Commerce & Industry**

Butterfly Conservation   1968
■   Manor Yard, East Lulworth, WAREHAM, Dorset, BH20 5QP.
    (hq)
    01929 400209   fax 01929 400210
    email info@butterfly-conservation.org.
    http://www.butterfly-conservation.org
    Chief Exec: Dr Martin Warren
▲   Company Limited by Guarantee; Registered Charity
Br   31
○   *B, *L, *Q; conservation of British wild butterflies, moths & their
    habitats; to research into their life needs; to set up reserves
    for the rare species
●   Conf - Mtgs - ET - Res - Exhib - Stat - Inf - PL
>   Butterfly Consvn Europe
M   12,000 i
    (Sub: £28)
¶   Local branch & regional NLs - irreg.   AR - 1; m only.

Buttonhook Society   1979
■   PO Box 1089, MAIDSTONE, Kent, ME14 9BA.   (hq)
    01622 752949
    email buttonhooksociety@tiscali.co.uk
    http://www.thebuttonhooksociety.com
    Chmn: Paul Moorehead
▲   Un-incorporated Society
Br   USA
○   *G; to encourage the research into, collection & preservation of
    buttonhooks & ancillary articles; to build up archives on the
    50,000 known buttonhooks researched
●   Mtgs - Res - Exhib - Inf - Lib - PL
M   c 230 i, UK / 140 i, o'seas
    (Sub: £18.50 UK / £21.50 Europe / £24.50 o'seas)
¶   The Boutonneur (NL) - 6.
    Compendium of Buttonhooks - in parts; priced individually.

**BVCA (British Private Equity & Venture Capital Association)
(BVCA)   1983**
■   Tower 3, 3 Clements Inn, LONDON, WC2A 2AZ.   (hq)
    020 7025 2950   fax 020 7025 2951
    email bvca@bvca.co.uk   http://www.bvca.co.uk
    Chief Exec: Peter Linthwaite
▲   Company Limited by Guarantee
○   *T; 'the public face of the industry providing services to its
    members, investors & entrepreneurs, as well as government
    & media'
●   Conf - Mtgs - ET - Res - Exhib - Stat - Expt - Inf - LG
M   180 f, 175 f (associate)
¶   Directory (LM) - 1; ftm, £10 nm.
    A Guide to Private Equity; free.
    Report of Investment Activity - 1; ftm, £50 nm.

Byron Society   1971
NR   Bay Trees, 35 Blackbrook Rd, FAREHAM, Hants, PO15 5DQ.
    (dir/p)
    01329 287336
    Hon Dir: Miss Maureen O'Connor
▲   Registered Charity
Br   2; 36
○   *A; to promote research into the life & work of the English poet
    Lord Byron (1788-1824)
M   i
¶   The Byron Jnl - 1.

4Children
NR   City Reach, 5 Greenwich View Place, LONDON, E14 9NN.
        (hq)
        020 7512 2112
        email info@4children.org.uk
        http://www.4children.org.uk
▲   Registered Charity
○   *W; to deliver & support innovative children's services ensuring
        that all children & families get the support they need in their
        community
M   org
✕   2004 Kids' Club Network

Cable Management Product Group
        a product association of BEAMA Installation, which is part of **BEAMA**

**Caernarvonshire Historical Society   (Cymdeithas Hanes Sir
Caernarfon) (CHS) 1939**
NR   County Offices, Shirehall St, CAERNARFON, LL55 1SH.   (hsb)
        01286 679088   fax 01286 679637
        Hon Sec: Ann Rhydderch
▲   Registered Charity
○   *L; to collect & preserve the history relating to the county of
        Caernarfon
●   Mtgs - VE
M   460 i, 10 org, UK / 20 i, o'seas
¶   Transactions (Jnl) - 1.

Café Society (CS) 1992
NR   Association House, 18c Moor St, CHEPSTOW, Monmouthshire,
        NP16 5DB.   (hq)
        01291 636331   fax 01291 630402
        Sec: Jim Winship
▲   Company Limited by Guarantee
○   *T; to promote quality standards in the coffee market in the UK
●   Conf - Mtgs - ET - Inf - LG - Promotion - Awards dinner
M   14 i, 68 f
¶   Café Culture Magazine - 4; ftm, £25 yr nm.

Cairngorms Chamber of Commerce
NR   PO Box 15, KINGUSSIE, Inverness-shire, PH21 1WF.
        01479 780539
        email info@cairngormschamber.org
        http://www.cairngormschamber.com
○   *C
        no further information supplied

Caithness Agricultural Society (CAS) 1830
■   An-Cala, Gills, WICK, Caithness, KW1 4YB.   (sp)
        01955 611266
        email wilmastewart2002@yahoo.com
        http://www.caithnessshow.co.uk
        Sec: Wilma Stewart
▲   Registered Charity
○   *F
●   Mtgs - Exhib - Comp - Agricultural show
<   Clydesdale Horse Soc; Highland Pony Soc; Shetland Pony Stud-
        Book Soc
M   c 400 i
        (Sub: £10 adult, £5 child)

Caithness Paperweight Collectors Club (CPCC) 1976
NR   Caithness Glass Ltd, PERTH, Perthshire, PH1 3TZ.   (hq)
        01738 637373   fax 01738 492300
        http://www.caithnessglass.co.uk
        Mgr: Caroline Clark
○   *G; for collectors of paperweights in traditional, contemporary,
        limited & open editions
M   c 6,500 i

Caithness & Sutherland Chamber of Commerce
NR   Bryn Tirion, Castlegreen Rd, THURSO, Caithness,
        KW14 7DN.   (sp)
        01847 892552   fax 01847 892552
        Sec: George Bruce
○   *C
✕   Caithness Chamber of Commerce

Caledonian Railway Association (CRA) 1983
NR   63 Andrew Drive, CLYDEBANK, Dunbartonshire, G81 1BU.
        (hsp)
        0141-952 7162
        http://www.crassoc.org.uk
        Sec: Douglas Hind
▲   Un-incorporated Society
Br   2
○   *G; to study the former Caledonian Railway Company
●   Mtgs - Res - Exhib - Inf - Lib - VE
M   310 i, 12 f, 7 org, UK / 16 i, o'seas
¶   The True Line (Jnl) - 4; ftm, £5 nm.   LM - 1; £3 m only.

Call Centre Association
        since 2005 **Customer Contact Association**

**Call Centre Management Association (UK) Ltd   (CCMAUK)
1995**
NR   PO Box 125, SANDBACH, Cheshire, CW11 2FF.   (hqa)
        01477 500826
        http://www.ccma.org.uk
        Sec: Roy Bailey
○   *P
●   Mtgs - ET
M   350 i, UK / 20 i, o'seas
¶   NL
✕   2001 (September) Call Centre Management Association

Calligraphy & Lettering Arts Society 1994
NR   54 Boileau Rd, LONDON, SW13 9BL.
        020 8741 7886
        email info@clas.co.uk   http://www.clas.co.uk
        Admin: Sue Cavendish
○   *A
M   1,500 i

Camanachd Association (CA) 1893
■   Alton House, 4 Ballifeary Rd, INVERNESS, IV3 5PJ.   (hq)
        01463 715931   fax 01463 226551
        email admin@shinty.com   http://www.shinty.com
        Chief Exec: Gill McDonald
▲   Un-incorporated Society
○   *S; governing body for the sport of shinty
Gp   Coaching; Youth development; Development
●   ET - Comp
>   Glasgow Celtic Soc; MacAulay Assn; Camanachd Referees'
        Assn
M   3,000 i, clubs
        (Sub: £10 i, £35 clubs)

**Cámara Chileno Británica de Comercio (British Chilean Chamber
of Commerce) 1917**
NR   Av El Bosque Norte 0125, Las Condes, SANTIAGO, Chile.
        (hq)
        56 (2) 370 4175   fax 56 (2) 370 4164
        http://www.britcham.cl
        Gen Mgr: Andrew Robshaw
○   *C
●   Mtgs - Comp - Expt - Inf - Lib
M   24 i, 130 f (in Chile)
¶   NL - 12; ftm.   Economic Report - 4; ftm.
        Directory of Members; ftm, £10.

Cámara de Comercio Argentino-Británica (CCAB) 1914
- ■ Av Corrientes 457 (Piso 10), CP (C1043AAE), BUENOS AIRES, Argentina. (hq)
  54 (11) 4394 2762   fax 54 (11) 4326 3860
  email info@ccab.com.ar   http://www.ccab.com.ar
  Chief Exec: Mónica Mesz
- ▲ Registered Charity
- ○ *C; to promote general trade & commerce between the UK & Argentina
- Gp Lawyers; Executive education; HHRR & IT
- ● Conf - Mtgs - ET - Exhib - Expt - Inf - LG
- M 140 f, Argentina
- ¶ NL - 26; ftm only.

Cámara de Comercio Británica AC (British Chamber of Commerce in Mexico) 1921
- NR Rio de la Plata 30, Col Cuauhtémoc, 06500 MEXICO DF, Mexico. (hq)
  52 (5) 256 09 01   fax 52 (5) 211 54 51
  email britcham@infoabc.com
  Dir Gen: Teresa de Lay
- ○ *C; to promote trade & investment between the UK & Mexico

Cámara de Comercio Británica en España
Spanish name of the **British Chamber of Commerce in Spain**

Cámara de Comercio Colombo Británica (British Colombian Chamber of Commerce) (CCCB) 1981
- NR Calle 95 No 13-55, Oficina 409, BOGOTÁ DC, Colombia. (hq)
  57 (1) 621 2401   fax 57 (1) 621 2431
  http://www.colombobritanica.com
  Exec Dir: Patricia Tovar
- ○ *C; to promote commerce & investment between Colombia & GB
- ● Conf - Mtgs - Exhib - Expt - Inf - Lib - VE - LG
- ¶ NL - 6; ftm.

Câmara de Comércio Luso-Británica
Portuguese name of the **British-Portuguese Chamber of Commerce**

Cámara de Comercio Uruguayo Británica (British-Uruguayan Chamber of Commerce) 1969
- NR Av Libertador Juan A Lavalleja 1641, Piso 2 Oficina 201, CP 11.100, MONTEVIDEO, Uruguay. (hq)
  598 (2) 908 0349   fax 598 (2) 900 0936
  email camurbri@netgate.com.uy
  http://www.camurbri.com.uy
  Sec: Armando Barrios
- ○ *C; to promote Anglo-Uruguayan commercial relations

Cámara Peruano-Británica
Spanish name of the **British-Peruvian Chamber**

Cámara Venezolana Británica de Comercio (CVBC) 1951
- NR Torre Metálica (Mezzanina 2), calle San Ignacio, Chacao, CARACAS, Venezuela. (hq)
  58 (212) 267 3112   fax 58 (212) 263 0362
  http://www.britcham.com.ve
  Gen Mgr: Helen Wadham
- ○ *C; to improve commercial relations between UK & Venezuela
- Gp Commercial dept; Events dept; Young executive section (to help develop business & English language skills in both a business & social environment)
- ● Conf - Mtgs - Res - Comp - Expt - Inf - Lib - VE - Overseas missions
- M 2 i, 22 f, UK / 55 i, 107 f, o'seas, 20 i (young execs section)
- ¶ Directory - 1.

Cambrian Archaeological Association (Cymdeithas Hynafiaethau Cymru) 1846
- NR Halfway House, Pont y Pandy, Halfway Bridge, BANGOR, Gwynedd, LL57 3DG. (memsec/p)
  01248 364865
  http://www.orchardweb.co.uk/cambrians/index.html
  Mem Sec: Frances Llewellyn
- ▲ Registered Charity
- ○ *L; to examine, preserve & illustrate the ancient monuments & remains of the history, language, manners, customs, arts & industries of Wales & the Marches
- Gp Research; Meetings
- ● Conf - Mtgs - Res - Comp - Lib - VE - LG
- < Coun for Brit Archaeology (CBA)
- M 600 i, 140 org, UK / 30 i, 30 org, o'seas
- ¶ Archaeologia Cambrensis - 1.   LM - 2 yrly.

Cambrian Railways Society
- ■ Oswald Rd, OSWESTRY, Shropshire, SY11 1RE. (hq)
  01691 671749
  email information@cambrian-railways-soc.co.uk
  http://www.cambrian-railways-soc.co.uk
  Sec: A M Hignett
- ▲ Company Listed by Guarantee, Registered Charity
- ○ *G; to acquire, preserve & restore any & all of the Cambrian Railways Company's infrastructure, buildings, lines & artifacts
- ● Mtgs - ET - Res - Exhib - Inf - VE
- M 488 i, UK / 5 i, o'seas
- ¶ Cambrian Line Magazine - 4; ftm, £1 nm.

Cambridge Antiquarian Society (CAS) 1840
- ■ 21 High St, West Wickham, CAMBRIDGE, CB21 4RY. (hsb)
  http://www.camantsoc.org
  Hon Sec: Janet Morris
- ▲ Registered Charity
- ○ *L; archaeology & history of the city & county of Cambridge
- ● Conf - Mtgs - ET - Inf - Lib - VE - LG (local)
- < Coun Brit Archaeology
- M 465 i, 52 affiliated socs, 85 subscribing org
- ¶ Proceedings - 1; ftm, £14.50 nm.   The Conduit - 1; ftm only.

Cambridge Bibliographical Society 1949
- ■ University Library, West Rd, CAMBRIDGE, CB3 9DR. (hsb)
  01223 333000   fax 01223 333160
  email nas1000@cam.ac.uk
  Hon Sec: N Smith
- ▲ Registered Charity
- ○ *L; to promote the study of bibliographical & palaeographical research
- ● Mtgs - VE
- M 150 i, 10 f, 50 org, UK / 45 i, 15 f, 120 org, o'seas
- ¶ Transactions - 1; £12.   Monographs - irreg; price varies.

Cambridge Paperweight Circle
since January 2004 the **Paperweight Collectors Circle**

Cambridge Philosophical Society (CPS) 1819
- NR Central Science Library, Arts School, Bene't St, CAMBRIDGE, CB2 3PY. (hq)
  01223 334743
  email philosoc@hermes.cam.ac.uk
  http://www.cambridgephilosophicalsociety.org
  Exec Sec: Mrs B Larner
- ▲ Registered Charity
- ○ *L; promotion of scientific enquiry
- ● Conf - Mtgs - Participation in upkeep & management of Scientific Periodicals Library of the University of Cambridge
  Office hours: Mon-Fri 0800-1615, Sat 0900-1300
- M 1,900 i
- ¶ Mathematical Proceedings [articles on original research] - 6. Biological Reviews [long reviews on the state of research in a particular field of Biology - NOT book reviews] - 4.

Cambridge Refrigeration Technology   (CRT)   1945
- ■ 140 Newmarket Rd, CAMBRIDGE, CB5 8HE.   (hq)
  01223 365101   fax 01223 461522
  email crt@crtech.demon.co.uk   http://www.crtech.co.uk
- ▲ Company Limited by Guarantee
- ○ *Q; research, development, testing, consultancy & information
  services relating to all types of refrigerated transport &
  storage
- Gp Refrigerated Transport Information Society
- ● Conf - ET - Res - Exhib - Inf - Lib - PL
- < Intl Inst Refrigeration (IIR); Amer Soc Heating, Refrigerating &
  Air-Conditioning Engrs Inc (ASHRAE); Assn Indep Res &
  Technology Orgs (AIRTO); BSRIA; Inst Refrigeration; Brit
  Refrigeration Assn
- M 5 i, 10 f, 10 org, UK / 6 i, 30 f, 2 org, o'seas
- ¶ NL - 4; ftm only.
  The Transport of Perishable Foodstuffs; £6.50.
  Cargo Companion (3 vol); ftm, £155 nm.

Cambridge Sheep Society   1978
- ■ Pharm House, Neston Rd, Willaston, NESTON, Cheshire,
  CH64 2TL.   (hsp)
  0151-327 5699
  email d.a.r.davies@liv.ac.uk
  Hon Sec: D Alun R Davies
- ▲ Registered Charity
- ○ *B
- ● Conf - Mtgs - Res - Exhib - SG - Stat - Expt - Inf
- < Nat Sheep Assn
- M 20 i
  (Sub: £15)
- ¶ NL - 3/4;   LM - 1;   AR - 1; all free.

Cambridge Society for the Application of Research   (CSAR)   1956
- ■ 10 Trumpington St, CAMBRIDGE, CB2 1QA.   (organising s)
  01223 333543   fax 01223 332988
  email barrythompson@enterprise.cam.ac.uk
  http://www.csar.org.uk
  Organising Sec: Dr Richard Freeman
- ▲ Un-incorporated Society
- ○ *L; to bring together & promote cooperation within & between
  the University of Cambridge & industry of all kinds with a
  view to the expeditious use of resources & research
- ● Mtgs - VE
- M 150 i, 16 f, 9 university colleges & depts
  (Sub: £25 i, £150 f & colleges/depts)

Cambridgeshire Association for Local History   (CALH)   1951
- NR PO Box 1112, Basham, CAMBRIDGE, CB21 4WP.   (hsp)
  01223 892430
  Hon Sec: Andrew Westwood-Bate
- ▲ Company Limited by Guarantee; Registered Charity
- ○ *L; to encourage the study of local history & impart information
  on it
- Gp Photographic recording
- ● Conf - Mtgs - Res - Exhib - VE
- < Cambridge Antiquarian Soc
- M 160 i, 10 org
- ¶ Review - 1.
- × 2006 Cambridgeshire Local History Society

Cambridgeshire Chambers of Commerce   (CCC)   1918
- NR Endeavour House, Vision Park, Histon, CAMBRIDGE,
  CB24 9ZR.   (hq)
  01223 237414
  http://www.cambridgeshirechamber.co.uk
  6 The Forum, Minerva Business Park, Lynch Wood,
  PETERBOROUGH, Cambs, PE2 6FT.
  01733 370809
  Chief Exec: John Bridge
- ▲ Company Limited by Guarantee
- Br Cambridge, Ely, Fenland, Huntingdonshire, Peterborough
- ○ *C
- Gp Technology; Retail; Professional; Policy
- ● Conf - Mtgs - ET - Exhib - Stat - Expt - Inf - Lib - Export
  documentation - Advice skills training
- < Brit Chams Comm
- M f

Cambridgeshire Local History Society
  since 2006 **Cambridgeshire Association for Local History**

Cambridgeshire Records Society   (CRS)   1972
- NR c/o Cambridgeshire Archives, Box RES 1009, Shire Hall,
  CAMBRIDGE, CB3 0AP.   (hsb)
  01223 717281   fax 01223 718823
  Hon Sec: Mrs Francesca Ashburner
- ▲ Un-incorporated Society
- ○ *L; to publish documentary sources relating to the history of
  Cambridgeshire & neighbouring areas
- M c 100 i, UK / c 20 i, o'seas
- ¶ Source material - 1.

Camera Club   1885
- NR 16 Bowden St, LONDON, SE11 4DS.   (hq)
  020 7587 1809
  http://www.thecameraclub.co.uk
  The Hon Secretary
- ▲ Un-incorporated Society
- ○ *G; to foster the art & science of photography by provision of
  affordable, high quality darkrooms & studio, exhibition
  gallery & courses
- ● Mtgs - ET - Exhib - SG - Inf - Lib
- M 320 i, 10 f, UK / 4 i, o'seas
- ¶ Club News - 12; free.

Campaign for Angling
  a campaign of the **Countryside Alliance**

Campaign against Arms Trade   (CAAT)   1974
- ■ 11 Goodwin St, LONDON, N4 3HQ.   (hq)
  020 7281 0297   fax 020 7281 4369
  email enquiries@caat.org.uk   http://www.caat.org.uk
  Coordinators (different people for enquiries)
- ▲ Un-incorporated Society
- ○ *K; information & campaigning about the arms trade
- ● Mtgs - Res - Exhib - Inf - Lib - Day schools
- M 15,000 i
- ¶ CAATnews; ftm, £1 nm.

Campaign for Better Transport   1973
- ■ 12-18 Hoxton St, LONDON, N1 6NG.   (hq)
  020 7613 0743
  email info@bettertransport.org.uk
  http://www.bettertransport.org.uk
  Exec Dir: Stephen Joseph
- ▲ Company Limited by Guarantee; Registered Charity
- ○ *K, *N; to develop sustainable transport policies reducing
  dependence on private cars & road-based transport modes;
  to campaign for their implementation
- Gp Road Block (a project to support groups campaigning against
  road building)
- ● Res - Inf
- × 2007 Transport 2000 Ltd

Campaign against Censorship (CAC) 1968
■ 25 Middleton Close, FAREHAM, Hants, PO14 1QN. (hsp)
 01329 284471
 http://www.dlas.org.uk
 Hon Sec: Mrs Mary M Hayward
▲ Un-incorporated Society
○ *K; to uphold freedom of speech & publication; to oppose censorship in all fields
● Inf - Lobbying
M [not available]
¶ NL - irreg.

Campaign for Community Banking Services 1997
■ 50 Roundwood Park, HARPENDEN, Herts, AL5 3AF. (dir/p)
 01582 764760 fax 01582 764760
 http://www.communitybanking.org.uk
 Hon Dir: Derek P G French
▲ Un-incorporated Society
○ *K; 'to promote the continued existence of convenient access to banking services within communities in order to sustain local commercial activity; to combat financial & social exclusion & assist the vulnerable, disabled & elderly'
● Res - Stat - Inf - LG - Lobbying financial service providers - Publicity
M 25 org

Campaign for Courtesy 1986
■ 240 Tolworth Rise South, SURBITON, Surrey, KT5 9NB. (hq)
 020 8330 3707
 email peter.foot1@btinternet.com
 http://www.campaignforcourtesy.org.uk
 Chmn: Peter G Foot,   Hon Sec: Mary Doyle
▲ Registered Charity
○ *K; to encourage courtesy & good manners; to encourage respect for others & their property; to encourage respect for themselves; to reject anti-social behaviour
● Mtgs - VE - LG - Seminars
M 1,000 i
¶ Courtesy Call (Jnl) - 4; free to subscibers to society.

Campaign for Dark Skies (CFDS) 1990
NR c/o Burlington House, Piccadilly, LONDON, W1J 0DU. (hq)
 email info@dark-skies.org
 Coordinator: Bob Mizon
Br 118 local officers
○ *K; a scientific (astronomical) pressure group set up to counter the increasing threat to the visibility of the night sky from waste upward artificial light
 Note: this is a campaign of the British Astronomical Association.

Campaign for the Defence of the Traditional Cathedral Choir
 since 2006 **Campaign for the Traditional Cathedral Choir**

Campaign against Drinking & Driving (CADD) 1986
NR PO Box 62, BRIGHOUSE, W Yorks, HD6 3YY. (hq)
 0845 123 5543
 http://www.cadd.org.uk
▲ Company Limited by Guarantee; Registered Charity
○ *K, *W; to support victims & families of those killed & injured by drunk & irresponsible drivers; to work for a reduction of deaths & injuries on the road
M i & f
¶ NL - 4.

Campaign for an English Parliament (TheCEP) 1998
■ Margarethe House (office 1), Eismann Way, CORBY, Northants, NN17 5ZB. (mail/address)
 07779 338343
 email admin@thecep.org.uk   http://www.thecep.org.uk
 Co Sec: Edward Higginbottom
▲ Company Limited by Guarantee
○ *K, *Z; to campaign for an English Parliament
● Conf - Mtgs - Res - Exhib - Inf - LG
M 1,700 i, UK / 30 i, o'seas
 (Sub: £20)
¶ Publicity leaflets - irreg.

Campaign against Euro-federalism (CAEF) 1991
■ PO Box 46295, LONDON, W5 2UG.
 email caef@caef.org.uk   http://www.caef.org.uk
▲ Un-incorporated Society
○ *K; the campaign is based on the rights of states to self-determination & national democracy.   The campaign opposes: Britain's membership of the European Union, joining the single currency, the EU constitution & charter of fundamental rights including a common foreign policy & European army
● Conf - Public mtgs
< Intl Alliance of Euro-critical Movements & Orgs (TEAM); Campaign for an Indep Britain; Anti Maastricht Alliance
M [not stated]
¶ The Democrat - 12.
 Democratic Broadsheet - irreg.
 Various pamphlets & leaflets.

Campaign for Freedom of Information 1984
§ 16 Baldwins Gardens (suite 102), LONDON, EC1N 7RJ. (hq)
 020 7831 7477 fax 020 7831 7461
 email admin@cfoi.demon.co.uk   http://www.cfoi.org.uk
 Dir: Maurice Frankel
 Campaigns against unnecessary official secrecy and for an effective Freedom of Information Act; presses for more disclosure in the private sector if the information is of public interest.

Campaign for Freedom from Piped Music (Pipedown) 1992
■ 1 The Row, Berwick St James, SALISBURY, Wilts, SP3 4TP. (mail address)
 01722 790622
 email newpipedown@btinternet.com
 http://www.pipedown.info
 Hon Sec: Nigel Rodgers
▲ Un-incorporated Society
Br Germany (associated), USA
○ *K; 'to campaign for the freedom in public spaces (shops, hospitals, doctors' surgeries, rail/bus stations, airports, trains, buses) from piped music (muzak), meaning music (of any sort) relayed nonstop around a room, building etc'
● Conf - Mtgs - Stat - Inf - LG - Co-ordinated letter writing campaigns - Lobbying Parliament for a bill - Handing out protest cards - Peaceful demonstrations - Listing muzak-free places
M 1,800 i, UK / 50 i, o'seas
¶ Newsletter - 4; ftm, £2 nm.

Campaign for Homosexual Equality (CHE) 1969
NR PO Box 342, LONDON, WC1X 0DU. (mail address)
 07702 326151 fax 020 8743 6252
 email secretary@c-h-e.org.uk
 Sec: Barry Cutler
▲ Un-incorporated Society
○ *K; 'promotion of equality in law & society for lesbians, gays & bisexuals'
● ET - Inf
M 150 i & affiliates
¶ Publications list available.

Campaign against Hysterectomy & Unnecessary Operations on Women   (CAH)   1995

■ The Maltings, 99 Saunders Lane, WOKING, Surrey, GU22 0NR.   (mail/add)
  01483 715435
  email sandra.simkin@virgin.net
  Dir: Sandra Simkin
▲ Un-incorporated Society
Br 4
○ *K; to campaign for legal protection against unnecessary surgery; to raise women's awareness of their right to choose what happens to their bodies; to provide women with information which will enable them to challenge ignorant decisions; to research into the consequences of unnecessary surgery
Gp Information; Informed consent; Legal
● Conf - Res - Inf
< Rights of Women
M i
¶ Information Sheets
  The Case against Hysterectomy.

Campaign for an Independent Britain   (CIB)   1989

NR Morton House, 3 Stamford Drive, GROBY, Lincs, LE6 0YD.
  07092 857684
  http://www.eurosceptic.org.uk
  Hon Sec: Mrs Petrina Holdsworth
▲ Un-incorporated Society
Br 20
○ *K; to halt the drive to political, economic & monetary union in the EC; to regain for Britain the rights, freedoms & powers of an independent nation
● Conf - Mtgs - ET - Res - Stat - Inf
< Anti-Common Market League; Campaign against Euro Federalism; Cheaper Food League; Labour Euro-Safeguards Campaign; Conservatives against a Federal Europe
M 3,000 i
¶ Independence - 4.   Leaflets.
  Common Fisheries Policy - End or Mend?
  There is an Alternative.   A Price not worth Paying.
  From Rome to Maastricht - a reappraisal of Britain's membership of the EC.

Campaign for Independent Food
  as Honest Food, a campaign of the **Countryside Alliance**

** Campaign for Industry
  Organisation lost; see Introduction paragraph 3

Campaign for Learning   1997

NR 19 Buckingham Street (basement), LONDON, WC2N 6EF.
  (hq)
  020 7930 1111   fax 020 7930 1551
  http://www.campaign-for-learning.org.uk
  Chief Exec: Susie Parsons
▲ Company Limited by Guarantee; Registered Charity
Br 3
○ *K; an independent voluntary organisation working for an inclusive society in which learning is valued, understood, freely available & accessible to everyone as of right; to stimulate learning that will sustain people for life
Gp Family learning; Workplace learning; Learning to learn in schools
● Conf - ET - Res - Inf - LG - Learning at Work day - Family Learning week
¶ Learning to Live (NL) - 4; [email].

** Campaign for National Community Service
  Organisation lost: see Introduction paragraph 3.

Campaign for Nuclear Disarmament   (CND)   1958

NR 162 Holloway Rd, LONDON, N7 8DQ.   (hq)
  020 7700 2393   fax 020 7700 2357
  email enquiries@cnduk.org   http://www.cnduk.org
▲ Un-incorporated Society
○ *K; works for international peace & disarmament & a world in which the vast resources now devoted to militarism are dedicated to the real needs of the human community
M i, org

Campaign for Philosophical Freedom   (CFPF)   1985

■ 12a Westover Rise, BRISTOL, BS9 3LU.   (hsp)
  http://www.cfpf.org.uk
  Hon Sec: Michael Roll
○ *K; a non-membership body campaigning to obtain a balance on all media & educational outlets; to disestablish the Church & make the second House of Parliament an elected chamber; to give a secular balance to all religious affairs departments; to challenge orthodox scientific thinking
● Res - Inf
¶ The Mode of Future Existence by Sir Oliver Lodge; free, please send sae.

Campaign against Political Correctness

NR Trevose House, Orsett St, LONDON, SE11 5PN.
  07092 040916   fax 07092 040916
  email info@capc.co.uk   http://www.capc.co.uk
  Co-founders: Laura & John Midgley
○ *K

Campaign for Press & Broadcasting Freedom   (CPBF)   1979

■ 23 Orford Rd (2nd floor), LONDON, E17 9NL.   (hq)
  020 8521 5932   fax 020 8521 5932
  email freepress@cpbf.org.uk   http://www.cpbf.org.uk
  Nat Sec: Jonathan Hardy
Br 2
○ *K; to campaign for diverse, democratic & representative media; to carry out research & generate debate on alternative forms of media free from state control or business domination
● Conf - Mtgs - ET - Res - Exhib - SG - Stat - Inf - LG
M 1,500 i, 50 org, UK / 50 i, o'seas
¶ Free Press - 6.

Campaign to Protect Rural England   (CPRE)   1926

NR 128 Southwark St, LONDON, SE1 0SW.   (hq)
  020 7981 2800   fax 020 7981 2899
  email info@cpre.org.uk   http://www.cpre.org.uk
  Chief Exec: Shaun Spiers
○ *G, *K; campaigning for the beauty, tranquility & diversity of the countryside
Gp Stop the drop; Planning; Housing & urban policy; Transport; Landscape; Natural resources; Farming & food
M i

Campaign for the Protection of Rural Wales   (Ymgyrch Diogelu Cymru Wledig)   (YDCW)   (CPRW)   1928

■ Tŷ Gwyn, 31 High St, WELSHPOOL, Powys, SY21 7YD.   (hq)
  01938 552525   fax 01938 552741
  email info@cprwmail.org.uk   http://www.cprw.org.uk
  Dir: Peter Ogden
▲ Registered Charity
Br 17
○ *G; to protect & improve the rural scenery & amenities in Wales
● Inf - Lib
¶ Rural Wales / Cymru Wledig - 3; ftm.

Campaign for Qualified Politicians
  alternative name of **Cognition**

© CBD Research Ltd · Beckenham · BR3 5JS · Tel 020 8650 7745 · Fax 020 8650 0768 · E-mail cbd@cbdresearch.com · www.cbdresearch.com

Campaign for Real Ale Ltd   (CAMRA)   1971
■   230 Hatfield Rd, ST ALBANS, Herts, AL1 4LW.   (hq)
      01727 867201   fax 01727 867670
      email camra@camra.org.uk   http://www.camra.org.uk
      Chief Exec: Mike Benner
▲   Company Limited by Guarantee
Br   200
○   *K; to promote quality, choice & value for money; to support
      the public house as a focus for community life; to maintain
      consumer rights & increase the appreciation of traditional
      beers & ciders
●   Conf - Mtgs - Res - Exhib - Comp - Stat - Lib - VE - LG
<   Eur Beer Consumers U (EBCU); Sustain; Nat Coun for Voluntary
      Orgs (NCVO)
M   79,000 i, UK / 1,000 i, o'seas
¶   What's Brewing - 12; ftm only.
      Good Beer Guide - 1; £10 m, £13.99 nm.
      Good Bottled Beer Guide - 1; £7.99 m, £9.99 nm.
      CAMRA's Good Cider Guide - 2/3 yrly; £8.99 m, £10.99 nm.
      Good Beer Guide to Germany; £10.99 m, £12.99 nm.

Campaign for Real Education   (CRE)   1987
■   12 Pembroke Sq, LONDON, W8 6PA.   (hsp)
      020 7937 2122   fax 020 7938 1638
      email cred@cre.org.uk   http://www.cre.org.uk
      18 Westlands Grove, Stockton Lane, YORK, YO31 1EF.
      01904 424134   (chmn/p).
      Hon Sec: Dr Vera Dalley,   Chmn: Nick Seaton
○   *E, *K; an association of parents, teachers & academics which
      campaigns for higher standards in state schools & colleges;
      to support individuals & groups with similar interests; to
      promote educational research & the dissemination of
      information
M   c 3,000 i, UK / c 30 i, o'seas

Campaign for Real Milk   (CAMILK)   1998
NR   1 Stoodley Barn, Holne, ASHBURTON, Devon, TQ13 7RY.
      (hsp)
      01364 631212
      email richard@copur.fsbusiness.co.uk
      Co-founder: Richard Copur
▲   Un-incorporated Society
○   *K; to promote raw un-pasteurised milk
●   Inf
<   Weston Price Foundation (www.realmilk.com) (USA)

Campaign for Real Recycling
NR   57 Prince St, BRISTOL, BS1 4QH.
      0117-942 0142   fax 0117-934 9944
      email www.realrecycling.org.uk
      Coordinator: Andy Moore
○   *K; to improve the quality of materials collected for recycling

Campaign for the Reform of Council Tax
      alternative name of **IsItFair (Campaign for the Reform of
      Council Tax)**

** **Campaign for the Restoration of the National Anthem & Flag**
      Organisation lost: see Introduction paragraph 3.

Campaign for Science & Engineering in the UK   (CASE)   1986
NR   29-30 Tavistock Square, LONDON, WC1H 9QU.   (hq)
      020 7679 4995
▲   Un-incorporated Society
○   *K; to communicate to the public, parliament & the government
      a proper appreciation of the economic & cultural benefits of
      scientific & technological research & development, with the
      consequent importance to the nation of adequate funding of
      research by government & industry
M   i, f & org
×   2005 Save British Science Society

Campaign for Shooting
      a campaign of the **Countryside Alliance**

Campaign against Stage Hypnosis   (CASH)   1994
■   52 Station Rd, Hesketh Bank, PRESTON, Lancs, PR4 6SP.
      (hsp/b)
      01772 813052
      Jt Secs: Connell Harper,   Nora Harper
○   *K; to inform the public of the abuse & dangers of stage
      hypnosis
●   Inf - LG
M   [not stated]

Campaign for State Education   (CASE)   1961
NR   98 Erlanger Rd, LONDON, SE14 5TH.
      07932 149942
      http://www.campaignforstateeducation.org.uk
      Sec: Keith Lichman
▲   Un-incorporated Society
○   *E, *K; to campaign for a fully comprehensive & locally
      accountable education system which enables all children to
      achieve their personal best in all areas of learning in a
      happy & secure environment; high quality early years
      education for all whose parents want it
●   Conf - Mtgs - Inf - Lobbying
¶   CASEnotes - 6; ftm.

Campaign for the Traditional Cathedral Choir   (CTCC)   1996
NR   49 Cambridge Rd, Oakington, CAMBRIDGE, CB24 3BG.
      (hsp)
      email ctcc@ctcc.org.uk   http://www.ctcc.org.uk
      Hon Sec: David Blumlein
▲   Un-incorporated Society
○   *K; to champion the ancient tradition of the all-male choir in
      cathedrals, chapels royal, collegiate churches, university
      chapels & similar ecclesiastical foundations; to encourage
      parish churches which maintain, or seek to establish, all-
      male voice choirs
●   Mtgs - Res - Campaigning
M   i
¶   Bulletin - 2; ftm, £2 nm.   NL - 2; ftm only.
×   2006 Campaign for the Defence of the Traditional Cathedral
      Choir

**Campden & Chorleywood Food Research Association
(CCFRA)   1919**
NR   Station Rd, CHIPPING CAMPDEN, Glos, GL55 6LD.   (hq)
      01386 842000
      Co Sec: J Wilkinson
▲   Company Limited by Guarantee
○   *Q; research & services for the food & allied industries (food
      packaging, machinery, manufacturers, distributors, retailers
      & growers, drink, cereals processing)
●   Conf - Mtgs - ET - Res - Exhib - SG - Stat - Inf - Lib - LG
M   800 f, UK / 200 f, o'seas
¶   Campden & Chorleywood NL - 12; free.
      Research Reports;   Guidelines;   Specifications;   Reviews;
      Symposium Proceedings - all irreg; prices vary.

Camping & Caravanning Club Ltd   1901
NR   Greenfields House, Westwood Way, COVENTRY, CV4 8JH.
       (hq)
       0845 130 7631
       http://www.campingandcaravanningclub.co.uk
       Dir Gen: Robert Louden
▲   Company Limited by Guarantee
○   *G; 'the promotion & servicing of the pastime of mobile
       recreational camping & caravanning'
Gp Association of Lightweight Campers; Boating Group; British
       Caravanners' Club; Camping Club Youth; Canoe Camping
       Club; Folk Song & Dance Group; Motor Caravan Section;
       Mountain Activity Section; Photographic Group; Trailer Tent &
       Folding Camper Group
●   Inf
<   Fédn Intl de Camping et de Caravanning (FICC)
M   c 400,000 i
¶   Camping & Caravanning Magazine - 12;
       Your Place in the Country (site guide) - 1;
       Your Big Sites Book (site guide) - 2 yrly; all ftm only.
       Carefree Camping & Caravanning Guide to Europe - 1.

Camping Club Youth
       a group of the **Camping & Caravanning Club**

Campoaign against Climate Change
NR   5 Caledonian Rd (top floor), LONDON, N1 9DX.
       020 7837 4473
○   *K

Can Makers   1981
NR   New Bridge St House, 30-34 New Bridge St, LONDON,
       EC4V 6BJ.   (hq)
       020 7072 4083   fax 020 7072 4020
       http://www.canmakers.co.uk
       Chmn: Gary Aslam
○   *T; promotion of beverage cans & can recycling
●   Conf - Res - Stat - Inf (on beverage cans, beer & soft drinks
       market)
<   Beverage Can Makers Europe (BCME)
M   8 f
¶   Thirst Choice - 2 yrly; free.

Canada-United Kingdom Chamber of Commerce   1921
NR   38 Grosvenor St, LONDON, W1K 4DP.   (hq)
       020 7258 6576   fax 020 7258 6594
       email info@canada-uk.org   http://www.canada-uk.org
       Exec Dir: Nigel Bacon
▲   Company Limited by Guarantee
○   *C, promotion of trade & investment between Canada & the
       UK in both directions
●   Conf - Mtg - Res - Inf
<   Canadian High Commission; Coun of Foreign Chams Comm
M   c 200 i, f & org
¶   NL - 6;   Membership Book - 1; both ftm only.

Canal Boatbuilders Association   (CBA)
■   Marine House, Thorpe Lea Rd, EGHAM, Surrey, TW20 8BF.
       (hq)
       0844 800 9575   fax 01327 340174
       email cba@britishmarine.co.uk   http://www.c-b-a.co.uk
       Sec: Samantha Clarke
▲   Un-incorporated Society
○   *T; for those in business connected with the inland waterways
       building or supply of narrowboats
●   Conf - Mtgs - ET - Res - Stat - Inf - LG
<   Brit Marine Fedn
M   110 f
¶   How to Buy a Boat - 1; free.

Canal Card Collectors Circle   (CCCC)   1978
■   18 Kilpatrick Way, Yeading, HAYES, Middx, UB4 9SX.   (hsp)
       020 8841 3788
       email ianjwilson@uwclub.net   http://www.gongoozler.org
       Hon Sec/Treas & Mem Sec: Ian J Wilson
       mobile: 0788 518 9765
▲   Un-incorporated Society
○   *G; the collection of post cards of canals & inland navigations
●   Mtg (Annual in June) - VE
<   Inland Waterways Assn
>   Shardlow Heritage Centre
M   55 i, 1 org, UK / 3 i, o'seas
¶   Gongoozler - 4; ftm, 50p nm.

Canary Council
       a group of the **National Council for Aviculture**

Cancer Genetics Group
       a group of the **British Society for Human Genetics**

Canine & Feline Behaviour Association   (CFBA)
NR   Applewood House, Ringshall Rd, Dagnall, BERKHAMSTED,
       Herts, HP4 1RN.
       0845 644 5993
       email mail@cfba.co.uk
○   *G; provides dog training & behaviour courses

Canoe Association of Northern Ireland   (CANI)
NR   Unit 2 River's Edge, 13-15 Ravenhill Rd, BELFAST, BT6 8DN.
       0870 240 5065
       http://www.cani.org.uk
       Sec: Mary Doyle
○   *S
●   Mtgs - Comp

Canoe Camping Club
       a group of the **Camping & Caravanning Club**

Canterbury Chamber of Commerce
       a branch of **Kent Invicta Chamber of Commerce**

Canterbury & York Society   1904
■   Borthwick Institute, University of York, Heslington, YORK,
       YO10 5DD.   (hsb)
       email cf13@york.ac.uk
       http://www.canterburyandyork.org
       Hon Sec: Dr C Fonge
▲   Registered Charity
○   *L; publication of the records of the medieval English church
●   Publishing
M   101 i, 141 libraries
¶   Annual Volume; prices vary (c £15 i, c £20 instns).

Capability Scotland   1946
NR   Westerlea, 11 Ellersly Rd, EDINBURGH, EH12 6HY.
       0131-337 9876   fax 0131-346 7864
       email ascs@capability-scotland.org.uk
       http://www.capability-scotland.org.uk
       Chief Exec: Alan D J Dickson
▲   Company Limited by Guarantee; Registered Charity
○   *W; to support children, young people & adults with a range of
       disabilities, providing a diverse range of services including
       community living, day & residential services, employment,
       respite/short breaks, therapy, education & learning, family
       support & activities

© CBD Research Ltd · Beckenham · BR3 5JS · Tel 020 8650 7745 · Fax 020 8650 0768 · E-mail cbd@cbdresearch.com · www.cbdresearch.com

Capel: the Chapels Heritage Society   (CAPEL)   1986
■   5 Cuffnell Close, Liddell Park, LLANDUDNO, LL30 1UX.   (hsp)
     01492 860449
     email obadiah1@btinternet.com
     http://www.capeli.org.uk
     Hon Sec: Rev Peter Jennings
▲   Registered Charity
○   *G, *L, *R; the study & preservation of the non-conformist
     heritage in Wales, with particular regard to chapel buildings
     & their records
●   Conf - Mtgs - Exhib - Inf - VE
M   c 300 i
¶   Capel NL - 2; ftm, £1 nm.

Captive Animals' Protection Society   (CAPS)   1957
■   PO Box 4186, MANCHESTER, Lancs, M60 3ZA.   (hq)
     0845 330 3911
     email info@captiveanimals.org
     http://www.captiveanimals.org
     Chief Exec: Pat Simpson
▲   Company Limited by Guarantee
○   *K; is opposed to the use of animals in entertainment;
     campaigns to end the captivity of animals in zoos, circuses &
     the exotic pet trade
●   ET - Inf
M   i
     (Sub: £12 , UK / £15, o'seas)
¶   Release - 2; ftm, £1.50 nm.

Car Park Appreciation Society   (CPAS)   2005
NR   1 Rowborough Close, Astwood Bank, REDDITCH, Worcs,
     B96 6DQ.   (hsp)
     01527 894088   fax 01527 522545
     email kevin@beresfordB96.freeserve.co.uk
     Sec/Pres: Kevin Beresford
▲   Un-incorporated Society
○   *G; to collect photographs & interesting data on car parks
     throughout Britain & the Irish Republic
●   Mtgs - VE
<   AA Insurance
M   2 i
¶   Car Parks of GB Calendar - 1; £8.
     Get Carter Calendar (the Gateshead car park) - 1; £6 m,
     £8 nm.
✕   nncs014

Car Rental Council of Ireland
IRL   5 Upper Pembroke St, DUBLIN 2, Republic of Ireland.
     353 (1) 676 1690   fax 353 (1) 661 9213
     email predmond@simi.ie
     http://www.carrentalcouncil.ie
     Chief Exec: Paul Redmond
○   *T

Caravan Club Ltd   1907
NR   East Grinstead House, EAST GRINSTEAD, W Sussex,
     RH19 1UA.   (hq)
     01342 326944   fax 01342 410258
     http://www.caravanclub.co.uk
     Dir Gen: Trevor Watson
○   *G; for touring caravanners; providing sites, travel &
     information services
<   Fédn Intle de Camping et Caravanning (FICC); Alliance of Intl
     Tourism (AIT); Fédn Intle Automobile (FIA); Soc of Motor Mfrs
     & Traders (SMMT)
M   323,000 i, UK / 1,000 i, o'seas
¶   Caravan Club Magazine - 12;
     Sites Directory & Map - 2 yrly;
         Site Supplement - 2 yrly (alt yrs to above); all ftm.
     Caravanning Europe [year] 2 vol - 1; £8.50 per vol m,
         (£9.99 nm).

Carbon Capture & Storage Association   (CCSA)
NR   35-37 Grosvenor Gardens, LONDON, SW1W 0BS.
     020 7821 0528   fax 020 7828 0310
     email info@ccsassociation.org
     http://www.ccsassociation.org
     Chief Exec: Jeff Chapman
○   *T; the capture & geological storage of carbon dioxide

Carbon Monoxide & Gas Safety Society   1995
§   Station Building, The Parade, CLAYGATE, Surrey, KT10 0PE.
     01372 466135   fax 01372 468965
     email office@co-gassafety.co.uk
     http://www.co-gassafety.co.uk
     Pres: Stephanie Trotter
     Known as **CO-Gas Safety**, the society campaigns to reduce
     accidents from carbon monoxide (CO) poisoning and other
     gas dangers.

Cardiff Naturalists' Society   (CNS)   1867
NR   36 Rowan Way, Lisvane, CARDIFF, CF14 0TD.   (hsp)
     029 2075 6869
     http://www.cardiffnaturalists.org
     Sec: Mike Dean
▲   Un-incorporated Society
○   *E, *L; to promote the study of the natural sciences & the
     conservation of the natural environment, with special
     reference to the counties of Glamorgan
M   i

Cardiomyopathy Association   (CMA)   1989
■   Unit 10 Chiltern Court, Asheridge Rd, CHESHAM, Bucks,
     HP5 2PX.   (hq)
     01494 791224   fax 01494 797199
     email info@cardiomyopathy.org
     http://www.cardiomyopathy.org
     Chmn: Peter McBride
▲   Registered Charity
Br   1
○   *K, *W; to provide accurate & up-to-date information about
     cardiomyopathy (a heart muscle disease) to patients, family
     members, doctors & medical staff
●   Conf - Mtgs - ET - Inf - Support through groups & individuals
     (one to on on telephone)
<   Children's Heart Fedn; GIG; Heart Transplant Families
     Together; NVCO
M   900 i, 5 org, UK / 21 i, o'seas
¶   NL - 2;   AR; both ftm.

Care of Collections Forum
     in 2005 merged with the Institute of Paper Conservation, the
     Photographic Materials Conservation Group, the Scottish Society for
     Conservation and Restoration & the United Kingdom Institute for
     Conservation of Historic & Artistic Works to form the **Institute of
     Conservation**

Care not Killing Alliance
     since 2007 **CNK Alliance Ltd (Care not Killing)**

Care Leavers Association   (CLA)
NR   23 New Mount St (suite F113), MANCHESTER, Lancs,
     M4 4DE.   (hq)
     0161-953 4047
     email info@careleavers.org   http://www.careleavers.org
     Sec: Jim Goddard
▲   Company Limited by Guarantee
○   *K, *W; 'to protect, promote & strengthen rights for care
     leavers; to challenge negative public perceptions of care
     leavers & children in care; to ensure care leavers receive the
     support services they require'
●   Conf - Mtgs - ET - Res - Inf - LG
M   50 i, 2 org, UK / 1 i, o'seas
¶   The Grapevine (NL) - 4; free.

Care Management Group
a group of the **Chartered Management Institute**

Career Development Group   1895
- ■ c/o CILIP, 7 Ridgmount St, LONDON, WC1E 7AE.   (hsb)
   07855 790716
   http://www.careerdevelopmentgroup.org.uk
   Hon Sec: Lorna Robertson
- ▲ Registered Charity
- Br 15 regional gps
- ○ *P
- ● Conf - Mtgs - ET - Res - Exhib
- < Library Assn
- M 5,000 i
- ¶ Impact - 10; £34 yr m (£39 o'seas, £98 USA).

Careers Writers' Association   (CWA)   1978
- ■ 32 Leyborne Avenue, LONDON, W13 9RA.   (hsp)
   020 8567 0796
   email sarah.marten@btinternet.com
   http://www.careerswriting.co.uk
   Sec: Sarah Marten
- ▲ Un-incorporated Society
- ○ *P; to promote the values of accuracy, clarity, impartiality, creativity & integrity in written & other forms of careers information
- ● Mtgs - ET
- M 28 i
- ¶ Booklet - 1.

Carers Association
- IRL Bolger House, Patrick St, TULLAMORE, Co Offaly, Republic of Ireland.
   email ceo@carersireland.com
   http://www.carersireland.com
   Chmn: Frank Goodwin
- ○ *W

Carers UK   1965
- ■ 20 Great Dover St, LONDON, SE1 4LX.   (hq)
   020 7378 4999   fax 020 7378 9781
   email info@carersuk.org   http://www.carersuk.org
   Chief Exec: Imelda Redmond
- ▲ Company Limited by Guarantee; Registered Charity
- Br 80
- ○ *W; to campaign for the rights of carers & to advise carers about their rights & entitlements to support
- ● ET - Inf - LG
   Helpline: 0808 808 7777 (Wed & Thurs 1000-1200 + 1400-1600)
- M 10,000 i, 569 f
- ¶ Caring (Jnl) - 4; m only.
   Publications list.

Caribbean-British Business Council   (CBBC)   1974
- NR 2 Belgrave Sq, LONDON, SW1X 8PJ.   (hq)
   020 7235 9484   fax 020 7823 1370
   email admin@cb-bc.org
   http://www.caribbean-council.org
   Exec Dir: David Jessop
- ▲ Un-incorporated Society
- Br Brussels
- ○ *T; to promote & support trade & investment between Britain & the Caribbean
- ● Conf - Mtgs - Exhib - Expt - Inf - LG
- M 8 i, 87 f, 3 org, UK / 3 f, o'seas
- ¶ Caribbean Briefing - 52; ftm, £210 yr nm.
   Caribbean Airline News - 6;   The Week in Europe;
   Weekly NL - 52; all ftm only.

Caring for Carers
   alternative name of **Crossroads**

Carlyle Society   1929
- ■ c/o Prof Ian Campbell, University of Edinburgh, David Hume Tower, George Sq, EDINBURGH, EH8 9JX.   (pres/b)
   0131-650 4284   fax 0131-650 6898
   email ian.campbell@ed.ac.uk
   Pres: Prof Ian Campbell
- ○ *A, *L; the study & encouragement of knowledge & information on the life & writing of the Carlyles - Thomas (1795-1881) & Jane (1801-1866)

Carmarthenshire Antiquarian Society   1905
- NR 63 Oaklands, Swiss Valley Park, LLANELLI, SA14 8DH.
   01554 773468
   http://www.carmants.org.uk
   Sec: Mrs Molly Rees

Carnival Band Secretaries League   (CBSL)   1936
- ■ 10 Stonyhurst Court, Shelton Lock, DERBY, DE24 9JZ.   (hsp)
   01332 690790
   email info@cbsl.org.uk   http://www.cbsl.org.uk
   Hon Sec & Treas: Moira Findlay
- ▲ Un-incorporated Society
- ○ *D; to promote the use of carnival marching showbands & the holding of band contests & arena displays at carnivals etc
- Gp Competitions (3-6 bands); Exhibitions (1-6 bands)
- ● ET - Exhib (1-5 bands) - Comp (3-5 bands) - Massed band displays - Cabaret
- M [not stated]

Carnival Glass Society   (CGS)   1982
- ■ PO Box 14, HAYES, Middx, UB3 5NU.   (mail/address)
   email pmphyllis@aol.com
   http://www.carnivalglasssociety.co.uk
   Sec: Phyllis Atkinson
- ▲ Company Limited by Guarantee
- ○ *G; for collectors of carnival glass & its accurate documentation; (Carnival Glass is mostly press moulded & sprayed, whilst hot, with metallic salts suspended in oil)
- M 300 i, UK / 6 i, o'seas
   (Sub: £18 UK / £24 o'seas)
- ¶ NL - 4; ftm only.

Carnival Guild
   alternative name of the **National Carnival Guild - the National Federation of Carnival Associations & Committees**

Carnivorous Plant Society   (CPS)   1978
- ■ 100 Lambley Lane, Burton Joyce, NOTTINGHAM, NG14 5BL.   (hsp)
   07528 342224
   email derek.c.petrie@btinternet.com
   http://www.thecps.org.uk
   NEC Gardeners World Coordinator: Derek Petrie
- ▲ Registered Charity
- ○ *H; to promote the growing & conservation of carnivorous plants
- ● Conf - Mtgs - ET - Exhib - Lib - PL - VE
- < R Horticl Soc

Carp Society   1983
- NR Horseshoe Lake, Burford Rd, LECHLADE, Glos, GL7 3QQ.   (hq)
   01367 253959   fax 01367 252450
   email info@thecarpsociety.com
   Commercial Mgr: David Mannall
- ○ *G; for those interested in fishing for carp
- ● Conf - Exhib
- M c 3,500 i
- ¶ Various.

© CBD Research Ltd · Beckenham · BR3 5JS · Tel 020 8650 7745 · Fax 020 8650 0768 · E-mail cbd@cbdresearch.com · www.cbdresearch.com

Carpet Foundation   2001
- ■ MCF Complex, 60 New Rd, KIDDERMINSTER, Worcs, DY10 1AQ.   (hq)
  01562 755568   fax 01562 865405
  email info@carpetfoundation.com
  http://www.carpetfoundation.com
  Chief Exec: Mike H Hardiman
- ▲ Company Limited by Guarantee
- ○ *T; British carpet industry; Registered Specialists (qualified independent retailers) & manufacturers
- ● Mtgs - Res - Stat - Inf - LG - Promoting public awareness of the benefits of carpet through the Quality Mark & media campaigns
- M 14 mfrs, 1,244 retailers, 5 associates
- ¶ NL - 4; ftm.

Carrier Bag Consortium
- ■ Gothic House (3rd floor), Barker Gate, NOTTINGHAM, NG1 1JU.
  0115-958 0403   fax 0115-948 3098
  email opinion@carrierbagtax.com
  http://www.carrierbagtax.com
  Contact: Peter Woodall
- ○ *K, *N, *T; a group of major UK carrier bag suppliers fighting the possibility of a carrier bag tax being imposed in the UK
- M f

Cartoonists' Club of Great Britain   (CCGB)   1960
- ■ 7 Gambetta St, LONDON, SW8 3TS.   (hsp/b)
  020 7720 1884
  email jedstone@tunamoon.demon.co.uk
  http://www.ccgb.org.uk
  Hon Sec: Jed Stone
- ▲ Un-incorporated Society
- ○ *P, *G; to champion the art & craft of the cartoon; to provide contact between members
- ● Conf - Mtgs - Exhib - Comp - PL - VE
- < Fedn Eur Cartoonist Orgs (FECO)
- M 200 i, UK / 10 i, o'seas
- ¶ The Jester (NL) - 12; ftm only.
  LM - 1; ftm, free on request nm.

Cartophilic Society of Great Britain Ltd   1938
- NR Ivy House, Ivy Farm, School Lane, Lower Heath, PREES, Shropshire, SY13 2BU.   (hsp)
  http://www.csgb.co.uk
  Gen Sec: Robin Short
- ▲ Company Limited by Guarantee
- Br 12
- ○ *G; 'propagating, enhancing & preserving the hobby of cigarette & trade card collecting'
- ● Conf - Mtgs - Res - Inf - Lib
- M 900 i, UK / 100 i, o'seas
- ¶ Cartophilic Notes & News - 6.

Casino Operators' Association of the UK   (COA(UK))   2001
- ■ 15 Livesey St, SHEFFIELD, S Yorks, S6 2BL.   (sb)
  0114-281 6209   fax 0114-281 6199
  email coa.generalsecretary@tiscali.co.uk
  http://www.casinooperatorsassociation.org.uk
  Gen Sec: Phil Lowther
- ▲ Company Limited by Guarantee
- ○ *T; formed from companies who felt the the British Casino Association was unable to represent adequately other than large company views. Those smaller companies have fundamentally different perspectives of the casino industry through experience & usually, a risk to their own capital
- ● Mtgs - Inf - LG
- M f

Caspari Foundation for Educational Therapy & Therapeutic Teaching   2000
- NR Caspari House, 1 Noel Rd, LONDON, N1 8HQ.   (hq)
  020 7704 1977   fax 020 7704 1783
  email casparihouse@btconnect.com
  http://www.caspari.org.uk
  Contact: Sister Bernadette Hunston
- ▲ Registered Charity
- ○ *E; to develop theory & practice of educational therapy as a treatment for those with learning difficulties; to promote the psychological insight of teachers in general into the emotional factors in learning & failing to learn
- ● Conf - Mtgs - ET - Inf - Lib - LG - Educational therapy - Lectures
- < Nat Children's Bureau
- M 80 i, 30 f, UK / 10 i, 5 f, o'seas, school services in corporate membership
- ¶ Educational Therapy & Therapeutic Teaching - 1; ftm, £10 nm.

Caspian Breed Society   (CBS(UK))   1999
- ■ Sparrow Farm, Lanhill, CHIPPENHAM, Wilts, SN14 6LX.   (hsp)
  01249 782246   fax 0871 251 3199
  email uk.caspian.society@virgin.net
  http://www.caspianbreedsociety.co.uk/
  Sec: Ronald J Scott
- ▲ Company Limited by Guarantee
- ○ *B; the promotion & preservation of the Caspian horse, an ancient breed from 3,000 BC
- Gp Horse breeding; Miniature horse
- ● Mtgs - Exhib - Breed show - Agricultural show promotion
- < Brit Horse Soc; Brit Assn of Equine Socs; Central Prefix Register
- M 102 i, UK / 30 i, o'seas
- ¶ CBS News (NL) - 6;   AR - 1; both free.

Caspian Horse Society   (CHS)   1987
- ■ Eglentyne, 6 Nuns Walk, VIRGINIA WATER, Surrey, GU25 4RT.   (hsp)
  01344 843352
  email rlharris@talk21.com
  http://www.caspianhorsesociety.org.uk
  Sec: Dr Rosemary Harris
- ▲ Company Limited by Guarantee; Registered Charity
- ○ *B
- ● Conf - Mtgs - Comp - Expt - LG
- < Intl Caspian Soc; Brit Horse Soc (Breeds C'ee); Central Prefix Register; Nat Equine Forum
- M 95 i
- ¶ The Caspian (Jnl) - 4; ftm.

Cast Iron Drainage Development Association   (CIDDA)
- ■ c/o Wyatt International Ltd, Wyatt House 72 Francis Rd, Edgbaston, BIRMINGHAM, B16 8SP.
  0121-454 8181
- ○ *T
  no further information supplied

Cast Metals Federation   (CMF)   2001
- NR National Metalforming Centre, 47 Birmingham Rd, WEST BROMWICH, W Midlands, B70 6PY.   (hq)
  0121-601 6397   fax 0121-601 6391
  email admin@cmfed.co.uk
  http://www.castmetalsfederation.com
  Chief Exec: John Parker
- ▲ Company Limited by Guarantee
- ○ *T; for the UK metal casting industry
- Gp Sections: Costs, Raw materials, Health & safety;
  Gps: Iron castings, brass & bronze; Investment castings; Light metals; Steel; Suppliers; Zinc
- ● Conf - Mtgs - Inf - LG
- < C'ee of Assns of Eur Foundries (CAEF); METCOM
- M c 200 f

Castlemilk Moorit Sheep Society   1973
NR   Hillcrest Farm, Coventry Rd, Berkswell, COVENTRY, CV7 7AZ
    (hsp)
    01676 535242
    http://www.castlemilkmoorit.co.uk
    Hon Sec: Sheila Cooper
○   *B; conservation & promotion of Britain's rarest sheep breed
●   Mtgs - Exhib - Livestock shows - Workshops
<   Rare Breeds Survival Trust
M   60 i
¶   NL - 3; ftm only.

Casualties Union   (CU)   1942
■   PO Box 1942, LONDON, E17 6YU.   (hsp)
    0870 007 0590   fax 0870 078 0590
    email hq@casualtiesunion.org.uk
    http://www.casualtiesunion.org.uk
    Hon Gen Sec: Caroline Thomas
▲   Registered Charity
Br   42; 2 o'seas
○   *W; to supply trained casualties for the training of first aid,
    nursing & rescue
Gp   Make-up; Acting; Staging
●   Conf - Mtgs - ET - Exam - Res - Comp - SG
M   440 i, UK / 8 i, o'seas
¶   Casualty Simulation - 4; ftm only.

Cat Fancy
    see **Governing Council of the Cat Fancy**

Catalogue Exchange
NR   151 High St, ILFRACOMBE, Devon, EX34 9EZ.
    01271 855545   fax 01271 866281
    http://www.catalogueexchange.co.uk
○   home shopping

Catenian Association   1908
NR   Copthall House (2nd floor), Station Sq, COVENTRY, Warks,
    CV1 2FY.   (hq)
    024 7622 4533
    http://www.thecatenians.com
    Admin: Mrs Jai Milward
▲   Company Limited by Guarantee; Registered Charity
Br   255; Australia, Eire, Hong Kong, Malta, S Africa, Zambia,
    Zimbabwe
○   *R; Catholic business & professional men
Gp   Benevolent & children's fund; Bursary fund
●   Conf - Mtgs - VE
M   9,500 i, UK / 1,000 i, o'seas
¶   Catena - 12.

**Catering Equipment Distributors Association of Great Britain
(CEDA)   1972**
NR   PO Box 683, INKBERROW, Worcs, WR7 4WQ.   (hsb)
    0560 261 8485
    email secretary@ceda.co.uk   http://www.ceda.co.uk
    Dir: Peter Kay (mobile: 0777 084 8798)
▲   Un-incorporated Society
○   *T; design, supply, installation & after-sales service of
    commercial kitchens & all catering equipment
Gp   CEDACARE (a catering equipment service initiative)
●   Conf - Mtgs - ET - Exhib - Stat - Inf - LG
M   80 f
¶   CEDA News - 4; free.

Catering Equipment Suppliers' Association   (CESA)   1994
NR   Westminster Tower, 3 Albert Embankment (ground floor),
    LONDON, SE1 7SL.   (hq)
    020 7793 3030   fax 020 7793 3031
    email enquiries@cesa.org.uk   http://www.cesa.org.uk
▲   Company Limited by Guarantee
○   *T; to promote cooperation between those engaged in the food
    service equipment industry
M   f

**Catering Managers Association of Great Britain & the Channel
Islands   (CMA)   1947**
NR   238 Nelson Rd, Whitton, TWICKENHAM, Middx, TW2 7BW.
    (hsp)
    020 8894 9103
    Sec: Paul Wenham
▲   Un-incorporated Society
○   *P
M   i & f
¶   Catering Manager - 4; ftm.

Cathedral Architects Association   (CAA)   1948
■   St Ann's Gate, Architects, The Close, SALISBURY, Wilts,
    SP1 2EB.   (hsb)
    01722 555200   fax 01722 555201
    email antony@stannsgate.com
    Hon Sec: Anthony Feltham-King
▲   Un-incorporated Society
○   *P; sharing sharing in relation to aesthetic, liturgical & technical
    issues particular to cathedrals & church buildings of similar
    status
●   Conf - VE - LG
M   80 i, UK / 10 i, o'seas
¶   Conference Notes & Proceedings - 1/2 yrly; ftm only.

Cathedral & Church Shops Association   (CCSA)
■   27 Wyedean Drive, Belmont, HEREFORD,
    HR2t08c@btinternet.com   (hsp)
    http://www.ccsa.org.uk
    Hon Sec: Mrs Alison Chambers
▲   Un-incorporated Society
○   *T; 'to extend the ministry of the church through the sale of
    Christian books & cards; by providing a presence in a church
    or cathedral; by making a 'bridge' into the worship building'
●   Conf - Mtgs - ET - Exhib
M   cathedrals & churches

Cathedral Organists' Association   (COA)   1946
■   19 The Close, SALISBURY, Wilts, SP1 2EB.   (hsb)
    Hon Sec: T Hone
▲   Un-incorporated Society
○   *P; interests & training of cathedral & collegiate church
    organists in the UK
●   Conf - Mtgs - ET - SG - VE - Empl - Liaison with the Church of
    England
M   127 i

CATHOLIC...
    for Catholic organisations, other than those listed below, please refer
    to the **Catholic Directory** published by Gabriel Communications.

Catholic Archives Society   (CAS)   1979
■   Innyngs House, Hatfield Park, HATFIELD, Herts, AL9 5PL.   (hsp)
    http://www.catholic-history.org
    Hon Sec: Margaret Harcourt Williams,
    Chmn: Judith Smeaton
▲   Un-incorporated Society
○   *L; to promote the care & preservation of archives of dioceses,
    religious orders, & other institutions of the Catholic Church in
    the UK & Ireland
●   Conf - ET - Inf - VE
M   200-250 i
    (Sub: £20)
¶   Catholic Archives - 1; ftm, £7 nm.   Bulletin - 1; ftm only.
    Occasional Papers - 1; £3-£5.
    Advice leaflets (see website) - 1/2; frre to download.

© CBD Research Ltd · Beckenham · BR3 5JS · Tel 020 8650 7745 · Fax 020 8650 0768 · E-mail cbd@cbdresearch.com · www.cbdresearch.com

Catholic Family History Society   (CFHS)   1983
■   14 Sydney Rd, ILFORD, Essex, IG6 2ED.   (mem/sp)
      020 8550 5543
      email kathmar247@btinternet.com
      http://www.catholic-history.org.uk/cfhs
      Mem Sec: Kathleen Black
▲   Registered Charity
Br   2
○   *G; to encourage research into the history of Catholic families
      in England, Wales & Scotland from the 16th to the 19th
      centuries
●   Conf - Mtgs
<   Fedn of Family History Socs
M   329 i, 15 f, 6 org, UK / 19 i, 2 f, 4 org, o'seasUK / 35 i, o'seas
      (Sub: £10 i & org, £15 f UK / £14 o'seas)
¶   Catholic Ancestor (Jnl) - 3; ftm.
      Publication - 1; on CD-ROM.

Catholic Medical Association   1923
■   Hospital of St John & St Elizabeth, 60 Grove End Rd, LONDON,
      NW8 9NH.   (hq)
      020 7266 4246   fax 020 7806 4001
      http://www.catholicdoctors.org.uk
      Hon Treas: I Jessiman
▲   Registered Charity
Br   29
○   *P; professional support in medical ethics; informed opinion
      about implications of developments in medicine & social
      policy
Gp   C'ees: Medical ethics, Standing parliamentary
●   Conf - Mtgs - SG - Inf - LG
<   Intl Fedn of Catholic Doctors (FIAMC); Eur Fedn of Catholic
      Doctors (FEAMC); Eur Doctors U
M   1,000 i, UK / 10 i, o'seas
¶   Catholic Medical Quarterly - 4.
×   2008 Guild of Catholic Doctors

Catholic Record Society   (CRS)   1905
NR   12 Melbourne Place, WOLSINGHAM, Co Durham,
      DL13 3EH.   (hsp)
      01388 527747
○   *L; publication of original documents & occasional
      monographs relating to the English Catholics from the
      Reformation to the end of the 19th century (but NOT
      genealogical)
M   350 i, 350 org
¶   Recusant History - 2.   Records & Monograph.

Catholic Truth Society   (CTS)   1868
§   40-46 Harleyford Rd, LONDON, SE11 5AY.
      020 7640 0042
      email info@cts-online.org.uk
      http://www.cts-online.org.uk
      A non-membership body of the Roman Catholic Church
      publishing & distributing books & tracts

Catholic Union of Great Britain   (CU)   1870
NR   St Maximilian Kolbe House, 63 Jeddo Rd, LONDON,
      W12 9EE.   (hsb)
      020 8749 1321   fax 020 8735 0816
      email phiggs@cathunion.fsnet.co.uk
      http://www.catholicunion.org
      Sec: Peter H Higgs
▲   Un-incorporated Society
○   *R; non-political association of Roman Catholic laity seeking to
      promote the common good & to uphold the Christian
      standpoint in public life
●   Conf - Inf - LG
M   1,700 i
¶   NL - 4; free.   AR; ftm only.

Cats Protection   (CP)   1927
NR   Chelwood Gate, HAYWARDS HEATH, Sussex, RH17 7TT.   (hq)
      0870 770 8650
      email cpl@cats.org.uk   http://www.ncac.cats.org.uk
      Chief Exec: Helen Ralston
▲   Registered Charity
○   *V; to rescue stray & unwanted cats & kittens to rehabilitate &
      re-home them; to encourage the neutering of all cats &
      kittens; to inform the public on their care
●   Helpline: 01403 221919
M   i

Cedar Foundation   1941
NR   31 Ulsterville Avenue, BELFAST, BT9 7AS.
      028 9066 6188   fax 028 9068 2400
      email info@cedar-foundation.org
      http://www.cedar-foundation.org
      Chief Exec: Stephen Mathews
▲   Company Limited by Guarantee; Registered Charity
○   *W; to provide quality support, care, accommodation & training
      services to enable disabled adults & children to participate in
      all aspects of community life

CEDIA UK Ltd   (CEDIA)   1986
■   Unit 2 Phoenix Park, ST NEOTS, Cambs, PE19 8EP.   (hq)
      01480 213744   fax 01480 213469
      email info@cedia.co.uk   http://www.cedia.co.uk
      Exec Dir: Wendy Griffiths
○   *T; for designers & installers of residential, custom integrated
      electronics that reflect people's lifestyles
●   Conf -ET - Exam - Res - Exhib - Stat - Inf
<   CEDIA Americas; CEDIA Asia Pacific
M   companies & manufacturers
      (Sub: £411.25 companies, £850 manufacturers)
¶   LM - ftm only.
      Red Book CEDIA Guide - every 18 months; £10 m only.
      Red Book (handout); 40p.
×   Custom Electronics Design & Installation Association

Cement Admixtures Association Ltd   (CAA)   1963
■   38a Tilehouse Green Lane, KNOWLE, W Midlands, B93 9EY.
      (sp)
      01564 776362   fax 01564 776362
      http://www.admixtures.org.uk
▲   Company Limited by Guarantee
○   *T; to encourage responsible use of admixtures in concrete,
      mortar & cement mixes
<   Eur Fedn of Cement Admixture Assns (EFCA)
M   12 f

Cementitious Slag Makers Association   (CSMA)   1985
NR   The Coach House, West Hill, OXTED, Surrey, RH8 9JB.   (hq)
      01708 682439
      email standards@ukcsma.co.uk
      http://www.ukcsma.co.uk
      Dir Gen: Denis Higgins
▲   Un-incorporated Society
○   *T; to promote the use of GGBS, ground granulated
      blastfurnace slag (a cementitious material widely used in
      concrete)
●   Conf - Res
M   4 f

Central Association of Agricultural Valuers (CAAV) 1910
NR Market Chambers, 35 Market Place, COLEFORD, Glos,
     GL16 8BD.   (hq)
     01594 832979   fax 01594 810701
     email enquire@caav.org.uk   http://www.caav.org.uk
     Sec & Adviser: Jeremy Moody
▲ Company Limited by Guarantee
Br 27
○ *P; representation & qualification of agricultural valuers
● Conf - Mtgs - ET - Exam - Stat - LG
M 2,100 i
¶ NL - 4;   Hbk - 1;   AR; all ftm only.
     LM; on website.
     Tenanted Farm Survey - 1; £10.
     Costings of Agricultural Operations - 1; ftm, £20 nm.
     Other professional publications.

Central Council for British Naturism (CCBN) 1964
NR 30-32 Wycliffe Rd, NORTHAMPTON, NN1 5JF.   (hq)
     01604 620361   fax 01604 230176
     email headoffice@british-naturism.org.uk
     http://www.british-naturism.org.uk
○ *G; promotion of physical, moral & mental wellbeing through
     indoor & outdoor recreation without clothes, either
     individually or socially in private grounds, premises or on
     official beaches
M i
     Note: trades as British Naturism

Central Council of Church Bell Ringers   1890
■ The Cottage, School Hill, Warnham, HORSHAM, W Sussex,
     RH12 3QN.   (hsp)
     01403 269743
     http://www.cccbr.org.uk
     Hon Sec: I H Oram
▲ Registered Charity
○ *G, *R; the ringing of bells for Christian worship, their
     maintenance & standards of change ringing
Gp Education; Towers & belfries; Restoration funds; Redundant
     bells; Records; Peal compositions; Publications; Public
     relations
● Conf - ET - Res - Exhib - Stat - Inf - Lib
M 27 i, 61 org, UK / 6 org, o'seas
¶ The Ringing World - 52; £1.60.

Central Dredging Association   (CEDA)
■ Institution of Civil Engineers, 1-7 Great George St, LONDON,
     SW1P 3AA.   (hsb)
     020 7665 2262   fax 020 7799 1365
     email adam.kirkup@ice.org.uk
     http://www.dredging.org
     Sec: Adam Kirkup
▲ Registered Charity
Br Africa, Belgium, Holland
○ *P; an independent, non-governmental society providing a
     forum for all those involved in activities related to dredging &
     who live or work in Europe, Africa, or the Middle East; it does
     not represent the interests of any particular industry sector
● Conf - Mtgs
< is a member of the World Organisation of Dredging
     Associations (WODA)
M i
     (Sub: 63)

Central Organisation for Maritime Pastimes & Support Services
    (COMPASS) 1990
■ 178 Woodfield Park, Cool Oak Lane, LONDON, NW9 7ND.
     (hq)
     020 8205 4492   fax 020 8200 6792
     Sec: Cmdr Gerald F Beck
▲ Registered Charity
○ *G; to promote character development of girls & boys through
     adventure & education using the practice of seafaring &
     seamanship
M c 3,000 i

Central & West Lancashire Chamber of Commerce & Industry
    since 2004 **North & Western Lancashire Chamber of**
    Commerce

CENTRE . . .
    see **'Centres, Bureaux & Research Institutes'** (Introduction 6)

CERAM Research Ltd   (CERAM) 1920
NR Queens Rd, Penkhull, STOKE-on-TRENT, Staffs, ST4 7LQ.   (hq)
     0845 025 0902
     email enquiries@ceram.com   http://www.ceram.com
▲ Company Limited by Guarantee
○ *Q; research, development, consultancy, testing, environmental
     & information services, materials & materials processing
     development, technology transfer
M f
     CERAM is the trading name of CERAM Research Ltd, a
     subsidiary of British Ceramic Research Ltd

Ceramic & Allied Trades Union
    since 2006 **Unity**

Ceramics Society
    a group of the **Institute of Materials, Minerals & Mining**

Cereal Ingredients Manufacturers' Association (CIMA) 1986
NR 6 Catherine St, LONDON, WC2B 5JJ.   (hq)
     020 7420 7106   fax 020 7836 0580
▲ Un-incorporated Society
○ *T
● Mtgs
< Food & Drink Fedn
M 6 f

Ceredigion Historical Society
    English name of **Cyndeithas Hanes Ceredigion**

Ceretas (BADCO) 1988
NR 88 Kingsway, Holborn, LONDON, WC2B 6AA.   (hsp)
     020 7841 1060   fax 020 7841 1001
     email info@ceretas.org.uk   http://www.ceretas.org.uk
     Chief Exec: Mary Bryce
▲ Company Limited by Guarantee
○ *P; *W; for people who work in home care
● Conf - Mtgs - ET - Workshops - Seminars
M 600 i, 50 f
¶ NL - 4; ftm.
     Good Practice Guidelines; £5 each or £60 for complete pack.
       Handling Service Users' Finances & Valuables.
       Caring for Staff.   Dementia.   Elder Abuse.
       Food Hygiene.   Managing Absence.   Medication.
       Personal & Professional Boundaries;   Personal Safety.
       Safe Hygiene Practice.   Staff Support, Supervision &
       Appraisal.
× 2004 (November) British Association of Domiciliary Care

CFA Society of the UK (CFA) 1956
■ 90 Basinghall St (4th floor), LONDON, EC2V 5AY.   (hq)
     020 7796 3000   fax 020 7796 3333
     email lcfaukstaff@cfauk.org   http://www.cfauk.org
     Chief Exec: Will Goodhart
▲ Company Limited by Guarantee
○ *P
● Conf - Mtgs - Exam - SG - Inf - VE
< CFA Inst
M 7,500 i
¶ Professional Investor - 4.   Report - 1; ftm.
     Headline Earnings Definition.
× 2007 (30 November) UK Society of Investment Professionals

© CBD Research Ltd · Beckenham · BR3 5JS · Tel 020 8650 7745 · Fax 020 8650 0768 · E-mail cbd@cbdresearch.com · www.cbdresearch.com

Chair Frame Manufacturers' Association (CFMA) 1940

■   Francis Vaughan House, Q1 Capital Point, Capital Business Park, Parkway, CARDIFF, CF3 2PU.   (hq)
    029 2077 8918   fax 029 2079 3508
    Chief Exec: Michael Bennett Spencer
○   *T; interests of manufacturers of upholstery frames & associated components
●   Conf - Mtgs - Exhib - Inf - Lib - VE - LG
<   Fedn of Small Businesses
M   18 f
¶   CFC   Contract Furnishing Concepts - 6; ftm, £21.50 yr nm.
    Note: This association is incorporated into the Association of Master Upholsterers.

Challenger Society for Marine Science 1903

■   National Oceanography Centre Room 346/10, Waterfront Campus, European Way, SOUTHAMPTON, Hants, SO14 3ZH.   (hsb)
    023 8059 5106   fax 023 8059 5107
    email jxj@noc.soton.ac.uk
    http://www.challenger-society.org.uk
    Exec Sec: Jennifer Jones
▲   Registered Charity
○   *L; to advance the study of marine science through research & education; to encourage a wider interest in the study of the seas & an awareness of their proper management
Gp British Group of Altimeter Specialists; Marine Chemistry Group; Ocean colour special interest group; Ocean modelling
●   Conf - Mtgs - ET - SG
<   Eur Fedn of Marine Science & Technology Socs (EFMS)
M   400 i, UK / 50 i, o'seas
    (Sub: £40 i, £20 student/retired)
¶   Ocean Challenge (Jnl) - 3;
    Challenger Wave (NL) - 12; 3; both ftm only.

Chamber Business Connections [Oldham]
    in 2004 merged with Manchester Chamber of Commerce & Industry to form the **Greater Manchester Chamber of Commerce**

Chamber of Commerce (Barnsley & Rotherham) Ltd 2006

NR Business Innovation Centre, Wilthorpe, BARNSLEY, S Yorks, S75 1JL.   (hq)
    01226 217770   fax 01226 215729
    http://www.brchamber.co.uk
    Chief Exec: John Lewis
▲   Company Limited by Guarantee
○   *C
<   Brit Chams Comm
M   f
×   2006 (Barnsley Chamber of Commerce & Industry
        (Rotherham Chamber of Commerce (merged 1 August)

Chamber of Commerce Herefordshire & Worcestershire
    trading name of the **Herefordshire & Worcestershire Chamber of Commerce Training & Enterprise**

Chamber of Commerce & Manufactures of Greenock
    original name of the **Greenock Chamber of Commerce**

Chamber of Commerce - Pembrokeshire 1990

NR Booth House, Llys Y Fran, Pembrokeshire, SA63 4RS.   (hq)
    01437 532533
○   *C
Gp various sub-c'ees
●   Conf - Mtgs - ET - Res - Exhib - SG - Expt - Inf - VE - LG - Web sites/pages for members
M   f

Chamber of Shipping Ltd 1975

■   Carthusian Court, 12 Carthusian St, LONDON, EC1M 6EZ.
    020 7417 2800   fax 020 7726 2080
    email stewart.conacher@british-shipping.org
    http://www.british-shipping.org/
    Sec: Stewart Conacher,   Asst Co Sec: Tim Springett
▲   Company Limited by Shares
○   *T; to protect & promote the interests of the British owners & managers of merchant ships
●   Mtgs - Stat - LG
<   Intl Cham of Shipping; Intl Shipping Fedn; EC Shipowners' Assn
M   120 f
¶   AR; ftm.

The Chamber - The Accredited Chamber of Commerce for Bedfordshire & Luton 1998

NR Business Competitiveness Centre, Kimpton Rd, LUTON, Beds, LU2 0SX.   (hq)
    01582 522448   fax 01582 522409
    email info@chamber-business.com
    http://www.chamber-business.com
    Chief Exec: Richard Lacy
▲   Company Limited by Guarantee
Br 3
○   *C
●   Conf - Mtgs - ET - Res - Exhib - Stat - Expt - Inf - Lib - LG
M   1,350 f
¶   Focus (Jnl) - 10.
×   2006 Chamber Business

Chambers of Commerce of Ireland
    see business name **Chambers Ireland**

Chambers of Commerce North West Ltd

NR International Business Centre, Delta Crescent, Westbrook, WARRINGTON, Cheshire, WA5 7WQ.
    01925 715166   fax 01925 715159
    email chamberofcommercenw@warrington-chamber.co.uk
    http://www.chambersofcommercenw.co.uk
○   *C
M   16 chambers in the North West
×   2005 North West Chambers of Commerce

Chambers Ireland (CCI) 1923

IRL 17 Merrion Sq, DUBLIN 2, Republic of Ireland.   (hq)
    353 (1) 661 2888   fax 353 (1) 661 2811
    email info@chambers.ie   http://www.chambers.ie
    Chief Exec: Ian Talbot
○   *C
    Chambers Ireland is the registered business name of the Chambers of Commerce of Ireland

Chambre de Commerce Française de Grande-Bretagne (CCFGB) 1883

NR Lincoln House (4th floor), 300 High Holborn, LONDON, WC1V 7JH.   (hq)
    020 7092 6600   fax 020 7092 6601
    email mail@ccfgb.co.uk   http://www.ccfgb.co.uk
    Managing Dir & Co Sec: Stéphane Bossavit
▲   Company Limited by Guarantee
Br 2; France
○   *C; business development between France & Britain
Gp Public relations; Business consultancy; Finance & administration
●   Conf - Mtgs - ET - Exam - Res - Exhib - Comp - SG - Stat - Expt - Inf - VE
<   U des Chambres de Commerce et de l'Industrie Françaises à l'Etranger; Franco-Scottish Business Club
M   531 f, UK / 70 f, o'seas
¶   Info (Jnl) - 6; ftm, £45 yr nm.
    The Franco-British Trade Directory - 1; ftm, £100 nm.
    The List of French Investments in the UK - 1:
        (book) £85 m, £120 nm.   (CD) £450 m, £700 nm.
    A range of practical & professional guides to daily & business life in Britain & France; ftm, £5-£30 nm.

Champagne Agents' Association   1908
NR   1 The Sanctuary, Westminster, LONDON, SW1P 3JT.
    Sec: D G Sills
○   *T
M   f

Channel Chamber of Commerce
NR   Shepway Business Centre, Shearway Rd, FOLKESTONE, Kent,
    CT19 4RH.
    01303 270022
    http://www.shepwaybc.co.uk
    Chief Exec: Peter Hobbs
○   *C

Channel Crossing Association   2001
NR   103 Station Rd, LYDD, Kent, TN29 9LJ.   (hsp/b)
    01797 329479
    email channelcrossings@aol.com
    http://www.channelcrossingassociation.com
    Sec: Andy King
▲   Company Limited by Guarantee
○   *S; to promote, organise & support Channel crossings by
    unorthodox craft & assisted Channel swims; to record & ratify
    successful attempts
M   i

Channel Swimming Association Ltd   (CSA)   1927
NR   381 New Ashby Rd, LOUGHBOROUGH, Leics, LE11 4ET.
    (hsp/b)
    01509 554137
    email swimsecretary@ntworls.com
    http://www.channelswimmingassociation.com
    Hon Sec: Dr Julie Bradshaw
▲   Company Limited by Guarantee
○   *S; the governing body for English Channel swimming
●   Inf - LG - Observing Channel swim attempts during Summer -
    Annual dinner
M   100 i, UK / 100 i, o'seas
¶   NL - 3.   Info pack - 1;   Hbk; both price on application.

Chapels Heritage Society
    alternative name of **Capel: the Chapels Heritage Society**

Chapels Society   1988
■   1 Newcastle Ave, BEESTON, Notts, NG9 1BT.   (hsp)
    0115-922 4930
    email website@adhscl.org.uk   http://www.britarch.ac.uk/
    chapelsoc
    Hon Sec: Robin Phillips
▲   Registered Charity
○   *K, *L; to foster the understanding, study & preservation of
    nonconformist (ie non-Anglican) places of worship & related
    buildings in the UK (includes Roman Catholic, Orthodox &
    Jewish)
●   VE - LG
<   Capel: the Chapels Heritage Soc; Coun for Brit Archaeology;
    Heritage Link
M   286 i, 1 f, 22 org, UK / 6 i, 1 org, o'seas£8   £12   £12
    £8   £12
¶   NL - 2; ftm.   LM; ftm.   AR; on website.
    Occasional publications.

Charcuterie Guild
    see **United Kingdom Charcuterie Guild**

CHARGE Family Support Group   1987
NR   Burnside, 50 Commercial St, Slaithwaite, HUDDERSFIELD,
    W Yorks, HD7 5JX.
    01484 8442020
    email cajthomas@btinternet.com
    http://www.chargesyndrome.org.uk
    Chair: Carol Thomas

Charities' Property Association   (CPA)   1976
■   Church House, Great Smith St, LONDON, SW1P 3AZ.   (hq)
    020 7222 1265   fax 020 7222 1250
    email info@charity-property.org
    http://www.charity-property.org
    Chmn: The Lord Cameron of Dillington
▲   Un-incorporated Association
○   *K; to monitor legislation, or changes in policy of public bodies,
    that may affect the property investments of charities
●   Conf - Mtgs - Inf - LG
M   100 charities
¶   NL - 4.

Charities' Tax Reform Group
    since 2007 **Charity Tax Group**

Charity Christmas Card Council   (4C)   1966
NR   49 Cross St, LONDON, N1 4LY.   (hq)
    0845 230 0046   fax 2545 230 0048
    email 4c@charitycards.org   http://www.charitycards.org
    Chief Exec: Neville C Bass
▲   Company Limited by Guarantee
○   *K; to raise funds for member charities by the design,
    publishing & marketing of charity Christmas cards to the
    corporate sector & abroad
Gp   Depts: Design & publishing, Marketing
●   Conf - Exhib - Stat - Design & publishing
M   96 charities
¶   Executive Range Catalogue - 1;   AR; both free.

Charity Finance Directors' Group   (CFDG)   1988
NR   Downstream Bldg (3rd floor), 1 London Bridge, LONDON,
    SE1 9BG.   (hq)
    0845 345 3192   fax 0845 345 3193
    email info@cfdg.org.uk   http://www.cfdg.org.uk
    Dir: Shirley Scott
▲   Company Limited by Guarantee; Registered Charity
○   *T; to assist in improving financial standards in the charity
    sector; to provide an additional focal point within the charity
    world to which others can refer for an informed view
●   Conf - Mtgs - ET - LG
M   900 i, 850 org
¶   Charity Finance Ybk - 1; ftm.

Charity Law Association   1992
NR   c/o Hempsons, The Exchange, Station Parade, HARROGATE,
    N Yorks, HG1 1DY.   (sb)
    01423 724105
    http://www.charitylawassociation.org.uk
    Sec: Catherine Rustomji
○   *P; 'to advance the understanding of charity law; to act as a
    forum for charity law specialists to consult & be consulted in
    the field'
Gp   Working parties: Responding to consultative documents;
    Examining areas of charity law in need of development
●   Mtgs - Joint project with NCVO & Liverpool University on the
    development of new legal structure for charities
M   600 f (solicitors, barristers, accountants, charities)

Charity Tax Group   (CTG)   1980
■   Church House, Great Smith St, LONDON, SW1P 3AZ.   (hq)
    020 7222 1265   fax 020 7222 1250
    email info@ctrg.org.uk   http://www.ctrg.org.uk
    Chmn: Mike Parkinson
▲   Un-incorporated Society
○   *K; to campaign to relieve the tax burden on charities,
    particularly VAT
●   Conf - Mtgs - Res - Inf - LG
<   Eur Charities' C'ee on VAT [ECCVAT]
M   350 charities
×   2007 Charities' Tax Reform Group

© CBD Research Ltd · Beckenham · BR3 5JS · Tel 020 8650 7745 · Fax 020 8650 0768 · E-mail cbd@cbdresearch.com · www.cbdresearch.com

Charles Close Society for the Study of Ordnance Survey Maps 1980

■ c/o The Map Library, British Library, 96 Euston Rd, LONDON, NW1 2DB. (mail address)
http://www.charlesclosesociety.org.uk
Hon Sec: Rob C Wheeler
▲ Registered Charity
○ *L; to promote interest in, & research into, the maps, plans & other activities of the Ordnance Surveys of Great Britain & Ireland.
The Society is named after Col Sir Charles Close, Director of the Ordnance Survey 1911-1922
● Mtgs - Res - Exhib - SG - Inf - VE
M 477 i, 6 f, 14 org, UK / 10 i, o'seas
¶ Sheetlines (Jnl/NL) - 3; ftm.
Publications mainly on the 1 inch Ordnance Survey maps.

Charles Lamb Society   1935

NR 80 Hall Lane, Great Chishill, ROYSTON, Herts, SG8 8SH.
Contact: R Healy
○ *L; to study the life, works & times of Charles Lamb (Elia) & his circle; to stimulate the Elian spirit of friendliness & humour

Charles Rennie Mackintosh Society   (CRM Soc)   1973

■ The Mackintosh Church, 870 Garscube Rd, GLASGOW, G20 7EL.   (hq)
0141-946 6600   fax 0141-946 7276
email info@crmsociety.com   http://www.crmsociety.com
Dir: Stuart Robertson
▲ Company Limited by Guarantee
Br 4
○ *G, *L; the conservation & improvement of the buildings & artifacts designed by Mackintosh & his contemporaries; the society's address is that of the only church designed by Mackintosh to be built
● ET - Exhib - SG - Inf - Lib - VE
< l'Assn Charles Rennie Mackintosh en Rousillon (Port Vendres)
M 1,257 i, UK / 311 i, o'seas
¶ Jnl - 2; ftm, £5 nm.

Charles Williams Society   1976

■ 35 Broomfield, Stacey Bushes, MILTON KEYNES, Bucks, MK12 6HA.   (hsp)
01908 316779
email charles_wms_soc@yahoo.co.uk
http://www.charleswilliamssociety.org.uk
Hon Sec: Dr R L Sturch
▲ Registered Charity
○ *A; research into, & encouragement of the study of, the life & work of the author, lay theologian & poet Charles Walter Stansby Williams (1886-1945)
● Conf - Mtgs - SG - Lib
< Alliance of Literary Socs
M 92 i, UK / 37 i, 3 org, o'seas
¶ Charles Williams Quarterly - 4.

Charlotte M Yonge Fellowship   (CMYF)   1995

■ 8 Anchorage Terrace, DURHAM, DH1 3DL.   (hsp)
0191-384 7857
email c.e.schultze@durham.ac.uk
http://www.cmyf.org.uk
Mem Sec: Dr Clemence E Schultze
▲ Un-incorporated Society
Br USA
○ *A; to provide a forum for all who enjoy reading the work of Charlotte M Yonge; to offer opportunities to learn more about her life & writings
● Conf - Mtgs - Res
< Alliance of Literary Socs
M 160 i, UK / 30 i, o'seas
¶ Review - 2; ftm.   Jnl - 1; £9.

Charmoise Hill Sheep Society

NR Llandinam Hall, LLANDINAM, Powys, SY17 5DN.   (chmn/p)
01686 688234
http://www.charmoisesheep.co.uk
Hon Sec: David Trow
○ *B
< Nat Sheep Assn
Note: also known as the Charmoise Sheep Society

Chart & Nautical Instrument Trade Association   (CNITA) 1918

NR 36 Broadway, LONDON, SW1H 0BH.
020 7340 6260
email info@cnita.com   http://www.cnita.com
○ *T; suppliers of equipment & information to national & merchant navies
Gp Admiralty chart agents; Magnetic compass manufacturers; Magnetic compass adjusters; Nautical publishers; Nautical instrument manufacturers & stockists
● Conf - Mtgs - Exam
< Brit Standards Instn
M 9 i, 14 f, UK / 19 f, o'seas
¶ LM - 1; ftm.

Charter 88
see **Unlock Democracy (incorporating Charter 88)**

Chartered Institute of Arbitrators   (CIArb)   1915

■ International Arbitration & Mediation Centre, 12 Bloomsbury Sq, LONDON, WC1A 2LP.   (hq)
020 7421 7444   fax 020 7404 4023
email info@ciarb.org   http://www.ciarb.org
Dir Gen: Michael Forbes-Smith
▲ Registered Charity
Br 13; 18
○ *P; promote & facilitate the determination of disputes by arbitration & alternate forms of dispute resolution
M i
¶ Arbitration (Jnl) - 4; ftm.
NL - 4;   LM - 1; both ftm.   AR - 1; free.

Chartered Institute of Architectural Technologists   (CIAT) 1965

■ 397 City Rd, LONDON, EC1V 1NH.   (hq)
020 7278 2206   fax 020 7837 3194
email info@ciat.org.uk   http://www.ciat.org.uk
Chief Exec: Mrs Francesca Berriman
▲ Company Limited by Guarantee
Br 15; Republic of Ireland, Hong Kong
○ *P; qualifying body for professionals in architectural technology
● Conf - Mtgs - ET - Res - Exhib - Comp - Inf - LG
M 6,500 i, UK / 500 i, o'seas
¶ Architectural Technology (Jnl) - 6; ftm, £2 nm.
Directory of Practices - 1;   Membership Booklet - 1;
The Architectural Technology Careers Hbk - 1;   AR - 1; all free.
✕ 2005 British Institute of Architectural Technologists

Chartered Institute of Bankers in Scotland   1875

NR Drumsheugh House, 38b Drumsheugh Gardens, EDINBURGH, EH3 7SW.   (hq)
0131-473 7777   fax 0131-473 7788
email info@ciobs.org.uk   http://www.ciobs.org.uk
○ *L, *P
M i

Chartered Institute of Building (CIOB) 1834
- ■ Englemere, Kings Ride, ASCOT, Berks, SL5 7TB.   (hq)
  01344 630700   fax 01344 630777
  email reception@ciob.org.uk   http://www.ciob.org.uk
  Chief Exec: Chris Blythe
- ▲ Incorporated by Royal Charter; Registered Charity
- Br 8; Australia, China, Hong Kong, Ireland, Malaysia, South Africa
- ○ *P; promotion of the science & practice of building
- Gp Architecture & Surveying Institute; Association of Building
  Conservation Management; FM Society
- ● Mtgs - ET - Exam - Res - Exhib - Comp - Inf - Lib - LG
- M 33,500 i, 470 f, UK / 7,650 i, o'seas
- ¶ Construction Manager - 10; ftm, £50 nm.   AR; free.
  Construction Information Quarterly - 4; £38 (£44 o'seas) m,
  £88 nm.
  Contact (NL) - 6; ftm only.

Chartered Institute of Environmental Health   (CIEH)   1883
- NR Chadwick Court, 15 Hatfields, LONDON, SE1 8DJ.   (hq)
  020 7928 6006
- ▲ Registered Charity
- ○ *P; the promotion of environmental health & dissemination of
  knowledge about environmental issues

Chartered Institute of Housing (CIoH) 1965
- NR Octavia House, Westwood Way, COVENTRY, Warks, CV4 8JP.
  (hq)
  024 7685 1700   fax 024 7669 5110
  email customer.services@cih.org   http://www.cih.org
  Chief Exec: Sarah Webb
- ▲ Registered Charity
- ○ *P; to promote the provision & management of good quality
  housing for all through education & continuing professional
  development
- ● Conf - Mtgs - ET - Exam - SG - LG
- M c 10,500 i, UK / c 1,000 i, o'seas
- ¶ Housing - 12; ftm.

Chartered Institute of Journalists (IOJ) 1890
- NR 2 Dock Offices, Surrey Quays Rd, LONDON, SE16 2XU.   (hq)
  020 7252 1187   fax 020 7232 2302
- ▲ Un-incorporated Society
- ○ *P; for all journalists - freelance, national & provincial
  newspaper, press & public relations, international,
  parliamentary & broadcasting
- M i
- ¶ The Jnl - 6; ftm only.

*Chartered Institute of Library & Information Professionals
styles itself **CILIP***

Chartered Institute of Linguists (IoL) 1910
- ■ Saxon House, 48 Southwark St, LONDON, SE1 1UN.   (hq)
  020 7940 3100   fax 020 7940 3101
  email info@iol.org.uk   http://www.iol.org.uk
  Chief Exec: John Hammond
- ▲ Company Limited by Guarantee
- ○ *P
- ● ET - Exam - Interpreting - Translating - Production
- M 5,000 i, UK / 1,500 i, o'seas
- ¶ The Linguist - 6; ftm, £39 yr nm.
- ✕ 2005-06 Institute of Linguists

Chartered Institute of Logistics & Transport in Ireland
- IRL 1 Fitzwilliam Place, DUBLIN 2, Republic of Ireland.
  353 (1) 676 3188   fax 353 (1) 676 4099
  email info@cilt.ie   http://www.cilt.ie
  Chief Exec: Colm Holmes
- ○ *P; to advance & promote the science & art of logistics &
  transport
- ✕ 2002 Chartered Institute of Transport in Ireland (merged)

Chartered Institute of Logistics & Transport in the UK (CILT(UK)) 1990
- NR Earlstrees Court, Earlstrees Rd, CORBY, Northants,
  NN17 4AX.   (hq)
  01536 740100
  http://www.ciltuk.org.uk
  Chief Exec: Steve Agg
- ▲ Company Limited by Guarantee; Registered Charity
- ○ *P; to promote & develop the concept of logistics & transport
- M i

Chartered Institute of Loss Adjusters   (CILA)   1942
- NR Warwick House, 65-66 Queen St, LONDON, EC4R 1EB.   (hq)
  020 7337 9960
  http://www.cila.co.uk
  Exec Dir: Graham Cave
- ▲ Un-incorporated Society
- Br Australia
- ○ *P
- ● Conf - ET - Exam - SG - Lib
- M 2,600 i, UK / 400 i, o'seas
- ¶ Jnl;   NL;   AR;   Books & Technical Bulletins - all irreg;
  prices vary.

Chartered Institute of Management Accountants   (CIMA) 1919
- NR 26 Chapter St, LONDON, SW1P 4NP.   (hq)
  020 8849 2251
  http://www.cimaglobal.com
- ○ *P; to promote the science of financial management & cost
  accounting
- M 137,000 i

Chartered Institute of Marketing   (CIM) 1911
- ■ Moor Hall, Cookham, MAIDENHEAD, Berks, SL6 9QH.   (hq)
  01628 427500   fax 01628 427499
  http://www.cim.co.uk
  Chief Exec: Rod Wilkes
- ▲ Incorporated by Royal Charter; Registered Charity
- Br 37; Australia, Ghana, Hong Kong, Kenya, Malaysia, Poland,
  Singapore
- ○ *P; 'the world's largest professional services body, which aims
  to provide marketers with best practice marketing knowledge
  & support to create long-term value for businesses'
  Areas of interest:
  Marketing, Sales, Direct marketing, CRM, Database marketing,
  sponsorship, Branding, Product marketing, Distribution,
  Market research, Marketing education, Marketing training
- Gp Groups:
  Construction industry; Financial services; Food, drink &
  agriculture; Medical marketing; National marketing group
  for learning & business support; Professional sales; Travel
  CIM Technology International; Hotel Marketing Association;
  Hotel Marketing Association Northern England
- ● Conf - Mtgs - ET - Exam - Res - Exhib - Stat - Inf - Lib
- < World Marketing Assn (WMA); Eur Marketing Coun (EMC); The
  CAM Foundation
- > CAM Foundation
- M 39,175 i, 75 f, org, UK / 16,035 i, o'seas
- ¶ the marketer - 10.
- ✕ 2004 (incorporated) Institute of Professional Sales

© CBD Research Ltd · Beckenham · BR3 5JS · Tel 020 8650 7745 · Fax 020 8650 0768 · E-mail cbd@cbdresearch.com · www.cbdresearch.com

Chartered Institute of Patent Attorneys   (CIPA)   1882
NR   95 Chancery Lane (3rd floor), LONDON, WC2A 1DT.   (hq)
       020 7405 9450
       email mail@cipa.org.uk   http://www.cipa.org.uk
       Press & PR: Peter Prowse
▲   Incorporated by Royal Charter
○   *P; protection of industrial property - patents, trade marks,
       designs, copyright
●   Conf - Mtgs - ET - Exam - Inf
M   2,800 i, UK / 220 i, o'seas
¶   CIPA (Jnl) - 12.   LM.
       Register of Patent Agents - 1.
       CIPA Directory of Patent Agents.
×   2006 Chartered Institute of Patent Agents

Chartered Institute of Personnel & Development   (CIPD)   1913
■   151 The Broadway, LONDON, SW19 1JQ.   (hq)
       020 8612 6200   fax 020 8612 6201
       email cipd@cipd.co.uk   http://www.cipd.co.uk
       Chief Exec: Geoff Armstrong
Br   48; Ireland
○   *P; promotion of the art & science of the management &
       development of people for the public benefit
●   Conf - Mtgs - ET - Exam - Res - Exhib - Inf - Lib - LG
<   Intl Fedn of Training & Devt Orgs; Wld [& Eur] Fedn of
       Personnel Mgt Assns; Eur Training & Devt Fedn
M   119,784 i, 5,046 f, UK / 4,000 i, o'seas
¶   People Management - 12.   AR.

Chartered Institute of Public Finance & Accountancy
       styles itself **CIPFA**

Chartered Institute of Public Relations   (CIPR)   1948
NR   Public Relations Centre, 32 St James's Square, LONDON,
       SW1Y 4JR.   (hq)
       020 7766 3333   fax 020 7766 3344
       email info@cipr.co.uk   http://www.cipr.co.uk
       Dir Gen: Colin Farrington
▲   Incorporated by Royal Charter
Br   13 regional
○   *P; to represent the PR industry
Gp   Construction & property; Corporate & financial; Education &
       skills; Government affairs; Health & medical; Internal
       comunications; International PR; Marketing &
       communications; Motor industry; Science, engineering &
       technology; Voluntary sector; Women in PR
●   Conf - ET - Exam - Res - Exhib - Lib
<   Global Alliance for PR & Communication Mgt; Confédn Eur de
       Relations Publiques (CERP)
M   7,800 i, UK / 377 i, o'seas
¶   Profile (Jnl) - 6; ftm, £55 yr nm.
       Annual Review; ftm, free online nm.
×   2005 Institute of Public Relations

Chartered Institute of Purchasing & Supply   (CIPS)   1932
■   Easton House, Easton on the Hill, STAMFORD, Lincs,
       PE9 3NZ.   (hq)
       01780 756777   fax 01780 751610
       email info@cips.org   http://www.cips.org
       Chief Exec: Simon Sperryn
▲   Registered Charity
Br   40; 16
○   *L, *P; raising standards in purchasing & supply chain
       management
●   Conf - ET - Exam - Res - EXhib - Inf - LG
M   27,600 i, UK / 18,100 i, o'seas
       (Sub: £125 UK / £88 o'seas)
¶   Supply Management - 26; ftm, £110 nm.

Chartered Institute of Taxation   (CIOT)   1930
NR   12 Upper Belgrave St, LONDON, SW1X 8BB.   (hq)
       020 7235 9381   fax 020 7235 2562
       http://www.tax.org.uk
▲   Registered Charity
○   *P; for tax advisers
M   i,000 i, UK & o'seas

**Chartered Institution of Building Services Engineers   (CIBSE)
1897**
NR   222 Balham High Rd, LONDON, SW12 9BS.   (hq)
       020 8675 5211   fax 020 8675 5449
       http://www.cibse.org
       Chief Exec: Julian Amey
▲   Registered Charity
Br   19; Australia, New Zealand, Republic of Ireland
○   *P; the art, science & practice of engineering services
       associated with the built environment (incl heating,
       ventilating, air conditioning, lighting, public health, internal
       transportation, electrical services)
Gp   Lighting; Electrical services; Thermal storage; Lifts; Information
       technology; Public health; Building Services Heritage
●   Conf - Mtgs - Res - ET - Exam - Exhib - Stat - Inf - LG
<   Fedn Heating & Air Conditioning Assns (REHVA); Commission
       Intle de l'Eclairage
M   12,000 i, UK / 3,000 i, o'seas
¶   Building Services Jnl - 12.
       Lighting Research & Technology - 4.
       Building Services Engineering Research & Technology - 4.
       AR.   Publications list available.

Chartered Institution of Wastes Management   (CIWM)   1898
NR   9 Saxon Court, St Peter's Gardens, NORTHAMPTON,
       NN1 1SX.   (hq)
       01604 620426   fax 01604 621339
       email ciwm@ciwm.co.uk   http://www.ciwm.co.uk
       Chief Exec: Steve Lee
▲   Company incorporated by Royal Charter; Registered Charity
Br   10
○   *L, *P; promotion of scientific, technical & practical aspects of
       wastes management
Gp   Waste collection; Street cleansing; Treatment & disposal;
       Reclamation; Recycling; Regulation
●   Conf - Mtgs - ET - Exhib - Inf - Lib - VE - LG
<   Eur C'ee Waste Mgt Org; WHO; Inst of Solid Wastes
       Assn (ISWA); Waste Mgt Ind Training & Advy Bd (WAMITAB);
       Soc for the Envt
M   6,123 i, 346 f, UK / 390 i, 8 f, o'seas
¶   Wastes Management (Jnl) - 12, ftm, £84 yr nm.
       News On-line (NL on Web page) - 52;   AR; both free.
       CIWM Register of Consultants - 1; ftm, £15 nm.
       Technical publications, Codes of practice, Advice notes.
       Note: The Institution administers a Registered Environmental
       Body - CIWM(EB)

**Chartered Institution of Water & Environmental Management
(CIWEM)   1895**
■   15 John St, LONDON, WC1N 2EB.   (hq)
       020 7831 3110   fax 020 7405 4967
       email admin@ciwem.org   http://www.ciwem.org
       Exec Dir: Nick Reeves
▲   Registered Charity; Incorporated by Royal Charter
Br   14 in UK; Hong Kong; Republic of Ireland
○   *P; to advance the science & practice of water & environmental
       management & sustainable development
Gp   Environment; Rivers & coastal; Scientific
●   Conf - Mtgs - ET - Exam - Exhib - SG - Inf - VE
<   Eur Water Assn (EWA); Water Envt Fedn (WEF)
M   9,900 i, UK / 1,300 i, o'seas
¶   Jnl - 4; ftm, £165 yr nm.
       Water & Environment Manager - 10; ftm, £98 yr nm.
       Manuals & handbooks - list available.

Chartered Insurance Institute   (CII)   1912

■ 42-48 High Rd, South Woodford, LONDON, E18 2JP.   (hq)
020 8989 8464   fax 020 8530 3052
email customer.serv@cii.co.uk   http://www.cii.co.uk
Head of Knowledge Services: Robert Cunnew
○ *P; for those working in the insurance & financial services
industry
● Conf - Mtgs - ET - Exam - Res - SG - Stat - Inf - Lib - LG
M 79,000i, UK / 13,000 i, o'seas

Chartered Management Institute   (CMI)   1992

NR Management House, Cottingham Rd, CORBY, Northants,
NN17 1TT.   (hq)
01536 204222   fax 01536 201651
email membership@managers.org.uk
http://www.managers.org.uk
Chief Exec: Ruth Spellman
▲ Company Limited by Guarantee; Registered Charity
Br 90; Hong Kong, Malaysia, Singapore, Sri Lanka
○ *P; to promote the art & science of management
Gp Care Management Group (CMG); Institute of Business
Consulting (IBC); Police Professional Network; Women in
Management (WiM)
● ET - Res - Inf - Lib - LG
< Eur Foundation for Mgt Devt; Conseil Eur du Comité Intl de
l'Org Scientifique (CECIOS)
M 65,000 i, 300 f, UK / 5,500 i, o'seas
¶ Professional Manager - 6; ftm, £3.60 nm.   AR; free.

Chartered Quality Institute   (CQI)   1919

■ 12 Grosvenor Crescent, LONDON, SW1X 7EE.   (hq)
020 7245 6722   fax 020 7245 6844
email info@thecqi.org   http://www.thecqi.org
Chief Exec: Simon Feary
▲ Company Limited by Guarantee; Registered Charity
Br 29; Australia, Hong Kong, Singapore
○ *L, *P; 'to promote the benefits of quality generally throughout
the UK & international marketplace by being an active &
vocal advocate of quality, by developing & disseminating
quality knowledge & practices & through the competent
quality professionals who are our members. We believe that
quality approaches are a fundamental prerequisite for
sustainable business where survival & success requires
innovation in product & service, combined with reduction in
cost & a socially responsible approach'
Gp Deming; Digital; Engineering; Financial services; Health &
social care; Integrated management; Medical technologies;
Nuclear; Pharmaceuticals; Standards development
● Conf - Mtgs - ET - Exam - Exhib - Res - Inf - Lib - LG
< Brit Quality Fedn; Inst of Customer Services; London Excellence;
Eur Org for Quality (EOQ)
M 4,091 i (members), 2,801 i (associates), 1,029 i (fellow), 144 f
(Subs: £117 (members), £97 (associates), £135 (fellows))
(Subs for f: on request)
¶ Quality World - 12; ftm, £66 nm.
Pharmaceutical quality group publications:
A: Good Quality Control Laboratory Practice;
B: Pharmaceutical Auditing;
C: Pharmaceutical Distribution;
D: Elements & Philosophy of Pharmaceutical QA;
E: Pharmaceutical Manufacturing;
F: Pharmaceutical Premises & Environment;
G: Cleaning Validation;
H: Pharmaceutical Packaging Validation;
I: Pharmaceutical Documentation;
J: Pharmaceutical Contract Manufacture; all £30.
Forward (e-newsletter).
Pocket guides; further information available on website.
× 2006 Institute of Quality Assurance

Chartered Society of Designers   (CSD)   1930

■ 1 Cedar Court, Royal Oak Yard, Bermondsey St, LONDON,
SE1 3GA.   (hq)
020 7357 8088   fax 020 7407 9878
email info@csd.org.uk   http://www.csd.org.uk
Chief Exec: Frank Peters
▲ Registered Charity
Br Regional Gps; Hong Kong
○ *P
Gp Design: Exhibition, Fashion, Graphic, Interactive, Interior,
Product, Textile
Design education; Design management
● Mtgs - ET - Res - Comp - SG - Expt - Inf - LG
< Design Assn
> Design Assn
M 3,000 i, UK / 250 i, o'seas
¶ The Designer - 4; ftm, £5 nm.
Various professional publications - list available.

Chartered Society of Physiotherapy   (CSP)   1894

■ 14 Bedford Row, LONDON, WC1R 4ED.   (hq)
020 7306 6666   fax 020 7306 6611
email enquiries@csp.org.uk   http://www.csp.org.uk
Chief Exec: Phil Gray
▲ Registered Charity; Un-incorporated Society
Br 4
○ *E, *P, *U; for chartered physiotherapists, students & assistants
Gp 35 clinical interest groups
● Conf - Mtgs - ET - Res - Exhib - Expt - Inf - Lib - Empl - LG
< Wld Confedn Physical Therapy (WCPT); Trades U Congress;
Alliance for Health Professionals; Allied Health Professions
Fedn (AHPF)
M 46,000 i, UK / 750 i, o'seas
(Sub: £276 (working), £127.44 (non-working),
£172.80 o'seas)
¶ Physiotherapy - 4; ftm, rates vary nm.   AR - 1; free.
Frontline - 26; ftm, £74.90 (UK), £110.20 o'seas.

Chatham House
alternative name of the **Royal Institute of International Affairs**

Chemical Business Association   (CBA)   1923

■ Lyme Building, Westmere Drive, Crewe Business Park, CREWE,
Cheshire, CW1 6ZD.   (hq)
01270 258200   fax 01270 258444
email cba@chemical.org.uk
http://www.chemical.org.uk
Dir: Peter Newport
○ *T; interests of chemical distributors & specialist service
companies
● Conf - Mtgs - ET - Exhib - Stat Inf - LG
< Fédn Européenne du Commerce Chimique (FECC); Alliance of
Industry Assns (AIA)
M 120 f
¶ Outlook (technical document) - 12; Outlook (NL) - 3;
both ftm only.
Where to Buy Directory - 1.
× 2006 (September) British Chemical Distributors & Traders
Association

Chemical Hazards Communication Society   (CHCS)   1994

■ PO Box 222, LYMINGTON, Hants, SO42 7GY.   (chmn/p)
0844 636 2427   fax 0844 636 2428
email chcs@chcs.org.uk   http://www.chcs.org.uk
Chmn & Mem Sec: Desmond Waight
▲ Un-incorporated Society
○ *P; to promote awareness of chemical hazards & improvements
in their identification & communication; to provide a forum
for sharing experiences, views & information; to promote the
need for specific training & aim toward setting of competency
standards
● Conf - Mtgs - Exhib - SG
M 450 i, UK / 20 i, o'seas
¶ NL - 3/4;   LM - 1; both ftm only.

Chemical & Industrial Consultants Association   (CICA)   1988
- ■ 19 St Annes Drive, Morda, OSWESTRY, Shropshire, SY10 9LU.   (hsp)
    01691 679967
    email secretary@chemical-consultants.co.uk
    http://www.chemical-consultants.co.uk
    Hon Sec: Martyn Bentley
- ▲ Un-incorporated Society
- ○ *L, *T; a networking group of independent, self-employed consultants serving the chemical & industrial community
- ● Mtgs - Res - Exhib - Inf
- M 40 i
    (Sub: £40)
- ¶ LM; on website.

Chemical Industries Association Ltd   (CIA)   1965
- ■ Kings Buildings, Smith Sq, LONDON, SW1P 3JJ.   (hq)
    020 7834 3399   fax 020 7834 8586
    email enquiries@cia.org.uk   http://www.cia.org.uk
    Chief Exec: Stephen Elliott
- ▲ Company Limited by Guarantee
- ○ *T; to represent UK chemical & allied industries to relevant shareholders; to support members in achieving economic, social & environmental sustainability, labour & technical fields affecting interests of members
- Gp GOSIP; Hydrogen fluoride, Speciality biocides
- ● Conf - Mtgs - Stat - Expt - LG
- < Eur Chemistry Ind C'ee (CEFIC);
- > Food Additives & Ingredients Assn; Nat Sulphuric Acid Assn
- M 135 f, 20 org
- ¶ CIA Matters - 10;   CIA Bulletin (email) - 52; both ftm only.AR & Accounts - 1; free.

Chemical Recycling Association   (CRA)   1998
- ■ 62 Lower St, STANSTED, Essex, CM24 8LR.   (hsp)
    01279 814035   fax 01279 814035
    email chemrecycass@aol.com
    Hon Sec: Roger Creswell
- ○ *T; to promote, protect, represent & otherwise assist the members engaged in the recovery, recycling &/or re-use of contaminated chemicals, including secondary fuels
- ● Mtgs - Stat - Inf - LG
- M 5 f
- ¶ NL - 4; ftm only.

Chemists' Defence Association   (CDA)
- NR 38-42 St Peter's St, ST ALBANS, Herts, AL1 3NP.   (hq)
    01727 832161   fax 01727 840858
    email npa@npa.co.uk   http://www.npa.co.uk
- ▲ Company limited by shares
- ○ *T; provision of legal advice & representation & professional indemnity
- M f
- ¶ AR.
    Note: CDA is a wholly-owned subsidiary of the National Pharmacy Association

Cherished Numbers Dealers Association
    a group of the **Retail Motor Industry Federation**

Yn Cheshaght Ghailckagh (the Manx Gaelic Society)   1899
- ■ 16 Hilary Rd, DOUGLAS, Isle of Man, IM2 3EG.   (hsp)
    01624 623821
    email bstowell@mcb.net   http://www.ycg.iofm.net
    Hon Sec: Dr T Brian Stowell
- ▲ Company Limited by Guarantee
- Br 102; Isle of Man
- ○ *K, *L; preservation & revival of Manx Gaelic
- ● Conf - Mtgs - ET - Inf - LG - Publishing books
- M 140 i, UK (incl 102 i, Isle of Man) / 13 i, o'seas
- ¶ Dhooraght (NL) - ftm only.

Cheshire Agricultural Society   (CAS)   1838
- NR Clay House Farm, Flittogate Lane, Tabley, KNUTSFORD, Cheshire, WA16 0HJ.   (hq)
    01565 650200   fax 01565 650540
    email info@cheshirecountyshow.org.uk
    http://www.cheshirecountyshow.org.uk
    Exec Dir: Nigel Evans
- ▲ Registered Charity
- ○ *F, *H; to encourage agricultural enterprise; to improve the breeding, rearing & health of livestock
- ● Exhib - Comp
- < Assn Show & Agricl Orgs
- M 1,300 i
- ¶ Schedule of Classes - 1; free.   AR; ftm only.
    Show Catalogue of Entries - 1; £3.
    Programme of Events - 1; £2.

Chess Scotland   (CS)   1884
- ■ 39 Morningside Park, EDINBURGH, EH10 5EZ.   (memsec/p)
    email membership@chessscotland.com
    http://www.chessscotland.com
    Mem Sec: George Anderson
- ▲ Registered Charity
- ○ *S; promotion & organisation of chess in Scotland
- M i & clubs
- ¶ Scottish Chess - 6.

Chester Archaeological Society   (CAS)   1849
- NR c/o Dr Peter Carrington, 27 Grosvenor St, CHESTER, CH1 2DD.   (hsb)
    01244 327750
    http://www.chesterarchaeolsoc.org.uk
    Hon Sec: Alan Williams (01244 310563)
- ▲ Registered Charity
- ○ *L; study of archaeology, history & architecture of Chester, Cheshire & N Wales
- Gp Fieldwork
- ● Conf - Mtgs - ET - Res - Exhib - Lib - VE
- < Coun of Brit Archaeology
- M 350 i, 40 org, UK / 5 i, 5 org, o'seas
- ¶ Jnl - 1/2 yrly, ftm, £8 nm.
    The Antiquary (NL) - 2; free.

Chester, Ellesmere Port & North Wales Chamber of Commerce   1920
- NR Willow House, Park West, Sealand Rd, CHESTER, CH1 4RW.   (hq)
    01244 669988   fax 01244 669989
    email info@cepnwchamber.org.uk
    http://www.cepnwchamber.org.uk
    Chief Exec: Bob Williams
- ▲ Company Limited by Guarantee
- ○ *C
- < Brit Chams Comm; Chams Comm NW

Chesterfield Canal Trust Ltd   (CCT)   1998
- NR 47 Whitecotes Park, Walton, CHESTERFIELD, Derbys, S40 3RT.   (mem/sec)
    01246 224068
    http://www.chesterfield-canal-trust.org.uk
    Mem Sec: Dave Fox
- ▲ Company Limited by Guarantee; Registered Charity
- ○ *G; to make the Chesterfield canal fully navigational
- ● Mtgs - Res - Exhib - SG - VE - LG - Campaigning - Physical restoration work
- < Inland Waterways Assn
- M i, f & org
- ¶ The Cuckoo (Jnl) - 4; ftm, £1 nm.
    Relevant information on the canal & associated activities.

Chesterton Society   (GKCSoc)   1964
- ■ 11 Lawrence Leys, Bloxham, BANBURY, Oxon, OX15 4NU. (hsp)
  01295 720869; 07766 711984 (mobile)
  fax 01295 720869
  email roberthughes11@talktalk.net
  Hon Sec: Rev Deacon Robert Hughes KCHS
- ▲ Registered Charity
- ○ *A; to promote interest & study of the works of G K Chesterton (1874-1936), critic, novelist & poet
- ● Lib
- M 250 i, UK / 50 i, o'seas
- ¶ G K Quarterly - 4; £2.

Chetham Society for the Publication of Remains Historical & Literary Connected with the Palatinate Counties of Lancaster & Chester   1843
- NR 77 Wellington St, PRESTON, Lancs, PR1 8TQ.   (hsp)
  01772 827835
  Hon Sec: Dr Alan Crosby
- ○ *L; to publish documents & monographs on the history of Lancashire & Cheshire
- ● Annual Mtg - Publication of records & monographs
- < Brit Records Assn
- M c 150 i, 100 universities & libraries, UK / 100 universities & libraries, o'seas
- ¶ Monograph / Record - c 1.

Cheviot Sheep Society   1891
- ■ Holm Cottage, LANGHOLM, Dumfriesshire, DG13 0JP.   (sp)
  01387 380222
  email info@cheviotsheep.org
  http://www.cheviotsheep.org
  Sec: Isobel J McVittie
- ▲ Registered Charity
- ○ *B
- ● Mtgs
- < Nat Sheep Assn
- M 122 i
  (Sub: £15 + £20)
- ¶ Flock Book 1.   NL.   AR.

Chichester Chamber of Commerce & Industry   (CCCI)
- ■ 3 Chapel St, CHICHESTER, W Sussex, PO19 1BU.
  01243 531765
  email office@chichestercci.org.uk
  http://www.chichestercci.org.uk
  Sec: Carylyn Webber-Walton
- ○ *C

Chief & Assistant Chief Fire Officers' Association
  since 2004 **Chief Fire Officers' Association**

Chief Building Surveyors Society   1975
- NR Property Services Client Support Unit, County Hall, WORCESTER, WR5 2NP.   (sb)
  01905 766476
  email jburton@worcestershire.gov.uk
  Sec: John Burton
- ○ *P; to share knowledge & experience & promote awareness of property maintenance & management within local government
- ● Mtgs - Stat - LG
- < Fedn Property Socs
- M c 80 i

Chief Cultural & Leisure Officers Association   (CLOA)   1976
- NR Park Farm, HETHERSETT, Norfolk, NR9 3DL.   (hq)
  0759 200 8710
  email sarahfoulkes@cloa.org.uk   http://www.cloa.org.uk
  Policy Officer: David Albutt
  Admin: Sarah Foulkes (sarahfoulkes@cloa.org.uk)
- ▲ Un-incorporated Society
- ○ *P; interest of arts, sports & recreation management; to represent chief leisure officers in England & Wales
- M 320 i & local authorities
- × 2003 Chief Leisure Officers Association

Chief Fire Officers' Association   (CFOA)   1974
- ■ 9-11 Pebble Close, Amington, TAMWORTH, Staffs, B77 4RD. (hq)
  01827 302300   fax 01827 302399
  email info@cfoa.org.uk
  Gen Mgr: Steve Currey
- ▲ Company Limited by Guarantee
- ○ *P; 'to reduce the loss of life, personal injury & damage to property & the environment by improving the quality of firefighting, rescue, fire protection & fire prevention in the UK'
- Gp Policy c'ees: Appliances, equipment & uniform; Communications & computing; Fire safety; Operations; Personnel & training; Health & safety
- ● Conf - Mtgs - ET - Res - Exhib - Comp - Inf - LG - Serving on standards groups (BSI, CEN & ISO)
- < Metrochiefs
- M 186 i
- × 2004 Chief & Assistant Chief Fire Officers' Association

Chief Fire Officers Association Ireland
- IRL c/o Fire Station, NENAGH, Co Tipperary, Republic of Ireland.
  353 (67) 31771
  Vice-Chmn: David Carroll
- ○ *P
- M i

Child Growth Foundation   (CGF)   1977
- ■ 2 Mayfield Ave, LONDON, W4 1PW.   (chmn/p)
  020 8995 0257   fax 020 8995 9075
  email cgflondon@aol.com
  http://www.heightmatters.org.uk
  Chmn: Tam Fry
- ▲ Registered Charity
- ○ *W; to seek regular growth assessment for every UK child; to ensure that every growth-related abnormality is immediately referred to an endocrine specialist for care of treatment
- ● Conf - Res
- M 1,100 i, UK / 25 i, o'seas
- ¶ NL - 2; ftm only.
  Publications list available.

Children 1st   1884
- ■ 83 Whitehouse Loan, EDINBURGH, EH9 1AT.   (hq)
  0131-446 2300   fax 0131-446 2339
  email info@children1st.org.uk
  http://www.children1st.org.uk
  Chief Exec: Anne Houston
- ▲ Registered Charity
- Br 30 (Scotland)
- ○ *K, *W, *Y; to give every child in Scotland a safe & secure childhood; to support families under stress; to protect children from harm & neglect; to protect their rights & interests; to help them recover from abuse
- ● Conf - ET - Exhib - Inf
  ParentLine Scotland - 0808 800 2222 - helpline for parents & carers
- ¶ AR - 1; free.
  Chldren 1st is the Royal Scottish Society for the Prevention of Cruelty to Children

© CBD Research Ltd · Beckenham · BR3 5JS · Tel 020 8650 7745 · Fax 020 8650 0768 · E-mail cbd@cbdresearch.com · www.cbdresearch.com

Children's Books History Society   (CBHS)   1969
NR   25 St Bernard's Close, BUCKFAST, S Devon, TQ11 0EP.   (sp)
    01364 643568
      email cbhs@abcgarrett.demon.co.uk
    Chmn: Mrs Pat Garrett
○   *G; to promote an appreciation of children's books; to study
    their history, bibliography & literary content
●   Conf - Mtgs - Exhib - VE - Biennial Harvey Darton Award
<   Library Assn; Osborne Collection (Toronto, Canada)
M   Libraries & Universities
¶   NL - 3; ftm, £4 nm.   Occasional papers - 1; ftm, £4 nm.

Children's Chronic Arthritis Association   (CCAA)   1990
■   Amber Gate, City Walls Rd, WORCESTER, WR1 2AH.   (hq)
    01905 745595   fax 01905 745703
      email info@ccaa.org.uk   http://www.ccaa.org.uk
    Gen Sec: Mrs Caroline Cox
▲   Registered Charity
○   *M, *W; to provide help & information for children with arthritis,
    their families & professionals involved in their care; to raise
    awareness of arthritis of childhood in the community
●   Conf - Mtgs - ET - Inf - Annual support weekend for children
    with arthritis & their families
M   2,000 i
¶   Joint Report (NL) - 2.
    Chat;   Chat 2;   Chat for Teachers; free on joining.

Children's Heart Association   (CHA)   1973
NR   26 Elizabeth Drive, Helmshore, ROSSENDALE, Lancs, BB4 4JB.
    01706 221988
      http://www.heartchild.info
▲   Registered Charity
Br   7 in Scotland
○   *W; to give support & understanding in everyday care & welfare
    to parents & families of children with heart disorders; to raise
    money for research into congenital heart disorders; to
    improve facilities & maintain improvements in hospitals
●   Mtgs - Inf - Family, teenage & young adult weekends - Fund
    raising
<   Heart Care
M   families
¶   Heart Beat - 2; free.
    Information pack; free for parents of a heart child.
×   2005 Association for Children with Heart Disorders

Children in Hospital Ireland
IRL   Carmichael Centre, Coleraine House, Coleraine St, DUBLIN 7,
    Republic of Ireland.
    353 (1) 878 0448   fax 353 (1) 873 5283
      email info@childreninhospital.ie
    Chief Exec: Mary O'Connor
○   *W

Children Living with Inherited Metabolic Diseases   (CLIMB) 2000
■   Climb Building, 176 Nantwich Rd, CREWE, Cheshire,
    CW2 6BG.   (hq)
    0800 652 3181
      email info@climb.org.uk   http://www.climb.org.uk
    Chief Exec: Steve Hannigan
▲   Company Limited by Guarantee; Registered Charity
Br   5
○   *W; to provide information & support on over 700 metabolic
    diseases for families & professionals
Gp   Metabolic
●   Conf - Mtgs - ET - Res - Inf
M   857 i, 52 org, UK / 64 i, 7 org, o'seas
¶   Climb Update - 4; £22 m.
    Climb book 100 metabolic diseases; £23.

Children's Rights Alliance for England   (CRAE)
NR   94 White Lion St, LONDON, N1 9PF.   (regd office)
    020 7278 8222   fax 020 7278 9552
      email info@crae.org.uk   http://www.crae.org.uk
○   *K

Children in Scotland   1983
■   Princes House, 5 Shandwick Place, EDINBURGH, EH2 4RG.
    (hq)
    0131-228 8484   fax 0131-228 8585
      email info@childreninscotland.org.uk
      http://www.childreninscotland.org.uk
    Chief Exec: Bronwen Cohen
○   *N, *W; Scotland's national agency for voluntary, statutory &
    professional organisations & individuals working with
    Scotland's children & their families
●   Conf - Mtgs - Res - SG - Stat - Inf - LG
<   Nat Children's Bureau; Children in Wales; Children in Northern
    Ireland
M   91 i, 373 org
¶   NL;   AR; both ftm.   Factsheets.
    List of publications on aspects of child & family policy.

Children's Services Research Group
    decision made to close 20 June 2008

Chilled Beam & Ceiling Association   (CCA)   1996
■   2 Waltham Court, Milley Lane, Hare Hatch, READING, Berks,
    RG10 9TH.   (hq)
    0118-940 3416   fax 0118-940 6258
      email info@feta.co.uk   http://www.feta.co.uk
    Dir Gen: C Sloan
○   *T; to promote the use of chilled beams & chilled ceilings &
    encourage best practice in their development & application
●   Mtgs
<   Heating, Ventilating & Air Conditioning Mfrs' Assn (HEVAC);
    Fedn Envtl Trade Assns (FETA)
M   14 f
¶   Chilled Ceilings (leaflet); free.
×   2008 Chilled Ceilings Association

Chilled Ceilings Association
    since 2008 **Chilled Beam & Ceiling Association**

Chilled Food Association Ltd   (CFA)   1989
■   PO Box 6434, KETTERING, Northants, NN15 5XT.   (hsb)
    01536 514365   fax 01536 515395
      email cfa@chilledfood.org   http://www.chilledfood.org
    Sec Gen: Miss Kaarin Goodburn
▲   Company Limited by Guarantee
○   *T; to represent the interests & promote the standards of the UK
    chilled food industry
Gp   C'ees: Executive, Technical
    Specialist working gps (transient)
●   Mtgs - ET - Res - SG -LG
<   Eur Chilled Food Fedn (ECFF); Food Northwest
>   North West Food Alliance
M   27 f, UK / 1 f, o'seas
¶   Best Practice Guidelines for the Production of Chilled Foods -
    irreg; £80 m, £100 nm.
    Handwash (training poster) - irreg; £10 m, £25 nm.
    Water Quality Management - irreg; £40, £55 nm.
    Regulatory Guidance - irreg.

Chillingham Wild Cattle Association Ltd   1939
■   Warden's Cottage, Chillingham, ALNWICK, Northumberland,
    NE66 5NP.   (sp)
    01668 215250
      http://www.chillingham-wildcattle.org.uk
    Sec: Mrs A E Widdows
▲   Company Limited by Guarantee; Registered Charity
○   *B; a registered charity set up to ensure the survival of the
    Chillingham wild cattle in their own environment at
    Chillingham Park, Northumberland
●   Conservation - Open to visitors
M   400 i, UK / 30 i, o'seas
    (Sub: £15)
¶   NL - 3;   AR - 1; both ftm, sae nm.
    History leaflet - 1; £1.

China-Britain Business Council   (CBBC)   1991
■   1 Warwick Row, LONDON, SW1E 5ER.   (hq)
   020 7802 2000   fax 020 7802 2029
   email enquiries@cbbc.org   http://www.cbbc.org
   Chief Exec: Stephen Phillips
▲   Company Limited by Guarantee
Br   7; China
○   *T; to promote British business in China through seminars,
   missions to & from China & offices in China
●   Conf - Mtgs - Res - Exhib - Expt - Inf - Lib - LG
<   Dept for Business Enterprise & Regulatory Reform (BERR)
M   426 i, 447 f
   (Sub: £427 i, £705-£2,937.50)
¶   China-Britain Trade Review - 10; ftm, £100 nm.

** China Society   1906

** 16 Bridge St, CHRISTCHURCH, Dorset, BH23 1EB.   (chmn & sp)
   01202 482717
   Chmn & Sec: Dr James Cantlie
▲   Un-incorporated Society
○   *L; 'to encourage interest on any aspect of China, past or
   present'
●   Mtgs - Lectures (at the Society of Antiquaries, London)
M   100 i, 5 f, UK / 5 i, o'seas
¶   NL - 4; ftm;   Booklets - 1.
   Organisation lost: see Introduction paragraph 3.

Chinese Takeaway Association (UK)   (CTAUK)   1993
■   40 Gerrard St, LONDON, W1D 5QE.   (mail add)
   07748 884387
   email chinesetauk@hotmail.com
   Chmn: Thomas Chan
▲   Company Limited by Guarantee
○   *T; Chinese takeaways in the UK
●   ET - Inf - LG
M   c 400 f

Chippendale Society   1963
NR   Last Cawthra Feather, 128 Sunbridge Rd, BRADFORD, W Yorks,
   BD1 2AT.   (hsb)
   01274 848800
   http://www.thechippendalesociety.co.uk
   Hon Sec: Simon Stell
▲   Registered Charity
○   *A, *L; to promote appreciation of the work of Thomas
   Chippendale (1718-1790) & the art of woodcarving
●   Mtgs - Exhib - Inf - VE to country houses - Lectures
M   400 i, 3 f, 2 org
¶   NL - 3/4; ftm.   Occasional publications.

Chiropractic Patients' Association   (CPA)   1966
■   8 Centre One, Lysander Way, Old Sarum Park, SALISBURY,
   Wilts, SP4 6BU.   (hq)
   01722 415027   fax 01722 415028
   email c.p.a@dial.pipex.com
   http://www.chiropatients.com
   Sec: Nastasya Blissett
▲   Registered Charity
Br   1
○   *K, *W; to support chiropractic; to advance knowledge &
   increase awareness of chiropractic treatment
●   Mtgs
<   Eur Fedn of Pro-Chiropractic Assns
M   923 i
¶   Back Chat (NL) - 3; ftm only.

Chocolate, Confectionery & Biscuit Council
   a group of **Food & Drink Industry Ireland**

Chocolate Society   1987
NR   Unit 6 Acton Business Park, LONDON, W3 7QE.   (hq)
   020 8743 2646
   email info@chocolate.co.uk   http://www.chocolate.co.uk
   Chmn: Alan Porter
▲   Company Limited by Guarantee
Br   3
○   *G; to promote awareness of & make available fine chocolate
●   ET - Exhib - Inf
M   5,000 i, UK / 500 i, o'seas
¶   NL.

Choice in Personal Safety   (CIPS)   1983
■   Mount House, Urra, Chop Gate, MIDDLESBROUGH,
   TS9 7HZ.   (chmn/p)
   01642 778302
   http://www.againstseatcompulsion.org
   Chmn: Don Furness
▲   Un-incorporated Society
○   *G, *K; campaigning to repeal the seatbelt compulsion
   legislation, which our research has shown to be actuallly
   inimical to personal safety & is thereby a malign interference
   with freedom of choice
●   Mtgs - LG
<   Soc for Individual Freedom; Assn of Brit Drivers
M   40 i, UK / 3 i, o'seas
¶   Minutes of Meetings - 5; free.

Choir Schools Association   (CSA)   1919
NR   Windrush, Church Rd, Market Weston, DISS, Norfolk,
   IP22 2NX.   (inf/officer)
   01359 221333
   email info@choirschools.org.uk
   http://www.choirschools.org.uk
   Information Officer
▲   Registered Charity
○   *A, *E
Gp   Bursary trust (to ensure that no child is denied a choristership
   on financial grounds)
●   Conf - Mtgs
M   44 schools, UK / 4 schools, o'seas
¶   Choir Schools Today - 1; ftm.

Chopin Society   1971
NR   44 Bassett Rd, LONDON, W10 6LJ.   (hsp)
   020 8960 4027
   email info@chopin-society.org.uk
   http://www.chopin-society.org.uk
   Sec: Gillian Newman
▲   Registered Charity
○   *D; the promotion & appreciation of the music of Chopin & of
   piano music in general; to support the development of young
   pianists
●   Mtgs - Exhib
<   Warsaw Chopin Soc (Poland); Chopin Foundation of the
   US (Miami, USA)
M   230 i
¶   NL - 4; free.

Christian Education   (CE)   2001
■   1020 Bristol Rd, Selly Oak, BIRMINGHAM, W Midlands,
   B29 6LB.   (hq)
   0121-472 4242   fax 0121-472 7575
   email enquiries@christianeducation.org.uk
   http://www.christianeducation.org.uk
   Chief Exec: Peter Fishpool
▲   Company Limited by Guarantee
Br   25
○   *P; 'to promote Christian concerns in education generally &
   religious education in schools particularly'
Gp   Study & research
●   Conf - ET - Res - Exhib - Comp - LG
M   4,500 i, 6,500 associated schools
¶   Publications list available.

© CBD Research Ltd · Beckenham · BR3 5JS · Tel 020 8650 7745 · Fax 020 8650 0768 · E-mail cbd@cbdresearch.com · www.cbdresearch.com

Christian Evidence Society (CES) 1870
- ■ 5 Vicarage Lane, CHELMSFORD, Essex, CM2 8HY.   (hsp)
  01245 478038
  http://www.christianevidenceociety.org.uk
  Admin: Canon Harry Marsh
- ▲ Company Limited by Guarantee; Registered Charity
- ○ *R; a non-membership body for 'the proclamation, defence & study of the Christian Faith'
- ¶ Booklets; details available on website.
  Note: The Christian Evidence Society does not provide grants.

Christian Social Order (CSO) 1965
- ■ 157 Vicarage Rd, LONDON, E10 5DU.   (hq)
  020 8539 3876   fax 020 8539 3876
  email keys@fsmail.net
  Sec: Ronald King
- ▲ Un-incorporated Society
- ○ *K, *R; to oppose organised naturalism by promoting a Christian social order
- Gp Pugin Gild
- ● Mtgs - Res - SG - Stat - Inf - Lib - PL
- M [not given]
- ¶ The Keys of Peter - 6; £5 (£6 o'seas).

Chromatographic Society
- NR c/o Meeting Makers, Jordanhill Campus, 76 South Brae Drive, GLASGOW, G13 1PP.   (hq)
  0141-434 1500   fax 0141-434 1519
  http://www.chromsoc.com
- ▲ Registered Charity
- ○ *L, *Q; to promote & disseminate knowledge on chromatography & separation techniques - gas, liquid, thin-layer & column liquid chromatography & capillary electrophoresis, supercritical fluids & HPLC
- M i

Church of England Guild of Vergers (CEGV) 1932
- NR 11 Church Row, Kirkgate, LEEDS, W Yorks, LS2 7HD.
  0113-244 1770
  email jeanne@jeannescott.wanadoo.co.uk
  http://www.societies.anglican.org/guild-of-vergers/
  Gen Sec: Jeanne Scott;   Shop: Iain Howell

Church of England Record Society 1991
- ■ c/o 13 Tarleton Gardens, LONDON, SE23 3XN.   (exec/sb)
  020 8699 0820
  http://www.coers.org
  Exec Sec: Miss Melanie Barber
- ▲ Registered Charity
- ○ *L; to promote interest & knowledge of the Church of England, from the 16th century onwards, by the publication of primary sources of information
- ● Mtgs - Publication (1 vol a year)
- M c 450 i & org
- ¶ Annual Volume - 1.

Church Lads' & Church Girls' Brigade (CL&CGB) 1891
- NR 2 Barnsley Rd, Wath-upon-Dearne, ROTHERHAM, S Yorks, S63 6PY.   (hq)
  01709 876535   fax 01709 878089
  email brigadesecretary@clcgb.org.uk
  http://www.clcgb.org.uk
  Brigade Sec: A Millward
- ▲ Company Limited by Guarantee; Registered Charity
- ○ *R; 'a uniformed voluntary organisation which, through a wide range of recreational, cultural & spiritual activities, seeks to equip young people & children for life & encourages them to be faithful members of the Church of England'
- ● Mtgs - ET - Comp - VE
- < Nat Coun of Voluntary Orgs; Nat Coun of Volunteer Youth Services
- M 5,000 i
- ¶ NL - 3;   AR; both ftm only.

Church Monuments Society (CMS) 1979
- ■ c/o Society of Antiquaries, Burlington House, Piccadilly, LONDON, W1J 0BE.   (mail/address)
  01837 851483   fax 01837 851483
  email churchmonuments@aol.com
  http://www.churchmonumentssociety.org
  The Honorary Secretary
- ▲ Registered Charity
- ○ *L; to promote the study & conservation of all church monuments both in the UK & abroad
- ● Conf - Mtgs - SG - Inf - VE
- M 398 i, 5 f, 43 org, UK / 18 i, 1 f, 25 org, o'seas
- ¶ Church Monuments (Jnl) - 1; ftm, £15 nm.
  NL - 2; ftm, £1.50 nm.

Churchill Society London   1990
- ■ Ivy House, 18 Grove Lane, IPSWICH, Suffolk, IP4 1NR.   (hq)
  01473 413533
  email secretary@churchill-society-london.org.uk
  http://www.churchill-society-london.org.uk
  Chmn: Mrs Pamela Timms,   Gen Sec: Mrs Judith O'Hanlon
- ▲ Un-incorporated Society
- ○ *G; the education re the causes & consequences of war, history of Churchill's life, & the encouragement of all the fine arts & crafts
- ● ET - Res - SG
- < www.englishadviser.co.uk
- M [not stated]
- ¶ All publications on website.

CIFE - Council for Independent Education (CIFE) 1973
- NR 1 Knightsbridge Green, LONDON, SW1X 7NW.   (hsp)
  020 8767 8666   fax 020 8767 9444
  email enquiries@cife.org.uk   http://www.cife.org.uk
  Hon Sec: Dr Norma R Ball
- ▲ Un-incorporated Society
- ○ *E, *P; for academic sixth form & tutorial colleges in the UK
- ● Conf - Mtgs - ET - Exam - Comp - Inf - LG - Provider of first attempt & retake GCSE & A+A/S level courses
- < Brit Accreditation Coun
- M 14 colleges
- ¶ LM & Guide to Courses - 1; free.
- ✕ 2006 Council for Independent Further Education

Cigarette Packet Collectors' Club of Great Britain   1980
- ■ Talisker, Vines Cross Rd, Horam, HEATHFIELD, E Sussex, TN21 0HF.   (hsp)
  01435 812453
  email bkr@horehamroad.wanadoo.co.uk
  http://www.cigarettepacket.com
  Hon Sec: Barry Russell
- ▲ Un-incorporated Society
- ○ *G; preservation of, & research into, the history of cigarette packets, tins & boxes; the collection of ephemera connected with the tobacco trade - packets of cigarette rolling papers (Rizla), tobacco trade price lists etc
- ● Mtgs - Lib - Auctions (qtrly)
- M 215 i, UK / 35 i, o'seas
- ¶ The Cigarette Packet - 4; ftm; £14 (25 EU) ($30 USA).
  Auction lists - 4; ftm.
  [subscription £14].

CILIP: Chartered Institute of Library & Information Professionals (CILIP) 1877
- ■ 7 Ridgmount St, LONDON, WC1E 7AE. (hq)
  020 7255 0500   fax 020 7255 0501
  email info@cilip.org.uk   http://www.cilip.org.uk
  Chief Exec: Bob McKee
- ▲ Registered Charity
- Br 12
- ○ *P; for librarians & information managers
- Gp Divns: Scottish Library Association, Welsh Library Association
  Special interest: Professional development; Subject interests;
  Employment sectors
  Online User Group
- ● Conf - Mtgs - ET - Exam - Inf - Empl - LG
- M 22,830 i, 461 f, UK / 999 i, 178 f, o'seas
- ¶ Update (Jnl) - 12.
  Gazette (NL) - 12.

Cine Guilds of Great Britain (CGGB) 1988
- ■ 72 Pembroke Rd, LONDON, W8 6NX. (sp)
  020 7602 8319   fax 020 7602 8319
  email cineguildsgb@btinternet.com
  Sec: Sally Fisher
- ▲ Un-incorporated Society
- ○ *P; maintaining levels of excellence in UK film-making crafts
- ● Mtgs - ET - Res - LG
- M 2,500 i in 7 guilds

Cinema Advertising Association Ltd (CAA) 1953
- NR 12 Golden Sq, LONDON, W1F 9JE. (hq)
  020 7534 6363   fax 020 7534 6464
- ▲ Company Limited by Guarantee
- ○ *T; for cinema advertising contractors in the UK & Eire
- M f

Cinema Exhibitors Association (CEA) 1912
- NR 22 Golden Sq, LONDON, W1F 9JW. (hq)
  020 7734 9551
  Chief Exec: John Wilkinson
- ▲ Un-incorporated Society
- Br 6
- ○ *T; interests of cinema exhibitors
- Gp Independent cinemas; Specialist exhibition
- ● Conf - Mtgs - ET - Stat - Inf - VE - LG - Liaison with production
  & distribution in UK & overseas
- < U Intle Cinémas; Media-Salles
- M c 180 f, UK / 5 f, o'seas
- ¶ NL - 6;   Guidance notes on operations;   AR; all free.

Cinema Organ Society (COS) 1952
- NR Dolby House, Barrington Gate, Holbeach, SPALDING, Lincs,
  PE12 7DA. (memsec/p)
  http://www.cinema-organs.org.uk
  Mem Sec: David Shepherd
  (david.shepherd@cinema-organs.org.uk)
- ○ *G; for those interested in the cinema (theatre) organ for
  entertainment
- M i

Cinema Theatre Association (CTA) 1967
- ■ 44 Harrowdene Gardens, TEDDINGTON, Middx, TW11 0DJ.
  (hsp)
  020 8977 2608
  http://www.cta-uk.org
  Hon Sec: Adam Unger
- ▲ Company Limited by Guarantee; Registered Charity
- Br 2
- ○ *D, *G, *K; promotes serious interest in all aspects of cinema
  buildings (architecture, lighting, film projection & stage
  facilities); promotes their study in terms of the history of
  entertainment, social & architectural history; campaigns for
  the preservation & continued use of cinemas for their original
  purpose
- ● Mtgs - Res - Inf - Lib - PL - VE - Lectures, talks & shows -
  Archive available for public research
- M 1,500 i
- ¶ Picture House - 1; ftm, £4.50 nm.
  CTA Bulletin - 6; ftm, £2 nm.

CIPFA - The Chartered Institute of Public Finance & Accountancy (CIPFA) 1885
- NR 3 Robert St, LONDON, WC2N 6RL. (hq)
  020 7543 5600   fax 020 7543 5700
  http://www.cipfa.org.uk
- ▲ Registered Charity
- ○ *P; professional accountancy body for public services (both
  public & private sectors) providing education & training in
  accountancy & financial management; to set & monitor
  professional standards
- M i

Circle of State Librarians
  since 2005 the **Network of Government Library & Information Scientists**

Circle of Wine Writers (CWW) 1960
- ■ Scots Firs, 70 Joiners Lane, CHALFONT ST PETER, Bucks,
  SL9 0AU. (admin/p)
  01753 882320
  email administrator@winewriters.org
  http://www.winewriters.org
  Admin: Andrea Warren
- ▲ Un-incorporated Society
- ○ *P; to improve the standard of writing, broadcasting & lecturing
  about wines & spirits; to promote wines & spirits of good
  quality & to comment adversely on faulty products & dubious
  practices; the Circle is open to all currently being published,
  including photographers
- ● Mtgs - ET - Comp - VE - Wine tastings
- M 195 i, UK / 83 i, o'seas
- ¶ Circle Update - 5.   LM (email only) - 12 ftm, £95 nm.
  [subscription £60].

** Circular Chess Society
  Organisation lost: see Introduction paragraph 3.

Circus Friends Association of Great Britain (CFA) 1934
- ■ Flat 3, 24 Devonshire Road, HASTINGS, E Sussex,
  TN34 1NE. (mem/sec/p)
  07812 647678
  email joditimmscfa@aol.com
  http://www.circusfriends.co.uk
  Mem Sec: Jodi Timms
- ▲ Un-incorporated Society
- ○ *G; to support traditional circus as a popular entertainment &
  valuable part of British culture
- ● Mtgs - Inf - Lib - VE - Video archive - Rallies to shows
- M 700 i, UK / 150 i, o'seas
- ¶ King Pole - 5; £27 yr.

© CBD Research Ltd · Beckenham · BR3 5JS · Tel 020 8650 7745 · Fax 020 8650 0768 · E-mail cbd@cbdresearch.com · www.cbdresearch.com

Circus Society   1983
NR   6 Sherwood Court, 372 London Rd, Langley, SLOUGH, Berks,
     SL3 7HX.   (pres p)
     01753 547081
     Pres: R Bartlett
▲   Un-incorporated Society
Br   9 areas
○   *P, *T; promotion of circus & circus artistes; to oppose anti-
     circus activities by various animal rights groups & local
     authorities
Gp   Circus: proprietors, artistes, artistes agents, friends &
     supporters, clowns, staff
●   Inf
M   100 i
¶   Circus News - 4.
     (Sub: £17)
     Note: any request for information should be accompanied by
     an sae.

Citizens Advice Bureaux   (NACAB)   1939
NR   Myddelton House, 115-123 Pentonville Rd, LONDON,
     N1 9LZ.   (hq)
     020 7833 2181C (admin)   fax 020 7833 4371
     http://www.citizensadvice.org.uk + adviceguide.org.uk
     Chief Exec: David Harker
▲   Registered Charity
Br   17
○   *K, *N, *W; provision of free, confidential & impartial advice &
     information on all subjects; social policy campaigning;
     lobbying
●   Conf - Mtgs - ET - Res - EXhib - Stat - Inf - Empl - LG
M   475 bureaux
¶   Mid Month NL - 12; m only.   Hbk; £6 m, £12 nm.   AR.
     Social Policy Reports - irreg.
     Registered name: National Association of Citizens Advice
     Bureaux

Citizens Advice Scotland   (CAS)   c 1940
NR   Spectrum House, 2 Powderhall Rd, EDINBURGH, EH7 4GB.
     (hq)
     0131-550 1000   fax 0131-550 1001
     email info@cas.org.uk   http://www.cas.org.uk
▲   Company Limited by Guarantee
○   *N, *W; supporting Scottish Citizens Advice Bureaux; provision
     of free, confidential & impartial information, guidance,
     counselling & support to all individuals

City Information Group   (CiG)   2002
■   PO Box 10017, HARLOW, Essex, CM20 9EY.
     01279 792079
     email admin@cityinformation.org.uk
     http://www.cityinformation.org.uk
     Chmn: Jill Fenton
▲   Company Limited by Guarantee; Registered Charity
○   *P; to promote, develop & advance the professional practice of
     collecting, collating & evaluating financial & business
     information
●   Mtgs - ET
M   500 i
¶   CIGLET (NL) - 4; ftm [past editions on website; free].
     Ybk - free.
     Note: was a special interest group of the Institute of Information
     Scientists

City Property Association   (CPA)   1904
NR   1 Warwick Row (7th floor), LONDON, SW1E 5ER.   (hq)
     020 7630 1782   fax 020 7630 8344
     http://www.londoncpa.com
▲   Un-incorporated Society
○   *T; interests of owners of property in the City of London
●   Mtgs - Inf - LG
<   Brit Property Fedn Ltd
M   125 f
¶   NL.   AR (incl LM).

City of Sheffield & District Chamber of Trade
     in 2004 merged with the **Sheffield Chamber of Commerce &
     Industry**

Civil Court Users Association   (CCUA)
NR   Warwick House, Birmingham New Rd, STRATFORD-upon-
     AVON, Warks, CV37 0BP.   (hq)
     0845 052 5336   fax 0845 052 5337
     http://www.ccua.org.uk
     Admin: Clare Green
○   *K; to liaise with debt collection companies & the Lord
     Chancellor's office; to encourage the updating of laws to
     benefit both debt collectors & debtors
●   LG
M   c 150 f

Civil Defence Association
NR   24 Paxton Close, MATLOCK, Derbyshire, DE4 3TD.
     01629 55738
     http://www.civildefenceassociation.org.uk
     Sec: Tim Essex-Lopresti

Civil Engineering Contractors' Association
     a member federation of the **Construction Confederation**

Clarice Cliff Collectors Club   (CCCC)   1982
NR   PO Box 2706, ECCLESHALL, Staffs, ST21 6WY.   (hsb)
     email information@claricecliff.com
     http://www.claricecliff.com
     Hon Sec: Leonard Griffin
▲   Un-incorporated Society
○   *G; for collectors of ceramics designed by Clarice Cliff between
     1927-1964
Gp   Websites: (1) public, (2) members only
●   Conf - Mtgs - Res - Exhib - SG - PL - VE
M   [confidential]
¶   NL - 4; ftm only.   NL [email] - 4; £25 yr.

Clarinet Heritage Society   (CHS)   1945
■   47 Hambalt Rd, LONDON, SW4 9EQ.   (hsp/b)
     020 8675 3877
     email chs@chello.se
     Hon Sec: Stephen Bennett
▲   Un-incorporated Society
Br   USA
○   *D, *K; to encourage the literature, repertoire, research, study &
     playing of clarinet music
Gp   Research (music, history, evolution & development); Recording
     & music publishing; Commissions; Teaching & study; Public
     relations & promotion
●   ET - Res - SG - Expt - Inf - Lib
M   500 i, UK / 400 i, Library of Congress, o'seas
¶   Sheet music, records, cassettes & CDs; £12-£15.

**Clarinet & Saxophone Society of Great Britain   (CASS GB)
1976**
■   12 Hanbury Close, Ingleby Barwick, STOCKTON-on-TEES,
     Cleveland, TS17 0UQ.   (hsp)
     0845 644 0187
     email membership@cassgb.org   http://www.cassgb.org
     Mem Sec: Andrew Smith
▲   Company Limited by Guarantee
○   *D, *Q; all aspects of the music for, & playing of, clarinet &
     saxophone
●   Conf - ET - Comp - Inf - Lib
M   1,410 i, UK / 120 i, o'seas
     (Sub: £35 i, UK / £30 i, o'seas)
¶   Clarinet & Saxophone - 4; ftm.

Clarsach Society
     English name of **Comunn na Clàrsaich**

Classic Motor Boat Association of Great Britain   (CMBA)   1998
NR   c/o Unit 1c Deacon Estate, Forstal Rd, AYLESFORD, Kent,
        ME20 7SP.
        01628 524169
        email jarretts@tiscali.co.uk   http://www.cmba-uk.com
        Contacts: Merle & Keith Jarrett

Classic Rally Association
NR   PO Box 633, NEWPORT, Monmouthshire, NP20 5ZX.   (hq)
        01633 263366
○   *S; for competitors in classic (car) rallies
M   i

Classical Association   (CA)   1904
■   Senate House, Malet St, LONDON, WC1E 7HU.   (hq)
        020 7862 8706   fax 020 7255 2297
        email office@classicalassociation.org
        http://www.classicalassociation.org
        Hon Sec: Prof D Cairns,   Admin: Miss Clare L Roberts
▲   Registered Charity
○   *E, *L; promotion of awareness of, & education in, the Classics
        & the ancient world
●   Conf - Publishing
<   Jt Assn of Classical Teachers
M   3,875 i, 70 f, UK / 700 i, 170 f, o'seas
¶   Classical Review (Jnl) - 2; £31 m, £88 nm.
        Classical Quarterly - 2; £29 m, £81 nm.
        Greece & Rome - 2; £25 m, £69 nm.

Clay Pigeon Shooting Association Ltd   (CPSA)   1928
NR   Edmonton House, Bisley Camp, Brookwood, WOKING, Surrey,
        GU24 0NP.   (hq)
        01483 485400   fax 01483 485410
        email info@cpsa.co.uk   http://www.cpsa.co.uk
        Chief Exec Officer: Phil Boakes
▲   Company Limited by Guarantee
○   *S; national governing body for the sport of clay target shooting
        in England
●   Mtgs - ET - Exam - Exhib - Comp - Inf - LG
<   Intl Clay Target Shooting Coun (ICTSC); Intl Shooting U (UIT);
        C'wealth Shooting Fedn (CSF); Fédn Intle de Tir aux Armes
        Sportives de Chasse; Brit Shooting Sports Coun
M   26,065 i, 170 f, 380 clubs, UK / 2,000 i, 30 org, o'seas
¶   Pull! - 10; ftm, £2 nm.

Clay Pipe Development Association Ltd   (CPDA)   1965
NR   Tree Tops, Bellingdon, CHESHAM, Bucks, HP5 2XL.   (hq)
        01494 791456   fax 01494 792378
        email cpda@aol.com   http://www.cpda.co.uk
        Sec & Consultant: L W Richardson
▲   Company Limited by Guarantee
○   *T; to foster the design, manufacture & sale of vitrified clay
        sewer & drain pipes & fittings, ducts for services & related
        products through research, representation, technical literature
        & direct advice
●   ET - Res - Inf - LG
<   Eur Clay Pipe Fedn (FEUGRES)
M   15 f
¶   Technical publications on clay pipes, relevant standards, design
        & construction of drains & sewers; list available.

Clay Roof Tile Council   (CRTC)
NR   Federation House, Station Rd, STOKE-ON-TRENT, Staffs,
        ST4 2SA.   (hq)
        01782 744631   fax 01782 744102
        email bcc@ceramfed.co.uk   http://www.clayroof.co.uk
        Sec: A McRae
▲   Un-incorporated Society
○   *T
●   Mtgs - Exhib - Inf
<   Brit Ceramic Confedn
M   7 f
¶   Promotional matter.

CLÉ - Irish Book Publishers' Association   (CL)É   1970
IRL   Guinness Enterprise Centre, Taylor's Lane, DUBLIN 8, Republic
        of Ireland.
        353 (1) 415 1210
        email info@publishingireland.com
        http://www.publishingireland.com
        Admin: Karen Kenny
○   *T
<   Fedn Eur Pubrs; Intl Pubrs Assn
        Irish name: Cumann Leabharfhoilsitheoin' Éireann

** CLEANAIR - Campaign for a Smoke-Free Environment
        Organisation lost; see Introduction paragraph 3

Cleaning & Hygiene Suppliers' Association Ltd   (CHSA)   1979
■   PO Box 770, MARLOW, Bucks, SL7 2SH.   (sb)
        01628 478273   fax 01628 478286
        email secretary@chsa.co.uk   http://www.chsa.co.uk
        Gen Sec: Graham G Fletcher
▲   Company Limited by Guarantee
○   *T; to represent manufacturers & distributors / suppliers to the
        cleaning industry
●   Mtgs - Res - Stat - Inf
<   Intl Sanitary Supply Assn; Brit Cleaning Coun
M   200 f
¶   AR; free.

Cleaning & Support Services Association   (CSSA)   1967
NR   Warnford Court, 29 Throgmorton St, LONDON, EC2N 2AT.
        (hq)
        020 7920 9632   fax 020 7256 9630
        http://www.cleaningindustry.org
        Dir Gen: Andrew Large
▲   Company Limited by Guarantee
○   *T
Gp   Membership; Marketing; Employment; Standards
●   Conf - Mtgs - Exhib - Comp - SG - Stat - Inf - LG
<   Wld Fedn of Bldg Services Contrs (WFBSC); Eur Fedn of
        Cleaning Inds (EFCI)
M   250 f, UK / 6 f, o'seas
¶   The Supporter (NL) - 12;   LM - 1; both ftm only.
        Code of Practice;   Membership Benefits;
        How to Profit from Contracting out;
        It Makes Sense to Choose a Member of the CSSA; all free.

Cleft Lip & Palate Association   (CLAPA)   1979
NR   Green Man Tower (1st floor), 332 Goswell Rd, LONDON,
        EC1V 7LQ.   (hq)
        020 7833 4883
        http://www.clapa.com
        Chief Exec: Rosanna Preston
▲   Registered Charity
○   *W; to provide advice & support to the parents of cleft lip &/or
        palate children & subsequently to the children themselves; to
        encourage research into craniofacial abnormalities
M   [not stated]

Cleveland Agricultural & Horticultural Society   1974
■   Stewart Park, The Grove, Marton, MIDDLESBROUGH, TS7 8AR.
        01642 312231   fax 01642 300276
        http://www.clevelandshow.co.uk
        Sec: Mrs M Dale
○   *F, *H; to hold the annual Cleveland Show on 4th Saturday in
        July
M   75 i

Cleveland Bay Horse Society (CBHS) 1884
■ York Livestock Centre, Murton, YORK, YO19 5GF. (hq)
01904 489731 fax 01904 489782
http://www.clevelandbay.com
Hon Sec: J F Stephenson
▲ Registered Charity
○ *B; preservation & promotion of Britain's only clean legged
native breed of horse
< sister socs in Australia & North America
M c 250 i, 1 f, UK / c 50 i, o'seas
¶ NL - 3/4; ftm only.   Magazine - 1; ftm, £5 nm.
Stud Book - 3 yrly; £15-£25.

Clinical Contract Research Association (CCRA) 1988
NR PO Box 1055, OADBY, Leics, LE2 4XZ.   (admin/b)
0116-271 9727 fax 0116-271 3155
○ *T; clinical research organisations
M f
✕ 2004 (replaced) Association of Independent Clinical Research
Contractors

Clinical Dental Technicians Association (CDTA) 1949
NR 12 Upper St North, NEW ASH GREEN, Kent, DA3 8JR. (hq)
01474 879430 fax 01474 872086
email cdta@btinternet.com http://www.cdta.org.uk
Chief Exec: Christopher James Allen
▲ Un-incorporated Society
Br 4
○ *T; to establish a class of denturists recruited, trained &
qualified from amongst experienced dental technicians to
supply dentures directly to the public
● Conf - Mtgs - ET - Exam - Exhib - SG - Inf - LG
< Intl Fedn of Denturists; Denturist Assn Canada
M 140 i
¶ NL - 4; free.

Clinical Genetics Society
a group of **British Society for Human Genetics**

Clinical Molecular Genetics Society
a group of the **British Society for Human Genetics**

Cloth Insignia Research & Collectors Society
alternative name of the **Military Heraldry Society**

Cloth Merchants Association 1934
■ c/o H Lesser & Sons (London) Ltd, Unit A, 43-53 Markfield Rd,
LONDON, N15 4QA. (sb)
020 8275 6400 fax 020 8275 6401
Sec: David Lesser
▲ Company Limited by Guarantee
○ *T
● Conf - Mtgs - Exhib - Expt - Inf - LG
M 10 f

Clothing Interest Group
a group of the **Defence Manufacturers Association**

Cloud Appreciation Society 2004
NR PO Box 81, SOMERTON, Somerset, TA11 9AY.
http://www.cloudappreciationsociety.org
Founder: Gavin Pretor-Pinney
○ *G
¶ Cloudspotters Guide.

Club Cricket Conference (CCC) 1915
NR 24-26 High St (top floor), HAMPTON HILL, Middx,
TW12 1PD. (hq)
020 8973 1612 fax 0870 143 2824
email enquiries@club-cricket.co.uk
http://www.club-cricket.co.uk
Hon Operations Mgr: Simon Dyson
○ *N, *S; 'wide ranging representational, advisory, procurement,
legal & other support services for over 1,500 recreational
cricket clubs & league members throughout the south /
south-east / Home Counties of England & Wales'
● Overseas tours
< Eur Cricket Coun; E&W Cricket Bd; League Cricket Conf
> Assn Cricket Umpires & Scorers (ACUS); Nat Playing Fields
Assn (NPFA)
M 312 i, 6 f, 1,500 clubs & leagues, UK / 1 f, o'seas
¶ Extra Cover (Jnl) - 4.
CCC Ybk - 1.

Clubs for Young People (CYP) 1925
■ 371 Kennington Lane, LONDON, SE11 5QY. (hq)
020 7793 0787 fax 020 7820 9815
email office@clubsforyoungpeople.org.uk
http://www.clubsforyoungpeople.org.uk
Chief Exec: Simon Antrobus
▲ Registered Charity
○ *Y; to enable young men & young women to achieve their
potential by providing them with opportunities to develop
their personal & social education from activities delivered
through a network of affiliated clubs
● ET - LG - Postitive activities incl Sports, arts, leadership training
for young PPU
< Clubs for Young People (Wales; Scotland; N Ireland)
M 400,000 i, 3,500 clubs
¶ Annual review.   NL - 4.
Various booklets & leaflets.
✕ 2005 National Association of Clubs for Young People

Clubs for Young People (NI) (CYP) 1940
■ 22 Stockmans Way, Musgrave Park Industrial Estate, BELFAST,
BT9 7JU. (hq)
028 9066 3321 fax 028 9066 3306
email post@cypni.net http://www.cypni.net
Chief Exec: Paul Curran
▲ Registered Charity; Un-incorporated Society
○ *Y; the headquarters for youth clubs & youth organisations in
Northern Ireland
Gp Youth sports: Soccer, Boxing, Swimming etc
● Mtgs - Comp - VE
< Clubs for Young People (UK; Scotland; Wales)
M 150 clubs
✕ 2007 Boys' & Girls' Clubs of Northern Ireland

Clubs for Young People Scotland (CYP) 1928
NR 88 Giles St, EDINBURGH, EH6 6BZ. (hq)
0131-555 1729 fax 0131-555 5921
email info@cypscotland.com
http://www.cypscotland.com
Chief Officer: Tom Leishman
▲ Company Limited by Guarantee
Br 5 local federations
○ *Y; to create & offer opportunities to young people
● Mtgs - Comp - SG - Lib - LG
< Eur Fedn of Youth Service Orgs (EFYSO); Clubs for Young
People (UK; Wales; N Ireland)
M 15,000 i
✕ 2007 Boys' & Girls' Clubs of Scotland

Clubs for Young People Wales   (CYP)
NR   Western Business Centre, Riverside Terrace, Ely Bridge,
        CARDIFF, CF5 5AS.
        029 2057 5705   fax 029 2057 5715
        email office@cypwales.org.uk
        http://www.cypwales.org.uk
        Admin: Shirley Higgins
▲   Registered Charity
○   *Y; to enable young men & young women to achieve their
        potential by providing them with opportunities to develop
        their personal & social education from activities delivered
        through a network of affiliated clubs
<   Clubs for Young People (UK; Scotland; N Ireland)

Clun Forest Sheep Breeders Society Ltd   1925
■   2 Upper Longwood, Eaton Constantine, SHREWSBURY,
        Shropshire, SY5 6SB.   (hsp)
        07968 218470   fax 01952 740731
        email davina@stanhope1.orangehome.co.uk
        http://www.clunforestsheep.co.uk
        Sec: Davina Stanhope
▲   Registered Charity
○   *B
M   180 i, UK / 2 i, o'seas
¶   Flock Book - 1; ftm.   Hbk - 3/4 yrly; free.

Clydesdale Horse Society   (CHS)   1870
NR   Kinclune, Kingoldrum, KIRRIEMUIR, Angus, DD8 5HX.   (hsp)
        01575 570900
        email secretary@clydesdalehorsesociety.com
        http://www.clydesdalehorsesociety.com
○   *B
M   i

CMT United Kingdom   1986
■   PO Box 5089, CHRISTCHURCH, Dorset, BH23 7ZX.   (hsp)
        0800 652 6316
        email secretary@cmt.org.uk   http://www.cmt.org.uk
        Sec: Mrs Karen Butcher
▲   Company Limited by Guarantee; Registered Charity
Br   10
○   *W; to offer support, advice & information to people affected by
        CMT (Charcot-Marie-Tooth Disease), a condition which
        affects the nerves in the arms and legs.
●   Conf - Inf
<   Wld Muscle Soc; LTCA; Neurological Alliance
M   1,200 i, UK / c 100 i, o'seas
        (Sub: £13 UK / £25 o'seas)
¶   Comment (NL) - 3   AR - 1; both ftm.

CNK Alliance Ltd (Care not Killing)   (CNK)   2006
■   PO Box 56322, LONDON, SE1 8XW.   (hq)
        020 7234 9680   fax 0871 900 4745
        email info@carenotkilling.org.uk
        http://www.carenotkilling.org.uk
        Co Sec: Charles Wookey
▲   Limited Liability Partnership
○   *K; a UK alliance of individuals & organisations bringing
        together groups concerned with human rights, healthcare,
        palliative care, as well as faith based organisations, with the
        aim of 1) promoting more & better palliative care;
        2) opposing euthanasia & assisted suicide; 3) influencing the
        balance of public opinion
●   Conf - Mtgs - ET - Res - Exhib - Inf - Lobbying & campaigning
<   Care Not Killing Scotland
M   400 +, 18 org, UK / 30 org, o'seas
        (Sub: £10 i, £1,500 org, UK / £50 org o'seas)
¶   NL - 4; free (on website).

Co-operatives UK Ltd   1869
NR   Holyoake House, Hanover St, MANCHESTER, M60 0AS.   (hq)
        0161-246 2900   fax 0161-831 7684
        email enquiries@cooperatives-uk.coop
        http://www.cooperatives-uk.coop
        Chief Exec: Dame Pauline Green
▲   An Industrial & Provident Society
Br   3
○   *T; national representational, promotional & advisory body for
        consumer co-operatives in the UK
●   Conf - ET - Exhib - Stat - Inf - LG - Legal registration of co-
        operatives & other social enterprises & charities
<   Intl Co-op Alliance
M   50 i, 450 f, 100 org
¶   Co-operatives - 3;   AR; both free.
        Co-operatives UK Briefing - 12; ftm only.

** Coach & Bus First Aid Association
        Organisation lost: see Introduction paragraph 3.

Coach Operators Federation   (COF)   1955
■   Oakwood, Radway, SIDMOUTH, Devon, EX10 8TW.
        0776 884 6138   fax 01395 513508
        http://www.cofed.net
        Sec: Ted Reece
▲   Un-incorporated Society
○   *T
●   Mtgs - VE - Empl - LG
M   5 i, 42 f, UK / 1 i, o'seas

Coach Tourism Council   (CTC)   1989
NR   10 Bermondsey Exchange, 179-181 Bermondsey St, LONDON,
        SE1 3UW.   (hq)
        0870 850 2839
        email admin@coachtourismcouncil.co.uk
        http://www.coachtourismcouncil.co.uk
        Chief Exec: Graham Beacom
▲   Un-incorporated Society
○   *T; promotion of travel & tourism by coach
●   Conf - Mtgs - ET - Res - Exhib - VE
<   Confedn of Passenger Transport; Visit Britain / London /
        England; Tourism Alliance
M   400 f, UK / 23 f, o'seas
¶   NL - 6; ftm only.   Ybk - 1; ftm, £40 nm.

**Coal Merchants Association of Scotland Ltd   (CMAS Ltd)
1913**
■   PO Box 9224, KILMACOLM, Renfrewshire, PA13 4YP.
        (mail/address)
        01505 874389   fax 01505 874389
        email norrie.johnstone@btinternet.com
        Sec: Norman Johnstone
▲   Company Limited by Guarantee
○   *T
●   Mtgs - SG
<   Solid Fuel Assn; Coal Merchants Fedn (GB) Ltd
M   130 i
¶   AR.

Coal Merchants Federation (Great Britain) Ltd   (CMF)   1934
■   7 Swanwick Court, ALFRETON, Derbys, DE55 7AS.   (hq)
        01773 835400   fax 01773 834351
        email cmf@solidfuel.co.uk
        http://www.coalmerchants.co.uk
        Gen Sec: Jim Lambeth
▲   Company Limited by Guarantee
Br   13
○   *T
●   Mtgs - ET - Res - Stat - Inf - LG
<   Solid Fuel Assn
M   850 f
¶   Coal Trader - 4; free.

Coalition for Medical Progress   (CMP)   2003
NR   Waterloo Business Centre, 117 Waterloo Rd, LONDON,
        SE1 8UL.   (hq)
        020 7921 0080
        email info@medicalprogress.org
        http://www.medicalprogress.org
        Dir: Jo Tanner
▲   Un-incorporated Society
○   *Q, *T; communications & public relations concerning the
        advancement of medicine via research
●   Conf - ET - Inf
M   14 f, 16 org
¶   Publicity / Explanatory booklets.

Coalition for the Removal of Pimping   (CROP)   1996
NR   34 York Rd, LEEDS, W Yorks, LS9 8TA.
        0113-240 3040
        email info@cropuk.org.uk   http://www.crop1.org.uk
        Sec: Alan Mastin Suggate
○   *K; to end the sexual exploitation of children and young people
        by pimps and traffickers

Coaters Group
        a group of **Performance Textiles Association**

Coble & Keelboat Society   (CKS)   1987
■   20 The Green, SALTBURN-by-the-SEA, N Yorks, TS12 1NF.
        (hsp)
        01287 623661
        email ae@readman1.plus.com
        http://www.coble-keelboatsociety.org
        Hon Gen Sec: A Edgar Readman
▲   Registered Charity
○   *G; preservation of traditional working boats of the North East
        coast of England
Gp   Preservers; Historians; Researchers
●   Mtgs - Inf
<   Sailing Smack Assn; 40+ Fishing Boat Assn; Bridlington Sailing
        Coble Presvn Soc; Sunderland Marine Sports Club; W Wales
        Maritime Heritage Soc
M   180 i, 400 org, 1 assn, UK / 6 i, o'seas
¶   The Coble & Keelboat Society (Jnl) - 2; ftm, 50p nm.
        Coblegram (NL) - 4; ftm only.

Cockburn Association - The Edinburgh Civic Trust   1875
NR   Trunk's Close, 55 High St, EDINBURGH, EH1 1SR.   (hq)
        0131-557 8686   fax 0131-557 9387
        http://www.cockburnassociation.org.uk
        Dir: Moira Tasker
○   *K; protection of the beauty of Edinburgh by the
        encouragement of enlightened planning & the preservation
        of good buildings of all ages
M   c 1,200 i

Coeliac Society of Ireland
IRL 4 North Brunswick St, DUBLIN 7, Republic of Ireland
        353 (1) 872 1471   fax 353 (1) 873 5737
        email coeliac@iol.ie   http://www.coeliac.ie
        Sec: Mary Thowig-Murray
○   *W

Coeliac UK   1968
■   Octagon Court (suites A-D), HIGH WYCOMBE, Bucks,
        HP11 2HS.   (hq)
        01494 437278   fax 01494 474349
        email info@coeliac.org.uk   http://www.coeliac.org.uk
        Contact: Jean Christopher
▲   Registered Charity
○   *W; to support the health, welfare & rights of coeliacs & those
        with dermatitis herpetiformis (DH); to promote & commission
        research into causes, alleviation, treatment, care & cure of
        these conditions; to educate the public & those in the
        appropriate sectors of health, government, commerce &
        industry
●   Helpline: 0870 444 8804 (Mon-Fri 1000-1600)
M   50,000 i
¶   Crossed Grain Magazine - 3.
        Food & Drinks Directory of the United Kingdom - 1.
        Publications list available.

Coffee Industry Association of Ireland
        a group of **Food & Drink Industry Ireland**

Coffee Trade Federation
        is winding up (2008)

**Cognition: Campaign for Qualified Politicians   (Cognition)
1998**
■   96 Broomfield Rd, SWANSCOMBE, Kent, DA10 0LT.   (asa)
○   *K; 'we believe that a new political qualification, covering
        business & financial studies, national & international current
        affairs & general knowledge, should become compulsory for
        all those wishing to stand for Parliament - such a
        qualification only being obtainable through involvement in
        the foregoing'
●   Mtgs - Stat - Lib
M   i, f & org
¶   Re: Cognition (NL) - 3.

Coir Association   1956
■   1 Gate Lodge Way, Noak Bridge, LAINDON, Essex,
        SS15 4AR.   (sp)
        01268 532797   fax 01268 272549
        email coirassociation@tiscali.co.uk
        Sec: David G Sunderland
○   *T; coir & allied products
●   Mtgs
M   4 f, UK / 7 f, o'seas
        (Sub: £95)
¶   LM - 1;   Panel of arbitrators;   AR; all ftm.

Coke Oven Managers Association   (COMA)   1915
NR   c/o R G Sargent, Universal Contractors Ltd, 1-3 Albion Place,
        DONCASTER, S Yorks, DN1 2EG.   (hsb)
        email richard@universalcontractors.co.uk
        http://www.coke-oven-managers.org
        Hon Gen Sec: R G Sargent
▲   Un-incorporated Society
Br   3 sections UK; 1 o'seas
○   *P; the science & technology of coal carbonisation, the recovery
        & chemical processing of by-products & peripheral
        technologies
Gp   Editorial c'ee
●   Conf - Mtgs - Stat - Inf
M   i & f
¶   Bulletin - 2; ftm.   COMA Ybk (incl LM); ftm.
        Technical publications; prices vary.

Cold Rolled Sections Association   (CRSA)   1946
NR   National Metalforming Centre, 47 Birmingham Rd,
        WEST BROMWICH, W Midlands, B70 6PY.   (sb)
        0121-601 6350   fax 0121-601 6373
        http://www.crsauk.com
○   *T; to sponsor research & promote use of cold rolled sections
●   Mtgs - Res - Inf

Cold Storage & Distribution Federation
since March 2008 **Food Storage & Distribution Federation**

Cold War Research Group
a group of **Subterranea Britannica**

Collections Trust   1977
NR   22 Hills Rd, CAMBRIDGE, CB2 1JP.   (hq)
01223 316028
email office@collectionstrust.org.uk
http://www.collectionstrust.org.uk
Chief Exec: Nick Poole
▲   Company Limited by Guarantee
○   *T; to support education by promoting standards & best
practice in museums
●   Mtgs - ET - Res - Inf - Standards
M   671 i & f, 5 org
¶   Collections News - 4;   AR - 1; both free.
✕   2008 MDA Europe

College of Emergency Medicine   (CEM)   1993
■   Churchill House, 35 Red Lion Square, LONDON,
WC1R 4SG.   (hq)
020 7404 1999   fax 020 7067 1267
email cem@emergencymedicine.uk.net
http://www.collemergencymed.ac.uk
Registrar: Dr Ruth Brown
▲   Company Limited by Guarantee; Registered Charity
○   *E, *M; the college has responsibility for the training &
academic standards of the speciality of emergency medicine
Gp   Emergency Medicine Trainees Association
●   Conf - ET - Exam - Res - LG
M   1,700 i, UK / 200 i, o'seas
✕   2008 British Association for Emergency Medicine (merged)
2005-06 Faculty of Accident & Emergency Medicine

College of Occupational Therapists
part of the **British Association of Occupational Therapists**

College of Operating Department Practitioners   (CODP)   1945
NR   197-199 City Rd, LONDON, EC1V 1JN.   (hq)
0870 746 0984   fax 0870 746 0985
http://www.aodp.org
Br   21
○   *P; those qualified in operating department practice; to protect
patients by self regulation & maintaining & improving
standards of practice & education in theatre practice
Gp   C'ees: Education, Patient care & management; Register of
qualified members
●   Conf - ET - Exhib - SG - Stat
<   Assn of Surgical Technologists (AST)(USA); Australasian Soc of
Anaesthetic Technicians (ASAT)
M   5,000 i, UK / 45 i, o'seas
¶   Technic - 12;   Code of Conduct; both ftm only.
Curriculum Framework for Operating Department
Practice; £12.
incoporating the Association of Operating Department
Practitioners

College of Optometrists   (BCO)   1980
NR   41-42 Craven St, LONDON, WC2N 5NG.   (hq)
▲   Registered Charity
○   *P; 'awards the sole registrable qualification in optometry in the
UK'
M   i

College of Piping   1944
NR   16-24 Otago St, GLASGOW, G12 8JH.   (hq)
0141-334 3587   fax 0141-587 6068
Principal: Robert Wallace
▲   Registered Charity
○   *D, *E; the teaching of the Highland Bagpipe; dissemination of
information on piping
●   Conf - Mtgs - ET - Exam - Res - Comp - Inf - Lib
M   200 i, UK / 100 i, o'seas
¶   The Piping Times - 12.

College of Psychiatry of Ireland   2009
IRL   Corrigan House, Fenian St, DUBLIN 2, Republic of Ireland.
(hq)
353 (1) 661 8450   fax 353 (1) 661 9835
email info@irishpsychiatry.ie
http://www.irishpsychiatry.ie
Senior Admin: Grace Smyth
○   *L, *M, *P
M   600 i

College of Radiographers
charitable non-membership subsidiary of the **Society of
Radiographers**

College of Teachers   1849
NR   Institute of Education, 20 Bedford Way, LONDON,
WC1H 0AL.   (hq)
020 7911 5536   fax 020 7612 6482
email info@cot.ac.uk   http://www.cot.ac.uk
Chief Exec & Registrar: Prof Ray Page
▲   Registered Charity
○   *E, *P; to promote sound learning & advance the interests of
education
Gp   Primary education; Secondary education; F/HE
●   Conf - Mtgs - ET - Exam
M   2,000 i, 100 schools, 20 org, UK / 200 i, 2 f, 12 org, o'seas
¶   Education Today (Jnl) - 4; ftm, from £110 yr nm.
NL - 4; ftm only (incl AR).

College of Vibrational Medicine Practitioner Association
NR   1 Rectory Rd, Tivetshall St Mary, NORWICH, Norfolk, NR15
2AL.
0845 478 6373
http://www.collegeofvibrationalmedicine.org.uk
○   *P; for trained pratitioners using pure vibrational, natural
frequencies to create balance, harmony & unity in body,
mind & spirit
●   ET - Workshops
M   i

Colloquium for Scottish Medieval & Renaissance Studies
alternative name of **Scottish Medievalists**

Colombian British Chamber of Commerce
English name of **Cámara de Comercio Colombo Británica**

Colonel Stephens Society   1985
NR   Cawdron House, 111 Charles St, MILFORD HAVEN,
Pembrokeshire, SA73 2HW.
http://www.colonelstephenssociety.org.uk
Sec: Guy Hardy
○   *G; for enthusiasts of the light and narrow gauge railways of
Col Holman F Stephens (1868-1931)

Colour Group (Great Britain) (CGGB) 1940
- ■ c/o Applied Vision Research Centre, The City University, LONDON, EC1V 7DD. (mail/address)
  email colourgroupgb@city.ac.uk
  http://www.colour.org.uk
  Hon Sec: Prof Lindsay MacDonald
- ▲ Registered Charity
- ○ *L; to encourage the study of colour in all its aspects; to promote education of the public in the field of colour; to further research into the uses of colour in art & science
- ● Conf - Mtgs - ET - Res - Exhib - Comp - Inf - Travel awards for students of colour - Mtgs are at the above address
- < Assn Intle de la Couleur (AIC); Commission Intle de l'Eclairage (CIE); Intl Soc of Colour Couns (ISCC)
- M 162 i, 14 f, UK / 19 i, o'seas
- ¶ NL - 12; ftm only.

Coloured Horse & Pony Society (CHAPS(UK)) 1983
- ■ 1 McLaren Cottages, Abertysswg, Rhymney, TREDEGAR, Gwent, NP22 5BH. (hsp)
  01685 845045   fax 01685 845045
  email admin@chapsuk.datanet.co.uk
  http://www.chapsuk.com
  Sec: Miss Lorraine Amor
- ▲ Company Limited by Guarantee
- ○ *B
- ● Shows - Issuing passports to horses - Studbook - Performance award scheme
- < Brit Horse Soc; Central Prefix Register
- M 1,200 i, UK / 12 i, o'seas
- ¶ A World of Colour - 3.

Combined Cadet Force Association (CCFA) 1952
- ■ Holderness House, 51-61 Clifton St, LONDON, EC2A 4OW. (hq)
  020 77426 8377   fax 020 7426 8378
  email acfa@armycadets.com
  http://www.armycadets.com
  Sec: Brig M Wharmby
- ▲ Company Limited by Guarantee; Registered Charity
- Br 280
- ○ *Y; a national youth organisation working in schools to develop leadership, citizenship & self belief; for young men & women aged 13-18
- ● Comp - Mtgs - ET - Comp - Stat - Inf - LG
- M 50,000 i
- ¶ Ybk - 1;   AR - 1; both free.

Combined Edible Nut Trade Association (CENTA) 1970
- ■ 62 Wilson St, LONDON, EC2A 2BU. (asa)
  020 7782 0007   fax 020 7782 0939
  email treenuts@compuserve.com
  http://www.centa.uk.com
  Sec: David G Sunderland
- ○ *T
- Gp Almonds; Brazil nuts; Cashews; Hazelnuts; Pistachios; Walnuts
- M 28 f, UK / 10 f, o'seas
  (Sub: £520)
- ¶ LM - 1;   Trade Reports;   AR - 1; all ftm.
  Terms & Conditions of Trading - on joining; ftm, £15 nm.
  Panel of Arbitrators - 1;
  List of Defaulters to Arbitration Awards - as arising; both ftm.

Combined Heat & Power Association (CHPA) 1968
- NR 35-37 Grosvenor Gardens, LONDON, SW1W 0BS. (hq)
  020 7828 4077   fax 020 7828 0310
  email info@chpa.co.uk   http://www.chpa.co.uk
  Dir: Phillip Piddington
- ▲ Company Limited by Guarantee
- ○ *T; to promote energy efficiency & environmental improvement through the provision of integrated energy services & the wider use of combined heat, power & community heating; the use of waste incineration
- ● Conf - Mtgs - Inf - Lib - LG
- M 15 i, 100 f
- ¶ CHPA Ybk; £35.
  Publications list available.

Combustion Engineering Association (CEA) 1932
- NR 1a Clarke St, Ely Bridge, CARDIFF, Glamorgan, CF5 5AL. (hq)
  029 2040 0670   fax 029 2055 5542
  http://www.cea.org.uk
- ▲ Registered Charity
- ○ *L, *Q; to further the cause of combustion engineering
- M i & f

Comedy Writers' Association UK (CWAUK) 1981
- NR 44 Cherry Ave, SWANLEY, Kent, BR8 7DU.
  01322 410742
  Contact: Mark Nicholson
- ○ +P
  since 1999 **British Society of Comedy Writers**

Comics Creators Guild (CCG) 1977
- NR 22 St James' Mansions, West End Lane, LONDON, NW6 2AA. (mail address)
  Sec: Ben Counter
- ▲ Un-incorporated Society
- ○ *P; for those working in the comic strip or graphic narrative medium; to promote this medium as an art form

Commemorative Collectors Society (CCS) 1972
- ■ Lumless House, 77 Gainsborough Rd, Winthorpe, NEWARK, Notts, NG24 2NR. (hsp)
  01636 671377
  Hon Sec: Steven N Jackson
- ▲ Un-incorporated Society
- ○ *A, *G; to research, publish & offer advice & information to members & manufacturers, on the design & issuing of all 'popular' commemorative items made from glass, ceramics, metal, wovens, paper & all printed materials etc
- ● Mtgs - ET - Res - Exhib - Stat - Inf - Lib - LG
- M 3,821 i, UK / 747 i, o'seas
  (Sub: £14 UK / £16 o'seas)
- ¶ Jnl - 4; ftm.   Review - irreg.

Commemoratives Museum Trust (CMT) 2003
- ■ Lumless House, 77 Gainsborough Rd, Winthorpe, NEWARK, Notts, NG24 2NR. (hq)
  01636 671377
  Chief Exec: Steven N Jackson
- ▲ Registered Charity
- ○ *A; to maintain & display a collection of commemorative items for information of private collectors, designers & historians
- ● ET - Res - Exhib - Inf
- M 489 i, UK / 218 i, o'seas

Comment on Reproductive Ethics (CORE)
- NR PO Box 4593, LONDON, SW3 6XE.
  020 7581 2623   fax 020 7581 3868
  http://www.corethics.org

© CBD Research Ltd · Beckenham · BR3 5JS · Tel 020 8650 7745 · Fax 020 8650 0768 · E-mail cbd@cbdresearch.com · www.cbdresearch.com   235

Commerce & Industry Group   (C&I)
NR   Woodbank House, 80 Churchgate, STOCKPORT, Cheshire,
       SK1 1YJ.
       0161-480 2918   fax 0161-968 1851
       email info@cigroup.org.uk   http://www.cigroup.org.uk
       Chmn: Sapna Bedi FitzGerald
○   *P; in-house solicitors
<   The Law Soc
       Commercial arm: C&I Group Services Ltd

Commercial Bar Association   (COMBAR)
NR   3 Verulam Buildings, LONDON, WC1R 5NT.
       020 7404 2022   fax 020 7404 2088
○   *P
M   598 i

** Commercial Boat Operators Association
       Organisation lost, see Introduction paragraph 3

Commercial Coarse Fisheries Association
       since Autumn 2005 **Professional Coarse Fisheries Association**

Commercial Farmers Group   (CFG)   1998
■   Church House, Horkstow, BARTON-upon-HUMBER, Lincs,
       DN18 6BG.   (hsb)
       01652 618329
       email henry.fell@tiscali.co.uk
       Sec: Henry Fell
▲   Un-incorporated Society
○   *F; 'agricultural lobbying'
●   Mtgs - Res - SG
M   22 i

Commercial Horticultural Association   (CHA)   1978
■   Stoneleigh Park, KENILWORTH, Warks, CV8 2LG.   (asa)
       024 7669 0330   fax 024 7669 0334
       email info@cha-hort.com   http://www.cha-hort.com
       Hon Sec: Dr Chris Wood,   Expt Promoter: Peter Grimbly
▲   Un-incorporated Society
○   *T; for manufacturers & suppliers of equipment, products &
       services to the commercial horticultural industry worldwide
●   Conf - Exhib - Expt - Lib - LG
M   120 f
¶   NL - 5; ftm only.
       Buyers' Guide: association details, members & what they
          provide - 1; free (also on website).

Commercial Radio Companies Association   (CRCA)   1973
NR   77 Shaftesbury Ave, LONDON, W1D 5DU.   (hq)
       020 7306 2603   fax 020 7470 0062
       email info@crca.co.uk   http://www.crca.co.uk
       Chmn: Lord John Eatwell
▲   Company Limited by Guarantee
○   *T; for commercial radio, representing UK commercial radio to
       government, the Regulator & the media
●   Conf - Mtgs - Res - LG - Negotiation with copyright bodies
<   Assn Eur des Radios
M   255 f
¶   Bulletin - 26; ftm only.   LM - updated; free.

Commercial Trailer Association   (CTA)   1980
NR   Forbes House, Halkin St, LONDON, SW1X 7DS.   (hq)
       020 7235 7000
○   *T; represents the interests of manufacturers of trailers over 3.5
       tonnes gross weight
M   f

Commissioning Specialists Association   (CSA)   1990
■   The Old House (2nd floor office suite), 24 London Rd,
       HORSHAM, W Sussex, RH12 1AY.   (hq)
       01403 754133   fax 01403 754134
       email office@csa.org.uk   http://www.csa.org.uk
       Sec: Julie Parker
▲   Un-incorporated Society
○   *T; for commissioning specialists within the construction industry
Gp   Commissioning for: Heating & ventilation, Air conditioning,
       Refrigeration
●   ET - Inf
M   208 i, 54 f, UK / 20 i, 4 f, o'seas
¶   Index (NL) - 4.   LM.   Guidance Notes.
       Commissioning Engineers Compendium; £12.50 m, £16 nm.
       Technical Memoranda; £7.50 m, £10 nm.

COMMITTEE . . .
       For details of official & non-official committees, other than the
       following, see the companion volume **'Councils, Committees &
       Boards'**

Committee on the Administration of Justice   (CAJ)   1981
■   45-47 Donegall St, BELFAST, BT1 2BR.   (hq)
       028 9096 1122   fax 028 9024 6706
       email info@caj.org.uk   http://www.caj.org.uk
       Dir: Mike Ritchie
▲   Company Limited by Guarantee
○   *G, *K; works for a just & peaceful society in Northern Ireland
       where the human rights of all are protected
●   Conf - ET - Res - Inf - Lib - Campaigning, lobbying & advising
<   Intl Fedn for Human Rights
M   180 i, 40 org, UK / 120 i, o'seas
¶   AR - 1.
       Publications list available.

Committee of Registered Clubs Associations   (CORCA)   1983
■   253-254 Upper St, LONDON, N1 1RY.   (hq)
       020 7226 0221   fax 020 7354 1847
       Sec: Kevin Smyth
○   *N; 'for separate club organisations who meet regularly for
       mutual benefit'
●   Mtgs - Stat - Empl - LG
M   8,000,000 i, 6 org
¶   CORCA-NJIC Wages Booklet - 1; 20p m, £2 nm.
       All Parliamentary Party Progress Report - 1; £2.

**Commons, Open Spaces & Footpaths Preservation Society
(Open Spaces Society)   1865**
■   25a Bell St, HENLEY-on-THAMES, Oxon, RG9 2BA.   (hq)
       01491 573535   fax 01491 573051
       email hq@oss.org.uk   http://www.oss.org.uk
       Gen Sec: Miss Kate Ashbrook
▲   Registered Charity
○   *K; to create & conserve common land, village greens, open
       spaces & rights of public access, in town & country, in
       England & Wales
●   Inf
M   2,460 i, local & national org, amenity groups, etc
¶   Open Space (Jnl) - 3; ftm only.
       Our Common Land (book); £14 m, £25 nm.
       Various other leaflets & publications.
       Note: the registered title of this organisation is Commons,
          Open Spaces & Footpaths Preservation Society; it is now
          better known under the title of Open Spaces Society

Communication Workers Union   (CWU)   1995
NR   150 The Broadway, LONDON, SW19 1RX.   (hq)
       020 8971 7200   fax 020 8971 7300
       http://www.cwu.org
       Gen Sec: Billy Hayes
○   *U; for people working in the postal & telecommunications
       industries
●   Conf - ET - Res - Stat - Lib - Empl - LG
<   U Network Intl; Labour Party; Trades U Congress
M   300,000 i
¶   Voice - 10; ftm.

Communications Management Association   (CMA)   1958
■   Ranmore House, 7 The Crescent, LEATHERHEAD, Surrey,
       KT22 8DY.   (hq)
       01372 361234   fax 01372 810810
       email cma@thecma.com   http://www.thecma.com
       Chief Exec: Glenn Powell
▲   Registered Charity
○   *P; for professionals & organisations focused on
       communications, networks & ICT, for business advantage
●   Conf - ET - Res - Exhib - SG - Stat - Inf - LG
<   Brit Computer Soc (BCS)
M   452 i, 75 f
       (Sub: £119.15 i, £595 f)
¶   Newsline (email) - 12;   Update (email) - 12; both free.
×   2007 Telecommunications Users' Association (merged October)

Community   2004
■   Swinton House, 324 Gray's Inn Rd, LONDON, WC1X 8DD.
       (hq)
       020 7239 1200   fax 020 7278 8378
       email info@community-tu.org
       http://www.community-tu.org
       Gen Sec: M Leahy
Br   480
○   *U
Gp   Steel, wire & domestic appliances; Betting shop workers; Social
       & voluntary workers; Textile, garment & leather workers;
       Equality; National League for the Blind & Disabled
●   Conf - Mtgs - ET - Res - Stat - Inf - Empl - LG
×   2004 (Iron & Steel Trades Confederation
                (National Union of Knitwear, Footwear & Apparel
                Trades
       ational Union of Domestic Appliances & General
                Operatives
       2008 (British Union of Social Work Employees

Community Composting Network   (CCN)
NR   67 Alexandra Rd, SHEFFIELD, S Yorks, S2 3EE.
       0114-258 0483
       http://www.communitycompost.org.uk
○   *H, *K, *N; promotes community composting at a national level
       & through local groups
●   Conf - Inf - Lib - LG
M   230 org
¶   The Growing Heap - 4.   Guide to Community Composting.

Community Development Finance Association   (cdfa)   2001
NR   Hatton Square Business Centre (Room 101), 16-16a Baldwins
       Gardens, LONDON, EC1N 7RJ.
       020 7430 0222
       email info@cdfa.org.uk   http://www.cdfa.org.uk
       Chief Exec: Bernie Morgan
▲   Company Limited by Guarantee
○   *T; for community development finance institutions -
       sustainable, independent financial institutions that provide
       capital & support to enable individuals to develop & create
       wealth in disadvantaged communities or under-served
       markets
●   Conf - Mtgs - ET - LG
M   5 i, 104 f
¶   Inside Out (survey of sector) - 1; £15, £15 +postage nm.
       Enterprise Communities (wealth beyond welfare); free.
       Money-go-Round: recycling finances, realising capital.
       Community Investment Relief Guide; £10 m, £12.50 nm.
       Guide to Building a CDFI;£200 m, £200 +postage nm.

Community & District Nursing Association UK   (CDNA)   1971
NR   Walpole House, 18-22 Bond St, Ealing, LONDON, W5 5AA.
       (hq)
       020 8231 0180   fax 020 8231 0187
       http://www.cdna-online.org.uk
       Dir: Anne Duffy
Br   40
○   *P, *U
●   Conf - Mtgs - ET - Exhib - SG - Empl - LG
M   5,090 i
¶   Nursing Care - 4; ftm, £1.20 nm.   Nurse Prescribing; £3.
       Key Issues in District Nursing 1, 2 & 3; £4.   AR.
       Innovations in Primary Health Care Nursing; £5.

Community Foundation Network   1991
NR   Arena House, 66-68 Pentonville Rd, LONDON, N1 9HS.   (hq)
       020 7713 9326   fax 020 7713 9327
       email network@communityfoundations.org.uk
       http://www.communityfoundations.org.uk
       Dir: Stephen Hammersley
▲   Company Limited by Guarantee; Registered Charity
○   *N; 'a support organisation for community trusts & foundations
       & those wishing to establish them in the UK'
●   Conf - Mtgs - Res - Stat - Inf - Lib - VE - LG
M   56 trusts / foundations
¶   NL - 4; ftm.
       Giving Shares & Securities: information pack for financial
       advisers; ftm.
       A Guide to European Funding; ftm.
       Community Foundations & Community Needs Assessment; ftm.
       Tackling Multiple Disadvantage; ftm.
       Changing the Future; ftm.
           Publications list available.

Community Hospitals Association   (CHA)   1969
NR   Meadow Brow, Broadway, ILMINSTER, Somerset, TA19 9RG.
       (hsb)
       01460 55951   fax 01460 53207
       Chief Exec: Mrs Barbara Moore
▲   Un-incorporated Society
○   *K, *M; promotion of community hospitals
●   Conf - Res - Stat - Inf - VE - LG
<   Assn for GP Maternity Care; Scot Assn of GP Community
       Hospitals
M   25 i, 10 org, 250 hospitals
¶   NL - 4; ftm.

Community Housing Cymru
NR Fulmar House, Beignon Close, Ocean Park, CARDIFF,
      CF24 5HF.
      029 2055 7400   fax 029 2055 7415
      email enquiries@chcymru.org.uk
      http://www.chcymru.org.uk
      Chief Exec: Nick Bennett
○ *W; housing associations
M 39 org
× 2006 Welsh Federation of Housing Associations

Community Matters
      alternative name of the **National Federation of Community
      Organisations**

Community Media Association   (CMA)   1983
NR 15 Paternoster Row, SHEFFIELD, S Yorks, S1 2BX.   (hq)
      0114-279 5219   fax 0114-279 8976
      email cma@commedia.org.uk
      http://www.commedia.org.uk
      Dir: Diane Reid
▲ Company Limited by Guarantee
○ *K, *N; to represent community media in the UK to
      government, regulators & industry
● Conf - Lib - LG
< Wld Assn of Community Radio Broadcasters (AMARC)
M 200 i, 300 f, UK / 10 i, 10 f, o'seas
¶ Airflash (Jnl) - 4; ftm only (subscription £5-£60).

Community Pharmacy Scotland
NR 42 Queen St, EDINBURGH, EH2 3NH.   (hq)
      0131-467 7766   fax 0131-467 7767
      email enquiries@communitypharmacyscotland.org.uk
      http://www.communitypharmacyscotland.org.uk
      Chief Exec: Harry McQuillan
○ *T; to represent community pharmacy owners throughout
      Scotland
M 1,117 i
× 2006 Scottish Pharmaceutical Federation (merged)2007
      Scottish Pharmaceutical General Council

Community Recycling Network UK   (CRN UK)
NR 57 Prince St, BRISTOL, BS1 4QH.
      0117-942 0142   fax 0117-934 9944
      email info@crn.org.uk   http://www.crn.org.uk
      Chief Exec: Andy Moore
○ to promote community based sustainable waste management

Community Self Build Scotland
      rumoured to have closed - we should appreciate confirmation.

Community Service Volunteers   (CSV)   1962
■ 237 Pentonville Rd, LONDON, N1 9NJ.   (hq)
      020 7278 6601   fax 020 7833 0149
      email information@csv.org.uk   http://www.csv.org.uk
      Chief Exec: Elisabeth Hoodless
▲ Company Limited by Guarantee; Registered Charity
Br 120
○ *W; to create opportunities for people to take an active part in
      the life of their community through volunteering, training &
      community action;Please note that CSV is NOT able to offer
      sponsorship or grants
Gp Retired & senior volunteers programme; Full-time volunteering,
      social care up to 12 months; Employee volunteering; Social
      action broadcasting; Education consultancy; Vocational
      training
● Conf - ET - Res - Exhib - Inf
M 229,000 i (per year)

Community Transport Association UK   (CTA)   1982
NR Highbank, Halton St, HYDE, Cheshire, SK14 2NY.
      0870 774 3586   fax 0870 774 3581
      email ctauk@communitytransport.com
      http://www.ctauk.org
      Chief Exec: Keith Halstead
▲ Company Limited by Guarantee; Registered Charity
Br 7
○ *W; any form of non-profit transport provision for people with
      mobility problems
Gp Dial-a-Ride; Rural transport; Community car scheme; Training
● Conf - Mtgs - ET - Exhib - Inf - Lib - PL - LG - Vehicle purchase
      scheme - Issue of minibus permits
< NCVO
M 1,250 org, UK / 10 org, o'seas
¶ Community Transport - 6; ftm, £21 nm.   AR; free.
      Publications list available.

Community & Youth Workers' Union   (CYWU)   1971
NR Transport House, 211 Broad St, BIRMINGHAM, B15 1AY.   (hq)
      0121-643 6221
      http://www.cywu.org.uk
      Nat Sec: Doug Nicholls
○ *U; trade union for full & part-time youth, community & play
      workers in the statutory or voluntary sector
< Unite, the Union
¶ Rapport - 6.

Companion Animal Behaviour Therapy Study Group
      a group of the **British Small Animal Veterinary Association**

Company Chemists' Association Ltd   (CCA)   1898
■ Garden Studios, 11-15 Betterton St, London, WC2H 9BP.   (hq)
      020 7470 8775   fax 020 7470 8776
      http://www.thecca.org.uk
      Chief Exec: Robert Darracott
▲ Company Limited by Guarantee
○ *T; for corporate bodies operating community pharmacy
      businesses
● Mtgs - LG
M 9 f

Company of Goldsmiths of Dublin   1637
IRL Assay Office, Dublin Castle, DUBLIN 2, Republic of Ireland.
      353 (1) 475 1286; 478 0323   fax 353 (1) 478 3838
      email hallmark@assay.ie
○ Controls & conducts the Assay Office

Compassionate Friends   (TCF)   1969
■ 53 North St, BRISTOL, BS3 1EN.   (hq)
      0845 120 3785   fax 0845 120 3786
      email info@tcf.org.uk   http://www.tcf.org.uk
      Chmn: Diana Youdale
▲ Company Limited by Guarantee; Registered Charity
Br Australia, Europe, New Zealand, USA
○ *W; to offer support & friendship to bereaved parents & their
      families through 250 local contacts
Gp Childless parents; POMC - parents of murdered children;
      Shadow of suicide; SIBBS - support in bereavement for
      brothers & sisters
● Mtgs - Inf - Lib - Annual weekend gathering - Personal &
      telephone support
      Helpline: 0845 123 2304
M 10,000 families, 100 f, 100 org, UK / 50 families, o'seas
¶ TCF NL - 4; £30 m only.

Competing Pipers Association   (CPA)   1976
NR Sunnybrae, Balkerach Street, DOUNE, Perthshire, FK16 6DE
      email secretary@competingpipers.com
      http://www.competingpipers.com
      Sec: Tracey Williams
○ *D; highland bagpipes

© CBD Research Ltd · Beckenham · BR3 5JS · Tel 020 8650 7745 · Fax 020 8650 0768 · E-mail cbd@cbdresearch.com · www.cbdresearch.com

Complementary Medical Association   (CMA)   1995
NR   Blackcleuch, Teviothead, HAWICK, Roxburghshire, TD9 0PU.
       (hq)
       http://www.the-cma.org.uk
▲   Un-incorporated Society
Br   2; Bulgaria, Georgia, India, Nepal, Portugal, S Africa
○   *P; a register of complementary medical practitioners & training
       organisations
●   Conf - ET - Exam - Res - Exhib - Comp - SG - Inf - VE - LG -
       Educational programmes to PhD level
M   15,000 i (worldwide), 10 f, 3 org, UK / 3 f, o'seas
¶   With Our Complements - 4.

Component Obsolescence Group   (COG)   1997
■   PO Box 314, HARPENDEN, Herts, AL5 4XL.   (asa)
       01582 762934   fax 01582 461928
       email info@cog.org.uk   http://www.cog.org.uk
       Chief Exec: Michael Trenchard
▲   Company Limited by Guarantee
○   *G; to provide a forum for industry professionals concerned
       with obsolescence of electronic, mechanical & software
       components in industries where equipment life is long
Gp   Website maintenance; Standardisation & guidance
●   Conf - Mtgs - ET - Exhib - Inf - LG
M   135 f, UK / 60 f, o'seas

Composites UK Ltd   1989
■   Sarum Lodge, St Anne's Court, Talygarn, PONTYCLUN,
       Glamorgan, CF72 9HH.   (hq)
       01443 228867   fax 01443 239083
       email info@compositesuk.org
       http://www.compositesuk.org
       Sec: Ken L Forsdyke
▲   Company Limited by Guarantee
○   *T; to enhance & promote the safe & effective use of
       composites
Gp   Aerospace Composites Group
●   Conf - ET - Exhib - Lib - LG
<   American Composites Mfrs' Assn
M   90 f
¶   Composites UK Bulletin - 4; free.
×   2007 (March) Composites Processing Association Ltd

Composting Association
       since 2008 **Association of Organics Recycling**

Composting Association of Ireland   (CR/Ea/)
IRL   Business Innovation Centre, Institute of Technology Campus,
       BALLINODE, Co Sligo, Republic of Ireland.
       email info@cre.ie   http://www.compostireland.ie
       Chmn: Fiacra Quinn
○   *T

Compulsory Annuity Purchase Protest Alliance   (CAPPA)   1999
NR   85 Oldfield Rd, SHEFFIELD, S Yorks, S6 6DU.   (mem/s/p)
       http://www.cappa.org.uk
       Mem Sec: Tony Davies
▲   Un-incorporated Society
○   *K; to seek reform of Finance Acts which compel private
       pension fund holders to buy an annuity at age 75

Computer Conservation Society   (CCS)   1988
NR   25 Comet Close, Ash Vale, ALDERSHOT, Hants, GU12 5SG.
       (hsp)
       http://www.computerconservationsociety.org
       Sec: Kevin Murrell
▲   Un-incorporated Society
Br   2
○   *G; conservation & restoration of historic computers; collection
       of archive material in history of computing, including
       hardware, software, publications & reminiscences
Gp   Working parties: Elliott 803; Elliott 401; Ferranti Pegasus; DEC;
       S100 BUS; Turing bombe
●   Mtgs - Working parties to restore historic computers
<   Parent Org: Brit Computer Soc, Science Museum South
       Kensington, Museum of Science & Ind in Manchester
M   c 700 i, 1 f, UK / c 25 i, o'seas
¶   Computer Resurrection (Jnl) - 3/4; ftm.

Computer & Peripherals Equipment Trade Association
       has closed

Comunn na Clàrsaich   (the Clarsach Society)   1931
NR   11 Granby Rd, EDINBURGH, EH16 5NP.   (admin p)
       0131-667 4645
       email clarsachs@blueyonder.co.uk
       http://www.clarsachsociety.co.uk
       Hon Sec: Mary Scott
▲   Registered Charity
Br   11
○   *D; to encourage the playing of the clarsach (Celtic harp); to
       preserve its place in the national life of Scotland, particularly
       among Gaelic speaking people
Gp   Wire strung harp
●   ET - Comp - Inf - Harp hire service to members - Organisation
       of the Edinburgh Harp Festival
<   An Comunn Gaidhealach
M   900 i, UK / 50 i, o'seas
¶   Branch newsletters - irreg; ftm only.
       Folios of Music (detailed catalogue on request).
       AR (incl list of harp makers).
       Diary of Events - 2; free to branches.

An Comunn Gaidhealach [The Highland Association]   1891
NR   109 Church St, INVERNESS, IV1 1EY.   (hq)
       01463 231226   fax 01463 715557
       http://www.ancomunn.co.uk
○   *L; promotion of the Gaelic language, literature, arts & music
M   c 2,500 i

Concert Artistes' Association   (CAA)   1897
■   20 Bedford St, LONDON, WC2E 9HP.   (hq)
       020 7836 3172   fax 020 7836 3172
       email office@the caa.org   http://www.thecaa.org
       Sec: Malcolm Knight,   Pres: Mark Wynter
○   *A, *D; for all those interested in the entertainment profession
       with particular reference to concerts, cabarets, radio,
       television & West End productions
       The association has its own West End club - the Club for Acts &
       Actors
Gp   General committee & several sub-committees; Trustees of the
       benevolent fund
●   Mtgs - ET - Exam - Exhib - Comp - SG - VE - Rehearsals, shows
       - Theatrical productions
<   Catholic Stage Gld
M   998 i, 1 guild, UK / 50 i, o'seas
¶   NL - 3;   Chairman's Report -1;   LM - 2 yrly; all ftm only.
       But - What do you do in the Winter? (book by Larry Parker); £8.

Concert Promoters Association   (CPA)   1986
NR   6 St Mark's Rd, HENLEY-on-THAMES, Oxon, RG9 1LJ.   (sp)
          01491 575060   fax 01491 414082
          email carolesmith.cpa@virgin.net
          Sec: Carole Smith
▲   Company Limited by Guarantee
○   *T; the interests of promoters of contemporary music concerts/
          tours in the UK
M   [not given]

**Conchological Society of Great Britain & Ireland   (CSGBI)
1876**
■   447B Wokingham Rd, Earley, READING, Berks, RG6 7EL.
          (hsp)
          Hon Sec: Rosemary Hill
▲   Registered Charity
○   *L; to promote the study of the mollusca in all its aspects;
          actively engaged in biographical distribution of marine &
          non-marine molluscs
●   Conf - Mtgs - Res - Stat
<   Brit Trust Consvn Volunteers; Coun Nature
M   280 i, 20 org, UK / 100 i, 20 org, o'seas
¶   Journal of Conchology - 2; ftm, £40 nm.
          Mollusc World - 3; ftm, £3 nm.
          Other occasional publications.

Concrete Block Association
          an affiliated association of the **British Precast Concrete
          Federation**

Concrete Bridge Development Group   (CBDG)   1992
NR   4 Meadows Business Park, Station Approach, Blackwater,
          CAMBERLEY, Surrey, GU17 9AB.   (hq)
          01276 608700   fax 01276 608701
▲   Company Limited by Guarantee
○   *T; to enhance the design, construction & management of
          concrete bridges
M   f & org

Concrete Manufacturers' Association of Ireland
IRL   Confederation House, 84/86 Lower Baggot St, DUBLIN 2,
          Republic of Ireland.
○   *T
          incorporated in the **Construction Industry Federation**

Concrete Pipeline Systems Association
          a product association of the **British Precast Concrete Federation**

Concrete Repair Association   (CRA)   1988
■   Tournai Hall, Evelyn Woods Rd, ALDERSHOT, Hants,
          GU11 2LL.   (asa)
          01252 357843   fax 01252 357831
          email cra@associationhouse.org.uk
          http://www.concreterepair.org.uk
          Sec: John G Fairley
▲   Company Limited by Guarantee
○   *T; to promote the practice of concrete repair
●   Conf - Mtgs - ET - Exhib - Inf - Seminars - Quality assurance &
          control system implementation
M   38 f
¶   LM - 3; free.
          Standard Method of Measurement; £5 m, £10 nm.
          Application & Measurement of Protective Coatings; free.
          Route to a Successful Concrete Repair; £2.50 m, £5 nm.

Concrete Sleeper Manufacturers' Association
          a product association of the **British Precast Concrete Federation**

Concrete Society   1966
■   4 Meadows Business Park, Station Approach, Blackwater,
          CAMBERLEY, Surrey, GU17 9AB.   (hq)
          01276 607140
          email enquiries@concrete.org.uk
          http://www.concrete.org.uk
▲   Company Limited by Guarantee
Br   20
○   *L, *T; to bring together all who are interested in concrete to
          exchange information, to encourage innovation, to promote
          excellence in design, construction, appearance &
          performance
Gp   Materials; Design; Construction
●   Conf - Mtgs - ET - Res - Inf - Lib - PL - LG - Annual awards -
          Advisory service
<   Fédn Intle du Beton; Eur Concrete Soc Network
M   1,000 i, 500 f
¶   Concrete (Jnl) - 10.
          Concrete Engineers International Jnl - 4.

Concrete Structures Group Ltd
          alternative name of **Construct**

Concrete Tile Manufacturers' Association
          an affiliated association of the **British Precast Concrete
          Federation**

Confederation of Aerial Industries Ltd   (CAI)   1978
NR   41A Market St, WATFORD, Herts, WD18 0PN.   (hq)
          01923 803030   fax 01923 803203
          email office@cai.org.uk   http://www.cai.org.uk
          Sec: Mrs Beverley K Allgood
▲   Company Limited by Guarantee
○   *T; for the aerial & satellite industry
●   ET - Exam - Exhib - LG
M   c 750 f
¶   Feedback - 4;   LM - 1;   Ybk - 1; Codes of practice; all free.

Confederation of British Industry   (CBI)   1965
NR   Centre Point, 103 New Oxford St, LONDON, WC1A 1DU.
          (hq)
          020 7379 7400
          http://www.cbi.org.uk
          Dir Gen: Richard Lambert
○   *T; employers organisation promoting the prosperity of British
          industry

Confederation of British Metalforming   (CBM)
NR   National Metalforming Centre, 47 Birmingham Rd, WEST
          BROMWICH, W Midlands, B70 6PY.   (hq)
          0121-601 6350   fax 0121-601 6373
          email info@britishmetalforming.com
          http://www.britishmetalforming.com
          Dir Gen: John Houseman
○   *T; manufacturers of fasteners, forgings & pressings
●   Conf - Mtgs - Inf
M   300 f

**   **Confederation of the British Security Industry**
          Organisation lost: see Introduction paragraph 3.

Confederation of British Service & Ex-Service Organisations (COBSEO) 1982

■ c/o GVAMP, The Baird Medical Centre, Gassiott House, St Thomas' Hospital, Lambeth Palace Rd, LONDON, SE1 7EP. (hsb)
020 7202 8322   fax 020 7928 0435
email sec.cobseo@btconnect.com
http://www.cobseo.org.uk
Co Sec: Michael Bray
▲ Company LImited by Guarantee
○ *N, *W; to represent, promote & further the interest of service & ex-service personnel of all ranks & their spouses & dependents
● Conf - Mtgs - Inf - LG
M 140 org
(Sub: '50)
¶ Bulletin - 4; ftm;   AR - 1.

Confederation of British Wool Textiles Ltd (CBWT) 1979

■ Textile House, Red Doles Lane, HUDDERSFIELD, W Yorks, HD2 1YF. (hq)
01484 346500   fax 01484 346501
email info@cbwt.co.uk   http://www.cbwt.co.uk
Dir Gen: John Lambert
▲ Company Limited by Guarantee
○ *T; representation of interests of the UK wool textile industry
● Conf - Mtgs - ET - Stat - Empl - LG
< Intl Wool Textile Org; Interlaine; Brit Apparel & Textiles Confedn
M 170 f

Confederation of Burial Authorities
since 2004-05 **Institute of Cemetery & Crematorium Management**

Confederation of Children's Services Managers
formerly (2005) Confederation of Education Service Managers, in 2007 merged with the children's element of the Association of Directors of Social Services to form the **Association of Directors of Children's Services**

Confederation of Co-operative Housing 1993

■ Fairgate House, 205 Kings Rd, Tyseley, BIRMINGHAM, W Midlands, B11 2AA.
0121-449 9588
http://www.cch.coop
Chmn: Nic Bliss
▲ Company Limited by Guarantee
○ *N; for all housing co-operatives & tenant controlled housing bodies

Confederation of Construction Specialists (CCS) 1983

■ 1 Walpole House, 2 Pickford St, ALDERSHOT, Hants, GU11 1TZ. (hq)
01252 312122   fax 01252 343081
email info@constructionspecialists.org
http://www.constructionspecialists.org
Group Dir: A R Gibbs
▲ Un-incorporated Society
○ *N, *T; central representative body for specialist building & civil engineering firms
● Conf - Mtgs - ET - Res - SG - Stat - Inf - Lib - LG - Advisory & consultancy service - Commercial intelligence service
< Construction Specialists Gp
M f & affiliated trade assns
¶ NL - 10; ftm.
Performance Bond; £10.   Certificate of vesting; £10.
Standard forms of contract & sub-contract; £5-£10.

Confederation of Dental Employers (CODE) 1978

■ Elm Tree House, Bodmin St, HOLSWORTHY, Devon, EX22 6BB. (hq)
01409 254354   fax 01409 254364
email info@codeuk.com   http://www.codeuk.com
Chief Exec: Dr Paul Mendlesohn
▲ Incorporated Society
○ *P; to represent the interests of practice owners in the UK
● Conf - ET - Res - Exhib - Inf - LG - Management services - Helpline
M 450 i, 8 f
¶ face2face - 4; ftm.

Confederation of Education Service Managers
in 2005 became the Confederation of Children's Services Managers, which in 2007 merged with the children's element of the Association of Directors of Social Services to form the **Association of Directors of Children's Services**

Confederation of English Fly Fishers (CEFF) 1974

NR 23 Smithson Close, Talbot Village, POOLE, Dorset, BH12 5EY. (hsp)
01202 537321   fax 07754 091923
email secretary@ceff.org.uk   http://www.ceff.org.uk
Hon Sec: Malcolm Price
○ *G; to foster all aspects of fly fishing; to promote the sport including respect for the environment
M c 5,000 i

Confederation of Forest Industries (ConFor) 1959

■ 59 George St, EDINBURGH, EH2 2JG.
0131-240 1410   fax 0131-240 1411
email mail@confor.org.uk   http://www.confor.org.uk
Chief Exec: Stuart Goodall
▲ Company Limited by Guarantee
○ *T; to represent the whole wood supply chain - growers, woodland managers, contractors, harvesters & primary & secondary processors
● Conf - Mtgs - Exhib - VE - LG
M 400 i, 1,300 f, 50 org
(Sub: varies)
¶ Forestry & Timber News - 6; ftm, £32 yr nm.
✕ 2006 Association of Timber Growers & Forestry Professionals

Confederation of Healing Organisations (CHO) 1981

■ c/o 18A Littleham Rd, EXMOUTH, Devon, EX8 2QG. (asa)
01584 890662
email diane.schooley@btinternet.com
http://www.confederation-of-healing-organisations.org
Sec: Mrs Diane Schooley
▲ Company Limited by Guarantee; Registered Charity
○ *K, *N; to advance public education in methods of healing; to promote research into the methods & effects of healing; to coordinate & represent member organisations
● Mtgs - Res - Inf
M 8,000 i in 12 org

Confederation of Long Distance Racing Pigeon Unions of Great Britain & Ireland

NR 20 Gorsey Lane, Banks, SOUTHPORT, PR9 8EH. (hq)
01704 232164
Hon Sec: Brian Newsome
○ *N, *S

Confederation of Paper Industries Ltd (CPI) 1999
NR 1 Rivenhall Rd, SWINDON, Wilts, SN5 7BD. (hq)
   01793 889600   fax 01793 878700
   email cpi@paper.org.uk   http://www.paper.org.uk
   Dir Gen: Dr Martin Oldman
▲ Company Limited by Guarantee
○ *N; the authoritative & effective voice of the UK's paper-related
   industries
Gp Corrugated; Papermaking; Recovered paper; Tissue
● Conf - Mtgs - ET - Stat - Inf - Empl - LG
< Confedn of Eur Paper Inds (CEPI); Fédn Eur des Fabricants de
   Carton Ondulé (FEFCO); Eur Recovered Paper Assn (ERPA)
M 100 f
¶ CPI News - 26;   Daily Data - daily;   MP's NL - 4;
   statistics (various); all ftm only.
   Annual Review - 1; free.

Confederation of Passenger Transport UK (CPT) 1974
NR Drury House, 34-43 Russell St, LONDON, WC2B 5HA. (hq)
   020 7240 3131   fax 020 7240 6565
   email cpt@cpt-uk.org   http://www.cpt-uk.org
   Dir Gen: Brian Nimick
▲ Company Limited by Guarantee
○ *T; representing bus & coach operators
● Conf - Mtgs - ET - Res - Exhib - SG - Stat - Inf - PL - LG
M 1,200 f
¶ Newsline (NL) - 10;   Annual review;
   Bulletins - irreg;   Hbk - 1; all ftm.

Confederation of Roofing Contractors Ltd (CRC) 1985
■ 72 Church Rd, Brightlingsea, COLCHESTER, Essex, CO7 0JF.
   (hq)
   01206 306600   fax 01206 306200
   email enquiries@corc.co.uk   http://www.corc.co.uk
   Chief Exec: Allan Buchan
▲ Company Limited by Guarantee
Br 4
○ *T; 'the main consumer protection organisation in the roofing
   industry'
● ET - Inf - Lib - LG
M 625 i, 625 f
¶ The Roofing Trades Jnl - 6; free.

**Confederation of Shipbuilding & Engineering Unions (CSEU)
1890**
NR 35 King St, LONDON, WC2E 8JG. (hq)
   020 7420 8957
   Gen Sec: J Wall
▲ Un-incorporated Society
Br 36
○ *U
● Empl
M 8 unions
¶ AR; ftm.

** **Confederation of Trades & Commerce**
   Organisation lost, see Introduction paragraph 6

**Confederation of Transcribed Information Services (COTIS)
1986**
■ Project Office, 67 High St, TARPORLEY, Cheshire, CW6 0DP.
   (admin)
   01829 733351   fax 01829 732408
   email administrator@cotis.org.uk
   http://www.cotis.org.uk
   Admin: Mrs S Jones
▲ Registered Charity
○ *N; to improve the provision & quality of information provided
   in formats other than normal print
● Mtgs - Inf - Workshops
M 12 i, 63 f, UK / 1 f, o'seas
¶ On Track (NL) - 3;   Basic Principles; both ftm, £1 nm.
   Guidelines; £5 each, (10% discount m):
      1: General Recording Technique;
      2: General Presentation;
      3: Reading Skills;
      4: Publicity;
      5: Computer;
      6: Recording Illustrations;
      7: Labelling & Packaging;
      8: How to Create a DIY Studio;
   Tapes; £8 each, (10% discount m):
      Technical Hints;
      Reading Masterclass.
      Describing Illustrations.

Confederation of UK Coal Producers (COALPRO) 1991
■ Confederation House, Thornes Office Park, Denby Dale Rd,
   WAKEFIELD, W Yorks, WF2 7AN. (hq)
   01924 200802   fax 01924 200796
   email db@coalpro.co.uk   http://www.coalpro.co.uk
   Dir Gen: David Brewer,   Gen Mgr: Mrs A Fellows
▲ Company Limited by Guarantee
○ *T; represents the majority of UK companies engaged in coal
   extraction
Gp Marketing & Development; Safety & Health; Opencast Mining;
   British Standards; Deep Mining
● Conf - Mtgs - Exhib - Stat - Inf - Lib - PL - LG - Liaison with
   European Commission - Liaison with associate organisations
   worldwide
< Worls Coal Inst; Euriscoal (Brussels); Combined Heat & Power
   Assn; Confedn of Brit Ind
M 21 f
¶ LM - 1.   Mines Database.
   Technical Information - 12.   AR.   NL - 12.

Confederation of West Midlands Chambers of Commerce 2002
NR Oak Tree Court, Binley Business Park, Harry Weston Rd,
   COVENTRY, Warks, CV3 2UN.
   024 7665 4336   fax 024 7645 4289
   http://www.westmidlandschambers.org
M 7 org

Conference Centres of Excellence (CCE)
NR 261 High St, DORKING, Surrey, RH4 1RL.
   0845 230 1414   fax 01306 876837
   http://www.cceonline.co.uk

Conference of Drama Schools (CDS) 1969
■ PO Box 34252, LONDON, NW5 1XJ. (hsp)
   020 7692 0032   fax 020 7692 0032
   email info@cds.drama.ac.uk   http://www.drama.ac.uk
   Exec Sec: Saul Hyman
▲ Company Limited by Guarantee
○ *P; to provide a voice for drama trainers; to give advice to
   prospective students
● Conf - Mtgs - ET - Res - Comp - Inf
< Nat Coun for Drama Training
M 21 f
¶ CDS Guide to Professional Training in Drama & Technical
   Theatre 1; free.
   CDS Guide to Careers Back Stage; free.

Conference of Heads of Irish Universities
since September 2005 **Irish Universities Association**

Conference Interpreters Group   (CIG)   1979
NR   10 Barley Mow Passage, LONDON, W4 4PH.   (hq)
       020 8995 0801   fax 020 8742 1066
       email ciglondon@aol.com
       http://www.cig-interpreters.com
       Sec: Andrew Brock
▲   Company Limited by Guarantee
○   *P; cooperative grouping of simultaneous interpreters
M   22 i
       No further information supplied.

Conference of Professional Dance Schools
a group of the **Council for Dance Education & Training (UK)**

Conflict Research Society   (CRS)   1963
■   28 Severn Drive, NEWPORT PAGNELL, Bucks, MK16 9DQ.
       (chmn/p)
       01908 611296
       http://www.conflictresearchsociety.org.uk
       Chmn: Gordon John Burt
▲   Registered Charity
○   *L, *Q; to promote research into, & the extension of knowledge
       about, conflict processes at all levels
M   c 80 i
¶   Jnl of the Conflict Research Society - 1; ftm, £10 nm
       (£15 o'seas).

Confraternity of Saint James   (CSJ)   1983
■   27 Blackfriars Rd, LONDON, SE1 8NY.
       020 7928 9988   fax 020 7928 2844
       email office@csj.org.uk   http://www.csj.org.uk
       Sec: Marion Marples
▲   Registered Charity
○   *G; a nondenominational organisation for all interested in the
       pilgrimage to Santiago de Compostela; to promote research
       into the history of the pilgrimage in Britain; to identify &
       safeguard works of art connected with St James & the
       pilgrimage
Gp   Research working party
●   Conf - Mtgs - Res - Exhib - SG - Inf - Lib - PL - VE - Concerts
<   European Assn Friends Road to St James
M   2,500 i, 15 org, UK / 300 i, 3 org, o'seas
¶   Bulletin - 4; ftm, £2.50 nm.
       Pilgrim Guides & other publications: list on application.

Congenital CMV Association   1986
■   111 Windmill Hill Lane, Kingsway, DERBY, DE22 3BN.   (hsp)
       01322 365528
       email congenitalcmv.association@ntlworld.com
       http://www.cmvsupport.org
       Coordinator: Mrs Carmen Burton
○   *W; the welfare & support of families with congenital
       cytomegalovirus (of the herpes virus group); to support
       research to aid medical staff & professionals
●   Res - Stat - Inf - Lib
M   80 i, 10 f, UK / 25 i, 10 f, o'seas
¶   NL - 4; ftm, free email nm.
       Information leaflets on Congenital CMV; free email.

** Congregational Union of Ireland
       Organisation lost, see Introduction paragraph 6

CONNECT   1972
NR   30 St George's Rd, LONDON, SW19 4BD.   (hq)
       020 8971 6000   fax 020 8971 6002
       email union@connectuk.org   http://www.connectuk.org
       Gen Sec: Adrian Askew
○   *U; working for managers & professionals in the
       communications sector

Connemara Pony Breeders Society
IRL   The Showgrounds, Hospital Rd, CLIFDEN, Co Galway, Republic
       of Ireland.
       353 (95) 21863
       email enquiries@cpbs.ie   http://www.cpbs.ie
○   *B

Conservatoires UK   (CBC)
■   c/o John Wallace, Royal Scottish Academy of Music & Drama,
       100 Renfrew St, GLASGOW, G2 3DB.   (chmn/b)
       Chmn: John Wallace
○   *D, *E; music education & training
●   Conf - Mtgs - SG - LG
<   Assn of Eur Conservatoires
M   7 conservatoires

**Consortium of Lesbian, Gay & Bisexual Transgendered Voluntary
& Community Organisations   (LGBT Consortium)**
NR   J111 Tower Bridge Business Complex, 100 Clements Rd,
       LONDON, SE16 4DG.   (hq)
       020 7064 8383   fax 020 7064 8382
       email jstewart@lgbtconsortium.org
       http://www.lgbtconsortium.org.uk
       Chief Exec: Mark Redman
▲   Company Limited by Guarantee; Registered Charity
○   *N
Gp   Lesbian; Gay; Bisexual; Transgendered
●   Conf - Res - Inf - Lib
M   c 400 i in 300 org

Consortium of Research Libraries in the British Isles
since 2008 **RLUK: Research Libraries UK**

Consortium of University Research Libraries
in 2004 was renamed CURL (Consortium of Research Libraries) & in
2008 became **RLUK: Research Libraries UK**

Constitutional Monarchy Association
part of the **Monarchist League**

Construct: Concrete Structures Group Ltd   (Construct)   1993
■   4 Meadows Business Park, Station Approach, Blackwater,
       CAMBERLEY, Surrey, GU17 9AB.   (hq)
       01276 38444   fax 01276 38899
       email enquiries@construct.org.uk
       http://www.construct.org.uk
       Exec Sec: Robin Holdsworth
▲   Company Limited by Guarantee
○   *T; for all specialist concrete contractors (concrete frame &
       other structures); to improve the efficiency of the concrete
       industry & thereby widening the market for concrete
Gp   Health & safety
●   Mtgs - ET - Inf
M   3 i, 76 f, 4 org (by negotiation)
       (Sub: £75-£3,500)
¶   Framework (NL); on website.   Ybk - 1; free.
       In-Situ Concrete Frames: a report; £5.
       Best Practice Guides (8); on website.
       Other publications; £10 - £60.

Construction Confederation (CC) 1817

NR 55 Tufton St, LONDON, SW1P 3QL. (hq)
 0870 898 9090 fax 0870 898 9095
 email enquiries@thecc.org.uk http://www.thecc.org.uk
 Chief Exec: Stephen Ratcliffe
▲ Un-incorporated Society
○ *N, *T; 'the predominant representative organisation for the UK construction industry'
Gp 5 member federations:
 British Woodworking Federation
 Civil Engineering Contractors Association
 Major Contractors Group
 National Contractors Federation
 National Federation of Builders & its
 House Builders Association
 Scottish Building Federation
● Conf - Mtgs - ET - Res - Exhib - SG - Stat - Inf - Empl - LG
M 5,000 f
¶ Construction Trends Survey - 4; £200 yr.

Construction Employers Federation Ltd (CEF) 1945

■ 143 Malone Rd, BELFAST, BT9 6SU. (hq)
 028 9087 7143 fax 028 9087 7155
 email mail@cefni.co.uk http://www.cefni.co.uk
 Dir: J Armstrong
▲ Company Limited by Guarantee
○ *T
Gp Private housing; Public authority housing; General contracting; Export; Civil engineering
● Conf - Mtgs - ET - Exhib - Stat - Expt - Inf - VE - Empl - LG
M 500 f
¶ Bulletin - 12; AR; both ftm.

Construction Equipment Association (CEA) 1942

■ Airport House, Purley Way, CROYDON, Surrey, CR0 0XZ. (asa)
 020 8253 4502 fax 020 8253 4510
 email cea@admin.co.uk http://www.coneq.org.uk
 Secs: Administration Services Ltd
▲ Un-incorporated Society
○ *T; to serve construction equipment manufacturers, their component & accessory suppliers & service providers
● Conf - Mtgs - Exhib - Stat - Expt - Inf - VE - LG
< C'ee for Eur Construction Eqpt (CECE); Fédn Eur de la Manutention (FEM)
M 100 f
¶ Newsline - 4; ftm.

Construction Fixings Association (CFA) 1977

■ 65 Deans St, OAKHAM, Rutland, LE15 6AF, (asa)
 01664 823687 fax 01664 823687
 email info@fixingscfa.co.uk
 http://www.fixingscfa.co.uk
 19 Hollytree Lane, Long Clawson, MELTON MOWBRAY, Leics, LE14 4NJ. (hsp)
 Gen Mgr: Mark Salmon
▲ Company Limited by Guarantee
○ *T; ensuring 'best fixings practice' among specifiers, distributors & installers of construction fixings
Gp Manufacturers (full members); Sellers within the UK (approved distributors); Sellers overseas (international members)
● Conf - Mtgs - ET - Inf
< Comité Eur de l'Outillage (CEO); Eur Tools C'ee
M 6 full members, 21 approved distbrs, UK; 2 f, o'seas
¶ Guidance Notes on the Correct Selection & Application of Fixings (a series of 10) - download from website; free.

Construction History Society 1981

■ c/o Library & Information Services Manager, CIB, Englemere, Kings Ride, ASCOT, Berks, SL5 8TB (sb)
 01344 630741 fax 01344 630764
 email michael.tutton@virgin.net
 http://www.constructionhistory.co.uk
 Sec: Michael Tutton
▲ Registered Charity; Un-incorporated Society
○ *L; to focus attention on the problems of historical information about the construction process becoming lost by default; to undertake a survey to establish the records available & their accessibility
● Conf - Mtgs - Lib
M 300 i
 (Sub: £25)
¶ Construction History Jnl - 1; ftm, price on application nm.
 NL - 4; ftm only.

Construction Industry Computing Association (CICA) 1973

NR National Computing Centre, Oxford House, Oxford Rd, MANCHESTER, M1 7ED. (hq)
 0161-242 2262
 email postmaster@cica.org.uk http://www.cica.org.uk
▲ Company Limited by Guarantee
○ *T; to promote the use of computers in the construction industry by advising all concerned
● Conf - Mtgs - ET - Exhib - Comp - SG - Inf - Lib - VE - Evaluation of software - Consultancy - Feasibility studies - Market research
< Intl Fedn Nat Construction Computer Users Gps
M 380 f, UK / 46 f, o'seas
¶ CICA Bulletin - 4; ftm only.
 Evaluation reports; Survey reports; prices vary.
 Publication list available.

Construction Industry Council (CIC) 1987

NR The Building Centre, 26 Store St, LONDON, WC1E 7BT. (hq)
 020 7399 7400 fax 020 7399 7425
 email cic@cic.org.uk http://www.cic.org.uk
 Chief Exec: Graham Watts
▲ Company Limited by Guarantee
○ *N, *T; to represent organisations in the built environment & to provide a forum for discussion, particularly for professional bodies
● Conf - Mtgs - Res - Inf - LG
M 34 full, 15 associate, 17 affiliate
¶ AR. Publications list available on website.

Construction Industry Federation

IRL Construction House, Canal Rd, DUBLIN 6, Republic of Ireland.
 353 (1) 406 6000 fax 353 (1) 496 6953
 email cif@cif.ie http://www.cif.ie
 Dir Gen: Tom Parlon
Br 13
○ *T
M c 3,000

Construction Industry Information Group (CIIG) 1962

NR 1 Ridgewood Drive, SUTTON COLDFIELD, W Midlands, B75 6TR. (mem s/p)
 http://www.ciig.org.uk
 Mem Sec: Paul James
○ *N, *P; to promote good practice in construction libraries & information services
Gp Freelance librarians
● Conf - VE
M 180 i
¶ NL - 12; Review - irreg; LM - 1; all ftm only.

© CBD Research Ltd · Beckenham · BR3 5JS · Tel 020 8650 7745 · Fax 020 8650 0768 · E-mail cbd@cbdresearch.com · www.cbdresearch.com

Construction Industry Research & Information Association (CIRIA)   1960

NR   Classic House, 174-180 Old St, LONDON, EC1V 9BP. (hq)
     020 7549 3300 fax 020 7253 0523
     email enquiries@ciria.org   http://www.ciria.org
     Chief Exec: Tim Broyd
▲   Company Limited by Guarantee
○   *Q; 'best practice research into issues relating to construction & the environment'
Gp Construction Ind Envt Forum (CIEF); Construction Productivity Network (CPN)
●   Conf - Mtgs - ET - Res
M   70 f, 500 subscribers
¶   Publications list available.

Construction Industry Trade Alliance   (CITA)

NR   PO Box 97, CARMARTHEN, SA31 1WT.
     0870 066 4404 fax 0870 066 4405
     email enquiries@cita.co.uk   http://www.cita.co.uk
     Gen Mgr: Tony Crosbie
○   *T; for builders & allied tradesmen within the contruction industry

Construction Industry Trading Electronically

this company is closing down ,please delete - June 2008

Construction Packed Products Association
    a product association of the **British Precast Concrete Federation**

Construction Plant-hire Association   (CPA)   1941

■   27-28 Newbury St, Barbican, LONDON, EC1A 7HU. (hq)
     020 7796 3366 fax 020 7796 3399
     email enquiries@cpa.uk.net   http://www.cpa.uk.net
     Chief Exec: Colin Wood
▲   Un-incorporated Society
○   *T; to represent the interests of plant hirers nationally
Gp Rail Plant Association; British Concrete Pumping Group
     Special Interest Groups: Construction hoist, Crane, Powered access, Shoring technology, Tower crane
●   Conf - Mtgs - Stat - Inf - LG
<   Intl Powered Access Fedn; Construction Confedn; Freight Transport Assn
>   Intl Powered Access Fedn
M   1,410 f
¶   The Bulletin - 4; free.   Plant Finder - 1; ftm, £30 nm.

Construction Products Association   (CPA)   2000

■   The Building Centre, 26 Store St, LONDON, WC1E 7BT. (hq)
     020 7323 3770 fax 020 7323 0307
     email enquiries@constructionproducts.org.uk
     http://www.constructionproducts.org.uk
     Chief Exec: Michael Ankers
▲   Company Limited by Guarantee
○   *N, *T; to represent the UK's manufacturers & suppliers of products to the construction industry
Gp Construction products manufacturers & distributors
●   Conf - Mtgs - Res - Exhib - Stat - Inf - LG
<   Coun of Eur Producers of Materials for Construction; CBI
M   22 f, 40 trade assns, 7 associates, 7 affiliates
¶   Construction Industry Forecasts - 2.
     Construction Markets Trends - 12.
     Construction Products Trade Survey - 4.
     Construction Products Briefing - 6.
     Weekly Notes - 52.   AR.

Construction Specialists Group

NR   1 Walpole House, 2 Pickford St, ALDERSHOT, Hants, GU11 1TZ.
     01252 312122 fax 01252 343081
     email constructiongroup@btconnect.com
○   *T; manufacturers, suppliers & installers of advanced systems & components, working for main contractors, owners & stakeholders
     This group includes the long standing Confederation of Construction Specialists & 2 organisations formed in 2001 - the Institute of Construction Specialists & the Construction Specialists Academy.
     The Confederation represents the interests of specialist construction companies;
     the Institute serves the interests of construction staff, & offers professional qualifications for management; the Academy 'provides contractual training needs of Institute candidates & general training needs of companies'.

Consumer Complaints Group
    a group of **Food & Drink Industry Ireland**

Consumer Credit Association   (CCA)   1978

NR   Queens House, Queens Rd, CHESTER, CH1 3BQ. (hq)
     01244 312044
     email cca@ccauk.org   http://www.ccauk.org
     Dir: Jack Bennett
▲   Company Limited by Guarantee
○   *T; 'main representative trade association for the home credit industry'
●   Conf - Mtgs - ET - SG - Inf - VE - LG - Provide regulated credit agreements & other documentation
<   Consumer Credit Assn (Republic of Ireland)
M   500 f
¶   CCA News - 4; ftm, £7.50 nm.   LM - 1; ftm only.   AR; free.
     Distributors of PSI Report.
     Note: Credit Consumer Association & CCA are trading names of CCA (UK) Advisory Services Ltd

Consumer Credit Trade Association   (CCTA)   1891

■   The Wave (suite 4), 1 View Croft Rd, SHIPLEY, W Yorks, BD17 7DU. (hq)
     0845 257 1166
     email info@ccta.co.uk   http://www.ccta.co.uk
     Chief Exec: Chris Oakes
▲   Company Limited by Guarantee
○   *T; to support businesses involved in consumer credit
●   Conf - Mtgs - ET - Res - Inf - LG
<   Eur Fedn of Finance House Assns (EUROFINAS)
M   20 i, 450 f
¶   Consumer Credit - 6; £24 m, £39 yr nm.
     Information leaflet - 6.

Consumer Electronics Distributors Association   (CEDA)

IRL Confederation House, 84/86 Lower Baggot St, DUBLIN 2, Republic of Ireland.
     353 (1) 605 1582 fax 353 (1) 638 1582
     email ceda@ibec.ie
     Dir: Tommy McCabe
○   *T
<   IBEC

Consumer Focus

NR   Artillery House (4th floor), Artillery Row, LONDON, SW1P 1RT.
     020 7799 7900

Consumer Health Information Consortium
    in December 2005 merged with the **Patient Information Forum**

Consumer Protection Association   (CPA)

NR   CPA House, 11 North Bridge St, SHEFFORD, Beds,
       SG17 5DQ.   (hq)
       01462 850062   fax 01462 817161
       email helpline@thecpa.co.uk   http://www.thecpa.co.uk
▲   Company Limited by Guarantee
○   *T; consumer protection; insurance backed guarantees

Consumers' Association   (CA)   1957

■   2 Marylebone Rd, LONDON, NW1 4DF.   (hq)
       020 7770 7000   fax 020 7770 7600
       email editor@which.co.uk   http://www.which.co.uk
       Chief Exec: Peter Vicary Smith,   Co Sec: Andrew Reading
▲   Registered Charity
○   *K, *Q; independent research & testing of consumer products &
       services; results published by CA's trading subsidiary Which?
       Ltd; campaigning on behalf of consumers
●   Res - Inf - Comparative testing of consumer goods & services
<   Consumers Us Intl; Bureau Européen des Unions de
       Consommateurs (BEUC)
M   982,000 i
¶   Which? - 12.   Which? Holiday - 4.
       Which? Gardening - 10.
       Which? Money - 12.   Which? Money - 6.
       Consumer Policy Review - 6.

Consumers Association of Ireland Ltd   1966

IRL   43-44 Chelmsford Rd, Ranelagh, DUBLIN 6, Republic of
       Ireland.
       353 (1) 497 8600
       email cai@consumerassociation.ie
       http://www.consumerassociation.ie
       Chief Exec: Dermott Jewell
○   *K

Consumers for Health Choice   1995

NR   Southbank House, Black Prince Rd, LONDON, SE1 7SJ.
       020 7463 0690
       http://www.healthchoice.org.uk
○   *K; for the right of consumers to have ready access to a wide
       range of natural health products, including vitamin & mineral
       supplements and health remedies.
M   i & f

Contact the Elderly   1965

■   15 Henrietta St, LONDON, WC2E 8QG.   (hq)
       020 7240 0630   fax 020 7379 5781
       email info@contact-the-elderly.org.uk
       http://www.contact-the-elderly.org.uk
       Dir: Roderick Sime
▲   Registered Charity
Br   280
○   *W; to alleviate the loneliness & isolation in people over 75 by
       promoting volunteer-led social groups meeting monthly
●   Mtgs
M   4,500 i
¶   Contact News (NL) - 2; free.   AR - 1.

Container Handling Equipment Manufacturers' Association
(CHEM)   1969

■   Hinchley, The Highlands, Painswick, STROUD, Glos, GL6 6SL.
       01452 814812   fax 01452 814812
       email enquiries@chem.uk.com
       http://www.chem.uk.com
       Technical Sec: David H Buxton
▲   Un-incorporated Society
○   *T; 'vehicles & equipment for the collection, transportation &
       handling of dry waste: to create standards for the interface of
       equipment with containers & to promote safe operations; to
       participate in the drafting of standards for equipment used in
       the collection & transportation of dry waste'
Gp   Technical c'ees for refuse collection vehicles (RCVs) of all types;
       skip loaders, hook loaders, static compactors
●   Mtgs - LG (DTI & Dept of Transport) - Liaison with standards
       institutes BSI & CEN
M   26 f

Contemporary Art Society   (CAS)   1910

NR   11-15 Emerald St, LONDON, WC1N 3QL.   (hq)
       020 7831 1243   fax 020 7831 1214
       email cas@contempart.org.uk
       http://www.contempart.org.uk
       Dir: Gill Hedley
▲   Company Limited by Guarantee; Registered Charity
○   *A; to acquire works of art by living artists for gift to public art
       galleries & museums; to promote collecting by individuals &
       companies
●   Exhib - VE
M   700 i, 96 org, UK / 100 i, o'seas
¶   NL - 2;   Events NL - 2;   AR - 1.

Contemporary Art Society for Wales   (CASW)   1937

■   Yr Hen Squbor, The Old Barn, FLEMINGSTON, Glamorgan,
       CF62 4QJ.   (memsec/p)
       http://www.casw.org.uk
       Mem Sec: Bernard Rees
▲   Registered Charity
○   *A; the purchase of contemporary art for free distribution to
       public galleries & museums throughout Wales
M   i, f, org

Contemporary Glass Society   (CGS)   1997

NR   c/o Broadfield House Glass Museum, Compton Drive,
       KINGSWINFORD, W Midlands, DY6 9NS.   (mail/address)
       01603 507737   fax 01603 507737
       email admin@cgs.org.uk   http://www.cgs.org.uk
       Admin: Pam Reekie
▲   Un-incorporated Society
○   *A; 'to encourage excellence in glass as a creative medium; to
       develop a greater public awareness & appreciation of
       contemporary glass world wide; for all those involved with
       glass in an artistic, technological, manufacturing &
       supportive capacity'
Gp   Glass makers
●   Conf - Mtgs - ET - Exhib
M   305 i, 15 f, UK / 10 i, o'seas
¶   Glass Network (NL) - 4; ftm only.

ContinYou   1992

NR   31-33 Bondway, Vauxhall, LONDON, SW8 1SJ.
       020 8709 9900   fax 020 8709 9933
       http://www.continyou.org.uk
       Chief Exec: Laurence Blackhall
○   to create learning opportunities
✕   2003 (Community Education Development Centre
       Education Extra

© CBD Research Ltd · Beckenham · BR3 5JS · Tel 020 8650 7745 · Fax 020 8650 0768 · E-mail cbd@cbdresearch.com · www.cbdresearch.com

Contract Flooring Association Ltd   (CFA)   1973
■   4c St Mary's Place, The Lace Market, NOTTINGHAM,
      NG1 1PH.   (hq)
      0115-941 1126   fax 0115-941 2238
      email info@cfa.org.uk   http://www.cfa.org.uk
      Chief Exec: Richard Catt,   Office Mgr: Mrs H E Tidmarsh
○   *T; to further the progress of flooring technology by education
      of all concerned
Gp   Contractors; Manufacturers; Distributors & consultants:
      Adhesives, Carpets, Rubber, Vinyl, Cork, Linoleum, Raised
      modular, Resin
●   Conf - Mtgs - ET - Res - Exhib - Inf - Lib - Empl
<   Nat Specialist Contrs Coun (NSCC)
M   500 f, UK / 5 f, o'seas
¶   The Contract Flooring Jnl - 10; ftm, £30 yr nm.

Contract Heat Treatment Association
      a group of the **Surface Engineering Association**

Contractor Support on Deployed Operations
      a group of the **Defence Manufacturers Association**

Contractors Mechanical Plant Engineers   (CMPE)   1957
■   c/o EA-Direct Ltd, 128 Arkleston Rd, PAISLEY, PA1 3TZ.   (usa)
      0870 720 2502   fax 0870 762 7332
      http://www.cmpe.co.uk
      Nat Sec: Wendy Pitches
▲   Un-incorporated Society
Br   15
○   *L; all aspects of mechanical plant used in the construction &
      building industries
●   Conf - Mtgs - ET
M   [not stated]

*Controls Manufacturers Association incorporating the Domestic Heating
      Controls Group*
      an association in the Energy section of **BEAMA Ltd**

Convenience Stores & Newsagents Association   (CSNA)   1988
IRL   Market Square, KILDARE TOWN, Co Kildare, Republic of
      Ireland.
      353 (45) 535051   fax 353 (45) 530016
      email info@csna.ie   http://www.csna.ie
      Chief Exec: Vincent Jennings
○   *T
✕   2006 (May) Irish Retail Newsagents Association

Convention of Scottish Local Authorities   (COSLA)   1975
NR   9 Haymarket Terrace, EDINBURGH, EH12 5XZ.   (hq)
      0131-474 9200   fax 0131-474 9292
      email enquiries@cosla.gov.uk   http://www.cosla.gov.uk
○   *N; the association for local authorities in Scotland
M   Councils in Scotland

Cookshop & Housewares Association
      a group of the **British Hardware Federation**

Copper Development Association   (CDA)   1933
■   5 Grovelands Business Centre, Boundary Way,
      HEMEL HEMPSTEAD, Herts, HP2 7TE.   (hq)
      fax 01442 275716
      email mail@copperdev.co.uk   http://www.cda.org.uk
      Dir & Co Sec: Angela Vessey
▲   Company Limited by Guarantee
○   *T; promotion of the correct use of copper & copper alloys
Gp   Brass Advisory Service; Copper Club; Copper in Architecture;
      Power Quality Partnership; UK Copper Board
●   Conf - Exhib - Comp - Inf - PL
<   Intl Copper Assn; Eur Copper Inst
M   8 f, UK / 2 f, o'seas

Coracle Society   1990
NR   3 Back Lane, Wereham, KING'S LYNN, Norfolk, PE33 9BB.
      (chmn/b)
      01366 500867
      email conwyrichards@hotmail.com
      http://www.coracle-fishing.net
      Chmn: Conwy Richards
▲   Un-incorporated Society
○   *G, *L; to promote the knowledge of coracles & allied craft,
      their making, use & study; to support the continuance of
      coracle fishing; to encourage the craft of coracle building
●   ET (courses) - Exhib - Comp - VE - Demonstrations - Seaboat
      construction - Use of hides as 'skin'
M   120 i, UK / 10 i, o'seas
¶   NL - 1; ftm only.

Cork Chamber of Commerce   1820
IRL   Fitzgerald House, Summerhill North, CORK, Republic of
      Ireland.
      353 (21) 450 9044   fax 353 (21) 450 8568
      email info@corkchamber.ie   http://www.corkchamber.ie
      Chief Exec: Conor Healy
○   *C

Cork Industry Federation   (CIF)   1966
■   13 Felton Lea, SIDCUP, Kent, DA14 6BA.   (hsp)
      020 8302 4801   fax 020 8302 4801
      http://www.cork-products.co.uk
      Hon Sec: Mrs Joy Bell
○   *N, *T; the umbrella organisation for all aspects of cork in the
      UK; decorative cork for floors & walls; industrial &
      construction materials (cork based); cork closures for wine &
      drinks industry
●   Mtgs - Res
<   Confédn Européenne du Liège
M   16 f
¶   LM.

Cornish Chamber of Mines & Minerals   (CCMM)   1917
■   Old Mine Offices, Wheal Jane, Baldhu, TRURO, Cornwall,
      TR3 6EE.   (regd/office/hsb)
      01872 560200   fax 01872 562000
      Sec: B J Ballard
▲   Company Limited by Guarantee
○   *T; to promote & protect mining (incl china clay & stone) in
      Cornwall & Devon
Gp   Legislation
●   Mtgs
<   CBI
M   15 i, 6 f, 2 org
¶   AR; ftm.

Cornish Language Board
      English name of **Kesva an Taves Kernewek**

Cornish Language Council (Cussel an Tavas Kernuack)   1988
NR   25 Hurland Rd, TRURO, Cornwall, TR1 2BU.   (hsp)
      01872 262667
      Sec: Mina Dresser
▲   Un-incorporated Society
○   *G, *K; to promote the Cornish language & research its past

Cornish Mining Development Association   (CMDA)   1948
NR   Roundway, Sennen, PENZANCE, Cornwall, TR19 7AW.   (hsp)
      Hon Gen Sec: Dr K Russ
○   *T; to encourage, develop & protect the metalliferous mining
      industry of GB particularly in Devon & Cornwall
M   c 150 i, f & org
¶   AR.

Cornish Pasty Association   (CPA)
NR   Cornwall Taste of the West, 7 The Courtyard, Trewolland Farm,
        LISKEARD, Cornwall, PL14 3NL.
        01579 349363
        Mgr: Angela Coombs
○   *T; Cornish pasty manufacturers & bakers
M   54 f
        no further information supplied

Cornwall Archaeological Society   (CAS)   1961
■   8 Minster Fields, Manaccan, HELSTON, Cornwall, TR12 6JG.
        (hsp)
        01326 231553
        http://www.cornisharchaeology.org.uk
        Hon Sec: Sallyann Stewart Ealey
▲   Registered Charity
○   *E, *L
Gp   Cornwall branch of Young Archaeolgists Club
●   Conf - Mtgs - ET - Res - VE
M   520 i, 2 org, UK / 20 i, o'seas
¶   Cornish Archaeology (Jnl) - 1; ftm, £20 nm.
        NL - 3; ftm only.

Cornwall Chamber of Commerce & Industry   (CCCI)   1988
NR   West Cornwall Enterprise Centre, Cardrew, REDRUTH,
        Cornwall, TR15 1SS.   (hq)
        01209 216006   fax 01209 765164
        email chamber@ccci.org.uk   http://www.ccci.org.uk
        Dir of Operations: Lyn Morris
▲   Company Limited by Guarantee
○   *C; to support Cornish industry
Gp   Export; Training courses; Information provision
●   Conf - Mtgs - ET - Expt - Inf - Lib - LG
<   Brit Chams Comm
M   160 f
¶   NL - 4; free.

Coronary Artery Disease Research Association   (CORDA)   1975
■   Chelsea Square, LONDON, SW3 6NP.   (hq)
        020 7349 8686   fax 020 7349 9414
        email corda@rbht.nhs.uk   http://www.corda.org.uk
        Exec Dir & Sec: Jennifer Jenks
▲   Company Limited by Guarantee; Registered Charity
○   *Q; to support high quality clinical research into the prevention
        of heart attacks & strokes through non-invasive techniques
●   Res

Coroners' Society of England & Wales   1846
NR   HM Coroner's Court, The Cotton Exchange, Old Hall St,
        LIVERPOOL, L3 9UF.   (hsb)
        0151-233 4708
        http://www.coroner.org.uk
        Hon Sec: André J A Rebello
▲   Un-incorporated Society
○   *P
●   Conf - Mtgs - Empl - LG
¶   Annual Report & Directory; m only.

Corporate Event Association
        in 2005 merged with the Incentive Travel & Meetings Association to
        form **Eventia Ltd**

Corporate Responsibility Coalition   (CORE)
NR   26-28 Underwood St, LONDON, N1 7JQ.
        020 7566 1665   fax 020 7490 0881
○   *K, *N; 'calling on the UK government to enact laws that will
        ensure making profits is done within the context of
        businesses' responsibilities to their stakeholders . . . are
        sustainable long-term'

Corporation of Insurance, Financial & Mortgage Advisers Ltd   (CIFMA)   1968
NR   5 Ollersett Lane, NEW MILLS, High Peak, Derbys, SK22 4JE.
        (hq)
        01663 746742
        Gen Sec: George Rogers
▲   Company Limited by Guarantee
○   *P, *T; for all practitioners in the insurance, mortgage &
        healthcare industry
●   Conf - Res - Inf - LG
M   c 700 i, c 300 f
¶   News & Views - irreg.   NL - 6.

Corps of Drums Society   1977
■   103 Clare Lane, EAST MALLING, Kent, ME19 6JB.   (hsp)
        01732 845207
        email info@corpsofdrums   http://www.corpsofdrums.com
        Hon Sec: Mrs Christine Fairfax
▲   Registered Charity
○   *D; to promote & preserve the tradition of drum & fife/flute
        music as demonstrated in the infantry of the British Army
●   Mtgs - ET
M   250 i, 2 f, 34 org, UK / 17 i, o'seas
¶   Drummers Call (Jnl) - 2; ftm, £3 nm.   NL - irreg; ftm.

Corrosion Prevention Association   (CPA)   1992
■   Tournai Hall, Evelyn Woods Rd, ALDERSHOT, Hants, GU11 2LL.
        01252 357843   fax 01252 357831
        email cpa@associationhouse.org.uk
        http://www.corrosionprevention.org.uk
        Sec: John Fairley
▲   Company Limited by Guarantee
○   *P
●   Seminars - Workshops
M   27 f
¶   Brochure;   LM (with areas of expertise);
        Special Feature Supplement;   all free.
        Reinforced Concrete: History, Properties & Durability; £5.
        Cathodic Protection of Reinforced Concrete: Status Report; £35.

Corrugated Packaging Association
        since 2004 the Corrugated Sector of the **Confederation of Paper
        Industries**

COSCA (Counselling & Psychotherapy in Scotland)   (COSCA)   1990
NR   16 Melville Terrace, STIRLING, FK8 2NE.   (hq)
        01786 475140
        email info@cosca.org.uk   http://www.cosca.org.uk
        Chief Exec: Brian Magee
▲   Company Limited by Guarantee; Registered Charity
○   *N, *W; to coordinate & promote development of training &
        good practice in counselling in Scotland; to encourage
        communication & cooperation between agencies &
        individuals engaged in similar activities
Gp   Gps who perform counselling services; Gps whose work
        includes some counselling skills
●   Conf - Mtgs - ET - LG
<   Eur Assn for Counselling
M   org
¶   Counselling in Scotland - 4; ftm, subscription nm.

Cosmetic, Toiletry & Perfumery Association Ltd   (CTPA)   1945
- ■ Josaron House, 5-7 John Princes St, LONDON, W1G 0JN.
     (hq)
     020 7491 8891   fax 020 7493 8061
     email info@ctpa.org.uk   http://www.ctpa.org.uk
     Co Sec: D A Hunter
- ▲ Company Limited by Guarantee
- ○ *T; representing cosmetic, toiletry & perfumery manufacturers,
     raw materials suppliers & contract services in the UK -
     technical & legislative advice member service only
- Gp Technical: Environment, Legal, Oral care, Packaging, Perfumery
     Scientific: Analytical, Cosmetic colourants, Cosmetic
       ingredients, Environmental legislation, Toxicology, Talc,
       (+c10 others)
- ● Conf - Mtgs - Expt - LG
- < Eur Cosmetic Tr Assn (COLIPA); CBI
- M 140 f
- ¶ NL - 12; ftm only.   Join Us;   AR; both free.
     Publications list available.

Costume Society   1966
- ■ c/o Moore Stephens, St Paul's House, 8 Warwick Lane,
     LONDON, EC4P 4BN.   (asa)
     http://www.costumesociety.org.uk
     Hon Sec: J Salen
- ▲ Registered Charity
- ○ *L; to promote the study of costume & its history; to help in the
     preservation of significant examples of historical &
     contemporary dress
- Gp Sub-c'ees: Programme, Symposium
- ● Conf - VE - Awards
- M 700 i, 100 libraries, UK / 150 i, 200 org, o'seas
- ¶ Costume (Jnl) - 1; £24.   NL - 2; ftm only.

Costume Society of Scotland   (CSS)   1965
- ■ 18 Grierson Crescent, EDINBURGH, EH5 2AX.   (hsp)
     0131-552 4968
     email cossocscotland@hotmail.com
     http://www.costumesocietyofscotland.org
     Chmn: Catriona Smyth
- ▲ Un-incorporated Society
- ○ *G, *L; to promote interest in, & study of, costume
- ● Mtgs - Exhib - VE
- < Costume Soc; Canadian Costume Museum & Archives of BC;
     Northern Soc of Costume & Textiles; Textile Soc; Cymdeithas
     Gwisgoedd a Thecstilau Cymru
- M 89 i, 6 museums etc, UK / 3 i, o'seas
- ¶ Bulletin - 1; ftm only.

Cot Death Society
   in 2004 activities were absorbed by the **Foundation for the Study
   of Infant Deaths**

Cotswold Sheep Society   1891
- ■ Hampton Rise, 1 High St, MEYSEY HAMPTON, Glos,
     GL7 5JE.   (hsb)
     01285 851197
     email info@cotswoldsheepsociety.co.uk
     http://www.cotswoldsheepsociety.co.uk
     Sec: Mrs Lucinda Foster
- ▲ Registered Charity
- ○ *B; conservation of the rare breed
- ● Mtgs - Exhib - Stat - Inf - Breeder workshops
- M 170 i, 8 org, UK / 5 i, o'seas
- ¶ NL - 4; ftm.   AR.
     Flock Book (incl LM) - 1; ftm, £3.50 nm.

Cottage Garden Society   (CGS)   1982
- NR Brandon, Main Rd, Betley, CREWE, Cheshire, CW3 9BH.
     (admin/p)
     01270 820940
     Admin: Clive Lane
- ▲ Un-incorporated Society
- ○ *H; to promote interest in cottage gardens & cottage garden
     plants
- M i

COUNCIL . . .
   For details of official & non-official councils, other than those
     listed below, see our companion volume **Councils,
     Committees & Boards** (note in introduction paragraph 6)

**Council for the Advancement of Arab-British Understanding
(CAABU)   1967**
- NR 1 Gough Square, LONDON, EC4A 3DE.   (hq)
     020 7832 1310   fax 020 7832 1329
     email caabu@caabu.org   http://www.caabu.org
     Dir & Chief Exec: Chris Doyle
- ▲ Company Limited by Guarantee
- ○ *X; 'Arab-British relations, Israel-Palestine, Iraq, War on Terror'
- Gp Education section (gives talks to schools); Parliamentary;
     Membership
- ● Conf - Mtgs - ET - Res - Exhib - Inf - LG
- ¶ Jnl - 6; £12 yr m, £20 yr nm.
     AR - 1; both free.

Council for Aluminium in Building   (CAB)   1995
- ■ Bank House, Bond's Mill, STONEHOUSE, Glos, GL10 3RF.
     (hq)
     01453 828851   fax 01453 828861
     http://www.c-a-b.org.uk
     Chief Exec: Justin Ratcliffe
- ▲ Company Limited by Guarantee
- ○ *T; to represent all companies who use aluminium products in,
     or supply to, the construction industry
- Gp Fabricators & installers; System companies; Specialist suppliers;
     General suppliers
- ● Conf - Mtgs - ET - Inf - LG
- < Construction Products Assn
- M 10,000 i, 100 f
- ¶ NL.   LM - updated.
     Technical publications; £10 m, £20 nm.

Council of British Archaeology   (CBA)   1944
- ■ St Mary's House, 66 Bootham, YORK, YO30 7BZ.   (hq)
     01904 671417   fax 01904 671384
     email info@britarch.ac.uk   http://www.britarch.ac.uk
     Dir: Dr Mike Heyworth
- ▲ Company Limited by Guarantee; Registered Charity
- Br 13
- ○ *G, *L, *N; to advance the study & care of Britain's historic
     environment; to improve public awareness of Britain's past
- Gp Research & conservation; Education; Publication; Industrial
     archaeology panel; Young archaeologists' club
- ● Conf - Mtgs - ET - Res - Exhib - Comp - Inf - Lib - VE - LG
- < Eur Forum of Heritage Assns
- M 6,000 i, 505 org, UK / 300 i, o'seas
- ¶ British Archaeology - 6; ftm, £25 yr nm.
     British & Irish Archaeological Bibliography - 2; free.
     Publications catalogue available.

Council on Commercial Diplomacy
   a group of the **Association of Certified Commercial Diplomats**

Council of Cricket Societies   (CofCS)   1969
NR   2 Jodrell Rd, WHALEY BRIDGE, High Peak, Derbys,
        SK23 7AN.   (hsp)
        01663 732866
        Hon Sec: Bob Wood
Br   25; Australia, New Zealand, South Africa, Zimbabwe
○   *S; to maintain interest in cricket during the 'off-season' period
●   Mtgs - Inviting speakers to address societies
M   c 3,000 i, UK / 1,000 i, o'seas
¶   NL - 1; ftm only.   NL of individual socs - irreg; free.

Council for Dance Education & Training (UK)   (CDET)   1978
■   Old Brewer's Yard, 17-19 Neal St, LONDON, WC2H 9UY.
        (hq)
        020 7240 5703   fax 020 7240 2547
        email info@cdet.org.uk   http://www.cdet.org.uk
        Dir: Sean Williams
▲   Company Limited by Guarantee; Registered Charity
○   *D; 'to advance the education of all persons & principally
        children, young people & students, in the art, practice &
        appreciation of the cultural significance of dance; to promote
        high standards in dance education & training'
Gp   Teaching society c'ee; Negotiation Board; Conference of
        Professional Dance Schools
●   Conf - Mtgs - ET - Res - Stat - Inf - LG - Accreditation &
        assessment service
M   20 i, 30 org
¶   UK Directory of Registered Dance Teachers - 1; ftm.
        Information sheets on dance education & training.
        AR - 1; ftm only.

Council of Docked Breeds   (CDB)   1991
NR   Marsburg, Whitehall Lane, THORPE le SOKEN, Essex,
        CO16 0AE.   (hsp/b)
        0700 078 1262
        email info@cdb.org   http://www.cdb.org
        Sec: Mrs Ginette Elliott
▲   Un-incorporated Society
○   *B, *V; to maintain the freedom of dog breeders to choose the
        docking option; to support the interests of owners & breeders
        (of traditional docked dog breeds) to government, the
        veterinary profession, the media & other interested parties
●   Inf - LG
<   is the UK branch of the Fedn of Field Sports Assns of the
        EU (FACE UK)
M   15,000 i, 500 socs
¶   Action pack sent on initial joining.

**Council of Gas Detection & Environmental Monitoring
(COGDEM)   1975**
■   Unit 11 Theobald Business Park, Knowle Piece, Wilbury Way,
        HITCHIN, Herts, SG4 0TY.   (hq)
        01462 434322   fax 01462 434488
        email cogdem@aol.com   http://www.cogdem.org.uk
        Admin: Leigh Greenham
▲   Company Limited by Guarantee
○   *T; to safeguard the standards of, & expand the market for, gas
        detection, gas analysis & environmental monitoring
        equipment & services
Gp   Sub-groups: Carbon monoxide, Industrial
●   Mtgs - ET - Exam - Exhib - SG - Stat - Inf - Lib - LG
M   33 f, 2 org, UK / 2 f, o'seas

Council for Hospitality Management Education   (CHME)   1979
■   School of Services Management, Bournemouth University,
        Talbot Campus, Fern Barrow, POOLE, Dorset, BH12 5BB.
        (chmn/b)
        Chmn: Prof Nigel Hemmington
▲   Un-incorporated Society
○   *E; to enhance the professional development & status of
        hospitality management education
Gp   Industrial tutors; Learning teaching & assessment; Placement
        Advisers for Tourism & Hospitality (PATH); Research
●   Conf - Mtgs - ET - Res - Comp - Inf - LG - Lobbying
<   Coun of Australian University Tourism & Hospitality
        Educ (CAUTHE); Nordic Tourism Res Assn (NOTRA)
M   1i, 28 universities & colleges, UK / 3 i, o'seas
¶   A Review of Hospitality Management Education in the UK - 1;
        ftm, £25 nm.
        AR - 1; free.

Council of Hunting Associations   (CHA)   2001
NR   The Hunting Office, The Old School, Bagendon, CIRENCESTER,
        Glos, GL7 7DU.
        01285 831470
        Sec: Brian Fanshawe
○   *K; to promote & protect the interests of those who hunt with
        dogs within the law
M   11 org

Council for Independent Archaeology   1989
NR   2 The Watermeadows, Swarkestone, DERBY, Derbys,
        DE73 7FX.   (hsp)
        01332 704148
        email skfoster@btopenworld.com
        http://www.independents.org.uk
        Hon Sec: Keith Foster
▲   Registered Charity; Un-incorporated Society
○   *L; the promotion of archaeology independent of government,
        especially amateur archaeology
●   Conf - Mtgs - ET - Res - Inf - VE - LG
M   200 i, UK / 20 i, o'seas
¶   NL - 4; ftm only.

Council for Independent Education
        alternative name of **CIFE**

Council for Independent Further Education
        since 2006 **CIFE - Council for Independent Education**

Council of Mortgage Lenders   (CML)   1989
NR   North West Wing, Bush House, Aldwych, LONDON,
        WC2B 4PJ.   (hq)
        0845 373 6771   fax 0845 373 6778
        http://www.cml.org.uk
▲   Un-incorporated Society
○   *T; interests of the UK residential mortgage market
●   Conf - Mtgs - ET - Res - Stat - Inf - Lib - LG
        Consumer information: 020 7438 8956
M   151 f
¶   [all on website]

Council of Organisations Registering Homeopaths
        organisation ceased

© CBD Research Ltd · Beckenham · BR3 5JS · Tel 020 8650 7745 · Fax 020 8650 0768 · E-mail cbd@cbdresearch.com · www.cbdresearch.com

Council for Registered Gas Installers (CORGI) 1991
NR 1 Elmwood, Chineham Park, Crockford Lane, BASINGSTOKE,
       Hants, RG24 8WG.   (hq)
       01256 372300
       email enquiries@corgi-group.com
       http://www.corgi-gas-safety.com
       Chief Exec: Mike Thompson,   Co Sec: Philippa Caine
▲ Company Limited by Guarantee
○ *T; the national watchdog for gas safety
● Inf - LG - Inspection of registered businesses - Dealing with
       customer complaints regarding gas safety - Gas safety
       publicity - Nationally accredited certification scheme for
       individual gas fitting operatives
M 52,000 f
¶ Gas Installer Magazine - 11; ftm.
       AR; free.

**Council for the Registration of Schools Teaching Dyslexic Pupils
(CReSTeD) 1993**
■ Greygarth, Littleworth, Winchcombe, CHELTENHAM, Glos,
       GL54 5BT.   (regd/office)
       01242 604852
       email admin@crested.org.uk   http://www.crested.org.uk
       Admin: Christine Hancock
▲ Registered Charity
○ *W; to register schools & other educational institutions
       providing facilities for & care of dyslexic pupils (those with
       learning difficulties)
● Mtgs - Inf
< Brit Dyslexia Assn; Dyslexia Action
M 85 schools
¶ Register of Schools that help Dyslexic Children - 1; free.

Council for Scottish Archaeology
       since 2008 **Archaeology Scotland**

Counselling 1998
■ 5 Pear Tree Walk, WAKEFIELD, W Yorks, WF2 0HW.   (regd off)
       email trustees@counselling.ltd.uk
       http://www.counselling.ltd.uk
       Dir: Yanina Ratcliffe (charity co-ordinator)
▲ Company Limited by Guarantee; Registered Charity
○ *W; to provide free counselling to those on low income
       throughout the UK; to maintain a website of counselling
       colleges & counselling related matters
● ET - Exam - Res - Stat - Inf
M 2,500 i, c 250 f
¶ Counselling NL - 12;   LM (website);   AR - 1; all free.

Counselling Children & Young People
       a group of the **British Association for Counselling &
Psychotherapy**

Country Doctors Association (CDA) 1998
NR 17 Symonds Rd, HITCHIN, Herts, SG5 2JJ.   (chmn/p)
       01462 434515
       http://www.countrydoctor.co.uk
       Chmn: Dr David Roberts
▲ Un-incorporated Society
○ *M; education & welfare & promotion of country doctors & their
       staff
Gp Dispensing by doctors; Rural welfare; Rural diseases; Zoonoses
● ET - Res - Stat
M i & f
¶ www.countrydoctor.co.uk; daily updates (no password
       required).

Country Gentlemen's Association Ltd (CGA) 1893
§ Chalke House, Station Rd, Codford, WARMINSTER, Wilts,
       BA12 0JX.   (hq)
       01985 850706   fax 01985 850378
       email enquiries@thecga.co.uk
       http://www.thecga.co.uk
       Chief Exec: William Harrison-Allan
       Supplier of goods and materials for estates, households, farms
       and gardens; advisor on agricultural, tax, financial and
       insurance matters.

Country Land & Business Association (CLA) 1907
NR 16 Belgrave Sq, LONDON, SW1X 8PQ.   (hq)
       020 7235 0511   fax 020 7235 4696
       email mail@cla.org.uk   http://www.cla.org.uk
▲ Un-incorporated Society
○ *P; the national association of owners of rural land &
       businesses in England & Wales
M I

Countryside Alliance 1997
NR The Old Town Hall, 367 Kennington Rd, LONDON,
       SE11 4PT.   (hq)
       020 7840 9200   fax 020 7793 8484
       email info@countryside-alliance.org
       http://www.countryside-alliance.org
       Pres: Baroness Ann Mallalieu
▲ Un-incorporated Society
○ *K; to champion & campaign for country sports, the countryside
       & the rural way of life
Gp Specialist campaigns for: Angling, Coursing, Falconry,
       Fisheries, Hunting, Rural issues, Shooting
       Honest Food - the Campaign for Independent Food
● ET - Res - Stat - Inf - VE - LG
< Fedn Eur Field Sports Gps (FACE)
M 80,000 i, 1,500 f, 320,000 org
¶ Country Sports - 4; ftm.

Countryside Alliance Ireland
NR Larchfield Estate, Bailliesmills Road, LISBURN, Co Antrim,
       BT27 6XJ.
       028 9263 9911   fax 028 9263 9922
       http://www.caireland.org
○ campaigning for the countryside, country sports and the rural
       way of life

Countryside Ireland 1970
IRL 100 Ballygall Road East, Glasnevin, DUBLIN 11, Republic of
       Ireland.
       353 (1) 834 8279
       email secretary@countrysideireland.com
       http://www.countrysideireland.com
       Hon Sec: Philip E de N Lawton
○ *S

Countryside Management Association (CMA) 1966
■ Writtle College, Lordship Rd, Writtle, CHELMSFORD, Essex,
       CM1 3RR.   (hq)
       01245 424116   fax 01245 420456
       http://www.countrysidemanagement.org.uk
       Admin: Mike Anderson
○ *P; to promote professional & sustainable management of the
       countryside & urban greenspace
● Conf - Mtgs - ET - LG
M i
¶ Ranger - 4; ftm, £5 nm.

Countrywide Holidays Association
       the activities of the CHA have been transferred to the
       Countryside UK Trust, which is outside the scope of this
       Directory

County Antrim Agricultural Association (Ballymena Show) (CAAA) 1898
- ■ The Showgrounds, Warden St, BALLYMENA, Co Antrim, BT43 7DR.   (hq)
028 2565 2666   fax 028 2565 2666
email ballymena.showoffice@virgin.net
Sec: Mrs Jane Lamont
- ▲ Registered Charity
- ○ *F; to encourage the breeding of all classes of farm stock; the cultivation of farm crops & products; to encourage cottage industries, agricultural & horticultural education
- ● Exhib - Comp
- < Assn Show & Agricl Orgs; NI Shows' Assn
- M 450 i

County Armagh Wildlife Society   (CAWS) 1952
- ■ Drumherriff Lodge, 37 Old Orchard Rd, LOUGHALL, Co Armagh, BT61 8JD.   (hsp)
028 3889 1317
http://www.armaghwild.mysite.wanadoo-members.co.uk/index.jhtml
Hon Sec: Dr J S Faulkner
- ▲ Un-incorporated Society
- ○ *L; the study of the natural history, botany, zoology & geology of County Armagh & Ireland
- Gp Butterfly & moth recording on behalf of Ulster Wildlife Trust in local nature reserve
- ● Mtgs - Stat - Lib - VE
- M c 80 i, 1 org
- ¶ AR; ftm.   LM.

County Education Officers of Two Tier Authorities
- ■ c/o Graham Badman, Kent County Council, Sessions House, County Hall, MAIDSTONE, Kent, ME14 1XQ.
01622 696550
- ○ *E
No further information supplied

County Surveyors' Society
styles itself **CSS**

Coventry & District Archaeological Society   (CADAS) 1965
- NR c/o 86 Potters Green Rd, COVENTRY, Warks, CV2 2AN.   (sp)
http://www.covarch.org.uk
- ▲ Un-incorporated Society
- ○ *L; to promote archaeology in the Coventry area; to care for Coventry heritage

Coventry & Warwickshire Chamber of Commerce   1997
- ■ Oak Tree Court, Binley Business Park, Harry Weston Rd, COVENTRY, Warks, CV3 2UN.   (hq)
024 7665 4321   fax 024 7645 0242
email info@cw-chamber.co.uk
http://www.cw-chamber.co.uk
Chief Exec: Louise Bennett
- ▲ Company Limited by Guarantee
- Br Rugby, Coventry & South, Mid & Northern Warwickshire
- ○ *C
- Gp Retail; Engineering & manufacturing; Professional & commercial; Building & construction; Transport; Hotel & leisure; Education
- ● Conf - Mtgs - ET - Exams - Res - Exhib - Stat - Expt - Inf - Lib - LG
- < BCC
- M 2,300 f
- ¶ C & W In Business - 6;   Update - 6; both ftm.
AR - 1; free.

Covered Conductors Association
a group of the **British Cables Association**

CP Sport England & Wales
- ■ Unit 5 Heathcoat Bldg, Nottingham Science & Technology Park, University Boulevard, NOTTINGHAM, NG7 2QJ.   (hq)
0115-925 7027   fax 0115-922 4666
http://www.cpsport.org
- ○ *S; for sportspeople with cerebral palsy

Craft Brewing Association   1995
- NR 49 Belper Rd, DERBY, DE1 3EP.
01332 347601
- ○ *P, *T; to uphold the tradition of private brewing to the highest standards
- M i & f

Craft Guild of Chefs   (CFA) 1965
- NR 1 Victoria Parade, by 331 Sandycombe Rd, RICHMOND, Surrey, TW9 3NB.   (hq)
020 8948 3870   fax 020 8948 3944
http://www.craftguildofchefs.com
Sec: Suzanne Barshall
- ○ *P; to increase standards of professional cooking through greater awareness, education & training
- M i

Craft Guild of Traditional Bowyers & Fletchers   (CGTBF) 1988
- ■ Yew Corner, 29 Batley Court, OLDLAND, S Glos, BS30 8YZ.   (clerk/p)
0117 932 3276   fax 0117 932 3276
email guildclerk@btinternet.com
http://www.bowyersandfletchersguild.org
Clerk; Mrs V M Soar
- ▲ Un-incorporated Society
- ○ *P; a forum for all involved in the manufacture of quality, traditional archery equipment; to maintain & improve the standard of bow & arrow making
- Gp Bowyers; Fletchers; Arrowsmiths; Stringmakers
- ● Conf - ET (incl apprentices) - Exam (for apprentices & established craftsmen before membership)
- M 35 i, UK / 10 i, o'seas
- ¶ News Booklet - 2;   Bulletin - irreg; both ftm only.

Craft Potters' Association of Great Britain   (CPA) 1957
- NR 25 Foubert's Place, LONDON, W1F 7QF.   (hq)
020 7437 7601
email admin@cpaceramics.co.uk
http://www.cpaceramics.co.uk
Sec: Tony Ainsworth
- ▲ Company Limited by Guarantee; Registered Charity
- ○ *A; promotion of high quality, hand-made ceramics, particularly work of original design & individual character made by members
- ● Conf - Mtgs - Exhib - VE
- M 150 fellows, 600 associates, 200 professional, UK / 50 associates, o'seas
- ¶ Ceramic Review - 6.
CPA News - 6.   Potters - 2 yrly.

Cranio Sacral Society
- NR 6 Clinton Rd (lwr gd floor), REDRUTH, Cornwall, TR15 2QE.
01209 211078
email mail@cranio-sacral.org.uk
http://www.cranio-sacral.org.uk
Hon Pres: Dr John E Upledger
- ○ *P; for practitioners of the Upledger CranioSacral therapy
- M c 130 i

© CBD Research Ltd · Beckenham · BR3 5JS · Tel 020 8650 7745 · Fax 020 8650 0768 · E-mail cbd@cbdresearch.com · www.cbdresearch.com

Craniofacial Society of Great Britain   2001

NR c/o The Faculty of Surgery, Royal College of Surgeons, 35-43
    Lincoln's Inn Fields, LONDON, WC2A 3PE.   (hsb)
    020 7869 6802
    email honsec@cfsgb.org.uk   http://www.cfsgb.org.uk
    Hon Sec: Sue Mildinhall
▲ Company Limited by Guarantee; Registered Charity
○ *M, *P; for those concerned with cleft lip & palate & other
    craniofacial anomalies
Gp Plastic surgeons; Orthodontists; Speech therapists; Maxillofacial
    surgeons; Nurses
● Conf - Mtgs - ET - Res
M 300 i, UK / 20 i, o'seas

Craniofacial Support Group
    alternative name of **Headlines**

Craniosacral Therapy Association of the UK   (CSTA)   1990

■ Monomark House, 27 Old Gloucester St, LONDON,
    WC1N 3XX.   (mail/address)
    0700 078 4735
    email secretary@craniosacral.co.uk
    http://www.craniosacral.co.uk
    Sec: Roger R James
▲ Un-incorporated Society
○ *P; to disseminate information about craniosacral therapy; to
    regulate training organisations
● Conf - Mtgs - ET - Res - Inf - Maintain a register of qualified
    members
M 450 i, 5 org
¶ The Fulcrum - 3; ftm, £18.50 yr nm.

Creator's Rights Alliance   (CRA)   2000

NR British Music House, 26 Berners Street, LONDON, W1T 3LR.
    (hq)
    020 7436 7296
    Chmn: David Ferguson
▲ Un-incorporated Society
○ *N; an alliance of the major organisations representing
    copyright creators & content providers throughout the media,
    particularly television, radio & the press
● Conf - Mtgs - Inf - LG
M 14 orgs
¶ Between a Rock & a Hard Place (the problems facing freelance
    creators in the media market place).
    Creators Have Rights (Video).

Credit Protection Association plc   (CPA)   1914

■ CPA House, 350 King St, LONDON, W6 0RX.   (hq)
    020 8846 0000   fax 020 8741 7459
    email info@cpa.co.uk   http://www.cpa.co.uk
    Hon Sec: O M Holmes
    Chmn & Managing Dir: David S Baber
Br Bolton, Bristol, Birmingham, Knaresborough, Newmarket,
    Falkirk
○ *T; for credit management services & debt recovery online
● Inf
< American Collectors Assn (USA); Credit Services Assn (UK)
M 3,500 f
¶ Business Informer - irreg; free.

Credit Services Association   (CSA)   1902

■ Wingrove House (2nd floor east), Ponteland Rd,
    NEWCASTLE upon TYNE, NE5 3AJ.   (hq)
    0191-286 5656   fax 0191-286 0900
    email info@csa-uk.com   http://www.csa-uk.com
    Exec Dir: Kurt Obermaier
○ *T
Gp Debt buyers & sellers
● Conf - Mtgs - ET - Exhib - LG - City & Guilds diploma course
    for the debt collection industry
< Fedn Eur Nat Collection Assns (ΓENCA)
M 260 f, UK / 46 f, o'seas
¶ NL - 6;   AR - 1; both ftm.
    Inside the Industry Report; £125 m, £250 nm.

Cremation Society of Great Britain   1874

■ 16-16a Albion Place (2nd floor), MAIDSTONE, Kent,
    ME14 5DZ.   (hq)
    01622 688292/3
    email info@cremation.org.uk
    http://www.cremation.org.uk
    Sec: R N Arber
▲ Registered Charity
○ *L; promotion of cremation; supply of technical & other
    information on every aspect of cremation & crematorium
    administration
● Conf - Stat - Inf - Lib - LG
< Intl Cremation Fedn
M i
¶ Pharos International (Jnl) - 4; £30.
    Directory of British Crematoria - 1; £23 (inserts)(£27 with
    binder).
    British Crematoria in Public Profile; £4.13.
    Directory of Pet Crematoria; £2.50.
    May Catholics choose Cremation?; 35p.
    AR & Accounts - 1; ftm only.
       Other prices on application.

Cri du Chat Syndrome Support Group

NR 5 Latimer Drive, Steeple View, LAINDON, Essex, SS15 4JD.
    0845 094 2725
    email info@criduchat.co.uk   http://www.criduchat.co.uk
    Nat Co-ordinator: Angela Stokes

Cricket & Hockey Association
    since 2006 **Sporting Goods Industry Association**

Cricket Memorabilia Society   (CMS)   1987

    Hon Sec: Steve Cashmore
▲ Un-incorporated Society
○ *G; the preservation of cricket memorabilia
● Mtgs - Res - Exhib - Inf - Valuations
M 850 i
¶ Jnl - 4; free.
    Directory of Collectors Interests - 2 yrly; ftm only.

Cricket Scotland   1908

NR National Cricket Academy, Ravelston, EDINBURGH,
    EH4 3NT.   (hq)
    0131-313 7420
▲ Un-incorporated Society
○ *S; governing body of cricket in Scotland
M i, clubs
× 2004 Scottish Cricket Union

Cricket Society   1945

NR PO Box 6024, LEIGHTON BUZZARD, Beds, LU7 2ZS.   (hsp)
    01525 370204
    email davidwood@cricketsociety.com
    http://www.cricketsociety.com
    Hon Sec: David Wood
▲ Un-incorporated Society
Br 3
○ *S; to encourage a love of cricket in all its spheres - for all ages
    & interests - playing, watching, reading or listening
● Mtgs - Lib
M 1,900 i, UK / 100 i, o'seas
¶ Jnl - 2; ftm, £3 nm.   News Bulletin - 8; ftm only.

Crime Concern 1988

NR Chapel House, Westmead Drive, Westlea, SWINDON, Wilts,
SN5 7UN.   (hq)
01793 863500   fax 01793 514654
email info@crimeconcern.org.uk
http://www.crimeconcern.org.uk
Chief Exec: Roger Howard
▲ Registered Charity
○ *K; to specialise in issues involving youth crime - criminality,
high crime neighbourhoods, business & town centre crime, &
rural crime, as well as hospital, passenger, school & women's
safety
● Conf - ET - Res - Exhib - Comp - Inf - Lib - LG
< Eur Forum for Urban Security; Intl Centre for the Prevention of
Crime
M 25 f
¶ Crime Concern Annual Review; free.
Various other publications.

Crime Reporters Association (CRA) 1945

NR c/o Jeff Edwards, Chief Crime Correspondent, Daily Mirror, 1
Canada Square, LONDON, E14 5AP.   (hsb)
020 7293 3000
Chmn: Jeff Edwards
○ *P; to represent crime reporters of the responsible media, in
consultations with Home Office & police organisations

Crime Writers Association (CWA) 1953

■ PO Box 273, BOREHAMWOOD, Herts, WD6 2XA.   (hsb)
email info@thecwa.co.uk   http://www.thecwa.co.uk
Sec: Liz Evans
▲ Company Limited by Guarantee
○ *P; for all involved in crime writing (authors, publishers, agents,
booksellers)
● Conf - Mtgs - Comp - Inf - Administration of: CWA Cartier
Diamond Dagger, CWA Non-fiction Gold Dagger, New Blood
Dagger, Ian Fleming Steel Dagger, Duncan Lawrie Dagger
(International Dagger) - Ellis Peters Award - Debut Dagger
< Mystery Writers of America
M 400 i, UK / 100 i, o'seas
¶ Red Herrings - 12;   LM - 1; both ftm only.

Crimean War Research Society 1983

■ 4 Castle Estate, RIPPONDEN, W Yorks, HX6 4JY.   (hsp)
01422 823529
http://www.crimeanwar.org/
Hon Sec: David Cliff
▲ Un-incorporated Society
○ *L, *G; to encourage research into all aspects of the Crimean
War, 1853-1856
● Conf - Mtgs - Res - Exhib - SG - Inf - Lib
M 250 i, UK / 100 i, o'seas
¶ The War Correspondent (Jnl) - 4; £15 UK (£20 o'seas) m only.

Criminal Bar Association (CBA) 1969

NR 289-293 High Holborn, LONDON, WC1V 7HZ.   (hq)
020 7242 1289   fax 020 7242 1107
email jbradley@barcouncil.org.uk
http://www.criminalbar.com
Admin: Julian Bradley
▲ Un-incorporated Society
○ *P; practising members of the Bar of England & Wales
● Conf - Mtgs - ET - Res - SG - Inf - Lib - Empl - LG
M c 3,000 i
¶ NL - 4; free.   Brochure.

Criminal Law Solicitors' Association 1990

NR New England House (Suite 2 Level 6), New England St,
BRIGHTON, E Sussex, BN1 4GH.   (hq)
01273 676725
Admin: Sue Johnson
▲ Un-incorporated Society
○ *P
M i

Critics' Circle 1913

NR 50 Finland Rd, LONDON, SE4 2JH.   (admin/b)
http://www.criticscircle.org.uk
Hon Gen Sec: William Russell
○ *P; critics of the performing arts

Crohn's in Childhood Research Association (CICRA) 1978

■ Parkgate House, 356 West Barnes Lane, MOTSPUR PARK,
Surrey, KT3 6NB.   (hq)
020 8949 6209   fax 020 8942 2044
email support@cicra.org   http://www.cicra.org
Chmn Bd of Trustees: Mrs Margaret Lee
▲ Registered Charity
○ *K, *W; to create wider awareness & understanding of Crohn's
disease & ulcerative colitis, particularly as it affects children &
young adults; to raise funds to support medical research
aimed at finding more effective treatments & eventual cure
Gp Children & youth; Health
● Conf - Mtgs - Res
M 3,000 i
¶ The Insider - 4.

Cromwell Association 1935

NR c/o The Cromwell Museum, Grammar School Walk,
HUNTINGDON, Cambs, PE29 3LF.   (mail address)
01480 375830
http://www.olivercromwell.org
▲ Un-incorporated Society
○ *L; to commemorate Oliver Cromwell (1599-1658); to
stimulate interest in Cromwell & the general history of the
British Isles & dependent territories from the birth of
Cromwell to the Restoration; to encourage scholarly study of
the period
● Conf - ET - Comp - Lib
M c 600 i, 6 libraries, UK / c 30 i, 1 library, o'seas
¶ Cromwelliana - 1; ftm.   NL - 2; ftm only.

Crop Circle Connector 1995

NR 11 Richmond Terrace, Clifton, BRISTOL, BS8 1AB.
http://www.cropcircleconnector.com

Crop Protection Association (CPA) 1928

NR 18-20 Cully Court, Orton Southgate, PETERBOROUGH,
Cambs, PE2 6XS.   (hq)
01733 367219   fax 01733 367212
http://www.cropprotection.org.uk
Chief Exec: Peter Sanguinetti
▲ Company Limited by Guarantee
○ *T; the responsible & safe manufacture & use of agrochemicals
with due regard for the interests of the community & the
environment
● Mtgs - Exam - Exhib - Stat - Inf
< Eur Crop Protection Assn (ECPA)
M 40 f
¶ Annual Review;   Hbk; both free.
Publications & other resources.

Croquet Association (CA) 1897

■ c/o Cheltenham Croquet Club, Old Bath Rd, CHELTENHAM,
Glos, GL53 7DF.   (hq)
01242 242318
email caoffice@croquet.org.uk
http://www.croquet.org.uk
Mgr: Elizabeth Larsson
▲ Un-incorporated Society
Br 9
○ *S; the governing body for the sport of croquet
● Conf - ET - Exam - Res - Comp - Stat - Inf - LG
< Wld Croquet Fedn; Eur Croquet Fedn
M 1,600 i, 160 clubs
(Sub: £37 i, UK / £32 i, £6.70 per mem clubs)
¶ The Croquet Gazette - 6.

© CBD Research Ltd · Beckenham · BR3 5JS · Tel 020 8650 7745 · Fax 020 8650 0768 · E-mail cbd@cbdresearch.com · www.cbdresearch.com

Crossroads: Caring for Carers   1974
- ■   33-35 Cathedral St (3rd floor), CARDIFF, CF11 9HB.
     0845 450 0350   fax 029 2022 8859
     email communications@crossroads.org.uk
     http://www.crossroads.org.uk
     10 Regent Place, RUGBY, Warks, CV21 2PN.   (regd/office).
     Chief Exec: Anne Roberts
- ▲   Company Limited by Guarantee; Registered Charity
- Br   126 (England & Wales)
- ○   *W; to provide practical support for carers; to supply trained
     support workers to relieve carers for essential breaks
- M   [not stated]
- ¶   AR & Accounts - 1.

Crossword Club   1978
- ■   Coombe Farm, Awbridge, ROMSEY, Hants, SO51 0HN.   (hsb)
     01794 524346   fax 01794 514988
     email bh@thecrosswordclub.co.uk
     http://www.thecrosswordclub.co.uk
     Sec: Brian Head
- ▲   Registered Business Name
- ○   *G; promotion of the art of the crossword - especially the
     setting & solving of puzzles of a high level of construction &
     difficulty
     NOTE: 'we do not offer non-members free advice on selling
     crosswords'
- M   c 700 i, 2 f, UK / c 50 i, 2 org, o'seas
- ¶   Crossword - 12; ftm only.   Hbk - irreg; free.
     Crossword Club Guide to Playfair; £1.25.

Croydon Chamber of Commerce & Industry   1891
- ■   The Lansdowne Building, 2 Lansdowne Rd, CROYDON, Surrey,
     CR9 2ER.   (hq)
     020 8263 2345   fax 020 8263 2352
     email info@croydonchamber.org.uk
     http://www.croydonchamber.org.uk
     Chief Exec: Matthew Sims
- ▲   Company Limited by Guarantee
- ○   *C
- ●   Mtgs - Exhib - Expt - Inf
- <   Brit Chams Comm; London Cham Comm & Ind (LCCI)
- M   400 i, f & org
- ¶   Business South - 10; ftm, £1.50 nm.
     Directory of Members - 1;   AR; both ftm only.

**Croydon Natural History & Scientific Society Ltd   (CNHSS)
1870**
- ■   96A Brighton Rd, SOUTH CROYDON, Surrey, CR2 6AD.   (hq)
     020 8688 3593
     http://www.greig51.freeserve.co.uk/cnhss
     Hon Sec: Brian Lancaster,   Co Sec: Paul W Sowan
- ▲   Company Limited by Guarantee; Registered Charity
- ○   *L; covering NE Surrey, NW Kent & southern London boroughs
- Gp   Archaeology; Botany & mycology; Entomology; Geology;
     Industrial studies; Local history; Meteorology; Ornithology
- ●   Conf - Mtgs - Res - Exhib - SG - Inf - Lib - VE - Museums
     The library may be visited by appointment only, contact Paul W
     Sowan 020 8688 3593
- <   Botanical Soc of the Brit Isles; Brit Assn for Local History; Coun
     for Brit Archaeology; Geologists' Assn
- M   344 i, 16 org
     (Sub: £13, £8 associates)
- ¶   Proceedings - irreg;   Bulletin - 2; ftm, prices vary nm.
     Croydon Church Townscape; £4.50.
     The River Wandle:
       Distribution of its flora; £1;
       The Non-conformist experience in Croydon; £1.
     From Palace to Washhouse: a study of the Old Palace,
       Croydon, from 1780 to 1887; £3.50.
     The Archbishop's town: the making of mediaeval
       Croydon; £2.95.
     Many other publications on Croydon & its history.

Cruising Association   (CA)   1908
- NR   CA House, 1 Northey St, Limehouse Basin, LONDON,
     E14 8BT.   (hq)
     020 7537 2828   fax 020 7537 2266
     email office@cruising.org.uk
     http://www.cruising.org.uk
     Hon Sec: Desmond Scott
- ▲   Company Limited by Guarantee
- ○   *S; an amateur organisation encouraging cruising in yachts &
     boats; protection of the interests of yachtsmen

Crusaders   1906
- NR   Kestin House, 45 Crescent Rd, LUTON, Beds, LU2 0AH.   (hq)
     01582 589850   fax 01582 721702
     Exec Dir: Matt Summerfield
- ▲   Registered Charity
- ○   *R, *Y; committed to sharing the Christian gospel with young
     people through interdenominational youth groups, overseas
     projects & holidays
- ●   Conf - ET - Exhib - Comp - SG - Inf
- <   Nat Youth Org; Evangelical Alliance
- M   20,000 i

Cruse Bereavement Care   (CRUSE)   1959
- ■   PO Box 800, RICHMOND, Surrey, TW9 1RG.   (hq)
     020 8939 9530
     email info@cruse.org.uk   http://www.cruse.org.uk
     Chief Exec: Debbie Kerslake
- ▲   Registered Charity
- Br   138 in UK (not Scotland)
- ○   *W; offers help to people bereaved by death, in any way,
     whatever their age, nationality or belief; also free counselling
     service, advice on practical matters & opportunities for
     contact with others through support groups
- ●   Conf - ET - Res - Stat - Inf - Lib - LG
- M   5,500 i (volunteers)
- ¶   Bereavement Care Jnl - 4; £19 m only.

Crystal & Healing Federation   (CHF)   1998
- ■   c/o 6 Buer Rd, LONDON, SW6 4LA.   (hsp)
     020 7736 0283
     email vhflondon@aol.com
     http://www.crystalandhealing.com
     Hon Sec: Henriette Maasdijk
- ○   *N; an umbrella organisation for crystal healing schools &
     graduates; also spiritual healing, stress therapy & Bach
     flower remedies
- ●   Mtgs - ET
- <   Brit Crystal Healers (BCH); Complementary Med Assn (CMA)
- M   115 i, 6 org
- ¶   Crystals & Healing for Everyone [book]; £5 m, £6 nm.
     Crystals Strong & Beautiful; £16 m.

Crystal Palace Foundation   (CPF)   1979
- ■   Crystal Palace Museum, Anerley Hill, LONDON, SE19 2BA.
     (hq)
     0788 933 8812   fax 0870 133 7920
     email crystalpalacefoundation@hotmail.com
     http://www.crystalpalacefoundation.org.uk
     Sec: David Britton,   Chmn: Melvyn Harrison
- ▲   Registered Charity
- ○   *G; to support the Crystal Palace Museum
- ●   ET - Res - Exhib - SG - Inf - Lib - PL - VE - Promotes education
     & research - Publishing work concerned with Crystal Palace
- <   Assn Indep Museums (AIM); Brit Assn Friends of Museums;
     Urban Parks Forum (UPF)
- M   700 i, 10 org, UK / 50 i, o'seas
- ¶   Crystal Palace Foundation News - 4; ftm only.
     New Crystal Palace Matters - 4; ftm, £1 nm.

CSS (CSS) 1885
NR Environment Services, County Hall, CHESTER, CH1 1SF.   (hsb)
    01244 972103
    email tom.mccabe@cheshire.gov.uk
    http://www.cssnet.org.uk
    Hon Sec: Tom McCabe
▲   Un-incorporated Society
Br 3
○   *P; to represent local authority chief officers, closely involved in
    crucial transport, waste management, environment,
    planning, energy & economic development issues
Gp C'ees: Engineering, Planning & regeneration, Transport,
    Environment, Finance
●   Conf - Mtgs - ET - Res - SG - Stat - LG
M   116 i, 221 honorary members, 43 special honorary members
¶   A wide variety of technical reports.
✕   County Surveyors' Society

CTC 1878
■   Parklands, Railton Rd, GUILDFORD, Surrey, GU2 9JX.   (hq)
    0844 736 8450   fax 0844 736 8454
    email cycling@ctc.org.uk   http://www.ctc.org.uk
    Dir: Kevin Mayne
▲   Company Limited by Guarantee; Registered Charity
○   *K, *S; campaigns for the rights of all cyclists - membership
    includes 3rd party insurance & legal aid
●   ET - Res - Comp - Inf - LG
M   i
    (Sub: £36 adults)
¶   Cycle - 6; ftm only.
✕   2007 Cyclists' Touring Club

Cue Sports Association
    since 2006 **Sporting Goods Industry Association**

Cued Speech Association UK   (CSAUK)   1980
■   9 Jawbone Hill, DARTMOUTH, Devon, TQ6 9RW.   (hq)
    01803 832784   fax 01803 835311
    email info@cuedspeech.co.uk
    http://www.cuedspeech.co.uk
    Chief Exec: Anne Worsfold
▲   Company Limited by Guarantee; Registered Charity
○   *W; to provide information & training in cued speech - an exact
    visual representation of spoken language by using 8 hand
    shapes in 4 positions to clarify the lip patterns of speech.
    Its use allows deaf children to think in English and so
    improve their literacy, lip-reading & speech; it can also help
    deafened & deaf adults
●   Conf - ET - Exam - Exhib - Inf
<   UK Coun on Deafness (UKCoD)
M   70 i
¶   NL - 4;   AR - 1; both free.
    The Cued Speech Research Book; £29.99
    Cued Speech Instructional Booklet; £6.
    Parents Booklet; £6.
    Cued Speech Explained by People who use it (DVD); £5.
    Cued Speech Instructional Video; £10.
    Application for membership; £10.

Cumann Leabharfhoilsitheoin' Éireann
    Irish name of **CLÉ - Irish Book Publishers' Association**

Cumann na Scríbheann nGaedhilge
    Irish name of the **Irish Texts Society**

Cumberland Agricultural Society   1836
■   Warcarr, Greenhead, BRAMPTON, Cumbria, CA8 7HY.   (sp/b)
    01697 747397   fax 01697 747397
    email secretary@cumberlandshow.co.uk
    http://www.cumberlandshow.co.uk
    Sec: Donella Rozario
▲   Un-incorporated Society with charitable status
○   *F
●   Mtgs - Exhib (Cumberland Agricultural Show) - Comp - Inf
M   c 1,000 i
¶   Catalogue - 1; £2.50.   Schedule - 1; free.

**Cumberland & Westmorland Antiquarian & Archaeological
Society   (CWAAS)   1866**
NR Westlands, Westbourne Drive, LANCASTER, LA1 5EE.   (hsp)
    01524 675234
    email eajones@skynow.net   http://www.cwaas.org.uk
    Hon Sec: Mrs M E MacClintock
▲   Registered Charity
○   *L; the study of the archaeology, history, genealogy, customs &
    traditions of the old counties of Cumberland, Westmorland &
    Lancashire north of the sands
Gp C'ees: Parish registers; Industrial archaeology; Regional;
    Research
●   Mtgs - Res - Inf - Lib - VE
<   Coun of Brit Archaeology
M   c 850 i, c 120 org
¶   Transactions - 1; ftm, £15 nm.   NL - 3; ftm only.
    Research series, Record series & Extra series - all irreg;
    prices vary.

Cumbria Chamber of Commerce   (CCC)   1999
NR Enterprise Centre, James St, CARLISLE, Cumbria, CA2 5DA.
    (hq)
    0845 226 0040   fax 0845 226 0050
    email contact@cumbriachamber.co.uk
    http://www.cumbriachamber.co.uk
    Chief Exec: Rob Johnston
▲   Un-incorporated Society
Br Barrow, Kendal, Whitehaven
○   *C; support & services for the Cumbrian business community
<   Chams Comm NW
M   f & org

** Curia Baronis
    Organisation lost, see Introduction paragraph 3

CURL: Consortium of Research Libraries in the British Isles
    since 2008 **RLUK: Research Libraries UK**

Curwen Institute   1972
■   56 Creffield Rd, COLCHESTER, Essex, CO3 3HY.   (hsp)
    email admin@johncurwensociety.org.uk
    http://www.johncurwensociety.org.uk
    Hon Sec: Yvonne Lawton
○   *E; to develop & extend the teaching of music in schools by
    means of a modern version of John Curwen's Tonic Sol-fa
    system
    The Institute is funded by the John Curwen Society.

Cussel an Tavas Kernuack
    Cornish name of the **Cornish Language Council**

© CBD Research Ltd · Beckenham · BR3 5JS · Tel 020 8650 7745 · Fax 020 8650 0768 · E-mail cbd@cbdresearch.com · www.cbdresearch.com

Customer Contact Association   (CCA)   1996
- ■ 20 Newton Place, GLASGOW, G3 7PY.   (hq)
      0141-564 9010   fax 0141-564 9011
      email cca@cca.org.uk   http://www.cca.org.uk
      Chief Exec: Anne Marie Forsyth
- ▲ Company Limited by Guarantee
- ○ *T; development & promotion of customer contact expertise
- Gp Industry council; Standards council; Foundation partners
- ● Conf - Mtgs - ET - Res - Exhib - Stat - Inf - Lib - LG
- M 800 f UK, 20 f o'seas
      (Sub: £20)
- ¶ In Touch - 4; ftm only.
- ✕ 2005 Call Centre Association

Cut the VAT Coalition   2008
- NR Gordon Fisher House, 14-15 Great James St, LONDON,
      WC1N 3DP.   (hq)
      020 7242 7583   fax 020 7405 0854
      email central@fmb.org.uk   http://www.fmb.org.uk/
      cutthevat
      Contact: Richard Hislop
- ○ *K; to reduce VAT on all maintenance & home improvement
      work

Cutlery & Allied Trades Research Association   (CATRA)   1952
- NR Henry St, SHEFFIELD, S Yorks, S3 7EQ.   (hq)
      0114-276 9736   fax 0114-272 2151
      email info@catra.org   http://www.catra.org
      Dir of Research: R C Hamby
- ▲ Company Limited by Guarantee
- ○ *Q; research & technology organisation, specialising in all
      aspects of domestic & industrial tools, blades, knives, cutters,
      surgical instruments, razors & shaving systems, kitchen
      gadgets & cookware
- Gp Cutting technology; Shaving; Blade manufacturing technology
- ● Res - Inf - Testing & product evaluation - Commercial
      consultancy
- M 15 f
- ¶ [numerous publications].

Cutout & Feeder Pillar Group
      a product association of BEAMA Installation, which is part of **BEAMA**

Cutty Sark Trust   1969
- ■ 2 Greenwich Church St, LONDON, SE10 9BG.   (hq)
      020 8858 2698   fax 020 8858 6976
      email enquiries@cuttysark.org.uk
      http://www.cuttysark.org.uk
      Hon Sec: Richard Doughty,   Admin: Gail Smith
- ▲ Registered Charity
- ○ *G; preservation & consercation of the Cutty Sark clipper ship
- M c 600 i
- ¶ NL - 1;   AR; both ftm only.
      This replaces the Maritime Trust which is now dormant

Cyclamen Society   1977
- NR Little Orchard, Church Rd, WEST KINGSDOWN, Kent,
      TN15 6LG.   (h/mem/p)
      http://www.cyclamen.org
      Mem Sec: Arthur Nicholls
- ▲ Registered Charity
- ○ *H; the study of the cyclamen species
- ● Conf - Res - Exhib - Comp - Inf - Lib - VE - Seed distribution
- M 1,200 i, UK / 200 i, o'seas
- ¶ Cyclamen Jnl - 2; ftm, c £2 nm.

Cycle Engineers' Institute   (CEI)   1896
- ■ 28 King St, SANDWICH, Kent, CT13 9BT.   (sp/b)
      01304 617161   fax 01304 617161
      Sec: Arthur H Lock
- ▲ Un-incorporated Society
- ○ *L; for the highest standards of design & manufacture of
      custom-built & made to measure bicycles
- Gp Designing; Building; Engineering methods
- ● Conf - Res - Inf
- < League Intl (cycle racing); Eur Inst of Cycle Engg
- M c 50 i, UK / 10 i, o'seas
- ¶ Proceedings - 6;   LM - 1;   Rules - irreg; all ftm only.

Cyclical Vomiting Syndrome Association UK
- ■ 77 Wilbury Hills Road, LETCHWORTH, Herts, SG6 4LD.   (hsp)
      0151-342 1660
      email info@cvsa.org.uk   http://www.cvsa.org.uk
      Chmn of Trustees: Dr Robin Dover
- ▲ Registered Charity
- ○ *W; 'cyclical vomiting syndrome: promotion of education,
      research, & offering support to sufferers & their families'
- ● Mtgs - ET - Inf
- M 300 i, UK / 20+ f, o'seas
- ¶ Bi-Annual NL - 2; ftm.

Cycling Time Trials   (CTT)   2002
- ■ 77 Arlington Drive, Pennington, LEIGH, Lancs, WN7 3QP.
      (hq/hsp)
      01942 603976   fax 01942 262326
      email phil.heaton@cyclingtimetrials.org.uk
      http://www.cyclingtimetrials.org.uk
      Nat Sec: Phil Heaton
- ▲ Company Limited by Guarantee
- Br 21
- ○ *S; governing body for road cycling time trials in UK (England,
      Wales, Channel Islands, Isle of Man)
- ● Conf - Mtgs - LG
- < Cent Coun for Physical Recreation
- M 998 clubs
- ¶ CTT Hbk - 1; £7.   AR - 1.

Cyclists' Touring Club
      since 2007 **CTC**

Cymdeithas Alawon Gwerin Cymru
      see **Welsh Folk Song Society (Cymdeithas Alawon Gwerin
      Cymru)**

Cymdeithas Amaethyddol Frenhinol Cymru Cyf
      Welsh name of the **Royal Welsh Agricultural Society Ltd**

Cymdeithas Cymru-Ariannin   1939
- ■ Rhos Helyg, 23 Maesyrefail, Penrhyn-coch, ABERYSTWYTH,
      Ceredigion, SY23 3HE.   (hsp)
      01970 828017
      email rhoshelyg@btinternet.com
      Sec: Ceris Gruffudd
- ▲ Registered Charity
- ○ *X; to form a link between Wales & the Welsh community in
      Chubut, Argentina; to organise & sponsor exchange visits for
      Welsh teachers, students & ministers of religion, &
      Argentinian students wishing to go to Wales to expand their
      educational horizon
- ● Mtgs - Exhib - Inf - Annual celebration to mark the landing of
      the first Welsh settlers in Chubut - Sponsorship of annual
      literary competition (in the Welsh lanugage) at the National
      Eisteddfod of Wales
- < Wales Intl
- M 231 i, 1 org, UK / 6 i, o'seas
- ¶ AR; free.
      Note: the name translates as the Wales-Argentine Society

Cymdeithas Ddawns Werin Cymru (Welsh Folk Dance Society (WFDS)) (CDdWC) 1949
- ■ Ffynnonlwyd, Trelech, CAERFYRDDIN, SA33 6QZ. (sec/p) 01994 484496
email dafydd.evans@ic24.net
http://www.welshfolkdance.org.uk
Sec: Dafydd M Evans
- ▲ Registered Charity
- Br 27; Australia, New Zealand, USA
- ○ *D; promoting Welsh folk dancing & music through the medium of Welsh language & English
- ● Conf - Mtgs - ET - Exam - Res - Exhib - Comp - SG - Inf - Lib - VE - Dancing displays - Publishing dance notations, records & tapes
- < Welsh Amat Music Fedn (WAMF)
- M 196 i, 67 families, 29 groups, UK / 21 i, o'seas
- ¶ Dawns (Jnl) - 1.   NL - 1.   Hbk.   AR (incl LM). Dance notations, records, tapes, CDs, videos & DVDs

Cymdeithas Ddrama Cymru
Welsh name of the **Drama Association of Wales**

Cymdeithas Defaid Torddu Cymreig Torwen
Welsh name of the **Badger Face Welsh Mountain Sheep Society**

Cymdeithas Hanes Ceredigion - Ceredigion Historical Society 1909
- ■ Penygeulan, Abermagwr, ABERYSTWYTH, Ceredigion, SY23 4AR. (hsb) 01974 261222
email nonbaskerville@onetel.com
Hon Sec: Mrs Eirionedd A Baskerville
- ▲ Registered Charity
- ○ *L; local history, antiquities & folklore of Ceredigion
- Gp Archaeological
- ● Mtgs - VE
- M 500+ i
- ¶ Ceredigion (Jnl) - 1.
County History, 3 vol; in course of publication.

Cymdeithas Hanes Sir Caernarfon
Welsh name of the **Caernarvonshire Historical Society**

Cymdeithas Hanes Sir Ddinbych - Denbighshire Historical Society 1950
- NR 1 Green Park, WREXHAM, Denbighshire, LL13 7YE. (hsp) 01978 353363
Hon Sec: David Jones
- ▲ Registered Charity
- ○ *L; study of the history of the old county of Denbighshire, including family history, folklore & archaeology
- ● Mtgs - VE
- M c 410 i & org
- ¶ Transactions - 1.

Cymdeithas Hynafiaethau Cymru
Welsh name of the **Cambrian Archaeological Association**

Cymdeithas yr Iaith Gymraeg (Welsh Language Society) 1962
- NR Penroc, Marine Terrace, ABERYSTWYTH, Ceredigion, SY23 2AZ. (hq) 01970 624501   fax 01970 627122
email swyddfa@cymdeithas.org
Contact: Dafydd Morgan Lewis
- ○ *K, *Z; 'a socialist organisation to ensure the future of the Welsh language'
- M [not given]

Cymdeithas Melinau Cymru
Welsh name of the **Welsh Mills Society**

Cymdieithas Defaid Llanwenog (Llanwenog Sheep Society) 1957
- ■ Nantygwyn, Llanfair Rd, LAMPETER, Ceredigion, SA48 8YJ. (hsb) 01570 423135
email llanwenogsheep@hotmail.com
http://www.llanwenog-sheep.co.uk
Sec: Miss Meinir Green
- ○ *B
- ● Conf - Mtgs - Exhib - Comp - Lib - VE
- < Nat Sheep Assn
- M 170 i
- ¶ Ybk;   NL;   LM;   AR; all ftm only.

Cyngor Gweithredu Gwirfoddol Cymru
Welsh name of the **Wales Council for Voluntary Action**

Cystic Fibrosis Trust 1964
- NR 11 London Rd, BROMLEY, Kent, BR1 1BY. (hq) 020 8464 7211   fax 020 8313 0472
http://www.cftrust.org.uk
Chief Exec: Rosie Barnes
- ▲ Registered Charity
- Br 97
- ○ *Q, *W; to fund hospital & university research into improved detection & treatment of cystic fibrosis; to provide a comprehensive support & advice network for people with cystic fibrosis & their families
- ● Conf - Mtgs - ET - Res - Exhib - Helpline 0845 859 1000
- < Intl Cystic Fibrosis (Mucoviscidosis) Assn (ICF(M)A)
- M 16,000 i
- ¶ CF Today;   CF Talk; both free.   Annual Review. Books, information leaflets, videos - list available.

Cystitis & Overactive Bladder Foundation (COB Foundation) 1994
- ■ 946 Bristol Road South, Northfield, BIRMINGHAM, W Midlands, B31 2LQ. (hq) 0121-476 1222
email info@cobfoundation.org
http://www.cobfoundation.org
- ▲ Registered Charity
- Br 35
- ○ *W; support for sufferers & their families; information dissemination to the medical profession on causes & treatments of, & research into, all forms of cystitis & overactive bladder
- ● Mtgs - Stat - Inf
- < Interstitial Cystitis Assn of America
- M 2,000 i
- ¶ A Wee Ray of Hope (NL) - 4.
- ✕ 2003 Interstitial Cystitis Support Group

© CBD Research Ltd · Beckenham · BR3 5JS · Tel 020 8650 7745 · Fax 020 8650 0768 · E-mail cbd@cbdresearch.com · www.cbdresearch.com

D&AD (D&AD) 1962

NR   9 Graphite Sq, Vauxhall Walk, LONDON, SE11 5EE.   (hq)
    020 7840 1120   fax 020 7840 0840
    email info@dandad.co.uk   http://www.dandad.org
    Chief Exec: Michael Hockney
▲   Registered Charity
○   *A, *P; to work on behalf of the design & advertising industries;
    to set standards of creative excellence & educate & inspire
    the next creative generation; to promote good design &
    advertising to the business area
●   Conf - ET - Exhib - Annual Congress
<   Art Directors Club of Europe (ADCE)
M   1,900 i, UK / 400 i, o'seas
¶   D&AD Annual & DVD Showreel - 1; ftm, £150 nm.
    D&AD Student Annual - 1; ftm, £10 nm.
    The Copy Book.   The Art Directors Book.
    The Commercials Book.   The Product Book.
    The Graphics book.

D H Lawrence Society 1974

■   24 Briarwood Ave, NOTTINGHAM, NG3 6JQ.   (hsp)
    0115-950 3008
    Hon Sec: Ron Faulks
▲   Registered Charity
○   *A; promotion of interest in the life & work of D H Lawrence
    (1885-1930) novelist, poet & essayist
●   Conf - Mtgs - Inf - Lib - VE
<   Assn of Literary Socs; societies in Australia, France, Italy, Japan,
    USA
M   126 i, UK / 75 i, o'seas
¶   Jnl - 1; ftm, £7 nm.   NL - 2; ftm, £2 nm.

Dad's Army Appreciation Society (DAAS) 1993

■   29 Brockley Rd, Leonard Stanley, STONEHOUSE, Glos, GL10
    3NB.   (hsp)
    email info@dadsarmy.co.uk   http://www.dadsarmy.co.uk
    Hon Sec (members): Tony Pritchard,
    Hon Sec (articles): Paul Carpenter
▲   Un-incorporated Society
○   *G; to promote & research the television series & share with
    like-minded people rare footage, photographs & information
Gp   Rare videos & photographs; Filming locations; Archives
●   Mtgs - Exhib - Inf - PL
M   1,540 i, UK / 51 i, o'seas
¶   NL [Permission to Speak Sir!] - 4; £8; UK m only.
    Dad's Army Companion (all the facts about the
    programme); £12 m, £14 nm.

Daffodil Society 1898

NR   105 Derby Rd, Bramcote, NOTTINGHAM, NG9 3GZ.   (hsp)
    0115-925 5498
    email rogerbb@lineone.net
    http://www.thedaffodilsociety.com
    Hon Sec: Mrs Terry Braithwaite
▲   Registered Charity
○   *H; cultivation & exhibition of the genus narcissus
●   Exhib - Regional meetings
<   R Horticl Soc
M   670 i, 220 org, UK / 123 i, o'seas
¶   Jnl - 1; NL - 1; ftm only.

Dairy Executives Association

IRL   33 Kildare St, DUBLIN 2, Republic of Ireland.
    353 (1) 676 1989   fax 353 (1) 676 7162
    email dairyexe@indigo.ie
    Gen Sec: Michael B McCann
○   *P; executives & managers in the dairy industry & agribusiness

Dairy Industry Association
    since 2004 **Dairy UK**

Dairy UK 1933

NR   93 Baker St, LONDON, W1U 6QQ.   (hq)
    020 7486 7244   fax 020 7847 4734
    email info@dairyuk.org   http://www.dairyuk.org
    Atholl House, 4 Torphichen St, EDINBURGH, EH3 6JQ.
    0131-229 1401
    8 Ranfurly Ave, BANGOR, Co Down, BT20 3SN.
    028 9147 1300
    Director General: Jim Begg
○   *T; body dealing with matters relating to manufacture &
    distribution of milk & milk products, & relating to wages &
    conditions of employees in the industry
M   f & org
×   2004 Dairy Industry Association
    2005 (Northern Ireland Dairy Association
    (Scottish Dairy Association

The Daisy Network 1995

■   PO Box 183, ROSSENDALE, Lancs, BB4 6WZ.   (mail/address)
    email daisy@daisynetwork.org.uk
    http://www.daisynetwork.org.uk
    Hon Sec: Mrs J Banks
▲   Registered Charity
○   *W; to support & inform those who have gone through a
    premature menopause, & their families
●   Conf - Inf
M   c 350 i, UK / 3 i, o'seas
    (Sub: £20)
¶   NL -4;   AR - 1; both ftm only.
×   Daisy Network Premature Menopause Support Group

Dalcroze Society UK (Inc) 1926

■   7 Canada Rise, Market Lavington, DEVIZES, Wilts,
    SN10 4AD.   (admin/p)
    01380 813198
    email admin.dalcroze@googlemail.com
    http://www.dalcroze.org.uk
    Admin: Greta Price,   Chmn: Nicola Gaines
▲   Registered Charity
○   *D; musical education through movement
●   ET - Exam
<   Institut Jaques Dalcroze (Geneva)
M   150 i, UK / i, o'seas
¶   NL - 2; ftm.   Publications list available.

Dales Pony Society (DPS) 1916

■   Greystones, Glebe Avenue, Great Longstone, BAKEWELL,
    Derbys, DE45 1TY.   (hsp)
    01629 640439   fax 01629 640439
    email dpssecretary@googlemail.com
    http://www.dalespony.org
    Hon Sec: Mrs J C Ashby
▲   Company Limited by Guarantee; Registered Charity
Br   CAnada, France, USA
○   *B
●   Conf - Comp - Inf
<   Nat Pony Soc; Brit Horse Soc
M   600 i, UK / 25 i, o'seas
    (Sub: £20)
¶   Dales Despatch - 2; ftm only.

Dalesbred Sheep Breeders' Association Ltd   1930
- ■ Brackenber Lane Farm, Brackenber Lane, Giggleswick, SETTLE, N Yorks, BD24 0EB.   (hsp)
  01729 822228
  email dalesbred@hotmail.com
  Sec: Jean E Bradley
- ○ *B
- ● Mtgs - Res - Exhib - Comp
- M 200 i
  (Sub: varies)
- ¶ Jnl - 5.   Flock Book - 1.

Dance UK Ltd   1982
- NR The Urdang, Old Finsbury Town Hall, Rosebery Avene, LONDON, EC1R 4QT.   (hq)
  020 7713 0730   fax 020 7833 2363
  email info@danceuk.org   http://www.danceuk.org
  Dir: Caroline Miller
- ▲ Company Limited by Guarantee; Registered Charity
- ○ *D, *W; 'the lead organisation for the dance profession; we work to create a diverse, dynamic & healthy future for dance & to build a stronger sense of a UK-wide dance community'
- Gp National Choreographers Forum; Communication & advocacy; Healthier dance practice; Professional development; Support & development of African dance
- ● Conf - Mtgs - ET - Res - Stat - Inf
- M 800 i, 130 f, UK / 50 i, 10 f, o'seas
- ¶ Dance UK News (Jnl) - 4.   Your Body Your Risk. Look Before You Leap. Choreography as Work. Dance Teaching Essentials. 18 information sheets.   Poster series. Warm Up Cool Down Posters.

Dancesport Scotland   1945
- NR 93 Hillfoot Drive, Bearsden, GLASGOW, G61 3QG.   (hsp)
  0141-563 2001
  http://www.dancesportscotland.org
  Exec Admin: Mrs Margo Fraser
- ○ *S; the governing body for ballroom & Latin American dancing in Scotland
- ✕ 2006 Scottish Dancesport

Danish-UK Chamber of Commerce   (DUCC)   1989
- ■ 55 Sloane St, LONDON, SW1X 9SR.   (hq)
  020 7259 6795
  email info@ducc.co.uk   http://www.ducc.co.uk
  Chief Exec: Martin Mortensen
- ▲ Company Limited by Guarantee
- ○ *C; to promote & assist the Anglo-Danish business community in both UK & Denmark
- Gp Managing Directors Network; Young Professionals Network (YPN); The Junior Chamber
- ● Mtgs
- M 150 i, 250 f
- ¶ Trade Directory - 1; free.

Daresbury Lewis Carroll Society   1970
- ■ Blue Grass, Clatterwick Lane, Little Leigh, NORTHWICH, Cheshire, CW8 4RJ.   (hsb)
  01606 891303 & 781731 (evgs)
  Hon Sec: Kenneth N Oultram
- ○ *L; to honour & promote the work of C L Dodgson (Lewis Carroll)
- ● Mtgs (in Daresbury, Carroll's birthplace)

Dartmoor Pony Society   (DPS)   1946
- NR Swn Yr Afon, Thornhill Rd, CWMGWILI, SA14 6PT.   (hsp)
  01269 844303
  http://www.dartmoorponysociety.com
  Hon Sec: Mrs Viv Brown
- ▲ Company Limited by Guarantee
- ○ *B
- ● Conf - Res - Exhib - Comp - Expt - Inf - Compilation of history of breed
- < Nat Pony Soc
- M 550 i, UK / 100 i, o'seas
- ¶ NL - 4.   Dartmoor Diary.

Dartmoor Preservation Association   (DPA)   1883
- ■ Old Duchy Hotel, Princetown, YELVERTON, Devon, PL20 6QF.   (pt/time hq)
  01822 890646
  email info@dartmoorpreservation.com
  http://www.dartmoorpreservation.com
  Chief Exec: James Paxman
- ▲ Registered Charity
- ○ *G, *K; protection, preservation & enhancement in the public interest of landscape, antiquities, flora & fauna, natural beauty & scientific interest of Dartmoor; preservation of Dartmoor Commons
- ● Mtgs - ET - Res - Exhib
- < Coun Protection Rural England (CPRE); Coun Nat Parks (CNP); Open Spaces Soc (OSS)
- M 2,400 i, UK / 30 i, o'seas
- ¶ Dartmoor Matters (NL) - 3; free.

Dartmoor Sheep Breeders Association   (DSBA)   1909
- ■ The Old Rectory, Clannaborough, CREDITON, Devon, EX17 6DA.   (hsp)
  01363 85205
  email greyface.dart@care4free.net
  http://www.greyface-dartmoor.org.uk
  Sec: Wilson Mitchell
- ▲ Registered Charity
- ○ *B; for breeders of Greyface Dartmoor sheep, farming & agriculture
- ● Inf
- M 250 i
- ¶ Flock Book - 1; ftm.

Darts Association
  since 2006 **Sporting Goods Industry Association**

Data Publishers Association   (DPA)   1970
- ■ Queens House, 28 Kingsway, LONDON, WC2B 6JR.   (hq)
  020 7405 0836   fax 020 7404 4167
  email christine@dpa.org.uk   http://www.dpa.org.uk
  Sec: Christine Scott
- ▲ Company Limited by Guarantee
- ○ *T; to represent data & directory publishers in the UK; to promote the interests of the industry both in print & electronic media
- ● Conf - Mtgs - Stat - LG
- < Eur Assn of Directory & Database Pubrs (EADP); Advertising Assn; Periodical Pubrs Assn; Digital Content Forum
- > Periodical Pubrs Assn
- M 80 f
- ¶ News in Brief - 12;   Members' Hbk - 1; both ftm, on request nm.
  AR; free.
- ✕ 2005 Directory & Database Publishers Association

David Hume Institute   1985
- NR 25 Buccleuch Place, EDINBURGH, EH8 9LN.   (hq)
  0131-667 9609   fax 0131-667 9609
  http://www.davidhumeinstitute.com
  Dir: Jeremy Peat
- ○ *L, *Q; to promote discourse & research on economic & legal aspects of public policy questions

© CBD Research Ltd · Beckenham · BR3 5JS · Tel 020 8650 7745 · Fax 020 8650 0768 · E-mail cbd@cbdresearch.com · www.cbdresearch.com

David Jones Society   1996
■   22 Gower Rd, Sketty, SWANSEA, SA2 9BY.   (hq)
      01792 206144   fax 01792 470385
      email anne.price-owen@davidjonessociety.org
      http://www.davidjonessociety.org
      Sec: Kirsty Black,   Dir: Dr Anne Price-Owen
▲   Un-incorporated Society
○   *A; to promote interest in the life & works of the painter-poet
      David Jones (1895-1974) & his sense of unity within the
      world & its people
Gp Visual arts; Literature; Theology
●   Conf - Mtgs - ET - Res - Exhib - Inf - Lib - PL - VE - Poetry
      readings - Seminars
M   250 i, 8 f, UK / 50 i, 4 f, o'seas
      (Sub: £20 i, £35 f)
¶   The David Jones Jnl - 2; £7.50 m, £10 nm.
      NL - 4.

Dawn Duellists' Society   (DDS)   1994
NR 3F2, 8 Thirlstane Rd, Marchmont, EDINBURGH, EH9 1AN.
      (hsp)
      email secretary@dawnduellists.co.uk
      http://www.dawnduellists.co.uk
      Sec: Matt Noel
▲   Un-incorporated Society
○   *S; revival of historically accurate swordplay from c1300-1900;
      to research teaching & practice of duelling techniques
●   Mtgs - ET - Res - Demonstrations
M   20 i, UK / 3 i, o'seas
¶   Information leaflets.

DBA - The Barge Association   (DBA)   1992
■   Island House, Moor Rd, CHESHAM, Bucks, HP5 1NZ.
      (mail/address)
      07000 227437 (07000 BARGES)   fax 0870 706 4033
      email info@barges.org   http://www.barges.org
      Hon Sec & Treas: Paul Whitehouse
▲   Company Limited by Guarantee
○   *G; support group for barge owners
Gp Continental cruising; Sailing barge; Thames
●   ET - Inf - LG - Liaison with navigation authorities, trade assns &
      other clubs - Arrangement of member discounts for goods &
      services
<   Eur Boating Assn
M   1,200 i, UK / 300 i, o'seas
      (Sub: £25 (Eur), £35 RoW)
¶   Blue Flag - 6; ftm.   Barge Buyers' Hbk.
×   2006-08 Dutch Barge Association

De Vere Society   1989
■   The Courtyard, 45 Royal York Crescent, Clifton, BRISTOL,
      BS8 4JS.   (hsp)
      0117-923 8993
      email malim@btinternet.com
      http://www.deveresociety.co.uk
      Hon Sec: R C W Malim
▲   Registered Charity
○   *A, *L, *Q; Shakespeare authorship question with 2
      propositions:
      a) that William Shakespeare (1564-1616) did not write any
      (or any significant part) of the works now attributed to him
      b) that Edward de Vere, 17th Earl of Oxford (1550-1604) is
      substantially the best candidate for (or plays a major role in)
      such authorship
●   Conf - Mtgs - ET - Res - Exhib - Inf - Lib - VE
<   Shakespeare Oxford Soc (USA)
M   150 i, UK / 60 i, o'seas
¶   NL - 3/4; ftm only.   Occasional study papers - irreg.
      Great Oxford Collection of Newsletter Essays 1996-2004;
      £12 m, £14 nm.

Deaf Broadcasting Council   (DBC)   1980
NR c/o 50 Clevedon Rd, LONDON, SE20 7QQ.   (chmn/p)
      fax 020 8676 0534
      email pennybes@aol.com
      http://www.deafcouncil.org.uk/dbc/
      Chmn: Penny Beschizza
▲   Registered Charity
○   *K; to ensure that that deaf people have access to TV & video &
      that the access is of suitable quality
●   LG
<   UK Coun on Deafness; Telecommunications Action Gp; Coun
      for the Advancement of Communication with Deaf People
M   350 i, 13 org
¶   Mailshot - 2.

Deaf Education through Listening & Talking   (DELTA)   1980
■   The Con Powell Centre, Alfa House, Molesey Rd, WALTON-on-
      THAMES, Surrey, KT12 3PD.   (hq)
      0845 108 1437
      email enquiries@deafeducation.org.uk
      http://www.deafeducation.org.uk
▲   Company Limited by Guarantee; Registered Charity
○   *W; a support group of teachers & parents of deaf & hearing-
      impaired children, providing information, advice & support to
      guide parents in helping their children develop normal
      speech & live independently in a hearing society
Gp Deaf children & families; Professionals who support them
●   Conf - Mtgs - ET - Res - Exhib - Stat - Inf
<   Alexander Graham Bell Assn Deaf & Hard of Hearing; Brit
      Academy Audiology; Brit Assn Educ Audiologists; Brit
      Cochlear Implant Users Assn; Elizabeth Foundation; Ewing
      Foundation
M   258 i
¶   Chat - 4;   Good Practice Guide; both ftm.
      Parents Guide 1; £10.   Parents Guide; £15.

Deafblind UK   1928
NR National Centre for Deafblindness, John & Lucille van Geest
      Place, Cygnet Rd, Hampton, PETERBOROUGH, Cambs,
      PE7 8FD.   (hq)
      01733 358100 (voice & minicom)   fax 01733 358356
      email info@deafblind.org.uk
      http://www.deafblind.org.uk
      Chief Exec: Jeff Skipp
▲   Registered Charity
○   *W; to further the interests of deafblind people by offering the
      full range of support services, education & training
●   Conf - ET - Exhib - Stat - Inf - VE
<   Brit Assn Disabled People
M   3,520 i
¶   Open Hand Magazine - 4.   Snippets (NL) - 52.
      Both publications are available in Braille, Moon, large print,
      tape or disk format.
      Annual Review; free.

DeafHear   1963
IRL 35 North Frederick St, DUBLIN 1, Republic of Ireland.
      353 (1) 817 5700   fax 353 (1) 878 3629
      email nad@iol.ie   http://www.deafhear.ie
      Chief Exec: Niall Keane
○   *W
×   2007 National Association for Deaf People

Debt Management Standards Association   (DEMSA)   2000
NR West Point, Westland Square, LEEDS, W Yorks, LS11 5SS.
      (chmn/b)
      0113-277 7610
      email info@demsa.co.uk   http://www.demsa.co.uk
      Chmn: Michael Land
○   *T
●   Mtgs - Inf
M   4 f

Defence Industry Security Association   (DISA)

NR   c/o CGP Associates Ltd, 2 Maple Park, Enigma Business Park,
　　　MALVERN, Worcs, WR14 1GQ.
　　　0870 458 9636
　　　http://www.thedisa.org.uk
○   *P

Defence Manufacturers Association   (DMA)   1976

■   Marlborough House, Headley Rd, GRAYSHOTT, Surrey,
　　　GU26 6LG.   (hq)
　　　01428 607788
　　　email enquiries@the-dma.org.uk
　　　http://www.the-dma.org.uk
　　　Dir Gen: Rear Admiral R G T Ward
　　　Co Sec: Elaine A Luck
▲   Company Limited by Guarantee
○   *T; to represent the interests of the British defence industry
Gp   Air Interest Group (AIRInG)
　　　British Industry Offset Group (BIOG)
　　　Clothing Interest Group (CLING)
　　　Contractor Support on Deployed Operations (CONDO)
　　　Defence Training Industry Group (DTIG)
　　　Exclusive Economic Zone Industry Group (EEZING)
　　　Export Group for Aerospace & Defence (EGAD)
　　　Industrial Participation Forum (IP Forum)
　　　Infrastructure Group (IG)
　　　Land Interest Group (LANDInG)
　　　Maritime Interest Group (MIG)
　　　Marketing Group of UK NBC Defence Capability (NBC UK)
　　　Section Five Special Interest Group
　　　UK Simulation & Training Action Group (UKSTAG)
●   Conf - Exhib - Expt - Inf - Lib - VE - LG
<   Eur Defence Inds Gp; Nat Defence Ind Coun; Defence Ind
　　　Coun; CBI
M   440 f
¶   Register of Members Products & Services - 1.
　　　Worldwide Directory on Defence & Security Prime Contractors -
　　　2 yrly.
　　　Export Opportunities Alerting Service NL - 52.
　　　DMA Annual Review; free.

Defence Training Industry Group
　　　a group of the **Defence Manufacturers Association**

Delius Society   1962

NR   8 Glisson Road, CAMBRIDGE, CB1 2HD.   (hsp)
　　　01223 302302
　　　http://www.delius.org.uk
　　　Hon Sec: Leslie Buckley
▲   Registered Charity
Br   3; 2 USA
○   *D; to develop a wider understanding & appreciation of Delius
　　　& his music; to encourage the performance, recording &
　　　publishing of his works
●   Mtgs - Res - VE
<   Delius Trust
M   380 i, 9 f, UK / 111 i, 17 f, o'seas
¶   Jnl - 2; ftm, £2-£3 nm.   NL - 2; ftm only.

Delphinium Society   1920

NR   2 The Grove, Ickenham, UXBRIDGE, Middx, UB10 8QH.
　　　(promotionsec/p)
　　　01895 464694   fax 0870 052 9321
　　　email promotions@delphinium.demon.co.uk
　　　http://www.delphinium.demon.co.uk
　　　Promotions Sec: Dr Roger D Beauchamp
▲   Registered Charity
Br   3
○   *H; the study of delphiniums in all their aspects - botanical,
　　　horticultural, genetic, physiological & general interest for
　　　non-specialists; investigation of species & their ecology; is
　　　also a forum for the more scientifically minded
Gp   Species & Breeders Communications Forum
●   ET - Exhib - Comp - Inf - VE
<   R Horticl Soc Jt Delphinium C'ee
M   c 600 i, c 20 affiliates, UK / c 150 i, o'seas
¶   Autumn Bulletin - 1 (Oct).   Delphiniums (Ybk) - 1.
　　　The Delphinium Garden; published on the 75th anniversary.

Democracy Movement

NR   72 Hammersmith Rd, LONDON, W14 8TH.   (hq)
　　　020 7603 7796   fax 020 7602 9699
　　　email mail@democracymovement.org.uk
　　　http://www.democracymovement.org.uk
Br   160
○   *K; a non-party campaign to keep the pound & stop the EU
　　　superstate
M   c 320,000 i

Denbighshire & Flintshire Agricultural Society Ltd   1839

■   1 Cross St, HOLYWELL, Flintshire, CH8 7LP.   (hq)
　　　01352 712131   fax 01352 712098
　　　email denbandflintshow@ukonline.co.uk
　　　http://www.denbighandflintshow.com
　　　Sec: Mrs V Johnstone
▲   Company Limited by Guarantee; Registered Charity
○   *F, *H; the encouragement of agriculture & horticulture by
　　　education, scientific research, experimental work & the
　　　holding of shows
Gp   Horses; Cattle; Sheep; Poultry; Bantams; Pigeons; Rabbits;
　　　Eggs; Horticulture; Floral art; Honey; WI; Merched y Wawr;
　　　Vintage machinery & cars; Classic cars & motorcycles
●   Mtgs - Comp - VE - Show
<   Assn of Show & Agricl Orgs; Various breed socs
M   1,200 i, 20 f
¶   Show Day Catalogue - 1.
　　　Show Schedule - 1.   AR.

Denbighshire Historical Society
　　　English name of **Cymdeithas Hanes Sir Ddinbych**

Dental Laboratories Association Ltd   (DLA)   1961

NR   44-46 Wollaton Rd, Beeston, NOTTINGHAM, NG9 2NR.   (hq)
　　　0115-925 4888   fax 0115-925 4800
　　　http://www.dla.org.uk
　　　Chief Exec: Richard Daniels
▲   Company Limited by Guarantee
Br   16
○   *T; interests of proprietors of dental laboratories; to represent
　　　views of dental technology to professional bodies &
　　　government
Gp   Education; Materials & technical standards; Business
　　　development
●   Conf - Mtgs - ET - Res - Exhib - SG - Stat - Inf - Empl
<   Fédn Eur des Patrons Prosthétistes Dentaires (FEPPD); Brit
　　　Dental Health Foundation (BDHF)
M   c 1,000 i
¶   Dental Laboratory (Jnl) - 12; ftm, £28 yr nm.
　　　DLA Directory - 1; ftm, £20 nm.   Year Planner - 1; free.

© CBD Research Ltd · Beckenham · BR3 5JS · Tel 020 8650 7745 · Fax 020 8650 0768 · E-mail cbd@cbdresearch.com · www.cbdresearch.com

Dental Practitioners Association   (DPA)   1954

- ◼ 61 Harley St, LONDON, W1G 8QU.   (hq)
  020 7636 1072   fax 020 7636 1086
  email info@uk-dentistry.org   http://www.uk-dentistry.org
  Chief Exec: Derek Watson
- ▲ Un-incorporated Society
- ○ *P, *U; the promotion of the welfare & interests of general
  dental practitioners, especially those working in high street
  practice
- ● Conf - Mtgs - Stat - Inf - Empl - LG
- < Eur U of Dentists (EUD)
- M 3,000 i, UK / 3 f, o'seas
- ¶ General Dental Practitioner - 6; ftm only.
- ✕ 2005 General Dental Practitioners Association

Dental System Suppliers Association   (DSSA)   1990

- NR c/o Geoff Emery, Elopak House, Rutherford Close, STEVENAGE,
  Herts, SG1 2EF.   (chmn/b)
  01483 245000
  Chmn: Geoff Emery
- ▲ Un-incorporated Society
- ○ *P, *T; promotion of & setting standards for management
  computer systems for dental surgeries
- Gp Dental surgeons; Suppliers of computer systems for dental
  surgeons & allied trades
- ● Exhib - Inf - LG
- M 5 f, 3 associates
- ¶ LM - updated; free.

Dental Technologists Association   (DTA)

- NR 3 Kestrel Court, Waterwells Drive, Waterwells Business Park,
  GLOUCESTER, GL2 2AT.
  0870 243 0753
  http://www.dta-uk.org
- ○ *P

Depression Alliance   (DA)   1979

- ◼ 212 Spitfire Studios, 63-71 Collier St, LONDON, N1 9BE.
  (hq)
  0845 123 2320
  email information@depressionalliance.org
  http://www.depressionalliance.org
  Sec: Paul Lanham
- ▲ Company Limited by Guarantee; Registered Charity
- Br 3
- ○ *W; information & understanding for anyone affected by
  depression
- ● Inf - Co-ordination of self-help groups, correspondence
  schemes & e-mail group
- M 2,500 i, UK & o'seas
- ¶ Various Booklets & Leaflets.

Depression UK   (D-UK)   1973

- ◼ c/o Self Help Nottingham, Ormiston House, 32-36 Pelham St,
  NOTTINGHAM, NG1 2EG.   (mail/address)
  email info@depressionuk.org
  http://www.depressionuk.org
  Hon Sec: Katie Wilkins
- ▲ Registered Charity
- ○ *W; support & encouragement for people with depression, &
  for their relatives & friends
- ● Conf - Res - Inf - Pen / phone friend schemes - Self help group
  support
- M 350 i, 1 org (NCVO), UK / 4 i, o'seas
  (Sub: £10)
- ¶ NL - 6; ftm, £1.50 each nm.   AR; free.
- ✕ 2007 (September) Fellowship of Depressives Anonymous

Derby Porcelain International Society   (DPIS)   1984

- ◼ PO Box 6997, COLESHILL, Warks, B46 2LF.   (hsp)
  01675 481293
  email a.varnam@farming.co.uk
  http://www.derby-porcelain.org.uk
  Hon Sec: Anthony Varnam
- ▲ Registered Charity
- ○ *G, *L; the history & research of Derbyshire ceramics from
  1748 to date
- ● Res - VE
- M 250 i, UK / 25 i, o'seas
  £25 UK / £35 o'seas)
- ¶ Jnl - 3; ftm, £10 nm.   NL - 2; ftm, £5 nm.

Derbyshire Agricultural & Horticultural Society Ltd   (DAHS)   1860

- ◼ 5 Willow Park Way, Weston Rd, Aston on Trent, DERBY,
  DE72 2DF.   (hsp)
  01332 793068   fax 01332 793068
  email info@derbyshirecountyshow.org.uk
  http://www.derbyshirecountyshow.org.uk
  Gen Sec: Mrs Anne James,
  Chmn: Edward Hicklin
- ▲ Registered Charity
- ○ *F, *H; farming & agriculture, horticulture & staging the
  Derbyshire County Show
- < Assn of Show & Agricl Orgs
- M 592 i
- ¶ Show Catalogue - 1; price varies.

Derbyshire Archaeological Society   (DAS)   1878

- NR 2 The Watermeadows, Swarkestone, DERBY, DE73 1JA.   (hsp)
  01332 704148
  email barbarafoster@talk21.com
  http://www.derbyshireas.org.uk
  Hon Sec: Barbara Foster
- ▲ Registered Charity
- ○ *L; to promote the study of archaeology & history of Derbyshire
- Gp Archaeological research; Architecture; Industrial archaeology;
  Local history; Vernacular architecture (Derbyshire Buildings
  Record)
- ● Mtgs - ET - Res - Lib - VE - LG (local)
- < Coun for Brit Archaeology; Assn for Indl Archaeology;
  Newcomen Soc
- M 502 i, 60 org
- ¶ Derbyshire Archaeological Jnl - 1; ftm, varies nm.
  Derbyshire Miscellany - 2; £4 m, £5 nm.
  Gazeteers of Industrial Archaeology - irreg.
  [subscription, £15].

Derbyshire Chamber & Business Link
  in 2008 merged with the Nottinghamshire Chamber of Commerce &
  Industry to form the **Derbyshire & Nottinghamshire Chamber**

Derbyshire Gritstone Sheepbreeders Society   (DGSS)   1906

- NR 5 Bridge Close, Waterfoot, ROSSENDALE, Lancs, BB4 9SN.
  (hsp)
  01706 228520
  Hon Sec: Mrs S Coppack
- ▲ Registered Charity
- ○ *B
- ● Mtgs - Society show & sale at Clitheroe
- < Nat Sheep Assn
- M 160 i
- ¶ NL - 1;   Booklet; both ftm only.

Derbyshire and Nottinghamshire Chamber of Commerce (DNCC) 1899
- ■ Commerce Centre, Canal Wharf, CHESTERFIELD, Derbys, S41 7NA. (hq)
  0845 601 1038   fax 01246 233228
  email info@dncc.co.uk   http://www.dncc.co.uk
  Chief Exec: George Cowcher
- ▲ Company Limited by Guarantee
- Br 2
- ○ *C; business support services incl training, business development & networking
- Gp Forums: Engineering, Skills, International trade;
  Councils: Derbyshire members, Nottinghamshire members
- ● Conf - Mtgs - ET - Exam - Res - Exhib - Expt - Inf - LG
- < Brit Chams Comm; E Midlands Cham Comm
- > Derbyshire Enterprise Agency
- M 3,600 f
- ¶ In Business - 12; ftm, £2.95 nm.
- × 2008 (Derbyshire Chamber & Business Link (Nottinghamshire Chamber of Commerce & Industry

Derbyshire Record Society (DRS) 1977
- ■ 57 New Rd, Wingerworth, CHESTERFIELD, Derbys, S42 6UJ. (treas/p)
  01246 231024
  Hon Treas: D G Edwards,   Hon Sec: Philip Riden
- ▲ Registered Charity
- ○ *L; publication of historical records relating to Derbyshire
- ● Res
- M 300 i, 15 org, UK / 15 i, o'seas
- ¶ NL - 2; ftm only.

Derry Chamber of Commerce
    alternative name of the **Londonderry Chamber of Commerce**

Design & Artists Copyright Society Ltd (DACS) 1983
- ■ 33 Great Sutton St, LONDON, EC1V 0DX. (hq)
  020 7336 8811   fax 020 7336 8822
  email info@dacs.org.uk   http://www.dacs.org.uk
  Chief Exec: Joanna Cave
- ▲ Company Limited by Guarantee
- ○ *A, *T; the copyright & collecting society for the visual arts in the UK; to administer & protect the rights of visual creators; membership is open to all artists & photographers
- Gp Artists copyright
- ● ET - Inf - LG - Collecting society
- < Eur Visual Artists (EVA); IFRRO; CISAC; Brit Copyright Coun
- M i
- ¶ AR - 1; free.

Design Association (DA) 2001
- ■ 1 Cedar Court, Royal Oak Yard, Bermondsey St, LONDON, SE1 3GA. (hq)
  020 7357 8282   fax 020 7407 9878
  email info@design-association.org
  http://www.design-association.org
  Chief Exec: Frank Peters
- ▲ Company Limited by Guarantee
- ○ *T; accreditation of design businesses
- ● ET - Stat - Expt
- < Chart Soc of Designers
- M f
- ¶ Various professional publications & practice documents.

Design Business Association (DBA) 1986
- NR 35-39 Old St, LONDON, EC1V 9HX.   (hq)
  020 7251 9229   fax 020 7251 9221
  email deborah.dawton@dba.org.uk
  http://www.dba.org.uk
  Chief Exec: Deborah Dawton
- ▲ Company Limited by Guarantee
- ○ *T; 'to demonstrate the contribution that design makes to society & to promote professional excellence in bringing together creativity & commerce'
- ● Conf - Mtgs - ET - Res - Exhib - Comp - Expt - Inf - LG
- M 200 f, UK / 2 f, o'seas

Design History Society (DHS) 1977
- ■ MoDA - Middlesex University, Cat Hill, BARNET, Herts, EN4 8HT.   (hsp)
  email z.hendon@mdx.ac.uk
  http://www.designhistorysociety.org
  Hon Sec: Zoe Hendon
- ▲ Registered Charity
- ○ *A; to promote the study of & research into, design history; to disseminate & publish the useful results; to exchange information with other bodies & individuals concerned with design history
- ● Conf - Mtgs - ET - Exhib - SG - Inf - VE
- M 200 i, 100 libraries & colleges, UK / 30 i, o'seas
- ¶ Jnl of Design History - 4;   NL - 4; both ftm.

Design & Industries Association (DIA) 1917
- NR c/o Derek Rothera & Co, Unit 15-16, 7 Wenlock Rd, LONDON, N1 7SL.
- ▲ Registered Charity
- ○ *P; to provide a forum for those engaged in education, design & industry with the common aim of raising the standards of design & the public awareness of the value of good design

Design & Technology Association (DATA) 1989
- NR 16 Wellesbourne House, Walton Rd, WELLESBOURNE, Warks, CV35 9JB.   (hq)
  01789 470007   fax 01789 841955
  email data@data.org.uk   http://www.data.org.uk
  Chief Exec: Richard Green
- ▲ Company Limited by Guarantee; Registered Charity
- ○ *E, *P; for all those involved in design & technology education & associated subject areas; to promote the advancement of education & in particular, but not exclusively, to support, encourage, promote, develop & maintain design & technological education in all its branches
- Gp Advisory groups: Primary, Secondary, Initial teacher education, Special educational needs
- ● Conf - Mtgs - ET - Res - Exhib - Stat - Inf (members only) - Lib - LG
- M 5,423 i, 54 f, UK / 118 i, o'seas
- ¶ DATA News - 3;   DATA Jnl - 3;   MODUS - 6; all ftm only. Designing Magazine - 3; £18 m, £21 nm.

Despatch Association (DA) 1985
- NR Lamb's End House, 36 Church Rd, Magdalen, KING'S LYNN, Norfolk, PE34 3DG.   (hq)
  01553 813479   fax 01553 813479
  email phil@despatch.co.uk   http://www.despatch.co.uk
  Chief Exec: Phillip Stone
- ▲ Un-incorporated Society
- ○ *T; to represent the despatch & courier industry
- ● Res - Inf - LG
- < Eur Express Assn
- M 250 f
- ¶ Despatches Magazine - 6; ftm, £1.10 nm.
  Despatches Magazine - online; ftm.

Desserts & Cake Mixes Association
    a sector of the **Food Processers Association**

© CBD Research Ltd · Beckenham · BR3 5JS · Tel 020 8650 7745 · Fax 020 8650 0768 · E-mail cbd@cbdresearch.com · www.cbdresearch.com

Deutsch-Britische Industrie- und Handelskammer
German name of the **German-British Chamber of Industry & Commerce**

Development Education Association   (DEA)   1993
NR   CAN Mezzanine, 32-36 Loman St, LONDON, SE1 0EH.   (hq)
         020 7922 7930   fax 020 7922 7929
         email dea@dea.org.uk   http://www.dea.org.uk
         Dir: Dr Douglas Bourn
▲   Company Limited by Guarantee; Registered Charity
○   *E, *N; an umbrella body working to support & promote
         greater awareness & understanding of global & international
         development issues in the UK; member organisations work
         within schools & education, youth organisations, community
         groups etc to bring a global perspective to learning at all
         ages
●   Conf - Mtgs - ET - Res - Inf - Lib - LG
M   45 centres, 230 org
¶   Development Education (Jnl) - 3.
         DEA Bulletin - 10;   Schools News (NL) - 2;
         Global Youth Work (NL) - 2;   AR;
         Worldlywise (adult education) (NL) - 2; all ftm only.

Development Studies Association   (DSA)   1978
NR   PO Box 108, BIDEFORD, Devon, EX39 6ZQ.   (admin/b)
         01288 331360
         email admin@devstud.org.uk   http://www.devstud.org.uk
         Exec Dir: Frances Hill
▲   Registered Charity
○   *G, *K; to connect & promote the development research
         community in the UK & Ireland
Gp   DSA Scotland
         Study groups: Ageing & development; Agriculture & rural
         development; Bridging research & policy, Conflict & human
         security, Corporate social responsibility, Design &
         development, Development ethics, Development
         management, Disasters & development, Economics, finance
         & trade, Environment, resources & sustainable development,
         European development policy, History & development, HIV/
         AIDS, Information technology & development, Livestock,
         Media & development, Multi-dimensional poverty, NGOs in
         development, Public engagement in development, Research
         students, Tourism & development, Urban policy, Women in
         development
●   Conf - Mtgs - ET - SG - Inf - LG
<   Brit O'seas NGOs for Devt; Devt Educ Assn; Eur Assn Devt
         Training Insts
M   1,000 i, 80 f, UK / 250 i, o'seas
¶   Jnl of International Development - 8; £52 yr m, £340 yr nm.

Development Trusts Association   (DTA)   1992
NR   33 Corsham St, LONDON, N1 6DR.   (hq)
         0845 458 8336   fax 0845 458 8337
         email info@dta.org.uk   http://www.dta.org.uk
         Dir: Steve Wyler
▲   Company Limited by Guarantee; Registered Charity
○   *N; to support existing development trusts & the creation of new
         ones
Gp   Forums: Coalfields, Coastal, Rural
●   Conf - Inf - VE - LG
<   Brit Urban Regeneration Assn; Indl Common Ownership
         Movement; Neighbourhood Initiatives Foundation
M   295 trusts, 140 associate m (local authorities, government
         agencies, businesses)
¶   Networker (NL) - 4; ftm.
         Other publications.

Development Trusts Association Scotland   2003
NR   54 Manor Place, EDINBURGH, EH3 7EH.
         0131 220 2456   fax 0131 220 3777
         email info@dtascot.org.uk   http://www.dtascot.org.uk
○   *K

Devon Archaeological Society   (DAS)   1929
■   Royal Albert Memorial Museum, Queen St, EXETER, Devon,
         EX4 3RX.   (hsb)
         http://www.groups.ex.ac/das/
▲   Registered Charity
○   *L, *Q; archaeological promotion & conservation within Devon
●   Conf - Mtgs - ET - Res - Exhib - SG - Inf - Lib - VE
M   940 i, 52 org, UK / 20 i, o'seas
¶   Proceedings - 1; ftm, £18 nm.   NL - 3; ftm only.
         Devon Archaeology - 1; ftm, from £1.50 nm (as available).

Devon Cattle Breeders' Society   (DCBS)   1884
■   Wisteria Cottage, Iddesleigh, WINKLEIGH, Devon,
         EX19 8BG.   (sp)
         01837 810942   fax 01837 810942
         http://www.redrubydevon.co.uk
         Sec: Andrew Lane
▲   Company Limited by Guarantee; Registered Charity
○   *B; to further the breeding of the Red Ruby Devon breed of
         cattle
●   Mtgs - Comp - Stat - Expt - Inf - Lib
<   Devon Cattle Breeder Socs in: Australia, New Zealand, Brazil &
         USA
M   c 400 i
¶   NL - 4;   AR; both ftm only.
         Davy's Devon Herd Book - 1.

Devon Closewool Sheep Breeders' Society   1923
■   c/o Holtom & Thomas, The Elms Office, Bishops Tawton,
         BARNSTAPLE, Devon, EX32 0EJ.   (sp)
         01271 326900
         http://www.devonclosewool.co.uk
         Sec: R F Y Smith
▲   Un-incorporated Society
○   *B
●   Comp
<   Nat Sheepbreeders Assn
M   65 i, 2 f
¶   Flock Book - 1; ftm, £2 nm.

Devon & Cornwall Longwool Flock Book Association   1977
NR   Peckham View, Kentisbeare, CULLOMPTON, Devon, EX15 2EY.
         01884 266201
         Sec: M J Britton
▲   Registered Charity
○   *B; breeding of pedigree longwool sheep; production of good
         lustre wool
●   Mtgs - Comp
M   60 i
¶   Flock Book - 1.

Devon & Cornwall Record Society   (DCRS)   1904
■   c/o Devon & Exeter Institution, 7 Cathedral Close, EXETER,
         Devon, EX1 1EZ.   (hsb)
         01392 274727
         http://www.cs.ncl.ac.uk/genuki/DEV/DCRS
         Admin: Mrs E Franceschini
▲   Registered Charity
○   *L; publication of local records, promotion of local historical
         studies & genealogical research
●   Res - Lib - Collection of transcripts of parish registers & other
         source material
M   500 i, 50 org, UK / 15 i, 40 org, o'seas, (org are libraries &
         institutions)
¶   Publications list available.

Devon County Agricultural Association (DCAA) 1872
NR Westpoint, Clyst St Mary, EXETER, Devon, EX5 1DJ. (hq)
    01392 446000   fax 01392 444808
    http://www.devoncountyshow.co.uk
    Co Sec: M Hosking
▲ Registered Charity
○ *F; promotion of agriculture, forestry, horticulture & commerce
    in Devon
● Agricultural shows, exhibitions & events
M 2,212 i, f & org
¶ Devon County Show Catalogue - 1.   DCAA Ybk; ftm only.
    Devon County Show Programme - 1.

Dexter Cattle Society 1892
■ RASE Offices (1st floor), STONELEIGH PARK, Warks,
    CV8 2LZ. (hq)
    024 7669 2300   fax 024 7669 2400
    email secretary@dextercattle.co.uk
    http://www.dextercattle.co.uk
    Sec: Sue Archer
▲ Company Limited by Guarantee; Registered Charity
Br 14; France, Germany, Ireland
○ *B; to promote the development of the breed & its markets
    (niche beef)
● Conf - Mtgs - ET - Res - SG - Stat - Expt
M 1,400 i, UK / 50 i, o'seas
¶ The Dexter Bulletin - 3;   Dexter NL - 3; both ftm only.

Diabetes Federation of Ireland
IRL 76 Lower Gardiner St, DUBLIN 1, Republic of Ireland.
    353 (1) 836 3022   fax 353 (1) 836 5182
    email info@diabetes.ie   http://www.diabetes.ie
    Hon Chmn: Dr Tony O'Sullivan
○ *W

Diabetes UK 1934
■ 10 Parkway, LONDON, NW1 7AA. (hq)
    020 7424 1000   fax 020 7424 1001
    email info@diabetes.org.uk
    http://www.diabetes.org.uk
    Chief Exec: Douglas Smallwood
▲ Registered Charity
Br 6
○ *W; to fund research into diabetes; to raise awareness of the
    seriousness of the condition; to provide information to people
    with diabetes, their families, healthcare professionals & the
    general public
Gp Healthcare professionals
● Conf - ET - Res - Exhib - Stat - Inf - Lib - PL - VE - LG
< Intl Diabetes Fedn (IDF)
M 180,000 i
¶ Balance - 6; ftm, £2.95 nm.
    Diabetic Medicine - 12.
    Diabetes Update (for healthcare professionals) - 4; ftm.

Diaconal Association of the Church of England 1988
NR 55 Vicarage Lane, Marton, BLACKPOOL, Lancs, FY4 4EF.
    0870 321 3260
    email secretary@dace.org   http://www.dace.org
    Sec: Revd Ann Wren

Dickens Fellowship 1902
■ 48 Doughty St, LONDON, WC1N 2LX. (hq)
    020 7405 2127   fax 020 7831 5175
    email dickensfellowship@btinternet.co.uk
    http://www.dickensfellowship.org
    Jt Hon Gen Secs: Mrs Lee Ault, Mrs Joan Dicks
▲ Un-incorporated Society
Br 15; 33 o'seas
○ *L; literary society for lovers of the works of Charles Dickens;
    preservation of buildings & objects associated with him
● Conf - Mtgs - Res - SG - Inf - VE
M i (branches are autonomous, numbers unknown)
¶ The Dickensian - 3; £12 m.

Diecasting Society (DCS) 1966
■ National Metalforming Centre, 47 Birmingham Rd,
    WEST BROMWICH, W Midlands, B70 6PY. (hq)
    0121-456 6103   fax 0870 138 9714
    email dcs@alfed.org.uk
    Sec: Will Savage
▲ Company Limited by Guarantee; Registered Charity
Br 3
○ *P; to advance the study of diecasting, the technology &
    methods, to promote research & disseminate the results
● Conf - Mtgs - ET - Exhib - SG - Inf - Lib - VE
M 153 i, 90 f, UK / 5 i, o'seas
¶ NL - 3; ftm only.
    Conference Proceedings - 2 yrly; £20.

Digital Content Forum (DCF) 2000
NR 131-151 Great Titchfield St, LONDON, W1W 5BB. (hq)
    020 7665 8440
    http://www.dcf.org.uk
    Chmn: Paul Jackson
○ *N
M 28 org

Digital & Screen Printing Association
    since 23 April 2008 **Prism**

Dignity in Dying 1935
NR 181 Oxford St, LONDON, W1D 2JT. (hq)
    020 7479 7730
    email info@dignityindying.org.uk
    http://www.dignityindying.org.uk
    Chief Exec: Deborah Annetts
▲ Un-incorporated Society
○ *K; to make it legal for a competent adult, who is suffering
    unbearably from an incurable illness, to receive medical help
    to die at their own considered & persistent request.
    The VES distributes forms for living wills in order to refuse
    unwanted life-prolonging treatment & advises on their usage
    (which is legally enforceable)
● LG
M 15,000 i
¶ NL - 4; ftm only.   Living Wills; £15.
× 2006 Voluntary Euthanasia Society

Dinosaur Society UK 1993
■ c/o Gnoll House, 15 Forster Rd, GUILDFORD, Surrey,
    GU2 9AE. (hsp)
    email editor@dinosaursociety.com
    http://www.dinosaursociety.com
    Chmn: Prof Richard T J Moody
▲ Registered Charity
○ *K; to raise the awareness & to advance public interest in
    dinosaur palaeontology
● Conf - ET - Exhib
M purely web-based; free.
¶ web-based.

Diplomatic Service Families Association   (DSFA)
NR Foreign & Commonwealth Office, Old Admiralty Building
    (Room 1/95), LONDON, SW1A 2PA.
    020 7008 0283
    email dsfa.enquiries@fco.gov.uk
    Chmn: Tina Attwood
○ *W

Dipterists Forum - the Society for the Study of Flies 1993
NR c/o BENHS, The Pelham-Clinton Building, Dinton Pastures
    Country Park, Hurst, READING, RG10 0TH.
    http://www.dipteristsforum.org.uk
○ *P, *G

© CBD Research Ltd · Beckenham · BR3 5JS · Tel 020 8650 7745 · Fax 020 8650 0768 · E-mail cbd@cbdresearch.com · www.cbdresearch.com

Direct Marketing Association (UK) Ltd   (DMA)   1992
NR   DMA House, 70 Margaret St, LONDON, W1W 8SS.   (hq)
        020 7291 3300
        http://www.dma.org.uk
▲   Company Limited by Guarantee
Br   3
○   *T; 'to raise the stature of the direct marketing industry, giving
        the consumer trust & confidence in direct marketing'
●   Conf - Mtgs - Res - Exhib - Stat - Expt - Inf - Lib - LG
M   680 f, UK / 40 f, o'seas

Direct Selling Association Ltd   (DSA)   1965
■   29 Floral St, LONDON, WC2E 9DP.   (hq)
        020 7497 1234   fax 020 7497 3144
        http://www.dsa.org.uk
        Dir: Richard M Berry
▲   Company Limited by Guarantee
○   *T; to represent companies who use independent salespeople to
        sell their products, by party plan or person to person, &
        whose marketing plans are legal & who have agreed to
        abide by the DSA codes of practice
●   Conf - Mtgs - Res - Stat - Inf - Lib - LG
<   Wld Fedn of Direct Selling Assns (USA); Fedn of Eur Direct
        Selling Assns (FEDSA)
M   41 f, 12 prospective f, 40 associates (suppliers of services)
¶   Shopping at Home: consumer guide including the DSA Code of
        Practice;
        A guide to earnings opportunities in direct selling (containing
        DSA Code of Business Conduct);
        Report - Independent Code Administration - 1; all free.
        Direct Selling, Consumer Goods in the UK (survey) - 1; ftm,
        £25 nm.
        Direct Selling: from door to door to network marketing; £17.99.

Directors Guild of Great Britain   (DGGB)   1983
NR   4 Windmill St, LONDON, W1T 2HZ.   (hq)
        020 7580 9131   fax 020 7580 9132
        http://www.dggb.co.uk
        Gen Sec: Piers Haggard
○   *P, *U; represents the interests of directors in all media: theatre,
        film, TV, ballet, opera, commercials, videos etc
Gp   Recorded media: Film, Television, Video, Radio
        Live media: Theatre, Opera, Dance
●   Conf - Mtgs - Res - Inf - Empl - LG - Events - Networking -
        Masterclasses
<   Fedn of Eur Film Directors (FERA), Informal Eur Theatre Meeting
        (IETM), Nat Campaign for the Arts (NCA)
M   1,000 i, 50 f, 22 org, UK / 20 i, o'seas
¶   Direct (NL) - 4.   LM - 2 yrly.
        Rates Cards (Schedule of rates of pay) - 1.
        Contract Guide - 1.
        Monitoring Report on Theatre Directors.

Directory & Database Publishers Association
        since 2005 **Data Publishers Association**

Disability Alliance   1974
■   Universal House, 88-94 Wentworth St, LONDON, E1 7SA.
        (hq)
        020 7247 8776 (1000-1600 hrs)   fax 020 7247 8765
        email office.da@dial.pipex.com
        http://www.disabilityalliance.org
        Chief Exec: Vanessa Stanislas,   Sec: David Fletcher
▲   Company Limited by Guarantee; Registered Charity
○   *K, *W; to break the link between poverty & disability by
        providing information to disabled people about their
        entitlements; to campaign for improvements to the social
        security system & for increases in benefits
●   ET - Inf - LG
M   380+ org
        (Sub: in price bands)
¶   Disability Rights Hbk 2008-09 - 1; £21 (£14.50 for individuals
        in receipt of benefits).
        Employment & Support Alliance Guide 2008-09; £7 (£2
        concessionary rate)

Disability Federation of Ireland   (DFI)
IRL   Fumbally Court, Fumbally Lane, DUBLIN 8, Republic of Ireland.
        353 (1) 454 7978   fax 353 (1) 454 7981
        email info@disability-federation.ie
        http://www.disability-federation.ie
        Chief Exec: John Dolan
○   *N, *W

Disability Sport England
        in 2005 became the events division of the **English Federation of
        Disability Sport**

Disabled Drivers' Association
        in 2005-06 merged with the Disabled Drivers Motor Club to form the
        Mobilise Organisation

Disabled Drivers' Motor Club
        in 2005-6 merged with the Disabled Drivers Association to form the
        Mobilise Organisation

Disabled Motorcyclists Association   (DMA)
NR   Ada House, 77 Thompson St, MANCHESTER, M4 5FY.
        0161-833 8817
        http://www.thedma.org.uk
        Sec: John Bowden

Disabled Motorists Federation   (DMF)   1955
■   Chester-le-Street CVS Volunteer Centre, Clarence Terrace,
        CHESTER-LE-STREET, Co Durham, DH3 3DQ.   (hsp)
        0191-416 3172   fax 0191-416 3172
        email jkillick2214@compuserve.com
        http://www.freewebs.com/dmfed
        Hon Sec: J E Killick
▲   Registered Charity
Br   11 affiliated clubs; Russia
○   *W; to provide motoring information to the disabled & their
        carers on all matters of disabled travel; to run social clubs &
        to negotiate with national bodies on all matters connected
        with disabled travel, not specialising in motoring
●   Mtgs - Inf - LG
M   c 2,000 i, 11 affiliated clubs
¶   The Way Ahead - 4; ftm, £1.25 nm.
        Publications list available.

Disablement Income Group Scotland   (DIG Scotland)   1966
NR   5 Quayside St, EDINBURGH, EH6 6EJ.   (hq)
        0131-555 2811   fax 0131-554 7076
        email info@digscotland.co.uk
        http://www.digscotland.org.uk
        Chmn: Mike Coveney,   Co Sec: Frank Cochrane
▲   Company Limited by Guarantee
○   *W; free welfare benefits information & advice service for
        disabled people & carers throughout Scotland
●   Talks to disability & carers' groups - Training for professionals -
        Advice clinics at hospital & cancer care centres
M   2,900 i, 15 org
¶   NL - 4; m only.
        AR & Chairman's Report.

Discovery Award England   (DAE)
- ■ St Mary's Church Hall, Wollaton Hall Drive, NOTTINGHAM, NG8 1AF.   (hq)
  0115-978 6988
  http://www.discoveryawardengland.co.uk
- ▲ Un-incorporated Society
- Br 100; Australia, Malta
- ○ *G; 'to foster & encourage the development of people over the age of 50, physically, mentally & spiritually - enables & encourages people to make choices about their own lives & increase their contribution to life by meeting personal challenges'
- ● Conf - Mtgs - VE
- M 525 i, UK / 5 i, o'seas
  Subs: £5
- ¶ AR; free.

Discrimination Law Association   (DLA)   1995
- ■ PO Box 7722, NEWBURY, Berks, RG20 4WD.   (hq)
  0845 478 6375
  email info@discriminationlaw.org.uk
  http://www.discriminationlaw.org.uk
  Co Sec: Sharon Morris
- ▲ Company Limited by Guarantee
- ○ *P; to promote good community relations by improving assistance & support to victims of discrimination; to advance education & training in the field of legal representation
- ● Conf - Mtgs - ET - Inf LG
- M 233 i, 41 f, 133 org
- ¶ Discrimination Law Briefings - 4; ftm, £20 each nm.
  Directory of Members - on-going; ftm only.
  Directory of Trainers - 2; free.
  NL - 4; ftm.   AR; ftm, £1 nm.

Dispensing Doctors Association Ltd   (DDA)   1997
- ■ Low Hagg Farm, Starfitts Lane, KIRKBYMOORSIDE, N Yorks, YO62 7JF.   (hsb)
  01751 430835   fax 01751 430836
  email office@dispensingdoctor.org
  http://www.dispensingdoctor.org
  Chief Exec: Dr David Baker
  Sec: Jeff Lee
- ▲ Company Limited by Guarantee
- ○ *P; for doctors providing pharmaceutical services in rural areas
- Gp Financial; Publicity
- ● Conf - ET - Inf - LG
- M c 2,400 i, 25 f
- ¶ Jnl - 4.

District Auditors Society
- NR c/o Sue Exton / Audit Commission, Millbank Tower (1st floor), Millbank, LONDON, SW1P 4HQ.   (pres/b)
  020 7828 1212
  Pres: Sue Exton
- ○ *P
- < Mtgs
- M i

District Courts Association
  wound up May 2007

District Surveyors Association Ltd
  registered name of **LABC**

District of Wigtown Chamber of Commerce   2006
- NR c/o Book Town Office, County Buildings, WIGTOWN, DG8 9JH.
  01671 403875
  email enquiries@dw-chamber.org.uk
  http://www.dw-chamber.org.uk
  Sec: Bobbie Ingram
- ○ *C

Docklands Business Club
  since 20 October 1999 (as Docklands Business Club & East London Chamber of Commerce) a branch of the **London Chamber of Commerce & Industry**

Doctor E F Schumacher Society   (Schumacher UK)   1978
- ■ The Create Environment Centre, Smeaton Rd, BRISTOL, BS1 6XN.   (hq)
  0117-903 1081   fax 0117-903 1081
  email admin@schumacher.org.uk
  http://www.schumacher.org.uk
  Dir: Richard St George
- ▲ Company Limited by Guarantee
- Br 3; Germany, India, Ireland, USA
- ○ *G; to promote the philosophy of Dr E F Schumacher; to promote human scale sustainable development in the UK & abroad
- Gp Schumacher book service
- ● Conf - ET - Res - Inf - VE - Presentation of annual Schumacher award
- < Members of the Schumacher Circle:
  Centre for Alternative Technology; Intermediate Technology; New Economics Foundation; Soil Association
- > Schumacher College
- M 500 i, 5 f, 5 org, UK / 50 i, o'seas
- ¶ Schumacher NL - 2; ftm, £2 nm.
  Schumacher Briefings - 2/3; ftm, £6-£8 nm.

Doctor Richard Bright Society
- NR c/o Richard Bright Renal Unit, Southmead Hospital, BRISTOL, BS11 5NR.   (mail address)
  Hon Sec: Diana Berry (0117-973 1937)
- ○ *G
- M c 30-40 i

Dogs Trust   1891
- ■ 17 Wakley St, LONDON, EC1V 7RQ.   (hq)
  020 7837 0006   fax 020 7833 2701
  email info@dogstrust.org.uk
  http://www.dogstrust.org.uk
  Chief Exec: Clarissa Baldwin
- ▲ Registered Charity
- Br 15
- ○ *V; 'working towards the day when all dogs can enjoy a happy life, free from the threat of unnecessary destruction'
- ● Conf - Mtgs - ET - Res - Exhib - Comp - Stat - Expt - Inf - PL
- M 15,825 i, 826 f, 262,775 supporters, UK / 96 i, 808 supporters, o'seas
- ¶ NL - 3; free.   AR; ftm only.
  Educational literature.
- ✕ 2003 National Canine Defence League

Doll Club of Great Britain
- NR 1 Chelsea Manor Street, LONDON, SW3 5RP.   (mail/address)
  Hon Sec: Mrs Margaret Towner
- ▲ Un-incorporated Society
- ○ *G; the study & appreciation of dolls, dolls houses & other nursery bygones of the past
- ● Mtgs - Comp - SG - VE
- M 150 i, UK / 20 i, o'seas
- ¶ Plangon - 4; ftm only.

© CBD Research Ltd · Beckenham · BR3 5JS · Tel 020 8650 7745 · Fax 020 8650 0768 · E-mail cbd@cbdresearch.com · www.cbdresearch.com

Dolmetsch Historical Dance Society   (DHDS)   1970
- ■ 17 Well Lane, Stock, INGATESTONE, Essex, CM4 9LT.   (hsp)
  01277 840473   fax 01277 840473
  email secretary@dhds.org.uk   http://www.dhds.org.uk
  Hon Sec: Mrs Jo Saunders
- ▲ Registered Charity
- ○ *A, *D, *G, *L, *Q; conducting & promoting original research
  into & practice of dance, from the 14th-19th centuries &
  allied subjects of music, literature, art, costume & social
  history
- ● Conf - Mtgs - Res - Inf
- M 94 i, UK / 21 i, o'seas
- ¶ Historical Dance (Jnl) - 2/3 yrly; ftm, £8 nm.
  NL - 3; ftm only.   Teaching Resource Packs.
  Summer School Booklets & CDs (dance instructions & music) -
  1; prices vary.
  Conference Proceedings - 2 yrly; prices vary.

Domestic Appliance Service Association   (DASA)   1978
- ■ 145-157 St John St, LONDON, EC1V 4PY.   (asa)
  0870 224 0343   fax 0870 224 0358
  email dasa@dasa.org.uk   http://www.dasa.org.uk
  Chmn: W Russell
- ▲ Un-incorporated Society
- ○ *T; repair & servicing of domestic appliances
- ● Mtgs - ET - Exhib - LG
- < Brit Quality Foundation; Electrical & Electronics Servicing
  Training Coun;Trade Assn Forum
- M 100 i, 30 f
- ¶ Orbit (NL) - 6; ftm only.   LM [website].

Domestic Fowl Trust   1974
- NR Station Rd, Honeybourne, EVESHAM, Worcs, WR11 7QZ.   (hq)
  01386 833083   fax 01386 833364
  email dlf@domesticfowltrust.co.uk
  http://www.domesticfowltrust.co.uk
  Chief Exec: Mrs Bernie Landshoff
- ○ *B; conservation of the domestic fowl & rare breeds of farm
  animals; marketing of poultry housing & equipment, hybrid &
  traditional breeds of poultry, books & gifts
- ● ET
- M 350 i, UK / 30 i, o'seas

Domestic Heating Controls Group
  incorporated in the Control Manufacturers Association in **BEAMA**

Domestic Water Treatment Association
  association in Energy section of **BEAMA Ltd**D17[S102UA]
  (06)Malcolm Dutton/0114-263 2431D17[S102UA]   (06)Malcolm
  Dutton/0114-263 2431

Doncaster Chamber   (DCCE)   1941
- ■ ICON, First Point Balby Carr Bank, DONCASTER, S Yorks,
  DN4 5JQ.   (hq)
  01302 341000   fax 01302 328382
  email enquiries@doncaster-chamber.co.uk
  http://www.doncaster-chamber.co.uk
  Chief Exec: Stephen Shore
- ▲ Company Limited by Guarantee
- ○ *C
- ● Conf - Mtgs - ET - Res - Exhib - Comp - Stat - Expt - Inf - Lib -
  VE - Empl - LG
- < Brit Chams Comm
- M 1,000 f
- ¶ Chamber News - 6;   Chamber Link - 6; both free.
- ✕ Doncaster Chamber of Commerce

Donizetti Society   1973
- ■ 146 Bordesley Rd, MORDEN, Surrey, SM4 5LT.   (hsp)
  020 8648 9364
  http://www.donizettisociety.com
  Hon Sec: J P Clayton
- ○ *D; to promote interest in the works of Gaetano Donizetti
  (1797-1848) & the music of his period
- M i

Donkey Breed Society   (DBS)   1967
- NR The Hermitage, Pootings, EDENBRIDGE, Kent, TN8 6SD.   (hsb)
  01732 864414   fax 01732 864414
  email carol@morse.freeserve.co.uk
  http://www.donkeybreedsociety.co.uk
  Sec: Carol Morse
- ○ *B; to encourage the use, appreciation, well being & protection
  of the donkey
- Gp Championship show; Shows & judges; Driving; Studbook;
  Welfare; Juniors
- ● Conf - ET - Comp - SG - Inf
- < Brit Horse Soc
- M c 1,000 i
- ¶ Magazine - 1.   NL - 4.

Donor Watch   1995
- ■ Turner House, 153 Cromwell Road, LONDON, SW5 0TQ.
  (hsp)
  020 7373 5560   fax 020 7373 5560
  email selbywhittingham@hotmail.com
  Sec-Gen: Dr Selby Whittingham
- ▲ Un-incorporated Society
- ○ *L; campaigning in support of fidelity to the conditions on
  which money, or objects, are given or bequeathed for the
  benefit of the public
- ● Campaigning
- M [not stated]
- ¶ NL - 2/3; ftm only.

Door & Hardware Federation   (DHF)   1970
- ■ 42 Heath St, TAMWORTH, Staffs, B79 7JH.
  01827 52337   fax 01827 310827
  email info@dhfonline.org.uk
  http://www.dhfonline.org.uk   (hq)
  Sec: Michael Skelding
- ▲ Company Limited by Guarantee
- ○ *T; to represent the interests of manufacturers & installers of
  industrial, pedestrian & garage doors; also manufacturers of
  locks & building hardware. It provides professionals in all
  sectors of the building industry with a single source for
  technical expertise to assure progress & maintenance of
  standards throughout the industry
- Gp Drive & control; Garage door; Hardware; Industrial door;
  Metal doorset; Repair & service
- ● Conf - Mtgs - ET - Res - Exhib - Inf - LG
- M 320 f
  (Sub: varies)
- ¶ Best Practice Guide (series) on [eg]: Thief resistant locks; Exit
  devices; Door & window bolts; Lock cylinders.
  Code of Practice on: Hardware for fire & escape doors; Rolling
  shutters; Repair & maintenance; FR metal doorsets
  List available.
- ✕ 2005 (Association of Building Hardware Manufacturers
  (Door & Shutter Manufacturers' Association

Door & Shutter Manufacturers Association
  in 2005 merged with the Association of Building Hardware
  Manufacturers to form the **Door & Hardware Federation**

Dorchester Agricultural Society (DAS) 1841
NR 27 Durngate St, DORCHESTER, Dorset, DT1 1 JP. (hq)
01305 264249   fax 01305 251643
email info@dorsetcountyshow.co.uk
http://www.dorsetcountyshow.co.uk
Sec: Samantha E Mackenzie-Green
▲ Company Limited by Guarantee; Registered Charity
○ *F
● Comp
M 1,500 i, 20 f

Dorothy L Sayers Society   1976
■ Rose Cottage, Malthouse Lane, HURSTPIERPOINT, W Sussex,
BN6 9JY.   (chmn/p)
01273 833444   fax 01273 835988
email jasmine@sayers.org.uk
http://www.sayers.org.uk/
Chmn: Christopher J Dean
▲ Registered Charity
○ *A; study of the life & works of Dorothy L Sayers;
encouragement & advice on production & research of her
works
● Conf - Res - SG - Inf
M 260 i, UK / 255 i, o'seas
¶ DLS Bulletin - 6; ftm.   Sidelights on Sayers - 2; £3.
Annual Proceedings - 1; £3.

Dorset Chamber of Commerce & Industry   (DCCI)   1949
NR Chamber House, Ling Rd, POOLE, Dorset, BH12 4NZ.   (hq)
01202 714800
http://www.dorsetbusiness.net
Chief Exec: Peter Scott
▲ Company Limited by Guarantee
○ *C
Note: is known as Dorset Business.

Dorset Down Sheepbreeders' Association   (DDSBA)   1906
■ Havett Farm, Dobwalls, LISKEARD, Cornwall, PL14 6HB.   (hsp)
01579 320273
email secretary@dorsetdownsheep.org.uk
http://www.dorsetdownsheep.org.uk
Breed Sec: Carolyn Opie
▲ Company Limited by Guarantee; Registered Charity
○ *B
● Mtgs - Exhib - Comp - Stat - Expt - Inf - VE - Annual breed sale
< Nat Sheep Assn
M 84 i, UK / 1 i, o'seas
¶ NL - 3/4; ftm only.   Breed Flock Book - 1; ftm, £5 nm.

**Dorset Horn & Poll Dorset Sheep Breeders' Association
(DHSBA) 1891**
■ Agriculture House, Acland Rd, DORCHESTER, Dorset,
DT1 1EF. (hq)
01305 262126   fax 01305 262126
email mail@dorsetsheep.org
http://www.dorsetsheep.org
Breed Sec: Mrs M Cowley
▲ Registered Charity
○ *B
● Mtgs - Comp - Expt - Inf - Breed show & sales
M 300 i
¶ Flock Book - 1; ftm, £20 nm.

**Dorset Natural History & Archaeological Society   (DNHAS)
1875**
■ 66 High West St, DORCHESTER, Dorset, DT1 1XA.   (hq)
01305 262735
email enquiries@dorsetcountymuseum.org
http://www.dorsetcountymuseum.org
Dir: Judy Lindsay
▲ Registered Charity
○ *A, *L; archaeology, local history, natural history & geology, art
& literature (including Thomas Hardy) of Dorset
Gp Natural history; Archaeology; Geology; Junior members
● Conf - Mtgs - ET - Res - Exhib - Comp - SG - Inf - Lib - PL - VE
- Conservation
M 1,900 i, 100 org
¶ Proceedings - 1.   AR.
Archaeological Monographs.   Dorset Series.
Note: The Dorset Record Society is a committee of DNHAS.

Dorset Record Society
a committee of the **Dorset Natural History & Archaeological
Society**

Double Harness Scurry Driving
since 2005 **Scurry Driving Association**

Dover District Chamber of Commerce & Industry   1850
NR White Cliffs Business Centre, Honeywood Rd, Whitfield,
DOVER, Kent, CT16 3EH.
01304 824955   fax 01304 822354
http://www.doverchamber.co.uk
Mgr: Julia Chambers
○ *C

Down's Syndrome Association   (DSA)   1970
NR Langdon Down Centre, 2A Langdon Park, TEDDINGTON,
Middx, TW11 9PS.   (hq)
0845 230 0372   fax 020 8682 4012
email info@downs-syndrome.org.uk
http://www.downs-syndrome.org.uk
▲ Company Limited by Guarantee; Registered Charity
○ *W; to help people with Down's syndrome to live full &
rewarding lives; to provide information, counselling &
support as well as being a resource to interested
professionals
M i, f & org

Down's Syndrome Scotland   1982
■ 158-160 Balgreen Rd, EDINBURGH, EH11 3AU.   (hq)
0131-313 4225   fax 0131-313 4285
email info@dsscotland.org.uk
http://www.dsscotland.org.uk
Dir: Pandora J Summerfield
▲ Registered Charity
Br 6
○ *W; a national support group giving information & support to
people with Down's Syndrome & their families in Scotland
● Conf - ET - Inf - Lib - Local group activities
M 1,200 i, 500 professionals
¶ Publications list available; 50p - £5.

© CBD Research Ltd · Beckenham · BR3 5JS · Tel 020 8650 7745 · Fax 020 8650 0768 · E-mail cbd@cbdresearch.com · www.cbdresearch.com

Dozenal Society of Great Britain   (DSGB)   1960
- 32 Lansdowne Crescent, CARLISLE, Cumbria, CA3 9EW. (gen/sp)
  01228 596834
  http://www.dozenalsociety.org.uk
  Gen Sec: Shaun Ferguson
- ▲ Un-incorporated Society
- ○ *K; 'following the introduction of place-value arithmetic it was recognised calculations to a divisible scale of twelve numerals would not only simplify the operations but allow a precise representation of the basic ratios required to define the physical world or manage our material affairs. The Society affirms this view with the object of unifying scientific & social practices'
- Gp Arithmetic & mathematics; Historical metrology; Metrication
- ● Res - Inf - Lib - Publishing - Cooperation with the British Weights & Measures Association providing technical information & informed criticism of attempts to impose decimal-metric methods in areas where they are inappropriate
- < Dozenal Soc of America (NY); Brit Weights & Measures Assn
- M 200 i, UK / 15 i, o'seas
- ¶ The Dozenal Jnl - 1.
  T.G.M. a coherent dozenal metrology.
  Booklets & reprints of salient articles.

Dracula Society   1973
- PO Box 30848, LONDON, W12 0GY.   (mail address)
  http://www.thedraculasociety.org.uk
  Chmn & Treas: Julia Kruk
- ○ *G; 'since it is named after the most evocative title in the entire genre, the Society naturally devotes a good deal of its attention to the book & its author, Bram Stoker. However vampires, werewolves, mummies & all the other monsters spawned by the Gothic genre fall within its field of interest, which also embraces stage & screen, adaptations & the sources of inspiration in myth & folklore; The society is not concerend with psychic research or occult ceremony of anykind'
- ● Mtgs - VE
- < The Vampire Empire (NY)
- M c 90 i, UK / c 20 i, o'seas
- ¶ Voices from the Vaults (NL) - 4; ftm only.

Drake Exploration Society   (DES)   1996
- 7 Rosewood Ave, BURNHAM-on-SEA, Somerset, TA8 1HD. (hsp)
  01278 783519
  email sfdsociety@aol.com
  http://www.indrakeswake.co.uk/society
  Founder: Michael Turner
- ▲ Un-incorporated Society
- ○ *G; to perpetuate the memory of Sir Francis Drake through research, fieldwork, lectures & publications
- ● Mtgs - Res - Exhib - SG - Inf - Lib - PL - VE - Illustrated lectures & fieldwork
- < Drake Navigator's Guild (USA)
- M 26 i, 2 f, 3 org, UK / 6 i, o'seas
  (Sub: £15)
- ¶ The Drake Broadside - 1;   The Drake NL - 1; both ftm.

Drama Association of Wales   (Cymdeithas Ddrama Cymru) (DAW)   1973
- The Old Library, Singleton Rd, Splott, CARDIFF, CF24 2ET.   (hq)
  029 2045 2200   fax 029 2045 2277
  email aled.daw@virgin.net   http://www.amdram.co.uk
  Admin: Gary Thomas
- ▲ Registered Charity
- ○ *A; to promote amateur theatre in Wales & worldwide; to encourage new writing
- ● Mtgs - ET - Res - Comp - SG - Inf - Lib (world's largest collection of playscripts) - LG - Publishing
- < Intl Amat Theatre Assn; Cent Coun for Amat Theatre; Nat Assn Youth Theatre; Wales Assn for the Performing Arts
- M 221 i, 16 f, 267 org, UK / 11 i, 1 f, 6 org, o'seas
- ¶ Dawn (NL) - 4; ftm.

Drama League of Ireland
- IRL The Mill Theatre, Dundrum, DUBLIN 14, Republic of Ireland.
  353 (1) 296 9343
  email dli@eircom.net   http://www.dli.ie
  Sec: Maura Lucey
- ○ *D; to promote amateur drama & theatre in Ireland

Draught Proofing Advisory Association Ltd   (DPAA)   1980
- PO Box 12, HASLEMERE, Surrey, GU27 3AH.   (hq)
  01428 654011   fax 01428 651401
  email dpaaassociation@aol.com
  http://www.dpaa-association.org.uk
  Dir: Gillian Allder
- ▲ Company Limited by Guarantee
- ○ *T; representing the draught proofing industry
- ● Mtgs - Inf - LG
- M f
- ¶ NL; m only.   LM.

Dress & Textile Specialists   (DATS)
- NR Furniture Textiles & Fashion, Victoria & Albert Museum, LONDON, SW7 2RL.   (hsb)
  020 7942 2673
  http://www.dressandtextilespecialists.org.uk
  Hon Sec: Edwina Ehrman
- ▲ Un-incorporated Society
- ○ *P; to support museum professionals working with costume & textile collections
- ● Conf - Mtgs - ET
- < Museums Assn
- M 88 i, 44 f
- ¶ NL - 2; ftm only.

Driffield Agricultural Society
- NR The Showground, Kelleythorpe, DRIFFIELD, E Yorks, YO25 9DN.
  01377 257494
  email office@driffieldshow.co.uk
  http://www.driffieldshow.co.uk
- ○ *F, *H
- ● Show
- M i & f

Drilling & Sawing Association Ltd   (DSA)   1984
- North Mill (suite 5.O), Bridge Foot, BELPER, Derbys, DE56 1YD.   (asa)
  01773 820000   fax 01773 821284
  email dsa@drillandsaw.org.uk
  http://www.drillandsaw.org.uk
  Sec: Hugh C Wylde
- ▲ Company Limited by Guarantee
- ○ *T; concrete drilling & sawing industry
- Gp Specialist drilling & sawing contractors; Suppliers of drilling & sawing equipment
- ● Mtgs - ET - Exhib - Inf - VE
- < Intl Assn of Concrete Drillers & Sawers
- M 100 f, UK / 5 org, o'seas
- ¶ Concrete Cutter (Jnl) - 2.   LM.   Brochure.

Drinking Fountain Association
alternative name of the **Metropolitan Drinking Fountain & Cattle Trough Association**

Drinks Industry Group of Ireland
- IRL Anglesea House, Anglesea Rd, Ballsbridge, DUBLIN 4, Republic of Ireland.
  353 (1) 668 0215   fax 353 (1) 668 0448
  http://www.drinksindustry.ie
  Hon Sec: Donal O'Keeffe
- ○ *T

Drivers' Alliance
NR e-Innovation Centre SE209, University of Wolverhampton,
     Priorslee, TELFORD, Shropshire, TF2 9FT.
     01952 288338
     http://www.driversalliance.org.uk
     Dir: Peter Roberts
○   *K

Driving Instructors Association (DIA) 1978
NR Safety House, Beddington Farm Rd, CROYDON, Surrey,
     CR0 4XZ. (hq)
     020 8665 5151   fax 020 8665 5565
     http://www.driving.org
     Sec: Tina Tutton
▲   Registered Charity
○   *P; to raise the standard of driver education & improve road
     safety by means of professional training
Gp Holders of Diploma in Driving Instruction; Specialist LGV & PCV
     instructors
●   Conf - Mtgs - ET - Exam - Res - Exhib - Comp - SG - Stat - Inf -
     Lib - VE
<   Soc of Motor Mfrs & Traders; Parliamentary Advy Coun for
     Traffic Safety; Intl Assn for Driver Education (IVV)
M   10,000 i, UK / 180 i, o'seas
¶   Driving Magazine - 6.
     Driving Instructor - 6.

Drogheda Chamber of Commerce
IRL Chamber House, Dublin Rd, DROGHEDA, Co Louth, Republic
     of Ireland.
     353 (41) 983 3544   fax 353 (41) 984 1609
     email enquiries@droghedachamber.com
     http://www.droghedachamber.com
     Pres: Eugene Kierans
○   *C

Drum Corps of the United Kingdom 1980
NR 3 Eridge Rd, HOVE, E Sussex, BN3 7QD.
     0845 688 8906   fax 0870 706 5608
     email admin@dcuk.org.uk   http://www.dcuk.org.uk
○   *D
M   c 1,500 i

Dry Stone Walling Association of Great Britain (DSWA) 1968
■   Westmorland County Showground, Lane Farm, Crooklands,
     MILNTHORPE, Cumbria, LA7 7NH.   (mail address)
     01539 567953
     http://www.dswa.org.uk
     Admin: Alison Shaw
▲   Registered Charity
Br 19
○   *G; to foster an interest in dry stone walling & dyking; to ensure
     that the best craftsmanship of the past is preserved
●   Mtgs - ET - Exam - Comp - Inf (send sae) - LG
M   1,200 i, 15 f, UK / 10 i, o'seas
¶   Waller & Dyker (Jnl) - 3; ftm, £2.50 nm.
     Register of Certificated Wallers/Dykers; free with sae.
     Building & Repairing Dry Stone Walls; £1.50.
     In There Somewhere; £5.   [all plus p&p].

Dublin Chamber of Commerce 1783
IRL 7 Clare St, DUBLIN 2, Republic of Ireland.
     353 (1) 644 7200   fax 353 (1) 676 6043
     email info@dublinchamber.ie
     http://www.dublinchamber.ie
     Chief Exec: Gina Quin
○   *C

Duchenne Family Support Group (DFSG) 1987
■   6 Laburnum Rd, SANDY, Beds, SG19 1HQ.   (hsp)
     01767 680644   Office 0870 241 1857   fax 0870 241
     1857
     email info@dfsg.org.uk   http://www.dfsg.org.uk
     Hon Sec: Mrs Ann Patterson
▲   Registered Charity
○   *W; is run by families for families affected by Duchenne
     muscular dystrophy (a severely disabling & life-limiting
     muscle wasting condition)
●   Conf - Mtgs - Inf - VE - National support network of parents,
     their families & professionals
     Helpline: 0800 121 4518
M   2,000 i, 230 org, UK / 40 i, 10 org, o'seas
¶   Duchenne News - 4; free.

Dugdale Society 1920
■   The Shakespeare Centre, Henley St, STRATFORD-upon-AVON,
     Warks, CV37 6QW.   (hq/hsb)
     01789 204016   fax 01789 296083
     email records@shakespeare.org.uk
     http://www.shakespeare.org.uk/dugdale
     Chmn: Prof C C Dyer,   Hon Sec: Mrs Cathy Millwood
▲   Registered Charity
○   *L; publication of original documents on history of
     Warwickshire (named after Sir William Dugdale, antiquary
     1605-1680)
●   Res
M   250 i, 70 org, UK / 50 org, o'seas
¶   Volumes & Occasional Papers - irreg; ftm, varies nm.
     AR.

Dumfries & Galloway Chamber of Commerce (DGCC) 1987
■   16 Buccleuch St, DUMFRIES, DG1 2AH.   (hq)
     01387 270866
     email admin@dgchamber.co.uk
     http://www.dgchamber.co.uk
     Admin: Sue Taylor
▲   Company Limited by Guarantee
○   *C
●   Mtgs - Inf - Seminars
<   Scot Chams Comm; Glasgow Cham Comm
M   2,400 i, 90 f
×   2001 Dumfries & Galloway Chamber of Trade & Commerce

**Dumfriesshire & Galloway Natural History & Antiquarian
Society (DGNHAS) 1862**
NR Merkland, Kirkmahope, DUMFRIES, DG1 1SY.   (hsp)
     01387 710274
     http://www.users.quista.net/dgnhas
     Hon Sec: John L Williams
▲   Registered Charity
○   *L
●   Mtgs - VE
M   300 i, 50 org, UK / 50 i, o'seas
¶   Transactions - 1.

Dun Horse & Pony Society (DHAPS) 1999
NR 4 Elderfield Rd, Kings Norton, BIRMINGHAM, W Midlands,
     B30 3PE.   (chmn/p)
     0121-451 3479
     http://www.dhaps-online.co.uk
     Chmn: Andrew Ward
○   *B; for those interested in dun horses & ponies (Palomino
     coloured, but with black mane & tail); to promote dun horses
     in all spheres of the horse industry
●   Comp - Horse show sponsorship
M   100 i
¶   The Dun Thing - 4;   The Dun Thing Update - 2/3;   DHAPS
     Hbk - 1; all ftm only.

© CBD Research Ltd · Beckenham · BR3 5JS · Tel 020 8650 7745 · Fax 020 8650 0768 · E-mail cbd@cbdresearch.com · www.cbdresearch.com

Dundalk Chamber of Commerce
IRL   Hagan House, Rampart Rd, DUNDALK, Co Louth, Republic of
        Ireland.
          353 (42) 933 6343   fax 353 (420 933 2085
          email info@dundalk.ie   http://www.dundalkchamber.ie
          Chief Exec: Bill Tosh
○   *C

Dundee & Angus Chamber of Commerce   1835
NR   11 City Quay, Camperdown St, DUNDEE, DD1 3JA.   (hq)
        01382 228545   fax 01382 228441
        http://www.dundeeandanguschamber.co.uk
        Chief Exec: Alan Mitchell
○   *C
●   Mtgs - Exhib - Expt - Inf - LG (local) - Business support
<   Brit Chams Comm; Assn Scot Chams Comm
M   750 f
¶   The Business - 6;   Annual Diary.
✕   2008 Dundee & Tayside Chamber of Commerce & Industry

Dundee & Tayside Chamber of Commerce & Industry
      since 2008 **Dundee & Angus Chamber of Commerce**

Durham County Agricultural Society   (DCAS)   1841
■   PO Box 58, CHESTER-le-STREET, Co Durham, DH3 3GB.   (hsp)
        0191-534 6482
        http://www.durhamcountyshow.co.uk
        Sec: Mrs C M Duke
○   *F, *H; to organise the Durham County Show

Durham County Local History Society   (DCLHS)   1964
■   21 St Mary's Grove, Tudhoe, SPENNYMOOR, Co Durham,
        DL16 6LR.   (hsp)
        01388 816209
        email johnbanham@tiscali.co.uk
        http://www.durhamweb.org.uk/dclhs
        Sec: Dr J D Banham
▲   Registered Charity
○   *L; to encourage & promote interest in the study of the history
        of County Durham, and of the North East in general
<   Brit Assn for Local History
M   232 i, 33 org, UK / 7 org, o'seas
        (Sub: £10 i, £20 org)
¶   Jnl - 2; ftm, £5 nm.
        Documentary series; prices vary.
        Durham Biographies (edited by Batho) vol 1-5; £25 set of 5.
        The Durham Crown Lordships (Reid).
        Durham City and its MPs (Heesom).
        Joseph Bouet's Durham; £10.
        The Lost Hills - history of papermaking in County
        Durham; £10.

Durham Wildlife Trust   (DWT)   1971
■   Rainton Meadows, Chilton Moor, HOUGHTON-le-SPRING,
        Tyne & Wear, DH4 6PU.   (hq)
        0191-584 3112   fax 0191-584 3934
        email mail@durhamwt.co.uk
        http://www.durhamwt.co.uk
        Dir: James Cokill
▲   Company Limited by Guarantee; Registered Charity
○   *K; protection of wild life & natural beauty of Durham County &
        Tyne & Wear south of the Tyne; management of the Trust's
        nature reserves
Gp   10 local groups; 26 nature reserves; 3 visitor centres
●   Conf - Mtgs - ET - Exhib - SG - Inf - VE
<   R Soc of Wildlife Trusts (UK Office)
M   8,500 i, 55 f
¶   Durham Wildlife - 3; tm, £1.50 nm.

Dutch Barge Association
      see **DBA - the Barge Association**

Dvořák Society for Czech & Slovak Music   1974
NR   13 Church LAne, Knutton, NEWCASTLE-under-LYME, Staffs,
        ST5 6DU.   (sp)
        http://www.dvorak-society.org
        Hon Sec: Dave Roberts
▲   Registered Charity
○   *D; 'to educate the public in the arts & sciences & in particular,
        the music of the Czech Republic & Slovakia'
●   Mtgs - ET - Res - Exhib - Inf - Lib - VE
<   Le Mouvement Janáček (France), Dvořák Soc (Czech Republic),
        Janáček Soc (Switzerland), Czech Music Socs (Czech Republic
        & USA), Martinů Soc (Czech Republic), Slovak Music
        Foundation, Czech Music Foundation, Smetana Soc (Czech
        Republic), Kmoch European Bands Soc (UK)
M   400 i, 7 f, 2 org, UK / 140 i, 9 f, 5 org, o'seas
¶   Czech Music - 1.
        NL - 4/5.   Ybk.

Dwarf Athletic Association United Kingdom   (DAAUK)   1993
■   PO Box 4269, DRONFIELD, Derbys, S18 9BG.
        01246 414238
        email office@daauk.org   http://www.daauk.org
○   *S; to make regular sporting opportunity accessible & enjoyable
        to anyone & everyone of restricted growth in the UK

Dylan Thomas Society of Great Britain   1977
■   Fernhill, 24 Chapel St, Mumbles, SWANSEA, Glam,
        SA3 4NH.   (chmn p)
        01792 363785
        Chmn: Mrs Cecily Hughes
Br   Australia, Canada
○   *G; to foster & stimulate interest in the work of Dylan Thomas
        (1914-1953) & the literature of Anglo-Welsh writers
●   Mtgs - VE
M   240 i, UK / 20 i, o'seas
¶   NL - 2; ftm, £1 nm.
        2003 commemorative publication: I Sang In My Chains, Essays
        & Poems in Tribute to Dylan Thomas; £10.

Dyslexia Association of Ireland   1972
IRL   Suffolk Chambers, 1 Suffolk St, DUBLIN 2, Republic of Ireland.
        353 (1) 679 0276   fax 353 (1) 679 0273
        email info@dyslexia.ie   http://www.dyslexia.ie
        Dir: Ann Hughes
○   *K, *W

Dyslexia Institute   (DI)   1974
■   Park House, Wick Rd, EGHAM, Surrey, TW20 0HH.   (hq)
        01784 222300   fax 01784 222333
        email info@dyslexiaaction.org.uk
        http://www.dyslexiaaction.org.uk
        Exec Dir: Mrs S Cramer
▲   Company Limited by Guarantee; Registered Charity
Br   27 dyslexia institutes
○   *E, *W; assessment of children & adults; teaching of dyslexic
        children & adults; teacher training
Gp   Assessment; Teaching
●   Conf - ET - Exhib - Comp - Inf - LG - Fund raising
<   Brit Dyslexia Assn
M   'friends'
¶   As We See It (NL) - 1; free.   Leaflets.
✕   2005 (July) Hornsby Dyslexia Charity (merged)

Dyslexia Scotland   1968
- ■ Stirling Business Centre, Wellgreen, STIRLING, FK8 2DZ.   (hq)
  01786 446650   fax 01786 471235
  email info@dyslexiascotland.org.uk
  http://www.dyslexiascotland.org.uk
  Chief Exec: Cathy Magee
- ▲ Company Limited by Guarantee; Registered Charity (Scotland)
- Br 13 (Scotland)
- ○ *K, *W; 'to enable & encourage dyslexic people, regardless of their age & abilities, to reach their potential in education, employment & life'
- ● Conf - Mtgs - ET - Stat - Inf - Lib - LG
  Resource centre of books, teaching materials, computer software, audio & visual aids
- M 700 i, 20 f
- ✕ 2004 Scottish Dyslexia Association

Dyspraxia Foundation   1987
- ■ 8 West Alley, HITCHIN, Herts, SG5 1EG.   (hq)
  01462 455016   fax 01462 455052
  email dyspraxia@dyspraxiafoundation.org.uk
  http://www.dyspraxiafoundation.org.uk
  Admin: Mrs Eleanor Howes
- ▲ Registered Charity
- Br 2
- ○ *W; to support individuals & families affected by dyspraxia (clumsy child syndrome); to promote better diagnosis & treatment facilities; to help professionals in health & education to assist those with dyspraxia
- Gp Adults with dyspraxia
  Helpline: 01462 454986 (Mon-Fri 1000-1300)
- ● Conf - Mtgs - Res - Exhib - Stat - Inf - LG
- M c 2,000 i
- ¶ Praxis Makes Perfect.   Information pack.
  Books & guides for parents; leaflets, booklets.

Dystonia Society   (TDS)   1983
- ■ Camelford House (1st floor), 89 Albert Embankment, LONDON, SE1 7TP.   (hq)
  0845 458 6211   fax 0845 458 6311
  email info@dystonia.org.uk
  http://www.dystonia.org.uk
  Chief Exec: Philip Eckstein
- ▲ Registered Charity
- Br 24
- ○ *M, *W; to raise awareness of dystonia, a neurological movement disorder; to support those affected by dystonia & provide information
- Gp Young Dystonia - support group for families
- ● Conf - Mtgs - Inf
  Helpline: 0845 458 6322
- < Eur Dystonia Fedn; Neurological Alliance
- M 3,000 i, UK / 115 i, o'seas
- ¶ NL - 4; free.

Dystrophic Epidermolysis Bullosa Research Association (DebRA)   1978
- NR 13 Wellington Business Park, Duke's Ride, CROWTHORNE, Berks, RG45 6LS.   (hq)
  01344 771961   fax 01344 762661
  email debra@debra.org.uk   http://www.debra.org.uk
- ○ *W; to help all people with Epidermolysis Bullosa (blistering of the skin) & their families; to fund research
- ● Conf - Res - SG - Inf
- < DEBRA Intl; DEBRA Europe
- ¶ NL - 4;   AR; both free.

© CBD Research Ltd · Beckenham · BR3 5JS · Tel 020 8650 7745 · Fax 020 8650 0768 · E-mail cbd@cbdresearch.com · www.cbdresearch.com

E A Bowles of Myddleton House Society
NR 2(A) Plough Hill, Cuffley, POTTERS BAR, Herts, EN6 4DR.
    http://www.eabowlessociety.org.uk
    Treas: A Pettitt
○ *G, *H; to commemorate the life & work of E A Bowles (1965-1954)

E F Benson Society   1984
■ The Old Coach House, High St, RYE, E Sussex, TN31 7JF.
    (hsp)
    01797 223114
    http://www.efbensonsociety.org
    Sec: Allan V Downend
▲ Un-incorporated Society
○ *A; furtherance of the knowledge & appreciation of the Benson family & particularly E F Benson (the author) & his works
● Mtgs - Exhib - VE - Walks
M 200 i, UK / 30 i, o'seas
¶ Dodo (Jnl) - 1; ftm, £4 nm.   NL - 4; ftm only.

EADA   (EADA)   1969
NR 3 Priory Rd, HASSOCKS, W Sussex, BN6 8PS.
    01273 846301
    http://www.eada.org.uk
▲ Un-incorporated Society
○ *S; the governing body for dancesport in England incl Modern, Latin-American, Sequence & Freestyle
● Mtgs - Comp
< Intl Dancesport Fedn
M 3,000 i, 5 specialist clubs
¶ AR - 1; ftm only.
✕ English Amateur Dancesport Association

Ealing Chamber of Commerce   1901
NR Grove Mews, 42 The Grove, LONDON, W5 5LH.
    020 8840 6332   fax 020 8579 0685
    email info@ealingchamber.org
    http://www.ealingchamber.org
    General Manager: Matthew Sims
Br Hammersmith & Fulham Chamber of Commerce
○ *C
< London Cham Comm & Ind

EAN Ireland
    since 2005 **GS1 Ireland**

EAN UK Ltd
    since February 2005 **GS1 UK**

Early Dance Circle   (EDC)   1984
■ Hunter's Moon, Orcheston, SALISBURY, Wilts, SP3 4RP.   (sp)
    01980 620339
    email dianacruic@aol.com
    http://www.earlydancecircle.co.uk
    Chmn: Diana Cruickshank
▲ Un-incorporated Society
○ *D; to promote & foster the knowledge, understanding & appreciation of dance & its context in European society up to the beginning of the 20th century
● Conf - Mtgs - ET - Res - SG - Inf - Advisory service
< Nat Early Music Assn (NEMA); Nat Resource Centre for Historical Dance (NRCHD)
M 166 i
¶ NL - 4; ftm only.
    Publications list available.

Early Education
    alternative name of the **British Association for Early Childhood Education**

Early English Text Society   (EETS)   1864
■ c/o Prof V A Gillespie, Lady Margaret Hall, OXFORD, OX2 6QA.   (exec sec b)
    01865 284066
    http://www.eets.org.uk
    Exec Sec: Prof V A Gillespie
▲ Un-incorporated Society
○ *L; printing of English texts earlier than 1558
M i, f & org
¶ 1 or 2 books per yr.

Earth Science Teachers' Association   (ESTA)   1968
■ 81A Birches Lane, Lostock Green, NORTHWICH, Cheshire, CW9 7SN.   (hsp)
    email rostodhunter@aol.com   http://www.esta-uk.org
    Hon Sec: Dr Rosalind Todhunter
▲ Registered Charity
Br 3
○ *E, *P; to encourage & support the teaching of earth science & geology at all levels as part of science & geography courses
Gp Education: Primary, Secondary, Teacher, Higher; Fieldwork
● Conf - Et - SG - Stat
M 740 i, UK / 60 i, o'seas
    (Sub: £32)
¶ Teaching Earth Sciences (Jnl) - 2; ftm only.

East of England Agricultural Society   1797
■ East of England Showground, PETERBOROUGH, Cambs, PE2 6XE.   (hq)
    01733 234451   fax 01733 370038
    email info@eastofengland.org.uk
    http://www.eastofengland.org.uk
    Chief Exec: Andrew Mercer
○ *F
● Conf - Exhib - Comp - SG - Inf - E of England Show
M c 8,000 i
¶ NL.   Show Catalogue.

East Hampshire Chamber of Commerce & Industry   (EHCCI)
NR Regional Business Centre, Harts Farm Way, HAVANT, Hants, PO9 1HR.
    023 9244 9449
    Sec: Andrew Gordon
○ *C

East Herts Archaeological Society   (EHAS)   1898
■ 11 St Leonards Close, Bengeo, HERTFORD, SG14 3LL.   (hsp)
    Hon Sec: Mrs G Pollard
▲ Registered Charity
○ *L; to promote interest in, & preservation of, archaeology in the county, old buildings & local history
Gp Old buildings survey
● Exhib - Inf - Lib - VE
< Coun Brit Archaeology; Hertfordshire Archaeol Trust
M 130 i
¶ Hertfordshire Archaeology - irreg; ftm, £15 nm.
    NL.   AR.
    A Century of Archaeology in East Herts; £9.95 (£4.95 paperback).

East Lancashire Chamber of Commerce & Industry   (ELCCI) 1991
- ■ Red Rose Court, Clayton Business Park, ACCRINGTON, Lancs, BB5 5JR.   (hq)
  01254 356400   fax 01254 388900
  email info@chamberelancs.co.uk
  http://www.chamberelancs.co.uk
  Chief Exec: Michael Damms
- ▲ Company Limited by Guarantee
- ○ *C; business support
- Gp Business support; International trade; Supply train; ICT; Training
- ● Conf - Mtgs - ET - Res - Exhib - Stat - Expt - Inf - LG
- < Brit Chams Comm; Chams Comm NW
- M 1,000 f
- ¶ Lancashire Business View - 6.

East London Chamber of Commerce
  since 25 May 1999 (as Docklands Business Club & East London Chamber of Commerce) a branch of the **London Chamber of Commerce & Industry**

East Lothian Antiquarian & Field Naturalists' Society (ELAFNS)   1924
- ■ 13 Stories Park, EAST LINTON, E Lothian, EH40 3BN.   (hsp)
  01620 860812
  email amc@eleutheria.madasafish.com
  http://www.el4.org.uk
  Sec: Allison Cosgrove
- ▲ Registered Charity
- ○ *L; antiquities, archaeology & natural history of the district
- ● Mtgs - Exhib - VE
- M 264 i, 11 org, UK / 1 org, o'seas
- ¶ Transactions (incl LM) - 3 yrly; ftm.   AR - 1; free.

Eastbourne & District Chamber of Commerce Ltd   (EDCC) 1892
- ■ 7 Hyde Gardens, EASTBOURNE, E Sussex, BN21 4PN.   (hq)
  01323 641144   fax 01323 730454
  email info@eastbournechamber.co.uk
  http://www.eastbournechamber.co.uk
  Co Sec: Mrs Christine Purkess
- ▲ Company Limited by Guarantee
- ○ *C
- ● Conf - Mtgs - ET - Exhib - Inf - LG
- M 600+ f
- ¶ NL - 12;   Directory - 1;   both ftm only.

Eastern Africa Association   (EAA)   1964
- ■ 2 Vincent St, LONDON, SW1P 4LD.   (hq)
  020 7828 5511   fax 020 7828 5251
  email jcsmall@eaa-lon.co.uk
  http://www.eaa-lon.co.uk
  Chief Exec: John C Small
- ▲ Company Limited by Guarantee
- Br Kenya, Uganda
- ○ *T; to facilitate the participation of firms & companies from other countries in the economic development of Kenya, Eritrea, Ethiopia, Burundi, Rwanda, Seychelles, Tanzania & Uganda
- ● Conf - Mtgs - Inf - LG
- < Brit African Business Assn
- M 30 i, 272 f, UK & o'seas
- ¶ The Eastern Africa NL - 8; m only.

Eating Disorders Association   (beat)   1989
- ■ Wensum House, 103 Prince of Wales Rd, NORWICH, Norfolk, NR1 1DW.   (hq)
  0870 770 3256   fax 01603 664915
  email info@b-eat.co.uk   http://www.b-eat.co.uk
  Chief Exec: Mrs Susan Ringwood
- ▲ Company Limited by Guarantee; Registered Charity
- Br UK-wide network of local help goups
- ○ *M, *W; to provide help & support for people affected by eating disorders, especially anorexia & bulimia nervosa; to provide training & help for professionals
- ● Conf - ET - Res - LG - Service specifications guidelines for treatment
  Helpline: 0845 634 1414 (Mon-Fri 1030-2030)
  Youthline (up to age 18): 0845 634 7650 (Mon-Fri 1600-2030)
  Text Service: 0778 620 1820
- ¶ Upbeat (Jnl) - 4; ftm.   Lists of treatment by area.
  European Eating Disorders Review (professional jnl).
  Note: Adopted working title 'beat' February 2007.

ECB Coaches Association
  alternative name of **England & Wales Cricket Board Coaches Association**

ECB Officials Association
  on 1 January 2008 merged with the Association of Cricket Umpires & Scorers to form the **England & Wales Cricket Board Association of Cricket Officials**

Ecclesiastical History Society   (EHS)   1962
- NR 32 Highfield Ave, Great Sankey, WARRINGTON, Cheshire, WA5 2TW.   (hsb)
  email stella@ravenna123.freeserve.co.uk
  http://www.ehsoc.org.uk
  Hon Sec: Dr Stella Fletcher
- ▲ Registered Charity
- ○ *L; study of ecclesiastical history & maintenance of relations between British historians & scholars abroad
- ● Conf - Res
- < Commission Intle d'Histoire Ecclésiastique Comparée (CIHEC)
- M 700 i, 35 colleges & Libraries, UK / 200 i, o'seas
- ¶ Studies in Church History - 1.

Ecclesiological Society   1839
- ■ 38 Rosebery Ave, NEW MALDEN, Surrey, KT3 4JS.   (hsp)
  http://www.ecclsoc.org
  Chmn: Trevor Cooper
- ▲ Registered Charity
- ○ *A, *L; the study of the arts, architecture & liturgy of the Christian church
- ● Conf - Mtgs - Inf - Lib - PL - VE
- M 1,00 i, 20 org, UK / 20 i, o'seas
- ¶ Ecclesiology Today - 2; ftm.
  Monographs & publications - irreg; prices vary.

© CBD Research Ltd · Beckenham · BR3 5JS · Tel 020 8650 7745 · Fax 020 8650 0768 · E-mail cbd@cbdresearch.com · www.cbdresearch.com

Eckhart Society   1987
- ■ Summa, 22 Tippings Lane, Woodley, READING, Berks, RG5 4RX.   (hsp)
  - 0118-969 0118
  - email ashleyyoung@aysumma.demon.co.uk
  - http://www.eckhartsociety.org
  - Hon Sec & Exec Dir: Ashley Young
  - Chmn: Christopher Glover (cgg@cgglover.com)
- ▲ Registered Charity
- ○ *G, *R; to promote understanding & appreciation of the writings of Meister Eckhart (1260-1327, a Dominican preacher) & their importance for Christian thought & practice; to facilitate scholarly research into Eckhart's life & works; to promote the study of Eckhart's teaching as a contribution to religious dialogue
- ● Conf - SG
- M 200 i, UK / 130 i, o'seas
  - (Sub: £20)
- ¶ The Eckhart Review - 1; ftm, £9.50 nm.
  - Tapes from annual conference - 1; £7.25 each.
  - CDs from annual conference - 1; £8.50 each.
  - Publications list available.

Economic History Society   1927
- NR Dept of Economic & Social History, University of Glasgow, Lilybank House, Bute Gardens, GLASGOW, G12 8RT.   (hq)
  - 0141-330 4662   fax 0141-330 4889
  - email ehsocsec@arts.gla.ac.uk   http://www.ehs.org.uk
  - Hon Sec: Prof P S Fearon
- ▲ Registered Charity
- ○ *L; to promote the study of economic & social history; to publish & sponsor publications
- Gp Urban; Financial; Transport
- ● Conf - Mtgs - ET - Res - Inf
- < Intl Historical Congress; Intl Economic History Assn
- M 1,500 i, libraries & colleges
- ¶ Economic History Review - 4; ftm only.   NL - 4.   AR.

Economic Research Council   (ERC)   1943
- ■ Baker Tilly, 65 Kingsway, LONDON, WC2B 6TD.   (mail address)
  - 020 7439 0271
  - http://www.ercouncil.org
  - Hon Secs: James Y Bourlet,   Dan Lewis
- ▲ Registered Charity
- ○ *L; to promote education in the science of economics with particular reference to monetary practice
- ● Mtgs - Res - Comp - SG - Dinners with talks
- M c 400 i, c 20 f, UK / c 30 i, o'seas
- ¶ Britain & Overseas - 4; £20.   Occasional Research Papers.

Economic & Social History Society of Ireland   1970
- IRL c/o Dept of Modern History, Trinity College, DUBLIN 2, Republic of Ireland.
  - 353 (1) 608 1020   fax 353 (1) 608 2291
  - email niall.ociosain@nuigalway.ie   http://www.eh.net/eshsi/
  - Sec: Dr Niall Ó'Ciosáin
- ○ *L, *P

Economic & Social Research Institute   (ESRI)   1960
- IRL Whitaker House, Sir John Rogerson's Quay, DUBLIN 2, Republic of Ireland.
  - 353 (1) 863 2000   fax 353 (1) 863 2100
  - email admin@esri.ie   http://www.esri.ie
  - Dir: Brendan J Whelan
- ○ *L

Economics, Business & Enterprise Association   (EBEA)   1946
- ■ The Forum, 277 London Rd, BURGESS HILL, W Sussex, RH15 9QU.   (hq)
  - 01444 240150   fax 01444 240101
  - email office@ebea.org.uk   http://www.ebea.org.uk
  - Chief Exec: Duncan Cullimore
- ▲ Registered Charity
- ○ *E, *L; supporting teachers & lecturers of economics, business studies & enterprise
- Gp Business studies; Economics; Enterprise
- ● Conf - Mtgs - ET - Inf
- M 1,410 i, 210 org
- ¶ Teaching Business & Education (Jnl) - 3; ftm, only.
  - EBEA News - monthly in term-time & online only; free.
- × 2008 (June) Economics & Business Education Association

Ectodermal Dysplasia Society   (EDS)   1984
- ■ 108 Charlton Lane, CHELTENHAM, Glos, GL53 9EA.
  - 01242 261332
  - email diana@ectodermaldysplasia.org
  - http://www.ectodermaldysplasia.org
  - Sec: Diana Perry,   Chmn: David Wyatt
- ▲ Registered Charity
- ○ *M, *W; to promote the health of people affected by ectodermal dysplasia & any related condition, & to support their families & carers; 'ectodermal dysplasias are heritable conditions in which there are abnormalities of two or more ectodermal structures such as the hair, teeth, nails, sweat glands, cranial-facial structure, digits & other parts of the body'
- ● Conf - Mtgs - Res - Inf
- M 332 i, UK / 79 i, o'seas
- ¶ NL - 4; ftm.

Edinburgh Bibliographical Society   (EBS)   1890
- ■ c/o Special Collections, Edinburgh University Library, George Square, EDINBURGH, EH9 9LJ.   (treas/b)
  - 0131-650 6864
  - email joseph.marshall@ed.ac.uk
  - http://www.mcs.qmuc.ac.uk/ebs/
  - Treas: Dr Joseph Marshall
- ▲ Registered Charity
- ○ *L; study of books & manuscripts, particularly those of Scottish interest
- ● Mtgs (at above address) - VE
- M c 200 i & org
- ¶ Transactions - 1; £15, UK / £20, o'seas.

Edinburgh Chamber of Commerce   1785
- ■ Capital House, 2 Festival Sq, EDINBURGH, EH3 9SU.   (hq)
  - 0131-221 2999   fax 0131-221 2998
  - email info@edinburghchamber.co.uk
  - http://www.edinburghchamber.co.uk
  - Chief Exec: Ron Hewitt
- ○ *C
- Gp Business training; Membership
- ● Conf - Mtgs - ET - Expt
- M 1,400 f
- × 2001 Edinburgh Chamber of Commerce & Enterprise
  - 2002 Management Association of South-East Scotland (merged)

Edinburgh Civic Trust
   alternative name of the **Cockburn Association**

Edinburgh Geological Society   1834
- NR 23 Summerfield Place, EDINBURGH, EH6 8AZ.   (hsp)
  - 0131-555 5488
  - email secretary@edinburghgeolsoc.org
  - http://www.edinburghgeolsoc.org
  - Hon Sec: Angus Miller
- ○ *L; to stimulate public interest in geology; advancement of geological knowledge

Edinburgh Highland Reel & Strathspey Society (EHRSS) 1881
■ 12 Comely Bank Terrace, EDINBURGH, EH4 1AS.   (sp)
0131-343 1923
http://www.highlandreel.co.uk
Sec: Nicola Foy
▲ Registered Charity
○ *D; to improve taste in traditional Scottish music, especially
highland reels & strathspeys by performing concerts
● Mtgs - Comp - Public concerts
M 50 i
(Sub: £20)
no further information supplied.

Edinburgh Mathematical Society (EMS) 1883
■ James Clerk Maxwell Building, Mayfield Rd, EDINBURGH,
EH9 3JZ.   (hsb)
0131-650 5040
email edmathsoc@maths.ed.ac.uk
http://www.maths.ed.ac.uk/~ems/
Hon Sec: Dr A D Gilbert
▲ Registered Charity
○ *L; advancement of mathematics, especially in Scotland
● Conf - Mtgs - Res - Lib
< Eur Mathematical Soc
M 360 i, UK / 60 i, o'seas
¶ Proceedings - 3; £18 yr m, £208 yr nm.

Edinburgh Sir Walter Scott Club   1894
■ 7 Dove Court, 16 Albert Terrace, EDINBURGH, EH10 5EA.
(hsp)
0131-447 6133
email secretary@walterscottclub.org.uk
http://www.eswsc.com
Hon Sec: Fraser Elgin
▲ Un-incorporated Society
○ *A; to keep alive & cherish the memory of Sir Walter Scott
● Mtgs
M 300 i, UK / 40 i, o'seas
¶ Bulletin - 1; free.

Edith Nesbit Society   1996
■ 21 Churchfields, WEST MALLING, Kent, ME19 6RJ.   (chmn/p)
email mccarthy804@aol.com
http://www.edithnesbit.co.uk
Chmn: Mrs Margaret McCarthy
▲ Un-incorporated Society
○ *A; to promote interest in the life & works of author Edith Nesbit
(1858-1924) & her friends
Gp Archives
● Mtgs - Res - Exhib - SG - VE
M 81 i, 2 org, UK / 3 i, o'seas
¶ NL - 4; ftm only.

Education Law Association   (ELAS)
NR 33 College Rd, READING, Berks, RG6 1QE.   (sp)
0118-966 9866
http://www.educationlawassociation.org.uk
Sec: Catherine Croft
○ *P
M c 320 i

Education Otherwise (EO) 1977
■ PO Box 325, KING'S LYNN, Norfolk, PE34 3XW.   (mail
address)
0870 730 0074
email enquiries@education-otherwise.org
http://www.education-otherwise.org
Co Sec: Pam Bellinger
▲ Company Limited by Guarantee; Registered Charity
Br local groups
○ *E, *K; self-help organisation offering support, advice &
information to families practising, or contemplating, home-
based education as an alternative to schooling.
We take our name from the Education Act which states that
parents are responsible for their children's education, 'either
by regular attendance at school or otherwise'
● Conf - Mtgs - Exhib - Comp - Inf - VE - Liaison with LEA's
M 4,500 families
¶ NL - 6;   Hbk - 1;   Contact List - 1;
School is Not Compulsory; all ftm only.
Publications list available [see website].

Educational Centres Association (ECA) 1920
■ 21 Ebbisham Drive, NORWICH, Norfolk, NR4 6HQ.
(chmn/p)
0844 249 5594   fax 01603 469292
email info@e-c-a.ac.uk   http://www.e-c-a.ac.uk
Chmn & Chief Exec: Bernard Godding
▲ Registered Charity
○ *E; promotion of lifelong learning
● Conf - Mtgs - Inf - LG
< Eur Assn Educ Adults; Community Sector Coalition; engage;
Nat Inst Adult Continuing Educ
> engage; Nat Inst Adult Continuing Educ
M i, f & org
¶ NL - 3;   AR; both ftm.

Educational Institute of Scotland (EIS) 1847
■ 46 Moray Place, EDINBURGH, EH3 6BH.   (hq)
0131-225 6244   fax 0131-220 3151
email enquiries@eis.org.uk   http://www.eis.org.uk
Gen Sec: Ronald A Smith
▲ Un-incorporated Society
Br 38
○ *E, *U; promotion of sound learning & the interests & welfare of
teachers
● Conf - Mtgs - ET - Empl
< Education Intl; Eur Trade U C'ee on Educ; TUC; STUC
M 60,685 i
¶ Scottish Educational Jnl - 6; ftm, £12 yr nm.

Educational Publishers Council
a group of the **Publishers Association**

Educational Software Publishers Association
a group of the **British Educational Suppliers Association**

Edward Thomas Fellowship   1980
■ 1 Carfax, Undercliff Drive, ST LAWRENCE, Isle of Wight,
PO38 1XG.   (hsp)
01983 853366
Hon Sec: Colin G Thornton
▲ Un-incorporated Society
○ *L; to perpetuate the memory of the writer Edward Thomas
(1878-1917); to preserve the countryside known to him; to
further interest in his life & work
● Conf - Mtgs - Res - VE
< Alliance of Literary Socs
M 450 i, 2 colleges, 1 museum, UK / 25 i, 1 library, o'seas
¶ NL - 2; ftm, £2 nm.

© CBD Research Ltd · Beckenham · BR3 5JS · Tel 020 8650 7745 · Fax 020 8650 0768 · E-mail cbd@cbdresearch.com · www.cbdresearch.com

EEF Ltd - the manufacturers' organisation   (EEF)   1896
NR   Broadway House, Tothill St, LONDON, SW1H 9NQ.   (hq)
    020 7222 7777   fax 020 7222 2782
    http://www.eef.org.uk
    Chief Exec: Gilbert Toppin
▲   Company Limited by Guarantee
○   *T; to represent employers in the manufacturing, engineering &
    technology industries
M   f
    'EEF & certain regional associations merged on 1 October
    2008 & subsequently transferred the entity's business to a
    new company EEF Ltd; it will conduct the business of the 'old'
    EEF & the regional associations under a new, unified
    structure'

Efficient Consumer Response Ireland
    a group of **Food & Drink Industry Ireland**

Egg Crafters Guild of Great Britain   1979
■   The Studio, 7 Hylton Terrace, NORTH SHIELDS, Tyne & Wear,
    NE29 0EE.   (hq)
    0191-258 3648   fax 0191-258 3648
    http://www.uk.geocities.com/eggcraftersguild/
    Chief Exec: Joan Cutts
▲   Un-incorporated Society
Br   30; 10 o'seas
○   *A, *G; to encourage the craft of egg decoration
●   Conf - Mtgs - ET - Exhib - SG
M   1,500 i, UK / 500 i, o'seas
¶   The Egg Crafter (NL) - 4; ftm.

Egypt Exploration Society   (EES)   1882
■   3 Doughty Mews, LONDON, WC1N 2PG.   (hq)
    020 7242 1880   fax 020 7404 6118
    email contact@ees.ac.uk   http://www.ees.ac.uk
    Sec: Dr Patricia A Spencer
▲   Company Limited by Guarantee; Registered Charity
Br   London, Manchester
○   *L; promotion of the study of the history & archaeology of
    ancient Egypt
●   Conf - Mtgs - Res - Lib - PL - VE - Archaeological excavations
M   2,608 i, 281 libraries
¶   Jnl of Egyptian Archaeology - 1; £40 m, £50 nm.
    Egyptian Archaeology - 2; £4.95.   AR; ftm.

Egyptian British Chamber of Commerce   (EBCC)   1981
■   PO Box 4EG, 299 Oxford St, LONDON, W1A 4EG.   (hq)
    020 7499 3100   fax 020 7499 1070
    email info@theebcc.com
    Sec-Gen: T Sherif
▲   Company Limited by Guarantee
○   *C; to promote commercial, industrial & tourist relations
    between Egypt & the UK
●   Conf - Mtgs - Exhib - Stat - Expt - Inf - Lib - LG
¶   Egyptian-British Trade - 4; free.
    Bulletin - trade opportunities - 26; ftm only.

EIS Association   (EISA)   1990
■   Erico House, 93-99 Upper Richmond Rd, LONDON,
    SW15 2TG.   (hq)
    020 8785 5560   fax 020 8785 5561
    email members@eisa.org.uk   http://www.eisa.org.uk
    Dir: Susan Phillips
▲   Company Limited by Guarantee
○   *T; to stimulate investment in the smaller company economy in
    the broadest sense but also specifically through the EIS
    (Enterprise Investment Scheme)
Gp   Tax committee; EISA Council
●   Inf - LG
M   80 f
¶   LM; [website].

Ekbom Support Group   (ESG)   1988
NR   42 Nursery Rd, Rainham, GILLINGHAM, Kent, ME8 0BE.   (hsp)
    http://www.ekbom.org.uk
    Coordinator: Mrs Beverley Finn
▲   Un-incorporated Society
○   *W; to support sufferers from Ekbom Syndrome (also known as
    Restless Legs Syndrome); to educate the medical profession;
    works with RLS UK a committee of professionals - doctors,
    consultants etc in the UK
●   Conf - Mtgs - Res - SG - Inf - Penfriend service
M   c 200 i. UK / 4 i, o'seas
¶   NL - 2; free.
    Note: please enclose an SAE when writing to the ESG.

eLearning Network   (eLN)   1989
NR   Thrift Cottage, Common Rd, HADLOW, Kent, TN11 0JE.
    (admin/b)
    01732 850650
    email info@elearningnetwork.org
    http://www.elearningnetwork.org
    Admin: Pat Straughan
▲   Un-incorporated Society
○   *G; to provide leadership in the application of technologies to
    learning; to provide an independent perspective on the issues
●   Conf - Mtgs - ET - Res - Inf
M   15 i, 84 f, 10 org

Electoral Reform Society Ltd   (ERS)   1884
■   6 Chancel St, LONDON, SE1 0UU.   (hq)
    020 7928 1622   fax 020 7401 7789
    email ers@reform.demon.co.uk
    http://www.electoral-reform.org.uk
    Chif Exec: Dr Ken Ritchie
▲   Company Limited by Guarantee
○   *K; to campaign for the introduction of the single transferable
    vote for all UK public elections & elections within common
    interest bodies; to provide election monitoring & voter
    education for emerging democracies internationally
Gp   Subsidiaries: Electoral Reform Ballot Services Ltd, Electoral
    Reform International Services Ltd; McDougall Trust
    (educational charity)
●   Conf - Mtgs - ET - Res - Exhib - SG - Stat - Inf - Lib - VE - LG -
    Votes At 16 Campaign
<   UNESCO; CVD (USA); NLGN; NCVO; Make Votes Count
M   2,300 i, 2 f, 6 org, UK / 40 i, 2 org, o'seas
¶   Representation: jnl of democracy & electoral systems - 4; ftm,
    £25 yr nm.
    ERS News - 4;   AR; both free.

Electric Boat Association   (EBA)   1980
■   150 Wayside Green, Woodcote, READING, Berks, RG8 0QJ.
    (sp)
    01491 681449
    email mail@eboat.org.uk   http://www.eboat.org.uk
    Hon Sec: Mrs B Penniall
▲   Un-incorporated Society
○   *T; to promote the technology & use of electrically-propelled
    boats worldwide
Gp   User group (boat owners)
●   Conf - Res - Exhib - Comp - SG - Stat - Expt - Inf - LG
M   c 400 i, 50 f
¶   Electric Boat News - 3; ftm, on application nm.

Electric Guitar Appreciation Society   (TEGAS)
NR   65 Stapleton Lane, Barwell, LEICESTER, LE9 8HE.
    01455 457928
    http://www.tegas.co.uk
    Founder / Pres: John Williams
○   *G, *D

Electric Heating & Ventilation Association
    association in the Energy section of **BEAMA Ltd**

Electric Railway Society   (ERS)   1946
■ 17 Catherine Drive, SUTTON COLDFIELD, W Midlands,
B73 6AX.   (hsp)
0121-354 8332
email iwfrew@tiscali.co.uk
http://www.electric-rly-society.org.uk
Hon Sec: Dr Iain D O Frew
▲ Un-incorporated Society
Br 2
○ *G; to study the history, development & practice of electric
railways incl rapid transit metro lines; to evaluate their
effectiveness in public transport in major cities throughout the
world
● Mtgs - Exhib - SG - PL - VE
< Rly Soc Sthn Africa; Asociacíon Uruguaya Amigos Riel; Pacific
Railroad Soc; Scot Intl Tramway Assn; Australian Electric
Traction Assn
M 271 i, 7 f, 4 org, UK / 105 i, 2 f, 3 org, o'seas
¶ The Electric Railway - 6; ftm, £13.00 nm.
[subscription £13.50].

Electric Security Fencing Federation
a group of the **Fencing Contractors' Association**

Electric Steel Makers' Guild   (ESMG)   1956
■ 193 Fitzwilliam St, Swinton, MEXBOROUGH, S Yorks,
S64 8RW.   (hsp)
01709 584135
Assistant Sec: John Kitchen
○ *T; improving steelmaking in electric arc furnaces (commercial
quantities only)
● Conf - Mtgs
M 51 i, UK / 3 i, o'seas

Electric Trace Heating Industry Council   (ETHIC)   1988
■ Oak Tree Lodge, 49 Biddulph Rd, CONGLETON, Cheshire,
CW12 3LQ.   (sp/b)
01260 274701
http://www.ethic-global.com
Sec: J W Young
▲ Un-incorporated Society
○ *T; communication between manufacturers, designers &
installers of electric trace heating equipment & the specifiers
& users of the equipment; the correct use of approved quality
equipment & industry specifications, standards & codes of
practice
● Mtgs - ET - Preparation of International Standards
< Energy Ind Coun; Electricity Assn; Brit Nat C'ee for Electroheat;
BSI
M 7 f

Electrical Contractors' Association   (ECA)   1901
NR Esca House, 34 Palace Court, LONDON, W2 4HY.   (hq)
020 7313 4800   fax 020 7221 7344
email electricalcontractors@eca.org.uk
http://www.eca.co.uk
○ *T; the association guarantees work of member firms in the UK
& Eire (but not Scotland) & that the job will be completed at
the original price if a member firm should run into difficulties
● Conf - Mtgs - ET - Inf - Empl
M f

Electrical Distributors Association   (EDA)   1914
■ Union House, Eridge Rd, ROYAL TUNBRIDGE WELLS, Kent,
TN4 8HF.   (hq)
01892 619990   fax 01892 619991
email info@eda.org.uk   http://www.eda.org.uk
Dir: Nigel Ellis
▲ Company Limited by Guarantee
○ *T
● Mtgs - ET - Stat
< Eur U of Electrical Whlsrs (EUEW)
M 30 f
¶ Ybk - 1; ftm, £59.50 nm.

Electrical & Electronic Retailers Association of Ireland
IRL Marina House, Clarence St, DÚN LAOGHAIRE, Co Dublin,
Republic of Ireland.
353 (1) 663 8700   fax 353 (1) 663 8704
Pres: John Kilkelly
○ *T

Electrical & Engineering Staff Association   (EESA)   1971
NR Hayes Court, West Common Rd, HAYES, Kent, BR2 7AU.   (hq)
020 8462 7755   fax 020 8315 8234
http://www.eesa.org.uk
○ *U
M i

Electrical Industries Federation of Ireland   (EIFI)   1934
IRL Unit H12 Centrepoint Business Park, Oak Rd, DUBLIN 12,
Republic of Ireland.
353 (1) 429 0088   fax 353 (1) 429 0090
email eifi@etci.ie   http://www.etci.ie
Hon Sec: Jimmy Whan
○ *T

Electrical Insulation Association   (EIA)   1911
■ PO Box 2462, STAFFORD, ST16 9AE.   (hq)
01785 661306
email jcgwheeler@tiscali.co.uk   http://www.eiauk.org +
http://www.insucon.org
Sec: Dr Jeremy C G Wheeler
▲ Un-incorporated Society
○ *T; laminates, mouldings, castings; liquid finishes, varnishes,
insulators, bushings for power engineering applications;
papers, cloths, fibres & film
Gp C'ees: Activites, Insucon Conference
● Conf - Mtgs - ET - VE
M 20 f
(£720)

Electricity Arbitration Association   (EAA)   1990
■ 5 Meadow Rd, Great Gransden, SANDY, Beds, SG19 3BD.
(hq)
01767 677043   fax 01767 677043
Sec: Donald H J Lester
○ *T; to provide dispute resolution services for the UK electricity
industry
M f

Electro-Technical Council of Ireland   (ETCI)
IRL Unit H12, Centrepoint Business Park, Oak Rd, DUBLIN 12,
Republic of Ireland.
353 (1) 429 0088   fax 353 (1) 429 0090
email admin@etci.ie   http://www.etci.ie
Chief Exec: Patrick Hession
○ *T

Electro-physiological Technologists' Association   (EPTA)   1949
NR c/o Department of Clinical Neurophysiology, Gt Ormond Street
Hospital, LONDON, WC1N 3JH.   (chmn/b)
Hon Sec: Kelly Dywer-St Pier
▲ Company Limited by Guarantee
○ *P; to promote a high standard of training & education in the
field of neurophysiology
● Conf - Mtgs - Exam - Exhib - SG - Empl
M 800 i
¶ Jnl of Electro-physiology & Technology - 4.

Electroheat Manufacturers' Association of BEAMA
a group of BEAMA Energy in **BEAMA**

© CBD Research Ltd · Beckenham · BR3 5JS · Tel 020 8650 7745 · Fax 020 8650 0768 · E-mail cbd@cbdresearch.com · www.cbdresearch.com

Elgar Society   1951
NR   2 Marriott's Close, HADDENHAM, Bucks, HP17 8BT.
   (mem/sp)
   email membership@elgar.org   http://www.elgar.org
   Mem Sec: David Morris
▲   Registered Charity
Br   10; Canada
○   *A; to promote the study, performance & appreciation of the
   works of Sir Edward Elgar & research into his life & music
Gp   Elgar Enterprises (trading company)
●   Conf - Mtgs - ET - SG - Inf - VE - Awards to young composers -
   Sponsorship of CDs & concerts - Grants for the hire of
   orchestral parts
M   1,700 i, UK / 50 i, o'seas
¶   The Elgar Jnl - 3;   The Elgar News - 3; both ftm only.

Elsie Jeanette Oxenham Appreciation Society   (EJO Society) 1989
■   32 Tadfield Rd, ROMSEY, Hants, SO51 5AJ.   (memsec/p)
   01794 517149
   email abbey@bufobooks.demon.co.uk
   http://www.bufobooks.demon.co.uk/abbeylnk.htm
   Mem Sec/Treas: Ruth Allen,   Editor: Fiona Dyer
▲   Un-incorporated Society
Br   Canada & USA, Australia & New Zealand
○   *A; to provide a postal meeting point for all who are interested
   in the work & collect the books of Elsie J Oxenham (1880-
   1960); to investigate the settings used for the books & the
   folk dances which form the backdrop to many of her titles
●   Inf - Lib - VE - Web pages with discussion board
<   Alliance of Literary Socs
M   470 i, 2 org, UK / 64 i, o'seas
¶   The Abbey Chronicle (Jnl) - 3; ftm only, £2-£3 back issues.
   LM (suppt to Jnl) - 1; ftm only.

EM Gauge Society Ltd
has asked to be removed from the Directory.

Embroiderers' Guild   1906
NR   Apartment 41 Hampton Court Palace, EAST MOLESEY, Surrey,
   KT8 9AU.   (hq)
   020 8943 1229   fax 020 8977 9882
   email administrator@embroiderersguild.com
   http://www.embroiderersguild.com
   Dir: Jane Sweet
▲   Registered Charity
Br   210
○   *A; to promote an understanding of embroidery history, design
   & technique ensuring the long-term future of this craft
Gp   Young Embroiderers (under 18s)
●   Mtgs - ET - Res - Exhib - Comp - SG - Inf - Lib - PL - VE
M   25,000 i
¶   Embroidery - 6.   NL - 2.
   Stitch with the Embroiderers' Guild - 6.
   The Workbook.   Ybk.
   Various other publications.

EMC Industry Association   (EMCIA)   2002
■   c/o Nutwood UK Ltd, Eddystone Court, De Lank Lane,
   St Breward, BODMIN, Cornwall, PL30 4NQ.   (asa)
   01208 851530   fax 01208 850871
   email emcia@emcia.org   http://www.emcia.org
   Sec: Alan Hutley
▲   Un-incorporated Society
○   *P, *T; for EMC (electromagnetic compatibility) product & service
   providers; EMC is defined as 'the ability of an equipment or
   system to function satisfactorily in its electromagnetic
   environment without introducing intolerable electromagnetic
   disturbances to anything in that environment'
●   Conf - Mtgs - Exhib - Expt - Inf - LG
M   35 i, 35 f

Emergency Medicine Trainees Association
an association within the **College of Emergency Medicine**

Emergency Planning Society   (EPS)   1993
■   The Media Centre, Culverhouse Cross, CARDIFF, CF5 6XS.
   (hq)
   0845 600 9587   fax 029 2059 0397
   email accounts@the-eps.org   http://www.the-eps.org
   Co Sec: John Liddell,   Operational Mgr: Dan Taylor
▲   Company Limited by Guarantee
Br   14
○   *P; to promote emergency planning & management in the UK
   (all functions relating to the preparation for the assessment of
   a response to emergencies for the benefit of people, property
   & the environment)
Gp   Society issues; Professional issues
●   Conf - Mtgs - ET - Exhib - SG - Inf - LG
<   Soc of Indl Emergency Services Officers (SIESO)
M   2,000 i
¶   Blue Print Magazine - 4; ftm only.

Emergency Response & Rescue Vessel Association   (ERRVA) 1979
■   Greystone Farm, Greystone Rd, ALFORD, Aberdeenshire,
   AB33 8ND.   (chmn/p)
   0845 241 1302
   http://www.errva.org.uk
   Chmn: David Kenwright
▲   Company Limited by Guarantee
○   *N, *T; to foster the effective use of standby ships.   Standby
   ships are specially equipped ships stationed at offshore
   installations to rescue people from the sea; to assist in the
   evacuation of installations in emergencies; to warn off ships
   which present a collision hazard
●   ET - Liaison with other industry bodies - To conduct trials & tests
   on any relevant equipment

Emergency Social Services Association   (ESSA)   1997
■   PO Box 6466, BRIDPORT, Dorset, DT6 3US.   (hsb)
   http://www.essauk.com
   Hon Sec: Terri Goodwin,   Treas: Sylvia Watkin
○   *P; to promote high standards in (& the significance of) out-of-
   hours social work
●   Conf - Mtgs
M   c 100 authorities
¶   ESSA News (NL) - 3; ftm only.

Employers Forum on Age   (EFA)   1996
NR   Downstream Bldg (3rd floor), 1 London Bridge, LONDON,
   SE1 9BG.   (hq)
   0845 456 2495   fax 020 7785 6536
   email efa@efa.org.uk   http://www.efa.org.uk
○   *N; to support member organisations in achieving an age-
   diverse workforce
M   f & org

Employers' Forum on Disability
§   Nutmeg House, 60 Gainsford St, LONDON, SE1 2NY.
   020 7403 3020   fax 020 7403 0404
   email enquiries@efd.org.uk   http://www.efd.org.uk
   Chief Exec: Susan Scott-Parker
   An unique network of organisations that share best practice on
   disability; to create a society where business and the public
   sector promote the economic and social inclusion of disabled
   people.

Employment Lawyers Association   (ELA)   1992
NR   PO Box 353, UXBRIDGE, Middx, UB10 0UN.
   01895 256972   fax 01895 256972
○   *P

ENABLE Scotland (ENABLE) 1954
NR 146 Argyle St (2nd floor), GLASGOW, G1 8BL. (hq)
    0141-226 4541 fax 0141-204 4398
    email enable@enable.org.uk
    http://www.enable.org.uk
▲ Registered Charity; Un-incorporated Society
Br 57
○ *W; to support people with learning difficulties & their families
    in Scotland; to achieve equal opportunities & better services
Gp ACE - national advisory committee of people with learning
    disabilities
● Conf - Mtgs - Inf - Lib - LG
< Inclusion Intl; Inclusion Europe; Disability Agenda Scotland;
    Learning Disability Alliance Scotland
M c 4,000 i
¶ Newslink (NL) - 4.   AR.

ENCAMS   (ENCAMS)
NR Elizabeth House, The Pier, WIGAN, Lancs, WN3 4EX. (hq)
    01942 612621 fax 01942 824778
    http://www.encams.org
    Chief Exec: Alan Woods
○ *K; long-term improvement of local environments - the
    durability of buildings & the quality of life for those who live
    in them

Encephalitis Society 1994
■ 7b Saville St, MALTON, N Yorks, YO17 7LL. (hq)
    01653 699599 fax 01653 604369
    email mail@encephalitis.info
    http://www.encephalitis.info
    Resource Centre Mgr: Elaine Dowall
▲ Company Limited by Guarantee; Registered Charity
○ *M, *W; to provide support, everyday advice & general
    information to families & carers of children or adults with
    encephalitis; to raise public awareness & gather more
    information to aid research into encephalitis.
    Contact between families in similar situations is encouraged so
    mutual experiences can be shared
● Conf - Mtgs - ET - Res - Inf
< Eur Org for Rare Disorders (EURORDIS); Children's Acquired
    Brain Injury Interest Gp (CABIIG); Contact-a-Family; Long-
    term Medical Conditions Alliance (LMCA); Neurological
    Alliance; Rare Disorders Alliance; R Assn for Disability &
    Rehabilitation (RADAR); UK Acquired Brain Injury
    Forum (UKABIF)
M 800 i
¶ NL - 3;   Annual Review; free.
    Note: Encephalitis Society is the operating name of the
    Encephalitis Support Group

Encephalitis Support Group
    registered name of the **Encephalitis Society**

Endurance GB (EGB) 2001
NR National Agricultural Centre, Stoneleigh Park, KENILWORTH,
    Warks, CV8 2RP. (hq)
    024 7669 8863 fax 024 7641 8429
    email enquiries@endurancegb.co.uk
    http://www.endurancegb.co.uk
    Chmn: Wendy Dunham
▲ Company Limited by Guarantee
Br 22
○ *S; to promote & enhance the sport of endurance (competitive
    long distance) riding in the UK . . . for all levels of rider
● Conf - Mtgs - ET - Exhib - Comp
< Brit Equestrian Fedn
M 2,200 i, UK / 100 i, o'seas
¶ Magazine - 4; ftm;
    Branch Group NL - 12;   AR - 1; all ftm only.

Energy Industries Council (EIC) 1943
NR Newcombe House, 45 Notting Hill Gate, LONDON,
    W11 3LQ. (hq)
    020 7221 2043 fax 020 7221 8813
    email info@eic-uk.com http://www.the-eic.com
    Chief Exec: Mike Major
▲ Company Limited by Guarantee
○ *T; manufacturers, contractors & financial institutions serving
    the oil, petrochemical, natural gas, coal, power & process
    industries
● Conf - Mtgs - Exhib - Expt - Inf - VE
< Fedn of Eur Petroleum & Gas Eqpt Mfrs
M 362 f
¶ NL - 17; m only.
    Catalogue of British Suppliers - 2 yrly; ftm, £45 nm.
    Technical publications, specification & datasheets.

Energy Institute (EI) 2003
■ 61 New Cavendish St, LONDON, W1G 7AR. (hq)
    020 7467 7100 fax 020 7255 1472
    email info@energyinst.org http://www.energyinst.org
    Chief Exec: Louise Kingham
▲ Registered Charity
Br 13; 5
○ *L, *Q; promotion of the safe, environmentally responsible &
    efficient supply & use of energy in all its forms & applications
Gp Discussion group
● Conf - Mtgs - ET - Exam - Res - Exhib - Comp - Stat - Inf - Lib -
    VE - LG
M 12,000 i, 1,300 f, UK & o'seas
    (Sub: £80 i, varies f)
¶ Petroleum Review - 12; ftm, £230 (UK) nm.
    Energy World - 11; ftm, £158 (UK) nm.
    Codes of Safe Practice.   Recommended Practices.
    AR; free via website.

Energy Intensive Users Group
NR Broadway House, Tothill St, London, SW1H 9NQ. (hq)
    020 7654 1536 fax 020 7222 2782
    http://www.eiug.org.uk
○ *K; campaigning for secure industrial energy supplies at
    internationally competitive prices
M f & org

Energy Networks Association
NR Dean Bradley House - 6th floor, 52 Horseferry Rd, LONDON,
    SW1P 2AF.
    020 7706 5100
○ *T; UK gas & electricity transmission & distribution licence
    holders
    Note: is one of the three associations formed by the closing of
    the Electricity Association

Energy Retail Association
NR 17 Waterloo Place (4th floor), LONDON, SW1Y 4AR.
    020 7930 9175
    http://www.energy-retail.org.uk
○ *T
    Note: was formed on the closing of the Electricity Association

Energy Systems Trade Association (ESTA) 1982
NR PO Box 77, BENFLEET, Essex, SS7 5EX. (hq)
    01268 569010
    Exec Dir: Alan Aldridge
▲ Company Limited by Guarantee
○ *T; to promote the efficient use of energy in industry, commerce
    & the public sector

© CBD Research Ltd · Beckenham · BR3 5JS · Tel 020 8650 7745 · Fax 020 8650 0768 · E-mail cbd@cbdresearch.com · www.cbdresearch.com

Enforcement Services Association   1906
■   Park House, 10 Park St, BRISTOL, BS1 5HX.   (accom address)
       0117-907 4771   fax 0117-915 4521
       email enquiries@ensas.org.uk
       http://www.ensas.org.uk
       Exec Dir: Vernon Phillips
▲   Un-incorporated Society
○   *P
●   Mtgs - ET - Exam - Res - Inf - LG
M   58 i, 30 f
¶   NL;   Ybk - 1; both free.

engage: National Association of Gallery Education   1988
NR   Rich Mix, 35-47 Bethnal Green Rd, LONDON, E1 6LA.   (hq)
       020 7729 5858   fax 020 7729 3688
       email info@engage.org   http://www.engage.org
       Dir: Jane Sillis
▲   Registered Charity
○   *A, *E, *G, *P; to promote greater understanding & enjoyment
       of the visual arts by engaging with the public, artists, galleries
       & educators
M   i, f & org
¶   engage review - 2; ftm.
       engagements - 4; ftm only.

Engineered Systems Product Group
       a product association of BEAMA Installation, which is part of **BEAMA**

Engineering Construction Industry Association   (ECIA)   1994
■   Broadway House, Tothill St, LONDON, SW1H 9NS.   (hq)
       020 7799 2000   fax 020 7233 1930
       http://www.ecia.co.uk
       Managing Dir: Michael Hockey
▲   Un-incorporated Society
Br   6 regions
○   *T
●   Mtgs - ET - Stat - Inf - Empl - LG
<   CBI; Engg Emplrs Fedn; Eur Construction Inst
M   c 300 f (employing 65,000 i)
¶
       Publications list available on wensite.

**Engineering Equipment & Materials Users' Association
(EEMUA)   1949**
■   10-12 Lovat Lane, LONDON, EC3R 8DN.   (hq)
       020 7621 0011   fax 020 7621 0022
       email info@eemua.org   http://www.eemua.org
       Exec Dir: C Tayler
▲   Company Limited by Guarantee
○   *L; for companies that use engineering equipment & materials
       in the construction, operation & management of chemical &
       petrochemical process plants, offshore rigs, power
       generation, storage & distribution & transport systems &
       similar industrial & production assets
Gp   Electrical; Mechanical (pressure equipment, storage tanks,
       piping & valve systems, rotating machinery); Materials
       technology; Inspection; Instruments & control
●   Mtgs - ET - SG - Inf - LG
>   Eur C'ee User Inspectorates
M   17 f, UK / 2 f, o'seas
¶   c 60 technical guides & handbooks.
       Free price list available.

Engineering Industries Association   (EIA)   1940
■   62 Bayswater Rd, LONDON, W2 3PS.   (hq)
       020 7298 6455   fax 020 7298 6456
       email head.office@eia.co.uk   http://www.eia.co.uk
       Pres: Sir Ronald Halstead
▲   Company Limited by Guarantee
Br   3 regions
○   *T; representation & promotion of the interests of the
       engineering manufacturing sector in UK, European & global
       markets
●   Conf - Mtgs - Exhib - Expt - Inf - VE - LG
M   400 f
¶   NL - 12;   Trade Leads - 12;   Buyers' Guide - 1; all ftm.

Engineering Integrity Society   (EIS)   1985
NR   18 Oak Close, BEDWORTH, Warks, CV12 9AJ.   (regd off)
       024 7673 0126   fax 024 7673 0126
       email eis@e-i-s.org.uk   http://www.e-i-s.org.uk
       Chmn: Dr Peter Blackmore
▲   Registered Charity
○   *P; 'to advance the education of persons working in the field of
       engineering by providing a forum for the interchange of
       ideas & information on integrity of engineering practice'
Gp   Durability & fatigue; Noise, vibration & human perception;
       Simulation, test & measurement
●   Conf - Mtgs - ET - Exhib
M   100 i, 37 f, UK / 26 i, o'seas
¶   Engineering Integrity (Jnl) - 2; ftm, £50 yr nm.
       EIS News (NL) - 2; free.

Engineering & Machinery Alliance   (EAMA)   2001
■   62 Bayswater Rd, LONDON, W2 3PS.   (hq)
       020 7298 6450   fax 020 7298 6430
       email eama@mta.org.uk   http://www.eama.info
       Sec: Rupert Hodges,   Chmn: Martin Walder
▲   Company Limited by Guarantee
○   *N, *T; for the engineering, production machinery, components
       & tooling manufacturing sectors in the UK
●   Res - Stat - LG
M   9 associations:
       British Automation & Robot Association
       British Paper Machinery Suppliers Association
       British Plastics Federation
       British Turned Part Manufacturers Association
       Confederation of British Metalforming
       Gauge & Tool Makers Association
       Manufacturing Technologies Association
       Picon Ltd
       Processing & Packaging Machinery Association
¶   Hbk - irreg; free.

Engineering Training Equipment Manufacturers' Association
       a group of the **British Educational Suppliers Association**

Engineers for Disaster Relief
       RedR - Engineers for Disaster Relief is the registered name of **RedR
       UK**

Engineers Hand Tools Association
       a group of the **Federation of British Hand Tool Manufacturers**

Engineers Ireland   1835
IRL   22 Clyde Rd, Ballsbridge, DUBLIN 4, Republic of Ireland.
       353 (1) 668 4341   fax 353 (1) 668 5508
       email info@engineersireland.ie
       http://www.engineersireland.ie
       Dir Gen: John Power
○   *P
M   c 22,000
       Note: Engineers Ireland is the operating name of the Institution
       of Engineers of Ireland

England Athletics 1880
NR Wellington House, Starley Way, Birmingham International Park,
    SOLIHULL, W Midlands, B37 7HE.   (hq)
    0121-781 7172   fax 0121-781 7205
    email info@englandathletics.org
    http://www.englandathletics.org
    Hon Sec: Walter Nicholls
○ *S; governing body for athletics in England; to control, promote
    & provide athletic competitions, coaching & training
M clubs

England Basketball (EBBA) 1936
NR PO Box 3971, SHEFFIELD, S Yorks, S9 9AZ.   (hq)
    0114-223 5693
    http://www.englandbasketball.co.uk
    Chief Exec: Keith Mair
▲ Company Limited by Guarantee
○ *S; to govern & promote the game of basketball
M 30,000 i, 1,000 clubs
¶ Zone Press - 6.   Competitions Hbk - 1.   AR.
    Note: Also known as the English Basketball Association.

England Handball Association (EHA) 1968
NR 40 Newchurch Rd, RAWTENSTALL, Lancs, BB4 7QX.   (hq)
    01706 229354   fax 01706 229354
    http://www.englandhandball.com
○ *S; national governing body for the sport
M i, schools & org
    Note: Registered as the British Handball Association.

England Hockey
NR The National Hockey Stadium, Silbury Boulevard, MILTON
    KEYNES, Bucks, MK9 1HA.   (hq)
    01908 544644
▲ Un-incorporated Society
○ *S; governing body for hockey in England (men, women &
    mixed)
M i, clubs & schools
✕ has replaced the English Hockey Association

England Indoor Cricket Association (BICA) 1997
■ 11a Harman Rd, SUTTON COLDFIELD, W Midlands,
    B72 1AH.   (hq)
    email info@ei8ca.co.uk   http://www.ei8ca.co.uk
    Chmn: Ashley Lawrence
▲ Company Limited by Guarantee
○ *S
● Comp - Inf
M [not stated]
    Note: Trades as Indoor Cricket England
✕ British Indoor Cricket Association

England Netball
    alternative name of the **All England Netball Association**

England Squash
    alternative name of the **Squash Rackets Association**

**England & Wales Cricket Board Association of Cricket Officials
(ECB ACO) 2008**
■ Lord's Cricket Ground, LONDON, NW8 8QZ.   (hq)
    020 7432 1240   fax 020 7289 5619
    email ecbaco@ecb.co.uk   http://www.ecb.co.uk/
    ecbaco
    Member Services Mgr: Sam Greaves
Br 39; ICC Europe
○ *S; all aspects of cricket officiating from playground to the test
    area, nationally & internationally
● Conf - Mtgs - ET - Exam
< England & Wales Cricket Bd (ECB); Marylebone Cricket
    Club (MCC)
M 5,654 i, UK / 200 i, o'seas
    £5-£22 UK / £10 o'seas)
¶ NL - 6; ftm, website nm.
    MCC Open Learning Manual - 1; £10 m, £15 nm.
✕ 2008 (Association of Cricket Umpires & Scorers
    (ECB Officials Association (merged 1 January)

**England & Wales Cricket Board Coaches Association   (ECB
Coaches Association) (ECB CA) 2002**
NR Warwickshire County Cricket Ground, Edgbaston,
    BIRMINGHAM, B5 7QX.   (hq)
    0121-440 4332   fax 0121-440 7605
    email coaches.association@ecb.co.uk
    http://www.ecbca.play-cricket.com
○ *S; ongoing education, development & support of cricket
    coaches at all levels in UK, Europe & overseas
● Conf - Mtgs - ET - Exhib - Inf - LG
M i

þa Engliscan Gesíþas   (the English Companions) 1966
NR Bottom Lane Farm, Bottom House, near LEEK, Staffs,
    ST13 7QL.   (hsp)
    01538 266440
    http://www.tha-engliscan-gesithas.org.uk
    Hon Sec: Harry Ball
▲ Company Limited by Guarantee
Br 16; Australia, Canada, New Zealand, Republic of Ireland, USA
○ *G; to encourage interest in the history & other aspects of Old
    English or the Anglo-Saxon period, its language, culture &
    traditions
Gp Living history; Local shire (scir) gps; Old English
    correspondence course
● Mtgs - ET - Res - Exhib - Comp - SG - Lib - VE - Lectures
M 544 i, UK / 42 i, o'seas
¶ Wiþowinde (Bindweed) (Jnl) - 3;
    Hrafnes Wisprung (Raven's Whisper) (NL) - 3; both ftm only.

English Apples & Pears Ltd (EAP) 1990
■ Bradbourne House, East Malling, WEST MALLING, Kent,
    ME19 6DZ.   (hq)
    01732 529781   fax 01732 529783
    http://www.englishapplesandpears.co.uk
▲ Company Limited by Guarantee
○ *H, *K, *T; 'to further the interests of shareholder members who
    are top fruit (apples & pears) growers in UK'
● Inf - PL
M 280 i

© CBD Research Ltd · Beckenham · BR3 5JS · Tel 020 8650 7745 · Fax 020 8650 0768 · E-mail cbd@cbdresearch.com · www.cbdresearch.com

English Association (EA) 1906
- University of Leicester, University Rd, LEICESTER, LE1 7RH. (hq)
  0116-252 3982   fax 0116-252 2301
  email engassoc@le.ac.uk   http://www.le.ac.uk/engassoc
  Sec: Helen Lucas
- ▲ Company Limited by Guarantee; Registered Charity
- Br Australia, South Africa
- ○ *L; promotion of knowledge & appreciation of English language & literature
- Gp Graduate students
- ● Conf
- M i & org
- ¶ NL - 3.   English - 3;   English 4-11 - 3.
  The Use of English - 3.
  Year's Work in English Studies - 1.
  Essays & Studies - 1.
  Year's Work in Critical & Cultural Theory - 1.

English Association of American Bond & Shareholders
- NR Broomfield Business Centre, 80-82 Broomfield Rd, CHELMSFORD, Essex, CM1 1SS.   (hq)
  01245 259911
  Sec: Navin Khattar
- ○ *G

English Association of Self Catering Operators (EASCO) 1985
- PO Box 567, HAYES, Middx, UB3 9EW.   (hsp)
  020 7078 7329   fax 0870 136 6638
  email info@englishselfcatering.co.uk
  http://www.englishselfcatering.co.uk
  Chief Exec: Martin Sach
- ▲ Un-incorporated Society
- ○ *T; to represent owners of self-catering accommodation businesses
- ● Mtgs - Res - Inf - LG
- < Fedn of Nat Self Catering Assns; Tourism Alliance
- M 25 i, 15 f

English Association for Snooker and Billiards (EASB)
- NR Martinet House, Martinet Rd, Thornaby, STOCKTON-on-TEES, N Yorks, TS17 0AS.
  0808 129 4040
  email info@nglishsnooker.com
  http://www.englishsnooker.com
  Sec: Peter Ainsworth
- ○ *S

English Baseball Association
- NR 7 Vanbrugh Rd, LIVERPOOL, L4 7TT.   (hsp)
  0151-476 1940
  Hon Sec: H Ashcroft
- ○ *S
- M 34 org

English Baseball Association (EBA) 1892
- NR 151 Blackmore Drive, West Derby, LIVERPOOL, L13 9EE
  http://www.englishbaseballassociation.co.uk
  Sec: Carl Nunnen
- ○ *S

English Basketball Association
  alternative name of **England Basketball**

English Boccia Association (EBA) 1999
- Unit 5 Heathcoat Bldg, Nottingham Science & Technology Park, University Boulevard, NOTTINGHAM, NG7 2QJ.   (hq)
  0115-925 7027
  http://www.cpsport.org
- ○ *S; to develop quality opportunities for players of all disabilities to participate in the sport of Boccia under the regulations of the International Boccia Commission (Boccia is a game akin to indoor bowls)
- ● ET - Res - Inf - Lib - Referee courses - Level 1 training courses
- < Intl Boccia Commission
- M i & org

English Bowling Association
  in 2007 merged with the English Women's Bowling Association to form **Bowls England**

English Bridge Union (EBU) 1936
- NR Broadfields, Bicester Rd, AYLESBURY, Bucks, HP19 8AZ.   (hq)
  01296 317200   fax 01296 317220
  email postmaster@ebu.co.uk   http://www.ebu.co.uk
  Gen Mgr & Co Sec: Barry Capal
- ▲ Un-incorporated Society
- ○ *S; governing body for the game of duplicate contract bridge
- Gp Bridge for All (learn & play programme)
- ● Conf - Mtgs - ET - Comp - SG - Stat - Inf - Lib
- < Wld Bridge Fedn; Eur Bridge League
- M 30,000 i, 1,100 clubs
- ¶ English Bridge - 6.   Club NL - 6.   County NL - 4.   .
  Really Easy. . . (7 titles).

English Carp Heritage Organisation (ECHO) 2001
- NR 16 The Parade, YATELEY, Hants, GU46 7UN.
  01252 861955
  email info@echocarp.co.uk   http://www.echocarp.co.uk
- ○ carp anglers

English Chess Federation (BCF) 1904
- The Watch Oak, Chain Lane, BATTLE, E Sussex, TN33 0YD. (hq)
  01424 775222   fax 01424 775904
  email office@englishchess.org.uk
  http://www.englishchess.org.uk
  Admin: Cynthia Gurney
- ▲ Un-incorporated Society
- ○ *S; the governing body for chess in England
- ● ET - Comp - Inf
- < Fédn Intl des Echecs
- > County assns
- M 1,600 i
- ¶ Chess Moves (NL) - 6.   Ybk.
- ✕ 2005 British Chess Federation

English Civil War Society Ltd (ECWS) 1980
- Flat 11 The Stables, Milton Park, PETERBOROUGH, PE6 7AF. (sb)
  01733 380177   fax 01733 380072
  http://www.english-civil-war-society.org
- ▲ Company Limited by Shares
- ○ *G; to further interest in 17th century English history; to organise & perform re-enactments of the English Civil War
- Gp The King's Army; The Roundhead Assn; Friends of the English Civil War Soc (supporting gp)
- ● Mtgs - Res - SG
- M c 3,000 i
- ¶ King's Army NL - 6;   Roundhead Association NL; both ftm only.
  Friends of the ECWS NL - 4.

English Clergy Association   (ECA)   1938
- ■ The Old School House, Norton Hawkfield, BRISTOL, BS39 4HB.   (chmn/p)
  01275 830017 (Mon-Thur 1100-1300)
  email benoporto-eca@yahoo.co.uk
  http://www.clergyassoc.co.uk
  Chmn: Rev J W Masding
- ▲ Registered Charity; Un-incorporated Society
- ○ *P, *R; a professional organisation for the clergy of the Church of England, & lay members supportive of the traditional place of the clergy
- ● Conf - Mtgs - Nominations for Clergy Holiday Grants - Monitoring the processes of legislation & other changes
- M 'no reliable figures available'
- ¶ Parson & Parish - 2; ftm, £6 yr nm.

English Community Care Association   (ECCA)   2004
- ■ Monmouth House (2nd floor), 38-40 Artillery Lane, LONDON, E1 7LS.   (hq)
  0845 057 7677   fax 0845 057 7678
  email info@ecca.org.uk   http://www.ecca.org.uk
  Chief Exec: Martin Green
- ▲ Company Limited by Guarantee; Registered Charity
- ○ *T; representative body for providers of continuing care homes registered under the 1984 Registered Homes Act; seeks to protect & promote high standards of treatment & care in the independent sector
- Gp Medical & rehabilitation units; Nursing homes; Residential homes
- ● Conf - Mtgs - Res - Stat - Inf
- M Care homes
- ¶ Bulletin;   AR;   both ftm.
- ✕ 2004 Independent Healthcare Association

English Companions
English name of þa **Engliscan Gesíþas**

English Cross Country Association   (ECCA)   1883
- ■ 22 Denham Drive, BASINGSTOKE, Hants, RG22 6LR.   (hsp)
  01256 328401   fax 01256 328401
  Sec: I S Byett
- ○ *S; to encourage & support cross-country running for men & women & organise national championships
- M clubs

English Curling Association   (ECA)   1971
- NR 14 Donnelly Drive, BEDFORD, Beds, MK41 9TU.   (sp)
  email development@englishcurling.co.uk
  http://www.englishcurling.co.uk
- ▲ Un-incorporated Society
- Br 3
- ○ *S; the sport of curling in England
- ● Mtgs - Comp - VE
- < Wld Curling Fedn; Eur Curling Fedn
- M c 130 i (England)
- ¶ Ybk - 1.

English Draughts Association   (EDA)   1897
- ■ 54 Mayfield Rd, RYDE, Isle of Wight, PO33 3PR.   (chmn/p)
  01983 565484
  email iancaws@msn.com   http://www.home.clara.net/davey
  Chmn: Ian H Caws
- ▲ Un-incorporated Society
- ○ *G, *S; to promote the game of draughts (checkers)
- ● Conf - Mtgs - Comp
- < Fédn Mondiale du Jeu de Dames; World Checkers/Draughts Fedn
- > County draughts assns
- M 200 i, UK / 35 i, o'seas
- ¶ English Draughts Jnl - 4; ftm, (50p back issues, nm).

English Federation of Disability Sport   (EFDS)
- NR Manchester Metropolitan University, Alsager Campus, Hassall Rd, Alsager, STOKE-on-TRENT, Staffs, ST7 2HL.
  0161-247 5294
  http://www.efds.co.uk
  Chief Exec: Colin Chaytors
- ○ *S
- ✕ 2005 Disability Sport England (merged)

English Folk Dance & Song Society   (EFDSS)   1932
- ■ Cecil Sharp House, 2 Regent's Park Rd, LONDON, NW1 7AY.   (hq)
  020 7485 2206   fax 020 7284 0534
  email info@efdss.org   http://www.efdss.org
  Chief Exec: Katy Spicer
- ▲ Company Limited by Guarantee; Registered Charity
- ○ *D, *G; 'putting English traditions into the hearts & minds of the people of England'
- ● ET - Res - Inf - Lib - PL
- M 3,500 i, 562 affiliates, UK & o'seas
- ¶ EDS (English Dance & Song) - 4; ftm, £2.50 nm.
  Folk Music Jnl - 1; ftm, £7.50 nm.
  Members' Quarterly; ftm only.

English Goat Breeders Association   (EGBA)   1978
- ■ Heathgate Farm, Gills Lane, Rooksbridge, AXBRIDGE, Somerset, BS26 2TZ.   (hsp)
  01934 750602
  http://www.egba.org.uk
  Hon Sec: Mrs J A Parry
- ▲ Registered Charity
- ○ *B; preservation & promotion of English goats
- ● Mtgs - Exhib - Inf - LG
- < Brit Goat Soc
- M c 90 i
- ¶ Jem - 6; ftm, 75p nm.

English Goethe Society   (EGS)   1886
- NR c/o Dept of German, King's College London, Strand, LONDON, WC2R 2LS.   (hsb)
  020 7848 2131   fax 020 7848 2089
  email matthew.bell@kcl.ac.uk
  http://www.englishgoethesociety.org
  Hon Sec & Treas: Dr Matthew Bell
- ▲ Registered Charity
- ○ *L; to promote the work & thought of Goethe, as well as other 18th century German writers & some later writers, notably Thomas Mann
- ● Conf - Mtgs - ET - Res - Comp
- < Goether-Gesellschaft (Weimar)
- M 150 i, UK / 20 i, o'seas
- ¶ Publications of the English Goethe Society - 1; ftm, £20 nm.

English Golf Union Ltd   (EGU)   1924
- ■ National Golf Centre, The Broadway, WOODHALL SPA, Lincs, LN10 6PU.   (hq)
  01526 354500   fax 01526 354020
  email info@englishgolfunion.org
  http://www.englishgolfunion.org
  Chief Exec: John Petrie
- ▲ Company Limited by Guarantee
- ○ *S; to promote, administer & encourage amateur golf in England; to maintain a uniform system of handicapping
- Gp Competitions; Coaching; Development
- ● ET - Comp - Inf - Development - Coaching
- < Eur Golf Assn; Cent Coun of Physical Recreation
- M 725,000 i
  (Sub: £4.50)
- ¶ Ybk - 1; £10.
- ✕ 2005 English Golf Union

© CBD Research Ltd · Beckenham · BR3 5JS · Tel 020 8650 7745 · Fax 020 8650 0768 · E-mail cbd@cbdresearch.com · www.cbdresearch.com

English Guernsey Cattle Society   (EGCS)   1884
NR   Scotsbridge House, Scots Hill, RICKMANSWORTH, Herts,
  WD3 3BB.   (hq)
  01923 695204   fax 01923 695215
  email office@guernseycattle.com
  http://www.guernseycattle.com
  Admin: Mrs K Jenkins
▲   Company Limited by Guarantee; Registered Charity
○   *B
●   Conf - Mtgs - SG
M   280 i, UK / 20 i, o'seas
¶   Guernsey Breeders NL - 3; ftm.

English Historic Towns Forum   (EHTF)   1987
NR   PO Box 22, BRISTOL, BS16 1RZ.   (hq)
  0117-975 0459   fax 0117-975 0460
  email ehtf@uwe.ac.uk   http://www.ehtf.org.uk
  Director: Chris Winter
▲   Un-incorporated Society
○   *K; to establish & encourage contact between local authorities
  having responsibility for the management of historic towns &
  cities, & between these authorities & other public, private &
  voluntary sector agencies
Gp   Built environment; Retail; Tourism; Transport
●   Conf - Mtgs - ET - Res - Exhib - SG - Inf - VE - LG
<   Eur Assn of Historic Towns & Regions (EAHTR)
M   i, f & org
¶   NL - 4;   AR; both free.
  Membership Directory - 1; ftm only.
  Publications list available on request.

English Indoor Bowling Association   (EIBA)   1971
■   David Cornwell House, Bowling Green, Leicester Rd, MELTON
  MOWBRAY, Leics, LE13 0FA.
  01664 481900   fax 01664 482888
  email enquiries@eiba.co.uk   http://www.eiba.co.uk
  Sec: S Rodwell
○   *S; indoor bowls (men only)
M   340 org
¶   Woods & Jack (NL) - 5.   Ybk; £3 m.

English Lacrosse Association   (ELA)   1996
NR   The Belle Vue Centre, Pink Bank Lane, MANCHESTER,
  M12 5GL.   (hq)
  0161-227 3626
  email info@englishlacrosse.co.uk
  Chief Exec: David Shuttleworth
▲   Company Limited by Guarantee
○   *S; the governing body for men's & women's lacrosse in Britain
M   c 4,000 i, c 100 org

English Pétanque Association
NR   c/o 7 Richard Walker Close, BURY ST EDMUNDS, Suffolk,
  IP32 7GX.
  email secretary@englishpetanque.org.uk
  http://www.englishpetanque.org.uk
  Nat Sec: Kevin Moss
○   *S

English Place-Name Society   (EPNS)   1923
■   School of English Studies, University of Nottingham,
  NOTTINGHAM, NG7 2RD.   (hq)
  0115-951 5919   fax 0115-951 5924
  email name-studies@nottingham.ac.uk
  http://www.nottingham.ac.uk/english/ins
  Hon Dir: Prof Richard Coates,   Hon Sec: Prof Turville-Petre
▲   Registered Charity
○   *L; to survey the place-names & field-names of England, county
  by county, & publish the results of the survey
●   Annual Meeting - Res - Inf - Lib
M   625 i
¶   The Place Names of [county] - 1; £35 m (£40 o'seas),
  £40 nm (£45 o'seas).
  Jnl - 1; ftm, £12 nm.   AR.

English Playing-Card Society   (EPCS)   1984
NR   Little Paddock, Charlton Mackrell, SOMERTON, Somerset,
  TA11 7BG.   (hsp)
  01458 223812
  email secretary@epcs.org   http://www.epcs.org
  Sec: Barney Townshend
▲   Un-incorporated Society
○   *G; to provide information for collectors & researchers of
  English playing cards & children's card games
●   Mtgs - Res - SG - Inf
<   Ephemera Soc
M   130 i
¶   NL (incl LM) - 3; £20 m.

English Poetry & Song Society   (EPSS)   1983
NR   76 Lower Oldfield Park, BATH, Somerset, BA2 3HP.   (hsp)
  email menistral@yahoo.co.uk
  Chief Exec: Richard Carder
○   *D; the promotion of English art song by performance,
  publication & recording
●   Mtgs - Res - Comp - Lib
<   Nat Fedn of Music Socs
M   50 i, UK / 2 i, o'seas
¶   NL & Song List - 2; £12 m.

English Pool Association   (EPA)   1979
NR   88 Crescent Rd, Hadley, TELFORD, Shropshire, TF1 4JX.   (sp)
  01952 641682
  email ivor.edwards22@blueyonder.co.uk
  http://www.epa.org.uk
  Gen Sec: Ivor Edwards
Br   46
○   *S; to organise, administer the game of pool in England
Gp   English Pool Referees Association
●   Mtgs - Exhib - Comp - LG - selection of national teams -
  organisation of fixtures & inter-league events
<   Wld Eight Ball Pool Fedn; Eur Eight Ball Pool Fedn
M   18,000 i
¶   Hbk - 1; ftm; £5 nm.

English Pool Referees Association
  a group of the **English Pool Association**

English Racketball   1998
■   50 Tredegar Rd, Wilmington, DARTFORD, Kent, DA2 7AZ.
  (hsp/b)
  01322 272200   fax 01322 289295
  email idw@kentsra.co.uk
  Hon Sec: Ian D W Wright
○   *S
<   is part of England Squash

English School [sport] Association
  no school sports associations are included in this directory - see
  controlling body for the sport concerned

English Schools' Badminton Association
  a group of **Badminton England**

English Short Mat Bowling Association   (ESMBA)
NR   Wytheford Hall AFrm, SHAWBURY, Shropshire, SY4 4JJ.   (hsp)
  Gen Sec: Herbie Bowden
○   *S; the playing of bowls on mats
●   Exhib - Comp
M   i

English Ski Council
  trades as **Snowsport England**

English Speaking Union of the Commonwealth   (ESU)   1918
NR   Dartmouth House, 37 Charles St, LONDON, W1J 5ED.   (hq)
     020 7529 1550   fax 020 7495 6108
     email esu@esu.org   http://www.esu.org
     Dir Gen: Mrs Valerie Mitchell
▲   Registered Charity
Br   40; 38 o'seas
○   *X; 'to promote international understanding & human
     achievement through the widening use of the English
     language throughout the world'
●   Conf - Mtgs - ET - Exhib - Comp - Inf - Lib - VE - Public
     speaking & debates - Youth exchange & work experience
     schemes - Cultural & literary events
<   English Speaking U (USA)
M   5,193 i, 57 f, UK / 449 i, o'seas
¶   Concord (Jnl) - 2;   ESU NL - 10; both ftm.

English Sports Association for People with Learning Disability
     in 2005 became the Mencap Sport division of **MENCAP**

English Table Tennis Association   (ETTA)   1926
■   Queensbury House (3rd floor), Havelock Rd, HASTINGS,
     E Sussex, TN34 1HF.   (hq)
     01424 722525   fax 01424 422103
     email admin@etta.co.uk   http://www.etta.co.uk
     Gen Sec: R H Sinclair,   Chief Exec: Richard Yule
▲   Company Limited by Guarantee
○   *S; governing body for the sport in England
●   Conf - Organisation of national championships
<   Intl Table Tennis Fedn; Eur Table Tennis U
M   40,000 i, 4,500 clubs
¶   Table Tennis News - 8; £2.75.

English Tiddlywinks Association   (ETwA)   1958
■   47 Swansholme Gardens, SANDY, Beds, SG19 1HL.   (chmn/p)
     01767 225744
     email ajdean47@msn.com09>etwa.org
     Chmn: Alan Dean,   Sec: Miss Sarah Knight
▲   Un-incorporated Society
○   *S; to promote the game of tiddlywinks throughout the UK
●   Comp
<   Intl Fedn Tiddlywinks Assns
M   80 i, UK / 5 i, o'seas
     (Sub: £6 UK / £10 o'seas)
¶   Winking World - 2; ftm, £3 nm.

English UK   2004
■   219 St John St, LONDON, EC1V 4LY.   (hq)
     020 7608 7960   fax 020 7608 7961
     email info@englishuk.com   http://www.englishuk.com
     Chief Exec: Tony Millns
▲   Registered Charity
○   *E, *P; British Council accredited English language teaching
     providers
Gp   Business English UK; Work Experience UK
●   Conf - ET - Res - Exhib - Inf - LG
<   Eur Fedn of Nat Assns for Teaching Mother Tongues to Foreign
     Students (ELITE); Assn of Language Teaching Orgs (ALTO)
M   330 f
¶   English UK News - 4;   English in the UK - 1; both free.
×   2004 (Association of Recognised English Language Services
     (British Association of State English Language Teaching

English Volleyball Association   (EVA)   1971
NR   Suite B Loughborough Technology Centre, Epinal Way,
     LOUGHBOROUGH, Leics, LE11 3GE.   (hq)
     01509 631699   fax 01509 631689
     email info@volleyballengland.org
     http://www.volleyballengland.org
     Chief Exec: Lisa Wainwright
○   *S; governing body for volleyball, beach volleyball and sitting
     volleyball
M   c 18,000 i
     Note: Volleyball England is the association's branded image

English Westerners Society   (EWS)   1954
■   130 The Keep, KINGSTON upon THAMES, Surrey, KT2 5UE.
     (hsp)
     email keg.cagb@btinternet.com
     http://www.english-westerners-society.org.uk
     Hon Sec: Kevin Galvin
▲   Un-incorporated Society
○   *G; study of the history of the American West, incl ethnological
     & cultural background
●   AGM only
<   Westerners Intl (USA)
M   150 i, UK / 55 i, o'seas
     (Sub: £'12.50)
¶   Tally Sheet - 3;   Brand Book - 1/3;
     Special publication - irreg; all ftm, prices vary nm.
     AR - 1; free.

English Wine Producers   (EWP)   1992
■   PO Box 5729, MARKET HARBOROUGH, Leics, LE16 8WX.
     01536 772264   fax 01536 772263
     email info@englishwineproducers.com
     http://www.englishwineproducers.com
     Contact: Julia Trustram Eve
○   *T
<   UK Vineyards Assn
M   c 20 i

English Women's Bowling Association
     in 2007 merged with the English Bowling Association to form **Bowls**
England

English Women's Indoor Bowling Association   (EWIBA)   1951
■   3 Moulton Business Park, Scirocco Close, Moulton Park,
     NORTHAMPTON, NN3 6AP.   (hq)
     01604 494163   fax 01604 494434
     email ewiba@btinternet.com   http://www.ewiba.com
     Nat Sec: Mrs Tricia Thomas
▲   Un-incorporated Society
○   *S; to promote & foster the game of flat green indoor bowls for
     women in England
●   ET - Comp
<   Wld Indoor Bowls Coun; Brit Isles Women's Indoor Bowls Coun
M   40,509 i, 309 clubs
     (Sub: £2.20 i, £35 clubs)
¶   Ybk (incl list of clubs); £2.50.

Enid Blyton Society   1995
NR   93 Milford Hill, SALISBURY, Wilts, SP1 2QL.
     01722 331937
     http://www.enidblytonsociety.co.uk

Entertainment & Leisure Software Publishers Association Ltd
(ELSPA)   1989
■   167 Wardour St, LONDON, W1F 8WL.   (hq)
     020 7534 0580   fax 020 7534 0581
     email info@elspa.com   http://www.elspa.com
     Dir Gen: Paul Jackson
▲   Company Limited by Guarantee
○   *T; for interactive consumer software publishers, including
     computer & video games
Gp   Publishers; Developers; Distributors; Duplicators; Suppliers;
     Hardware Mfrs; Trade & Consumer Media; Legal
●   Conf - ET - Res - Exhib - Stat - Expt - Inf - LG - Anti piracy
     (crime unit) - Accreditation (duplicators)
<   Video Standards Couns: VUD (Germany); SELL (France); ISF-E
M   120 f, 4 org
¶   The Britsoft Book

Entertainment Retailers Association   (ERA)   1988
- ■ Colonnade House, 2 Westover Rd, BOURNEMOUTH, Dorset, BH1 2BY.
  01202 292063   fax 01202 292067
  email admin@eraltd.org   http://www.eraltd.org
  Dir Gen: Kim Bayley
- ▲ Company Limited by Guarantee
- ○ *T; for retailers of music, video & computer games
- ● Conf - Mtgs - Res - Stat - Inf - LG
- < Global Entertainment Retailers Alliance (GLOBAL); Nat Assn of Rack Merchandisers (USA) (NARM)
- M [not stated]
- ¶ ERA Ybk - 1; ftm, £25 nm.
- × 2006 (July) British Association of Record Dealers

Envelope Makers' & Manufacturing Stationers' Association
Secretariat in Alexandria, VA, USA

Environment & Planning Law Association
a group of the **Law Society of Northern Ireland**

Environmental Communicators' Organisation   (ECO)   1972
- ■ 8 Hooks Cross, Watton-at-Stone, HERTFORD, SG14 3RY. (chmn p)
  01920 830527   fax 01480 830538
  Chmn: Alan Massam,   Hon Sec: Barbara Jefferies
- ▲ Un-incorporated Society
- ○ *K; promotion of conservationist ideas among professional journalists & broadcasters
- ● Res - Inf - PR support for green orgs
- < Brit Naturalists Assn
- M 300 i
- ¶ NL - irreg.

Environmental Health Officers' Association   1949
- IRL 39A Main St, BRAY, Co Wicklow, Republic of Ireland.
  353 (1) 276 1211   fax 353 (1) 276 4665
  http://www.ehoa.ie
- ○ *P

Environmental Industries Commission Ltd   (EIC)   1995
- NR 45 Weymouth St, LONDON, W1G 8ND. (hq)
  020 7935 1675   fax 020 7486 3455
  email info@eic-uk.co.uk   http://www.eic-uk.co.uk
  Chief Exec: Adrian Wilkes
- ○ *N, *T; to represent the UK's environmental technology sector
- ● Conf - Mtgs - Res - Exhib - Expt - Inf - Lib - LG
- M 295 f, UK / 5 f, o'seas
- ¶ Envirotech News EU - 4;   Envirotech News UK - 12; both ftm, £135 nm.

Environmental Industries Federation Ltd
no longer in existence

Environmental Investigation Agency   (EIA)   1984
- NR 62-63 Upper St, LONDON, N1 0NY. (hq)
  020 7354 7960   fax 020 7354 7961
  email info@eia-international.org
  http://www.eia-international.org
  Chmn: Allan Thornton
- ▲ Company Limited by Guarantee
- Br USA
- ○ *K; 'an independent, non-profit organisation fighting to protect endangered wildlife & the natural world. Working closely with governments, enforcement agencies & other organisations, EIA develops effective long-term solutions to environmental problems'
- ● Res - Lib - PL - LG - Undercover investigations
- M 10,000 i
- ¶ NL - 2.   Various publications.

Environmental Noise Barrier Association
a group of the **Fencing Contractors' Association**

Environmental Protection UK   1898
- ■ 44 Grand Parade, BRIGHTON, E Sussex, BN2 9QA. (hq)
  01273 878770   fax 01273 606626
  email admin@environmental-protection.org.uk
  http://www.environmental-protection.org.uk
  Chief Exec: Philip Mulligan
- ▲ Registered Charity
- Br 10
- ○ *K; to achieve our vision of a cleaner, healthier, quieter world; focusing on air quality & climate change, noise & land quality
- ● Conf - Mtgs - ET - Res - Inf - Lib - LG
- < Intl U of Air Pollution Prevention & Envtl Protection Assns (IUAPPA); Eur Envt Bureau (EEB)
- M 322 i, 95 f, 262 org
  (Sub: £60 i, variable f & org)
- ¶ Briefing (NL) - 12;   AR - 1; both ftm only.
  Pollution Control Hbk - 1; £76 m, £95 nm.
  Information leaflets & booklets; £12-£20.
  Reports on various topics - irreg.
- × 2007 (October) National Society for Clean Air & Environmental Protection

Environmental Services Association   (ESA)   1969
- ■ 154 Buckingham Palace Rd, LONDON, SW1W 9TR. (hq)
  020 7824 8882   fax 020 7824 8753
  email info@esauk.org   http://www.esauk.org
  Chief Exec: Dirk Hazell
- ▲ Company Limited by Guarantee
- ○ *T; for the waste management industry (including collection, treatment, disposal, recovery, recycling, & use of waste in the commercial & industrial sectors), specialist equipment manufacturers, & consultants
- Gp Plant & equipment mfrs; Consultants; Overseas; Affiliates
- ● Conf - Mtgs - ET - Res - Exhib - SG - Expt - Inf - Lib - VE - LG - Annual lunch & AGM
- < Fedn Waste Mgt & Envtl Services (FEAD); Confedn of Brit Ind (CBI); UN GlobalCompact
- M 250 f
- ¶ Guidelines; ftm, prices vary nm.   AR; free.
- × 2001 Energy from Waste Association (merged)

Environmental & Technical Association for the Paper Sack Industry   (ETAPS)
- NR 24 Grange St, KILMARNOCK, Ayrshire, KA1 2AR. (hq)
  01563 570518   fax 01563 572728
  email npc@natpack.org.uk
  http://www.papersacks.org.uk
  Sec: Allan Glen
- ▲ Un-incorporated Society
- ○ *T; for paper sack producing companies
- ● Mtgs - Exhib - Inf
- M 6 f, UK / 2 f, o'seas

Environmental Transport Association
alternative name of **ETA Services Ltd**

Ephemera Society   (Ephsoc)   1975
- ■ PO Box 112, NORTHWOOD, Middx, HA6 2WT.
  01923 829079   fax 01923 825207
  Admin: Valerie Jackson-Harris
- ▲ Un-incorporated Society
- Br 1; Australia, Austria, Canada, USA
- ○ *G; the conservation, study & presentation of printed & handwritten ephemera (the minor transient documents of everyday life)
- ● Mtgs - Inf - VE - Bazaars
- < Foundation for Ephemera Studies
- M 700 i, f & org
- ¶ The Ephemerist - 4;   Members' Hbk - updated; both ftm only. (Sub: £25 Eur, £30 RoW)

Epilepsy Action
working name of the **British Epilepsy Association**

Epilepsy Action Scotland   (EAS)   1954
■   48 Govan Rd, GLASGOW, G51 1JL.   (hq)
     0141-427 4911   fax 0141-419 1709
     email enquiries@epilepsyscotland.org.uk
     http://www.epilepsyscotland.org.uk
     Chief Exec: Susan Douglas-Scott
▲   Company Limited by Guarantee; Registered Charity
Br 10
○   *W; to provide information, support & advice for people with
     epilepsy, their families, carers & professionals involved in
     their care
●   Conf - Mtgs - ET - Exam - Exhib - Inf - LG
<   Intl Bureau for Epilepsy; Mobility Intl; Jt Epilepsy Coun (UK &
     Ireland)
M   632 i
¶   Epilepsy News (NL) - 2.   Factsheets;   AR.
     Note: this organisation trades as Epilepsy Scotland

Epiphytic Plant Study Group   (EPSG)   1968
NR 31 Ribble Drive, Barrow-upon-Soar, LOUGHBOROUGH, Leics,
     LE12 8LJ.   (hsp)
     01509 413541
     email john@jhorobin.freeserve.co.uk
     http://www.epiphytes.co.uk
     Sec: John F Horobin
▲   Un-incorporated Society
○   *H; to foster an interest in epiphytic plants; to circulate
     information about such plants that would not otherwise be
     readily available
M   175 i, UK & o'seas
¶   Epiphytes (Jnl) - 4.

Eppynt Hill & Beulah Speckled Face Sheep Society
NR The Firs, 63 Garth Rd, BUILTH WELLS, Brecknockshire,
     LD2 3NH.
     01982 553726
     http://www.beulahsheep.co.uk
     Sec: D J Jones
○   *B

Equestrian Federation of Ireland
     see **HorseSport Ireland**

Equine Behaviour Forum   (EBF)   1978
NR 12 Allermuir Rd, Colinton, EDINBURGH, EH13 0HE.   (hsp)
     http://www.gla.ac.uk/external/ebf/
     Publicity & Marketing Offr: Sonia Davidson
▲   Un-incorporated Society
○   *L; to exchange information on the behaviour of horses in all
     situations
●   Lib (advice)
M   c 300 i, UK / c 50 i, o'seas
¶   Equine Behaviour - 4.

Equine Shiatsu Association
NR Hill Farm House, Mill Rd, STANFORD, Beds, SG18 9JH.
     01462 811933
     http://www.equineshiatsuassociation.com
○   *V

Equine Sports Massage Association   (ESMA)
NR Haycroft Barn, Lower Wick, DURSLEY, Glos, GL11 6DD.
     01453 511814
     http://www.equinemassageassociation.co.uk
○   *V

Equitoy: the association for toy importers   1950
■   Somers, Mounts Hill, BENENDEN, Kent, TN17 4ET.   (asa)
     01580 240819   fax 01580 241109
     Sec: Alan Milne
▲   Un-incorporated Society
○   *T
●   Conf - Mtgs - Exhib - LG - Lobbying European Commission -
     Advice on toy safety
M   c 2 i, 100 f, UK / 1 f, o'seas
¶   LM - updated.
     Advice on toy safety & importing quality procedures - updated
     on law or regulations change.
×   2006 British Toy Importers Association

Ergonomics Society   (ES)   1949
■   Elms Court, Elms Grove, LOUGHBOROUGH, Leics,
     LE11 1RG.   (hq)
     01509 234904   fax 01509 235666
     email ergsoc@ergonomics.org.uk
     http://www.ergonomics.org.uk
     Chief Exec: David O'Neill
▲   Company Limited by Guarantee; Registered Charity
○   *L; promotes ergonomics & the work of ergonomists, whose
     anatomical, physiological & psychological knowledge can
     help solve problems that arise between people, their working
     environment & the things they use
Gp Professional affairs board; Regional & special interest groups
●   Conf - Mtgs - Exhib - Inf - VE - LG
     Providing ergonomics information to young people through
     www.ergonomics4schools.com
<   Intl Ergonomics Assn
M   1,100 i, 59 f, UK / 300 i, o'seas
¶   The Ergonomist NL - 12; ftm only.
     Comsultancy Register.
     Applied Ergonomics - 6; £80 m.
     Behaviour & Information Technology - 6; £50 m, £192 nm.
     Ergonomics - 15; £50 m, £805 nm.
     Ergonomics in design - 4; £29 m.
     International Jnl of Injury Control & Safety Promotion - 4;
        £51.50 m, £60 nm.
     Jnl of Sports Sciences - 12; £60.
     Theoretical Issues in Ergonomics - 6; £50 m, £166 nm.
     Work & Stress - 4; £50 m, £13 nm.

Eriskay Pony Society
NR Carsaig, Gauls of Murthly, nr DUNKELD, Perthshire, PH1 4HT.
     01350 728063
     http://www.eriskaypony.com
     Sec: Jeanette Seaman
○   *B
M   c 130 i

**ERoSH, the National Consortium for Sheltered Housing
     (ERoSH)   1997**
■   PO Box 2616, CHIPPENHAM, Glos, SN15 1WZ.   (hq)
     01249 654249   fax 01249 654249
     email info@shelteredhousing.org
     http://www.shelteredhousing.org
     Hon Sec: Linda Milton
○   *W
●   Conf - ET - Comp - Inf

Esperanto-Asocio de Skotlando
     Esperanto name of the **Scottish Esperanto Association**

Esperanto Association of Britain (Esperanto-Asocio de Britio) (EAB) 1904

- ■ Esperanto House, Station Rd, Barlaston, STOKE-on-TRENT, Staffs, ST12 9DE.   (hq)
  0845 230 1887   fax 01782 372229
  email eab@esperanto-gb.org
  http://www.esperanto-gb.org
  Hon Sec: Geoffrey Sutton
- ▲ Registered Charity
- ○ K; to advance the education of the public in the international language Esperanto in the furtherance of international communication without discrimination & of the natural right of all people & peoples, their languages & cultures to be treated equally
- ● Conf - ET - Exam - Res - SG - Inf - Lib - LG
- < Universala Esperanto-Asocio (UEA)
- M 460 i
- ¶ La Brita Esperantisto (Jnl) - 2; ftm, £2.40 nm.
  EAB Update (NL) - 4; ftm only.

Essex Agricultural Society   1858

- ■ c/o Writtle Agricultural College, Lordship Lane, Writtle, CHELMSFORD, Essex, CM1 3RR.   (hq)
  01245 424113
  Sec: Heather Tarrant
- ▲ Company Limited by Guarantee; Registered Charity
- ○ *F; to promote & advance agriculture for the benefit of the public through education & publicity; sponsorship of the County Farms competition & County Ploughing Championship (not the Essex Show)
- ● ET - Exhib - Comp - Ploughing match - Farms competition
- M 350 i
- ¶ NL - 4;   AR; both free.

Essex Archaeological & Historical Congress   (EAHC)   1964

- ■ Roseleigh, Epping Rd, EPPING, Essex, CM16 5HW.   (hsp)
  01992 813725
  email pmd2@ukonline.co.uk
  http://www.essexhistory.net/essexcongress.htm
  Hon Sec: Mrs Pauline Dalton
- ▲ Registered Charity
- ○ *L; to advance the education of the public in archaeology, history & conservation in Essex
- ● Conf - Mtgs - Res - Exhib - Inf
- < Brit Assn for Local History (BALH); Coun Brit Archaeology
- M 95 org
- ¶ Essex Jnl - 2; £10 yr (£5 each).   NL - 3;   AR; both ftm.

Essex Chambers of Commerce   (ECCI)   1997

- NR 8-9 St Peter's Court, COLCHESTER, Essex, CO1 1WD.   (hq)
  01206 765277   fax 01206 578073
  email info@essexchambers.co.uk
  http://www.essexchambers.co.uk
  County Exec: John Clayton
- ▲ Company Limited by Guarantee
- ○ *C, *N
- ● Conf - Mtgs - ET - Exam - Res - Exhib - Comp - Expt - Inf - Lib - VE - LG
- < Brit Chams Comm
- M 2,500 f including affiliated chambers
- ¶ Business Plus - 12; ftm & enquirers.
  Essex Chambers Directory (incl LM/firms) - 1; ftm, £30 nm.

Essex Society for Archaeology & History   (ESAH)   1852

- ■ 2 Landview Gardens, ONGAR, Essex, CM5 9EQ.   (hsp)
  01277 363106
  email leach1939@yahoo.co.uk   http://www.essex.ac.uk/history/esah
  Hon Sec: Dr Michael Leach
- ▲ Registered Charity
- ○ *L; study of, & promotion of interest in, archaeology & history of the historic County of Essex
- Gp Essex Place-names Project
- ● Conf - Mtgs - ET - Res - Lib - VE
- < Coun Brit Archaeology; Scole C'ee; Stdg Conf on London Archaeology; Brit Assn for Local History
- > various local history societies
- M 380 i, 60 academic bodies, UK / 20 academic bodies, o'seas
  (Sub: £20 i, £25 academic bodies)
- ¶ Essex Archaeology & History - 1; ftm, £18 nm.
  Essex Archaeology & History News - 3; ftm, £1 nm.

Essex Wildlife Trust Ltd   (EWT)   1959

- ■ Abbotts Hall Farm, Great Wigborough, COLCHESTER, Essex, CO5 7RZ.   (hq)
  01621 862960   fax 01621 862990
  email admin@essexwt.org.uk
  http://www.essexwt.org.uk
  Sec: Valerie M Crookes
- ▲ Company Limited by Guarantee; Registered Charity
- ○ *G; nature conservation
- ● ET - VE
- < The Wildlife Trusts
- M 17,500 i, 470 f, UK / 9 i, o'seas
- ¶ Essex Wildlife - 3; free.

Estuarine & Coastal Sciences Association   (ECSA)   1971

- NR c/o Dr Jim Wilson, Dept of Zoology, Trinity College, DUBLIN 2, Republic of Ireland.   (sb)
  00 (353) 1 608 1640
  email jwilson@tcd.ie   http://www.ecsa-coast.org
  Sec: Dr Jim Wilson
- ▲ Registered Charity
- ○ *L, *P, *Q; to promote knowledge & understanding of estuaries & brackish waters in order to prevent environmental deterioration; to encourage resource management for the public benefit
- M i & f

ETA Services Ltd   (ETA)   1990

- NR 68 High St, WEYBRIDGE, Surrey, KT13 8BL.   (hq)
  0845 389 1010
  email eta@eta.co.uk   http://www.eta.co.uk
  Dir: Andrew Davis
- ▲ Company Limited by Guarantee
- ○ *K; 'for an environmentally sustainable transport policy for Britain; to provide an innovative range of quality & competitive services directly to those on the move (Breakdown)'
- Gp Insurance - travel, motor, house & home, cycle; Road rescue; Vehicle inspection; Carbon neutral products; Membership
- ● Conf - Mtgs - Res - Inf - LG
- < Carplus; Slower Speed Initiative
- M 18,000 i, 500 f
- ¶ Going Green - 4.   Car Buyer's Guide - 1.
  also known as the Environmental Transport Association

Ethical Trading Initiative (ETI) 1998
- ■ Cromwell House (2nd floor), 14 Fulwood Place, LONDON, WC1V 6HZ. (hq)
  020 7841 5180   fax 020 7831 7852
  email eti@eti.org.uk   http://www.ethicaltrade.org
  Dir: Dan Rees
- ▲ Company Limited by Guarantee
- ○ *K; an alliance of companies, NGOs & trade unions committed to working together to identify & promote good practice in the implementation of codes of labour practice
- ● Conf - Mtgs - ET - Res - Inf - LG
- M c 50 orgs
- ¶ Various occasional publications.

Eton Fives Association (EFA) 1930
- ■ 3 Bourchier Close, SEVENOAKS, Kent, TN13 1PD. (hsp)
  01732 458775
  email efa@etonfives.co.uk   http://www.etonfives.co.uk
  Hon Sec: Mike Fenn
- ▲ Company Limited by Guarantee
- ○ *S; to promote & encourage the playing of Eton Fives both at school & adult level
- ● Comp - Inf
- M 550 i, 70 org, UK / 25 i, 8 org, o'seas
- ¶ NL - 1.   AR - 1; both ftm only.

EURISOL-UK Ltd (UK Mineral Wool Association) (EURISOL-UK) 1985
- ■ PO Box 35084, LONDON, NW1 4XE. (hq)
  020 7935 8532   fax 07006 065950
  email info@eurisol.com   http://www.eurisol.com
  Sec Gen: C Dunn-Meynell
- ▲ Company Limited by Guarantee
- ○ *T; interests of manufacturers of glass wool & rock wool; to promote the usage of mineral wool products for thermal & acoustic insulation & fire protection in building, industry & commerce
- ● Mtgs - Exhib - LG
- M 5 f
- ¶ Technical publications & general guidance notes for home insulation.

European Association of Copper Clad Laminate Manufacturers
  as a part of BEAMA Energy is a group of **BEAMA**

European Associations
For information about associations with members throughout Europe see our advertisement for our **Directory of European Industrial & Trade Associations, Directory of European Professional & Learned Societies and Directory of Pan European Associations**

European-Atlantic Group (E-AG) 1954
- ■ 4 St Pauls Way, LONDON, N3 2PP. (hq)
  020 8632 9253   fax 020 8343 3532
  email info@eag.org.uk   http://www.eag.org.uk
  Dir: Justin Glass
- ▲ Registered Charity
- ○ *K; to promote closer relations between the European & Atlantic countries by providing a regular forum in Britain for informed discussion of their problems & possibilities for better economic & political cooperation with each other & the rest of the world
- ● Conf - Mtgs - ET - LG
- M 1,000 i, 20 f
  Subs: £29 i, £250 f.
- ¶ European-Atlantic Jnl - 2.
  NL - 2.   Elma Dangerfield Prize - 1.

The European Atlantic Movement (TEAM) 1958
- NR Cloverdown, Green Hill, HIGH WYCOMBE, Bucks, HP13 5QH. (chmn/p)
  Chmn: Laurence Smy
- ▲ Registered Charity
- ○ *K; 'to encourage research & disseminate information about the European & Atlantic communities & their institutions.'
- ● Conf - SG - VE
- < Atlantic Coun
- M 95 i, 25 schools, UK / 35 i, o'seas
- ¶ Publications list available.

European Catering Association (GB)
  since 2006 **Association for Catering Excellence**

European Information Association (EIA) 1991
- NR Central Library, St Peter's Sq, MANCHESTER, M2 5PD. (hq)
  0161-228 3691   fax 0161-236 6547
  email eia@libraries.manchester.gov.uk
  http://www.eia.org.uk
  Hon Sec: Angela Stogia
- ▲ Registered Charity
- ○ *P; to develop, coordinate & improve access to European Union information
- ● Conf - Mtgs - ET - Exhib - Inf - Liaison with European Union institutions
- M i, f & org
- ¶ Publications on various subjects linked to European information.

European Liquid Roofing Association
  since 2005-06 **European Liquid Waterproofing Association**

European Liquid Waterproofing Association (ELWA) 1979
- NR c/o Liquid Plastics Ltd, Iotech House, Miller St, PRESTON, Lancs, PR1 1TA.
  01772 255041   fax 01772 255674
  email info@elwassociation.org.uk
  http://www.elwassociation.org.uk
- ▲ Company Limited by Guarantee
- ○ *T; for manufacturers of liquid applied waterproofing systems
- Gp Roofing; Car park decks; Balconies & walkways; Bridge decks
- ● Mtgs - ET - Inf - Drafting industry standards & technical guidance notes
- M 21 f
- ¶ LM.
- × 2005-06 European Liquid Roofing Association

European Movement of the United Kingdom Ltd   1948
- NR Southbank House (room 203), LONDON, SE1 7SU. (hq)
  020 3176 0543
  email info@euromove.org.uk
  http://www.euromove.org.uk
- ▲ Company Limited by Guarantee
- Br 50
- ○ *K; to campaign for support for, & understanding of, the European Union & other European institutions
- ● Conf - Mtgs - SG - Inf
- M 2,500 i

Europilots - the Association of Licensed Deep Sea Pilots   1972
- ■ 2 Dormy Avenue, Mannamead, PLYMOUTH, Devon, PL3 5BY.
  01752 262845   fax 01752 262845
  email secretary@europilots.org.uk
  http://www.europilots.org.uk
  Sec: Captain John Hunt
- ▲ Un-incorporated Society
- ○ *P
- ● Liaison with maritime authorities
- M 30 i
  Sub: £84.

© CBD Research Ltd · Beckenham · BR3 5JS · Tel 020 8650 7745 · Fax 020 8650 0768 · E-mail cbd@cbdresearch.com · www.cbdresearch.com

Evacuees Reunion Association   (ERA)   1996
NR   The Mill Business Centre, Mill Hill, GRINGLEY-on-the-HILL,
       Notts, DN10 4RA.   (hq)
       01777 816166
       email era@evacuees.org.uk   http://www.evacuees.org.uk
       Chief Exec: James Roffey
▲   Registered Charity
○   *W; to relieve the physical & mental suffering of former
       evacuees of the Second World War; to advance the
       education of the public on the subject of child evacuation
       during the War
●   Conf - Mtgs - ET - Res - Exhib - SG - Inf - VE
M   3,500 i, UK / 100 i, o'seas
¶   The Evacuee - 12; ftm, 50p nm.

Evaluation International   (EI)   1963
■   East Malling Enterprise Centre, New Rd, EAST MALLING, Kent,
       ME19 6BJ.   (hsb)
       0845 644 4602   fax 01732 897453
       email info@evaluation-international.com
       http://www.evaluation-international.com
       Mgr: Peter Russell,   Sec: Dr Derek Cornish
▲   Company Limited by Guarantee
○   *T; to commission independent evaluations of instruments, for
       measurement & control, on behalf of member companies
       who are instrument users
Gp   Technical panel
●   Conf - Mtgs - Res - Exhib - Stat - Inf - Lib - LG - Preparation of
       instrumentation guides
<   Intl Instrument Users' Assn; WIB (Netherlands); EXERCA
       (France)
M   10 f, UK / 75 f, o'seas
¶   Electronic NL - 6; free.
       Instrument Evaluation Reports - 20; ftm only.
       Instrument Selection Guides - 20; ftm, £50-£200 each nm.

Evangelical Alliance UK   (EAUK)   1846
NR   186 Kennington Park Rd, LONDON, SE11 4BT.   (hq)
       020 7207 2100 (Mon-Fri 0900-1700)   fax 020 7207
       2150
       email info@eauk.org   http://www.eauk.org
       Gen Dir: Rev Joel Edwards
▲   Registered Charity
Br   England, Wales, Northern Ireland
○   *N, *R; providing a voice for evangelical Christians to
       government, the media & society
Gp   Alliance commission on unity & truth among evangelicals;
       Reaching older people; Stewardship forum; Evangelical
       coalition on drugs;
       Networks: Care for pastors, Disability; EA youth & children
●   Conf - Inf - LG
<   Wld Evangelical Fellowship; Eur Evangelical Alliance
M   38,000 i, 6,000 churches, 725 org
¶   idea (Jnl) - 6;
       Leaders-digest.com - 6 (online); both ftm only.

Event Horse Owners Association
NR   Wolfhamcote Barn, Flecknoe, RUGBY, Warks, CV23 8AU.
       email chris.gillespie@fsmail.net   http://www.ehoa.org
       Sec: Chris Gillespie

Event Services Association   (TESA)   1991
NR   Association House, 18c Moor St, CHEPSTOW, Monmouthshire,
       NP16 5DB.   (hq)
       01291 636331   fax 01291 630402
       email info@tesa.org.uk   http://www.tesa.org.uk
       Dir: Jim Winship
○   *T
Gp   Security; Mobile units; Fireworks; Electrics; Event organisers &
       venues
●   Mtgs - Inf - LG
M   20 i, 180 f, UK / 4 f, o'seas
¶   Event Organiser - 6; ftm, £48 nm.

Event Supplier & Services Association   (ESSA)   2008
■   ESSA House, Uplands Business Park, Black Horse Lane,
       LONDON, E17 5QJ.   (secretariat)
       01442 285812,   0845 122 1880   fax 01442 875551
       email info@essa.uk.com   http://www.essa.uk.com
       Sec: Trevor Foley
▲   Un-incorporated Society
○   *T; for contractors working in partnership with organisers &
       venues to promote quality & value for exhibitors thus raising
       the profile of exhibitions as a medium
●   Conf - Mtgs - ET - Res - Exhib - Inf - LG
<   Events Ind Alliance (EIA)
×   2008 (Association of Exhibition Contractors
              (British Exhibition Contractors' Association

Eventia Ltd   (EVENTIA)   2006
■   Charles House (6th floor), 148-149 Great Charles St,
       BIRMINGHAM, B3 3HT.   (hq)
       0121-212 1400   fax 0121-212 3131
       email info@eventia.org.uk   http://www.eventia.org.uk
       Exec Dir: Izania Downie
       Project Dir: Tony Rogers
▲   Company Limited by Guarantee
○   *T; for organisations providing events, business meetings &
       conferences, motivational experiences, training &
       communications activity, inventive travel programmes,
       celebratory functions, corporate hospitality
Gp   Education; CSR; Awards; Regulations & representation;
       Membership
●   Conf - Mtgs - ET - Exhib - LG - Annual awards ceremony &
       dinner
<   Business Visits & Events Partnership
M   14 i, 206 f, UK / 51 f, o'seas
       (Sub: £100 enrolment, £75 i, & by turnover c £350-£1.000)
¶   Ybk - 1.
×   2008 (British Association of Conference Destinations
       2006 (Corporate Event Association
              (Incentive Travel & Meetings Association

Events Industry Alliance   (EIA)   2006
■   119 High St, BERKHAMSTED, Herts, HP4 2DJ.   (hq)
       01442 873331   fax 01442 875551
       email info@eventsindustryalliance.com
       http://www.eventsindustryalliance.com
       Sec: Trevor Foley
▲   Company Limited by Share
○   *N, *T; a marketing alliance for trade organisations within the
       exhibition industry; works with contractors, organisers &
       venues to raise the profile of exhibitions as a medium
●   Conf - Mtgs - ET - Res - Inf - LG
M   no members
¶   Exhibition Standard - 5; ftm.

Events Sector Industry Training Organisation   (ESITO)   1995
NR   Tetford House, East Road, Tetford, HORNCASTLE, Lincs,
       LN9 6QQ.   (hq)
       01507 533639
       Admin: Peggy Glendinning
▲   Company Limited by Guarantee
○   *N; forum for training & development in the events sector:
       which comprises conferences, meetings, exhibitions, outdoor
       events, events services, incentive & business travel & venues.
       Also acts as the coordinating body for pursuing these issues
       & the development of occupational standards & NVQs with
       government departments, educational bodies, NTOs & other
       organisations
●   ET - Exam - SG - Inf - LG
<   Business Tourism Partnership (BTP); Association for Conferences
       & Events (ACE)
M   6 org, UK / 3 org, o'seas
¶   AR; ftm.

Excellence Ireland Quality Association   (EIQA)   1969
IRL   9 Appian Way, Ranelagh, DUBLIN 6, Republic of Ireland.
    353 (1) 660 4100   fax 353 (1) 660 4280
    email info@eiqa.com   http://www.eiqa.com
    Chmn: Paul O'Grady
○   *L, *P
✕   2004 Excellence Ireland

Exclusive Economic Zone Industry Group
    a group of the **Defence Manufacturers Association**

Executives' Association of Great Britain Ltd   (EAGB)   1929
NR   Kent Innovation Centre, Thanet Reach Business Park,
    Millennium Way, BROADSTAIRS, Kent, CT10 2QQ.   (hq)
    07957 151787
    http://www.eagb.biz
    Dir of Operations: Jo Gideon
Br   4; Canada, South Africa, USA
○   *P; business contacts & opportunities for networking
●   Conf - Mtgs
<   Intl Coordinators' Conf of Executives Assns
M   250 f, UK / 5,000 f, o'seas
¶   Bulletin - 12;   NL - 4;   Ybk - 1; all ftm only.

Exercise Movement & Dance Partnership   (EMDP)
NR   1 Grove House, Foundry Lane, HORSHAM, W Sussex,
    RH13 5PL.
    01403 266000
    http://www.emdp.org
○   *A; the governing body for the modernisation plan for
    movement & dance

Exeter Chamber of Commerce (1992) Ltd   1992
■   10 Southernhay West, EXETER, Devon, EX1 1JG.
    (admin/office)
    01392 431133   fax 01392 278804
    email enqiries@exeterchamber.co.uk
    http://www.exeterchamber.co.uk
    Hon Sec: Michael Martin
▲   Company Limited by Guarantee
○   *C
●   Mtgs - Inf
M   350 f
¶   LM - 1;   AR - 1; both ftm.

Exhibition Study Group   (ESG)   1980
NR   46 Thorncliffe Rd, Norwood Green, SOUTHALL, Middx,
    UB2 5RQ.   (mem/sp)
    Mem Sec: Alan Sabey
▲   Un-incorporated Society
○   *G; collectors of memorabilia of national & international
    exhibitions & world fairs (souvenirs, books, commemorative
    china, postcards etc).
●   Conf - Res - Exhib - SG - Book publishing
M   100 i, UK / 5 i, o'seas
¶   Jnl - 4.

Exhibition Venues Association
    in 2006 merged with the **Association of Event Venues**

Exmoor Horn Sheep Breeders' Society   1906
■   Kitridge Farm, WITHYPOOL, Somerset, TA24 7RY.   (hsp)
    01643 831593
    email info@exmoorhornbreeders.co.uk
    http://www.exmoorhornbreeders.co.uk
    Sec: Mrs Gina Rawle
○   *B; to further the breeding of Exmoor sheep & their crosses
●   Mtgs - Exhib - Inf - VE
<   Nat Sheep Assn
M   152 i
¶   NL - 4;   Flock Book - 1; £2.

Exmoor Pony Society   1921
■   Woodmans, Brithem Bottom, CULLOMPTON, Devon,
    EX15 1NB.   (hsp)
    01884 839930
    email secretary@exmoorponysociety.org.uk
    http://www.exmoorponysociety.org.uk
    Sec: Sue McGeever
▲   Company Limited by Guarantee; Registered Charity
○   *B
●   Comp - Inf
M   600 i, UK / 25 i, o'seas
¶   NL - 1; ftm only.

Exmouth Chamber of Trade & Commerce   1896
NR   c/o The Tourist Information Bureau, Alexandra Terrace,
    EXMOUTH, Devon, EX8 1NZ.   (hq)
    01395 275133
    Sec: Simon Wood
▲   Un-incorporated Society
○   *C
M   c 150 i & f
¶   NL - 4; ftm.

Experimental Psychology Society   (EPS)   1946
■   c/o Dr C Jarrold, Dept of Experimental Psychology, University of
    Bristol, 12a Priory Rd, BRISTOL, BS8 1TU.   (hsb)
    email c.jarrold@bristol.ac.uk   http://www.eps.ac.uk
    Hon Sec: Dr C Jarrold
▲   Registered Charity
○   *P; for the furtherance of scientific enquiry within the field of
    psychology & cognate subjects
●   Mtgs - Res - Inf
M   c 600 i
¶   Quarterly Jnl of Experimental Psychology - 12.

Expert Witness Institute   (EWI)   1996
NR   7 Warwick Court (1st floor), LONDON, WC1R 5DJ.   (hq)
    0870 366 6367
    email info@ewi.org.uk   http://www.ewi.org.uk
▲   Company Limited by Guarantee
○   *P; the support of the proper administration of justice & the
    early resolution of disputes through fair & unbiased expert
    evidence; to encourage the use by lawyers of experts
●   Conf - Mtgs - ET - Inf - LG - Helpline
M   c 1,200 i & org
¶   NL - 3/4; ftm only.

Explosives Industry Group   (EIG)
NR   Centrepoint, 103 New Oxford St, London, WC1A 1DU.
    020 7395 8063   fax 020 7497 2597
    email info@eig.org.uk   http://www.eig.org.uk
    Sec: Brig Charles Smith
○   *T

Export Group for Aerospace & Defence
    a group of the **Defence Manufacturers Association**

Extruded Sealants Association
NR   18 Furness Avenue, Simonstone, BURNLEY, Lancs, BB12 7SU.
    (sp)
    01282 771260
    Sec: Paul Liles
○   *T
M   f

© CBD Research Ltd · Beckenham · BR3 5JS · Tel 020 8650 7745 · Fax 020 8650 0768 · E-mail cbd@cbdresearch.com · www.cbdresearch.com

Fabian Society   1884
NR   11 Dartmouth St, LONDON, SW1H 9BN.   (hq)
020 7227 4900
○   *Q
M   i

Fabricated Access Covers Trade Association   (FACTA)   1995
■   42 Heath St, TAMWORTH, Staffs, B79 7JH.
01827 52337   fax 01827 310627
email info@facta.org.uk   http://www.facta.org.uk
Sec: Michael Skelding
○   *T; for manufacturers of fabricated access (manhole) covers
●   Mtgs - Res - Inf - British & European Standards
M   11 f
(Sub: £750)
¶   FACTA Specification.

Facilities Management Association   (FMA)   1995
NR   Charter House, 13-15 Carteret St, LONDON, SW1H 9DJ.
(hq)
0796 042 8146
email info@fmassociation.org.uk
http://www.fmassociation.org.uk
○   *T; for organisations / companies engaged in the provision of
facility management services to clients
M   f

Factoring Services Group
since 2005 **Group Auto Union UK & Ireland Ltd**

Factors & Discounters Association
since 2007 **Asset Based Finance Association**

Faculty of Accident & Emergency Medicine
since 2005-06 the **College of Emergency Medicine**

Faculty of Actuaries in Scotland   1856
NR   18 Dublin St, EDINBURGH, EH1 3PP.
0131-240 1300   fax 0131-240 1313
○   *P; for the actuarial profession, life assurance, pensions &
general insurance, investment

Faculty of Advocates   1682
NR   Advocates' Library, Parliament House, EDINBURGH, EH1 1RF.
(hq)
0131-226 5071   fax 0131-225 3642
http://www.advocates.org.uk
○   *P; the practice of Scots law in all its aspects
M   i

Faculty of Astrological Studies   1948
NR   BM Box 7470, LONDON, WC1N 3XX.   (pres/b)
07000 790143   fax 07000 790143
http://www.astrology.org.uk
○   *P; study of basic natal astrology
M   c 2,000 i

Faculty of Building
since 2005 the **BRE Trust**

Faculty of Church Music   1956
■   27 Sutton Park, Blunsdon, SWINDON, Wilts, SN26 7BB.   (hsp)
020 8675 0180
Hon Gen Sec: Rev Geoffrey Gleed,   Asst Hon Sec: M N
Gretason
▲   Un-incorporated Soc
○   *D, *P; to raise the standard of church music, both practical &
theoretical
●   Exam
M   i
¶   NL - 2; ftm.

Faculty of Dental Surgery   1947
NR   at the Royal College of Surgeons, 35-43 Lincoln's Inn Fields,
LONDON, WC2A 3PE.   (hq)
020 7869 6810
○   *E, *L; advancement of science & art of dentistry

Faculty of Family Planning & Reproductive Healthcare of the RCOG
since 2007 **Faculty of Sexual & Reproductive Healthcare**

Faculty of Forensic & Legal Medicine   (FFLM)   2006
■   116 Gt Portland St (3rd floor), LONDON, W1W 6PJ.
020 7580 8490
email info@fflm.ac.uk   http://www.fflm.ac.uk
Registrar: Dr George Fernie
○   *M, *P; forensic and legal medicine

Faculty of General Dental Practice (UK)
NR   at the Royal College of Surgeons, 35-43 Lincoln's Inn Fields,
LONDON, WC2A 3PE.
020 7312 6754
○   *M, *P

Faculty of Healthcare Counsellors & Psychotherapists
a group of the **British Association for Counselling &
Psychotherapy**

Faculty of Homeopathy   1950
■   Hahnemann House, 29 Park Street West, LUTON, Beds,
LU1 3BE.   (hq)
0870 444 3955   fax 0870 444 3960
email info@trusthomeopathy.org
http://www.trusthomeopathy.org
Chief Exec: Sally Penrose
▲   Un-incorporated Society
Br   20
○   *L, *M, *P; to promote the academic & scientific development of
homeopathy; the Faculty regulates the education, training &
practice of homeopathy by doctors, veterinary surgeons,
dentists, nurses, midwives, pharmacists & other statutorily
regulated healthcare professionals
●   Conf - Mtgs - ET - Exam - Res - Exhib - SG - Inf - Lib - LG
<   Liga Medicorum Homoeopathica Internationalis (LIGA); Eur
C'ee for Homeopathy
M   800 i, UK / 300 i, o'seas
¶   Homeopathy Jnl - 4;   Simile (LM) - 4;
Membership Directory - 18 months; all ftm only.

Faculty of Occupational Medicine   (FOM RCP)   1978

■　6 St Andrew's Place, Regent's Park, LONDON, NW1 4LB.　(hq)
　　020 7317 5890　fax 020 7317 5899
　　email fom@facoccmed.ac.uk
　　http://www.facoccmed.ac.uk
　　Chief Exec: Nichola Wilkins
▲　Registered Charity
○　*L, *P; to promote high standards in the training & practice of
　　occupational medicine
●　Conf - Mtgs - ET - Exam - Exhib - LG
<　EU of Med Specialities/section of Occupational Medicine; R
　　Coll of Physicians of London
M　1,700 i
¶　NL;　eletters;　Periodicals;　AR - 1.
　　Guidance on Ethics for Occupational Physicians; £25 nm.
　　Guidance on Alcohol & Drug Misuse in the Workplace; £26
　　nm.

Faculty of Pharmaceutical Medicine of the Royal College of Physicians of the United Kingdom

NR　1 St Andrew's Place, LONDON, NW1 4LB.

Faculty of Public Health   1972

NR　4 St Andrew's Place, LONDON, NW1 4LB.　(hq)
　　020 7935 0243　fax 020 7224 6973
　　http://www.fph.org.uk
　　Chief Exec: Paul Scourfield
○　*M, *N; is a joint faculty of the Royal Colleges of Physicians in
　　the UK & shares in their efforts for the advancement of
　　medical knowledge & care in the field of public health &
　　medicine (the prevention of disease & the prolonging of life)
×　2003 Faculty of Public Health Medicine

Faculty of Royal Designers for Industry   1936

NR　8 John Adam St, LONDON, WC2N 6EZ.　(hq)
　　020 7930 5115　fax 020 7839 5805
　　email melanie.andrews@rsa.org.uk
○　*P; 'the distinction of Royal Designer for Industry (RDI) was
　　established by the Royal Society of Arts in 1936, to be
　　conferred on persons who have achieved sustained
　　excellence in aesthetic & efficient design for industry. Persons
　　holding the distinction are members of the Faculty'

Faculty of Sexual & Reproductive Healthcare of the RCOG   1993

■　27 Sussex Place, LONDON, NW1 4RG.　(hq)
　　020 7724 5534
　　http://www.fsrh.org
　　Co Sec: Corin Jones
▲　Company Limited by Guarantee; Registered Charity
○　*P; to maintain & develop standards of care & training of all
　　providers of family planning & reproductive health care; to
　　advance knowledge in the discipline & encourage research;
　　to give academic status to the discipline
●　Conf - ET - Exam - Res - Inf (m only) - Essay competition for
　　medical undergraduates
<　R Coll of Obstetricians & Gynaecologists
M　11,000 i, UK / 300 i, o'seas
¶　Journal of Family Planning & Reproductive Healthcare - 4;
　　President's NL - 4;　AR;
　　Recommendations for Clinical Practice - 1/2; all ftm.
×　2007 Faculty of Family Planning & Reproductive Healthcare

Fair Organ Preservation Society   (FOPS)   1958

NR　Gaythorpe, Blacketts Wood Drive, CHORLEYWOOD, Herts,
　　WD3 5QQ.　(memsec/p)
　　email memsec@fops.org
　　Mem Sec: Norman Rogers
▲　Un-incorporated Society
Br　Australia, USA
○　*D, *G; promotion & encouragement of all forms of interest in,
　　& the preservation of, fair organs & mechanical musical
　　instruments
●　Conf - Mtgs - Res - Stat - Inf - VE - Register of organs available
　　for events, nationwide
　　Archives held within the National Fairground Archive at the
　　University of Sheffield, (email: fairground@sheffield.ac.uk)
M　650 i, UK / 85 i, o'seas
¶　The Key Frame - 4; ftm only.
　　On Display (128 pages 205 photos).

Fair Play for Children Association   (FPFC)   1972

■　32 Longford Rd, BOGNOR REGIS, W Sussex, PO21 1AG.
　　(hsp)
　　0845 330 7635
　　email fairplay@arunet.co.uk　http://www.arunet.co.uk/
　　fairplay/
　　Hon Sec: Jan Cosgrove
▲　Company Limited by Guarantee; Registered Charity
○　*K; a campaign for more, safer & better play facilities &
　　services for children. The FPFC Charitable Trust (same
　　address) provides information on training in play & safety for
　　children
●　Conf - ET - Inf - LG
¶　Playaction - 4; ftm, £4 nm.
　　Playaction Guides - irreg; ftm, 3 1st class stamps+SAE nm.

Fairground Association of Great Britain   (FAGB)   1976

NR　5 Crooks Lane, STUDLEY, Warks, B80 7QX.　(ed/p)
　　Editor: Graham Downie
▲　Un-incorporated Society
○　*G; to record, study & publish history & current information on
　　the British fairground industry

Fairground Society   1962

■　66 Carolgate, RETFORD, Notts, DN22 6EF.　(chmn/b)
　　01777 702872
　　http://www.fairgroundsociety.co.uk
　　PO Box 549, Tweedale, TELFORD, TF7 5WA.　(mem/s)
　　Chmn: Jack Schofield,　Sec: Steven Smith
　　Mem Sec: S Harris
▲　Un-incorporated Society
○　*G; to promote interest in the British fairground heritage &
　　history of fairs
●　Mtgs - Exhib - Inf - VE - Archive
M　c 800 i
¶　The Platform - 4; ftm.

Fairyworld   1999

■　117 Hadfield Rd, NORTH WALSHAM, Norfolk, NR28 0BE.
　　(hq)
　　01692 404539
　　email thefairyworld@aol.com
　　http://www.thefairyworld.co.uk
　　Editor: Graham Newton
▲　Un-incorporated Society
○　*G; 'an international association for everyone who loves fairy
　　folk & angels; Fairyworld aims to bring back harmony to the
　　earth'
Gp　Fairies; Angels
●　Mtgs - Inf
M　1,100 i, UK / 25 i, o'seas
　　(Sub: £12)
¶　Fairyworld News - 4; m only.
×　2007 Fairy Ring

© CBD Research Ltd · Beckenham · BR3 5JS · Tel 020 8650 7745 · Fax 020 8650 0768 · E-mail cbd@cbdresearch.com · www.cbdresearch.com

Falkland Islands Association   1976
NR c/o Falkland House, 14 Broadway, LONDON, SW1H 0BH.
     (hq)
     0845 260 4884
     http://www.fiassociation.com
▲ Un-incorporated Society
Br 2
○ *K, *W; 'to support the wish of the people of the Falkland
     Islands to decide their own future for themselves without
     being subjected to pressure direct, or indirect, from any
     quarter'
M c 850 i & f, UK / c 120 i & f, o'seas
¶ NL - 2.

Falklands Conservation   1979
NR 1 Princes Avenue, LONDON, N3 2DA.   (hq)
     020 8343 0831   fax 020 8343 0831
     http://www.falklandsconservation.com
▲ Registered Charity
Br Falkland Islands
○ *Q; research & study of the flora & fauna of the Falkland
     Islands; to protect & preserve the sites of scientific importance
     & outstanding natural beauty in the islands & surrounding
     seas
● ET - Res - Exhib - Inf - LG
< Intl U for the Consvn of Nature (IUCN); Birdlife Intl
M c 600 i & f
¶ NL - 12;   AR.

Fall Arrest Safety Equipment Training   (FASET)   2000
■ PO Box 138, WHITCHURCH, Shropshire, SY13 3AD.
     01948 780652
     email enquiries@faset.org.uk   http://www.faset.org.uk
     Sec: Stephen Kennefick
▲ Company Limited by Guarantee
○ *T; a trade association & training body for the safety net rigging
     & fall arrest industry
● Mtgs - ET - Stat - LG
< Nat Access & Scaffolding Confedn (NASC)
M 32 f
¶ [publications on website].

Falsely Accused Carers & Teachers   (FACT)   2000
■ PO Box 3074, CARDIFF, CF3 3WZ.   (hsp)
     029 2077 7499
     email info@factuk.org   http://www.factuk.org
     Hon Sec: Michael Barnes
Br 10
○ *K; 'we support carers & teachers (& their families) who have
     been falsely accused or wrongly convicted of child abuse; we
     also campaign for justice, lobby for change in the criminal
     justice system, & seek to raise awareness of issues relating to
     false allegations of abuse'
● Conf - Mtgs - Inf - LG - Prison support - Lobbying
M 500 i, UK / 100 i, o'seas
¶ FACTion - 12; ftm only.

Families Anonymous   (FA)   1980
■ Doddington & Rollo Community Association, Charlotte Despard
     Ave, LONDON, SW11 5HD.   (hq)
     0845 120 0660   fax 020 7498 1990
     email office@famanon.org.uk
     http://www.famanon.org.uk
▲ Un-incorporated Society
Br 66; 23 countries
○ *W; to support families & friends of drug abusers by weekly
     meetings
● Mtgs (totally confidential)
M c 750 i
¶ The FA NL - 4; 50p.   Publications list available.

Families Need Fathers   (FNF)   1974
■ 134 Curtain Rd, LONDON, EC2A 3AR.   (hq)
     0870 760 7111   fax 020 7739 3410
     email fnf@fnf.org.uk   http://www.fnf.org.uk
     Chief Exec: Jon Davies,   Sec: Ian Julian
▲ Company Limited by Guarantee; Registered Charity
Br 29
○ *K; to provide support, advice & information on children's
     issues to parents, following separation / divorce
● Conf - Mtgs - ET - Res - Inf - LG
M 2,750 i, UK / 30 i, o'seas
¶ McKenzie Magazine (Jnl) - 6; ftm, £25 nm.

Family Doctor Association   (FDA)   2007
■ FDA House, 9 York St, HEYWOOD, Lancs, OL10 4NN.
     01706 620920   fax 01706 691880
     email admin@family-doctor.org.uk
     http://www.family-doctor.org.uk
     Chief Exec: Moira Auchterlonie
▲ Registered Charity
○ *M, *P; to improve he quality of care provided for patients in
     family doctor practices in the UK
● Conf - Mtgs ET - Inf - LG
M i
✕ 2007 (September) Small Practices Association

Family Education Trust (Family & Youth Concern)
     is a non-membership body & therefore outside the scope of this
     directory.

Family Farmers' Association   (FFA)   1979
■ Osborne Newton, Aveton Gifford, KINGSBRIDGE, Devon,
     TQ7 4PE.   (chmn b/p)
     01548 852794   fax 01548 852794
     Chmn: Mrs Pippa Woods
▲ Un-incorporated Society
○ *F, *K; to represent the family farmer; to prevent the decline of
     rural areas; to make farming more accessible to new
     entrants
● LG
M 250 i
¶ NL - 4; ftm.

Family Holiday Association   (FHA)   1975
§ 16 Mortimer St, LONDON, W1T 3JL.
     020 7436 3304   fax 020 7323 7299
     http://www.fhaonline.org.uk
     Dir: John McDonald
     Charity specialising in helping provide holidays for families and
     children in need.

Family Law Association of Scotland   (FLA)   1989
■ 52-54 Albert St, ABERDEEN, AB25 1XS.   (hsb)
     01224 593100   fax 01224 593200
     email anne@mcintoshmctaggart.com
     http://www.mcintoshmctaggart.com
     Sec: Anne G McTaggart (of McIntoshMcTaggart)
▲ Un-incorporated Society
○ *P; for solicitors involved in family law
● Conf - Mtgs - ET - Inf
M 300 i

Family Law Bar Association   (FLBA)   1947
NR 289-293 High Holborn, LONDON, WC1V 7HZ.   (hsb)
     020 7242 1289   fax 020 7831 7144
     http://www.flba.co.uk
     Admin: Carol Harris
▲ Un-incorporated Society
○ *P; for members of the Bar practising in the field of family law
     & cases involving children
M c 1,300 i

Family Matters Institute   (FMI)   1998
§   Moggerhanger Park, Moggerhanger, BEDFORD, MK42 3RW.
      (hq)
      01767 641002   fax 01767 641515
      email family@familymatters.org.uk
      http://www.familymatters.org.uk
      Chief Exec: Matt Buttery
      An educational charity specialising in research and training
        programmes to strengthen marriage and family life in
        Britain.

Family Mediation Scotland
      on 1 April 2008 merged with Relate Scotland to form **Relationships
Scotland

Family Mediators' Association   (FMA)   1988
■   Grove House, Grove Rd, BRISTOL, BS6 6UN.   (hq)
      0117-946 7062   fax 0117-946 7181
      email info@fmassoc.co.uk   http://www.fmassoc.co.uk
      Chmn: Linda Glees
▲   Registered Charity
○   *P; to provide assistance through mediation for adults &
        children who are affected by family breakdown
Gp   Family mediators; Family mediator professional consultants;
        Family mediation training faculty
●   Conf - Mtgs - ET - Res
      Helpline: 0808 200 0033
<   UK Coll of Family Mediators
>   ADR [alternative dispute resolution] Gp
M   250 i
¶   NL - 4;   LM; both free.

Family Planning Association   (FPA)   1930
■   50 Featherstone St, LONDON, EC1Y 8QU.   (hq)
      020 7608 5240   fax 0845 123 2349
      http://www.fpa.org.uk
      Contact: Julie Bentley
▲   Registered Charity
Br   6
○   *W; to improve the sexual health & reproductive rights of all
        people throughout the UK
●   ET - Res - Inf - Lib - LG - Sexual Health Direct
      SHD Helpline: 0845 122 8690 (Mon-Fri 0900-1800)
<   Intl Planned Parenthood Fedn
M   1,000 i
¶   Publications catalogue available.

Family Rights Group   (FRG)   1974
■   The Print House, 18 Ashwin St, LONDON, E8 3DL.   (hq)
      020 7923 2628   fax 020 7923 2683
      http://www.frg.org.uk
      Chief Exec: Cathy Ashley
▲   Company Limited by Guarantee; Registered Charity
○   *W; to promote policies which fully involve families in decisions
        about their own children; to advise parents & relations whose
        children are known to social services; to promote good
        practice by social workers & solicitors working with families
●   Conf - ET - Res - LG
      Advice line: 0800 731 1696 (Mon-Fri 1000-1200 + 1330-
        1530)
¶   Family Matters - 2;   Conference NL - 3;   AR; all ftm.

Family Welfare Association   (FWA)   1869
§   501-505 Kingsland Rd, LONDON, E8 4AU.
      020 7254 6251
      http://www.fwa.org.uk
      Chief Exec: Helen Dent
      Tackles some of the most complex and difficult issues facing
        families, including domestic abuse, mental health problems,
        learning disabilities and severe financial hardship; works with
        whole families to help them find solutions to their problems.

Fan Manufacturers' Association   (FMA)   1979
■   2 Waltham Court, Milley Lane, Hare Hatch, READING, Berks,
      RG10 9TH.   (hq)
      0118-940 3416   fax 0118-940 6258
      email info@feta.co.uk   http://www.feta.co.uk/
      Dir Gen: C Sloan
○   *T; interests of fan manufacturers, irrespective of the final
        application of their products. The association covers fans &
        similar air moving devices of any type & size & for any
        application, including: heating, ventilating, air conditioning,
        industrial processing, fume & dust removal, pneumatic
        conveying, combustion, heat transfer, drying, mines & tunnel
        ventilation, power generation or any other purpose involving
        movement & control of air or other gases as defined in
        Eurovent Terminology Document ref 1/1 paragraph 2 &
        within the scope of British Standard 848/1979
Gp   Technical & Economic committees
●   Mtgs - ET - Res - Exhib - Stat - Expt - Inf
<   HEVAC; BSI; Fedn Envtl Tr Assns (FETA)
M   30 f

**Fanderson: the official Gerry Anderson Appreciation Society
      1981**
■   PO Box 12, BRADFORD, W Yorks, BD10 0YE.   (mail address)
      http://www.fanderson.org.uk
      Sec: Nick Williams
▲   Un-incorporated Society
○   *G; to promote the appreciation & preservation of Gerry
        Anderson productions - Thunderbirds & UFO & other TV
        series
●   Conf - ET - Res - Exhib - Comp - Inf - PL
M   1,000 i, UK / 400 i, o'seas
¶   FAB - 4; ftm only.

Farm
      has closed

Farm Machinery Preservation Society Ltd   (FMPS)   1968
■   6 Lordship Rd, WRITTLE, Essex, CM1 3EH.   (chmn/p)
      01245 420168
      Chmn: H W Preston
▲   Company Limited by Guarantee
○   *G, *K; to promote interest in & knowledge of vintage
        agriculture & horticulture machinery
●   Mtgs - Exhib - VE
<   Fedn of Brit Historic Vehicle Clubs
M   330 i
¶   NL - 4; free.

Farm Retail Association
      in 2004 merged with the National Association of Farmers' Markets to
      form the **National Farmers' Retail & Markets Association**

Farm Tractor & Machinery Trade Association   (FTMTA)
IRL   Unit 3, Road D, Tougher's Business Park, Newhall, NAAS,
        Co Kildare, Republic of Ireland
        353 (45) 409309   fax 353 (45) 409308
        email info@ftmta.ie   http://www.ftmta.ie
        Chief Exec: Gary Ryan
○   *F, *T; farm & garden machinery industry

Farmers for Action   (FFA)   2000
NR   Old Llanishen Farm, Llangovan, MONMOUTH, NP25 4BU.
        01291 690224
        email secretary@farmersforaction.org
        http://www.farmersforaction.org
○   *F, *K; to secure a sustainable level of income for farmers &
        growers

© CBD Research Ltd · Beckenham · BR3 5JS · Tel 020 8650 7745 · Fax 020 8650 0768 · E-mail cbd@cbdresearch.com · www.cbdresearch.com

Farmers Club   1842
- ■ 3 Whitehall Court, LONDON, SW1A 2EL.   (hq)
  020 7930 3557   fax 020 7839 7864
  http://www.thefarmersclub.com
  Chief Exec & Sec: Air Commodore Stephen Skinner
- ▲ a not-for-profit organisation
- ○ *F; social club for those interested in agriculture; furthers
  knowledge of agriculture by educational activities
- ● Mtgs - Inf
- M 5,700 i
- ¶ Jnl - 6; ftm, £20 yr nm.

Farmers' Union of Wales   (FUW)   1955
- NR Llys Amaeth, Plas Gogerddan, ABERYSTWYTH, Ceredigion,
  SY23 3BT.   (hq)
  01970 820820   fax 01970 820821
  http://www.fuw.org.uk
- ○ *F; to represent the interests of Welsh agriculture & rural Wales
- M 12,000 i

Farming and Countryside Education   (FACE)
- NR Arthur Rank Centre, Stoneleigh Park, Warwickshire,
  CV8 2LZ.   (HQ)
  024 7685 8261
  http://www.face-online.org.uk
- ○ *E

Farming & Wildlife Advisory Group   (FWAG)   1962
- ■ National Agricultural Centre, Stoneleigh Park, KENILWORTH,
  Warks, CV8 2RX.   (hq)
  024 7669 6699   fax 024 7669 6760
  email info@fwag.org.uk   http://www.fwag.org.uk
  Managing Dir: Andy Ormiston
- ▲ Company Limited by Guarantee; Registered Charity
- Br 55
- ○ *F; provision of environmental & conservation advice &
  technical support to farmers & land managers throughout
  England, Scotland, Wales & Northern Ireland
- ● Conf - Mtgs - Res - Exhib - Comp - SG - Stat - Inf - VE - LG
- M i, c 17 f
- ¶ AR.   Booklets.

Farms for Schools   (FFS)
- ■ Unit 4c Topland Farm, Cragg Rd, MYTHOLMROYD, W Yorks,
  HX7 5RW.   (hq)
  01422 882708   fax 01422 885533
  email amanda-marsden@farmsforschools.org.uk
  http://www.farmsforschools.org.uk
  Chief Exec: Gary Richardson
- ▲ Registered Charity
- ○ *E, *F; 'to ensure that school trips to farms are safe, enjoyable
  & educationally worthwhile'
- ● Conf - Mtgs - ET - Inf
- < an initiative of the Nat Farmers' U
- M 140 farms
- ¶ NL - 4; free.

Farnborough Air Sciences Trust   (FAST)   1990
- NR Trenchard House, 85 Farnborough Rd, FARNBOROUGH,
  Hants, GU14 6TF.   (hq)
  01252 375050
- ▲ Registered Charity
- ○ *K; to establish an air sciences centre & museum detailing
  research done at the Royal Aircraft Establishment 1918-1990
- ● Mtgs - ET - Res - Inf - Lib - PL - LG
- M 700+ i, 5 f
- ¶ Fast News - 4; ftm, £2.50 nm.

Fastener & Engineering Research Association   (FERA)
- NR National Metalforming Centre, 47 Birmingham Road, WEST
  BROMWICH, W Midlands, B70 6PY.
  0121-601 6350   fax 0121-601 6373
  http://www.fera.org.uk
- ○ *P

Fawcett Society   1866
- NR 1-3 Berry St, LONDON, EC1V 0AA.   (hq)
  020 7253 2598   fax 020 7253 2599
  http://www.fawcettsociety.org.uk
- ▲ Company Limited by Guarantee
- Br local gps
- ○ *K; campaign for equality of women
- ● Conf - Res - LG
- M 2,000 i, 100 org
- ¶ Towards Equality - 4.
  Campaign reports.   AR.

**FCA Membership Ltd (Forestry Contracting Association
Membership Ltd)   (FCA)   1992**
- ■ PO Box 11443, ELLON, AB41 7WX.   (hq)
  0870 042 7999
  email members@fcauk.com   http://www.fcauk.com
  Chmn: Donald MacLean
- ▲ Company Limited by Guarantee
- ○ *T; covers all parts of the forestry industry
- Gp Arboriculture; British horse loggers; Charcoal & coppice;
  Timber haulage
- ● Conf - Mtgs - ET - Res - Exhib - Inf
- M 967 i, 382 f
- ¶ FCA News - 6; ftm only.

Federation of Active Retirement Associations   (FARA)
- IRL Shamrock Chambers, 1-2 Eustace St, DUBLIN 2, Republic of
  Ireland.
  353 (1) 679 2142   fax 353 (1) 679 2142
  email fara@eircom.net   http://www.fara.ie
- ○ *W

Federation of Aerospace Enterprises in Ireland   (FAEI)
- IRL Confederation House, 84-86 Lower Baggot St, DUBLIN 2,
  Republic of Ireland.
  353 (1) 605 1562   fax 353 (1) 638 1562
  email info@faei.ie   http://www.faei.ie
  Exec: Mark MacAuley
- ○ *P
- < IBEC

Federation of Aerospace Support Services   (FASS)   2000
- NR Charter House, White Gates, Clyst Rd, Topsham, EXETER,
  Devon, EX3 0DB.   (hsp/b)
  01392 875809   fax 01392 875809
  email jc@fass.org.uk   http://www.fass.org.uk
  Chief Exec: Jon Cousens
- ▲ Company Limited by Guarantee
- ○ *T; the supply of temporary workers to the aircraft maintenance
  industry
- ● Mtgs - ET - LG
- M 16 f, UK / 1 f, o'seas
- ¶ FASS Information - 1; free.

Federation of Artistic & Creative Therapy   (FACT)   1994
- § 29-33 Old St, LONDON, EC1V 9HL.
  020 7490 4140
  http://www.factmultisensory.org
  Finds ways of learning and communicating for profoundly
  disabled children and young people through the
  development of individually tailored programmes of multi-
  sensory therapy, play and educational activities.

Federation of Artistic Roller Skating
- NR 10 The Broadway, THATCHAM, Berks, RG19 3JA.
  01635 877322   fax 01635 877323
  http://www.fars.co.uk
- ○ *S

Federation of Associations for Country Sports in Europe (FACE(UK))   1977
NR   c/o Countryside Alliance, The Old Town Hall,
         367 Kennington Rd, LONDON, SE11 4PT.   (hsb)
         020 7840 9200   fax 020 7793 8899
         Sec: Col T P B Hoggarth
▲   Un-incorporated Society
○   *K; to support, maintain & promote the rights of all field
         sportsmen in the UK; it assists authorities by providing expert
         advice & information & monitors subsequent proposals &
         decisions
         This is the UK branch, the FACE hq is in Brussels
●   Mtgs - Inf - LG - Political lobbying in Europe
<   FACE-Europe
M   19 org
¶   Brochure.

Federation of Astronomical Societies   (FAS)   1974
NR   Chegwyn House, 6 Broomcroft Drive, PYFORD, Surrey,
         GU22 8NS.   (memsec/p)
         01932 341036
         http://www.fedastro.org.uk
         Mem Sec: John Axtell
▲   Un-incorporated Society
Br   Gibraltar
○   *N; to help & advise local astronomical societies
●   Inf - Conventions
<   Assn for Astronomy Educ
M   170 org
¶   FAS NL - 4; ftm only.   Hbk - 1; ftm, £4 nm.
         Astrocalendar - 1.

Federation of Authorised Energy Rating Organisations
         has ceased trading.

Federation of Automatic Transmission Engineers   (FATE) 1978
NR   c/o Chris Lockett, Carvers Transmission Ltd, Unit 21 Turner St,
         Denton, MANCHESTER, M34 3EG.   (mail address)
         0161-320 3400
         http://www.fedauto.co.uk
         Sec: Chris Lockett
○   *T; for rebuilders of automatic transmissions
●   Conf - Mtgs - ET - Res - Exhib - Expt - Inf - Lib
M   c 50 f

Federation of Bakers   (FOB)   1942
■   6 Catherine St, LONDON, WC2B 5JW.   (hq)
         020 7420 7190   fax 020 7379 0542
         email info@bakersfederation.org.uk
         http://www.bakersfederation.org.uk
         Dir: Gordon Polson
▲   Un-incorporated Society
○   *T; representation of the UK's leading bakeries; a £3 billion
         industry producing 80% of the nation's bread
●   Conf - Mtgs - ET - Stat - Inf - LG
<   Assn Intle de la Boulangerie Industrielle (AIBI); Food & Drink
         Fedn; CBI
M   44 f
¶   LM;   AR.
         Information Sheets 1-21 (on various aspects of bread & bread-
         making).
         Health & Safety publications:
         Breathe Easy: a training video; £49.34.
         Federation Safety Memoranda; £96.44 (the set).
         Safety Information Notes; ftm.
         Publications list available.

Federation of Bloodstock Agents (GB) Ltd   (FBA)   1978
NR   9 Paddocks Drive, NEWMARKET, Suffolk, CB8 9BE.   (hsb)
         01638 561116   fax 01638 560332
         http://www.bloodstock-agencies.com
○   *T; to represent bloodstock agents in Great Britain
●   Mtgs - Liaison with horseracing industry through British
         Horseracing Board
M   f

Fédération Britannique des Alliances Françaises   (FBAF) 1905
NR   1 Dorset Sq, LONDON, NW1 6PU.   (hq)
         020 7223 6439
         http://www.alliancefrancaise.org.uk
▲   Registered Charity
○   *X; to widen access to French language & culture by offering
         French classes & social & cultural events about France
<   Alliance Française
M   i, org UK & o'seas

Federation of British Aquatic Societies   (FBAS)   1938
NR   44 Weekes Rd, RYDE, Isle of Wight, PO33 2TL.   (chmn/p)
         01983 613575
         http://www.fbas.co.uk
         Chmn: Les Pearce
▲   Un-incorporated Society
○   *N; all aspects of fishkeeping, breeding, & showing

Federation of British Artists   (FBA)   1961
■   17 Carlton House Terrace, LONDON, SW1Y 5BD.   (hq)
         020 7930 6844   fax 020 7839 7830
         http://www.mallgalleries.org.uk
         Co Sec: John Sayers
▲   Company Limited by Guarantee; Registered Charity
○   *A; to provide exhibition facilities for member societies
●   Conf - Mtgs - Exhib - Comp - SG - Commissions bureau
M   9 org:
         Hesketh Hubbard Art Society
         New English Art Club
         Pastel Society
         Royal Institute of Oil Painters
         Royal Institute of Painters in Water Colours
         Royal Society of British Artists
         Royal Society of Marine Artists
         Royal Society of Portrait Painters
         Society of Wildlife Artists
¶   NL.   Catalogues of each society's exhibitions.

Federation of British Bonsai Societies   (FOBBS)   1962
NR   32 Giles Close, Hedge End, SOUTHAMPTON, Hants,
         SO30 2TH.   (sp)
         01489 789962
         email paul@eslinger.com   http://www.fobbsbonsai.co.uk
         Hon Sec: Paul Eslinger
▲   Company Limited by Guarantee
○   *H, *N; to educate & promote the ancient art of bonsai
         (training of miniature trees in pots)
Gp   Friends of the National Bonsai Collection
●   ET - Exhib - Comp - Inf - PL
<   Eur Bonsai Assn (EBA); R Horticl Soc
M   45 org
¶   NL (published by the EBA) - 6.

Federation of British Cremation Authorities
         since 2007 **Federation of Burial & Cremation Authorities**

© CBD Research Ltd · Beckenham · BR3 5JS · Tel 020 8650 7745 · Fax 020 8650 0768 · E-mail cbd@cbdresearch.com · www.cbdresearch.com

**Federation of British Engineers' Tool Manufacturers   (FBETM)
1943**
NR   c/o Institute of Spring Technology Ltd, Henry St, SHEFFIELD,
     S Yorks, S3 7EQ.   (hq)
     0114-278 9143   fax 0114-275 5573
     http://www.britishtools.com
     Sec Gen: M A Ponikowski
○   *T
●   Conf - Mtgs - Exhib - Stat - Expt - Inf - LG - Standardisation
<   ECTA; BSI; ISO
M   80 f
¶   News Bulletin - 4; ftm.

Federation of British Fire Organisations   (FOBFO)   1963
NR   London Rd, MORETON-in-MARSH, Glos, GL56 0RH.   (asa)
     01608 812500
     Contact: Colin Simpson
○   *N, *T; to promote the services of constituent member
     organisations, both nationally & internationally in the fight
     against fire

**Federation of British Hand Tool Manufacturers   (FBHTM)
1944**
■   c/o 62 Bayswater Rd, LONDON, W2 3PS.   (MTA/hq)
     020 7298 6400   fax 020 7298 6430
     email fbhtm@mta.org.uk   http://www.britishtools.co.uk
     Dir Gen (MTA): Graham Dewhurst
▲   Un-incorporated Society
○   *T; interests of manufacturers of hand tools
Gp   Construction Fixings Association (q.v.); Engineers Hand Tools
     Association; Horticultural & Contractors Tools Association;
     Woodworkers, Builders & Miscellaneous Tools Association
●   Conf - Mtgs - ET - Res - Exhib - Stat - Expt - Inf - LG
<   Comité Eur de l'Outillage (CEO);
M   30 f

**Federation of British Historic Vehicle Clubs Ltd   (FBHVC)
1988**
■   Stonewold, Berrick Salome, WALLINGFORD, Oxon,
     OX10 6JR.   (sp)
     01865 400845   fax 01865 400845
     email secretary@fbhvc.co.uk   http://www.fbhvc.co.uk
     Sec: Rosy Pugh
▲   Company Limited by Guarantee
○   *G, *K; 'to uphold the freedom to use old vehicles on UK
     roads'
●   Conf - Res - Inf - LG
<   Fén Intle des Vehicles Anciens (FIVA)
M   i, f, c 500 org
     (Sub: £12 i, £46 f, 35p (per mem) org)
¶   NL - 6; ftm only.

**Federation of British Port Wholesale Fish Merchants
Associations   1928**
■   Wharncliffe Rd, Fish Docks, GRIMSBY, Lincs, DN31 3QJ.   (s/b)
     01472 350022   fax 01472 240775
     email ce@grimsbyfma.com
     Sec: Steve Norton
▲   Company Limited by Guarantee
○   *N; a federation of fish merchants associations collective
     lobbying on behalf of the seafood industry
●   Inf - LG
>   Grimsby (& Hull) Fish Merchants Assn(s)
M   7,200 f

Federation of Building Specialist Contractors   (FBSC)   1970
NR   Unit 9 Lakeside Industrial Estate, STANTON HARCOURT, Oxon,
     OX29 5SL.   (hq)
     01865 883508
▲   Un-incorporated Society
○   *T; for specialist sub-contractors in the building industry
M   f

Federation of Burial & Cremation Authorities   (FBCA)   1924
■   41 Salisbury Rd, CARSHALTON, Surrey, SM5 3HA.   (sb)
     020 8669 4521
     Sec: D McCallum
○   *T; practice of cremation & administration & operation of
     crematoria
●   Conf - Mtgs - Res - ET - Exhib - Stat - Inf
M   18 f, 183 org (mainly local authorities)
¶   Resurgam - 4; ftm.   Code of practice.
     Technical leaflets & booklets.   AR.
×   2007 Federation of British Cremation Authorities

Federation of Chefs Scotland   (FCS)   1994
■   2 Helenslee Court, Kirktonhill, DUMBARTON, G82 4HT.
     (ce/p)
     01698 232603   fax 01698 232527
     email nthomson@motherwell.co.uk
     http://www.scottishchefs.com
     Chief Exec: Neil Thomson
▲   Un-incorporated Society
○   *P; promoting excellence in the art of professional cookery
●   Conf - Exhib - Comp
<   Wld Assn Chefs Socs (WACS)
M   250 i, 10 f
     (Sub: £25 i, £5,000 f)
¶   Sizzle - 4; free.

Federation of Chemical Associations
     This organisastion is dormant

Federation of Children's Book Groups   (FCBG)   1968
■   2 Bridge Wood View, Horsforth, LEEDS, W Yorks, LS18 5PE.
     (hq)
     0113-258 8910
     email info@fcbg.org.uk   http://www.fcbg.org.uk
     Hon Secs: Sinead & Martin Kromer
▲   Registered Charity
Br   40
○   *A; 'to bring children & good books together; to foster a love of
     books & reading in children'
●   Conf - Mtgs - Exhib - Comp - Inf - Children's Book Award
M   110 i, 125 f (libraries, schools, publishers etc), 40 groups, UK /
     3 i, o'seas
¶   NL - 3; 50p m only.
     Booklists; ftm, 15p nm.

**Federation of City Farms & Community Gardens   (FCFCG)
1980**
■   The GreenHouse, Hereford St, Bedminster, BRISTOL,
     BS3 4NA.   (hq)
     0117-923 1800   fax 0117-923 1900
     email admin@farmgarden.org.uk
     http://www.farmgarden.org.uk
     Dir: Jeremy Iles
▲   Company Limited by Guarantee; Registered Charity
○   *F, *H, *V; supports, promotes & represents city farms,
     community gardens & similar organisations across the UK
●   Conf - Exhib - Inf - Lib - LG
<   Eur Fedn City Farms; CEE; NCVO; Soil Assn; Thrive; Nat Soc of
     Allotment & Leisure Gardens; HDRA; Greenspace
M   300 org
¶   Growing Places (Members NL) - 4; ftm only.
     Public NL - 2;   AR; both free.

Federation of Clinical Scientists   (FCS)
NR   c/o ACB, 130-132 Tooley St, LONDON, SE1 2TU.   (hq)
     020 7403 8001   fax 020 7403 8006
     email admin@acb.org.uk   http://www.acb.org.uk
○   *U
M   i

Federation of Clothing Designers & Executives (FCDE) 1943

■ c/o Mr A Cannon Jones, Fashion Design Technology,
London College of Fashion, 100 Curtain Rd, LONDON,
EC2A 3AA. (hsb)
http://www.fcde.org.uk
Hon Gen Sec: A Cannon Jones
▲ Un-incorporated Society
Br 3
○ *T; technical federation for the garment industry (working &
independent members) covering manufacture, IT, retail,
design technology, & utilities
● Conf - Mtgs - VE - Social
M 130 i, London College of Fashion, UK / 10 i, o'seas

Federation of Cocoa Commerce (FCC) 1929

NR Cannon Bridge House, 1 Cousin Lane, LONDON, EC4R 3XX.
(hq)
020 7379 2884   fax 020 7379 2389
email fcca@liffe.com   http://www.cocoafederation.com
Secretariat: Silde Lauand
▲ Company Limited by Guarantee
○ *T; to promote, protect & regulate the cocoa trade
● Conf - Mtgs - ET - Res - SG - Inf - Arbitration system for
settlement of disputes without resort to the courts
< Intl Cocoa Trade Fedn (ICTF); Eur Community Cocoa Trade
Org (ECCTO)
M c 100 f
¶ News Reports - ftm daily via email.   Contract Book.

Federation of Commercial Audiovisual Libraries Ltd   (FOCAL) 1985

NR Pentax House, South Hill Ave, SOUTH HARROW, Middx,
HA2 0DU. (hq)
020 8423 5853   fax 020 8933 4826
email info@focalint.org   http://www.focalint.org
Gen Mgr: Julie Lewis
Comml Mgr: Anne Johnson
▲ Company Limited by Guarantee
○ *T; for audio-visual libraries, researchers, producers & facility
houses, promoting the use of library footage, stills & sound in
programming, advertising, corporate videos, multi media
projects etc.
● Conf - Mtgs - ET - Res - Stat - Inf - Informing users of footage
where to go for footage & advice - Helping to find film
researchers
M 100 i, 100 f, UK / 25 i, 75 org, o'seas
¶ Archive Zones - 4; ftm, £50 yr nm.
LM - 1; ftm, £25 nm.
Note: Also uses the name FOCAL International Ltd

Federation of Commodity Associations (FCA) 1943

NR GAFTA House, 6 Chapel Place, Rivington St, LONDON,
EC2A 3SH. (hq)
020 7814 9666   fax 020 7814 8383
Sec: Mrs Pamela Kirby Johnson
▲ Company Limited by Guarantee
○ *N, *T; to protect the interests of European commodity
associations
Gp C'ees: Legal & arbitration; Shipping; Taxation
● Mtgs - ET - SG - Expt - Inf
< Intl Cham of Comm; Freight Transport Assn
M c 100 f & org
¶ Book of Rules & Regulations (incl LM); m only.

Federation of Communication Services (FCS) 1981

■ Burnhill Business Centre, Providence House, Burrell Row,
BECKENHAM, Kent, BR3 1AT. (hq)
020 8249 6363   fax 0870 120 5927
email fcs@fcs.org.uk   http://www.fcs.org.uk
Chief Exec: Mrs Jacqui Brooks
▲ Company Limited by Guarantee
○ *T; communication service providers delivering telephony
services & products via fixed, mobile, IP & radio
Gp Business radio; Critical national infrastructure; Installers; Fixed
service provision; Numbering; VOIP; Mobile takeback; DECT
guard band licensees; Number portability
● Conf - Mtgs - Inf - LG
< Trade Assn Forum
> Eur Mobile Messaging Assn; Onsite Communications Assn;
Direct Marketing Assn
M 350 f, 2 org
(Sub: £500 f, £315 org)
¶ FCS Bulletin - 3.

Federation for Community Development Learning   (FCDL) 1977

NR The Circle (3rd floor), 33 Rockingham Lane, SHEFFIELD,
S Yorks, S1 4FW.
0114-253 6770   fax 0114-253 6771
email info@fcdl.org.uk   http://www.fcdl.org.uk
Head of Agency: Janice Marks
▲ Company Limited by Guarantee; Registered Charity
○ *E; to support the development of communities through the
advancement & promotion of community development
learning at local, regional & national levels; to create
relevant opportunities for good quality training &
qualifications
Gp Support for Ubuntu - the national training network for Black
Minority Ethnic practitioners who share an interest in
promoting & developing community development from Black
perspectives
● Conf - Mtgs - ET - Res - Inf - Lib
M 43 i, 133 f
¶ Federation News (NL) - 4; ftm only.
Resource Packs for the Community Development
Programme; £54 m, £60 nm.
Get Accredited (guidance pack); £9 m, £10 nm.
[see website for other publications].
× 2003 (1 April) Federation of Community Work Training Groups

Federation against Copyright Theft   (FACT) 1982

NR Europa House, Church Street, OLD ISLEWORTH, Middx,
TW7 6DA. (hq)
020 8568 6646   fax 020 8560 6364
email bc@fact-uk.org.uk   http://www.fact-uk.org.uk
▲ Company Limited by Guarantee
○ *N; copyright protection of motion pictures
Gp Data Federation
< Motion Picture Assn
M 20 f

Federation of Crafts & Commerce (FCC) 1983

■ Federation House, 4 The Briars, Waterberry Drive,
WATERLOOVILLE, Hants, PO7 7YH. (hq)
023 9223 7010   fax 023 9223 2120
Gen Sec: David Pinnock
▲ Company Limited by Guarantee
○ *T; provision of management services for small & medium sized
businesses
Gp Credit management; Debt recovery; Advisory services; Status
checks etc
● Inf - Status enquiry - Debt recovery - Legal advisory services &
many other similar services
M 1,000 i & f

© CBD Research Ltd · Beckenham · BR3 5JS · Tel 020 8650 7745 · Fax 020 8650 0768 · E-mail cbd@cbdresearch.com · www.cbdresearch.com

Federation for Detached Youth Work   (FDYW)
NR   c/o NYA, Eastgate House, 19-23 Humberstone Rd, LEICESTER,
      LE5 3GJ.
      0116-242 7490
      http://www.detachedyouthwork.info
○   Youth work in which both the initial contact and building of
      retalionships are developed on the street, free from the
      constraints of centre-based work

Federation of Dredging Contractors   1950
NR   c/o Alliotts, 9 Kingsway, LONDON, WC2B 6XF.   (asa)
      020 7240 9971   fax 020 7240 9692
      Sec: N Armstrong
○   *T; to further the interests of the UK dredging industry
M   3 f

Federation of Drug & Alcohol Professionals   (FDAP)   1984
NR   Unit 84, 95 Wilton Rd, LONDON, SW1V 1BZ.   (hq)
      0873 763 6139
      http://www.fdap.org.uk
▲   Company Limited by Guarantee
○   *P, *W; to contribute to the relief of poverty, sickness & distress
      among persons suffering from addiction to drugs of any
      kind; to develop alcohol & drug abuse counselling as a
      professional specialism
●   Conf - Mtgs - ET - Inf - LG
<   Nat Assn of Alcohol & Drug Abuse Counsellors (USA)
M   c 1,000 i

Federation of Drum Reconditioners
      2004 merged with the Association of Drum Manufacturers & the Rigid
      Intermediate Bulk Container Association to form the **Industrial
      Packaging Association**

Federation of Engine Re-Manufacturers   (FER)   1937
NR   59 Mewstone Ave, Wembury, PLYMOUTH, Devon, PL9 0JT.
      (sb)
      01752 863681   fax 01752 863682
      http://www.fer.co.uk
○   *T; for engine reconditioners & their suppliers; to discourage
      unscrupulous traders
●   Mtgs - ET - Exhib - Comp - VE - LG
M   f

Federation of Engineering Design Companies Ltd
      has closed

Federation of English Language Course Organisations Ltd
      was the second title of the Association of Recognised English
      Language Services, which on 12 May 2004 amalgamated with the
      British Association for State English Language Teaching to become
      English UK

Federation of Entertainment Unions   (FEU)   1990
■   c/o Equity, Upper St Martin's Lane, LONDON, WC2H 9EG.
      (sp)
      email entertainment.unions.googlemail.com
      Sec: Paul Evans
○   *U, *N
Gp   Committees: European; Training & equal opportunities; Film &
      electronic media
●   Mtgs - LG
M   170,000 i in 7 org

Federation of Environmental Trade Associations   (FETA)   1977
■   2 Waltham Court, Milley Lane, Hare Hatch, READING, Berks,
      RG10 9TH.   (hq)
      0118-940 3416   fax 0118-940 6258
      email info@feta.co.uk   http://www.feta.co.uk
      Dir Gen: C Sloan
○   *N, *T; 'common action concerning environmental control in
      buildings'
M   11 assns:
      Association of Ductwork Contractors & Allied
          Services
      British Flue & Chimney Manufacturers' Association
      British Refrigeration Association
      Building Controls Industry Association
      Chilled Beam & Ceiling Association
      Fan Manufacturers' Association
      Heat Pump Association
      Heating, Ventilating & Air Conditioning Manufacturers'
          Association
      Hose Manufacturers & Suppliers Association
      Residential Ventilation Association
      Smoke Control Association

Federation of Ethical Stage Hypnotists   (FESH)   1979
NR   The Maltings, Old Malton Rd, Staxton, SCARBOROUGH,
      N Yorks, YO12 4SB.   (hsp)
      07515 355747
      http://www.fesh.co.uk
      Chmn: Ken Webster
○   *P
M   14 i

Federation of Family History Societies   (FFHS)   1974
■   PO Box 8857, LUTTERWORTH, Leics, LE17 9BJ.   (admin/b)
      01455 203133
      email info@ffhs.org.uk   http://www.ffhs.org.uk
      Jt Admin: Maggie Loughran,   Philippa McCray
▲   Company Limited by Guarantee; Registered Charity
○   *G, *L, *N; to bring together societies with a common interest in
      genealogy, heraldry & allied subjects
●   Conf - ET
M   163 org, UK / 54 org, o'seas

Federation of Garden & Leisure Equipment Exporters Ltd
      alternative name of **GARDENEX**

Federation for Healthcare Science   2002
NR   12 Coldbath Sq, LONDON, EC1R 5HL.
      020 7833 5807
      http://www.fedhcs.net
○   *P

Federation of Heating Spares Stockists   (FHSS)   1981
NR   PO Box 672, SHIFNAL, Shropshire, TF11 8YH.   (sp)
      0844 636 0696
      email enquiries@heat-spares.co.uk
      http://www.heat-spares.co.uk
○   *T
M   f

Federation of Holistic Therapists (FHT) 1962
NR 18 Shakespeare Business Centre, Hathaway Close, EASTLEIGH, Hants, SO50 4SR.   (hq)
    0870 420 2022   fax 023 8062 2499
    email info@fht.org.uk   http://www.fht.org.uk
▲ Company Limited by Guarantee
○ *P; to promote & maintain the highest standards of professionalism in holistic therapies (aromatherapy, reflexology, massage) & health & fitness therapies & beaty therapies
Gp Association of Therapy Lecturers; Health & Beauty Employers Federation; International Council of Health Fitness & Sports Therapists; International Council of Holistic Therapists; International Federation of Health & Beauty Therapists; Professional Association of Clinical Therapists
● Conf - ET
M 21,000 i
¶ The International Therapist - 6; ftm only.

Federation of Image Consultants Ltd (TFIC) 1988
NR 13 Dunstable Rd, Studham, DUNSTABLE, Beds, LU6 2QG. (regd/off)
    07010 701018
    Pres: Sue Donnelly
▲ Company Limited by Guarantee
Br New Zealand
○ *P; personal presentation, appearance & image development for men, women, business clients & corporations
● Conf - Mtgs - Exam - Exhib - Inf
< Assn of Image Consultants Intl (AICI)(USA)
M 200 i, UK / 6 i, o'seas
¶ TFIC News - 2.   Image Update - 2.

Federation of Independent Advice Centres
    the operating name of **AdviceUK**

Federation of Independent Detectorists (FID) 1982
NR 44 Heol Dulais, Birchgrove, SWANSEA, W Glam, SA7 9LT. (hsp)
    01792 814615   fax 01792 814615
    email fid.pro@detectorists.net
    http://www.fid.newbury.net
    Hon Sec: Colin Hanson
▲ Un-incorporated Society
Br 2
○ *G; for those interested in recreational metal detecting
Gp Emergency call out for veterinary tranquilliser dart recovery
● Conf - Exhib - Comp - Inf - LG - Insurance - Advice line - Free recovery service (metal items)
M 5,000 i, UK / 750 i, o'seas
¶ NL - 4; ftm only.

Federation of Independent Mines of Great Britain (FIM) 1948
■ 14 Moorland Avenue, BARNSLEY, S Yorks, S70 6PQ.   (hsp)
    01226 244437
    email d7l7b7@gmail.com
    Hon Sec: Douglas Bulmer
▲ Un-incorporated Society
○ *T; to represent the interests of coal producers & associated industry
● Mtgs - ET - Exam - Stat - Expt - Inf - LG - Advice on legal matters (common, employment & mining law)
> Coal Pro, Wakefield
M 12 f, 2 museums

Federation of Independent Practitioner Organisations (FIPO)
NR 14 Queen Anne's Gate, LONDON, SW1H 9AA.
    020 7222 0975
    email info@fipo.org   http://www.fipo.org
○ *M, *N; to represent medical professional organisations in Britain that have private practice committees

Federation of Inline Speed Skating   (FISS)
NR 23 Seaton Rd, Thorpe Astley, LEICESTER, LE3 3SU.
    email fissinfo@inlinespeed.co.uk
    http://www.inlinespeed.co.uk
    Gen Sec: Cass Porter
○ *S

Federation of Internet Traders   (FIT)   2000
NR Oceana House, 39-49 Commercial Rd, SOUTHAMPTON, Hants, SO15 1GA.
    email info@fitraders.com   http://www.fitraders.com
○ *T

Federation of Irish Beekeepers' Associations   (FIBKA)
IRL Ballinakill, ENFIELD, Co Meath, Republic of Ireland.
    353 (46) 954 1433
    email mgglee@eircom.net
    http://www.irishbeekeeping.ie
    Hon Sec: Michael Gleeson
○ *F

Federation of Irish Fishermen   2007
IRL Fitzwilliam Business Centre, 26/27 Upper Pembroke St, DUBLIN 2, Republic of Ireland.
    353 (1) 637 3937   fax 353 (1) 662 0635
    email info@fif.ie   http://www.fif.ie
○ *T

Federation of Irish Nursing Homes
    in January 2008 merged with the Irish Nursing Homes Organisation to from **Nursing Homes Ireland**

Federation of Irish Renderers
    a group of **Food & Drink Industry Ireland**

Federation of Irish Societies   (FIS)   1971
NR 95 White Lion St, LONDON, N1 9PF.   (hq)
    020 7833 1226   fax 020 7833 3214
○ *X; to promote the interests of the Irish community in GB through welfare, cultural & youth activities

Federation of Jewellery Manufacturers of Ireland
IRL Marina House, Clarence St, DÚN LAOGHAIRE, Republic of Ireland.
    353 (1) 663 8700   fax 353 (1) 663 8704
    http://www.fjmi.com
    Chmn: Joe Harbourne
    Sec: Ida Kiernan
○ *T

Federation of Licensed Victuallers Associations   (FLVA)   1992
■ 126 Bradford Rd, BRIGHOUSE, W Yorks, HD6 4AU.   (hq)
    01484 710534   fax 01484 718647
    email admin@flva.fsbusiness.co.uk
    http://www.flva.co.uk
    Chief Exec: Tony Payne
○ *T; to offer help & advice to members with any problems arising from the day-to-day running of their business, whether as tenants, free traders or lessees
● Conf - Mtgs - Inf - LG
< UK & Ireland Licensed Trade Assn
M 700 i, 9 f
¶ NL - 4; free.
    Publicans Guide to the Health & Safety Act; ftm onlyGuidance Notes:
      Employment Law;
      General Food Hygiene Regulations;
      Disability Audit;
      Contracts of Employment; all ftm only.

© CBD Research Ltd · Beckenham · BR3 5JS · Tel 020 8650 7745 · Fax 020 8650 0768 · E-mail cbd@cbdresearch.com · www.cbdresearch.com

Federation of Local History Societies
IRL Winter's Hill, KINSALE, Co Cork, Republic of Ireland.   (sp)
       http://www.homepage.eircom.net/~localhist/index.html
     Sec: Dermot Ryan
○   *G

Federation of Manufacturing Opticians   (FMO)   1917
■   199 Gloucester Terrace, LONDON, W2 6LD.   (hq)
       020 7298 5123   fax 020 7298 5120
       email info@fmo.co.uk   http://www.fmo.co.uk
     Contact: the Hon Sec
▲   Company Limited by Guarantee
○   *N, *T; a federation for the ophthalmic optical manufacturing &
       distributing industry consisting of 4 trade associations each
       concerned with a separate branch of the industry
Gp   Optra Exhibitions UK; Optical Equipment Manufacturers' &
       Suppliers' Association; Optical Frame Importers' &
       Manufacturers' Association; Ophthalmic Lens Manufacturers'
       & Distributors' Association
●   Conf - Mtgs - Exhib
<   EUROM
M   152 f, UK / 1 f, o'seas
¶   In-Focus (NL) - 3;   AR (incl LM) - 1; both ftm only.

Federation of Master Builders   (FMB)   1941
■   Gordon Fisher House, 14-15 Great James St, LONDON,
       WC1N 3DP.   (hq)
       020 7242 7583   fax 020 7405 0854
       email central@fmb.org.uk
       http://www.findabuilder.co.uk
     Dir Gen: Richard Diment
▲   Company Limited by Guarantee
Br   11
○   *T; for the construction industry
●   Conf - Mtgs - ET - Exhib - Inf - Lib - VE - Empl - LG
<   Eur Bldrs Fedn
M   13,000 f
¶   Masterbuilder - 12; ftm, £3.50 each nm.

Federation of Museums & Art Galleries of Wales
■   c/o Barbara Bartl, Newport Museum & Art Gallery,
       John Frost Square, NEWPORT, NP20 1PA.   (hsb)
       01633 656656
       http://www.welshmuseumsfederation.org.uk
     Hon Sec: Barbara Bartl
▲   Un-incorporated Society
○   *P; to encourage the highest professional standards within the
       museum profession in Wales
●   Mtgs - ET
<   Museums Assn
M   30 i, 20 f
¶   Y Mag - 2; ftm.

Federation of Music Services
NR   7 Courthouse St, OTLEY, W Yorks, LS21 3AN.
       01943 463311
○   *D; 'to advance the education of the public in the art of music'
M   130+ org

Federation of National Self Catering Associations   (FoNSCA)
1996
■   c/o EASCO, PO Box 567, HAYES, Middx, UB3 9EW.
       (v-chmn/b)
       020 7078 7329
       email ce@englishselfcatering.co.uk
     Vice-Chmn: Martin Sach
○   *T; furthering the interests of self catering holiday
       accommodation providers; promoting the use of self catering
       accommodation & maintaining standards within the sector
●   Mtgs - Inf - LG
M   4 org, UK / 1 org, o'seas

Federation of Oils, Seeds & Fats Associations Ltd   (FOSFA)
1970
■   20 St Dunstan's Hill, LONDON, EC3R 8NQ.   (hq)
       020 7283 5511
       http://www.fosfa.org
     Chief Exec: Stuart Logan
▲   Company Limited by Guarantee
○   *N, *T
Gp   Oils & fats; Oilseeds & HPS groundnuts
●   Mtgs - ET - Res - Inf - LG
<   African Groundnut Coun (AGC); Amer Oil Chemists
       Soc (AOCS); AOAC Intl; Argentine Oil Ind Chamber (CIARA);
       Deutscher Verband des Grosshandels mit Ölen, Fetten und
       Ölrohstoffen eV (GROFOR); Eur Oleochemicals & Allied
       Products Gp (APAG); Intl Assn of Seed Crushers (IASC);
       Fishmeal & Fish Oil Org (IFFO); Intl Margarine Assn
       Countries Europe (IMACE); Malayan Edible Oil Mfrs
       Assn (MEOMA); Nat Inst Oilseed Products (NIOP); Nat
       Renderers Assn (NRA); Netherlands Oils, Fats & Oilseeds Tr
       Assn (NOFOTA); Palm Oil Refiners Assn Malaysia (PORAM);
       Seed Crushers & Oil Processors Assn (SCOPA)
M   800 f
¶   NL - 4.   FOSFA International Manual.   Contracts.
     Rules of Arbitration.   Codes of Practice.

Federation of Ophthalmic & Dispensing Opticians   (FODO)
1985
■   199 Gloucester Terrace, LONDON, W2 6LD.   (hq)
       020 7298 5151   fax 020 7298 5111
       email optics@fodo.com   http://www.fodo.com
     Chief Exec: David Hewlett
▲   Company Limited by Guarantee
○   *T; representation of optical employers & businesses including
       both dispensing & ophthalmic practices; 'FODO represents
       all of the high street companies & most of the large groups'
Gp   FODO educational charity
●   Mtgs - SG - Stat - Empl - LG
<   Eur Coun of Optometry & Optics
M   140 f
¶   Optics at a Glance - 1;   Vouchers at a Glance - 1;
     Opticians in Business - 12;
     Hbk (inc AR & accounts) - 1; all free.

Federation of Overseas Property Developers, Agents & Consultants
   in 2008 was incorporated into the **National Association of Estate
   Agents** *as NAEA International incorporating FOPDAC*

Federation of Petroleum Suppliers Ltd   (FPS)   1979
■   6 Royal Court, Tatton St, KNUTSFORD, Cheshire, WA16 6EN.
       (hq)
       01565 631313   fax 01565 631314
       email info@fpsonline.co.uk   http://www.fpsonline.co.uk
     Chief Exec: Susan Hancock
▲   Company Limited by Guarantee
Br   9; Republic of Ireland
○   *T; interests of oil distribution industry (including heating oil &
       delivery to commercial sites for agricultural, marine &
       industrial use)
Gp   FPS Forecourt Division
●   Conf - Mtgs - Comp - ET - Exhib - Stat - Inf - LG
M   3 i, 230 f, UK / 30 f, o'seas
¶   Publication - 5; ftm, single complimentary copies only nm.
×   2006 Garage Watch (merged)

Federation of Piling Specialists (FPS) 1964
■ 83 Copers Cope Rd, BECKENHAM, Kent, BR3 1NR. (asa)
    020 8663 0947   fax 020 8663 0949
    email fps@fps.org.uk   http://www.fps.org.uk
    Sec: Dianne Jennings
▲ Company Limited by Guarantee
○ *T; specialist subcontractors carrying out all aspects of
    foundation construction & design
● Mtgs
< Eur Fedn of Foundation Contrs; Nat Specialist Contrs Coun;
    Ground Forum
M 18 f
¶ LM.

Federation of Plastering & Drywall Contractors (FPDC) 1950
■ 8-9 Ludgate Square, LONDON, EC4M 7AS. (hq)
    020 7634 9480   fax 020 7248 9263
    email admin@fpdc.org   http://www.fpdc.org
    Chief Exec: Emma Tomlin
▲ Company Limited by Guarantee
○ *T
● Conf - Mtgs - ET - Res - Stat - LG
< Nat Specialist Contrs Coun
M 250 f
¶ Specialist Building Finisher - 6; free.
✕ 2005-06 Scottish Plastering & Drylining Association (merged)

Federation of Private Residents' Associations (FPRA) 1971
■ 59 Mile End Rd, COLCHESTER, Essex, CO4 5BU. (hq)
    0871 200 3324; 01206 855888   fax 020 8989 3153
    email info@fpra.org.uk   http://www.fpra.org.uk
    Chief Exec: Robert Levene
▲ Company Limited by Guarantee
○ *K; advice to members on leasehold & freehold management
    issues
● Mtgs - Inf - LG
M 500 org
¶ NL - 4; ftm only.
    Information pack (advice on forming a residents'
    association); £10.

**Federation of Professional Associations in Guidance
(FedPAG) 2000**
■ c/o ACEG - 19 Lawrence Leys, Bloxham, BANBURY, Oxon,
    OX15 4NU. (hsp)
    01295 720809   fax 01295 720809
    email alan@aceg.org.uk   http://www.fedpag.org
    Admin: Alan Vincent
○ *N, *P; for professionals working in career guidance

Federation of Racecourse Bookmakers 2003
NR 19 Culm Valley Way, UFFCULME, Devon, EX15 3XZ.
    01884 841859   fax 01184 841859
    email comments@frb.org.uk   http://www.frb.org.uk
    Sec: B Newland
▲ Company Limited by Guarantee
○ *N; to act on behalf of the Association of Racecourse
    Bookmakers, the National Association of Bookmakers, and
    the Rails Bookmakers Association on matters of mutual
    interest

Federation of Recorded Music Societies (FRMS) 1936
■ 18 Albany Rd, Hartshill, STOKE-on-TRENT, Staffs, ST4 6BB.
    (hsp)
    01782 251460
    http://www.thefrms.co.uk
    Hon Sec: Tony Baines
▲ Company Limited by Guarantee
Br 210 affiliated societies
○ *D, *N; to promote the development & extension of societies or
    organisations using recorded music as part of their activities
● Conf - Mtgs
M 12,000 i, UK / 80 i, o'seas
¶ Bulletin - 2; £1.75.

**Federation of the Retail Licensed Trade Northern Ireland
(FRLTNI) 1872**
NR 91 University St, BELFAST, BT7 1HP. (hq)
    028 9032 7578   fax 028 9032 7578
    email enquiries@ulsterpubs.com
    http://www.ulsterpubs.com
    Chief Exec: Nicola Carruthers
▲ Un-incorporated Society
○ *T; promotion of the licensed trade; advice & information for
    members
● Conf - Mtgs - ET - Res - Inf - LG
< UK & Ireland Licensed Trade Assn
M 1,200 i
¶ Federation section within Catering & Licensing Review - 12; ftm.

Federation of Road Racing Motorcyclists
NR Numeric House, 98 Station Rd, SIDCUP, Kent, DA15 7BY.

Federation of Road Surface Treatment Associations (FoRSTA)
NR PO Box 986, CHESTER, CH4 8XD.
    01244 677648   fax 01244 680141
    http://www.rsda-gb.co.uk/forsta.htm
    Sec: Alistair Jack
○ *N, *T

Federation of Scottish Aquaculture Producers
NR 15 Shielhill Park, STANLEY, Perthshire, PH1 4QT.
    01738 828170
    Exec Dir: R J Slaski
○ *N; to represent the marine fish, trout & independent salmon
    smolt producers in Scotland

Federation of Scottish Theatre Ltd   (FST)
NR c/o Theatre Workshop, 34 Hamilton Place, EDINBURGH,
    EH3 5AX. (hq)
    0131-220 6393   fax 0131-220 6373
    email fst@scottishtheatre.org
○ *N, *P; to act as the voice of theatre in Scotland; to work with
    unions, the Scottish Arts Council, local authorities & other
    organisations to further interests & development of the
    theatre industry in Scotland
M f

Federation of Services for Unmarried Parents & their Children
    since 2005-06 **National Federation of Services for Unmarried
    Parents & their Children**

Federation of Sidecar Clubs (FOSC) 1958
NR 107 Silverweed Rd, Walderslade, CHATHAM, Kent, ME5 0RF.
    (mem/sp)
    email EddieCheer@aol.com   http://www.sidecars.org.uk
    Mem Sec: Ted Cheer
○ *N, *G; sidecars & motorcycle combinations
● Conf - Mtgs - Exhib - Stat - Inf - Lib - Rallies
M c 400 i
¶ Outlook.

Federation of Small Businesses (FSB) 1974
■ Press & Parliamentary Office, 2 Catherine Place, LONDON,
    SW1E 6HF. (hq)
    020 7592 8100   fax 020 7828 5919
▲ Company Limited by Guarantee
Br 200; Belgium, Gibraltar
○ *K, *T; lobby organisation for small businesses
● Conf - Mtgs - Stat - Inf - Lib - LG
< Eur Alliance for Small Businesses (ESBA)
M 215,000 f
¶ First Voice - 6.

© CBD Research Ltd · Beckenham · BR3 5JS · Tel 020 8650 7745 · Fax 020 8650 0768 · E-mail cbd@cbdresearch.com · www.cbdresearch.com

Federation against Software Theft   (FAST)   1984
NR   York House, 18 York Rd, MAIDENHEAD, Berks, SL6 1SF.   (hq)
    01628 622121
    http://www.fastiis.org
▲   Company Limited by Guarantee
○   *T; protecting the interests of member companies from
    copyright infringement; to counter software piracy & increase
    public awareness of the damage to investment & innovation
    from unauthorised copying - to promote the legal use of
    software

Federation of Specialist Restaurants   (FSR)   2006
■   PO Box 416, SURBITON, Surrey, KT1 9BJ.   (hq)
    020 8399 4831
    email groveint@aol.com   http://www.fedrest.com
    Sec: Colleen Grove
▲   Un-incorporated Society
○   *T; to publicise & further the interests of UK restaurants offering
    a specialist cuisine
●   Res - Stat - Inf - PL
>   Gld of Bangladeshi Restarateurs
M   1,000 f
¶   Mood Food Magazine - 12; ftm only.
    Publications on www.moodfoodmag.com

Federation of Sports & Play Associations   (FSPA)   1919
■   Federation House, STONELEIGH PARK, Warks, CV8 2RF.   (hq)
    024 7641 4999   fax 024 7641 4990
    email admin@sportsandplay.com
    http://www.sportsandplay.com

    Head of Membership & Communications: Jane Montgomery
▲   Company Limited by Guarantee
○   *N, *S, *T; to represent the sports goods & play industries
Gp   Specialist:
    Angling Trades Association Ltd
    Association of Play Industries
    Association of Professional Sales Agents (Sports
      & Leisure Industries)
    British Association of Seating Equipment Suppliers
    British Golf Industry Association
    British Rootzone & Top Dressing Manufacturers Association
    European Golf Industry Association
    Golf Consultants Association
    Inflatable Play Manufacturers Association
    Play Providers Association
    Professional Anglers Association
    Professional Darts Players Association
    Sports & Fitness Equipment Association
    Sports & Play Construction Association
    General:
    Register of Play Inspectors International Ltd
●   Conf - Mtgs - ET - Exam - Res - Exhib - Stat - Expt - Inf - Lib -
    LG
<   Wld Fedn of the Sporting Goods Ind (WFSGI); Fedn of the Eur
    Sporting Goods Ind
>   Profl Darts Corporation (PDC)
M   991 f in 16 assns
¶   Sportslife - 4; ftm, £1.75 each nm.
    Membership Directory - 1; free.
✕   2006 Sports Industries Federation

Federation of Stadium Communities   (FSC)   1991
NR   Vale Park Enterprise Centre (suite 20), Hamil Rd, Burslem,
    STOKE-on-TRENT, Staffs, ST6 1AW.   (hq)
    01782 831900
    http://www.stadiumcommunities.org
    Chief Exec: Judy Crabb
▲   Company Limited by Guarantee; Registered Charity
○   *K; to improve the quality of life of those communities that exist
    in the shadow of sports stadia; to encourage & assist the
    formation of constructive partnerships between sports clubs,
    local communities, local authorities & other interested parties
●   Conf - Mtgs - ET - Res - Inf - LG - Advocacy - Representation -
    Consultancy
M   245 community groups
¶   The Shadow NL - 4;   AR; both free.

Federation of Street Traders Unions
NR   Unit 1 Balmoral Trading Estate, River Rd, BARKING, Essex,
    IG11 0EG.   (hq)
    020 8591 1004
    Hon Sec: Wally Watson
○   *T

Federation of Swiss Societies in the UK   (FOSSUK)   1949
NR   Swiss Embassy, 16-18 Montagu Place, LONDON, W1H 2BQ.
    020 7616 6000   fax 020 7724 7001
    email info@swiss-societies.co.uk
    http://www.swiss-societies.co.uk
○   *X
M   25 org

Federation of Synagogues   1887
NR   65 Watford Way, LONDON, NW4 3AQ.   (hq)
    020 8202 2263   fax 020 8203 0610
    email info@federationofsynagogues.com
    http://www.federationofsynagogues.com
    Chief Exec: Dr Eli Kienwald
▲   Registered Charity
○   *R; to provide services to Orthodox rabbis; to assist
    congregations in erection, reconstruction or redecoration of
    synagogues; to assist in maintenance of Orthodox religious
    instruction.   Is also a burial society providing an orthodox
    Jewish funeral to its members & others of the Jewish faith

Federation of Tax Advisers   (FTA)   1997
■   Oakdene House, Kenton, EXETER, Devon, EX6 8NN.
    01626 891222   fax 01626 891555
    email admin@fta.co.uk   http://www.fta.uk.com
    Managing Dir & Sec: P T Harmsworth
▲   Company Limited by Guarantee
○   *P; to offer support to tax advisers
●   ET - Exam - Inf - LG
M   720 i
¶   NL - 12; ftm only

Federation of Technological Industries   (FTI)   2003
NR   Tuscan House (ground floor), Beck Court,
    Cardiff Gate Business Park, CARDIFF, CF23 8RP.
    0870 850 6120
    http://www.fti.org.uk
    Chmn & Sec: Fred Howarth
○   *K; traders of mobile phones & computer chips

Federation of Tour Operators (FTO) 1969

■ 14-16 Sussex Rd, HAYWARDS HEATH, W Sussex, RH16 4EA. (hq)
  01444 457900   fax 01444 457901
  email general@fto.co.uk   http://www.fto.co.uk
  Dir Gen: Andrew Cooper
▲ Company Limited by Guarantee
○ *I; co-ordination of industry activity in the areas of crisis management, health & safety & responsible tourism; representation of tour operating sector, demonstration of benefits to consumers
● Mtgs - Res - Stat - LG
< Intl Fedn Tour Operators
M 10 f

Federation for Ulster Local Studies Ltd (FULS) 1975

■ 18 Ardmore Avenue, DOWNPATRICK, Co Down, BT30 6JU. (treas/p)
  028 4461 2986
  email info@fuls.org.uk   http://www.fuls.org.uk
  Hon Sec: William Devlin
▲ Company Limited by Guarantee; Registered Charity
○ *G, *N; to promote the study & recording of the history, antiquities & folk life of Ulster; to develop co-operation & communications between local historical groups & between the groups & relevant voluntary organisations
● Conf - Mtgs - ET - SG - VE - LG
< Fedn of Local History Socs (Republic of Ireland)
M 94 org
  (Sub: £30)
¶ Due North - 2; £1.50 m, £3 nm.

Federation of Water Fitness Professionals

please delete entry

Federation of Wholesale Distributors (FWD) 1918

NR 9 Gildredge Rd, EASTBOURNE, E Sussex, BN21 4RB. (hq)
  01323 724952   fax 01323 732820
▲ Un-incorporated Society
○ *T; interests of food & drink wholesalers in the UK
M f

Federation of Window Cleaners (FWC) 1947

■ Summerfield House, Harrogate Rd, Reddish, STOCKPORT, Cheshire, SK5 6HQ. (hq)
  0161-432 8754   fax 0161-947 9033
  email info@f-w-c.co.uk   http://www.f-w-c.co.uk
  Gen Sec: Beryl Murray
▲ Un-incorporated Society
○ *T; an employers' trade association for self-employed window cleaners
● Mtgs - ET - Exhib - Comp - Inf - LG
M 1,600 f
¶ Window Talk (Jnl) - 4; free.
× 2006 (1 January) National Federation of Master Window & General Cleaners

Federation of Women's Institutes of Northern Ireland (WI) 1932

■ Federation House, 209-211 Upper Lisburn Rd, BELFAST, BT10 0LL. (hq)
  028 9030 1506 & 028 9060 1781   fax 028 9043 1127
  email wini@btconnect.com
  Gen Sec: Mrs Irene A Sproule
▲ Registered Charity
Br 190 (NI)
○ *W; 'confidence building: encouraging women to reach their potential, giving opportunities to meet other women, learn new skills & provide new opportunities'
● Conf - Mtgs - Exhib - Comp
< Associated Countrywomen of the Wld (ACWW)
M 7,000+ i
¶ Ulster Countrywoman - 10; 85p.

Federation of Worker Writers & Community Publishers (FWWCP) 1976

NR Burslem School of Art, Queen St, STOKE-on-TRENT, Staffs, ST6 3EJ. (hq)
  01782 822327
  Coordinator: Tim Diggles
▲ Company Limited by Guarantee
○ *A, *N; to make writing & publishing more accessible
● Conf - ET - Res - Inf
M org

Federation of Zoological Gardens of Great Britain & Ireland (Zoo Federation)
  since 2004 **British & Irish Association of Zoos & Aquariums**

Fèisean nan Gàidheal 1991

NR Meall House, Portree, ISLE of SKYE, IV51 9BZ.   (hq)
  01478 613355   fax 01478 613399
  email fios@feisean.org   http://www.feisean.org
  Chief Exec: Arthur Cormack
▲ Company Limited by Guarantee
○ *A, *D; the promotion of Gaelic arts tuition with emphasis on young people
M i & org

Fell Pony Society (FPS) 1898

■ Ion House, Great Asby, APPLEBY-in-WESTMORLAND, Cumbria, CA16 6HD.   (hsp)
  01768 353100   fax 01768 353100
  http://www.fellponysociety.org
  Sec: Elizabeth Parkin
▲ Company Limited by Guarantee
Br Germany, Netherlands
○ *B
● Mtgs - Exhib - Comp - Inf
< Brit Assn Equine Socs; Nat Pony Soc; Brit Horse Soc; Brit Central Prefix Register
M 1,020 i, UK / 80 i, o'seas
¶ Stud Book - 1; price varies.

Fell Runners Association (FRA) 1970

■ 8 Leygate View, New Mills, HIGH PEAK, Derbys, SK22 3EF. (sp)
  01663 746476
  email alan.brentnall@btinternet.com
  http://www.fellrunners.org.uk
  Sec: Alan Brentnall
▲ Un-incorporated Society
○ *S; the governing body of fell-running in England; to encourage & promote fell-running; to provide services to competitors; to establish regulations for the the conduct of clubs, competitors & race organisers
● Comp
< UK Athletics; Wld Mountain Running Assn
M 6,500 i & org
¶ The Fell Runner - 3;
  Hbk & Fixtures Calendar - 1; both ftm only.

Fellowship of Cycling Old-Timers (FCOT) 1965

■ 5 Avocet Close, South Oulton Broad, LOWESTOFT, Suffolk. (sp)
  01502 563262
  http://www.fcot.co.uk
  Gen Sec: Sian Charlton
▲ Un-incorporated Society
○ *G; for cyclists of age 50 & up who wish to stay cycling or return to it; to keep in touch with old cycling friends
● Mtgs
M 1,160 i, UK / 60 i, o'seas
¶ Fellowship News - 4; ftm, £2 nm.

Fellowship of Depressives Anonymous
  since September 2007 **Depression UK**

© CBD Research Ltd · Beckenham · BR3 5JS · Tel 020 8650 7745 · Fax 020 8650 0768 · E-mail cbd@cbdresearch.com · www.cbdresearch.com

Fellowship of Independent Evangelical Churches (FIEC) 1922
■ 39 The Point, Rockingham Rd, MARKET HARBOROUGH, Leics,
   LE16 7QU.   (hq)
   01858 434540   fax 01858 411550
   email admin@fiec.co.uk   http://www.fiec.org.uk
   Gen Sec: Richard J Underwood
▲ Registered Charity
Br 495
○ *R; establish & strengthen independent evangelical churches &
   uphold & proclaim the Christian Gospel
Gp Prepared for service - a training course for Christian ministry;
   Pastors' Association - supporting, equipping & setting standards
   for ministers & their churches
● Conf - Mtgs - ET - Inf
< Affinity
M 23,000 i, 495 churches, UK / 700 i, o'seas
¶ Together - 2; ftm only.   Churches Hbk - 3 yrly; £10.
   FIEC Directory - 2 yrly; £6 m, £9 nm.

**Fellowship of Makers & Researchers of Historical Instruments
(FoMRHI) 1975**
NR c/o Lewis Jones, London Metropolitan University,
   41 Commercial Rd, LONDON, E1 1LA.   (hsb)
   020 7320 1841   fax 020 7320 1830
   email ljones@lgu.ac.uk
   Hon Sec: Lewis Jones
○ *L; to promote authenticity in the making, restoration & use of
   historical musical instruments
● Conf - Res - SG - Inf
M 700 i, UK & o'seas
¶ FoMRHI Quarterly - 4; ftm only.   LM - 1 (updates - 4).
   Note: Information is only given to persons writing theses if they
   are members.

Fellowship of Postgraduate Medicine (FPM) 1919
■ 12 Chandos St, LONDON, W1G 9DR.   (hq)
   020 7636 6334   fax 020 7436 2535
   email admin@fpm-uk.org
   Chief Exec: Prof Donald Singer
▲ Registered Charity
○ *E, *P; promotion of postgraduate medical education (NOT
   personal assistance)
M c 60 i
¶ Postgraduate Medical Jnl - 12.

Fellowship of the White Boar
   alternative name of the **Richard III Society**

Fencing Contractors' Association Ltd (FCA) 1942
■ Hillside Grange, Warren Rd, TRELLECH, Monmouthshire,
   NP25 4PQ.   (hq)
   0700 056 0722   fax 01600 860888
   email info@fencingcontractors.org
   http://www.fencingcontractors.org
   Chief Exec: Wendy A Baker
▲ Incorporated under the Industrial & Provident Societies Act.
○ *T; contracting, supplying & manufacturing for fencing & safety
   barriers
Gp Incorporating:
   Association of Safety Fencing Contractors
   Electric Security Fencing Federation
   Environmental Noise Barrier Association
   Gate Automation & Access Barrier Association
● Conf - Mtgs - Inf - Empl - LG
M 230 f
¶ NL - 4; ftm only.   LM; free.

Feng Shui Society (FSS) 1993
NR 377 Edgware Rd, LONDON, W2 1BT.   (asa)
   0845 257 9988
   email info@fengshuisociety.org.uk
   http://www.fengshuisociety.org.uk
   Chmn: Raymond Catchpole
▲ Un-incorporated Society
Br 12
○ *G, *P; 'the only independent, not for profit professional body
   regulating regulating the professional practice of feng shui in
   the UK'
● Conf - Mtgs - ET - Exam - Res - Exhib - SG - Inf - Lib - PL - VE -
   LG
M 400 i, UK / 100 i, o'seas
¶ Feng Shui News; ftm only.

FeRFA: the Resin Flooring Association (FeRFA) 1969
■ 16 Edward Rd, FARNHAM, Surrey, GU9 8NP.   (hq)
   01252 714250
   email secretariat@ferfa.org.uk   http://www.ferfa.org.uk
   Hon Sec: Lisa Hennessey
▲ Company Limited by Guarantee
○ *T; UK manufacturers, contractors & associated companies
   involved in industrial resin systems
Gp Technical working parties
● Conf - Mtgs - Exhib - Comp - LG
M 82 f
¶ Technical Guidance Notes.

Fertility Care Scotland 1976
■ 196 Clyde St, GLASGOW, G1 4JY.   (hq)
   0141-221 0858
   email info@fertilitycare.org.uk
   http://www.fertilitycare.org.uk
▲ Registered Charity
Br 16
○ *M, *W; to promote the Billings ovulation method of natural
   family planning
Gp Educational presentations & resourcing; Teaching Billings
   ovulation method; Fertility/infertility awareness; Natural
   family planning tuition
● Mtgs - ET - Exam - Inf
< Wld Org Ovulation Method Billings (WOOMB)
M 70 i

Fertilizer Association of Ireland 1967
IRL c/o 151 Thomas St, DUBLIN 8, Republic of Ireland.
   353 (1) 612 1200
   http://www.fertilizer-assoc.ie
   Pres: Terry Carroll
○ *T; for farmers, agribusiness, fertilzer manufacturers

Ffederasiwn Cerddoriaeth Amatur Cymru
   Welsh name of the **Welsh Amateur Music Federation**

Ffestiniog Railway Society Ltd (FRSL) 1954
NR Harbour Station, PORTHMADOG, Gwynedd, LL49 9NF.   (hq)
   fax 0870 052 0091
○ *G; conservation of the Ffestiniog Railway
M i
   This is not the same organisation as the Ffestiniog Railway
   Company.

**Fibre Bonded Carpet Manufacturers' Association (FBCMA)
1968**
NR Tower House, 269 Walmersley Rd, BURY, Lancs, BL9 6NX.
   (asa)
   0161-761 5231   fax 0161-761 3001
   Sec & Treas: C A Nuttall
▲ Un-incorporated Society
○ *T; for manufacturers of fibre-bonded carpets
● Conf - Mtgs - Res - Inf - LG
< Intl Standards Org; Comité Eur de Normalisation; BSI
M 9 f

Fibre Cement Manufacturers' Association Ltd   (FCMA)   1984
■　5a The Maltings, Stowupland Rd, STOWMARKET, Suffolk,
　　IP14 5AG.　(hq)
　　01449 676053　fax 01449 770028
　　Sec-Gen: Tony Hutchinson
▲　Company Limited by Guarantee
○　*T; fibre cement building products, their technical development
　　& safe utility
Gp　Technical; Health & safety
●　Res - Inf - LG
M　1 f

Fibreoptic Industry Association   (FIA)   1990
■　The Manor House, High St, BUNTINGFORD, Herts,
　　SG9 9AB.　(hq)
　　01763 273039　fax 01763 273255
　　email jane@fiasec.demon.co.uk
　　http://www.fia-online.co.uk
　　Co Sec: Jane Morrison
▲　Company Limited by Guarantee
○　*T; to facilitate the development & professionalism of the UK's
　　fibre optic industry; to represent end users of fibre optics,
　　installers, distributors, training providers, consultants &
　　component manufacturers
●　Mtgs - ET - SG - Inf
M　5 i, 210 f, UK / 5 i, o'seas
¶　NL - 6;　Members' Guide to Products & Services (2000);
　　both free.
　　Technical publications; ftm (website password); prices vary nm.

Fibromyalgia Association UK   (FMA UK)   1994
■　PO Box 206, STOURBRIDGE, W Midlands, DY9 8YL.　(hq)
　　0845 345 2322　fax 01384 895005
　　email fmauk@hotmail.com　http://www.fmauk.org
　　Chmn: Pam Stewart
▲　Registered Charity
Br　90
○　*W; to make people aware of fibromyalgia & its effects, to both
　　the public at large & to health professionals that are
　　responsible for diagnosing & treating people with the
　　condition
●　Conf - Mtgs - Res - Comp - Inf - LG
　　Fibromyalgia benefits helpline: 0845 345 2343 (Mon-Fri 1000-
　　1600)
＞　Local support groups in UK & NI
M　[not stated]
¶　Family Magazine - 12; £16.50 yr.

Field Studies Council   (FSC)   1943
■　Preston Montford, Montford Bridge, SHREWSBURY, Shropshire,
　　SY4 1HW.　(hq)
　　01743 852100　fax 01743 852101
　　email fsc.headoffice@field-studies-council.org
　　http://www.field-studies-council.org
　　Chief Exec: A D Thomas,　Sec & Treas: C J Bayliss
▲　Company Limited by Guarantee; Registered Charity
Br　17
○　*E, *L; promotion of environmental understanding for all
　　environmental & special course operators
●　ET - Res - SG - VE
M　4,000 i, UK / 250 i, o'seas
¶　Field Studies Magazine - 2; ftm only.　AR; free.
　　Catalogue of publications; on request.

Fields in Trust
　　operating name of the **National Playing Fields Association**

Fife Agricultural Association   (FAA)
NR　Chesterhill, Boarhills, ST ANDREWS, Fife, KY16 8PP.　(hsp)
　　01334 880518
　　Sec: Louise Roger
▲　Registered Charity
○　*F
●　Exhib
M　600 i

Fife Chamber of Commerce & Enterprise Ltd   1988
NR　Wemyssfield House, Wemyssfield, KIRKCALDY, Fife, KY1 1XN.
　　(hq)
　　01592 201932　fax 01592 641187
　　email info@fifechamber.co.uk
　　http://www.fifechamber.co.uk
　　Chief Exec: Alan Russell
▲　Un-incorporated Society
○　*C
M　f

Film Distributors' Association   (FDA)   1915
■　22 Golden Sq, LONDON, W1F 9JW.　(hq)
　　020 7437 4383　fax 020 7734 0912
　　http://www.launchingfilms.com
　　Chief Exec & Sec: Mark Batey
▲　Company Limited by Guarantee
○　*T
●　Mtgs - Inf - LG - Liaison with all industry & other bodies where
　　distributor interests are concerned
＜　Intl Fedn Film Distributor Assns (FIAD)
M　13 f

Film & Video Institute
　　alternative name of the **Institute of Amateur Cinematographers**

Filtration Society   1964
■　5 Henry Dane Way, Newbold Coleorton, COALVILLE, Leics,
　　LE67 8PP.　(hsp)
　　01530 223124　fax 01530 223124
　　email r.j.wakeman@lineone.net　http://www.filtsoc.com
　　Sec: Prof Richard Wakeman
▲　Registered Charity
Br　8 o'seas
○　*L; filtration, separation & related processes; design,
　　manufacture & use of filtration equipment & processes
●　Conf - Mtgs - ET - Res - Exhib - Lib - VE
M　400 i, UK / 870 i, o'seas
¶　Jnl - 4.

Finance Industry Standards Association
NR　24 Boston Rd, SLEAFORD, Lincs, NG34 7ET.
　　01529 305698　fax 01529 308755
　　http://www.fisa.co.uk
　　Gen Sec: J Harper
○　*T; an advisory body representing lenders & brokers
M　c 270 i & f

Finance & Leasing Association   (FLA)   1992
NR　15-19 Imperial House, Kingsway, LONDON, WC2B 6UN.
　　(hq)
　　020 7836 6511　fax 020 7420 9600
　　email info@fla.org.uk　http://www.fla.org.uk
　　Dir Gen: Stephen Sklaroff
▲　Company Limited by Guarantee
○　*T; to represent companies providing consumer credit, business
　　finance & leasing & motor finance
Gp　Divns: Asset finance & leasing, Consumer finance, Motor
　　finance
●　Conf - Mtgs - ET - Exam - Stat - LG
＜　Eur Fedn of Finance House Assns (EUROFINAS); Eur Fedn Eqpt
　　Leasing Co Assns (LEASEUROPE)
M　100 f, 56 associates
¶　Annual Survey of Business Finance.
　　Code of Practice.　AR; free.
　　Early Settlement Rebate (leaflet).

© CBD Research Ltd · Beckenham · BR3 5JS · Tel 020 8650 7745 · Fax 020 8650 0768 · E-mail cbd@cbdresearch.com · www.cbdresearch.com

Financial Services Ireland   (FSI)   1968
IRL   Confederation House, 84/86 Lower Baggot St, DUBLIN 2,
        Republic of Ireland.
        353 (1) 605 1586   fax 353 (1) 638 1586
        email fsi@ibec.ie   http://www.fsi.ie
        Dir: Brendan Kelly
○   *T
<   IBEC

Fine Art Trade Guild   1910
■   16-18 Empress Place, LONDON, SW6 1TT.   (hq)
        020 7381 6616   fax 020 7381 2596
        email info@fineart.co.uk   http://www.fineart.co.uk
        Managing Dir: Christrose Sumner
▲   Company Limited by Guarantee
○   *T; for the picture trade & fine art publishing
Gp   Art galleries; Suppliers to the fine arts; Picture framers; Picture
        restorers; Fine art printers; Artists
●   Conf - Mtgs - ET - Exam - Exhib - Comp - Expt - Inf - Lib - LG
M   [delete]
¶   Art Business Today (Jnl) - 5; ftm, £25 yr nm.
        The Directory - 1; ftm, £52.50 nm.
        LM (on disk); £141 m only.
        The Artist's Guide to Selling Work; ftm, £9.99 nm.
        Starting up a Gallery & Frame Shop; £14.99 nm.

Fingerprint Society   1974
■   c/o Robert Doak, Humberside Police Fingerprint Bureau, Police
        HQ, HULL, HU5 5SF.   (sb)
        01482 220518   fax 01482 220545
        email robert.doak@humberside.pnn.police.uk
        http://www.fpsociety.org.uk
        Sec: Robert Doak
▲   Un-incorporated Society
○   *P; to advance the study & application of fingerprints & to
        facilitate the co-operation among persons interested in this
        field of personal identification
●   Conf - Mtgs - ET
M   291 i, 10 f, 7 universities, UK / 260 i, o'seas
¶   Fingerprint Whorld - 4; ftm.

Finnish-British Chamber of Commerce   2001
NR   177-179 Hammersmith Rd, LONDON, W6 8BS   (hq)
        020 8741 6352   fax 020 8846 9265
        email admin@fbcc.co.uk   http://www.fbcc.co.uk
        Gen Mgr: Mrs Hely Abbondati
▲   Company Limited by Guarantee
○   *C; to promote & develop trade & other economic relations
        between Finland & Great Britain; to retain direct contacts with
        & express the views of members to both the Finnish & British
        governments
●   Mtgs - Expt - Inf - VE - Junior Chamber of Commerce
M   f

Fire Brigade Society   (FBS)   1963
■   4 Burway Meadow, Alrewas, BURTON upon TRENT, Staffs,
        DE13 7EB.   (gsp)
        http://www.thefirebrigadesociety.co.uk
        Gen Sec: Steve Dodge
Br   14; worldwide
○   *G; 'for people who have an interest in all matters 'fire &
        rescue''
●   Mtgs - Lib - VE
M   800 i, 12 orgs, UK / 100 i, o'seas
¶   Fire Cover - 4; ftm only.

Fire Brigades' Union   (FBU)   1918
■   68 Coombe Rd, KINGSTON upon THAMES, Surrey, KT2 7AE.
        (hq)
        020 8541 1765   fax 020 8546 5187
        Gen Sec: Matt Wrack
○   *U; for all uniformed fire service personnel
M   c 45,605 i

Fire Extinguishing Trades Association
        in 2007 merged with the Association of British Fire Trades, the British
        Fire Protection Systems Association & the Fire Industry Confederation
        to form the   **Fire Industry Association**

**Fire Fighting Vehicles Manufacturers' Association   (FFVMA)
1970**
NR   25 Westfield Rd, GUILDFORD, Surrey, GU1 1RR.   (sec/b)
        01483 506678
        http://www.ffvma.org.uk
○   *T; interests of manufacturers of fire appliances & pumps
M   f

Fire Industry Association   (FIA)   2007
NR   Thames House, 29 Thames St, KINGSTON upon THAMES,
        Surrey, KT1 1PH.   (hq)
        020 8549 5855   fax 020 8547 1564
        email info@fia.uk.com   http://www.fia.uk.com
▲   Company Limited by Guarantee
○   *T; mfrs & specialist distributors of fire extinguishers of all types,
        incl portable fire fighting eqpt & fittings
Gp   Mfrs: Fire extinguisher, Fittings & hose; Servicing companies
●   Conf - Mtgs - ET - Exam - Exhib - Inf - LG - Standards
<   Eur C'ee Mfrs Fire Protection & Safety Eqpt & Fire Fighting
        Vehicles (Europe); Fire Ind Coun; Fire Protection Assn; BSI
M   85 f, UK / 5 f, o'seas
¶   LM; free.
        Guide to the servicing of portable fire extinguishers.
×   2007 (Association of British Fire Trades
        (British Fire Protection Systems Association
        (Fire Extinguishing Trades Association
        (Fire Industry Confederation

Fire Industry Confederation
        in 2007 merged with the Association of British Fire Trades, the British
        Fire Protection Systems Association & the Fire Extinguishing Trades
        Association to form the **Fire Industry Association**

Fire Mark Circle   (FMC)   1934
NR   3 Bow Meadow Cottage, Bow Hill, WATERINGBURY, Kent,
        ME18 5EE.   (chmn/p)
        01622 812643
        http://www.firemarkcircle.com
        Chmn: Mrs Elizabeth Drewe
▲   Un-incorporated Society
○   *G; for persons interested in the origin & history of fire
        insurance companies, their fire marks, fire brigades & all that
        pertains to the past of fire insurance
●   Conf - Mtgs - Res - Inf - Lib - Valuation of collections
<   Fire Mark Circle of America
M   200 i, UK / 2 i, o'seas
¶   FMC News - 2;
        Membership List, Rarity Guide, both 2 yrly; all ftm.

Fire Officers Association   (FOA)   1994
NR   London Rd, MORETON-in-MARSH, Glos, GL56 0RH.   (hq)
        01608 652023
        email foa@fireofficers.org.uk
        http://www.fireofficers.org.uk
        Gen Sec: Graham Setterfield
○   *U; the efficiency & status of the fire service; to maintain the
        conditions of service of its employees
●   LG
M   2,500 i
¶   Magazine - 4; ftm only.

Fire Protection Association   (FPA)   1946
NR   London Rd, MORETON-in-MARSH, Glos, GL56 0RH.   (hq)
　　　01608 812500　fax 01608 812501
　　　email fpa@thefpa.co.uk　http://www.thefpa.co.uk
　　Managing Dir: Jonathan O'Neill
▲　Company Limited by Guarantee
○　*L, *P; the UK's national fire safety organisation, providing
　　authoritative advice, information & training on all aspects of
　　fire safety
●　ET - Res - Exhib - Stat - Inf - Lib - LG
<　Confedn of Fire Protection Assns - Europe (CFPA-Europe)
M　3,500 i, UK / 1,500 f, o'seas
¶　Fire Prevention (Jnl) - 12.
　　Fire Protection Ybk.　Handbooks - 1.
　　Technical publications & CDs on aspects of fire fighting;
　　catalogue available.

Fire & Rescue Suppliers Association   (FIRESA)
NR   Thames House, 29 Thames St, KINGSTON upon THAMES,
　　Surrey, KT1 1PH.
　　　020 8549 5855　fax 020 8547 1564
　　　http://www.firesa.org.uk
　　Sec: D Smith
○　*T

Fire Service Preservation Group   (FSPG)   1968
NR   50 Old Slade Lane, IVER, Bucks, SL0 9DR.　(hsp)
　　　01753 652207
　　　email admin@firespg.freeserve.co.uk
　　　http://www.firespg.freeserve.co.uk
　　Treas: Andrew Scott
▲　Un-incorporated Society
Br　12
○　*G; for those interested in the history of the fire service, the
　　preservation of fire engines & associated equipment.
　　Appliances owned by the group & its members date from
　　1730 to 1987
●　Mtgs
<　Fedn Brit Historic Vehicles Clubs
M　c 600 units, UK / 6 units, o'seas
¶　Off the Run - 12; ftm only.

Fire Sprinkler Association Ltd
　　since March 2007 **Residential Sprinkler Associates**

First Division Association   (FDA)   1918
NR   8 Leake St, LONDON, SE1 7NN.　(hq)
　　　020 7401 5566
　　　email info@fda.org.uk　http://www.fda.org.uk
　　Gen Sec: Jonathan Baume
○　*U; the union of choice for senior managers & professionals in
　　public service
Gp　Association of Revenue & Customs
●　Conf - Mtgs - Res - Empl - LG
M　17,000 i
¶　Public Service Magazine - 6; ftm, £22.95 yr nm.
×　Association of First Division Civil Servants

Fish Veterinary Society
　　a group of the **British Veterinary Association**

Fisheries Society of the British Isles   (FSBI)   1967
NR   Martineau Johnson, 1 Colmore Sq, BIRMINGHAM, B4 6AA.
　　　http://www.fsbi.org.uk
○　to encourage, promote and support all branches of fish biology
　　and fisheries science and conservation

Fishermen's Association Ltd   1995
■　McColl & Associates Ltd, 11 Burns Rd, ABERDEEN,
　　AB15 4NT.　(sb)
　　　01224 313473　fax 01224 310385
　　　email roddy@mccollassociates.com
　　Secs: Roddy McColl (McColl & Associates Ltd)
Br　4
○　*T; a trade protection association for the fishing industry
●　Conf - Mtgs - ET - Inf - LG
<　Shellfish Assn of GB
>　NI Fish Producers Org; Scot Ship Chandlers' Assn; S Devon &
　　Channel Shellfish Fishermen's Assn
M　220 i
¶　FAL NL - 3.　FAL Ybk & Diary - 1.

Fitness Industry Association   (FIA)   1991
NR   Castlewood House, 77-91 New Oxford St, LONDON,
　　WC1A 1PX.　(hq)
　　　020 7420 8560　fax 020 7420 8561
　　　email info@fia.org.uk　http://www.fia.org.uk
　　Chief Exec: Andrée Deane
▲　Company Limited by Guarantee
○　*T; for the health & fitness industry
Gp　Educational establishments; Operators; Sports centres;
　　Suppliers; Students; Individuals
●　Conf - Mtgs - ET - Res - Exhib - Comp - SG - Stat - Expt - Inf -
　　Lib - VE - Empl - LG
<　Intl Health, Racquet & Sportsclubs Assn
M　1,600 clubs
¶　Leisure Management - 12;　Health Club Management - 12;
　　Leisure Opportunities - 24;　CBI - 12;
　　On Track Magazine - 4;　all ftm.

Fitness League   1930
NR   6 Station Parade, SUNNINGDALE, Berks, SL5 0EP.　(hq)
　　　01344 874787
　　　http://www.thefitnessleague.com
▲　Registered Charity
○　*G; the provision of exercise & movement to music classes for
　　all ages & abilities
M　i

Fitness Northern Ireland   1953
NR   The Robinson Centre, Montgomery Rd, BELFAST, BT6 9HS.
　　(hq)
　　　028 9070 4080
　　Chmn: Eileen Boyd
▲　Company Limited by Guarantee
○　*G; exercise for women & men of all ages
M　[not stated]

Fitness Products Association
　　since 2006 **Sporting Goods Industry Association**

Fitness Scotland
　　in 2004 merged with the **Scottish Gymnastics Association**

**Fjord Horse National Stud Book Association of Great Britain
(FHNSAofGB)   1984**
■　Cilyblaidd Manor, Pencarreg, LLANYBYDDER, Carmarthenshire,
　　SA40 9QL.　(hsp/b)
　　　0870 415 5541
　　　email info@fjord-horse.co.uk
　　　http://www.fjord-horse.co.uk
　　Sec: L D Moran
▲　Company Limited by Guarantee
○　*B; to promote, preserve & verify the fjord horse in GB in
　　accordance with the Mother Stud Book in Norway; to act as
　　the official Passport Issuing Authority in the UK
●　Mtgs - Res - Exhib - Stat - Inf
<　Fjordhesteavlen i Danmark; Brit Horse Soc
M　106 i, UK / 24 i, o'seas
¶　Jnl - 1.
×　Fjord Horse Society of GB

Flag Institute   1971
■　38 Hill St, LONDON, W1J 5NS.　(mem/sec/p)
　　email membership@flaginstitute.org
　　http://www.flaginstitute.org
　　Gen Sec: Mike Kearsley
▲　Un-incorporated Society
○　*L; research & publication of information of all types on flags of
　　all countries, periods & kinds - the technical term is
　　vexillology
●　Mtgs - Res - Inf - Lib
<　Fédn Intle des Assns Véxillologiques
M　c 500 i, f & org
¶　Flagmaster - 4; ftm.

Flat Glass Council   (FGC)   1977
■　44-48 Borough High St, LONDON, SE1 1XB.　(hq)
　　0845 257 7957　fax 0870 042 4266
　　email nrees@ggf.org.uk　http://www.ggf.org.uk
　　Nat Sec: Nigel Rees
▲　Company Limited by Guarantee
○　*N; formal liaison with the UK & EEC flat glass manufacturers
　　on behalf of glaziers, merchants & flat glass processors; the
　　Council deals with wage negitiations with unions
●　Mtgs - ET - Stat - Inf - Empl
M　200 f
¶　Code of Practice: Window Installation Safety.
　　Note: The FGC is the employers' organisation in the Glass and
　　Glazing Federation. The Council forms, with the three trade
　　unions concerned (GMBU, AMICUS-AEEU & GPMU) the
　　National Joint Council for the Flat Glass Industry
　　Negotiations are manifest in the NLA & Manual of Training

Flat Glass Manufacturers Association   (FGMA)
■　Prescot Rd, ST HELENS, Merseyside, WA10 3TT.　(sb)
　　01744 28882　fax 01744 692444
　　Sec Gen: Phil Brown
▲　Un-incorporated Society
○　*T; to support & promote interests of flat glass manufacturers in
　　the UK
●　LG
M　1 f

Flat Roofing Alliance   (FRA)   1997
■　Roofing House, 31 Worship St, LONDON, EC2A 2DX.　(hq)
　　020 7448 3857　fax 020 7256 2125
　　email info@fra.org.uk　http://www.fra.org.uk
　　Dir/Co Sec: William A Jenkins
▲　Company Limited by Guarantee
○　*T; for flat roofing contractors & manufacturers; promoting &
　　extending the proper use of reinforced bituminous bitumen
　　membranes; to promote the use of approved contractors
●　Mtgs - ET - Inf - Lib - Empl - LG
<　Construction Products Assn; Nat Specialist Contrs Coun
M　100 f (on completion of a one-year assessment period)
¶　Roofing Hbk(in 31 individual sheets, available separately); ftm,
　　£25 nm.
　　Householders Guide to Flat Roofing; free.

Fleece Washers & Dyers Association   (FWA)   1935
NR　423 Upper Elmers End Rd, BECKENHAM, Kent, BR3 3DA.
　　(mail address)
○　*T
●　Mtgs - Inf - Lib
M　4 f

Flexible Packaging Association
　　since 2007 **Packaging & Industrial Films Association**

Flintshire Historical Society   (FHS)   1911
■　69 Pen-y-Maes Avenue, RHYL, Denbighshire, LL18 4ED.　(hsp)
　　01745 332220
　　Hon Sec: Mrs N P Parker
▲　Registered Charity
○　*L; archaeology & history of Flintshire
●　Mtgs - VE - 6 winter lectures
<　Coun of Brit Archaeology
M　382 i, 34 org, UK / 4 i, 12 org, o'seas
¶　Jnl; £7.50 m, £21 nm.

Floatation Tank Association of the UK & Eire   (FTA)   1988
NR　Floatopia, 97 Devonshire Rd, LONDON, W14 2HU.
　　020 8994 0708
　　http://www.floatationtankassociation.net
▲　Un-incorporated Society
Br　USA
○　*G; to promote & disseminate information on floatation (a
　　method of deep relaxation & stress management) & on
　　accredited public float centres
●　Stat - Inf
M　20 f

Flood Protection Association
NR　10 Cavalry Ride, NORWICH, Norfolk, NR3 1UA.
　　01603 6334400
　　Chmn: Ron Whitehead
○　*T; for manufacturers of flood walls & water barriers, as well as
　　advisers on flood insurance & risk
M　f

Flower Import Trade Association
■　68 First Avenue, Mortlake, LONDON, SW14 8SR.
　　020 8939 6473　fax 020 8878 9983
○　*T
　　no further information supplied

Flowers & Plants Association Ltd   (F&PA)   1984
■　260-277 Flower Market, New Covent Garden Market,
　　LONDON, SW8 5NB.　(hq)
　　020 7738 8044　fax 020 7738 8083
　　email info@flowers.org.uk　http://www.flowers.org.uk
　　Chief Exec: Andrew Caldecourt
▲　Company Limited by Guarantee
○　*H, *T; to promote commercially grown cut flowers &
　　houseplants; to work on behalf of the horticulture industry
●　ET - Res - Exhib - Comp - Stat - Inf - Lib - PL
<　Links with equivalent orgs worldwide
M　c 200 f, UK & o'seas
¶　NL - 4; ftm only.
　　Leaflets & Factsheets - irreg; ftm, (nm please send sae).

Flydressers Guild   1967
■　Woryem, Blackgate Lane, HENFIELD, E Sussex, BN5 9HA.
　　(hsp)
　　01273 493473
　　email woryem@globalnet.co.uk　http://www.the-fdg.org
　　Chmn: A Middleton
▲　Un-incorporated Society
○　*G, *T; 'teaching the art of tying artificial flies for fishing'
●　Mtgs - ET - Exhib - Comp
M　2,200 i, UK / 200 i, o'seas
¶　The Flydresser - 4; ftm, £3 nm.

Flying Farmers Association   (FFA)   1974
NR   Moor Farm, West Heslerton, MALTON, N Yorks, YO17 8RU.
      (hsb)
      01944 738281   fax 01944 738240
      http://www.ffa.org.uk
      Hon Sec: Paul A Stephens
▲   Company Limited by Guarantee
○   *P; to safeguard members' special interests as aircraft, or
      airstrip, owners by representation on the General Aviation
      Safety Council
●   Mtgs - Inf - VE - LG (Civil Aviation Authority) - Insurance
M   c 370 i
¶   NL;   LM;   Map of Members' Airstrips; all m only.

FM Society
      a specialist group of the **Chartered Institute of Building**

FOCAL International Ltd
      alternative name of**Federation of Commercial Audiovisual
      Libraries Ltd**

Folio Society   1947
§   44 Eagle St, LONDON, WC1R 4FS.
      020 7400 4200
      http://www.foliosociety.com
      Run by booklovers for booklovers, creating beautiful editions of
      the world's greatest books.

Folk Music Society of Ireland   1971
IRL   63 Merrion Sq, DUBLIN 2, Republic of Ireland.
      353 (1) 661 9699
      Chmn: Dr Seóirse Bodley
○   *D

FolkArts England
NR   PO Box 296, MATLOCK, Derbys, DE4 3XU.
      01629 827014   fax 01629 821874
      email info@folkarts-england.org
○   *G; music: folk, acoustic, roots & traditional

Folklore of Ireland Society   1926
IRL   UCD School of Irish Celtic Studies, Newman Building, Belfield,
      DUBLIN 4, Republic of Ireland.
      353 (1) 716 8216   fax 353 (1) 716 1144

Folklore Society   1878
■   c/o The Warburg Institute, Woburn Sq, LONDON,
      WC1H 0AB.   (hq)
      020 7862 8564   fax 020 7862 8565
      Sec: Prof James Grayson
○   *L; systematic comparative study of oral traditions & cultures
●   Conf - Mtgs - Res - Exhib - Inf - Lib
M   c 500 i, c 600 org
¶   Folklore - 3.   FLS News - 3; ftm.
      New Books in Folklore - 2.   Current Folklore - 2.

Followers of Rupert   1983
■   29 Mill Rd, LEWES, E Sussex, BN7 2RU.   (hsp)
      01273 480339   fax 01273 480339
      email rupertsecretary@btinternet.com
      http://www.rupertthebear.org.uk
      Hon Sec: John Beck
▲   Un-incorporated Society
Br   5
○   *A, *G; for all interested in the literature concerning Rupert
      Bear, his artists & storytellers
●   Annual meeting
M   1,150 i, UK / 100 i, o'seas
      (Sub: £25 UK / £30 Europe / £35 rest of world)
¶   NL (+ special issues) - 4;   Rupert Calendar - 1; all ftm only.

Folly Fellowship   1988
NR   36 Longfield Drive, Rodley, LEEDS, W Yorks, LS12 1JX.
      (mem/s)
▲   Registered Charity
Br   6; Netherlands
○   *G; preservation, protection, promotion, conservation of follies,
      grottoes & garden buildings
●   Conf - Mtgs - ET - Res - Exhib - Comp - Inf - Lib - PL - VE
<   Fountain Soc
M   c 850 i, f & org, UK / c 250 i, f & org, o'seas
¶   Follies - 4.

Food Additives & Ingredients Association   (FAIA)   1977
■   10 Whitchurch Close, MAIDSTONE, Kent, ME16 8UR.   (exec
      sec/p)
      01622 682119   fax 01622 682119
      email rbr1@btconnect.com   http://www.faia.org.uk
      Exec Sec: Richard Ratcliffe
○   *T; 'to encourage a positive attitude [to food additives], through
      clear understanding of food additives & ingredients among
      identified key audiences including manufacturers, retailers,
      health professionals, regulatory authorities & consumers'
●   Mtgs - Inf (members only) - LG
<   Fedn Eur Food Additives & Food Enzymes Inds (ELC)
M   25 f

Food from Britain Fast Track
      questionnaire returned unopened, marked 'please delete'

Food & Chemical Allergy Association   1976
§   27 Ferringham Lane, Ferring, WORTHING, W Sussex,
      BN12 5NB.   (hs/chmn/p)
      Chmn: Mrs Ellen Rothera
      Support for people with allergy-induced illness. Publishes the
      booklet 'Understanding Allergies'; £2 with A5 sae.

Food Development Association
■   c/o Dewberry Redpoint, Apex House, London Rd, Northfleet,
      GRAVESEND, Kent, DA11 9JA.
      0870 746 6396
      email fda@dewberryredpoint.co.uk
      http://www.fdaonline.co.uk
      no further information supplied

Food & Drink Federation   (FDF)   1973
■   6 Catherine St, LONDON, WC2B 5JJ.   (hq)
      020 7836 2460   fax 020 7836 0580
      http://www.fdf.org.uk
      Dir Gen: Melanie Leech
▲   Company Limited by Guarantee
○   *M, *T; to represent, promote & further the interests of the UK
      food manufacturing industry with government, EEC
      institutions & other decision making bodies
●   Conf - Mtgs - SG - Stat - Lib
<   Confédn des Inds Agro-Alimentaires; CBI
M   150 f, 12 trade associations

© CBD Research Ltd · Beckenham · BR3 5JS · Tel 020 8650 7745 · Fax 020 8650 0768 · E-mail cbd@cbdresearch.com · www.cbdresearch.com

Food & Drink Industry Ireland   1968

IRL Confederation House, 84/86 Lower Baggot St, DUBLIN 2,
     Republc of Ireland.
     353 (1) 605 1500   fax 353 (1) 638 1500
     http://www.fdii.ie
     Dir: Paul Kelly
○   *T; food, drink & non-food grocery manufacturers & suppliers
Gp Associations: Coffee Industry, Dairy Industries, Margarine, Pig
     Meat, Soap, Soup, Spirits, Tea
     Committees: Infant nutrition
     Councils: Biscuit industry, Chocolate, confectionery & biscuit,
     Technical
     Groups: Consumer complaints, Jams & jellies & marmalade,
     Sugar users,
     Advisory Committee on the Marketing of Infant Formula
     Efficient Consumer Response Ireland; Federation of Irish
     Renderers; Food Ingredient Suppliers of Ireland; HR Circle;
     Irish Cold Storage Federation; Irish Forest Industry Chain;
     Meat Industry Ireland
<   IBEC

Food Ingredient Suppliers of Ireland
   a group of **Food & Drink Industry Ireland**

Food Processors Association   (FPA)   2001

NR 6 Catherine St, LONDON, WC2B 5JJ.   (hq)
     020 7420 7106   fax 020 7836 0580
     email john.lepley@fdf.org.uk   http://www.fdf.org.uk
     Exec Sec: John Lepley
○   *N, *T; to represent members' common interests & issues,
     particularly contaminants, labelling & the environment
Gp Desserts & Cake Mixes Association
     Pickles & Sauces Association
     Soup, Gravy & Produce Processors Association
     UK Sweet Spreads Association

Food Processors & Suppliers Group
   a group of **Food & Drink Industry Ireland**

Food Storage & Distribution Federation   (FSDF)   1911

■   7 Diddenham Court, Lamb Wood Hill, Grazeley, READING,
     Berks, RG7 1JS.   (hq)
     0118-988 4468   fax 0118-988 7035
     email info@fsdf.org.uk   http://www.fsdf.org.uk
     Chief Exec: John Hutchings
▲   Company Limited by Guarantee
○   *T; represents & covers all aspects of food storage & distribution
     in the UK; it includes frozen, chilled & ambient sectors
●   Conf - Inf - LG
M   150 f
¶   NL - 4; free.   Information Broadsheet - 12; ftm only.
     Guide/Directory - 2 yrly; ftm, £35 nm.
     RFIC Fire Prevention Guide; ftm, £43 nm.
     RFIC Storage & Handling of Frozen Foods; ftm, £12 nm.
     RFIC Guidance on the Assessment of Fire Risk; ftm, £17 nm.
     CSDF Material Handling Safety Guide; ftm, £50 nm.
     CSDF Fire Risk Minimisation Guidance; ftm, £75 nm.
     CSDF Business Continuity Guide; ftm, £50 nm.
✕   2008 (March) Cold Storage & Distribution Federation

Foodservice Consultants Society International (UK)   (FCSI (UK))

■   Bourne House, Horsell Park, WOKING, Surrey, GU21 4LY.
     01483 761122   fax 01483 750991
     email admin@fcsi.org.uk   http://www.fcsi.org.uk
     Chmn: Richard Wedgbury
▲   Un-incorporated Society
○   *P; 'to promote professionalism in foodservice & hospitality
     consulting while returning maximum benefits to all members'
●   Conf - Mtgs - ET - Exam - Exhib - Comp - VE
M   136 i

Foodservice Packaging Association   (FPA)   1969

NR The Old Rectory, Bletchingdon, KIDLINGTON, Oxon, OX5
     3DH.   (hq)
     01869 351139   fax 01869 350231
     email admin@foodservicepackaging.org.uk
     Contact: Martin Kersh
▲   Un-incorporated Society
○   *T; to promote both the concept & the marketing of disposables
     manufactured in the UK for use in industry, public service &
     the home
Gp Technical c'ees
●   Mtgs - Exhib - Inf
M   60 f
¶   NL - 3/4;
     Booklets on: Drinking vessels, Napkins, Plates & bowls;
     Serviettes; Straws; all free.

Football Association of Ireland   (FAI)

IRL National Sports Campus, Abbotstown, DUBLIN 15, Republic of
     Ireland.
     353 (1) 899 9500   fax 353 (1) 899 9501
     http://www.fai.ie
     Chief Exec: John Delaney
○   *S

Football Association Ltd   (FA)   1863

NR 25 Soho Sq, LONDON, W1D 4FA.   (hq)
     020 7745 4545   fax 020 7745 5545
     email info@thefa.com   http://www.thefa.com
     Chief Exec: Brian Barwick
▲   Company Limited by Guarantee
○   *S; the governing body for English football; to promote, control,
     organise & administer Association Football in England
●   Conf - Exam - Comp - Stat - PL - LG
<   U des Assns Eur de Football (UEFA); Fédn Intle de Football
     Assns (FIFA)
>   County Football Assns; Football Clubs
M   30 org
¶   The FA Ybk - 1. The FA Hbk - 1.
     The FA Annual Review; free.

Football Association of Wales Ltd   (FA of Wales)   1876

NR 11-12 Neptune Court, Vanguard Way, CARDIFF, CF24 5PJ.
     (hq)
     029 2043 5830   fax 029 2049 6953
     email dcollins@faw.co.uk   http://www.faw.org.uk
     Sec Gen: David Collins
○   *S; administration of Association Football in Wales

Football League Ltd   1888

NR Edward VII Quay, Navigation Way, PRESTON, Lancs, PR2 2YF.
     (hq)
     0870 442 0 1888   fax 0870 442 1188
     email fl@football-league.co.uk
     http://www.football-league.co.uk
     Chmn: Sir Brian Mawhinney
▲   Company Limited by Guarantee
Br   2
○   *S
M   72 clubs
¶   NL - weekly during season.   Hbk - 1; ftm, £13.50 nm.
     Fixture Booklet - 1; ftm, £4.50 nm.

Football Supporters' Federation (FSF) 2002
NR The Fans' Stadium - Kingsmeadow, Jack Goodchild Way,
422A Kingston Rd, KINGSTON upon THAMES, Surrey,
KT1 3PB. (sb)
0870 277 7777
http://www.fsf.org.uk
Sec: Mike Williamson
▲ Un-incorporated Society
Br England national; Welsh national
○ *S; representing to the Government & football authorities the
views & concerns of football supporters at all levels of the
game; information interchange between member clubs on
best practice & crisis management
Gp Insurance scheme offered for personal accident & late
cancellation of matches
● Conf - Mtgs - Res - Exhib - LG
> Nat Assn of Disabled Supporters; The Football Programme
Directory
M 110,000 in 120 supporters clubs UK / 75 i, o'seas
¶ FSF News - 4.   .
FSF Members NL - 4.
× 2002 (Football Supporters Association
(National Federation of Football Supporters' Clubs

Football Writers' Association
NR c/o Paul Hetherington, Daily Star, The Northern & Shell Building,
10 Lower Thames St, LONDON, EC3R 6EN.
http://www.footballwriters.co.uk
Chmn: Paul Hetherington
○ *P

Forecourt Equipment Federation (FEF) 1969
■ PO Box 35084, LONDON, NW1 4XE. (asa)
020 7935 8532   fax 07006 065950
email office@fef.org.uk   http://www.fef.org.uk
Sec: C Dunn-Meynell
○ *T; includes liaising with government departments on safety,
weights & measures legislation & regulation
● Mtgs - Res - Inf - LG
M 11 f

Foreign Bird Federation 1933
NR 4 St Andrews Drive, Tividale, OLDBURY, W Midlands,
B69 1PR. (sec/p)
01384 258154
http://www.foreignbirdfederation.co.uk
Sec: Bryan Reed
○ *G; for keepers of foreign birds
Gp Foreign Bird League
● Mtgs - Exhib - Comp - VE
M i
(Sub: £12).
¶ Foreign Birds - 4; ftm.

Foreign Bird League
see **Foreign Bird League**

Foreign Press Association in London (FPA) 1888
■ 11 Carlton House Terrace, LONDON, SW1Y 5AJ. (hq)
020 7930 0445   fax 020 7925 0469
email secretariat@foreign-press.org.uk
http://www.foreign-press.org.uk
Dir: Christopher Wyld
▲ Un-incorporated Society
○ *P; to assist foreign correspondents based in the UK in their
work by arranging briefings, visits etc
● Mtgs - ET - VE - LG
M 200 i, UK / 500 i, o'seas

Forensic Science Society (FSSoc) 1959
■ Clarke House, 18a Mount Parade, HARROGATE, N Yorks,
HG1 1BX. (hq)
01423 506068   fax 01423 566391
email president@forensic-science-society.co.uk
http://www.forensic-science-society.co.uk
Hon Sec: Shirley Marshall
▲ Registered Charity
○ *L; to advance the study, application & standing of forensic
science
● Conf - Mtgs - ET - Exam - Inf
< California Assn of Criminalists
M 1,750 i, 83 f, UK / 405 i, 13 f, o'seas
¶ Science & Justice - 4;   Interfaces - 4; ftm.

**Foresight, the Association for the Promotion of Preconceptual
Care 1978**
NR 178 Hawthorn Rd, BOGNOR REGIS, W Sussex, PO21 2UY.
(hq)
01243 868001   fax 01243 868180
http://www.foresight-preconception.org.uk
Founder & Dir: Mrs Belinda Barnes,   Sec: Julia Martin
▲ Registered Charity
Br 32; 12 o'seas
○ *W; promotion &/or execution of preconceptual care to
overcome infertility, miscarriage, perinatal death, prematurity,
low birth weight, malformation &/or compromised health in
mother or baby
● Conf - Mtgs - ET - Res - Exhib - SG - Stat - Inf - Lib - LG
M c 2,500 i, UK / c 250 i, o'seas
¶ NL - 3; ftm only.

Forestry Contracting Association Membership Ltd
styles itself **FCA Membership Ltd**

Forestry & Timber Association
was the trading name of the Association of Timber Growers &
Forestry Professionals which in 2006 became the **Confederation of
Forest Industries (ConFor)**

Fork Lift Truck Association (FLTA) 1972
■ Manor Farm Buildings, Lasham, ALTON, Hants, GU34 5SL.
(hq)
01256 381441   fax 01256 381735
email mail@fork-truck.org.uk
http://www.fork-truck.org.uk
Chief Exec: David Ellison
▲ Company Limited by Guarantee
○ *T; to promote the industry for customers, dealers,
manufacturers & suppliers; to raise standards of education,
training & health & safety; to provide advice & guidance on
operational & related matters
● Conf - Mtgs - ET - Exhib - Inf - VE - LG
< Consolidated Fork Truck Services (CFTS); Fork Lift Apprentices
Trust (FLAT)
M 380 f, UK / 10, o'seas
(Sub: varies)
¶ Uplift (NL) - 4; free.
Manuals on:
Health & Safety; Legislationn & Registration;
Personal Policies & Procedures; Technical Bulletins.
List of publications available + CDs & DVDs & other items.

Formula Air Racing Association (FARA) 1972
■ c/o Chadwick International, 137 High Holborn, LONDON,
WC1V 6PW. (hsb)
020 7269 0920   fax 020 7269 0929
email chadwick@chadwick-international.com
Contact: Andrew Chadwick
▲ Company Limited by Guarantee
○ *S; promotion & management of formula air racing in the UK
● Comp - LG - Races in UK & Europe
< FGédn Aeronautique Intle (PAKIS); R Aero Club, London
M 6 i

© CBD Research Ltd · Beckenham · BR3 5JS · Tel 020 8650 7745 · Fax 020 8650 0768 · E-mail cbd@cbdresearch.com · www.cbdresearch.com

Fort Cumberland & Portsmouth Militaria Society (FC&PMS) 1964

■ 5 Herne Rd, Cosham, PORTSMOUTH, Hants, PO6 3PB. (hsp)
  023 9242 3649
  Sec: Allan Dickenson
▲ Registered Charity
○ *G; preservation of historical buildings; popularising local
  military history; maintaining Fort Cumberland Guard: display
  group re-enacting drill of 1830-40 & 1860 Royal Marines
  incl musket & cannon firing & drum corps drill
Gp Fort Cumberland Guard
● Mtgs - ET - Res - Exhib - Inf - Lib - PL - VE
< UK Fortifications Club
M 40 i, 2 f

Fort William & District Chamber of Commerce

NR Lochaber College, An Aird, FORT WILLIAM, PH33 7AN.
  01397 874487
  email info@hubnuts.co.uk
  http://www.fortwilliam-choc.co.uk
  Sec: Lindsey Wade
○ *C

Fortress Study Group (FSG) 1975

■ 6 Lanark Place, LONDON, W9 1BS. (hsp)
  020 7286 5512
  Hon Sec: W H Clements
▲ Registered Charity
○ *G, *L; the study of fortification since the introduction of artillery
● Conf - Res - SG - Inf - Lib
< Intl Fortress Coun
M c 750 i, 50 f
¶ Fort (Jnl) - 1; Casemate (NL) - 3; both ftm only.

Forty Plus (40+) Fishing Boat Association 1995

NR Hillcrest, 63 Birch Hill Crescent, ONCHAN, Isle of Man,
  IM3 3DA. (founder/p)
  01624 627568
  email mike@mcb.net http://www.homepages.mcb.net/
  40fba
  20 Briavels Grove, Ashley Hill, BRISTOL, BS6 5JJ.
  0797 124 4943.
  Co-Founders: Michael Craine, Mike Smylie
○ *G; to encourage research into the historical & social elements
  of fishing boats; to represent their owners; to encourage
  liaison between boat owners, museums, heritage centres,
  trusts, businesses & other organisations in the promotion of
  the importance of our islands' fishing boat heritage
● Res - Exhib - Stat - Inf - PL - LG - Compiling register of all boats
  over 40 years old
M 520 i, 50 f, 20 org, UK / 10 i, o'seas
¶ Fishing Boats (NL) - 3; £10 m, £15 nm.

Forum of Private Business (FPB) 1977

■ Ruskin Chambers, Drury Lane, KNUTSFORD, Cheshire,
  WA16 6HA. (hq)
  01565 634467 fax 0870 241 9570
  email info@fpb.org http://www.fpb.org
  Chief Exec: Philip Orford
▲ Company Limited by Guarantee
Br 2
○ *K; business support organisation, working with small &
  medium-sized privately-owned businesses
Gp Members helpline; Legal expenses insurance; 24-hour legal
  helpline; Telecoms; Card processing; Business insurance;
  Utilities; Invoice finance; Asset finance; Non-core purchasing;
  D+O insurance; Payroll; Business monitoring
● Conf - Res - Exhib - Stat - Inf - LG
< Eur Assn of Small & Medium-sized Enterprises (UEAPME)
> Brit Cheque Cashers Assn; Garden Centre Assn; Health Food
  Mfrs' Assn; Nat Soc Allied & Indep Funeral Dirs; etc
M 600,000 i, 25,000 f, 21 org
¶ eNewsletter - 52. Referendum [NL] - 4. AR - 1; all ftm.
  Employmenr Guide - 1; £185 m, £415 nm.
  Health & Safety Guide - 1; £105 m, £205 nm.
  Costs, Controls & Profit (guide); £95 m, £155 nm.

Fostering Network 1974

NR 87 Blackfriars Rd, LONDON, SE1 8HA. (hq)
  020 7620 6400 fax 020 7620 6401
  email info@fostering.net http://www.fostering.net
  Chief Exec: Robert Tapsfield
▲ Registered Charity
Br 46 local groups
○ *W; to improve the quality of service given to children in care;
  to bring together representatives of organisations &
  authorities concerned with fostering
Gp Assessment of foster carers; Relatives & friends as foster carers
● Conf - Mtgs - ET - Res - SG - Stat - Inf - Lib - LG - Advice &
  mediation service
M 21,500 i, 213 local authorities, 145 org
¶ Foster Care - 4. AR.
  Publication & resources catalogue available.
✕ 2001 National Foster Care Association

Foundation & Aided Schools National Association (FASNA) 1992

■ 11 The Orchard, Blackheath, LONDON, SE3 0QS. (hsp)
  020 8318 0872
  email fasna@fasna.org.UK http://www.fasna.org.uk
  Gen Sec: George Phipson
▲ Company Limited by Guarantee; Registered Charity
○ *E, *P; to provide educational & professional support for
  headteachers & governors of foundation & voluntary aided
  schools
● Conf - ET
M 800 schools
¶ NL - 3; ftm only.

Forum for Clothing & Textiles
  alternative name of **ASBCI**

Foundation for the Built Environment
  since 2005 the **BRE Trust**

Foundation for the Study of Infant Deaths   (FSID)   1971
- ■ Artillery House, 11-19 Artillery Row, LONDON, SW1P 1RT. (hq)
     020 7222 8001   fax 020 7222 8002
     email office@fsid.org.uk   http://www.fsid.org.uk
     Chief Exec: Joyce Epstein
- ▲ Registered Charity
- Br 8 regional devt offices
- ○ *K, *M, *Q; to raise funds for research into the causes & prevention of cot death; to support bereaved parents; to disseminate information about cot death & infant care
- ● Conf - Res - SG - Stat - Inf - LG
     Helpline: 020 7233 2090 (Mon-Fri 0900-2300; Sat-Sun 1800-2300)
- < Assn of Med Res Charities (AMRC)
- > SIDS Intl; Eur Soc for Preventing Infant Death (ESPID)
- M 12,000 i on mailing list
- ¶ FSID (NL) - 1; free.
     Various information books & leaflets; see website.
- × 2004 Cot Death Society (absorbed)

Foundry Equipment & Supplies Association Ltd   (FESA)   1925
- ■ National Metalforming Centre, 47 Birmingham Rd, WEST BROMWICH, W Midlands, B70 6PY.   (hsb)
     email secretary@fesa.org.uk   http://www.fesa.org.uk
     Sec: Andrew Turner
- ▲ Company Limited by Guarantee
- ○ *T
- ● Conf - Exhib - Expt
- < Comité Européen des Matériels et Produits pour la Fonderie (CEMAFON)
- M 28 f

Fountain Society   1986
- ■ High House, BUCKNELL, Shropshire, SY7 0AA.   (hsp)
     01547 530750
     email fs-secretary@fountainsoc.org.uk
     http://www.fountainsoc.org.uk
     Hon Sec: Ian Hay-Campbell
- ▲ Registered Charity
- ○ *K; to promote the provision, conservation & restoration of fountains, cascades & water features in both the public & private sector
- ● Conf - Mtgs - Res - Comp - VE
- M 290 i, 10 f, 12 org, UK / 12 i, o'seas
- ¶ NL - 4;   Bibliography - 3 yrly; both ftm only.
     Creating a Fountain - 2 yrly; ftm, £3 nm.   AR; free.

Fragile X Society   1990
- ■ Rood End House, 6 Stortford Road, GREAT DUNMOW, Essex, CM6 1DA.   (hq)
     01371 875100
     email info@fragilex.org.uk   http://www.fragilex.org.uk
     Dir: Amanda Cherry
- ▲ Registered Charity
- ○ *W; to provide support & information to families affected by Fragile X syndrome; to raise awareness & assist & encourage research
- ● Conf - Inf
- M 1,490 families, 155 associates, UK / 100 families, o'seas
     Subs: associates, £15 / families £30, o'seas
- ¶ NL - 3;   AR; free.
     Various publications.

Francis Bacon Society Inc   1886
- ■ Flat 1 Lee House, 75A Effra Rd, LONDON, SW19 8PS.   (hsp)
     http://www.baconsocietyinc.org
     Hon Sec: Gerald Salway
- ▲ Company Limited by Guarantee; Registered Charity
- ○ *L; to promote the study of the works of Francis Bacon, (Baron Verulam of Verulam) 1561-1626, as a philosopher, statesman & poet; to examine evidence of his authorship of the plays ascribed to Shakespeare; to investigate his connection with other works of the Elizabethan period
- ● Mtgs - Res - Lib
- M 90 i, UK / 50 i, o'seas
- ¶ Baconiana (Jnl) - irreg; on website.

Francis Brett Young Society   (FBY Soc)   1979
- ■ 92 Gower Road, HALESOWEN, W Midlands, B62 9BT.   (hsp)
     0121-422 8969
     http://www.fbysociety.co.uk
     Hon Sec: Mrs J Hadley
- ▲ Registered Charity
- ○ *A; to collate research done on the life & work of Francis Brett Young; to promote his works, & the work of promising writers born in Halesowen
- ● Mtgs - ET - Res - Inf - VE - Speakers on Brett Young provided on request
- < Alliance Literary Socs
- M 189 i, 8 org, 6 org, UK / 10 i, o'seas
- ¶ Jnl - 2; ftm.

Franco-British Chamber of Commerce & Industry   (FBCCI)   1872
- NR 31 rue Boissy d'anglas, F-75008 PARIS, France.
     33 (1) 53 30 81 30   fax 33 (1) 53 30 81 35
     email information@francobritishchamber.com
     http://www.francobritishchamber.com
     Catherine Le Yaouanc
- ○ *C; 'to assist companies to promote & develop their activities from both sides of the channel'
- ● Conf - Mtgs - ET - Exam - Res - Expt - Inf - Lib - LG
- < Coun Brit Chams Comm Continental Europe (COBCOE)
- M 750 f
- ¶ NL - 3; ftm only.

Franco-British Society   1944
- NR 2 Dovedale Studios, 465 Battersea Park Rd, LONDON, SW11 4LR.   (hq)
     020 7924 3511   fax 020 7924 3511
     email execsec@francobritishsociety.org.uk
     http://www.francobritishsociety.org.uk
     Chmn: The Rt Hon The Baroness Shepherd of Northwold
- ▲ Company Limited by Guarantee; Registered Charity
- ○ *X; an educational charity for the encouragement of British understanding of French artistic, scientific, social & economic achievements, through travel, personal contacts & meetings
- M i

Franco-Scottish Society of Scotland   (FSSS)   1895
- ■ 127 Dundee Rd, Broughty Ferry, DUNDEE, DD5 1DU.   (hsp)
     01382 775022
     http://www.franco-scottish.org.uk
     Hon Sec: Françoise Pérombelon
- ▲ Registered Charity
- Br 7; Canada, France
- ○ *X; promotion of knowledge of all matters of Franco-Scottish interest & of Franco-Scottish friendship & understanding through cultural, educational & social activities & personal contacts
- ● Mtgs - ET - Comp - VE
- < Assn Franco-Ecossaise (France); Franco-Scottish Soc (Canada)
- M c 300 i, UK / c 200 i, o'seas
     (Sub: £18-£20)
- ¶ Bulletin - 1; ftm.

© CBD Research Ltd · Beckenham · BR3 5JS · Tel 020 8650 7745 · Fax 020 8650 0768 · E-mail cbd@cbdresearch.com · www.cbdresearch.com

Free Trade League   (FTL)   1905
- 1 Fern Dene, Templewood, LONDON, W13 8AN.   (hsp)
  020 8997 6868
  email john.heffernan@virgin.net
  http://www.freetradeleague.org.uk
  Hon Sec: John Heffernan
- ▲ Un-incorporated Society
- ○ *K; 'to promote the economic & political case for unilateral UK trade policy of dismantling protection'
- ● Mtgs - VE
- M i, f & org
- ¶ The Free Trader - 1.

Freedom Association Ltd   (TFA)   1975
- PO Box 3394, FARINGDON, Oxon, SN7 7FN.   (hq)
  0845 833 9626
  email mail@tfa.net   http://www.tfa.net
  Office Mgr: Mrs Vicki Stevens
- ▲ Company Limited by Guarantee
- ○ *K, 'a political pressure group campaigning for individual freedom & national independence'
- ● Conf - Mtgs - Political lobbying
- M 4,000 i, UK / 1,000 i, o'seas
- ¶ Freedom Today (Jnl) - 6; ftm, £3 nm.

Freedom Organisation for the Right to Enjoy Smoking Tobacco (FOREST)   1981
- NR Sheraton House, Castle Park, CAMBRIDGE, CB3 0AX.   (hq)
  01223 370156
  email contact@forestonline.org
  http://www.forestonline.org
  Dir: Simon Clark
- ▲ Company Limited by Guarantee
- ○ *K; to promote equal rights for smokers
- ● Res - Inf - LG - Media lobbying
- M i, uk & o'seas
- ¶ Various research papers & information sheets.

Freelance Hair & Beauty Federation Ltd   (FHBF Ltd)   1993
- The Business Centre, Kimpton Rd, LUTON, Beds, LU2 0LB.   (hq)
  01582 431783
  email enquiries@fhbf.org.uk   http://www.fhbf.org.uk
  Dir: Sheila Abrahams
- ○ *T
- ● Conf - ET - Inf
- M [not disclosed]
- ¶ Highlights (NL) - 4; ftm only.

Freemen of England & Wales   (FEW)   1964
- Richmond House, Beech Close, Oversley Green, ALCESTER, Warks, B49 6PP.   (hsp)
  01789 762574
  Hon Sec: R E Leek
- ▲ Registered Charity
- ○ *N; interests of the freemen of the cities & boroughs of England & Wales; to advance the knowledge of the history & legal custom of the boroughs & the legal institution of freedom
- Gp Freemen's Guilds; Groups of freemen of towns & cities in England & Wales
- ● Mtgs - ET - Res - LG
- M 425 i, 41 guilds
- ¶ Freemen of England & Wales (NL) - 4; ftm only.

Freemen & Guilds of the City of Chester
- NR The Guildhall, Watergate St, CHESTER, CH1 2LA.   (hq)
  01244 320431
- ▲ Un-incorporated Society
- ○ *N; founded in the 14th century the guild upholds & promotes the history of the individual craft companies; to support the Lord Mayor & Chester Council by participating in their civic & cultural duties
- M i

Freight Transport Association   (FTA)   1889
- Hermes House, St John's Rd, TUNBRIDGE WELLS, Kent, TN4 9UZ.   (hq)
  01892 526171   fax 01892 534989
  email enquiries@fta.co.uk   http://www.fta.co.uk
  Chief Exec: Theo de Pencier
- ▲ Company Limited by Guarantee
- Br 5; Brussels (Belgium)
- ○ *T; interests of companies in the transport industry
- Gp British Shippers Council; Utilities Group
- ● Conf - Mtgs - ET - Res - Exhib - Stat - Inf - VE - LG - Support services
- < Intl Road Transport U (IRU)
- M 14,000 f
- ¶ Freight - 12; ftm, £25 yr nm.   Ybk - 1; ftm, £34 nm.
  International Manual - 1; ftm, £60 nm.

French Chamber of Commerce in Great Britain
  English name of **Chambre de Commerce Française de Grande-Bretagne**

Fresh Produce Consortium (UK)   (FPC)   1993
- NR Minerva House, Minerva Business Park, Lynch Wood, PETERBOROUGH, Cambs, PE2 6FT.   (hq)
  01733 237117   fax 01733 237118
  email info@freshproduce.org.uk
  http://www.freshproduce.org.uk
  Chief Exec: Nigel R Jenney
- ▲ Company Limited by Guarantee
- ○ *T; to develop the competitive performance of the produce & floral industries of the UK
- Gp Divisions: Importers, Wholesale, Floral, Technical, Business services, Retail, Freshfel, Growers & potato packers
- ● Conf - Mtgs - ET - Res - Exhib - VE - LG - Promotion of consumption of fresh produce through education in schools & the wider community
- < Freshfel Europe; Produce Marketing Assn (USA)
- M 1,000 f
- ¶ Hbk - 1.

Freshwater Biological Association   (FBA)   1929
- The Ferry House, Far Sawrey, AMBLESIDE, Cumbria, LA22 0LP.   (hq)
  01539 442468   fax 01539 446914
  email info@fba.org.uk   http://www.fba.org.uk
  Dir: Dr Michael Dobson
- ▲ Company Limited by Guarantee; Registered Charity
- Br 2
- ○ *L, *Q; to advance freshwater science & encourage as many people as possible to adopt it as the best way to understand, protect & manage our precious water resources
- Gp Cooperative Research Partnership; FBA NE regional group
- ● Conf - ET - Res - Inf - Lib
- < Eur Fedn of Freshwater Science (EFFS); Inst of Biology
- M 1,550 i & f
  (Sub: £30 students, £35 i, £300 f)
- ¶ Freshwater Reviews (Jnl) - 2; free online, £22 print m, £40 online, £65 online & print nm.
  Scientific & Special Publications - irreg.
  Publications list available.

Friedreichs Ataxia Society of Ireland
- IRL San Martino, Mart Lane, Foxrock, DUBLIN 18, Republic of Ireland.
  353 (1) 289 4788   fax 353 (1) 289 8845
  email ataxia@eircom.net   http://www.ataxia.ie
- ○ *W

Friends of Alan Rawsthorne   1989

■   30 Florida Avenue, Hartford, HUNTINGDON, Cambs,
      PE29 1PY.   (sp)
      01480 456931
      email apkmusicprom@ntlworld.com
      http://www.musicweb-international.com/rawsth/
      Sec: Andrew P Knowles
▲   Un-incorporated Society
○   *D; promotion of music by Alan Rawsthorne, British composer
      1905-1971
●   Mtgs - Inf - Lib - Concerts
M   70 i, 5 org
¶   The Creel (Jnl) - 1.   The Sprat (NL) - irreg.

** **Friends of Alfred Williams**
      Organisation lost; see Introduction paragraph 3.

Friends of Arthur Machen   1986

NR   Stable Cottage, Priest Bank Rd, Kildwick, KEIGHLEY, N Yorks,
      BD20 9BH.   (hsp)
      http://www.machensoc.demon.co.uk
▲   Company Limited by Guarantee; Registered Charity
○   *A; to honour the life & work of writer Arthur Machen (1863-
      1947); to support research students, publishers, writers etc
      interested in Machen's work
M   i, libraries & universities

Friends of Blue   (FOB)   1973

■   PO Box 122, DIDCOT D O, Oxon, OX11 0YN.   (hsp)
      01235 816266
      http://www.fob.org.uk
      Sec: Arthur C Roberts
▲   Un-incorporated Society
○   *G; to promote study & interest of ceramics with under-glaze
      blue decoration, made by transfer print, a technique
      developed in Britain during the last two decades of the
      eighteenth century
●   Res
M   407 i, UK / 53 i, o'seas
¶   Bulletin - 4; ftm only.
      True Blue (1998); £9.50 m, £11.50 nm.

Friends of Cathedral Music   (FCM)   1956

■   27 Old Gloucester St, LONDON, WC1N 3XX.   (hq)
      email info@fcm.org.uk   http://www.fcm.org.uk
      Hon Sec: Roger Bishton
▲   Registered Charity
○   *D, *R; to safeguard the heritage of cathedral music; to
      increase public knowledge & appreciation of cathedral
      music; to encourage high standards in choral & organ music
●   Mtgs - Exhib - Inf - Awards of grants to cathedral authorities to
      assist in maintaining choral services
M   2,700 i, 30 org, UK / 300 i, o'seas
¶   Cathedral Music Singing in Cathedrals: a listing of choral
      services in the UK - 2; ftm, £3.50 nm.

Friends of Classics   (FoC)

■   51 Achilles Rd, LONDON, NW6 1DZ.
      020 7431 5088   fax 020 7431 5129
      email classics@friends-classics.demon.co.uk
      http://www.friends-classics.demon.co.uk
      Exec Sec: Jeannie Cohen
○   *G

Friends of Coleridge   1986

■   11 Castle St, NETHER STOWEY, Somerset, TA5 1LN.   (hsp)
      01278 733338
      http://www.friendsofcoleridge.com
      87 Richmond Rd, Montpelier, BRISTOL, BS6 5EP.
         0117-942 6366.   (conf organiser)
      Hon Sec: Mrs Shirley M Watters
      Conf Org: Graham Davidson
▲   Registered Charity
Br   Canada, USA (Mems worldwide)
○   *A, *L; to promote the work of Samuel Taylor Coleridge (1772-
      1834); to support Coleridge Cottage with the National Trust
●   Conf - Mtgs - SG - VE
M   250 i, 3 org, UK / 65 i, 2 org, o'seas
¶   The Coleridge Bulletin - 2; ftm.
      Conference brochure - 2 yrly (even yrs); free.

Friends of Dr Watson   (FDW)   1996

NR   13 Crofton Avenue, ORPINGTON, Kent, BR6 8DU.   (mem/sec)
      Mem Sec: R J Ellis
Br   Belgium
○   *G; to promote interest in the life, times & work of Dr John H
      Watson MD (from the Sherlock Holmes stories by Arthur
      Conan Doyle) & the society of the period; to study the
      medical aspects of Conan Doyle's work
●   Res - Comp - Inf - VE - Annual dinner - Maiwand luncheon - Dr
      Watson Day
<   Franco-Midland Hardware Co (an international Sherlock
      Holmes study group)
M   33 i, 2 f, UK / 19 i, 1 f, o'seas
¶   The Formulary (Jnl) - 2; £4 (US$8) m, £6 (US$12) nm.
      Watson's Wanderings; £4 (US$8) m, £6 (US$12) nm.
      Watson's Wanderings Again; £4 (US$8) m, £6 (US$12) nm.
      The London Practice; £4 (US$8) m, £6 (US$12) nm.
      The Maiwand Luncheon Monograph;   Watson's Weapons;
      The Maiwand Dispatch No 1;   From Netley to Maiwand;
         all £5 m (US$10), £7 nm (US$14).
      5th Birthday Annual; ftm, £5 nm (US$10).   AR; free.

Friends of the Dymock Poets   (FDP)   1993

NR   122 Preston New Rd, BLACKBURN, Lancs, BB2 6BU.
      (mem/s/p)
      01531 634796
      email jeff@jeffcooper.me.uk
      http://www.dymockpoets.co.uk
      Mem Sec: Jeff Cooper
○   *A; to foster an interest in the group of poets associated with
      the Dymock area in Gloucestershire before the First World
      War (Lascelles Abercrombie, Rupert Brooke, John Drinkwater,
      Robert Frost, Wilfrid Gibson & Edward Thomas)
●   Conf - Mtgs
<   Alliance of Literary Socs
M   325 i, UK / 25 i, o'seas
¶   NL - irreg;   Dymock Poets & Friends - 1; both ftm only.

Friends of the Earth   (FOE)   1971

■   26-28 Underwood St, LONDON, N1 7JQ.   (hq)
      020 7490 1555   fax 020 7490 0881
      email info@foe.co.uk   http://www.foe.co.uk
      Exec Dir: Andy Atkins
▲   Company Limited by Guarantee; Registered Charity
Br   12
○   *K; environmental issues
●   ET - Res - Stat - Inf - PL
<   Friends of the Earth Intl
M   c 100,000 i
¶   Earth Matters - 3; Friend - 3; both ftm only.
      Publications list available.

© CBD Research Ltd · Beckenham · BR3 5JS · Tel 020 8650 7745 · Fax 020 8650 0768 · E-mail cbd@cbdresearch.com · www.cbdresearch.com

Friends of Friendless Churches   1957
■   St Ann's Vestry Hall, 2 Church Entry, LONDON, EC4V 5HB.
    (hsb)
    020 7236 3934
    email office@ancientmonumentssociety.org.uk
    http://www.friendsoffriendlesschurches.org.uk
    Chmn: Roger Evans,   Hon Dir: Matthew Saunders
▲   Registered Charity
○   *K; the ownership of 38 disused but architecturally important
    places of worship
●   Inf
<   Ancient Monuments Soc (working partnership)
M   2,000 i
¶   AR;   Appeals.

Friends Historical Society   (FHS)   1903
NR   c/o The Quakers Library, 173-177 Euston Rd, LONDON,
    NW1 2BJ.   (hsb)
    http://www.quaker.org.uk
    Clerk, Treas & Mem Sec: Brian Hawkins
▲   Un-incorporated Society
○   *L; history of the Quakers
●   Conf - Mtgs
¶   Jnl - 1; ftm, £6 nm.   NL - 2; ftm only.
    Meeting Houses in Britain (1999); David Butler.

Friends of the Lake District   (FLD)   1934
NR   Murley Moss, Oxenholme Rd, KENDAL, Cumbria, LA9 7SS.
    (hq)
    01539 720788   fax 01539 730355
    Exec Dir: Andrew Forsyth
▲   Registered Charity
○   *K; protect & cherish the landscape & natural beauty of the
    Lake District & Cumbria
●   Conf - Mtgs - Exhib - Inf - VE - Joint action with other societies
    for protection of the environment
<   CPRE; Nat Trust; Ramblers' Assn; Coun Nat Parks
M   i & org
¶   NL - 2;   Conserving Lakeland - 2; both ftm only.

Friends of Medieval Dublin   (FMD)   1975
IRL   c/o Medieval History Dept, Trinity College, DUBLIN 2, Republic
    of Ireland.
    353 (1) 608 1801   fax 353 (1) 608 3995
    Hon Sec: Stuart Kinsella
○   *L

Friends of Mendelssohn   (F of M)   1995
NR   35 Northcourt Avenue, READING, Berks, RG2 7HE.   (hq)
    0118-987 1479
    Founder & Dir: Mrs Pam Gulliver
▲   Un-incorporated Society
○   *D; to promote the music of Felix Mendelssohn & his
    contemporaries; to campaign for higher standards in
    performances & recordings of such work
Gp   Team Mendelssohn (sporting events for charity)
●   Mtgs - Res - SG - Inf - Lib - VE
M   20 i

Friends of the National Bonsai Collection
    a group of the **Federation of British Bonsai Societies**

Friends of the National Collections of Ireland
IRL   Ivy House, ATHBOY, Co Meath, Republic of Ireland.
    353 (46) 943 2114
    Hon Sec: Jennifer Waldron-Lynch
○   *A

Friends of the National Libraries   (FNL)   1931
■   c/o Dept of Manuscripts, The British Library, 96 Euston Rd,
    LONDON, NW1 2DB.   (hsb)
    020 7412 7559
    http://www.friendsofnationallibraries.org.uk
    Hon Sec: Michael Borrie
▲   Registered Charity
○   *G; to promote the acquisition by national libraries of printed
    books, manuscripts & records of historical, literary, artistic,
    architectural, musical or suchlike interest by grants for
    purchases, channelling benefactions & legacies & public
    appeals
●   Mtgs - VE
M   c 700 i, 100 f
¶   AR.

Friends of the Pianola Institute   (FPI)   1985
■   111A Station Rd, WEST WICKHAM, Kent, BR4 0PX.   (asa)
    http://www.pianola.org
    Chmn: Keith Daniels
▲   Un-incorporated Society
○   *D; for supporters of the Institute, which exists to promote
    pianolas & music for pianolas
Gp   Pianola roll production
●   Mtgs - Res - Concerts - Roll & record production
M   65 i, UK / 15 i, o'seas
¶   Jnl - 1; ftm, £10 nm.   NL - 4; ftm only.

Friends of Real Lancashire   (FoRL)   1992
■   1 Belvidere Park, GREAT CROSBY, Lancs, L23 0SP.   (chmn/p)
    0151-928 2770
    email csd@forl.co.uk   http://www.forl.co.uk
    Chmn: C S Dawson
○   *G; to promote the true identity of the ancient & geographical
    county of Lancashire
●   Inf - LG
<   Assn of Brit Counties
M   660 i, 13 f, 8 org
¶   The Lancastrian - 1; ftm, £150 nm.   NL - 3; free (sae nm).

Friends of the Red Squirrel   2002
§   c/o Northumberland Wildlife Trust, The Garden House, St
    Nicholas Park, Gosforth, NEWCASTLE upon TYNE,
    NE3 3XT.   (mail/address)
    0191 284 6884
    A campaign to protect the red squirrel: 0845 347 9375

Friends of St Bride Library   (FSBL)
■   c/o St Bride Library, Bride Lane, Fleet St, LONDON,
    EC4Y 8EE.   (hq)
    020 7353 4660   fax 020 7583 7073
    email friends@stbride.org   http://www.stbride.org
    Hon Sec: Stephen Lubell
▲   Registered Charity (as pt of the St Bride Foundation)
○   *G, *K; to promote, support, improve, & raise money to
    safeguard the future of the St Bride Library (contains
    collections on printing & allied subjects - paper, binding,
    design, typography, typefaces, calligraphy, illustration &
    printmaking)
●   Conf - Mtgs - Exhib - Lectures
<   St Bride Foundation
M   c 2,000 i
¶   The Ravilious Notebook; Caroline Archer & Robert Harling.
    The Nymph and the Grot; James Mosley.
    Typefounders London A-Z; Justin Howes & Nigel Roche.
×   2004 (April) Friends of St Bride Printing Library

Friends of War Memorials
    since 2004 the **War Memorials Trust**

Friesian Horse Association of Great Britain & Ireland (FHAGBI) 1995
■ Harbours Hill Farm, Hanbury Rd, STOKE PRIOR, Worcs, B60 4AG. (hsp)
   01527 821276
   email fhagbi.events@btinternet.com
   http://www.fhagbi.co.uk
   Pres: Jane Slevin,   Co Sec: Julian Atkins
▲ Company Limited by Guarantee
○ *B
● ET -Exam - Comp - Annual horse inspections - Show & dressage/driving events
< Het Friesch Paarden-Stamboek (Netherlands) (mother studbook)
M c 200 i,
   (Sub: £50)
¶ Phrysko - 12;   NL - 4; both ftm only.

Frontier
   operating name of the **Society for Environmental Exploration**

Frozen & Chilled Potato Processors' Association (FCPPA) 1972
NR 6 Catherine St, LONDON, WC2B 5JJ. (hq)
▲ Un-incorporated Society
○ *T; to raise the standard & quality of raw materials; to exchange ideas & information
● Mtgs - Res - Stat - Inf - LG
< Food & Drink Fedn (FDF); Potato Processors' Assn (PPA)
M 10 f

Fund for the Replacement of Animals in Medical Experiments (FRAME) 1969
■ Russell & Burch House, 96-98 North Sherwood St, NOTTINGHAM, NG1 4EE. (hq)
   0115-958 4740   fax 0115-950 3570
   email frame@frame.org.uk   http://www.frame.org.uk
   Chmn of the Trustees: Prof Michael Balls
   Admin Mgr: Dr David Vowles
▲ Registered Charity
○ *K; to promote, research & develop the use of alternative methods in medical & related research, which refine, reduce or replace the use of laboratory animals
● Conf - ET - Res - Inf
M 500 i, 50 f org, UK / 5 f, o'seas
¶ ATLA Jnl - 6; £126 yr.   AR - 1; ftm.
   Frame News - 3 (with) Friends of Frame - 3; £15.

Funeral Furnishing Manufacturers Association (FFMA) 1939
■ 11 Fentham Close, Hampton in Arden, SOLIHULL, W Midlands, B92 0BE. (sb)
   01675 443718
   http://www.ffma.co.uk
   Sec: Sue Bullock
▲ Un-incorporated Society
○ *T; 'to promote the provision of coffins & other services to funeral directors; legal, technical & environmental issues are also under constant discussion'
● Conf - Mtgs - Exhib - LG
M 38 f

Furniture History Society (FHS) 1964
■ 1 Mercedes Cottages, St John's Rd, HAYWARDS HEATH, W Sussex, RH16 4EH.   (msp)
   01444 413845   fax 01444 413845
   email furniturehistorysociety@hotmail.com
   http://www.furniturehistorysociety.org
   Mem Sec: Dr Brian Austen
▲ Registered Charity
○ *L; the study of the history of furniture & furnishings on a worldwide basis
● Conf - Mtgs - ET - Res - SG - VE
M 1,200 i, 30 f, 80 org, UK / 300 i, 30 f, 70 org, o'seas
¶ Furniture History - 1;   NL - 4;   AR; all ftm.

Furniture Industry Research Association (FIRA) 1949
■ Maxwell Rd, STEVENAGE, Herts, SG1 2EW.   (hq)
   01438 777700   fax 01438 777800
   email info@fira.co.uk   http://www.askfira.co.uk
   Managing Dir: Hayden Davies
▲ Company Limited by Guarantee
Br China, Malaysia
○ *Q; research, consultancy & commercial services for the furniture industry including testing, customer care, lean manufacturing & the furniture ombudsman'
● Conf - Mtgs - ET - Res - Exhib - Inf - VE - LG - Testing - Consultancy
M 340 f, UK / 20 f, o'seas
¶ Ask FIRA News - 4;   Ybk;
   Club Green News - 2   AR; all free.

Further Education Research Association (FERA) 1973
NR External Affairs Office, University of Worcester, Henwick Grove, WORCESTER, WR2 6AJ.   (chmn/b)
   01905 855145   fax 01905 855132
   email g.elliott@worc.ac.uk   http://www.fera.uk.net
   Chmn: Prof Geoffrey Elliott
▲ Un-incorporated Society
○ *E, *L, *Q; research within & about further education (post 16)
● Conf - Mtgs - ET - Res - Inf
× (incorporated) National Association for Staff Development in the Post-16 Sector

Futon Association of Britain (FAB) 1994
NR 24 Beauchamp Rd, LONDON, SW11 1PQ.
   http://www.futonsonline.co.uk
▲ Un-incorporated Society
○ *T; promotion & education on all matters concerning futon furniture
● ET - Stat - Inf - Lib
< Futon Assn Intl (FAI)
M 20 i, 15 f

Futures & Options Association (FOA) 1993
NR 36-38 Botolph Lane (2nd floor), LONDON, EC3R 8DE.   (hq)
   020 7929 0081   fax 020 7621 0223
   http://www.foa.co.uk
   Chief Exec: Anthony Belchambers
○ *T; for the derivatives industry; to monitor & respond to regulatory & tax changes; to heighten industry & product awareness
M f

© CBD Research Ltd · Beckenham · BR3 5JS · Tel 020 8650 7745 · Fax 020 8650 0768 · E-mail cbd@cbdresearch.com · www.cbdresearch.com

GA Retail
    a group of the **Giftware Association**

Gaelic Athletic Association   1884
IRL   Croke Park, DUBLIN 3, Republic of Ireland.
        353 (1) 836 3222   fax 353 (1) 836 6420
        email info@gaa.ie   http://www.gaa.ie
○   *S; promotion of Gaelic football, hurling, handball and
        rounders

Gallipoli Association   1969
■   Earleydene Orchard, Earleydene, ASCOT, Berks, SL5 9JY.
        (hsp)
        01344 626523
        http://www.gallipoli-association.org
        Hon Sec: J C Watson Smith
▲   Un-incorporated Society
○   *G; to keep alive the memory of the Gallipoli campaign of
        1915; for those interested in the campaign
●   Mtgs - VE - 2 lunches a year - Tour to Dardanelles
M   c 1,000 i, UK & o'seas
¶   The Gallipolian - 3; ftm.

Galloway Cattle Society of Great Britain & Ireland   1877
■   15 New Market St, CASTLE DOUGLAS, Kirkcudbrightshire,
        DG7 1HY.   (hq)
        01556 502753   fax 01556 502753
        email info@gallowaycattlesociety.co.uk
        http://www.gallowaycattlesociety.co.uk
        Sec: Dorothy J Goldie
▲   Registered Charity
○   *B; to promote & keep pure Galloway cattle
Gp   Farmers; Small holding-farms; Farmers' markets
●   Exhib
M   500 i, UK / 150 i, o'seas
¶   Jnl - 1; free.   Herd Book - 1; £10.

Galpin Society   1946
■   37 Townsend Drive, ST ALBANS, Herts, AL3 5RF.   (chmn/p)
        http://www.galpinsociety.org
        Chmn of Trustees: Graham Wells
▲   Registered Charity
○   *L, *Q; the study of the history, construction, development & use
        of musical instruments
●   Conf - Mtgs - Res
M   400 i, UK / 600 i, o'seas, c 300 universities & libraries
        worldwide
¶   Jnl - 1; ftm.   NL - 3; ftm only.

Galton Institute   1907
■   19 Northfields Prospect, Northfields, LONDON, SW18 1PE.
        (hq)
        020 8874 7257
        email betty.nixon@talk21.com
        http://www.galtoninstitute.org.uk
        Gen Sec: Betty Nixon
▲   Company Limited by Guarantee; Registered Charity
○   *L, *Q; to study the effects of hereditary & environmental
        factors on inborn human qualities; to promote a responsible
        attitude to parenthood; Population problems
●   Conf - ET - Res
<   Inst Biology
M   300 i, UK / 100 i, o'seas
¶   NL - 4; m only.
        Proceedings of Conference (book) - 1; ftm, £5 nm.

Galvanizers Association   (GA)   1949
■   56 Victoria Rd, Wren's Court, SUTTON COLDFIELD,
        W Midlands, B72 1SY.   (hq)
        0121-355 8838   fax 0121-355 8727
        email ga@hdg.org.uk   http://www.galvanizing.org.uk
        Gen Mgr: David M Baron
▲   Company Limited by Guarantee
○   *T; to provide technical & marketing services for the hot dip
        galvanizing industry in the UK & Ireland
●   Conf - Mtgs - ET - Res - Exhib - Stat - Inf - Lib - VE
M   37 f, UK / 48 f, o'seas
¶   Hot Dip Galvanizing (Jnl) - 4; free (1st 10 copies ftm).
        Brochure: Engineers' & Architects' Guide to Hot Dip
        Galvanising (2001); £1.50 m, £5 nm.

Galway Chamber of Commerce & Industry
IRL   Commerce House, Merchants Rd, GALWAY, Republic of
        Ireland.
        353 (91) 563536   fax 353 (91) 561963
        email info@galwaychamber.com
        http://www.galwaychamber.com
        Chief Exec: Michael Coyle
○   *C

GAMBICA
        alternative name of the **Association for Instrumentation,
        Control, Automation & Laboratory Technology**

Game Conservancy Trust / Game Conservancy Ltd   (GCT / GCL)   1980
NR   Burgate Manor, FORDINGBRIDGE, Hants, SP6 1EF.   (hq)
        01425 652381   fax 01425 655848
        email info@gct.org.uk   http://www.gct.org.uk
        Chief Exec: Teresa Dent
▲   Registered Charity
○   *Q; research & advice into conservation & habitat of all game
        species.   Associated research in agriculture, arable insects,
        songbirds & pesticides/herbicides
M   i, f & org

Game Farmers Association   (GFA)   1918
■   Colnbrook, Withington, CHELTENHAM, Glos, GL54 4BW.
        (sec&treas/p)
        01242 890372   fax 01242 890372
        email jimatgfa@btinternet.com
        Sec & Treas: E J Day
▲   Un-incorporated Society
○   *F
●   Mtgs - ET - Seminars
<   in close co-operation with the Nat Gamekeepers Assn
M   179 i, 29 f, UK / 3 f, o'seas
¶   Game Farming NL - 4; ftm only.

Garage Equipment Association   (GEA)   1945
■   2-3 Church Walk, DAVENTRY, Northants, NN11 4BL.   (hq)
        01327 312616   fax 01327 312606
        email name@gea.co.uk   http://www.gea.co.uk
        Chief Exec: Dave Garratt
▲   Company Limited by Guarantee
○   *T; represents the interests of all sectors of the garage
        equipment industry; manufacturing, servicing, installation,
        selling & distribution of garage equipment & provision of
        training
Gp   Manufacturers; Distributors; Service; MOT liaison; Code of
        Practice; Exhibitions
●   Mtgs - Exhib - Stat - LG
<   Eur Garage Eqpt Assn (EGEA)
M   115 f
¶   The World of Emissions (on emission testing).

Garage Watch Ltd
in 2006 became the Forecourt division of the **Federation of Petroleum Suppliers**

Garden Centre Association Ltd   (GCA)   1979
■   Leafield Technical Centre, Leafield, WITNEY, Oxon,
OX29 9EF.   (hq)
01993 871456   fax 01993 871458
email info@gca.org.uk   http://www.gca.org.uk
▲   Company Limited by Guarantee
○   *T
●   Conf - Comp - SG - Inf
<   Intl Garden Centre Assn
M   160 f, 183 associate f
¶   GCA Ybk - 1; ftm, £50 nm

Garden History Society   (GHS)   1965
NR   70 Cowcross St, LONDON, EC1M 6EJ.
020 7608 2409   fax 020 7490 2974
email enquiries@gardenhistorysociety.org
http://www.gardenhistorysociety.org
Chmn: Dr Colin Treen
▲   Registered Charity
○   *H, *L; to promote study into the history of gardening &
horticulture in all aspects; to protect historic gardens
Gp   Conservation
●   Conf - Mtgs - Res - Exhib - Stat - Inf - VE - Advising on
restoration & preservation of historic gardens
<   ICOMOS; Civic Trust; CPRE; Brit Assn for Local History
M   1,800 i, UK / c 250 i, o'seas, also university & civic libraries
¶   Garden History (Jnl) - 2.   NL - 3.

Garden & Landscape Designers Association   (GLDA)
IRL   PO Box 10954, DUBLIN 18, Republic of Ireland.
353 (1) 294 0092   fax 353 (1) 283 8043
email info@glda.ie   http://www.glda.ie
○   *G, *P

Garden Media Guild   (GMG)   1991
■   Katepwa House, Ashfield Park Avenue, ROSS-on-WYE,
Herefords, HR9 5AX.   (hq)
01989 567393   fax 01989 567676
email info@gardenmediaguild.co.uk
http://www.gardenmediaguild.co.uk
Hon Sec: Michael Howes,   Admin: Gill Hinton
▲   Un-incorporated Society
○   *P; to raise the quality of garden writing, photography &
broadcasting
Gp   Writers; Broadcasters; Lecturers; Photographers (Garden
Photographers Assn); Photo libraries; Photographic
collections
●   Comp - ET - Annual awards ceremony
M   312 i, + 35 associates, 14 probationary, 19 retired
(Sub: £55 full, £75 associates, £411.25 probationery,
£18 retired)
¶   News - 4; ftm only;   Ybk - 1; ftm, £150 nm.
×   2007 Garden Writers' Guild

Garden Organic
working name of the **Henry Doubleday Research Association**

Garden Writers' Guild
since 2007 the **Garden Media Guild**

**GARDENEX: the Federation of Garden & Leisure Manufacturers
Ltd   (GARDENEX)   1961**
NR   The White House, High St, BRASTED, Kent, TN16 1JE.   (hq)
01959 565995   fax 01959 565885
email info@gardenex.com   http://www.gardenex.com
Chief Exec: Amanda Sizer Barrett
▲   Company Limited by Guarantee
○   *T; to promote the export of British manufactured products,
services, plants etc in international markets
M   f

Gardening for the Disabled Trust & Garden Club   1973
■   PO Box 285, TUNBRIDGE WELLS, Kent, TN2 9JD.   (hsp)
http://www.gardeningforthedisabledtrust.org.uk
○   *G, *H; a charity to encourage disabled people of all ages to
enjoy gardening as a creative hobby
●   Planning & building special gardens
M   i & org
¶   NL - 4.

Gas Forum   1994
NR   Gemserv, Centurion House (7th floor), 24 Monument St,
LONDON, EC3R 8AJ.   (hq)
020 7090 1030
▲   Company Limited by Guarantee
○   *T; for companies shipping gas through the national gas
pipeline system & those supplying gas to industrial,
commercial & domestic customers

Gascon Cattle Society   1990
NR   1 Goval Farm Cottages, Dyce, ABERDEEN, AB21 0HS.   (hsp)
email kirsteenrankin@btinternet.com
Sec: Kirsteen Rankin
▲   Un-incorporated Society
○   *B; promotion of the Gascon breed of beef cattle
●   Mtgs - Res - Exhib
<   UPRA Gasconne (France)
M   10 i, UK / 300 i, o'seas
¶   NL - 4;   Ybk - 1; both free.

Gaskell Society   1985
■   Far Yew Tree House, Chester Rd, Tabley, KNUTSFORD,
Cheshire, WA16 0HN.   (hsp)
01565 634668
email joanleach@aol.com   http://www.gaskellsociety.co.uk
Sec: Mrs Joan Leach
▲   Registered Charity
Br   2; Japan
○   *A; to promote interest in Mrs Elizabeth Cleghorn Gaskell's life
& writings
●   Conf - Mtgs - SG
<   Alliance of Literary Socs
M   500 i, UK / 120 i, o'seas
¶   Jnl - 1.   NL - 2.

Gasket Cutters' Association   (GCA)   1993
NR   105 St Peter's St, ST ALBANS, Herts, AL1 3EJ.   (asa)
01727 896084   fax 01727 896026
email info@gcassociation.co.uk
▲   Un-incorporated Society
○   *T; interests of companies cutting gaskets & associated
conversion processes
●   Conf - Mtgs - SG - Inf - LG
M   30 f
¶   The Informer - 4; ftm only.

Gate Automation & Access Barrier Association
a group of the **Fencing Contractors' Association**

Gaucher's Association   1991
NR   3 Bull Pitch, DURSLEY, Glos, GL11 4NG.   (hq)
01463 549231   fax 01463 549231
email ga@gaucher.org.uk   http://www.gaucher.org.uk
Exec Sec: Tanya Collin-Histed
▲   Company Limited by Guarantee; Registered Charity
○   *M, *W; information & support group for people with
Gaucher's disease (abnormal storage of lipids) & their
families
●   Conf - Mtgs - Res - Inf - LG
M   494 i, 454 f, UK / 30 i, 272 f, o'seas
¶   Gauchers News - 2; free.

Gauge & Tool Makers Association (GTMA) 1942
■ 3 Forge House, Summerleys Rd, PRINCES RISBOROUGH,
   Bucks, HP27 9DT. (hq)
   01844 274222   fax 01844 274227
   email gtma@gtma.co.uk   http://www.gtma.co.uk
▲ Un-incorporated Society
○ *T
Gp Metrology; Mould & die; Special purpose machinery; Press tool;
    Tool & workholding eqpt
● Conf - Mtgs - ET - Exhib - Stat - Expt - Inf - Lib - VE
< Intl Special Tooling Assn
M 320 f
¶ GTMA Directory of Gauging & Toolmaking Products &
   Services - 1; ftm.

Gemmological Association of Great Britain (Gem-A) 1925
NR 27 Greville St, LONDON, EC1N 8TN. (hq)
    020 7404 3334
    http://www.gem-a.info
    Chief Exec: Jack Ogden
▲ Company Limited by Guarantee; Registered Charity
○ *L, *P; to promote the study of gemmology & provide
   continuous professional development to members

Gender Trust 1990
NR Community Base, 113 Queens Rd, BRIGHTON, E Sussex,
    BN1 3XG. (hq)
    01273 234024
    email info@gendertrust.org.uk
    http://www.gendertrust.org.uk
    Trust Admin: Rosemary Turner
▲ Registered Charity
Br 12
○ *W; information & support for transsexual people, their families
   & partners
Gp Gender; Transsexual
● Conf - ET - Inf - Telephone service
   Helpline: 0845 231 0505
M 450 i, 2 f, 20 org, UK / 6 i, o'seas
¶ Membership magazine - 4; £29 yr m only.
   Employers Guide;   Sex Reassignment Surgery;
   Standards of Care;   all £2.50.
   Gender Trust Guide; £6 m, £8 nm.

General Aviation Manufacturers & Traders Association Ltd
   in 2004 merged with the Business Aircraft Users Association to form
   the **British Business & General Aviation Association**

General Council of County Councils
   since 2007 the **Association of County & City Councils**

General Council for Massage Therapy (GCMT) 2002
■ 27 Old Gloucester St, LONDON, WC1N 3XX. (hsb)
   0870 850 4452
   email gcmt@btconnect.com   http://www.gcmt.org.uk
   Sec: Isabel Hoxworth
▲ Un-incorporated Society
○ *N, *P; for the self-regulation of massage therapy in the UK; to
   bring together organisations engaged in representing, or
   teaching, massage therapy, for the protection of the public
● Mtgs - ET - Res - SG - If - LG
> CTHA; LCSP; MTI; MTIGB; PACT; SMTO
M 670 i, 6 org

General Council & Register of Consultant Herbalists Ltd
   trading name of the **International Register of Consultant
   Herbalists & Homoeopaths**

General Council & Register of Naturopaths (GCRN) 1967
NR Goswell House, 2 Goswell Rd, STREET, Somerset, BA16 0JG.
    (hsb)
    0870 745 6984
    http://www.naturopathy.org.uk
    Sec: M W F Szewiel
▲ Company Limited by Guarantee
○ *L, *P; to register suitably qualified naturopathic practitioners; to
   set minimum standards for the training of practitioners for
   the benefit of the public
● Conf - ET - LG
M 310 i, UK / 19 i, o'seas
¶ Register of Practitioners Members - 1.

General Dental Practitioners Association
   since 2005 **Dental Practitioners Association**

General Federation of Trade Unions (GFTU) 1899
■ Central House, Upper Woburn Place, LONDON, WC1H 0HY.
   (hq)
   020 7387 2578   fax 020 7383 0820
   email gftuhq@gftu.org.uk   http://www.gftu.org.uk
   Gen Sec: Michael Bradley
▲ Un-incorporated Society
○ *N; a federation of unions providing benefits & services to
   affiliates
● Conf - Mtgs - ET - Res - Stat - Inf - Lib - LG
M 35 unions
¶ Federation Jnl - 2/3;   Federation News - 2/3;
   Report - 2 yrly; all free.

General Insurance Market Research Association
   a special interest group of the **Association of Users of Research
   Agencies**

Genetic Interest Group (GIG) 1990
■ 4D Leroy House, 436 Essex Rd, LONDON, N1 3QP. (hq)
   020 7704 3141   fax 020 7359 1447
   email mail@gig.org.uk   http://www.gig.org.uk
   Dir: Alastair Kent
▲ Registered Charity
○ *M; to improve services for all people with genetic disorders; to
   increase understanding & knowledge of human genetics
● Conf - Mtgs - ET - Inf - LG
< Eur Alliance of Genetic Support Groups
M 120 org
¶ GIG Today (NL) - 4;   AR; both free.

Genetics Society 1919
NR Roslin Biocentre, Wallace Building, ROSLIN, Midlothian,
    EH25 9PP. (hq)
    0131-200 6391   fax 0131-200 6394
    email mail@genetics.org.uk
    http://www.genetics.org.uk
    Exec Officer: Christine Fender
▲ Registered Charity
○ *L; Gene structure, function & regulation; Cell & development
   genetics; Evolutionary, ecological & population genetics;
   Genomics; Applied & quantitative genetics; Corporate
   genetics & biotechnology
● Conf - Mtgs - Inf
< Intl Genetics Fedn (IGF); Fedn Eur Genetics Socs (FEGS);
   Inst Biology (IoB); BioSciences Fedn (BSF)
M 2,000 i, UK / 300 i, o'seas
¶ Heredity - 12; £28 m, £138 nm.
   Genes & Development - 24; £128 m.

GeneWatch
NR 60 Lightwood Rd, BUXTON, Derbys, SK17 7BB.
    01298 24300
    email mail@genewatch.org   http://www.genewatch.org
○ *K

Genito-Urinary Physicians Colposcopy Group
  a special interest group of the **British Association for Sexual Health & HIV**

Geographical Association   (GA)   1893
■ 160 Solly St, SHEFFIELD, S Yorks, S1 4BF.   (hq)
    0114-296 0088   fax 0114-296 7176
    email info@geography.org.uk
    http://www.geography.org.uk
    Chief Exec: Dr David Lambert
▲ Registered Charity; Un-incorporated Society
Br 39
○ *E, *L, *P; to further the learning & teaching of geography
Gp Phase c'ees: Early years & primary, Secondary, Post-16 & HE
    Working gps: Assessment & examinations, Citizenship,
    Education for sustainable development, ICT, Independent
    schools, International, Learning outside the classroom,
    Physical geography, Teacher education
● Conf - Mtgs - ET - Res - Exhib - Comp - SG - Inf - VE - LG
< Coun of Brit Geography; Coun for Subject Teaching Assns
M 3,155 i, 3,271 groups (schools, universities etc}
    (Sub: £22-25-£99.50 i, £76.25-£131.50 groups)
¶ Geography - 3;   Primary Geographer - 3;
    Teaching Geography - 3;   GA Magazine - 3; all ftm.

Geographical Society of Ireland   1934
IRL School of Geography, Planning & Environmental Policy,
    E001 Newman Bldg, University College Dublin, Belfield,
    DUBLIN 4, Republic of Ireland.
    353 (1) 716 8179   fax 353 (1) 269 5597
    Sec: Dr Niamh Moore
○ *L

Geological Society   1807
■ Burlington House, Piccadilly, LONDON, W1J 0BG.   (hq)
    020 7434 9944
    http://www.geolsoc.org.uk
    Exec Sec: Edmund Nickless
○ *L; furtherance of all aspects of geological science
Gp British Geophysical Association; British Society for
    Geomorphology; Joint Association for Quaternary Research;
    Joint Association of Geoscientists for International
    Development; Joint Committee for Palaeontology.Irehole
    research, Coal geology, Engineering, Environment,
    Environmental & industrial geophysics, Forensic geoscience,
    Gaia: Earth systems science, Geochemistry, Geological
    curators, Geological remote sensing, Geoscience
    information, History of geology, Hydrogeological, Marine
    studies, Metamorphic studies, Mineral deposits studies,
    Petroleum, Tectonic studies, Volcanic & magmatic studies

Geologists' Association   (GA)   1858
NR Burlington House, Piccadilly, LONDON, W1J 0DU.   (hq)
    020 7434 9298
    Exec Sec: Mrs Sarah Stafford
▲ Registered Charity
○ *G, *L; to promote awareness of our geological heritage; to
    promote interest in & the study of geology & its allied
    sciences, at all levels

George Borrow Society   1991
■ 1 Holywell Close, Meads, EASTBOURNE, E Sussex,
    BN20 7RX.   (hsp)
    01323 737209   fax 01323 737209
    email adakyns@yahoo.co.uk
    http://www.clough5.fsnct.co.uk
    Hon Sec: Andrew Dakyns
▲ Un-incorporated Society
○ *A; to promote the knowledge of the life & works of the English
    author George Borrow (1803-81), best known for his novels
    'Lavengro', 'The Romany Rye', 'The Bible in Spain' & 'Wild
    Wales'
● Conf - Mtgs - Res - Annual memorial lecture
< Alliance of Literary Socs; Centre of East Anglian Studies, UEA,
    Norwich; Friends of Brompton Cemetery
M 128 i, 11 libraries, UK / 33 i, 2 orgs, o'seas
¶ George Borrow Bulletin - 2; ftm, £4 nm.

George Eliot Fellowship   1930
■ 12 Fair Isle Drive, NUNEATON, Warks, CV10 7LJ.   (hsp)
    email blueyorkshirecat@yahoo.co.uk
    http://www.george-eliot-fellowship.com
    Hon Sec: Elizabeth Mellor
▲ Registered Charity
Br Japan, USA
○ *A; to honour George Eliot & to promote interest in her life &
    writings; to encourage collection of her books & manuscripts
    & other ephemera connected with her
● Mtgs - Res - Comp - SG - Inf - VE
< Alliance Literary Socs
M 357 i, 6 org, UK / 243 i, 1 org, o'seas
¶ George Eliot Review - 4; ftm, £10 nm.   NL - 4; ftm only.
    Those of Us Who Loved Her: the men in George Eliot's
    life; £7.50 m.
    Pitkin Guide to George Eliot; £3.50.

George Formby Society   (GFS)   1961
NR 52 Windrush Drive, HINCKLEY, Leics, LE10 0NY.   (contact/p)
    Contact: Andrew Gatherer
▲ Un-incorporated Society
○ *G; to perpetuate the music & memory of George Formby, MBE
● Conf - Mtgs
M c 850 i
¶ Vellum - 4; ftm only.

George MacDonald Society   1981
NR 10 Appian Court, Parnell Rd, LONDON, E3 2RS.   (regd/add)
    http://www.george-macdonald.com
    Sec: Roger Bardet
▲ Registered Charity
○ *A; to promote public interest & knowledge in the life & works
    of George MacDonald (1824-1905), author
● Conf - Mtgs - Res - Exhib - Inf - Lib - VE
M 74 i, 16 org, UK / 78 i, org, o'seas
¶ North Wind - 1.   Orts (NL).

Georgian Group   1937
NR 6 Fitzroy Sq, LONDON, W1T 5DX.   (hq)
    0871 750 2936
▲ Registered Charity; Un-incorporated Society
○ *G; preservation & appreciation of buildings of the Georgian
    period (18th century) & those in the classical style
M i & f
¶ Jnl - 1.   NL - 3.   AR.

© CBD Research Ltd · Beckenham · BR3 5JS · Tel 020 8650 7745 · Fax 020 8650 0768 · E-mail cbd@cbdresearch.com · www.cbdresearch.com

German-British Chamber of Industry & Commerce   1971
- ■ 16 Buckingham Gate, LONDON, SW1E 6LB.   (hq)
  020 7976 4100   fax 020 7976 4101
  email mail@ahk-london.co.uk
  http://www.germanbritishchamber.co.uk
  Dir-Gen: Ulrich Hoppe
  Contact: Thesy Lobitzer (020 7976 4112)
- ▲ Company Limited by Guarantee
- ○ *C; promotion of trade & investment between Germany & the United Kingdom
- Gp Business: Information, Partner search, Promotion; Legal; Marketing services; Trade Fairs; Green Dot; VAT refund
- ● Conf - Res - Exhib - Expt - Inf
- < AHK Deutsche Auslandshandelskammern (Germany)
- M 640 f, 60 org (chambers of commerce), UK / 140 f, 60 org, o'seas
- ¶ Publication details by request.
  Note: the German title is - Deutsch-Britische Industrie- und Handelskammer.

German History Society   1979
- NR c/o Annika Mombauer, Dept of History, Open University, Walton Hall, MILTON KEYNES, Bucks, MK7 6AA.   (hsb)
  http://www.germanhistorysociety.org
  Sec: Annika Mombauer
- ▲ Un-incorporated Society
- ○ *L; academic research on German history
- ● Conf - Res
- M c 200 i, UK / c 50 i, o'seas
- ¶ German History - 4.

German Railway Society   (GRS)   1980
- ■ Shalimar, 10 Beechwood Rd, MIRFIELD, W Yorks, WF14 9JX.
  (hsp)
  01924 495929
  email mrdransfield@beechwoodroad.freeserve.co.uk
  Sec: P Dransfield
- ▲ Un-incorporated Society
- Br 6 groups
- ○ *G; for enthusiasts & modellers of German & Austrian railways
- ● Mtgs - Exhib - Lib
- M c 800 i
- ¶ Merkur - 4; ftm only.

Gestalt Association UK
  former name of the **British Gestalt Society**

Giftware Association   (The GA)   1947
- ■ Federation House, 10 Vyse St, BIRMINGHAM, B18 6LT.   (hq)
  0121-237 1104   fax 0121-237 1106
  http://www.ga-uk.org
  Chief Exec: Isabel Martinson
- ○ *T; promotion & provision of supporting business services to British manufacturers, importers & distributors of giftware
- Gp GA Retail
- ● Conf - Res - Comp - Expt - Inf - LG
- < Brit Jewellery, Giftware & Finishing Fedn
- M 1,500 i, f & org
- ¶ Newsline - 2.

Gilbert & Sullivan Society   (G&SS)   1924
- NR 7 Mace Walk, CHELMSFORD, Essex, CM1 2GE.   (mem/sp)
  http://www.gilbertandsullivansociety.org.uk
  Mem Sec: John Tritton
- ▲ Registered Charity
- Br 11; Australia, Canada, Israel, South Africa, USA
- ○ *D; to inform, educate & entertain all who are interested in the works of Gilbert & Sullivan & the Savoy operas
- Gp Music; Theatre; Opera; Appreciation Society
- ● Conf - Mtgs - ET - Res - Inf - Lib
- < Nat Fedn Music Socs
- M 1,000 i, UK / 500 i, o'seas
- ¶ Gilbert & Sullivan News - 3; ftm, (or £2 each), £8 yr nm (£12 o'seas).

** **Gilt-Edged Market Makers' Association**
  Organisation lost: see Introduction paragraph 3.

GIMA (1999) Ltd   (GIMA)   1977
- NR 225 Bristol Rd, Edgbaston, BIRMINGHAM, B5 7UB.   (hq)
  0121-446 5213   fax 0121-446 5215
  email info@gima.org.uk
  Dir: Neil Gow,   Sec: Rebecca Abbott
- ○ *T; represent manufacturers of garden products
- ● Conf - Mtgs - ET - Res - SG - Stat
- M 140 f
- ¶ NL;   LM; both m only.   AR; ftm.

Gin & Vodka Association of Great Britain   (GVA)   1991
- ■ Cross Keys House, Queen St, SALISBURY, Wilts, SP1 1EY.   (hq)
  01722 415892   fax 01722 415840
  email gva@ginvodka.org.uk   http://www.ginvodka.org
  Dir Gen: Edwin Atkinson
- ▲ Company Limited by Guarantee
- ○ *T; to protect & promote the interests of the gin & vodka trades generally both at home & abroad; to prevent any malpractices or abuses that might arise in connection with the production, importation or sale of gin or vodka
- ● Stat - Inf - LG
- < Confédn Eur des Producteurs de Spiritueux (Brussels)
- M 29 f
- ¶ NL - 4;   AR; both ftm.

Gingerbread (an Association for One Parent Families) Ltd
  1 June 2007 merged with the National Council of One Parent Families to form **One Parent Families / Gingerbread**

Girlguiding UK   1910
- ■ 17-19 Buckingham Palace Rd, LONDON, SW1W 0PT.   (hq)
  020 7834 6242   fax 020 7828 8317
  email chq@girlguiding.org.uk
  http://www.girlguiding.org.uk
  Chief Exec: Denise King
- ▲ Registered Charity
- Br 7
- ○ *Y; to help girls & young women to develop emotionally, mentally, physically & spiritually so that they can make a positive contribution to the community & the wider world
- Gp Rainbow Guides (5-7 yrs) (in Ulster 4-7); Brownie Guides (7-10 yrs); Guide (10-14 yrs); Ranger Guides; Young leaders; Adult leaders
- ● Mtgs - ET
- < Wld Assn Girl Guides & Girl Scouts
- M 600,000 i
- ¶ Guiding - 12; ftm (16+yrs only); £2 nm.   AR - 1.
  Note: registered as the Guide Association.

Girls' Brigade England & Wales   1893
- NR PO Box 196, 129 Broadway, DIDCOT, Oxon, OX11 8XN.   (hq)
  01235 510425   fax 01235 510429
  http://www.girlsbrigadeew.org.uk
  Nat Dir: Miss Ruth E Gilson
- ▲ Registered Charity
- Br 966; 55 o'seas
- ○ *R, *Y; acts as the National Council for England & Wales with regard to the spiritual & personal development of girls & young women
- ● Conf - Mtgs - ET - Exhib - Comp - Stat - VE
- < Girls' Brigade Intl Coun
- M 31,782 i, 996 f, UK / 55 f, o'seas
- ¶ The View - 6.   AR.

Girls' Schools Association (GSA) 1973
NR 130 Regent Rd, LEICESTER, LE1 7PG.   (hq)
0116-254 1619   fax 0116-255 3792
email office@gsa.uk.com   http://www.gsa.uk.com
Gen Sec: Sheila Cooper
▲ Company Limited by Guarantee
○ *E, *P; policy & administration of independent girls' schools
● Conf - Mtgs - ET - Res - Exhib - Inf - VE - LG
M c 212 schools; c 88 associates & o'seas

Girls Venture Corps Air Cadets (GVCAC) 1964
■ 1 Bawtry Gate, SHEFFIELD, S Yorks, S9 1UD.   (hq)
0114-244 8405   fax 0114-244 8419
email gvcac@toucansurf.com   http://www.gvcac.org.uk
Corps Dir: Mrs B Layne
▲ Company Limited by Guarantee; Registered Charity
Br 30
○ *W, *Y; uniformed youth organisation for girls aged 11-20 who
are interested in aviation, sport, Duke of Edinburgh Award,
community service, & leadership skills
● Conf - Mtgs - Exam - Comp - VE - LG
< Air Training Corps; Army Cadet Force; RAF WARMA; NCYVYS;
CCPR
M 800 i
¶ Circuit - 2; ftm.

GIST Support UK 2000
■ 67 Between Streets, COBHAM, Surrey, KT11 1AA.   (chmn/p)
01932 862090
email judith@ndrobinson.plus.com
http://www.gistsupportuk.com
Chmn: Judith K Robinson
▲ Un-incorporated Society
○ *G, *W; to promote & protect the physical & mental health of
sufferers of gastro-intestinal stromal tumours (GISTs) & their
carers in the UK, through provision of emotional support,
education & practical advice; to increase awareness of the
needs of GIST patients & their carers
● Conf - Mtgs - ET - Inf - LG - email, mailtalk & phone support
< GIST Support Intl (GSI); The Liferaft Gp; Sarcoma UK
M [not stated]
¶ GIST Patient guide;   GIST Support leaflet;
Gist Patient Passport; all free.

Glamorgan History Society 1957
NR Ruthin Fach, St Mary Hill, BRIDGEND, Glamorgan,
CF35 5EB.   (treas/b)
01656 860552
http://www.glamorganhistory.org
Treas: Keith Jones
○ *L; promote the study of the history of Glamorgan
M i & org

Glasgow Agricultural Society (GAS) 1898
NR The Faulds, Kilmany, CUPAR, Fife, KY15 4PT.   (sp)
01382 330710   fax 01382 330710
Sec: Miss Mardy Whiteford
○ *B, *F, *G; to promote & encourage the breeding & showing of
horses & ponies; to organise the national stallion show
annually (for in-hand Clydesdales, Highlands, Shetlands &
mountain & moorland horses & ponies); farrier competitions
< Nat Pony Soc; Highland Pony Soc; Clydesdale Horse Soc;
Shetland Pony Studbook Soc
M 394 i

Glasgow Archaeological Society (GAS) 1856
NR c/o Dept of Archaeology, University of Glasgow, GLASGOW,
G12 8QQ.   (hsp)
http://www.glasarchsoc.co.uk
Mem Sec: S Hunter
▲ Registered Charity
○ *L; promotion of & interest in archaeology, particularly in
Glasgow & West of Scotland
● Conf - Mtgs - Res - Exhib - Inf - VE
< Coun Brit Archaeology
M 325 i, 2 f, 5 org, UK / 20 i, o'seas
¶ Scottish Archaeological Jnl - 2; ftm, £18 nm.
Bulletin - 2; ftm, £5 nm.

Glasgow Chamber of Commerce 1783
■ 30 George Square, GLASGOW, G2 1EQ.   (hq)
0141-204 2121   fax 0141-221 2336
email chamber@glasgowchamber.org
http://www.glasgowchamber.org
Chief Exec: Richard Cairns
○ *C; interests of the business community of Glasgow & West of
Scotland
● Mtgs - Stat - Expt - Inf - LG
< Assn Brit Chams Comm; Assn Scot Chams Comm
M 2,000 f
¶ Glasgow Business Jnl - 6.   Diary & Directory - 1.

Glasgow Mathematical Association (GMA) 1927
NR Mathematics Dept, University of Glasgow, University Gardens,
GLASGOW, G12 8QW.   (treas/b)
Hon Treas: Dr F H Goldman
▲ Un-incorporated Society
○ *L; to stimulate study & teaching of mathematics at all levels; to
provide a forum for professional mathematicians, especially
teachers, to exchange ideas
M i

Glasgow Natural History Society 1851
NR c/o Zoology Museum, Graham Kerr Building, University of
Glasgow, GLASGOW, G12 8QQ.
http://www.glasgownaturalhistory.org.uk
▲ Registered Charity
○ *L

Glass Association 1983
NR 150 Braemar Rd, SUTTON COLDFIELD, W Midlands, B73 6LZ.
http://www.glassassociation.org.uk
Mem Sec: Pauline Wimpory
○ *G, *P; for all interested in glass & glassmaking

The Glass Circle 1937
■ 66 Corringham Rd, LONDON, NW11 7BX.   (hsp)
020 8455 7348
email secretary@glasscircle.org
http://www.glasscircle.org
Hon Sec: Marianne Scheer
▲ Un-incorporated Society
○ *G; to promote the study, understanding, appreciation & history
of artistic & collected glass
● Conf - Mtgs - Exhib - Lib - VE
M 405 i, 4 f, 6 org, UK / 70 i, 4 org, o'seas
¶ Glass Circle New - 4; ftm, £5 nm.
Glass Circle Jnl - 2; ftm, £20 nm.

© CBD Research Ltd · Beckenham · BR3 5JS · Tel 020 8650 7745 · Fax 020 8650 0768 · E-mail cbd@cbdresearch.com · www.cbdresearch.com

Glass & Glazing Federation   (GGF)   1977
■   44-48 Borough High St, LONDON, SE1 1XB.   (hq)
     0870 042 4255   fax 0870 042 4266
     email info@ggf.org.uk   http://www.ggf.org.uk
     Chief Exec: Nigel Rees
▲   Company Limited by Guarantee
○   *T; interests of companies engaged in glazing (glass & plastics),
     including solar control, leaded & stained glass, shopfronts,
     patent glazing, double glazing, merchanting, laminating,
     toughening, bending, conservatories manufacturing of sealed
     units, mirrors, compounds, all flat glass processing, external
     relations with government & all other relevant bodies
Gp Home improvements; Glazing executive; Specialist interests;
     Fire resistant glazing
●   Conf - Mtgs - ET - Exhib - Empl - LG
M   600 f
     (Sub: according to turnover)
¶   NL (email) - 10; ftm only.   AR - 1; free.
     Glazing Manual - updated; £50 m, £100 nm.
     Publications CDs & DVDs list available.

Glenn Miller Society   1950
■   3 Pine View Close, Verwood, WIMBORNE, Dorset, BH21 6NN.
     Contact: Brenda Martin
○   *D, *G

Global Commons Institute   (GCI)   1991
NR 37 Ravenswood Rd, LONDON, E17 9LY.   (hq)
     020 8520 4742
     Exec Dir: Aubrey Meyer
○   *K: 'GCI is concerned with global warming & climate change;
     our focus is the promotion of 'Contraction & Convergence'
     (C&C). C&C is a global greenhouse gas emissions
     management framework based on the principles of
     precaution & equity. These principles make possible an
     effective overall response to global climate change'

Glosa Education Organisation   (GEO)   1987
■   PO Box 18, RICHMOND, Surrey, TW9 2GE.   (hsp)
     020 8288 0257
     http://www.glosa.org
     Hon Sec: Sabine Asenkerschbaumer,
     Mem Sec: Wendy Ashby
▲   Registered Charity
Br 5 o'seas
○   *E, *X, to promote the international language Glosa; to put
     speakers & penfriends in touch with each other; to provide
     teaching materials & establish study centres worldwide
●   Mtgs - ET - Inf - Penfriends service
M   180 i, 6 org, UK / 150 i, 10 org, o'seas
¶   Plu Glosa Nota - 4; £6.50 yr.
     Dictionaries & textbooks; £1 - £10.95.

Gloucester Cattle Society   1972
■   Hillfields Lodge, Lighthorne, WARWICK, CV35 0BQ.   (sp)
     01926 651147
     http://www.gloucestercattle.org.uk
     Sec: Gill Heaven
▲   Un-incorporated Society
○   *B; recording, support & development of the breed of
     Gloucester cattle
●   Inf
<   Rare Breeds Survival Trust
M   140 i

Gloucestershire Chamber of Commerce & Industry   1902
■   Chargrove House, Main Rd, Shurdington, CHELTENHAM, Glos,
     GL51 5GA.   (hq)
     01242 864164
     email john.cripps@gloscci.org   http://www.gloscci.org
     Managing Dir: John Cripps
Br 2
○   *C
Gp Retail; Industrial; Business club
<   Bristol Cham Comm & Ind
M   500 i & f

**Gloucestershire Old Spot Pig Breeders' Club   (GOSPBC)
1992**
■   Freepost (GL442), CIRENCESTER, Glos, GL7 5BR.   (hsp)
     01285 860229
     email mail@oldspots.org.uk   http://www.oldspots.org.uk
     Sec: Richard Lutwyche
▲   Un-incorporated Society
○   *B
●   ET - Expt - Inf - VE
M   300 i, UK / 10 i, o'seas
¶   Spot Press (NL) - 4.

**Gloucestershire Society for Industrial Archaeology   (GSIA)
1964**
■   Oak House, Hamshill, Coaley, DURSLEY, Glos, GL11 5EH.
     (hsp)
     01453 860595
     email ray.wilson@coaley.net   http://www.gsia.org.uk
     Hon Sec: Dr R Wilson
▲   Registered Charity
Br 1
○   *L; to stimulate interest in, to record, to study & where
     appropriate to preserve, items of industrial archaeology
     especially in the county of Gloucestershire
●   Conf - Mtgs - Res - Exhib - SG - Inf - PL - VE
<   Assn Industrial Archaeology
M   215 i, 1 f, 7 org, UK / 1 i, o'seas
¶   Jnl - 1; ftm, £9 nm.   NL - 4; free.

**Glued Laminated Timber Association   (GLULAM/GLTA)
1988**
■   Chiltern House, Stocking Lane, HIGH WYCOMBE, Bucks,
     HP14 4ND.   (hq)
     01494 565180   fax 01494 565487
     http://www.glulam.co.uk
     Sec: Mrs P M Presland
○   *T; an independent trade association of manufacturers,
     distributors & suppliers of glulam
●   Promotion of glued laminated timber - Publication of technical
     information
M   f

GM Freeze
NR 50 South Yorkshire Buildings, Silkstone Common, BARNSLEY,
     S Yorks, S75 4RJ.
     0845 217 8992
     email enquiry@gmfreeze.org   http://www.gmfreeze.org
     Campaign coordinator: Eve Mitchell
○   campaign for government freeze on genetically modified crops
     and foods

** **Go Outdoors - Outdoor Industries Association
     Organisation lost; see Introduction paragraph 3**

Goat Veterinary Society
     a group of the **British Veterinary Association**

Golden Guernsey Goat Society   1986
NR   Gelli Isaf, Rhydcymerau, LLANDEILO, Carmarthenshire,
       SA19 7PY.
       01558 685060
       email gellisaf@hotmail.com
       http://www.goldenguernseygoat.org.uk
       Sec: Mrs Carole Lovell
○   *B

Goldfish Club   1942
■   24 Bridgewater Drive, Great Glen, LEICESTER, LE8 9DX.   (hsp)
       0116-259 2105
       email richardshepherd@dsl.pipex.com
       Hon Sec: Richard Shepherd
▲   Un-incorporated Society
Br   Australia, Canada, N Zealand, USA
○   *G; to advance the equipment for aircrew ditching in the sea
●   Annual Reunion - Dinner
M   400 i, UK / 85 i, o'seas
¶   The Goldfish Club (NL) - 4; ftm only.

Golf Club of Great Britain   (GCGB)   1986
NR   5 Sage Yard, Douglas Rd, SURBITON, Surrey, KT6 7TS.   (hq)
       020 8390 3113
○   *S; to promote golfing activities for members & their guests
M   i & org

Golf Club Managers' Association   (GCMA)   1933
■   7a Beaconsfield Rd, WESTON-super-MARE, Somerset,
       BS23 1YE.   (hq)
       01934 641166   fax 01934 644254
       email hq@gcma.org.uk   http://www.gcma.org.uk
       Chief Exec: Keith Lloyd
▲   Un-incorporated Society
Br   17 regions
○   *N, *P, *S; to provide support & help to secretaries, secretary/
       managers & owners of golf clubs in the UK
●   Conf - Mtgs - ET - Exhib - Stat - Inf - Lib - Empl
M   2,500 i, UK / 50 i, o'seas
¶   Golf Club Management - 12; ftm, £5 each (£55 yr) nm.
       Members' Hbk - 1; ftm only.
×   2007 Association of Golf Club Secretaries

Golf Consultants Association   (GCA)   1999
NR   Federation House, STONELEIGH PARK, Warks, CV8 2RF.
       024 7641 4999   fax 024 7641 4990
       email gca@sportsandplay.com
       http://www.golfconsultants.org.uk
       Sec: Jacqui Baldwin
▲   Un-incorporated Society
○   *P, S; to provide a point of reference for those requiring
       independent professional golf consultancy services world-
       wide
●   Conf - Mtgs
<   a group of the Fedn of Sports & Play Assns (FSPA)
M   12 i

Golf Union of Wales   (WGU)   1895
NR   Catsash, NEWPORT, Monmouthshire, NP18 1JQ.   (hq)
       01633 436040   fax 01633 430843
       email office@golfunionwales.org
       http://www.golfunionwales.org
       Chief Exec: Richard Dixon
○   *S; the governing body for golf in Wales
●   Mtgs - ET - Res - Comp - SG - Stat - Inf - VE
<   Coun Nat Golf Unions; Eur Golf Assn
M   62,000 i, 159 affiliated clubs
¶   Ybk; free.   Information leaflets.
×   2007 (Welsh Golfing Union
             (Welsh Ladies' Golf Union

Golfing Union of Ireland   1891
IRL   Carton House, MAYNOOTH, Co Kildare, Republic of Ireland.
        353 (1) 505 4000   fax 353 (1) 505 4001
        email 09>gui.ie
        Gen Sec: Seamus Smith
○   *S

Good Gardeners' Association   (gGA)   1960
NR   4 Lisle Place, WOTTON-under-EDGE, Glos, GL12 7AZ.   (hsb)
       01453 520322
       email info@goodgardeners.org.uk
       http://www.goodgardeners.org.uk
       Hon Sec: Matt Adams
▲   Registered Charity
○   *H; a membership based charity for people who want to grow
       & eat nutritious food; to promote the concept of 'moving
       beyond organic'; no dig gardening & the use of compost
●   Conf - ET - Res
M   300 i, 5 f, 10 org, UK / 5 i, o'seas
¶   NL - 4; ftm only.

Goon Show Preservation Society   (GSPS)   1972
■   114 Fountains Rd, IPSWICH, Suffolk, IP2 9TW.   (sp)
       07825 699539
       email johnrepsch@hotmail.com
       Sec: Tina Hammond,   Chief Exec: John Repsch
▲   Un-incorporated Society
Br   6; Australia, Canada, Germany, Japan, S Africa, USA
○   *; to ensure that as many Goon Show recordings & other
       related information / recordings / articles as possible are
       archived; to meet like-minded people
Gp   Archive recordings: Audio, video & print
●   Mtgs - Res
<   Goon Appreciation Socs: Perth & Victoria (Australia)
M   456 i, UK / 92 i, o'seas
       (Sub: £10 UK / £11 o'seas)
¶   NL - 4.

** Gooseberry Society
       Organisation lost: see Introduction paragraph 3

Governing Council of the Cat Fancy   (GCCF)   1910
■   5 King's Castle Business Park, The Drove, BRIDGWATER,
       Somerset, TA6 4AG.   (hq)
       01278 427575
       Office Mgr: Miss Jackie Beeson
○   *V
●   Registration of pedigree cats - Licensing of cat shows for
       pedigree cats
M   143 cat clubs

Gower Society   1947
■   The Orchard, Perriswood, Penmaen, SWANSEA, Glam,
       SA3 2HN.   (hsp)
       01792 371665
       Hon Sec: Mrs Ruth Ridge
▲   Registered Charity
○   *L; promotion of knowledge of the history & conservation of the
       physical aspects of the Lordship of Gower
Gp   Planning search; Publication; Footpaths; Working party;
       Programmes
●   Conf - Mtgs - ET - Inf - VE - LG - Archives - Weekly excursions -
       Clearing footpaths
<   Nat Trust; Campaign Protection Rural Wales; Ramblers' Assn
M   1,700 i
¶   Jnl - 1; ftm, £5.95 nm.   Guide to Gower; £4.95.
       Gower Walks; £3.   Butterflies of Gower; £2.50.
       Gower Way (leaflet); 75p.   Gower in Focus; £15.
       Vernacular Gower; £8.50 (hardback) £4.50 (paperback)
       The Castles of Gower;   Edgar Evans of Gower;
          The Churches & Chapels of Gower; all £3.50.

© CBD Research Ltd · Beckenham · BR3 5JS · Tel 020 8650 7745 · Fax 020 8650 0768 · E-mail cbd@cbdresearch.com · www.cbdresearch.com

Grain & Feed Trade Association Ltd   (GAFTA)   1971
- ■ GAFTA House, 6 Chapel Place, Rivington St, LONDON, EC2A 3SH.   (hq)
   020 7814 9666   fax 020 7814 8383
   email post@gafta.com   http://www.gafta.com
   Dir-Gen: Mrs Pamela Kirby Johnson
- ○ *T; to promote international trade in grains, animal feeding-stuffs, pulses & rice
- Gp Shippers; Brokers; Crushers; Dealers & manufacturers; Grain, protein, feeding stuffs & marine & animal products; Pulses
- ● Conf - Mtgs - ET - Res - Exhib - SG - Stat - Inf - Arbitration - Contracts
- M c 900 f in 80 countries
- ¶ NL - 6; ftm, £2 nm.   Forms of Contract.
   Hbk - 1;   AR - 1; both ftm.

Grand Lodge of Antient Free & Accepted Masons of Scotland (The Grand Lodge of Scotland)   1736
- NR Freemason's Hall, 96 George St, EDINBURGH, EH2 3DH.   (hq)
   0131-225 5577   fax 0131-225 3953
   email gladmin@grandlodgescotland.org
   http://www.grandlodgescotland.com
   Grand Sec: David M Begg
- Br 658
- ○ *N; freemasonry
- ● Mtgs - Lib - VE
- < Scot Museums Coun
- M 26,000 i, UK / 12,000 o'seas
- ¶ Ybk - 1; £10.

Grand National Archery Society   (GNAS)   1861
- ■ Lilleshall National Sports Centre, NEWPORT, Shropshire, TF10 9AT.   (hq)
   01952 677888   fax 01952 606019
   email enquiries@gnas.org   http://www.gnas.org
   Chief Exec: David Sherratt
- ▲ Company Limited by Guarantee
- Br clubs
- ○ *S; national governing body for the sport of archery in all its forms; to act as the contact office for all clubs in the UK
- Gp Clubs: Target, Field, Popinjay, Flight, Clout, Recurve, Compound
   Bow types: Olympic, Compound, Long bow, Cross bow
- ● Conf - Mtgs - Exhib - Comp
- < Fédn Intle de Tir à l'Arc (FITA); Brit Olympic Assn (BOA); Brit Paralympic Assn
- M 25,000+ i, 1,100 clubs
- ¶ Archery UK - 4; ftm, £4.25 nm.

Grand Priory of the Most Venerable Order of the Hospital of St John of Jerusalem   1888
- NR The Chancery, St John's Gate, St John's Lane, Clerkenwell, LONDON, EC1M 4DA.   (hq & museum)
   The St John Ambulance - offers first aid training for industry, commerce & & general public; also responsible for Public first aid duties; Ophthalmic Hospital in Jerusalem (eye hospital); Care of the elderly; Community care

Grandparents Action Group   (GAG)   2001
- NR 7 Hilda Hook Close, Madeley, TELFORD, Shropshire, TF7 4HU.   (hq)
   01952 582621   fax 01952 582621
   Chmn: Mrs Pamela Wilson,   Sec: Mrs Denise Matekie
- ○ *G, *K; to help grandparents maintain & protect the relationship between grandchildren & grandparents when contact is an issue
- ● Conf - Res - Stat - Inf - LG
- M 208 i

Grandparents' Association   1987
- ■ Moot House, The Stow, HARLOW, Essex, CM20 3AG.   (hq)
   01279 428040   fax 01279 428040
   email info@grandparents-association.org.uk
   http://www.grandparents-association.org.uk
   Chief Exec: Mrs Lynn Chesterman
- ▲ Registered Charity
- ○ *K, *W; to work with all grandparents for the best interests of children; we particularly support those who are denied contact with their grandchildren, who are raising their grandchildren or who have childcare responsibilities
- Gp Support groups in some areas; Information; Hearings
- ● Conf - Mtgs - ET - Support groups (grandparents & toddlers)
   Helpline: 0845 434 9585
- < Children's Rights Alliance for England; Nat Coun for Voluntary Child Care Organisations; Nat Coun for Voluntary Organisations
- M 1,085 i, 182 f, 8 org, 20 social services
   (Sub: £20 i, £225 f, £50 org, £200 social services)
- ¶ Grandparent Times (NL) - 3;   AR; both free.
   Specialist publications; £4.40 m, £5.75 nm.
      Relative Values . . . Missing out on Contact?
      Relative Values . . . The Best Interests of the Child?
      An Evaluation of the Grandparent & Toddler Group Initiative.

Grantham Chamber of Commerce   1961
- NR Springfield House, Springfield Rd, GRANTHAM, Lincs, NG21 7BG.
   01476 568970   fax 01476 575758
   Sec & Chief Exec: Mrs J S P Smith
- ▲ Company Limited by Guarantee
- ○ *C
- ● Expt - Inf - Lib
- < Brit Chams Comm
- M 20 f

Graphical, Paper & Media Union
   since 2004 a sector of Amicus, now **Unite the Union**

Grassroots Action on Food & Farming
   'we do not need an entry''

Great Britain Basketball
   organisation replaced 2006 by the **British Basketball Federation**

Great Britain Diving Federation   (GBDF)   1993
- NR 6 Derwent Ave, Wilsden, BRADFORD, W Yorks, BD15 0LY.
   (admin/dir/p)
   01535 273633
   http://www.diving-gbdf.com
   Admin Dir: Mrs Lesley Grist
- ▲ Un-incorporated Society
- ○ *S
- ● Conf - ET - Comp - Inf
- < Cent Coun for Physical Recreation (CCPR); Scot Amat Swimming Assn (SASA)
- M 850 i

Great Britain Luge Association
- NR 61 West Malvern Rd, MALVERN, Worcs, WR14 4NF.
   01684 576604
   http://www.gbla.org.uk
   Sec Gen: Mark Armstrong
- ○ *S; luge racing

Great Britain Postcard Club   (GBPCC)   1961
- ■ 34 Harper House, St James Crescent, LONDON, SW9 7LW. (hsp)
    020 7771 9404
    email drenebrennan@yahoo.co.uk
    Chief Exec: Drene Brennan
- ▲ Un-incorporated Society
- ○ *G, *X; postcard collecting; world friendship
- ● Conf - Res - Comp
- < Clubs in USA: Disney, Duneland, Metropolitan, San Francisco; Sunshine; Tuscan; Webfoot
- M 200 i, UK / 100 i, o'seas
- ¶ Postcard World - 6; £10 yr m.

Great Britain Racquetball Federation   (GBRF)   1984
- NR 78 Suffolk Drive, WOODBRIDGE, Suffolk, IP12 2TP. (hsp)
    01394 461069
- ▲ Un-incorporated Society
- ○ *S; to promote the game of racquetball

Great Britain Target Shooting Federation
    since 2007 **British Shooting**

Great North of Scotland Railway Association   (GNSRA)   1964
- ■ 19 Seafield Terrace, PORTSOY, Banffshire, AB45 2QB. (hsp)
    Hon Sec: G Boardman
- ▲ Un-incorporated Society
- ○ *G; study, acquisition & preservation of documents, illustrations & information relating to the railway
- Gp Specialist groups according to the research on hand
- ● Mtgs - Res - Exhib - Inf - VE
- M 315 i, 5 org, UK / 3 i, o'seas
- ¶ Great North Review - 4; (Index every 5 yrs); LM - 1; all ftm.

Great Northern Railway Society   (GNR Society)   1981
- ■ 57 North Rd, GLOSSOP, Derbys, SK13 7AU. (hsp)
    01457 852851
    http://www.gnrs.150m.com
    Hon Sec: Peter Hall
- ▲ Un-incorporated Society
- ○ *G; historical research & study of the former Great Northern Railway & its joint lines from inception to present day
- ● Mtgs - Res - Exhib - SG - Inf - PL
- M c 300 i, UK / 5 i, o'seas
- ¶ GN News (Jnl) - 6; ftm only.
    Booklets with information on coaches, wagons etc; prices vary.

Great Western Society Ltd   (GWS)   1961
- ■ DIDCOT, Oxon, OX11 7NJ. (hq)
    01235 817200   fax 01235 510621
    email didrlyc@globalnet.co.uk
    http://www.didcotrailwaycentre.org.uk
    Sec: F Cooper
- ▲ Company Limited by Guarantee; Registered Charity
- Br 8
- ○ *G; study of history, equipment & operation of the former Great Western Railway; preservation of items of interest - locomotives, rolling stock, buildings, etc
- ● Conf - Mtgs - ET - Res - Exhib - SG - Inf - VE
- < Assn of Independent Museums; Heritage Railways; Assn of Brit Transport & Engineering Museums; Transport Trust
- M 4,520 i, UK / 120 i, o'seas
- ¶ Great Western Echo - 4; ftm, £1 nm.
    NL - 7;   AR; both ftm only.

Greater Altrincham Chamber of Commerce, Trade & Industry
    since September 2005 **Altrincham & Sale Chamber of Commerce**

Greater London Industrial Archaeology Society   (GLIAS) 1968
- ■ 14 Mount Rd, BARNET, Herts, EN4 9RL. (hsp)
    email secretary@glias.org.uk   http://www.glias.org.uk
    Hon Sec: Brian James-Strong
- ▲ Company Limited by Guarantee; Registered Charity
- ○ *L; informing the public of London's industrial history, & the preparation of photographic & documentary records of industrial monuments in Greater London
- Gp Recording
- ● Res - SG - Inf - VE - Lectures - Walks
- < Assn Indl Archaeology (AIA); Coun for Brit Archaeology
- M c 600 i, c 50 org
- ¶ London's Industrial Archaeology (Jnl) - irreg; ftm.
    NL - 6; free.

Greater Manchester Chamber of Commerce   1820
- NR Lee House, 90 Great Bridgewater St, MANCHESTER, M1 5JW. (hq)
    0161-245 4800
    email info@gmchamber.co.uk
    http://www.gmchamber.co.uk
    Chief Exec: Angie Robinson
- ▲ Company Limited by Guarantee
- ○ *C; promotion of trade & industry & provision of specialist information & representation for NW England
- < Chams Comm NW
- M f
- × 2004 (Chamber Business Connections [Oldham] (Manchester Chamber of Commerce & Industry

Greek Institute   1969
- ■ 34 Bush Hill Rd, LONDON, N21 2DS. (hsp)
    020 8360 7968   fax 020 8360 7968
    email info@greekinstitute.co.uk
    http://www.greekinstitute.co.uk
    Dir: Dr Kypros Tofallis
- Br 20
- ○ *L; to promote modern Greek studies in UK
- ● Mtgs - Exam - Res - ET - Comp - Inf - VE
- M 20 i, f
- ¶ Anglo-Greek Review - 4; ftm.

Green Alliance Trust   1978
- NR 36 Buckingham Palace Rd, LONDON, SW1W 0RE. (hq)
    020 7233 7433   fax 020 7233 9033
    email ga@green-alliance.org.uk
    http://www.green-alliance.org.uk
    Dir: Guy Thompson
- ▲ Registered Charity
- ○ *K; to promote sustainable development by ensuring that the environment is at the heart of decision-making
- Gp Environment
- ● Conf - Mtgs - Res - Inf - LG
- < Eur Envt Bureau
- M 450 i, 100 f, 30 org, UK
- ¶ Parliamentary NL - 26.
    Inside Track - 4.   AR.

Green Lane Association   (GLASS)   1995
- NR PO Box 918, PETERBOROUGH, Cambs, PE1 9DX.
    email glass@glass-uk.org   http://www.glass-uk.org
    Chmn: D Codrai
- ▲ Un-incorporated Society
- Br 12
- ○ *G, *K; to promote & protect vehicular rights of way & unsurfaced highways
- ● Mtgs - ET - Res - Exhib - SG - LG
- < Brit Trust for Consvn Volunteers (BTCV); Land Access & Recreation Assn (LARA)
- M 520 i, 20 org
- ¶ Green Lanes - 4;   Northern Bulletin - 4;
    Southern Bulletin - 4; all ftm only.

© CBD Research Ltd · Beckenham · BR3 5JS · Tel 020 8650 7745 · Fax 020 8650 0768 · E-mail cbd@cbdresearch.com · www.cbdresearch.com

Greenock Chamber of Commerce 1813
NR   The Business Store, 75-81 Cathcart St, GREENOCK,
      Renfrewshire, PA15 1DE.   (hq)
      01475 715555   fax 01475 715566
      email hugh.bunten@greenock-chamber.org.uk
      http://www.greenock-chamber.org.uk
      Exec Admin: Hugh Bunten
▲   Un-incorporated Society
○   *C; to promote local business, both home & export trade
●   Mtgs - ET - Inf - LG - Networking events
<   Brit & Scot Chams Comm
M   150 f
¶   Bulletin - 4;   AR.
✕   Chamber of Commerce & Manufactures of Greenock

GreenSpace
NR   Caversham Court, Church Rd, Caversham, READING, Berks,
      RG4 7AD.
      0118-946 9060   fax 0118-946 9061
○   *H, *K; to create 'a network of easily accessible, safe, attractive
      & welcoming parks, gardens & green spaces'

Greenwich, Bexley & Lewisham Chamber of Commerce
    since July 2007 **South East London Chamber of Commerce**

Greeting Card Association (GCA) 1919
■   United House, North Rd, LONDON, N7 9DP.   (hq)
      020 7619 0396   fax 020 7607 6411
      email gca@max-publishing.co.uk
      http://www.greetingcardassociation.org.uk
      Admin: Sharon Little
▲   Company Limited by Guarantee
○   *T; to promote, protect & celebrate the greeting card industry
●   Mtgs - ET - Inf - LG
M   320 f
¶   Progressive Greetings - 12; £50 yr.

Gregorian Association 1870
NR   26 The Grove, Ealing, LONDON, W5 5LH.
      020 8840 5832
      http://www.beaufort.demon.co.uk/chant.htm
      Chmn: Greg Macartney
○   *D; for those interested in singing the Gregorian chant

Greyhound Action 1997
NR   PO Box 127, KIDDERMINSTER, Worcs, DY10 3UZ,
      01562 745778   fax 0870 138 3993
      email info@greyhoundaction.org.uk
      http://www.greyhoundaction.org.uk
○   campaigning for the abolition of greyhound racing

Grieg Society of Great Britain 1992
■   c/o The Royal Norwegian Embassy, 25 Belgrave Sq, LONDON,
      SW1X 8QD.   (mail address)
      01634 714434   fax 01634 714434
      Chmn: Beryl Foster,   Mem Sec: Audrey Banker
▲   Un-incorporated Society
○   *A; to promote interest & encourage appreciation of the music
      of Edvard Hagerup Grieg (1843-1907) & other Norwegian
      composers
●   Conf - Mtgs - Res - Exhib - Inf - Lib - Recitals & concerts
<   Intl Grieg Soc (Bergen, Norway);
      Grieg Soc(s) in: Oslo (Norway), Moscow (Russia), Münster &
      Leipzig (Germany), Tokyo (Japan), Groningen (Netherlands),
      New York (USA), Tokyo (Japan)
M   100 i, UK / 8 i, o'seas
¶   The Grieg Companion (Jnl) - 1; ftm, £3 nm.
      NL - 3; ftm only.

Grimsby & Cleethorpes Chamber of Trade
    a local chamber of the **Hull & Humber Chamber of Commerce,
    Industry & Shipping**

Ground Forum (GF) 1992
■   83 Copers Cope Rd, BECKENHAM, Kent, BR3 1NR.   (asa)
      020 8663 0947   fax 020 8663 0949
      email gforum@ground-forum.org.uk
      http://www.ground-forum.org.uk
      Hon Sec: Dianne Jennings
▲   Un-incorporated Society
○   *T; all aspects of geotechnical engineering (site investigation,
      foundation construction, tunnelling, ground improvement &
      remediation, geoenvironmentalism)
●   Mtgs - LG
<   Construction Ind Coun (CIC)
M   9 org

Ground Limestone Producers Association
IRL   Confederation House, 84/86 Lower Baggot St, DUBLIN 2,
      Republic of Ireland.
○   *T; producers of ground limestone for agricultural use
<   IBEC

Group-Analytic Society (London) (GAS) 1952
■   102 Belsize Lane, LONDON, NW3 5BB.   (hq)
      020 7435 6611
▲   Registered Charity
○   *P; promotion & development of group analysis as a treatment,
      prophylaxis & science

Group Auto Union UK & Ireland Ltd 1974
NR   Roydsdale House, Roydsdale Way, Euroway Trading Estate,
      BRADFORD, W Yorks, BD4 6SE.   (hq)
      01274 654600   fax 01274 654610
      http://www.gau.co.uk
○   *T; a specialist business group for independent motor factors
M   f
✕   2005 Factoring Services Group

Group for Education in Museums (GEM) 1948
NR   Primrose House, 193 Gillingham Rd, GILLINGHAM, Kent,
      ME7 4EP.   (hq)
      01634 312409
▲   Un-incorporated Society
Br   8
○   *E; to promote educational work in museums & related
      institutions; to foster the highest standards in museum
      education
M   i

Group for Solicitors with Disabilities
    a group of the **Law Society of England & Wales**

Group Travel Organisers Association (GTOA) 1992
■   Beech Croft, Weston-under-Lizard, SHIFNAL, Shropshire,
      TF11 8JT.   (hsp)
      01952 860269   fax 0844 736 5822
      email gen.sec@gtoa.co.uk   http://www.gtoa.co.uk
      Gen Sec: Michael Tebbutt
▲   Un-incorporated Society
Br   6
○   *T; for group travel organisers & travel trade suppliers
●   Conf - Mtgs - SG - VE - LG
M   213 i, 370 org, UK / 2 f, o'seas
¶   GTOA News - 4;   Hbk - 3 yrly;   AGM Report - 1;
      NL (to the 6 branches) - 4; all ftm.

Growing Media Association   (GMA)
- ■ Horticulture House, 19 High St, Theale, READING, Berks, RG7 5AH.   (hq)
  0118-930 3132   fax 0118-932 3453
  email info@the-hta.org.uk
  http://www.growingmedia.co.uk
  Chief Exec: Tim Briercliffe
- ▲ Un-incorporated Society
- ○ *T; the development, production, marketing & sale of growing media & soil improvers in the UK & Ireland
- ● Mtgs - Inf - LG
- M 24 f
- ¶ NL - 4; ftm only.

GS1 Ireland
- IRL The Nutley Building, Merrion Rd, DUBLIN 4, Republic of Ireland.
  353 (1) 208 0660   fax 353 (1) 208 0670
  email info@gs1ie.org   http://www.gs1ie.org
  Chief Exec: Jim Bracken
- ○ *T; the article number industry
- < IBEC
- × 2005 EAN Ireland

GS1 UK   1976
- NR Staple Court, 11 Staple Inn Buildings, LONDON, WC1V 7QH.   (hq)
  020 7092 3500   fax 020 7681 2290
  email info@gs1uk.org   http://www.gs1uk.org
  Chief Exec: Steve Coussins
- ▲ Company Limited by Guarantee
- ○ *T; dedicated to the development of global data standards for the supply chain
- ● Conf - Mtgs - ET - Res
- < GS1
- M 17,000 f
- ¶ GSQ - 4; ftm.
  e-Highlights (email NL) - 4; ftm only.
- × 2005 (February) Association for Standards & Practices in Electronic Trade - EAN UK Ltd

Guernsey Chamber of Commerce   1808
- NR 16 Glategny Esplanade (suite 3), ST PETER PORT, Guernsey, GY1 1WN.   (hq)
  01481 727483   fax 01481 710755
  email director@chamber.guernsey.net
  http://www.chamber.guernsey.net
  Dir: Mike Collins
- ▲ Company Limited by Guarantee
- ○ *C; to link together the members of the business community so that they can speak with an authoritative voice on matters concerning the trade, industry & commerce in the Isle of Guernsey
- ● Mtgs - Inf - LG
- < Brit Chams Comm
- M c 600 f (Guernsey)
- ¶ Contact - 12; ftm (extra copies £2.50), £2.50 nm.

Guernsey Growers Association   (GGA)   1894
- ■ Landes du Marche, VALE, Guernsey, GY6 8DE.   (hq)
  01481 253713   fax 01481 254015
  Sec: Mrs V Mechem
- ○ *F; the farming & growing of crops under glass & in the open
- ● Conf - Mtgs - Exhib - Comp - Stat - Inf - VE
- M 150 i & f (mainly local growers)
- ¶ NL.   Ybk.   AR.

Guide Association
  registered name of **Girlguiding UK**

Guide Dogs for the Blind Association   (GDBA)   1934
- NR Hillfields, Burghfield, READING, Berks, RG7 3YG.   (hq)
  0118-983 5555
  http://www.gdba.org.uk
  Chief Exec: Bridget Wall
- ▲ Registered Charity
- ○ *W; to enhance the mobility, independence & quality of life of sight impaired people by providing guide dogs & other services
- M i

Guild of Agricultural Journalists   1946
- ■ Isfield Cottage, Church Rd, CROWBOROUGH, E Sussex, TN6 1BN.   (hsp/b)
  01892 610628
  Hon Gen Sec: Don Gomery
- ▲ Registered Charity
- ○ *P
- ● Conf - Mtgs - ET - Comp - VE - LG
- < Intl Fedn Agricl Journalists (IFAJ)
- M 600 i, UK / 13 i, o'seas
- ¶ NL - 4.   AR.   Ybk.

Guild of Air Pilots & Air Navigators of London   (GAPAN)   1929
- ■ Cobham House, 9 Warwick Court, Gray's Inn, LONDON, WC1R 5DJ.   (hq)
  020 7404 4032
  http://www.gapan.org
  Clerk: Paul J Tacon
- ▲ Livery Company - un-incorporated association
- Br Australia, Hong Kong, N Zealand
- ○ *E, *P; a livery company of the City of London; achievement of air safety through the highest standards for pilots & navigators
- Gp C'ees: Technical & air safety, Education & training, Trophies & awards;
  Benevolent Fund Board of Management [for airmen & their dependents]
- ● Conf - Mtgs - ET - Res - SG - VE - LG
- M 1,700 i, UK / 500 i, o'seas
- ¶ Guild News (Jnl) - 6; ftm only.

Guild of Air Traffic Control Officers   (GATCO)   1954
- NR Central Admin Facility, 4 St Mary's Rd, Bingham, NOTTINGHAM, NG13 8DW.   (hq)
  01949 876405
  http://www.gatco.org
  Pres: Richard Dawson
- ▲ Un-incorporated Society
- Br 5
- ○ *P
- Gp C'ees: Technical; Professional
- ● Conf - Mtgs - Exhib - SG - Inf - LG
- < Intl Fedn of Air Traffic Control Assns (IFATCA); Flight Safety C'ee; Gen Aviation Safety Coun; Parliamentary Advy Coun on Transport Safety (PACTS)
- M 2,250 i, 29 f, UK / 150 i, 3 f, o'seas
- ¶ Transmit (Jnl) - 4.   LM - 8.   AR.

Guild of Antique Dealers & Restorers   (GADAR)   1989
- NR 2 Willow Cottages, Hereford Rd, SHREWSBURY, Shropshire, SY3 7QL.   (hq)
  01743 271852
  http://www.gadar.co.uk
  Sec: Maureen Edmondson
- ▲ Un-incorporated Society
- ○ *T; to facilitate & offer advice on: repairs & restoration to all antiques, & valuations for insurance & probate
- ● Res - Comp - Stat
- M 150 i, UK / 10 i, o'seas
- ¶ NL - 4; ftm only.

© CBD Research Ltd · Beckenham · BR3 5JS · Tel 020 8650 7745 · Fax 020 8650 0768 · E-mail cbd@cbdresearch.com · www.cbdresearch.com

Guild of Architectural Ironmongers   (GAI)   1961

- ■ 8 Stepney Green, LONDON, E1 3JU.   (hq)
  020 7790 3431   fax 020 7790 8517
  email info@gai.org.uk   http://www.gai.org.uk
  Chief Exec: Gary Amer
- ▲ Company Limited by Guarantee
- ○ *T; the best possible materials & service for use in each project
- ● Conf - Mtgs - ET - Exam - Exhib - SG - Inf
- < Door & Hardware Inst (USA); Construction Products Assn (CPA)
- M 190 full members (distributors), 90 associates (manufacturers)
- ¶ Architectural Ironmongery Jnl - 4; ftm.   Ybk - 1.
  Guild News - 4;   Education Prospectus - 1;
  AR - 1; all ftm.

Guild of Aviation Artists   (GAvA)   1971

- NR Trenchard House, 85 Farnborough Rd, FARNBOROUGH,
  Hants, GU14 6TF.   (hq)
  01252 513123
- ○ *A, *P; encouragement of Aviation Art in all its forms
- ● Conf - Mtgs - ET - Exhib - Comp - SG - Inf - PL - VE
- < R Aero Club
- M i

Guild of Battlefield Guides   2003

- NR Cooper's Court, Moreton, ONGAR, Essex, CM5 0LE.
  01277 890470
  http://www.battlefieldguides.co.uk
  Sec: Graeme Cooper
- ○ *P;

Guild of Bricklayers   1932

- ■ 83 Windsor Rd, Ashton-in-Makerfield, WIGAN, Lancs,
  WN4 9ET.   (treas/p)
  01942 724927
  email barry@walton120.freeserve.co.uk
  http://www.guild-of-bricklayers.org.uk
  Nat Treas: Barry Walton
- ▲ Registered Charity
- ○ *T
- ● Conf - Mtgs - ET - Comp
- M 500 i, 5 colleges
- ¶ Jnl - 1;   NL - 1; both free.

Guild of British Camera Technicians   (GBCT)   1978

- NR c/o Panavision, Metropolitan Centre, Bristol Rd, GREENFORD,
  Middx, UB6 8GD.   (hq)
  020 8813 1999   fax 020 8813 2111
  email admin@gbct.org   http://www.gbct.org
  Co Sec & Office Mgr: Christine Henwood
- ○ *P; for professionally recognised camera technicians with the
  film, TV & video industry
- ● Conf - ET - Exhib
- M 500 i, UK / 50 i, o'seas
- ¶ GBCT TECHS Magazine - 6; ftm, £12 yr.

Guild of British Coach Operators   (1985)

- ■ PO Box 5657, SOUTHEND-on-SEA, Essex, SS1 3WT.   (hq)
  email admin@coach-tours.co.uk
  http://www.coach-tours.co.uk
  Admin: Richard Delahoy
- ▲ Company Limited by Guarantee
- ○ *T; to increase public recognition of the role that coaches play
  in tourism & public transport; to establish working
  relationships with organisations & bodies involved in
  transport
- < Intl Motor Coach Gp (USA)
- M 21 f

Guild of British Découpeurs   (GBD)   1999

- ■ Chimneys, 18 Pembridge Close, Charlton Kings,
  CHELTENHAM, Glos, GL52 6XY.   (sp)
  01242 235302
  http://www.decoupageguild.co.uk
  Sec: Mrs Madeleine Smith
- ○ *A, *G; to provide information & education in the art &
  authentic techniques of découpage (the art of applying
  decorative paper cut-outs to surfaces)
- ● Mtgs - ET - Inf - PL
- M 35 i, UK / 290 i, o'seas
- ¶ Shortcuts - 2; ftm only.

Guild of British Film & Television Editors   (GBFE)   1966

- ■ 72 Pembroke Rd, LONDON, W8 6NX.   (hsp)
  020 7602 8319   fax 020 7602 8319
  Sec: Sally Fisher
- ○ *P
- ● Conf - Res - Exhib - Inf - VE - Film shows
- < BECTU
- M 91 i, UK / 8 i, o'seas
- ¶ NL - irreg.
- ✕ 2005-06 Guild of British Film Editors

Guild of British Tie Makers
   a group of the **British Clothing Industry Association**

Guild of Builders & Contractors   (GBC)   1994

- ■ Crest House, 102-104 Church Rd, TEDDINGTON, Middx,
  TW11 8PY.   (hq)
  020 8977 1105   fax 020 8943 3151
  email info@buildersguild.co.uk
  http://www.buildersguild.co.uk
  Dir: E A Goddard
- ▲ Company Limited
- ○ *T; for individuals & firms who are actively engaged in the
  building industry, who are experienced & knowledgeable &
  trade with integrity
- ● Mtgs - Stat - Inf - LG
- M 800 i, 2,000 f
  (Sub: £75)
- ¶ NL - 6; ftm only.

Guild of Business Travel Agents
   since 2005 **Guild of Travel Management Companies**

Guild of Catholic Doctors - Guild of St Luke, Sts Cosmas & Damian
   since 2008 **Catholic Medical Association**

Guild of Church Braillists   (GoCB)   1911

- ■ 5 North St, SOUTHPORT, Merseyside, PR9 9HX.   (regd/office)
  01363 860141
  http://www.gocb.org
  Sec: Mary Hazlewood
- ▲ Registered Charity
- ○ *P, *R; to advance the Christian religion in particular by
  transcribing Christian literature from print into braille; to
  increase the number of Christian books in the National
  Library for the Blind
- ● ET - Lib
- M i (blind proof readers, Braille consultants, transcribers)
- ¶ AR - 1; free.

Guild of Church Musicians   (GCM)   1888
■ St Katharine Cree, 86 Leadenhall St, LONDON, EC3A 3DH.
   (hsb/regd/office)
   01883 743168
   http://www.churchmusicians.org
   Gen Sec: John Ewington
▲ Registered Charity
Br Australia
○ *L; to promote the highest standards in church music & liturgy
● Conf - Mtgs - ET - Exam (for Archbishop's certificate in church
   music & in public worship; Fellowship of Guild of Church
   Musicians)
< University of Newcastle (NSW)
M 720 i, UK / 80 i, o'seas
¶ Laudate - 3; ftm;   Ybk - 1; both ftm.

Guild of Cleaners & Launderers   (GCL)   1949
NR 7 Churchill Court, 58 Station Rd, NORTH HARROW, Middx,
   HA2 7SA.   (hsb)
   0845 600 1838
   email enquiries@gcl.org.uk   http://www.gcl.org.uk
   Gen Sec: Mrs Sandra Pearce
▲ Registered Charity
Br 9
○ *P; examining body of the textile care industry & joint awarding
   body with SVQs/NVQs
Gp Laundry & dry cleaning
● Conf - Mtgs - Exam - Inf - Lib
M 450 i, UK / 25 i, o'seas
¶ NL - 6.   Retail Sales Garment Cleaning.
   Textiles for Launderers & Drycleaners.
   The After Care of Silk.   Stain Removal Guide.
      Other publications.

Guild of Colon Hydrotherapists   2003
NR 12 Chapel Close, Leavesden, WATFORD, Herts, WD25 7AR.
   07825 517231
   email colonicinfo2@yahoo.co.uk
   http://www.colonic-association.com

** Guild of Curative Hypnotherapists
   Organisation lost; see Introduction paragraph 3.

Guild of Drama Adjudicators   (GODA)   1947
■ 25 The Drive, Bengeo, HERTFORD, Herts, SG14 3DE.   (hsp)
   01992 581993
   email jo.godasec@talktalk.net
   http://www.amdram.co.uk/goda
   Hon Sec: Mrs Joan Crossley
▲ Registered Charity
○ *P; to supply qualified adjudicators to all organisations
   promoting amateur drama
● Conf - Mtgs - ET - Inf - Adjudication at drama festivals
M 125 i
¶ News & Views - 3; ftm only.   Asides - 1; free.
   A Directory of Drama Adjudicators - 1; free.

Guild of Enamellers   (GE)   1978
■ c/o 60 Deane Croft Rd, Eastcote, PINNER, Middx, HA5 1SP.
   (puboffr/p)
   020 8868 8853
   email erika.speel@yahoo.co.uk
   http://www.guildofenamellers.org
   Publicity Officer: Erika Speel
▲ Un-incorporated Society
Br 7
○ *A; to promote the craft of enamelling on metal; to exert a
   progressive influence on standards of workmanship & design
● Conf - Mtgs - ET - Res - Exhib - Lib - PL - VE
M 200 i, UK / 5 i, o'seas
   (Sub: £20 UK / £28 o'seas)
¶ Jnl - 4; ftm, on request, nm.

Guild of Erotic Artists
■ Beaumont Hall Studios, Beaumont Hall Lane, Redburn Rd,
   ST ALBANS, Herts, AL3 6RN.   (hq)
   01582 791661
   http://www.theguildoferoticartists.com
   Sec: Colin Ballard
○ *A
Gp Artists; Models; Photographers; Sculptors & bodycasters;
   Corporate; Patrons
● Mtgs - ET - Exhib - SG - Inf - PL - Demonstrations of artists'
   skills including photography, sketching, bodycasting, shibari,
   life model drawing, body painting etc
M 160 i, 5 f, UK / 6 i, o'seas
¶ Jade - 6; ftm, £35 nm.

Guild of Fine Food Retailers   (GFFR)   1995
■ Guild House, Station Rd, WINCANTON, Somerset, BA9 9FE.
   (hq)
   01963 824464   fax 01963 824651
   email bobfarrand@finefoodworld.co.uk
   http://www.finefoodworld.co.uk
   Nat Dir: Bob Farrand
▲ Company Limited by Guarantee
○ *T; to champion the cause of speciality food retailers &
   producers
● ET - Res - Exhib - Comp - LG - Cheese training to NVQ
   standard - Great Taste Awards - World Cheese Awards
< UK Cheese Gld; UK Charcuterie Gld
M 1,250 i, UK / 50 i, o'seas
¶ Fine Food Digest - 10; ftm, leese - 1; ftm, £3.50 nm.

Guild of Food Writers   (GFW)   1984
■ 255 Kent House Rd, BECKENHAM, Kent, BR3 1JQ.   (admin/p)
   020 8659 0422
   email admin@gfw.co.uk   http://www.gfw.co.uk
   Admin: Jonathan Woods
▲ Un-incorporated Society
○ *P; to contribute to the growth of public interest in, & knowledge
   of, the subject of food; to campaign for improvements in the
   quality of food
● Conf - Mtgs - ET - Comp - VE - LG
M 360 i
¶ LM - 1; ftm, £190 nm.

Guild of Freemen of the City of London   1908
■ PO Box 1202, KINGSTON upon THAMES, Surrey, KT2 7XB.
   (mail address)
   020 8541 1435   fax 020 8541 1455
   email clerk@guild-freemen-london.co.uk
   Clerk: Brig M I Keun
▲ Company Limited by Guarantee; Registered Charity
○ *G, *W; within the City of London: to support traditions &
   institutions, to promote fellowship & good citizenship, to help
   the needy & underprivileged & to support & promote
   education & training
● ET - VE - Charity work & benevolence
< Hon Company of Freemen of the City of London of N America
M 3,000 i, UK / 200 i, o'seas
¶ The Freeman (Jnl) - 1; ftm, £7.50 nm.   AR; ftm only.

Guild of Glass Engravers   1975
■ 87 Nether St, LONDON, N12 7NP.   (hq)
   020 8446 4050
   http://www.gge.org.uk
   Sec: Mrs Christine Reyland
▲ Registered Charity
Br 9
○ *A, *G, *P; to promote the highest quality of creative design &
   craftsmanship among glass engravers & advance the
   education of the public in the art of glass engraving & other
   forms of surface decoration on glass
● Conf - Mtgs - ET - Exhib - Assessments
M 380 i, UK / 53 i, o'seas
¶ NL - 4; ftm only.

© CBD Research Ltd · Beckenham · BR3 5JS · Tel 020 8650 7745 · Fax 020 8650 0768 · E-mail cbd@cbdresearch.com · www.cbdresearch.com

Guild of Health Ltd   1904

- ■ c/o St Marylebone Parish Church, 17 Marylebone Rd, LONDON, NW1 5LT.   (mail/address)
  020 7563 1389
  email gohealth@freeuk.com   http://www.gohealth.org.uk
  Chmn: Rev Roger Hoath
- ▲ Company Limited by Guarantee; Registered Charity
- Br 25
- ○ *W; to bring together Christian people (clergy, laity, health care professionals) with a concern for healing, wholeness & 'finding God in all things'
- ● Conf - Mtgs - Prayer & meditation - Workshops - Retreats - Seminars - Literature
- < Retreat Assn
- M 350 i
- ¶ Way of Life (Jnl) - 4; ftm, £8 yr nm.   AR - 1; ftm only.

Guild of Health Writers   1994

- ■ Dale Lodge, 88 Wensleydale Rd, HAMPTON, Middx, TW12 2LX.   (chmn/p)
  020 8941 2977   fax 020 8941 2977
  email admin@healthwriters.com
  http://www.healthwriters.com
  Chmn: Caroline White
- ○ *P; for journalists dedicated to providing accurate, broad-based information about health & related subjects to the public
- Gp Ageing; Children's health; Complementary medicine; Fitness; General medicine; Health & education; Medical ethics; Mental health; Mind body medicine; Preventative medicine; Psychology & psychotherapy; Relationships; Women's health
- ● Mtgs - ET - Comp
- M c 230 i
- ¶ Health Writer - 4; ftm only.

Guild of Healthcare Pharmacists

Guild of Healthcare Pharmacists
  an autonomous professional body within **Unite the Union**

Guild of International Butler Administrators & Personal Assistants   1981

- ■ 12 Little Bornes, Dulwich, LONDON, SE21 8SE.   (dir/b)
  020 8670 5585
  http://www.ivorspencer.com
- ▲ Un-incorporated Society
- Br USA, Hong Kong
- ○ *P; to promote the British butler worldwide; to encourage the highest standards among British trained butlers throughout the world
- ● Mtgs - ET - Exam - Comp - Expt - Inf - VE - Empl - Speakers bureau - Placement service
- < Toastmasters for Royal Occasions; Gld Intl Profl Toastmasters
- M 60 i, UK / 75 i, o'seas
- ¶ NL - 2; ftm only.

Guild of International Professional Toastmasters   1990

- ■ 12 Little Bornes, Dulwich, LONDON, SE21 8SE.   (pres/b)
  020 8670 5585
  http://www.ivorspencer.com
- ▲ Un-incorporated Society
- ○ *P; to organise banquets worldwide & to advise companies & embassies on protocol on these occasions; to lecture on the art of after-dinner speaking; to train toastmasters & butlers
- ● Conf - ET - International award for Best After-Dinner Speaker of the Year
- < Toastmasters for Royal Occasions
- M 20 i

Guild of Letting & Management   (GLM Ltd)   1997

- ■ 64 High St, HODDESDON, Herts, EN11 8ET.   (hq)
  01992 479949   fax 01992 451340
  email info@guild-let.co.uk   http://www.guild-let.co.uk
  Chief Exec: Asunta Crolla
- ▲ Company Limited by Guarantee
- Br 2
- ○ *P; for property management letting agents & landlords
- ● Conf - ET - Exam - Inf - LG
- M 75 i, 400 f, 100 org

Guild of Location Managers   1989

- NR PO Box 58010, LONDON, W10 6UZ.
  email admin@golm.org.uk   http://www.golm.org.uk
  Sec: Rikke Dakin
- < a consitutent member of Ciné Guilds of Great Britain

Guild of Mace-Bearers   1950

- ■ 54 Winifred Rd, COULSDON, Surrey, CR5 3JE.   (sb)
  020 8668 5997   fax 020 8407 3062
  http://www.civicprotocol.com
  Guild Clerk: Peter Townsend
- ▲ Un-incorporated Society
- ○ *P; to uphold & preserve the customs of the civic & corporate life of the country & Commonwealth & the dignity of the office of mayor; to offer advice on such matters
- ● Conf - ET - Inf
- M 260 i, UK / 1 i, o'seas
- ¶ The Mace-Bearer - 3;   LM - 1; both ftm only.
  The Manual of the Mace; £10 m only.

Guild of Master Craftsmen   (GMC)   1974

- ■ 166 High St, LEWES, E Sussex, BN7 1XU.   (hq)
  01273 478449   fax 01273 478606
  email theguild@thegmcgroup.com
  http://www.guildmc.com
  Jt Secs: Jennifer & Jonathan Phillips
- ▲ Company Limited by Guarantee
- ○ *A, *P, *T; for skilled craftspeople & professionals
- ● Inf - Legal advice - Debt collection - Assistance to members in finding work - Promotional material Insurance & financial services - Discounts on business expenses
- M 15,000 i
- ¶ All journals below are supplied at a discount to members: Woodturning.   Woodcarving.   Woodworking plans & projects. Furniture & Cabinetmaking.   Outdoor Photography.   Black & White Photography.   Knitting. The Dolls' House Magazine.
  Healthy & Organic Living.

Guild of Motoring Writers Ltd   (GOMW)   1944

- ■ 40 Baring Rd, BOURNEMOUTH, Dorset, BH6 4DT.   (gen/sec)
  01202 422424   fax 01202 422424
  email generalsec@gomw.co.uk
  http://www.gomw.co.uk
  Gen Sec: Patricia Lodge
- ▲ Company Limited by Guarantee
- ○ *P; for automotive editorial professionals; to raise the standard of motoring journalism & encourage motoring, motorsport & road safety
- ● Two annual outings for classic & notable vehicles - Annual awards dinner
- M 350 i, UK / 50 i, o'seas
  (Sub: £95 UK / £70 o'sea)
- ¶ NL - 12; ftm.
  Who's Who in the Motor Industry - 1; ftm, £90 nm.

Guild of Musicians & Singers   1993
NR   8 Clave St, LONDON, E1W 3XQ.   (sp)
    020 7488 3650
    http://www.musiciansandsingers.org.uk
    Sec-Gen: Michael Newman-Horwell
○   *L, *P; for professional & amateur musicians; to promote a high
    standard of musical performance
●   Mtgs - Concerts - Lectures & talks
M   c 200 i
¶   NL - 2.

Guild of One-Name Studies   (GOONS)   1979
■   14 Charterhouse Buildings (Box G), Goswell Rd, LONDON,
    EC1M 7BA.   (mail address)
    0800 011 2182
    email guild@one-name.org   http://www.one-name.org
    Sec: Mrs Kirsty Gray
▲   Registered Charity
○   *L; study of surnames & family history
●   Conf - Mtgs - Lib - e-Lib - Registration of one-name studies
M   2,000 i
¶   Jnl of One-Name Studies - 1; ftm, £2 nm.
    Register of One-Name Studies - 1; ftm, £2 nm.

Guild of Pastoral Psychology   (GPP)   1937
NR   13 Ascot Lodge, Greville Place, LONDON, NW6 5JD.
▲   Registered Charity
○   *P; for all those interested in the relation between religion &
    depth psychology; especially that of C G Jung & his followers
●   Conf - Mtgs - SG - Lib
M   500 i, 30 org, UK / 30 i, o'seas
¶   Pamphlets - 5;   List of groups - 1; both ftm only.
    Printed lectures - 3/4.   Cassette recordings;   AR.

Guild of Photographers UK   (GP)   1988
■   Moorlinch, BRIDGWATER, Somerset, TA7 9DD.   (hq)
    01278 723217
    Dir: Joan Roberts
▲   Un-incorporated Society
○   *P; training & qualifying photographers in the skills of wedding
    & portrait photography
●   ET - Exam - Comp - Inf
<   Wedding & Portrait Photographers Intl (USA)
M   300 i, UK / 4 i, o'seas

Guild of Polyglots   1987
■   191 Westcombe Hill, LONDON, SE3 7DR.   (mail address)
▲   Un-incorporated Society
○   *G; for people interested in speaking languages other than
    their native tongue
●   Mtgs - ET - Exam - SG - Lib - VE
M   77 i, 2 f
¶   NL; ftm only.

Guild of Professional Beauty Therapists Ltd   (GPBT)   1994
■   320 Burton Rd, DERBY, DE23 6AF.   (hq)
    0845 217 7383   fax 0845 217 7387
    email info@beautyguild.com
    http://www.beautyguild.com
    Managing Dir: Paul Archer
▲   Limited Company
○   *P; to represent the interests of professional beauty therapists &
    salon owners
●   ET - Res - Exhib - Comp - Stat - Inf - LG
M   6,000 i
¶   Guild Gazette - 6;   Beautyguild Bulletin (email NL) - 26.

Guild of Professional Estate Agents   (GPEA)   1993
NR   121 Park Lane, LONDON, W1K 7AG.   (hq)
    020 7629 4141   fax 020 7629 2329
    email theguild@property-platform.com
    http://www.property-platform.com
    Man Dir: Malcolm Lindley
▲   Company Limited by Guarantee
○   *T; for independent estate agencies
●   Marketing
M   400 f
¶   The Property Magazine - 12.

Guild of Professional Teachers of Dancing   (GPTD)   1973
■   43 Telfer Rd, Radford, COVENTRY, CV6 3DG.   (hsp)
    024 7659 7907
    Gen Sec: Terry Perkins
Br   4
○   *U; an independent trade union representing teachers of
    dancing, movement to music & dramatic arts
Gp   Teachers of dance & movement to music; Ballroom; Stage;
    Aerobics; Keep fit; Irish dance; Indian dance; Western line
    dancing; Dramatic arts
●   Conf - Mtgs - ET - Exhib - Comp - Inf - Empl - LG
M   1,200 i, UK / 10 i, o'seas
¶   Tempo - 4; ftm only.

Guild of Professional Toastmasters   1963
■   32 Shearman Rd, Blackheath, LONDON, SE3 9TN.   (hsp)
    020 8852 4621
    email rgrosse@guild-of-toastmasters.co.uk
    http://www.guild-of-toastmasters.co.uk
    Hon Sec: Robert Grosse
▲   Un-incorporated Society
○   *; for toastmasters, masters of ceremonies & compères
Gp   Profl Toastmasters' Academy
●   Conf - Mtgs - ET - Exam
M   25 i

Guild of Professional Videographers   (GPV)   1991
■   11 Telfer Rd, Radford, COVENTRY, Warks, CV6 3DG.   (hq)
    024 7627 2548   fax 024 7627 2548
    email mail@professionalvideographers.co.uk
    http://www.professionalvideographers.co.uk
    Sec: Mrs Ann Middleton
▲   Company Limited by Guarantee
○   *P; to assist members with legal problems; advise on training;
    advise on grants available to small/medium business
●   Mtgs - ET - Exam - Inf
M   140 i, 10 f, UK / 25 i, 3 f, o'seas
¶   [all communications to members is sent by email].

Guild of Professional Wedding Services
    There are local guilds in various parts of the UK.

Guild of Psychotherapists   1974
■   47 Nelson Sq, Blackfriars Rd, LONDON, SE1 0QA.   (hq)
    020 7401 3260   fax 020 7401 3472
    email info@guildofpsychotherapists.org.uk
    http://www.guildofpsychotherapists.org.uk
    Hon Sec: Alison Kings
▲   Registered Charity
○   *P; training in psychoanalytic psychotherapy
●   Conf - Mtgs - ET - SG - Lib - Low-cost clinic for Southwark,
    Lambeth & Lewisham
<   UK Coun for Psychotherapy (UKCP)
M   260 i

© CBD Research Ltd · Beckenham · BR3 5JS · Tel 020 8650 7745 · Fax 020 8650 0768 · E-mail cbd@cbdresearch.com · www.cbdresearch.com

Guild of Q Butchers   (Q butchers)   1997
NR   Algo Business Centre, 24 Gleneam Rd, PERTH, PH2 0NJ.   (hq)
     01738 450443 (24-hr answering service)
     fax 01738 449431
     email qbutcher@rossmuir.co.uk
     http://www.guildofqbutchers.co.uk
     Contact: Chief Exec
▲   Company Limited by Guarantee
○   *T; for progressive independent meat retailers (members'
     premises are subject to independent inspection by EFSIS)
Gp Specialists: Sausage, Cooked meat, Deli, B-B-Q, Meal
●   Mtgs - Comp - Promotion
M   300 f
¶   Q News - 4; ftm only.

Guild of Railway Artists   1979
■   45 Dickins Rd, WARWICK, CV34 5NS.   (admin p)
     01926 499246
     http://www.railart.co.uk
     Chief Exec: F P Hodges
▲   Un-incorporated Society
○   *A; to forge a link between artists depicting railway subjects
●   Mtgs - Exhib - Inf
<   Assn of Rly Presvn Socs
M   158 i, UK / 6 i, 1 org
¶   Wheel & Palette - 4; ftm.

Guild of Registered Tourist Guides   (GRTG)   1950
■   Guild House, 52D Borough High St, LONDON, SE1 1XN.   (hq)
     020 7403 1115   fax 020 7378 1705
     http://www.blue-badge-guides.com
     Gen Mgr: Mehmet Ahmet
▲   Un-incorporated Society
○   *P; the national professional association of qualified Blue
     Badge tourist guides
●   Conf - ET - Exhib - Inf - Lib - LG
<   Wld Fedn of Tourist Guides Assns(WFTGA); Fedn of Eur Guides
     Assns (FEG); Visit London
M   700 i, 38 org, UK / 2 i, o'seas
     (Sub: £194)
¶   Guide Post - 12; free.   Guild Directory - 1; ftm, £10 nm.
     Guide's Guide - 1; ftm, £8 nm.

Guild of Shareholders
NR   PO Box 192, UPMINSTER, Essex, RM14 3WB.   (admin/office)
     01708 855113
▲   Company Limited by Guarantee
○   *K; to enable shareholders to influence the way their
     companies are run

Guild of Straw Craftsmen   1989
NR   Higher Bejowan, Quintrell Downs, NEWQUAY, Cornwall,
     TR8 4LJ.   (mem/sp)
     01726 860296
     email guildinfo@strawcraftsmen.co.uk
     http://www.strawcraftsmen.co.uk
     Mem Sec: Gillian Nott
▲   Un-incorporated Society
○   *G; to promote straw craft in all its many facets; to bring straw
     artists & workers together to develop the craft
●   Conf - Mtgs - ET - Exam - Res - Exhib - Comp - SG - Inf - Lib -
     PL - VE
M   100 i, UK / 40 i, o'seas
¶   Guild News (NL) - 2; ftm, £1.50 nm.

Guild of Stunt & Action Coordinators   (SCAG)   1986
■   72 Pembroke Rd, LONDON, W8 6NX.   (hsb)
     020 7602 8319   fax 020 7602 8319
     email stunts.uk@btinternet.com
     Sec: Sally Fisher
▲   Un-incorporated Society
○   *P; film stunt coordinators
●   Mtgs - ET - LG
M   25 i

Guild of Taxidermists   1976
■   c/o Lancashire County Museums, Stanley St, PRESTON, Lancs,
     PR1 4YP.   (hq)
     http://www.taxidermy.org.uk
     Hon Sec: Duncan Ferguson,   Chmn: Lawrence Dowson
○   *P; to raise standards & awareness of taxidermy in the UK
●   Conf - Mtgs - ET - Exam - Exhib
<   Eur Taxidermy Fedn
M   190 i, UK / 10 i, o'seas
¶   Jnl - 1; ftm, £5 nm.

Guild of Television Cameramen   1972
NR   1 Churchill Rd, Whitchurch, TAVISTOCK, Devon, PL19 9BU.
     (admin/p)
     01822 614405   fax 01822 615785
     http://www.gtc.org.uk
     Admin Officer: Sheila Lewis
○   *P; improve the art & craft of television cameramen for
     broadcast television
M   c 1,200 i

Guild of Theatre Prompters
■   191 Westcombe Hill, LONDON, SE3 7DB.
○   *P
M   i

Guild of Travel Management Companies   (GTMC)   1967
NR   Queens House, 180-182 Tottenham Court Rd, LONDON,
     W1T 7PD.   (hq)
     020 7637 1091   fax 020 7580 6593
▲   Company Limited by Guarantee
○   *T; to speak for business travellers & the agents who act for
     them
M   f
×   2005 Guild of Business Travel Agents

Guild of Travel & Tourism   1995
■   Suite 193 Temple Chambers, 3-7 Temple Avenue, LONDON,
     EC4Y 0DB.   (hq)
     020 7583 6333
     email nigel.bishop@traveltourismguild.com
     http://www.traveltourismguild.com
     Chief Exec: Nigel Bishop
▲   Company Limited by Guarantee
○   *P; 'to promote the interests & needs of people within the travel
     industry & those organisations involved in transport, travel &
     tourism'
Gp Travel industry trade assn
●   Mtgs - Seminars
M   i, f
¶   The Travel Business (NL) - 4; free.

Guillain Barré Syndrome Support Group   (GBS)   1985
■   Lincolnshire County Council Offices, Eastgate, SLEAFORD,
     Lincs, NG34 7EB.   (hq)
     01529 304615   fax 01529 304615
     email admin@gbs.org.uk   http://www.gbs.org.uk
     Sec: Mrs Helen Howell
▲   Registered Charity
Br 4
○   *W; to support sufferers of the disease & their families; to
     promote research & treatment
Gp GBS; CIDP (Chronic Inflammatory Demyelinating
     Polyneuropathy); Miller Fisher & other related neuropathies;
     Specialists in those who are children; Pregnant; Diabetic
●   Conf - ET - Res - Inf
<   Guillain Barré Syndrome Foundation Intl
M   1,300 i
     (Sub: £18 + £7.50 concessions)
¶   Reaching Out (Jnl) - 1; ftm.
     In the Know (NL) - 3; free.
     Information leaflets / posters / booklets; free.

Gulf Veterans Association   (GVA)   1994
■   MEA House (4th floor), Ellison Place, NEWCASTLE upon TYNE,
     NE1 8XS.   (hq)
     0191-230 1065   fax 0191-260 2558
     email larry@gvanewcastle.freeserve.co.uk
     http://www.gulfveteransassociation.co.uk
     Chmn: Larry Cammock
▲   Un-incorporated Society
○   *K; to support & act for all members & their families whether
     they were Army, Navy, RAF or civilians, who fought in the
     Gulf War & service personnel who have served in that area
     since
Gp Service pensions; Crisis advocate
●   Res - Inf - LG
<   Nat Vietnam & Gulf War Veterans Coalition; Nat Gulf War
     Resource Centre
M   2,000 i, UK / 500 i, o'seas

Gun Trade Association Ltd   (GTA)   1896
■   PO Box 43, TEWKESBURY, Glos, GL20 5ZE.   (hq)
     01684 291868   fax 01684 291864
     email enquiries@guntradeassociation.com
     http://www.guntradeassociation.com
     Dir: John Batley
▲   Company Limited by Guarantee
○   *T; interests of the sporting firearms, ammunition, accessories
     industry & those providing related services; liaison with proof
     authorities, police & other government agencies
Gp Joint Venture C'ee - organises British Pavilion at overseas trade
     fairs
●   Conf - Mtgs - ET - Res - Exhib - Stat - Expt - Inf - LG
<   Brit Shooting Sports Coun; Standing Conf on Countryside
     Sports; Eur Inst for Hunting & Sporting Guns; Wld Forum on
     the Future of Sport Shooting Activities
M   550 i & f, UK / 10 f (associates), o'seas
¶   NL - 6; ftm only.

Gut Trust   1991
■   Unit 5, 53 Mowbray St, SHEFFIELD, S Yorks, S3 8EN.   (hq)
     0114-272 3253
     email info@ibsnetwork.org.uk   http://www.thegutrust.org
     Sec: P J Nunn
▲   Company Limited by Guarantee; Registered Charity
○   *K, *M, *W; a self-help organisation for people with irritable
     bowel syndrome
Gp Local self-help; Befriender/penpal scheme; Media list; Reviewer
     list
●   Conf - ET - Res - Exhib - Comp - Inf
<   Nat Coun Voluntary Orgs (NCVO); Long-term Medical
     Conditions Alliance (LMCA); Patients Forum
M   3,000 i, 10 f, 18 org, UK / 50 i, o'seas
¶   Gut Reaction - 4; ftm only.   Factsheets; ftm, £1 each nm.
     [back copies of Gut Reaction; £2.50 m, £5 nm].
     Registered as the IBS Network.

**Gwartheg Hynafol Cymru   (Ancient Cattle of Wales)   (GHC/
ACW)   1981**
■   Croesheddig Newydd, Pentre'r Bryn, LLANDYSUL, Ceredigion,
     SA44 6NB.   (hsp)
     01545 560255
     http://www.ghc-acw.org
     Hon Sec: Sian Ioan
▲   Un-incorporated Society
○   *B; the breeding of Welsh cattle of colours other than black
M   30 i
¶   NL - irreg; free.

Gwent Wildlife Trust   (GWT)   1963
■   Seddon House, Dingestow Court, MONMOUTH, NP25 4DY.
     (hq)
     01600 740358   fax 01600 740299
     email gwentwildlife@cix.co.uk
     http://www.wildlifetrust.org.uk/gwent
     Chief Exec: Julian Branscombe
▲   Registered Charity
○   *L
Gp Education; Reserves; Conservation; Membership; Local groups;
     Volunteers
●   ET - Inf - VE
M   7,200 i, 10 f, 20 org, UK / 3 i, o'seas
¶   Local News - 3;   Supplement in Natural World - 3;   Annual
     Review;   all free.

Gypsum Products Development Association   (GPDA)   1889
■   PO Box 35084, LONDON, NW1 4XE.   (asa)
     020 7935 8532   fax 07006 065950
     email office@gpda.com   http://www.gpda.com
     Sec: C Dunn-Meynell
○   *T
●   Mtgs - Inf
<   Eurogypsum
M   4 f

Gypsy Cob Society
NR Chywoon Farm, Church Brough, KIRKBY STEPHEN, Cumbria,
     CA17 4EJ.
     01768 341319
     email info@gypsycobsociety.org
○   *B

© CBD Research Ltd · Beckenham · BR3 5JS · Tel 020 8650 7745 · Fax 020 8650 0768 · E-mail cbd@cbdresearch.com · www.cbdresearch.com

H G Wells Society   (HGWS)   1960

NR   Flat 3 / 27b Church Rd, LONDON, NW4 4EB.   (hsp)
      http://www.hgwellsusa.50megs.com
      Hon Gen Sec: Mark Egerton
▲   Un-incorporated Society
○   *A, *L; to promote an interest in, & appreciation of the life,
      work & thought of Herbert George Wells (1866-1946)
●   Conf - Lib
<   Alliance of Literary Socs
M   100 i, UK / 100 i, o'seas
¶   The Wellsian (Jnl) - 1.
      NL - 2; both ftm only.

Hackney Horse Society   1883

■   Fallowfields, Little London, Heytesbury, WARMINSTER, Wilts,
      BA12 0ES.   (hq)
      01985 840717   fax 01985 840616
      email dawn@hackney-horse.org.uk
      http://www.hackney-horse.org.uk
      Sec: Mrs Dawn Hicketts
▲   Registered Charity
○   *B; improvement of breeding of Hackney horses & ponies;
      harness & driving horses
●   Exhib - Comp
M   650 i, 28 org, UK / 50 i, o'seas
¶   Hackney Stud Book - 5 yrly; £30.   Ybk - 1; £12.

Haemochromatosis Society   1990

■   Hollybush House, Hadley Green Rd, BARNET, Herts,
      EN5 5PR.   (hq)
      020 8449 1363   fax 020 8449 1363
      email info@haemochromatosis.org.uk
      http://www.haemochromatosis.org.uk
      Dir: Mrs Janet Fernau
▲   Company Limited by Guarantee; Registered Charity
○   *W; to provide support, awareness & information for families
      affected by this iron overload genetic disorder & to the
      medical profession; to promote awareness at all levels as
      early diagnosis prevents serious complications
●   Res (support) - Inf - Support for members
M   1,000 i
¶   NL - 4;   Hbk;   Venesection record card;
      Information leaflet; all free.

Haemophilia Society United Kingdom   1950

■   Petersham House, 57A Hatton Garden, LONDON,
      EC1N 8JG.   (hq)
      020 7831 1020   fax 020 7405 4824
      email info@haemophilia.org.uk
      http://www.haemophilia.org.uk
      Chief Exec: Chris James
▲   Registered Charity
Br   17 groups
○   *W; the national patient organisation for people with
      haemophilia & related bleeding disorders, including von
      Willebrand's, in the UK; to ensure that people with these
      disorders receive the best quality of care & support
●   Conf - Mtgs - Inf
      Helpline: 0800 018 6068 (Mon-Fri 1000-1600)
>   Wld Fedn of Hemophilia; Eur Haemophila Consortium
M   4,000 i, UK / 122 i, o'seas
¶   Haemophilia Quarterly - 4;
      HQ too! (NL for young people) - 4;   AR- 1; free.
      Publications list available.

Haflinger Society of Great Britain   (HSGB)   1970

■   11 Northumberland Place, RICHMOND, Surrey, TW10 6TS.
      (hsp)
      020 8948 6599
      http://www.haflingersgb.com
      Sec: Carolyn Hallett
▲   Registered Charity
○   *B; to promote the breeding of the Haflinger horse & publish
      the pedigrees of those in Great Britain
●   Mtgs - Comp - Inf - Young stock inspections - Breed Show
<   Wld Haflinger Fedn
M   c 400 i
¶   Focus on Haflingers (NL) - 4; ftm only.

Hairdressing & Beauty Suppliers Association Ltd   (HBSA)
1926

■   Greenleaf House, 128 Darkes Lane, POTTERS BAR, Herts,
      EN6 1AE.   (hq)
      01707 649499   fax 01707 649497
      http://www.hbsa.uk.com
      Chief Exec: David Macklin
▲   Company Limited by Guarantee
○   *T; for manufacturers & suppliers of professional hair & beauty
      products
Gp   Wig makers
●   Conf - Mtgs - ET - Exhib
M   120 f
¶   HBSA News - 6; ftm only.

Hairline International: the Alopecia Patients' Society   1995

NR   Lyons Court, 1668 High Street, KNOWLE, W Midlands,
      B93 0LY.   (hq)
      http://www.hairlineinternational.com
      Dir & Founder: Elizabeth Steel
▲   Un-incorporated Society
○   *K, *W; to provide information & support for all hair loss
      patients, including those who have alopecia or suffer from
      trichotillomania (compulsive hair-pulling)
●   Inf
M   i
¶   NL - 4

Hakluyt Society   1846

NR   c/o The Map Library, The British Library, 96 Euston Rd,
      LONDON, NW1 2DB.   (mail/address)
      01428 641850
      email office@hakluyt.com   http://www.hakluyt.com
      Admin: Richard Bateman
▲   Registered Charity
○   *L; 'to advance education by the publication of records of
      voyages, travels, naval expeditions & other geographical
      material & to promote public knowledge of these matters'
●   Mtgs
<   American Friends of the Hakluyt Soc
M   810 i, 350 org, UK / 1,454 i, o'seas
¶   Volumes - 2/3.   NL - 1.   AR.   LM.
      Text of Annual Lecture.
      Publications list available.

Hallé Concerts Society (The Hall)é 1858
■ The Bridgewater Hall, Lower Mosley St, MANCHESTER,
M1 5HA. (hq)
0161-237 7000   fax 0161-237 7029
http://www.halle.co.uk
Chief Exec: John Summers
▲ Company Limited by Guarantee
○ *D; promotion of Hallé orchestra, the Hallé choir & Hallé
emsembles through management of Hallé concerts
Gp Symphony concerts; Recitals
● Mtgs - Lib
< Assn of Brit Orchestras
M i & f
¶ NL - 4;   AR - 1.

Halliwick Association of Swimming Therapy   1952
■ c/o ADKC Centre, Whitstable House, Silchester Rd, LONDON,
W10 6SB. (chmn/b)
020 8968 7609   fax 020 8968 7609
http://www.halliwick.org.uk
Sec: Eric Dilley
▲ Registered Charity
Br 22; 2 o'seas
○ *S, *W; to teach swimming to people with disabilities using the
'Halliwick' method; to provide training for volunteers &
professionals in the basic methods of 'Halliwick'; to organise
galas at club, regional & national level
● Mtgs - ET (training courses) - Exam - Res - Comp
< Intl Halliwick Assn (IHA)
M i & org
¶ Swimming for People with Disabilities (hbk).
Rainbow Series: Instructors & Students Guides.
Leaflets.   Videos.

Halon Users National Consortium Ltd
has closed.

Hammer Circle: the Association of British Hammer Throwers 1952
NR 10 Pershore Close, BEDFORD, MK41 8NS.   (hsp)
http://www.hammer-circle.co.uk
Hon Sec: Darren Kerr
○ *S; support & promotion of British hammer throwing
● ET - Stat - Lib
< Midland Counties Athletic Assn; Amateur Athletic Assn
M 200 i, UK / 3 i, o'seas
¶ AR; ftm.

Hammersmith & Fulham Chamber of Commerce
a branch of the London Chamber of Commerce & Industry based at
the offices of the **Ealing Chamber of Commerce**

Hamper Industry Trade Association Ltd
dissolved.

Hampshire Down Sheep Breeders Association   (HDSBA) 1889
■ Rickyard Cottage, Denner Hill, GREAT MISSENDEN, Bucks,
HP16 0HZ. (hsp/b)
01494 488388   fax 01494 488388
email richard@rickyard.plus.com
http://www.hampshiredownsociety.org.uk
Sec: Richard J Davis
▲ Company Limited by Guarantee; Registered Charity
Br 4
○ *B
● Mtgs - Res - Exhib - Inf
< Nat Sheep Assn
M 140 i, 20 f, UK / 40 i, 4 org, o'seas
¶ NL - 6; ftm only.   Flock Book - 1; ftm, £10 nm.

Hampshire Field Club & Archaeological Society   (HFC)   1885
NR Mottisfont Court, High Street, WINCHESTER, Hants,
SO23 8ZF. (Sec/b)
01963 846044
http://www.fieldclub.hants.org.uk
Sec: Alex Lewis
▲ Registered Charity
○ *L, *Q; archaeology, history & natural history of Hampshire
Gp Archaeology; Landscape; Local history; Historic buildings;
New Forest
● Conf - Mtgs - ET - Res - Lib - VE
M 577 i, 79 org
¶ NL - 2.   Monographs - ad hoc.   Hampshire Studies - 1.

Handbag Liners & Repairers Association   (HLRA)   1972
■ 76c The Avenue, BECKENHAM, Kent, BR3 2ES.   (mail address)
○ *T
● Mtgs - Exhib
M 13 f

Handbell Ringers of Great Britain   (HRGB)   1967
NR 87 The Woodfields, Sanderstead, SOUTH CROYDON, Surrey,
CR2 0HJ. (hsp)
020 8651 2663   fax 020 8651 2663
email info@hrgb.org.uk   http://www.hrgb.org.uk
Hon Sec: Mrs Sandra Winter
▲ Registered Charity
Br 8 regions
○ *D; to encourage & develop the art of handbell tune ringing (as
distinct from change ringing); also hand-chime & belleplate
ringers
● Concerts, rallies, workshops & seminars
< Making Music (the Nat Fedn of Music Socs)
M 3,500 i
¶ Reverberations - 2;   Regional NLs - irreg; both ftm only.

Handcycling Association   (HCAUK)   1999
■ 4 Monty Place, Fenton, STOKE-on-TRENT, Staffs, ST4 3RQ.
(chmn/p)
01782 593647
http://www.handcyclinguk.org.uk
Chmn: Marcus Asbury
○ *S
M 120 i

Handley Page Association   (HPA)   1979
■ 16 Guernsey Drive, FLEET, Hants, GU51 2TG.   (hsp)
01252 626996
Hon Sec: A H Fraser-Mitchell
▲ Un-incorporated Society
○ *G, *L, *Q; to keep alive the memories of the Handley Page
companies, their founder & their aircraft; to encourage new
ideas & development in aeronautics & promote their
application in the spirit of Sir Frederick Handley Page
● Mtgs - Comp - Inf - PL - VE
M 400 i, 1 f, 2 org, UK / 20 i, o'seas
¶ NL - 6; ftm.   LM; £1 m.   Video; £13 m only.

© CBD Research Ltd · Beckenham · BR3 5JS · Tel 020 8650 7745 · Fax 020 8650 0768 · E-mail cbd@cbdresearch.com · www.cbdresearch.com

Hansard Society Ltd   1944
- ■ 40-43 Chancery Lane, LONDON, WC2A 1JA.   (hq)
  020 7438 1222   fax 020 7438 1229
  email hansard@hansard.lse.ac.uk
  http://www.hansardsociety.org.uk
  Chief Exec: Fiona Booth
- ▲ Registered Charity
- Br Scotland
- ○ *L, *Z; an independent, non-partisan political research & education charity; it aims to strengthen parliamentary democracy & encourage greater public involvement in politics
- Gp Programmes: Hansard Society Scotland, Citizenship education, Parliament & government, Edemocracy, Study & scholars
- ● Conf - ET - Res - LG - Public meetings - Mock elections
- M 356 i
  (Sub: £20 UK / £45 o'seas)
- ¶ Audit of Political Engagement - 1.
  No Overall Control? the impact of a 'hung parliament' on British Politics (2008).
  Other publications available.

Hardy Orchid Society   (HOS)   1993
- ■ The Windmill, Vennington, Westbury, SHREWSBURY, Salop, SY5 9RG.
  http://www.hardyorchidsociety.org.uk
  Mem Sec: Mrs Celia Wright

Hardy Plant Society   (HPS)   1957
- NR Little Orchard, Great Comberton, PERSHORE, Worcs, WR10 3DP.   (hq)
  01386 710317   fax 01386 710117
  email admin@hardy-plant.org.uk
  http://www.hardy-plant.org.uk
  Admin: Mrs Pam Adams,
- ▲ Registered Charity
- Br 45
- ○ *H; cultivation of hardy herbaceous plants (excluding rock plants)
- Gp Half hardy; Hardy geranium; Pulmonaria; Peony; Variegated plants; Correspondents
- ● Conf - Mtgs - Exhib - SG - PL - VE
- M 11,000 i, 10 org, UK / 500 i, 2 org, o'seas
- ¶ The Hardy Plant (Jnl) - 2;   NL - 3;   Seed distribution list - 1; all ftm only.

Harleian Society   1869
- ■ College of Arms, Queen Victoria St, LONDON, EC4V 4BT.
  (hsb)
  020 7236 7728   fax 020 7248 6448
  http://www.harleian.co.uk
  Hon Sec: T H S Duke
- ▲ Registered Charity
- ○ *L; transcribing, printing & publishing heraldic visitations of counties, parish registers or any manuscripts relating to family history, genealogy or heraldry
- M 210 i & org, UK / 105 i & org, o'seas
- ¶ Publications - irreg (c 1); free to subscribers, £25 (i), £30 (instns), £35 nm.

Harness Goat Society   (HGS)   1986
- ■ Meadow Court Farm, Alfrick, WORCESTER, WR6 5HY.
  (chmn/p)
  01886 832294
  email harnessgoatsociety.uk@virgin.net
  http://www.harnessgoats.co.uk
  Sec: Mrs Angela Rickerby
- ▲ Un-incorporated Society
- ○ *V; the driving of goats & their welfare
- ● Mtgs - Exhib
- < Brit Goat Soc
- M 60 i, UK / 6 i, o'seas
  Sub: £15.
- ¶ Harness Goat Society - 4; ftm, £3 nm.
  Training Your Harness Goat; £2 m, £3 nm.ltion Leaflet No 1: History;ltion Leaflet No 2: Where to Find Harness & Carts

Harrogate Chamber of Trade & Commerce   1896
- ■ PO Box 8, Dept DBA19, HARROGATE, N Yorks, HG2 8XB.
  01423 879208   fax 01423 870025
  email info@harrogatechamber.org
  http://www.harrogatechamber.org
  Chief Exec & Hon Sec: Brian L Dunsby
- ▲ Un-incorporated Society
- ○ *C
- Gp Focus groups: Business development; Promoting Harrogate; Town centre; Traffic & transport; Waste disposal
- ● Mtgs - Exhib - VE - Liaison with local government
- M 250 f
- ¶ Review (NL) - 12; ftm, free samples to enquirers.

Harry Roy Appreciation Society   (HRAS)   1972
- ■ 43 Repton Close, LUTON, Beds, LU3 3UL.   (memsec/p)
  01582 574946
  Mem Sec: Pauline Wolsey
- ▲ Un-incorporated Society
- ○ *G; for all appreciative of the Harry Roy Dance Band (1930's & 1940's), his musicians & vocalists
- ● Mtgs - Res - Stat - Inf
- M 90 i, UK / 6 i, o;seas
  (Sub: £5)
- ¶ The Bugle Call Rag - 4; free.

Harveian Society of Edinburgh   1782
- NR c/o Prof Dr Kelvin Palmer, Dept of Gastroenterology, Western General Hospital, EDINBURGH, EH4 2XU.   (sb)
  0131-537 1000
  Sec: Dr Kelvin Palmer
- ○ *L

Harveian Society of London   1831
- ■ Lettsom House, 11 Chandos St, LONDON, W1G 9EB.   (hq)
  020 7580 1043
  Exec Sec: Col Richard Kinsella-Bevan
- ○ *L; advancement of medical science
- ● Mtgs - VE
- M i

Hat Pin Society of Great Britain   1980
- NR PO Box 809, HORSHAM, W Sussex, RH12 9EA.   (mail address)
  http://www.hatpinsociety.org.uk
  Chmn: Valerie Pugh
- ▲ Un-incorporated Society
- ○ *G; collecting hat pins & hat pin holders
- ● Mtgs
- < Amer Hatpin Soc
- M 196 i, UK / 34 i, o'seas
- ¶ NL - 4; ftm only.

Havergal Brian Society   (HBS)   1974
■   39 Giles Coppice, LONDON, SE19 1XF.   (hsp)
       020 8761 8134
       email damian_rees@yahoo.com
       http://www.havergalbrian.org
     Sec: Damian Rees
▲   Registered Charity
○   *D; promote knowledge & appreciation of the works of William
       Havergal Brian (1876-1972) English composer & writer on
       music
●   Publication of Brian's music, studies of Brian's work & his own
       writing on music - Concerts - Recordings
M   167 i, 2 org, UK / 47 i, o'seas
       (Sub: £12 i, varies o'seas)
¶   NL - 6; ftm, 50p nm.
     Havergal Brian's Gothic Symphony - two studies; £10.
     The Complete Music for Solo Piano; £11.
     Havergal Brian on Music, Vol 1: British Music; £17.95 m,
       £19.95 nm, (paperback £8.50 m, £9.50 nm) (in association
       with Toccata Press).

Hawick Archaeological Society   (HAS)   1856
NR   Orrock House, Stirches Rd, HAWICK, Roxburghshire,
       TD9 7HF.   (hsp)
       01450 375546
     Hon Sec: I W Landles
▲   Un-incorporated Society
○   *L, *Q; antiquities & natural history of Hawick & district
M   i

Hawk & Owl Trust   (HOT)   1969
NR   PO Box 100, TAUNTON, Somerset, TA4 2WX.   (asa)
       0870 990 3889
       http://www.hawkandowl.org
     Dir: Linda Bennett
▲   Company Limited by Guarantee; Registered Charity
○   *K, *V; conservation & protection of all birds of prey, including
       owls in the wild & their habitats
Gp   Barn Owl Conservation Network
●   Conf - Mtgs - ET - Res - Exhib - SG - Stat - Inf - PL - LG
<   Birdlife Intl
M   6,000 i, 3 f, 40 org, UK / 98 i, 20 org, o'seas
¶   Peregrine (NL) - 2.   Adopt a Box (NL) - 2.
     Various publications.

Haydn Society of Great Britain   1979
■   2 Aldcliffe Mews, LANCASTER, LA1 5BT.   (dir/p)
       01524 61553   fax 01524 61553
       email d.mccaldin@lancaster.ac.uk
       http://www.haydnsocietyofgb.netfirms.com
     Dir: Prof Denis McCaldin
▲   Un-incorporated Society
○   *A; to promote a wider knowledge & understanding of the
       music of Joseph Haydn
●   Conf - Res - Exhib - Inf - Lib - VE
<   Burgenland Haydn Festival (Eisenstadt, Austria)
M   240 i, 1 f, 10 org, UK / 10 i, 1 org, o'seas
¶   Jnl - 1; ftm, nm by arrangement.

HDRA - the Organic Organisation
     alternative name of the **Henry Doubleday Research Association**

Headlines, the Craniofacial Support Group   1993
NR   128 Beesmoor Rd, Frampton Cotterell, BRISTOL, BS36 2JP.
       01454 850557
       email info@headlines.org.uk
       http://www.headlines.org.uk
     Admin: Gil Ruff
○   *W
×   Cranio Facial Support Group

Headmasters' & Headmistresses' Conference   1869
NR   12 The Point, Rockingham Rd, MARKET HARBOROUGH, Leics,
       LE16 7QU.   (sb)
       01858 469059
       http://www.hmc.org.uk
     Sec: G S Lucas
○   *P; for headmasters & headmistresses of Independent schools
●   Conf - Mtgs - ET - Stat - Inf - LG
<   Indep Schools Coun; Secondary Heads Assn
M   250 i, UK / 80 i, o'seas

Headteachers' Association of Scotland
     since 1 August 2008 **School Leaders Scotland**

Headway - the Brain Injury Association   (HEADWAY)   1979
■   4 King Edward Court, King Edward St, NOTTINGHAM,
       NG1 1EW.   (hq)
       0115-924 0800   fax 0115-958 4446
       email info@headway.org.uk
       http://www.headway.org.uk
     Chief Exec: Peter McCabe
▲   Registered Charity
Br   115
○   *K, *M, *W; to provide information, support & services to
       people with acquired brain injuries, their families, carers &
       related professionals
●   Conf
<   Eur Brain Injury Soc; Brain Injured & Families Eur Confedn (BIF)
M   800 i, 11 f, UK / 40 org, o'seas
¶   Headway News - 4; £2.25.
     Noticeboard (NL) - 6; ftm only.
     Publications on varying aspects of head injury; list available.

Health & Beauty Employers Federation   (HBEF)   1969
■   18 Shakespeare Business Centre, Hathaway Close, EASTLEIGH,
       Hants, SO50 4SR.   (hq)
       0870 420 2022
       email info@fht.org.uk   http://www.fht.org.uk
     Exec Sec: Mrs Jacqueline M Palmer
○   *T; representing owners & managers of health & beauty therapy
       establishments incl: saunas, health hotels, beauty clinics etc
●   Conf - Exhib - Inf
<   part of the Fedn of Holistic Therapists
M   [not stated]

Health & Beauty Group
     a group of **Food & Drink Industry Ireland**

Health Care Supply Association   1960
NR   c/o Eugene Cooke, NHS Blood & Transplant, 500
       North Bristol Park, Northway - Filton, BRISTOL, BS34 7QH.
       (sb)
       0117-021 7303
       email eugene.cooke@nhsbt.nhs.uk
     Sec: Eugene Cooke
▲   Un-incorporated Society
Br   12
○   *P; to promote the work of health care supplies staff at all levels
●   Conf - Mtgs - ET - Exhib - LG - Seminars - Annual awards
<   Chart Inst of Purchasing & Supply
M   720 i
¶   Official Procurement Guide - 1; ftm, £50 nm.
×   2006 Health Care Supplies Association

Health Food Institute   (IHFR)   1979
NR   Gothic House, Barker Gate, NOTTINGHAM, NG1 1JU.   (hsb)
      0115-941 4188
      http://www.healthfoodinstitute.org.uk
▲   Company Limited by Guarantee
○   *P; to increase knowledge & education in nutritional & health
      matters; to promote & maintain standards in nutrition &
      health food retailing
●   Conf - Mtgs - ET - Exam - Res - Exhib - Stat - Inf - LG
M   200 i
¶   Jnl - 1.

Health Food Manufacturers' Association   (HFMA)   1965
NR   1 Wolsey Rd, EAST MOLESEY, Surrey, KT8 9EL.   (hq)
      020 8481 7100   fax 020 8481 7101
      email hfma@hfma.co.uk   http://www.hfma.co.uk
      Dir: David Adams
▲   Un-incorporated Society
○   *T; interests of manufacturers of health foods & allied products
Gp   Food supplements; Herbal; Health foods
●   Conf - Mtgs - SG - Expt - Inf - LG
<   Intl Alliance of Dietary/Food Supplement Assns (IADSA); Eur
      Fedn of Health Product Mfrs Assn (EHPM)
M   c 150 f
¶   NL;   LM; both ftm only.

Health & Medical Public Relations Association
      has ceased to exist.

Health & Safety Sign Association   (HSSA)   1994
NR   Box 377, REDHILL, Surrey, RH1 2RZ.   (mail/add)
      http://www.hssa.co.uk
○   *T; for manufacturers of safety & other statutory signs
●   LG
M   f

Healthcare Financial Management Association   (HFMA)   1950
NR   Albert House (suite 32), 111 Victoria St, BRISTOL, BS1 6AX.
      (hq)
      0117-929 4789   fax 0117-929 4844
      http://www.hfma.org.uk
      Chief Exec: Mark Knight
▲   Registered Charity
Br   14
○   *P; for accountants engaged in healthcare financial
      management in the UK
●   Conf - Mtgs - ET - Res - Exhib - Inf
<   Eur Healthcare Mgt Assn; HFMA (USA)
M   4,000 i
¶   Healthcare Finance - 10; ftm.   Ybk - 1.   AR - 1.

Healthcare People Management Association   (HPMA)   1974
■   Gothic House, 3 The Green, RICHMOND, Surrey, TW9 1PL.
      (admin/b)
      020 8334 4530   fax 020 8332 7201
      http://www.hpma.org.uk
      Exec Dir: Alex O'Grady
▲   Un-incorporated Society
Br   10
○   *P; to bring together healthcare professionals to enable them to
      develop, influence & promote high quality human resource
      management in the NHS
●   Conf - Mtgs - Res - Comp - LG
M   288 i, 320 f, UK / 1,000 f, o'seas)
      (Sub: £45 i, £500 f, £350 NHS trust, UK / £1,000 f, o'seas)
¶   Network - 12; ftm only.
✕   2005 Association of Healthcare Human Resource Management

HealthWatch   1988
NR   Box BM HealthWatch, LONDON, WC1N 3XX.   (B Monomarks)
      020 8789 7813
      http://www.healthwatch-uk.org
      Press & Inf Officer: Michael E Allen
▲   Registered Charity
○   *K; to provide reliable information about health matters,
      especially treatments, whether orthodox or alternative
●   Mtgs - Inf
M   141 i
¶   NL - 4.

Hearing Concern   1947
NR   The Resource Centre, 356 Holloway Rd, LONDON, N7 6PA.
      (hq)
      020 7700 8177   fax 020 7700 8211
      email info@hearingconcern.org.uk
      http://www.hearingconcern.org.uk
      Chief Exec: Damian Barry
▲   Charity Limited by Guarantee; Registered Charity
Br   3
○   *W; to improve the quality of life for people who are deaf or
      hard of hearing; is a volunteer-led organisation
Gp   Hearing advisory service; Broadcasting c'ee; Resource centres
●   ET - Exhib - Inf - VE
<   Intl Fedn of the Hard of Hearing; UK Coun on Deafness; Nat
      Coun for Voluntary Orgs
M   1,671 i, 34 f, 90 org, UK / 5 org, o'seas
¶   AR - 1; free.

Heart of England Fine Foods   (HEFF)   1998
■   PO Box 1, MUCH WENLOCK, Shropshire, TF13 6WH.   (hq)
      01746 785185   fax 01746 785186
      email office@heff.co.uk   http://www.heff.co.uk
      Chief Exec: Karen Davies
▲   Private Limited Company
○   *T; organisation for the promotion of West Midlands food &
      drink
●   Conf - Mtgs - Inf
M   236 f

Heart Line Association   1980
■   Community Link, Surrey Heath House, Knoll Rd, CAMBERLEY,
      Surrey, GU15 3HH.   (hq)
      01276 707636   fax 01276 707642
      http://www.heartline.org.uk
      Office Mgr: Pamela Lawrence
▲   Registered Charity
Br   20
○   *W; support for families with children who have heart
      conditions
●   Support groups
M   1,400 i
¶   NL - 4; free.   Heart Children: a practical handbook; £6.

Heart UK   1986
■   7 North Rd, MAIDENHEAD, Berks, SL6 1PE.   (hq)
      01628 628638
      http://www.heartuk.org.uk
      Chief Exec: Michael Livingston
▲   Company Limited by Guarantee; Registered Charity
○   *K, *W; support & information for people at high risk of
      premature coronary heart disease, especially families with
      inherited (genetic) blood cholesterol or triglyceride problems
Gp   Diet & Lifestyle help-line, dieticians & other health professionals
      respond to members' enquiries by phone & post
●   Conf - ET - Res - SG - Stat - Inf - LG - Publications - Lectures -
      Professional training
<   Nat Heart Forum; Genetic Interest Gp; Parliamentary Food &
      Health Forum; Long Term Medical Conditions Alliance
M   c 1,500 i
¶   Digest - 6; ftm, £2.50 nm.

Heat Pump Association   (HPA)   1994

■ 2 Waltham Court, Milley Lane, Hare Hatch, READING, Berks,
   RG10 9TH.   (hq)
   0118-940 3416   fax 0118-940 6258
   email info@feta.co.uk   http://www.feta.co.uk
   Dir Gen: C Sloan
○ *T; promotes the benefits & proper use of heat pumps & heat
   pump technology by increasing the awareness of heat pumps
   as a means of using energy efficiently, cost effectively & with
   the minimum impact on the environment
● Mtgs - Comp - Inf
< Fedn of Envtl Tr Assns (FETA)
M 21 full members, 12 associate

Heat Transfer & Fluid Flow Service   (HTFS)   1968

NR c/o AspenTech Ltd, C1 Reading International Business Park,
   Basingstoke Rd, READING, Berks, RG2 6DT.   (hq)
   0118 922 6405   fax 0118 922 6401
   email htfs@aspentech.com   http://www.htfs.com
   Dir: T Ralston
▲ Company Limited by Guarantee
Br National Engineering Laboratory, E Kilbride
○ *Q; heat exchange design & associated fluid flow equipment
Gp Heat exchangers: Shell & tube, Air-cooled, Cryogenic, Plate fin;
   Condensers; Boilers; Furnaces; Refrigeration & air
   conditioning plant; Fired heaters
● Conf - Mtgs - Res - Software
M 40 f, UK / 100 f, o'seas
¶ NL;   AR; both ftm.

Heather Society   1963

■ Tippitiwitchet Cottage, Hall Rd, Outwell, WISBECH, Cambs,
   PE14 8PE.   (admin p)
   01945 774077
   email admin@heathersociety.org.uk
   http://www.heathersociety.org.uk
   Admin: Dr E Charles Nelson,   Hon Sec: Jean Julian
▲ Registered Charity
Br 13; USA
○ *H; study, research & development of heather varieties
Gp Technical c'ee responsible for trials at Harlow Carr, Harrogate
   & RHS Garden, Wisley; also for compiling the International
   Register of Heather Names
● Conf - Res - ET - Exhib - Comp - Inf - PL (slides only) - VE
< R Horticl Soc; Nederlandse Heidevereniging Ericultura;
   Gesellschaft der Heidefreunde; N Amer Heather Soc
M 1,500 i, 125 f, 15 university libraries, UK / 100 i, 12 f, 15
   university libraries, o'seas
¶ News Bulletin - 3.   Ybk; ftm only.

Heating Oil Buyers Association

n
   has been incorporatedd with Oilbuyers Ltd (a company offering
   analyst services to heating oil users) & is therefore outside the
   scope of this directory scope of this directory

Heating, Ventilating & Air Conditioning Manufacturers' Association Ltd   (HEVAC)   1962

■ 2 Waltham Court, Milley Lane, Hare Hatch, READING, Berks,
   RG10 9TH.   (hq)
   0118-940 3416   fax 0118-940 6258
   email info@feta.co.uk   http://www.feta.co.uk
   Dir Gen: C Sloan
○ *T; interests of heating, ventilating & air conditioning equipment
   manufacturers
Gp Air conditioning; Air curtains; Air distribution; Fan coils; Filters;
   House ventilation; Humidity; Noise & vibration control
● Mtgs - ET - Exhib - Comp - SG - Stat - Expt - Inf
< Fedn of Envtl Trade Assns (FETA)
M 118 f
¶ NL - 12; ftm only.

Heating & Ventilating Contractors' Association   (HVCA)   1904

■ Esca House, 34 Palace Court, LONDON, W2 4JG.   (hq)
   020 7313 4900   fax 020 7727 9268
   email contact@hvca.org.uk   http://www.hvca.org.uk
Br 9 in 11 regions
○ *T; refrigeration & air unit conditioning, home heating, duct
   work, ventilation, service & facilities
Gp Central services; Commercial & legal; Communications &
   public affairs; Education & training; Employment affairs;
   Finance; Membership services; Publications; Specialist group
   services; Technical & safety
   Building Engineering Services Competence Accreditation
   Ltd (BESCA), 0800 652 5533 info@besca.org.uk
M f
¶ HVCA Newslink (NL).

Heavy Transport Association   (HTA)   1983

■ Century House, High St, Tattenhall, CHESTER, CH3 9PX.   (hsb)
   01829 771774   fax 01829 773109
   email info@hta.uk.net   http://www.hta.uk.net
   Sec: John B Dyne
▲ Un-incorporated Society
○ *T; to promote the interests of the heavy haulage industry
Gp Working Groups: HTA-DfT-HA liaison; Self-escorting - Strategic
   sites & water - Preferred policy
● Mtgs
< Eur Assn of Heavy Haulage Transport & Mobile Cranes (ESTA)
M 91 f, UK / 3 f, o'seas
¶ Heavy Talk (NL) - 4;   Members' Hbk - 2 yrly; both ftm.

Hebe Society   1985

■ 20 Beech Farm Drive, MACCLESFIELD, Cheshire, SK10 2ER.
   (hsp)
   01625 611062
   http://www.hebesoc.org
   Hon Sec: Tony Hayter
▲ Registered Charity
○ *H; a specialist plant society encouraging the cultivation &
   conservation of Hebe, Parahebe & all other New Zealand
   native plants
● Mtgs - Exhib - Plant collections
< New Zealand Alpine Garden Soc; R Horticl Soc; Tatton Garden
   Soc
M 263 i, 22 f, libraries & arboreta, UK / 21 i, o'seas
   (Sub: £8 i, £15 f)
¶ Hebe News (NL) - 4; ftm, £2 nm (with Index & Author index).
   Cultivation of Hebes & Parahebes; price as below -
   Bibliogrpahy of books on Hebes & other New Zealand native
   plants (incl in new members' starter pack), ftm, £1
   nm.Cultivation of Hebes & Parahebes; ftm, £1 nm.

Hebridean Sheep Society   1986

■ Coney Grey, Gun Lane, Sherington, NEWPORT PAGNELL,
   Bucks, MK16 9PE.   (hsp)
   01908 611092
   email info@hebrideansheep.org.uk
   http://www.hebrideansheep.org.uk
   Hon Sec: Helen Brewis
○ *B
● ET - Exhib - Comp - Stat - Inf
< Nat Sheep Assn
M 300 i, UK / 2 i, o'seas
¶ The Black Sheep (Ybk) - 1;   NL - 4; both ftm only.

Hedge Laying Association of Ireland

IRL Miskaun, BALLINAMORE, Co Leitrim, Republic of Ireland.
   00 (353) 86 302 8790
○ *G

© CBD Research Ltd · Beckenham · BR3 5JS · Tel 020 8650 7745 · Fax 020 8650 0768 · E-mail cbd@cbdresearch.com · www.cbdresearch.com

Hedgeline   1998
NR   1 Applebees Meadow, HINCKLEY, Leics, LE10 0FL.   (admin/p)
 0870 240 0627
 http://www.hedgeline.org
 Admin: Max Ayriss
▲   Un-incorporated Society
Br   Regional & local
○   *K; for the legislative control of hedge nuisance
●   Political lobbying
M   c 3,700 i
¶   Hedgeline - irreg; free.

Helensburgh & Lomond Chamber of Commerce   1997
NR   c/o Allied Surveyors, 13 Colquhoun St, HELENSBURGH,
 G84 8AN.
 07504 978441
 email info@helensburghchamber.org
 http://www.helensburghchamber.org
 Chief Exec: Susan Mathieson
○   *C
M   40 f

Hellenic Society
 alternative name of the **Society for the Promotion of Hellenic
 Studies**

Help International Plant Protein Organisation   (HIPPO)   1999
NR   The Old Vicarage, Llangynog, CARMARTHEN, SA33 5BS.   (hq)
 01267 241547
 email hippocharity@aol.com
 Dir: Neville Heath Fowler
▲   Registered Charity
○   *K; 'Third World' aid designed to encourage use of vegetable
 protein foods for direct human consumption instead of
 livestock products, for reasons of efficiency, ecology, health &
 animal welfare
●   Mtgs - Inf
M   120 i, UK / 10 i, o'seas
¶   Hippo News (NL) - irreg; free.

Henkeepers' Association   2006
■   Church Lane, Troston, BURY St EDMUNDS, Suffolk, IP31 1EX.
 (hsp)
 01359 268322
 email info@henkeepersassociation.co.uk
 http://www.henkeepersassociation.co.uk
 Sec: Francine Raymond
▲   Company Limited by Guarantee
○   *G; to inform & support henkeepers who keep small flocks in
 their garden for pleasure
●   Inf
M   60 i

Henry Bradshaw Society   (HBS)   1890
■   5a Green Place, OXFORD, OX1 4RF.   (hsp)
 http://www.henrybradshawsociety.org
 Hon Sec: Peter Jackson
▲   Registered Charity
○   *L; editing of liturgical texts from manuscripts or rare printed
 books
●   Res - Inf
<   Alcuin Club; Societas Liturgica; Soc for Liturgical Study
M   83 i, 59 org, UK / 68 i, 79 org, o'seas
¶   Edition series; Subsidia series - irreg; prices vary.
 AR; ftm only.

Henry Doubleday Research Association   (HDRA)   1958
NR   Garden Organic Ryton, Wolston Lane, COVENTRY, Warks,
 CV8 3LG.   (hq)
 024 7630 3517   fax 024 7663 9229
 email enquiry@gardenorganic.org.uk
 http://www.gardenorganic.org.uk
 Chief Exec: Myles Bremner
▲   Company Limited by Guarantee; Registered Charity
Br   60
○   *F, *H, *Q; to research & promote organic horticulture & food
●   Conf - ET - Res - Inf - Lib - VE
M   30,000 i, UK / 700 i, o'seas
¶   NL - 4;   AR; both ftm.   Books & pamphlets; prices vary.
 Mail order catalogue - 1; free.
 Note: Garden Organic is the working name of the Henry
 Doubleday Research Association (also known as HDRA - the
 Organic Organisation)

Henry Williamson Society   (HWS)   1980
■   7 Monmouth Rd, DORCHESTER, Dorset, DT1 2DE.   (hsp)
 01305 264092
 http://www.henrywilliamson.co.uk
 Farm Cottage, Scotch Meadows, ALLENHEADS,
 Northumberland, NE47 9JQ.
 Sec: Sue Cumming,   Chmn: Andrew Sanders
▲   Registered Charity
○   *L; to encourage interest & a deeper understanding of the life &
 work of the 20th century English writer Henry Williamson
 (1895-1977)
●   Mtgs - Comp - SG - VE
M   525 i, 5 libraries, UK / 21 i, o'seas
¶   Jnl - 1;   NL - 1; both ftm, (subn £12).

Henty Society   1977
■   205 Icknield Way, LETCHWORTH, Herts, SG6 4TT.   (hsp)
 http://www.hentysociety.org
 Hon Sec: David Walmsley
▲   Un-incorporated Society
○   *A; to further study the life & work of George Alfred Henty
 (1832-1902) Victorian writer & war correspondent
Gp   Biographical research; Biographical study; Publications of rare
 work
●   Conf - Res - Exhib - SG - Inf
<   Alliance Literary Socs
M   90 i, UK / 55 i, o'seas
¶   Bulletin - 2;   Literary Supplements - occasional.
 Bibliographical Research (for UK, Canadian & American
 editions) - 1; all ftm only.

Heraldry Society   1950
NR   PO Box 772, GUILDFORD, Surrey, GU3 3ZX.   (hq)
 01483 237373
 email secretary@theheraldrysociety.com
 http://www.theheraldrysociety.com
 Sec: Melvyn Jeremiah
▲   Company Limited by Guarantee; Registered Charity
○   *L; heraldry, armory, chivalry & genealogy
●   Conf - Exam - Exhib - Lib - VE
M   900 worldwide
¶   The Heraldry Gazette - 4; ftm only.
 Coat of Arms - 2.

Heraldry Society of Scotland   1977
- ■ 25 Craigentinny Crescent, EDINBURGH, EH7 6QA.   (treas/p)
  0131-553 2232
  http://www.heraldry-scotland.co.uk
  Treas: Stuart G Emerson
- ▲ Registered Charity
- ○ *L; to encourage the study & practice of heraldry in Scotland,
  taking into account its European & international context
- ● Conf - Mtgs - Res - Inf - Lib - VE
- < Heraldry Soc (London)
- M c 300 i, UK / c 100 i, o'seas
- ¶ The Double Tressure (Jnl) - 1; ftm.
  Tak Tent (NL) - 1/2;   LM - irreg; both m only.
  Special publications - irreg.

Herb Society   1927
- ■ Sulgrave Manor, Sulgrave, BANBURY, Oxon, OX17 2SD.   (hq)
  01295 768899
  email info@herbsociety.org.uk
  http://www.herbsociety.org.uk
  Chmn: John Baylis,   Sec: Flick Kingston
- ▲ Company Limited by Guarantee; Registered Charity
- ○ *G, *H; promotion of knowledge & use of herbs
- ● Conf - Mtgs - ET - Exhib - Comp - Inf - Lib - VE
- < R Horticl Soc; Henry Doubleday Res Assn
- M 1,750 i, UK / 258 i, o'seas
  (Sub: £25, £22.5 concession)
- ¶ Herbs - 4; £20 yr m.

** Herb Trust
  Organisation lost: see Introduction paragraph 3

Herbert Howells Society   1987
- ■ 32 Barleycroft Rd, WELWYN GARDEN CITY, Herts, AL8 6JU.
  (hsp)
  01707 335315
  email andrew.millinger@virgin.net
  Hon Sec: Andrew Millinger
- ▲ Un-incorporated Society
- Br USA
- ○ *D; to commemorate the life & work of Herbert Howells (1892-
  1983); to encourage the performance, recording &
  publication of his music
- ● Inf - Working with publishers, recording companies & concert
  promoters
- M 200 i, 2 f, UK / 100 i, o'seas
- ¶ NL - 1; ftm.

Herdwick Sheep Breeders' Association   (HSBA)   1916
- ■ c/o The Old Stables, Redhills, PENRITH, Cumbria, CA11 0DT.
  (hsp)
  01768 869533
  http://www.herdwick-sheep.com
  Sec: G F Brown
- ○ *B
- < Nat Sheep Assn
- M 150 i
- ¶ Flock Book - 2 yrly.

Hereford Cattle Society   1878
- ■ Hereford House, 3 Offa St, HEREFORD, HR1 2LL.   (hq)
  01432 272057   fax 01432 377529
  email postroom@herefordcattle.org
  http://www.herefordcattle.org
  Sec: D E Prothero
- ▲ Company Limited by Guarantee; Registered Charity
- ○ *B
- ● Conf - Exhib - Expt
- < 21 other Hereford Cattle Societies throughout the world
- M 850 i, UK / 860 i, o'seas
- ¶ Jnl - 1; ftm, £5 nm.

Herefordshire & Worcestershire Chamber of Commerce   1839
- NR Severn House, Prescott Drive, Warndon Business Park,
  WORCESTER, WR4 9NE.   (hq)
  0845 641 1641   fax 0845 641 4641
  http://www.hwchamber.co.uk
  Chief Exec: Mike Ashton
- ○ *C
- ● Conf - Mtgs - ET - Res - Stat - Expt - Inf - Lib - LG - Business
  advice - Seminars - Training & Enterprise Council (TEC)
  services
- < Brit Chams Comm
- M c 2,700 f
- ¶ New Direction (Jnl) - 6.
  Note: uses title of Chamber of Commerce Herefordshire &
  Worcestershire

Heritage Afloat   (HA)   1994
- ■ 9 Strode St, EGHAM, Surrey, TW20 9BT.   (mem/sp)
  http://www.heritageafloat.org.uk
  Mem Sec: Bernard Hales,
  Publicity Officer: Hannah Cunliffe
- ○ *K, *G; preservation, history & interest in old & historic vessels
- ● Mtgs - Inf - LG
- M 57 i, 28 f, UK / 1 i, o'seas
- ¶ NL; free.

Heritage Railway Association   (HRA)   1996
- ■ 10 Hurdeswell, Long Hanborough, WITNEY, Oxon,
  OX29 8DH.   (press offr/p)
  01993 883384
  email john.crane@hra.gb.com
  http://www.heritagerailways.com
  Press Officer: John Crane
- ▲ Company Limited by Guarantee
- ○ *N, *T; for the heritage railway movement - heritage railways,
  railway centres, tramways & railway preservation groups
- ● Conf - Mtgs - Comp - Inf - LG
- < Eur Fedn of Museum & Tourist Rlys (FEDECRAIL)
- M 337 i, 149 f, 97 org, UK / 13 i, o'seas
  (Sub: £17.63 i, varies f & org)
- ¶ Sidelines - 6;   Broadlines - 6;   Guidelines - irreg;
  Information papers - irreg; all ftm only.
  Note: please state specific information needed & enclose an
  sae.

Herpes Viruses Association   (HVA)   1983
- ■ 41 North Rd, LONDON, N7 9DP.   (hq)
  0845 123 2305
  http://www.herpes.org.uk
  Dir: Marian Nicholson
- ▲ Registered Charity
- ○ *W; to supply information, advice & counselling to people with
  herpes simplex (cold sores, whitlow & genital sores)
- Gp Shingles Support Society (provides information of self-help
  therapies & drugs to patients with Post-Herpetic Neuralgia, &
  their GPs)
- ● Conf - Mtgs - Res - Stat - Inf - Lib - Counselling & advice to
  people with herpes viruses - Provision of correct information
  to the media
- < Skin Care Campaign; All Party Parliamentary Gp on Skin; Brit
  Assn for Sexual Health & HIV (BASHH)
- M 1,000 i, 12 f, 20 clinics, UK / 30 i, o'seas
- ¶ SPHERE (NL) - 4; ftm.
  Herpes Simplex - A Guide; £1 m, 30p in bulk nm.

Herring Buyers Association Ltd   (HBA)   1976
- NR 36 Springfield Terrace, South Queensferry, EDINBURGH,
  EH30 9XF.   (hq)
  0131-331 1222
- ○ *T

© CBD Research Ltd · Beckenham · BR3 5JS · Tel 020 8650 7745 · Fax 020 8650 0768 · E-mail cbd@cbdresearch.com · www.cbdresearch.com

Hertfordshire Agricultural Society   1801
- ■   The Showground, Dunstable Rd, REDBOURN, Herts, AL3 7PT. (hq)
  01582 792626   fax 01582 794027
  email office@hertsshow.com
  http://www.hertsshow.com
  Sec: Mike Harman
- ▲   Company Limited by Guarantee; Registered Charity
- ○   *F, *H; to promote a better understanding of farming, agriculture & the country way of life in Hertfordshire
- ●   Exhib (Organising the County Agricultural Show)
- <   Brit Show Jumping Assn; other breed societies
- M   300 i
- ¶   NL - 2;   AR - 1; both ftm only.
  Show Catalogue - 1; £3.   Show Schedule - 1; free.

Hertfordshire Chamber of Commerce & Industry   1971
- NR   4 Bishops Square Business Park, HATFIELD, Herts, AL10 9NE. (hq)
  01707 398400
  http://www.hertschamber.com
  Chief Exec: Tim Hutchings
- ▲   Company Limited by Guarantee
- ○   *C

Hesketh Hubbard Art Society
  a member of the **Federation of British Artists**

Heyday   2006
- NR   Astral House, 1268 London Rd, LONDON, SW16 4ER.   (hq)
  0845 685 0555
  email signup@heyday.org.uk   http://www.heyday.org.uk
  Dir: Ailsa Ogilvie
- ▲   Registered Charity
- ○   *K; 'a membership organisation promoting modern retirement'
- ●   Conf - Mtgs - ET - Res - Exhib - Comp - SG - Stat - Inf - Lib - VE - Empl - LG
- ¶   Heyday Magazine - 6.
  Note: has replaced the Association of Retired & Persons over 50

High Friction Surfacing Association
  in 2008 merged with the Road Surface Dressing Association & the Slurry Surfacing Contractors Association to form the **Road Surface Treatments Association**

High Sheriffs' Association of England & Wales   1970
- ■   Barn Lea, Lime Grove, West Clandon, GUILDFORD, Surrey, GU4 7UT.   (hsp)
  01483 223773   fax 01483 223773
  email secretary@highsheriffs.com
  Hon Sec: J P Hargrove
- ▲   Company Limited by Guarantee
- ○   *P; to protect, promote & strengthen the ancient Office & traditions of the High Sheriffs
- ●   Conf - Mtgs - ET - Comp - SG - Inf - LG
- M   950 i, UK / 3 i, o'seas
- ¶   The High Sheriff - 2; ftm, £20 yr nm.
  Note: also known as the Shrievalty Association

Higher Education Liaison Officers' Association   (HELOA)   1990
- ■   HELOA Office, University of Essex, Wivenhoe Park, COLCHESTER, Essex, CO4 3SQ.   (hq)
  01206 873423   fax 0871 661 5779
  email heloa@essex.ac.uk   http://www.heloa.ac.uk
  Sec: Jennifer Williams
- ▲   Un-incorporated Society
- Br   9 regional groups
- ○   *P; to provide information & assistance to students, parents & careers advisers on entry to higher education in the UK; to advise government & other organisations on needs & attitudes of students & their parents to higher education
- ●   Conf - ET - LG
- M   739 i

Highland Association
  English name of **Comunn Gaidhealach**

Highland Cattle Society   (HCS)   1884
- ■   c/o Stirling Auction Mart, Kildean, STIRLING, FK9 4UB.   (hq)
  01786 446866   fax 01786 446022
  email info@highlandcattlesociety.com
  http://www.highlandcattlesociety.com
  Breed Sec: Miss Hazel M McFadzean
- ▲   Registered Charity
- ○   *B
- ●   Exhib (Society's annual shows)
- M   890 i, UK / 50 i, o'seas
  (Sub: £64.41 (incl VAT))
- ¶   Jnl -1; ftm £5+ nm.   NL - 3; free.
  AR; ftm only.

Highland Mule Breeders Association
  a group of the **Highland & Islands Sheep Health Association Ltd**

Highland Pony Society   (HPS)   1923
- ■   Grosvenor House, Shore Rd, PERTH, PH2 8BD.   (hq)
  01738 451861   fax 01738 451861
  http://www.highlandponysociety.com
  Sec: Mrs Susie Robertson
- ▲   Company Limited by Guarantee; Registered Charity
- ○   *B; to keep the purity of the breed; to promote breeding for use in farm work, forestry, riding or driving & for sporting & show purposes
- ●   Conf - Mtgs - ET - Res - Comp - Expt - Inf - VE
- <   Nat Pony Soc
- M   1,500 i, UK / 100 i, o'seas
- ¶   Stud Book - 1.

Highland Railway Society
- ■   Ringmarsh Cottage, Horsington Marsh, TEMPLECOMBE, Somerset, BA8 0EL.   (h/treas/p)
  01963 370697   fax 01963 370697
  http://www.hrsoc.org.uk
  Treas: J Roake
- ▲   Un-incorporated Society
- ○   *G; study & recording of all aspects of the Highland Railway Company
- ●   Mtgs - Lib - PL
- M   280 i, 10 org, UK / 15 i, o'seas
- ¶   Highland Railway Jnl - 4; ftm only.

Highlands & Islands Sheep Health Association Ltd   (HISHA)   1988
- ■   Drummondhill, Stratherrick Rd, INVERNESS, IV2 4JY.   (hq)
  01463 713687   fax 01463 713687
  email info@hisha.org.uk   http://www.hisha.org.uk
  Sec: Eleanor A Fraser
- ▲   Company Limited by Guarantee
- ○   *B, *F; to create awareness of the dangers & financial implications of enzootic abortion of ewes (EAE)
- Gp   Highland Mule Breeders Association
- ●   Mtgs - Inf - Promotion of the availability of the EAE-free stock of members
- <   Scot Agricl Org Soc (SAOS)
- M   240 i, 1 org
- ¶   HISHA NL - 3/4;   AR - 1;
  List of Accredited Flocks - 1; all ftm only.

Highway Electrical Manufacturers & Suppliers Association (HEMSA) 1998
■ Bowden House, 1 Church St, HENFIELD, W Sussex, BN5 9NS. (hq)
  01273 491146   fax 01273 491147
  email hemsa@bowden-house.co.uk
  http://www.highwayelectrical.org.uk/hemsa/
  Chief Exec: Gareth Pritchard
▲ Company Limited by Guarantee
○ *T; for manufacturers & suppliers to the highway electrical industry
● Conf - Mtgs - ET - Res - Exhib - Inf - LG
M c 30 f

Hill Radnor Flock Book Society (HRFBS) 1949
NR c/o Montague Harris & Co, 16 Ship St, BRECON,
  Brecknockshire, LD3 9AD.   (hsb)
  01874 623200
  http://www.hillradnor.co.uk
  Sec: John A Lewis
▲ Un-incorporated Society
○ *B; to keep the rare breed alive
● Mtgs - Annual show & sale
< Nat Sheep Assn
M 45 i
¶ Flock Book - 1.

Hilliard Society of Miniaturists 1982
NR Priory Lodge, 7 Priory Rd, WELLS, Somerset, BA5 1SR.   (hq)
  01749 674472
  email hilliardsociety@aol.com
  http://www.art-in-miniature.org
  Exec Sec: Pamela Taylor
▲ Un-incorporated Society
○ *A; to promote & inform on contemporary & modern miniature paintings
● Exhib - VE
M c 250 i
¶ NL - 2; ftm, £2 nm.

HIPS (97) (HIPS (97)) 1997
■ White Cottage, Elstronwick, Burton Pidsea, HULL, HU12 9BP. (hsp)
  01964 670614   fax 0870 912 5369
  email abcraven@breathe.com
  Organiser: A B Craven
○ *G, *K; to support victims of failed home income plans (HIPS) originally set up in 1991; is also involved with modern equity release schemes (now regulated) & sale & rent schemes (un-regulated)
● Inf - LG
< Nat Pensioners Convention; Struggle against Financial Exploitation (SAFE)
M 120 i
¶ HIPS (97) NL - 4; free.
✕ National Support Group for Victims of Failed Home Income Plans

Hispanic & Luso Brazilian Council 1943
■ Canning House, 2 Belgrave Sq, LONDON, SW1X 8PJ.   (hq)
  020 7235 2303   fax 020 7838 9258
  email enquiries@canninghouse.com
  http://www.canninghouse.com
  Dir Gen: Veronica Scott,   Chmn: David V Thomas
▲ Registered Charity
○ *E, *X; promotion of closer relations between the UK & the Hispanic & Luso Brazilian countries
Gp Depts: Corporate (Monica Caro), Culture & education (Larissa Litchfield), Library & information (Alan Biggins)
● Conf - ET - Exhib - Expt - Inf - Lib - LG
M i, f & schools
¶ British Bulletin of Publications on Latin America, Spain & Portugal - 2;   NL - 52;
  Cultural Programme - 4;   AR - 1; all ftm.
  Information Leaflets on Special Events.

Historic Aircraft Association (HAA) 1979
■ 17 Ravensdale Ave, LEAMINGTON SPA, Warks, CV32 6NQ. (hsp)
  http://www.haa-uk.aero
  Sec: Stuart Powney
○ *G, *K; to further the preservation of historic aircraft in a flying condition (which involves the provision of a flight safety service to the public, the authorities, owners & display organisers)
Gp Register of Pilots
● Mtgs - ET - Inf
< Eur Fedn of Light, Experimental & Vintage Aircraft (EFLEVA); R Aero Club; Aircraft Owners & Pilots Assn (AOPA)
M 170 i, UK / 10 i, o'seas

Historic Artillery (HA) 1987
■ 23 Viewside Close, Corfe Mullen, WIMBORNE, Dorset, BH21 3ST.   (hsp)
  01202 690224
  email richardbarton@caving5.freeserve.co.uk
  Sec: Richard Barton
▲ Un-incorporated Society
○ *G; research into the science of artillery in history; promotion of historical re-enactment for educational purposes
Gp Field research; Workshop; Research into siege weapons & techniques; Computer database; Artillery Association GB
● Res - SG - Inf - VE - Re-enactment
< Siege Warfare in the Midlands; Coalhouse Fort Project
M 20 i, 2 org

Historic Canoe & Kayak Association (HCKA) 1989
■ 48 Russell Way, HIGHAM FERRERS, Northants, NN10 8EJ. (hsp)
  01933 314672   fax 01933 314672
  email jteam@btinternet.com
  http://www.uk.geocities.com/hcka@btinternet.com
  Hon Sec: J F Pearton
▲ Un-incorporated Society
○ *G; to promote an interest in historic canoes & kayaks
● Res - Inf - Displaying historic craft
> R Marines Museum
M i
¶ Paddles Past (Jnl) _ 4; ftm.   LM - 1.
  [subscription £13].

Historic Caravan Club (HCC) 1993
NR 29 Linnet Close, Lodgefield Park, HALESOWEN, W Midlands, B62 8TW.   (hsp)
  0121-561 5742
  email bbissechcc@aol.com   http://www.hcclub.co.uk
  Hon Sec: Barbara Bissell
▲ Un-incorporated Society
Br 9 area coordinators
○ *G; to encourage the rescue, restoration, display & use of trailer caravans up to 1960, including horse-drawn ancestors of the touring caravan
● Mtgs - Res - Exhib - Inf - Provision of displays at vintage rallies
< Fedn of Brit Historic Vehicle Clubs; Assn of Caravan & Camping Exempted Orgs
M 210 i, UK / 3 i, 4 org, o'seas
¶ Wanderer (NL) - 8;   LM - 1;   Register of Member's Caravans - 1;   all ftm only.
  Membership Hbk - free on joining.
  Historic Caravan Scene (Jnl) - irreg; ftm, £2.25 each nm.

© CBD Research Ltd · Beckenham · BR3 5JS · Tel 020 8650 7745 · Fax 020 8650 0768 · E-mail cbd@cbdresearch.com · www.cbdresearch.com

Historic Commercial Vehicle Society (HCVS) 1957
- ■ Iden Grange, Cranbrook Rd, STAPLEHURST, Kent, TN12 0ET.
  (hsp)
  01580 892929   fax 01580 893227
  email hcvs@btinternet.com   http://www.hcvs.co.uk
  Snr Exec Officer & Vice-Pres: Michael J Banfield
- ▲ Company Limited by Guarantee; Registered Charity
- Br 11
- ○ *G; to promote the study & preservation of historic commercial
  vehicles over 20 years old
- ● Mtgs - Inf - Lib - LG
- < Intl Historic Vehicle Org (IHVO)
- M 3,500 i, UK / 60 i, o'seas
- ¶ Historic Commercial News - 9; ftm, £2.50 nm.   AR.

Historic Endurance Rallying Organisation (HERO) 1996
- NR Ynysymaerdy Farm Cottage, Ynysymaerdy Rd, Britton Ferry,
  NEATH, SA11 2TS.
  01639 820864   fax 01639 812863
  email enquiries@hero.org.uk   http://www.hero.org.uk
  Gen Sec: Lynn Nedin
- ○ long distance motor rallies for vintage, historic and classic cars

Historic Houses Association (HHA) 1973
- ■ 2 Chester St, LONDON, SW1X 7BB.   (hq)
  020 7259 5688
  email info@hha.org.uk   http://www.hha.org.uk
  Dir Gen: Nick Way
- ○ *K, *N; an association of owners & guardians of historic
  houses, parks, gardens & places of interest (& their
  associated contents) of Great Britain; formed to promote &
  safeguard their legitimate interests so far as they are
  consistent with the interests of the nation
- ● Conf - Mtgs - Res - Exhib - Inf - Cooperation with art galleries
  & museums - Seminars
- < U Historic Houses
- M 1,500 i, 20,000 friends
- ¶ Historic House - 4.   Jnl; ftm.
  Technical papers & guidelines.

Historic Society of Lancashire & Cheshire (HSLC) 1848
- ■ Flat 4 / 3 Bramhall Rd, Waterloo, LIVERPOOL, L22 3XA.   (hsb)
  0151-920 8213
  email rch2949@yahoo.co.uk   http://www.hslc.org.uk
  Hon Sec: Roger Hull
- ▲ Registered Charity
- ○ *L; to promote the study of any aspect of the history of
  Lancashire & Cheshire
- ● Mtgs - Lib
- M 266 i, 127 org
- ¶ Transactions - 1.

Historical Association (HA) 1906
- NR 59a Kennington Park Rd, LONDON, SE11 4JH.   (hq)
  020 7735 3901   fax 020 7582 4989
  email enquiry@history.org.uk   http://www.history.org.uk
  Chief Exec: Madeline Stiles
- ▲ Company Limited by Guarantee; Registered Charity
- Br 59
- ○ *E, *P; 'to bring together people who share an interest in, &
  love for, the past'; to promote the study & teaching of history
  at all levels
- ● Conf - Mtgs - ET - VE
- M 5,300 i, 500 f, 2,000 schools, UK / 400 i, o'seas
- ¶ The Historian - 4.   History - 4.
  Teaching History - 4.   Primary History - 3.
  Annual Bulletin of Historical Literature.
  Pamphlets.   AR.

Historical Breechloading Smallarms Association (HBSA)
1973
- ▣ BCM HBSA, LONDON, WC1N 3XX.   (mail/address)
  01376 563684
  email general.secretary@hbsa-uk.org
  http://www.hbsa-uk.org
  Gen Sec: Chris Smith
- ▲ Company Limited by Guarantee
- Br 4
- ○ *G; to study the history, development, conservation,
  preservation & use of breechloading smallarms, ammunition
  & related items; to act as the national supervisory body for
  the sporting & competitive use of historical breechloading
  smallarms
- ● Conf - Mtgs - ET - Res - Exhib - Comp - LG
- < Nat Rifle Assn
- M 350 i, 50 affiliates
  (Sub: £35 i, £50 affiliates)
- ¶ Jnl - 1; ftm, £3.55 nm.   Report - 3; ftm, £2 nm.

Historical Diving Society (HDS) 1990
- NR 29 Pringle Croft, Woodend, CHORLEY, Lancs, PR6 7UL.
  (mem/sp)
  01737 249961
  email info@thehds.com   http://www.thehds.com
  Mem Sec: Una Smillie
- ▲ Registered Charity
- ○ *G; to provide a forum for all interested in the history of
  underwater descent, including all aspects of diving
  (commercial, amateur, naval, military, experimental &
  scientific)
- Gp Sections: Bibliophile, Film; Working historical equipment
- ● Conf - Mtgs - Exhib - Lib
- M i, f & org
- ¶ Historical Diving Times (NL) - 3; ftm.
  Membership Register - 1; ftm only.

Historical Maritime Society (HMS) 1995
- ■ 2 Mount Zion, Brownbirks St, Cornholme, TODMORDEN,
  Lancs, OL14 8PG.
  01706 819248
  http://www.hms.org.uk
  Contact: Chris Jones
- ○ historical research and re-enactment group recreating the Royal
  Navy

Historical Medical Equipment Society (HMES) 1996
- ■ Streams, West Kington, CHIPPENHAM, Wilts, SN14 7JE.   (hsp)
  01249 782218
  email drtgcsmith@aol.com
  Hon Sec: Dr Tim Smith
- ▲ Un-incorporated Society
- ○ *G; the study of old medical & surgical items & the history of
  medicine
- ● Conf - Mtgs - Inf - VE
- M 90 i, UK / 20 i, o'seas
- ¶ Bulletin - 2; ftm, £2 nm.

Historical Metallurgy Society Ltd (HMS) 1962
- ■ 267 Kells Lane, Low Fell, GATESHEAD, Tyne & Wear,
  NE9 5HU.   (hsb)
  0191-482 1037   fax [by arrangement]
  email cranconsult@btinternet.com
  http://www.hist-met.org
  Hon Gen Sec: David Cranstone
- ▲ Company Limited by Guarantee; Registered Charity
- ○ *L; study, research & preservation of the historical &
  archaeological evidence of the extraction, smelting &
  working of metals & the manufacture of metal objects
- ● Conf
- < Inst Materials
- M 340 i, 31 org, UK / 170 i, 42 org, o'seas
- ¶ Historical Metallurgy (Jnl) - 2.   NL - 3.

Historical Model Railway Society   (HMRS)   1950
NR   Midland Railway Centre, Butterley Railway Station, RIPLEY,
     Derbys, DE5 3QZ.   (hq)
     01773 745959
     email studycentremanager@hmrs.org.uk
     http://www.hmrs.org.uk
     Chmn: T Johnson
▲   Registered Charity
○   *G; for the study & recording of information relating to all the
     railways of the British Isles; public education on matters
     concerning these railways; construction, operation,
     preservation & public exhibition of models depicting them.
     (Nothing to do with toys)
●   Mtgs - ET - Res - Exhib - Comp - SG - Inf - Lib - PL - VE
M   1,900 i, UK & o'seas
¶   HMRS Jnl - 4;   HMRS News - 6; both ftm.
     North Eastern Record:
        Volume 1: Infrastructure;
        Volume 2: Rolling Stock;
        Volume 3: Locomotives;
     The Locomotives of the Stockton & Darlington Railway;
     British Railways Mark 1 Coaches;
        [all above; £24.95.]
     Private Owner Wagons from the Ince Waggon & Ironworks Co;
     Oil on the Rails;
     Brunel's Cornish Viaducts;
        [all above; £19.95.]
     Locomotives of the Hull & Barnsley Railway; £5.95.
     GWR Iron Minks; £4.50.
     British Railway Brakevans & Ballast Ploughs; £12.95.
     Modelling Historic Architecture; £8.95.
     William Bradshaw - a Leicestershire railway
        photographer; £11.95.
        [Special discounts are available to members]

History of Anaesthesia Society   (HAS)   1986
■   49 Howey Lane, FRODSHAM, Cheshire, WA6 6DD.   (hsp)
     01928 731888
     email gasflo@btinternet.com
     http://www.histansoc.org.uk
     Hon Sec: Dr Anne M Florence
▲   Un-incorporated Society
○   *L; to promote interest & study in the worldwide history of
     anaesthesia
●   Mtgs
<   Brit Soc for the History of Medicine (BSHM)
M   318 i, UK / 82 i, o'seas
     (Sub: £20)
¶   Proceedings - 2; ftm, £6 nm.

History Curriculum Association   (HCA)   1990
NR   Windover, Punnetts Town, HEATHFIELD, E Sussex, TN21 9DS.
     (dir/p)
     01435 830109
     Dir: Chris McGovern
▲   Un-incorporated Society
○   *G, *K; to restore the history curriculum within the UK education
     system
●   Res - SG - Inf - LG
<   Granted a statutory right to be consulted on the National
     Curriculum
M   supporters

History of Education Society (UK)   (HES(UK))   1967
■   c/o Faculty of Education, University of Winchester,
     WINCHESTER, Hants, SO22 4NR.   (hsb)
     01962 827125
     email secretary@historyofeducation.org.uk
     http://www.historyofeducation.org.uk
     Sec: Dr Stephanie Spencer
▲   Registered Charity
○   *L; to study & research into the history of education; to support
     students
●   Conf - ET - Res
<   Intl Standing Conf for History of Education (ISCHE)
M   155 i, UK / 45 i, o'seas
     (Sub: £25)
¶   History of Education Jnl - 6; £50 m, £299 nm.
     History of Education Researcher - 2; ftm only.

Hitchin Chamber of Commerce & Industry   (HCCI)
■   c/o 27 Churchyard, HITCHIN, Herts, SG5 1HP.   (chmn/b)
     01462 453335
     Chmn: Alan Doggett
▲   Un-incorporated Society
○   *C
●   Mtgs - ET - LG
M   [not stated]
×   Hitchin & District Chamber of Commerce.

HL7 UK Ltd   2000
NR   PO Box 7230, HOOK, Hants, RG27 9WX.
     0870 011 2866   fax 0870 011 2867
     http://www.hl7.org.uk
○   *P, *T; to support the development, promotion &
     implementation of HL [Health Level] healthcare standards, in
     order to meet the needs of healthcare organisations,
     professionals & healthcare software suppliers in the UK

Holiday Centres Association   (HCA)   1935
■   The Coppice, Rowe Close, Devonshire Park, BIDEFORD, Devon,
     EX39 5XX.   (hq)
     01237 421347
     email holidaycentres@aol.com
     http://www.holidaycentres.com
     Chief Exec: David Howell
▲   Company Limited by Guarantee
○   *T; interests of holiday centres
●   Conf - Mtgs - Res - Stat - Inf - LG
<   Music Users Coun of Europe; Tourism Alliance
M   53 f
¶   NL - 2; ftm only.   LM - 1; free.

Holistic Healers Association   1998
NR   3 MacLean Grove, Stewartfield, EAST KILBRIDE, G74 4TJ.
     01355 276410
     email holistic-healers-association.co.uk
     Contact: K Lawrence
○   *P
M   900 i
     no further information supplied

Holstein UK   1909
NR   Scotsbridge House, Scots Hill, RICKMANSWORTH, Herts,
     WD3 3BB.   (hq)
     01923 695200
     http://www.holstein-uk.org
     Admin: Jacky Palmer
○   *B
M   c 10,000 i

Home Beer & Wine Manufacturers Association
     no longer in existence

© CBD Research Ltd · Beckenham · BR3 5JS · Tel 020 8650 7745 · Fax 020 8650 0768 · E-mail cbd@cbdresearch.com · www.cbdresearch.com

Home Builders Federation   (HBF)   1947

NR   Byron House, 7-9 St James's St, LONDON, SW1A 1DW.   (hq)
       020 7960 1600   fax 020 7960 1601
       http://www.hbf.co.uk
       Chief Exec: Robert Ashmead
       Head of Media Relations: Pierre Williams
▲   Un-incorporated Society
Br   8
○   *T; to ensure a favourable economic, political & planning
       climate in the UK in which private housebuilders can operate
Gp   Planning; Political; Technical; Public relations; Taxation; Europe
●   Conf - Mtgs - ET - Stat - LG
<   Intl Housing Assn; Eur U Developers & Housebuilders
M   800 f
¶   House Builder Magazine - 10;   NL - 4; both ftm.
✕   2005 (April) House Builders Federation

Home Business Alliance   (HBA)   1984

■   Werrington Business Centre, 86 Papyrus Rd, PETERBOROUGH,
       Cambs, PE4 5BH.   (hq)
       0871 474 1015   fax 0871 474 1016
       email info@homebusiness.org.uk
       http://www.homebusiness.org.uk
       Chmn: Leonard Tondel,   Sec: Marion Owen
○   *T; 'production & exchange of information on successful
       business methods for business owners & home businesses -
       to expand existing businesses & set up new ones'
M   i
¶   The Boss (NL).

Home Decoration Retailers' Association
   a group of the **British Hardware Federation**

Home Education Advisory Service   (HEAS)   1995

■   PO Box 98, WELWYN GARDEN CITY, Herts, AL8 6AN.
       (mail address)
       01707 371854   fax 01707 338467
       email enquiries@heas.org.uk   http://www.heas.org.uk
       Sec: Mrs Brenda Holliday
▲   Company Limited by Guarantee; Registered Charity
○   *E; advice & information on education at home instead of
       school
●   Conf - ET - Inf - Lib - Subscribers' advice line
M   [not stated]
¶   HEAS Bulletin - 4; ftm only.
       HEAS Introductory Information Pack; £2.50.
       HEAS Resources Book;   Home Education Hbk; both £8.75.
       Home Education Overseas; £1.50
       Information leaflets:
          Special Education Needs; £1.50.
          Examinations;   Dyslexia; both £1.
       Maths Pack; £9.75.

Home Laundering Consultative Council   (HLCC)   1966

NR   5 Portland Place, LONDON, W1B 1PW.   (hq)
       020 7636 7788   fax 020 7636 7515
       http://www.care-labelling.co.uk
       Sec: A Mansell
○   *T; promotion & administration of a uniform system of care-
       labelling, both nationally & internationally
●   Mtgs - Inf
<   GINETEX
M   70 f, c 70 trade assns & educational bodies with an interest in
       care-labelling
¶   LM;   AR.   Other publications.

Homeless Link   2001

■   10-13 Rushworth St (1st floor), LONDON, SE1 0RB.   (hq)
       020 7960 3010   fax 020 7960 3011
       email info@homelesslink.org.uk
       http://www.homeless.org.uk
       Chief Exec: Jenny Edwards,   Co Sec: Alex Botha
▲   Company Limited by Guarantee; Registered Charity
○   *K, *N; relief of poverty, sickness & need caused by, or resulting
       in, a condition of homelessness
●   Conf - Mtgs - ET - Res - LG
M   25 i, 450 f
       Sub: £42 i, £10-£1,056 f)
¶   Connect - 4; ftm, £28 yr nm.
       Members Mailing - 12; ftm only.   AR - 1; free.
       Various books & guides; listed on website.

Homeopathic Medical Association   (HMA)   1985

■   7 Darnley Rd, GRAVESEND, Kent, DA11 0RU.   (hq)
       01474 560336   fax 01474 327431
       email info@the-hma.org   http://www.the-hma.org
       Coun Sec: Mrs Parm Randhawa
▲   Company Limited by Guarantee
○   *M, *P; 'members must have passed a qualifying examination
       at a college approved by the Council &/or proved their
       worthiness to practise the art & science of Homoeopathy...
       members are bound by a strict code of ethics & practice &
       obliged to carry professional indemnity insurance'
●   Conf
M   i
¶   Homeopathy International (Jnl) - 4; £25.

Homes for Scotland

NR   5 New Mart Place, EDINBURGH, EH14 1RW.   (hq)
       0131-455 8350   fax 0131-455 8360
       email info@homesforscotland.com
       http://www.homesforscotland.com
       Exec Dir: Bruce Black
▲   Company Limited by Guarantee
Br   1
○   *T; to promote the long-term interests of the Scottish home
       building industry; to create awareness of the economic,
       social & environmental significance of home builders;
       interests include planning, water & drainage, design,
       environmental quality
Gp   Housing planning
●   Mtgs - Inf - LG
M   160 f
¶   NL - 12; ftm only.
✕   SHBA Ltd (Homes for Scotland)

Honest Food - the Campaign for Independent Food
   a campaign run by the **Countryside Alliance**

Honey Association   (HA)   1940

■   Crescent House, 34 Eastbury Way, SWINDON, Wilts,
       SN25 2EN.   (asa)
       01793 727387   fax 01793 726486
       email info@honeyassociation.com
       http://www.honeyassociation.com
       Sec: Walter J Anzer
▲   Company Limited by Guarantee
○   *T; interests of British honey importers & packers
●   Mtgs - PR - Technical services
<   Eur Fedn Honey Packers & Distributors (FEEDM)
M   16 f

Hong Kong Association   1961
■   Swire House, 59 Buckingham Gate, LONDON, SW1E 6AJ.
      (hq)
      020 7963 9447   fax 020 7828 6331
      email info@hkas.org.uk   http://www.hkas.org.uk
      Exec Dir: Capt Robert Guy
▲   Company Limited by Guarantee
○   *T, *X; to nurture the business & commercial relationship
      between the Hong Kong SAR & the UK
●   Mtgs - LG
<   Hong Kong Soc
M   100 f

Honorable Society of King's Inns   1200
IRL   Henrietta St, DUBLIN 1, Republic of Ireland.
      353 (1) 874 4840   fax 353 (1) 872 6048
      email info@kingsinns.ie   http://www.kingsinns.ie
○   *P

**Honourable Society of Cymmrodorion   (Anrhydeddus
Gymdeithas y Cymmrodorion)   1751**
NR   30 Eastcastle St, LONDON, W1W 8DJ.   (hsb)
      020 7631 0502
      email aelodau1751we@yahoo.co.uk
      http://www.cymmrodorion1751.org.uk
      Hon Sec: John Samuel
▲   Registered Charity
○   *L; encouragement of the literature, arts & sciences of Wales
●   Mtgs - Res - Lib
M   c 800 i, c 80 org, UK / 30 i, 40 org, o'seas
¶   Transactions - 1; £25.

The Honourable The Irish Society   1613
■   Salters' Hall, 4 Fore St, LONDON, EC2Y 5DE.   (hq)
      020 7786 9876   fax 020 7786 9877
      email charlesf@irishsociety.co.uk
      Sec: C J H Fisher
▲   Charity incorporated by Royal Charter
○   *W; to aid & support the economic status of both institutions &
      individuals in Co Londonderry (Northern Ireland), through
      grant aid & charitable donations; to support cross-community
      self-help initiatives & educational projects, as well as
      individuals & small groups who apply for financial assistance
●   Mtgs - VE - Sets up presentation meetings in the City of London
      for those in Northern Ireland seeking investment
<   The Corporation of the City of London
M   membership confined to the Court of Common Council in the
      City of London

Hop Merchants Association   (HMA)   1917
■   Charles Faram & Co Ltd, Monkfield Lane, Newland, MALVERN,
      Worcs, WR13 5BB.   (pres/b)
      01905 830734
      Chmn: Paul Corbett
▲   Un-incorporated Society
○   *T; to promote the interests of members trading in hops grown
      in England
      no further information supplied

Hopkins Society   1990
NR   41 North Drive, RHYL, Flintshire, LL18 4SW.   (mem/sp)
      Mem Sec: Imelda Jones
▲   Un-incorporated Society
○   *A; for those interested in the work & life of Gerard Manley
      Hopkins, English poet & priest
M   i

Horatian Society   1934
■   c/o John S C Eidinow, Merton College, OXFORD, OX1 4JD.
      (mail/add)
      Hon Sec & Treas: J S C Eidinow
▲   Un-incorporated Society
○   *A; 'the poet Horace & his works'
●   Annual dinner
M   200 i
¶   AR (incl LM); ftm only.

Horse Rangers Association (Hampton Court) Ltd   (HRA)   1954
■   Royal Mews, Hampton Court Rd, EAST MOLESEY, Surrey,
      KT8 9BW.   (hq)
      020 8979 4196   fax 020 8941 3310
      email admin@horserangers.com
      http://www.horserangers.com
      Dir: Jackie Bryans
▲   Registered Charity
Br   4
○   *Y; a uniformed youth organisation enabling young people to
      learn stable management & to ride; it also offers a riding for
      the disabled section
Gp   Riding for the disabled, throughout the week in term time
●   ET
<   Brit Horse Soc; Riding for the Disabled Assn
M   400 i

**Horserace Writers & Photographers Association   (HWPA)
1927**
■   68 Dale St, YORK, YO23 1AE.   (pres/p)
      07789 983903
      email will.hayler@gmail.com   http://www.hwpa.co.uk
      Pres: Will Hayler
▲   Un-incorporated Society
Br   3
○   *P; to represent the interests of all racing media (TV, radio,
      newspapers, photographers) within the racing industry
●   Derby awards lunch (London, 1st Monday in December)
<   Nat Turf Writers Assn (USA)
M   303 i
¶   NL - 4/5.   Derby Awards brochure - 1.

Horseracing Sponsors Association   (HSA)   1993
NR   Stirling Way, BOREHAMWOOD, Herts, WD6 2AZ.   (hq)
      020 8207 4114
      http://www.horseracingsponsors.com
▲   Company Limited by Guarantee
○   *T; to provide practical help & advice for race sponsors; to work
      with racecourses to attract new sponsors; to represent
      sponsors within the industry

HorseSport Ireland
IRL   Beech House, Millennium Park, Osberstown, NASS, Co Kildare,
      Republic of Ireland.
      353 (45) 850 800
      email efi@horsesport.ie   http://www.horsesport.ie
      Chief Exec: Damian McDonald
○   *B, *T
✕   Equestrian Federation of Ireland

Horticultural Association of Retail Traders Ltd
has closed

Horticultural & Contractors Tools Association
      a group of the **Federation of British Hand Tool Manufacturers**

© CBD Research Ltd · Beckenham · BR3 5JS · Tel 020 8650 7745 · Fax 020 8650 0768 · E-mail cbd@cbdresearch.com · www.cbdresearch.com

Horticultural Exhibitors' Association   (HEA)   1946
- The Cottage, Cow Green, Bacton, STOWMARKET, Suffolk,
  IP14 4HJ.   (hsp)
  01449 782013   fax 01449 782013
  email secretary@h-e-a.freeserve.co.uk
  http://www.h-e-a.co.uk
  Hon Sec: Mrs Sarah Clare
○ *T; interests of horticultural producers & suppliers who exhibit at
  horticultural & agricultural shows
Gp Categories of membership: Floral, Sundries, Associate
● Mtgs
M 182 f, show organisers
  (Sub: £55)
¶ NL - 4;   Hbk - 1; both ftm only.

Horticultural Trades Association   (HTA)   1899
- Horticulture House, 19 High St, Theale, READING, Berks,
  RG7 5AH.   (hq)
  0118-930 3132
  http://www.the-hta.org.uk
  Dir Gen: David Gwyther
▲ Company Limited by Guarantee
○ *H, *T; to represent the UK garden industry; to promote the
  profitable growth of its retail & grower members
Gp Association of British Conifer Growers; Association of Liner
   Producers (ALP); Association of Professional
   Landscapers (APL); British Heather Growers (BHG); British
   Rose Group; Tree & Hedging Group
● Conf - Mtgs - ET - Exam - Res - Exhib - Stat - Inf - Lib - VE - LG
M 3,000 f
¶ HTA News - 12; ftm, £2 nm.   AR; free.

Horticulture Research International Association
no longer exists

Hose Manufacturers' & Suppliers' Association   (HMSA)   1999
- 2 Waltham Court, Milley Lane, Hare Hatch, READING, Berks,
  RG10 9TH.   (hq)
  0118-940 3416   fax 0118-940 6258
  email info@feta.co.uk   http://www.feta.co.uk
  Dir Gen: Cedric Sloan
○ *T; the manufacture or supply of quality flexible hoses to the
  heating, ventilating & air conditioning industry
● Mtgs - Inf
< Heating & Ventilating Mfrs' Assn (HEVAC); Fedn Envtl Tr
  Assns (FETA)
M 4 f

Hospital Broadcasting Association
the trading name of **National Association of Hospital
Broadcasting Organisations**

Hospital Caterers Association   (HCA)   1948
- New Cross Hospital, Wednesfield Rd, WOLVERHAMPTON,
  WV10 0QP.   (hsb)
  01902 307999
  email sandra.roberts@rwh-tr.nhs.uk
  http://www.hospitalcaterers.org
  Hon Sec: Mrs Sandra Roberts
Br 17
○ *P; to promote & improve the standards of catering in hospitals
  & healthcare; in Great Britain, Northern Ireland & elsewhere;
  to ensure the education & training of persons engaged in
  healthcare catering services & the improvement of their
  professional interests & status
● Conf - Mtgs - ET - Exhib - Comp - Inf - Lib - LG
< Healthcare Catering Intl
M 700+ i
¶ Hospital Caterer (Jnl) - 6.   Hospital Caterer Ybk - 1.
  Hygiene Good Practice Guide.
  Food Service Standards at Ward Level: good practice guide.

Hospital Consultants & Specialists Association   (HCSA)   1948
NR 1 Kingsclere Rd, Overton, BASINGSTOKE, Hants, RG25 3JA.
   (hq)
   01256 771777
   http://www.hcsa.com
   Head of Admin: Steve George
▲ Un-incorporated Society
○ *P, *U; to promote, protect & advance the interests of
  consultants in their relationship with hospital authorities & the
  progress of medical practice in the NHS
● Conf - Mtgs - SG - Stat - Inf - Empl
< TUC
M 3,000 i
¶ HCSA News.

Hospital & Medical Care Association   (HMCA)   1978
- Beech Hall, KNARESBOROUGH, N Yorks, HG5 0EA.   (hq)
  01423 866985   fax 01423 866586
  email hmca@hmca.co.uk   http://www.hmca.co.uk
  Hon Sec: Ian Cook
○ *T; provides benefits for members of membership groups; is
  authorised & regulated by the Financial Services Authority

Hostelling International Northern Ireland   (HINI)   1931
- 22-32 Donegall Rd, BELFAST, BT12 5JN.   (hq)
  028 9032 4733   fax 028 9031 5889
  http://www.hini.org.uk
  Gen Sec: Ken Canavan
▲ Company Limited by Guarantee; Registered Charity
○ *Y; to promote an appreciation of the countryside among
  young people through provision of hostel accommodation
Gp Fell walking
● Conf - Mtgs - Exhib - Inf - VE
< Intl Youth Hostel Fedn (IYHF)
M 6,500 i
¶ AR; free.
× Youth Hostel Association of Northern Ireland

Hot Water Association   (HWA)   2007
NR 17 Victoria Rd, Saltaire, SHIPLEY, W Yorks, BD18 3LQ.   (sb)
   01274 583355   fax 01274 583355
   email info@hotwater.org.uk
   http://www.hotwater.org.uk
▲ Un-incorporated Society
○ *T; domestic hot water storage (vented & unvented cylinders)
× 2007 (Manufacturers of Domestic Unvented Systems
   (Waterheater Manufacturers Association

Hotel Booking Agents Association   (HBAA)   1997
- 3000 Cathedral Hill, GUILDFORD, Surrey, GU2 7YB.   (asa)
  0845 603 3349   fax 01483 243501
  email secretariat@hbaa.org.uk
  http://www.hbaa.org.uk
  Exec Dir: Peter Ducker
▲ Company Limited by Guarantee
○ *T; to represent the hotel venue conference community
Gp Agents; Hotels & venues
● Conf - Mtgs - ET - Inf - VE - LG
M 240 f
  (Sub: £250,000)
¶ Code of Working Practice.

Hotel & Catering International Management Association
since 2007 the **Institute of Hospitality**

Hound Trailing Association   (HTA)   1906
- ■ Ash Cottage, Blencow, PENRITH, Cumbria, CA11 0DB.
  (hsp/b)
  01768 483686
  email hta.margaret@btopenworld.com
  http://www.houndtrailing.org.uk
  Sec: Margaret Baxter
- ▲ Company Limited by Guarantee
- ○ *S; hound racing following aniseed scent; a traditional
  Cumbrian sport (not a blood-sport)
- ● Mtgs - Comp
- M c 1,000 i
- ¶ Ybk; £2.50.   AR; free.

House Builders Association
  an association in the National Federation of Builders, in the
  Construction Confederation

House Builders Federation
  since April 2005 **Home Builders Federation**

Houses, Castles & Gardens of Ireland
- IRL 16A Woodlands Park, BLACKROCK, Co Dublin, Republic of
  Ireland.
  353 (1) 288 9114
  email info@castlesgardensireland.com
  http://www.gardensireland.com
  Chmn: Bartle D'Arcy
- ○ *G

Housing Institute of Ireland   1989
- IRL c/o 50 Merrion Sq, DUBLIN 2, Republic of Ireland.
  353 (1) 661 8334   fax 353 (1) 661 0320
  Co-ordinator: Sally Blair
- ○ *P

Housman Society   1973
- ■ 80 New Rd, BROMSGROVE, Worcs, B60 2LA.   (chmn/p)
  01527 874136
  email info@housman-society.co.uk
  http://www.housman-society.co.uk
  Chmn: J C Page
- ▲ Registered Charity
- Br 1; Japan, USA
- ○ *L; to foster interest in & promote knowledge of A[lfred]
  E[dward] Housman (1865-1959), his sister Clemence &
  brother Laurence
- ● Mtgs - Res - Exhib - Inf - Lib - VE - Publications
- < Alliance of Literary Socs
- M 300 i, UK / 40 i, o'seas
  (Sub: £10)
- ¶ Housman Jnl - 1; ftm, £6 nm.   NL - 2; free.
  The Name & Nature of Poetry.
  Unkind to Unicorns.   Housman's Places.
  A Westerly Wanderer.   Three Bromsgrove Poets.
  Soldier I Wish You Well.

Hovercraft Club of Great Britain Ltd   (HCGB)   1966
- ■ 26 Milverton Close, Lostock, BOLTON, Lancs, BL6 4RR.   (hsp)
  01204 841248
  email info@hovercraft.org.uk
  http://www.hovercraft.org.uk
  Chmn: Jim Lyne,   Vice-Chmn: Chris Barlow
- ▲ Company Limited by Guarantee
- Br 7
- ○ *G, *S; construction & development of light sports hovercraft;
  including regulation of design & construction safety
- Gp Competitions; Cruising & coastal events; Specialist publications
- ● Conf - Mtgs - Comp - Inf - Lib/Archive - National hovercraft
  series racing - Cruising events (river & coastal) - Coastal
  racing
- < Wld Hovercraft Fedn; Eur Hovercraft Fedn
- > Hovercraft Museum
- M 700 i, 10 f, 5 org, UK / 30 i, 2 f, o'seas
- ¶ Light Hovercraft - 12; ftm, £2.50 nm.   AR - 1; free.
  Inland Racing Competition Regulation - 1; ftm; £4 nm.
  Racing Construction Regulation - 1; ftm, £4 nm.
  Cruising Construction Regulations - 1; ftm, £4 nm.
  Coastal Racing Construction Regulations - 1; ftm, £4 nm.
  Guide to Making Model Hovercraft - irreg; £6.
  Hovercraft Construction Guide - irreg; £17.
  Guideline to Safe Operation of Cruising Hovercraft; £3.
  Hover Humour; £1.50.

Hovercraft Museum Trust   (HMT)   1986
- ■ HMS Daedalus, Chark Lane, LEE-on-the-SOLENT, Hants,
  PO13 9NY.   (hq)
  023 9255 2090
  email warwick@hovercraft-museum.org
  http://www.hovercraft-museum.org
  Mgr: W Jacobs
- ▲ Registered Charity
- ○ *L, *Q; to promote the hovercraft educational museum trust
- ● Conf - Mtgs - ET - Res - Exhib - Comp - Stat - Expt - Inf - Lib -
  PL - VE - LG Lectures - Open days - Restoration
- < Brit Aviation Presvn Coun
- M 400 i, 50 f
  (Sub: £25)
- ¶ Hovercraft Museum NL - 4; £20.
- ✕ 2004-06 Hovercraft Society & Hovercraft Museum Trust

Howard League for Penal Reform   1921
- NR 1 Ardleigh Rd, LONDON, N1 4HS.   (hq)
  020 7249 7373
  http://www.howardleague.org
  Dir: Frances Crook
- ▲ Company Limited by Guarantee; Registered Charity
- ○ *K; advancement of constructive penal & social policies
- ● Conf - Mtgs - ET - Res - VE - LG
- < John Howard Soc of: Canada / S Australia / British Columbia
- M 3,000 i, 50 f, 50 org, UK / 300 i, 10 f, 10 org, o'seas
- ¶ HLM: Howard League Magazine - 4.
  Missing the Grade: Education for Children in Prison.
  Suicide & Self Harm Prevention (4 reports).
  Children in Prison (10 reports).

HR Circle
  a group of **Food & Drink Industry Ireland**

HR Society Ltd   1970
NR   Bridge House, Church Rd, BURNHAM-on-CROUCH, Essex,
        CM0 8BZ.   (hq)
        01621 781035   fax 01621 782327
        email network@hrsociety.co.uk
        http://www.hrsociety.co.uk
        Sec: Mrs Sheila Nutt
▲   Company Limited by Guarantee; Registered Charity
○   *L; to promote the study & advancement of education in the
        field of manpower policy (human resources) management,
        planning & utilisation
Gp   Financial services special interest
●   Conf - Mtgs - ET - Res - SG - Inf
M   63 i, 22 f
¶   Manpower News - irreg; ftm only.   AR - 1; free.
        Spotlight (NL) - 4; ftm & free to Health Service.

Huguenot Society of Great Britain & Ireland   1885
■   Huguenot Library, University College London, Gower St,
        LONDON, WC1E 6BT.   (college/library)
        020 7679 5199
        email library@ucl.ac.uk
        http://www.huguenotsociety.org.uk
        Hon Sec: Barbara Julien
▲   Registered Charity
○   *L; collection & publication of information on the history &
        genealogy of the Huguenots, particularly those who took
        refuge in the British Isles; their influence on the culture,
        politics & economy of Britain & Ireland
Gp   Irish section (Dublin)
●   Conf - Mtgs - Res - Inf - Lib - VE
M   1,086 i, 107 libraries, UK / 245 i, o'seas
¶   Proceedings - 1; ftm, £8 nm.   NL - 2; ftm only.
        Quarto Series - irreg; £5-£11 m, £12-£24 nm.
        CD Roms of some of the above; £17.50 m, £19.99 nm.
            As a set: £125 m, £150 nm.
        Microfiches of Quarto Series 1-47; £4 (each) m, £5 (each) nm.
        New series - irreg; £10-£15 m, £15-£15 nm.

**Hull & Humber Chamber of Commerce, Industry & Shipping
1837**
■   34-38 Beverley Rd, HULL, HU3 1YE.   (hq)
        01482 324976   fax 01482 213962
        email info@hull-humber-chamber.co.uk
        http://www.hull-humber-chamber.co.uk
        Chief Exec: Dr Ian Kelly
▲   Company Limited by Guarantee
Br   2
○   *C
Gp   Grimsby & Cleethorpes Chamber of Trade; Bridlington
        Chamber of Trade
●   Conf - Mtgs - ET - Res - Exhib - Expt - Inf - LG
<   Brit Chams Comm; Yorkshire & Humber Chams Comm
>   Brit Caribbean Cham Comm
M   1,440 f, UK / 100 f, o'seas
        (Sub: £99-£800 UK / £99 o'seas)
¶   Business Intelligence - 6; ftm.

Human Genetics Alert   (HGA)
■   c/o 22B St Kilda's Rd, LONDON, N16 5BZ.   (hsp)
        020 7502 7516   fax 020 7502 7516
        email david.king@hgalert.org   http://www.hgalert.org
        Sec: David King
▲   Company Limited by Guarantee
○   *K; a watch-dog group for human genetics
●   Inf
M   30 i
¶   Human Genetics NL - 6.

Human Rights Society
        closed December 2008

Humane Slaughter Association   (HSA)   1911
NR   The Old School, Brewhouse Hill, WHEATHAMPSTEAD, Herts,
        AL4 8AN.   (hq)
        01582 831919   fax 01582 831414
        email info@hsa.org.uk   http://www.hsa.org.uk
        Sec: Donald Davidson
▲   Registered Charity
○   *V; promotion of humane methods of slaughter; introduction of
        reforms in cattle markets; welfare of animals in transit
●   ET - Res - Exhib - Inf - Lib - LG
M   605 i, 30 f, UK / 20 i, o'seas
¶   AR.   NL; both ftm.
        Numerous educational booklets, technical notes, videos.

Humanist Association of Ireland   1993
IRL Rose Cottage, Coach Road, Balrothery, BALBRIGGAN,
        Co Dublin, Republic of Ireland.
        353 (1) 841 3116
        http://www.irish-humanists.org
        Pres: Justin Keating
○   *K
×   2004 Association of Irish Humanists

Humanist Society of Scotland   (HSS)   1989
        Sec: Peter Macdonald
▲   Registered Charity (Scotland)
○   *G; 'to promote in Scotland the principles & practice of
        humanism defined as the moral, intellectual & social
        development of individuals & the community free from
        theistic, religious & dogmatic beliefs & dogmas'
Gp   Register of officiants for humanistic, non-religious funerals,
        weddings & namings
●   Conf - Mtgs - ET - Res - Exhib - Comp - SG - Inf - LG - Legal
        weddings, funerals & namings
<   Intl Humanist & Ethical U (IHEU)
M   3,000 i
        (Sub: £20)
¶   Humanité - 4; ftm, £2.50 nm.

Humanities Association   (Hums)   1984
NR   Humanities Wirral Education Centre, Acre Lane,
        BROMBOROUGH, Wirral, CH62 7BZ.   (hsp)
        0151-346 6503
        http://www.hums.org.uk
        Sec: Deirdre Smith
○   *P; development of humanities learning
●   Conf - Mtgs - Exhib - LG
<   Devt Educ Assn
M   130 i, UK / 5 i, o'seas
¶   Humanities Too;   Humanities Now; both available on website.

Hundred Group of Finance Directors
NR   c/o Julian Heslop, GlaxoSmithKline plc, 980 Great West Rd,
        BRENTFORD, Middx, TW8 9GS.   (chmn/b)
        Chmn: Julian Heslop
○   *P; finance directors
M   i
        no further information supplied

Hunter Archaeological Society   1912
■   Royd Farm, Carr Rd, Deepcar, SHEFFIELD, S Yorks, S36 2NR.
        (hsp)
        0114-288 2640
        http://www.shef.ac.uk/archaeology/hunter/
        Hon Sec: Dr Ruth Morgan
▲   Registered Charity
○   *L; to study & preserve the archaeology & history of S Yorkshire
        & N Derbyshire
●   Mtgs - VE - Field work
M   200 i
¶   Transactions - biennial;   NL; both ftm.

Hunterian Society   1819

NR   c/o Betty Smallwood, Lettsom House, Chandos St, LONDON, W1G 9EB.   (hsb)
       http://www.hunteriansociety.org.uk
       Hon Sec: Neil Weir
▲   Registered Charity
○   *L; the cultivation & promotion of the science & practice of medicine
       The society was formed to commemorate the surgeon & anatomist John Hunter
●   Mtgs
M   490 i
¶   Transactions - 1.

Hunting Association of Ireland

IRL   Friarstown Lodge, KILMALLOCK, Co Limerick, Republic of Ireland.
         email hunting@hai.ie
○   *S

Huntingdonshire Chamber of Commerce last D18
         a local chamber of **Cambridgeshire Chambers of Commerce**

Huntingdonshire Local History Society   1959

■   2 Croftfield Rd, Godmanchester, HUNTINGDON, Cambs, PE29 2ED.   (memsec/p)
       01480 411202
       email huntslocalhistory@yahoo.com
       http://www.huntslhs.org.uk
       Mem Sec: Mrs Mary Hopper
▲   Registered Charity
Br   1
○   *L; to promote the advancement of public education through the study of local history in the former County of Huntingdonshire (now part of Cambridgeshire)
●   Mtgs - Res - Exhib - SG - VE
<   Cambridge Antiquarian Soc
M   c 200 i
¶   NL - 2;   AR.
       Records of Huntingdon - 1; (special Oliver Cromwell edition available).

Huntington's Disease Association   (HDA)   1971

■   Neurosupport Centre, Norton St, LIVERPOOL, L3 8LR.   (hq)
       0151-298 3298   fax 0151-298 9440
       email info@hda.org.uk   http://www.hda.org.uk
       Chief Exec: Cath Stanley
▲   Company Limited by Guarantee; Registered Charity
Br   34
○   *W; to provide help & support to sufferers of the disease; to promote research
●   Conf - Mtgs - ET - Res - Inf - Family counselling service - Support groups - Films - Speakers available
<   Intl Huntington's Disease Assn
M   8,000 i
¶   NL - 2;   AR;   Factsheets; all free.
       Case Notes for Professionals; £8.50.
       Physicians Guide to the Management of Huntington's Disease; £5.75.
       Publications list available.

Hurdy-Gurdy Society   (HGS)   1982

■   47 Tudor Gardens, STONY STRATFORD, Bucks, MK11 1HX.   (hsp)
       01908 565339
       email michaelpmuskett@beeb.net
       Hon Sec: Michael Muskett
▲   Un-incorporated Society
Br   80
○   *D, *G; to further the knowledge of the hurdy-gurdy, its history, construction, playing techniques & repertoire
●   ET - Res - Inf - Regional playing days
M   80 i, 1 f, UK / 6 i, 2 f, o'seas
¶   Jnl - 4.   LM - 1.

Hurlingham Polo Association   (HPA)   1874

NR   Manor Farm, Little Coxwell, FARINGDON, Oxon, SN7 7LW.   (hq)
       01367 242828   fax 01367 242829
       email enquiries@hpa-polo.co.uk
       http://www.hpa-polo.co.uk
       Chief Exec: David Woodd
Br   affiliated clubs in British Isles & Commonwealth
○   *S; to act as the governing body for polo in the UK
●   Inf
<   Fedn of Intl Polo
M   2,000 i, 50 org, UK / 28 org, o'seas
¶   HPA Ybk (Blue Book) - 1; ftm, £10 nm.
       HPA Arena Ybk - 1; ftm, £10 nm.

Hydrographic Society UK   2004

■   PO Box 103, PLYMOUTH, Devon, PL4 7YP.   (hq)
       01752 223512   fax 01752 223512
       email helen@ths.org.uk   http://www.ths.org.uk
       Mgr & Co Sec: Helen Atkinson
▲   Company Limited by Guarantee; Registered Charity
Br   5; Ireland, Middle East, International
○   *L; to promote the development & understanding of hydrography & hydrographic learning; to facilitate the exchange of ideas & practices
●   Conf - Mtgs - Exhib - Inf - Publications
<   Intl Fedn of Hydrographic Socs; UK GeoForum
M   c 475 i, c 60 f, UK / c 110 i, c 30 f, o'seas
¶   Soundings - 4; free. - 4; ftm, £70 yr nm.
       Conference/Seminar Proceedings - irreg; £5.
       Proceedings of seminars & symposia; & Special Publications; £3.50. £50.
       Publications list available; free.
       Note: in 2004 the Hydrographic Society was incorporated as the Hydrographic Society UK.
       in 2005 the Hydrographic Society restructured & became the International Federation of Hydrographical Societies (& as such is outside the scope of this directory).
×   2004 Hydrographic Society

Hymn Society of Great Britain & Ireland   1936

■   99 Barton Rd, Scotforth, LANCASTER, LA1 4EN.   (hsp)
       01524 66740   fax 01524 66740
       email robcanham@haystacks.fsnet.co.uk
       http://www.hymnsocietygbi.org.uk
       Hon Sec: Rev Robert A Canham
▲   Registered Charity
○   *A, *L; to promote the use of hymns in Christian worship; research into hymnody
Gp   Art & literature; Educational; General interest & hobbies; Learned, scientific & technical societies; Research organisations; Religious organisations
●   Conf - Res - SG - Inf
<   Hymn Soc in the USA & Canada
M   369 i, 54 libraries, UK / 72 i, o'seas
¶   Bulletin - 4; ftm, £2.50 nm.   NL - 4; free.
       Festival of Hymns (booklet) - 1; ftm, £2.50 nm.
       Occasional Papers - irreg; ftm, £2.50 nm.   AR - 1; free.

© CBD Research Ltd · Beckenham · BR3 5JS · Tel 020 8650 7745 · Fax 020 8650 0768 · E-mail cbd@cbdresearch.com · www.cbdresearch.com

Hyperactive Children's Support Group   (HACSG)   1977

■ 71 Whyke Lane, CHICHESTER, W Sussex, PO19 7PD.   (hsp/b)
  01243 539966
  email hyperactive@hacsg.org.uk
  http://www.hacsg.org.uk
  Dir & Founder: Mrs Sally Bunday
▲ Registered Charity
Br London
○ *K; to support,advise & provide information for parents, carers
  & professionals interested in ADHD/hyperactivity & autistic
  spectrum disorders; to promote research & disseminate
  information on the rule of diet & nutrition
● Conf - ET - Inf
< Foresight; Autism Unravelled; FAB-Food & Behaviour Res;
  Sustain; Food Cmsn; Brain Bio-Centre
M 450 i, 50 f, 10 org, UK / 12 i, o'seas
¶ Jnl - 3; £15 m, £2 each nm.
  ADHD / Hyperactive Children: A Guide for Parents; ftm, £6 nm.
  Introductory pack; free.

Hypermobility Syndrome Association   (HMSA)   1992

■ PO Box 1122, Nailsea, BRISTOL, Somerset, BS48 2YZ.   (hsp)
  0845 345 4465
  email info@hypermobility.org
  http://www.hypermobility.org
  Sec: Cathy Elliott
▲ Registered Charity
○ *W; to provide information & support for those affected by the
  inheritable syndrome; to promote knowledge &
  understanding within the medical profession & general public
< Brit Coalition Heritable Disorders (Connective Tissue)
M 400 i, UK / 60 i, o'seas

Hysterectomy Association   1998

■ The Gables, Acreman Close, Cerne Abbas, DORCHESTER,
  Dorset, DT2 7JU.   (hq)
  0871 781 1141
  email info@hysterectomy-association.org.uk
  http://www.hysterectomy-association.org.uk
  Dir: Linda Parkinson-Hardman
▲ Un-incorporated Society
○ *M, *W; to provide impartial, clear & timely information &
  support to women who have, or who are thinking of having,
  a hysterectomy
● ET - Res - Inf
< Nat Coun for Voluntary Orgs; Brit Assn for Counselling &
  Therapy
M 1,000 i, UK / 500 i, o'seas
¶ The Pocket Guide to Hysterectomy; £7.
  101 Handy Hints for a Happy Hysterectomy; £7.

IA: the Ileostomy & Internal Pouch Support Group (IA) 1956
- ■ 1-5 Mill Rd, BALLYCLARE, Co Antrim, BT39 9DR. (nat/sec/p)
  0800 018 4724   fax 028 9332 4606
  email info@iasupport.org   http://www.iasupport.org
  Nat Sec: Mrs Anne Demick
- ▲ Registered Charity
- Br 55
- ○ *W; to help people return to full & active lives following surgery
  for the removal of the colon; to promote research into the
  causes of inflammatory bowel diseases (ulcerative colitis &
  Crohn's disease)
- Gp Internal pouch; Trained visitors; Welfare
- ● Conf - Mtgs - Res - Exhib - Inf - VE - LG
  Helpline: 0800 018 4724
- < Intl Ostomy Assn (IOA); Eur Ostomy Assn (EOA)
- M 10,000 i, 25 f
- ¶ ia Jnl - 4; ftm.   The Ostomy Book; £10.
  The ia Journal, omnibus edition [Hbk]; £5.
  Leaflets on various aspects of ileostomy; free.

IBS Network
  registered name of the **Gut Trust**

ICC United Kingdom
  alternative name of the **International Chamber of Commerce -
  UK National Committee**

Ice Cream Alliance Ltd (ICA) 1945
- NR 3 Melbourne Court, Pride Park, DERBY, DE24 8LZ.   (hq)
  01332 203333   fax 01332 203420
  email info@ice-cream.org   http://www.ice-cream.org
  Chief Exec: Mark Gossage
- ▲ Company Limited by Guarantee
- Br 10
- ○ *T; to protect, inform & represent the UK ice cream industry
- ● Conf - Mtgs - Res - Exhib - Comp - Inf - Lib - PL - VE - LG
- M 800 i, f, 1 org, UK / 100 i, f & org, o'seas
- ¶ Ice Cream - 11; £110 m.

Ice Hockey Players Association
  has folded

Ice Hockey UK (IHUK) 1991
- NR 19 Heather Avenue, Rise Park, ROMFORD, Essex, RM1 4SL.
  (hq)
  07917 194 264   fax 01708 725241
  http://www.icehockeyuk.co.uk
  Contact: Andy French
- ▲ Company Limited by Guarantee
- ○ *S; national governing body for the sport of ice hockey
- Gp Training; Officials; Juniors; National team; Under 18; Under
  20; Women; Senior men
- ● ET - Exam - Comp - Inf - PL - LG
- < Intl Ice Hockey Fedn; Brit Olympic Assn; UK Sport; Cent Coun
  for Physical Recreation (CCPR); English / Scottish Ice Hockey
  Assn(s)
- M 10,000 i, 65 clubs, 3 regions
- ¶ Weekly Media Services; m only.
  Ice Hockey Annual - 1.
- × 1999 (1 July) British Ice Hockey Association

Icelandic Horse Society of Great Britain Ltd (IHSGB) 1986
- ■ 50 Locksley Close, NORTH SHIELDS, Tyne & Wear,
  NE29 8EN.   (sp)
  0191-289 2364
  http://www.ihsgb.co.uk
  Chmn: Ian Pugh,   Sec: Elaine Rannie
- ▲ Registered Charity
- ○ *B; to encourage, promote & improve the breeding & use of the
  Icelandic horse
- Gp Breeding; Sports; Youth
- ● Conf - Mtgs - ET - Exhib - Comp - EXpt - Inf - Lib - VE
- < Intl Fedn of Icelandic Horse Assns (FEIF)
- M 300 i
- ¶ Sleipnir (Jnl) - 6; £32 yr m.

Icelandic Sheep Breeders of Britain
  alternative name of the **British Icelandic Sheep Breeders Group**

ICHCA International Ltd (ICHCA) 2003
- NR 85 Western Rd (suite 2), ROMFORD, Essex, RM1 3LS.   (hq)
  01708 735295
  http://www.ichcainternational.co.uk
  Co Sec: Mrs Rosemary Neilson
- ▲ Company Limited by Guarantee
- ○ *T; to promote efficient & economic movement of goods from
  origin to destination by air, rail, road & sea

ICOM Energy Association (ICOM) 2004
- ■ 36 Holly Walk, LEAMINGTON SPA, Warks, CV32 4LY.   (hq)
  01926 463940   fax 01926 423284
  email petermccree@icomenergyassociation.org.uk
  http://www.icomenergyassociation.org.uk
  Chief Exec: Peter McCree
- ▲ Company Limited by Guarantee
- ○ *T; manufacturers & distributors of combustion equipment
  including boilers, burners, air heaters, radiant heaters,
  controls
- Gp Air heaters; Boilers (commercial); Boilers (industrial process);
  Burners; Controls; Radiant heaters; Water heaters
- ● Mtgs - Stat - LG
- M 44 f
- × 2004 (May) British Combustion Equipment Manufacturers
  Association

ICRA (ICRA) 1999
- NR 12-13 Ship St, BRIGHTON, E Sussex, BN1 1AD.
  http://www.icra.org.uk
- < Family Online Safety Institute
- × 2008 Internet Content Rating Association

ICSA (Irish Cattle & Sheep Farmers' Association) (ICSA)
- IRL 9 Lyster House, Lyster Square, PORTLAOISE, Co Laois, Republic
  of Ireland.   (hq)
  353 (57) 866 2120   fax 353 (57) 866 2121
  email info@icsaireland.com
  http://www.icsaireland.com
  Gen Sec: Eddie Punch
- ○ *F

ICT Ireland (ICT) 2001
- IRL Confederation House, 84/86 Lower Baggot St, DUBLIN 2,
  Republic of Ireland.
  353 (1) 605 1527   fax 353 (1) 638 1527
  email info@ictireland.ie   http://www.ictireland.ie
  Dir: Kathryn Raleigh
- ○ *T; to represent companies in the information &
  communications technology sector
- < IBEC
- M 300 f

© CBD Research Ltd · Beckenham · BR3 5JS · Tel 020 8650 7745 · Fax 020 8650 0768 · E-mail cbd@cbdresearch.com · www.cbdresearch.com

IdeasUK 1987
NR Williams House, 11-15 Columbus Walk, Atlantic Wharf,
CARDIFF, CF10 4BZ. (hq)
0870 902 1658 fax 029 2049 8403
email info@ideasuk.com http://www.ideasuk.com
▲ Company Limited by Guarantee; Registered Charity
○ *K; to promote the benefits of employee suggestion schemes to
industry, commerce & the public sector
Gp Sectors: Financial services, Utilities, Government depts
● Conf - Mtgs - ET - Comp - Stat - Inf
M i, f, government depts
¶ News - 4; LM; Annual Survey; all ftm only.
Suggestion Schemes: the management tool of the 90's (1995).

IGA-UK
reported to us as having closed

Ileostomy & Internal Pouch Support Group
alternative name of the **IA**

Imaginative Book Illustration Society (IBIS) 1995
NR 50 Lauderdale Mansions, Lauderdale Rd, LONDON,
W9 1NE. (hsp)
http://www.bookillustration.org
Hon Sec: Robin Greer
○ *A; 'to study & research imaginatively illustrated books, mainly
in the English language'
● Conf - Mtgs - Exhib
M 200 i, 80 f, UK / 80 i, 20 f, o'seas
¶ IBIS Studies - 3.
IBIS Jnl - 2 yrly.

Immigration Law Practitioners' Association (ILPA) 1984
■ Lindsey House, 40-42 Charterhouse St, LONDON,
EC1M 6JN. (hq)
020 7251 8383 fax 020 7251 8384
email info@ilpa.org.uk http://www.ilpa.org.uk
Gen Sec: Alison Harvey
▲ Company Limited by Guarantee
○ *P
● Conf - Mtgs - ET - Res - LG
M 589 i, 398 f, 125 org
¶ [on website}

Imperial Society of Knights Bachelor (ISKB) 1908
■ 1 Throgmorton Avenue, LONDON, EC2N 2BY. (hq)
020 7374 8974 fax 020 7374 8968
email iskb99@supanet.com http://www.iskb.co.uk
Clerk to the Council: Richard L Jenkins
▲ Registered Charity
○ *W; 'participation by its members in the UK & Commonwealth
in charitable work compatible with upholding the status &
dignity of Knights Bachelor'
● Mtgs - Inf - Lib - Annual service of dedication
¶ Chivalry - 1/2; free.
The Story of the Knights Bachelor; ftm.

Imperial Society of Teachers of Dancing (ISTD) 1904
NR Imperial House, 22-26 Paul St, LONDON, EC2A 4QE. (hq)
020 7377 1577
http://www.istd.org
Chief Exec: Jon Singleton
▲ Registered Charity
Br 10; 37 countries o'seas
○ *D, *P; professional society for teachers of dancing & an
examination board
Gp Ballroom; Latin-American; Sequence; Classical Greek dance;
Imperial Ballet; Modern; Tap; National dance; Scottish
dance; Disco; Freestyle; Rock'n'Roll; Cecchetti ballet; Jazz;
Dance research; Natural movement
● Conf - Mtgs - ET - Exam - Res - Exhib - Comp - Inf - Lib
< Brit Coun of Ballroom Dancing; Coun for Dance Educ &
Training; CCPR (movement & dance divn)
M 7,000 i, UK / 2,900 i, o'seas
¶ Dance - 6; ftm only.

** Implanted Defibrillator Association of Scotland
Organisation lost: see Introduction paragraph 3

Imported Tobacco Products Advisory Council (ITPAC) 1974
NR Rondle Wood House, Milland, LIPHOOK, Hants, GU30 7LA.
(hsp)
07900 197888 fax 01730 821397
email wyndham@carverw.com
Sec-Gen: Wyndham H Carver
▲ Un-incorporated Society
○ *T; to represent the interests of importers of cigars, tobaccos &
cigarettes to government & other relevant bodies; to provide
inforamtion on tobacco & the industry
● Mtgs - Res - Inf - LG
M 11 f, UK / 1 f, o'seas

Imported Tyre Manufacturers' Association (ITMA) 1979
■ 5a Pindock Mews, LONDON, W9 2PY. (hsp)
020 7289 1043 fax 020 7286 9859
email prt@itma-europe.com
http://www.itma-europe.com
Dir: Peter Taylor
▲ Company Limited by Guarantee
○ *T; for tyre importers & manufacturers in the UK
● Mtgs - Stat - Inf - LG
< Tyre Ind Fedn (TIF)
M 20 f

INCA - Institute for Numerical Computation & Analysis (INCA) 1980
IRL 7-9 Dame Court, DUBLIN 2, Republic of Ireland.
353 (1) 402 8535 fax 353 (1) 402 8540
email jm@incaireland.org http://www.incaireland.org
Sec: Diarmuid Herlihy
○ *Q; to promote research & development in scientific &
engineering computation & analysis

Incentive Travel & Meetings Association
in 2006 merged with the Corporate Event Association to form
Eventia Ltd

Inclusion Ireland (National Association for People with an Intellectual Disability)
IRL Unit C2, The Steelworks, Foley St, DUBLIN 1, Republic of
Ireland.
353 (1) 855 9891 fax 353 (1) 855 9904
email info@inclusionireland.ie
http://www.inclusionireland.ie
Chief Exec: Deirdre Carroll
○ *W
× National Association for the Mentally Handicapped of Ireland

Incontact (INCONTACT) 1989

■ SATRA Innovation Park, Rockingham Rd, KETTERING, Northants, NN16 9JH.   (hq)
  01536 533255   fax 01536 533240
  email info@incontact.org   http://www.incontact.org
  Exec Dir: Lesley Woolnough
▲ Company Limited by Guarantee; Registered Charity
○ *G, *K,*W; campaigns for people living with bladder & bowel control problems; to raise awareness & improve the understanding of continence issues
● Res - Inf - LG -
< UK Continence Alliance (UKCA)
M 2,000 i
    (Sub: £20, £10 (concession))
¶ Incontact - 3; ftm.

Incorporated Association of Organists (IAO) 1913

■ 19 The Poplars, Gosforth, NEWCASTLE upon TYNE, NE3 4AE.   (hsp)
  0191-285 7303
  http://www.iao.org.uk
  Gen Sec & Chief Exec: Dr Peter Chatfield
▲ Company Limited by Guarantee; Registered Charity
Br 80; 10 (inc Australia, N Zealand, S Africa)
○ *D, *E; to promote the education & enjoyment of all who love the (pipe) organ & its music, players & listeners alike; to encourage training & education to improve standards at all levels
● Conf - Mtgs - ET
M 6,000 i, UK / 1,000 i, o'seas
    (Sub: £22 UK / £24.10 o'seas)
¶ Organists' Review - 4; ftm.

Incorporated Association of Preparatory Schools (IAPS) 1892

■ 11 Waterloo Place, LEAMINGTON SPA, Warks, CV32 5LA.   (hq)
  01926 887833   fax 01926 888014
  email iaps@iaps.org.uk   http://www.iaps.org.uk
  Chief Exec: David Hanson
▲ Company Limited by Guarantee
○ *E, *P; 'independent education of boys & girls (up to 13) for entrance to independent secondary schools'
● Conf - Mtgs - ET
< Independent Schools Coun
M 540 schools, UK / 30 schools, o'seas
¶ Independent Schools Ybk.   Prep School Magazine.

Incorporated Guild of Hairdressers, Wigmakers & Perfumers 1882

■ Archway House, Langdale Rd, BARNSLEY, S Yorks, S71 1AQ.   (hq)
  01226 786555   fax 01226 786555
  email info@hairguild.co.uk   http://www.hairguild.co.uk
  Master: Bill Shaw
▲ Company Limited by Guarantee
○ *P; to promote & advise the hairdressing industry
● Conf - Mtgs - Exam - Comp - Inf - LG
M 580 i
¶ NL - 4;   AR - 1; ftm only.

Incorporated National Association of British & Irish Millers Ltd (NABIM) 1878

NR 21 Arlington St, LONDON, SW1A 1RN.   (hq)
  020 7493 2521
  http://www.nabim.org.uk
  Sec: N F Bennett
▲ Company Limited by Guarantee
○ *T; for UK flour millers
● Conf - Mtgs - ET - Exam - Stat - Inf - LG
M 32 f
¶ Facts & Figures - 1; ftm.

Incorporated Phonographic Society (IPS) 1872

■ c/o The Bishopsgate Institute, 230 Bishopsgate, London, EC2M 4QH.   (mtgs address)
  020 8907 8249   fax 020 8907 5820
  email marysorene@ntlworld.com
  http://www.the-ips.org.uk
  Gen Admin: Mary Sorene
▲ Company Limited by Guarantee
○ *P; to maximise members' skill in all systems of shorthand & typewriting schools
Gp Reporters; Secretaries; Teachers of secretarial skills; Shorthand users
● Mtgs - Exam - SG - Inf
M 250 i, UK / 50 i, o'seas
¶ IPS Jnl - 4; ftm, £5 yr nm.

Incorporated Society of British Advertisers Ltd (ISBA) 1900

■ Langham House, 1B Portland Place, LONDON, W1B 1PN.   (hq)
  020 7291 9020
  email answers@isba.org.uk   http://www.isba.org.uk
  Dir Gen: Mike Hughes
▲ Company Limited by Guarantee
○ *T; to represent the collective interests of British advertisers to government, regulators & the media; to provide expert advice & guidance on advertising effectively & efficiently
● Conf - Mtgs - Inf - LG
< Wld Fedn of Advertisers; Advertising Assn
M 400 f
¶ AR - 1; free.

Incorporated Society of Musicians (ISM) 1882

■ 10 Stratford Place, LONDON, W1C 1AA.   (hq)
  020 7629 4413   fax 020 7408 1538
  email membership@ism.org   http://www.ism.org
  Chief Exec: Deborah Annetts
▲ Company Limited by Guarantee
○ *P; to promote the art of music; to maintain the honour & interests of the music profession
Gp Professional private music teachers; Performers & composers; Musicians in education
● Conf - Mtgs - ET - LG
M 4,800 i, 120 f, UK
¶ Music Jnl - 12; ftm, £32 nm.
  Register of Professional Private Music Teachers - 1; ftm, £20 nm.
  Ybk (incl LM) - 1; ftm, £40 nm.   AR; free.
  Publications list available.

Incorporated Society of Organ Builders (ISOB) 1947

NR Smithy Steads, Cragg Vale, HEBDEN BRIDGE, W Yorks, HX7 5SQ.   (hq)
  fax 0870 139 3645
  email admin1@isob.co.uk   http://www.isob.co.uk
○ *P, *T
● Conf - Mtgs - Inf - VE
M 190 i, UK / 9 i, o'seas
¶ Jnl - irreg.   LM - 1; free.   AR; ftm only.

Incorporated Society for Psychical Research
  now **Society for Psychical Research**

Incorporated Society of Registered Naturopaths (ISRN) 1934

NR 70 Kingston Avenue, Liberton, EDINBURGH, EH16 5SW.   (hsp)
  0131-644 3435
  http://www.naturecuresociety.org
  Hon Sec: Mrs May Thomson
▲ Company Limited by Guarantee
○ *P; alternative therapy offering naturopathic, dietary & manipulative therapy & advice
● Conf - ET - Exam
< Brit Naturopathic Assn
M 40 i, UK / 5 i, o'seas
¶ Publications list available.

© CBD Research Ltd · Beckenham · BR3 5JS · Tel 020 8650 7745 · Fax 020 8650 0768 · E-mail cbd@cbdresearch.com · www.cbdresearch.com

Incorporation of Plastic Window Fabricators & Installers (IPWFI) 1991
NR The Media Centre, 7 Northumberland St, HUDDERSFIELD,
      W Yorks, HD1 1RL.   (hq)
      0844 800 4125   fax 0844 800 4185
      email ipwfi@aol.co.uk   http://www.ipwfi.co.uk
▲ Company Limited by Guarantee
○ *T; for the window industry
Gp Insurance to the consumer of window companies
● Conf - Exhib
M 2,000 f

Independent Age
      the operating name of the **Royal United Kingdom Beneficent
      Association**

Independent Association of Telecommunications Users Ltd
      alternative name of the Telecommunication Users' Association which
      in October 2007 merged with the **Communications Management
      Association**

Independent Authors Special Interest Group
      a group of the **Institute of Scientific & Technical
      Communicators**

Independent Banking Advisory Service (IBAS) 1993
■ Somersham, HUNTINGDON, Cambs, PE28 3WD.   (hq)
      01487 843444   fax 01487 740607
      email helpdesk@ibas.co.uk   http://www.ibas.co.uk
      Exec Officer: Sara Cummings
▲ Un-incorporated Society
○ *K; independent advice & case investigation on all matters
      relating to banking, mortgage shortfall, & banking
      procedures & charging structures
● Res - Stat - Inf - LG
M [confidential]

Independent Battery Distributors Association (IBDA) 1991
■ 3 Blakeley Dene, Raby Mere, WIRRAL, Cheshire, CH63 0QE.
      (hsp)
      0151-334 2040   fax 0151-334 2040
      email jgferris@tesco.net   http://www.ibda.co.uk
      Hon Sec: J Godfrey Ferris
▲ Un-incorporated Society
○ *T; for battery manufactures & independent distributors of
      automotive & industrial batteries in the UK
● Conf - Mtgs - ET - Inf - LG
< Automotive Aftermarket Liaison Gp
M 2 i, 26 f
      (Sub: £400 f)
¶ IBDA NL - 4; ftm, £5 nm.   LM; ftm, £20 nm.
      Battery User Guides; ftm, £5 nm.   AR; ftm.
      Information booklets; ftm, £5 nm.

Independent Broadcasters of Ireland (IBI)
IRL Hume House, Pembroke Rd, Ballsbridge, DUBLIN 4, Republic of
      Ireland.
      353 (1) 500 6616
      email lisa@ibireland.ie   http://www.ibireland.ie
      Chmn: Willie O'Reilly
○ *T

** Independent Business League
      Organisation lost, see Introduction paragraph 6

Independent Children's Homes Association (ICHA) 2004
■ PO Box 99, HEBDEN BRIDGE, W Yorks, HX7 9AA.   (hq)
      0845 467 8152
      email admin@icha.co.uk   http://www.icha.org.uk
      Exec Officer: Roy Williamson,   Admin: Gail Williamson
○ *W; for all independent providers of social care for children;
      works to raise professional standards through shared work
      experience
● Conf - Mtgs - ET - Res - EXhib - SG - Stat - Inf - LG
M 70+ f
¶ NL - 4;   Hbk - 1; both free.
      Weekly Electronic Bulletin - 52; ftm only.
× 2004 National Association of Independent Resources for
      Children

Independent Consultants Consortium (ICON) 1980
■ 101 Amersham Rd, BEACONSFIELD, Bucks, HP9 2EH.   (hsp)
      01494 673581
      email icon@chiltime.co.uk   http://www.icon.uk.net
      Hon Sec: John Holroyd
▲ Un-incorporated Society
Br 2
○ *P, *T; a national umbrella for independent management
      consultants & consultancies
Gp 3 regional groups
● Conf - ET - Inf
M 33 f
¶ ICON NL - 2; free.

Independent Family Brewers of Britain (IFBB) 1993
NR Spring Cottage Offices, 28 Spring Lane, GREAT HORWOOD,
      Bucks, MK17 0QW.   (asa)
      01296 714745
      http://www.familybrewers.co.uk
▲ Company Limited by Guarantee
○ *N, *T; to represent nationally & internationally the common
      interests of Britain's independent family-controlled brewers;
      to protect traditional brewery tenancies (the Tied House
      system) from potential EC legislation
< all members are also members of the British Beer & Pub Assn
M f

Independent Federation of Nursing in Scotland (IFON) 1995
NR Huntershill Village, 102 Crowhill Rd, Bishopbriggs, GLASGOW,
      G64 1RP.   (hq)
      0141-772 9222   fax 0141-762 3776
      email ifoninscotland@aol.com
      http://www.ifonscotland.org
      Gen Sec: Mrs Irenee F O'Neill
Br 6
○ *U; 'is a nursing union with a solely Scottish identity, run by
      health care professionals for health care professionals'
Gp Health care professionals: Un-qualified, Qualified
● Conf - ET - Exhib - Empl
M i
¶ Nursing Scotland - 6; ftm only.

**Independent Fire Engineering & Distributors Association
(IFEDA)**
NR Unit 203 Solent Business Centre, Millbrook Rd West, Millbrook,
      SOUTHAMPTON, Hants, SO15 0HW.
      023 8051 3326
      http://www.ifeda.org
○ *T

Independent Footwear Retailers Association   (IFRA)   1950
■   Runnymede Malthouse, off Hummer Rd, EGHAM, Surrey,
      TW20 9BD.
      0870 330 8620   fax 0870 330 8621
      email ifra@shoeshop.org.uk
      http://www.shoeshop.org.uk
      Chief Exec: David Pryke
○   *T
●   Conf - Mtgs - ET - Exhib - SG - Stat - Lib - VE - Empl
<   Footwear Distbrs' Fedn; Soc Shoe Fitters; Nat Shoe Retailers'
      Assn (USA)
M   250 f
¶   NL - 4; ftm only.

Independent Games Developers Trade Association
      alternative name of **Tiga**

Independent Garage Association
      a group of the **Retail Motor Industry Federation**

Independent Group of Analytical Psychologists   (IGAP)
NR   PO Box 22343, LONDON, W13 8GP.   (hsp)
      020 8933 0353   fax 020 8933 0645
      email office@igap.co.uk   http://www.igap.co.uk
      Sec: Clare Craig
▲   Company Limited by Guarantee; Registered Charity
○   *P; Jungian analysis
●   ET - SG
M   49 i, UK / 9 i, o'seas

Independent Healthcare Association
      since 2004 the **English Community Care Association**

Independent Midwives' Association   (IMA)   1985
■   PO Box 539, ABINGDON, Oxon, OX14 9DF.   (hsp)
      0845 460 0185
      http://www.independentmidwives.org.uk
      Sec: Andrya Prescott
○   *P; support group for midwives working independently, giving
      women informed choices in childbirth, home, hospital or
      water births
●   Mtgs - Exhib - SG - Stat - Inf
<   Intl Confedn of Midwives; Assn of Radical Midwives
M   88 i
¶   Register of Independent Midwives - 2 yrly; ftm, send sae nm.

Independent Motor Trade Factors Association Ltd   (IFA)   1977
NR   9 Church St, ST AUSTELL, Cornwall, PL25 4AT.   (hq)
      01726 70440
      http://www.imtfa.co.uk
      Sec: Gretal Taylor
○   *T
M   f

Independent Pilots Association   (IPA)   1992
■   The Priory, HAYWARDS HEATH, W Sussex, RH16 3LB.   (hq)
      01444 441149   fax 01444 441192
      email office@ipapilot.com   http://www.ipapilot.com
      Sec: Capt Noel Baker
▲   Company Limited by Guarantee
Br   1
○   *P; for aviation pilots & flight engineers
●   Conf - Mtgs - ET - Res - Inf - LG
>   Indep Pilots Fedn
M   1,230 i, UK / 330 i, o'seas
¶   Skypointer - 4; ftm only.

Independent Print Industries Association   (IPIA)   1990
■   Unit 9 Business Innovation Centre, Staffordshire
      Technology Park, Beaconside, STAFFORD, ST18 0AR.   (hq)
      0844 902 0214   fax 0844 902 0215
      email info@ipia.org.uk   http://www.ipia.org.uk
      Chief Exec: Andrew Pearce
▲   Un-incorporated Society
○   *T; for print managers, brokers, distributors, & outsourcers of
      print as well as trade manufacturers of print & print related
      products & services
Gp   Trade printers; Print managers; Brokers; Distributors &
      outsourcers; Software suppliers to the printing industry;
      Suppliers of office & computer consumables; Papermakers &
      merchants
●   Conf - Mtgs - ET - Exhib - Inf
<   Document Mgt Inds Assn (DMIA)(USA)
M   165 f, UK / 4 f, o'seas
¶   Innovation in Print - 6; free.

Independent Publishers Advisory Council
      a group of the **Periodical Publishers Association**

Independent Publishers Guild   (IPG)   1962
■   PO Box 12, Llain, WHITLAND, Dyfed, SA34 0WU.   (mail)
      01437 563335   fax 01437 562071
      email info@ipg.uk.com   http://www.ipg.uk.com
      Exec Dir: Bridget Shine
▲   Company Limited by Guarantee
○   *T; 'providing a forum for the exchange of ideas & information'
      for directors of independent publishing companies
●   Conf - Mtgs - Exhib - Inf - VE - Book industry communication
<   National Book Committee
M   419 f
¶   email bulletin- 52; ftm only.

Independent Retailers Confederation   (IRC)   1991
NR   Quintus Public Affairs, 36 Broadway, SW1H 0BH.   (hsb)
      020 7340 6260   fax 020 7340 6261
      http://www.independent-retailers.co.uk
      Sec: Richard Maugham
○   *N, *T; a group of independent trade associations which meet
      to exchange information & views on matters affecting small
      independent retailers
M   12 trade associations
×   2003 Independent Food Retailers Confederation

Independent Safety Consultants Association   (ISCA)   1985
NR   The Old Bakehouse, Fullbridge, MALDON, Essex, CM9 4LE.
      (hsb)
      01621 874938   fax 01621 851756
      email isca@isca.org.uk   http://www.isca.org.uk
      Sec: Mrs Caroline Head,   Chmn: Howard Hall
▲   Un-incorporated Society
○   *P, *T; for safety consultancies giving safety advice & guidance;
      some consultancies give specialist help for asbestos,
      construction etc
●   Mtgs
M   5 i, 11 f

Independent Schools Association   (ISA)   1895
■   Boys' British School, East St, SAFFRON WALDEN, Essex,
      CB10 1LS.   (hq)
      01799 523619
      http://www.isaschools.org.uk
      Gen Sec: Mrs J Le Poidevin
▲   Company Limited by Guarantee
○   *E; promotion of interests of independent schools
●   Conf - Mtgs - Comp - SG - Inf
<   Indep Schools Jt Coun; ISIS
M   300 i (heads of independent schools), UK / 3 i, o'seas
¶   Directory - 1.

© CBD Research Ltd · Beckenham · BR3 5JS · Tel 020 8650 7745 · Fax 020 8650 0768 · E-mail cbd@cbdresearch.com · www.cbdresearch.com

Independent Schools' Bursars Association   (ISBA)   1932
NR   Unit 11-12 Manor Farm, Cliddesden, BASINGSTOKE, Hants,
    RG25 2JB.   (hq)
    01256 330369   fax 01256 330376
    email office@theisba.org   http://www.theisba.org.uk
    Gen Sec: J R B Cook
▲   Registered Charity
○   *P; the advancement of education by the promotion of efficient
    & effective administration & ancillary services at independent
    schools
●   Conf - Mtgs - ET - SG - Inf
<   Indep Schools Coun (ISC)
M   852 schools, UK / 30 schools, o'seas
¶   The Bursar's Review - 3;   Bulletin (NL) - 10; both ftm only.

Independent Schools Council   (ISC)   1974
NR   St Vincent House, 30 Orange St, LONDON, WC2H 7HH.   (hq)
    020 7766 7070   fax 020 7766 7071
    email office@isc.co.uk   http://www.isc.co.uk
    Chief Exec: David Lyscom
▲   Company Limited by Guarantee
○   *E, *N; the policy & management of independent education
Gp   Independent Schools Council information & advice
    service (ISCias)
●   ET
M   1,300 schools within 7 orgs:
    Association of Governing Bodies of Independent
      Schools
    Girls' Schools Association
    Headmasters' & Headmistresses' Conference
    Incorporated Association of Preparatory Schools
    Independent Schools Association
    Independent Schools Bursars' Association
    Society of Headmasters & Headmistresses of Independent
      Schools

Independent Schools Council Information Service
    is the **Independent Schools Council** information & advice service.

Independent Sports Retailers Association
    since 2006 **Sporting Goods Industry Association**

Independent Surveyors Association   (ISA)
NR   Broadbury, OKEHAMPTON, Devon, EX20 4NH.
    01837 871700   fax 01837 871700
    email mail@surveyorsweb.co.uk
    http://www.surveyorsweb.co.uk

Independent Theatre Council (Ltd)   (ITC)   1974
■   12 The Leathermarket, Weston St, LONDON, SE1 3ER.   (hq)
    020 7403 1727   fax 020 7403 1745
    email admin@itc-arts.org   http://www.itc-arts.org
    Chief Exec: Charlotte Jones
▲   Company Limited by Guarantee
○   *T; management association for the performing arts
●   Conf - ET - Advice service & networking for members
M   644 i, f & org
¶   NL - 6; ftm only.   AR - 1.
    The ITC Practical Guide for Writers & Companies; £5.
    Working in Schools; £5.
    Equal Opportunities - policy into practice; £5 each (£12 the set):
      Race;   Disability;   Sexuality;   Gender.

**Independent Training Standards Scheme & Register
(ITSSAR)   1990**
NR   Armstrong House, 28 Broad St, WOKINGHAM, Berks,
    RG40 1AB.   (hq)
    0118-989 3229
    http://www.ittsar.org.uk
    Chmn: Lynda Dobson
▲   Company Limited by Guarantee
○   *E; fork lift truck accreditation scheme
●   ET
M   3,000 i, 200 f

Independent Turner Society   1988
■   Turner House, 153 Cromwell Road, LONDON, SW5 0TQ.
    020 7373 5560   fax 020 7373 5560
    email selbywhittingham@hotmail.com
    http://www.jmwturner.org
    Hon Sec: Dr Selby Whittingham
▲   Un-incorporated Society
○   *K; campaigning for a proper Turner gallery for J M W Turner's
    bequest
●   Campaigning
M   [not stated]
¶   Jnl - irreg;   NL - 2/3; both ftm only.

Independent Tyre Distributors Network   (ITDN)   1985
NR   Unit 9 Cranmere Rd, Exeter Rd Industrial Estate,
    OKEHAMPTON, Devon, EX20 1UE.
    01837 54243   fax 01837 54043
    http://www.itdn.org.uk
    Dir: Mrs J Dawe
○   *T

Independent Valuers Association
NR   PO Box 12, PAIGNTON, Devon, TQ3 1ZA.   (hsp)
    01803 872265
    Founder: Bill Simpson
○   *P; for valuers of antiques & works of art & security advisers

Independent Warranty Association   (IWA)   1990
NR   20 Billing Rd, NORTHAMPTON, NN1 5AW.   (hq)
    01604 604511   fax 01604 604512
    email enquiries@iwa.biz   http://www.iwa.biz
○   *T; 'provision of insurance backed guarantees for home
    improvement products such as - double glazing,
    conservatories bathrooms, loft conversions, kitchens,
    driveways & block paving'
M   f

**Independent Waste Paper Processors Association   (IWPPA)
1975**
■   Heritage House, Vicar Lane, DAVENTRY, Northants,
    NN11 4GD.   (hq)
    01327 703223   fax 01327 300612
    email info@iwppa.co.uk   http://www.ippwa.co.uk
    Sec: D J Symmers
▲   Un-incorporated Society
○   *T; to represent a significant part of the independent sector of
    waste paper merchants; to promote & widen the use of
    recovered paper, both within the UK & other world markets
●   Mtgs - Expt - LG
<   Bureau of Intl Recycling (BIR); Eur Recovered Paper Assn (ERPA)
M   83 f, UK / 4 f, o'seas

Indian Military Historical Society   (IMHS)   1983
■   33 High St, Tilbrook, HUNTINGDON, Cambs, PE28 0JP.   (hsp)
    01480 860437
    email imhs@mcclenaghan.waitrose.com
    Hon Sec: A N McClenaghan
▲   Un-incorporated Society
○   *G; to act as a forum for the dissemination of knowledge of
    uniforms, medals, badges, buttons & other militaria, as well
    as the history of service in India both before & after
    independence (India, Pakistan & Bangladesh)
●   Res - Inf
M   190 i, 5 org, UK / 80 i, 2 org, o'seas
¶   Durbar - 4; ftm only.

Indoor Cricket England
▲   Company Limited by Guarantee
    trading name of the **England Indoor Cricket Association**

Industrial Agents Society   (IAS)   1975

NR   c/o Mark Webster, Cushman & Wakefield, 43-45 Portman
        Square, LONDON, W1A 3BG.   (chmn/b)
        http://www.shedshifters.co.uk
        Chmn: Mark Webster
▲   Un-incorporated Society
○   *P; commercial surveyors & agents whose principal business
        activity is wholly or mainly the buying, selling or development
        of business space, including industrial & warehouse property
●   Conf - Mtgs - VE
M   900 i
¶   NL - 2.   Members Directory - 1.

Industrial Cleaning Machine Manufacturers Association
   (ICMMA)

NR   PO Box 12492, SOLIHULL, W Midlands, B91 9AX.
        (mail/address)
        0121-703 0636
        http://www.icmma.org.uk
○   *T; for manufacturers of industrial & commercial cleaning
        equipment, including pressure washers, carpet & upholstery
        cleaners, vacuum cleaners (wet & dry), mechanical sweeping
        machines, scrubber driers for floor surfaces, & stem cleaning
        equipment for hygiene cleaning
M   f

Industrial Commercial Energy Association
    see **ICOM Energy Association**

Industrial Law Society

NR   18 Grays Mead, Sible Hedingham, HALSTEAD, Essex,
        CO9 3NY.
        01787 463838
        http://www.industriallawsociety.org.uk
○   *L, *P
●   [Hours 1000-1300]

Industrial Locomotive Society   (ILS)   1946

■   Topham, 14 Leigh Lane, Bramshall, UTTOXETER, Staffs,
        ST14 5DN.   (hsp)
        email enquiries@industrial-loco.org.uk
        http://www.industrial-loco.org.uk
        Hon Sec: Allen Civil
▲   Un-incorporated Society
○   *G; historical research into railways other than main line
        railways (incl military railways & associated industrial
        archaeology)
●   Mtgs - Res - Lib - PL
M   210 i, 10 org, UK / 30 i, 4 org, o'seas
¶   The Industrial Locomotive - 4; ftm, £3 nm.

Industrial Packaging Association   (IPA)   2004

■   PO Box 110, KNARESBOROUGH, N Yorks, HG5 8ZX.   (ceo/b)
        07770 633320   fax 01423 867098
        email info@theipa.co.uk   http://www.theipa.co.uk
        Chief Exec: Phil Pease
▲   Un-incorporated Society
○   *T; for the industrial industry - kegs, drums, intermediate bulk
        containers (IBCs)
Gp   Steel / Plastic / Fibre drum manufacturing; IBC Manufacturing;
        Used container; Re-conditioning & recycling
●   Mtgs - ET - Inf
<   Intl Plastics Packaging (ICPP); Eur Steel Drum Mfrs (SEFA); Eur
        Plastics Packaging Assn (EUPC)
M   28 f, UK / 2 f, o'seas
×   2004 (Association of Drum Manufacturers
            (Federation of Drum Reconditioners
            (Rigid Intermediate Bulk Container Association

Industrial Participation Forum
    a group of the **Defence Manufacturers Association**

Industrial & Power Association   (IPA)

NR   Brunel Building, James Watt Ave, Scottish Enterprise
        Technology Park, EAST KILBRIDE, G75 0QD.
        01355 272630   fax 01355 272633
        http://www.ipa-scotland.org.uk
○   aims to help society meet its needs for clean and affordable
        energy by bringing the experience, skills and technologies of
        Scotland to the world power market

Industrial Railway Society   (IRS)   1949

NR   4 Fernbrook Drive, HARROW, Middx, HA2 7EB.   (hsp)
        email news@irsociety.co.uk   http://www.irsociety.co.uk
        Hon Sec: Edward Knotwell
▲   Un-incorporated Society
○   *G; study & record all aspects of industrial railways & their uses
Gp   Rail mounted cranes; Non-locomotive worked railway lines &
        small mines; Ex-British Rail locomotives engaged in industrial
        use; Tunnelling contractors using rail transport; Ministry of
        Defence railways; Coal-mining railways
●   Mtgs - Res - Lib - PL - VE (many visits take place abroad)
M   950 i, UK / 50 i, o'seas
¶   Industrial Railway Record - 4.
        Bulletin - 6.   Books.

Industrial Rope Access Trade Association   (IRATA)   1989

■   Tournai Hall, Evelyn Woods Rd, ALDERSHOT, Hants,
        GU11 2LL.   (asa)
        01252 357839   fax 01252 357831
        email info@irata.org   http://www.irata.org
        Sec: John G Fairley
▲   Company Limited by Guarantee
○   *T
●   Conf - Mtgs - ET - Exam - Inf - LG
M   24 i, 44 f, UK / 3 i, 16 f, o'seas
¶   Directory;   Brochure; both free.
        Guidelines: on the use of rope access methods for industrial
            purposes; £10 m, £45 nm.
        International Guidelines: on the use of rope access methods for
            industrial purposes; £10 m, £45 nm.
        General Requirements: for certification of personnel engaged in
            industrial rope access methods; £10 m, £45 nm.

Industrial & Single Phase Product Group
    a product association of BEAMA Installation, which is part of **BEAMA**

Industrial Textiles Manufacturers Group
    a group of the **Performance Textiles Association**

Industrial Tyre Association   (ITA)   1977

■   33 Marshfield Way, BATH, BA1 6HD.   (sp)
        01225 420577
        Sec: Paul Hayward
▲   Un-incorporated Society
○   *T; for all industrial tyre applications, both solid and pneumatic
●   Mtgs - Stat - Inf

Industry Council for Packaging & the Environment   (Incpen)
   1974

■   Soane Point, 6-8 Market Place, READING, Berks, RG1 2EG.
        (hq)
        0118-925 5991
        http://www.incpen.org
▲   Company Limited by Guarantee
○   *T; to study the environmental & social impacts of packaging;
        members are international companies involved in all aspects
        of the distribution of packaged goods
Gp   Trade; Environment
●   Conf - Mtgs - ET - Res - Exhib - Stat - Inf - LG
<   Eur Org for Packaging & the Envt (EUROPEN)
M   25 f
¶   NL - 11; ftm only.
        Factsheets;   AR; both free.

© CBD Research Ltd · Beckenham · BR3 5JS · Tel 020 8650 7745 · Fax 020 8650 0768 · E-mail cbd@cbdresearch.com · www.cbdresearch.com

Industry Research & Development Group
IRL Confederation House, 84/86 Lower Baggot St, DUBLIN 2,
      Republic of Ireland.
      353 (1) 605 1608   fax 353 (1) 661 1095
      email irdg@iol.ie   http://www.irdg.ie
      Managing Dir: Dick Kavanagh
○   *T; Irish-owned & multinational companies from all
      manufacturing sectors
<   IBEC

Infant & Dietetic Foods Association Ltd (IDFA) 1986
■   6 Catherine St, LONDON, WC2B 5JJ. (hq)
      020 7420 7112   fax 020 7836 0580
      email idfa@fdf.org.uk   http://www.idfa.org.uk
      Dir Gen: Roger Clarke
▲   Company LImited by Guarantee
○   *T; manufacturers & suppliers of special foods for special
      requirments (infant formulae, weaning, medical, sports foods
      & drinks, & slimming foods)
●   Mtgs - Res - SG - Inf - LG
<   Intl Soc for Dietetic Foods (ISDI); Assn of Infant & Dietetic Foods
      in the EEC (IDACE); Food & Drink Fedn
M   14 f

Infant Nutrition Executive Committee
      a group of **Food & Drink Industry Ireland**

Infant Nutritional Technical Committee
      a group of **Food & Drink Industry Ireland**

Infection Control Nurses Association of GB
      since 1 October 2007 **Infection Prevention Society**

Infection Prevention Society (IPS) 1960
■   c/o Fitwise Management Ltd, Drumcross Hall, BATHGATE,
      W Lothian, EH48 4JT. (asa)
      01506 811077   fax 01506 811477
      email info@fitwise.co.uk   http://www.ips.uk.net
      Hon Sec: Philip Pugh
▲   Company Limited by Guarantee; Registered Charity
Br   12
○   *P; to promote the advancement of infection control &
      prevention for the benefit of the community as a whole, & in
      particular the provision of training courses, accreditiation
      schemes, etc
Gp Mental health interest; Audit & surveillance
      Community infection control practitioners network
●   Conf - Mtgs - ET - Res - Exhib - SG - Inf - LG
<   Intl Fedn of Infection Control (IFIC)
M   1,320 i, 32 f, UK / 153 i, o'seas
      (Sub: £70 i, £1,500 f)
¶   Community Audit Tool (booklet & CD); £25.
      [All the following are £5 m, £10 nm]:
      Hand Decontamination Guidelines;
      Guidelines for Preventing Intravascular Catheter related
      Infection.
      Infection Control Guidance for General Practice.
      Enteral Feeding.
      Asepsis: preventing healthcare associated infection.
      Prevention of Infection in the Home (home hygiene booklet).
✕   2007 (1 October) Infection Control Nurses Association of GB

Infertility Network UK
■   Charter House, 43 St Leonards Rd, BEXHILL-on-SEA, E Sussex,
      TN40 1JA. (hq)
      http://www.infertilitynetworkuk.com
▲   Company Limited by Guarantee; Registered Charity
○   *K, *W; to provide essential support services & information on
      developments in infertility research; to represent patients'
      views; to campaign to raise awareness of the impact of
      infertility & improve access to treatment
●   Conf - Mtgs - ET - Res - Stat - Inf - LG
      Support line: 0800 008 7464
M   [not stated]
¶   Fact sheets.
      A Journey through Infertility (video).

Inflatable Play Manufacturers Association (IPMA) 1990
NR Federation House, STONELEIGH PARK, Warks, CV8 2RF.
      024 7641 4999   fax 024 7641 4990
      http://www.ipma.uk.com
      Co Sec: Deborah Holt
▲   Company Limited by Guarantee
○   *T
●   Mtgs - ET - Stat - Expt - Inf - LG
M   15 f

Infrastructure Group
      a group of the **Defence Manufacturers Association**

Inland Shipping Group
      a group of the **Inland Waterways Association**

Inland Waterways Association (IWA) 1946
NR Island House, Moor Rd, CHESHAM, Bucks, HP5 1WA. (hq)
      01494 783453
      http://www.waterways.org.uk
      Exec Dir: Neil Edwards
▲   Company Limited by Guarantee; Registered Charity
Br   35
○   *K; to ensure the restoration, conservation, retention &
      development of the navigable waterways of the British Isles &
      their fullest commercial & recreational use
Gp Inland Shipping Group
●   Conf - Mtgs - ET - Res - Exhib - Comp - SG - Stat - Inf - VE - LG
      - Conservation & restoration work
<   Boating Alliance
M   18,000 i, 100 f, 200 org, UK / 300 i, f & org, o'seas
¶   Waterways - 3.   Inland Waterways Guide - 1.
      Wide variety of regional, local & specialist publications.

Inland Waterways Association of Ireland 1954
IRL Ballymakenny, DROGHEDA, Co Louth, Republic of Ireland.
      http://www.iwai.ie
○   *G

Inland Waterways Protection Society Ltd (IWPS) 1958
■   Top Lock House, 7 Lime Kiln Lane, Marple, STOCKPORT,
      Cheshire, SK6 6BX. (chmn/p)
      0161-427 7402: 07710 361093
      email ian@theedgars.co.uk   http://www.brocross.com/
      iwps/index.htm
      Chmn: Ian Edgar
▲   Company Limited by Guarantee; Registered Charity
○   *K; for the restoration, preservation & development of the
      inland waterways of Great Britain
●   Waterway restoration & development (specifically the Bugsworth
      canal basin at the head of the Peak Forest Canal)
M   300 i, 20 f, 10 org
¶   174 (NL) - 4; ftm, 50p nm.
      Note: 174 is the number of the last remaining Peak Forest
      Tramway wagon

Inn Sign Society (ISS) 1960
NR   9 Denmead Drive, Wednesfield, WOLVERHAMPTON,
     W Midlands, WV11 2QS.   (hsp)
     01902 721808
     http://www.innsignsociety.com
     Hon Sec: Alan Rose
▲   Un-incorporated Society
○   *G; the study of the inn sign (pub sign), its origin, history, the
     stories connected with individual signs
●   Inf
M   360 i, 5 f, UK / 7 i, o'seas
¶   At the Sign of [...] - 4; ftm only.

Insolvency Lawyers' Association   (ILA)   1989
■   Valiant House, 4-10 Heneage Lane, LONDON, EC3A 5DQ.
     (sb)
     020 7397 6405
     email ila@skadden.com   http://www.ilauk.org
     Sec: Peter Joyce
▲   Company Limited bu Guarantee
○   *P; a special interest group providing a forum for lawyers
     specialising in insolvency administration
●   Conf - Mtgs - ET - Inf - LG
M   291 i, 21 org, UK / 4 i, o'seas
¶   Insolvency Intelligence - 12;   Bulletins [email] - 26.

Insolvency Practitioners Association   (IPA)   1961
■   Valiant House, 4-10 Heneage Lane, LONDON, EC3A 5DQ.
     (hq)
     020 7623 5108   fax 020 7623 5127
     http://www.insolvency-practitioners.org.uk
     Chief Exec: D Kerr
○   *P; members act as trustees, liquidators, receivers,
     administrators etc
     no further information supplied

Institiúid Bitheolaíochta na h'Éireann
     Irish name of the **Institute of Biology of Ireland**

Institiúid Ceimice na h'Éireann
     Irish name of the **Institute of Chemistry of Ireland**

INSTITUTE ...
     Other than the bodies listed below, organisations entitled
     'Institute' that have no voluntary membership structure but
     carry out serious research will be found in our publication
     Centres, Bureaux & Research Institutes

** Institute of Account Executives & Book-keepers
     Organisation lost: see Introduction paragraph 3

Institute of Accounting Technicians in Ireland   (IATI)
IRL   Burlington House, Burlington Rd, DUBLIN 4, Republic of
     Ireland.
     353 (1) 637 7363   fax 353 (1) 637 7357
     email info@iati.ie   http://www.iati.ie
     Chief Exec: Gay Sheehan
○   *P

Institute of Acoustics   (IoA)   1974
■   77a St Peter's St, ST ALBANS, Herts, AL1 3BN.   (hq)
     01727 848195   fax 01727 850553
     email ioa@ioa.org.uk   http://www.ioa.org.uk
     Chief Exec: Kevin Macan-Lind
▲   Company Limited by Guarantee
Br   10
○   *L, *P; the art, science & technology of acoustics
Gp   Acoustics: Building, Physical, Musical, Underwater
     Noise: Electro, Environmental, Industrial, Speech
●   Conf - Mtgs - ET - Exam - Exhib - Lib
<   Intl Inst Noise Control - Engg (I-INCE); Intl Congress
     Acoustics (ICA); Eur Acoustics Assn (EAA)
M   3,100 i, 30 org, UK / 300 i, o'seas
¶   Acoustics Bulletin - 6; ftm, £20 each nm.
     Register of Members - 1; ftm, £10 nm.
     Buyers Guide - 1; ftm; £15 nm.

Institute of Actuaries   1848
■   Staple Inn Hall, High Holborn, LONDON, WC1V 7QJ.   (hq)
     020 7632 2100   fax 020 7632 2111
     email institute@actuaries.org.uk
     http://www.actuaries.org.uk
     Pres: Nigel B Masters
     Chief Exec: Caroline M Instance
▲   Incorporated by Royal Charter 1884
Br   2
○   *P; the controlling body (along with the Faculty of Actuaries in
     Edinburgh) for the actuarial profession
Gp   Continuous mortality investigation;
     Boards: Life (insurance), Pensions, General insurance, Finance
     investment & risk management, Education & continuing
     professional development
●   Conf - Mtgs - ET - Exam - Res - Lib - Technical guidance -
     Issuance of practising certificates
     The Education Executive, Careers & Library are at:
     4 Worcester St, Oxford, OX1 2AW.   01865 268200
<   Intl Actuarial Assn
>   Faculty of Actuaries in Scotland
M   10,270 i, UK / 5,067 i, o'seas
¶   British Actuarial Jnl - 3.
     Annals of Actuarial Science - 2.
     Professional Standards Directory - updated.

Institute of Administrative Management   (IAM)   1915
NR   6 Graphite Sq, Vauxhall Walk, LONDON, SE11 5EE.   (hq)
     020 7091 2600   fax 020 7091 2619
     email info@instam.org   http://www.instam.org
     Chief Exec: David Woodgate
▲   Registered Charity
○   *P; to promote & develop, for the public benefit, the science of
     administrative management in all branches
●   Conf - ET - Exam - Res - Exhib - Stat - Inf
M   4,500 i, UK / 4,500 i, o'seas
¶   Manager: the British Jnl of Administrative Management - 6; ftm,
     £45 yr nm.   AR - 1.
     Publications list available.

Institute of Advanced Motorists Ltd   (IAM)   1956
NR   510 Chiswick High Rd, LONDON, W4 5RG.   (hq)
     020 8996 9600   fax 020 8996 9601
     email enquiries@iam.org.uk   http://www.iam.org.uk
     Chief Exec: C T Bullock
▲   Company Limited bu Guarantee; Registered Charity
Br   208
○   *K; to make a major contribution to road safety through the
     skill, attitude & responsibility, shown by motorists &
     motorcyclists, in the test for membership
Gp   IAM fleet training (for company personnel)
●   Exam - IAM Fleet Training Ltd (for training of company
     personnel) - Advanced Driving (IAM Group Services Ltd)
M   112,000 i, UK / 1,000 i, o'seas
¶   Advanced Driving - 3; ftm.
     How to be an Advanced Motorist; £7.99.
     How to be an Advanced Motorcyclist; £7.99.

© CBD Research Ltd · Beckenham · BR3 5JS · Tel 020 8650 7745 · Fax 020 8650 0768 · E-mail cbd@cbdresearch.com · www.cbdresearch.com

Institute of Advertising Practitioners in Ireland   (IAPI)   1964
IRL   8 Upper Fitzwilliam St, DUBLIN 2, Republic of Ireland.
         353 (1) 676 5991   fax 353 (1) 661 4589
         email info@iapi.com   http://www.iapi.ie
         Chief Exec: Sean McCrave
○   *P

** Institute for African Alternatives
         Organisation lost: see Introduction paragraph 3

Institute of Agricultural Secretaries & Administrators   (IAgSA) 1967
■   National Agricultural Centre, Stoneleigh Park, KENILWORTH,
      Warks, CV8 2LG.   (hq)
      024 7669 6592   fax 024 7641 7937
      email iagsa@iagsa.co.uk   http://www.iagsa.co.uk
      Sec: Mrs Charlotte O'Kane
▲   Company Limited by Guarantee
Br   29
○   *P, *T; to promote & encourage professional excellence in rural
      business administration
Gp   Agriculture
●   Conf - Mtgs - ET - LG
M   900 i, 20 f
¶   Jnl - 1;   Bulletin - 12; both ftm only.
      Directory - 1.

Institute of Amateur Cinematographers   (IAC)   1932
■   Global House, 1 Ashley Avenue, EPSOM, Surrey, KT18 5AD.
      (hq)
      01372 822812
      email admin@theiac.org.uk   http://www.theiac.org.uk
      Chmn: Linda Gough
▲   Registered Charity
○   *G; 'non-commercial organisation to assist amateur movie
      makers'
Gp   Film Library
●   ET - Comp - Inf - Lib
M   2,000 i
      (Sub: £37.50)
¶   Film & Video Maker - 6; ftm only.
      Note: Generally known as IAC - The Film & Video Institute

Institute of Animal Technology   (IAT)   1965
NR   5 South Parade, Summertown, OXFORD, OX2 7JL.
      (asa/regd/office)
      email secretary@iat.org.uk   http://www.iat.org.uk
▲   Company Limited by Guarantee
Br   16
○   *P, *V; to advance & promote excellence in the care & welfare of
      animals in science
●   Conf - ET - Exam
<   Eur Fedn of Animal Technologists (EFAT); Amer Assn of
      Laboratory Animal Science (AALAS)
M   2,100 i, 60 f, UK / 50 i, o'seas
¶   Jnl of Animal Technology & Welfare - 3.
      Bulletin - 12.

Institute of Archaeologists of Ireland   (IAI)
IRL   63 Merrion Sq, DUBLIN 2, Republic of Ireland.
      353 (1) 662 9517
      email iaireland@eircom.net   http://www.iai.ie
      Chmn: Eoin Halpin
○   *L

Institute of Architectural Ironmongers   (IAI)
■   8 Stepney Green, LONDON, E1 3JU.   (hq)
      020 7790 3431   fax 020 7790 8517
      email info@gai.org.uk   http://www.iai.uk.com
      Chief Exec: Gary Amer
▲   Un-incorporated Society
Br   8
○   *P; interests of individual architectural ironmongers
●   Conf - Mtgs - ET
M   350 i
¶   Guildnews - 4; (IAI has own entry).

Institute of Art & Law   (IAL)
NR   Pentre Moel, Crickadarn, BUILTH WELLS, Powys, LD2 3BX.
      (hq)
      01982 56066   fax 01982 560604
      email info@ial.uk.com   http://www.ial.uk.com
      Dir: Ruth Redmon-Cooper
○   *L, *P; for those interested in all aspects of transacting in art
●   Mtgs - Seminars (speakers incl academics, practitioners,
      government officials & museum directors) - Publishing
M   i, org
¶   Art Antiquity & Law [Jnl] - 4.
      Commentary on the Unidroit Convention by Lyndel V Prott.
      Art Treasures & War by Wojciech Kowalski.

Institute of Asphalt Technology   (IAT)   1966
NR   Paper Mews Place, 290 High St, DORKING, Surrey,
      RH4 1QT.   (hq)
      01306 742792   fax 01306 888902
      email secretary@instofasphalt.org
      http://www.instofasphalt.org
      Sec: Anthony Pelham Morter
▲   Company Limited by Guarantee
Br   9; Republic of Ireland
○   *P; to encourage & promote improvements in the practice,
      knowledge & standards of asphalt technology
●   Conf - Mtgs - ET - Exam - Exhib - Lib - PL - VE
M   15,900 i UK / 88 i, o'seas
¶   Asphalt Professional - 6; ftm, on request (tel) nm.
      Sampling Bituminous Materials (training video 1).
      Hot Rolled Asphalt Production Laying & Compaction (training
      video 2).

Institute of Assessors & Internal Verifiers   (IAV)   1998
■   PO Box 148, WIRRAL, Cheshire, CH62 7WB.   (mail/address)
      0151-334 8215   fax 0151-334 2623
      email office@iavltd.co.uk   http://www.iavltd.co.uk
      Chief Exec: Mr Homan
▲   Company Limited by Guarantee
○   *P; for assessors & internal verifiers involved with national
      training / national vocational qualifications (NVQs)
●   Conf - Mtgs - ET - Res - Inf - LG
M   3,500 i, 200 i
¶   Best Practice (Jnl) - 4.

Institute of Association Management   (IAM)   1933
NR   1 Queen Anne's Gate, Westminster, LONDON, SW1H 9BT.
      (hq)
      0870 330 8624   fax 0870 330 8614
      email iam@iofam.org.uk   http://www.iofam.org.uk
      Pres: John Wilkinson
▲   Un-incorporated Society
○   *P; to represent & support 'executives, managers & staffs of
      trade & professional associations, medical institutes,
      chambers of commerce & similar bodies'
Gp   Computers; Europe; Assn mgt companies; Govt liaison
●   Conf - Mtgs - ET - Inf - VE - LG
M   370 i, 30 f, UK
¶   Association Executive - 4; ftm, £30 nm.   Hbk & LM - 1; ftm.

**Institute of Auctioneers & Appraisers in Scotland   (IAAS)
1926**
NR   Rural Centre, West Mains, Ingliston, NEWBRIDGE, Midlothian,
        EH28 8NZ.   (hq)
        0131-472 4067   fax 0131-472 4067
        email iaas@fsmail.net
        http://www.auctioneersscotland.co.uk
        Exec Sec: W Andrew Wright
▲   Company Limited by Guarantee
○   *P; for livestock & fine arts auctioneers, agricultural valuers &
        estate agents
Gp   Land agents; Fine art auctioneers & valuers
●   Conf - ET - LG
<   Eur Assn of Livestock Markets
M   290 i, 35 f

Institute of Automotive Engineer Assessors   (IAEA)   1932
■   Brooke House, 24 Dam St, LICHFIELD, Staffs, WS13 6AB.   (hq)
        01543 266906   fax 01543 257848
        http://www.iaea.org.uk
        Sec: P A Grice
▲   Company Limited by Guarantee; Registered Charity
Br   8
○   *P; to promote & develop for public benefit the science, design,
        manufacture & related technology of motor vehicles & their
        repair
●   Exam - Res - Inf
<   FIEA
M   1,250 i, UK / 50 i, o'seas
¶   NL - 6; ftm.

Institute of Bankers in Ireland   1898
IRL   1 North Wall Quay, DUBLIN 1, Republic of Ireland.   (hq)
        353 (1) 611 6500   fax 353 (1) 611 6565
        http://www.bankers.ie
        Chief Exec: Anthony Walsh
○   *P

Institute of Barristers' Clerks   (IBC)   1922
NR   289-293 High Holborn, LONDON, WC1V 7HZ.   (admin/b)
        020 7831 7144
        http://www.ibc.org.uk
▲   Registered Charity
○   *P
●   Conf - Mtgs - ET - Inf
M   850 i
¶   Mailshot (with job vacancies) - 52; £10 for 6 months.

Institute of Biology   (IOB)   1950
■   9 Red Lion Court, LONDON, EC4A 3EF.   (hq)
        020 7936 5900   fax 020 7936 5901
        email info@iob.org   http://www.iob.org
        Chief Exec: Prof Alan D B Malcolm
▲   Registered Charity
Br   17; Hong Kong
○   *L, *P; to advance the science & practice of the biological
        sciences; to advance education & encourage the study of the
        biological sciences & their applications
●   Conf - Mtgs - ET - Exam - Exhib - Comp - Inf - VE - LG
<   Intl U of Biological Sciences (IUBS); Eur Countries Biologists
        Assn (ECBA); Science Coun; Royal Instn; Brit Assn for the
        Advancement of Science; Save Brit Science
M   15,800 i, 6 f, 76 org, UK / 1,331 i, o'seas
¶   Jnl of Biological Education - 4.
        Biologist - 6.   AR - 1.
        Publications list available.

**Institute of Biology of Ireland   (Institiúid Bitheolaíochta na
h'Éireann) of Ireland)   1965**
IRL   National University of Ireland, MAYNOOTH, Co Kildare,
        Republic of Ireland.
        email ibi@nuim.ie   http://www.nuim.ie/ibi
○   *P

Institute of Biomedical Science   (IBMS)   1912
NR   12 Coldbath Square, LONDON, EC1R 5HL.   (hq)
        020 7713 0214   fax 020 7436 4946
        email mail@ibms.org   http://www.ibms.org
        Chief Exec: Alan Potter
▲   Registered Charity
Br   48; 5 o'seas
○   *L, *P; promotes the scientific study & development of
        biomedical science
●   Conf - Mtgs - ET - Exam - Res - Comp - Inf - LG
<   Eur Professions in Biomedical Science; Eur Confedn of
        Laboratory Science
M   15,000 i, 74 f, UK / 1,000 i, o'seas
¶   Biomedical Scientist - 12.
        British Jnl of Biomedical Science - 4.
        Science & educational leaflets.   AR.

Institute of Bookbinding & Allied Trades   (IBAT)   1904
NR   c/o Clerkenwell Conference Centre, Clerkenwell Green,
        LONDON, EC1R 0NA.   (mtgs)
        http://www.ibat.org.uk
▲   Un-incorporated Society
○   *P. *U; to promote the exchange of information within the
        bookbinding industry & improve the standards of training
●   Mtgs - ET - Inf - VE
<   Worshipful Company of Stationers
M   130 i
¶   Quarterly Magazine.   LM - 1;   AR; both ftm only.

Institute of Brewing & Distilling   (IBD)   1886
NR   33 Clarges St, LONDON, W1J 7EE.   (hq)
        020 7499 8144   fax 020 7499 1156
        email enquiries@ibd.org.uk   http://www.ibd.org.uk
        Contact: The Secretary
▲   Registered Charity
○   *P; for the advancement of education & professional
        development in the science & technology of brewing,
        distilling & related industries
●   Conf - Mtgs - ET - Exam - Exhib - Comp - Lib
M   1,925 i, UK / 1,950 i, o'seas
¶   The Brewer & Distiller - 12; ftm, £60 (£75 o'seas) nm.
        Jnl of the Institute of Brewing - 4; ftm only.
        Brewing & Distilling Directory - 1; ftm only.
×   2005 Institute & Guild of Brewing

Institute of British Geographers
    with the **Royal Geographical Society**

Institute of British Organ Building   (IBO)
■   13 Ryefields, Thurston, BURY ST EDMUNDS, Suffolk, IP31 3TD.
        01359 233433
        http://www.ibo.co.uk
        Admin: Carol Levey
○   *T; for builders of pipe organs
M   420 i, UK / 40 i, o'seas
¶   Ybk.

Institute of Broadcast Sound   (IBS)   1977
■   PO Box 208, HAVANT, Hants, PO9 9BQ.   (mail add)
        030 0400 8427 (option 1)   fax 0870 762 2835
        email ibs-info@ibs.org.uk   http://www.ibs.org.uk
        Co Sec: Malcolm Johnson
▲   Company Limited by Guarantee; Registered Charity
○   *P; to promote the excellence of professional sound for radio &
        television broadcasting; to provide a continuing forum for
        such objectives
●   Conf - Mtgs - ET - Exhib - Inf - Lib - LG
M   750 i, 35 f, UK / 30 i, 1 f, o'seas
        (Sub: £60 i, £325 f, UK / £83 i, o'seas)
¶   Line Up - 5; ftm, £45 (UK), £55 (Eur), £65 (RoW), nm.

© CBD Research Ltd · Beckenham · BR3 5JS · Tel 020 8650 7745 · Fax 020 8650 0768 · E-mail cbd@cbdresearch.com · www.cbdresearch.com

Institute of Builders' Merchants   (IoBM)   1968
- ■ Touchwood, 2 Oak View Rise, Harlow Wood, MANSFIELD, Notts, NG18 4UT.   (hq)
01623 633228   fax 01623 427693
http://www.instbm.co.uk
Dir: Dave Saunders
- Br   6
- ○ *P; improvement of technical & general knowledge of persons engaged in the trade of builders' merchant
- ● ET
- < Bldrs Merchants Fedn; Worshipful Company of Bldrs Merchants
- M   800 i

Institute of Business Administration Ltd   (IAM)   1947
- NR   16 Park Crescent, LONDON, W1B 1BA.   (hq)
http://www.ibauk.org
- ○ *P; for company secretaries & administrators in medium & small size organisations

Institute of Business Advisers
in 2007 merged with the Institute of Management Consultancy to form the **Institute of Business Consulting**

Institute of Business Analysts & Consultants   1983
- IRL   7 Forest Park, SWORDS, Co Dublin, Republic of Ireland.
353 (1) 810 7685
email secretary@inbusans.ie   http://www.inbusans.ie
- ○ *P

Institute of Business Consulting   (IBC)   2007
- ■ 25 Savoy Court (4th floor), Strand, LONDON, WC2R 0EZ.
(hq)
020 7421 0580   fax 020 7497 0463
email ibc@ibconsulting.org.uk
http://www.ibconsulting.org.uk
Dir: Lynda Purser
- ▲ Registered Charity
- ○ *P; for those offering management consultancy, business advice, business consulting, professional standards
- Gp   Consultancy purchasing; Internal business consulting
- ● Conf - Mtgs - ET - Res - Exhib - Comp - SG - Stat - Inf - Lib - PL - LG
- < Intl Coun of Insts of Mgt Consultancy
- > Chart Mgt Inst
- M   i, f
- ¶ Business Consultant (NL) - 4; ftm only.
- × 2007 (Institute of Business Advisers (Institute of Management Consultancy

Institute of Business Ethics   (IBE)   1986
- NR   24 Greencoat Place, LONDON, SW1P 1BE.   (hq)
020 7798 6040
http://www.ibe.org.uk
Dir: Philippa Foster Back
- ▲ Registered Charity
- ○ *T; to clarify ethical issues involved in business; to identify & promulgate best business practice
- ● Conf - Mtgs - ET - Res - Lib
- M   25 i, 60 f, 10 org, UK / 2 f, o'seas
- ¶ Various publications available.

Institute of Car Fleet Management   (ICFM)   1992
- NR   PO Box 314, CHICHESTER, W Sussex, PO20 9WZ.   (hq)
01462 744914
http://www.icfm.com
- ○ *P

Institute of Career Guidance Ltd   (ICG)   1922
- NR   Copthall House (3rd floor), 1 New Rd, STOURBRIDGE, W Midlands, DY8 1PH.   (hq)
01384 445630   fax 01384 440830
email hq@icg-uk.org   http://www.icg-uk.org
Admin: Ruth Weston
- ▲ Company Limited by Guarantee
- ○ *P; awarding body for the career guidance sector
- ● Conf - ET - Exhib - Lib
- M   3,000 i, 17 f
- ¶ Careers Guidance Today - 6; ftm, £27.50 yr nm.
Front-Line - 6; ftm only.
Vacancy Bulletin (Portico) - 26; £10 m, £40 nm.

Institute of Carpenters   (IOC)   1890
- NR   Carpenters' Hall (3rd floor D), 1 Throgmorton Ave, LONDON, EC2N 2BY.   (asa)
020 7256 2700   fax 020 7256 2701
email info@instituteofcarpenters.com
http://www.instituteofcarpenters.com
Chmn: Trevor Greeves
- ○ *P; to encourage the highest standards of carpentry & joinery work; to promote & enhance the role & status of skilled craftsmen & women
- M   3,000 i
- ¶ Jnl - 4; ftm.

Institute of Cast Metals Engineers   (ICME)   1904
- ■ National Metalforming Centre, 47 Birmingham Rd, WEST BROMWICH, W Midlands, B70 6PY.   (hq)
0121-601 6979   fax 0121-601 6981
email info@icme.org.uk   http://www.icme.org.uk
Dir: Dr Pam Murrell
- ▲ Registered Charity
- Br   7
- ○ *P; to provide professional development programmes for individuals employed in the global cast metal industry
- Gp   Working gps (technical, educational & training) investigating various topics
- ● Mtgs - ET - Inf - Lib - PL
- < Wld Foundrymen Org; Engg Coun
- M   1,207 i, UK / 90 i, o'seas
- ¶ Foundry Trade Jnl - 10; ftm, £179 (237 RoW) nm.
Diecasting World - 2; £38 (£56 RoW).
Foundry Ybk & Castings Buyers Guide - 1; £151.
AR - 1; free.

Institute of Cemetery & Crematorium Management   (ICCM)   1913
- ■ City of London Cemetery, Aldersbrook Rd, LONDON, E12 5DQ.   (hq)
020 8989 4661   fax 020 8989 6112
email julie@iccm.fsnet.co.uk   http://www.iccm-uk.com
Chief Exec: Tim Morris
- ▲ Company Limited by Guarantee
- Br   8
- ○ *P; to promote professional training, education & consultancy for UK burial & cremation authorities
- ● Conf - Mtgs - ET - Exam - Exhib - Lib
- < Intl Cremation Fedn
- M   680 i, 305 f, UK / 10 i, o'seas
- ¶ The Jnl - 4; ftm, £4 yr nm.
- × 2004-05 Confederation of Burial Authorities

Institute of Certified Book-Keepers (ICB) 1996
NR 1 Northumberland Ave, LONDON, WC2N 5BW.   (hq)
    0845 060 2345
    http://www.book-keepers.org
    Chief Exec: Garry Carter
▲ Company Limited by Guarantee
Br 32; 11 countries
○ *P; to set standards in book-keeping
Gp Members in practice
● Exam
< ICB Intl
M 100,000 i, 5 f, 54 colleges & training org, UK / 604 i, o'seas
¶ Invoice - 4.

Institute of Certified Public Accountants in Ireland   (CPA) 1943
IRL 17 Harcourt St, DUBLIN 2, Republic of Ireland.
    353 (1) 425 1000   fax 353 (1) 425 1001
    email cpa@cpaireland.ie   http://www.cpaireland.ie
    Chief Exec: Eamonn Siggins
Br 3 Wellington Park, Belfast, BT9 6DJ.
    048 9092 3390
○ *P

Institute of Chartered Accountants in England & Wales (ICAEW) 1880
■ Chartered Accountants' Hall, PO Box 433, LONDON, EC2P 2BJ.   (hq)
    020 7920 8100
    http://www.icaew.co.uk
    Chief Exec: Michael Izza
▲ Registered Charity
○ *P
M i, f & org
¶ Accountancy (Jnl) - 12.   LM.   AR.

Institute of Chartered Accountants in Ireland   1888
IRL Burlington House, Burlington Road, DUBLIN 4, Republic of Ireland.   (hq)
    353 (1) 637 7200   fax 353 (1) 668 0842
    email ca@icai.ie   http://www.icai.ie
Br 11 Donegall Square South, Belfast, BT1 5JE.
    028 9032 1600
○ *P

Institute of Chartered Accountants of Scotland   (ICAS)   1854
NR 21 Haymarket Yards, EDINBURGH, EH12 5BH.   (hq)
    0131-347 0100   fax 0131-347 0105
    email enquiries@icas.org.uk   http://www.icas.org.uk
    Chief Exec & Sec: Des Hudson
Br 7 area committees
○ *P
● Conf - Mtgs - ET - Exam - Res - SG - Inf - Lib - LG
< Intl Fedn of Accountants (IFAC); Intl Accounting Standards C'ee (IASC); Fédn des Experts Comptables Eur (FEE); Auditing Practices Bd (APB)
M 15,208 i
¶ CA Magazine - 12; ftm.
    Directory of Insolvency Permit Holders - 1.
    Research Publications; prices vary.

Institute of Chartered Foresters   (ICF)   1925
■ 59 George St, EDINBURGH, EH2 2JG.   (hq)
    0131-240 1425   fax 0131-240 1425
    email icf@charteredforesters.org
    http://www.charteredforesters.org
    Exec Dir: Shireen Chambers
▲ Registered Charity
○ *L, *P
● Conf - ET - Exam - Res - Inf - VE - LG
< Soc for the Envt
M i
¶ The Chartered Forester - 4;   Forestry Jnl - 5.
    Register of Consultants - 1;   AR; all ftm.
    Forestry - 4; £40 m, £230 nm.

Institute of Chartered Secretaries & Administrators   (ICSA) 1891
NR 16 Park Crescent, LONDON, W1B 1AH.   (hq)
    020 7580 4741
    http://www.icsa.org.uk
▲ Registered Charity
○ *P; law & practice of secretaryship & administration
M i

Institute of Chartered Shipbrokers   (ICS)   1920
NR 85 Gracechurch St, LONDON, EC3V 0AA.   (hq)
    020 7623 1111
    http://www.ics.org.uk
▲ Royal Charter
○ *P
M i, f

Institute of Chemistry of Ireland   (Institiúid Ceimice na h'Éireann)   1950
IRL PO Box 9322, Cardiff Lane, DUBLIN 2, Republic of Ireland.
    email info@instituteofchemistry.org
    http://www.instituteofchemistry.org
    Hon Sec: Dr J P Ryan
○ *L; the professional body representing chemists in Ireland

Institute of Chiropodists & Podiatrists   1938
■ 27 Wright St, SOUTHPORT, Merseyside, PR9 0TL.   (hq)
    01704 546141   fax 01704 500477
    email secretary@iocp.org.uk   http://www.iocp.org.uk
    Sec: Mrs S M Kirkham
▲ Company Limited by Guarantee
Br 25
○ *P
M i
¶ Podiatry Review.

Institute of Civil Defence & Disaster Studies
    on 1 January 2009 the Institute of Civil Defence & Disaster Studies & the Institute of Emergency Management amalgamated to form the **Institute of Civil Protection & Emergency Management**

Institute of Civil Protection & Emergency Management (ICPEM)   1938
NR PO Box 698, CAMBERLEY, Surrey, GU15 3WY.   (hq)
    01305 767560   fax 01305 767560
    Sec:
○ *P; advancement of civil protection, emergency management & disaster studies (natural events, terrorism, catastrophes & system failure)
● Conf - ET - Res - Lib - LG
< Intl Civil Defence Org
M i & org
¶ Alert (Jnl).
× 2009 (Institute of Civil Defence & Disaster Studies (Institute of Emergency Management

Institute of Clay Shooting Instructors   (ICSI)   1987
NR 4 Holmlands Crescent, Durham Moor, DURHAM, DH1 5AR.   (mem sec/p)
    http://www.icsi.org.uk

Institute of Clay Technology
    since 2005 the International Clay Technology Association, within the Ceramics Society, a group of the **Institute of Materials, Minerals & Mining**

Institute of Clayworkers   (ICW)
NR Federation House, Station Rd, STOKE-ON-TRENT, Staffs, ST4 2SA.   (hq)
    01782 744631   fax 01782 744102
    email bcc@ceramfed.co.uk
    Sec: A McRae
    A benevolent fund, awarding long service medals

Institute of Clerks of Works of Great Britain Inc   (ICW)   1882
- ■ Equinox, 28 Commerce Rd, Lynch Wood, PETERBOROUGH, Cambs, PE2 6LR.   (hq)
  01733 405160   fax 01733 405161
  email info@icwgb.co.uk   http://www.icwgb.org
  Gen Sec: Rachel Morris
- ▲ Company Limited by Guarantee
- Br 20; Hong Kong
- ○ *P; examining & qualifying body for clerks of works in the UK & overseas
- Gp Building construction
- ● Conf - Mtgs - Res - Exhib - Inf - VE - LG
- > Brit Standards Inst; Construction Ind Coun
- M 1,579 i, UK / 183 i, o'seas
- ¶ Site Recorder (Jnl) - 12;   LM - 1; both ftm.

Institute of Clinical Research   (ICR)   1978
- ■ Institute House, Boston Drive, BOURNE END, Bucks, SL8 5YS. (hq)
  0845 521 0056   fax 01628 530641
  http://www.icr-global.org
  Chief Exec: Dr John Hooper
- ▲ Company Limited by Guarantee
- ○ *P
- ● Conf - Mtgs - ET - Exam - Exhib
- M 3,980 i, UK / 1,048 i, o'seas
- ¶ Clinical Research Focus - 11; ftm only.   AR; free.

Institute of Commercial Management Ltd   (ICM)   1979
- ■ The Fusee, 20a Bargates, CHRISTCHURCH, Dorset, BH23 1QL.   (hq)
  01202 490555   fax 01202 490666
  email icm@icm.ac.uk   http://www.icm.ac.uk
  Chief Exec: Prof Tom Thomas
- ▲ Company Limited by Guarantee; Registered Charity
- ○ *E, *P; 'educational foundation supporting business, personal & professional development'
- Gp Provision of expert technical assistance & consultancy services in the fields of trade, tourism & professional development
- ● Conf - ET - Exam
- M 12,400 i

Institute for Communications Arbitration & Forensics
no longer exists

** Institute of Community Development
Organisation lost: see Introduction paragraph 3

Institute for Complementary Medicine
since 2008 **Institute for Complementary & Natural Medicine**.

Institute for Complementary & Natural Medicine   (ICM)   1982
- NR Can-Mezzanine, 32-36 Loman St, LONDON, SE1 0EH.   (hq)
  020 7922 7980   fax 020 7922 7981
  http://www.i-c-m.org.uk
- ▲ Registered Charity
- ○ *P; to make known information, to encourage research & promote high standards in practice & training in complementary medicine
- ● Conf - ET - Inf - LG
- M i, 600 org
- ¶ ICNM Jnl - 4.
- ✕ 2008 Institute for Complementary Medicine

Institute of Concrete Technology   (ICT)   1972
- NR 4 Meadows Business Park, Station Approach, Blackwater, CAMBERLEY, Surrey, GU17 9AB.   (hq)
  01276 607140   fax 01276 607141
  http://www.ict.concrete.org.uk
  Pres: R Gaimster,   Hon Sec: C D Nessfield
- ▲ Company Limited by Guarantee
- Br 1; Ireland, South Africa
- ○ *P; to promote the advancement of concrete technology
- ● Conf - Mtgs - ET - Exam
- M 420 i, UK / 210 i, o'seas
- ¶ NL - 4.   Ybk.   Members Hbk.

Institute of Conflict Management   (ICM)   2000
- NR 840 Melton Rd, Thurmaston, LEICESTER, LE4 8BN.   (asa)
  0116-269 1049   fax 0116-264 0141
  email icm@associationhq.org.uk
  http://www.conflictmanagement.org
  Chief Exec: Stuart Hex
- ▲ Company Limited by Guarantee
- ○ *P; to develop, monitor & promote professional standards for the effective prevention & management of aggression & conflict at work
- ● Conf - Mtgs - ET - Res - Exhib - Inf - LG - Training provision of the National Foundation Certificate for Managing Work-related Violence - Quality award process for training in the management of work related violence
- M 350 i
- ¶ ICM NL - 4.

Institute of Conservation   (ICON)   2005
- NR Downstream Bldg (3rd floor), 1 London Bridge, LONDON, SE1 9BG.   (hq)
  020 7785 3805   fax 020 7785 3806
  http://www.icon.org.uk
  Chief Exec: Alastair McCapra,
  Admin Officer: Diane Copley
- ○ *P
- ✕ 2005 (Care of Collections Forum
    (Institute of Paper Conservation
    (Photographic Materials Conservation Group
    (Scottish Society for Conservation & Restoration
    (United Kingdom Institute for Conservation of
    (Historic & Artistic Works

Institute for the Conservation of Historic & Artistic Works in Ireland   (ICHAWI)
- IRL 1 Lower Grand Canal St, DUBLIN 2, Republic of Ireland.
  email ichawi@eircom.net   http://www.ichawi.org
  Hon Sec: Maighréad McParland
- ○ *P

Institute of Construction Management   (ICM)   1970
- NR 69 Adur Avenue, SHOREHAM-by-SEA, W Sussex, BN43 5NL.
  01273 453392
  http://www.the-icm.com
  Sec: D Charlton
- ▲ Company Limited by Guarantee
- Br 9; Hong Kong
- ○ P; construction & site management & knowledge of all modern construction methods
- ● Conf - Mtgs - ET - Exam - Inf - VE
- < Construction Ind Coun
- M c 700 i & f
- ¶ Viewpoint (NL) - 4; ftm only.

Institute of Construction Specialists (IOCS) 2001

- ■ 1 Walpole House, 2 Pickford St, ALDERSHOT, Hants, GU11 1TZ. (hq)
  01252 312122 fax 01252 343081
  email info@constructionspecialists.org
  http://www.constructionspecialists.org
  Group Dir: A R Gibbs
- ▲ Un-incorporated Society
- ○ *P; for managers & administrative & supervisory staff of specialist construction firms; to focus on training & accreditation
- ● ET - Exam - Comp
- < Construction Specialists Gp
- M i
- ¶ IOCS/CCS NL - 10; ftm only.

Institute of Consumer Affairs (ICA) 1974

- NR 134 Trinity Rd, LONDON, SW17 7HS. (chmn/p)
  020 8767 6887
  http://www.icanet.org.uk
  Mem Sec: Jacqui King
- ○ *P; a network of consumer advisers & others working in consumer protection & consumer affairs. To raise the quality of services to consumers through better information, advice & education; to improve consumer protection
- ● Conf - Mtgs - ET - Inf
- M 150 i
- ¶ Help & Advice - 6; m only.

Institute of Consumer Sciences (incorporating Home Economics)

has closed

Institute of Contemporary Arts (ICA) 1947

- NR 12 Carlton House Terrace, LONDON, SW1Y 5AH. (hq)
  http://www.ica.org.uk
- ○ *A, *D; a centre for contemporary cultural activities, incl film, theatre, dance, lectures & visual arts

Institute of Continuing Professional Development

- NR Grosvenor Gardens House, 35-37 Grosvenor Gardens, LONDON, SW1W 0BS.
  020 7828 1965 fax 020 7828 1967
  http://www.cpdinstitute.org
  Mem Mgr: Jane Guest
- ○ *E

Institute of Copywriting (IOC) 1992

- § Overbrook Business Centre, Poolbridge Rd, Blackford, WEDMORE, Somerset, BS28 4PA.
  0800 781 1715
  http://www.inst.org/copy/
  Part of the Learning Institute, which offers over 25 vocational courses.

Institute of Corrosion (ICorr) 1975

- NR Corrosion House, Vimy Court, Vimy Rd, LEIGHTON BUZZARD, Beds, LU7 1FG. (hq)
  01525 851771
  http://www.icorr.org
  Hon Sec: Dr Steve Mabbutt
- ▲ Registered Charity
- Br 8; Republic of Ireland
- ○ *L *P; study & advice concerning corrosion engineering problems & corrosion prevention
- ● Conf - Mtgs - ET
- M 1,450 i, 40 f, UK / 150 i, 1 f, o'seas
- ¶ Corrosion Science - 12. Corrosion Management - 6.
  UK Corrosion (conference papers) - 1.

Institute of Cost & Executive Accountants (ICEA) 1958

- NR Akhtar House, 2 Shepherd's Bush Rd, LONDON, W6 7PJ. (hq)
  020 8749 7126 fax 020 8749 7127
  email icea@enta.net http://www.icea.enta.net
  Sec Gen: Dr Sushil K das Gupta
- ▲ Company Limited by Guarantee; Registered Charity
- Br 14; 23 o'seas
- ○ *P; ' modern professional accounting institute, producing tomorrow's accountants to take financial decisions'
- Gp Small business; Public practice; Local government
- ● Conf - Mtgs - ET - Exam - Res - Exhib - SG - Inf - Lib - LG
- < Eur Accounting Assn; Coun for Educ in the C'wealth; Brit Accounting Assn; Foundation for Science & Technology in the UK
- M c 2,000 i, UK / c 2,000 i, o'seas
- ¶ Executive Accountant - 4.

Institute of Couriers

- NR Green Man Tower, 332 Goswell Rd, LONDON, EC1V 7LQ.
  0845 601 0245
  http://www.ioc.uk.com
- ○ *T

Institute of Credit Management (ICM) 1939

- ■ The Water Mill, Station Rd, South Luffenham, OAKHAM, Rutland, LE15 8NB. (hq)
  01780 722900 fax 01780 721333
  email info@icm.org.uk http://www.icm.org.uk
  Dir Gen: Philip King
- ▲ Company Limited by Guarantee; Registered Charity
- Br 26
- ○ *P; for those employed in credit management, credit finance & ancillary services
- ● Conf - Mtgs - ET - Exam - Res - Exhib - Inf - Lib - LG
- < Fedn of Eur Credit Mgt Assns (FECMA)
- M 9,000 i, UK / 300 i, o'seas
- ¶ Credit Management - 12; ftm, £75 yr nm.
  AR - 1; ftm.

Institute of Customer Service (ICS) 1997

- NR 2 Castle Court, St Peter's St, COLCHESTER, Essex, CO1 1EW. (hq)
  01206 571716 fax 01206 546688
  email enquiries@icsmail.co.uk
  http://www.instituteofcustomerservice.com
  Chief Exec: David Parsons
- ▲ Company Limited by Guarantee
- Br 10
- ○ *P; to develop & spread authoritative knowledge & good practice, define national professional & occupational standards & provide professional recognition to individuals in the customer service industry
- ● Conf - Mtgs - ET - Res - Exhib - Stat - Inf - VE - LG
- M 3,000 i, 180 f
- ¶ Customer First - 5; ftm, £4.95 nm.
  Research publications - irreg; prices vary.

© CBD Research Ltd · Beckenham · BR3 5JS · Tel 020 8650 7745 · Fax 020 8650 0768 · E-mail cbd@cbdresearch.com · www.cbdresearch.com

Institute of Decontamination Sciences (IDSc) 2004

NR   Chesterfield Royal Hospital, Calow, CHESTERFIELD, Derbys, S44 5BL. (hsb)
01246 513069
email idsc.admin@googlemail.com
http://www.idsc-uk.co.uk
Dir of Admin: Kath Saxelby
▲   Un-incorporated Society
Br   8
○   *P; for staff & management in the field of decontamination & sterile services
Gp Conference c'ee; Education
●   Conf - Mtgs - ET - Exhib - Promotion of research & development
<   Eur Fedn of Hospital Sterile Services
>   Eur Fedn of Hospital Sterile Services
M   370 i, 15 f, UK / 8 i, o'seas
¶   Jnl - 4; ftm, £25 each nm.
Ybk - 1; ftm, £55 nm.
Technical Vocational Training Programme; £18.
Standards & Practices; £25.
×   2004 Institute of Sterile Services Management

Institute of Demolition Engineers (IDE) 1971

■   69 Poplicans Rd, Cuxton, ROCHESTER, Kent, ME2 1EJ. (hsp)
01634 294255   fax 01634 294255
email info@ide.org.uk   http://www.ide.org.uk
Sec: Mrs Valerie J Stroud
▲   Registered Charity
○   *P; to advance the science of demolition engineering, the use of effective techniques in the industry & safer methods of working; to provide a qualifying body in the industry
●   Conf - Mtgs - ET - Exam - Inf - LG
M   317 i, UK / 7 i, o'seas
¶   Demolition Engineer - 3; complimentary.

Institute of Designers in Ireland 1972

IRL The Digital Hub, Roe Lane, Thomas St, DUBLIN 8, Republic of Ireland.
353 (1) 489 3650
email idi@indigo.ie   http://www.idi-design.ie
Pres: Barry Sheehan
○   *A, *P

Institute of Direct Marketing (IDM) 1987

NR   1 Park Rd, TEDDINGTON, Middx, TW11 0AR. (hq)
020 8977 5705   fax 020 8943 2535
email enquiries@theidm.com   http://www.theidm.com
▲   Registered Charity
○   *P; direct marketing training & education for members
●   ET - Exam - Lib
<   Direct Marketing Assn
M   5,000 i, UK / 200 i, o'seas
¶   Jnl of Interactive Marketing - 4.

Institute of Directors (IoD) 1903

NR   116 Pall Mall, LONDON, SW1Y 5ED. (hq)
020 7839 1233   fax 020 7930 1949

Institute of Directors in Ireland

IRL Heritage House, Dundrum Office Park, DUBLIN 14, Republic of Ireland.
353 (1) 296 4093   fax 353 (1) 296 4127
email info@iodireland.ie   http://www.iodireland.ie
Sec: Ralph MacDarby
○   *P

Institute of Domestic Heating & Environmental Engineers (IDHEE) 1964

■   Unit 35A New Forest Enterprise Centre, Chapel Lane, Totton, SOUTHAMPTON, Hants, SO40 9LA. (hq)
023 8066 8900   fax 023 8066 0888
email admin@idhee.co.uk   http://www.idhee.org.uk
Exec Chmn: Bill Bucknell
▲   Un-incorporated Society
Br   Ireland, New Zealand
○   *P; to raise the standard of domestic heating & environmental engineering
Gp Renewable energy; Consulting & design engineers
●   Conf - Mtgs - ET - Exam - Exhib - LG
M   781 i, 31 f, UK / 64 i, 3 f, o'seas
¶   Comfort Engineering - 4; ftm, £5 nm.
Technical Hbk - 1; ftm, £7.50 nm.

Institute of Ecology & Environmental Management (IEEM) 1991

NR   43 Southgate St, WINCHESTER, Hants, SO23 9EH. (hq)
01962 868626   fax 01962 868625
email enquiries@ieem.net   http://www.ieem.net
Exec Dir: Dr Jim R Thompson
▲   Company Limited by Guarantee
Br   8 regional sections
○   *P; to promote & support professionalism in the fields of ecology & environmental management
●   Conf - Mtgs - ET - Res - Exhib - Comp - Stat - Lib - LG
<   Intl Consvn U (IUCN); Eur Fedn of Assns of Envtl Profls (EFAEP); Soc for the Envt (SOCENV); EUROPARC; EUROSITE
M   3,500 i, UK / 200 i, o'seas
     (Sub: £120 UK / £80 o'seas)
¶   In Practice (Jnl) - 4; ftm; £30 yr nm.
Members Directory - 1; [on website].
Conference Proceedings - 2; £21.
Technical Guidance.   AR - 1.

Institute of Economic Affairs Ltd (IEA) 1957

NR   2 Lord North St, LONDON, SW1P 3LB. (hq)
020 7799 3745
http://www.iea.org.uk
Dir Gen: John Blundell
▲   Registered Charity
○   *L; extension of public understanding of economic principles in their application to practical problems
●   Conf - ET - Lib
M   2,000 i, 500 f, UK / 500 i, 5 f, o'seas
¶   Economic Affairs - 4; ftm.   Hobart Papers.
Hobart Paperbacks.   Research Monographs.
Series on Environment.   Choice in Welfare.
Health Series.   Religion 2 Liberty.   Occasional Papers.
Publications are irreg & prices vary.
Videos.   Conferences.   Lectures.

Institute of Educational Assessors 2005

NR   29 Bolton St, LONDON, W1J 8GP. (hq)
http://www.ioea.org.uk
○   *P

Institute of Electrolysis Ltd
2004 merged with the British Association of Electrolysists to form the
British Institute & Association of Electrolysis

Institute of Emergency Management
on 1 January 2009 the Institute of Emergency Management & the Institute of Civil Defence & Disaster Studies amalgamated to form the
Institute of Civil Protection & Emergency Management

Institute of Employment Rights (IER) 1989

■ The People's Centre, 50-54 Mount Pleasant, LIVERPOOL,
  L3 5SD. (hq)
  0151-702 6925   fax 0151-702 6935
  email office@ier.org.uk   http://www.ier.org.uk
  Dir: Carolyn Jones,
  Admin & Publications Officer: Megan Dobney
▲ Company Limited by Guarantee; Registered Charity
○ *Q; 'an independent organisation or think-tank acting as a
  focal point for the spread of new ideas in the field of the
  Labour movement & labour law'
● Conf - ET - Res - Inf - Publishing
M 406 i, 55 f, 290 org, UK / 6 i, 3 f, o'seas
¶ Books on various aspects of labour law - 8; £6.50 m, £20 nm.

Institute of Entertainment & Arts Management
   since 2006 the **Institute of Entertainment & Arts Professionals**

Institute of Entertainment & Arts Professionals (IEAP) 1982

■ 17 Drake Close, HORSHAM, W Sussex, RH12 4UB.   (admin/p)
  0870 241 7248   fax 0870 241 7248
  email admin@ieap.co.uk   http://www.ieap.co.uk
  Admin: Shirley Carpenter
  Pres: Bob Bustance
▲ Company Limited by Guarantee
Br Northern & Southern areas
○ *D; for managers & managements throughout local
  government, commercial & subsidised sectors of the arts,
  entertainment & related leisure interests
● Conf - Mtgs - ET - Exhib - Comp - Stat - Inf - VE
M 290 i
¶ NL - 12;   Ybk - 1; both ftm only.
✕ 2006 Institute of Entertainment & Arts Management

Institute of Environmental Management & Assessment (IEMA) 1999

NR St Nicholas House, 70 Newport, LINCOLN, LN1 3DP.   (hq)
  01522 540069   fax 01522 540090
  email info@iema.net   http://www.iema.net
  Chief Exec: Russell Foster
○ *P; to promote & develop the best practice standards in
  environmental management, auditing & assessment
● Conf - Mtgs - ET - Exam - Exhib - Inf - Lib
M 7,620 i, 310 f, UK / 1,245 i, 26 f, o'seas

Institute of Explosives Engineers (IExpE) 1974

NR Wellington Hall 289, Cranfield University, Defence Academy of
  the UK, Shrivenham, SWINDON, Wilts, SN6 8LA.   (hq)
  01793 785322   fax 01793 785972
  email info@iexpe.org   http://www.iexpe.org
  Sec: Gillian Bonar
Br 13
○ *P; the qualifying body for explosives engineers
Gp Quarrying; Tunnelling & shaft sinking; Excavation & land
  clearance; Demolition; Underwater work; Pyrotechnics;
  Offshore oil operations; High explosives trials; Film & special
  effects
● Conf - Mtgs - ET - Exam - Res - Exhib - SG - Inf - LG
< Eur Fedn Explosives Engineers
M 758 i, 31 i (company), 20 f, UK / 145 i, 4 f, o'seas
¶ Explosives Engineering - 4.

Institute of Export (IoE) 1935

■ Export House, Minerva Business Park, Lynch Wood,
  PETERBOROUGH, Cambs, PE2 6FT.   (hq)
  01733 404400   fax 01733 404444
  email institute@export.org.uk   http://www.export.org.uk
  Chmn: Lesley Batchelor
▲ Company Limited by Guarantee; Registered Charity
Br 8; Hong Kong
○ *P; 'we are the only professional body in the UK offering
  recognised qualifications in international trade'
Gp Education & training; Examinations
● ET - Exam - Exhib
M 3,000 i, 100 f, UK / 500 i, o'seas
¶ Pathfinder Business - 6; ftm, £3.95 nm.

Institute for Family Business   (IFB)

NR 32 Buckingham Palace Rd, LONDON, SW1W 0RE.   (hq)
  020 7630 6250   fax 020 7630 6251
  email info@ifb.org.uk   http://www.ifb.org.uk
  Dir Gen: Grant E Gordon
○ *T

Institute of Field Archaeologists (IFA)   1982

■ SHES, University of Reading, Whiteknights, PO Box 227,
  READING, Berks, RG6 6AB.   (hq)
  0118-931 6446   fax 0118-378 6448
  email admin@archaeologists.net
  http://www.archaeologists.net
  Admin: Alex Llewelyn,   Chief Exec: Peter Hinten
▲ Company Limited by Guarantee
○ *L, *P; to advance the practice of archaeology & allied
  disciplines by the promotion of professional standards &
  ethics
Gp Area: Scotland, Wales, East Midlands
  Special interest: Buildings Archaeology Group, Marine affairs,
  Finds, Diggers Forum, Illustration & surveying, Geophysics,
  Forum for information standards in heritage
● Conf - Mtgs - ET - Res - Exhib - Inf
< Irish Assn Profl Archaeologists; Assn Archaeol Illustrators &
  Surveyors
M 61 f
  (Sub: depends on income / turnover)
¶ The Archaeologist (Jnl) - 4.ftm, £5 nm.
  Ybk & Directory - 1; ftm, £30 nm.   AR - 1; ftm, £5 nm.
  Professional Practice Papers - irreg; ftm, £10 nm.
  Standards Guidance Documents;ftm, £30 nm.
  JIS - 52; £15 or email free, c£20 per month nm.

Institute of Financial Accountants   (IFA) 1916

■ Burford House, 44 London Rd, SEVENOAKS, Kent,
  TN13 1AS.   (hq)
  01732 458080
  http://www.ifa.org.uk
  Chief Exec: J M Dean
▲ Company Limited by Guarantee
○ *P; for accountants in commerce, industry & private practice
M i

Institute of Financial Planning (IFP) 1987

NR Whitefriars Centre, Lewins Mead, BRISTOL, BS1 2NT.   (hq)
  0117-945 2470   fax 0117-929 2214
  email enquiries@financialplanning.org.uk
  http://www.financialplanning.org.uk
  Chief Exec: Nick Cann
▲ Company Limited by Guarantee
Br 12
○ *P; to promote understanding & recognition of the financial
  planning profession (those who offer objective assistance to
  clients in organising their personal & business affairs)
● Conf - Mtgs - ET - Exam - Res - Exhib - Comp - SG - Inf - Lib -
  LG
< Intl CFP Coun; Financial Planning Assn (FPA)(USA)
M 1,250 i, UK / 50 i, o'seas
¶ Financial Planner - 4; ftm only.

© CBD Research Ltd · Beckenham · BR3 5JS · Tel 020 8650 7745 · Fax 020 8650 0768 · E-mail cbd@cbdresearch.com · www.cbdresearch.com

Institute of Financial Services   (ifs)   1879
NR   ifs House, 4-9 Burgate Lane, CANTERBURY, Kent, CT1 2XJ.
      (hq)
      01227 818609
      http://www.ifslearning.ac.uk
      Chief Exec: Gavin Shreeve
▲   Registered Charity
Br   72 local centres; 6 o'seas
○   *L, *P; education & training of financial services staff
●   Conf - Mtgs - ET - Exam - Res - Exhib - Comp - SG - Inf - Lib
M   42,000 i
¶   Financial World - 12.
      ifs News - 12.   Syllabus.   Catalogue.   AR.
      Publications list available.
      Note: The parent body of the ifs is the Chartered Institute of
      Bankers; the ifs develops & delivers qualifications for which
      the CIB acts as an assessing & awarding body

Institute for Fiscal Studies   (IFS)   1969
■   7 Ridgmount St, LONDON, WC1E 7AE.   (hq)
      020 7291 4800
      email mailbox@ifs.org.uk   http://www.ifs.org.uk
      Dir: Robert Chote
▲   Company Limited by Guarantee; Registered Charity
○   *Q; promotion of research & understanding of the economic &
      social implications of existing taxes & different fiscal systems
●   Conf - ET - Res - SG - Stat - Inf
M   600 i, 100 f, 100 org, UK / 100 i, 50 org, o'seas
¶   Fiscal Studies (Jnl) - 4; ftm, £237 nm.
      Reports & Commentaries - 15; ftm, c £40 each nm.
         Briefing Notes - 15;   NL - 4; Working Papers - 20;
            [last three publications online].

Institute of Fisheries Management   (IFM)   1969
■   22 Rushworth Ave, West Bridgford, NOTTINGHAM, NG2 7LF.
      (treas/p)
      0115-982 2317   fax 0115-982 6150
      email info@ifm.org.uk   http://www.ifm.org.uk
      Exec Sec: Valerie Holt
▲   Un-incorporated Society
Br   11
○   *L, *P; management of freshwater aquatic environment
●   Conf - Mtgs - ET - Exam - LG
<   is a constituent body of the Soc for the Envt
M   900 i, 5 f, 40 org, UK / 40 i, o'seas
¶   Fish - 4; ftm only.

Institute of Food Science & Technology   (IFST)   1964
NR   5 Cambridge Court, 210 Shepherds Bush Rd, LONDON,
      W6 7NJ.   (hq)
      020 7603 6316
      email info@ifst.org   http://www.ifst.org
      Chief Exec: Helen G Wild
▲   Company Limited by Guarantee; Registered Charity
Br   7
○   *L, *P; application of science & technology to every aspect of
      food
●   Conf - Mtgs - ET - Exam - VE - LG
<   Intl U of Food Science & Technology (IUFOST); UK Fedn for
      Food Science & Technology (UKFFOST); Parliamentary Food
      & Health Forum; Eur Food Law Assn (UK section); Science
      Coun; Foundation for Science & Technology
M   2,221 f, UK / 335 f, o'seas
¶   International Jnl of Food Science & Technology - 10;
      £21 (£13 online) m, £936 yr nm (UK).
      Food Science & Technology - 4; ftm, £96 yr nm.
      Keynote - 11; ftm.

Institute of Food Science & Technology of Ireland   1975
IRL   PO Box 10071, DUBLIN 2, Republic of Ireland.
      email ifsti@hotmail.com   http://www.ifsti.com
      Hon Sec: Dr Lisa O'Connor
○   *L

**Institute of Football Management & Administration   (IFMA)
1990**
NR   The Camkin Suite, 1 Pegasus House, Pegasus Court,
      Tachbrook Park, WARWICK, CV34 6LW.   (hq)
      01926 831556   fax 01926 429781
      email ifma@lmasecure.com
      http://www.leaguemanagers.com
      Chmn: Andy Daykin
▲   Registered Trade Union
○   *S; for all key staff in 92 FA Premier & Football League football
      clubs
●   Conf - Mtgs - ET - Exhib - SG - Inf
M   708 i
¶   Centre Circle - 4; free.

Institute of Fundraising   1983
■   12 Lawn Lane, Park Place, LONDON, SW8 1UD.   (hq)
      020 7840 1000   fax 020 7840 1001
      email info@institute-of-fundraising.org.uk
      http://www.institute-of-fundraising.org.uk
      Sec: Lindsay Boswell
▲   Registered Charity
○   *P; to advance, or promote, the efficiency of organisations
      established for charitable purposes throughout the UK; to
      promote higher standards of administration of fund-raising
      for charitable purposes
●   Conf - ET - Inf
M   [not stated]
¶   Update - 11; ftm only.   LM; m only.   Ybk; ftm.
      List of Consultants; ftm.   AR; free.

Institute of Geologists of Ireland
IRL   c/o Dept of Geology, University College Dublin, Belfield,
      DUBLIN 4, Republic of Ireland.
      353 (1) 716 2085   fax 353 (1) 283 7733
      email info@igi.ie   http://www.igi.ie
○   *P

Institute of Grocery Distribution   (IGD)   1909
NR   Grange Lane, Letchmore Heath, WATFORD, Herts,
      WD25 8GD.   (hq)
      01923 857141   fax 01923 852531
      email igd@igd.com   http://www.igd.com
      Chief Exec: Joanne Denney-Finch
○   *L, *P, *Q; supply chain management in the food and grocery
      industry
M   665 f

Institute of Groundsmanship   (IOG)   1934
NR   28 Stratford Office Village, Walker Avenue, Wolverton Mill East,
      MILTON KEYNES, Bucks, MK12 5TW.   (hq)
      01908 312511   fax 01908 311140
      email iog@iog.org   http://www.iog.org
      Chief Exec: Patrick Gosset
▲   Company Limited by Guarantee
Br   39
○   *P
●   Conf - Mtgs - ET - Exam - Res - Exhib - Inf - Lib - Empl
M   i & org
¶   The Groundsman - 12.

Institute of Group Analysis   (IGA)   1971
■   1 Daleham Gardens, LONDON, NW3 5BY.   (hq)
      020 7431 2693   fax 020 7431 7246
      email iga@igalondon.org.uk
      http://www.groupanalysis.org
      Chmn: Marcus Page
▲   Company Limited by Guarantee; Registered Charity
Br   8
○   *P; a teaching institution for group-analytic psychotherapy; to
      promote group analysis; to train in group analysis
Gp   Clinical section
●   Conf - Mtgs - ET - Res - SG - Lib
M   300 i
¶   Dialogue (NL) - 3;   AR - 1; both ftm only.

Institute of Guidance Counsellors (IGC) 1968
IRL 17 Herbert St, DUBLIN 2, Republic of Ireland.
      353 (1) 676 1975   fax 353 (1) 661 2551
      email igc@eircom.net   http://www.igc.ie
      PRO: M Gleeson
○   *P

Institute & Guild of Brewing
     since 2005 the **Institute of Brewing & Distilling**

Institute of Health Promotion & Education (IHPE) 1962
■ Oral Health & Development, University Dental Hospital, Higher
     Cambridge St, MANCHESTER, M15 6FH. (hsp)
     0161-275 6610   fax 0161-275 6299
     email anthony.blinkhorn@man.ac.uk
     http://www.ihpe.org.uk
     Hon Sec: Prof A S Blinkhorn
▲ Un-incorporated Society
○ *L; for all interested in health promotion & education
Gp Professional educators
M 600 i, 150 f, UK / 100 i, 50 f, o'seas
¶ Jnl - 4; ftm, £36 yr nm.

Institute of Health Record & Information Management (IHRIM) 1948
NR 141 Leander Drive, Castleton, ROCHDALE, Lancs,
     OL11 2XE. (hq)
     01706 868481   fax 01706 868481
     email ihrim@zen.co.uk   http://www.ihrim.co.uk
     Office Mgr: Gordon Nicholson
▲ Un-incorporated Society
○ *P; the promotion of excellence & professionalism in the
     management of health records & information to enable
     delivery of high quality health care professions
● Conf - ET - Exam - Exhib - SG - Inf
< Intl Fedn of Health Records Orgs (IFHRO); NHS Inf Authority
M 735 i, 20 f, UK / 50 i, o'seas
¶ Jnl - 4; ftm.

Institute of Healthcare Engineering & Estate Management (IHEEM) 1943
NR 2 Abingdon House, Cumberland Business Centre,
     Northumberland Rd, PORTSMOUTH, Hants, PO5 1DS. (hq)
     023 9282 3186
     http://www.iheem.org.uk
     Chief Exec: John Long
▲ Company Limited by Guarantee; Registered Charity
Br 14; Hong Kong, Ireland
○ *L, *P; for all those working in the healthcare engineering &
     estates field; the Institute is nominated by the Engineering
     Council
Gp Sterilisation, Architects; Diagnostic imaging section
● Conf - Mtgs - ET - Exhib - Lib
< Intl Hospital Fedn; Intl Fedn of Hospital Engg; Engg Coun
M 2,200 i, 60 f, UK / 150 i, 5 f, o'seas
¶ Health Estate Jnl - 10. Ybk. AR.
     Guide to Commissioning.

Institute of Healthcare Management (IHM) 1902
■ 18-21 Morley St, LONDON, SE1 7QZ. (hq)
     020 7620 1030   fax 020 7620 1040
     email enquiries@ihm.org.uk   http://www.ihm.org.uk
     Chief Exec: Sue Hodgetts,   Sec: Roger Morris
▲ Registered Charity
Br 12
○ *M, *N, *P; ' to support managers whose excellence in
     management contributes to excellence in healthcare; to
     improve standards in healthcare management'
Gp Armed forces; Estates & facilities management; Independent
     sector; Primary care
● Conf - Mtgs - ET - Exam - Res
M i
¶ Health Management - 6; ftm, £55-£70 nm.
✕ Institute of Health Care Management

Institute of Heraldic & Genealogical Studies (IHGS) 1961
■ 79-82 Northgate, CANTERBURY, Kent, CT1 1BA. (hq)
     01227 768664   fax 01227 765617
     email ihgs@ihgs.ac.uk   http://www.ihgs.ac.uk
     Principal: Cecil R Humphery-Smith
▲ Registered Charity
↻ *E, *P, *Q; to study the history & structure of the family
     genealogy, heraldry & their applications for historical
     research; family history research for genetical inherited
     diseases
● ET - Exam - Res - Lib
< Intl Confedn of Genealogy & Heraldry; Fedn of Family History
     Socs
M 240 i, UK / 30 i, o'seas
¶ Family History (Jnl) - 4; ftm, £15 yr nm.

Institute of Highway Incorporated Engineers (IHIE) 1965
■ De Morgan House, 58 Russell Square, LONDON,
     WC1B 4HS. (hq)
     020 7436 7487   fax 020 7436 7488
     email information2@ihie.org.uk   http://www.ihie.org.uk
     Sec: Miss J M Walker
▲ Company Limited by Guarantee
Br 15
○ *P; interests of engineers & technicians in landbased highways
     & transportation
● Conf - Mtgs - Exam - Exhib - Comp - VE
< Engg Coun; Construction Ind Coun
M 3,000 i, UK / 100 i, o'seas
¶ Highways [magazine].   AR - 1.

Institute of Historic Building Conservation (IHBC) 1981
■ Jubilee House, High St, TISBURY, Wilts, SP3 6HA. (hsp)
     01747 873133   fax 01747 871718
     http://www.ihbc.org.uk
     Sec: Dr Richard Morrice
○ *P; to promote the successful preservation & enhancement of
     the historic built environment in the UK
M c 1,750 i
¶ Context - 5; ftm, £50 yr nm.

Institute of Holistic Therapies 1976
■ Oakwood, Kirkdale Court, KIRKBYMOORSIDE, N Yorks,
     YO62 6HN. (hsp)
     01751 430626
     email laroche17@tiscali.co.k
     http://www.holisticdoctors.co.uk + hypnosistraining.co.uk
     Sec: Mrs Eileen Jones
▲ Un-incorporated Society
Br Internet based only
○ *P; 'to register all holistic therapists & to offer them malpractice
     insurance cover'
● ET - Exam - Exhib
< La Roche Intl Coll
M 275 i, UK / 220 i, o'seas

Institute of Home Inspectors (IHI) 2006
NR c/o Barnard Cottage, DUNCOTE, Northants, NN12 8AH.
     (hsp)
     http://www.ihi.org.uk
     Hon Sec: Anthony Douglas
▲ Company Limited by Guarantee
Br 20
○ *P; licensed home inspectors & those studying to be licensed
     home inspectors
M 6,000 i
¶ email NL.

© CBD Research Ltd · Beckenham · BR3 5JS · Tel 020 8650 7745 · Fax 020 8650 0768 · E-mail cbd@cbdresearch.com · www.cbdresearch.com

Institute of Home Safety   (IHS)   1976
NR   21 Tuckers Nook, Maxey, PETERBOROUGH, PE6 9EH.   (hsp)
 01778 344297
 http://www.instituteofhomesafety.co.uk
 Sec: Sheila Merrill
○   *E, *W; accident prevention in the home & its environs (inc
 outbuildings, gardens, ponds etc); to provide a forum & point
 of contact for the development, dissemination & exchange of
 ideas & information
●   Conf - Mtgs - ET - Exhib - Comp - Inf - LG - Organisation of
 campaigns etc on home safety & accident prevention
<   R Soc for Prevention of Accidents (RoSPA); Child Accident
 Prevention Trust (CAPT); London Home & Water Safety
 Coun (LHWSC); Inst of Safety & Public Protection (ISPP); Brit
 Safety Soc (BSS)
M   70 i
¶   NL - 4.   AR.

Institute of Horticulture   (IOH)   1985
■   9 Red Lion Court, LONDON, EC4A 3EF.   (hq)
 020 7936 5957   fax 020 7936 5958
 email ioh@horticulture.org.uk
 http://www.horticulture.org.uk
 Admin Mgr: Mary Porter
▲   Registered Charity
Br   8
○   *P; to promote the profession of horticulture
Gp   Advisory & research; Amenity horticulture; Commercial
 horticulture; Education
●   Conf - Mtgs - ET - Comp - Inf - VE - LG
M   1,600 i, 10 f, UK / 65 i, o'seas
¶   The Horticulturist (Jnl) - 4; ftm, £84 yr nm.
 Come Into Horticulture (careers booklet);
 Education & Training Courses in Horticulture;   AR.

Institute of Hospitality   1971
■   Trinity Court, 34 West St, SUTTON, Surrey, SM1 1SH.   (hq)
 020 8661 4900   fax 020 8661 4901
 http://www.instituteofhospitality.org
 Chief Exec: Philippe Rossiter
▲   Company Limited by Guarantee; Registered Charity
Br   20; Australia, Cyprus, Ghana, India, Malta, New Zealand, Sri
 Lanka, Zambia
○   *P; to promote & maintain the highest professional & ethical
 standards for management, education & training in the
 international hotel & catering industry
●   ET - Exam - Res - SG - Inf - Lib - LG
<   Eur Coun on Hotel, Restaurant & Institutional Educ
 (EuroCHRIE); Profl Assns Res Network (PARN); CBI; FAB;
 Coun for Hospitality Mgt Educ (CHME)
M   8.500 i, 5 f, 65 colleges, UK / 1,500 i, 'o;seas
¶   Hospitality - 4.   Hospitality Ybk - 1;   AR - 1;
 Management Guides - 4; all ftm.
✕   2007 Hotel & Catering International Management Association

Institute of Ideas
NR   Academy of Ideas, Signet House, 49-51 Farringdon Rd,
 LONDON, EC1M 3JP.
 020 7269 9220   fax 020 7269 9235
 email academy@instituteofideas.com
 http://www.instituteofideas.com

Institute of Imagination
NR   House of William Blake, 17 South Molton St, LONDON,
 W1K 5QT.
 020 7495 5654
 http://www.ioi.org.uk

Institute of Incorporated Public Accountants
IRL   Unit 2 Abbey Moat House, NAAS, Co Kildare, Republic of
 Ireland.
 353 (45) 895936   fax 353 (45) 895830
 email info@iipa.ie   http://www.iipa.ie
○   *P

Institute for Independent Business   (IIB)   1984
NR   Clarendon House, Bridle Path, WATFORD, Herts, WD17 1UB.
 (hq)
 01923 239543
 email info@iib.org.uk   http://www.iib.org.uk
 Principal: Linden P Dyason
▲   Company Limited by Guarantee; Registered Charity
Br   4; India, USA
○   *T; to provide practical advice to the independent business
 sector
Gp   Small to medium-sized businesses
●   Conf - Mtgs - ET - Exam - Res - SG - Expt - Inf - Support for
 experienced executives wishing to become management
 consultants
M   950 f, UK / 30 f, o'seas
¶   Independent Business Today - 4.

Institute of Indirect Taxation   (IIT)   1991
■   Suite G1, The Stables, Station Road West, OXTED, Surrey,
 RH8 9EE.   (hq)
 01883 730658   fax 01883 717778
 email enquiries@theiit.org.uk   http://www.theiit.org.uk
 Sec Gen: Terry Davies
▲   Company Limited by Guarantee
○   *P; to qualify, regulate & represent practitioners & research in
 VAT, customs, excise, stamp taxes, other indirect taxes
●   Conf - ET - Exam - LG - Lib - Mtgs
<   Academy of Experts
M   615 i, UK / 50 i, o'seas
¶   Indirect Tax Voice - 9; ftm.

Institute for Individual Psychology
 see **Adlerian Society (UK) & Institute for Individual
 Psychology**

Institute of Industrial Engineers   (IIE)
IRL   PO Box 790, Sandyford, DUBLIN 18, Republic of Ireland.
 353 (1) 294 3156   fax 353 (1) 294 3131
 email enquiries@iie.ie   http://www.iie.ie
 Hon Sec: Daniel Vaughan
○   *P

Institute of Information Security Professionals   (IISP)   2006
NR   83 Victoria St, LONDON, SW1H 0HW.
 0845 612 3828
 email info@instisp.com   http://www.instisp.com

Institute of Insurance Brokers   (IIB)
NR   Higham Business Centre, Midland Rd, HIGHAM FERRERS,
 Northants, NN10 8DW.   (hq)
 01933 410003   fax 01933 410020
 email inst.ins.brokers@iib-uk.com
 http://www.iib-uk.com
 Dir Gen: Andrew Paddick,   Sec: Barbara Bradshaw
▲   Company Limited by Guarantee
○   *P; for independent insurance broking businesses
●   Conf - Mtgs - ET - Exam - Res - Exhib - Comp - SG - Inf - Lib -
 LG
M   1,100 f

Institute of Internal Auditors - UK & Ireland   (IIA)
NR   13 Abbeville Mews, 88 Clapham Park Rd, LONDON, SW4 7BX.
 020 7498 0101
 email info@iia.org.uk   http://www.iia.org.uk
 Chief Exec: Mrs Gail Easterbrook
○   *P
M   i
¶   Internal Auditing & Business Risk - 12.
 Various other publications.

Institute of International Licensing Practitioners Ltd (IILP) 1969
- ■ 1 Samian Way, DORCHESTER-on-THAMES, Oxon, OX10 7JS. (asa)
  01865 340828   fax 01865 340828
  email enquiries@iilp.net   http://www.iilp.net
  Sec: James Hunt.   Chmn: Mike Kerr
- ▲ Company Limited by Guarantee
- ○ *P; assistance to companies, or individuals, to obtain the service of a qualified licensing practitioner; to set, promote & maintain high standards of professional practice amongst those engaged in licensing, technology transfer & commercialising invention; to promote the wider understanding of the value of licensing in international business as a marketing & business development tool
- ● Conf
- M i, f, org

Institute of International Marketing (IIM) 2008
- ■ PO Box 70, LONDON, E13 0UU.   (hq)
  0870 042 2072
  email info@iim-org.com   http://www.iim-org.com
  Dir Gen: C Oham
- Br Netherlands, Nigeria, South Africa, USA
- ○ *P; to promote & encourage all aspects of international marketing
- ● Conf - ET - Exam - Res - SG - VE - Seminars
- M 85 i, 3 f, UK / 718 i, 5 f, o'seas
  (Sub: £75 i)
- ¶ Jnl of International Marketing - 1; ftm.
  NL (email) - 4; ftm.   Membership Hbk.
  Dictionary of International Marketing (4th ed); £15 m, £20 nm.
  A Guide to Marketing in Europe.
  A Guide to Marketing in North America (4th ed) £10 m, £15 nm.
  Other books available.
- ✕ 2008 Association of International Marketing

Institute of International Trade of Ireland
- IRL 28 Merrion Sq, DUBLIN 2, Republic of Ireland.
  353 (1) 661 2182   fax 353 (1) 661 2315
  email iiti@irishexporters.ie   http://www.irishexporters.ie
  Dir: John F Whelan
- ○ *T

Institute of Inventors (II) 1964
- NR 19-23 Fosse Way, Ealing, LONDON, W13 0BZ.   (hq)
  020 8998 3540; 6372
  http://www.instituteofinventors.com
  Pres: Michael V Rodrigues
- ▲ Un-incorporated Society
- ○ *L
- Gp Sifting c'ee;
  Depts: Online database patent research, Patent drafting, CAD design development
- ● Exam - Res - Inf - LG - Patent searching - New invention design & development - Invention investor marriage
- M i & f
- ¶ New Invention List - 12.

Institute of IT Training
- NR Westwood House, Westwood Business Park, COVENTRY, Warks, CV4 8HS.   (hq)
  0845 006 8858
  Chief Exec: Colin Steed
- ▲ Company Limited by Guarantee
- ○ *P; for IT trainers
- ● ET
- M 3,500 i, UK / 250 i, o'seas

Institute for Jewish Policy Research (JPR) 1996
- NR 79 Wimpole St, LONDON, W1G 9RY.   (hq)
  020 7935 8266
  Exec Dir: Antony Lerman
- ▲ Registered Charity
- ○ *Q; 'an independent think tank which informs & influences policy, opinion & decision making on issues affecting Jewish life worldwide'
- ● Conf - Res - Inf - Development & dissemination of policy proposals - Promotion of public debate
- M i & org
- ¶ Patterns of Prejudice (Jnl) - 4.
  JPR Reports & Policy Papers.
  Antisemitism in the World Today; (Internet publication)

Institute of Leadership & Management (ILM) 1947
- NR 1 Giltspur St, LONDON, EC1A 9DD.   (hq)
  020 7294 2470
  http://www.i-l-m.com
  Chief Exec: Penny de Valk
- ▲ Company Limited by Guarantee; Registered Charity
- ○ *P; to improve leadership & management performance through a flexible range of learning & development solutions
- ● Conf - ET - Exam - Inf
- M 24,000 i
- ¶ Modern Management - 6.

Institute of Legal Cashiers & Administrators (ILCA) 1978
- ■ Marlowe House (2nd floor), 109 Station Rd, SIDCUP, Kent, DA15 7ET.   (hq)
  020 8302 2867   fax 020 8302 7481
  email info@ilca.org.uk   http://www.ilca.org.uk
  Exec Sec: Margaret Macdonald
- ○ *P; to promote the status of the legal cashier & administrator
- ● Conf - Mtgs - ET - Exam - Res - Exhib - Comp - Inf
- < Inst Legal Accountants Ireland
- M 3,000 i
- ¶ Legal Abacus - 6; ftm, £30 yr nm.

Institute of Legal Executives (ILEX) 1963
- ■ Kempston Manor, Kempston, BEDFORD, MK42 7AB.   (hq)
  01234 841000   fax 01234 853982
  email info@ilex.org.uk   http://www.ilex.org.uk
  Chief Exec: Mrs Diane Burleigh
- ▲ Un-incorporated Society
- Br 19; Bermuda, Gibraltar, Kenya
- ○ *P; for legal executives (lawyers employed by, or working for, solicitors in private practice, or employed as such in governmental, public, commercial or other departments or undertakings)
- Gp Lawyers; Press; Colleges; MP's
- ● Conf - Mtgs - Exam - Res - Exhib - Comp
- M 24,000 i
- ¶ Legal Executive Jnl - 12; ftm.
  AR; free.

Institute of Legal Secretaries & PAs (ILS) 1990
- NR 9 Unity St, BRISTOL, BS1 5HH.   (hq)
  0117-927 7007   fax 0117-929 3887
  email info@institutelegalsecretaries.com
  http://www.institutelegalsecretaries.com
  Chief Exec: Emma Stacey
- ▲ Un-incorporated Society
- ○ *P; to provide for the professional recognition of members by the quality of their qualifications, standard, skills & expertise; to further the knowledge of law & legal procedure
- Gp Legal: Secretaries, PAs, Receptionists
- ● Conf - ET - Exam - Res - Exhib - Inf - LG
- < Nat Assn of Licensed Paralegals
- M c 2,000 i
- ¶ Dedicated - 4; ftm only.

Institute of Leisure & Amenity Management
  in 2007 merged with the National Association for Sports Development to form the **Institute for Sport, Parks & Leisure**

© CBD Research Ltd · Beckenham · BR3 5JS · Tel 020 8650 7745 · Fax 020 8650 0768 · E-mail cbd@cbdresearch.com · www.cbdresearch.com

Institute of Leisure & Amenity Management Ireland Ltd   (ILAM)
IRL   The Old Barracks, Main St, CLANE, Co Kildare, Republic of
      Ireland.
      353 (45) 861201   fax 353 (45) 893195
      email info@ilam.ie   http://www.ilam.ie
      Chief Exec: Kilian Fisher
○   *P

Institute of Licensed Trade Stock Auditors   (ILTSA)   1953
NR   Brockwell Heights, Brockwell Lane Triangle, SOWERBY BRIDGE,
      HX6 3PQ.   (hsp)
      01422 833003   fax 01422 316641
      email dianeswift@iltsa.co.uk   http://www.iltsa.co.uk
▲   Company Limited by Guarantee
Br   300
○   *P; to support licensed trade stock auditors in the UK
●   Mtg (AGM) - ET - Exam
M   395 i
¶   The Stock Auditor - 6; ftm, £2 each nm.
      Taking Stock Book; £18.   LM - 1; free.

Institute of Linguists
      since 2005-06 the **Chartered Institute of Linguists**

Institute of Logistics & Transport
      since 2004 **Chartered Institute of Logistics & Transport in the
      UK**

**Institute of Machine Woodworking Technology Ltd
(IMWoodT)   1952**
■   St Keynes, Bowl Rd, CHARING, Kent, TN27 0HB.   (hsp)
      01233 713768   fax 01233 713768
      email imwoodt@tesco.net   http://www.imwoodt.org.uk
      Hon Sec: John Fryer
Br   4; 1
○   *E, *L; theory & practice of machine woodworking technology
Gp   Health & safety
●   Conf - Mtgs - ET - Exhib - Comp - Inf - VE
M   i, 1 f
¶   Woodworking Technology - 1; ftm.   AR; ftm only.

Institute of Maintenance & Building Management
      in April 2008 merged with the **Association of Building Engineers**

Institute of Management Consultancy
      in 2007 merged with the Institute of Business Advisers to form the
      Institute of Business Consulting

Institute of Management Consultants & Advisers   (IMCA)
IRL   19 Elgin Rd, Ballsbridge, DUBLIN 4, Republic of Ireland.
      353 (1) 634 9636
      email info@imci.ie   http://www.imci.ie
      Sec: Brian Flanagan
○   *P

**Institute for the Management of Information Systems   (IMIS)
1978**
NR   5 Kingfisher House, New Mill Rd, ORPINGTON, Kent,
      BR5 3QG.   (hq)
      0700 002 3456   fax 0700 002 3023
      email central@imis.org.uk   http://www.imis.org.uk
      Chief Exec: Ian M Rickwood
▲   Registered Charity
Br   6; Malta, Malaysia, Zambia, Zimbabwe
○   *P; to advance the interests of the management of information
      systems / information technology profession
Gp   Outsourcing; Women in Technology (WIT)
●   Conf - Mtgs - ET - Exam - LG
M   3,255 i, 40 f, UK / 7,411 i, 20 f, o'seas
¶   IMIS Jnl - 6; free.
      IT Skills Trend Report Summary; free.

Institute of Management Services   (IMS)   1978
NR   Brooke House, 24 Dam St, LICHFIELD, Staffs, WS13 6AB.   (hq)
      01543 266909
      http://www.ims-productivity.com
▲   Registered Charity
○   *P; productivity improvement; work study; O&M & related areas
M   4,000 i

Institute of Management Specialists   (IMS)   1971
■   Warwick Corner, 42 Warwick Rd, KENILWORTH, Warks,
      CV8 1HE.   (asa)
      01926 855498   fax 01926 513100
      email info@group-ims.com   http://www.group-ims.com
      Pres/Hon Sec: Prof H J Manners
○   *P; for those in industrial, business, commercial, professional,
      educational & technical fields, who provide a service to
      senior departmental management
<   Academy of Execs & Administrators; Academy of Multi-Skills;
      Inst of Manufacturing; Profl Business & Technical Mgt
M   [not stated]
¶   The Management Specialist (Jnl) - 3; £2 m, £7 nm.

Institute of Manufacturing   (IManf)   1978
■   Warwick Corner, 42 Warwick Rd, KENILWORTH, Warks,
      CV8 1HE.   (asa)
      01926 855498   fax 01926 513100
      email info@group-ims.com   http://www.group-ims.com
      Pres/Hon Sec: Prof H J Manners
○   *P; to develop recognition of the professional role of the
      manufacturer in industry
●   ET - Exam
<   Inst of Mgt Specialists; Profl Business & Technical Mgt
¶   Manufacturing (Jnl) - 1; £2 m, £7 nm.
      Manufacturing Management - 1; £2 m, £7 nm.

**Institute of Marine Engineering, Science & Technology
(IMarEST)   1889**
NR   80 Coleman St, LONDON, EC2R 5BJ.   (hq)
      020 7382 2600   fax 020 7382 2670
      email info@imarest.org   http://www.imarest.org
      Sec: Keith Read
▲   Registered Charity
Br   14; 33 o'seas
○   *L, *P; to promote the scientific development of marine
      engineering, science & technology: marine, offshore &
      subsea engineering, naval architecture & ship construction,
      marine science & marine technology
Gp   Marine, offshore & subsea engineering; Naval architecture &
      ship construction; Marine science & technology
●   Conf - Mtgs - ET - Exhib - Inf - Lib - LG
<   Engg Coun (EC); Intl Maritime Org (IMO); W Eur Confedn of
      Maritime Technology Societies (WEMT)
M   10,073 i, UK / 6,067 i, o'seas
¶   Marine Engineers Review - 10.
      Jnl of Offshore Technology - 6.
      Maritime IT & Electronics - 6.
      Transactions (after each technical meeting).
      IMarEST News - 12.   AR.
      Technical publications & CD ROMs - catalogue available.
      Member prices on request.

Institute of Master Tutors of Driving   (IMTD)   1957
■   12 Queensway, Poynton, STOCKPORT, Cheshire, SK12 1JG.
      (hsp)
      01625 872708
      email rogersimtd@btinternet.com   http://www.imtd.org.uk
      Sec: Bernard E Rogers
▲   Un-incorporated Society
○   *P; to represent trainers of drivers, & drivers of large goods
      vehicles, motorcyclists & road safety teachers
●   Conf - Mtgs - ET - Res - SG - Inf - LG
M   70 i, UK / 10 i, o'seas
      (Sub: £100 UK / £50 o'seas)
¶   Teaching Deaf People to Drive; free.

Institute of Masters of Wine   (IMW)   1953

NR   Mapfre House, 2-3 Philpot Lane, LONDON, EC3M 8AN.   (hq)
     020 7621 2830   fax 020 7929 2302
     email enquiries@mastersofwine.org
     http://www.mastersofwine.org
     Exec Dir: Jane Carr
Br   Australia, USA
○   *P; to promote the attainment & maintenance of high standards
     of technical knowledge & achievement by those making their
     livelihood in the wine & spirit trade
M   229 i
¶   Jnl of Wine Research - 3.   NL - 12.   LM - 1.

Institute of Materials, Minerals & Mining   (IOM3)   1869

■   1 Carlton House Terrace, LONDON, SW1Y 5DB.   (hq)
     020 7451 7300   fax 020 7839 1702
     email admin@iom3.org   http://www.iom3.org
     Chief Exec: Dr B A Rickinson
▲   Registered Charity
Br   4
○   *L, *P; the professional body for all involved in the field of
     materials, minerals & mining; to promote the science & study
     of all aspects of the science, technology & use of materials &
     minerals
Gp   Materials divisions:
        The Ceramics Society (includes the
           International Clay Technology Association);
        The British Composites Society;
        Light Metals Division;
        The Polymer Society;
        The Iron & Steel Society;
        Materials Science & Technology Division;
     Minerals & Mining divisions:
        International Mining & Minerals Association
           represents 4 resources divisions;
     Applications divisions:
        Automotive Division;
        Biomedical Applications Division
        Casting Division
        Electronic applications Division
        IOP: The Packaging Society
        Surface Engineering Division:
           Corrosion Committee
           Society for Adhesion & Adhesives;
     Multidisciplinary Groups
●   Conf - Mtgs - ET - Exam - Exhib - Comp - SG - Stat - Inf - Lib -
     VE - Empl
<   Fedn of Eur Materials Socs
M   i & f
¶   Materials World - 12; ftm, £55 yr nm.
     The Packaging Professional - 6; ftm, £40 yr nm.
     Clay Technology - 6; ftm, £35 yr nm.   AR - 1; free.
×   2006 Institute of Packaging
            Institute of Clay Technology

Institute of Mathematics & its Applications   (IMA)   1964

■   Catherine Richards House, 16 Nelson St, SOUTHEND-on-SEA,
     Essex, SS1 1EF.   (hq)
     01702 354020   fax 01702 354111
     email post@ima.org.uk   http://www.ima.org.uk
     Exec Dir: David Youdan
▲   Registered Charity
Br   6
○   *E, *L, *P; for qualified & practising mathematicians; to
     promote mathematics in industry, business, the public sector,
     education & research
Gp   Computational fluid dynamics; Computational science &
        engineering education; Environment; Numerical analysis;
        Management
●   Conf - Mtgs - Comp - LG
<   Eur Mathematical Soc; Eur Mechanics Soc; Coun of
        Mathematical Sciences
M   4,400 i, UK / 400 i, o'seas
¶   Mathematics Today - 6; ftm, £90 yr nm.
     IMA Jnl of Applied Mathematics.
     IMA Jnl of Numerical Analysis.
     Mathematical Medicine & Biology: a Jnl of the IMA.
     IMA Jnl of Mathematical Control & Information.
     IMA Jnl of Management Mathematics.
     Teaching Mathematics & its Applications: an international Jnl of
        the IMA.
     [prices vary with print &/or online access & discounts for the
        number taken].

Institute of Maxillofacial Prosthetists & Technologists   (IMPT) 1962

NR   c/o M J Pilley, Prosthesis Clinic, Leicester Royal Infirmary,
     LEICESTER, LE1 5WW.   (hsb)
     Contact: Mark Townend
▲   Company Limited by Guarantee; Registered Charity
○   *L, *M, *P; to establish, oversee & maintain the study & science
        of maxillofacial prosthetics & technology for the benefit of
        patients requiring prosthetic rehabilitation for trauma, burns,
        cancer, congenital deformity etc
●   Conf - Mtgs - ET - Exam - Res - SG - Lib - LG
M   i

Institute of Measurement & Control   (InstMC)   1944

■   87 Gower St, LONDON, WC1E 6AF.   (hq)
     020 7387 4949
     email ceo@instmc.org.uk   http://www.instmc.org.uk
     Sec: P J Martindale
▲   Registered Charity
Br   20; Hong Kong
○   *P; to promote for the public benefit the general advancement
        & application of the science & practice of measurement &
        control technology
Gp   Aviation; Measurement science & technology; Systems & control
        technology; Systems & management; Safety; Standards;
        Weighing
●   Conf - Mtgs - ET - Exhib - LG
<   Intl Measurement Confedn (IMEKO); UK Automatic Control
        Coun (UKAC); Foundation for Science & Technology
M   3,000 i, 130 f, UK / 400 i, o'seas
¶   Transactions - 7.   Measurement & Control - 10.
     Interface (NL) - 2.   Ybk.

© CBD Research Ltd · Beckenham · BR3 5JS · Tel 020 8650 7745 · Fax 020 8650 0768 · E-mail cbd@cbdresearch.com · www.cbdresearch.com

Institute of Medical Illustrators   (IMI)   1968
- ■ Medical Illustration Dept, St Lukes Hospital, Little Horton Lane, BRADFORD, W Yorks, BD5 0NA.   (hsb)
01274 365325   fax 01274 365661
email carol.fleming@bradfordhospital.nhs.uk
http://www.imi.org.uk
Hon Sec: Carol M Fleming
- ▲ Company Limited by Guarantee; Registered Charity
- ○ *T, *P; to promote the role of the medical illustrator as a professional member of a multi-skilled team offering clinical illustrative & communication services for the benefit of patient & client
- Gp Medical: Photographers, Artists, Videographers, Graphic designers, Multi-media specialists
- ● Conf - Mtgs - ET - Exhib - Comp - LG
- < Coun for the Accreditation of Medical Illustration Practitioners (CAMP); Fedn of Healthcare Science (FHCS)
- M 370 i, 25 f, UK / 25 i, o'seas
(Sub: £110 i, £252 f)
- ¶ Jnl of Visual Communication in Medicine (Vision) - 4; ftm, 580 nm.
IMI News - 4; ftm only.

Institute of Metal Finishing   (IMF)   1925
- NR Exeter House, 48 Holloway Head, BIRMINGHAM, B1 1NQ. (hq)
0121-622 7387   fax 0121-666 6316
email exeterhouse@instituteofmetalfinishing.org
http://www.uk-finishing.org.uk
Business Devt Mgr: Ken Hoare
- ▲ Registered Charity
- Br 8
- ○ *L; theory & practice of all aspects of metal finishing
- Gp Aluminium; Organic; Printed circuit; Electroforming
- ● Conf - Mtgs - ET - Exam - Exhib - SG - Inf - Lib - VE
- M 1,200 i, 62 f, UK / 345 i, 3 f, o'seas
- ¶ Transactions - 6.

Institute of Money Advisers   2006
- ■ Stringer House, 34 Lupton St, Hunslet, LEEDS, W Yorks, LS10 2QW.   (hq)
0113-270 8444   fax 0113-270 2111
http://www.i-m-a.org.uk
Admin: Carole Robertson
- ▲ Registered Charity
- ○ *P, *W; for money advisers (ie those who advise debtors); to provide a range of services
- ● Conf - Mtgs - ET - Exhib - Stat - Inf - LG
- < NCVO; ASA
- M 600 i
- ¶ Quarterly Account - 4; ftm, £30 nm.   AR - 1; ftm only.
- × 2005 Money Advice Association

Institute of the Motor Industry (Inc)   (IMI)   1920
- ■ Fanshaws, Brickendon, HERTFORD, SG13 8PQ.   (hq)
01992 511521   fax 01992 511548
email imi@motor.org.uk   http://www.motor.org.uk
Chief Exec: Sarah Sillars
Dir Marketing: N C Beaven
- ▲ Company Limited by Guarantee
- Br Australia, Malaysia
- ○ *P
- ● Conf - Mtgs - ET - Exam - Res - Stat - Inf
- M 25,160 i, UK / 3,100 i, o'seas
- ¶ Motor Industry Magazine - 10; ftm, £4 nm.

Institute of Musical Instrument Technology   (IMIT)   1961
- NR 11 Kendall Avenue South, SOUTH CROYDON, Surrey, CR2 0QR.   (hsp)
http://www.imit.org.uk
Hon Sec: Malcolm Dalton
- ▲ Company Limited by Guarantee
- ○ *L, *P; for those engaged in musical instrument design, manufacture, repair or education
- ● Conf - Mtgs - Exam - Lib - VE
- M 215 i, UK / 5 i, o'seas
- ¶ Jnl - c 1;   Soundings - 4;   LM - 1; all ftm.

Institute for Numerical Computation & Analysis
styles itself **INCA - Institute for Numerical Computation & Analysis**

Institute of Operations Management   (IOM)   1969
- NR Earlstrees Court, Earlstrees Rd, CORBY, Northants, NN17 4AX.   (hq)
01536 7401056   fax 01536 7401016
email iom@iomnet.org.uk   http://www.iomnet.org.uk
Chief Exec: J D Tayler
- ▲ Company Limited by Guarantee; Registered Charity
- Br 10
- ○ *P; operations supply chain & production management in manufacturing & service industries
- Gp Special interest: 1) Pharmaceutical, toiletries & chemicals; 2) Advanced planning & scheduling; 3) Lean & Agile; 4) Product support & services; 5) Retail; 6) Health
- ● Conf - Mtgs - ET - Exam - Inf - Lib - VE - Qualification awarding body
- M 4,000 i, 15 f, UK / 100 i, o'seas
- ¶ Control - 8.

Institute for Optimum Nutrition   (ION)   1984
- ■ Avalon House, 72 Lower Mortlake Rd, RICHMOND, Surrey, TW9 2JY.   (hq)
0870 979 1122
http://www.ion.ac.uk
- ▲ Registered Charity
- ○ *K; to help the public achieve optimum nutrition & optimum health through an education programme &/or one-to-one consultations for advanced assessment of personal nutrition needs
- ● Conf - ET - Exam - Res - Exhib - Inf - Lib - Courses
- M 3,700 i
- ¶ Optimum Nutrition - 4.
Specialised magazine on diet & health; ftm.

Institute for Outdoor Learning   (IOL)   1970
- NR The Barn, Plumpton Old Hall, Plumpton, PENRITH, Cumbria, CA11 7YE.   (hq)
01768 885800   fax 01768 885801
email institute@outdoor-learning.org
http://www.outdoor-learning.org
Managing Dir: Karen J Brush
- ▲ Registered Charity
- Br regional groups
- ○ *P; to support, develop & promote learning through outdoor experiences
- Gp Development training; Research forum
- ● Conf - Mtgs - ET - Res - Exhib - SG - Stat - Inf - Lib - LG
- < CCPR; Engl Outdoor Coun; SPRITO
- M 1,100 i, 140 f, 60 org, UK / 36 i, 10 f, 3 org, o'seas
- ¶ Jnl of Adventure Education & Outdoor Learning - 2; £22 m, £25 nm.
Horizons Magazine - 4; £17.65 m, £26 nm.
NL - 12; ftm only.
Outdoor Sourcebook - 1; £8 95 m, £9.95 nm.
Guide to Careers in Outdoor Learning - 1; £8 m, £9 nm.

Institute of Packaging
since 2005 IOP: The Packaging Society, a group of the **Institute of Materials, Minerals & Mining**

Institute of Paper Conservation
in 2005 merged with the Care of Collections Forum, Photographic Materials Conservation Group, Scottish Society for Conservation & Restoration & United Kingdom Institute for Conservation of Historic & Artistic Works to form the **Institute of Conservation**

Institute of Paper, Printing & Publishing International 1992

■ Runnymede Malthouse, off Hummer Rd, EGHAM, Surrey, TW20 9BD. (hq)
0870 330 8625   fax 0870 330 8615
http://www.ip3.org.uk
Dir Gen: David Pryke
○ *P; for those employed in, or closely associated with, the paper industry
● Conf - Mtgs - ET - Exam - Inf - Lib - VE
M i
¶ NL - 4; ftm only.
Various other publications - details on request.

Institute of Paralegal Training (ILT) 1976

NR Berkeley Square Hosue (2nd floor), Berkeley Sq, LNDON, W1J 6BD. (hq)
020 887 1420
Sec Gen: A Y Ibberson
○ *P; 'for persons of education, ability & experience who desire to qualify as legal secretaries &/or administrators & to secure professional status'
● ET - Exam - Inf - Examination Board for Legal Secretaries
M i
¶ Examination Papers.

Institute of Patentees & Inventors (IPI) 1919

NR PO Box 39296, LONDON, SE3 7WH. (hq)
0871 226 2091   fax 020 8293 5920
email enquiries@invent.org.uk
http://www.invent.org.uk
▲ Company Limited by Guarantee
○ *L; assistance & advice to inventors on protection & commercialising of inventions, encouragement of inventive talent & industrial innovation
● Mtgs - ET - Exhib - Inf
< Intl Fedn Inventors' Assns (IFIA)
M 830 i, 12 f, UK / 28 i, o'seas
¶ Future & the Inventor - 4; ftm.

Institute of Payroll & Pensions Management
since September 2006 the **Institute of Payroll Professionals**

Institute of Payroll Professionals (IPP) 1985

■ Shelly House, Farmhouse Way, Monkspath, SOLIHULL, W Midlands, B90 4EH. (hq)
0121-712 1000   fax 0121-712 1001
email info@payrollprofession.org
http://www.payrollprofession.org
Chief Exec: Lindsay Melvin
▲ Company Limited by Guarantee
○ *P
Gp IPP Consult; Representations to government by the Pay & Policy Team
● Conf - Mtgs - ET - Exam - Res - Exhib - SG - LG - Advisory service for members
M 5,000 i, UK / 300 i, o'seas
(Sub: £116 UK / £142 o'seas)
¶ Payroll Professional - 10; ftm, £100 nm.
× 2006 (Sept) Institute of Payroll & Pensions Management

Institute of Physics (IoP) 1919

NR 76 Portland Place, LONDON, W1B 1NT. (hq)
020 7470 4800   fax 020 7470 4848
email physics@iop.org   http://www.iop.org
Chief Exec: Julia King
▲ Registered Charity
Br 13
○ *L, *P; advancement of knowledge of physics, pure & applied, & the elevation of the profession of physicist
Gp 44 specialist subject groups; 4 professional groups
● Conf - Mtgs - ET - Stat - LG
M i
¶ Jnl of Physics:
A Mathematical & General Physics - 24.
B Atomic, Molecular & Optical Physics - 24.
C Condensed Matter - 51.
D Applied Physics - 12.
G Nuclear & Particle Physics - 12.
Publications list on website.

Institute of Physics & Engineering in Medicine (IPEM) 1982

NR Fairmount House, 230 Tadcaster Rd, YORK, YO24 1ES. (hq)
01904 610821
http://www.ipem.ac.uk
Gen Sec: R W Neilson
○ *L; advancement of physics & allied physical sciences applied to medicine & biology

Institute of Piping (InstP) 1960

NR 16-24 Otago St, GLASGOW, G12 8JH. (hq)
0141-334 3587   fax 0141-587 6068
Hon Sec: Robert Wallace
○ *D; examination & certification of pipers

Institute of Place Management (IPM) 2008

NR 1 Queen Anne's Gate, LONDON, SW1H 9BT.
020 7227 3593
http://www.placemanagement.org
○ to support people committed to developing, managing and making places better

Institute of Plumbing & Heating Engineering (IPHE) 1906

NR 64 Station Lane, HORNCHURCH, Essex, RM12 6NB. (hq)
01708 472791
▲ Company Limited by Guarantee; Registered Charity
○ *L, *P, *T; 'to advance the science & practice of plumbing & heating engineering in the public interest'
M i & f
× 2004 (June) Institute of Plumbing

Institute of Practitioners in Advertising (IPA) 1917

■ 44 Belgrave Sq, LONDON, SW1X 8QS. (hq)
020 7235 7020   fax 020 7245 9904
email info@ipa.co.uk   http://www.ipa.co.uk
Sec: Geoffrey Russell
▲ Company Limited by Guarantee
Br 2
○ *P, *T; the professional & trade organisation for UK advertising & marketing agencies
● Conf - Mtgs - ET - Res - Exhib - Stat - Inf - Lib - Empl - LG
< Eur Assn of Communications Agencies
M 272 f
¶ see website

Institute of Professional Auctioneers & Valuers

IRL 129 Lower Baggot St, DUBLIN 2, Republic of Ireland.
353 (1) 678 5685   fax 353 (1) 676 2890
email info@ipav.ie   http://www.ipav.ie
Chief Exec: Fintam McNamara
○ *P
M c 700

© CBD Research Ltd · Beckenham · BR3 5JS · Tel 020 8650 7745 · Fax 020 8650 0768 · E-mail cbd@cbdresearch.com · www.cbdresearch.com

Institute of Professional Designers   (IPD)   1963
NR   Piccotts End Farm, 117 Piccotts End Rd, HEMEL HEMPSTEAD,
        Herts, HP1 3AU.   (hq)
        01442 245513
        Pres/Sec: Gerald Wiedman
▲   Un-incorporated Society
○   *A, *P; environmental design incl architecture, interior design &
        website design
Gp   Interior designers; Architects; Landscape architects; Graphic
        designers; Designers
●   Inf
M   250 i, UK / 200 i, o'seas
¶   Calendar - 1; free.

Institute of Professional Goldsmiths   (IPG)   1984
■   PO Box 668, RICKMANSWORTH, Herts, WD3 0EQ.   (admin)
        020 3004 9806   fax 07092 882157
        email info@ipgold.org.uk   http://www.ipgold.org.uk
        Admin Sec: Emma Lister
○   *P; to establish & maintain the highest standards of
        craftsmanship
●   Mtgs - VE
M   i

Institute of Professional Investigators Ltd   (IPI)   1976
NR   Runnymede Malthouse, off Hummer Rd, EGHAM, Surrey,
        TW20 9BD.   (hq)
        0870 330 8622   fax 0870 330 8612
        http://www.ipi.org.uk
○   *P
M   i
        no further information supplied

Institute of Professional Sales
        in 2004 merged with the **Chartered Institute of Marketing**

Institute of Professional Soil Scientists   (IPSS)   1991
NR   Macaulay Land Use Research Institute, Craigiebuckler,
        ABERDEEN, AB15 8QH.
        01224 318611   fax 01224 208065
        http://www.soilscientist.org
        Sec: J H Gauld
○   to promote and enhance the status of soil science and allied
        disciplines

Institute of Professional Sport
        since 2007 **Professional Players Federation**

Institute of Professional Willwriters   (IPW)   1991
■   Trinity Point, New Rd, HALESOWEN, W Midlands, B63 3HY.
        (hq)
        0845 644 2042   fax 0845 644 2043
        email office@ipw.org.uk   http://www.ipw.org.uk
        Chmn: Paul Sharpe
▲   Un-incorporated Association
○   *P; for individuals & organisations who specialise in will-writing
●   Conf - ET - Exam
<   Fedn of Small Businesses
M   500 i, UK / 2 i, o'seas
¶   IPW Jnl - 12; ftm.

Institute of Psychoanalysis   1924
■   Byron House, 112A Shirland Rd, LONDON, W9 2EQ.   (hq)
        020 7563 5000   fax 020 7563 5001
        http://www.psychoanalysis.org.uk
        Chief Exec: N M Hall
▲   Company Limited by Guarantee; Registered Charity
○   *L; the theory & practice of Freudian psychoanalytic treatment
Gp   British Psycho-Analytical Society; London Clinic of Psycho-
        Analysis
●   Conf - Mtgs - ET - Exam - SG - Inf - Lib - Empl - Clinic
<   Intl Psychoanalytical Assn; Eur Psychoanalytical Fedn
M   352 i, UK / 97 i, o'seas
¶   International Jnl of Psychoanalysis - 6.   AR.

Institute of Public Administration   (IPA)   1957
IRL   57-61 Lansdowne Rd, DUBLIN 4, Republic of Ireland.   (hq)
        353 (1) 240 3600   fax 353 (1) 668 9135
        email information@ipa.ie   http://www.ipa.ie
        Dir Gen: John Cullen,
○   *P; Irish public sector management development agency
●   ET - Lib - Res
¶   Publications list available

Institute of Public Loss Assessors   (IPLA)   1965
NR   c/o Henry Dony Associates, 9-10 Ye Corner, Bushey,
        WATFORD, Herts, WD19 4BS.   (hsb)
        01923 225201
        http://www.lossassessors.org.uk
▲   Company Limited by Guarantee
○   *P; for all qualified persons who prepare on behalf of public &
        corporate bodies claims arising from insured losses, statutory
        claims, malicious claims & third party claims
●   Conf - Mtgs - Inf
M   200 i, UK / 10 i, o'seas

Institute of Public Relations
        since 2005 the **Chartered Institute of Public Relations**

Institute of Public Rights of Way Management   (IPROW)
■   PO Box 78, SKIPTON, N Yorks, BD23 4UP.   (mail/address)
        07000 782318
        email iprow@iprow.co.uk   http://www.iprow.co.uk
        Exec Offr: Mrs L S Smith
▲   Un-incorporated Society
○   *P; for all working with public rights of way
●   Conf - ET - Inf - LG
M   360 i
¶   Waymark - 4; ftm only.
×   2007 Institute of Public Rights of Way Officers

Institute of Public Sector Management   (IPSM)   1997
NR   45 Cherry Tree Rd, AXMINSTER, Devon, EX13 5GG.   (hq)
        01297 35423
        email info@ipsm.org.uk   http://www.ipsm.org.uk
        Hon Sec: Derek Wolfe
▲   Company Limited by Guarantee
○   *P; for managers working in the public services, voluntary
        bodies & community enterprises
Gp   Risk management; Balanced scorecard
●   Conf - ET - Res - Inf - LG
M   300 i
¶   Topics - 4; ftm only.

**Institute of Qualified Professional Secretaries Ltd   (IQPS)
1957**
■   24-28 St Leonards Rd (Suite 464), WINDSOR, Berks,
        SL4 3BB.   (hq)
        0844 800 0182   fax 01753 775798
        email office@iqps.org   http://www.iqps.org
        Mem Devt Mgr: Jackie Wood
▲   Company Limited by Guarantee
Br   11
○   *P; establishment of status of qualified secretaries &
        administrators within the professions, commerce, industry &
        colleges
●   Conf - Mtgs - ET - Exhib - Comp - Inf
<   Intl Assn Admin Profls (US)
M   1,500 i, UK / 50 i, o'seas
¶   Career Secretary (Jnl) - 4; ftm, £60 yr nm.

Institute of Quality Assurance
        since 2006 the **Chartered Quality Institute**

Institute of Quarrying (IQ) 1917
■ 7 Regent St, NOTTINGHAM, NG1 5BS.   (hq)
    0115-945 3880   fax 0115-948 4035
    email mail@quarrying.org   http://www.quarrying.org
    Sec: Lyn Bryden
▲ Company Limited by Guarantee; Registered Charity
Br 13; Australia, Malaysia, New Zealand, Hong Kong, South
    Africa,
○ *P; to improve the standards of business, technical &
    environmental performance in quarrying
● Conf - Mtgs - ET - Exam - VE
M 2,850 i, UK / 2,500 i, o'seas
¶ Quarry Management - 12.

Institute of Race Relations (IRR) 1958
NR 2-6 Leeke St, LONDON, WC1X 9HS.   (hq)
    020 7837 0041
    email info@irr.org.uk   http://www.irr.org.uk
▲ Company Limited by Guarantee; Registered Charity
○ *Q; promotion of research, making available information &
    advice on proposals concerned with race relations & racial
    justice in Britain & internationally
M i

Institute of Refractories Engineers (IRE) 1961
NR Joan Royd Cottage, Penistone, SHEFFIELD, S Yorks, S36 9DA.
    (sp)
    01226 762578   fax 01226 762673
    email alanhey@ireng.org   http://www.ireng.org
    Sec & Treas: Alan Hey
▲ Un-incorporated Society
Br 9; Australia, South Africa
○ *P; promotion of refractories engineering & technology - high
    temperature materials required in: iron & steel, cement,
    chemical & petrochemical, glass, incineration, power,
    ceramics & domestic uses
● Conf - Mtgs - ET - Inf - Assessment Centre (NVQs in refractories
    installation)
< Inst of Materials; Soc Glass Technology; Inst of Brit Foundrymen
M c 600 i, UK / c 420 i, o'seas
¶ Refractories Engineer - 6.

Institute of Refrigeration (IoR) 1899
NR Kelvin House, 76 Mill Lane, CARSHALTON, Surrey, SM5 2JR.
    (hq)
    020 8647 7033   fax 020 8773 0165
    email ior@ior.org.uk   http://www.ior.org.uk
    Sec: Miriam Rodway
▲ Registered Charity
Br 8
○ *L, *P; to advance refrigeration standards & services
Gp Service engineers' section; Intl Refrigeration C'ee
● Mtgs - ET - Inf
< Intl Inst Refrigeration; Amer Soc Heating Refrigerating Air
    Conditioning Engrs
M 1,900 i, UK / 200 i, o'seas
¶ Proceedings - 1.   NL.

Institute of Registration Agents & Dealers (MIRAD) 1977
■ PO Box 333, SOUTHPORT, Merseyside, PR9 7GW.   (hsb)
    01704 320000   fax 01704 322222
    email enquiries@mirad.co.uk   http://www.mirad.co.uk
    Hon Sec: Ordan Heaton
○ *T; dealers in vehicle registration number plates
● Mtgs - Res - Exhib - Comp - Inf - LG
M 52 f
    (Sub: £184)

Institute of Remedial Treatment Surveyors
    since 2005 **Institute of Specialist Surveyors & Engineers**

Institute of Residential Property Management (IRPM) 2002
■ 178 Battersea Park Rd, LONDON, SW11 4ND.   (secretariat)
    020 7622 5092   fax 020 7498 6153
    email info@irpm.org.uk   http://www.irpm.org.uk
    Contact: The Executive Secretary
▲ Un-incorporated Society
○ *P; 'founded as a means of delivering a portable professional
    qualification in residential property management to
    individuals working in the sector, & one which would be
    accepted by all those operating within it'
● Exam
< Sponsors: Assn Residential Managing Agents (ARMA), Assn
    Retirement Housing Mgrs(ARHM); Property Mgrs Assn
    Scotland (PMAS)
M 688 i
¶ Members' NL - 3; ftm only.
    [LM on website].

Institute of Revenues, Rating & Valuation (IRRV) 1882
NR 41 Doughty St, LONDON, WC1N 2LF.   (hq)
    020 7831 3505
○ *P; rating & local revenues administration; valuation for rating
    & general purposes; valuation appeals
M i

Institute of Risk Management (IRM) 1986
■ Lloyd's Avenue House, 6 Lloyd's Ave, LONDON, EC3N 3AX.
    (hq)
    020 7709 9808   fax 020 7709 0716
    email enquiries@theirm.org   http://www.theirm.org
    Chief Exec Officer: Steve Fowler
▲ Company Limited by Guarantee
○ *P; 'the world's leading provider of professional risk
    management education'
Gp Central government; Charities; Financial services enterprise
    risk; Innovation, value creation & opportunity; Legal risk; Loss
    management; Operational risk; People, communication &
    behaviour; PPP/PFI; Risk in information systems & e-business;
    Strategic risk management; Transport & logistics
● Conf - Mtgs - ET - Exam - Exhib - SG - Lib
< Intl Fedn of Risk Mgt Assns (IFRIMA)
M 2,000 i, UK / 500 i, o'seas
¶ InfoRM - 6;   InfoRm e-supplement; both ftm only.
    AR - 1; free.

Institute of Road Safety Officers Ltd (IRSO) 1971
NR Pin Point, Rosslyn Crescent, HARROW, Middx, HA1 2SU.   (hq)
    0870 010 4442
    email irso@dbda.co.uk   http://www.irso.org.uk
    Hon Sec: Mrs Kathy Saunders
▲ Company Limited by Guarantee
Br 13
○ *P; to receive, analyse & disseminate information to members
    relating to road safety education, training & publicity
    programmes
● Conf - Mtgs - ET - Exam - Exhib - LG
< Parliamentary Advisory Coun on Transport Safety
M 400 i
¶ InRoads (Jnl) - 4; ftm, £50 nm.   AR; free.

Institute of Road Transport Engineers
    a sector of the **Society of Operations Engineers**

Institute of Roofing (IoR) 1981
NR Roofing House, 31 Worship St, LONDON, EC2A 2DX.   (hq)
    020 7448 3194   fax 020 7448 3195
    email info@instituteofroofing.org.uk
    http://www.instituteofroofing.org
    Chmn: Mike Harris
▲ Company Limited by Guarantee
○ *P; for individuals working in the roofing industry
● Conf - Mtgs - ET - Exam
M 1,086 i, UK / 3 i, o'seas
¶ IoR Bulletin (NL) - 4; ftm only.

© CBD Research Ltd · Beckenham · BR3 5JS · Tel 020 8650 7745 · Fax 020 8650 0768 · E-mail cbd@cbdresearch.com · www.cbdresearch.com

Institute of Safety in Technology & Research   (ISTR)   1981
NR   Bocyde, Weston Rd - Loxton, AXBRIDGE, N Somerset,
       BS26 2XD.   (mem/sb)
       01934 750915
       Mem Sec: M A Cheshire
O   *P; for safety professionals working in organisations engaged in
       research activities
●   Conf - Mtgs
M   204 i, UK / 1 i, o'seas
¶   ISTR Bulletin - 3;   Ybk; both ftm only.

Institute of Sales & Marketing Management   (ISMM)   1966
■   Harrier Court, LOWER WOODSIDE, Beds, LU1 4DQ.   (hq)
       01582 840001   fax 01582 849142
       email sales@ismm.co.uk   http://www.ismm.co.uk
       Chmn: Sheila Watson-Challis
▲   Company Limited by Guarantee
O   *P; to represent sales people & companies with a sales force
●   Conf - Mtgs - ET - Exam - Res - Government accredited
       awarding body for sales qualifications
M   [not divulged]
¶   Winning Edge - 10; ftm, £95 yr nm.

Institute of Sales Promotion Ltd   (ISP)   1933
NR   Arena House, 66-68 Pentonville Rd, LONDON, N1 9HS.   (hq)
       020 7837 5340   fax 020 7837 5326
       email enquiries@isp.org.uk   http://www.isp.org.uk
       Dir-Gen: Edwin Mutton
▲   Company Limited by Guarantee
O   *P; to promote the promotional marketing industry in the UK
Gp   Legal advisory service; Coupon c'ee; Education; Promoters
●   Conf - Mtgs - ET - Exam - Res - Exhib - Stat - Inf - Lib - LG
<   Eur Promotional Marketing Alliance; Eur Assn of
       Communication Agencies; CBI; Advertising Assn
M   850 i, 250 f
¶   ISP email - 12; ftm only.   AR - 1.

Institute of Science & Technology   (IST)   1954
■   Kingfisher House, 90 Rockingham St, SHEFFIELD, S1 4EB.   (hq)
       0114-276 3197   fax 0114-272 6354
       http://www.istonline.org.uk
       Hon Sec: A Taylor
▲   Company Limited by Guarantee
O   *L, *P; to advance knowledge of science laboratory techniques;
       to promote professional standing of laboratory technicians,
       technical speicalists, managerial staff
●   Conf - ET - Exam - Exhib - Inf
M   1,100 i, UK / 100 i, o'seas
¶   Science Technology - 4; ftm only.

Institute of Scientific & Technical Communicators   (ISTC)   1972
NR   Airport House, Purley Way, CROYDON, Surrey, CR0 0XZ.
       (hsp)
       020 8253 4506
       email istc@istc.org.uk   http://www.istc.org.uk
       Sec: Carol Hewitt
▲   Company Limited by Guarantee
O   *P; communication & presentation of scientific & technical
       information
Gp   Independent Authors Special Interest Gp (IASIG); Irish; Middle
       East
●   Conf - ET
<   Intl Coun for Technical Communication (INTECOM)
M   c 1,000 i, 21 f, UK / c 75 i, o'seas
¶   Communicator (Jnl) - 4; ftm, £35 (£40 EU, £43 RoW) nm.
       ISTC Hbk on Professional Communication & Information
       Design; £20 (available through Amazon).

Institute of Security Management   (ISecM)   1988
■   17 Hough Rd, Kings Heath, BIRMINGHAM, B14 6HL.   (hsp)
       0121-444 5006   fax 0121-444 5006
       http://www.i-s-m.co.uk
       Nat Sec: David Fell
O   *P; members are from various specialist groups employed in
       the industry incl: Armed forces, UK police services,
       Commercial & industrial security, MOD, Banks, Exhibition,
       Electronic security alarms, PCTV, Radio
●   Conf - Mtgs - ET - LG
<   Jt Securities Ind Coun (JSIC); Security Systems & Alarms
       Inspection Bd (SSAIB)
M   150 i, UK / 20 i, o'seas
¶   NL - 4.

Institute of Sheet Metal Engineering   (ISME)   1946
■   PO Box 2242, STAFFORD, ST17 0WH.   (hq)
       01785 716886   fax 01785 716886
       email isme@onetel.com   http://www.isme.org.uk
       Hon Sec: O W Pinfold
▲   Registered Charity
O   *L; theory & practice of sheet metal forming & fabrication
Gp   Sheet forming technology; Education
●   Conf - Mtgs - Exhib - Comp - SG - Inf - VE - Lectures
<   Confedn of Brit Metalforming
M   100 i, 25 f, UK / 8 i, o'seas
¶   Oracle - 4.

Institute of Shopfitting   (IOS)
NR   Central Office, 35 Hayworth Rd, Sandiacre, NOTTINGHAM,
       NG10 5LL.   (hq)
       0115-949 0641   fax 0115-949 1664
       http://www.central-office.co.uk/ios/
       Sec: David R Winson
O   *P

Institute for Small Business & Entrepreneurship   (ISBE)   1993
■   3 Ripon Rd (2nd floor), HARROGATE, N Yorks, HG1 2SX.   (hq)
       01423 500046   fax 01423 500046
       email info@isbe.org.uk   http://www.isbe.org.uk
       Admin: G E Wareham
▲   Company Limited by Guarantee; Registered Charity
O   *Q; to promote excellence in eduation, research & practice in
       small business & entrepreneurship
●   Conf - Workshops & Seminars
M   380 i, UK / 130 i, o'seas
       (Sub: £40)
¶   Small Business Issues (NL) - 4; free online.
×   2005 Institute of Small Business Affairs

Institute for Social Inventions   1985
NR   12a Blackstock Mews, Blackstock Rd, LONDON, N4 2BT.
       (mtgs address)
       020 7359 8391   fax 020 7354 3831
       http://www.globalideasbank.org
       Contact: Nick Temple
O   *K; to promote social inventions - new imaginative non-
       technological solutions to social problems
●   Conf - Mtgs - ET - Res - Comp - Inf - Lib - Workshop courses in
       state schools - £1,000 awards for best ideas
M   400 members & subscribers
¶   Social Inventions Annual Book - 1; £15 m only.
       Note: The Institute runs the Global Ideas Bank see -
       www.globalideasbank.org

Institute of Sound & Communications Engineers   (ISCE)
NR   PO Box 7966, READING, Berks, RG6 7WY.   (hq)
  0118-954 2175   fax 0118-954 2175
  http://www.isce.org.uk
  Secretariat: Rosalind Wigmore
▲   Company Limited by Guarantee
◠   *I , *P; supports technicians, managers & designers in the
  performing arts & public address industries
●   Conf - Mtgs - ET - Exam - Exhib - Lib
M   250 i, 16 f, UK / 20 i, o'seas
¶   Public Address (NL) - irreg.

Institute of Specialist Surveyors & Engineers   (ISSE)   1989
NR   Essex House, High St, CHIPPING ONGAR, Essex, CM5 9EB.
  (hq)
  0800 915 6363
  http://www.isse.org.uk
  Chmn: Derek Spring
▲   Company Limited by Guarantee
◯   *P; professional advice on timber infestations (woodworm and
  rot) and various forms of damp problems in buildings;
  assistance in finding reliable surveyors & treatment specialists
M   c 200 i
✕   2005 Institute of Remedial Treatment Surveyors

Institute of Spiritualist Mediums   (ISM)   1956
NR   132 Reading Rd South, Church Crookham, FLEET, Hants,
  GU52 6AL.   (sp)
  http://www.ism.org.uk
  Asst Sec: Christine Jones
▲   Registered Charity
◯   *E; to improve the standard of mediumship & the work of
  spiritualist mediums

Institute for Sport, Parks & Leisure   (ISPAL)   2007
NR   Abbey Business Centre, 1650 Arlington Business Park, Theale,
  READING, Berks, RG7 4SA.   (hq)
  0844 418 0077
  email info@ispal.org.uk   http://www.ispal.org.uk
  Chief Exec: Sue Sutton
▲   Registered Charity
Br   13
◯   *P; representing the public, private & voluntary sectors of leisure
  - sports centres, arts & entertainment complexes, parks,
  gardens & playgrounds, museums & tourist attractions,
  health & fitness clubs, countryside recreation
Gp   Children's play; Cultural activities; Sports services; Tourism &
  visitor attractions; Leisure education & training; Parks, open
  spaces & countryside
●   Conf - Mtgs - ET - Exam - Res - Exhib - Comp - SG - Stat - Inf -
  Lib - LG
M   5,000 i
¶   INFORM - 4; ftm.
✕   2007 (Institute for Leisure & Amenity Management
  (National Association for Sports Development

Institute of Sport & Recreation Management   (ISRM)   1921
NR   Sir John Beckwith Centre for Sport, Loughborough University,
  LOUGHBOROUGH, Leics, LE11 3TU.   (hq)
  01509 226474
  email info@isrm.co.uk   http://www.isrm.co.uk
  Chief Exec: Ralph Riley
◯   *P; for those involved in sport & recreation facility management
  & operation (including swimming baths)

Institute of Spring Technology   (IST)   1997
■   Henry St, SHEFFIELD, S Yorks, S3 7EQ.
  0114-276 0771   fax 0114-252 7997
  email ist@ist.org.uk   http://www.ist.org.uk
  Managing Dir: Andrew Watkinson
▲   Company Limited by Guarantee
◯   *E, *L, *P, *Q, *T; spring design, testing & consultancy
●   ET - Res - Exhib - Inf - Lib - VE
<   Intl Wire & Machinery Assn; Eur Spring Fedn; Fastener & Engg
  Res Assn
M   100 i, UK / 120 i, o'seas
¶   IST Technology NL - 4;   UKSMA NL - 4; both ftm only.
  UKSMA Member Guide - 1;   IST Member Guide - 1; both
  free.

Institute of Sterile Services Management
  since 2004 the **Institute of Decontamination Sciences**

** Institute of Stock Auditors & Valuers
  Organisation lost: see Introduction paragraph 3.

Institute of Swimming   (IOS)   1975
■   Harold Fern House, Derby Square, LOUGHBOROUGH, Leics,
  LE11 5AL.   (hq)
  01509 618746
  email istc@swimming.org.uk
  http://www.swimming.org.uk
  Admin: Jane Nickerson
▲   Company Limited by Guarantee
Br   12; Eire, International
◯   *P, *S; for qualified swimming teachers & coaches
●   Conf - Mtgs - ET - Res - Exhib - Inf - Lib - LG
<   Fedn of Water Fitness Profls; Amat Swimming Assn;
  Synchronised Swimming Coaches Assns
M   13,000 i, UK / 1,000 i, o'seas
¶   Swimming Times - 12; ftm, £1.70 nm.   LM - 2 yrly; ftm.
✕   2008 Institute of Swimming Teachers & Coaches

Institute of Swimming Pool Engineers Ltd   (ISPE)   1978
NR   PO Box 3083, NORWICH, Norfolk, NR6 7YL.   (hq)
  01603 499959
  http://www.ispe.co.uk
▲   Company Limited by Guarantee
◯   *P; design, construction & maintenance of swimming pools &
  spas, both public & private
Gp   Education & training to the swimming pool industry
●   Conf - ET - Exam - Exhib - SG - Inf
M   830 i, UK / 30 i, o'seas
¶   ISPE Magazine - 4; free.   Hbk.
  Home study course training manuals.
  Swimming Pool Industry Directory & Specifier (SPidas).
  Technical Papers (20 titles to date; £6-£13) incl:
   Water treatment for pool operators.
   Heat pumps.   Ozone.
   Domestic & commercial spas.
   Heat losses from indoor & outdoor pools.

Institute of Tourist Guiding   2002
NR   Coppergate House, 16 Brune St, LONDON, E1 7NJ.   (hq)
  020 7953 1257   fax 020 7953 1357
  email office@itg.org.uk   http://www.itg.org.uk
  Pres: Alan Frost
◯   *P; to achieve and maintain recognition of the profession of
  tour guiding

Institute of Trade Mark Attorneys   (ITMA)   1934

■   Canterbury House, 2-6 Sydenham Rd, CROYDON, Surrey,
      CR0 9XE.   (hq)
      020 8686 2052   fax 020 8680 5723
      email tm@itma.org.uk   http://www.itma.org.uk
      Co Sec: Mrs Margaret J Tyler
▲   Company Limited by Guarantee
○   *P
●   Conf - Mtgs - ET - Exam - LG
M   970 i, UK / 500 i, o'seas
¶   NL - 12;   Information - 12;   AR - 1; all ftm only.
      LM - 1; ftm, £10 nm.

Institute of Traffic Accident Investigators   (ITAI)   1990

NR   Column House, London Rd, SHREWSBURY, Shropshire,
      SY2 6NW.   (admin/office)
      0845 621 2066   fax 0845 621 2077
      email admin@itai.org   http://www.itai.org
      Admin: Anna Maria Rudy
▲   Company Limited by Guarantee
○   *P; representation, communication, education, & regulation in
      traffic accident investigation
●   Conf - ET - Exam - Res - VE
M   750 i, UK / 60 i, o'seas
¶   Impact (Jnl) - 3; ftm, £10 nm.   Contact (NL) - 6; ftm only.

Institute of Training & Occupational Learning   (ITOL)   2000

NR   49 Seymour Terrace, LIVERPOOL, L3 5PE.   (hq)
      0151-707 8424   fax 0151-703 7843
      http://www.itol.org
▲   Un-incorporated Society
○   *P; training, assessment & vocational education
●   ET - Exam - Res - Inf - Lib
¶   Training & Learning - 12.

Institute of Transactional Analysis   (ITA)   1977

■   Broadway House, 149-151 St Neots Rd, Hardwick,
      CAMBRIDGE, CB23 7QJ.   (hq)
      0845 009 9101
      email admin@ita.org.uk   http://www.ita.org.uk
      Chmn; Jean Lancashire
▲   Company Limited by Guarantee; Registered Charity
○   *P; the education of the public in the study, theory & practice of
      transactional analysis - a theory of personality & social
      psychology within a humanistic tradition
Gp   Clinical; Counselling; Educational; Organisational
●   Conf - Mtgs - ET - Exam - SG - Counselling - Therapy -
      Coaching
<   Eur Assn Transactional Analysis; UK Coun for Psychotherapy
M   1,200 i, 20 f, UK / 40 i, o'seas
      (Sub: £33-£286 i, £25-£260 f)
¶   ITA News (NL) - 6; ftm, £16.50 nm.
      Transactions (Jnl) - 2; ftm only.   AR - 1; ftm only.

Institute of Translation & Interpreting   (ITI)   1986

NR   Fortuna House, South Fifth St, MILTON KEYNES, Bucks,
      MK9 2EU.   (hq)
      01908 325250
      email info@iti.org.uk   http://www.iti.org.uk
      Chief Exec: Alan Wheatley
▲   Company Limited by Guarantee
○   *P; for translators & interpreters; has a structure of regional
      group, language & subject networks
Gp   Subject networks: Medicine, Law, Insurance, Finance & trade,
      Book translators, Media, arts & tourism, Information
      technology, Patents, Construction
●   Conf - Mtgs - ET - Exhib - SG - Expt - Inf
<   Intl Fedn of Translators (FIT)
M   2,240 i, 93 f, UK / 480 i, 5 f, o'seas
¶   ITI Bulletin - 6; ftm.   LM - 1.   AR - 1; free.
      Conference Proceedings - 1.   Leaflets & factsheets - irreg.

Institute of Transport Administration   (IoTA)   1944

NR   The Old Studio, 25 Greenfield Rd, Westoning, BEDFORD,
      MK45 5JD.   (hq)
      01525 634940   fax 01525 750016
      email director@iota.org.uk   http://www.iota.org.uk
      Pres; Dr Michael Asteris
○   *P; to improve & develop the knowledge & efficiency of
      members in the skills of transport management
M   i
¶   Transport Management (Jnl) - 6.

Institute of Transport Management   (ITM)   1977

NR   14-20 George St, BIRMINGHAM, W Midlands, B12 9RG.   (hq)
      0121-440 5222
      Chmn: William Gavin
▲   Registered Charity
○   *P
M   i

Institute of Travel Management Ltd   (ITM)   1956

NR   Waters Green House, Waters Green, MACCLESFIELD,
      Cheshire, SK11 6LF.   (hq)
      01625 430472   fax 01625 439183
      email secretariat@itm.org.uk
      Nat Chmn: Louise Innes
▲   Company Limited by Guarantee
Br   6; Ireland
○   *P; for those involved in the planning & procurement of
      business travel services
Gp   Supplier c'ee (representatives of short-haul airlines,
      international & independent hotels & surface transportation)
●   Conf - Mtgs - ET - Exhib - SG - LG
<   Chart Inst Purchasing & Supply (CIPS)
M   312 i, 284 f, UK / 38 i, 16 f, o'seas
¶   Newsline - 4;   ITM Ybk - 1; both ftm only.

Institute of Travel & Tourism   (ITT)   1956

NR   PO Box 217, WARE, Herts, SG12 8WY.   (hq)
      0870 770 7960
▲   Company Limited by Guarantee
○   *P
M   i & f

Institute of Trichologists (Inc)   (IT)   1902

NR   24 Langroyd Rd (ground floor), LONDON, SW17 7PL.
      (regd off)
      0870 607 0602
      http://www.trichologists.org.uk
      Chmn: Mrs Marilyn Sherlock
▲   Company Limited by Guarantee
○   *L, *P; the treatment & care of human hair & scalp in health &
      disease
●   ET - Exam - Res
M   220 i, UK / 20 i, o'seas
¶   The Trichologists - 2.

Institute for Turnaround   (IFT)   2000

NR   The Bridge, 12-16 Clerkenwell Rd, LONDON, EC1M 5PQ.
      020 7324 6244   fax 020 7253 5029
      email info@instituteforturnaround.com
      http://www.instituteforturnaround.com
      Chief Exec: Christine Elliott
▲   Company Limited by Guarantee
○   *P; for rehabilitators of under-performing organisations
×   2008 Society of Turnaround Professionals

Institute of Value Management   (IVM)   1966
- ■ 1-3 Birdcage Walk, LONDON, SW1H 9JJ.   (hsp)
  0870 902 0905
  email secretary@ivm.org.uk   http://www.ivm.org.uk
  Hon Sec: D W Hurst
- ▲ Company Limited by Guarantee
- Br 6
- ○ *P; 'driving for sustainable worth in all sectors'
- ● Conf - Mtgs - ET - G - Inf - LG
- M 180 i, 16 f, UK / 21 i, o'seas
  Subs: £70 i. £575 f
- ¶ Value Jnl - 3; ftm, £25 nm.
  Value Management is a style of management particularly
  dedicated to motivating people, developing skills &
  promoting synergies & innovation, with the aim of
  maximising overall performance

Institute of Vehicle Engineers
  since 2005-06 the **Society of Automotive Engineers - UK**

Institute of Vehicle Recovery   (IVR)   1984
- ■ Bignell House (top floor), Horton Rd, WEST DRAYTON, Middx,
  UB7 8EP.   (hq)
  01895 436426
- ▲ Company Limited by Guarantee
- ○ *P; interests of persons engaged in motor vehicle recovery; to
  promote technical training & improve the standard of safety
  in motor vehicle recovery
- ● ET - Exam - Res - Exhib - SG
- M 700 i, UK / 56 i, o'seas
- ¶ NL; ftm.

Institute of Videography   (IOV)   1985
- NR PO Box 625, LOUGHTON, Essex, IG10 3GZ.
  020 8502 3817   fax 020 8508 9211
  email info@iov.co.uk   http://www.iov.co.uk
  Exec Coordinator: Kevin Cook
- Br 16
- ○ *P; video production & training
- ● Conf - Comp - Mtgs - SG - ET - Inf - Exhib - VideoSkills
  workshops
- M 800 i, 50 f
- ¶ Focus Magazine - 12.

Institute of Vitreous Enamellers & Vitreous Enamel Association (IVE)   1934
- NR 39 Sweetbriar Way, Heath Hayes, CANNOCK, Staffs,
  WS12 2US.   (hsp)
  01543 450596
  email info@ive.org.uk   http://www.ive.org.uk
  Admin Sec: Angela Nutting
- ▲ Company Limited by Guarantee
- ○ *L, *P; exchange of technical information on vitreous
  enamelling
- ● Conf - Mtgs - ET - Inf - Lib - VE - LG - Advice on environment,
  health & safety
- < Intl Enamellers Inst; Eur Enamellers Authority
- M 65 i, 29 f, UK / 15 i, 5 f, o'seas
- ¶ The Vitreous Enameller (Jnl) - 4.
  Atlas of Enamel Defects.   Buyer's Guide.
  Classification of Adhesion of Vitreous Enamel to Steel.

Institute for Volunteering Research
- NR Regent's Wharf, 8 All Saints Street, LONDON, N1 9RL.
  0845 305 6979
- ○ *Q; 'to develop knowledge & understanding of volunteering in
  a way that is relevant to practitioners & policy makers'

Institute of Welfare   (IWO)   1945
- ■ Newland House (2nd floor), 137-139 Hagley Rd, Edgbaston,
  BIRMINGHAM, WztzMidlands, B16 8UA.   (hq)
  0121-454 8883   fax 0121-454 7873
  email info@instituteofwelfare.co.uk
  Chmn: Austin Griffiths
- ○ *P; for welfare officers in industry, commerce, social
  organisations, national & local government departments
- ● Conf - Mtgs - ET - Res
- M c 2,500 i
- ¶ Welfare World - 4.

Institute of Welsh Affairs   (IWA)   1987
- ■ 4 Cathedral Rd (2nd Floor), CARDIFF. CF11 9LJ.   (hq)
  029 2066 0820
  email wales@iwa.org.uk   http://www.iwa.org.uk
  Dir: John Osmond
- ▲ Registered Charity
- Br 5
- ○ *P; to promote the prosperity of Wales, its industry & people by
  encouraging debate upon & research into economic, social &
  cultural issues
- ● Conf - Mtgs - Res
- M 1,100 i, 150 f, UK / 50 i, o'seas
  (Sub: £40 i, from £250 f, UK / £50 i, o'seas)
- ¶ Agenda - 3; ftm, £5.
  Miscellaneous Research Reports;   Proceedings;   Discussion
  papers.

Institute of Wood Science   (IWSc)   1955
- NR Carpenters' Hall (3rd floor D), 1 Throgmorton Ave, LONDON,
  EC2N 2BY.   (hq)
  020 7256 2700   fax 020 7256 2701
  email info@iwsc.org.uk   http://www.iwsc.org.uk
  Dir: Duncan King
- ▲ Company Limited by Guarantee; Registered Charity
- ○ *P; to advance & encourage the scientific, technical, practical &
  general knowledge of timber & wood-based materials
- M i & f
- ¶ Jnl - 2;   NL - 2.

Institution of Agricultural Engineers   (IAgrE)   1938
- ■ Barton Rd, Silsoe, BEDFORD, MK45 4FH.   (hq)
  01525 861096   fax 01525 861660
  email secretary@iagre.org   http://www.iagre.org
  Chief Exec: Christopher R Whetnall
- ▲ Company Limited by Guarantee; Registered Charity
- Br 13
- ○ *L, *P; for engineers, managers, scientists & technologists in
  agriculture & allied industries (incl forestry, food processing,
  agrochemicals & amenity industries)
- Gp Agro-industrial products; Amenity & ecological engineering;
  Food technology; Forestry engineering; Horticultural
  engineering; Machinery management; Overseas
  development; Pioneering technology; Precision in farming;
  Renewable energy; Soil & water management; Vehicles;
  Young engineers
- ● Conf - Mtgs - Inf - Lib
- < Intl Commission of Agricl Engg (CIGR); Eur Soc of Agricl Engrs
  (EurAgEng)
- M 1,700 i, 15 f, UK / 200 i, o'seas
- ¶ Landwards - 4; ftm, £52 nm.

Institution of Analysts & Programmers   (IAP)   1971
- ■ 36 Culmington Rd, LONDON, W13 9NH.   (hq)
  020 8567 2118
  http://www.iap.org.uk
  Dir Gen: Michael Ryan
- ○ *P; systems analysis & computer programming
- M c 3,000 i, UK / c 500 i, o'seas
- ¶ NL - 4;   LM;   AR.

** Institution of British Engineers
  Organisation lost: see Introduction paragraph 3

© CBD Research Ltd · Beckenham · BR3 5JS · Tel 020 8650 7745 · Fax 020 8650 0768 · E-mail cbd@cbdresearch.com · www.cbdresearch.com

Institution of Chemical Engineers (IChemE) 1922

- Davis Building, 165-189 Railway Terrace, RUGBY, Warks, CV21 3HQ. (hq)
  01788 578214   fax 01788 560833
  http://www.icheme.org
  Chief Exec: Dr Trevor J Evans
▲ Registered Charity
Br Australia, Malaysia, Singapore
○ *L, *P; the professional qualifying body for process & chemical engineers
● Conf - ET - Exhib - Products & services for qualified chemical engineers & those interested in chemical engineering as a career
M 18,168 i, UK / 7,455 i, o'seas
¶ The Chemical Engineer (tce) - 12 ftm, £165 (UK) (£180 RoW) nm.
  Chemical Engineering Research & Design - 12;
    (members) print & online; £120 (UK) £140 (RoW).
    (members) online only; £50 (UK+RoW).
    (non-members) print & online £721 (UK) £742 (RoW).
  Process Safety & Environmental Protection - 6;
    (members) print & online; £80 (UK) £100 (RoW).
    (members) online only; £40 (UK+RoW).
    (non-members) print & online; £448 (UK) £464 (RoW).
  Food & Bioproducts Processing - 4;
    (members) print & online; £50 (UK) £70 (RoW).
    (members) online only; £30 (UK+RoW).
    (non-members) £278 (UK) £294 (RoW).

Institution of Civil Engineering Surveyors (ICES) 1969

NR Dominion House, Sibson Rd, SALE, Cheshire, M33 7PP. (hq)
  0161-972 3100   fax 0161-972 3118
  email admin@ices.org.uk   http://www.ices.org.uk
  Admin: Simeon Payne & Serena Ronan
▲ Company Limited by Guarantee; Registered Charity
○ *P; the qualification & regulation of geospatial engineering surveyors (land surveyors) & commercial managers (quantity surveyors)
Gp Commercial management, including:
  Construction economics; Construction law; Cost engineering; Estimating; Planning; Procurement engineering, Project management, Quantity surveying.
  Geospatial engineering surveyors, including:
  Cartography; Dimensional control; Geographical information systems; Hydrographic surveying; Land / engineering surveyors; Photogrammetrists; Remote seeking.
● Conf - Mtgs - ET - Exam - Res - Exhib - Stat - Inf - Lib
< Intl Fedn Surveyors (FIG); Construction Ind Coun; Instn Civil Engrs
M 3,100 i, UK / 400 i, o'seas
¶ Civil Engineering Surveyor (Jnl) - 12.
  Construction & Law Review - 1.
  Reference Manual for Construction Plant - 3/4 yrly.

Institution of Civil Engineers (ICE) 1818

NR One Great George St, LONDON, SW1P 3AA. (hq)
  020 7222 7722
  Chmn: Prof Quentin Leiper
Br Intl local assns: Australia, France, Hong Kong, India, Indonesia, Ireland, Netherlands, Qatar, Saudi Arabia, Sri Lanka, USA
  Branches: Belgium, Cayman Islands, Poland, Switzerland
○ *L, *P
Gp British Geotechnical Assn; Soc for Earthquake & Civil Engineering Dynamics
● Conf - Mtgs - ET - Exam - Res - Exhib - Comp - Inf - Lib - LG - Register of engineers for disaster relief - Dispute resolution service - Recruitment subsidiary - Panel for historical engineering works - Archives - Audio-visual collection - Guided tours of building available - Rooms available for external bookings
< Intl C'ee on Large Dams; Intl Assn for Hydraulic Res; Intl Cmsn on Irrigation & Drainage; Intl Soc of Trenchless Technology; Permanent Intl Assn of Navigation Congresses; Central Dredging Assn; Standing C'ee on Structural Safety
M 60,891 i, UK / 14,162 i, o'seas

Institution of Commercial & Business Agents (ICBA) 2008

NR Arbon House, 6 Tournament Court, Edgehill Drive, WARWICK, CV34 6LG.
  01926 417774   fax 01926 417789
  email info@icba.uk.com   http://www.icba.uk.com
○ *P; estate agents specialising in the commercial sector
< Is a subsidiary of the National Association of Estate Agents, a division of the National Federation of Property Professionals

Institution of Diagnostic Engineers 1983

- 7 Weir Rd, Kibworth, LEICESTER, LE8 0LQ. (hq)
  0116-279 6772   fax 0116-279 6884
  email admin@diagnosticengineers.org
  http://www.diagnosticengineers.org
  Admin: Karen Seiles
▲ Company Limited by Guarantee; Registered Charity (as Society of Diagnostic Engineers)
○ *P; engineers involved in diagnosing faults in machines, plant, & systems.
  Specialist areas: Vibration analysis, condition monitoring, engine health
Gp Society of Diagnostic Engineers - maintains a register of professional engineers who are entitled to use the designation P.Eng.
● Conf - ET - Exhib - VE
M 1,500 i, 20 f, UK / 500 i, o'seas
¶ Diagnostic Engineering - 6; ftm, £60 nm.

Institution of Diesel & Gas Turbine Engineers (IDGTE) 1913

- Bedford Heights, Manton Lane, BEDFORD, MK41 7PH. (hq)
  01234 214340   fax 01234 355493
  email enquiries@idgte.org   http://www.idgte.org
  Dir Gen: Peter Tottman
▲ Un-incorporated Society
Br Canada
○ *L; the advancement of diesel & gas engines, gas turbines & related products & technology
Gp Working gps: Diesel engines, Gas turbines
● Conf - Mtgs - ET - Exhib - Inf - Lib - VE
M 457 i, 60 f, UK / 101 i, 58 f, o'seas
¶ The Power Engineer - 4; ftm (extra copies £15), £30 nm.
  The Power Engineer (Operational Report) - 1; ftm (extra copies £25), £50 nm.

Institution of Economic Development Ltd (IED) 1983

NR PO Box 796, NORTHAMPTON, NN4 9TS. (hq)
  01604 87461311
  Chmn: Neil Robertson
○ *P
M 1,000 i
¶ Economic Development - 4.

Institution of Electrical Engineers
in 2006 merged with Institution of Incorporated Engineers to form the
Institution of Engineering & Technology

Institution of Engineering Designers (IED) 1945

- Courtleigh, Westbury Leigh, WESTBURY, Wilts, BA13 3TA. (hq)
  01373 822801   fax 01373 858085
  email ied@ied.org.uk   http://www.ied.org.uk/
  Sec: E K Brodhurst
▲ Company Limited by Guarantee; Registered Charity
Br 13; Malta, Hong Kong
○ *P; to advance education in engineering, product design & CADD; Licensed body of the Engineering Council
Gp Computer aided design (CAD); Product design
● Conf - Mtgs - ET - Exhib - Comp - SG - Stat - Inf - Lib - VE
M 4,920 i, UK / 410 i, o'seas
¶ The Engineering Designer - 6; ftm, £39 yr nm.

Institution of Engineering & Technology (IET) 1871
- ■ Savoy Place, LONDON, WC2R 0BL. (hq)
  020 7240 1871 fax 020 7497 7735
  http://www.theiet.org
  Chief Exec: Robin McGill
- ▲ Registered Charity
- Br 47; 53 o'seas
- ○ *L, *P; to promote the advancement of science, engineering & technology; to act as the voice of the profession; to set standards of qualifications standards of qualifications
- Gp 40 technical interest groups grouped under: Communications engineering, Computing & control, Electronic systems & software, Information professional, Management, Manufacturing, Power, Transport
- ● Conf - Mtgs - ET - Exhib - Comp - Inf - Lib - PL - VE - LG
- M c 150,000 i & f
- ¶ Engineering & Technology (Jnl) - 22.
  Electronic Letters
  Wiring Matters
  Flipside (for teenagers).
  Student & Graduate Magazine.
- ✕ 2004-05 (Institution of Electrical Engineers (Society of Engineers)
  2006 (Institution of Incorporated Engineers

Institution of Engineers of Ireland
  registered name of **Engineers Ireland**

Institution of Engineers & Shipbuilders in Scotland (IESIS) 1857
- NR Clydeport Building, 16 Robertson St, GLASGOW, G2 8DS. (hq)
  0141-248 3721 fax 0141-221 2698
- ○ *L, *P
- M i

Institution of Environmental Sciences Ltd (IEnvSc) 1971
- ■ 38 Ebury St (suite 7), LONDON, SW1W 0LU. (hq)
  020 7730 5516 fax 020 7730 5519
  Hon Sec: Mrs J R Blumhof
- ▲ Company Limited by Guarantee; Registered Charity
- ○ *L, *P; to promote, sponsor, & organise research & interdisciplinary action, consultation & coordination into all matters concerning environmental sciences
- Gp Education c'ee
- ● Conf - ET - Accreditation of university courses - Publications - Careers advice
- < Science Coun
- M 780 i, 8 f, 6 org, UK / 65 i, o'seas
- ¶ The Environmental Scientist - 6.

Institution of Fire Engineers (iFE) 1918
- ■ London Rd, MORETON-in-MARSH, Glos, GL56 0RH. (hq)
  01608 812580
- ▲ Company Limited by Guarantee; Registered Charity
- Br 20; 18 countries o'seas
- ○ *L, *P; to promote, encourage & improve the science & practice of fire extinction, fire prevention & fire engineering
- ● Conf - Mtgs - ET - Exam - Res - Exhib - Inf
- M 7,000 i, UK / 4,500 i, o'seas
- ¶ Fire Engineers Jnl - 6; ftm.
  Hbk for Fire Engineers. How did it start?
  Fire Technology - Chemistry Combustion.
  Fire Technology - Calculations.
  Dictionary of Fire Technology.
  Guide to Examinations of the IFE.
  Principles of Fire Investigation.

Institution of Gas Engineers & Managers (IGEM) 1863
- NR Charnwood Wing - Holywell Park, Ashby Rd, LOUGHBOROUGH, Leics, LE11 3GR. (hq)
  01509 282728 fax 01509 283110
  email general@igem.org.uk http://www.igem.org.uk
  Chief Exec & Sec: John Williams
- ▲ Registered Charity
- Br 10; Brazil, Hong Kong
- ○ *L, *P; licensed to accredit engineers to chartered, incorporated & technician levels; provides a focus & technical standards for the gas industry
- Gp Sections: Information, Membership, Technical
- ● Conf - Mtgs - ET - Exhib - Comp - SG - Inf - Lib - PL - LG
- < Intl Gas U (IGU); Accredited by Engg Coun (UK)
- M 4,846 i, 114 f, UK / 394 i, 12 f, o'seas
- ¶ International Gas Engineering & Management (Jnl) - 10.
- ✕ 2001 Institution of Gas Engineers

Institution of Highways & Transportation (IHT) 1930
- ■ 119 Britannia Walk, LONDON, N1 7JE. (hq)
  020 7336 1550
  http://www.iht.org
  Chief Exec: Mary Lewis
- ▲ Company Limited by Guarantee; Registered Charity
- Br 18; Hong Kong, Malaysia, Republic of Ireland
- ○ *P
- ● Conf - Mtgs - ET - Exhib - Expt - Inf - VE - LG
- M 9,514 i, 19 f, UK / 1,166 i, o'seas
- ¶ Transportation Professional - 10; ftm, £58.

Institution of Incorporated Engineers
  in 2006 merged with Institution of Electrical Engineers to form the
  Institution of Engineering & Technology

Institution of Lighting Engineers (ILE) 1924
- NR Regent House, Regent Place, RUGBY, Warks, CV21 2PN. (hq)
  01788 576492
- ▲ Company Limited by Guarantee; Registered Charity
- ○ *P
- M i & f

Institution of Mechanical Engineers (IMechE) 1847
- NR 1 Birdcage Walk, LONDON, SW1H 9JJ. (hq)
  020 7222 7899
  Dir Gen: Sir Michael Moore
- ▲ Registered Charity
- ○ *L, *P; 'to create the natural professional home for all involved in mechanical engineering'

Institution of Nuclear Engineers
  on 1 January 2009 merged with the British Nuclear Energy Society to form the **Nuclear Institute**

Institution of Occupational Safety & Health (IOSH) 1945
- NR The Grange, Highfield Drive, WIGSTON, Leics, LE18 1NN. (hq)
  0116-257 3100 fax 0116-257 3101
  http://www.iosh.co.uk
- ▲ Incorporated by Royal Charter; Registered Charity
- Br 23; 2
- ○ *P; for those professionally involved in occupational safety & health
- Gp Construction; Public services; Offshore; Healthcare
- ● Conf - Mtgs - ET - Res - Exhib - Inf - Lib - PL - VE - LG
- M 26,500 i, UK / 2,500 i, o'seas
- ¶ Safety & Health Practitioner - 12. Jnl - 2 yrly.
  Various other publications.

© CBD Research Ltd · Beckenham · BR3 5JS · Tel 020 8650 7745 · Fax 020 8650 0768 · E-mail cbd@cbdresearch.com · www.cbdresearch.com

Institution of Planning Supervisors   (IPS)   1995
NR   Heriot-Watt Research Park, EDINBURGH, EH14 4AP.   (hq)
      0131-449 4646
▲   Company Limited by Guarantee
○   *P; to improve health & safety in the construction industry
      particularly in relation to the Construction (Design &
      Management) Regulations 1994 (CDM) & to the role of
      planning supervisor
M   i

Institution of Plant Engineers
      a sector of the **Society of Operations Engineers**

Institution of Railway Operators   2000
NR   PO Box 128, BURGESS HILL, W Sussex, RH15 0UZ.
      01444 248931   fax 01444 246392
      http://www.railwayoperators.org
○   *P

Institution of Railway Signal Engineers   (IRSE)   1912
■   1 Birdcage Walk (4th floor), Westminster, LONDON,
      SW1H 9JJ.   (hq)
      020 7808 1180
      http://www.irse.org
      Chief Exec: Colin H Porter
▲   Registered Charity
Br   worldwide
○   *L, *P; railway signalling & telecommunications
●   Conf - Mtgs - ET - Exam - Exhib - SG - Inf - Lib - VE
M   2,500 i, UK / 1,000 i, o'seas
¶   NL - 6.   Proceedings - 1.
      Various books.

Institution of Structural Engineers   (IStructE)   1908
NR   11 Upper Belgrave St, LONDON, SW1X 8BH.   (hq)
      020 7235 4535   fax 020 7235 4294
      email mail@istructe.org.uk   http://www.istructe.org.uk
      Chief Exec & Sec: Dr Keith J Eaton
▲   Incorporated by Royal Charter; Registered Charity
Br   18; Australia, Barbados, Hong Kong, N Zealand, Nigeria,
      Singapore, S Africa, Trinidad & Tobago
○   *L, *P
●   Conf - Mtgs - ET - Exam - Comp - SG - Inf - Lib
M   16,300 i, UK / 6,600 i, o'seas
¶   The Structural Engineer (Jnl) - 23.
      Publications list available.

Instock Footwear Suppliers' Association   (IFSA)   1947
NR   Marlone House, Churchill Way, Fleckney, LEICESTER,
      LE8 8UD.   (hq)
      0116-240 3232   fax 0116-240 2762
▲   Un-incorporated Society
○   *T; those distributing footwear (from manufacturers to retailers)
●   Mtgs - LG
M   10 f
¶   NL; ftm only.

Insulated Render & Cladding Association Ltd   (INCA)   1981
■   PO Box 12, HASLEMERE, Surrey, GU27 3AH.   (hq)
      01428 654011   fax 01428 651401
      email incaassociation@aol.com
      http://www.inca-ltd.org.uk
      Dir: Gillian Allder
▲   Company Limited by Guarantee
○   *T
●   Mtgs - Inf - LG - Seminars
M   58 f
¶   NL; m only.   LM.   Technical literature.

Insulating Concrete Formwork Association   1992
NR   PO Box 72, BILLINGSHURST, W Sussex, RH14 0FD.
      0845 812 0000
      http://www.icfinfo.org.uk

Insurance Financial & Legal Services Association
      a group of the **British Marine Federation**

Insurance Institute of Ireland
IRL   39 Molesworth St, DUBLIN 2, Republic of Ireland.   (hq)
      353 (1) 677 2582   fax 353 (1) 677 2621
      email iii@iol.ie   http://www.insurance-institute.ie
      Chief Exec: Denis Hevey
○   *P

Intellect   1994
NR   Russell Square House, 10-12 Russell Square, LONDON,
      WC1B 5EE.
      020 7331 2000   fax 020 7331 2040
      email john.park@intellectuk.org
      http://www.intellectuk.org
      Co Sec: John Park
▲   Un-incorporated Society
○   *N, *T; interests of the information technology, electronics,
      communications, defence electronics, office technology &
      document management, software & services industries
Gp   Councils for: Telecommunications & radio, Information
      technology, Aerospace & defence, Naval & maritime, Office
      technology, Components & manufacturing;
      Group: Defence policy;
      Advisory groups: Commercial, Engineering services, Publicity,
      Research, Mobile telephone, Skills & training, Health, safety
      & environment
      Business Function Groups: Human Resources, Legal &
      contracts, Marketing, Quality
      Industry Groups: Financial services, Utilities, Defence,
      Government, Healthcare; Justice & emergency services
●   Conf - Mtgs - Exhib - Stat - Expt - Inf - LG
<   EECA; EICTA; FRMB; EDIG; CEN; CENELEC; ETSI; NIAG;
      NATO
M   1,000+ f
¶   Publications list available.

Intellectual Property Lawyers Association   1982
NR   c/o Rowan Freeland, Simmons & Simmons, CityPoint, 1
      Ropemaker St, LONDON, EC2Y 9SS.
      020 7628 2020
      http://www.ipla.org.uk
      Sec: Rowan Freeland
○   *P

Intelligent Membrane Trade Association   (IMA)
NR   PO Box 74, Stretford, MANCHESTER, M32 0XN.   (sb)
      0161-865 8913   fax 0161-866 9859
      email ima.uk@icopal.com   http://www.imaroofer.com
      Sec: Tony Burke
○   *T; for roof waterproofing contractors
M   200 f

Intensive Care Society   (ICS)   1970
■   Churchill House, 35 Red Lion Square, LONDON,
      WC1R 4SG.   (hq)
      020 7280 4350   fax 020 7280 4369
      email admin@ics.ac.uk   http://www.ics.ac.uk
      Hon Sec: Dr Bruce Taylor
▲   Company Limited by Guarantee; Registered Charity
○   *P; to promote & develop the medical speciality of intensive
      care
Gp   Conferences; Education & training; Scientific or other systematic
      research
●   Conf - ET - Res - Exhib
<   Eur Soc of Intensive Care (ESICCM); Ir Intensive Care Soc;
      ICNARC;
M   2,450 i, UK / 100 i, o'seas
      (Sub: varies)
¶   JICS (Jnl) - 4; ftm.   AR; free.

Interactive Media in Retail Group   (IMRG)   1990
NR   25 Floral St, LONDON, WC2E 9DS.
         0700 046 4674   fax 0700 039 4674
         email market@imrg.org   http://www.imrg.org

Interflora
NR   Interflora House, SLEAFORD, Lincs, NG34 7TB.   (hq)
         0870 904 5459
○   *T
M   f
         No further information supplied.

Interlay, the Association of Block Paving Contractors
         an affiliated association of the **British Precast Concrete
         Federation**

Intermediary Mortgage Lenders Association   (IMLA)   1988
NR   North West Wing (3rd floor), Bush House, Aldwych, LONDON,
         WC2B 4PJ.   (hsb)
         020 7438 8942   fax 0845 373 6778C
         email julie.dover@cml.org.uk   http://www.imla.org.uk
         Sec: Julie Dover
▲   Company Limited by Guarantee
○   *T
●   Mtgs
M   32 f
¶   LM - 1; free.

International Association of Animal Therapists   (IAAT)   1991
NR   Tyringham Hall, Cuddington, AYLESBURY, Bucks, HP18 0AP.
         (hq)
         01844 290512   fax 01844 290474
         email therapyenquiry@aol.com   http://www.iaat.org.uk
         Sec: Latie Lawrence
▲   Company Limited by Guarantee
○   *P, *V; animal physiotherapy
●   Mtgs - ET - Exam - Expt
M   40 i, UK / 20 i, o'seas
✕   2005 National Association of Animal Therapists

**International Association of Auto Theft Investigators (UK
Branch)   (IAATI UK)**
NR   Chapelside, Plain Rd, Smeeth, ASHFORD, Kent, TN25 6QL.
         (sec/p)
         01737 761950
         email mail@iaati.org.uk   http://www.iaati.org.uk
         Sec: Michael Hinchliffe
Br   Europe (several); Australia, S Africa, USA
○   *P; to provide an exchange of technical information &
         development; to cooperate with all law enforcement agencies
         & associations involved in prevention, detection &
         suppression of vehicle crime
●   Conf - VE - ET - LG
<   Intl Assn Auto Theft Investigators
M   380 i, UK / 4,000 i, o'seas

International Bond & Share Society   (IBSS)   1978
■   167 Barnett Wood Lane, ASHTEAD, Surrey, KT21 2LP.   (hsp)
         01372 276787
         email secretary@scripophily.org
         http://www.scripophily.org
         Hon Sec: Philip Atkinson
○   *G; the study, buying & selling, exchanging & promoting the
         knowledge of scripophily (collectable bond, stock & share
         certificates)
M   i

**International Chamber of Commerce - UK National Committee
(ICC United Kingdom)   1920**
NR   12 Grosvenor Place, LONDON, SW1X 7HH.   (hq)
         020 7838 9363
         http://www.iccuk.net
         Dir: Andrew Hope
○   *T; to represent interests of world business to governments &
         intergovernmental organisations
Gp   Air transport; Arbitration; Banking technique & practice;
         Competition law; Computing telecommunications &
         information policy; Environment; Financial services;
         Insurance; Intellectual property; International commercial
         practice; Marketing; Multinationals & investment; Sea
         Transport; Taxation; Trade policy; Trade regulations
●   Conf - Mtgs - LG
M   f
¶   Business Bulletin (NL) - 6:   AR; both free.
         Publications list available.

International Clay Technology Association
         a committee of the Ceramics Society, a group of the **Institute of
         Materials, Minerals & Mining**

**International Consulting Economists' Association   (ICEA)
1986**
■   45 Sorrel Bank, Linton Glade, CROYDON, Surrey, CR0 9LW.
         (hsb)
         020 8651 1380
         email secretariat@icea.co.uk   http://www.icea.co.uk
         Secretariat: Mrs Turhan Donegan
▲   Un-incorporated Society
○   *P; international economic consultancy; economic issues;
         development aid
Gp   Agricultural & rural development; Aid & evaluation;
         Construction; Education; Energy; Environment & water; EU
         integration; Finance; Health; Industry; Infrastructure;
         Irrigation; Manufacture; Migration; Private sector; Tourism;
         Trade; Transport; Urban; Other
●   Mtgs
M   126 i, UK / 18 i, o'seas
¶   NL - 2;   LM - 1; both ftm only.

International General Produce Association Ltd   (IGPA)   1876
NR   GAFTA House, 6 Chapel Place, Rivington St, LONDON,
         EC2A 3SH.
         020 7814 9666   fax 020 7814 8383
         email igpa@gafta.com   http://www.igpa.com
         Sec: Pamela Kirby Johnson
○   *T; a contract issuing body for international trade in herbs,
         spices, essential oils, aromatic chemicals & general produce
M   i, f & org
¶   Hbk.

**International Glassfibre Reinforced Concrete Association
(GRCA)   1975**
NR   4 Meadows Business Park, Station Approach, Blackwater,
         CAMBERLEY, Surrey, GU17 9AB.   (hq)
         01276 607140
▲   Company Limited by Guarantee
○   *T; the development of GRC industry for the benefit of
         suppliers, manufacturers, users & specifiers; GRC is a
         composite of alkali resistant glass fibres & concrete/sand
         matrix (thin high strength concrete)
M   f

International Guild of Knot Tyers   1982
NR   PO Box 3540, CHESTER, CH1 9FU.   (hsp)
         email sec@igkt.net   http://www.igkt.net
         Hon Sec: Dave Walker
▲   Registered Charity
Br   16; 7
○   *G; all aspects of knot-tying & associated ropework
M   573 i, 5 f, 5 org, UK / 629 i, 1 f, o'seas
¶   Knotting Matters (NL) - 4.
         Membership Hbk - 18 months; m only.

© CBD Research Ltd · Beckenham · BR3 5JS · Tel 020 8650 7745 · Fax 020 8650 0768 · E-mail cbd@cbdresearch.com · www.cbdresearch.com

International Language [Ido] Society of Great Britain (ILSGB)   1910
- ■ 24 Nunn St, LEEK, Staffs, ST13 8EA.   (hsp)
  http://www.idolinguo.org.uk
  Hon Sec: David Weston
- ▲ Un-incorporated Society
- ○ *X; to promote the use of Ido as an international language
- ● Mtgs - Inf
- < Uniono por la Linguo Internaciona Ido
- M 20 i, UK / 16 i, o'seas

International Law Association   (ILA)   1873
- NR Charles Clore House, 17 Russell Square, LONDON, WC1B 5JD.   (hq)
  020 7323 2978   fax 020 7323 3580
  http://www.ila-hq.org
  Sec Gen: David Wyld
- ○ *L; study, elucidation & advancement of international law, both public & private
- M c 4,000 i

International Marine Contractors Association   (IMCA)   1972
- ■ 5 Lower Belgrave St, LONDON, SW1W 0NR.   (hq)
  020 7824 5520   fax 020 7824 5521
  email imca@imca-int.com   http://www.imca-int.com
  Chief Exec: Hugh Williams
- ▲ Un-incorporated Society
- Br Africa, Americas, Asia, Europe, Middle East, Pacific
- ○ *T
- Gp Marine; Diving; Safety & legislation; ROV; Survey vessels; Training certification & personal competence
- ● Conf - Mtgs - ET - Exam - LG
- M f
- ¶ IMCA NL - 4; free.

International Masonry Society   1986
- ■ Shermanbury, Church Rd, WHYTELEAFE, Surrey, CR3 0AR. (hsp)
  020 8660 3633   fax 020 8668 6983
  http://www.masonry.org.uk
  Hon Sec: Dr K Fisher
- ▲ Registered Charity
- ○ *L; the science & technology of masonry materials, their interaction & the finished structure; covers all forms of masonry, mortar & ancillary components
- ● Conf - Mtgs - ET
- M 200 i, 23 f, UK / 100 i, 1 f, o'seas
- ¶ Masonry International (Jnl) - 3; £53 m, £64 nm.
  Proceedings - irreg.   AR; free.
- × 2008 (1 January) British Masonry Society

International Mining & Materials Association
     a group of the **Institute of Materials, Minerals & Mining**

International Otter Survival Fund   (IOSF)   1993
- ■ 7 Black Park, BROADFORD, Isle of Skye, IV49 9DE.   (hq)
  01471 822487   fax 01471 822487
  email iosf@otter.org   http://www.otter.org
  Chief Exec: Grace Yoxon
- ▲ Company Limited by Guarantee; Registered Charity
- Br Belarus, Sri Lanka
- ○ *K, *V; 'to conserve otters by safeguarding areas of good habitat & supporting people working in research & rehabilitation worldwide'
- Gp Toxicology
- ● Conf - ET - Res - Inf - Lib - PL
- M 5,500 i, 25 f, 6 org, UK / 420 i, o'seas
  (Sub: £22 i, £200 f, £100 org UK / £28 i o'seas)
- ¶ Proceedings of the European Otter Conference (2007); £35 nm.

International Pen Friends   (IPF)   1967
- ■ PO Box 42, BERWICK-upon-TWEED, TD15 1RU.
  (UK/coordinator)
  01289 331335   fax 01289 331335
  email ipfatuk@aol.com
  UK Coordinator: Mrs Pamela Walker
- ▲ Company Limited by Guarantee
- Br worldwide
- ○ *G, *X; promotion of international correspondence for all age groups
- Gp Sections: Youth (schools service); Language students
- ● Comp - Supply of a pen friend service for all age groups; apply in writing to address above
- M 4,000 i, UK / 250,000 i, o'seas
- ¶ People & Places - 2; £5 each.

International Register of Consultant Herbalists & Homoeopaths (IRCH)   1960
- ■ 1 Institute Row, Townshend, HAYLE, Cornwall, TR27 6AQ. (hsb)
  01736 850941
  email office@gmail.com   http://www.irch.org
  Hon Sec: Marilyn Scott
- ▲ Company Limited by Guarantee
- ○ *M, *P; to promote the interest of herbal medicine; to be a teaching school providing secondary education
- ● Conf - Mtgs - ET - Exam - Res
- < Eur Herbal Practitioners Assn; Brit Herbal Medicine Assn
- M 30 i
  (Sub: £260)
- ¶ Journal of Natural Medicine - 4.
  Note: trades as the General Council & Register of Consultant Herbalists Ltd

International Society of Typographic Designers   (ISTD)   1928
- ■ PO Box 725, TAUNTON, Somerset, TA2 8WE.   (hsp)
  020 7436 0984   fax 020 7637 7352
  email mail@istd.org.uk   http://www.istd.org.uk
  Chmn: Jonathan Doney
- ▲ Company Limited by Guarantee
- Br Ireland, Lebanon, South Africa
- ○ *P; to promote the highest standards of typographic design
- ● Conf - Mtgs - ET - Exam - Exhib - SG - Inf - VE - Student assessment programme for direct entry
- < Intl Congress of Graphic Design Assns
- M 580 i, UK / 75 i, o'seas
- ¶ Typographic - 2; ftm, £12 nm.

International Steel Trade Association   (ISTA)
- ■ Broadway House, Tothill St, LONDON, SW1H 9NQ.   (hq)
  020 7799 2662   fax 020 7799 2468
  email hbailey@steeltrade.co.uk
  http://www.steeltrade.co.uk
  Dir: Hugh W Bailey
- ○ *T; to look after the interests of international steel traders
- ● Mtgs - ET - VE - LG
- M 99 f
- ¶ AR.

International Stress Management Association UK   (ISMA UK) 1984

- ■ PO Box 491, Bradley Stoke, BRISTOL, BS34 9AH.   (hsp)
  0117-969 7284
  email stress@isma.org.uk   http://www.isma.org.uk
  Chmn: Ann McCracken
- ▲ Company Limited by Guarantee; Registered Charity
- Br Australia, Brazil, Eire, Hong Kong, India, Netherlands, Russia, USA
- ○ *P; to promote sound knowledge & best practice in the prevention & reduction of human stress
- Gp Trainers & consultants working with organisations to carry out:
  Primary - Risk assessment
  Secondary - Workshop & training in stress awareness
    & reduction
  Tertiary - Work with people experiencing stress
- ● Conf - Mtgs - LG
- M 550 i
  (Sub: £80)
- ¶ Stress News - 4; ftm, £35 yr nm.

International Underwriting Association of London   (LIRMA) 1991

- NR London Underwriting Centre, 3 Minster Court, Mincing Lane, LONDON, EC3R 7DD.
  020 7617 4444
- ▲ Company Limited by Guarantee
- ○ *T; for international reinsurance & non-marine insurance companies in the international wholesale market

Internet Advertising Bureau: the trade association for online advertising   (IAB)

- NR 14 Macklin St, LONDON, WC2B 5NF.
  020 7050 6969
- ○ *T; interests of the UK internet industry
- M c 450 f

Internet Content Rating Association
  since 2008 **ICRA**

Internet Service Providers' Association   (ISPA UK)   1995

- ■ 28 Broadway, LONDON, SW1H 9JX.   (hq)
  0870 050 0710   fax 0871 594 0298
  email secretariat@ispa.org.uk   http://www.ispa.org.uk
  Sec: Nicholas Lansman
- ▲ Company Limited by Guarantee
- ○ *T; to promote the development of the internet industry
- ● Conf - Mtgs - Res - LG
- < EuroISPA; IWF
- M 159 f
- ¶ Electronic NL - 12; (hardcopy) - 2; both free.

Interpave, the Precast Concrete Paving & Kerb Association
  a product association of the **British Precast Concrete Federation**

Intumescent Fire Seals Association   (IFSA)   1982

- NR 20 Park St, PRINCES RISBOROUGH, Bucks, HP27 9AH.   (hq)
  01844 276928
  http://www.ifsa.org.uk
  Sec: Mrs Christine Barfield
- ▲ Un-incorporated Society
- ○ *T; promotion of benefits both technical & commercial arising from the use of intumescent fire & smoke seals
- Gp Representation on BSS, ISO & CEN standards c'ees
- ● Conf - Mtgs - ET - Res - Expt - Inf
- M 14 f
- ¶ Technical Information Sheets 1-5 - updated.
  IFSA Code.

Inverness Chamber of Commerce   1893

- ■ PO Box 5512, INVERNESS, IV2 3ZE.   (hq)
  01463 718131   fax 01463 231523
  email info@inverness-chamber.co.uk
  http://www.inverness-chamber.co.uk
  Chief Exec: Stewart Nicol
- ▲ Company Limited by Guarantee
- ○ *C
- ● Mtgs - Exhib - LG
- < Aberdeen & Grampian Cham Comm; Scot Chams Comm
- M 319 f
- ¶ inbusiness - 4.   LM; ftm only.

Invertebrate Conservation Trust
  alternative name of **Buglife**

Investment Management Association   (IMA)   1959

- NR 65 Kingsway, LONDON, WC2B 6TD.   (hq)
  020 7831 0898
  Office Mgr: Carolyn Smith
- ○ *T; to improve the regulatory, fiscal & legal environment for unit trusts & investment funds; to increase public awareness of collective investments
- ● Conf - Mtgs - ET - Exam - Res - Stat - Inf - LG
- M f

Investment Property Forum   (IPF)   1988

- ■ New Broad Street House, 35 New Broad St, LONDON, EC2M 1NH.   (hq)
  020 7194 7920   fax 020 7194 7921
  email ipfoffice@ipf.org.uk   http://www.ipf.org.uk
  Exec Dir: Sue Forster
- ▲ Company Limited by Guarantee
- ○ *P; 'to improve the awareness, understanding & efficiency of property as an investment, for its members & other interested parties, including government
- ● Conf - Mtgs - ET - Exam - Res - Stat - Inf - VE - LG - Social lunches & dinners
- M 1,900 i (by invitation only)
- ¶ Investment Property Focus - 3; ftm, on special request nm.
  Annual Review, Report & Accounts - 1; free.

Investor Relations Society   (IR Society)   1980

- ■ Bedford House, 3 Bedford St, LONDON, WC2E 9HD.   (hq)
  020 7379 1763   fax 020 7240 1320
  email enquiries@irs.org.uk   http://www.irs.org.uk
  Communications Mgr: Richard Knight
- ▲ Company Limited by Guarantee
- ○ *N; to promote excellence in investor relations
- ● Conf - Mtgs - ET - Exam - Res - Exhib - Comp - SG - Stat - Inf - Lib - VE - LG
- M 560 i, c 370 f, UK / 60 i, o'seas
  (Sub: £350 or £500)
- ¶ Informed (Jnl) - 4; ftm, £5 nm.
  IR Essentials Guidebooks - irreg; ftm, £15 nm.

Involvement & Participation Association   (IPA)   1884

- NR 42 Colebrooke Row, LONDON, N1 8AF.   (hq)
  020 7354 8040
  http://www.ipa-involvement.com
- ▲ Company Limited by Guarantee; Registered Charity
- ○ *E, *Q; improvement of business performance through involving employees in the operation of the organisation
- M i & f

IOP: The Packaging Society
  a group of the **Institute of Materials, Minerals & Mining**

IPPA - the Early Childhood Organisation   (IPPA)   1969
IRL   Unit 4, Broomhill Business Complex, Broomhill Rd, Tallaght,
          DUBLIN 24, Republic of Ireland.
          353 (1) 463 0010   fax 353 (1) 463 0045
          email info@ippa.ie   http://www.ippa.ie
O   *W; playgroups, parent & toddler groups, full day care groups,
          after-school & out-of-school groups
M   2,400 i & org

Iran Society   1936
■   2 Belgrave Sq, LONDON, SW1X 8PJ.   (hq)
          020 7235 5122   fax 020 7259 6771
          email info@iransociety.org   http://www.iransociety.org
          Hon Sec: Robert McKenzie,
          Chmn: Hugh Arbuthnott
▲   Registered Charity
O   *X; 'to promote learning & advance education regarding Iran,
          its people & culture; no contemporary party politics form any
          part of the Society's activities'
●   Mtgs - Lectures
M   396 i, 10 f
¶   Jnl - 1, free.

Irish Airline Pilots' Association   1946
IRL   Corballis Park, DUBLIN AIRPORT, Co Dublin, Republic of
          Ireland.
          353 (1) 844 5272   fax 353 (1) 844 6051
          email admin@ialpa.net   http://www.ialpa.net
O   *P

Irish Amateur Boxing Association   (IABA)
IRL   National Boxing Stadium, South Circular Rd, DUBLIN 8,
          Republic of Ireland.   (hq)
          353 (1) 453 3371   fax 353 (1) 454 0777
          http://www.iaba.ie
          Hon Sec: Séan Crowley
O   *S

Irish Anti-Vivisection Society   1970
IRL   PO Box 13, GREYSTONES, Co Wicklow, Republic of Ireland.
          353 (1) 282 0154
          http://www.irishantivivisection.org
          Sec: Heather Finnegan
O   *K, *V

Irish Association of Corporate Treasurers
IRL   PO Box 10104, LUCAN, Co Dublin, Republic of Ireland.
          353 (1) 610 8574   fax 353 (1) 621 3494
          email info@treasurers.ie   http://www.treasurers.ie
O   *P

Irish Association for Counselling & Psychotherapy   (IACP)
IRL   21 Dublin Rd, BRAY, Co Wicklow, Republic of Ireland.
          353 (1) 272 3427
          email iacp@irish-counselling.ie
          http://www.irish-counselling.ie
O   *P

Irish Association for Cultural, Economic & Social Relations   1938
NR   120 Haberton Park, BELFAST, BT9 6TU.
          email info@irish-association.org
          http://www.irish-association.org
          Pres: Prof Pauline Murphy
O   *K, *X; to foster understanding between Irish people of different
          traditions

Irish Association of Distributive Trades Ltd
IRL   Rock House, Main St, BLACKROCK, Co Dublin, Republic of
          Ireland.
          353 (1) 288 7584   fax 353 (1) 283 2206
          Dir Gen: Tara Buckley
O   *T; represents food wholesalers in Ireland

Irish Association for Economic Geology
IRL   c/o The Geological Survey of Ireland, Beggars Bush,
          Haddington Rd, Ballsbridge, DUBLIN 4, Republic of Ireland.
          353 (1) 678 2000   fax 353 (1) 678 2589
O   *L; mineral exploration, mining geology & petroleum geology

Irish Association for Industrial Relations   1971
IRL   c/o Dept of Personnel & Employment Relations, University of
          Limerick, LIMERICK, Republic of Ireland.
          353 (61) 202091
          Hon Sec: Dr Noel Harvey
O   *P

Irish Association of International Express Carriers   (IAIEC)
IRL   c/o 28 South Frederick St, DUBLIN 2, Republic of Ireland.
          353 (1) 676 5633   fax 353 (1) 676 5641
          email michael.darcy@darcysmyth.ie
O   *T

Irish Association of Investment Managers   1986
IRL   35 Fitzwilliam Place, DUBLIN 2, Republic of Ireland.
          353 (1) 676 1919   fax 353 (1) 676 1954
          email info@iaim.ie   http://www.iaim.ie
          Sec Gen: Ann Fitzgerald
O   *P; institutional investors in the Irish market

Irish Association of Pension Funds   (IAPF)   1973
IRL   Slane House, 25 Lower Mount St, DUBLIN 2, Republic of
          Ireland.
          353 (1) 661 2427   fax 353 (1) 662 1196
          email info@iapf.ie   http://www.iapf.ie
          Sec: Marie Collins
O   *T

Irish Association of Pigmeat Processors
          a group of **Food & Drink Industry Ireland**

Irish Association of Social Workers   1971
IRL   114-116 Pearse St, DUBLIN 2, Republic of Ireland.
          353 (1) 677 4838   fax 353 (1) 671 5734
          email iasw@eircom.net   http://www.iasw.ie
O   *P

Irish Association for Spina Bifida & Hydrocephalus
IRL   Old Nangor Rd, Clondalkin, DUBLIN 22, Republic of Ireland.
          353 (1) 457 2329   fax 353 (1) 457 2328
          email info@iasbah.ie   http://www.iasbah.ie
          Chief Exec: George Kennedy
O   *W; to provide information, support & advice to people with
          spina bifida &/or hydrocephalus

Irish Astronomical Society   1937
IRL   PO Box 2547, DUBLIN 14, Republic of Ireland.
          email ias1937@hotmail.com
          http://www.irishastrosoc.org
O   *L

Irish Auctioneers & Valuers Institute   (IAVI)   1922
IRL   38 Merrion Sq, DUBLIN 2, Republic of Ireland.   (hq)
          353 (1) 661 1794   fax 353 (1) 661 1797
          email info@iavi.ie
          Chief Exec: Alan A Cooke
O   *P

Irish Bankers' Federation
IRL   Nassau House, Nassau St, DUBLIN 2, Republic of Ireland.
          353 (1) 671 5311   fax 353 (1) 679 6680
          email ibf@ibf.ie   http://www.ibf.ie
          Chief Exec: Pat Farrell
O   *P

Irish Basketball Association
since 2003 **Basketball Ireland**

Irish BioIndustry Association   (IBIA)
IRL   Confederation House, 84-86 Lower Baggot St, DUBLIN 2,
        Republic of Ireland.
        353 (1) 605 1584   fax 353 (1) 638 1584
        email matt.moran@ibec.ie   http://www.ibec.ie/ibia
        Dir: Matt Moran
○   *P
<   IBEC

Irish Book Publishers' Association
alternative name of **CLÉ**

Irish Bowling Association   (IBA)   1904
■   2 Oronsay Crescent, LARNE, Co Antrim, BT40 2HD.   (hsp)
        Hon Sec: Tom McGarel
▲   Un-incorporated Society
○   *S; regulating & organising men's outdoor flat green bowls in
        Ireland
Gp   Irish Bowls Coaches Association; Irish Bowls Umpires
        Association
●   Mtgs - Comp - Inf
<   Wld Bowls; Eur Bowls U; Brit Isles Bowls Coun; NI C'wealth
        Games Coun; NI Sports Forum; NI Sports Trust
>   Bowling League of Ireland; NI Bowling Assn; NI Private Greens
        League; NI Provincial Bowling Assn
M   5,200 i, 125 clubs
¶   Ybk.

Irish Bowls Coaches Association
a group of the **Irish Bowling Association**

Irish Bowls Umpires Association
a group of the **Irish Bowling Association**

Irish Brewers Association
IRL   Confederation House, 84-86 Lower Baggot St, DUBLIN 2,
        Republic of Ireland.
        353 (1) 660 1011   fax 353 (1) 660 1717
        http://www.irishbrewersassociation.ie
○   *T
<   IBEC

Irish Bridge Union
IRL   8 Orchardstown Pk, DUBLIN 14, Republic of Ireland.
        353 (1) 494 7726
        161 Moss Rd, Lambeg, Lisburn, Co Antrim, BT27 4LG.
        Jt Hon Secs: Mrs K Downes & Dr A Hill
○   *G

Irish Business & Employers Confederation   (IBEC)   1993
IRL   Confederation House, 84/86 Lower Baggot St, DUBLIN 2,
        Republic of Ireland.
        353 (1) 605 1500   fax 353 (1) 638 1500
        http://www.ibec.ie
        Dir Gen: Turlough O'Sullivan
○   *T, *N

Irish Cancer Society   1963
IRL   43-45 Northumberland Rd, DUBLIN 4, Republic of Ireland.
        353 (1) 231 0500   fax 353 (1) 231 0555
        email info@irishcancer.ie   http://www.cancer.ie
        Chief Exec: John McCormack
○   *W

Irish Cattle & Sheep Farmers' Association
see title **ICSA**

Irish Cellular Industry Association
IRL   Confederation House, 84-86 Lower Baggot St, DUBLIN 2,
        Republic of Ireland.
        353 (1) 605 1656   fax 353 (1) 638 1656
        email icia@ibec.ie   http://www.icia.ie
        Dir: Tommy McCabe
○   *T
<   IBEC

Irish Chamber of Shipping
IRL   Port Centre, Alexandra Rd, DUBLIN 1, Republic of Ireland.
        353 (1) 855 9011   fax 353 (1) 855 9022
        Dir: B W Kerr
○   *N

Irish Chemical Marketers Association   (ICMA)
IRL   Confederation House, 84-86 Lower Baggot St, DUBLIN 2,
        Republic of Ireland.
        353 (1) 605 1563   fax 353 (1) 638 1563
        Dir: Matt Moran
○   *P
<   IBEC

Irish Chiropodists/Podiatrists Organisation
IRL   c/o Ard na Gréine, Flynn's Cross, BALLINCOLLIG, Co Cork,
        Republic of Ireland.
        353 (21) 487 4560
        Gen Sec: Finbarr Dalton
○   *P

Irish Clothing & Textiles Alliance   (ICATA)
IRL   Confederation House, 84/86 Lower Baggot St, DUBLIN 2,
        Republic of Ireland.
        353 (1) 605 1529   fax 353 (1) 638 1529
        email icata@ibec.ie   http://www.ibec.ie/icata
        Dir: Sean Beary
○   *T
<   IBEC

Irish Co-operative Organisation Society Ltd   (ICOS)
IRL   84 Merrion Sq, DUBLIN 2, Republic of Ireland.
        353 (1) 676 4783   fax 353 (1) 662 4502
        http://www.icos.ie
        Sec: Seamus O'Donohoe
○   *N; for the co-operative movement in Ireland

Irish Cold Storage Federation
IRL   Confederation House, 84-86 Lower Baggot St, DUBLIN 2,
        Republic of Ireland.
        353 (1) 605 1500   fax 353 (1) 638 1500
        http://www.ibec.ie/icsf
○   *T
<   IBEC

Irish College of General Practitioners
IRL   4-5 Lincoln Place, DUBLIN 2, Republic of Ireland.
        353 (1) 676 3705   fax 353 (1) 676 5850
        email info@icgp.ie   http://www.icgp.ie
        Hon Sec: Dr Fiona Graham
○   *P
M   2,600

Irish Commercial Horticultural Association
IRL   c/o Irish Farm Centre, Naas Rd, DUBLIN 12, Republic of
        Ireland.
        353 (1) 450 0266   fax 353 (1) 456 5146
        http://www.ifa.ie
        Exec Sec: Kieran Leddy
○   *F, *H; for growers of vegetables, fruit & ornamental plants

Irish Computer Society   1972
IRL   Crescent Hall, Mount Street Crescent, DUBLIN 2, Republic of
        Ireland.
        353 (1) 644 7820   fax 353 (1) 662 0224
        email info@ics.ie   http://www.ics.ie
        Chief Exec: Jim Friars
○   *P

Irish Concrete Federation
IRL   8 Newlands Business Park, Naas Rd, Clondalkin, DUBLIN 22,
        Republic of Ireland.
        353 (1) 464 0082   fax 353 (1) 464 0087
        email info@irishconcrete.ie   http://www.irishconcrete.ie
        Chief Exec & Sec: John Maguire
○   *T

Irish Concrete Society
IRL   Platin, DROGHEDA, Co Louth, Republic of Ireland.
        353 (41) 987 6466   fax 353 (41) 987 6400
        email secretary@concrete.ie   http://www.concrete.ie
        Hon Sec: Marie O'Donovan
○   *P, *T

Irish Conference of Professional & Service Associations   1946
IRL   93 St Stephen's Green, DUBLIN 2, Republic of Ireland.
        353 (1) 830 3833   fax 353 (1) 830 3331
        Hon Sec: John Healy
○   *N

Irish Congress of Trade Unions   (ICTU)   1959
IRL   31-32 Parnell Sq, DUBLIN 1, Republic of Ireland.
        353 (1) 889 7777   fax 353 (1) 887 2012
        email congress@ictu.ie   http://www.ictu.ie
        4-6 Donegal St Place, Belfast BT1 2FM.
        Gen Sec: David Begg
○   *N, *U
        Note: There are 57 unions affiliated to ICTU; full details are
        contained in 'Administration Yearbook & Diary' (see
        Introduction 3 (c)).

Irish Contract Cleaning Association
IRL   Confederation House, 84/86 Lower Baggot St, DUBLIN 2,
        Republic of Ireland.
        Sec: Sonya Higgins
○   *T; for companies in the commercial cleaning field
<   IBEC

Irish Corrugated Packaging Association
IRL   Confederation House, 84-86 Lower Baggot St, DUBLIN 2,
        Republic of Ireland.
○   *T
<   IBEC

**Irish Cosmetics, Detergents & Allied Products Association
(ICDA)**
IRL   Confederation House, 84-86 Lower Baggot St, DUBLIN 2,
        Republic of Ireland.
        353 (1) 605 1624   fax 353 (1) 638 1624
        email info@icda.ie   http://www.icda.ie
○   *T; to represent the industry & keep it updated on all relevant
        EU rules & regulations
<   IBEC

Irish Council against Blood Sports   1966
IRL   PO Box 88, MULLINGAR, Co Westmeath, Republic of Ireland.
        353 (44) 934 9848
        email icabs@eircom.net
        http://www.banbloodsports.com
        PRO: Aideen Yourell
○   *K

Irish Council for Civil Liberties   (ICCL)   1976
IRL   DMG Business Centre, 9-13 Blackhall Place, DUBLIN 7,
        Republic of Ireland
        353 (1) 799 4504
        email info@iccl.ie   http://www.iccl.ie
        Admin: Dawn Quinn
○   *K

Irish Countrywomen's Association   (ICA)   1910
IRL   58 Merrion Rd, Ballsbridge, DUBLIN 4, Republic of Ireland.
        (hq)
        353 (1) 668 0453   fax 353 (1) 660 9423
        email office@ica.ie   http://www.ica.ie
        Hon Sec: Peg McMeel
○   *G

Irish Creamery Milk Suppliers Association   (ICMSA)
IRL   John Feely House, Dublin Rd, LIMERICK, Republic of Ireland.
        353 (61) 314677   fax 353 (61) 315737
        email icmsa@eircom.net   http://www.icmsa.ie
        Gen Sec: Ciaran Dolan
○   *F; for family farms

Irish Dairy Industries Association
        a group of **Food & Drink Industry Ireland**

Irish Deaf Society   (IDS)   1981
IRL   30 Blessington St, DUBLIN 7, Republic of Ireland.
        353 (1) 860 1878   fax 353 (1) 860 1960
        email info@irishdeafsociety.ie
        http://www.irishdeafsociety.ie
        Chief Exec: Kevin Stanley
○   *W

Irish Deer Farmers & Venison Association
IRL   Ballinea, MULLINGAR, West Meath, Republic of Ireland.   (hsp)
        353 (86) 256 7398
        email highdell@esatclear.ie
        Sec: Fiona Crowe
○   *F, *T

Irish Dental Association   (IDA)   1922
IRL   Unit 2 Leopardstown Office Park, Sandyford, DUBLIN 18,
        Republic of Ireland.
        353 (1) 283 0499   fax 113 (1) 283 0515
        http://www.dentist.ie
        Sec Gen: Donal St A Atkins
○   *P

Irish Direct Marketing Association   (IDMA)
IRL   8 Upper Fitzwilliam St, DUBLIN 2, Republic of Ireland.
        353 (1) 661 0470   fax 353 (1) 830 8914
        email info@idma.ie   http://www.idma.ie
        Chmn: Alex Pigot
○   *T

Irish Draught Horse Society (GB) Ltd   (IDHS(GB))   1980
■   The Forge, Avenue B 10th St, STONELEIGH PARK, Warks,
        CV8 2LG.
        0845 230 0399
        email administrator@idhsgb.com
        http://www.irishdraughthorsesociety.com
        Admin: Carol Malin,   Jenny Beardsmore
▲   Company Limited by Guarantee; Registered Charity
○   *B
●   Conf - Mtgs - ET - Comp - Inf
<   Brit Horse Soc; The Showing Coun
M   850 i
        (Sub: £35)
¶   NL - 4; free.   Ybk - 1; ftm, £7 nm.

Irish Educational Publishers Association
IRL c/o Gill & Macmillan Ltd, Hume Avenue, Park West,
DUBLIN 12, Republic of Ireland.
353 (1) 500 9509   fax 353 (1) 500 9598
email hmahony@gillmacmillan.ie
Sec: Hubert Mahony
○ *T

Irish Engineering Enterprises Federation   (IEEF)
IRL Confederation House, 84/86 Lower Baggot St, DUBLIN 2,
Republic of Irelsnd.
353 (1) 605 1624   fax 353 (1) 638 1624
http://www.ibec.ie/ieef
Dir: Marian Byron
○ *T

Irish Epilepsy Association
see **Brainwave, the Irish Epilepsy Association**

Irish Exporters Association   (IEA)
IRL 28 Merrion Sq, DUBLIN 2, Republic of Ireland.
353 (1) 661 2182   fax 353 (1) 661 2315
email iea@irishexporters.ie   http://www.irishexporters.ie
Chief Exec: John F Whelan
○ *T

Irish Family History Society   1984
IRL PO Box 36, NAAS, Co Kildare, Republic of Ireland.
email ifhs@eircom.net
http://www.homepage.eircom.net/~ifhs/
Chmn: Mary Beglan
○ *G

Irish Family Planning Association   (IFPA)   1969
IRL 60 Amiens St, DUBLIN 1, Republic of Ireland.
353 (1) 806 9444   fax 353 (1) 806 9445
email post@ifpa.ie   http://www.ifpa.ie
Chief Exec: Niall Behan
○ *W

Irish Farmers' Association   1972
IRL Irish Farm Centre, Bluebell, DUBLIN 12, Republic of Ireland.
353 (1) 450 0266   fax 353 (1) 455 1043
email postmaster@ifa.ie   http://www.ifa.ie
Gen Sec: Michael Berkery
○ *F

Irish Federation of Sea Anglers   1953
IRL H O'Rorke, Sports HQ - 13 Joyce Way, Park West Business
Park, DUBLIN 12, Republic of Ireland.
353 (1) 280 6873   fax 353 (1) 280 6873
http://www.ifsa.ie
Hon Sec: H O'Rorke
○ *G, *S

Irish Federation of University Teachers   (IFUT)   1965
IRL 11 Merrion Sq, DUBLIN 2, Republic of Ireland.
353 (1) 661 0910   fax 353 (1) 661 0909
email ifut@eircom.net   http://www.ifut.ie
Gen Sec: Daltún Ó Ceallaigh
○ *E, *P

Irish Film Institute
IRL 6 Eustace St, Temple Bar, DUBLIN 2, Republic of Ireland.
353 (1) 679 5744   fax 353 (1) 677 8755
email info@irishfilm.ie   http://www.irishfilm.ie
Dir: Mark Mulqueen
○ *A
✕ 2003 Film Institute of Ireland

Irish Finance Houses Association Ltd
IRL ICB House, Newstead, Clonskeagh Rd, DUBLIN 14, Republic of
Ireland.
353 (1) 260 7222   fax 353 (1) 260 0336
http://www.ifha.ie
Sec Gen: Séamus Ó Tighearnaigh
○ *T

Irish Fish Processors & Exporters Association
IRL c/o T F Geoghegan, 25 Kincora Ave, Clontarf, DUBLIN 3,
Republic of Ireland.
353 (1) 833 7882
Sec: T F Geoghegan
○ *T

Irish Fish Producers' Organisation
IRL 77 Sir John Rogerson's Quay, DUBLIN 2, Republic of Ireland.
353 (1) 640 1850   fax 353 (1) 640 1851
email ifpo@ifpo.ie   http://www.ifpo.ie
Chief Exec: Lorcán Ó Cinnéide
○ *T

Irish Fishermen's Organisation Ltd   1974
IRL Cumberland House, Fenian St, DUBLIN 2, Republic of Ireland.
353 (1) 661 2400   fax 353 (1) 661 2424
email irishfish@eircom.net
○ *N, *T

Irish Football Association Ltd   (IFA)   1880
■ 20 Windsor Ave, BELFAST, BT9 6EG.   (hq)
028 9066 9458
email info@irishfa.com   http://www.irishfa.com
Chief Exec: Howard J C Wells
▲ Company Limited by Guarantee
○ *S; governing body for Association football in Northern Ireland
● Mtgs - ET - Exam - LG
< Fédn Intle Football Assns (FIFA); U of Eur Football Assns (UEFA)
M [not stated]
¶ IFA Magazine - 2; £2.50.

Irish Forestry Industry Chain
a group of **Food & Drink Industry Ireland**

Irish Franchise Association
IRL 30 Tolka Valley Business Park, Ballyboggan Rd, Glasnevin,
DUBLIN 11, Republic of Ireland.
353 (1) 499 1091   fax 353 (1) 830 3913
http://www.irishfranchiseassociation.com
Chief Exec: Michael Bradley
○ *T

Irish Genealogical Research Society   (IGRS)   1936
NR 18 Stratford Avenue, RAINHAM, Kent, ME8 0EP.   (.)
http://www.igrsoc.org
Br 1; Eire
○ *L
● Mtgs - Res - Lib
M 350 i, 20 org, UK / 550 i, 20 org, o'seas
¶ The Irish Genealogist - 1; £16.   NL - 2; ftm only.

Irish Geological Association
IRL c/o Beggar's Bush, Haddington Rd, DUBLIN 4, Republic of
Ireland.
353 (1) 678 2000
http://www.ucd.ie/geology/IGA
Pres: Barry Long
○ *L

© CBD Research Ltd · Beckenham · BR3 5JS · Tel 020 8650 7745 · Fax 020 8650 0768 · E-mail cbd@cbdresearch.com · www.cbdresearch.com

Irish Georgian Society   (IGS)   1958
IRL   74 Merrion Sq, DUBLIN 2, Republic of Ireland.
         353 (1) 676 7053   fax 353 (1) 662 0290
         email info@igs.ie   http://www.igs.ie
○   *K, *L

Irish Girl Guides
IRL   27 Pembroke Park, DUBLIN 4, Republic of Ireland.
         353 (1) 668 3898   fax 353 (1) 660 2779
         email info@irishgirlguides.ie
         http://www.irishgirlguides.ie
         Chief Exec: Linda Peters
○   *Y

Irish Grain & Feed Association
IRL   19 Carrick Hill, PORTLAOISE, Co Laois, Republic of Ireland.
         353 502 67022   fax 353 502 68690
         email info@eorna.ie   http://www.eorna.ie
         Dir: Deirdre Webb
○   *T; manufacturers of compound animal feed & grain importers
         & traders

Irish Grassland Association
IRL   Curraghclooney, BALLYLOOBY, Co Tipperary, Republic of
         Ireland.
         email secretary@irishgrassland.com
         http://www.irishgrassland.com
○   *P
●   Conf
M   c 1,000

Irish Hardware & Building Materials Association
IRL   Elmville, Upper Kilmacud Rd, Dundrum, DUBLIN 14, Republic
         of Ireland.
         353 (1) 298 0969   fax 353 (1) 298 6103
         email info@ihbma.ie   http://www.ihbma.ie
         Sec Gen: James Goulding
○   *T

Irish Health Services Management Institute
IRL   Hume Street Hospital, DUBLIN 2, Republic of Ireland.
         Hon Sec: Edward J Byrne
○   *P

Irish Hereford Breed Society
IRL   Harbour St, MULLINGAR, Co Westmeath, Republic of Ireland.
         353 (44) 934 8855   fax 353 (44) 934 8949
         http://www.irishhereford.com
         Sec: Laurence Feeney
○   *B

Irish Hockey Association   1893
IRL   Newstead, University College Dublin, Belfield, DUBLIN 4,
         Republic ofIreland.   (mail/address)
         353 (1) 716 3261   fax 353 (1) 716 3260
         email info@hockey.ie   http://www.hockey.ie
         Sec: Joan Morgan
○   *S
✕   2001 (Irish Hockey Union
         (Irish Ladies Hockey Association

Irish Homing Union   (IHU)   1895
NR   38 Ballynahatty Rd, Shaws Bridge, BELFAST, BT8 8LE.   (gen
         s/p)
         028 9064 4231
         email kenmcconaghie38@btinternet.com
         http://www.irishhomingunion.com
         Gen Sec: Ken McConaghie
○   *N, *S; to regulate the sport of pigeon racing in Ireland
M   3,318 i in 121 clubs

Irish Hospital Consultants Association
IRL   Heritage House, Dundrum Office Park, DUBLIN 14, Republic of
         Ireland.
         353 (1) 298 9123   fax 353 (1) 298 9395
         email info@ihca.ie
         Sec Gen: Finbarr Fitzpatrick
○   *P

Irish Hospitality Institute   (IHI)   1966
IRL   8 Herbert Lane, DUBLIN 2, Republic of Ireland.
         353 (1) 662 4790   fax 353 (1) 662 4789
         email info@ihi.ie   http://www.ihi.ie
         Chief Exec: Natasha Kinsella
○   *P
✕   2005 Irish Hotels & Catering Institute

Irish Hotels & Catering Institute
         since 2005 **Irish Hospitality Institute**

Irish Hotels Federation
IRL   13 Northbrook Rd, DUBLIN 6, Republic of Ireland.
         353 (1) 497 6459   fax 353 (1) 497 4613
         email info@ihf.ie   http://www.ihf.ie
         Chief Exec: John Power
○   *T

Irish Hydro Power Association
IRL   c/o Joseph Stewart & Co, Corn Mills, BOYLE, Co Roscommon,
         Republic of Ireland.
         353 (71) 967 0100
         http://www.irishhydro.com
         Chmn: Darrell Nightingale
○   *T; for producers of hydroelectric power; to press for its greater
         use

Irish Institute of Credit Management   (IICM)   1980
IRL   121 Lower Baggot St, DUBLIN 2, Republic of Ireland.
         353 (1) 676 7822
         email iicm@indigo.ie   http://www.iicm.ie
         Chief Exec: Declan Flood
○   *P

Irish Institute of Pensions Managers   1989
IRL   Insurance House, 39 Molesworth Street, DUBLIN 2, Republic of
         Ireland.
         353 (1) 662 0320   fax 353 (1) 677 2621
         http://www.iipm.ie
         Sec: Geoffrey McMaster
○   *P

Irish Institute of Purchasing & Materials Management   (IIPMM)
IRL   5 Belvedere Place, DUBLIN 1, Republic of Ireland.
         353 (1) 855 9257   fax 353 (1) 855 9259
         email iipmm@iipmm.ie   http://www.iipmm.ie
○   *P; the pursuit of excellence in purchasing & materials
         management

Irish Institute of Training & Development   1969
IRL   4 Sycamore House, Millennium Business Park, NAAS,
         Co Kildare, Republic of Ireland.
         353 (45) 881166   fax 353 (45) 881192
         email info@iitd.com   http://www.iitd.ie
○   *P

Irish Institution of Surveyors   (IIS)
IRL   36 Dame St, DUBLIN 2, Republic of Ireland.
         353 (1) 677 4797
         email iissecretary@eircom.net
         http://www.irish-surveyors.ie
         Sec: Vera Destac
○   *P
M   c 320

Irish Insurance Federation   (IIF)
IRL   Insurance House, 39 Molesworth St, DUBLIN 2, Republic of
        Ireland.
        353 (1) 676 1820   fax 353 (1) 676 1943
        email fed@iif.ie   http://www.iif.ie
        Chief Exec: Michael Kemp
○   *T

Irish International Freight Association
IRL   Strand House, Strand St, MALAHIDE, Co Dublin, Republic of
        Ireland.
        353 (1) 845 5411   fax 353 (1) 845 5433
        email iifa@eircom.net   http://www.iifa.ie
        Hon Sec: Michael Slevin
○   *P

Irish Internet Association   1997
IRL   The Digital Hub, 101 James St, DUBLIN 8, Republic of Ireland.
        353 (1) 542 4154
        email info@iia.ie   http://www.iia.ie
        Chief Exec: Irene Gahan
○   *T
M   c 700 f

Irish Kidney Association   (IKA)
IRL   Donor House, Block 43A Park West, Crumlin, DUBLIN 12,
        Republic of Ireland.
        353 (1) 688 9788
        email info@ika.ie   http://www.ika.ie
        Hon Sec: Vera Frisby
Br   24
○   *W

Irish Ladies' Golf Union   1983
IRL   103-105 Q House, 76 Furze Rd, Sandyford Industrial Estate,
        DUBLIN 8, Republic of Ireland.
        353 (1) 293 4833   fax 353 (1) 293 4832
        email info@ilgu.ie   http://www.ilgu.ie
        Chief Exec: Sinead Heraty
○   *S

Irish Landscape Institute   (ILI)   1993
IRL   PO Box 11068, DUBLIN 2, Republic of Ireland.
        353 (1) 662 7409
        http://www.irishlandscapeinstitute.com
        Sec: Lucy Carey
○   *P

Irish League of Credit Unions   (ILCU)
IRL   33-41 Lower Mount St, DUBLIN 2, Republic of Ireland.
        353 (1) 614 6700   fax 353 (1) 614 6701
        email info@creditunion.ie   http://www.creditunion.ie
        Sec: John O'Halloran
○   *N

Irish Legal History Society   (ILHS)   1988
■   c/o Dr David Capper, School of Law, Queens University Belfast,
        BELFAST, BT7 1NN.   (hsb)
        028 9097 3473   fax 028 9097 3376
        email d.capper@gov.ac.uk
        Hon Sec: Dr David Capper
▲   Un-incorporated Society
Br   Republic of Ireland
○   *L; to study of the administration of law & of the development
        of law in Ireland, both pre- & post-partition
●   Conf - Mtgs -ET - Exhib - SG - Inf - Lib
<   informal links with Selden & Stair Societies
M   100 i, UK / 180 i, o'seas
¶   Books & Occasional Papers.

Irish Linen Guild
        To promote Irish linen, a virtual organisation with no address or
        telephone.

Irish Management Institute   (IMI)   1952
IRL   National Management Centre, Sandyford Rd, DUBLIN 16,
        Republic of Ireland.
        353 (1) 207 8400   fax 353 (1) 295 5150
        email reception@imi.ie   http://www.imi.ie
        Chief Exec: Dr Tom McCarthy
○   *P

Irish Marine Federation
IRL   Confederation House, 84/86 Lower Baggot St, DUBLIN 2,
        Republic of Ireland.
○   *T
<   IBEC

Irish Maritime Law Association   (IMLA)   1963
IRL   c/o Matheson Ormsby Prentice, 70 Sir John Robertson's Quay,
        DUBLIN 2, Republic of Ireland.
        353 (1) 232 3333
        email helen.noble@mop.ie
        http://www.irishmaritimelaw.com
        Hon Sec: Helen Nobleer
○   *N

Irish Master Printers' Association   1919
IRL   Sheridan House, 33 Parkgate St, DUBLIN 8, Republic of
        Ireland.
        353 (1) 677 9116   fax 353 (1) 677 9144
        email barbara@rnan.ie
        Chief Exec: Neville Galloway
○   *T

Irish Masters of Beagles Association   1949
IRL   3 Iveragh Rd, Whitehall, DUBLIN 9, Republic of Ireland.
        Hon Dec: Aileen Byrne
○   *S; hare hunting

Irish Medical Devices Association   (IMDA)   1995
IRL   Confederation House, 84/86 Lower Baggot St, DUBLIN 2,
        Republic of Ireland.
        353 (1) 605 1529   fax 353 (1) 638 1529
        email imda@ibec.ie
        Dir: Sharon Higgins
○   *T
<   IBEC
M   85 f

Irish Medical Organisation   (IMO)   1936
IRL   10 Fitzwilliam Place, DUBLIN 2, Republic of Ireland.   (hq)
        353 (1) 676 7273   fax 353 (1) 661 2758
        email imo@imo.ie   http://www.imo.ie
        Chief Exec: George McNeice
○   *P, *U

Irish Mining & Exploration Group   (IMEG)
IRL   Confederation House, 84/86 Lower Baggot St, DUBLIN 2,
        Republic of Ireland.
        Dir: Sean Beary
○   *T
<   IBEC

Irish Mining & Quarrying Society
IRL   Room G16A, UCD School of Geological Sciences, Belfield,
        DUBLIN 4, Republic of Ireland.
        353 (1) 716 2185
        Hon Sec: Brian Burke
○   *P

Irish Moiled Cattle Society
NR   7 The Terrace, Martinstown, DORCHESTER, Dorset, DT2 9JY.
        (mail/address)
○   *B

© CBD Research Ltd · Beckenham · BR3 5JS · Tel 020 8650 7745 · Fax 020 8650 0768 · E-mail cbd@cbdresearch.com · www.cbdresearch.com

Irish Mortgage Council
IRL   Nassau House, Nassau Street, DUBLIN 2, Republic of Ireland.
     353 (1) 677 7612   fax 353 (1) 677 7652
     email imc@ibf.ie   http://www.mortgagecouncil.ie
○   *T
✕   2003 Irish Mortgage & Savings Association

Irish Mountain Training Board
     a group of the **Mountaineering Council of Ireland**

Irish Municipal, Public & Civil Trade Union   (IMPACT)
IRL   Nerney's Court, DUBLIN 1, Republic of Ireland.
     353 (1) 817 1500   fax 353 (1) 817 1501
     http://www.impact.ie
     Gen Sec: Peter McLoone
○   *U
M   c 54,000

Irish Museums Association
IRL   89 Merrion Sq, DUBLIN 2, Republic of Ireland.
     353 (1) 663 3579
     http://www.irishmuseums.org
     Sec: Karin Stierle
○   *G, *P; for all working or interested in museums

Irish National Federation against Copyright Theft   (INFACT) 1982
IRL   PO Box 5344, DUBLIN 7, Republic of Ireland.
     353 (1) 882 8565   fax 353 (1) 882 8594
     email infact@iol.ie
     Dir Gen: Brian Finnegan
○   *T

Irish National Teachers Organisation   (INTO)   1868
IRL   35 Parnell Sq, DUBLIN 1, Republic of Ireland.
     353 (1) 804 7700
     email info@into.ie   http://www.into.ie
     23 College Gardens, BELFAST, BT9 6BS.
     028 9038   1455 fax 028 9066 2803 (Northern office)
     Gen Sec: John Carr
○   *P

Irish Naturist Association   (INA)   1965
IRL   PO Box 1077, Churchtown, DUBLIN 14, Republic of Ireland.
     353 (86) 837 0395   fax 353 (86) 837 0395
     http://www.irishnaturism.org.ie
     Pres: Pat Gallagher
○   *G

Irish Nurses' Organisation   (INO)
IRL   Whitworth Building, North Brunswick St, DUBLIN 7, Republic of Ireland.
     353 (1) 664 0600   fax 353 (1) 664 0466
     email ino@ino.ie   http://www.ino.ie
     Gen Sec: Liam Doran
○   *P
M   c 30,000

Irish Nursing Homes Organisation
     in January 2008 merged with the Federation of Irish Nursing Homes to form **Nursing Homes Ireland**

Irish Offshore Operators Association
IRL   Tramway House, Dartry Rd, DUBLIN 6, Republic of Ireland.
     353 (1) 497 5716   fax 353 (1) 497 5886
     email iooa@tramway.ie   http://www.iooa.ie
     Chmn: Fergus B Cahill
○   *T

Irish Organic Farmers & Growers Association   (IOFGA)
IRL   Main St, NEWTOWNFORBES, Co Longford, Republic of Ireland.
     353 (43) 42495
     email info@iofga.org   http://www.iofga.org
○   *F; for those interested in farming organically

Irish Peatland Conservation Council
IRL   Bog of Allen Nature Centre, Lullymore, RATHANGAN, Co Kildare, Republic of Ireland.
     353 (45) 860133   fax 353 (45) 860481
     email bogs@ipcc.ie   http://www.ipcc.ie
     Sec: Dr Ruth McGrath
○   *K

Irish Pharmaceutical & Chemical Manufacturers Association
     since 2004 **PharmaChemical Ireland**

Irish Pharmaceutical Healthcare Assn   (IPHA)
IRL   Franklin House, 140 Pembroke Rd, DUBLIN 4, Republic of Ireland.   (hq)
     353 (1) 660 3350   fax 353 (1) 668 6672
     email info@ipha.ie   http://www.ipha.ie
     Chief Exec: Anne Nolan
○   *T

Irish Pharmaceutical Union
IRL   Butterfield House, Butterfield Ave, Rathfarnham, DUBLIN 14, Republic of Ireland.
     353 (1) 493 6401   fax 353 (1) 493 6407
     email info@ipu.ie   http://www.ipu.ie
     Sec Gen: Seamus Feely
○   *T

Irish Planning Institute   1975
IRL   The Courtyard (3rd floor), 25 Great Strand St, DUBLIN 1, Republic of Ireland.
     353 (1) 878 8630   fax 353 (1) 878 8682
     http://www.irishplanninginstitute.ie
     Hon Sec: Philip Jones
○   *P

Irish Playwrights & Screenwriters Guild   1969
IRL   Art House, Curved St, Temple Bar, DUBLIN 2, Republic of Ireland.
     353 (1) 670 9970   fax 353 (1) 492 3808
     email david.kavanagh@script.ie   http://www.script.ie
     Chief Exec: David Kavanagh
○   *P

Irish Printing Federation   (IPF)   1899
IRL   Confederation House, 84-86 Lower Baggot St, DUBLIN 2, Republic of Ireland.
     353 (1) 605 1500   fax 353 (1) 638 1500
     Dir: Terry Cummins
○   *T
<   IBEC

Irish Professional Conservators' & Restorers' Association   1982
IRL   PO Box 9185, DUBLIN 4, Republic of Ireland.   (mail address)
     http://www.ipcra.org
▲   Un-incorporated Society
○   *P

Irish Professional Photographers' Association
IRL   5 Naas Rd Business Park, Muirfield Drive, DUBLIN 12, Republic of Ireland.
     353 (1) 429 8648
     email ippa@irishphotographers.com
     Hon Sec: Mick Quinn
○   *P

Irish Property & Facility Management Association   (5PFMA) 1989
IRL   5 Wilton Place, DUBLIN 2, Republic of Ireland.
         353 (1) 676 5500   fax 353 (1) 676 1412
         email info@ipfma.com   http://www.ipfma.com
         Sec: Tony Smith
○   *P

Irish ProShare Association   (IPSA)
IRL   Confederation House, 84-86 Lower Baggot St, DUBLIN 2,
         Republic of Ireland.
○   *P
<   IBEC

Irish Radio Transmitters Society   (IRTS)   1932
IRL   PO Box 462, DUBLIN 9, Republic of Ireland.
         http://www.irts.ie
         Sec: Noel Walsh
○   *G

Irish Real Tennis Association   (IRTA)
IRL   c/o Turnberry, Carrigaline Rd, DOUGLAS, Co Cork, Republic of
         Ireland.
         353 (87) 226 0032
         http://www.irishrealtennis.ie
         Sec: Ted Neville
○   *S

Irish Recorded Music Association   (IRMA)
IRL   IRMA House, 1 Corrig Avenue, DÚN LAOGHAIRE, Co Dublin,
         Republic of Ireland.
         353 (1) 280 6571   fax 353 (1) 280 6579
         email info@irma.ie   http://www.irma.ie
         Sec: Clive Leacy
○   *T

Irish Red Cross Society
IRL   16 Merrion Sq, DUBLIN 2, Republic of Ireland.
         353 (1) 676 5135   fax 353 (1) 661 4461
         email info@redcross.ie   http://www.redcross.ie
         Chmn: David Andrews
○   *W

Irish Retail Newsagents Association
         since May 2006 **Convenience Stores & Newsagents Association**

Irish Road Haulage Association   1973
IRL   Gowna PLaza (suite 6), Bracetown Business Park, CLONEE,
         Co Meath, Republic of Ireland.
         353 (1) 801 3380   fax 353 (1) 825 3080
         email info@irha.ie   http://www.irha.ie
         Pres: Vincent Caulfield
○   *T

Irish Rugby Football Union   (IRFU)   1874
IRL   62 Lansdowne Rd, DUBLIN 4, Republic of Ireland.   (hq)
         353 (1) 647 3800   fax 353 (1) 647 3801
         http://www.irishrugby.ie
         Chief Exec: P R Browne
○   *S

Irish Sailing Association
IRL   3 Park Rd, DÚN LAOGHAIRE, Co Dublin, Republic of Ireland.
         353 (1) 280 0239   fax 353 (1) 280 7558
         email info@sailing.ie   http://www.sailing.ie
         Sec Gen: Paddy Boyd
○   *S

Irish Security Industry Association   (ISIA)   1972
IRL   Unit 1 / IDA Industrial Estate, BALBRIGGAN, Co Dublin,
         Republic of Ireland.
         353 (1) 690 5736   fax 353 (1) 690 5739
         email info@isia.ie   http://www.isia.ie
         Exec Dir: Barry Brady
○   *P, *T

Irish Seed Trade Association
IRL   Marina House, Clarence St, DÚN LAOGHAIRE, Co Dublin,
         Republic of Ireland.
         353 (1) 663 8700   fax 353 (1) 663 8704
         email ista@fmco.ie
         Sec: Patrick O'Mara
○   *T

Irish Ship Agents' Association   (ISAA)
IRL   Ormonde House, 26 Harbour Row, CÓBH, Co Cork, Republic
         of Ireland.
         353 (21) 481 3180   fax 353 (21) 481 1849
         email isaa1@eircom.net
         Pres: Monnie Cliffe
○   *T

Irish Small & Medium Enterprises Association   (ISME)
IRL   17 Kildare St, DUBLIN 2, Republic of Ireland.
         353 (1) 662 2755   fax 353 (1) 661 2157
         email info@isme.ie   http://www.isme.ie
         Sec: Helen Johnston
○   *T

Irish Society
         see the **Honourable The Irish Society**

Irish Society for Archives   1970
IRL   c/o UCD Archives, James Joyce Library, University College
         Dublin, Bellfield, DUBLIN 4, Republic of Ireland.   (mem/sb)
         Hon Mem Sec: Olivia McCormack
○   *L

Irish Society for Autism   (ISA)   1963
IRL   Unity Building, 16-17 Lower O'Connell St, DUBLIN 1, Republic
         of Ireland.
         353 (1) 874 4684   fax 353 (1) 874 4224
         email autism@isa.iol.ie   http://www.autism.ie
         Hon Sec: Nuala Matthews
○   *W

Irish Society of Chartered Physiotherapists
IRL   c/o Royal College of Surgeons, St Stephen's Green, DUBLIN 2,
         Republic of Ireland.
         353 (1) 402 2148   fax 353 (1) 402 2160
         email info@iscp.ie   http://www.iscp.ie
         Chief Exec: Helen McGrath
○   *P

Irish Society of Occupational Medicine   (ISOM)
IRL   PO Box 7453, Ballsbridge, DUBLIN 4, Republic of Ireland.
         email isom@eircom.net   http://www.iol.ie/~isom
         Hon Sec: Dr Fiona Donnelly
○   *P

Irish Society for the Prevention of Cruelty to Animals   (ISPCA) 1949
IRL   Derryglogher Lodge, KEENAGH, Co Longford, Republic of
         Ireland.
         353 / (43) 25035   fax 353 (43) 25024
         email info@ispca.ie   http://www.ispca.ie
         Pres: Pegeen McAllister
○   *V

© CBD Research Ltd · Beckenham · BR3 5JS · Tel 020 8650 7745 · Fax 020 8650 0768 · E-mail cbd@cbdresearch.com · www.cbdresearch.com

**Irish Society for the Prevention of Cruelty to Children   (ISPCC)
1956**
IRL   29 Lower Baggot St, DUBLIN 2, Republic of Ireland.
        353 (1) 676 7960
        email ispcc@ispcc.ie   http://www.ispcc.ie
        Chief Exec: Paul Gilligan
○   *W

Irish Society of Public Health Medicine
IRL   c/o Dr Pasqueline Lyng, Vergemount Hall, Clonkeagh,
        DUBLIN 6, Republic of Ireland.
        353 (1) 268 0300
        Hon Sec: Dr Elaine Martin
○   *P

Irish Software Association   (ISA)
IRL   Confederation House, 84/86 Lower Baggot St, DUBLIN 2,
        Republic of Ireland.
        353 (1) 605 1582   fax 353 (1) 638 1582
        email isa@ibec.ie   http://www.software.ie
        Dir: Shane Dempsey
○   *P
<   IBEC

Irish Spirits Association
        a group of **Food & Drink Industry Ireland**

Irish Sudden Infant Death Association   (ISIDA)   1976
IRL   Carmichael House, 4 North Brunswick St, DUBLIN 7, Republic
        of Ireland.
        353 (1) 873 2711   fax 353 (1) 872 6056
        email kibnsidr@iol.ie   http://www.iol.ie/~isidansr/
        home.htm
        Sec: Frank Dowling
○   *W

Irish Taxation Institute   1967
IRL   South Block, Longboat Quay, Grand Canal Harbour,
        DUBLIN 2, Republic of Ireland.
        353 (1) 663 1700   fax 353 (1) 668 8387
        email info@taxireland.ie   http://www.taxireland.ie
        Chief Exec: Mark Redmond
○   *P
×   2003 Institute of Taxation in Ireland

Irish Taxi Drivers' Federation
IRL   48 Summerhill Parade, DUBLIN 1, Republic of Ireland.
        353 (1) 855 5682   fax 353 (1) 836 4155
        Sec: Martin J Morris
○   *P

Irish Tea Association
        a group of **Food & Drink Industry Ireland**

Irish Texts Society (Cumann na Scríbheann nGaedhilge)   1898
§   69a Balfour St, LONDON, SE17 1PL.   (hsp)
        http://www.irishtextssociety.org
        Hon Sec: Seán Hutton
        The promotion of Irish literature; publishes annotated texts in
        Irish with English translations & related commentaries

Irish Thoroughbred Breeders Association   (ITBA)
IRL   Greenhills, KILL, Co Kildare, Republic of Ireland.
        353 (45) 877543   fax 353 (45) 877429
        email info@itba.ie   http://www.itba.ie
        Sec: Anne O'Connor
○   *P

Irish Timber Growers Association   (ITGA)   1971
IRL   17 Castle St, DALKEY, Co Dublin, Republic of Ireland.
        353 (1) 235 0520   fax 353 (1) 235 0416
        email info@itga.ie   http://www.itga.ie
        Hon Sec: D Bergin
○   *T; private woodland owners

Irish Tourist Industry Confederation   (ITIC)
IRL   17 Longford Terrace, MONKSTOWN, Co Dublin, Republic of
        Ireland.
        353 (1) 284 4222   fax 353 (1) 280 4218
        email itic@eircom.net   http://www.itic.ie
        Chief Exec: Eamonn McKean
○   *N, *T

Irish Translators and Interpreters Association   1986
IRL   Irish Writers' Centre, 19 Parnell Square, DUBLIN 1, Republic of
        Ireland.
        353 (1) 872 1302   fax 353 (1) 872 6282
        http://www.translatorsassociation.ie
        Chmn: Annette Schiller
○   *P

Irish Travel Agents Association   1971
IRL   Heaton House (3rd floor), 32 South William St, DUBLIN 2,
        Republic of Ireland.
        353 (1) 679 4179   fax 353 (1) 671 9897
        email info@itaa.ie
        Chief Exec: Simon Nugent
○   *P
M   365 f

Irish Tyre Industry Association
IRL   PO Box 5387, DUBLIN 13, Republic of Ireland.
        353 (1) 832 4295   fax 353 (1) 832 3129
        http://www.itia.ie
        Chief Exec: Jack Farrell
○   *T

Irish Universities Association   (IUA)   1997
IRL   48 Merrion Square, DUBLIN 2, Republic of Ireland.
        353 (1) 676 4948   fax 353 (1) 662 2815
        email iua@iua.ie   http://www.iua.ie
        Dir: Michael McGrath
M   7 universities
×   2005 (September) Conference of Heads of Irish Universities

Irish Vocational Education Association   (IVEA)   1902
IRL   99 Marlborough Rd, Donnybrook, DUBLIN 4, Republic of
        Ireland.
        353 (1) 496 6033   fax 353 (1) 496 6460
        email info@ivea.ie   http://www.ivea.ie
        Gen Sec: Michael Moriaty
○   *E

Irish Waste Management Association   (IWMA)   1999
IRL   Confederation House, 84/86 Lower Baggot St, DUBLIN 2,
        Republic of Ireland.
        353 (1) 605 1672   fax 353 (1) 638 1672
        email iwma@ibec.ie
○   *T

Irish Wheelchair Association   1960
IRL   Áras Chúchulain, Blackheath Drive, Clontarf, DUBLIN 3,
        Republic of Ireland.
        353 (1) 818 6400   fax 353 (1) 833 3873
        email info@iwa.ie   http://www.iwa.ie
○   *W; to improve the lives of people with physical disabilities in
        Ireland

Irish Women's Bowling Association   (IWBA)   1947
■   30 Cromlyn Fold, HILLSBOROUGH, Co Down, BT26 6SD.
     (hsp)
     028 9268 8254
     email jeanfleming2006@btinternet.com
     http://www.iwba.co.uk
     Hon Sec: Mrs Jean Fleming
○   *S; to encourage the sport of bowls for women
<   Wld Bowls Ltd; Eur Bowls U; Brit Isles Coun (England, Scotland,
     Wales & Jersey)
M   2,400 i

Irish Writers' Union   1986
IRL   Irish Writers' Centre, 19 Parnell Square, DUBLIN 1, Republic of
       Ireland.
       353 (1) 872 1302   fax 353 (1) 872 6282
       http://www.ireland-writers.com
       Hon Sec: Sam McAughtry
○   *A

Irish Youth Hostels Association (An Óige)   (IYHA)
IRL   61 Mountjoy St, DUBLIN 7, Republic of Ireland.
       353 (1) 830 4555   fax 353 (1) 830 5808
       email mailbox@anoige.ie   http://www.anoige.ie
○   *Y; to help all, but especially young people, to a love &
     appreciation of the countryside, particularly by providing
     simple hostel accommodation for them whilst on their travels
<   Intl Youth Hostel Fedn (IYHF)

Iron & Steel Society
     a group of the **Institute of Materials, Minerals & Mining**

Iron & Steel Trades Confederation
     in 2004 merged with the National Union of Knitwear, Footwear &
     Apparel Trades to form **Community**

IsItFair (Campaign for Reform of Council Tax)
NR   Willow Cottage, Church Lane, Headley, BORDEN, Hants,
       GU35 8PJ.
       01428 712680
       http://www.isitfair.co.uk
       Contact: Christine Melsom
○   *K; campaign to reform the council tax & replace it with one
     based on ability to pay

Isle of Man Chamber of Commerce   1956
■   17 Drinkwater St, DOUGLAS, Isle of Man, IM1 1PP.   (hq)
     01624 674941   fax 01624 663367
     email enquiries@iomchamber.org.im
     http://www.iomchamber.org.im
     Chief Exec: Mrs Barbara O'Hanlon
▲   Company Limited by Guarantee
○   *C
●   Mtgs - Expt - Inf - Lib - LG - Seminars
<   Brit Chams Comm
M   370 f, 5 org
¶   Members Classified Directory 2004-05; ftm, £25 nm.

**Isle of Man Natural History & Antiquarian Society
     (IOMNHAS)   1879**
NR   Stream Cottage, Ballacrye, BALLAUGH, Isle of Man, IM7 5AV.
       (hsp)
       Sec: Mrs C J Bryan
▲   Registered Charity
○   *L, 'the advancement of knowledge of natural science, human
     history & cultural development in the Isle of Man & counties
     related thereto'

Isle of Wight Chamber of Commerce, Tourism & Industry   1910
NR   Mill Court, Furrlongs, NEWPORT, Isle of Wight, PO30 2AA.
       (hq)
       01983 520777   fax 01983 554555
       email chamber@iwchamber.co.uk
       http://www.iwchamber.co.uk
       Chief Exec: Kevin Smith
▲   Company Limited by Guarantee
○   *C; business support services
●   Conf - Mtgs - ET - Res - Expt - Inf - Lib - PL - VE - LG
<   Brit Chams Comm (BCC)
M   800 f
¶   Island Business - 12; ftm, £2.25 nm.
     Chamber Directory - 1; ftm. [TBA nm].

Isle of Wight Natural History & Archaeological Society   1919
■   Salisbury Gardens, Dudley Rd, VENTNOR, Isle of Wight,
     PO38 1EG.   (hq/Thurs am)
     01983 855385
     email iwnhas@btinternet.com   http://www.iwnhas.org
     Hon Sec: Mrs Lorna Snow
▲   Registered Charity
○   *L; to promote study of the natural history & archaeology of the
     Isle of Wight (incl the conservation of the flora & fauna & all
     objects of special archaeological & geological interest)
Gp   Access to the countryside; Archaeology; Bat; Botany;
       Conservation working parties; Entomology; Geology;
       Mammals, reptiles & amphibians; Marine & freshwater;
       Ornithology
●   Mtgs - ET - Res - Exhib - Lib - PL - VE - LG (local)
M   c 400 i, UK / 1 i, o'seasls
     (Sub: £15, £20 family)
¶   Proceedings - 1; ftm, £12 nm.   Bulletin - 2; ftm only.
     Isle of Wight Birds - 1; ftm, £8 nm.

Islington Chamber of Commerce & Trade Ltd   (ICCT)   1924
■   40 Bowling Green Lane, LONDON, EC1R 0NE.   (hq)
     020 7970 5670   fax 020 7415 7090
     email admin@islchamber.org.uk
     http://www.islchamber.org.uk
     Mgr: Andrew Mortimer
▲   Company Limited by Guarantee
○   *C
●   Mtgs - ET - Inf - LG
M   370 f
     (Sub: £110-£500)
¶   NL - 12; ftm.

Italian Chamber of Commerce & Industry for the UK
NR   1 Princes St, LONDON, W1B 2AY.   (hq)
       020 7495 8191   fax 020 7495 8194
       email info@italchamind.org.uk
       http://www.italchamind.org.uk
       Sec: Giorgio Giaccardi
○   *C
M   400 f

© CBD Research Ltd · Beckenham · BR3 5JS · Tel 020 8650 7745 · Fax 020 8650 0768 · E-mail cbd@cbdresearch.com · www.cbdresearch.com

ITS United Kingdom   1993

■ Tower Bridge Business Centre (suite 312), 46-48 East Smithfield, LONDON, E1W 1AW.   (hq)
    020 7709 3003   fax 020 7709 3007
    email mailbox@its-uk.org.uk   http://www.its-uk.org.uk
    Chief Exec: Mrs Jennie Martin
▲ Company Limited by Guarantee
○ *T; for UK companies involved in Intelligent Transport Systems - the use of electronic systems & services to provide online route guidance; to improve traffic control & the capacity of roads as an alternative to building new ones, including road charging
Gp Intelligent transport systems: Education, System architecture, Millennium project, Government consultation
● Conf - Mtgs - ET - Res - Exhib - SG - Expt - Inf - Lib - VE - LG
< ITS America; Eur Road Transport Informatics Coordination & Devt Org (ERTICO)
M 80 f, 25 org, UK / 5 org, o'seas
¶ ITS Focus - 4; ftm.

IWO   (IWO)   1946

■ 4 Carlton Court, Team Valley, GATESHEAD, Tyne & Wear, NE11 0AZ.   (hq)
    0191-422 0088   fax 0191-422 0087
    email info@iwo.org.uk   http://www.iwo.org.uk
    Chief Exec: Mrs Lynn Cooper
Br 9
○ *P; for people working in the water industry
● Conf - Mtgs - Exhib - SG - VE
< Engg Coun; Amer Water Works Assn
M 2,000 i, 40 f, UK / 50 i, o'seas
¶ Jnl - 4; ftm, £25 yr nm.

J B Priestley Society   1997
- ■ 54 Framingham Rd, SALE, Cheshire, M33 3RJ.   (hsp)
  0161 962 1477
  email rodslater@ukonline.co.uk
  http://www.jbpriestley-society.com
  Hon Sec: Rod Slater
- ▲ Un-incorporated Society
- ○ *A; appreciation of the works of the English writer J B Priestley (1894-1984)
- ● Mtgs - Exhib - VE - Walks - Archive - Links with drama groups
- M 205 i, 2 f, 4 org, UK / 15 i, o'seas
- ¶ Jnl - 1.   NL - 2.

Jacob Sheep Society Ltd   (JSS)   1969
- ■ Oaktree Farm, Buttermilk Lane, Yarningale Common, CLAVERDON, Warks, CV35 8HP.
  01926 842413   fax 0870 165 1353
  http://www.jacobsheep.freeserve.co.uk
  Sec: Louise Smith
- ▲ Company Limited by Guarantee; Registered Charity
- ○ *B
- ● Mtgs - Exhib - Expt - Inf - VE
- < Nat Sheep Assn
- M 730 i, UK / 24 i, o'seas
- ¶ Jacob Jnl - 3.   Flock Book - 1; £10.

James Hilton Society   (JHS)   2000
- ■ 49 Beckingthorpe Drive, Bottesford, NOTTINGHAM, NG13 0DN.   (hsp)
  Hon Sec: J R Hammond
- ▲ Un-incorporated Society
- ○ *A; to promote interest in the life & work of the novelist & scriptwriter James Hilton (1900-1954), author of Goodbye Mr Chips, Lost Horizon & Random Harvest
- ● Conf - Mtgs - Res - VE
- < Alliance of Literary Socs
- M 70 i, UK / 5 i, o'seas
- ¶ James Hilton (NL) - 4; £10 yr m only.

Jams, Jellies & Marmalades Group
     a group of **Food & Drink Industry Ireland**

Jane Austen Society   1940
- ■ 9 Nicola Close, SOUTH CROYDON, Surrey, CR2 6NA.   (hsp)
  http://www.janeaustensociety.org.uk
  Hon Sec: Maureen Stiller
- ▲ Registered Charity
- Br 12; Australia, Canada, USA
- ○ *A; to foster the appreciation & study of the life, work & times of Jane Austen
- ● Conf - Mtgs - ET - Res - Comp - SG - VE
- < Jane Austen Memorial Trust
- M 1,700 i, UK / 300 i, o'seas
- ¶ NL - 2;   AR - 1; both ftm only.

Japan Society   1891
- ■ Swire House, 59 Buckingham Gate, LONDON, SW1E 6AJ.   (hq)
  020 7828 6330   fax 020 7828 6331
  email info@japansociety.org.uk
  http://www.japansociety.org.uk
  Exec Dir: Captain Robert Guy
- ▲ Company Limited by Guarantee; Registered Charity
- ○ *T, *X; to promote learning & advance education with regard to Japan, its culture & people; to provide resources & support to schools teaching about Japan
- ● Mtgs - ET - Exhib - Inf - Lib - VE - LG
- M 750 i, 250 f, 20 org, UK / 30 i, 30 f, o'seas
- ¶ Proceedings - 1; ftm only.
  Britain and the 're-opening ' of Japan: the Treaty of Yedo of 1858 & the Elgin Mission (2008); £10.
  Biographical Portraits Vol IV.
  Japan Experiences.
- × 2007 Japan 21 (merged)

Japan Society of Scotland   1986
- ■ c/o T Steward, 21/5 Leopold Place, EDINBURGH, EH7 5LB.   (treas/p)
  0131-558 1489   fax 0131-557 9029
  http://www.japansocietyofscotland.org.uk
  Chmn: Prof Stuart Picken
- ▲ Registered Charity
- ○ *X; to foster knowledge & understanding of Japan; to develop & improve relations between Japan & Scotland
- ● Mtgs - VE
- < Japan Soc
- M 100 i, 2 f, 40 students
  (Sub: £15 i, £200 f, £7.50 students)
- ¶ NL - 3; ftm only.

Japanese Chamber of Commerce & Industry in the United Kingdom   (JCCI)   1959
- ■ Salisbury House (5th floor), 29 Finsbury Circus, LONDON, EC2M 5QQ.   (hq)
  020 7628 0069   fax 020 7374 2280
  email chamber@jcci.org.uk
  Sec-Gen: M Takahashi
- ▲ Company Limited by Guarantee
- ○ *C; promotion of UK-Japan economic relations & of the interests of Japanese business in the UK
- ● Mtgs - ET - Expt - Inf - LG
- < Coun of Foreign Chams Comm in the UK
- M 312 f (Japanese owned companies in the UK)
- ¶ JCCI Review (NL) - 4; free.
  Thames (NL in Japanese) - 4;   Members' Directory - 1;
  Economic Trends UK (report in Japanese) - 4; all ftm only.

Japanese Garden Society
- NR Woodzened, Longdene Rd, HASLEMERE, Surrey, GU27 2PQ.
  http://www.jgs.org.uk
  Hon Sec: Mrs Kira Dalton
- ○ *G
- M i
  no further information supplied

Japanese Knotweed Alliance   1999
- NR CABI, Nosworthy Way, WALLINGFORD, Oxon, OX10 8DE.
  01491 829361
  http://www.cabi.org/japaneseknotweedalliance/
  PR & Corporate Communication Mgr: Sarah Wilson
- ○ to highlight the problems posed by Japanese knotweed and to promote its control with natural predators

Jazz Piano Teachers Association   (JAPTA)   2001
NR   70 Culverden Rd, LONDON, SW12 9LS.   (hsp)
    020 8675 0335
    email info@japta.org.uk   http://www.japta.org.uk
    Hon Sec: Robert Webb
▲   Un-incorporated Society
○   *D, *P; for jazz education relating especially to piano
●   ET
M   c 300 i, c 10 f, c 5 org
¶   NL - 2; on web.

Jerome K Jerome Society   (JKJ Society)   1984
■   c/o Fraser Wood (Midlands) Ltd, 15/16 Lichfield St, WALSALL,
    W Midlands, WS1 1TS.   (hsb)
    01922 629000   fax 01922 721065
    email aag@fraser-wood.co.uk@jeromekjerome.com
    Hon Sec: Tony Gray
▲   Registered Charity
○   *A; to research & study the life & works of Jerome Klapka
    Jerome (1859-1927)
●   VE - Annual dinner (May), Christmas concert
M   180 i, 10 f, UK / 10 i, o'seas
¶   Idle Thoughts (NL) - 2; ftm.

Jersey Cattle Society of the UK   (JCS)   1878
NR   Scotsbridge House, Scots Hill, RICKMANSWORTH, Herts,
    WD3 3BB.   (hq)
    01923 695203   fax 01923 695303
    email jcsoffice@jerseycattle.org
    http://www.jerseycattle.org
    Sec: Steve Baker
○   *B
M   700 i

Jersey Chamber of Commerce & Industry Inc   1768
NR   Chamber House, 25 Pier Rd, ST HELIER, Jersey,
    Channel Islands, JE1 4HF.   (hq)
    01534 724536   fax 01534 734942
○   *C
M   f

Jersey Farmers' Union   (JFU)   1919
NR   22 Seale St, ST HELIER, Jersey, Channel Islands, JE2 3QG.
    (hq)
    01534 733581   fax 01534 733582
○   *F

Jewellery Distributors' Association of the UK   (JDA)   1970
NR   Federation House, 10 Vyse St, BIRMINGHAM, B18 6LT.   (hq)
    0121-236 3921
    email secretariat@jda.org.uk   http://www.jda.org.uk
    Sec: Lynn Snead
▲   Company Limited by Guarantee
○   *T; to represent the wholesalers, importers & distributors of
    precious & fashion jewellery & silverware who sell to high
    street jewellery shops
●   Conf - Mtgs - Exhib - Expt - Inf - LG
<   Brit Jewellery, Giftware & Finishing Fedn
M   80 f, UK / 2 f, o'seas
¶   The Distributor - 2; free.

Jewish Historical Society of England   (JHSE)   1893
NR   33 Seymour Place, LONDON, W1H 5AP.   (hq)
    020 7723 5852   fax 020 7723 5852
    email info@jhse.org   http://www.jhse.org
    Contact: The Administrator
○   *L; research into Jewish history
●   Conf - Cultmgs - Res - Comp - Lib
M   i
¶   Transactions - 2 yrly.
    Bulletin, AR & Accounts - 1; ftm only.

Jockeys Association of Great Britain Ltd
    registered name of the rebranded (2008) **Professional Jockeys
    Association**

Johann Strauss Society of Great Britain   1964
■   12 Bishams Court, Church Hill, CATERHAM, Surrey,
    CR3 6SE.   (hsp)
    01883 349681
    Hon Sec: Mrs V E Coates
▲   Un-incorporated Society
○   *D; recording, study, & appreciation of the music of the Strauss
    family & their Viennese contemporaries
●   Mtgs - Exhib - SG - Lib
<   11 sister societies worldwide
M   500 i, UK / 100 i, o'seas
¶   Vienna Music - 2; ftm, £5 nm.   NL - 6; ftm only.

John Bradburne Memorial Society
■   PO Box 32, LEOMINSTER, Herefords, HR6 0YB.
    01568 760632
    email info@johnbradburne.com
    http://www.johnbradburne.com
    Dir & Sec: Celia Brigstocke
○   *G, *W; to support the Mutemwa Leprosy Settlement,
    Zimbabwe, in memory of John Bradburne (1921-1979), who
    worked at the settlement; to disseminate information on John
    Bradburne, poet, pilgrim & prophet

John Buchan Society   1979
■   Barnack, Goring Rd, STEYNING, W Sussex, BN44 3GF.   (hsp)
    01903 813603
    email diana@durden.clara.co.uk
    http://www.johnbuchansociety.co.uk
    Hon Sec: Mrs Diana Durden
▲   Registered Charity
○   *A; to promote a wider understanding & appreciation of the life
    & works of John Buchan (1875-1940)
●   Conf - Mtgs - Res - Inf - VE
<   Alliance of Literary Socs; Biggar Museum Trust
M   430 i, UK / 70 i, o'seas
¶   The John Buchan Jnl - 2; ftm, £4 nm.   NL - 2; ftm only.

John Clare Society   1981
■   9 The Chase, ELY, Cambs, CB6 3DR.   (hsp)
    01353 668438
    Contact: Sue Holgate
▲   Un-incorporated Society
○   *A, *G, *L; to promote the study of the life & work of the poet
    John Clare (1793-1864) & the collection, preservation &
    exchange of items of literary & biographical interest
    associated with him
●   Conf - ET - Res - VE
<   Alliance of Literary Socs
M   i & org

John Curwen Society
    Funding body of the **Curwen Institute**

John Hampden Society (JHS) 1992

NR   Little Hampden, Cryers Hill, HIGH WYCOMBE, Bucks,
     HP15 6JS.   (hq)
     01494 562279
     email enquiries@johnhampden.org
     http://www.johnhampden.org
     Hon Sec: Mrs Anthea Coles
▲   Registered Charity
Br   Australia, New Zealand, USA
○   *G, *L; to make better known the character & achievements of
     the 17th century Parliamentarian John Hampden; to
     stimulate research into his life & times
●   Res - Exhib - Inf - Lib - PL - VE - Lectures - Preservation &
     renovation of monuments & artifacts connected with John
     Hampden
<   English Civil War Soc; Hampden (Maine) Histl Soc
M   130 i, UK / 12 i, o'seas
¶   The Patriot (NL) - 4.
     John Hampden & His Times (brochure).
     John Hampden of Buckinghamshire: the people's hero.
     The Controversy of John Hampden's Death.
     In the Steps of the Patriot (leaflet).

John Innes Manufacturers Association (JIMA) 1975

■   PO Box 8, Dept CBD, HARROGATE, N Yorks, HG2 8XB.   (asa)
     01423 879208   fax 01423 870025
     email info@johninnes.info   http://www.johninnes.info
     Sec & PRO: Brian L Dunsby
▲   Un-incorporated Society
○   *T; to represent the leading independent UK manufacturers of
     John Innes loam-based composts (or potting mixes)
●   Mtgs - Inf - Advertising & PR - Quality standards
M   8 f
¶   Benefits of John Innes loam based compost (leaflet) - 1;
     ftm & consumers.
     Technical Data Sheets (set of 19); ftm & trade enquirers.

John Masefield Society 1992

■   The Frith, LEDBURY, Herefords, HR8 1LW.   (chmn/p)
     01531 633800
     http://www.ies.sas.ac.uk/cmps/projects/masefield/society/
     jmsws.htm
     Chmn: Peter Carter,   Sec: Robert Vaughan
▲   Registered Charity
○   *A; to stimulate interest in the life & works of the poet & novelist
     John Masefield (1878-1967) Poet Laureate 1930-1967
●   Readings - Lectures - Festivals - Screenings - Walks
M   160 i, 2 org
¶   Jnl - 1; ftm, £3 nm.   NL - 2.

John Meade Falkner Society 1999

■   Greenmantle, 75 Main St, Kings Newton, MELBOURNE,
     Derbys, DE73 8BX.   (founder/p)
     01332 865315
     email nebuly@hotmail.co.uk
     http://www.johnmeadefalknersociety.co.uk
     Founder & Hon Sec: Kenneth Hillier
▲   Un-incorporated Society
○   *A; to promote a wider understanding & appreciation of the life
     & works of John Meade Falkner (1858-1932)
●   Mtgs - Res - Inf - VE
<   Alliance of Literary Societies
M   34 i, UK / 15 i, o'seas
¶   Jnl - 1; ftm, £2 nm.   NL - 3; ftm only.

John Moore Society 1988

■   3 Normandy Close, Hampton Magna, WARWICK,
     CV35 8UB.   (hsp)
     01926 494368
     email phillrobbins@yahoo.co.uk
     http://www.gloster.demon.co.uk/JMCM/jmoore.html
     Mem Soc: Phillip Robbins
▲   Un-incorporated Society
○   *A; to promote the life & works of John Moore, the 20th century
     conservation pioneer & author of the 'Brensham Trilogy',
     who was concerned about threats to the countryside
●   Mtgs - ET - Exhib - Inf - Lib - VE
M   150 i, 2 org, UK / 10 i, o'seas
¶   Jnl - 2; ftm, £3.50 nm.

** John Polidori Literary Society

     Organisation lost: see Introduction paragraph 3.

John Snow Society

NR   c/o Caitlyn Booth Royal Institute of Public Health, 28 Portland
     Place, LONDON, W1B 1DE.
     020 7291 8359   fax 020 7291 8383
     http://www.johnsnowsociety.org
○   *L; to promote the life & works of Dr John Snow, the pioneer of
     epidemiological method & celebrated anaesthetist

Johnson Society 1910

■   Johnson Birthplace Museum, Breadmarket St, LICHFIELD,
     Staffs, WS13 6LG.   (hq)
     01543 264972
     Hon Gen Sec: Mrs Norma Hooper
▲   Registered Society
○   *L, study of life, works & times of Dr Samuel Johnson,
     preservation of his birthplace, books, manuscripts etc
●   Mtgs - VE
M   i & org
¶   Transactions - 1; ftm.

Johnson Society of London (JSL) 1928

■   16 Laurier Rd, LONDON, NW5 1SG.   (hsp)
     email memsec@johnsonsocietyoflondon.org
     http://www.johnsonsocietyoflondon.org
     Mem Sec & Treas: Christopher T W Ogden
▲   Un-incorporated Society
○   *L; 'to 'Johnsonise the land' (Boswell); to promote the study of
     Samuel Johnson, his works, his circle, his contemporaries &
     his times'
M   i
¶   The New Rambler - 1; ftm, £5 nm.
     The New Idler - 2-4; ftm only.

Joinery Managers Association

NR   Central Office, 35 Hayworth Rd, Sandiacre, NOTTINGHAM,
     NG10 5LL.
     0115-949 0641
     http://www.central-office.co.uk/jma/
     Dir: David R Winson

Joint Animal By-Products Parliamentary & Advisory Committee

     no longer in existence

© CBD Research Ltd · Beckenham · BR3 5JS · Tel 020 8650 7745 · Fax 020 8650 0768 · E-mail cbd@cbdresearch.com · www.cbdresearch.com

Joint Association of Classical Teachers   (JACT)   1962
- ■ Senate House, Malet St, LONDON, WC1E 7HU.   (hq)
  020 7862 8719   fax 020 7255 2297
  email office@jact.org   http://www.jact.org
  Hon Sec: Alan Clague,   Chmn: Prof Thomas Harrison
- ▲ Registered Charity
- ○ *E, *P; to promote the teaching of the classics in schools; to support those who teach classics
- ● Conf - Mtgs - ET - Exam - Comp - Inf - LG
- < Classical Assn; Brit School at Athens
- > Assn for Latin Teaching (ARLT)
- M 1,308 i, UK / 93 i, o'seas
  (Sub: £40 UK / £42 o'seas)
- ¶ Jnl of Classics Teaching -3; ftm only.
  Omnibus Magazine - 2; ftm, £8.20 (UK), £10 (RoW).

Joint Association of Geoscientists for International Development
a group of the **Geological Society**

Joint Association for Quaternary Research
a group of the **Geological Society**

Joint Committee for Palaeontology
a group of the **Geological Society**

Joseph Conrad Society (UK)   1973
- NR c/o POSK, 238-246 King St, LONDON, W6 0RF.   (hq)
  020 8741 1940
  email theconradian@aol.com
  http://www.josephconradsociety.org
  Sec: Hugh Epstein
- ▲ Registered Charity
- ○ *A, *L; to promote the study of all aspects of the work & life of Joseph Conrad (1857-1924)
- ● Conf - Res - Comp - Lib
- < Joseph Conrad Soc(s) of America & France; Tokyo Conrad Gp (Japan)
- M 50 i, UK / 100 i, o'seas
- ¶ The Conradian - 2; £20.
  Note: the hq is run by the staff of the Polish Library.

Joseph Williamson Society   1989
- NR Williamson Tunnels Heritage Centre, The Old Stableyard, Smithdown Lane, LIVERPOOL, L7 3EE.
  0151-709 6868   fax 0151-709 8156
  http://www.williamsontunnels.co.uk
- ○ *G; for all interested in the tunnels dug under Liverpool at the instigation of the millionaire Joseph Williamson during the early 19th century to give unemployment to men returning from the Napoleonic Wars

Josephine Butler Society   (JBS)   1869
- ■ 4 The Hedges, Penenden Heath, MAIDSTONE, Kent, ME14 2JW.   (hsp)
  01622 679630
  http://www.jbs-webeden.co.uk
  Hon Correspondence Sec: Mrs Jenni Paterson
- ▲ Un-incorporated Society
- ○ *K; 'to promote an equal, moral standard of morality & sexual responsibility between men & women; to expose the traffic in persons & exploitation of prostitution by third parties; to examine existing & proposed legislation in matters relating to prostitution'
- ● Conf - Mtgs - Res - SG - Inf - Lib - LG
- < Intl Abolitionist Fedn; Intl Coun Women; C'wealth Countries League; Nat Coun Women; Women's Coun; Nat Assn Women's Orgs
- M c 80 i
- ¶ News & Views - 1.

Judo Scotland   1949
- NR Adventure Centre, South Platt Hill, Ratho, NEWBRIDGE, EH28 8AA.   (hq)
  0131-333 2981
  email info@judoscotland.com
  http://www.judoscotland.com
  Chief Exec: Colin McIver
- ▲ Company Limited by Guarantee
- ○ *S; governing body for Judo in Scotland
- ● ET - Exam - Comp - Stat
- < Brit Judo Assn
- M 6,000 i, 125 org
- ¶ Judo News - 3; ftm only.
- × 2002 (May) Scottish Judo Federation

Junior Lawyers Division
a group of the **Law Society of England & Wales**

Junk Rig & Advanced Cruising Rig Association   1980
- NR 373 Hunts Pond Rd, Titchfield, FAREHAM, Hants, PO14 4PB.
  01329 842613   fax 01329 315232
  http://www.junkrigs.com
  Sec: Robin Blain

Jussi Björling Appreciation Society   (JBAS)   1988
- ■ Glenaire, 58 Mill Rd, CROWLE, N Lincs, DN17 4LN.   (hsp)
  01724 710334
  email erik.wimbles@btinternet.com
  Sec: Erik Wimbles
- ▲ Un-incorporated Society
- ○ *D; the appreciation of the life, career, art & recordings of the Swedish tenor Jussi Björling (1911-1960)
- ● Conf - VE - Stat - Res
- < Jussi Björling Soc, USA
- M 50 i, UK / 4 i, o'seas
- ¶ NL - 4; ftm only.

Just William Society   1995
- NR 7 Willoughby Rd, BRIDGWATER, Somerset, TA6 7LY.
  01278 421958
  email heardaboutwilliambrown@yahoo.co.uk
  http://www.justwilliamsociety.co.uk
  Sec: Ray Heard

Justice Awareness & Basic Support   (JABS)   1994
- ■ 1 Gawsworth Rd, Golborne, WARRINGTON, Cheshire, WA3 3RF.   (hq)
  01942 713565   fax 01942 713565
  email jackie@jabs.org.uk   http://www.jabs.org.uk
  Founder & Nat Co-ordinator: Jacqueline Fletcher
- ○ *K; 'JABS neither recommends nor advises against vaccinations but aims to promote understanding about immunisations & offer basic support to any parent whose child has a health problem after vaccination'; it is a voluntary support group
- ● Inf

Justices' Clerks' Society   (JCS)   1839
- NR Port of Liverpool Building (2nd floor), Pier Head, LIVERPOOL, L3 1BY.   (hq)
  0151-255 0790   fax 0151-236 4458
  email secretariat@jc-society.co.uk
  http://www.jc-society.co.uk
  Chief Exec: Sid Brighton
- ▲ Company Limited by Guarantee
- Br 16
- ○ *P; promotion of science of law, especially as administered by Justices of the Peace in the UK
- ● Conf - Mtgs - LG
- M i
- ¶ The Justices' Clerk Jnl - 4; ftm.
  Good practice guides; prices vary.

Kaolin & Ball Clay Association (UK) (KaBCA) 2000
■ Par Moor Centre, Par Moor, PAR, Cornwall, PL24 2SQ. (hsb)
01726 811328   fax 01726 811200
http://www.kabca.org
Sec: George Muskett
▲ Company Limited by Guarantee
○ *T; to represent the interests of both ball clay & china clay
producers
Gp Minerals searches
● Mtgs - LG
M 5 f

Karg-Elert Archive (KES) 1987
■ 38 Lyndhurst Ave, TWICKENHAM, Middx, TW2 6BX. (hsp)
020 8894 6859   fax 020 8894 6859
email anthony@caldicott247.fslife.co.uk
http://www.karg-elert-archive.org.uk
Chmn: Anthony Caldicott
○ *D; to further the appreciation, performance & recording of the
music of Sigfrid Karg-Elert (1877-1933) composer & organist
● Res - Inf - Performances
< Karg-Elert Gesellschaft (Germany)
M 45 i, UK / 15 i, o'seas
¶ NL - 2; ftm, 50p nm.   Review - 1; ftm, 50p nm.

Keats-Shelley Memorial Association (Inc) (KSMA) 1906
■ Bedford House, 76a Bedford St, LEAMINGTON SPA, Warks,
CV32 5DT. (hsp)
01926 427400   fax 01926 335133
http://www.keats-shelley.co.uk
Hon Sec: David Leigh-Hunt
▲ Company Limited by Guarantee; Registered Charity
Br Italy
○ *A; to encourage interest in the works of John Keats & Percy
Bysshe Shelley & other Romantic writers; to maintain the
house in which Keats died at 26 Piazza di Spagna (Rome), as
a museum in honour of romantic poets in Italy
● Conf - Mtgs - Comp - Inf - Lib
< Alliance Literary Socs
M i
¶ Annual Review - 1; price on application.

Keep Fit Association (KFA) 1956
NR 1 Grove House, Foundry Lane, HORSHAM, W Sussex,
RH13 5PL. (hq)
01403 266000
email kfa@keepfit.org.uk   http://www.keepfit.org.uk
Sec: Lyn Davis
Br 70
○ *G; 'to enable people of all ages to enjoy a total body
experience; to be able to sample the vitality, energy & variety,
improved stamina, strength & suppleness; develop balance,
agility, coordination & rhythm, to participate in the physical &
mental challenge'
Gp Youth Moves (keep fit for ages 5-16)
● Conf - Mtgs - ET - Exhib - Comp
¶ Quarterly Publication - 3.   NL - 6.
Your Move Magazine - 2.

Keighley & Worth Valley Railway Preservation Society
(KWVRPS) 1962
NR The Railway Station, Haworth, KEIGHLEY, W Yorks,
BD22 8NJ. (hq)
01535 645214   fax 01535 647317
http://www.kwvr.co.uk
▲ Un-incorporated Society
○ *G; preservation of the line as an operating steam passenger
railway
● Running the railway by volunteers
M i

Keith Murray Collectors Club 2000
NR PO Box 2706, ECCLESHALL, Staffs, ST21 6WY. (hsb)
Hon Sec: Leonard Griffin
○ *G; for collectors of ceramics designed by Keith Murray

Kempe Society 1984
■ 41 York Avenue, CROSBY, Merseyside, L23 5RN. (hsp)
0151-924 6345
email collinsp79@hotmail.com
http://www.churchmousewebsite.co.uk
Hon Sec: Philip N H Collins
▲ Un-incorporated Society
○ *A; to encourage the fitting recognition of Charles Kempe
(stained glass painter); to advocate sensitive re-use of glass
at risk from redundant or demolished churches
Gp County recorder section
● Conf - Res - Exhib - PL
< Ecclesiological Soc; Victorian Soc
M 300 i, UK / 20 i, o'seas
¶ Wheatsheaf (NL) - 4; ftm only.
Complete Corpus of Kempe Glass in the UK; £15.

Kennel Club (KC) 1873
■ 1-5 Clarges St, LONDON, W1J 8AB. (hq)
0870 606 6750
http://www.thekennelclub.org.uk
Chief Exec: R Smart
○ *B; to promote the general improvement of dogs, dog shows,
field trials, working trials & obedience classes
Gp Classification of breeds; Registration of pedigrees, transfers,
etc; Registration of societies & associations; Publications;
Crufts Dog Show; Discipline; Awards; Discover dogs
● Mtgs - Exhib - Inf
M 700 i
¶ Kennel Club Ybk - 1; ftm.   Kennel Gazette - 12; ftm.
Kennel Club Stud Book - 1; ftm.
Breeds Record Supplement (7 groups) - 4; ftm.

Kensington & Chelsea Chamber of Commerce (KCCC)
NR The Crypt, St Luke's Church, Sydney St, LONDON, SW3 6NH.
020 7795 0304   fax 020 7795 0306
email kccc@kccc.co.uk   http://www.kccc.co.uk
Admin: Antoinette Pardo
○ *C

Kent Archaeological Society (KAS) 1857
■ The Museum, St Faith's Street, MAIDSTONE, Kent,
ME14 1LH. (hq)
http://www.kentarchaeology.org.uk
Hon Gen Sec: Andrew Moffat
▲ Registered Charity
○ *L; 'study & publication of, & education in, all aspects of
archaeology & history of the ancient county of Kent'
Gp Records; Buildings; Fieldwork; Churches; Place names;
Education; Library; Visual records
● Conf - Res - Exhib - SG - Lib - PL - VE
< to some 193 UK & overseas institutions
M c 1,500 i & org
¶ Archaeologia Cantiana - 1; ftm.   NL - 3; ftm only.
Kent Record Series & Monograph Series - c 1; prices vary.

Kent County Agricultural Society   (KCAS)   1923
NR   County Showground, Detling, MAIDSTONE, Kent, ME14 3JF.
     (hq)
     01622 630975   fax 01622 630978
     email info@kentshowground.co.uk
     http://www.kentshowground.co.uk
     Gen Mgr: David Geoff
▲   Company Limited by Guarantee; Registered Charity
○   *F, *H; improvement of agriculture, forestry, horticulture & allied
     industries: rural crafts, breeding of livestock & the
     demonstration of improved methods
Gp Livestock; Show jumping; Agricultural demonstrations; Bee
     garden; English wine; British food; Forestry; Cherry & soft
     fruit show; Flower show; Crafts; Farming fayre; Trade stands
●   Conf - Mtgs - ET - Exhib - Organisation of the Kent County
     Show
<   Assn Show & Agricl Orgs; Breed Socs
M   2,348 i, 438 f
¶   Kent View - 2; ftm, £1 nm.

Kent & East Sussex Railway Co Ltd   (K&ESR)   1961
■   Tenterden Town Station, Station Rd, TENTERDEN, Kent,
     TN30 6HE.   (hq)
     01580 765155   fax 01580 765654
     email enquiries@kesr.org.uk   http://www.kesr.org.uk
     Co Sec: N Pallant
▲   Company Limited by Guarantee; Registered Charity
○   *G; restoration & operation of vintage railway rolling stock for
     the education & benefit of others; operation of a heritage
     railway as a tourist attraction
Gp Restoration, Maintenance, Engineering
●   Conf - Running a tourist railway - Maintenance of rolling stock
<   Heritage Rly Assn; S E England Tourist Bd; Visit Kent
>   Norwegian Locomotive Trust; Tenterden Terrier Trust
M   2,200 i
     (Sub: £23)
¶   Tenterden Terrier - 3; ftm, £2 nm.
✕   2004 Tenterden Railway Co Ltd

Kent Invicta Chamber of Commerce   1900
■   Ashford Business Point, Waterbrook Avenue, Sevington,
     ASHFORD, Kent TN24 0LH.   (hq)
     01233 503838   fax 01233 503687
     http://www.kentinvictachamber.co.uk
     Chief Exec: Jo James
▲   Company Limited by Guarantee
Br Canterbury, Maidstone
○   *C
●   Conf - Mtgs - Exhib - Expt - Inf - VE - LG
M   600 f
¶   Chamber Update - 12; free.   Diary (inc LM).
✕   2005 Ashford (Kent) Chamber of Commerce, Industry &
     Enterprise

Kentish Cobnuts Association   1991
NR   Apple Trees, Comp Lane, St Mary's Platt, SEVENOAKS, Kent,
     TN15 8NR.   (hsp)
     01732 882734
     http://www.kentishcobnutsassociation.co.uk
     Hon Sec: Alexander Hunt
▲   Un-incorporated Society
○   *T; to promote the growing & marketing of Kentish cobnuts
●   Mtgs - ET - Exhib - VE
M   150 i, UK / 10 i, o'seas
¶   The Cobweb (NL) - 4; free.   Information pack; £5.
     Pruning Kentish Cobnuts; £3.
     In a Nutshell by Meg Game; £5.

Kerry Hill Flock Book Society   1899
■   The Bramleys, Broadheath, PRESTEIGNE, Powys, LD8 2HG.
     (hsp)
     01544 267353   fax 01544 267353
     email kerryhillsheep@excite.co.uk
     http://www.kerryhill.net
     Sec: Mrs Pam Chilman
▲   Registered Charity
○   *B; breeding and marketing of pedigree Kerry Hill sheep
●   Exhib - Inf - Mtgs
M   140 i
¶   Kerry Hill Flock Book - 1; £10

Kesva an Taves Kernewek (Cornish Language Board)
■   16 Trelawney Rd, CALLINGTON, Kernow (Cornwall),
     PL17 7EE.   (hsp)
     01579 382511
     email mpiercekernow@hotmail.com
     http://www.kesva.co.uk
     Sec: Mrs M Pierce
○   *L; promotion of the Cornish language
●   Mtgs - ET - Exam - Res - Inf
M   [not stated]
¶   Books, dictionaries & academic texts.

Keygraphica
     wound up September 2008

Kids' Clubs Network
     since 2004 **4children**

Kilvert Society   1948
NR   30 Bromley Heath Avenue, Downend, BRISTOL, BS16 6JP.
     (hsp)
     email kilvertsociety@here.communigate.co.uk
     Hon Sec: Alan Brimson
▲   Un-incorporated Society
○   *L; to foster an interest in the Rev Francis Kilvert, his work, diary
     & the countryside he loved
●   Conf - Mtgs - Res - Inf - Lib (archives) - PL - VE - Church
     services - Conducted walks
<   William Barnes Soc; Alliance of Literary Socs; John Clare Soc
M   484 i, 3 socs, 4 libs, UK / 116 i, o'seas
¶   Jnl - 3; ftm only.

Kinesiology Federation   (KF)   1991
■   PO Box 28908, DALKEITH, Midlothian, EH22 2YQ.   (admin/p)
     0845 260 1094
     email kfadmin@kinesiologyfederation.org
     http://www.kinesiologyfederation.org
     Admin: Joyce Couper
▲   Company Limited by Guarantee
○   *M, *N, *P; an organisation representing the many varied types
     of kinesiology (a holistic complementary system of natural
     healing based on muscle testing to identify & facilitate the
     release of blocks in the body's vital energies, drawing on
     principles from traditional Chinese medicine)
●   Inf
<   Brit Complementary Medicine Assn
M   378 i, 5 org, UK / 7 i, 2 org, o'seas
¶   KF Today (NL); ftm only.

King's Army
     a group of the **English Civil War Society Ltd**

Kingston Chamber of Commerce   (KCoC)   1903
NR   River Reach House, 31-35 High St, KINGSTON upon THAMES,
      Surrey, KT1 1LF.   (hq)
      020 8541 4441   fax 020 8541 4445
      email chiefexecutive@kingstonchamber.co.uk
      http://www.kingstonchamber.co.uk
      Chief Exec: Lisa Gagliani
▲   Company Limited by Guarantee
○   *C
Gp   Small/medium businesses
●   Mtgs - ET - Expt
M   500 i & f
¶   Eureka - 6; free.

Kipling Society   1927
■   6 Clifton Rd, LONDON, W9 1SS.   (hsp)
      020 7286 0194   fax 020 7286 0194
      email jane@keskar.fsworld.co.uk
      http://www.kipling.org.uk
      Hon Sec: Jane Keskar
▲   Registered Charity
Br   USA
○   *A, *L; to extend the knowledge of Rudyard Kipling (1865-
      1936), his life & works; for anyone interested in his prose &
      verse
●   Mtgs - Inf - Lib (housed at the City University [London])
M   519 i, 90 universities/libraries
¶   The Kipling Jnl - 4; ftm.
      [membership £22].

Kitchen Bathroom Bedroom Specialists Association   (KBSA)
1977
NR   Unit L4A Mill 3, Pleasley Vale Business Park, MANSFIELD, Notts,
      NG19 8RL.   (hq)
      01905 621787   fax 01905 621887
      email info@kbsa.co.uk   http://www.kbsa.co.uk
▲   Company Limited by Guarantee
○   *T; for the independent kitchen, bedroom & bathroom specialist
Gp   Kitchens; Bedrooms; Bathrooms; Fitted interiors
●   Conf - Mtgs - ET - Res - Exhib - Inf - LG
<   CBI; METO; NHIC; NKBA
M   i & f

Kite Society   (KSGB)   1979
■   PO Box 2274, Great Horkesley, COLCHESTER, Essex,
      CO6 4AY.   (hq)
      01206 271489
      email info@thekitesociety.org.uk
      http://www.thekitesociety.org.uk
▲   Un-incorporated Society
Br   5
○   *S; to promote adult kiteflying activities
●   Conf - Res - Exhib - Comp - PL - VE
M   3,500 i, 40 f, UK / 400 i, 30 f, o'seas
¶   The Kiteflier (NL) - 4.

Klinefelter's Syndrome Association   (KSA)
■   56 Little Yeldham Rd, Little Yeldham, HALSTEAD, Essex,
      CO9 4QT.
      0845 230 0047
      email secretary@ksa-uk.co.uk   http://www.ksa-uk.co.uk
▲   Registered Charity
○   *W; gives support & information to adults & parents / carers of
      children with Klinefelter's Syndrome
●   Conf - Mtgs - Inf - Activity weekends
M   140 i
¶   A Guide for Adults; 42p postage.
      A Guide for Parents; 42p postage.
      NL - 4; free.

Kmoch European Bands Society   (KEBS)   1973
■   1 Keelton Close, Bicton Heath, SHREWSBURY, Shropshire,
      SY3 5PS.   (hsp)
      01743 354784
      Hon Sec: K J Bladon
Br   Czech Republic, Sweden
○   *D; history, performance & all aspects of music played by
      military & brass bands in Central Europe
●   Mtgs - Res - Inf - VE
M   90 i, 2 org, UK / 60 i, 4 org, o'seas
¶   Ceska Muzika (Jnl) - 1; ftm, £4 nm.
      Blasmusik Bulletin - 3.

Knights of Royal England   (National Jousting Association)
1985
NR   Beechenwood Farm, Spode Lane, Cowden, EDENBRIDGE,
      Kent, TN8 7HP.   (hq)
      01342 850392   fax 01342 850392
      http://www.knightsroyal.co.uk
      Pres: Jeremy Richardson
▲   Un-incorporated Society
○   *S; to promote, perform & preserve mediaeval jousting & its
      associated history by staging tournaments, educating &
      entertaining
●   Mtgs - ET - Exhib - Comp - Expt - Inf - PL
M   88 i, UK / 19 i, o'seas

Knitting & Crochet Guild   1978
NR   108 Park Lane, KIDDERMINSTER, Worcs, DY11 6TB.
      (mem/sec/p)
      01562 754367
      email guild@blueyonder.co.uk
      http://www.knitting-and-crochet-guild.org.uk
      Mem Sec: Mrs Anne Budworth
▲   Registered Charity
Br   33; Australia, Canada, New Zealand, USA
○   *G; for handknitters, machine knitters, crocheters; to preserve
      the best of the old whilst exploring the new
●   ET - Lib
M   850 i, UK / 50 i, o'seas
¶   Slip Knot - 4;   Hbk - 1;   Assorted Supplements - 4;
      all ftm only.

Knitting Industries' Federation   (KIF)   1970
NR   12 Beaumanor Rd, LEICESTER, LE4 5QA.   (hq)
      0116-266 3332   fax 0116-266 3335
      email directorate@knitfed.co.uk
      Dir: Mrs Anne Carvell
▲   Company Limited by Guarantee
○   *T; promotion of the interests of the textile knitting & hosiery
      industry in the UK; is a non-profit making organisation
Gp   Dyeing & finishing
●   Mtgs - Expt - Inf - Empl - LG
<   EURATEX; Brit Clothing Ind Assn (BCIA); Brit Apparel & Textile
      Confedn
>   Brit Narrow Fabrics Assn (BNFA)
M   280 f
¶   Bulletin - 6;   IR Bulletins - 4;
      Health & Safety Bulletin - 2; all ftm only.
      Knitstats - 1; ftm.   AR; free.

Knowsley Chamber of Industry & Commerce
NR   Business Resource Centre, Admin Rd, KNOWSLEY, Merseyside,
      L33 7TX.
      0151-477 1356   fax 0151-549 1357
      email info@knowsleychamber.org.uk
      http://www.knowsleychamber.org.uk
      Chief Exec: Paula James
○   *C
<   Chams Comm NW

© CBD Research Ltd · Beckenham · BR3 5JS · Tel 020 8650 7745 · Fax 020 8650 0768 · E-mail cbd@cbdresearch.com · www.cbdresearch.com

L P Gas Association (LPGA) 1970
NR   Unit 14 Bow Court, Fletchworth Gate, Burnsall Rd, COVENTRY,
        Warks, CV5 6SP.   (hq)
        02476 711601
        email mail@lpga.co.uk   http://www.lpga.co.uk
        Dir Gen: Tom Fidell
▲   Company Limited by Guarantee
○   *T
●   Conf - Mtgs - Exhib - Stat - Inf - LG
<   Eur LPG Assn (AEGPL)
M   162 f, UK / 2 f, o'seas
¶   NL - 4; ftm only.   AR.
      Codes of Practice (36 to date) - irreg; prices on application.

Laban Guild for Movement & Dance
NR   Creekside, LONDON, SE8 3DZ.
        020 8691 8600   fax 020 8691 8400
        email info@laban.org   http://www.labanguild.f9.co.uk
▲   Registered Charity
○   *D; the promotion & advancement of the study of human
        movement recognising the contribution made by Rudolf
        Laban
Gp   Dance; Movement analysis; Dance notation; Movement/dance
        therapy; Dance in education; Movement for actors; Action
        profiling
●   Conf - Mtgs - ET - Exam - Exhib
<   Motus Humanus (USA); Eurolab (Europe); Foundation for
        Community Dance (UK)
M   240 i, 35 org, UK / 60 i, 25 org, o'seas
¶   Movement & Dance - 4.

LABC (LABC) 2005
■   137 Lupus St, LONDON, SW1V 3HE.   (hq)
        020 7641 8737   fax 020 7641 8739
        email info@labc.uk.com   http://www.labc.uk.com
        Sec & Chief Exec: Paul Everall
▲   Company Limited by Guarantee
○   *P; for local authority building control departments in England
        & Wales; to promote the design & cosntruction of buildings
        that are safe, accessible & environmentally efficient, to
        comply with the building regulations
●   Mtgs - ET - LG
<   Consortium of Eur Bldg Control; Construction Ind Coun;
        UK Green Bldg Coun; Bldg Control Alliance; Bldg Control
        Performance Standards Advy Gp
M   c 4,000 i
¶   Sitelines - 4; LABC Outlook - 12; both free.
      National Directory of Services (LM) - 1; ftm, £15 nm.
      Directory of Local Authority Building Control - 1; ftm only.
      Note: LABC is the trading of the District Surveyors Association
        Ltd

Labologists Society   1958
NR   87 Cambridge Rd, BIRMINGHAM, B13 9UG.   (hsp)
        http://www.labology.org.uk
        Chmn/Sec: D C Adams
▲   Un-incorporated Society
○   *G; research into history of breweries & social history
        connected with the brewing trade. Collection of beer, wines,
        spirits & soft drinks labels, as well as advertising matter
        relating to old breweries

Laboratory Animal Science Association (LASA) 1976
■   PO Box 3993, TAMWORTH, Staffs, B78 3QU.   (asa)
        01827 259130   fax 01827 259188
        email lasa@btconnect.com   http://www.lasa.co.uk
        Admin: Sue Millington
▲   Registered Charity
○   *P, *V; welfare of animals in laboratory science; to promote
        refinement of scientific procedures
Gp   Sections: Management, Animal health & nutrition, Toxicology &
        pathology, Alternatives, Ethics, Transgenic animals
●   Conf - Mtgs - ET - Comp - SG - LG
<   Fedn of Eur Laboratory Animal Science Assns
M   289 i, 14 f, UK / 63 i, 2 f, o'seas
¶   Laboratory Animals (Jnl) - 4;   NL - 4;   AR; all ftm only.

Laboratory Animals Veterinary Association
      is a group of the **British Veterinary Association**

Labour behind the Label   (LBL)
■   10-12 Picton St, BRISTOL, BS6 5QA.   (hq)
        0117-944 1700   fax 0117-942 0164
        email info@labourbehindthelabel
        http://www.labourbehindthelabel.org
        Office Mgr: Bee Hayes
▲   Not for profit organisation
○   K; campaigning towards improvement in rights of working
        conditions for people in the international garment industry
●   Conf - ET - Res - Inf - Empl - Lobbying - Appeals - fundraising
<   Clean Clothes Campaign Intl
M   229 i, 23 org, UK / 14 i, o'seas
        (Sub: £10-£20 i, £50 org)
¶   Action Update - 6; ftm only.

Lace Guild   1976
NR   The Hollies, 53 Audnam, STOURBRIDGE, W Midlands,
        DY8 4AE.   (hq)
        01384 390739   fax 01384 444415
        email hollies@laceguild.org   http://www.laceguild.org
        Hon Chmn: Sue Dane,   Hon Sec: Sara Ruks
▲   Registered Charity
○   *G; to promote understanding of all aspects of lace &
        lacemaking by hand
●   Conf - Mtgs - ET - Exam - Res - Exhib - Comp - SG - Inf - Lib -
        PL
M   c 4,888 i, 30 org, UK / c 1,000 i, 20 org, o'seas
¶   Lace (NL) - 4; £23 (£27 EU, £31 RoW), m only.   AR - 1; ftm
        only.
      Young Lacemaker - 4; £5 (£8 EU, £9 RoW), m only.

Lace Society   1968
NR   PO Box 14463, HENLEY-in-ARDEN, Warks, B95 8AQ.
        email thelacesociety@gmail.com
        http://www.thelacesociety.org.uk
▲   Un-incorporated Society
○   *A; to further interest in lace & lace making
●   Conf - ET - Exhib - Inf - Lib
M   850 i, UK / 36 i, o'seas
¶   Lacemaking (NL) - 4;   AR; both ftm only.

Ladder Stabiliser Manufacturers Association
      since 2005 **Ladder Systems Manufacturers Association**

Ladder Systems Manufacturers Association   (LASMA) 1997
NR   c/o 33 Fulford Cross, YORK, YO1 4PB.   (sb)
        Contact; The Secretary
▲   Un-incorporated Society
○   *T
●   Inf - LG
M   3 f
×   2005 Ladder Stabiliser Manufacturers Association

**Ladies' Association of British Barbershop Singers   (LABBS)
1976**
▲   Un-incorporated Society
○   *A; to encourage & promote singing in 4-part harmony in the
      UK, through education & friendship

Ladies' Golf Union   (LGU)   1893
■   The Scores, ST ANDREWS, Fife, KY16 9AT.   (hq)
      01334 475811   fax 01334 472818
      email info@lgu.org   http://www.lgu.org
      Chief Exec: Shona Malcolm
Br   4
○   *S; the governing body for women's amateur golf in the UK,
      Ireland & overseas; to uphold the rules of the game
●   Mtgs - Lib
<   [too many to list]
M   c 2,760 clubs (representing c 209,000 lady members)
¶   LGU Hbk - 1; £3.

Lakeland Dialect Society   (LDS)   1939
NR   Gale View, Main St, Shap, PENRITH, Cumbria, CA10 3NH.
      (hsp)
      01931 716386
      email lakespeak@galeview.freeserve.co.uk
      http://www.lakelanddialectsociety.org
      Hon Sec: Mrs Jean M Scott-Smith
▲   Un-incorporated Society
○   *L; to study origins & history of dialect, folklore & songs, local
      customs & traditions; to encourage interest in the use of
      dialect speech & writing all particular to the former counties
      of Cumberland, Westmorland & Furness district of Lancashire
      (now encompassed by the modern county of Cumbria)
●   Mtgs - Comp - Inf - Lib - Church service conducted in dialect
      (2-yrly, next June 2006) - Talks & lectures by arrangement
>   Yorkshire Dialect Soc; Northumbrian Language Soc,
      Edwin Waugh Soc
M   264 i, 3 org, 4 colleges & libraries, UK / 9 i, 7 colleges &
      libraries, o'seas
¶   The Jnl - 1; ftm, £1.50 nm.
      Lakeland Treasury 1998; £5 m, £5.50 nm.
      Lakeland Gems 1999; (tape) £5 m, £5.50 nm, (CD) £11 m,
      £11.50 nm.
      Old Fell Side (Kendal) 1991; £5 m, £5.50 nm.
      Susannah Blamire (18th century poet) 1994; £2 m, £2.50 nm.
      Hoosta Ga'an On?, 2002; £7 m, £7.50 nm.

Lanarkshire Chamber of Commerce   2003
■   Barncluith Business Centre, Townhead St, HAMILTON, Lanarks,
      ML3 7DP.
      01698 426882   fax 01698 891916
      email info@lanarkshirechamber.org
      http://www.lanarkshirechamber.org
      Chief Exec: Douglas Millar
○   *C
      Note: was formed in 2003 from a merger of Clyde Vale,
      Hamilton & Clydesdale, Motherwell & District & East Kilbride
      Chambers & the Cambuslang & Rutherglen Business Group

Lancashire Archaeological Society   1975
NR   12a Carleton Avenue, Fulwood, PRESTON, Lancs, PR2 6YA.
      01772 709187
      email bil_shannon@msn.com
      http://www.lancsarchsoc.org.uk
      Sec: Mrs Mavis Shannon

Lancashire Authors' Association   (LAA)   1909
NR   22 Meadowfields, BLACKBURN, Lancs, BB2 4JH. BL5 2BJ.   (sp)
      01254 56788
      Contact: E Ashworth
▲   Un-incorporated Society
○   *L; for writers & lovers of Lancashire literature & history
●   Mtgs - Comp - Lib
M   c 220 i, c 30 libraries & org, UK / c 20 i, c 10 libraries &
      org, o'seas
¶   The Record (Jnl) - 4; ftm only.

Lancashire & Cheshire Antiquarian Society   (LCAS)   1883
■   59 Malmesbury Rd, Cheadle Hulme, CHEADLE, Cheshire,
      SK8 7QL.   (hsp)
      0161-439 7202
      email morrisgarratt@sky.com   http://www.landcas.org.uk
      Hon Sec: Morris Garratt
▲   Un-incorporated Society
○   *L, *Q; for the study of all aspects of the history of the Counties
      Palatine of Lancashire & Cheshire, from antiquity to the
      present day: archaeology, architecture, social, economic &
      industrial history
●   Conf - Mtgs - Res - Lib (housed at Manchester Central
      Reference Library) - VE - Making representations concerning
      listed buildings, conservation areas & major planning
      applications
M   171 i, f & org, UK / c 150 i, f & org, o'seas
¶   Transactions - 1; ftm, £18 nm.

Lancashire Parish Register Society   (LPRS)   1897
■   13 Corrie Drive, Kearsley, BOLTON, Lancs, BL4 8RG.
      (h/treas/p)
      email jr.corrie@ntlworld.com   http://www.genuki.org.uk/
      big/eng/LAN/lprs
      Hon Treas: Mrs Jackie Roberts
▲   Registered Charity
○   *G, L; to transcribe, index & publish the pre-1837 parochial
      registers of ancient Lancashire
●   Mtgs - Transcribing & publishing parish registers
<   Fedn Family History Societies
M   320 i, 55 libraries, UK / 35 i, 30 libraries, o'seas
      (Sub: £25 i, £35 libraries)
¶   NL - irreg; ftm only.
      Printed Parish Registers - 2; £18 to i, £28 libraries).

**Lancashire & Yorkshire Railway Preservation Society   (LYRPS)
1960**
NR   The Railway Station, Haworth, KEIGHLEY, W Yorks,
      BD22 8NJ.   (hq)
      http://www.lyrtrust.org.uk
▲   Registered Charity
○   *G; to seek, preserve &/or restore to working order rolling
      stock & other items of the Lancashire & Yorkshire Railway, its
      connections & records
●   Mtgs

Lancashire & Yorkshire Railway Society   (LYRS)   1950
■   31 Enfield Close, Hilton, DERBY, DE65 5HT.   (hsp)
      01283 730544
      http://www.lyrs.org.uk
      Hon Sec: Martin Nield
▲   Un-incorporated Society
○   *G; to create a permanent record of the 75 years existence of
      The Lancashire & Yorkshire Railway
●   Mtgs - Exhib - Inf - PL - VE
M   671 i, 23 org, UK / 27 i, o'seas
¶   Focus - 3;   NL - 4; both free.

**Lancaster District Chamber of Commerce, Trade & Industry
1897**
■   Commerce House, Fenton St, LANCASTER, LA1 1AB.   (hq)
      01524 381331   fax 01524 389505
      email info@lancaster-chamber.org.uk
      http://www.lancaster-chamber.org.uk
      Chief Exec: Mrs Ann Morris
▲   Company Limited by Guarantee
○   *C
Gp   Industry; Commerce; Retail & retail promotion; Transport
      policy; Economic
      Policy: Transport, Economic development, Finance, Tourism
●   Mtgs - ET - Expt - Inf - Lib - LG
<   N & Wstn Lancs Cham Comm; Chams Comm NW
M   454 f
¶   Business Matters - 12; free.

Land Based Colleges Aspiring to Excellence
alternative name of **Landex**

Land Drainage Contractors Association   (LDCA)   1985
NR   NAC Stoneleigh Park, Stoneleigh, KENILWORTH, Warks,
        CV8 2LG.   (hq)
        01327 263264   fax 01327 263265
        email secretary@ldca.org   http://www.ldca.org
        Sec: Bruce Brockway
▲   Company Limited by Guarantee
○   *T; contractors in agricultural drainage, pipeline utilities &
        highway, & sports turf drainage
Gp   Contractors; Trade manufacturers & suppliers; Consultants
●   Conf - Mtgs - ET - Exhib - VE - LG - Demonstrations
M   70 f
¶   NL - 4; ftm.
        Specifications (at £25 each) for:
        Field drainage.
        Pipeline re-instatement.
        Sports turf drainage.

Land's End - John O'Groats Association   1983
NR   18 Coberley Ave, Davyhulme, MANCHESTER, Lancs,
        M41 8QE.   (h/mem/p)
        http://www.landsendjohnogroats.com
        Mem Sec: Don Dyer
▲   Un-incorporated Society
○   *G, *K; to support, or assist or organise, attempts by the public
        to make a continuous journey from Land's End to John
        O'Groats (or vice versa), in compliance with the law & other
        statutory provisions, for social or recreational purposes
●   Mtgs - Inf
M   c 200 i, UK / 8 i, o'seas
¶   Quo Vadis? (Jnl) - 3; ftm only.   LM - irreg.

Land Interest Group
    a group of the **Defence Manufacturers Association**

Landex - Land Based Colleges Aspiring to Excellence   1950
■   Kingston Maurward College, DORCHESTER, Dorset,
        DT2 8PY.   (sb)
        http://www.landex.org.uk
        Company Sec: David Henley
▲   Un-incorporated Society
○   *P; to support the role & work of UK colleges engaged in the
        provision of further & higher education & training in land
        based & associated subjects
●   Conf - Mtgs - ET - SG - Inf - LG
<   Assn of Colleges
M   34 colls; 8 associate colls
×   2008 Napaeo - the Association for Land Based Colleges

Landlife   1975
NR   National Wildflower Centre, Court Hey Park, LIVERPOOL,
        L16 3NA.   (hq)
        0151-737 1819   fax 0151-737 1820
        email info@landlife.org.uk   http://www.landlife.org.uk
        Chief Exec: Grant Luscombe
▲   Company Limited by Guarantee; Registered Charity
○   *K; a charity taking action for a better environment by creating
        new opportunities for wildlife & encouraging people to enjoy
        them
Gp   Suppliers of wildflower seeds & plants
●   Res - PL - VE
>   Lady Bird Johnson Wildflower Ctr (Texas, USA)
M   200 i
¶   Natterjack News - 2;   AR - 1;
        Wildflower Seed Catalogue - 2 yrly; all free.
        Wildflower Seed & Plant Catalogue - 1.

Landlords' Association of Northern Ireland   (LANI)   1989
NR   197 Lisburn Rd, BELFAST, BT9 7EJ.
        028 9066 7233
        email info@lani.org.uk   http://www.lani.org.uk
○   landlords of private residential accommodation
<   Nat Fedn Residential Landlords

Landor Society of Warwick
    closed November 2008

Landscape Institute   (LI)   1929
NR   33 Great Portland St, LONDON, W1W 8QG.   (hq)
        020 7299 4500   fax 020 7299 4501
        http://www.landscapeinstitute.org
○   *L, *P; the advancement of all aspects of the arts & sciences of
        landscape architecture & management
M   i

Landscape Research Group   (LRG)   1966
■   PO Box 53, Horspath, OXFORD, OX33 1WX.   (asa)
        email admin@landscaperesearch.org
        http://www.landscaperesearch.org
        Chmn: Dr George Revill,   Sec: Dr S Shuttleworth
        Admin: Mrs Pauline Graham
▲   Company Limited by Guarantee; Registered Charity
○   *L; to promote the study of & interest in landscape, landscape
        research & the human environment
●   Conf - Res
M   117 i, 40 f, 150 org, UK / 65 i, 5 f, 90 org, o'seas
¶   Landscape Research Jnl - 4; ftm, £35 nm.   LM.
        Landscape Research Extra (NL) - 3; ftm only

Latex Allergy Support Group
NR   PO Box 27, FILEY, N Yorks, YO14 9YH.
        07071 225838
        http://www.lasg.co.uk
○   *W
●   Helpline: 07071 225838 (Mon-Fri 1900-2200 hrs)

Latin American Association   1986
NR   Priory House, Kingsgate Place, LONDON, NW6 4TA.   (hq)
        020 7372 8653   fax 020 7372 5650
        email admin@casalatina.org.uk
        http://www.casalatina.org.uk
        Chmn: Javier Sanchez
▲   Registered Charity
○   *X; to help Latin-American people living in London by providing
        free/low cost services & a space for events
Gp   Legal advice; Nursery; Psychotherapy; Library; English &
        Spanish classes
●   ET - Exhib - Inf - Lib
M   120 i

**Latin Mass Society for the Preservation of the Tridentine Rite of
    Mass   (LMS)   1965**
■   11-13 Macklin St, LONDON, WC2B 5NH.   (hq)
        020 7404 7284   fax 020 7831 5585
        email thelatinmasssociety@snmail.co.uk
        http://www.latin-mass-society.org
▲   Registered Charity
Br   22
○   *R; preservation & restoration of the Tridentine Rite of Mass in
        the Catholic Church
●   Arranging masses
<   Intl Fedn of Una Voce (Switzerland)
M   4,000 i, UK / 300 i, o'seas
¶   NL - 4; ftm only; and selected bookshops; £1.95 each.

Laurel & Hardy Appreciation Society - Sons of the Desert   1972
NR   63 Wollaston Close, GILLINGHAM, Kent, ME8 9SH.   (hsp)
    01634 371550
    http://www.laurelandhardy.org
    Pres: Robert S Lewis
▲   Un-incorporated Society
◯   *G; founded (in the USA in 1965 & in the UK in 1972) to
    perpetuate the spirit & genius of Laurel & Hardy
●   Conf - VE
<   worldwide Laurel & Hardy Fan Club
M   6,000 i, UK / 10,000 i, o'seas
¶   The Laurel & Hardy Magazine - 4.

Laurence-Moon-Bardet-Biedl Society   (LMBBS)   1987
■   1 Blackthorn Avenue, Southborough, TUNBRIDGE WELLS, Kent,
    TN4 9YA.   (hsp)
    01633 664163
    email chris.humphreys4@ntlworld
    http://www.lmbbs.org.uk
    Sec: Mrs Julie Sales
▲   Registered Charity
◯   *W; 'to support sufferers, families, carers of the syndrome; to
    inform professionals about LMBBS, through our web page,
    leaflets & our family conference'
●   Conf - ET
<   Genetic Interest Gp; Contact-a-Family
M   200 i, UK / 50 i, o'seas
¶   NL - 2;   Conference Report - 1; both free.
    More than meets the eye (medical leaflet);
    LMBBS child at school;   Introducing LMBBS;
    Who are we & how can we help; all free.

Law Centres Federation   (LCF)   1978
■   293-299 Kentish Town Rd (3rd floor), LONDON, NW5 2TJ.
    (hq)
    020 7428 4400   fax 020 7428 4401
    email info@lawcentres.org.uk
    http://www.lawcentres.org.uk
    Dir: Julie Bishop,   Chmn: John Fitzpatrick
▲   Company Limited by Guarantee; Registered Charity
Br   57
◯   *N, *W; to encourage the development of publicly funded legal
    services for those most disadvantaged in society; to provide
    support & development services to Law Centres
●   Conf - Inf - LG
<   Advice Services Alliance; Nat Coun for Voluntary Orgs
M   51 org
¶   Law Centres providing Equal Access for All.
    LCF Promoting Equal Access for All.   AR.

The Law Society of England & Wales   (The Law Society)   1825
NR   Law Society's Hall, 113 Chancery Lane, LONDON,
    WC2A 1PL.   (hq)
    020 7242 1222
    email contact@lawsociety.org.uk
    http://www.lawsociety.org.uk
    Chief Exec: Des Hudson
◯   *P; solicitors
Gp   Association of Muslim Lawyers; Association of Women
    Solicitors; Black Solicitors Network; Commerce & Industry
    Group; Group for Solicitors with Disabilities; Junior Lawyers
    Division; The Law Society's European Group; Society of Asian
    Lawyers; Solicitors in Local Government; Solicitor Sole
    Practitioners Group
M   i & f

Law Society's European Group
    a group of the **Law Society of England & Wales**

Law Society of Ireland   1830
IRL   Blackhall Place, DUBLIN 7, Republic of Ireland.   (hq)
    353 (1) 672 4800   fax 353 (1) 672 4801
    email general@lawsociety.ie   http://www.lawsociety.ie
◯   *P

Law Society of Northern Ireland   1922
■   40 Linenhall St, BELFAST, BT2 8BA.   (hq)
    028 9023 1614   fax 028 9023 2606
    email info@lawsoc-ni.org   http://www.lawsoc-ni.org
    Chief Exec: Alan Hunter
◯   *L, *P; by Royal Charter & Statute, the governing body of
    solicitors in Northern Ireland
Gp   Association of Collaborative Family Lawyers; Environment &
    Planning Law Association; Solicitors' Criminal Bar Associaton
    Lawyers: Company & commercial; Employment
●   Conf - Mtgs - ET - Exam - Res - Stat - Inf - Lib - Empl
<   Intl Bar Assn; C'wealth Bar Assn
M   2.200 i, 575 f
¶   The Writ (NL) - 10; ftm only.
    Solicitors of the Supreme Court of Northern Ireland: List - 2 yrly;
    m only.
    Legal Aid Solicitors List (NL) - 1; free.

Law Society of Scotland   1949
NR   26 Drumsheugh Gardens, EDINBURGH, EH3 7YR.   (hq)
    0131-226 7411   fax 0131-225 2934
    email lawscot@lawscot.org.uk
    http://www.lawscot.org.uk
◯   *L, *P
M   i

Lawn Tennis Association   (LTA)   1888
NR   The National Tennis Centre, 100 Priory Lane, Roehampton,
    LONDON, SW15 5JQ.   (hq)
    020 8487 7000   fax 020 8487 7301
    http://www.lta.org.uk
    Chief Exec: R Draper
◯   *S; promotion of the game of lawn tennis
●   Conf - Mtgs - ET - Exam - Res - Exhib - Comp - Stat - Inf
<   Intl Tennis Fedn; Eur Tennis Assn; Brit Olympic Assn; Central
    Coun Physical Recreation
M   82,000 i, 2,500 clubs, 3,000 schools
¶   Ace & Volley - 11.   British Tennis - 11.
    LTA Hbk - 1; ftm.   AR.

Lawn Tennis Writers Association   (LTWA)   1950
NR   Cedar Lodge, Howe Rd, WATLINGTON, Oxon, OX9 5ER.
    (hsp)
    01491 612042   fax 01491 614104
    http://www.ltwa.org.uk
    Hon Sec: Henry Wancke
◯   *P, *S

Lead Contractors Association   (LCA)   1984
■   Centurion House, 36 London Rd, EAST GRINSTEAD, W Sussex,
    RH19 1AB.   (hq)
    01342 317888   fax 01342 303200
    email rwr@lca.gb.com   http://www.lca.gb.com
    Sec: R W Robertson
▲   Un-incorporated Society
◯   *T; specialist leadwork contractors
Gp   Quality standards; Quality assessment & training
●   Conf - Mtgs - ET - Comp
<   Lead Sheet Assn; Plumbing & Heating Ind Alliance; Summit
    Skills
M   90 f
¶   Quarterly NL;   Annual Directory; both free.

Lead Sheet Association   (LSA)   1926
■   Unit 10 Archers Park, Branbridges Rd, East Peckham,
    TONBRIDGE, Kent, TN12 5HP.   (hq)
    01622 872432   fax 01622 871649
    email leadsa@globalnet.co.uk
    http://www.leadsheetassociation.org.uk
    Co Sec: Mrs B Hawkes
▲   Company Limited by Guarantee
◯   *T
●   ET - Exam - Res - Stat - Inf - Lib
M   4 f
¶   Publications list available.

© CBD Research Ltd · Beckenham · BR3 5JS · Tel 020 8650 7745 · Fax 020 8650 0768 · E-mail cbd@cbdresearch.com · www.cbdresearch.com

Lead Smelters & Refiners Association   (LSRA)   1967
■   17A Welbeck Way, LONDON, W1G 9YJ.   (hq)
     020 7499 8422   fax 020 7493 1555
     email mcdermott@ldaint.org   http://www.ldaint.org
     Sec: Dr David Wilson
○   *T
     No further information supplied

League against Cruel Sports Ltd   (LACS)   1924
NR   Sparling House, 83-87 Union St, LONDON, SE1 1SG.   (hq)
     020 7403 6155
○   *K, *V; to campaign for the protection of animals from cruel
     sports
M   i

**League for the Exchange of Commonwealth Teachers   (LECT)
1901**
NR   7 Lion Yard, Tremadoc Rd, LONDON, SW4 7NQ.   (hq)
     020 7498 1101   fax 020 7720 5403
○   *E, *X; to promote friendly & educational understanding
     through the interchange of teachers between countries of the
     Commonwealth
M   i & org

League Managers Association   (LMA)   1990
■   The Camkin Suite, 1 Pegasus House, Pegasus Court,
     Tachbrook Park, WARWICK, CV34 6LW.   (hq)
     01926 831556   fax 01926 429781
     email lma@lmasecure.com
     http://www.leaguemanagers.com
     Chief Exec: Richard Bevan
▲   Un-incorporated Association
○   *P; for managers at all 92 FA Premier & Football League
     football clubs
●   Mtgs - ET - Exam - SG
M   150 i
¶   Centre Circle - 4; free.   LMA NL - 12; ftm only.

** **League of Professional Craftsmen Ltd**
     Organisation lost, see Introduction paragraph 6

Learning on Screen: the Society for Screen-Based Learning
     since April 2004 has become part of **British Universities Film &
     Video Council**

Leasehold Enfranchisement Association   (LEA)   1988
■   52-3 Kingsway Court, 1st Avenue, HOVE, E Sussex,
     BN3 2LQ.   (chief exec/p)
     01273 705432   fax 01273 735101
     email enfranchiseinfo@yahoo.co.uk
     http://www.leaseadvise.org
     Chief Exec: Shula Rich
▲   Un-incorporated Society
○   *K; 'abolition of leasehold ownership of flats & houses, plus
     easy fair access to freeholds for leaseholders'
●   Conf - Mtgs - ET - Res - SG - Inf - LG
M   8,000 i
¶   Escaping the Leasehold Trap (video); £6 m, £10 nm.

Leather Producers' Association   (LPA)   1919
■   8 Queensberry Rd, KETTERING, Northants, NN15 7HL.   (hq)
     01536 483668   fax 01536 416771
     Sec: Jack Purvis
▲   Company Limited by Guarantee
○   *T; employee relations within the leather producing industry
●   Empl
M   23 f
¶   Leather Technician's Hbk.

Leeds Chamber of Commerce   1851
NR   White Rose House, 28a York Place, LEEDS, W Yorks, LS1 2EZ.
     (hq)
     0113-247 0000   fax 0113-247 1111
     email info@leedschamber.co.uk
     http://www.leedschamber.co.uk
     Chief Exec: Gary Williamson
▲   Company Limited by Guarantee
○   *C
¶   ML - 1.   NL - 6.
     Note: The Leeds Chamber was established in 1785 and was
     the first body in the country to bear the name 'Chamber of
     Commerce'. It was refounded in 1851.

Leek Growers' Association Ltd   (TLGA)
■   133 Eastgate, LOUTH, Lincs, LN11 9QG.   (asa)
     01507 602427   fax 01507 607165
     email crop.association@pvga.co.uk
     http://www.british-leeks.co.uk
     Sec: Mrs Jayne Dyas
○   *T; to provide technical, commercial & marketing information
     for growers
●   Conf - Mtgs - Res - Exhib - Stat - Inf - LG
M   120 f

Left-Handers Association   (LHA)
■   Sterling House, 18 Avenue Rd, BELMONT, Surrey, SM2 6JD.
     (hq)
     020 8770 3722   fax 020 8715 1220
     email enquiries@anythingleft-handed.co.uk
     http://www.anythingleft-handed.co.uk
     Organiser: Lauren Milsom
▲   Un-incorporated Society
○   *G
●   ET - Res - Stat - Inf - LG
<   Left-Handers Club
M   i
¶   The Left-Hander - 12.

Left Handers Club   (LHC)   1990
■   Sterling House, 18 Avenue Rd, BELMONT, Surrey, SM2 6JD.
     (hq)
     020 8770 3722   fax 020 8715 1220
     email enquiries@anythingleft-handed.co.uk
     http://www.anythingleft-handed.co.uk
     Dir: Lauren Milsom
▲   Un-incorporated Society
○   *G; provide support, advice & information for left-handers to
     increase awareness of their needs, particularly in schools; to
     promote research & consideration in product design &
     manufacture
M   i & schools
¶   The Left-Hander (NL).

Legal Aid Practitioners Group
NR   10 Greycoat Place, LONDON, SW1P 1SB.
     020 7960 6068   fax 020 7960 6168
     http://www.lapg.co.uk
○   *P

Legal Defence Union Ltd   (LDU)
NR   Athas House, Inchbare, By EDZELL, Angus, DD9 7QL.
     01356 648480 (Advice Line)
     http://www.ldu.org.uk
     Chief Exec & Company Sec: Prof David O'Donnell
○   to protect the interests of all solicitors in Scotland

Legal Software Suppliers Association   (LSSA)   1996
- ■ River Cottage, Water Lane, North Witham, GRANTHAM, Lincs, NG33 5LJ.   (hq)
  01476 860417   fax 01476 737449
  email sec@lssa.co.uk   http://www.lssa.co.uk
  Sec: Roger M Hancock
- ▲ Un-incorporated Society
- ○ *T; regulatory body for suppliers of software to legal firms & businesses
- ● Conf - Mtgs - ET - Exhib - Inf
- M 25 f
- ¶ NL - 4; free on website.

** **Legalise Cannabis Campaign**
Organisation lost: see Introduction paragraph 3

Leicester Longwool Sheepbreeders' Association   (LLSBA) 1883
- ■ White Lodge Farm, Gaddesby Lane, Frisby on the Wreake, MELTON MOWBRAY, Leics, LE14 2PA.   (hsp)
  http://www.leicesterlongwoolsheepassociation.co.uk
  Chmn: Barry Enderby,   Sec: Mrs S Hatton
- ▲ Un-incorporated Society
- Br Australia, New Zealand, America
- ○ *B; preservation & conservation of the rare breed of which a 85% are scrapie resistant
- ● Mtgs - Inf - VE
- < Rare Breeds Survival Trust; Nat Sheep Assn
- > Rare Breeds Survival Trust (RBST); Nat Sheep Assn
- M 60 i, UK / 5 i, o'seas
  (Sub: £35)
- ¶ NL - 4;   Flock Book (LM) - 1;   AR - 1; all ftm only.

Leicestershire Agricultural Society Ltd   (LAS Ltd)   1833
- ■ The Show Office, Dishley Grange Farm, Derby Rd, LOUGHBOROUGH, Leics, LE11 5SF.   (hq)
  01509 646786   fax 01509 646787
  email info@leicestershireshow.co.uk
  http://www.leicestershireshow.co.uk
  Show Admin: J A Hardy-Smith
- ▲ Company Limited by Guarantee; Registered Charity
- ○ *F, *G
- Gp BSJA showjumping; Cattle; Goats; Horse & pony; Sheep; Dog show; Trade stands; Pigeon & poultry; Heavy horse; Private driving; Funfair; Army
- ● Comp - ET - Leicestershire County Show
- < Various breed socs
- M c 400 i
- ¶ NL - 2;   AR - 1; both free.

Leicestershire Archaeological & Historical Society   (LAHS) 1855
- NR The Guildhall, Guildhall Lane, LEICESTER, LE1 5FQ.   (hq)
  0116-270 3031
  http://www.le.ac.uk/lahs/
  Hon Sec: Dr Alan D McWhirr
- ▲ Registered Charity
- ○ *L; study of archaeological history & preservation of historical buildings in Leicestershire
- Gp Historic buildings; Archaeology
- M i & org
- ¶ NL - 2; ftm.   Transactions - 1; ftm.

Leicestershire Chamber of Commerce   1860
- ■ Charnwood Court, 5b New Walk, LEICESTER, LE1 6TE.   (hq)
  0116-247 1800   fax 0116-247 0430
  email leics@chamberofcommerce.co.uk
  http://www.chamberofcommerce.co.uk
  Managing Dir: Martin Traynor
- ▲ Company Limited by Guarantee
- ○ *C
- ● Mtgs - ET - Res - Stat - Expt - Inf - LG
- < Brit Chams Comm
- M 1,800 f
- ¶ Chamber News - 12.
  Directory - 1.

Leisure Boat Builders Association
a group of the **British Marine Federation**

Leisure Management Contractors Association   (LMCA)   1990
- NR c/o Avalon Leisure Ltd, 141C High St, STREET, Somerset, BA16 0EX.   (sb)
  01458 446878
  email secretary@lmca.info
  Sec: Peter Gilpin
- ○ *T; companies servicing UK local authorities for the furtherance of sport, health & leisure activities
- ● Mtgs - Conf - Inf

Leisure & Outdoor Furniture Association   (LOFA)
- ■ 113 Worcester Rd, CHICHESTER, W Sussex, PO19 4EE.   (asa)
  01243 839593   fax 01243 839467
  http://www.lofa.com
  Sec: Richard Plowman
- ○ *T
- M f
  no further information supplied

Leisure Studies Association   (LSA)   1975
- NR Chelsea School, University of Brighton, EASTBOURNE, E Sussex, BN20 7SP.   (mem sb)
  01323 640357
  Admin: Myrene McFee
- ▲ Registered Charity
- ○ *P; an independent body of researchers, planners, policymakers, administrators & practitioners interested in leisure issues

Leith Chamber of Commerce   1786
- NR Capital House, 2 Festival Sq, EDINBURGH, EH3 9SU.   (hq)
  0131-221 2999   fax 0131-221 2998
  http://www.edinburghchamber.co.uk/member_services/leith_chamber
  Sec: John Kennedy
- ○ *C
- ● Mtgs - ET
- < Edinburgh Cham Comm
- M f
- ¶ Business Comment - 4.

Leopold Stokowski Society   (LSS)   1978
- ■ 12 Market St, DEAL, Kent, CT14 6HS.   (hsp)
  01304 389134   fax 01304 389134
  email leopold.stokowski@yahoo.co.uk
  http://www.stokowskisociety.net
  Sec: Christine Athalie Ducrotoy
- ▲ Un-incorporated Society
- Br Japan, New Zealand, USA
- ○ *D; promotion of Leopold Stokowski's work
- ● Conf - Mtgs - ET - Exhib - Inf - VE
- M 250 i, 6 org, UK/ 250 i, o'seas
- ¶ Toccata (Jnl) - 3; £6 m, £8 nm.

© CBD Research Ltd · Beckenham · BR3 5JS · Tel 020 8650 7745 · Fax 020 8650 0768 · E-mail cbd@cbdresearch.com · www.cbdresearch.com

Let's Face It   (LFI)   1984
■   72 Victoria Avenue, WESTGATE-on-SEA, Kent, CT8 8BH.   (hq)
      01843 833724   fax 01843 835695
      email chrisletsfaceit@aol.com
      http://www.lets-face-it.org.uk
      Chief Exec: Christine Piff
▲   Registered Charity
Br 26; 8 o'seas
○   *W; to give patient & family support when coping with facial
      disfigurement; to advise on surgeons, prosthetics & other
      services
      Incl the junior 'Let's Face It'
Gp Facial cancer; Burns; Accidents; Bells Palsy; Congenital
      disfigurement; Acne; Facial hair; Dysmorphobia
●   Mtgs - SG - Inf
M   c 1,700 i
¶   Lets Face It; £2.50.   NL - 3; £10 yr.
      Me & My Face; 75p.   Leaflets.

Letter Box Study Group   (LBSG)   1976
■   13 Amethyst Ave, Davis Estate, CHATHAM, Kent, ME5 9TX.
      (hsp)
      01634 861714
      email enquiry@lbsg.org   http://www.lbsg.org
      Hon Sec: Mrs Avice Harms
○   *G; to collect, disseminate & record information on letter boxes
      at home & abroad, particularly those of historical importance
      & rarity
●   Conf - Res - Inf
M   c 800 i
¶   NL - 4; ftm only.

Letter File Manufacturers' Association
      a group of the **British Office Supplies & Services Federation**

Leukaemia CARE   1967
NR 1 Birch Court, Blackpole Estate, WORCESTER, WR3 8SG.   (hq)
      01905 755977   fax 01905 755166
      email info@leukaemiacare.org.uk
      http://www.leukaemiacare.org.uk
      Chief Exec: Tony Gavin
▲   Registered Charity
○   *W; to provide vital care & support services to those whose lives
      are affected by leukaemia & allied blood disorders, including
      the welfare of families & carers as well as the sufferers
      themselves
●   Mtgs - Inf - Support via CARE line 0800 169 6680
M   6,200 i, 220 f, 600 org
¶   Focus (NL) - 2.
      Booklets: Insight   Care; all free.
      Framework (AR); ftm, charged to nm.

Lewis Carroll Society   1969
■   50 Lauderdale Mansions, Lauderdale Rd, LONDON,
      W9 1NE.   (hsp)
      email alanwhite@tesco.net
      http://www.lewiscarrollsociety.org.uk
      Sec: Alan White
▲   Registered Charity
○   *A, *G; to promote interest in the life of Charles Lutwidge
      Dodgson (1832-1898); to study works produced under his
      real name & under his famous pseudonym, Lewis Carroll
●   Conf - Mtgs - ET - Res - Exhib - Comp - SG - Inf - VE
<   Lewis Carroll Socs: Australia, Canada, Japan, N America
M   250 i, UK / 150 i, o'seas
¶   The Carrollian (Jnl) - 2; ftm, £10 issue nm.
      Bandersnatch (NL) - 4; ftm, prices vary nm.
      Lewis Carroll Review - 4; ftm, £1 issue nm.

LGcommunications
      abbreviated name of the **Association of Local Government
      Communications**

Liberation - incorporating the Movement for Colonial Freedom   1954
■   9 Arkwright Rd, Hampstead, LONDON, NW3 6AB.   (hq)
      020 7435 4547   fax 020 7435 4547
      email liberation@btinternet.com
      http://www.liberationorg.co.uk
      Gen Sec: Mrs Maggie Bowden
▲   Un-incorporated Society
○   *K; an anti-racist, anti-imperialist organisation for peace &
      social justice concerned with Africa, Asia, Caribbean & Latin
      America
Gp UN; NGO; Women; Racism; Somalis; Sudanese
●   Conf - ET - Res
M   c 1,000 i
¶   Liberation - 6; £2.   AR - 1; free.

Libertarian Alliance   1967
NR 2 Lansdowne Row (suite 35), LONDON, W1J 6HL.
      (accom/add)
      0870 242 1712
      email admin@libertarian.co.uk
      http://www.libertarian.co.uk
      Dir: Dr Sean Gabb
○   *K; 'leading radical pro-free market & civil libertarian group.
      Campaigning for social & economic freedom'
●   Conf - Mtgs - Seminars
<   Intl Soc for Individual Liberty; Libertarian Intl
¶   Free Life (Jnl) - 4.
      c 700 publications in print - list available.

Liberty: National Council for Civil Liberties   (Liberty)   1934
■   21 Tabard St, LONDON, SE1 4LA.   (hq)
      020 7403 3888   fax 020 7407 5354
      http://www.liberty-human-rights.org.uk
      Dir: Shami Chakrabarti
▲   Registered Charity
○   *K; campaigns to extend & defend civil liberties
●   Conf - Mtgs - Res - Inf - Lib - Lobbying - Test case work in UK &
      European courts
<   Intl League of Human Rights
M   7,000 i
¶   Liberty - 4; ftm.   AR.
      Publications list available.

Librarians' Christian Fellowship   (LCF)   1976
■   34 Thurlestone Ave, ILFORD, Essex, IG3 9DU.   (hsp)
      020 8599 1310
      email secretary@librarianscf.org.uk
      http://www.librarianscf.org.uk
      Hon Sec: Graham Hedges
▲   Un-incorporated Society
Br 9
○   *R; 'to enable Christian librarians to consider issues in
      librarianship from a standpoint of the Christian faith...'
Gp C'ee for Overseas Library Development
●   Conf - Mtgs - Res - Exhib - SG - Inf - Lib - VE
<   Chart Inst of Library & Ind Profls; Christian Res Assn;
      Evangelical Alliance; Universities & Colleges' Christian
      Fellowship
M   330 i, UK / 30 i, o'seas
¶   Christian Librarian - 4; ftm, £20 nm.

Librarians of Institutes & Schools of Education   (LISE)   1954
NR Education Library, University of Bristol, 35 Berkeley Square,
      BRISTOL, BS8 1JA.   (sb)
      email sue.chubb@bris.ac.uk
      http://www.www2.worc.ac.uk/lise/
      Sec: Sue Chubb
▲   Registered Charity
Br 28
○   *P; promotes information provision for students, teachers,
      researchers & others engaged in education
●   Conf - Mtgs - ET - Res
M   c 60 f
¶   Education Libraries Jnl - 3.

Library Association of Ireland
IRL   53 Upper Mount St, DUBLIN 2, Republic of Ireland.
         353 (87) 776 8054
         http://www.libraryassociation.ie
         Hon Sec: M Plaice
○   *P

Library Campaign: supporting friends & users of libraries   1984
■   22 Upper Woburn Place, LONDON, WC1H 0TB.
         (mail address)
         0845 450 5946   fax 0845 450 5947
         email librarycam@aol.com
         http://www.librarycampaign.com
         Sec: Andrew Coburn
▲   Registered Charity
○   *K; to advance the lifelong education of the public by the
         promotion, support, assistance & improvement of libraries
         throughout the activities of friends & users' groups
●   Conf - LG
>   UNISON; NASUWT
M   600 i, 10 f, 50 org
         (Sub: £15 i, £100 f, on application org)
¶   The Campaigner (NL) - 2/3; ftm, £30 yr nm.

**Licensed Animal Slaughterers & Salvage Association
(LASSA)   1917**
NR   Hopwood House, Nottingham Rd, Somercotes, ALFRETON,
         Derbys, DE55 4JJ.   (hq)
         01773 602212
         email sydgrotier@aol.com
         Sec: Syd G Grotier
▲   Un-incorporated Society
○   *T; to represent the knacker industry
●   Mtgs - ET - SG - Inf - LG
<   Jt Animal By-Products Parliamentary & Advy C'ee
M   35 i, 75 f, 1 org
¶   NL - 4; ftm only.

Licensed Taxi Drivers' Association Ltd   (LTDA)   1967
NR   Taxi House, Woodfield Rd, LONDON, W9 2BA.   (hq)
         020 7286 1046   fax 020 7286 2494
○   *W; the wellbeing of taxi drivers & their families
M   i

Licensed Vintners' Association   1817
IRL   Anglesea House, Anglesea Rd, Ballsbridge, DUBLIN 4, Republic
         of Ireland.
         353 (1) 668 0215   fax 353 (1) 668 0448
         http://www.lva.ie
         Chief Exec: Donal O'Keeffe
○   *T

Licensing Executives Society Ltd   (LES)   1968
■   c/o Northern Networking Ltd, 1 Tennant Avenue,
         College Milton South, East Kilbride, GLASGOW, G74 5NA.
         (hsb)
         01355 244966   fax 01355 249959
         email LES@glasconf.demon.co.uk
         http://www.bi.les.europe.org
         Hon Sec: Dr John M Roe
▲   Company Limited by Guarantee
○   *P; the successful commercialisation of technology & intellectual
         property rights by licensing or transfer
Gp   Brands; Education; EC Laws; Healthcare; IT & commerce
●   Conf - Mtgs - ET - LG
<   Licensing Executives Soc Intl (LESI)
M   635 i, UK/ 10,000 i, o'seas
¶   News Exchange - 6.   Les Nouvelles - 6.
         LM (LESI) -1.   AR (LESI) - 1.

LIFE   (LIFE)   1970
NR   LIFE House, 1 Mill St, LEAMINGTON SPA, Warks, CV31 1ES.
         (hq)
         01926 421587   fax 01926 336497
         email info@lifecharity.org.uk
         http://www.lifecharity.org.uk
▲   Registered Charity
○   *W; full welfare service before, during & after birth including
         accommodation for homeless mothers; full education service
         in schools & to other groups; research information on all
         reproductive issues

Life Academy   1964
■   9 Chesham Rd, GUILDFORD, Surrey, GU1 3LS.   (hq)
         01483 301170   fax 01483 300981
         email info@life-academy.co.uk
         http://www.life-academy.co.uk
         Chief Exec: Stuart Royston
○   *E, *W; planning & preparation for retirement & life change;
         incl social circumstances, leisure, health, career development
         & training of trainers to assist such guidance
Gp   Retirement; Mid-life planning; Post retirement; Pre-retirement
         education
●   ET - Post-graduate certificate & Masters Programme in Pre-
         Retirement Education & Planning - Introduction to life-
         planning level 3 qualification
M   i & corporate
¶   NL.   Your Retirement - 1.   AR.
         Resource lists & other publications available.
×   2005 Pre-Retirement Association of Gt Britain & N Ireland

Life Insurance Association Ltd
         in 2005 merged with the Society of Financial Advisers to form the
         Personal Finance Society

Lifeboat Enthusiasts' Society   (LBES)   1964
■   13 West Way, Petts Wood, ORPINGTON, Kent, BR5 1LN.   (hsp)
         01689 829068
         Hon Sec: John G Francis
▲   Registered Charity
○   *G; to bring together all with a keen interest in lifeboats & the
         lifeboat service, past & present
●   Res - Stat - PL - Lifeboat modelling
<   R Nat Lifeboat Instn
M   744 i, UK / 29 i, o'seas
¶   NL - 3; ftm only.   Annual Hbk - 1; ftm, £5 nm.

Lift & Escalator Industry Association   (LEIA)   1997
■   33-34 Devonshire St, LONDON, W1G 6PY.   (hq)
         020 7935 3013   fax 020 7935 3321
         email enquiries@leia.co.uk   http://www.leia.co.uk
         Managing Dir: D M Fazakerley
▲   Company Limited by Guarantee
○   *T; interests of manufacturers & distributors of lifts, escalators &
         passenger conveyors & equipment therefor
Gp   Lifts; Escalators; Passenger conveyors
●   Mtgs - ET - Inf - Technical cooperation on high standard of
         design & safety - Standardisation
M   f

© CBD Research Ltd · Beckenham · BR3 5JS · Tel 020 8650 7745 · Fax 020 8650 0768 · E-mail cbd@cbdresearch.com · www.cbdresearch.com

Lifting Equipment Engineers Association   (LEEA)   1944
- ■ 3 Osprey Court, Kingfisher Way, Hinchingbrooke Business Park, HUNTINGDON, Cambs, PE29 6FN.   (hq)
  01480 432801   fax 01480 436324
  http://www.leea.co.uk
  Chief Exec: Derrick Bailes
- ▲ Company Limited by Guarantee
- ○ *T; interests of specialists engaged in design, manufacture, testing, examination, inspection, sale, repair, maintenance & hire of lifting equipment
- Gp Technical; Examination; Registration
- ● Conf - Mtgs - ET - Exam - Exhib - SG - Inf - Lib
- M 163 f, UK / 115 f, o'seas
  (Sub: £880 f, UK / £780 f, o'seas)
- ¶ Bulletin - 8;   LM;   AR - 1; all ftm only.
  Lifting Engineers Hbk; £8 m, £20 nm.
  Lifting Equipment - a user's pocket guide; £8.
  Code of Practice for Safe Use of Lifting Equipment; £81 m, £135 nm.
  Hand Chain Blocks & Lever Hoists in the Offshore Environment; £10 m, £15 nm.

Light Aircraft Association   (LAA)   1946
- ■ Turweston Aerodrome, BRACKLEY, Northants, NN13 5YD. (hq)
  01280 846786   fax 01280 846780
  email office@laa.uk.com   http://www.laa.uk.com
  Chmn: Roger Hopkinson,   Sec: Bob Littledale
- ▲ Company Limited by Guarantee
- ○ *G, *S; the representative body in the UK for amateur aircraft construction, recreational & sport flying; encourages amateur design; promotes clubs & light aviation's infrastructure
- Gp Engineering (to administer & regulate amateur aircraft construction)
- ● Conf - Mtgs - ET - Res - Inf - Lib - LG - Annual international air rally
- < R Aero Club; Sports Council
- M 8,500 i
- ¶ Light Aviation (Jnl) - 12; ftm, £5 each nm.
- ✕ 2007 Popular Flying Association

Light Music Society   1957
- ■ Lancaster Farm, Chipping Lane, Longridge, PRESTON, Lancs, PR3 2NB.   (chmn/p)
  01772 783646   fax 01772 786026
  email hilary.ashton@talk21.com
  http://www.lightmusicsociety.com
  Sec & Librarian: Mrs H Ashton
- ▲ Un-incorporated Society
- ○ *D; to act as the backing organisation for the Library of Light-Orchestral Music; this music is available for hire by members & provides an archive of the kind of music played by popular orchestras for over a one hundred years
- ● Mtgs - Inf - Lib
- M 385 i, UK / 15 i, o'seas
- ¶ NL - 3/4; ftm only.

Light Rail Transit Association   (LRTA)   1938
- NR 8 Berwick Place, WELWYN GARDEN CITY, Herts, AL7 4TU. (mail/address)
  0117-951 7785
  email office@lrta.org   http://www.lrta.org
  Chmn: David F Russell
- ▲ Un-incorporated Society
- ○ *K; to advocate the retention & development of public transport, especially light rail transit & tramways
- ● Mtgs - Inf - Lib - VE - Duplication of books & videos on tramways
- < Confedn of Passenger Transport (fixed track section); UITP
- M c 1,800 i, UK / c 1,500 i, o'seas
- ¶ Tramways & Urban Transit - 12.

Lighting Association Ltd   (LA)   1970
- NR Stafford Park 7, TELFORD, Shropshire, TF3 3BQ.   (hq)
  01952 290905   fax 01952 290906
  email enquiries@lightingassociation.com
  http://www.lightingassociation.com
  Co Sec & Chief Exec: Keven Verdun
- ▲ Company Limited by Guarantee
- ○ *T; for all sectors of the lighting industry
- Gp Luminaire manufacturers; Lighting distributors; Component manufacturers & suppliers; Lamp suppliers & producers
- ● Mtgs - ET - Exhib - Comp - SG - Stat - Expt - Inf - Lib - LG - Seminars - Accreditation - Certification laboratories
- < C'ee Eur Luminaire Mfrs Assn (CELMA)
- > Furniture Ind Res Assn (FIRA); Profl Lighting & Sound Assn (PLASA)
- M 218 f, UK / 12 f, o'seas
- ¶ LA News & Views - 12;   Lighting News - 2;
  Buyers Guide - 1;   AR - 1; all ftm only.

Lighting Industry Federation Ltd   (LIF)   1969
- NR Westminster Tower (Ground Floor), 3 Albert Embankment, LONDON, SE1 7SL.   (hq)
  020 7793 3020   fax 020 7793 3003
  email info@lif.co.uk   http://www.lif.co.uk
  Dir: Eddie Taylor
- ○ *T
- M f

Limbless Association   1983
- ■ Queen Mary's Hospital, Roehampton Lane, LONDON, SW15 5PN.   (hq)
  020 8788 1777   fax 020 8788 3444
  http://www.limbless-association.org
- ▲ Company Limited by Guarantee; Registered Charity
- ○ *W; for the welfare of people of all ages who have been born without limb(s), or who have had amputations, their carers & the professionals involved with their care; to promote policy matters & monitor NHS services for limbless people
- ● Conf - Res - Inf
- < R Assn for Disability & Rehabilitation
- M 3,000 i, 13 f, UK / 100 i, o'seas
- ¶ Step Forward - 4; ftm, amputees, carers & professionals.

Limerick Chamber of Commerce   1815
- IRL 96 O'Connell St, LIMERICK, Republic of Ireland.
  353 (61) 415180   fax 353 (61) 415785
  email info@limerickchamber.ie
  http://www.limerickchamber.ie
  Chief Exec: Maria Kelly
- ○ *C

Lincoln Longwool Sheep Breeders' Association   1892
- NR Lincolnshire Showground, Grange de Lings, LINCOLN, LN2 2NA.   (hq)
  01522 568660   fax 01522 730033
  http://www.lincolnlongwools.co.uk
  Sec: Ruth Mawer
- ▲ Registered Charity
- ○ *B
- ● Mtgs - Exhib - Comp - Stat - Expt - Inf
- M 87 i
- ¶ Jnl - 6.   Flock Book - 1.

Lincoln Record Society   (LRS)   1910
- ■ Lincoln Cathedral Library, Minster Yard, LINCOLN, LN2 1PX. (treas/b)
  01522 561640
  http://www.lincoln-record-society.org.uk
  Treas: Ken Hollamby
- ▲ Registered Charity
- ○ *L; publication of historical records relating to the ancient county & diocese of Lincoln
- ● Res
- M 175 i, 70 org, UK / 9 i, 43 org, o'seas
- ¶ Lincoln Record Society - 1; £18 m, £25-£30 nm.

Lincoln Red Cattle Society   (LRCS)   1895
NR   Lincolnshire Showground, Grange de Lings, LINCOLN,
       LN2 2NA.   (hq)
       01522 511395   fax 01522 730033
       http://www.lincolnredcattlesociety.co.uk
       Sec: Mrs L Newboult
▲   Registered Charity
○   *B
●   Mtgs - Exhib - Comp - Stat - Inf
<   Nat Cattle Assn
M   108 i, 1 f, 2 org, UK / 4 i, o'seas
¶   Jnl - 6.   Herd Book - 1.

Lincolnshire Agricultural Society   1869
NR   Lincolnshire Showground, Grange de Lings, LINCOLN,
       LN2 2NA.   (hq)
       01522 522900 & 524240   fax 01522 520345
       http://www.lincolnshireshowground.co.uk
       Chief Exec & Sec: S A C Frere-Cook
▲   Company Limited by Guarantee; Registered Charity
○   *F; to stage county agricultural shows incl all aspects of
       agriculture, forestry, horticulture & conservation
●   Conf - Mtgs - ET - Exhib - Comp - Annual show
M   i, f, org
¶   Show catalogue.   AR.
       Programme & prize list schedule.

Lincolnshire Chamber of Commerce & Industry   1889
NR   Commerce House, Outer Circle Rd, LINCOLN, LN2 4HY.   (hq)
       01522 523333   fax 01522 546667
○   *C
M   c 1000 i, f & org

Lindsay Society for the History of Dentistry   1963
■   Dunelm, Black Dyke Lane, Upper Poppleton, YORK,
       YO26 6PT.   (hsp)
       01904 794929
       email stuartrobson367@btinternet.com
       http://www.bda.org.uk
       Hon Sec: Dr J Stuart Robson
▲   Un-incorporated Society
○   *L; to study all aspects of the history of dentistry - including oral
       diseases, education of dentists & other staff, economic effects
       in the development of dental treatments & history of leading
       personalities in the development of dental sciences
●   Conf - Mtgs - ET - VE
<   Brit Dental Assn; Brit Soc for the History of Medicine
>   Henry Noble Dental Res Gp
M   100 i, 4 f, UK / 30 i, o'seas
       (Sub: £22 i, £100 f, UK / £27 i, o'seas
¶   Dental Historian (Jnl) - 3; ftm, £15 nm.

Linguistics Association of Great Britain   (LAGB)   1959
NR   c/o Dr David Willis, Selwyn College, Grange Rd, CAMBRIDGE,
       CB3 9DQ.   (hsb)
       http://www.lagb.org.uk
       Hon Sec: Dr David Willis
▲   Un-incorporated Society
○   *L; to promote the study of linguistics
Gp   C'ee for linguistics in education; C'ee for endangered
       languages
●   Conf - Mtgs - ET - Res - LG
M   600 i
¶   Jnl of Linguistics - 3.

Linnean Society of London   1788
NR   Burlington House, Piccadilly, LONDON, W1J 0BF.   (hq)
       020 7434 4479   fax 020 7287 9364
       email info@linnean.org   http://www.linnean.org
       Exec Sec: Dr Ruth Temple
▲   Registered Charity
○   *L; the science of natural history in all its branches
●   Conf - Mtgs - Lib
M   1,700 i, UK / 800 i, o'seas
¶   The Linnean - 4; ftm, (internet; free nm).
       Biological Jnl.   Botanical Jnl.   Zoological Jnl.

Lipizzaner National Stud Book Association of Great Britain
■   Cilyblaidd Manor, Pencarreg, LLANYBYDDER, Carmarthenshire,
       SA40 9QL.   (hsp)
       0870 908 9080
       email info@lipizzanerhorse.com
       http://www.lipizzanerhorse.com
       Sec: L Moran
▲   Company Limited by Guarantee
○   *B; to register & verify the pure bred Lipizzaner in the UK
●   Inf
<   Lipizzaner Intl Fedn (LIF); Brit Horse Soc
M   i

Lipizzaner Society of Great Britain   (LSGB)   1982
■   Starrock Stud, Leopards' Lair, Homelands, Bish Mill,
       SOUTH MOLTON, Devon, EX36 4EH.   (chmn/p)
       01769 551773
       email lsgb@lipizzaner.co.uk   http://www.lipizzaner.co.uk
       Chmn: Una Harley,   Hon Sec: Mary Kibblewhite
▲   Company Limited by Guarantee
○   *B; to register pure-bred & part-bred Lipizzaner horses
●   Mtgs - ET - Comp - Inf - Lib - VE - LG - Issuing of EU equine
       passports -
<   Intl Lipizzaner U; Brit Horse Soc (BHS); Spanish Riding School of
       Vienna
M   131 i
       (Sub: £20)
¶   NL - 2; ftm only.
       The Lipizzaner (published by J A Allen); £5.99.

Liquid Food Carton Manufacturers' Association
       since 2007 **Alliance for Beverage Cartons & the Environment**

Lisburn Chamber of Commerce   1961
NR   3a Bridge St, LISBURN, Co Antrim, BT28 1XZ.   (hq)
       028 9266 6297   fax 028 9266 6297
       email lisburnchamber@btconnect.com
       Hon Sec: S Baird
▲   Un-incorporated Society
○   *C
●   Conf - Mtgs - Inf - VE - LG
<   NI Cham Comm & Ind
M   120 f
¶   News Sheet - 4; free.

List & Index Society   (LIS)   1965
NR   c/o The National Archives, Ruskin Avenue, Kew, RICHMOND,
       Surrey, TW9 4DU.   (sec/b)
       020 8876 3444   fax 020 8878 8905
       email listandindexsociety@nationalarchives.gov.uk
▲   Un-incorporated Society
○   *L; to distribute unpublished Public Record Office search room
       lists & indexes
M   50 i, 50 org, UK / 25 i, 70 org, o'seas
¶   Lists & indexes:
       Standard series - 1;
       Special series - irreg; all prices on application.

Listed Property Owners Club   (LPOC)   1994
■   Freepost, SITTINGBOURNE, Kent, ME9 7TE.   (hsp)
01795 844939   fax 01795 844862
email info@lpoc.co.uk   http://www.lpoc.co.uk
Managing Dir: Peter Anslow
▲   Company Limited by Guarantee
○   *G; assistance & information for the owners of listed buildings
Gp   Legal information; VAT information; Insurance policy
●   Conf - Exhib - Inf
M   2,423 i, 229 f
¶   Listed Heritage - 6; ftm only.

Liszt Society   1951
NR   14 Mardley Dell, WELWYN, Herts, AL6 0UR.
01438 717724   fax 01438 717724
email secretary@lisztsoc.org.uk
http://www.lisztsoc.org.uk
Mem Sec: Andrew King
▲   Company Limited by Guarantee; Registered Charity
○   *D; to foster & promote interest in the music of Franz Liszt
●   Res - Inf - Lib (Books, CDs, tapes) - Recitals - Talks -
Masterclasses
M   190 i, UK / 80 i, o'seas
¶   Jnl - 1.   NL - 4.   Occasional piano scores.

**Lithuanian Association in Great Britain Ltd   (Britanjos
Lietuviai)   1947**
NR   Headley Park Club, Picketts Hill, BORDON, Hants,
GU35 8TE.   (hq)
email yaldyba@yahoo.co.uk
▲   Company Limited by Guarantee
Br   12
○   *W; promotion of welfare, social & cultural activities for
Lithuanians in Great Britain
Gp   Lithuanian Youth Association in GB
●   Conf - Mtgs - Exhib - SG - Lib
<   Lithuanian Wld Community
M   c 800 i, 10 org
¶   Europos Lietuvis - 52.   Lynes (Youth NL) - 4.

Little Theatre Guild of Great Britain   (LTG)   1946
NR   181 Brampton Rd, CARLISLE, Cumbria, CA3 9AX.   (sp)
http://www.littletheatreguild.org
○   *D; encouragement of establishment & work of little theatres

Liverpool Chamber of Commerce & Industry   (LCCI)   1850
NR   1 Old Hall St, LIVERPOOL, L3 9HG.   (hq)
0151-227 1234   fax 0151-236 0121
email chamber@liverpoolchamber.org.uk
http://www.liverpoolchamber.org.uk
Chief Exec: Jack Stopforth
▲   Company Limited by Guarantee
Br   2; China
○   *C; represents, promotes & supports the business community of
Merseyside
●   Conf - Mtgs - ET - Exam - Res - Exhib - Comp - Stat - Expt - Inf
- Lib - VE - LG
<   Eurochambers; Brit Chams Comm; Chams Comm NW
M   50 i, 1,550 f
¶   Liverpool Chamber - 6; ftm, £3 nm.

Livestock Auctioneers Association   (LAA)   1954
NR   Cobblethwaite, Wreay, CARLISLE, Cumbria, CA4 0RZ.   (hq)
01697 475433   fax 01697 475423
email chris.dodds@laa.co.uk   http://www.laa.co.uk
Sec: Chris Dodds
▲   Un-incorporated Society
Br   13
○   *T; 'all matters pertaining to the sale by auction of cattle, sheep
& pigs in England & Wales'
Gp   Conditions of sale sub-c'ee; (Working parties as required)
●   Mtgs - Stat - Inf - LG
<   Association Européenne des Marchés aux Bestiaux (Brussels)
M   13 i (associates), 216 f
¶   NL - as required; m only.   Report - 1; ftm, postage nm.
Directory of Markets in England, Wales & Scotland - 3 yrly; ftm,
£25 nm.
Conditions of sale - as required; ftm, £10 nm.

Livestock Traders Association of Great Britain Ltd   (LTA)   1918
■   The Orchard, North Kilworth, LUTTERWORTH, Leics,
LE17 6HG.   (hsp)
01858 880714   fax 01858 880714
Hon Sec: D G W Ward
▲   Company Limited by Guarantee
○   *T; interests of livestock traders & cattle & sheep salesmen in
the farming industry
●   LG
M   35 i, 15 f

Living Streets   1929
NR   31-33 Bondway, LONDON, SW8 1SJ.   (hq)
020 7820 1010   fax 020 7820 8208
email info@pedestrians.org.uk
http://www.livingstreets.org.uk
Chief Exec: Tony Armstrong
▲   Registered Charity
Br   91
○   *K; to promote the interests & safety of people on foot
●   Conf - Mtgs - Res - LG
<   Intl Fedn of Pedestrians; Fedn of Eur Pedestrian Assns
M   c 1,200 i, 50 org
¶   Walk (Jnl) - 4; ftm.   AR; free.
Registered name: Pedestrians Association

Llanwenog Sheep Society
English name of **Cymdieithas Defaid Llanwenog**

Lleyn Sheep Society
NR   Gwyndy, Bryncroes, Sarn, PWLLHELI, Gwynedd, LL53 8ET.
01758 730366
http://www.lleynsheep.com
Sec: Mrs G Roberts
○   *B
M   c 700 i

Lloyd's Market Association   (LMA)   2001
NR   Suite 358, 1 Lime St, LONDON, EC3M 7DQ.
020 7327 3333   fax 020 7327 4443
email lma@lmalloyds.com   http://www.lmalloyds.com
Chief Exec: David Gittings
○   *N, *P; 'to promote the interests of the Society of Lloyds & to
represent the interests of underwriters, managers & members
of the Association'
Gp   4 underwriting committees: Aviation, Marine, Non-marine &
Motor

Lloyd's Names Association
NR   Kenton House, Oxford St, MORETON in MARSH, Glos,
GL56 0LA.

LMCA (Long-term Medical Conditions Alliance)
since 2008 **Long-term Conditions Alliance**

Loan Market Association (LMA)

NR 10 Upper Bank St, LONDON, E14 5JJ. (hq)
    020 7006 6007   fax 020 7006 3423
    email lma@cliffordchance.com
    http://www.lma.eu.com
    Exec Dir: Clare Dawson
▲   Company Limited by Guarantee
○   *T; 'embraces all aspects of the primary & secondary
    syndicated loan markets in Europe'
●   Conf - Mtgs - ET - Inf - LG (regulatory & fiscal issues) -
    Seminars - Provision of recommended standard
    documentation & secondary loan pricing data
<   Asia Pacific Loan Market Assn; Loan Syndications & Trading
    Assn Inc
M   77 f, 3 courtesy mems, UK / 122 f, 5 courtesy mems, o'seas
¶   LMA News - 2; free.

Local Authorities Research & Intelligence Association (LARIA) 1974

■   1 Henderson Close, Great Sankey, WARRINGTON, Cheshire,
    WA5 3JJ. (admin/p)
    01925 723539   fax 01925 721548
    email admin@laria.gov.uk   http://www.laria.gov.uk
    Hon Sec: Christine Collingwood,   Admin: Doris Besford
○   *P; to promote the role & practice of research within the field of
    local government; to provide a supporting network for those
    conducting or commissioning research
●   Conf - ET - Res - SG - LG
M   1,045 i, 271 local authorities
¶   Laria News - 3; ftm.
    Note: is a Registered Friendly Society.

Local Authority Caterers' Association (LACA) 1990

■   Bourne House, Horsell Park, WOKING, Surrey, GU21 4LY.
    (hq)
    01483 766777   fax 01483 751991
    email admin@laca.co.uk   http://www.laca.co.uk
    Admin: Vic Laws
▲   Un-incorporated Society
Br 9
○   *T; to promote professionalism in local authority catering
Gp Representation on c'ees of relevant professional bodies
●   Conf - Mtgs - ET - Exhib - Comp - LG
M   700 i, 250 f
¶   NL - 4; ftm.   Reports & Hbk (incl LM) - 1; ftm.

Local Authority Civil Enforcement Forum (LACEF)

NR Brighton & Hove City Council, Priory House, PO Box 2929,
    BRIGHTON, E Sussex, BN1 1PS.
    01273 291876   fax 01273 291881
    email barrie.minney@brighton-hove.gov.uk
    http://www.lacef.org.uk
    Chmn: Barrie Minney

Local Authority PVC-u Frame Advisory Group (LAPFAG) 1988

NR 3 Fairways Drive, WHITCHURCH, Shropshire, SY13 1TX.
    01978 352353   fax 01978 661795
    email tony.hailes@lapfag.org.uk
    http://www.lapfag.org.uk
    Treas/Sec: Tony Hailes

Local Authority Road Safety Officers' Association (LARSOA) 1974

NR Road Safety Group, Guild House, Cross St, PRESTON, Lancs,
    PR1 8RD   (hsb)
    01772 534663
    http://www.larsoa.org.uk
    Hon Sec: Alan Fisher
▲   Un-incorporated Society
○   *P; a national forum for road safety education, training,
    publicity & the School Crossing Patrol Service
M   all local authorities except London

Local Government Association (LGA) 1997

NR Local Government House, Smith Sq, LONDON, SW1P 3HZ.
    (hq)
    020 7664 3131   fax 020 7664 3030
    email info@lga.gov.uk   http://www.lga.gov.uk
    Chief Exec: Brian Briscoe
○   *P; 'to enable local authorities to speak with one voice &
    promote the cause for democratic local communities which
    are prosperous, safe, healthy & environmentally friendly'
Gp Sparcity Partnership
●   Conf - Mtgs - Inf - Empl - LG
M   480 local authorities
¶   First - 52; ftm.

Local Government Reform Society Ltd

has closed

Local Government Technical Advisers Group (TAG) 1995

■   Bluewaters, Andurn, Down Thomas, PLYMOUTH, Devon,
    PL9 0AT. (hsb)
    01752 863053   fax 01752 863778
    email tag-1@rfconsultancy.co.uk
    http://www.tagonline.co.uk
    Nat Sec: Roy Fairclough
▲   Un-incorporated Society
Br 8 regions
○   *P; the provision of coordinated & comprehensive services to
    local & central government & its agencies in the
    management & operation of all areas of technical services -
    regeneration, environment, waste, transportation, coastal &
    fluvial management, climate change & operations
Gp Climate change; Coastal & fluvial management; Highways;
    Transportation; Waste
●   Conf - Mtgs - ET - VE - LG
<   Construction Ind Coun
M   200 i, 10 f, 100 local govt
¶   The Bulletin - 4/6; on website.

Locomotive & Carriage Institution (Loco & Carr Inst) 1911

NR 34 Camp St, DERBY, DE1 3SD.   (gsp)
    01332 295378
    Gen Sec: A J Spencer
▲   Un-incorporated Society
○   *L; the advancement of knowledge & information in all aspects
    of modern railway operation

Locomotive Club of Great Britain (LCGB) 1949

■   58 Osprey Rd, BIGGLESWADE, Beds, SG18 8HE.   (chmn/p)
    01767 220271   fax 01767 220271
    email p.crossman@ntlworld.com
    http://www.lcgb.org.uk
    Sec: P S Crossman
▲   Un-incorporated Society
Br 8
○   *G; railway history & operation & all other aspects
●   Mtgs - Res - Exhib - SG - Lib - VE
M   c 600 i, UK / c 200 i, o'seas
¶   Jnl - 10; free.

© CBD Research Ltd · Beckenham · BR3 5JS · Tel 020 8650 7745 · Fax 020 8650 0768 · E-mail cbd@cbdresearch.com · www.cbdresearch.com

Locomotive 6201 'Princess Elizabeth' Society Ltd   (PELS)   1963
- ■ 39 Newton St, MILLOM, Cumbria, LA18 4DR.   (chmn/p)
  01229 775215   fax 01229 775215
  Chmn: Clive Mojonnier
- ▲ Company Limited by Guarantee
- ○ *G; to preserve & operate on British Rail main lines (passed for
  steam operation) the 'Princess Elizabeth' 6201. This
  locomotive was preserved because of its record non-stop
  runs between London-Glasgow-London, 16-17 November
  1936 & was the forerunner of non-stop steam operation
  between the two cities; the locomotive is available for private
  charter
- ● AGM - Open days at the East Lancs Railway, Bury -
  Preservation of the engine
- < Mainline Steam Locomotive Operators Ltd; Assn Rly Presvn Socs
- M 160 i, UK / 6 i, o'seas
- ¶ NL - 4; ftm only.

Locus Association
- ■ c/o Quintus Public Affairs, Buchanan House, 3 St James's
  Square, LONDON, SW1Y 4JU.   (asa)
  020 7930 9788   fax 020 7976 1680
  email harriet@quintuspa.com
  http://www.locusassociation.co.uk
  Sec: Harriet Crosthwaite
- ○ *T; to increase opportunities & reduce barriers to fair trade
  between the public & private sector, particularly in the use of
  PSI (public sector information)

London Anglers' Association   (LAA)   1884
- NR Izaak Walton House, 2A Hervey Park Rd, LONDON, E17 6LJ.
  (hq)
  020 8520 7477   fax 020 8520 7477
  email admin@londonanglers.net
  http://www.londonanglers.net
  Chmn/Sec: A E Hodges
- ▲ Un-incorporated Society
- ○ *S; to promote the sport of fair angling & to provide fishing
  facilities for members
- ● Comp
- M 3,000 i
- ¶ AR - 1; free.

London Appreciation Society   (LAS)   1932
- NR 45 Friars Avenue, Friern Barnet, LONDON, N20 0XG.
  (chmn/p)
  Chmn: Anthea H Gray
- ▲ Un-incorporated Society
- ○ *G; a secular, non-political & non-profit-making organisation
  for adults interested in the past, present & future of London
- ● Guided walks, visits & lectures
- M c 580 i
- ¶ Blue Book (programme of events) - 2; ftm only.
  Note: the Society has a seven-year waiting list.

London Bullion Market Association   (LBMA)   1987
- NR 13 Basinghall St, LONDON, EC2V 5BQ.   (hq)
  020 7796 3067   fax 020 7796 2112
  Chief Exec: Stewart Murray
- ▲ Company Limited by Guarantee; Registered Charity
- ○ *T; to promote the interests of the London (gold & silver) bullion
  market
- ● Conf - ET - Stat - LG - Liaison with regulatory authority
- M 63 f
- ¶ Alchemist (NL) - 4; free.
  Brochure; ftm, single copy free nm.

London Chamber of Commerce & Industry   (LCCI)   1881
- ■ 33 Queen St, LONDON, EC4R 1AP.   (hq)
  020 7248 4444   fax 020 7489 0391
  email lc@londonchamber.co.uk
  http://www.londonchamber.co.uk
  Chief Exec: Colin Stanbridge
- ▲ Company Limited by Guarantee
- Br Croydon Chamber of Commerce & Industry; Docklands
  Business Club & East London Chamber of Commerce; Ealing
  Chamber of Commerce; Hammersmith & Fulham Chamber
  of Commerce; Westminster Chamber of Commerce
- ○ *C
- Gp Asian Business Assn; Defence & security gp; Property &
  construction gp; Women in business gp
- ● Conf - Mtgs - ET - Stat - Expt - Inf - Lib - LG - Networking -
  Seminars
- < Intl Chams Comm; Brit Chams Comm
- M 3,000 f
- ¶ London Business Matters (Jnl) - 12; ftm.
  Directory of Members - 1; ftm, £155 nm.   AR & Accounts.

London Cornish Association   (LCA)   1898
- ■ 26 Sharrow Vale, HIGH WYCOMBE, Bucks, HP12 3HB.   (hsp)
  01494 531703   fax 01494 531703
  http://www.londoncornish.co.uk
  Hon Sec: Dr Francis Dunstan
- Br 19; Australia, Canada, N Zealand, South Africa, USA
- ○ *G; to encourage fellowship & social activities among Cornish
  people in London & the Home Counties, & to provide a link
  to Cornish associations worldwide.
- Gp Family History; 'Old Cornwall'
- ● Conf - Mtgs - Research - SG - Lib - VE
- < 19 in UK and Cornish Associations in Australia, Canada, N
  Zealand, S Africa, & USA
- M 230 i, UK / 50 i, o'seas
- ¶ NL - 6; ftm.
  Ybk (incl LM).

London Councils   (ALG)   1995
- ■ 59½ Southwark St, LONDON, SE1 0AL.   (hq)
  020 7934 9999
  email info@londoncouncils.gov.uk
  http://www.londoncouncils.gov.uk
  Contact: Pauline McMahon
- ▲ Company Limited by Guarantee
- ○ *N; consultation with government & the European Union over
  matters relating to local authorities & the services provided by
  them
- Gp Equalities; Housing; Education; Environment; Employment;
  Social services; Health; Voluntary sector; Asylum seekers; Arts
  & leisure; Police; Local government; Crime; Training; Greater
  London Authority
- ● Conf - Mtgs - Res - Stat - Inf - LG
- M 33 London councils
- ¶ London Government Directory - 1.
  Directory of Funded Organisations - 1.
  London Bulletin - 6.
  London Housing Magazine - 6.
  Survey of Londoners - 1.
  Making Allowances Report - 1.
- × 2006 Association of London Government

London Cycling Campaign   (LCC)   1978
- NR 2 Newhams Row (Off Bermondsey St), LONDON, SE1 3UZ.
  (hq)
  020 7234 9310
  email office@lcc.org.uk   http://www.lcc.org.uk
  Dir: Simon Brammer
- Br 33
- ○ *K
- ● Conf - Mtgs - Exhib - Inf - Lib - LG
- M c 9,000 i
- ¶ London Cyclist - 6.

London District Surveyors Association   (LDSA)
NR   c/o Lola Majekodunmi, Neighbourhoods & Regeneration,
       Hackney Building Control, 263 Mare St, LONDON,
       E8 3HT.   (hsb)
       http://www.londonbuildingcontrol.org.uk
       Hon Sec: Lola Majekodunmi
Br   34
○   *P; 'uniformity of interpretation & operation of the Building
       Regulations in London'
Gp   C'ees: Education & training, Electrical & mechanical, Fire safety
       & means of escape, LANTAC, Licensing, Management &
       legislation, Publications & seminars, Safety at sports grounds,
       Technical & foundations
●   Mtgs - ET - SG - Inf - LG
<   District Surveyors Assn
M   33 i

London Fish Merchants (Billingsgate) Ltd   (LFMA)   1923
NR   Office 36 Billingsgate Market, Trafalgar Way, LONDON,
       E14 5ST.   (hq)
       020 7515 2655   fax 020 7538 2618
○   *T; to promote Billingsgate Market; to help merchants in any
       sphere of their business
M   f
¶   AR.

London Fish & Poultry Retailers Association
       a branch association of the **National Federation of Fishmongers**

London Food Link
       a group of **Sustain**

London General Shipowners' Society
       incorporated in the **London Shipowners' & River Users' Society**

London Harness Horse Parade Society   1885
■   Oakley Farm, Merstham, REDHILL, Surrey, RH1 3QN.   (hq)
       01737 646132   fax 01737 645121
       http://www.lhhp.co.uk
       Sec: Mrs J E Shearman
▲   Company Limited by Guarantee; Registered Charity
○   *V; improvement of general condition & treatment of horses &
       ponies employed for transport
●   Annual parade on Easter Monday at the South of England
       Centre, Sussex.

London Investment Banking Association   (LIBA)   1988
NR   6 Frederick's Place, LONDON, EC2R 8BT.   (hq)
       020 7796 3606   fax 020 7796 4345
       email liba@liba.org.uk   http://www.liba.org.uk
       Dir Gen: Jonathan Taylor
▲   Un-incorporated Society
○   *T; for firms active in the investment banking & securities
       industry; to represent members' interests to authorities in the
       UK & Europe
●   Mtgs - SG - LG
<   Intl Coun of Securities Assns (ICSA)
M   50 f
¶   AR; free.

** London Jute Association
       Organisation lost: see Introduction paragraph 3

London Library   1841
■   14 St James's Sq, LONDON, SW1Y 4LG.   (hq)
       020 7930 7705   fax 020 7766 4766
       email membership@londonlibrary.co.uk
       http://www.londonlibrary.co.uk
       Librarian: Inez T P A Lynn
○   *G; a research library of books in the humanities, with lending
       service to subscribing members
●   Res - Lib
M   8,200 i, 250 org
¶   AR; ftm only.

London Mathematical Society   (LMS)   1865
■   De Morgan House, 57-58 Russell Sq, LONDON, WC1B 4HS.
       (hq)
       020 7637 3686   fax 020 7323 3655
       email lms@lms.ac.uk   http://www.lms.ac.uk
       Exec Sec: P Cooper
▲   Registered Charity
○   *L; to promote & extend mathematical knowledge
●   Conf - Mtgs - Stat - Inf - Lib - LG
<   19 mathematical societies in other countries
M   c 1,700 i, UK / c 800 i, o'seas
       Subs: £43.50
¶   Proceedings - 6; £88 m, £719 nm.   Jnl - 6; £88 m, £719
       nm.
       Bulletin - 6; £44 m, £286 nm.
       NL - 11;   Hbk - 2 yrly;   AR; all ftm only.

London Mayors' Association   (LMA)   1901
■   c/o Freeman Box & Co, 8 Bentinck St, LONDON, W1U 2BJ.
       (chmn/b)
       020 7486 9041   fax 020 7224 1336
       email rjd432@aol.com
       http://www.londonmayors.org.uk
       Chmn: Councillor Robert Davis
▲   Company Limited by Guarantee
○   *P; to represent the Mayors, Lord Mayors & former Mayors &
       Lord Mayors of the London Boroughs
●   Mtgs - VE
M   600 i
¶   NL - 4; free.
       Mayoral Directory - 1; £55 (for 7).

London Medieval Society   (LMS)   1945
■   3 Rothwell St, LONDON, NW1 8YH.   (hsp)
       020 7722 1040
       email gopa.roy.robertson@gmail.com
       http://www.the-lms.org
       Hon Sec: Dr G Roy
▲   Un-incorporated Society
○   *L; promotion of research & study of the culture & civilisation of
       the Middle Ages
●   Conf - Mtgs - Inf - Research encouragement
<   Inst of Romance Studies (University of London)
M   30 i
       (Sub: £20)

London & Middlesex Archaeological Society   (LAMAS)   1855
■   c/o Museum of London, London Wall, LONDON,
       EC2Y 5HN.   (regd address)
       020 7600 3699   fax 020 7600 1058
       http://www.lamas.org.uk
       Hon Sec: Jackie Keily
▲   Registered Charity
○   *L; to promote the study of the local history & archaeology of
       the metropolitan area of London
Gp   C'ees: Archaeological research, Historic buildings, Local history
●   Conf - Mtgs - Res - Inf - Lib - LG
M   651 i
¶   [Visit website for full information]

© CBD Research Ltd · Beckenham · BR3 5JS · Tel 020 8650 7745 · Fax 020 8650 0768 · E-mail cbd@cbdresearch.com · www.cbdresearch.com

London Money Market Association   (LMMA)   1998
NR   c/o Investec Bank (UK) Ltd, 2 Gresham St, LONDON,
　　　EC2V 7QP.   (hsb)
　　　020 7597 4485   fax 020 7597 4491
　　　Hon Sec: Mrs Kathy Cong
○   *T; to monitor the liquidity of the Sterling Money Market; to
　　　consider matters of policy interest to members; to promote
　　　good relations with the Treasury & the Bank of England
●   Mtgs - Inf
M   c 20 f

London Motor Cab Proprietors' Association   (LMCPA)   1909
■   c/o Richmond Road Cab Centre, 195 Richmond Rd, LONDON,
　　　E8 3NJ.   (hq)
　　　020 7275 7589
　　　Sec: Raymond Kinzler
▲   Un-incorporated Society
○   *T; taxi fleet proprietors operating within the licensed London
　　　taxi trade
●   Mtgs - Stat - VE - LG
<   London Taxi Bd
M   50 f

London Natural History Society   (LNHS)   1858
■   19 Mecklenburgh Square, LONDON, WC1N 2AD.   (hsp)
　　　020 7837 7800
　　　http://www.lnhs.org.uk
　　　Hon Sec: Dr John Edgington
▲   Registered Charity
○   *L, *Q; conservation & study of natural history in the London
　　　area; recording of species & habitats found there
Gp Botany; Ecology; Entomology; Ornithology
●   Conf - Mtgs - Res - Lib - VE
M   1,000 i, 20 org
　　　(Sub: £20)
¶   The London Naturalist - 1; ftm, £8 nm.
　　　London Bird Report - 1; ftm, £8 nm.
　　　Ornithological Bulletin - 6;   NL - 6;   both m only.

**London Private Hire Car Association Ltd   (Graded Private Hire
Companies)   1994**
NR   Talbot House, 204-226 Imperial Drive, HARROW, Middx,
　　　HA2 7HH.   (hq)
　　　07956 329288   fax 01442 380607
　　　http://www.lphca.co.uk
　　　Chmn: Steve Wright
○   *T; for private hire, chauffeur & mini cab companies

London Record Society   1964
■   PO Box 300, HERTFORD, SG13 9EF.   (hsb)
　　　fax 020 7862 8793
　　　email londonrecordsoc@btinternet.com
　　　http://www.londonrecordsociety.org.uk
　　　Hon Sec: Dr Helen Bradley
▲   Registered Charity
○   *L; publication of an annual series of carefully edited
　　　transcripts, abstracts & lists of original sources for the history
　　　of London; stimulation of public interest in the archives of
　　　London
●   Mtgs
M   126 i, 72 f & org, UK / 21 i, 85 f & org, o'seas
¶   Annual volume; £18 m, £23 instns, UK / £20 m,
　　　£25 instns, o'seas

London Rice Brokers' Association   (LRBA)   1869
NR   4 St Georges Yard, FARNHAM, Surrey, GU9 7LW.   (hq)
　　　01252 727677
　　　email lrba@lrba.co.uk   http://www.lrba.co.uk
　　　Sec: Michael French
○   *T; establishment of contract forms on which rice business is
　　　transacted
M   i & f
¶   Monthly Rice Circular - 12.

**London Shipowners' & River Users' Society (incorporating the
London General Shipowners' Society)   1811**
■   Carthusian Court, 12 Carthusian St, LONDON, EC1M 6EZ.
　　　(hq)
　　　020 7417 2830   fax 020 7600 1534
　　　Sec: D W Chard
○   *T; representative body protecting & promoting the interests of
　　　London river users
M   f

London Society   1912
■   Mortimer Wheeler House, 46 Eagle Wharf Rd, LONDON,
　　　N1 7ED.   (hq)
　　　020 7253 9400
　　　email info@londonsociety.org.uk
　　　http://www.londonsociety.org.uk
　　　Hon Sec: Patrick Gaskell-Taylor
▲   Registered Charity
○   *K; is active in reviewing & commenting on the planning &
　　　development of London, as well as conservation; to stimulate
　　　appreciation of London; to encourage excellence in planning
　　　& development & to preserve its amenities & the best of its
　　　buildings; it reviews planning proposals & considers planning
　　　applications
●   Res - Inf - Lib - VE
M   812 i, 10 f, 28 org, UK & o'seas
　　　(Sub: £6 i & £9 f UK, £12 i & f o'seas)
¶   Jnl - 2; ftm only.

London Stock Exchange plc   1676
NR   10 Paternoster Square, LONDON, EC4M 7LS.   (hq)
　　　020 7797 1000
　　　http://www.londonstockexchange.com
　　　Chief Exec: Mrs Clara Furse
○   *P; to provide a central market in securities
M   f

London Subterranean Survey Association   (LSSA)   1968
■   98 Cambridge Gardens, LONDON, W10 6HS.   (hsp)
　　　020 8968 1360
　　　email wolstan-dixie@hotmail.co.uk
　　　Hon Sec: Roger Morgan
▲   Un-incorporated Society
○   *L; to promote the discovery & recording of natural & man-
　　　made features of subterranean London; to promote the
　　　utilisation of subterranean space & to minimise its conflict
　　　with surface developments
●   Res - Inf - Lib - PL - VE
<   Subterranea Britannica
M   20 i, 1 org

London Swing Dance Society   (LSDS)   1986
■   22 Bessingby Rd, RUISLIP, Middx, HA4 9BX.   (hq)
　　　01895 613703
　　　email swinguk@zetnet.co.uk
　　　http://www.swingdanceuk.com
　　　Dir & Founder: Simon Selmon
▲   Company Limited by Guarantee
○   *D, *G; to support & promote swing dance events, classes &
　　　performances
●   Mtgs - Exhib - Comp
M   c 400 i

London Topographical Society (LTS) 1880
- ■ 36 Old Deer Park Gardens, RICHMOND, Surrey, TW9 2TL. (hsp)
  020 8940 5419
  email patfrazer@yahoo.co.uk   http://www.topsoc.org
  Hon Sec: Patrick Frazer
- ▲ Registered Charity
- ○ *L, *Q; publication of facsimiles of scarce printed or manuscript maps & views of London; research on these & other topographical subjects
- ● Res - Publication
- M c 1,100 i & f
- ¶ London Topographical Record (Jnl) - 5 yrly.   NL - 2.

London Underground Railway Society (LURS) 1961
- ■ 54 Brinkley Rd, WORCESTER PARK, Surrey, KT4 8JF. (sp)
  020 8330 1855
  http://www.lurs.org.uk
  Sec: Eric Felton
- ▲ Un-incorporated Society
- ○ *G; study of the railways of London Transport, its predecessors & successors & other underground railways in London
- Gp Modelling; Visits
- ● Mtgs - Inf - VE
- M c 900 i, UK / 50 i, o'seas
- ¶ Underground News - 12; ftm (on sale at the London Transport Museum).

London Vintage Taxi Association (LVTA) 1978
- NR 51 Ferndale Crescent, Cowley, UXBRIDGE, Middx, UB8 2AY.
  http://www.lvta.co.uk
  Contact: Mem Sec
- ○ *G; for collectors & enthusiasts
- ● Mtgs - Inf - Archive - Provision of vintage taxis for special events & films, TV etc
- ¶ MAgazine - 6; ftm.

London Welsh Association (LWA) 1920
- ■ 157-163 Gray's Inn Rd, LONDON, WC1X 8UE. (hq)
  020 7837 3722   fax 020 7837 6268
  email administrator@lwcentre.demon.co.uk
  http://www.londonwelsh.org
  Hon Sec: Olwen Evans,   Admin: Huw Jackson
- ▲ Registered Charity
- ○ *D, *E; to promote Welsh culture & language
- Gp London Welsh Male Voice Choir; Gwalia Choir; London Welsh Chorale
- ● Mtgs - ET - Comp
- M 1,500 i
  (Sub: £35)
- ¶ Cymry Llundain - London Welshman - 4; ftm, £2 nm.

Londonderry Chamber of Commerce 1885
- ■ Chamber of Commerce House, 1 St Columb's Court, Bishop St, LONDONDERRY, BT48 6PT. (hq)
  028 7126 2379   fax 028 7128 6789
  email info@londonderrychamber.co.uk
  http://www.londonderrychamber.co.uk
  Chief Exec: Janice Tracey
- ▲ Company Limited by Guarantee
- ○ *C; the business representation body to drive & develop economic development in the Northwest region; areas of interest - tourism, infrastructure, skills business development & information
- Gp Business Information & Guidance Service; NWCCI - Cross Border Lobby Gp
- ● Conf - Mtgs - ET - Stat - Expt - Inf - LG
- < Cham of Comm Ireland
- M 310 f
- ¶ NL - 4;   Ybk - 1;   AR - 1; all free.

Lone Twin Network (LTN) 1989
- ■ PO Box 5653, BIRMINGHAM, B29 7JY.   (mail/address)
  Chmn: Jill Deeley
- ○ *W; n informal, unfunded network for people whose twin has died
- ● Conf - Inf
- M i
  (Sub: £18 UK / £20 o'seas)
- ¶ Spring Newssheet 0 1;   Autumn NL - 1;   LM ; ftm only.

Long-term Conditions Alliance (LTCA) 1989
- ■ 202 Hatton Square, 16 Baldwins Gardens, LONDON, EC1N 7RJ. (hq)
  020 7813 3637   fax 020 7405 5300
  email info@ltca.org.uk   http://www.ltca.org.uk
  Admin: Pia Charles
- ▲ Company Limited by Guarantee; Registered Charity
- ○ *N; 'an umbrella body working with member organisations towards better lives for people with long-term health conditions; it aims to gain recognition of people's needs & ensure resources are available to meet them'
- ● Conf - Mtgs - ET - Res - LG
- M 110 org
- ¶ Connect (NL) - 4;   AR - 1;   LM; all free.
- ✕ 2005 Long-term Medical Conditions Alliance
  2007 LMCA

Long Distance Walkers Association Ltd (LDWA) 1972
- ■ Speedwell Farm Bungalow, Nettle Bank, WISBECH, Cambs, PE14 0SA. (hsp)
  email secretary@ldwa.org.uk   http://www.ldwa.org.uk
  Hon Sec: Katie Hunt
- ▲ Company Limited by Guarantee
- Br 40
- ○ *G; furthering the interests of people who enjoy long distance walking
- ● Mtgs - Challenge & social walks, long distance paths
- < Ramblers Assn
- M 6,500 i
- ¶ Strider - 3; ftm only.
  Database of Long Distance Paths (on website).

Longhorn Cattle Society 1878
- ■ 3 Eastgate, Stoneleigh Park, STONELEIGH, Warks, CV8 2LG. (hq)
  0845 017 1027
  email secretary@longhorncattlesociety.com
  http://www.longhorncattlesociety.com
  Sec: Debbie Dann
- ▲ Registered Charity
- ○ *B; registration of pedigree longhorn cattle & their promotion, improvement & marketing
- ● Conf - Mtgs - ET - Exhib - Comp - SG - Expt - Inf - PL - VE
- < Nat Beef Assn (NBA); Rare Breeds Survival Trust (RBST)
- M 510 i, UK / 10 i, o'seas
- ¶ Jnl - 1;   NL - 6;   List of A1 Bulls - 2 yrly;   Rules; AGM Report; all ftm.
  Herd Book - 1; ftm, £3 nm.

Lonk Sheep Breeders Association (LSBA) 1905
- NR 51 Glen View Rd, BURNLEY, Lancs, BB11 2QW. (hsp)
  Hon Sec: Mrs Jeanette Shorrock
- ▲ Registered Charity
- ○ *B
- ● Mtgs - Exhib - Shows & sales
- < Nat Sheep Assn
- M 77 i
- ¶ Flock Book - irreg.

© CBD Research Ltd · Beckenham · BR3 5JS · Tel 020 8650 7745 · Fax 020 8650 0768 · E-mail cbd@cbdresearch.com · www.cbdresearch.com

LOOK (LOOK) 1991
- ■ Queen Alexandra College, 49 Court Oak Rd, Harborne, BIRMINGHAM, B17 9TG. (hq)
  0121-428 5038   fax 0121-428 5038
  http://www.look-uk.org
  Inf Officer: Jane Benham
- ▲ Registered Charity
- ○ *W; the national federation of families with visually impaired children; to support parents &/or carers of children with visual problems
- ● ET - Inf - Lib - Welfare support - Linking families with similar disabilities
- M [not stated]
- ¶ NL - 4; ftm.
  registered name: National Federation of Families with Visually Impaired Children

Lord's Day Observance Society
has become Day One Christian Ministries & is therefore outside the scope of this Directory.

Lotteries Council 1979
- NR 21 Bristow Close, Great Sankey, WARRINGTON, WA5 8EU. (mail/address)
  http://www.lotteriescouncil.org.uk
  Exec Officer: Mrs Judith Horner (01925 710880)
- ○ *T; for any person or organisation who is engaged in activities connected with the promotion of lawful lotteries
- ● Conf - Mtgs - Inf - LG
- M c 150 i, f & org
- ¶ Lottery Magazine - 4.   Code of Conduct.
  The Acts Combined.

Low Incomes Tax Reform Group (LITRG) 1998
- NR Chartered Institute of Taxation, 12 Upper Belgrave St, LONDON, SW1X 8BB. (hq)
  020 7235 9381   fax 020 7235 2562
  http://www.litrg.org.uk
  Chmn: John Andrews
- ▲ Registered Charity
- ○ *K; the tax problems of those on low incomes
- ● ET - Res - LG
  Helpline (TaxHelp for Older People): 0845 601 3321
- M 20 i
- ¶ Older People on Low Incomes:
  The case for a friendlier tax system.
  The taxman's response; both irreg.

Lowe Syndrome Association (UK Contact Group) (LSA) 1983
- ■ 29 Gleneagles Drive, Penwortham, PRESTON, Lancs, PR1 0JT. (hsp)
  01772 745070
  email info@lowesyndrome.org
  http://www.lowesyndrome.org
  UK Contact Family: Mr David & Mrs Julie Oliver
- ▲ Un-incorporated Society
- ○ *W; to provide mutual support & information among families; Lowe Syndrome is a rare genetic condition which only affects boys, causing physical & mental handicaps & medical problems
- ● Conf - Res - Inf
- < Contact-a-Family
- M 15 i, UK / 350 i, o'seas
- ¶ NL - 3;   Family Directory - 1; both ftm only.

Loyal Company of Town Criers (LCTC) 1994
- ■ Bellringer House, Blackbird Way, Biddulph, STOKE-on-TRENT, Staffs, ST8 7UH. (hsp)
  01782 516434   fax 01782 516434
  email oyezman2002@yahoo.com
  Hon Sec: John Robinson
- ○ *G; to promote & encourage the appointment of town criers; to maintain the standards & conduct of their ancient office
- ● Conf - Mtgs - Res - Exhib - Comp - Expt - Inf - VE
- < Pacific Northwest Company of Town Criers (Canada); Public Criers of Victoria (Canada)
- M 100 i, UK / 10 i, o'seas
  (Sub: £26 UK / £20 o'seas)
- ¶ The Scroll (NL) - 2; ftm only.

Luing Cattle Society Ltd 1965
- ■ Wester Drumlochy, Lornty, BLAIRGOWRIE, Perthshire, PH10 6TD. (sp)
  01250 879162
  email secretary@luing-cattle.ndo.co.uk
  http://www.luingcattlesociety.co.uk
  Sec: Johnny Mackey
- ▲ Registered Charity
- ○ *B; a native beef-breed from the Island of Luing off the west coast of Scotland
- ● Mtgs - Comp - Stat - Inf - VE
- M 320 i, 6 f, UK / 15 i, o'seas
- ¶ The Luing Jnl - 1;   Luing News - 3; both free.
  AR; ftm only.

Lupus UK 1990
- NR St James House, Eastern Rd, ROMFORD, Essex, RM1 3NH. (hq)
  01708 731251   fax 01708 731252
  email headoffice@lupusuk.org.uk
  http://www.lupusuk.org.uk
  Dir: Chris Maker
- ▲ Registered Charity
- Br 30 regional gps
- ○ *W; to support those who suffer with the disease Systemic Lupus Erythematosus; fundraising for research & welfare support; advice for members & those seeking diagnosis
- ● Conf - Mtgs - Res
- < Eur Lupus Fedn; Long Term Medical Conditions Alliance; Brit League Against Rheumatism; Brit Assn of Dermatologists
- M 7,500 i, UK / 100 i, o'seas
- ¶ Factsheets; free.   Publications list available.

Lusitano Breed Society of Great Britain (LBSGB) 1984
- NR Carreg Dressage, Abercegir, MACHYNLLETH, Powys, SY20 8NW. (hsp)
  01650 511800
  http://www.lusobreedsociety.co.uk
- ▲ Company Limited by Guarantee
- ○ *B; promotion & registration of the Lusitano (Portuguese) horse
- Gp Classical riding; Training; Dressage
- ● ET - Comp - Inf
- < Associação Portuguesa de Craidores do Cavalo Puro Sangue Lusitano (Lisbon)
- M 250 i, UK / 10 i, o'seas
- ¶ Luso News - 3; ftm, £3.50 each nm.   NL - 3/4.

Lute Society   1956

■ Southside Cottage, Brook Hill, Albury, GUILDFORD, Surrey,
   GU5 9DJ.   (hsp/b)
   01483 202159   fax 01483 203088
   email lutesoc@aol.com   http://www.lutesoc.co.uk
   Sec: Christopher Goodwin
▲ Un-incorporated Society
○ *D; to spread information on the lute, other related instruments
   & their music
● Mtgs - Res - Comp - Inf - PL - Publication of music, working
   drawings of instruments
M   350 i, 10 libraries, UK / 400 i, 50 libraries, o'seas
¶ The Lute (Jnl) - 1; with Lute News - 4; £33 (subscription only).
   Catalogue available of booklets & music.

Lutheran Council of Great Britain   (LC)   1955

NR 30 Thanet St, LONDON, WC1H 9QH.   (hq)
    020 7554 2900   fax 020 7383 3081
    http://www.lutheran.org.uk
    Gen Sec: Rev Thomas Bruch
○ *R
¶ The Lutheran Link - 3.

Lutyens Trust   1985

■ Goddards, Abinger Common, DORKING, Surrey, RH5 6JH.
   (hq)
   01306 730487
   http://www.lutyenstrust.org.uk
   Chmn: Martin Lutyens
▲ Registered Charity
○ *A; to protect the spirit & substance of the work of the architect
   Sir Edwin Lutyens
¶ NL - 3; ftm only.
   Guidebook to Goddards (the Trust's house designed by Sir
   Edwin Lutyens)

Lymphoedema Support Network   (LSN)

■ St Luke's Crypt, Sydney St, London, SW3 6NH.
   020 7351 0990   fax 020 7349 9809
   http://www.lymphoedema.org/lsn/
○ *W
   no further information supplied

Lymphoma Association   1986

NR PO Box 386, AYLESBURY, Bucks, HP20 2GA.   (hq)
    01296 619400   fax 01296 619414
    email information@lymphoma.org.uk
    http://www.lymphoma.org.uk
    Chief Exec: Melanie Burfitt
▲ Registered Charity
○ *W; to provide information & emotional support to anyone with
   Lymphatic cancer, their families, carers & friends
Gp Non-Hodgkin's lymphoma; Hodgkin lymphoma
● Conf - Exhib - Inf - Lib
   Helpline: 0808 808 5555; www.lifesite.info (for young adults)
M   2,125 i
¶ Lymphoma NL - 4;
   Lymphoma Fundraising News - 4; both ftm only.
   Booklets (designed to help patients to cope with their
       illness & treatments):
   Lymphomas (a general booklet for Hodgkin); £2.
   Low Grade Hodgkin Lymphomas; £2 (both; £25 for 15
   copies).
   Hodgkin Lymphoma; £3 (£25 for 10 copies).
   Videos:
   Hodgkin lymphoma & its treatments; £10.
   Understanding non-Hodgkin lymphoma; £10.
   Publications list available.

© CBD Research Ltd · Beckenham · BR3 5JS · Tel 020 8650 7745 · Fax 020 8650 0768 · E-mail cbd@cbdresearch.com · www.cbdresearch.com

Mac Technology Association (MTA-UK) 2007
- ■ 14 Anson Way, BICESTER, Oxon, OX26 4UH.   (hq)
  0871 717 7264   fax 0871 717 7265
  email nfo@mactechnology.org.uk
  http://www.mactechnology.org.uk
  Exec Dir: Robert Peckham
- ▲ Company Limited by Guarantee
- ○ *T; companies and individuals who sell, support, maintain or
  consult on Apple computers, MacOS applications,
  peripherals and related services
- Gp IT support; IT consultancy
- ● Conf - Mtgs - ET - Exhib - Inf
- < Indep Tr Assn of Computer Specialists (ITACS); Profl Computing
  Assn; CompTIA; Brigantia; Integra
- M 64 i, 8 f, 12 org, UK / 2 i, o'seas
  (Sub: £100 i, £200 f, £50 org)
- ¶ Member Update - 52; ftm (email).
  General News - 12; free (email).
- × 2004 Mac-Dealer Association

Macclesfield Chamber of Commerce & Enterprise   (MCCE) 1994
- NR Churchill Chambers, Churchill Way, MACCLESFIELD, Cheshire,
  SK11 6AS. (hq)
  01625 665940   fax 01625 665941
  email info@macclesfieldchamber.co.uk
  http://www.macclesfieldchamber.co.uk
  Chief Exec: John Lamond
- ▲ Company Limited by Guarantee
- ○ *C
- ● Mtgs - Inf - LG
- < Brit Chams Comm; Chams Comm NW
- M 500 f
- ¶ Chamberlink (NL) - 6.   Directory - 1.

Macedonian Society of Great Britain   1989
- NR The Hellenic Centre, 16-18 Paddington St, LONDON,
  W1U 5AS. (regd/office)
  020 7487 5060   fax 020 7486 4254
  http://www.macedonia.org.uk
- ○ *G; for the further education of the public in aspects of
  Macedonian culture, art, language & life

Machinery Ring Association of England and Wales   (MRA)
- NR Hall Moor Farm, Shipton Rd, Wigginton, YORK, YO32 2RQ.
  01904 471419   fax 01904 471423
  email info@ridingsmachineryring.co.uk
  http://www.machineryrings.org.uk
  Sec: Andrew Whittam

Machinery Users' Association (Inc) (MUA) 1887
- NR 11 Moorfields High Walk, LONDON, EC2Y 9DP. (hq)
  020 7638 4383
  http://www.mua.co.uk/association.htm
- ▲ Company Limited by Guarantee
- ○ *P; representations to government on property rating &
  valuation matters
- M 5 i, 60 f
- ¶ NL - 4; ftm only.

Macular Disease Society (MDS) 1987
- ■ PO Box 1870, ANDOVER, Hants, SP10 9AD.   (hq)
  01264 350551   fax 01264 350558
  email info@maculardisease.org
  http://www.maculardisease.org
  Chief Exec: Tom Bremridge
- ▲ Company Limited by Guarantee; Registered Charity
- ○ *W; to provide information, help, support & practical advice to
  people with Macular Disease (loss of central vision due to
  scarring of the retina - the most common cause of registrable
  blindness in the UK), health professionals & the general
  public
- ● Conf - Mtgs - Res - Exhib - LG
  Helpline: 0845 241 2041
- < AMD Alliance Intl
- M 17,500 i in 173 gps
- ¶ Side View (NL) - 4;   Digest (Jnl) - 1; both ftm only.
  [subscription: i (£15 UK / £30 o'seas), professionals
  (eyehealth) £50-£100.

Made-up Textiles Association Ltd
since 2004 **Performance Textiles Association**

Magic Circle   1905
- NR Centre for the Magic Arts, 12 Stephenson Way, LONDON,
  NW1 2HD. (hq)
  020 7387 2222   fax 020 7387 5114
  http://www.themagiccircle.co.uk
  Sec: Chris Pratt
- ○ *A, *P; to advance the art of magic
- ● Mtgs - ET - Exam - Res - Comp - Exhib - Lib
- M 1,500 i
- ¶ The Magic Circular - 12; ftm only.

Magic Lantern Society   1976
- ■ South Park, Galphay Rd, Kirkby Malzeard, RIPON, N Yorks,
  HG4 3RX. (hsp)
  email lmh.smith@magiclanternsocy.demon.co.uk
  http://www.magiclantern.org.uk
  Hon Sec: L M H Smith
- ▲ Un-incorporated Society
- ○ *G
- ● Conf - Mtgs - Res - Exhib - Inf - Lib
- < Magic Lantern Soc US & Canada
- M 260 i, 10 f, UK / 120 i, o'seas
- ¶ Jnl;   NL; both ftm.

Magistrates' Association   1920
- NR 28 Fitzroy Sq, LONDON, W1T 6DD. (hq)
  020 7387 2353   fax 020 7383 4020
  email secretariat@magistrates-association.org.uk
  http://www.magistrates-association.org.uk
  Chief Exec: Sally J Dickinson
- ▲ Registered Charity (incorporated by Royal Charter)
- Br 60
- ○ *P; supports magistrates in their duties; contributes towards
  their training
- ● Conf - Mtgs - ET - Inf - LG
- M 28,500 i
- ¶ The Magistrate - 10; £24 yr m.   AR.

Magna Carta Society
has been disbanded

Maidenhead & District Chamber of Commerce   1905
- ■ 29-31 Risborough Rd, MAIDENHEAD, Berks, SL6 7YT. (mail/address)
   01628 670573   fax 01628 670573
   email admin@maidenhead.org.uk
   http://www.maidenhead.org.uk
   Sec: Lynda Morten
- ▲ Un-incorporated Society
- ○ *C
- M 400 i & f
   no further information supplied

Maidstone & Mid Kent Chamber of Commerce & Industry (Maidstone Chamber)
   is a branch of the **Kent Invicta Chamber of Commerce**

Mail Competition Forum
- NR c/o DX Network Services Ltd, DX House, Ridgeway, IVER, Bucks, SL0 9JQ.
   01753 630630   fax 01753 631631
   Sec: David Sibbick
- ○ *T; for non-Royal Mail delivery companies

Mail Consolidators Association   (MCA)
- NR 4 Kingsmill Business Park, Chapel Mill Rd, KINGSTON-upon-THAMES, Surrey, KT1 3GZ.   (chmn/b)
   020 8439 1177   fax 020 8439 1144
   email nst@imxuk.co.uk   http://www.themca.org.uk
   Chmn: Nicholas Street
- ○ *T; for consolidators of international mail
- ● Mtgs
- M 25 f

Mail Order Traders' Association of Great Britain   (MOTA) 1941
- NR PO Box 51909, LONDON, SW99 0WZ.   (hsb)
   020 7735 3410   fax 020 7735 9592
   email mota@mota.org.uk   http://www.mota.org.uk
   Chief Exec: Mark Hogarth
- ▲ Un-incorporated Society
- ○ *T; to represent the major home shopping companies in GB
- ● Mtgs - Res - Stat - LG - Operation of a code of practice
- < Eur Mail Order Traders' Assn; Advertising Assn (AA); Brit Retail Consortium (BRC)
- M 7 f
- ¶ LM - as required.

Mail Users' Association Ltd   (MUA)   1975
- NR 70 Main Rd, EMSWORTH, Hants, PO10 8AX.   (hsb)
   01243 370840   fax 01243 370840
   http://www.mailusers.co.uk
   Sec: Jeremy Partridge
- ○ *T; to work on behalf of its members for improvements in the postal services

Mainline Steam Locomotive Operators Ltd
   'please delete from your files/records' (Richard Dodd, Secretary 2008)

Maize Growers Association   (MGA)   1988
- NR Town Barton Farm, Sandford, CREDITON, Devon, EX17 4LS. (hq)
   01363 775040
   http://www.maizegrowersassociation.co.uk
   Admin: June Howard
- ▲ Company Limited by Guarantee
- ○ *F; a farmer managed group providing technology to maximise the profitability of growing forage crops, particularly maize
- ● Conf - Res - Comp - Inf - VE
- M c 900 i & f
- ¶ MGA Times - 12;   Maize Grower - 2;
   Technical Notes - agronomy / ruminant - 12; all ftm only.

Major Contractors Group
   a member federation of the **Construction Confederation**

Major Projects Association   (MPA)   1982
- NR Egrove Park, Kennington, OXFORD, OX1 5NY.   (hq)
   01865 422581   fax 01865 326068
   http://www.majorprojects.org
   Mgr: Manon Bradley
- ○ *L, *P; to explore specific, mainly industrial, projects
- M c 70 f

Making Music   1935
- NR 2-4 Great Eastern St, LONDON, EC2A 3NW.   (hq)
   0870 903 3780   fax 0870 903 3785
   email info@makingmusic.org.uk
   http://www.makingmusic.org.uk
   Chief Exec: Robin M Osterley
- ▲ Company Limited by Guarantee; Registered Charity
- Br 13
- ○ *D; to represent & assist the UK's voluntary music sector
- Gp Choirs; Orchestras; Music clubs
- ● Conf - ET - Inf - LG
- < Nat Music Coun, Assn Brit Orchestras, Nat Campaign for the Arts, Voluntary Arts Network, Scottish Arts Lobby
- M c 2,300 org
- ¶ Making Music News - 4; free.
   Annual Review;   Guide to Member Services; both ftm.
   Orchestral Catalogue.   Choral Catalogue.
   Chamber Music Catalogue.   Information sheets; ftm only.

Malacological Society of London   (Malsoc)   1893
- ■ c/o Ecology Research Group, Canterbury Christ Church University, North Holmes Rd, CANTERBURY, Kent, CT1 1QU.   (hsb)
   01227 767700   fax 01227 470442
   email j.a.trigwell@canterbury.ac.uk
   http://www.malacsoc.org.uk
   Hon Sec: Dr J Trigwell
- ▲ Registered Charity
- ○ *L; study of molluscs from pure & applied aspects
- ● Conf - Res
- M c 230 i
- ¶ Jnl of Molluscan Studies - 4 (with supplements); ftm.
   Bulletin - 2; ftm only.

Malcolm Muggeridge Society   2003
- ■ Pilgrim's Cottage, Pike Rd, EYTHORNE, Kent, CT15 4DJ. (sb/p)
   01304 831964
   email info@malcolmmuggeridge.org
   http://www.malcolmmuggeridge.org
   Sec: David Williams
- ▲ Un-incorporated Society
- ○ *A, *G; to promote interest in the work of the author, journalist, broadcaster, Christian apologist & soldier/spy, Malcolm Muggeridge 1903-1990
- ● Conf - Mtgs - Inf - Lib - VE
- M 105 i, UK / 110 i, o'seas
   (Sub: £15)
- ¶ The Gargoyle (Jnl) - 4; ftm, £5 nm.

Malcolm Saville Society   1994
- ■ 6 Redcliffe St, LONDON, SW10 9DS.   (msp)
   email mystery@witchend.com   http://www.witchend.com
- ▲ Un-incorporated Society
- ○ *A, *G; to celebrate the life & work of this popular children's author (1901-1982); to stimulate awareness of his books
- ● Mtgs - Lib - Themed walks based on the novels - Book search service
- M 370 i, UK / 12 i, o'seas
- ¶ Acksherley! - 3;   Peewit! (LM) - 1; both ftm only.
   AGM Souvenir programme; price varies.

© CBD Research Ltd · Beckenham · BR3 5JS · Tel 020 8650 7745 · Fax 020 8650 0768 · E-mail cbd@cbdresearch.com · www.cbdresearch.com

Maling Collectors' Society
NR   PO Box 1762, NORTH SHIELDS, Tyne & Wear, NE30 4YJ.
     http://www.maling-pottery.org.uk
○   *G; for collectors of Maling pottery

Malone Society   1906
■   Institute of English Studies, Senate House, Malet St, LONDON,
     WC1E 7HU.   (hq)
     020 7862 8679
     email wim.van-mierlo@sas.ac.uk
     http://www.ies.sas.ac.uk/malone
     Exec Sec: Prof John Creaser
▲   Registered Charity
Br   Australia, Canada, Japan, Switzerland
○   *A, *D, *L; to publish editions of 16th & 17th century plays from
     manuscript, photographic facsimile editions of printed plays
     of the period, & editions of original documents relating to
     Renaissance theatre & drama
●   ET - Inf - Lib
<   Shakespeare Assn of America
M   238 i, UK / 432 i, o'seas
¶   Books - 1 or 2 yr; ftm.   AR - 1; free.
     [subscription £20]

Malt Distillers Association of Scotland   (MDAS)   1874
■   1 North St, ELGIN, Moray, IV30 1UA.   (asa)
     01343 544077   fax 01343 548523
     email mdas@grigor-young.co.uk
     Secs: Grigor & Young (solicitors & estate agents)
○   *T; interests of the pot still malt whisky industry
M   f

Maltsters' Association of Great Britain   (MAGB)   1827
NR   31b Castle Gate, NEWARK, Notts, NG24 1AZ.   (hq)
     01636 700781
     email info@magb.org.uk   http://www.ukmalt.com
▲   Un-incorporated Society
○   *T; 'to promote & safeguard the UK malting industry'
Gp   Malt exporters
●   Conf - Mtgs - ET - Exam - Res - Stat - Expt - LG
<   Euromalt
M   14 f
¶   AR; ftm only.

Malvern Spa Association   (MSA)   1998
■   24 Assarts Lane, MALVERN, Worcs, WR14 4JR.   (treas)
     http://www.malvern-hills.co.uk/malvernspa/
     Chmn: Rose Garrard,   Treas: John Bibby
○   *G, *K; to conserve, protect and restore the springs, wells and
     fountains of the Malvern Hills.

Mammal Society   1954
NR   3 The Carronades, New Road, SOUTHAMPTON, Hants,
     SO14 0AA.   (hq)
     023 8023 7874
     email enquiries@mammal.org.uk
     http://www.abdn.ac.uk/mammal/
     Admin Officer: Sarah Gardner
▲   Company Limited by Guarantee; Registered Charity
○   *L, *Q; to protect British mammals, halt the decline of
     threatened species & advise on all issues affecting British
     mammals; to study mammals, identify the problems they
     face & promote conservation & other policies based on
     sound science
●   Conf - Mtgs - ET - Res - Inf - Study of conservation needs of
     threatened species - Trap loan scheme for members
<   IVCN; Wildlife & Countryside Link
M   2,200 i, UK / 100 i, o'seas
¶   Mammal Review - 4.   Mammal News - 4.
     Mammalaction News [youth group NL] - 4.
     Other publications.

Mammillaria Society
NR   22 Stirling Rd, CHICHESTER, W Sussex, PO19 7DS.
     email admin@mammillaria.co.uk
     http://www.mammillaria.co.uk
     Sec: Chris Baker
○   *H; promoting and furthering the study of the cactus genus
     mammillaria

Management Consultancies Association   (MCA)   1956
■   60 Trafalgar Sq, LONDON, WC2N 5DS.   (hq)
     020 7321 3990   fax 020 7321 3991
     email mca@mca.org.uk   http://www.mca.org.uk
     Chief Exec: Peter Hill
▲   Company Limited by Guarantee
○   *P, *T; to maintain standards within the UK management
     consultancy sector
Gp   HR directors; Marketing director; Finance directors; Public
     sector interest; Statistics interest
●   Conf - Mtgs - ET - Res - Exhib - Stat - Inf - LG
<   Eur Fedn of Mgt Consultancy Assns (FEACO)
M   65 f
¶   Spectra (Jnl) - 4;   Electronic NL - 12;   Careers Guide;
     Corporate brochure; all free.
     The UK Consulting Industry Report - 1.
     MCA book series; £16.99 (published by Hodder & Stoughton).

Managing & Marketing Sales Association   (MAMSA)   1979
■   PO Box 11, SANDBACH, Cheshire, CW11 3GE.   (hq)
     01270 625339   fax 01270 625339
     email info@mamsasbp.org.uk
     http://www.mamsasbp.org.uk
     Chief Exec: M Whitaker
▲   Company Limited by Guarantee
○   *P; examination board for sales marketing; management;
     business studies & communications
●   Exam
M   1,000 i, UK / 17,000 i, o'seas
¶   Nexus - 1.

Manchester Chamber of Commerce & Industry
     in 2004 merged with Chamber Business Connections to form the
     Greater Manchester Chamber of Commerce

Manchester Geographical Society   1884
■   Friends Meeting House, 6 Mount St, MANCHESTER, M2 5NS.
     (hq)
     0161-834 2965
     http://www.mangeogsoc.org.uk
     Hon Sec: Dr B P Hindle
▲   Registered Charity
○   *E, *L, *Q; to promote all branches of geographical science
●   Mtgs - Inf - Library on permanent loan to the University of
     Manchester
<   R Geographical Soc; Geographical Assn
M   160 i
¶   North-West Geography (Jnl) - 4; free.   AR - 1; ftm only.

**Manchester Literary & Philosophical Society   (LIT & PHIL)
1781**
NR   MMU Business School, Aytoun St, MANCHESTER, M1 3GH.
     (hq)
     0161-247 6774   fax 0161-247 6773
     http://www.manlitphil.co.uk
     Hon Sec: Mrs Patricia Verdin
▲   Company Limited by Guarantee; Registered Charity
○   *A, *L; 'to promote the advancement of education & the
     widening of public interest in, & appreciation of, any form of
     literature, science, the arts & public affairs...'
Gp   Sections: Arts, Science & technology, Social philosophy, Young
     people
●   Conf - Mtgs - Lib
M   c 500 i
¶   Manchester Memoirs - 1.   NL - 12.   AR.
     John Dalton Bibliography, Vol 2.

Manchester Medical Society (MMS) 1834
- John Rylands University Library, Oxford Rd, MANCHESTER, M13 9PP.   (hq)
  0161-273 6048   fax 0161-272 8046
  email admin@mms.org.uk   http://www.mms.org.uk
  Chmn: Dr R F T McMahon
- ▲ Registered Charity
- ○ *L, *M; to cultivate & promote all branches of medicine, & of all related schemes
- Gp Medicine; Anaesthesia; Odontology; Primary care; Surgery; Pathology; Paediatrics; Psychiatry; Public health medicine; Imaging
- ● Mtgs - ET - Lib
- M 2,100 i

Mangold Hurling Association
- NR c/o 11 Orchard Lane, Wembdon, BRIDGWATER, Somerset, TA6 7QY.
  email mail@mangoldhurling.co.uk
  http://www.mangoldhurling.co.uk
  Contact: John Ennals
- ○ *G, *S

Manic Depression Fellowship Ltd
  since 2005 **MDF - the BiPolar Organisation**

Manila Hemp Association (MHA) 1910
- NR c/o John Harrison, 25 Beaufort Court, Admirals Way, LONDON, E14 9XL.   (hsb)
  020 7538 5383   fax 020 7538 2007
  Chmn: John Harrison
- ○ *T; trading in manila hemp & abaca
- M 20 i, 12 f, UK / 3 i, 3 f, o'seas
- ¶ AR; free.

Manorial Society of Great Britain (MSGB) 1906
- 104 Kennington Rd, LONDON, SE11 6RE.   (hq)
  020 7735 6633   fax 020 7582 7022
  email manorial@msgb.co.uk   http://www.msgb.co.uk
  Hon Exec Chmn: Robert A Smith
- ○ *L; historical research, manorial rights, legal liability, insurance, estate management, genealogy, armigerous devices
- ● Conf
- M i & f
- ¶ Bulletin - 2; ftm only.   NL - 12; m only.
  The House of Lords (1992).
  The House of Commons (1996).
  Manorial Law (1996).
  The Monarchy (1998).
  Labour & the House of Lords (1998).
  Land Tenures & Customs of Manors (1673, reprinted 1999).
  Britain & Europe (1999).
  Millennium Book (2000).
  The Land Registration Bill (2002).
  Blood Royal (2002).
  The Land Registration Act (2005).

** **Mansfield & District Chamber of Trade & Commerce**
  Organisation lost: see Introduction paragraph 3

Manufacturers' Agents' Association of Great Britain & Ireland Inc (MAA) 1909
- Unit 16 Thrales End, HARPENDEN, Herts, AL5 3NS.   (hq)
  01582 767618   fax 01582 766092
  email prw@themaa.co.uk   http://www.themaa.co.uk
  Sec: Paul Wakeling
- ▲ Company Limited by Guarantee
- ○ *T; independent manufacturers' (commission) agents
- ● Conf - Mtgs - ET - Stat - Res - Inf - LG - Legal advice
- < Intl U of Comml Agents & Brokers (Amsterdam)
- M 900 i
- ¶ Agents News - 12.
  The Commission Agent.   20 Legal Questions Agents Ask.

Manufacturers of Domestic Unvented Systems (MODUS)
  in 2007 merged with the Waterheater Manufacturers Association to form the **Hot Water Association**

Manufacturing Science Finance Union
  in January 2004 became Amicus, now **Unite the Union**

Manufacturing Technologies Association (MTA) 1919
- 62 Bayswater Rd, LONDON, W2 3PS.   (hq)
  020 7298 6400   fax 020 7298 6430
  email info@mta.org.uk   http://www.mta.org.uk
  Dir Gen: Graham Dewhurst
- ▲ Company Limited by Guarantee
- Br 2 o'seas
- ○ *T; to represent companies in the machine tool sector & related technologies
- Gp Equipment importers; Equipment manufacturers
- ● Mtgs - ET - Exhib - Stat - Expt - LG - Technical support
- M 252 f
- ¶ Various technical publications.

Manx Gaelic Society
  English name of Yn **Cheshaght Ghailckagh**

Manx Loaghtan Sheep Breeders Group (MLSBG) 1988
- Cannons, Huntley Rd, Tibberton, GLOUCESTER, GL19 3AB   (hsp)
  email kempsoncannons@aol.com
  http://www.manxloaghtansheep.org
  Sec: Carol Kempson
- ▲ Un-incorporated Society
- ○ *B
- ● Workshops
- < Rare Breed Survival Trust
- M 72 i, 3 f, 1 org, UK / 1 i, o'seas
- ¶ NL - 3; ftm only.

Manx National Farmers' Union (MNFU) 1947
- NR Agriculture House, Ballafletcher Farm Rd, TROMODE, Isle of Man, IM4 4QL.   (sp)
  01624 662204   fax 01624 662204
  email manx-nfu@talk21.com   http://www.manx-nfu.org
- ▲ Un-incorporated Society
- Br 3
- ○ *F
- ● Mtgs - LG
- M c 360 i

Map Curators Group
  a group of the **British Cartographic Society**

Map Design Group
  a group of the **British Cartographic Society**

** **Marchigiana Cattle Society**
  Organisation lost: see introduction paragraph 3

© CBD Research Ltd · Beckenham · BR3 5JS · Tel 020 8650 7745 · Fax 020 8650 0768 · E-mail cbd@cbdresearch.com · www.cbdresearch.com

Marfan Association UK   1984
- ■ Rochester House, 5 Aldershot Rd, FLEET, Hants, GU51 3NG. (hq)
  01252 810472   fax 01252 810473
  email marfan@tinyonline.co.uk
  http://www.marfan-association.org.uk
  Chmn: Mrs Diane Rust
- ▲ Registered Charity
- ○ *W; offering support to patients with Marfan syndrome, which affects the cardiovascular system, causing near-sightedness & skeletal abnormalities; working alongside the many medical sectors involved in patient care; educating patients, doctors, the public, the Dept of Health & the Government; undertaking & sponsoring research projects
- ● Conf - ET - Res - Exhib - Stat - Inf - LG
- < Intl Fedn of Marfan Syndrome Orgs; Eur Marfan Support Network
- M 1,500 families
- ¶ In Touch (Jnl) - 2.
  Publications list available.

Margarine Manufacturers Association of Ireland
  a group of **Food & Drink Industry Ireland**

Margarine & Spreads Association   (MSA)
- ■ 6 Catherine St, LONDON, WC2B 5JJ.   (hq)
  020 7836 2460   fax 020 7836 0580
  http://www.margarine.org.uk
  Sec: Juliet Howarth
- ▲ Un-incorporated Society
- ○ *T
- < Intl Fedn Margarine Assns (IFMA); EEC Margarine Mfrs Assn (IMACE); Food & Drink Fedn
- M 8 f
- ¶ AR; ftm only.

Margery Allingham Society   1987
- ■ 9 Bailey St, Castle Acre, KING'S LYNN, Norfolk, PE32 2AG. (gen/sec)
  http://www.margeryallingham.org.uk
  2B Hiham Green, WINCHELSEA, E Sussex, TN36 4HB.
  01797 222363   fax 01797 222363. (hon/mem/sec).
  Gen Sec: Mrs Marianne Van Hoeven
- ▲ Un-incorporated Society
- ○ *A, *G; to bring together all interested in the life & work of Margery Allingham, a queen of crime & one of the greatest detective story writers of the 'Golden Age'
- ● Conf - VE
- M 120 i, UK / 12 i, o'seas
- ¶ The Bottle Street Gazette - 2; ftm.

Margery Kempe Society   1999
- NR 1a Auckland Rd, LONDON, SW11 1EW.   (hsp)
  020 7924 5868
  email c.maddern@gold.ac.uk
  Hon Sec: Dr Carole Maddern
- ○ *G; to further learned research into the English mystic Margery Kempe (c1373-c1440); to further historical & literary research in this field
- ● Conf
- M 30 i

Marie Stuart Society   1992
- ■ Copeland, 3 Barley Close, Little Eaton, DERBY, DE21 5DJ. (hsp)
  email syd@qcinternet.co.uk
  http://www.marie-stuart.co.uk
  Sec: Syd Whitehead
- ▲ Registered Charity
- Br 3
- ○ *G; study & research into the life & times of Mary Queen of Scots (1542-1587)
- ● Mtgs - Res - Exhib - Comp - Inf - Lib - PL - LG
- M 134 i, UK / 30 i, o'seas
- ¶ Jnl - 3; ftm only.

Marine Biological Association of the United Kingdom   (MBA) 1884
- ■ The Laboratory, Citadel Hill, PLYMOUTH, Devon, PL1 2PB. (regd/office)
  01752 633331   fax 01752 262043
  email sec@mba.ac.uk   http://www.mba.ac.uk
  Dir & Sec: Prof Colin Brownlee
- ▲ Registered Charity
- ○ *L, *Q; studies in various aspects of marine biology & biological oceanography, pollution, taxonomy, physiology, molecular biology & biochemistry
- Gp Biochemists; Biologists; Library; Molecular biologists; Physiologists
- ● Mtgs - ET - Res - Inf - Lib - SG - VE
- M 808 i, 10 f, UK / 196 i, 1 f, o'seas (Sub: £35-£425)
- ¶ Jnl - 6; ftm, £95 m, £688 nm.
  IMBA Global Marine Environment (NL) - 2; ftm, £2.50 each nm.
  [subscription £95 yr].

Marine Chemistry Group
  a group of the **Challenger Society for Marine Science**

Marine Conservation Society   (MCS)   1983
- NR Unit 3 Wolf Business Park, Alton Rd, ROSS-ON-WYE, Herefords, HR9 5BU.   (hq)
  01989 566017   fax 01989 567815
  email info@mcsuk.org   http://www.mcsuk.org
  Dir of Consvn: Mrs Samantha Fanshawe
  Operations Mgr: Mrs Pamela Bridgewater
- ▲ Company Limited by Guarantee; Registered Charity
- ○ *K, *L; 'the only UK based charity devoted exclusively to the protection of the marine environment; it believes that decisions affecting our seas & coasts should be based on sound scientific principles & implemented by environmentally sensitive management'
- ● Conf - ET - Res - Inf - PL - VE - LG - Volunteer work
- < Sea at Risk; Sea Turtle Survival; Wildlife & Countryside Link
- M 5,200 i, UK / 200 i, o'seas
- ¶ Marine Conservation (Jnl) - 4; ftm.

Marine Engine & Equipment Manufacturers' Association (MEEMA)   1960
- NR 56 Braycourt Ave, WALTON-on-THAMES, Surrey, KT12 2BA. (hsp)
  01932 224910
  Sec: Mrs Alison Banks
- ○ *T; manufacturers, wholesalers & retailers of marine engines & related equipment including personal watercraft
- < a group association within the British Marine Federation
- M 100 f
- ¶ LM; ftm, on request nm.

Marine Industries Leadership Council
  a group of the **Shipbuilders & Shiprepairers Association**

Marine Institute   1941
- IRL Rinville, ORANMORE, Co Galway, Republic of Ireland.
  353 91 387 200
  email institutemail@marine.ie   http://www.marine.ie
  Pres: Desmond Branigan   (353 (1) 660 0737)
- ○ *G; to promote greater awareness among the people of Ireland of their maritime history & of the sea
  Maritime Institute of Ireland

Marine Leisure Association   (MLA)   2005
- ■ Burrwood, 24 Peterscroft Avenue, Ashurst, SOUTHAMPTON, Hants, SO40 7AB.   (hq)
  023 8029 3822   fax 023 8029 3888
  email info@marineleisure.co.uk
  http://www.marineleisure.co.uk
  Gen Sec: Mrs Brigid Howells
- ▲ Company Limited by Guarantee
- ○ *S, *T; to market & promote training, charter & holidays afloat
- Gp Training; Charter; Holidays
- ● Conf - Mtgs - ET - Exam - Exhib - Stat - Expt - Inf - LG
- < Brit Marine Fedn (BMF); R Yachting Assn (RYA) - training only; Air Travel Organiser Licence (ATOL) - holidays only
- M 150 f, UK / 25 f, o'seas
- ¶ Brochure - 1; free.
- ✕ 2005 (Association of Bonded Sailing Companies
      (National Federation of Sea Schools
      (Yacht Charter Association
      all merged September 2005

Marine Sector Advisory Group
    a group of the **Shipbuilders & Shiprepairers Association**

Marine Society & Sea Cadets   (MSSC)   2004
- ■ 202 Lambeth Rd, LONDON, SE1 7JW.   (hq)
  020 7654 7000   fax 020 7928 8914
  email info@ms-sc.org   http://www.sea-cadets.org
  Chief Exec: Jeremy Cornish
- ▲ Registered Charity
- Br 400
- ○ *E, *W; to raise public awareness of the Royal & Merchant Navies, & the maritime world in general; to provide support for those who go to sea & enhance the well-being of professional sailors; to be responsible for the activities of the Sea Cadet Corps, open to young people 10-18 years old
- Gp Sea Cadet Corps
- ● ET - Lib - Nautical/maritime youth training (sponsored by Royal Navy training ships)
- < Intl Sea Cadet Assn (ISCA)
- M 16,000 i, UK / 1,200 i, o'seas
- ¶ The Seafarer (Jnl) - 6; £25 yr m, £3 each nm.
  AR - 1; ftm only.
- ✕ 2004 (Marine Society
      (Sea Cadet Associaton (merged November)

Marine Trades Association   (MTA)   1960
- NR 5 Beoley Close, SUTTON COLDFIELD, W Midlands, B72 1EJ. (sp)
  http://www.britishmarine.co.uk
- ▲ Un-incorporated Society
- ○ *T; retailing, distributing, wholesaling & manufacturing marine equipment
- ● Conf - ET - Exhib (annual 2-day) - Expt
- < an association within the British Marine Federation
- M 312 f
- ¶ Ybk.

Maritime Information Association   (MIA)   1971
- ■ 18 Durrington Avenue, LONDON, SW20 8NT.   (sec/p)
  http://www.maritime-information.net
  Chmn: Barbara Jones
- ▲ Un-incorporated Society
- ○ *L; contact with marine librarians, information workers & others with an interest in the maritime world
- ● Conf - Mtgs - VE - Lectures
- ¶ NL - 4;   LM - 1.
  Maritime Information: a guide to sources.

Maritime Interest Group
    a group of the **Defence Manufacturers Association**

Maritime Trust
    is now dormant

Market Research Quality Standards Association   (MRQSA) 1996
- NR Pendowrick, Pendower Rd, Veryan, TRURO, Cornwall, TR2 5QL.   (hsp)
  01872 501373
  email pettrevjac@aol.com
  Sec: Peter Jackson
- ▲ Company Limited by Guarantee
- ○ *P; to develop quality standards for market research services; to develop schemes by which organisations can be assessed to these standards
- ● Conf - liaison with bodies in associated fields
- M 5 org

Market Research Society   (MRS)   1946
- ■ 15 Northburgh St, LONDON, EC1V 0JR.   (hq)
  020 7490 4911   fax 020 7490 0608
  email info@marketresearch.org.uk
  http://www.mrs.org.uk
  Dir Gen: David Barr
- ▲ Company Limited by Guarantee
- Br Scotland
- ○ *P, *T; for professional researchers & other engaged (or interested) in market, social & opinion research & for company partner organisations
- ● Conf - Mtgs - ET - Exam - Res - Exhib - Inf - Lib - LG
- < Intl Cham Comm (UK): Eur Fedn of Assns of Market Res Orgs (EFAMRE); Advertising Assn
- M 7,300 i, UK / 700 i, o'seas
- ¶ Research - 12; ftm.   MRS News - 8; ftm only.
  International Jnl of Market Research - 6; ftm.
  Research Buyers Guide - 1; ftm.   AR - 1; ftm only.
- ✕ 2006 (incorporated) British Market Research Association

Marketing Communication Consultants Association   1989
- NR 4 New Quebec St, LONDON, W1H 7RF.   (hq)
  020 7535 3550   fax 020 7535 3551
  email info@mcca.org.uk   http://www.mcca.org.uk
  Chmn: Graham Kemp
- ○ *T; practitioners in promotional marketing & communication
- M c 50 f
- ✕ 2002 Sales Promotion Consultants Association

Marketing Group of UK NBC Defence Capability
    a group of the **Defence Manufacturers Association**

Marketing Institute [Ireland]
- IRL South County Business Park, Leopardstown, DUBLIN 18, Republic of Ireland.
  353 (1) 295 2355   fax 353 (1) 295 2453
  email info@mii.ie   http://www.mii.ie
- ○ *P

Marketing Society
- IRL PO Box 58, BRAY, Co Wicklow, Republic of Ireland.
  353 (1) 276 1995
  email info@marketingsociety.ie
  http://www.marketingsociety.ie
  Chmn: Kay McCarthy
- ○ *P

Marketing Society Ltd   1959
- NR 1 Park Rd, TEDDINGTON, Middx, TW11 0AR.   (hq)
  020 8973 1700
  http://www.marketing-society.org.uk
  Chief Exec: Hugh Burkitt
- ▲ Company Limited by Guarantee
- ○ *P; 'for senior marketers'
- ● Conf - Mtgs - Inf
- M 3,500 i
- ¶ Market Leader - 4.

© CBD Research Ltd · Beckenham · BR3 5JS · Tel 020 8650 7745 · Fax 020 8650 0768 · E-mail cbd@cbdresearch.com · www.cbdresearch.com

Marlowe Society 1955

- ■ 27 Melbourne Court, Randolph Avenue, LONDON, W9 1BJ. (hsp)
  email valerie.colin-russ@marlowe-society.org
  http://www.marlowe-society.org
  Hon Sec: Valerie Colin-Russ
- ▲ Company Limited by Guarantee; Registered Charity
- ○ *A, *G; to present Christopher Marlowe in his true light as a great poet-dramatist; to stimulate research into his life & work, into the lives of his friends & associates & the era in which he lived
- ● Mtgs - Res - Exhib - Lib - VE - Annual MArlowe Day (usually in Canterbury) - Biennial commemoration at the Marlowe memorial window in Poet's Corner, Westminster Abbey
- M 138 i, 2 schools, UK / 46 i, o'seas
  (Sub: £15 i, £200 (1-off) schools, UK / £20 i, o'seas)
- ¶ NL - 3; ftm, £3 (UK), £3.50 (Eur), £4 (RoW).
  Note: 'this is not the same as the Marlowe [Dramatic] Society of Cambridge which was founded by Rupert Brooke & is devoted to performing plays'.

Marquee Hirers Group
a group of the **Performance Textiles Association**

MARQUES the Association of European Trade Mark Owners (MARQUES) 1988

- NR 840 Melton Rd, Thurmaston, LEICESTER, LE4 8BN. (asa)
  0116-264 0080 fax 0116-264 0141
  email info@marques.org http://www.marques.org
  Co Sec: Robert Seager
- ▲ Company Limited by Guarantee
- ○ *T; representing on a Pan-European basis the interests of owners of trade marks & associated intellectual property
- ● Conf - Mtgs - Inf - LG
- M 50 f, UK / 250 f, o'seas
- ¶ Marques News Sheet - 10; ftm only.
- ✕ Association of European Brand Owners

Marquetry Society 1952

- NR 14 Buntingsdale Rd, MARKET DRAYTON, Shrops, TF9 1LT. (hsp)
  01630 656550
  http://www.marquetry.org
  Hon Gen Sec: Neil Micklewright
- ▲ Un-incorporated Society
- Br 29; 8
- ○ *G; to foster the craft of marquetry
- ● Mtgs - Exhib (annual + members competitions) - Inf - PL
- < Crafts Coun; Voluntary Arts Network
- M c 500 i, UK / c 150 i, o'seas
- ¶ The Marquetarian - 4; ftm, £2 nm.

MARS (M.A.R.S.)

- NR 34 Wycliffe Road, Battersea, LONDON, SW11 5QR.
  email info@mars.org.uk http://www.mars.org.uk
- ○ *G

Martial Arts Development Commission (MADEC) 1992

- NR PO Box 416, WEMBLEY, Middx, HA0 3WD. (hq)
  0870 770 0461
  http://www.madec.org
  Chmn: Richard Thomas
- ▲ Un-incorporated Society
- ○ *S; to act as a forum for the martial arts; to promote & develop the practice & administration of the martial arts in the UK
- Gp Aikido, Budo, Capoeira, Judo, Ju jitsu, Karate, Kalarippayat, Kendo, Kobudo, Kyudo, Kung fu, Tai chi, Taekwondo, Tang soo do, Thai boxing, Kick boxing, Wu shu, Wing Chun
- ● Conf - Mtgs - ET - Comp - Inf
- < Nat Coun for Voluntary Orgs (NCVO); Sport & Recreation Ind Trg Org (SPRITO)
- M 14,000 i, 100 org
- ¶ Various leaflets on: Disciplines, Safety, Weapons (send large sae).

Mary Rose Society 1978

- NR c/o The Mary Rose Trust, College Rd, HM Naval Base, PORTSMOUTH, Hants, PO1 3LX. (hq)
  023 9275 0521
  http://www.maryrose.org
  Chmn: Nicholas Braddock
- ○ *G; support of the Mary Rose (King Henry VIII's flagship)

Mary Webb Society 1972

- ■ 8 The Knowe, Willaston, NESTON, Cheshire, CH64 1TA. (hsp)
  0151-327 5843
  email suehigginbotham@yahoo.co.uk
  http://www.marywebbsociety.co.uk
  Sec: Sue Higginbotham
- ▲ Un-incorporated Society
- ○ *A, *G; to honour the memory of the author Mary Webb; to further appreciation of her works & the Shropshire countryside about which she wrote
- ● Mtgs - Exhib - VE
- < Alliance of Literary Socs
- M 157 i, UK / 9 i, o'seas
- ¶ Jnl - 1; ftm, £3 nm. NL - 2/3; free.

Masham Sheep Breeders Association (MSBA) 1986

- ■ Oak Bank, Bentham, LANCASTER, LA2 7DW.
  01524 261606
  Sec: Mrs V J Lawson
- ▲ Company Limited by Guarantee
- ○ *B; 'quality female sheep'
- ● Mtgs - Exhib
- < Nat Sheep Assn
- M 80 i
- ¶ NL - 4; ftm only. LM; ftm.

Massenet Society 1972

- NR Flat 2, 79 Linden Gardens, LONDON, W2 4EU.
  020 7229 7060
  Founder & Dir: Stella J Wright
- Br USA
- ○ *D; to promote a wider knowledge of the music of Jules Massenet (1842-1912) the French composer
- ● Lib
- ¶ NL. Jnl.

Mast Action UK: the National Campaign for the Sensible Siting of Masts (MAUK) 2000

- ■ PO Box 312, WALTHAM CROSS, Herts, EN7 5ZE.
  01707 872920
  email headoffice@mastaction.co.uk
  http://www.mastaction.co.uk
  Coordinators: Chris Mangat, Julie Matthew
- ○ *K; for control in the raising of masts for telephone & other purposes

Master Carvers Association (MCA) 1897

- ■ Unit 2, 15b Vandyke Rd, LEIGHTON BUZZARD, Beds, LU7 2QD. (hsb)
  01525 851594 fax 01525 851594
  email info@mastercarvers.co.uk
  http://www.mastercarvers.co.uk
  Hon Sec: Paul Ferguson
- ▲ Un-incorporated Society
- ○ *A, *T; promotion & protection of the interests of wood carving, stone carving & modelling generally
- ● Conf - Inf - Empl
- M 37 f, UK / 2 f, o'seas
- ¶ NL - irreg; ftm only. LM; free.

Master Chefs of Great Britain (MCGB) 1980

■ Woodmans, Brithem Bottom, CULLOMPTON, Devon, EX15 1NB. (hsp)
01884 35104   fax 01884 35105
email mcgb@masterchefs.co.uk
http://www.masterchefs.co.uk
Chmn: Gerald Roser
Sec: Susan M McGreever
○ *P; to provide a forum for the exchange of culinary ideas; to further the profession through the training & guidance of young chefs; to promote all that is best about British cuisine & the produce available
● Mtgs - ET - Culinary demonstrations
M 240 i, 22 f, UK / 5 i, o'seas
¶ Masterchefs - 4; ftm, £3 nm.

Master Craftsmen's Association & Retail Export Group   (MCA)

NR c/o Henry Poole & Co Ltd, 15 Savile Row, LONDON, W1S 3PJ. (hsb)
020 7734 5985   fax 020 7287 2161
Sec: Alex Cook
▲ Un-incorporated Society
○ *T; to export 'bespoke' handmade gentlemen's suits, shirts, shoes etc
Gp Bespoke: tailors, shoemakers, shirtmakers; Woollen / trimming merchants
● ET - Expt
M 35 f

Master Locksmiths' Association (MLA) 1958

NR 5d Great Central Way, Woodford Halse, DAVENTRY, Northants, NN11 3PZ. (hq)
01327 262255   fax 01327 262539
email admin@locksmiths.co.uk
http://www.locksmiths.co.uk
Chief Exec: Lorraine Stanley
▲ Company Limited by Guarantee
○ *P, *T
● Conf - Mtgs - ET - Exam - Exhib - Inf - Lib - LG - Locktesting - Professional consultancy
M 1,000 i, 350 f, UK / 100 i, o'seas
¶ Keyways - 6; ftm only.

Master Photographers Association Ltd (MPA) 1952

■ 1 Chancery Lane, DARLINGTON, Co Durham, DL1 5QP. (hq)
01325 356555   fax 01325 357813
email enquiries@mpauk.com   http://www.thempa.com
Chief Exec: Colin R Buck
○ *T; represents professional photographers
M f
no further information supplied

Masters of Deerhounds Association (MDHA) 1951

NR Broford Farm, DULVERTON, Somerset, TA22 9DW. (hsp)
Sec: Guy Everard
▲ Company Limited by Guarantee; Registered Charity
○ *S; control & regulation of deer hunting with hounds
M 3 hunts in England (Devon & Somerset, Tiverton, Quantock)

Masters of Draghounds & Bloodhounds Association

NR RMA Sandhurst - Blacklands Farm, Milford Rd, ELSTEAD, Surrey, GU8 6LA. (chmn/p)
01252 703304
http://www.bloodhoundhunting.co.uk
Chmn: Pat Sutton
○ *G, *S; for followers of the sport - hounds following artificial scent laid down by a runner or mounted rider

Masters of Foxhounds Association (MFHA) 1881

■ Overley Barn, Daglingworth, CIRENCESTER, Glos, GL7 7HX. (hq)
01285 653001   fax 01285 653559
http://www.mfha.org.uk
Dir: Alastair Jackson
○ *S; the governing body of foxhunting
M i (past & present masters of foxhounds only)

Mastic Asphalt Council (MAC) 1995

■ PO Box 77, HASTINGS, E Sussex, TN35 4WL. (hq)
01424 814400   fax 01424 814446
email masphaltco@aol.com
http://www.masticasphaltcouncil.co.uk
Dir & Sec: J K Blowers
▲ Company Limited by Guarantee
○ *T; represents mastic asphalt contractors & manufacturers providing a free technical service to specifiers
Gp Specialist mastic asphalt contractors
● Conf - Mtgs - ET - Exhib - Comp - SG - Inf - VE - Empl - LG (via NSCC)
< Eur Mastic Asphalt Assn (EMAA); Nat Specialist Contrs Coun (NSCC)
M 72 f (contractors), 6 f (manufacturing), 21 associates
¶ The New Technical Guide (incl Roofing, Flooring, Paving, Tanking); ftm, £30 nm.
[the Guide is produced as an A4 loose-leaf ring-binder]

Materials Handling Engineers Association (MHEA) 1938

■ 2B Hills Lane, ELY, Cambs, CB6 1AY, (hq)
01353 666298   fax 01353 666298
email pw@mhea.co.uk   http://www.mhea.co.uk
Sec: Peter Webster
▲ Un-incorporated Society
○ *T; manufacturers & users of bulk & continuous handling eqpt
● Conf - Mtgs - Expt through ISHAB - LG
< permanent member of Intl Solids Handling Advy Bd (ISHAB)
M 27 f
¶ Online NL - 3; ftm.
Recommended Practice for Troughed Belt Conveyors.

MatheMagic 1999

■ 1 Straylands Grove, YORK, YO31 1EB.
email info@mathemagic.org + qed@enterprise.net
http://www.mathemagic.org
Dir: John Bibby
▲ Un-incorporated Society
○ *E; to popularise maths & numeracy
Gp Adult basic skills; Multicultural mathematics
● Conf - Exhib - Comp - PL - VE - Maths Funfairs
< Adults Learning Mathematics
M 300 i, UK / 20 i, o'seas
¶ NL

Mathematical Association (MA) 1871

NR 259 London Rd, LEICESTER, LE2 3BE. (hq)
0116-221 0013   fax 0116-212 2835
email office@m-a.org.uk   http://www.m-a.org.uk
Admin: Marcia Murray
▲ Registered Charity
Br 20
○ *E, *P; to improve mathematical education
Gp Library; Publications; Teaching; Problem bureau; Careers; Schools & industry; Diplomas; Universities; Society of Young Mathematicians (http://www.syms.org.uk)
● Conf - Mtgs - ET - Exam - Exhib - Comp - Lib - LG
< Intl Congress on Mathematical Educ; Coun of Subject Teaching Assns; R Soc Mathematical Instruction (sub c'ee); Standing Conf of Assns concerned with Mathematical Education in Schools
M 5,000 i worldwide UK / 500 i, 300 f, o'seas
¶ [publishes a range of mathematics books & jnls].

© CBD Research Ltd · Beckenham · BR3 5JS · Tel 020 8650 7745 · Fax 020 8650 0768 · E-mail cbd@cbdresearch.com · www.cbdresearch.com

Max Wall Society   2003
- ■ 11 Milland Rd, HAILSHAM, E Sussex, BN27 1TG.   (h/mem/sp)
    email (09>maxwall.org
    Mem Sec: Jean Barham
- ▲ Un-incorporated Society
- ○ *G; for all interested in the life & performing career of Max[well George Lorimer] Wall (1908-1990), actor & comedian & to perpetuate his memory
- ● Exhib - Lectures - Annual dinner
- M   c 150 i
- ¶   Wallpaper; ftm only.

McCarrison Society   1965
- NR c/o IBCHN, London Metropolitan University, North London Campus, 166-222 Holloway Rd, LONDON, N7 8DB. (chmn/b)
    020 7133 2926   fax 020 7133 2453
    email michael@macrawf.demon.co.uk
    http://www.mccarrisonsociety.org.uk
    Chmn: Prof Michael A Crawford
- ▲ Registered Charity
- Br 2
- ○   L, *P; research & dissemination of knowledge on nutrition & health; areas of interest include the rise in mortality from non-communicable diseases, mental ill-health & the widening inequality of health
- Gp Dietetics; Nutrition; Cardiology; Cancer; Comparative pathology; Epidemiology; Diseases of Western & developing countries
- ●   Conf - Mtgs - ET - Res - Comp - SG - LG
- <   Mother & Child Foundation
- M   250 i, UK / 50 i, o'seas
- ¶   Nutrition & Health - 4.

MCPS-PRS Alliance
- NR 29-33 Berners St, LONDON, W1T 3AB.   (hq)
    020 7580 5544   fax 020 7306 4455
    http://www.mcps-prs-alliance.co.uk
- ○   *T; collection of royalties for the music industry
- M   2 org:
    Mechanical Copyright Protection Society Ltd
    Performing Right Society Ltd

McTimoney Chiropractic Association   (MCA)   1979
- NR Crowmarsh Gifford, WALLINGFORD, Oxon, OX10 8DJ.   (hq)
    01491 829211   fax 01491 829492
    email services@mctimoney-chiropractic.org
    http://www.mctimoney-chiropractic.org
    Sec: Christine Chalmers,   Chmn: Dr Christina Cunliffe
- ○   *P; promotion of McTimoney chiropractic
- Gp Chiropractic; Private sector education (McTimoney chiropractic college)
- ●   Conf - ET - Exam - Res - Exhib - Inf - PL
- M   500 i, UK / 10 i, o'seas
- ¶   Background (NL) - 4; ftm only.
    Directory of Practitioners - 1; ftm, £7.10 nm.
    Information leaflets & college prospectus.

MDA Europe
    since 2008 **Collections Trust**

MDF - the BiPolar Organisation   (MDF)   2005
- NR Castle Works, 21 St George's Rd, LONDON, SE1 6ES.   (hq)
    0845 634 0540   fax 020 7793 2639
    email mdf@mdf.org.uk   http://www.mdf.org.uk
- ▲ Company Limited by Guarantee; Registered Charity
- ○   *W; to support those with manic depression & their carers & friends; to encourage research into the illness; to educate the public & caring professions
- M   c 150 self-help groups
- ¶   Pendulum - 4; ftm.
    Group News.
    Factsheets & literature.
- ×   2005 Manic Depression Fellowship Ltd

Meat Industry Ireland
    a group of **Food & Drink Industry Ireland**

Meath Archaeological and Historical Society
- IRL Spiddal, Nobber, Co Meath, Republic of Ireland.
    353 (46) 52236
    http://www.community.meath.ie/mahs/

MeCCSA with AMPE
    since 2008 **Media, Communications & Cultural Studies Association**

Mechanical Copyright Protection Society Ltd
    a member of the **MCPS-PRS Alliance**

Mechanical & Metal Trades Confederation   (METCOM)   1989
- ■ National Metalforming Centre, 47 Birmingham Rd, WEST BROMWICH, W Midlands, B70 6PY.   (hq)
    0121-601 6350   fax 0121-601 6387
    http://www.metcom.org.uk
    Managing Dir: Brian Huxley
- ▲ Company Limited by Guarantee
- ○   *N; a federation of trade associations in the mechanical engineering & metal industries
- ●   Mtgs - ET - Stat - LG
- <   Confedn Brit Ind
- M   4,000 f, 34 org

Mechanical Organ Owners Society   (MOOS)   1976
- ■ 27 Silvergate, Blickling, NORWICH, Norfolk, NR11 6NN. (hsp)
    01263 732776
    email info@moos.org.uk   http://www.moos.org.uk
    Sec: Robert Wichall
- ▲ Un-incorporated Society
- ○   *G; to promote an interest in all types of mechanical organs (fair, street & dance); to protect owners' interests regarding the playing & legislation of organ display vehicles
- ●   Res - Exhib - Inf - VE - LG
- <   Kring van Draaiorgelvrienden (Dutch Organ Soc); Fair Organ Presvn Soc
- M   250 i, UK / 30 i, 1 org (Nat Museum of Mechanical Musical Instruments (Netherlands)
- ¶   Vox Humana (Jnl) - 4; ftm. (subscription £12 (£15 o'seas)).

Medau Society   1952
- NR 1 Grove House, Foundry Lane, HORSHAM, W Sussex, RH13 5PL.   (hq)
    01403 266000
    email office@medau.org.uk   http://www.medau.org.uk
    Admin: Lynda Bridges
- ▲ Company Limited by Guarantee
- ○   *G, *S; to train & support Medau Movement teachers; (for women (devised by Hinrich Medau) using hoops, clubs & balls)
- ●   Mtgs - ET - SG - Inf
- <   Sport England; Cent Coun of Physical Recreation (CCPR)
- M   2,200 i, UK / 7 i, o'seas
- ¶   Medau News - 2;   AR; both ftm only.

Media, Communications & Cultural Studies Association (MeCCSA) 1999

■   c/o Prof Peter Golding, Dept of Social Sciences, Loughborough University, LOUGHBOROUGH, Leics, LE11 3TU.   (hsb)
    01509 222451
    email p.golding@lboro.ac.uk   http://www.meccsa.org.uk
    Hon Sec: Prof Peter Golding
○   *P; for all who teach or research in higher education in media, communications & cultural studies whether in arts, humanities or social science departments
Gp Media policy network; Media practice section; Postgraduate network; Women's media studies network
●   Conf - Mtgs - SG - LG
M   c 70 i, c 60 instns
    Sub: c £25 i, c £100-£300 instns
✕   2008 MeCCSA with AMPE
    2006 Association of Media Practice Educators (merged)

Media Education Association   (MEA)   2006

■   c/o 21-22 Poland St (2nd floor), LONDON, W1F 8QQ.
    email info@mediaedassociation.org.uk
    http://www.mediaedassociation.org.uk
    Sec: Terry Bolas
○   *P; to support media teachers, promote media literacy work, and raise the status of media education

Media Research Group   (MRG)

■   Red Lion House, West Dean, SALISBURY, Wilts, SP5 1JF.
    (admin/p)
    01794 341337
    email sallyhiddleston@mrg.org.uk
    http://www.mrg.org.uk
    Admin: Sally Hiddleston
    Jt Chmn: David Lucas,   Keith Donaldson
○   *P; 'to recognise & promote importance of media research, its validity, directness & development'
●   Conf - Mtgs - ET - Res
M   i
    (Sub: £45)

Media Society Ltd   (MS)   1973

NR Flat 1, 24 Park Rd, LONDON, NW1 4SH.   (hsp)
    http://www.themediasociety.co.uk
    Admin: Dorothy Josem
▲   Registered Charity
○   *P; for people working in the media & public life
●   Mtgs
<   Chart Inst of Journalists
M   300 i

Mediators Institute Ireland   1992

IRL Montana House, Whitechurch, DUBLIN 16, Republic of Ireland.
    353 (1) 284 7121   fax 353 (1) 493 0595
    http://www.themii.ie
○   *P

mediawatch-uk: campaigning for decency & accountability in the media 1965

■   3 Willow House, Kennington Rd, ASHFORD, Kent, TN24 0NR.   (hq)
    01233 633936   fax 01233 633836
    email info@mediawatchuk.org
    http://www.mediawatchuk.org
    Dir: John C Beyer
▲   Un-incorporated Society
Br 40; Australia
○   *K; 'to uphold good standards of programme content in TV & radio; to strengthen the law against obscenity in the media'
●   Conf - ET - Res - Inf - LG
M   8,000 i, 175,000 org, UK / 100 i, o'seas
¶   newsbrief - 3; 50p.
    Children and the Media (booklet); £1.

Medical Action for Global Security   (MEDACT)   1992

NR The Grayston Centre, 28 Charles Sq, LONDON, N1 6HT.   (hq)
    020 7324 4739
○   *K; for doctors & other health professionals committed to preventing war & promoting peace & global security

Medical Artists Association of Great Britain & Northern Ireland (MAA)   1949

NR Medical Illustration UK Ltd, Charing Cross Hospital, LONDON, W6 8RF.   (hsb)
    http://www.maa.org.uk
○   *A; to promote & facilitate the acquisition & dissemination of knowledge of the graphic & plastic arts as applied to the illustration of medicine
M   c 80 i

Medical Council on Alcohol   (MCA)   1967

■   3 St Andrew's Place, LONDON, NW1 4LB.   (hq)
    020 7487 4445   fax 020 7935 4479
    email mca@medicouncilalcol.demon.co.uk
    http://www.medicouncilalcol.demon.co.uk
    Sec & Medical Dir: Dr Guy Ratcliffe
▲   Registered Charity
○   *L, *M, *P; to ioimprove medical understanding of alcohol related problems - particularly for medical students & medical practitioners. Members are from most, if not all, specialities within medicine
Gp C'ees: Education, Executive, Journal
●   Conf - Mtgs - ET - Comp - Inf - Lib
<   R Coll of Physicians of London; Alcohol Health Alliance
>   Eur Soc of Biomedical Res on Alcohol (ESBRA)
M   280 i, 20 f, UK / 5 i, o'seas
    (Sub: £50 i, £28 f)
¶   Alcohol & Alcoholism (Jnl) - 6; £45 m, £520 nm.
    Alcoholis (NL) - 4; ftm, £3 nm.
    Alcohol & Health: a handbook for medical students & practitioners; free to students; £12 for qualified practitioners.

Medical Defence Union   (MDU)   1885

NR 230 Blackfriars Rd, LONDON, SE1 8PJ.   (hq)
    020 7202 1500   fax 020 7202 1666
    http://www.the-mdu.com
    Chief Exec: Dr Michael Saunders
▲   Company Limited by Guarantee
○   *N; provision of medico-legal advice, assistance & indemnity to doctors, dentists, nurses & other healthcare professionals in the UK & Eire
●   Conf - ET - LG - Workshops - Presentations
M   c 90,000 i
¶   Jnl - irreg; ftm only.   AR; free.
    Training packages; m only.

Medical & Dental Defence Union of Scotland   (MDDUS)   1902

NR Mackintosh House, 120 Blythswood St, GLASGOW, G2 4EA.
    (hq)
    0141-221 5858   fax 0141-228 1208
    email info@mddus.com   http://www.mddus.com
    Chief Exec: Prof Gordon Dickson
▲   Company Limited by Guarantee
○   *M; professional indemnity for doctors & dentists
Gp Risk management; Education for primary care staff
●   Conf - ET - Inf - LG
<   Physician Insurers Assn of America (PIAA)
M   22,000 i
¶   Summons (Jnl) - 4;   AR; both free.

© CBD Research Ltd · Beckenham · BR3 5JS · Tel 020 8650 7745 · Fax 020 8650 0768 · E-mail cbd@cbdresearch.com · www.cbdresearch.com

Medical Equestrian Association   (MEA)   1984
NR   Ravenscroft Hall, King St, BYLEY, Cheshire, CW10 9LE.   (hsp)
       01606 835480
       http://www.medequestrian.co.uk
       Hon Sec: Dr J Trelawny
▲   Registered Charity
Br   links with similar gps in Eire, Australia, New Zealand, Sweden,
       USA
○   *K, *M; to maintain & improve medical cover at equestrian
       events - Pony Club, riding clubs, British eventing, carriage
       driving, flat & jump racing
●   Mtgs - ET - VE
M   150 i, UK / 50 i, o'seas

Medical Ethics Alliance   (MAEA)   1999
■   79 Friar St (suite 240), WORCESTER, WR1 2NT.
       (mail/address)
       01905 352967   fax 01905 352967
       email worcestercoles@aol.com
       http://www.medethics-alliance.org
       Hon Sec: Dr F Leahy
▲   Registered Charity
○   *K, *P; to promote discussion on medical ethics within & without
       the medical profession
●   Conf - Mtgs - Exhib - SG - Inf - LG
<   affiliated to all organisations listed as members
M   60 i, 3,000 f via 6 org:
       Guild of Catholic Doctors
       First Do No Harm
       HOPE (Healthcare Opposed to Euthanasia)
       Muslim Doctors & Dentists Association
       Nurses Opposed to Euthanasia
       World Federation of Doctors
¶   Ethics & Wisdom in Medicine - 3; [online Jnl].
       Conferences papers - 2; prices vary.

Medical Journalists' Association   (MJA)   1967
NR   Fairfield, Cross in Hand, HEATHFIELD, E Sussex, TN21 0SH.
       (hsp)
       01435 868786   fax 01435 865714
       email pigache@tiscali.co.uk   http://www.mja-uk.org
       Hon Sec: Philippa Pigache
▲   Un-incorporated Society
○   *M, *P; to improve the quality of medical journalism &
       understanding between medical healthcare professionals, the
       media & the public
●   Mtgs - ET - Awards
M   390 i, UK / 2 i, o'seas
¶   MJA News (NL) - 5; ftm only.
       Directory of Members with contacts - 1; ftm,
       £450 (commercial), £200 (charities & academics).

Medical Officers of Schools Association   (MOSA)   1884
NR   Amherst Medical Practice, 21 St Botolph's Rd, SEVENOAKS,
       Kent, TN13 3AQ.   (hsb)
       01732 459255   fax 01732 450751
       email honsec@mosa.org.uk   http://www.mosa.org.uk
       Hon Sec: Dr Neil Arnott
▲   Un-incorporated Society
○   *L, *P; promotion of school health
●   Conf - Mtgs - ET - Inf - Empl
<   Eur U of School & University Health & Medicine
M   c 400 i
¶   NL - 4; free.
       Handbook of School Health - 5-6 yrly.

Medical Protection Society Ltd   (MPS)   1892
NR   33 Cavendish Sq, LONDON, W1G 0PS.   (hq)
       010 7399 1300
       http://www.medicalprotection.org
▲   Company Limited by Guarantee
○   *P; a not-for-profit mutual association run exclusively for, &
       largely by, doctors, dentists & other healthcare professionals
●   ET - Inf - Wide range of medico-legal services (professional
       indemnity for adverse awards of costs & damages in medical
       negligence cases)
<   Physician Insurers Assn of America
M   100,000 i UK / 125,000 i, o'seas
¶   Casebook (Jnl) - 2;   Medico-legal booklets;   AR; all free.

Medical Research Society   (MRS)
NR   Box 118, Dialysis Centre, Addenbrooke's Hospital, Hills Rd,
       CAMBRIDGE, CB2 2QQ.   (hsb)
       http://www.medres.org
       Academic Sec: Dr Afzal Chaudhry
▲   Registered Charity
○   *L; exchange of information on medical research
Gp   Association of Young Medical Scientists (AYMS)
●   Conf - Mtgs - ET - Comp - LG
<   Biological Coun
M   350 i
¶   Clinical Science - 12; ftm, £90 yr nm.

Medical Science Historical Society   (MSHS)   1982
■   117 Woodland Drive, Cassiobury, WATFORD, Herts,
       WD17 3DA.   (hsp)
       01923 231704
       Hon Sec: Hilda Taylor
▲   Registered Charity
○   *L; to further education in the history of diagnostic medical
       sciences; to provide a forum for everyone with an interest in
       the history of the medical laboratory
●   Mtgs
<   Brit Soc History Medicine
M   i
¶   Jnl - 1 (Summer);   NL - 2 (Spring & Autumn).

Medical Society of London   1773
■   Lettsom House, 11 Chandos St, LONDON, W1G 9EB.   (hq)
       020 7580 1043
       Registrar: Col Richard Kinsella-Bevan
○   *L; the advancement of medicine & surgery
●   Mtgs - Inf
M   i
¶   Transactions - 1.

Medical Women's Federation   (MWF)   1917
NR   Tavistock House North, Tavistock Sq, LONDON, WC1H 9HX.
       (hq)
       020 7387 7765   fax 020 7388 9216
       http://www.medicalwomensfederation.org.uk
○   *P; to further the careers of women doctors
M   i
¶   Medical Woman.   AR; both ftm.

Medico-Legal Society   1901
NR   c/o XPL Publishing, 99 Hatfield Rd, ST ALBANS, Herts, AL1 4EG.
       http://www.medico-legalsociety.org.uk
▲   Registered Charity
○   *L; the dissemination of medico-legal knowledge in all its
       aspects

Medieval Dress & Textile Society   (MEDATS)
NR   PO Box 948, GUILDFORD, Surrey, GU1 9AH.   (sec)
       http://www.medats.org.uk
       Sec: Karen Watts
○   *L
●   Mtgs

Medieval Settlement Research Group (MSRG) 1986

■ School of Archaeology & Ancient History, University of Leicester, University Rd, LEICESTER, LE1 7RH.   (hsb)
0116-252 2617   fax 0116-252 5005
email njc10@le.ac.uk   http://www.britarch.ac.uk/msrg/
Hon Sec: Dr Neil Christie
▲ Registered Charity
○ *L; to advance knowledge of settlements, especially those dating between the 5th & 16th centuries; to offer advice & information to those conducting research into settlement history; to influence national policy on the survey, conservation & excavation of medieval settlement sites; to encourage the preservation of settlement sites wherever possible.
● Conf - Mtgs - Res - VE
M 430 i, 55 org
¶ AR - 1; ftm, back numbers to 2004; £5 each nm.

Medieval Siege Society

NR 11-12 Wrotham Rd, GRAVESEND, Kent, DA11 0PE.
email secretary@medieval-siege-society.co.uk
http://www.medieval-siege-society.co.uk
Sec: Chris Broome-Smith

Meet-a-Mum Association (MAMA) 1979

NR 24 Celandine Rd, WORCESTER, WR5 3SP.   (hq)
01905 764498
http://www.mama.co.uk
Contact: Paul Perrett
▲ Registered Charity
Br 68
○ *W; to support mums & mums-to-be feeling isolated or suffering with post-natal depression by putting them in touch with others; offers support through the national helpline 020 8768 0123 (Mon-Fri 0700-2200)
● Mtgs - ET - Exhib - SG - Inf - LG
< Telephone Helplines Assn
M 3,000 i
¶ Behind the Painted Smile: an insight into postnatal depression. Lifting the Veil of Silence on Emotional Problems after Childbirth.
Publications list available.

Meetings Industry Association (MIA) 1991

NR PO Box 515, KELMARSH, Northants, NN6 9XW.   (hq)
0845 230 5508   fax 0845 230 7708
email info@mia-uk.org   http://www.mia-uk.org
Chief Exec: Jane Evans
▲ Company Limited by Guarantee
○ *P, *T; meetings & conference industry
● Conf - Mtgs - ET - Res - Exhib
M 450 f
¶ NL - 12;   Magazine - 4; both free.
UK Conference Market Survey - 1; £135 m, £165 nm.
Buyers' Directory of Members - 1; free.   AR - 1; ftm only.

Megalithic Society (incorporating the Stonehenge Society) 1997

■ 25A Whitehill, BRADFORD-on-AVON, Wilts, BA15 1SQ.   (hq)
01225 862482
email terence.meaden@stonehenge-avebury.net
http://www.stonehenge-avebury.net
Chief Exec: Terence Meaden
▲ Un-incorporated Society
Br 2
○ *G, *K; to promote interest in & the preservation & security of the ancient stones of Britain; is also concerned with crop circles
Gp Avebury; Stonehenge
● Mtgs - ET - Res - Inf - PL - VE
< Stonehenge Soc
M 50 i
¶ The Complete Guidebook to Avebury; £8 m, £10 nm.

Melton Mowbray Pork Pie Association

NR PO Box 5540, MELTON MOWBRAY, Leics, LE13 1YU.
01664 569388
http://www.mmppa.co.uk
○ *T; makers of Melton Mowbray pork pies
M 7 f

Men of the Stones (MOS) 1947

NR Beech Croft, Weston-under-Lizard, SHIFNAL, Shropshire, TF11 8JT.   (chmn/p)
01952 850269
http://www.menofthestones.org.uk
▲ Registered Charity
○ *K; a society advocating the use of stone & other natural & local building materials; to encourage craftsmanship & preservation of the good architectural qualities of Stamford & other places in the limestone belt

Mencap (MENCAP) 1946

NR 123 Golden Lane, LONDON, EC1Y 0RT.   (hq)
020 7454 0454   fax 020 7696 5540
email information@mencap.org.uk
http://www.mencap.org.uk
▲ Registered Charity
○ *W; 'is the leading charity working with children & adults with learning disabilities in England, Wales & Northern Ireland; it campaigns to ensure that persons with such a disability live the fullest life possible; it undertakes research into issues affecting people with a learning disability
Gp Divn: National Federation of Gateway Clubs
● Conf - Mtgs - ET - Res - Exhib - Inf - LG
M i & gps
¶ Publications list available.
Mencap is the Royal Society for Mentally Handicapped Children & Adults
× 2005 English Sports Association for People with Learning Disabilities (merged as Mencap Sport)

Ménière's Society 1984

■ The Rookery, Surrey Hills Business Park, Wotton, DORKING, Surrey, RH5 6QT.   (hq)
01306 876883   fax 01306 876057
email info@menieres.org.uk
http://www.menieres.org.uk
Dir: Mrs Natasha Harrington-Benton
▲ Registered Charity
○ *W; to help those with the symptoms of Ménière's disease: vertigo (nausea), fluctuating & increasing deafness & tinnitus
● Conf - Mtgs - Res - Stat - Inf
Helpline: 0845 120 2975
M 5,400 i, 139 org, UK / 53 i, 10 org, o'seas
¶ NL - 4;   Contact List - 4;   Information sheets; AR; all ftm only.

Meningitis Association of Scotland 1991

NR 9 Edwin St, GLASGOW, G51 1ND.
0141-427 6698
http://www.menscot.org
Chmn: Mrs E E McKiernan

© CBD Research Ltd · Beckenham · BR3 5JS · Tel 020 8650 7745 · Fax 020 8650 0768 · E-mail cbd@cbdresearch.com · www.cbdresearch.com

Meningitis Research Foundation   1989
- ■ Midland Way, Thornbury, BRISTOL, BS35 2BS.   (hq)
  01454 281811   fax 01454 281094
  email info@meningitis.org   http://www.meningitis.org
  Chief Exec: Christopher Head
- ▲ Company Limited by Guarantee; Registered Charity
- Br 3; Republic of Ireland
- ○ *M, *Q; to promote research into the causes & treatment of all
  forms of meningitis & associated infections, & the
  dissemination of knowledge gained by such research; to
  advance the education of the public in the causes, treatment
  & prevention of meningitis & associated infections; to help
  relieve distress to individuals & families caused by death &
  damage through meningitis & associated infections
- ● Conf - ET - Res - Exhib - G - Stat - Inf - PL - VE
  Helpline: 0808 800 3344 (24-hours)
- < Assn of Med Res Charities (AMRC); Telephone Helpline
  Assn (THA)
- M 5,500 i, UK / 100 i, o'seas
- ¶ Microscope (NL) - 3;   AR - 1; both free.
  Awareness Literature:
    Baby Watch; Tot Watch; Get it Sussed;
    Race against Time.
  Materials for health professionals to help in the diagnosis &
  treatment of meningitis & septicaemia.

Mental After Care Association
  since July 2005 **Together**

Mental Health Ireland
- IRL 6 Adelaide St, DÚN LAOGHAIRE, Co Dublin, Republic of
  Ireland.
  353 (1) 284 1166   fax 353 (1) 284 1736
  email info@mentalhealthireland.ie
  http://www.mentalhealthireland.ie
- ○ *W

Mental Health Nurses Association   (MHNA)   1975
- ■ Cals Meyn, Grove Lane, Hinton, CHIPPENHAM, Wilts,
  SN14 8HF.   (hq)
  07918 630403
  email brian.rogers@unitetheunion.org
  http://www.amicus-mhna.org
  Profl Officer: Brian Rogers
- ○ *P, *U; representing the professional & labour relations needs of
  community mental health nurses
- ● Conf - Mtgs - ET - Res - Inf - Lib - Empl - LG
- < Unite
- M 4,000 i
- ¶ Mental Health Nursing - 6; ftm, £72.45 (i),£108.75 (instns) nm.

**Merchant Navy Locomotive Preservation Society Ltd
    (MNLPS)   1965**
- NR 12 Inglewood Ave, Heatherside, CAMBERLEY, Surrey,
  GU15 1RJ.   (hsp)
  01276 514000
  http://www.clan-line.org.uk
  Sec: R F Abercrombie
- ▲ Registered Charity
- ○ *G, *K; to preserve, maintain, operate & foster an interest in the
  ex-British Railways Southern Region 'Merchant Navy' Class
  locomotive no. 35028 'Clan Line'
- ● Mtgs - ET - Exhib - Comp - Maintenance of the locomotive -
  Special excursion runs
- M i
- ¶ Southern Express (Jnl).

Mercia Cinema Society   1980
- ■ 29 Blackbrook Court, Durham Rd, LOUGHBOROUGH, Leics,
  LE11 5UA.   (Admin/p)
  01509 218393
  email mervyn.gould@virgin.net
  http://www.merciacinema.org.uk
  Administrator: Mervyn Gould
- ▲ Registered Charity
- ○ *G; To promote & publish research into picture house history
- ● Conf - Res - Inf - Lib - Publishing
- M 205 i,UK/ 5 i, o'seas
  (Sub: £10 UK / £15 o'seas)
- ¶ The Mercia Bioscope - 4; ftm, £2.50 nm.
  Various books on cinemas of specific areas.

Merioneth Agricultural Society   (MAS)   1868
- ■ Tir y Dail, Cader Rd, DOLGELLAU, Gwynedd, LL40 1SG.   (hsp)
  01341 422837   fax 01341 422837
  email sioesir@aol.com   http://www.sioesir.org.uk
  Hon Sec: E Douglas Powell
- ▲ Registered Charity
- ○ *F; promotion of agriculture by staging an annual county show
- ● Exhib - Comp - Merioneth County Show
- M 400 i
- ¶ Show catalogue - 1; £2.

Merseyside Industrial Heritage Society   (MIHS)   1970
- NR 14 Ardern Lea, Alvanley, FRODSHAM, Cheshire, WA6 9EQ.
  http://www.mihs.org.uk
- ▲ Un-incorporated Society
- ○ *K, *L; to foster an interest in the study & conservation of the
  industrial heritage of Merseyside
- M i & org

Merton Chamber of Commerce   1992
- NR Tuition House (5th floor), 27-37 St George's Rd, LONDON,
  SW19 4EU.
  020 8944 5501   fax 020 8286 2552
  email info@mertonchamber.co.uk
  http://www.mertonchamber.co.uk
  Chief Exec: Diana Sterck
- ▲ Company Limited by Guarantee
- ○ *C
- ● Mtgs - ET - Exhib - Inf - LG - Business support services
- M 350 f
- ¶ NL - 4; free.   LM - 1; ftm, £5 nm.

**Metal Cladding & Roofing Manufacturers Association Ltd
    (MCRMA)**
- NR 18 Mere Farm Rd, Prenton, WIRRAL, Cheshire, CH43 9TT.
  0151-652 3846   fax 0151-653 4080
  email mcrma@compuserve.com
  http://www.mcrma.co.uk
- ○ *P

Metal Finishing Association
  a group of the **Surface Engineering Association**

Metal Gutter Manufacturers Association Ltd   (MGMA)
- NR 18 Mere Farm Rd, Prenton, WIRRAL, Cheshire, CH43 9TT.
  0151-652 3846   fax 0151-653 4080
  http://www.mgma.co.uk
- ○ *T

Metal Packaging Manufacturers Association   (MPMA)   1914
■   The Stables, Tintagel Farm, Sandhurst Rd, WOKINGHAM,
     Berks, RG40 3JD.   (hq)
     0118-978 8433
     email enquiries@mpma.org.uk   http://www.mpma.org.uk
     Dir: N J Mullen
▲   Company Limited by Guarantee
○   *T; interests of companies involved directly, or indirectly, in the
     production of light metal containers, closures & components
     (including cans, & tinplate items)
Gp   Business c'ees: Open top, Closures, General line, Technical,
     Food contact
     Service/advisory c'ees: Environment, Health & safety, Public
     relations
●   Mtgs - Exhib - Stat - Inf
<   Eur Metal Packaging (EMPAC)
M   23 f (full), 18 f (associate)

Metalforming Machinery Makers' Association Ltd   (MMMA)
■   The Cottage, Down End, Hook Norton, BANBURY, Oxon,
     OX15 5LW.   (hq)
     01608 737129   fax 01295 253333
     email rayjelf@mmma.org.uk
     http://www.mmma.org.uk
     Co Sec: Ray Jelf
▲   Company Limited by Guarantee
○   *N, *T; to act as the central organisation promoting the interests
     of companies involved in the manufacture & sale of
     metalforming machinery & ancillary products in the UK
●   Exhib - Inf
<   a METCOM organisation
M   35 f
     (Sub: £400)
¶   Hbk.

Metalworking Fluid Product Stewardship Group
     a group of the **United Kingdom Lubricants Association Ltd**

Metamorphic Association   1979
NR   159 Bembrook Rd, HASTINGS, E Sussex, TN34 3PD.   (hq)
     0870 770 7984 (recorded information only)
     email metamorphicassoc@cs.com
     http://www.metamorphicassociation.org
▲   Registered Charity
○   *P; to promote awareness, understanding & use of the
     metamorphic technique - a unique & simple approach to
     self-healing & personal development through the contact with
     the spinal reflex points in the feet
●   Conf - Mtgs - ET - Exhib - Inf
M   c 350 i
¶   NL - 4;   Bulletin - 4; both ftm only.
     Programme of Activities - 2; ftm, on request for sae.

Metric Martyrs
NR   PO Box 526, SUNDERLAND, SR1 3YS.
     0191 565 7143   fax 0191 565 2004
     email metricmartyrs@btconnect.com
     http://www.metricmartyrs.co.uk
○   *K;

**Metropolitan Drinking Fountain & Cattle Trough Association
1859**
■   Oaklands, 5 Queenborough Gardens, CHISLEHURST, Kent,
     BR7 6NP.   (hsp)
     020 8467 1261
     email dfa@tesco.net   http://www.drinkingfountains.org
     Sec: Ralph P Baber
▲   Registered Charity
○   *G; to promote the provision of drinking water for people &
     animals in the UK & overseas; to keep an archive of
     materials, artifacts, drinking fountains, cattle troughs & other
     installations
M   25 i
     Note: Also known as the Drinking Fountain Association.

Metropolitan Public Gardens Association   (MPGA)   1882
NR   348 London Rd, MITCHAM, Surrey, CR4 3ND.   (sp)
     020 8648 9469
     http://www.mpga.org.uk
     Sec: Mrs J K Bellamy
▲   Registered Charity
○   *G; the protection, preservation & acquiring for permanent
     preservation for public use of gardens, disused burial
     grounds, churchyards, open spaces, areas of land adjoining
     roads & footpaths, or any land situated within the
     Metropolitan Police District; the encouragement of window
     boxes, provision of seats & the planting of trees
●   AGM - Res - Exhib - Comp (via London in Bloom) - SG - LG
<   London in Bloom
M   100 i
¶   Ybk (AR) - 1; free.

**Meuse Rhine Issel Cattle Society of the United Kingdom
(MRI)   1971**
NR   Castlemoor Farm, Four Oaks, NEWENT, Glos, GL18 1LU.
     (sp/b)
     01531 890730   fax 01531 890939
     email office@mri.org.uk   http://www.mri.org.uk
     Sec: Mrs Niki Ford
▲   Registered Charity
Br   N Zealand
○   *B, *F
●   Conf - Mtgs - Exhib - Stat - Expt - Inf - Semen sales
<   R Assn Brit Dairy Farmers; Nat Cattle Assn (Dairy)
M   72 i, UK / 3 i, o'seas
¶   MRI NL - 3;   Herdbook - 1; £10; both m only.

Meyrick Society   1890
■   38 Downs Hill, BECKENHAM, Kent, BR3 5HB.   (hsp)
     020 8650 4527
     email robin@peterdaleltd.com
     Hon Sec: Robin Dale
○   *G, *L; promotion of the study of antiques, arms & armour
●   Mtgs
M   25 i

Micro & Anophthalmic Children's Society   (MACS)   1993
■   22 Lower Park St, HOLYHEAD, Anglesey, LL65 1DU.   (hsp)
     0800 169 8088
     email enquiries@macs.org.uk   http://www.macs.org.uk
     Sec: Lynda Rhodes
▲   Registered Charity
○   *W; a support group for children born with anophthalmia
     (absence of eyes), microphthalmia (small eyes) & coloboma
     (a structural defect of the eyes)
●   Conf - Mtgs
<   Contact a Family
M   300 i, UK / 120 i, o'seas
¶   NL;   AR; both free.

Microtome Manufacturers Association   (MMA)   1976
■   10 Montcalm Close, Hayes, BROMLEY, Kent, BR2 7LZ.   (hsp)
▲   Un-incorporated Society
○   *T
●   Mtgs - Stat
M   34 f
¶   Notes - 2/3;   Report - 1.

© CBD Research Ltd · Beckenham · BR3 5JS · Tel 020 8650 7745 · Fax 020 8650 0768 · E-mail cbd@cbdresearch.com · www.cbdresearch.com

Microwave Technologies Association (MTA) 1978
■ Norfolk Glen, Love Lane, IVER, Bucks, SL0 9QZ.   (hq)
  01753 652939   fax 01753 652939
  email jennipher@microwaveassociation.org.uk
  http://www.microwaveassociation.org.uk
  Chmn: Jennipher Marshall-Jenkinson
▲ Un-incorporated Society
○ *T; to promote & advise on all aspects of microwave &
  microwave related products to trade, hotels, caterers &
  consumers
Gp Individual membership; Corporate membership
● Mtgs - ET - Exhib - Inf
< Food Standards Authority
M 50 i, 20 f
¶ NL - 6; ftm only.

**Mid Yorkshire Chamber of Commerce & Industry Ltd   (MYCCI)
1853**
■ The Stable Block, Lockwood Park, Brewery Drive,
  HUDDERSFIELD, W Yorks, HD4 6EN.   (hq)
  0844 980 0045   fax 01484 483699
  email info@mycci.co.uk   http://www.mycci.co.uk
  Chmn: Eddie Rodgers
▲ Company Limited by Guarantee
Br 3; 1
○ *C
● Conf - Mtgs - ET - Exhib - Expt - LG - Export documentation
< Brit Chamber of Commerce
M 1,500 f
¶ Close Up - 4; free.

Middle East Association   (MEA)   1961
■ Bury House, 33 Bury St, LONDON, SW1Y 6AX.   (hq)
  020 7839 2137   fax 020 7839 6121
  email mail@the-mea.co.uk   http://www.the-mea.co.uk
  Sec: Graham Green
▲ Company Limited by Guarantee
○ *T; to promote trade & investment between the UK & the Middle
  East (all Arab states, Iran, Turkey, Afghanistan, Ethiopia &
  Eritrea) on behalf of its members
Gp Law sub group
● Conf - Mtgs - Exhib - Stat - Expt - Inf - Lib - VE - LG
M c 70 i, 350 f
¶ Information Digest - 24;   Hbk - 1;   AR; free.
  Information sheets.

Middle White Pig Breeders CLub   1990
■ Benson Lodge, 50 Old Slade Lane, IVER, Bucks, SL0 9DR.
  (hsp)
  01753 654166
  email miranda@middlewhites.freeserve.co.uk
  Hon Sec: Mrs Miranda M Squire
○ *B; promotion of the traditional breed
● Exhib (occasional) - Expt -Inf
< Brit Pig Assn (BPA)
M c 110 i
  (Sub: £15)
¶ NL - 4.

**Midlands Asthma & Allergy Research Association   (MAARA)
1968**
■ No 1 Mill, The Wharf, Shardlow, DERBY, DE72 2GH.   (hq)
  01332 799600   fax 01332 792200
  email enquiries@maara.org   http://www.maara.org
▲ Registered Charity
○ *Q; to research into asthma & allergy
Gp Aerobiology research
● Mtgs - Res
< Intl Assn of Aerobiology; Brit Aerobiology Fedn
M 300 i
¶ [see website]

Midlands Club Cricket Conference   (MCCC)   1947
■ 65 Tilesford Close, Monkspath, SOLIHULL, W Midlands,
  B90 4YF.   (hsp)
  0121-744 6746
  email murray.ali@gmail.com   http://www.mccc.co.uk
  Hon Sec: A Murray
▲ Un-incorporated Society
○ *S; to foster & maintain club cricket in the Midlands
Gp Fixture bureau; Tours bureau; Club insurance; Competitions for
  various age groups
● Comp - Inf
< England & Wales Cricket Bd
M c 500 clubs and leagues
¶ NL - 3;   Ybk - 1

Midlothian & East Lothian Chamber of Commerce   (MELCC)
NR 42/3 Hardengreen Business Park, Dalhousie Rd, DALKIETH,
  Midlothian, EH22 3NU.   (hq)
  0131-654 1234   fax 0131-654 6259
  email info@met.org.uk   http://www.melcc.org.uk
  Mgr: Laura Socha
▲ Company Limited by Guarantee
○ *C

Migraine Action Association   1958
NR 27 East St, LEICESTER, LE1 6NB.   (hq)
  0116 275 8317   fax 0116 254 2023
  email info@migraine.org.uk
  http://www.migraine.org.uk
▲ Registered Charity
○ *Q; promotion of research into causes & cure of migraine;
  information & assistance to sufferers
● Conf - Res - Inf - Migraine Action Week (September)
M c 36,000 i
¶ NL - 4.   Various booklets & leaflets.

Milestone Society   2001
■ Hollywell House, Hollywell Lane, Clows Top, KIDDERMINSTER,
  Worcs, DY14 9NR.   (hsp)
  01299 832338
  email john113atkinson@btinternet.com
  http://www.milestone-society.co.uk
  Hon Sec: John Atkinson
▲ Registered Charity
○ *G; to identify, record, research, conserve & interpret for public
  benefit the milestones & other waymarkers of the British Isles
● Conf - Mtgs - Res - Inf - PL
M 500 i, 15 f, UK / 3 i, o'seas
  (Sub: £10 i, £15 f UK / £20 i, o'seas
¶ Milestones & Waymarkers; ftm, £5 nm.
  NL - 2; ftm, £2 nm.   On the Ground - 1; ftm, £3 nm.

**Military Heraldry Society (The Cloth Insignia Research &
Collectors Society)   (M Her S)   1951**
■ Windyridge, 27 Sandbrook, Ketley, TELFORD, Shropshire,
  TF1 5BB.   (publicityofficer)
  01952 270221
  email billbowbagins@hotmail.com
▲ Un-incorporated Society
○ *G; collectors of cloth formation signs (shoulder sleeve insignia,
  shoulder titles, regimental & unit flashes & similar items)
● Mtgs - Res - Inf - Lib
M 250 i, UK / 140 i, o'seas
¶ The Formation Sign - 4; free.

Military Historical Society (MHS) 1948
- ■ c/o National Army Museum, Royal Hospital Rd, LONDON, SW3 4HT. (mail addr)
  020 7730 0717
  email herbert99@blueyonder.co.uk
  http://www.militaryhistsoc.plus.com
  99 Douglas Rd, SURBITON, Surrey, KT6 7SD. (mem/sec).
  Mem Sec: W J Herbert
- ▲ Registered Charity
- Br 4
- ○ *G; the study of the history of the uniformed services of the Crown, of uniforms, weapons, & all aspects of military history
- ● Conf - Mtgs - Res - Exhib - Comp - VE
- M 680 i, 20 org, UK / 20 i, 5 org, o'seas
  (Sub: £15)
- ¶ Bulletin - 4; ftm, £4 each nm.
  Special publication - irreg; ftm, £6.

Military Vehicle Trust (MVT) 1970
- ■ Meadowhead Cottage, Beaumaris Ave, BLACKBURN, Lancs, BB2 4TP. (hsp)
  01254 202253
  http://www.mvt.org.uk
  Gen Sec: Simon P Bromley
- ▲ Company Limited by Guarantee; Registered Charity
- Br 43
- ○ *G; preservation & restoration of military vehicles
- ● Mtgs - Exhib - Inf - Lib - PL - VE - LG - Shows - Film hire
- < Danish Soc Military Vehicle Presvn (FMKB), Belgian Military Vehicle Trust, MOVT, Swiss Club Romand, VHSP
- M 6,616 i, UK / 421 i, o'seas
- ¶ Windscreen - 4; ftm, £3.50 nm.
  Greensheet (NL) - 6; ftm only.

Milking Equipment Association (MEAA) 1941
- ■ Samuelson House, Forder Way, Hampton, PETERBOROUGH, Cambs, PE7 8JB. (hq)
  0845 644 8748   fax 01733 314767
  email dg@aea.uk.com
  Sec: Roger Lane-Nott
- ▲ Company Limited by Guarantee
- ○ *T; representing manufacturers of equipment used by the dairy farming industry
- M 5 f
- × 2007 Milking Machine Manufacturers' Association

Milking Machine Manufacturers' Association
  since 2007 **Milking Equipment Association**

Milton Keynes & North Bucks Chamber of Commerce 1994
- NR World Trade Center @ The Hub, 9 Rillaton Walk, CENTRAL MILTON KEYNES, Bucks, MK9 2FZ. (hq)
  01908 259000   fax 01908 246799
  http://www.mk-chamber.co.uk
- ○ *C
- ● ET - Inf
- < Brit Chams Comm; TEC Nat Coun
- M 1,500 f
- ¶ Opportunity (Jnl) - 6.   AR - 1; both free.

Mind (the mental health charity) (MIND) 1946
- ■ Granta House, 15-19 Broadway, LONDON, E15 4BQ. (hq)
  020 8519 2122   fax 020 8522 1725
  email contact@mind.org.uk   http://www.mind.org.uk
  Contact: The Chief Exec
- ▲ Registered Charity
- ○ *W; works for everyone with experience of mental distress
- ● Conf - ET - Res - Exhib - Inf - Lib - LG - Advice service & legal network
  MINDinfoline: 020 8522 1728   (Outer London 0845 766 0163)
- < Wld Fedn for Mental Health
- M c 1,200 i
- ¶ Publications list available.

Mineral Industry Research Organisation (MIRO) 1974
- ■ Concorde House, Trinity Park, SOLIHULL, W Midlands, B37 7UQ. (hq)
  0121-635 5225   fax 0121-635 5226
  email mail@miro.co.uk   http://www.miro.co.uk
  Dir: A Gibbon
- ▲ Company Limited by Guarantee
- ○ *Q; technology transfer brokerage & research facilitation that identifies, promotes & manages innovative technology research projects on exploration, mining, extraction & processing of primary & secondary raw materals
- Gp Research panels
- ● Conf - Res - Inf - LG
- M 25 f, UK / 7 f, o'seas
- ¶ Miro News - 6;   AR; both ftm.

Mineralogical Society of Great Britain & Ireland (MINSOC) 1876
- NR 12 Baylis Mews, Amyand Park Rd, TWICKENHAM, Middx, TW1 3HQ. (hq)
  020 8891 6600   fax 020 8891 6599
  email info@minersoc.org   http://www.minersoc.org
  Gen Sec: Dr Mark Hodson
- ▲ Registered Charity
- ○ *L; advancing the knowledge of the science of mineralogy & its application to other subjects including crystallography, geochemistry, petrology, environmental science & economic geology
- Gp Clay minerals; Geochemistry; Applied mineralogy; Metamorphic studies; Mineral physics; Volcanic & magmatic studies
- ● Conf - Mtgs - ET - SG - Exhib - Inf - Lib - VE - LG
- < Intl Mineralogical Assn; Eur Mineralogical U; Foundation for Science & Technology; Geological Soc; R Society
- M c 900 i
- ¶ Publications list available on request.

Minerals Engineering Society (MES) 1958
- ■ 2 Ryton Close, Blyth, WORKSOP, Notts, S81 8DN. (hsp)
  01909 591787   fax 01909 591940
  email hon.sec.mes@lineone.net
  http://www.mineralsengineering.org
  Hon Sec: A W Howells
- ▲ Company Limited by Guarantee; Registered Charity
- Br 3; Australia, Canada, New Zealand, South Africa, USA
- ○ *L, *P; to disseminate the science of minerals processing
- ● Conf - Mtgs
- < American Coal Preparation Soc; Australian Coal Preparation Soc
- M 410 i, 4 f, UK / 30 i, o'seas
  (Sub: £14-£20 i, £100 f)
- ¶ MQR - 6; ftm.

Miners' & Industrial Lamp Manufacturers' Association (MILMA) 1934
- ■ c/o Wolf Safety Lamp Co, Saxon Road Works, 62-92 Saxon Rd, SHEFFIELD, S Yorks, S8 0YA. (sec/b)
  0114-255 1051   fax 0114-255 7988
  Sec: John N M Jackson
- ▲ Un-incorporated Society
- ○ *T; manufacturers of mining & industrial portable lamps - including safety lamps
- ● Mtgs - Expt - LG - Participation in British, European & International Standards Committees
- M 6 f

© CBD Research Ltd · Beckenham · BR3 5JS · Tel 020 8650 7745 · Fax 020 8650 0768 · E-mail cbd@cbdresearch.com · www.cbdresearch.com

Miniature Armoured Fighting Vehicle Association (MAFVA) 1965

■ 45 Balmoral Drive, HOLMES CHAPEL, Cheshire, CW4 7JQ. (hsp)
  01477 535373   fax 01477 535892
  email mafvahq@aol.com   http://www.mafva.net
  Pres & Sec: G E Gary Williams
▲ Un-incorporated Society
Br 52; 59 o'seas
○ *G; for makers & collectors of model AFVs & other military vehicles & equipment
● Mtgs - Res - Exhib - Comp - Stat - Inf - VE
M 4,060 i, f & org, UK / 2,600 i, f & org, o'seas
¶ Tankette - 6.
  NL (county groups) - 7; ftm only.

Miniature Mediterranean Donkey Association (MMDA) 1996

■ Holebrook Farm, Cheriton Bishop, EXETER, Devon, EX6 6HL. (hsp)
  01647 281642
  http://www.miniature-donkey-assoc.com
  Sec: Penny Cooke
▲ Company Limited by Guarantee
○ *B; care, welfare, education & promotion of the breed
Gp Register & stud book of the UK
● ET - Stat - Expt - Inf - Lib - LG
< Nat Miniature Donkey Assn (USA)
M 150 i, UK / 4 i, o'seas
¶ Little People (NL) - 6; ftm only.

Mining Association of the United Kingdom (MAUK) 1946

■ 78 Copt Heath Drive, Knowle, SOLIHULL, W Midlands, B93 9PB. (hsb)
  01564 205079   fax 01564 205079
  email mail@mauk.org.uk   http://www.mauk.org.uk
  Sec: R A Fenton
▲ Company Limited by Guarantee
○ *T; to promote & foster the mining metals & minerals worldwide
● LG
< Euromines (Brussels); CBI Minerals C'ee
M 3 i, 16 f, 4 org
¶ AR - 1; ftm.

Minor Counties Cricket Association (MCCA) 1895

NR Blueberry Haven, 20 Boucher Rd, BUDLEIGH SALTERTON, Devon, EX9 6JF. (sp)
  01395 445216   fax 01395 445216
  email geoffe1@btinternet.com
  Sec: G R Evans
▲ Un-incorporated Society
○ *S
● Cricket matches
< England & Wales Cricket Bd
M 280 i, 20 county cricket clubs
¶ Minor Counties Cricket Annual - 1; ftm, £8 nm.

Minor Metals Trade Association 1973

NR Angel Gate, 326A City Rd, LONDON, EC1V 2PT. (asa)
  020 8330 7456   fax 020 8330 7447
  email secretariat@mmta.co.uk   http://www.mmta.co.uk
  Sec: N Barry Jaynes
▲ Company Limited by Guarantee
○ *T; regulation of trading relationships in the trading of minor metals
● Conf - Mtgs - LG
M 35 f, UK / 35 f, o'seas

MIRA Ltd (MIRA) 1946

NR Watling St, NUNEATON, Warks, CV10 0TU.   (hq)
  024 7635 5000   fax 024 7635 5355
  http://www.mira.co.uk
  Managing Dir: J R Wood
▲ Company Limited by Guarantee
○ *Q
Gp Aerodynamics; Durability; Noise; Vehicle safety; Ride & handling; Engines & transmissions; Vehicle analysis; Proving ground
● Conf - Mtgs - Res - SG - Inf - Lib
< Assn Indep Res & Technology Orgs
M 85 f
¶ Automobile Abstracts - 12.
  Automotive Business News - 25.
  Research Reports; ftm.   AR; free.

MIRAD, the Institute of Registration Dealers & Agents is now the acronym for the **Institute of Registration Agents & Dealers**

Miscarriage Association (MA) 1982

■ c/o Clayton Hospital, Northgate, WAKEFIELD, W Yorks, WF1 3JS.   (hq)
  01924 200799   fax 01924 298834
  email info@miscarriageassociation.org.uk
  http://www.miscarriageassociation.org.uk
  Nat Dir: Ruth Bender Atik
▲ Company Limited by Guarantee; Registered Charity
Br 50+
○ *M, *W; to provide information & support to women & their partners who have had a miscarriage, ectopic or molar pregnancy; to promote good practice in the way pregnancy loss is managed in hospitals & the community
Gp Special register
● Support group meetings - Inf
M 200 volunteer support contacts, 45 support gps
¶ NL - 4; ftm.   AR.
  Information leaflets; prices vary.

Mixed Wood-chip Suppliers Association (MWSA)

■ Kingsway House, Wrotham Rd, Meopham, GRAVESEND, Kent, DA13 0AU.   (sp)
○ *T
● Mtgs - ET - Stat
M 7 f

Mobile Data Association (MDA) 1994

■ PO Box 9347, SLEAFORD, Lincs, NG34 4DA.   (mail addr)
  0870 225 5632
  email info@themda.org   http://www.themda.org
  Operations Dir: Martin Ballard
▲ Company Limited by Guarantee
○ *T; to increase awareness of mobile applications
● Conf - Mtgs - Stat - Expt - LG
M 65 f, UK / 15 f, o'seas

Mobile Electronics & Security Federation (MESF) 1977

NR PO Box 3750, BRAINTREE, Essex, CM77 8DZ.   (hq)
  0870 863 5210
  email advice@mesf.org.uk   http://www.mesf.org.uk
○ *T; for the aftermarket mobile electronics industry - security (incl electronic & mechanical devices), mobile media (incl audio & in-car entertainment), telematics (incl fleet management & tracking) & communications (incl cellular & mobile radio), van lining & racking, & towing equipment
● Mtgs - ET - Exam - Exhib - Comp - Inf - LG
M i & org

Mobile Industry Crime Action Forum   (MICAF)   2000
NR   PO Box 28353, LONDON, SE20 7WJ.
      020 8778 9864   fax 020 8659 9561
      email micaf@tuff.co.uk   http://www.micaf.co.uk
      Exec Sec: Jack Wraith
▲   Un-incorporated Society
○   *T; to provide a forum for the exchange of information &
      research in mobile handset abuse & theft
Gp   Administrative Board;
      Mobile phone & theft technical group; Crime prevention group;
      Cooperation working group
●   Conf - Mtgs - ET - SG - Stat - Inf - LG
<   TUFF Ltd
M   30 i, 14 f

Mobile Marketing Association
      an international organisation based in the USA

Mobile Operators Association   2003
NR   Russell Square House, 10-12 Russell Square, LONDON,
      WC1B 5EE.
      020 7331 2015   fax 020 7931 2047
      email info@ukmoa.org
      http://www.mobilemastinfo.com
○   *T; mobile phone network operators
M   5f

Mobile & Outside Caterers Association
      since 2005 **Nationwide Caterers Association**

Mobilise Organisation   1922
■   Ashwellthorpe, NORWICH, Norfolk, NR16 1EX.   (hq)
      01508 489449   fax 01508 488173
      email enquiries@mobilise.info
      http://www.mobilise.info
      Chmn: Douglas Campbell
▲   Registered Charity
Br   50 area representatives
○   *W; to promote & protect the interests & welfare of physically
      disabled drivers; assistance regarding car conversions, ferry
      concessions, reduced RAC subscriptions, general information
●   Mtgs - ET - Exam - LG
M   14,500 i, 7 f
¶   Mobilise - 6; ftm, £2.50 each nm.
×   2005-6 (Disabled Drivers Association
              (Disabled Drivers' Motor Club

Model Electronic Railway Group   (MERG)   1967
■   Dingle Bank, Elmhurst Walk, Goring-on-Thames, READING,
      Berks, RG8 9DE.   (hsp)
      01491 872566
      email secretary@merg.org.uk   http://www.merg.org.uk
      Hon Sec: Howard Watkins
▲   Un-incorporated Society
○   *G; to promote & foster interest in the application of
      electronics, including computers, to railway modelling
●   Mtgs - ET - Exhib - Inf - Lib - VE
M   800 i, UK / 80 i, o'seas
¶   Jnl - 4;
      Technical Bulletins (downloadable from web) - irreg;
      both ftm only.

Model Railway Club   (MRC)   1910
■   Keen House, 4 Calshot St, LONDON, N1 9DA.   (hq)
      020 7837 2542
      http://www.themodelrailwayclub.org
      Chmn: Peter Mann
▲   Company Limited by Guarantee
○   *G; the modelling & study of railways
●   Conf - Mtgs - ET - Exhib - SG - Inf - Lib
<   Chiltern Model Rly Assn
M   c 200 i
¶   Bulletin - 6; ftm only.

Model Yachting Association   (MYA)   1911
NR   5A Cuckoo Lane, Stubbington, FAREHAM, Hants, PO14 3PJ.
      (sp)
      01329 665880
      http://www.mya-uk.org.uk
      Sec: Chris Durant
▲   Un-incorporated Society
○   *G, *S; to promote the design, construction & racing of model
      sailing boats; to act as the model yacht racing authority for
      the UK
●   Mtgs - Comp - Settling conditions, venues & dates for national
      & international competitions
<   Intl Sailing Fedn/Radio Sailing Divn (ISAF/RSD); R Yachting
      Assn; Cent Coun of Physical Recreation (Water Recreation
      Divn)
M   1,600 i & clubs
¶   Acquaint - 4;   Ybk - 1; both ftm, £2.50 each nm.

Modern Churchpeople's Union   (MCU)   1898
■   MCU Office, 9 Westward View, Aigburth, LIVERPOOL,
      Merseyside, L17 7EE.   (hq)
      0151-726 9730
      email office@modchurchunion.org
      http://www.modchurchunion.org
      Gen Sec: Revd Jonathan Clatworthy
▲   Registered Charity
○   *R; an Anglican society for the study & advancement of liberal
      theological thought
●   Conf - Mtgs - ET - SG
<   Inclusive Church
M   550 i, 130 org, UK / 10 i, 90 org, o'seas
¶   Modern Believing - 4; ftm, £6 each nm.
      Signs of the Times (NL) - 4; ftm, 50p each nm.

Modern Humanities Research Association   (MHRA)   1920
■   1 Carlton House Terrace, LONDON, SW1Y 5DB.   (hsb)
      01225 385404
      email d.c.gillespie@bath.ac.uk   http://www.mhra.org.uk
      Hon Sec: Prof David Gillespie
▲   Registered Charity
Br   Washington (DC)
○   *L, *Q; advanced studies & research in modern & medieval
      languages & literature (incl English)
●   Res
<   Intl Fedn Modern Languages Literatures
M   200 i, 50 f, UK / 100 i, 50 f, o'seas
      (Sub: £27)
¶   Modern Language Review - 4; £27 (US$51).
      Publications list available on request.

Modern Masonry Alliance
      an affiliated association of the **British Precast Concrete
      Federation**

Modern Pentathlon Association of Great Britain Ltd
      registered name of **Pentathlon GB**

Modern Studies Association   (MSA)   1972
NR   14 Fontstane St, MONIFIETH, Angus, DD5 4LE.   (sp)
      http://www.msa-scotland.org.uk
▲   Un-incorporated Society
○   *E, *P; to promote & enhance teaching of modern studies in
      Scottish schools
●   Conf - ET - Res - Comp
M   i

© CBD Research Ltd · Beckenham · BR3 5JS · Tel 020 8650 7745 · Fax 020 8650 0768 · E-mail cbd@cbdresearch.com · www.cbdresearch.com

Modular & Portable Building Association Ltd   (MPBA)   1938
- ■   PO Box 99, CAERSWS, Powys, SY17 5WR.   (mail addr)
    0870 241 7687   fax 01686 4304005
    email mpba@mpba.biz   http://www.mpba.biz
    Chief Exec: Mrs Jackie Maginnis
- ▲   Company Limited by Guarantee
- ○   *T; to promote the modular & portable buildings industry & companies involved in the supply of products & services to the industry
- Gp   C'ees: Technical, Health & safety & hire
- ●   Conf - Mtgs - ET - Res - Exhib - LG
- M   c 110 f
- ✕   2004 (March) National Prefabricated Building Association

Momentum - the Northern Ireland ICT Federation (MOMENTUM)
- NR   NiSoft House, Ravenhill Business Pk, Ravenhill Rd, BELFAST, BT6 8AW.
    028 9045 0101   fax 028 9045 2123
    http://www.momentumni.org

Monarchist League   1943
- ■   PO Box 5307, BISHOP'S STORTFORD, Herts, CM23 3DZ. (mail/address)
    01279 465551   fax 01279 466111
    http://www.monarchy.net
    Contact: The Secretary
- ▲   Un-incorporated Society
- Br   22; Australia, USA
- ○   *G; to promote, support & defend the monarchical system of government in the UK & abroad
- Gp   Bulgaria; Egypt; Portugal; Heraldry
- ●   Mtgs - Inf - Lib - LG
- <   cooperates with c 100 monarchist organisations worldwide
- M   4,500 i, UK / 500 i, o'seas
- ¶   Monarchy (Jnl) - 4.   The Crown (Jnl) - 4.
    Note: The Constitutional Monarchy Association is part of the League.

Money Advice Association
    since 2005 **Institute of Money Advisers**

Monmouthshire Antiquarian Association   1847
- NR   1 Brunel Avenue, High Cross, NEWPORT, Monmouthshire, NP10 0DN.
    01633 894338
    Hon Sec: Mrs G V Jones
- ○   *L

Monmouthshire Show Society Ltd   1790s
- NR   Parclands House, Raglan, USK, Monmouthshire, NP15 2BX. (hsb)
    01291 691160   fax 01291 691161
    http://www.monmouthshow.co.uk
    Management Sec: Mrs K Spencer
- ▲   Registered Charity
- ○   *F; to produce the Monmouthshire agricultural show; to promote the welfare of animals
- ●   Mtgs - ET - Exhib - Comp
- M   350 i

Montessori Society (AMI) UK   (Mont Soc)   1935
- ■   26 Lyndhurst Gardens, LONDON, NW3 5NW.   (hq)
    020 7435 7874
    email montessori.ami.uk@tiscali.co.uk
    http://www.montessori-uk.org
    Mem Sec: Mrs Elizabeth Hood
- ▲   Un-incorporated Society
- ○   *E; promotion of the philosophy of Dr Maria Montessori with regard to child development & general attitude to life
- ●   Conf - Exhib - Inf
- <   Assn Montessori Intle (AMI)
- M   300 i, UK / 50 i, o'seas
- ¶   Montessori Direction - 2; free.

Monumental Brass Society   1887
- ■   Stocks, Lyth Bank, SHREWSBURY, Shropshire, SY3 0BE.   (hsp)
    email davidinstocks@yahoo.co.uk
    http://www.mbs-brasses.co.uk
    Hon Sec: David J Fry
- ▲   Registered Charity
- Br   12; 2 in USA
- ○   *L; study & preservation of monumental brasses, indents of lost brasses & incised slabs
- ●   Conf - Mtgs - Res - Stat - Inf - VE - Advice & assistance to Church authorities on care & repair of brasses
- M   c 500 i, 50 org
- ¶   Portfolio - irreg;   Transactions - 1;   Bulletin - 3;   AR - 1;   LM - irreg; all ftm only.

Moorland Association   1987
- NR   16 Castle Park, LANCASTER, LA1 1YG.   (hsb)
    01524 846846
    http://www.moorlandassociation.org
    Sec: R M N Gillibrand
- ▲   Un-incorporated Society
- ○   *K; to conserve heather moorland in England & Wales
- ●   Conf - Mtgs - ET
- M   i & f

Moray Chamber of Commerce
- NR   12-14 Greyfriars St, ELGIN, Morayshire, IV30 1LF.
    01343 563540   fax 01343 563542
    email chamber@moray.gov.uk
    Dir: James Johnston
- ○   *C

** Morgan Horse Association
    Organisation lost, see Introduction paragraph 6

Morganatic Society
- NR   191 Westcombe Hill, LONDON, SE3 7DB.
- ○   *G; 'for mutual sympathy for the lesser-born persons in morganatic relationships''
- ●   Mtgs - LG

Morris Federation   (MF)   1971
- ■   28 Fairstone Close, HASTINGS, E Sussex, TN35 5EZ.   (hsp)
    01424 436052
    email sec@morrisfed.org.uk
    http://www.morrisfed.org.uk
    Hon Sec: Fee Lock
- ▲   Un-incorporated Society
- Br   400+; 6
- ○   *D, *G; to encourage & maintain interest in Morris dancing
- Gp   Notation; Archive; Publicity; Step-dance
- ●   Conf - Mtgs - Res - Inf - Lib - PL - LG - Public dance displays
- <   Folk Arts England; Engl Folk Dance & Song Soc
- M   30 i, 350 org, UK / 2 i, 3 org, o'seas
- ¶   NL - 4; ftm only.

Morris Ring   1934
- ■   70 Greengate Lane, Birstall, LEICESTER, LE4 3DL.   (hsp)
    Bagman: Charlie Corcoran
- ○   *G; practice & performance of English men's ritual dance (Morris, sword-dancing & mumming)
- ●   Conf - Mtgs - ET - Res - Exhib - SG - Inf
- M   180 clubs & 60 associates, UK / 6 o'seas
- ¶   Ring Directory (list of clubs) - 1.
    List of books, tapes & equipment available.

Mortar Industry Association (MIA) 1998
- ■ Gillingham House, 38-44 Gillingham St, LONDON, SW1V 1HU. (hq)
   024 7963 8000
   http://www.mortar.org.uk
   Chmn: David Rawson
- ▲ Company Limited by Guarantee
- ○ *T; the manufacture, use & applications of building mortars
- Gp C'ees: Technical, Marketing
- ● Mtgs - Res - SG - Inf - LG
- < UK Cast Stone Assn; Eur Mortar Industry Assn
- M 30 f
- ¶ Various publications & guides to the uses of mortar; free. Video.

Mothers Apart from Their Children (MATCH) 1979
- ■ BM Box No 6334, LONDON, WC1N 3XX.   (mail address)
   email enquiries@matchmothers.org
   http://www.matchmothers.org
   Chmn: Penny Cross, Hon Sec: Penny Cooper
- ▲ Un-incorporated Society
- ○ *G, *W; run by & for mothers who are, or have been, separated from their children in a wide variety of circumstances
- ● Mtgs - LG - Email support groups
- M 220 i
- ¶ NL - 4.

Mothers' Union (MU) 1876
- § Mary Sumner House, 24 Tufton St, LONDON, SW1P 3RB.   (hq)
   020 7222 5533   fax 020 7222 1591
   email mu@themothersunion.org
   http://www.themothersunion.org
   Chief Exec: Reg Bailey
   A Christian organisation with over 3.6 million members worldwide promoting marriage and family life.

Motor Accident Solicitors Society (MASS) 1991
- ■ 54 Baldwin St, BRISTOL, BS1 1QW.   (hq)
   0117-929 2560   fax 0117-904 7220
   email office@mass.org.uk   http://www.mass.org.uk
   Exec Dir: Jane Loney
- ▲ Un-incorporated Society
- ○ *P; for solicitors who specialise in road traffic accident claims, providing advice & assistance to claimants; 'MASS promotes the highest standards of legal services through education & representation in the pursuit of justice for the victims of road traffic accidents'
- ● Conf - Mtgs - ET - Inf - LG
- M 170 f
- ¶ MASS Newsletter - 4; ftm, £50 nm.
   Accident Advice Leaflets;   Accident Report Forms; both ftm.

Motor Caravanners' Club Ltd 1960
- ■ 22 Evelyn Close, TWICKENHAM, Middx, TW2 7BN.   (hq)
   020 8893 3883   fax 020 8893 8324
   email info@motorcaravanners.eu
   http://www.motorcaravanners.eu
   Sec: Colin Reay
- ▲ Company Limited by Guarantee
- Br 27; Europe & rest of world
- ○ *G; to promote & develop motor-caravanning
- Gp Walking; American motor homes; Photography; European rallies
- ● Mtgs - Exhib - Inf - VE - LG
- < Fédn Intle de Camping & de Caravanning
- M 11,500 i, UK / 100 i, o'seas
- ¶ Motor Caravanner - 12;   Buyers Guide;   Sites List - 1; all ftm.

Motor Cycle Industry Association Ltd (MCIA) 1973
- ■ 1 Rye Hill Office Park, Birmingham Rd, Allesley, COVENTRY, Warks, CV5 9AB.   (hq)
   024 7640 8000   fax 024 7640 8001
   http://www.mcia.co.uk
   Chief Exec: Mark Foster
- ▲ Company Limited by Guarantee
- ○ *T
- Gp Manufacturers & importers of machines; Accessory & component manufacturers; Factors; Associates
- ● Conf - Mtgs - Res - Exhib - Stat - Expt - Inf - LG
- < Intl Motorcycle Mfrs Assn; Nat Motorcycle Coun; RoSPA; ACEM
- M 150 f
- ¶ Revolutions (NL) - 4; ftm.   LM.   AR.

Motor Industry Public Affairs Association Ltd (MIPAA) 2005
- ■ Little Grange, Church St, West Grimstead, SALISBURY, Wilts, SP5 3RE.   (gsp)
   01722 711295   fax 01722 711295
   email hyaxley@supanet.com   http://www.mipaa.com
   Gen Sec: Heather Yaxley
- ▲ Company Limited by Guarantee
- ○ *P; for those engaged in communications in the motor industry
- ● Mtgs - ET - SG - Inf - VE - Job search service - Mentoring programme
- M 460 i, UK / 10 i, o'seas
- ¶ The News (NL) - 4;   Directory - 1; both ftm.
- × 2005 (November) Motor Industry Public Affairs Association

Motor Neurone Disease Association 1979
- ■ PO Box 246, NORTHAMPTON, NN1 2PR.   (hq)
   01604 250505   fax 01604 624726
   http://www.mndassociation.org
   Chief Exec: Dr Kirstine Knox
- ▲ Registered Charity
- Br 100
- ○ *W; the support of people with MND & their carers; to research into the causes & treatment of the disease
- ● Conf - Mtgs - ET - Res - Inf - Lib - Loan of equipment - Helpline
- < Intl Alliance of ALS/MND Assns; Assn of Medical Res Charities
- M c 6,500 i
- ¶ Thumbprint (NL) - 4; free.
   MND Association News (NL) - 12; ftm only.   AR - 1; free.
   International Exchange (NL) - 3.

Motor Schools Association of Great Britain Ltd (MSA) 1935
- NR 101 Wellington Road North, STOCKPORT, Cheshire, SK4 2LP.
   (hq)
   0161-429 9669
- ○ *T; all aspects of learning to drive, driving, advanced driving & road safety
- M i

Motor Sports Association UK (MSAUK) 1979
- NR Motor Sports House, Riverside Park, Colnbrook, SLOUGH, Berks, SL3 0HG.   (hq)
   01753 765000   fax 01753 682938
   http://www.msauk.org
- ▲ Company Limited by Guarantee
- ○ *S; the governing body for motor sport in the UK
- < Fédn Automobile Intle (FIA)

Motor Vehicle Dismantlers Association of Great Britain (MVDA) 1943
- ■ 33 Market St, LICHFIELD, Staffs, WS13 6LA.   (hq)
   01543 254254   fax 01543 254274
   email mail@mvda.org.uk   http://www.mvda.org.uk
   Sec: Duncan Wemyss
- ▲ Un-incorporated Society
- ○ *T
- ● Conf - Mtgs - ET - Inf - LG
- < Eur Vehicle Dismantlers Assn (EGARA)
- M 217 f, UK / 8 f, o'seas
- ¶ Automotive Recycling & Disposal UK - 4; free.

© CBD Research Ltd · Beckenham · BR3 5JS · Tel 020 8650 7745 · Fax 020 8650 0768 · E-mail cbd@cbdresearch.com · www.cbdresearch.com

Motorcycle Action Group   (MAG(UK))   1973
- ■ PO Box 750, RUGBY, Warks, CV21 3ZR.   (hq)
  01788 570065   fax 01788 570052
  http://www.mag-uk.org
- ▲ Company Limited by Guarantee
- ○ *K; to protect the rights & interests of motorcyclists; to
  safeguard the tradition & future of motorcycling in the UK; to
  promote positive aspects of motorcycling
- ● Conf - Mtgs - Res - Exhib - SG - Stat - Inf - LG
- < Intl Coalition of Motorcyclists (ICOM); Fédn Eur de
  Motocyclistes Assns (FEMA); links with other motorcycle assns
  & gps worldwide
- M 25,000 i, 40 f, 270 clubs, / 80 i, o'seas
- ¶ The Road - 6; ftm, £2 nm.
  Network for Regions (NL) - 12; ftm, £10 yr nm.

Motorcycle Retailers Association
a group of the **Retail Motor Industry Federation**

Motorcycle Rider Training Association
a group of the **Retail Motor Industry Federation**

**Motoring Organisations' Land Access & Recreation Association
(LARA)   1986**
- ■ PO Box 142, NEWCASTLE upon TYNE, NE3 5YP.   (devt/offr/p)
  0191-236 4086
  email laragb@mac.com   http://www.laragb.org
- ▲ Un-incorporated Society
- ○ *N, *S; an umbrella organisation of motor sport groups -
  promoting responsible use of the environment for motor
  sports & recreation
- ● Conf - Mtgs - Res - Inf - LG - Liaison with local & county
  authorities & with sporting, recreational & rights of way
  groups
- M 330,000 i, in 11 org
- ¶ Access Guide; ftm.   Conference papers.   Leaflets; Codes of
  Conduct; all free.

Motorsport Industry Association Ltd   (MIA)   1994
- NR Federation House, STONELEIGH PARK, Warks, CV8 2RF.   (hq)
  024 7669 2600   fax 024 7669 2601
  email info@the-mia.com   http://www.the-mia.com
- ○ *T; to represent, promote & protect the interests of the British
  motorsport industry
- M f

Mountain Bothies Association   (MBA)   1965
- NR c/o Henderson Black & Co, 22 Crossgate, CUPAR, Fife,
  KY15 5HW.   (asa)
  01334 656666   fax 01334 656278
  email mba@hendersonblack.co.uk
  http://www.mountainbothies.org.uk
  Gen Sec: Peter King
- ▲ Company Limited by Guarantee; Registered Charity
- Br 9 areas
- ○ *W; to maintain simple shelters in remote country for the use &
  benefit of all who love wild & lonely places
- Gp Renovation work on old & derelict buildings in remote areas
- ● Renovation & maintenance work parties
- < Scot Rights of Way & Access Soc; Mountaineering Coun
  Scotland; NE Mountain Trust
- M c 3,000 i
- ¶ NL - 4; ftm.   AR - 1; ftm, on request nm.
  Members Hbk - 1; ftm only.
  Volunteer's Hbk - 1; ft volunteers, on request nm.

Mountain Leader Training Association   (MLTA)
- ■ Siabod Cottage, CAPEL CURIG, Conwy, LL24 0ES.   (hq)
  01690 720120   fax 01690 720248
  email info@mlta.co.uk   http://www.mlta.co.uk
  Devt Officer: Phillip Thomas
- ○ *S; to provide on-going training for leaders who hold MLTUK
  leaderships awards; to provide communication between
  membership of training boards & provide leadership in the
  mountains
- Gp Leaders of mountaineering groups who have, or are engaged
  in obtaining, MLTUK leadership awards
- ● Conf - ET - Inf
- < Mountain Leader Training UK
- M 1,900 i
  (Sub: £15)
- ¶ NL (e-NL) - irreg; free.

Mountaineering Council of Ireland   (MCI)   1972
- IRL Sport HQ, 13 Joyce Way, Park West Business Park, DUBLIN 12,
  Republic of Ireland.   (hq)
  353 (1) 625 1115   fax 353 (1) 625 1116
  email info@mountaineering.ie
  http://www.mountaineering.ie
  Chief Officer: Stuart Garland
- ▲ Company Limited by Guarantee
- Br N Ireland
- ○ *S; to promote mountaineering, including hill walking, rock
  climbing, rambling, bouldering & alpinism; to preserve &
  maintain the mountaineering environment
- Gp Irish Mountain Training Board; Access & Conservation
  Committee; Youth Steering Group
- ● Comp - Conf - ET - Inf - LG - Lib
- < U Intle des Assns d'Alpinisme; Eur Ramblers Assn
- M 1,400 i, 130 clubs (7,600 i)
- ¶ Irish Mountain Log - 4; ftm.

Mountaineering Council of Scotland   (MCofS)   1970
- ■ The Old Granary, West Mill St, PERTH, PH1 5QP.   (hq)
  01738 492942   fax 01738 442095
  email info@mountaineering-scotland.org.uk
  http://www.mcofs.org.uk
  Senior Officer: David Gibson
- ▲ Company Limited by Guarantee
- ○ *S; representative body for Scotland's hill walkers, climbers &
  ski-mountaineers; the national sports governing body for
  sport climbing; to provide information on mountain safety
  matters
- Gp Mountain safety; Membership services; Environment & Access
- ● ET - Comp - Inf - LG
- < UK & Ireland Mountaineering Co-ordination Gp
- M 3,000 i, 35 f, 130 org
  (Sub: £27.30 i, £60 f, £13 org (per capita))
- ¶ The Scottish Mountaineer - 4; ftm, £3,15 nm.
  The Scottish Club Huts List - 1;   AR - 1; both free.
  Club Safety & Liaibility Guidance - 2 yrly; free.
  Publications on mountain safety, wild camping & environmental
  issues; free.

**Mounted Games Association of Great Britain   (MGAGB)
1984**
- NR Wyelands Cottage, 59 St Johns Rd, BUXTON, Derbys,
  SK17 6XA.   (hsb)
  01298 24292   fax 01298 24292
  email mary@mgagb.co.uk   http://www.mgagb.co.uk
  Chief Exec: Mrs Mary Worth
- ▲ Company Limited by Guarantee
- ○ *S, *Y; to organise & promote mounted games events for young
  riders
- ● Mtgs - Comp
- < Intl Mounted Games Assn (IMGA)
- M 1,400 i
- ¶ Pony Express - 4; ftm.   Hbk - 1.

Movement for Colonial Freedom
incorporated in the organisation **Liberation**

Movers Institute (TMI)   (TMI)   1937
NR   Tangent House, 62 Exchange Rd, WATFORD, Herts,
       WD18 0TG.   (hq)
       01923 699480   fax 01923 699481
       email info@bar.co.uk   http://www.bar.co.uk
       Sec. Robert D Syers
▲   Company Limited by Guarantee
○   *T; training, educational & accreditation for the removals &
       storage industry
Gp National & European domestic moves; Overseas; Commercial
●   Conf - Mtgs - ET - Exam - Comp - SG - Inf - VE
<   Brit Assn of Removers (BAR)
M   1,300 i
¶   Moving News - 4; ftm only.

Moving Image Society
       alternative name of **BKSTS**

MRSA Support Group
NR   46 Great Stone Rd, Northfield, BIRMINGHAM, W Midlands,
       B31 2LS.
       0121-476 6583
       email info@mrsasupport.co.uk
       http://www.mrsasupport.co.uk
       Contact: Tony Field

Mull & Iona Chamber of Commerce   1992
NR   Ceann Cuin, DERVAIG, Isle of Mull, PA75 6QR.   (sb)
       http://www.mullchamber.org
       Sec: Georgia O'Neill
○   *C

Multi Vintage Wine Growers Society   (MVWGS)   1985
■   191 Westcombe Hill, LONDON, SE3 7DR.   (hsp)
▲   Un-incorporated Society
○   *G; for anyone interested in wine growing techniques
●   Mtgs - Stat - VE - LG
M   23 i
¶   Jnl - irreg; m only.

Multiple Births Foundation   (MBF)   1988
■   Hammersmith House Level 4, Queen Charlotte's & Chelsea
       Hospital, Du Cane Rd, LONDON, W12 0HS.   (hq)
       020 8383 3519   fax 020 8383 3041
       email mbf@imperial.nhs.uk
       http://www.multiplebirths.org.uk
       Dir: Jane Denton,   Admin: Marian Patterson
▲   Registered Charity
○   *P, *W; to offer support to parents of twins, triplets & more; to
       offer advice & training to the professions concerned with
       them
Gp Medical (paediatricians, obstetricians, GPs); Nursing (midwives,
       health visitors); Education (teachers, psychologists)
●   Conf - Mtgs - ET - Stat - Inf - Lib - PL
¶   NL - 4; £10/£15 yr m.   AR.   Publications list available.

Multiple Sclerosis National Therapy Centres   1993
■   Bradbury House, 155 Barkers Lane, BEDFORD, MK41 9RX.
       (MS/Centre)
       01234 325781   fax 01234 365242
       email info@ms-selfhelp.org
       http://www.ms-selfhelp.org
       Admin: Mrs V Woods
▲   Company Limited by Guarantee; Registered Charity
○   *N, *W; to administer the MS therapy centres throughout the
       country which provide therapy, support & information to all
       MS sufferers & their families
●   ET - Inf
M   35 centres
¶   NL (to all MS centres) - 2/3.
×   2002 Federation of Multiple Sclerosis Therapy Centres
       2003 National Multiple Sclerosis Therapy Centres

**Multiple Sclerosis Society of Great Britain & Northern Ireland
      (MS Society)   1953**
NR   372 Edgware Rd, LONDON, NW2 6ND.   (hq)
       020 8438 0700   fax 020 8438 0701
       email info@mssociety.org.uk
       http://www.mssociety.org.uk
       Chief Exec: Mike O'Donovan
▲   Registered Charity
Br   360
○   *M, *W; to advise & assist anyone affected by MS
●   Conf - Mtgs - Res - Inf
>   MS Trust
M   c 44,000 i
¶   MS Matters - 6; ftm.
       Publications list available.

Multiple Sclerosis Society of Ireland
IRL   80 Northumberland Rd, DUBLIN 4, Republic of Ireland.
       353 (1) 678 1600   fax 353 (1) 678 1601
       email info@ms-society.ie   http://www.ms-society.ie
       Chief Exec: Anne Winslow
○   *W

MultiService Association Ltd   (MSA)   2003
■   PO Box 9378, NEWARK, Notts, NG24 9FE.   (sp)
       01400 281298   fax 01400 282326
       email info@msauk.biz   http://www.msauk.biz
       Sec: Martyn Harvey
▲   Company Limited by Guarantee
○   *T; the only trade association representing shoe repairers &
       associated trades - key cutting, engraving & watch repairs
●   ET - Exhib - Comp - Inf - Lib
<   Cutting Edge - represents suppliers to the trade
>   Cutting Edge
M   350 i, 6 f, UK / 5 i, o'seas
¶   Shoe Service - 4; free.

Murray Grey Beef Cattle Society Ltd   1973
■   Pen-Twyn, Llangenny, CRICKHOWELL, Brecknockshire,
       NP8 1HD.   (hq)
       01873 810547   fax 01873 810547
       email info@murray-grey.co.uk
       http://www.murray-grey.co.uk
       Sec: Mrs Rosemary Kent
▲   Company Limited by Guarantee; Registered Charity
○   *B; to promote research into improvement of the breed; to
       maintain the purity of the breed
●   Mtgs - Exhib - Comp - VE
M   50 i, UK / 4 i, o'seas
¶   NL - 3;   Herdbook - 1;   Ybk - 1.

Muscular Dystrophy Campaign   1961
■   61 Southwark St, LONDON, SE1 0HL.   (hq)
       http://www.muscular-dystrophy.org
▲   Company Limited by Guarantee; Registered Charity
○   *M, *W; to raise funds for & to manage medical research into
       muscular dystrophy & allied neuromuscular diseases;
       practical advice & support to affected families
<   Eur Alliance of Muscular Dystrophy Assns
M   c 2,000 i
¶   Target MD (NL) - 4; ftm.   AR; free.

Muscular Dystrophy Ireland
IRL   71-72 North Brunswick St, DUBLIN 7, Republic of Ireland.
       353 (1) 872 1501   fax 353 (1) 872 4482
       email info@mdi.ie   http://www.mdi.ie
○   *W
×   2000-2002 Muscular Dystrophy Society of Ireland

© CBD Research Ltd · Beckenham · BR3 5JS · Tel 020 8650 7745 · Fax 020 8650 0768 · E-mail cbd@cbdresearch.com · www.cbdresearch.com

Museum Ethnographers Group   (MEG)   1976
- ■ Plymouth City Museum & Art Gallery, Drake Circus,
  PLYMOUTH, Devon, PL4 8AJ.   (hsb)
  email tabitha.cadbury@plymouth.gov.uk
  http://www.museumethnographersgroup.org.uk
  Hon Sec: Tabitha Cadbury
- ▲ Registered Charity
- ○ *P; to encourage good practice in the curatorship of
  ethnographic collections in the UK; to encourage research &
  the exchange of information
- ● Conf - Mtgs - ET - Inf - VE
- M [not stated]
  (Sub: £20-25 i, £30 f, UK / £27-32 i, £37 f o'seas)
- ¶ Jnl of Museum Ethnography - 1; ftm (£25 back issues),
  £30 nm.
  Occasional Papers; prices vary.

Museum Professionals Group   (MPG)   1937
- NR c/o David Rice, Gloucester City Museum, Brunswick Rd,
  GLOUCESTER, GL1 1HP.   (treas/b)
  http://www.museumprofessionalsgroup.org
  Treas: David Rice
- ▲ Un-incorporated Society
- ○ *P; to campaign on issues relevant to all junior museum
  professionals
- ● Conf - Mtgs - ET - Res
- M 100 i, 40 org, UK / 10 org, o'seas

Museums Action Movement
  alternative name of **National Heritage**

Museums Association   (MA)   1889
- ■ 24 Calvin St, LONDON, E1 6NW.   (hq)
  020 7426 6970   fax 020 7426 6961
  email info@museumsassociation.org
  http://www.museumsassociation.org
  Dir: Mark Taylor
- ▲ Registered Charity
- ○ *A, *P; the interests of museum people, museums & their
  collections
- ● Conf - Mtgs - ET - Inf - LG
- M 5,000 i, 250 f, 600 instns, UK & o'seas
- ¶ Museums Jnl - 12.   Museum Practice - 4.
  Museums Ybk (a directory of museums & galleries of the British
  Isles).
  Ethics Guidelines.   Museum briefings.   AR.

Mushroom Growers' Association   (MGA)   1945
- NR c/o Snowcap Mushrooms Ltd, Broadway, Yaxley,
  PETERBOROUGH, Cambs, PE7 3EF.   (hq)
- ▲ Un-incorporated Society
- ○ *F, *T; for growers, suppliers, scientists & academic institutions;
  provides technical advice & information
- ● Conf - Mtgs - Exhib - Stat - Inf - VE - LG
- M c 250 f
- ¶ Mushroom Jnl - 6.

Music Education Council   (MEC)   1975
- NR 54 Elm Rd, Hale, ALTRINCHAM, Cheshire, WA15 9QP.
  (admin/p)
  0161-928 3085   fax 0161-929 9648
  email ahassan@easynet.co.uk   http://www.mec.org.uk
  Admin: Anna Hassan
- ▲ Registered Charity
- ○ *D, *E; promote & advance the education & training of the
  public in music
- ● Conf - Inf
- < Intl Soc for Music Educ (ISME)
- M c 50 i, 170 org
- ¶ NL - 6.

Music Industries Association   (MIA)   1882
- ■ Ivy Cottage Offices, Finch's Yard, Eastwick Rd,
  GREAT BOOKHAM, Surrey, KT23 4BA.   (hq)
  01372 750600   fax 01372 750515
  email office@mia.org.uk   http://www.mia.org.uk
  Chief Exec: Paul McManus
- ▲ Company Limited by Guarantee
- ○ *D, *T; for the musical instrument industry: represents
  manufacturers, wholesalers, distributors, retailers, educators,
  publishers etc of musical instruments, accessories &
  amplification eqpt
- Gp All types & genres of musical instuments & associated products
- ● Conf - Mtgs - ET - Res - Exhib - Stat - Expt - Inf
- < Nat Assn of Music Merchants (USA)
- M 350 f
  (Sub: £500)
- ¶ NL - 26; ftm only.

Music Managers Forum   (MMF)
- NR British Music House, 26 Berners St, LONDON, W1T 3LR.
  0870 8507 800
- ○ *P

Music Masters' & Mistresses' Association   (MMA)   1903
- ■ St Edmund's School, CANTERBURY, Kent, CT2 8HU.
  (admin/b)
  01227 475600
  http://www.mma-online.org.uk
  Admin: Carol Hawkins
- ▲ Company Limited by Guarantee
- ○ *E, *P; advancement of musical education in independent
  schools; a professional forum for teachers of music
- ● Conf - Mtgs - Inf
- M c 950 i, UK / c 10 i, o'seas
- ¶ Jnl - 3;   LM - 1; both ftm only.

Music Producers Guild UK Ltd   (MPG)   1986
- ■ 71 Avenue Gardens, LONDON, W3 8HB.   (hq)
  020 3110 0060
  http://www.mpg.org.uk
  Co Sec: Penny Ganz,   Chmn: Mike Howlett
- ▲ Company Limited by Guarantee
- Br affiliates in 10 countries o'seas
- ○ *T; to represent producers, engineers, remixers & mastering
  engineers to the music industry
- ● Mtgs - ET - LG
- < Eur Sound Directors Assn (ESDA); Assn ofProfl Recording
  Services (APRS); Jt Audio Media Services (JAMES)
- M 400 i
- ¶ NL (online); free.

Music Publishers' Association Ltd   (MPA)   1881
- ■ British Music House (6th floor), 26 Berners St, LONDON,
  W1T 3LR.   (hq)
  020 7580 0126   fax 020 7637 3929
  email info@mpaonline.org.uk
  http://www.mpaonline.org.uk
  Chief Exec: Stephen Navin
- ▲ Company Limited by Guarantee
- ○ *T; to represent the interests of music publishers to government,
  the music industry, the media & the public
- ● Conf - Mtgs - ET - Inf - LG
- < Intl Confedn of Music Publishers; Brit Music Rights
- M c 200 f
- ¶ Music Copyright Matters - 4; ftm only.
  Distributor's List - 1; ftm, £10 nm.
  LM - 1; ftm, £10 nm.   Code of Fair Practice.

Musical Box Society of Great Britain   (MBSGB)   1962
- ■ PO Box 373, WELWYN, Herts, AL6 0WY.   (hsb)
    email mail@mbsgb.org.uk   http://www.mbsgb.org.uk
- ○ *D, *G; preservation of musical boxes & all other forms of
    mechanical musical instruments, including automata;
    research into their history & dovolopment
- ● Conf - Mtgs - Res - Exhib - SG - Inf - VE
- M c 250 i, UK / 350 i, o'seas
    (Sub: £24)
- ¶ The Music Box - 4; ftm only.

Musicians' Union   (MU)   1893
- NR 60-62 Clapham Rd, LONDON, SW9 0JJ.   (hq)
    020 7582 5566   fax 020 7582 9805
    email info@musiciansunion.org.uk
    http://www.musiciansunion.org.uk
- Br 74
- ○ *U
- Gp Sections: Folk, Jazz, Session, Theatre; Freelance orchestral;
    Teachers' register;
    British Music Writers' Council
- ● Conf - Mtgs - ET - Exhib - Stat - Inf - Empl - LG - Careers
    service - Lobbying
- < Intl Fedn Musicians (FIM)
- M 31,000 i
- ¶ Musician (Jnl) - 4; free.
    Section NL - 4;   Branch NL - 12; both ftm only.

Mutton Renaissance Campaign   2004
- ■ c/o NSA, The Sheep Centre, MALVERN, Worcs, WR13 6PH.
    01684 892661
    http://www.muttonrenaissance.org.uk
- ○ *K, *F; to encourage the use of meat from traceable farm
    assured sheep that are at least two years old

Muzzle Loaders Association of GB   (MLAGB)   1952
- NR Goodform Ltd, 7 Olympus Court, Tachbrook Park, WARWICK,
    CV34 6RZ.   (mem/sb)
    01926 458198
    http://www.mlagb.com
- Br 29
- ○ *G; for collectors, shooters & students of muzzle loading
    firearms
- Gp Rifle; Pistol; Clay pigeon
- ● Mtgs - Comp
- < Muzzle Loading Assns Intl C'ee (Paris); Brit Shooting Sports
    Coun; Nat Rifle Assn
- M 1,900 i, 180 clubs, UK / 17 i, 3 clubs, o'seas
- ¶ Black Powder (NL) - 4; ftm.

MVRA Ltd   (MVRA Ltd)   1988
- NR Glenfield Business Park, Philips Rd, BLACKBURN, Lancs,
    BB1 5QH.   (hq)
    0870 458 3051   fax 0870 458 3052
    email enquiry@mvra.com   http://www.mvra.com
    Managing Dir: Mike Monaghan,
    PR & Communications: Barbara Herbert
- ▲ Company Limited by Guarantee
- ○ *T; a motor trade body representing motor vehicle repairers
- Gp Car; Commercial; Motorcycle
- ● LG
- M 2,200 i
- ✕ 2002-03 Motor Vehicle Repairers' Association

Myalgic Encephalopathy Association   (MEA)   1976
- ■ 7 Apollo Office Court, Radclive Road, GAWCOTT, Bucks,
    MK18 4DF.   (hq)
    01280 818968   fax 01280 821602
    email meconnect@meassociation.org.uk
    http://www.meassociation.org.uk
    Admin: Gill Briody
- ▲ Company Limited by Guarantee; Registered Charity
- ○ *W; to serve the needs of people with ME/CFS & their families
    & carers
- ● Conf - Res
- < Nat Coun of Voluntary Orgs (NCVO); Long-Term Med
    Conditions Alliance (LMCA)
- M 6,800 i
- ¶ Perspectives - 4.
    [subscription £18]

Myasthenia Gravis Association   (MGA)   1976
- ■ Southgate Business Centre (1st floor), Normanton Rd, DERBY,
    DE23 6UQ.   (hq)
    01332 290219   fax 01332 293641
    email mg@mga-charity.org   http://www.mgauk.org
    Chmn: Peter Finney
- ▲ Registered Charity
- ○ *W; to provide advice & support for sufferers, carers & the
    medical profession; to fund research into improved
    treatment; (an auto-immune disease characterised by
    fluctuating, sometimes fatal, muscle weakness)
- ● Conf - Mtgs - ET - Res - Exhib - Inf
    Helpline: 0800 919922
- < Neurological Alliance
- M 9,000 i, UK / 270 i, o'seas
- ¶ MGA News - 4; free.   Medical Companion; ftm, £2.50 nm.
    AR; ftm only.   Information leaflets; free.

Myositis Support Group
- NR 146 Newtown Rd, Woolston, SOUTHAMPTON, Hants,
    SO19 9HR.
    023 8044 9708   fax 023 8039 6402
    email info@myositis.org.uk   http://www.myositis.org.uk
- ○ *W; inflamation of muscles

Myotonic Dystrophy Support Group   (MDSG)   1985
- ■ 35a Carlton Hill, Carlton, NOTTINGHAM, NG4 1BG.
    0115-987 5869
    email mdsg@tesco.net   http://www.mdsguk.org
    Nat Co-ordinator: Margaret Bowler
- ▲ Registered Charity
- ○ *W; to give support to families & professionals concerning
    myotonic dystrophy
- ● ET - Res - Exhib - Helpline
- < Muscular Dystrophy Campaign; Contact-a-Family; LMCA;
    NCVO
- M 35 i, UK / 20 i, o'seas
- ¶ NL - 3; ftm.

© CBD Research Ltd · Beckenham · BR3 5JS · Tel 020 8650 7745 · Fax 020 8650 0768 · E-mail cbd@cbdresearch.com · www.cbdresearch.com

Naace (Naace) 1984
- ■ PO Box 6511, NOTTINGHAM, NG11 8TN. (hq)
  0870 240 0480 fax 0870 241 4115
  email office@naace.org http://www.naace.co.uk
  Gen Mgr: Bernadette Brooks
- ▲ Company Limited by Guarantee; Registered Charity
- ○ *P; 'advancing education through ICT'
- ● Conf - Mtgs - ET - Res - Exhib - SG - Inf - LG
- M 3,100 i, 115 f
- ¶ NL - 52; Jnl - 2; both ftm only.
- × 2004 (Computer Education Group
  (Micros & Primary Education

NABAS (the Balloon Association) Ltd (NABAS) 1988
- ■ Katepwa House, Ashfield Park Avenue, ROSS-on-WYE,
  Herefords, HR9 5AX. (hq)
  01989 762204 fax 01989 567676
  email admin@nabas.co.uk http://www.nabas.co.uk
  Admin: Gill Hinton
- ▲ Company Limited
- ○ *T; to coordinate the party & promotional balloon decorating
  industry, both latex & foil
- Gp Decorators; Retailers; Manufacturers; Wholesalers
- ● Conf - Mtgs - ET - Exhib - Comp - Inf
- M 720 f
- ¶ Balloonies (NL) - 4; LM - 2; both ftm.

NACRO - National Association for the Care & Resettlement of Offenders 1966
- NR Park Place, 10-12 Lawn Lane, LONDON, SW8 1UD. (hq)
  020 7840 7200 fax 020 7840 7240
  http://www.nacro.org.uk
- ○ *W

NAEA International incorporating FOPDAC
a group of the **National Association of Estate Agents**

NAEGA - promoting adult guidance on learning & work (NAEGA) 1982
- ■ c/o Meeting Makers Ltd, Jordanhill Campus,
  76 Southbrae Drive, GLASGOW, G13 1PP. (asa)
  0141-434 1500 fax 0141-434 1519
  email admin@naega.org.uk http://www.naega.org.uk
  Chmn: Ann Ruthven
- ▲ Company Limited by Guarantee
- Br 10
- ○ *E; to promote adult career guidance & provide development
  opportunities for people who deliver it
- Gp Career guidance managers, practitioners & others
- ● Conf - Mtgs - ET - Inf - LG
- M 300 i, 400 f
  (Sub: £50 i, £150-£250 f)
- ¶ e NL - 4; ftm only. AR - 1; Occassional publications; see
  website for updates & articles; all free.
- × 2006 National Association of Educational Guidance for Adults

NAGALRO: Professional Association for Children's Guardians & Children & Family Reporters & Independent Social Workers (NAGALRO) 1989
- ■ PO Box 264, ESHER, Surrey, KT10 0WA.
  01372 818504 fax 01372 818505
  email nagalro@globalnet.co.uk
  http://www.nagalro.com
  Principal Admin: Karen Harris
- ▲ Company Limited by Guarantee
- ○ *P
- ● Conf - Mtgs - Inf - LG
- M 900 i
- ¶ Seen & Heard - 4; ftm.

Nail Patella Syndrome UK (NPS UK)
- NR PO Box 26415, East Kilbride, GLASGOW, G74 1YW.
  0800 121 8298
  http://www.npsuk.org

Napaeo - the Association for Land Based Colleges
since 2008 **Landex**

Napoleonic Association Ltd (NA) 1975
- ■ 16 Little Kimble Walk, Hedge End, SOUTHAMPTON, Hants,
  SO30 0JQ. (sec/p)
  01489 783224
  email celia.norris@ntlworld.co
  http://www.napoleonicassociation.org
  Co Sec: Celia Norris
- ▲ Company Limited by Guarantee
- ○ *G, *L; to promote interest & study in military history 1792-
  1815 & to re-enact such history
- Gp Research; Wargames; Re-enactment
- ● Res - Battle re-enactment & shows - Research conferences
- < Muzzle Loaders Assn of GB
- M 600 i, UK / 20 i, o'seas

Napoleonic Society 1969
- ■ 157 Vicarage Rd, LONDON, E10 5DU. (hq)
  020 8539 3876 fax 020 8539 3876
  email keys@fsmail.net
  Sec: Ronald King
- ▲ Un-incorporated Society
- ○ *L, *Q; to foster interest & understanding of French history
  1756-1945
- ● Res - SG - Inf - Lib - PL
- ¶ Napoleon.
  Note: Please note this is NOT a re-enactment or fancy costume
  society.

NARA - Association of Property & Fixed Charge Receivers (NARA) 1995
- ■ PO Box 553, WORCESTER, WR2 6WY. (admin/sb)
  0870 600 1925 fax 0870 600 1925
  http://www.nara.org.uk
  Admin: Dag Smith
- ○ *P; to promote the interests of receivers who are NOT
  administrative receivers; incl LPA & fixcd charge receivers
  (agricultural receivers, receivers of book debt & court
  appointed receivers)
- × 2008 Non-Administrative Receivers Association

Narcolepsy Association United Kingdom   (UKAN)   1981
- ■ PO Box 13842, PENICUIK, Midlothian, EH26 8WX.
     (mail/address)
     0845 450 0394
     email info@narcolepsy.org.uk
     http://www.narcolepsy.org.uk
- ▲ Registered Charity
- Br 20
- ○ *W; to support research into the causes & treatment of
     narcolepsy (a sleep disorder characterised by excessive
     daytime sleepiness); to provide support & information for
     sufferers & their families; to press for recognition of
     narcolepsy as a disability by the DoE & DSS
- ● Inf - LG
- < Eur Narcolepsy Assn (ENA); Neurological Alliance; Long-term
     Med Conditions Alliance (LMCA); Genetic Interest Gp (GIG);
     Nat Coun of Voluntary Orgs (NCVO)
- M 700 i, 1 f, 4 org, UK / 50 i, o'seas
- ¶ Catnap (Jnl) - 4; ftm, 50 p each nm.
     Reports:
          1. Medication for Narcolepsy; £1.50 m, £2.25 nm.
          2. Narcolepsy: a layman's guide; £1 m, £1.50 nm.
          3. Narcolepsy: care & treatment; £1.80 m, £2.70 nm.
     Personal Experiences; £2 m, £3 nm.

Narrow Bandwidth Television Association   (NBTVA)   1975
- ■ 1 Lucknow Ave, Mapperley Park, NOTTINGHAM, NG2 5AZ.
     (hsp)
     0115-962 1453
     http://www.nbtv.org
     Chmn: Jeremy Jago
- ▲ Un-incorporated Society
- ○ *G; for those interested in amateur television - construction of
     apparatus, transmission & reception & the history of
     television
- ● Conf - ET - Res - Exhib
- < Brit Amat TV Club
- M 100 i, UK / 50 i, o'seas
- ¶ NBTV (NL) - 4; £5 yr m.

Narrow Gauge Railway Society   (NGRS)   1951
- NR 4 Park Mews, Park Gate, SOUTHAMPTON, Hants,
     SO31 1ED.   (hsp)
     http://www.ngrs.org
     Sec: Iain McCall
- ▲ Un-incorporated Society
- ○ *G
- ¶ Narrow Gauge - 4.   Narrow Gauge News - 6.

nasen   (nasen)   1992
- ■ Nasen House, 4-5 Amber Business Village, Amber Close,
     Amington, TAMWORTH, Staffs, B77 4RP.   (hq)
     01827 311500   fax 01827 313005
     email welcome@nasen.org.uk
     http://www.nasen.org.uk
     Chief Exec Officer: Lorraine Peterson
- ▲ Company Limited by Guarantee; Registered Charity
- Br 65
- ○ *E, *P; to promote the development of children & young people
     with special educational needs
- ● Conf - Mtgs - ET - Res - Exhib - SG - Inf - LG
- < NCVO; COSTA; Nat Children's Bureau
- M 5,059 i, f, UK / 79 i, o'seas
     (Sub: £66 i, £85 f, UK / £115 i, £105 EU)
- ¶ British Journal for Special Education - 4; ftm.
     Support for Learning - 4; ftm.
     Special (NL) - termly; ftm, £12 nm (£15 o'seas).
     Publications list available.
- × 2004-05 National Association for Special Educational Needs

NATFHE - the University & College Lecturers' Union
     in 2006 merged with the Association of University Teachers to form
     the **University & College Union**

National Access & Scaffolding Confederation   (NASC)   1943
- ■ Carthusian Court, 12 Carthusian St, LONDON, EC1M 6EZ.
     (hq)
     020 7397 8120   fax 020 7397 8121
     email enquiries@nasc.org.uk   http://www.nasc.org.uk
     Managing Dir: Robin James
- ▲ Company Limited by Guarantee
- ○ *T; for the access & scaffolding industry; members provide
     products & services including the supply & erection, hire, sale
     & manufacturing of: access & scaffolding equipment,
     formwork & falsework & temporary suspended access
     systems
- ● Inf - LG
- < Nat Specialist Contrs Coun; Access Ind Forum
- > Specialist Access Engg & Maintenance Assn (SAEMA); Fall Arrest
     Safety Eqpt Training (FASET)
- M 180 f
- ¶ NASC Ybk (incl LM - 1.
     SG4:05 - Preventing falls in scaffolding & falsework; £25.
     SG4: You - User guide to SG4:05; £5.
     Guide to Good Practice for Scaffolding with Tubes &
          Fittings; £105.
     Technical & Safety Guidance Notes; prices vary.

**National Accordion Organisation of the United Kingdom
(NAO)   1947**
- ■ 17 Marsh Mill Village, THORNTON CLEVELEYS, Lancs,
     FY5 4JZ.   (hsb)
     01253 822046
     email naouk@accordions.com
     http://www.accordions.com/nao
     Hon Sec: Gina Brannelli
- ▲ Registered Charity
- ○ *D; to promote accordion playing through competition
- ● Mtgs - Exam (through the British Academy of Accordionists
     (BCA) at address above) - Comp
- < Confédn Intle des Accordéonistes (CIA)
- M 700 i
     (Sub: £15)
- ¶ NL - 12;   Ybk - 1; both ftm only.

National Acquisitions Group   (NAG)   1986
- ■ 12-14 King St, WAKEFIELD, W Yorks, WF1 2SQ.   (hq)
     01924 383010   fax 01924 383010
     email nag@btconnect.com   http://www.nag.org.uk
     Hon Sec: Eileen Hiller
- ▲ Un-incorporated Society
- ○ *P; to stimulate, coordinate & publicise developments
     concerning the acquisition of library materials; to provide a
     forum for their discussion
- ● Conf - Mtgs - ET - Res - VE
- M 5 i, 450 f, UK / 15 f, o'seas
- ¶ Directory of Acquisitions Librarians; £60 m, £80 nm.
     Publications list available.

National Acrylic Painters' Association   (NAPA)   1985
- ■ 134 Rake Lane, Wallasey, WIRRAL, Merseyside, CH45 1JW.
     (hq)
     0151-639 2980   fax 0151-639 2980
     http://www.napauk.org
     Sec: Anthony F Patrick
     (email:anthony@patrick1766.freeserve.co.uk)
- ▲ Un-incorporated Society
- Br USA
- ○ *A, *G, *P; the promotion of the use of acrylic paint as a
     medium of excellence & innovation for professional fine art
     painters
- ● Exhib - PL
- < Fine Art Tr Gld
- M 100 i, UK / 300 i, ISAP, o'seas
- ¶ International (NL) - 2; ftm, £1 nm.
     Exhibition Catalogue - 1; £1.

© CBD Research Ltd · Beckenham · BR3 5JS · Tel 020 8650 7745 · Fax 020 8650 0768 · E-mail cbd@cbdresearch.com · www.cbdresearch.com

National Acupuncture Detoxification Association   (NADA)   1988
NR   The People's Centre, 50-54 Mount Pleasant, LIVERPOOL,
        L3 5SD.   (hq)
        0151-702 6959
        http://www.nadauk.com
▲   Un-incorporated Society
Br   Europe, Australia, Canada, India, Mexico, Nepal, Russia,
        Trinidad, USA
○   *P; to treat substance abuse, compulsive behaviour, attention
        deficient disorder & stress management
M   1,000 i, UK / 10,000 i, o'seas
¶   NL - 2; ftm only.
✕   2001-02 National Auricular Acupuncture Detoxification
        Association

National Adult School Organisation   (NASO)   1899
NR   Riverton, 370 Humberstone Rd, LEICESTER, LE5 0SA.   (hq)
        0116-253 8333   fax 0116-251 3626
        email gensec@naso.org.uk   http://www.naso.org.uk
▲   Registered Charity
Br   10
○   *E; to promote learning for life for those aged 50+ through the
        medium of informal, non-vocational study in discussion
        groups
●   Conf - Mtgs - ET - Exhib - SG - VE - Residential schools
<   Nat Coun Voluntary Orgs (NCVO)
M   1,078 i
¶   One & All - 10.   AR.
        Study Hbk (title varies) - 1.
        Discussion leaflets & Training papers - sets of 12.

**National Advisory Service for Parents of Children with a Stoma
(NASPCS)   1988**
NR   51 Anderson Drive, Valley View Park, DARVEL, Ayrshire,
        KA17 0DE.   (chmn p)
        01560 322024
        email john@stoma.freeserve.co.uk
        http://www.naspcs.co.uk
        Chmn: John Malcolm
▲   Registered Charity
○   *W; parental self-help group for those with children who have
        serious bladder & bowel problems
●   Res - Stat - Inf
<   Intl Ostomy Assn
M   440 i, 12 f, 60 org, UK / 20 i, 4 org, o'seas
¶   NL - 4; free.   Contact list - 1; ftm only.

National Alcohol Producers Association   (NAPA)   1982
■   4 Stour Close, KESTON, Kent, BR2 6BX.   (hsb)
        01689 889583
        email dhw@dhward.com
        Chmn & Gen Sec: David H Ward
▲   Un-incorporated Society
○   *T; UK producers of neutral alcohol for drinks & industrial use.
        Neutral alcohol is distilled from agricultural crops, the main
        market being in the production of spirit drinks (gin & vodka)
        & a growing potential for use in biofuel production
●   Mtgs - Stat - Inf
<   U Eur des Producteurs d'Alcools (UEPA); Confédn Eur des
        Producteurs de Spiritueux (CEPS); Gin & Vodka Assn; Scotch
        Whisky Assn
M   5 f (full), 7 f (associates)
✕   2008 (1 January) Neutral Alcohol Producers Association

National Alliance of Women's Organisations   (NAWO)   1989
NR   Davina House (Suite 405), 137-149 Goswell Rd, LONDON,
        EC1V 7ET.   (hq)
        020 7490 4100
        email info@nawo.org.uk   http://www.nawo.org.uk
        Hon Sec: Janet Harris
▲   Registered Charity; Un-incorporated Society
○   *N; brings together widely diverse women's organisations to
        achieve equality & justice for all women
M   org

National Amateur Bodybuilders Association   (NABBA)   1950
NR   PO Box 1186, BRIERLEY HILL, W Midlands, DY5 2GL.   (hq)
        01384 898578   fax 01384 898579
        http://www.nabba.co.uk
▲   Un-incorporated Society
○   *S; the controlling body for bodybuilding contests for men &
        women; promotion of weight-training as a means of health &
        fitness
M   i & clubs

National Ankylosing Spondylitis Society   (NASS)   1976
NR   Unit 0.1, One Victoria Villas, RICHMOND, Surrey, TW9 2GW.
        (hq)
        020 8948 9117   fax 020 8940 7736
        email nass@nass.co.uk   http://www.nass.co.uk
        Dir: Fergus Rogers
▲   Registered Charity
Br   110
○   *W; patient education & support
●   Conf - Mtgs - ET - Res - Inf
<   Ankylosing Spondylitis Intl Fedn; Brit League against
        Rheumatism; Brit Soc of Rheumatology
M   7,000 i, UK / 400 i, o'seas
¶   AS News - 2; free.
        Guidebook for Patients - 1; free.
        Living with Ankylosing Spondylitis.
        Physiotherapy (cassette tape).
        Fight Back (physiotherapy video + DVD); £12
        Other publications available.

National Anti-Vivisection Society   (NAVS)   1875
§   Millbank Tower, Millbank, LONDON, SW1P 4QP.   (hq)
        020 7630 3340   fax 020 7828 2179
        http://www.navs.org.uk
        Dir: Jan Creamer
        To promote awareness of the inequity of experiments or
        processes causing suffering or distress to living creatures and
        to obtain legislation totally prohibiting all such experiments.
        The society is affiliated to The Animal Defenders & Animal +
        World Show.

National Approved Premises Association   (NAPA)   1942
NR   PO Box 13682, CRADLEY HEATH, W Midlands, B62 2DY.
        0121-550 6444
        http://www.napa-uk.org
        Dir: Mike Short
○   *W; to support and develop approved residential provision for
        offenders
M   c 300 i
✕   2007 National Association of Probation & Bail Hostels

National Arabidopsis Society   (NAS)   1999
■   81 Park View, Collins Rd, LONDON, N5 2UD.   (asa)
○   *L
●   Conf - Mtgs - VE
M   i

National Arenas Association   (NAA)   1991
NR   Trent FM Arena, Bolero Square, The Lace Market,
        NOTTINGHAM, NG1 1LA.   (chmn/b)
        email naa@blueyonder.co.uk
        http://www.nationalarenasassociation.com
        Chmn: Geoff Huckstep
○   *T; managers of concert & event venues
M   15 f

National Art Collections Fund (The Art Fund) 1903
- ■ Millais House, 7 Cromwell Place, LONDON, SW7 2JN. (hq)
    020 7225 4800   fax 020 7225 4848
    email info@artfund.org   http://www.artfund.org
- ○ *A; the UK's leading art charity; to help museums, art galleries, historic houses & other public collections to acquire works of art, either by grants or through gifts & bequests.
    The Art Fund is independent of government & receives no public funding
- ● Funding
- M i
- ¶ Art Quarterly - 4;   Review - 1; both ftm only.

National Association for Able Children in Education   (NACE)
- ■ PO Box 242, Arnolds Way, OXFORD, OX2 9FR.
    01865 861879   fax 01865 861880
    email info@nace.co.uk   http://www.nace.co.uk
    Dir: Joanna Raffan
- ○ *E; to help education professionals to improve classroom practice for able, gifted & talented pupils
- M c 2,000 i

National Association of Accordion & Fiddle Clubs
- ■ 7 Lathro Lane, KINROSS, KY13 8RX.
    01577 862337
    Sec: Lorna Mair
- ○ *D
- M 76 clubs
    no further information supplied

National Association of Adult Placement Services   (NAAPS)
- NR 602 The Cotton Exchange, Old Hall St, LIVERPOOL, L3 9LQ. (hq)
    0151-227 3499   fax 0151-236 3590
    http://www.naaps.co.uk
- ▲ Registered Charity
- ○ *W; to promote & develop adult placement as a resource offering vulnerable adults the opportunity to live in a normal domestic setting, as part of a family & of a local community
- ● Conf - Mtgs - ET - Inf
- M 2,000+ i, 150+ SSDs
- ¶ Publications list available.

National Association of Advanced Motorcycle Instructors
- ▲ Company Limited by Guarantee
    Closed

National Association of Advisers for Computers in Education
    in 2004 merged with the Micros & Primary Education & Computer Education Group to form **Naace**

National Association of Advisers & Inspectors in Design & Technology   (NAAIDT) 1992
- NR Waterton Technology Centre, BRIDGEND, Glamorgan, CF31 3WT. (hsp)
    01656 669381
    email bob.cater@naaidt.org.uk   http://www.naaidt.org.uk
    Admin: Bob Cater
- ▲ Un-incorporated Society
- ○ *P; promotes the teaching of design & technology in schools
- < Standing Conf Schools' Science & Technology
- M 315 i & f
- ¶ NL.   Conference Report - 1.
    Safety Training for Teachers.   Occasional papers.

National Association of Advisory Officers for Special Educational Needs (NAAOSEN) 1983
- ■ 22 St Peter's St, SANDWICH, Kent, CT13 9BW. (hsp)
    01304 620179
    email linda.samson@kent.gov.uk
    http://www.naaosen.org.uk
    64 Glossop Rd, Marple Bridge, Stockport, SK6 5EL.
        0161-427 0803.   (treas)
    Hon Sec: Linda Samson, Treas: Sue Woodgate
- ○ *P
- ● Conf - LG
- < Nat Assn Educl Inspectors, Advisers & Consultants
- M i
- × 2005-06 National Association of Advisory Officers for Special Education

National Association of Aerial Photographic Libraries (NAPLIB) 1989
- NR c/o RCAHMS, John Sinclair House, 16 Bernard Terrace, EDINBURGH, EH8 9NX. (hq)
    email naplib@rspsoc.org   http://www.rspsoc.org
    Hon Sec: Kevin McLaren
- ○ *L; promote the use & preservation of aerial photography
- ● Conf - Inf - VE
- < Remote Sensing & Photogrammetry Soc
- M 47 i, 31 f, UK / 1 i, o'seas
- ¶ NAPLIB Flyer - 4; ftm only.
    NAPLIB Directory of Aerial Photographic Collections in the UK; £10 m, £15 nm.
    The Care & Storage of Photographs: recommendations for good practice; £2.50 m, £5 nm.

National Association of Agricultural Contractors   (NAAC) 1893
- ■ Samuelson House, 62 Forder Way, Hampton, PETERBOROUGH, Cambs, PE7 8JS. (hq)
    08456 448750   fax 01733 352806
    email jill.hewitt@naac.co.uk   http://www.naac.co.uk
    Chief Exec: Mrs Jill Hewitt
- ▲ Company Limited by Guarantee
- ○ *F,*H, *T; for UK contractors who supply land-based services to farmers, government, local authorities, sports & recreational facilities
- Gp Crop spraying; Amenity; Livestock; Mobile feed mill+mix; Mobile seed processors
- ● Conf - Mtgs - ET - Inf & advice - LG
- < Confédn Eur des Entrepreneurs de Travaux Techniques Agricoles et Rurales (CEETAR)
- M i & f (numbers confidential)
- ¶ Contracting Bulletin - 12; ftm only.
    ProContractor - 2; free.
    Contractors Directory [Ybk] - 1; ftm only.

National Association of Almshouses 1946
- ■ Billingbear Lodge, Maidenhead Rd, WOKINGHAM, Berks, RG40 5RU. (hq)
    01344 452922   fax 01344 862062
    email naa@almshouses.org
    http://www.almshouses.org
    Dir: A P De Ritter
- ▲ Registered Charity
- ○ *W; to advise members on any matters concerning almshouses & the welfare of the elderly
- ● Conf - Mtgs - Res - Exhib - SG - VE - LG
- < Age Concern; Charities Working Party
- M 1,800 almshouses
- ¶ The Almshouses Gazette - 4; £1;   AR - 1; £1.
    Also known as the Almshouse Association.

National Association of Animal Therapists
    since 2005 the **International Association of Animal Therapists**

© CBD Research Ltd · Beckenham · BR3 5JS · Tel 020 8650 7745 · Fax 020 8650 0768 · E-mail cbd@cbdresearch.com · www.cbdresearch.com

National Association for Areas of Outstanding Natural Beauty (NAAONB)

NR   The Old Police Station, Cotswold Heritage Centre, NORTHLEACH, Glos, GL54 3JH.
01451 862007
http://www.aonb.org.uk
Sec: Jill Smith
○   *G

National Association of Bank & Insurance Customers (NABIC) 1992

NR   PO Box 15, CALDICOT, Monmouthshire, NP26 5YD.   (sb)
email enquiries@lemonaid.net   http://www.lemonaid.net
Sec: Janet Saunders
▲   Un-incorporated Society
Br   3; France, Germany, Holland, Italy, Spain, USA
○   *K, *N; 'independent watchdog group for private & commercial users of bank & insurance services'
Gp   Banks; Banking; Insurance; Customer protection; Consumer protection
●   Conf - ET - Res - SG - Stat - Inf - Lib - LG
<   Eur U of Financial Service Users; Nat Assn of Mortgage Victims; Anti-poverty Forum
M   5,000 i, 15,000 f, 100 org, UK / 100 i, 250 f, 10 org, o'seas
¶   Money Minder - 12; ftm only.
Reports & Statistics - irreg; on application.

National Association for Bikers with a Disability (NABD) 1991

NR   Unit 20 The Bridgewater Centre, Robson Avenue, Urmston, MANCHESTER, Lancs, M41 7TE.   (hq)
0870 759 0603
email office@thenabd.org.uk   http://www.nabd.org.uk
▲   Registered Charity
Br   32; Republic of Ireland
○   *W; to help disabled people enjoy motorcycling to the full; to organise & finance adaptions to motorcycles, trikes & scooters to suit the disability of the rider; help with licensing, insurance & general access to motorcycling events; to ensure that when it comes to motorcycling 'a disability is not a handicap'.
●   Conf - Mtgs - ET - Res - Exhib - Comp - Inf - VE - LG - Annual National Rally
<   Motorcycle Action Group (MAG); Brit Motorcyclist Fedn (BMF)
M   2,000 i, 30 f, 70 org, UK / 20 i, o'seas
¶   Open House - 4; ftm, donation nm.

National Association of Boat Owners (NABO) 1991

■   Mill House End Farm, Grape Lane, Croston, LEYLAND, Lancs, PR26 9HB.   (hsp)
email gen.sec@nabo.org.uk   http://www.nabo.org.uk
Freepost (BM8367), B31 2BR.
Gen Sec: Richard Carpenter
▲   Un-incorporated Society
○   *G; representation of private boat owners on Britain's inland waterways
●   Stat - Inf - LG & representation to statutory bodies & waterway authorities
<   Intl Navigation Assn
M   2,500 i & org
¶   NABO News - 7; ftm only.

National Association of Bookmakers Ltd (NAB) 1932

NR   19 Culm Valley Way, UFFCULME, Devon, EX15 3XZ.   (hq)
01884 841859
http://www.nab-bookmakers.co.uk
○   *T; for on-course bookmakers

National Association of Brass Band Conductors (NABBC) 1946

■   30 Havant Rd, Horndean, WATERLOOVILLE, Hants, PO8 0DT.   (hsp)
023 9259 8162
http://www.nabbc.org.uk
Hon Sec: Ted Howard
▲   Un-incorporated Society
Br   6
○   *G; the promotion of brass band music & conductors
●   Conf - Mtgs - Comp - Lib - Assistance to members wishing to study adjudication & conducting
M   300 i
¶   The Conductor - 4; ftm, £2.50 yr nm.

National Association of British & Irish Millers
see the **Incorporated National Association of British & Irish Millers**

National Association of British Market Authorities (NABMA) 1919

NR   The Guildhall, OSWESTRY, Salop, SY11 1PZ.   (hq)
01691 680713   fax 01691 671080
email nabma@nabma.com   http://www.nabma.com
Chief Exec: G Wilson
○   *N, *T; to constitute a medium of communication between members & others in promoting & administering matters of common interest relating to markets, fairs, abattoirs & cold stores
Gp   Section c'ees: Livestock & abattoirs, Retail markets, Wholesale markets
●   Conf - Mtgs - Exhib - Inf - VE - LG
<   Assn of Town Centre Mgt; Eur Assn of Livestock Markets; Wld U of Whls Markets
M   135 local authorities
¶   AR; ftm.

National Association of Building Co-operatives Society Ltd (NABCO)

IRL 33 Lower Baggot St, DUBLIN 2, Republic of Ireland.
353 (1) 661 2877   fax 353 (1) 661 4462
http://www.nabco.ie
○   *N

National Association of Caravan Owners (NACO) 1996

NR   Leisurefame House, 37 Clacton Rd, St OSYTH, Essex, CO16 8RA.
01255 820321
http://www.nacoservices.com
▲   Company Limited by Guarantee
○   *T; to represent the owners of static holiday caravans
¶   The Holiday Caravanner (Jnl) - 3.

National Association of Care Catering (NACC) 1986

NR   Meadow Court, Faygate Lane, Faygate, HORSHAM, W Sussex, RH12 4SJ.
0870 748 0180   fax 0870 748 0181
email info@thenacc.co.uk   http://www.thenacc.co.uk
Nat Sec: Ros Speight
○   *T; to promote & enrich the standard of catering within the care sector
M   c 500 i

National Association for the Care & Resettlement of Offenders
alternative name of **NACRO**

National Association of Careers & Guidance Teachers
since January 2006 **Association for Careers Education & Guidance**

National Association of Catering Butchers   (NACB)   1983
NR   224 Central Markets, LONDON, EC1A 9LH.   (hq)
    020 7248 1896   fax 020 7329 0658
    email info@nacb.co.uk   http://www.nacb.co.uk
    Sec: Liz Murphy
○   *T; to raise the standard of catering butchery
M   c 30 f

National Association of Cattle Foot Trimmers
NR   Berthlwyd, Maestmeillion, LLANDYSUL, Ceredigion,
    SA44 4NG.   (treas/p)
    01545 590590
    http://www.nacft.co.uk
    Treas: Andrew Tyler
    Sec: Steve Jones (01829 781476)
○   *P; for cattle hoof trimmers

National Association of Child Contact Centres   (NACCC)   1985
■   Minerva House, Spaniel Row, NOTTINGHAM, NG1 6EP.   (hq)
    fax 0845 450 0420
    email contact@naccc.org.uk   http://www.naccc.org.uk
    Chief Exec: Yvonne Kee
▲   Company Limited by Guarantee; Registered Charity
○   *N, *W; to keep over 2,000 children a week in touch with both
    parents through a network of child contact centres
●   Helpline: 0845 450 0280 (0900-1300 Mon-Fri)
M   c 300 centres
¶   Ben's Story: an introduction to child contact centres (a children's
    book); £2 m, £2.50 nm.
    AR.

National Association for Child Support Action   (NACSA)   1993
NR   PO Box 4454, DUDLEY, W Midlands, DY1 9AN.
    (mail/address)
    email admin@nacsa.co.uk   http://www.nacsa.co.uk
▲   Company Limited by Guarantee
○   *K; to help & support parents who have problems with the
    Child Support Agency
Gp   specialist advisers
●   Res - Inf - LG
¶   NACSA News - 4; ftm only.

National Association for Children of Alcoholics   (NACOA)
§   PO Box 64, Fishponds, BRISTOL, BS16 2UH.
    0117-924 8005   fax 0117-924 2928
    http://www.nacoa.org.uk
●   Helpline: 0800 358 3456
    Providing information, advice and support to children of
    alcoholics and people concerned with their welfare.

National Association of Chimney Engineers Ltd   (NACE)   1982
■   PO Box 849, Metheringham, LINCOLN, LN4 3WU.   (hq)
    01526 322555   fax 01526 323181
    email info@nace.org.uk   http://www.nace.org.uk
    Sec: Michael Carr
▲   Company Limited by Guarantee
○   *T; to promote & develop the safe installation & construction of
    all types of chimney & chimney lining in domestic properties
Gp   Competent persons register; Code of practice development
●   ET - Exhib - Inf - LG
M   15 installers, 7 associates
¶   Flueways (NL) - 4; ftm only.

National Association of Chimney Sweeps   (NACS)   1982
■   Unit 15 Emerald Way, Stone Business Park, STONE, Staffs,
    ST15 0SR.   (hq)
    01785 811732   fax 01785 811712
    email nacs@chimneyworks.co.uk
    http://www.nacs.org.uk
    Admin: Mrs Amanda Pulfer
○   *T; to promote the use of professional sweeps to clean &
    maintain chimneys; to advise public of chimney safety
●   Conf - Mtgs - ET - Exam - Exhib - LG
<   Europäische-Schornsteinfegermeister-Föderation; Co-Gas
    Safety; HETAS; OFTEC; Solid Fuel Assn; Nat Fireplace Assn;
    Nat Energy Foundation
M   235 i, 16 f, UK / 2 f, o'seas
¶   Chimney Jnl - 3; ftm.

National Association of Choirs   (NAC)   1920
■   612 Lightwood Rd, Lightwood, STOKE-on-TRENT, Staffs,
    ST3 7EQ.   (hsp)
    email rhodeswf@ntlworld.com
    http://www.nationalassociationofchoirs.org.uk
    Gen Sec: Frank Rhodes
▲   Registered Charity
Br   25 areas
○   *D, *N; to promote, develop & maintain public education in, &
    appreciation of, the art & science of music & in particular
    choral music
●   Conf - Mtgs - Inf - Lib
<   Tonsil
M   13 i, 16 f, 500 org
¶   NAC News & Views - 3; ftm, £2 nm.
    NAC Ybk - 1; ftm, £2 nm.

National Association of Cider Makers   (NACM)   1920
■   c/o 6 Catherine St, LONDON, WC2B 5JJ.   (hq)
    020 7420 7106
    email info@cideruk.com   http://www.cideruk.com
    Sec: John Lepley
▲   Un-incorporated Society
○   *T; interests of makers of cider & perry
Gp   Technical (incl manufacture, packaging & labelling)
●   Mtgs - LG
<   Assn des Inds des Cidres et Vins de Fruits de l'EU (AICV); Food
    & Drink Fedn
M   8 f, 2 affiliated org
    SW of England Cidermakers Association
    Three Counties Cider & Perry Association
¶   Cider - 2.   LM; on request.

**National Association of Cigarette Machine Operators
(NACMO)   1968**
■   Cherwell Tobacco, Unit 2 Waymills Industrial Estate,
    WHITCHURCH, Shropshire, SY13 1TT.   (hsb)
    01948 663322   fax 01948 663671
    Gen Sec: Michael G White
▲   Company Limited by Guarantee
Br   5
○   *T; for cigarette vending machine operators & protection of
    their interests
Gp   Tobacco distribution
●   Conf - Mtgs - Stat - Inf
<   Europäischer Tabakwaren-Grosshandels-Verband eV (ETG)
M   [not available]
¶   NL - 4; free.

National Association of Citizens Advice Bureaux
    the registered name of **Citizens Advice Bureaux**

National Association of Clinical Tutors (NACT) 1969
NR Norfolk House East, 499 Silbury Boulevard, MILTON KEYNES,
      Bucks, MK9 2AH.
      01908 488033   fax 01296 715255
      email office@nact.org.uk   http://www.nact.org.uk
      Hon Sec: Dr Peter Harrison
▲ Registered Charity
○ *E, *P; to support medical education in running postgraduate
      medical education in teaching hospitals
Gp Clinical tutors; Foundation programme training directors
● Conf - Mtgs - ET
M 480 i
¶ Directory of Postgraduate Medical Centres (with gazetteer) - 1;
      ftm, £60 nm.

National Association of Clubs for Young People
      since 2005 **Clubs for Young People**

National Association of Co-operative Officials (NACO) 1917
■ 6a Clarendon Place, HYDE, Cheshire, SK14 2QZ.   (hq)
      0161-351 7900   fax 0161-366 6800
      email info@nacoco-op.org   http://www.naco.coop
      Gen Sec: Neil Buist
▲ Registered Trade Union
Br 31
○ *U
● Conf - ET - Empl - LGl - LG
< Trs U Congress (TUC); Soc for Coop Studies; Cooperatives UK
M 2,450 i
¶ Co-operative Official - 4;   Grapevine NL - irreg;
      AR - 1; all free.

**National Association for Colitis & Crohn's Disease (NACC)
1979**
NR 4 Beaumont House, Sutton Rd, ST ALBANS, Herts, AL1 5HH.
      (hq)
      01727 830038   fax 01727 862550
      http://www.nacc.org.uk
      Dir: Richard Driscoll
▲ Registered Charity
Br 70
○ *W; to provide support & information to patients & families with
      ulcerative colitis & Crohn's disease; to fund research into the
      cause & cure of these conditions
Gp NACC in contact listening ear service; Welfare fund
● Conf - Mtgs - Res - Inf
      Infoline: 0845 130 2233
M c 30,000 i
¶ NL - 4.   AR; free.

**National Association of Commercial Finance Brokers
(NACFB) 1993**
NR 3 Silverdown Office Park, Fair Oak Close, EXETER, Devon,
      EX5 2UX.   (hq)
      email admin@nacfb.org   http://www.nacfb.org
      Chief Exec: Keith Heron
▲ Company Limited by Guarantee
○ *P; for commercial mortgage, lease & asset finance, factoring &
      invoice discounting brokers
● Conf - Mtgs - ET - Exhib - LG
M 500 i, 350 f
¶ Niche Commercial - 12.

** **National Association of Complaints Personnel, Health Ltd**
      Organisation lost: see Introduction paragraph 3.

National Association of Councillors (NAC) 1959
NR Gateshead MBC, Civic Centre, GATESHEAD, Tyne & Wear,
      NE8 1HH.   (hsb)
      0191-433 3000   fax 0191-477 9253
      email info@nac.uk.com   http://www.nac.uk.com
      Nat Sec: Councillor Peter Mole
○ *P; to represent the interests of local government councillors
¶ The Councillor - 2.   Bulletin - 2.

National Association of Councils for Voluntary Service
      since 14 June 2006 **National Associaton for Voluntary &
      Community Action**

**National Association of Counsellors, Hypnotherapists &
Psychotherapists (NACHP) 1977**
■ PO Box 719, Burwell, CAMBRIDGE, CB25 0NX.   (hq)
      01638 741363   fax 01638 744190
      email mail@nachp.org   http://www.nachp.org
      Chmn: James Hammond,   Co Sec: Sarah Anderson
▲ Company Limited by Guarantee; Registered Charity
○ *P; to provide information to the general public in the fields of
      counselling, hypnotherapy & psychotherapy; to provide
      accreditation of qualified & ethical persons
Gp Counsellors; Hypnotherapists; Psychotherapists; Trans-gender
      issues; Education/training; Information
● Conf - Mtgs - ET - Inf
      Helpline: 0870 850 5383
< UK Confedn of Hypnotherapy Orgs
M 102 i, UK / 2 i, o'seas
¶ NL - 4; ftm only.

**National Association of Credit Hire Operators   (NACHO)
2002**
NR 3 Stead Close, HAYLING ISLAND, Hants, PO11 9BE.
      023 9235 8026
      http://www.nacho.org.uk
      Sec: Barry Bromley
○ *T; to represent the vehicle credit hire industry
M 25 f

National Association for Deaf People
      since May 2007 **DeafHear**

National Association of Deafened People (NADP) 1984
■ PO Box 50, AMERSHAM, Bucks, HP6 6XB.   (mail/address)
      0845 055 9663, 07527 211348 (SMS)
      fax 01305 262591
      email enquiries@nadp.org.uk   http://www.nadp.org.uk
      Hon Sec: Paul Tomlinson
▲ Registered Charity
○ *W; to promote the interests & welfare of people with a
      profound or total acquired hearing loss
● Conf - Exhib - Inf - Local support groups
< member of UK Council on Deafness
M 500 i
      (Sub: £15)
¶ Network (NL) - 4; ftm only.
      Information Booklet; ftm, £2.50 nm.
      An Introduction to Cochlear Implants; ftm, £5 nm.

**National Association of Decorative & Fine Arts Societies
(NADFAS) 1968**
■ NADFAS House, 8 Guilford St, LONDON, WC1N 1DA.   (hq)
      020 7430 0730   fax 020 7242 0686
      email enquiries@nadfas.org.uk
      http://www.nadfas.org.uk
      Chief Exec: David Bell
▲ Company Limited by Guarantee; Registered Charity
Br 338; Belgium, France, Germany, Netherlands, New Zealand,
      Spain
○ *A; to educate the public in the cultivation, appreciation &
      study of the decorative & fine arts
Gp Church recorders; Heritage volunteers; Young arts
● Mtgs - ET - SG - VE
< Assn of Australian Decorative & Fine Arts Soc
M c 90,000 i, 370 societies
¶ NADFAS Review - 4; ftm, £2.50 nm.
      Inside Churches; £15.95.   Stained Glass + Monograms;
      £12.50.
      Behind the Acanthus: the NADFAS story; £20.

National Association for Dentistry in Health Authorities & Trusts
      no longer in existence

** National Association of Deputising Doctors
 Organisation lost: see Introduction paragraph 3

**National Association for the Education of Sick Children
 (NAESC) 1993**
§ Open School, 18 Victoria Park Sq, LONDON, E2 0PF.   (hq)
   020 8980 8523
   email naesc@ednsick.demon.co.uk
   http://www.sickchildren.org.uk
   NAESC (also known as 'Present') works to ensure that all
   children and young people get the education they need when
   they are sick.

**National Association for the Education, Training & Support of
 Blind & Partially Sighted People   (OPSIS) 1992**
■ c/o Queen Alexandra College, Court Oak Rd, Harborne,
   BIRMINGHAM, B17 9TG.   (hq)
   0121-428 5037   fax 0121-428 5048
   email opsis@dircon.co.uk   http://www.opsis.org.uk
   Chief Exec: Mike Brace
○ *N, *W; to exert influence on policymakers, raise standards &
   improve the quality of services for visually impaired people
Gp Housing; Schools
● Conf - Mtgs - ET - Exhib - Inf - LG - Welfare & support for
   visually impaired people
< VISION 2020
M 7 org

National Association of Educational Guidance for Adults
  since 2006 **NAEGA - promoting adult guidance on learning &
  work**

National Association of Educational Inspectors, Advisers & Consultants
  since November 2005 **Association of Professionals in Education
  & Children's Trusts**

**National Association for Environmental Education (UK)
 (NAEE) 1960**
■ University of Wolverhampton, Walsall Campus, Gorway Rd,
   WALSALL, W Midlands, WS1 3BD.   (hq)
   01922 631200
   email info@naee.org.uk   http://www.naee.org.uk
   Hon Sec: Sue Fenoughty
▲ Registered Charity
○ *E, *L, *P; 'for all interested in education & the environment'
● Conf - Mtgs - ET - Res - SG - Inf
M 2,000 i, 12 local org, UK / i, o'seas
   (Sub: £25 i, £30 f, UK / £40 i, £50 f, o'seas)
¶ Environmental Education - 3; £25 yr m, £6 each nm.

National Association of Estate Agents   (NAEA) 1962
■ Arbon House, 6 Tournament Court, Edgehill Drive, WARWICK,
   CV34 6LG.   (hq)
   01926 496800   fax 01926 417788
   email info@naea.co.uk   http://www.naea.co.uk
   Hon Sec: Peter Bolton King
▲ Company Limited by Guarantee
Br 48
○ *P; cooperation among estate agents & protection of public
   against fraud, misrepresentation & malpractice
Gp Institution of Commercial & Business Agents
   National Association of Valuers & Auctioneers
   NAEA International incorporating the Federation of Overseas
   Property, Agents & Consultants (FOPAC)
● Conf - Mtgs - ET - Exam - Res - Exhib - Lib
< Intl Consortium of Real Estate Agents (ICREA);
   Is a division of the National Federation of Property Professionals
M 10,000 i
¶ The Estate Agent - 8; ftm.

National Association Family Information Services   (NAFIS)
NR City Reach (5th floor), 5 Greenwich View Place, LONDON,
    E14 9NN.   (hq)
    020 7515 9000   fax 020 7515 9001
    email info@familyinformationservice.org.uk
    http://www.familyinformationservices.org.uk
    Chief Exec: Karen Ramshaw
○ *W; to link & promote children's information services in GB
● Inf
M i
¶ Bulletins (email) - 52.
   NAFIS National Quality Standards (a guide).

National Association of Farmers' Markets
  in 2004 merged with the Farm Retail Association to form the
  National Farmer's Retail & Markets Association

**National Association of Farriers, Blacksmiths & Agricultural
 Engineers   (NAFBAE) 1902**
NR The Forge, Avenue B 10th St, STONELEIGH PARK, Warks,
    CV8 2LG.   (hq)
    024 7669 6595   fax 024 7669 6708
    email nafbaehq@nafbae.org   http://www.nafbae.org
Br 28
○ *T
● Conf - Mtgs - ET - Exhib - Comp - Inf - Empl
M 1,300 i
¶ Forge - 6; ftm, £5.90 nm.

National Association of Field Studies Officers   (NAFSO) 1969
■ CEES Stibbington Centre, Church Lane, Stibbington,
   PETERBOROUGH, PE8 6LP.
   01780 782386   fax 01780 783835
   email office@nafso.org.uk   http://www.nafso.org.uk
   Chmn: Chas Matthews
▲ Un-incorporated Society
○ *P; for field studies officers in education & all interested in the
   environment, natural history & historical sites & buildings
Gp Field studies; Education; Environmental; Heritage education;
   Ecology; Geography; History; Outdoor education; Geology
● Conf - Mtgs - ET - Res - Exhib - SG - Stat - Inf - Lib - VE - LG
< Outdoor Coun; Nat Assn of Envtl Educ; Inst of Outdoor
   Learning
M 150 i, UK/ 5 i, o'seas
   (Sub: £35)
¶ Jnl - 1; ftm; £5 nm.   NL - 3 (electronic); free.
   Topical publications - 1; ftm, c £5 nm.   AR - 1.
   Note: the enquiry address is open for 1 day a week

National Association of Fine Art Education   (NAFAE)
NR SASS, Northumbria University, Lipman Building (room 123),
    Sandyford Rd, NEWCASTLE upon TYNE, NE1 8ST.
    0191-227 3105
    email secretary@nafae.org.uk   http://www.nafae.org.uk
    Sec: Helen Baker

National Association of Fire Officers   (NAFO) 1942
NR Hayes Court, West Common Rd, HAYES, Kent, BR2 7AU.   (hq)
    020 8462 7755   fax 020 8315 8234
○ *U

**National Association of Fisheries & Angling Consultatives
 (NAFAC)**
NR 106 Icknield Port Rd, Edgbaston, BIRMINGHAM, B16 0AA.
    0121-454 2886
    http://www.nafac.co.uk
    Sec: John Williams
○ *G, *N; for local fisheries & angling consultatives in coarse
   game fishing

© CBD Research Ltd · Beckenham · BR3 5JS · Tel 020 8650 7745 · Fax 020 8650 0768 · E-mail cbd@cbdresearch.com · www.cbdresearch.com

National Association of Flower Arrangement Societies (NAFAS) 1959
NR Osborne House, 12 Devonshire Square, LONDON, EC2M 4TE.   (hq)
020 7247 5567   fax 020 7247 7232
email flowers@nafas.org.uk   http://www.nafas.org.uk
▲ Registered Charity
○ *A; promotion of the art & practice of flower arranging
Gp Demonstrators; Teachers; Judges & speakers
● Conf - Mtgs - ET - Exam - Exhib - Comp - SG - Lib - PL - VE
< Wld Assn of Flower Arrangers (WAFA); R Horticl Soc
¶ The Flower Arranger - 4.

National Association of Funeral Directors   (NAFD)   1905
■ 618 Warwick Rd, SOLIHULL, W Midlands, B91 1AA.   (hq)
0845 230 1343   fax 0121-711 1351
email info@nafd.org.uk   http://www.nafd.org.uk
Chief Exec: Alan Slater
▲ Un-incorporated Society
○ *T; to protect the interests of members by means of formulating policy with regard to the statutory, legal, economic, health & safety, commercial, educational & other matters affecting funeral service
● Conf - Mtgs - ET - Exam - Exhib - Stat - Inf - LG
< Eur Fedn Funeral Services; Fédn Intle des Assns des Thanatologues; Coun of Brit Funeral Service
M 3,382 f, UK / 37 f, o'seas
¶ The Funeral Director Monthly - 12; ftm; £48 nm, £72 (Europe), £90 row.
× 2004 (1 January) Funeral Standards Council (absorbed).

National Association of Gallery Education
    alternative name of **engage**

National Association for Gifted Children   (NAGC)   1967
NR Challenge House (suite 14), Sherwood Drive, Bletchley, MILTON KEYNES, Bucks, MK3 6DP.   (hq)
email amazingchildren@nagcbritain.org.uk
http://www.nagcbritain.org.uk
Dir: Denise Yates
Br 26
○ *W; to help, support & encourage gifted & talented children & their families & all others involved in their education & welfare
M c 2,000 i, 500 schools
¶ Gifted & Talented (Jnl) - 1.
    NL - 3;   AR - 1; both ftm only.

** **National Association for Gifted Children in Scotland**
    Organisation lost: see Introduction paragraph 3

National Association of Goldsmiths of GB & Ireland   (N.A.G.) 1894
■ 78a Luke St, LONDON, EC2A 4XG.   (hq)
020 7613 4445   fax 020 7613 4450
email nag@jewellers-online.org.
http://www.jewellers-online.org
Chief Exec: Michael J Hoare
▲ Company Limited by Guarantee
○ *T; to represent the interests of retail jewellers (incl goldsmiths, silversmiths & horologists) in the UK & Ireland
Gp Jewellery sector
● Conf - ET - Res - Exhib - Inf - Lib - LG - Promotional services
M 3,000 f
¶ The Jeweller (Jnl) - 6; ftm.
    n:gauge (NL) - 12.
    Note: The abbreviation for this association must have full stops.

National Association of Governors & Managers
    in 2005 renamed the National Association of School Governors which, in 2006, merged with the National Governors' Council to form the **National Governors' Association**

National Association of Head Teachers   (NAHT)   1897
■ 1 Heath Sq, Boltro Rd, HAYWARDS HEATH, W Sussex, RH16 1BL.   (hq)
01444 472472   fax 01444 472473
email info@naht.org.uk   http://www.naht.org.uk
Gen Sec: Mick Brookes
○ *E, *P, *U; for head teachers, deputy head teachers & leaders, principals & vice-principals, of schools & colleges in state maintained & the private sector from nursery to tertiary level
M c 30,500 i

National Association of Health Stores   (NAHS)   1931
NR PO Box 14177, TRANENT, E Lothian, EH34 5WX.   (sb)
01875 341408
email info@nahs.co.uk   http://www.nahs.co.uk
▲ Un-incorporated Society
○ *T; for independent & other specialist health food retailers
● Mtgs - ET - Stat - Inf - Empl - LG
M i representing retail outlets
¶ NL - 4/8 weekly; free.

National Association of Healthcare Fire Officers   (NAHFO) 1973
■ c/o Peter Aldridge, Estates Dept, Ashley Wing, St James's, Beckett St, LEEDS, W Yorks, LS9 7TF.   (hsb)
http://www.nahfo.org
Gen Sec: Peter Aldridge
○ *P; to promote & encourage the highest standards of fire safety in Health Service premises
● Conf - Mtgs - ET - SG - Stat - VE - LG - Liaison with NHS Estates & Fire & Local Authorities on development of legislation & all matters relating to fire safety in healthcare
< Brit Fire Services Assn; UNISON
× 2006 National Association of Hospital Fire Officers

National Association for Healthcare Security
■ c/o Penny van der Bijl, Somerset Partnership, Little Court, BERROW, Somerset, TA8 2NF.
email enqs@nahs.org.uk   http://www.nahs.org.uk
○ *P
M c 70 i

National Association for Higher Education in the Moving Image (NAHEMI)   1963
NR c/o Sara Jolly, ATRiuM, University of Glamorgan, Adam St, CARDIFF, CF24 2HX.   (sb)
http://www.nahemi.org
Sec: Sara Jolly
○ *A, *E

National Association of Homeopathic Groups   (NAHG)   1982
■ 11 Wingle Tye Rd, BURGESS HILL, W Sussex, RH15 9HR.   (hsp)
01444 236848
email homoeopathy@platform11.org.uk
Nat Admin: Mrs Mary Mitchell
▲ Un-incorporated Society
○ *K, *M, *N
M 20 i, 10 org

National Association of Hospital Broadcasting Organisations (HBA)   1970
- ■ 54 St Annes Close, WINCHESTER, Hants, SO22 4LQ.   (hsp)
      0870 321 6003
      email secretary@hbauk.com   http://www.hbauk.com
      Hon Sec: Nigel Dullard
- ▲ Company Limited by Guarantee; Registered Charity
- Br 12
- ○ *W; support & representation of hospital broadcasters
- ● Conf - Mtgs - ET - Inf - LG - Liaison with NHS, Copyright collecting societies
- M i, 6 f, 230 org
      (Sub: £15 i, £300 f, £37 org)
- ¶ On Air - 6;   AR - 1; both ftm only.
      Note: the trading name of this association is Hospital Broadcasting Association

National Association of Hospital & Community Friends
      since April 2006 **Attend**

National Association of Hospital Fire Officers
      since 2006 **National Association of Healthcare Fire Officers**

National Association of Hospital Play Staff   (NAHPS)   1975
- ■ 143 Gresham Rd, STAINES, Middx, TW18 2AG.   (inf/officer/p)
      http://www.nahps.org.uk
      Admin: Sue Pallot
- ▲ Registered Charity
- ○ *W; support & information for staff who lead therapeutic play for hospital patients under 21 years; to campaign & advise on high quality hospital play services
- ● Conf - Mtgs - ET - Inf - Empl
- M c 450 i
- ¶ Jnl - 2.   NL - 2.   AR.
      Expert Articles & Reading List.
      Salary & other information; free.

National Association of Hot Foil Printers
      since 2005 the **Association of Hot Foil Printers**

National Association of Independent Resources for Children
      since 2004 **Independent Children's Homes Association**

National Association of Independent Travel Agents Ltd
      since May 2005 **Advantage**

National Association of Investigators & Process Servers (NAIPS)
- NR 33 Greenville Drive, Low Moor, BRADFORD, W Yorks, BD12 0PT.   (hsb)
- ○ *P
- ● Conf - Mtgs
- < Assn Brit Investigators; Nat Assn Retired Police Officers
- M 32 i

National Association of Karate & Martial Art Schools (NAKMAS)   1990
- ■ Rosecraig, Bullockstone Rd, HERNE BAY, Kent, CT6 7NL.   (hq)
      01227 370055   fax 01227 370056
      email admin@nakmas.org.uk
      http://www.nakmas.org.uk
      Dir of Operations: Sandra J Beale
- ▲ Un-incorporated Society
- Br 1,200; 500 clubs o'seas
- ○ *S; to act as the governing body for martial arts; to provide training courses & vocational & NVQ qualifications
- Gp Autistic Martial Arts
- ● Mtgs - ET - Exam - Exhib - Comp - LG
- < Cent Coun of Physical Recreation
- M 73,000 i, 1,200 f, 400 org, UK / 2,000 i, o'seas
      (Sub: varies i, £99.45 f & org)
- ¶ NAKMAS Review - 6; ftm, £2.99 nm.
      NAKMAS Annual Review - 1; ftm, £2.99 nm,
      Martial Arts Code of Safety.
      Codes of Ethics & Child Protection Procedures.

National Association of Kebab Shops
      company dissolved

National Association of Ladies' Circles of Great Britain & Ireland   (NALC)   1936
- ■ Marchesi House, 4 Embassy Drive, Edgbaston, BIRMINGHAM, B15 1TP.   (hq)
      0121-456 0304
      email headquarters@ladies-circle.org.uk
      http://www.ladies-circle.org.uk
      Admin: Aileen Axcell
- Br 280
- ○ *W; 'non-political, non-sectarian organisation for women aged 18-45 for fun, friendship & fund-raising
- Gp Social activities; Community service projects; Fundraising
- ● Conf - Mtgs - VE
- < Ladies' Circle Intl
- M 2,300 i
      (Sub: £42.50)
- ¶ The Circler - 2; ftm only.

National Association of Language Advisers   (NALA)   1969
- ■ c/o Redcar & Cleveland ICT Centre, Corporation Rd, REDCAR, Cleveland, TS10 1HA.   (hsb)
      01642 286688
      http://www.nala.org.uk
      Hon Sec: Jim McElwee
- ○ *P; for modern foreign language (MFL) advisers, consultants & inspectors (public & private sectors) who work with schools & colleges in the UK to promote the quality of MFL teaching & learning
- ● Conf - Mtgs - ET - Res - Inf - LG
- M c 250 i
- ¶ NALA Update - 3; ftm only.
      Report on Members' Annual Trends Survey - 1; ftm; (from Centre for Information on Language Teaching & Research, 20 Bedfordbury, London, WC2N 4LB).

National Association of Laryngectomee Clubs   (NALC)   1976
- ■ 152 Buckingham Palace Rd, LONDON, SW1W 9TR.   (hq)
      020 7730 8585   fax 020 7730 8584
      http://www.laryngectomy.org.uk
      Gen Sec: Vivien Reed
- ▲ Registered Charity
- Br 95
- ○ *W; to promote the welfare & rehabilitation of laryngectomy patients & their families; to be of assistance to professionals working in the field
- Gp Cancer of the larynx
- ● Conf - Mtgs - ET - Res - Inf
- < MacMillan Cancer Support
- M 4,500 i, 95 clubs, UK / 500 i, o'seas
      (Sub: £20)
- ¶ Publications list available.

© CBD Research Ltd · Beckenham · BR3 5JS · Tel 020 8650 7745 · Fax 020 8650 0768 · E-mail cbd@cbdresearch.com · www.cbdresearch.com

National Association of the Launderette Industry Ltd (NALI) 1955
■ Hamilton House, Mabledon Place, LONDON, WC1H 9BB. (hq)
   020 7554 8500
   http://www.nali.co.uk
   Sec: Mrs J Cowan
▲ Company Limited by Guarantee
○ *T; for launderette operators & supplier companies to the trade
● Mtgs - Exhib - SG - Stat - Inf - LG
M 586 i, 56 f
¶ Launderette & Cleaning World - 4; ftm.

National Association for Leisure Industry Certification (NAFLIC) 1988
NR PO Box 752, SUNDERLAND, Co Durham, SR3 1XX. (hsp)
   0191-523 9498   fax 0191-523 9498
   email mccleisure@lineone.net   http://www.naflic.org.uk
   Gen Sec: Neil R McCullough
▲ Un-incorporated Society
○ *T; to promote safety in the leisure industry
● Conf - Mtgs - Exhib - Inf - LG
M 34 f, UK / 2 f, 1 org, o'seas

National Association of Licensed Opencast Operators (NALOO) 1988
NR Thrislington Industrial Estate, West Cornforth, FERRYHILL,
   Co Durham, DL17 9EU. (regd off)
▲ Company Limited by Guarantee
○ *T; to promote the interests of those concerned with licensed
   opencast coal mining operations
M f

National Association of Licensed Paralegals (NALP) 1987
■ 73 Shenley Rd, LONDON, SE5 8NE. (hsb)
   020 7252 7545
   email info@nationalparalegals.com
   http://www.nationalparalegals.com
   Hon Sec: Amanda Hamilton
▲ Company Limited by Guarantee
○ *P; national regulatory & professional body for paralegals;
   provides educational & qualifying requirements, training,
   professional status & licensing to all those working or seeking
   to work as paralegals in solicitors' offices or within
   commerce, industry or the public sector
Gp Community & voluntary sector paralegals group; Paralegal
   advocacy group; Private paralegal practitioners; Vocational
   training
● Conf - Mtgs - ET - Exam - Res - Exhib - SG - Inf - VE - Empl -
   LG
> Inst Legal Secs & PAs
M c 4,000 i, UK / c 250 i, o'seas
¶ The Paralegal (Jnl) - 4; ftm only.
✕ 2005 National Association of Paralegals

National Association of Licensing & Enforcement Officers (NALEO) 1985
NR 3 Tyne Close, LIVERPOOL, L4 1XP.
   0151-933 4301
   http://www.naleo.org.uk
   Hon Sec: John Thompson
○ *P; for those concerned with Hackney carriage & private vehicle
   hire legislation & licensing enforcement
● Mtgs - ET
✕ 2007-08 National Association of Taxi & Private HGire Licensing
   & Enforcement Officers

National Association for Literature Development (NALD) 1994
■ PO Box 49657, LONDON, N8 7YZ. (mail/address)
   020 7272 8386
   email director@nald.org   http://www.nald.org
   Dir: Melanie Abrahams
▲ Company Limited by Guarantee
○ *P; for literature professionals & those working in writng &
   reading & developing literature audiences
● Conf - Mtgs - ET - Inf
< The Literature Consortium
M 200 ii, 110 f
   (Sub: £30 - £50)
¶ Literature professional (online pdf) - 4; ftm.

National Association of Local Councils (NALC) 1947
NR 109 Great Russell St, LONDON, WC1B 3LD. (hq)
   020 7637 1865   fax 020 7436 7451
   email nalc@nalc.gov.uk   http://www.nalc.gov.uk
▲ Un-incorporated Society
○ *N; to promote interests of parish, community & town councils;
   to assist them in the performance of their duties; to promote
   social, cultural & recreational life of parishes & villages
● Conf - Mtgs - ET - Exhib - Inf - Empl - LG
< Intl U Local Authorities
M 10,000 parish, community & town councils in England & Wales
¶ Local Council Review.   Various other publications.

National Association of Local Councils in Wales
   in 2004 merged with the Wales Association of Community & Town
   Councils to form **One Voice Wales**

National Association of Local Government Arts Officers (NALGAO) 1997
■ Oak Villa, off Amman Rd, Lower Brynamman, AMMANFORD,
   Carmarthenshire, SA18 1SN. (hq)
   01269 824728   fax 01269 824728
   email nalgao@aol.com   http://www.nalgao.org +
   http://www.nalgao-goodcompanion.org.uk
   Admin: Pete Bryan
▲ Registered Charity
○ *A, *P; for logal government arts officers & those in the creative
   industries sector
Gp Local authority arts officers &those working in the creative
   industries sector
● Conf - Mtgs - ET - Res - SG - Stat - Inf - VE - LG
< Arts at the Heart - 3.
M 45 i, 333 f, 34 org
¶ NL - 3; ftm only.

National Association for Managers of Student Services in Colleges (NAMSS)
■ PO Box 529, WESTON-super-MARE, Somerset, BS23 9EQ.
   01934 811275   fax 01934 811275
   Admin: Tina Philp
○ *P

National Association of Master Bakers (NAMB) 1887
NR 21 Baldock St, WARE, Herts, SG12 9DH. (hq)
   01920 468061   fax 01920 461632
   Chief Exec: David Smith
○ *T; to represent craft bakery businesses in England & Wales
M f

National Association of Master Letter Carvers   (NAMLC)
1920
- ■ c/o NAMM, 1 Castle Mews, RUGBY, Warks, CV21 2XL.   (hq)
  01788 542264   fax 01788 542276
  Sec: John Smith
- ▲ Un-incorporated Society
- ○ *P; to preserve & promote hand carved lettering in stone, marble & granite
- ● Mtgs - Empl
- M 50 i
- ¶ LM; free.

National Association of Mathematics Advisers   (NAMA)   1974
- NR PO Box 51, Glos, GL12 7XA.
  email enquiries@nama.org.uk   http://www.nama.org.uk
  Hon Sec: Brian Robinson
- ▲ Un-incorporated Society
- ○ *E, *P; to disseminate information & ideas on all subjects relating to maths education; to promote specific policies on maths education
- ● Conf - ET - SG - LG
- M 350 i
- ¶ NL - 3; ftm.

National Association for Medical Education Management
(NAMEM)   1975
- ■ Education Centre, Southend University Hospital, WESTCLIFF-on-SEA, Essex, SS0 0RY.   (hsp)
  01702 385082
  email jsharpe@southend.nhs.uk
  http://www.namem.org.uk
  Locum Sec: Mrs Judi Sharpe
- ○ *N, *P; organisation & administration of postgraduate medical training for dentists & doctors
- ● Conf - Mtgs - ET - SG
- < Nat Assn Clinical Tutors (NACT)
- > NAMPS; Middlesex University
- M 250 i
- ¶ NL - 2.   AR - 1.   LM - 1.
  Reference Hbk - 1.   Training Programme 3-yr course; £1,200.
  Council Hbk - 1.

National Association of Memorial Masons   (NAMM)   1907
- ■ 1 Castle Mews, RUGBY, Warks, CV21 2XL.   (hq)
  01788 542264   fax 01788 542276
  email enquiries@namm.org.uk
  http://www.namm.org.uk
  Pres: Penny Lymn Rose
- ▲ Company Limited by Guarantee
- ○ *T; interests of memorial masonry industry (natural stone memorials)
- ● Conf - Mtgs - ET - Exam - Res - Exhib - Comp - Inf - VE - Empl - LG
- < Intl Monument Fedn; EURO-ROC; Coun of Brit Funeral Services; Confedn of Burial Authorities (UK)
- M 25 i, 400 f, UK / 5 i, 25 f, o'seas
- ¶ Review (Jnl) - 4; ftm only.

National Association for Mental After-Care in Residential Care Homes   (MARCH)   1989
- ■ 10 Holmwood Avenue, UDDINGSTON, Lanarkshire, G71 7AJ.   (hq)
  01698 815400
  email ian@silverwellshouse.co.uk
  http://www.march.org.uk
  Sec: Ian Strachan
- ▲ Company Limited by Guarantee; Registered Charity
- ○ *W; to relieve those persons who are, or who have been, suffering from a mental disorder; to secure & enhance their quality of life & assist in the prevention of further episodes of acute illness
- Gp Dementia care (EMI); Respite care
- ● Conf - Mtgs - ET - Res - Exhib - SG - Stat - Inf - LG
- M 70 i
- ¶ MARCH Mental Health Circular - 4; ftm, £2.50 nm.

National Association for the Mentally Handicapped of Ireland
now named **Inclusion Ireland**

National Association of Microwave Engineers   (NAME)
- NR 5 Bournemouth Drive, SEAHAM, Co Durham, SR7 8HB.
  email nameoffice@ntlworld.com
- ○ *T
  no further information supplied.

National Association of Mining History Organisations
(NAMHO)   1979
- NR Peak District Mining Museum, The Pavilion, MATLOCK BATH, Derbys, DE4 3NR.   (hq)
  01629 583834
  http://www.namho.org
  Hon Sec: S Bassham
- ▲ Registered Charity
- ○ *L, *N; for learned & research organisations; to promote development of knowledge of mining history
- ● Conf - Res - SG - Inf - VE - LG - Field meetings - Formation of codes of practice
- < Assn of Indl Archaeology; Brit Cave Res Assn; Nat Caving Assn
- M 7 f, 73 org, UK / 1 org, o'seas
- ¶ NL - 3; ftm, £1 nm.   Mining Heritage Guide; £5 m, £6 nm.
  Code of Practice for: Mineral collecting, Removal of artefacts, Mine exploration; free for sae please.   Publicity leaflet.

National Association of Mortgage Victims
- NR PO Box 1869, Cheadle, STOKE-on-TRENT, Staffs, ST10 4WA.
  01889 507394
  http://www.namv.org.uk
- ○ *K

National Association of Music Educators   (NAME)   1947
- ■ Gordon Lodge, Snitterton Rd, MATLOCK, Derbys, DE4 3LZ. (hq)
  01629 760791   fax 01629 760791
  email musiceducation@name.org.uk
  http://www.name.org.uk
  Admin: Helen Fraser
- ▲ Company Limited by Guarantee; Registered Charity
- ○ *D, *E; for all involved in the furtherance of musical education
- Gp Music curriculum: Primary, Secondary; Initial teacher training & higher education; Advisers, inspectors, consultants; Corporate members
- ● Conf - Mtgs - ET - Res - Inf - LG
- < Music Educ Coun; Fedn of Music Services; Scot Assn of Music Educators; Welsh Music Inf Centre (CAGAC)
- M 556 i, 53 org, UK / 4 i, o'seas
- ¶ Name magazine - 3; ftm, £3.50 nm.
  Postbag (NL) - 4; ftm, £1 nm.

National Association of Musical Instrument Repairers
(NAMIR)   1993
- ■ 42 Marine Parade, HYTHE, Kent, CT21 6AN.   (hsp)
  email secretary@namir.org.uk   http://www.namir.org.uk
  Hon Sec: Chris McNeilly
- ▲ Un-incorporated Society
- ○ *P; to encourage a high standard of workmanship & customer care; to provide a means of information exchange on techniques & parts availability; to provide technical backup where required; to advance technical skills by cooperation with manufacturers; to act as arbitrator in the event of a dispute between repairer & customer
- Gp Woodwind; Brass; Strings; Baroque instruments; Suppliers
- ● Conf - Mtgs - ET - Inf - VE
- < Nat Assn of Profl Band Instrument Repair Technicians (NAPBIRT (USA))
- M 136 i, 6 f, UK / 12 i, o'seas
- ¶ The Intrepid Repairer - 4; ftm.

© CBD Research Ltd · Beckenham · BR3 5JS · Tel 020 8650 7745 · Fax 020 8650 0768 · E-mail cbd@cbdresearch.com · www.cbdresearch.com

National Association of Nappy Services   (NANS)   1992
NR   Unit 1 Hall Farm, Mill Lane, South Moreton, DIDCOT, Oxon,
    OX11 9AH.
    0121-693 4949
    http://www.changeanappy.co.uk
    Contact: Ian Rapley
▲   Un-incorporated Society
○   *T; for cotton nappy laundering services
●   Conf - Mtgs - Exhib - Inf - LG
    Helpline: 0121-693 4949
<   Real Nappy Assn
M   30 f

**National Association of NFU Group Secretaries   (NAGS)
1947**
NR   Woodside Industrial Estate, Llanbadoc, USK, Monmouthshire,
    NP15 1SS.   (hsb)
    01291 672715   fax 01291 673835
    Gen Sec: Andy Hilditch
▲   Un-incorporated Society
○   *T; 'to represent the business & welfare interests of agents of
    the NFU Mutual & Farming Union Secretaries to their
    principals, & otherwise promote the prosperity of their
    business'
Gp   Education; Financial services; Insurance; IT & group services
●   Conf - Mtgs - ET - SG - Stat - Inf - Empl
M   430 i, 300 f
¶   NL - 4; ftm.

National Association of Non-Principals
    since 2004 **National Association of Sessional GPs**

National Association of Nurses for Contraception & Sexual Health
NR   5 Rectory Close, Drayton Bassett, TAMWORTH, Staffs,
    B78 3UH.
    07511 639650
○   *M, *P

**National Association of Official Prison Visitors   (NAOPV)
1924**
NR   Azure House, 10 Imperial Ave, WESTCLIFF-on-SEA, Essex,
    SS0 8NE.   (hsp)
    01702 345083
    Gen Sec: Ian Currie
Br   40
○   *W
●   Conf - Mtgs - LG (Home Office)
M   1,400 i
¶   NL - 2; ftm.
✕   2003 National Association of Prison Visitors

**National Association of Ovulation Method Instructors UK
(NAOMI)   1978**
■   The Billings Method Centre, 4 Southgate Drive, CRAWLEY,
    W Sussex, RH10 6RP.   (pres/p)
    01444 881744   fax 01444 881744
    http://www.billingsnaomi.org
    Pres: Dr Helen Davies
▲   Registered Charity
○   *P; to provide information & authentic literature on the Billings
    Ovulation Method of natural family planning to achieve, or
    avoid, a pregnancy
●   ET (for qualifications to instruct) - Inf - Lib
<   Wld Org of the Ovulation Method Billings (WOOMB)
M   i

National Association of Paper Merchants   (NAPM)   1920
NR   PO Box 2850, NOTTINGHAM, NG5 2WW.   (hq)
    0115-841 2129
    email info@napm.org.uk   http://www.napm.org.uk
    Dir: Tim Bowler
▲   Un-incorporated Society
○   *T
●   Conf - Mtgs - Stat - Inf - Lib - LG
M   21 f

National Association of Paralegals
    since 2005 **National Association of Licensed Paralegals**

**National Association of Park Home Residents   (NAPHR)
1982**
■   Flat B, 38 Abergele Rd, COLWYN BAY, LL29 7PA.   (hq)
    01492 535677
    email jim@naphr.org   http://www.naphr.org
    Chmn: Jim Winchester
▲   Un-incorporated Society
○   *G; voluntary advisory group serving the interests of park home
    / mobile home owner occupiers on permanently licensed
    parks
Gp   Mobile home law
●   Inf
M   10,000 i
¶   NAPHR NL - irreg; ftm.

**National Association for Pastoral Care in Education   (NAPCE)
1982**
NR   175 Butt Lane, Allesley, COVENTRY, Warks, CV5 9FD.   (hq)
    07531 453670
    email base@napce.org.uk   http://www.napce.org.uk
    Chmn: Jae Bray
▲   Registered Charity
Br   13
○   *E, *W; 'promoting pastoral care & personal-social education'
●   Conf - Mtgs - ET - Res - Comp - Inf
M   800 i, 1,200 org, UK / 50 i, o'seas
¶   Pastoral Care in Education (Jnl) - 4; ftm, £4 each nm.
    AR; free.

National Association for Patient Participation   (N.A.P.P.)   1978
NR   10 Rosegarth Avenue, Aston, Sheffield, S26 2DD.
    (mail/address)
    Hon Sec: Audrey Hoggard
▲   Registered Charity
○   *W; to develop & maintain patient participation at surgeries &
    health care centres; to facilitate improved networking of
    patients within primary care groups; individuals can affiliate
●   Conf - Mtgs - ET - LG
M   c 200 groups
¶   NL - 4; m only.
    Note: it is a legal requirement that this Association uses full
    stops in its abbreviation

National Association of Pension Funds Ltd   (NAPF)   1923
NR   NIOC House, 4 Victoria St, LONDON, SW1H 0NX.   (hq)
    020 7808 1300
    http://www.napf.co.uk
○   *T

**National Association for People Abused in Childhood
(NAPAC)   1997**
■   42 Curtain Rd, LONDON, EC2A 3NH.
    http://www.napac.org.uk
▲   Registered Charity
○   *W
●   Helpline: 0800 085 3330
    no further information supplied

National Association of Percussion Teachers (NAPT) 1984
- ■ 11 Mallard Close, Kempshott, BASINGSTOKE, Hants, RG22 5JP. (hsp)
  01256 329009
  email wendy@waba4.co.uk   http://www.napt.org.uk
  Hon Sec: Wendy Harding
- ○ *D, *P; for teachers, instructors & players of percussion instruments
- Gp Percussion teachers & performers
- ● Conf - ET - Lib
- M 200 i, 8 f, UK / 10 i, o'seas
- ¶ NL - 3; ftm only.

National Association for Pre-Paid Funeral Plans (NAPFP) 1993
- NR 15 Riverside Drive, SOLIHULL, W Midlands, B91 3HH. (hq)
  0121-705 5133
  http://www.napfp.co.uk
  Sec: Nigel Burton
- ▲ Un-incorporated Society
- ○ *T; to serve the interests of members in providing pre-paid funeral plans for clients (incl ensuring the security of funds entrusted for this purpose) & maintaining a high standard of integrity in the marketing & selling of such plans
- ● Inf - LG
- M 9 f
- ¶ Code of Practice - 1;   AR - 1;
  Independent Chairman's Report on Adherence to Code of Practice - 1; all ftm.

National Association for Premenstrual Syndrome (NAPS) 1984
- ■ 41 Old Rd, EAST PECKHAM, Kent, TN12 5AP. (hq)
  0870 777 2178   fax 0870 777 2178
  email naps@pms.org.uk   http://www.pms.org.uk
  Chief Exec: Christopher Ryan
- ▲ Registered Charity
- ○ *W; to provide support, help & information to women who suffer pre-menstrual syndrome & their families; works to promote better understanding of the condition & its treatment
- ● Conf
  Helpline: 0870 777 2177
- < Long-term Med Conditions Alliance
- M c 850 i
- ¶ NL - 12;   Understanding PMS.
  Diet books & other publications.

National Association of Press Agencies Ltd (NAPA) 1983
- ■ c/o Mercury Press Agency, Unit 218 Century Buildings, Tower St, LIVERPOOL, L3 4BJ. (asa)
  0870 609 1935
  http://www.napa.org.uk
  The Administrator
- ▲ Company Limited by Guarantee
- Br 46; 3
- ○ *T; for news & photographic agencies, established correspondents for all leading newspapers, magazines, TV & broadcasting outlets
- ● Conf - Mtgs
- M 46 f, UK / 3 f, o'seas
- ¶ NAPA Hbk - 1.

National Association of Primary Care (NAPC) 1998
- NR Lettsom House, 11 Chandos St, Cavendish Sq, LONDON, W1G 9DP. (hq)
  020 7636 7228   fax 020 7636 1601
- ○ *N; for all practices working as Primary Care Groups
- ●
  Helpline: 020 7636 1677 (Mon-Fri 0900-1700)
- M org

National Association of Primary Care Educators UK (NAPCE) 1990
- NR DTE House, Hollins Mount, BURY, Lancs, BL9 8AT. (hq)
  0161-796 1212
  email napce@btinternet.com   http://www.napce.net
  Chmn: Dr Stephen Holmes
- ▲ Registered Charity
- ○ *E, *M, *P
- ● Conf - Mtgs - ET
- ¶ NL - 4; free.
  List of publications available.

National Association for Primary Education (NAPE) 1980
- ■ Moulton College, Moulton, NORTHAMPTON, NN2 8PR. (hq)
  01604 647646   fax 01604 647660
  email nationaloffice@nape.org.uk
  http://www.nape.org.uk
  Gen Sec: John Coe
- ▲ Registered Charity
- Br 4
- ○ *E; partnership between parents & teachers & any other interested individuals, in the promotion & provision of primary & pre-school education; the professional development of all who work with primary children
- ● Conf - Mtgs - ET - Res - Exhib - SG - Inf - Lib - LG
- < Design & Technology Assn
- M a network of c 2,500
- ¶ Newsbrief (NL) - 3;   NAPE News - 3; both ftm only. Primary First - 3; ftm, £5 each nm.

National Association of Private Ambulance Services (NAPAS) 1987
- ■ 21 Bassenhally Rd, WHITTLESEY, Cambs, PE7 1RN. (hsp)
  01733 350916   fax 01733 350112
  email napas@ambulanceservices.co.uk
  http://www.ambulanceservices.co.uk
  Nat Dir: Peter A Littledyke
- ▲ Un-incorporated Society
- Br 53; 3 Republic of Ireland
- ○ *P; to ensure standards in the provision of independent, private & professional ambulance & ambulance aid in the UK & throughout Europe
- Gp Equestrian; Boxing; Motor sport; Pop concerts; Repatriation; NHS contracting; Rave parties; Club medics; Ambulance services: Air, Rail, Road, Ice sports; Advisory & contingency for all events & business
- ● Conf - Mtgs - ET - Res - SG - Stat - Inf - Lib - PL - LG
- < Brit Ambulance Services Panel; DTI Foresight
- M 53 f, UK / 3 f, o'seas
- ¶ NAPAS News & Views - 4; ftm only.
  NAPAS Code of Practice & Annual Members Audit - 1; ftm, 4x1st class stamps, nm.

National Association of Probation & Bail Hostels
  since 2007 **National Approved Premises Association**

National Association of Probation Officers (NAPO) 1912
- NR 3-4 Chivalry Rd, LONDON, SW11 1HT. (hq)
  020 7223 4887   fax 020 7223 3503
  email info@napo.org.uk   http://www.napo.org.uk
- ○ *P, *U

National Association of Professional Inspectors & Testers (NAPIT) 1992
- NR Mill 3 (4th floor), Pleasey Vale Business Park, MANSFIELD, Notts, NG19 8RL.
  0870 444 1392   fax 0870 444 1427
  http://www.napit.org.uk
  Chief Exec: John Andrews
- ○ inspectors and testers of electrical, plumbing, heating and ventilation systems

© CBD Research Ltd · Beckenham · BR3 5JS · Tel 020 8650 7745 · Fax 020 8650 0768 · E-mail cbd@cbdresearch.com · www.cbdresearch.com

National Association of Professionals concerned with Language Impairment in Children (NAPLIC) 1986
NR 29 Franklands Drive, Rowtown, ADDLESTONE, Surrey, KT15 1EG.
  http://www.naplic.org.uk
  Chmn: John Parrott
○ teachers, speech and language therapists and other professionals

National Association for Providers of Activities for Older People (NAPA) 1997
■ Bondway Commercial Centre (5th floor), Unit 5 12, 71 Bondway, LONDON, SW8 1SQ.   (hq)
  020 7078 9375   fax 020 7735 9634
  email sylvie@napa-activities.co.uk
  http://www.napa-activities.net
  Strategic Dir: Mrs Sylvie Silver
▲ Company Limited by Guarantee; Registered Charity
○ *W; to provide activities for older people, essential to the maintenance of physical & psychological health & well-being; to provide education & training; to support individuals who provide activities, whether in home or care settings
● ET - Res - Inf
M 660 i
¶ NAPA NL - 3; ftm.

National Association of Public Golf Courses   (NAPGC)   1927
■ 12 Newton Close, REDDITCH, Worcs, B98 7YR.   (hsp)
  01527 542106   fax 01527 455320
  email eddiemitchell@blueyonder.co.uk
  http://www.napgc.org.uk
  Hon Sec: Ed Mitchell
▲ Un-incorporated Society
○ *S; to represent public pay & play golf courses in the UK
M 100 clubs & members
¶ Annual Competitions Review - 1; ftm.   Ybk.

National Association of Railway Clubs   (NARC)   1952
■ 2 Romsey Rd, EASTLEIGH, Hants, SO50 9FE.   (hq)
  023 8032 2686   fax 023 8039 9736
  email narcsrmb@aol.com
  http://www.railsocialclubs.co.uk
  Gen Sec: Malcolm Brown
▲ Un-incorporated Society
Br 180
○ *N; fo sports & community clubs
M [not stated]

National Association of Range Manufacturers   1933
NR c/o Preston & Thomas Ltd, Woodville Engineering Works, Heron Rd, Rumney, CARDIFF, Glamorgan, CF3 3YF.   (sb)
  029 2079 3331   fax 029 2077 9195
  Sec: Simon Preston
○ *T; interests of makers & suppliers of equipment for fried fish & chip restaurants

National Association of Re-enactment Societies   (NARES)   1991
NR Alma House, 72 Cow Close Rd, LEEDS, W Yorks, LS12 5PD.   (hsp)
  0113-229 6759
  email des1622@ntlworld.com
  Conact: Des Thomas
▲ Un-incorporated Society
○ *G, *N; to represent the interests of British re-enactors
● Conf - Mtgs - ET - Res - Exhib - SG - Inf - PL
M 5,000 i, 25 f
¶ Retrospection - 4; ftm, £1 nm.

National Association of Reformed Offenders
  alternative name of **Unlock**

National Association of Registered Home Inspectors (NARHI) 2006
NR 1 Gleneagles House, Vernongate, DERBY, DE1 1UP.
  01332 225016
  http://www.narhi.org
  Chmn: Hugh Dunsmore-Hardy
○ *P; to promote the role of the home inspector and energy assessor

National Association of Registered Petsitters
NR PO Box 1433, OXFORD, OX4 9AU.
  0845 230 8544
  email info@dogsit.com   http://www.dogsit.com
  Chmn: Robin Taylor
○ *G

National Association for the Relief of Paget's Disease (NARPD) 1973
NR 323 Manchester Rd, Walkden, Worsley, MANCHESTER, M28 3HH.   (hq)
  0161-799 4646   fax 0161-799 6511
○ *W; to support & inform sufferers of Paget's disease of bone, & their carers; to raise awareness of the disease among the medical profession & the public at large; to support & raise funds for research

National Association of Retired Police Officers   (NARPO) 1919
NR 38 Bond St, WAKEFIELD, W Yorks, WF1 2QP.   (hq)
  01924 362166   fax 01924 372088
  email narpo.org.uk
  Chief Exec: Mike Thornton
▲ Un-incorporated Society
Br 120
○ *P; 'to safeguard the rights of members & promote measures for their welfare with particular regard to pensions'
● Conf - Mtgs - Inf - Pension matters - Appeals & benefits
< Public Services Pensioners Coun
M 100,000 i
¶ Magazine - 4; ftm only.

National Association of Road Transport Museums   (NARTM) 1982
■ PO Box 5141, BURTON upon TRENT, Staffs, DE15 0ZF.   (chmn/b)
  http://www.nartm.org.uk
  Chmn: Dennis Talbot
▲ Un-incorporated Society
Br 25
○ *G, *N; to assist the development of volunteer-operated road transport museums by the exchange of information & expertise. To monitor the introduction of legislation which may affect the continued operation of historic road vehicles
Gp Vehicle database - listing historic buses & coaches in collections
● Mtgs - Stat - Inf - VE - LG
< Fedn Brit Historic Vehicle Clubs
M c 60 org
¶ The Bulletin - 4; ftm only.

National Association of Rooflight Manufacturers   (NARM) 1988
■ 43 Clare Croft, Middleton, MILTON KEYNES, MK10 9HD.   (hq)
  01908 692325
  email admin@narm.org.uk   http://www.narm.org.uk
  Sec: Lorraine Cookham
○ *T; represents manufacturers of rooflights & raw materials in the UK; to enhance & improve standards within the UK & Europe on all types of rooflight products; to provide assistance to architects & other specifiers
Gp Technical c'ee
● Mtgs
< Construction Products Assn
M 7 f, UK / 4 f, o'seas
  (Sub: £2,500 UK / £1,250 o'seas)
¶ Publications available on website only.

National Association of Round Tables of Great Britain & Ireland   (RTBI)   1927
- ■ Marchesi House, 4 Embassy Drive, Edgbaston, BIRMINGHAM, B15 1TP.   (hq)
  0121-456 4402
  email hq@roundtable.org.uk
  http://www.roundtable.org.uk
  Admin: Maureen Huggins
- ○ *W, *X; service to community through cultivation of highest ideals in business, professional & civic traditions
- M   c 10,000 i

National Association of School Governors
  in 2006 merged with the National Governors' Council to form the
  National Governors' Association

National Association of Schoolmasters Union of Women Teachers   (NASUWT)   1919
- ■ Hillscourt Education Centre, Rose Hill, Rednal, BIRMINGHAM, B45 8RS.   (hq)
  0121-453 6150   fax 0121-457 6208
  email nasuwt@mail.nasuwt.org.uk
  http://www.teachersunion.org.uk
  Gen Sec: Chris Keates
- Br   360; Cyprus, Germany, Gibraltar, Guernsey, Jersey
- ○ *E, *P, *U
- ● Conf - Mtgs - ET - Res - Exhib - Comp - Empl - LG
- <   Educ Intl
- M   265,202 i
- ¶   Teaching Today - termly; ftm.

National Association of Screen Make-up Artists & Hairdressers (NASMAH)   2000
- ■ 68 Sarsfield Rd, PERIVALE, Middx, UB6 7AG.   (chmn/p)
  020 8998 7494   fax 020 8998 7494
  email info@nasmah.co.uk   http://www.nasmah.co.uk
  Sec: Angela Seyfang,   Chmn: Sandra Exelby
- ○ *P; to raise the standards of make-up artists & hairdressers in this country; to improve training & raise the profile of members in the media industry
- Gp   Training; Seminars; Master classes; Courses
- ● ET
- M   200 i
- ¶   NL - 4; free.

National Association of Security Dog Users   (NASDU)   1996
- ■ Unit 11 Boundary Business Centre, WOKING, Surrey, GU21 5DH.   (mailink/address)
  01483 888588   fax 01483 486335
  email info@nasdu.co.uk   http://www.nasdu.co.uk
  Co Sec: Steve Hill
- ▲ Company Limited by Guarantee
- ○ *P; to achieve, promote & maintain national standards for all trainers, handlers & dogs within the security industry; for those who are concerned the care, health, safety & welfare of dogs within the industry
- Gp   Training sub-c'ee; Detection dogs (incl drugs & explosives)
- ● Conf - Mtgs - ET - Exam - Res - Inf - LG - Annual working security dogs trials
- <   Brit Inst of Profl Dog Trainers; Skills for Security
- M   200+ i, 60 f, 10 org, UK / 10 i, o'seas
- ¶   NL - 4; ftm, £2 nm.   Code of Practice; £25.
  Pocket Reference Guide; £5.
  Underpinning Knowledge Pack; £25 m, £32.50 nm.
  Trainers Pack; £150 m only.

National Association of Seed Potato Merchants
  in 2006 merged with the Scottish Potato Trades Association to form the **British Potato Trades Association**

National Association of Sessional GPs   (NASGP)   1997
- NR   PO Box 188, CHICHESTER, W Sussex, PO19 2ZA.   (hsp)
  fax 01243 536428
  email info@nasgp.org.uk   http://www.nasgp.org.uk
  Chief Exec: Richard Fieldhouse
- ▲ Company Limited by Guarantee
- ○ *P; voluntary organisation supporting sessional (salaried & freelance) general practitioners
- Gp   GPs: salaried; Freelance/locum
- ● Inf
- M   1,500 i
- ¶   The Sessional GP - 6; ftm, £5 nm.
- ×   2004 National Association of Non-Principals

National Association of Shopfitters   (NAS)   1919
- ■ 411 Limpsfield Rd, The Green, WARLINGHAM, Surrey, CR6 9HA.   (hq)
  01883 624961
  http://www.shopfitters.org
  Dir: R Hudson
- Br   4
- ○ *T
- ● Conf - Mtgs - Comp - Stat - Expt - Inf
- <   Intl Shopfitting Org; Australian Shopfitters Assn; NZ Shopfitters Assn
- M   f

National Association for Small Schools   (NASS)   1978
- ■ Quarrenden, Upper Red Cross Rd, GORING-on-THAMES, Berks, RG8 9BD.   (nat/coord/p)
  01491 873548
  email mbenford@bigfoot.com
  http://www.smallschools.org.uk
  Sec: Barbara Taylor
- ○ *E, *K, *N; to advance the case for retaining small local schools, mainly those threatened with closure; to promote good practice in both school & community
- ● Conf - Res - Inf
- <   Interskola (education in sparsely populated areas)
- >   Human Scale Education; Village Retail Services Assn
- M   600 i & gps, UK / 15 i & gps, o'seas
- ¶   NL - 2.

National Association of Social Workers in Education (NASWE)   1884
- NR   c/o National Children's Bureau, 8 Wakley St, LONDON, EC1V 7QE.   (gsp)
  020 7843 6000
  http://www.naswe.org.uk
  Gen Sec: Jacqui Newvell
- ▲ Un-incorporated Society
- ○ *E, *P; for all education welfare officers & education social workers working for a local education authority
- ● Conf - Mtgs - ET - LG
- <   UNISON
- M   c 500 i
- ¶   The Education Social Worker - 3; ftm, on request nm.

National Association of Sole Practitioners
  see **Solicitor Sole Practitioners Group**

National Association for Special Educational Needs
  since 2004-05 **nasen**

© CBD Research Ltd · Beckenham · BR3 5JS · Tel 020 8650 7745 · Fax 020 8650 0768 · E-mail cbd@cbdresearch.com · www.cbdresearch.com

National Association of Specialist Computer Retailers (NASCR) 1988
■ West Orchard, Waddingham Rd, SOUTH KELSEY, Lincs, LN7 6PN.   (hq)
01652 678876   fax 01652 678876
http://www.nascr.net
Chmn: Mrs Jenny Stimson
▲ Un-incorporated Society
○ *T; to represent independent computer retailers & other companies involved in the computer industry; to promote fair practices within the industry & for the consumer; to clarify new legislation
● Conf - Mtgs - Exhib - LG
> NBG
M 68 f
(Sub: £75)
¶ NASCR NL; ftm only.

National Association for Sports Development
in 2007 merged with the Institute for Leisure & Amenity Management to form the **Institute for Sport, Parks & Leisure**

National Association of Stable Staff   (NASS)   1975
■ 74 High St, SWADLINCOTE, Derbys, DE11 8HS.   (hq)
01283 211522   fax 01283 550821
email office@naoss.co.uk   http://www.naoss.co.uk
Chief Exec: Jim Cornelius
○ *U; for racing stable staff
● Conf - Mtgs - ET - Comp - SG - Stat
< GFTU
M 1,600 i
¶ Stable Talk - 4; free.
✕ 2007 (September) Stable Lads Association

National Association for Staff Development in the Post-16 Sector
in 2007 merged with the **Further Education Research Association**

National Association of Steel Stockholders   (NASS)   1928
■ The Citadel (1st floor), 190 Corporation St, BIRMINGHAM, B4 6QD.   (hq)
0121-200 2288   fax 0121-236 7444
email info@nass.org.uk   http://www.nass.org.uk
Dir Gen: Bryan Holden
○ *T
Gp Product Gps: General steels, Strip mill coil & sheet, Bright & engineering steels, Stainless steels, Tubes, Plate & processing
Specialist c'ee: Health & safety
● Conf - Mtgs - ET - Exhib - SG - Stat - Inf - VE - LG
< EUROMETAL; is a member of Metals Forum
M 113 f
¶ NASS News (NL) - 4.   LM.   AR.
Steel & Its Distribution.
Safety Guidelines for Steel Stockholders & Processors.
Beating the Odds [&] Moving Steel by Crane (health & safety video).

National Association for the Support of Victims of Stalking & Harassment   (NASH)   1993
NR PO Box 1309, KENILWORTH, Warks, CV8 2YJ.
01926 850089
Dir: Evonne von Heussen-Countryman
○ *W; to support & advise the victims of stalking & harassment, in any circumstances, & their families; to provide expert witnesses in court cases
Note: Please enclose an SAE when writing to the Association.

National Association of Supported Employment
2006 merged with the Association for Supported Employment to form the **British Association for Supported Employment**

National Association of Supporting Artistes Agents   (NASAA)
NR 373-377 Clapham Rd, LONDON, SW9 9BT.
email chair@nasaa.org.uk
Chmn: Sarah Dickinson
○ *T

National Association of Swimming Clubs for the Handicapped (NASCH)   1965
NR The Willows, Mayles Lane, WICKHAM, Hants, PO17 5ND.
01329 833689
http://www.nasch.org.uk
Nat Coordinator: Mike O'Leary
○ *S; to promote swimming & swimming clubs for people with disabilities

National Association of Taxi & Private Hire Licensing Enforcement Officers
since 2007-08 **National Association of Licensing & Enforcement Officers**

National Association of Teachers of Dancing Ltd   (NATD) 1906
■ 44-47 The Broadway, THATCHAM, Berks, RG19 3HP.   (hq)
01635 868888   fax 01635 872301
email info@natd.org.uk   http://www.natd.org.uk
Sec: Mrs Lyn Foster
▲ Company Limited by Guarantee
Br worldwide
○ *D, *P; to promote & improve the art of dancing in all its forms - ballroom, theatrical & social
Gp Ballroom; Latin American; Classic & sequence; Ballet; Tap; Modern stage; Acrobatic; Disco free-style; Rock'n'roll; National dance; Dance & exercise; Country & Western; Contemporary dance; Street
● Conf - Mtgs - ET - Exam
M 2,500 i, UK / 500 i, o'seas
¶ NL - 4; free.   AR - 1; ftm only.
Mail shots - new dances etc - irreg; ftm.

National Association of Teachers of Religious Education (NATRE)   1985
NR 1020 Bristol Rd, Selly Oak, BIRMINGHAM, W Midlands, B29 6LB.   (hq)
0121-472 4242   fax 0121-472 7575
email retoday@retoday.org.uk   http://www.natre.org.uk
Gen Sec: Peter Fishpool
▲ Un-incorporated Society
○ *E, *P, *R; for teachers of religious education in schools & colleges
Gp Examinations & assessment
● Conf - Mtgs - ET - Res - Comp - LG
< Eur Fedn Teachers of Religious Educ
M 2,500 i
¶ Resource - 3; ftm only.
✕ 2008 Professional Council for Religious Education

National Association of Teachers of Travellers   (NATT)   1980
NR Newham Traveller Education Service, Credon Centre, Kirton Rd, LONDON, E13 9BT.   (pres/b)
020 8430 6279
http://www.natt.org.uk
Pres: Anthea Wormington
▲ Company Limited by Guarantee; Registered Charity
○ *E, *P; to promote access to educational opportunities for Gypsies & Travellers as a recognised ethnic group under the Race Relations Act
● Conf - Mtgs - Inf
< Eur Fedn Educ Children Occupational Travellers (EFECOT)
M 200 i
¶ NL - 3; free.   Information Mail Out - 3; ftm only.

National Association for the Teaching of Drama   (NATD)   1977
■   The Kingstone School, Broadway, BARNSLEY, S Yorks, S70 6RB.
   01226 738591
   email k.fechter@barnsley.org
   Admin: Kirsty Fechter
○   *A, *E; the advancement of young people through drama; to encourage & promote the development of drama at all levels of education; to provide support for all involved with drama in education
●   Conf - Mtgs - ET - SG - LG
<   Standing Conf of Young Peoples Theatre (SCYPT)
M   c 120 i
¶   Jnl for Drama in Education - 2; ftm.
   Publication arising from Annual Conference.
   Other occasional publications.

National Association for the Teaching of English   (NATE)
■   50 Broadfield Rd, SHEFFIELD, S Yorks, S8 0XJ.   (hq)
   0114-255 5419   fax 0114-255 5296
   email info@nate.org.uk   http://www.nate.org.uk
   Co Sec: Lyn Fairfax
▲   Registered Charity
Br   13 regions
○   *E, *P; to improve the teaching of English at all levels of education; to provide a national voice on all aspects of education concerning English concerning English
●   Conf - Mtgs - Exhib - SG - Inf
M   [not stated]
¶   English, Drama, Media - 3; ftm, £10 per issue nm.
   NATE Classroom - 3; ftm, £6.50 per issue nm.
   NATE News - 3; ftm only.

National Association for Teaching English & other Community Languages to Adults   (NATECLA)   1976
■   South Birmingham College (room HA205), Hall Green Campus, Cole Bank Rd, BIRMINGHAM, B28 8ES.   (hq)
   0121-688 8121   fax 0121-694 5062
   email co-ordinator@natecla.fsnet.co.uk
   http://www.natecla.org.uk
   Coordinator: Cathy Burns
▲   Un-incorporated Society
Br   10
○   *E, *K, *P; campaigning, information, training for ESOL & other language tutors
●   Conf - ET - Inf - LG
M   489 i, 122 org
¶   NATECLA News - 3; ftm, £2 nm.
   Language Issues [Jnl] - 2; £10 m (£20 instns), £15 nm (£30 instns).

National Association of Tenants Organisations   (NATO)
IRL   35 Meath Place, DUBLIN 8, Republic of Ireland.
   353 (1) 454 3842   fax 353 (1) 454 3842
   Gen Sec: Matt Larkin
○   *G

National Association of Theatre Nurses
   since April 2005 the **Association for Perioperative Practice**

National Association for Therapeutic Education   (NATE)   1995
■   59 Birdham Rd, CHICHESTER, W Sussex, PO19 8TB.   (hsp)
   01243 776042
   email john.tierney@virgin.net
   Dir: John Tierney
▲   Un-incorporated Society
○   *E, *P; to promote understanding of therapeutic education; to provide a focus for workers in the field
●   Mtgs - Res - LG - Lobbyists
M   c 95 i

National Association of Toastmasters   (NAT)   1952
■   Durfold Cottage, Buckhorn Weston, GILLINGHAM, Dorset, SP8 5HS.   (hsp)
   01963 370604
   http://www.natuk.com
   Hon Sec: Peter Craft
▲   Un-incorporated Society
○   *P; provision of toastmasters for all types of functions worldwide
●   Conf - Mtgs - Exhib
M   62 i
   (Sub: £145)

National Association of Toy & Leisure Libraries   (Play Matters)   (NATLL)   1972
NR   68 Churchway, LONDON, NW1 1LT.   (hq)
   020 7255 4600   fax 020 7255 4602
   email admin@playmatters.co.uk
   http://www.natll.org.uk
▲   Registered Charity
○   *W; to promote the principle that play DOES matter for the developing child; to offer a supportive service to parents & extend the opportunity for shared play in the home;   Leisure libraries extend this concept to adults with special needs
●   Conf - ET - Exhib - Inf - Making available & lending appropriate toys at local level, through toy libraries
<   Intl Toy Libraries Assn
M   c 1,000 libraries
¶   Play Matters (Jnl) - 4; ftm, £1 nm.   AR.
   Publications list available.

National Association of Tree Officers   (NATO)
NR   PO Box 734, MANCHESTER, M60 3UB.
   0161-281 6122   fax 0161-281 6122
   email admin@nato.org.uk   http://www.nato.org.uk
   Admin: David Williams
○   *P

National Association of Tripe Dressers   (NATD)
NR   1 Tuscan Court, 18 The Esplanade, TELSCOMBE CLIFFS, E Sussex, BN10 7HF.   (hsp)
   01273 585422
   Hon Sec: Mrs Jean Beavis
○   *T
●   Mtgs
M   4 f

National Association of UK Regionally Important Geological Sites   (UKRIGS)   1999
■   National Stone Centre, Porter Lane, Middleton, WIRKSWORTH, Derbys, DE4 4LS.   (hsb)
   01384 443644
   email info@ukrigs.org.uk   http://www.ukrigs.org.uk
   Hon Sec: Dr Cheryl Jones
▲   Un-incorporated Society
○   *N; conservation of all the UK important geological & germorphological sites
●   Con f- ET - Res - Inf - VE - LG
M   38 f, 5 org
   (Sub: £5 f, £25 org)
¶   NL - 4; free.

© CBD Research Ltd · Beckenham · BR3 5JS · Tel 020 8650 7745 · Fax 020 8650 0768 · E-mail cbd@cbdresearch.com · www.cbdresearch.com

National Association of Valuers & Auctioneers (NAVA) 1988
- ■ Arbon House, 6 Tournament Court, Edgehill Drive, WARWICK, CV34 6LG. (hsb)
  01926 496800
  http://www.nava.org.uk
  Hon Sec: Peter Bolton King
- ▲ Company Limited by Guarantee
- ○ *P; valuers & auctioneer firms giving independent, impartial valuation advice & asset sales services to business & the public, for finance, company restructuring, insurance, insolvency, asset transfer & probate purposes (covers everything from drawing pins through antiques, plant, machinery to aeroplanes & house sales)
- Gp Insolvency; Fine arts & antiques; Plant & machinery
- ● Conf - Mtgs - ET - Exam - Res - Exhib - Lib
- < Intl Consortium of Real Estate Agents (ICREA);
  Is a subsidiary of the National Association of Estate Agents, a division of the National Federation of Property Professionals
- M 279 i
- ¶ The Gavel (NL) - 4; free.

National Association of Victim Support Schemes
Registered name of **Victim Support**

National Association of Village Shops 2000
- NR Steamer Point, 29 West St, LEWES, E Sussex, BN7 2NZ.
  01273 473422 fax 01273 483109
  email alan.wyle@srcc.org.uk
  http://www.villageshops.org.uk
  Chmn: Alan Wyle
- ○ *T; promoting village shops and rural post offices

National Association for Voluntary & Community Action (NAVCA) 1991
- ■ The Tower, Furnival Square, SHEFFIELD, S Yorks, S1 4QL. (hq)
  0114-278 6636 fax 0114-278 7004
  email navca@navca.org.uk http://www.navca.org.uk
  Chief Exec: Kevin Curley
- ▲ Company Limited by Guarantee; Registered Charity
- ○ *N, *W; to promote, support & develop an effective local voluntary sector; the national forum of local infrastructure organisations
- ● Conf - Mtgs - ET - Inf - LG
- < Nat Coun Voluntary Orgs (NCVO); Standing Conf for Community Devt (SCCD)
- M 350 local infrastructure org
- ¶ NACVS Circulation - 6.
  AR; free. Occasional publications.
- × 2006 (14 June) National Association of Councils for Voluntary Service

National Association of Voluntary Service Managers (NAVSM) 1968
- NR c/o Janet Lloyd, E Kent NHS & Social Care Ptnrship Trust, Littlebourne Rd, CANTERBURY, Kent, CT1 1AZ. (chmn/b)
  01227 812020
  http://www.navsm.org.uk
  Chmn: Janet Lloyd
- ▲ Un-incorporated Society
- ○ *P, *W; for voluntary managers & volunteers in the field of health & social care
- ● Conf - Mtgs - ET - Stat - Inf - LG
- < Volunteer Centre UK
- M 135 i
- ¶ NL - 6; free. AR.

National Association of Waste Disposal Officers (NAWDO)
- NR c/o Cassie Hart-Fisher, East Riding of Yorkshire Council, County Hall, BEVERLEY, HU17 9BA.
  http://www.nawdo.org
  Sec: Cassie Hart-Fisher
- ○ *P
- M i

National Association of Widows (NAW) 1971
- ■ 48 Queen's Rd (3rd floor), COVENTRY, Warks, CV1 3EH. (hq)
  024 7663 4848
  email inf@nawidows.org.uk
  http://www.nawidows.org.uk
  Nat Chmn: Jean Sargent
- ▲ Company Limited by Guarantee; Registered Charity
- Br 34
- ○ *W; run by & for widows & widowers; to provide friendship & support; there are local branches nationwide & headquarters membership is available where there is no local branch
- ● Conf - Mtgs - Comp - LG
  Office hours: 0900-1600 Mon-Fri
- M 3,000 i

National Association of Wine & Beermakers (Amateur) (NAWB(A)) 1961
- ■ 2 St Ives Close, Digswell, WELWYN, Herts, AL6 0BB. (hsp)
  01438 716906
  email secretary@nawb.org.uk http://www.nawb.org.uk
  Sec: Peter Robinson
- ▲ Un-incorporated Society
- ○ *G; to promote the art of home wine & beermaking
- ● Conf - Mtgs - ET - Comp
- M 237 i, 62 org
- ¶ News & Views (NL) - 3; ftm only.

National Association of Women's Clubs (NAWC)
- NR 5 Vernon Rise, King's Cross Rd, LONDON, WC1X 9EP. (hq)
  020 7837 1434 fax 020 7713 0727
  Chmn: Christine Burton
- Br 300
- ○ *E; to advance education & provide facilities for recreation or other leisure time occupations for women, without distinction of political, religious or other opinions
- ● Conf - Mtgs - Comp - SG
- < NCVO; Nat Coun Women; Women's Nat Commission
- M c 7,000 i
- ¶ NL - 6; ftm. Club History; 75p m. AR; ftm, 50p nm.

National Association of Women Pharmacists (NAWP) 1905
- ■ c/o The Office Manager, Royal Pharmaceutical Society of GB, 1 Lambeth High St, LONDON, SE1 7JN. (mail address)
  01453 759516
  email enquiries@nawp.org.uk http://www.nawp.org.uk
  Hon Sec: Mrs Brenda Ecclestone
- ▲ Un-incorporated Society
- Br 3
- ○ *P
- ● Conf - ET - VE
- M c 300 i
- ¶ NL - 4; ftm.

National Association of Writers in Education (NAWE) 1987
- NR PO Box 1, Sheriff Hutton, YORK, YO60 7YU. (mail/address)
  01653 618429
  email info@nawe.co.uk http://www.nawe.co.uk
  Dir: Paul Munden
- ▲ Company Limited by Guarantee
- ○ *A; to promote & support the development of creative writing of all genres in all educational settings
- ● Conf - ET - Res - Inf - LG
- M c 800 i, c 100 f
- ¶ Writing in Education - 3; ftm only.

National Association of Writers' Groups (NAWG) 1995
- ■ 40 Burstall Hill, BRIDLINGTON, E Yorks, YO16 7GA. (hq)
  01262 609228
  Chmn: Mike Wilson
- ▲ Registered Charity, Un-incorporated Society
- ○ *A, *N; to support writers' groups
- ● Conf - Mtgs - ET - Comp - SG - Inf
- M 160 i, f & org
- ¶ Link Magazine - 6; ftm only.

National Association of Youth & Community Education Officers (NAYCEO) 1942
- ■ c/o Barbican Post Office, Barbican Rd, LOOE, Cornwall, PL13 1EZ.
  01503 265300
  Exec Sec: Mike Williams
- ▲ Un-incorporated Society
- ○ *E, *P, *Y
- Gp Professional Services; Social Action; International; Women's Issues
- ● Conf - Mtgs - ET - Exhib - Inf - VE - Empl
- < Nat U of Teachers
- M i
- ¶ AR; ftm.   Policy statements - irreg; ftm.

National Association for Youth Drama   (NAYD)
- IRL 34 Upper Gardiner St, DUBLIN 1, Republic of Ireland.
  353 (1) 878 1301   fax 353 (1) 878 1302
  email info@nayd.ie   http://www.youthdrama.ie
  Dir: Orlaith McBride
- ○ *D, *Y

National Association for Youth Justice   (NAYJ) 1995
- ■ 4 Spring Close, Ratby, LEICESTER, LE6 0XD.   (hsp)
  0116-238 8354
  email enquiries@nayj.org.uk   http://www.nayj.org.uk
  Admin & Devt: Ken Hunnybun
- ○ *K; to promote the rights of, & justice for, children in trouble; to campaign for the development & implementation of policies & practice consistent with this purpose
- ● Conf - Mtgs - ET - Liaison with children's orgs
- > Regional organisations & observers from NI, Scotland & Wales
- M 200 i, associated regional orgs
- ¶ Youth Justice; ftm, £30 nm. (published jointly with Russell House Publishing).

National Association of Youth Orchestras   (NAYO) 1961
- ■ Central Hall, West Tollcross, EDINBURGH, EH3 9BP.   (hq)
  0131-221 1927
  email admin@nayo.org.uk   http://www.nayo.org.uk
  Hon Sec: Keith Horsfall
- ▲ Registered Charity
- ○ *D; to represent youth orchestras throughout the UK; to foster their development
- Gp Festivals of British Youth Orchestras; European Youth Music Week
- ● Conf - Mtgs - ET - Comp - Inf - Lib - VE - LG
- < Intl Arbeitskreis für Musik; Eur Assn Youth Orchestras; Brit Assn of Symphonic Bands & Wind Ensembles; Scot Arts Lobby; Music Educ Coun; Assn of Brit Orchestras; Voluntary Arts Network; Inc Soc of Musicians
- M 4 i, 12 f, 128 org, UK / 1 i, 2 org, o'seas
- ¶ Full Orchestra (NL) - 3; ftm only.   AR - 1.
  Directory of Youth & Student Orchestras, 2002; ftm, £5.50 nm.
  Youth Orchestra Tours Guide; ftm only.

National Association of Youth Theatres   (NAYT) 1982
- ■ The Arts Centre, Vane Terrace, DARLINGTON, Co Durham, DL3 7AX.   (hq)
  01325 363330   fax 01325 363313
  email nayt@btconnect.com   http://www.nayt.org.uk
  Chief Exec: Jill Adamson
- ▲ Company Limited by Guarantee; Registered Charity
- ○ *D; supports the development of Youth Theatre activity; is open to any group or individual using theatre techniques in their work with young people, outside of formal education
- ● Conf - ET - Inf - Big Youth Theatre Festival (4-day workshop & performance programme)
- < Nat Coun for Voluntary Youth Service (NCVSI); Nat Assn of Clubs for Young People (NACYP); Nat Operatic & Dramatic Assn (NODA); Nat Assn Youth Drama (NAYD); Promote Youth Theatre Scotland; Nat Coun of Voluntary Orgs (NCVO)
- M 838 i, youth theatres & groups, UK / 9, o'seas
- ¶ Bulletin - 12;   AR; both ftm only.
  The Big Youth Theatre Manual; £19.99.
  Playing a Part: a study of the impact of youth theatre on the personal, social & political development of young people; £10.

National Asthma Campaign
  since 2004 **Asthma UK**

National Auricula & Primula Society (Midland & West Section) (NAPS) 1901
- NR 9 Church St, Belton, LOUGHBOROUGH, Leics, LE12 9UG.   (hsp)
  01530 222458   fax 01530 222458
  email david.tarver@btinternet.com
  http://www.auriculaandprimula.org.uk
  Hon Sec: David Tarver
- ▲ Un-incorporated Society
- ○ *H; to encourage & extend the cultivation of auriculas & primulas; to preserve & improve accepted standards
- ● Conf - Mtgs - Res - Exhib - Comp - Inf - PL - LG
- < R Horticl Soc
- M c 600 i
- ¶ NL - 2; 25p.   Argus [Ybk] - 1.

National Auricula & Primula Society (Northern) 1872
- ■ 27 Temple Rhydding Drive, Baidon, SHIPLEY, W Yorks, BD17 5PX.   (hsp)
  http://www.auriculas.org.uk
  Hon Sec: R Taylor
- ▲ Un-incorporated Society
- ○ *H; to encourage the growing & exhibition of Auriculas & Primulas
- ¶ Ybk.

National Auricula & Primula Society (Southern) 1876
- ■ 67 Warnham Court Rd, CARSHALTON BEECHES, Surrey, SM5 3ND.   (hsp)
  Hon Sec: L E Wigley
- ○ *H; breeding & cultivation of auriculas, primroses, polyanthuses & other hardy primula species
- ● Exhib - Comp - Inf - Plant sales
- M 400 i, UK / 10 i, o'seas
- ¶ Offsets (NL) - 1; free.   Ybk; ftm, £4 nm.

© CBD Research Ltd · Beckenham · BR3 5JS · Tel 020 8650 7745 · Fax 020 8650 0768 · E-mail cbd@cbdresearch.com · www.cbdresearch.com

National Autistic Society   (NAS)   1962
NR   393 City Rd, LONDON, EC1V 1NG.   (hq)
    020 7833 2299   fax 020 7833 9666
    email nas@nas.org.uk   http://www.nas.org.uk
▲   Company Limited by Guarantee; Registered Charity
Br   45
○   *W; to provide: 1) specialist schools & adult services for people
    with autistic spectrum disorder, 2) supported employment; to
    promote awareness with central government & the public; to
    offer information, advice & support to people with autism &
    their families & carers
●   Conf - ET - Inf - Lib - LG
    Helpline: 0845 070 4004
M   i & org
¶   Publications list available.

National Backpain Association   (BackCare)   1968
■   16 Elmtree Rd, TEDDINGTON, Middx, TW11 8ST.   (hq)
    020 8977 5474   fax 020 8943 5318
    email info@backcare.org.uk
    http://www.backcare.org.uk
    Chief Exec: Mrs Sash Newman
▲   Company Limited by Guarantee; Registered Charity
Br   30
○   *Q, *W; to educate people on how to avoid preventable back
    pain; to support those living with back pain; to promote
    research into causes & treatment of back pain
●   ET - Res - Inf - LG
<   NCVO; Assn of Medical Res Charities (AMRC); Long-term
    Medical Conditions Alliance (LMCA); Arthritis & Musculo-
    Skeletal Alliance (ARMA)
M   4,000 i, 200 f, UK / 100 i, o'seas
¶   Talkback - 4; ftm, £3.95 nm.
    Various books & leaflets.

National Baton Twirling Association   (NBTA)   1982
NR   17 Gard Close, TORQUAY, Devon, TQ2 8QU.   (hsp)
    01803 324175
    http://www.nbta.org.uk
    Sec: Denise Pearse
○   *S; to promote the sport of baton twirling & associated activities
●   Mtgs - ET - Exam - Comp
<   Nat Baton Twirling Assn Europe; Nat Baton Twirling Assn
    Intl (USA)
M   c 1,500 i
¶   News Direct (NL) - 4; ftm only.

National Baton Twirling Association of Scotland   (NBTA Scotland)
NR   Morningside Medical Practice, 2 Morningside Place,
    EDINBURGH, EH10 5ER.
    http://www.twirlscotland.com
    Sec: Anne Crandles
○   *G

National Bed Federation Ltd   (NBF)   1912
■   High Corn Mill, Chapel Hill, SKIPTON, N Yorks, BD23 1NL.
    (hq)
    0845 055 6406   fax 0845 055 6407
    email info@bedfed.org.uk   http://www.bedfed.org.uk
    Exec Dir: Jessica Alexander
▲   Company Limited by Guarantee
○   *T; interests of manufacturers of beds & mattresses & their
    suppliers
●   Conf - Mtgs - Exhib - Stat - Inf - VE - LG
M   112 f, UK & o'seas

National Beef Association   (NBA)   1998
■   Mart Centre, Tyne Green, HEXHAM, Northumberland,
    NE46 3SG.   (hq)
    01434 601005   fax 01434 601008
    email helen@nationalbeefassociation.com
    http://www.nationalbeefassociation.com
    Sec: Helen Dobson
▲   Company Limited by Guarantee; Registered Charity
○   *F,*T; development & sustainability of beef cattle production
    within the UK
●   Conf - Mtgs - ET - Expt - LG
M   2,600 i, 70 f
    (Sub: £50 i, £200 f)
¶   Beef Farmer - 4; ftm, £3 nm.   NL - 52; ftm only.

National Begonia Society   (NBS)   1948
NR   7 Brabraham Rd, Sawston, CAMBRIDGE, CB22 3DQ.   (hsp)
    01223 834202
    http://www.national-begonia-society.co.uk
    Hon Sec: Alan Harris
○   *H; improved cultivation of begonias & their hybridisation
●   Mtgs - ET - Comp
<   R Horticl Soc
M   c 500 i, f & org
¶   Bulletin - 3; ftm only.

National Bingo Game Association Ltd   (NBGA)   1986
NR   Lexham House, 75 High St North, DUNSTABLE, Beds,
    LU6 1JF.   (hq)
    01582 860900
    email info@nationalbingo.co.uk
    http://www.nationalbingo.co.uk
    Chief Exec: Paul Talboys
▲   Company Limited by Guarantee
○   *T; administration of the game
●   Administration
M   f
¶   AR.

National Brickmakers Federation
    2006-7 amalgamated into the **Brick Development Association**

National Bursars Association   (NBA)
NR   140 Wood St, RUGBY, Warks, CV21 2SP.   (hq)
    01788 573300   fax 01788 571812
    email bursarsassoc@btinternet.com
    http://www.nba.org.uk
    Chief Exec: William Simmonds
○   *P; for school bursars, business managers & senior
    administrative staff
M   i

National Campaign for the Arts   (NCA)   1985
■   1 Kingly St, LONDON, W1B 5PA.   (hq)
    020 7287 3777   fax 020 7287 4777
    email nca@artscampaign.org.uk
    http://www.artscampaign.org.uk
    Dir: Louise de Winter
▲   Company Limited by Guarantee
○   *A, *D, *K; the only independent lobbying organisation which
    exists to represent the interests of the whole arts sector in all
    its diversity.
    It is funded entirely by its members to ensure its independence
●   Conf - ET - Res - ST - LG
M   c 500 i, 500 org
¶   NCA News - 4; ftm; £5 nm.
    Friday Briefing (email) - 52; ftm only.

National Campaign for Firework Safety (NCFS) 1969
NR   118 Long Acre, Covent Garden, LONDON, WC2E 9PA.   (hq)
        020 7836 6703
        email ncfs@cgsystem.co.uk   http://www.cgsystem.co.uk
        Dir: Noël Tobin
▲   Registered Charity
Br   12; N Zealand
○   *K; to amend the 1875 Explosives Act & 1976 & 1992
        Fireworks Acts; to license fireworks for use by trained people
        for organised displays only, to dis-allow sale of fireworks to
        un-licensed individuals
Gp   Fireworks; Consumers; Safety
●   Conf - Mtgs - Res - Exhib - Stat - Inf - LG
<   Fire Brigades U; Age Concern; Cats Protection League; Canine
        Defence League; Nat Civil Defence Org
>   Confedn of Brit Ind (CBI)
M   100,000 i, 15 org
¶   [see website].

National Campaign for real Nursery Education (NCNE) 1965
NR   c/o Tachbrook Nursery School, Aylesford St, LONDON,
        SW1V 3RN.   (mail address)
        email ncea@yahoo.co.uk
        Contact: Tess Robson
○   *E, *K; promoting & defending state funded nursery education
        nationally
M   i

National Campaign for the Sensible Siting of Masts
        alternative name of **Mast Action**

National Campaign for Water Justice (NCWJ) 1992
■   25 Brooklyn Close, CARSHALTON, Surrey, SM5 2SL.   (hq)
        020 8773 9743   fax 020 8773 9743
        Gen Sec: Tony May,   Chmn: Neil Fishpool
Br   40; Canada, France, USA
○   *K; 'for the re-instatement of the core business of water supply
        & sewerage services into public hands; for the lowering of all
        water charges; to stop the abuses of the water industry such
        as high salaries to the selected few; to campaign against the
        bringing in of measured water & forced installation of water
        meters where they are not wanted'
Gp   Advice on: Water law, Political (legislative issues), Complaints
        against the industry, Matters related to people on state
        benefits, the retired & aged, & water matters overseas
●   Conf - Mtgs - Res - Stat - Inf - Lib - LG
<   U Associates US; Canadian Envtl Law Assn; Nat Consumer
        Coun
M   38,250 i, 18 f, 36 org, UK / 14 i, o'seas
¶   Justice Bulletin - irreg; free.
        Membership Joining Book - 4; free.

National Cancer Alliance (NCA) 1995
NR   PO Box 579, OXFORD, OX4 1LB.   (hq)
        01865 793566   fax 01865 251050
        email nationalcanceralliance@btinternet.com
        http://www.nationalcanceralliance.co.uk
        Chief Exec: Dr Becky Miles
▲   Company Limited by Guarantee; Registered Charity
○   *N; an alliance of patients, carers & health professionals
        working together to improve the treatment & care of all
        cancer patients in Britain
M   i

National Candida Society 1997
NR   PO Box 151, ORPINGTON, Kent, BR5 1UJ.
        01689 813039
        email info@candida-society.org.uk
        http://www.candida-society.org.uk
        Dir: Dr Christine Tomlinson
○   *M

National Caravan Council Ltd   (NCC) 1939
NR   Catherine House, Victoria Rd, ALDERSHOT, Hants,
        GU11 1SS.   (hq)
        01252 318251   fax 01252 322596
        email info@nationalcaravan.co.uk
        http://www.nationalcaravan.co.uk
        Dir Gen: Graham Beacon
▲   Company Limited by Guarantee
○   *G; interests of the caravan industry
Gp   National Park Homes Council; Manufacturers; Traders; Park
        operators; Supplies & services; Holiday caravan distributors
●   Conf - Mtgs - ET - Exhib - Stat - Inf - LG
<   Eur Caravan Fedn
M   23 i, 500 f, UK / 10 f, o'seas
¶   The Business - 4;   NL - 12; AR; all ftm.

National Care Association   (NCA) 1981
■   45-49 Leather Lane, LONDON, EC1N 7TJ.   (hq)
        020 7831 7090   fax 020 7831 7040
        email info@nca.gb.com   http://www.nca.gb.com
        Chief Exec: Sheila Scott
▲   Company Limited by Guarantee
○   *N, *T; to represent providers of care to local & national
        government; to provide services to members to allow them to
        concentrate on the people they care for
Gp   Children's services; Domiciliary care; Nursing care; Older
        people; Younger adults
●   Conf - Mtgs - ET - Exhib - Inf - LG
M   2,000 i
¶   NL - 12;   Homeowners Manual;   Health & Safety Manual;
        Working Safely (Employees' Hbk).
×   2005 National Care Homes Association

National Care Homes Association
        since 2005 **National Care Association**

**National Carnival Guild - the National Federation of Carnival
        Associations & Committees   (Carnival Guild) 1964**
NR   54 Rokesly Avenue, LONDON, N8 8NR.   (chmn/p)
        020 8340 7339
        Chmn: Gordon P Rathbone
○   *G; promotion of carnival; cooperation between carnival
        associations

National Carpet Cleaners Association Ltd   (NCCA) 1968
NR   62c London Rd, OADBY, Leics, LE2 5DH.   (hq)
        0116-271 9550   fax 0116-271 9588
        email info@ncca.co.uk   http://www.ncca.co.uk
        Co Sec: Paul Pearce
▲   Limited Company
Br   3
○   *T; as well as carpets also incl soft furnishings (curtains &
        upholstery), fire & flood restoration
Gp   Fire & flood divn
●   Conf - ET - Exam - Res - Exhib - Inf - Lib - PL - LG
<   Brit Cleaning Coun; Carpet & Upholstery Cleaners Assn of
        Australia [& South Africa]; Assn of Specialists in Cleaning &
        Restoration (USA)
M   c 550 f
¶   NL - 12; ftm.

National Cattle Association (Dairy)
■   Brick House, Risbury, LEOMINSTER, Herefords, HR6 0NQ.
        01568 760632   fax 01568 760523
        email timbrigstocke@hotmail.com
        Sec: Tim Brigstocke
▲   Un-incorporated Society
○   *B, *N; to represent the interests of dairy cattle breed societies
●   Conf - Mtgs - Et - Stat - Inf - LG
M   11 breed societies

National Caving Association
        since 1 January 2004 **British Caving Association**

© CBD Research Ltd · Beckenham · BR3 5JS · Tel 020 8650 7745 · Fax 020 8650 0768 · E-mail cbd@cbdresearch.com · www.cbdresearch.com

National Cavy Club (NCC) 1890
NR 79 Thornhill Gardens, HARTLEPOOL, TS26 0JF. (hsp)
 01429 264294
 email nationalcavyclub@yahoo.co.uk
 http://www.nationalcavyclub.co.uk
 Hon Sec: Mrs Pauline Avery
▲ Un-incorporated Society
○ *G, *V; to promote & encourage the breeding, keeping &
 exhibiting of all varieties of cavies (guinea pigs)
● Mtgs - Exhib - Comp - Inf
M c 575 i, UK / 5 i, o;seas
¶ Newsflash (NL) - 2; ftm only. NCC Hbk - 2 yrly; ftm, £4 nm.
 Cavies (Jnl) - 12; £30 yr (the official organ for the club but not
 published by it).

National Childbirth Trust (NCT) 1956
NR Alexandra House, Oldham Terrace, LONDON, W3 6NH. (hq)
 0870 770 3237 (admin), 0870 444 8707 (enquiries)
 fax 0870 770 3237
 email enquiries@national-childbirth-trust.co.uk
 http://www.nctpregnancyandbabycare.com
 Chief Exec: Belinda Phipps
▲ Registered Charity
Br 336
○ *W; 'the NCT wants all parents to have an experience of
 pregnancy, birth & early parenthood that enriches their lives
 & gives them confidence in being a parent; it runs antenatal
 classes & provides information on maternity issues,
 breastfeeding & postnatal support'
Gp Postnatal support; Home birth; Caesarean
● Mtgs - ET - Res - Exhib - Inf - LG
< Intl Childbirth Education Assn; Unicef Baby Friendly Initiative;
 Baby Milk Action; Consumer Congress; Nat Alliance
 Women's Orgs; Nat Children's Bureau; Nat Coun Voluntary
 Orgs (NCVO); Nat Coun Women; Women's Nat Cmsn
M 42,000 i
¶ New Generation (Jnl) - 4; Local NLs - varies; all ftm.
 NCT Sales Catalogue (with sales goods); free.

National Childminding Association (NCMA) 1977
NR Royal Court, 81 Tweedy Rd, BROMLEY, Kent, BR1 1TG. (hq)
 0845 880 0044
 email info@ncma.org.uk http://www.ncma.org.uk
 Chief Exec: Liz Bayram
▲ Registered Charity
Br 2 (North & South)
○ *W; promotes quality registered childminding for children,
 families & communities
● Conf - Mtgs - ET - Res - SG - Inf - Lib - VE - LG
M c 47,000 i
¶ Who Minds - 4; ftm. AR.
 Publications list available.

National Children's Nurseries Association 1988
IRL Unit 12C, Bluebell Business Park, Old Naas Rd, DUBLIN 12,
 Republic of Ireland.
 353 (1) 460 1138 fax 353 (1) 460 1185
 email info@ncna.ie http://www.ncna.net
○ *P

**National Childrenswear Association of Great Britain & Ireland
(NCWA) 1940**
NR 5 Portland Place, LONDON, W1B 1PW. (hq)
 020 7631 5445 fax 020 7631 3443
 email info@ncwa.co.uk http://www.ncwa.co.uk
 Co Sec: Elizabeth Fox
▲ Company Limited by Guarantee
○ *T; all sectors of the children's wear industry
Gp Retailers; Manufacturers; Distributors; Accredited agents
● Conf - Mtgs - ET - Exhib - Inf - LG - Seminars
< BKCEC; BSSA; BCIA
M c 600 f

National Chinchilla Society (NCS) 1955
■ 101 Simmondley Lane, GLOSSOP, Derbys, SK13 6LU. (hsp)
 01457 856945
 email chillaquip@freeserve.com
 http://www.natchinsoc.co.uk
 Hon Sec: Paul S Spooner
▲ Un-incorporated Society
Br 4
○ *B; to promote good husbandry practice in the breeding of
 animals known as Chinchilla Lanigera & Chinchilla
 Brevicaudata & with any mutant form of these animals
● Conf - Mtgs - ET - Exhib - Stat - Inf
M c 150 i
 (Sub: £15 UK / £20 o'seas)
¶ Gazette - 6; ftm only.
 Guide to Quality Chinchilla; Show Rules.

National Chrysanthemum Society (NCS) 1846
■ 317 Plessey Rd, BLYTH, Northumberland, NE24 3LJ.
 01670 353580
 http://www.ncsuk.info
 Mem Sec: Peter Fraser
▲ Registered Charity
Br 6
○ *H; to encourage the growing of chrysanthemums to the
 highest standard
● Conf - Mtgs - Exam - Exhib - Comp - SG - National Register of
 Chrysanthemums
< R Horticl Soc
M 4,000 i, 1,000 org, UK / 300 i, o'seas
¶ Bulletin - 2. Ybk.
 List of specialist publications available.

National Churchwatch 1999
NR Endeavour, 8 Commercial Rd, SHEPTON MALLET, Somerset,
 BA4 5DH.
 01749 344992
 http://www.nationalchurchwatch.com
 Nat Co-ordinator: Nick Tolson
○ *K; to encourage all sections of the community to work together
 to protect places of worship and the people who frequent
 them

National Coastwatch Institution
■ Heron's Flight, Church Lane, Fritton, GREAT YARMOUTH,
 Norfolk, NR31 9EZ. (hq)
 0845 460 1202
 email jwt.fritton@btinternet.com http://www.nci.org.uk
 Gen Sec: John Turlington
○ *K; set up by the Sea Safety Group (UK) to re-open the coastal
 look-out stations closed by the government as a money-
 saving idea in the 'age of satellite installations'
M 15,000 39 stations

National Cochlear Implant Users Association (NCIUA)
■ PO Box 260, HIGH WYCOMBE, Bucks, HP11 1FA.
 (mail/address)
 email alison.Heath@hotmail.com
 http://www.nciua.demon.co.uk
 Sec: Alison Heath
▲ Registered Charity
Br 10 local support groups for parents & users
○ *K; campaigning for adequate funds for cochlear implants for
 the deaf; to support users
● Conf - Inf
< EURO-CIU
M 403 i, 12 f, 10 org
¶ NCIUA NL - 4; ftm only.
 Cochlear Implants: a collection of experiences of users of all
 ages; ftm, £2 nm.

National Community Boats Association 1985
NR c/o The Yorkshire Waterways Museum, Dutch River Side,
    GOOLE, E Yorks, DN14 5TB. (hq)
    01405 765704 fax 01405 765704
    email staff@national-cba.co.uk
    http://www.national-cba.co.uk
○ *W; to provide community groups (schools, hospitals, youth
    clubs, etc) with access to the UK & European inland
    waterways

**National Confederation of Parent-Teacher Associations
   (NCPTA) 1956**
NR 39 Shipbourne Rd, TONBRIDGE, Kent, TN10 3DS. (hq)
    01732 375460
    email info@ncpta.org.uk http://www.ncpta.org.uk
    Chief Exec: D W Butler
▲ Company Limited by Guarantee; Registered Charity
○ *E, *K; to promote cooperation between home & school
● Conf - ET - Res - LG
< Eur Parents Assn
M 12,000 org
¶ PTA - 3; News & Views - 3; AR; all ftm only.

National Consortium for Sheltered Housing
   alternative name of **ERoSH**

National Consumer Federation (NCF) 2001
■ 24 Hurst House, Penton Rise, LONDON, WC1X 9ED. (hsp)
    020 7837 8545
    email secretary@ncf.info http://www.ncf.info
    Hon Sec: Hugh Jenkins
▲ Company Limited by Guarantee; Registered Charity
○ *K, *N; to promote grassroot consumer interests & provide a
    channel for consumer opinion & representation
Gp Communications; Consumer affairs; Food; Personal finance;
    Utilities
● Mtgs - ET - Res - Inf
M 130 i, 20 f, 50 org
    (Sub: £20 i, £500 f, £200 org)

National Contractors Federation
   a member federation of the **Construction Confederation**

National Cooperage Federation (NCF) 1919
■ 34 Maitland Rd, KIRKLISTON, W Lothian, EH29 9AP. (hsp)
    0131-333 3314
    email john@gaffney113.wanadoo.co.uk
    Hon Sec: John Gaffney
▲ Un-incorporated Society
○ *T; interests of employers of coopers in the UK
● Mtgs - Trade tests for apprentices
M 42 f
¶ AR - 1; free.

NATIONAL COUNCIL ...
   For details of bodies whose names begin thus, other than the
   following, see the companion volume **'Councils, Committees &
   Boards' (Introduction paragraph 6)**

National Council for Aviculture Ltd (NCA) 1955
■ Davies House, Spring Gardens, NORTHAMPTON, NN1 1DR.
    (hq)
    01604 624549 fax 01604 627108
    email info@nca.uk.net http://www.nca.uk.net
    Sec: David Whittaker
▲ Un-incorporated Society
○ *N; coordination body representing aviculturists in the UK
Gp British Bird Council; Budgerigar Society; Canary Council;
    Foreign Bird Federation
● Mtgs - Exhib - Comp
M 29,000 i

National Council for Civil Liberties
   registered name of **Liberty**

**National Council for the Conservation of Plants & Gardens
   (NCCPG) 1978**
■ 12 Home Farm, Loseley Park, GUILDFORD, Surrey,
    GU3 1HS. (hq)
    01483 447540 fax 01483 458933
    email info@nccpg.org.uk http://www.nccpg.com
    Exec Officer: Genevieve Melbourne Webb
▲ Company Limited by Guarantee; Registered Charity
Br 41
○ *H, *N; to conserve the heritage of our garden plants built up
    during the past 400 years. This is achieved through
    NCCPG's 650 National Plant Collections in which some
    100,000 garden plants are maintained in safe cultivation
Gp 650+ National Plant Collections
● Mtgs - Res - Exhib - Inf - PL - VE
< works closely with RBG, Kew, R Horticl Soc, NTS & Engl
    Heritage
M 4,500 i, 100 f, 100 org, UK / 100 i, o'seas
¶ Plant Heritage (Jnl) - 2.
    The National Plant Collections Directory.
    Publications list available.

National Council for the Divorced & Separated (NCDS) 1974
NR 68 Parkes Hall Rd, Woodsetton, DUDLEY, W Midlands,
    DY1 3SR. (hsp)
    07041 478120
    email info@ncds.org.uk http://www.ncds.org.uk
▲ Registered Charity
Br 75; Ireland
○ *W; welfare of all persons divorced, separated or bereaved
● Conf - Mtgs - Inf - VE
< NCDS Trust (a charity)
M 6,000 i
¶ NL - 4.
    Note: Also known as NCDS Phoenix.

National Council for Housing & Planning
   see **ROOM at RTPI**

National Council for Hypnotherapy (NCH) 1973
NR PO Box 14542, STUDLEY, Warks, B91 9HH. (mail)
    0800 756 6375
    email admin@hypnotherapists.org.uk
    http://www.hypnotherapists.org.uk
    Admin: Brenda Bentley
▲ Un-incorporated Society
○ *P; to provide a register of competent hypnotherapists
● Conf - Mtgs - ET - Exam - Res - Inf - LG - Referrals register
< Foundation for Integrated Medicine; Nat Gld of Hypnotists
M c 800 i
¶ Jnl - 4. LM. AR.

** **National Council on Inland Transport**
   Organisation lost: see Introduction paragraph 3

National Council for Metal Detecting (NCMD) 1981
■ 51 Hilltop Gardens, Denaby, DONCASTER, S Yorks,
    DN12 4BA. (sp)
    01709 868521
    email trevor.austin@ncmd.co.uk http://www.ncmd.co.uk
    Gen Sec: Trevor Austin
▲ Un-incorporated Society
Br 150; USA
○ *G; the encouragement & defence of the hobby of recreational
    metal detecting
● Mtgs - Comp - LG
< Cent Coun Physical Recreation (CCPR)
M 5,000 i, UK / 150 i, o'seas
¶ Reports of Executive Committee Meetings - 3/4; free.
    Reports of meetings with government bodies.

National Council of Psychotherapists (NCP) 1971
- ■ PO Box 7219, HEANOR, Derbys, DE75 9AG. (hsb)
  0845 230 6072 fax 01773 711031
  email ncphq@btinternet.com http://www.ncphq.co.uk
  Sec: Brian Jackson
- ▲ Un-incorporated Society
- Br 1; Singapore
- ○ *P; to represent & protect registered members & the general public in the field of psychotherapy & hypnotherapy
- Gp Psychotherapy; Hypnotherapy; Critical incident de-briefing
- ● Conf - ET - Exam - Res
- < Intl Coun of Psychotherapists
- M 653 i, UK / 37 i, o'seas i, o'seas
  (Sub: £70 UK / £125 o'seas)
- ¶ Fidelity (Jnl) - 4; ftm.
  AR; ftm only.

National Courier Association (NCA) 1989
- ■ 9 Woodside, Ecton Lane, Sywell, NORTHAMPTON, NN6 0DG. (hsp)
  0845 603 7813
  email theadministrator@thenca.co.uk
  http://www.thenca.co.uk
  Admin: Lyn Cox, Chmn: Mike McCartney
- ▲ Company Limited by Guarantee
- ○ *T; network of independent courier companies completing same-day work throughout the UK, which intertrade with each other
- Gp Same day courier companies
- ● Mtgs
- M 95 f

National Crossbow Federation of Great Britain (NCFGB) 1964
- NR 24 Ivy Rd, POYNTON, Cheshire, SK12 1BE. (gensec/p)
  01625 877900
  email graeme@ethel975.freeserve.co.uk
  Gen Sec: Graeme Peatfield
- ▲ Un-incorporated Society
- ○ *S; to promote competitive amateur crossbow shooting at national & club level in the British Isles
- ● Mtgs - ET - Comp - Inf - Lib - VE - LG
- < Wld Crossbow Shooting Assn (WCSA)
- M c 70 i
- ¶ NL - 4; ftm.
- × British Crossbow Society

National Dahlia Society (NDS) 1881
- NR 48 Vickers Rd, Ash Vale, ALDERSHOT, Hants, GU12 5SE. (sp)
  01252 693003
  Gen Sec: David Kent
- ▲ Registered Charity
- ○ *H; to encourage, improve & extend the cultivation of the dahlia

National Dance Teachers Association (NDTA) 1988
- ■ PO Box 4099, LICHFIELD, Staffs, WS13 6WX. (hq)
  01543 308618 fax 01543 308618
  email office@ndta.org.uk http://www.ndta.org.uk
  Chmn: Veronica Jobbins
- ▲ Company Limited by Guarantee; Registered Charity
- ○ *D, *P; to support teachers in schools & colleges to deliver dance within the school curriculum
- ● Conf - ET - Inf - LG
- M 484 i, 266 f, UK / 12 i, 1 f, o'seas
  (Sub: £35.50 i, £75 f)
- ¶ Dance Matters - 3; ftm, £4 50 each nm.

National Day Nurseries Association (NDNA) 1991
- ■ National Early Years Enterprise Centre, Longbow Close, HUDDERSFIELD, W Yorks, HD2 1GQ. (hq)
  01484 407070 fax 01484 407060
  email info@ndna.org.uk http://www.ndna.org.uk
  Chief Exec: Purnima Tanuku
- ▲ Registered Charity
- ○ *T; to represent children's day nurseries across the UK; to give information, training & support their families & communities
- ● Conf - ET - EXhib - Inf
- M [not stated]
- ¶ Nursery News.

National Deaf Children's Society (NDCS) 1944
- NR 15 Dufferin St, LONDON, EC1Y 8UR. (hq)
  020 7490 8656 fax 020 7251 5020
  email ndcs@ndcs.org.uk http://www.ndcs.org.uk
  Chief Exec: Susan Daniels
- ▲ Company Limited by Guarantee; Registered Charity
- Br 120
- ○ *E, W, *Y; to inform & advise deaf children & young people & their carers
- Gp Technology Inf Centre (London); Services delivery (London)
- ● Conf - ET - Res - Exhib - Inf - Lib
  Helpline: 0808 800 8880 (Mon-Fri 0010-1700, Tues-1900)
- M 14,000 i
- ¶ Talk - 6; £10. AR. Publications list available.

National Deafblind & Rubella Association
alternative name of **Sense**

National Dog Wardens Association (NDWA) 1987
- NR Haffield Lodge, Gloucester Rd, Corse, STAUNTON, Glos, GL19 3RA.
  Pres: Sue Bell
- Br 12; Bermuda, France, Gibraltar, USA
- ○ *P; for workers in the field of animal control
- ● Conf - Mtgs - ET - Res - Exhib - Stat - Inf - VE - LG
- < Nat Animal Control Assn America
- M i, f, & org
- ¶ Dog Warden News - 4.

National Drama (ND) 1989
- NR West Barn, Church Farm, Happisburgh, NORWICH, Norfolk, NR12 0QY. (chmn/p)
  01692 650066
  http://www.nationaldrama.co.uk
  Chmn: Patrice Baldwin
- ▲ Un-incorporated Society
- ○ *D, *P; for people who work with young people (all ages) in drama & theatre
- Gp Teachers (all sectors of education); Theatre educators; Theatre workers; Workers with people with special needs
- ● Conf - Mtgs - ET - Res - Inf - LG
- M c 650 i, UK & o'seas
- ¶ Drama (Jnl) - 2; ftm. Reflections (NL) - 3; ftm only.
  Drama Research.

National Drama Festivals Association (NDFA) 1964
- ■ NODA House, 58-60 Lincoln Rd, PETERBOROUGH, Cambs, PE1 2RZ. (hsb)
  0870 770 2480 fax 0870 770 2490
  email secretary@ndfa.org.uk http://www.ndfa.org.uk
  Hon Sec: Bronwen Stanway
- ▲ Registered Charity
- ○ *D; to encourage & support the amateur theatre in all its forms & through the organisation of drama festivals
- ● Drama festivals - Play writing competitions - Representation, coordination & liaison
- < Nat Operatic & Dramatic Assn (NODA)
- M 45 i, 44 festival organisers, 23 associate org, UK / 11, 1 festival organiser, 1 org, o'seas
  (Sub: £12 i, £30 organisers, £18 org)
- ¶ NL - 4; Directory (incl festival details) - 1; both ftm only.

National Dried Fruit Trade Association (UK) Ltd   (NDFTA) 1942
- ■ 18 Lichfield Rd, WOODFORD GREEN, Essex, IG8 9ST.   (hq)
  020 8506 2379   fax 020 8506 2379
  email cathy@ndfta.co.uk   http://www.ndfta.co.uk
  Sec / Treas: Mrs Cathy Grant
- ▲ Company Limited by Guarantee
- ○ *T; all matters connected with the dried fruit trade (mainly currants, sultanas, raisins, apricots, peaches, pears, dates & prunes)
- Gp Sub-c'ees: Technical, Public relations
- ● Conf - Mtgs - Res - Stat - Inf - VE - LG
- < Fédn Eur du Commerce en Fruits Secs, Conserves, Epices et Miel (FRUCOM);
- M 22 f, UK / 14 f, o'seas

National Early Music Association   (NEMA)   1981
- ■ 126 Shanklin Drive, LEICESTER, LE2 3QB.   (admin/p)
  0116-270 9984
  http://www.nema-uk.org
  Admin: John Bence
- ▲ Registered Charity
- Br 11
- ○ *D, *N; to bring together organisations & individuals, both professional & amateur, involved in the whole range of early music
- Gp Dance; Music; Theatre; Coordinating bodies
- ● Conf - ET - Inf
- < UK Early Music Forum
- M c 300 i, f & org
- ¶ Early Music Performer - 2.

National Eczema Society   (NES)   1976
- ■ Hill House, Highgate Hill, LONDON, N19 5NA.   (hq)
  020 7281 3553   fax 020 7281 6395
  email info@eczema.org   http://www.eczema.org
  Chief Exec: Margaret Cox
- ▲ Company Limited by Guarantee; Registered Charity
- ○ *W; to (1) provide people with independent & practical advice about treating & managing eczema; & (2) raise awareness of the needs of eczema sufferers with healthcare professionals, teachers & the government
- ● Conf - Mtgs - ET - Res (support & fund) - Exhib - Comp - SG - Inf - VE
- M 6,000 i, 8 corporate
  (Sub: £20 i, £6,000 corporate)
- ¶ Exchange (Jnl) - 4; ftm only.
  Information Sheets 3-10, 11-25; ftm, £7 nm.
  Guides & Booklets; ftm, £2.50 nm.
  Publications order form available.

National Edible Oil Distributors Association   (NEODA)
- NR PO Box 259, BECKENHAM, Kent, BR3 3YA.   (hq)
  020 8776 2644   fax 020 8249 5402
  http://www.neoda.org.uk
  Sec: Lynda Simmons
- ▲ Un-incorporated Society
- ○ *T; of trades concerned in the supply of frying media & suchlike material
- ● Conf - Mtgs - Inf
- < Food & Drink Fedn; Fedn Oils, Seeds Fats Assns (FOSFA)
- M 70 f
- ¶ LM; ftm only.   AR.

National Egg Marketing Association Ltd   (NEMAL)   1935
- ■ 89 Charterhouse St (2nd floor), LONDON, EC1M 6HR.   (hq)
  020 7608 3760   fax 020 7608 3860
  email Louisa.Platt@britisheggindustrycouncil.com
  http://www.britegg.co.uk
  Sec: Louisa Platt
- ▲ Company Limited by Guarantee
- ○ *T; interests of those who pack & market eggs
- ● Mtgs - LG
- < Brit Egg Ind Coun
- M 53 f

National Endometriosis Society   (NES)   1981
- NR 50 Westminster Palace Gardens, 1-7 Artillery Row, LONDON, SW1P 1RR.   (hq)
  020 7222 2781   fax 020 7222 2786
  http://www.endo.org.uk
  Chief Exec: Robert Music
- ▲ Company Limited by Guarantee
- Br 50+
- ○ *K; support for women suffering from endometriosis; raising money for research into the disease; information to health professionals
- ● Conf - Mtgs - Res - Inf
  Helpline: 0808 808 2227
- M c 2,500 i
- ¶ NL - 4;   AR - 1; both ftm only.
  Publications list available.

National Energy Action   (NEA)   1981
- NR St Andrew's House, 90-92 Pilgrim St, NEWCASTLE upon TYNE, NE1 6SG.   (hq)
  0191-261 5677   fax 0191-261 6496
  email info@nea.org.uk   http://www.nea.org.uk
- ▲ Registered Charity
- ○ *K; promotes energy efficiency services to tackle the heating & insulation problems of low-income households
- ● Conf - Mtgs - ET - Res - Lib
- < Nat Coun of Voluntary Orgs
- M 242 org
- ¶ Energy Action - 4; ftm, £25 nm.   NL - 6; ftm only.
  AR - 1; free.   Other publications.

National Entertainment Agents Council   (NEAC)   1978
- NR PO Box 112, SEAFORD, E Sussex, BN25 2DQ.   (gsb)
  0870 755 7612   fax 0870 755 7613
  email info@neac.org.uk   http://www.neac.org.uk
  Gen Sec: Chris Bray
- ▲ Un-incorporated Society
- Br 4
- ○ *P, *T
- ● Conf - Mtgs - ET - Inf - LG
- < Nat Outdoor Events Assn
- M 100 f
- ¶ The Agent - 24; ftm only.

National Exhibitors Association   (NEA)   1988
- ■ 29a Market Sq, BIGGLESWADE, Beds, SG18 8AQ.   (hq)
  01767 316255   fax 01767 316430
  http://www.eou.org.uk
  Sec Gen: Peter Cotterell
- ▲ Un-incorporated Society
- ○ *T
- ● Conf - ET
- M 70 f

National Family Mediation   (NFM)   1982
- ■ Margaret Jackson Centre, 4 Barnfield Hill, EXETER, Devon, EX1 1SR.   (hq)
  01392 271610   fax 01392 271945
  email general@nfm.org.uk   http://www.nfm.org.uk
  Chief Exec: Jane Robey
- ▲ Registered Charity
- Br 50
- ○ *W; to help those involved in family breakdown to communicate better with one another & reach their own decisions about some or all of the issues arising from separation, divorce, children, property & finance
- Gp Divorce; Mediation; Families
- ● ET - Mediation
- M 60 services
- ¶ The Bulletin - 4; free.   AR - 1.

© CBD Research Ltd · Beckenham · BR3 5JS · Tel 020 8650 7745 · Fax 020 8650 0768 · E-mail cbd@cbdresearch.com · www.cbdresearch.com

National Fancy Rat Society   (NFRS)   1976
NR   PO Box 24207, LONDON, SE9 5ZF.   (hsb)
　　　email secretary@nfrs.org　　http://www.nfrs.org
　　　Hon Sec: Estelle Sandford
▲   Un-incorporated Society
○   *B; to promote the care of the Fancy Rat (Domesticus Rattus
　　　Norvegicus) as a pet & exhibition animal
●   Conf - Mtgs - ET - Res - Exhib - Comp - Inf - Lib
<   Amer Fancy Rat & Mouse Assn; Amer Rat, Mouse & Hamster
　　　Soc; Svenska Råttsällskapet; Sydsveriges Maädjursvänner;
　　　Finnish Rat Soc
M   c 800 i
¶   Pro-rat-a (NL) - 6; ftm, £3 nm.

**National Farmers' Retail & Markets Association Ltd   (FARMA)
1979**
NR   12 Southgate St, WINCHESTER, Hants, SO23 9EF.   (hq)
　　　0845 458 8420   fax 0845 456 5156
　　　email justask@farma.org.uk   http://www.farma.org.uk
　　　Exec Sec: Rita Exner
▲   Co-operative under Industrial & Provident Society rules
○   *F, *K, *T; 'representing direct sales to customers through farm
　　　shops, pick-your-own, farmers' markets, home delivery, on-
　　　farm catering & farm entertainment'
●   Conf - Mtgs - ET - Res - Exhib - Comp - SG - Stat - Inf - Lib - PL
　　　- VE - LG
M   650 f, UK / 10 f, o'seas
¶   Retail Farmer - 4; ftm only.
　　　LM (farmers' markets): http://www.farmersmarkets.net
　　　LM (farm shops): http://www.farmshopping.net
　　　LM (pick your own): http://www.pickyourown.info
×   2004 (Farm Retail Association
　　　　　(National Association of Farmers' Markets

National Farmers Union of England & Wales   (NFU)   1908
■   Agriculture House, Stoneleigh Park, STONELEIGH, Warks,
　　　CV8 2TZ.   (hq)
　　　024 7685 8500   fax 020 7685 8501
　　　http://www.nfuonline.com
　　　Dir Gen: Richard Macdonald,　Sec: Lucilla Evers
▲   Un-incorporated Society
Br   8; Brussels
○   *F, *H; to represent & promote the interests of farmers &
　　　growers & others with an interest in agriculture, horticulture &
　　　the countryside
●   Conf - Mtgs - ET - Res - Exhib - Comp - SG - Stat - Inf - VE - LG
<   Intl Fedn of Agricl Producers (IFAP); Gen Confedn of Agricl Co-
　　　operatives in the EU (COGECA); Eur Confedn of
　　　Agriculture (CEA); Nat Pig Assn; Taste of the West; Dairy
　　　Coun
M   136,573 i (incl countryside mems)
¶   British Farmer & Grower - 12; ftm, £55 yr nm.
　　　NFU Horticulture - 3;　NFU Professional - 12;
　　　NFU Countryside - 12; NFU Farming Wales - 12; all ftm only.
　　　nfuonline.com (hosting various publications).

National Farmers Union of Scotland
　　see **NFU Scotland**

National Federation of Access Centres
　　since 2006 **National Network of Assessment Centres**

National Federation of Anglers   (NFA)   1903
NR   National Water Sports Centre, Adbolton Lane, Holme
　　　Pierrepont, NOTTINGHAM, NG12 2LU.   (hq)
　　　0115-981 3535   fax 0115-981 9039
　　　email office@nfadirect.com   http://www.nfadirect.com
　　　Chief Exec Officer: Paul Baggaley
▲   Un-incorporated Society
Br   8 regions
○   *G, *K, *S; the governing body for freshwater angling; to
　　　promote & protect angling through education, development
　　　& performance programmes; to promote the conservation &
　　　development of fisheries; to represent freshwater angling at
　　　local, national & international levels
●   Conf - Mtgs - Comp
<   Confédn Intle de la Pêche Sportive (CIPS); FIPS
M   3,320 i (direct members), 330 clubs (with individual members)
¶   Link (NL) - 4; ftm only.   AR - 1; free.

National Federation of Badger Groups
　　since 2005 **Badger Trust**

National Federation for Biological Recording   (NFBR)   1985
NR   122 Link Rd, Anstey, LEICESTER, LE7 7BX.
　　　0116-212 5075
　　　email darwyn.sumner@ntlworld.com
　　　http://www.nfbr.org.uk
　　　Sec: Darwyn Sumner
▲   Un-incorporated Society
○   *G, *P; wildlife recording - the recording of the natural world
　　　(species & habitats)
●   Conf - Mtgs - ET - Res
M   c 200 i
¶   NL - 3;　Conference Proceedings - 1; both ftm.

**National Federation of the Blind of the United Kingdom
(NFBUK)   1947**
■   Sir John Wilson House, 215 Kirkgate, WAKEFIELD, W Yorks,
　　　WF1 1JG.   (hq)
　　　01924 291313   fax 01924 200244
　　　email nfbuk@nfbuk.org   http://www.nfbuk.org
▲   Registered Charity
Br   20
○   *K, *W; for the welfare of all blind people
●   Conf - Mtgs - Exhib - Comp - SG - Inf
<   Wld Blind U; Eur Blind U; NCVO; Disability Alliance; RNIB;
　　　Disabled Living Foundation
M   c 1,400 i & associates
¶   Viewpoint - 2;　Fedtalk tape - 4;　AR; free.

National Federation of Bridleway Associations   (NFBA)   1989
NR   Baxenden House, Manchester Rd, ACCRINGTON, Lancs,
　　　BB5 2RU.   (treas/p)
　　　email nfba@righttoride.org.uk
　　　http://www.rightsofway.org.uk
　　　Chmn: Sue Hogg
▲   Un-incorporated Society
○   *K; to protect & defend existing & non-definitive bridleways &
　　　higher rights of way; to encourage the formation of bridleway
　　　groups throughout England & Wales; to pursue claims for
　　　statutory definition of bridleways
●   Mtgs - Res - Inf - LG
<   Rights of Way Review Committee
>   Local Bridleway Assns; Local Riding Gps
M   6 i, 20 org
¶   Seminar Proceedings - 1; £5.

National Federation of Builders
　　a member federation of the **Construction Confederation**

National Federation of Bus Users
　　since 2005 **Bus Users UK**

National Federation of Carnival Associations & Committees
alternative name of the **National Carnival Guild - the National Federation of Carnival Associations & Committees**

National Federation of Cemetery Friends   (NFCF)   1986
- ■ 42 Chestnut Grove, SOUTH CROYDON, Surrey, CR2 7LH. (sec/p)
  - 020 8651 5090
  - email gwyneth1@btinternet.com
  - http://www.cemeteryfriends.org.uk
  - Hon Sec: Gwyneth Stokes
- ▲ Un-incorporated Society
- ○ *N; provides a forum for the exchange of information & views on the conservation of cemeteries & their appropriate development for educational & recreational purposes
- ● Inf - Advises potential groups
- M 80 groups (Friends)
- ¶ NL - 2; ftm only.

National Federation of Community Organisations   (Community Matters)   1945
- NR 12-20 Baron St, LONDON, N1 9LL.   (hq)
  - 020 7837 7887   fax 020 7278 9253
  - email communitymatters@communitymatters.org.uk
  - http://www.communitymatters.org.uk
  - Nat Dir: David Tyler
- ▲ Company Limited by Guarantee; Registered Charity
- ○ *N, *W; to promote & support action by ordinary people in response to society, education & recreational needs in their neighbourhood & community, resulting in healthy, sustainable communities in which everyone can play their full part
- Gp Local Federation of Community Organisations
- ● Conf - Mtgs - ET - Res - Inf - LG - Advice & consultancy
- < Nat Coun for Voluntary Orgs; Charity Tax Reform Gp; Wales Coun for Voluntary Assns
- M 1,156 org
- ¶ Community - 6; ftm, £15 nm.
  Community Extra; ftm, £15 nm.   NL; free.
  Other publications available.

National Federation of Demolition Contractors   (NFDC)   1941
- ■ 1A New Rd, STAINES, Middx, TW18 3DH.   (hq)
  - 01784 456799   fax 01784 461118
  - email info@demolition-nfdc.com
  - http://www.demolition-nfdc.com
  - Chief Exec: Howard Button
- ▲ Company Limited by Guarantee
- Br 5
- ○ *T; for the demolition & dismantling industry
- ● Conf - Mtgs - ET - Stat - Empl - LG
- < Eur Demolition Assn (EDA)
- M 167 f
  - (Sub: £1,500)
- ¶ Demolition & Dismantling Jnl - 4;   Ybk - 1.

National Federation of Eighteen Plus Groups
since 2006 **National Federation of Plus Areas of Great Britain**

National Federation of Enterprise Agencies   (NFEA)   1993
- NR 12 Stephenson Court, Fraser Rd, Priory Business Park, BEDFORD, MK44 3WH.   (hq)
  - 01234 831623   fax 01234 831625
  - email enquiries@nfea.com   http://www.nfea.com + smallbusinessadvice.org.uk
  - Chief Exec: George Derbyshire
- ○ *N; for local enterprise agencies & other like-minded organisations, in England; it forms a network of independent not-for-profit local agencies committed to responding to the needs of small & growing businesses by providing a comprehensive range of quality services
- Gp Business Volunteer Mentors Association
- M c 130 f
- ¶ Best Practices Jnl - 1.   NL - 4.   Bulletin - 12.
  Various publications.

National Federation of Families with Visually Impaired Children
registered name of **LOOK**

National Federation of Fish Friers Ltd   (NFFF)   1913
- NR New Federation House, 4 Greenwood Mount, Meanwood, LEEDS, W Yorks, LS6 4LQ.   (hq)
  - 0113-230 7044   fax 0113-230 7010
  - email mail@federationoffishfriers.co.uk
  - http://www.federationoffishfriers.co.uk
  - Gen Sec: Mrs A M Kirk
- ▲ Company Limited by Guarantee
- ○ *T
- ● Conf - Mtgs - ET - Exhib - Inf - LG
- M c 2,500 i
- ¶ Fish Friers Review - 12; ftm.

National Federation of Fishermen's Organisations   (NFFO)   1977
- NR 30 Monkgate, YORK, YO31 7PF.   (hq)
  - Chief Exec: Barrie C Deas
- ○ *T; to represent fishermen & their interests, locally, nationally & within the European Community
- M c 1,200 i in 40 org
- ¶ NL - 6.   NFFO Official Ybk & Diary - 1.

National Federation of Fishmongers   (NFF)   1932
- NR PO Box 9639, COLCHESTER, Essex, CO5 9WR.   (hq)
  - 01376 571391
  - email info@fishmongersfederation.co.uk
  - http://www.fishmongersfederation.co.uk
  - Pres: David Ridley
- Br London Fish & Poultry Retailers Association
- ○ *T; interests of retail fishmongers

National Federation of Glaziers   (NFG)   1991
- ■ 27 Old Gloucester St, LONDON, WC1N 3XX.   (hq)
  - 020 7404 3099
  - Chmn: A C Jones
- ▲ Un-incorporated Society
- ○ *T; to provide information & assistance on glass products in relation to window & conservatory installation
- ● Inf - Vetting of individuals & companies in the field - Arrangement of insured guarantees (as introducer) of approved schemes - Helpline for members
- M 170 f
- ¶ Commitment to Good Practice.

National Federation of Inland Wholesale Fish Merchants   (NFIWFM)
- NR Office 36 Billingsgate Market, Trafalgar Way, LONDON, E14 5ST.
  - 020 7515 2655   fax 020 7517 3531
- ○ *T; to promote inland fish merchants
- M f

National Federation of Master Window & General Cleaners
since 1 January 2006 **Federation of Window Cleaners**

National Federation of Meat & Food Traders   1888
- NR 1 Belgrove, ROYAL TUNBRIDGE WELLS, Kent, TN1 1YW.   (hq)
  - 01892 541412   fax 01892 535462
  - email info@nfmft.co.uk
  - Chief Exec: Graham Bidston
- ○ *T
- M f
- ¶ Food Trader - 10; ftm.   Ybk.

© CBD Research Ltd · Beckenham · BR3 5JS · Tel 020 8650 7745 · Fax 020 8650 0768 · E-mail cbd@cbdresearch.com · www.cbdresearch.com

National Federation of Plus Areas of Great Britain   (Plus)   1941
NR   210 Commerce House, High St, SUTTON COLDFIELD,
         W Midlands, B72 1AB.   (hq)
         http://www.plusgroups.org.uk
         Admin Officer: Mrs Christine George
         Hon Gen Sec: Francis Wellington
Br   50 gps
○   *N, *Y; a multi-activity social group for ages 18-35, run by
         members for the members
●   Conf - Mtgs - ET - VE
M   c 1,000 i
¶   Plus News - 4; ftm only.
✕   2006 National Federation of Eighteen Plus Groups

National Federation of Property Professionals
         Umbrella organisation, see the **National Association of Estate
         Agents** and the **Association of Residential Letting Agents**

National Federation of Residential Landlords
         merged in 2008 with the **National Landlord's Association**

National Federation of Retail Newsagents   1919
NR   Yeoman House, Sekforde St, LONDON, EC1R 0HF.   (hq)
         020 7253 4225   fax 020 7250 0927
         email info@nfrn.org.uk   http://www.nfrn.org.uk
         Nat Pres: Mahendra Jadeja
▲   Un-incorporated Society
Br   209; 20 o'seas (incl Republic of Ireland)
○   *T
●   Conf - Mtgs - ET _ Res - Exhib - Stat - Inf - LG - CTN World
         Exhib
M   18, 603 i, UK / 469 i, o'seas
¶   Retail Newsagent - 52; £1.50.
         Retail Express - 26; free.   The FED - 12; ftm, £1.95 nm.
         Members Business Guide - 1;   AR - 1; both ftm only.

**National Federation of Retirement Pensions Associations
(Pensioners' Voice)**
         reported to us as having closed - we should appreciate
         confirmation.

National Federation of Roofing Contractors   (NFRC)   1943
NR   Roofing House, 31 Worship St, LONDON, EC2A 2DY.   (hq)
         020 7638 7663   fax 020 7256 2125
         email info@nfrc.co.uk   http://www.nfrc.co.uk
         Chief Exec: Ray Horwood
Br   6; Ireland
         Scottish section: PO Box 28011, Edinburgh, EH16 6WN.
         0131-448 0266   fax 0131-440 4032
         email jmckinney@support-services.fsbusiness.co.uk
         Sec: John McKinney
○   *T; for the roofing trade (includes manufacturers, suppliers &
         service providers); ensures (through its vetting procedure &
         code of practice) that high standards of workmanship & high
         quality materials are used
Gp   Construction; Roofing
●   Conf - Mtgs - ET - Res - Comp - Inf - VE - Empl - LG
<   Intl Fedn of Roofing Contrs (IFD); Nat Home Improvement
         Coun (NHIC); Nat Specialist Contrs Coun (NSCC);
         Constructors' Liaison Gp (CLG)
M   c 900 f
¶   Update (NL) - 6; ftm only.
         Annual Directory - 1; ftm, £35 nm.
         Technical Bulletins; prices vary.   AR - 1; free.

National Federation of Royal Mail & BT Pensioners
         see **Unite: the National Federation of Royal Mail & BT
         Pensioners**

National Federation of Sea Anglers   (NFSA)   1904
NR   Hamlyn House (Level 5), Mardle Way, BUCKFASTLEIGH,
         Devon, TQ11 0NS.   (hq)
         01364 644643   fax 01364 644486
         email ho@nfsa.org.uk   http://www.nfsa.org.uk
         Devt Officer: David Rowe
○   *S; the recognised governing body for the sport of sea angling;
         to look after sea anglers & clubs
M   i in clubs
¶   NL - 4; free.

National Federation of Sea Schools
         in September 2005 merged with the Association of Bonded Sailing
         Companies & the Yacht Charter Association to form the **Marine
         Leisure Association**

**National Federation of Services for Unmarried Parents & their
         Children   (Treoir)   1976**
IRL   14 Gandon House, Custom House Sq, IFSC, DUBLIN 1,
         Republic of Ireland.
         353 (1) 670 0120   fax 353 (1) 670 0199
         http://www.treoir.ie
         Chief Exec: Margaret Dromey
○   *W
✕   2005-06 Federation of Services for Unmarried Parents & their
         Children

National Federation of Shopmobility   (NFS)   1987
NR   PO Box 6641, CHRISTCHURCH, Dorset, BH23 9DQ.   (hq)
         0845 644 2446   fax 0845 644 4442
         email info@shopmobilityuk.org.uk
         http://www.justmobility.co.uk
○   *K; to assist groups to establish shopmobility schemes
         throughout the country by providing information, advice &
         contacts
         Shopmobility is a free mobility equipment loan scheme -
         equipment is loaned daily
●   Conf - Mtgs - Inf
M   300 schemes representing 720,000 users
¶   NFS Review - 2;   AR; both ftm only.
         NFS Directory - 2.   NFS Guidelines - 1.

National Federation of Solo Clubs   (Solo NFSC)   1965
NR   PO Box 2278, NUNEATON, Warks, CV11 5YX.   (sp)
         024 7673 6499
         Nat Sec: Mavis Marsden
▲   Registered Charity
Br   53
○   *W; to provide friendship, social activities & welfare facilities for
         widowed, divorced, separated & single people over 21; to
         offer help & comfort to the bereaved & lonely
●   Mtgs - Holidays - Day trips - Dancing - Skittles - Ten pin
         bowling - Social gatherings
M   3,500 i

National Federation of Spiritual Healers   (NFSH)   1955
■   Old Manor Farm Studio, Church St, SUNBURY-on-THAMES,
         Middx, TW16 6RG.   (hq)
         01932 7831647
         email office@nfsh.org.uk   http://www.nfsh.org.uk
▲   Registered Charity
○   *P; for potential & established spiritual healers; 'NFSH is not
         associated with any religion'
●   Conf - Mtgs - Res - Exhib - SG - Inf - National Healer Referral
         Service - Distance healing
         Helpline: 0845 123 2777
M   c 5,000 i
¶   Healing Today (Jnl) - 4;   Regional NLs - 4;   AR; all ftm.

National Federation of Sub-Postmasters (NFSP) 1897
NR   Evelyn House, 22 Windlesham Gardens, SHOREHAM-by-SEA,
　　 W Sussex, BN43 5AZ.   (hq)
　　 01273 452324   fax 01273 465403
　　 email admin@nfsp.org.uk   http://www.nfsp.org.uk
　　 Gen Sec: George Thomson
▲   Un-incorporated Society
Br   95
○   *U
●   Conf - Mtgs - ET - Res - Exhib - Inf - Empl - LG
M   c 14,000 i
¶   The Subpostmaster (Jnl) - 12.   Hbk - 3 yrly.
　　 Branch Secretaries Circular - 24.   AR.

National Federation of SwimSchools
NR   c/o STA, Anchor House, Birch St, WALSALL, W Midlands,
　　 WS2 8HZ.
　　 01922 645097
　　 http://www.nfswimschools.co.uk
○   *S

**National Federation Terrazzo, Marble & Mosaic Specialists
(NFTMMS) 1932**
■   PO Box 2843, LONDON, W1A 5PG.   (hsp)
　　 0845 609 0050   fax 0845 607 8610
　　 email info@nftmms.co.uk   http://www.nftmms.co.uk
　　 Sec: Brian James
▲   Un-incorporated Society
○   *T; interests of manufacturers & fixers of terrazzo, working &
　　 laying of natural stone & mosaic
Gp   Associate membership for suppliers of goods & services to full
　　 members
●   Mtgs - Inf - VE - Provision of technical information (free) -
　　 Technical Inspection service (chargeable)
<   Brit Standards Inst; Trade Assn Forum
M   c 50 f
¶   Technical Specifications for Terrazzo & Marble - irreg; free.

National Federation of Women's Institutes (NFWI) 1915
■   104 New Kings Rd, LONDON, SW6 4LY.   (hq)
　　 020 7371 9300   fax 020 7736 3652
　　 email hq@nfwi.org.uk   http://www.thewi.org.uk
　　 Gen Sec: Mrs Jana Osborne
▲   Registered Charity
Br   c 6,500
○   *G; to enable women to improve & develop conditions of rural
　　 life; to advance their education in citizenship, cultural
　　 subjects, home economics & social welfare
●   Mtgs - ET - Social & community work
M   200,000 i
¶   WI Life - 8; ftm.

**National Federation of Young Farmers' Clubs (England &
Wales) (NFYFC) 1932**
NR   YFC Centre, NAC, Stoneleigh Park, KENILWORTH, Warks,
　　 CV8 2LG.   (hq)
　　 024 7685 7200   fax 024 7685 7229
　　 email post@nfyfc.org.uk   http://www.nfyfc.org.uk
　　 Contact: The Chief Exec
▲   Registered Charity
○   *F, *Y; to advance knowledge of agriculture, rural life,
　　 countryside issues & home crafts
●   Conf - Mtgs - Comp - LG
M   c 20, 500 i
¶   Ten 26 - 4; ftm only.

National Ferret Welfare Society (NFWS) 1989
NR   1 The Terrace, Loddiswell, KINGSBRIDGE, Devon, TQ7 4RH.
　　 (treas/p)
　　 01548 550156
　　 email herbielye@aol.com   http://www.nfws.250free.com
　　 Treas: Mrs B Lyo
○   *V; to promote the welfare of ferrets
●   Inf - Annual show (open)
<   Countryside Alliance (CA)
M   c 300
¶   NL - 3.   Information booklet - 1. .

National Field Archery Society (NFAS) 1973
NR   3 Coombe St, BRUTON, Somerset, BA10 0EP.   (hsp)
　　 01749 813056
　　 email general.secretary@nfas.net   http://www.nfas.net
　　 Gen Sec: Ralph Ashdown
▲   Company Limited by Guarantee
○   *S; promotion of archery in woodland
●   Exhib - Comp
M   c 4,500 i
¶   NFAS NL - 6; ftm only.

National Fillings Association (NFA) 1963
■   c/o HLM Secretaries Ltd, Prospect House, Sunderland Rd,
　　 ALTRINCHAM, Cheshire, WA14 5ET.   (asa)
　　 0845 638 6417   fax 0845 638 6418
　　 email nfa@hlmsecretaries.co.uk
　　 Sec: Chris Varley
▲   Un-incorporated Society
○   *T; upholstery fibre processors & manufacturers of curled hair,
　　 cotton felt, flock & felt, polyester fibre
●   Mtgs - ET
M   10 f

National Fireplace Association (NFA) 1970
■   PO Box 583, HIGH WYCOMBE, Bucks, HP15 6XT.   (hq)
　　 0845 643 1901   fax 0845 643 1902
　　 email enquiry@nfa.org.uk   http://www.nfa.org.uk
　　 Sec: Peter Heath
▲   Company Limited by Guarantee
○   *T; to represent the interests of retailers, manufacturers &
　　 importers of fires, fireplaces & stoves
●   Exhib - Inf - LG - Marketing the products - Negotiating with
　　 standards authorities of the EU on regulation
M   260 f, org
　　 (Sub: £250)
¶   Technical leaflets; ftm, £5 each nm:
　　 Open fires for coal & wood.
　　 Chimney problems & how to cure them.
　　 Air supply for open fires.
　　 Lining old chimneys.
　　 Fuels for your fire.
　　 Coal & log effect gas fires.
　　 Roomheaters & stoves.
　　 Fireplace safety, maintenance & chimney sweeping.
　　 Masonry chimneys, their design & construction.
　　 Fireplace surrounds, their construction & installation.

National Forum of Engineering Centres (NFEC) 1993
NR   22 Yorkshire St, MORECAMBE, Lancs, LA3 1QE.   (hq)
　　 01524 401044
　　 http://www.nfec.org.uk
▲   Registered Charity
○   *E
M   f & org
✕   2003 National Forum for Engineering in Colleges

National Forum for Risk Management in the Public Sector
　　 alternative name of **ALARM**

          © CBD Research Ltd · Beckenham · BR3 5JS · Tel 020 8650 7745 · Fax 020 8650 0768 · E-mail cbd@cbdresearch.com · www.cbdresearch.com

National Foundation for Educational Research in England & Wales (NFER) 1946
- ■ The Mere, Upton Park, SLOUGH, Berks, SL1 2DQ. (hq)
  01753 574123 fax 01753 691632
  email enquiries@nfer.ac.uk http://www.nfer.ac.uk
  Chief Exec: Sue Rossiter
- ▲ Company Limited by Guarantee; Registered Charity
- Br 2
- ○ *E, *Q; provision of educational research services, information & results; development of assessment tests & methods
- ● Conf - Mtgs - ET - Res - Inf - Lib
- M c 200 org
- ¶ Publications list available.

National Fox Welfare Society (NFWS) 1993
- NR 135 Higham Rd, RUSHDEN, Northants, NN10 6DS. (coordinators/p)
  01933 411996
- ○ *V; to rescue & rehabilitate sick & injured foxes; to provide advice to the public on any aspect of fox behaviour or problems; to recommend, or provide, an effective deterrent

National Franchised Dealers Association
   a group of the **Retail Motor Industry Federation**

National Fruit Wine, Mead & Liqueur Producers Association 2003
- NR 3 Grange Rd, TRING, Herts, HP23 5JP. (hsp)
  email bsreid@aol.com
  Hon Sec: Brian S Reid
- ▲ Un-incorporated Society
- ○ *T; 'to improve the quality & image of fruit wines, meads & liqueurs in the UK'
- ● Mtgs - Exhib - Comp - VE
- < Intl Assn Cider & Fruit Wine Producers
- M 12 f

National Game Dealers' Association (NGDA) 1979
- ■ Pollards Farm, Clanville, ANDOVER, Hants, SP11 9JE. (chmn/b)
  01264 730294 fax 01264 730780
  Chmn: Chris Chappel
- ▲ Un-incorporated Society
- Br Scotland
- ○ *T; to safeguard & promote the commercial interests of the members; to encourage best practice in the industry
- ● Conf - Mtgs - ET - Res - Exhib - Stat - Expt - Inf - LG
- M 1 i, 36 f, 1 org
- ¶ Various publications.

National Gamekeepers Organisation (NGO) 1997
- ■ PO Box 107, BISHOP AUCKLAND, Co Durham, DL14 9YW. (hq)
  01388 665899 fax 01388 665899
  http://www.nationalgamekeepers.org.uk
  Mem Sec: Ann Robinson-Ruddock
- ○ *P
- Gp Moorland branch
- M 12,400 i

National Gardens Scheme Charitable Trust (NGS) 1927
- ■ Hatchlands Park, East Clandon, GUILDFORD, Surrey, GU4 7RT. (hq)
  01483 211535 fax 01483 211537
  email ngs@ngs.org.uk http://www.ngs.org.uk
  Chief Exec: Mrs Julia Grant
- ▲ Company Limited by Guarantee; Registered Charity
- ○ *G, *H, *W; a non-membership body concerned to arrange the opening of gardens of quality, character & interest to raise money for beneficiary charities such as: 1) Queen's Nursing Institute, 2) Macmillan Cancer Support, 3) the careership scheme of the National Trust, 4) Perennial Fund, 5) the Royal Fund for Gardeners' Children, 6) Crossroads, 7) Help the Hospices, 8) Marie Curie Cancer Care; & many others chosen by garden owners
- ● Exhib - Arrangement of opening (to the public) of nearly 3,500, mostly private, gardens in England & Wales on advertised days to raise money
- ¶ The Yellow Book, 2008; £7.99. (formerly known as Gardens of England & Wales open for Charity).

National Gerbil Society (NGS) 1971
- NR 373 Lynmouth Ave, MORDEN, Surrey, SM4 4RY. (sp)
  020 8241 8942 fax 0870 160 0843
  email jackie@gerbils.co.uk http://www.gerbils.co.uk
  Sec: Jackie Roswell
- ▲ Un-incorporated Society
- ○ *G; to promote Gerbils & Jirds as pets, breeding & exhibition animals
- ● Mtgs - Exhib - Comp - Inf - PL - VE
- < Intl Gerbil Fedn
- M 200 i, 1 f, UK / 11 i, 3 org, o'seas
- ¶ The Nibbler - 4; Ybk; both ftm only.

National Golf Clubs' Advisory Association (NGCAA) 1922
- NR The Threshing Barn, Homme Castle Barns, Shelsley Walsh, WORCESTER, WR6 6RR. (hq)
  01886 812943
  http://www.ngcaa.org.uk
  Sec: Michael Shaw
- ▲ Un-incorporated Society
- ○ *N, *S; provision of advice, especially legal advice, to affiliated golf clubs
- ● Inf
- M 1,200 golf clubs
- ¶ NL - 6; Ybk (incl AR & LM); both ftm only.

National Governors' Association 2006
- NR SBQ1 (2nd floor), 29 Smallbrook Queensway, BIRMINGHAM, B5 4HG. (hq)
  0121-643 5787 fax 0121-633 7141
  http://www.nga.org.uk
  Chief Exec: Jean McEntire
- ▲ Company Limited by Guarantee; Registered Charity
- ○ *E; to represent the governor's view
- Gp Governing bodies of schools
- ● Publications
- M c 6,000 i, 600 org
- × 2006 (National Association of School Governors
  (2005 Nat Assn of Governors & Managers
  (National Governers' Council

National Grammar Schools Association (NGSA) 1986
- NR 18 Leomansley Rd, LICHFIELD, Staffs, WS13 8AW. (sb/p)
  01543 251517
  http://www.ngsa.org.uk
  Hon Sec: Mrs Jenny Jones
- ○ *K; to support selective education as a parental option within the State education sector; to offer support & advice to grammar schools under threat of closure or reorganisation

National Greyhound Racing Club Ltd   (NGRC)   1928
NR   Procter Hosue, 1 Procter St, LONDON, WC1V 6DW.   (hq)
      0845 077 0825   fax 0845 071 0801
      email mail@ngrc.org.uk   http://www.ngrc.org.uk
▲   Company Limited by Guarantee
○   *S; the judicial & administrative body for greyhound racing
M   racecourses
¶   Various publications.

National Group on Homeworking
¶   Publications available.
      Closed November 2008

National Guild of Removers & Storers   1993
NR   PO Box 690, CHESHAM, Bucks, HP5 1WR.   (hq)
      01494 792279   fax 01494 792111
      http://www.ngrs.org.uk
      Hon Chmn: Jonathan Bramwell
○   *T
●   Conf - Mtgs - LG
<   Assn Relocation Agents; Nat Register of Approved Removers &
      Storers
M   c 200 f
¶   The Professional Remover - 6; free.

National Hairdressers' Federation   (NHF)   1942
■   1 Abbey Court, Fraser Rd, Priory Business Park, BEDFORD,
      MK44 3WH.   (hq)
      0845 345 6500   fax 01234 838875
      email enquiries@nhf.info   http://www.nhf.biz
      Gen Sec: Eileen Lawson
▲   Un-incorporated Society
Br   52
○   *T; for self-employed hairdressing, beauty therapists & salon
      owners
●   Conf - Mtgs - Comp - SG - Empl - LG
<   Org Mondiale de la Coiffure
M   7,250 i, 30 f, UK / 30 i, o'seas
¶   Salon Focus - 6; ftm only.

National Harmonica League   (NHL)   1975
NR   112 Hag Hill Rise, Taplow, MAIDENHEAD, Berks, SL6 0LT.
      (chmn/p)
      01628 604069
      Chmn: Dr Roger Trobridge
▲   Un-incorporated Society
○   *D; for anyone interested in the harmonica, whether a player or
      not
●   Mtgs - ET - Comp - Inf
<   Intl Harmonica Org
M   c 400 i
¶   Harmonica World - 6; ftm, £1.50 nm.

National Health Service Consultants' Association   1976
NR   Hill House, Great Bourton, BANBURY, Oxon, OX17 1QH.
      (chmn p)
      01295 750407   fax 01295 750407
      email nhsca@pop3.poptel.org.uk
      http://www.nhsca.org.uk
      Pres: Peter Fisher,   Chmn: Prof Allyson Pollock
○   *P

National Hedge Laying Society   (NHLS)   1978
NR   88 Manor Rd, TODDINGTON, Beds, LU5 6AJ.   (hsb)
      01525 873795
      email nhls.enquiries@googlemail.com
      http://www.hedgelaying.org.uk
      Hon Sec: Allan Portas
▲   Registered Charity
○   *F, *K; to encourage the art of hedge laying & to keep local
      styles in existence; to encourage landowners to manage
      hedges by laying
●   ET - Exhib - Comp - PL - LG
M   450 i
      (Sub: £15)
¶   NL - 3; ftm, £1 nm.

**National Heritage: the Museums Action Movement   (NH)
1971**
■   NH Administration Centre, Rye Rd, HAWKHURST, Kent,
      TN18 5DW.   (hq)
      01580 752052   fax 01580 755670
      email liz@lizm.eclipse.co.uk
      http://www.nationalheritage.org.uk
      Admin: Liz Moore
▲   Registered Charity
○   *A, *G; to support museums & galleries in the United Kingdom;
      to represent their visitors & users
●   Mtgs - Inf - Research/survey collection
M   i, f, museums
¶   Museum News.   AR.

National Hillclimb Association
■   3 Perryfield Rd, Southgate, CRAWLEY, E Sussex, RH11 8AA.
      (mem/sp)
      Mem Sec: Lin Cooper,
      Contact: Nigel Glover (01305 764432)
○   *S; motor-cycle hillclimbs
      No further information supplied

National Historic Ships   (NHSC)   1992
NR   Park Row, Greenwich, LONDON, SE10 9NF.   (hq)
      020 8312 8558
      http://www.martyn.heighton@nationalhistoricships.org.uk
      http://www.nationalhistoricships.org.ul
      Head of Secretariat: Martyn Heighton
○   *L; to secure the long time preservation of a sample of ships
      representing important aspects of UK maritime history
Gp   Technical c'ee (people with specialist skills & knowledge in ship
      preservation)
●   Conf - Mtgs - Res - Inf - PL - LG
<   Nat Maritime Museum
M   [not stated]
×   2006 National Historic Ships Committee

National Home Improvement Council   (NHIC)   1974
■   Roofing House, 31 Worship St, LONDON, EC2A 2DY.   (hq)
      020 7448 3853   fax 020 7256 2125
      email info@nhic.org.uk   http://www.nhic.org.uk
      Exec Dir: Roman N Russocki
▲   Company Limited by Guarantee
○   *T; to be the home imrovement industry's principal interface
      with government, ensuring that housing policies & public
      funding are directed at home & environmental improvement
      & fuel policy issues; to promote to homeowners the benefits
      of renovating & maintaining houses to the highest possible
      standards of energy efficiency
●   Mtgs - ET - Res - Comp - Stat - Inf - VE - LG
M   20 f, 20 org
¶   Progress - 2.

© CBD Research Ltd · Beckenham · BR3 5JS · Tel 020 8650 7745 · Fax 020 8650 0768 · E-mail cbd@cbdresearch.com · www.cbdresearch.com

National Hop Association   (NHA)
NR   The Basement, 754 Fulham Rd, LONDON, SW6 5SH.
     (press/office)
     020 7384 1333   fax 020 7384 0335
     email rupert@randr.co.uk   http://www.hops.co.uk
○   *F, *N; to represent the hop growers of England, through the 5
     producer groups
●   Mtgs - Res - Stat - Expt - Inf - PL
M   5 gps

National Horse Brass Society   (NHBS)   1975
■   Woodbine Cottage, Tarrington, HEREFORD, HR1 4HZ.   (hq)
     01432 890404
     http://www.horse-brass-society.org.uk
     Gen Sec: Steve Pink
▲   un-incorporated Society
○   *G; to bring together people interested in horse brasses
●   Mtgs - VE - Archives
M   c 450 i
¶   Jnl - 2;   NL - 2;   Directory - 1; all ftm.
     Reference works - 1½-2 yrly; c £10.

National Housing Federation   1935
NR   25 Procter St, LONDON, WC1V 6NY.   (hq)
     020 7067 1010   fax 020 7067 1011
     email info@housing.org.uk   http://www.housing.org.uk
     Chief Exec: Jim Coulter
▲   Company Limited by Guarantee
Br   10
○   *N; to promote housing associations; to provide advice in
     formation
●   Conf - Mtgs - ET - Res - Exhib - Stat - Inf - LG
<   Intl Fedn Housing & Planning; Comité Européen Co-ordination
     de l'Habitat Social
M   1,380 housing assns
¶   Housing Today - 51; ftm, prices on application nm.
     Ybk.   AR; free.

National Ice Skating Association of UK Ltd   (NISA)   1879
NR   Grains Building, High Cross St, Hockley, NOTTINGHAM,
     NG1 3ax.   (hq)
     0115-988 8060   fax 0115-988 8061
     email nisa@iceskating.org.uk
     http://www.iceskating.org.uk
     Chief Exec: Keith Horton
▲   Company Limited by Guarantee
○   *S; to develop ice skating in all its disciplines; to optimise
     individual achievement at every level
●   Comp - Inf
<   Intl Skating U (ISU)(Switzerland)
M   4,500 i, 84 clubs
¶   Ice Link (Jnl) - 6; free.

National Information Forum   (NIF)   1981
■   33 Highshore Rd, LONDON, SE15 5AF.   (hq)
     020 7708 5943
     http://www.nif.org.uk
     Dir: Ann Darnbrough
▲   Company Limited by Guarantee; Registered Charity
○   *K; 'committed to making information more accessible &
     available to all disabled or elderly people, refugees & any
     other groups who have difficulty in getting information'
●   Conf - Mtgs - ET - Inf - LG
M   100 org
¶   Alf Morris - People's Parliamentarian; £10 m, £20 nm.
     Information Sheets (emailed) - irreg; ftm only.

**National Institute of Adult Continuing Education (England &
Wales)   (NIACE)   1949**
■   Renaissance House, 20 Princess Road West, LEICESTER,
     LE1 6TP.   (hq)
     0116-204 4200
     email enquiries@niace.org.uk   http://www.niace.org.uk
     Dir: Alan Tuckett
▲   Company Limited by Guarantee; Registered Charity
○   *E, *N; a national centre for cooperation, enquiry, research,
     information & consultation in the field of continuing
     education for adults
●   Conf - Mtgs - Res - Exhib - SG - Stat - Inf - Lib - LG
<   Eur Assn of Adult Educ; Intl Coun of Adult Educ
M   c 250 i, 480 org
¶   Publications list available.

National Institute of Carpet & Floorlayers Ltd   (NICF)   1978
■   4d St Mary's Place, The Lace Market, NOTTINGHAM,
     NG1 1PH.   (hq)
     0115-958 3077   fax 0115-941 2238
     email info@nicfltd.org.uk   http://www.nicfltd.org.uk
○   *T; to give competent fitters a form of recognition so that
     retailers, contractors & customers can identify them
●   ET - Exam - Exhib - Inf - Conciliation of complaints
M   500 i, 100 f (manufacturers as patrons, retailers as associates)
¶   Installation Manual; £50 m, £75 nm.

National Institute of Medical Herbalists Ltd   (NIMH)   1864
■   Elm House, 54 Mary Arches St, EXETER, Devon, EX4 3BA.   (hq)
     01392 426022   fax 01392 498963
     email info@nimh.org.uk   http://www.nimh.org.uk
     Hon Sec: Anne Varley
▲   Company Limited by Guarantee
○   *L, *P, *Q; a professional body of practising medical herbalists;
     research & education in herbal medicine
●   Conf - Mtgs - ET - Res - Inf - Lib - LG
<   Eur Herbal Practitioners Assn; Brit Herbal Medicine Assn
M   575 i, UK / 120 i, o'seas
¶   Herbal Thymes (NL) - 4; ftm only.   LM - 1; free.

National Insulation Association   (NIA)   2002
■   2 Vimy Court, Vimy Rd, LEIGHTON BUZZARD, Beds,
     LU7 1FG.   (hq)
     01525 383313   fax 01525 854918
     email info@nationalinsulationassociation.org.uk
     http://www.nationalinsulationassociation.org.uk
     Chief Exec: Neil Marshall
▲   Company Limited by Guarantee
○   *T; to represet the manufacturers, installers & associate
     members of cavity wall insulation, draught proofing & other
     innovative solutions
Gp   Installers; Manufacturers; Surveyors; Scheme managers
●   Conf - Mtgs - Exhib - Inf - LG
<   Bldgs Efficiency Fedn (BEEF)
M   99 i, 11 f, 5 associate
     (Sub: £1173.83 i, £3523.83 f & org)
¶   The Installer - 3;   In-House NL - 6/10; both ftm only.
     LM - updated; free.

National Irish Safety Organisation   (NISO)
IRL   A11 Calmount Park, Ballymount, DUBLIN 12, Republic of
     Ireland.
     353 (1) 465 9760   fax 353 (1) 465 9765
     email info@niso.ie
○   *P

National Joint Utilities Group   (NJUG)   1977
NR   28 Broadway, Westminster, LONDON, SW1H 9JX.   (hq)
    020 7340 1423
    email info@njug.co.uk
    Chief Exec: Richard Wakelen
○   *N, *T; the forum for objects of mutual interest in distribution
    engineering activities for the gas, electricity, water & cable
    telecommunications industries; to coordinate reports /
    responses on behalf of the utilities
Gp   Electricity industry; Gas industry; Telecommunications; Water
    industry
●   Conf - Mtgs - Res - Exhib
<   Assn Geographic Inf
M   f & org
¶   Bulletin - 2; free.
    Specialist reports; prices vary (free to £10).   AR.

National Jousting Association
    alternative name of **Knights of Royal England**

National Jumblers Federation   (NJF)
NR   347 Kingston Rd, Ewell, EPSOM, Surrey, KT19 0BS.   (hsp)
    020 8393 3342
    email truedvd@aol.com
    Sec: David True
○   *G, *T; acts in the interests of autojumblers, bike jumblers &
    boat jumblers
M   i & f
¶   Jnl - 6.

National Karting Association Ltd   (NKA)   1993
■   Devonia, Long Road West, Dedham, COLCHESTER, Essex,
    CO7 6ES.   (hsp/b)
    01206 322726   fax 01206 322726
    email nka@nationalkarting.co.uk
    http://www.nationalkarting.co.uk
    Co Sec: Mrs Linda D Barton
▲   Company Limited by Guarantee
Br   USA
○   *S, *T; to help circuit owners in the aspects of health & safety &
    promotion
Gp   Safety coordination
●   Mtgs - ET - LG
<   Motor Activities Trg Coun; [& a proposed Kart Forum body]
M   c 100 i
¶   NL - 4;   NKA Guideline; both ftm.

National Kidney Federation   1978
NR   The Point, Coach Rd, WORKSOP, Notts, S81 8BW.
    (regd/office)
    01909 544999   fax 01909 481723
    email nkf@kidney.org.uk   http://www.kidney.org.uk
▲   Registered Charity
○   *W; to promote the welfare of persons suffering from kidney
    disease or renal failure & those relatives & friends who care
    for them
●   Conf - Inf - LG
    Helpline: 0845 601 0209
<   Eur Kidney Patients' Assn (CEAPIR)
M   500 i, 65 org
¶   Kidney Life - 4; £12.
    Conference Report - 1;   AR & Accounts - 1; both free.

National Landlords' Association   (NLA)   1973
■   22-26 Albert Embankment, LONDON, SE1 7TJ.   (hq)
    020 7840 8900   fax 0871 237 7535
    email info@landlords.org.uk
    http://www.landlords.org.uk
    Chief Exec: David Salusbury
▲   Company Limited by Guarantee
○   *K; to protect & promote the interests of private residential
    landlords
●   Conf - Mtgs - ET - Exhib - Inf - LG
M   14,000 i, f
    (Sub: £88 i, £128 f)
¶   UK Landlord - 6; ftm, £50 nm.
    Landlord Development Manual - 1; ftm, £3 nm.
×
    2008 National Federation of Residential Landlords
    2004 Small Landlords' Association

National League of the Blind & Disabled
    a section of **Community**

National Library for the Blind
    now the national library service of the **Royal National Institute for
    the Blind**

National Limousine & Chauffeur Association   (1997)   NLCA
■   Wishbone Garage, Calverley Green Rd, Altofts, WAKEFIELD,
    W Yorks, WF6 2JS.   (hsb)
    07886 563724
    email info@nlca.co.uk   http://www.nlca.co.uk
    Chmn: Peter Wright
▲   Company Limited by Guarantee
Br   4
○   *T; to ensure the safe & legal operation of limousines &
    chauffeur driven cars throughout the UK
●   Conf - Mtgs - ET - Res - Exhib - LG
M   i & f
    (Sub: £60 i, £120 f)
¶   New items on web - 12; ftm only.
×   2007 (January) National Limousine Association

National Literacy Association   (NLA)   1993
NR   87 Grange Rd, RAMSGATE, Kent, CT11 9QB.   (hq)
    01843 239952
    email mail@nla.org.uk   http://www.nla.org.uk
    Dir & Sec: Jo Klaces
▲   Registered Charity
○   *K; a charity working to eliminate illiteracy amongst children &
    young people
●   ET - Res - Stat - Inf - Lib - LG
<   Assn Educl Psychologists; Assn of Teachers & Lecturers; Brit
    Dyslexic Assn; Brit Educl Suppliers Assn [& 9 other
    educational bodies]
M   64 i, 298 org
¶   NL - 4; free.   AR - 1; board members only.
    The Guide to Literacy Resources 7th ed - 1.
    Literacy & ICT: cutting edge practice in the primary school - 1.

National Market Traders Federation   (NMTF)   1899
■   Hampton House, Hawshaw Lane, Hoyland, BARNSLEY, S Yorks,
    S74 0HA.   (hq)
    01226 749021   fax 01226 740329
    email enquiries@nmtf.co.uk   http://www.nmtf.co.uk
    Gen Sec: Joe Harrison
▲   Un-incorporated Society
Br   125
○   *T; representation of market traders at local, national &
    international level
●   Conf - Exhib - LG - Promotion events
<   World U of Whls Market Retail Section (WUWM)
M   35,000 i
    (Sub: £76)
¶   Federation News - 6; free.

© CBD Research Ltd · Beckenham · BR3 5JS · Tel 020 8650 7745 · Fax 020 8650 0768 · E-mail cbd@cbdresearch.com · www.cbdresearch.com

National Metal Trades Federation
 has closed.

National Microelectronics Institute   (NMI)   1997
NR   Innovation Centre (1st floor), Broad Quay, BATH, Somerset,
        BA1 1UD.   (hq)
        email info@nmi.org.uk   http://www.nmi.org.uk
        Chief Exec: Derek Boyd
▲   Company Limited by Guarantee
○   *N, *T; to provide a mechanism for collaboration between
        members, educational organisations, regional bodies &
        government
●   Mtgs - ET - LG
M   [not stated]

National Motorcycle Council   (NMC)   1985
NR   3 The Quadrant, COVENTRY, Warks, CV1 2DY.   (hq)
        247 655 3838
        http://www.nmc.org.uk
        Secretariat: Craig Carey-Clinch
○   *N; liaison between various sectional interests within
        motorcycling
●   Inf - LG
<   Parliamentary Advisory C'ee on Transport Safety (PACTS)
M   i, f & org

National Mouse Club   (NMC)   1895
NR   44 Speeton Avenue, BRADFORD, W Yorks, BD7 4NQ.   (hsp)
        01274 574205
        http://www.nationalmouseclub.co.uk
        Hon Sec: Brian Cookson
▲   Un-incorporated Society
○   *B; to promote breeding & exhibition of fancy mice
●   Mtgs - Exhib - Comp - Inf
M   150 i, UK / 5 i, o'seas
¶   NMC News - 12; £20 yr m, £2 each nm.   Ybk; ftm only.

National Network of Assessment Centres   (NNAC)
NR   The Royal National College, College Rd, HEREFORD,
        HR1 1EB.   (hq)
        01432 376635
        email access@rncb.ac.uk   http://www.nnac.org
○   *N, *W; for physically or sensorily disabled people; to advise
        colleges & universities about teaching, learning strategies &
        enabling devices to ensure access to the curriculum for all
        students
M   centres
✕   2006 National Federation of Access Centres

National Newspapers of Ireland   (NNI)
IRL   Clyde Lodge, 15 Clyde Rd, DUBLIN 4, Republic of Ireland.
        353 (1) 668 9099   fax 353 (1) 668 9872
        email nni@cullencommunications.ie   http://www.nni.ie
○   *T; the representative body of Ireland's daily & weekly
        newspapers

National Obesity Forum   (NOF)   2000
NR   6a Gordon Rd (1st floor), NOTTINGHAM, NG2 5LN.
        0115-846 2109   fax 0115-846 2329
        email info@nof.uk.com
        http://www.nationalobesityforum.org.uk
○   *P; for health care professionals concerned in raising
        awareness of the growing impact of obesity on the National
        Health Service
M   i
¶   Via their webpage

National Off-Licence Association
IRL   Block D - Unit 8, Nutgrove Office Park, Rathfarnham,
        DUBLIN 14, Republic of Ireland
        353 (1) 296 2326   fax 353 (1) 296 2451
        email admin@noffla.ie   http://www.noffla.ie
        Admin: Reggie Walsh
○   *T

National Office of Animal Health Ltd   (NOAH)   1986
■   3 Crossfield Chambers, Gladbeck Way, ENFIELD, Middx,
        EN2 7HF.   (hq)
        020 8367 3131   fax 020 8363 1155
        email noah@noah.co.uk   http://www.noah.co.uk
        Chief Exec: Philip Sketchley
▲   Company Limited by Guarantee
○   *T, *V; for manufacturers of licensed animal medicines in the
        UK (incl pet & farm animals)
Gp   Code of Practice C'ee for the Promotion of Animal Medicines
●   Conf - Mtgs - ET - Res - Exhib - Stat - Inf - LG - Conducts
        research sales survey on behalf of members & non-members
        - Media relations on behalf of members
<   Intl Fedn Animal Health (IFAH); Intl Fedn Animal Health (IFAH-
        Europe)
M   32 i, 12 f
¶   Compendium of Data Sheets IOC Animal Medicines - 1.
        (also available online: www.noahcompendium.co.uk).
        Poisoning in Veterinary Practice, 1992; £3.
        Animal Medicine Record Book, 1999; £3.50.
        Briefing documents & reports; free.

National Operatic & Dramatic Association   (NODA)   1899
NR   NODA House, 58-60 Lincoln Rd, PETERBOROUGH, Cambs,
        PE1 2RZ.   (hq)
        0870 770 2480   fax 0870 770 2490
        email everyone@noda.org.uk   http://www.noda.org.uk
        Chief Exec: Tony Gibbs
▲   Registered Charity
○   *A, *D, *N; 'national umbrella body for amateur operatic &
        dramatic societies'
●   Conf - Mtgs - ET (Summer school for amateur operatic &
        dramatic students with professional tutors)
<   Intl Theatre Exchange (UK branch of IATA)
M   2,500 i, 2,500 org
¶   NODA National News - 4; ftm, £2.50 each nm.

National Organisation of Beaters & Pickers Up   (NOBs)   2005
NR   28 Butts Rd, Chiseldon, SWINDON, Wilts, SN4 0NW.
        01793 741113
        http://www.nobs.org.uk
        Chief Exec: Neil Dale
○   *G; for those interested in working with gamekeepers & shoot
        captains as beaters, pickers-up or loaders

National Organisation for Counselling Adoptees & their Parents
(NORCAP)
   see Adults Affected by Adoption - NORCAP

**National Organisation for Phobias, Anxiety, Neuroses,
   Information & Care   (NO PANIC)**
■   93 Brands Farm Way, TELFORD, Shropshire, TF3 2JQ.   (hsp)
        01952 590005   fax 01952 270962
        email ceo@nopanic.org.uk   http://www.nopanic.org.uk
        Chief Exec: Colin M Hammond
▲   Registered Charity
Br   Ireland
○   *W; the relief & rehabilitation of those people suffering from
        panic attacks, phobias, obsessive compulsive disorder,
        related anxiety disorders & tranquilliser withdrawal; to
        provide support to sufferers & their families &/or carers
●   Conf - ET - Inf - Telephone recovery course - Advice & support
        Helpline: 0808 808 0545 (0010-2200 daily)
M   2,700 i, UK / 100 i, o'seas
¶   NL - 24; ftm.
        No Panic: the facts [about the charity].
        Information booklets [on specific problems]; £1.50 each.
        Books; £5 - £12 each.   Audio & Visual aids; £2 - £14.

National Organisation for Pupil Referral Units   2004
NR   Somerset County Council, County Hall, TAUNTON, Somerset,
       TA1 4DY.
       01823 358163
       email secretary@prus.org.uk   http://www.prus.org.uk
       Sec: Jacky Mackenzie
O   *E; the provision of suitable education for pupils of compulsory
       school age who, because of illness etc are unable to attend
       a mainstream school

National Organisation for the Treatment of Abusers   (NOTA)
1991
NR   PO Box 356, HULL, HU12 8WR.   (hq)
       01482 896990   fax 01482 896990
       email notaoffice@aol.com   http://www.nota.co.uk
▲   Registered Charity
Br   12; Eire
O   *K, *P; to protect potential victims of sexual aggression through
       developing & promoting professional practice with both sex
       offenders (regardless of their age or gender)... & by direct
       work with their victims & non-abusing family members
●   Conf - Mtgs - ET - Res - LG
<   Assn for the Treatment of Abusers (USA)
M   c 1,200 i
¶   Jnl of Sexual Aggression - 2.   NOTA News - 4.
       Annual Conference Audio Tapes - 1.

National Orthophobics Group
■   81 Park View, Collins Rd, LONDON, N5 2UD.
O   *W
M   5 i

National Osteoporosis Society   (NOS)   1986
■   Manor Farm, Skinners Hill, Camerton, BATH, Somerset,
       BA2 0PJ.   (hq)
       01761 471771   fax 01761 471104
       email info@nos.org.uk   http://www.nos.org.uk
       Chief Exec: Mrs Claire L Severgnini
▲   Registered Charity
Br   130 regional support groups
O   *W; to provide help & support for sufferers of osteoporosis; to
       encourage the medical professions, government etc to work
       together towards improving treatment & prevention; to
       support research
●   Conf - Mtgs - ET - Res - Inf - LG - Advice & reassurance to
       people with medical queries through the helpline staffed by
       specialised nurses, booklets etc
<   Eur Foundation for Osteoporosis & Bone Disease; Intl
       Osteoporosis Foundation; Nat Coun Women
M   25,000 i
       (Sub:£15)
¶   Osteoporosis News (NL) - 4; ftm only.
       Osteoporosis Review - 4; ftm only.   AR; free.

National Outdoor Events Association   (NOEA)   1979
■   7 Hamilton Way, WALLINGTON, Surrey, SM6 9NJ.   (hq)
       020 8669 8121   fax 020 8647 1128
       email secretary@noea.org.uk   http://www.noea.org.uk
       Gen Sec: John W Barton
▲   Un-incorporated Society
O   *T; for local authorities, show organisers & suppliers of
       equipment & services for the outdoor events industry
M   262 f
¶   Ybk; free.   Code of Practice for Outdoor Events; £22.

National Outsourcing Association   (NOA)
NR   44 Wardour St, LONDON, W1D 6QZ.   (hq)
       020 7292 8686   fax 020 7287 2905
       email admin@noa.co.uk   http://www.noa.co.uk
▲   Company Limited by Guarantee
∩   *T; to develop experience & professionalism in all areas of
       business technology outsourcing - in particular outsourcing of
       telecommunications & computing networks; to promote the
       business advantages of outsourcing
●   Conf - Mtgs - Res - Inf - LG - Promotion & lobbying
M   f
¶   Business Technology Outsourcer - 2; free.

National Packaging Council   (NPC)   1999
NR   24 Grange St, KILMARNOCK, Ayrshire, KA1 2AR.   (hq)
       01563 570518   fax 01563 572728
       email npc@natpack.org.uk   http://www.natpack.co.uk
       Sec: Allan Glen
O   *N, *P; administrative & management services for trade
       associations involved in the packaging industry
Gp   British Packaging Association; Environmental & Technical
       Association for the Paper Sack Industry; Sheet Plant
       Association;
●   Conf - Mtgs - ET - Exhib - Comp - Inf - VE - LG
M   180 f, UK / 10 f, o'seas

National Park Homes Council
       a division of the **National Caravan Council**

National Pawnbrokers Association   (NPA)   1892
NR   Chiltern Court 37 St Peters Avenue, Caversham, READING,
       Berks, RG4 7DH.   (asa)
       0118-947 7385
       http://www.thenpa.co.uk
       Sec Gen: Des Milligan
▲   Company Limited by Guarantee
O   *T
●   Conf - Mtgs - Res - Exhib - Comp - Stat - Inf - VE - LG -
       Insurance - Legal, financial, operations, publicity advice -
       New business promotion & assistance
<   Nat Cham Tr; Soc Assn Execs: Glasgow Pawnbrokers Assn
M   c 450 f
¶   NPA Times - 4;   AR & Accounts - 1; both free.
       Leaflets:
           Pawnbrokers Guide;   Using a Pawnbroker; both ftm.

National Pensioners' Convention   (NPC)   1990
■   19-23 Ironmonger Row, LONDON, EC1V 3QP.   (hq)
       020 7553 6510   fax 020 7553 6511
       email admin@npcuk.org   http://www.npcuk.org
       Gen Sec: Joe Harris
       Admin: Alison Purshouse
▲   Un-incorporated Society
Br   500 affiliated groups
O   *K, *N; umbrella organisation for pensioner organisations,
       regional pensioner liaison forums, charities & trade union
       retired members associations
●   Mtgs - ET - Res - Inf - LG
<   AGE: the Eur Older People's Platform
M   1,200 i, 100 f, 400 org
¶   The Message - 4; ftm, 10p per copy nm.
       Pension credit for beginners; 50p.
       Women - 'Wise-up' on Pensions; £1.

© CBD Research Ltd · Beckenham · BR3 5JS · Tel 020 8650 7745 · Fax 020 8650 0768 · E-mail cbd@cbdresearch.com · www.cbdresearch.com

National Pest Technicians Association (NPTA) 1993
■ NPTA House, Hall Lane, Kinoulton, NOTTINGHAM,
  NG12 3EF. (hq)
  01949 81133   fax 01949 823905
  email officenpta@aol.com   http://www.npta.org.uk
  Sec: John A Davison
  Admin Officer: Mrs Julie Gillies
▲ Company Limited by Guarantee
○ *P; to promote the role of pest controller
● Conf - Mtgs - ET - Exhib - Inf
M c 900 i & f
¶ Today's Technician - 4; ftm, £4 each nm.

National Pharmacy Association (NPA) 1921
NR 38-42 St Peter's St, ST ALBANS, Herts, AL1 3NP. (hq)
  01727 832161   fax 01727 840858
  email npa@npa.co.uk   http://www.npa.co.uk
▲ Company Limited by Guarantee
○ *T; for community retail pharmacists
M f
✕ 2005 National Pharmaceutical Association

National Philatelic Society (NPS) 1899
■ British Postal Museum & Archive, Freeling House, Phoenix
  Place, LONDON, WC1X 0DL. (hq)
  email nps@ukphilately.org.uk
  http://www.ukphilately.org.uk/nps
  Hon Gen Sec: Peter Mellor
▲ Un-incorporated Society
○ *G; promotion & encouragement of philately
● Mtgs - Lib
< Assn of Brit Philatelic Socs
M 600 i, 1 org, UK / 50 i, o'seas
¶ The Stamp Lover - 6; ftm, £17 yr nm.

National Phobics Society (NPS) 1970
■ Zion Community Resource Centre, 339 Stretford Rd, Hulme,
  MANCHESTER, M15 4ZY. (hq)
  0844 477 5774   fax 0161-227 9862
  email info@phobics-society.org.uk
  http://www.phobics-society.org.uk
  Chief Exec: Glenmoure Kingsley-Nunes
▲ Registered Charity
Br self-help groups & therapists
○ *W; to support anyone affected by anxiety disorders (phobias,
  panic attacks, obsessive/compulsive disorders)
Gp Mental health; Anxiety disorders
● Conf - ET - Inf - Support groups - One to one therapy services -
  Helpline services - On-line service
M 6,000 i, 1,000 f, 20 self-help gps, UK / 25 i, o'seas
¶ Anxious Times (NL) - 4; ftm only.

National Piers Society (NPS) 1979
NR 11 Bloomesley Close, NEWTON AYCLIFFE, Co Durham,
  DL5 4XQ. (pro/p)
  01325 318317; 01472 350404
  email timmickleburgh2002@yahoo.co.uk
  http://www.piers.co.uk
  Hon Sec: Louise Foster
▲ Company Limited by Guarantee; Registered Charity
○ *G, *K; promoting interest in the preservation & continued
  enjoyment of seaside piers
● Res - Inf - PL - VE - LG
< Paddle Steamer Preservation Soc
M i & f
¶ Piers (Jnl) - 4; ftm.   Good Piers Guide.
  Guide to British Piers, 3rd ed.

National Pig Association (NPA) 1999
NR Agriculture House, STONELEIGH PARK, Warks, CV8 2LZ. (hq)
  024 7685 8784   fax 024 7865 8786
  email npa@npanet.org.uk   http://www.npa-uk.org.uk
  Exec Dir: Stewart Houston
▲ Company Limited by Guarantee
○ *B, *T; for the UK pig industry
Gp Allied industry; Campaigns
● Conf - Mtgs - ET - LG
M 1,300 i, 100 f

National Pigeon Association (NPA) 1918
NR 27 Highclere Rd, QUEDGELEY, Glos, GL2 4HD. (hsp)
  01452 720783
  email grahamgiddings@aol.com
  http://www.nationalpigeonassociation.co.uk
  Sec: Graham Giddings
▲ Un-incorporated Society
○ *B, *G; organising body for issue of rings & exhibitions of fancy
  pigeons (NOT racing pigeons)
● Mtgs - Exhib
< Entente Européenne d'Aviculture et de Cuniculture
M c 150 org
¶ Feathered World - 12; £21 yr.

National Pipe Organ Register
  a group of the **British Institute of Organ Studies**

National Playbus Association 1974
■ Brunswick Court, Brunswick Square, BRISTOL, BS2 8PE. (hq)
  0117-916 6580   fax 0117-916 6588
  email playbus@playbus.org.uk
  http://www.playbus.org.uk
  Chief Exec: Geoffrey Riddick
▲ Company Limited by Guarantee; Registered Charity
○ *N, *W, *Y; a national umbrella organisation which supports the
  work of locally based community groups who make use of
  covered vehicles to provide services
● Conf - ET - Inf - Project support & development
< Nat Coun Voluntary Orgs (NCVO); Scot Coun Voluntary
  Orgs (SCVO); Nat Coun Voluntary Child Care
  Orgs (NCVCCO)
M c 230 org
¶ Busfare - 3.   AR.
  Information sheets & specialist publications; prices vary.

National Playing Fields Association (NPFA) 1925
■ 2D Woodstock Studios, 36 Woodstock Grove, LONDON,
  W12 8LE. (hq)
  020 8735 3380   fax 020 8735 3397
  email info@fieldsintrust.org   http://www.fieldsintrust.org
  Dir: Alison Moore-Gwyn
▲ Registered Charity
Br 4
○ *K; charity committed to the protection & preservation of
  recreational space
● Conf - ET - Inf - LG
M 600 i, f & org
¶ The Six Acre Standard; £25.   Taking a Lead; £12.95.
  Playwork - a guide for trainers; £10.
  Impact Absorbing Surfaces for Children's Playgrounds; £15.
  Play Safety Guidelines; £11.95.   NPFA Cost Guide; £25.
  NOTE: uses the operating name of Fields in Trust

National Pony Society (NPS) 1893
■ Willingdon House, 7 The Windmills, St Mary's Close, ALTON, Hants, GU34 1EF.   (hq)
01420 88333   fax 01420 80599
email info@nationalponysociety.org.uk
http://www.nationalponysociety.org.uk
Chief Exec: Mrs Caroline Nokes
▲ Registered Charity
○ *B, *V; to encourage the breeding, registration & improvement of British riding ponies (incl mountain & moorland ponies); to foster the welfare of ponies in general
Gp Breed societies; Veterinary & animal welfare gps
● Conf - Mtgs - ET - Comp - Inf - LG
< Brit Driving Soc; Brit Show Pony Soc; Brit Equine Welfare C'ee; Central Prefix Register
M 3,000 i
(Sub: £32)
¶ Review - 1; ftm, £10 nm.   NL - 3; ftm only.
Stud Book.   AR; free.   Judges List & Rules.
Show Schedule; free.   Show Catalogue.

National Portage Association (NPA) 1983
NR Kings Court 17 School Rd, Hall Green, BIRMINGHAM, W Midlands, B28 8JG.
email npa@portageuk.freeserve.co.uk
http://www.portage.org.uk
▲ Company Limited by Guarantee; Registered Charity
Br Regional
○ *E, *W; to support families caring for children with special needs by promoting & supporting portage educational home visiting services
Gp Training & Monitoring; Information & Publicity; Ethics
● Conf - Mtgs - ET - Exhib - Inf
M 400 i, 77 groups, UK / 3 i, 1 group, o'seas
¶ Portage Post NL - 3; ftm.   AR - 1; free.
Conference Proceedings - 1; £11.74.
Publications list available from:
PO Box 3075, Yeovil, BA21 3FB or
npa@portageuk.freeserve.co.uk

National Portraiture Association (NPA) 1972
NR 59-60 Fitzjames Avenue, LONDON, W14 0RR.   (hq)
020 7602 0892   fax 020 7602 6705
email enquiries@natportrait.com
http://www.natportrait.com
Dir: William H Deeves
▲ Un-incorporated Society
○ *A; acquisition of fine portrait commissions in all media
● Bursaries for talented children

** National Pot Leek Society
Organisation lost; see Introduction paragraph 3

National Prefabricated Building Association
since March 2004 the **Modular & Portable Building Association**

National Private Hire Association (NPHA) 1993
NR 8 Silver St, BURY, Lancs, BL9 0EX.   (hq)
0161-280 2800   fax 0161-280 7787
Gen Sec: Bryan M Roland
▲ Company Limited by Guarantee
○ *T; for private hire & hackney carriage companies & drivers; to raise standards in the trade, both actual & as perceived by the public
Gp NPH QA - ISO 9002 consultancy
● Conf - ET - Exhib - Inf - LG - Legal guidance - Representations in court
M 50 i, 600 f, 66 local org
¶ Private Hire & Taxi Monthly - 12.

National Pure Water Association (NPWA) 1960
■ 42 Huntington Rd, YORK, YO31 8RE.   (hsp)
020 8220 9168
http://www.npwa.org.uk
Vice-Chmn: Ian Packington
○ *K; to oppose the use of public water supplies for the purpose of mass medication, particularly fluoridation; to protect the public water supplies from any form of pollution or contamination, deliberate or accidental
● Inf - Supporting local groups with similar aims
M [not stated]
¶ NL - 2/3; free.

National Quoits Association (NQA) 1986
NR 54 Park Avenue, Shiremoor, NEWCASTLE upon TYNE, NE27 0LG.   (hsp)
01947 841100
Pres: Peter Brown
○ *S; the governing body for the traditional & ancient game of quoits
M i & leagues

National Register of Access Consultants (NRAC) 2000
■ 70 South Lambeth Rd, LONDON, SW8 1RL.   (hq)
020 7735 7845   fax 020 7840 5811
email info@nrac.org.uk   http://www.nrac.org.uk
Chief Exec: Sarah Langton-Lockton
○ *P; accreditation of individuals in the access/inclusive environments sector
Gp Specialists for building types; Countryside; Designer; Expert witness; Policy & strategy; Signage & wayfinding; Trainer; Transport; Web accessibility
● Conf - Accreditation of individuals - Services to members
M 200 i, + 150 affiliates (i & org)
¶ email NL - m only.

National Register of Hypnotherapists & Psychotherapists (NRHP) 1985
■ 18 Carr Rd (1st floor), NELSON, Lancs, BB9 7JS.   (hq)
01282 716839
email admin@nrhp.co.uk   http://www.nrhp.co.uk
Chmn: Sir Bill Connor
▲ Company Limited by Guarantee
○ *P; a free referral service (by post, email, telephone) for members of the public seeking qualified hypnotherapists.   All members trained by a UKCP recognised training organisation, with on-going supervision, adhere to a code of practice & carry appropriate insurance
● Conf - ET
< Eur Assn for Hypno Psychotherapy; Eur Assn for Hypno Psychotherapy; UK Coun for Psychotherapy; Brit Assn for Counselling & Psychotherapy
M 450 i, UK / 10 i, o'seas
(Sub: £140, UK / £52 o'seas)
¶ NL - 3; ftm only.   LM (by area); free on request.
Directory of Practitioners - 1; ftm, £7 nm.

National Register of Personal Trainers (NRPT) 1991
NR PO Box 3455, MARLOW, Bucks, SL7 1WG.
0870 200 6010
email info@nrpt.co.uk   http://www.nrpt.co.uk
○ *P
M c 600 i

National Register of Property Preservation Specialists
■ 11 Greenland Rd, BARNET, Herts, EN5 2AL.
07876 192249
http://www.nrpps.co.uk
Contact: Mr Smith
○ *P
M c 180 i

© CBD Research Ltd · Beckenham · BR3 5JS · Tel 020 8650 7745 · Fax 020 8650 0768 · E-mail cbd@cbdresearch.com · www.cbdresearch.com

National Rheumatoid Arthritis Society (NRAS) 2001

NR Unit B4 Westacott Business Centre, Littlewick Green,
    MAIDENHEAD, Berks, SL6 3RT. (hq)
    01628 823524
    email enquiries@rheumatoid.org.uk
    http://www.rheumatoid.org.uk
    Chmn: Ailsa Bosworth
▲ Registered Charity
○ *G, *K; is patient-led & focuses on rheumatoid arthritis; to
    provide an advisory & information service on all aspects of
    the disease
Gp Expert patient network
● Inf
    Helpline: 0800 298 7650
M c 850 i
¶ NL - 3; ftm only (subscription £15). AR.
    Information leaflet.

National Rifle Association (NRA) 1860

■ c/o National Shooting Centre, Bisley Camp, Brookwood,
    WOKING, Surrey, GU24 0PB. (hq)
    01483 797777 fax 01483 797285
    email info@nra.org.uk http://www.nra.org.uk
    Chmn: John Jackman, Sec Gen: Glynn Algar
▲ Registered Charity
○ *S; to promote rifle & pistol shooting
● Mtgs - ET - Exhib - Comp - Stat - Inf - Lib - PL - LG
< Brit Shooting Sports Coun; GB Target Shooting Fedn
M 4,500 i, 1,100 org, UK / 42 org, o'seas
¶ Jnl - 3; ftm.

National Roller Hockey Association of England Ltd (NRHA)
1909

NR 136 Canterbury Rd, HERNE BAY, Kent, CT6 5RX. (sp)
    http://www.nrha.co.uk
    Sec: Aileen Barker
○ *S; governing body for roller hockey
M i & clubs
¶ NL - 12. Coaching Manual. AR.

National Rounders Association (NRA) 1943

NR 55 Westland Gdns, Westfield, SHEFFIELD, S Yorks, S20 8ES.
    (office/address)
    0114-248 0357 fax 0870 052 0396
    email nraoffice@btopenworld.com
    http://www.nra-rounders.co.uk
    Contact: Alan Fergus
▲ Voluntary Organisation
○ *S; national governing body for game of rounders; trustees of
    the rules of rounders worldwide
Gp International teams at 8 age groups (ladies)
● Mtgs - ET - Exam - Res - Comp - Inf - LG
< Cent Coun for Physical Recreation (CCPR); Sports Coach
    UK (SCUK)
M c 10,000 i, c 800 org
¶ Publications list on request.

National Sawmilling Association
    no longer in existence.

National School Band Association (NSBA) 1952

NR 52 High St, Abergwynfi, PORT TALBOT, Glamorgan,
    SA13 3YW. (execoffr/p)
    http://www.nsba.org.uk
    Exec Officer: Craig Roberts
▲ Registered Charity
○ *D; to encourage an interest in music, through the playing of
    brass & woodwind instruments in schools
M i & schools

National Search & Rescue Dog Association (NSARDA)

NR 3 Strawberry Hill Rd, The Haulgh, BOLTON, Lancs, BL2 1DP.
    email secretary@nsarda.org.uk
    http://www.nsarda.org.uk
○ *G; provision of dogs for searching for people in mountain
    areas, crime scenes & other emergencies

National Secular Society (NSS) 1866

■ 25 Red Lion Sq, LONDON, WC1R 4RL. (hq)
    020 7404 3126 fax 0870 762 8971
    email admin@secularism.org.uk
    http://www.secularism.org.uk
    Exec Dir: Keith Porteus Wood
▲ Company Limited by Guarantee
○ *K; to campaign for secularism (incl free speech, freedom from
    religious discrimination & other civil liberties) & for an end to
    religious privilege (incl no public finding of an established
    church, of sectarian schools & of faith-based social services)
● LG - Campaigning
< Intl Ethical & Humanist U; Liberty; Amnesty Intl; Abortion Law
    Reform Assn; Network for Peace
M 2,090 i, 31 org, UK / 45 i, o'seas
¶ Bulletin - 3; Newsline (email) - 52; AR - 1; all free.

National Security Inspectorate (NSI) 2001

■ Sentinel House, 5 Reform Rd, MAIDENHEAD, Berks, SL6 8BY.
    (hq)
    0845 006 3003 fax 01628 773367
    email nsi@nsi.org.uk http://www.nsi.org.uk
    Chief Exec: Andrew White
▲ Company Limited by Guarantee
○ *N; an independent regulatory & certification body approving &
    regulating firms concerned with installation, service &
    maintenance of security systems - intruder alarms, CCTV,
    access control & alarm receiving centres; inspection of
    companies providing 'people based' services in the security
    industry; inspection of companies designing, installing,
    commissioning & maintaining fire detection systems
● Conf - Mtgs - Exhib - Inf - LG - Inspection services
< BSI; Security Ind Training Org; Security Ind Bd; Jt Security Ind
    Coun
M 1,100 f
¶ Network NL - 3; free.
    Technical Memoranda - irreg; ftm only.
    Regulatory Documents - irreg; £9.

National Sewerage Association (NSA) 1995

■ 98 Alric Ave, NEW MALDEN, Surrey, KT3 4JW. (hsp)
    020 8942 9391 fax 020 8942 9391
    email nsa@tinyonline.co.uk http://www.sewerage.org
    Sec: Mrs V A Gibbens
▲ Un-incorporated Society
○ *T; to improve the professional standards of firms carrying out
    sewer surveys, cleaning, monitoring, repairs & renovation
Gp Contractors: CCTV sewer inspection, Flow monitoring,
    Blockage clearance & cleaning; Associated manufacturers
● Mtgs - ET - Inf - LG - Liaison with water companies & WRc on
    national standards for the industry
M 32 f
¶ Members Directory - on request; free.

National Sheep Association (NSA) 1892

NR The Sheep Centre, MALVERN, Worcs, WR13 6PH. (hq)
    01684 892661
    http://www.nationalsheep.org.uk
○ *B, *T; expansion of UK sheep industry
M f

National Small-Bore Rifle Association   (NSRA)   1903
NR   Lord Roberts Centre, Bisley Camp, Brookwood, WOKING,
        Surrey, GU24 0NP.   (hq)
        01483 485505   fax 01483 476392
        email info@nsra.co.uk   http://www.nsra.co.uk
▲   Registered Charity
○   *S; promotion of .22 target shooting & air rifle shooting & .177
        airgun shooting
M   i & clubs
¶   The Rifleman - 4; ftm.

National Small Schools Forum   (NSSF)
NR   Old Sodbury School, 44 Church Lane, Old Sodbury, BRISTOL,
        BS37 6NB.   (treas/b)
        email cwilliams0@btinternet.com
        http://www.www.nssf.co.uk
        Treas: Chris Williams
○   *E; promotes high quality education in small schools with
        primary pupils
M   c 1,000 i

**National Society of Allied & Independent Funeral Directors
(SAIF)   1989**
■   SAIF Business Centre, 3 Bullfields, SAWBRIDGEWORTH, Herts,
        CM21 9DB.   (hq)
        01279 726777   fax 01279 726300
        email info@saif.org.uk   http://www.saif.org.uk
        Acting Chief Exec: Alun Tucker
▲   Un-incorporated Society
○   *P, *T; to promote, project & assist the interests of independent
        funeral directors
●   Conf - Mtgs - ET - Res - Exhib - SG - LG
<   Independent Funeral Directors College
M   600 f
¶   SAIFinsight (NL) - 12; free.
        Note: also known as the Society of Allied & Independent
        Funeral Directors

**National Society of Allotment & Leisure Gardeners Ltd
(NSALG)   1930**
■   O'Dell House, Hunters Rd, CORBY, Northants, NN17 5JE.
        (hq)
        01536 266576   fax 01536 264509
        email natsoc@nsalg.org.uk   http://www.nsalg.org.uk
        Sec: Geoff Stokes
○   *G, *H; to ensure that allotments & leisure gardens are
        available to all who require them
●   Conf - Inf
<   NCVO
M   85,000 i, 1,700 org
¶   Allotment & Leisure Gardener - 4; ftm, £2 nm.

*National Society for Children & Adults with Learning Disabilities & their
Families*
        see **Rescare - National Society for Children & Adults with
        Learning Disabilities & their Families**

**National Society (Church of England) for Promoting Religious
Education   1811**
NR   Church House, Great Smith St, LONDON, SW1P 3NZ.   (hq)
        020 7898 1518
        http://www.natsoc.org.uk
        Gen Sec: Canon John Hall
▲   Registered Charity
○   *R; to support all involved in religious education in schools,
        colleges & churches in England & Wales
M   i & schools

National Society for Clean Air & Environmental Protection
        since October 2007 **Environmental Protection UK**

**National Society for Education in Art & Design   (NSEAD)
1888**
■   The Gatehouse, Corsham Court, CORSHAM, Wilts,
        SN13 0BZ.   (hq)
        01249 714825   fax 01249 716138
        email johnsteers@nsead.org   http://www.nsead.org
        Sec: Dr John Steers
▲   Un-incorporated Society
○   *E, *P, *U; to promote & defend art & design education & the
        interests of teachers
Gp   Boards: Editorial, Teacher education, Information &
        communications technology
●   Conf - ET - Res - Inf - Empl
<   Intl Soc for Educ through Art
M   c 2,500 i
¶   International Jnl of Art & Design Education - 3; ftm.
        Start - 4; ftm (some categories); £30 nm.

National Society for Epilepsy   (NSE)   1892
■   Chesham Lane, CHALFONT ST PETER, Bucks, SL9 0RJ.   (hq)
        01494 601300   fax 01494 871927
        Chief Exec: Graham Faulkner
▲   Company Limited by Guarantee; Registered Charity
○   *W; to advance research, treatment, care, understanding &
        support for people with epilepsy
●   ET - Res - Exhib - Inf
        Helpline: 01494 601400
M   i
¶   Epilepsy Review (Jnl) - 3; ftm only.   AR - 1; free.

National Society of Master Thatchers   (NSMT)   1977
■   13 Parkers Hill, Tetsworth, THAME, Oxon, OX9 7AQ.   (hsp)
        01844 281208   fax 01844 281208
        Sec & Chief Exec: Marjorie Sanders
▲   Company Limited by Guarantee
○   *T; the protection & promotion of thatch for the benefit of
        members & the thatch owning public
Gp   Thatching; Thatched property ownership; Thatching advice
●   Conf - Mtgs - ET
M   120 i, 3 f, 3 org
¶   The Thatcher's Standard - 4; ftm, £12.50 yr nm.
        Hbk: a practical guide to thatch & thatching in the 21st
        century; £12.50.
        Guidance Notes:
        Fire & Thatch; £5.50.
        Conservation Issues & the Maintenance of Cereal
        Varieties for Thatching; £5.50.

**National Society of Painters, Sculptors & Printmakers   (NS)
1930**
■   122 Copse Hill, LONDON, SW20 0NL.   (hsp)
        020 8946 7878
        http://www.nationalsociety.org
        Hon Sec: Gwen Spencer
▲   Registered Charity
○   *A; 'formed in 1930 to meet a growing desire among artists of
        every creed & outlook for an annual exhibition in London
        which would embrace all aspects of art under one roof,
        without prejudice or favour to anyone'
●   Mtgs - Exhib
M   83 i, UK / 1 i, o'seas
¶   NL - 2; ftm only.

National Society for Phenylketonuria (United Kingdom) Ltd (NSPKU) 1973
- ■ PO Box 26642, LONDON, N14 4ZF.   (mail/address)
  020 8634 3010   fax 0845 004 8341
  email info@nspku.org   http://www.nspku.org
  Sec: Eric Lange
- ▲ Company Limited by Guarantee; Registered Charity
- ○ *W; the welfare of persons suffering from Phenylketonuria & allied (amino acid) disorders, their families & carers
- Gp Medical advisory panel (provides a link with the medical profession & a voice in decisions on standards on PKU treatment)
- ● Conf - Mtgs - Inf
- < Eur Soc for Phenylketonuria (ESPKU); Genetic Interest Gp (GIG)
- M 1,130 i, 5 f, 1 org, UK / 50 i, 10 org, o'seas
  (Sub: £17 i, £25 f, UK / £25 i, £33 f, o'seas)
- ¶ Publications on treatment, diet, & children; 25p - £30.

National Society for the Prevention of Cruelty to Children (NSPCC) 1884
- ■ 42 Curtain Rd, LONDON, EC2A 3NH.   (hq)
  020 7825 2500   fax 020 7825 2525
  email info@nspcc.org.uk   http://www.nspcc.org.uk
  Dir & Chief Exec: Mary Marsh
- ▲ Registered Charity
- ○ *K, *W; to prevent child abuse & neglect in all its forms
- ● ET - Res - Inf - Lib - LG
  Child protection helpline: 0800 800 5000
- M voluntary workers
- ¶ Publications catalogue & some full text publications available on website.

National Society of Professional Hypnotherapists   (NSPH) 1990
- NR Kennard, Shawfield Lane, BLAIRGOWRIE, Perthshire, PH10 6GW.   (hq)
  01250 874384
  email nwblair@nsph-hypnotherapy.co.uk
  http://www.nsph-hypnotherapy.co.uk
  Hon Sec: Neil Watson
- ▲ Un-incorporated Society
- ○ *P
- ● Mtgs - ET - Exam - Res - Exhib - SG - Inf
- M 100 i, UK / 6 i, o'seas
- ¶ NSPH Members Jnl - 4; ftm only.

National Society for the Promotion of Punctuality   (NSPP)
- ■ 81 Park View, Colins Rd, LONDON, N5 2UD.   (asa)
- ○ *K; to increase public awareness of the importance of punctuality; 'being late may be fashionable but it is also rude'
- ● Mtgs - Stat - VE
- M 52 i
- ¶ Stopwatch (Jnl) - 12.

National Society for Research into Allergy   (NSRA) 1980
- NR 2 Armadale Close, Hollycroft, HINCKLEY, Leics, LE10 0SZ. (hsp/b)
  01455 250715
  email eunicerose@donald.com
  http://www.all-allergy.co.uk
  Hon Sec: Mrs Eunice L Rose
- ▲ Registered Charity
- Br New Zealand, USA
- ○ *K, *Q; to promote the awareness of allergic diseases; to research into the causes of allergic diseases & methods of safe treatment; to offer help & advice to people suffering from allergy-intolerance
- Gp Asthma; Eczema; Migraine; Crohn's; ME; Food & chemical intolerance; Allergy
- ● Mtgs - ET - Res
- M c 1,000 i, UK / c 100 i, o'seas
- ¶ Reaction - 3; ftm, £5 nm.
  Is it anything you ate? - 1; ftm (on joining), £10 nm.
  Publications list available.

National Society of Teapot & Kettle Collectors
- ■ 81 Park View, Collins Rd, LONDON, N5 2UD.
- ○ *G
- Gp Miniature teapots
- ● Mtgs - Exhib - PL
- M 56 i
- ¶ Spouting (Jnl) - 6; ftm only.
- × 2008 National Society of Teapot Collectors

National Specialist Contractors Council   (NSCC) 1992
- NR Royal London House, 22-25 Carthusian St, LONDON, EC2A 1DX.   (hq)
  0844 249 5351   fax 0844 249 5352
  http://www.nscc.org.uk
  Chief Exec Officer: Suzannah Nichol
- ▲ Company Limited by Guarantee
- Br Scottish section: PO Box 28011, Edinburgh, EH16 6WN.
  0131-448 0266   fax 0131-440 4032
  Sec: Alan McKinney
- ○ *T; the sub-contract sector of the construction industry
- ● Conf - Mtgs - ET - Res - SG - Stat - Inf - LG
- M 30 associations
- ¶ Bulletin - 2;   AR; both ftm only.
  Check It - 2; ftm, £10 nm.

National Sprint Association Ltd   (NSA) 1958
- NR 8 King George Gardens, Chapel Allerton, LEEDS, W Yorks, LS7 4NS.   (chmn/p)
  0113-295 6949
  Chmn: Tony Hodgson
- ○ *S; organisation of motorcycle & three-wheeler standing-start quarter-mile sprints (& record attempts) in a straight line, not circuits
- < Auto-Cycle U

National Stallion Association   (NaStA) 1981
- NR School Farm, School Lane, Pickmere, KNUTSFORD, Cheshire, WA16 0JF.
  01565 733222
  email info@nationalstallion.org.uk
  http://www.nasta.fsnet.co.uk
  Sec: John Kelcher
- ○ *
- M 9 org

National Stoolball Association
  since 28 September 2008 **Stoolball England**

National Street Rod Association
- NR 8 Punchbowl Lane, BOSTON, Lincs, PE21 8HU.   (contact/p)
  01205 310885
  Contact: Dave Biggadyke
- ○ *G
- M 2,000 i

National Street Van Association   (NSVA) 1974
- NR 84 Melthorne Drive, RUISLIP, Middx, HA4 0TR.   (mem/sp)
  020 8582 0877
  http://www.nsva.co.uk
  Mem Sec: George Meacher
- ○ *G; for owners of vans

National Sugar Art Association
- NR 16 Mentieth Drive, DUNFERMLINE, Fife, KY11 8RR.
  01383 727751
  Chmn: Sheila Tasker
- ○ *A

National Support Group for Victims of Failed Home Income Plans
  former name of **HIPS (97)**

National Sweet Pea Society (NSPS) 1900
- ■ 8 Wolseley Rd, Parkstone, POOLE, Dorset, BH12 2DP. (hsp)
  01202 734088
  email bg.bulstrode@btinternet.com
  http://www.sweetpeas.org.uk
  Hon Sec: Janet Bulstrode
- ▲ Registered Charity
- ○ *H; to promote the growing of the sweet pea & to further its development
- ● Conf - Exhib - Comp
- < R Horticl Soc
- M 1,100 i, 10 f, 300 affiliated socs, UK / 50 i, o'seas
- ¶ NSPS Annual. Bulletin (Spring & Autumn) - 2. Schedule of Exhibitions - 1. Judges' Rules. Enjoy Sweet Peas.

National Taxi Association (NTA) 1960
- NR Infirmary St, Newtown, CARLISLE, Cumbria, CA2 7AA. (hsb)
  01228 598740
  email secretary@national-taxi-association.co.uk
  Admin Officer: Wayne Casey
- ▲ Company Limited by Guarantee
- ○ *N, *P, *T; the Hackney carriage trade
- ● Conf - Mtgs - Exhib - LG
- M c 70 trade org

National Tortoise Club of Great Britain 1975
- ■ 2 Laith Close, Cookridge, LEEDS, W Yorks, LS16 6LE. (chief/exec/p)
  0113-267 7587
  Chief Exec: Mrs B Waller
- Br worldwide
- ○ *B, *G; exchange of information on all aspects of tortoise keeping & breeding (incl the American Box, Greek & all Mediterranean & other species)
- ● Mtgs - ET - Helpline - Inf - SG - Talks - Box Tortoise (help & advice) - Speaker available for talks incl radio & TV
- M i (numbers expanding)
- ¶ Care sheets & data; prices on application. [NL under review]. Note: as this is a voluntary body run by experts all enquiries must be accompanied by a pre-paid envelope &/or donation.
  NO personal visits to address - letters & phone calls ONLY.

National Traction Engine Trust 1954
- ■ 153 Micklefield Rd, HIGH WYCOMBE, Bucks, HP13 7HA. (hsp)
  01494 521727   fax 01494 521727
  email suejackson@themutual.net
  Gen Sec: Mrs Susan Jackson
- ▲ Registered Charity
- ○ *G; preservation, restoration & maintenance of steam driven traction engines & steam driven road vehicles; training in operation & maintenance of steam driven vehicles
- ● Conf - Mtgs - Res - Exhib - Comp - Inf - VE
- < Fedn of Brit Historic Vehicle Clubs
- M 3,100 i, 60 affiliated gps
- ¶ Steaming - 4; ftm, £22 nm.
  Code of Practice for the better organisation of Traction Engine rallies, incorporating the Rally Authorisation Scheme.
  Code of Practice for Traction Engines & Similar Vehicles.

National Trailer & Towing Association Ltd (NTTA) 1976
- ■ Plestowes Barnes, Hareway Lane, BARFORD, Warks, CV35 8DD.
  01926 335445   fax 01926 335445
  email info@ntta.co.uk   http://www.ntta.co.uk
  Exec Admin: David Millington
- ▲ Company Limited by Guarantee
- ○ *T; to represent the trailer & towbar industries on British, European & Industrial Standards Committees
- Gp Training courses; NVQ qualifications; Consultancy; Expert witness; Inspection & report
- ● Conf - Mtgs - ET - Exhib - Inf - LG
- < BSI; ISO; SMMT
- M 170 f, 2 org
- ¶ NTTA News - 4; ftm only.

National Trainers Federation (NTF) 1975
- NR 9 High St, Lambourn, HUNGERFORD, Berks, RG17 8XN. (hq)
  01488 71719   fax 01488 73005
  email info@racehorsetrainers.org
  http://www.racehorsetrainers.org
  Chief Exec: Rupert Arnold
- ○ *T; to promote the interests of racehorse trainers within the racing industry
- M c 550 i

National Trolleybus Association (NTA) 1963
- ■ 24 Heath Farm Rd, FERNDOWN, Dorset, BH22 8JW. (editor/p)
  email editor.tm@btinternet.com
  http://www.trolleybus.co.uk/nta
  Editor: Carl Isgar
- ▲ Company Limited by Guarantee; Registered Charity
- ○ *G; to preserve & to promote interest in trolleybuses
- ● Mtgs - Stat - PL
- < Transport Trust; Assn of Indep Museums
- M 554 i, f & org
- ¶ Trolleybus Magazine - 6; ftm only.
  Is involved in Trolleybooks, a joint publishing venture with the British Trolleybus Society.

National Trust for Ireland (An Taisce) 1948
- IRL Tailor's Hall, Back Lane, DUBLIN 8, Republic of Ireland.
  353 (1) 454 1786   fax 353 (1) 453 3255
  email info@antaisce.org   http://www.antaisce.org
- ○ *G

National Trust for Places of Historic Interest or Natural Beauty 1895
- NR 32 Queen Anne's Gate, LONDON, SW1H 9AB. (hq)
  01793 817400   fax 01793 817401
  email enquiries@thenationaltrust.org.uk
  http://www.nationaltrust.org.uk
  Dir: Fiona Reynolds
- ▲ Registered Charity
- ○ *G; to preserve places of historic interest or natural beauty permanently for the nation to enjoy; as a charity independent of government, the Trust protects forests, woods, fens, farmland, downland, moorland, islands, archaeological remains, villages - for ever, for everyone
- M c 3,500,000 i

National Trust for Scotland (NTS) 1931
- NR 28 Charlotte Sq, EDINBURGH, EH2 4ET. (hq)
  0131-243 9300   fax 0131-243 9301
  email information@nts.org.uk   http://www.nts.org.uk
  Chmn: Shonaig MacPherson
- ▲ Registered Charity
- ○ *G; to protect & promote Scotland's national & cultural heritage for present & future generations to enjoy
- ● Care of properties & opening them to the public - Inf (on matters relating to the Trust only) - VE
- < Europa Nostra
- M 270,000 i
- ¶ Jnl - 4;   Ybk - 1; both ftm only.

© CBD Research Ltd · Beckenham · BR3 5JS · Tel 020 8650 7745 · Fax 020 8650 0768 · E-mail cbd@cbdresearch.com · www.cbdresearch.com

National Tyre Distributors Association (NTDA) 1930
NR 8 Temple Square, AYLESBURY, Bucks, HP20 2QH. (hq)
      0870 900 0600 fax 0870 900 0610
      email mail@ntda.co.uk http://www.ntda.co.uk
      Dir: Richard Edy
○ *T; for companies in the tyre specialist & fast fit trade
Gp Divisions: Training services; Technical services;
      Specialist c'ees: Tyre Wholesalers Group; Approved tyre
      repairers
● Conf - Mtgs - ET - Exhib - Comp - Stat - Inf - LG
< BIPAVER
M 450 f, UK / 1 f, o'seas
¶ NTDA News - 12; AR; both ftm only.
      Directory of Members & Ybk - 1; ftm, £25 nm.

*National Union of Domestic Appliances & General Operatives
    in 2006 merged with* **Community**

National Union of Journalists (NUJ) 1907
NR 308-312 Gray's Inn Rd, LONDON, WC1X 8DP. (hq)
      020 7278 7916 fax 020 7837 8143
      email info@nuj.org
      Gen Sec: Jeremy Dear
○ *U
M c 35,000 i

*National Union of Knitwear, Footwear & Apparel Trades
    in 2004 merged with the Iron & Steel Trades Confederation to form*
Community

National Union of Marine, Aviation & Shipping Transport Officers
    since October 2006 **Nautilus UK**

National Union of Mineworkers (NUM) 1944
NR Miners' Offices, 2 Huddersfield Rd, BARNSLEY, S Yorks,
      S70 2LS. (hq)
      01226 215555
      Sec: Steve Kemp
○ *U
● Conf - Mtgs
< TUC; Labour Party
M c 3,500 i
¶ The Miner - 4; ftm.

National Union of Residents' Associations (NURA) 1921
■ 20 Park Drive, ROMFORD, Essex, RM1 4LH. (chmn/p)
      01708 749119 fax 01708 736213
      Chmn: Ian Wilkes
○ *K
● Mtgs - LG
M c150 org
¶ NURA NL - irreg; ftm.
      Simple Guide to Planning Applications; £5.25.

National Union of Students (NUS) 1922
NR Centro 3 (2nd floor), 19 Mandela St, LONDON, NW1 0DU.
      (hq)
      0871 221 8221 fax 020 7263 5713
      email nusuk@nus.org.uk http://www.nusonline.co.uk
      Chief Exec: Matt Hyde
▲ Un-incorporated Society
○ *U
Gp Scotland; Wales; N Ireland
● Conf - Res - Inf - LG - Campaigns
M 5,000,000 i in 700+ student unions

National Union of Teachers (NUT) 1870
NR Hamilton House, Mabledon Place, LONDON, WC1H 9BD.
      (hq)
      020 7388 6191
▲ Un-incorporated Society
○ *U; to promote state education & protect & improve the
      salaries, working conditions & status of the teaching
      profession in England & Wales
● Conf - ET - Res - Exhib - Inf - Empl - LG
< Educ Intl; TUC
M c 250,000 i
¶ The Teacher - 8. Education Review - 2.

National Vegetable Society (NVS) 1960
NR 5 Whitelow Rd, Heaton Moor, STOCKPORT, Cheshire,
      SK4 4BY. (hsp)
      0161-442 7190
      email d.hampsey@ntlworld.com
      http://www.nvsuk.org.uk
      Webmaster: David Hampsey
Br 5
○ *H; to advance the education of the public in the cultivation &
      improvement of vegetables
● Mtgs - Exam - Exhib - Comp - Inf - Lib - Displays at shows
< R Horticl Soc
M 2,500 i
¶ Bulletin - 4; Directory - 1; AR; all ftm.
      Growing leaflets (13); 40p each m.
      Judges Guide; £3.50 m.

National Vintage Tractor & Engine Club (NVTEC) 1965
■ Eastfields, North Wheatley, RETFORD, Notts, DN22 9BK. (hsp)
      01427 880238
      email p.scarborough@lineone.net
      http://www.nvtec.co.uk
      Sec: Pat Scarborough
▲ Un-incorporated Society
Br 33; France, Germany, Norway, USA
○ *G; study & preservation of agricultural tractors, machines &
      implements & all associated equipment
● Cobnf - Mtgs - ET - Exhib - Comp - Inf - VE - LG
< Soc Ploughmen; Traction Engine Trust; Nat Farmers' U
M 61000 i
¶ Vaporising - 4; ftm only.

*National Wardens' Association
    since 2005* **NWA - an association of housing & support
managers**

National Women's Register (NWR) 1960
NR 3A Vulcan House, Vulcan Road North, NORWICH, Norfolk,
      NR6 6AQ. (hq)
      01603 406767 fax 01603 407003
      email office@nwr.org http://www.nwr.org
      Co Sec & Organiser: Gaynel Munn
▲ Company Limited by Guarantee; Registered Charity
Br c 450; Australia, Belgium, South Africa, Zimbabwe
○ *G; for women of all ages who wish to participate in wide-
      ranging discussions leading to friendship & other activities
Gp Correspondence magazine; Penfriends; House exchange;
      Research bank; Postal Book
● Conf - Mtgs - ET - Res - Exhib - Comp
M c 7,500 i
¶ Register - 2; ftm only.

National Wool Textile Export Corporation   (NWTEC)   1940
NR   Lloyds Bank Chambers, 43 Hustlergate, BRADFORD, W Yorks,
      BD1 1PH.   (hq)
      01274 724235
      Dir: Peter Ackroyd
▲   Company Limited by Guarantee
○   *T; promotion & protection of the export trade of the British
      wool textile industry
M   c 250 f
¶   'All publications for m only'.
      Note: also known (principally abroad) as the British Wool Textile
      Export Corporation

National Youth Choirs of Great Britain   (NYCGB)   1979
NR   Pelaw House, University of Durham, Leazes Rd, DURHAM,
      DH1 1TA.   (sb)
      0191-3334 8110 (weekdays 0900-1700)
      email office@nycgb.net
      Hon Sec: Carl Browning
▲   Registered Charity
○   *D
●   Mtgs - ET - Exam - VE - Concerts
M   i

National Youth Council of Ireland   (NYCI)   1967
IRL   3 Montague St, DUBLIN 2, Republic of Ireland.
      353 (1) 478 4122   fax 353 (1) 478 3974
      email info@nyci.ie   http://www.youth.ie
      Dir: Mary Cunningham
○   *Y; to represent & support the interests of voluntary youth
      organisations
M   c 40 orgs

National Youth Federation
IRL   20 Dominick Street Lower, DUBLIN 1, Republic of Ireland.
      353 (1) 872 9933   fax 353 (1) 872 4183
      email info@nyf.ie   http://www.youthworkireland.ie
      Chief Exec: Diarmuid Kearney
○   *Y
      Note: Trades under the name Youth Work Ireland

Nationwide Caterers Association Ltd   (NCASS)   1987
■   Association House, 89 Mappleborough Rd, Shirley, SOLIHULL,
      W Midlands, B90 1AG.   (hq)
      0121-603 2524   fax 0121-474 3938
      email enq@ncass.org.uk   http://www.ncass.org.uk
      Managing Dir: Bob Fox
▲   Company Limited by Guarantee
○   *T; for caterers & suppliers - mobile caterers, static caterers
      (sandwich bars, takeaways) & suppliers to the trade
Gp   Technical c'ee
●   Conf - Exam - State - LG
M   600 i, 100 f
      (Sub: £189 caterers, £400 suppliers)
¶
      NL - 4; free.
      Profitable Mobile Catering - 1; £20.
      The Events Directory - 1; £20 m, £40 nm.
      Annual Industry Guide - 1; £20.
      [subscription: £174 i, £350 f].
×   2005 Mobile & Outside Caterers Association

** **Natural Family Planning Teachers Association**
      Oganisation lost; see Introduction paragraph 3

Natural Gas Vehicle Association   (NGVA)   1992
■   36 Holly Walk, LEAMINGTON SPA, Warks, CV32 4LY.   (hq)
      01926 462900   fax 01925 450459
      email info@ngva.co.uk   http://www.ngva.co.uk
      Marketing Mgr: Caroline Taylor
▲   Company Limited by Guarantee
Br   Brussels
○   *T; to stimulate the use of natural gas & biomethane as vehicle
      fuels
Gp   C'ees: Technical; Marketing; Government relations
●   Conf - Mtgs - ET - Res - Expt - Inf
<   Intl Natural Gas Vehicle Assn; Eur Natural Gas Vehicle Assn;
      Japan & USA Gas Vehicle Assn
M   30 f
¶   NGV News - 4.

Natural History Society of Northumbria   (NHSN)   1829
■   The Hancock Museum, NEWCASTLE upon TYNE, NE2 4PT.
      (hq)
      0191-232 6386   fax 0191-232 2177
      email nhsn@ncl.ac.uk   http://www.nhsn.ncl.ac.uk
      Sec: David C Noble-Rollin
▲   Registered Charity
○   *L; to encourage the study of natural history in all its branches;
      to protect the natural environment & local flora & fauna
Gp   Natural history library & archives
●   Mtgs - Res - Lib (open for public access) - VE - LG - Field mtgs -
      Lectures
M   900 i, UK / 4 i, o'seas
¶   Bulletin - 3.   Transactions - 3 (2-yrly);   AR; all ftm.

Natural Sausage Casings Association   (NSCA)   1953
NR   Wychwood Cottage, 38 High St, RISELEY, Beds, MK44 1DX.
      (asa)
      01234 709022   fax 01234 709749
      Sec: Digby Morgan-Jones
○   *T; for those involved in the natural casings industry in the UK;
      to cooperate with any other organisation worldwide with
      similar objectives
●   Mtgs - LG - Statistical information for members
<   Eur Natural Casings Assn
M   13 f + 1f (Eire)

Natural Sciences Collections Association   (NatSCA)   2003
■   Dept of Entomology, The Natural History Museum,
      Cromwell Rd, LONDON, SW7 5BD.   (hsb)
      020 7942 5196   fax 020 7942 5229
      email p.brown@nhm.ac.uk   http://www.nhm.ac.uk/
      hosted_sites/natsca
      Chmn: Paul A Brown,   Sec: Claire Stringer
▲   Registered Charity
○   *N, *P; to represent natural science collections & associated
      museum staff
●   Conf - Mtgs - ET - VE - LG
<   Inst of Consvn (UK); Nat Biodiversity Network
>   Geology Curators Gp
M   c 200 i, c 50 org
      (Sub: £25 i, £30 org)
¶   NatSCA News - 4; ftm, £5 nm.

Nature in Art Trust   1982
■   Wallsworth Hall, Twigworth, GLOUCESTER, GL2 9PA.   (hq)
      01452 731422   fax 01452 730937
      email enquiries@nature-in-art.org.uk
      http://www.nature-in-art.org.uk
      Chmn: Dr David H Trapnell
▲   Company Limited by Guarantee; Registered Charity
○   *A; to collect & display fine, decorative & applied art inspired
      by nature in all media & from any period or culture; to
      provide learning opportunities for young people & adults
●   Conf - Mtgs - ET - Exhib - Comp - SG - Inf - Lib - VE
<   Accredited by Museums, Libraries & Archives Council
M   c 1,200 i
¶   Nature in Art - 4; ftm.

Nautical Archaeology Society (NAS) 1972

- Fort Cumberland, Fort Cumberland Rd, PORTSMOUTH, Hants, PO4 9LD. (hq)
  023 9281 8419   fax 023 9281 8419
  email nas@nasportsmouth.org.uk
  http://www.nasportsmouth.org.uk
  Chmn: George Lambrick
- ▲ Registered Charity
- Br 7; 20 countries
- ○ *G, *L, *Q; to further research into all aspects of nautical & maritime archaeology; to bring together all people interested in our maritime heritage
- Gp Ancient technologists; Archaeologists; Avocationals; Conservators; Historians; Naval architects; Researchers; Sports divers; Students
- ● Conf - Mtgs - ET - Res - Exhib - Comp - Inf - Lib - VE - LG
- < Inst of Naval Archaeology (INA)
- > The Dive Connection (TDC)
- M 500 i, 50 f, UK / 300 i, 25 f, o'seas
- ¶ International Jnl of Nautical Archaeology - 2; ftm, £16 each nm.
  Nautical Archaeology NL - 4; ftm.
  NAS Monograph Series - irreg.
  [subscription £45].

Nautical Heritage Association (NHA)

- c/o The Secretary, PO Box 212, HASTINGS, E Sussex, TN35 5WT. (hsb)
  01424 200958
  http://www.nautical-heritage.org.uk
  Hon Sec: David Renno
- ▲ Registered Charity
- ○ *G, *L; to support, enhance & promote the work of the Nautical Museums Trust & the Shipwreck & Coastal Heritage Centre
- ● Res - Exhib - Restoration - Talks
- M 120 i
  Sub: £6)

Nautical Institute (NI) 1972

- NR 202 Lambeth Rd, LONDON, SE1 7LQ. (hq)
  020 7928 1351   fax 020 7401 2817
  email sec@nautinst.org   http://www.nautinst.org
  Chief Exec: C P Wake
- ▲ Company Limited by Guarantee; Registered Charity
- Br 40 worldwide
- ○ *P; to promote a high standard of knowledge among those in control of sea-going vessels including non-displacement craft. Open to all qualified mariners
- ● Conf - ET - Inf - Lib
- < Sea Vision UK; UK Maritime Forum
- M 6,500 i in 110 countries
- ¶ Publications list available.

Nautilus UK 1936

- Oceanair House, 750-760 High Rd, LONDON, E11 3BB. (hq)
  020 8989 6677   fax 020 8530 1015
  email enquiries@nautilusuk.org
  http://www.nautilusuk.org
  Gen Sec: Brian Orrell
- ▲ Un-incorporated Society
- ○ *U
- ● ET - Res - Inf - Empl - LG
- < Eur Transport Workers' Fedn (ETF); Intl Transport Workers' Fedn (ITF); Trs U Congress (TUC)
- M 18,700 i
- ¶ The Telegraph - 12; ftm, £40 nm.
- × 2006 (October) National Union of Marine, Aviation & Shipping Transport Officers

Naval Defence Group
a group of the **Shipbuilders & Shiprepairers Association**

Naval Dockyards Society 1996

- NR 44 Lindley Avenue, SOUTHSEA, Hants, PO4 9NU.
  023 9286 3799
  http://www.navaldockyards.moonfruit.com
  Sec: Dr Ann Coats
- ○ *G
- ● Conf - Mtgs - VE
- ¶ NL - 2

Naval Historical Collectors & Research Association (NHCRA) 1988

- 9 Lyngate Gardens, Lyngate Rd, NORTH WALSHAM, Norfolk, NR28 0NE. (mem/sp)
  email wilkinsonA44@hotmail.com
  http://www.nhcra-online.org
  Mem Sec: Anthony C Wilkinson
- ▲ Un-incorporated Society
- ○ *G; collecting naval medals & memorabilia; research into naval battles, ships & personnel
- ● Scientific, systematic research - PL
- M 400 i, 5 f, 12 org, UK / 40 i, o'seas
- ¶ The Review (Jnl) - 4; ftm, £15 nm (£17 EU) (£20 o'seas) or £3.50 each.
  Note: the association is a non-profit-making body in support of worthy naval causes & charities

Navy Records Society (NRS) 1893

- c/o Pangbourne College, PANGBOURNE, Berks, RG8 8LA. (hsb)
  http://www.navyrecordssociety.com
  Hon Sec: R H A Brodhurst
- ▲ Registered Charity
- ○ *L; editing & publishing manuscripts & rare works illustrating the history, administration, organisation or social life of the Navy
- ● Publishing
- M c 650 i, c 150 org
- ¶ NL - 1;   AR - 1.
  1 or 2 vols each year.

Needleloom Underlay Manufacturers' Association (NUMA) 1957

- NR Tower House, 269 Walmersley Rd, BURY, Lancs, BL9 6NX. (asa)
  0161-761 5231   fax 0161-761 3001
  Sec & Treas: C A Nuttall
- ▲ Un-incorporated Society
- ○ *T; manufacturers of needled underfelts & allied industries
- ● Conf - Mtgs - Inf
- < BSI
- M 5 f

Neil Munro Society 1996

- NR 4 Randolph Rd, GLASGOW, G11 7LG. (chmn/p)
  email ronnierenton@googlemail.com
  http://www.neilmunro.co.uk
  Chmn: Ronnie Renton
- ▲ Un-incorporated Society
- ○ *A; to promote interest in the life & works of Neil Munro (1863-1930) Scottish novelist, journalist & poet
- ● Conf - Mtgs - Res - Exhib - Comp - Lib - VE
- < Alliance Literary Socs
- M 160 i, 2 f, UK / 15 i, o'seas
- ¶ Paragraphs (NL) - 2; ftm only.

Nelson Society   1981
NR   68 Stamshaw Rd, PORTSMOUTH, Hants, PO2 8LS.
       (mem/sec)
       Mem Sec: Andrea Green
▲   Registered Charity
Br   6
○   *G; to promote interest in, & appreciation of, the outstanding
       qualities of leadership & patriotism displayed by Admiral
       Lord Nelson
●   Conf - Mtgs - Res - Exhib - Lib - VE
M   c 1,000 i
¶   The Nelson Dispatch - 4.

Neonatal Society   (NNS)   1959
NR   c/o Dr Nikki Robertson, UCL, Dept of Obstetrics &
       Gynaecology, 86-96 Chenies Mews, LONDON,
       WC1E 6HX.   (hsb)
       020 7679 6052
       Sec: Dr Nikki Robertson
○   *Q; 'a research society with members from clinical & basic
       science disciplines relating to perinatology'
●   Conf - Mtgs - Res - Exhib
M   c 280 i, UK / c 90 i, o'seas
¶   NL - 3.   Hbk.

Nerine & Amaryllid Society   (NAAS)   1997
NR   2 The Grove, Ickenham, UXBRIDGE, Middx, UB10 8QH.   (hsp)
       01895 464694   fax 0870 052 9312
       http://www.nerine.org.uk
       Sec: Dr Roger D Beauchamp
▲   Un-incorporated Society
○   *H; for the general study & promotion of interest in, the plant
       family Amaryllidaceae
●   Exhib - Inf - is the International Cultivar Registration
       Authority (ICRA) for Nerine
<   R Horticl Soc
       is an Agency of the Intl Soc for Horticl Science (ISHS)
M   c 130 i, UK / c 5 i, o'seas
¶   Amaryllids - 3;   LM - 1;   AR; all ftm only.
       [subscription; £10 single, £15 joint & overseas].

Netball Northern Ireland   (NINA)   1951
■   City of Lisburn Racquets Club, 36 Belfast Rd, LISBURN,
       Co Antrim, BT27 4AS.   (hq)
       07845 875802   fax 028 9266 8215
       email mckeown_392@hotmail.com
       http://www.netballnorthernireland.org
       Hon Sec: Louise McKeown
○   *S; to develop netball in NI
<   Intl Fedn Netball Assns (IFNA); Fedn Eur Netball Assns (FENA)
>   NI Clubs Netball Assn (NICNA); NI Schools Netball
       Assn (NISNA)
M   c 1,500 i, 30 clubs

Netball Scotland   1946
NR   Central Chambers (suite 196), 93 Hope St, GLASGOW,
       G2 6LD.   (hq)
       0141-572 0114   fax 0141-248 5566
       http://www.netballscotland.com
▲   Un-incorporated Society
○   *S; promotion & playing of netball in Scotland
M   c 2,000 i & org

Netherlands-British Chamber of Commerce   1891
■   Imperial House, 15-19 Kingsway, LONDON, WC2B 6UN.
       (hq)
       020 7539 7960
       email info@nbcc.co.uk   http://www.nbcc.co.uk
       Dir: M van Deursen
Br   2; Netherlands
○   *C
●   Conf - Mtgs - Res - Exhib - Expt - Inf - VE
M   200 i, UK / 200 i, o'seas
¶   In Touch - 4; ftm.   Ybk; ftm.
       Other publications & directories.

**Network for Alternative Technology & Technology Assessment
(NATTA)   1976**
■   c/o EERU, Faculty of Technology, Open University, Walton Hall,
       MILTON KEYNES, Bucks, MK7 6AA.   (hq)
       01908 654638 (24-hr answering machine)
       fax 01908 654052
       email s.j.dougan@open.ac.uk
       http://www.eeru.open.ac.uk/natta/rol.html
       Coordinator: Ms Tam Dougan,
       Editor: Prof David Elliott
▲   Un-incorporated Society
○   *E; renewable energy (water, solar, wind power) & related
       energy issues
●   Conf - ET
M   500 i
¶   Renew (NL) - 6; (prices to m = £18 waged, £12 non-waged,
       £50 libs & instns, £6 airmail supplement).
       Renewables, Past, Present & Future: a review of government
       policy & the development of the UK Renewable Energy
       Programme 1994-97 by Dave Elliott; £10.
       Various other publications.

**Network of Government Library & Information Specialists
(NGLIS)   1925**
■   c/o Kate Pritchard, Defra Information Management Divn, Area
       1E 3-8 Whitehall Place, LONDON, SW1A 2HH.   (sb)
       020 7270 8261
       email k.pritchard@defra.gsi.gov.uk
       http://www.nglis.org.uk
       Sec: Kate Pritchard
▲   Un-incorporated Society
○   *P; to promote networking with colleagues working in the
       information sector
●   Conf - Mtgs - ET - Inf - VE
<   C'ee of Departmental Librarians (CDL); Govt Libaries & Inf
       Gp (GLIG)
M   494 i
¶   The Network (Jnl) - 2; ftm.
✕   2005 Circle of State Librarians

Network of Independent Forensic Accountants   (NIFA)   1999
■   4 Pavilion Court, 600 Pavilion Drive, Northampton Business
       Park, NORTHAMPTON, NN4 7SL.   (sb)
       0845 609 6091   fax 01604 662681
       email nifa@nifa.co.uk   http://www.nifa.co.uk
       Sec: Clive Adkins
▲   Company Limited by Guarantee
○   *P, *T; to provide accounting & litigation support
●   Conf
M   15 i, 15 f
¶   NIFA News - 4; free.

Neuroblastoma Society   1982
NR   Beech Lodge - 22 Penrose Way, Four Marks, ALTON, Hants,
       GU34 5BG.   (sp)
       01420 563826
       email secretary@neuroblastoma.org.uk
       http://www.nsoc.co.uk
       Hon Sec: Dennis Bignell
       Chmn: Stephen Smith (01904 633744)
▲   Registered Charity
○   *K, *W; to raise funds for UK based research into
       neuroblastoma (a children's cancer); to offer support for
       families affected by neuroblastoma
●   Res - SG - Social fundraising events
M   c 350-400 i
¶   Neuroblastoma News - 4.
       Neuroblastoma - a booklet for parents - every 3-4 years.

© CBD Research Ltd · Beckenham · BR3 5JS · Tel 020 8650 7745 · Fax 020 8650 0768 · E-mail cbd@cbdresearch.com · www.cbdresearch.com

Neurofibromatosis Association   1981
NR   Quayside House, 38 High St, KINGSTON upon THAMES,
     Surrey, KT1 1HL.   (hq)
     020 8439 1234   fax 020 8439 1200
     Gen Sec: Mark Stevens
▲   Registered Charity
○   *W; a self-help group providing advice & information; to
     establish & maintain a network of family support workers; to
     sponsor research through fund raising
<   Intl Neurofibromatosis Assn (NFA); Neurological Alliance;
     Genetic Interest Gp; Neurofibromatosis Assn Australia
     (NFAA)
M   1,667 i, UK / 31 i, o'seas
¶   Factsheets & videos.   Publications list available.

Neurological Alliance   1994
NR   Stoke House, 240 City Rd, LONDON, EC1V 2PR.   (hq)
     020 7566 1540
     email admin@neural.org.uk
     Co-Chmn: Maggie Alexander,   Andrew Russell
▲   Company Limited by Guarantee; Registered Charity
○   *N, *W; unites charities working to raise the profile of
     conditions & needs of people with neurological conditions &
     their carers; to raise the standards of care & improve lives
●   Conf - Mtgs - LG - Lobbying/campaigning
M   c 60 org
¶   Publications list available.

Neutral Alcohol Producers Association
     since 1 January 2008 **National Alcohol Producers Association**

New Baxter Society
NR   c/o Reading Museum & Art Gallery, Blagrave St, READING,
     Berks, RG1 1QH.
     http://www.rpsfamily.demon.co.uk
○   *G; to promote interest in George Baxter (1804-1867) colour
     picture printer, his licensees & nineteenth century colour
     printing century colour printing

**New Canterbury Literary Society - Richard Aldington Society
(NCLS)   1973**
NR   2B Bedford Rd, ST IVES, Cornwall, TR26 1SB.   (hsp)
     http://www.imagists.org
     Hon Sec: David Wilkinson
○   *A; to promote interest in the life & writings of the author
     Richard Aldington (1892-1962)

New English Art Club
     a member of the **Federation of British Artists**

New Forest Agricultural Show Society   1920
NR   The Showground, New Park, BROCKENHURST, Hants,
     SO42 7QH.   (hq)
     01590 622400   fax 01590 622637
     email info@newforestshow.co.uk
     http://www.newforestshow.co.uk
▲   Company Limited by Guarantee; Registered Charity
○   *F, *H; to promote & encourage the development of agriculture,
     forestry, equestrianism & horticulture... & to encourage the
     breeding of stock

New Forest Pony Breeding & Cattle Society   (NFPB&CS)   1891
NR   The Corner House, Ringwood Rd, BRANSGORE, Hants,
     BH23 8AA.   (hsp)
     01425 672775
     http://www.newforestpony.com
     Sec: Jane Murray
▲   Company Limited by Guarantee; Registered Charity
○   *B
●   Mtgs - Exhib - Comp - Expt
<   Stud Book Societies in: Australia, Belgium, Denmark, Finland,
     France, Germany, Holland, Norway, Sweden, USA
M   c 1,400 i
¶   Stud Book - 1.   Leaflets.   AR.
     Celebration of New Forest Ponies.

New Producers Alliance   (NPA)   1992
NR   7.03 Tea Building, 56 Shoreditch High St, LONDON, E1 6JJ.
     (hq)
     020 7613 0440
     email queries@npa.org.uk
     http://www.newproducer.co.uk
     Chief Exec: David Pope
▲   Registered Charity
○   *P; to train & support new filmmakers
●   Mtgs - ET - Inf - Lib
<   Brit Film Inst
M   1,000 i
¶   New Producer - 12; ftm only.

New Under Ten Fishermen's Association Ltd   (NUTFA)   2008
NR   PO Box 10109, COLCHESTER, Essex, CO1 9GF.
     01206 797373   fax 01206 861114
     email info@nutfa.org   http://www.nutfa.org
▲   Company Limited by Guarantee
○   *T; 'a non-profit-making body representing the under 10m &
     non-sector, that require representation at national &
     European levels, regarding any issues that affect fish stocks
     & fishermen's livelihoods'
●   Mtgs
M   300+ i

Newark & Nottinghamshire Agricultural Society   1799
■   The County Showground, Winthorpe, NEWARK, Notts,
     NG24 2NY.   (hq)
     0870 224 1035   fax 0870 224 1036
     email info@newarkshowground.com
     http://www.newarkshowground.com
     Chief Exec: Adrian M Johnston
▲   Company Limited by Guarantee; Registered Charity
○   *F; to promote agriculture through the County Show, held
     annually on the 2nd weekend of May
●   Annual show - Hire of venue, halls & catering business
<   Nat Outdoor Events Assn; Derbyshire & Nottinghamshire Cham
     Comm
M   500 i, 40 f, 40 org
¶   NL - 2; free.   AR - 1; ftm only.

Newbury and District Agricultural Society
NR   Newbury Showground, Priors Court Rd, Hermitage,
     THATCHAM, Berks, RG18 9QZ.
     01635 247111
     http://www.newburyshow.co.uk
     Gen Mgr: Rebecca Elvin
○   *F

**Newcomen Society for the Study of the History of Engineering &
Technology   (The Newcomen Society)   1920**
NR   Science Museum, LONDON, SW7 2DD.   (hq)
     020 7371 4445   fax 020 7371 4445
     email office@newcomen.com
     http://www.newcomen.com
     Exec Sec: R M Swann
○   *L; the study of the history of engineering & technology

Newman Association   1942
NR   20-22 Bedford Row, LONDON, WC1R 4JS.   (mail/address)
      email secretary@newman.org.uk
      http://www.newman.org.uk
      Contact: The Secretary
▲   Company Limited by Guarantee; Registered Charity
Br   20
○   *E, *R; educational & religious organisation
●   Conf - Mtgs
<   Pax Romana
M   830 i
¶   The Newman - 3; ftm, £1 nm.

**Newport & Gwent Chamber of Commerce, Enterprise &
Industry   (ngb2b)   1870**
■   Unit 30 Enterprise Way, NEWPORT, Monmouthshire,
      NP20 2AQ.   (hq)
      01633 222664   fax 01633 222301
      email info@ngb2b.co.uk   http://www.ngb2b.co.uk
      Managing Dir: David Russ
▲   Company Limited by Guarantee
○   *C
●   Conf - Mtgs - ET - Exhib - Expt - Inf - Lib - VE - LG -
      Commercial services
<   Brit Chams Comm; Chamber Wales; SW Chams Gp
>   Chambers of Commerce: Chepstow & Monmouth; Newport
      Cham Tr
M   c 450 org
¶   Chamber Chat - 4; free.   AR - 1; free.
      South Wales Business Directory - 1; ftm.
      Note: since May 2000 trades under the name ngb2b at the
      same address.
✕   2005 Newport & Gwent Chamber of Commerce & Industry

Newspaper Conference   1920
■   St Andrew's House, 18-20 St Andrew St, LONDON,
      EC4A 3AY.   (hq)
      020 7632 7400   fax 020 7632 7401
      http://www.newspapersoc.org.uk
      Sec: Paul Sinker
○   *P; comprises London editors & political correspondents of
      regional newspapers in membership of the Newspaper
      Society; meets 3 or 4 times a year with senior politicians
●   Conf - Mtgs
M   23 i

Newspaper Publishers Association Ltd   (NPA)   1906
■   St Andrew's House (8th floor), 18-20 St Andrew St, LONDON,
      EC4A 3AY.   (hq)
      020 7632 7430   fax 020 7632 7431
      Dir: David Newell
▲   Company Limited by Guarantee
○   *T; for British national newspaper publishers
M   f

Newspaper Society   1836
■   St Andrew's House, 18-20 St Andrew St, LONDON,
      EC4A 3AY.   (hq)
      020 7632 7400   fax 020 7632 7401
      email ns@newspapersoc.org.uk
      http://www.newspapersoc.org.uk
      Dir: David Newell
▲   Un-incorporated Society
○   *P, *T; 'the voice of Britain's regional press; to represent &
      promote the interests of over 1,300 local & regional titles'
Gp   Political, Editorial & Regulatory Affairs (PERA); Marketing;
      Communications; Finance & administration
●   Conf - Mtgs - ET - Res - Exhib - SG - Stat - Inf - LG - Legal
      advice - Issuing of press ID cards - Press/Rota passes
<   Wld Assn Newspapers (WAN); Eur Newspaper Publishers Assn
      (ENPA); Advertising Assn (AA); Newspaper Conf; Young
      Newspaper Executives Assn (YNEA)
M   f
¶   NS News (NL) - 52.   Headlines (Magazine) - 6.
      Production Jnl - 12.   Commercial Update - 4.
      Headlines & Production Jnl are both available by annual
      subscription.

Newstead Abbey Byron Society
NR   Acushla, Halam Rd, SOUTHWELL, Notts, NG25 0AD.
      (chmn/p)
      01636 813818
      Chmn: P K Burslow
○   *G; for all interested in the life & works of the poet Lord
      George Gordon Byron (1788-1824)
<   Mtgs - VE

NFU Scotland   (NFUS)   1913
■   Rural Centre, West Mains, Ingliston, NEWBRIDGE, Midlothian,
      EH28 8LT.   (hq)
      0131-472 4000   fax 0131-472 4010
      http://www.nfus.org.uk
      Chief Exec: James Withers
Br   72
○   *F, *H, *P; agriculture in all its branches
●   Conf - Mtgs - ET - Res - Exhib - Comp - SG - Stat - Inf - Lib - VE
      - Empl - LG
<   C'ee Agricl Orgs in the EU (COPA); Intl Fedn Agricl Producers
M   12,000 i
¶   Scottish Farming Leader Update - 4/6; ftm.

NHS Alliance   1998
NR   Rossington Hosue, West Carr Rd, RETFORD, Notts,
      DN22 7SW.   (hq)
      01777 869080
      http://www.nhsalliance.org
○   *P; to represent primary care groups & trusts to government; to
      provide networking opportunities & develop & spread good
      practice

NHS Confederation
      on 14 January 2008 merged with the Ambulance Service Association
      to form the **Ambulance Service Network**

NHS Support Federation   1989
NR   113 Queens Rd, BRIGHTON, E Sussex, BN1 3XG.   (hq)
      01273 234822
      http://www.nhscampaign.org
○   *K
M   c 5,000 i in groups

NHS Trusts Association   (NHSTA)
NR   PO Box 45734, LONDON, SW16 5JW.
      020 8679 2471   fax 020 8765 4818
      http://www.nhsta.org.uk
      Chief Exec: Dr David Tod
✕   2006 Association of Primary Care Groups & Trusts

© CBD Research Ltd · Beckenham · BR3 5JS · Tel 020 8650 7745 · Fax 020 8650 0768 · E-mail cbd@cbdresearch.com · www.cbdresearch.com

NIAB (NIAB) 1919
NR Huntingdon Rd, CAMBRIDGE, CB3 0LE.   (hq)
       01223 342200   fax 01223 277602
       email info@niab.com   http://www.niab.com
Br   8 regional trials centres
○   *F, *H, *Q; improvement of crop varieties & seeds
●   Conf - Mtgs - ET - Exam - Res - Exhib - Stat - Inf - Lib - PL - LG
M   c 4,300 i
¶   Jnl.   AR.
       Publications list available.

NISA Today's (Holdings) Ltd   (NISA)   1978
NR Waldo Way, Normanby Enterprise Park, SCUNTHORPE, Lincs,
       DN15 9GE.
       01724 282028
       http://www.nisa-todays.com
○   *T; to support independent retailers & wholesalers in food &
       drink markets, through buying power, marketing &
       distribution services
M   f

NO2ID (NO2ID) 2004
NR PO Box 412, 19-21 Crawford St, LONDON, W1H 1PJ.
       (mail/add)
       0700 580 0651
       email enquiries@no2id.net   http://www.no2id.net
       Nat Co-ordinator: Phil Booth
▲   Un-incorporated Society
○   *K; 'to research, evaluate & raise public awareness of the issues
       around ID cards, identity registers & unique identifiers,
       including biometrics; to lobby & campaign against any such
       legislation or schemes that would prove detrimental to UK
       citizens, including initiatives that would involve
       comprehensive data sharing without the fully informed &
       explicit consent of the individual'
●   Conf - Mtgs - ET - Res - Exhib - Comp - Stat - Inf - LG
<   Eur Social Forum
M   20,000 i, 80 org
¶   NO2ID (email NL) - 26; free.

Noctis: the voice of the nighttime economy   (BEDA)   2008
NR 5 Waterloo Rd, STOCKPORT, Cheshire, SK1 3BD.
       0161-476 8380   fax 0161-429 7214
       http://www.noctisuk.org
       Exec Dir: Paul Smith
○   *T; for owners & operators of late licensed property -
       discotheques, clubs, bars, & live music venues, as well as
       suppliers & product manufacturers for the industry
¶   Night.
✕   2008 (Bar Entertainment & Dance Association
       (British Entertainment & Discotheque Association

NOF Energy Ltd   (NOF Energy)   2006
■   Pennine House (3rd floor), WASHINGTON TOWN CENTRE,
       Tyne & Wear, NE37 1EP.   (hq)
       0191-417 4254   fax 0191-417 4257
       http://www.nofenergy.co.uk
       Chief Exec: Geroge Rafferty
▲   Company Limited by Guarantee
○   *T; business support for the oil, gas & associated energy related
       sectors
Gp Sub-sea North East; Intl steering gp
●   Conf - Mtgs - Res - Exhib - Expt - Inf - VE
<   Aberdeen & Grampian Cham Comm
M   275 f, UK / 7 f, o'seas
¶   News 4 Energy - 4;   NOF Energy Directory (2007-08) - 1;
       NOF Energy Subsea Production Wallchart (2008) -1;
       NOF Energy North Sea Map (2007) - 1; all free.
✕   2006 (October) Northern Offshore Federation

Noise Abatement Society   (NAS)   1959
NR 26 Brunswick Terrace (flat 2), HOVE, E Sussex, BN3 1HJ.   (hq)
       01273 823850
       email n_a_s@nbtconnect.com
       http://www.noiseabatementsociety.com
       Dir: Peter Wakeham
▲   Registered Charity
○   *K; to reduce noise from all sources to tolerable & reasonable
       levels
Gp Helpline: 0800 389 1380
●   Conf - Mtgs - ET - Res - Exhib - SG - Stat - Inf - LG
M   11,000 i, 128 f, 250 org
¶   NL - 4; ftm only.

Non-Administrative Receivers Association
       since 2008 **NARA**

Non-Ferrous Alliance   (NFA)   1995
NR National Metalforming Centre, 47 Birmingham Rd,
       WEST BROMWICH, West Midlands, B70 6PY.   (hq)
       0121-601 6363   fax 0870 138 9714
       http://www.nfalliance.org.uk
▲   Un-incorporated Society
○   *T; UK non-ferrous metals
●   Conf - Mtgs - ET - Stat - LG
M   280 f in 9 org:
       Aluminium Federation
       British Non-Ferrous Metals Federation
       Cobalt Development Institute
       International Molybdenum Association
       International Tungsten Industry Association
       Lead Development Association International
       Nickel Institute
       Titanium Information Group
       Zinc Information Centre

NORCAP
       see **Adults Affected by Adoption - NORCAP**

Norfolk Chamber of Commerce & Industry   1896
NR 9 Norwich Business Park, Whiting Rd, NORWICH, Norfolk,
       NR4 6DJ.   (hq)
       01603 625977   fax 01603 633032
       email info@norfolkchamber.co.uk
       http://www.norfolkchamber.co.uk
       Chief Exec: Caroline Williams
▲   Company Limited by Guarantee
Br   Great Yarmouth, King's Lynn
○   *C
Gp C'ees: Tax & business finance, Business law, Transportation,
       International trade, POAC, TAC
●   Mtgs - Stat - Expt - Inf - LG - Interpreting
<   Brit Netherlands Cham Comm; Brit Chams Comm (BCC)
M   2,000 f
¶   Business Magazine - 12; ftm.   AR; free.

Norfolk Horn Breeders Group
NR 2 Leighs Lodge Cottages, Willows Green, CHELMSFORD,
       Essex, CM3 1QJ.
       01245 361371
       email info@norfolkhornbreeders.co.uk
       Sec: Kerry Long

Norfolk Naturalists' Trust
       registered name of the **Norfolk Wildlife Trust**

Norfolk & Norwich Archaeological Society (NNAS) 1846
■ 64 The Close, NORWICH, Norfolk, NR1 4DH. (hsp)
   01493 661270
   email duodiscus2@aol.com   http://www.nnas.info
   Hon Sec: M Gooch
▲ Registered Charity
○ *L; study of the archaeology, history, architecture & antiquities
   of Norfolk
Gp Young archaeologists; Walking
● Conf - Mtgs - ET - Lib (at 64 The Close, Norwich) - VE
< Coun Brit Archaeology
M 400 i, 100 f, 10 org, UK / 50 org, o'seas
   (Sub: £16 i, UK / £20 others)
¶ Norfolk Archaeology - 1; ftm, £20 nm.

Norfolk Record Society (NRS) 1923
NR 29 Cintra Rd, NORWICH, Norfolk, NR1 4AE. (hsp)
   01603 436046
   email nrs@norfolkrecordsociety.org.uk
   http://www.norfolkrecordsociety.org.uk
   Hon Sec: Dr G A Metters
▲ Registered Charity
○ *L; publication of historical record material relating to the
   County of Norfolk
● Lectures to accompany launch of each new volume
< Fedn of Norfolk Historical & Archaeol Socs
M c 350 i
¶ 1 publication each year; ftm, £18 nm.

Norfolk Wildlife Trust (NWT) 1926
■ Bewick House, 22 Thorpe Rd, NORWICH, Norfolk, NR1 1RY.
   (hq)
   01603 625540
   http://www.norfolkwildlifetrust.org.uk
   Dir: Brendan Joyce
▲ Registered Charity
○ *E, *G; to protect & enhance Norfolk's wildlife & wild places;
   the trust looks after 40 nature reserves & owns 10 km of
   coastline, 9 Norfolk Broads & 5 ancient woodlands
● Mtgs - ET - Exhib - Stat - Inf - VE
< The Wildlife Trusts (R Soc Nature Consvn)
M 17,500 i, c 100 f
¶ Tern (NL) - 3;   Events Listings - 3;   AR; all free.
   Note: the registered name is the Norfolk Naturalists' Trust

North Country Cheviot Sheep Society 1946
■ Wallacehall West, Waterbeck, LOCKERBIE, Dumfriesshire,
   DG11 3HR. (sp)
   01461 600646
   email secretary@nc-cheviot.co.uk
   http://www.nc-cheviot.co.uk
   Sec: Alison Brodie
▲ Registered Charity
○ *B
● Mtgs - Exhib - Comp - Inf - Shows
< Nat Sheep Assn
M 400 i, UK / 6 i, o'seas
¶ Flock Book - 1; £5 m, £7.50 nm.   Brochures.

North Devon Chamber of Commerce & Industry (NDCCI) 1994
NR Queens House (2nd floor), BARNSTAPLE, Devon, EX32 8HJ.
   (hq)
   0845 337 2892
   email infondcci.com   http://www.ndcci.com
   Co Sec: Mrs Sophia Mayo
▲ Company Limited by Guarantee
○ *C
Gp Manufacturers; Directors; Tourism & services
● Conf - Mtgs - ET - Exhib - Stat - Inf - Empl - LG
< SW Cham Comm; Brit Chams Comm
M 258 f
¶ NL - 4;   AR; both free.   LM; £15 m, £60 nm.

North East Chamber of Commerce, Trade & Industry 1995
NR Aykley Heads Business Centre, Aykley Heads, DURHAM,
   DH1 5TS. (local/office)
   0191-386 1133   fax 0191-386 1144
   email information@ne-cc.com
▲ Company Limited by Guarantee
○ *C
M f

North of England Horticultural Society (NEHS) 1911
NR 4A South Park Rd, HARROGATE, N Yorks, HG1 5QU. (hq)
   01423 561049   fax 01423 536880
   email info@flowershow.org.uk
   http://www.flowershow.org.uk
   Co Sec: Jane Kitchen
▲ Registered Charity
○ *G, *H; organisation of Harrogate spring & autumn flower
   shows
● Exhib
M 150 i
¶ Show leaflet - 2; free.   Show Catalogue - 2.

North of England Institute of Mining & Mechanical Engineers (NEIMME) 1852
NR Neville Hall, Westgate Rd, NEWCASTLE upon TYNE,
   NE1 1SE. (hq)
   0191-232 2201   fax 0191-232 2201
   email office@mininginstitute.org
   http://www.mininginstitute.org.uk
   Hon Sec & Treas: J S Porthouse
▲ Registered Charity
○ *L, *Q; to advance & promote the science & technology of
   mining engineering & other allied branches of engineering,
   particularly coal mining
● Conf - Mtgs - SG - Lib - VE
< Inst of Materials, Minerals & Mining (NE)
M c 400 i

North of England Mule Sheep Association (NEMSA) 1980
■ Eslaforde, Wear View, Frosterley, BISHOP AUCKLAND,
   Co Durham, DL13 2RB. (regd off)
   01388 527411   fax 01388 526728
   email info@nemsa.co.uk   http://www.nemsa.co.uk
   Sec: Mrs Dorothy L Bell
Br 9
○ *B; to promote the North of England mule ewe lamb as a
   breeding sheep (a cross of 2 contrasting pure breeds; a
   Bluefaced Leicester ram to either a Swaledale or
   Northumberland type Blackface dam)
● Mtgs - Exhib - Comp - Stat - Expt - Inf
< Nat Sheep Assn
M c 1,000 i
¶ Mule News (Jnl) - 1;   Sales booklet - 1; both free.

North of England Rosecarpe Horticultural Society (ROSECARPE) 1938
■ 6 Stoneylea Close, Crawcrook, RYTON, Tyne & Wear,
   NE40 4EZ. (hsp)
   0191-413 8026
   email morrosa@talktalk.net
   http://www.rosecarpe.8k.com
   Sec: Mrs Rosamund Robinson
▲ Un-incorporated Society
○ *H; to encourage, improve & extend the cultivation of flowers &
   the art of flower arranging, information on show exhibits &
   on all garden enquiries
Gp Carnations; Daffodils; Roses; Sweet peas
● Mtgs - Exhib - Inf - VE - Spring bulb show
   Show Sec: Morris Robinson, 0191-413 8026
< Nat Sweet Peas Soc; Brit Nat Carnation Soc; Nthn Daffodil Soc
M 150 i
   Sub: £3
¶ News Bulletin - 10;   Ybk; both ftm only.
✕ 2007 North of England Rose, Carnation & Sweet Pea
   Horticultural Society

© CBD Research Ltd · Beckenham · BR3 5JS · Tel 020 8650 7745 · Fax 020 8650 0768 · E-mail cbd@cbdresearch.com · www.cbdresearch.com

North of England Zoological Society   (Chester Zoo)   1934
- ■ Cedar House, Caughall Rd, UPTON by CHESTER, Cheshire,
     CH2 1LH.   (hq)
     01244 380280   fax 01244 371273
     email marketing@chesterzoo.co.uk
     http://www.chesterzoo.org
     Chief Exec: Prof Gordon McGregor Reid
- ▲ Company Limited by Guarantee; Registered Charity
- ○ *B, *E, *V; a conservational & educational charity dedicated to
     breeding & supporting rare & endangered species &
     increasing knowledge of fauna & flora worldwide
- ● Conf - Mtgs - ET - Res - SG - Lib - VE
- < Wld Assn Zoos & Aquariums (WAZA); Intl U Conservation of
     Nature (IUCN); Eur Assn Zoos & Aquaria (EAZA); Assn
     Leading Visitor Attractions (ALVA); Fedn Zoological Gardens
     GB & Ireland
- M 10,000+ i
- ¶ Chester Zoo Life (Jnl) - 4; ftm, £1 nm.
     Guide Book & Map; £3 (£4 by post).   AR; ftm, £5 nm.

**North Hampshire Chamber of Commerce & Industry
(NHCCI)   1998**
- NR Business Support Centre Deanes Bldg, London Rd,
      BASINGSTOKE, Hants, RG21 7YP.   (hq)
      01256 352275   fax 01256 479391
      email office@nhcci.co.uk   http://www.nhcci.co.uk
      Co Sec: Valerie Cloke,   Chief Exec: John Horrocks
- Br 2
- ○ *C

North of Ireland Potato Marketing Association   1935
- NR 80 Hazel Bank Rd, Aughafatten, BALLYMENA, Co Antrim,
      BT42 2LP.   (hq)
      Sec: Laura Hamill
- ▲ Company Limited by Guarantee
- ○ *T; interests of potato merchants & exporters (both ware & seed
     potatoes)
- ● Mtgs - Exhib - Expt - Inf - VE
- < Eur U Potato Merchants; Brit Potato Trs Consortium
- M 10 f
- ¶ NL - 5-6; ftm only.   LM - 1.   AR; ftm only.

North Kent Chamber of Commerce   1891
- NR Stirling House, Sunderland Quay, Medway City Estate,
      ROCHESTER, Kent, ME2 4HN.   (hq)
      01634 311411   fax 01634 311450
      email general@northkentchamber.org
      http://www.northkentchamber.org
      Managing Dir: Tracey Manley
- ▲ Company Limited by Guarantee
- Br Kent Thameside:
      Management Suite, Upper Rose Gallery, Bluewater,
      GREENHITHE, Kent, DA9 9ST.
      01322 381333   fax 01322 381555
      Swale:
      St George's Business Park, Eurolink Industrial Estate,
      SITTINGBOURNE, Kent, ME10 3TB.
      01795 432602
- ○ *C
- ● Conf - Mtgs - ET - Expt
- < Brit Chams Comm
- M c 400 f
- ¶ Business Chat - 6;   Diary - 1; both free.

North London Chamber of Commerce
- NR Enfield Business Centre, 201 Hertford Rd, ENFIELD, Middx,
      EN3 5JH.
      020 8443 4464   fax 020 8443 3822
      email chamber@nlcc.co.uk   http://www.nlcc.co.uk
- ○ *C

North Ronaldsay Sheep Fellowship
- NR Walmer Hall, Dob Lane, Little Hoole, PRESTON, Lancs,
      PR4 4SU.
      01772 613928
      http://www.nrsf.moonfruit.com
      Sec: Anne Lane
- ○ *B

North of Scotland Grassland Society   1961
- NR Gowanwell, Crudie, TURRIFF, Aberdeenshire, AB53 5QR.
      (hsp)
      01261 851416   fax 01261 851416
      Hon Sec: Iain Taylor
- ▲ Registered Charity
- ○ *F; research into methods & management of grass & forage
     crops

North Somerset Agricultural Society   1840
- NR c/o NFU Office (suite 1), 6 Alexandra Rd, CLEVEDON,
      Somerset, BS21 7QE.   (sb)
      0845 634 2464   fax 01275 3406588
      email office@nsas.org.uk   http://www.nsas.org.uk
      Sec: Tim Ledbury
- ▲ Company Limited by Guarantee; Registered Charity
- ○ *F; to promote agriculture & rural issues
- Gp Annual agricultural show; Annual ploughing match & produce
      show
- ● Mtgs - ET - Exhib (agricultural & produce shows) - Comp
     (ploughing match)
- < Assn of Show & Agricl Orgs (ASAO)
- M 500 i
- ¶ NL - 12; ftm, £15 nm.
     [subscription £15].

**North Staffordshire Chamber of Commerce & Industry
(NSCCI)   1861**
- ■ Commerce House, Festival Park, STOKE-on-TRENT, Staffs,
     ST1 5BE.   (hq)
     01782 202222   fax 01782 202448
     email membership@nscci.co.uk   http://www.nscci.co.uk
     Membership Services Mgr: Mark Brammar
- ▲ Company Limited by Guarantee
- ○ *C
- Gp Export club; Manufacturing; Professional services network
- ● Mtgs - ET - Res - Expt - Inf - LG
- < Brit Chams Comm
- M 1,070 f
- ¶ Focus - 4; ftm, £30 nm.
     International Trade News;
     Business Bulletin - 6; both ftm only.

North West Area Board Association
closed 2007

North West Chambers of Commerce
     since 2005 **Chamber of Commerce North West Ltd**

North West London Chamber of Commerce Ltd   (NWLCC)
- ■ Enterprise House, 297 Pinner Rd, HARROW, Middx,
     HA1 4HS.   (hq)
     020 8427 2884   fax 020 8861 5709
     email info@nwlchamber.org.uk
     http://www.nwlchamber.org.uk
     Sec: Mrs Vandona Patel
- ▲ Company Limited by Guarantee
- ○ *C
- ● Conf - Mtgs - ET - Inf - Networking
- < London Cham Comm & Ind
- M f
- ¶ NL - 4; free.

North West Timber Trade Association   (NWTTA)   1972
■   Forest View, Blakemere Lane, NORLEY, Cheshire, WA6 6NS.
     (hsp)
        email secretary@nwtta.org   http://www.nwtta.org
     Sec: Alison Cunningham
▲   Un-incorporated Society
○   *T; importers, agents & merchants for timber
●   Mtgs - Stat - Inf - VE
<   Timber Tr Fedn
M   64 f

**North & Western Lancashire Chamber of Commerce
    (NWLCC)   1916**
NR   9-10 Eastway Business Village, Oliver's Place, Fulwood,
     PRESTON, Lancs, PR2 9WT.   (hq)
        01772 653000   fax 01772 655544
        email info@lancschamber.co.uk
        http://www.lancschamber.co.uk
     Chief Exec: Babs Murphy
▲   Company Limited by Guarantee
○   *C
M   f
×   2004 Central & West Lancashire Chamber of Commerce &
     Industry

**North Western Model Railway Clubs Association   (NWMRCA)
    1968**
NR   67 Norwood Rd, SOUTHPORT, Lancs, PR8 6HQ.   (hsp)
        http://www.nwmrca.org.uk
     Sec: Peter Mills
▲   Un-incorporated Society
○   *G, *N; to provide a link between model railway clubs in the
     North West
●   Conf - Exhib - Conf - Inf
M   c 50 clubs
¶   North West Notes - 12;   NL - 4; both ftm.

North Yorkshire Moors Historical Railway Trust   (NYMR)   1967
NR   Pickering Station, PICKERING, N Yorks, YO18 7AJ.   (hq)
        01751 473799   fax 01751 476970
        email admin@nymrpickering-fsnet.co.uk
        http://www.northyorkshiremoorsrailway.com
     Gen Mgr: Philip Benham
▲   Registered Charity
○   *G; to advance the education of the public in the history &
     development of railway locomotion by the maintenance, in
     working order, of the historic & scenic railway line between
     Grosmont & Pickering
●   ET
<   Assn of Rly Presvn Socs
M   c 7,225 i, 50 f
¶   Moors Line - 4; ftm, £1.20 nm.

Northamptonshire Archaeological Society   1974
NR   2 Bolton House, Wootton Hall Park, NORTHAMPTON,
     NN4 8BP.
        01604 700493
        http://www.northants-archaeology.org.uk
     Hon Sec: Andy Chapman
○   *L; to study of the archaeology of the County
●   Mtgs - VE
M   i
¶   Northamptonshire Archaeology (Jnl).

**Northamptonshire Chamber of Commerce, Training &
    Enterprise   1991**
NR   Opus House, Anglia Way, Moulton Park, NORTHAMPTON,
     NN3 6JA.   (hq)
        01604 490490   fax 01604 670362
     Chief Exec: Stephen Smith
○   *C
M   c 1,300 i & f

Northamptonshire Natural History Society   1876
NR   The Humfrey Rooms, 10 Castilian Terrace, NORTHAMPTON,
     NN1 1LD.   (hq)
        01604 602242
     Sec: C T Sampson
○   *G; to promote research into the natural history & allied
     sciences of the County
●   Mtgs - Res
M   i & org
¶   Jnl.

Northamptonshire Record Society   1920
NR   Wootton Hall Park, Mereway, NORTHAMPTON, NN4 8BQ.
        (hq)
        01604 762297
        http://www.northamptonshirerecordssociety.org.uk
     Sec: Leslie C Skelton
▲   Registered Charity
○   *L, *Q; the pursuit of the history of Northamptonshire in all its
     forms
●   Mtgs - Lib - Lectures
M   500 i, 130 org, UK / 80 families, o'seas
¶   Northamptonshire Past & Present (Jnl) - 1; £3.
     Publications list available.

Northern Cricket Union of Ireland   (NCU)   1886
■   181 Belvoir Drive, BELFAST, BT8 7DS.   (gsp)
        028 9064 7328
        email ncu.cricket@btinternet.com
     Gen Sec: Bryan Milford
▲   Un-incorporated Society
○   *S; the governing body for cricket in Belfast & Counties Antrim,
     Down & Armagh
●   Mtgs - ET - Comp
<   Ir Cricket U
M   50 clubs, 45 schools
¶   Hbk - 1;   AR - 1.

Northern Ireland Agricultural Producers' Association   (NIAPA)
NR   15 Molesworth St, COOKSTOWN, Co Tyrone, BT80 8NX.
        028 8676 5700
○   *T

**Northern Ireland Amusement Caterer's Trade Association
    (NIACTA)**
NR   58 Mallusk Rd, Hyde Park Industrial Estate, NEWTOWNABBEY,
     Co Antrim, BT36 4PX.
        028 9084 8731
○   *T

Northern Ireland Archery Society   (NIAS)
NR   PO Box 282, CRAIGAVON, Co Armagh, BT67 0YA.   (mail add)
        email admin@nias.co.uk
     Chmn: Hugh Irvine
○   *S; governing body of the sport of archery in NI

**Northern Ireland Association for the Care & Resettlement of
    Offenders   (NIACRO)   1971**
NR   Amelia House, 4 Amelia St, BELFAST, BT2 7GS.   (hq)
        028 9032 0157
○   *W; to assist with the rehabilitation of offenders; to work with
     those at risk of criminal involvement & thereby prevent crime

Northern Ireland Association of Christian Teachers   (NIACT)
NR   4 Bolea Park, LIMAVADY, Co Londonderry, BT49 0SH.
        email fred@capple.demon.co.uk   http://www.niact.org.uk
○   *P, *R; to support Christians employed in education in Northern
     Ireland

© CBD Research Ltd · Beckenham · BR3 5JS · Tel 020 8650 7745 · Fax 020 8650 0768 · E-mail cbd@cbdresearch.com · www.cbdresearch.com

Northern Ireland Association for Mental Health 1959
NR 80 University St, BELFAST, BT7 1HE.   (hq)
      028 9032 8474
      email info@niamh.co.uk
      Chief Exec: Alan Ferguson
▲ Company Limited by Guarantee
○ *W; all aspects of mental health & mental illness

Northern Ireland Association for the Study of Psychoanalysis (NIASP) 1988
NR 136 Groomsport Rd, BANGOR, Co Down, BT20 5PE.
      028 9443 2882
      Sec: Mrs Anne Anderson
▲ Registered Charity
○ *P
Gp Child psychotherapy; Group psychotherapy
● Conf - Mtgs - ET - Res - SG
< Brit Confedn Psychotherapy (BCP); Intl Psychoanalytic Assn (IPA)
M c 20 i

Northern Ireland Athletic Federation (NIAF) 1935
NR Athletics House, Old Coach Rd, BELFAST, BT9 5PR.   (hq)
      028 9060 2707   fax 028 9030 9939
      email info@niathletics.org   http://www.niathletics.org
      Hon Sec: John Allen
○ *S; men's & women's athletics in NI
< Intl Assn of Athletic Fedns; UK Athletics
M 45 clubs
¶ Ybk.   AR.

Northern Ireland Bankers' Association
      no longer in existence

Northern Ireland Bat Group (NIBG) 1985
NR 33 Glebe Manor, NEWTOWNABBEY, Co Antrim, BT36 6HF.
      (hsp)
      07989 354592
      email NI.Bats@gmail.com   http://www.bats-ni.org.uk
      Hon Sec: James McCrory
▲ Un-incorporated Society
○ *V; to promote bat conservation in Northern Ireland by
      educating & advising the public; to monitor numbers &
      investigate aspects of bat biology
● ET - Res - Exhib - LG
M 71 i
¶ NL - 4; ftm only.

Northern Ireland Chamber of Commerce & Industry   (NICCI) 1783
NR 22 Great Victoria St, BELFAST, BT2 7BJ.   (hq)
      028 9024 4113
      email mail@northernirelandchamber.com
      http://www.northernirelandchamber.com
      Chief Exec: Frank Hewitt
○ *C

Northern Ireland Childminding Association 1990
NR 16-18 Mill St, NEWTOWNARDS, BT23 4LU.
      028 9181 1015   fax 028 9182 0921
      http://www.nicma.org
      Dir: Bridget Nodder
○ *P
M c 2,500 i

Northern Ireland Council for Voluntary Action (NICVA) 1938
NR 61 Duncairn Gardens, BELFAST, BT15 2GB.   (hq)
      028 9087 7777   fax 028 9087 7799
      http://www.nicva.org
      Chief Exec: Seamus McAleavey
▲ Company Limited by Guarantee; Registered Charity
○ *N, *W; resource & development body serving the voluntary
      sector in Northern Ireland
M i, f & org

Northern Ireland Countryside Staff Association   (NICSA) 1992
NR c/o Park Amenities Dept, Belfast City Council, Malone House,
      Barnett Demesne, BELFAST, BT9 5PB.   (chmn/b)
      028 9066 2259
      http://www.nicsa.co.uk
      Contact: Orla Maguire
○ *P; for all staff involved in promotion & conservation of the
      natural heritage of Northern Ireland

Northern Ireland Cycling Federation   (NICF) 1949
■ 10 Cairndore Avenue, NEWTOWNARDS, Co Down,
      BT23 8RF.   (hsp)
      028 9181 7396
      http://www.nicyclingfederation.com
      Hon Sec: Anthony Mitchell
▲ Un-incorporated Society
○ *S; sporting body for cyclists in Northern Ireland
● Comp
< Cycling Ireland
M 200 i
¶ Ybk; ftm.
✕ 2007 (1 Jan) Cycling Ulster (amalgamated)

Northern Ireland Dairy Association
      since 2005 **Dairy UK** (Northern Ireland branch)

Northern Ireland Deer Society   (NIDS) 1989
NR 14 Glenaan Park, BANGOR, Co Down, BT20 4SN.   (h/treas/p)
      028 9145 5818
      Sec: Dave McCullough
▲ Un-incorporated Society
○ *V; to protect the welfare of deer & their habitat; to advance the
      study of deer, their distribution & ecology for their better
      management & humane control
● Mtgs - Res - Exhib - Inf - VE
M i

Northern Ireland Federation of Housing Associations (NIFHA) 1977
NR 38 Hill St, BELFAST, BT1 2LB.   (hq)
      028 9023 0446   fax 028 9023 8057
      email info@nifha.org   http://www.nifha.org
      Dir & Co Sec: Christopher Williamson
▲ Company Limited by Guarantee
○ *N; 'to represent & promote housing associations in Northern
      Ireland; to support them in the provision of high quality,
      affordable housing for the benefit of the community'
● Conf - Mtgs - ET - Res - Exhib - SG - Stat - Inf - VE - LG
< Intl Co-operative Alliance; Eur Liaison C'ee for Social Housing
      (CECODHAS)
M 45 housing org
¶ AR.

Northern Ireland Food & Drink Association   (NIFDA)
NR Belfast Mills, 71-75 Percy St, BELFAST, BT13 2HW.
      028 9024 1010   fax 028 9024 0500
      email mbell@nifda.co.uk   http://www.nifda.co.uk
○ *T

Northern Ireland Fruit Growers Association   (NIFGA) 1942
NR 52 Teagy Rd, Annaghmore, PORTADOWN, Co Armagh,
      BT62 1LX.   (chmn/p)
      07787 150512
      Chmn: Dermot Morgan
○ *T; promotion of fruit growing

Northern Ireland Grain Trade Association Ltd   (NIGTA) 1966
NR 27 Berwick View, MOIRA, Co Down, BT67 0SX.   (hq)
      028 9261 1044   fax 028 9261 1979
      email doris@leemanpr.demon.co.uk
      Sec: Doris Leeman
○ *T
M 30 f

Northern Ireland Hotels Federation 1922
NR The McCune Building, 1 Shore Rd, BELFAST, BT15 3PG.   (hq)
      028 9077 6636   fax 028 9077 1899
      email office@nihf.co.uk
      Chief Exec: Janet Gault
▲ Un-incorporated Society
○ *T; private sector business in the hospitality industry - hotel,
      guesthouses, restaurants, commercial & trade suppliers

**Northern Ireland Local Government Association   (NILGA)
1973**
NR 123 York St, BELFAST, BT15 1AB.   (hq)
      028 9024 9286   fax 028 9023 3328
      email office@nilga.org   http://www.nilga.org
      Chief Exec: Heather Moorhead
▲ Un-incorporated Society
○ *N; represents the interests of local authorities in Northern
      Ireland
● Conf - Mtgs - SG - Empl - LG
< LEIB; Local Authorities Coordinating Body on Food & Trading
      Standards (LACOTS)
M c 150 icils
¶ The Councillors' Hbk - 4 yrly; free.
      NL - 4;   AR - 1; both free.

**Northern Ireland Master Butchers Association   (NIMBA)
1937**
■ 38 Oldstone Hill, MUCKAMORE, Co Antrim, BT41 4SB.   (sp)
      028 9446 5180
      Sec: Harry Marquess
▲ Un-incorporated Society
○ *T
● Mtgs - Comp - Inf - Empl - LG
M 200 i
¶ N.I. Master Butchers - 4.

**Northern Ireland Master Plumbers' Association   (NIMPA)
1931**
■ 38 Hill St, BELFAST, BT1 2LB.   (asa)
      028 9032 1731   fax 028 9024 7521
      email crawfordsedgwick@excite.com
      Sec: W A Crawford
▲ Un-incorporated Society
○ *T
● Conf - Mtgs - ET - Empl
< Scot & NI Plumbing Employers' Fedn
M 118 f
¶ Plumbheat - 10; ftm only.

Northern Ireland Meat Exporters Association   (NIMEA)   1980
NR Lissue House, 31 Ballinderry Rd, LISBURN, Co Down,
      BT28 2SL.   (hq)
      028 9262 2510
      email nimea@aol.com   http://www.nimea.co.uk
      Chief Exec: Cecil Mathers
▲ Company Limited by Guarantee
○ *T; to represent all EU approved meat exporting companies in
      Northern Ireland
Gp Plants: Slaughter, Cutting, Processing
● Conf - Mtgs - ET - Expt - Inf - LG
< UECBV (Brussels, Belgium)
M 17 f

**Northern Ireland Mixed Marriage Association   (NIMMA)
1974**
NR 28 Bedford St, BELFAST, BT2 7FE.
      028 9023 5444   fax 028 9043 4544
      email nimma@nireland.com   http://www.nimma.org.uk
▲ Registered Charity
○ *W; for the mutual support & help of people involved in or
      about to be involved in a mixed (Catholic / Protestant)
      marriage
● Inf - 'helping the clergy to understand the concept &
      practicalities of mixed marriage' - Influencing the attitudes of
      the community to mixed marriage
< Assn Interchurch Families
M 80 i
¶ Newssheet / Update - 4; ftm only.
      Mixed Marriage in Ireland: A companion to those involved, or
      about to be involved, in a mixed marriage; £3.50.

Northern Ireland Oil Federation
NR 11 Ballyblack Road East, NEWTOWNARDS, Co Down,
      BT22 2BD.
      0845 600 2105   fax 028 9186 3459
      email david@nioil.com   http://www.nioil.com
      Contact: David Blevings
○ *T

Northern Ireland Orienteering Association
NR 31 Pond Park Avenue, LISBURN, Co Antrim, BT28 3HL.
      07797 725398
      http://www.niorienteering.org.uk
      Devt Officer: Helen Baxter
○ *S
M i

Northern Ireland Polymers Association   2002
NR c/o Polymer Processing Research Centre, Queen's University of
      Belfast, Ashby Bldg, Strandmills Rd, BELFAST, BT9 5AH.
      Chmn: Brian McCann
○ *T

Northern Ireland Potato Breeders Association   (NIPBA)   1996
NR 38-40 Carnlea Rd, BALLYMENA, Co Antrim, BT43 6TS.   (hq)
      028 2568 5533
      Chmn: R J Cherry
▲ Company Limited by Guarantee
○ *T; interests of breeders of new varieties of potatoes for home &
      overseas markets

Northern Ireland Poultry Federation
NR c/o O'Kane Poultry Ltd, 170 Larne Rd, BALLYMENA, Co Antrim,
      BT42 9XX.   (chmn/b)
      028 2564 1111   fax 028 2565 8498
      Chmn: W P O'Kane
○ *T
M f

Northern Ireland Public Service Alliance   (NIPSA)   1971
NR 54 Wellington Park, BELFAST, BT9 6DP.   (hq)
      028 9066 1831   fax 028 9066 5847
      http://www.nipsa.org.uk
      Gen Sec: John Corey
Br 250
○ *U; representing non-industrial grades of civil & public servants
● Conf - Mtgs - ET - Inf - Lib - Empl
M 44,000 i
¶ NIPSA News (newspaper) - 11;   Bulletins;   AR;
      Rule Book & Constitution - 1; all free.

© CBD Research Ltd · Beckenham · BR3 5JS · Tel 020 8650 7745 · Fax 020 8650 0768 · E-mail cbd@cbdresearch.com · www.cbdresearch.com

Northern Ireland Shows' Association   (NISA)   1983
■   The King's Hall, Balmoral, BELFAST, BT9 6GW.   (hsb)
     028 9066 5225   fax 028 9066 1264
     email karen@kingshall.co.uk
     Hon Sec: Colin McDonald
○   *F, *N; to represent all agricultural shows in Northern Ireland
●   Conf - Mtgs - ET - Exhib - Comp
M   15 agricultural org (N Ireland)

Northern Ireland Timber Trade Association   (NITTA)   1939
NR   13 Churchill Drive, CARRICKFERGUS, Co Antrim, BT38 7LH.
      (hsp/b)
      028 9336 2784   fax 028 9332 9011
      Liaison Officer: T G Rankin
▲   Un-incorporated Society
○   *T; to promote the imported timber industry
●   Conf - Mtgs - ET - Stat - Empl
<   Timber Trade Fedn UK; Nat Sawmill Assn; Timber Res & Devt
     Assn
M   17 f

Northern Ireland Transplant Association   1991
NR   Eagle Lodge, 51 Circular Rd, BELFAST, BT4 2GA.   (hq)
      028 9076 1394
      email nitransplants@email.com   http://www.nita.org.uk
      Hon Sec: Beverly Robinson
▲   Registered Charity
○   *W; to give support, advice & aid to those concerned with
     organ transplantation; to promote the organ donor card &
     registration scheme
●   Conf - Mtgs - ET - Inf - VE - LG
M   160 i (NI only)
¶   NL - 2; ftm only.

Northern Ireland Volleyball Association   (NIVA)   1970
NR   UUJ Sports Centre, Shore Rd, NEWTOWNABBEY, Co Antrim,
      BT37 0QB.   (mail address)
      028 9036 6373   fax 0870 432 2559
      http://www.nivb.com
      Pres: Paddy Murphy
○   *S; the organisation of the sport of volleyball in Ireland
¶   Hbk - 1; ftm.

Northern Ireland Women's Aid Federation   (NIWAF)   1978
NR   129 University St, BELFAST, BT7 1HP.   (hq)
      028 9024 9041   fax 028 9023 9296
      email info@womensaidni.org
      Dir: Annie Campbell
▲   Company Limited by Guarantee; Registered Charity
○   *K, *W; to challenge attitudes & beliefs which perpetuate
     domestic violence; it seeks to promote healthy & non-abusive
     relationships
Gp   Advice; Outreach; Refuge; Aftercare; Education & awareness
      on domestic violence
●   Conf - Mtgs - ET - Exhib - Stat - Inf - Lib - LG
     Helpline 0800 917 1414 (24-hr)
<   Eur Women's Lobby (EWL); Women against Violence (WAVE);
     Women's Aid Fedn England / Scotland / Wales / Eire
M   11 groups
¶   List of publications on request.

Northern Mill Engine Society   (NMES)   1966
■   84 Watkin Rd, Clayton-le-Woods, CHORLEY, Lancs, PR6 7PX.
     (hsp)
     01257 265003
     http://www.nmes.org
     Hon Sec: John Phillp
▲   Company Limited by Guarantee; Registered Charity
○   *G, *L; preservation of steam engines used to drive the textile
     mills of Lancashire & Yorkshire
●   Mtgs - Exhib - Operation of Bolton Steam Museum
M   230 i, 4 f, 4 org, UK / 5 i, 1 org, o'seas
¶   The Flywheel - 3;   NL - 4; both ftm.

Northern Mine Research Society   (NMRS)   1960
■   Winshaw Barn, Chapel-le-Dale, INGLETON, N Yorks,
     LA6 3AT.   (pres/p)
     http://www.nmrs.co.uk
     Pres: Sallie Bassham
▲   Registered Charity
○   *G, *L; encourages research & publication covering all aspects
     of mining history & related topics in Britain
●   Conf - Mtgs - Res - Inf - Lib - VE
<   Nat Assn of Mining History Orgs (NAMHO); Assn Indl
     Archaeology (AIA)
M   425 i, UK / 8 i, o'seas
¶   NL - 4; ftm only.
     British Mining Monograph - 1; ftm, £13 nm.
     British Mining Memoirs - 1; ftm, £13 nm.

Northern Offshore Federation
     since 2006 **NOF Energy**

Northumberland & Newcastle Society   1924
NR   Jesmond Methodist Church, St George's Terrace, Jesmond,
      NEWCASTLE upon TYNE, NE2 2DL.   (hq)
      0191-281 6266
      email secretary@nandnsociety.org.uk
      http://www.nandnsociety.org.uk
○   *G; conservation & preservation of buildings & the countryside

Northumbrian Pipers' Society   (NPS)   1928
■   Park House, Lynemouth, MORPETH, Northumberland,
     NE61 5XQ.   (hsp)
     01670 860215
     email secretary@northumbrianpipers.org.uk
     http://www.northumbrianpipers.org.uk
     Hon Sec: Julia Say
▲   Un-incorporated Society
○   *D; to foster & encourage the playing, study, manufacture &
     development of Northumbrian pipes & their music &
     traditional Northumbrian music in general
●   Mtgs - ET - Res - Comp
M   650 i, UK / 150 i, o'seas
¶   NPS NL - 4; ftm only.   NPS Magazine - 1; ftm, £4 nm.

Norwegian-British Chamber of Commerce   1906
NR   Charles House, 5 Lower Regent St, LONDON, SW1Y 4LR.   (hq)
      020 7930 0181   fax 020 7930 7946
      http://www.norwegian-chamber.co.uk
      Gen Mgr: Anni Glesaaen
▲   Company Limited by Guarantee
○   *C
●   Conf - Mtgs
M   c 800 i & f
¶   Ybk & LM - 1; ftm, £25 nm.

Not Forgotten Association   1920
§   2 Grosvenor Gdns (4th floor), LONDON, SW1W 0DH.   (hq)
     020 7730 2400   fax 020 7730 0020
     http://www.nfassociation.org
     A charity providing recreation for disabled ex-service men and
     women, such TV sets and licences, holidays and day trips,
     and in-house entertainment in care homes.

Notaries' Society   1907
NR   PO Box 226 Melton, WOODBRIDGE, Suffolk, IP12 1WX.   (hq)
      01394 380436
○   *P; for public notaries

Nottinghamshire Chamber of Commerce & Industry
     in 2008 mered with Derbyshire Chamber & Business Link to form
     Derbyshire & Nottinghamshire Chamber

Nottinghamshire Local History Association   (NLHA)   1953
■   6 Cornwall Road, RETFORD, Notts, DN22 6SH.   (hsp)
      01777 702475
      Chmn: Margaret Woodhead,   Hon Sec: Colin Whitham
▲   Registered Charity
○   *G; to encourage interest in the local history of
        Nottinghamshire
●   Mtgs - Publishing works on Nottinghamshire local history
M   149 i, 51 org
¶   Nottinghamshire Historian (Jnl) - 2; ftm, £2 nm.

Nuclear Industry Association   (NIA)   1962
■   Carlton House, 22A St James's Square, LONDON,
      SW1Y 4JH.   (hq)
      020 7766 6640   fax 020 7839 1523
      email info@niauk.org   http://www.niauk.org
      Chief Exec: Keith Parker
▲   Company Limited by Guarantee
○   *T; UK civil nuclear industry
●   Conf - Mtgs - ET - Exhib - Expt - Inf - LG
<   Brit Energy Assn
M   87 f
¶   Industry Link (NL) - 4;   Trade Directory - 1;
      Educational Booklets;   AR; all free.

Nuclear Institute
NR   Allan House, 1 Penerley Rd, LONDON, SE6 2LQ.   (hq)
         020 8695 8220
○   *L; the application & advancement of nuclear engineering
        technology & allied fields
●   Conf - Mtgs - Inf
M   i
¶   Jnl - 6; ftm.
×   2009 (British Nuclear Energy Society
           (Institution of Nuclear Engineers (merged 1 January)

Nuclear Stock Association Ltd   (NSA)   1952
NR   15 Orchard Way, Cowbit, SPALDING, Lincs, PE12 6XA.   (hq)
         01406 380993 (mobile: 07713 161153)
      Sec: Sarah Troop
○   *H, *T; the maintenance & supply of high health status indexed
        propagation material for soft & tree fruit propagation
Gp   Working gps: Strawberry, rubus & ribes; Tree fruits c'ee
●   Mtgs - VE - LG
M   i
¶   AR - 1; ftm only.
      Note: is a limited company registered as a Friendly Society

Nurse Directors Association   (NDA)   2002
NR   PO Box 1140, HEMEL HEMPSTEAD, Herts, HP1 9BS.
         01442 391123
         email ndamail@ntlworld.com   http://www.nda-uk.org
      Chief Exec: Anne McPherson
○   *P

Nurses Opposed to Euthanasia
   a group with the **Society for the Protection of Unborn Children**

Nursing Homes Ireland   (NHI)   2008
IRL   G6 Centrepoint Business Park, Oak Rd, DUBLIN 12,
         Republic of Ireland.
         353 (1) 429 2570
         http://www.nhi.ie
○   *N
×   2008 (Federation of Irish Nursing Homes
           (Irish Nursing Homes Organisation

Nutrition Society   1941
NR   10 Cambridge Court, 210 Shepherds Bush Rd, LONDON,
         W6 7NJ.   (hq)
         020 7602 0228
         email office@nutsoc.org.uk
○   *L, *P; to advance the scientific study of nutrition & its
        application to the maintenance of human & animal health

**NWA - an association of housing & support managers
      (NWA)   1985**
■   Katepwa House, Ashfield Park Avenue, ROSS-on-WYE,
      Herefords, HR9 5AX.   (hq)
      01989 566699   fax 01989 567676
      email nwa@assocmanagement.co.uk
      http://www.shelteredhousingmanagers.co.uk
      Treas: Gwen Hassall
      Admin: Gill Hinton
▲   Company Limited by Guarantee
○   *P; for the support of wardens & scheme managers of sheltered
        housing & for people with an interest in older people
●   Conf - Mtgs - Inf (members only) - VE - LG
M   1,350 i, 66 f
¶   The Voice - 4; ftm, £1 nm.
×   2005 National Wardens' Association

Nystagmus Network   1984
■   13 Tinsley Close, Claypole, NEWARK, Notts, NG23 5BS.
      (Inf/Offr/p)
      01636 627004
      email info@nystagmusnet.org
      http://www.nystagmusnet.org
      Information Officer: Paul White
▲   Registered Charity
○   *W; to promote help, support & information to all those
        affected by the eye condition Nystagmus (characterised by
        jerky eye movements which nearly always impair vision)
●   Conf - ET - Res - Exhib - Inf
      Helpline: 01392 272573
<   Look; Contact a family; Albino Fellowship
M   500 i, 20 org
¶   Focus (NL) - 4;   Parent Pack; both ftm only.
      Understanding Nystagmus (booklet); ftm.
      Tales of Northwick (book).   Information sheets; ftm.
      Publications list available.

© CBD Research Ltd · Beckenham · BR3 5JS · Tel 020 8650 7745 · Fax 020 8650 0768 · E-mail cbd@cbdresearch.com · www.cbdresearch.com

Observer's Pocket Series Collectors' Society (OPSCS) 1993
NR   10 Villiers Rd, KENILWORTH, Warks, CV8 2JB.   (hsp)
      01926 857047
      http://www.observersbooksociety.co.uk
      Hon Sec: Alan Sledger
▲   Un-incorporated Society
○   *G; 'to promote the interest in & collecting of Observer's &
      other related books published by Frederick Warne'
●   Mtgs
M   550 i, UK / 15 i, o'seas
¶   OPSCS Magazine - 4; ftm only.

Obstetric Anaesthetists Association (OAA) 1969
■   PO Box 3219, LONDON, SW13 9XR.   (regd off)
      020 8741 1311   fax 020 8741 0611
      email secretariat@oaa-anaes.ac.uk
      http://www.oaa-anaes.ac.uk
▲   Company Limited by Guarantee; Registered Charity
○   *P; highest standards of anaesthetic practice in the care of
      mother & baby
●   Conf - Mtgs - ET - Res - Exhib - Inf
M   1,925 i, UK / 343 i, o'seas
      (Sub: £90)
¶   Pencil Point (NL) - 4; ftm only.
      International Jnl of Obstetric Anesthesia - 4; ftm, £127 nm..

Occupational & Environmental Diseases Association (OEDA) 1993
NR   PO Box 26, ENFIELD, Middx, EN1 2NT.   (sp)
      020 8360 8490
      http://www.oeda.demon.co.uk
      Mgt C'ee: Dr Nancy Tait
▲   Registered Charity
○   *W; to help those suffering from, & those working to identify &
      prevent, industrial diseases
●   Res - SG - Inf
¶   Asbestos Facts;   Publications list available.

Occupational Pensioners Alliance (OPA) 2003
■   Carlton House, 42-44 West St, DUNSTABLE, Beds, LU6 1TA.
      (exec/b)
      01582 663880   fax 01582 475775
      email rogerturner@pensioneronline.com
      http://www.opalliance.org.uk
      Exec Officer: Roger Turner
▲   Un-incorporated Society
○   *K; to develop & promote policies that are in the interests of
      occupational pension schemes; to influence national &
      European policy making
●   Mtgs - LG - Campaigning to government on all issues affecting
      occupational pensions
<   Nat Pensioners' Convention
M   [not stated]

OCD Action 1991
■   Davina House (Suite 506-507), 137-149 Goswell Rd,
      LONDON, EC1V 7ET.   (hq)
      0870 360 6232   fax 020 7253 5277
      email info@ocdaction.org.uk
      http://www.ocdaction.org.uk
      Chmn: Peter Jennings
▲   Registered Charity
○   *W; to advance awareness, research, understanding &
      treatment of obsessive compulsive disorder & associated
      disorders; to offer support & advice to sufferers, their families
      & interested professionals
●   Conf - Inf
M   1,200 i
¶   NL - 3;   Information booklet; free.
      Challenging OCD - 1; free.
      [subscription £17 yr].

Ocean Liner Society (OLS) 1987
NR   27 Old Gloucester St, LONDON, WC1N 3XX.   (hsp)
      http://www.ocean-liner-society.com
▲   Un-incorporated Society
○   *G; to promote interest in passenger ships past & present (incl
      line service or cruising, ferries with overnight accommodation
      & sailing or cargo ships carrying passengers)
●   Mtgs - Res - Exhib - Lib - PL - VE
M   400 i, 40 f, 10 org, UK / 200 i, 20 f, 5 org, o'seas
¶   Sea Lines (Jnl) - 4; ftm.

Oesophageal Patients Association 1985
NR   22 Vulcan House, Vulcan Rd, SOLIHULL, West Midlands,
      B91 2JY.   (regd/office)
      0121-704 9860
      Chmn: David Kirby
○   *W; support group for people with oesophageal cancer

Offa's Dyke Association (ODA) 1969
■   West St, KNIGHTON, Powys, LD7 1EN.   (hq)
      01547 528753
      Chmn: Sophie Andreas,   Hon Sec: Ian Bapty
▲   Registered Charity
○   *G; to provide a link between walkers, tourists, historians,
      conservationists & those who live & work on the Welsh
      Border; to provide visitors with information about the area &
      specifically the Offa's Dyke Path
●   Mtgs - ET - Exhib - Inf - PL - Footpath maintenance - Tourist
      Information centre (on behalf of Visit Wales)
<   None formal but close links with: local authorities, CADW
      (Welsh Historic Monuments), Countryside Coun for Wales,
      English Heritage, Natural England,
M   1,000 i & org
¶   NL - 3; ftm only.   Accommodation list - 1; ftm, £4.50 nm.
      Strip maps of Offa's Dyke Path; £5 a set of 10.
      Route Notes N to S, S to N; £2 each.
      List available of other publications.

Offenders Tag Association (OTA) 1982
NR   128 Kensington Church St, LONDON, W8 4BH.   (hq)
      020 7221 7166   fax 020 7792 9288
      email ota@stacey-international.co.uk
      http://www.offenderstag.co.uk
      Chmn: Tom Stacey,   Sec: M A Carruthers
▲   Un-incorporated Society
○   *K; penal reform lobby group
●   Inf - LG
M   30 i

Office Products & Stationery Association
      a group of the **British Office Supplies & Services Federation**

Officers' Association (OA) 1920
§   Mountbarrow House (1st floor), 6-20 Elizabeth St, LONDON,
      SW1W 9RB.   (hq)
      http://www.officersassociation.org.uk
      A registered charity for the relief of distress amongst those who
      have, or have had, a commission in HM Forces, or their
      families

Offshore Contractors' Association (OCA) 1995

NR 58 Queens Rd, ABERDEEN, AB15 4YE. (hq)
01224 326070 fax 01224 326071
email admin@oca-online.co.uk
http://www.oca-online.co.uk
Chief Exec: Bill Murray
▲ Company Limited by Guarantee
○ *T; to represent the UK's Oil & gas contracting industry
● Mtgs - Res - Exhib - Stat - Inf - Lib -Empl - LG
M c 70 f
¶ NL - 12; Brochure; both free.
Guidance Notes - irreg; prices vary.

Offshore Engineering Society (OES) 1987

■ c/o Institution of Civil Engineers, 1 Great George St, LONDON, SW1P 3AA. (hq)
020 7665 2262 fax 020 7799 1325
email oes@ice.org.uk http://www.oes.org.uk
Sec: Adam Kirkup
▲ Registered Charity
○ *P, *T; offshore engineering
● Conf - Mtgs
< is an associated society of the Institution of Civil Engineers
M i & f
(Sub: £16.50 i, from £72 f)
¶ List of publications available.

Offshore Industry Liaison Committee (OILC) 1992

NR 49 Carmelite St, ABERDEEN, AB11 6NQ. (hq)
01224 210118 fax 01224 210095
email gensec@oilc.org http://www.oilc.org
Gen Sec: Jake Molloy
○ *U; for offshore workers
● Conf - ET
M i [not stated]
¶ Blowout (Jnl) - 4; ftm, £1 nm.
Flareoff (supplement) - 4; free.

Oil & Colour Chemists' Association (OCCA) 1918

■ 967 Harrow Rd, WEMBLEY, Middx, HA0 2SF. (hq)
020 8908 1086
Gen Sec: C Pacey-Day
▲ Company Limited by Guarantee; Registered Charity
Br 12; 7 o'seas
○ *L; science & technology of paint, printing ink & allied industries
● Conf - Mtgs - ET - Exhib
< Coating Socs Intl (CSI)
M 1,550 i, UK / 1,650 i, o'seas
¶ Surface Coatings International - 6.
UK Surface Coatings Hbk - 1.

Oil Firing Technical Association for the Petroleum Industry (OFTEC) 1991

■ Foxwood House, Dobbs Lane, Kesgrave, IPSWICH, Suffolk, IP5 2QQ. (hq)
0845 658 5080 fax 0845 658 5181
email enquiries@oftec.org http://www.oftec.org
Dir Gen: Jeremy Hawksley
▲ Company Limited by Guarantee
Br Republic of Ireland
○ *T; to provide technical services for the oil firing industry
Gp Oil: companies, distbrs, eqpt mfrs
● Conf - Mtgs - ET - Exam - Exhib - Stat - LG - Testing & approval of oil firing equipment - Register of approved technicians
< Eurofuel
M 150 f, UK / 1 f, o'seas

Oil & Gas UK 2007

NR 232-242 Vauxhall Bridge Rd (2nd floor), LONDON, SW1V 1AU.
020 7802 2400 fax 020 7802 2401
email info@oilandgasuk.co.uk
http://www.oilandgasuk.co.uk
Admin: Alexa Chaffer
Br Aberdeen, Brussels
○ *T
Note: the correct (registered) title of the organisation is the United Kingdom Offshore Oil & Gas Industry Association Ltd.

Oil Recycling Association (ORA) 1998

■ 62 Lower St, STANSTED, Essex, CM24 8LR. (hsp)
01279 814035 fax 01279 814035
email oilrecyclingasso@aol.com
Hon Sec: Roger Creswell
▲ Company Limited by Guarantee
○ *T; for those engaged in the recovery & recycling of lubricants, fuels & other liquid wastes which are no longer fit for their original purpose and arise mainly from the servicing of automotive engines & other mechanical equipment;
The recovery & recycling of other garage wastes such as oil filters, catalysts, batteries & other products
Gp Allied shipping services
● Mtgs - Res - Stat - Inf - LG
M 29 f
¶ NL - 4; ftm only.

Old Bottle Club of Great Britain (OBCofGB) 1975

NR Elsecar Heritage Centre, BARNSLEY, S Yorks, S74 8HJ. (hq)
01226 745156
Hon Sec: Alan Blakeman
Br 40
○ *G; recovery & study of antique bottles & containers pre 1911
● Conf - Mtgs - Res - ET - Exhib - Comp - Inf - VE
M c10,000 i
¶ British Bottle Review - 4.

Old Gaffers Association

NR 6 Chatham Place, RAMSGATE, Kent, CT11 7PT. (hsp)
01843 582997
Hon Sec: Robert Holden
○ *G; for owners of 'gaff-rigged' (mainly 19th century) sailing craft

Old Lawn Mower Club 1990

NR PO Box 5999 Apsley Guise, MILTON KEYNES, MK17 8HS. (mail address)
email enquiry@oldlawnmowerclub.co.uk
http://www.oldlawnmowerclub.co.uk
Contact: Membership Secretary
▲ Un-incorporated Society
○ *G; promotes the collection, preservation & display of old lawnmowers
● Mtgs - Exhib - Inf
M 300 i, UK / 15 i, o'seas
¶ Grassbox (NL) - 4; ftm only.

Old Time Dance Society 1984

■ 31 Dexter Way, MIDDLEWICH, Cheshire, CW10 9GH. (hsp)
01606 834492
email fredboast@btinternet.com
http://www.oldtimedance.co.uk
Pres: Fred Boast
▲ Un-incorporated Society
○ *D; to keep Old Time Dancing & its music alive; to help form new old time dance clubs
● Conf
M 1,450 i, UK / 40 i, o'seas
(Sub: £15 (couple) UK / £27 (couple) o'seas)
¶ NL - 8; AR; both ftm only.
✕ 2005 Society for the Preservation & Appreciation of Old Time Music & Dancing (Old Time Society)

© CBD Research Ltd · Beckenham · BR3 5JS · Tel 020 8650 7745 · Fax 020 8650 0768 · E-mail cbd@cbdresearch.com · www.cbdresearch.com

Old Time Society
originally the shortened title of the Society for the Preservation & Appreciation of Old Time Music & Dancing, which in 2005 changed its name to **Old Time Dance Society**

Omnibus Society   (OS)   1929
- ■ 185 Southlands Rd, BROMLEY, Kent, BR2 9QZ.
  http://www.omnibussoc.org
  Hon Sec: A J Francis
- ▲ Registered Charity
- Br 5
- ○ *G; study of passenger road transport; understanding of traffic, engineering & methods of operating buses, coaches, trolleybuses & tramcars
- Gp Photographic register; Central timetable collection; Ticket collection; Route recording schemes; Historical research
- ● Mtgs - Res - SG - Inf - Lib - VE
- M 960 i, UK / 10 i, o'seas
- ¶ The Omnibus Magazine - 6;   Members' Bulletin - 6; both ftm.

On Site Massage Association   (OSMA)   1992
- ■ PO Box 8031, READING, Berks, RG6 9DX.   (hq)
  0118-927 2750
  email info@aosm.co.uk   http://www.aosm.co.uk
  Principal: Pauline Baxter
- ○ *P; 'a form of acupressure massage where the client sits on a specially designed chair, with no clothes removed or aids used. The sequence takes just 20 minutes & leaves the client feeling relaxed & alert'
- ● Conf - ET - Exhib - Work in therapy centres & offices
- < Brit Complementary Medicine Assn (BCMA); Complementary Medicine Assn (CMA); Embody, Complementary Therapists Assn
- M 550 i
- ¶ In Touch (NL) - 4; £20 yr.

One Hundred & Sixty (160) Characters Association
- NR 10 Upper Close, FOREST ROW, E Sussex, RH18 5DX.
  01342 825169
  http://www.160characters.org
- ○ *T; mobile messaging technologies & communications services
- M c 23 f

One Parent Families / Gingerbread   2007
- ■ 255 Kentish Town Road, LONDON, NW5 2LX.   (hq)
  020 7428 5400   fax 020 7482 4851
  email info@oneparentfamilies.org.uk
  http://www.oneparentfamilies.org.uk
- ▲ Registered Charity
- Br 2
- ○ *W; to give support & help to lone parent families
- ● Mtgs
  Helpline: 0800 018 5026 (Mon-Fri 0900-1700, Wed 0900-2000)
- M 11,000 i
- ¶ NL - 4; ftm only.   e-newsletter - 12; ftm only.   AR.
- ✕ 2007 (Gingerbread
  (National Council of One Parent Families (merged 1 June)

One Parent Families Scotland   (OPFS)   1944
- ■ 13 Gayfield Sq, EDINBURGH, EH1 3NX.   (hq)
  0131-556 3899
  http://www.opfs.org.uk
  Dir: Sue Robertson
- ▲ Company Limited by Guarantee, Registered Charity
- ○ *W; to promote & provide support, information & services for single parent families within Scotland
- ● Conf - ET - Res - Inf
  Helpline: 0800 018 5026
- M c 430 i & org
- ¶ Various factsheets; free.

One Voice Wales   (OVW)   2004
- ■ 24 College St, AMMANFORD, Carmarthenshire, SA18 3AF.
  (hq)
  01269 595400   fax 01269 598510
  email admin@onevoicewales.org.uk
  http://www.onevoicewales.org.uk
  Chmn: Cllr Isgoed Williams,   Chief Exec: Simon White
- ▲ Un-incorporated Society
- Br 13 area committees
- ○ *N; representative body for community & town councils in Wales
- ● Conf - Mtgs - Empl - LG
- M 509 councils
- ¶ The Voice - 4; £2. only, (discount on bulk purchase).
- ✕ 2004 (National Association of Local Councils in Wales
  (Wales Association of Community & Town Councils

One World Linking Association
see **UK One World Linking Association**

Online Content UK   2001
- ■ Mayfair House, 14-18 Heddon St, LONDON, W1B 4DA.   (hq)
  0845 123 5717
  http://www.onlinecontentuk.org
  Dir: Elizabeth Varley
- ▲ Un-incorporated Society
- ○ *P; for UK based new media editorial professionals; to support the editorial community within the new media & technology industries
- ● Conf - Mtgs - ET - Email discussion list - Industry job & resources lists
- M 215 i, UK / 10 i, o'seas

Online User Group
a group of **CILIP**

Onsite Communications Association   (OSCA)   1963
- NR 25 Shelley Lane, HAREFIELD, Middx, UB9 6HP.   (sb/p)
  01895 473551   fax 0870 831 6161
  Sec Gen: Derek Banner
- ▲ Un-incorporated Society
- ○ *T; manufacturers & suppliers of radio paging & local communications eqpt
- ● Conf - Mtgs - Exhib - Inf - LG
- M i & f

Open Canoe Association   (OCA)
- NR 12 De Verdun Avenue, BELTON, Leics, LE12 9TY.   (mem/sp)
  http://www.opencanoe.org
  Mem Sec: Alan Jones
- ○ *S

Open Canoe Sailing Group   (OCSG)
- NR 94 Dunnocksfold Rd, Alsager, STOKE-on-TRENT, Staffs, ST7 2TW.
  http://www.ocsg.org.uk
  Sec: Dave Seddon
- ○ *S; for those who use sails on canoes & kayaks

Open Spaces Society
the working title of the **Commons, Open Spaces & Footpaths Preservation Society**

Operational Research Society (ORSoc) 1948
■ Seymour House, 12 Edward St, BIRMINGHAM, W Midlands, B1 2RX. (hq)
0121-233 9300 fax 0121-233 0321
email email@theorsociety.com
http://www.theorsociety.com
Sec & Gen Mgr: Gavin Blackett
▲ Company Limited by Guarantee; Registered Charity
Br 10 regions
○ *L; the advancement of the knowledge & applications of operational research
Gp Agricultural & natural resources; Community OR; Criminal justice; Decision analysis; Defence; Financial services; Forecasting; Health & social services; Independent consultants; Information systems; Local search; Mathematical programming; OR+strategy; OR for developing countries; Problem structuring methods; Productivity measurement; Simulation; System dynamics (SD+)
● Conf - Mtgs - ET - Res - Exhib - SG - Inf - Lib - Careers information - Publicity for OR grants
< Intl Fedn of Operational Res Socs (IFORS); Assn of Eur OR Socs (EURO)
M 2,290 i, UK / 310 i, o'seas
(Sub: £63)
¶ Jnl - 12; ftm, institutional only nm.
Inside OR - 12 ftm only.
& for m at £8 each extra:
O.R. Insight - 4; £150 nm.
European Jnl of Information Systems - 6; £190 nm.
Knowledge Management Research & Practice - 4; £108 nm.
Jnl of Simulation - 4; £90 nm.

Ophthalmic Lens Manufacturers' & Distributors' Association (OLMADA) 1950
■ 199 Gloucester Terrace, LONDON, W2 6LD. (hq)
020 7298 5123 fax 020 7298 5120
email info@fmo.co.uk
▲ Company Limited by Guarantee
○ *T; prescription spectacles
● Conf - Mtgs - Exhib - Inf - LG
< Fedn Mfrg Opticians
M 85 f
¶ AR; ftm only.

Ophthalmological Products Trade & Industry Conference (OPTIC (UK)) 1984
NR PO Box 363, DORKING, Surrey, RH4 3XQ. (hq)
01306 741367
Contact: Mrs M Wright
○ *N
no further information supplied

OPTIC (UK)
see **Ophthalmological Products Trade & Industry Conference**

Optical Equipment Manufacturers' & Suppliers' Association (OEMSA) 1990
■ 199 Gloucester Terrace, LONDON, W2 6LD.
020 7298 5123 fax 020 7298 5120
email info@fmo.co.uk
Contact: the Hon Sec
▲ Un-incorporated Society
○ *T
● Mtgs
< Fedn Mfrg Opticians
M 18 f

Optical Frame Importers' & Manufacturers' Association (OFIMA) 1983
■ 199 Gloucester Terrace, LONDON, W2 6LD. (hq)
020 7405 8101 fax 020 7831 2797
email info@fmo.co.uk
Contact: the Hon Sec
○ *T; companies importing & distributing spectacle frames manutactured outside the UK
● Mtgs
< Fedn Mfrg Opticians
M 45 f
¶ AR; ftm only.

Optimum Population Trust (OPT) 1991
NR 12 Meadowgate, Urmston, MANCHESTER, M41 9LB. (hq)
0797 637 0221
http://www.optimumpopulation.org
Chmn & Chief Exec: Martin Chilcott
○ *K; research into & campaigning for sustainable population numbers for the UK & world

Optra Exhibitions UK (OEUK) 1968
■ 199 Gloucester Terrace, LONDON, W2 6LD. (hq)
020 7298 5123 fax 020 7298 5120
email info@fmo.co.uk
Contact: the Hon Sec
▲ Un-incorporated Society
○ *T; formulating the ophthalmic optical trades policy on exhibitions
● Mtgs - Exhib
< Fedn Mfrg Opticians
M c 40 f

Oral History Society
■ c/o Dept of History, University of Essex, COLCHESTER, Essex, CO4 3SQ. (hq)
email rob.perks@bl.uk http://www.oralhistory.org.uk
c/o British Library Sound Archive, 96 Euston Rd, LONDON, NW1 2DB.
020 7412 7405 fax 020 7412 7441 (hsb)
Sec: Robert Perks
▲ Registered Charity
○ *L; study & writing of history through the words of people who experienced it
Gp Local history; Social history; Political history; Reminiscence; Care of the elderly; Archives
● Conf - Mtgs - Res - Inf
M 600 i, 300 org
¶ Oral History - 2.

Orchid Society of Great Britain (OSGB) 1950
NR 103 North Rd, Three Bridges, CRAWLEY, W Sussex, RH10 1SQ. (hsp)
01293 528615
http://www.orchid-society-gb.org.uk
Hon Sec: Mrs Val Micklewright
▲ Registered Charity
Br 3
○ *H; support & encouragement in amateur orchid growing; orchid conservation
● Mtgs - Exhib - Comp - Inf - Lib - PL - VE - Conservation of orchids by redistribution of deceased members' plants
< R Horticl Soc; American Orchid Soc; Barbara Everard Trust for Orchid Consvn
M 1,011 i, 25 org, UK / 69 i, 45 org, o'seas
¶ Jnl - 4; ftm only.
Orchid Cultivation Booklet; ftm, £3 nm.

Order of Malta 1174
IRL St John's House, 32 Clyde Rd, DUBLIN 4, Republic of Ireland.
353 (1) 614 0033 fax 353 (1) 668 5288
email omac@orderofmalta.ie
http://www.orderofmalta.ie
○ *W

© CBD Research Ltd · Beckenham · BR3 5JS · Tel 020 8650 7745 · Fax 020 8650 0768 · E-mail cbd@cbdresearch.com · www.cbdresearch.com

Order of Woodcraft Chivalry   (OWC)   1916
■   7 The Enterdent, GODSTONE, Surrey, RH9 8EG.   (hsp)
     01883 744200
     Hon Sec: Vivienne Cluff
▲   Un-incorporated Society
Br   3
○   *G; family outdoor activities as a means of character
     development, self-sufficiency & initiative in adults as well as
     children
Gp   Camping in adverse conditions for survival skills; Country
     dancing; Woodcraft
●   Inf - VE
¶   Pine Cone (Jnl) - 4; ftm, £6 nm.

Orders & Medals Research Society   (OMRS)   1942
■   PO Box 1233, HIGH WYCOMBE, Bucks, HP11 9BW.   (hsb)
     01494 441207
     email generalsecretary@omrs.org.uk
     http://www.omrs.org.uk
     Gen Sec: P M R Helmore
▲   Un-incorporated Society
Br   10; Australia, Canada, Hong Kong, New Zealand
○   *G; to foster an interest in orders, decorations & campaign
     medals; to publish the results of members' researches
Gp   Ribbon collectors; Miniature medal collectors
●   Mtgs - Res - Lib - Annual convention
M   1,850 i, 63 f, 39 org, UK / 753 i, 17 f, 22 org, o'seas
¶   Orders & Medals - 4;   LM - 2 yrly; both ftm only.

Ordnance Society   (OS)   1988
NR   3 Maskell Way, FARNBOROUGH, Hants, GU14 0PU.
     (mem/sp)
     01252 521201
     http://www.freespace.virgin.net/ordnance.society/
     Mem Sec: Ian McKenzie
▲   Un-incorporated Society
○   *G; to study all aspects of the history of ordnance, artillery &
     ammunition

Orff Society UK   1964
■   7 Rothesay Ave, RICHMOND, Surrey, TW10 5EB.   (hsp)
     020 8876 1944   fax 020 8876 1944
     email orffsocuk@btconnect.com   http://www.orff.org.uk
     Hon Sec: Margaret Murray
▲   Un-incorporated Society
○   *D, *E; to promote the experience & understanding of Carl
     Orff's approach to music education; a creative way of
     teaching music to groups using voices in speech/singing,
     movement/dance & all percussion in early stages
●   Conf - ET - Exam - Inf - Lib - Workshops
<   Carl-Orff & Orff-Schulwerk associations & societies worldwide
M   135 i, 1 f, 8 universities, UK / 11 i, 2 universities,
     9 schools, o'seas
¶   Orff Times - 2; ftm only.

The Organ Club   1926
NR   92 The Hawthorns, Charvil, READING, Berks, RG10 9TS.
     (memsec/p)
     http://www.organclub.org
     Mem Sec: Mark Jameson
○   *D; to promote & develop public education in organs & organ
     music; to promote study & research
●   Mtgs - Inf - Lib - PL - VE
M   500 i, UK / 60 i, o'seas
¶   Jnl - 3.   NL - 6;   AR - 1;   Hbks - irreg.

Organic Food Federation   (OFF)   1986
NR   31 Turbine Way, Eco Tech Business Park, SWAFFHAM, Norfolk,
     PE37 7XD.   (hq)
     01760 720444
     http://www.organicfoodfed.com
     Exec Sec: Julian Wade
▲   Company Limited by Guarantee
○   *F, *T; for processors, producers & retailers of organic food
●   Mtgs - ET - Exhib - Stat - LG
<   UK Register of Organic Food Standards ([UKROPS] A division of
     DEFRA)
M   c 380 f

Organic Living Association   1971
■   St Mary's Villa, Hanley Swan, WORCESTER, WR8 0EA.   (sp)
     fax 01684 310703
     Dir & Sec: Dennis C Nightingale-Smith
▲   Un-incorporated Society
○   *K; to integrate the production & consumption of food crops
     grown on healthy, naturally fertilised soil; to disseminate
     knowledge of nutrition, alternative medicine, conservation &
     self-sufficient community living
●   Mtgs - Inf - VE
M   200 i, UK / 10 i, o'seas
¶   NL - 6; free.
     Note: please send sae for information.

Organic Organisation
     is an alternative title for the **Henry Doubleday Research
     Association**

Organisation of Horsebox & Trailer Owners
NR   Whitehill Farm, Hamstead Marshall, NEWBURY, Berks,
     RG20 0HP.   (hq)
     01488 657651
     email info@horsebox-rescue.co.uk
     http://www.horsebox-recue.co.uk
○   *G; membership covers a road rescue/repair service & tyre
     network for horsebox breakdown problems

Oriental Ceramic Society   (OCS)   1921
■   PO Box 517, CAMBRIDGE, CB21 5BE.   (hq)
     01223 881328   fax 01223 881328
     email ocslondon@btinternet.com
     http://www.ocs-london.com
     The Society of Antiquaries, Burlington House, LONDON,
     W1J 0BF.   (regd/office)
     Admin: Mrs Mary Painter
▲   Company Limited by Guarantee; Registered Charity
○   *A, *G; to increase the knowledge & appreciation of ceramics
     & all the arts of Asia; to provide a link between collectors,
     curators, scholars & others with like interests
●   Conf - Mtgs - Res - Exhib - SG - VE
M   440 i, UK / 500 i, o'seas, & Libraries, museums & other
     ceramic societies
¶   Transactions - 1; ftm only.
     (Sub: £55 (home), £50 (o'seas), £100 (corporate),
     £100 (benefactor) £25 (under-25 & curators)).

Original Pearly Kings & Queens Association   (OPKA)   1975
§   c/o St Martin's in the Field, Trafalgar Square, LONDON,
     WC2N 4JJ.
     Supporting the church of St Martin's in the Field and raising
     money for charities

Orkney Chamber of Commerce
NR   PO Box 6202, KIRKWALL, Orkney, KW15 1YG.
○   *C
     No further information supplied

Orkney Heritage Society   1979
- ■ Moan House, HARRAY, Orkney, KW17 2LE.   (hsp)
      01856 771391
      email tunguska@tiscali.co.uk
      http://www.orkneycommunities.co.uk/OHS
      Hon Sec: Lynn Campbell
- ○ *G

Ornamental Aquatic Trade Association   (OATA)   1991
- NR Wessex House, 40 Station Rd, WESTBURY, Wilts, BA13 3TN.
      (hq)
      0870 043 4013   fax 01373 301236
      email info@ornamentalfish.org
      http://www.ornamentalfish.org
      Chief Exec: Keith Davenport
- ▲ Company Limited by Guarantee
- ○ *T; for the ornamental fish industry
- ● ET - Stat - Inf
- M c 700 f
- ¶ The Voice (NL) - 4;   OATA Worldwide NL - 12;
      LM - 1; all ftm only.   Handbooks.
      Publications list available.

Ornithological Society of the Middle East   (OSME)   1967
- NR c/o The Lodge, SANDY, Beds, SG19 2DL.   (mail/address)
      01636 703512   fax 01442 822623
      email secretary@osme.org   http://www.osme.org
      Sec: John Bartlet,   Chmn: Keith Betton
- ▲ Registered Charity
- ○ *G; recording, conservation study of wild birds in the Middle
      East
- ● Conf - ET - Res - SG - Lib - LG
- M 429 i, 3 f, 68 org, UK / 325 i, o'seas
- ¶ Sandgrouse - 2; ftm, £5 nm.

Orthodontic Technicians Association   (OTA)   1971
- ■ Centre for Dental Technology, Room T018 CSHS, UWIC,
      Western Ave, Llandaff, CARDIFF, CF5 2YB.   (hsb)
      029 2041 6899   fax 029 2041 6898
      email jlewis@uwic.ac.uk   http://www.orthota.co.uk
      Hon Sec: Jeff Lewis
- ▲ Un-incorporated Society
- ○ *P; to encourage the study, improve the practice & advance the
      knowledge of the science of orthodontic laboratory
      techniques
- Gp Education sub-c'ee
- ● Conf - Mtgs - ET - Exhib - Comp - Inf - PL - Empl - LG
- < Brit Orthodontic Soc (BOS)
- M 250 i, UK / 5 i, 3 f, o'seas
- ¶ NL - 4;   Proceedings - 1; both ftm only.

Oscar Wilde Society   (OWS)   1990
- NR Kambah, Harcourt Hill, OXFORD, OX2 9AS.   (memsec/p)
      http://www.oscarwildesociety.co.uk
      Mem Sec: Cressida Battersby
- ▲ Un-incorporated Society
- ○ *A; to further interest in & knowledge of, the life & works of
      Oscar Wilde
- ● Conf - Mtgs - ET - Res - Exhib - Comp - Inf - VE - Lib
- < Alliance of Literary Socs
- M 210 i, UK / 75 i, o'seas
- ¶ The Wildean (Jnl) - 2; ftm, £6 nm.
      Intentions (NL) - 5; ftm only.

Osteopathic Sports Care Association   (OSCA)   1995
- NR 88 Great Northern Rd, DUNSTABLE, Beds, LU5 4BT.   (chmn/p)
      01582 608400
      email oscasecretary@hotmail.co.uk
      http://www.osca.org.uk
      Chmn: Jonathan Betser
- ▲ Un-incorporated Society
- ○ *M; osteopathic education, promotion & sports care
- Gp Sub-c'ees: Conferences, Periodical, Post graduate education
- ● Conf - Mtgs - ET - Res - Inf - VE
- < in partnership with Nat Sports Medicine Inst
- M c 250 i
- ¶ Still Improving Sport - 4.

**Outdoor Advertising Association of Great Britain Ltd   (OAA)
1982**
- NR Summit House, 27 Sale Place, LONDON, W2 1YR.   (hq)
      020 7973 0315   fax 020 7973 0318
      email enquiries@oaa.org.uk   http://www.oaa.org.uk
      Chief Exec: Alan James
- ○ *T; for UK poster contractors
- M f
      No further information supplied

Outdoor Advertising Council
- ■ Collingwood, 2 Bell Barn Rd, Stoke Bishop, BRISTOL,
      BS9 2DA.   (hsp)
      0117-904 7235   fax 0117-904 7236
      Sec: Chris Thomas
- ▲ Un-incorporated Society
- ○ *N
- ● Conf - Mtgs - ET - LG
- M c 300 f

Outdoor Media Association
- IRL Arena House, Arena Road, Seaford Ind Est, DUBLIN 18,
      Republic of Ireland.
      353 (1) 201 6760
      http://www.oma.ie5
      Dir: Su Duff

Outdoor Swimming Society.   (OSS)
- NR c/o Milk Studios, 34 Southern Row, LONDON, W10 5AN.
      http://www.outdoorswimmingsociety.com
- ○ *G, *S; for all who enjoy swimming in Britain's lakes, rivers,
      lidos & the sea

Outdoor Writers' & Photographers' Guild   (OWG)   1980
- ■ PO Box 520, Bamber Bridge, PRESTON, Lancs, PR5 8LF.   (hsp)
      01772 321243   fax 0870 137 8888
      email info@owg.org.uk   http://www.owg.org.uk
      Hon Sec: Terry Marsh
- ▲ Un-incorporated Society
- ○ *P; to promote a high professional standard among writers who
      specialise in outdoor activities; to provide a forum for
      members to meet, includes writers, photographers,
      illustrators, broadcasters
- ● ET - VE - Awards to members - Press trips
- M 160 i, UK / 5 i, o'seas
- ¶ Outdoor Focus - 4;
      Electronic Media Bulletin - 6; both ftm only.
- × 2007 Outdoor Writers' Guild

© CBD Research Ltd · Beckenham · BR3 5JS · Tel 020 8650 7745 · Fax 020 8650 0768 · E-mail cbd@cbdresearch.com · www.cbdresearch.com

Ovacome: the ovarian cancer support network   1996
- ■ PO Box 6294, LONDON, W1A 7WJ.   (hq)
       020 7299 6654   fax 020 7631 4674
       email ovacome@ovacome.org.uk
       http://www.ovacome.org.uk
       Trustee: Adrian Dickinson
- ▲ Registered Charity
- ○ *W; a nationwide support group for all those affected by ovarian cancer - sufferers, families, carers & health professionals
- ● Conf - Mtgs - ET - Res - Inf - LG
       Support line: 0845 371 0554
- M 1,700 i, 100 hospitals, care professionals
- ¶ NL - 3;   AR; both free.

Ovarian Cancer Support Network
   see **Ovacome: the ovarian cancer support network**

Over Fifties Association   (TOFFS)   1990
- NR 29 Hill Court, Hanger Lane, LONDON, W5 3DF.   (hq)
       020 8998 2065
       Chmn: Eric Bellenie
- ○ *K; to abolish age discrimination; to establish training centres; to encourage cooperative commercial ventures

Overeaters Anonymous   (OA)   1960
- ■ PO Box 19, Stretford, MANCHESTER, M32 9EB.   (mail address)
       0700 078 4985
       http://www.oagb.org.uk
- Br 200; worldwide
- ○ *W; to help compulsive eaters & people with eating disorders to recover using the 12 steps adopted from Alcoholics Anonymous
- ● Conf - Mtgs
- M i [unknown]
- ¶ Lifeline - 12.

Overseas Press & Media Association   (OPMA)   1965
- NR CRI-Media Ltd, PO Box 3345, COVENTRY, Warks, CV6 6YD. (asa)
       024 7636 1888   fax 024 7636 3916
       http://www.opma.co.uk
       Hon Sec: Cara-Lyn Reynolds
- ▲ Company Limited by Guarantee
- ○ *T; to promote the interests of advertising representatives of media from overseas
- ● Mtgs - ET
- M c 150 f
- ¶ Overseas Press & Media Guide - 1.

Overseas Territories Association
   see **United Kingdom Overseas Territories Association**

Owner Drivers Society   (ODS)   1948
- NR 21 Buckingham Palace Rd, LONDON, SW1W 0PN.   (hq)
       020 7834 6541   fax 020 7931 0822
       Sec: T Owen
- ▲ Un-incorporated Society
- ○ *T; taxi drivers' representatives
- ● LG
- < Nat Taxi Assn
- M 1,800 i

Oxford Down Sheep Breeders Association   (ODSBA)   1889
- NR Hillfields Lodge, LIGHTHORNE, Warks, CV35 0BQ.   (hsp)
       01926 650098
       email secretay@oxforddownsheep.org.uk
       http://www.oxforddownsheep.org.uk
       Sec: PAul Froehlich
- ▲ Company Limited by Guarantee; Registered Charity
- ○ *B
- ● Mtgs - Exhib - Comp - Stat - Inf
- < Nat Sheep Assn
- M 70 i, 2 f, UK / 1 i, o'seas
- ¶ Flock Book - 1; £7.
       The Oxford Down - One Hundred Years of Breeding; £5.

Oxford Sandy & Black Pig Society   (OSB)   1985
- NR Lower Coombe Farm, Blandford Rd, Coombe Bissett, SALISBURY, Wilts, SP5 4LJ.   (hsp)
       01722 718263
       email osbpigs@homecall.co.uk
       Hon Sec/Treas: Mrs Heather Royle
- ○ *B; to promote one of the oldest British pig breeds
- ● Mtgs - Exhib - Comp - Inf - Agricultural shows
- M c 100 i
- ¶ NL - 6/8; free.   Herdbook - 1; ftm.

Oxford University Archaeological Society   (OUAS)   1911
- NR Institute of Archaeology, Beaumont St, OXFORD, OX1 2PG. (mail address)
       email archsoc@herald.ox.ac.uk
       http://www.geocities.com/ouarchsoc
       Contact: The President
- ▲ Un-incorporated Society
- ○ *L; investigation of local antiquities
- Gp Excavations; Roman / Anglo-Saxon / Mediaeval archaeology
- M i

Oxfordshire Architectural & Historical Society   (OAHS)   1839
- NR 7A Burford Rd, CHIPPING NORTON, Oxon, OX7 5EB.   (hsp)
       email secretary@oahs.org.uk   http://www.oahs.org.uk
       Sec: Valerie Davies
- ▲ Registered Charity
- ○ *L; study of local history, archaeology & architecture
- Gp Victorian; Listed buildings c'ee; Oxford City & County Archaeological Forum
- ● Mtgs - Lib - VE
- < Coun Brit Archaeology
- M 600 i, 150 org, UK / 10 i, 10 org, o'seas
- ¶ Oxoniensia (Jnl) - 1; ftm, £12 nm.

Oxfordshire Record Society   (ORS)   1919
- NR Bodleian Library, OXFORD, OX1 3BG.   (mail add)
- ▲ Registered Charity
- ○ *L; to publish edited texts of local history documents relating to the County of Oxford

P G Wodehouse Society (UK)   1995
NR   26 Radcliffe Rd, CROYDON, Surrey, CR0 5QE.   (mem/sp)
        http://www.eclipse.co.uk/wodehouse
       Mem Sec: Christine Hewitt
▲   Un-incorporated Society
○   *A; to promulgate the enjoyment of the writings of
        P G Wodehouse (1881-1975)
¶   Wooster Sauce - 4; ftm only.

**PACE: Professional Association for Catering Education   (PACE)
2003**
■   Thomas Danby College, Roundhay Rd, LEEDS, W Yorks,
        LS7 3BG.   (sb)
        0113-284 6408   fax 0113-240 1967
        email info@keepinpace.org.uk
        http://www.keepinpace.org.uk
       Chief Exec: Jim Armstrong (0788 776 8524)
▲   Company Limited by Guarantee
Br   6 regional
○   *N, *P; to encourage catering educational institutions to work
        together to manage the challenges of continual change
        within hospitality & catering education
●   Conf - Mtgs - ET - Res - Exhib - Comp - Inf - LG
M   c 500 i, f & org
       Note: PACE is the trading name of Keep in Pace Ltd
✕   2003 National Association for Heads of Hospitality Education

**Pacific Islands Society of the United Kingdom & Ireland
(PISUKI)   1981**
NR   3 Wood St, New Bradwell, MILTON KEYNES, MK13 0AZ.
        (chmn/p)
       Mem Sec: Mrs Dorothy Prince
▲   Un-incorporated Society
○   *X; for Pacific Islanders in the UK & Ireland & to bring together
        all those interested in, or concerned with, the islands
●   Conf - Mtgs - Inf - Social activities especially for islanders
        temporarily in UK
M   c 300 i & f, 16 org
¶   The Outrigger (NL) - 3/4; ftm.

Packaging Federation   (PF)   1995
■   1 Warwick Row, LONDON, SW1E 5ER.   (regd/office)
        020 7808 7217   fax 020 7808 7218
        email dicksearle@packingingfedn.co.uk
        http://www.packagingfedn.co.uk
       Chief Exec: Dick Searle
▲   Company Limited by Guarantee
○   *T; to represent members, who are the major packaging firms,
        on economic & environmental issues
●   Mtgs - LG
M   f

Packaging & Industrial Films Association   (PIFA)   1973
■   Gothic House (3rd floor), Barker Gate, NOTTINGHAM,
        NG1 1JU.   (hq)
        0115-959 8389   fax 0115-959 9326
        email pifa@pifa.co.uk   http://www.pifa.co.uk
       Chief Exec: David Tyson
▲   Company Limited by Guarantee
○   *T; producers & distributors of plastic packaging & industrial
        films
●   Mtgs - ET - Stat - LG
<   Plast Euro Film; Brit Plastics Fedn; Packaging Fedn
M   55 f, UK / 4 f, o'seas
¶   PIFA Annual review - 1; ftm, £25 nm.
       PIFA Annual Statistical Report - 1; £25 m, £50 nm.
✕   2007 Flexible Packaging Association (merged

Packaging Society
        alternative name of IOP: The Packaging Society, a division of the
        Institute of Materials, Minerals & Mining)

Paddle Steamer Preservation Society   (PSPS)   1959
■   PO Box 365, WORCESTER, WR3 7WH.   (asa)
       Hon Sec: John Anderson
▲   Company Limited by Guarantee; Registered Charity
Br   5
○   *G, *K; to encourage interest in paddle steamers; retention of
        existing services & preservation of the society's own steamers
Gp   Models
●   Conf - Mtgs - Res - Exhib - VE - Special cruises
<   Transport Trust
M   3,400 i, UK / 100 i, o'seas
¶   Paddle Wheels - 4; ftm.

Paediatric First Aid Association   (PFAA)   2006
NR   178 Marlborough Way, ASHBY de la ZOUCH, Leics,
        LE65 2QH.
        07976 207997
        http://www.pfaa.org.uk
○   *P; approval body for paediatric first aid training

Pagan Federation   (PF)   1971
NR   BM Box 7097, LONDON, WC1N 3XX.   (mail address)
        07986 034387
        http://www.paganfed.org
▲   Un-incorporated Society
○   *G; to promote & defend pagan traditions
●   Conf - Mtgs - ET - Inf - VE - LG
M   c 4,000 i, UK / 200 i, o'seas
¶   Pagan Dawn - 4;   AR; ftm.
       Various information packs.

Paget Gorman Society
■   43 Westover Rd, FLEET, Hants, GU51 3DB.   (hq)
        01252 621183
        email contact.pgs@ntlworld.com   http://www.pgss.org
       Admin Sec: Mike Simpson
▲   Registered Charity
○   *W; to support the use of Paget Gorman signed speech by
        speech therapists in schools, special schools, special units &
        hospital units
●   Conf - Mtgs - ET - Exam - Res - Awarding of qualifications
M   1,000 i, UK / 100 i, o'seas
¶   NL - 1; free.

Pain Society (the British Chapter of IASP)
        since 2004 **British Pain Society**

Paint & Powder Finishing Association
        a group of the **Surface Engineering Association**

Paint Research Association   (PRA)   1926
NR   14 Castle Mews, High St, HAMPTON, Middx, TW12 2NP.   (hq)
        020 8487 0800   fax 020 8487 0805
        http://www.pra.org.uk
▲   Company Limited by Guarantee
○   *Q; research, technology & information services for the
        coatings & related industries
●   Conf - Mtgs - ET - Res - Exhib - Stat - Inf - Lib
<   Assn Indep Res & Technology Orgs
M   100 f, UK / 75 f, o'seas

Painting & Decorating Association   2002
■   32 Coton Rd, NUNEATON, Warks, CV11 5TW.   (hq)
        024 7635 3776   fax 024 7635 4513
        http://www.paintingdecoratingassociation.co.uk
▲   Un-incorporated Society
○   *T; for professional painters & decorators in GB
●   Conf - Mtgs - ET - Exhib - Comp - LG
M   2,400 f

© CBD Research Ltd · Beckenham · BR3 5JS · Tel 020 8650 7745 · Fax 020 8650 0768 · E-mail cbd@cbdresearch.com · www.cbdresearch.com

Palaeontographical Society (PAISoc) 1847

■ Dept of Palaeontology, The Natural History Museum, Cromwell Rd, LONDON, SW7 5BD. (hsb)
020 7942 5552 fax 020 7942 5546
email p.barrett@nhm.ac.uk http://www.nhm.ac.uk/hosted_sites/palsoc/
Secs: Dr P Barrett & Dr S Long
▲ Registered Charity
○ *L, *Q; promotion of study of geology through publication of monographs on British fossil fauna & flora
● Mtgs - ET - Res - Publication of monographs
M 144 i, 210 f, 110 org
(Sub: £33 i, £110 org)
¶ Monographs - 1; £33 m, £210 nm.

Palaeontological Association 1957

NR c/o Dr T J Palmer, Institute of Geography & Earth Sciences, University of Wales Aberystwyth, ABERYSTWYTH, Ceredigion, SY23 3BD. (exec/offr)
http://www.palass.org
Exec Officer: Dr T J Palmer
▲ Registered Charity
○ *L, *Q; to study palaeontology (life of the past) & its allied sciences
● Conf - Mtgs - Res - Inf - PL
M c 1,200 i, c 700 f, UK / c 500 i, o'seas
¶ Palaeontology - 6; £28 yr m, £55 per part nm.

Pali Text Society (PTS) 1881

NR c/o CPI Antony Rowe Ltd, Unit 4 Pegasus Way, Bowerhill Industrial Estate, MELKSHAM, Wilts, SN12 6TR. (hq)
0117-955 4100 (Mon/Wed/Fri 1900-1600) fax 0117-955 4100
email pts@palitext.com http://www.palitext.com
Admin: Karen Wendland
▲ Registered Charity
○ *L, *Q, *R; promoting the study of Pali by publishing Pali texts in Roman characters, translations & ancillary work; funding research students
● Res - Inf - Lib - Publishing
M c 570 i
¶ Jnl - irreg. List of Issues; free.
NL - 2; AR; both ftm only.

Palmerston Forts Society (PFS) 1984

NR Fort Nelson, Portsdown Hill Rd, FAREHAM, Hants, PO17 6AN. (hq)
http://www.palmerstonforts.org.uk
023 9266 0261 (0900-1700 hrs) (chmn/b)
Chmn: Geoffrey M Salvetti
▲ Registered Charity; Un-incorporated Society
○ *G, *L; a forum for research into the field of Victorian fortification & artillery; to offer advice to government & local authorities on Victorian fortifications
Gp Portsdown artillery volunteers
● Conf - Mtgs - ET - Res - Exhib - SG - Inf - Lib - PL - Artillery re-enactment (authentic Victorian gun drills on period pieces)
M i

Pancreatic Society of GB & Ireland

NR c/o Mr Ross Carter, 12-14 Alexandra Parade, Glasgow Royal Infirmary, GLASGOW, G31 2ER. (sb)
0141-211 5129
http://www.pancsoc.org.uk
Sec: Ross Carter
▲ Registered Charity
○ *L
● Conf - ET - Res - SG
M 180 i, UK / 20 i, o'seas

Paper Agents Association (PAA) 1924

■ 48 Courtmoor Ave, FLEET, Hants, GU52 7UE. (dir/p)
01252 680449 fax 07092 386132
email info@paa.org.uk http://www.paa.org.uk
Dir: John R Paine
▲ Un-incorporated Society
○ *T; to promote a better & closer understanding among accredited agents & mill owned sales offices in the UK & Eire representing overseas paper & board makers; to represent legitimate overall best interests in the local market
Gp Publications & fine papers; Corrugated case materials; Packaging, industrial & other papers; Carton boards, industrial & other boards
● Mtgs - Stat - LG
< Confedn Paper Inds
M 42 f

Paper Federation of Great Britain Ltd
since 2004 the Papermaking Sector of the **Confederation of Paper Industries**

Paper Industry Technical Association Ltd (PITA) 1920

■ 5 Frecheville Court, BURY, Lancs, BL9 0UF. (hq)
0161-764 5858 fax 0161-764 5353
email info@pita.co.uk http://www.pita.co.uk
Chief Exec: Graham Toft
▲ Company Limited by Guarantee; Registered Charity
○ *P; for all involved in the pulp, paper, converting & allied industries
Gp Environmental; Engineering; Papermaking; Raw materials; Coating; Finishing
● Conf - Mtgs - ET - SG - Inf - VE
M 1.097 i, 138 f, UK / 150 i, o'seas
¶ Paper Technology - 12; ftm, £100 yr nm.
PITA Ybk - 1; ftm only.
The Essential Guide to Aqueous Coating of Paper & Board (textbook); £75 m, £85 nm.

Paper Makers' Allied Trades Association (PMATA) 1931

■ 24 Beatrice Rd, Worsley, MANCHESTER, M28 2TN. (hsp)
0161-794 5734 fax 0161-793 0827
Hon Sec: D G McNay
▲ Un-incorporated Society
○ *T; fostering good relations between the paper industry & its suppliers
● Golf competitions - Annual dinners
M 200 i, 78 f

Paperweight Collectors Circle (PCC) 1981

■ PO Box 941, Comberton, CAMBRIDGE PDO, CB23 7GQ. (mail/address)
01223 264656
http://www.paperweightcollectorscircle.org.uk
Sec: Angela Faulkner
▲ Un-incorporated Society
○ *G; for collectors of paperweights; to promote the art of paperweight makers
● Mtgs - Exhib - VE
< Paperweight Collectors Assn (USA)
M 200 i, UK / 30 i, o'seas
¶ NL - 4; ftm only.
× 2004 (January) Cambridge Paperweight Circle

Parallel Traders Association

NR c/o Clintons, 55 Drury Lane, LONDON, WC2B 5SQ. (asa)
020 7379 6080
Contact: Gary Lux
○ *T

Parenteral Society
since March 2006 **Pharmaceutical & Healthcare Sciences Society**

Parents at Work
in 2004 merged with New Ways to Work to form **Working Families**

Parity   1986
■ Constables, Windsor Rd, ASCOT, Berks, SL5 7LF.   (hsp)
    01344 621167
    http://www.parity-uk.org
    Hon Sec: David Yarwood
▲ Registered Charity
○ *K; to promote & protect the equal rights of men & women to
    the enjoyment of all civil, political, economic, social &
    cultural rights under the law
Gp Human rights; Legal; Parliamentary; Pensions; Research
● Mtgs - Res - Inf - Identifying & monitoring unequal treatment of
    men & women under law - Promoting legal activities
M c 300 i, 2 trade unions, UK / c 5 i, o'seas
¶ NL - 4.   Information sheets - irreg.

**Parkinson's Disease Society of the United Kingdom   (PDS)
1969**
NR 215 Vauxhall Bridge Rd, LONDON, SW1V 1EJ.   (hq)
    020 7931 8080
    Chief Exec: Linda Kelly
▲ Company Limited by Guarantee; Registered Charity
Br 250
○ *W; welfare, research, education of the public & help to
    patients & their relatives
Gp YAPPERS: Young Alert Parkinsonians, Partners & Relatives (a
    support group)
● Conf - Mtgs - ET - Res - Stat - Inf - Lib - PL
< Eur Parkinson's Disease Soc (EPDA)
M 27,000 i

Parrot Society UK   1967
■ 92a High St, BERKHAMSTED, Herts, HP4 2BL.   (hq)
    01442 872245   fax 01442 872245
    email les.rance@theparrotsocietyuk.org
    http://www.theparrotsocietyuk.org
    Sec: Les A Rance
▲ Registered Charity
○ *B, *G; to promote the breeding & keeping of all parrot-like
    birds
● Conf - Mtgs - Exhib - Inf - VE - LG
< Soc for the Protection of Aviculture
M 4,777 i, UK / 171 i, o'seas
¶ The Magazine of the Parrot Society UK - 12; £16 yr m only.

Parson Woodforde Society   1968
■ 22 Gaynor Close, WYMONDHAM, Norfolk, NR18 0EA.   (hsp)
    email editor@parsonwoodforde.org.uk
    http://www.parsonwoodforde.org.uk
    Mem Sec: Mrs A Elliott
▲ Registered Charity
○ *A; to extend & develop the knowledge of the life of the
    eighteenth century diarist James Woodforde (1740-1803) &
    of the society in which he lived
● Mtgs - Res
< Alliance of Literary Societies
M 390 i, UK / 10 i, o'seas
¶ Jnl - 4;   NL - 4; both ftm only.
    [15 volumes of diary material]; £20-£25 (available from the
    President).

Partially Sighted Society   (PSS)   1973
NR Queen's Rd, DONCASTER, S Yorks, DN1 2NX.   (hq)
    01302 323132
    Sec: Norman Stenson
▲ Company Limited by Guarantee
Br 10
○ *W; to help visually impaired people to make the best use of
    remaining sight; to raise public awareness of the problems
    associated with visual impairment
● Inf - Supply of aids & equipment to help in daily living
M i, f & clubs
¶ Oculus - 4.   AR.

Passenger Shipping Association
since 2007 **Association of Cruise Experts**

Passive Fire Protection Federation   (PFPF)   1995
■ Tournai Hall, Evelyn Woods Rd, ALDERSHOT, Hants,
    GU11 2LL.   (asa)
    01252 357841   fax 01252 357831
    http://www.pfpf.org
    Sec: John G Fairley
○ *T; 'the primary measure integrated within the constructional
    fabric of a biulding to provide inherent fire safety &
    protection by responding against heat, smoke & flame to
    maintain the fundamental requiremnets of building
    compartmentation, structural stability, fire separation & a safe
    means of escape'
M 21 f

Pastel Society
a member of the **Federation of British Artists**

**Pathological Society of Great Britain & Ireland   (Path
Society)   1906**
■ 2 Carlton House Terrace, LONDON, SW1Y 5AF.   (sb)
    020 7976 1260   fax 020 7930 2981
    email admin@pathsoc.org   http://www.pathsoc.org
    Pres: Prof D A Levison,   Gen Sec: Prof C S Herrington
▲ Registered Charity
○ *L; 'dedicated to understanding disease'
● Conf - ET - Exhib
M 1,039 i, UK / 294 i, o'seas
    (Sub: £48 (full members), £10 (concessions))
¶ Jnl of Pathology - 12; £54 m, £678 nm.   NL - 2; ftm only.

Patient Information Forum   (PiF)   1997
■ Handel House, 13 Park Rd, MANCHESTER, M8 4HT.   (chmn/p)
    07824 605352
    email secretary@pifonline.org.uk
    http://www.pifonline.org.uk
    Pres: Mark Duman
▲ Un-incorporated Society
Br 13
○ *M, *N; for those producing, developing, disseminating &
    researching high quality information for patients, carers, their
    families & others
● Conf - Mtgs - ET - Res - Inf - LG - Quality, appraisal,
    accreditation - Consulting
M 778 i, UK / 2 i, o'seas
¶ [subscription, £50 yr].
× 2005 (December) Consumer Health Information Consortium
    (merged)

Patients Association   1963
§ PO Box 935, HARROW, Middx, HA1 3YJ.   (hq)
    020 8423 9111   fax 020 8423 9119
    email mailbox@patients-association.com
    http://www.patients-association.org.uk
● Helpline: 0845 608 4455
    Promotes the voice of patients by offering them an opportunity
    to share their experiences of health services, and uses this
    knowledge to work with the NHS and other healthcare
    providers in improving services.

Patients' Voice for Medical Advance
NR PO Box 504, DUNSTABLE, Beds, LU6 2LU.
    01582 873108
    http://www.patientsvoice.org.uk
○ *K; 'a patients' group which supports the humane use of
    animals & genetic technology, where necessary, in medical
    research'
× 2005 Seriously Ill for Medical Research

© CBD Research Ltd · Beckenham · BR3 5JS · Tel 020 8650 7745 · Fax 020 8650 0768 · E-mail cbd@cbdresearch.com · www.cbdresearch.com

Pattern, Model & Mould Manufacturers Association (PMMMA) 1954
NR   National Metalforming Centre, 47 Birmingham Rd,
      WEST BROMWICH, W Midlands, B70 6PY. (hq)
      0121-601 6976
      http://www.pmmma.co.uk
      Sec: Andrew Turner
▲   Un-incorporated Society
○   *T
Gp   Mould makers; Pattern makers
●   Mtgs - Exhib - Inf - LG
<   Wld Foundrymen Org; Inst Cast Metals Engrs
M   40 i & f
¶   Patternmaking News - 4.

Patton Historical Society 1985
■   Blue Grass, Clatterwick Lane, Little Leigh, NORTHWICH,
      Cheshire, CW8 4RJ. (hsp)
      01606 891303 & 781731 (evgs)
      Hon Sec: Kenneth N Oultram
○   *L; to commemorate the life & times of US General George S
      Patton who was based in Cheshire in World War II

Payroll Alliance 1985
NR   Tolley House, 2 Addiscombe Rd, CROYDON, Surrey,
      CR9 5AF. (hq)
      020 8401 1828
○   *P

Peace Pledge Union (PPU) 1934
■   1 Peace Passage, LONDON, N7 0BT. (hq)
      020 7424 9444
      Admin: Annie Bebington
▲   Un-incorporated Society
○   *K; promotion of pacifism & nonviolent solution to
      international, national & local conflict

Peak District Mines Historical Society Ltd (PDMHS) 1959
■   Peak District Mining Museum, The Pavilion, MATLOCK BATH,
      Derbys, DE4 3NR. (regd office)
      01629 583834
      email mail@peakmines.co.uk   http://www.pdmhs.com +
      peakmines.com
      Hon Sec: Nigel Nix
▲   Company Limited by Guarantee; Registered Charity
○   *L; to promote, encourage & further the study of & research
      into the mines & mineralogy of the Peak district & adjacent
      areas in England; to catalogue, collect, collate, publish & sell
      material & inforamtion & service, or interest to the members
      & general public
Gp   Mining museum; Archaeology & conservation
●   Mtgs - Res - Exhib - Inf - Lib - VE - Preservation of artifacts -
      Peak District Mining Museum
<   Nat Assn of Mining Hist Orgs (NAMHO)
M   450 i, 10 org, UK / 12, o'seas
¶   Mining History (Jnl) - 2; ftm, £8 nm.   NL - 4; ftm only.

Peak & Northern Footpaths Society (PNFS) 1894
■   Taylor House, 23 Turncroft Lane, Offerton, STOCKPORT,
      Cheshire, SK1 4AB. (hq)
      0161 480 3565   fax 0161 429 7279
      email mail@peakandnorthern.org.uk
      http://www.peakandnorthern.org.uk
      Chmn: David Bratt
▲   Registered Charity
○   *K; preservation, maintenance & defence of public rights of
      way, commons & open spaces in the Northern & Midland
      counties of England
●   Conf - Mtgs - Inf - LG
<   Brit Trust for Consvn Volunteers (BTCV); Open Spaces Soc;
      Ramblers Assn; NW Coun for Sport; Byways & Bridleways
      Trust
M   c 1,000 i, 80 org
¶   Signpost - 4; ftm.   AR; ftm, £2 nm.

Pedestrians Association
    registered name of **Living Streets**

Peel Society
NR   2 Sunningdale, TAMWORTH, Staffs, B77 4NW.
      http://www.thepeelsociety.org.uk
○   *G; Sir Robert Peel (1788-1850), founder of the Metropolitan
      Police; hence the names 'Bobbies' & 'Peelers'

Pelargonium & Geranium Society 1970
■   8 Ingswell Avenue, Notton, WAKEFIELD, W Yorks, WF4 2NG.
      (hsp)
      01226 722187
      Hon Sec: David Steele
▲   Un-incorporated Society
Br   11
○   *H; to promote interest in the cultivation & hybridisation of
      pelargoniums & geraniums by amateurs & professionals
●   Conf - Mtgs - ET - Exhib - Comp - SG - Stat - VE - Lectures -
      Advisory panel for information
×   2008 (merged) British & European Geranium Society
      British Pelargonium & Geranium Society

Pembrokeshire Agricultural Society (PAS) 1784
■   Show Office, County Showground, Withybush,
      HAVERFORDWEST, Pembrokeshire, SA62 4BP. (hq)
      01437 764331   fax 01437 767203
      Gen Mgr: Malcolm Crossman
▲   Registered Charity
○   *F, *H; agricultural show
●   Conf - Mtgs - Exhib
M   i

Pembrokeshire Chamber of Commerce
    see**Chamber of Commerce - Pembrokeshire**

Pembrokeshire Historical Society (PHS) 1983
■   Dolau, Dwrbach, FISHGUARD, Pembrokeshire, SA65 9RN.
      (hsp)
      01348 873316
      Hon Sec: Mrs Anne Eastham
▲   Un-incorporated Society
○   *L, *Q; to promote interest in & research into subjects of
      historical, archaeological, artistic, genealogical &
      architectural importance in the heritage of Pembrokeshire
●   Conf - Mtgs - VE
>   Pembrokeshire Family History Soc; Pembrokeshire local history
      societies
M   250 i
¶   PHS Jnl - 1; £5 m, £6 nm.

Penguin Collectors' Society (PCS) 1974
NR   31 Myddelton Sq, LONDON, EC1R 1YB. (regd/office)
      020 7278 8064
      Sec/Treas: Michael Fowle
▲   Company Limited by Guarantee
Br   Australia, Canada, USA etc
○   *G; to encourage the study, research & collection of Penguin
      books; to publish relevant material
●   Conf - Res - Publication
M   350 i, UK / 50 i, o'seas
¶   The Penguin Collector - 2.
      List of publications available on request.

Pennine Way Association 1971
NR   49 Hedley Hill Terrace, WATERHOUSES, Co Durham,
      DH7 8AZ. (sp)
      http://www.penninewayassociation.co.uk
      Sec: Doug Moffatt
○   *G; to protect the Penine Way; to campaign for upkeep &
      refurbishment of signs, sits & bridges

Pensions Action Group
NR   36 Seaside Avenue, Minster on Sea, SHEERNESS, Kent,
         ME12 2NN.
         01795 875835
         Andrew Parr
○   *G, *K; a protest group on the wind-up of company pension
         schemes

Pensions Management Institute   (PMI)   1976
■   PMI House, 4-10 Artillery Lane, LONDON, E1 7LS.   (hq)
         020 7247 1452   fax 020 7375 0603
         email enquiries@pensions-pmi.org.uk
         http://www.pensions-pmi.org.uk
         Chief Exec: Vince Linnane
▲   Company Limited by Guarantee
Br   9; Ireland
○   *P
Gp   Pensions professionals; Trustees
●   Conf - Mtgs - ET - Exam - Res - Exhib - Inf - LG
M   4,700 i, UK / 160 i, o'seas
¶   PMI News - 12;   PMI Technical News - 4; both ftm only.

Pentathlon GB   (MPAGB)   1948
■   Norwood House, University of Bath, Claverton Down, BATH,
         BA2 7AY.   (hq)
         01225 386808   fax 01225 386995
         email admin@pentathlongb.org
         http://www.pentathlongb.org
         Admin Sec: Skip Peacey,   Chief Exec: Peter Hart
○   *S; organisation of modern pentathlon (a compilation of 5
         different events, fencing, swimming, shooting, cross-country
         running & riding)
●   Comp
<   U Intle Pentathlon Moderne (UIPM)
M   4,400 i, 80 clubs, UK / 25 i, o'seas
¶   Points per Second (NL) - 4; ftm only.
         Registered name: Modern Pentathlon Association of Great
         Britain Ltd

Penzance Chamber of Commerce
NR   Sycamores, Relubbus Lane, St Hilary, PENZANCE, Cornwall,
         TR20 9EG.   (sb)
         01736 762888
         http://www.penzance.co.uk/chamber
         Sec: A Vinnac
○   *C

People & Dogs Society   (PADS)   1988
■   45B Ashgap Lane, NORMANTON, W Yorks, WF6 2DT.   (hsp)
         01924 897732   fax 01977 677968
         email pads@btinternet.com   http://www.padsonline.org
         Hon Sec: Mrs K Le Seelleur
▲   Registered Charity
○   *V; to encourage high standards of dog ownership; to help
         people with problem dogs or dog-related problems
●   ET - Exhib - Comp - Inf - Dog shows - Confidential advice line
<   Telephone Helplines Assn (associate mem)
M   [not stated]
¶   Pawprints - 3; m only.
         Code of Caring (leaflets on dog care);   Factsheets; both free.

PEP & ISA Managers' Association
         since 2007 **Tax Incentivised Savings Association**

PERA   1946
NR   Pera Innovation Park, MELTON MOWBRAY, Leics, LE13 0PB.
         (hq)
         01664 501501
         http://www.pera.com
▲   Company Limited by Guarantee
○   *Q; to promote innovation & productivity within technology &
         manufacturing led organisations through the application of
         current & future thinking & technology transfer practices
M   c 500 f
¶   Pera Abstracts - 5;   Technical Reports - irreg; both ftm only.

Percussive Arts Society   (PAS)
■   25 Copperfield Rd, Cheadle Hulme, CHEADLE, Cheshire,
         SK8 7PN.   (msp)
         0161-439 5757
         http://www.pas.org
         Mem Sec: Ron Baker
○   *D, *P; for teachers, instructors & players of percussive
         instruments
●   ET - Inf
<   Percussive Arts Soc (USA)
M   i
¶   Percussive Notes - 4; ftm.

Percy Grainger Society   (PGS)   1978
■   6 Fairfax Crescent, AYLESBURY, Bucks, HP20 2ES.   (hsp)
         01296 428609   fax 01296 581185
         email pgsoc@percygrainger.org.uk
         http://www.percygrainger.org.uk
         Sec: Barry P Ould
▲   Un-incorporated Society
○   *D; to promote & develop interest in the life & works of the
         Australian composer & pianist Percy Aldridge
         Grainger (1882-1961)
●   Inf - Lib (music & sound archives) - PL
<   Intl Percy Grainger Soc (USA); Friends of Percy Grainger
         Museum (Melbourne, Australia)
M   120 i, 10 f, UK / 300 i, 15 f, o'seas
¶   The Grainger Society Jnl - 2;   Random Round (NL) - 2;
         In a Nutshell - 4;   (subscription for all 3, £14 m, £18 nm).

Performance Textiles Association Ltd   (PTA)   1919
■   36 Broadway, LONDON, SW1H 0BW.   (asa)
         020 7340 6265   fax 020 7340 6261
         email info@performancetextiles.org.uk
         http://www.performancetextiles.org.uk
         Sec: Michael Skelding
▲   Company Limited by Guarantee
○   *T; all facets of the textile industry from production, through
         conversion, manufacture & on to use (includes awnings,
         banners & flags, inflatables, ropes, cords & slings, shower
         curtains, tarpaulins, tents, webbing, & welding curtains
Gp   Association of Inflatable Manufacturers, Operators, Designers
         & Suppliers; Coaters Group; Industrial Textiles Manufacturers
         Group; Marquee Hire Group; Reusable Healthcare Textile
         Association; Suppliers Group
●   Conf - Mtgs - ET - Res - Exhib - Inf - LG - British & European
         Standards
M   250 f
         (Sub: varies)
¶   Performance Textiles - 3;
         Safe Use of & Operation of Marquees & Temporary Structures;
         Business Guide & Ybk - 1;   all free.
×   2004 Made-up Textiles Association

Performing Artists' Media Rights Association
         in 2007 merged with **Phonographic Performance Ltd**

Performing Right Society Ltd
         a member of the **MCPS-PRS Alliance**

© CBD Research Ltd · Beckenham · BR3 5JS · Tel 020 8650 7745 · Fax 020 8650 0768 · E-mail cbd@cbdresearch.com · www.cbdresearch.com

Periodical Publishers Association - Interactive (PPAi) 1998
NR Queen's House, 28 Kingsway, LONDON, WC2B 6JR. (hq)
020 7404 4166
○ *T; for online content providers
< Is a division of the Periodical Publishers Association & a member of theAssociation of Online Publishers

Periodical Publishers Association of Ireland
IRL 25 Denzille Lane, DUBLIN 2, Republic of Irelnad.
353 (1) 667 5579
email grace@ppa.ie   http://www.ppa.ie
Chief Exec: Grace Aungier
○ *T

Periodical Publishers Association Ltd (PPA) 1913
NR Queen's House, 28 Kingsway, LONDON, WC2B 6JR. (hq)
020 7404 4166   fax 020 7404 4167
email info1@ppa.co.uk   http://www.ppa.co.uk
Chief Exec: Ian Locks
▲ Company Limited by Guarantee
○ *T; interests of the UK magazine publishing industry
Gp Association of Publishing Agencies; PPA Scotland; PPA Ireland
C'ees: Ad marketing, B2B media, Copyright, Credit management, Editorial public affairs, Environmental, Finance, Newstrade, PPA Interactive, Parliamentary & legal affairs, Production & technology, Subscriptions
Postal contract gp; Independent Publishers Advisory Council
● Conf - Mtgs - ET - Res - Exhib - Comp - SG - Stat - Expt - Inf - Lib - PL - VE - LG
< is linked with: Publishers Assn (books), Newspaper Soc (newspapers), Newspaper Pubrs Assn (daily newspapers) to form the UK Publishing Media
Online Publishing Assn (US)
M c 400 f
¶ List of publications available.

Permaculture Association (Britain) (PcA) 1984
NR BCM Permaculture Association, LONDON, WC1N 3XX. (mail address)
0845 458 1805 & 01132 307461
Coordinator: Andrew Goldring
▲ Registered Charity
○ *F; sustainable design & implementation in agriculture, forestry, housing & energy
Gp Projects network; Designers' register; Teachers' register; Permaculture design courses; Permaculture diploma
● Conf - ET - Res - Exhib - Inf
M 800 i, UK / 50 i, o'seas
¶ Permaculture Works (Jnl) - 4; ftm.

Permanent Show Organisers Association (PSOA)
NR Lordsbridge Arena, Wimpole Rd, Preston, CAMBRIDGE, CB23 7AE.
01223 262343
Chmn: Mr N Bargh;   Dir: Simon Bates

Permanent Way Institution (PWI) 1884
■ 11 Caraway Place, Meir Park, STOKE-on-TRENT, Staffs, ST3 7FE. (hq)
01782 397880
Gen Sec: Brian Newman
▲ Company Limited by Guarantee
Br 20; Australia, Ireland, Malaysia, S Africa
○ *L, *P; management, construction & maintenance of railway permanent way & works
Gp Sub-c'ees: Technical (training & education), Textbooks
● Conf - Mtgs - Exhib - VE
< Verband Deutscher Eisenbahn-Ingenieure (VDEI); U of Eur Railway Engineer Assns (UEEIV)
M c 4,000 i
¶ Jnl & Report of Proceedings - 4.   British Railway Track. The Permanent Way Institution - the first 100 years, 1884-1984.
New Tracks to the Cities.   Evolution of Permanent Way.

Permit Trainers Association 1973
■ Drewitts, Warninglid, HAYWARDS HEATH, W Sussex, RH17 5TB. (hq)
01444 461235   fax 01444 461485
email freddie@pta.eclipse.co.uk
Chmn: Frederick Gray
Hon Sec: J Payne (01398 371244)
▲ Company Limited by Guarantee
○ *P; for racehorse owners & trainers; training of National Hunt racehorses which are family owned
M 300 i

Pernicious Anaemia Society
NR PO Box 245, BRIDGEND, Glam, CF31 9FB.
0845 658 0322
http://www.pernicious-anaemia-society.org
○ *W

Personal Computer Association
since 2004 **Professional Computing Association**

Personal Computer Direct Marketers' Association
a group of the **Professional Computing Association**

Personal Finance Society (PFS) 1972
NR 42-48 High Rd, South Woodford, LONDON, E18 2JP. (hq)
020 8530 0852   fax 020 8530 3052
http://www.thepfs.org
Managing Dir: Simon Holt
▲ Company Limited by Guarantee
○ *P; representing the interests of all those who give & support personal financial advice
● Conf - Mtgs - ET - SG - LG
× 2005 (Life Insurance Association Ltd (Society of Financial Advisers

Personal Injuries Bar Association (PIBA) 1995
NR No 5 Chambers, Fountain Court, Steelhouse Lane, BIRMINGHAM, B4 6DR. (sb)
0121-606 0500   fax 0121-606 1501
email tn@no5.com   http://www.piba.org.uk
Sec: Tim Newman
▲ Un-incorporated Society
○ *P; to represent the Personal Injury Bar of England & Wales; to provide education & training to barristers in the field of personal injuries
● Conf - Mtgs - ET - Inf - LG
M c 1,100 i
¶ NL - 3/4; ftm.
Personal Injuries Hbk (published by Sweet & Maxwell).

Personal Managers Association Ltd (PMA) 1950
■ PO Box 63819, LONDON, N1P 1HL. (hq)
0845 602 7191
email info@thepma.com
Liaison Sec: Angela Adler
○ *P; for those variously operating in the entertainment & publishing industries as personal managers, theatrical agents, literary or authors' agents
● Mtgs
M 125 f

Personal Safety Association (PSA)
NR 32 Cheam Place, CARDIFF, Glamorgan, CF14 5DD. (hq)
029 2075 2508
email mark@ppts.co.uk
Sec: L Hicks
○ *P; 'to offer the UK & Ireland's only open college network accreditations & BTEC qualifications in conflict management & personal safety'
● ET - Exam - Res - Inf
M i, f & org
¶ NL - 6; ftm only.

Personal Safety Manufacturers Association
a group of the **British Safety Industry Federation**

Perthes Association   1976
■ PO Box 773, GUILDFORD, Surrey, GU1 1XN.   (hq)
   01483 306637 (admin) 01483 534431 (helpline)
   email admin@perthes.org.uk   http://www.perthes.org.uk
   Dir: Lisa Grant
▲ Registered Charity
○ *W; to help & advise families with children suffering from
   Perthes disease (a potentially crippling disease of the hip) &
   other forms of osteochondritis as well as multiple epiphyseal
   dysplasia
● Comp - Inf - VE - Children's Christmas party - Contact register
   - Equipment loan for members (subject to availability)
< Contact a Family
M c 1,000 i
¶ NL - 4; ftm only.   Hbk; ftm.
   Layman's Guide to Osteochondritis; ftm.
   Your Child in an Immobilising Plaster: a few hints; ftm.
   Leaflets; ftm, one free copy nm.

Perthshire Agricultural Society   (PAS)   1867
■ 26 York Place, PERTH, PH2 8EH.   (hq)
   01738 623780   fax 01738 621206
   email secretary@perthshow.co.uk
   http://www.perthshow.co.uk
   Sec: Neil C Forbes
▲ Company Limited by Guarantee
○ *F; promotion of agriculture & organisation of 2-day
   agricultural show
● ET - Agricultural show
M 750 i

Perthshire Chamber of Commerce   (PCC)   1871
NR Algo Business Centre, Glenearn Rd, PERTH, PH2 0NJ.   (hq)
   01738 450401   fax 01738 450402
   email info@perthshirechamber.co.uk
   http://www.perthshirechamber.co.uk
   Pres: Mike Beale
▲ Company Limited by Guarantee
○ *C
● Mtgs - Expt - Inf - Lib - LG
< Scot Cham Comm
M c 400 f
¶ NL - 12;   AR; both ftm.

Perthshire Society of Natural Science   (PSNS)   1867
■ Perth Museum & Art Gallery, George St, PERTH, PH1 5XX.
   (mail/address)
   Hon Sec: Miss R Fothergill
▲ Registered Charity
○ *L; the study & research of natural history & natural sciences
   incl photography, archaeology, history, botany, ornithology;
   the study of the natural environment & its conservation
M i

Pesticide Action Network   (PAN UK)
NR Development House, 56-64 Leonard St, LONDON, EC2A 4LT.
   020 7065 0905   fax 020 7065 0907
   email admin@pan-uk.org   http://www.pan-uk.org
○ *K; to publicise & eliminate the dangers of, & exposure to, toxic
   pesticides & their presence in the environment

Pet Care Trust   1951
■ Bedford Business Centre, 170 Mile Rd, BEDFORD, MK42 9TW.
   01234 273933
   Chief Exec: Janet Nunn
▲ Registered Charity
○ *T; retail pet trade; manufacturers & wholesalers of pet foods &
   accessories; dog groomers; boarding kennels & catteries
Gp Manufacturers; Retailers; Wholesalers; Groomers; Boarding
   kennels & catteries
● Conf - Mtgs - ET - Exam - Exhib - Stat - Expt - LG
M 1,500 f
¶ NL - 6.   Ybk.

Pet Food Manufacturers' Association Ltd   (PFMA)   1969
■ 20 Bedford St, Covent Garden, LONDON, WC2E 9HP.   (hq)
   020 7379 9009   fax 020 7379 8008
   email info@pfma.org.uk   http://www.pfma.org.uk
   Chief Exec: Michael Bellingham
▲ Company Limited by Guarantee
○ *T
● Mtgs - Inf - VE - LG - Seminars - Symposia
< Eur Pet Food Mfrs Assn (FEDIAF)
M 50 f

Pet Fostering Service Scotland   (PFSS)   1985
■ PO Box 6, CALLANDER, Perthshire, FK17 8ZU.   (mail address)
   01877 331496 (referral phone)
   Chmn: Anne Docherty
▲ Registered Charity
○ *G, *W; provision of short-term care of pets belonging to
   people who have to go into hospital or other short-term care
   in emergencies
< SCAS; The Blue Cross
M 300 i
¶ Booklet.

Pet Health Council   (PHC)   1979
NR 20 Bedford St, LONDON, WC1E 9HP.   (hq)
   020 7379 6546
▲ Company Limited by Guarantee
○ *N; *V; to promote pet health in relation to human health
● Inf
M 11 org:
   Associaton of Pet Behaviour Counsellors
   British Small Animal Veterinary Association
   British Veterinary Association
   National Office of Animal Health
   Peoples Dispensary for Sick Animals
   Pet Care Trust
   Pet Food Manufacturers Association
   Pets as Therapy
   Royal College of Nursing -Complementary Therapies
      Forum
   Royal Pharmaceutical Society of GB
   Society for Companion Animal Studies
¶ Leaflets.

Pet Product Retailers Association
a group of the **British Hardware Federation**

Peter Warlock Society   1963
NR 31 Hammerfield House, Cale St, LONDON, SW3 3SG.   (hsp)
   020 7589 9595   fax 020 7589 9595
   http://www.peterwarlock.org
   Hon Sec: Malcolm Rudland
▲ Registered Charity
○ *D; to increase the knowledge of all aspects of the life & works
   of composer Peter Warlock (1894-1930); Philip Arnold
   Heseltine, an Anglo-Welsh music critic & composer used the
   (now better known) name when he composed
● Mtgs - Comp - Inf - Lib - Publishing complete edition of
   Warlock's works
M 250 i, UK / 35 i, o'seas
¶ NL - 2.   Society Edition of Songs, 9 vols.

Peterborough Chamber of Commerce
   a local chamber of **Cambridgeshire Chambers of Commerce**

Peterborough Royal Foxhound Show Society   (PRFSS)   1878
- ■ East of England Showground, PETERBOROUGH, Cambs,
   PE2 6XE.   (hq)
   01733 234451   fax 01733 370038
   Sec: Andrew Mercer
- ○ *B; breeding & showing of foxhounds

Petfood Association of Ireland
   a group of **Food & Drink Industry Ireland**

Petrol Retailers Association
   a group of the **Retail Motor Industry Federation**

Petroleum Exploration Society of Great Britain   (PESGB)   1965
- NR 9 Berkeley St (5th floor), LONDON, W1J 8DW.   (hq)
   020 7408 2000
   http://www.pesgb.org.uk
   Pres: Chris Flavell
- ▲ Registered Charity
- ○ *L; to promote, for the public benefit, education in the scientific
   & technical aspects of petroleum
- ● Conf - ET - Exhib - Inf - VE
- < Amer Assn Petroleum Geologists (AAPG); SEG
- M 5,300 i, UK / 600 i, o'seas
- ¶ NL - 12; ftm only.

Pewter Society   1918
- ■ 37 Hurst Lane, BOLLINGTON, Cheshire, SK10 5LT.   (hsp)
   email secretary@pewtersociety.org
   http://www.pewtersociety.org
   Hon Sec: John Swindell
- ▲ Un-incorporated Society
- ○ *A, *G; to stimulate interest in, & preservation of, old pewter
- ● Mtgs - Res - Inf - Lib
- M 150 i, 10 org, UK / 90 i, o'seas
- ¶ Jnl - 2;   NL - 2;   LM; all ftm only.

Pharmaceutical & Healthcare Sciences Society   (PHSS)   1981
- ■ 6a Kingsdown Orchard, Hyde Rd, SWINDON, Wilts,
   SN2 7RR.   (hq)
   01793 824254   fax 01793 832551
   email info@phss.demon.co.uk   http://www.phss.co.uk
   Business Devt Mgr: Mrs June T Prout
- ▲ Un-incorporated Society
- ○ *L, *P; for research, development, manufacture & control of
   pharmaceutical & healthcare products; with representatives
   from academia, pharmaceutical industries, medical devices,
   pharmaceutical packaging, equipment suppiers &
   biotechnology
- Gp Aseptic process filtration; Autoclave validation; Cleanroom
   particle monitoring systems; Dry heat sterilisation; Freeze
   drying; LAL users; Parenteral GMP inspection; RABS
- ● Conf - ET - Exhib - Inf - LG
- M 700 i, UK / 289 i, o'seas
   (Sub: £90)
- ¶ European Jnl of Parenteral & Pharmaceutical Sciences - 4; ftm.
   NL - 4; free on website.   LM (on disc) - 1; ftm only.
   Technical monographs.   Publications Catalogue.
- × 2006 (March) Parenteral Society

**Pharmaceutical Information & Pharmacovigilance Association
(PIPA)   1980**
- NR PO Box 254, HASLEMERE, Surrey, GU27 7XT.   (mail address)
   email pipa@pipaonline.org
   Administrator: 0753 189 9537
- ○ *P; to maintain & develop professional standards in all aspects
   of information work in the pharmaceutical industry
- M i
- × 2005 Association of Information Officers in the Pharmaceutical
   Industry

Pharmaceutical Society of Ireland   1875
- IRL 18 Shrewsbury Rd, DUBLIN 4, Republic of Ireland.
   353 (1) 218 4000   fax 353 (1) 283 7678
   email info@pharmaceuticalsociety.ie
   Admin Sec: Dr Ambrose McLoughlin
- ○ *T

Pharmaceutical Society of Northern Ireland   (PSNI)   1925
- ■ 73 University St, BELFAST, BT7 1HL.   (hq)
   028 9032 6927   fax 028 9043 9929
   email info@psni.org.uk   http://www.psni.org.uk
   Dir: Trevor Patterson,   Pres: Raymond Anderson
- ▲ Un-incorporated Society
- ○ *P; registration & regulatory body for the practice of Pharmacy
   in Northern Ireland
- ● Mtgs - ET - Exam - LG
- M 1,836 i, 539 f, UK / 87 i, o'seas
   (Sub: £345 i, £142 f UK / £158 i o'seas)

PharmaChemical Ireland
- IRL Confederation House, 84-86 Lower Baggot St, DUBLIN 2,
   Republic of Ireland.
   353 (1) 605 1584   fax 353 (1) 638 1584
   email matt.moran@ibec.ie
   http://www.pharmachemicalireland.ie
   Dir: Matt Moran
- ○ *T
- < IBEC
- M 55 f
- × 2004 Irish Pharmaceutical & Chemical Manufacturers
   Association

Philatelic Traders Society Ltd   (PTS)   1946
- ■ PO Box 371, FLEET, Hants, GU52 6ZX.   (hq)
   01252 628006   fax 01252 684674
   email info@philatelic-traders-society.co.uk
   http://www.philatelic-traders-society.co.uk
   Sec: J M Czuczman
- ▲ Company Limited by Guarantee
- ○ *G, *T; organisation of stamp dealers, auctioneers, philatelic
   publishers & philatelic accessory dealers; to promote the
   hobby of philately
- ● organisation of two national stamp exhibitions in London by
   Stampex Ltd (a wholly owned subsidiary)
- M 300 f, UK / 200 i, o'seas
- ¶ PTS News - 6; ftm only.   Directory - 1; ftm, £10 nm.

Philip Larkin Society   (PLS)   1995
- ■ PO Box 44, HORNSEA, E Yorks, HU18 1WP.   (sb)
   email secretary@philiplarkin.com
   http://www.philiplarkin.com
   Hon Sec: Andrew Eastwood
- ▲ Registered Charity
- ○ *A, *G; to promote awareness of the life & work of the poet,
   writer & Hull University librarian Philip Larkin (1922-1985) &
   his literary contemporaries
- Gp Publishing sub-c'ee
- ● Conf - Mtgs - Res - Exhib - VE
- < Alliance Literary Socs
- M 250 i, UK / 50 i, o'seas
- ¶ About Larkin - 2; ftm, £7 each nm.   Monographs.

Philological Society 1842

- ■ Dept of Africa, School of Oriental & African Studies, Thornhaugh St, LONDON, WC1H 0XG. (hsb)
  020 7898 4653   fax 020 7898 4399
  email secretary@philsoc.org.uk
  http://www.philsoc.org.uk
  Hon Sec; Dr Lutz Marten
- ▲ Company Limited by Guarantee; Registered Charity
- ○ *L, *Q; the study of the structure, the affinities & the history of languages
- ● Conf - Mtgs - Res
- M 618 i
- ¶ Transactions - 3.
  Publications of the Philological Society - irreg.

Philosophical Society of England (PhS) 1913

- ■ 6 Craghall Dene Avenue, NEWCASTLE upon TYNE, NE3 1QR. (hsb)
  0191-284 1223
  email thephilosophicalsociety@yahoo.co.uk
  http://www.philsoc.co.uk
  Chmn: Michael Bavidge
- ○ *L, *R; the study & discussion of the philosophy of religion & 'English thought'
- M 110 i, UK / 60 i, o'seas
- ¶ The Philosopher - 2; ftm, £15 m.

Phoenix Camping Club 1999

- ■ 88 Charfield Drive, Eggbuckland, PLYMOUTH, Devon, PL6 5PS. (hsp)
  01752 518669
  email sue-britt@btinternet.com
  Sec: Sue Britten
- ▲ Un-incorporated Society
- ○ *G; a national singles camping club for anyone who lives & camps alone in motor caravan, caravan, tent or trailer tent
- ● Mtgs
- < ACCEO
- M 190 i
  (Sub: £10)
- ¶ NL - 6; ftm only.
  Note: Please enclose a large SAE with all enquiries

Phonographic Performance (Ireland) Ltd (PPI) 1968

- IRL 1 Corrig Avenue, DÚN LAOGHAIRE, Co Dublin, Republic of Ireland.
  353 (1) 280 5977   fax 353 (1) 280 6579
  email info@ppiltd.com   http://www.ppiltd.com
- ○ *T; collects royalties originating from the broadcasting of sound recordings

Phonographic Performance Ltd (PPL) 1934

- NR 1 Upper James St, LONDON, W1F 9DE. (hq)
  020 7534 1000   fax 020 7534 1111
  email info@ppluk.com   http://www.ppluk.com
  Chief Exec: Fran Nevrkla
- ▲ Company Limited by Guarantee
- ○ *T; licenses recorded music & music videos for public performance, broadcast & new media use
- M i & f
- ✕ 2007 (merged) Performing Artists' Media Rights Association & Association of United Recording Artists

Photo Imaging Council (PIC) 2002

- ■ Airport House, Purley Way, CROYDON, Surrey, CR0 0XZ. (hq)
  020 8253 4507   fax 020 8253 4510
  email pic@admin.co.uk   http://www.pic.uk.net
  Co Sec: Mrs Pamela Hyde
- ▲ Company Limited by Guarantee
- ○ *T; to represent & promote the interests of the photographic & imaging industry in the UK to government, the media, external organisations & the general public
- Gp Manufacturing; Marketing; Photo wastes; Export
- ● Conf - Mtgs - Exhib - Comp - Stat - Expt - LG
- < Brit Brands Gp
- M 110 f

Photographic Alliance of Great Britain (PAGB) 1930

- ■ Cavendish House, 2 Tumbling Hill, PONTEFRACT, W Yorks, WF8 3SA.
  email hgtate@tesco.net
  http://www.pagb-photography-uk.co.uk
  Hon Sec: Howard G Tate
- ▲ Un-incorporated Society
- ○ *N; to coordinate the interests of the 15 photographic federations in the UK
- ● Mtgs - Exhib - Comp - SG- Inf - Provision of services & awards to the Federations - Confers patronage to exhibitions
- < Fédn Intle de l'Art Photographique (FIAP)
- > c 1,000 UK Camera Clubs
- M 25 i, 15 federations
- ¶ NL - 2; ftm, £5 nm.   Hbk - 2; ftm, £10 nm.

Photographic Collectors' Club of Great Britain (PCCGB) 1977

- ■ 5 Buntingford Rd, Puckeridge, WARE, Herts, SG11 1RT. (regd/office)
  01920 821611   fax 01920 821611
  email info@pccgb.com   http://www.pccgb.com
  Mem Sec: Diana Balfour
- ▲ Company Limited by Guarantee
- ○ *A, *G; to promote the study & collection of historical photographic equipment & images
- ● Mtgs - SG - Inf - VE - Major Fair (London, May)
- < Exacta Circle; Half Frame Gp; Voigtlander Verein; Kodak Brownie
- M 930 i, UK / 85 i, 5 org, o'seas
  (Sub: £30 i, UK / £32-£40, o'seas)
- ¶ Photographica World (Jnl) - 4;   Tailboard (NL) - 6; Postal Auction - 3;   Members' Hbk (LM) - 1; all ftm only, on application nm.

Photographic Materials Conservation group
in 2005 merged with the Care of Collections Forum, the Institute of Paper Conservation, the Scottish Society for Conservation & Restoration & the United Kingdom Institute for Conservation of Historic & Artistic Works to form the **Institute of Conservation**

Photoluminescent Safety Products Association (PSPA) 1991

- NR PO Box 377, REDHILL, Surrey, RH1 2RZ. (mail add)
  01737 763400   fax 01737 728818
  email pspa@pspa.org.uk   http://www.pspa.org.uk
- ▲ Company Limited by Guarantee
- ○ *T; promotes use & knowledge of photoluminescent products in the field of safety
- M 14 f, UK / 8 f, o'seas

Photonics Cluster

- NR Faraday Wharf, Holt St, Aston Science Pk, BIRMINGHAM, B7 4BB.
  0121-260 6020
  http://www.photonicscluster.org
- ○ *T; is the business network for the UK's photonics industry

Physical Education Association of the United Kingdom
in 2006 merged with the British Association of Advisers & Lecturers in Physical Education to form the **Association for Physical Education**

© CBD Research Ltd · Beckenham · BR3 5JS · Tel 020 8650 7745 · Fax 020 8650 0768 · E-mail cbd@cbdresearch.com · www.cbdresearch.com

Physio First 1952

NR   Cedar House, The Bell Plantation, Watling St, TOWCESTER, Northants, NN12 6GX.
01327 354441
http://www.physiofirst.org.uk
Gen Sec: Paul Donnelly
○   *P; to promote the highest standards of clinical practice in physiotherapy

Physiological Society 1876

NR   Peer House, Verulam St, LONDON, WC1X 8LZ.   (hq)
020 7269 5710
http://www.physoc.org
Chief Exec: Dr Michael Collis
▲   Company Limited by Guarantee; Registered Charity
○   *L, *M; to promote the advancement of physiology; to contribute to the understanding of biomedical & related sciences; to aid the prevention & treatment of disease, disability & malfunction of physical processes in all forms of life
●   Mtgs - ET - Res - SG - LG
M   c 2,000 i, UK / c 500 i, o'seas
¶   Jnl of Physiology - 24.   Experimental Physiology - 6.
Magazine - 6;   AR;   Monographs;   Study guides;   Books; prices vary.

Pianoforte Tuners' Association (PTA) 1913

■   PO Box 1312, LIGHTWATER, Surrey, GU18 5UB.   (mail)
0845 602 8796   fax 0845 602 8796
email secretary@pianotuner.org.uk
http://www.pianotuner.org.uk
Sec: Mrs Annette Summers
▲   Un-incorporated Society
○   *P
●   Conf - Mtgs - ET - Exam - Inf - Lib - VE
M   200 i, UK / 10 i, o'seas
¶   NL - 12; ftm.   Ybk; ftm, £2 nm.

Pick's Disease Support Group (PDSG) 1993

■   3 Fairfield Park, LYME REGIS, Dorset, DT7 3DS.   (hsp)
01297 445488
email penelope@pdsg.org.uk   http://www.pdsg.org.uk
Hon Sec: Penelope K Roques
▲   Registered Charity
○   *W; for carers of people with frontotemporal dementia - Pick's disease, frontal lobe degeneration, corticostal degeneration & alcohol related dementia
●   Conf - Mtgs - ET - VE
<   Nat Hospital Devt Foundation
M   600 i, 50 org, UK / 700 i, 50 org, o'seas
¶   NL - 4; free.

Pickles & Sauces Association
a sector of the **Food Processors Association**

Picon Ltd (PICON) 1993

■   PO Box 300, HITCHIN, Herts, SG4 8WJ.   (hq)
01483 412000   fax 01483 412001
email info@picon.co.uk   http://www.picon.com
Chief Exec: Tim Webb
▲   Company Limited by Guarantee
○   *T; for manufacturers & suppliers to the printing, publishing, paper making paper converting industries (including plastics film)
Gp   Division: British Paper Machinery Suppliers Association
●   Mtgs - Exhib - Stat - Expt - VE - LG
<   Eur C'ee of Printing & Paper Converting Machinery (EUMAPRINT); Paper Ind Technical Assn (PITA)
M   150 f
¶   British Paper Machinery News - 2; free.
✕   2007 Association of Printing Machinery Importers (merged)

Pictish Arts Society (1988)

■   Pictavia, Haughmuir, BRECHIN, Angus, DD9 6RL. (visitor/centre)
email admin@pictart.org   http://www.pictart.org
Hon Sec: Stewart Mowatt
▲   Registered Charity (Scotland)
○   *G; the study, research, development & preservation of Pictish arts, crafts & language; to advance the education of the public in all aspects of the early history of Scotland & in particular the Picts in Scotland
●   Conf - Mtgs (Winter) - ET - Lib - VE
M   200 i, 10 org, UK / 18 i, o'seas
¶   Jnl - 1; ftm, £5 nm.   NL - 4; ftm only.

Picture Research Association (PRA) 1977

■   c/o Scala, 1 Willow Court, off Willow St, LONDON, EC2A 4QB.   (mail/address)
020 7739 8544
Chmn: Charlotte Lippmann
○   *P; for all those involved in picture research, editing, management & supply
Gp   Freelance register; Members advisory service
●   Conf - Mtgs - ET - Inf
M   250 i, UK / 30 i, o'seas
¶   Montage - 4.   Bulletin (NL) - 12.

Pig Veterinary Society
a group of the **British Veterinary Association**

Pigging Products & Services Association (PPSA) 1990

■   PO Box 2, STROUD, Glos, GL6 8YB.   (hsb)
01285 760597   fax 01285 760470
email ppsa@ppsa-online.com
http://www.ppsa-online.com
Exec Sec: Gill Hornby
▲   Company Limited by Guarantee
Br   USA
○   *T; to promote the knowledge of pipeline pigging & its related products & services by providing a channel of communication between members themselves, users & other interested parties
Pigs are devices inserted into & travel throughout the length of a pipeline driven by the product flow
●   Conf - ET - Inf - PL
M   10 i, 17 f, UK / 5 i, 49 f, o'seas
¶   Pigging Industry News - 3; free.
Buyers' Guide & Directory of Members - 1; free.
An Introduction to Pipeline Pigging; ftm, £25 ($50 o'seas).

Pike & Shot Society (P&SS) 1973

NR   91 Symons Ave, LEIGH-on-SEA, Essex, SS9 5QD.   (hsp)
email bill.ray@supanet.com
http://www.pikeandshotsociety.org
Hon Sec: Bill Ray
▲   Un-incorporated Society
○   *G, *L; study of the military history of the Renaissance & 17th century (c1495-1721) including: flags, banners, arms & armour, tactics & strategy, wars, armies & war-gaming
●   Res
M   250 i, UK / 50 i, o'seas
¶   The Arquebusier - 6; ftm only.

Pilates Institute

NR   The Sail Loft, Limehouse Court, 3-11 Dod St, LONDON, E14 7EQ.
0870 111 0166
email info@pilates-institute.com
http://www.pilates-institute.com
○   *P; training in the practice of the pilates method of body alignment

The Pilgrims   1902
- ■ Allington Castle, MAIDSTONE, Kent, ME16 0NB.   (hq)
    01622 606404   fax 01622 606402
    email sec@pilgrimsociety.org
    Hon Sec: M P S Barton
- ▲ Un-incorporated Society
- ○ *X; promotion of Anglo-American good fellowship
- ● Dinners & receptions
- < The Pilgrims of the USA
- M 1,000 i, UK / 50 i, o'seas
- ¶ NL - 2;   LM & Rules - 2 yrly; free.

Pillbox Study Group & United Kingdom Fortifications Club   1989
- ■ 12 Castle Close, Reffley Estate, KING'S LYNN, Norfolk,
    PE30 3EP.   (hsp)
    01553 675053
    http://www.pillbox-study-group.org.uk
    Hon Treas & Mem Sec: Thomas Bell
- ▲ Un-incorporated Society
- ○ *G; study of fortifications of all periods in the UK, with special
    interest in those of the 20th century
- ● SG - Inf
- < Fortress Study Gp
- M 250 i, UK / 5 i, o'seas
    (Sub: £7.50 UK / £10 o'seas)
- ¶ Loopholes - 3; ftm only.
- ✕ 2008 United Kingdom Fortifications Club (merged)

Pinball Owners' Association   (POA)   1976
- ■ Kilndown, 31 Earlsmead Crescent, Cliffsend, RAMSGATE, Kent,
    CT12 5LQ.   (mail address)
    email poa@dial.pipex.com
    http://www.dspace.dial.pipex.com/poa/
    Mem Sec: Philip Crow
- ▲ Un-incorporated Society
- ○ *G, *S; to promote the playing, collecting & ownership of
    pinball & other coin operated machines
- ● Comp - Exhib (Annual show) - Inf - Spares & specialist goods
    sales
- M 470 i, 15 f, UK / 50 i, 10 f, o'seas
- ¶ Pinball Player - 10; £16 m, £20 nm.

Piobaireachd Society   1902
- NR 16-24 Otago St, GLASGOW, G12 8JH.   (hq)
    0141-334 3587   fax 0141-587 6068
    Hon Sec: Dugald MacNeill
- ▲ Un-incorporated Society
- ○ *D, *G; the encouragement & dissemination of the
    piobaireachd & its playing

Pipe Jacking Association   (PJA)   1973
- ■ 10 Greycoat Place, LONDON, SW1P 1SB.   (hq)
    0845 070 5201   fax 0845 070 5202
    email secretary@pipejacking.org
    http://www.pipejacking.org
    Sec: Andrew K Marshall
- ▲ Company Limited by Guarantee
- ○ *T; to represent the leading contractors, pipe suppliers &
    machine manufacturers in the pipe jacking & microtunnelling
    industry in the UK
- Gp Tunnelling; Tunnelling machinery; Pipe manufacture
- ● Conf - Mtgs - ET - Inf
- M 21 f
- ¶ NL - 2.
    Guide to Best Practice for the Installation of Pipe Jacks &
    Microtunnels; £35 nm.
    An Introduction to Pipe Jacking & Microtunnelling
    Design £9.50 nm.

Pipe Roll Society   1883
- ■ c/o The National Archive, Ruskin Avenue, KEW, Surrey,
    TW9 4DU.
    020 8876 3444   fax 020 8878 8905
    Contact: David Crook
- ▲ Registered Charity
- ○ *L; 'the enlargement of the public knowledge of medieval
    English history by the publication of the Pipe Rolls &
    associated records of medieval English government & other
    manuscripts of national importance prior to 1350'
- No further information supplied.

Pipedown
    alternative name of the **Campaign for Freedom from Piped
    Music**

Pipeline Industries Guild Ltd   (PIG)   1957
- ■ 14-15 Belgrave Sq, LONDON, SW1X 8PS.   (hq)
    020 7235 7938   fax 020 7235 0074
    email hqsec@pipeguild.co.uk
    http://www.pipeguild.co.uk
    Dir Gen: Cheryl Burgess
- ▲ Company Limited by Guarantee
- Br 7; Republic of Ireland
- ○ *T; science & practice of aspects of the pipeline engineering
- Gp Technical panels: Onshore, Offshore, Utilities
- ● Conf - Mtgs - ET - Exhib - Comp/Awards - Expt - Inf - Lib - LG
- < Fedn of Wld Pipeline Assns
- M 900 i, 220 f, UK / 250 i, 20 f, o'seas
- ¶ Pipeline Industry Directory - 1; ftm, £50 nm.

Pipers' Guild   1932
- NR 25 Dorothy Curtice Court, London Rd, Copford, COLCHESTER,
    Essex, CO6 1DX.   (sb/p)
    email sec@pipersguild.org   http://www.pipersguild.org
    Sec: Anne Jones
- ○ *G; for those interested in making, selling & playing bamboo
    pipes

Pira International   1929
- ■ Cleeve Rd, LEATHERHEAD, Surrey, KT22 7RU.   (hq)
    01372 802000   fax 01372 802238
    email infocentre@pira.co.uk   http://www.piranet.com
    Managing Dir: Michael Hancock
- ▲ Company Limited by Guarantee
- ○ *Q; consultancy & research into paper, packaging, printing &
    publishing
- Gp Printing & publishing; Paper & board; Packaging
- ● Conf - ET - Res - Inf - Lib
- ¶ [Publications catalogue on website].

Pizza, Pasta & Italian Food Association   (PAPA)   1977
- NR Association House, 18c Moor St, CHEPSTOW, Monmouthshire,
    NP16 5DB.   (hq)
    01291 636331   fax 01291 630402
    email enq@papa.org.uk   http://www.papa.org.uk
    Dir: Jim Winship
- ○ *T; to promote better standards & knowledge in the industry
- ● Mtgs - Inf - VE - Promotions - Insurance schemes - Financial
    advice
- < Nat Assn of Pizza Operators (USA)
- M 52 i, 680 f, UK / 13 i, 36 f, o'seas
- ¶ Magazine - 6; ftm, £48 nm.   PAPA Ybk - 1; ftm.

© CBD Research Ltd · Beckenham · BR3 5JS · Tel 020 8650 7745 · Fax 020 8650 0768 · E-mail cbd@cbdresearch.com · www.cbdresearch.com

Plain English Campaign 1979   (PEC)
- ■   PO Box 3, New Mills, HIGH PEAK, Derbys, SK22 4QP.   (hq)
    01663 744409   fax 01663 747038
    email info@plainenglish.co.uk
    http://www.plainenglish.co.uk
    Mgr: Tony Maher
- ▲   Company Limited by Guarantee
- ○   *K; to persuade government departments, local councils &
    companies to write forms, leaflets, letters & agreements
    clearly & to set them out clearly & logically
- ●   Conf - ET - Res - Exhib - Comp - LG
- M   1,000 i, 500 f
- ¶   Plain English (Jnl) - 4; free.
    List available on request.

Plainsong & Mediæval Music Society   (PMMS)   1888
- ■   19 The Close, SALISBURY, Wilts, SP1 2EB.   (hq)
    email pmms@rscm.com
    Chmn: Prof John Harper
- ▲   Registered Charity
- ○   *D, *L; the advancement of education in plainsong & mediæval
    music
- ●   Publication of scholarly books & facsimiles
- M   i & libraries
- ¶   Plainsong & Medieval Music (Jnl) - 2; ftm.

Planning Disaster Coalition
- NR   c/o FOE, 26-28 Underwood St, LONDON, N1 7JQ.
    020 7566 1649
    http://www.planningdisaster.co.uk
- ○   *K; against the government's plans to remove community
    voices from the planning process
- M   17 org

Planning & Environment Bar Association   (PEBA)
- NR   Landmark Chambers, 180 Fleet St, LONDON, EC4A 2HG.
    (sb)
    020 7430 1221
    http://www.peba.info
    Sec: Christopher Boyle
- ○   *P

Planning Officers Society   1997
- NR   PO Box 842, AYLESBURY, Bucks, HP20 9DY.   (sb)
    01296 422161
    http://www.planningofficers.org.uk
    Sec: Chris Swanwick
- ○   *P

Plantagenet Medieval Archery & Combat Society
(Plantagenet Society)   1976
- ■   37 Willowslea Rd, WORCESTER, WR3 7QP.   (sp)
    01905 455192
    email mike@mkerslake.freeserve.co.uk
    http://www.plantagenet.org.uk
    Sec: Mike Kerslake
- ▲   Un-incorporated Society
- ○   *G; re-enactment of medieval tourneys, sieges, foot combat,
    archery, music & dance
- Gp   Archers; Knights; Musicians; Dancers
- ●   Re-enactments & entertainment
- M   60 i

Plantlife International: the wild plant conservation charity
- NR   14 Rollestone St, SALISBURY, Wilts, SP1 1DX.   (hq)
    01722 342730
    email enquiries@plantlife.org.uk
    http://www.plantlife.org.uk
    Devt Mgr: Lisa Clements
- ▲   Registered Charity
- ○   *K; 'the in-situ conservation of wild plants'
- ●   Res - LG - Conservation of wild plants
- M   125,000 i
- ¶   Plantlife - 3; ftm, on request nm.

Plastics & Board Industries Federation   (PBIF)   2001
- ■   15A London Rd, MAIDSTONE, Kent, ME16 8LY.   (pubrs/office)
    01483 277387
    email turner13@btconnect.com   http://www.pbif.co.uk
    Sec: Michael Turner
- ▲   Company Limited by Guarantee
- ○   *T; for companies who either manufacture products which
    involve high frequency welding of PVC, or converting other
    types of plastic or board, or who are suppliers to those
    manufacturers & the trade (including: automotive, flexible
    structures & marquees, inflatables, nursery goods,
    promotional &* presentation products
- ●   Inf
- M   50 f, UK / 13 f, o'seas
    (Sub: £12,000 UK / £1,300 o'seas)
- ¶   Plastics & Board Jnl (insert in SPDI (Screen Process & Digital
    Image) - 4; online www.pbif.co.uk - 2.

Plastics Historical Society   (PHS)   1986
- ■   PO Box 52473, London, NW3 9BZ.   (mail/address)
    020 8302 0684
    email memb.sec@plastiquarian.com
    http://www.plastiquarian.com
    Mem Sec: Deborah Jaffé,   Hon Sec: Jen Cruse
- ▲   Un-incorporated Society
- ○   *L; to study all historical aspects of plastics & other polymers; to
    record current developments
- ●   Conf - Mtgs - Res - Exhib - Inf - Lib at the (Institute of Materials
    Minerals & Mining) - VE
- <   Inst Materials, Minerals & Mining
- M   175 i, 25 org, UK / 50 i, o'seas
- ¶   Plastiquarian - 2; ftm, £10 nm.   NL - 6; ftm, £3 nm.

Plastics Ireland
- IRL   Confederation House, 84/86 Lower Baggot St, DUBLIN 2,
    Republic of Ireland.
    353 (1) 605 1574   fax 353 (1) 638 1574
    http://www.plasticsireland.ie
    Dir: Marian Byron
- ○   *T
- <   IBEC
- M   50 f

Plastics Window Federation
- NR   Federation House, 85-87 Wellington St, LUTON, Beds,
    LU1 5AF.   (hq)
    01582 456147
    http://www.pwfed.co.uk
- ▲   Company Limited by Guarantee
- ○   *T; manufacturers & installers of plastics (PVCU) windows for
    domestic & commercial use

Play Matters
    campaign title of the **National Association of Toy & Leisure
    Libraries**

Play Providers Association   (PPA)   2005
- ■   Federation House, STONELEIGH PARK, Warks, CV8 2RF.   (hq)
    024 7641 4999   fax 024 7641 4990
    email ppa@playproviders.org
    http://www.playproviders.org.uk
- ▲   Company Limited by Guarantee
- ○   *T; for indoor operators of children's play centres
- ●   Mtgs
- <   a group of the Federation of Sports & Play Assns (FSPA)
- M   f

Player Piano Group (PPG) 1959
- ■ Strets, Church Rd, LINGFIELD, Surrey, RH7 6AH. (hsp)
  Hon Sec: Tony Austin
- ▲ Un-incorporated Society
- ○ *D, *G; to foster interest in the player piano & the reproducing piano; their history, mechanisms & musical virtues
- ● Mtgs - VE
- < Automatic Musical Instrument Collectors Assn Intl (AMICA); Ned Pianola Vereniging; NW [& S Wales & the West] Player Piano Assn[s]; Gesellschaft Selbspielende Musikinstrumente eV; Australian Collectors Mechanical Musical Instruments; Perferons la Musique; Pianola Inst
- M 273 i, 5 org, UK / 26 i, 5 org, o'seas
- ¶ The Bulletin - 4; ftm only.

Player-Playwrights 1947
- ■ 37 Woodvale Way, LONDON, NW11 8SQ. (hsp)
  http://www.playerplaywrights.co.uk
  Hon Sec: Christine Strickett
- ▲ Un-incorporated Society
- ○ *A; to promote the writing & appreciation of theatre in all its forms
- ● Mtgs - Comp - Reading & performing new texts & trying to get them before the public
- M 125 i
  (Sub: £10 to join + £6 annually)
- ¶ NL & Programmes - 3.

Pleasure Horse Society Ltd 2003
- NR Victoria House, Desborough St, HIGH WYCOMBE, Bucks, HP11 2NF.
  01494 601042
  email info@pleasurehorsesociety.co.uk
  Contact: Chris Stroud
- ○ *G; for all horse owners

Plymouth Chamber of Commerce & Industry (PCCI) 1813
- NR 22 Lockyer St, PLYMOUTH, Devon, PL1 2QW. (hq)
  01752 220471
  http://www.plymouth-chamber.co.uk
  Dir of Operations & Co Sec: Sally Perdrisat
- ▲ Company Limited by Guarantee
- ○ *C
- Gp Membership consultation, policy & representation; Membership services & marketing
- ● Mtgs - ET - Res - Exhib - Expt - Inf - VE - LG - Representation of members' views
- M 900 f
- ¶ NL - 12.   LM - 12.   Ybk.

POA: the Professional Trades Union for Prison, Correctional & Secure Psychiatric Workers (POA) 1939
- NR Cronin House, 245 Church St, LONDON, N9 9HW. (hq)
  020 8803 0255
  http://www.poauk.org.uk
  Gen Sec: Brian Caton
- Br 4
- ○ *U
- Gp Prison officers; Nurses & ancillary staff in special hospitals
- ● Conf - Mtgs - ET - Res - Stat - Inf - Lib - VE - Empl
- < TUC; Coun Civil Service Us; EUROFEDOP
- M 33,500 i
- ¶ Gatelodge - 6.
- × 2007 Prison Officers Association

Poetry Society (Inc) (PS) 1909
- ■ 22 Betterton St, LONDON, WC2H 9BX. (hq)
  020 7420 9880   fax 020 7240 4818
  email info@poetrysociety.org.uk
  http://www.poetrysociety.org.uk
  Dir: Jules Mann
- ▲ Company Limited by Guarantee; Registered Charity
- ○ *A; promotion of poets & poetry
- ● ET - Res - Exhib - Comp - Inf
- M c 4,000 i & org
- ¶ The Poetry Review - 4.   The Poetry News - 4.

Point-to-Point Owners & Riders Association (PPORA) 1977
- NR The Coach House, Mill Rd, Sturry, CANTERBURY, Kent, CT2 0AJ. (hsb)
  01227 713080   fax 01227 713088
  http://www.ppora.co.uk
- ▲ Un-incorporated Society
- ○ *G, *S
- M i
- ¶ Between the Flags - 2.

Police Federation of England & Wales (PFEW) 1919
- ■ Federation House, Highbury Drive, LEATHERHEAD, Surrey, KT22 7UY. (hq)
  01372 352000   fax 01372 352039
  email polfed@polfed.org   http://www.polfed.org
  Gen Sec: Ian Rennie
- Br 43 branch boards
- ○ *U; a staff association to consult & negotiate on terms & conditions of service for police officers in the ranks of constable to chief inspector
- ● Conf - Empl
- M i
- ¶ Police - 12; free to branches.

Police Federation for Northern Ireland (PFNI) 2008
- ■ 77-79 Garnerville Rd, BELFAST, BT4 2NX. (hq)
  028 9076 4200
  email secretary.pfni@btconnect.com
  Sec: Stevie McCann
- ▲ Un-incorporated Society
- ○ *P; representative body concerned with welfare & efficiency of police officers in Northern Ireland
- ● Conf - Mtgs - ET - Res - Inf - Empl - LG
- < Standing C'ee of Police in Europe
- M 8,000 i
  Sub: £15
- ¶ Police Beat - 4; ftm only.

Police History Society (PHS) 1985
- ■ 64 Nore Marsh Rd, WOOTTON BASSETT, Wilts, SN4 8BH. (hsp)
  01793 853635
  email stevebridge100@btinternet.com
  http://www.policehistorysociety.co.uk
  Hon Sec: Steve Bridge
- ▲ Registered Charity
- ○ *G; promotion of interest in police history
- Gp Police museum curators
- ● Conf - Res - Re-publication of historical sources of police history
- M c350 i
- ¶ Jnl - 1; ftm, £5 nm.   NL - 4;   LM - 2/3 yrly; both ftm only.
  Monographs - irreg; prices vary.

© CBD Research Ltd · Beckenham · BR3 5JS · Tel 020 8650 7745 · Fax 020 8650 0768 · E-mail cbd@cbdresearch.com · www.cbdresearch.com

Police Insignia Collectors Association of Great Britain   (PICA GB)   1975
- ■ 8 Foxon Lane Gdns, CATERHAM, Surrey, CR3 5SN.   (mem/sp)
  http://www.pica.co.uk
  Hon Mem Sec: Tony Collman
- ○ *G; to foster comradeship through a mutual interest in police insignia; to instruct, inform & interest all collecting police insignia
- ● Swap mtgs
- M 600 i, UK / 150 i, o'seas.
- ¶ PICA Magazine - 3; ftm only.

Police Professional Network
  a group of the **Chartered Management Institute**

Police Superintendents' Association of England & Wales   1921
- NR 67a Reading Rd, PANGBOURNE, Berks, RG8 7JD.   (hq)
  0118-984 4005   fax 0118-984 5642
  email enquiries@policesupers.com
  http://www.policesupers.com

  Pres: Chief Superintendent Ian Johnston
- Br 44
- ○ *P; for police superintendents & chief superintendents in England & Wales
- Gp Business Areas: BCU (Basic Command Unit) liaison; Command resilience; Crime; Diversity; Human resources; Operational policing; Panel of friends; Roads policing
- ● Conf - Mtgs - Res - Stat - Inf - Empl - LG
- M 1,510 i
- ¶ The Superintendent - 3; free.

Polish Society   1996
- ■ Ashcroft House, Chalton Rd, BRIDGE of ALLAN, Stirlingshire, FK9 4EF.   (chmn/p)
  01786 832793
  Chmn: Prof Peter D Stachura
- ▲ Un-incorporated Society
- ○ *L, *X; an academic discussion forum for Polish history, culture & contemporary affairs
- ● Conf - Mtgs - ET - Res
- M 25 i
- ¶ NL - 3; ftm only.

Polite Society
  former (1996) & alt name of the **Campaign for Courtesy**

Political Cartoon Society
- NR 32 Store St, LONDON, WC1E 7BS.
  020 7580 1114
  http://www.politicalcartoon.co.uk
- ○ *G; to promote the political cartoon as an educational, amusing & informative force
- ● Exhib
- ¶ NL - 4; ftm.

Political Studies Association of the United Kingdom   (PSA)   1950
- NR School of Policy Studies, University of Ulster, NEWTOWNABBEY, Co Antrim, BT37 0QB.   (hq)
  028 9036 8896   fax 028 9036 6847
  http://www.psa.ac.uk
  Hon Sec: Prof Paul Carmichael
- ▲ Registered Charity
- ○ *L; promotion of the development of political studies
- ● Conf - Mtgs - ET - Res - SG - Stat - LG
- M i & f
- ¶ Many publications available

Politics Association   (PA)   1969
- NR Old Hall Lane, MANCHESTER, M13 0XT.   (hq)
  0161-256 3906   fax 0161-256 3906
  email politicass@btconnect.com
  http://www.politics-association.org.uk
  Contact: Steve Buckley
- ▲ Registered Charity
- Br 6
- ○ *E; to promote the study & teaching of the theory & practice of politics
- Gp Politics Association Resources Centre (PARC) - teaching resources, publishing, printing
- ● Conf - Mtgs - ET - Exam - Res - Comp - Inf - LG
- < Hansard Soc for Parliamentary Government
- M c 1,300 i
- ¶ Talking Politics (Jnl) - 4.

** Poll Holstein Breeders Club
  (Organisation lost: see Introduction paragraph 3)

Polymer Machinery Manufacturers' & Distributors' Association Ltd   (PMMDA)   1966
- ■ PO Box 2539, RUGBY, Warks, CV23 9YF.   (asa)
  0870 241 1474   fax 05602 094484
  email pmmda@pmmda.org.uk
  http://www.pmmda.org.uk
  C'ee Sec: Nikki Williams,   Pres: Brian Stinton
- ▲ Company Limited by Guarantee
- ○ *T; support to plastics machinery suppliers in the UK
- Gp Export; Technical; Health & safety
- ● ET - Exhib - SG - Stat - Expt - Inf - LG - Sponsorship of 'Modern Apprentice'
- < Brit Plastics Fedn
- M c 80 f
- ¶ Buyers Guide to. . .
  Granulators;   Chillers;   Robots;   Dryers;   Temperature Control;   all 2 yrly; free.

Polymer Society
  a group of the **Institute of Materials, Minerals & Mining**

Ponies Association (UK) Ltd   (Ponies(UK))   1988
- ■ Chesham House, 56 Green End Rd, SAWTRY, Cambs, PE28 5UY.   (hq)
  01487 830278   fax 01487 832086
  email info@poniesuk.org   http://www.poniesuk.org
  Chmn: Mrs Davina Whiteman
- ▲ Company Limited by Guarantee; Registered Charity
- ○ *G; to promote equestrian events & the training of horse & rider
- ● Conf - ET - Comp
- M 4,500 i
- ¶ NL - 2 + by email; ftm only.

Pony Breeders of Shetland Association   (PBSA)
- NR 5 Dale Park, DUNROSSNESS, Shetland, ZE2 9JH.   (treas/p)
  http://www.shetlandponybreeders.com
- ○ *B

The Pony Club   (Pony Club)   1929
- ■ Stoneleigh Park, KENILWORTH, Warks, CV8 2RW.   (hq)
  024 7669 8300
  http://www.pcuk.org
  Chief Exec: Mrs Judy E Edwards
- ▲ Registered Charity
- Br 347; 15 countries
- ○ *S, *Y; an international voluntary youth organisation for those interested in ponies & riding
- Gp Mounted games; Tetrathlon; Polo; Polocrosse; Show jumping; Eventing; Dressage; Racing
- ● Conf - ET - Exam - Exhib - Comp - VE
- M 36,000 i, UK / 104,500 i, o'seas
- ¶ Ybk.   Instructors Hbk.
  Manual of Horsemanship.   All Rule Books - 1.

Pony Riders Association (PRA) 1991
NR 131 The Butts, FROME, Somerset, BA11 4AQ.
   http://www.ponyriders.org.uk
   Mem Sec: Gina Coltman
O *G; for adults with ponies

Pool Promoters Association (PPA) 1933
NR 100 Old Hall St, LIVERPOOL, L3 9TD.   (asa)
   0151-237 7777   fax 0151-237 7676
   Sec: W Roger S Calvert
▲ Un-incorporated Society
O *T; to coordinate dealings with the government & football
   authorities; to deal generally with enquiries from the public &
   the media
● Mtgs - Comp - Stat - Inf - LG
M 2 f

Pop & Rock Fans' Association (PRFA) 1997
■ 11 South Block Peabody Buildings, Brodlove Lane, LONDON,
   E1W 3DY.   (hsb)
   0798 047 7454
   email gothamcity8@yahoo.co.uk
   Pres: Michael Blackett
▲ Un-incorporated Society
Br 2; USA
O *D, *K; to give record buying fans a voice & platform within the
   music industry on a wide variety of interests - CD prices,
   tickets, merchandise, venue conditions etc
● Conf - Mtgs - Campaigning/marching
M 40 i
¶ Pop & Rock Fanzine - 12; £1.50 m, £2 nm.

Popular Flying Association
   since 2007 **Light Aircraft Association**

Porcupine Marine Natural History Society (PMNHS) 1977
■ Cherry Cottage, 11 Ballyhaft Rd, NEWTOWNARDS, Co Down,
   BT22 2AW.   (exec officer)
   http://www.pmnhs.co.uk
   Exec Officer: Julia Nunn
▲ Un-incorporated Society
O *L; marine natural history, taxonomy, biogeography; (named
   after the first marine biology deep-sea research vessel,
   HMS Porcupine)
● Conf - Mtgs - ET - Res - Field survey
M [not stated]
¶ NL - 3; ftm.

**Portable Electric Tool Manufacturers Association (PETMA)
1942**
■ PO Box 35084, LONDON, NW1 4XE.   (asa)
   020 7935 8532   fax 07006 065950
   email office@petma.org.uk
   Sec: C Dunn-Meynell
O *T
● Mtgs - Res - Inf
< Eur Power Tool Assn (EPTA)
M 2 f

Portland Sheep Breeders Group
NR Huish Barns, Winterborne Zelston, BLANDFORD FORUM,
   Dorset, DT11 9ES.
   01929 459082   http://www.portlandsheep.org.uk
   Sec: Tessa Hucklesby
O *B
M c 200 i

Portman Group (TPG) 1990
■ 7-10 Chandos St, LONDON, W1G 9DQ.   (hq)
   020 7907 3700   fax 020 7907 3710
   email info@portmangroup.org.uk
   http://www.portmangroup.org.uk
   Chief Exec: David Poley
O *K; a drinks industry initiative against alcohol misuse
● Conf - Mtgs - ET - Res - Stat - Inf
M 8 f, 2 org

Ports & Terminals Group   (PTG)
■ 28-29 Threadneedle St, LONDON, EC2R 8AY.
   020 7628 2555   fax 020 7638 4376
   email info@maritimeindustries.org
   http://www.maritimeindustries.org
   Dir: Ken Gibbons
O *T; port development, supply chain management & related
   security systems
< Soc of Maritime Inds

**Portsmouth & South East Hampshire Chamber of Commerce &
Industry (P&SEHCC&I) 1879**
NR Regional Business Centre, Harts Farm Way, HAVANT, Hants,
   PO9 1HR.   (hq)
   023 9244 9449   fax 023 9244 9444
   email sehants@chamber.org.uk
   http://www.chamber.org.uk
▲ Company Limited by Guarantee
O *C
● Conf - Mtgs - ET - Res - Exhib - Expt - Inf - Lib - LG -
   Networking - Commercial services
< Brit Chams Comm
> E Hants Cham Comm
M 800 f, 100 org
¶ Business News - 10; ftm.

**Portuguese Chamber - the Portuguese UK Business Network
1980**
■ 11 Belgrave Square (4th floor), LONDON, SW1X 8PP.   (hq)
   020 7201 6638
   Chief Exec: John Newgas
▲ Company Limited by Guarantee
Br representative offices in Midlands & Scotland; Lisbon (Portugal)
O *C
Gp Industry; Financial; Construction; Import/Export; Legal;
   Consultancy; Design; Marketing; Freight/Transport; Services
● Conf - Mtgs - Res - SG - Stat - Expt - Inf - LG
M 240 f & org, UK / 105 f & org, o'seas
¶ Tradewinds (NL) - 3; ftm.
   Directory & Ybk; ftm.

Post Office Vehicle Club (POVC) 1962
■ 32 Russell Way, LEIGHTON BUZZARD, Beds, LU7 3NG.   (hsp)
   01525 382129
   email povehclub@aol.com   http://www.povehclub.org.uk
   Hon Sec: Francis J Weston
O *G; for people interested the operations & fleets of the General
   Post Office & its successors, the Post Office, BT & Royal Mail
Gp Preservation & archives; Modern fleet
● Inf - VE
< Roads & Road Transport Hist Assn
M 200 i
   (Sub: £10 UK / £26 o'seas)
¶ Post Horn - 12; f6m, £12 nm.
   Books on various types of vehicle; c £10-14.

© CBD Research Ltd · Beckenham · BR3 5JS · Tel 020 8650 7745 · Fax 020 8650 0768 · E-mail cbd@cbdresearch.com · www.cbdresearch.com

Post Tensioning Association   (PTA)   1984
NR   Riverside House, 4 Meadows Business Park, Station Approach,
        Blackwater, CAMBERLEY, Surrey, GU17 9AB.   (hq)
        01726 606800
▲   Un-incorporated Society
○   *T; post-tensioned concrete
●   Mtgs - SG - Technical developments in conjunction with other
        technical committees & bodies
M   10 f
        Note: a new chairman is due to be elected in January 2007

Postal History Society   (PHS)   1936
■   99 North End Rd, LONDON, NW11 7TA.   (hsp)
        020 8458 7353   fax 020 8209 1980
        email smithhans963@aol.com
        Sec: Hans Smith
▲   Un-incorporated Society
○   *G, *L, *Q; the study of written communication, with special
        emphasis on the postal services of the world
●   Conf - Mtgs - Res - Exhib - Comp - Inf - Lib - Publications
<   British Philatelic Federation
M   322 i
        (Sub: £24 GB, £27 (Europe), £30 (RoW))
¶   Postal History Jnl - 4; ftm only.

Postcard Traders' Association   (PTA)   1976
NR   24 Parry Rd, Sholing, SOUTHAMPTON, Hants, SO19 0HU.
        (hsp)
        email ptasec@postcard.co.uk   http://www.postcard.co.uk
        Hon Sec: Derek Popplestone
▲   Un-incorporated Society
○   *T; to encourage the hobby of picture postcard collecting
        worldwide
●   Exhib - Comp - Inf - Organisation of the Picture Postcard Show
M   160 f, UK / 21 f, o'seas
¶   News - 4; ftm only.

Postwatch
        'On 1 October 2008 Postwatch joined with energywatch & the
        Welsh, Scottish & National Consumer Councils to form
        Consumer Focus, the new champion for consumers' interests
        in England, Scotland Wales, & for post, in Northern Ireland.'
        See website: consumerfocus.org.uk
        To make a consumer complaint telephone 0845 404 0506,
        or see the Consumer Direct website: consumerdirect.gov.uk/
        [Information culled from the Consumer Focus website].

Potato Processors Association   (PPA)
NR   6 Catherine St, LONDON, WC2B 5JJ.   (hq)
▲   Un-incorporated Society
○   *T
●   Mtgs
<   U Eur Inds Transformation Pomme de Terre; Food & Drink Fedn
M   11 f, 1 org

Poultry Club of Great Britain   (PCGB)   1877
■   Keeper's Cottage, 40 Benvarden Rd, Dervock, BALLYMONEY,
        Co Antrim, BT53 6NM.   (gsp)
        028 2074 1056
        email info@poultryclub.org   http://www.poultryclub.org
        Gen Sec: Mrs A Bachmet
▲   Registered Charity
○   *B, *F; to promote high standards in the keeping & breeding of
        purebred poultry
●   ET - Exhib - Inf
M   c 1,400 i & org
¶   NL - 4;   Ybk - 1; both ftm only.

Power Fastenings Association Ltd   (PFA)   1978
■   42 Heath St, TAMWORTH, Staffs, B79 7JH.   (hq)
        01827 52337   fax 01827 310827
        email info@powerfastenings.org.uk
        http://www.powerfastenings.org.uk
        Sec: Alain Skelding
▲   Company Limited by Guarantee
○   *T; to represent the major manufacturers & suppliers of
        branded, power-driven tools & collated fasteners
●   Mtgs - Res - Inf - LG - British & European Standards
M   7 i
        (Sub: £750)
¶   Using Power Fastener Driving Tools Safely; 20p m,
        1 copy free nm.

Powys Society   1967
■   25 Mansfield Rd, TAUNTON, Somerset, TA1 3NJ.   (hsp)
        01823 278177
        http://www.powys-society.org
        Hon Sec: Peter Lazare
▲   Registered Charity
○   *A, *G; to establish public recognition of the writings, thought &
        contribution to the arts of the Powys family, particularly the
        brothers John Cowper, Theodore & Llewelyn & their close
        circle of friends: Louis Wilkinson, James Hanley, T E Lawrence
        & Sylvia Townsend Warner
●   Conf - Mtgs - Lib
<   Powys Soc of N America
M   200 i, UK / 150 i, o'seas
¶   The Powys Journal - 1.   The Powys NL - 3.   LM - 3 yrly.
        A Powys Checklist (list of publications by the Powys family &
        circle) - irreg.

Prader-Willi Syndrome Association (UK)   (PWSA (UK))   1981
■   125a London Rd, DERBY, DE1 2QQ.   (welfare/coord/p)
        01332 365676   fax 01332 360401
        email admin@pwsa.co.uk   http://www.pwsa.co.uk
        Welfare Services Coordinator: Jacquie Wood
        Hon Sec: Julian Courtauld
▲   Registered Charity
Br   6
○   *W; to promote care, welfare & treatment of people with
        Prader-Willi syndrome; to offer support & information to
        carers & professionals
●   Conf - Mtgs - ET - Inf - Lib
<   Intl Prader-Willi Syndrome Org
M   1,500 i, UK / 130 i, o'seas
¶   Publications list available.

Prayer Book Society   (PBS)   1975
■   The Studio, Copyhold Farm, Lady Grove, Goring Heath,
        READING, Berks, RG8 7RT.   (chmn/b)
        0118-984 2582
        http://www.pbs.org.uk
        Chmn: Prudence Dailey
▲   Registered Charity
Br   44; Portugal, S Africa
○   *R; to uphold the worship & doctrine of the Church of England
        as enshrined in the Book of Common Prayer; to spread the
        use of the Book of Common Prayer & to see that it is used
●   Conf - Mtgs - ET - Comp - Inf
M   i
¶   NL - 4.   The Journal - 2.   Faith & Worship - 2.

Pre Basic Growers Association   (PBGA)
- ■ 1 St Fillans Grove, Aberdour, BURNTISLAND, Fife, KY3 0XG. (hsp)
  01383 860695
  email wjrennie@btinternet.com
  Hon Sec: William John Rennie
- ▲ Un incorporated Society
- ○ *T; represents the interests of early generation, high grade seed potato growers
- ● Conf - SG - LG
- M 60 i
- ✕ 2007 Virus Tested Stem Cutting Growers Association

Pre Eclampsia Society   (PETS)   1981
- NR Rhianfa, Carmel, CAERNARFON, Gwynedd, LL54 7RL. (trustee/p)
  01702 205088
  email dawnjames@clara.co.uk
  http://www.pre-eclampsia-society.org.uk
  Founder: Dawn James,   Trustee: Sharon Copping
- ▲ Registered Charity
- ○ *W; self-help & support group for women suffering from, or who have suffered from, pre-eclampsia / eclampsia, & others interested in the condition
- ● Res - Comp - Stat - Inf - Lib
- M 200 i
- ¶ NL - 4; ftm only.

Pre-Raphaelite Society   (PRS)   1988
- ■ 37 Larchmere Drive, Hall Green, BIRMINGHAM, B28 8JB. (sp)
  email info@pre-raphaelitesociety.org
  http://www.pre-raphaelitesociety.org
  Sec: Barry C Johnson
- ▲ Registered Charity
- ○ *A; the study of the lives & art of the Pre-Raphaelite Brotherhood
- ● VE - Lectures - Seminars
- M 350 i, UK & o'seas
- ¶ The Review of the PRS - 3.

Pre-Retirement Association of Gt Britain & N Ireland
   since 2005 **Life Academy**

Pre-School Learning Alliance   (PLA)   1961
- NR 188 York Way, LONDON, N7 9AD.   (hq)
  020 7697 2534   fax 020 7700 0319
  email info@pre-school.org.uk
  http://www.pre-school.org.uk
  Chmn (Nat Exec C'ee): Judith Thompson
- ▲ Registered Charity
- Br 300
- ○ *E; links 16,000 pre-schools & 500,000 young children & their families in England
- ● Conf - Mtgs - ET - Exam - Res - Exhib - Comp - Stat - Inf - Lib - PL - VE - Empl - LG
- < Wld Org for Early Childhood Education (OMEP)
- M 500,000 i (children), 16,000 gps
- ¶ Under Five (NL) - 10.   AR; free.
  Guide to Training [lists courses] - 1.
  Leaflets; free.   Publications list available.

Precast Concrete Paving & Kerb Association
   alternative name of Interpave, a product association of the **British Precast Concrete Federation**

Precast Flooring Federation
   a product association of the **British Precast Concrete Federation**

Prefabricated Access Suppliers' & Manufacturers' Association (PASMA)   1978
- ■ PO Box 168, LEEDS, LS11 9WW.   (hsp)
  0845 230 4041   fax 0845 230 4042
  email info@pasma.co.uk   http://www.pasma.co.uk
- ▲ Company Limited by Guarantee
- ○ *T; the safe use of alloy access towers
- ● Conf - Mtgs - ET - Exam - Exhib
- < Access Ind Forum
- M 40 i, 220 f
- ¶ Operators Code of Practice; £5.
  Guide to Safe Use of Mobile Access (DVD); £35.

Prehistoric Society   1935
- NR c/o Institute of Archaeology, 31-34 Gordon Sq, LONDON, WC1H 0PY.   (mail address)
  http://www.prehistoricsociety.org
  Admin Sec: Dr Tessa Machling
- ○ *L; study of prehistory & its interpretation & conservation

Premature Menopause Support Group
   see **Daisy Network**

Premenstrual Society   (Premsoc)   1986
- NR PO Box 429, ADDLESTONE, Surrey, KT15 1DZ.   (h chmn b)
  01932 872560 (1100-1800 hrs)
  Chmn: Dr Michael G Brush
- Br 10
- ○ *W; information & support for individual sufferers from premenstrual syndrome (PMS) & period pains (dysmenorrhoea)
- ● Conf - ET - Res - Inf
- M 500 i
- ¶ NL - 2; ftm only.   Leaflets.
  Selfhelp for PMS (booklet); free (sae please).

Premium Rate Association   (PRA)   1997
- NR Elite House, 25 South St, READING, Berks, RG1 4QU.   (hq)
  0118-956 7956
  email info@praltd.co.uk   http://www.praltd.co.uk
  Chief Exec: Suzanne Gillies
- ▲ Company Limited by Guarantee
- ○ *T; for companies involved in the premium rate telephone industry
- Gp Telecommunications
- ● Mtgs - Res - LG - Liaison with regulators (ICSTIS, OFCOM)
- M 35 f
- ¶ NL - 4.

Presbyterian Historical Society of Ireland   (PHSI)   1906
- ■ Church House, Fisherwick Place, BELFAST, BT1 6DW.   (hq)
  028 9032 2284   fax 028 9041 7307
  Hon Secs: Dr A W G Brown & James Moffett
- ▲ Registered Charity
- ○ *L; to collect & preserve the materials & to promote knowledge of the history of the Presbyterian Church in Ireland & of its constituent congregations
- ● Mtgs - Lib
- M 400 i, UK / 50 i, o'seas
- ¶ Bulletin - 1; ftm, £2 nm.
  Fasti of the General Assembly of the Presbyterian Church in Ireland 1840-1910; 3 parts; £2 per part.
  Publications list available.

© CBD Research Ltd · Beckenham · BR3 5JS · Tel 020 8650 7745 · Fax 020 8650 0768 · E-mail cbd@cbdresearch.com · www.cbdresearch.com

Press Standards Board of Finance Ltd   (PRESSBOF)   1990
- ■ 21 Lansdowne Crescent, EDINBURGH, EH12 5EH.   (sb)
   0131-535 1064   fax 0131-535 1063
   email info@pressbof.org.uk
   Sec & Treas: J B Raeburn
- ▲ Company Limited by Guarantee
- ○ *N, *T; coordination & finance of self-regulation in the newspaper & magazine publishing industry in the UK
- ● Mtgs - LG
- M 5 org
- ¶ Code of Practice; ftm.

Pressed Flower Guild   1983
- ■ 383 Leasowe Rd, Moreton, WIRRAL, Merseyside, CH46 2RF.
   (hsp)
   0151-638 1706
   Hon Sec: Mrs C Foster
- ▲ Un-incorporated Society
- ○ *H; to raise the standard of pressed flowers; to arrange teaching & seminar facilities
- ● Conf - Mtgs - ET - Exam - Res - Exhib - Comp - SG - Inf - Lib - VE
- < R Horticl Soc
- M c 150 i
- ¶ NL - 4;   LM - 1; both ftm only.
- ✕ 2000-02 Pressed Flower Craft Guild

Pressure Gauge & Dial Thermometer Association   (PGDT) 1951
- ■ Heathcote House, 136 Hagley Rd, Edgbaston, BIRMINGHAM, B16 9PN.   (asa)
   0121-454 4141   fax 0121-454 4949
   email info@pgdt.org   http://www.pgdt.org
   Exec Sec: Mrs Sharon J Parker
- ▲ Un-incorporated Society
- ○ *T; to promote the industry; to participate in the preparation & amendment of European & inter-nation standards
- ● Mtgs - Stat
- M 16 f
- ✕ 2003-04 British Pressure Gauge Manufacturers Association

Pressure Sensitive Manufacturers Association
merged into the **British Printing Industries Federation**

Prestressed Concrete Association
a product association of the **British Precast Concrete Federation**

Primary Care Dermatology Society   (PCDS)   1994
- ■ 12 Thorpe Rd, NORWICH, Norfolk, NR1 1RY.   (secretariat)
   01603 252525
   email pcds@pcds.org.uk   http://www.pcds.org.uk
   Chmn: Dr Stephen Kownacki,   Dr Elizabeth Ogden
- ▲ Company Limited by Guarantee
- Br Republic of Ireland
- ○ *M
- ● Conf - Mtgs - ET
- < Brit Assn Dermatologists
- M 580 i, 13 f, UK / 80 i, o'seas
- ¶ PCDS Bulletin - 4; free.

Primary Care Rheumatology Society
- NR PO Box 42, NORTHALLERTON, N Yorks, DL7 8YG.
   01609 774794   fax 01609 774726
   http://www.pcrsociety.org.uk

Primary Immunodeficiency Association   (PiA)   1989
- ■ Alliance House, 12 Caxton St, LONDON, SW1H 0QS.   (hq)
   020 7976 7640   fax 020 7976 7641
   email info@pia.org.uk   http://www.pia.org.uk
   Chief Exec: Chris Hughan
- ▲ Registered Charity
- ○ *W; to promote the wellbeing of people with primary immunodeficiencies
- Gp Personal support; Medical advisory panel
- ● Conf - Mtgs - Res - Inf - LG
- < Intl Patient Org for Primary Immunodeficiencies (IPOPI); AMRC
- M c 1,500
- ¶ Insight - 4; subscription only.
   Various publications; ftm, 50p - £2 nm.

Primate Society of Great Britain   (PSGB)   1967
- ■ c/o Dr Colleen Schaffner, Psychology Dept, University of Chester, CHESTER, CH1 4BJ.   (hsb)
   01244 513476   fax 01244 392823
   email secretary@psgb.org   http://www.psgb.org
   Sec: Dr Colleen Schaffner,
   Pres: Prof Ann MacLaren
- ▲ Registered Charity
- ○ *L; research into & general awareness of primate biology, evolution, conservation & management
- Gp Working parties: Conservation, Captive care
- ● Conf - Mtgs - ET - Res - Inf - LG
- < Intl Primatological Soc; Eur Primatological Fedn; Inst Biology
- M 265 i, 10 f, UK / 20 i, 10 f, o'seas
- ¶ Primate Eye - 3; £25 m, £30 nm.

Princess Gwenllian Society
- ■ 158 Lake Rd East, Roath Park, CARDIFF, CF23 5NQ.
   http://www.princessgwenllian.co.uk
   Sec: Mrs Mallt Anderson
- ○ *G; to commemorate Gwenllian (c1282-1337), daughter of Llewellyn the last ruling Prince of Wales'

Principals' Professional Council   1920
- ■ 1 Heath Sq, Boltro Rd, HAYWARDS HEATH, W Sussex, RH16 1BL.   (hsb)
   01444 472499
   Sec: Dr Michael Thrower
- ▲ Un-incorporated Society
- Br 9
- ○ *E, *P; committed to the strong mutual support of its members working with other organisations for the promotion & development of the further education sector
- Gp Colleges of Agriculture & Horticulture
- ● Conf - Mtgs - ET - LG
- < a council of the National Association of Head Teachers
- M 750 i
- ¶ Newslink (NL) - 5;   Life Members (NL) - 2;
   Hbk (incl LM) - 1; all ftm only.

Printed Postage Impression Study Circle
a group of the **British Postmark Society**

Printing Historical Society   (PHS)   1964
- ■ c/o St Bride Library, Bride Lane, Fleet St, LONDON, EC4Y 8EE.   (hq)
   email secretary@printinghistoricalsociety.org.uk
   Hon Sec: Philip Wickens
- ▲ Registered Charity
- ○ *L; history of printing & preservation of historical printing equipment; history of the book
- ● Conf - Mtgs - ET - Res - VE - Recording & preserving antique equipment
- M i & libraries
- ¶ Jnl - 2;   NL - irreg; both ftm.

Printmakers Council (PMC) 1965

NR Ground Floor Unit, 23 Blue Anchor Lane, LONDON,
  SE16 3UL. (hq)
  020 7237 6789
▲ Registered Charity
○ *A; promotion of printmaking & the art & work of
  contemporary printmakers & new & experimental techniques;
  to aid young & unestablished artists

Prism - Association of Print Specialists & Manufacturers 1934

NR Association House, 7a West St, REIGATE, Surrey, RH2 9BL.
  (hq)
  01737 240792   fax 01737 240770
  email info@prismuk.org   http://www.prismuk.org
  Manager: John Keith
▲ Company Limited by Guarantee
○ *T; to improve the profitability & competitiveness of UK imaging
  specialists, serving the POS, graphics, industrial, garment &
  textile markets
< Fedn of Eur Screen Printers Assns (FESPA)
M 114 f
✕ 2008 (23 April) (Digital &) Screen Printing Association

Prison Advice & Care Trust (PACT) 1975

NR City Cloisters (suite C5), 196 Old St, LONDON, EC1V 9FR.
  (hq)
  020 7490 3139
  Dir: Andy Keen-Downs
▲ Company Limited by Guarantee; Registered Charity
○ *W; to offer advice, information & emotional support to families
  & friends of those in prison
● Mtgs
M i
¶ Leaflets;   Information booklets;   AR.

Prison Governors Association (PGA) 1987

NR Cleland House (room 217), Page St, LONDON, SW1P 4LZ.
  (hq)
  020 7217 8591   fax 020 7217 8923
  http://www.prisongovernors.org.uk
  Gen Sec: C P A Bushell
▲ Un-incorporated Society
Br c 150
○ *P; to represent the industrial relations & professional interests
  of prison governors (operational managers & senior
  operational managers in England, Wales, Scotland &
  Northern Ireland
Gp Northern Ireland (separate prison services), Scotland
● Conf - Mtgs - Empl - LG
M 1,200 i
¶ The Key - 4; ftm only.

Prison Officers Association
  since 2007 styles itself **POA**

Prisoners Abroad 1978

■ 89-93 Fonthill Rd, LONDON, N4 3JH.   (hq)
  020 7561 6820   helpline: 0808 172 0098   fax 020 7561
  6821
  email info@prisonersabroad.org.uk
  http://www.prisonersabroad.org.uk
  Chief Exec: Pauline Crowe
▲ Registered Charity
○ *W; to offer support for British citizens in prison outside the UK
  & their families. Information on foreign criminal justice
  systems, prison conditions & transfer
● Inf - Practical support - Survival grants - Pen-pal scheme -
  Resettlement assistance
¶ NL - 3;   AR - 1; both free.
✕ 2003 (April) National Council for the Welfare of Prisoners
  Abroad

Private Libraries Association (PLA) 1956

■ Ravelston, South View Road, PINNER, Middx, HA5 3YD.
  email dchambrs@aol.com   http://www.plabooks.org
  Hon Sec: S J Brett,   Hon Ed: David Chambers
▲ Registered Charity; Un-incorporated Society
○ *A, *G; encouragement of buying & private ownership of
  books; publication of books of relevance to book collectors
● Mtgs - VE
< [in liaison with the Chart Inst of Library & Inf Profls]
M 370 i, 30 f, UK / 150 i, 100 f, o'seas
¶ The Private Library - 4; ftm, £25 nm.   NL - 4.
  Private Press Books (check list of work of private presses in the
  western world) - 1; £10 m, £16 nm.
  Members' Volume - 2/3 yrly; ftm, £30-£50 nm.
  Exchange List - 4.

Private Wagon Federation (PWF) 1977

NR Homelea, Westland Green, Little Hadham, WARE, Herts,
  SG11 2AG.   (hsp)
  01279 843487
  email geoffrey.pratt@btconnect.com
  Sec Gen: Geoffrey Pratt
○ *T
Gp Railway wagon: Building; Hiring; Owners; Repairers
M 5 org

Probation Association 2008

NR 83 Victoria St, LONDON, SW1H 0HW.   (hq)
  020 3008 7930   fax 020 3008 7931
  http://www.probationboards.co.uk
  Chief Exec: Christine Lawrie
▲ Company Limited by Guarantee
○ *P, U; for members of probation boards in England & Wales
M 42 probation boards
✕ 2008 (1 April) Probation Boards' Association

Probation Boards' Association
  since 1 April 2008 the **Probation Association**

Probation Managers Association (PMA) 1980

NR Hayes Court, West Common Rd, HAYES, Kent, BR2 7AU.   (sb)
  020 8462 7755
○ *U; for managers in probation service - provides professional
  advice & support & full range of trade union functions
M i

Processed Vegetable Growers' Association Ltd (PVGA) 1970

■ 133 Eastgate, LOUTH, Lincs, LN11 9QG.   (hq)
  01507 602427   fax 01507 600689
  email postbox@pvga.co.uk
  Chief Exec: M P Riggall
○ *F, *H
● Mtgs - Res - Stat - Expt - Inf - LG - Provision of administration &
  secretarial services - Contract negotiation support
M [i, f]
¶ Specialist market surveys in UK & Europe - prices vary.

Processing & Packaging Machinery Association (PPMA) 1987

■ New Progress House, 34 Stafford Rd, WALLINGTON, Surrey,
  SM6 9AA.   (hq)
  020 8773 8111   fax 020 8773 0022
  email administrator@ppma.co.uk
  http://www.ppma.co.uk
  Chief Exec: Chris Buxton
▲ Company Limited by Guarantee
○ *T; for manufacturers of machinery used in processing &
  packaging food, cosmetics, pharmaceuticals, beverages etc
● Conf - Mtgs - ET - Exhib - Stat - Expt - Inf - Lib - PL - LG
< Confedn Packaging Machinery Assns (COPAMA); European
  Sector Gp (EUROPAMA)
M 310 f
¶ Machinery Update - 6;
  PPMA Machinery Directory - 1; both ftm only.

Processors & Growers Research Organisation   (PGRO)   1944
- ■ The Research Station, Great North Rd, THORNHAUGH, Cambs, PE8 6HJ.   (hq)
  01780 782585   fax 01780 783993
  email info@pgro.org   http://www.pgro.org.uk
  Dir & Sec: G P Gent
- ▲ Registered Charity
- ○ *H, *Q; research into the production & harvesting of peas & beans for both vegetable & protein use
- Gp Agronomy; Biology; Botany
- ● Conf - ET - Res - SG - Inf - Lib - VE - Advisory & technical services
- M 3,003 i, 135 f, 30 org, UK / 8 i, 33 f, 17 org, o'seas
- ¶ NL - 2; ftm.   AR; ftm, £2 nm.
  Information sheets - 8/10; m only.

Procurators Fiscal Society   1930
- NR c/o Emma Knox, Crown Office, 25 Chambers St, EDINBURGH, EH1 1LA.   (hsb)
  email fdasecretary@copfs.gsi.gov.uk
  Sec: Emma Knox
- ○ *P; [in Scotland the Procurator Fiscal is the name for the public prosecutor who also does the same work as a Coroner elsewhere]
  is a division of the Association of First Division Civil Servants

Producers Alliance for Cinema & Television   (PACT)   1991
- NR Procter House, 1 Procter St, LONDON, WC1V 6DW.   (hq)
  020 7067 4367
  http://www.pact.co.uk
- ○ *P, *T; for independent film & television producers in the UK
- M f

Production Managers Association   1991
- NR Ealing Studios, Ealing Green, LONDON, W5 5EP.   (hq)
  020 8758 8699
  Admin: Caroline Fleming
- ○ *P; for film, TV & video production managers
- < Producers Alliance for Cinema & Television (PACT)
- M c 180 i
- ¶ The Bottom Line - 6.
  Directory of Members - 1.

Production Services Association   (PSA)   1994
- ■ PO Box 2709, BATH, BA1 3YS.   (hq)
  01225 332668   fax 01225 332701
  email admin@psa.org.uk   http://www.psa.org.uk
  Gen Mgr: Andy Lenthall
- ▲ Company Limited by Guarantee
- ○ *T; to make representations to government & the EU on matters affecting the live music, events & entertainment industry
- Gp Training & qualification development in the BTEC award system
- ● Conf - ET - Exhib - LG
- M c 500

Professional Anglers Association Ltd   (PAA)
- ■ Federation House, STONELEIGH, Warks, CV8 2RF.   (hq)
  024 7641 4999   fax 024 7641 4990
  email paa@sportsandplay.com   http://www.paauk.com
  Sec: Shaun Gilbert
- ▲ Company Limited by Guarantee
- ○ *P; to represent accredited angling coaches
- ● ET
- < a group of the Fedn of Sports & Play Assns (FSPA)
- M 130 i

Professional Association of Alexander Teachers   (PAAT)   1987
- ■ The Big Peg (room 706), 120 Vyse St, BIRMINGHAM, B18 6NF.   (hq)
  01743 356274
  http://www.paat.org.uk
  Hon Sec: Liz Tunnicliffe
- ▲ Un-incorporated Society
- ○ *P; to support members who are teachers of the Alexander Technique; to promote the Alexander Technique which provides a practical means for change by bringing about an improvement in physical balance & coordination
- ● ET
- M 48 i
- ¶ Pamphlets.

Professional Association for Catering Education
  styles itself **PACE**

Professional Association for Children's Guardians & Children & Family Reporters & Independent Social Workers
  alternative name of **NAGALRO**

Professional Association of Clinical Therapists
  a committee of the **Federation of Holistic Therapists**

Professional Association of Legal Services   (PALS)   2002
- NR 2 Cowan Close, BURNHAM-on-SEA, Somerset, TA8 2TG.
  email secretary@thepals.org.uk
- ○ *P; to represent licensed agents & consultants in England & Wales
- ● Inf
- M i

Professional Association of Nursery Nurses
  on 28 February 2008 merged with the Professional Association of Teachers and Professionals Allied to Teaching to become **Voice**

Professional Association of Teachers
  on 28 February 2008 merged with Professionals Allied to Teaching and the Professional Association of Nursery Nurses to become **Voice**

Professional Associations Research Network   (PARN)   1998
- ■ 16 Great George St, BRISTOL, BS1 5RH.   (hq)
  0117-929 4515   fax 0117-934 9623
  email info@parnglobal.com
  http://www.parnglobal.com
  Dir: Andy Friedman
- ▲ Company Limited by Guarantee
- ○ *N, *P; 'the centre of expertise on issues relating to professionalism & the professionalisation of professional bodies. To provide a research enriched network for professional associations & a range of specialist knowledge based services'
- Gp CPD Network; Consultancy & information services
- ● Conf - ET - Res - Inf - Lib - Consultancy - Publications - Networking
- M 150 org
- ¶ CPD Spotlight (NL) - 12; ftm only.
  PARN Members News Update - 12; ftm only
  PARN Research Publications - 2; ftm, £50-£95 nm.

Professional Boatmans Association   1991
- NR 48 Loveys Rd, Yapton, ARUNDEL, W Sussex, BN18 0HG.   (hq)
  01243 551927
  http://www.pba.org.uk
  Sec: Daniel Parker

Professional Bodyguard Association   (PBA)   1985
NR   PO Box 532, DURHAM, DH1 9DW.   (hq)
      07970 948811
      http://www.professionalbodyguardassociation.co.uk
      Hon Sec: M J Tombs
▲   Un-incorporated Society
○   *P; for the training of bodyguards
●   ET
<   Amer Soc of Law Enforcement Trainers (ASLET)
M   1,000 i, UK / 300 i, o'seas

**Professional Business & Technical Management   (PBTM)
1983**
■   Warwick Corner, 42 Warwick Rd, KENILWORTH, Warks,
      CV8 1HE.   (asa)
      01926 855498   fax 01926 513100
      email info@group-ims.com   http://www.group-ims.com
      Pres & Hon Sec: Prof H J Manners
○   *P; to provide a link between business & technology; to keep
      members informed of new developments, controls, methods,
      techniques & education in business & technical fields
Gp   Business; Technology; Management
●   ET - Exam
<   Inst Management Specialists; Inst Manufacturing
M   [not stated]
¶   Professional Business & Technical Management (Jnl) - 3; £3 m,
      £7 nm.

Professional Charter Association   (PCA)   1991
■   The Glass Works, Penns Rd, PETERSFIELD, Hants, GU32 2EW.
      (hq)
      01730 710425   fax 01730 710423
      email info@ybdsa.co.uk   http://www.ybdsa.co.uk
      Chmn: Robin Milledge
○   *T; to represent professional skippers & vessel owners whose
      principal activity is skippered charter in domestic waters
●   Mtgs - LG - Social events
<   Yacht Brokers, Designers & Surveyors Assn
M   25 f
¶   [in the YBDSA Ybk - 2 yrly.]

Professional Coarse Fisheries Association   (PCFA)   2005
■   Federation House, STONELEIGH, Warks, CV8 2RF.   (hq)
      024 7641 4999 ext 204   fax 024 7641 4990
      email enquiries@pcfa.co.uk   http://www.pcfa.co.uk
      Assn Mgr: Milly Durrant
▲   Un-incorporated Society
○   *T; professional coarse fisheries in the UK
Gp   Fishery managers
●   Conf - Mtgs - ET - Res - SG - Stat - LG
<   Angling Foundation; Brit Disabled Anglers Assn; Nat Fedn of
      Anglers
>   Fedn of Sports & Play Assns
M   i, f & org
      (Sub: £100)
¶   FSPA Members' Directory - 1; free.
      (www.sportsandplay.com)
×   2005 Commercial Coarse Fisheries Association

Professional Computing Association   (PCA)   1993
■   PO Box 48, ROYSTON, Herts, SG8 6JS.   (hq)
      0845 634 9245   fax 0845 635 9247
      email admin@pcauk.org   http://www.pcassocietion.org
      Exec Dir: Keith Warburton
▲   Company Limited by Guarantee
○   *T; to promote, represent & provide services & information for
      businesses in the personal computer marketplace; to provide
      consumer advice & protection
Gp   Personal Computer Direct Marketers' Association; Payment
      protection scheme
●   Conf - Mtgs - ET - Inf - LG
M   155 f, 2 org
¶   Interface (NL) - 12; ftm, £50 nm.   AR; ftm.
      EMC Guidance Notes (notes on EC Guidelines); ftm, £30 nm.
×   2004 Personal Computer Association

Professional Contractors Group Ltd   (PCG)   1999
NR   Heathrow Boulevard, 280 Bath Rd, WEST DRAYTON, Middx,
      UB7 0DQ.   (hq)
      0845 125 9899   fax 020 8622 3200
      email admin@pcg.org.uk   http://www.pcg.org.uk
      Chmn: David Ramsden
▲   Company Limited by Guarantee
○   *T; to represent the interests & to promote the use of
      independent contractors & consultants, & to ensure the sector
      retains a professional image; to make representations to
      Government for legislation affecting independent contractors;
      to help members cope with the burden of new legislation,
      particularly IR35; to oppose IR35
Gp   Aberdeen Working Party (AWP); Associate members
●   Conf - Mtgs - LG - Legal / accounting / tax technical advice
<   Assn Technology Staffing Cos (ATSCO); Confedn Brit Ind (CBI);
      Fedn Small Businesses (FSB); Inst Chart Accountants (ICAEW);
      Inst Directors (IoD); Recruitment & Employment
      Confedn (REC); Tax Faculty / Inst Taxation
M   c 14,000 f
¶   NL (email only) - irreg; ftm.

Professional Council for Religious Education
      since 2008 the **National Association of Teachers of Religious
Education**

Professional Cricketers' Association   (PCA)   1967
NR   5 Utopia Village, 7 Chalcot Rd, LONDON, NW1 8LH.   (hq)
      020 7449 4221   fax 020 7586 8520
      Chief Exec: Sean Morris
○   *S; for current & past professional cricketers
M   420 i

Professional Darts Players Association   (PDPA)
■   Federation House, STONELEIGH PARK, Warks, CV8 2RF.   (hq)
      024 7669 3360   fax 024 7641 4990
      http://www.pdpa.co.uk
      Chmn: Peter Manley
○   *P
<   a group of the Fedn of Sports & Play Assns (FSPA)
M   i

Professional Footballers Association   (PFA)   1907
■   20 Oxford Court, Bishopsgate, MANCHESTER, M2 3WQ.   (hq)
      0161-236 0575   fax 0161-228 7229
      email info@thepfa.co.uk
      http://www.givemefootball.com
      Chief Exec: Gordon Taylor
○   *U
●   Conf - Mtgs - ET - Res - Empl - LG
<   Intl Assn of Football Players Us (FIFPro)
M   4,000 i
¶   The Players Jnl - 4;   The Players Club - 4;   AR; all ftm only.

Professional Footballers' Association Scotland   (PFA Scotland)
NR   Woodside House, 20-23 Woodside Place, GLASGOW, G3 7QF.
      0141-582 1301   fax 0141-582 1303
      email info@pfascotland.co.uk
      http://www.pfascotland.co.uk
      Sec: Fraser Wishart

Professional Gardeners' Guild (PGG) 1977
■ 34 Fitz Rd, COCKERMOUTH, Cumbria, CA13 0AN. (hsp/b)
  01900 824377
  email svetasker@sparker4.fsnet.co.uk
  Hon Sec: Sue Tasker
▲ Un-incorporated Society
Br 4; Ireland, USA, worldwide
○ *H, *P; to promote & encourage professional contact,
  communication & cooperation between gardeners,
  exchanging ideas & information on all aspects of
  professional gardening, including the use of both new
  technology & traditional skills; to promote gardening as a
  profession, & the better management & maintenance of
  gardens & designed landscapes, especially those of historic,
  horticultural & botanical value
● Conf - Mtgs - ET - Res - Exhib - Comp - SG - Stat - Inf - VE -
  Empl - LG - Training bursary - Job opportunities - Advice -
  Industry representation
< Historic Houses Assn; Nat Trust; English Heritage; Garland
M 800+ i, c 10 f, c 30 org, UK / 100+ i, o'seas
¶ The Professional Gardener (Jnl) - 4; £25 m, £36 nm,
  £40 companies, £48 libraries.

Professional Golfers' Association (1GA) 1901
■ Centenary House, The Belfry, SUTTON COLDFIELD,
  W Midlands, B76 9PT. (hq)
  01675 470333   fax 01675 477888
  Chief Exec: Sandy Jones
Br 7 regions
○ *P, *S; to promote interest in golf
Gp Tournament section; Membership services; Development section
● Conf - Mtgs - ET - Exam - Comp - Stat - Inf - Lib - PL - Empl -
  Securing sponsorship for members tournaments
M 6,500 i, 1,200 trainees, UK / 900 i, o'seas
¶ Profile (Jnl) - 12; ftm, £35 yr nm.
  The PGA Ybk - 1; ftm only.   Regional Hbks - 1; ftm only.

Professional Guild of After Dinner Speakers 1983
■ 12 Little Bornes, Dulwich, LONDON, SE21 8SE. (dir/b)
  020 8670 5585
  http://www.ivorspencer.com
▲ Un-incorporated Society
○ *P; 'engages the finest after dinner speakers on an international
  basis for clients worldwide'
● Conf - Mtgs
< Gld of Profl After Dinner Speakers; Gld of Intl Profl
  Toastmasters
M 15 i

Professional Jockeys Association (PJA) 1969
■ 39b Kingfisher Court, Hambridge Rd, NEWBURY, Berks,
  RG14 5SJ. (hq)
  01635 44102   fax 01635 37932
  email info@thepja.co.uk   http://www.thepja.co.uk
  Sec: Ann Saunders,   Chief Exec: Josh Apiafi
▲ Company Limited by Guarantee
○ *P, *S; to promote facilities for professional jockeys; to negotiate
  on their behalf with racing authorities
M i
  Registered name: Jockeys Association of Great Britain Ltd

Professional Lighting & Sound Association (PLASA) 1977
■ Redoubt House, 1 Edward Rd, EASTBOURNE, E Sussex,
  BN23 8AS. (hq)
  01323 524120   fax 01323 524121
  email info@plasa.org   http://www.plasa.org
  Exec Dir: Ruth Rossington
▲ Company Limited by Guarantee
○ *T; to serve the entertainment, leisure, communication &
  architectural industries
● Exhib - Expt - Inf - Lib - VE - LG - Members deliver technical &
  creative solutions to clients & projects worldwide
< Wld Entertainment Technology Fedn (WETF)
M 60 i, 457 f, 7 educational, 10 affiliates
¶ Lighting & Sound International - 11; ftm, £30 yr nm.
  Lighting & Sound America - 12; ftm, controlled nm.   AR; ftm.
  Membership News - 12;   Standards News - 12; both ftm only.

**Professional Photographic Laboratories Association (PPLA)
1984**
NR Wisteria House, 28 Fulling Mill Lane, WELWYN, Herts,
  AL6 9NS.
  0870 240 4542
▲ Company Limited by Guarantee
○ *P, *T; to support professional photographic & imaging centres
● Conf - Exhib - Inf - Lib - VE
< Photo Marketing Assn Intl (USA)
M 250 f
¶ Lablink (NL) - 6; ftm.

Professional Plant Users Group (PPUG)
NR c/o Landscape Institute, 33 Great Portland St, LONDON,
  W1W 8QG.
  020 7299 4500
○ *H, *P; professional & trade bodies using plants in landscaping

Professional Players Federation (PPF)
NR 10 Bow Lane (3rd floor), LONDON, EC4M 9AL. (hq)
  020 7236 5148   fax 020 7329 3355
  http://www.ppf.org.uk
  Gen Sec: Simon Taylor
▲ Un-incorporated Society
○ *P, *S; for professional sports players' organisations
● Conf - Mtgs - Res - Stat - LG
M 14 org
✕ 2007 Institute of Professional Sport

Professional Rugby Players Association (PRA) 1998
NR Regal House (7th floor), London Rd, TWICKENHAM, Middx,
  TW1 3QS. (hq)
  020 8831 7930
  Chief Exec: Damien Hopley
○ *P, *S; to represent professional Rugby Union players
● Mtgs
M i

Professional Services Marketing Group
NR Regent House (Studio 3), 18 Lombard Rd, LONDON,
  SW11 3RB. (asa)
  020 7924 6047
  http://www.psmg.co.uk
  Admin: Carol Strath

Professional Speakers Association (PSA)
NR 12 Russell Close, UTTOXETER, Staffs, ST14 8HZ. (hq)
  0845 370 0504   fax 0845 370 0503
  http://www.professionalspeakers.org
  Admin Mgr: Sue Cliff
○ *T
● Mtgs
M i

*Professional Trades Union for Prison, Correctional & Secure Psychiatric
  Workers*
  alternative name of **POA**

Professionals Allied to Teaching
 on 28 February 2008 merged with the Professional Association of Nursery Nurses amd the Professional Association of Teachers to become **Voice**

Promota (UK) Ltd (Promotional Merchandise Trade Association) 1958
- ■ Concorde House, Trinity Park, SOLIHULL, W Midlands, B37 7UQ. (asa)
 0845 371 4345 fax 0845 371 4336
 email info@promota.co.uk   http://www.promota.co.uk
 Sec: Annette Scott
- ▲ Company Limited by Guarantee
- ○ *T; 'to promote & further the interests of businesses engaged in the promotional merchandise trade'
- ● Conf - Exhib
- M 735 f, UK / 108 f, o'seas
- ¶ Promota Bulletin - 6; ftm.

Promotional Merchandise Trade Association
 alternative name of **Promota (UK) Ltd**

Property Care Association (PCA) 2006
- NR Lakeview Court, Ermine Business Park, HUNTINGDON, Cambs, PE29 6XR. (hq)
 0870 121 6737 fax 01480 417587
 email pca@property-care.org
 http://www.property-care.org
 Chief Exec: Yasmin Chopin
- ○ *T; structural waterproofing, damp proofing, timber preservation, structural maintenance, flooding
- Gp Structural Waterproofing Group
- ✕ 2006 Brit Wood Preserving & Damp-proofing Assn

Property Consultants Society Ltd (PCS) 1954
- NR 1 Surrey St (basement office), ARUNDEL, W Sussex, BN18 9DT. (hq)
 01903 883787 fax 01903 889590
 email pcs@p-c-s.org.uk
 Sec: David J May
- ▲ Company Limited by Guarantee
- ○ *P; a central organisation for qualified surveyors, architects, valuers, auctioneers, land & estate agents, master builders & constructional engineers who practise as consultants
- ● Stat - Inf
- M 550 i, UK / 70 i, o'seas
- ¶ NL - 4;   LM - irreg;   AR - 1; all ftm only.

Proprietary Acoustic Systems Manufacturers (PASM)
- NR Adam St, off Lever St, BOLTON, Lancs, BL3 2AP.
 01204 380074 fax 01204 380957
 email info@pasm.org.uk   http://www.pasm.org.uk
- ○ *T; for manufacturers of proprietary acoustic (sound-proofing & insulation) products
- M 9 f

Proprietary Association of Great Britain (PAGB) 1919
- ■ Vernon House, Sicilian Ave, LONDON, WC1A 2QS. (hq)
 020 7242 8331 fax 020 7405 7719
 email info@pagb.co.uk   http://www.pagb.co.uk
 Co Sec: Marion Fergusson
- ▲ Company Limited by Guarantee
- ○ *T; to represent manufacturers of branded over-the-counter (OTC) medicines & food supplements
- ● Conf - Mtgs - ET - Exam - Res - Inf - LG
- M 40 f, 35 f associates
- ¶ This Week (NL) - 52; ftm only.   AR; free.

Prospect 2001
- NR New Prospect House, 8 Leake St, LONDON, SE1 7NN. (hq)
 020 7902 6600
 http://www.prospect.org.uk
 Gen Sec: Paul Noon
- ○ *P, *U; interests & professional knowledge of members in the UK Civil Service & public & private sectors
- ● Conf - Mtgs - ET - Res - Inf - Lib - Empl - Campaigning
- M c 102,000 i

Prostate Cancer Support Association (PSA) 1995
- ■ BM Box 9434, LONDON, WC1N 3XX. (asa)
 0845 601 0766
 email psasec@atlworld.com
 http://www.prostatecancersupport.info
 Hon Sec: Philip Barnard
- ▲ Registered Charity
- Br 4
- ○ *N, *W; regional & local self-help & support groups; it is managed by & for men with prostate cancer, their families & those who are interested in improving the care & support of those affected by this form of cancer
- ● Mtgs - Inf
- < USTOOI Intl; Prostate Cancer Support Fedn
- M 229 i
 (Sub: £12)
- ¶ NL - 1; ftm.

Protestant Alliance (PA) 1845
- NR 77 Ampthill Rd, FLITWICK, Beds, MK45 1BD. (hsp/b)
 01525 712348 fax 01525 712348
 Sec: Dr S J Scott-Pearson
- ○ *R; Protestant theology & history
- M i

Protestant Reformation Society (PRS) 1827
- NR PO Box 47, RAMSGATE, Kent, CT11 9XB. (hsp)
 01843 580542
 Gen Sec: Dr D A Scales
- ○ *R; to promote the religious principles of the Reformation
- M i
- ¶ NL - 3.

Protestant Truth Society (Inc) (PTS) 1889
- NR 184 Fleet St, LONDON, EC4A 2HJ
 020 7405 4960
 email info@protestant-truth.org
 Sec: G Rae
- ▲ Company Limited by Guarantee; Registered Charity
- ○ *K, *R; 'for the promotion & protection of the Protestant reformed faith'
- ● Conf - Mtgs - Exhib - Comp - VE - Providing preachers for church services & deputation meetings
- M 55 i
- ¶ Protestant Truth - 6.

Provincial Booksellers Fairs Association (PBFA) 1974
- ■ The Old Coach House, 16 Melbourn St, ROYSTON, Herts, SG8 7BZ. (hq)
 01763 248400 fax 01763 248921
 email info@pbfa.org   http://www.pbfa.org
 Admin: Ms Becky Wears
- ▲ Un-incorporated Society
- ○ *T; to promote interest in the collection & sale of antiquarian & secondhand books by organising book fairs, exhibitions, lectures & seminars; to publish books on book collecting
- ● Conf - Exhib - Inf - Book fairs
 Book fairs information: 01763 249212
- M 703 f, UK / 47 f, o'seas
- ¶ NL - 10; ftm only.
 Calendar of Book Fairs - 1; Fair Catalogues; both free.
 Book Collecting; ABC of Book Collecting; both £12.95
 Directory of Antiquarian & Second Hand Booksellers - 1; ftm, £4.00 nm.

Provincial Hospital Services Association   (PHSA)   1919
§   14 St Cuthbert's Street, BEDFORD, MK40 3JU.   (hq)
      01234 267371   fax 01234 218174
      http://www.phsa.org.uk
      A not-for-profit insurance company specialising exclusively in
      corporate and individual healthcare plans.

Provision Trade Federation   (PTF)   1976
■   17 Clerkenwell Green, LONDON, EC1R 0DP.   (hq)
      020 7253 2114   fax 020 7608 1645
      email info@provtrade.co.uk
      http://www.provtrade.co.uk
      Dir Gen: Mrs Clare Cheney
▲   Company Limited by Guarantee
○   *T; for the provision trade & allied trades in the UK
Gp   Bacon & pigmeat; Canned foods; Chilled & processed meats;
      Dairy products; Export; Speciality cheese; Yoghurt & short life
      dairy products
●   Mtgs - Stat - Inf - LG - Annual dinner
<   Food & Drink Fedn (FDF); EUCOLAIT; Tr Assn Forum
M   130 f
¶   Ybk; free.

PSHE Association   2007
■   8 Wakley St, LONDON, EC1V 7QE.   (hq)
      020 7843 1916
      email info@pshe-association.org.uk
      http://www.pshe-association.org.uk
      Mgr: Sarah Smart
▲   Company Limited by Guarantee
○   *P; to raise the status, quality and impact of PSHE (Personal
      Social Health & Economic) education
Gp   Teachers; Local authority advisers
●   Conf - Mtgs - ET - Res - Inf - Lib - LG
<   DCSF - Dept for Children Schools & Families
M   226 i, 577 f, 112 org

Psoriasis Association   1968
■   Dick Coles House, 2 Queensbridge, NORTHAMPTON,
      NN4 7BF.   (hq)
      01604 251620   fax 01604 251621
      email mail@psoriasis.demon.co.uk
      Chief Exec: Mrs Gladys Edwards
▲   Registered Charity
Br   12
○   *W; all matters relating to psoriasis & psoriatic arthritis
●   Conf - Res - Inf - LG
<   Eur Psoriasis Assns (EUROPSO); Assn Med Res
      Charities (AMRC); Long Term Med Conditions Alliance
      (LMCA); Nat Coun Voluntary Orgs
M   5,020 i, 10 f, UK / 80 i, o'seas
¶   Psoriasis (Jnl) - 4; ftm.

Psoriasis & Psoriatic Arthritis Alliance   (PAPAA)   2007
NR   PO Box 111, ST ALBANS, Herts, AL2 3JQ.   (hq)
      0870 770 3212   fax 0870 770 3213
      email info@papaa.org   http://www.papaa.org
      Chief Exec: David Chandler
▲   Company Limited by Guarantee; Registered Charity
○   *W; to raise awareness of & help people with psoriatic arthritis
      & its associated skin disorder, psoriasis
●   Conf - ET - Exhib - Inf - LG
<   Intl Fedn Psoriasis Assns; All Party Parliamentary Gp for Skin;
      Brit League against Rheumatism
M   [subscribers]
¶   Skin 'n' Bones Connection (Jnl) - 2; £3.
      Psoriatic Care Fact File - ongoing; £9.50.
      Leaflets & booklets.
✕   2007 (Psoriatic Arthropathy Alliance
          (Psoriasis Support Trust

Psoriatic Arthropathy Alliance
      in 2007 joined with the Psoriasis Support Trust to form the **Psoriasis
      & Psoriatic Arthritis Alliance**

PSP Association   1994
NR   PSP House, 167 Watling St West, TOWCESTER, Northants,
      NN12 6BX.
      01327 322410   fax 01327 322412
      email psp@pspeur.org   http://www.pspeur.org
      Chief Exec: Jane Hardy
○   *W; PSP - progressive supranuclear palsy, the progressive death
      of neurons in the brain

Psychiatric Rehabilitation Association   (PRA)   1959
■   Bayford Mews, Bayford St, LONDON, E8 3SF.   (hq)
      020 8985 3570   fax 020 8986 1334
      email ppra528898@aol.com
      http://www.pra-services.4mg.com
      Chief Exec: Mirella Manni
▲   Registered Charity
Br   14
○   *W; to promote mental health & improve attitudes towards the
      mentally ill
Gp   Art training; Computer training; Counselling; European
      networking; Stress management
●   ET - Exam - Res - Exhib - SG - Inf - VE - Provision of day
      centres, work programmes, residential care
M   2,000 i
¶   NL - 4; ftm, £10 yr nm.   AR - 1; free.

Psychological Society of Ireland   1970
IRL   CX House, 2A Corn Exchange Place, Poolbeg St, DUBLIN 2,
      Republic of Ireland.
      353 (1) 474 9160   fax 353 (1) 474 9161
      email info@psihq.ie   http://www.psihq.ie
○   *P

Public & Commercial Services Union   (PCS)   1998
■   160 Falcon Rd, LONDON, SW11 2LN.   (hq)
      020 7924 2727   fax 020 7924 1847
      email info@pcs.org.uk   http://www.pcs.org.uk
      Gen Sec: Mark Serwotka
▲   Un-incorporated Society
Br   1,000
○   *U; to represent civil & public servants
●   Conf - Mtgs - ET - Res - Inf - Empl - LG
<   Public Services Intl (PSI); Trade Union Congress (TUC)
M   320,000 i
¶   PCS View - 12; ftm only.   AR - 1; free.
✕   2005 (merged) Association of Magisterial Officers

** Public Contractors Association
      Organisation lost: see Introduction paragraph 3.

Public Fundraising Regulatory Association   (PFRA)   2001
■   Unit 11 Europoint, 5-11 Lavington St, LONDON, SE1 0NZ.
      (hq)
      020 7401 8452   fax 020 7928 2925
      email info@pfra.org.uk   http://www.pfra.org.uk
      Chief Exec: Michael Aldridge
▲   Company Limited by Guarantee
○   *K, *N; to regulate the 'face-to-face' fundraising by charities &
      professional fundraising organisations; works with local
      authorities to ensure that fundraising sites are used
      appropriately
●   Mtgs - Res - SG - Stat - Inf - LG - Accreditation scheme -
      Monitoring of compliance - Complaints processing &
      resolution - Mystery shopping
M   1 i, 16 f, 114 org
¶   AR - 1; free.

Public Management & Policy Association   (PMPA)   1998
NR   3 Robert St, LONDON, WC2N 6RL.
      020 7543 5600
○   *P; for managers & policy-makers within the public services; is
      managed by the Chartered Institute of Public Finance &
      Accountancy

Public Monuments & Sculpture Association   (PMSA)   1991
■   c/o Courtauld Institute of Art, Somerset House, Strand,
      LONDON, WC2R 0RN.   (hq)
      020 7485 4688
      email pmsa@pmsa.org.uk   http://www.pmsa.org.uk
      Chief Exec: Jo Darke
▲   Company Limited by Guarantee; Registered Charity
○   *A, *G, *L; to record, preserve, research & enhance public
      appreciation of all aspects of public sculpture & monuments
Gp National Recording Project (NRP); Save our Sculpture
      Campaign; Custodians Handbook; The Sculpture Journal;
      the Marsh Award for public sculpture
●   Conf - Mtgs - Res - Inf - VE
<   Ancient Monuments Soc; Art & Architecture; Brit Sundial Soc;
      Fountain Soc; Historic GArdens Foundation; Landscape &
      Arts Network; R Brit Soc Sculptors; Soc of Portrait Sculptors;
      Twentieth Century Soc
M   228 i, UK / 10 i, 35 f, o'seas
¶   The Sculpture Jnl - 2; ftm, £35 nm.
      Public Sculpture of Britain (a series of volumes describing in
      detail the national heritage of public sculpture); £19.95 -
      £52.95.

Public Relations Consultants Association   (PRCA)   1969
NR Willow House, Willow Place, LONDON, SW1P 1JH.   (hq)
      020 7233 6026
      http://www.prca.org.uk
      Dir Gen: Patrick Barrow
▲   Company Limited by Guarantee
○   *P; the maintenance of ethics & standards throughout the
      industry
Gp Government; Market sector; Finance directors c'ee; Scottish
      Public Relations Consultants Assn
●   Conf - Mtgs - ET - Res - Comp - Inf - Lib - Empl
<   Intl C'ee of Public Relations Consultancies Assns Ltd (ICO)
M   160 f
¶   Public Relations Consultancy (Ybk) - 1.

Public Relations Consultants Association (Ireland)   (PRCA)
IRL 78 Merrion Square, DUBLIN 2, Republic of Ireland.
      353 (1) 661 8004   fax 353 (1) 676 4562
      email info@prca.ie   http://www.prca.ie
      Chmn: Mark Cahalane
○   *P
M   34 f

Public Relations Institute of Ireland   (PRII)   1953
IRL 78 Merrion Sq, DUBLIN 2, Republic of Ireland.
      353 (1) 661 8004   fax 353 (1) 676 4562
      email info@prii.ie   http://www.prii.ie
      Chief Exec: Gerry Davis
○   *P

Public Sector People Managers' Association   (PPMA)   1975
NR Mount Lavina, 195 Canterbury Rd, BIRCHINGTON, Kent,
      CT7 9AH.   (hq)
      01843 848050
      email john.tonks@ppma.org.uk   http://www.ppma.org.uk
      Exec Officer: John Tonks
▲   Un-incorporated Society
Br 17
○   *P
Gp Recruitment training & development; Industrial relations &
      conditions of service; Performance review organisation &
      planning; Equal opportunities
●   Conf - Mtgs - ET - Res - Exhib - Comp - SG - Stat - Inf - Empl
<   Inst Personnel Managers Assn (USA)
M   500 i
¶   NL - 4;   AR; both free.   Various technical publications.
✕   2006 Society of Chief Personnel Officers in Local Government

Public Services Network   (PSnet)   2001
■   19 Shepperton Close, Great Billing, NORTHAMPTON,
      NN3 9NT.   (regd off)
      01604 401726   fax 01604 414366
      email ossie@psnet.org.uk   http://www.psnet.org.uk
      Exec Dir: Oswald A Dodds
▲   Company Limited by Guarantee
Br 10
○   *P; promotion of best practice in management & delivery of
      public services
●   Conf - Mtgs - ET - Res - Exhib - SG - Inf - LG
M   100 public bodies
      (Sub: £15 retired, £900 f, £450 public bodies)
¶   Publications on web.

Publicity Club of London   (PCL)   1913
NR Sheraton House, 15-19 Great Chapel St, LONDON,
      W1F 8FN.   (chmn/b)
      020 7734 5666   fax 020 7734 9666
      http://www.thepcl.co.uk
○   *P; a cross-discipline organisation with members from
      advertising, direct marketing, marketing, new media, PR &
      the media in the London area
●   Mtgs - Exhib - VE
M   500 i

Publishers Association   (PA)   1896
■   29b Montague St, LONDON, WC1B 5BW.   (hq)
      020 7691 9191   fax 020 7691 9199
      email mail@publishers.org.uk
      http://www.publishers.org.uk
      Chief Exec: Simon Juden
▲   Company Limited by Guarantee
○   *T; to represent interests of UK publishers in books, book
      related material & journals to governments, other bodies in
      the trade & the public at large
Gp Educational Publishers Council (EPC); Academic & Professional
      Publishers; Trade Publishers Council; International
●   Conf - Mtgs - Exhib - Stat - Expt - Inf - LG
M   180 f
¶   LM (CAPP) - 1;   LM (EPC) - 1; both free.
      Book Trade Year Book - 1; £10 m, £50 nm.

Publishers Licensing Society   (PLS)   1981
■   37-41 Gower St, LONDON, WC1E 6HH.   (hq)
      020 7299 7730   fax 020 7299 7780
      email pls@pls.org.uk   http://www.pls.org.uk
      Chief Exec: Dr Alicia Wise,   Mgr: Caroline Elmslie
▲   Company Limited by Guarantee
○   *T; formed jointly by the Association of Learned & Professional
      Society Publishers, the Periodical Publishers Association & the
      Publishers Association to protect & enforce publishers' rights
      in copyright of all published works (by means of
      reprographic reproduction); to distribute royalties from such
      reproduction
<   Intl Fedn of Reproduction Rights Orgs; Copyright Licensing
      Agency
M   1,800 f
¶   PLS Plus (NL) - 3;   AR - 1; both ftm only.

Publishing Scotland   1973
NR   Scottish Book Centre, 137 Dundee St, EDINBURGH,
        EH11 1BG.   (hq)
        0131-228 6866   fax 0131-228 3220
        email enquiries@publishingscotland.org
        http://www.publishingscotland.org
        Chief Exec: Marion Sinclair
▲   Registered Charity
○   *T; to provide information, advice, consultancy, training,
        marketing & promotional services
Gp   Scot Book Marketing Gp (publicity & marketing service for
        booksellers in Scotland)
●   ET - Inf - LG - Attending bookfairs, both domestic & overseas;
        Marketing & export advice; Promotional services
M   72 f
¶   Directory of Publishing in Scotland - 1; £9.99.
×   2007 Scottish Publishers Association

Pugin Gild   1974
■   157 Vicarage Rd, LONDON, E10 5DU.   (hq)
        020 8539 3876   fax 020 8539 3876
        email keys@fsmail.net
        Sec: Ronald King
▲   Un-incorporated Society
○   *L; to promote Christian architecture, crafts & guild system
●   Res - SG - Inf - Lib - PL

Pugin Society   1995
■   33 Montcalm House, Westferry Rd, LONDON, E14 3SD.   (hsp)
        020 7515 9474
        email pamcole@madasafish.com
        http://www.pugin-society.org
        Hon Sec: Pam Cole
▲   Registered Charity
○   *G; to study the work of Augustus Welby Pugin (181201852) &
        other designers of the Victorian period; to report on buildings
        at risk (eg churches being demolished or changed from
        original design)
●   Mtgs - Res - Exhib - Inf - VE - Annual 4-day study tour
<   Victorian Soc; Pugin Foundation (Australia)
>   Enniscorthy Pugin Soc (Ireland)
M   460 i, UK / 40 i, o'seas, also corporate
        (Sub: £15 i, UK / £25 i, o'seas / corporate)
¶   True Principles - 1; ftm, £5 nm.
        Present State - 1; ftm, £5 nm.

Pullet Hatcheries Association   (PHA)   1985
■   89 Charterhouse St (2nd floor), LONDON, EC1M 6HR.   (hq)
        020 7608 3760   fax 020 7608 3860
        email Louisa.Platt@britisheggindustrycouncil.com
        http://www.britegg.co.uk
        Sec: Louisa Platt
▲   Company Limited by Guarantee
○   *T
●   Mtgs - LG
M   8 f

Pullet Rearers Association   (PRA)   1983
■   89 Charterhouse St (2nd floor), LONDON, EC1M 6HR.   (hq)
        020 7608 3760   fax 020 7608 3860
        email Louisa.Platt@britisheggindustrycouncil.com
        http://www.britegg.co.uk
        Sec: Louisa Platt
▲   Company Limited by Guarantee
○   *T; for pullet rearers & shell egg producers
●   Mtgs - LG
<   Brit Egg Ind Coun; Pullet Hatcheries Assn
M   13 f

Pulmonary Hypertension Association   (PHA)
NR   Unit 3a Enterprise Court, Farfield Park, MANVERS, S Yorks,
        S63 5DB.
        01709 761450   fax 01709 761450
        http://www.phassociation.uk.com
○   *M

Pulp & Paper Fundamental Research Society   (FRC)   c1984
■   5 Frecheville Court, BURY, Lancs, BL9 0UF.   (hq)
        0161-764 5858   fax 0161-764 5353
        email frc@pita.co.uk   http://www.ppfrs.org.uk
▲   Company Limited by Guarantee; Registered Charity
○   *Q; to promote research & education in the pulp & paper
        industry; its principal activity is the organising of four-yearly
        symposia, alternately in the universities of Oxford &
        Cambridge
●   Conf
M   10 i, UK / 6 i, o'seas
¶   Proceedings of each symposia - 4 yrly; £135.

Pump Distributors Association   (PDA)   1985
■   5 Chapelfield, Orford, WOODBRIDGE, Suffolk, IP12 2HW.
        (chief exec/p)
        fax 01394 450181
        email pumps@the-pda.com   http://www.the-pda.com
        Chief Exec: Ian Castle
▲   Un-incorporated Society
○   *T; to represent firms who distribute industrial pumps, install
        pumps & repair them
Gp   Pump training in conjunction with the British Pump
        Manufacturers' Association
●   Conf - Mtgs - ET - Inf
M   28 f, UK / 1 f, o'seas
¶   NL - 2; free.

Punch & Judy College of Professors
■   2 Pembury Road, WORTHING, W Sussex, BN14 7DN.
        01903 200 364
        email enquiries@punchandjudy.org
        http://www.punchandjudy.org
        Coordinator: Glyn Edwards
○   *D
<   Worldwide Friends of Punch & Judy
M   12 i

Purine Metabolic Patients Association   (PUMPA)   1992
■   Pumpa Purine Research Unit, South Wing (3rd floor), St
        Thomas' Hospital, LONDON, SE1 7EH.   (hq)
        020 7188 1276
        email info@pumpa.org.uk   http://www.pumpa.org.uk
▲   Registered Charity
○   *W; to increase awareness of the 28 genetic nucleotide
        disorders under the PUMPA umbrella which include
        compulsive self-biting, kidney disease & fatal infections; to
        improve diagnosis & develop treatments Europe-wide
Gp   Patient contact Lesch-Nyhan disease; Familial juvenile gout
●   Conf - Mtgs - ET - Res
<   Intl Fedn of Clinical Chemists; Contact a Family; Lesch-Nyhan
        Action C'ee
M   i
¶   Publications list available on request.

Pushkin Club   1954

■   5A Bloomsbury Sq, LONDON, WC1A 2TA.   (meeting room)
     020 7269 9770
     Co-Chmn: Lucy Daniels,   Richard McKane
▲   Un-incorporated Society
○   *A; Russian culture, particularly literature
●   Mtgs - Inf - Lectures - Recitals [in English, in Russian or
     bilingual]
M   c 80 i
¶   Programme - 1; free.
     Note: In 2007 will move to: 5a Bloomsbury Sq, LONDON,
     WC1A 2LP.

Pygmy Goat Club   1982

NR Solomons Farm, Latchley, GUNNISLAKE, Cornwall,
     PL18 9AX.   (sp)
     01822 834474
     http://www.pygmygoatclub.org
     Sec: Mrs Margaret Thompson
▲   Un-incorporated Society
○   *B
●   Mtgs - Exhib - Inf - Shows
M   500 i, org, UK / 4 i, o'seas
¶   Pygmy Goat Notes - 4; ftm only.   Herdbook - 1.
     Pygmy Goat Hbk.   Members Hbk - 1; ftm only.

© CBD Research Ltd · Beckenham · BR3 5JS · Tel 020 8650 7745 · Fax 020 8650 0768 · E-mail cbd@cbdresearch.com · www.cbdresearch.com

QG Business Solutions Ltd
registered name of the **Quality Guild**

Quad Racing Association UK   (QRA UK)
NR   74 Roman Way, ANDOVER, Hants, SP10 5JJ.
01264 354259
email tonynash@quadriding.com
http://www.quadriding.com
Sec: Tony Nash
○   *S; for all interested in quad bike racing
●   Mtgs

Quality British Celery Association   (QBC)
■   133 Eastgate, LOUTH, Lincs, LN11 9QG.   (asa)
01507 602427   fax 01507 607165
email crop.association@pvga.co.uk
Sec: Mrs Jayne Dyas
○   *T; to provide technical, commercial & marketing information
for growers
●   Conf - Mtgs - Res - Exhib - Stat - Inf - LG
M   120 f

Quality Guild   (QG)   1994
■   Westwinds, Lambley Bank, Scotby, CARLISLE, Cumbria,
CA4 8BX.   (hq)
01228 631681
email blightowler@qgbiz.co.uk   http://www.qgbiz.co.uk
Managing Dir: Brian Lightowler
▲   Company Limited by Guarantee
○   *T; a network of quality assessed businesses
●   Inf - Business advice
M   250 f
(Sub: £315-£500)
Registered name: QG Business Solutions Ltd

Quality Meat Scotland   (QMS)
■   Rural Centre, West Mains, Ingliston, NEWBRIDGE, Midlothian,
EH28 8NZ.   (hq)
0131-472 4040
email info@qmscotland.co.uk
http://www.qmscotland.co.uk
Chief Exec: Uel Morton
▲   Non-Departmental Public Body
○   *T; marketing & development of Scottish red meat industry
●   Conf - Mtgs - ET - Res - Exhib - Comp - Stat - Expt - Inf - PL -
VE - LG
¶   Corporate Plan - 3 yrly; free.

Quality Methods Association
no longer active

Quality Milk Producers Ltd   1954
NR   Scotsbridge House, Scots Hill, RICKMANSWORTH, Herts,
WD3 3BB.   (hq)
01923 695266
▲   Company Limited by Guarantee
○   *T; marketing, advertising & representation for Channel Islands
(Gold Top) milk producers
●   Conf - Exhib - Comp - Stat - Expt - Inf - Promotion
M   600 i
¶   Gold Top News - 3; m only.

Quarry Products Association   (QPA)   1982
■   Gillingham House, 38-44 Gillingham St, LONDON,
SW1V 1HU.   (hq)
020 7963 8000
email info@qpa.org   http://www.qpa.org
Dir Gen: Simon van der Byl
▲   Company Limited by Guarantee
Br   3
○   *T; for the aggregates, asphalt, ready-mixed concrete, mortar,
lime & silica-sand industries
●   Conf - Mtgs - ET - Res - Exhib - Stat - Inf - Lib - PL - LG
<   Eur Asphalt Producers Assn; Eur Ready-Mixed Concrete Org;
Eur Aggregates Assn
M   c 140 f
¶   The Aggregates Industry at a Glance (fact file).
Voice of the Quarrying Industry (a profile of the QPA & its
work).
General:
What's in a Quarry (Video); £15.
Quarrying in Depth - recycling.
Environmental:
Directory of Restoration: a compendium of examples.
Shifting Ground (Video); £35.
Managers' Guide to the video; £3.25.
Lime:
Lime Stabilisation Manual; £6.   Leaflets.
Marine:
Aggregates from the Sea (video) & (booklet); free.
Health & Safety:
Clearing Blocked Crushers; £6.75.
Code of Practice for Safeguarding Machinery; £7.50.
Record Book for the Recording of Explosives kept in:
Quarries' Blasting Sites; £3.
Quarries' Explosives Stores; £3.
Safety booklets; 30p each.
Publications list available.

Queen's English Society   (QES)   1972
NR   The Clergy House, Hide Place, LONDON, SW1P 4NJ.   (hsp)
020 7630 1819
http://www.queens-english-society.com
Hon Sec: G J Hardwick
▲   Registered Charity
Br   4
○   *K; to promote & uphold the use of good English; to encourage
the enjoyment of the language; to defend the precision,
subtlety & richness of the language against debasement,
ambiguity & other forms of misuse
●   Conf - Mtgs
M   695 i, UK / 84 i, o'seas
¶   Quest (Jnl) - 4.

Queen's Nursing Institute   (QNI)   1887
§   3 Albemarle Way, LONDON, EC1V 4RQ.
020 7490 4227   fax 020 7490 1269
email mail@qni.org.uk   http://www.qni.org.uk
An independent non-membership body promoting the highest
standards of nursing for the benefit of the community &
public health.

Quekett Microscopical Club   (QMC)   1865
■   90 The Fairway, SOUTH RUISLIP, Middx, HA4 0SQ.
(subn/manager/p)
email secretary@quekett.org.   http://www.quekett.org
Subscription Manager: Peter Thomas
▲   Registered Charity
○   *L; all aspects of light microscopes
●   Mtgs
M   360 i, UK / 60 i, o'seas
¶   The Quekett Jnl of Microscopy - 2.   Bulletin - 2.

Quilling Guild   1982

■ 33 Mill Rise, Skidby, COTTINGHAM, E Yorks, HU16 5UA.
(hsp)
01482 843721   fax 01482 840783
email guild@quilling.karoo.co.uk
http://www.quilling-guild.co.uk
Sec: Paul Jenkins
▲ Registered Charity
○ *A, *G; to promote the art form / craft (a.k.a. paper filigree or paper rollwork) where paper is rolled and applied to create pictures
● Mtgs - Exhib - Comp - Inf - Archive of antique & modern work
M 600 i, UK / 100 i, o'seas
(Sub: £18 UK / £24 o'seas)
¶ Quillers Today (NL) - 3.

Quilt Art
a group of the **Quilters' Guild of the British Isles**

Quilt Association   1995

■ The Minerva Arts Centre, High St, LLANIDLOES, Powys, SY18 6BY.
01686 413467
email quilts@quilt.org.uk   http://www.quilt.org.uk
Exhib Organiser: Mrs Doreen Gough
▲ Company Limited by Guarantee; Registered Charity
○ *G; the exhibition of Welsh quilts, both antique & contemporary; education connected with quilting, its history & artistry
● Conf - Mtgs - ET - Exhib - SG - VE
> Mid-Wales branch of Embroiderers' Gld; Welsh Heritage Quilters
M 150 i, UK / 25 i, o'seas
¶ NL - 2;   AR;   both ftm only.

Quilters' Guild of the British Isles   1979

■ St Anthony's Hall, Peaseholme Green, YORK, YO1 7PW.   (hq)
01904 613242   fax 01904 632394
email info@quiltersguild.org.uk
http://www.quiltersguild.org.uk
Admin: Carol Bowden
▲ Company Limited by Guarantee; Registered Charity
Br 17 regions
○ *G; to promote the study & art of the techniques & heritage of patchwork, quilting & appliqué & of their future use & development
Gp British Quilt Study Group; Quilt Art
● Conf - ET - Res - Exhib - Comp - SG - Inf - Lib - VE
< Eur Quilting Assn
M c 6,500 i, UK / c 200 i, o'seas
¶ The Quilter - 4;   Hbk - 1;   NL (Regional) - 3; all ftm only.

Quoted Companies Alliance   (QCA)   1992

■ 6 Kinghorn St, LONDON, EC1A 7HW.   (hq)
020 7600 3745   fax 020 7600 8288
email mail@quotedcompaniesalliance.co.uk
http://www.quotedcompaniesalliance.co.uk
Chief Exec: John Pierce
▲ Company Limited by Guarantee
○ *N; for smaller quoted companies (SQCs) which are listed on the London Stock Exchange & are outside the FTSE 350 Index, including those on AIM + FWS Market Group
¶ QCA Voice - 4.

© CBD Research Ltd · Beckenham · BR3 5JS · Tel 020 8650 7745 · Fax 020 8650 0768 · E-mail cbd@cbdresearch.com · www.cbdresearch.com

R S Surtees Society   (RSSS)   1983
- ■ Manor Farm House, Nunney, FROME, Somerset, BA11 4NJ.
  01373 836937
  http://www.r.s.surteessociety.org
  Chief Exec: Helen Lady Pickthorn,   Sec: Jeremy Lewis
- ▲ Un-incorporated Society
- Br USA
- ○ *A, *L; for those interested in the life & works of R S Surtees
  (1803-64), the sporting writer of the 'Jorrocks' stories;
  keeping the works in print
- ● Exhib - Publishing
- < Selwood Foundation
- M c 4,000 i

Rabbit Welfare Association   (RWA)   1996
- NR PO Box 603, HORSHAM, W Sussex, RH13 5WL.
  (mail/address)
  0870 046 5249 (helpline)
  Chief Exec: Rachel Todd
- ▲ Un-incorporated Society
- ○ *B; to promote the keeping of rabbits as house pets; to raise
  interest in rabbit medicine within the veterinary profession
- Gp Coordinators: Rabbits; Pets; Houserabbits
- ● Conf - Mtgs - ET - Exhib - Inf
- M 3,500 i, f & org
- ¶ Rabbiting On - 4;   Hbk; both ftm.

Race Walking Association   (RWA)   1907
- ■ Hufflers, Heard's Lane, Shenfield, BRENTWOOD, Essex,
  CM15 0SF.   (hsp)
  01277 220687   fax 01277 212380
  email racewalkingassociation@btinternet.com
  http://www.racewalkingassociation.btinternet.co.uk
  Hon Gen Sec: Peter J Cassidy
- ▲ Un-incorporated Society
- ○ *S; organisation, management, control & development of race
  walking (within the territory of England Athletics - England,
  the Isle of Man & the Channel Islands)
- ● Conf - Mtgs - ET - Exam - Comp - SG - Stat - Inf - VE
- < England Athletics
- M 120 clubs & county org
- ¶ Race Walking Record - 12; £20 (UK), £30 (Europe),
  £40 (o'seas).
  Hbk.

Racecourse Association Ltd   (RCA)   1907
- NR Winkfield Rd, ASCOT, Berks, SL5 7HX.   (hq)
  01344 625912
  Chmn: David Thorpe
- ▲ Company Limited by Guarantee
- ○ *S, *T; to promote & represent the interests of racecourse
  owners
- Gp Publicity & Marketing
- ● Mtgs - Exhib - Inf
- M 58 f (racecourses)
- ¶ AR; free.

Racehorse Owners Association Ltd   (ROA)   1945
- ■ 60 St James's St, LONDON, SW1A 1LE.   (hq)
  020 7408 0903   fax 020 7408 1662
  email info@roa.co.uk   http://www.racehorseowners.net
  Sec: Keely Brewer
- ▲ Company Limited by Guarantee
- ○ *S; representation of all racehorse owners in negotiation with
  the British Horseracing Authority, Horserace Betting Levy
  Board, the government & other bodies in racing in the UK &
  abroad
- ● Conf - Mtgs - Res - SG - Stat - Inf - LG
- M c 7,250 i & f
- ¶ Thoroughbred Owner & Breeder - 12; ftm, £42 nm.

Racehorse Transporters Association   (RTA Ltd)   1967
- ■ Folly House, Lambourn, HUNGERFORD, Berks, RG17 8QG.
  (chmn/p)
  01488 71700   fax 01488 73208
  email merrick@lrtltd.demon.co.uk
  Chmn: Merrick E D Francis,
  Sec: Miss Philippa Gillie (00 353 872 116719)
- ▲ Company Limited by Guarantee
- ○ *T; 'the RTA is the trade association member of the British
  Horseracing Authority Industry Committee, which represents
  the majority of all UK & Irish transporters & shipping agents;
  the association is available to help & advise members on any
  subject of horse transport'
- ● Mtgs - ET - Inf - LG
- < Brit Horseracing Auth Ind C'ee Ltd; Nat Trainers Fedn;
  Thoroughbred Breeders Assn
- M 90 f, UK / 15 f, o'seas (Republic of Ireland)

Rachmaninoff Society   1990
- ■ 2 Boundary Lane, Mossley, CONGLETON, Cheshire,
  CW12 3HZ.   (mem sec/p)
  01260 272073
  email Charles@neilmac.co.uk
  http://www.rachmaninoff.org
  Mem Sec: Charles McAllister
- ▲ Registered Charity
- Br North America
- ○ *D; furtherance of public knowledge, interest & appreciation of
  the life, art & music of Sergei Vassilyevich Rachmaninoff
  (1873-1943)
- ● Conf - Res - Inf
- M 200 i, UK / 200 i, o'seas
  (Sub: £15)
- ¶ The Bells - a music jnl - 2;   Update (NL) - 1; both ftm only.

Racket Sports Association
  since 2006 **Sporting Goods Industry Association**

Radical Statistics Group   1975
- ■ 27/2 Hillside Crescent, EDINBURGH, EH7 5EF.
  email admin@radstats.org.uk   http://www.radstats.org.uk
  Admin: Alistair Cairns
- ▲ Un-incorporated Society
- ○ *P; for statisticians & research workers with a common concern
  about the political assumptions & implications of much of
  their work & an awareness of the actual & potential use of
  statistics & its techniques. The group is independent from
  other organisations... members are radical in the sense of
  being committed to helping to build a more free, egalitarian
  & democratic society
- Gp Radical Statistics Health Gp
- ● Conf - Res - SG - Stat
- M c 300 i, 30 librarians
- ¶ Radical Statistics - 3; £12.
  Jnl;   NL.

Radio Academy   1983
NR   5 Market Place, LONDON, W1W 8AE.   (hq)
       020 7255 2010   fax 020 7255 2029
       email info@radioacademy.org
       http://www.radioacademy.org
       Dir: John Bradford
▲   Registered Charity
Br   11
○   *P; dedicated to the encouragement, recognition & promotion
       of excellence throughout the UK radio industry
Gp   Administrates for: Student Radio Association
●   Conf - Mtgs - ET - Res - Comp
>   Student Radio Assn
M   c 1,800 i & f
¶   Off Air (NL) - 4; ftm only.   AR - 1; free.
       Directory - 1; ftm.

**Radio, Electrical & Television Retailers' Association Ltd
(RETRA)   1942**
■   Retra House, St John's Terrace, 1 Ampthill St, BEDFORD,
       MK42 9EY.   (hq)
       01234 269110
       email retra@retra.co.uk   http://www.retra.co.uk
       Chief Exec: Bryan Lovewell
▲   Company Limited by Guarantee
○   *T; for electrical & electronics retailers, renters & service
       businesses; to represent small independents together with
       regional & national multiples
Gp   Conference; Training; Legal; Advice; Representation; Lobbying;
       Visits & excursions; Stationery & business supplies;
       Information; Meetings
●   Conf - Mtgs - ET - Comp - Inf - VE - LG
<   Eur Fedn Electronics Retailers (EFER); Retailers' Forum
M   1,500 i, 4,000 f
¶   Alert (NL) - 10.   Ybk.   AR.
       Safety in Electrical Testing.   Directory - 1.

Radio Society of Great Britain   (RSGB)   1913
NR   3 Abbey Court, Fraser Rd, Priory Business Park, BEDFORD,
       MK44 3WH.   (hq)
       01234 832700   fax 01234 831496
       http://www.rsgb.org.uk
▲   Company Limited by Guarantee
○   *G; all activities concerned with the advancement of amateur
       radio & the science of communication
<   Intl Amat Radio U (IARU); Inst of Electrical Engrs
M   c 26,000 i, UK / c 2,500 i, o'seas, 700 affiliated clubs & org
¶   Radcom - 12.   Various other publications.

Radionic Association Ltd   (RA)   1943
■   Baerlein House, Goose Green, Deddington, BANBURY, Oxon,
       OX15 0SZ.   (hq)
       01869 338852   fax 01869 338852
       email secretary@radionic.co.uk
       http://www.radionic.co.uk
       Sec: Miss Rebecka Blenntoft
▲   Company Limited by Guarantee
○   *M, *P, *Q; to promote the study & practice of radionics
●   Con f- ET - Exam - Res - Inf - Lib
<   Confedn of Healing Orgs
M   i
       (Sub: £25 i, UK / £31 i, o'seas)
¶   The Radionic Jnl - 4; ftm, £5 nm.

Radnorshire Society   1930
■   Pool House, Discoed, PRESTEIGNE, Powys, LD8 2NW.
       (mail address)
       http://www.radnorshiresociety.org.uk
       Hon Sec: Mrs S Cole
▲   Registered Charity
○   *L; history & culture of Radnorshire (pre-1974 county, now part
       of Powys)
●   Mtgs - Lib
M   350 i, 20 org, UK / 10 i, o'seas
¶   Transactions - 1; ftm, back issues £1 m, £5 nm.

Rail Freight Group   (RFG)   1990
NR   Monticello House, 45 Russell Square, LONDON, WC1B 4JP.
       (hq)
       020 7907 4646
       http://www.rfg.org.uk
       Admin Mgr: Phillippa O'Shea
▲   Company Limited by Guarantee
○   *K; promotion & development of freight by rail
●   Conf - Mtgs - Res - Inf - Lib - LG - Media relations - Press
       releases - Political lobbying
M   145 f, UK / 5 f, o'seas
¶   Rail Freight Group News - 6; free.   Hbk - 1; ftm.

Rail Industry Contractors Association   (RICA)   1999
NR   Gin Gan House, Thropton, MORPETH, Northumberland,
       NE65 7LT.
       01669 620569
       http://www.rica.uk.com
○   *T; to represent suppliers of labour & other suppliers & services
       to the railway industry
●   Mtgs - Liaison within rail industry - Lobbying
M   50 f
×   2006 Association of On-Track Labour Suppliers

Rail, Maritime & Transport Union   (RMT)
NR   Unity House, 39 Chalton St, LONDON, NW1 1JD.
       020 7387 4771
       email info@rmt.org.uk   http://www.rmt.org.uk
       Gen Sec: Bob Crow
○   *U
M   c 73,000 i

Rail Plant Association
       is a group of the **Construction Plant-hire Association**

Railfuture
       is the title used for campaigning purposes by the **Railway
Development Society**

Rails Bookmakers Association
NR   PO Box 42, TADWORTH, Surrey, KT20 5YT.
       01737 216376   fax 01737 356141
       email rba@frb.org.uk
       http://www.rba-bookmakers.co.uk
       Chmn: Robin Grossmith
○   *T; bookmakers who operate from the members' rail on British
       rececourses
<   Fedn Racecourse Bookmakers

Railway & Canal Historical Society   (R&CHS)   1954
■   3 West Court, West St, OXFORD, OX2 0NP.   (hsp)
       01865 240514
       email secretary@rchs.org.uk   http://www.rchs.org.uk
       Hon Sec: Matthew Searle
▲   Company Limited by Guarantee; Registered Charity
Br   6
○   *G, *L; to encourage the study of the history of transport, with
       particular reference to railways & canals but including
       associated modes of transport such as river navigations,
       roads, docks, coastal shipping, ferries & by air
Gp   Air transport; Pipelines; Railway chronology; Road transport;
       Tramroads; Waterways
●   Mtgs - Res - Inf - PL - VE
M   780 i, 2 f, 3 org, UK / 16 i, 1 org, o'seas
¶   Jnl - 3;   Bulletin - 6; both ftm.

© CBD Research Ltd · Beckenham · BR3 5JS · Tel 020 8650 7745 · Fax 020 8650 0768 · E-mail cbd@cbdresearch.com · www.cbdresearch.com

Railway Correspondence & Travel Society (RCTS) 1928
NR 6 Sandpiper Rd, IPSWICH, Suffolk, IP2 9HX. (hsp)
    01473 404683
    http://www.rcts.org.uk
    Hon Sec: John Day
▲ Un-incorporated Society
Br 27
○ *G; railway history, operation & development
Gp Photographic
● Conf - Mtgs - Exhib - Stat - Inf - Lib - VE - Publication of
    specialist histories involving research on locomotives
< 6 railway socs in UK; 30 o'seas
M 3,000 i
¶ The Railway Observer - 12; ftm.
    A wide range of books on railway subjects.

Railway Development Society Ltd (RDS) 1978
NR 33 Station Court, Aberford Rd, Garforth, LEEDS, LS25 2QQ.
    (hq)
    0113-286 4844
    email info@railfuture.org.uk   http://www.railfuture.org.uk
    Chmn: Mike Crowhurst
▲ Company Limited by Guarantee
Br 17
○ *K; to gain improvements to the railways; to provide the public
    with a modern joined-up transport system; to fight for
    environmentally friendly transport
Gp Freight; Passenger; International; Reopenings; Policy & lobbying
● Conf - Mtgs - SG - Inf - VE - LG
< Transport 2000
M 3,400 i, 10 f, 80 org, UK / 10 i, o'seas
¶ Railwatch - 4.
    Note: Uses title Railfuture for all campaigning purposes.

Railway Enthusiasts Society (Rail Europe) 1963
■ PO Box 1, Thornton, BRADFORD, W Yorks, BD13 3QD. (hsb)
    07974 651105   fax 01274 830520
    email raileurope@blueyonder.co.uk
    http://www.rail-europe.co.uk
    Hon Sec: Dale W Fickes
▲ Un-incorporated Society
○ *G; to further an interest in railways, particularly modern
    traction, with similar enthusiasts throughout Europe
● VE
< Utd Travel Associates
M 80 i, UK / 2 i, o'seas
    (Sub: £25, UK / 40 ($60) o'seas)
¶ European Rail News (NL) - 5/6; £15 m (2004).

Railway Forum
■ 12 Grosvenor Place, LONDON, SW1X 7HH. (hq)
    020 7259 6543   fax 020 7259 6544
    email railinfo@railwayforum.com
    http://www.railwayforum.com
○ *T; 'railway industry strategic think tanks & lobby group
    representing passenger & freight train operating companies,
    infrastructure providers, service companies & equipment
    suppliers'

Railway Industry Association (RIA) 1875
■ 22 Headfort Place, LONDON, SW1X 7RY. (hq)
    020 7201 0777   fax 020 7235 5777
    email ria@riagb.org.uk   http://www.riagb.org.uk
    Dir Gen: Jeremy Candfield,   Dir: G Coomb
▲ Un-incorporated Society
○ *T; to promote the interests of British rail industry
    manufacturers, contractors & specialist service providers,
    both in the UK & overseas
● Conf - Mtgs - Exhib - Expt - Inf - LG
< Eur Fedn of Rly Trackworks Contrs; U des Inds Ferroviaires Eur;
    Confedn Brit Ind; Rly Forum
M 140 f
¶ UK Railway Suppliers Directory.
    Technical Specifications.

Railway Preservation Society of Ireland (RPSI) 1964
■ PO Box 171, LARNE, Co Antrim, BT40 1UU. (regd off)
    028 2826 0803   fax 028 2826 0803
    email rpsitrains@hotmail.com
    http://www.steamtrainsireland.com
    Hon Sec: Paul McCann
▲ Company Limited by Guarantee; Registered Charity
Br Republic of Ireland
○ *G, *K; to preserve, maintain & operate mainline steam
    locomotives & vintage rolling stock on the main line railways
    of Ireland
● Mtgs
< Heritage Rly Assn (HRA)
M 700 i, UK / 300 i, o'seas
¶ Five Foot Three (Jnl) - 1; ftm, £3 nm.

Railway Ramblers (RR) 1978
■ 27 Sevenoaks Rd, Brockley, LONDON, SE4 1RA. (mem/sp)
    http://www.railwayramblers.org.uk
    Mem Sec: Peter Walker
○ *G; exploration & documentation of disused railways - mainly
    in the UK
● VE
M 583 i, 2 org, UK / 3 i, o;seas
    (Sub: £8 i, £24 org, UK / £12 i, o'seas)
¶ Railway Ramblings - 4; ftm only.

Railway Study Association (RSA) 1909
NR 37 Charlwood Rd, BURGESS HILL, W Sussex, RH15 0RJ. (hsp)
    01444 246379   fax 01444 246392
    email info@railwaystudyassociation.org
    http://www.railwaystudyassociation.org
    Hon Sec: Steven Saunders
▲ Un-incorporated Society
○ *G; 'to be the most effective forum in Great Britain for
    promoting a broad understanding of all aspects of the
    railway industry'
● Conf - Mtgs - VE
M 830 i, 32 f, UK / 12 i, o'seas
¶ NL - irreg.   Ybk.

Ramblers' Association (RA) 1935
■ Camelford House (2nd floor), 87-90 Albert Embankment,
    LONDON, SE1 7TW. (hq)
    020 7339 8500   fax 020 7339 8501
    email ramblers@ramblers.org.uk
    http://www.ramblers.org.uk
    Chief Exec: Tom Franklin
▲ Registered Charity
Br 3
○ *G, *K, *S; to encourage walking; to protect footpaths; to
    campaign for freedom to roam in open country; to defend
    the beauty of the countryside
● Conf - Mtgs - ET - Res - Exhib - Inf - Lib (maps) - LG
M i

Randolph Caldecott Society 1983
■ Blue Grass, Clatterwick Lane, Little Leigh, NORTHWICH,
    Cheshire, CW8 4RJ. (hsb)
    01606 891303 & 781731 (evgs)
    Hon Sec: Kenneth N Oultram
○ *A, *G; to promote the work of Randolph Caldecott, the 19th
    century artist & illustrator; to liaise with the American-based
    society
● Mtgs (at Caldecott's birthplace in Chester)

Ranulf Higden Society 1992
NR History, Keele University, KEELE, Staffs, ST5 5BG. (hq)
      fax 01782 583195
      Contact: Miss Amanda Roberts (01782 733196)
○ *A; to promote interest, understanding & research into
      documents written in Medieval Latin & Anglo Norman (with
      particular emphasis on north western England).   Ranulf
      Higden was a Benedictine monk & English chronicler who
      died in 1364
M   c 75 i

Ranunculaceae Society 2003
IRL 24 Lambourne Wood, Brennanstown Rd, Cabinteely,
      DUBLIN 18, Republic of Ireland.   (hsp)
      353 (1) 289 2721   fax 353 (1) 289 2721
      email ranunculaceae@eircom.net
      http://www.buttercupsonline.com
      Admin Sec: Claire Gloster
○ *H; to foster interest in plants belonging to the buttercup family
      - Ranunculaceae
● Conf - Mtgs (irreg) - VE
< R Horticl Soc
M   15 i, 1 f, 1 org, Republic of Ireland / 65 i, o'seas
¶ NL - 4; ftm, £2 nm.

Rapid Prototyping & Manufacturing Association 1995
NR Institution of Mechanical Engineers, Engineering Programmes,
      1 Birdcage Walk, LONDON, SW1H 9JJ.
      020 7304 6837
      Exec: Charlotte Newman
○ *T
M   250 i

Rapra Technology Ltd 1919
NR Shawbury, SHREWSBURY, Shropshire, SY4 4NR.   (hq)
      01939 250383   fax 01939 251118
      email info@rapra.net   http://www.rapra.net
▲ Private Limited Company
○ *Q; 'independent research, technology & information
      consultancy specialising in plastics & rubber'
● Conf - ET - Res - Inf
< Assn of Indep Res & Technology Orgs (AIRTO)
M   f
¶ over 1,200 titles.
      Note: is a company in the Smithers Group

Rare Breeds Survival Trust (RBST) 1973
■ Stoneleigh Park, KENILWORTH, Warks, CV8 2LG.   (hq)
      024 7669 6551   fax 024 7669 6706
      email enquiries@rbst.org.uk   http://www.rbst.org.uk
      Chief Exec: Richard Clarke
▲ Company Limited by Guarantee; Registered Charity
○ *B, *K; the preservation, conservation & promotion of native
      breeds of British farm livestock
● Conf - Res - Exhib - SG - Stat - Inf - Lib - PL - LG
< Rare Breeds Intl
M   9,500 i, 114 org, UK / 260 i, o'seas
¶ The Ark - 4; ftm.

Rare Poultry Society (RPS) 1969
■ Danby, The Causeway, Congresbury, BRISTOL, BS49 5DJ.
      (hsp)
      01934 833619
      Hon Sec: Mrs Anne Merriman
▲ Un-incorporated Society
○ *G, *K; for the preservation of over 60 rare & endangered
      breeds of poultry
● Exhib - Inf
< Poultry Club of GB; Fedn of Poultry Clubs
M   204 i, UK / 3 i, o'seas
      (Sub: £10)
¶ NL - ; 4.

Rating Surveyors' Association 1909
NR c/o Hartnell Taylor Cook, 12/13 Conduit St, LONDON,
      W1S 2XH.   (hsb)
      020 7788 3809
      email martin.davenport@btc.uk.com
      http://www.ratingsurveyorsassociation.org
      Hon Sec: Martin Davenport
▲ Un-incorporated Society
○ *P; to represent experienced Chartered Surveyors who
      specialise in the field of business rates, in both the public &
      private sector
● Mtgs - Inf - VE - LG
< R Instn of Chart Surveyors
M   350 i
¶ NL - 2;   LM;   President's Report (AR) - 1.

Rationalist Association (RPA) 1899
■ 1 Gower St, LONDON, WC1E 6HD.   (hq)
      020 7436 1151
      email info@newhumanist.org.uk
      http://www.newhumanist.org.uk
      Editor: Caspar Melville
▲ Registered Charity
○ *K; publishing & campaigning in the area of secular humanism
      & non-religious thought; for artists, non-religious, free
      thinkers - philosophy, science & culture
● Conf - Publishing
M   2,190 UK / 310 i, o'seas
¶ The New Humanist (Jnl) - 6; £18.
× 2005-06 Rationalist Press Association

Rationalist Press Association Ltd
      since 2005-06 the **Rationalist Association**

Ray Society 1844
■ c/o Dept of Zoology, Natural History Museum, Cromwell Rd,
      LONDON, SW7 5BD.   (hsb)
      020 7942 5532   fax 020 7942 5433
      email nje@nhm.ac.uk   http://www.scientificbooks.co.uk
      Hon Sec: Dr Nicholas John Evans
▲ Registered Charity
○ *L; publication of original texts of scientific interest & merit
      which would not otherwise be published because of lack of
      commercial; works usually (but not exclusively) relate to
      British flora & fauna
      Founded in memory of English naturalist John Ray (1627-1705)
● ET - Res - Publication of scientific books/monographs of
      original works, translations & facsimiles on natural history
M   c 200 i, UK / c 50 i, o'seas
¶ Volumes (bound books 700-900 pages) - c 1; prices vary.
      AR - 1; ftm, £1 nm.

Raynaud's & Scleroderma Association 1982
■ 112 Crewe Rd, Alsager, STOKE-on-TRENT, Staffs, ST7 2JA.
      (hq)
      01270 872776   fax 01270 883556
      email info@raynauds.org.uk
      http://www.raynauds.org.uk
      Dir: Mrs Anne H Mawdsley
▲ Registered Charity
○ *W; to promote better communication between doctors &
      patients; to put patients in touch with each other in order to
      exchange ideas; to raise funds for research
Gp Sufferers; Health professionals; General public
● Conf - Mtgs - Res
< Brit Soc of Rheumatology; Arthritis & Musculoskeletal
      Alliance (ARMA)
M   6,000 i
¶ Hot News (NL) - 4; ftm.
      Raynaud's: your questions answered; £4.
      Journey of Discovery; £12.
      Scleroderma - The Inside Story; £5.99.

© CBD Research Ltd · Beckenham · BR3 5JS · Tel 020 8650 7745 · Fax 020 8650 0768 · E-mail cbd@cbdresearch.com · www.cbdresearch.com

Re-Solv (the Society for the Prevention of Solvent & Volatile Substance Abuse) 1984
- ■ 30A High St, STONE, Staffs, ST15 8AW.
  01785 817885
  http://www.re-solv.org
  Chmn: Gerald Soane,   Dir: Steve Lambert
- ▲ Company Limited by Guarantee; Registered Charity
- Br 3 regions
- ○ *K; the only national charity dealing with all aspects of solvent & volatile substance abuse (VSA)
- ● Conf - ET - Res - Inf
- M c 30 i, 50 assns, 220 health authorities etc
- ¶ NL - 6; free.
  Publications & videos, list available.

REACH: the Association for Children with Hand or Arm Deficiency (REACH) 1978
- ■ PO Box 54, HELSTON, Cornwall, TR13 8WD.   (hq)
  0845 130 6225   fax 0845 130 0262
  email reach@reach.org.uk   http://www.reach.org.uk
  Nat Coordinator: Mrs Sue Stokes
- ▲ Registered Charity
- Br 15; Eire
- ○ *W; to support families of upper limb deficient children
- ● Conf - Mtgs - Exhib - Inf
- M 1,053 i, UK / 53 i, o'seas
- ¶ Within Reach - 4;   Introductory Booklet;
  Guide to Artificial Arms;   AR; all free.

Reading Association of Ireland
- IRL Education Dept, St Patrick's College, Drumcondra, DUBLIN 9, Republic of Ireland.
  353 (1) 884 2072
  http://www.reading.ie
  Sec: Celine Fitzpatrick
- ○ *K

Record Society of Lancashire & Cheshire (LCRS) 1878
- NR c/o Greater Manchester County Record Office, 56 Marshall St, New Cross, MANCHESTER, M4 5FU.   (mail/address)
- ○ *L; publication of original documents relating to the two counties
  Note: The GMCRO hosts the society's site but staff cannot answer any queries regarding the Society's membership or publications.

Records Management Society of Great Britain (RMS) 1983
- NR Benchmark Communications, 14 Blandford Sq, NEWCASTLE upon TYNE, NE1 4HZ.   (hq)
  0191-244 2839   fax 0191-245 3802
- ▲ Un-incorporated Society
- Br 7 regional groups
- ○ *P; 'to encourage the highest standards in records management: the systematic control, organisation, access & protection of an organisation's information (whether it be on tape, disk, paper or film) from its creation through its use to its permanent retention or legal destruction'
- Gp Orgs covered by the Public Record Acts
- ● Conf - Mtgs - ET - Exhib - SG - VE - LG
- M 700 i, 250 f
- ¶ Bulletin - 6.   NL - 6.

Records, Racing & Rally Association
  see **Royal Aero Club - Records, Racing & Rally Association**

RECOUP - maximising efficient plastics recycling 1990
- NR 1 Metro Centre, Welbeck Way, Woodston, PETERBOROUGH, Cambs, PE2 7UH.
  01733 390021   fax 01733 390031
  email enquiry@recoup.org   http://www.recoup.org
- ○ *K; a charity promoting best practice in the recycling of plastics - pots, tubs trays & film
- < Inf

Recreation Managers' Association of Great Britain
  has closed.

Recruitment & Employment Confederation (REC) 2000
- ■ 15 Welbeck St, LONDON, W1G 9XT.   (hq)
  020 7009 2100   fax 020 7935 4112
  email info@rec.uk.com   http://www.rec.uk.com
  Chief Exec: Kevin Green
- ▲ Company Limited by Guarantee
- ○ *P, *T; for the recruitment industry
- Gp Childcare; Construction; Drivers; Engineering; Healthcare; Hospitality; Interim management; IT & Communications; Media; Search & selection; Security
- ● Conf - Mtgs - ET - Exam - Res - Stat - Inf - LG
- M 5,000 i, 8,000 f
- ¶ Recruitment Matters - 4.

Recruitment Society 1978
- ■ 211-212 Piccadilly, LONDON, W1J 9HF.   (hsb)
  020 7917 1728
  email admin@recruitmentsociety.org.uk
  http://www.recruitmentsociety.org.uk
  Admin: Richard Taylor,   Chmn: Steve Huxham
- ▲ Un-incorporated Society
- ○ *P; to provide a forum for discussion of best practice in recruitment
- ● Conf - Mtgs
- M 300 i

Red Poll Cattle Society 1888
- ■ 52 Border Cot Lane, Wickham Market, WOODBRIDGE, Suffolk, IP13 0EZ.   (hq)
  01728 747230   fax 01728 748226
  email secretary@redpoll.co.uk   http://www.redpoll.org
  Sec: Mrs T J Booker
- ▲ Registered Charity
- ○ *B
- ● Stat - Expt - Inf
- M 314 i, f & org, UK / 31 i, f & org, o'seas
- ¶ NL - 4; m only.   Herd Book - 1; ftm, £10 nm.

Redbridge Chamber of Commerce
- NR The Teachers Centre, Melbourne Rd, ILFORD, Essex, IG1 4HT.   (hq)
  0845 270 2009   fax 0845 249 9981
  email chamber@redbridgechamber.co.uk
  http://www.redbridgechamber.co.uk
  Sec: Mrs Vibeke Gardiner,   Chmn: Julie Woodward
- ▲ Company Limited by Guarantee
- ○ *C
- ● Conf- Mtgs - ET- Stat - Inf
- M c 200 f

RedR UK (RedR) 1980
- ■ 250A Kennington Lane, LONDON, SE11 5RD.   (hq)
  020 7840 6000
  email info@redr.org   http://www.redr.org.uk
  Chief Exec: Martin McCann
- ▲ Company Limited by Guarantee; Registered Charity
- Br Sri Lanka, Sudan
- ○ *W; an international NGO which provides training & recruitment services for the disaster relief sector, supporting other NGOs and their staff.
- Gp The security programmes; Recruitment; General training; Membership
- ● ET - Res - Inf - PL
- < RedR Intl; People in Aid, ALNAP
- M c 1,400 i
- ¶ NL - 3.   AR.
  Engineering in Emergencies: a practical guide.
  Note: RedR UK is the operating name of RedR - Engineers for Disaster Relief

Referees' Association   (The RA)   1908
- ■   1 Westhill Rd, Coundon, COVENTRY, Warks, CV6 2AD.   (hq)
  024 7660 1701   fax 024 7660 1556
  email ra@footballreferee.org
  http://www.footballreferee.org
  Gen Sec: Arthur Smith
- ▲   Un-incorporated Society
- ○   *S; interests of all grades of Football Association registered referees & assistant referees
- ●   Conf - Mtgs - ET - Supplies - Members' insurance - Help & advice
- <   Football Assn
- M   c 35,000 i
  (Sub: £15 UK / £13 o'seas)

Referenda Society   1991
- ■   29 Cleves Walk, ILFORD, Essex, IG6 2NQ.   (regd office)
  020 8500 4074
  email info@directvotes.info
  Dir: G Munnery
- ○   *K; to campaign for the introduction of a referenda voting system by which the electorate can express an opinion on issues of public concern & interest & secure the appropriate legislation
- ●   Campaigning
- <   Direct Votes
- M   i
- ¶   Introducing Direct Democracy; free for sae.

Refined Bitumen Association Ltd   (RBA)   1968
- ■   Harrogate Business Centre, Hammerain House, Hookstone Avenue, HARROGATE, N Yorks, HG2 8ER.   (hq)
  01423 876361   fax 01423 873999
  http://www.bitumenuk.com
  Press enquiries: HMPR, 14A Eccleston St, LONDON, SW1W 9LT.
      020 7730 2212,   Fex 020 7730 2213.
  Sec: Chris Southwell
- ▲   Company Limited by Guarantee
- ○   *T; to represent the bitumen supply industry in the UK; to increase knowledge of the engineering properties of bitumen & the development of the applications in which bitumens are used
- Gp   Technical c'ee
- ●   Mtgs - ET - Res - SG - Inf - LG - Sponsoring research into bituminous materials for use in the construction & maintenance of highways & airfields
- <   Eurobitume; Quarry Products Assn; Road Surface Dressing Assn (RSDA)
- M   f
- ¶   Technical bulletins on specific subjects - irreg; free.

Refined Sugar Association   (RSA)   1891
- NR   154 Bishopsgate, LONDON, EC2M 4LN.   (hq)
  020 7377 2113   fax 020 7247 2481
  http://www.sugarassociation.co.uk
  Sec: N Durham
- ○   *T; rules & contract conditions for the white sugar trade
- Gp   Arbitrators; Rules & contract conditions
- ●   Mtgs - ET - Inf - Empl - LG
- M   40 f, UK / 70 f, o'seas
- ¶   Rules & Regulations; £35 m, £60 nm.

Refractory Users Federation   (RUF)   1945
- ■   Broadway House (5th floor), Tothill St, LONDON, SW1H 9NS.   (asa)
  020 7799 2000
- ▲   Un-incorporated Society
- ○   *T; for contractors involved in refractory work of all types incl furnace installation & boiler setting
- ●   Mtgs - ET - Inf - Empl - LG
- <   Engg Construction Ind Assn
- M   10 f

Refrigerated Transport Information Society
  a group of **Cambridge Refrigeration Technology**

Regency Society of Brighton & Hove   1945
- ■   85 Furze Croft, Furze Hill, HOVE, E Sussex, BN3 1PE.   (hsp)
  01273 737434
  email john-small@waitrose.com
  http://www.regencysociety.org
  Hon Sec: John Small
- ▲   Registered Charity
- ○   *A, *K; preservation of historic architecture of Brighton & Hove; to promote interest in architecture & urban design
- ●   Mtgs - Res - Exhib - VE
- <   Georgian Gp; Civic Trust; Fedn of Sussex Amenity Socs; 20th Century Soc; Victorian Soc
- M   c 400 i, 5 org
- ¶   AR; free.

Regia Anglorum   (Regia)   1980
- NR   9 Durleigh Close, Headley Park, BRISTOL, BS13 7NQ.   (hq)
  0117-964 6818
  email events@regia.org   http://www.regia.org
  Business Mgr: J Kim Siddorn
- ▲   Un-incorporated Society
- Br   40; Australia, Canada, Denmark, Germany, Italy, N Zealand, USA
- ○   *D, *G; to accurately re-create the life & times of the Saxons, Vikings, Cymru, Scots, Normans & other inhabitants of the islands of Britain between the reigns of Alfred the Great & Richard the Lionheart
- Gp   Archery; Arms & armour; Battle re-enactment; Carpentry & house-building techniques; Early music; Folkdance; Hunting; Permanent site in Kent; Ships & the sea
- ●   Conf - Mtgs - ET - Res - Exhib - Inf - PL - LG
- <   Nat Assn Re-enactment Socs; Engliscan Gesíþas; York Archaeological Trust
- M   650 i, UK / 100 i, o'seas
- ¶   Chronicle (NL) - 4; ftm only.   Clamavi - irreg.

Regional Newspapers Association of Ireland   (RNAI)   1919
- IRL   Sheridan House, 33 Parkgate St, DUBLIN 8, Republic of Ireland.
      353 (1) 677 9116   fax 353 (1) 677 9144
- ○   *T; the representative body of Ireland's weekly regional newspapers

Regional Studies Association   (RSA)   1965
- ■   PO Box 2058, SEAFORD, E Sussex, BN25 4QU.   (hq)
  01323 899698   fax 01323 899798
  email rsa@mailbox.ulcc.ac.uk
  http://www.regional-studies-assoc.ac.uk
  Chief Exec: Sally Hardy
- ▲   Registered Charity
- Br   11; Ireland, Poland, Hungary
- ○   *E, *L; to promote education & studies in regional planning
- Gp   International regional research
- ●   Conf - Mtgs - SG - Inf
- M   450 i, 170 org, UK / 110 i, 17 org, o'seas
- ¶   Regional Studies - 9;   NL - 6;   AR; all ftm.

Register of Apparel & Textile Designers   (RATD)   1985
- NR   5 Portland Place, LONDON, W1B 1PW.   (hq)
  020 7636 5577   fax 020 7636 7515
  Mgr: Laurian Davies
- ○   *T; to assist manufacturers of clothing & textiles in the UK & overseas; to offer a help & advice service to designers by holding up-to-date lists of designers by speciality;
  The Register is jointly sponsored by the British clothing industry & UK Fashion Exports
- ●   Conf - Mtgs - ET - Res - Exhib - Expt - Inf - Lib - VE - Empl - LG
- M   i
- ¶   NL - 12; ftm only.

© CBD Research Ltd · Beckenham · BR3 5JS · Tel 020 8650 7745 · Fax 020 8650 0768 · E-mail cbd@cbdresearch.com · www.cbdresearch.com

Register of Chinese Herbal Medicine (RCHM) 1987
- ■ Office 5 Ferndale Business Centre, 1 Exeter St, NORWICH, NR2 4QB. (hq)
  01603 623994   fax 01603 667557
  email herbmed@rchm.co.uk   http://www.rchm.co.uk
  Sec: Emma Farrant
- ○ *P; to register & regulate fully qualified practitioners of traditional Chinese herbal medicine across the UK; to safeguard & promote their interests
- ● Conf - ET - Res - Exhib - Inf - LG
- < Eur Herbal & Traditional Medicine Practitioner Assn (EHPA)
- M 400 i
- ¶ RCHM Jnl - 2; ftm, £25 yr nm.
  NL - c 6; ftm only.

Register of Independent Professional Turfgrass Agronomists (RIPTA) 2002
- NR c/o Peter Jones Associates Ltd, 65 Crow Lane, HUSBORNE CRAWLEY, Beds, MK43 0XA. (hsb)
  01525 280573
  http://www.ripta.co.uk
  Register Administrator: Peter Jones
- ▲ Un-incorporated Society
- ○ *P; ; to give independent advice on growing & tending turf
- ● Inf
- M 16 i

Register of Professional Turners
- NR The Workshop, Moor Close Lane, Over Kellet, CARNFORTH, Lancs, LA6 1DF. (chmn/p)
  01524 735882
  Chmn: Malcolm Cobb
- ○ *P; woodturners
- M 215 i

Registered Nursing Home Association Ltd (RNHA) 1968
- ■ John Hewitt House, Tunnel Lane (off Lifford Lane), Kings Norton, BIRMINGHAM, B30 3JN. (hq)
  0121-451 1088   fax 0121-486 3175
  http://www.rnha.co.uk
  Chief Exec: Frank E Ursell
- ▲ Company Limited by Guarantee
- Br 35
- ○ *P; improvement of standards of care & techniques in registered nursing homes
- ● Conf - Mtgs - ET - Res - SG - Stat - Inf - VE - Joint efforts with DH & DSS.
- M 1,600 nursing homes, clinics & hospitals
- ¶ Courier (NL) - 6;   Nursing Home News - 6; both ftm only.
  Reference Book - 1; ftm.
  Care Assistant Training Manual; ftm, £50 nm.
  Business Management / Nursing Management Manuals; both ftm only.

Reiki Association (TRA) 1991
- NR Westgate Court, Spittal, HAVERFORDWEST, Pembs, SA62 5QP. (coordinator/p)
  0770 427 0727
  email enquiries@reikiassociation.org.uk
  http://www.reikiassociation.org.uk
  Contact: Sonia Thornton
- ▲ Company Limited by Guarantee
- ○ *P, *W; for Reiki practitioners & masters with the focus of Usui Shiki Ryoho Reiki; to offer information to the public about Reiki treatments
- ● Conf - Mtgs - ET - Exhib - Inf
- M 936 i, UK / 31 i, o'seas
- ¶ Touch - 4; ftm only.
  Reiki Magazine International - 6; £26 yr m, £45 yr nm.

Relate Scotland
on 1 April 2008 merged with Family Mediation Scotland to form
Relationships Scotland

Relationships Scotland 2008
- ■ 18 York Place, EDINBURGH, EH1 3EP. (hq)
  0845 119 2020   fax 0845 119 6089
  email enquiries@relationships-scotland.org.uk
  http://www.relationships-scotland.org.uk
  Contact: Graeme Hutchinson
  Chmn: Jim Wallace,   Chief Exec: Stuart Valentine
- ▲ Company Limited by Guarantee
- ○ *N, *W; a coordinating body for 24 affiliated family mediation services operating throughout Scotland; responsible for the promotion & development of a confidential counselling service to those in marriage & other intimate relationships
- ● Conf - Mtgs - ET - Res - Stat - Inf - Lib - LG
  Mon-Fri 0900-1700 - local services on website
- < Nat Family Mediation
- M 24 org
- ¶ NL - 2.   AR.
  Various guidance leaflets & training videos.
- × 2008 (Family Mediation Scotland
      (Relate Scotland (merger 1 April)

Relatives & Residents Association 1992
- ■ 24 The Ivories, 6-18 Northampton St, LONDON, N1 2HY. (hq)
  020 7359 8148   fax 020 7226 6603
  email advice@relres.org   http://www.relres.org
  Chief Exec: Gillian Dalley
- ▲ Company Limited by Guarantee; Registered Charity
- ○ *W; to support & advise older people, & their relatives & friends, who are in, or considering, long term care; to promote good practice in homes through local groups, publications & training
- ● Conf - Mtgs (local gps) - ET - Inf
  Advice line: 020 7359 8136
- M c 300 i
- ¶ NL - 2; ftm, £1 nm.
  Publications list available.

Religious Drama Society (Radius) 1929
- ■ 7 Lenton Rd, The Park, NOTTINGHAM, NG7 1DP. (hq)
  email office@radius.org.uk   http://www.radius.org.uk
  Editor: Margaret Hunt
- ▲ Registered Charity
- ○ *R; to promote drama which explores faith & the human condition
- ● Conf - ET - Comp - Inf - Lib - VE
- M 200 i, 30 org, UK / 20 i, o'seas
- ¶ Radius Performing (Jnl) - 4; ftm, £1 nm.

Religious Society of Friends (Quakers) (Quakers) 1650
- NR 173-177 Euston Rd, LONDON, NW1 2BJ. (hq)
  020 7663 1000
  Recording Clerk: Elsa Dicks
- ▲ Registered Charity
- Br 475; Worldwide
- ○ *R; pastoral work; witness to Quaker beliefs
- ● Conf - Mtgs - Inf - Lib - Supporting international representatives
- M 16,978 i, (13,309 attenders)
- ¶ Quaker News - 4.   Quaker Monthly - 12.
  Quaker Projects - 2;   Books - irreg.

Remote Gambling Association (RGA) 2005
- ■ Regency House, 1-4 Warwick St, LONDON, W1B 5LT.
  020 7479 4040
  email chawkswood@rga.eu.com   http://www.rga.eu.com
  Chief Exec: Clive Hawkswood
- ○ *T
- M 34 online betting and poker sites
  no further information supplied

Remote Imaging Group   (RIG)
■   PO Box 2001, DARTMOUTH, Devon, TQ6 9QN.   (msp)
        email membership@rig.org.uk   http://www.rig.org.uk
▲   Company Limited by Guarantee
○   *G; to promote interest & disseminate information pertaining to
        the reception & display of 'remote images' namely weather
        satellites; to liaise with official bodies, eg AMSAT-UK, the
        Dept of Trade & Industry, the European Space Agency, Nat
        Oceanic & Atmospheric Administration (US), the Radio
        Society of Great Britain, etc
●   Conf - Exhib - Inf
M   1,250 i, UK / 536 i, o'seas

Remote Sensing & Photogrammetry Society   (RSPSoc)   2001
■   School of Geography, University of Nottingham,
        NOTTINGHAM, NG7 2RD.   (hq)
        0115-951 5435   fax 0115-951 5249
        email rspsoc@nottingham.ac.uk   http://www.rspsoc.org
        Hon Gen Sec: Dr Philippa Mason
▲   Company Limited by Guarantee; Registered Charity
○   *L; to educate the public in remote sensing & photogrammetry
Gp Special interest: Archaeology, Education, Geological remote
        sensing, GIS, Modelling & advanced techniques, Ocean
        colour, Synthetic aperture radar
●   Conf - Mtgs - ET - Inf
<   Intl Soc of Photogrammetry & Remote Sensing (ISPRS)
M   1,200 i, 65 f
¶   RSPSoc NL - 4;   AR; both ftm only.
        International Jnl of Remote Sensing - 22; £55 m (2003).
        The Photogrammetric Record - 4; ftm, £150 nm.
        Annual Conference Proceedings (CD-ROM) - 1; ftm, £10 nm.

Renal Association   1950
■   Durford Mill, PETERSFIELD, Hants, GU31 5AZ.   (secretariat)
        0870 458 4155   fax 0870 442 9940
        Hon Sec: Dr Lorraine Harper
▲   Company Limited by Guarantee; Registered Charity
○   *L; to advance, collate & disseminate knowledge of renal
        function & structure; to seek means for the prevention &
        treatment of renal disorders
●   Conf - Mtgs - ET - Exhib
M   950 i, 16 f

Renewable Energy Association   (REA)   2001
■   17 Waterloo Place, LONDON, SW1Y 4AR.   (hq)
        020 7747 1830   fax 020 7925 2715
        email info@r-e-a.net   http://www.r-e-a.net
        Chief Exec: Philip Wolfe
▲   Company Limited by Guarantee
○   *T; to secure the best legislative & regulatory controls for
        expanding renewable energy production in the UK
Gp Biomass; Bioenergy; Solar; Ocean energy; Renewable transport
        fuels
●   Conf - Mtgs - SG - Stat - LG
M   400 i, f & org
¶   Renewables Ybk - 1.
×   2005 (British BioGen
            (Renewable Power Association (December)
    2006 (British Association of Biofuels & Oils
            (British Photovoltaic Association (April)

Renfrewshire Chamber of Commerce   1964
NR Bute Court, St Andrews Drive, Glasgow Airport, PAISLEY,
        Renfrewshire, PA3 2SW.
        0141-847 5450   fax 0141-847 5499
        email info@renfrewshirechamber.com
        http://www.renfrewshirechamber.com
        Chief Exec: Norman Simpson
▲   Company Limited by Guarantee
○   *C
    no further information supplied

Rescare   1984
NR Steven Jackson House, 31 Buxton Rd - Heaviley, STOCKPORT,
        Cheshire, SK2 6LS.   (HQ)
        0161-474 7323   fax 0161-480 3668
        email office@rescare.org.uk   http://www.rescare.org.uk
        Chmn: Richard S Jacobson
○   *W; support & information for families of children & adults with
        learning disabilities & their families
●   Helpline: 0161-477 1640
¶   Resnews - 4.

Research Defence Society   (RDS)   1908
■   25 Shaftesbury Ave, LONDON, W1D 7EG.   (hq)
        020 7287 2818   fax 020 7287 2627
        email admin@rds-net.org.uk
        http://www.rds-net.org.uk
        Exec Dir: Dr Simon Festing
▲   Industrial & Provident Society
○   *L; 'to make known the facts about experimental research
        involving use of animals; to emphasise importance &
        necessity of such experiments; to give guidance on the
        prevention of suffering of experimental animals'
●   Inf - LG - Public education
<   Eur Biomedical Res Assn
M   10,000 i, 50 f, 100 org
¶   NL - 4; free.

Research & Development Society   (R&D)   1962
■   6-9 Carlton House Terrace, LONDON, SW1Y 5AG.   (hq)
        020 7451 2513   fax 020 7930 2170
        email rdsociety@royalsociety.org   http://www.rdsoc.org
        Admin Sec: Scott Keir
▲   Company Limited by Guarantee
○   *P; 'to promote networking between people involved in R & D
        management & related professions over the whole range of
        science, engineering & technology; to disseminate current
        new ideas in science & technology, related management &
        business development, & science policy'
●   Conf - Mtgs
M   150 i, 45 f, UK / 5 f, o'seas
        (Subs: £60 i, £600 f)
¶   LM - 1; ftm only.   AR; free.
        Note: the society was incorporated in 1961

Research Libraries UK
    operates as **RLUK**

Residential Boat Owners Association   (RBOA)   1963
■   PO Box 267, ELY, Cambs, CB7 9EP.   (mail add)
        http://www.rboa.org.uk
        Chmn: Rex Walden
▲   Un-incorporated Society
○   *K; to further the interests of boat dwellers on the coasts, rivers
        & canals of Britain; to safeguard & increase the number of
        residential moorings; to encourage high standards of safety
        of boats & their moorings & good relations between
        members & landlords & local authorities; to encourage
        mobile boats to cruise
●   Mtgs
M   i, f & org
¶   Soundings (NL) - 4; ftm.   Living Afloat; £8.50.
        A Home Afloat (leaflet); free.

Residential Landlords Association
NR 1 Roebuck Lane, SALE, Cheshire, M33 7SY.
        0845 666 5000   fax 0845 665 1845
        http://www.rla.org.uk

© CBD Research Ltd · Beckenham · BR3 5JS · Tel 020 8650 7745 · Fax 020 8650 0768 · E-mail cbd@cbdresearch.com · www.cbdresearch.com

Residential Sprinkler Associates (RSA) 2007

■ Mill House, Mill Lane, Padworth, READING, Berks, RG7 4JX. (hsb)
   0118-971 2322   fax 0118-971 3015
   email info@firesprinklers.org.uk
   http://www.firesprinklers.org.uk
   Admin: Sir George Pigot
▲ Un-incorporated Society
○ *T; to provide support for the residential fire sprinkler contractor, especially in the fields of training, administration & technical advice
Gp Technical c'ee
● ET - Exam - Inf - LG
M 43 f
   (Sub: £250)
✕ 2007 (March) Fire Sprinkler Association

Residential Ventilation Association (RVA) 2000

■ 2 Waltham Court, Milley Lane, Hare Hatch, READING, Berks, RG10 9TH.   (hq)
   0118-940 3416   fax 0118-940 6258
   email info@feta.co.uk   http://www.feta.co.uk
   Dir Gen: Cedric Sloan
○ *T; the responsible provision of suitable ventilation products for all applications in the home
● Mtgs - SG - Inf
< Heating & Ventilating Mfrs' Assn (HEVAC); Fedn Envtl Trade Assns (FETA)
M 19 f

Resin Flooring Association
   alternative name of **FeRFA**

Resolution 1982

NR PO Box 302, ORPINGTON, Kent, BR6 8QX.   (hq)
   01689 820272   fax 01689 896972
   email info@resolution.org.uk
   http://www.resolution.org.uk
   Chmn: Godfrey Freeman
Br 40 regional groups
○ *P; solicitors working in the area of family law & marriage breakdown, who have adopted a conciliatory, rather than a litigious approach to family law
Gp Working parties & c'ees: Mediation, Legal aid, Education, Training, Procedure, Children; Child Support Act
M 5,000 i
¶ NL - 6.   Precedents for Consent Orders - updated.
✕ 2005 Solicitors Family Law Association

Resource Use Institute Ltd (RUI) 1969

NR 19 West End, Kinglassie, LOCHGELLY, Fife, KY5 0XG.   (hsb)
   01592 882248
   http://www.rui.co.uk
   Sec: Miss Isabel Soutar
▲ Company Limited by Guarantee
Br 3
○ *L; to encourage new thinking, especially in science, technology & economics; the management of innovation
Gp Clay minerals; Resource economics; Mathematical chemistry; Land utilisation
● Res
M 18 i, UK / 1 i, o'seas

Restaurant Association

   no longer in existence

Restaurant Property Advisors Society (RPAS) 1990

NR c/o Restaurant Property, Berkeley Square House (2nd floor), Berkeley Square, LONDON, W1J 6BD.   (sb)
   020 7629 9922
   http://www.rpas.org.uk
   Sec: David Rawlinson
▲ Un-incorporated Society
○ *P; 'professionals specialising in the sale, acquisition, letting, valuation, rent review & lease renewal advice on restaurants & other licensed properties'
● Conf - Mtgs
M 58 i

Restaurants Association of Ireland

IRL 11 Bridge Court, City Gate, Saint Augustine St, DUBLIN 8, Republic of Ireland.
   353 (1) 677 9901   fax 353 (1) 671 8414
   email info@rai.ie
   Chief Exec: Henry O'Neill
○ *T

Restricted Growth Association (RGA) 1970

NR PO Box 1024, PETERBOROUGH, Cambs, PE1 8GX. (mail/address)
   01733 759458 (office & helpline)
   email office@restrictedgrowth.co.uk
   Assn Mgr: Angela Belcher
▲ Registered Charity
○ *Q, *W; to promote the general welfare of persons of restricted growth; to investigate the causes & mitigate their medical condition
M i

Retail Book, Stationery & Allied Trade Employees Association (RBA)

NR 22 Borough Fields Shopping Centre, Wootton Bassett, SWINDON, Wilts, SN4 7AX.
   01793 841414
   http://www.the-rba.org
○ *U
   Note: Generally known as the Retail Book Association

Retail Bridalwear Association Ltd (RBA) 1995

■ 106 Broad Street Mall, READING, Berks, RG1 7QA.   (hq)
   01494 445155   fax 01494 445155
   email rba@fsmail.net   http://www.rbaltd.org.uk
   Sec: Philip Rathkey
▲ Company Limited by Guarantee
○ *T; an association of independent bridal & formalwear retailers committed to the highest standards of customer service where the bride & groom can buy with confidence
● Mtgs - ET - SG - VE - LG - Annual awards
> Brit Bridalwear Assn
M 100 i
¶ LM on website

Retail Confectioners & Tobacconists Association Ltd (RCTA) 1976

NR c/o Levicks, 3 Lloyd Rd, BROADSTAIRS, Kent, CT10 1HY.   (hq)
   Contact: Michael Collier
○ *T; 'providing a distribution service of product to members; liaison with trade & industry on issues parochial to the CTN sector in tobacco, confectionery & ancillary fields'

Retail Ireland

IRL Confederation House, 84/86 Lower Baggot St, DUBLIN 2, Republic of Ireland.
   353 (1) 605 1586   fax 353 (1) 638 1559
   http://www.retailireland.ie
   Dir: Torlach Denihan
○ *T
< IBEC

Retail Markets Alliance
NR Hampton House, Hawshaw Lane, Hoyland, BARNSLEY, s Yorks,
      S74 0HA   (sb)
      01226 749021
      email joe.harrison@nmtf.co.uk
      Chief Exec: Joe Harrison
◔ *T
M   org:
      Association of Town Centre Management
      National Association of British Market Authorities
      National Farmers' Retail & Markets Association
      National Market Traders' Federation

Retail Motor Industry Federation   (RMI)   1913
NR 201 Great Portland St, LONDON, W1W 5AB.   (hq)
      020 7580 9122
      http://www.rmif.co.uk
◯ *T; interests of those selling & servicing new & used cars, trucks
      & motorcycles & other related activities
Gp Cherished Numbers Dealers Association; Independent Garage
      Association; Motorcycle Retailers Association; Motorcycle
      Rider Training Association; National Franchised Dealers
      Association; Petrol Retailers Association; Society of Motor
      Auctions;
      Bodyshop Services Division
M   f
¶   Motor Retailer - 12.
      Forecourt - 12.
      Recovery Operator - 4.

Rethink   1972
■ 89 Albert Embankment (15th floor), LONDON, SE1 7TP.   (hq)
      0845 456 0455
      email info@rethink.org   http://www.rethink.org
      Chief Exec: Paul Jenkins
▲ Registered Charity
Br 9 in England, 1 Northern Ireland
◯ *W; to help everyone affected by severe mental illness, recover
      a better quality of life
Gp 350 mental health services; 30 local support groups; National
      advice service
● Mtgs - Res - Inf - LG
      Advice service: 020 7840 3188
<   Mental Health Providers' Forum; Mental Health Alliance; NHS
      Confedn
M   c 6,000 i
¶   Publications list on www.mentalhealthshop.org

Retread Manufacturers Association   (RMA)   1938
NR PO Box 320, CREWE, Cheshire, CW2 6WY.   (hq)
      01270 561014   fax 01270 668801
      http://www.retreaders.org.uk
▲ Un-incorporated Society
◯ *T; for the UK retread tyre industry & associated businesses
● Conf - Mtgs - ET - Exam - Res - Exhib - SG - Stat - Inf - VE - LG
<   Intl Assn of Retreading & Dealer Assns (BIPAVER); Eur Tyre
      Recycling Assn (ETRA); Soc of Assn Execs (SAE); Tyre Ind
      Coun (TIC); Brit Tyre Ind Fedn (BTIF)
M   110 f, UK / 6 f, o'seas
¶   The Retreader (published in Tyres & Accessories) - 12.
      LM - updated.   AR.
      Manual of Operating Standards.

Retreat Association   (RA)   1989
■ The Central Hall, 256 Bermondsey St, LONDON, SE1 3UJ.
      (hq)
      020 7357 7736   fax 0871 715 1917
      email info@retreats.org.uk   http://www.retreats.org.uk
      Dir: Alison MacTier
▲ Registered Charity
◯ *G, *N, *R; a federation of Christian retreat groups
● Conf - Mtgs - ET - Inf - Promoting retreats & offering advice
      about spiritual direction & training
M   7 retreat gps each with own members:
      Association for Promoting Retreats
      Baptist Union Retreat Group
      Catholic Network for Retreats & Spirituality
      Methodist Retreat & Spirituality Network
      Quaker Retreat Group
      United Reformed Church Silence & Retreat Network
      affiliates of the Retreat Associaton
¶   Retreats - 1.   2 copies ftm m, £5.50 nm.
      Information leaflets.

**Retroreflective Equipment Manufacturers' Association
(REMA)   1977**
NR 9 Cavendish Rd, LYTHAM ST ANNES, Lancs, FY8 2PX.   (hsp)
      01253 722598   fax 01253 722598
      email info@rema.org.uk   http://www.rema.org.uk
      Hon Sec: John Lloyd
▲ Un-incorporated Society
◯ *T; manufacturers of road & other safety products that employ
      wholly retroreflective surfaces in their construction or form
Gp Road studs; Temporary markings; High visibility clothing; Road
      cones & cylinders; Road danger lamps; Retroreflective
      materials; Barriers & temporary signs; Marker posts & street
      furniture
● Mtgs - SG - Inf - LG
M   32 f
¶   LM - 1; free.

Rett Syndrome Association   (RSA)   1985
■ Langham House West, Mill St, LUTON, Beds, LU1 2NA.
      01582 98910   fax 01582 724129
      email info@rettsyndrome.org.uk
      http://www.rettsyndrome.org.uk
      Hon Chmn: Linda Partridge
▲ Registered Charity
◯ *M, *W; 'Rett syndrome is a complex neurological disorder that
      occurs mostly in females; the charity offers help & advice to
      all families & professionals; to raise funds for research'
● Fund raising - Specialist clinics - Facilitates local support groups
<   Intl Rett Syndrome Assn
M   i
¶   NL - 4.

Returned Volunteer Action   (RVA)   1966
■ 76 Wentworth St, LONDON, E1 7SA.   (hq)
      020 7247 6406
      email retvolact@lineone.net
      Hon Sec: A C Symes
▲ Company Limited by Guarantee; Registered Charity
◯ *W; to help returned volunteers & development workers
      evaluate their overseas experience; to encourage those
      seeking overseas placements to examine their personal
      expectations & motivations
● ET - Inf
M   350 i, 250 org
¶
      Introduction to Volunteering Overseas; £4.
      Publications list available; free.

Reuseable Healthcare Textile Association
      a group of the **Performance Textiles Association**

RGDATA   (RGDATA)
IRL   Rock House, BLACKROCK, Co Dublin, Republic of Ireland.
        353 (1) 288 7584   fax 353 (1) 283 2206
        email rgdata@rgdata.ie   http://www.rgdata.ie
        Dir Gen: Tara Buckley
○   *T; the representative body for the independent retail grocery
        sector in Ireland

Rhea & Emu Association   (REA)
NR   31 Newbold Rd, KIRKBY MALLORY, Leics, LE9 7QG.   (hsp)
        01455 823344   fax 01455 823344
        email margaret@leicestershireemus.com
        Sec: Margaret Dover
○   *B; for keepers of rhea (Pampas ostrich) & emus
●   Mtgs
M   40 i, UK / 1 i, o'seas

Rheumatoid Arthritis Surgical Society
        a specialist society of the **British Orthopaedic Association**

Rice Association   (RA)   1989
NR   21 Arlington St, LONDON, SW1A 1RN.   (hq)
        020 7493 2521
▲   Un-incorporated Society
○   *T; processors, packers & users of rice in the UK
●   Mtgs - LG
<   Food & Drink Fedn
M   16 f
¶   LM; free.

Richard Aldington Society
        alternative name of the **New Canterbury Literary Society**

Richard III Society - Fellowship of the White Boar   1924
■   Gorsedene, Bagshot Rd, Knaphill, WOKING, Surrey,
        GU21 2SF.   (hsp)
        email information@richardiii.net   http://www.richardiii.net
        Hon Sec: Jane Trump
▲   Un-incorporated Society
Br   15; America, Australia, Canada
○   *G, *L; to promote historical research into life & times of King
        Richard III & to secure re-assessment of his role in English
        history
●   Conf - Mtgs - Res - Inf - Lib - VE
M   3,000 i, UK / 1,000 i, o'seas
¶   The Ricardian - 1; ftm, £16 nm.
        The Ricardian Bulletin - 4; ftm only.

Richard Jefferies Society   1950
■   Pear Tree Cottage, Longcot, FARINGDON, Oxon, SN7 7SS.
        (hsp)
        01793 783040
        Hon Sec: Jean Saunders
▲   Registered Charity
○   *A; to promote study & interest in the life & works of Richard
        Jefferies, naturalist & writer, & concern for places intimately
        connected with him in Wiltshire, Sussex & Surrey
●   Mtgs - Res - Inf - Lib - PL - VE - Book sales - Care of memorials
M   c 300 i & org
¶   Jnl - 1; ftm, £1.50 nm.   NL - 2;   AR; both ftm.

Richard Strauss Society   1991
NR   104 Church Rd, RICHMOND, Surrey, TW10 6LW.   (treas/p)
        http://www.richard-strauss-society.co.uk
        Treas: Nigel Coles
▲   Registered Charity; Un-incorporated Society
○   *D; the life & works of Richard Strauss
●   Conf - SG - VE
M   100 i, UK / 2 i, o'seas
¶   NL - 3/4; ftm only.

Richmond Chamber of Commerce   1908
NR   River Reach House (2nd floor) 31-15 High St, KT1 1LF.   (hq)
        020 8541 4441
        http://www.richmondchamberofcommerce.co.uk
        Pres: Christina Jackson
○   *C
●   Conf - Mtgs - ET - Stat - Inf - LG
<   West London Enterprise Agency; Richmond in Business
✕   2005 Richmond Borough Chamber of Commerce

Rider Haggard Society   (RHS)   1984
■   27 Deneholm, Monkseaton, WHITLEY BAY, Tyne & Wear,
        NE25 9AU.   (hsp)
        0191-252 4516
        email rb27allen@blueyonder.co.uk
        http://www.riderhaggardsociety.org.uk
        Hon Sec: Roger Allen
▲   Un-incorporated Society
○   *A; to futher the works of Rider Haggard (1856-1925) &
        provide access to his books, his life & his influence on others
●   Mtgs - Res - Comp - Inf - VE
<   Alliance of Literary Socs
M   70 i, UK / 30 i, o'seas
        (Sub: £9 UK / £10 o'seas
¶   The Haggard Jnl - 4; ftm.
        Illustrated Guide to Fiction of Rider Haggard; £15.
        Illustrated Guide to Non-Fiction of Rider Haggard; £16.
        Haggardiana (ephemera folder); £16 m, £25 nm.

Riding for the Disabled
        a discipline member of the **British Equestrian Federation**

Riding for the Disabled Association   1969
■   Norfolk House, 1a Tournament Court, Edgehill Drive,
        WARWICK, CV34 6LG.   (hq)
        0845 658 1082   fax 0845 658 1083
        email info@rda.org.uk   http://www.rda.org.uk
        Chief Exec: Ed Bracher
▲   Company Limited by Guarantee; Registered Charity
○   *W; to improve the lives of people with special needs, by
        enabling them to ride &/or carriage drive for the benefit of
        their health & general wellbeing
●   Conf - Mtgs - ET - Exam - Comp - LG
<   Fedn of Riding for the Disabled Intl; Brit Equestrian Fedn; Nat
        Equine Welfare Coun
M   18,500 i (volunteers), 25,000 i (riders)
¶   RDA News - 3; free (not Summer).

Riggit Galloway Cattle Society
NR   Sherberton Farm, Princetown, YELVERTON, Devon, PL20 6SF.
        01364 631276
        http://www.riggitgallowaycattlesociety.co.uk
        Sec: Anton Coaker
○   *B

Rights of Women   (ROW)   1975
■   52-54 Featherstone St, LONDON, EC1Y 8RT.   (hq)
        020 7251 6575/6   fax 020 7490 5377
        email info@row.org.uk
        http://www.rightsofwomen.org.uk
        Dir: Ranjit Kaur
▲   Un-incorporated Society
○   *K; to advise & inform women of their legal rights & promote
        the interests of women in relation to the law
●   Conf - Mtgs - Res - Inf - Legal advice/referral
        Advice: 020 7251 8887 (Mon 1100-1300, Tues 1000-1200)
<   Advice UK
M   150 i, 50 f

Rigid Intermediate Bulk Container Association
        in 2004 merged with the Association of Drum Manufacturers & the
        Federation of Drum Reconditioners to form the **Industrial**
        Packaging Association

Ring of Tatters   1980
- ■ 7 Oakfield, Caerleon, NEWPORT, Mon, NP18 3DP.
  (mem/sec/p)
  http://www.ringoftatters.org.uk
  Mem Sec: Jean Johnston
- ○ *G; to promote interest in & knowledge of the lacemaking craft
  of tatting
- ● Mtgs - ET - Exhib - Comp - Lib
- M 800 i, 400 i
- ¶ NL - 2; £6.75 m only.

**River Association for Freight & Transport (incorporating
   AMLBO)   (RAFT)   2000**
- NR Tamesis House, 35 St Philip's Avenue, WORCESTER PARK,
  Surrey, KT4 8JS.   (hq)
  020 8330 6446   fax 020 8330 7447
  email raft@tamgroup.co.uk
  Sec: N Barry Jaynes
- ○ *T; for operation on & around the River Thames
- Gp Lighterage; Passenger boats; Wharves
- ● Mtgs - Comp - LG
- M 12 f

River Thames Alliance   2003
- NR c/o Environment Agency (Thames Region), Kings Meadow
  House, Kings Meadow Rd, READING, Berks, RG1 8DQ.
  0118-953 5527
  http://www.riverthamesalliance.com
  Contact: Juliet King
- ○ *G, *K; to help manage the future of the non-tidal Thames
- M 78 org

River Thames Society   (RTS)   1962
- ■ 23a Cuxham Rd, WATLINGTON, Oxon, OX49 5JW.   (admin p)
  01491 612456
  http://www.riverthamessociety.org.uk
  Admin: Mrs Helen Batten
- ▲ Company Limited by Guarantee; Registered Charity
- Br 5
- ○ *G; encouragement of interest in the river & preservation &
  development of its amenities & natural beauty
- ● Conf - Mtgs - Exhib - Lib (at River & Rowing Museum, Henley-
  on-Thames)
- < Inland Waterways Assn; Ramblers Assn
- M c 1,200 i, f & org, UK / 2 i, o'seas
- ¶ Thames Guardian - 4.

RLUK: Research Libraries UK   (RLUK)   1985
- ■ Maugham Library, King's College London, Chancery Lane,
  LONDON, WC2A 1LR.   (dir b)
  020 7848 2737
  http://www.rluk.ac.uk
  Exec Dir: Anne Poulson
- ▲ Company Limited by Guarantee; Registered Charity
- ○ *P; to increase the ability of research libraries to share
  resources for the benefit of the local, national & international
  research community
- ● Res - Lib
- < Ligue des Bibliothéques Européennes de Recherche (LIBER);
  Digital Presvn Coalition; Counting Online use of Networked
  Electronic Resources (COUNTER)
- M 29 research libraries
- ¶ AR - 1.
- × 2004 Consortium of University Research Libraries
  2008 CURL: Consortium of Research Libraries in the British
  Isles

RNID   (RNID)   1911
- NR 19-23 Featherstone St, LONDON, EC1Y 8SL.   (hq)
  0808 808 0123 (voice)   0808 808 9000 (textphone)
  fax 020 7296 8199
  email informationline@rnid.org.uk
  http://www.rnid.org.uk
- ▲ Registered Charity
- Br 7 offices
- ○ *W; works to provide services for deaf & hard of hearing
  people; seeks to raise public awareness of the issues
  surrounding deafness
- ● ET - Res - Exhib - Inf - Lib
  Services for deaf people: Typetalk, the national telephone relay
  service; Sound Advantage, providing assistive devices
- M 37,624 i & org
- ¶ One in Seven - 6

Road Block
  a project of the **Campaign for Better Transport**

Road Emulsion Association Ltd   (REAL)   1928
- NR September House, Plantation Way, STORRINGTON, W Sussex,
  RH20 4JF.   (hq)
  01903 746584
  http://www.rea.org.uk
  Consultant & Sec: John Keayes
- ▲ Company Limited by Guarantee
- ○ *T; to promote the interests of producers & suppliers of road
  emulsion materials
- ● Conf - Mtgs - Inf - LG
- < Intl Bitumen Emulsion Fedn (IBEF); Asphalt Emulsion Mfrs
  Assn (AEMA)
- M 6 f

Road Haulage Association Ltd   (RHA)   1945
- ■ 35 Monument Hill, WEYBRIDGE, Surrey, KT13 8RN.   (hq)
  01932 841515
  http://www.rha.net
  Chief Exec: Roger King
- ▲ Company Limited by Guarantee
- Br 4
- ○ *T; to represent Britain's professional hire-or-reward hauliers
- Gp National Agricultural, Foods & Tipping; Livestock carriers; Milk
  carriers; Car transporters; Express parcels; Tankers
- ● Conf - Mtgs - ET - Exhib
- < Intl Road Transport U
- M 10,000 f
- ¶ Roadway - 12; ftm.   Road Haulage Manual - 2 yrly; ftm.

Road Locomotive Society   (RLS)   1937
- NR PO Box 1878, ANDOVER, Hants, SP10 9AU.
  01332 781485
- ▲ Registered Charity
- ○ *G; to encourage education & research into the history of self
  propelling steam engines & vehicles (other than those
  running on rails) & portable engines

Road Records Association   (RRA)   1888
- NR 135 Beaconsfield Rd, ENFIELD, Middx, EN3 6AY.   (chmn/p)
  01992 762121
  http://www.rra.org.uk
  Gen Sec: Brian Edrupt
- ○ *S; verification of road cycling records
- ● Dinner (triennial)
- M 500 i, UK / 6 i, o'seas

© CBD Research Ltd · Beckenham · BR3 5JS · Tel 020 8650 7745 · Fax 020 8650 0768 · E-mail cbd@cbdresearch.com · www.cbdresearch.com

Road Rescue Recovery Association   (RRRA)   1987

■ Hubberts Bridge Rd, Kirton Holme, BOSTON, Lincs,
   PE20 1TW.   (hq)
   01205 290622   fax 01205 290611
   email linda@recovery.co.uk   http://www.rrra.co.uk
   Chmn: Nigel Howarth
▲ Company Limited by Guarantee
○ *T;
● Mtgs - ET - Exam - Res - Exhib - Inf - LG - Shows
M 31 i, 448 f
¶ Jnl - 4; ftm, £2.95 nm.   NL - 2; ftm only.
   Ybk - 1; free.   LM - irreg.   AR; ftm only.

Road Roller Association   (RRA)   1974

NR Invicta, 9 Beagle Ridge Drive, Acomb, YORK, YO24 3JH.
   (memsec/p)
   email info@r-r-a.org.uk   http://www.r-r-a.org.uk
   Mem Sec: Mrs D Rayner
○ *G; preservation, study of history & manufacture of road rollers
   & road making equipment, especially steam road rollers
● Mtgs - ET - Res - Exhib - Inf - Lib - PL - VE
< Nat Traction Engine Trust; Transport Trust; Fedn British Historic
   Vehicles Clubs
M 500 i, 8 f
¶ Rolling - 4; ftm.

Road Runners Club   (RRC)   1951

NR 7 Bellway Court, Grosvensor Rd, WESTCLIFF-on-SEA, Essex,
   SS0 8EP.   (treas/p)
   Hon Treas: Elaine Oddie
○ *S; road running & long distance running & racing
● Mtgs - Comp - Road running course measurement - Standards
   scheme for road runners - Insurance for road runners
M i
¶ NL - 3; ftm only.

Road Safety Markings Association   (RSMA)   1976

■ Unit 35 Corringham Rd Industrial Estate, Corringham Rd,
   GAINSBOROUGH, Lincs, DN21 1QB.   (hq)
   01427 610101   fax 01427 610106
   email rsma@dial.pipex.com
   Nat Dir: George Lee
▲ Un-incorporated Society
○ *T; provision of road/traffic safety markings, both vertical &
   horizontal (incl: thermoplastic, paint, road studs, road tapes)
   Is an NVQ assessment centre
Gp Road marking forum; Client/contractor partnership gp; Health
   & safety forum; Promoting health & safety to industry;
   Marketing; Technical; Contracting; Ad hoc projects
● Conf - Mtgs - ET - Res - Exhib - SG - Stat - Inf - LG - is an NVQ
   assessment centre
< Intl Road Fedn
M 75 f, 5 org
¶ Standard Issue (NL) - 4.
   Update your Road Markings (CD); ftm.
   Whose Job is it Anyway? (video).
   Top Marks - 1;   Stanspec 2006 (CD).
   RSMA Safety Code of Practice (CD) - 1.

Road Surface Dressing Association Ltd
   in 2008 merged with the Slurry Surfacing Contractors Association &
   the High Friction Surfacing Association to form the **Road Surface
   Treatments Association**

Road Surface Treatments Association   (RSTA)   2008

■ Westwood Park, London Rd, Little Horkesley, COLCHESTER,
   Essex, CO6 4BU.   (hq)
   01206 274052   fax 01206 274053
   email enquiries@rsta-uk.org   http://www.rsta-uk.org
   Consultant Dir: John Baxter
▲ Company Limited by Guarantee
○ *T; highways maintenance - to promote quality, workforce
   competence & safe working practices
● Conf - Mtgs - ET - Exhib - Stat
< Road Users Alliance
M 67 f
   (Sub: £1,000)
¶ Code of Practice for Surface Dressing; £30 m, £50 nm; and
   Code of Practice for Signing in at Surface Dressing Sites; both
   free to download.
   Pocket Guide to Road Note 39; £5 m, £8 nm.
× 2008 (Road Surface Dressing Association
      (High Friction Surfacing Association
      (Slurry Surfacing Contractors Association

Road Transport Fleet Data Society   (Fleet Data)   1980

NR 18 Poplar Close, BIGGLESWADE, Beds, SG18 0EW.   (hsp)
   email info@fleetdata.co.uk
   Hon Sec: P Jarman
▲ Un-incorporated Society
○ *G; interest in vehicles of local & national government, public
   service fleets, power & water industries etc; research on
   vehicles & operators which no longer exist
● Res - SG - Inf - Lib - PL - VE - Compilation of photographic &
   related items
M 90 i
¶ Council Vehicle News - 4;   Ybk - irreg;
   Public Utilities Bulletin - 4; all ftm only.
   Vehicle Operator Lists - irreg.
   British Military Serials - irreg.
   Note: NO trade enquiries please!

RoadPeace, UK's charity for road crash victims   1992

■ G4b Shakespeare Business Centre, 245a Coldharbour Lane,
   LONDON SW9 8RR.   (hq)
   0845 450 0355
   email info@roadpeace.org   http://www.roadpeace.org
▲ Registered Charity
○ *K, *W; offers vital information & assistance to bereaved &
   injured road victims; advocates for their rights & justice;
   highlights road danger issues
● Conf - Mtgs - ET - Res - Exhib - Stat - Inf - Lib - LG
< Eur Fedn of Road Crash Victims (NGO of UN); PACTS;
   Transport 2000; Safer Streets Coalition, Slower Speeds
   Initiative
M 2,000 i, 300 f, 50 org, UK / 30 i, o'seas

Roads & Road Transport History Association Ltd   (RRTHA)   1992

■ 21 The Oaklands, DROITWICH, Worcs, WR9 8AD.   (hsp)
   email ernquiries@rrtha.org.uk   http://www.rrtha.org.uk
   Hon Sec: P Jaques
▲ Company Limited by Guarantee
○ *G; to promote the study of the history of roads, road
   passenger transport & the carriage of goods
● Conf - Mtgs - Res - SG - Inf - VE
M 100 i, 16 org
¶ NL - 4; m only.   Symposium Papers - 1; £3.

Robert Bloomfield Society   2000

NR 71 Spenser Rd, BEDFORD, MK40 2BE.   (sp)
   Contact: Hugh Underhill
○ *A; English shoemaker & poet 1766-1823

Robert Burns World Federation Ltd   1885
■   Dean Castle Country Park, KILMARNOCK, Ayrshire,
      KA3 1XB.   (hq)
      01563 572469   fax 01563 572469
      email admin@robertburnsfederation.com
      http://www.robertburnsfederation.com
      Chief Exec: Mrs Shirley Bell
▲   Company Limited by Guarantee; Registered Charity
○   *A, *E; to stimulate the teaching & study of Scottish literature,
      history, art, music & language through competitions; to
      conserve buildings & places associated with Robert
      Burns (1759-1796) & his contemporaries
●   Conf - Mtgs - ET - Comp - Inf - LG
M   356 i, 6 f, 249 org, UK / 67 i, 54 org, o'seas
¶   Burns Chronicle - 3; ftm, £5 nm.   AR.

Robert Farnon Society   (RFS)   1956
■   Stone Gables, Upton Lane, Seavington St Michael, ILMINSTER,
      Somerset, TA19 0PZ.   (hsp)
      01460 242226   fax 01460 242226
      http://www.rfsoc.org.uk
      Hon Sec: David Ades
▲   Un-incorporated Society
○   *D; a musical appreciation society for lovers of light orchestral
      & film music; to keep members informed of all aspects of
      Robert Farnon's work in radio, TV, films, records etc; to
      encourage & publicise the work of other similar musicians
      from light classics to jazz
●   Mtgs (in London April & November) - Res - Stat - Inf
M   750 i, UK / 100 i, o'seas
¶   Journal into Melody - 4; £15 yr.

Robert Louis Stevenson Club   (RLS Club)   1920
■   17 Heriot Row, EDINBURGH, EH3 6HP.   (hsp)
      0131-556 1896   fax 0131-556 1896
      email mail@stevenson-house.co.uk
      http://www.rlsclub.org.uk
      Correspondence Sec: John W S McFie
▲   Registered Charity
○   *A, *G; to foster an interest in the life & works of Robert Louis
      Stevenson (1850-94)
●   Mtgs - Inf - VE
M   282 i, 2 f, UK / 64 i, 2 org, o'seas
      (Sub: £20 i, £26 org UK / £26 i, £34 org o'seas)
¶   RLS Club News - 2; ftm only.

Roller Coaster Club of Great Britain   (RCCGB)   1988
■   PO Box 235, UXBRIDGE, Middx, UB10 0TF.   (hq)
      01895 259802   fax 01895 259802
      email rccgb@rccgb.co.uk
      Chmn: Andy Hine
○   *G; to unite roller-coaster enthusiasts from all over the world; to
      encourage amusement parks & manufacturers to create &
      build new, exciting & daring rides
Gp   Historians photo library
●   Mtgs - Res - Exhib - Comp - Stat - Inf - PL - Annual coach tour
      of coasters in Europe & the USA
<   Intl Assn of Amusement Parks & Attractions (IAAPA)
M   1,300 i, 21 f, 1 org, UK / 100 i, 17 f, 1 org, o'seas
      (Sub: £25 i, £30 f, £25 org UK / £35 i, £40 f,
      £35 org o'seas)
¶   AIRtime (Jnl) - 6; ftm only.
      Yearly Survey (Report) - 1; ftm, £3 nm.

Roman Finds Group
NR   Centre for Archaeology, Fort Cumberland, PORTSMOUTH,
      Hants, PO4 9LD.
      023 9285 6700
      http://www.romanfinds.org.uk
      Gen Sec: Nicola Hembrey
○   *G; for all interested in Roman artifacts
●   Mtgs
M   i
¶   NL - 2

Roman Society
      alternative name of the **Society for the Promotion of Roman
      Studies**

Romantic Novelists Association   (RNA)   1960
NR   Bonnyton House, Arbirlot, ARBROATH, Angus, DD11 2PY.
      (hsp)
      01241 874131   fax 01241 874131
      email eileen@eileenramsay.f9.co.uk
      http://www.rna-uk.org
      Chmn: Catherine Jones,   Hon Sec: Eileen Ramsay
▲   Un-incorporated Society
○   *A; to raise the prestige of the genre & the professionalism of
      romantic novelists
Gp   New Writers Scheme (for unpublished writers)
●   Conf - Mtgs - Comp - Inf
M   700 i, UK / 20 i, o'seas
¶   RNA News - 4.

Romany Society   1996
■   10 Haslam St, BURY, Lancs, BL9 6EQ.   (hsp)
      0161-764 7078   fax 01625 504515
      email romany@macclesfield.gov.uk
      Hon Sec: John Thorpe
▲   Un-incorporated Society
○   *G; to celebrate the life & work of the Rev G Bramwell Evens -
      'Romany of the BBC'; to ensure that his ground-breaking
      natural history broadcasting is remembered by future
      generations; to promote interest in the natural world by all &
      particularly the young
●   Mtgs - Res - Inf - Lib - VE
<   Alliance Literary Socs
M   241 i, 3 org, UK / 2 i, o'seas
¶   Romany Magazine - 1;   NL - seasonal; both ftm only.

Romney Sheep Breeders' Society   1895
■   2 Woodland Close, WEST MALLING, Kent, ME19 6RR.   (sp)
      01732 845637
      email alan.t.west@btinternet.com
      http://www.romneysheepuk.com
      Sec: Alan West
▲   Company Limited by Guarantee
○   *B
Gp   Registration of members; Registration of animals; Official
      society records; Export promotion
●   Mtgs - Exhib - Expt
<   Nat Sheep Assn
M   120 i, 60 org
¶   The Romney Flock Book - 1;   The Romney Hbk - irreg;
      both free.

Ronald Stevenson Society   (RSS)   1993
■   3 Chamberlain Rd, EDINBURGH, EH10 4DL.   (hsp)
      fax 0131-229 9298
      email info@ronaldstevensonsociety.org.uk
      http://www.ronaldstevensonsociety.org.uk
      Chmn: Philip Hutton,   Hon Sec: Iain Colquhoun
▲   Un-incorporated Society
Br   Luxembourg, Switzerland
○   *D; to publish & promote the performance & recording of the
      music of Ronald Stevenson, Scottish composer, pianist &
      writer
Gp   Pianists; Singers; Chamber players; Conductors
●   Conf - Res - Summer symposium - Concerts & recitals -
      Publication of Stevenson's music
<   Scot Music Inf Centre; Nat Lib
      Scotland; Scot Poetry Lib; Scot Arts Coun
M   105 i, 3 org, UK / 25 i, o'seas
¶   NL - 3; ftm, subscribers only nm.
      Catalogue of Publications.

© CBD Research Ltd · Beckenham · BR3 5JS · Tel 020 8650 7745 · Fax 020 8650 0768 · E-mail cbd@cbdresearch.com · www.cbdresearch.com

Roofing Industry Alliance   (RIA)   1997
- ◼ Roofing House, 31 Worship St, LONDON, EC2A 2DX.   (hq)
  020 7448 3857   fax 020 7256 2125
  Co Sec: William A Jenkins
- ▲ Company Limited by Guarantee
- ○ *N, *T; to provide an umbrella organisation to bring together
  the various associations within the roofing industry; to
  provide a collective forum to work with construction skills to
  improve training in the roofing industry
- ● ET - LG

ROOM at RTPI   (ROOM)   1900
- NR 41 Botolph Lane, LONDON, EC3R 8DL.   (hq)
  020 7929 9494   fax 020 7929 9490
  email room@rtpi.org.uk   http://www.room.org.uk
- ▲ Registered Charity
- ○ *K, *N; to bring together all those involved in housing planning
  & regeneration on an equal footing, to share information,
  debate the issues, influence policy & contribute to best
  practice

Rotating Electrical Machines Association
   an association in the Power section of **BEAMA Ltd**

Rotherham Chamber of Commerce
   on 1 August 2006 merged with the Barnsley Chamber of Commerce
   & Industry to form the **Chamber of Commerce (Barnsley &
   Rotherham) Ltd**

Rough Fell Sheep Breeders Association   (RFSBA)   1926
- ◼ High Newstead Farm, Jervaulx, Masham, RIPON, N Yorks,
  HG4 4PJ.   (sp)
  01677 460241
  http://www.roughfellsheep.co.uk
  Sec: Amanda Croft
- ○ *B
- ● Mtgs - Res - Exhib - Inf
- M c 200 i
- ¶ Flock Book - 1.

Rough & Smooth Collie Training Association   (RSCTA)   1991
- ◼ 1 Leigh Lane, Bramshall, UTTOXETER, Staffs, ST14 5DN.   (hsp)
  01889 568090
  email jean@rscta.co.uk   http://www.rscta.co.uk
  Hon Sec: Mrs Jean Tuck
- ▲ Un-incorporated Society
- ○ *B; to preserve, promote & enhance the Rough & Smooth Collie
  as a working breed through the establishment & support of
  working events & tests
- ● ET
- M 83 i
  (Sub: £5)
- ¶ NL - 3; ftm, £1 nm.   LM - 1; ftm only.

Round Tower Churches Society   (RTCS)   1973
- ◼ Crabbe Hall, Burnham Market, KING'S LYNN, Norfolk,
  PE31 8EN.   (hsp)
  01328 738237
  http://www.roundtowers.org.uk
  Hon Sec: Mrs E M Stilgoe
- ▲ Registered Charity
- ○ *G; promotion of interest, research & preservation of round
  tower churches
- ● Res - Exhib - SG - Inf - Lib - VE - Lectures, slide shows &
  organised tours to churches
- M 520 i, 55 parochial church councils, UK / 6 i, o'seas
- ¶ Magazine - 4; ftm, 50p nm.

Roundhead Association
   a group of the **English Civil War Society Ltd**

Roussin Sheep Society   1989
- NR Mount Pleasant Farm, Hatherleigh, OKEHAMPTON, Devon,
  EX20 3LN.   (sp)
  01837 810006
  Sec: Andrea Molyneux
- ○ *B
- < Nat Sheep Assn

**Routemaster Operators & Owners Association   (Routemaster
Association)   1988**
- NR 6 Silverdale Grove, RUSHDEN, Northants, NN10 6UG.
  01933 316844
  http://www.routemaster.org.uk
  Sec: Mike Fuller
- ○ *G; for operators & owners of Routemaster buses, suppliers of
  parts or services & anyone else with a genuine interest in
  their operation or preservation
- M c 400
- ¶ Routemaster Magazine

Royal Academy of Arts   (RA)   1768
- NR Burlington House, Piccadilly, LONDON, W1J 0BD.   (hq)
  020 7300 8000   fax 020 7300 8001
  http://www.royalacademy.org.uk
  Sec & Chief Exec: Charles Saumarez Smith
- ▲ Registered Charity
- ○ *A; to promote the creation, enjoyment and appreciation of the
  visual arts through exhibitions, education and debate
- Gp Friends of the Royal Academy
- ● ET - Exhib - Lib
- < Amer Associates of the R Academy Trust; R Scot Academy; R
  Hibernian Academy
- M 80 i & c 85,000 friends
- ¶ R A Magazine - 4; ftm.   AR.

Royal Academy of Dance   (RAD)   1920
- NR 36 Battersea Sq, LONDON, SW11 3RA.   (hq)
  020 7326 8000   fax 020 7924 3129
  email info@rad.org.uk   http://www.rad.org.uk
  Chief Exec: Luke Rittner
- ▲ Registered Charity
- Br 83 o'seas
- ○ *D, *E, *P; to improve the standards of dance teaching
  worldwide; to provide the opportunity for largest number of
  children to learn & enjoy ballet
- Gp Benesh Institute
- ● Conf - ET - Exam - Comp - Inf - Lib - PL
- M 13,000 i, UK & o'seas
- ¶ Dance Gazette - 3.
  UK Diary (with Dance Gazette).   AR.

Royal Academy of Dramatic Art   (RADA)   1904
- § 62-64 Gower St, LONDON, WC1E 6ED.   (hq)
  020 7636 7076   fax 020 7323 3865
  http://www.rada.org
  To train actors, stage managers & technical staff for
  professional stage, film & television.

Royal Academy of Engineering   (RAEng)   1976
- ◼ 3 Carlton House Terrace, LONDON, SW1Y 5DG.   (hq)
  020 7766 0600   fax 020 7930 1549
  email administrator@raeng.org.uk
  http://www.raeng.org.uk
  Chief Exec: P D Greenish
- ▲ Registered Charity
- ○ *L, *N; promotion of excellence in engineering in the UK;
  promotion of engineering education
- ● Conf - Mtgs - ET - Res - SG - VE - LG
- < Eur Coun of Applied Sciences & Engg (Euro-CASE); Coun of
  Academies of Engg & Technological Services (CAETS)
- M 1,259 i, UK / 87 i, o'seas
  (Sub: £210)
- ¶ Ingenia - 4;   NL - 4; both free.

Royal Academy of Medicine in Ireland   1882
IRL   Frederick House, 19 South Frederick Street, DUBLIN 2, Republic
    of Ireland
       353 (1) 633 4820   fax 353 (1) 676 4918
       email secretary@rami.ie   http://www.rami.ie
    Gen Sec: Dr John O'Connor
○   *M, *P

Royal Academy of Music   (RAM)   1822
NR   Marylebone Rd, LONDON, NW1 5HT.   (hq)
       020 7873 7373   fax 020 7873 7374
       http://www.ram.ac.uk
    Principal: Prof Jonathan Freeman-Attwood
▲   Registered Charity
○   *D, *P; the further education & training of musicians
    (performers of classical music & jazz, opera & music theatre;
    composers)
●   ET - Res - Exhib - Inf - Lib - VE - Public concerts
<   University of London
M   i
¶   Diary of Events - 3; free.
    Prospectus (details of classes & entry arrangements); free.

Royal Aero Club - Records, Racing & Rally Association   (3R's)   1982
NR   Ballagarraghy, ST JOHNS, Isle of Man, IM4 3LH.   (chmn/p)
       01624 801027
       http://www.airraceuk.co.uk
    Chmn: Geoffrey Boot,   Sec: Judy Hanson
▲   Company Limited by Guarantee
○   *S; national handicap air racing
●   Comp
<   Fédn Aeronautique Intl; R Aero Club
M   59 i

Royal Aero Club Trust   1998
NR   Kimberley House, Vaughan Way, LEICESTER, LE1 4SG.   (regd
    off)
       0116-253 1051   fax 0116-251 5939
       email administrator@royalaeroclubtrust.org
       http://www.royalaeroclubtrust.org
    Hon Treas & Sec: Peter Crispin
▲   Company Limited by Guarantee; Registered Charity
○   *G; to advance the course of air sport & aviation
Gp   Flying for youth: Bursary scheme, Airsport information data
    bank; Conservation of memorabilia; National photographic
    competition
●   Conf - ET - Res - Comp - SG - PL
<   R Aero Club UK
¶   AR

Royal Aero Club of the UK
■   Radford Barn, Radford Semele, ROYAL LEAMINGTON SPA,
    Warks, CV31 1UT.   (hq)
       01926 332713   fax 01926 335206
       email secretary@royalaeroclub.org
       http://www.royalaeroclub.org
    Sec: Diana M King
▲   Company Limited by Guarantee
○   *G, *N, *S; the coordinating body of British airsport
●   Comp - LG
<   EAS; FAI
M   160 i, 6 f, 20 org, UK / 5 i, o'seas
¶   NL - 4; ftm.
    Annual Award Ceremony Report - 1; ftm (on application nm).

Royal Aeronautical Society   (RAeS)   1866
■   4 Hamilton Place, LONDON, W1J 7BQ.   (hq)
       020 7670 4300   fax 020 7499 6230
       email raes@aerosociety.com
       http://www.aerosociety.com
    Chief Exec: Keith Mans
▲   Registered Charity
Br   37; Australia, Cyprus, France, Germany, Hong Kong, Ireland,
    Kenya, Malaysia, New Zealand, Pakistan, Singapore,
    South Africa, UAE, Zimbabwe
○   *L, *P; for the global aerospace community; for the general
    advancement of aeronautical art, science & engineering &
    for promoting that species of knowledge which distinguishes
    the profession of aeronautics
Gp   Aerodynamics; Aerospace medicine; Air law; Air power; Air
    transport; Airworthiness & maintenance; Avionics & systems;
    Environment; Flight operations; Flight simulation; Flight test;
    General aviation; Historical; Human factors; Human
    powered; Licensed engineers; Management studies;
    Propulsion; Rotorcraft; Space; Structures & materials; UAV;
    Weapons systems & technology
●   Conf - Mtgs - ET - Res - Comp - Inf - Lib - PL - VE - LG -
    Careers service
M   15,000 i, 101 f, UK / 4,500 i, 15 f, o'seas
¶   Aeronautical Jnl - 12; £39 yr m, £25 yr nm.
    Aerospace International - 12; ftm, £95 yr nm.
    Aerospace Professional - 12; ftm only.

Royal African Society   1901
NR   36 Gordon Square, LONDON, WC1H 0PD.   (hq)
       020 3073 8335   fax 020 3073 8340
       email ras@soas.ac.uk
       http://www.royalafricansociety.org
    Sec: Gemma Haxby
Br   3
○   *X; to spread information about the peoples & countries of
    Africa; to develop public interest in African problems; to
    serve as a link between the peoples of UK & Africa
●   Conf - Mtgs - Lib
M   599 i, 23 f, UK / 157 i, 2 f, o'seas
¶   African Affairs - 4.

Royal Agricultural Society of the Commonwealth   (RASC)   1957
■   Royal Highland Centre, Ingliston, EDINBURGH, EH28 8NF.
    (hq)
       0131-335 6200   fax 0131-335 6229
       email rasc@commagshow.org
       http://www.commagshow.org
    Hon Sec: Charles Runge
▲   Company Limited by Guarantee; Registered Charity
Br   1
○   *F, *N; a federation of national agricultural societies within the
    British Commonwealth, to encourage interchange of
    knowledge & experience in the practice & science of
    agriculture
●   Conf - Organising cooperation & exchange between member
    societies
M   12 org, UK / 31 org, o'seas
¶   NL - 4; ftm.   Biennial Conference Report - 2 yrly.

Royal Agricultural Society of England   (RASE)   1840
■   Stoneleigh Park, KENILWORTH, Warks, CV8 2LZ.   (hq)
       024 7669 6969   fax 024 7669 6900
       email info@rase.org.uk   http://www.rase.org.uk
    Chmn: Hugh Oliver-Bellasis,   Sec: Richard Wood
▲   Registered Charity
○   *F; to be the independent voice for the agricultural industry &
    rural economy
●   Conf - ET - Res - Exhib - Lib - VE - LG
>   Arthur Rank Centre (ARC); Farming & Countryside
    Education (FACE)
M   5,935 i, UK / 8 i, o'seas
¶   Jnl - 1; ftm, £35 nm.
    Rural Matters - 4; ftm only.

Royal Air Force Historical Society   (RAFHS)   1986
- ■ Silverhill House, Coombe, WOTTON-under-EDGE, Glos, GL12 7ND.   (hsp)
  01453 843362
  Mem Sec: Dr Jack Dunham
- ▲ Registered Charity
- ○ *L; to serve as a focus of interest in the history of the Royal Air Force & its precursor services, their operations, policies & personalities
- ● Seminars (2 a yr) - AGM
- M 860 i, UK / 55 i, o'seas
- ¶ Jnl (proceedings of seminars & AGM) - 2/3; ftm, back issues £10 (hardback), £5 (softback).

Royal Air Forces Association   (RAFA)   1943
- ■ 117½ Loughborough Rd, LEICESTER, LE4 5ND.   (hq)
  0116-266 5224
  http://www.rafa.org.uk
  Sec Gen: Edward Jarron
- ▲ Un-incorporated Society
- Br 502; 27 countries o'seas
- ○ *W; the welfare of serving & ex-serving members of the RAF & Commonwealth Air Forces & their dependents
- ● Conf - Mtgs - ET
- M 100,000 i
- ¶ Air Mail - 4;   AR; both free.

Royal & Ancient Golf Club   (R&A)   1754
- NR St Andrews, FIFE, KY16 9JD.   (hq)
  01334 460000   fax 01334 460001
  http://www.randa.org
  Sec: Peter Dawson
- ▲ Un-incorporated Society
- ○ *S; governing body for rules of golf & amateur status for all countries of the world apart from the USA & Canada
- Gp Organisers of golf championships; Rules of golf seminars
- ● Conf - Mtgs - Exam - Exhib - Comp - Lib - PL
- < Wld Amat Golf Coun
- M 2,400 unions & assns worldwide
- ¶ R&A News Bulletin - 2; free.
  A Course for all Seasons: a guide to golf course management.
  Practical Greenkeeping (textbook) by J Arthur.

Royal Anthropological Institute of Great Britain & Ireland   (RAI)   1843
- ■ 50 Fitzroy St, LONDON, W1T 5BT.   (hq)
  020 7387 0455
  http://www.therai.org.uk
  Hon Sec: Dr Eric Hirsch
- ▲ Company Limited by Guarantee; Registered Charity
- ○ *L; to promote the study of the science of man
- ● Conf - Res - Inf - Lib - PL - Fundraising
- M c 1,000 i, UK / c 500 i, o'seas
- ¶ Jnl - 4.   Anthropology Today - 6.
  Anthropological Index Online (free Internet bibliographic service).

Royal Archaeological Institute   (RAI)   1844
- ■ c/o Society of Antiquaries, Burlington House, Piccadilly, LONDON, W1J 0BE.   (hq)
  0116-243 3839   fax 0116-243 3839
  email admin@royalarchaeolinst.org
  http://www.royalarchaeolinst.org
  Admin: Caroline Raison
- ▲ Registered Charity
- ○ *L; all aspects of archaeology & history of architecture but mainly that of GB
- ● Conf - Mtgs - Res - Comp - VE
- M c 1,700 i, 384 libraries & org
- ¶ Archaeological Jnl - 1; ftm; £65 nm.   NL - 2; free.
  Index to Jnl; prices on application.

Royal Army Veterinary Corps Division
  a group of the **British Veterinary Association**

Royal Asiatic Society of Great Britain & Ireland   (RAS)   1823
- NR 14 Stephenson Way, LONDON, NW1 2HD.   (hq)
  020 7388 4539
  email info@royalasiaticsociety.org
  http://www.royalasiaticsociety.org
  Dir: Dr B Murtagh
- ▲ Registered Charity
- ○ *L; to provide a forum for those who are interested in the history, languages, cultures & religions of Asia
- ● Mtgs - Lib
- M c 500 i, UK / c 300 i, o'seas
- ¶ Jnl - 3; ftm.

Royal Association of British Dairy Farmers   (RABDF)   1876
- ■ Dairy House, Unit 31, Stoneleigh Deer Park, Stareton, KENILWORTH, Warks, CV8 2LY.   (hq)
  0845 458 2711   fax 0845 458 2755
  email office@rabdf.co.uk   http://www.rabdf.co.uk
- ▲ Registered Charity
- ○ *T, *V; to represent the interests of dairy farmers & the dairy farming industry
- ● Conf - Mtgs - Exam - Exhib - Comp - SG - Inf - VE - LG
  Dairy Event (http://www.dairyevent.co.uk)
- M 2,000 i
- ¶ Milk Digest - 6;
  Dairy Farming Event Showguide - 1; both ftm.

Royal Association for Deaf People   (RAD)   1841
- § 18 Westside Centre, London Rd, Stanway, COLCHESTER, Essex, CO3 8PH.   (hq)
  0845 688 2525
  email info@royaldeaf.org.uk
  http://www.royaldeaf.org.uk
  Chief Exec: Tom Fenton
  A registered charity promoting the welfare and interests of deaf people whose first or preferred language is sign language.

Royal Association for Disability & Rehabilitation   (RADAR)   1977
- NR 12 City Forum, 250 City Rd, LONDON, EC1V 8AF.   (hq)
  020 7250 3222
  email radar@radar.org.uk   http://www.radar.org.uk
  Chief Exec: Liz Sayce
- ▲ Registered Charity
- ○ *K, *N, *W; to promote change by empowering disabled people to achieve our rights and expectations and by influencing the way that we, as disabled people, are viewed as members of society
- ● Inf
- M c 600 i & org
- ¶ Bulletin - 12.   A Guide to RADAR.   AR & Accounts.
  Publications list available.

Royal Astronomical Society   (RAS)   1820
- NR Burlington House, Piccadilly, LONDON, W1J 0BQ.   (hq)
  020 7734 4582; 3307   fax 020 7494 0166
  email info@ras.org.uk   http://www.ras.org.uk
- ▲ Registered Charity
- ○ *L; the leading UK body for astronomy & astrophysics, geophysics, solar & solar-terrestrial physics & planetary sciences
- ● Conf - Mtgs - Res - Comp - Lib - PL - Empl - LG - Support for educational activities - Awards grants & prizes
- < IAU; EAS; Science Coun
- > Brit Sundial Soc; Brit Geophysical Assn (BGA)
- M 2,037 i, UK / 1,236 i, o'seas
- ¶ Astronomy & Geophysics (Jnl) - 6; ftm.
  Monthly Notices - 36 [9 volumes of 4 issues each];
  Geophysical Journal International - 12 [4 volumes of 3 issues each]; prices for both on application.

Royal Bath & West of England Society   1777
NR   The Showground, SHEPTON MALLET, Somerset, BA4 6QN.
     (hq)
     01749 822200   fax 01749 823169
     http://www.bathandwest.co.uk
     Chief Exec: Jane Guise
▲   Company Limited by Guarantee; Registered Charity
○   *F; for the encouragement of agriculture, arts, manufacture,
     commerce
●   Conf - Exhib (agricultural shows) - Events & exhibition centre
M   2,141 i
¶   NL - 2;   Annual Review & Report - 1; both free.
     Show Programme - 1;   Show Catalogue; both ftm.
     Note: commonly known as the Bath & West

Royal Birmingham Society of Artists   (RBSA)   1814
■   4 Brook St, St Paul's, BIRMINGHAM, B3 1SA.   (hq)
     0121-236 4353   fax 0121-236 4555
     email secretary@rbsa.org.uk   http://www.rbsa.org.uk
     Hon Sec: Simon Davis
▲   Registered Charity
○   *A; to advance the public education in (& the practice of) art,
     particularly painting, sculpture, ceramics & printing
●   Mtgs - ET - Res - Exhib - Inf
M   127 i & associates
¶   NL - 4; ftm & Friends.

**Royal Botanical & Horticultural Society of Manchester & the
Northern Counties   (RBS)   1827**
§   60 Glebelands Rd, KNUTSFORD, Cheshire, WA16 9DZ.   (sb)
     01565 633917
     Hon Sec: James R Goodchild
     A charity providing funds for the Tatton Garden Society & local
     horticultural societies, as well as judges for local shows,
     speakers, advice, etc.

Royal British Legion   1921
■   48 Pall Mall, LONDON, SW1Y 5JY.   (hq)
     020 7973 7200
     Dir Gen: Chris Simpkins
▲   Registered Charity
Br 101
○   *K, *W; to assist needy ex-servicemen & women & their
     families; to ensure the maintenance of war pensions, war
     widows pensions & associated allowances
Gp Attendants company (security & car parking); RBL poppy
     factory; Poppy appeal; Training company
●   Conf - Mtgs - Comp - Inf
<   Brit C'wealth Ex-Services League; Wld Veterans Fedn; Coun of
     British Service & Ex-service Orgs
M   398,132 i, UK & o'seas
¶   The Legion (Jnl) - 12;   AR;   Publicity leaflets &
     posters; all free.

Royal British Legion Scotland   (RBLS)   1921
NR   New Haig House, Logie Green Rd, EDINBURGH, EH7 4HR.
     (hq)
     0131-557 2782   fax 0131-557 5819
     email lao@rblscotland.org   http://www.rblscotland.org
     Legion affairs officer: George Ross
▲   Registered Charity
Br 214 in Scotland
○   *K, *W; to safeguard the welfare, interests & memory of those
     who have served in the armed forces, & their dependents
Gp War pensions claims & appeals
●   Conf - Mtgs - Inf - VE _ LG
<   Brit C'wealth Ex-Services League; Earl Haig Fund (Scotland);
     Officers Assn Scotland; Scot Ex-Services Charitable Orgs
M   50,000 i, 88 private clubs
¶   Scottish Legion News - 4; ftm.

Royal British Society of Sculptors   (RBS)   1904
NR   108 Old Brompton Rd, LONDON, SW7 3RA.   (hq)
     020 7373 8615
     email info@rbs.org.uk   http://www.rbs.org.uk
     Dir: Anne Rawcliffe-King
▲   Registered Charity
○   *A, *P; to advance the art & practice of sculpture
●   Mtgs - Exhib - Inf - Lib
M   c 500 i

Royal Caledonian Curling Club   (RCCC)   1838
■   Cairnie House, Ingliston Showground, NEWBRIDGE,
     Midlothian, EH28 8NB.   (hq)
     0131-333 3003   fax 0131-333 3323
     email office@royalcaledoniancurlingclub.org
     http://www.royalcaledoniancurlingclub.org
     Chief Exec Officer: Colin Grahamslaw
     Finance & Admin Mgr: Alastair Hibbert
▲   Company Limited by Guarantee
Br Canada
○   *S; governing body for the sport of curling throughout Scotland
     & mother club of curling throughout the world
●   Conf - Mtgs - ET - Comp - Stat - Lib
<   Wld Curling Fedn (WCF); Eur Curling Fedn (ECF)
M   13,000 i, 562 clubs, UK / 20 assns, o'seas
¶   RCCC Annual - 1; £6.   RCCC Rules of the Game - 1; £1.

Royal Caledonian Horticultural Society   (RCHS)   1809
NR   17 Jordan Lane, EDINBURGH, EH10 4RA.   (hsp)
     0131-478 2141
     http://www.rchs.co.uk
     Sec: Alison Murison
▲   Registered Charity
○   *H; the encouragement & advancement of horticulture in all its
     forms
●   Mtgs - Exhib - Comp - Inf - VE - Lectures - Awards
<   R Horticl Soc (London)
¶   Preview - 3.   Caledonian Gardener - 1.

Royal Cambrian Academy of Art   (RCA)   1881
■   Crown Lane, CONWY, LL32 8AN.   (hq)
     01492 593413   fax 01492 593413
     email rca@rcaconwy.org   http://www.rcaconwy.org
     Hon Sec: Tim Pugin,   Curator: Gill Bird
▲   Company Limited by Guarantee; Registered Charity
○   *A; to promote the arts of painting, engraving & sculpture &
     other forms of art in Wales
●   Mtgs - Exhib - Art classes
M   120 i
¶   Summer Exhibition Catalogue - 1; £1.   AR 1; ftm, £1 nm.

Royal Celtic Society   1820
■   23 Rutland St, EDINBURGH, EH1 2RN.   (asa)
     0131-228 6449   fax 0131-229 6987
     email gcameron@stuartandstuart.co.uk
     Hon Sec & Treas: J Gordon Cameron
▲   Registered Charity
○   *G; to promote interest in the history, traditions, arts & music of
     Scotland & in Scottish Gaelic
●   Mtgs - One-off grants to assist with the aims of the society
M   200 i, UK / 10 i, o'seas
¶   AR; m only.

Royal Choral Society   (RCS)   1872
NR   Studio 9, 92 Lots Rd, LONDON, SW10 0QD.   (hq)
         020 7376 3718   fax 020 7376 3719
         email virginia@royalchoralsociety.co.uk
         http://www.royalchoralsociety.co.uk
         Admin: Virginia Edwyn-Jones
▲   Registered Charity
○   *D; 'we are an amateur choir, singing to a professional
         standard; we work with professional orchestras & promoters'
●   Mtgs - Concerts
<   Making Music (Nat Fedn Music Socs)
M   c 200 i
¶   Summer NL.

Royal College of Anaesthetists   1948
NR   Churchill House, 35 Red Lion Square, LONDON,
         WC1R 4SG.   (hq)
         020 7092 1500
         email info@rcoa.ac.uk
○   *L; advancement of art & science of anaesthetics

Royal College of General Practitioners   (RCGP)   1952
■   14 Prince's Gate, LONDON, SW7 1PU.   (hq)
         020 7581 3232   fax 020 7225 3047
         email info@rcgp.org.uk   http://www.rcgp.org.uk
         Hon Sec: Dr Maureen Baker
▲   Registered Charity
○   *L, *P; to encourage & maintain high standards of general
         medical practice
●   Conf - Mtgs - ET - Exam - Res - Exhib - SG - Inf - Lib - LG
M   17,500 i, UK / 1,300 i, o'seas
¶   Jnl - 12; ftm, £124 nm.   Members' Reference Book - 1; ftm.

Royal College of Midwives   (RCM)   1881
NR   15 Mansfield St, LONDON, W1G 9NH.   (hq)
         020 7312 3535   fax 020 7312 3536
         http://www.rcm.org.uk
         Gen Sec: Dame Karlene Davis
▲   Company Limited by Guarantee; Registered Charity
Br   5
○   *P, *U; to advance the art & science of midwifery
●   Conf - Mtgs - ET - Inf - Lib - VE - Empl - LG
<   Intl Confedn Midwives; WHO Collaborating Centre for
         Midwifery
M   c 36,000 i, UK / 7000 i, o'seas
¶   Jnl - 12.

Royal College of Nursing of the United Kingdom   (RCN)   1916
NR   20 Cavendish Sq, LONDON, W1G 0RN.   (hq)
         020 7409 3333
         http://www.rcn.org.uk
         Chief Exec & Gen Sec: Dr Peter Carter
▲   Registered Charity
○   *M, *P; to act as the voice of nursing in the UK; to campaign on
         behalf of nurses & nursing; to promote the interests of nurses
         & patients by working with government, the professional
         bodies, trade unions & voluntary organisations
●   Conf - Empl - ET - Exhib - LG - Lib - Res
<   Intl Coun of Nurses (ICN); Eur Fedn of Public Service Us (EPSU);
         C'wealth Nurses Fedn (CNF); Standing C'ee of Nurses (PCN)
M   390,000 i
¶   Nursing Standard - 52.   RCN Bulletin - 26; both ftm.

**Royal College of Obstetricians & Gynaecologists   (RCOG)
1929**
■   27 Sussex Place, LONDON, NW1 4RG.   (hq)
         020 7772 6200   fax 020 7772 6359
         email coll.sec@rcog.org.uk   http://www.rcog.org.uk
         Chief Exec: Helen Moffatt
▲   Registered Charity
○   *L, *Q
●   Conf - Mtgs - ET - Exam - Res - Exhib - SG - Stat - Inf - Lib - LG
M   4,000 i, UK / 6,000 i, o'seas
         (Sub: £380 UK / £85 o'seas)
¶   BJOG: an international Jnl of Obstetrics & Gynaecology - 12.
         The Obstetrician & Gynaecologist - 4.

Royal College of Ophthalmologists   1988
NR   17 Cornwall Terrace, LONDON, NW1 4QW.   (hq)
         020 7935 0702   fax 020 7935 9838
         http://www.rcophth.ac.uk
         Hon Sec: Larry Benjamin
○   *L; advancement of study & practice of ophthalmology
Gp   Ophthalmology; Medicine
●   Conf - Mtgs - ET - Exam
M   2,800 i, UK / 950 i, o'seas
¶   Eye (Jnl) - 6.   College News (NL) - 4.   LM - 1.

Royal College of Organists   (RCO)   1864
NR   PO Box 56357, LONDON, SW16 7XL.
         0560 076 7208
         email admin@rco.org.uk   http://www.rco.org.uk
         Gen Mgr: Mrs Kim Gilbert
▲   Registered Charity
Br   4
○   *D; to promote the arts of organ-playing, choir-training &
         related activities
●   Conf - Mtgs - ET - Exam - Res - Exhib - Comp - SG - Inf - Lib -
         PL - VE - Empl
         The College isd open during term time Mon-Fri 1000-1700
<   Inc Soc of Musicians (corporate member); R School of Church
         Music
M   2,479 i, 102 f, UK / 836 i, o'seas
¶   RCO News (Jnl) - 4.

Royal College of Paediatrics & Child Health   (RCPCH)   1996
NR   5-11 Theobalds Rd, LONDON, WC1X 8SH.   (hq)
         020 7092 6000   fax 020 7092 6001
         email enquiries@rcpch.ac.uk   http://www.rcpch.ac.uk
         Chief Exec: Len Tyler
▲   Registered Charity
○   *L; to advance education in child health & paediatrics; to
         relieve sickness by promoting improvements in paediatric
         practice; to promote research & publish the results
Gp   Accident & emergency; Allergy; Computer information &
         technology; Clinical genetics; Immunology & infectious
         diseases; International child health; Nutrition & metabolism;
         Oncology & haematology; Psychiatry & psychology;
         Radiology & imaging
         British Association for Community Child Health; British
         Association for Paediatric Nephrology; British Association of
         Perinatal Medicine; British Paediatric Cardiac Association;
         British Paediatric Neurology Association; British Paediatric
         Pathology Association; British Paediatric Respiratory Society;
         British Society for Paediatric Dermatology; British Society for
         Paediatric Endocrinology & Diabetes; British Society for
         Paediatric Gastroenterology & Nutrition
●   Conf - Mtgs - ET - Exam - Res
<   Intl Paediatric Assn; Conf of Eur Specialists in Paediatrics
M   7,194 i, UK / 1,625 i, o'seas
¶   NL - 4; ftm.   Hbk; ftm, £20 nm.
         Archives of Disease in Childhood - 12; ftm, £218
         (£95+VAT online) nm.
         Cherub Bulletin - 4;   Guideline Appraisal - irreg;   AR - 1;
         all free.
         British National Formulary for Children - 1: free to those
         prescribing to children.

Royal College of Pathologists   (RCPath)   1962
NR   2 Carlton House Terrace, LONDON, SW1Y 5AF.   (hq)
    020 7451 6700   fax 020 7451 6701
    email info@rcpath.org   http://www.rcpath.org
    Chief Exec: Daniel Ross
▲   Registered Charity
○   *P, *Q; to advance the science & practice of pathology
●   Conf - Exam
M   5,000 i, UK / 2,500 i, o'seas
¶   Bulletin - 4; ftm, £60 nm.   Hbk - 2 yrly; ftm only.

Royal College of Physicians of Edinburgh   (RCPE)   1681
NR   9 Queen St, EDINBURGH, EH2 1JQ.   (hq)
    0131-225 7324   fax 0131-220 3939
    http://www.rcpe.ac.uk
    Chief Exec: Elaine Tait
▲   Registered Charity
○   *L, *P; to promote the highest standards of practice in internal
    medicine & related specialities wherever its fellows, collegiate
    members & members practise
●   Conf - Mtgs - ET - Exam - Res - Exhib - Lib - VE - LG
M   2,168 fellows, 1,917 collegiate m, 73 affiliates, UK /
    2,623 fellows, 609 collegiate m, 7 affiliates, o'seas
¶   The Journal - 4;   The Bulletin (NL) - 12 (online); both ftm.

Royal College of Physicians of Ireland
IRL   Frederick House, 19 South Frederick St, DUBLIN 2, Republic of
    Ireland.
    353 (1) 863 9700   fax 353 (1) 672 4707
    email info@rcpi.ie   http://www.rcpi.ie
○   *M, *P

Royal College of Physicians of London   (RCP)   1518
■   11 St Andrew's Place, Regent's Park, LONDON, NW1 4LE.
    (hq)
    020 7224 1539   fax 020 7487 5218
    email info@rcplondon.ac.uk
    http://www.rcplondon.ac.uk
    Chief Exec: Martin Else
▲   Registered Charity
Br   12
○   *L, *P; to set & improve standards in education & training; to
    ensure quality of care for patients; to influence the delivery of
    care; to provide professional leadership & influence
    government; to involve patients & the public
Gp   Faculty of Occupational Medicine; Faculty of Public Health;
    Faculty of Pharmaceutical Medicine; Faculty of Forensic
    Medicine;
    Jt C'ee for Higher Medical Training
●   Conf - Mtgs - ET - Exam - Exhib - Inf - Lib - LG
<   Eur Assn of Med Specialists (EUMS)
M   18,900 i (fellows & members), UK / 2,700 i (fellows), o'seas
¶   Clinical Medicine (Jnl) - 6; ftm, £120 nm (UK).
    LM - 1; ftm, price on application nm.   AR; free.

**Royal College of Physicians & Surgeons of Glasgow
(RCPSGlasg)   1599**
■   232-242 St Vincent Street, GLASGOW, G2 5RJ.   (hq)
    0141-221 6072
    http://www.rcpsg.ac.uk
    Chief Exec: Dr James Miller
▲   Registered Charity
○   *L, *P; to set & maintain standards of practice in medicine,
    surgery & dental surgery; to conduct postgraduate
    examinations & organise training & educational events for
    physicians, surgeons & dentists at all stages of their careers
Gp   Dental faculty; Faculty of travel medicine
●   Mtgs - ET - Exam - Res - Lib
<   Intl Assn of Coll & Academy Presidents; Fedn of R Colls of
    Physicians in the UK; Senate of Surgery of GB & Ireland
M   c 4,100 i, UK / 2,300 i, o'seas
¶   Bulletin - 3; ftm, on application nm.
    News & Views - 3;   AR; both free.

Royal College of Psychiatrists   (RCPsych)   1971
■   17 Belgrave Sq, LONDON, SW1X 8PG.   (hq)
    020 7235 2351   fax 020 7245 1231
    email rcpsych@rcpsych.ac.uk   http://www.rcpsych.ac.uk
    Registrar: Prof Sue Bailey
▲   Registered Charity
○   *L, *M, *P; to advance the science & practice of psychiatry &
    related subjects
Gp   Faculties:
    Academic psychiatry; Addictions; Child & adolescent psychiatry;
    Forensic psychiatry; General & community psychiatry; Liaison
    psychiatry; Psychiatry of learning disability; Psychiatry of old
    age; Psychotherapy; Rehabilitation & social psychiatry
●   Conf - ET - Exam - Res - Inf - VE - LG
<   Wld Psychiatric Assn
M   6,941 i, UK / 1,729 i, o'seas
¶   British Journal of Psychiatry - 12.
    Psychiatric Bulletin - 12.
    Advances in Psychiatric Treatment - 6.

Royal College of Radiologists   1975
■   38 Portland Place, LONDON, W1B 1JQ.   (hq)
    020 7636 4432   fax 020 7323 3100
    email enquiries@rcr.ac.uk   http://www.rcr.ac.uk
    Exec: Andrew Hall
○   *L, *M, *P; the science & practice of radiology & oncology
M   5,820 i, UK / 1,580 i, o'seas
¶   Clinical Radiology (Jnl) - 12.   Clinical Oncology (Jnl) - 8.NL -
    4;   AR - 1.

**Royal College of Speech & Language Therapists   (RCSLT)
1945**
NR   2 White Hart Yard, LONDON, SE1 1NX.   (hq)
    020 7378 1200
    email postmaster@rcslt.org   http://www.rcslt.org
    Chief Exec: Kamini Gadhok
▲   Registered Charity
○   *P; the governing body for speech & language therapy in the
    UK
Gp   all acquired or developmental conditions affecting
    communication
●   Conf - Mtgs - ET - Exam - Res - Exhib - SG - Stat - Inf - Lib - PL
    - Empl
<   Intl Assn of Logopedics & Phoniatrics (AILP); Standing Liaison
    C'ee of EC Speech & Language Therapists & Logopedists
    (CPLOL)
M   10,031 i, UK / 418 i, o'seas
¶   European Journal of Disorders of Communication - 4; ftm.
    Communicating Quality (professional standards).
    Bulletin - 12 (supplements - 24); ftm.
    LM.   AR; ftm only.
    Publications list available.

Royal College of Surgeons of Edinburgh   (RCSEd)   1505
NR   Nicolson St, EDINBURGH, EH8 9DW.   (hq)
    0131-527 1600   fax 0131-557 6406
    email information@rcsed.ac.uk   http://www.rcsed.ac.uk
    Chief Exec: Alison Rooney
▲   Registered Charity
○   *L, *P; a body incorporated by royal charter, concerned with
    education & training for medical & surgical practice & the
    maintenance of high standards of professional competence
    & conduct; includes both surgery & dental surgery
Gp   Faculties: Dental surgery, Pre-hospital care, Health informatics,
    Sport & exercise medicine
●   Conf - ET - Exam - Inf - Lib - LG
M   7,800 i, UK / 5,500 i, o'seas
¶   Jnl - 6;   NL - 4.

© CBD Research Ltd · Beckenham · BR3 5JS · Tel 020 8650 7745 · Fax 020 8650 0768 · E-mail cbd@cbdresearch.com · www.cbdresearch.com

Royal College of Surgeons of England   (RCS)   1800
NR   35-43 Lincoln's Inn Fields, LONDON, WC2A 3PE.   (hq)
    020 7405 3474
    http://www.rcseng.ac.uk
    Chief Exec: David Munn
▲   Registered Charity
○   *L, *P; an independent professional body committed to
    promoting & advancing the highest standards of surgical
    care for patients
M   i

Royal College of Surgeons in Ireland   (RCSI)   1784
IRL   123 St Stephen's Green, DUBLIN 2, Republic of Ireland.   (hq)
    353 (1) 402 2100   fax 353 (1) 402 2460
    http://www.rcsi.ie
    Chief Exec: Michael Horgan
○   *P

Royal College of Veterinary Surgeons   (RCVS)   1844
■   Belgravia House, 62-64 Horseferry Rd, LONDON,
    SW1P 2AF.   (hq)
    020 7222 2001   fax 020 7222 2004
    email admin@rcvs.org.uk   http://www.rcvs.org.uk
    Registrar: Miss J C Hern
▲   Incorporated Statutory Body
○   *L, *P, *V
●   ET - Exam - Stat - Inf - Lib
M   16,137 i, UK / 2,606 i, o'seas
¶   NL - 3; ftm & online.   Register of Members - 1; ftm, £40 nm.
    Directory of Veterinary Practices - 1; £65.
    Guide to Professional Conduct - 1; free online; printed
        copies £15 m,   £20 nm.
    List of Veterinary Nurses - 1; £10.   AR; free.

Royal Cornwall Agricultural Association   (RCAA)   1793
■   The Royal Cornwall Showground, WADEBRIDGE, Cornwall,
    PL27 7JE.   (hq)
    01208 812183   fax 01208 812713
    email info@royalcornwall.co.uk
    http://www.royalcornwall.co.uk
    Sec: C P Riddle
▲   Registered Charity
○   *F; to promote agriculture
Gp   C'ees for: Poultry, Dogs, Fur, Bees, Honey, Pigeons, Cage birds,
    Goats, Horticulture
●   Mtgs - Exhib - Comp
<   Most livestock breed societies
M   6,500 i, c 750 f
¶   Show Catalogue - 1; £4.00.   AR; ftm only.
    Souvenir Programme - 1; £3.00.

Royal Dublin Society   (RDS)   1731
IRL   Ballsbridge, DUBLIN 4, Republic of Ireland.   (hq)
    353 (1) 668 0866   fax 353 (1) 660 4014
    email info@rds.ie   http://www.rds.ie
○   *L

Royal Economic Society   (RES)   1890
■   Sch of Economics & Finance, University of St Andrews,
    ST ANDREWS, Fife, KY16 9AL.   (hsb)
    01334 462479   fax 01334 462444
    email royaleconsoc@st-andrews.ac.uk
    http://www.res.org.uk
    Sec-Gen: Prof John Beath
▲   Registered Charity
○   *L
●   Conf - ET - Res - Inf
<   Intl Economic Assn
M   1,500 i, UK / 1,700 i, o'seas
¶   The Economic Jnl - 8.   NL - 4; both ftm.
    New editions of economic classics.

Royal Entomological Society of London   (REntSoc)   1833
NR   The Mansion House, Chiswell Green Lane, ST ALBANS, Herts,
    AL2 3NS.   (hq)
    01727 899387   fax 01727 894797
    http://www.royensoc.co.uk
    Registrar: W H F Blakemore
○   *L
M   i

**Royal Environmental Health Institute of Scotland   (REHIS)
1983**
■   3 Manor Place, EDINBURGH, EH3 7DH.   (hq)
    0131-225 6999   fax 0131-225 3993
    email contact@rehis.org   http://www.rehis.org
    Sec & Chief Exec: Tom Bell
▲   Incorporated by Royal Charter
○   *P; covers food safety, housing, health & safety, pollution, public
    health, waste management
●   Conf - Mtgs - ET - Exam - Res - Exhib - SG - Stat - Inf - Lib - VE
    - LG
<   Intl Fedn of Envtl Health
M   1,000 i, UK / 100 i, o'seas
¶   Environmental Health Scotland - 6;
    Congress Proceedings - 1;   AR- 1; all ftm only.

Royal Faculty of Procurators in Glasgow   (RFPG)   pre-1668
■   12 Nelson Mandela Place, GLASGOW, G2 1BT.   (hq)
    0141-332 3593   fax 0141-332 4714
    email library@rfpg.org   http://www.rfpg.org
    Chief Exec: John McKenzie
▲   Royal Charter
○   *P; to provide a library, an education programme & auditing
    services for members
●   Mtgs - ET - Comp - Lib - Management of charitable funds
M   1,400 i, 200 f

**Royal Forestry Society of England, Wales & Northern Ireland
(RFS)   1882**
NR   102 High St, TRING, Herts, HP23 4AF.   (hq)
    01442 822028   fax 01442 890395
    email rfshq@rfs.org.uk   http://www.rfs.org.uk
    Chief Exec: Dr J E Jackson
▲   Company Limited by Guarantee; Registered Charity
Br   21 divisions
○   *L; promoting the wise management of trees & woods;
    advancement of knowledge & practice of forestry &
    arboriculture; promotion of sustainable forestry
●   Mtgs - Exam - Lib - VE
M   4,235 i, 280 f
¶   Quarterly Jnl of Forestry - 4; ftm, £2.50 nm.

**Royal Geographical Society (with the Institute of British
Geographers)   (RGS-IBG)   1830**
NR   1 Kensington Gore, LONDON, SW7 2AR.   (hq)
    020 7591 3000   fax 020 7591 3001
    http://www.rgs.org
    Dir & Sec: Dr Rita Gardner
▲   Registered Charity
○   *L, *Q; to advance geographical science and support its
    practitioners
M   i, f & org

Royal Glasgow Institute of the Fine Arts   (RGI)   1861
■   5 Oswald St, GLASGOW, G1 4QR.   (asa)
    0141-248 7411   fax 0141-221 0417
    email rgi@robbferguson.co.uk
    http://www.rgiscotland.co.uk
    Sec: Mrs Lesley Nicholl
▲   Company Limited by Guarantee; Registered Charity
○   *A; to encourage & promote contemporary art
●   Exhib
M   1,100 i

Royal Guernsey Agricultural & Horticultural Society
NR 3 Cornet St, ST PETER PORT, Guernsey, GY1 1BZ.
    01481 720711
    Sec: Joan de Garis
○ *F, *H
M c 100 i

Royal Highland & Agricultural Society of Scotland   (RHASS)
1784
■ Royal Highland Centre, Ingliston, EDINBURGH, EH28 8NB.
    (hq)
    0131-335 6200   fax 0131-335 6229
    email info@rhass.org.uk   http://www.rhass.org.uk
    Chief Exec: R J Jones,   Sec: A J Thomson
▲ Registered Charity
○ *F; promotion of agriculture & allied industries in Scotland
● Conf - Mtgs - ET - Exhib - Comp - Inf - Lib - LG
< R Agricl Soc of the C'wealth
M 14,000 i, UK / 50 i, o'seas
    (Sub: £48)
¶ Royal Highland Review - 3; ftm only.
    Royal Highland Show Guide - 1.
    Royal Highland Show Catalogue - 1.

Royal Highland Education Trust   (RHET)   1999
■ Royal Highland Centre, Ingliston, EDINBURGH, EH28 8NB.
    (hq)
    0131-335 6227   fax 0131-333 5236
    email rhetinfo@rhass.org.uk   http://www.rhet.org.uk
    Chmn: J F Warnock,   Sec: A J Thomson
▲ Registered Charity
○ *F; information service for schools & the public about the
    economic & environmental realities of farming, forestry &
    food production in Scotland
Gp Local initiative bodies available for school-farm links
● Inf
¶ Sprouts (NL) - 3.

Royal Historical Society   (RHistS)   1868
NR University College London, Gower St, LONDON, WC1E 6BT.
    (hq)
    020 7387 7532
    Exec Sec: Susan Carr
○ *L; promote the study of history by the publication of
    documentary, bibliographical & reference material
M i

Royal Horticultural Society   (RHS)   1804
■ 80 Vincent Sq, LONDON, SW1P 2PE.   (hq)
    0845 260 5000
    http://www.rhs.org.uk
    Dir Gen: Inga Grimsey
▲ Registered Charity
Br 4 gardens: Harlow Carr (N Yorks); Hyde Hall (Essex); Rosemoor
    (Devon); Wisley (Surrey)
○ *H; the encouragement & improvement of the science, art &
    practice of horticulture in all its branches
● Conf - Mtgs - ET - Exam - Res - Exhib - Comp - Inf - Lib
M 335,000 i, 3,000 org, UK & o'seas
¶ The Garden (Jnl) - 12; ftm, £3.50 each nm.
    Numerous manuals & reference works.

Royal Horticultural Society of Ireland   (RHSI)   1830
IRL Cabinteely House, The Park, Cabinteely, DUBLIN 18, Republic
    of Ireland.
    353 (1) 235 3912   fax 353 (1) 235 3912
    email info@rhsi.ie   http://www.rhsi.ie
○ *H

Royal Humane Society   (RHS)   1774
NR Brettenham House, Lancaster Place, LONDON, WC2E 7EP.
    (hq)
    020 7836 8155   fax 020 7836 8155
    email info@royalhumanesociety.org
    http://www.royalhumanesociety.org.uk
    Sec: Dick Wilkinson
▲ Registered Charity
○ *W; to encourage the saving of human life; to present awards
    for bravery in so doing
● Mtgs - Res - Lib
< R Humane Socs: Australasia, Canada, New South Wales, New
    Zealand
M i & f
¶ Short History of the Society;   Medals of the Society.
    Saved from a Watery Grave;   AR.

Royal Incorporation of Architects in Scotland   (RIAS)   1916
■ 15 Rutland Sq, EDINBURGH, EH1 2BE.   (hq)
    0131-229 7545   fax 0131-228 2188
    email admin@rias.org.uk   http://www.rias.org.uk
    Sec: Neil Baxter
▲ Registered Charity
○ *L, *P; for architects, professional advisory services
Gp Competitions; Exhibitions; Bookshop & gallery; Library;
    Professional section for architects & public
● Conf - Mtgs - ET - Res - Exhib - Comp - Lib - PL - LG
< R Inst Brit Architects (RIBA)
M 3,500 i, 500 f
¶ Chartered Architect - 4.   e-bulletins - 12.

Royal Institute of the Architects of Ireland   (RIAI)   1839
IRL 8 Merrion Sq, DUBLIN 2, Republic of Ireland.
    353 (1) 676 1703   fax 353 (1) 661 0948
    email info@riai.ie   http://www.riai.ie
○ *P

Royal Institute of British Architects   (RIBA)   1834
■ 66 Portland Place, LONDON, W1B 4AD.   (hq)
    020 7580 5533   fax 020 7255 1541
    email info@inst.riba.org   http://www.architecture.com
    Dir Gen: Richard Hastilow
○ *L, *P; to advance architecture by demonstrating public benefit,
    & promoting excellence in the profession
● Conf - Exam - Exhib - Comp - Inf - Lib - PL - LG
M 30,000 i
¶ RIBA Jnl - 12; ftm.   AR - 1; free.
    Architecture Periodicals Index - 4.
    RIBA Directory of Practices - 1 (printed & on-line).
    RIBA Directory of Members - 1; ftm (on-line only).
    RIBA International Directory of Practices - 1 (on-line only).

Royal Institute of International Affairs (RIIA) 1920
NR Chatham House, 10 St James's Sq, LONDON, SW1Y 4LE.
    (hq)
    020 7957 5700   fax 020 7957 5710
    email contact@chathamhouse.org.uk
    http://www.chathamhouse.org.uk
    Dir: Dr Robin Niblett
▲ Registered Charity
○ *L; for the discussion, research & analysis of international
    affairs; the provision of information on & analysis of
    international issues with the object of stimulating informal
    debate among decision-makers & the wider public
Gp Research programmes:
    Africa; Americas; Asia; Energy, environment & development;
      Europe; International economics; International law;
      International security; Middle East; Russia & Eurasia; Global
      trends - food supply project
● Conf - Mtgs - Res - SG - Lib
< Instns of international affairs
M 1,700 i, 300 f
¶ The World Today (Jnl) - 12.
    International Affairs (Jnl) - 6; ftm.
    Chatham House NL - 12.   AR.
    Publications list available.
    Note: Chatham House is both the name of the building and the
    name by which the Institute is widely known.

Royal Institute of Navigation (RIN) 1947
NR 1 Kensington Gore, LONDON, SW7 2AT.   (hq)
    020 7591 3130   fax 020 7591 3131
    email info@rin.org.uk   http://www.rin.org.uk
    Dir: Gp Capt D W Broughton
▲ Registered Charity
Br 2
○ *L; the advancement of the art & science of navigation by land,
    sea, air & in space (includes animal & bird navigation)

Royal Institute of Oil Painters
    a member of the **Federation of British Artists**

Royal Institute of Painters in Water Colours
    a member of the **Federation of British Artists**

Royal Institute of Philosophy 1925
NR 14 Gordon Sq, LONDON, WC1H 0AR.   (hq)
    020 7387 4130
    Sec: James Garvey
▲ Company Limited by Guarantee; Registered Charity
○ *L; to promote the study of philosophy & the encouragement of
    original work
M i

Royal Institute of Public Health
    in October 2008 merged with the Royal Society (for the Promotion) of
    Health to form the **Royal Society for Public Health**

Royal Institution of Chartered Surveyors (RICS) 1868
■ 12 Great George St, LONDON, SW1P 3AD.   (hq)
    0870 333 1600   fax 020 7334 3811
    email contactrics@rics.org   http://www.rics.org
    Chief Exec: John Armstrong
▲ Un-incorporated Society
○ *P
M i & f
    no further information supplied

Royal Institution of Cornwall (RIC) 1818
■ Royal Cornwall Museum, 25 River St, TRURO, Cornwall,
    TR1 2SJ. (hq)
    01872 272205   fax 01872 240514
    email enquiries@royalcornwallmuseum.org.uk
    http://www.royalcornwallmuseum.org.uk
    Dir: Hilary Bracegirdle
▲ Registered Charity
○ *L; furtherance of Cornish studies; maintenance of the Museum
● Mtgs - ET - Exhib - Inf - Lib - PL - VE
M 714 i, UK / 25 i, o'seas
¶ RIC Jnl - 1;   NL - 2; both ftm.

Royal Institution of Great Britain (RI) 1799
NR 21 Albemarle St, LONDON, W1S 4BS.   (hq)
    020 7409 2992
Br Davy Faraday Research Laboratory
○ *L, *Q; advancement of the public understanding of science; to
    research into solid state chemistry
M i & f
¶ Elements - 4.
    No further information supplied

Royal Institution of Naval Architects (RINA) 1860
NR 10 Upper Belgrave St, LONDON, SW1X 8BQ.   (hq)
    020 7235 4622   fax 020 7259 5912
    email hq@rina.org.uk   http://www.rina.org.uk
    Chief Exec: Trevor Blakeley
▲ Registered Charity
Br Europe (14), Asia Pacific, Australia, Middle East
○ *L, *P; advancement of the art & science of naval architecture,
    as applied to ship design & other related activities
Gp Small craft; High speed craft; Historical; Young members
● Conf - Mtgs - ET - Exhib - Comp - SG - Inf - Lib - LG
< W Confedn of Maritime Technology Socs (WEMT)
M 4,100 i, UK / 2,400 i, o'seas
¶ The Naval Architect - 10.   Ship & Boat Intl - 10.
    Offshore Marine Technology - 4.
    Warship Technology - 5 (included with The Naval Architect).
    Ship Repair & Conversion Technology - 4.
    Significant Ship - 1.   Significant Small Craft - 1.

Royal Institution of South Wales (RISW) 1835
■ c/o Swansea Museum, Victoria Rd, SWANSEA, Glam,
    SA1 1SN. (hq)
    01792 653763   fax 01792 652585
    email swanseamuseum@swansea.gov.uk
    http://www.risw.org.uk
    Hon Sec: Wendy Norris,   Pres: Gwyneth Davies
▲ Registered Charity
○ *L; created as a literary & philosophical institution; nowadays,
    acts as a friends group of Swansea Museum
Gp Education; Publication; Collection
● Conf - Mtgs - Et - Res - Exhib - Comp - Inf - PL - VE
M 400 i, 4 org
¶ Minerva: Jnl of Swansea History - 1; £5 m, £6 nm.
    The Remarkable James Livingstone; £5.
    Welsh Ceramics In Context: Pt 1; £27.50 (softback),
      £39.95 (hardback).
    Welsh Ceramics in Context: Pt 2; £39.50 (softback),
      £55 (hardback).

Royal Irish Academy (RIA) 1785
IRL 19 Dawson St, DUBLIN 2, Republic of Ireland.   (hq)
    353 (1) 676 2570   fax 353 (1) 676 2346
    email admin@ria.ie   http://www.ria.ie
    Sec: H B Clarke
○ *L
M 320

Royal Irish Academy of Music   (RIAM)   1848
IRL   36 Westland Row, DUBLIN 2, Republic of Ireland.
    353 (1) 676 4412   fax 353 (1) 662 2798
    email info@riam.ie   http://www.riam.ie
    Sec: Dorothy Shiel
○   *D, *E

Royal Irish Automobile Club   (RIAC)   1901
IRL   34 Dawson St, DUBLIN 2, Republic of Ireland.
    353 (1) 677 5141 (Motor Sport Dept: 677 5628)
    fax 353 (1) 671 0793
    email info@riac.ie   http://www.riac.ie
    Sec: A T M Sinclair
○   *G

Royal Isle of Wight Agricultural Society   (RIWAS)   1882
NR   Central House, 48/49 High St, NEWPORT, Isle of Wight,
    PO30 1SE.   (hq)
    01983 826275   fax 01983 826275
    email info@riwas.org.uk   http://www.riwas.org.uk
    Hon Sec: Mrs Rosemary Edwards
▲   Company Limited by Guarantee; Registered Charity
○   *F; to promote farming & agriculture & organisation of the Isle
    of Wight County Show
●   Exhib - Shows
M   540 i, UK / 1 i, o'seas
¶   NL - 4;   AR; both ftm only.

**Royal Jersey Agricultural & Horticultural Society   (RJA&HS)
1833**
■   Royal Jersey Showground, La Route de la Trinité, TRINITY,
    Jersey, Channel Islands, JE3 5JP.   (hq)
    01534 866555   fax 01534 865619
    email society@royaljersey.co.uk
    http://www.royaljersey.co.uk
    Chief Exec: James W Godfrey
▲   Registered Charity
○   *B, *F, *H
●   Conf - Mtgs - Exhib - Comp - Expt - Inf - LG
M   1,000 i, 20 f, 10 org, UK / 200 i, o'seas
¶   Jersey at Home - 1; ftm, £5 nm.

Royal Lancashire Agricultural Society   (RLAS)   1767
NR   South Planks Farm, Garstang Rd, Barton, PRESTON, Lancs,
    PR3 5AB.   (hq)
    01995 643215   fax 01995 640894
    email info@rlas.co.uk   http://www.rlas.co.uk
    Hon Sec: Wendy George
▲   Company Limited by Guarantee; Registered Charity
○   *F; promotion of agriculture; to organise the annual show
●   Exhib (annual show)
M   450 i
¶   Rural Review (NL) - 2; m only.   Show Catalogue - 1.   AR.

Royal Life Saving Society UK   (RLSS UK)   1891
■   River House, High St, Broom, ALCESTER, Warks, B50 4HN.
    (hq)
    01789 773994   fax 01789 773995
    email lifesavers@rlss.org.uk
    http://www.lifesavers.org.uk
    Chief Exec: Di Standley
▲   Company Limited by Guarantee; Registered Charity
Br   50
○   *K, *W; educating people in preventing the loss of life through
    drowning, choking & heart attacks
●   ET - Comp - Inf - LG
<   Intl Lifesaving Fedn; Inst Sport & Recreational Mgt
M   13,000 i, 1,400 org
¶   Lifesavers Magazine - 4; ftm & supporters.

Royal Manx Agricultural Society   1858
■   Alpines, Curragh Rd, ST JOHNS, Isle of Man, IM4 3LN.   (hsb)
    01624 801850
    email royalmanx@manx.net
    Sec: Mrs Christine A Pain
▲   Company Limited by Guarantee
○   *F, *H; to organise an annual agricultural show
●   Mtgs - Exhib - Comp - VE - LG - Schools competition with
    'greenfingers' bias
<   Brit Show Jumping Assn; Clydesdale Horse Soc of GB &
    Ireland; Shire Horse Assn; Holstein UK Premier Show; R
    Gardeners Benevolent Assn
M   100 i

Royal Martyr Church Union   (RMCU)   1906
■   7 Nunnery Stables, ST ALBANS, Herts, AL1 2AS.   (hsp)
    01727 856626
    Hon Sec & Treas: E D Roberts
▲   Un-incorporated Society
○   *G, K; to promote the restoration of King Charles I's name to
    its proper place & fitting observance in the worldwide
    Anglican Communion's calendar; to maintain the principles
    of faith, loyalty & liberty for which the King died; open to
    anyone interested in the heroic & stirring times of King
    Charles I
●   Mtgs - Annual remembrance service on the nearest Thursday to
    30 January at St Mary's Cathedral, Palmerston Place,
    Edinburgh & on the nearest Saturday to 30 January in
    St Mary-le-Strand, London WC2
M   85 i, UK / 6 i, o'seas
¶   Royal Martyr Annual - 1; ftm, on application nm.

Royal Medical Society   (RMS)   1736
■   Potterrow, 5/5 Bristo Sq, EDINBURGH, EH8 9AL.   (hq)
    0131-650 2672   fax 0131-650 2672
    email enquiries@royalmedical.co.uk
    http://www.royalmedical.co.uk
    Sec: Mrs Elizabeth Singh,   Snr Pres: Beci Evans
▲   Registered Charity
○   *L; the medical student society of Edinburgh
Gp   Museum; Library; Learning resource centre
●   Mtgs - ET - Comp - SG - Inf - Lib - PL
M   300 i
¶   Res Medica (Jnl) - 2.

Royal Meteorological Society   (RMetS)   1850
NR   104 Oxford Rd, READING, Berks, RG1 7LL.   (hq)
    0118-956 8500   fax 0118-956 8571
    email info@rmets.org   http://www.rmets.org
    Chief Exec: Prof Paul Hardaker
▲   Registered Charity
○   *L; promotion of all aspects of the science of meteorology
    (including the application of the discipline to agriculture,
    aviation, hydrology, marine transport & oceanography)
M   i, f & org

Royal Microscopical Society   (RMS)   1839
NR   37/38 St Clements, OXFORD, OX4 1AJ.   (hq)
    01865 248768   fax 01865 791237
    email info@rms.org.uk   http://www.rms.org.uk
    Exec Dir: Rob Flavin
▲   Registered Charity
○   *L; 'publication & discussion of research in fields of
    improvement in construction & mode of application of
    microscopes, & those branches of science where microscopy
    is important'
Gp   Cytometry; Cell biology; Electron microscopy; Light microscopy;
    Materials science
●   Conf - Mtgs - ET - Exhib
<   Intl Fedn Socs Histochemistry & Cytochemistry; Intl Fedn Socs
    Electron Microscopy
M   c 900 i, UK / 500 i o'seas
¶   Jnl of Microscopy - 12.
    In Focus - 4; ftm.

© CBD Research Ltd · Beckenham · BR3 5JS · Tel 020 8650 7745 · Fax 020 8650 0768 · E-mail cbd@cbdresearch.com · www.cbdresearch.com

Royal Miniature Society
alternative name of the **Royal Society of Miniature Painters, Sculptors & Engravers**

Royal Musical Association   (RMA)   1874
■   4 Chandos Rd, Chorlton-cum-Hardy, MANCHESTER, M21 0ST.   (hsp/b)
0161-861 7542   fax 0161-861 7543
email jeffrey.dean@stingrayoffice.com
http://www.rma.ac.uk
Sec: Dr Jeffrey Dean
▲   Company Limited by Guarantee; Registered Charity
Br   2
○   *D, *L; art, science & history of music
●   Conf - Mtgs
<   Amer Musicological Soc; Soc for Musicology in Ireland
M   900 i, UK / 85 i, o'seas
¶   Jnl - 2; ftm, £109 nm.
NL - 2; ftm, £10 nm.
RMA Research Chronicle - 1; price varies.
RMA Monographs; price varies.

Royal National Institute of the Blind   (RNIB)   1868
NR   105 Judd St, LONDON, WC1H 9NE.   (hq)
020 7388 1266   fax 020 7388 2034
http://www.rnib.org.uk
Dir Gen: Lesley-Anne Alexander
▲   Registered Charity
Br   9
○   *W; 'works for blind & partially sighted people throughout the UK.   We have over 60 different services to help people at all stages of their lives'
●   Inf - Talking book service - Tape & braille services - Holidays - Residential homes - Training, rehabilitation & help in finding jobs
M   subscribers

Royal National Lifeboat Institution   (RNLI)   1824
NR   West Quay Rd, POOLE, Dorset, BH15 1HZ.   (hq)
0845 122 6999
http://www.rnli.org.uk
Chief Exec: Andrew Freemantle
○   *W; to save lives at sea around the coasts of UK & Ireland
●   Conf - Mtgs - Exhib - Inf - PL - VE
<   Intl Lifeboat Fedn
M   200,000+ i
¶   The Lifeboat - 4; ftm.   AR; free.

Royal National Rose Society   (RNRS)   1876
NR   Gardens of the Rose, Chiswell Green, ST ALBANS, Herts, AL2 3NR.   (hq)
01727 850461   fax 01727 850360
http://www.rnrs.org
Gen Mgr: Brian Gill
▲   Company Limited by Guarantee; Registered Charity
○   *H
●   Res - Exhib - Inf - Lib - PL
M   c 10,000 i & org
¶   The Rose (Jnl) - 3.
How to Grow Roses - irreg.

Royal Naval Association   (RNA)   1950
NR   Semaphore Tower (room 209), PP70, HM Naval Base, PORTSMOUTH, Hants, PO1 3LT.   (hq)
023 9272 2983
http://www.royal-naval-association.co.uk
Gen Sec: Cdr Paddy McClurg
▲   Registered Charity
Br   450; 10 o'seas
○   *W; 'to further the efficiency of the Service in which members of the association have served or are serving, by fostering the esprit de corps & preserving the traditions of the Service; ... to relieve members of the association who are in conditions of real hardship or distress'
●   Conf - Mtgs - VE
M   i
¶   NL - 4;   Circular - 11;   Ybk;   AR; all ftm.

Royal Naval Bird Watching Society   (RNBWS)   1946
NR   16 Cutlers Lane, Stubbington, FAREHAM, Hants, PO14 2JN.   (hsp)
07717 368300
email francisward@btopenworld.com
http://www.rnbws.org.uk
Hon Sec: Cdr Frank Ward
▲   Registered Charity
○   *G; forum for exchange of information & observation of seabirds & land birds at sea & onboard ships whilst at sea
Gp   Seabird distribution database
●   Res - PL of seabirds: c/o Lt Cmdr G D Lewis RN, 40 Pondfield Rd, Saltash, Cornwall, PL12 4UA.
M   180 i, org, UK / 60 i, org, o'seas
¶   NBWS Bulletin - 2; ftm, £1 each nm.
Sea Swallow - 1; ftm, £8 nm.

Royal Navy Enthusiasts' Society   (RNES)   1977
■   7 Valley Rd, PEACEHAVEN, E Sussex, BN10 8AE.   (hq)
01273 589187
Chmn: Dave Palmer
▲   Un-incorporated Society
○   *G; collection of memorabilia & ephemera of the Royal Navy from 1600 to the present day
Gp   Collectors: Cap tallies, Branch badges; Historians: Nelson, his ships & men, World Wars I & II; Photographs of ships; the Royal Navy & other navies
●   Mtgs - Res
<   Fedn of Naval Assns
M   145 i, UK / 4 i, o'seas
¶   Excalibur (NL) - 12; free.

Royal Norfolk Agricultural Association   (RNAA)   1847
■   Norfolk Showground, Dereham Rd, New Costessey, NORWICH, Norfolk, NR5 0TT.   (hq)
01603 748931   fax 01603 748729
http://www.royalnorfolkshow.co.uk
Show Mgr: Mrs Sarah de Chair
○   *F; the improvement of livestock & plants, agricultural machines & implements; encouragement of skills & education in agriculture & horticulture
●   ET - Res - Exhib - Comp - Annual show covering livestock (horses, cattle, pigs, sheep, goats, driving & showjumping); Small livestock (poultry, rabbits, cavies, cage birds & dogs); Agricultural machinery & general trade stands
<   Assn Show & Agricl Orgs (ASAO); Breed Socs
M   4,000 i
¶   Jnl;   Prize List - 1;   NL;   AR; all ftm.
Catalogue - 1; £5.

Royal Northern Agricultural Society   (RNAS)   1843
- ■ Auchcairnie Farm, LAURENCEKIRK, Aberdeenshire, AB30 1ER.   (sp)
  01561 340221
  email secretary@rnas.org.uk   http://www.rnas.org.uk
  Sec: Alison M Argo
- ▲ Registered Charity
- ○ *F; to improve agricultural production & the rural economy in all its branches
- ● Conf - Res - Exhib - VE
- M 525 i

Royal Numismatic Society   (RNS)   1836
- ■ Dept of Coins & Medals, British Museum, Great Russell St, LONDON, WC1B 3DG.   (hsb)
  020 7323 8173   fax 020 7323 8267
  email info@numismatics.org.uk
  http://www.numismatics.org.uk
  Jt Secs: Vesta Sarkhosh Curtis,   Sam Moorhead
- ▲ Registered Charity
- ○ *L; to promote & support numismatic research
- ● Mtgs - Lib
- M 420 i, 21 org, UK / 500 i, 54 org, o'seas
- ¶ The Numismatic Chronicle (Jnl) - 1; ftm.
  Special publications - irreg.

Royal Odonto-Chirurgical Society of Scotland   1867
- NR c/o Royal College of Surgeons of Edinburgh, Nicolson St, EDINBURGH, EH8 9DW.
  0131 527 1600   fax 0131 557 6406
  Hon Sec: Y Maidment
- ○ *P

Royal Over-Seas League   (ROSL)   1910
- ■ Over-Seas House, Park Place, St James's St, LONDON, SW1A 1LR.   (hq)
  020 7408 0214   fax 020 7499 6738
  email info@rosl.org.uk   http://www.rosl.org.uk
  Dir Gen: Robert F Newell
- ▲ Royal Charter
- Br 19; Australia, Canada, Hong Kong, New Zealand, Thailand & Switzerland
- ○ *X; private membership-based London club which encourages the arts in the youth of the Commonwealth; to increase the knowledge & interest in the Commonwealth
- ● Conf - Mtgs - Comp (music & art) - Exhib - VE - Residential club-house - Lectures
- M 12,814 i, UK / 10,038 i, o'seas
- ¶ Overseas - 4; ftm, £7.50 nm (£10 o'seas).

Royal Pharmaceutical Society of Great Britain   (RPSGB)   1841
- NR 1 Lambeth High St, LONDON, SE1 7JN.   (hq)
  020 7735 9141   fax 020 7735 7629
  email enquiries@rpsgb.org   http://www.rpsgb.org
  Chief Exec & Registrar: Jeremy Holmes
- ▲ Un-incorporated Society
- ○ *L, *P; to lead, regulate, develop & represent the profession of pharmacy
- ¶ Pharmaceutical Jnl - 52.   Hospital Pharmacist - 10.
  Tomorrow's Pharmacist - 1. Communities - 12.
  International Jnl of Pharmacy Practice - 4.
  Publications list available of pharmacopoeia, textbooks & handbooks on various aspects of pharmacy practice.

Royal Philatelic Society London   (RPSL)   1869
- ■ 41 Devonshire Place, LONDON, W1G 6JY.   (hq)
  020 7486 1044
  http://www.rpsl.org.uk
  Hon Sec: Mrs Christine Earle
- ▲ Registered Charity
- ○ *L, *T; for collectors & philatelic traders interested in the advancement & study of philately & postal history
- ● Mtgs - Lib
- M c 2,200 i
- ¶ The London Philatelist (Jnl) - 10; ftm, £20 nm.
  Books & booklets.

Royal Philharmonic Society   (RPS)   1813
- ■ 10 Stratford Place, LONDON, W1C 1BA.   (hq)
  020 7491 8110   fax 020 7493 7463
  email admin@royalphilharmonicsociety.co.uk
  http://www.royalphilharmonicsociety.org.uk
  Gen Admin: Rosemary Johnson
- ▲ Registered Charity
- ○ *D; to promote excellence, creativity & understanding in classical music
- ● Lectures - Scholarships - Awards - Commissioning new music
- M 700 i, 8 f, UK / 30 i, o'seas
- ¶ RPS Annual Lecture Text - 1.

Royal Philosophical Society of Glasgow   (RPSG)   1802
- ■ PO Box 8268, GLASGOW, G46 7BR.   (sb)
  email info@royalphil.org   http://www.royalphil.org
  Pres: Dr Felicity Grainger
- ▲ Company Limited by Guarantee; Registered Charity
- ○ *L; lectures & discussion on all branches of arts & science
- ● Mtgs
- M 700 i
  (Sub: £20)
- ¶ Summaries of lectures published on website.

Royal Photographic Society of Great Britain   (RPS)   1853
- NR Fenton House, 122 Wells Rd, BATH, Somerset, BA2 3AH.   (hq)
  01225 325733
  email reception@rps.org   http://www.rps.org
  Dir Gen: Stuart Blake
- ▲ Company Limited by Guarantee; Registered Charity
- Br 18
- ○ *L; to promote the art & science of photography in all aspects
- Gp Archaeology & heritage; Audio visual; Colour; Contemporary; Creative; Digital imaging; Film & video; Historical; Holography; Imaging science; Medical; Nature; Travel; Visual art; Visual journalism
- ● Mtgs - ET - Res - Exhib - Comp - Inf
- M 7,972 i, 102 f, UK / 1,271 i, 104 f, o'seas
- ¶ RPS Journal - 10; ftm, £65 yr nm (£70 o'seas).
  Imaging Science Journal - 4; ftm.
  Group & Regional NLs - 1/2; ftm only.

Royal Pigeon Racing Association   (RPRA)   1896
- ■ The Reddings, CHELTENHAM, Glos, GL51 6RN.   (hq)
  01452 713529   fax 01452 857119
  email gm@rpra.org   http://www.rpra.org
  Gen Mgr: Peter Bryant
- Br 13
- ○ *B, *S; control & administration of long distance pigeon racing
- ● Conf - Mtgs - Exhib - Comp - Stat - Inf - LG
- < Fédn Colombophile Intle (FCI); Confedn of Long Distance Pigeon Us of GB (CLDPUGB)
- M 33,000 i, 2,000 clubs
- ¶ British Homing World - 52; 55p m.

© CBD Research Ltd · Beckenham · BR3 5JS · Tel 020 8650 7745 · Fax 020 8650 0768 · E-mail cbd@cbdresearch.com · www.cbdresearch.com

Royal School of Church Music   (RSCM)   1927
- ■ 19 The Close, SALISBURY, Wilts, SP1 2EB.   (hq)
  01722 424848
  email enquiries@rscm.com   http://www.rscm.com
  Dir: Mr Lindsay Gray
- ▲ Company Limited by Guarantee; Registered Charity
- Br 52; Australia, Canada, N Zealand, S Africa, USA
- ○ *D, *L; training, advice & resources for all concerned with music in worship - singers, organists, instrumentalists, clergy & congregation
- ● ET - Exam - Comp - SG - Inf - Lib - Publishing & retailing church music & training material
- M 2,158 i, 4,260 org, UK / 787 i, 1,137 org, o'seas
- ¶ Church Music Quarterly - 4; ftm.   AR.

Royal Scottish Academy   (RSA)   1826
- ■ The Mound, EDINBURGH, EH2 2EL.   (hq)
  0131-225 6671   fax 0131-220 6016
  email info@royalscottishacademy.org
  http://www.royalscottishacademy.org
  Academy Coordinator: Pauline Costigane
- ▲ Registered Charity
- ○ *A; promotion & furtherance of the fine arts in Scotland (painting, sculpture, architecture & printmaking)
- ● Exhib - Comp - Lib
- M 104 academicians, 30 hon mems
- ¶ Exhibition Catalogue - 1.
- ✕ 2006 Royal Scottish Academy of Painting, Sculpture & Architecture

Royal Scottish Academy of Music & Drama   (RSAMD)   1847
- NR 100 Renfrew St, GLASGOW, G2 3DB.   (hq)
  0141-332 4101   fax 0141-332 8901
  email registry@rsamd.ac.uk   http://www.rsamd.ac.uk
  Principal: John Wallace
- ▲ Company Limited by Guarantee; Registered Charity
- ○ *D; an international conservatoire for degree courses in music & drama; to act as an arts & conference venue
- < St Andrews University; Glasgow University; The Piping Centre
- M [none]
- ¶ Drama NL - 4;   Events Brochure - 4;
  Events Brochure - 4;   Prospectus - 1; all free.

Royal Scottish Academy of Painting, Sculpture & Architecture since 2006 the **Royal Scottish Academy**

Royal Scottish Automobile Club (Motor Sport) Ltd since 2004-05 **RSAC Motorsport Ltd**

Royal Scottish Country Dance Society   (RSCDS)   1923
- NR 12 Coates Crescent, EDINBURGH, EH3 7AF.   (hq)
  0131-225 3854   fax 0131-225 7783
  email info@rscds.org   http://www.rscds.org
  Sec: Elspeth Gray
- ▲ Registered Charity
- Br 170
- ○ *D; to preserve & further the practice of traditional Scottish country dancing
- ● Mtgs - Exam
- M c 17,000 i
- ¶ Bulletin - 1; ftm.   Scottish Country Dancer - 2.

Royal Scottish Forestry Society   (RSFS)   1854
- ■ Hagg-on-Esk, CANONBIE, Dumfriesshire, DG14 0XE.   (hq)
  01387 371518   fax 01387 371418
  email rsfs@lumison.co.uk   http://www.rsfs.org
  Admin Dir: Andrew Little
- ▲ Registered Charity
- Br 6
- ○ *H, *L; to advance all areas of forestry
- Gp Silviculture; Trees, woods & people; Forest for a 1000 years
- ● Conf - Mtgs - ET - Exhib - Comp - SG - Lib - VE - LG
- < Forestry Ind Coun (FIC)
- M 950 i, 50 f, UK / 50 i, 10 f, o'seas
- ¶ Scottish Forestry - 4; ftm, £52 (£67 o'seas).

Royal Scottish Geographical Society   (RSGS)   1884
- ■ Graham Hills Building, 40 George St, GLASGOW, G1 1QE. (hq)
  0141-552 3330   fax 0141-552 3331
  email rsgs@strath.ac.uk   http://www.rsgs.org
  Dir & Sec: Dr David M Munro
- ▲ Registered Charity
- Br 14
- ○ *E, *L; to advance the science of geography & create a greater understanding of the wider world
- ● Conf - Mtgs - ET - Exhib - Comp - Inf - Lib - PL - VE - LG
- M 2,500 i
- ¶ Scottish Geographical Jnl - 4; ftm, £44 nm (£95 instns). GeogScot (NL) - 3; ftm, £2 nm.   AR.

Royal Scottish Pipe Band Association   (RSPBA)   1930
- NR 45 Washington St, GLASGOW, G3 8AZ.   (hq)
  0141-221 5414   fax 0141-221 1561
  http://www.rspba.org
  Chief Exec: Ian Embelton
- ▲ Registered Charity
- Br 12
- ○ *D, *G
- ● Conf - ET - Comp - Lib
- M c 650 pipe bands
- ¶ The Pipe Band - 4.

Royal Scottish Society of Arts (Science & Technology)   (RSSA)   1821
- ■ 29/3 East London St, EDINBURGH, EH7 4BN.   (hsp)
  0131-556 2161
  email secretary@rssa.org.uk   http://www.rssa.org.uk
  Hon Sec: Mrs Jane Ridder-Patrick
- ▲ Registered Charity
- ○ *L; 'for the promotion of the 'useful arts' - science, technology, engineering, manufacturing'
- ● Mtgs - VE
- M 180 i

Royal Scottish Society of Painters in Water Colours   (RSW)   1878
- ■ 5 Oswald St, GLASGOW, G1 4QR.   (asa)
  0141-248 7411   fax 0141-221 0417
  email rsw@robbferguson.co.uk
  http://www.thersw.org.uk
  Sec: Mrs Lesley Nicholl
- ▲ Registered Charity
- ○ *A; to develop & encourage the art of painting in watercolour
- ● Exhib
- M 120 i

The Royal Society   1660
- ■ 6-9 Carlton House Terrace, LONDON, SW1Y 5AG.   (hq)
  020 7451 2500
  http://www.royalsociety.org
  Exec Sec: Stephen Cox
- ▲ Registered Charity
- ○ *L, *Q; 'to recognise excellence in science; to support leading edge scientific research & its applications: to stimulate international interaction; to further the role of science, engineering & technology in society; to promote education & the public's understanding of science; to provide independent authoritative advice on matters relating to science; to encourage research into the history of science
- ● Mtgs - Res - Exhib - SG - Stat - Inf - Lib - PL - Grants for research & travel overseas - Appointments
- < Intl Coun for Science (ICSU); Eur Science Foundation (ESF)
- M 1,200 i, UK / 100 i, o'seas
- ¶ Philosophical Transactions:
  (Series A - Mathematical & Physical Sciences.
  (Series B - Biological Sciences); prices vary.
  Proceedings (Series A & B); prices vary.
  Science & Public Affairs - 1.   NL; ftm.
  Notes & Records - 2; ftm.   Ybk.
  Biographical Memoirs of Fellows - 1.
  List of Fellows 1660-2000.
  Obituaries of Fellows 1830-2000.
  Numerous reports & papers.

Royal Society of Antiquaries of Ireland   (RSAI)   1849
- IRL 63 Merrion Sq, DUBLIN 2, Republic of Ireland.
  353 (1) 676 1749   fax 353 (1) 676 1749
  http://www.rsai.ie
  Exec Sec: Colette Ellison
- ○ *L

Royal Society of Architects in Wales   (RSAW)
- NR Bute Building, King Edward VII Avenue, Cathays Park, CARDIFF, Glamorgan, CF10 3NB.
  029 2087 4753   fax 029 2087 4926
  email rsaw@inst.riba.org
  http://www.architecture-wales.com
  Dir: Liz Walder
- ▲ Registered Charity
- ○ *P
- ● Conf - Mtgs - Comp - LG
- < R Inst Brit Architects
- M 854 i
- ¶ Touchstone - 2; £5.
  Note: the RSAW is constituted as the regional organisation of the Royal Institute of British Architects in Wales

Royal Society for the encouragement of Arts, Manufactures & Commerce   (RSA)   1754
- ■ 8 John Adam St, LONDON, WC2N 6EZ.   (hq)
  020 7930 5115   fax 020 7839 5805
  email general@rsa.org.uk   http://www.thersa.org
  Chief Exec: Matthew Taylor
- ▲ Registered Charity
- Br 11; 4 o'seas
- ○ *A, *E, *L, *P; the RSA's 21st century mission is to:
  encourage enterprise
  move towards a zero waste society
  develop a capable population
  foster resilient communities
  advance global citizenship
- Gp Examples of projects: Design Directions; Environment Awards Forum; Intellectual Property Charter; Opening Minds
- ● Conf - Mtgs - Res - Exhib - Comp - SG - Lib - Archive (200 years of RSA history) - Lectures
- M 20,500 i, 15 f, UK / 2,500 i, o'seas
- ¶ The RSA Jnl - 5.
  Note: Also known as the Royal Society of Arts.

Royal Society for Asian Affairs   1901
- ■ 2 Belgrave Sq, LONDON, SW1X 8PJ.   (hq)
  020 7235 5122
  http://www.rsaa.org.uk
  Sec: Neil Porter
- ▲ Registered Charity
- ○ *L; culture & current affairs of Asian countries, from the Near East to China & Japan
- ● Conf (occasional) - Mtgs - Lib - PL
- ¶ Asian Affairs (Jnl) - 3; ftm, £55 i (£125 instns), nm.

Royal Society of British Artists
a member of the **Federation of British Artists**

Royal Society of Chemistry   (RSC)   1980
- ■ Burlington House, Piccadilly, LONDON, W1J 0BA.   (hq)
  020 7437 8656   fax 020 7437 8883
  email library@rsc.org   http://www.rsc.org
  Sec Gen: Dr Richard Pike
- ▲ Registered Charity
- Br 35; 8 o'seas
- ○ *L; to advance the chemical sciences
- Gp Specialist subject groups are controlled by the following divisions:
  Analytical, Dalton, Education, Faraday, Industrial, Perkin
- ● Conf - Mtgs - ET - Exam - SG - Stat - Inf - Lib
- < Intl U of Pure & Applied Chemistry; Fedn of Eur Chemical Socs; Eur Communities Chemistry Coun
- M 34,721 i, UK / 7,714 i, o'seas
- ¶ The Analyst.   Analytical Abstracts.
  Annual Reports on the Progress of Chemistry:
  Section A;   Section B;   Section C.
  Catalysts & Catalysed Reactions.   Chemical Communications.
  Chemical Hazards in Industry.
  Physical Chemistry Chemical Physics.
  Chemical Society Reviews.   Chemical World.
  Chromatography Abstracts.   CrystEngComm.
  Dalton Transactions.   Education in Chemistry.
  Faraday Discussions.   Geochemical Transactions.
  Green Chemistry.   Hazards in the Office.
  Issues in Environmental Science & Technology.
  Jnl of Analytical Atomic Spectrometry.
  Jnl of Environmental Monitoring.
  Jnl of Materials Chemistry.   Lab on a Chip.
  Laboratory Hazards Bulletin.   Mass Spectrometry Bulletin.
  Methods in Organic Synthesis.   Natural Products Reports.
  Natural Products Updates.   New Jnl of Chemistry.
  Organic & Biomolecular Chemistry.   New Pesticide Outlook.
  Photochemical & Photobiological Sciences.
  PhysChemComm.   Russian Chemical Reviews.
  University Chemistry Education.
  [Reduced member prices are available for all RSC publications].

Royal Society of Edinburgh   (RSE)   1783
- NR 22-26 George St, EDINBURGH, EH2 2PQ.   (hq)
  0131-240 5000   fax 0131-240 5024
  http://www.rse.org.uk
  Gen Sec: Prof Geoffrey Boulton
- ▲ Registered Charity
- ○ *L; the achievement of learning & useful knowledge in Scotland.   'The Society is unique in the UK as it encompasses all branches of learning - science, arts, letters, the professions, technology, industry & commerce'
- ● Conf - Mtgs - SG - LG - Awards research fellowship, prizes & prize lectureships - Schemes to interest young people in science & technology
- M c 1,200 i (fellows by election only)
- ¶ Transactions: Earth Sciences - 4.
  Proceedings Section A (Mathematics) - 6.
  RSE News - 4;   AR.   Ybk (inc LM).

Royal Society of Health
in October 2008 merged with the Royal Institute of Public Health to form the **Royal Society for Public Health**

© CBD Research Ltd · Beckenham · BR3 5JS · Tel 020 8650 7745 · Fax 020 8650 0768 · E-mail cbd@cbdresearch.com · www.cbdresearch.com

Royal Society of Literature   (RSL)   1820
- ■   Somerset House, Strand, LONDON, WC2R 1LA.   (hq)
      020 7845 4676
      email info@rslit.org   http://www.rslit.org
      Sec: Maggie Fergusson
- ▲   Registered Charity
- ○   *A; to sustain & encourage all that is perceived as best, whether traditional or experimental, in English letters
- ●   Conf - Mtgs - Comp
- M   450 fellows, 420 members, 10 org
- ¶   News from the RSL - 1.

Royal Society of Marine Artists
   a member of the **Federation of British Artists**

Royal Society of Medicine   (RSM)   1805
- ■   1 Wimpole St, LONDON, W1G 0AE.   (hq)
      020 7290 2900   fax 020 7290 2909
      email membership@rsm.ac.uk   http://www.rsm.ac.uk
      Chief Exec: Ian Balmer
- ▲   Registered Charity
- ○   *L; 'for the cultivation & promotion of physic & surgery & of the branches of science connected with them'
- Gp   Sections:
      Accident & emergency medicine, Anaesthesia, Black & ethnic minority health, Cardiothoracic, Catastrophes & conflict, Clinical, Clinical forensic & legal medicine, Clinical immunology & allergy, Clinical neurosciences, Coloproctology, Communication in healthcare, Comparative medicine, Dermatology, Endocrinology & diabetes, Epidemiology & public health, Food & health, General practice with primary healthcare, Geriatrics & gerontology, History of medicine, Hypnosis & psychosomatic medicine, Laryngology & rhinology, Learning disability, Lipids in clinical medicine, Maternity & the newborn, Medical genetics, Nephrology, Obstetrics & gynaecology, Occupational medicine, Odontology, Oncology, Open, Ophthalmology, Orthopaedics, Otology, Paediatrics & child health, Palliative care, Pathology, Pharmaceutical medicine & research, Plastic surgery, Psychiatry, Quality in health care, Radiology, Respiratory medicine, Rheumatology & rehabilitation, Sexual health & reproductive medicine, Sleep medicine, Sports & exercise medicine, Surgery, Telemedicine & e-health, Transplantation, United services, Urology, Vascular medicine, Venous
- ●   Conf - Mtgs - ET - Lib
- M   17,000 i, UK / 4,000 i, o'seas
- ¶   Jnl - 12;   Calendar - 1;   AR; all ftm only.

Royal Society for Mentally Handicapped Children & Adults
   alternative name of **Mencap**

Royal Society of Miniature Painters, Sculptors & Gravers (RMS)   1895
- ■   3 Briar Walk, Putney, LONDON, SW15 6UD.   (exec/sp)
      020 8785 2338
      email info@royal-miniature-society.org.uk
      http://www.royal-miniature-society.org.uk
      115 Vale Rd, CHESHAM, Bucks, HP5 3HP.
         01494 772362.   (hsp)
      Exec Sec: Mrs Phyllis Rennell
      Hon Sec: Helen White
- ▲   Registered Charity
- ○   *A, *P; to esteem, protect & practice the traditional 16th century art of miniature painting, emphasising the infinite patience needed for its fine techniques
- ●   Exhib
- M   c 120 i
- ¶   100th Anniversary Book; £40.
      Annual Exhibition Catalogue - 1; £3.50.
      Note: is more usually known as the Royal Miniature Society.

Royal Society of Musicians of Great Britain   (RSM)   1738
- §   10 Stratford Place, LONDON, W1C 1BA.   (hq)
      020 7629 6137   fax 020 7629 6137
      http://www.royalsocietyofmusicians.co.uk
      A charity to provide assistance to those working in the music profession and their dependents, when in need, because of accident, illness or old age.

Royal Society for Nature Conservation
   since 2004 the **Royal Society of Wildlife Trusts**

Royal Society of Painter-Printmakers   (RE)   1884
- ■   48 Hopton St, LONDON, SE1 9JH.   (hq)
      020 7928 7521
      http://www.banksidegallery.com
      Pres: Hilary Paynter
- ▲   Registered Charity
- ○   *A; to promote printmaking through exhibitions
- ●   ET - Exhib - SG - Inf - Lib
- M   i

Royal Society of Portrait Painters
   a member of the **Federation of British Artists**

Royal Society for the Prevention of Accidents   (RoSPA)   1916
- NR   Edgbaston Park, 353 Bristol Rd, BIRMINGHAM, B5 7ST.   (hq)
      0121-248 2000   fax 0121-248 2001
      email help@rospa.com   http://www.rospa.com
      Chief Exec: Tom Mullarkey
- ▲   Company Limited by Guarantee; Registered Charity
- Br   3
- ○   *E, *K; accident prevention
- ●   Conf - Mtgs - ET - Exam - Exhib - Stat - Inf - Lib - PL - LG
- <   La Prévention Routière Intle
- M   6,905 i, f & org
- ¶   RoSPA Bulletin - 12.
      Occupational Safety & Health - 12.
      Safety Express - 6.   Staying Alive - 4.
      Care on the Road - 6.   Safety Education - 3.

Royal Society for the Prevention of Cruelty to Animals (RSPCA)   1824
- NR   Wilberforce Way, Southwater, HORSHAM, W Sussex, RH13 9RS.
      030 0123 4555   fax 030 3123 0284
      http://www.rspca.org.uk
      Chief Exec: Mark Watts
- ○   *K; to, by all lawful means, prevent cruelty, promote kindness & alleviate suffering of animals
- ●   24-Hour Cruelty Line: 030 0123 4999
- M   i

Royal Society for the Promotion of Health
   in October 2008 merged with the Royal Institute of Public Health to form the **Royal Society for Public Health**

Royal Society for the Protection of Birds   (RSPB)   1889
- NR   The Lodge, SANDY, Beds, SG19 2DL.   (hq)
      01767 680541
      http://www.rspb.org.uk
      Chief Exec: Graham Wynne
- ▲   Registered Charity
- ○   *G, *K; conservation & protection of wild birds; 'RSPB works for a healthy environment rich in birds & wildlife'
- ●   Conf - Res - Lib - PL
- <   Birdlife Intl
- M   1,036,869 i
- ¶   Birds - 4.

Royal Society for Public Health   (RSPH)   2008
NR   Market Towers (3rd floor), 1 Nine Elms Lane, LONDON,
        SW8 5NQ.   (hq)
        020 3177 1600   fax 020 3177 1601
        email info@rsph.org.uk   http://www.rsph.org.uk
        Chief Exec: Prof Richard Parish
▲   Registered Charity
○   *E, *L; to improve public health & to support the public health
        workforce
●   Conf - Exam - LG
<   Intl U for Health Promotion & Educ; Eur Public Health Alliance;
        Wld Fedn of Public Health Assns; Amer Public Health Assn
M   6,000 i
¶   Public Health - 12.
        Perspectives in Public Health - 6.
×   2008 (Royal Institute of Public Health
                (Royal Society [for the Promotion] of Health
                        merged October

Royal Society of St George   1894
■   127 Sandgate Rd, FOLKESTONE, Kent, CT20 2BH.   (hq)
        01303 241795   fax 01303 211710
        email info@rssg.u-net.com
        http://www.royalsocietyofstgeorge.com
        Chmn: James Newton
▲   Registered Charity
Br   40; c 40
○   *K, *W; 'the premier patriotic society of England, standing for
        loyalty & patriotic service to our nation & within our
        communities, with duty to our sovereign who as head of state
        transcends all party, political & personal ego & ambitions'
Gp   C'ees: Policy, Events; Charitable trust
●   Conf - Mtgs - ET - Lib - VE
<   about 40 affiliated socs o'seas
M   10,000 i
¶   England's Standard - 3; ftm, £2.50 nm.

**Royal Society of Tropical Medicine & Hygiene   (RSTM&H)
1907**
■   50 Bedford Square, LONDON, WC1B 3DP.   (hq)
        020 7580 2127   fax 020 7436 1389
        email mail@rstmh.org   http://www.rstmh.org
        Admin: Caryl Guest
▲   Registered Charity
○   *L; 'study of diseases & hygiene of man & other animals in
        warm climates'
●   Mtgs
M   827 i, UK / 2,067 i, o'seas
¶   Transactions - 12;   Ybk - 1; both ftm.

Royal Society of Ulster Architects   (RSUA)   1901
NR   2 Mount Charles, BELFAST, BT7 1NZ.   (hq)
        028 9032 3760   fax 028 9023 7313
        email info@rsua.org.uk   http://www.rsua.org.uk
        Hon Sec: Paul Crowe,   Sec: Gillian Lendrum
▲   Registered Charity
○   *P
●   Conf - Mtgs - ET - Exhib - Comp - VE
<   R Inst Brit Architects
M   750 i
¶   Perspective (Jnl) - 6; ftm, £4.50 nm.   Ybk; ftm, £25 nm.

Royal Society of Wildlife Trusts   (RSWT)   1912
■   The Kiln, Waterside, Mather Rd, NEWARK, Notts, NG24 1WT.
        (hq)
        01636 677711   fax 01636 670001
        http://www.rswt.org
        Chief Exec: Stephanie Hilborne
▲   Registered Charity
Br   47 wildlife trusts
○   *K, *N; to promote wildlife conservation in the UK; The Wildlife
        Trusts is the umbrella group for the 47 local wildlife trusts
Gp   Community Recycling & Economic Development Programme;
        Social, Economic & Environmental Development Programme
●   Conf - Mtgs - ET - Res - Stat - Inf - LG - Land management
<   Eur Envtl Bureau; NCVO; Wildlife Link
M   c 260,000 i
¶   Natural World - 3;   Watchword - 3; both ftm only.   AR.
×   2004 Royal Society for Nature Conservation

Royal Statistical Society   (RSS)   1834
NR   12 Errol St, LONDON, EC1Y 8LX.   (hq)
        020 7638 8998
        http://www.rss.org.uk
▲   Registered Charity
○   *L

Royal Stuart Society   1926
NR   24 Park St, SALISBURY, Wilts, SP1 3AU.   (hsp)
        http://www.royalstuartsociety.com
        Principal Sec: Roger Davies
▲   Un-incorporated Society
○   *G; for all who have an interest in the members of the Royal
        House of Stuart, their descendants & supporters; to promote
        research in, & further knowledge of, Stuart history; to uphold
        rightful monarchy & oppose republicanism; to arrange
        commemorations, lectures & other activities as shall advance
        these objects
●   Conf - Mtgs - Res - VE - LG - Lectures - Commemorative &
        social events
<   Intl Monarchist League
M   i
¶   NL - 3; ftm only.
        Royal Stuart Papers - 2; ftm, £3 each nm.
        Royal Stuart Review - 1; ftm, £3 each nm.

Royal Surgical Aid Society   (RSAS)   1862
§   47 Great Russell St, LONDON, WC1B 3PB.   (hq)
        020 7637 4577   fax 020 7323 6878
        http://www.agecare.org.uk
        Operating as **AgeCare**, the charity RSAS is committed to
        advancing of excellence in residential care for older people
        and ensuring dignity, respect and individual choice is
        paramount in the care provided

Royal Television Society   (RTS)   1927
NR   Kildare House (5th floor), 3 Dorset Rise, LONDON,
        EC4Y 8EN.   (hq)
        020 7822 2810   fax 020 7822 2811
        http://www.rts.org.uk
○   *L

© CBD Research Ltd · Beckenham · BR3 5JS · Tel 020 8650 7745 · Fax 020 8650 0768 · E-mail cbd@cbdresearch.com · www.cbdresearch.com

Royal Town Planning Institute   (RTPI)   1914
NR   41 Botolph Lane, LONDON, EC3R 8DL.   (hq)
    020 7929 9494   fax 020 7929 9490
    email online@rtpi.org.uk   http://www.rtpi.org.uk
    Sec Gen: Robert Upton
▲   Registered Charity
Br   13; various countries o'seas
○   *L, *P; to advance the science & art of town planning in all its
    aspects (including local, regional & national planning) for the
    benefit of the public
Gp   Planning service
●   Conf - Mtgs - ET - Res - SG - Inf - Lib - LG
<   Eur Coun of Town Planners; C'wealth Assn of Planners; Urban
    Design Alliance
M   18,000 i
¶   Various papers.

Royal Ulster Academy of Arts   (RUA)
NR   9-13 Waring St, BELFAST, BT1 2DX.   (hq)
    028 9032 0819
    http://www.rua.webcorono.com
    Admin: Karin Bamford
○   *A, *P

Royal Ulster Agricultural Society   (RUAS)   1826
■   The King's Hall, Balmoral, BELFAST, BT9 6GW.   (hq)
    028 9066 5225   fax 028 9066 1264
    email general@kingshall.co.uk
    http://www.balmoralshow.co.uk
    Chief Exec: Colin McDonald
▲   Registered Charity
○   *F; to promote agriculture, industries, sciences & the arts
●   Conf - Exhib - Organisation of the Balmoral Show (the national
    agricultural show in NI) & of the Royal Ulster Winter Fair, a
    dairy orientated event
<   R Agricl Soc of the C'wealth
M   3,500 i
¶   NL.   Hbk.   AR.

**Royal United Kingdom Beneficent Association   (RUKBA)
1863**
§   6 Avonmore Rd, LONDON, W14 8RL.   (hq)
    020 7605 4200   fax 020 7605 4201
    http://www.independentage.org.uk
    Operating as Independent Age, the charity RUKBA exists to help
    older people on low incomes live with dignity and peace of
    mind

**Royal United Services Institute for Defence & Security Studies
(RUSI)   1831**
NR   Whitehall, LONDON, SW1A 2ET.   (hq)
    020 7930 5854   fax 020 7321 0943
    email defence@rusi.org   http://www.rusi.org
    Dir: Prof Michael Clarke
▲   Registered Charity
Br   Qatar; USA (Washington DC)
○   *L, *P, *Q; the study, analysis & debate of matters concerning
    natural & international defence & security; is a professional
    association of the Armed Forces
Gp   International security studies; Military sciences & homeland
    security & resilience
●   Conf - Mtgs - Res - SG - Inf - Lib - LG
M   4,500 i, 300 f, 200 org, UK / 1,000 i, 50 f, 32 org, o'seas
¶   RUSI Jnl - 6.   HSR Monitor - 10;
    RUSI Defence Systems - 3.   Whitehall Papers - 6.
    Newsbrief - 12.   Various other publications.

Royal Warrant Holders Association   1840
■   1 Buckingham Place, London, SW1E 6HR.   (hq)
    020 7828 2268   fax 020 7828 1668
    email warrants@rwha.co.uk
    http://www.royalwarrant.org
    Sec: Richard Peck
○   *T; to unite in one body all who hold a Royal Warrant of
    Appointment; the maintenance of the highest standards of
    craftsmanship & service
M   c 870 f

Royal Watercolour Society   (RWS)   1804
■   48 Hopton St, LONDON, SE1 9JH.   (hq)
    020 7928 7521   fax 020 7928 2820
    email info@banksidegallery.com
    http://www.royalwatercoloursociety.co.uk
    Pres: Richard Sorrell
▲   Registered Charity
○   *A; to spread the knowledge of watercolour painting; to act as
    a showcase for the best of watercolour either by members or
    annually by non-members in open competition
Gp   Friends of the RWS
●   ET - Exhib
M   84 i
¶   NL - 3; ftm only.

**Royal Welsh Agricultural Society Ltd   (Cymdeithas Amaethyddol
Frenhinol Cymru Cyf)   (RWAS)   1904**
■   Royal Welsh Showground, Llanelwedd, BUILTH WELLS, Powys,
    LD2 3SY.   (hq)
    01982 553683   fax 01982 553563
    email requests@rwas.co.uk   http://www.rwas.co.uk
    Chief Exec: David Walters,   Sec: Barrie Jones
▲   Company Limited by Guarantee
○   *B, *F, *H; to promote agriculture, horticulture, forestry &
    conservation in Wales
Gp   R Welsh Agricl Winter Fair; R Welsh Smallholders' & Garden
    Festival
●   Conf - Mtgs - Exhib - Comp - Agricultural shows
M   12,500 i
¶   Jnl - 1;   Show Programme; both ftm.
    Show Catalogue.

Royal Yachting Association   (RYA)   1875
NR   RYA House, Ensign Way, HAMBLE, Hants, SO31 4YA.   (hq)
    023 8060 4100   fax 023 8060 4299
    email admin@rya.org.uk   http://www.rya.org.uk
▲   Company Limited by Guarantee
○   *S; for UK sailors, windsurfers, powerboat racers, motorboaters
    & personal watercraft users
<   Boating Alliance

Royal Yachting Association Scotland   (RYAS)
NR   Caledonia House, 1 Redheughs Rigg, South Gyle,
    EDINBURGH, EH12 9DQ.
    0131-317 7388   fax 0131-317 8566
    email admin@ryascotland.org.uk
    http://www.ryascotland.org.uk
    Hon Sec: Stewart Boyd
○   *S; the promotion of sailing in Scotland
¶   NL - 12.
    no further information supplied

Royal Zoological Society of Scotland   (RZSS)   1909
NR   134 Corstorphine Rd, EDINBURGH, EH12 6TS.   (hq)
　　0131-334 9171   fax 0131-314 0384
　　email info@rzss.org.uk
　　http://www.edinburghzoo.org.uk
　　Chief Exec: David Windmill
▲　Registered Charity
○　*L, *V; 'to promote, facilitate & encourage the study of zoology
　　& kindred subjects; to foster an interest in animal life'
Gp Edinburgh Zoo; Highland Wildlife Park
●　Mtgs - ET - VE - Care & conservation of wildlife
<　Intl U Consvn Nature & Natural Resources; World Assn Zoos &
　　Aquariums; Eur Assn Zoos & Aquaria; Brit & Ir Assn Zoos &
　　Aquariums
M　15,000 i, 85 f
¶　Life Links (NL) - 3; free.   Guide Book; £5.   AR; free.

RSAC Motorsport Ltd   1982
NR   PO Box 3333, GLASGOW, G20 2AX.   (hq)
　　0141-946 5045   fax 0141-946 5045
　　email mail@rsacmotorsport.co.uk
　　http://www.rsacmotorsport.co.uk
▲　Company Limited by Guarantee
○　*S; for the development of motor sport in Scotland;
　　authorisation of motoring events on the public highway in
　　Scotland
Gp Development; Event organising c'ees
●　Mtgs - Comp - Inf
<　Motor Sports Assn UK
M　2 f, 40 clubs
¶　NL - 2.   Ybk.
×　2004-05 Royal Scottish Automobile Club (Motor Sport) Ltd

Rubber Stamp Manufacturers' Guild   (RSMG)
■　Farringdon Point, 29-35 Farringdon Rd, LONDON,
　　EC1M 3JF.   (hq)
　　0845 450 1565   fax 020 7405 7784
　　email info@rsmg.org.uk   http://www.rsmg.org.uk
　　Sec: Philippa Morrell
▲　Company Limited by Guarantee
○　*T; rubber stamps, daters, marking devices
●　Conf - Mtgs - Exhib - SG - Inf
<　an affiliate of the British Office Supplies & Services Fedn
M　f

Rudolf Kempe Society
NR   58 Waterside, STRATFORD-upon-AVON, Warks, CV37 6BA.
　　(dir/p)
　　01789 298869
○　*D; for those interested in the life & work of Rudolf Kempe
　　(1910-1976), the German conductor

Rugby Fives Association   (RFA)   1927
■　66 Brayburne Avenue, Clapham, LONDON, SW4 6AA.
　　020 7627 8303
　　http://www.rfa.org.uk
　　Gen Sec: Andy Pringle
▲　Company Limited by Guarantee
○　*S; governing body of the game of Rugby fives
●　Exhib - Comp - Inf - LG
M　600 i, 100 org
¶　NL - 2;   Hbk - 1;   Pocket Book - 1; all ftm only.

Rugby Football League   (RFL)   1895
NR   Red Hall, Red Hall Lane, LEEDS, W Yorks, LS17 8NB.   (hq)
　　0844 477 7113   fax 0844 477 0013
　　email enquiries@rfl.uk.com   http://www.rfl.uk.com
　　Chief Exec: Nigel Wood
○　*S; governing body of rugby league football in the UK
Gp Brit Amat Rugby League Assn
<　Rugby League Intl Fedn
M　professional clubs
¶　Guide - 1; ftm.

Rugby Football Union   (RFU)   1871
NR   Rugby House, Rugby Rd, TWICKENHAM, Middx, TW1 1DS.
　　(hq)
　　0870 405 2000   fax 0870 405 2009
　　http://www.rfu.com
　　Chief Exec: Francis Baron
○　*S; promotion, encouragement & extension of Rugby Union
　　football
●　Conf - Mtgs - ET - Exam - Comp - Inf - Organisation of
　　international matches
<　Intl Rugby Football Bd
M　2,000 clubs, 3,500 schools, UK / 70 unions & clubs, o'seas
¶　RFU Hbk (incl Laws of the Game).   Laws of the Game.
　　Numerous specialised publications.

Rugby Memorabilia Society
NR   PO Box 57, HEREFORD, HR1 9DR.
　　http://www.rugby-memorabilia.co.uk
○　*G, *S

Rural Crafts Association   (RCA)   1970
■　Heights Cottage, Brook Rd, Wormley, GODALMING, Surrey,
　　GU8 5UA.   (hq)
　　01428 682292   fax 01428 685969
　　email ruralcraftsassociation@btinternet.com
　　http://www.ruralcraftsassociation.co.uk
　　Chief Exec: Trevor Sears
▲　Company Limited by Guarantee
○　*A; to encourage men & women to make & sell their work &
　　skills; to uphold the quality of work; to encourage the growth
　　of small craft businesses & provide employment on a long-
　　term basis
●　Exhib - Inf - Provision of a forum for the sale members' work
M　600 i, UK / 15 i, o'seas
¶　NL - 6.   Directory - 1.

Rural Design & Building Association
　　since 2004 **Rural & Industrial Design & Building Association
　　Ltd**

**Rural & Industrial Design & Building Association Ltd   (RIDBA)
1956**
■　5a The Maltings, Stowupland Rd, STOWMARKET, Suffolk,
　　IP14 5AG.   (hq)
　　01449 676049   fax 01449 770028
　　email secretary@ridba.org.uk   http://www.ridba.org.uk
　　Nat Sec: A M Hutchinson
▲　Company Limited by Guarantee
Br　4
○　*F, *T; an independent organisation covering all aspects of rural
　　building, both industrial & agricultural
Gp Construction group
●　Conf - Mtgs - SG - Inf - VE - LG
<　Nat Specialist Contractors Coun; Advy C'ee on Roofwork
M　240 i, 60 f, UK / 4 i, o'seas
¶　Countryside Building - 4; ftm, £25 nm.
×　2004 Rural Design & Building Association

Rural Shops Alliance   (RSA)   2001
NR   The Little Keep, Bridport Rd, DORCHESTER, Dorset,
　　DT1 1SQ.   (hq)
　　01305 259911   fax 01305 259384
　　email info@rural-shops-alliance.co.uk
　　http://www.rural-shops-alliance.co.uk
　　Chief Exec: Ken Parsons
▲　Company Limited by Guarantee
○　*T; to be the campaigning voice of the independent rural
　　retailer; to provide practical support, particularly in terms of
　　retail best practice
●　Mtgs - ET - Res - SG - Inf - LG
M　7,200 f
¶　Rural Retailer - 4; ftm.

© CBD Research Ltd · Beckenham · BR3 5JS · Tel 020 8650 7745 · Fax 020 8650 0768 · E-mail cbd@cbdresearch.com · www.cbdresearch.com

Rural Theology Association   (RTA)   1981
- ■ The Vicarage, 28 Park Avenue, WITHERNSEA, E Yorks, HU19 2JU.   (hsp/b)
  01964 611462
  email secretary@rural-theology.org.uk(09>rural-theology.org.uk
  Sec: Stephen Cope
- ▲ Registered Charity
- ○ *R
- ● Conf - Res - SG - Inf
- M i, f & org
  (Sub: £15 i, £30 f & org)
- ¶ Rural Theology (Jnl) - 2; ftm, £7.50 nm.
  NL - 2;   LM - 1; both ftm.

Ruskin Society   1997
- ■ 49 Hallam St, LONDON, W1W 6JP.   (hsp)
  020 7580 1894
  email c.gamble@zen.co.uk   http://www.lancs.ac.uk/fass/centres/ruskin/links.htm
  Chmn: Dr Malcolm Hardman,   Vice Chmn: Dr C J Gamble
- ▲ Un-incorporated Society
- ○ *A; to promote an interest in the life & ideals of John Ruskin (1819-1900) & to relate his thought to the present day
- ● Mtgs - VE
- < The Ruskin Foundation (Bowland College, University of Lancaster)
- M 130 i, UK / 5 i, o'seas
- ¶ NL - irreg; ftm only.

Ruskin Society of Oxford   1985
- NR 351 Woodstock Rd, Summerfield Rd, OXFORD, OX2 7NX.
  (hsp/b)
  01865 310987
  Hon Sec: Miss O Forbes-Madden
- ▲ Un-incorporated Society
- ○ *A, *L; to promote interest in John Ruskin (1819-1900); in his philosophy, artistic guidance & economic recommendations; his connection with his contemporaries
- ● Res - SG - Inf - VE
- < Brit-Italian Soc; R Soc Literature
- M c 35 i
- ¶ The Ruskin Gazette - 1; ftm.
- × Ruskin Society of London

Russell Society
- NR 78 Leconfield Rd, LOUGHBOROUGH, Leics, LE11 3SQ.
  (sec/p)
  01509 263507
  http://www.russellsoc.org
  Gen Sec: Dr Frank Ince
- ○ *L; named after Sir Arthur Russell (1878-1964) mineralogist; the principal aims are the study, recording & conservation of mineralogical sites & material
- ● Mtgs
- M c 500 i
- ¶ Jnl - irreg.   NL - 2; ftm.

Russo-British Chamber of Commerce   (RBCC)   1916
- ■ 42 Southwark St, LONDON, SE1 1UN.   (hq)
  020 7403 1706   fax 020 7403 1245
  email infolondon@rbcc.com   http://www.rbcc.com
  Chief Exec: Stephen Dalziel
- ▲ Company Limited by Guarantee
- Br Russia
- ○ *C; facilitation & promotion of trade between Russia & Britain
- ● Conf - Mtgs - LG
- < Russian Fedn Cham Comm & Ind
- M 250 f, UK / 300 f, Russia
- ¶ Bulletin - 10/12.   Observer - 52; both free.

Rutland Agricultural Society   1830
- NR Chard Farm, Main St, TILTON on the HILL, Leics, LE7 9LF.   (hq)
  0116-259 7466
  email jo@rutlandshow.fsnet.co.uk
  http://www.rutlandcountyshow.co.uk
- ○ *F; organise Rutland county show
- ● Mtgs
- M i

Rutland Boughton Music Trust   1978
- ■ 25 Bearton Green, HITCHIN, Herts, SG5 1UN.   (sb/p)
  01462 434318 & 0770 358 4152 (mobile)
  email boughtontrust@aol.com
  http://www.rutlandboughtonmusictrust.org.uk
  Admin: Ian Boughton
- ▲ Registered Charity
- ○ *D; to promote an interest in the composer Rutland Boughton (1878-1960) by encouraging performances & sponsoring recordings of his finest works
- ● Mtgs - Exhib - Lib
- M 200 i
- ¶ NL - 1/2; free.

Rutland Local History and Record Society   1970
- NR Rutland County Museum, Catmose St, OAKHAM, Rutland, LE15 6HW.   (hq)
  01572 758440   fax 01572758445
  http://www.rutlandhistory.org
  Sec: Jill Kimber
- ○ *L; to promote the study of the history & archaeology of the ancient County of Rutland

Ryeland Flock Book Society   (RFBS)   1903
- ■ Holly Cottage, Playley Green, Redmarley D'Abitot, GLOUCESTER, GL19 3NB.   (hq/hsp)
  01531 650400
  http://www.ryelandfbs.com
  Sec: Mrs Anne M Jones
- ▲ Company Limited by Guarantee
- ○ *B
- ● Mtgs - Exhib - Inf
- < Nat Sheep Assn
- M 300 i, UK / 7 i, o'seas
- ¶ NL - 4;   AR - 1; both ftm only.
  Hbk; ftm, £5.10 nm.   Flock Books - 1; ftm, £5. nm.

SAA - the Society for All Artists 1992
- ■ PO Box 50, NEWARK, Notts, NG23 5GY.   (hq)
  01949 844050   fax 01949 844051
  http://www.saa.co.uk
  Chmn: John Hope-Hawkins
- ▲ Un-incorporated Society
- ○ *A; to inform, encourage & inspire all who want to paint, from the complete beginner to those whose profession depends on it
- ● Exhib - Comp - Inf
- M 41,000 i, 923 clubs, UK / 1,244 i, o'seas
- ¶ Paint (NL) - 6;   SAA Home Shopping Catalogue - 4; both ftm only.

SACRO, safeguarding communities - reducing offending (SACRO) 1971
- NR 1 Broughton Market, EDINBURGH, EH3 6NU.   (hq)
  0131-624 7270
- ○ *K, *W; to make communities safer in Scotland by reducing conflict & offending & by influencing change in criminal justice & social policy
- M i

SAD Association (SADA) 1987
- ■ PO Box 989, STEYNING, W Sussex, BN44 3HG.
  (mail address)
  01903 814942   fax 01903 879939
  http://www.sada.org.uk
  Sec: Marie Walters
- ▲ Registered Charity
- ○ *W; to offer advice & support for sufferers of Seasonal Affective Disorder (SAD)
- ● Inf
- < Mind; R Coll of Psychiatry
- M c 1,500 i, UK / i, o'seas
- ¶ NL - 3; ftm.

Safe Home Income Plans (SHIP) 1994
- ■ 83 Victoria St, LONDON, SW1H 0HW.   (hsp)
  020 3178 4395
  email info@ship-ltd.org   http://www.ship-ltd.org
  Dir Gen: Andrea Rozario
- ▲ Company Limited by Guarantee
- ○ *T; a non-profit trade association dedicated to safe equity release plans including lifetime mortgages & home reversions
- ● Mtgs - Stat - Inf - LG
- M 21 f

Safe Speed (SS) 2001
- NR Coast View, Hunting Hill, TAIN, Ross-shire, IV19 1PE.
  01862 893030
  email carmstrong@safespeed.org
  http://www.safespeed.org.uk
  Sec: Claire Armstrong
- ○ *K; campaigning for the removal of speed cameras, for improved driving standards & safe speeds set by drivers
- M 150 i

SAFE: Struggle against Financial Exploitation (SAFE)
- § 69 Sutton Rd, Heston, HOUNSLOW, Middx, TW5 0PN.   (hq)
  020 8630 9990
  http://www.safe-online.org
  a Parliamentary Working Group highlighting the serious issues related to cases, concerned with fraud & deception, seemingly condoned by banks & other government institutions

Safety Assessment Federation (SAFed) 1995
- NR Unit 4 / 70 South Lambeth Rd (first floor), Vauxhall, LONDON, SW8 1RL.   (hq)
  020 7582 3208   fax 020 7582 3456
  email info@safed.co.uk   http://www.safed.co.uk
  Chief Exec: Richard Hulmes
- ▲ Company Limited by Guarantee
- ○ *T; representing companies that undertake independent safety inspection & certification of engineering & manufacturing plant & equipment
- Gp SAFed Type Approval Service (STAS)
- ● Mtgs - Stat - LG
- < Eur Confedn of Orgs for Testing, Inspection, Certification & Prevention (CEOC)
- M 13 f, UK / 2 f, o'seas
- ¶ Guidelines on/for:
  the Thorough Examination & Testing of Lifts (LG1).
  Periodicity of Examinations of Pressure Systems (PSG1).
  the Periodic Testing & Examination of Fixed Low Voltage Electrical Installations at Quarries.
  Shell Boilers - Guidelines for the Examination of:
  Longitudinal Seams of Shell Boilers.
  Welding Procedures & Welding Guidelines on Approval Testing.

Safety & Reliability Society 1980
- NR Clayton House, 59 Piccadilly, MANCHESTER, M1 2AQ.   (hq)
  0161-228 7824
  Sec: J Christodoulou
- Br 5
- ○ *P; to provide a forum for the exchange of information on safety & reliability engineering; to establish professional & educational standards for safety & reliability engineers

Sailing Barge Association (SBA)
- NR PO Box 5191, BOURNEMOUTH, Dorset, BH1 3WZ.
  (mail/address)
  01202 552582
  email sba@ffbs.co.uk
  http://www.sailingbargeassociation.co.uk
  Sec: Frank Morris
- ▲ Un-incorporated Society
- ○ *T; to keep Thames sailing barges working
- M 28 i, 13 f, 3 org
- ¶ NL - 4; ftm only.

Sailing Smack Association (SSA) 1991
- NR 11 Butt Lane, MALDON, Essex, CM9 5HD.
  email info@ssa-uk.org   http://www.ssa-uk.org
  Mem Sec: Hilary Halajko
- < RYA

Saint
In the entries below Saint is put in full (rather than St) in order to keep them in their correct alphabetical order in the directory.

Saint Albans District Chamber of Commerce 1907
- ■ Suite 19 STANTA Business Centre, 3 Soothouse Spring, ST ALBANS, Herts, AL3 6PF.   (hq)
  01727 863054   fax 01727 851200
  email lisa@stalbans-chamber.co.uk
  http://www.stalbans-chamber.co.uk
  Gen Mgr: Lisa Bates
- ▲ Company Limited by Guarantee
- ○ *C
- ● Mtgs - Conf - Inf
- M 250 f
- ¶ Chamber Bulletin - 6;   Ybk - 1; both ftm only.

© CBD Research Ltd · Beckenham · BR3 5JS · Tel 020 8650 7745 · Fax 020 8650 0768 · E-mail cbd@cbdresearch.com · www.cbdresearch.com

Saint Albans & Hertfordshire Architectural & Archaeological Society (SAHAAS) 1845
- ■ 24 Monks Horton Way, ST ALBANS, Herts, AL4 9AF. (hsp)
  01727 851734
  email admin@stalbanshistory.org.uk
  http://www.stalbanshistory.org
  Sec: Bryan Hanlon
- ▲ Registered Charity
- ○ *L; to preserve, record & disseminate information about sites & buildings of archaeological & historical importance as well as historical documents & records
- Gp Archaeology; Architecture & local history; 17th century research
- ● Conf - Mtgs - Res - Exhib - SG - Inf - Lib - PL - VE
- < Coun Brit Archaeology; Brit Assn Local History
- M 500 i, 10 org, UK / 5 i, o'seas
- ¶ Hertfordshire Archaeology - 1; ftm, prices vary nm.
  NL - 3; ftm only.
  History of the Society 1845-1995; £2 m, £3 nm.
  Research Reports - irreg; prices vary.

Saint Andrew's Ambulance Association 1882
- ■ St Andrew's House, 48 Milton St, GLASGOW, G4 0HR. (hq)
  0141-332 4031 fax 0141-332 6582
  email firstaid@staaa.org.uk http://www.firstaid.org.uk
  Chmn of Council: Rudy Crawford
- ▲ Registered Charity
- Br 11
- ○ *W; first aid training & services in Scotland
- Gp Volunteer Corps
- ● ET - Services for public events
- M 1,600 i
- ¶ First Aid Manual (8th ed); £9.90. AR - 1; free.

Saint Andrew Society 1902
- NR PO Box 84, EDINBURGH, EH3 8LG. (mail add)
  http://www.st-andrew.org.uk
- ○ *K, *N; to promote the study and celebration of all things Scottish
- M i

Saint Austell District Chamber of Commerce & Industry
- NR Semball House, West Hill, ST AUSTELL, Cornwall, PL25 5ET.
  01726 69094
- ○ *C

Saint Dunstan's 1915
- § 12-14 Harcourt St, LONDON, W1H 4HD. (hq)
  020 7723 5021 fax 020 7262 6199
  email enquiries@st-dunstans.co.uk
  http://www.st-dunstans.co.uk
  Rehabilitation, training & settlement of ex-service men & women with very significant loss of sight.

Saint Helens Chamber Ltd 1989
- ■ Technology Campus, ST HELENS, Merseyside, WA9 1UE. (hq)
  01744 742000 fax 01744 742001
  email info@sthelenschamber.com
  http://www.sthelenschamber.com
  Chief Exec: Kath Boullen
- ▲ Company Limited by Guarantee
- ○ *C
- ● Conf - Mtgs - ET - Inf - Business advice
- < Brit Chams Comm; Chams Comm NW
- M 1,100 f
- ¶ Comment - 3; Comment Extra - 6; AR; all free.

Saint John Ambulance 1887
- NR 27 St John's Lane, LONDON, EC1M 4BU. (hq)
  0870 0104 950
- ▲ Registered Charity
- ○ *W; the first aid, transport & care charity; to provide caring services in support of community needs
- M i

Saintpaulia & Houseplant Society 1956
- ■ 93 St Margarets Avenue, RUSHDEN, Northants, NN10 9YQ. (mem/sp)
  01933 358180
  email pjcollins13@btinternet.com
  Mem Sec: Pat Collins
- ▲ Un-incorporated Society
- ○ *H; to encourage the growing of beautiful house plants; special interest is in Saintpaulias (African violets) & the very wide range of houseplants now available
- ● Mtgs - Comp - Lib - Srping leaf for members to enlarge their collections
- < Gesneriad Soc; R Horticl Soc; African Violet Soc of America
- M 180 i, UK / 20 i, o'seas
  (Sub: £8 UK / £10 o'seas)
- ¶ Bulletin - 4; ftm only.

Salers Cattle Society of the United Kingdom Ltd 1986
- ■ Brook House Farm, Norbury, WHITCHURCH, Shropshire, SY13 4HY. (sp)
  01948 667223 fax 01948 667448
  email johncrowe@salers-cattle-society.co.uk
  http://www.salers-cattle-society.co.uk
  Sec: John M Crowe
- ▲ Company Limited by Guarantee
- ○ *B
- ● Conf - Mtgs - Exhib - Comp - Inf - VE
- < Intl Salers Fedn; Nat Beef Assn
- M 180 i
- ¶ Salers Jnl - 1; free.
  NL - 4; Herd Book - 1; both ftm only.

Sales Institute of Ireland
- IRL 68 Merrion Sq, DUBLIN 2, Republic of Ireland.
  353 (1) 662 6904 fax 353 (1) 662 6968
  email info@salesinstitute.ie http://www.salesinstitute.ie
- ○ *P

Salisbury & District Chamber of Commerce & Industry (1912) 1912
- ■ 7 Scots Lane, SALISBURY, Wilts, SP1 3TR. (hq)
  01722 322708 fax 01722 341508
  email mail@salisburychamber.org.uk
  http://www.salisburychamber.org.uk
  Chief Exec: Loretta Lupi
- ▲ Company Limited by Guarantee
- ○ *C
- ● Mtgs - ET - Exhib - Inf - VE - LG - Networking - Economic partner with local government - Lobbying
- M 350 f
- ¶ Journal Business - 4; enewsletter - 12; both free.

Salmon Processors & Smokers Group
  a group of the **Scottish Salmon Producers' Organisation**

Salmon & Trout Association (S&TA) 1903
- ■ Fishmongers' Hall, London Bridge, LONDON, EC4R 9EL. (hq)
  020 7283 5838 fax 020 7626 5137
  email hq@salmon-trout.org
  http://www.salmon-trout.org
  Chief Exec: Paul Knight
- ▲ Company Limited by Guarantee; Registered Charity
- ○ *S; safeguarding the salmon & trout fisheries of the UK & game fishing & angling
- M i, f & org

Salt Association (SA) 1970
NR PO Box 125, KENDAL, Cumbria, LA8 8XA. (hsp)
    01539 568005 fax 01539 568999
    http://www.saltsense.co.uk
    Gen Sec: Peter Sherratt
▲ Un-incorporated Society
○ *T; promoting the use of salt for domestic, catering, water-
    softening, industrial & de-icing uses; to monitor related
    medical & environmental issues
● Mtgs - Res - Stat - Inf - LG - Promoting the use of salt
< Eur Salt Producers Assn; Salt Inst (USA); Food & Drink Fedn
M 6 f
¶ Facts on Salt; free.
✕ Salt Manufacturers' Association

Salt Manufacturers' Association
    renamed the **Salt Association**

Saltire Society 1936
■ 9 Fountain Close, 22 High St, EDINBURGH, EH1 1TF. (hq)
    0131-556 1836 fax 0131-557 1675
    email saltire@saltiresociety.org.uk
    http://www.saltiresociety.org.uk
    Admin: Mrs Kathleen Munro
▲ Registered Charity (Scotland)
Br 9
○ *K; preservation of the best in Scottish tradition &
    encouragement of development of Scottish cultural life
Gp Publications; Housing design; Education; Literature; Arts &
    crafts; Civil engineering; Science
● Conf - Mtgs - Exhib - SG - Scots Songs
M 1,057 i, 35 f
¶ AR; ftm.

Salvation Army 1865
§ 101 Newington Causeway, LONDON, SE1 6BN. (hq)
    020 7367 4500
    http://www.salvationarmy.org.uk
    A church demonstrating its Christian principles through social
    welfare provision, with programmes including homeless
    centres, drug rehabilitation centres, schools, hospitals and
    medical centres.

The Samaritans 1953
§ The Upper Mill, Kingston Rd, EWELL, Surrey, KT17 2AF. (hq)
    020 8394 8300 fax 020 8394 8301
    email admin@samaritans.org
    http://www.samaritans.org
    Chief Exec: Dominic Rudd
● Helpline: 08457 90 90 90
    Available 24 hours a day to provide confidential emotional
    support for people who are experiencing feelings of distress
    or despair, including those which may lead to suicide.

SAMM - Support After Murder & Manslaughter
NR Scotia House (1st floor), 33 Finsbury Sq, LONDON,
    EC2A 1PL. (hq)
    020 7638 4040 fax 020 7638 4050
    email samm@victimsupport.org.uk
    http://www.samm.org.uk
    Sec: Avril Sanders Royle
▲ Registered Charity
○ *W; to offer understanding & support to families & friends who
    have been bereaved as a result of murder & manslaughter,
    through the mutual support of others who have suffered a
    similar tragedy
● ET - Inf - LG
M 2,000 i
¶ Report & Financial Statement.

SANE (SANE) 1986
■ Cityside House (1st floor), 40 Adler St, LONDON, E1 1EE.
    (hq)
    020 7375 1002 fax 020 7375 2162
    email info@sane.org.uk http://www.sane.org.uk
    Chief Exec: Marjorie Wallace
▲ Registered Charity
○ *K, *W; to raise awareness of mental illness & campaign to
    improve services; to initiate & fund research into the causes
    of serious mental illness; to provide information & support to
    those experiencing mental health problems through its
    helpline, SANELINE
Gp SANELINE: 0845 767 8000 (1800-2300 hrs, every day)
    Prince of Wales International Centre for SANE Research,
    Warneford Hospital, Oxford
● Res - Inf - Helpline
¶ SANE News - NL; Medical Methods of Treatment;
    Talking Treatments; Schizophrenia;
    Manic Depression; Phobias; Obsessions;
    Depression; Anxiety; all free.

**Sanitary Medical Disposal Services Association (SMDSA)
1993**
NR 111 Wollaston Rd, IRCHESTER, Northants, NN29 7DD. (hsb)
    01933 311223 fax 01993 311223
    email info@smdsa.com http://www.smdsa.com
    Sec: Martin Foulser
▲ Company Limited by Guarantee
○ *T; interests of companies involved in the collection & disposal
    of sanitary & medical waste materials
M 33 f

SAPERE (SAPERE) 1992
NR Westminster Institute of Education, Oxford Brookes University,
    Harcourt Hill Campus, OXFORD, OX2 9AT. (hq)
    01865 488340 fax 01865 488356
    email admin@sapere.net http://www.sapere.net
    Chmn: Paul Cleghorn
▲ Registered Charity
○ *E; to promote philosophy for children; to train teachers
Gp Education; Thinking skills; Teaching; Emotional literacy;
    Citizenship education
● Conf - ET - Res - Inf - Teacher training - Projects - Courses
< Intl Coun for Philosophical Inquiry with Children
M 650 i
¶ NL - 4; ftm only.
    SAPERE = Society for the Advancement of Philosophical Enquiry
    & Reflection in Education

Sarcoidosis & Interstitial Lung Association (SILA) 1993
■ c/o Chest Clinic Office, 2nd floor Admin Block, King's College
    Hospital, LONDON, SE5 9RS. (mail/address)
    020 7237 5912
    email info@sila.org.uk http://www.sila.org.uk
    Hon Sec: Heather Walker
▲ Registered Charity25
○ *W; to raise public awareness of sarcoidosis & the effect it has
    on sufferers, patients & friends; to give support & practical
    advice to those affected; to promote research & to identify
    those most at risk
● Mtgs - Res - Inf
< Eur Assn of Patients Orgs for Sarcoidosis & Other
    Granulomatous Disorders (EPOS); Long-term Conditions
    Alliance
M 150 i, UK / 2 i, o'seas
    (Sub: £12)
¶ NL - 2; ftm, (free on website).
    So You Have Sarcoidosis! by Rose Bartholomew-Thomas; ftm,
    large sae nm.

© CBD Research Ltd · Beckenham · BR3 5JS · Tel 020 8650 7745 · Fax 020 8650 0768 · E-mail cbd@cbdresearch.com · www.cbdresearch.com

Satellite & Cable Broadcasters' Group   (SCGB)   1983
- ■ Gainsborough House, 81 Oxford St, LONDON, W1D 2EU. (hq)
  07894 206515
  Exec Dir: Kerry Neilson
- ▲ Un-incorporated Society
- ○ *T; for satellite & cable programme providers
- ● Mtgs - Res - LG
- < Advertising Assn; Brit Screen Advy Coun; Skillset
- M 20 f

SATIPS - Support & Training in Prep Schools   (SATIPS)   1953
- ■ Cherry Trees, Stebbing, GREAT DUNMOW, Essex, CM6 3ST. (admin/p)
  01371 856823   fax 01371 856823
  http://www.satips.com
  Admin: Mrs Pat Harrison
- ▲ Company Limited by Guarantee; Registered Charity
- ○ *E; professional support for staff in independent schools
- Gp Art; Classics; Design & technology; Drama; English; Geography; History; Information & communications technology; Maths; Modern languages; Music; Personal & social education with health; Physical education; Pre-prep & nursery; Religious studies; Science; Senior management; Special needs; Years 3 & 4 teachers
- ● Conf - Mtgs - ET - Exhib - Comp - SG - Inf
- M c 100 i, c 450 schools, UK / c 10 i, c 10 schools, o'seas
- ¶ Prep School - 3; ftm, £10 yr nm. (published with the Inc Assn of Preparatory Schools).
  NL - 3; ftm only.   Broadsheets - 3; ftm, £5 each nm.
- × Society of Assistants Teaching in Preparatory Schools Ltd

Saudi-British Society   1986
- NR 1 Gough Square, LONDON, EC4A 3DE.   (sp)
  01372 842788
  email secretary@saudibritishsociety.org.uk
  http://www.saudibritishsociety.org.uk
  Hon Sec: Ionis Thompson
- ▲ Registered Charity
- Br Saudi Arabia
- ○ *X; to promote Saudi-British understanding & educational & cultural contacts
- ● Mtgs - ET
- M 200 i, 50 f, UK / 50 i, 8 f, o'seas

Save Britain's Heritage   (SAVE)   ]975
- NR 70 Cowcross St, LONDON, EC1M 6EJ.   (hq)
  020 7253 3500   fax 020 7253 3400
  email office@savebritainsheritage.org
  http://www.savebritainsheritage.org
  Sec: William Palin
- ▲ Registered Charity
- ○ *K; to campaign for the preservation & re-use of historic buildings; to prevent their loss through demolition or neglect
- ● Res - Exhib
- M c 350 i
- ¶ NL - 1; ftm only.
  SAVE Britain's Heritage 1975-2005: thirty years of campaigning; £20.
  Who Cares Wins: the Buildings at Risk Register (2004); £12.
  Publications list available.

Save British Science Society
  since 2005 the **Campaign for Science & Engineering in the UK**

Save our Building Societies   (SoBS)   2000
- NR 8 Belmont Court, Belmont Hill, ST ALBANS, Herts, AL1 1RB. (hsp)
  01727 847370
  email info@sobs.org.uk   http://www.sobs.org.uk
- ○ *K
- M 1,000 i
- ¶ NL - irreg;   Press releases; both free.

Save our Parsonages   (SOP)   1994
- ■ Flat Z / 12-18 Bloomsbury St, LONDON, WC1B 3QA.   (dir/p)
  020 7636 4884
  email ajsjennings@hotmail.com
  http://www.saveourparsonages.co.uk
  Dir: Anthony J S Jennings
- ▲ Un-incorporated Society
- ○ *K; a support group for historic, or traditional, parsonages remaining in church use
- ● Conf - Mtgs - Res - Inf
- < Rural Theology Assn; Engl Clergy Assn
- M 150 i, UK / 1 i, o'seas
- ¶ NL - 1; ftm, £2 nm.

Saxifrage Society
- NR The Gardens, 12 Vicarage Lane - Grasby, BARNETBY, N Lincs, DN38 6AU.   (mem/sp)
  http://www.saxifraga.org
  Mem Sec: Mark Childerhouse
- ○ *H; for all interested in the growing of the genus Saxifraga

SBGI   (SBGI)   1905
- ■ 36 Holly Walk, LEAMINGTON SPA, Warks, CV32 4LY.   (hq)
  01926 334357   fax 01926 450459
  email mail@sbgi.org.uk   http://www.sbgi.org.uk
  Chief Exec: John Stiggers
- ○ *T; operates two divisions: HHIC (Heating & Hotwater Industry Council) & SBGI Utility Networks
- Gp Appliance manufacturers; Gas suppliers, shippers & transporters; Gas storage operators; Distribution & transmission equipment manufacturers & contractors; Service providers; Metering & control manufacturers; Ancillary products
- ● Conf - Mtgs - Exhib - Stat - Expt - LG - Provides a wide range of support services
- M 170 f
- ¶ Gas Business - 4.   Review of Activities - 1.
  Directory of Products & Services - 1.
- × 2008 Society of British Gas Industries

Scala - Serving Construction & Architecture in Local Authorities (SCALA)   1973
- ■ Hillside, St Mary Church, COWBRIDGE, Glamorgan, CF71 7LT.   (hq)
  01446 771209   fax 01446 772580
  email policy@scala.org.uk   http://www.scala.org.uk
  Sec: Stephen Dodsworth
- ▲ Company Limited by Guarantee
- ○ *P; development, design & management of the public sector estate
- Gp Design forum: design & related issues; Practice forum: Professional & legal issues
- ● Conf - Mtgs - ET - LG
- M 290 i
- ¶ SCALAnews (NL) - 5; ftm only.
  Building Maintenance Expenditure by Local Authorities; £60 m, £80 nm.
  Appointment of Consultants Document; £30 m, £38 nm.
- × 2008(?) Society of Chief Architects of Local Authorities

Schizophrenia Association of Great Britain
  closed 15 June 2007

Schizophrenia Ireland
- IRL 38 Blessington St, DUBLIN 7, Republic of Ireland.
  353 (1) 860 1620   fax 353 (1) 860 1602
  email info@sirl.ie   http://www.sirl.ie
  Dir: John Saunders
- ○ *W
- × 1997 Schizophrenia Association of Ireland

School Journey Association (SJA) 1911
§   48 Cavendish Rd, LONDON, SW12 0DH. (hq)
    0845 658 1063   fax 0845 658 1064
    http://www.sjatours.org
    A travel organisation, run by teachers and ex-teachers,
    promoting educational travel for school pupils to centres In
    the UK and Europe.

School Leaders Scotland (SLS) 1936
■   University of Strathclyde, Jordanhill Campus, Southbrae Drive,
    GLASGOW, G13 1PP. (hq)
    0141-950 3298   fax 0141-950 3434
    email sls@strath.ac.uk   http://www.sls-scotland.org.uk
    Gen Sec: Ken Cunningham
▲   Un-incorporated Society
○   *E, *P; professional support for members in being effective
    leaders in the provision of the highest quality learning for
    young people; to influence the educational policies of the
    Scottish government & local authorities
●   Conf - ET - Exhib - LG
<   Assn of School & College Leaders (ASCL)
M   500 i
    (Sub: £318)
¶   Scottish Leader - 4;   Scottish Bylines - 4; both ftm.
×   2008 (1 August) Headteachers' Association of Scotland

School Library Association (SLA) 1937
■   Unit 2 Lotmead Business Village, SWINDON, Wilts, SN4 0UY.
    (hq)
    01793 791787   fax 01793 791786
    email info@sla.org.uk   http://www.sla.org.uk
    Chief Exec: Tricia Adams
▲   Registered Charity
Br   15
○   *E; promotion of development of the school library as central to
    literacy & the curriculum
●   Conf - Mtgs - ET - Lib - LG
<   Intl Assn School Libraries (IASL); Intl Fedn Library Assns (IFLA)
M   3,200 i
    (Sub: £75)
¶   The School Librarian (Jnl) - 4; ftm, £95 nm.
    Practical Guidelines.   Booklists.

Schoolhouse Home Education Association
NR PO Box 18044, GLENROTHES, Fife, KY7 9AD.
    01307 463120
○   *E; home education in Scotland

Schools Music Association (SMA) 1938
■   71 Margaret Rd, NEW BARNET, Herts, EN4 9NT. (regd off)
    020 8440 6919   fax 020 8440 6919
    email maxwellpryce@educamas.free-online.co.uk
    http://www.schoolsmusic.org.uk
    Hon Sec: Maxwell Pryce
▲   Registered Charity
Br   14 regions
○   *D, *E; to promote the musical education of young people by
    supporting those who work with them
●   Conf - Mtgs - ET - Res - SG - Inf
<   Inc Soc Musicians (ISM), Music Educ Coun (MEC)
M   i, f & org
¶   Bulletin - 3;   Register of Members - 1;   AR; all ftm only.

Schoolwear Association (SA) 2006
■   c/o AIS, Sheward House, Cranmore Ave, Shirley, SOLIHULL,
    W Midlands, B90 4LF.
    0121-683 1415
    email info@schoolwearassociation.co.uk
    http://www.schoolwearassociation.co.uk
    Sec: Joyce Daly
∩   *T; for school uniform manufacturers, suppliers and retailers
M   200 f

Schubert Society of Britain 1957
■   German YMCA, 35 Craven Terrace, LONDON, W2 3EL. (sb)
    020 7723 5684
    email u.bauer@german-ymca.org.uk
    http://www.german-ymca.org.uk/schubert.htm
    Sec: Udo Bauer
▲   Registered Charity
○   *D; for those interested in the life & works of the Austrian
    composer Franz Schubert (1797-1828)
●   Schubertiades - Gives young musicians an opportunity to
    perform in London
<   sponsored by the German YMCA in London
M   60 i, 5 org
¶   Concert programmes.

Schumacher UK
    alternative name of the **Doctor E F Schumacher Society**

Science, Engineering & Manufacturing Technologies Alliance
NR 14 Upton Rd, WATFORD, Herts, WD18 0JT.
    01923 238441
    http://www.semta.org.uk
    Chief Exec: Philip Whiteman
○   *T

Science, Technology, Engineering, Medicine Public Relations Association (STEMPRA) 1992
■   38 Trinity Court, 254 Gray's Inn Rd, LONDON, WC1X 8JZ.
    (treas/p)
    email info@stempra.org.uk   http://www.stempra.org.uk
    Treas: Dr Robert Walker
▲   Un-incorporated Society
○   *P; for press & public relations people who work in, with, or for,
    all the scientific societies
●   Conf - Mtgs - ET - VE - LG
M   88 i
    (Sub: £15)
¶   NL - 4.

Scientific Alliance 2001
NR St John's Innovation Centre, Cowley Rd, CAMBRIDGE,
    CB4 0WS.
    01223 421242
    email info@scientific-alliance.org
    http://www.scientific-alliance.org
    Dir: Martin Livermore
○   *K; a campaign aiming to bring together scientists & non-
    scientists to have rational discussions & debates on the
    challenges facing the environment today

Scientific Exploration Society Ltd (SES) 1969
■   30 Orchard Lane, AMERSHAM, Bucks, HP6 5AA. (exec/dir/p)
    01747 853353   fax 01747 851351
    email ses@ses-explore.org   http://www.ses-explore.org
    Exec Dir: Mrs Yvonne Konieczna
    Hon Pres: Col John Blashford-Snell
▲   Registered Charity
Br   1 (01494 722229)
○   *L; to enable advancement of knowledge through the initiation
    & support of challenging, scientific expeditions to remote
    areas of the world
●   Mtgs - Expeditions overseas
<   Just a Drop (water aid charity)
M   100 i, 10 f, UK; 150 i, o'seas
¶   Sesame (Jnl) - 2; ftm only.

Scientific Instrument Society (SIS) 1983
- ■ 90 The Fairway, SOUTH RUISLIP, Middx, HA4 0SQ. (hq)
  email sis@sis.org.uk   http://www.sis.org.uk
  Exec Officer: Peter Thomas
- ▲ Registered Charity
- ○ *G, *L; for all interested in scientific instruments from antiques to the latest electronic devices (collectors, antiques trade, museum staff, professional historians & enthusiasts)
- ● Conf - Mtgs - VE - Lectures
- M 250 i, UK / 350 i, o'seas
- ¶ Bulletin - 4; ftm.

Scientists for Global Responsibility (SGR) 1992
- ■ Ingles Manor, Castle Hill Avenue, FOLKESTONE, Kent, CT20 2RD. (hq)
  01303 851965
  email info@sgr.org.uk   http://www.sgr.org.uk
  Exec Dir: Dr Stuart Parkinson
- ▲ Un-incorporated Society
- ○ *K, *Q; promoting ethical science & technology
- Gp Built environment & sustainable development; Climate change & energy; Emerging technologies; Security & disarmament
- ● Conf - Res - SG - Inf
- < Intl Architects Designers Planners for Social Responsibility (ARC-PEACE);Intl Network of Engrs & Scientists for Global Responsibility (INES)
- M 950 i, UK / 15 i, o'seas
- ¶ SGR NL - 2; ftm, £3.50 nm.   AR; ftm only.
  Publications list available.

Scleroderma Society 1982
- ■ 6 Portishead House, Westbourne Park Rd, LONDON, W2 5UP.
  020 7229 4750
  http://www.sclerodermasociety.co.uk
  Sec: S Holloway
- ○ *W
- M 300 i
- ¶ NL - 4; ftm only.

Scoliosis Association (UK) (SAUK) 1981
- NR 2 Ivebury Court, 323-327 Latimer Rd, LONDON, W10 6RA. (hq)
  020 8964 5343   fax 020 8964 5343
  email sauk@sauk.org.uk   http://www.sauk.org.uk
  Chmn: Stephanie Clark
- ▲ Registered Charity
- Br Regional
- ○ *W; to put people with scoliosis (curvature of the spine) in touch with each other; to make available to parents of children with scoliosis the experience of others in this field
- ● Mtgs - Inf
  Helpline: 020 8964 1166
- M 3,000 i
- ¶ Backbone - 2.   NL Index.   AR.
  Scoliosis Hbk.   Shona's Story.
  Clothes to Suit.   A Twist of Fate.

Scope 1952
- NR 6 Market Rd, LONDON, N7 9PW. (hq)
  020 7619 7100
  http://www.scope.org.uk
  Chief Exec: Jon Sparkes
- ▲ Company Limited by Guarantee; Registered Charity
- ○ *E, *W; the disability organisation in England & Wales whose focus is people with cerebral palsy; with the aim that disabled people achieve equality, and a society in which they are valued and have the same human & civil rights as everyone else
- ● Conf - Res - Exhib - Inf - Lib - Campaigns
  Helpline: 0808 800 3333
- < Capability Scotland; Cedar Foundation (NI)
- M 208 groups
- ¶ Disability Now - 12; ftm.   Reports.   AR; free.
  Publications list available.

Scotch Half Bred Association (SHBA)
- NR Greenend, St Boswells, MELROSE, Roxburghshire, TD6 9ES. (sp)
  01835 824207
  Sec: Nesta D Todd
- ○ *B
- M f

Scotch Malt Whisky Society Ltd (SMWS) 1983
- NR The Vaults, 87 Giles St, EDINBURGH, EH6 6BZ. (hq)
  0131-554 3451   fax 0131-553 1003
  email vaults@smws.com   http://www.smws.co.uk
- ▲ Company Limited by Guarantee
- ○ *G; club for anyone who enjoys single malt whisky
- M i

Scotch Mule Association
- NR Bogside Cottage, Ochiltree, CUMNOCK, Ayrshire, KA18 2QF. (hsp)
  01292 591821
  email scotchmule.association@yahoo.co.uk
  http://www.scotchmule.co.uk
  Sec: George Allan
- ▲ Registered Charity
- ○ *B; to promote the breed of Mule sheep
- < Nat Sheep Assn

Scotch Whisky Association (SWA) 1942
- ■ 20 Atholl Crescent, EDINBURGH, EH3 8HF. (hq)
  0131-222 9200   fax 0131-222 9237
  email contact@swa.org.uk
  http://www.scotch-whisky.org.uk
  Chief Exec: Gavin Hewitt
- ▲ Company Limited by Guarantee
- Br 2
- ○ *T; protection promotion of Scotch whisky; including legal protection, public affairs, international trade issues & promoting responsible attitudes to alcohol
- ● Conf - Mtgs - ET - Res - Exhib - Stat - Expt - Inf - VE - LG
- < Confédn Eur des Producteurs de Spiritueux (CEPS); CBI; Scot Coun Devt & Ind; Scotland Europa
- M 54 f
- ¶ Scotch Whisky: questions & answers.   Annual Review - 1.
  Scotch at a Glance.   Statistical report - 1.
  Distilleries to Visit Guide.   Distillery Map - 1.
  Scotch Whisky: matured to be enjoyed responsibly.

Scotland-Russia Forum 2003
- ■ 9 South College St, EDINBURGH, EH8 9AA. (hq)
  0131-668 3635
  email info@scotlandrussiaforum.org
  http://www.scotlandrussiaforum.org
  Chmn: Jennifer Carr
- ▲ Registered Charity
- ○ *X; to promote mutual understanding between Scotland & Russia & its neighbours
- ● Mtgs - ET - Exhib - Lib
- M [not stated]
- ¶ SRF Review - 2; ftm, £1.50 nm.

ScotlandIS 2000
- NR Geddes House (suite 41), Kirkton North, LIVINGSTON, W Lothian, EH54 6GU. (hq)
  01506 472200   fax 01506 472209
  email info@scotlandis.com   http://www.scotlandis.com
  Exec Dir: Polly Purvis
- ▲ Company Limited by Guarantee
- Br 2
- ○ *T; design & development of Scottish quality software, IT & creative technology
- Gp Quality; Aberdeen area; Advanced technologies; Year 2000
- ● Conf - Mtgs - ET - Res - Exhib - Comp - SG - Stat - Expt - Inf - LG
- M 344 f

Scots Language Society (SLS) 1972
- ■ Blackford Lodge, Blackford, AUCHTERARDER, Perthshire, PH4 1QP. (admin/p)
  01764 682315   fax 0870 428 5086
  email mail@lallans.co.uk   http://www.lallans.co.uk
  Admin: John Law
- ▲ Registered Charity
- Br 2
- ○ *L; celebration & preservation of the Scots language
- ● Conf - Mtgs - Res - Comp - Inf
- < Scot Poetry Lib Assn
- M 350 i, 30 org, UK / 50 i, 10 org, o'seas
- ¶ Lallans (Jnl, in Scots Language) - 2; ftm, £6.50 each nm.

Scottish Adoption Association Ltd 1923
- § 16 Constitution St, EDINBURGH, EH6 7DF.   (hq)
  0131-553 5060   fax 0131-553 6422
  http://www.scottishadoption.org
  A charity offering information, counselling and support to anyone who has adopted, has been adopted or is interested in adoption.

Scottish Aeromodellers Association (SAA) 1943
- NR PO Box 1621, JOHNSTONE, Renfrewshire, PA9 1YN.
  (mail add)
  http://www.saaweb.org.uk
  Sec: Elliot Balfour
- ○ *G; flying radio controlled model aircraft
- ● Mtgs - Exam - Exhib - Comp - Inf - VE
- < Brit Model Flying Assn; Scottish Sports Council
- M 1,700 i in 50 clubs
- ¶ Airtime - 4; ftm.

Scottish Agricultural Arbiters Association (SAAA) 1926
- NR c/o Turcan Connell, Princes Exchange, 1 Earl Grey St, EDINBURGH, EH3 9EE.   (asa)
  0131-228 8111
  Sec: Malcolm Strang Steel
- ▲ Un-incorporated Society
- ○ *F, *P; professional interests of agricultural arbiters & valuers
- Gp Agricultural arbiters & valuers
- ● Conf - Mtgs - ET - LG
- M 243 i, 5 org
- ¶ LM - 1; ftm only.

Scottish Agricultural Organisation Society Ltd (SAOS) 1905
- NR Rural Centre, West Mains, Ingliston, NEWBRIDGE, Midlothian, EH28 8NZ.   (hq)
  0131-472 4100   fax 0131-472 4101
  http://www.saos.co.uk
  Chief Exec: James Graham
- ○ *F, *N, *T; to promote agriculture & rural cooperation in Scotland
- M 15 i (personal), 80 i (business)
- ¶ NL - 4;   AR (incl LM) - 1.

Scottish Amateur Football Association (SAFA) 1909
- NR Hampden Park, GLASGOW, G42 9DB.   (hq)
  0141-620 4550
  http://www.scottishamateurfa.co.uk
  Sec: Hugh Knapp
- ○ *S
- Gp Association football as played by amateurs: Saturday, Sunday, Youth, Summer
- ● Mtgs - Comp - Inf
- < Scot Football Assn
- M 65,000 i, 3,000 clubs
- ¶ Hbk - 1.   AR; ftm only.

Scottish Amateur Music Association (SAMA) 1956
- § 18 Craigton Crescent, ALVA, Clackmannanshire, FK12 5DS. (hsp)
  01259 760249
  email secretary@sama.org.uk   http://www.sama.org.uk
  Hon Sec: Margaret W Simpson
  Week-long courses offer the amateur musician, both of school age and adult years, tuition and experience of string orchestras and wind and brass bands. Chamber music and recorder ensemble playing are catered for on weekend courses. Indigenous Scottish music is encouraged and promoted by the Traditional Scots Fiddle School and the biennial Scots Song Recital Competition.

Scottish Amateur Rowing Association (SARA) 1881
- NR 41 Dumyat Ave, Cambuspark, TULLIBODY, Clackmannanshire, FK10 2RY.
  01259 216923
  http://www.scottish-rowing.co.uk
  Pres: Mary Massaro
- ▲ Un-incorporated Society
- ○ *S; governing body for rowing in Scotland
- ● Conf - Mtgs - Exam - Comp - VE
- < represented internationally by the Amateur Rowing Association (ARA)
- M 32 clubs
- ¶ Rowing Action - 4; free (donations from nm please).

Scottish Amateur Swimming Association
    the registered name of **Scottish Swimming**

Scottish Anglers National Association Ltd (SANA) 1880
- ■ The National Game Angling Academy, The Pier, Loch Leven, KINROSS, KY13 8UF.   (hq)
  01577 861116   fax 01577 864769
  email admin@sana.org.uk   http://www.sana.org.uk
  Sec: Alastair Wallace
- ▲ Company Limited by Guarantee
- ○ *S; governing body for game angling in Scotland
- ● Conf - Mtgs - ET - Exam - Exhib - Comp - Inf - LG
- < FIPS Mouche; Scot Sports Assn
- M 195 i, 20 f, 420 org
    (Sub: £25 i, £60 f, £34 associates)
- ¶ SANACAST (NL) - 4;   Hbk & AR; Information leaflets; all free.

Scottish Archery Association (SAA) 1949
- ■ Glenearn Cottage, Edinburgh Rd, PORT SETON, E Lothian, EH32 0HQ. (hsp)
  01355 268211
  http://www.scottisharchery.org.uk
  Admin: Mrs J Dunlop
- ▲ Un-incorporated Society
- ○ *S; to promote the sport of archery incl target, field, flight, clout & all types of bow including Olympic, compound & longbow
- M i

Scottish Assessors' Association (SAA) 1854
- ■ c/o 235 Dumbarton Rd, CLYDEBANK, G81 4XT.   (sb)
  0141-562 1260   fax 0161-562 1255
  email david.thomson@dab-vjb.gov.uk
  http://www.saa.gov.uk
  Sec: David C Thomson
- ▲ Un-incorporated Society
- ○ *P; to promote uniformity in operating the provisions of the Lands Valuation (Scotland) Acts & the Representation of the People Acts
- ● Conf - ET - Mtgs - LG
- M 94 i

© CBD Research Ltd · Beckenham · BR3 5JS · Tel 020 8650 7745 · Fax 020 8650 0768 · E-mail cbd@cbdresearch.com · www.cbdresearch.com

Scottish Association for Country Sports   (SACS)   1994
- ■ Netherholme, Netherburn, LARKHALL, Lanarkshire,
       ML9 3DG.   (hq)
       01698 885206   fax 01698 885206
       email sacs@netherholm.sol.co.uk
       http://www.sacs.org.uk
       Dir: Ian Clark
- ▲ Un-incorporated Society
- ○ *K, *S; To represent all who take part in country sports in the
       UK; to protect the environment on which they depend
- ● Conf - Mtgs - ET - Exhib - Stat - Inf - LG
- M 15,000 i
- ¶ SACS Jnl- 4; ftm..

Scottish Association of Family History Societies   (SAFHS)   1986
- NR 77 Erskine Hill, Polmont, FALKIRK, FK2 0UH.
        email scots@safhs.org.uk   http://www.safhs.org.uk
        Publications: Margaret Mackay
        Sec & Treas: Kenneth Nisbet
- ▲ Registered Charity
- ○ *G, *N; to promote the study of Scottish family history,
       genealogy & local history; to coordinate the work of member
       societies
- ● Conf - Mtgs - ET - Res - Exhib - Comp - LG
- M 45,000 i, org, UK / 39,000, org, o'seas
- ¶ Bulletin - 2; ftm only.

Scottish Association of Geography Teachers   (SAGT)   1970
- ■ 42 Culzean Crescent, Newton Mearns, GLASGOW,
       G77 5TA.   (hsp)
       0141-639 8134   fax 0141-943 0216
       email ssmith@boclair.e-dunbarton.sch.uk
       Gen Sec: Sheree Smith
- ▲ Registered Charity
- ○ *E, *P; geographical education
- ● Conf - Comp - VE
- < Coun for Brit Geography
- M 670 i, UK / 10 i, 20 org, o'seas
- ¶ Jnl - 1.   NL - 3.   Occasional Papers - 1.

Scottish Association of Health Councils
-     has been replaced by the Scottish Health Council, for further
       details see the companion volume 'Councils, Committees &
       Boards' (Introduction paragraph 6)

Scottish Association of Landlords
- ■ 22 Forth St, EDINBURGH, EH1 3LH.   (hq)
       0131-270 4774
       email info@scottishlandlords.com
       http://www.scottishlandlords.com
- ▲ Company Limited by Guarantee
- ○ *T
       no further information supplied

Scottish Association of Law Centres   (SALC)   1993
- ■ c/o Govan Law Centre, 47 Burleigh St, GLASGOW,
       G51 3LB.   (sb)
       0141-440 2503
       http://www.govanlc.com/salc
       Sec: Mike Dailly
- ▲ Un-incorporated Society
- ○ *P
- ● Conf - Mtgs - ET - Inf - LG
- < Advice Services Alliance
- M 8 f
- ¶ SALC Briefing - 1; free.

Scottish Association of Local Sports Councils   (SALSC)   1979
- NR Flat 2/L 2 Lorne St, HELENSBURGH, Dunbartonshire,
        G84 8TT.   (hsb)
        0723 087 1456
        email oliver@salsc.org.uk   http://www.salsc.org.uk
        Admin: Oliver Barsby
- ○ *N, *S
- M district sports councils in Scotland

Scottish Association for Marine Science   (SAMS)   1885
- NR Dunstaffnage Marine Laboratory, OBAN, Argyllshire,
        PA37 1QA.   (hq)
        01631 559000   fax 01631 559001
        email info@sams.ac.uk   http://www.sams.ac.uk
        Sec: Allison Dawson
- ▲ Company Limited by Guarantee; Registered Charity
- ○ *Q; research & education in marine science
- M i, f, org

Scottish Association of Master Bakers   (SAMB)   1891
- ■ Atholl House, 4 Torphichen St, EDINBURGH, EH3 8JQ.   (hq)
       0131-229 1401   fax 0131-229 8239
       http://www.samb.co.uk
       Chief Exec: Kirk Hunter
- ▲ Company Limited by Guarantee
- ○ *T; craft bakery trade & employers association
- Gp Training & education; Industrial relations; Technical; Member
        services
- ● Conf - Mtgs - ET - Res - Comp - SG - Inf - Lib - VE - Empl - LG
- < CBI; UK Baking Ind Consultative C'ee
- M 600 i, 400 f, UK / 10 i, o'seas
- ¶ NL - c17.   Ybk.

Scottish Association of Meat Wholesalers   (SAMW)   1977
- ■ c/o BLP Consultancy, 38 North Meggetland, EDINBURGH,
       EH14 1XG.   (asa)
       0131-443 2180   fax 0131-443 2180
       email ianranderson@btinternet.com
       http://www.scottish-meat-wholesalers.org.uk
       Exec Mgr: Ian Anderson
- ▲ Company Limited by Guarantee
- ○ *T; to represent the views of members, on issues affecting the
       Scottish meat industry, to government & other agencies
- ● Conf - Mtgs - Expt - Inf - LG
- < Eur Livestock & Meat Trading U (UECBV)
- M 39 f
- ¶ NL - 12; ftm only.

Scottish Association for Mental Health   (SAMH)   1967
- § Cumbrae House, 15 Carlton Court, GLASGOW, G5 9JP.   (hq)
       0141-568 7000
       http://www.samh.org.uk
       Company Sec: Patricia Aniello
       Works to support people who experience mental health
       problems, homelessness, addictions and other forms of
       social exclusion.

Scottish Association for Metals   (SAM)   1974
- NR 11 Craig's Court, TORPHICHEN, W Lothian, EH48 4NU.   (hsp)
        01506 634184
        email haywood.jim@btinternet.com
        http://www.scottishmetals.org
        Hon Sec: Jim Haywood
- ▲ Registered Charity
- ○ *L; the development, performance & processing of metals &
       related materials
- ● Conf - Mtgs - VE
- < Inst of Materials
- M 180 i

Scottish Association for Music Education   (SAME)
- ■ c/o Graeme Wilson, Auchterderran Centre, Woodend Rd, CARDENDEN, Fife, KY5 0NE.
  01592 568612   fax 01592 568612
  email nickie.mcguire@blueyonder.co.uk
  Sec: Graeme Wilson
- ○ *E; for all who are concerned in promoting music in education

Scottish Association of Painting Craft Teachers   (SAPCT)   1955
- ■ 16 Riverside Gardens, MUSSELBURGH, E Lothian, EH21 6NW.   (hsp)
  0131-665 2735
  email brownjeff178@aol.com   http://www.sapct.org
  Nat Sec: Jeff Brown
- ▲ Un-incorporated Society
- ○ *P; to advance education of painting & decorating; to liaise with other relevant bodies
- ● Mtgs - ET - Exhib - Comp - VE
- < Assn Painting Craft Teachers
- M 57 i
- ¶ Artisan - 3; ftm (in liaison with the PCTA in England).

Scottish Association of Psychoanalytical Psychotherapists   1972
- NR c/o SIHR, 172 Leith Walk, EDINBURGH, EH6 5EA.
  0131-454 3240   fax 0131-454 2341
  email info@sihr.org.uk   http://www.sihr.org.uk

Scottish Association for Public Transport   (SAPT)   1970
- ■ 11 Queens Crescent, GLASGOW, G4 9AS.   (hq)
  0776 038 1729
  email mail@sapt.org.uk   http://www.sapt.org.uk
  Chmn: Dr John McCormick,   Sec: Alastair Reid
- ▲ Un-incorporated Society
- Br 2
- ○ *K; to promote an integrated, socially inclusive, public transport
- ● Conf - Mtgs
- < Transport 2000; Transform Scotland
- M 120 i, 20 f, 10 org
- ¶ Scottish Transport Matters - 4; ftm, £80 yr nm.
  Transport Papers; £1.   AR - 1; ftm only.

Scottish Association of Sign Language Interpreters   (SASLI) 1981
- NR Baltic Chambers (suite 317-319), 50 Wellington St, GLASGOW, G2 6HJ.   (hq)
  0141-202 0790   fax 0141-202 0792
  email mail@sasli.org.uk   http://www.sasli.org.uk
  Dir: Iain Whyte
- ▲ Registered Charity
- ○ *P
- ● Conf - Mtgs - ET - Exam - Stat
- < Eur Forum of Sign Language Interpreters
- M 38 i

Scottish Association of Speech & Drama Adjudicators   (SASDA)
- NR 104 Argyle Rd, SALTCOATS, Ayrshire, KA21 5NE.
  01294 552807   fax 01294 559274
  email admin:sasda.org.uk   http://www.sasda.org.uk
  Admin: Jim Gibson
- ○ *P

Scottish Association of Spiritual Healers   (SASH)   1980
- ■ 46 Wood Place, Eliburn Souith, LIVINGSTON, W Lothian, EH54 6SZ.   (hsb)
  01506 411801
  email maureennic@aol.com
  http://www.scottishhealers.bravehost.com
  Pres: Maureen Nicoll
- ▲ Registered Charity
- Br 10
- ○ *P, *W; to provide spiritual & hands-on healing
- ● Mtgs - ET - Exam - SG
- < Confedn of Healers Org; Alliance of Healers Assns
- M 149 i
  (Sub: £12, £10 concessions)

Scottish Association for the Study of Offending   (SASO)
- NR Association Management Solutions, PO Box 2781, GLASGOW, G61 3YL.
  0141-560 4092
  email cameron@a-m-s-online.com
  http://www.sastudyoffending.org.uk
  Admin: Irene Cameron
- Br 10
- ○ *K, *L; to study & research the causes of delinquency & crime & its treatment & prevention
- < Mtgs - Res
- M i

Scottish Association for Volunteer Management
dead 2008

Scottish Association of Young Farmers Clubs   (SAYFC)   1938
- NR Young Farmers Centre, Ingliston, EDINBURGH, EH28 8NE.   (hq)
  0131-333 2445   fax 0131-333 2488
  email natsec@sayfc.org   http://www.sayfc.org
  Nat Sec: Fiona Bain
- ○ *F, *Y

Scottish Athletics Ltd   (SA)   2001
- NR 9a South Gyle Crescent, EDINBURGH, EH12 9EB.   (hq)
  0131-539 7320
  email admin@scottishathletics.org.uk
  http://www.scottishathletics.org.uk
  Chief Exec: Geoff Wightman
- ▲ Company Limited by Guarantee
- ○ *S; governing body for athletics in Scotland (incl track & field, road running, cross country & hill running)
- Gp Athletes; Coaches; Officials
- ● Mtgs
- M 12,000 i, 150 clubs
- ¶ PB (NL) - 4.   AR - 1.

Scottish Auto Cycle Union   (SACU)   1913
- NR 28 West Main St, UPHALL, W Lothian, EH52 5DW.   (hq)
  01506 858354   fax 01506 855792
  email office@sacu.co.uk   http://www.sacu.co.uk
  Sec: Robert Young
- ▲ Company Limited by Guarantee
- ○ *S; governing for motorcycle sport in Scotland

© CBD Research Ltd · Beckenham · BR3 5JS · Tel 020 8650 7745 · Fax 020 8650 0768 · E-mail cbd@cbdresearch.com · www.cbdresearch.com

Scottish Badminton Union   (SBU)   1901
- ■ Cockburn Centre, 40 Bogmoor Place, GLASGOW, G51 4TQ. (hq)
  0141-445 1218   fax 0141-425 1218
  email enquiries@badmintonscotland.org.uk
  http://www.badmintonscotland.org.uk
  Chief Exec: Anne Smillie
- ○ *S
- Gp SBU Coaching C'ee; Scottish Schools Badminton Union
- ● Mtgs - Comp
- < Intl Badminton Fedn; Eur Badminton U
- M c 12,000 i, 560 clubs
- ¶ Scottish Badminton - 4 (each season); free to clubs, £6 nm.
  Note: uses the trading name Badminton Scotland

Scottish Basketball Association
  former name of **Basketball Scotland Ltd**

Scottish Basketmakers' Circle
- NR 18 Burns-Begg Crescent, Balfron, GLASGOW, G63 0NR.
  http://www.scottishbasketmakerscircle.org
  Mem Sec: Di Hannah
- ○ *G; to promote basketmaking in Scotland
- ● Mtgs - Exhib
- M i
- ¶ NL - 4.

Scottish Beekeepers Association   (SBA)   1912
- ■ 20 Lennox Row, EDINBURGH, EH5 3JW.   (gensec/p)
  0131-552 3439
  email secretary@scottishbeekeepers.org.uk
  http://www.scottishbeekeepers.org.uk
  Gen Sec: Mrs Bron Wright
- ▲ Registered Charity
- Br 40
- ○ *G; to promote beekeeping within Scotland
- ● Conf - Mtgs - ET - Exam - Res - Exhib - Comp - SG - Stat - Inf - Lib - VE - LG
- < Coun of Nat Beekeepers Assns (CONBA)
- M 1,200 i, UK / 40 i, o'seas
- ¶ The Scottish Beekeeper - 12; ftm only.

Scottish Beer & Pub Association   (SBPA)   1906
- NR 6 St Colme St, EDINBURGH, EH3 6AD.
  0131-225 4681
  http://www.scottishpubs.co.uk
  Chief Exec: Patrick Browne
- ○ *T
- < Brit Beer & Pub Assn
- M 13 f

Scottish Borders Chamber of Commerce
- NR Unit 127 Ettrick Riverside, Dunsdale Rd, SELKIRK, TD7 5EB.
  01750 505058   fax 01750 505001
  email enquiries@borderschamber.org.uk
  http://www.broderschamber.org.uk
  Pres: David Sturrock
- ○ *C

Scottish Bowling Association   (SBA)   1892
- ■ National Centre for Bowling Northfield, Hunters Avenue, AYR, KA8 9AL.   (hq)
  01292 294623
  email scottishbowling@btconnect.com
  http://www.scottish-bowling.co.uk
  Pres: William Cook
- ○ *S; to control & foster the level green game of bowls
- ● Comp
- < Brit Isles Bowls Coun; Wld Bowls Ltd
- M c 75,000 i, 900 org
- ¶ Bowls for the Beginner - 1.
  Ybk - 1.   Laws of the Game - 1.

Scottish Brass Band Association   (SBBA)
- ■ 71 Tantallon Drive, PAISLEY, Renfrewshire, PA2 9HS.   (sp)
  http://www.sbba.org.uk
  Sec: Tom Allan
- ▲ Registered Charity
- ○ *D; the development of brass bands in Scotland
- ● Mtgs - ET - Res - Exhib - Comp
- < Eur Brass Band Assn
- > Nat Youth Brass Bands of Scotland; Scot Borders Brass Band Assn; Nthn Counties Brass Band Assn
- M 2,500 i, 80 brass bands, 15 youth bands
- ¶ SBBA Ybk - 1; £10 m.

Scottish Building Contractors Association   (SBCA)   1869
- NR 4 Woodside Place, GLASGOW, G3 7QF.   (hq)
  0141-353 5050   fax 0141-332 2928
  email sbca@btinternet.com
  http://www.scottishcontractors.com
  Pres: Craig McKillop
- ▲ Un-incorporated Society
- ○ *T
- ● Conf - Mtgs - Inf - VE
- < Scot Construction Industry Gp
- M 21 i, 37 f
- ¶ NL - 4;   AR; both ftm only.   LM; free.

Scottish Building Federation
- ■ Crichton House, 4 Crichton's Close, Holyrood, EDINBURGH, EH8 8DT.   (hq)
  0131-556 8866   fax 0131-558 5247
  email info@scottish-building.co.uk
  http://www.scottish-building.co.uk
  Chief Exec: Michael Levack
- ○ *N, *T
- ● Conf - Mtgs - ET - Exhib - SG - Inf - Empl
- < Construction Confedn
- M c 800 f
- ¶ Magazine - 4;   Bulletin - 36;   Directory; all ftm;   AR.

Scottish Business in the Community   (SBC)   1982
- NR Livingstone House (1st floor east), 43a Discovery Terrace, Heriot-Watt Research Park, EDINBURGH, EH14 4AP.   (hq)
  0131-451 1100   fax 0131-451 1127
  email info@sbcscot.com   http://www.sbcscot.com
  Chief Exec: Samantha Barber
- ▲ Company Limited by Guarantee; Registered Charity
- ○ *K, *T; to support, broker & challenge businesses to continually improve their positive impact on society to ensure a successful, sustainable economy & environment
- Gp Community; Environment; Marketplace; Workplace
- ● Conf - ET - LG
- < Business in the Community
- M 80 f
- ¶ NL - 3;   LM;   AR - 1; all free.

Scottish Canoe Association   (SCA)   1939
- ■ Caledonia House, South Gyle, EDINBURGH, EH12 9DQ.   (hq)
  0131-317 7314   fax 0131-317 7319
  email general.office@canoescotland.com
  http://www.canoescotland.com
  Admin: Mrs Margaret Winter
- ○ *S; governing body of the sport of canoeing in Scotland
- Gp Access; Canoe polo; Canoe surf; Coaching; Marathon racing; Slalom; Sprint; Touring; White water racing; Canoe sailing
- ● Mtgs - ET - Comp - Inf - Coaching - Tests, proficiency certificates & instructors' awards
- < Brit Canoe U; C'wealth Canoe Fedn; Intl Canoe Fedn
- M 2,200 i & org
- ¶ Scottish Paddler - 4; ftm.   Ybk.

Scottish Carriage Driving Association
NR   Woodfield, Balmullo, ST ANDREWS, Fife, KY16 0AN.
        0845 226 9498
        email secretary@scda.co.uk   http://www.scda.co.uk
        Sec: Simon Sanders
○   *S; carriage driving

Scottish Cashmere Producers Association   (SCPA)   1986
NR   77 Davidson Drive, Northfield, ABERDEEN, AB16 7QS   (hsp)
        01224 692359
        email scpa@thefibrelab.co.uk
        http://www.cashmere-scotland.co.uk
        Sec: Hilary Redden
▲   Company Limited by Guarantee
○   *T; to set & encourage the acceptance of quality standards for
        Scottish cashmere goats
●   Mtgs - ET - Comp - Inf - LG
M   50 i, 4 f, UK / 2 i, o'seas
¶   SCPA Bulletin - 2; ftm only.

Scottish Catholic Historical Association   (SCHA)   1950
NR   c/o Dr A Newby, School of Divinity History & Philosophy,
        Crombie Annexe, Meston Walk, University of Aberdeen,
        OLD ABERDEEN, AB24 3FX.   (sb)
        email a.newby@abdn.ac.uk
        Sec: Dr Andrew G Newby
▲   Registered Charity
○   *L; to study the history of the Catholic church in Scotland
●   Conf - Res
M   270 i, c 80 org, UK / c 30 i, o'seas
¶   Innes Review - 2.

Scottish Chambers of Commerce   1946
NR   30 George Square, GLASGOW, G2 1EQ.   (hq)
        0141-204 8316   fax 0141-221 2336
        email admin@scottishchambers.org.uk
        http://www.scottishchambers.org.uk
        Chief Exec: Liz Cameron
▲   Un-incorporated Society
Br   20 chams
○   *C, *N; business support
●   Conf - Mtgs - LG
<   Scotland Europa
M   9,000 f
¶   Business Survey - 4; ftm, varies nm.   AR - 1; free.
        National Directory - 1.

Scottish Childminding Association   (SCMA)   1990
NR   7 Melville Terrace, STIRLING, FK8 2ND.   (hq)
        01786 445377   fax 01786 449062
        email information@childminding.org
        http://www.childminding.org
        Chief Exec: Anne McNellan
▲   Company Limited by Guarantee; Registered Charity
○   *P; 'to promote quality childminding; building confident
        children within a family childcare experience'
●   Conf - Mtgs - ET - Exhib - Stat - Inf - LG
<   Intl Family Day Care Org
M   i
¶   Childminding - 4;   AR; both free.

Scottish Chiropractic Association
NR   Laigh Hatton Farm, Old Greenock Rd, BISHOPTON,
        Renfrewshire, PA7 5PB.
        01505 863151
        http://www.sca-chiropractic.org
○   *P

** **Scottish Church History Society**
        Organisation lost, see Introduction paragraph 3

Scottish Clay Target Association Ltd   (SCTA)   2000
■   PO Box 7588, PERTH, PH1 4WD.   (mail add)
▲   Company Limited by Guarantee
○   *S; 'to promote the art of clay target shooting in Scotland at all
        levels, from novice to international'
●   ET - Comp - Organised series of shoots & selection shoots for
        team selection for national team
<   Intl Coun Clay Pigeon Shooting GB & I; Brit Intl Clay Target
        Shooting Fedn; Scot Target Shooting Fedn
M   1,080 i
¶   NL - 4;   Annual Bulletin; both ftm only.

Scottish Committee of Optometrists   (SCO)   1935
NR   5 St Vincent St, EDINBURGH, EH3 6SW.   (hsb)
        0131-220 4542
        email sco-online.org
        Admin: Lorna Cameron
▲   Un-incorporated Society
○   *P; represents interests of optometrists in Scotland
●   Conf - Mtgs - ET - Res - LG
<   General Optical Coun; Brit Coll Optometrists; Assn
        Optometrists; Eyecare Information Service
M   740 i
¶   Look North - 4; free.

Scottish Community Drama Association   (SCDA)   1926
■   5 York Place (1st floor), EDINBURGH, EH1 3EB.   (hq)
        0131-557 5552
        email headquarters@scda.org.uk
        http://www.scda.org.uk
        Contact: The National Chair
▲   Un-incorporated Society
Br   28
○   *G, *N; to act as the umbrella body for encouragement of
        amateur & community theatre in Scotland
Gp   Festivals; Playwriting; Youth activities
●   Conf - Mtgs - ET - Exhib - Comp - Inf - Lib - LG - Theatre
        Maker
<   Intl Amat Theatre Assn (IATA); Intl Theatre Exchange (ITE); Indep
        Theatre Coun; Scot Coun for Voluntary Orgs (SCVO)
M   700 i, 175 org
        (Sub: £17 i, £45 org)
¶   Scene Magazine - 4; free.

Scottish Consortium for Learning Disability
NR   Adelphi Centre Room 16, 12 Commercial Rd, GLASGOW,
        G5 0PQ.
        0141 418 5420   fax 0141 429 1142
○   *N
M   12 org

Scottish Contaminated Land Forum   (SCLF)   1997
■   Jacobs (attn: Dave Cooke), 95 Bothwell St, GLASGOW,
        G2 7HX.   (chmn/b)
        0141-243 8095
        email sclf@jacobs.com   http://www.chem.gla.ac.uk/sclf/
        index.html
        Contact: Dave Cooke
▲   Un-incorporated Society
○   *G; discussion of all aspects of contaminated land
●   Mtgs - ET - SG

Scottish Corn Trade Association Ltd   (SCTA)   1969
■   77/2 Hanover St, EDINBURGH, EH2 1EE.   (asa)
        0131-225 7773   fax 0131-226 4448
▲   Company Limited by Guarantee
○   *T; promotion of the interests of the grain trade
●   Mtgs - LG - Annual dinner
<   UKASTA; GAFTA
M   80 f

© CBD Research Ltd · Beckenham · BR3 5JS · Tel 020 8650 7745 · Fax 020 8650 0768 · E-mail cbd@cbdresearch.com · www.cbdresearch.com

SCOTTISH COUNCIL ...
For details of bodies whose names begin thus, other than those
entered below, see the companion volume **'Councils, Committees
& Boards'** (Introduction paragraph 6)

Scottish Council on Deafness   (SCOD)   1927
- ■ Central Chambers (suite 62 1st floor), 93 Hope St, GLASGOW, G2 6LD.   (hq)
  0141-248 2474 & 0141-248 2477 (text)   fax 0141-248 2479
  email admin@scod.org.uk   http://www.scod.org.uk
  Dir: Lilian Lawson
- ▲ Registered Charity
- ○ *N, *W; to act on behalf of agencies & organisations working with deaf people in Scotland by forming strategic alliances, developing policy initiatives & using them to improve the human & civil rights of deaf people living in Scotland
- ● Conf - Mtgs - ET - Res - Inf - LG
- M 80 org
- ¶ NL - 4; ftm only.   Bulletin - 12; ftm, £5 yr nm.
  Directory; online only.   AR - 1; ftm.

Scottish Council for Development & Industry   (SCDI)   1931
- ■ Campsie House, 17 Park Circus Place, GLASGOW, G3 6AH.   (hq)
  0141-332 9119   fax 0141-333 0039
  email enquiries@scdi.org.uk   http://www.scdi.org.uk
  Chief Exec: Dr Lesley Sawers
- ▲ Company Limited by Guarantee
- Br 4
- ○ *K; an independent, non-political membership network, which strengthens Scotland's competitiveness by influencing government policies to encourage sustainable, economic prosperity; membership is from manufacturing & service sectors, universities & colleges, trade associations, local enterprise companies, the churches & trade unions
- Gp Business information; Public policy; Trade development; Education/industry links
- ● Conf - Mtgs - Res - Stat - Expt - Inf - LG
- M 1,300 f
- ¶ Pointer - 10; £45 m, £90 nm.
  Indicator - 6; ftm only.   AR; free.
  Annual Survey of Scottish Export Sales - 1; ftm only.

Scottish Council for National Parks   (SCNP)   1990
- ■ The Barony, Glebe Rd, KILBIRNIE, Ayrshire, KA25 6HX.   (chmn/p)
  01505 682447   fax 0870 051 6410
  email rgmaund@thebarony.demon.co.uk
  http://www.scnp.org.uk
  Chmn: Robert Maund,   Sec: Kate Walsham
- ▲ Registered Charity
- ○ *F, *K; to promote the establishment of National Parks in Scotland with adequate powers & finance to ensure good management of the landscape, tourism & the local economy
- ● Conf - ET - Res - Exhib - Inf - PL - LG
- < Intl U for the Consvn of Nature; Campaign for National Parks: Scot Environment Link
- > Assn for the Protection of Rural Scotland; Camping & Caravan Club; Friends of Loch Lomond & the Trossachs; Ramblers Assn; Save Your Regional Park Campaign
- M 71 i, 22 org, UK / 4 i, o'seas
  Subs: £10 (single), £16 couple, UK / varies, o'seas
- ¶ NL - 4;   AR & Accounts; both free.

Scottish Council for Single Homeless   (SCSH)   1974
- ■ Wellgate House, 200 Cowgate, EDINBURGH, EH1 1NQ.   (hq)
  0131-226 4382
  email enquiries@scsh.demon.co.uk
  http://www.scsh.co.uk
  Dir: Robert Aldridge
- ▲ Registered Charity
- ○ *K, *W; to promote awareness about the causes, nature & extent of single homelessness; to identify means of preventing & alleviating homelessness & to collaborate with all appropriate agencies
- ● Conf - Mtgs - ET - Res - Exhib - Inf - Lib - LG
- < Fédn Eur des Assns Nationaux Travaillant avec les Sans-Abris (FEANTSA); Shelter; Age Concern Scotland
- M 90 i, 200 org, UK / 5 org, o'seas
- ¶ Briefing Papers; free.
  Publications list available.

Scottish Council for Voluntary Organisations   (SCVO)   1943
- ■ 15 Mansfield Place, EDINBURGH, EH3 6BB.   (hq)
  0131-556 3882   fax 0131-556 0279
  email enquiries@scvo.org.uk   http://www.scvo.org.uk
  Chief Exec: Martin Sime
- ▲ Company Limited by Guarantee; Registered Charity
- Br 3
- ○ *N, *W; an independent organisation working at a national level to provide services to voluntary & community groups throughout Scotland
- Gp Parliamentary information & advisory service; Policy officers network; Social inclusion partnership team; Equal project strengthening the social economy; Voluntary management development unit; New deal; IT services
- ● Conf - Mtgs - ET - Res - Stat - Inf - Lib - LG
- < Scotland Europa; Civicus
- M 1,200 i & org
- ¶ Third Force News & Inform (jt information pack) - 48; ftm, £110 nm.
  Work packs;   Handbooks;   Directories;   AR.
  Publications list available.

Scottish Countryside Rangers' Association   (SCRA)   1974
- NR Pitcairn Centre, Moidart Drive, Coul, GLENROTHES, Fife, KY7 6ET.
  http://www.scra-online.co.uk
- ▲ Un-incorporated Society
- ○ *P; countryside ranger services in Scotland
- M i & f

Scottish Covenanter Memorials Association   1966
- ■ Lochnoran House, AUCHINLECK, Ayrshire, KA18 3JW.   (hsp)
  01290 425594
  email info@covenanter.org.uk
  http://www.covenanter.org.uk
  Hon Sec: Dane Love
- ▲ Registered Charity
- ○ *G; to preserve monuments & memorials to the Scottish Covenanters (mainly 1638-1689); to erect new memorials to commemorate Covenanters or events
- ● Lib - Annual mtg - Annual dinner - Irregular religious services (Conventicles)
- M 360 i, UK / 40 i, o'seas
- ¶ NL - 3; ftm only.

Scottish Cremation Society
- NR Glasgow Crematorium, Tresta Rd, GLASGOW, G23 5AA.
  0141-946 2895
  Sec: John Gordon

Scottish Cricket Union
since 2004 **Cricket Scotland**

Scottish Crofting Foundation (SCF) 1986

NR Lochalsh Business Park, Auchtertyre, KYLE of LOCHALSH,
    IV40 8EG. (hq)
    01599 566365
    email hq@crofting.org
    http://www.croftingfoundation.co.uk
    Chief Exec: Patrick Krause
▲ Un-incorporated Society
○ *F; to develop, promote & encourage crofting
M i & f
¶ The Crofter - 4.

Scottish Croquet Association (SCA) 1974

NR 2 St Leonard's Bank (2F3), EDINBURGH, EH8 9SQ.
    (matchsec/p)
    0131-667 4216
    http://www.scottishcroquet.org.uk
    Match Sec: Fergus McInnes
▲ Un-incorporated Society
○ *S; promotion, development & organisation of croquet in
    Scotland
● ET - Comp
< Wld Croquet Fedn; Eur Croquet Fedn
M 130 i, 9 org
¶ Bulletin - 4. Ybk.

Scottish Cycling (SC) 1953

NR The Velodrome, Meadow Bank Stadium, London Rd,
    EDINBURGH, EH7 6AD. (hq)
    0131-652 0187 fax 0131-661 0474
    email info@scottishcycling.com
    http://www.scuonline.org
▲ Company Limited by Guarantee
○ *S; governing body for cycle sport in Scotland
Gp Cycling; Mountain biking; Sports; Coaching
● ET - Comp - Inf - Coaching & leadership - Scottish Mountain
    Bike Leader Award (SMBLA) Scheme
< Brit Cycling Fedn; Sportscotland
M c 2,4000 i, 100 clubs
¶ NL - 12; free. Hbk - 1. AR.
    Note: Scottish Cycling is the trading name of the Scottish
    Cyclists' Union

Scottish Daily Newspaper Society (SDNS) 1915

NR 48 Palmerston Place, EDINBURGH, EH12 5DE. (hq)
    0131-220 4353 fax 0131-220 4344
    email info@sdns.org.uk
    Dir: Jim Raeburn
○ *T; represents daily & Sunday newspapers in Scotland
● Mtgs - LG
M 7 f

Scottish Dairy Association
    since 2005 **Dairy UK** (Scottish branch)

Scottish Dance Teachers Alliance (SDTA) 1934

NR 101 Park Rd, GLASGOW, G4 9JE. (hq)
    0141-339 8944 fax 0141-357 4994
    email info@thesdta.com http://www.thesdta.com
    Pres: Andrew Cowan
○ *D, *P; for professional teachers of dancing: ballet, tap,
    modern, jazz, highland, Scottish national, sequence,
    ballroom, Latin American, line-dancing, baton twirling &
    cheerleading, disco; rock'n'roll
● Conf - Mtgs - ET - Exam - Comp - SG - Expt - Inf - Provision of
    examinations in all forms of [above] dancing
< Scot Official Bd of Highland Dancing (SOBHD); Brit Dance
    Coun (BDC); Coun for Dance Educl Trg (CDET)
M 500 i, UK / 450 i, o'seas
¶ Alliance News - 4; AR; both ftm only.

Scottish Dancesport
    since 2006 **Dancesport Scotland**

Scottish Darts Association (SDA) 1971

NR 213 Bonnyview Drive, ABERDEEN, AB16 7EY. (regd off)
    01224 692535
    email scotdarts@aol.com http://www.scottishdarts.com
    Chmn: Len Mutch
○ *S

Scottish Decorators Federation (SDF) 1878

■ Castlecraig Business Park, Players Rd, STIRLING, FK7 7SH.
    (hq)
    01786 448838 fax 01786 450541
    http://www.scottishdecorators.co.uk
    Chief Exec: Ian H Rogers
○ *T
● Conf - Mtgs - ET - Comp - Inf - Lib - Empl - LG
M f
¶ NL - 4; free. Ybk - 1; ftm.
    Wage agreement information - 1; free.

Scottish Disability Sport (SDS) 1963

■ Caledonia House, South Gyle, EDINBURGH, EH12 9DQ. (hq)
    0131-317 1130 fax 0131-317 1075
    email admin@scottishdisabilitysport.com
    http://www.scottishdisabilitysport.com
    Chief Exec: Gavin MacLeod, Admin: Caroline Ellis
▲ Company Limited by Guarantee; Registered Charity
Br 15 (Scotland)
○ *S, *W; national governing & coordinating body of all sports for
    all people with a disability in Scotland
Gp Committees: Local development; Sports; Athletes; Medical
● Conf - Mtgs - ET - Res - Comp - SG - Inf - LG
M 5,500 i, 8 org
¶ Changing with the Times (NL) - 3; AR; both free.

Scottish Dowsing Association

NR 14 Scott Drive, LARGS, Ayrshire, KA30 9PA.
    01475 674364
    Sec: G Harper

Scottish Dyslexia Association
    since 2004 **Dyslexia Scotland**

Scottish Ecological Design Association (SEDA) 1991

NR 15 High St, BELFORD, Northumberland, NE70 7NG.
    http://www.seda2.org
    Development Officer: Mary Kelly
○ *K

Scottish Economic Society (SES) 1954

NR Sch of Accounting & Economics, Napier University,
    Craiglockhart Campus, EDINBURGH. EH14 1DJ. (sec/b)
    http://www.scotecsoc.org
    Sec: Dr Linda Juleff
▲ Registered Charity
○ *L; to promote the study & teaching of economics
¶ Scottish Journal of Political Economy - 5.

Scottish Educational Research Association (SERA) 1971

NR c/o PDU, University of Strathclyde, Faculty of Education,
    Jordanhill Campus, Southbrae Drive, GLASGOW, G13 1PP.
    0141-950 3208 fax 0141-950 3210
    email admin@sera.ac.uk http://www.sera.ac.uk
    Admin: Jan Bissett
▲ Registered Charity
○ *E; to promote educational research; to debate about the
    contribution that research can make to enhanced practice

© CBD Research Ltd · Beckenham · BR3 5JS · Tel 020 8650 7745 · Fax 020 8650 0768 · E-mail cbd@cbdresearch.com · www.cbdresearch.com

Scottish Employers' Council for the Clay Industries   (SECCI)
NR   c/o Raeburn Brick Ltd, East Avenue, Blantyre, GLASGOW,
        G72 0JB.   (pres/b)
        01698 828888
      Pres: J M Raeburn
○   *T; manufacturers of all types of bricks, building & refractory,
        field drain pipes etc
M   f

Scottish Engineering   1991
■   105 West George St, GLASGOW, G2 1QL.   (hq)
        0141-221 3181   fax 0141-204 1202
        email consult@scottishengineering.org.uk
        http://www.scottishengineering.org.uk
      Chief Exec: Peter T Hughes
○   *T; employers' association
Gp   Representation; Employment law; Industrial tribunal advice &
        representation; Personnel procedures & practices; Health &
        safety advice &/or consultation; Employment information &
        statistics; Supervisor & management development
●   Mtgs - ET - SG - Stat - Inf - Lib - VE - Empl - LG - Forums &
        seminars
<   Engg Employers' Fedn
M   350 f
¶   Quarterly Review.   Hbk.   Information sheets.   AR.

Scottish Environment Link   1987
NR   2 Grosvenor House, Shore Road, PERTH, PH2 8BD.   (hq)
        01738 630804   fax 01738 643290
        email enquiries@scotlink.org   http://www.scotlink.org
      Chief Officer: Jen Anderson
▲   Registered Charity
○   *N; 'voluntary organisations working together to care for &
        improve Scotland's heritage for people & nature'
M   31 org
¶   The Link (NL) - 4.

**Scottish Environmental & Outdoor Education Centres Association
Ltd   (SOEC)   1947**
§   Loaningdale House, Carwood Rd, BIGGAR, Lanarks,
        ML12 6LX.   (hq)
        01899 221115   fax 01899 220644
        http://www.soec.org.uk
      Runs four Scottish Outdoor Education Centres across Scotland
        and is the country's largest provider of residential outdoor
        education.

Scottish Equestrian Association
      a discipline member of the **British Equestrian Federation**

**Scottish Esperanto Association   (Esperanto-Asocio de
Skotlando)   (SEA)   1908**
■   47 Airbles Crescent, MOTHERWELL, Lanarks, ML1 3AP.   (hsp)
        01698 263199
        email secretary@skotlando.org   http://www.skotlando.org
      Hon Sec: David W Bisset
▲   Registered Charity
○   *E, *X; to promote & teach Esperanto
Gp   Young people
●   Conf - Mtgs - ET - Exam - Res - Exhib - SG - Inf - Lib - LG
<   Esperanto Assn of Britain
>   Scot Esperanto Study Weekend
M   100 i, 10 org, UK / 10 i, o'seas
¶   Scottish Esperanto Bulletin - 2; ftm, £1 nm.
      Esperanto en Skotlando - 2; ftm, £4 nm.

Scottish Federation of Baton Twirling
NR   55 Springkell Ave, Maxwell Park, GLASGOW, G41 4DP.
        0141-424 0109
        http://www.sfbt.org.uk
      Pres: David Wood;   Sec: Tony Pratt
○   *S

Scottish Federation of Housing Associations Ltd   (SFHA)   1976
NR   Pegasus House, 375 West George St, GLASGOW, G2 4LW.
        (hq)
        0141-332 8113   fax 0141-332 9684
        email sfha@sfha.co.uk   http://www.sfha.co.uk
      Chief Exec: Jacqui Watt
▲   Company Limited by Guarantee
Br   Glasgow, Dundee
○   *N; advisory & representative body for housing associations in
        Scotland
Gp   Teams: Policy & practice, Consultancy, Training & events; Lintel
        Trust (charitable)
●   Conf - Mtgs - ET - Exhib - Inf - LG
M   400 f, 100 org
¶   Federation Focus (Jnl) - 10.
      Federation Digest - 10.
      SFHA Directory - 1.   SFHA Diary - 1.

**Scottish Federation of Meat Traders Associations   (SFMTA)
1917**
■   8-10 Needless Rd, PERTH, PH2 0JW.   (hq)
        01738 637472   fax 01738 441059
        email info@sfmta.co.uk   http://www.sfmta.co.uk
      Chief Exec: Douglas Scott
▲   Company Limited by Guarantee
○   *T; for independent meat retailers in Scotland
      In 2000 the SFMTA Training organisation became Food
        Training Services, which in 2003 became Scottish Meat
        Training
●   Conf - Mtgs - ET - Exam - Exhib - Comp - Inf - Empl - LG
M   420 f
¶   NL - 12; ftm only.

Scottish Federation of Sea Anglers   (SFSA)   1960
NR   Unit 62 Evans Business Centre, Mitchelston Drive, Mitchelston
        Industrial Estate, KIRKCALDY, KY1 3NB.   (hq)
        01592 657520   fax 01592 657520
        http://www.fishsea.co.uk
      Sec/Admin: Mrs Margaret McCallum
▲   Un-incorporated Society
○   *S; governing body of the sport of sea angling in Scotland
Gp   Competitions; Coaching; Conservation
●   Mtgs - ET - Comp - Inf - LG
<   Sportscotland
M   155 i, 30 clubs
¶   NL - 4; ftm.   SFSA Hbk - 1; ftm, £4 nm.

Scottish Fencing
NR   589 Lanark Rd, EDINBURGH, EH14 5DA.   (regd off)
        0131-453 9074   fax 0131-453 9079
        email admin@scottish-fencing.com
        http://www.scottish-fencing.com
      Exec Admin: Lorraine Rose
○   *S; the governing body in Scotland for the sport of fencing
M   c 750 i

Scottish Fiddle Society   2002
NR   28 Arnott Gardens, EDINBURGH, EH14 2LB.
        0131-443 6631
        email watson-alan@tiscali.co.uk
        http://www.thescottishfiddlesociety.org.uk
      Admin: Alan Watson
○   *D; to support, enrich and encourage a burgeoning Scottish
        fiddle music scene

Scottish Field Archery Association (SFAA) 1966
■ 7 The Cottages, Threemiletown, LINLITHGOW, W Lothian,
   EH49 6NG. (hsp)
   01506 830063   fax 01506 830063
   email jimgreig@msn.com
   http://www.scottishfieldarchery.co.uk
   Hon Sec: James B Greig
▲ Company Limited by Guarantee
○ *S; 'to foster & encourage good fellowship among those who
   take up the sport of IFAA based field archery'
● Mtgs - ET - Comp
< Intl Field Archery Assn
M 250 i, 12 clubs
¶ NL - 4; ftm only.

Scottish Field Studies Association Ltd (SFSA) 1964
NR Kindrogan Field Studies Centre, Enochdhu, BLAIRGOWRIE,
   Perthshire, PH10 7PG.
   01250 870150
   http://www.field-studies-council.org
▲ Registered Charity
○ *E; to study all aspects of natural sciences, natural history &
   conservation
< Field Studies Coun
M i & org

Scottish Fishermen's Federation (SFF) 1973
NR 24 Rubislaw Terrace, ABERDEEN, AB10 1XE. (hq)
   01224 646944   fax 01224 647058
   email sff@sff.co.uk   http://www.sff.co.uk
   Chief Exec: Bertie Armstrong
▲ Un-incorporated Society
○ *N, *T; to preserve & promote the collective interests of
   fishermen's associations
< Assn Nat Fishing Orgs EEC (EUROPECHE)
M 8 org

Scottish Fishermen's Organisation (SFO) 1973
NR 601 Queensferry Rd, EDINBURGH, EH4 6EA.
   0131-339 7972   fax 0131-339 6662
   email info@scottishfishermen.co.uk
   http://www.scottishfishermen.co.uk
   Chief Exec: Iain McSween
○ *N

** **Scottish Flour Millers Association**
   organisation lost, see Introduction paragraph 3

Scottish Food & Drink Federation (SFDF) 1999
NR 4a Torphichen St, EDINBURGH, EH3 8JQ. (hq)
   0131-229 9415   fax 0131-229 9407
   email sfdf@sfdf.org.uk   http://www.sfdf.org.uk
   Dir: Flora McLean
○ *T; to represent the interests of the food & drink manufacturing
   industry in Scotland
● Conf - Mtgs - Inf - LG
< Food & Drink Fedn; Scot Civic Forum
M 75 f
¶ NL - 12;   AR; both ftm.

Scottish Food Trades Association (SFTA) 1889
NR c/o Accredited Training, 69 Aberdalgie Rd, GLASGOW,
   G34 9HY. (hsb)
   0141-773 2100
   email sfta@firemail.co.uk
   Sec: Mrs Mari McTear
▲ Un-incorporated Society
Br 4
○ *T; the networking platform for the Scottish food industry
● Mtgs
M 100 i, 50 f

Scottish Football Association Ltd (SFA) 1873
■ Hampden Park, GLASGOW, G42 9AY. (hq)
   0141-616 6000   fax 0141-616 6001
   email info@scottishfa.co.uk   http://www.scottishfa.co.uk
   Chief Exec: Gordon Smith
▲ Company Limited by Guarantee
○ *S; to promote, foster & develop in all its branches the game of
   Association Football in Scotland
● Conf - Mtgs - ET - Exam - Comp - Stat - Inf
< FIFA; UEFA
M 77 clubs
¶ Hbk; ftm, £10 nm (£2p&p).
   Laws of the Game; ftm, £4 nm.   AR; ftm, £5 nm.

Scottish Football League (SFL) 1890
■ Hampden Park, GLASGOW, G42 9EB. (hq)
   0141-620 4160   fax 0141-620 4161
   email info@scottishfootballleague.com
   http://www.scottishfootballleague.com
   Chief Exec: David Longmuir
▲ Un-incorporated Body
○ *S; to promote & extend the game of Association Football in
   Scotland
● Conf - Mtgs - ET - Res - Comp - Stat - Inf - Provision of League
   championships & League cup competitions
< Intl Football League Bd; Scot Football Assn
M 30 clubs
¶ Hbk (incl list of clubs & referees) - 1; £10.
   Fixture Book - 1; £3.

Scottish Freshwater Group (SFG)
■ Dr Laurence Carvalho, Centre for Ecology & Hydrology,
   Edinburgh Bush Estate, PENICUIK, EH26 0QB. (sb)
   0131-445 4343
   http://www.ceh.ac.uk/sci_programmes/water/
   scottish_freshwater_group.html
   Sec: Dr Laurence Carvalho
○ *P; an informal forum for the exchange of information on
   current issues & research related to Scottish freshwaters
● Conf - Mtgs
M 350 i, 20 org

Scottish Gaelic Texts Society (SGTS) 1934
■ c/o McLeish Carswell, 29 St Vincent Place, GLASGOW,
   G1 2DT. (hsb)
   0141-248 4134   fax 0141-226 3118
   http://www.sgts.org.uk
   Hon Sec: Miss A F Wilson
▲ Registered Charity
○ *L; to promote the publication of texts in the Scottish Gaelic
   language, accompanied by introductions, English translations
   & glossaries
● Res
M 120 i, 10 org, UK / 20 i, 10 org, o'seas
¶ Various publications.

Scottish Gamekeepers Association (SGA) 1997
NR PO Box 7477, PERTH, PH2 7YE. (hsp)
   01738 587515   fax 01738 587516
   email sga1@btconnect.com
   http://www.scottishgamekeepers.co.uk
   Sec: Hazel Donnelly
▲ Un-incorporated Society
○ *P; to promote the work of gamekeepers, stalkers, ghillies &
   rangers; to educate them in good practice; to promote their
   welfare
● Conf - Mtgs - ET - Res - Comp - Inf - VE - LG
M 2,500 i, 500 f, 25 org, UK / 500 i, o'seas
¶ Scottish Gamekeeper (Jnl) - 4.

© CBD Research Ltd · Beckenham · BR3 5JS · Tel 020 8650 7745 · Fax 020 8650 0768 · E-mail cbd@cbdresearch.com · www.cbdresearch.com

Scottish Games Association **(SGA)** **1946**
NR 54 Crawford Gardens, ST ANDREWS, Fife, KY16 8XQ.
      (pres/p)
      01334 476305
      http://www.highlandgames-sga.com
      Pres: Ian Grieve
▲ Company Limited by Guarantee
○ *S; to encourage & foster the highest standards of ethics &
      performance in open athletics & traditional Highland games
● Mtgs - Comp
M 65 full members, 5 associate members, 4 committees
¶ Ybk.

Scottish Genealogy Society **1953**
NR 15 Victoria Terrace, EDINBURGH, EH1 2JL.
      0131-220 3677   fax 0131-220 3677
      email enquiries@scottishgenealogy.com
      http://www.scottishgenealogy.com
      Hon Sec: Ken Nisbet
▲ Registered Charity
○ *L, *Q; to promote research into Scottish family history
● Mtgs - Inf - Lib
M i, org
¶ The Scottish Genealogist - 4; ftm.
      Lists of pre 1855 Monumental Inscriptions.

Scottish Glass Society **1979**
■ PO Box 29329, GLASGOW, G20 2BA.
      http://www.scottishglasssociety.com
      Hon Sec: Siobhan Healy
○ *G; to promote the development of the art and craftsmanship
      of glass making in Scotland
M c 180 i

Scottish Gliding Union Ltd **(SGU)** **1934**
■ The Scottish Gliding Centre, Portmoak Airfield, Scotlandwell, by
      KINROSS, KY13 9JJ.   (hq)
      01592 840543
      http://www.portmoak.force9.co.uk
      Hon Sec: Bruce Marshall,   Chmn: John Williams
▲ Company Limited by Guarantee
○ *S; provision & promotion of gliding activities to members & the
      public
Gp Disabled facilities; Flying for disabled
● ET (training of glider pilots) - Trial flight option for members of
      the public
< Brit Gliding Assn
M 250 i
      Note: The trading name is the Scottish Gliding Centre.

Scottish Golf Union Ltd **(SGU)** **1920**
NR The Duke's, ST ANDREWS, Fife, KY16 8NX.   (hq)
      01334 466477   fax 01334 462361
      email sgu@scottishgolf.org   http://www.scottishgolf.org
      Chief Exec: Hamish Grey
○ *S; governing body of amateur golf in Scotland
● Mtgs - ET - Comp - VE - LG
< Intl Golf Fedn; Eur Golf Assn; Coun of Nat Golf Us
> Scot Golf Envt Gp (wholly owned subsidiary)
M 260,000 i, 650 clubs in Scotland
¶ Scottish Golfer - 8;   Ybk; both free.
× 2004 (February) Scottish Golf Union

Scottish Grocers' Federation **(SGF)** **1918**
■ 222 Queensferry Rd, EDINBURGH, EH4 2BN.   (hq)
      0131-343 3300   fax 0131-343 6147
      email info@scotgrocersfed.co.uk
      http://www.scottishshop.org.uk
      Chief Exec: John Drummond
▲ Company Limited by Guarantee
○ *T; for independent convenience retailers in Scotland
● Conf - Mtgs - ET - SG - Stat - Inf - LG
< Intl Fedn of Grocers' Assns (IFGA)
M 600 f
¶ Retail News - 12;   Retail Outlook (Ybk) - 1.

Scottish Gymnastics Association **(SGA)** **1890**
NR Airthrey Castle, University of Stirling, STIRLING, FK9 4LA.   (hq)
      01786 466232   fax 01786 466246
      email info@scottishgymnastics.org
      http://www.scottishgymnastics.org
      Chief Exec: Mike Roberts
▲ Company Limited by Guarantee
○ *S
M i
× 2004 (July) Fitness Scotland (merged)

Scottish Handball Association **(SHA)**
NR National Sports Centre Inverclyde, Burnside Rd, LARGS,
      N Ayrshire, KA30 8RW.   (sb)
      01475 687804
      http://www.scottishhandball.com
○ *S

Scottish Hang Gliding & Paragliding Federation **(SHPF)**
1973
NR Noble Lodge, Ballencrieff Toll, BATHGATE, W Lothian,
      EH48 4LD.   (hsp)
      email bob@shpf.co.uk   http://www.shpf.co.uk
      Sec: Robert Matthews
○ *S; to promote the sports of hang gliding & paragliding in
      Scotland
M i & clubs
¶ The Flying Scot (NL) - 4.

Scottish Hazards Campaign Group **1993**
NR 113 Kingsknowe Rd North, EDINBURGH, EH14 2DQ.   (hsp)
      0131-477 0817
      email info@scottishhazards.co.uk
      http://www.scottishhazards.co.uk
      Sec: Kathy Jenkins
▲ Un-incorporated Society
○ *K; to campaign for improved worker health & safety
      throughout Scotland
● Conf - Mtgs - ET - Res
M 30 i, 10 org

** Scottish Hereford Breeders Association**
      Organisation lost, see Introduction paragraph 3

Scottish History Society **(SHS)** **1886**
■ School of History, St Katharine's Lodge, The Scores,
      ST ANDREWS, Fife, KY16 9AL.   (hsb)
      01337 831996
      email kcs7@st-andrews.ac.uk
      http://www.scottishhistorysociety.org
      Hon Sec: Dr Katie Stevenson
▲ Registered Charity
○ *L; 'to discover & print, in a series of annual volumes,
      unpublished documents illustrating the history of Scotland'
● Conf - Mtgs - ET - Res - Comp
< R Histl Soc (Brit Nat C'ee)
M 380 i, 175 f
      (Sub: £20 i, £25 f)
¶ Annual Volume (back copies available; prices vary).

Scottish Hockey Union **(SHU)** **1989**
■ 589 Lanark Rd, EDINBURGH, EH14 5DA.   (hq)
      0131-453 9070   fax 0131-453 9079
      email info@scottish-hockey.org.uk
      http://www.scottish-hockey.org.uk
      Chief Exec: Brent Deans
▲ Company Limited by Guarantee
○ *S; the national governing body for the sport of hockey in
      Scotland
Gp Youth Commission
● Mtgs - ET - Exam - Exhib - Comp - Inf - LG
< Intl Hockey Fedn (FIH); Eur Hockey Fedn (EHF)
M 6,000 i, 165 clubs
¶ Hockey Scotland - 2; free.

Scottish Homing Union (SHU)
NR 231a Low Waters Rd, HAMILTON, Lanarks, ML3 7QN. (hq)
01698 286983
email enquiries@shuonline.co.uk
http://www.shuonline.co.uk
Sec: Linda Brooks
○ *N, *S; the governing body for members who race & show racing pigeons in Scotland

Scottish Huntington's Association 1989
NR St James Business Centre (suite 135), Linwood Rd, PAISLEY, PA3 3AT. (hq)
0141-848 0308   fax 0141-887 6199
email sha-admin@hdscotland.org
http://www.hdscotland.org
Sec: Ann Carruthers
▲ Company Limited by Guarantee; Registered Charity
Br 9
○ *W; to help sufferers of Huntington's disease & their families; to help people at risk of developing the disease
Gp Professional interest
● Conf - Mtgs - ET - Res - Inf - Lib
< Intl Huntington's Disease Assn
M 1,000 i
¶ Books:
A Physician's Guide to the Management of Huntington's Disease.
Behavioural Problems in Huntington's Disease.
Huntington's Disease: What's it all about? A guide for young people (aged 14+).
Other publications available.

Scottish Ice Skating Association (SISA) 1981
NR The Ice Sports Centre, Riversdale Crescent, EDINBURGH, EH12 5XN. (hq)
0131-337 3976   fax 0131-337 9239
email office@sisa.org.uk   http://www.sisa.org.uk
Admin: John MacDonald
▲ Un-incorporated Society
○ *S; promotion of amateur ice skating in Scotland
Gp Skating: Recreational; Ice dancing; Figures & free; Pairs; Exhibition; Show; Precise
● Exam - Exhib - Comp - Courses & grade test
< Nat Ice Skating Assn UK Ltd
M 546 i, 22 affiliated clubs
¶ Scottish Skate Update - 4.
Members' Hbk - 1.   Event Programme - 4.

Scottish Icelandic Horse Association
NR 39 Bartongate Drive, EDINBURGH, EH4 8BE. (mem/sp)
0131-317 1675
email info@siha.org.uk   http://www.siha.org.uk
Mem Sec: Susan Irvine
○ *B

Scottish Independent Advocacy Alliance (SIAA) 2002
■ Melrose House, 69a George St, EDINBURGH, EH2 2JG. (hq)
0131-260 5380   fax 0131-260 5381
email enquiry@siaa.org.uk   http://www.siaa.org.uk
Dir: Shaben Begum
▲ Company Limited by Guarantee; Registered Charity
○ *N; to promote, support & defend independent advocacy throughout Scotland
● Conf - Mtgs - ET - Res - Stat - Inf - LG
M 100 org
(Sub: £100)
¶ Abouth Advocacy (Jnl) - 4;   AR - 1.

Scottish Indoor Bowling Association (SIBA) 1936
■ 1 Nursery Lane, MAUCHLINE, Ayrshire, KA5 6EH. (hsp)
01290 551067   fax 01290 551067
email gordon.siba@o2mail.co.uk
http://www.bowls-siba.co.uk
Hon Sec: Gordon Woods
▲ Un-incorporated Society
○ *S
● Mtgs - Comp
< Wld Indoor Bowls Coun; Brit Isles Indoor Bowls Coun
M 60,000 i (Scotland only)
¶ Bowls International - 12.
World Bowls - 12.   Scots Bowler - 12.

Scottish Industrial Heritage Society (SIHS) 1984
NR 58 Kenningknowes Rd, STIRLING, FK7 9JG. (sp)
http://www.sihs.co.uk
Contact: C D Bates
▲ Company Limited by Guarantee; Registered Charity
○ *L; the study of the history & development of industry in Scotland
● Conf - Mtgs - Inf - VE
< Assn for Indl Archaeology
M 120 i, 10 f, 5 org, UK / 1 i, 1 f, o'seas
¶ SIHS Review (NL) - 2.
Guide to Scottish Industrial Heritage (Hbk).

Scottish Inland Waterways Association (SIWA) 1971
■ 5 Calder Rd, Bellsquarry, LIVINGSTON, W Lothian, EH54 9AA. (hsp)
01506 417685
http://www.siwa.org.uk
Sec: Ann Street
▲ Registered Charity
○ *G, *K, *N; to preserve & rehabilitate Scottish inland waterways; to coordinate local canal societies; to promote the use of waterways for leisure & commercial purposes
● Mtgs - Exhib - Inf - VE
< Inland Waterways Assn
M 137 i, 18 org

Scottish Intensive Care Society (SICS) 1991
NR Dept of Anaesthesia, Walton Building, Royal Infirmary, Castle St, GLASGOW, G4 0SF. (hsb)
0141-211 4000
http://www.scottishintensivecare.org.uk
Hon Sec: Dr Malcolm Booth

Scottish Ju-Jitsu Association (SJJA) 1979
NR 3 Dens St, DUNDEE, DD4 6BU. (hq)
01382 458262   fax 01382 458262
http://www.sjja.eu
Gen Sec: Robert G Ross
▲ Un-incorporated Society
Br 20; Spain, USA
○ *S; governing body for the sport in Scotland
Gp Ju Jitsu (un-armed combat); Ko-Ryu (traditional schoools of combat)
● Conf - Mtgs - ET - Exam - Res - Exhib - Comp - Inf - Lib - VE - LG
< Nippon Jujitsu & Kobudo Intl; Amer Self-Defence Assn; Hon Tai Yoshin Ryu; Scot Sports Coun; Sportscotland; Scot Sports Assn; Fedn of Scot School Sports Assn
M 800 i, 20 org, UK / 150 i, 3 org, o'seas
¶ Samuri NL - 6;   Scottish Jujitsu - 4; both ftm only.

© CBD Research Ltd · Beckenham · BR3 5JS · Tel 020 8650 7745 · Fax 020 8650 0768 · E-mail cbd@cbdresearch.com · www.cbdresearch.com

Scottish Justices Association (SJA) 2007
- ■ c/o 78 Cairnfield Place, ABERDEEN, AB15 5NA. (hsp)
  email secretary@scottishjustices.org
  http://www.scottishjustices.org
  Sec: Susan Kirkwood
- ▲ Un-incorporated Society
- ○ *N, *P; to assist Justices of the Peace in Scotland in performing their judicial duties
- ● Mtgs - LG
- < C'wealth Magistrates & Justices Assn
- M open to all JPs in Scotland
- ¶ The Scottish Justice - 2/4; ftm only.

Scottish Kennel Club (SKC) 1881
- NR Paterson House, Eskmills Park, Station Rd, MUSSELBURGH, E Lothian, EH21 7PQ. (hq)
  0131-665 3920   fax 0131-653 6937
  email info@scottishkennelclub.org
  http://www.scottishkennelclub.org
  Sec: Myra Orr
- ○ *B; to promote dogs, canine education & responsible dog ownership
- M i

Scottish Labour History Society (SLHS) 1961
- NR 18 Sackville Avenue, GLASGOW, G13 1NG. (sec/p)
  http://www.slhs.org.uk
  Sec: George Rawlinson
- ○ *G; study, discussion, publication & exhibition of the history of the Scottish, British & international labour & working class movements
- ● Conf - Exhib - SG
- M 200 i, 80 org, UK / 2 i, 20 org, o'seas
- ¶ Scottish Labour History - 1.

Scottish Ladies' Golfing Association (SLGA) 1904
- NR The Den, 2 Dundee Rd, PERTH, PH2 7DW. (hq)
  01738 442357   fax 01738 442380
  email secretary@slga.co.uk   http://www.slga.co.uk
  Sec: Dr Sheila Hartley
- ○ *S
- ● ET - Comp - Inf
- < Ladies' Golf U
- M 38,000 i, 420 org
- ¶ Ybk; £3.

Scottish Landowners Federation
since 2004 **Scottish Rural Property & Business Association**

Scottish Language Dictionaries (SLD) 2002
- ■ 27 George Sq, EDINBURGH, EH8 9LD. (hq)
  0131-650 4149   fax 0131-650 4149
  email mail@scotsdictionaries.org.uk
  http://www.scotsdictionaries.org.uk
  Dir: Dr Christine Robinson
- ▲ Company Limited by Guarantee; Registered Charity
- ○ *L, *Q; 'we research Scots language as it is spoken & used in writing, & use our results to update the nation's record of one of Scotland's indigenous languages; we also support the use of Scots in the community & promote it internationally as part of Scottish culture'
- ● Res - Inf
- M 135 i, 4 org, UK / 6 i, o'seas
- ¶ NL - 2.
  Compact Scottish National Dictionary (hardback) £157.50 m, £175 nm / (paper) £108 m, £120 nm.
  Concise Scots Dictionary (hardback) £22.50 m, £25 nm / (paper) £13.50 m, £14.99 nm.
  Scots Thesaurus (paper) £13.50 m, £14.99 nm.
  Pocket Scots Dictionary (paper); £5.40 m, £5.99 nm.
  Essential Scots Dictionary (paper); £7.20 m, £7.99 nm.
  Dictionary of the Scots Language (www.dsl.ac.uk); free.

Scottish Law Agents Society (SLAS) 1884
- ■ 166 Buchanan St, GLASGOW, G1 2LW. (sb)
  0141-332 3536   fax 0141-353 3819
  email secretary@slas.co.uk   http://www.slas.co.uk
  Sec: Michael Sheridan
- ▲ Un-incorporated Society
- ○ *P; for Scottish solicitors; central legal practice, legal policy & research
- Gp Conveyancing; Litigation; Legal aid; Legal education & training
- ● Conf - Mtgs - ET - Res - SG - Stat - Inf - Lib - VE - LG
- M 2,000 i, 30 org
  (Sub: £70 i, £40 org)
- ¶ The Scottish Law Gazette - 6ftm, £10 nm.
  Memorandum Book - 1; ftm, £5 nm.

Scottish Legal Action Group (Scolag) 1975
- NR 148 Muirdrum Ave, GLASGOW, G52 3AP. (admin)
  056 0072 7138   fax 056 0072 7138
  email admin@scolag.org   http://www.scolag.org
  Convenor: Robert Sutherland
- ▲ Company Limited by Guarantee; Registered Charity
- ○ *P; to explain the law; to promote the use of legal services (& changes in the law & legal system) so as to benefit disadvantaged members of society & promote equal access to justice
- ● Conf - LG
- M [not stated]
- ¶ SCOLAG (Jnl) - 12; £42 i, (£18 students, £68 business, £47 voluntary orgs).

Scottish Library Association
a division of **CILIP**

Scottish Licensed Trade Association (SLTA) 1880
- NR 10 Walker St, EDINBURGH, EH3 7LA. (hq)
  0131-225 5169   fax 0131-220 4057
  email theslta@aol.com   http://www.slta.info
  Sec: Colin Wilkinson
- ▲ Un-incorporated Society
- Br 7
- ○ *T; represents all sections of the licensed trade in Scotland
- ● Conf - Mtgs - ET - Exam - Exhib - Inf - LG
- < UK & Ireland Licensed Tr Assn
- M 3,000 i, 40 f
- ¶ Scottish Licensee (Jnl) - 4; free.

Scottish Local Authority Network of Physical Education (SLANOPE) 1974
- ■ Auchterderran Centre, Woodend Rd, CARDENDEN, Fife, KY5 0NE. (hsb)
  0845 155 5555 ext 442015   fax 01592 583175
  Hon Sec: David Maiden
- ○ *P; to facilitate physical education networking in local authority education departments in Scotland
- ● Conf - Mtgs - ET
- M 84 i, 31 local authorities, 9 associates

Scottish Local History Forum
- ■ c/o Dept of Scottish History, University of Edinburgh, 17 Buccleuch Place, EDINBURGH, EH8 9LN. (hsb)
  fax 0131-650 4042
  http://www.slhf.gcal.ac.uk
  Admin: Doris Williamson
- ○ *N; for Scottish local history societies & local historians

Scottish Massage Therapists Organisation Ltd   (SMTO)   1992
■   70 Lochside Rd, Bridge of Don, ABERDEEN, AB23 8QW.   (hsb)
01224 822960   fax 01224 822960
email smto@scotmass.co.uk
http://www.scotmass.co.uk
Chmn: Maggie Brooks-Carter,   Sec: Nicola Brooks
▲   Company Limited by Guarantee
○   *M, *P; for massage therapists, remedial & sports massage
therapists, advanced remedial massage therapists,
manipulative therapists, on-site massage therapists, clinical
aromatherapists & reflexologists in the UK, primarily in
Scotland
●   Conf - Mtgs - ET - Res - Exhib - Inf - Continuing professional
development for members
>   Black Isle Complementary Therapies; Scottish Massage Schools
Ltd; Western School of Massage
M   500 i, 5 org, UK / 5 i, o'seas
¶   On the Massage Scene - 3; ftm, £2.50 nm.
Directory of therapists.

Scottish Master Slaters & Roof Tilers Association   (SMSRTA)
NR   c/o Scottish Building Federation, Crichton House, 4
Crichton's Close - Holyrood, EDINBURGH, EH8 8DT.
0131-556 8866   fax 0131-558 5247
Sec: Ken Fish
○   *T
M   21 f

Scottish Master Wrights & Builders Association   (SMWBA) 1885
NR   Blairtummock Lodge, Campsie Glen, GLASGOW, G66 7AR.
(asa)
01360 770583
http://www.smwba.org.uk
Sec/Treas: David Milliken
○   *T
M   i

Scottish Medievalists: the Colloquium for Scottish Medieval & Renaissance Studies   1958
■   12 Brougham Place, EDINBURGH, EH3 9JX.   (hsp)
0131-229 1038
email mr-scotmed@anonymous.org.uk
Hon Sec: Mairi Robinson
▲   Scottish Charity
○   *L; to further the study of & promote interest in, Scottish history,
particularly the period before 1707
●   Conf - Res - Inf - SG
M   201 i, UK / 24 i, o'seas
(Sub: £5)

Scottish Microbiology Society
NR   Glasgow Dental School & Hospital, 378 Sauchiehall St,
GLASGOW, G2 3JZ.
0141-211 9752
email g.ramage@dental.gla.ac.uk
http://www.scottish-microbiology.org.uk
Sec: Dr Gordon Ramage
○   *L

Scottish Military Historical Society
the society was disbanded on 2 February 2008

Scottish Modern Pentathlon Association   (SPMA)   1990
■   Currie Gilmour & Co, 41-43 Warrender Park Rd, EDINBURGH,
EH9 1EU.   (dir p)
0177 164 4855
http://www.pentathlon-scotland.org
Dir/Admin: Rachel Caughey
▲   Company Limited by Guarantee
○   *S; the governing body in Scotland of the sport & the sports
pursuits which comprise the modern pentathlon; to provide
services to individuals, clubs & other bodies with an interest
in such sports
●   ET - Comp - Coaching
<   Modern Pentathlon Assn GB
M   i

Scottish Motor Neurone Disease Association   1981
■   76 Firhill Rd, GLASGOW, G20 7BA.   (hq)
0141-945 1077   fax 0141-945 2578
email info@scotmnd.co.uk   http://www.scotmnd.org.uk
Chief Exec: Craig Stockton
▲   Company Limited by Guarantee; Registered Charity
Br   4 (Scotland)
○   *W; to help the motor neurone disease patient live as full &
normal a life as possible
●   Conf - Mtgs - ET - Res - Inf - Lib - Care research - Equipment
loan service - Fundraising - Counselling service - Holiday
caravan - Small grants scheme
<   Intl Alliance of MND Assns
M   800 i
¶   Aware (NL) - 3; ftm.   AR; ftm.
Infofact (leaflets); free.
Publications list available.

Scottish Motor Racing Club Ltd   (SMRC)   1946
NR   Birch House, Duncrievie, by Glenfarg, PERTH, PH2 9PD.   (sp)
01577 830133
http://www.smrc-uk.com
Competition Sec: Chris Edwards
▲   Company Limited by Guarantee
○   *S; organisation of motor racing at Knockhill & Ingliston race
circuits
●   Mtgs - Comp
M   i

Scottish Motor Trade Association Ltd   (SMTA)   1903
■   Palmerston House, 10 The Loan, SOUTH QUEENSFERRY,
EH30 9NS.   (hq)
0131-331 5510   fax 0131-331 4296
email info@smta.co.uk   http://www.smta.co.uk
Chief Exec: Douglas Robertson
▲   Company Limited by Guarantee
○   *T
●   Conf - LG
M   i & f
¶   Monthly Bulletin;   AR & Accounts;   both ftm only.

Scottish Museums Federation   1932
NR   National Galleries of Scotland, The Mound, EDINBURGH,
EH2 2EL.
http://www.smf-online.org
Sec: Helen Smailes
○   *P; for all who manage & work in museums in local authorities,
universities, national & independent museums of Scotland
●   Mtgs

© CBD Research Ltd · Beckenham · BR3 5JS · Tel 020 8650 7745 · Fax 020 8650 0768 · E-mail cbd@cbdresearch.com · www.cbdresearch.com

Scottish Music Hall & Variety Theatre Society, incorporating the Sir Harry Lauder Society   (SMH&VTS)   1979
- ■ 69 Langmuirhead Rd, Auchinloch, KIRKINTILLOCH, G66 5DJ.   (hsp)
  0141-578 4108
  email bob.bain@ntlworld.com
  Hon Sec: Bob Bain
- ▲ Un-incorporated Society
- ○ *A; the Scottish variety theatre & music hall - past, present & future
- ● Exhib - VE - Staging shows
- M 260 i, UK / 16 i, o'seas
- ¶ Stagedoor - 4; ftm only.
- ✕ 2002-03 Scottish Music Hall Society

** Scottish Musical Instrument Retailers Association
   Organisation lost: see Introduction paragraph 3.

Scottish National Federation for the Welfare of the Blind   (SNFWB)   1917
- ■ Redroofs, Balgavies, by FORFAR, Angus, DD8 2TH.   (hsp)
  01307 830265   fax 01307 830265
  email secyj@snfwb.wanadoo.co.uk
  http://www.snfwb.org.uk
  Hon Sec: John Duncan
- ▲ Registered Charity
- ○ *W; to promote the education & social wellbeing of blind & partially sighted people throughout Scotland
- ● Conf - Mtgs - ET - Inf
- > most local authorities & volunteer organisations dealing with the visually impaired in Scotland
- M 52 org
- ¶ AR; free.

Scottish Neuroscience Group   (SNG)   1971
- NR Dept of Biology, St Andrews University, Bute Medical Building, Queens Terrace, ST ANDREWS, Fife, KY16 9TS.   (sb)
  01334 463503
  Sec & Treas: Prof Keith Sillar
- ○ *L, *P; incl neuroethology, electrophysiology, neuroanatomy, neurochemistry, pharmacology, muscle physiology

Scottish Newspaper Publishers Association   (SNPA)   1920
- ■ 48 Palmerston Place, EDINBURGH, EH12 5DE.   (hq)
  0131-220 4353   fax 0131-220 4344
  email info@snpa.org.uk   http://www.snpa.org.uk
  Dir: Jim Raeburn
- ▲ Un-incorporated Society
- ○ *T; representing the weekly newspaper industry in Scotland
- ● Conf - Mtgs - ET - Res - Empl - LG
- < Newspaper Soc
- M 26 f
- ¶ NL - 2; free.   LM (on Internet).   AR; free.

Scottish & Northern Ireland Plumbing Employers' Federation   (SNIPEF)   1923
- ■ 2 Walker St, EDINBURGH, EH3 7LB.   (hq)
  0131-225 2255
  http://www.snipef.org
  Dir & Sec: Robert D Burgon
- ▲ Company Limited by Guarantee
- ○ *T; the national trade association for all types of firms involved with the plumbing & domestic heating industry
- Gp Association of Installers of Unvented Hot Water Systems (Scotland & NI)
- ● Conf - Mtgs - ET - Exhib - Comp - Inf
- M 800 f
- ¶ Plumb Heat - 3.   SNIPEF Ybk.

Scottish Official Highland Dancing Association   (SOHDA)   1947
- NR 16 Renshaw Rd, BISHOPTON, Renfrewshire, PA7 5HN.   (sp)
  0779 300 5283
  email admin@sohda.org.uk   http://www.sohda.org.uk
  Sec: Kirsten Donaldson
- ○ *G, *P; for all interested in learning & teaching Highland dancing & keeping the dances alive

Scottish Optoelectronics Association   (SOA)   1994
- ■ Geddes House, Kirkton North, LIVINGSTON, W Lothian, EH54 6GU.   (hq)
  01506 497228
  email soa@optoelectronics.org.uk
  http://www.optoelectronics.org.uk
  Chief Exec: Chris Gracie
- ▲ Un-incorporated Society
- ○ *T; to represent the optoelectronics community in Scotland
- Gp Displays; Optical components / modules / systems; Measurement & instrumentation
- ● Mtgs - Exhib - Stat - Expt - Inf - VE - LG
- < Optoelectronics Ind Devt Assn (USA); Optoelectronics Ind & Technology Devt Assn (Japan); Photonics Ind Devt Assn (Taiwan); Singapore Photonics Assn; Optech net Deutschland; Korean Assn Photonics Ind Devt; Optoelectronics Inds Australia
- M 50 f, 30 university depts
- ¶ Membership Directory; on-line.   AR - 1; ftm only.

Scottish Organic Producers Association   (SOPA)   1988
- NR SFQC, Royal Highland Centre, 10th Avenue, Ingliston, EDINBURGH, EH28 8NF.   (hq)
  0131-335 6606   fax 0131-335 6601
  email info@sopa.org.uk   http://www.sopa.org.uk
  Chmn: John Hamilton
- ○ *T; strengthening the prosperity & sustainability of members' businesses by being the champion of the development of organic food & farming in Scotland
- ● Mtgs
- M c 450 i

Scottish Organisation for Practice Teaching   (ScOPT)   1999
- NR PO Box 21163, ALLOA, Clackmannanshire, FK10 9BD.   (mail/address)
  0845 643 4061
  email enquiries@scopt.co.uk   http://www.scopt.co.uk
  Admin: Tara Hamilton
- ○ *P; to promote practice learning and teaching in social work practice

Scottish Orienteering Association   (SOA)   1962
- NR 6 Newark Crescent, AYR, KA7 4HP.   (hsp)
  http://www.scottish-orienteering.org
  Hon Sec: Mel Perry
- ▲ Un-incorporated Society
- ○ *S; to promote & coordinate the sport of orienteering in Scotland
- ● Comp
- < Brit Orienteering Fedn; Intl Orienteering Fedn
- M 1,400 i, UK / 15 i, o'seas
- ¶ Score (NL) - 6.   AR.

Scottish Ornithologists' Club (SOC) 1936

- ■ Scottish Birdwatching Resource Centre, Waterston House, ABERLADY, W Lothian, EH32 0PY. (hq)
  01875 871330
  http://www.the-soc.org.uk
  Office Mgr: Wendy Hicks
- ▲ Registered Charity
- Br 14
- ○ *L; study of Scottish ornithology & protection of rare birds
- ● Conf - Mtgs - Res - SG - Lib
- M 2,800 i, 100 org, UK / 300 i, 50 org, o'seas
- ¶ Scottish Birds (Jnl).   Scottish Bird News.
  Scottish Bird Report.
  Scottish Raptor Monitoring Scheme Report.

Scottish Otolaryngological Society (SOS) 1910

- NR c/o David Simpson, Stobhill Hospital, Balornock Rd, GLASGOW, G21 3UZ. (hsb)
  0141-201 3161
  http://www.scottish-otolaryngological-society.scot.nhs.uk
  Hon Sec/Treas: David Simpson
- ▲ Registered Charity
- ○ *P; the study & advancement of otology, rhinology & laryngology & all allied branches of medical science by the continuing education of members & their trainees
- ● Conf - Mtgs - ET - Acting as an advisory body on otolaryngological matters to other organisations
- M 90 i

Scottish Parent Councils Association (SPCA) 1992

- ■ Newall Terrace, DUMFRIES, DG1 1LW. (hq)
  01387 260428   fax 01387 260428
  email info@scottishparents.com
  http://www.scottishparents.com
  Office Mgr: Jennifer Gallacher
- ▲ Company Limited by Guarantee; Registered Scottish Charity
- ○ *E; to promote & encourage partnership in education
- ● Conf - Mtgs - ET - Res - Exhib - Comp - SG - Inf - VE - LG
- × 2008 Scottish School Board Association

Scottish Pelagic Fishermen's Association (SPFA) 1932

- ■ 1 Frithside St, FRASERBURGH, Aberdeenshire, AB43 9AR. (hq)
  01346 510714   fax 01346 510714
  email spfa@btconnect.com
  Sec: Derek Duthie
- ▲ Company Limited by Guarantee
- Br 3
- ○ *T; to promote & protect the interests of owners of boats engaged in fishing for pelagic fish
- ● Mtgs - LG
- < Scot Fishermen's Fedn
- M 51 i
- ¶ NL - 4; ftm.   AR.

Scottish Pensions Association (SOAPA)

- NR 207 The Pleasance, EDINBURGH, EH8 9RU. (hq)
  0131-668 1001
- ○ *K, *W

Scottish Pétanque Association (SPA) 1985

- NR 208 Union Grove, ABERDEEN, AB10 6TP. (sp)
  0771 124 9616
  http://www.scottishpetanque.org
  Sec: Lynn Jenkins
- ○ *S; the governing body in Scotland for the playing of pétanque
- ● ET - Inf
- M c 300 i
- ¶ NL - 3; free.

Scottish Pharmaceutical Federation
  merged 2006 with the Scottish Pharmaceutical General Council, since 2007 **Community Pharmacy Scotland**

Scottish Pharmaceutical General Council
  since 2007 **Community Pharmacy Scotland**

Scottish Pipers Association (SPA) 1920

- ■ 69 Kirkland St, GLASGOW, G20 6SU. (pres/p)
  0141-946 2137
  Pres: Miss J E Campbell
- ▲ Un-incorporated Society
- ○ *D; 'the study & practice of the great Highland bagpipe'
- ● Mtgs - Comp - Recitals of bagpipe music - Ceilidhs
- M 120 i, UK / 20 i, o'seas

Scottish Piping Society of London (SPSL) 1932

- ■ 9 Queens Rd, CHESHAM, Bucks, HP5 3AE. (pres/p)
  email adam@scottishpipingsocietyoflondon.com
  http://www.scottishpipingsocietyoflondon.com
  Pres: Adam Sanderson
- ▲ Registered Charity
- ○ *G; to further interest in solo piping of the great Highland bagpipe
- ● Mtgs - ET - Comp
- M 250 i, 6 i, o'seas
- ¶ NL - 12; free.

Scottish Place-Name Society (SPNS) 1996

- NR c/o School of Scottish Studies, University of Edinburgh, 27 George Sq, EDINBURGH, EH8 9LD. (hsb)
  http://www.spns.org.uk
  Sec: Alison Drummond
- ▲ Registered Charity
- ○ *L; to advance & encourage research in & understanding of place-names & their essential contribution to the languages, history & culture of Scotland
- M i
- ¶ NL

Scottish Plant Owners Association (SPOA) 1950

- NR 302 St Vincent St, GLASGOW, G2 5RZ. (sb)
  0141-248 3434   fax 0141-221 1226
  email info@spoa.org.uk   http://www.spoa.org.uk
  Sec: Graham Bell
- ○ *T; for civil engineering, building & plant hire contractors
- ● Maintains a schedule of rates prepared from an annual survey of rates obtained in the market by members - Sponsors a form of agreement suitable for the transaction of plant hire
- M 260 f
- ¶ Schedule of Rates & Handbook - 1.

Scottish Plastering & Drylining Association
  in 2005-6 merged with the **Federation of Plastering & Drywall Contractors**

Scottish Poetry Library (SPL) 1984

- ■ 5 Crichtons Close, Canongate, EDINBURGH, EH8 8DT. (hq)
  0131-557 2876   fax 0131-557 8393
  email reception@spl.org.uk   http://www.spl.org.uk
  Dir: Dr Robyn Marsack
- ▲ Registered Charity
- Br 13
- ○ *A, *E; a reference & lending library (free to public) for Scottish & international poetry, mainly of the 20th century
- ● Lib - Events during the Edinburgh International Festival - Visits to schools & other orgs - Monthly workshops for practising poets
- < Scot Lib Inf Coun (SLIC)
- M 700 i, 100 schools, colleges & libraries, UK / 50 i, o'seas
- ¶ NL - 2; ftm, (donation) nm.
  Scottish Poetry Index (ongoing series indexing poetry magazines) - irreg.

© CBD Research Ltd · Beckenham · BR3 5JS · Tel 020 8650 7745 · Fax 020 8650 0768 · E-mail cbd@cbdresearch.com · www.cbdresearch.com

Scottish Police Federation   (SPF)   1919
NR 5 Woodside Place, GLASGOW, G3 7QF.   (hq)
      0141-332 5234   fax 0141-331 2436
      http://www.spf.org.uk
      Gen Sec: Calum Steele
Br 8
○   *P; staff association, covering constable to chief inspector
M 16,000 i

Scottish Potato Trades Association
      in 2006 merged with the National Association of Seed Potato
      Merchants to form the **British Potato Trades Association**

Scottish Potters' Association   (SPA)
NR 4 Springfield Terrace, ARBROATH, Angus, DD11 1EL.
      (chmn/p)
      01241 439714
      email chairman@scottishpotters.org
      http://www.scottishpotters.org
      Chmn: Fran Marquis-Faulkes
▲ Un-incorporated Society
○   *G, *P; the promotion of Scottish potters & ceramics; open to
      professional & amateur potters
● Mtgs - Exhib - VE - Workshops
M 60 i
¶   NL - 4; ftm.

Scottish Prayer Book Society   (SPBS)
■ 32 Compton Avenue, GLASGOW, G44 5TH.   (hsp)
      http://www.scottish-prayer-book.co.uk
      Hon Sec: Mrs Paula R Fleetwood
▲ Registered Charity
○   *G, *K, *R; to keep in print & promote the use of the 1929
      Scottish Prayer Book, one of the official service books of the
      Scottish Episcopal Church
● Mtgs
< Prayer Book Soc
M 175 i
¶   Scottish NL - 4.

Scottish Pre-School Play Association   (SPPA)   1967
NR 21 Granville St, GLASGOW, G3 7EE.   (hq)
      0141-221 4148   fax 0141-221 6043
      email info@sppa.org.uk   http://www.sppa.org.uk
      Chief Exec: Ian McLaughlan
▲ Company Limited by Guarantee; Registered Charity
Br 5
○   *W; to promote the development of quality care & education in
      pre-school groups which respect the rights, responsibilities &
      needs of all children & their parents
Gp Information & advice; Insurance; Grants; Training; Field staff;
      Publications
● Conf - Mtgs - ET - Res - Comp - Inf - Empl - LG
< Pre-school assns of England, Wales, Nthn Ireland & Ireland;
      Pre-School Learning Alliance
M 15 i, 26 f, 1,400 member gps
¶   First Five - 4; ftm.
      Learning & Development: an introduction to childcare in an
      early years setting; £38 m, £58 nm.
      Publications list available.

Scottish Print Employers Federation   (SPEF)   1910
NR 48 Palmerston Place, EDINBURGH, EH12 5DE.   (hq)
      0131-220 4353   fax 0131-220 4344
      email info@spef.org.uk   http://www.spef.org.uk
      Dir: Jim Raeburn
▲ Un-incorporated Society
Br 4
○   *T
Gp Printing; Binding; Ancillary
● Conf - Mtgs - ET - Inf - Lib - Empl - LG - Legal advisory service
< Intergraf
M 100 f
¶   NL - 2;   Directory (on internet);   AR; all free.

Scottish Public Relations Consultants Association
      a regional group of the **Public Relations Consultants Association**

Scottish Publishers Association
      since 2007 **Publishing Scotland**

Scottish Pure Water Association
      July 2008 'Organisation is currently suspended. The issue (to
      use the public water supply for mass medication) is off the
      agenda of the Scottish Government'

Scottish Quality Salmon
      since 2006 the **Scottish Salmon Producers' Organisation**

Scottish Rafting Association   (SRA)
NR The Coachyard, Chapel St, Aberfeldy, Perthshire, PH15 2AS.
      01887 829292
      http://www.scottish-rafting-association.org.uk
      Chmn: Alistair Leitch
○   *S

Scottish Railway Preservation Society   (SRPS)   1961
■ Bo'ness Station, Union St, BO'NESS, W Lothian, EH51 9AQ.
      (hq)
      01506 825855   fax 01506 828766
      http://www.srps.org.uk
      Hon Sec: Iain Gent
▲ Company Limited by Guarantee; Registered Charity
○   *G; 'to obtain, restore, display & run a working railway; to
      preserve all aspects of Scottish railway history'
      The railway operates under title of Bo'ness & Kinnel Railway
● Mtgs - Exhib - SG - Operating the railway
< Heritage Rly Assn
M 1,200 i
¶   Blastpipe - 4; ftm.

Scottish Record Industry Association   (SRIA)   1988
NR c/o Alexander Sloan, 1 Atholl Place, EDINBURGH, EH3 8HP.
      (hq)
      0131-228 7979
○   *T; for all business people working within the music industry in
      Scotland; to keep local industry aware of national &
      international changes
M f

** Scottish Record Society

Scottish Records Association   (SRA)   1977
NR Royal College of Physicians & Surgeons, 232-242 St Vincent St,
      GLASGOW, G2 5RJ.   (hsb)
      0141-227 3234   fax 0141-221 1804
      email carol.parry@rcpsglasg.ac.uk
      http://www.scottishrecordsassociation.org
      Sec: Mrs Carol Parry
▲ Registered Charity
○   *L; the preservation & use of historical records in Scotland
● Conf - Inf - VE
< Scot Coun on Archives; Nat Coun on Archives
M 276 i, 67 org, UK / 8 i, 11 org, o'seas
¶   Scottish Archives (Jnl) - 1; ftm, £25 nm.   NL - 2.

Scottish Reformation Society   (SRS)   1851
NR   The Magdalen Chapel, 41 Cowgate, EDINBURGH, EH1 1JR.
  (hq)
    0131-220 1450   fax 0131-220 1450
    email ashbethany35@hotmail.com
    http://www.magdalenchapel.org
    Sec & Lecturer: Rev A Sinclair Horne
▲   Registered Charity
Br   2
○   *R; 'to promote a witness to the Reformation in its history,
    theology & principles'
●   Mtgs - ET - Res - SG - Inf - VE - Reformation tours
<   Utd Protestant Coun
M   400 i, UK / 40 i, o'seas
¶   The Bulwark - 4.

Scottish Renewables Forum   (SRF)   1996
NR   49 Bath St (3rd floor), GLASGOW, G2 2DL.   (hq)
    0141-353 4980   fax 0141-353 4989
    email info@scottishrenewables.com
    http://www.scottishrenewables.com
    Chief Exec: Jason Ormiston
▲   Company Limited by Guarantee
○   *T; renewable enery
●   Conf - Mtgs - Exhib - LG
<   Brit Hydropower Assn; Brit Wind Energy Assn
>   Renewable Energy Gp(s): Aberdeen, Highland, Orkney,
    Shetland; Hebridean Renewable Energy Partnership
M   14 i, 252 f

Scottish Retail Consortium   (SRC)   1999
NR   PO Box 13737, GULLANE, E Lothian, EH31 2WX.
    0870 609 3631   fax 0870 609 3631
    http://www.brc.org.uk/srcdefaultnew.asp
    Chmn: Ken Mackenzie
○   *T
M   f

Scottish Rifle Association   (SRA)   1886
NR   164 Ledi Drive, Bearsden, GLASGOW, G61 4JX.   (hsp)
    0141-942 2390
    email mabooonscotland@ntlworld.com
    http://www.scottishrifleassociation.org.uk
    Hon Sec: Allan Mabon
▲   Registered Charity; Un-incorporated Society
○   *S; the governing body for full-bore target rifle shooting in
    Scotland
●   Comp
<   Nat Rifle Assn; Scot Target Shooting Fedn
M   180 i, 20 org

Scottish Rights of Way & Access Society   (ScotWays)   1845
■   24 Annandale St, EDINBURGH, EH7 4AN.   (hq)
    0131-558 1222   fax 0131-558 1222
    email info@scotways.com   http://www.scotways.com
    Sec: Judith Lewis
▲   Company Limited by Guarantee; Registered Charity
○   *G, *K; protection of public rights of way & outdoor access
    rights in Scotland
Gp   Legal; Fund-raising; Publicity; Projects; Walks
●   Res - Stat - Inf - VE - LG - Maintain National Catalogue of
    Rughts of Way - Heritage Paths Project
M   2,105 i, 463 org
¶   NL - 2;   AR - 1; both free.
    Access Rights & Rights of Way: a guide to the law in
    Scotland; £7.50, £10 nm.
    Rights of Way: the authority of case law; £5.
    Scottish Hill Tracks, revised 4th ed (2004); £12 m, £16 nm.

Scottish Rock Garden Club   (SRGC)   1933
■   PO Box 14063, EDINBURGH, EH10 4YE.   (mail address)
    http://www.srgc.org.uk
    Sec: L Mills
▲   Registered Charity
Br   affiliated groups
○   *H; to promote the cultivation of alpine & peat garden plants
●   Conf - Mtgs - Exhib - Comp - SG - Inf - Lib - PL - VE
<   Amer Rock Garden Soc; Caledonian Horticl Soc; R Horticl Soc;
    Nthn Horticl Soc; Alpine Garden Soc
M   4,500 i, UK / in 38 countries o'seas
¶   The Rock Garden (Jnl) - 2;   Secretary's Page - 2;   Ybk - 1;
    all ftm only.

Scottish Rugby Union plc   (SRU)   1873
NR   Murrayfield, EDINBURGH, EH12 5PJ.   (hq)
    0131-346 5000   fax 0131-346 5001
    http://www.scottishrugby.org
    Sec: Graham Ireland
○   *S; administration of Rugby in Scotland; the development of the
    game at all levels in schools, clubs, district, national &
    international
M   i & clubs
¶   SRU Hbk - 1.   SRU Laws Book - 1.

Scottish Rural Property & Business Association   (SRPBA)   1906
■   Stuart House, Eskmills, MUSSELBURGH, E Lothian,
    EH21 7PB.   (hq)
    0131-653 5400   fax 0131-653 5401
    http://www.srpba.com
▲   Company Limited by Guarantee
Br   5
○   *F; 'working for: high standards of land management; the
    owners of rural land in Scotland; the rural economy & those
    who depend upon it'
●   Conf - Mtgs - Inf - VE - LG
<   Eur Landowners Org (ELO)
M   2,600 i, 200 f
¶   Land Business - 6; ftm only.
    Ybk.   NL.
×   2004 Scottish Landowners Federation

Scottish Salmon Producers' Organisation   (SSPO)
NR   Durn, Isla Rd, PERTH, PH2 7HG.   (hq)
    01738 587000   fax 01738 621454
    email enquiries@scottishsalmon.co.uk
    http://www.scottishsalmon.co.uk
    Chief Exec: Scott Landsburgh
○   *T; salmon farming
Gp   Salmon Processors & Smokers Group
M   f
×   2006 Scottish Quality Salmon

Scottish Salmon Smokers Association
    Organisation closed c 2008

Scottish School Board Association
    since 2008 **Scottish Parent Councils Association**

Scottish Schoolsport Federation   (SSF)   1988
■   5 Mount Rich Place, DINGWALL, Ross-shire, IV15 9RU.   (hsp)
    01349 867924
    email alan.clark@highland.gov.uk
    http://www.scottishschoolsportfederation.org
    Sec: Alan Clark
○   *N, *S; concerned with school sports, extra-curricular activities
    & international school sport Federation (ISF) events
Gp   Education; Schools organisations; Sports organisations
●   Conf - Mtgs - Comp - LG
<   Scot Sports Assn
M   14 assns, 18 local authorities
    (Sub: £50)

© CBD Research Ltd · Beckenham · BR3 5JS · Tel 020 8650 7745 · Fax 020 8650 0768 · E-mail cbd@cbdresearch.com · www.cbdresearch.com

Scottish Seafood Processors Federation Ltd   1986
NR   South Esplanade West, ABERDEEN, AB11 9FJ.   (hq)
        01224 897744
        http://www.scottishseafoodprocessors.org
▲   Company Limited by Guarantee
Br   7
○   *T
●   Mtgs - ET - LG
M   180 f
¶   Ybk & Diary.

Scottish Secondary Teachers' Association   (SSTA)   1946
■   14 West End Place, EDINBURGH, EH11 2ED.   (hq)
        0131-313 7300   fax 0131-346 8057
        email info@ssta.org.uk   http://www.ssta.org.uk
        Gen Sec: David Eaglesham
Br   32
○   *E, *U
●   Conf - Mtgs - ET - Res - SG - Inf - Empl - LG
<   Education Intl (EI); Eur Tr U C'ee for Education (ETUCE); Scot Tr
        U Congress
M   9,500 i
¶   NL - 4/5;   Bulletin - 5/6.

Scottish Security Association   (SSA)   1996
NR   PO Box 308, GLASGOW, G44 4BH.   (mail address)
        01236 738739
        http://www.scottishsecurityassociation.co.uk
        Sec: William Watson
▲   Un-incorporated Society
○   *P; to develop & foster members engaged in all aspects of
        security & safety
●   Conf - Mtgs - Exhib - Comp - Lib - VE - LG - Social events
M   50 i (Scotland)
¶   LM - 1; ftm only.

Scottish Seed & Nursery Trade Association   (SSNTA)   1917
■   18 Tulloch Terrace, PERTH, PH1 2PG.
        01738 564733
        Sec: Donna McNicol
▲   Un-incorporated Society
○   *T; for all those involved in the Scottish seed trade (agricultural,
        horticultural, wholesale, retail, nursery traders & landscape
        contractors)
●   Mtgs - VE
<   Attends mtgs of Agricl Industries Fedn (AIF) & UK Plant Varieties
        & Seeds Advisory Body (UKSAB)
M   f

Scottish Ship Chandlers Association   (SSCA)   1955
■   McColl & Associates Ltd, 11 Burns Rd, ABERDEEN,
        AB15 4NT.   (sb)
        01224 313473   fax 01224 310385
        email roddy@mccollassociates.com
        Secs: McColl & Associates Ltd
○   *T; trade protection
●   Mtgs
M   14 f

Scottish Ski Club   (SSC)   1907
■   44 Broomvale Drive, GLASGOW, G77 5NW.   (hsp)
        email secretay@scotski.org.uk   http://www.scotski.org.uk
        Hon Sec: Alan Forbes
▲   Un-incorporated Society
○   *S; promotion of skiing; support for competitive ski racing
Gp   Alpine; Racing; Touring
●   Mtgs - ET - Comp - Inf - Lib - VE
<   Snowsport GB; Snowsport Scotland
M   1,100 i, UK / 50 i, o'seas
        (Sub: £33)
¶   Jnl - 1;   NL - 4; both ftm only.

Scottish Society for Autism   1968
NR   Hilton House, Alloa Business Park, Whins Rd, ALLOA,
        Clackmannanshire, FK10 3SA.   (hq)
        01259 720044   fax 01259 720051
        email autism@autism-in-scotland.org.uk
        http://www.autism-in-scotland.org.uk
        Chief Exec: John McDonald
▲   Registered Charity
○   *W; to provide care, support & education for peoples of all
        ages with autism throughout Scotland
●   Conf - Mtgs - ET - Inf - Lib - Residential school for children -
        Respite care & family support - Adult accommodation &
        community houses
M   662 i, 37 schools & housing org
¶   In Touch (Jnl) - 2; ftm, £3 nm.
        Jigsaw (NL) - 3;   AR - 1; both free.

Scottish Society for Conservation & Restoration
        in 2005 merged with the Care of Collections Forum, Institute of Paper
        Conservation, Photographic Materials Conservation Group, United
        Kingdom Institute for Conservation of Historic & Artistic Works to form
        the **Institute of Conservation**

Scottish Society for Contamination Control   (S2C2)   1986
NR   Suite 20 Atrium Business Centre, North Caldeen Rd,
        COATBRIDGE, Lanarks, ML5 4EF.
        0844 800 7809   fax 0844 800 7810
        email admin@s2c2.co.uk   http://www.s2c2.co.uk
▲   Registered Charity
○   *K; to advance the education of the public in matters relating to
        the practice & science of contamination control as applicable
        to a wide range of industries - cleanroom design, classroom
        suppliers, pharmaceutivcal & medical devices, biotechnology,
        hospitals etc
M   c 1,000 i

Scottish Society for Crop Research   (SSCR)   1981
NR   c/o Scottish Crop Research Institute, Invergowrie, DUNDEE,
        DD2 5DA.   (hq)
        01382 562731
        email bill.macfarlane.smith@scri.ac.uk
        http://www.sscr.scri.ac.uk
        Hon Sec: Dr Bill Macfarlane Smith
○   *F, *Q; crop research & plant breeding
Gp   Combinable crops; Potatoes; Soft fruit

Scottish Society of the History of Medicine   (SSHM)   1948
NR   1 Exchange Crescent, Conference Square, EDINBURGH,
        EH3 8UL.   (regd/office)
        http://www.st-andrews.ac.uk/~sshm/
▲   Registered Charity
○   *L; to further the general history of medicine, with special
        reference to Scottish medicine

Scottish Society for the History of Photography   (SSHoP)
NR   Boyd Orr Building (room 415), University of Glasgow,
        GLASGOW, G12 8QQ.
        http://www.sshop.arts.gla.ac.uk

Scottish Society for Northern Studies   (SSNS)   1968
NR   Celtic & Scottish Studies, University of Edinburgh,
        27 George Sq, EDINBURGH, EH8 9LD.   (hq)
        http://www.northernstudies.org.uk
○   *L; the study the inter-relationships between the Scandinavian,
        Celtic & Scottish cultures
M   i & org
¶   Northern Studies (Jnl) - 1.

Scottish Society of Playwrights (SSP) 1973

NR 10 Torphichen Place, Haymarket, EDINBURGH, EH3 0DU.
   http://www.scottishsocietyofplaywrights.co.uk
   Sec: Clare Duffy
○ *A; to develop & promote the interests & craft of professional
   playwrights & playwriting within Scottish theatre & also
   abroad

Scottish Society for the Prevention of Cruelty to Animals (ScottishSPCA) 1839

■ Braehead Mains, 603 Queensferry Rd, EDINBURGH,
   EH4 6EA. (hq)
   0300 099 9999   fax 0131-339 4777
   email enquiries@scottishspca.org
   http://www.scottishspca.org
   Chief Exec: Stuart Earley
▲ Company Limited by Guarantee; Registered Charity
Br 12
○ *K, *V; to prevent cruelty to animals & to promote kindness in
   their treatment
● ET - Inf - PL - Inspectors investigate complaints of cruelty -
   Animal welfare & re-homing centres - Education officers give
   talks to schools
< Wld Soc for the Protection of Animals
M 33,150 i
   (Sub: £36)
¶ Friends Magazine - 2;   Information leaflets;   AR - 1.

Scottish Society for the Protection of Wild Birds 1927

NR Scottish Natural History Library, Foremount House,
   KILBARCHAN, Renfrewshire, PA10 2EZ.
   01505 702419
   Sec: Dr J A Gibson
○ *K, *L
   no further information supplied

Scottish Society for Psychical Research (SSPR) 1987

■ 5 Church Wynd, Kingskettle, by CUPAR, Fife, KY15 7PS.   (vp/p)
   01337 830387   fax 01337 830387
   email archie.lawrie@ukgateway.net
   http://www.sspr.co.uk
   Vice Pres: Archie Lawrie
▲ Registered Charity
○ *Q; investigating the paranormal in Scotland
Gp Investigation; Historical research
● Mtgs - Res - SG - Inf - Library including audio & video tapes
M 225 i, UK / 5 i, o'seas
¶ Psi Report - 9; ftm, £1 nm.

Scottish Society of Rehabilitation

   has been disbanded

Scottish Solar Energy Group (SSEG) 1980

NR Sch of the Built & Natural Environment, Glasgow Caledonian
   University, Cowcaddens Rd, GLASGOW, G4 0BA. (treas/b)
   0141-331 3897
   email s.burek@gcal.ac.uk   http://www.sseg.org.uk
   Treas: Dr Stas Burek
○ *P; to encourage the use of solar energy in Scotland
● Conf - Mtgs - VE - Seminars
M i
¶ NL - 1.
   Published papers.

Scottish Spina Bifida Association (SSBA) 1964

NR The Dan Young Building, 6 Craighalbert Way, CUMBERNAULD,
   G68 0LS.   (hq)
   01236 794500   fax 01236 736435
   email mail@ssba.org.uk   http://www.ssba.org.uk
   Chief Exec: Andrew H D Wynd
▲ Company Limited by Guarantee; Registered Charity
Br 5
○ *W; to increase public awareness & understanding of
   individuals with spina bifida, hydrocephalus & related
   disorders; to aim to secure provision for their special needs &
   those of their families
Gp Spina bifida; Hydrocephalus
● Mtgs - ET - Res - Exhib - SG - Inf - VE - Empl - LG
   Family support services: 0845 911 1112
< Intl Fedn for Spina Bifida & Hydrocephalus; Assn for Spina
   Bifida & Hydrocephalus
M 3,800 i, 20 f, 10 org, UK / 20 i, o'seas
¶ talkBACK - 4; ftm, on request nm.
   Publications list available.

Scottish Sporting Car Club (SSCC) 1932

NR 18 Ayr Road, Giffnock, GLASGOW, G46 6RY.   (sp)
   http://www.scottishsportingcarclub.org.uk
   Company Limited by Guarantee
   Sec: Charles Turner
○ *S; organisation of motor sport events
M i

Scottish Sports Association (SSA) 1983

■ Caledonia House, South Gyle, EDINBURGH, EH12 9DQ.   (hq)
   0131-339 8785
   email mail@info-ssa.org.uk
   http://www.scottishsportsassociation.org.uk
   Policy Director: Chris Robison
▲ Company Limited by Guarantee
○ *N, *S; to promote cooperation among governing bodies &
   organisations of sport in Scotland in consultation with (& as
   an independent consultative body to) Sportscotland
● Conf - Mtgs - Res - Inf - LG
M c 52 org
¶ Bulletin - 12; ftm.

Scottish Sports Horse

NR Bickramside Farm, Oakley, DUNFERMLINE, Fife, KY12 9LF.
   (admin/p)
   0870 770 8880
   http://www.scottishsportshorse.org
   Contact: Jackie Aird
○ *B; to promote the breeding of the very best sport horses and
   ponies for the Olympic disciplines of dressage, showjumping
   and eventing

Scottish Squash Ltd 1937

NR Caledonia House, 1 Redheughs Rigg, South Gyle,
   EDINBURGH, EH12 9DQ. (hq)
   0131-317 7343   fax 0131-317 7734
   email info@scottishsquash.org
   http://www.scottishsquash.org
   Chief Operating Officer: Kim Atkinson
▲ Company Limited by Guarantee
○ *S; the national governing body for the sport of squash in
   Scotland
< Wld Squash Fedn (WSF); Eur Squash Fedn (ESF); Scot Sports
   Assn (SSA)
M i & clubs

© CBD Research Ltd · Beckenham · BR3 5JS · Tel 020 8650 7745 · Fax 020 8650 0768 · E-mail cbd@cbdresearch.com · www.cbdresearch.com

Scottish Stone Liaison Group (SSLG)
- ■ 16 Rocks Rd, CHARLESTOWN, Fife, KY11 3EN. (hq)
  01383 872006
  email jane.milroy@sslg.co.uk   http://www.sslg.co.uk
  Chief Exec: Colin Tennant,   Admin: Jane Milroy
- ▲ Registered Charity
- ○ *G, *K; to advance the education of the public about the stone built heritage of Scotland; to assist in production of guidance on use of stone for specifiers
- ● Conf - Mtgs - ET - Res - SG - Inf - LG
- M 31 i, 15 f, 11 associates
- ¶ NL; free.

Scottish Sub Aqua Club (ScotSAC) 1953
- NR The Cockburn Centre, 40 Bogmoor Place, GLASGOW, G51 4TQ. (hq)
  0141-425 1021   fax 0141-425 1021
  email hq@scotsac.com   http://www.scotsac.com
  Admin: Hazel McBride & Sharon McKenzie
- ▲ Un-incorporated Society
- Br 70+; Eire
- ○ *S; governing body for sub-aqua diving in Scotland
- Gp Boat handling (rigid inflatable boats)
- ● Conf - Mtgs - ET - Exam - Comp - Lib
- < Scot Sports Coun
- M c 2,000 i
- ¶ Scottish Diver - 6; ftm, £2.50 nm.

Scottish Support for Learning Association (SSLA)
- ■ 11 Mayshade Rd, LOANHEAD, Midlothian, EH20 9HJ. (hsp/p)
  email info@ssla.org.uk   http://www.ssla.org.uk
  Sec: Sheena Richardson
- ▲ Registered Charity
- ○ *P; to support professionals working with children & young people
- ● Conf - Mtgs - ET - Inf - LG
- < Ir Support for Learning Assn (ISLA); Scot Dyslexia Assn; Afasic Scotland; Enquire
- M c 200 i, c 16 f, 4 org

Scottish Surfing Federation (SSF) 1976
- NR c/o MowaT, Achlibster, WESTERDALE, Caithness, KW12 6UP. (chmn/b)
  01847 841300
  http://www.scottishsurfingfederation.com
  Chmn: Andy Bain
- ○ *S; promotion of surfing in Scotland

Scottish Swimming Ltd (SASA) 1888
- NR National Swimming Academy, University of Stirling, STIRLING, FK9 4LA. (hq)
  01786 466520   fax 01786 466521
  email info@scottishswimming.com
  http://www.scottishswimming.com
  Chief Exec: Ashley Howard
- ▲ Company Limited by Guarantee
- Br 4
- ○ *S; governing body for swimming, masters, diving, water polo, open water & synchronised swimming in Scotland
- Gp Swimming, Diving, Open water, Masters, Disability, Synchronised
- ● Mtgs - ET - Exam - Comp - Inf
- < Fédn Intle de Natation Amateur (FINA); League Eur de Natation (LEN); C'wealth Games Coun for Scotland (CGCS); Amat Swimming Fedn of GB (ASFGB); Sportscotland; Scot Sports Coun (SSC)
- M 160 clubs
- ¶ Bank of Scotland Learn to Swim Syllabus; £29.99.
  Bank of Scotland Learn to Swim (Adult & Child Syllabus); £35.
  National Swimming Award Pack; £10 m.
  Note: Scottish Swimming is the trading name of the Scottish Amateur Swimming Association Ltd

Scottish Table Tennis Association (STTA) 1935
- NR Caledonia House, South Gyle, EDINBURGH, EH12 9DQ. (hq)
  0131-317 8077   fax 0131-317 8224
  email graham@ttscotland.com
  http://www.ttscotland.com
  Admin: Graham Stuart
- ▲ Un-incorporated Society
- ○ *S; governing body for table tennis in Scotland
- Gp Veterans
- ● ET - Comp - Stat - Inf
- < Intl Table Tennis Fedn; Eur Table Tennis U; C'wealth Table Tennis Fedn
- M 1,500 i
- ¶ The Bulletin - 5/6.
  Note: trades as Table Tennis Scotland.

Scottish Target Shooting Federation 1886
- NR 77 Malbet Park, Liberton, EDINBURGH, EH16 6WB. (hsp)
  0131-664 9674
  http://www.stfs.org.uk
  Hon Sec: Colin R Aitken
- ○ *S
- M 4 org
  No further information supplied

Scottish Tenants Organisation (STO)
- NR Claymore House (suite 633), 145 Kilmarnock Rd, Shawlands, GLASGOW, G41 3JA. (hq)
  0787 671 8111
  email contact@scottishtenants.org.uk
  http://www.scottishtenants.org.uk
- ○ *K, *W; campaigns for the rights of tenants
- M c 100 org

Scottish Text Society (STS) 1882
- ■ School of English, University of Nottingham, University Park, NOTTINGHAM, NG7 2RD. (editorial/sb)
  0115-957 5922
  email editorialsecretary@scottishtextsociety.org
  http://www.scottishtextsociety.org
  Editorial Sec: Dr Nicola R Royan
- ▲ Registered Charity
- ○ *L; to further the study & teaching of Scottish literature by publishing editions of original texts (mediaeval period to the 18th century)
- ● AGM
- M 45 i, 52 f, UK / 17 i, 120 f, o'seas
- ¶ Annual volume; ftm, £30 nm.   AR; ftm only.

Scottish Timber Trade Association (STTA) 1910
- NR Office 14 John Player Building, Stirling Enterprise Park, Springbank Rd, STIRLING, FK7 7RP. (asa)
  01786 451623   fax 01786 473112
  email mail@stta.org.uk   http://www.stta.org.uk
  Sec: David Sulman
- ○ *T
- M f
  Note: is a regional association of the Timber Trade Federation.

Scottish Tourism Forum (3TF) 1994
- ■ 29 Drumsheugh Gardens, EDINBURGH, EH3 7RN. (hq)
  0131-220 6321   fax 0131-220 5905
  email mail@stforum.co.uk   http://www.stforum.co.uk
  Chief Exec: Iain Herbert
- ▲ Company Limited by Guarantee
- ○ *N; to represent tourism industry interests with government & public agencies
- ● Conf - Mtgs - Res - LG
- M 165 f
- ¶ News Digest - 52;   NL - 4;   AR - 1; all ftm only.
  LM - on website; free.

Scottish Tourist Guides Association   (STGA)   1960
■   Norrie's House, 18b Broad St, STIRLING, FK8 1EF.   (hq)
    01786 447784   fax 01786 451953
    email info@stga.co.uk   http://www.stga.co.uk
    Chmn: Toni McPherson
▲   Company Limited by Guarantee
○   *P; for tourist guides in Scotland
Gp   Blue Badge members; Regional affiliates; Site affiliates
●   Conf - ET - Exhib - SG - Inf - VE - Tourist guide accreditation
<   Wld Fedn Tourist Guide Assns; Eur Fedn of Tourist Guides
>   Scot Tourism Forum
M   475 i
¶   Guidelines - 12;   Guide List (guide directory) - 1.

Scottish Trades Union Congress   (STUC)   1897
NR   333 Woodlands Rd, GLASGOW, G3 6NG.   (hq)
    0141-337 8100
    email info@stuc.org.uk
    Gen Sec: Grahame Smith
○   *U
●   Conf
M   c 700,000 i
¶   AR.   LM.   Agenda.

Scottish Tramway & Transport Society   (STTS)   1951
NR   PO Box 7342, GLASGOW, G51 4YQ.   (mail/address)
    email stts.glasgow@virgin.net
    http://www.stts-glasgow.co.uk
    Gen Sec: Hugh McAulay
▲   Registered Charity
○   *G; recording of history of the development of public transport
    in Scotland, especially trams, trolleybuses & buses; to support
    preservation schemes
●   Mtgs - Res - Exhib - VE
<   Tramway Museum Soc
M   165 i, UK / 20 i, o'seas
¶   Scottish Transport - 1; £3.95.
    Occasional publications and videos.

Scottish Transport Studies Group   (STSG)   1984
■   26 Palmerston Place, EDINBURGH, EH12 5AL.   (chmn/b)
    0870 350 4202   fax 0871 250 4200
    email admin@stsg.org   http://www.stsg.org
    Chmn: Gordon Hill
▲   Registered Charity
○   *G, *L, *N; to stimulate interest in, & awareness of, the
    transport function & its importance for the Scottish economy
    & society
Gp   Publication
●   Conf - Mtgs - Res - SG - Stat - Inf
M   80 i, 20 f, 10 org
    (Sub: £30 i, £60-£500 org)
¶   Scottish Transport Review - 4; ftm £30 nm.
    Occasional Papers - irreg; ,ftm, £30 nm.

Scottish Tug of War Association   (STOWA)   1981
NR   47 Finlay Avenue, EAST CALDER, W Lothian, EH53 0RP.   (hsp)
    01506 881650
    http://www.scottish-tug-of-war.co.uk
    Sec: Gary Gillespie
○   *S

Scottish Vernacular Buildings Working Group   (SVBWG)
NR   c/o D Kidd, National Museums of Scotland, Chambers St,
    EDINBURGH, EH1 1JF.
    http://www.svbwg.org.uk
    Treas: D Kidd
○   *G; for all interested in the smaller traditional buildings of
    Scotland

Scottish Vintage Vehicle Federation   (SVVF)   1973
■   4 Plockton Terrace, DUNDEE, DD2 4TS.   (hsp)
    01382 643083
    http://www.svvf.org.uk
    Sec: John Hyman
○   *N
M   100 orgs representing 6,700 individuals

Scottish Volleyball Association   (SVA)   1963
NR   48 The Pleasance, EDINBURGH, EH8 9TJ.   (hq)
    0131-556 4633   fax 0131-557 4314
    http://www.scottishvolleyball.org
    Chief Exec: Margaret Ann Fleming
○   *S; to promote, develop & control volleyball in Scotland
M   i, schools & clubs

Scottish White Fish Producers' Association Ltd   (SWFPA)   1944
NR   c/o MacRae Stephen & Co, 40 Broad St, FRASERBURGH,
    Aberdeenshire, AB43 9AH.   (asa)
    01346 514545
    http://www.fishnewseu.com
    Sec: George A MacRae
▲   Company Limited by Guarantee
○   *T; represents the trade & political interests of members, locally,
    nationally & internationally
<   Scot Fishermen's Fedn

Scottish Wholesale Association   (SWA)   1940
NR   30 McDonald Place, EDINBURGH, EH7 4NH.   (hq)
    0131-556 8753   fax 0131-558 1623
    email info@scottishwholesale.co.uk
    http://www.scottishwholesale.co.uk
    Exec Dir: Kate Salmon
○   *T; food, grocery & drink wholesale industry in Scotland
Gp   Committee for Licensed Active Negotiations (CLAN); Scottish
    Trade Activity Group (STAG); Scottish Wholesale Association
    Security (SAS)
●   Conf - Mtgs - ET - LG
<   Fedn Whls Distbrs; Scot Grocers' Fedn; Scot Licensed Tr Assn
M   37 f, 80 associate members
¶   NL - 4; Ybk; both free.

Scottish Wild Land Group   (SWLG)   1982
■   8 Hartington Place, EDINBURGH, EH10 4LE.   (hsp)
    0131-229 2094 (evenings)
    email enquiries@swlg.org.uk   http://www.swlg.org.uk
    Co-ordinator: Alistair Cant
▲   Registered Charity; Un-incorporated Society
○   *K; to protect wild land in Scotland against intrusive
    developments; to ensure any development is done sensitively
    & sustainably
<   Scot Envt Link
M   450 i, UK / 10 i, o'seas
¶   Wild Land News - 3; ftm, 50p nm.

Scottish Wildlife Trust Ltd   (SWT)   1964
NR   3 Kirk Cramond, EDINBURGH, EH4 6HZ.   (hq)
    0131-312 7765   fax 0131-312 8705
    email enquiries@swt.org.uk   http://www.swt.org.uk
    Chief Exec: Simon Milne
▲   Company Limited by Guarantee; Registered Charity
Br   3 regional offices
○   *K; to conserve all forms of wild life & habitats in Scotland
●   ET - Res - Management of wildlife reserves
<   UK Wildlife Trusts
M   19,000 i, 34 f, 51 org
¶   Scottish Wildlife - 3.   AR.

© CBD Research Ltd · Beckenham · BR3 5JS · Tel 020 8650 7745 · Fax 020 8650 0768 · E-mail cbd@cbdresearch.com · www.cbdresearch.com

Scottish Wirework Manufacturers' Association (SWMA) 1908
- ■ c/o Wm Reid & Sons (Wireworkers) Ltd, 162 Glenpark St, GLASGOW, G31 1PG.   (hsb)
  0141-554 6987   fax 0141-556 4483
  Sec: Ian W Reid
- ○ *T
- M 17 f

Scottish Women's Bowling Association 1936
- NR Office 2, Commercial Centre, Stirling Enterprise Park, STIRLING, FK7 7RP.   (hq)
  01786 449012
  http://www.scottishwomensbowling.co.uk
  Sec: Ms Anna Marshall
- ▲ Company Limited bu Guarantee
- ○ *S; to foster, encourage, promote & develop the sport of Outdoor Bowling for Women
- M 42 clubs

Scottish Women's Football (SWF) 1972
- ■ Hampden Park, GLASGOW, G42 9DF.   (hq)
  0141-620 4580   fax 0141-620 4581
  email swf@scottish-football.com
  http://www.scottishwomensfootball.com
  Exec Admin: Maureen McGonigle
- ○ *S
- Gp Leagues: Senior, Universities, Under 19, Under 17, Under 13, Under 11
- ● Conf - Mtgs - ET - Comp
- M 4,000 i
- ¶ NL - 2;   Club Secretary Lists - irreg; both free.

Scottish Women's Indoor Bowling Association (SWIBA) 1961
- NR Troscons, Watson St, Letham, FORFAR, DD8 2QB.   (hsp)
  01307 818238
  Hon Sec: Anne Easton
- ▲ Un-incorporated Society
- ○ *S
- ● Mtgs - Comp - National & international championship teams
- < Brit Isles Women's Indoor Bowls Coun; Wld Indoor Bowls Coun
- M 18,000 i, 56 clubs
- ¶ Ybk.

Scottish Women's Rural Institutes (SWRI) 1917
- ■ 42 Heriot Row, EDINBURGH, EH3 6ES.   (hq)
  0131-225 1724   fax 0131-225 8129
  email swri@swri.demon.co.uk
  Gen Sec: Mrs Anne Peacock
- ▲ Registered Charity
- Br 886
- ○ *G; non-political, non-sectarian organisation providing educational, recreational & social opportunities for those who live & work in the country or are interested in country life
- ● Conf - Mtgs - ET - Exhib - Comp - Lib
- < Associated Countrywomen of the World
- M 23,000 i
- ¶ Scottish Home & Country - 12; £1.

Scottish Working Trials Society
- NR East Lodge, Gledswood, MELROSE, Roxburghshire, TD6 9DN.
  01896 822619
  http://www.workingtrials.co.uk
  Treas: Ann Bedford
- ○ *G; or all interested in sheep dog trials

Scottish Youth Hostels Association   (SYHA) 1932
- NR 7 Glebe Crescent, STIRLING, FK8 2JA.
  01786 891400   fax 01786 891333
  email info@syha.org.uk   http://www.syha.org.uk
  Gen Sec: Keith Legge
- ▲ Company Limited by Guarantee; Registered Charity
- Br 5
- ○ *Y; to help all, but especially young people, to experience & appreciate the Scottish countryside & places of historic & cultural interest in Scotland, & to promote their health, recreation & education, particularly by providing low cost accommodation for them on their travels
- ● Conf - Mtgs - Exhib - Comp - Stat - Inf - Empl - Activity holidays - Foreign travel
- M 44,745 i, 1,000 org, clubs & schools
- ¶ AR; free.   Guides & books.   Publicity pamphlets.

Scout Association 1908
- ■ Gilwell Park, Bury Rd, LONDON, E4 7QW.   (hq)
  020 8433 7100   fax 020 8433 7103
  email info.centre@scout.org.uk
  http://www.scout.org.uk
  Sec: David Shelmerdine
- ▲ Registered Charity
- Br 7,373
- ○ *Y; the purpose of scouting is to promote the development of young people in achieving their full physical, intellectual, social & spiritual potentials, as individuals, as responsible citizens & as members of their local, national & international communities
- Gp Beaver Scouts (6-8 years); Cub Scouts (8-10$\frac{1}{2}$); Scouts (10$\frac{1}{2}$-15); Explorer Scouts (15-18); Scout Network (18-25)
- ● Conf - Mtgs - ET - Exhib - Comp - VE - Activities (camping, creative, faith)
- < Wld Scout Org
- M 453,278 i
  (Sub: £19.10)
- ¶ Scouting - 62; ftm.   AR - 1; free.

Scout & Guide Graduate Association (SAGGA) 1957
- NR 15 Weatheroak Close, Webheath, REDDITCH, Worcs, B97 5TF.   (chmn/p)
  01527 455352
  email chairman@sagga.org.uk   http://www.sagga.org.uk
  Chmn: Sally Payne
- ▲ Registered Charity
- Br 6
- ○ *N, *Y; to provide service to the scout & guide movements; to promote scout & guide cooperation
- ● Conf - Mtgs - ET - SG - VE - Service work
- < Scout Assn; Girl Guiding UK
- M 250 i, UK & o'seas
- ¶ News & Ideas - 4; ftm only.

Scouting Ireland 2004
- IRL Larch Hill, DUBLIN 16, Republic of Ireland.
  353 (1) 495 6300   fax 353 (1) 495 6301
  http://www.scouts.ie
  Nat Sec: Michael Devins
- ○ *Y
- < World Org of the Scout Movement
- M 40,000 i

Scrabble Clubs (UK) 1993
- ■ Mattel House, Vanwall Business Park, Vanwall Rd, MAIDENHEAD, Berks, SL6 4UB.   (hq)
  01628 500000   fax 01628 500075
  email philip.nelkon@mattel.com
  Mgr: Philip Nelkon
- ○ *G
- ● Conf - Comp - Inf
- M 500 clubs, UK / 400 clubs, o'seas
- ¶ Scrabble Club News - 4; ftm.

Screen Printing Association (UK) Ltd
   since 23 April 2008 **Prism**

Screen Producers Ireland   1987
IRL   77 Merrion Square, DUBLIN 2, Republic of Ireland.
      353 (1) 662 1114   fax 353 (1) 661 9949
      http://www.screenproducersireland.com
      Chief Exec: Sean Stokes
○   *T
✕   2003 Film Makers Ireland

Sculptors' Society of Ireland   (SSI)
IRL   37 North Great George's St, DUBLIN 1, Republic of Ireland.
      353 (1) 872 2296
      email info@sculptors-society.ie
      http://www.sculptors-society.ie
      Dir: Toby Dennett
○   *A; to promote contemporary sculpture
M   420
      Uses the trading name of Visual Artists Ireland

Scurry Driving Association   (SDA)
■   Willoughby House, 42 Church Lane, Manby, LOUTH, Lincs,
      LN11 8HL.   (sp)
      http://www.scurrydrivers.co.uk
      Sec: Carole Davenport
▲   Company Limited by Guarantee
○   *S; a competitive sport in which a driven pair of ponies
      complete a course of obstacles, the winner being the pair
      with the fastest overall time
●   ET - Exhib - Comp - Inf
M   40 i
¶   NL - 3; ftm, £3 nm.
      Leaflet with rules.
✕   2005 Double Harness Scurry Driving

Sea Cadet Association
   in November 2004 merged with the Marine Society to form the
   Marine Society & Sea Cadets

Sea Cadet Corps
   see the **Marine Society & Sea Cadets**

Sea of Faith Network (UK)   (SoF)   1989
NR   3 Belle Grove Place, Spital Tongues, NEWCASTLE upon TYNE,
      NE2 4LH.   (mail add)
      email john.pearson@unn.ac.uk   http://www.sofn.org.uk
      Chmn: John Pearson
▲   Un-incorporated Society
Br   26 groups
○   *L, *R; exploring & promoting religious faith as a human
      creation
●   Conf - Local group meetings for study & discussion
<   Sea of Faith Networks Australia, NZ
M   526 i, UK / 47 i, o'seas
¶   sofia - 6; ftm, £15 nm.   NL - 6.
      Agenda of Faith; £2.50.
      A Reasonable Faith: introducing the Sea of Faith
         Network; £2 m, free nm.
      Time and Tide: Sea of Faith beyond the Millennium; £7.

Seabird Group   1966
■   c/o BTO, The Nunnery, THETFORD, Norfolk, IP24 2PU.
      (mail/address)
      email seabird@bto.org   http://www.seabirdgroup.org.uk
      Sec: Alan Leitch (to end 2008)
▲   Registered Charity
○   *I; to promote & help coordinate the study & conservation of
      seabirds
●   Conf - Res
M   331 i, 30 f, 4 org
         (Sub: £10 i, £15 f, £15 org)
¶   Seabird (Jnl) - 1.   NL - 3; both ftm only.

Seafood Scotland   1999
NR   18 Logie Mill, Logie Green Rd, EDINBURGH, EH7 4HG.
      0131-557 9344
      email enquiries@seafoodscotland.org
      http://www.seafoodscotland.org
      Chief Exec: Libby Woodhatch
○   *T

Seal Conservation Society   (SCS)   1996
NR   9 Todds Hill, SAINTFIELD, Co Down, BT24 7AR.
      028 4482 1107
      email info@pinnipeds.org   http://www.pinnipeds.org
○   *K; to protect & conserve pinnipeds (seals, sea-lions &
      walruses) worldwide

Sealed Knot Ltd   (SK)   1968
■   Burlington House, Botleigh Grange Business Park, Hedge End,
      SOUTHAMPTON, SO30 2DF.   (asa)
      0845 209 1556
      email lesley.barnes@clarkewillmott.com
      http://www.thesealedknot.org.uk
      Chief Exec: Arthur Jackson
▲   Company Limited by Guarantee; Registered Charity
○   *G; promotes education & research into history
Gp   Living history; Cavalry; Artillery; Medical services
●   Exhib - Inf - Re-enactment of 17th century life & military
      displays
M   4,500 i
         (Sub: £20)
¶   Orders of the DAy - 6; ftm, prices on application nm.

Seasonal Affective Disorder Association
   alternative name of the **SAD Association**

Seasoning & Spice Association   (SSA)   1992
NR   6 Catherine St, LONDON, WC2B 5JJ.   (hq)
      020 7836 2460   fax 020 7836 0580
      email ssa@fdf.org.uk
      http://www.seasoningandspice.org.uk
▲   Un-incorporated Society
○   *T; represents seasoning & spice processors based in the UK
●   Mtgs
<   Eur Spice Assn (ESA); Food & Drink Fedn
M   22 f

**SEBDA - the Social, Emotional & Behavioural Difficulties
   Association   (SEBDA)   1952**
NR   The Triangle (room 211), Exchange Square, MANCHESTER,
      M4 3TR.   (hq)
      0161-240 2418   fax 0161-240 5601
      email admin@sebda.org   http://www.sebda.org
      Exec Dir: Barbara Knowles
▲   Registered Charity
Br   6
○   *P; for all professionals working with children with emotional &/
      or behavioural difficulties & their families
●   Conf - Mtgs - ET - LG
<   Nat Children's Bureau; Young Minds
M   1,100 i, UK / 60 i, o'seas
¶   Emotional & Behavioural Difficulties (Jnl) - 3; ftm.
      Sebda News - 12.
      Publications list available.

**Second World War Aircraft Preservation Society   (SWWAPS)
   1976**
NR   Lasham Airfield, ALTON, Hants, GU34 5SS.   (hq)
▲   Un-incorporated Society
○   *G; a private collection available to the public to preserve
      aircraft, in a museum environment, that would otherwise be
      lost to our aviation heritage; includes artifacts & components
●   Mtgs - ET - Inf - Lib
<   Brit Aviation Presvn Coun (BAPC)
M   43 i

© CBD Research Ltd · Beckenham · BR3 5JS · Tel 020 8650 7745 · Fax 020 8650 0768 · E-mail cbd@cbdresearch.com · www.cbdresearch.com

Secondary Heads Association
  since 2006 **Association of School & College Leaders**

Section Five Special Interest Group
  a group of the **Defence Manufacturers Association**

Securities & Investment Institute   1992
NR   8 Eastcheap, LONDON, EC3M 1AE.   (hq)
  020 7645 0600   fax 020 7645 0601
  http://www.sii.org.uk
  Chief Exec: Simon Culhane
▲   Company Limited by Guarantee; Registered Charity
○   *P; for qualified & experienced practitioners of good standing in
  securities, derivatives & related areas of investment business;
  to set & improve standards through training & qualifications
●   Conf - Mtgs - ET - Exam - Res - Lib - LG
M   16,000 i, UK / 1,000 i, o'seas
¶   Securities & Investment Review (Jnl) - 6; ftm.
  LM - 2; ftm.   Report & Accounts - 1; free.
×   2004 Securities Institute

Security Institute of Ireland   1981
IRL   Swords Business Park, SWORDS, Co Dublin, Republic of Ireland
  353 (1) 840 4466   fax 353 (1) 840 8855
  email sii@eircom.net   http://www.sii.ie
○   *P

Security Manufacturers' Export Council
  a group of the **British Security Industry Association**

Sedum Society   1987
■   8 Percy Gardens, CHOPPINGTON, Northumberland, NE62
  5YH.   (sp)
  01670 817901
  email ray@sedumray.ndo.co.uk
  http://www.cactus-mail.com/sedum/
  Sec/Chmn/Editor: Ray Stephenson
▲   Un-incorporated Society
○   *H; to preserve as many species, sub-species, varieties, forms &
  cultivars in cultivation as possible
●   Res - Exhib - SG - Inf - Lib -PL
<   Brit Cactus & Succulent Soc
M   70 i, UK / 140 i, o;seas
  (Sub: £10 UK / £15 o'seas)
¶   NL - 4; ftm.   Occasional booklets.

Seed Crushers & Oil Processors Association
■   PO Box 259, BECKENHAM, Kent, BR3 3YA.   (hq)
  020 8776 2644; 020 8398 5955   fax 020 8249 5402
  http://www.scopa.org.uk
  Sec: Angela Bowden
▲   Un-incorporated Society
○   *T
<   Intl Assn Seed Crushers (IASC); Eur Seed Crushers & Oil
  Processors' Assn (FEDIOL); FOSFA; Food & Drink Fedn
M   13 f
¶   AR.

Seeing Dogs Alliance   1979
NR   116 Potters Lane, Send, WOKING, Surrey, GU23 7AL.   (hq)
  01483 765556
  email info@seeingdogs.org.uk
  http://www.seeingdogs.org.uk
  Sec: Chris Parker
▲   Registered Charity
○   *W; to train guide dogs for blind people; to give instruction in
  the use of alternative mobility aids where guide dogs are not
  suitable
M   i
¶   Lead On - 3.

Sefton Chamber of Commerce & Industry Ltd   1993
NR   150 Lord St, SOUTHPORT, Merseyside, PR9 0NP.   (hq)
  01704 531710   fax 01704 539255
  email mail@seftonchamber.com
  http://www.seftonchamber.com
  Chief Exec: Steve Dickson
▲   Company Limited by Guarantee
○   *C
●   Conf - Mtgs - ET - Res - Exhib - SG - Stat - Expt - Inf - Lib - VE -
  LG - Video Conference; 01704 549673
<   NI Cham Comm; Business Link Merseyside; Chams Comm NW
M   600 f, 6 org
¶   Chamber News - 6; ftm only.
  Business to Business Flyer - 12.
  Sefton Business Directory - 2; ftm.

Selborne Society   1885
■   89 Daryngton Drive, GREENFORD, Middx, UB6 8BH.
  (regd/add)
  020 8578 3181
  http://www.biochem.ucl.ac.uk/~dab/selborne.html
  Hon Sec: R.J. Hall
▲   Company Limited by Guarantee; Registered Charity
○   *E, *G; to promote interest in conservation & natural history,
  especially among children; to maintain Perivale Wood Nature
  Reserve
●   Mtgs - Res - Exhib - Lib - VE
M   800 i
¶   Jnl Pioneers of Conservation (2004); £2 m, £3 nm.Wildlife in
  the Suburbs (3rd ed); £2 m,£3 nm.

Selden Society   1887
■   c/o Law Building, Queen Mary University of London,
  Mile End Rd, LONDON, E1 4NS.   (hq)
  020 7882 5136   fax 020 8981 8733
  email selden-society@qmul.ac.uk
  http://www.selden-society.qmul.ac.uk
  Sec: Victor Tunkel
▲   Registered Charity
○   *L, *Q; history of English law
●   Res - Inf - Advice to public bodies, libraries, the media &
  general public on questions of legal history, history of courts,
  the profession, institutions, manuscripts, family & local
  history, etc
<   Assn Intle de l'Histoire de Droit
M   380 i, 165 f & org, UK / 1,080 i, f & org, o'seas
¶   Main series - annual volume.
  Volumes in supplementary series - irreg; prices vary.
  Hbk (incl LM & Rules) - 5 yrly.
  Lectures - irreg.   AR - 1.

SELECT   1900
■   The Walled Garden, BUSH ESTATE, Midlothian, EH26 0SB.
  (hq)
  0131-445 5577
  email admin@select.org.uk   http://www.select.org.uk
  Managing Dir: D N McGuiness
▲   Un-incorporated Society
Br   7
○   *T; to represent the electrical, electronic & communications
  systems industry in Scotland; membership categories incl
  electrical installation, safety & security systems, information
  technology, telecommunications, electronics & controls
●   Conf - Mtgs - ET - Exhib - Comp - SG - Inf - Empl - LG
<   Intl Assn of Electrical Contractors
M   550 f
¶   Cabletalk - 6.   NL - 12.   AR.   LM - 1.

Selective Mutism Information & Research Association (SMIRA)
NR   13 Humberstone Drive, LEICESTER, LE5 0RE.
    0116-212 7411
    http://www.selectivemutism.co.uk
    Sec: Lindsay Whittington
○   *W; for sufferers & parents of the rare childhood condition
    characterised by 'a consistent failure to speak in specific
    situations in which there is an expectation for speaking'
●   Mtgs

Self Defence Federation (SDF) 2000
NR   Unit 12 fusion@magna, Magna Way, Templeborough,
    ROTHERHAM, S Yorks, S60 1FE.
    01709 789422
    email daveturtonsdf@hotmail.com
    http://www.selfdefencefederation.co.uk
    Head: Dave Turtons
○   *G; for all interested in various methods of self-defence
M   c 3,000 i, 30 clubs

Self Storage Association Ltd (SSAUK)
■   Priestley House, The Gullet, NANTWICH, Cheshire,
    CW5 5SZ.   (hq)
    01270 623150   fax 01270 623471
    email admin@ssauk.com   http://www.ssauk.com
    Chief Exec: Rodney Walker
▲   Company Limited by Guarantee
○   *T
●   Conf - Mtgs - ET - Exhib - Stat - Inf - LG
M   229 f, UK / 12 f, o'seas
    (Sub: £650)
¶   Focus Magazine - 4; ftm, £4 nm.

Sense - National Deafblind & Rubella Association 1955
■   101 Pentonville Rd, LONDON, N1 9LG.   (hq)
    0845 127 0060   fax 0845 127 0062
    email info@sense.org.uk   http://www.sense.org.uk
    Chief Exec: Richard Brook
▲   Registered Charity
Br   11 regions
○   *K, *W; to support & campaign for children & adults who are
    deafblind & their families
●   ET - Inf - Lib
M   350 i
¶   Talking Sense - 3; ftm.

Seriously Ill for Medical Research
    since 2005 **Patients' Voice for Medical Advance**

Services, Industrial, Professional & Technical Union
    styles itself **SIPTU**

Serving Construction & Architecture in Local Authorities
    alternative name of **Scala**

Sevenoaks & District Chamber of Commerce 1910
■   The Quadrant, 5 Victoria Rd, SEVENOAKS, Kent, TN13 1YD.
    (hq)
    01732 455188   fax 01732 455188
    email info@sevenoakschamber.com
    http://www.sevenoakschamber.com
    Admin: Mrs Avril Ferguson
▲   Company Limited by Guarantee
○   *C
●   Conf - Mtgs - Inf
M   120 f
    (Sub: £90-£155)
¶   NL - 4; on website

Seventeen Fortyfive / 1745 Association 1946
■   Ferry Cottage, Corran, Ardgour, FORT WILLIAM, Highland,
    PH33 7AA.   (hsp)
    01855 841306
    http://www.1745Association.org.uk
    Hon Sec: Miss C W H Aikman
▲   Registered Charity; Un-incorporated Society
○   *L; the study of Jacobite history; erection of memorials on
    historical sites
●   Conf - VE
M   350 i, 1 f, UK / 50 i, 1 org (Alliance France-Ecosse), o'seas
¶   The Jacobite - 3;   AR - 1; ftm only.

Seventeenth Century Life & Times 2000
NR   Fern Cottage, 91 High St, ALTON, Hants, GU34 1LG.
    01420 541731
    http://www.17thcenturylifeandtimes.com
    Events Coordinator: Geoffrey Thorne
▲   Un-incorporated Society
○   *G; 17th century (mainly English civil war) civilian & military
    living history re-enactment
●   Mtgs - ET - Res - Exhib - SG - Inf - VE
<   Nat Assn of Re-enactment Socs
M   130 i
¶   The Scrichowl - 2; ftm only.

Sewing Machine Trade Association Ltd (SMTA) 1939
■   Runnymede Malthouse, off Hummer Rd, EGHAM, Surrey,
    TW20 9BD.   (hq)
    0870 330 8610   fax 0870 330 8611
○   *T; interests of sewing machine dealers & allied interests in the
    UK & Eire
●   Conf - Mtgs - ET - Exhib - Inf - VE
M   360 f, UK / 3 f, o'seas
¶   Shuttle Plus - 4; free.

Sexaholics Anonymous (SA) 1991
NR   PO Box 1914, BRISTOL, BS99 2NE.   (mail/address)
    07000 725463
    http://www.sauk.org
▲   Un-incorporated Society
○   *M, *W; offers a 12-step programme of recovery for those who
    want to stop their self-destructive sexual thinking & behaviour
●   Mtgs

Sexual Dysfunction Association 1995
■   Emblem House (suite 301), London Bridge Hospital,
    27 Tooley St, LONDON, SE1 2PR.   (asa)
    0870 774 3571
    email info@sda.uk.net   http://www.sda.uk.net
    Chmn: Dr Graham Jackson
▲   Registered Charity
○   *M, *W; to raise awareness of the causes & treatments of male
    & female sexual dysfunction
●   Inf
<   Eur Sexual Dysfunction Alliance (ESDA)
M   i
    (Sub: £15)
¶   NL - 2; free.   AR; free.

Sexual Freedom Coalition (SFC) 1996
■   BCM Box Lovely, LONDON, WC1N 3XX.   (mail)
    07770 884985
    email mail@sfc.org.uk   http://www.sfc.org.uk
    Chmn: Dr Tuppy Owens
▲   Un-incorporated Society
○   *K; 'to represent supporters & campaign groups who revere sex
    & want to be free to enjoy seeing, hearing, reading & doing
    as we please, so long as nobody is exploiting anyone else'
●   Conf - LG
>   TLC; Outsiders Trust; Leydig Trust

© CBD Research Ltd · Beckenham · BR3 5JS · Tel 020 8650 7745 · Fax 020 8650 0768 · E-mail cbd@cbdresearch.com · www.cbdresearch.com

Shakespeare Reading Society   (SRS)   1874
- ■ 123 Lynton Rd, LONDON, W3 9HN.   (hsp)
  020 8992 0772
  Hon Sec: Mrs Frances J Hughes
- ▲ Un-incorporated Society
- ○ *A, *L; to read & study the works of Shakespeare
- ● Mtgs - Res - VE - Reading of plays - Lectures - Acting
  workshops
- M 50 i
- ¶ Annual programme; free.

Shared Care Network   1988
- ■ Units 63-66 Easton Business Centre, Felix Rd, BRISTOL,
  BS5 0HE.   (hq)
  0117-941 5361   fax 0117-941 5362
  email enquiries@sharedcarenetwork.org.uk
  http://www.sharedcarenetwork.org.uk
  Chief Exec: Candy Smith
- ▲ Registered Charity
- Br 8
- ○ *N, *W; to support the development of family based short-term
  care services in England, Wales & Northern Ireland
  Family based care services link disabled children to support
  families willing to offer occasional care. The network
  supports 300 schemes organising family based short breaks
- ● Conf - ET - Res - Inf - LG - Campaigning
- M 300 services
- ¶ Annual Review; free.

Shark Angling Club of Great Britain   (SACGB)   1953
- ■ Middletons Corner, The Quay, EAST LOOE, Cornwall,
  PL13 1DX.   (hq)
  01503 262642
  email lindareynolds@sacgb.freeserve.co.uk
  http://www.sharkanglingclubofgreatbritain.org.uk
  Sec: Linda Reynolds
- ○ *S; to promote shark angling in GB, including reef fishing,
  mackerel trips, evening conger trips
- ● Res - Comp - SG - Stat - Inf - Lib
- < Intl Game Fishing Assn
- M 500 i, UK / 50 i, o'seas
- ¶ NL - 2; ftm only.

Shaw Society   1941
- NR 1 Buckland Court, 37 Belsize Park, LONDON, NW3 4EB.
  (memsec/p)
  020 7794 7014
  email shawsociety@blueyonder.co.uk
  http://www.shawsociety.org.uk
  Mem Sec: Evelyn Ellis
- ▲ Un-incorporated Society
- ○ *A, *L; study of the life & work of George Bernard Shaw; to
  promote interest in his work & provide 'a rallying point for
  the cooperation & education of kindred spirits & a forum for
  their irreconcilable controversies'
- ● Mtgs - Inf - Performances at Shaw's house at Ayot St Lawrence
  (Herts)
- M c 90 i, 10 libraries, UK / c 40 i, 100 libraries, o'seas
- ¶ The Shavian - 2; ftm, donation nm.   NL - 3; ftm.
  News-sheet for meetings - 10; free to attendees.

Sheep Veterinary Society
  a group of the **British Veterinary Association**

Sheet Plant Association   (SPA)
- NR 24 Grange St, KILMARNOCK, Ayrshire, KA1 2AR.   (hq)
  01563 570518   fax 01563 572728
  email npc@natpack.org.uk
  http://www.sheetplant.org.uk
  Sec: Allan Glen
- ○ *T; to represent the interests of corrugated converters
- ● Conf - ET - Exhib - Comp - Inf
- < Fédn Français du Cartonnage; Assn of Indep Corrugated
  Converters (USA)
- M 65 f, UK / 5 f, o;seas

Sheffield Chamber of Commerce & Industry   (SCCI)   1857
- ■ Albion House, Savile St, SHEFFIELD, S Yorks, S4 7UD.   (hq)
  0114-201 8888   fax 0114-272 0950
  email info@scci.org.uk   http://www.scci.org.uk
  Chief Exec: Nigel Tomlinson
- ▲ Company Limited by Guarantee
- ○ *C
- Gp Black & minority ethnic; Manufacturers; Retailers; Women in
  business
- ● Conf - ET - Res - Expt - Inf - VE
- < Brit Chams Comm
- M 1,800 f
- × 2004 City of Sheffield & District Chamber of Trade (merged)

Sheila Kaye-Smith Society   (SK-S)   1987
- ■ 22 The Cloisters, St Johns Rd, ST LEONARDS-on-SEA, E Sussex,
  TN37 6JT.   (hsp)
  01424 422139
  Hon Sec: Miss Christine Hayward
- ○ *A; to stimulate & widen interest in the life & work of this
  English writer & novelist (1887-1956)
- ● Mtgs - VE
- < Alliance of Literary Societies (ALS)
- M 56 i
- ¶ The Gleam (Jnl) - 1;   NL - 1.
  Occasional papers & books.

Shellfish Association of Great Britain   (SAGB)   1908
- NR Fishmongers' Hall, London Bridge, LONDON, EC4R 9EL.   (hq)
  020 7283 8305
  email sagb@shellfish.org.uk   http://www.shellfish.org.uk
  Dir: Dr Peter Hunt
- ○ *T; for the UK shellfish industry (catching, cultivating & selling)
- M f

Shelter   1966
- § 88 Old St, LONDON, EC1V 9HU.   (hq)
  0844 515 2000   fax 0844 515 2030
  email info@shelter.org.uk   http://www.shelter.org.uk
  Scotiabank House (4th floor), 6 South Charlotte St,
  EDINBURGH, EH2 4AW.
  Chief Exec: Adam Sampson
- ● Helpline: 0808 800 4444
  Gives advice, information and advocacy to people in housing
  need, and campaigns for lasting political change to end the
  housing crisis for good.

Sherlock Holmes Society of London   1951
- ■ 41 Sandford Rd, CHELMSFORD, Essex, CM1 6DE.   (pro/p)
  01245 284006
  email rojerjohnson@yahoo.co.uk
  http://www.sherlock-holmes.org.uk
  13 Crofton Avenue, ORPINGTON, Kent, BR6 8DU.
  01689 811314.   (mem/sp).
  PR Officer: Roger Johnson,   Mem Sec: Robert Ellis
- ▲ Un-incorporated Society
- ○ *A, *G; 'a spoof literary society devoted to the lives & works of
  Sherlock Holmes & Dr John Watson'
- ● Mtgs - VE
- M c 1,000 i
- ¶ Sherlock Holmes Journal - 2; ftm only.

Shetland Cattle Breeders' Association   (SCBA)   2000
- NR Renwick Mill, Renwick, PENRITH, Cumbria, CA10 1JH.
  (mem/sp)   http://www.shetlandcattle.org.uk
  Mem Sec: Barry Allen
- ○ *B

Shetland Cattle Herd Book Society
- NR Shetland Rural Centre, Staneyhill, LERWICK, Shetland,
  ZE1 0NA.
  01595 696300   fax 01595 696305
- ▲ Registered Charity
- ○ *B

Shetland Cheviot Marketing Society   1986
- ■ Toog, VIDLIN, Shetland, ZE2 9QB.   (hsb)
  01806 577227
  Sec: James A Johnson
- ▲ Un-incorporated Society
- ○ *B
- ● Mtgs
- M 100 i

Shetland Flock Book Society   1926
- NR Lonabrek, Aith, BIXTER, Shetland, ZE2 9ND.   (hsp)
  01595 810343
  Sec: James P Nicolson
- ▲ Registered Charity
- ○ *B; to encourage the breeding of pure Shetland sheep; to ensure that all Shetland Flock Book sheep comply with the breed standards
- ● Mtgs - Comp
- M 116 i

Shetland Livestock Marketing Group   (SLMG)
- ■ Shetland Rural Centre, Staneyhill, LERWICK, Shetland, ZE1 0NA.   (hq)
  01595 696300   fax 01595 696305
  email hazel_slmg@hotmail.co.uk
  http://www.shetlandagriculture.com
  Sec: Peter Duncan
- ○ *F; to promote and market agriculture in Shetland
- ● Mtgs - Inf - LG
- < Shetland Flock Health Assn
- M 300 i
- ✕ 2003 Shetland Agricultural Association

Shetland Pony Stud-Book Society   (SPSBS)   1890
- NR Shetland House, 22 York Place, PERTH, PH2 8EH.   (hq)
  01738 623471   fax 01738 442274
  http://www.shetlandponystudbooksociety.co.uk
  Pres: G N Hurst
- ▲ Company Limited by Guarantee; Registered Charity
- ○ *B
- Gp Pony Breeders of Shetland; Ridden & Driven Performance Award Schemes
- ● Expt - Inf
- M 2,200 i, UK / 120 i, o'seas
- ¶ Shetland Pony Stud Book - 1.   Magazine - 1.

Shetland Sheep Society   1986
- NR The Fold, East Torrington, MARKET RASEN, Lincs, LN8 5SE.   (hsp)
  01673 857363
  http://www.shetland-sheep.org.uk
  Hon Sec: Mrs Maureen Turner
- ○ *B; promotion of Shetland sheep & their products, meat & wool
- ● Conf - Mtgs - ET - Exhib - Comp - Expt - Inf - VE
- M 375 i, UK / 25 i, o'seas
- ¶ The Shetland Breed - 4; ftm only.
- ✕ 2002 (October) Shetland Sheep Breeders Group

Shiatsu Society (UK)   1981
- ■ PO Box 4580, RUGBY, Warks, CV21 9EL.   (hq)
  0845 130 4560   fax 01788 555052
  email admin@shiatsusociety.org
  http://www.shiatsusociety.org
  Chmn: David Home
- ▲ Company Limited by Guarantee
- ○ *P; for students, practitioners & teachers of Shiatsu - the use of finger &/or palm pressure - as a natural healing discipline
- ● Conf - Mtgs - ET - Exam - Res - Exhib - Comp - SG - Stat - Inf - Lib - PL - Empl - VE - LG
- < Eur Shiatsu Fedn
- M 1,850 i, UK / 52 i, o'seas
- ¶ NL - 4; £43 yr.   Guide to Shiatsu.   GP leaflet.
  Shiatsu in the NHS.   Schools Booklet.

Shingles Support Society
- ▲ Registered Charity
  a group of the **Herpes Viruses Association**

Ship Stamp Society   (SSS)   1970
- ■ 10 Heyes Drive, LYMM, Cheshire, WA13 0PB.   (hsp)
  01925 758435
  email brad666sss@freenetname.co.uk
  Hon Sec: T Broadley
- ▲ Un-incorporated Society
- Br 1
- ○ *G; for collectors of postage stamps with ship interest
- ● Mtgs - Res - Exhib - Inf
- < Intl Fedn of Maritime Philately; Brit Thematic Assn
- M 180 i, UK / 108 i, o'seas
- ¶ The Log Book - 12.   LM & Reports; m only.

Shipbuilders & Shiprepairers Association   (SSA)   1989
- ■ Marine House, Meadlake Place, Thorpe Lea Rd, EGHAM, Surrey, TW20 8BF.   (hq)
  01784 223770   fax 01784 223775
  email office@ssa.org.uk   http://www.ssa.org.uk
  Chief Exec: Mike Albans-Jackson
- Br 2
- ○ *T; to support UK shipbuilding, shiprepair, conversion, disposal, design, operation & key supply chain such as electical, propulsion, mechanical / pressure / fluid systems, naval architecture & safety
- Gp Marine Industries Leadership Council (MILC); Marine Sector Advisory Group (MSAG); Naval Defence Group
- ● Conf - Mtgs - Res - Exhib - SG - Stat - Inf - Lib - PL - VE - LG - Health & safety - Project management - Technology/ translation
- < C'ee of Eur Shipyard Assns; R Inst Naval Architects; Lloyds Register; Yorkshire Forward
- > Best Practice Club; Business Enterprise Regulations & Reform; Ministry of Defence; SEMTA
- M 108 f, UK / 2 f, o'seas
- ¶ Circular - 52; ftm only.   Reports - irreg; m only.
  NL - 4;   Ybk - 1;   LM - on web; all free.

Shire Horse Society   (SHS)   1878
- ■ East of England Showground, PETERBOROUGH, Cambs, PE2 6XE.   (hq)
  01733 234451   fax 01733 370038
  http://www.shire-horse.org.uk
  Sec: Andrew Mercer
- ○ *B; to promote the breed of English cart-horse
- Gp Judges: In-hand, Turnout
- ● Mtgs - ET - Exhib - Comp - Stat - Expt - Inf - VE - LG - National Shire Horse Show
- M i, f & org
- ¶ List of Breeders, Exhibitors & Local Societies - 2;
  NL;   List of Shows - 1;   AR;
  Panel of Judges - 1;
  Notes for Overseas Breeders - irreg; all free.

Shooters' Rights Association   (SRA)   1984
- ■ PO Box 3, CARDIGAN, Ceredigion, SA43 1BN.   (hq)
  01239 698607   fax 01239 698614
  Sec: Richard Law
- ▲ Un-incorporated Society
- ○ *K; provision of public liability & legal costs insurance; assistance in difficulties encountered with respect to gun licence grant or renewal
- ● Res - Exhib - Comp - Inf - Lib
- M 3,285 i, 85 f, 115 org, UK / 29 i, o'seas

© CBD Research Ltd · Beckenham · BR3 5JS · Tel 020 8650 7745 · Fax 020 8650 0768 · E-mail cbd@cbdresearch.com · www.cbdresearch.com

Shop & Display Equipment Association   (SDEA)   1947
- ■ 24 Croydon Rd, CATERHAM, Surrey, CR3 6YR.   (hq)
     01883 348911   fax 01883 343435
     email enquiries@sdea.co.uk
     http://www.shopdisplay.org
     Dir: Lawrence Cutler
- ▲ Un-incorporated Society
- ○ *T; for manufacturers, distributors & importers of shop fittings & retail display equipment
- ● Conf - Mtgs - Exhib - Stat - Expt - Inf - LG
- M 202 f
- ¶ Shoptalk (NL) - 4;   LM - 1;   PR Planner - 1;
     Confidential Circulars - 52;   all ftm only.
     SDEA Directory of Shopfittings & Display - 1; ftm, £10 nm.

Shorthorn Society of the United Kingdom of GB & I   1875
- ■ 4th Street, Stoneleigh Park, KENILWORTH, Warks, CV8 2LG.
     (hq)
     024 7669 6549   fax 024 7669 6729
     email shorthorn@shorthorn.co.uk
     http://www.shorthorn.co.uk
     Sec: Frank Milnes
- ○ *B
- Gp Red Cattle Genetics (semen company)
- ● Mtgs - Res - Exhib - Comp - Stat - Expt - Inf - PL - VE - Empl - Breed societies
- < Wld Shorthorn Coun
- M 280 i, UK / 250 i, o'seas
- ¶ Shorthorn Jnl - 1.   NL - 4.
     Coates Herd Book - 1.

Showmen's Guild of Great Britain   1889
- NR 41 Clarence St, STAINES, Middx, TW18 4SY.   (hq)
     01784 461805   fax 01784 461732
     http://www.www.showmensguild.com
- ○ *T; interests of travelling showmen & protection of the industry
- M f

Shrievalty Association
     alternative name of the **High Sheriffs' Association of England & Wales**

Shropshire Archaeological & Historical Society   (SAHS)   1877
- ■ Glebe House, Vicarage Rd, SHREWSBURY, Shropshire,
     SY3 9EZ.   (hsp)
     01743 236914   fax 01743 351255
     email s.baugh@virgin.net
     http://www.discovershropshire.org.uk
     Sec: G C Baugh
- ▲ Registered Charity
- ○ *L; archaeological research, local history & publication of parish registers
- ● Mtgs - Lib - VE
- < Coun Brit Archaeology
- M 316 i, 33 universities & libraries, UK / 3 i, 11 org, o'seas
     (Sub: £14 UK / £18 o'seas)
- ¶ Shropshire History & Archaeology (Transactions) - 1;
     ftm, varies nm.
     NL - 2; ftm only.

Shropshire Chamber of Commerce & Enterprise Ltd   1962
- ■ Trevithick House, Stafford Park 4, TELFORD, Shropshire,
     TF3 3BA.   (hq)
     01952 208200   fax 01952 208208
     email enquiries@shropshire-chamber.co.uk
     http://www.shropshire-chamber.co.uk
     Chief Exec: Nick Graham
- ▲ Company Limited by Guarantee
- ○ *C
- Gp Networking; Policy & representation
- ● Inf
- < Brit Chams Comm; Confedn W Midlands Chams Comm
- M i
- ¶ Shropshire Business Matters - 6; free.
- ✕ 2005 Shropshire Chamber of Commerce, Training & Enterprise

**Shropshire Sheep Breeders Association & Flock Book Society
(SSBA)   1882**
- ■ Gibshiel, Tarset, HEXHAM, Northumberland, NE48 1RR.   (hsp)
     01434 240235
     email shropshire_sheep@hotmail.com
     http://www.shropshire-sheep.co.uk
     Sec: Jane Wilson
- ▲ Registered Charity
- ○ *B
- ● Mtgs - ET - Exhib - Comp - Expt - Inf - PL - LG
- M 110 i, UK / 1 i, o'seas
- ¶ Shroptalk (NL) - 4; ftm; £10 yr nm.

**Shropshire & West Midlands Agricultural Society   (SWMAS)
1875**
- ■ The Agricultural Showground, Berwick Rd, SHREWSBURY,
     Shropshire, SY1 2PF.   (hq)
     0870 957 6444
     http://www.westmidshow.co.uk
     Chmn: David Tudor
- ▲ Company Limited by Guarantee; Registered Charity
- ○ *F; to promote agriculture & industry
- Gp Horse; Cattle; Sheep; Machinery & arable farming;
     Horticulture; Conservation
- ● Exhib - Comp - 2 day county show
- M 4,000 i, 400 f, 50 org
- ¶ Show Programme - 1; ftm, £2 nm.   AR; ftm; £2 nm.
     Schedule(s) - 1; free.   Catalogue - 1; £2.50.

Siambr Fasnach Gorllewin Cymru
     Welsh name of the **West Wales Chamber of Commerce**

Sickle Cell Society   1979
- NR 54 Station Rd, LONDON, NW10 4UA.   (hq)
     020 8961 7795   fax 020 8961 8346
     email info@sicklecellsociety.org
     http://www.sicklecellsociety.org
     Dir: Dr Asa'ah Nkohkwo
- ▲ Registered Charity
- ○ *W; to help & support families affected by sickle cell disorders;
     to educate the general public & health professionals about
     the problems of sickle cell disorders
- ● Conf - Exhib - Inf - Provides financial assistance, educational
     grants & holiday & recreational opportunities
- M 150 i
- ¶ News Review - 4.   AR.
     Information leaflets (publications list available); free.

Side Saddle Association   (SSA)   1974
- ■ 17 Halls Green, WESTON, Herts, SG4 7DR.   (hsp)
     01462 790960
     email urquhart@clara.net
     http://www.sidesaddleassociation.co.uk
     Hon Gen Sec: Mrs Siobhan Urquhart
- ▲ Un-incorporated Society
- Br 15; Australia, Austria, Belgium, Canada, Eire, France,
     Germany, Japan, Netherlands, New Zealand, Northern
     Ireland, South Africa, Spain, Sweden, USA
- ○ *G; to encourage & promote the art of riding side saddle, & the
     furtherance of the interests of side saddle riders all over the
     world
- ● Conf - Mtgs - ET - Exam - Exhib - Comp - Inf
- < Brit Horse Soc
- M 1,300 i
- ¶ NL - 3.   Shows & Fixture List - 1.
     Members' Hbk - 1.

** Siege Group
     Organisation lost: see Introduction paragraph 3.

Siegfried Sassoon Fellowship
NR   PO Box 11, COWBRIDGE, Vale of Glamorgan, CF71 7XT.
       (mail/address)
       http://www.sassoonfellowship.org
       Hon Sec: Deborah Fisher
○   *G; for all intetrested in the llife & works of the poet & novellist
       Siegfried Sassoon (1886-1967) & the literature of the first
       World War
M   i

SIESO   (SIESO)   1973
NR   Practice Protection, Deloitte Touche LLP, Hill House,
       1 Little New St, LONDON, EC4A 3TR.   (sp)
       020 7303 5543
       email sieso@sieso.org.uk   http://www.sieso.org.uk
       Sec: Kevin Brear
▲   Un-incorporated Society
Br   4
○   *P; for managers & those involved in the prevention, of &
       response to, industrial & commercial emergencies
Gp   Industrial safety: health, safety & environment; Crisis
       management; Risk assessment; Statutory regulations; EU &
       government legislation
●   Conf - ET - Exhib - SG - Inf - VE - LG
<   Nat Steering C'ee for Warning & Informing the Public; Civil
       Contingencies Coordination Alliance
M   300 i, UK / 20 i, o'seas
       Full title: Society of Industrial Emergency Services Officers

SIFA   (SIFA)   1994
NR   10 East St, EPSOM, Surrey, KT17 1HH.
       01372 721172   fax 01372 745377
       email sifa@sifa.co.uk   http://www.sifa.co.uk
       Managing Dir: Ian Muirhead
○   *P; financial advisers who are partly or wholly owned by
       solicitors or accountants, or who have close links with the
       professions
✕   2003-04 Solicitors for Independent Financial Advice

Silhouette Collectors Club   1965
■   Flat 5/13 Brunswick Sq, HOVE, E Sussex, BN3 1EH.   (hsp)
       01273 735760
       Hon Sec: Miss Diana B Joll
○   *A; for collectors & anyone interested in the silhouette from
       1760 to the present
●   Res - VE
M   68 i, UK / 3 i, o'seas
¶   NL - 3; ftm only.

Silica & Moulding Sands Association   (SAMSA)   1941
■   Gillingham House, 38-44 Gillingham St, LONDON,
       SW1V 1HU.   (hq)
       020 7963 8000
       http://www.samsa.org.uk
       Dir: Brian James
▲   Company Limited by Guarantee
○   *T; to promote the continuity of supply of indigenous silica &
       industrial sand for the consumer industries
Gp   Environment & planning; Health & safety training
●   Conf - Mtgs - Stat - Inf - LG
<   A constituent body of the Quarry Products Assn
       Assn of Eur Producers of Silica (EUROSIL); Indl Minerals Assn of
       Europe (IMA-EUROPE)
M   11 f

Silk Association of Great Britain   (SAGB)   1970
NR   5 Portland Place, LONDON, W1B 1PW.   (hq)
       020 7636 7788   fax 020 7636 7515
       email sagb@dial.pipex.com   http://www.silk.org.uk
▲   Company Limited by Guarantee
○   *T; to promote the use of & knowledge of real silk
●   Mtgs - Stat - Inf - LG
<   Intl Silk Assn; Brit Apparel & Textile Confedn
M   35 f
¶   Serica (NL) - 4; ftm.

Silver Society
NR   Box 246 / 2 Landsdowne Row, LONDON, W1J 6HL.
       (mail/address)
       email secretary@the silversociety.org
       http://www.thesilversociety.org
○   *G; to widen the appreciation of silver of all periods, also gold
       & platinum
¶   Jnl - 1.

Silver Spoon Club of Great Britain   (SSC)   1989
NR   Daniel Bexfield Antiques, 26 Burlington Arcade, LONDON,
       W1J 0PU.   (ed/b)
       Jnl Editor: Daniel Bexfield
▲   Un-incorporated Society
○   *G; to assist & support connoisseurs & collectors of antique &
       other fine silver spoons & related table silver
Gp   Historical; Research; Marketing; Instruction
●   Res - Comp - SG - Stat - Inf - Lib
M   175 i, UK / 25 i, o'seas
¶   The Finial (Jnl) - 6.
       Note: all activities are carried out by post.

Simplified Spelling Society
       since 2007 the **Spelling Society**

Sing for Pleasure   (SfP)   1964
NR   Bolton Music Centre, New York, BOLTON, Lancs, BL3 4NG.
       (hq)
       01204 333540
       email admin@singforpleasure.org.uk
       http://www.singforpleasure.org.uk
       Admin: Vicky Williams
▲   Registered Charity
Br   Regional c'ees
○   *D, *G; for conductors, teachers, singers & children interested
       in choral music
●   Conf - Mtgs - ET - SG - Inf - VE
<   À Coeur Joie; Europa Cantat; Brit Fedn Young Choirs; NCVO;
       Tonsil
M   650 i, 100 choirs
¶   NL - 2; ftm.   Sheet Music - 3; ftm.
       AR; ftm.   Summer & Weekend Course Brochures.

Singapore United Kingdom Association   (SUKA)   1988
NR   c/o Singapore Tourist Board, Grand Buildings, 1-3 Strand,
       LONDON, WC2N 5HR.
       email secretary@suka.org   http://www.suka.org
       ontact: Mem Sec
○   *X

Single Ply Roofing Association   (SPRA)   1994
NR   Roofing House, 31 Worship St, LONDON, EC2A 2DY.   (hq)
       0115-914 4445   fax 0115-974 9827
       email enquiries@spra.co.uk   http://www.spra.co.uk
       Sec: Jim Hooker
▲   Un-incorporated Society
○   *T; to provide independent technical advice to clients &
       designers on polymeric roofing membranes & to ensure the
       membership comply with membership criteria
●   Mtgs - ET - Comp - Inf
<   Brit Flat Roofing Coun; Construction Products Assn; Nat
       Specialist Contrs Coun; Roofing Ind Alliance; RIBA CPD
       Providers Network
M   75 f
¶   Brochure;   Design Guide; both free.

Single Travellers' Action Group
       This organisation closed in 2006

SIPTU (Services, Industrial, Professional & Technical Union) (SIPTU) 1990
IRL Liberty Hall, DUBLIN 1, Republic of Ireland.
    353 (1) 858 6300   fax 353 (1) 874 9466
    email info@siptu.ie   http://www.siptu.ie
    Gen Sec: Joe O'Flynn
○ *U; to represent workers in both the public & private sector in
    almost every industry in Ireland & at virtually every level
M 276,000 i
    Ireland's largest trade union

Sir Arthur Sullivan Society   (SASS)   1977
■ 2 Wherry Way, Dobwalls, LISKEARD, Cornwall, PL14 4NS.   (sp)
    email shturnbull@aol.com
    http://www.sirarthursullivansociety.co.uk
    Sec: Stephen Turnbull
▲ Registered Charity
○ *A, *D, *G, *L; to advance the education of the public in &
    promote the performance of, the music of Sir Arthur Sullivan
    (1842-1900) & other contemporaneous British composers
● Conf - Mtgs - ET - Res - Exhib - Comp - SG - Inf - Lib - VE
M 400 i, 15 org, UK / 80 i, 5 org, o'seas
¶ Magazine - 3; ftm, £2 nm (back numbers only).
    NL - 1/2; ftm only.

Sir Harry Lauder Society
    incorporated in the **Scottish Music Hall & Variety Theatre
    Society**

Sir Joseph Banks Society
NR 7 Bridge St, HORNCASTLE, Lincs, LN9 5HZ.
    Life Pres: David N Robinson
○ *G; to stimulate interest in the life & achievements of Sir Joseph
    Banks (1744-1820), English botanist & President of the Royal
    Society from 1778 to 1819; the genus Banksia
    commemorates his work in botany
● ET - Res - Inf
M i
¶ NL.   Publications.

Sira Ltd   1918
■ South Hill, CHISLEHURST, Kent, BR7 5EH.   (hq)
    020 8467 2636   fax 020 8468 1705
    email info@sira.co.uk   http://www.sira.co.uk
    Chief Exec: Steve Pickering
▲ Company Limited by Guarantee
○ *Q; Design, manufacture, marketing of instrumentation &
    control equipment; Innovation of new instrumentation
    techniques; Development of solutions to instrument &
    measurement problems; Electro optical design; Safety
    certification
● Conf - ET - Res
< airto
M c 40 f, UK / 10 f, o'seas

Sittingbourne & Kemsley Light Railway Ltd   (SKLR)   1969
■ 51 Russell Drive, WHITSTABLE, Kent, CT5 2RG.   (hsp)
    01227 792498   fax 01277 794963
    email mail@nickw.enterprise-plc.com
    http://www.sklr.net
    Hon Sec: N G Widdows
▲ Registered Charity
○ *G; railway preservation & operation
● Exhib - Railway operation
< Heritage Rly Assn; Kent [& Swale] Museum[s] Gp; Swale
    Heritage Assn; Swale Tourism Assn
M 350 i
¶ NL - 6; ftm.

Ski Club of Great Britain   1903
NR The White House, 57-63 Church Rd, Wimbledon, LONDON,
    SW19 5SB.   (hq)
    020 8410 2000   fax 020 8410 2001
    email skiers@skiclub.co.uk   http://www.skiclub.co.uk
    Chief Exec: Caroline Stuart-Taylor
○ *S; sport & recreation of skiing - cross-country, downhill, ski
    mountaineering & snowboarding
M c 26,000 i, f & org

Ski Council of Wales
    see under trading name: **Snowsport Cymru/Wales**

Skibob Association of Great Britain   (SAGB)   1966
NR 2-4 Langhorne Gardens, FOLKESTONE, Kent, CT20 2EA.
    (regd office)
    01303 251444   fax 01303 255167
    email admin@skibob.org.uk   http://www.skibob.org.uk
    Chmn: Richard Platt
▲ Un-incorporated Society
○ *S; promoting the sport of skibobbing
● ET - Comp - VE
< Fédn Intle de Skibob
M 500 i
¶ NL - 1; free.

Sleep Apnoea Trust Association   (SATA)
NR 12a Bakers Piece, KINGSTON BLOUNT, Oxon, OX39 4SW.
    0845 606 0685
    email sata.admin@tiscali.co.uk
    http://www.sleep-apnoea-trust.org
    Chmn: Brian Spires
○ *W; to improve the lives of sleep apnoea patients, their partners
    & their families
¶ Sleep Matters (NL) - 4.

Sleep Council   1995
NR High Corn Mill, Chapel Hill, SKIPTON, N Yorks, BD23 1NL.
    (hq)
    0845 058 4595   fax 0845 055 6407
    email info@sleepcouncil.org.uk
    http://www.sleepcouncil.com
▲ Company Limited by Guarantee
○ *T; 'promotes the benefits of a good bed to a good night's
    sleep to the consumer & media on behalf of bed
    manufacturers & retailers'
● Inf - Advertising
M 5,000 f
¶ Marketing Newz - 3; free.

**Sliding Glass Window Distributors Association   (SGWDA)
1980**
■ 10 Montcalm Close, Hayes, BROMLEY, Kent, BR2 7LZ.
    (mail address)
○ *T
● Conf
M f
¶ Runners - 6; ftm only.

Slurry Surfacing Contractors Association
    in 2008 merged with the Road Surface Dressing Association & the
    High Friction Surfacing Association to form the **Road Surface
    Treatments Association**

SMAE Fellowship (Association of British Physiotherapists) (SMAE) 1919

NR   New Hall, 149 Bath Rd, MAIDENHEAD, Berks, SL6 4LA.   (hq)
    01628 621100
    Principal: Michael J Batt
▲   Un-incorporated Society
○   *P; to promote professionalism & training in physiotherapy & sports injuries; covers surgical chiropody, podiatric medicine & complementary medicine
<   SMAE Institute
M   i

Small Charities Coalition (SCC)

NR   24 Stephenson Way, LODNON, NW1 2DP.   (hq)
    020 7391 4812
    email smallcharities.org.uk
    Chief Exec: Patrick Cox
○   *K; to level the playing field between the large & small charity orgs by providing access to resources and inf. to the public about the importance ofS Char's'small'= less than £1m income and where no member of staff is paid more than£50,000 pa(!!)

Small Electrical Appliance Marketing Association   (SEAMA) 1981

■   Airport House, Purley Way, CROYDON, Surrey, CR0 0XZ. (asa)
    020 8253 4508   fax 020 8253 4510
    email seama@admin.co.uk   http://www.seama.org.uk
    Sec: T Faithfull
▲   Un-incorporated Society
○   *T
●   Conf - Mtgs - SG - Stat - Inf - LG
M   12 f (22 brand names)
¶   LM; free.   Retailers Guide to Service - 1; ftm & retailers.

Small Farms Association (SFA) 1987

■   Ley Coombe Farm, Modbury, IVYBRIDGE, Devon, PL21 0TU. (chmn/p)
    01548 830302
    http://www.small-farms-association.co.uk
    Chmn: Philip Hosking
▲   Un-incorporated Society
○   *F; for those who are interested in the conservation of the countryside, particularly farmers who farm less than 250 acres, & also practise less intensive traditional methods of farming that are sympathetic to the needs of the environment & its wildlife
Gp   Steering group for marketing
●   Conf - Mtgs - ET - VE - LG
M   250 i
¶   NL - 12; ftm, on request nm.

Small Firms Association (SFA)

IRL   Confederation House, 84/86 Lower Baggot St, DUBLIN 2, Republic of Ireland.
    353 (1) 605 1500   fax 353 (1) 638 1602
    email info@sfa.ie   http://www.sfa.ie
    Dir: Patricia Callan
○   *T
<   IBEC
M   8,000 f

Small Landlords' Association
    since 2004 the **National Landlords' Association**

Small Practices Association
    since September 2007 **Family Doctor Association**

Small Woods Association (SWA) 1988

NR   Green Wood Centre, Station Rd, Coalbrookedale, TELFORD, Shropshire, TF8 7DR.   (hq)
    01952 432769   fax 01952 433082
    http://www.smallwoods.org.uk
    Exec Dir: Russell Rowley
▲   Company Limited by Guarantee; Registered Charity
○   *K, *N; to advance education in the conservation of small woodlands
Gp   Policy development; Training; Marketing; Information line
●   Conf - Mtgs - ET - Exhib - SG - Inf - VE - LG
M   700 i, 100 f, 50 org, UK / 10 i, 5 org, o'seas
¶   Smallwoods - 4.
    Small Woods Information Pack.
    Woodland Initiatives Register.

Smoke Control Association (SCA)

■   2 Waltham Court, Milley Lane, Hare Hatch, READING, Berks, RG10 9TH.   (hq)
    0118-940 3416   fax 0118-940 6258
    email info@feta.co.uk   http://www.feta.co.uk
    Dir-Gen: C Sloan
○   *T; specialist smoke control section of the HEVAC Association.   Develops & promotes high standards of quality, design, safety & workmanship in the industry & publishes standards for smoke control
Gp   Technical
●   Mtgs - Exhib - Stat - LG
<   Fedn Envtl Tr Assns (FETA)
M   22 f

Snack, Nut & Crisp Manufacturers Association Ltd (SNACMA) 1983

NR   6 Catherine St, LONDON, WC2B 5JJ.   (hq)
    020 7420 7220   fax 020 7420 7221
    email esa@esa.org.uk   http://www.esa.org.uk
    Sec Gen: Steve Chandler
▲   Company Limited by Guarantee
○   *T; to collaborate with industry players & external stakeholders in order to develop & grow sevoury snacks in the UK
Gp   Technical working group, Commercial working group, PR task force
●   Mtgs - ET - Stat - Inf - LG
<   Confedn Food & Drink Inds EU (CIAA); Food & Drink Fedn
M   7 f
¶   NL - 12; ftm.

Snowsport Cymru/Wales 1994

■   Cardiff Ski & Snowsport Centre, 198 Fairwater Rd, Fairwater, CARDIFF, CF5 3JR.   (hq)
    029 2056 1904   fax 029 2056 1924
    email info@snowsportwales.net
    http://www.snowsportwales.net
    Chief Exec: Robin Kellen
▲   Company Limited by Guarantee
○   *S; the governing body of skiing and snowboarding in Wales
●   Mtgs - ET - Exam - Comp - VE - LG
<   Snowsport GB
    is managed by the Ski Council of Wales
>   Ski Clubs in Wales; John Nike Ski Centre (Llandudno)
M   350 i, 1 f, 5 clubs schools, corporate support
      (Sub: £48 i, £70 f, £3 (per head) clubs)
¶   NL - 4;   AR - 1;   Website Updates - 12; all ftm.
    Snowsport Cymru/Wales is the trading name of the Ski Council of Wales

© CBD Research Ltd · Beckenham · BR3 5JS · Tel 020 8650 7745 · Fax 020 8650 0768 · E-mail cbd@cbdresearch.com · www.cbdresearch.com

Snowsport England   (ESC)   1979
- ■ Area Library Bldg, Queensway Mall, The Cornbow, HALESOWEN, W Midlands, B63 4AJ.   (hq)
  0121-501 2314   fax 0121-585 6448
  email info@snowsportengland.org.uk
  http://www.snowsportengland.org.uk
  Chief Exec: Tim Fawke
- ▲ Company Limited by Guarantee
- ○ *S; governing body of the sport in England; to promote & develop the sport within England & for English skiers
- ● Conf - Mtgs - ET - Exam - Exhib - Comp - Inf - VE - National Coaching Scheme (training & coaching instructors, officials & competitors) - Responsibility for standards, rules & regulations for the sport within England
- < Snowsport GB
- M 3,000 i, 15 f, 150 org
  Note: Snowsport England is the trading name of the English Ski Council Ltd

Snowsport GB   1981
- ■ Hillend, Biggar Rd, MIDLOTHIAN, EH10 7EF.   (hq)
  0131-445 7676   fax 0131-445 4949
  email info@snowsportgb.com
  http://www.snowsportgb.com
  Chief Exec: Mark Simmers
- ▲ Company Limited by Guarantee
- ○ *S; governing body for skiing & snowboarding in the UK
  The primary role is the selection, training & management of British teams
- Gp Alpine, Snowboard, Freestyle, Nordic
- ● ET
- < Intl Ski Fedn (FIS)
- > Snowsport England; Snowsport Scotland; Snowsport Wales
- M org
- ¶ Year Planner; free.
  Note: Snowsport GB is the trading name of the British Ski & Snowboard Federation.

Snowsport Industries of Great Britain   (SIGB)   1987
- ■ 3 Coalhill, The Shore, EDINBURGH, EH6 6RH.   (asa)
  0131-555 3820   fax 0131-553 7488
  email sigb@raremanagement.co.uk
  http://www.snowlife.org.uk
  Mgrs (Rare Management): Mike Jardine & Lesley Beck
- ▲ Company Limited by Guarantee
- ○ *T; for the ski & snowboard industry
- Gp Exhibition organisation
- ● Res - Exhib - Stat - Inf
- M 200 f
- ¶ e NL - 12; ftm only.   Exhibition Catalogue - 1; ftm, £5 nm.

Snowsport Scotland   (SNSC)   1963
- NR Hillend, Biggar Rd, MIDLOTHIAN, EH10 7EF.   (hq)
  0131-445 4151   fax 0131-445 4949
  email info@snowsportsctoland.org
  http://www.snowsportscotland.org
  Chief Exec: Jane Harvey
- ▲ Company Limited by Guarantee
- ○ *S; national governing body for skiing & snowboarding
- Gp Clubs (include) Skiing: Disabled, nordic, alpine, freestyle; Snowboarding
- ● Mtgs - ET - Exam - Comp - LG
- < Fédn Intle de Ski; Brit Ski & Snowboard Fedn; Scot Sports Assn
- M 7,000 i, 10 f, 40 clubs, UK / 20 i, o'seas
- ¶ Snowsport News - 4.
  Scottish Snowsport Hbk - 1.   AR.

Snuff Bottle Society   1969
- NR Pitts Deep, 3 Quay Rd, CHRISTCHURCH, Dorset, BH23 1BU.   (hq)
  01202 469050   fax 01202 469050
  Pres: Michael Kaynes
- ▲ Un-incorporated Society
- ○ *G; for all interested in the collecting, sale & exchange of snuff bottles
- M 50 i, UK / 40 i, o'seas
- ¶ Snuff Bottle Review - irreg.

Snuff - Narcotic Inhaler Followers & Aficionados
- ■ 191 Westcombe Hill, LONDON, SE3 7DR.
- Gp Snuff Users
- ● Conf
- M 10 i
- ¶ The Sniffer (Jnl) - 6; ftm only.

Social Care Association   (SCA)   1949
- ■ 350 West Barnes Lane, Motspur Park, NEW MALDEN, Surrey, KT3 6NB.   (hq)
  020 8949 5837   fax 020 8949 4384
  email sca@socialcaring.co.uk
  http://www.socialcaring.co.uk
  Chief Exec: Nicholas Johnson
- ▲ Company Limited by Guarantee
- Br 2
- ○ *P; to promote high standards in social care services
- ● Conf - ET - Exhib - Inf - LG
- M 4,000 i, 100 f
- ¶ Social Caring - 4.

Social, Emotional & Behavioural Difficulties Association styles itself **SEBDA**

Social History Curators Group   (SHCG)   1975
- ■ c/o The Bridewell, Bridewell Alley, NORWICH, Norfolk, NR2 1AQ.   (sb)
  01603 614018
  email enquiry@shcg.org.uk   http://www.shcg.org.uk
  Sec: Hannah Maddox
- ▲ Registered Charity
- ○ *P; to raise standards of curatorship in museums; interest in all aspects of social history
- ● Conf - ET - SG - VE - LG
- < Museums Assn; Collections Trust
- M 170 i, 123 f, UK / 8 i, o'seas
  (Sub: £16 i, £38 f, UK / £26 i, o'seas)
- ¶ Social History in Museums (Jnl) - 1; ftm, £7.50 nm.
  News - 3; ftm only.

Social History Society   (SHS)   1976
- ■ Centre for Social History, Furness College, LANCASTER, LA1 4YG.   (hq)
  01524 592547   fax 01524 846102
  email l.persson@lancaster.ac.uk
  http://www.socialhistory.org.uk
  Admin Sec: Linda Persson
- ▲ Registered Charity
- ○ *P; to encourage the study of the history of society
- ● Conf
- M 250 i, UK / 100 i, o'seas
- ¶ Cultural & Social History - 3; ftm only.

Social Policy Association   (SPA)
- NR Centre for the Analysis of Social Policy, University of Bath, BATH, Somerset, BA2 7AY.   (hsb)
  01225 385838   fax 01225 386381
  email t.m.ridge@bath.ac.uk
  http://www.social-policy.com
  Hon Sec: Tess Ridge
- ○ *P; for academics & practitioners working in social policy

Social Research Association (SRA) 1978

■ 24-32 Stephenson Way, LONDON, NW1 2HX. (hq)
  020 7388 2391
  email admin@the-sra.org.uk http://www.the-sra.org.uk
  Chief Exec: Dr Nigel Goldie
▲ Company Limited by Guarantee; Registered Charity
Br 3
○ *P; to advance the conduct, application & development of
  social research
Gp C'ees: Training, Events;
  Working gps: Commissioning & funding, Dissemination
● Conf - Mtgs - ET - Res
M 1,000 i, UK / 30 i, o'seas
¶ SRA News (NL) - 4; e-bulletin - 12; both ftm only.
  Ethical Guidelines; ftm, £10 nm.
  Data Protection Act 1998: guidelines for social research; ftm,
  £10 nm.
  Commissioning Social Research: a good practice guide; ftm,
  £10 nm.

** Socialist Business Values Association

Organisation lost, see Introduction paragraph 3

Socialist Environment & Resources Association (SERA) 1973

NR 1 London Bridge, Downstream Bldg (2nd floor), LONDON,
  SE1 9BG. (hq)
  020 7022 1985
  email enquiries@sera.org.uk http://www.sera.org.uk
  Nat Co-ordinator: Melanie Smallman
▲ Company Limited by Guarantee
○ *K; 'an environmental pressure group, affiliated to the Labour
  Party'
Gp Transport; Energy; Waste
● Conf - Mtgs - Inf - LG
< Labour Party
M 992 i, 23 f, 45 org, UK
¶ New Ground - 2; ftm.

Socialist Health Association (SHA) 1930

■ 22 Blair Rd, East Chorlton, MANCHESTER, Lancs, M16 8NS.
  (hq)
  0870 013 0065
  email admin@sochealth.co.uk
  http://www.sochealth.co.uk
  Dir: Martin Rathfelder
▲ Un-incorporated Society
Br 6
○ *K; to defend & extend the NHS; to develop the Labour Party's
  health policies; to encourage debate about politics & health
● Conf - Mtgs - SG
< Brit Labour Party
M 800 i, 100 org, UK / 10 i, o'seas
¶ Socialism & Health (Jnl) - 2/3; free.

La Société Guernesiaise 1882

■ Candie Gardens, ST PETER PORT, Guernsey, GY1 1UG. (hq)
  01481 725093 fax 01481 726248
  email societe@cwgsy.net http://www.societe.org.gg
  Sec: Mrs Lawney Martin
▲ Incorporated Society
○ *L; all aspects of natural science, archaeology, history, folklore,
  language, geography, geology, genealogy, nature
  conservation, etc of Guernsey & its islands
Gp Archaeology; Astronomy; Botany; Climate change;
  Entomology; Family history; Geology & geography; Historic
  buildings; History & philology; Marine biology & Zoology;
  Nature conservation; Ornithology
● Res - Lib - VE - LG
< Alderney Wildlife Trust; Bat Gp; Friends of Priaulx Library;
  Guernsey Conservation Volunteers; La Comité d'la Culture
  Guernésiase; La Société Sercquiaise; Meteorological
  Observatory; NCCPG (Guernsey gp), WEA
M 1,150 i, 65 f, (260, UK / 110, foreign)
¶ Transactions - 1; ftm, £10 nm. NL - 3; ftm only.

Société Jersiaise 1873

■ 7 Pier Rd, ST HELIER, Jersey, Channel Islands, JE2 4XW. (hq)
  01534 758314 fax 01534 888262
  email societe@societe-jersiaise.org
  http://www.societe-jersiaise.org
  Sec: Mrs Pauline J Syvret
▲ Registered Charity
○ *L; the study of the history, language, geology, natural history &
  antiquities of Jersey
Gp Archives; History; Bibliography; Numismatics; Garden history
● Mtgs - ET - Res - Exhib - SG - Inf - Lib - VE - Preservation
< Museums Assn
M 3,500 i
¶ Bulletin - 1; ftm, £15 nm.

Society of Academic & Research Surgery (SARS) 1953

NR Royal College of Surgeons, 35-43 Lincoln's Inn Fields,
  LONDON, WC2A 3PE. (hsb)
  020 7869 6640 fax 020 7869 6644
  email sars@rcseng.ac.uk
  http://www.surgicalresearch.org.uk
  Hon Sec: Linda Slater
○ *L; to provide for the interchange of information about research
  related to surgery & surgical disease
● Conf - Mtgs - Res
M 600 i
¶ Summaries of papers given at meetings are published in the
  British Journal of Surgery.

Society of Adhesion & Adhesives
  a group of the **Institute of Materials, Minerals & Mining**

Society for Advanced Legal Studies 1997

NR Charles Clore House, 17 Russell Square, LONDON,
  WC1B 5DR. (hq)
  020 7862 5865 fax 020 7862 5855
  email sals@sas.ac.uk http://www.ials.sas.ac.uk/sals/
  society.htm
  Sec: Julian Harris
○ *Q; to facilitate legal research at an advanced level; to
  engender collaboration between scholars & those involved in
  the practice of law
M 1,000+ i
¶ Amicus Curiae (Jnl) - 4; ftm, £75 nm.

Society for the Advancement of Anaesthesia in Dentistry (SAAD) 1957

NR 21 Portland Place, LONDON, W1B 1PY. (hq)
  020 7631 8893
  email saad@aagbi.org http://www.saad.org.uk
  Exec Sec: Fiona Wraith
▲ Registered Charity
○ *L; to research into the applications of methods of pain &
  anxiety control in dentistry
● Conf - ET - Courses - Lectures
< Intl Fedn of Dental Anaesthesiology Socs
M 1,700 i, UK / 300 i, o'seas
¶ SAAD Digest - 4.

Society for the Advancement of Games & Simulations in Education & Training (SAGSET) 1970

NR 11 Lloyd St, RYTON, Tyne & Wear, NE40 4DJ. (hsp)
  0191-413 2262 fax 0191-413 2262
  email peter@j-walsh.freeserve.co.uk
  http://www.simulations.co.uk/sagset/
  Admin: Peter Walsh
▲ Un-incorporated Society
○ *E; to develop games, simulations & all forms of interactive
  learning in education & training
● Conf - Mtgs - ET - Inf
< ISAGA, ABSEL
M 71 i, 26 f & org, UK / 26 i, 23 f & org, o'seas
¶ Interact - 3.
  International Simulation & Gaming Research Ybk.

© CBD Research Ltd · Beckenham · BR3 5JS · Tel 020 8650 7745 · Fax 020 8650 0768 · E-mail cbd@cbdresearch.com · www.cbdresearch.com

Society for the Advancement of Philosophical Enquiry & Reflection in Education
    rationale behind the name **SAPERE**

Society for All Artists
    styles itself **SAA**

Society of Allied & Independent Funeral Directors
    alternative name of the **National Society of Allied & Independent Funeral Directors**

Society for Anaerobic Microbiology   1975
NR c/o Dr Mark Wilks, Microbiology, Pathology & Pharmacy Bldg,
    80 Newark St, LONDON, E1 2ES.   (sb)
    020 3246 0295
    email m.wilks@qmul.ac.uk   http://www.clostridia.net/sam/
    Sec: Dr Mark Wilks
▲ Company Limited by Guarantee
○ *P
● Conf - Mtgs - ET
M 200 i, UK / 68 i, o'seas
¶ NL - 2; free.
    Proceedings of Biennial Meetings - 1/2 yrly; free to delegates, £20.

Society of Ancients   (SOA)   1965
NR Twin Oaks, The Drive, Ifold, LOXWOOD, W Sussex,
    RH14 0TE.   (hsp)
    01403 752973
    email davidedwards30@hotmail.com
    http://www.soa.org.uk
    Sec: David Edwards
▲ Un-incorporated Society
○ *G; to promote the study of ancient & mediæval military history & wargaming therein (3000 BC - 1500 AD)
● Conf - Exhib - Comp
M 872 i, UK / 446 i, o'seas
¶ Slingshot - 6.

Society for Anglo-Chinese Understanding Ltd   (SACU)   1965
NR 16 Portland St, CHELTENHAM, Glos, GL52 2PB.   (hq)
    01229 472010
    email info@sacu.org   http://www.sacu.org
    Chmn: David Clare
▲ Company Limited by Guarantee; Registered Charity
Br 5
○ *X; to promote friendship & understanding between the peoples of Britain & China
● Mtgs - ET - Lib - Inf on China related events in Britain - Inf about China for schools, playgroups & local groups
M 340 i, 4 org
    Subs:£15 i, £22 org
¶ China Eye - 4; ftm, £1 nm.   Hbk.   AR.
    Education pack on request.

Society of Antiquaries of London   1707
■ Burlington House, Piccadilly, LONDON, W1J 0BE.   (hq)
    020 7734 0193
    Gen Sec: David Gaimster
▲ Registered Charity
○ *L; promotion of antiquarian interests, particularly archaeological investigation & the preservation of historic buildings
● Conf - Mtgs - Res - Lib
M 1,700 i, UK / 300 i, o'seas
¶ Antiquaries Jnl - 1.
    Research reports;   Occasional papers; prices vary.

Society of Antiquaries of Newcastle upon Tyne   (SANT)   1813
■ The Black Gate, Castle Garth, NEWCASTLE upon TYNE,
    NE1 1RQ.   (hq)
    0191-261 5390
    email admin@newcastle-antiquaries.org.uk
    http://www.newcastle-antiquaries.org.uk
    Sec: Dr N Hodgson,   Mem Sec: Mrs S Walter
▲ Registered Charity
○ *L; the study & preservation of antiquities & historical records particularly relating to the old counties of Northumberland & Durham & Newcastle upon Tyne
● Conf - Mtgs - Res - Lib - VE - One-day workshop (annual) - Workshops (10 evenings)
M 600 i, 100 f, UK / 20 i, 20 f, o'seas
¶ Archaeologia Aeliana - 1.
    Occasional research publications & guide books.

Society of Antiquaries of Scotland   1780
■ National Museums Scotland, Chambers St, EDINBURGH,
    EH1 1JF.   (hq)
    0131-247 4115 & 4133   fax 0131-247 4163
    email administration@socantscot.org
    http://www.socantscot.org
    Dir: Simon Gilmour
▲ Registered Charity
○ *L; archaeology, history & antiquities of Scotland
● Conf - Mtgs - Res - VE - LG
< Built Environment Forum Scotland; The Archaeology Forum
M 3,000 i, UK / 600 i, o'seas
    (Sub: £60)
¶ Proceedings - 1; ftm, £60 nm.   NL - 2; ftm only.
    Books - irreg; prices vary.

Society for Applied Microbiology   (Sfam)   1931
NR School of Life Sciences, Kingston University, Penrhyn Rd,
    KINGSTON upon THAMES, Surrey, KT1 2EE.   (hq)
    email info@sfam.org.uk   http://www.sfam.org.uk
    Hon Gen Sec: Dr Mark Fielder
▲ Registered Charity; Un-incorporated Society
○ *L; to advance the study of microbiology, in its application to the environment, agriculture & industry
Gp Special interest groups: Bioengineering, Educational development, Environmental, Food safety & technology, Infection, Prevention & treatment, Molecular biology
● Conf - Publishing
< Intl U Microbiology Socs; Fedn Eur Microbiology Socs; Inst of Biology; Foundation for Science & Technology; UK Nat C'ee for Microbiology
M 1300 i, UK / 500 i, o'seas
¶ Jnl of Applied Microbiology - 12; [with] Letters in Applied Microbiology - 12.
    NL - 4.   Environmental Microbiology - 6.

Society for Applied Philosophy   (SAP)   1982
■ c/o Jon Cameron, RIISS, Humanity Manse 19 College Bounds,
    University of Aberdeen, ABERDEEN, AB24 3UG.   (admin)
    01224 272343
    Admin: Jon Cameron,   Chmn: Prof David Archard
    Hon Sec: Dr John Tasioulas
▲ Registered Charity
○ *L; to promote philosophical research into practical problems of social & ethical concern
● Conf - Funding academic activity
M 80 i, UK / 45 i, o'seas
    (Sub: £25)
¶ Jnl of Applied Philosophy - 4; ftm, £70 nm.

Society of Archer-Antiquaries   (SAA)   1956
- ■ Yew Corner, 29 Batley Court, OLDLAND, S Glos, BS30 8YZ.
    (hsp/b)
    0117-932 3276
    email bogaman@btinternet.com
    http://www.societyofarcher-antiquaries.org
    Hon Soc: Hugh D Hewitt Suur
- ▲ Registered Charity
- Br Australia, Germany, Italy, Netherlands, USA
- ○ *L; the study of the history & development of the bow & arrow
    across the world
- ● Mtgs - Res - Inf - Lib
- M 227 i, UK / 161 i, o'seas
- ¶ Jnl - 1;   NL - 3; both ftm only.

**Society of Architectural Historians of Great Britain   (SAHGB)
1956**
- NR c/o RCAHMS, 16 Barnard Terrace, EDINBURGH, EH8 9NX.
    (hsb)
    email secretary@sahgb.org.uk   http://www.sahgb.org.uk
    Hon Sec: Simon Green
- ▲ Company Limited by Guarantee; Registered Charity
- ○ *L; to encourage an interest in the history of architecture
- ¶ Architectural History - 1.   NL - 3.

Society of Architectural Illustration Ltd   (SAI)   1975
- ■ Rosemary Cottage, Bletchinglye Lane, ROTHERFIELD, E Sussex,
    TN6 3NN.   (hq)
    01892 852578
    email info@sai.org.uk   http://www.sai.org.uk
    Admin: Heather Coe
- ▲ Registered Charity
- ○ *A, *P; for members of the design profession specialising in
    illustration of architectural subjects
- Gp Illustrators; Photographers; Model makers
- ● Conf - Mtgs - ET - Exhib - Comp
- M 178 i, UK / 8 i, o'seas
- ¶ Viewpoint - 2;   NL - 4; both free.
    LM; on application & by region.   AR.
- ✕ Society of Architectural Illustrators

Society of Archivists   1947
- NR Prioryfield House, 20 Canon St, TAUNTON, Somerset,
    TA1 1SW.   (hq)
    01823 327030   fax 01823 371719
- ▲ Company Limited by Guarantee; Registered Charity
- Br 10; Republic of Ireland
- ○ *P; for archivists, archive conservators & records managers; for
    the effective management of record systems including the
    retrieval of information from them
- Gp Records management; Preservation & conservation; Specialist
    repositories; Film & sound; Archives in education;
    Information technology
- ● Conf - Mtgs - ET - Exam - Res - Exhib - Stat - Inf - Lib - VE -
    Empl - LG
- < Intl Coun Archives
- M 1,915 i
- ¶ Jnl - 2.   NL - 12.   Career Opportunities - 26.

Society for Army Historical Research   (SAHR)   1921
- NR c/o National Army Museum, Royal Hospital Rd, LONDON,
    SW3 4HT.   (accom address)
    http://www.sahr.co.uk
- ▲ Registered Charity
- ○ *L; research into the history & traditions of the British Army, the
    land forces of the Empire, Dominions & Commonwealth &
    ancillary units attached thereto
- ● Mtgs - Res - VE - Publishing members' research - Lecture series
- M 930 i, 20 org, UK / 40 i, 10 org, o'seas
- ¶ Jnl - 4.   Special issues - irreg; ftm only.

Society of Artists' Agents   (SAA)   1992
- ■ 31 Eleanor Rd, LONDON, E15 4AB.   (admin/p)
    0845 050 7600
    email membershipsecretary@the saa.com
    http://www.ssahub.com
    Admin: Delphine Lebourgeois
- ▲ Un-incorporated Society
- ○ *T; to promote the use of illustration & improve the working
    practices between clients, agents & artists
- ● Mtgs
- < Pro-Action
- M 11 f
- ¶ Originals - 1; ftm.

Society of Asian Lawyers
    a group of the **Law Society of England & Wales**

Society of Assistants Teaching in Preparatory Schools Ltd
    now known as **SATIPS - Support & Training in Prep Schools**

Society of Authors   (SoA)   1884
- ■ 84 Drayton Gardens, LONDON, SW10 9SB.   (hq)
    020 7373 6642   fax 020 7373 5768
    email info@societyofauthors.org
    http://www.societyofauthors.org
    Gen Sec: Mark Le Fanu
- ○ *U
- Gp Academic writers; Broadcasting; Children's writers & illustrators;
    Educational writers; Medical writers; Translators Association
- ● Conf - Mtgs - Inf - Empl - LG
- M 8,000 i
- ¶ The Author - 4.

Society of Authors in Scotland
- ■ c/o The Society of Authors, 84 Drayton Gardens, LONDON,
    SW10 9SB.
    020 7373 6642   fax 020 7373 5768
    email anguskonstam@aol.com
    Sec: Angus Konstam
- ▲ Company Limited by Guarantee
- ○ *A; the Scottish branch of the Society of Authors
- ● Mtgs - ET - VE
- < Soc Authors
- M 450 i
- ¶ Occasional NL - irreg.

Society for the Autistically Handicapped
    alternative name of **Autism Independent UK**

Society of Automotive Engineers - UK   (SAE-UK)   1881
- ■ 9 Tixall Rd, BIRMINGHAM, W Midlands, B28 0RU.   (hq)
    0121-270 6592
    email info@sae-uk.org   http://www.sae-uk.org
    Chief Exec: Dr Anthony McDonagh-Smith
- ▲ Registered Charity
- ○ *L; dedicated to the furtherance of mobility engineering in the
    fields of automotive, aerospace, naval, agricultural & others
- ● Conf - Mtgs - ET - Comp - Inf
- < Soc of Automotive Engrs-Intl
- > Soc of Automotive Engrs - Intl (SAE-Intl)
- M 2,000 i, 100 f, 20 org
- ¶ Vehicle Technology - 4; £60 m.   Members' Hbk - 1; ftm only.
- ✕ 2005-06 Institute of Vehicle Engineers

© CBD Research Ltd · Beckenham · BR3 5JS · Tel 020 8650 7745 · Fax 020 8650 0768 · E-mail cbd@cbdresearch.com · www.cbdresearch.com

Society of Automotive Historians in Britain (SAH) 1977

■ Acorns, Oak Lane, Easterton, DEVIZES, Wilts, SN10 4PD.
(chmn/p)
01380 812649
email m_jeal@tiscali.co.uk
Chmn: Malcolm Jeal
▲ Un-incorporated Society
○ *G; to encourage research, preservation, recording,
compilation & publication of historical facts concerning the
worldwide development of the automobile & related items
● Conf - Res - Res - Lib - PL
< American Histl Soc
> Veteran Car Club of GB
M c 100 i, UK / c 900 i, o'seas
(Sub: £30)
¶ SAHB Times - 4; free.
Aspects of Motoring History - 1; ftm, £5 nm.
in USA:
SAH Jnl - 6; SAH Review - irreg; both ftm only.

Society for Back Pain Research
a specialist society of the **British Orthopaedic Association**

Society of Batrachologists 1995

■ 3 Hughes Stanton Way, MANNINGTREE, Essex, CO11 2HQ.
(hsp)
○ *L
● Conf - VE
M 85 i, 1 org
¶ Ribbit Road (Jnl) - 4.

Society of Bookbinders (SOB) 1974

NR 73 Lyncombe Hills, BATH, Somerset, BA2 4PH. (chmn/p)
http://www.societyofbookbinders.com
Acting Chmn: Tim Gulliford
▲ Registered Charity
Br 8, overseas
○ *L, *T; to advance the art, craft & science of bookbinding, book
restoration & conservation
¶ Bookbinder (Jnl) - 1. NL - 3.

Society of Border Leicester Sheep Breeders 1896

■ Rock Midstead, ALNWICK, Northumberland, NE66 2TH. (hsp)
01665 579326 fax 01665 579326
email info@borderleicesters.co.uk
http://www.borderleicesters.co.uk
Sec: Ian J R Sutherland
▲ Registered Charity
○ *B
● Mtgs - Exhib - Expt - Inf
< Nat Sheep Assn
M 250 i, 10 f, UK / 5 i, o'seas
¶ Jnl - 1. Flock Book - 1; £15. AR.

Society of Botanical Artists (SBA) 1985

■ 1 Knapp Cottages, Wyke, GILLINGHAM, Dorset, SP8 4NQ.
(hq)
01747 825718 fax 01747 826835
email info@soc-botanical-artists.org
http://www.soc-botanical-artists.org
Exec Sec: Mrs Pamela Henderson
▲ Company Limited by Guarantee; Registered Charity
○ *A, *P; to paint & record for the benefit of art, botany,
conservation & horticulture
● Exhib
M 140 i, UK / 13 i, o'seas
¶ Annual Exhibitions Catalogue - 1; £5.

Society of British Aerospace Companies Ltd (SBAC) 1916

NR Salamanca Square, 9 Albert Embankment, LONDON,
SE1 7SP. (hq)
020 7091 4500 fax 020 7091 4545
email post@sbac.co.uk http://www.sbac.co.uk
Pres: Alex Dorrian
▲ Un-incorporated Society
○ *T; UK aerospace & overseas airport development industries
● Conf - Mtgs - Res - Exhib - Stat - Expt - Inf - Lib - PL - VE - LG -
Organises the Farnborough Intl Air Show
< Eur Assn of Aerospace Inds (AECMA)
M 250 f
¶ What's New in UK Aerospace (NL) - 4; Capability Brochure - 1;
Members' E-Bulletin - 26; Annual Review; all ftm.

Society of British Gas Industries
since 2008 **SBGI**

Society of British Neurological Surgeons (SBNS) 1926

■ at the Royal College of Surgeons, 35-43 Lincoln's Inn Fields,
LONDON, WC2A 3PE. (hq)
020 7869 6892 fax 020 7869 6890
email admin@sbns.org.uk http://www.sbns.org
Admin: Suzanne Murray
○ *P; interests of neurosurgery & neurosurgeons
● Conf - Mtgs - Exam - Res - LG
< WFNS; EANS
M c 400 i
¶ NL - 3.

Society of British Theatre Designers (SBTD) 1971

■ 55 Farringdon Rd, LONDON, EC1M 3JB. (regd/office)
020 7242 9200
email admin@theatredesign.org.uk
http://www.theatredesign.org.uk
Jt Hon Secs: Sophie Jump & Iona McLeish
▲ Registered Charity
○ *P; to enhance the standing of British theatre design at home &
abroad; to support designers in their working lives
● Conf - Exhib (4-yrly) - Inf
< Intl Org of Scenographers (OISTAT); Assn of Brit Theatre
Technicians (ABTT)
M 300 i, 10 org, UK / 10 i, o'seas
(Sub: £60 i, £200 org, UK / £67.50 i, o'seas)
¶ The Blue PAges (NL) - 4; ftm only.

Society of British Water & Wastewater Industries (SBWWI) 1986

■ 38 Holly Walk, LEAMINGTON SPA, Warks, CV32 4LY. (hq)
01926 831530 fax 01926 831931
email hq@sbwwi.co.uk http://www.sbwwi.co.uk
Exec Dir: Carol Hickman
▲ Un-incorporated Society
○ *T; for manufacturers, contractors, suppliers, consultants &
other organisations involved in the UK water & wastewater
industry
Gp Sections: Commercial, Technical
Groups: Export, Health & safety, Leakage, Specialist products
● Conf - Mtgs - Exhib - Stat - Inf - LG
M 90 f

Society of Business Economists (SBE) 1953
■ Dean House, Vernham Dean, ANDOVER, Hants, SP11 0JZ. (sec/p)
   01264 737552
   email admin@sbe.co.uk   http://www.sbe.co.uk
   Sec: Katie Abberton
▲ Company limited by Guarantee
○ *P; applications of economics in business & industry
Gp Forecasting; Statistics; Industrial economics
● Conf - Mtgs - SG
< Intl Fedn Assns Business Economists (IFABE); Assn Française
   Economistes d'Entreprise (AFEDE); Canadian Assn Business
   Economists (CABE); Nat Assn Business
   Economists (NABE)(USA)
M 600 i, UK / 50 i, o'seas
¶ The Business Economist (Jnl) - 3; ftm, £38 nm (£45 outside
   Europe).

Society of Business Practitioners (SBP) 1956
■ New House, Warmingham Rd, Warmingham, SANDBACH,
   Cheshire, CW11 3QP.   (hq)
   01270 526339   fax 01270 526339
   Pres: M Whitaker
▲ Company Limited by Guarantee
Br China, Hong Kong, New Zealand, Singapore
○ *P; professional quailifications for all aspects of management
● ET - Exam
M 3,000 i, UK / 9,000 i, o'seas
¶ Nexus - 1.

Society of Cable Telecommunication Engineers (SCTE) 1945
NR 41A Market St, WATFORD, Herts, WD18 0PN.   (hq)
   01923 815500   fax 01923 803203
   http://www.scte.org.uk
   Sec: Mrs Beverley Allgood
▲ Un-incorporated Society
○ *L, *P; to raise the standard of broadband engineering in the
   telecommunications industry
● Mtgs - ET - Exam - Exhib - Inf
< Intl SCTE (America)
M c 700 i, 100 f
¶ Broadband (Jnl) - 4;   Ybk; both free.

Society Campaigning for the Removal of Exasperating Automated Switchboards (SCREAMS) 2003
NR 191 Westcombe Hill, LONDON, SE3 7DR.
○ *K
M 49 i
¶ Human Voices (NL) - 4.

Society for Cardiological Science & Technology (SCST) 1948
■ Sovereign House (suite 4), 22 Gate Lane, SUTTON COLDFIELD,
   W Midlands, B73 5TT.   (admin)
   0845 838 6037   fax 0121-355 2420
   email admin@scst.org.uk   http://www.scst.org.uk
   Hon Sec: Peter Lewis
▲ Registered Charity
○ *P; to support clinical physiologists within cardiology
● ET - Exam - LG
M 1,500 i

Society for Cardiothoracic Surgery in Great Britain & Ireland (SCTS) 1933
■ at the Royal College of Surgeons, 35-43 Lincoln's Inn Fields,
   LONDON, WC2A 3PE.   (asa)
   020 7869 6893   fax 020 7869 6890
   email sctsadmin@scts.org   http://www.scts.org
   Hon Sec: Graham Cooper
▲ Registered Charity
○ *P; cardiothoracic surgery
● Conf - ET - Exhib - Empl - LG
M 492 i, UK / 53 i, o'seas
× Society of Cardiothoracic Surgeons of Great Britain & Ireland

Society of Chartered Surveyors (SCS)
IRL 5 Wilton Place, DUBLIN 2, Republic of Ireland.
   353 (1) 676 5500   fax 353 (1) 676 1412
   email info@scs.ie   http://www.scs.ie
   Hon Sec: Pauline Daly
○ *P

Society of Cheese Connoisseurs (SCC) 1985
■ 10 Montcalm Close, Hayes, BROMLEY, Kent, BR2 7LS.
   (mail address)
○ *G
● Mtgs - VE - Tastings
M 25 i
¶ Mousetrap! (incl AR) - 1;   NL - 4; both ftm only.

Society of Chemical Industry (SCI) 1881
NR 14-15 Belgrave Square, LONDON, SW1X 8PS.   (hq)
   020 7598 1500
   http://www.soci.org
▲ Registered Charity
○ *L; 'an interdisciplinary network connecting industry, research &
   consumer affairs at all levels throughout the world; provides
   opportunities for forward-looking people in the process &
   materials technologies, energy, water, agriculture, food,
   pharmaceuticals, materials, construction & environmental
   protection areas to exchange ideas & gain new perspectives
   on markets, technologies, strategies & people'

Society of Chief Architects of Local Authorities
   since 2008 **Scala - Serving Construction & Architecture in Local Authorities**

Society of Chief Librarians (SCL) 1996
■ c/o Fiona Williams, Libraries & Heritage, City of York Council,
   Library Square, YORK, YO1 7DU.   (hsb)
   01904 553316
   email fiona.williams@york.gov.uk   http://www.goscl.com
   Hon Sec: Fiona Williams
▲ Un-incorporated Society
○ *P; the development of the public library service; to influence
   statutory, financial & other decisions which relate to the
   effectiveness of public library services
● Conf - Mtgs - Res - SG - Stat - LG
< Quality Forum [for library & information services]; Share the
   Vision
M 122 i
¶ Fines & Charges in Public Libraries in England & Wales - 1.

Society of Chief Officers of Trading Standards in Scotland (SCOTSS) 1975
NR Trading Standards Service, John Muir House, HADDINGTON,
   E Lothian, EH41 3HA.   (hsb)
   01620 827365
   email tmcauley@eastlothian.gov.uk
   http://www.scotss.org.uk
   Sec: Tony McAuley
▲ Un-incorporated Society
○ *P; coordination of trading standards & consumer protection in
   Scotland
< Trading Standards Inst
M 33 i

Society of Chief Personnel Officers in Local Government
   since 2006 **Public Sector People Managers' Association**

Society of Chief Quantity Surveyors in the Public Sector
   since 2003 **Society of Construction & Quantity Surveyors**

© CBD Research Ltd · Beckenham · BR3 5JS · Tel 020 8650 7745 · Fax 020 8650 0768 · E-mail cbd@cbdresearch.com · www.cbdresearch.com

Society of Chiropodists & Podiatrists   (SCP)   1945
NR   1 Fellmonger's Path, Tower Bridge Rd, LONDON, SE1 3LY.
        (hq)
        020 7234 8620   fax 0845 450 3721
        email scp1@scpod.org   http://www.feetforlife.org
        Chief Exec: Joanna Brown
▲   Un-incorporated Society
Br   40
○   *P, *U; registered podiatrists
M   10,000 i
¶   Podiatry Now - 12.   British Journal of Podiatry - 4.

Society of Cirplanologists   1955
■   26 Roe Cross Green, Mottram, HYDE, Cheshire, SK14 6LP.
        (hsp)
        01457 763485
        Sec: E A Rose
▲   Un-incorporated Society
○   *L; study, collection, preservation of circuit plans, mainly
        Methodist
●   Informal annual mtg
M   100 i, UK / 5 i, o'seas
¶   Cirplan - 2; £1.50.

**Society of Clinical Perfusion Scientists of Great Britain & Ireland
1974**
■   at the Royal College of Surgeons, 35-43 Lincoln's Inn Fields,
        LONDON, WC2A 3PE.   (hq)
        020 7869 6891
        Admin: Ms Valerie Campbell
○   *P

Society of Clinical Psychiatrists   (SCP)   1958
■   Chapel Garth, Westway, Crayke, YORK, YO61 4TE.   (hsp)
        01347 823042
        email dermot.ward@talktalk.net   http://www.scpnet.com
        Hon Sec: Dr M T Haslam
▲   Un-incorporated Society
○   *P; to promote good practice in psychiatry; to undertake studies
        in related matters
Gp   Suspended doctors support
●   Conf - Mtgs - Res - SG - LG
M   50 i, UK / 5 i, o'seas
        (Sub: £20)
¶   NL - updated on web.

Society for Co-operative Studies
        see the **United Kingdom Society for Co-operative Studies**

Society of Coat Hook Collectors   (SCHC)   1976
■   76c The Avenue, BECKENHAM, Kent, BR3 5EF.   (hsp)
▲   Un-incorporated Society
○   *G
●   Conf - Mtgs
M   i

Society for Companion Animal Studies   (SCAS)   1979
NR   The Blue Cross, Shilton Rd, BURFORD, Oxon, OX18 4PF.   (hq)
        01993 825597   fax 01993 825598
        email info@scas.org.uk   http://www.scas.org.uk
        Dir: Jo-Ann Fowler
▲   Registered Charity
Br   Australia, France, Japan, Netherlands, New Zealand,
        Singapore, Spain & USA
○   *E, *V, *W; to study the nature of the bond between people &
        companion animals
Gp   Pet bereavement support; Research advisory panel
●   Conf - ET - Res - Exhib - Inf - Lib
<   Intl Assn of Human-Animal Interaction Orgs (IAHAIO)
M   361 i, 58 f, UK / 25 i, o'seas
¶   Jnl - 4; ftm, £2.50 nm.
        When a Pet Dies [learning pack]; £58.
        Children & Pets; £5.99.

Society for Computers & Law   (SCL)   1973
NR   10 Hurle Crescent, Clifton, BRISTOL, BS8 2TA.   (hq)
        0117-923 7393   fax 0117-923 9305
        http://www.scl.org
        Gen Mgr: Ruth Baker
▲   Company Limited by Guarantee; Registered Charity
○   *L; to study the development of the law and practice regulating
        IT
M   1,676 i, 68 org
¶   Computers & Law - 3.

**Society for Computing & Technology in Anaesthesia   (SCATA)
1987**
■   21 Portland Place, LONDON, W1B 1PY.   (hq)
        email mail@scata.org.uk   http://www.scata.org.uk
        Sec: Paul Cooper
▲   Registered Charity
○   *L, *M, *P; to promote research into the use of computing &
        technology in anaesthetic practice
●   Conf - Mtgs - ET - Res - SG - LG
<   Eur Soc for Computing & Technology Anaesthesia & Intensive
        Care; Assn Anaesthetists GB & Ireland
M   325 i, UK / 25 i, o'seas

Society of Construction Law   (SCL)   1983
NR   67 Newbury St, WANTAGE, Oxon, OX12 8DJ.   (hq)
        01235 770606   fax 01235 770580
        http://www.scl.org.uk
        Sec: Jocelyn Taylor
▲   Registered Charity
○   *L; to promote the study & advancement of education in the
        theory & practice & application of construction law
<   Eur Soc Construction Law
M   2,090 i
¶   NL - 9; ftm only.   Papers (after meetings); ftm.

Society of Construction & Quantity Surveyors   (SCQS)   1973
■   24 Pennine Rise, Scissett, HUDDERSFIELD, W Yorks, HD8 9JE.
        (ch/exec/p)
        01484 863686
        http://www.scqs.org.uk
        Chief Exec: Brian Kirkham
▲   Company Limited by Guarantee
○   *P; interchange of information on quantity surveying, building
        economics, types of contract, government regulations & all
        other matters affecting the built environment in the public
        sector
●   Conf - Mtgs - ET - Res - SG - Stat - LG
<   Fedn Property Socs
M   224 i
¶   NL - 4; free.   Ybk - 1; ftm, £5 nm.

Society of Consulting Marine Engineers & Ship Surveyors   1920
■   202 Lambeth Rd, LONDON, SE1 7JW.   (hq)
        020 7261 0869   fax 020 7261 0871
        email sec@scmshq.org   http://www.scmshq.org
        Sec: Paul Owen
▲   Company Limited by Guarantee
○   *P; for consulting marine engineers, naval architects & ship
        surveyors
●   Mtgs - Inf - Social events
<   Fedn of Eur Maritime Assns of Surveyors & Consultants
        (FEMAS)
M   252 i, UK / 137 i, o'seas
¶   Jnl; m only.

Society for Cooperation in Russian & Soviet Studies   (SCRSS) 1924
- ■ 320 Brixton Rd, LONDON, SW9 6AB.   (hq)
    020 7274 2282   fax 020 7274 3230
    email ruslibrary@scrss.org.uk   http://www.scrss.org.uk
    Sec: Jean Turner
- ▲ Registered Charity
- ○ *X; to promote studies in the language, culture & history of
    Russia & other republics of the former USSR
- Gp Music; Russian/Soviet literature; History; Art; Visual aids;
    Lawyers & architects
- ● Conf - Mtgs - ET - Res - Exhib - Inf - Lib - PL
- < Russian State Centre for Intl Co-operation in Science & Culture;
    St Petersburg Assn for Intl Co-operation
- M 400 i, 18 f, 4 org, UK / 2 i, o'seas
- ¶ SCRSS Information Digest - 3; ftm, £1+p&p nm.
    Publicity brochure.   AR.

Society of Cosmetic Scientists   (SCS)   1948
- ■ GT House, 24-26 Rothesay Rd, LUTON, Beds, LU1 1QX.   (hq)
    01582 726661   fax 01582 405217
    email ifscc.scs@btconnect.com   http://www.scs.org.uk
    Sec Gen: Mrs Lorna Weston
- ▲ Un-incorporated Society
- ○ *P; to promote the scientific status of the cosmetic industry
- ● Conf - Mtgs - ET (courses) - Exam - Exhib
- < Intl Fedn Socs Cosmetic Chemists (IFSCC)
- M 950 i
- ¶ International Jnl of Cosmetic Science - 6;
    NL - 9/10;   AR;   all ftm only.

Society of County Treasurers   (SCT)   1903
- NR Shire Hall, WARWICK, CV34 4RA.   (hsb)
    01926 410410
    http://www.sctnet.org
    Hon Sec: David Clarke
- ▲ Un-incorporated Society
- ○ *P; financial management, personnel & other matters affecting
    local government in England & Wales
- Gp Local government finance
- ● Mtgs - SG - Stat - LG
- M 37 i
- ¶ Standard Spending Indicators - 1.
    Precept Return - 1.   AR.

Society for Court Studies   1995
- ■ PO Box 57089, LONDON, EC1P 1RF.   (hq)
    email admin@courtstudies.org
    http://www.courtstudies.org
    Mem Admin: Helen Jones
- ▲ Un-incorporated Society
- Br USA
- ○ *L; stimulate the study of royal courts from 1400 to the present
- ● Conf - Mtgs
- M 240 i & f
- ¶ The Court Historian (Jnl) - 2.

Society of Crisp Packet Collectors   (SCPC)
- ■ 81 Park View, Collins Road, LONDON, N5 2UD.
    Hon Sec: V Salis
- ○ *G
- ● Mtgs - Exhib
- M 11 i
- ¶ Blue Bag - irreg, ftm only.

Society of Dairy Technology   (SDT)   1943
- ■ PO Box 12, APPLEBY-in-WESTMORLAND, Cumbria,
    CA16 6YJ.   (hq)
    01768 354034
    http://www.sdt.org
    Exec Dir: Maurice Walton
- ▲ Company Limited by Guarantee; Registered Charity
- Br 15; 1
- ○ *L, *F, *P; the advancement of dairy science & technology
- Gp Milk & milk products processing, manufacture & distribution;
    Supply of dairy plant & equipment; Dairy - education,
    advisory, research
- ● Conf - Mtgs - ET
- < Intl Dairy Fedn (through the UK Dairy Assn)
- M 450 i, UK / 30 i, o'seas
- ¶ International Jnl of Dairy Technology - 4; ftm, £230 nm.NL - 4;
    AR; both ftm only

Society for Dance Research   (SDR)   1983
- ■ c/o Dr Helen Julia Minors, School of Arts, Southlands College,
    Roehampton University, LONDON, SW15 5SL.   (hsb)
    020 8392 3420
    email h.minors@roehampton.ac.uk
    http://www.dancebooks.co.uk/sdr-uk/
    Sec: Dr Helen Julia Minors
- ▲ Registered Charity
- ○ *D; to further research in dance history, anthropology, analysis
    & criticism in both theatre & social forms
- ● Conf - Mtgs - ET - Res - Inf
- M c 170 i, c 20 org, UK / c 40 i, o'seas
- ¶ Dance Research Jnl - 2; £30 m, £35 nm o'seas.

Society of Decorative Art Curators   (SODAC)
- ■ 127 Dale St, LIVERPOOL, L2 2JH.   (hsb)
    0151-478 4262
    Mem Sec: Pauline Rushton
- ▲ Un-incorporated Society
- ○ *P
    No further information supplied.

Society of Designer Craftsmen   (SDC)   1888
- NR 24 Rivington St, LONDON, EC2A 3DU.   (hq)
    020 7739 3663
    email info@societyofdesignercraftsmen.org.uk
    http://www.societyofdesignercraftsmen.org.uk
- ▲ Registered Charity
- ○ *A; to promote professional practice by designer-craftsmen of
    all kinds
- ● Conf - Res - Exhib - SG - Inf
- M 800 i, UK / 13 i, o'seas
- ¶ The Designer Craftsman - 1;   NL - 4; both ftm only.

Society of Diagnostic Engineers
a division of the **Institution of Diagnostic Engineers**

Society of District Council Treasurers
- NR c/o Graham Soulsby, Kettering Borough Council, Municipal
    Offices, KETTERING, Northants, NN15 7QX.
    01536 5334213
    email grahamsoulsby@kettering.gov.uk
    http://www.socdct.co.uk
    Vice-Pres & Sec: Graham SOulsby
- ○ *P

© CBD Research Ltd · Beckenham · BR3 5JS · Tel 020 8650 7745 · Fax 020 8650 0768 · E-mail cbd@cbdresearch.com · www.cbdresearch.com

Society of Dyers & Colourists   (SDC)   1884
NR   PO Box 244, Perkin House, 82 Grattan Rd, BRADFORD,
      W Yorks, BD1 2JB.   (hq)
      01274 725138   fax 01274 392888
      http://www.sdc.org.uk
      Chief Exec: Susie Hargreaves
Br   7; Bangladesh, China, India (Mumbai & Tirupur), Pakistan
      (Karachi & Lahore), Sri Lanka
○   *L, *P; science & technology of colour & colouration
¶   Coloration Technology - 6.   The Colourist - 4.
      Colour Index - online.
      Textbooks & technical publications.

**Society for Earthquake & Civil Engineering Dynamics
      (SECED)   1969**
NR   Institution of Civil Engineers, One Great George St, LONDON,
      SW1P 3AA.   (hq)
      020 7222 7722   fax 020 7222 7500
      email secretary@seced.org.uk   http://www.seced.org.uk
      Chmn: Dr Paul Greening
○   *L, *Q; the better design of structures subject to dynamic loads
      from earthquakes & other sources
M   i & org
¶   NL - 4.

** **Society for Economic Analysis Ltd**
      Organisation lost: see Introduction paragraph 3.

Society of Editors   1999
◼   University Centre, Granta Place, Mill Lane, CAMBRIDGE,
      CB2 1RU.   (hq)
      01223 304080
      http://www.societyofeditors.co.uk
      Exec Dir: Bob Satchwell
▲   Company Limited by Guarantee
Br   11
○   *P; to represent editors in national, regional & local
      newspapers, magazines, broadcasting, new media,
      journalism, education & media law; to protect & promote the
      freedom of the media & the general right to the freedom of
      expression
●   Conf - Mtgs - ET - Res - LG
<   Wld Assn of Newspapers
M   475 i
¶   Briefing - 12; ftm only.

Society for Editors & Proofreaders   (SfEP)   1988
NR   Erico House, 93-99 Upper Richmond Rd, LONDON,
      SW15 2TG.   (Admin)
      020 8785 5617   fax 020 8785 5618
      email administration@sfep.org.uk
      http://www.sfep.org.uk
      Exec Sec: Justina Amenu
▲   Un-incorporated Society
○   *P; to foster & encourage high standards of editing &
      proofreading
●   Conf - Mtgs - ET
M   1,315 i, 49 f, 30 org, UK / 35 i, 2 f, 5 org, o'seas
¶   NL - 6; ftm only.   Directory - 1; free.

Society of Education Consultants   (SEC)   1990
◼   25 Dickenson Rd, LONDON, N8 9ER.   (hsb)
      0845 345 7932
      email enquiries@sec.org.uk   http://www.sec.org.uk
      Hon Sec: Patrick Allan
▲   Un-incorporated Society
○   *P; to support education management consultants
●   Conf - ET
M   140 i, 12 f, UK / 10 i, o'seas
¶   NL - 6;   Education - 52; both ftm only.

**Society for Education, Music & Psychology Research
      (SEMPRE)   1972**
NR   University of Roehampton, Sch of Education (rm QB110),
      Roehampton Lane, LONDON, SW15 5PJ.   (hsb)
      020 8392 3701
      http://www.sempre.org.uk
      Sec: Prof Adam Ockelford
○   *D, *N; to bring together researchers in the field of music
      education & similar fields
●   Conf - Res
M   157 i, 82 f, UK /130 i, 461 f, o'seas
¶   Psychology of Music (Jnl) - 2; ftm only.

Society for Effective Affective Learning
      Ceased to trade with effect from 30 June 2007

**Society of Electrical & Mechanical Engineers serving local
      government   (SCEME)   1951**
◼   32 Discovery Rd, Bearsted, MAIDSTONE, Kent, ME15 8HF.
      (hsp)
      07884 342315
      email tanswellc@gmail.com   http://www.sceme.org
      Hon Sec: Charles Tanswell
▲   Un-incorporated Society
○   *P; representing all aspects of building service engineering in
      local government in the UK
Gp   Sub-c'ees: Electrical, Energy, Maintenance, Professional matters
●   Conf - Mtgs - LG
M   25 i, 54 f
      (Subs: £10 i, £30 f)

Society for Endocrinology   1946
◼   22 Apex Court, Woodlands, Bradley Stoke, BRISTOL,
      BS32 4JT.   (hq)
      01454 642200   fax 01454 642222
      http://www.endocrinology.org
      Chmn: Prof John Wass
▲   Registered Charity
○   *L; advancement of public education in endocrinology
●   Conf - ET - Exhib - Publishing
<   Intl Soc of Endocrinology; Eur Soc of Endocrinology;
      BioScientifica Ltd
M   1,400 i, UK / 400 i, o'seas
¶   Jnl of Endocrinology - 12.   Endocrine Related Cancer - 4.
      Jnl of Molecular Endocrinology - 6. The Endocrinologist - 4.

Society of Engineers
▲   Company Limited by Guarantee
      in 2004-05 merged with the Institution of Electrical
      Engineers, which in 2006 merged with the Institution of
      Incorporated Engineers to form the **Institution of
      Engineering & Technology**

Society for the Environment   2004
NR   The Old School House, 212 Long St, ATHERSTONE, Warks,
      CV9 3SU.
      0845 337 2951   fax 01827 717064
      email enquiries@socenv.org   http://www.socenv.org.uk
      Chief Exec: David Hickie
○   *P; working to deliver a sustainable future for everyone
●   Conf - Mtgs - Inf - Awards
M   17 org

Society of Environmental Engineers   (SEE)
◼   The Manor House, High St, BUNTINGFORD, Herts,
      SG9 9AB.   (asa)
      01763 271209   fax 01763 273255
      email office@environmental.org.uk
      http://www.environmental.org.uk
      Chief Exec: Prof Raymond Clark
○   *P; engineering & technical aspects of the environment
M   i & f
¶   Jnl - 4.   NL - 9/10.

Society for Environmental Exploration   1989
NR   50-52 Rivington St, LONDON, EC2A 3QP.   (hq)
        020 7613 2422   fax 020 7613 2992
        email info@frontier.ac.uk   http://www.frontier.ac.uk
        Managing Dir: Ms Eibleis Fanning
▲   Company Limited by Guarantee
◯   *L, *N, *Q; an international environmental research,
        conservation & natural resource development non-
        governmental organisation (NGO), operating long-term
        biodiversity & socio-economic field programmes in important
        threatened tropical habitats
        Note: operates as Frontier

Society of Equestrian Artists   (SEA)   1978
NR   The Flat / Red House, Woolston Rd, NORTH CADBURY,
        Somerset, BA22 2DW.   (sp)
        email sec@equestrianartists.co.uk
        http://www.equestrianartists.co.uk
        Hon Sec: Debbie Burt
▲   Registered Charity
◯   *A
●   Mtgs - ET - Exhib - Comp - Inf
M   c 450 i, UK / c 25 i, o'seas
¶   NL - 3/4; ftm only.

Society of Euphobics   1997
■   311 Courtenay House, 9-15 New Park Rd, LONDON,
        SW2 4UN.   (mail/add)
◯   *W; for people with a fear of good news
●   Mtgs - Lib - VE
M   237 i

Society of Event Organisers   1996
■   29a Market Sq, BIGGLESWADE, Beds, SG18 8AQ.   (hq)
        01767 316255   fax 01767 316430
        http://www.eou.org.uk
        Gen Mgr: Peter Cotterell
▲   Un-incorporated Society
◯   *P, *T; for organisers of events in companies & associations;
        events include meetings, conferences, exhibitions, incentive
        travel, training, corporate hospitality etc
●   Conf - Mtgs - ET - Inf - VE - Seminars
M   150 f
¶   Event Organisers Update - 10; free to anyone involved in
        events.

Society for Existential Analysis   1988
■   BM Existential, LONDON, WC1N 3XX.   (mail address)
        email info@existentialanalysis.co.uk
        http://www.existentialanalysis.co.uk
        Chmn: Paul McGinley
▲   Registered Charity
◯   *L; a forum for the analysis of existence from philosophical &
        psychological perspectives (membership consists mostly of
        psychotherapists, counsellors, psychologists & philosophers)
●   Conf - Inf - Directory of Existential Psychotherapists
M   350 i, UK / 25 i, o'seas
¶   Jnl - 2.

Society for Experimental Biology   (SEB)   1923
NR   3 The Carronades, New Rd, SOUTHAMPTON, Hants,
        SO14 0AA.   (hq)
        023 8022 4824   fax 023 8022 6312
        http://www.sebiology.org
        Chier Exec: Christine Trimmer
▲   Company Limited by Guarantee; Registered Charity
Br   2
◯   *L, *Q; to embrace all disciplines of experimental biology; to
        support & promote experimental biology in all its branches,
        to both the scientific community & the general public
●   Conf - Mtgs - ET - Exhib - LG
M   1,350 i, UK / 450 i, o'seas
¶   Jnl of Experimental Botany.   The Plant Jnl.
        Bulletin (NL).   Plant Biotechnology.
        Publications list available.

Society of Expert Witnesses   (SEW)   1996
■   PO Box 345, NEWMARKET, Suffolk, CB8 7TU.   (hq)
        0845 702 3014   fax 01638 668656
        email helpline@sew.org.uk   http://www.sew.org.uk
        Sec: Richard Cory-Pearce
▲   Company Limited by Guarantee
◯   *P; to promote excellence in all aspects of the service provided
        by expert witnesses; to cooperate with other bodies with
        similar aims
●   Conf - SG - Inf

Society of Financial Advisers
        in 2005 merged with the Life Insurance Association to form the
        Personal Finance Society

Society of Fine Art Auctioneers & Valuers   (SOFAA)   1973
■   2 Kingfisher Court, Bridge Rd, EAST MOLESEY, Surrey,
        KT8 9HL.   (hsp)
        07803 303125
        email secretary@sofaa.org   http://www.sofaa.org
        Sec: Robbie Barry
▲   Un-incorporated Society
◯   *P; promotion & maintenance of standards in the valuation &
        sale of antiques & fine art
●   Conf - LG
M   i & f

Society of Floristry Ltd   (SOF)   1951
NR   Wilcot Chapel, Kinton, SHREWSBURY, Shropshire, SY4 1AZ.
        (sp)
        0870 241 0432
        email info@societyoffloristry.org.uk
        http://www.societyoffloristry.org
        Sec: Lucy Todman
▲   Company Limited by Guarantee
◯   *H, *P; for professional florists
●   Conf - Mtgs - Exam - Exhib - Comp - SG - Inf
M   1,044 i, UK / c 20 i, o'seas
¶   Focal Point - 4; ftm only.   Hbk.
        Publications list available.

Society for Folk Life Studies   1961
■   548 Wilbraham Rd, MANCHESTER, M21 9LB.   (hsb)
        0161-881 8640
        Hon Sec: Dr Eddie Cass
◯   *L; to study traditional & changing ways of life in Great Britain
        & Ireland with particular interest in regional culture
●   Conf - Res - SG
M   c 400 l & instns
¶   Folk Life: a jnl of ethnological studies - 1; ftm.   NL.

Society of Food Hygiene & Technology   (SOFHT)   1979
■   The Granary, Middleton House Farm, Tamworth Rd,
        MIDDLETON, Staffs, B78 2BD.   (hq)
        01827 872500   fax 01827 875800
        email admin@sofht.co.uk   http://www.sofht.co.uk
        Admin: Claudette Schlitter
▲   Company Limited by Guarantee
Br   1
◯   *L, *P
●   Mtgs - ET - Exhib - Inf
M   700 i, 130 f, UK / 30 i, o'seas
¶   SOFHT Focus (Jnl) - 3;   Diary; both ftm only.   NL.

Society for French Studies   (SFS)   1947
NR   French Studies - School of Humanities, University of
        Birmingham, Edgbaston, BIRMINGHAM, B15 2TT.   (hsb)
        email s.m.forcer@bham.ac.uk   http://www.sfs.ac.uk
        Hon Sec: Dr Stephen Forcer
◯   *L; to promote French studies in universities & institutions of
        comparable standing in the British Isles & Commonwealth
M   i & org
¶   French Studies (with French Studies Bulletin) - 4.

© CBD Research Ltd · Beckenham · BR3 5JS · Tel 020 8650 7745 · Fax 020 8650 0768 · E-mail cbd@cbdresearch.com · www.cbdresearch.com

Society of Friends of King Richard III
- ■ 7 Askrigg House, Bouthwaite Drive, YORK, YO26 4TJ. (chmn/p)
  01904 790265
  email sandra.wadley@yahoo.co.uk
  http://www.silverboar.org
  Chmn: Sandra Wadley
- ▲ Un-incorporated Society
- ○ *G; to support King Richard III, to clear & support his name in York, his city
- ● Mtgs - Res - VE
- M 300 i, UK / 50 i, o'seas
  (Sub: £10 i, UK £18 i, o'seas)
- ¶ Silver Boar (Jnl) = 4; free.

Society of the Friends of St George's & Descendants of the Knights of the Garter   1931
- NR 1 The Cloisters, Windsor Castle, WINDSOR, Berks, SL4 1NJ. (hsb)
  01753 860629   fax 01753 620165
  email friends@stgeorges-windsor.org
  http://www.stgeorges-windsor.org
- ▲ Registered Charity
- Br Australia, Canada, New Zealand, USA
- ○ *G; to help maintain the fabric & beauty of St George's Chapel, Windsor Castle; to promote interest & knowledge of the history & traditions of the Order of the Garter
- M 3,800 i, UK / 1,500 i, o'seas
- ¶ AR - 1; ftm, £2.

Society of Garden Designers   (SGD)   1981
- ■ Katepwa House, Ashfield Park Avenue, ROSS-on-WYE, Herefords, HR9 5AX.   (hq)
  01989 566695   fax 01989 567676
  email info@sgd.org.uk   http://www.sgd.org.uk
  Admin: Gill Hinton
- ▲ Company Limited by Guarantee
- Br 11 regional groups
- ○ *P; to promote professional standards in garden design
- Gp Education policy c'ee
- ● Conf - Mtgs - ET - Exhib - Inf - Lib - VE
- < R Horticl Soc
- M 1,600 i, UK / 60 i, o'seas
- ¶ Garden Design Jnl - 10; ftm, £45 (£62 o'seas) nm.

Society of Garlic Growers, Processors & Packers   (SGPP)   1998
- ■ 191 Westcombe Hill, LONDON, SE3 7DR.
- ○ *T
- ● Mtgs - Tastings
- M i
- ¶ NL - 3; ftm only.

Society of Genealogists   (SoG)   1911
- NR 14 Charterhouse Buildings, Goswell Rd, LONDON, EC1M 7BA.   (hq)
  020 7251 8799   fax 020 7250 1800
  email events@sog.org.uk   http://www.sog.org.uk
  Chief Exec: June Perrin
- ▲ Company Limited by Guarantee; Registered Charity
- ○ *G, *L; to promote & foster the study of genealogy
- Gp Computers in genealogy
- ● Conf - Mtgs - ET - Lib - VE
- < Fedn of Family History Socs
- M 13,500 i, UK / 1,500 i, o'seas
- ¶ Genealogists' Magazine - 4.
  Computers in Genealogy - 4.   AR.

Society for General Microbiology   (SGM)   1945
- ■ Marlborough House, Basingstoke Rd, Spencers Wood, READING, Berks, RG7 1AG.   (hq)
  0118-988 1800   fax 0118-988 5656
  email admin@sgm.ac.uk   http://www.sgm.ac.uk
  Exec Sec: Dr R S S Fraser
- ▲ Company Limited by Guarantee; Registered Charity
- Br Ireland
- ○ *L; to promote the art & science of microbiology
- Gp Education; Eukaryotes; Irish; Prokaryotes; Virus
- ● Conf - Mtgs - Exhib - Inf - LG
- < Fedn of Eur Microbiological Socs (FEMS); Intl U of Microbiological Socs
- M 3,925 i, UK / 1,380 i, o'seas
- ¶ Jnl of General Virology - 12; £106 m, £1,000 nm.
  Microbiology - 12; £106 m, £1,000 nm.
  Microbiology Today - 4; ftm, £76 nm.
  Jnl of Medical Microbiology - 12; £60 m, £780 nm.
  International Journal of Systematic & Evolutionary Microbiology - 6; £106 m, £715 nm.

Society of Glass Technology   (SGT)   1916
- ■ 12 o'clock Court (Unit 9), 21 Attercliffe Rd, SHEFFIELD, S4 7WW.   (hq)
  0114-263 4455   fax 0114-263 4411
  email info@sgt.org   http://www.sgt.org
  Hon Sec: John Henderson
- ▲ Registered Charity
- Br 6; India, USA
- ○ *L; all aspects of the history, art, science, manufacture, after-treatment & use of glass of any & every kind
- Gp Technical c'ees - Analysis & properties; Basic science & technology; Engineering; Glass batch, furnaces & refractories; Handmade glassware
- ● Conf - Mtgs - Lib - VE
- < Intl Cmsn on Glass; Eur Soc Glass Science & Technology
- M 350 i, 70 f, UK / 150 i, 20 f, o'seas
- ¶ Glass Technology - 6.
  Physics & Chemistry of Glasses - 6.
  Borate Glasses, Crystals & Melts 4; £40 m. £60 nm.
  Ceramics & Glass: a basic technology.
  Bosc d'Antic on Glassmaking; £20 m, £25 nm.
  Early 19th Century Glassmaking in Austria & Germany; £20 m, £25 nm.
  Crystallisation 2003; £40 m, £60 nm.
  ESG 2004; £40 m, £60 nm.
  Monographs & Topical issues in glass.
  Specialist publications on aspects of glass technology.

Society of Graphic Fine Art   (SGFA)   1919
- NR 27 Lorne Avenue, CROYDON, Surrey, CR0 7RQ.   (hsp)
  email enquiries@sgfa.org.uk   http://www.sgfa.org.uk
- ○ *P; to promote good drawing skills through exhibitions
- ● Exhib
- M i

Society of Greeting & Visiting Card Collectors   (SGVCC)   1986
- ■ 76c The Avenue, BECKENHAM, Kent, BR3 5EF.
- ▲ Un-incorporated Society
- ○ *G
- ● Mtgs - Exhib
- M i

Society of Greyhound Veterinarians
  a group of the **British Veterinary Association**

Society of Headmasters & Headmistresses of Independent Schools (SHMIS) 1961
■ 12 The Point, Rockingham Rd, MARKET HARBOROUGH, Leics, LE16 7QU. (hq)
01858 433760
Gen Sec: Dr David Richardson
▲ Company Limited by Guarantee
○ *E, *P; to maintain high standards of education in member schools; to facilitate the sharing of ideas; to ensure genuine independence
● Conf - Mtgs - ET - Inf - LG
< Indep Schools Coun (ISC)
M 100 i
¶ NL - 1; LM - 1; Hbk - 1.

Society of Health Education & Health Promotion Specialists (SHEPS) 1982
NR c/o Asst Director of Policy & Public Health, Sheffield Health, 5 Old Fulwood Rd, SHEFFIELD, S10 1EX. (Chmn/b)
0114-271 1305
http://www.hj-web.co.uk/sheps/
Chmn: Frances Cunning
▲ Un-incorporated Society
○ *P; 'policy & practice of health promotion & public health'
● Conf - Mtgs - ET - Res - SG - Inf - Empl - LG
< UK Public Health Assn
M 300-400 i
¶ 'A range of ad hoc publications are produced - often in the form of policy / discussion papers'

Society of Heraldic Arts (SHA) 1987
NR 12 Ridgeway, OTTERY St MARY, Devon, EX11 1DT. (hsp)
01404 811091
email sha.hon-sec@tiscali.co.uk
http://www.heraldic-arts.com
Hon Sec: Kevin Arkinstall
▲ Un-incorporated Society
○ *P; for heraldic artists & craftsmen
● Mtgs - Res - Inf - VE
M i
¶ The Heraldic Craftsman - 4; ftm, £1.50 nm.

Society for the History of Alchemy & Chemistry (SHAC) 1937
■ Dept of Science & Technology Studies, University College London, Gower St, LONDON, WC1E 6BT. (hsb)
email secretary@ambix.org http://www.ambix.org
Hon Sec: Dr Georgette Taylor
▲ Registered Charity
○ *L; all aspects of the history of alchemy & chemistry from the earliest times
● Mtgs - Res - Comp
M 82 i, UK / 94 i, o'seas; 133 f, UK/o'seas
(Sub: £27 i, £142 f)
¶ Ambix - 1 vol in 3 pts each yr

Society for the History of Astronomy
is a group of the **Birmingham & Midland Institute**

Society for the History of Natural History (SHNH) 1936
NR The Natural History Museum, Cromwell Rd, LONDON, SW7 5BD. (hsb)
email info@shnh.org http://www.shnh.org
Hon Sec: Sara Joynes
▲ Registered Charity
○ *L; study of the history & bibliography of all branches of natural history
● Conf
M 600 i
¶ Archives of Natural History - 2. NL - 3.
Sherborn Facsimiles (of rare natural history texts) - irreg; price varies.
Special publications & conference papers.

Society of Homeopaths 1978
■ 11 Brookfield, Duncan Close, Moulton Park, NORTHAMPTON, NN3 6WL. (hq)
0845 450 6611 fax 0845 450 6622
email info@homeopathy-soh.org
http://www.homeopathy-soh.org
Chief Exec: Paula Ross
▲ Company Limited by Guarantee
○ *P; to promote homoeopathy in the Hahnemannian tradition
● Conf - Mtgs - ET - Res - Inf - LG
< Coun for Complementary & Alternative Medicine; Eur Coun for Classical Homeopathy; Intl Coun for Classical Homeopathy
M 2,250 i, UK / 85 i, o'seas
¶ Register of Homeopaths (LM).

Society of Hospital Linen Service & Laundry Managers (SHLSLM) 1951
■ c/o Linen Services Manager, Royal Blackburn Hospital, Haslingden Rd, BLACKBURN, Lancs, BB2 3HH.
01254 733136
email lynn.fort@elht.nhs.uk
http://www.linenmanager.co.uk
Hon Sec: Lynn Fort
▲ Un-incorporated Society
Br 8; Republic of Ireland
○ *P
● Conf - Mtgs - ET - Exhib - Inf - LG
M 74 i
Sub: £35
¶ Ybk; ftm, 20 nm.

Society of Incentive & Travel Executives (SITE)
§ 12-15 Hanger Green (1st floor), LONDON, W5 3EL. (hq)
020 8998 2667 fax 020 8998 2669
http://www.site-intl.org
Dir: Paul Miller
UK chapter of an international, not-for-profit, professional association devoted to the pursuit of excellence in incentives.

Society of Independent Brewers (SIBA) 1980
■ PO Box 101, THIRSK, N Yorks, YO7 4WA. (asa)
0845 337 9158
email secretariat@siba.co.uk http://www.siba.co.uk
Chief Exec: Julian Grocock
▲ Company Limited by Guarantee
Br 7 regions
○ *T; to represent the small independent brewers
Gp Training; Marketing; Political; Commercial
● Conf - Mtgs - ET - Comp - Inf - LG
< Food & Drink Fedn
M 220 f
¶ SIBA Jnl - 6; ftm only.

Society of Independent Roundabout Proprietors (SIRP) 1985
■ 66 Carolgate, RETFORD, Notts, DN22 6EF. (hsb)
01777 702872
http://www.sirp.co.uk
Sec: Jack Schofield
○ *G, *T; owners & operators (both professional & semi-professional) of vintage fairground equipment (wood-framed, hand-turned, steam driven, pre-war) & vintage slot-machines
● Mtgs
M 100 i

© CBD Research Ltd · Beckenham · BR3 5JS · Tel 020 8650 7745 · Fax 020 8650 0768 · E-mail cbd@cbdresearch.com · www.cbdresearch.com

Society of Indexers   (SI)   1957

NR   Woodbourn Business Centre, 10 Jessell St, SHEFFIELD, S Yorks,
　　　S9 3HY.   (hq)
　　　0114-244 9561   fax 0114-244 9563
　　　email info@indexers.org.uk
　　　http://www.indexers.org.uk
　　　Sec: Judith Menes,　　Admin: Wendy Burrow
▲　　Un-incorporated Society
○　　*L, *P; promotes standards & instruction on techniques for all
　　　　forms of indexing
●　　Conf - Mtgs - ET - Exam - Inf - Register of Indexers
<　　Soc of Indexers in: Australia / America / China / South Africa;
　　　　Indexing & Abstracting Soc of Canada
M　　850 i, 16 f, UK / 60 i, 1 f, o'seas
¶　　The Indexer - 2; ftm, £50 yr nm.
　　　SIdelights - 4;　　LM - 1; both ftm only.
　　　Indexers Available - 1; free to publishers, £4.50 nm.
　　　Occasional papers on aspects of indexing - irreg; prices vary.

Society for Individual Freedom   (SIF)   1945

■　　PO Box 744, BROMLEY, Kent, BR1 4WG.   (chmn/p)
　　　01424 713737
　　　http://www.individualist.org.uk
　　　Chmn: M Plumbe
▲　　Un-incorporated Society
○　　*K; to campaign & lobby on issues of personal freedom
●　　Conf - Mtgs
M　　c 200 i
¶　　The Individual - 3/4; ftm, £1 nm.
　　　Books & tracts - irreg.

Society of Industrial Emergency Service Officers
　　　full name of **SIESO**

Society of Information Technology Management   (SOCITM)
1986

NR   F19 Moulton Business Park, Redhouse Rd, NORTHAMPTON,
　　　NN3 6AQ.   (hq)
　　　01604 497774   fax 01604 497610
　　　email enquiries@socitm.gov.uk
　　　http://www.socitm.gov.uk
　　　Managing Dir: Adrian Hancock
▲　　Un-incorporated Society
○　　*P; ICT managers working in and for the public sector
M　　1,900 i

Society for International Folk Dancing   (Interfolk)   (SIFD)
1946

NR   5 South Rise, CARSHALTON, Surrey, SM5 4PD.   (shop/p)
　　　020 8395 1400
　　　email mail@sifd.org　　http://www.sifd.org
　　　Shop: Alison Scrimshaw
▲　　Registered Charity
○　　*D; to preserve folk dances of all peoples & to make them
　　　　known; to encourage the practice of them in traditional form
●　　Mtgs - ET - Public dances - Day & summer schools
<　　Cent Coun of Physical Recreation; English Folk Dance & Song
　　　　Soc
>　　Israel Dance Inst; Welsh Circle Dance Assn
M　　400 i
¶　　SIFD News - 12; ftm only.

Society of International Treasurers
　　　was dissolved 31 December 2007

Society of Irish Foresters   1942

IRL Enterprise Centre, BALLINTOGHER, Co Sligo, Republic of
　　　Ireland.
　　　353 (71) 916 4434   fax 353 (71) 913 4904
　　　email sif@eircom.net
　　　http://www.societyofirishforesters.ie
　　　Sec: Clodagh Duffy
○　　*P; to advance & spread the knowledge of forestry in all its
　　　　aspects

Society of the Irish Motor Industry   (SIMI)

IRL 5 Upper Pembroke St, DUBLIN 2, Republic of Ireland.
　　　353 (1) 676 1690   fax 353 (1) 661 9213
　　　email info@simi.ie　　http://www.simi.ie
○　　*T

Society for Italic Handwriting   (SIH)   1952

■　　203 Dyas Ave, Great Barr, BIRMINGHAM, B42 1HN.　(hsp)
　　　0121-244 8006
　　　email nickthenibs@hotmail.co.uk
　　　http://www.nickthenibs.co.uk
　　　Sec: Nicholas Caulkin
▲　　Registered Charity
○　　*A; to promote the use of Italic handwriting
●　　Mtgs - Exhib - Comp - SG - Inf - Lib
M　　500 i, 3 f, 30 schools, UK / 200 i, o'seas
¶　　Jnl - 4.

Society of Jewellery Historians   (SJH)   1977

NR   Scientific Research, British Museum, LONDON, WC1B 3DG.
　　　fax 01588 620558
　　　http://www.societyofjewelleryhistorians.ac.uk
　　　Sec: Mo Cerrone
▲　　Registered charity
○　　*L; to stimulate interest in jewellery of all ages & cultures
M　　i, f & org
¶　　Jewellery Studies - occasional.
　　　Jewellery History Today - 3.

Society of King Charles the Martyr   (SKCM)   1894

■　　22 Tyning Rd, Winsley, BRADFORD-on-AVON, Wilts,
　　　BA15 2JJ.　(hsp)
　　　01225 862965
　　　Chmn: Robin Davies
▲　　Un-incorporated Society
Br　　Australia, USA
○　　*R; observance of 30 January in commemoration of King
　　　　Charles I's martyrdom & upholding the principles (the prayer
　　　　book & episcopacy) for which he died
●　　Mtgs - Services
M　　150 i, UK / 350 i, o'seas
¶　　Church & King - 2; ftm.

Society for Landscape Studies   (SLS)   1979

■　　c/o Dept of Geography, University of Exeter, Amory Building,
　　　Rennes Drive, EXETER, Devon, EX4 4RJ.　(hsp)
　　　01392 263330   fax 01392 264358
　　　email d.c.harvey@exeter.ac.uk
　　　http://www.landscapestudies.com
　　　Hon Sec: Dr David Harvey
▲　　Registered Charity
○　　*G, *L; 'to secure a more penetrating comprehension of
　　　　landscape evolution & an overall narrative account of
　　　　landscape, prehistory & history, together with an
　　　　understanding of how this has influenced & may usefully
　　　　guide the management of the present-day landscape'
●　　Conf
<　　Coun Brit Archaeology
M　　370 i, 140 org, UK / 14 i, o'seas
¶　　Landscape History - 1.

Society of Laundry Engineers & Allied Trades Ltd   (SLEAT)
1907

■　　Suite 7 Southernhay, 207 Hook Rd, CHESSINGTON, Surrey,
　　　KT9 1HJ.　(asa)
　　　020 8391 2266   fax 020 8391 4466
　　　email admin@sleat.co.uk　　http://www.sleat.co.uk
　　　Sec: David M Hart
▲　　Company Limited by Guarantee
○　　*T; to promote, support & protect the welfare & interest of
　　　　laundry engineers & allied trades
●　　Exhib - LG
<　　Eur Laundry & Dry Cleaning Machinery Mfrs Org
M　　43 f

Society of Law Accountants in Scotland   (SOLAS)
NR   7 Sidlaw Terrace, BIRKHILL, Angus, DD2 5PY.
        01382 580131   fax solas.admin@hotmail.co.uk
        email solas.admin@hotmail.co.uk
        http://www.solas.co.uk
        Admin: Moira Shepherd
◯   *P

Society of Leather Technologists & Chemists Ltd   (SLTC)   1897
NR   18 Kinross Drive, Bletchley, MILTON KEYNES, Bucks,
        MK3 7UD.   (hsp)
        01908 372115
        email tova.irving@talktalk.net   http://www.sltc.org
        Hon Sec: Mrs Tova Irving
▲   Company Limited by Guarantee; Registered Charity
Br   2; Australia, South Africa
◯   *L; to promote the theoretical & practical interests of leather
        manufacturers, hide & skin trades, machinery, chemical &
        dye & finish manufacturers, & allied industries
<   Intl U Leather Technologists & Chemists Socs (IULTCS)
¶   Jnl - 6.

**Society of Legal Scholars in the United Kingdom & Ireland
   (SLS)   1908**
■   School of Law, University of Southampton, Highfield,
        SOUTHAMPTON, SO17 1BJ.   (hsb)
        023 8059 4039   fax 023 8059 3024
        email s.j.thomson@soton.ac.uk
        http://www.legalscholars.ac.uk
        Hon Sec: Prof Stephen Bailey, Admin Sec: Mrs S J Thomson
▲   Registered Charity
◯   *P; to advance legal research & education
Gp   Law: Company, Comparative, Competition, Consumer,
        Contract & commercial, Criminal justice, Environmental,
        European, Family, Human rights & civil liberties, Immigration
        & refugee, Information technology, Intellectual property,
        International, Jurisprudence, Labour, Legal education, Legal
        history, Maritime media, Medical, Practice, Profession &
        ethics, Property & trusts, Public, Restitution, Tax, Torts
●   Conf - Mtgs - ET - Res - LG
M   2,800 i, 33 f, UK / 190 i, o'seas
¶   Legal Studies (Jnl) - 4;   The Reporter (NL) - 2; both ftm only.

Society of Leisure Consultants & Publishers   (SOLCAP)   1989
■   1 Sandringham Close, Tarleton, PRESTON, Lancs, PR4 6UZ.
        (dir/b)
        01772 816046
        Dir: J B A Sharples
▲   Un-incorporated Society
◯   *T; to represent consultants, publishers & commercial interests
        in the leisure industry (entertainment, recreation, tourism,
        hotels, catering, marketing, publicity, sport & public relations)
●   Conf - Mtgs - Exhib - Inf - VE
M   38 i, 10 f, UK / 1 i, 1 f, o'seas
¶   NL - 2; ftm, £2 nm.   LM - 1; ftm, £5 nm.

Society of Ley Hunters   (SOL)   2000
■   9 Mawddwy Cottages, Minllyn, Dinas Mawddwy,
        MACHYNLLETH, SY20 9LW.   (hsp)
        01650 531354
        email leyhunter@googlemail.com
        http://www.leyhunter.org
        17 Victoria St, CHELTENHAM, Glos, GL50 4HV.   (mem/sp)
        Hon Sec: Laurence Main,   Mem Sec: Gerald Frowley
▲   Un-incorporated Society
◯   *G; the study of leys (straight alignments of ancient sites in the
        andscapes), their meanings & purposes & other related
        mysteries
●   Mtgs - VE
M   c 170 i
        (Sub: £12.50 UK / £18 o'seas)
¶   NL - 4; ftm only.

Society for Libyan Studies   1969
■   c/o Institute of Archaeology, 31-34 Gordon Sq, LONDON,
        WC1H 0PY.   (pt-time)
        email shirleystrong@btcoonect.com
        http://www.britac.ac.uk/institutes/libya/form.html
        Sec: Mrs S K Strong
▲   Registered Charity
◯   *L; study & research into history, archaeology, geography &
        geology of Libya
●   Conf - Mtgs - Res - Exhib - SG - Inf
M   199 i, 38 org, UK / 66 i, 74 org, o'seas
        (Sub: £25)
¶   Libyan Studies (AR); ftm, £30 nm.

Society of Licensed Conveyancers   1988
■   Chancery House, 110 High St, CROYDON, Surrey,
        CR0 1ND.   (hq)
        020 8681 1001
        http://www.conveyancers.org.uk
        Chief Exec: N F Ewert Evans
▲   Company Limited by Guarantee
◯   *P; for licensed conveyancers in England & Wales
●   Conf - Mtgs - Inf - LG - Referral of the public to a local licensed
        conveyancer - Provision of compulsory professional
        development courses
M   400 i
¶   The Licensed Conveyancer - 4.

Society of Limners   (SLm)   1986
■   16 Tudor Close, HOVE, E Sussex, BN3 7NR.   (admin/p)
        01273 770628
        email rgeast.limners@ntlworld.com
        Administrator: Richard East
▲   Un-incorporated Society
◯   *A; to promote & encourage interest in miniature painting,
        calligraphy & silhouette painting
●   Conf - ET - Exhib
<   Wld Fedn Miniaturists
M   140 i, 2 org, UK / 5 i, 1 org, o'seas
¶   NL - 3, ftm, £1.50 nm.

Society for Lincolnshire History & Archaeology   (SLHA)   1974
■   Jews' Court, Steep Hill, LINCOLN, LN2 1LS.   (hq)
        01522 521337   fax 01522 521337
        email slha@lincolnshirepast.org.uk
        http://www.lincolnshirepast.org.uk
        Admin: Rodney E Callow
▲   Registered Charity
Br   2
◯   *L; local history, archaeology & industrial archaeology of
        Lincolnshire
Gp   Archaeology; Industrial archaeology; Local history; Publications
●   Conf - Mtgs - Res - SG - Lib - VE
<   Coun for Brit Archaeology; Brit Assn for Local History; Assn for
        Indl Archaeology
M   550 i, 65 f, UK / 3 i, 22 f, o'seas
¶   Jnl - 1; ftm, £10 nm.   Magazine - 4; ftm, £1.60 nm.
        Bulletin - 4;   AR - 1; both ftm only.

© CBD Research Ltd · Beckenham · BR3 5JS · Tel 020 8650 7745 · Fax 020 8650 0768 · E-mail cbd@cbdresearch.com · www.cbdresearch.com

Society of Local Authority Chief Executives & Senior Managers (SOLACE) 1973
■ Hope House, 45 Great Peter St, LONDON, SW1P 3LT.   (hq)
   0845 601 0649
   Dir Gen: David Clark
▲ Company Limited by Guarantee; Registered Charity
Br 12
○ *P; for senior managers in local government in the UK; to develop & strengthen the UK local government sector
Gp Ad hoc enquiries; E-Government & IT; Electoral matters; Health; Human resources; International; Management practice; Transformational change; Urban planning & policy
● Conf - Mtgs - ET - Res - Exhib - SG - Empl - LG
< Local Govt Mgrs Australia; Soc Local Govt Mgrs (NZ); Inst Local Govt Mgrs (S Africa); Intl City Mgrs Assn (USA)
M 930 i, 8 f, UK / 20 i, o'seas
¶ Running Elections.   Healthy Living Report. Sing When You're Winning - E-Government. Chance or Choice - Risk Management.

Society of Local Council Clerks   (SLCC)   1974
■ 8 The Crescent, TAUNTON, Somerset, TA1 4EA.   (hq)
   01823 253646   fax 01823 253681
   email treasurer@slcc.co.uk   http://www.slcc.co.uk
   Chief Exec: Nick Randle
▲ Un-incorporated Society
Br 45
○ *P, *U; for clerks & managers of town, parish & community coucils in England & Wales
● Conf - ET - Exam - Inf - Empl - LG
< Intl Inst of Municipal Clerks
M 3,500 i
¶ The Clerk (Jnl) - 6; ftm, £5 nm.

Society of London Art Dealers   (SLAD)   1932
■ Ormond House, 3 Duke of York St, LONDON, SW1Y 6JP.   (hq)
   020 7930 6137   fax 020 7321 0685
   email office@slad.org.uk   http://www.slad.org.uk
   Dir Gen: Christopher Battiscombe
▲ Un-incorporated Society
○ *T; to promote & protect the good name & interests of the art trade throughout the UK & to enhance public confidence in responsible art dealing
● Mtgs - ET - Exhib - Inf - LG - Seminars - VAT & Droit de Suite helpline
< Confédn Intle Négociants en Oeuvres d'Art (CINOA); Fedn Eur Art Galleries Assns (FEAGA); Brit Art Market Fedn
M 115 f
¶ NL - 4; ftm only.
   Society of London Art Dealers Directory - 1; free.
   Society of London Art Dealers Survey - 2 yrly; ftm only.

Society of Maritime Industries   1966
NR 28-29 Threadneedle St, LONDON, EC2R 8AY.   (hq)
   020 7628 2555   fax 020 7638 4376
   email info@maritimeindustries.org
   http://www.maritimeindustries.org
   Chief Exec: John C Murray
▲ Company Limited by Guarantee
○ *T; 'the voice of the UK maritime business sector, promoting & supporting companies which build, refit & modernise warships, & which supply equipment & services for all types of commercial & naval ships, ports & terminals infrastructure, offshore oil & gas, & marine science & technology
Gp Association of British Offshore Industries; Association of Marine Scientific Industries; British Marine Equipment Association; British Naval Equipment Association; Ports & Terminals Group
● Conf - Mtgs - ET - Exhib - SG - Stat - Expt - LG
M 200 f

Society of Martial Arts
NR 69 Piccadilly, MANCHESTER, M1 2BS.
   0161-702 1660
   http://www.societyofmartialarts.org
▲ Company Limited by Guarantee; Registered Charity
○ *E, *Q; to promote the educational & research aspects of martial arts; to offer degrees & postgraduate qualifications in martial arts

Society of Master Saddlers (UK) Ltd   1966
■ Green Lane Farm, Stonham, STOWMARKET, Suffolk, IP14 5DS.   (hq)
   01449 711642   fax 01449 711642
   http://www.mastersaddlers.co.uk
   Chief Exec: Mrs H Morley
▲ Company Limited by Guarantee
○ *T; representing manufacturers, retail & craft saddlers without retail premises; training & apprenticeship
Gp Registered qualified saddle fitters
● ET - Exhib - Comp - Inf
M 300 f
¶ NL - 2.   Members List & Ybk - 1.
   Leaflets.

Society of Medical Writers   (SOMW)   1985
NR 30 Dollis Hill Lane, LONDON. NW2 6JE.   (treas/p)
   http://www.somw.org.uk
   Finance Officer: Dr Richard Cutler
▲ Un-incorporated Society
○ *A; to encourage good standards of writing within the medical professions
● Conf - ET - Comp
< Assn Broadcasting Doctors; Media Medics
M 200 i, UK / 25 i, o'seas
¶ The Writer (Jnl) - 2; ftm only.
✕ 2001 General Practitioners Writers Association

Society for Medicines Research   (SMR)   1966
NR 840 Melton Rd, Thurmaston, LEICESTER, LE4 8BN.   (asa)
   0116-269 1048   fax 0116-264 0141
   email secretariat@smr.org.uk   http://www.smr.org.uk
   Hon Sec: Dr Phillip Cowley
▲ Registered Charity
○ *P; to provide a forum for those interested in medicines research; to further the education of such persons to the ultimate benefit of the general public in the field of the relief of sickness
Gp Medicinal chemistry; Biology; Pharmacology; Medicine; Pharmacy; Toxicology; Clinical
● Conf - Mtgs - ET (one-day scientific mtgs)
< Eur Fedn of Medicinal Chemistry (EFMC)
M 525 i, UK / 25 i, o'seas
¶ SMR NL - 2; ftm only.

Society for Medieval Archaeology   (SMA)   1957
NR Dept of Archaeology, University of Sheffield, Northgate House, West St, SHEFFIELD, S Yorks, S1 4ET.   (hsb)
   0114-222 2920
   http://www.medievalarchaeology.org
   Hon Sec: Dr Dawn Hadley
○ *L; archaeology in the British Isles in the post-Roman period
M i & org

Society of Messengers-at-Arms & Sheriff Officers   1922
NR 11 Alva St, EDINBURGH, EH2 4PH.   (hq)
   0131-225 9110   fax 0131-220 3468
   email admin@smaso.ednet.co.uk
   http://www.smaso.org
   Admin Sec: Alan Hogg
○ *P; professional officers of court (messengers-at-arms or sheriff-officers) who are employed by private firms dealing with service & enforcement of court papers & decrees
< U Intle des Huissiers de Justice & Officiers Judicaires
M 25 f

Society of Metaphysicians Ltd   (SofM)   1944
■   Archers' Court, Stonestile Lane, The Ridge, HASTINGS,
    E Sussex, TN35 4PG.   (hq)
    01424 751577   fax 01424 751577
    email newmeta@btinternet.com
    http://www.metaphysicians.org.uk
    Gon Soc: Carrie Yuen
▲   Company Limited by Guarantee
Br   Belgium, Nigeria, USA
○   *L; development & application of the science of fundamental
    laws (infinitely based or absolute) - neometaphysics, electro-
    imaging, radiesthesia, extra-sensory perception, Zener tests
Gp   Radiation from living organisations (AURA); Mnemonics - effect
    of mind on physical processes
●   ET - Res - SG - Inf - Lib - VE
>   Hasting Holistic Health Clinic
M   2,318 i, 6 org, UK / 1,500 i, o'seas
    (Sub: £50 UK / £60 o'seas)
¶   Neometaphysical Digest - 1; ftm, £4 nm.

Society of Model Aeronautical Engineers Ltd
    the registered name of the **British Model Flying Association**

Society of Model & Experimental Engineers   (SM&EE)   1898
NR   Marshall House, 28 Wanless Rd, LONDON, SE24 0HW.   (hq)
    email secretary@sm-ee.co.uk   http://www.sm-ee.co.uk
▲   Company Limited by Guarantee
○   *G; to support & encourage builders of medels & experimental
    devices
¶   Jnl - 6.

Society of Model Shipwrights   (SMS)   1975
■   5 Lodge Crescent, ORPINGTON, Kent, BR6 0QE.   (hsp)
    01689 827213
    Hon Sec: Peter Rogers
▲   Un-incorporated Society
○   *G; to promote research into & construction of true scale
    models of ships & boats of all periods; to preserve the skills
    of model shipwrightry
●   Mtgs - Res - Exhib - Comp
M   c 80 i, UK / 3 i, o'seas
¶   The Log (NL) - 12; ftm only.

Society of Motor Auctions
    a group of the **Retail Motor Industry Federation**

Society of Motor Manufacturers & Traders Ltd   (SMMT)   1902
NR   Forbes House, Halkin St, LONDON, SW1X 7DS.   (hq)
    020 7235 7000   fax 020 7235 7112
    http://www.smmt.co.uk
    Chief Exec: Paul Everitt
▲   Company Limited by Guarantee
○   *T; to support & promote the interests of the UK automobile
    industry at home & abroad
M   f

**Society for Mucopolysaccharide Diseases   (MPS Society)
1982**
■   MPS House, Repton Place, White Lion Rd, AMERSHAM, Bucks,
    HP7 9LP.   (hq)
    0845 389 9901   fax 0845 389 9902
    email mps@mpssociety.co.uk
    http://www.mpssociety.co.uk
    Chief Exec: Mrs Christine Lavery
▲   Registered Charity
○   *W; to support those affected by the disease, their families &
    carers; to bring about public awareness of MPS & related
    diseases; to support research
●   Conf - ET - Res - Exhib - Stat - Inf - VE
<   Nat Coun for Voluntary Orgs
M   800 families, 6 f, 12 org, UK / 100 i, 3 f, o'seas
¶   NL - 4.   AR.
    Booklets on specific diseases: Hurler, Scheie & Hurler/Scheie,
    Morquio, Sanfilippo, Maroteaux/Lamy etc.

Society of Museum Archaeologists   (SMA)   1976
NR   Dept of Archaeology & Numismatics, National Museum,
    Cathays Park, CARDIFF, CF10 3NP.   (hsb)
    029 2057 3274
    http://www.socmusarch.org.uk
    Hon Sec: Elizabeth Walker
Br   1 regional group in Scotland
○   *P; to promote the interests of archaeology in museums
    throughout the UK
●   Conf - SG
<   Museums Assn
M   250 i, 60 org, UK / 2 i, 2 org, o'seas
¶   The Museum Archaeologist - 1; ftm.   NL - 2; ftm.
    Publications list available.

Society for Music Analysis   (SMA)
■   c/o Dr Edward Venn, LICA (Music), Lancaster University,
    LANCASTER, LA1 4YW.   (admin/b)
    http://www.sma.ac.uk
    Treas & Admin: Dr Edward Venn
▲   Registered Charity
○   *D, *L, *P; is the leading organisation dedicated to the theory &
    practice of musical analysis
●   Conf - Mtgs - ET
M   i
¶   NL - 2.

Society for Name Studies in Britain & Ireland   (SNSBI)   1991
NR   Medical Library, Sch of Medical Sciences, University of Bristol,
    University Walk, BRISTOL, BS8 1TD.   (hsb)
    email secretary@snsbi.org.uk   http://www.snsbi.org.uk
    Hon Sec: Miss Jennifer Scherr
▲   Registered Charity
○   *L; to research into place names, personal names & surnames
    of GB & Ireland
●   Conf - Res - Comp - SG - Inf
M   200 i, 5 org, UK / i & org, o'seas
¶   NOMINA (Jnl) - 1.   NL.

Society for Nautical Research   (SNR)   1910
■   6 Ashmeadow Rd, Arnside, CARNFORTH, Lancs, LA5 0AE.
    (hsb)
    01524 761616   fax 01524 761616
    email honsecretary.snr@btinternet.com
    http://www.snr.org.uk
    National Maritime Museum, Greenwich, LONDON,
    SE10 9NF. (regd office).
    Hon Sec: Peter Winterbottom
▲   Company Limited by Guarantee; Registered Charity
○   *L, *Q; to research into all matters relating to seafaring &
    shipbuilding in all ages & among all nations & into the
    language & customs of the sea & other subjects of nautical
    interest
Gp   Provides the Chairman of the HMS Victory Advisory Technical
    C'ee, & in partnership with the Royal Navy oversees the
    continuing preservation, restoration & conservation of the
    ship
●   Conf (with the British Commission for Maritime History) - Res -
    EXhib - LG - Sponsorship of N A M Rodger's Naval History of
    Britain (in 3 vol) - The recording of small watercraft
M   1,000 i, 95 org, UK / 300 i, 220 org, o'seas
    (Sub: £37)
¶   The Mariner's Mirror - 4; ftm, £12.95 each nm..
    Bibliography of Mariner's Mirror (index) - 5 yrly.
    NL - 4; ftm only.

Society of Numismatic Artists & Designers   (SNAD)   1992
NR   108 Brompton Rd, LONDON, SW3 1JJ.   (hsp)
    020 7373 5554
    http://www.snad.org
    Sec: Jane McAdam-Freud
▲   Un-incorporated Society
○   *P; to raise the quality of coin design in the UK
●   Mtgs - Exhib - Empl
M   20 i, UK / 3 i, o'seas

© CBD Research Ltd · Beckenham · BR3 5JS · Tel 020 8650 7745 · Fax 020 8650 0768 · E-mail cbd@cbdresearch.com · www.cbdresearch.com

Society of Nursery Nursing Practitioners (SNN) 1991

- ■ 40 Archdale Rd, LONDON, SE22 9HJ. (hq)
  020 8693 0555   fax 07092 342170
  email info@snn.uk.com   http://www.snn.uk.com
  Chief Exec: Prof R A Herbert-Blankson
- ▲ Company Limited by Guarantee
- Br 6; 20 o'seas
- ○ *P; 'the only professional examining body for all those who look after children & young people'
- Gp Graduates (GSNNP); Associates (ASNNP); Fellows (FSNNP)
- ● Conf - Mtgs - ET - Exam - Res - Exhib - Comp - SG - Stat - Expt - Inf - Lib - VE - LG
- M 60 i, UK / 210 i, o'seas
- ¶ Nursery Nursing Practitioner - 4; ftm, £1.50 nm.   NL - irreg.
  NL - irreg.

Society of Occupational Medicine (SOM) 1935

- NR 6 St Andrew's Place, Regent's Park, LONDON, NW1 4LB. (hq)
  020 7486 2641   fax 020 7486 0028
  email admin@som.org.uk   http://www.som.org.uk
  Chief Exec: Hilary Todd
- ▲ Registered Charity
- Br 11 regional gps
- ○ *L; for doctors working in any capacity in occupational health in any field (incl government agencies & the armed forces) concerned with the protection of the health of people at work & the prevention of occupational diseases & injuries
- ● Conf - Mtgs - Res - Exhib - Inf - VE - LG
- M 1,800 i, UK / 100 i, o'seas
- ¶ Occupational Medicine Journal - 8; ftm.
  NL - 4;   Hbk - 2 yrly;   AR - 1; all ftm only.

Society for Old Testament Study (SOTS) 1917

- ■ St Stephen's House, 16 Marston St, OXFORD, OX4 1JX. (hsb)
  01865 613512   fax 01865 613513
  email john.jarick@theology.ox.ac.uk
  http://www.sots.ac.uk
  Hon Sec: Dr John Jarick
- ▲ Un-incorporated Society
- ○ *L; the promotion & coordination of Old Testament studies in GB & Ireland
- ● Conf
- M 301 i, UK/ 158 i, o'seas
- ¶ NL & LM - 1; ftm only.   Book List - 1; ftm, £23 nm.

Society of Olympic Collectors (SOC) 1984

- ■ 19 Hanbury Path, Sheerwater, WOKING, Surrey, GU21 5RB. (hsp)
  Hon Sec: Miss P Burger
- ▲ Un-incorporated Society
- ○ *G; to collect, collate & distribute information about philatelic & other memorabilia items related to the Olympic games
- ● Res - Exhib - Inf - Lib - VE
- < Assn Brit Philatelic Socs
- M 91 i, UK / 117 i, o'seas
- ¶ Torch Bearer (Jnl) - 4; ftm, £2 each nm.

Society of Operations Engineers (SOE) 2000

- NR 22 Greencoat Place, LONDON, SW1P 1PR. (hq)
  020 7630 1111   fax 020 7630 6677
  email soe@soe.org.uk   http://www.soe.org.uk
  Chief Exec: Nick Jones
- ▲ Company Limited by Guarantee; Registered Charity
- ○ *P; for engineers in the road transport, plant & engineer surveying industries
- Gp Professional sectors: Institute of Road Transport Engineers; Institution of Plant Engineers; Bureau of Engineer Surveyors
- ● Conf - Mtgs - ET - Comp - Inf - VE
- < Engg Coun; NICEIC; NCSIIB
- M 4,862 i, 16 f, UK / 684 i, o'seas
- ¶ The Plant Engineer (Jnl) - 6.
  Transport Engineer (Jnl).
  Various guides.   AR.

Society of Orthopaedic Medicine 1983

- ■ PO Box 204, WOOLTON, Merseyside, L25 7RL. (hq)
  0845 680 1608   fax 0845 680 1618
  email admin@somed.org   http://www.somed.org
  Exec Dir: Julia Kermode
- ▲ Company Limited by Guarantee; Registered Charity
- ○ *P; to promote orthopaedic medicine for public benefit through education & research
- ● Conf - Mtgs - ET - Res
- < Cyriax Org; Orthopaedic Medicine Intl; Ir Soc of Orthopaedic Medicine
- M 1,000 i, UK / 300 i, o'seas
  (Sub: £30 UK / £35 o'seas)
- ¶ International Musculskeletal Medicine Jnl - 3;   NL - 2;
  Members Directory; all ftm only.

Society of Parliamentary Agents (SPA) 1844

- NR Bircham Dyson Bell, 50 Broadway, LONDON, SW1H 0BL. (hsb)
  020 7783 3425
  email robbieowen@bdb-law.co.uk
  Hon Sec: Robbie Owen
- ▲ Un-incorporated Society
- ○ *P
  No further information supplied.

Society of Parsley Cultivators

- ■ 191 Westcombe Hill, LONDON, SE3 7RR.
- ○ *H
- ● Mtgs - Stat - VE
- M f

Society for Pattern Recognition
see full title **British Machine Vision Association & Society for Pattern Recognition**

Society of Pension Consultants (SPC) 1958

- ■ St Bartholomew House, 92 Fleet St, LONDON, EC4Y 1DG. (hq)
  020 7353 1688   fax 020 7353 9296
  email john.mortimer@spc.uk.com
  http://www.spc.uk.com
  Sec: John Mortimer
- ▲ Company Limited by Guarantee
- Br 3
- ○ *T; interests of organisations providing advice on & services to schemes & funds for the provision of retirement benefits
- Gp Compliance forum
- ● Mtgs - Inf - LG
- < Occupational Pension Schemes Jt Working Gp
- M 133 f
- ¶ SPC News - 6; ftm only.   LM - 1;   AR; both free.

Society of Personnel Directors Scotland (SPDS)

- NR Angus House, Orchardbank Business Park, FORFAR, Angus, DD8 1AX.
  01307 476111   fax 01307 476140
  email robertsonh@angus.gov.uk
  http://www.spds.org.uk
  Sec: Hugh Robertson
- ○ *P; to represent personnel in local government in Scotland

Society of Pharmaceutical Medicine (SPM) 1987

- NR 9 Red Lion Court, LONDON, EC4A 3EF. (hq)
  020 7936 5980   fax 020 7936 5901
  email spm@iob.org   http://www.socpharmed.org
  Exec Sec: Victoria Wood
- ▲ Registered Charity
- ○ *P; to promote the acquisition & dissemination of knowledge concerning the action & development of medicinal agents & their application in therapeutics
- ● Conf
- M 100 i, UK / 20 i, o'seas
- ¶ International Jnl of Pharmaceutical Medicine - 4.

Society of Ploughmen Ltd   1972
- ■ Quarry Farm, Loversall, DONCASTER, S Yorks, DN11 9DH.
  (hq)
  01302 852469   fax 01302 859880
  email info@ploughmen.co.uk
  http://www.ploughmen.co.uk
  Exec Dir: Ken Chappell
- ▲ Company Limited by Guarantee
- ○ *F; to promote the art & skill of ploughing the land; to promote the annual British National Ploughing Championship
- ● Comp
- < Wld Ploughing Org
- M 1,000 i, 250 org
- ¶ NL - 2; ftm only.

Society for Popular Astronomy   (SPA)   1953
- ■ 36 Fairway, Keyworth, NOTTINGHAM, NG12 5DU.   (hsp)
  email info@popastro.com   http://www.popastro.com
  Hon Sec: Guy Fennimore
- ○ *G, *L; to promote the knowledge & study of astronomy in a popular manner
- Gp Sections: Meteors, Comets, Aurorae, Planets, Moon, Sun, Variable stars, Deep-sky objects, Lunar occultations
- ● Mtgs - ET - Res - Comp - Stat - Inf - VE - Weekend courses
- < Brit Astronomical Assn
- M 3,100 i, 60 org, UK / 70 i, 4 org, o'seas
- ¶ Popular Astronomy (Jnl) - 4; ftm, price on application nm.
  Circular (NL) - 6; ftm only.

Society of Portrait Sculptors   (SPS)   1953
- ■ 50A Hyde St, WINCHESTER, Hants, SO23 7DY.
  01962 860904
  email sps@portrait-sculpture.org
  http://www.portrait-sculpture.org
  Hon Sec: Robert Hunt
- ▲ Registered Charity
- ○ *A; 'portrait & figurative sculpture'
- ● Exhib (annual)
- M 30 i, UK / 2 i, o'seas
- ¶ Catalogue - 1; ftm, £6 nm.

Society for Post-Medieval Archaeology   (SPMA)   1967
- NR School of Archaeology & Ancient History, University of Leicester, University Rd, LEICESTER, LE1 7RH.
  0116-252 2846
  http://www.spma.org.uk
  Hon Sec: Dr Audrey Horning
- ▲ Company Limited by Guarantee
- ○ *L; to study evidence of British & Colonial history of the post-medieval period before industrialisation
- ● Conf - Res - Lib - VE - LG
- < Soc Histl Archaeology (USA)
- M 462 i, 219 org
- ¶ Post-Medieval Archaeology (Jnl); ftm.   NL - 2; free.

Society of Practising Veterinary Surgeons
a group of the **British Veterinary Association**

Society for the Preservation & Appreciation of Old Time Music & Dancing
since 2005 **Old Time Dance Society**

Society for the Preservation of Beers from the Wood   (SPBW)   1963
- ■ 46 The Fairway, DEVIZES, Wilts, SN10 5DX.   (chmn/p)
  01380 726378
  email chairman@spbw.com
  Chmn: Chris Callow
- ▲ Un-incorporated Society
- Br 20; Turkey, USA
- ○ *K; to stimulate the brewing & encourage the drinking of traditional draught beers, drawn direct from the cask by gravity or by handpump or other appropriate methods & to support those brewers who, by their policy, assist in the society's aims
- ● Conf - Mtgs - Exhib (at beer festivals) - Comp (London Pub of the Year) - Stat
- M 600 i, UK / 300 i, o'seas
  (Sub: £5 i, £15 f, UK / £10 i, £15 f, o'seas
- ¶ Pint in Hand - 4; ftm only.

Society for the Prevention of Solvent & Volatile Substance Abuse
alternative name of **Re-Solv**

Society of Procurement Officers in Local Government   (SOPO)   1997
- ■ SBV Ltd, Rosecroft, Holbrook Rd, Harkstead, IPSWICH, Suffolk, IP9 1BP.   (hsp/b)
  01473 327952
  Chief Exec: Peter Howarth
- ▲ Company Limited by Guarantee
- Br 12 regions
- ○ *P; to provide procurement guidance & promote strategic procurement within local government; to provide a forum & network
- ● Conf - Mtgs - ET - Exhib - Inf - LG
- < Chart Inst of Purchasing & Supply
- M 2,400 i, 13 f
- ¶ enewsletter - 52; free.   Annual Ybk - 1; ftm, £200 nm.

Society for Producers & Composers of Applied Music   (PCAM)   1982
- ■ Birchwood Hall, Storridge, MALVERN, Worcs, WR13 5EZ.
  (admin/p/b)
  01886 884204
  email bobfromer@onetel.com   http://www.pcam.co.uk
  Admin: Bob Fromer
- ▲ Un-incorporated Society
- ○ *T; music producers &/or composers working primarily in commissioned film, advertising & television programme music
- Gp Television c'ee
- ● Mtgs - ET - Res - Inf
- < sister organisations in Australia, Germany, Spain, USA
- M 90 f, UK / 3 f, o'seas
- ¶ The Bugle (NL) - 4.   PCAM Directory - 1.

Society of Professional Accountants   (SPA)   1996
- ■ 95 High St, GREAT MISSENDEN, Bucks, HP16 0AL.   (hq)
  01494 864414   fax 01494 864454
  email mail@spa.org.uk   http://www.spa.org.uk
  Chmn: Peter J D Mitchell
- ▲ Un-incorporated Society
- ○ *P; for chartered accountants who have a qualification issued by a recognised professional accountancy institute (ICAEW, ICAI, IAS, ACCA, CIMA); such individuals in practice
- ● Inf - LG
- < ICAEW
- M 1,800 i, 1,500 f
- ¶ NL;   LM;   AR; all ftm.

© CBD Research Ltd · Beckenham · BR3 5JS · Tel 020 8650 7745 · Fax 020 8650 0768 · E-mail cbd@cbdresearch.com · www.cbdresearch.com

Society of Professional Engineers Ltd (SPE) 1969
- ■ Lutyens House, Billing Brook Rd, Weston Favell, NORTHAMPTON, NN3 8NW. (regd off)
  01604 415729   fax 01604 415729
  email christine.braybrook@abe.org.uk
  http://www.professionalengineers-uk.org
  Chief Exec: David R Gibson
- ▲ Company Limited by Guarantee
- ○ *P; 'to promote the concept of the professional engineer & to place on a register those deemed to be so qualified'
- ● Mtgs - Exhib
- M 150 i, UK / 400 i, o'seas
- ¶ The Professional Engineer - 4; free.

** Society of Professional Licensed Taxi Drivers**

Society for Promoting Christian Knowledge (SPCK) 1698
- § 36 Causton St, LONDON, SW1P 4ST. (hq)
  020 7592 3900   fax 020 7592 3939
  http://www.spck.org.uk
  An Anglican mission agency working in the UK and around the world to help people to grow in the Christian faith through the ministries of Christian education and literature.

Society for Promoting the Training of Women (SPTW) 1859
- ■ c/o Vine Hall Farm, Bethersden, ASHFORD, Kent, TN26 3JY. (hsp)
  email sec.sptw@btinternet.com   http://www.sptw.org
  Hon Sec: Mrs Michelle Bennett
- ▲ Registered Charity
- ○ *W; to make interest free loans to women (18+) undertaking full time (very occasionally part-time) training for a career
- ● ET
- M 50 i
- ¶ AR; ftm, free nm (for sae).

Society for the Promotion of Byzantine Studies (SPBS) 1983
- NR c/o Dr Antony Eastmond, Courtauld Institute of Art, Somerset House, Strand, LONDON, WC2R 0RN. (hsb)
  http://www.byzantium.ac.uk
  Hon Sec: Dr Antony Eastmond
- ▲ Registered Charity
- ○ *L; to further the study & knowledge of the history of the Byzantine Empire & its neighbours
- ● Conf - Mtgs - Res - PL - VE
- < Assn Intle des Études Byzantines (AIEB)
- M i
- ¶ Bulletin - 1.

Society for the Promotion of Hellenic Studies (Hellenic Society) (SPHS) 1879
- ■ Senate House, Malet St, LONDON, WC1E 7HU. (hq)
  020 7862 8730   fax 020 7862 8731
  email office@hellenicsociety.org.uk
  http://www.hellenicsociety.org.uk
  Sec: Rachel Doyle,   Pres: Prof Malcolm Schofield
  Hon Sec: Dr Pantelis Michelakis
- ▲ Registered Charity
- ○ *L; to study the Greek language, literature, history & art in the ancient, Byzantine & modern periods
- ● Conf - Res - Comp - Lib - PL
- < Brit School at Athens
- M 3,000 i, UK / 1,000 org, o'seas
  (Sub: £22 student, £41 full mem, £200 corporate, £60 libraries & schools)
- ¶ Jnl of Hellenic Studies - 1; ftm only.
  Archaeological Reports - 1; ftm, £11 nm.
  Note: the Library is owned in common with the Society for the Promotion of Roman Studies & the Institute of Classical Studies of the University of London.

Society for the Promotion of New Music (SPNM) 1943
- ■ St Margaret's House, 18-20 Southwark St (4th floor), LONDON, SE1 1TJ. (hq)
  020 7407 1640   fax 020 7403 7652
  email spnm@spnm.org.uk   http://www.spnm.org.uk
  Admin: Isobel Anderson
- ▲ Registered Charity
- ○ *D; to help composers by presenting new works in workshop & concert performances
- ● Conf - ET - Exhib - Comp - SG - Inf
- < Intl Soc for Contemporary Music (ISCM)(British section)
- M 1,500 i, f & org, UK / 100 i, f & org, o'seas
- ¶ New Notes (contemporary music brochure) - 12.
  Beat Magazine - 4.

Society for the Promotion of Roman Studies (Roman Society) 1910
- ■ Senate House, Malet St, LONDON, WC1E 7HU. (hq)
  020 7862 8727   fax 020 7862 8728
  email office@romansociety.org
  http://www.romansociety.org
  Sec: Dr Fiona K Haarer
- ▲ Company Limited by Guarantee; Registered Charity
- ○ *L; to promote the study of the history, archaeology, literature & art of Italy & the Roman Empire, from the earliest times down to c AD 700
- ● Conf - Mtgs - Lib
- < Fédn Intle des Assns d'Études Classiques
- M 2,100 i, 250 org, UK / 650 i, 950 org, o'seas
- ¶ Jnl of Roman Studies - 1; ftm, £60 yr nm.
  Jnl of Roman Studies Monographs - irreg; prices vary.
  Britannia - 1; ftm, £60 yr nm.
  Britannia Monographs - irreg; prices vary.   AR; free.

Society of Property Researchers (SPR) 1987
- ■ St Mary's, Gandish Rd, EAST BERGHOLT, Suffolk, CO7 6UR. (mem/sp)
  01206 298205   fax 01206 298683
  email ftrott@sprweb.com   http://www.sprweb.com
  Mem Sec: Fiona Trott
- ▲ Un-incorporated Society
- ○ *P
- ● Mtgs - Res - VE
- M 500 i, UK / 30 i, o'seas
- ¶ LM - 1;   SPR Property Review & Digest No 1 & 2 (1993); both ftm only.
  The Adequacy & Accuracy of Commercial Property Data, Working Paper No 1: The Need for Property Data (1995);
  Local Area Analysis & Portfolio Construction (1994);
  Property Indices Report (1994);   all ftm, £20 nm.
  Survey of Salaries & Benefits - 2 yrly; ftm, £30 nm.

Society for the Protection of Ancient Buildings (SPAB) 1877
- ■ 37 Spital Sq, LONDON, E1 6DY. (hq)
  020 7377 1644   fax 020 7247 5296
  email info@spab.org.uk   http://www.spab.org.uk
  Sec: Philip Venning
- ▲ Registered Charity
- ○ *K, *L; to promote the conservative repair of historic buildings; the SPAB must be notified of all applications to demolish in whole or part any listed building in England & Wales
- Gp Mills section; SPAB in Scotland
- ● Conf - Mtgs - ET - Exhib - Inf - Lib - VE - LG
- < Jt C'ee of Nat Amenity Socs
- M 8,500 i
- ¶ SPAB News - 4;   Wind & Watermill - 4; both ftm.

Society for the Protection of Aviculture
  merged, probably in 2007, with the **National Council for Aviculture Ltd**

Society for the Protection of Life from Fire   1836
§   15 Mallow Close, HORSHAM, W Sussex, RH12 5GA.   (hq)
      http://www.splf.org.uk
      Sec: Michael Gale
      The Society exists to give recognition to people who perform
      acts of bravery in rescuing others from the life-threatening
      effects of fires.

Society for the Protection of Unborn Children   (SPUC)   1967
NR   3 Whitacre Mews, Stannary St, LONDON, SE11 4AB.   (hq)
      020 7091 7091   fax 020 7820 3131
      email information@spuc.org.uk
      http://www.spuc.org.uk
      Gen Sec: Paul Tully
Br   141
○   *K; to affirm, defend & promote the existence & value of
      human life from the moment of conception
Gp   Conservative Group, Muslim Division, No Less Human, Nurses
      Opposed to Euthanasia, Patients First Network, Silent No
      More, SPUC Evangelicals
●   Conf - Mtgs - ET - Res - Comp - Inf - LG
M   45,000 i
¶   Pro-Life Times - 2.

Society for Psychical Research   (SPR)   1882
NR   49 Marloes Rd, LONDON, W8 6LA.   (hq)
      020 7937 8984
      http://www.spr.ac.uk
      Sec: Peter M Johnson
▲   Company Limited by Guarantee; Registered Charity
○   *Q; 'to further systematic, scientific investigation of certain
      paranormal phenomena which are apparently inexplicable
      on any generally recognised hypothesis - telepathy & all
      forms of paranormal cognition, poltergeists, apparitions,
      alleged movement of objects without contact; any other
      phenomena which appear to be paranormal. The Society
      does not hold or express views'
Gp   ESP C'ee; Physical phenomena; Research advisory; Publications
●   Conf - Lectures - Res - Inf - Lib
M   1,100 i
¶   Jnl - 4.   Proceedings - irreg.
      Paranormal Review Magazine - 4.
✕   Incorporated Society for Psychical Research

Society of Public Information Networks
      ceased trading 31 March 2008

Society of Publishers in Ireland   (SPI)   2002
IRL   c/o Verba Editing House, 4 Donore Rd Industrial Estate,
      DROGHEDA, Co Louth, Republic of Ireland.
      353 (41) 987 1000   fax 353 (41) 987 1000
      email info@the-spi.com   http://www.the-spi.com
      Sec: Rachel Pierce
○   *T
      A networking society for all those working in the publishing
      trade and related industries, organising informal social
      events to promote greater understanding throughout the
      industry.

Society of Radiographers   (SoR)   1920
■   207 Providence Square, Mill St, LONDON, SE1 2EW.   (hq)
      020 7740 7200   fax 020 7740 7204
      email info@sor.org   http://www.sor.org
      Chief Exec: Richard Evans
▲   Company Limited by Guarantee
○   *P, *U; the Society & College exist to promote & develop the
      science & practice of radiography (including both diagnostic
      & therapeutic disciplines); it is the recognised trade union for
      those engaged in radiography & related activities
Gp   College of Radiographers (charitable non-membership
      subsidiary)
●   Conf - Mtgs - ET - Exam - Res - Exhib - Comp - SG - Stat - Lib -
      VE - Empl - LG
<   Intl Soc Radiographers & Radiological Technologists; Alliance
      Health Profls
M   21,729 i, UK / 244 i, o'seas
¶   Radiography (Jnl) - 4;   Synergy (NL) - 12; both ftm.
      Imaging & Oncology - 1; free to all in radiological &
      oncological communities.

Society for Radiological Protection   (SRP)   1963
■   PO Box 117, BUCKFASTLEIGH, Devon, TQ11 0WA.
      (admin/off)
      01364 644487   fax 01364 644492
      email admin@srp-uk.org   http://www.srp-uk.org
      Hon Sec: Bryan Smith
▲   Registered Charity
○   *L, *P; the scientific, technological, medical & legal aspects of
      radiological protection
●   Conf - Mtgs
<   Intl Radiation Protection Assn
M   1,491 i, f & org
¶   Jnl - 4; ftm, £340 yr nm.

Society of Recorder Players   (SRP)   1937
NR   21 Bereweeke Ave, WINCHESTER, Hants, SO22 6BH.   (hsp)
      01962 868862
      email secretary@srp.org.uk   http://www.srp.org.uk
      Sec: Bob Whitmarsh
▲   Registered Charity
Br   50; Ireland
○   *D; 'education of the public in the study, practice &
      appreciation of the art of music & in particular the repertoire
      & playing of recorders'
●   Conf - Mtgs - ET - SG - Exams for certificate for teaching &
      conducting - Workshops - Biennial competition for young
      professionals
M   1,250 i, 4 org, UK / 30 i, o'seas

Society of Registered Naturopaths
      see the **Incorporated Society of Registered Naturopaths**

Society for Renaissance Studies   (SRS)   1967
■   c/o Dr Gabriele Neher, Dept of Art History, Lakeside Arts
      Centre, University of Nottingham, NOTTINGHAM,
      NG7 2RD.   (hsp)
      email gabriele.neher@nottingham.ac.uk
      http://www.rensoc.org.uk
      Hon Sec: Dr Gabriele Neher
▲   Registered Charity
○   *L; study of all aspects of the Renaissance
●   Conf - Mtgs - ET - Exhib
<   Renaissance Soc of America (RSA)
M   c 600 i
¶   Renaissance Studies (Jnl) - 5; £25-£38 m.

© CBD Research Ltd · Beckenham · BR3 5JS · Tel 020 8650 7745 · Fax 020 8650 0768 · E-mail cbd@cbdresearch.com · www.cbdresearch.com

Society for Reproduction & Fertility   2001
NR Procon Conferences Ltd, Tattersall House, East Parade,
    HARROGATE, N Yorks, HG1 5LT.   (regd off)
    01423 564488   fax 01423 701433
    email srfsecretariat@procon-conferences.co.uk
    http://www.srf-reproduction.org
    Gen Sec: John Parrington
▲   Company Limited by Guarantee; Registered Charity
○   *L; to enhance the knowledge of reproductive processes in man
    & animals

Society for Reproductive & Infant Psychology   (SRIP)   1980
NR Sch of Healthcare Studies, University of Leeds, 15 Hyde Terrace,
    LEEDS, W Yorks, LS2 9LT.   (hsb)
    0113-343 1281
    email j.hirst@leeds.ac.uk   http://www.srip.ac.uk
    Sec: Janet Hirst
▲   Registered Charity
○   *M; to promote the scientific study, both pure & applied, of all
    psychological & behavioural matters related to human
    reproduction
●   Conf - Mtgs - ET - Res - Comp
M   140 i, UK / 38 i, o'seas
¶   Journal of Reproductive & Infant Psychology - 4.

Society for Research into Higher Education Ltd   (SRHE)   1964
NR 76 Portland Place, LONDON, W1B 1NT.   (hq)
    020 7637 2766   fax 020 7637 2781
    email srheoffice@srhe.ac.uk   http://www.srhe.ac.uk
    Dir: Helen Perkins
▲   Company Limited by Guarantee; Registered Charity
○   *L; to advance understanding of higher education

Society for Research into Hydrocephalus & Spina Bifida
(SRHSB)   1957
■   Gagle Brook House, Chesterton, BICESTER, Oxon,
    OX26 1UF.   (hsb)
    email hsec@srhsb.org   http://www.srhsb.org
    Hon Sec: Dr Hazel C Jones
▲   Registered Charity
○   *L, *Q; to advance education & promote research into
    hydrocephalus & spina bifida; to bring together workers in
    different fields so that they may be aided in their joint effort
    to prevent, cure or alleviate these conditions
●   Conf - Res
M   56 i, UK / 200 i, o'seas
¶   Cerebrospinal Fluid Research - 1;   NL - 3;   AR - 1;
    Prospectus - 1; m only, £60 yr (£30 yr senior members).

Society for the Responsible Use of Resources in Agriculture & on
the Land   (RURAL)   1983
■   Chester House, 12 Hillbury Rd, Alderholt, FORDINGBRIDGE,
    Hants, SP6 3BQ.   (hq)
    01425 652035
    http://www.rural.org.uk
    Dir: Brig H J Hickman
○   *F; to assist the policy makers in the field of land use,
    agricultural & rural management; to form opinions; to
    reconcile competing rural interests; information policy
    development
●   Conf - Mtgs - SG - Discussion groups
M   180 i, 29 f
¶   RURAL Briefing; £15 yr.   Network opportunities.

Society for Sailing Barge Research   (SSBR)   1963
■   5 Cox Rd, Alresford, COLCHESTER, Essex, CO7 8EJ.   (hsp)
    01206 825317
    email john.white6@talk21.com
    http://www.sailingbargeresearch.org.uk
    Hon Sec: John White
▲   Un-incorporated Society
○   *G; research into the sailing barge, the men who built & sailed
    them & the ports from which they sailed
●   Res - Exhib - PL
M   340 i, 10 org, UK / 10 i, o'seas
¶   Topsail (Jnl) - 1;   NL - 2; both ftm only.

Society of Sales & Marketing   (SSAM)   1980
■   40 Archdale Rd, LONDON, SE22 9HJ.   (hq)
    020 8693 0555   fax 0709 234 2170
    email info@ssam.co.uk   http://www.ssam.co.uk
    Chief Exec: Prof R A Herbert-Blankson
▲   Company Limited by Guarantee
Br 12; 70 o'seas
○   *P; to encourage the study & practice of selling, sales
    management, retail management, marketing & international
    trade & services
●   Conf - Mtgs - ET - Exam - Res - Exhib - Comp - SG - Stat - Expt
    - Inf - Lib - LG
<   Soc of Nursery Nursing Practitioners
M   500 i, UK / 4,000 i, o'seas
¶   Sales & Marketing Today; ftm, £1.50 nm.   NL.

Society of Schoolmasters & Schoolmistresses   (SOSS)   1798
■   c/o Miss Sarah Brydon, SGBI, Queen Mary House, Manor Park
    Rd, CHISLEHURST, Kent, BR7 5PY.   (hsb)
    020 8468 7997   fax 020 8468 7200
    email sgbi@fsmail.net
    Case Officer: Miss Sarah Brydon
▲   Registered Charity
○   *W; 'to give assistance to necessitous schoolmasters,
    schoolmistresses & their dependents'
●   Mtgs
M   14 i

Society of Scottish Artists   (SSA)   1891
NR 2 Wemyss Avenue, GLASGOW, G77 6AR.   (sp)
    0141-616 2566
    email ssa@tanglewebs.co.uk   http://www.s-s-a.org
    Sec: Noreen Sharkey Paisley
▲   Registered Charity
○   *A; to mount an annual exhibition reflecting the adventurous
    spirit of Scottish art; to promote international exhibition &
    exchange
●   Exhib
M   350 i, UK / 10 i o'seas
¶   SSA NL - 4; free.
    The SSA: the last 100 years; £15.
    Exhibition Catalogue (incl LM) - 1.

Society of Scribes & Illuminators   (SSI)   1921
■   6 Queen Sq, LONDON, WC1N 3AR.   (mail address)
    email gillianhazeldine@austwick-yorks.net
    http://www.calligraphyonline.org
    Sec: Gillian Hazeldine
▲   Un-incorporated Society
○   *A; to perpetuate a tradition of craftsmanship in the production
    of manuscript books & documents; to encourage the practice
    & influence of calligraphy & fine letterings
Gp 64 fellows; 28 advanced calligraphers on 3-yr scheme
●   Mtgs - ET - Exhib - SG - Inf - Lib
M   700 i, UK / 200 i, o'seas
¶   The Scribe (Jnl) - 1; ftm.   NL.   LM.

Society of Sexual Health Advisers   (SSHA)
- ■   35 King St, Covent Garden, LONDON, WC2E 8JG.   (hq)
  07919 324716
  email info@ssha.info   http://www.ssha.info
  Nat Officer: Carol English
- ▲   Company Limited by Guarantee
- ○   *P, *U; for health advisers working in departments of genito-urinary medicine & sexual health
- ●   Conf - Mtgs - ET - Res - Empl - LG - Professional website
- <   a professional section of Unite, the Union
- M   300 i
- ¶   SSHA NL - 2; ftm only.

Society of Share & Business Valuers   1996
- NR   1 Winchester Rd, BROMLEY, Kent, BR2 0PZ.   (hsb)
  020 8466 7924   fax 020 8466 7637
  http://www.ssbv.org
  Sec: J W Hallam
- ○   *P

Society of Shoe Fitters   1959
- ■   c/o The Anchorage, 28 Admirals Walk, HINGHAM, Norfolk, NR9 4JL.   (hsp)
  01953 851171   fax 01953 851190
  email secretary@shoefitters-uk.org
  http://www.shoefitters-uk.org
  Sec: Laura West
- ▲   Un-incorporated Society
- ○   *P; training people to fit shoes correctly to a recognised qualification
- ●   Mtgs - ET - Exam - Exhib - Inf - VE - LG - Providing foot health education material - Helpline
- M   223 i, 9 f, UK/ 10 i, o'seas
  (Suib: £10.50 i, £150 f, UK / £50 i, o'seas
- ¶   LM; on website, £5 nm.   Leaflets; £5 per 100.

Society for the Social History of Medicine   (SSHM)   1969
- ■   School of History Classics and Archaeology, University of Edinburgh, William Robertson Building, 50 George Square, EDINBURGH, EH8 9JY.   (hsb)
  email gayle.davis@ed.ac.uk   http://www.sshm.org
  Sec: Dr Gayle Davis
- ▲   Registered Charity
- ○   *L; to promote the study of all aspects of the social history of medicine, having reference to the patients as well as the practitioner & to health as well as disease
- ●   Conf - Mtgs - ET - Res - Comp - SG - Inf
- M   189 i, UK / 158 i, o'seas
- ¶   Social History of Medicine (Jnl) - 3; £37 m, £101 nm, (2005).

Society for Social Medicine   (SSM)   1957
- ■   NYCRIS, Level 6 Bexley Wing, St James' University Hospital, LEEDS, W Yorks, LS9 7TF.   (hsb)
  email admin@socsocmed.org.uk
  http://www.socsocmed.org.uk
  Hon Sec: Dr Amy Downing
- ▲   Un-incorporated Society
- ○   *L; concerned with all aspects of social medicine including epidemiology & the study of medical & health needs of society, provision & organisation of health services & prevention of disease
- ●   Conf - Mtgs
- <   Eur Public Health Assn
- M   1,250 i, UK / 70 i, o'seas
- ¶   NL - 4;   AR; both ftm only.

Society of Solicitors in the Supreme Courts of Scotland (SSCSoc)   1784
- ■   SSC Library, Parliament House, 11 Parliament Sq, EDINBURGH, EH1 1RF.   (hq)
  0131 225 6268   fax 0131 225 2270
  email enquiries@ssclibrary.co.uk
  http://www.ssclibrary.co.uk
  Sec: Ian L S Balfour
- ○   *P; to maintain a practitioners' law library; to express opinions on current legal questions; to maintain a fund for widows & orphans
- ●   Inf - Lib
- <   part of the College of Justice in Scotland
- M   300 i, UK / 6 i, o'seas

Society for South Asian Studies
on 1 October 2007 merged with the **British Association for South Asian Studies**

Society of Sports Therapists   1990
- ■   16 Royal Terrace, GLASGOW, G3 7NY.   (hq)
  0845 600 2613   fax 0141-332 5335
  email admin@society-of-sports-therapists.org
  http://www.society-of-sports-therapists.org
  Chmn: Prof Graham N Smith
- ▲   Company Limited by Guarantee
- ○   *P; *S
- ●   Mtgs - Exam - LG
- M   3,500 i
- ¶   Sports Therapy (Jnl) - 1.   NL - 6.

Society of Stars   1995
- NR   55 Denham Lane, Chalfont St Peter, GERRARDS CROSS, Bucks, SL9 0EW.   (hq)
  01494 872817
- ▲   Company Limited by Guarantee; Registered Charity
- ○   *W; celebrity support for children & adults with cerebral palsy

Society for Storytelling   (SfS)   1993
- ■   PO Box 2344, READING, Berks, RG6 7FG.   (mail)
  0118-935 1381
  email admin@sfs.org.uk   http://www.sfs.org.uk
  Sec: David England
- ▲   Company Limited by Guarantee; Registered Charity
- ○   *A; to increase awareness of the art, practice & value of oral storytelling; to provide information of storytelling, storytellers & events
- Gp   Education; Health & therapy; Storytelling in organisations
- ●   Conf - ET - Inf - Lib - Co-ordination of events
- <   Assn Festival Organisers; FATE; Lapidus; Mythstories Museum; Scottish Storytelling Centre; The Telling Place
- >   ACE; Bit Crack; FATE; Fibs & Fables; Mythstories Museum; Scot Storytelling Centre; The Telling Place
- M   569 i, 16 org, UK / 18 i, o'seas
- ¶   Storylines Magazine - 4; ftm only.
  Directory of Storytellers - 1 £7.50 m, £11.50 nm.
  Talkshop Catalogue - 1; free.
  Booklets on the theory & practice of storytelling - irreg.
  Factsheets of useful information & booklists - irreg; £1.35.

Society of Stress Managers (the Association for Professional Stress Managers & Life Support Managers)
- NR   10 Wimborne Ave, Chadderton, OLDHAM, Lancs, OL9 0RN. (hq)
  0161-652 2284
  email petermatthews@manageyourstress.co.uk
  http://www.manageyourstress.co.uk
  Sec: Peter Matthews
- ○   *P
- M   i

© CBD Research Ltd · Beckenham · BR3 5JS · Tel 020 8650 7745 · Fax 020 8650 0768 · E-mail cbd@cbdresearch.com · www.cbdresearch.com

Society for the Study of Addiction to Alcohol & other Drugs (SSA) 1884
- ■ 19 Springfield Mount, LEEDS, W Yorks, LS2 9NG.   (hq)
  0113-295 2787   fax 0113-295 2787
  email membership@addiction-ssa.org
  http://www.addiction-ssa.org
  Sec: Prof John Strang
- ▲ Company LImited by Guarantee; Registered Charity
- ○ *L; to expand & promote the scientific understanding of addiction & the problems related to it; to advance the use of the evidence-base in policy & practice
- ● Conf - Mtgs - ET - Res - Comp
- M 300 i, UK / 110 i, o'seas
  (Sub: £85)
- ¶ Addiction - 12; ftm, £335 nm.
  Addiction Biology - 4; ftm, £244 nm.

Society for the Study of Animal Breeding
  a group of the **British Veterinary Association**

Society for the Study of Artificial Intelligence & Simulation of Behaviour (SSAISB) 1964
- NR Chichester C1-209, Sch of Science & Technology, University of Sussex Falmer, BRIGHTON E Sussex, BN1 9QH.
  01273 678448
  http://www.aisb.org.uk
  Sec: Louise Dennis
- ○ *L; to promote the study of artificial intelligence, simulation of behaviour & the design of intelligent systems

Society for the Study of Flies
  see **Dipterists Forum - the Society for the Study of Flies**

Society for the Study of Human Biology (SSHB) 1958
- ■ Dept of Human Sciences, Loughborough University, LOUGHBOROUGH, Leics, LE11 3TU.   (hsb)
  01509 228486
  email p.griffiths@lboro.ac.uk   http://www.sshb.org
  Hon Sec: Dr Paula Griffiths
- ▲ Company Limited by Guarantee
- ○ *L; to advance the study in all its branches, of the biology of human populations & of humans as a species, particularly human variability, adaptability & ecoloy, auxology, environmental physiology, epidemiology & ageing
- ● Conf - Mtgs - Symposium
- < Inst Biology
- M 114 i, UK / 66 i, o'seas
- ¶ Annals of Human Biology - 6; ftm, £36 yr nm.
  Symposium Proceedings - 1; price varies (published by Taylor & Francis).

Society for the Study of Labour History (SSLH) 1960
- ■ Dept of History, University of Exeter, Queen's Drive, EXETER, Devon, EX4 4QJ.   (conf/s/b)
  email m.reiss@ex.ac.uk   http://www.sslh.org.uk
  Conf Sec: Matthias Reiss
- ▲ Registered Charity
- ○ *L; 'an exploration into the working lives & politics of 'ordinary' people; the emphasis is on British labour history, though comparative & international studies are not neglected'; preservation of labour archives
- Gp Archives & resources c'ee; Editorial Advy Bd (Labour History Review)
- ● Conf - Mtgs - Res - Comp - SG
- ¶ Labour History Review - 3; £24 m.

Society for the Study of Subterranean Survival (SSSS) 1982
- ■ Beau Lodge, Kelsey Lane, BECKENHAM, Kent, BR3 3NF.   (hsp)
- ▲ Un-incorporated Society
- ○ *L
- ● Conf - Mtgs - SG - Lib - VE
- ¶ Survival Underground - 2; ftm only.

Society of Sussex Downsmen
  since 2005 **South Downs Society**

Society of Teachers of the Alexander Technique (STAT) 1958
- NR Linton House (1st floor), 39-51 Highgate Rd, LONDON, NW5 1RS.   (hq)
  0845 230 7828   fax 020 7482 5435
  email office@stat.org.uk   http://www.stat.org.uk
- ▲ Registered Charity
- ○ *P; to ensure the highest standards of teacher training & professional practice of the Alexander Technique

Society of Teachers of Speech & Drama (STSD) 1951
- ■ 73 Berry Hill Rd, MANSFIELD, Notts, NG18 4RU.   (regd/office)
  01623 627636
  email ann.k.Jones@btinternet.com
  http://www.stsd.org.uk
  Gen Sec: Mrs Ann K Jones
- ▲ Company Limited by Guarantee
- Br 34; 16 countries o'seas
- ○ *E; the teaching of speech & drama & other theatrical skills; to support & encourage students in training
- Gp Teaching: Communication skills, Speech & drama, Theatre skills;
  Business communication & presentation; Correction of speech problems; Lecturing; Workshops; Conferences; Amateur & professional theatre
- ● Conf - ET - Exhib - Comp - SG - Inf
- < Nat Campaign for the Arts; Central Coun of Amat Theatre
- > Voice Network; Engl Speaking Bd; Gld of S African Teachers of Speech & Drama;Australian Speech & Drama Assns; New Zealand Speech Assn
- M 750 i, 18 f, UK / 98 i, 1 f, o'seas
- ¶ Speech & Drama (Jnl) - 2; ftm, £7 nm.   NL - 3; ftm only.

Society of Technical Analysts Ltd (STA) 1969
- NR Dean House, Vernham Dean, ANDOVER, Hants, SP11 0LA.   (hq)
  0845 003 9549
- ▲ Company Limited by Guarantee
- ○ *P; to promote the use & understanding of technical analysis amongst the public & investment community; to maintain professional standards in the subject & to set an examination to allow competency to be measured & proven

Society of Television Lighting Directors (STLD) 1974
- NR 223 Cressex Rd, HIGH WYCOMBE, Bucks, HP12 4QE.   (memsec/p)
  email secretary@stld.org.uk   http://www.stld.org.uk
  Mem Sec: Graham Rimmington
- ▲ Un-incorporated Society
- ○ *P; an apolitical society for the free exchange of ideas in all aspects of the television profession (incl techniques & reports on the use & design of equipment both to manufacturers & members)
- ● Mtgs (also regional) - ET - Exhib - VE
- M i
- ¶ Television Lighting - 4; ftm only.

Society of Theatre Consultants (STC) 1964
- ■ 27 Old Gloucester St, LONDON, WC1N 3XX.   (asa)
  020 7419 8767
  http://www.theatreconsultants.org.uk
  Chmn: Michael Houlden
- ▲ Un-incoporated Society
- ○ *P; for specialist consultants in the field of theatre building design & management & the design & integration of specialist theatre equipment
- ● Conf - Mtgs - ET
- M i
  (Sub: £100, UK / £60 o'seas)
- ¶ Occasional.

Society for Theatre Research   (STR)   1948
NR   PO Box 53971, LONDON, SW15 6UL.   (mail/address)
         http://www.str.org.uk
         Hon Secs: Eileen Cottis,   Valerie Lucas
▲   Registered Charity
Br   Northern
○   *L, *Q; to foster research into the history & practice of the
         British theatre
●   Mtgs - Res - SG - VE - Research awards (£4,000 yr) - Annual
         Theatre Book Prize - Administration of annual William Poel
         Festival & the Edward Gordon Craig memorial lecture
<   Intl Fedn for Theatre Res; Theatres Trust
M   400 i, 80 f, UK / 150 i, 150 f, o'seas
¶   Theatre Notebook - 3; £18 m (£19.50 o'seas),
         £6 back issue nm.
         NL - 2;   AR; both ftm only.
         Books on various aspects of the British theatre.

Society of Ticket Agents & Retailers   (STAR)
NR   PO Box 43, LONDON, WC2H 7LD.   (mail/address)
         0870 603 9011
         email info@s-t-a-r.org.uk   http://www.s-t-a-r.org.uk
         Sec: Jonathan Brown
○   *T

Society of Trust & Estate Practitioners   (STEP)   1991
■   Artillery House (South), 11-19 Artillery Row, LONDON,
         SW1P 1RT.   (hq)
         020 7340 0500   fax 020 7340 0501
         email step@step.org   http://www.step.org
         Chief Exec: David Harvey
▲   Company Limited by Guarantee
Br   29; 30
○   *P; for those involved at senior level with trusts & estates - from
         the legal, accountancy, corporate trust, banking, insurance &
         related professions
●   Conf - Mtgs - ET - Inf - LG
M   5,388 i, UK / 8,745 i, o'seas
¶   STEP Jnl - 4;   Trust Qaurterly Review - 4;
         STEP USA Jnl - 3; all ftm, all £345 yr nm.

Society of Turnaround Professionals
         since 2008 **Institute for Turnaround**

Society for Underwater Technology Ltd   (SUT)   1966
NR   80 Coleman St, LONDON, EC2R 5BJ.   (hq)
         020 7382 2601   fax 020 7382 2684
         email info@sut.org   http://www.sut.org.uk
         Hon Sec: M Crawford,   Chief Exec: Ian Gallett
▲   Registered Charity
Br   2; Australia (Melbourne, Perth), Brazil, Malaysia, USA
○   *L; to promote the understanding & use of the underwater
         environment; the development of the techniques & tools to
         explore, study & exploit the oceans & the earth beneath
Gp   Diving & submersibles; Education & training; Environmental
         forces; Marine renewable energies; Ocean resources;
         Offshore site investigation & geotechnics; Policy advisory;
         Subsea engineering & operations; Underwater robotics;
         Underwater science
●   Conf - Mtgs - ET - Inf - LG
M   868 i, 109 f
¶   Underwater Technology (Jnl) - 4.
         SUT News - 8.   Ybk - 2 yrly.
         Conference proceedings - irreg.

**Society of Wedding & Portrait Photographers   (SWPP/BPPA)
1988**
■   6 Bath St, RHYL, Flintshire, LL18 3EB.   (hq)
         01745 356935
         email enquiries@swpp.co.uk
         Chief Exec: Phil Jones
▲   Company Limited by Guarantee
○   *P
●   Conf - Mtgs - ET - Exam - Exhib - Comp - Inf
M   6,500 i
¶   Professional Imagemaker.

Society for the Welfare of Horses & Ponies   (SWHP)   1973
NR   The Horse Hospital, Coxstone, St Maughan's, MONMOUTH,
         NP25 5QF.   (hq)
         01600 750233   fax 01600 750468
         email swhp@swhp.co.uk   http://www.swhp.co.uk
         Chmn: Jenny MacGregor
▲   Registered Charity
○   *G, *K; to take into care sick, injured & abused horses &
         ponies, returning them to health & loaning them to homes
         suitable for their age, fitness & capabilities
●   SG - LG - Care of horses on site & on loan
<   Nat Equine Welfare Coun
M   1,200 i, UK / 10 i, o'seas
¶   NL - 2; free.

**Society of West Highland & Island Historical Research
(SWHIHR)   1972**
■   Hebridean Centre, ISLE OF COLL, Argyllshire, PA78 6TB.
         (hsp)
         01879 230444   fax 01879 230357
         email swhihr@ntlworld.com
         Sec: Douglas Young
▲   Un-incorporated Society
○   *L; to encourage research into the history of the West Highlands
         & Islands; to make the results available to the public in an
         attractive format
●   Res - (Submissions of work are welcomed)
M   120 i, UK / 35 i, o'seas
         (Sub: £10 i, £15 f, UK / £20 i o'seas)
¶   West Highland Notes & Queries - 2; ftm, £5 nm.

Society of Wildlife Artists
         a member of the **Federation of British Artists**

Society of Will Writers & Estate Planning Practitioners   1994
■   Eagle House, Exchange Rd, LINCOLN, LN6 3JZ.   (hq)
         01522 687888   fax 01522 694666
         email info@willwriters.com   http://www.willwriters.com
         Dir Gen: Brian W McMillan
▲   Company Limited by Guarantee
Br   13
○   *P; 'a non-profit-making self-regulatory organisation whose
         primary objects are the advancement, education & ethical
         standards within the will-writing profession'
●   Conf - Mtgs - ET - Exam - Res - SG - Inf - LG
M   1,600 i, UK / 10 i, o'seas
¶   Testament (NL) - 12; ftm only.

Society of Women Artists   (SWA)   1855
NR   1 Knapp Cottages, Wyke, GILLINGHAM, Dorset, SP8 4NQ.
         (hq)
         01747 825718   fax 01747 826835
         email pamhenderson@dsl.pipex.com
         http://www.society-women-artists.org.uk
         Exec Sec: Mrs Pamela Henderson
▲   Company Limited by Guarantee; Registered Charity
○   *A; a non-political, non-feminist society for the encouragement
         of women artists
Gp   Painting in all media; Drawing; Sculpture in all media;
         Engraving; Lithography; Ceramics; Miniature work
●   Exhib
M   142 i
¶   Illustrated Exhibition Catalogue - 1; ftm, £3.50 nm.

© CBD Research Ltd · Beckenham · BR3 5JS · Tel 020 8650 7745 · Fax 020 8650 0768 · E-mail cbd@cbdresearch.com · www.cbdresearch.com

Society of Wood Engravers (SWE) 1920
- ■ The Old Governor's House, Norman Cross, PETERBOROUGH, Cambs, PE7 3TB. (gen sec/p)
  01733 242833
  http://www.woodengravers.co.uk
  Gen Sec: Geraldine Waddington
- ▲ Un-incorporated Society
- Br 1 o'seas
- ○ *A; for those interested in all aspects of wood engraving
- ● Conf - Mtgs - ET - Res - Exhib - Inf - Publications
- M 70 i, UK / 10 i, o'seas
  (subscribers: 350 i, 30 org, UK / 50 i, 30 org, o'seas)
- ¶ Multiples (NL) - 6.

Society of Writers to Her Majesty's Signet (WSSociety) 1594
- NR Signet Library, Parliament Sq, EDINBURGH, EH1 1RF. (hq)
  0131-225 4923 & 220 3426 (general enquiries)
  fax 0131-220 4016
  email library@wssociety.co.uk
  http://www.signetlibrary.co.uk
- ▲ Un-incorporated Society
- ○ *P; private society of qualified Scottish solicitors
- Gp Signet Library (mainly Scottish law); Training & education (courses & seminars for members & non-members); Function & conference facilities letting
- ● Conf - ET - SG - Inf - Lib (current & historical material, mainly appertaining to Scotland) - Liaison with other legal bodies
- M i UK & o'seas
- ¶ Signet NL - 3; ftm only.   AR.

Society of Young Mathematicians
  the youth group of the **Mathematical Association**

Socio-Legal Studies Association (SLSA) 1989
- NR c/o Sally Wheeler, School of Law, Queen's University Belfast, BELFAST, BT7 1NN. (hsb)
  Sally Wheeler
- ▲ Un-incorporated Society
- ○ *E, *L
- ● Conf - ET - SG
- M i
- ¶ Socio-legal NL - 3; ftm only.   LM - 1.

Sociological Association of Ireland
- IRL Department of Sociology, University College Cork, Safari, Donovan's Rd, Cork, Republic of Ireland
  353 (0) 21 490 3756
  email sai@ucd.ie   http://www.sociology.ie
- ○ *P; for all concerned with theoretical & empirical issues in the social sciences

Soil Association Ltd 1946
- ■ South Plaza, Marlborough St, BRISTOL, BS1 3NX. (hq)
  0117-314 5000   fax 0117-314 5001
  email info@soilassociation.org
  http://www.soilassociation.org
  Dir: Patrick Holden,   Sec: Roger Mortlock
- ▲ Registered Charity
- Br 5
- ○ *E, *F, *H; 'plays a crucial role in transforming attitudes to food & farming in the UK & internationally; we work with the public, farmers, growers, food processors, retailers, consumers & policy makers. Our mission is to bring about change by creating a growing body of public opinion that understands the links between farming practice & food & between plant, animal, human & environmental health'
- ● Conf - ET - Res - Stat - Inf - Lib - PL - LG
- < Intl Fedn Organic Agricl Movements
- M 18,000 i, 4,500 f, UK / 100 i, o'seas
- ¶ Living Earth - 3; ftm, £2 nm.
  Organic Farming - 4; ftm only.

Soil & Groundwater Technology Association (SAGTA)
- NR c/o Halcrow Group Ltd, Griffin House, 135 High St, CRAWLEY, W Sussex, RH10 1DQ.
  01293 434500   fax 01293 434599
  email laidlerd@halcrow.com   http://www.sagta.org.uk
  Sec: Doug Laidler
- ○ *L; to address the technical challenges associated with the management of landholdings which are potentially contaminated

SOLACE
  see **Society of Local Authority Chief Executives & Senior Managers**

Solar Energy Society (UK-ISES) 1974
- NR PO Box 489, ABINGDON, Oxon, OX14 4WY. (hq)
  07760 163559   fax 01235 484684
  email info@uk-ises.org   http://www.uk-ises.org
- ○ *L, *P; as the UK section of the International Solar Energy Society it aims to further the use of all forms of renewable energy
- Gp all renewable energy technologies
- ● Conf - Mtgs - ET - Inf - LG
- < Intl Solar Energy Soc
- M i & f

Solar Trade Association Ltd (STA) 1978
- ■ National Energy Centre, Davy Avenue, Knowlhill, MILTON KEYNES, Bucks, MK5 8NG. (hq)
  01908 442290   fax 01908 665577
  email enquiries@solar-trade.org.uk
  http://www.solartrade.org.uk
  Chief Exec: David Matthews
- ▲ Company Limited by Guarantee
- ○ *T; to promote widespread use of solar energy technology; to encourage excellence within the UK solar energy industry
- Gp Working groups: Technial; Training
- ● Conf - Mtgs - ET - Exhib - Stat - Inf - LG
- < Eur Solar Thermal Inf Fedn (ESTIF)
- M 168 f, UK / 1 f, o'seas
  (Sub: £100 - £1,600)
- ¶ e-NL - 12 ftm only.Code of Ethical Practice - irreg;   The Sun's Abundant Energy (information sheet) - irreg; both free.

Soldiers, Sailors, Airmen & Families Association (SSAFA) 1885
- § 19 Queen Elizabeth St, LONDON, SE1 2LP. (hq)
  0845 130 0975
  email info@ssafa.org.uk   http://www.ssafa.org.uk
  Chief Exec: Andrew Cumming
  Provides support for the serving men & women in today's armed forces, those who have served, & their families & dependents.

Sole Practitioners Group
  see **Solicitor Sole Practitioners Group**

Solicitor Sole Practitioners Group (SPG) 1990
- ■ Buckland Manor, LYMINGTON, Hants, SO41 8NP. (hsb)
  01590 672595   fax 01590 671466
  http://www.spg.uk.com
  Hon Sec: Edmund Clive Sutton
- ▲ Un-incorporated Society
- ○ *P; o protect the interests of sole practitioner solicitors
- ● Conf - Mtgs - ET - LG - Liaison with The Law Society
- < The Law Soc
- M 4,000 i
- ¶ Solo Magazine - 3; free.
- × 2006-08 National Association of Sole Practitioners

Solicitors' Criminal Bar Association
  a group of the **Law Society of Northern Ireland**

Solicitors Family Law Association
   since 2005 **Resolution**

Solicitors in Local Government
   a group of the **Law Society of England & Wales**

Solid Fuel Association   (SFA)   1993
■   7 Swanwick Court, ALFRETON, Derbys, DE55 7AS.   (hq)
   01773 835400   fax 01773 834351
   http://www.solidfuel.co.uk
   Gen Manager: Jim Lambeth
▲   Company Limited by Guarantee
○   *T; promotion of solid fuel
Gp   Approval Coal Merchants Scheme - coal trade code to
   guarantee service to domestic solid fuel customers
●   Mtgs - ET - Exam - Res - Exhib - Stat - Inf - Lib - LG - Advice on
   solid fuel heating
M   2 f
¶   Various technical publications & videos.

Solids Handling & Processing Association Ltd   (SHAPA)   1981
■   20 Elizabeth Drive, Oadby, LEICESTER, LE2 4RD.   (hq)
   0116-271 3704   fax 0116-271 3704
   email shapaltd@aol.com   http://www.shapa.co.uk
   Gen Sec: John Whitehead
▲   Company Limited by Guarantee
○   *T; representing companies/universities involved in the
   handling & processing of particulate solids particularly in the
   process industries; members' interests incl: Abrasion resistant
   equipment; Blowers/compressors; Bulk storage & handling;
   Centralised vacuum cleaning; Control systems; Dryers/
   coolers; Dust filters; Feeders; Grinding & milling machinery;
   Instrumentation; Intermediate bulk containers; Load cells;
   Mechanical conveyors/elevators; Mixers; Pneumatic
   handling; Process plant; Sack/bag systems; Sieves/screens;
   Silos, hoppers, bins & tanks & dischargers; Valves; Weighing
   machinery
Gp   Marketing; Technical; Commercial
●   Mtgs - Expt - LG - Scholarship award
<   permanent member of Intl Solids Handling Advy Bd (ISHAB)
M   97 i, 94 f, 3 universities
¶   NL - 3.

Solihull Chamber of Commerce & Industry   (SCCI)   1990
■   Wellington House, Starley Way, SOLIHULL, W Midlands,
   B37 7HE.   (hq)
   0121-781 7384   fax 0121-781 7385
   email info@solihull-chamber.com
   http://www.birminghamchamber.org.uk
   Dir: Jane Jackson
▲   Company Limited by Guarantee
○   *C
●   Mtgs - ET - Res - Stat - Expt - Inf - Lib - VE - LG
<   Birmingham Cham Comm; Brit Chams Comm
M   450 f
¶   Chamberlink - 10;   AR; both ftm.

Solvents Industry Association   (SIA)   1986
NR   19 Heathdene Rd, LONDON, SW16 3NZ.
   email info@sia-uk.org.uk   http://www.sia-uk.org.uk
   Sec: Terry Badcock
▲   Company Limited by Guarantee
○   *T; a technical organisation dealing with legislation relating to
   Customs & Excise, health, safety & the environment
Gp   Responsible care (SIASHE); HSE gp on classification (SCHIP);
   Eur Chemical Ind - Hydrocarbon Solvent Producers
   Assn (CEFIC-HSPA)
●   Conf - Mtgs - Stat - LG
<   Eur Solvents Ind Gp (ESIG); Hydrocarbon Solvents Producers
   Assn (HSPA)
M   21 f

**Somerset Archaeological & Natural History Society   (SANHS)
   1849**
NR   The Castle, Castle Green, TAUNTON, Somerset, TA1 4AA.
   (hq)
      01823 272429
▲   Registered Charity
○   *L
Gp   Archaeology; Local history; Historic buildings; Natural history
●   Conf - Mtgs - ET - Res - SG - Lib - PL - VE
M   654 i, 42 org, UK / 4 i, 14 org, o'seas
¶   Proceedings - 1.   NL - 2.

Somerset Chamber of Commerce & Industry Ltd
NR   Equity House, Blackbrook Park Avenue, TAUNTON, Somerset,
   TA1 2PX.
   01823 444924   fax 01823 444924
   http://www.somerset-chamber.co.uk
   Office Mgr: Brenda Dilley

Somerset Record Society   1889
■   c/o Somerset Studies Library, Paul St, TAUNTON, Somerset,
   TA1 3XZ.   (hsb)
   01823 340300   fax 01823 340301
   Hon Sec: David Bromwich
▲   Registered Charity; Un-incorporated Society
○   *L; publication of historical records (not parish registers) of
   Somerset
●   Annual mtg
M   121 i, 53 org, UK / 4 i, 68 org, o'seas
¶   Occasional volume - c 1; ftm, prices vary nm.

Songbird Survival   (SBS)
■   PO Box 311, DISS, Norfolk, IP22 1WW.   (hq)
   01379 641715
   email dawn-chorus@songbird-survival.org.uk
   http://www.songbird-survival.org.uk
   Dir: K A McDougall
▲   Registered Charity
○   *K; to protect & enhance the population of UK songbirds &
   other small birds by research & education
●   Mtgs - Res - Exhib - Stat - Inf - VE - LG
M   1,800 i
¶   Songbird Survival (NL) - 4; ftm only.

Sonic Arts Network   (SAN)   1979
NR   The Jerwood Space, 171 Union St, LONDON, SE1 0LN.   (hq)
   020 7928 7337   fax 020 7928 7338
   email phil@sonicartsnetwork.org
   http://www.sonicartsnetwork.org
▲   Registered Charity
○   *D; a performance, information & education resource for those
   interested in experimental approaches to sound & the ways in
   which new technology is transforming the nature & practice
   of music; aims to raise awareness & innovate new
   approaches to sonic art
●   Conf - ET - Exhib - Inf - 'Commissioning, encouraging &
   promoting new & exciting work' - 'Raising awareness of
   sonic art through information, opportunity & education'
M   400 i, 50 f, UK / 100 i, 20 f, o'seas
¶   Diffusion - 12;   Jnl - 1; both ftm.

© CBD Research Ltd · Beckenham · BR3 5JS · Tel 020 8650 7745 · Fax 020 8650 0768 · E-mail cbd@cbdresearch.com · www.cbdresearch.com

Sound Sense   1990
- ■ Riverside House, Rattlesden, BURY ST EDMUNDS, Suffolk, IP30 0SF.   (hq)
  email info@soundsense.org   http://www.soundsense.org
  Chief Exec: Kathryn Deane
- ▲ Company Limited by Guarantee; Registered Charity
- ○ *D, *G, *N; for community musicians
- Gp Health; Cultural diversity; Campaigns
- ● Conf - Res - Inf - LG
- < Intl Soc for Music Educ
- M 380 i, 95 org, UK / 20 i, o'seas
  (Sub: £35 i, £90 org UK / £50 i o'seas)
- ¶ Sounding Board - 4; ftm [back issues £5].
  Bulletin Board - 12; ftm only.
  Publications list available.

Soup, Gravy & Produce Processors Association
  a sector of the **Food Processers Association**

Soup Manufacturers Association of Ireland
  a group of **Food & Drink Industry Ireland**

Source Testing Association   (STA)   1996
- ■ Unit 11 Theobald Business Park, Knowle Piece, Wilbury Way, HITCHIN, Herts, SG4 0TY.   (hq)
  01462 457535   fax 01462 457157
  email dave.curtis@s-t-a.org   http://www.s-t-a.org
  Dir: Dave Curtis
- ▲ Company Limited by Guarantee
- ○ *T; research into aspects of emission monitoring
- Gp Task Groups: Health & safety, Management, Quality, Small business, Technical, Training & personal development
- ● Conf - Mtgs - ET - Res - Exhib - Inf - Seminars - Company endorsement
- M 102 f, UK / 3 f, o'seas
- ¶ STA Communicator (NL) - 2; free.

South Cheshire Chamber of Commerce & Industry Ltd   2001
- NR Enterprise House, Wistaston Road Business Centre, CREWE, Cheshire, CW2 7RP.   (hq)
  01270 504700   fax 01270 504701
  email info@sccci.co.uk
  http://www.southcheshirechamber.co.uk
- ○ *C
- ● Mtgs - ET - Exhib - Stat - Expt - Inf - Lib
- M f

South Devon Chamber of Commerce   (SDCC)   1995
- ■ Torbay Innovation Centre, Vantage Point, PAIGNTON, Devon, TQ4 7EJ.   (chmn/b)
  01803 540683
  email info@southdevonchamber.co.uk
  http://www.southdevonchamber.co.uk
  Admin: Brenda Hooper,   Chmn: Christian Seiflow-Moran
- ▲ Company Limited by Guarantee
- ○ *C
- Gp Branches: Brixham, Paignton, Torquay
- ● Conf - Mtg - Inf
- M 200 f
- ¶ NL - 4;   Directory/Ybk - 5 yrly; both ftm, prices on application nm.
  Note: is also known as Torbay Chamber of Commerce

South Devon Herd Book Society   (SDHBS)   1891
- NR Westpoint, Clyst St Mary, EXETER, Devon, EX5 1DJ.   (hq)
  01392 447494   fax 01392 447495
  email info@sdhbs.org.uk   http://www.sdhbs.org.uk
  Breed Sec: Caroline Poultney
- ▲ Registered Charity
- Br Australia, Canada, New Zealand, South Africa, USA
- ○ *B
- ● Conf - Mtgs - Res - Exhib - Comp - Stat - SG - Expt - Inf - VE - LG
- < S Devon Cattle Socs in: Australia, Canada, New Zealand, S Africa, USA
- M 630 i, UK / 10 i, o'seas
- ¶ Jnl - 1.   NL - 12.   Herd Book - 2 yrly.

South Downs Society   (SDS)   1923
- NR 2 Swan Court, Station Rd, PULBOROUGH, W Sussex, RH20 1RL.   (hq)
  01798 875073   fax 01798 873108
  http://www.southdownssociety.org.uk
- ○ *G; preservation of character & beauty of the South Downs, including their ancient monuments & public rights of way
- ● Conf - Mtgs - Exhib - Lib - VE - Illustrated talks
- M i
- × 2005 Society of Sussex Downsmen

South East London Chamber of Commerce   2007
- NR Unit 4 Harrington Way, Warspite Rd, LONDON, SE18 5NR. (hq)
  020 8317 3365   fax 020 8854 8273
  http://www.selondonchamber.org
  Co Sec: Adrian Hollands
- ▲ Company Limited by Guarantee
- ○ *C; chamber of commerce for the London boroughs of Bexley, Bromley, Greenwich & Lewisham
- ● Conf - Mtgs - ET - Inf - LG
- M 600 f
- × 2007 (July) Greenwich, Bexley & Lewisham Chamber of Commerce

South of England Agricultural Society   (SEAS)   1967
- NR The South of England Centre, Ardingly, HAYWARDS HEATH, W Sussex, RH17 6TL.   (hq)
  01444 892700   fax 01444 892888
  email seas@btclick.com   http://www.seas.org.uk
- ▲ Registered Charity
- ○ *H, *F; to promote agriculture, horticulture & forestry
- ● Conf - Mtgs - ET - Exhib - Spring Garden Show (May) - South of England Show (June) - Autumn Show (October) - Fast Food & Drink (December)
- M 3,000 i, 1,000 f
- ¶ Four Seasons News - 2; ftm only.

South Place Ethical Society   (SPES)   1793
- NR Conway Hall, 25 Red Lion Sq, LONDON, WC1R 4RL.   (hq)
  020 7242 8034   fax 020 7242 8034
  http://www.ethicalsoc.org.uk
- ▲ Registered Charity
- ○ *L; study & dissemination of ethical principles based on humanism; the cultivation of a rational & humane way of life
- M i & org
- ¶ Ethical Record - 10; ftm.   AR.
  Conway Memorial Lecture - 1; ftm.

** South Wales Mountain Sheep Breeders' Society
  Organisation lost: see Introduction paragraph 3

South West Coast Path Association (SWCPA) 1973
■ Bowker House, Lee Mill Bridge, IVYBRIDGE, Devon, PL21 9EF. (hsp)
   01752 896237   fax 01752 893654
   email info@swcp.org.uk   http://www.swcp.org.uk
   Admin: Liz Wallis
▲ Registered Charity
○ *K; to promote the interests of users of the South West coast path, Britain's longest national trail
● Mtgs - Exhib - Inf - PL - LG
M 5,000 i, 20 org, UK / 150 i, o'seas
¶ The South West Coast Path Guide - 1; ftm, £8 nm.
   NL - 2;   AR; both ftm only.

South Western Circle 1962
NR 43 Raymond Rd, PORTSMOUTH, Hants, PO^ 4RB.   (mem sec/p)
   email peterswiftderby@tiscali.co.uk   http://www.lswr.org
▲ Un-incorporated Society
○ *G; historical society for the London & South Western Railway & its successors
● Mtgs - Res - Inf - PL
M 500 i, UK / 25 i, o'seas
¶ South Western Circular - 4;   Monographs; both ftm.

Southampton & Fareham Chamber of Commerce & Industry (SFCCI) 1851
■ Bugle House, 53 Bugle St, SOUTHAMPTON, Hants, SO14 2LF.   (hq)
   023 8022 3541   fax 023 8022 7426
   email info@soton-chamber.co.uk
   http://www.soton-chamber.co.uk
   Dir Gen: Jimmy Chestnutt
▲ Company Limited by Guarantee
○ *C
● Conf - Mtgs - ET - Expt - Inf
M 1,000 i & f
¶ Chamber News - 12; ftm.

Southdown Sheep Society 1890
■ Meens Farm, Capps Lane, All Saints, HALESWORTH, Suffolk, IP19 0PD.   (hsb)
   01986 782416
   email secretary@southdownsheepsociety.co.uk
   http://www.southdownsheepsociety.co.uk
   Sec: Gail Sprake
▲ Company Limited by Guarantee; Registered Charity
○ *B
● Res - Exhib - Expt - Inf - LG
< Nat Sheep Assn; Rare Breeds Survival Trust
M 300 i
¶ The Southdown Flock Book - 2 yrly; ftm, £15 nm.
   The Southdown Year Book - 1; ftm, £5 nm.
   The Southdown Sheep; £20+£5p&p

Southern Counties Folk Federation (SCoFF) 1966
NR 11 Redmoor Close, Bitterne, SOUTHAMPTON, Hants, SO19 4DH.   (sp)
   Sec: David Nixon
○ *D, *G, *N

Southern Counties Heavy Horse Association (SCHHA) 1970
■ 74 Burnham Rd, Durrington, WORTHING, E Sussex, BN13 2NJ.   (hsp)
   01903 692532
   Hon Sec: Sharon Rumbelow
▲ Un-incorporated Society
○ *B, *F, *G, *V; to promote the heavy horse & preserve the art of horse ploughing
Gp Show horses & drays for promotional work; Working horses for ploughing & working demonstrations
● Mtgs - Exhib - Working demonstrations - Members' events
< Shire Horse Soc
M c 400 i & org
¶ NL - 4.   AR.

Southern Counties Historic Vehicle Preservation Trust (SCHVPT) 1962
■ 2 Dower Walk, Gossops Green, CRAWLEY, W Sussex, RH11 8EN.   (inf officer/p)
   01293 529264
   http://www.brmmbrmm.com/schvpt/
   Inf Officer: A Urben
▲ Registered Charity
○ *G, *L; to preserve historic vehicles & machinery
● Mtgs - Exhib - Inf - Lib - PL
< Nat Traction Engine Trust; Transport Trust; Historic Vehicles Clubs Jt C'ee; Historic Comml Vehicles Soc
M 300 i, 2 f, 3 org, UK / 2 i, o'seas
¶ News Circular - 12; ftm only.
   Traction Engine Register - 3 yrly; £4 m only.

Southern Staffordshire Chamber of Commerce & Industry (SSCCI) 2001
■ Fradley Business Centre, Fradley Park, LICHFIELD, Staffs, WS13 8NF.   (hq)
   0845 071 0191   fax 01543 441697
   http://www.sscci.co.uk
   Chief Exec: Peter Ralphs
▲ Company Limited by Guarantee
Br 56
○ *C
Gp Three divisions:
   Chase; Burton & District; Lichfield & Tamworth
● Mtgs - ET - Exhib - Stat - Expt - Inf - LG
M [not stated]

Southwark Chamber of Commerce
NR South Bank Technopark (room 1A07), LONDON, SE1 6LN.
   0845 680 1946
   http://www.southwarkcommerce.com
   Chamber Sec: Nancy Hammond
○ *C

SOVA (SOVA) 1975
■ Chichester House, 37 Brixton Rd, LONDON, SW9 6DZ.   (hq)
   020 7793 0404
▲ Registered Charity
Br 41
○ *W; 'to train local volunteers & involve them in work with offenders, ex-offenders & their families; we believe that everybody is touched by crime & that members of the community have a contribution to make in preventing & reducing crime'
Gp Literacy & numeracy tuition; Employment training; Befriending
● Conf - ET - Stat
M 644 i
¶ AR; free.

Soya Protein Association (SPA) 1973
NR 6 Catherine St, LONDON, WC2B 5JJ.   (hq)
   020 7836 2460   fax 020 7836 0580
○ *T; to disseminate information on vegetable proteins for human consumption
● Mtgs - Inf
M 5 f

© CBD Research Ltd · Beckenham · BR3 5JS · Tel 020 8650 7745 · Fax 020 8650 0768 · E-mail cbd@cbdresearch.com · www.cbdresearch.com

Spa Business Association Ltd   (SpaBA)   1921
- ■ Philpot House (suite 5-6), Station Rd, RAYLEIGH, Essex, SS6 7HH.   (hq)
  0870 780 0787   fax 01268 745881
  email info@spabusinessassociation.co.uk
  http://www.spabusinessassociation.co.uk
  Sec: Mike Fitch
- ▲ Company Limited by Guarantee
- ○ *T; for the mutual benefit of all persons employed in, dependent upon or supplying the spa industry
- Gp Consultant, Day spas, Destination spas, Education provider, Hotel spas, Other, Product house, Recruitment, Salon, Spa towns, Spa travel, Suppliers
- ● Conf - Mtgs - ET - Res - Exhib - Comp - Stat - Inf
- < Eur Spas Assn
- M 10 i, 62 f
  (Sub: £61-69 i, £1,000 f)
- × 2004 British Spas Federation

Spanish Chamber of Commerce in Great Britain
- NR 126 Wigmore St, LONDON, W1U 3RZ.
  020 7009 9071   fax 020 7009 9089
  email info@spanishchamber.co.uk
  http://www.spanishchamber.co.uk
- ○ *C
- M 225 i & f, UK / 118 i & f, Spain

Sparsity Partnership for Authorities Delivering Rural Services
a group of the **Local Government Association**

Speakability   1979
- ■ 1 Royal St, LONDON, SE1 7LL.   (hq)
  020 7261 9572   fax 020 7928 9542
  email speakability@speakability.org.uk
  http://www.speakability.org.uk
  Chief Exec: Melanie Derbyshire
- ▲ Registered Charity
- Br 91
- ○ *K, *W; to support people & carers living with aphasia (loss of communication skills as a result of a stroke, head injury or other neurological condition)
- ● Mtgs - ET - Inf - Ve - LG - Campaigning for improved services for people with communication impairments
- < Aphasia Alliance
- M 3,953 i, 26 f, 509 org, UK / 38 i, o'seas
- ¶ Publications list on website.
  Annual Review; free.

Specialised Organic Chemicals Sector Association
  closed

Specialist Access Engineering & Maintenance Association (SAEMA)   1972
- ■ c/o 19 Joseph Fletcher Drive, Wingerworth, CHESTERFIELD, Derbys, S42 6TZ.   (hsp)
  01246 224175
  email enquiries@saema.org   http://www.saema.org
  Sec: Trevor Fennell
- ▲ Un-incorporated Society
- ○ *T; for companies involved in the design, manufacture, installation & maintenance of facade access systems
- ● Mtgs
- < Nat Access & Scaffolding Confedn
- M 26 f
  (Sub: £1,500)
- ¶ Ybk - 1.

Specialist Anglers Alliance   (SAA)   2001
- ■ 41 Crofts Path, HEMEL HEMPSTEAD, Herts, HP3 8HB.   (hsp)
  01442 398022   fax 01442 398044
  email secretary@saauk.org   http://www.saauk.org
  Sec: Michael Heylin
- ▲ Un-incorporated Society
- ○ *G, *K, *S; to defend the angling rights of all members; to campaign for a cleaner water environment; to provide a unified body for all specialist anglers; to combat anti-angling propaganda
- ● Res - SG - Inf - LG - Representation on British Record Fish Committees
- < Anglers' Consvn Assn; Inst Fisheries Mgt; Nat Fedn Anglers
- M 650 i, 4 f, 14 org, UK / 15 i, o'seas
- ¶ New Specialist Angler - 2; ftm, £2.50 nm.
  NL - 2; ftm only.

Specialist Cheesemakers' Association   (SCA)   1989
- ■ 17 Clerkenwell Green, LONDON, EC1R 0DP.   (hq)
  020 7253 2114   fax 020 7608 1645
  email info@provtrade.co.uk
  http://www.specialistcheesemakers.co.uk
  Sec: Mrs Clare Cheney
- ▲ Company Limited by Guarantee
- ○ *T; to encourage excellence in cheesemaking, promote speciality cheeses & represent the interests of members to Government & the media
- ● Mtgs - Res - Exhib - Inf - VE - LG
- < Amer Cheese Soc; Ir Cheesemakers Assn; Stilton Cheesemakers Assn; Farmhouse Cheesemakers Assn
- M 235 f, UK / 20 f, o'seas
- ¶ SCA NL - 4; ftm only.
  Guide to the Finest Cheeses of Britain & Ireland; £5.95.

Specialist Engineering Contractors Group   (SEC group)   1992
- ■ Esca House, 34 Palace Court, LONDON, W2 4JG.   (hq)
  020 7313 4919   fax 020 7727 9268
  email pmattison@hvca.org.uk
  http://www.secgroup.org.uk
- ▲ Un-incorporated Society
- ○ *N, *T; represents six trade associations (with a total membership of 8,000 companies) in the specialist engineering sector of the construction industry (including mechanical, electrical, plumbing, steel & lifts) to the government & other industry bodies
- M 6 associations:
  Association of Plumbing & Heating Contractors
  British Constructional Steelwork Association
  Electrical Contractors Association
  Electrical Contractors Association of Scotland
    (this trades as SELECT)
  Heating & Ventilating Contractors Association
  Lift & Escalator Industry Association
- ¶ Guides on contractual & legal matters (these can be obtained from HVCA Publications on 01768 860405).

Spectroscopy & Dynamics Group
a special interest group within the Faraday division of the **Royal Society Chemistry**

Speedway Control Board   (SCB)   1940
- NR ACU House, Wood St, RUGBY, Warks, CV21 2YX.
  01788 565603   fax 01788 552308
  email office.scb@lineone.net
  http://www.british-speedway.co.uk
- ○ *S; governing body of speedway motorcycle racing in GB
- M i & clubs

Spelling Society (TSS) 1908
NR 4 Valletta Way, Wellesbourne, WARWICK, CV35 9TB.
(mem/sp)
http://www.spellingsociety.org
Mem Sec: John Gledhill
○ *K; to raise awareness of the problems caused by the
irregularity of English spelling; to promote remedies to
improve literacy, including spelling reform
× 2007 Simplified Spelling Society

SPHERE
journal and alternative name of the **Herpes Viruses Association**

Spinal Injuries Association (SIA) 1974
NR SIA House, 2 Trueman Place, Oldbrook, MILTON KEYNES,
MK6 2HH.   (hq)
0845 678 6633   fax 01908 608492
email sia@spinal.co.uk   http://www.spinal.co.uk
▲ Company Limited by Guarantee
○ *W; the national charity for spinal cord injured people & their
families; controlled & run by people who are themselves
paralysed, its aim is to enable spinal cord injured people to
control their lives & achieve their goals
Gp Helpline service; Publications
● Conf - Inf - Lib - LG
Helpline: 0800 980 0501
< Brit Coun of Disabled People; Dial UK; ADAIP; RADAR; NCVO
M 6,000 i, 500 org, UK / 400 i, o'seas
¶ Forward (NL) - 6.   AR.
Moving Forward: a guide to living with spinal cord injury.
Other publications available.

Spinal Injuries Scotland (SIS) 1962
■ Festival Business Centre, 150 Brand St, GLASGOW,
G51 1DH.   (hq)
0800 013 2305   fax 0141-427 9258
email info@sisonline.org   http://www.sisonline.org
Chmn: Adrian O'Donnell
▲ Registered Charity
○ *K, *W; to offer information, advice & education to those with
spinal cord injuries, their families & carers
● Conf - ET - Exhib - Inf - VE - LG
M 750 i
¶ Newsline - 4; free.

Spiritualist Association of Great Britain (SAGB) 1872
NR 33 Belgrave Sq, LONDON, SW1X 8QB.   (hq)
020 7235 3351   fax 020 7245 9706
http://www.spiritualistassociation.org.uk
▲ Company Limited by Guarantee; Registered Charity
○ *R; spiritualist healing; proof of survival after death
● Mtgs - Res
M c 900 i, UK / c 200 i, o'seas
¶ Service - 3; ftm, £1 nm.

Spiritualists' National Union (SNU) 1890
NR Redwoods, Stansted Hall, STANSTED, Essex, CM24 8UD.   (hq)
0845 458 0768
http://www.snu.org.uk
Gen Sec: Charles S Coulston
▲ Company Limited by Guarantee; Registered Charity
Br 15
○ *R; to promote the religion & religious philosophy of
Spiritualism
Gp Spiritualists' Lyceum Union (youth movement); The Arthur
Findlay College (residential training school)
● Conf - Mtgs - ET - Exam - Res - SG - Inf - Lib
M 2,200 i, 382 churches, UK / 80 i, 8 churches, o'seas
¶ Ybk & Diary.

SPLINTA
■ PO Box 398, STEVENAGE, Herts, SG1 9DR.
07831 805455
http://www.splintacampaign.co.uk
Nick Salmon
○ *K; are against sellers' pack on house sales

Spode Society 1986
NR c/o The Spode Museum Trust, Church St, STOKE-on-TRENT,
Staffs, ST4 1BX.   (editor/b)
01782 744011
○ *G; to increase knowledge of the Spode/Copeland factory & its
wares
● Mtgs - Res - VE
M c170 i, the Museum, UK / c20 i, o'seas
¶ Spode Society Review - 2; ftm only.

Spohr Society of Great Britain 1969
■ 123 Mount View Rd, SHEFFIELD, S Yorks, S8 8PJ.   (hq)
0114-258 5420   fax 0114-258 5420
email chtutt@yahoo.co.uk
http://www.spohr-society.org.uk
Chmn: Keith Warsop,   Sec: Chris Tutt
▲ Un-incorporated Society
○ *D; to promote the music of the German composer Louis Spohr
(1784-1859) through recordings, broadcasts & live
performances; to research into his life & music
● Mtgs - Res - Inf - Loan of performing material - Promoting
recordings
< Intle Louis Spohr Gesellschaft (Germany)
M 47 i, UK / 25 i, o'seas
Subs: £6 UK, £10 o'seas
¶ Spohr Jnl - 1; ftm, £1.50 nm.   NL - 4; ftm, 40p each nm.

Spoken Word Publishing Association
since 2004 **Audiobook Publishing Association**

Sport Horse Breeding of Great Britain (SHB(GB)) 1886
■ 96 High St, EDENBRIDGE, Kent, TN8 5AR.   (hq)
01732 866277
http://www.sporthorsegb.co.uk
Sec: Miss C Burdock
▲ Registered Charity
○ *B; to support the horse industry by way of incentives for
breeders, education, information & high standard grading
schemes & shows
Gp Council; C'ees: Show, Brood mare, Stallion
● Conf - Mtgs - ET - Exhib - Comp - Stat - Inf - Lib
< Wld Breeding Fedn for Sport Horses
M 3,000 i
¶ NL - 1.   Hbk - 1.   Sales List - 12.
Show List - 1.   Show Secretaries List - 1.   Judges List - 1.
Stallion List - 1.   Rulebook - 1.

Sporting Goods Industry Association (SGIA) 2006
NR Federation House, STONELEIGH PARK, Warks, CV8 2RF.   (hq)
024 7641 4999   fax 024 7641 4990
email info@sgiauk.com   http://www.sgiauk.com
○ *T; to promote, develop & protect the interests of
manufacturers, wholesalers & distributors of sporting goods
● Mtgs - Inf - LG
< a group of the Federation of Sports & Play Associations (FSPA)
M 22 f
× 2007 Sports Manufacturers & Retailers Trade Association
2006 (merged):
Bowls Group
Cricket & Hockey Association
Cue Sports Association
Darts Association
Fitness Products Association
Independent Sports Retailers Association
Racket Sports Association
Sports Textiles & Footwear Association

© CBD Research Ltd · Beckenham · BR3 5JS · Tel 020 8650 7745 · Fax 020 8650 0768 · E-mail cbd@cbdresearch.com · www.cbdresearch.com

Sports Coach UK
NR   114 Cardigan Rd, Headingley, LEEDS, W Yorks, LS6 3BJ.
       0113-274 4082   fax 0113-275 5019
       email coaching@sportscoachuk.org
       http://www.sportscoachuk.org
       Chmn: Heather Crouch
○   *S; to develop & implement a coaching system for all coaches
       at every level

Sports & Fitness Equipment Association   (SAFEA)   1990
■   Federation House, STONELEIGH PARK, Warks, CV8 2RF.   (hq)
       024 7641 4999   fax 024 7641 4990
       email safea@sportsandplay.com
       http://www.safea.co.uk
▲   Company Limited by Guarantee
○   *T; for companies engaged in the supply & installation of sports
       hall, games, fitness & gymnasium equipment (incl physical
       education in schools)
●   Conf - Mtgs - Exhib - Inf - Lib - LG
<   a group of the Fedn of Sports & Play Assns (FSPA)
M   20 f

Sports Industries Federation
       since 2006 **Federation of Sports & Play Associations**

Sports Journalists' Association of Great Britain   (SJA)   1948
NR   c/o Start2Finish Event Management, Unit 92 Capital Business
       Centre, 22 Carlton Rd, SOUTH CROYDON, Surrey,
       CR2 0BS.   (asa)
       020 8916 2234   fax 020 8916 2235
       http://www.sportsjournalists.co.uk
○   *P, *S; for journalists who specialise in sport
●   Conf - Mtgs - Educ - Inf - LG (through UK Sport & Sport
       England) - Careers advice - Promotion of annual Sports
       Journalists of the Year & Sportsman, Sportswoman & Sports
       Team of the Year Awards
<   Assn Intle de la Presse Sportive (AIPS); U Eur de la Presse
       Sportive (UEPS)
M   550 i
¶   Bulletin - 2;   NL - 3/4;   Hbk; all free.
×   2003 Sports Writers Association of Great Britain

Sports Manufacturers & Retailers Trade Association
       since 2007 the **Sporting Goods Industry Association**

Sports Massage Association   (SMA)   1999
NR   1 Woodville Terrace, LYTHAM, Lancs, FY8 5QB.   (hq)
       0870 005 2678   fax 0870 005 2679
       email info@thesma.org   http://www.thesma.org
○   *P; to establish & maintain the ethical, professional &
       educational standards of practitioners so as to give
       confidence to the general & sporting public, the medical
       profession & government agencies that practitioners are
       suitably trained
●   Conf - Mtgs - ET - Exam - Res
M   i

Sports & Play Construction Association   (SAPCA)   1997
NR   Federation House, STONELEIGH PARK, Warks, CV8 2RF.   (hq)
       024 7641 6316   fax 024 7641 4773
       email info@sapca.org.uk   http://www.sapca.org.uk
       Chief Exec: Christopher Trickey
▲   Company Limited by Guarantee
○   *T; 'the recognised UK trade association for the sports facility
       construction industry'
Gp   Principal contractors (inc multi-sport, natural sportsturf, pitch,
       play surfaces, tennis court, track divisions)
       Surfacing contractors; Ancillary contractors; Manufacturers &
       suppliers; Professional services
●   Conf - Mtgs - ET - Res - Exhib - SG - Stat - Expt - Inf - VE - LG
<   a group of the Sports Industries Federation
>   Brit Assn Landscape Inds (BALI); Brit Paralympic Assn (BPA);
       England & Wales Cricket Bd (ECB); Inst of
       Groundsmanship (IOG); Intl Assn for Sports & Leisure
       Facilities (IAKS); Intl Sports Engg Assn (ISEA); Intl Tennis
       Fedn (ITD); Lawn Tennis Assn (LTA); Nat Playing Fields
       Assn (NPFA); Nat Trainers Fedn NTF); Oxford Playing Fields
       Assn (OPFA); Quarry Products Assn (QPA); Recreation Mgrs
       Assn (RMA); Sports Coun of NI (SCNI); Sports Rurf Res
       Inst(STRI); UK Athletics (UKA); Waste Resources Action
       Programme (WRAP)
M   170 f, 30 org, UK / 10 f, 4 org, o'seas
×   2002-04 Sports & Play Contractors' Association

Sports Pony Studbook Society   (SPSS)
NR   Bernwode Stud, Sock Farm, Chilthorne Domer, YEOVIL,
       Somerset, BA22 8QZ.
       01935 840029
○   *B

Sports Textiles & Footwear Association
       since 2006 **Sporting Goods Industry Association**

Sports Turf Research Institute   (STRI)   1929
■   St Ives Estate, BINGLEY, W Yorks, BD16 1AU.   (hq)
       01274 565131   fax 01274 561891
       email anne.wilson@stri.org.uk   http://www.stri.co.uk
       Head of External Affairs: Anne Wilson,
       Chief Exec: Dr Gordon McKillop
▲   Company Limited by Guarantee
Br   13
○   *Q, *S; independent non-profit-making research & advisory
       service: sports field & golf course management &
       construction; research on sports turf surfaces
Gp   Golf course ecology & land management; Golf course
       architecture & design; Sports turf construction & irrigation
●   Conf - ET - Res - Exhib - Inf - Lib - VE
<   Sports Coun; All sports governing bodies
M   150 i, 200 f, 1,900 org, UK / 120 i, 15 f, 200 org, o'seas
       [above are subscribers not members]
¶   Jnl of Turfgrass & Sports Surface Science - 1; ftm, £28 nm.
       International Turfgrass Bulletin - 4; ftm, £55 yr nm.
       STRI Green Pages Trade Directory; online only.
       Various publications on turf related issues, available from their
       specialist online & mail order book service.

**Sportsmans Association of Great Britain & Northern Ireland
(SAGBNI)   1996**
NR   2 Clockhouse Place, LONDON, SW15 2EL.   (hq)
       020 8789 1211   fax 020 8789 1211
       email mike.wells@sagbni.co.uk
       http://www.sportsmansassociation.org.uk
       Gen Sec: M B Wells
▲   Un-incorporated Society
○   *K; 'to campaign against the ban on target pistol shooting &
       for freedom of choice & fair & effective firearms legislation'
●   Res - Inf - LG
<   Brit Shooting Sports Coun
M   c 3,000 i, 14 f
¶   NL - 12; ftm only.

Spotted Horse & Pony Society (SHAPS) 1992
■ Spout Farm, Wilday Green, Barlow, DRONFIELD, Derbys,
    S18 7SH. (hsp)
    Chmn/Sec: Marlyn Pollard
▲ Un-incorporated Society
○ *B
● Exhib Comp Stat Inf PL LG
M c 100 i, 1 f, UK / 10 i, o'seas
¶ NL - 4; ftm only.

** **Spotted Pony Breed Society**

Sprayed Concrete Association (SCA) 1976
■ Tournai Hall, Evelyn Woods Rd, ALDERSHOT, Hants,
    GU11 2LL. (asa)
    01252 357842 fax 01252 357831
    email sca@associationhouse.org.uk
    http://www.sca.org.uk
    Sec: John G Fairley
○ *T; to promote & foster the use of sprayed concrete, otherwise
    known as 'gunite' or 'shotcrete'
● Conf - Mtgs - ET - Res - Exhib
< Eur Fedn of Nat Assns of Specialist Contrs & Material Suppliers
    for the Construction Ind (EFNARC)
M 40 f
¶ LM; free.   Technical Data Sheets; ftm, £1 each nm.
    An Introduction to Sprayed Concrete.
    EFNARC Specification for Sprayed Concrete; £10.
    Seminar Papers & other technical publications; list available.

Square Dance Callers Club of Great Britain (SDCCGB) 1955
■ 2 Crossbridge Cottages, Thornborough Rd, Thornton,
    MILTON KEYNES, Bucks, MK17 0HE. (hsp)
    01280 816940
    email graybo@freenet.co.uk
    Hon Sec: Susie Kelly
▲ Un-incorporated Society
○ *D; to promote & further American square & round dancing by
    the provision & instruction of callers & teachers
● Mtgs - ET - SG - Lib
< Intl Assn of Square Dance Callers (CALLERLAB-USA)
M 170 i, UK / 10 i, o'seas
¶ NL - 6; ftm.

Squash Rackets Association (England Squash) 1929
■ National Squash Centre, Rowsley St, MANCHESTER,
    M11 3FF. (hq)
    0161 231 4499 fax 0161 231 4231
    email enquiries@englandsquash.com
    http://www.englandsquash.com
    Chief Exec: Nick Rider
▲ Company Limited by Guarantee
○ *S; the governing body for squash in England
< Wld Squash Fedn; Eur Squash Fedn
M 25,000 i, 1,000 clubs, UK / 10 i, o'seas

Squash Wales Ltd 2005
■ St Mellons Country Club, St Mellons, CARDIFF, Glamorgan,
    CF3 2XR. (hq)
    01633 681646 fax 01633 680998
    email squashwales@squashwales.co.uk
    http://www.squashwales.co.uk
    Finance & Office Mgr: Sue Evans
▲ Company Limited by Guarantee
○ *S; the governing body of squash in Wales
● ET - Regulation
< Wld Squash Fedn; Eur Squash Fedn; C'wealth Games Coun for
    Wales; Welsh Sports Assn
M 3,170 i, 122 clubs
¶ NL - 3/4.   Fixture List - 1.

St ...
    see **Saint ...**

Stable Lads Association
since September 2007 **National Association of Stable Staff**

Staff & Educational Development Association (SEDA)
■ John Foster House, 36 Gordon Square, LONDON, WC1H 0PF.
    020 7380 6767 fax 020 7387 2655
    email office@seda.ac.uk http://www.seda.ac.uk
○ *P; for staff & educational developers

**Staffordshire Archaeological & Historical Society (SAHS)
1959**
■ 29 Boldmere Drive, Boldmere, SUTTON COLDFIELD,
    W Midlands, B73 5ES. (hsp)
    0121-350 3497
    email sahs@britishlibrary.net   http://www.sahs.uk.net
    Hon Gen Sec: James Debney
▲ Registered Charity
Br 1
○ *L, *Q; the study, investigation, description & preservation of
    antiquities & historical records, particularly of Staffordshire
Gp Sub-c'ees: Editorial, Survey & excavation
● Mtgs - Res - SG - VE - Publishing results of research -
    Archaeological excavations - Standing historical buildings
    survey
< Coun for Brit Archaeology
M 180 i, 70 org
¶ Annual Transactions - 1; ftm.

**Staffordshire & Birmingham Agricultural Society (SBAS)
1800**
NR County Showground, Weston Rd, STAFFORD, ST18 0BD. (hq)
    01785 258060
○ *F; promotion of agriculture through the County Show & the
    National Primestock Show
● Conf - Exhib - Comp
M 1,500 i
¶ Showground News - 1;   AR; both ftm only.

Staffordshire Parish Registers Society (SPRS) 1900
■ 35 Middlefield Lane, Hagley, STOURBRIDGE, W Midlands,
    DY9 0PY. (chmn/p)
    01562 882210 fax 01562 882210
    email chair@sprs.org.uk http://www.sprs.org.uk
    Chmn: Dr Peter D Bloore
▲ Registered Charity
○ *L; publication in printed form of Staffordshire parish registers,
    mainly to 1837
● Mtgs (AGM) - Res - Transcription & printing of parish registers
M 280 i, 10 libraries, UK / 5 i, 5 libraries, o'seas
¶ Registers (up to 1837) - 2/3; prices vary.

Staffordshire Record Society 1879
■ c/o William Salt Library, Eastgate St, STAFFORD, ST16 2LZ.
    (hsb)
    Hon Sec: Matthew Blake
▲ Registered Charity
○ *L; the editing & printing of original documents relating to the
    County of Stafford & the publication of articles relating to the
    history of the county
M i, f & org
¶ Collections for a history of Staffordshire - irreg; ftm,
    prices vary nm.

© CBD Research Ltd · Beckenham · BR3 5JS · Tel 020 8650 7745 · Fax 020 8650 0768 · E-mail cbd@cbdresearch.com · www.cbdresearch.com

Stage Management Association (SMA) 1954

■ 55 Farringdon Rd, LONDON, EC1M 3JB. (hq)
020 7242 9250 fax 020 7242 9303
email admin@stagemanagementassociation.co.uk
http://www.stagemanagementassociation.co.uk
Chmn: Liz Burton-King
▲ Company Limited by Guarantee
○ *P; to support & represent professional stage management in the UK
Gp Professionally working stage managers (full members); Recent graduates (provisional members); Student members (on NCDT accredited courses); Non-professional associates
● ET - Inf - VE
< Stage Mgrs Assn (USA); Indep Theatre Coun
M 620 i
¶ Cue Line (NL) - 6; ftm only.
SMA Guide to Props & Propping; £4.50 m, £7 nm.
Freelist (LM available for work) - 12; free.
Stage Management: a career guide, free.
Stage Management Notes.   Notes for Company Managers. [prices available on website].
A Stage Manager's Guide to. . .
  . . . the West End Agreement;
  . . . the Provincial Commercial Contract;
  . . . the Subsidised Repertory Agreement;
   all £2 m, £3.50 nm.

Stair Society 1935

■ 6 The Glebe, Manse Road, DIRLETON, E Lothian, EH39 5FB. (hsp)
01620 850264
email stairsecretary@btinternet.com
http://www.stairsociety.org
Sec: Thomas H Drysdale
▲ Un-incorporated Society
○ *L; to encourage the study & to advance the knowledge of the history of Scots law
● Mtgs - Publication of original documents - Reprinting & editing of works of sufficient rarity or importance
M 259 i, 66 f & org, 14 students, UK / 35 i, 78 f & org, o'seas
¶ AR; free.

Stalin Society 1991

■ BM Box 2521, LONDON, WC1N 3XX.   (mail/address)
020 8571 9723 fax 020 8571 9723
http://www.stalinsociety.org.uk
Chmn: Harpal Brar
○ *G, *L; research into the history of the USSR under Joseph Stalin (1879-1953) [Iosif Vissarionovich Dzhugashvili]
● Mtgs - Res
M [not stated]
¶ List of research presentations; on request.

Standardbred and Trotting Horse Association of Great Britain & Ireland (STAGBI)

■ Little Craig, LLANDEGLEY, Powys, LD1 5UD.
01597 850033
http://www.standardbred.org
▲ Company Limited by Guarantee
○ *B
no further information supplied

Statewatch

NR PO Box 1516, LONDON, N16 0EW.   (hq)
020 8802 1882
○ *K; a civil liberties group concerned with secrecy laws & the public's 'right to know'

Statistical & Social Inquiry Society of Ireland (SSISI) 1847

IRL c/o ESRI, Whitaker Square, Sir John Rogerson's Quay, DUBLIN 2, Republic of Ireland.   (hsb)
email sean.lyons@esri.ie   http://www.ssisi.ie
Hon Sec: Seán Lyons
○ *L; to promote the study of statistics, jurisprudence, & social & economic science

Statisticians in the Pharmaceutical Industry (PSI) 1977

■ Association House, South Park Rd, MACCLESFIELD, Cheshire, SK11 6SH.   (regd/office)
01625 267882 fax 01625 267879
email admin@psiweb.org   http://www.psiweb.org
Exec Sec: Dan Hollingshurst
▲ Company Limited by Guarantee
○ *P; to promote professional standards of statistics in the pharmaceutical industry
● Conf - Mtgs - ET - SG - Stat
< Eur Fedn of Statisticians in the Pharmaceutical Ind
M 834 i, 306 f, UK / 211 i, 148 f, o'seas
¶ Pharmaceutical Statistics (Jnl) - 4; free (electronic).
Spin (NL) - 4;   LM - 1;   AR; all ftm only.

Statistics User Council
since 2005 is the Statistics User Forum of the **Royal Statistical Society**

Statute Law Society 1968

NR 21 Goodwyns Vale, LONDON, N10 2HA.   (hsb)
020 8883 1700
http://www.statutelawsociety.org
Admin: Mary Block
▲ Registered Charity
○ *K, *L; to educate the legal profession & the public about the legislative process, with a view to encouraging improvements in statute law
● Conf - Lectures
M i & f
¶ The Statute Law Review - 4.

Steam Boat Association of Great Britain (SBA) 1971

■ Awelon, 28 Colley Lane, SANDBACH, Cheshire, CW11 4HE. (hsp)
01270 765837
email p.g.cuthbert@classicfm.net
http://www.steamboat.org.uk
Hon Sec: Dr Peter F Cuthbert
▲ Un-incorporated Society
○ *G, *L; to foster & encourage steam boating & the building, development, preservation & restoration of steam boats & steam machinery
Gp Heritage Steam Boats Sub-Committee
● Mtgs - Exhib - Inf - Cruising events throughout the year
< Eur Steamboat Fedn; Inland Waterways Assn; R Yachting Assn
> The SBA Heritage Steam Boat Trust
M 1163 i
 (Sub: £18 (£12 under 18s)
¶ The Funnel - 4; ftm only.
The Steamboat Register (CD-ROM; £5.
Catalogue Reprints:
 LIFU Engineering (1910); £3.50.
 A G Mumford (1900); £8.
 Lune Valley Engineering (1909); £5.
 Simpson Strickland (7th ed); £5.
 Escher Wyss & Co (extract); £2.   All +P&P.

Steam Car Club of Great Britain

NR 1113 Leeds Rd, Woodkirk, DEWSBURY, W Yorks, WF12 7JN. (hsp)
01924 475193
email sccgbsec@tiscali.co.uk   http://www.steamcar.net
Sec: Christopher Busk
○ *G; for all owners of steam cars & steam cycles
M i
¶ The Steam Car - 4; ftm.

Steam Plough Club   (SPC)   1966
■   Old Station House, Twyford, READING, Berks, RG10 9NA.
      (hsp)
      0118-934 0381
      http://www.steamploughclub.org.uk
      Hon Sec: John Billard
▲   Un-incorporated Society
○   *G; to encourage & expand interest in the use of steam plough
      cultivation by demonstration, discussion & archive research
●   Mtgs - ET - Res - Comp - SG - Stat - Inf - Lib - PL - VE
<   Nat Traction Engine Club; Fedn Brit Historic Vehicle Clubs
M   400 i
¶   Steam Plough Times - 4; ftm, £1 nm.

Steel Construction Institute   (SCI)   1986
■   Silwood Park, ASCOT, Berks, SL5 7QN.   (hq)
      01344 623345
      http://www.steel-sci.org
      Dir: G H Couchman
▲   Company Limited by Guarantee
○   *L; to promote the proper & effective use of steel in
      construction, both offshore & onshore
Gp Computing: Structural analysis, CAD/CAE technical information
      database; Multi-media, Internet site development
      Design development & advisory: Technical advice to industry,
      Offshore & onshore engineering;
      Education: organises courses on all aspects of steel design
●   Conf - ET - Res - Inf - Lib - VE
M   50 i, 800 f, UK / 30 i, 150 f, o'seas
¶   New Steel Construction - 6.   SCI News (NL) - 4.
      Range of technical publications; £15-£50.   Ybk.   AR.

Steel Lintel Manufacturers' Association   (SLMA)   1978
■   Corus Strip Products, PO Box 10, NEWPORT, Monmouthshire,
      NP19 4XN.   (sb)
      01633 755113
      email info@slma.co.uk   http://www.slma.co.uk
      Sec: Dr Clive Challinor
○   *T; steel lintels used for construction applications
●   Mtgs
M   4 f

Steel Window Association   (SWA)   1967
NR The Building Centre, 26 Store St, LONDON, WC1E 7BT.   (hq)
      020 7637 3571
      http://www.steel-window-association.co.uk
Br 1
○   *T; represents manufacturers of steel windows & associated
      products
M   f

Stephenson Locomotive Society   (SLS)   1909
■   3 Cresswell Court, HARTLEPOOL, Teesside, TS26 0ES.
      email stephenson@stephensonloco.org.uk
      http://www.stephensonloco.org.uk
      Mem Sec: M A Green
Br 15
○   *G, *L; study of railways, particularly locomotives
●   Mtgs - Lib - PL - VE
M   c 700 i & org
¶   SLS Jnl - 6; ftm.

STEPS   (STEPS)   1980
NR Warrington Lane, LYMM, Cheshire, WA13 0SA.   (hq)
      0871 717 0045   fax 01925 750270
      email info@steps-charity.org.uk
      http://www.steps-charity.org.uk
      Founder & Dir: Sue Banton,   Office Mgr: Anna Dorman
▲   Registered Charity
Br 25
○   *W; a charity which gives support, contact, help, advice &
      information to families with children with lower limb
      abnormalities (club foot, congenital dislocated hip (CDH),
      developmental dysplasia of the hip (DDH), lower limb
      deficiency)
●   Conf - Inf - Register of families for contact
<   Contact-a-Family (GB)
M   1,200 i, 10 org
¶   NL - 4; ftm.   AR; free.
      Handbooks for parents:
      CDH/DDH Splints.
      CDH/DDH Plasters.
      Lower Limb Deficiency.
      Talipes.

Stereoscopic Society   (Stereo Society)   1893
■   32 Orkney Close, HINCKLEY, Leics, LE10 0TA.   (hsp)
      01455 635520
      http://www.stereoscopicsociety.org.uk
      Hon Sec: Neville Jackson
▲   Un-incorporated Society
○   *L; 3D photography, graphics & computer graphics; the
      advancement of stereo images
Gp Transparencies; Prints; Computer
●   Conf - Mtgs - Exhib - Comp - Lib - VE - Workshops - Auctions
<   Intl Stereoscopic U; Photographic Alliance of GB; Photographic
      Soc of America (Stereo Divn)
M   527 i, UK / 81 i, o'seas
¶   Jnl of Stereo Imaging - 4; ftm, £2 each nm.

Steroid Aid Group
      The secretary has died & the future of the Group is uncertain
      (19 Aug 2008)

Stewart Society   1899
■   53 George St, EDINBURGH, EH2 2HT.   (asa)
      0131-220 4512   fax 0131-220 4512
      email info@stewartsociety.org
      Sec: Mrs I Crichton
▲   Registered Charity
Br Australia, Canada, Europe, Far East, N Zealand, USA
○   *G, *L; research into the Stewart family & its history
●   Res - Lib - VE
M   320 i, UK / 391 i, o'seas
¶   The Stewarts (Jnl) - 1; ftm, £5 nm.   NL - 2; free.

Stickler Syndrome Support Group   (SSSG)   1989
■   PO Box 371, WALTON-on-THAMES, Surrey, KT12 2YS.   (hq)
      01932 267635
      email info@stickler.org.uk   http://www.stickler.org.uk
      Hon Pres & Sec: Mrs Wendy Hughes
▲   Registered Charity
○   *W; to raise awareness of Stickler syndrome amongst the
      medical profession & the general public
●   Conf
<   Genetic Interest Gp; Long Term Conditions Alliance; Nat Coun
      for Voluntary Orgs
M   400 families, 160 profls, UK / 40 families, o'seas
¶   Information Booklets; ftm.
      Stickler Syndrome: the elusive syndrome; £16.99 m,
      £19.99 nm.

© CBD Research Ltd · Beckenham · BR3 5JS · Tel 020 8650 7745 · Fax 020 8650 0768 · E-mail cbd@cbdresearch.com · www.cbdresearch.com

Stiff Man Syndrome Support Group   (SMS/SPS)   1998
- 75 Normandy Ave, BEVERLEY, E Yorks, HU17 8PF.   (hsp)
  01482 868881
  email liz.blows@smssupportgroup.co.uk
  http://www.smssupportgroup.co.uk
  Hon Sec: Liz Blows
- ▲ Registered Charity
- ○ *W; for sufferers with a compromised auto-immune system, causing rigidity, spasms, anxiety & startle response symptoms
- ● Res - Stat - Inf
- M c 100 i
- ¶ NL - 6.

Stillbirth & Neonatal Death Society   (SANDS)   1978
- 28 Portland Place, LONDON, W1B 1LY.   (hq)
  020 7436 7940   fax 020 7436 3715
  email support@uk-sands.org   http://www.uk-sands.org
  Dir: Neal Long
- ▲ Registered Charity
- ○ *M, *W; to provide support for anyone affected by the death of a baby; to improve quality of care & services to bereaved families; to promote research or change in practice that could help reduce the loss of babies lives
- ● ET - Inf - LG
  Helpline: 020 7436 5881
- M c 1,000 i, f
  (Sub: £8-£16 i, £40 f UK / £24 i, o'seas)
- ¶ NL - 3.   AR.   Support leaflets.
  Pregnancy Loss & the Death of a Baby (guidelines for professionals).
  Understanding Pregnancy Loss.   When a Baby Dies.
  Saying Goodbye to Your Baby.

Stilton Cheese Makers' Association   (SCMA)   1936
- PO Box 384a, SURBITON, Surrey, KT5 9YL.   (asa)
  020 8255 1334   fax 020 8255 1335
  email nigelwhite@msn.com
  http://www.stiltoncheese.com
  Sec: Nigel White
- ▲ Un-incorporated Society
- Br USA
- ○ *T; to promote marketing of Stilton cheese - to protect the use of the 'Stilton' trade name & device
- ● Mtgs - ET - Res - Exhib - Stat - Expt - Inf - LG
- < Cheese Importers Assn of America; Dairy UK
- M 6 f
- ¶ Recipe leaflets & information leaflets; free.

Stirling Engine Society   1997
- NR PO Box 5909, CHELMSFORD, Essex, CM1 2FG.   (hsp)
  http://www.stirlingengines.org.uk
  Chmn: Ken Boak
- ○ *G; hot air engines
- M i
- ¶ Stirling News - 4.

Stockport Chamber of Commerce & Industry
  the Stockport office of the **Greater Manchester Chamber of Commerce**

Stoke-on-Trent Museum Archaeological Society   (SOTMAS)   1959
- The Potteries Museum, Bethesda St, Hanley, STOKE-on-TRENT, Staffs, ST1 3DW.   (hq)
  01782 232323
  Hon Sec: Mrs R Helen Outram
- ▲ Un-incorporated Society
- ○ *Q; to promote & encourage research into the archaeology in N Staffordshire
- ● Mtgs - ET - Res - Inf - Lib - VE
- < Coun Brit Archaeology; Coun for Indep Archaeology
- M c 60 i, UK / 1 i, o'seas
- ¶ Staffordshire Archaeological Studies - irreg.
  NL - 3; free.

Stone Federation Great Britain   (SFGB)   1974
- Channel Business Centre, Ingles Manor, Castle Hill Avenue, FOLKESTONE, Kent, CT20 2RD.   (hq)
  01303 856123   fax 01303 856117
  email enquiries@stone-federationgb.org.uk
  http://www.stone-federationgb.org.uk
  Dir: Jane Buxey
- ▲ Un-incorporated Society
- ○ *N, *T; to further the natural stone industry; to coordinate all aspects of the industry & provides specifiers & users with a first point of contact for information, advice & guidance in sourcing an appropriate material
- Gp British Slate Association; Contractors Group; Marble & Granite Group; Quarry Forum; Stone Cleaning & Surface Repair Group
- ● Conf - Mtgs - ET - Res - Exhib - Comp - Inf - VE - LG - Courses & seminars (RIBA & CPD approved) on stone
- M 200+ f, UK / 5 f, o'seas
- ¶ Stone Specifiers Guide - 1; ftm, price varies nm.
  Codes of Practice on the design & Installation of:
    Kitchen Worktops; £25 m, £45 nm.
    Internal Flooringors; £30 m, £50 nm.
    Modern Practical Masonry by E G Warland; £22 m, £30 nm.

Stone Roofing Association   1995
- NR Ceunant, CAERNARFON, Gwynedd, LL55 4SA.   (hsb)
  01286 650402   fax 07092 307784
  email terry@slateroof.co.uk
  http://www.stoneroof.org.uk
  Chmn: Ted Hughes
- ▲ Un-incorporated Society
- ○ *T; to support the manufacturers of stone slates in the UK; to act as a point of reference for users & specifiers with the stone slate industry
- ● Mtgs - Inf
- M 20 f

Stonehenge Society
  incorporated in the **Megalithic Society**

Stoolball England   1979
- NR 53 Kings Rd, HORSHAM, W Sussex, RH13 5PP.   (hsp)
  01403 252419
  http://www.stoolball.co.uk
  Sec: Kay Price
- ○ *S
- × 2008 (September) National Stoolball Association

Stop Climate Change Coalition
- NR 2 Chapel Place (1st floor), LONDON, EC2A 3DQ.
  020 7729 8732
- ○ *K
- M org

Storage Equipment Manufacturers' Association   (SEMA)   1970
- NR National Metalforming Centre, 47 Birmingham Rd, WEST BROMWICH, W Midlands, B70 6PY.   (hq)
  0121-601 6350   fax 0121-601 6387
  email enquiry@sema.org.uk   http://www.sema.org.uk
  Sec: David B Corns
- ▲ Company Limited by Guarantee
- ○ *T
- Gp Technical
- ● Mtgs - ET - Exhib - Stat - Inf - Issuing codes of practice for the design, manufacture & use of storage equipment
- < Brit Materials Handling Fedn; Fédn Européenne de la Manutention; METCOM
- M 22 f
- ¶ Various codes of practice & guidelines on storage equipment - irreg; prices vary.

Storage & Handling Equipment Distributors' Association (SHEDA) 1978
- ■ Heathcote House, 136 Hagley Rd, Edgbaston, BIRMINGHAM, B16 9PN. (hq)
   0121-454 4141   fax 0121-454 4949
   email sp@heathcote-coleman.co.uk
   http://www.sheda.org.uk
   Sec: Mrs Sharon J Parker
- ▲ Un-incorporated Society
- ○ *T; to support & protect the reputation, status & interests of storage equipment distributors
- ● Mtgs - ET - Exhib
- < Storage Eqpt Mfrs Assn (SEMA)
- M 60 f
- ¶ SHEDA News - 4; free.   LM; ftm.

Stove Industry Alliance   (SIA)
- NR Hasely Manor, Birmingham Road, WARWICK, CV35 7LS.
   02476 247246
- ○ *T; to promote the advantages of stoves as heating appliances

Strategic Planning Society   1967
- NR Buxton House, 7 Highbury Hill, LONDON, N5 1SU.   (hq)
   0845 056 3663   fax 0845 056 3663
   email enquiries@sps.org.uk   http://www.sps.org.uk
- ▲ Company Limited by Guarantee; Registered Charity
- ○ *P; to foster & promote research, innovation & best practice in strategic thought & action
- Gp Corporate strategy; Financial services; Innovation & corporate venturing; Knowledge economy; Public sector; Risk; SMEs; Technology, media &telecoms (TMT); Utilities; Voluntary sector
- ● Conf - Mtgs - ET - Res - Inf
- < Eur Strategic Planning Fedn (ESPLAF)
- M 1,300 i, 50 f, UK / 200 i, 20 f, o'seas
- ¶ Long Range Planning (Jnl) - 6;   Strategy - 4; both ftm only.
   Email NL - 12; free.

Strathspey Railway Association Ltd   (SRA)   1972
- NR Spey Lodge, Aviemore Station, Dalfaber Rd, AVIEMORE, Inverness-shire, PH21 1ET.   (hq)
- ▲ Company Limited by Guarantee
- ○ *G; to support the operation of the railway by provision of staff, maintenance of stock & restoration of relics
- Gp Permanent way; Signalling; Locomotive engineering; Carriage & wagon; Civil engineering works; Publicity; Marketing
- ● Mtgs - ET - Res - Exhib - Inf - Lib - VE
- M 730 i, 2 org, UK / 20 i, o'seas
- ¶ The Strathspey Express - 2; ftm.

Straw Bale Building Association   (SBBA (WISE))   1998
- ■ c/o Hollinroyd Farm, Butts Lane, TODMORDEN, Lancs, OL14 8RJ.   (hsp)
   Contact: Chug Tugby (01442 825421)
   Hon Sec: B Rowan
- ▲ Un-incorporated Society
- ○ *G; for people who build, live in or are interested in buildings made of straw bales
- Gp Intl straw bale building; Research & testing; Volunteer opportunities
- ● Conf - ET - Res - Inf - Lib - PL - VE - Networking
- < Global Straw Bale Network; Eur Straw Bale Network
- M 45 i, 5 f, UK / 7 i, o'seas
- ¶ The Last Straw (Jnl) - 4;   Baling Out (NL) - 4.

Street Sled Sports Racers   (SSSprint)   1995
- ■ 3a Canal St, OXFORD, OX2 6BQ.   (chmn/b)
   01865 311179   fax 01865 426007
   email dingboston@oxfordstuntfactory.com
   http://www.streetluge.co.uk
   Chmn: David Boston
- ▲ Un-incorporated Society
- ○ *S; the regulation, safety, promotion & supply of all facets of street luging & land luging
- ● Mtgs - ET - Res - Comp - Inf - LG
- M i
- ¶ NL - 8/10.

Strict Baptist Historical Society   (SBHS)   1960
- ■ 33 Addison Rd, CATERHAM-on-the-HILL, Surrey, CR3 5LU.   (hsp)
   01883 341909
   email thesecretary@sbhs.org.uk
   http://www.strictbaptisthistory.org.uk
   Hon Sec: Pauline Johns
- ▲ Registered Charity
- ○ *L; all matters of Particular Baptist & Strict Baptist history
- ● Mtgs - Inf - Lib
- M 125 i, UK / 3 i, o'seas
   (Sub: £7)
- ¶ Bulletin - 1; ftm, £1 nm.   NL - 1; free.

Stroke Association   1899
- § Stroke House, 240 City Rd, LONDON, EC1V 2PR.   (hq)
   020 7566 0300   fax 020 7490 2686
   email stroke@stroke.org.uk   http://www.stroke.org.uk
   Chief Exec: Jon Barrick
- ● Helpline: 0845 303 3100
   Funds research into prevention, treatment and better methods of rehabilitation, and helps stroke patients directly through its rehabilitation and support services.

Structural Precast Association
   a product association of the **British Precast Concrete Federation**

Structural Waterproofing Group
   a group of the **Property Care Association**

Struggle against Financial Exploitation
   since 2007 **SAFE**

Student Radio Association
   administrated by the **Radio Academy**

Sub-Aqua Association   (SAA)   1976
- NR Space Solutions Business Centre, Sefton Lane, Maghull, LIVERPOOL, L31 8BX.   (hq)
   0151-287 1001
   email admin@saa.org.uk   http://www.saa.org.uk
   Contact: Irene Sartorius
- ▲ Registered Charity
- Br 350
- ○ *S
- Gp Boat handling; Chartwork & navigation; Marine life identification; Nautical archaeology
- ● Conf - Mtgs - ET - Exam - Res - Exhib - Inf
- < R Yachting Assn; Marine Conservation Soc; Nautical Archaeol Soc
- M 6,000 i
- ¶ Scuba World - 12.
   Introduction to SAA - on enrolment; free.

© CBD Research Ltd · Beckenham · BR3 5JS · Tel 020 8650 7745 · Fax 020 8650 0768 · E-mail cbd@cbdresearch.com · www.cbdresearch.com

Subsea UK   2004
- ■ The Innovation Centre, Aberdeen Science & Energy Park, Exploration Drive, ABERDEEN, AB23 8GX.   (hq)
  01224 355355
  email admin@subseauk.com   http://www.subseauk.com
  Co Sec: Trish Burrell
- ▲ Company Limited by Guarantee
- ○ *T; to act as the focal point for the entire British sub-sea industry; to increase business opportunities in the sector
- ● Conf - Mtgs - Exhib - Expt - Inf - LG
- M c 800 f
  (Sub: see website)
- ¶ NL - 4; free.
  Publications on website.

Subsidence Forum
- ■ Tournai Hall, Evelyn Woods Rd, ALDERSHOT, Hants, GU11 2LL
  01252 357843   fax 01252 357831
  http://www.subsidenceforum.org.uk
- ○ *N, *T
  no further information supplied

Subterranea Britannica   (SUB.BRIT)   1974
- NR 14 Maple Close, Sandford, WAREHAM, Dorset, BH20 7QD.
  (hsp)
  email secretary@subbrit.org.uk
  http://www.subbrit.org.uk
  Sec: Roger Starling
- ○ *L; the study & investigation of all man-made & man used underground places
- Gp Cold War Research Group
- ● Conf - Mtgs - Res - SG - Inf - VE
- < Coun Brit Archaeology; Nat Assn Mining History Socs
- M 819 i, 22 org, UK & o'seas
- ¶ Bulletin Subterranea Britannica - irreg;
  Subterranea - 2/3; both ftm only.

Sudden Death Support Association   (SDSA)   1994
- ■ Yew Tree Farm, Part Lane, Swallowfield, READING, Berks, RG7 1TB.   (hq)
  0118-988 8099   fax 0118-988 8099
  Sec: Mrs Sarah Firth
- ▲ Registered Charity
- ○ *W; to help anyone who has suffered a bereavement through sudden death
- ● Mtgs - Befriending service

Suffolk Agricultural Association   (SAA)   1831
- NR Trinity Park, Felixstowe Rd, IPSWICH, Suffolk, IP3 8UH.   (hq)
  01473 707110
  http://www.suffolkshow.co.uk
  Exec Dir: Christopher Bushby
- ▲ Registered Charity
- ○ *F; to improve agriculture (incl forestry, horticulture & allied industries); to develop & improve agricultural instruments & machinery
- ● Conf - Mtgs - Exhib
- M c 3,500 i
- ¶ Suffolk Scene - 3; free.

Suffolk Chamber of Commerce, Industry & Shipping Incorporated   1884
- NR Felaw Maltings, South Kiln, 42 Felaw St, IPSWICH, Suffolk, IP1 2DE.   (hq)
  01473 680600   fax 01473 603888
  email info@suffolkchamber.co.uk
  http://www.suffolkchamber.co.uk
- ▲ Company Limited by Guarantee
- ○ *C
- Gp International Trade; Transport; Business Library; Training; Home & economic affairs; Ipswch Port; Ipswich Chamber
- ● Conf - Mtgs - ET - Exhib - Expt - Inf - Lib
- < Brit Chams Comm
- M f

Suffolk Horse Society   1877
- ■ The Market Hill, WOODBRIDGE, Suffolk, IP12 4LU.   (hq)
  01394 380643
  email sec@suffolkhorsesociety.org.uk
  http://www.suffolkhorsesociety.org.uk
  Chmn: Christopher Bushby
- ▲ Company Limited by Guarantee; Registered Charity
- ○ *B; to promote the Suffolk breed of heavy horse
- ● Stat - Inf - Maintenance of stud book
- M 1500 i
- ¶ Suffolk Horse Magazine - 3; ftm, £3.50 nm.

Suffolk Institute of Archaeology & History   (SIA)   1848
- ■ Flat 514 Neptune Marina, 1 Coprolite St, IPSWICH, Suffolk, IP3 0BN.   (hsp)
  01473 250422
  http://www.suffolkarch.org.uk
  Hon Sec: John Fairclough
- ▲ Registered Charity
- ○ *L; the study of the archaeology & history of Suffolk
- Gp Archaeological field gp
- ● Mtgs - ET - Res - Exhib - Inf - Lib - VE
- < Coun Brit Archaeology
- M 790 i, 61 org, UK / 8 i, 20 org, o'seas
- ¶ Proceedings - 1;   NL - 2; both ftm.

Suffolk Records Society   (SRS)   1958
- ■ Westhorpe Lodge, Westhorpe, STOWMARKET, Suffolk, IP14 4TA.   (hsp)
  01449 781078   fax 01449 780335
  email claire@ejbarker.co.uk
  http://www.suffolkrecordssociety.com
  Hon Sec: Claire Barker
- ▲ Registered Charity
- ○ *L; publication of documents relating to Suffolk & its people in all periods
- ● Publication
- M 348 i, 90 f
  (Sub: £12.50 i)
- ¶ Annual volume; ftm.

Suffolk Sheep Society   1886
- NR Unit 1, Woodside Road East, BALLYMENA, Co Antrim, BT42 4QJ.   (hq)
  028 2563 2342
  http://www.suffolksheep.org
- ○ *B
- M i, f, org

Sugar Association of London   (SAOL)   1882
- NR 154 Bishopsgate, LONDON, EC2M 4LN.   (hq)
  020 7377 2113   fax 020 7247 2481
  http://www.sugarassociation.co.uk
  Sec: N Durham
- Br 2
- ○ *T; supervisors of raw sugar cargoes; provision of rules & contract conditions for the raw sugar trade
- Gp Supervisors of raw sugar cargoes; Arbitrators; Rules & contract conditions
- ● Mtgs - ET - Inf - Empl - LG
- M 40 f, UK / 60 f, o'seas
- ¶ Rules & Regulations; £35 m, £60 nm.

Sugar Traders Association of the UK   (STAUK)   1952
■ c/o C Czarnikow Sugar Ltd, 24 Chiswell St, LONDON, EC1Y 4SG.   (hsb)
020 7972 6631   fax 020 7972 6699
email sugartraders@sugartraders.co.uk
http://www.sugartraders.co.uk
Hon Sec: David Clark
▲ Un-incorporated Society
○ *T; to promote, support, develop, protect & maintain the trade in sugar
● Mtgs - LG
< Assn Profl Orgs Sugar Tr EU (ASSUC)
M 12 f, 5 org

Sugar Users Group
a group of **Food & Drink Industry Ireland**

Sunbed Association   1995
■ Chess House, 105 High St, CHESHAM, Bucks, HP5 1DE.   (hq)
01494 785941   fax 01494 786791
email info@sunbedassociation.org.uk
http://www.sunbedassociation.org.uk
Sec: Kathy Banks
▲ Company Limited by Guarantee
○ *T; interests of sunbed manufacturers, operators & hirers
● Mtgs - ET - Stat - Inf - LG - Printed merchandise
< Eur Sunlight Assn
M 1,000 f
¶ NL - 2; ftm only.   LM - 12; free.

Sunday Shakespeare Society   (SSS)   1874
■ 308 Copperfield, CHIGWELL, Essex, IG7 5JZ.   (hsp)
020 8501 2841
http://www.sundayshakespeare.weebly.com
Hon Sec: Susan E Taylor
▲ Un-incorporated Society
○ *A, *G; to encourage the study of Shakespeare's plays by dramatic readings by members on Sundays
● Mtgs
M 41 i
¶ NL - 12;   Programme - 1; both free.

Superintendents' Association of Northern Ireland   (PSANI)   1972
■ PSNI College, Garnerville, Garnerville Rd, BELFAST, BT4 2NX.   (hq)
028 9092 2201   fax 028 9092 2169
email mail@psani.org   http://www.psani.org
▲ Un-incorporated Society
○ *P; representing the interests of superintendents in the police service of Northern Ireland
● Conf - Mtgs - Empl - LG
M 100 i

Superyacht UK
NR Marine House, Thorpe Lea Rd, EGHAM, Surrey, TW20 8BF.   (hq)
01784 473377   fax 01784 429678
email info@superyachtuk.com
http://www.superyachtuk.com
Sec: Sarah Johnson
○ *T; designers, builders, suppliers & service providers of yachts over 24 metres load length
< Brit Marine Fedn

Support Dogs
■ 21 Jessops Riverside, Brightside Lane, SHEFFIELD, S Yorks, S9 2RX.
0114-261 7800   fax 0114-261 7555
email supportdogs@btconnect.com
http://www.support-dogs.org.uk
▲ Registered Charity
○ *W; the only organisation worldwide that trains dogs to help disabled people with everyday tasks & also to recognise & predict an epileptic seizure

Support after Murder & Manslaughter
styles itself **SAMM**

Support Society for Children of High Intelligence
is no longer functioning

Support & Training in Prep Schools
alternative name of **SATIPS**

Supporters of Nuclear Energy   (SONE)   1998
NR c/o 1-7 Great George St, LONDON, SW1P 3AA.   (hq)
020 7665 2046
email sec@sone.org.uk   http://www.sone.org.uk
▲ Company Limited by Guarantee
○ *K; promotion of nuclear energy policy
● Conf - Mtgs - Inf - LG
M 280 i
¶ NL - 12; free on website.

Supporting Adults affected by Adoption
see **Adults Affected by Adoption - NORCAP**

Surf Life Saving Association of Great Britain Ltd   (SLSGB)   1955
■ 19 Southernhay West (1st floor), EXETER, Devon, EX1 1PJ.   (hq)
01392 218007   fax 01392 217808
email mail@slsgb.org.uk
http://www.surflifesaving.org.uk
Nat Sec: Kate Morgan
▲ Company Limited by Guarantee; Registered Charity
○ *K, *S; promotion of beach & surf safety; provision of community service by voluntary lifeguards on British beaches; promotion of surf life saving as a competitive sport
Gp Commissions: Technical, Powercraft, Sport, Youth development
● Conf - Mtgs - ET - Exam - Comp - Stat - Inf - LG
< Intl Life Saving
M 4,000 i, 25 f, 75 org
¶ Swim & Save - 12.

Surface Engineering Association   (SEA)   1997
■ Federation House, 10 Vyse St, BIRMINGHAM, B18 6LT.   (hq)
0121-237 1123   fax 0121-237 1124
email info@sea.org.uk   http://www.sea.org.uk
Chief Exec: D Elliot
▲ Company Limited by Guarantee
○ *T
Gp British Surface Treatment Suppliers Association; Contract Heat Treatment Association; Metal Finishing Association (& its division the British Electroless Nickel Society); Paint & Powder Finishing Association
Process technology; Organic coating equipment; Health, safety & environment
● Conf - Mtgs - ET - Res - Exhib - Comp - SG - Stat - Inf - VE - LG
< Aluminium Finishing Assn (AFA)
M c 400 f
¶ SEA News - 4;   Watchword - 4; both ftm.

© CBD Research Ltd · Beckenham · BR3 5JS · Tel 020 8650 7745 · Fax 020 8650 0768 · E-mail cbd@cbdresearch.com · www.cbdresearch.com

Surfers against Sewage (SAS)
- Unit 2 Wheal Kitty Workshops, ST AGNES, Cornwall, TR5 0RD.   (hq)
  01872 553001   fax 01872 552615
  email info@sas.org.uk   http://www.sas.org.uk
  Campaigns Dir: Richard Hardy
- ▲ Company Limited by Guarantee
- ○ *K; campaign for clear, safe recreational waters
- ● ET - Res - Campaigning - Fundraising (including selling merchandise)
- M c 9,000 i, 200 f, UK / 100 i, o'seas
- ¶ Pipeline (NL) - 4; ftm only.

Surgical Dressings Manufacturers Association (SDMA) 1936
- Fernbank, 17 The Crescent, Holymoorside, CHESTERFIELD, Derbys, S42 7EE.   (sb)
  01246 568175   fax 01246 568175
  email sdma@nigelb.fsworld.co.uk
  http://www.sdma.org.uk
  Sec: Dr Nigel Brassington
- ▲ Un-incorporated Society
- ○ *T; operates in the area of wound care products & associate products, including bandages, hip protectors, first aid kits & disposable medical devices
- ● Mtgs - SG - Inf - LG - Consideration of legislative measures - Discussions with government departments - Networking
- M 17 f
- ¶ Industry Code of Practice - irreg; fre.

Surrey Archaeological Society (SyAS) 1854
- NR Castle Arch, GUILDFORD, Surrey, GU1 3SX.   (hq)
  01483 532454   fax 01483 532454
  email info@surreyarchaeology.co.uk
  http://www.surreyarchaeology.org.uk
  Hon Sec: David Calow
- ▲ Company Limited by Guarantee; Registered Charity
- ○ *L; archaeology, history & antiquities of Surrey (including those parts now in Greater London)
- Gp Artefacts & Archives Research Group; Local History Group; Medieval Studies Forum; Prehistoric Group; Roman Studies Group; Surrey Industrial History Society; Villages Study Group
- ● Conf - ET - Res - SG - Lib - PL - VE
- < Brit Assn Local History; Coun Brit Archaeology; Field Studies Coun
- M 787 i, 126 org, UK / 5 i, 38 org, o'seas
- ¶ Surrey Archaeological Collections - 1.
  Bulletin - 9.   AR.

Surrey Chambers of Commerce Ltd
- NR Hollywood House, Church Steet East, WOKING, Surrey, GU21 6HJ.   (hq)
  01483 726655   fax 01483 740217
  email info@surrey-chambers.co.uk
  http://www.surrey-chambers.co.uk
  Chief Exec: Louise Punter
- ▲ Company Limited by Guarantee
- Br 3
- ○ *C; representing chambers in Surrey
- Gp Regional offices: East, Guildford & Spelthorne
- ● Conf - Mtgs - ET - Res - Exhib - SG - Stat - Expt - Inf - Lib - LG
- < Brit Chams Comm
- M 3,300 f
- ¶ The Chamber - 6;   NL - 12; both ftm only.
  Members Directory - 1; ftm, £65 nm.

Surrey County Agricultural Society (SCAS) 1829
- 8 Birtley Courtyard, Bramley, GUILDFORD, Surrey, GU5 0LA.   (hq)
  01483 890810   fax 01483 890820
  email scas@surreycountyshow.co.uk
  http://www.surreycountyshow.co.uk
  Chief Exec: Mrs Sonia Ashworth
- ▲ Company Limited by Guarantee; Registered Charity
- ○ *F, *H; to promote agriculture, farming, breeding, horticulture, conservation & environment
- Gp Farming; Horticulture; Agriculture; Breeding (animals)
- ● Comp - Mtgs - Exhib
- < ASAO
- M 379 i, 3 f, 1 school
- ¶ AR - 1; free.

Surrey Industrial History Society
a group of the **Surrey Archaeological Society**

Surrey Record Society (SRS) 1913
- c/o Surrey History Centre, 130 Goldsworth Rd, WOKING, Surrey, GU21 6ND.   (hsb)
  01483 518737   fax 01483 518738
  email mpage@surreycc.gov.uk
  Hon Sec: Michael Page
- ▲ Registered Charity
- ○ *L; to publish records relating to areas within the ancient county of Surrey (including those parts now in Greater London)
- ● Publication
- < Brit Records Assn
- M 149 i, 55 org, UK / 4 i, 17 org, o'seas
  (Sub: £5)
- ¶ Record volumes; ftm, prices vary nm.   AR; ftm.

Surtees Society (SS) 1834
- Dept of History, 43 North Bailey, DURHAM, DH1 3EX.   (hsb)
  0191-334 1040   fax 0191-334 1041
  email surtees.society@dur.ac.uk
  http://www.surteessociety.org.uk
  Hon Sec: Dr Michael Stansfield
- ▲ Registered Charity
- ○ *L; publication of unedited historical manuscripts illustrative of the intellectual, moral, religious or social condition of the ancient Kingdom of Northumbria (those parts of England & Scotland between the Humber & Firth of Forth in the east & the Mersey & the Clyde to the west)
  Named after Robert Surtees 1779-1834, antiquary & topographer
- ● Publication
- M 225 i & org
- ¶ Annual Volume - 1; ftm (subscription £25), £50 nm.

Survey Association
familiar name of the **United Kingdom Land & Hydrographic Survey Association**

Sussex Archaeological Society 1846
- Bull House, 92 High St, LEWES, E Sussex, BN7 1XH.   (hq)
  01273 486260
  http://www.sussexpast.co.uk
  Chief Exec: John Manley
- ▲ Company Limited by Guarantee; Registered Charity
- Br 6
- ○ *L; to further interest in & knowledge of the history & archaeology of Sussex
- Gp Sussex archaeology forum; Sussex history forum; Archaeological excavations
- ● Conf - Mtgs - ET - Res - Exhib - SG - Inf - Lib - PL - VE - LG - Opens to the public society-owned museums, sites & properties
- M 2,102 i, 123 org, UK / 12 i, 69 org, o'seas
- ¶ Sussex Past & Present - 3.
  Sussex Archaeological Collections - 1.

Sussex Cattle Society   1879
NR   Station Rd, ROBERTSBRIDGE, E Sussex, TN32 5DG.   (hq)
       01580 880105
○   *B; Sussex & Sussex cross cattle
M   i

Sussex Chamber of Commerce & Enterprise   1945
NR   Greenacre Court, Station Rd, BURGESS HILL, W Sussex,
       RH15 9DS.   (hq)
       0845 678 8867   fax 01444 259255
       email information@sussexenterprise.co.uk
       http://www.sussexenterprise.co.uk
       Chief Exec: Mark Froud
▲   Company Limited by Guarantee
○   *C; as the Chamber of Commerce & Business Link for Sussex to
       help Sussex business prosper & develop
Gp   International services; Important advice services; Employee
       development advice; Membership organisation
●   Conf - Mtgs - ET - Res - Exhib - Stat - Expt - Inf - LG
<   Brit Chams Comm
M   2,500 f
¶   Business Edge - 10.
       Business Directory - 1.
       Note: Trades as Sussex Enterprise.

Sussex Enterprise
       the trading name of **Sussex Chamber of Commerce &
       Enterprise**

Sussex Industrial Archaeology Society   (SIAS)   1967
■   42 Falmer Avenue, Saltdean, BRIGHTON, E Sussex,
       BN2 8FG.   (hsp)
       01273 271330
       email sias@ronmartin.org.uk   http://www.sussexias.co.uk
       Gen Sec: R G Martin
▲   Registered Charity
○   *L; recording, repairing & preserving documentary & other
       recordings & sites of economic & industrial activity in Sussex
Gp   Breweries & malthouses; Brickmaking; Fuel & power;
       Icehouses; Limekilns; Mills; Railways; Water supply
●   Conf - Mtgs - Res - Exhib - SG - Inf - VE - LG
<   Assn for Indl Archaeology; British Brick Soc; S E Region Indl
       Archaeology Conf; Sussex Archaeological Soc
M   340 i, 23 org, UK / 3 i, o'seas
       Sub: £10
¶   Sussex Industrial History - 1; ftm, £4.25 nm.
       NL - 4; ftm, 50p nm.

Sussex Record Society   (SRS)   1901
■   Barbican House, High St, LEWES, E Sussex, BN7 1YE.   (hq)
       01273 405739
       http://www.sussexrecordsociety.org
       Hon Sec: P M Wilkinson
▲   Registered Charity
○   *L; transcribing & publishing in book form documents relating
       to the County of Sussex
●   Publication
M   268 i, 47 org, UK / 11 i, 39 org, o'seas
¶   Sussex Record Society [volume...] - 1; ftm, prices vary nm.
       NL - 1;   LM - irreg;   AR - 1; all ftm.

**Sustain: the Alliance for Better Food & Farming   (SUSTAIN)
1999**
■   94 White Lion St, LONDON, N1 9PF.   (hq)
       020 7837 1228   fax 020 7837 1141
       email sustain@sustainweb.org
       http://www.sustainweb.org
       Coordinator: Jeanette Longfield
▲   Registered Charity
○   *F, *K, advocates food & agricultural policies & practices that
       enhance the health & welfare of people & animals, improve
       the working & living environment, promote equity & enrich
       society & culture
       Represents about 100 national public interest organisations
       working at international, national, regional & local level
Gp   Projects & campaigns:
       Children's Food Campaign; Eat Somerset; Farming & Trade
       Project; Food Access Network; Food & Mental Health; Food
       Facts; Good Food on the Public Plate; Good Food Training
       for London; London Food Link; The Orchard Project;
       Sustainable Food
●   Conf - ET - Res - Stat - Inf - LG
M   100 org
¶   Publication list available.

Sustainable Food
       a group of **Sustain**

**Sutherland Society (the UK organisation for cranial osteopathy)
1970**
NR   Church Street Practice, 15a Church St, BRADFORD-on-AVON,
       Wilts, BA15 1LN.   (mem/sb)
       http://www.cranial.org.uk
       Mem Sec: Stephanie Brown
○   *P; named for W G Sutherland, founder of osteopathy in the
       cranial field

Sutton Business Federation
       since 2004 **Sutton Chamber**

Sutton Chamber   1936
NR   Quadrant House, The Quadrant, SUTTON, Surrey, SM2 5AS.
       (hq)
       020 8642 9661
       http://www.suttonchamber.biz
       Chmn: Paul Cawthorne
▲   Company Limited by Guarantee
○   *C; for the London Borough of Sutton
●   Mtgs - ET - Exhib - Inf
×   2004 Sutton Business Federation

Swaledale Sheep Breeders Association   (SSBA)   1920
NR   The Shooting Lodge, High Shipley, Eggleston,
       BARNARD CASTLE, Co Durham, DL12 0DP.   (sp)
       01833 650516
       http://www.swaledale-sheep.com
○   *B
●   Mtgs - Inf
<   Nat Sheep Assn
M   i
¶   Flock Book - 1; ftm only.

© CBD Research Ltd · Beckenham · BR3 5JS · Tel 020 8650 7745 · Fax 020 8650 0768 · E-mail cbd@cbdresearch.com · www.cbdresearch.com

Swaziland Society   1991
NR   4 Sybil's Way, HOUGHTON CONQUEST, Beds, MK45 3AQ.
       01234 742815
       http://www.swazisoc.com
       Sec: Vera Robbins
▲   Un-incorporated Society
○   *X; developing & strengthening educational, cultural, economic
       & social ties between Britain & Swaziland; to foster friendship
       & uderstanding between the peoples of the two countries
●   Mtgs - VE - Social gatherings - Financial assistance to
       development projects in Swaziland
M   160 i, UK / 86 i, o'seas
¶   Focus on Swaziland - 3; ftm.
       [subscription £18 (double), £12 (single).]

Swedenborg Society   1810
■   20-21 Bloomsbury Way, LONDON, WC1A 2TH.   (hq)
       020 7405 7986   fax 020 7831 5848
       email richard@swedenborg.org.uk
       http://www.swedenborg.org.uk
       Sec: Richard Lines
▲   Company Limited by Guarantee; Registered Charity
○   *A, *L; printing & publication of works of Emanuel Swedenborg
       (1688-1772), the Swedish philosopher, scientist & theologian
●   Conf - Mtgs - Res - Exhib - Lib - PL
<   Swedenborg Publishers International
M   500 i, UK / 350 i, o'seas
       Subs: £5.
¶   Journal of the Swedenborg Society - 1; £9.50.
       Things Heard & Seen (NL) - 3;   AR; both free.

Swedish Chamber of Commerce for the United Kingdom   1906
NR   5 Upper Montagu St, LONDON, W1G 0AZ.   (hq)
       020 7224 8001
○   *C; to promote trade between Great Britain & Sweden

**Swimming Pool & Allied Trades Association Ltd   (SPATA)
1961**
NR   4 Eastgate House, East St, ANDOVER, Hants, SP10 1EP.   (hq)
       01264 356210   fax 01264 332628
       email admin@spata.co.uk   http://www.spata.co.uk
       Managing Dir: Allen Brobyn,   Pres: Bob Spring
▲   Company Limited by Guarantee
○   *T; interests of contractors & manufacturers of equipment &
       accessories for swimming pools & spas
●   Conf - Mtgs - ET - Exhib - Inf - Lib
<   is part of the British Swimming Pool Federation
M   220 f, UK / 14 f, o'seas
¶   Various publications on standards for installations, water
       treatment for swimming pools & spas.

Swimming Teachers' Association Ltd   (STA)   1932
NR   Anchor House, Birch St, WALSALL, W Midlands, WS2 8HZ.
       (hq)
       01922 645097   fax 01922 720628
       email sta@sta.co.uk   http://www.sta.co.uk
▲   Company Limited by Guarantee; Registered Charity
Br   16; Australia, Hong Kong, Singapore, Taiwan
○   *E, *S; 'to save lives by the teaching of swimming, lifesaving &
       survival techniques'
●   Conf - Mtgs - ET - Exam
<   Intl Fedn of Swimming Teachers Assns (IFSTA)
M   5,000 i
¶   Swim & Save - 6; ftm, £18 yr nm (UK) (£24 Europe).

Swindon Chamber of Commerce & Industry
       is part of **Thames Valley Chamber of Commerce & Industry**

Swiss Railways Society
NR   28 Appletree Lane, REDDITCH, Worcs, B97 6SE.   (mem/sec)
       Mem Sec: Martin Fisher
○   *G; for all interested in rail journeys, particularly through
       Switzerland
●   Mtgs - VE
M   i
       (Sub: £15)
¶   Swiss Express

Synchronised Swimming Coaches Association
       please delete record

Synthetic Fibre Rug, Mat & Carpet Association   (SFRMA)   1965
■   Kingsway House, Wrotham Rd, Meopham, GRAVESEND, Kent,
       DA13 0AU.   (hsp)
▲   Un-incorporated Society
○   *T
●   Conf - Mtgs - Stat - Lib
M   8 f
¶   NL - 6;   AR; both ftm only.
×   2003 Synthetic Fibre Rug Manufacturers Association

Systematics Association   1937
NR   CABI Bioscience, Bakeham Lane, EGHAM, Surrey, TW20 9TY.
       (hsb)
       01491 829080
       Sec: Dr Zofia Griffiths
○   *L; for the study of systematics (the classification of organisms)
       in relation to general biology & evolution
●   Conf - Mtgs - ET - Inf
M   i

T E Lawrence Society (TELS) 1985
■ PO Box 728, OXFORD, OX2 6YP.   (mail address)
    email info@telsociety.org   http://www.telsociety.org.uk
    Sec: Ian Heritage,   Chmn: Peter Leney
▲ Registered Charity
Br 3; Japan, Netherlands, USA
○ *A; to promote interest & research into the life & works of
    T E Lawrence (Lawrence of Arabia), 1888-1935
● Conf - Mtgs - Res - Exhib - Inf - Lib - VE
M 348 i, UK / 235 i, o'seas
¶ Jnl - 2; ftm, £8 nm.   NL - 4; ftm only.
    [subscription £18 UK]

Table Soccer Players Association   (TSPA) 1954
NR 68 Gresham Drive, Chadwell Heath, ROMFORD, Essex,
    RM6 4TS.   (sp)
    020 8270 1028
    email jeff.jordan1@ntlworld.com
    Sec: Jeff Jordan
Br 7 (regional)
○ *S; to play & promote Subbuteo (a type of table soccer) at
    national & international level
Gp Subbuteo Collectors Club
● Conf - Mtgs - Exhib - Comp - VE - TV & radio work
M 32 i
¶ The Bulletin - 12; ftm, 50p issue nm.
    Playing Rules Official Book - 1; ftm, £1.20 nm.
    National B&W Premier League Fixture Book - 1;
    LM;   Hbk; all ftm only.

Table Tennis Association of Wales   (TTAW) 1921
NR 7 Hopkins Close, Thornbury, BRISTOL, BS35 2PX.   (hsp)
    Sec: John Fraser
○ *S
Gp Sub-c'ees: Coaching, Veteran, Selection, Umpires,
    Management, Computer ranking
M i & org

Table Tennis Scotland
    the trading name of the **Scottish Table Tennis Association**

Tai Chi Union for Great Britain   (TCUGB) 1991
NR 5 Corunna Drive, HORSHAM, W Sussex, RH13 5HG.   (hsp)
    01403 257918
    http://www.taichiunion.com
    Sec: Peter Ballam
○ *S; for instructors in the art of Tai Chi in all its aspects - self-
    defence, meditation & health
● inf
M c 400 i
¶ Tai Chi Tuan & Oriental Arts - 4.

**Talking Newspaper Association of the United Kingdom
(TNAUK) 1974**
■ National Recording Centre, HEATHFIELD, E Sussex,
    TN21 8DB.   (hq)
    01435 866102   fax 01435 865422
    email info@tnauk.org.uk   http://www.tnauk.org.uk
    Chief Exec: Tim McDonald
▲ Registered Charity
○ *M, *W; to provide 230 national newspapers & magazines on
    tape, e mail, CD-ROM & bulletin board service to blind,
    visually impaired & disabled people
● Inf
M c 11,500 i

Tall Persons Club GB & Ireland   (TPC) 1991
■ Spectrum House, Dunstable Rd, Redbourn, ST ALBANS, Herts,
    AL3 7PR.   (hq)
    07000 825512
    email admin@tallclub.co.uk   http://www.tallclub.co.uk
    The Director
▲ Company Limited by Guarantee
Br Links with clubs in Europe & USA
○ *K; to provide information for & to promote the interests of
    those who are taller than average; includes practical,
    medical, psychological & social aspects
Gp Little Big Ones (for tall children & their parents)
● Mtgs - ET - Stat - Inf - VE
< Links with Tall Clubs in Europe & USA
M 1,000 i
¶ 6 ft+ - 4; ftm.
    Tall Suppliers Directory - 2; ftm, £35 nm.

Tallis Group
NR 51 Vernon Ave, LONDON, SW20 8BN.   (hsp)
    020 8715 7659
    Pres: Edward Clark
○ *D

Talybont Welsh Sheep Society   2002
■ c/o Montague Harris & Co, 16 Ship St, BRECON,
    Brecknockshire, LD3 9AD.   (hsb)
    01874 623200
    Sec: John A Lewis
< Nat Sheep Assn
M c 40

Talyllyn Railway Preservation Society   (TRPS) 1950
■ Wharf Station, TYWYN, Merioneth, LL36 9EY.   (hq)
    01654 710472   fax 01654 711755
    email secretary@talyllyn.co.uk
    http://www.talyllyn.co.uk
    Hon Sec: John S Robinson
▲ Un-incorporated Society
Br 8
○ *G; operation of the Talyllyn Railway as an example of a
    steam-operated narrow-gauge railway built in the 19th
    century
● Mtgs - ET - Exhib - VE - Practical work on railway by volunteers
> Talyllyn Holdings Ltd; Talyllyn Rly Co; Narrow Gauge Rly
    Museum Trust
M 3,700 i, UK / 110 i, o'seas
¶ Talyllyn News - 4; ftm.   AR.

Tamworth Breeders' Group
NR Broad Leaze, Boyton, WARMINSTER, Wilts, BA12 0SS.
    01985 850208
○ *B; for breeders of Tamworth pigs

Tandem Club of the United Kingdom   (TC) 1971
■ 25 Hendred Way, ABINGDON, Oxon, OX14 2AN.
    01235 525161
    email secretary@tandem-club.org.uk
    http://www.tandem-club.org.uk
    Hon Sec: Peter Hallowell
▲ Un-incorporated Society
Br 50; Holland
○ *S; to encourage & assist tandem cycling
Gp Techncal; Disabilities liaison
● Mtgs - Comp - Inf
< Cycling Time Trials
M 3,500 i, UK / 500 i, o'seas
    (Sub: £10)
¶ Tandem Club Jnl - 6.

© CBD Research Ltd · Beckenham · BR3 5JS · Tel 020 8650 7745 · Fax 020 8650 0768 · E-mail cbd@cbdresearch.com · www.cbdresearch.com

Tank Storage Association   (TSA)   1978
NR   Black Dog Farm, Waverton, CHESTER, CH3 7PB.   (dir/p)
    01244 335627   fax 01244 332198
    email tsa@tankstorage.org.uk
    http://www.tankstorage.org.uk
    Dir: Dr K H M Bray
▲   Company Limited by Guarantee
○   *T; to represent companies operating in the UK whose main
    business is the storage of bulk liquids for third parties
●   Mtgs - LG
<   Fedn of Eur Tank Storage Assns (FETSA)
M   13 f

Tapestry Frame Manufacturers' Association   (TFMA)   1991
■   81 Park View, Collins Rd, LONDON, N5 2UD.
○   *T
●   Mtgs
M   11 f
¶   In the Frame (NL) - 1.

Tarot Association of the British Isles   (TABI)   1999
■   PO Box 14555, CRADLEY HEATH, W Midlands, B62 2FT.
    (treas/p)
    email treasurer@tabi.org.uk   http://www.tabi.org.uk
    Treas: Louise Underhill,   Sec: Jane Booth
▲   Un-incorporated Society
○   *G; to promote tarot in a positive, contructive way
●   Conf - ET - Comp - SG - Inf
<   Spiritual Workers Assn
M   300 i, UK / 50 i, o'seas
    (Sub: £20 UK / £22,50 o'sea)

Tattoo Club of Great Britain   1975
NR   389 Cowley Rd, OXFORD, OX4 2BS.   (hq)
    01865 716877   fax 01865 775610
    email tcgb@tattoo.co.uk   http://www.tattoo.co.uk
    Pres: Lionel Titchener
○   *G; for tattoo artists & enthusiasts interested in furthering
    greater understanding of tattoo art
Gp TCGB Engineering is the manufacturing division of tattooing
    equipment supplied to trade worldwide
●   Mtgs - Res - Exhib
<   Brit Tattoo Artists Fedn
M   2,500 i, UK / 1,500 i, o'seas
¶   Tattoo International - 6.

Taunton Chamber of Commerce
■   12F Fore St (1st floor), TAUNTON, Somerset, TA1 3TP.   (hq)
    01823 353353   fax 01823 353353
    email office@taunton-chamber.co.uk
    http://www.taunton-chamber.co.uk
    Admin Officer: J Burden
○   *C
●   Mtgs - Exhib - Inf - VE - LG - Promotional services
<   Brit Chams Comm; Bristol Cham Comm & Initiative
M   c 200 f
¶   Business News (Jnl) - 12; ftm only.

Tax Incentivised Savings Association   (TISA)   1998
NR   Dakota House, 25 Falcon Court, Preston Farm Business Park,
    STOCKTON-on-TEES, Co Durham, TS18 3TX.   (hq)
    01642 666999
    http://www.tisa.co.uk
    Dir Gen: Tony Vine-Lott
▲   Company Limited by Guarantee
○   *T; to encourage consultation on existing & future regulations
    with government, HM Treasury, Inland Revenue, statutory
    regulating authorities & other relevant organisations
●   Conf - Mtgs - ET - Res - Stat - Inf - LG
M   c 115 f
×   2007 PEP & ISA Managers' Association

TaxPayers' Alliance   (TPA)   2004
NR   43 Old Queen St, LONDON, SW1H 9JA.
    0845 330 9554
    email info@taxpayersalliance.com
    http://www.taxpayersalliance.com
    Chief Exec: Matthew Elliott
○   *K; for a lowering of the tax rates

** Tea Buying Brokers Association of London
    Organisation lost: see Introduction paragraph 3.

Teachers' Union of Ireland
IRL   73 Orwell Rd, Rathgar, DUBLIN 6, Republic of Ireland.
    353 (1) 492 2588   fax 353 (1) 492 2953
    email tui@tui.ie   http://www.tui.ie
    Gen Sec: Peter MacMenamin

Technical & Legal Committee
    a group of **Food & Drink Industry Ireland**

Ted Heath Musical Appreciation Society   (THMAS)
NR   Flat 15 Ynysderwe House, PONTARDAWE, Glamorgan,
    SA8 4AA.   (mem/sp)
    01792 830691
    Mem Sec: Mrs P (Jackie) Jones
○   *D; for all interested in the music of the bandleader Edward
    (Ted) Heath (1902-1969)banleader
M   i
¶   Jnl - 4.

Teeswater Sheep Breeders' Association Ltd   (TSBA)   1949
■   Wodencroft, Cotherstone, BARNARD CASTLE, Co Durham,
    DL12 9UQ.   (hq)
    01833 650032
    http://www.teeswater-sheep.co.uk
    Sec: Mrs M S Braithwaite
▲   Company Limited by Guarantee
○   *B; registration of pedigrees & promotion of Teeswater sheep
●   Mtgs - Exhib - Recording lambs for the Flock Book
M   80 i
¶   Flock Book - 1; ftm.

Telecare Services Association   (TSA)   1994
NR   Membership Services Centre, Wilmslow House (suite 8),
    Grove Way, WILMSLOW, Cheshire, SK9 5AG.   (hq)
    01625 520320
    email admintelecare.org.uk
    The Secretary
▲   Company Limited by Guarantee
○   *T; to set standards for providers; to improve the available
    hardware & software
Gp Technical; Education; Training
●   Conf - Mtgs - ET - Exhib - Stat - LG
M   126 f
¶   NL - 8; ftm only.
×   2005 Association of Social Alarms Providers

Telecommunications Heritage Group   (THG)   1987
■   Dalton House, 60 Windsor Avenue, LONDON, SW19 2RR.
    (hsp)
    020 8099 1699
    email membership@thg.org.uk   http://www.thg.org.uk
    Mem Sec: Alex Clark
▲   Un-incorporated Society
○   *L; to promote the study & preservation of telephone &
    telegraph apparatus & related literature
●   Mtgs - ET - Res - Exhib - SG - Inf - Lib - VE
M   450 i
¶   THG Jnl - 4; ftm only.

Telecommunications Industry Association
    in 2006 became the Communications & Information
    Technology Association, which has now closed.

Telecommunications & Internet Federation   (TIF)
IRL   Confederation House, 84-86 Lower Baggot St, DUBLIN 2,
        Republic of Ireland.
        353 (1) 605 1533   fax 353 (1) 638 1533
        http://www.tif.ie
        Dir: Tommy McCabe
○   *T; companies involved in fixed, mobile, wireless, fixed wireless,
        satellite & cable based service provisions, outsourcing &
        internet service provision
<   IBEC
M   70 f

Telecommunications UK Fraud Forum Ltd   (TUFF)   2000
NR   PO Box 28353, LONDON, SE20 7WJ.   (hq)
        020 8778 9864   fax 020 8659 9561
        email tuff@tuff.co.uk   http://www.tuff.co.uk
        Chief Exec: Jack Wraith
▲   Company Limited by Guarantee
○   *G, *T; to provide a forum for the exchange of information
        between telecom companies in respect to fraud & crime; to
        provide training for the telecom professional
Gp   Communications & operations; Training; Technical research &
        programs; Premium rate services
●   Mtgs - ET - Exam - Res - SG - Inf - LG
<   Ir Telecommunications Fraud Forum
M   150 i, 45 f, 5 org
¶   The Jnl - 2; ftm only.   In the Frame (NL) - 5; free.

Telecommunications Users' Association
in October 2007 merged with the **Communications Management
Association**

Telephone Helplines Association   (THA)   1996
■   9 Marshalsea Rd, LONDON, SE1 1EP.   (hq)
        020 7089 6321   fax 020 7089 6320
        email info@helplines.org.uk
        http://www.helplines.org.uk
        Chief Exec: Rekhha Wadhwani
▲   Company Limited by Guarantee; Registered Charity
Br   1
○   *T, *W; to promote & support the development of helpline
        services
●   Conf - Mtgs - ET - Res - LG - Development services
M   500 f, UK / 5 f, o'seas
        (Sub: £63,000 UK / £200 o'seas)
¶   Digital Exchange - 12;   Annual Review - 1; both free.
        THA Directory - 2; £22.
        Quality Standard Workbook.

Television & Radio Industries Club   (TRIC)   1931
NR   Hill Farm, Margaretting Rd, GALLEYWOOD, Essex, CM2 8TS.
        (hq)
        01245 290480   fax 01245 265963
        email info@tric.org.uk   http://www.tric.org.uk
        Sec: George Stone
○   *P
        no further information supplied

Telework Association   (TA)   1993
NR   31 Tidmarsh Rd, Leek Wootton, WARWICK, CV35 7QR   (hq)
        0800 616008
        email enquiries@telework.org.uk
        http://www.telework.org.uk
        Devt Dir: Shirley Borrett
▲   Company Limited by Guarantee
○   *G; the use of information technology (IT) &
        telecommunications for the development of local (particularly
        rural) economies, incl the use of shared facilities in local
        centres (telecottages); for telecottages (telecentres) &
        teleworkers (people who work from home)
●   Conf - Res - Inf & advice line - Networking with mem
M   2,000 i, 100 f, UK / 100 i, 20 f, o'seas
¶   Teleworker (Jnl) - 6; £34.50 yr.
        Teleworking Handbook - 1; £16.
        Note: The Telework Association is the trading name of the
        Telecottage Association
×   2002 Telework, Telecottage & Telecentre Association

Ten Sixty Six Enterprise   1993
NR   Summerfields Business Centre, Bohemia Rd, HASTINGS,
        E Sussex, TN34 1UT.   (hq)
        01424 205500   fax 01424 205501
        http://www.1066enterprise.co.uk
        Chief Exec: Graham Marley
▲   Company Limited by Guarantee
○   *C; the chamber of commerce for the Hastings & St Leonards
        area, the enterprise agency for Hastings & Rother
M   f

Tenant Farmers' Association Ltd   (TFA)   1981
■   5 Brewery Court, Theale, READING, Berks, RG7 5AJ.   (hq)
        0118-930 6130   fax 0118-930 3424
        email tfa@tfa.org.uk   http://www.tfa.org.uk
        Chief Exec: George Dunn
▲   Company Limited by Guarantee
Br   9
○   *F
Gp   Listed land agents; Professional legal advice
●   Conf - Mtgs - Exhib - Stat - Inf - VE - LG
M   c 4,000 i
        (Sub: dependent on size of farm)
¶   TFA News Sheet - 6;   Briefing Notes - 52;
        Information Sheets - irreg;   all ftm only.

**Tenants & Residents Organisations of England   (TAROE)
1997**
NR   Federation House, St John's Avenue, Newsome,
        HUDDERSFIELD, W Yorks, HD4 6JP.   (hsb)
        01484 223466   fax 01484 223478
        http://www.taroe.org
        Sec: Cora Carter
▲   Company Limited by Guarantee
○   *N; the representative body of tenants & residents groups,
        associations & federations in England relating to housing
●   Conf - Mtgs - Inf - Lib - Support for tenants
<   Intl U of Tenants
M   10 i, 90 org

Tennis & Rackets Association   (TandRA)   1907
NR   The Queen's Club, Palliser Rd, West Kensington, LONDON,
        W14 9EQ.   (hq)
        020 7386 3447
        http://www.tennisandrackets.com
        Chmn: P G Mallinson
○   *S; to act as the national governing body in Great Britain in all
        matters connected with the games of real tennis & rackets
Gp   Rackets; 'Real' tennis

© CBD Research Ltd · Beckenham · BR3 5JS · Tel 020 8650 7745 · Fax 020 8650 0768 · E-mail cbd@cbdresearch.com · www.cbdresearch.com

Tennis Scotland 1895
- 177 Colinton Rd, EDINBURGH, EH14 1BZ.   (hq)
  0131-444 1984   fax 0131-444 1973
  http://www.tennisscotland.org
  Chief Exec: James Campbell
- ▲ Registered Charity
- ○ *S; controlling body of the game in Scotland
- ● Mtgs - ET - Comp
- < Lawn Tennis Assn
- M 9 district org
- ¶ Scottish Tennis - 4/6; free.

Tennis Wales
- NR Welsh National Tennis Centre, Ocean Way, Ocean Park,
  CARDIFF, CF24 5HF.   (hq)
  029 2046 3335
  email info@tenniswales.org.uk
  Exec Dir: Peter Hybart
- ○ *S; to promote & develop tennis in Wales
- ● Mtgs - ET - Exam - Comp - Coaching
- < Lawn Tennis Assn
- M 85 clubs

Tennyson Society 1960
- Tennyson Research Centre, Central Library, Free School Lane,
  LINCOLN, LN2 1EZ.   (hsb)
  01522 552862   fax 01522 552858
  email kathleen.jefferson@lincolnshire.gov.uk
  http://www.tennysonsociety.org.uk
  Hon Sec: Miss K Jefferson
- ▲ Registered Charity
- Br USA
- ○ *A, *L; life & work of Alfred, Lord Tennyson
- ● Conf - Mtgs - Exhib - Res - Inf - Lib - VE
- < City University, New York (Victorian C'ee)
- M 150 i, 20 universities & academic bodies, UK / 200 i,
  130 universities, o'seas
- ¶ Tennyson Research Bulletin - 1; ftm.   AR.
  Monographs & Occasional Papers (2 series) - 1; ftm.
  Tape recordings & gramophone records.

Tenpin Bowling Proprietors Association of Great Britain (TBPA) 1966
- 4 Goodacre Drive, Chandlers Ford, EASTLEIGH, Hants,
  SO53 4LG.   (hsp)
  023 8026 1313   fax 023 8026 1313
  email jashbridge@tiscali.co.uk
  http://www.gotenpin.co.uk
  Gen Sec: John Ashbridge
- ▲ Un-incorporated Society
- ○ *S, *T; to promote & develop tenpin bowling; to ensure that
  members accept international standards of the sport
- ● Mtgs - SG - Inf - Lib - LG
- M 44 f

Tenterden Railway Co Ltd
   since 2004 **Kent & East Sussex Railway Co Ltd**

Tertiary Research Group (TRG) 1969
- NR 81 Crofton Lane, ORPINGTON, Kent, BR5 1HB.   (hsp)
  email david@fossil.ws   http://www.trg.org
  Hon Sec: David Ward
- ○ *L; to bring together amateur and professional geologists with
  an interest in the Tertiary period worldwide

Test Card Circle: an association of trade test devotees
   we do not consider that our organisation requires inclusion in
   your directory

Textile Finishers' Association (TFA) 1989
- Textile House, Red Doles Lane, HUDDERSFIELD, W Yorks,
  HD2 1YF.   (hq)
  01484 346500   fax 01484 346501
  Sec: John Lambert
- ▲ Company Limited by Guarantee
- ○ *T
- ● Mtgs - Inf - LG
- < BATC; Eur Textile Finishing Assn
- M 30 f

Textile Institute International 1910
- St James's Buildings (1st floor), 79 Oxford St, MANCHESTER,
  M1 6FQ.   (Intl hq)
  0161-237 1188   fax 0161-236 1991
  email tiihq@texi.org.uk   http://www.texi.org
  Hon Sec: David Wooliscroft
- ▲ Registered Charity
- Br 2; 7 worldwide
- ○ *L, *P; for people involved in the textile, clothing & footwear
  industries worldwide
- Gp Design & product marketing; Finishing; Fibre Science;
  Industrial; Engineering & technical; Textiles; Knitting;
  Marketing; Narrow fabrics; Quality; Floorcoverings;
  Weaving; Yarn; Management & economics; Human
  resources; Young members
- ● Conf - Mtgs - Res - Exhib - Comp - SG - Stat - Inf - Lib - VE -
  LG
- M 1,601 i, 48 f UK / 1,495 i, 51 f, o'seas
- ¶ Journal of the Textile Institute - 6; £60 m, £99 nm.
  Textile Progress - 4; c £30 m, £45 nm.
  Textiles Magazine - 4; ftm, £45 nm.
  TI News (NL) - 4;   Membership Directory - 1;
  LM (web-based) - continuous;   AR; all ftm only.

Textile Recycling Association (TRA) 1913
- PO Box 965, MAIDSTONE, Kent, ME17 3WD.   (sp)
  0845 600 8276   fax 0845 600 8276
  email info@textile-recycling.org.uk
  http://www.textile-recycling.org.uk
  Nat Liaison Mgr: Alan Wheeler
- ○ *T; interests of persons trading in discarded textiles
- Gp Recyclatex (bonded textile recycling scheme)
- ● Conf - Mtgs - Inf - LG
- < Bureau of Intl Recycling
- M 45 f, UK / 4 f, o'seas
- ¶ Bulletins; m only.   LM;   AR; both free.
  Recyclatex leaflet for local authorities.
  Recyclatex booklet for schools.

Textile Services Association (TSA) 1886
- NR 7 Churchill Court, 58 Station Rd, NORTH HARROW, Middx,
  HA2 7SA.   (hq)
  020 8863 7755
  email tsa@tsa-uk.org
  Chief Exec: Murray Simpson
- ▲ Company Limited by Guarantee
- ○ *T; for the drycleaning, laundry & textile rental industry
- M i & f

Textile Society: for the study of the history, art & design of textiles   1981

■ 8 Hillside, Denby Dale, HUDDERSFIELD, W Yorks, HD8 8QZ. (hsp)
email info@textilesociety.org.uk
http://www.textilesociety.org.uk
Sec: Katina Bill
▲ Registered Charity
○ *A; to unite scholars, designers, teachers, practitioners, artists, collectors & others who share an interest in the study of textile art, design & history
Gp Collectors (advice on private collections)
● Conf - Mtgs - ET - Inf - VE
M 350 i, 61 universities & museums, UK / 25 i, o'seas (Sub: £18 i, £35 org)
¶ Text (Jnl) - 1; ftm, £6 nm.   NL - 3;   AR; both ftm only.

Thalidomide Society Ltd   1963

Coordinator: Vivien Kerr
tel 01462 438212; info@thalsoc.demon.co.uk
▲ Company Limited by Guarantee; Registered Charity
○ *W; to provide support & information to thalidomide & similarly impaired people
● Mtgs - Inf
M 300 i
¶ NL - 2; ftm, £10 nm.
Note: contact by telephone or email only.

Thames Boating Trades Association   (TBTA)   1993

NR 51 New Rd, BOURNE END, Bucks, SL8 5BT.   (hsp)
01628 524376
email paul@thewagtail.co.uk
Hon Sec: Paul Wagstaffe
▲ Un-incorporated Society
○ *T; to liaise with the British Marine Federation & with members; the area covered is from the source of the Thames to the Barrier (approx 15 miles from each bank)
● Mtgs - ET
< Brit Marine Fedn
M 80 f
¶ Boatyards, Marinas & Services around the River Thames - 2 yrly; free.

Thames & Chilterns Vineyards' Association   (T&CVA)   1988

■ c/o Brightwell Vineyard, Rush Court, WALLINGFORD, Oxon, OX10 8LJ.   (chmn/p)
01491 836586
http://www.brightwines.co.uk
Chmn: Bob Nielsen
▲ Un-incorporated Society
○ *T; to promote public interest in & knowledge of the wines of the region; membership is open to people interested in English wine
Gp Commercial vineyards; Amateur growers
● Conf - Mtgs - ET - Comp - SG - Inf - VE
< Confédn Eur Viticulture Indep; UK Vineyards Assn; English Wine Producers
M c 100 i, 25 f
¶ NL - 4;   AR; both ftm only.

Thames Hire Cruiser Association
a group of the **British Marine Federation**

Thames & Medway Canal Association

■ Meadow View, Hodsoll Street, SEVENOAKS, Kent, TN15 7LA. (hsp)
01732 823725
Chmn: Brian Macnish
○ *G; to restore the Thames & Medway Canal to navigation
no further information supplied

Thames Valley Chamber of Commerce & Industry   (TVCCi)   1993

NR 467 Malton Ave, SLOUGH, Berks, SL1 3SB.   (hq)
01753 870500
Chief Exec: Paul Briggs
▲ Company Limited by Guarantee
Br 8
○ *C
Gp Branch Chams Comm at: Aylesbury, Bracknell, Heathrow, High Wycombe, Newbury, Oxford, Reading, Wokingham
● Conf - Mtgs - ET - Exhib - Stat - Expt - Inf - Lib - LG
< Brit Chams Comm
M c 2,500 f
¶ Business Jnl - 6.   CCi News - 12. Directory - 1.

Thanet & East Kent Chamber Ltd

NR Kent Innovation Centre, Millennium Way, BROADSTAIRS, Kent, CT10 2QQ.
01843 609289
http://www.tekc.co.uk
Admin: Kay Tift
○ *C

The . . .
Except for 3 exceptions the word **The** has not been used to start any organisation's title; this controls the left-hand margin of the text & puts the emphasis on the first noun of the title.

Theosophical Society in England   (TS)   1888

■ 50 Gloucester Place, LONDON, W1U 8EA.   (hq)
020 7563 9817   fax 020 7935 9543
email office@theosoc.org.uk
http://www.theosoc.org.uk
Nat Pres: Eric McGough
▲ Un-incorporated Society
○ *L; to form a nucleus of the universal brotherhood of humanity without distinction of race, creed, sex, caste or colour; to encourage study of comparative religion, philosophy & science; investigation of unexplained laws of nature & the powers latent in man
● Conf - Mtgs - SG - Inf - Lib - VE
M 900 i
¶ Insight - 4; ftm, £10 UK, £15 o'seas
Note: is a section of the International Theosophical Society (1875), Adyar, Madras 20, India.

Thermal Insulation Contractors Association   (TICA)   1957

NR TICA House, Allington Way, Yarm Road Business Park, DARLINGTON, Co Durham, DL1 4QB.   (hq)
01325 466704   fax 01325 487691
email enquiries@tica-acad.co.uk
http://www.tica-acad.co.uk
Chief Exec: Ralph Bradley
▲ Company Limited by Guarantee
○ *T; for companies involved in industrial thermal insulation & asbestos removal
Gp ACAD - Asbestos control & abatement division; IETA - Insulation & environmental training agency
● Conf - Mtgs - ET - Inf - Empl - LG
< Wld Insulation & Acoustics Congress Org (WIACO); Fédn Eur des Syndicats d'Entreprises d'Isolation (FESI)
M 220 f, UK / 2 f, o'seas
¶ ACADdemy (asbestos removal) - 4; ftm, on application nm.
FESI - European Insulation Standards; on application.
Health & Safety Handbook for Operatives.
Man-made Mineral Fibre (1990 IOM Report).

© CBD Research Ltd · Beckenham · BR3 5JS · Tel 020 8650 7745 · Fax 020 8650 0768 · E-mail cbd@cbdresearch.com · www.cbdresearch.com

Thermal Insulation Manufacturers & Suppliers Association (TIMSA) 1978

- ■ Tournai Hall, Evelyn Woods Rd, ALDERSHOT, Hants, GU11 2LL.   (asa)
  01252 357844   fax 01252 357831
  email info@associationhouse.org.uk
  http://www.timsa.org.uk
  Sec: J G Fairley
- ○ *T; to improve standards of thermal insulation contributing to energy conservation & fuel efficiency
- Gp Building insulation; Technical; Publicity; Acoustics
- ● Mtgs - LG
- < Thermal Insulation Contractors Assn
- M 18 i, 4 i (associates)
- ¶ Insulation (Jnl) - 6.   Hbk & Directory - 3; free.

Thermal Spraying & Surface Engineering Association (TSSEA) 1984

- ■ 38 Lawford Lane, Bilton, RUGBY, Warks, CV22 7JP.   (hq)
  0870 760 5203   fax 0870 760 5206
  email info@tssea.org   http://www.tssea.co.uk
  Sec: Dr Andrew T Cole
- ▲ Company Limited by Guarantee
- ○ *T; to promote the use & development of thermal (metal) spraying techniques used 1: to provide corrosion resistant coatings to structural steelwork, 2: to confer specific surface properties (wear/corrosion resistance, thermal protection, restore size)
- Gp Health & safety; Euro-international standards
- ● Conf - Mtgs - ET - Exhib - SG - Inf - LG
- < Inst of Materials
- M 10 i, 75 f, 2 org, UK / 10 f, 1 org, o'seas
- ¶ Coatings (NL) - 4; free.

Thermostatic Mixing Valves Association
  association in the Energy section of **BEAMA Ltd**

Thimble Society of London 1981

- ■ 1 Cathcart St, LONDON, NW5 3BL.   (hq)
  020 7419 9562
  http://www.thimblesociety.com
  Sec: Bridget McConnel
- ○ *G; collection of antique sewing articles & thimbles
- ● Conf - Mtgs - Res - Inf
- M 600 i, UK / 100 i, o'seas
- ¶ Magazine - 3.

Thomas Hardy Society Ltd 1968

- ■ PO Box 1438, DORCHESTER, Dorset, DT1 1YH. (accom/address)
  01305 251501   fax 01305 251501
  email info@hardysociety.org
  http://www.hardysociety.org
  Sec: Mike Nixon,   Chmn: Dr Anthony Fincham
- ▲ Company Limited by Guarantee; Registered Charity
- ○ *A; promotion, study & appreciation of the works of Thomas Hardy
- ● Conf - Mtgs - Res
- M 800 i, UK / 400 i, o'seas; universities, UK & o'seas
- ¶ The Thomas Hardy Jnl - 3; ftm, £4 nm.

Thomas Lovell Beddoes Society 1994

- ■ 9 Amber Court, BELPER, Derbys, DE56 1HG.   (chmn/p)
  01773 828066   fax 01773 828066
  email john@beddoes.demon.co.uk
  http://www.phantomwooer.org
  Sec: Christine Hunkinson
- ▲ Registered Charity
- ○ *A; to promote interest in the life & work of the poet Thomas Lovell Beddoes (1803-1849)
- Gp the study of Maria Edgeworth
- ● Conf - Mtgs - Res - Exhib - VE
- < Alliance of Literary Societies
- > Walter Savage Landor Soc
- M 70 i, 5 f, UK / 10 i, o'seas
- ¶ NL - 1; ftm, £4.50 nm.

Thomas Merton Society of Great Britain & Ireland (TMS-GBI) 1993

- NR 2 Western Villas, Western Rd, CREDITON, Devon, EX17 3NA. (mem/sp)
  01363 772816
  email the.margin@virgin.net
  http://www.thomasmertonsociety.org
  Mem Sec: Stephen Dunhill
- ▲ Un-incorporated Society
- ○ *A; to encourage the study of the life & works of Thomas Merton (1915-1968) poet, monk & prophet
- ● Conf - Mtgs - Res - Inf - Lib
- < Intl Thomas Merton Soc (USA)
- M 300 i
  (Sub: £12)
- ¶ The Merton Jnl - 2; ftm, £4 nm.
  Conference Papers - 2 yrly; £12.99 m.

Thoresby Society 1889

- NR Claremont, 23 Clarendon Rd, LEEDS, W Yorks, LS2 9NZ.   (hq)
  0113-247 0704
  http://www.thoresby.org.uk
- ▲ Registered Charity
- ○ *L; history of Leeds & its neighbourhood
- ● Mtgs - Lib - VE - Publishing
- M 461 i, 54 libraries, UK / 6 i, 42 libraries, o'seas
- ¶ Annual Volume; ftm, price on application nm.

Thoroton Society of Nottinghamshire 1897

- ■ Little Dower House, Station Rd, BLEASBY, Notts, NG14 7FX. (hsp)
  01636 830284
  email bjcast@aol.com   http://www.thorotonsociety.org.uk
  Hon Sec: Barbara Cast
- ▲ Registered Charity
- ○ *L; to promote & foster study of the history, archaeology & antiquities of Nottinghamshire
- Gp Record; Archaeological
- ● Mtgs - Res - VE
- M c 500 i
- ¶ NL - 4;   Transactions - 1;   AR - 1; Record Series; all ftm.

Thoroughbred Breeders' Association (TBA) 1917

- ■ Stanstead House, 8 The Avenue, NEWMARKET, Suffolk, CB8 9AA.   (hq)
  01638 661321
  http://www.thetba.co.uk
  Chief Exec: Louise Kemble
- ▲ Registered Charity
- ○ *B; the science of maintaining the thoroughbred horse in Great Britain
- ● Mtgs - ET - Res - Expt - Inf - Lib - VE - LG - Prizes & awards
- < Eur Fedn of Thoroughbred Breeders' Assns (EFTBA);
  is a member of the Brit Horse Ind Confedn
- M 2,400 i, UK / 400 i, o'scas
- ¶ Thoroughbred Owner & Breeder;
  Thoroughbred Stallion Guide; both ftm.

Three Counties Agricultural Society   (TCAS)   1797
- ■ The Showground, MALVERN, Worcs, WR13 6NW.   (hq)
  01684 584900
- ▲ Company limited by Guarantee
- ○ *F, *H; promotion of agriculture & horticulture in the shires of Gloucester, Hereford & Worcester
- Gp C'ees: Livestock, Flower, Dog Show
- ● Conf - Mtgs - ET - Exhib - Comp - Shows
- M c 5,500 i & f
- ¶ Members' News;   AR; both ftm.

Three Counties Cider & Perry Association   (3CCPA)   1993
- ■ Gregg's Pit, Much Marcle, LEDBURY, Herefords, HR8 2NL. (hsp)
  01531 660687
  email helen.woodman@hotmail.co.uk
  http://www.thethreecountiesciderandperry
  association.co.uk
  Hon Sec: Helen Woodman
- ▲ Un-incorporated Society
- ○ *T; for top quality cider & perry makers
- ● Mtgs - ET - Comp - VE
- < Nat Assn of Cider Makers (NACM)
- M c 80 i, f & org
- ¶ NL - 4;   Technical Bulletin - 1;   LM - 1; all ftm only.

THRIVE   1978
- NR Geoffrey Udall Centre, Trunkwell Park, Beech Hill, READING, RG7 2AT.   (hq)
  0118-988 5688   fax 0118-988 5677
  email info@thrive.org.uk   http://www.thrive.org.uk
  Chief Exec: Nicola Carruthers
- ▲ Company Limited by Guarantee; Registered Charity
- Br 4 gardens
- ○ *W; to promote the use of horticulture & gardening in therapy, rehabilitation, vocational training, leisure & employment for all disabled people (includes people with mental health problems, sensory, physical or learning disabilities)
- Gp Service for projects; Training service; Full-time volunteers; Garden advisory service; Advisory committee of blind gardeners
- ● ET - Exam - Res - Inf - Lib - PL
- < R Horticl Soc
- M 800 i, 40 org, UK / 120 i, o'seas
- ¶ Growth Point - 4; ftm, £10 nm.
  Come Gardening (braille & tape only) - 4; £5 m only.
  Leaflets; prices vary.

Thyroid Eye Disease Charitable Trust   (TEDct)   1990
- ■ PO Box 2954, CALNE, Wilts, SN11 8WR.   (hq)
  0844 800 8133
  email ted@tedct.co.uk   http://www.tedct.co.uk
  Contact: Margaret Russell
- ▲ Registered Charity
- Br 13 support groups
- ○ *M, *W; to provide information, care & support to those affected by the disease; to promote better awareness of the condition amongst the medical profession & the general public
- Gp Medical helpline of consultants
- ● Conf - ET - Res - Inf
- < Thyroid Fedn Intl; Brit Thyroid Assn
- M c 700 i
- ¶ NL - 4; free.

Tiga: the Independent Games Developers Association (TIGA)   2001
- NR 1 London Wall, LONDON, EC2Y 5EB.
  0845 094 1095   fax 0845 094 1095
  email info@tiga.org   http://www.tiga.org
  Chief Exec: Richard Wilson
- ○ *T; for the computer games industry
- M 157 f

Tile Association   (TTA)   2000
- ■ 83 Copers Cope Rd, BECKENHAM, Kent, BR3 1NR.   (hq)
  020 8663 0946   fax 020 8663 0949
  email info@tiles.org.uk   http://www.tiles.org.uk
  Exec Officer: Mrs Lesley Day
- ▲ Company Limited by Guarantee
- ○ *T; to represent manufacturers, suppliers & tiling contractors in the UK wall & floor tile industry
- Gp Tile adhesive & accessory mfrs; Distributors, retailers & agents of wall & floor tiles; Tiling contractors
- ● Conf - Mtgs - Exam - Inf - Empl - LG
- < Ceram-Unie; CET; EUF
- M 750 f

Tiles & Architectural Ceramics Society   (Tile Society)   (TACS)   1981
- ■ Oakhurst, Cocknage Rd, Rough Close, STOKE-on-TRENT, ST3 7NN.   (mail/address)
  01782 397996
  http://www.tilesoc.org.uk
  Sec: Kath Adams
- ▲ Registered Charity
- ○ *G, *L; the national society responsible for the study & protection of tile & architectural ceramics
- ● Conf - Res - Exhib - SG - Inf - VE - Tile location index
- M c 420 i, f & org
- ¶ Jnl - 1;   Glazed Expressions - 2;   NL - 4;   all ftm, charged to nm.
  Tour Notes.   Tile Bibliography - up-dated.

Timber Arbitrators Association   (TAA)
- NR The Building Centre, 26 Store St, LONDON, WC1E 7BT.   (hq)
  020 3205 0067
- ○ *P
- < a division of the Timber Trade Federation
- M 11 i

Timber Decking Association Ltd   (TDA)   1999
- ■ 5 Flemming Court, CASTLEFORD, W Yorks, WF10 5HW.   (hq)
  01977 558147
  email info@tda.org.uk   http://www.tda.org.uk
  Dir: Steve Young
- ▲ Company Limited by Guarantee
- ○ *T; technical & advice organisation established to set standards for the quality of materials & installation good practice in the UK; operates 'Deckmark'- a quality assurance scheme for products & contractors involved in timber deck design & construction
- Gp Manufacturing; Preservatives & coating; Design installation; Forestry & sawmilling
- ● ET - Stat - PL - LG - Promotion of standards
- < Wood Protection Assn
- M 43 f, 3 org, UK / 3 f , o'seas
- ¶ The Timber Decking Manual; ftm, £32 nm.
  An Introduction to Creating Quality Decks; free.
  Parapet Design; ftm, £5 nm.
  Statutory Regulations; free.
  Decking - the essential guide for DIY; £5.99.

Timber Packaging & Pallet Confederation   (TIMCON)   1940
- NR 840 Melton Rd, Thurmaston, LEICESTER, LE4 8BN.   (asa)
  0116-264 0579   fax 0116-264 0141
  email timcon@associationhq.org.uk
  http://www.timcon.org
  Exec Sec: Miss Sharon Hutchinson
- ▲ Company Limited by Guarantee
- ○ *T; to represent the timber packaging industry
- ● Conf - Mtgs - ET - Exhib - Stat - Inf
- < Eur Fedn of Wooden Pallet & Packaging Mfrs (FEFPEB); Brit Nat C'ee for EPAL - Eur Pallet Assn)(BREPAL)
- M 110 f, UK / 20 f, o'seas

Timber Research & Development Association
operates as **TRADA Technology Ltd**

Timber Trade Federation (TTF) 1893
NR The Building Centre, 26 Store St, LONDON, WC1E 7BT. (hq)
    020 3205 0067
    email ttf@ttf.co.uk   http://www.ttf.co.uk
    Chief Exec: John White
○ *T; 'the voice of the UK timber industry'
Gp Forests Forever

Time Haiku 1994
■ Basho-an, 105 King's Head Hill, LONDON, E4 7JG. (hsp)
    020 8529 6478
    email facey@aol.com
    Sec: Erica Facey
▲ Un-incorporated Society
○ *A; to promote haiku & related forms (Japanese poetry & prose); to increase accessibility through education
● ET - Yearly reading
M 50-200 i
    (Sub: £10 UK / £12 o'seas)
¶ Time Haiku - 2; ftm.

Timeshare Consumers Association (TCA) 1997
■ Nornay, BLYTH, Notts, S81 8HG. (hq)
    01909 591100 fax 01909 591338
    email info@timeshare.org.uk
    http://www.timeshare.org.uk
    Chmn: Sandy Grey
○ *G; to help make timeshare an enjoyable, value-for-money form of holidaying for consumers
    No further information supplied

TimeWatch
NR Willow House, Brompton Road, Newton-le-Willows, BEDALE, N Yorks, DL8 1SJ
    email info@timewatch.org   http://www.timewatch.org
    Contact: George Chaplin
○ *G; to protect ancient monuments and landscapes, particularly the Thornborough Henges (Yorkshire) the most important site between Stonehenge & the Orkneys, which is subject to extensive quarrying

Tissue Viability Society 1981
■ 21 Wilson St, CARDIFF, Glamorgan, CF24 2NZ. (hq)
    email tissue.viability@btinternet.com
    http://www.tvs.org.uk
    Professional Adviser: Michael Clark
▲ Registered Charity
○ *L, *M; to disseminate information relating to the development of wound prevention & healing (tissue viability); to raise awareness of classic & contemporary research to tissue viability; to provide examples of all aspects of peer accepted best practice
● Conf - Mtgs - ET - Res - Exhib - Inf
< Eur Wound Mgt Assn
M 1,100 i, 100 f, UK / 50 i, 20 f, o'seas
    (Sub: £30 i, £140 f, UK / £40 i, o'seas)
¶ Jnl of Tissue Viability - 4; ftm, £70 nm.

Toastmasters of England 1971
■ 12 Little Bornes, Dulwich, LONDON, SE21 8SE. (pres/b)
    020 8670 5585
    http://www.ivorspencer.com
▲ Un-incorporated Society
○ *T; to organise & arrange authentic banquets with traditional ceremonies here & abroad; to act as promotional advisers to firms of repute; to engage only members of the Guild of International Professional Toastmasters for special engagements in the USA, Canada, Japan, New Zealand, & Australia
● Conf - Mtgs - Expt - VE
< Gld Intl Profl Toastmasters
M 20 i

Toastmasters of Great Britain 1970
■ 12 Little Bornes, Dulwich, LONDON, SE21 8SE. (hq)
    020 8670 5585
    http://www.ivorspencer.com
▲ Un-incorporated Society
○ *T; to act as advisers to firms of repute; to promote for them special traditional banquets with authentic ceremonies in Europe (incl Ireland).
    The only toastmasters engaged are from the Guild of International Professional Toastmasters
● Conf - Mtgs - Expt - VE
< Gld Intl Profl Toastmasters
M 20 i

Toastmasters for Royal Occasions 1970
■ 12 Little Bornes, Dulwich, LONDON, SE21 8SE. (pres/b)
    020 8670 5585
    http://www.ivorspencer.com
▲ Un-incorporated Society
○ *T; officiate as toastmasters in this country & abroad on Royal & State occasions
● Conf - Mtgs - SG - Expt - VE
< Gld Intl Profl Toastmasters
M 20 i

Tobacco Alliance
    since 2006-08 **Tobacco Retailers' Alliance**

Tobacco Industry Employers' Association (TIEA)
■ Astwick House, Croughton, BRACKLEY, Northants, NN13 5LL. (hq)
    01869 811400 fax 01869 811311
    email tiea93@hotmail.com
    Mgr & Sec: John L Hadley
○ *T
● Mtgs - ET - SG - Employee relations - Safety & health
M 4 f

Tobacco Manufacturers' Association (TMA) 1940
■ Burwood House (5th floor), 14-16 Caxton St, LONDON, SW1H 0ZB. (hq)
    020 7544 0100 fax 020 7544 0117
    email information@the-tma.org.uk
    http://www.the-tma.org.uk
    Chief Exec: Christopher Ogden
▲ Un-incorporated Society
○ *T; for companies manufacturing tobacco products in the UK
● Mtgs - Inf - LG
< Confedn of the Eur Community's Cigarette Mfrs (CECCM)
M 3 f
¶ Briefing - 3 to 4; free.

Tobacco Retailers Alliance 1984
■ PO Box 61705, LONDON, SW1H 0XS. (hq)
    0800 008282
    http://www.tobaccoalliance.org.uk
    Nat Spokeswoman: Audrey Wales
○ *K; to raise awareness of the issue of tobacco smuggling & the detrimental effects this has on independent retailers
● Conf - Mtgs - Res - VE - LG
M 17,000 i
✕ 2006-08 Tobacco Alliance

Toc H
    is closing down

Together: working for wellbeing   1879
- ■ 12 Old St, LONDON, EC1V 9BE.   (hq)
    020 7780 7300   fax 020 7780 7301
    email contactus@together-uk.org
    http://www.together-uk.org
    Chief Exec: Liz Felton
- ▲ Registered Charity
- ○ *W; provides high quality services in the community, hospitals & prisons for people with mental health needs & their carers
- M c 150 i
- ¶ AR; free.
- ✕ 2005 (July) Mental After Care Association

Token Corresponding Society   (TCS)   1972
- ■ 89 Gillards Close, Rockwell Green, WELLINGTON, Somerset, TA21 9DX.   (sp)
    email davidyoungco@yahoo.co.uk
    Editor: David Young
- ▲ Un-incorporated Society
- ○ *G; for all interested in British tokens, tickets, tallies & checks
- ● Res
- M 180 i, UK / 12 i, o'seas
- ¶ Bulletin - 4; m only.

Tolkien Society   (TS)   1969
- NR 655 Rochdale Rd, Walsden, TODMORDEN, Lancs, OL14 6SX.   (h/mem/sp)
    email tolksoc@tolkiensociety.org
    http://www.tolkiensociety.org
    Mem Sec: Maria Kershaw
- ▲ Registered Charity; Un-incorporated Society
- Br 23; Australia, Brazil, Canada, Germany, Italy, Malta, Mexico, Netherlands, Taiwan, USA
- ○ *A; to promote research into the life & works of J R R Tolkien
- Gp The Tolkien Collector (book collecting); Quettar (linguistics); Nigglings (fiction)
- ● Conf - Mtgs - Exhib - Lib - Archives
- < Alliance of Literary Socs
- M 613 i, 3 org, UK / 502 i, 18 org, o'seas
    (Sub: £21 i, £23 f & org, UK / £24-29, o'seas airmail)
- ¶ Mallorn (Jnl) - 1;
    Anon Hen (NL) - 6; both ftm, £22 nm (UK).

✶✶ Tool & High Speed Steel Suppliers Association
    Organisation lost: see Introduction paragraph 3.

Tools for Self Reliance   (TFSR)   1979
- ■ Netley Marsh, SOUTHAMPTON, Hants, SO40 7GY.   (hq)
    023 8086 9697
    Chief Exec: Janice Kidd
- ▲ Company Limited by Guarantee; Registered Charity
- Br 65
- ○ *K; volunteers refurbish & ship handtools & sewing machines to village development groups in some of the poorest communities in Africa
- ● Conf - Exhib - Collection of tools
- M 300 i, UK / 50 i, o'seas
- ¶ Forging Links - 3.   AR - 1.

Tools & Trades History Society   (TATHS)   1983
- ■ Woodbine Cottage, Budleigh Hill, EAST BUDLEIGH, Devon, EX9 7DT.   (mem/sp)
    01395 443030
    email membership@taths.org.uk   http://www.taths.org.uk
    Mem Sec: W Rose
- ▲ Registered Charity
- ○ *G, *L; 'to further the knowledge & understanding of hand-tools & the trades & persons that used them'
- ● Conf - Mtgs - Exhib - Inf - Lib - VE
- M 348 i, 21 org, UK / 58 i, 9 org, o'seas
- ¶ Tools & Trades (Jnl) - 1; ftm, £15 nm.   NL - 4; ftm.

Torbay Chamber of Commerce
alternative name of the **South Devon Chamber of Trade & Commerce**

Tornado & Storm Research Organisation   (TORRO)   1974
- NR PO Box 972, Thelwall, WARRINGTON, Cheshire, WA4 9DP.   (hsp)
    07813 075509
    email sam.hall@torro.org.uk   http://www.torro.org.uk
    Hon Sec: Samantha Hall
- ▲ Un-incorporated Society
- ○ *L, *Q; to research into severe weather in the UK; to document, archive & research severe weather events: Tornadoes & other whirlwinds; Severe thunderstorms & hail; Heavy rain, floods, snowstorms & blizzards; Ball lightning & other lightning incidents. To educate the general public but not limited to severe weather forecasts
- Gp Divisions: Ball lightning, Blizzards & heavy snowfalls, Coastal impacts, Hailstorm, Ligtning impacts, Tornado, Thunderstorm census, Weather disasters, Extreme rainfall, Flashfloods
- ● Conf - Mtgs - ET - Res - Stat - Inf - Lib - PL
- < Intl Jnl of Meteorology
- M c 400 worldwide
- ¶ International Jnl of Meteorology - 10; ftm, £38 nm.
    Convection - 2;   Members' Hbk - 1; both ftm only.
    [subscription £39.50].

Tortoise Trust   1986
- ■ BM Tortoise, LONDON, WC1N 3XX.   (asa)
    email tortoisetrust@aol.com   http://www.tortoisetrust.org
- ○ *V; provides sanctuary & hospital facilities for tortoises; educational material relating to tortoise welfare & conservation; carries out conservation projects overseas
- M i, f & org
- ¶ Jnl - 4.   NL - 6.
    Guide to Tortoises & Turtles - 1.

Tory Reform Group   (TRG)   1975
- ■ 83 Victoria St, LONDON, SW1H 0HW.   (hq)
    020 3008 4991
    email trg@trg.org.uk   http://www.trg.org.uk
    Contact: The Director
- ○ *K, *Z; to influence Conservative Party policy
- ● Conf - Mtgs - Res - Inf - LG
- M 'confidential'
- ¶ Reformer (Jnl) - 2.   Policy Papers - irreg.

Tourette Syndrome (UK) Association   (TSA(UK))   1980
- ■ Southbank House, Black Prince Rd, LONDON, SE1 7SJ.   (hq)
    020 7793 2356
    email enquiries@tsa.org.uk   http://www.tsa.org.uk
    Chief Exec: Judith Kidd
- ▲ Company Limited by Guarantee; Registered Charity
- ○ *W; to support people with the neurological disorder Tourette Syndrome throughout their lives, delivering appropriate information, practical help & opportunities for social contact; to educate & inform health & social care & other statutory agencies
- ● Conf - Mtgs - ET - Res - Inf
- M 660 i
    (Sub: £20)
- ¶ NL - 4;   AR; both ftm only.
    Leaflets; free.
    Trading as Tourettes Action.

Tourism for All UK
- ■ c/o Vitalise, Shap Rd Industrial Estate, Shap Rd, KENDAL, Cumbria, LA9 6NZ.
    0845 124 9973
    email info@tourismforall.org.uk
    http://www.tourismforall.org.uk
    Information Officer: Carrie-Ann Fleming
- ○ *K; accessible tourism
    no further information supplied

© CBD Research Ltd · Beckenham · BR3 5JS · Tel 020 8650 7745 · Fax 020 8650 0768 · E-mail cbd@cbdresearch.com · www.cbdresearch.com

Tourism Alliance   2001

NR Centre Point, 103 New Oxford St, LONDON, WC1A 1DU. (hq)
     020 7395 8246   fax 020 7395 8178
     email kurt.janson@tourismalliance.com
     http://www.tourismalliance.com
     Policy Dir: Kurt Janson
▲   Company Limited by Guarantee
○   *T; to work with & lobby government on all issues related to the growth of tourism & its contribution to the British economy
●   Conf - Mtgs - LG
M   46 org
¶   NL - 12;   AR - 1; both free.

Tourism Concern   1989

NR Stapleton House, 277-281 Holloway Rd, LONDON, N7 8HN.   (hq)
     020 7133 3800   fax 020 7133 3331
     email info@tourismconcern.org.uk
     http://www.tourismconcern.org.uk
     Inf Officer: Francesca Leadlay
▲   Company Limited by Guarantee; Registered Charity
○   *G, *K; 'a UK-based organisation campaigning worldwide for just & sustainable tourism - tourism that is fairly traded'
●   Conf - ET - Res - Exhib
<   Ecumenical Coalition on Third World Tourism (ECTWT); Third World European Network (TEN)
M   i
¶   Tourism in Focus - 4.   Being There.
     The Good Alternative Travel Guide.

Tourism Management Institute   (TMI)   1997

■   18 Cuninghill Avenue, INVERURIE, Aberdeenshire, AB51 3TZ.   (hsp)
     01467 620769
     email secretary@tmi.org.uk   http://www.tmi.org.uk
     Hon Sec: Cathy Guthrie
▲   Company Limited by Guarantee
○   *P; 'the professional voice for tourism destination managers'
Gp Panels: Education & training, Marketing, ICT
●   Conf - ET - LG
M   230 i, 14 f, UK / 3 i, o'seas
¶   The Tourism Manager (NL) - 3;   LM (website);
     TMI online (email NL) - 4; all m only.

Tourism Society Ltd   1977

NR Trinity Court, 34 West St, SUTTON, Surrey, SM1 1SH.   (hq)
     020 8661 4636
     email admin@tourismsociety.org
     http://www.tourismsociety.org
     Exec Dir: Flo Powell
▲   Company Limited by Guarantee
○   *P; networking organisation for professionals working, or interested in, tourism
Gp Association Tourism Teachers & Trainers (ATTT); Tourism Society Consultants' Group (TSCG)
●   Conf - Mtgs - Comp - Expt - Journal production
M   1,110 i, 2 f, UK / 100 i, o'seas
¶   Tourism - 4; ftm, £85 nm.
     Membership Executive - 1; free; £85 nm.

Town & Country Planning Association   (TCPA)   1899

NR 17 Carlton House Terrace, LONDON, SW1Y 5AS.   (hq)
     020 7930 8903   fax 020 7930 3280
▲   Registered Charity
○   *K; to promote a national policy of land-use planning

Townswomen's Guilds   (TG)   1929

■   Tomlinson House (1st floor), 329 Tyburn Rd, BIRMINGHAM, B24 8HJ.   (hq)
     0121-326 0400   fax 0121-326 1976
     email tghq@townswomen.org.uk
     http://www.townswomen.org.uk
     Office Mgr: David Brotherton
▲   Registered Charity
○   *G, *K; a charitable organisation to educate women
Gp Sports & creative leisure; Public affairs; National events
●   Conf - Mtgs - ET - Exhib - Comp - Stat - Inf - Lib - VE
M   i
¶   Townswoman - 4.

Towpath Action Group   (TAG)   1988

■   23 Hague Bar, NEW MILLS, High Peak, Derbys, SK22 3AT. (hsp)
     01663 742198
     email andyscreen@towpath.org.uk
     http://www.towpath.org.uk
     Sec: Andrew Screen
▲   Un-incorporated Society
○   *G, *K; campaign for better access on the towpaths of the country's canals
●   Inf - Campaigning & pressure gp activities
<   Inland Waterways Assn; Parliamentary Waterways Gp
M   150 i, 10 org
¶   NL - 4; £4 yr (£3 students, pensioners).

Toy Retailers Association   (TRA)   1950

■   Waterfront Enterprise Centre, Lea Rd, GAINSBOROUGH, Lincs, DN21 1LX.   (hq)
     0870 753 7437   fax 0870 706 0042
     email enquiries@toyretailersassociation.co.uk
     http://www.toyretailersassociation.co.uk
     Sec: Derek Markie
▲   Company Limited by Guarantee
○   *T
●   Conf - Exhib - Inf - LG
M   f
×   2004 British Association of Toy Retailers

Tracheo-Oesophageal Fistula Support   (TOFS)   1982

■   St George's Centre, 91 Victoria Rd, Netherfield, NOTTINGHAM, NG4 2NN.   (hq)
     0115-961 3092   fax 0115-961 3097
     email info@tofs.org.uk   http://www.tofs.org.uk
     Hon Sec: Duncan Jackson
▲   Registered Charity
○   *W; 'to offer support & information to the families & carers of babies born with tracheo-oesophageal fistula (TOF), oesophageal atresia (OA) & related conditions; the group enables families to benefit from the friendship of other parents who have experienced the particular stresses of caring for these children - as well as the joy when problems have been overcome'
●   Conf - Res - Inf - Support
M   1,016 i, 40 f, UK / 120 i, 13 f, o'seas
¶   Chew (NL) - 4;   AR; both free.
     We Just Want Our Daughter to Live; £9.99 m, £14.99 nm.
     The TOF Child; £9.99 m, £14.99 nm.

TRADA Technology Ltd   (TRADA)   1995
■ Stocking Lane, Hughenden Valley, HIGH WYCOMBE, Bucks,
  HP14 4ND.   (hq)
  01494 569600   fax 01494 565487
  email information@trada.co.uk   http://www.trada.co.uk
  Chief Exec: Andrew Abbott
▲ Company Limited by Guarantee
○ *Q; technical advice relating to the correct use of timber in
  construction
● Conf - ET - Res - Exhib - Inf - PL
M i, f & org
¶ Ybk;   AR; both ftm.   Numerous technical publications.
  Note: carries out all the activities of the Timber Research &
  Development Association.

Trade Association Forum   (TAF)   1997
NR Centre Point, 103 New Oxford St, LONDON, WC1A 1DU.
  (hq)
  020 7395 8238   fax 020 7395 8178
  http://www.taforum.org
  Manager: Stuart Bean
○ *N; promotion of trade associations & best practice in the UK
● Conf - Mtgs - ET - Res - Comp - Inf - LG
< CBI
M 300 trade associations
¶ Managing Trade Associations by Mark Boleat; £25.

Trade Marks Patents & Designs Federation   (TMPDF)   1920
■ 63-66 Hatton Garden (5th floor), LONDON, EC1N 8LE.   (hq)
  020 7242 3923   fax 020 7242 3924
  email admin@tmpdf.org.uk
  Sec: Sheila Draper
▲ Company Limited by Guarantee
○ *T; to express the views of industry on intellectual property
  matters
● Mtgs - LG
< UNICE; CBI
M 50 f
¶ Trends & Events - 1; free.

Trade & Professional Publishers Association   1976
IRL 31 Deansgrange Rd, BLACKROCK, Co Dublin, Republic of
  Ireland.
  353 (1) 289 3305   fax 353 (1) 289 6406
  Chmn: David Markey
○ *T

Trade Publishers Council
  a group of the **Publishers Association**

Trade Union Badge Collectors Society   (TUBCS)   1979
■ 6 Leven Close, LINSLADE, Beds, LU7 2XS.   (hsp)
  email adge1@hotmail.co.uk
  Sec: Adrian Heffernan
▲ Un-incorporated Society
○ *G; to collect old & new trade union badges
Gp Pre trade union amalgamation badges; Foreign badges
● Res - Exhib - Inf - Lib
M i

Trades Union Congress   (TUC)   1868
NR Congress House, 23-28 Great Russell St, LONDON,
  WC1B 3LS.   (hq)
  Gen Sec: Brendan Barber
○ *U

Trading Standards Institute   (TSI)   1892
■ 1 Sylvan Court, Sylvan Way, Southfields Business Park,
  BASILDON, Essex, SS15 6TH.   (hq)
  0845 608 9400   fax 0845 608 9425
  email institute@tsi.org.uk   http://www.tsi.org.uk
  Chief Exec: Ron Gainsford
▲ Company Limited by Guarantee
○ *L, *P; to offer expertise & unique services to the wider
  consumer affairs sector & to businesses in consumer markets
Gp History pen circle (historical metrology)
● Conf - Mtgs - ET - Exam - Res - Exhib - Comp - SG - Stat - Inf -
  Lib - VE - LG
M 3,500 i
¶ Trading Standards Today - 12.
  Trading Standards Appointments - 12.

Traditional Cosmology Society   (TCS)   1984
■ c/o School of Scottish Studies, University of Edinburgh,
  27 George Sq, EDINBURGH, EH8 9LD.   (h/pres/b)
  0131-650 4152   fax 0131-650 4163
  email e.lyle@ed.ac.uk   http://www.tradcos.co.uk
  Pres: Emily Lyle
▲ Registered Charity
○ *L; to explore myth, religion & cosmology across cultural &
  disciplinary boundaries; to increase our understanding of
  world views past & present
● Conf - Mtgs - Res
M 106 i, UK / 56 i, o'seas
¶ Cosmos (Jnl) - 2; ftm, £25 yr nm.

Traditional Farmfresh Turkey Association   (TFTA)   1985
■ PO Box 3041, EASTBOURNE, E Sussex, BN21 9EN.
  (admin/sp)
  01323 419671   fax 01323 419671
  Admin Sec: Mrs E J Peters
○ *T; marketing & promoting slower growing breeds of turkey,
  reared to full maturity, dry plucked & hung like a game bird
  for at least seven days
M 50 f

Traditional Housing Bureau
  an affiliated association of the **British Precast Concrete
  Federation**

**Traditional Music & Song Association of Scotland   (TMSA)
1966**
■ 30-38 Dalmeny St, EDINBURGH, EH6 8RG.   (hq)
  0131-555 2224
  email office@tmsa.org.uk   http://www.tmsa.org.uk
  Nat Dir: Kay Thomson
▲ Company Limited by Guarantee; Registered Charity
Br 11
○ *A; the promotion, presentation & preservation of Scotland's
  traditional music & song, through educational workshops,
  concerts, festivals; to act as the source of information on
  traditional music in Scotland
● Mtgs - ET - Comp - Inf - Concerts, festivals & events promoting
  traditional music & song in Scotland
M 617 i, 24 org
  (Sub: £15-20 i, £30 org)

**Traditional Youth Marching Bands Association   (TYMBA)
1983**
NR 37 Stoneywell Rd, Anstey Heights, LEICESTER, LE4 1AT.
  (memsec/p)
  0116-235 3812
  http://www.tymba.org.uk
  Mem Sec: Richard Warrington
Br 3
○ *G; to advance the education & training of young people &
  their leaders in all aspects of traditional banding

© CBD Research Ltd · Beckenham · BR3 5JS · Tel 020 8650 7745 · Fax 020 8650 0768 · E-mail cbd@cbdresearch.com · www.cbdresearch.com

Traffic Management Contractors Association   (TCMA)   1898
NR   Highlands Lane, HENLEY-on-THAMES, Oxon, RG9 4EL.   (hq)
     020 8973 1777   fax 020 8973 1777
     http://www.tmca.org.uk
     Sec: P Crickmay.   Chmn: R Pearson
▲   Company Limited by Guarantee
○   *T; traffic management on high speed roads
●   Conf - Mtgs - Exhib - LG
M   12 f
¶   Notes for Guidance - irreg; ftm, £2 nm.

Trail Riders Fellowship   (TRF)   1970
■   PO Box 196, DERBY, DE1 9EY.   (hsp)
     01483 535644
     email trfmemsec@aol.com   http://www.trf.org.uk
     Hon Sec: P R Cody
Br   44
○   *G, *K; 'a national, voluntary & non-competitive body formed
     by motorcyclists to preserve our heritage of green lanes &
     our right to use them'
●   Mtgs - Res - Exhib - Inf - VE - LG
<   Brit Motorcycle Fedn (BMF); Land Access & Recreation
     Assn (LARA); Motorcycle Action Gp (MAG); Nat Motorcycle
     Coun (NMC)
M   3,000 i
¶   Trail (Jnl) - 12;   TRF Hbk - 1; both ftm only.

Train Collectors Society   (TCS)   1978
NR   PO Box 13891, REDDITCH, Worcs, B97 9FN.   (mail)
     email memsec@traincollectors.co.uk
     http://www.traincollectors.co.uk
     Mem Secs: Andy & Elaine Hyelman
▲   Un-incorporated Society
○   *G; collection & restoration of model trains of any make, any
     age, any gauge
●   Mtgs - Exhib - Gatherings in Biggleswade, Sandy & Leicester
M   470 i, UK / 30 i, 2 org, o'seas
¶   TCS News - 4; £18 yr (£22 Europe)(£25 world) m only.
     Spares Directory (loose-leaf or CD) 2003; ftm.
     Archive CDs TCS News; £10 m, £20 nm.

Trakehner Breeders Fraternity   (TBF)   1989
NR   Whitehouse Farm, Learnside, HOUGHTON-le-SPRING,
     Tyne & Wear, DH4 6QJ.   (sec/p)
     07900 413886
     email mail@learnsideequestrian.co.uk
     http://www.trakehnerbreeders.com
     Co Sec: Bev Brown
▲   Company Limited by Guarantee
○   *B; registration & promotion of the Trakehner horse in the UK
●   Mtgs - Inf - VE
<   Trakehner Verband (Germany)
M   220 i
     Note: the Fraternity's marketing name is Trakehners UK.

Tralee Chamber of Commerce
IRL   20 Denny St, TRALEE, Co Kerry, Republic of Ireland.
     353 (66) 712 1472
     email tralcham@iol.ie
     Admin: Bernie Griffin
○   *C

Tramway & Light Railway Society   (TLRS)   1938
■   47 Soulbury Rd, LEIGHTON BUZZARD, Beds, LU7 2RW.   (hsp)
     01525 377215
     Hon Sec: G R Tribe
▲   Registered Charity
○   *G; for those interested in tramways & light railways; to retain
     historic tramway archives; to encourage tramway modelling
M   i
¶   Tramfare - 6.

Tramway Museum Society   (TMS)   1955
■   National Tramway Museum, Crich, MATLOCK, Derbys,
     DE4 5DP.
     01773 854321
     Hon Sec: I M Dougill
▲   Company Limited by Guarantee; Registered Charity
○   *G; preservation & demonstration of the tramcar for museum
     purposes (by mobile operation in a period setting) &
     associated historical research
●   Exhib - Res - Inf - Museum
<   Assn Indep Museums; Assn Brit Transport & Engg Museums;
     Transport Trust; Heart of England Tourist Bd
M   c 1,800 i
¶   Jnl - 4;   Contact (NL) - 12;   AR; all ftm.
     Tramway Museum Guidebook.

Trans-Antarctic Association   1960
NR   British Antarctic Survey, Madingley Rd, CAMBRIDGE,
     CB3 0ET.   (hsb)
     01223 221400 (switchboard)
○   *L, *Q; furthering research in subjects relating to Antarctica
●   Awarding grants
M   5 i (committee of management), UK / i, o'seas.

Transform Scotland
NR   5 Rose St, EDINBURGH, EH6 6RD.
     0131-243 2690
     email info@transformscotland.org.uk
     http://www.transformscotland.org.uk
     Dir: Colin Howden
○   *K; sustainable transport

Transfrigoroute UK Ltd   (TUK)   1984
NR   39a Meneage St, HELSTON, Cornwall, TR13 8RB.   (hq)
     01326 569657   fax 01326 563859
     email secretary@transfrigoroute.co.uk
     http://www.transfrigoroute.com
     Sec: Liam E W Olliff
▲   Company Limited by Guarantee
Br   24 o'seas
○   *T; promotes & coordinates the interests of operators & users of
     temperature-controlled transport
●   Conf - Mtgs - Res - Stat - Expt - Inf - LG
<   Transfrigoroute Intl
M   c 120 f
¶   TUK Talk (NL).   Code of Conduct.

Translators Association   (TA)   1958
■   84 Drayton Gardens, LONDON, SW10 9SB.   (hq)
     020 7373 6642   fax 020 7373 5768
     email inf0@societyofauthors.org
     http://www.societyofauthors.org
     Sec: Sarah Baxter
○   *P, *U; a specialist unit of the Society of Authors, exclusively
     concerned with the interests & problems of writers who
     translate foreign literary, dramatic or technical work into
     English for publication or performance
●   Mtgs - Inf
<   Fédn Intle des Traducteurs (FIT); Eur Coun of Literary Translators
     Assns (CEATL)
M   420 i, UK / 60 i, o'seas
¶   The Author - 4.   In Other Words - 2.

Transparency International (UK)   (TI(UK))   1994
■ Downstream Bldg (3rd floor), 1 London Bridge, LONDON,
    SE1 9BG.   (hq)
      020 7785 6356   fax 020 7785 6355
      email info@transparency.org.uk
      http://www.transparency.org.uk
    Chmn: Laurence Cockcroft
    Co Sec: Mrs J Lanigan
▲ Company Limited by Guarantee; Registered Charity
○ *K; a non-profitmaking, independent, non-governmental
    organisation dedicated to increasing government
    accountability & to curbing national & international
    corruption
● Conf - Mtgs - Res
< Transparency International (Berlin)
M c 150 i, c 25 f
¶ (for publications see website)

Transplant Support Network   1995
NR 6 Kings Meadow Drive, WETHERBY, W Yorks,LS22 7FS.
      0800 027 4490   fax 01937 585434
      http://www.transplantsupportnetwork.org.uk
○ *W; to provide support (usually over the telephone) for patients
    & families & all concerned with transplants & mechanical
    implants

Transport Association   (TA)   1955
NR PO Box 374, LEATHERHEAD, Surrey, KT22 2EY.   (sb)
      0750 778 5845
      email marion@transportassociation.org.uk
      http://www.transportassociation.org.uk
    Sec: Peter Acton
○ *T
● Conf - Mtgs
M c 60 f

Transport & General Workers' Union
      in May 2007 merged with Amicus to form **Unite the Union**

Transport 2000 Ltd
      since 2007 **Campaign for Better Transport**

Transport Research & Information Network
      on 1 January 2004 merged with the **Association of Community
      Rail Partnerships**

Transport Salaried Staffs' Association   (TSSA)   1897
NR 10 Melton St, LONDON, NW1 2EJ.   (hq)
      020 7387 2101
    Gen Sec: Gerry Doherty
○ *U; for clerical, supervisory, professional & technical employees
    of British & Irish railways, London Regional Transport, British
    Waterways Board & allied undertakings, hotels, docks & road
    haulage

Transport Ticket Society   (TTS)   1945
NR 6 Breckbank, Forest Town, MANSFIELD, Notts, NG19 0PZ.
      (hsp)
    Mem Sec: D Randell
▲ Un-incorporated Society
○ *G, *L; study of transport tickets & theory & practice of fare
    collection
● Mtgs - Res - Exhib - SG - Inf - Lib
< Roads & Road Transport History Conference
M i, f & org
¶ Jnl - 12; ftm only.   Various occasional papers.

Transport Trust   (TT)   1965
■ 202 Lambeth Rd, LONDON, SE1 7JW.   (hq)
      020 7928 6464   fax 020 7928 6565
      email hq@thetransporttrust.org.uk
    Dir Gen: Col Anthony Walker
▲ Registered Charity
○ *G; to facilitate the preservation of items of transport of
    historical & technical interest (road, rail, air & water)
    including books, papers, ephemera & photographs
Gp Railways; Road transport; Air (civil & military); Inland
    waterways; Coastal waters
● Conf - Res - Inf - Lib - VE
< Heritage Railways (AIRPS); Assn Brit Transport Museums; The
    Maritime Trust; Vintage Sports-Car Club (VSCC); The
    Shuttleworth Trust
M 600 i, 20 f, 150 org
¶ The Transport Digest (Jnl) - 3; ftm, 'normally free' nm.

Transport-Watch   2004
■ 12 Redland Drive, NORTHAMPTON, NN2 8QE.   (hq)
      01604 847438   fax 01604 455074
      email enquiries@transport-watch.co.uk
      http://www.transport-watch.co.uk
    Dir: Paul F Withrington
▲ Company Limited by Guarantee
○ *Q; 'research & development reference transport policy,
    particularly road & rail'
Gp Congestion charging; Rail; Rapid transit; Traffic management;
    Transport policy
● Res - Stat
M 10 i, UK / 1 i, o'seas

Transport on Water Association   (TOW)   1975
NR Basin South, Gate 14, Woolwich Manor Way, LONDON,
    E16 2QY.   (hq)
      020 7476 2424
    Hon Dir: L Faram
▲ Registered Charity
○ *K; to promote the use of river & canals for commercial traffic
● Inf - LG
M 200 i, 21 f

Transverse Myelitis Society   (TMS)
NR 35 Avenue Rd, BRENTFORD, Middx, TW8 9NS.   (sec/p)
      020 8568 0350
      http://www.myelitis.org.uk
    Sec: Lew Gray
▲ Registered Charity
○ *W; to provide information & support to TM sufferers, their
    carers & families
< Transverse Myetitis Assn (intl/US)
M 400 i

Travel Retail Forum
      see **United Kingdom Travel Retail Forum**

Travel Trust Association Ltd   (TTA)   1993
■ Albion House (3rd floor), High St, WOKING, Surrey,
    GU21 1BE.   (hq)
      0870 889 0577   fax 01483 730746
      email steve.clark@traveltrust.co.uk
      http://www.traveltrust.co.uk
    Dir: Stephen Jeffrey Clark
▲ Company Limited by Guarantee
○ *T; 'for the travel industry & regulatory body, coupled with
    commercial negotiations with suppliers'
Gp Travel agents; Tour organisers
● Conf - Mtgs - ET - Res - Exhib - Stat - Inf - VE - LG
< Inst Travel & Tourism (ITT)
M 460 f
¶ NL - 4;   Fax Publications - 52; both ftm.

© CBD Research Ltd · Beckenham · BR3 5JS · Tel 020 8650 7745 · Fax 020 8650 0768 · E-mail cbd@cbdresearch.com · www.cbdresearch.com

Treacher Collins Family Support Group
NR 114 Vincent Rd, NORWICH, Norfolk, NR1 4HH.
　　01603 433736　fax 01603 433736
　　http://www.treachercollins.net
　　Sec: Sue Moore
○　*W; for sufferers of the syndrome which causes facial
　　malformation & severe hearing loss

Trebuchet Society　1998
■　23 Viewside Close, Corfe Mullen, WIMBORNE, Dorset,
　　BH21 3ST.　(hsp)
　　01202 690224
　　email richardbarton@caving5.freeserve.co.uk
　　Sec: Richard Barton
▲　Un-incorporated Society
○　*G; research into early weaponry; designing & building replica
　　weaponry; experiments into the effectiveness of early
　　weaponry
Gp　Field research; Workshop; Research into trebuchet science;
　　Computer database
●　Res - SG - Inf - PL - VE
<　Coalhouse Fort Project; Artillery Assn GB
M　6 i, 2 org

Tree Council of Ireland　1985
IRL　Seismograph House, Rathfarnham Castle, DUBLIN 14, Republic
　　of Ireland.
　　353 (1) 493 1313　fax 353 (1) 493 1317
　　email trees@treecouncil.ie　http://www.treecouncil.ie
　　Pres: Dorothy Hayden
○　*H

Tree & Hedging Group
　　a group of the **Horticultural Trades Association**

Trekking & Riding Society of Scotland　(TRSS)　1992
■　Bruaich-na-h'Abhainne, Maragowan, KILLIN, Perthshire,
　　FK21 8TN.　(hsp)
　　01567 820909　fax 01567 820909
　　email trss@btinternet.com
　　http://www.ridinginscotland.com
　　Chief Exec: Mrs Susan Howard
▲　Un-incorporated Society
○　*T; to encourage & assist in the development of all forms of
　　equestrian tourism in Scotland; to set & maintain standards
　　of excellence
●　Conf - Mtgs - ET - Exam - Res - Exhib - SG - Stat - Inf - LG
<　Brit Horse Soc (Scotland); Scot Equestrian Assn; Scot Tourism
　　Forum
M　c 70 f
¶　Promotional brochure by Scottish Tourist Board.

Trevithick Society　1935
■　PO Box 62, CAMBORNE, Cornwall, TR14 7ZN.　(asa)
　　01209 716811
　　Hon Sec: George B Wilson
▲　Registered Charity
Br　2
○　*G, *L; the study of the history of technology in Cornwall & the
　　preservation of buildings, machinery & sites connected with
　　mining, engineering, china clay workings, transport, & any
　　other industry carried on elsewhere where there are Cornish
　　connections
●　Mtgs - ET - Res - PL - Organisation of King Edward Mine Ltd,
　　which is responsible for the last group of remaining mine
　　buildings at Camborne which are Grade II* listed; these are
　　installed with historic tin extraction & separation machines &
　　other relevant artifacts
<　Assn Indl Archaeology (AIA); Nat Assn of Mining History Orgs
M　400 i, 4 f, UK / 20 i, o'seas
¶　Jnl - 1; ftm, £5 nm.　NL - 4; ftm, £1.50 nm.

Triathlon England　2007
NR　PO Box 25, LOUGHBOROUGH, Leics, LE11 3WX.　(hq)
　　01509 226161　fax 01509 226165
　　email info@triathlonengland.org
　　http://www.triathlonengland.org
　　Dir: Mark Barfield
▲　Company Limited by Guarantee
Br　9
○　*S; to govern, administer & develop the sport of triathlon by
　　providing opportunities for athletes of all ages & abilities to
　　compete at the highest level
<　Brit Triathlon Fedn

Tricycle Association　(TA)　1928
■　54 Bassnage Rd, HALESOWEN, W Midlands, B63 4HQ.　(hsp)
　　0121-550 3644
　　email normfenn@hotmail.com
　　http://www.tricycleassociation.org.uk
　　Nat Sec: Norman Fenn
○　*G, *S; to provide social & competitive activities for members.
　　Membership is open to all past & present riders of the
　　tricycle; defined as a humanly propelled machine making
　　three tracks when in motion
●　Mtgs - Exhib - Comp - VE
<　Cycling Time Trials; Road Records Assn
M　400 i, UK / 35 i, o'seas
¶　Gazette - 4; ftm only.

**Trigeminal Neuralgia Association United Kingdom　(TNA
UK)　1999**
■　PO Box 234, OXTED, Surrey, RH8 8BE.　(hq)
　　01883 370214
　　email tna@ntlbusiness.com　http://www.tna.org.uk
　　Chmn: David Rose,　Sec: Janet Bruten
▲　Registered Charity
○　*W; to provide information & support to members; to raise
　　awareness of TN (an extremely severe facial pain which tends
　　to come & go without warning) amongst medical
　　professionals and general public
●　Conf - Mtgs - ET - Exhib - SG - Stat - Inf - Lib - LG
<　informal affiliation to TNS USA & TNSA Australia
M　815 i, UK / 15 i, o'seas
¶　NL - 3;　Contact list (voluntary entries) - 1; both ftm only.
　　Medical books; £17.50 each,　Information leaflets; free.

Trollope Society　1987
■　Maritime House, Old Town, Clapham, LONDON, SW4 0JW.
　　(hq)
　　020 7720 6789
　　email info@trollopesociety.org
　　http://www.trollopesociety.org
　　Chmn: Priscilla Hungerford,
　　PA: Pelham Ravenscroft
▲　Registered Charity
○　*A; to produce the first complete, uniform, edition of the novels
　　of Anthony Trollope; to serve as a forum for discussions
●　VE - Annual dinner - Lecture
M　1,200 i, UK / 500 i, USA
¶　Trollopiana Jnl - 3;　Mailing - 3; ftm.

Tropical Agriculture Association　(TAA)　1979
■　3 Sandy Mead, BOURNEMOUTH, Dorset, BH8 9JY.　(mem/sp)
　　01202 397085
　　email membership-secretary@taa.org.uk
　　http://www.taa.org.uk
　　Mem Sec: J B Davis
▲　Registered Charity
Br　Regions: Southwest, Scotland & Borders, London & South East,
　　East Anglia
○　*F; the promotion, practice, education & research in tropical
　　agriculture
●　Conf - Mtgs - ET - Inf - VE
M　1,150 i, 12 f, UK / 350 i, o'seas
¶　TAA(UK) NL - 4; ftm, £2 nm.

Tropical Forest Forum
no longer in existence

Tropical Growers' Association Ltd   (TGA Ltd)   1907
■   20 St Dunstan's Hill (1st floor), LONDON, EC3R 8NQ.   (hq)
        020 7283 2707   fax 020 7623 1310
        email stuart.logan@fosfa.org
        Co Sec: Stuart R Logan,   Hon Sec: Philip D Gatland
▲   Company Limited by Guarantee
○   *T; for all concerned with tropical commodities & plantation
        interests
Gp   Council
●   Mtgs
<   Fedn of Oils, Seeds & Fats Assns Ltd (FOSFA)
>   Malaysian Palm Oil Bd
M   50 i, 5 f, 5 Associates, UK / 1 f, 3 associates, o'seas
        (Sub: £15 i, £50 f, £30 associates UK)
¶   [nil in public domain]

Trussed Rafter Association   (TRA)
NR   PO Box 571, CHESTERFIELD, Derbyshire, S40 9DH.
        01246 230036   fax 01246 230036
        http://www.tra.org.uk
○   *T; for trussed rafter manufacturers, industry suppliers &
        professionals involved in roof design & construction
        no further information supplied

Trust for Training & Education in Building Maintenance
alternative name of **Upkeep**

TT Riders Association   (TTRA)   1907
■   Mountainview, Glen Maye, PEEL, Isle of Man, IM5 3BJ.   (hsp)
        01624 843695
        email frances@thorpiom.freeserve.co.uk
        http://www.ttra.co.uk
        Hon Sec & Treas: Frances Thorp
▲   Registered Charity
○   *S; 'the continuance of the Isle of Man TT races; the creation of
        a social & charitable association of all those who take part,
        have taken part & those who race no more'
Gp   Isle of Man TT race riders; Sidecar passengers
●   Conf - Stat - Inf - Lib
<   Intl Historic Racing Org; Auto-Cycle U; Fédn Intle
        Motocyclisme; Manx Grand Prix Riders Assn; Amer Historic
        Motorcycle Racing Assn
M   1,270 i, UK / 411 i, o'seas
¶   NL - 2; ftm.

Tuberous Sclerosis Association   (TSA)   1977
■   PO Box 12979, Barnt Green, BIRMINGHAM, B45 5AN.   (sb)
        0121-445 6970
        email diane.sanson@tuberous-sclerosis.org
        http://www.tuberous-sclerosis.org
        Head of Development & Support Services: Mrs Fiona McGlynn
▲   Company Limited by Guarantee; Registered Charity
○   *W; to support & help sufferers & their families; to raise
        awareness of & to encourage research into the causes of the
        disease
●   Conf - ET - Res - Inf
<   Tuberous Sclerosis Intl (associations in 25 countries)
M   1,500 i, UK / 100 i, 25 org, o'seas
¶   Scan (NL) - 3;   Medical Brochure;   Factsheets; all free.
        Publications list available.

Tue Iron Manufacturers Association   (TIMA)   1994
NR   81 Park View, Collins Rd, LONDON, N5 2UD.   (asa)
▲   Un-incorporated Society
○   *T; 'the tue iron is a nozzle attached to a bellows, used in a
        forge to fan flames to a high heat'
●   Mtgs - ET - Exhib
M   17 f
¶   Hot Air (NL) - 4.

Tug of War Association   (TOWA)   1958
NR   57 Lynton Rd, CHESHAM, Bucks, HP5 2BT.   (hsp)
        01494 783057   fax 01494 792040
        email peter@tugofwar.co.uk   http://www.tugofwar.co.uk
        Sec: Peter Craft
○   *S; controlling body of the game of tug-of-war in Britain

Turfgrass Growers Association Ltd   (TGA)   1995
■   133 Eastgate, LOUTH, Lincs, LN11 0QG.   (asa)
        01507 607722   fax 01507 600101
        email info@turfgrass.co.uk   http://www.turfgrass.co.uk
        Co Sec: Tim Mudge
▲   Company Limited by Guarantee
○   *T; turf growers for domestic & commercial use
Gp   Producers; Suppliers of goods & services
●   Conf - Mtgs - Exhib
M   60 f

Turkey Club UK   2000
NR   Colts Farmhouse, Whithorn, NEWTON STEWART,
        Wigtownshire, DG8 8HA.   (hsb)
        01988 600763
        Hon Sec & Treas: Janice Houghton-Wallace
○   *B; to conserve & promote the standards breeds of turkey; to
        encourage & assist with advice anyone wishing to keep
        turkeys; to establish a higher profile for the turkey as an
        exhibition bird & utility species of poultry (provider of eggs &
        meat)
Gp   Breeders of the original standard breeds of turkey
●   ET - Exhib - Comp - Inf - VE
<   Poultry Club of GB
M   200 i
¶   NL - 4;   Ybk - 1; both ftm only.
        a turkey column in 'Fancy Fowl' - 12.

Turkish-British Chamber of Commerce & Industry
■   Bury House (2nd floor), 33 Bury St, LONDON, SW1Y 6AU.
        (hq)
        020 7321 0999
        http://www.tbcci.org
○   *C
        No further information supplied

Turner Society   1975
■   BCM Box Turner, LONDON, WC1N 3XX.   (mail address)
        http://www.turnersociety.org.uk
▲   Registered Charity
○   *A; to promote interest in the life, work & influence of the
        painter J M W Turner (1775-1851)
●   Mtgs - VE
M   c 500 i & org, UK / c 100 i & org, o'seas
¶   Turner Society News - 3; ftm only.

© CBD Research Ltd · Beckenham · BR3 5JS · Tel 020 8650 7745 · Fax 020 8650 0768 · E-mail cbd@cbdresearch.com · www.cbdresearch.com

Turner Syndrome Support Society (UK) (TSSS) 1979
NR   13 Simpson Court, 11 South Avenue, Clydebank Business Park,
        CLYDEBANK, G81 2NR.   (hq)
        0141-952 8006   fax 0141-952 8025
        email turner.syndrome@tss.org.uk
        http://www.tss.org.uk
        Exec Officer: Arlene Smyth
▲   Registered Charity
○   *W; information & support for those who have Turner syndrome
        (genetic abnormality incl short stature & lack of ovarian
        function, it affects only females & is caused by complete, or
        partial deletion, of the X chromosome in some, or all cells, of
        the body) their families & health professionals involved in
        their care
●   Conf - Mtgs - ET - Res - Comp - Inf
        Helpline: 0845 230 7520
M   750 i, 20 org, UK / 10 i, o'seas
¶   Turner Syndrome - lifelong guidance & support;
        Talking About Turner Syndrome (video);
            both minimum donation £5 (UK), £10 (o'seas).
        Talking About Turner Syndrome (booklet); minimum donation
            £1 (UK), £3 (o'seas).
        Information leaflets: publications list available.

Twentieth Century Society   1979
■   70 Cowcross St, LONDON, EC1M 6EJ.   (hq)
        020 7250 3857   fax 020 7251 8985
        email administrator@c20society.org.uk
        Dir: Catherine Croft
▲   Registered Charity
○   *G; preservation of architecture (post 1914); to stimulate public
        interest in the subject
●   Conf - ET - Res - VE
M   1,950 i, 50 f, 50 org, UK / 60 i, o'seas
        (Sub: £35 i, £180 f, £90 org, UK / £42 i, o'seas)
¶   Jnl - 1; ftm, £20 nm.   NL - 3; ftm, £4.50 nm.

TWI Ltd
        trading name of the **Welding Institute**

Twins & Multiple Births Association   (TAMBA)   1978
■   2 The Willows, Gardner Rd, GUILDFORD, Surrey, GU1 4PG.
        (hq)
        0870 770 3305   fax 0870 770 3303
        email enquiries@tamba.org.uk
        http://www.tamba.org.uk
        Dir: Keith Reed
▲   Registered Charity
○   *W; to provide information & mutual support networks for
        families of twins, triplets & more, highlighting their unique
        needs to all involved in their care
Gp   Supertwins; Infertility; Bereavement; One parent families;
        Special needs; Support groups
●   Conf - Mtgs - ET - Res - SG - Inf - PL
<   Intl Soc for Twin Studies
M   6,000 families
¶   Twins, Triplets & More - 4; ftm, £2.50 nm.   AR.
        Specialist Support Group NLs - irreg.

Tyre Industry Council
        since 2008 **TyreSafe**

Tyre Recovery Association   (TRA)   2004
NR   6 Bath Place, Rivington St, LONDON, EC2A 3JE.
        020 7457 5040   fax 020 7972 9008
        email info@tyrerecovery.org.uk
        http://www.tyrerecovery.org.uk
        Sec: Peter Taylor
○   *T

Tyre Wholesalers Group
        a committee of the **National Tyre Distributors Association**

TyreSafe   1989
NR   6 Bath Place, Rivington Place, LONDON, EC2A 3JE.   (hq)
        020 7457 5016
        http://www.tyresafety.org
▲   Un-incorporated Society
○   *T; improving tyre safety awareness
●   Mtgs - ET - Res - Stat - Inf - PL - LG
<   Brit Rubber Mfrs Assn; Imported Tyre Mfrs Assn
¶   Annual Report; free.
✕   2008 Tyre Industry Council

UK ...

see **United Kingdom ...**

[All organisations whose names begin with 'UK' or 'United Kingdom'
are printed & filed as 'United Kingdom' to avoid the confusion of two
separate sequences]

UK EInformation Group   (UKeiG)   1978

- ■ The Old Chapel - Walden, West Burton, LEYBURN, N Yorks,
  DL8 4LE.   (admin/hq)
  01969 663749   fax 01969 663749
  email info@ukeig.co.uk   http://www.ukeig.co.uk
  Hon Sec: Christine A Baker
- ▲ Registered Charity
- ○ *P; to encourage communication & the exchange of knowledge
  about electronic information
- ● Conf - ET - Inf
- < is a special interest group (SIG) of CILIP
- M 1,650 i, 105 f, UK / 50 i, o'seas
- ¶ eLucidate (Jnl) - 6; ftm only.
- ✕ 2004-05 UK Online User Group

UK Organisation for Cranial Osteopathy

see the **Sutherland Society (the UK organisation for cranial
osteopathy**

UKinbound   1977

- ■ 388 The Strand (3rd floor), LONDON, WC2R 0LT.   (hq)
  020 7395 7500   fax 020 7240 6618
  http://www.ukinbound.org
  Chief Exec: Stephen Dowd
- ○ *T; representing tour operators & suppliers to Britain
- ● Conf - Mtgs - ET - Exhib - Stat
- M 250 f
- ¶ Hbk & LM - 1.
- ✕ 2004 (November) British Incoming Tour Operators Association

UKRIGS

see **National Association of UK Regionally Important
Geological Sites**

UKspace   1975

- ■ PO Box 423, FLEET, Hants, GU51 9BD.   (hsb)
  email secgenukspace@btinternet.com
  http://www.sbac.co.uk
  Sec Gen: Paul Flanagan
- ▲ Un-incorporated Society
- ○ *N, *T; to grow the share of the global space market; to
  promote greater awareness of commercial space in
  government & media; to provide the primary forum for the
  space industry to dialogue with government & shareholders
- Gp Sector C'ees; Earth observation; Navigation; Research &
  technology; Satellite telecoms
- ● Conf - Mtgs - SG - Expt - LG
- < Eurospace; Intellect; Soc Brit Aerospace Cos
- M 19 f
- ¶ Brochures & policy papers - irreg; all ftm.
- ✕ 2006 United Kingdom Industrial Space Committee

Ukulele Society of Great Britain

- NR 43 Finstock Rd, LONDON, W10 6LU.   (sp)
  020 8960 0459
  email m@gicman.com   http://www.usgb.co.uk
  Sec: Fred Pearson
- ▲ Un-incorporated Society
- ○ *D; for all interested in the playing of ukuleles & ukulele banjos
- M i
  No further information supplied.

Ulster Angling Federation   (UAF)   1937

- NR 6 Beech Green, Doagh, BALLYCLARE, Co Antrim, BT39 0QB
  (asst/sp)
  028 9334 0884   fax 028 9334 0884
  email phyllis.glenn@lineone.net
  Assistant Sec: Phyllis Glenn,   Hon Sec: Allan Kilgore
  Devt Officer: Newell McCreight (028 9084 4636)
- ▲ Company Limited by Guarantee
- ○ *S; representative body for game angling in Northern Ireland;
  to conserve the aquatic environment; to prevent water
  pollution
- ● Mtgs - ET - Inf - LG
- < N Atlantic Salmon Consvn Org; Salmon & Trout Assn;
  Countryside Alliance
- M 10,000 i, 80 clubs
- ¶ The Ulster Angler - 1; ftm.

Ulster Archaeological Society   (UAS)   1935

- ■ c/o School of Geography, Archaeology & Palaeoecology,
  Queen's University Belfast, 42 Fitzwilliam St, BELFAST,
  BT9 6AX.   (mail/add)
  http://www.uarcsoc.org
  Hon Sec: K Pullin
- ▲ Registered Charity
- ○ *L; to further in every way the study of the past, particularly in
  Ulster
- Gp Field survey
- ● Mtgs - Lectures - Fieldtrips
- M c 300 i
  (Sub: £15)
- ¶ Ulster Jnl of Archaeology - 1; ftm, £15 nm.
  NL - 4; ftm only.

Ulster Architectural Heritage Society   (UAHS)   1967

- ■ 66 Donegall Pass, BELFAST, BT7 1BU.   (hq)
  028 9055 0213   fax 028 9055 0214
  email info@uahs.org.uk   http://www.uahs.org.uk
  Chmn: Peter O Marlow,   Hon Sec: Séan Hagan
- ▲ Company Limited by Guarantee; Registered Charity
- ○ *A, *K, *L; to promote & encourage appreciation of good
  architecture of all periods (from prehistoric to the
  contemporary) in the nine counties of Ulster; to encourage
  the preservation & restoration of buildings of merit or
  importance; to increase the public awareness of the beauty,
  history & character of local neighbourhoods
- ● Conf - Mtgs - ET - Res - SG - Inf - Lib - VE - LG
- M 1,200 i
- ¶ Books, Monographs, Essays, Lists & Surveys; £2-£24.
  List of publications available.

Ulster Automobile Club Ltd   (UAC)   1925

- ■ 29 Shore Rd, HOLYWOOD, Co Down, BT18 9HX.   (hq)
  028 9042 6262   fax 028 9042 1818
  email office@ulsterautomobileclub.co.uk
  http://www.ulsterautomobileclub.co.uk
  Hon Sec: Tom Allison
- ▲ Company Limited by Guarantee
- ○ *S; organisation promotion of motor sport events
- Gp Communications team (radio); Competitions c'ee (event
  organisation)
- ● Comp - VE
- < Fédn Intle des Véhicules Anciens (FIVA); Motor Sports Assn -
  UK (MSA-UK); Assn of NI Car Clubs (ANICC)
- M 250 i, UK / 30 i, o'seas
- ¶ Wheelspin - 2; ftm, on request, nm.

Ulster Chemists' Association   (UCA)   1901
- ■ 5 Annandale Avenue, BELFAST, BT7 3JH.   (hq)
      028 9069 0456   fax 028 9059 0457
      http://www.uca.org.uk
      Sec: Adrienne Clugston
- ▲ Un-incorporated Society
- ○ *P, *T; for retail pharmacy in Northern Ireland
- ● Conf - Mtgs - ET - Inf - Liaison with trade - Assistance to small
      businesses
- < Nat Pharmaceutical Assn
- M 487 i
- ¶ NI Pharmacy in Focus - 12; ftm only.

Ulster Coarse Fishing Federation   (UCFF)   1975
- ■ 29 Georgian Villas, OMAGH, Co Tyrone, BT79 0AT.   (hsp)
      028 8224 5363
      email victor.refausse@swc.ac.uk
      Hon Sec: Victor Refausse
- ▲ Un-incorporated Society
- ○ *S; to promote & develop coarse angling in Northern Ireland
- ● ET - Comp - LG
- < Nat Coarse Fishing Fedn of Ireland
- M 500 i, 10 org
- ¶ Calendar of Events - 1; £2.50.

Ulster Farmers Union   (UFU)   1918
- ■ 475 Antrim Rd, BELFAST, BT15 3DA.   (hq)
      028 9037 0222   fax 028 9037 1231
      email info@ufuhq.com   http://www.ufuhq.com
      Chief Exec: Clarke Black
- ▲ Un-incorporated Society
- Br 25
- ○ *F; to defend the rights & promote the interests of farmers
- ● Conf - Mtgs - ET - Res - SG - Stat - Inf - Lib - LG
- M 12,000 i
- ¶ Farming News - 5.

Ulster Federation of Rambling Clubs   (UFRC)   1980
- ■ 10 Strangford Ave, BELFAST, BT9 6PG.   (chmn/p)
      028 9266 6358
      email secretary@ufrc-online.co.uk
      http://www.ufrc-online.co.uk
      Hon Sec: Ronnie Carser
- ▲ Un-incorporated Society
- ○ *S; 'to encourage recreational walking, appreciation & respect
      for the countryside'
- ● Mtgs - ET - LG
- < Ramblers' Assn
- M 29 org

Ulster Folk Life Society   (UFLS)   1961
- NR c/o Ulster Folk & Transport Museum, Cultra, HOLYWOOD,
      Co Down, BT18 0EU.   (mail address)
      Hon Sec: Mrs Hilary Maginnis
- ▲ Registered Charity
- ○ *L; study of the folklife, customs & traditions of Ulster
- ● VE
- M c 100 i
- ¶ Ulster Folklife (Jnl) - 1.

Ulster Genealogical & Historical Guild
      the membershp body of the **Ulster Historical Foundation**

Ulster Historical Foundation   (UHF)   1956
- ■ Cotton Court, 30 Waring St, BELFAST, BT1 2ED.   (hq)
      028 9033 2288   fax 028 9023 9885
      email enquiry@uhf.org.uk
      http://www.ancestryireland.com
      Exec Dir: Fintan Mullan
- ▲ Registered Charity
- ○ *P, *Q; publishers of Irish historical, genealogical, educational
      & academic texts; also genealogical research professionals
      offering bespoke research services
- Gp Genealogical researchers; Publications; GU membership,
      accounts & administration; Sales & marketing
- ● Conf - ET - Res - Inf - VE - Publishing
- < Fedn of Families Hist Socs; Family Hist Coun (Republic of
      Ireland); Brit Assn of Ir Studies
- M 800 i, 20 org, UK / 1,000 i, 25 org, o'seas
      (Sub: £30)
- ¶ Familia: Ulster Genealogical Review - 1; ftm, £5.99 m.
      Directory of Irish Family History - 1; fm, £6.99 nm.
      The foundation's mambership body is the Ulster Genealogical
      & Historical Guild

Ulster Launderers Association   (ULA)   1912
- NR Standard Laundry, 475-477 Antrim Rd, BELFAST, BT12 6LU.
      (hsb)
      028 9062 7295
      Hon Sec: Geoffrey Wood
- ○ *T; interests of commercial launderers & cleaners in N Ireland
- ● Mtgs - SG - LG
- M 6 f

Ulster Place-Name Society   (UPNS)   1952
- NR Irish & Celtic Studies, Sch of Languages Literatures & Arts,
      Queen's University, BELFAST, BT17 1NN.
      028 9097 3689   fax 028 9097 5298
      email townlands@qub.ac.uk
      http://www.ulsterplacenames.org
- ○ *L; to undertake a survey of Ulster place-names
- ¶ Ainm (jnl)

Ulster-Scots Language Society   (USLS)   1992
- NR 68-72 Great Victoria St (2nd floor), BELFAST, BT2 7BB.
      028 9043 6716
      email usls@ulster-scots.com   http://www.ulster-scots.com
- ▲ Registered Charity
- ○ *L; to record, promote & uphold the use of Ulster-Scots
      language in writing, education & speech; to promote Ulster-
      Scots cultural traditions
- M c 250 i, UK / c 50 i, o'seas
- ¶ Ullans (Jnl) - 1.

Ulster Society of Organists & Choirmasters   1918
- NR 8c Beechwood House, Woolland Drive, NEWTOWNABBEY,
      Co Antrim, BT37 9SF.   (hsb)
      http://www.dnausers/dnetzMNU/usoc
      Hon Secs: Stephen & Carolyn Hamill
- ▲ Un-incorporated Society
- ○ *D; to promote the interests of church musicians
- ● Conf - Mtgs - ET - VE
- < Inc Assn Organists (UK)
- M 180 i
- ¶ NL - 12; m only.

**Ulster Society for Prevention of Cruelty to Animals   (USPCA)
1836**
- ■   PO Box 103, BELFAST, BT6 8US.   (hq)
    028 3083 0361   fax 028 3083 0024
    email enquiries@uspca.co.uk   http://www.uspca.co.uk
    Chief Exec: Stephen Philpott
- ▲   Company Limited by Guarantee; Registered Charity
- ○   *K, *V; care & prevention of cruelty to animals through
    education & inspectorate vigilance
- ●   ET - VE - Shelters for homeless animals
- <   Wld Soc Protection of Animals
- M   1,000 i
    (Sub: £10)
- ¶   AR; free.

**Ulster Society for the Protection of the Countryside   (USPC)
2537**
- ■   22 Donegall Rd, BELFAST, BT12 5JN.   (hq)
    028 9024 9006
    email uspcinfo@tiscali.co.uk
    Hon Sec: Ian Lamont
- ▲   Un-incorporated Society
- ○   *K, *N; to safeguard the beauty of Northern Ireland; to
    campaign for the protection of Northern Ireland's countryside
- Gp   Access the Countryside
- ●   Conf - Mtgs - Exhib - Inf - LG
- <   NI Envt Link
- >   Cyclists' Touring Club of NI; Ulster Fedn of Rambling Clubs;
    Youth Hostel Assn of NI
- M   240 i, 5 org
- ¶   The USPC Countryside Recorder (NL) - 2;   AR; both free.

Ulster Teachers' Union   (UTU)   1919
- ■   94 Malone Rd, BELFAST, BT9 5HP.   (hq)
    028 9066 2216   fax 028 9066 3055
    email office@utu.edu   http://www.utu.edu
    Gen Sec: Avril Hall-Callaghan
- ○   *P, *U
- ●   Conf - Mtgs - ET
- <   ICTU
- M   6,500 i
- ¶   UTU News - 4;   NL - 12;   AR; all free.

Ulster Women's Hockey Union   (UWHU)   1896
- ■   The Hockey Office, The House of Sport, Upper Malone Rd,
    BELFAST, BT9 5LA.   (hq)
    028 9038 3818   fax 028 9068 2757
    email lorrainethompson@houseofsport.net
    http://www.hockeyulster.org
    Hon Sec: Mrs Norma Gartside
- ▲   Un-incorporated Society
- ○   *S; governing body of the sport
- ●   Administration of women's hockey
- <   Ir Hockey Assn
- M   51 clubs

Undeb Badminton Cymru
    Welsh name of the **Welsh Badminton Union**

UNIFI
    since 2004 the finance & business services sector of Amicus, now
    Unite the Union

Union of Country Sports Workers   (UCSW)   1977
- ■   PO Box 129, BANBURY, Oxon, OX17 2HX.   (hsp)
    01295 712719   fax 01295 712719
    email office@ucsw.org   http://www.ucsw.org
    Chmn: Alex Ford,   Sec/Admin: Phillippa White
- ○   *U; to represent anyone employed in country sports, either
    directly or indirectly, full-time or part-time
- ●   Empl - LG - Stands at country fairs, game fairs - Lobbying
- M   4,500 i
- ¶   Livin' Country - 3; ftm, £2 nm.

Union of Democratic Mineworkers   (UDM)   1985
- NR   Berry Hill Lane, MANSFIELD, Notts, NG18 4JU.   (hq)
    01623 626094   fax 01623 642300
    Nat Pres: N Greatrex,   Gen Sec: M L Stevens
- ○   *U; operating in the UK coal mining industry
- M   i

Union for Education Professionals
    alternative name of **Voice**

Union of Senior Revenue Officials
    since 2005 the **Association of Revenue and Customs**

Union of Shop, Distributive & Allied Workers   (USDAW)   1947
- ■   188 Wilmslow Rd, MANCHESTER, M14 6LJ.   (hq)
    0161-224 2804
    Gen Sec: John Hannett
- ○   *U; interests of workers in retail, distribution & manufacturing
- M   c 360,000 i
- ¶   Arena (Jnl) - 4.

Union of UK Unicyclists   (UUU)   2001
- NR   24 Park Parade, CAMBRIDGE, CB5 8AL.
    http://www.unicycle.org.uk
    Chmn: Paul Royle
- ○   *S

Union of UK Unicyclists   (UUU)   2001
- NR   40 Park Hill Court, Beeches Rd, LONDON, SW17 7LX.
    (chmn/p)
    email chairperson@unicycle.org.uk
    Chmn: Paul Royle
- ○   *S; to promote all unicycle events; to further recognition of the
    sport
- ●   Mtgs - ET - Exam - Events
- M   i, clubs

Union of Women Teachers
    see **National Association Schoolmasters Union of Women
    Teachers**

Unison   (UNISON)   1993
- NR   1 Mabledon Place, LONDON, WC1H 9AJ.   (hq)
    0845 355 0845
    Gen Sec: Dave Prentis
- ○   *U
- M   i

Unitarian Historical Society   (UHS)   1915
- NR   223 Upper Lisburn Rd, BELFAST, BT10 0LL.   (hq)
    Sec: Rev David Steers
- ○   *L; study of history of Unitarian & kindred movements;
    preservation of records & antiquities
- M   i & libraries
- ¶   Transactions - 1.

Unite - CMA Sector
    a sector of **Unite the Union**

Unite: the National Federation of Royal Mail & BT Pensioners
- ■   Unit 6 Imperial Court, Laporte Way, LUTON, Beds, LU4 8FE.
    01582 721652   fax 01582 450906
    email info@pensioneronline.com
    http://www.pensioneronline.com
    Nat Chmn: Jill Ipey
- ○   *U
- M   102,569 i, UK / 225 i, o'seas
- ¶   Unite - 12; £1.10.

© CBD Research Ltd · Beckenham · BR3 5JS · Tel 020 8650 7745 · Fax 020 8650 0768 · E-mail cbd@cbdresearch.com · www.cbdresearch.com

Unite the Union (Amicus section)
NR   35 King St, Covent Garden, LONDON, WC2E 8JG.   (hq)
       0845 850 4242
       http://www.unitetheunion.org.uk
       Gen Sec: Derek Simpson
○   *U; to improve members' standard of living & quality of life
       through efficient relationships with employers & government
Gp   Aerospace; Chemicals & pharmaceuticals; Civil air transport;
       Community & not for profit; Construction & contracting;
       Education; Electrical engineering, electronics & IT; Energy;
       Equalities; Finance & business services; Food, drink &
       tobacco; FPA (Fedn of Profl Assns) - for professional &
       managerial staff); General industries; Graphical, paper &
       media; Guild of Healthcare Pharmacists; Health; Local
       authorities; MoD & government depts; Motor components;
       Motor vehicles; Process including offshore oil & gas;
       Railways, buses & ferries; Servicing; Shipbuilding; Steel,
       metals & foundry; Unite - CMA Sector (for communications
       profls)
M   i
×   2004 (Amicus-MSF
              (Graphical, Paper & Media Union
              (Manufacturing Science & Finance Union
              (UNIFI (all merged as Amicus)
       2007 (Amicus
              (Transport & General Workers' Union (merging)

Unite the Union (T&G section)
NR   Transport House, 128 Theobald's Rd, LONDON, WC1X 8TN.
       (hq)
       020 7611 2500   fax 020 7611 2555
       email tgwu@tgwu.org.uk
       http://www.unitetheunion.org.uk
       Gen Sec: Tony Woodley
○   *U
Gp   Food & agriculture; Manufacturing; Services; Transport;
       Women, race & equalities
M   i
×   2007 (Transport & General Workers' Union
              (Amicus (merging)

United Chiropractic Association   (UCA)   2000
■   17 Fore St, IVYBRIDGE, Devon, PL21 9AB.   (hq)
       01752 896223   fax 01752 896223
       email admin@united-chiropractic.org
       http://www.united-chiropractic.org
       Contact: Melissa Sandford
○   *M, *P; to represent principle-centred chiropractic (wellness
       based)
●   Conf - Mtgs - ET - Res
M   150 i, UK / 10 i, o'seas

United Counties Agricultural Society   1895
■   The Showground, Nantyci, CARMARTHEN, SA33 5DR.   (hq)
       01267 232141   fax 01267 221884
▲   Registered Charity
○   *F, *H; covers Cardiganshire, Carmarthenshire &
       Pembrokeshire
●   Exhibitions & shows

United Grand Lodge of England
NR   Freemasons' Hall, 60 Great Queen St, LONDON,
       WC2B 5AA.   (hq)
       020 7539 2930
○   *G

**United Kingdom Acquired Brain Injury Forum   (UKABIF)
1998**
■   PO Box 355, PLYMOUTH, Devon, PL3 4WD.   (mail)
       01752 601318
       email ukabif@btconnect.com   http://www.ukabif.org.uk
       Chmn: Prof Mike Barnes,   Exec Offr: Chloë Hammond
▲   Registered Charity
○   *K, *L; the advancement of education in the subject of children
       & adults with acquired brain injury; the relief of disability of
       people with acquired brain injury, by education rather than
       as a provider of direct services
●   Conf - Mtgs - ET - Inf - LG
M   100 i, 150 f
       Subs: £25 i, £75 f.
¶   Directory of Rehabilitation Services;
       NL - 4;   AR;   all ftm.

United Kingdom Alliance   (UKA)   1853
NR   176 Blackfriars Rd, LONDON, SE1 8ET.   (hsb)
       07985 011029
       email douglas.sinclair@ntlworld.com
       Gen Sec: Douglas Sinclair
○   *K; advising on the dangers of alcohol & drug abuse
●   Conf - Comp - Seminars for senior school pupils in House of
       Commons committee rooms
M   c 400 i
¶   AR; ftm, £2 nm.

United Kingdom Alliance of Dance Teachers   (UKA)   1902
■   Centenary House, 38-40 Station Rd, BLACKPOOL, Lancs,
       FY4 1EU.   (hq)
       01253 408828   fax 01253 408066
       email info@ukadance.co.uk
       http://www.ukadance.co.uk
       Chief Exec: David Roberts
▲   Company Limited by Guarantee
○   *D; to further the development of dance & movement in all its
       forms; to provide a syllabus & examination service
●   Conf - Mtgs - ET - Exam - Exhib - Comp - SG - Inf - LG
<   Brit Coun of Ballroom Dancing; Scot Official Bd Highland
       Dancing; Brit Keep Fit Confedn; Stage Dance Coun; CCPR;
       Coun for Dance Educ & Trg (CDET)
M   i

**United Kingdom Alliance of Wedding Planners   (UKAWP)
2006**
NR   7 Churchfield Rd, COGGESHALL, Essex, CO6 1QE.
       (co-fdr/b)
       01376 561544
       email info@ukawp.com   http://www.ukawp.com
       Co-founder: Bernadette Chapman
▲   Company Limited by Guarantee
○   *P; to promote professionalism in wedding planning
M   22 f (full & associate)

**United Kingdom Aluminium Packaging Recycling Organisation
(Alupro)   1989**
■   1 Brockhill Court, Brockhill Lane, REDDITCH, Worcs,
       B97 6RB.   (hq)
       01527 597757   fax 01527 594140
       http://www.alupro.org.uk
○   *T; to promote recycling of aluminium foil & cans working with
       local authorities & private sector companies
●   Conf - Mtgs - ET - Res - Comp - Stat - PL - Provision of
       educational materials to schools, groups etc to set up a
       recycling initiative
M   350 centres
¶   Campaign NL - 4; ftm, on application nm.

United Kingdom eHealth Association   (UKeHA)   1999
NR   5 Ashbury Drive, Hawley, CAMBERLEY, Surrey, GU17 9HH
        (treas/p)
        01276 35130   fax 01276 37193
        email treasurer@ukeha.co.uk   http://www.ukeha.co.uk
        Treas: Mike McCurry
▲   Company Limited by Guarantee
○   *P; to encourage improvement in health care delivery through
        the application of telecommunications technology
M   90 i & f
✕   UK Telemedicine Association

United Kingdom Association of Cancer Registries
NR   National Cancer Intelligence Centre, Office for National
        Statistics, 1 Drummond Gate, LONDON, SW1V 2QQ.   (asa)
        020 7533 5257
        Co Chmn: Dr Anna Gavin,   Dr Monica Roche
○   *W; to provide a complete coverage of cancer data

United Kingdom Association of Celebrity Assistants
        see **Association of Celebrity Assistants (UK)**

United Kingdom Association for European Law   1974
■   King's College London, Strand, LONDON, WC2R 2LS.   (hq)
        020 7722 9746
        email eva.evans@kcl.ac.uk   http://www.ukael.org
        Admin: Mrs Eva Evans,   Pres: Sir Christopher Bellamy
▲   Registered Charity
○   *P
●   Conf
<   Fédn Intle du Droit Européen (FIDE)
M   200 i, 20 f, UK / 35 i, o'seas
¶   Conference publications - irreg.

United Kingdom Association of the FIS
        since 2003 a sector of the **Agricultural Industries Confederation**

**United Kingdom Association of Fish Meal Manufacturers
        (AFMM)   1917**
NR   c/o United Fish Products Ltd, Greenwell Place, ABERDEEN,
        AB12 3AY.   (hq)
        01225 854444
        email secretariat@iffo.net
○   *T; the production & use of fish meal & fish oil in the UK

**United Kingdom Association of Fish Producer Organisations
        (UKAFPO)   1988**
■   2 St Wilfred Rd, BRIDLINGTON, E Yorks, YO16 4DJ.   (hsp)
        07742 252033
        email sue.willson@fishproducers.org
        Sec: Mrs S J Willson
▲   Friendly Society
○   *N, *T; to promote & develop cooperation between & the
        interests of fish producer organisations, both in the UK &
        other parts of the EU
●   Mtgs - LG
M   9 f

**United Kingdom Association of Frozen Food Producers
        (UKAFFP)   1959**
NR   6 Catherine St, LONDON, WC2B 5JJ.   (hq)
        020 7420 7180
▲   Un-incorporated Society
○   *T; represents the interests of frozen food manufacturers
        especially in the field of legislation
M   f
¶   RFIC Guide to the Storage & Handling of Frozen Foods.

**United Kingdom Association of Letting Agents   (UKALA)
        1997**
■   59 Mile End Rd, COLCHESTER, Essex, CO4 5BU.   (hq)
        01206 853741   fax 01206 851616
        email ukala@sys3internet.net   http://www.ukala.org.uk
        Gen Sec: John Peartree
▲   Company Limited by Guarantee
Br c 500
○   *T; for letting agents & managing agents
●   ET - Stat - LG
M   206 i, 206 f
¶   Letting Update (Jnl) - 4; ftm, £75 yr nm.

**United Kingdom Association of Manufacturers of Bakers' Yeast
        (UKAMBY)   1973**
■   6 Catherine St, LONDON, WC2B 5JJ.   (hq)
        020 7420 7109   fax 020 7836 0580
        email grace.foyle@fdf.org.uk
        Exec Sec: Grace Foyle
▲   Un-incorporated Society
○   *T
●   Mtgs
<   Comité des Fabricants de Levure de Panification de
        l'U Eur (COFALEC); Food & Drink Fedn
M   3 f

**United Kingdom Association of Preservation Trusts   (APT)
        1989**
NR   Alhambra House (9th floor), 27-31 Charing Cross Rd,
        LONDON, WC2H 0AU.   (hq)
        020 7930 1629
        Chmn: Colin Johns
        Co-ordinator: Louise Bailey
▲   Registered Charity
Br 9
○   *N; to encourage & assist building preservation trusts; to
        expand their capacity to preserve the built heritage
●   Conf - Mtgs - SG - Inf - LG
M   c 275 trusts
¶   NL - 2.   Guidance Notes - irreg.

**United Kingdom Association of Professional Engineers
        (UKAPE)   1969**
NR   Hayes Court, West Common Rd, HAYES, Kent, BR2 7AU.   (hq)
        020 8462 7755
        http://www.ukape.org
○   *U; interests of engineers holding management, executive,
        supervisory, design & research appointments
M   i

**United Kingdom Association of Proposal Management
        Professionals   (UKAPMP)   2001**
NR   3 North Street Workshops, STOKE sub HAMDON, Somerset,
        TA14 6QR.   (chiefexec/b)
        01935 825200
        Chief Exec Officer: Pat Thomas
Br Netherlands, USA
○   *P; 'to advance the arts, sciences & technology of new business
        acquisition & to promote the professionalism of those
        engaged in those pursuits'
●   Conf - Mtgs - ET - Exam - Res - Exhib - Stat - Inf - LG
M   c 200 i, UK / c 1,600 i, o'seas
¶   Jnl - 2; ftm only.

United Kingdom Association of Suggestion Schemes
        alternative name of **Ideas UK**

United Kingdom Athletics Ltd   (UKA)   1991
NR   Athletics House, Central Boulevard, Blythe Valley Park,
        SOLIHULL, B90 8AJ.   (hq)
        0121-713 8400   fax 0121-713 8452
▲   Company Limited by Guarantee
○   *S; governing body for track & field athletics
M   clubs

© CBD Research Ltd · Beckenham · BR3 5JS · Tel 020 8650 7745 · Fax 020 8650 0768 · E-mail cbd@cbdresearch.com · www.cbdresearch.com

United Kingdom Bartenders Guild (UKBG) 1933

■ Rosebank, Blackness, LINLITHGOW, W Lothian, EH49 7NL. (admin/p)
01506 834448 fax 01506 834373
Admin Officer: Jim Slavin
▲ Un-incorporated Society
Br 4; 1 o'seas
○ *P; interests of bartenders
● Mtgs - ET - Exam - Exhib - Comp
< Intl Bartenders' Assn
M 600 i, UK / 15 i, o'seas

United Kingdom Bodybuilding & Fitness Federation (UKBFF)

NR PO Box 231, Waterloo, LIVERPOOL, L22 9WW. (admin)
0151-931 4090
email admin@ukbff.co.uk http://www.ukbff.co.uk
Admin: Wanda Tierney
▲ Company Limited by Guarantee
○ *S
< Intl Fedn of Body Builders (IFBB)

United Kingdom Botswana Society (UKBS) 1980

NR 29 Tournay Rd, LONDON, SW6 7UG. (hsp)
020 7385 7031
Hon Sec: Mrs Fay Pearson, Chmn: M R B Williams
▲ Un-incorporated Society
○ *X; to encourage & strengthen ties between Britain & Botswana
● Mtgs
M 380 i, 10 f, UK / 5 i, o'seas
¶ NL - 4; ftm only.

United Kingdom Brain Tumour Society
since 2004 **Brain Tumour UK**

United Kingdom Bungee Club 1989

NR Magna Science Adventure Centre, Sheffield Rd,
Templeborough, ROTHERHAM, S Yorks, S60 1DX. (hq)
07000 286433 fax 01924 849452
email enquiries@ukbungee.co.uk
http://www.ukbungee.co.uk
Dir: Jon Nicholls
Br 2
○ *G, *S; 'thrill-seeking, fun, overcoming your fears'; for all
interested in bungee jumping (filming, stunt jumpers &
riggers); the group does not accept people with high blood
pressure, heart or neurological conditions, dizziness /
epilepsy, pregnancy, asthma, or diabetes
< CityPaintball.com
M 30,000 i

United Kingdom Cartridge Remanufacturers Association (UKCRA) 1994

NR 1a Sandwich St, Walken, Worsley, MANCHESTER, M28 3XN.
(asa)
01706 525050 fax 01706 647440
email info@ukcra.com http://www.ukcra.com
Sec: Laura Heywood
▲ Company Limited by Guarantee
○ *T; for remanufactures & component suppliers to the toner &
inkjet industry; to provide laser printer users with proven high
quality products that are cost effective & environmentally
friendly alternatives to imported toner cartridges
Gp Laser toner cartridge re-manufacters; Inkjet cartridge refillers
● Mtgs
M 2,000 i, 40 f
✕ 2003 United Kingdom Cartridge Recyclers Association

United Kingdom Cast Stone Association (UKCSA) 1991

NR 15 Stone Hill Court, The Arbours, NORTHAMPTON,
NN3 3RA. (hq)
01604 405666
http://www.ukcsa.co.uk
▲ Un-incorporated Society
○ *T; for manufacturers of cast stone construction materials
M 8 f

United Kingdom Catamaran Racing Association (UKCRA)

NR 9 Daniels Court, Island Wall, WHITSTABLE, Kent, CT5 2AJ.
01227 282625
email dewhirst@btinternet.com
http://www.catamaran.co.uk
Chmn: Nick Dewhirst
○ *S

United Kingdom Charcuterie Guild 1989

■ Guild House, Station Rd, WINCANTON, Somerset, BA9 9FE.
(hq)
01963 824464 fax 01963 824651
email info@finefoodworld.co.uk
http://www.finefoodworld.co.uk
Nat Dir: Bob Farrand
○ *E; product training for staff involved in retailing charcuterie
● ET
< Gld of Fine Food Ltd
¶ Good Cheese Magazine - 1; £3.50.

United Kingdom Chasers & Riders Ltd 1999

NR St Tinnivers, Beckley, OXFORD, OX3 9UU. (hq)
01865 351688
email dt@ukchasers.com http://www.ukchasers.com
▲ Company Limited by Guarantee
Br 2
○ *G; 'to help you enjoy your horse more by providing riding
which is as varied, safe & enjoyable as possible. We provide
a nationwide network of xc courses & equestrian centres
providing competitions, facilities & safe off road riding for all
members'
● ET - Comp - Inf
M 30,000+ i, 50 farms & equestrian centres, 10 riding clubs
¶ UK Chasers Handbook - 1; ftm only.
NL & Competitions Calendar - 2; free.
Holidays with your Horse; free.

United Kingdom Cheese Guild & UK Charcuterie Guild 1989

■ Guild House, Station Rd, WINCANTON, Somerset, BA9 9FE.
(hq)
01963 824464 fax 01963 824651
email info@finefoodworld.co.uk
http://www.finefoodworld.co.uk
Nat Dir: Bob Farrand
○ *E; product training for staff involved in retailing cheese &
charcuterie
● ET
< Gld of Fine Food Ltd
¶ Good Cheese Magazine - 1; £3.50.

United Kingdom Chrysanthemum Growers' Association Ltd (UKCGA) 1966

■ 30 Pern Drive, Botley, SOUTHAMPTON, Hants, SO30 2GW.
(hsp)
01489 786638 fax 01489 798827
Sec: Mrs Veronica Mason
▲ Un-incorporated Society
○ *H, *T; for commercial chrysanthemum growers; to further
research
● Mtgs - SG
M 4 i, 12 f
¶ NL - irreg; LM; AR; all ftm.
✕ 2005 All Year Round Chrysanthemum Growers' Association

United Kingdom Cleaning Products Industry Association (UKCPI)
- ■ Century House (1st floor suite), Old Mill Place, TATTENHALL, Cheshire, CH3 9RJ.   (hq)
  01829 770055
  Dir-Gen: Dr Andrew N Williams
- ▲ Un-incorporated Society
- ○ *T; interests of UK producers of cleaning, hygiene & surface care products
- Gp Technical; Packaging; Legal; Industrial & institutional products
- ● Mtgs - Stat - Inf - LG - Detergent Industry Information Bureau
- < Assn Intle de la Savonnerie, de la Détergence et des Produits d'Entretien (AISE); Chemical Industries Assn (CIA)
- M c 45 f

United Kingdom Clinical Pharmacy Association   (UKCPA) 1981
- ■ Alpha House, Countesthorpe Rd, WIGSTON, Leics, LE18 4PJ. (hq)
  0116-277 6999   fax 0116-277 6272
  email admin@ukcpa.com   http://www.ukcpa.org
  Sec: Graeme Hall
- ▲ Un-incorporated Society
- ○ *M, *P; to foster the concepts & practice of pharmaceutical care for the benefit of patients & public
- Gp Cardiology; Community pharmacy; Critical care; Diabetes; Education & training; Emergency care; Gastroenterology / Hepatology, care of the elderly; Infection management; Leadership development; Pain management; Quality & risk management; Respiratory; Surgery & theatres
- ● Conf - Mtgs - ET - Res - Exhib - SG - Inf - LG
- M 2,000 i, 23 f, 4 hospitals, UK / 60 i, 1 hospital, o'seas
- ¶ In Practice (NL) - 4; ftm only.   Practice Guides; £2.50.
  Symposia Abstract Booklet - 2; ftm, £7 nm.

United Kingdom Coloured Pencil Society
- NR White Meadows, Horton, DEVIZES, Wilts, SN10 3DB.   (sp)
  http://www.ukcps.co.uk
  Sec: Pat Heffer
- ○ *A

United Kingdom Competitive Telecommunications Association (UKCTA)
- NR 10 Fitzroy Square, LONDON, W1T 5HP.
  0870 801 8000
- ○ *T; 'to foster a more competitive fixed telecommunications market in the UK'
- M f

United Kingdom Computer Measurement Group   (UKCMG) 1981
- ■ Kebbell House (suite A1), Carpenders Park, WATFORD, Herts, WD19 5BE.   (asa)
  020 8421 5330   fax 020 8421 5457
  email ukcmg@ukcmg.org.uk   http://www.ukcmg.org.uk
  Sec: Mike Ley
- ○ *P; for information technology professionals
- M i, f & org
- ¶ e NL.

United Kingdom Confederation of Hypnotherapy Organisations (UKCHO)   1998
- ■ Albany House (suite 404), 324-326 Regent St, LONDON, W1B 3HH.   (hq)
  0800 952 0560
  http://www.ukcho.org.uk
  Co Sec: Peter Matthews
- ▲ Company Limited by Guarantee
- ○ *N, *P
- < Conf - Mtgs - ET - Res - LG
- M 8 org
- ¶ NL - irreg.

United Kingdom Consortium for Photonics & Optics
- NR Geddes House, Kirkton North, LIVINGSTON, W Lothian, EH54 6GU.   (hq)
  01506 497228   fax 01506 497229
  http://www.ukcpo.org
  Sec: Chris Gracie
- ▲ Un-incorporated Society
- ○ *T

United Kingdom Council for Psychotherapy   (UKCP)   1992
- NR Edward House (2nd floor), 2 Wakley St, LONDON, EC1V 7LT.   (hq)
  020 7014 9955   fax 020 7014 9977
  email info@psychotherapy.org.uk
  http://www.psychotherapy.org.uk
  CEO: Valerie Tufnell
- ▲ Registered Charity
- ○ *P; to promote & maintain the profession of psychotherapy
- Gp Analytical psychology; Behavioural & cognitive psychotherapy; Experiential constructivist therapies; Family / couple / sexual & systemic therapy; Humanistic & integrative psychotherapy; Therapy with children
- ● Conf - Mtgs - ET - Inf - LG
- < Eur Assn for Psychotherapy; Brit Assn for Counselling
- M 6,500 i, 80 f
- ¶ The Psychotherapist (NL) - 2; ftm only.
  National Register of Psychotherapists - 1.
  Directory of Member Organisations & Training Courses - 1.

United Kingdom Dance & Drama Federation   (UKDDF)   1989
- NR 18 Ashbourne Grove, Hanley, STOKE-on-TRENT, Staffs, ST1 5QW.
  01782 257820
  email info@ukddf.co.uk   http://www.ukddf.co.uk
  Pres: Gloria Harrison
- ▲ Un-incorporated Society
- ○ *D; an examination body offering a full dance & drama syllabus for qualified & professional teachers of dance
- ● ET - Exam
- < Gld of Profl Teachers of Dancing; Hong Kong Jazz Soc
- > [all dance bodies & teacher orgs are able to join]
- M c 55 i
- ¶ NL - 4; m only.

United Kingdom Education & Research Networking Association
  the trading name of the JNT association, which since 2007 trades as JANET(UK);is not a membership body & is therefore outside the scope of this directory.

United Kingdom Egg Producers Association Ltd   (UKEP)   1972
- ■ Kings House, Maunsel Rd, North Newton, BRIDGWATER, Somerset, TA7 0BP.
  01278 661280   fax 01278 661009
  email ukep@chicken-doctor.demon.co.uk
  http://www.laidinbritaineggs.co.uk
  Sec: David Spackman
- ▲ Company Limited by Guarantee
- ○ *T; for British egg producers
- ● Stat - Inf - LG
- M 90 i
- ¶ UKEP/LIB Hotwire - 12; ftm only.

United Kingdom Employee Assistance Professionals Association (UKEAPA)   1991
- NR 3 Moors Close, Ducklington, WITNEY, Oxon, OX28 5HY.   (asa)
  0800 783 7616
  Sec: Jane Timms
- ○ *P; the advancement of education in the field of employee assistance programmes (EAPs); the encouragement of growth & development of EAPs in all workplaces
- M 100 i, 50 f

© CBD Research Ltd · Beckenham · BR3 5JS · Tel 020 8650 7745 · Fax 020 8650 0768 · E-mail cbd@cbdresearch.com · www.cbdresearch.com

United Kingdom Environmental Law Association (UKELA) 1986

- The Brambles, Cliftonville, DORKING, Surrey, RH4 2JF. (exec/dir)
  01306 501320
  email vicki-elcoate@ntworld.com   http://www.ukela.org
  Exec Dir: Vicki Elcoate
- ▲ Company Limited by Guarantee; Registered Charity
- ○ *L, *P; to promote the enhancement & conservation of the environment; to advance the education of the public relating to the development, teaching, application & practice of law relating to the environment
- Gp Climate change; Contaminated land; Environmental due diligence; Environmental litigation Northern Ireland; Insurance; NAaure conservation; Water
- ● Conf - Mtgs - ET - Res - SG - Inf
- < Eur Envtl Law Assn
- M [not stated]
- ¶ Environmental Law (Jnl) - 6; ftm only.   AR; free.

United Kingdom Environmental Mutagen Society (UKEMS) 1977

- NR 1 Atholl Place, EDINBURGH, EH3 8HP. (asa)
  email info@ukems.org   http://www.ukems.org
  Sec: Peter Jenkinson
- ▲ Registered Charity
- ○ *L; the advancement of genetic toxicology by research, discussion & developing methodology

United Kingdom Excellence Federation

no longer exists

United Kingdom Fashion Exports 1983

- 5 Portland Place, LONDON, W1B 1PW. (hq)
  020 7636 5577
  http://www.5portlandplace.org.uk
  Dir: Paul Alger
- ▲ Company Limited by Guarantee
- ○ *T; to promote UK exports of clothing & accessories
- ● Conf - Mtgs - ET - Exhib - Comp - Expt - Inf - Lib - Seminars
- M c 750 f
- ¶ The Exporter - 12.

United Kingdom Federation of Jazz Bands (UKFJB) 1977

- Wallsend Community Centre, Vine St, WALLSEND, Tyne & Wear, NE28 6JE. (hq)
  0191-262 8536   fax 0191-262 8536
  email m.paxton@ukjazzbands.com
  http://www.ukjazzbands.com
  Nat Sec & Chief Exec: Mrs Margaret Paxton
- ▲ Registered Charity
- Br 5
- ○ *D; 'to advance the musical education of children throughout the UK by helping to train them in the playing of marching band instruments & by means of concerts & exhibitions at which such children may perform as bands to advance the aesthetic education of the public'
- ● Mtgs - ET - Exhib - Comp - VE - LG
- M 6,940 i
- ¶ [on website only]

United Kingdom Federation of Smaller Mental Health Agencies 1996

- Findon House, 110 Ellis Rd, CROWTHORNE, Berks, RG45 6PH. (hsp)
  01344 772025
  email ukfed@ontheside.org   http://www.ukfed.org.uk
  Hon Sec: Tony Heyes
- ▲ Company Limited by Guarantee
- ○ *W; to support small mental health groups to work together by coordination & information
- ● Inf - LG
- M 30 i, 2200 org
- ¶ Small Voices (NL)

United Kingdom Flat Glass Manufacturers' Association
see **Flat Glass Manufacturers Association**

United Kingdom Forest Products Association (UKFPA) 1996

- NR Office 14 John Player Building, Stirling Enterprise Park, Springbank Rd, STIRLING, FK7 7RP. (hq)
  01786 449029   fax 01786 473112
  email dsulman@ukfpa.co.uk   http://www.ukfpa.co.uk
  Sec: David Sulman
- ▲ Company Limited by Guarantee
- ○ *T; to represent the British timber industry - harvesting companies, sawmillers, merchants & other processors of British home grown timber & forest products
- Gp Harvesting & contracting; Wood supply; Health & safety; Training; Environmental; Technical & devt
- ● Mtgs - ET - Res - Exhib - SG - Inf - VE - LG
- M 116 f
- ¶ LM;   AR - 1.

United Kingdom Fortifications Club
in 2008 amalgamated with the Pillbox Study Group to become the
Pillbox Study Group & United Kingdom Fortifications Club

United Kingdom Forum for Environmental Industries 2000

- NR c/o Gill Nowell, Envirolink Northwest, Spencer House, 91 Dewhurst Rd, Birchwood, WARRINGTON, Cheshire, WA3 7PG. (secretariat)
  01925 813200   fax 01925 819031
  email info@ukfei.co.uk   http://www.ukfei.co.uk
  Co-ordinator: Gill Nowell,   Chmn: Jackie Seddon
- ▲ Company Limited by Guarantee
- ○ *T; an informal group acting as a conduit for the environmental sector between regions & nations of the UK & central government
- Gp Sub-groups: Biomass, Exports, New markets for recyclates, Skills
- ● Mtgs - Expt - Inf - LG
- M RDA's/DA's, Trade Associations, Enabling bodies

United Kingdom Gout Society 2002

- NR PO Box 527, LONDON, WC1V 7YP.
  email info@ukgoutsociety.org
  http://www.ukgoutsociety.org

United Kingdom Hand Knitting Association (UKHKA) 1991

- NR Lloyds Bank Chambers, 43 Hustlergate, BRADFORD, W Yorks, BD1 1PH. (hq)
  01274 724235
  http://www.ukhandknitting.com
  Dir: Ann Thomson-Krol
- ○ *K, *T; to create a desire to knit
- ● Mtgs - ET - Res - Exhib
- M 9 f
- ¶ LM.
- × 2007 (January) British Hand Knitting Confederation

United Kingdom Harp Association (UKHA) 1964

- 27 Donovan Ave, Muswell Hill, LONDON, N10 2JU. (memsec/p)
  020 8365 2285
  http://www.ukharp.net
  Mem Sec: Philip Sefton
- ○ *P, *T; for harpists, harp makers & repairers & harp enthusiasts, includes players of non-pedal harps (the clarsach), Paraguayan harp & metal strung harps
- ● Mtgs - Inf
- M c 400 i, UK / c 100 i, o'seas
- ¶ Magazine - 4; £15 yr m.   Directory - 2 yrly; ftm only.

United Kingdom Homecare Association (UKHCA) 1988

NR Group House, 52 Sutton Court Rd, SUTTON, Surrey,
      SM1 4SL. (hq)
      020 8288 5291   fax 020 8288 5290
      email enquiries@ukhca.co.uk   http://www.ukhca.co.uk
      Chief Exec: Lesley Rimmer
▲ Company Limited by Guarantee
○ *N, *W; professional association to promote highest standards
      of domiciliary care
● Conf - Mtgs - ET - Exhib - LG
< Jt Advy Gp on Domiciliary Care; Nat Coun Voluntary Orgs
      (NCVO); Continuing Care Conference (CCC); Care Forum
      Wales; Indep Care Orgs Network (ICON)
M 1,600 f
¶ The Homecarer (NL) - 6; ftm.

United Kingdom Horse Shoers Union (UKHSU) 2002

■ 3 Roughdown Villas Road, HEMEL HEMPSTEAD, Herts,
      HP3 0AX.
      01442 248657
      Sec: Martin Humphrey
○ *U
      no further information supplied

United Kingdom Housekeepers Association (UKHA) 1985

■ Flat 7 / 14-15 Molyneux St, LONDON, W1H 5HQ. (hsp)
      fax 020 7724 7378
      email lynn.yambao@virgin.net   http://www.ukha.co.uk
      Sec: Lynn K D Yambao
Br 4
○ *P
● Conf - Mtgs
< Intl Exec Housekeepers Assn
M i
      (Sub: £30 i, £75 associates)

United Kingdom Industrial Space Committee
      since 2006 **UKspace**

United Kingdom Industrial Sugar Users Group (UKISUG)

■ 20-22 Stukeley St, LONDON, WC2B 5LR.
      020 7430 0356   fax 020 7831 6014
      email info@ukisug.org.uk   http://www.ukisug.org.uk
      Sec: Richard Laming
○ *T; for industrial users of sugar: manufacturers of confectionery,
      chocolate, cakes, biscuits, soft drinks, fruit juices & ice cream
● Mtgs
< C'ee Indl Users Sugar (CIUS)
M f

United Kingdom Industrial Vision Association (UKIVA) 1992

■ PO Box 25, ROYSTON, Herts, SG8 6TL.
      01763 261419   fax 01763 261961
      email info@ukiva.org   http://www.ukiva.org
      Admin: Don Braggins
▲ Company Limited by Guarantee
○ *T; to promote the use of vision technology by the
      manufacturing industry in Britain
M 40 f, UK / 3 f, o'seas
¶ NL - 2;   LM; both free.
      21 Financial Justifications for using Machine Vision.
      Guide to Machine Vision; free to qualifying applicants.

United Kingdom Institute for Conservation of Historic & Artistic Works
      *in 2005 merged with the Care of Collections Forum, Institute of Paper
      Conservation, Photographic Materials Conservation Group & Scottish
      Society for Conservation & Restoration to form the* **Institute of
      Conservation**

**United Kingdom & Ireland Society of Cataract & Refractive
Surgeons (UKISCRS)**

NR PO Box 598, STOCKTON-ON-TEES, Co Durham, TS20 1WY.
      (hq)
      01642 651208   fax 01642 651208
      email ukiscrs@onyxnet.co.uk   http://www.ukiscrs.org.uk
      The Secretary
▲ Company Limited by Guarantee
○ *P; promotion & dissemination of knowledge of cataract &
      refractive surgery to interested healthcare professionals
● Conf - Mtgs - ET
< Eur Soc of Cataract & Refractive Surgeons (ESCRS)
M 500 i
¶ Jnl of Cataract & Refractive Surgery - 12; ftm, priced nm.
      NL - 2; ftm only.

United Kingdom Irrigation Association (UKIA) 1980

■ c/o Moorland House, Hayway, RUSHDEN, Northants,
      NN10 6AG. (regd/off)
      01427 717627
      http://www.ukia.org
      Exec Sec: Melvyn Kay
▲ Company Limited by Guarantee
○ *F, *H
Gp Agriculture; Horticulture; Mains water; Sports turf & amenity
● Conf - Mtgs - ET - Inf - LG
M 350 i, UK / 50 i, o'seas
¶ Irrigation News (Jnl) - 2.
      Monographs (Conference Proceedings).

** **United Kingdom Jute Association**
      Organisation lost: see Introduction paragraph 3

**United Kingdom Land & Hydrographic Survey Association
(TSA) 1979**

NR Northgate Business Centre, 38 Northgate, NEWARK-on-TRENT,
      Notts, NG24 1EZ. (hq)
      01636 642840   fax 01636 642841
      email office@tsa-uk.org.uk   http://www.tsa-uk.org.uk
      Sec Gen: Rory Stanbridge
○ *T; to give a focus for private sector businesses in land &
      hydrographic survey
● Mtgs - Inf
M 120 f
¶ NL;   Members Directory; both free.
      Note: Is commonly known as The Survey Association

United Kingdom Literacy Association (UKLA) 1961

■ Attenborough Building (4th floor), University of Leicester,
      LEICESTER, LE1 7RH. (hq)
      email admin@ukla.org   http://www.ukla.org
      Hon Sec: Lyn Overall
▲ Registered Charity
○ *E; for professionals interested in the teaching & learning of
      language, literacy & communication
● Conf - ET - Res - Exhib - LG - Book awards
< Intl Reading Assn
M 500 i, 100 f, 80 schools
¶ Journal of Research in Reading - 3;   Literacy - 3;
      Language & Literacy News - 3; all ftm.

United Kingdom Locksmiths Association (UKLA) 2005

■ 370 Cranbrook Rd, Gants Hill, ILFORD, Essex, IG2 6HY.
      020 8590 7111   fax 020 8550 7703
      email info@uklocksmithsassociation.co.uk
      Sec: Adam Jackson
▲ Company Limited by Guarantee
○ *P; training students to become qualified locksmiths
● ET - Inf
M 200 i, 5 f
      (Sub: £175)
¶ via website.

© CBD Research Ltd · Beckenham · BR3 5JS · Tel 020 8650 7745 · Fax 020 8650 0768 · E-mail cbd@cbdresearch.com · www.cbdresearch.com

United Kingdom Lubricants Association Ltd   (UKLA)   1968
- ■ Berkhamsted House, 121 High St, BERKHAMSTED, Herts, HP4 2DJ.   (hq)
  01442 230589   fax 01442 259232
  email enquiries@ukla.org.uk   http://www.ukla.org.uk
  Exec Dir: Rod G Parker
- ▲ Company Limited by Guarantee
- ○ *T; for the UK lubricants industry
- Gp Metalworking Fluid Product Stewardship Gp
- ● Conf - Mtgs - Stat - Inf - VE - LG
- < Indep U of the Eur Lubricants Ind (UEIL)
- M 100 f, UK / 2 f, o'seas
- ¶ Lube (Jnl) - 6; free.
- × 2005 (1 January) British Lubricants Federation

United Kingdom Magnetics Society
- NR Grove Business Centre, Grove Technology Park, WANTAGE, Oxon, OX12 9FA.   (asa)
  01235 770652
- ○ *L; 'to represent both industrial & academic interests in all field of magnetics'
  No further information supplied

United Kingdom Maize Millers' Association   1997
- NR 21 Arlington St, LONDON, SW1A 1RN.   (hq)
  020 7493 2521
  Sec: Alex Waugh
- ▲ Un-incorporated Society
- ○ *T; for the UK maize milling industry
- ● Mtgs - LG
- < Euromaiziers
- M 4 f

United Kingdom Maritime Pilots' Association   (UKMPA)   1884
- ■ Transport House, 128 Theobald's Rd, LONDON, WC1X 8TN.   (hq)
  020 7611 2570   fax 020 7611 2757
  email ukmpa@tgwu.org.uk   http://www.ukmpa.org
  Sec: John A Pretswell
- ▲ Un-incorporated Society
- ○ *P; interests of maritime pilots of ports of Great Britain & Northern Ireland
- < Intl Maritime Pilots' Assn; Eur Maritime Pilots' Assn; Unite - T & G section
- M 500 i

United Kingdom Metering Forum
- NR Gemserv, Centurion House (7th floor), 24 Monument St, LONDON, EC3R 8AJ.
  020 7090 1000
- ○ *T

United Kingdom Metric Association   (UKMA)   2000
- ■ 34 Wroxham Gardens, LONDON, N11 2BA.   (hsp)
  020 8374 6997; 07880 542950
  email secretary@metric.org.uk   http://www.ukma.org.uk
  Sec: Derek Pollard
- ▲ Un-incorporated Society
- ○ *K; a non-political organisation which supports the use of the international metric system (SI) for all official, trade, health, safety, educational, media, legal & contractual purposes in the UK. It believes that the universal adoption of the metric system is in the best interests of the British Public
- Gp Cookery; Education; PR; Retail; Transport
- ● Conf - Res - SG - Inf - LG
- < US Metric Assn (USMA)
- M 80 i, UK / 5 i, o'seas
- ¶ NL - 4;   AR - 1; both ftm only.
  Technical Reports; £6.25 m, £12.50 nm.

United Kingdom Mineral Wool Association
    alternative name of **EURISOL-UK Ltd**

United Kingdom Money Transmitters Association   (UKMTA)   2005
- NR Unit 8, 42 Braganza St, LONDON, SE17 3RJ.
  020 7735 6222   fax 020 7735 6222
  email dominic.thorncroft@ukmta.org
  http://www.ukmta.org
  Chmn: Dominic Thorncroft
- ▲ Company Limited by Guarantee
- ○ *T; to represent businesses registered with HM Revenue & Customs for the purposes of money transfer
- M 250 f

United Kingdom National Defence Association Ltd   (UKNDA)   2007
- NR PO Box 819, PORTSMOUTH, Hants, PO1 9FF.
  http://www.uknda.org.uk
  Gen Sec: David Robinson,   Chief Exec: John Muxworthy
- ▲ Company Limited by Guarantee
- ○ *K; a campaign for the full funding of the UK's armed forces for the defence of this country & throughout the world
- M i, f & org
  (Sub: £12i, f & org varies, £100 life)

United Kingdom Newsletter & Electronic Publishers Association
    since 2006 **United Kingdom Specialised Information Publishers Association**

United Kingdom Noise Association   (UKNA)   2000
- ■ PO Box 551, CHATHAM, Kent, ME4 9AJ.   (hq)
  01634 8638524
  email info@ukna.org.uk   http://www.ukna.org.uk
  Chmn: John Stewart
- ▲ Un-incorporated Society
- ○ *K; campaigns for action against noise
- ● Conf - Mtgs - Res - Exhib - Inf - LG
- M 200 i, 40,000 org

United Kingdom Offshore Operators Association Ltd
    since 2007 **Oil & Gas UK**

United Kingdom One World Linking Association   (UKOWLA)   1992
- ■ The Glade Centre, Frog Lane, ILMINSTER, Somerset, TA19 0AP.   (hq)
  01460 55449   fax 01460 55753
  email info@ukowla.org.uk   http://www.ukowla.org.uk
  Sec: Ian Croxford
- ▲ Company Limited by Guarantee; Registered Charity
- ○ *X; to support, promote & encourage communities in the UK to develop partnership links with communities in the South (Africa, Asia, Latin America, the Caribbean)
- ● Conf - Mtgs - ET - Res - LG
- M [not stated]
  (Sub: £15 i, £95 f, £30 org)
- ¶ Owl - 4; ftm only.

United Kingdom Online User Group
    since 2005 the **UK eInformation Group**

United Kingdom Onshore Operators Group   (UKOOG)   1986
- ■ Shepherds, CRANBROOK, Kent, TN17 3EN.   (hq)
  01202 780333   fax 01202 780444
  Sec: Phill Jones
- ▲ Company Limited by Guarantee
- ○ *T; for UK onshore oil & gas operators licensed under UK Landward   Licences (Petroleum Production Act 1934)
  no further information supplied

United Kingdom Onshore Pipeline Operators' Association (UKOPA)
- Pipelines Maintenance Centre, Ripley Rd, AMBERGATE, Derbys, DE56 2FZ.
  01773 852003   fax 01773 856456
  http://www.ukopa.co.uk
  Sec: Phill Jones
  No further information supplied

United Kingdom Overseas Territories Association   (UKOTA)   1998
- NR c/o British Virgin Islands Government Office, 15 Upper Grosvenor St, LONDON, W1K 7PJ.   (hq)
  020 7355 9570   fax 020 7355 9575
- ▲ Un-incorporated Society
- ○ *N, *W; to provide a forum for discussion for residents of British overseas territories on issues of common interest in the relevant areas
- ● Conf - Mtgs - Inf
- M 9 territories

United Kingdom Paint Horse Association
- NR Olde Walnut Tree Farm, Pristow Green Lane, Tibenham, NORWICH, NR16 1PU.
  01379 674551
  http://www.ukpha.co.uk
- ○ *B

United Kingdom Paintball Sports Federation   (UKPSF)   1991
- ■ 5 Waingap Crescent, Whitworth, ROCHDALE, Lancs, OL12 8PX.   (chiefexec/p)
  0845 130 4252
  Chief Exec: Steven Bull
- ▲ Un-incorporated Society
- ○ *S; to promote the sport of paintball (the firing of paint 'blobs')
- Gp Players' Council
- ● Exhib - Comp - Inf - LG
- M 850 i, 175 f, 2 org, UK / 50 i, 10 f, o'seas
- ¶ Paintball UK (NL) - 4.   Paintball Games in Woodlands. Millennium Site Guide - 1.
  Code of Practice.   Site Survey - 1.

United Kingdom Parking Enforcement Agency
- has become Parkforce: the UK Parking Enforcement Agency - 'leading the way in the parking control industry with clients nationwide'.

United Kingdom Petroleum Industry Association   (UKPIA)   1978
- NR 9 Kingsway, LONDON, WC2B 6XF.   (hq)
  020 7240 0289
- ▲ Company Limited by Guarantee
- ○ *T; represents oil companies involved in the supply, refining & distribution of oil in the UK
- M f
  Note: the correct title of the Association is - UK Petroleum Industry Association
  see note under UK. . .

United Kingdom Polarity Therapy Association   (UKPTA)   1996
- NR Monomark House, 27 Old Gloucester St, LONDON, WC1N 3XX.   (mail/address)
  0700 705 2748
  email info@ukpta.org.uk   http://www.ukpta.org.uk
- ▲ Un-incorporated Society
- ○ *P; 'for those who practice & teach the therapeutic system called Polarity Therapy developed by Dr Randolph Stone; to promote this form of therapy - a true holistic approach to health & healing employing a person's own energy to heal at physical, mental & emotional levels'
- M i & schools

United Kingdom Polocrosse Association Ltd   (UKPA)   1986
- ■ Grove House Farm, Main Rd, Wharncliffe Side, SHEFFIELD, S35 0DQ.   (hsp)
  01226 765126   fax 01226 370105
  email nfo@polocrosse.org.uk
  http://www.polocrosse.org.uk
  Hon Sec: Susan Brookes
- ▲ Company Limited by Guarantee
- ○ *S; to control & administer the game of Polocrosse (a team game played on horseback)
- ● Mtgs - ET - Comp - VE
- < Intl Polocrosse Coun; Brit Horse Soc
- M 500 i
- ¶ NL - 4;   Magazine - 1;   Ybk - 1; all ftm.

United Kingdom Practical Shooting Association   (UKPSA)   1977
- ■ PO Box 7057, Preston, WEYMOUTH, Dorset, DT4 4EN.   (mail add)
  07010 703845   fax 0870 765 7721
  http://www.ukpsa.co.uk
  Sec: Alan B Phillips
- ▲ Registered Charity
- ○ *S; to administer the sport of practical shooting in the UK
- ● Comp - LG
- < Intl Practical Shooting Confedn (IPSC); Brit Assn for Shooting & Conservation (BASC); Nat Rifle Assn (NRA)
- M [not stated]
- ¶ DVC - 1;   eDVC - 9; both ftm only.

United Kingdom Preserve Manufacturers' Association
  since 2003-04 the UK Sweet Spreads Association, one of the four associations within the **Food Processors Association**

United Kingdom Public Health Association   (UKPHA)   1988
- NR 94 White Lion St, LONDON, N1 9PF.   (hq)
  020 7713 8910   fax 020 3051 1769
  email info@ukpha.org.uk   http://www.ukpha.org.uk
  Chief Exec: Angela Mawle
- ▲ Company Limited by Guarantee; Registered Charity
- Br 11
- ○ *K, *P; to eliminate inequalities in health, promote sustainable development & combat anti-health forces
- Gp Alcohol & violence; Devolution; Food & nutrition; Health & sustainable environments; Health visiting & public health
- ● Conf - Mtgs - Res - Exhib - SG - LG
- M 1,000 i, 200 org, UK / 100 i, o'seas

United Kingdom Pyrotechnics Society   (UKPS)   2006
- NR Cliffe-Torn Lodge, Newland, Drax, SELBY, N Yorks, YO8 8PS.
  email secretary@pyrosociety.org.uk
  http://www.pyrosociety.org.uk
  Sec: Jon Williams
- ▲ Company Limited by Guarantee
- ○ *G; to represent the heritage, science, history and art of pyrotechnics in the UK
- ¶ Spark

United Kingdom Quality Ash Association   (UKQAA)   1997
- ■ Regent House, Bath Avenue, WOLVERHAMPTON, W Midlands, WV1 4EG.
  01902 810087   fax 01902 810187
  email enquiries@ukqaa.org.uk
  http://www.ukqaa.org.uk
  Technical Dir: Dr Lindon Sear
- ▲ Un-incorporated Society
- ○ *T; to represent the interests of producers & users of fly ash from coal fired power stations, eg the construction industry - use of fly ash in concrete fill, grouting; road construction
- ● Conf - Mtgs - ET - Res - Exhib - Inf - Lib
- < Eur Ash Assn (ECOBA)
- M 17 f
- ¶ Datasheets;   Case Studies;   Best Practice Guides - all irreg; all free.

© CBD Research Ltd · Beckenham · BR3 5JS · Tel 020 8650 7745 · Fax 020 8650 0768 · E-mail cbd@cbdresearch.com · www.cbdresearch.com

United Kingdom Rainwater Harvesting Association (UK-RHA) 2004

- Business Centre, Rio Drive, Collingham, NEWARK, Notts, NG23 7NB. (hq)
  01636 894900   fax 01636 894909
  email info@ukrha.org   http://www.ukrha.org
  Co Sec: Terry Nash
- ▲ Company Limited by Guarantee
- ○ *T; to represent the rainwater harvesting industry in the UK
- Gp Industry liaison; Best practice; Marketing
- ● Conf - Mtgs - ET - Res - Exhib - SG - Stat - Inf - LG
- M 20 f
  (Sub: £500)

United Kingdom Renderers' Association (UKRA) 1966

- NR c/o Pharo Communications Ltd, 10th St, Stoneleigh Park, KENILWORTH, Warks, CV8 2LG.
  024 7641 8704
  email info@ukra.co.uk   http://www.ukra.co.uk
  Technical Dir: David Green
- ○ *T; to promote good practice & to raise the profile of the rendering industry
- M f

United Kingdom Resilient Flooring Association (UKRFA)

- c/o Bunkers, 7 The Drive, HOVE, E Sussex, BN3 3JS. (asa)
  01273 329797
  Sec: R J M Crawt
- ○ *T; manufacturers of vinyl & linoleum
- ● Mtgs - Inf (on vinyl & linoleum only)
- M 9 f

United Kingdom Revenue Protection Association (UKRPA) 1997

- NR Gemserv, Centurion House (7th floor), 24 Monument St, LONDON, EC3R 8AJ. (hsb)
  020 7090 1000
  http://www.ukrpa.org.uk
- ▲ Un-incorporated Society
- ○ *T; for companies involved in investigating & dealing with theft of electricity &/or interference with meters
- Gp Publicity c'ee; Technical c'ee
- ● Conf - Mtgs - ET - Inf - LG
- < Intl Utilities Revenue Protection Assn (IURPA)
- M 16 f

United Kingdom Rocketry Association (UKRA) 1996

- NR 105 Thomas Way, Lakesview International Business Park, Hersden, CANTERBURY, Kent, CT3 4NH. (mail address)
  email enquiries@ukra.org.uk   http://www.ukra.org.uk
  Sec: Jonathan Rhodes
- ▲ Un-incorporated Society
- ○ *G; to promote amateur rocketry in the UK; to provide a link between groups & individuals interested in rocketry in the UK; to create a recognised safety code & certification & achievement programme
- ● Mtgs - ET - Exam - Exhib - LG - Annual flying events - Monthly club meetings
- < Brit Model Flying Assn (BMFA)
- M 200 i, 7 org
- ¶ UKRA Hbk - 1.   10.9.8 - 4.

United Kingdom Roundabout Appreciation Society (UKRAS) 2003

- PO Box 12810, Astwood Bank, REDDITCH, Worcs, B97 9BH.
  07815 630416   fax 01527 522545
  email info@roundaboutsofbritain.com
  http://www.roundaboutsofbritain.com
- ▲ Un-incorporated Society
- ○ *G; to collect data & other information on traffic islands, roundabouts & all traffic gyratory systems
- ● Mtgs - VE
- M 30 i
- ¶ Roundabouts of GB Calendar [for 26 towns] - 1; £5 m, £8 nm.
  Roundabouts of Britain (book); £7.99.
  Roundabouts from the Air (book); £8.99.

United Kingdom Science Park Association (UKSPA) 1984

- Chesterford Research Park, Little Chesterford, SAFFRON WALDEN, Essex, CB10 1XL. (hq)
  01799 532050   fax 01799 532049
  email info@ukspa.org.uk   http://www.ukspa.org.uk
  Chief Exec: Anthony P Wright
- ▲ Company Limited by Guarantee
- ○ *L, *N; 'to assist in the planning, development, operation & management of science parks / technology parks & incubators linked to universities & other institutes of higher education; to stimulate the growth of technology & knowledge based firms through the transfer of technology'
- ● Conf - Mtgs - ET - Res - Stat - Inf - LG
- < Intl Assn of Science Parks (IASP); World Alliance for Innovation (WAINOVA); Assn of Universities Res & Indl Links (AUKUL)
- M 60,000 i, 2,600 f
- ¶ Innovation into Success (Jnl) - 4; ftm, £4.95 nm.
  Annual Directory of Science Parks; ftm (£25 2nd copy), £50 nm.
  Evaluation of the Past & Future Economic Contribution of the UK Science Park Movement; £35 m, £75 nm.
  Planning, Development & Operation of Science Parks; £20.
  Best Practice Guides - irreg; £20 each or £60 the set.

United Kingdom Security Shredding Association (UKSSA) 1997

- Unit C Stowe Court, Stowe St, LICHFIELD, Staffs, WS13 6AQ. (hq)
  0800 634 0212
  email admin@ukssa.org.uk   http://www.ukssa.org.uk
  Sec: Dean Murphy
- ▲ Company Limited by Guarantee
- ○ *T; to promote the interests of security shredding & confidential document destruction industries together with legal requirements at local & national levels
- ● Conf - Mtgs - ET - Inf - LG - National industrial standards
- M 10 f

United Kingdom Serials Group (UKSG) 1978

- NR PO Box 5594, NEWBURY, Berks, RG20 0YD. (admin p)
  01635 254292   fax 01635 253826
  email alison@uksg.org   http://www.uksg.org
  Business Manager: Alison Whitehorn
- ○ *L, *P; 'to promote & assist discussion & research on serials & their management between all interested parties in the information industry'
- ● Conf - Mtgs - ET - Res - Exhib - Stat - Inf
- M c 600 org
- ¶ Serials (online Jnl) - 3; £72+VAT m only.

United Kingdom Shareholders' Association Ltd   (UKSA)   1992
■ BM UKSA, LONDON, WC1N 3XX.   (mail add)
   0870 706 0600
   email uksa@uksa.org.uk   http://www.uksa.org.uk
   Chmn: Martin White,   Dir: Roger Lawson
   Nat Sec: Toby Keynes (membership@uksa.org.uk)
▲ Company Limited by Guarantee
Br 6
○ *K, *W; to promote improved standards of corporate
   governance for the benefit of the UK economy including all
   shareholders; to represent the interests of private
   shareholders; to assist private shareholders exercise their
   responsibilities as joint owners of their companies
Gp Company activities group
● Mtgs - ET - Res - SG - VE - LG
< Euroshareholders (Eur Shareholders Gp)
M 500 i, 10 org, UK / 10 i, o'seas
   (Sub: £50 i)
¶ UKSA Update (NL) - 6; ftm only.
   Numerous policy papers available on website.

United Kingdom Sibelius Society   1984
NR 51 Vernon Ave, LONDON, SW20 8BN.   (hsp)
   020 8715 7659
   Pres: Edward Clark
▲ Un-incorporated Society
○ *D; to explore & promulgate Sibelius' achievement in 20th
   century music
● Conf - Mtgs - Concerts - Seminars
M 120 i, UK / 40 i, o'seas
¶ NL - 4; free.

United Kingdom Simulation Training & Action Group
   a group of the **Defence Manufacturers Association**

United Kingdom Skateboardin Association   (UKSA)
NR 113 Broomstick Hall Rd, WALTHAM ABBEY, Essex, EN9 1LP.
   (hsp)
   Sec: Dave CArlin
○ *DS
● Mtgs - Comp
M i

United Kingdom Skeptics   (UK Skeptics)   1988
■ 10 Crescent View, LOUGHTON, Essex, IG10 4PZ.   (hsp)
   http://www.skeptic.org.uk
   Contact: Mike Hutchinson
▲ Un-incorporated Society
○ *K, *L; a non-membership body providing a rational, scientific
   response to paranormal &/or pseudoscientific claims; to
   inculcate critical thinking & an understanding of science
Gp Remote viewing; Crystal power; Crop circles; Anti-gravity;
   Perpetual motion; Hypnotic regression (past lives); Re-
   incarnation; Health fraud; Astrology; ESP; Creationism (anti-
   evolution theories); Spoon bending; Fire-walking
● Conf - Res - Inf
¶ The Skeptic - 4; £15 yr.

United Kingdom Social Investment Forum   (UKSIF)   1991
NR Holywell Centre, 1 Phipp St, LONDON, EC2A 4PS.
   020 7749 9950
   email info@uksif.org   http://www.uksif.org
   Chief Executive: Penny Shepherd,   Admin: Louise Hopper
▲ Company Limited by Guarantee
○ *L; to promote sustainable & responsible finance
M 200 f, i & org

United Kingdom Society for Co-operative Studies   (SCS)   1967
NR Holyoake House, Hanover St, MANCHESTER, M60 0AS.   (hq)
   0161-246 3553
   email richard.bickle@cooptel.net
   http://www.co-opstudies.org
   Sec: Richard Bickle
▲ Registered Charity
○ *L, *Q; to promote the knowledge & study of the co-operative
   movement
● Conf - Mtgs - Res
M 184 i, 42 org
¶ Jnl - 3; ftm, £10 nm.

United Kingdom Society of Investment Professionals
   since 30 November 2007 **CFA Society of the UK**

United Kingdom Society for Trenchless Technology   (UKSTT)
■ 38 Holly Walk, LEAMINGTON SPA, Warks, CV32 4LY.   (hq)
   01926 330935
   http://www.ukstt.org.uk
▲ Company Limited by Guarantee; Registered Charity
○ *P; to advance the science & practice of trenchless technology
   for public benefit; to promote education, training, study &
   research in trenchless technology
● Conf - Mtgs - ET - Exhib - Expt - Inf - LG
< Intl Soc for Trenchless Technology
¶ UKSTT News (NL) - 6; ftm.

United Kingdom Software Metrics Association   (UKSMA)
■ c/o Xchanging (Attn: Rob Ratcliff), Walter Burke Way,
   Chatham Maritime, CHATHAM, Kent, ME4 4RQ.   (chmn/b)
   01634 887890
   email rob.ratcliff@xchanging.com
   http://www.uksma.co.uk
   Chmn: Rob Ratcliff
▲ Company Limited by Guarantee
○ *P; for organisations & individuals involved in the development,
   promotion or use of software metrics
● Conf - Mtgs - ET - Exam - Res - Exhib - SG - Inf - Lib
M i, f
¶ NL - 4; ftm, £10 nm.

**United Kingdom Specialised Information Publishers
Association   (SIPA UK)**
NR Cliveden House, 19-22 Victoria Villas, RICHMOND, Surrey,
   TW9 2JX.   (hq)
   020 8288 7415   fax 020 8288 7415
   email uksipa@btconnect.com
   http://www.sipaonline.com
   Dir: Karen Hindle
▲ Un-incorporated Society
Br USA (New England, New York, North California, South
   California, Southeast, Washington DC)
○ *T; for producers of specialised business information, both
   newsletters & online, based in the UK
● Conf - Mtgs - ET - Inf
< is the UK chapter of Specialized Information Publishers Assn
   (USA)
M 70+ f
× 2006 United Kingdom Newsletter & Electronic Publishers
   Association

United Kingdom Spill Association   (UKSPILL)   2004
■ Keepers Cottage, Acton Scott, CHURCH STRETTON, Shropshire,
   SY6 6QN.   (hsb)
   0870 486 8980
   email info@ukspill.org   http://www.ukspill.org
   Exec Dir: Roger M Mabbott
▲ Company Limited by Guarantee
○ *T; for the UK oil spill industry, spill contractors, equipment
   manufacturers & consulting companies
● Conf - Mtgs - Exhib - Expt - Inf - LG
< Soc of Marine Inds
M 10 i, 80 f, 10 org
× 2004 British Oil Spill Control Association

   © CBD Research Ltd · Beckenham · BR3 5JS · Tel 020 8650 7745 · Fax 020 8650 0768 · E-mail cbd@cbdresearch.com · www.cbdresearch.com

United Kingdom Spoon Collectors Club (UKSCC) 1980
- ■ 72 Edinburgh Rd, NEWMARKET, Suffolk, CB8 0QD. (hsp)
  01638 665457
  email david.cross340@ntlworld.com
  Hon Sec: David S Cross
- ▲ Un-incorporated Society
- Br 6; Australia, N Zealand, South Africa, USA
- ○ *G; for those interested in collecting spoons (souvenir or antique)
- ● Mtgs - AGM (October)
- M 200 i
- ¶ Club Magazine - 4; subscription varies (£12- £1).

United Kingdom Sports Association for People with Learning Disability (UKSA) 1980
- ■ 12 City Forum (1st floor), 250 City Rd, LONDON, EC1V 2PU. (hq)
  020 7490 3057   fax 020 7251 8861
  email info@uksportsassociation.org
  http://www.uksportsassociation.org
  Nat Dir: Mrs Tracey McCillen
- ▲ Registered Charity
- ○ *N; the National Governing Body of sport in the UK for people with learning disabilities; to co-ordinate, promote & develop sport & recreational opportunities for all people with learning disability in the UK
- ● Conf - Mtgs - Inf - VE - LG
- < Intl Paralympic C'ee; Intl Sports Fedn for Persons with Intellectual Disability (INAS-FID); Brit Paralympic Assn; Disability Sport NI; Mencap Sport; Scot Disability Sport; Welsh Sports Assn for People with Learning Disability
- ¶ Coaching People with Learning Disability; £8.

United Kingdom Spring Manufacturers Association (UKSMA) 1948
- ■ Henry St, SHEFFIELD, S Yorks, S3 7EQ. (hq)
  0114-276 0542   fax 0114-252 7997
  email uksma@uksma.org.uk   http://www.uksma.org.uk
  Managing Dir: Andrew Watkinson
- ▲ Company Limited by Guarantee
- ○ *T
- ● Conf - Mtgs - ET - Res - Inf - Lib - VE
- < Eur Spring Fedn
- M c 100 f
- ¶ Directory of British Spring Manufacturers - 1; free.

United Kingdom Steel 1967
- ■ Broadway House, Tothill St, LONDON, SW1H 9NQ. (hq)
  020 7222 7777   fax 020 7222 3531
  email enquiries@uksteel.org.uk
  http://www.uksteel.org.uk
  Dir: Ian Rodgers
- ○ *T; representation of UK steel producing & processing companies
- Gp Tubes product (incorporating members of the former British Welded Steel Tube Assn)
- ● Conf - Mtgs - Stat - Expt - Inf - LG - Provision of detailed information on steel specifications to specifiers & users of steel
- < is a division of EEF
- > Energy Intensive Users Gp; Brit Metallurgical Plant Constructors Assn
- M 30 f
- ¶ LM;   Annual Statistics; AR; all free.
  Steel specifications [book & On-line]
- ✕ 2003 UK Steel Association

United Kingdom Sustainable Development Association (UK-SDA) 2008
- ■ Business Centre, Rio Drive, Collingham, NEWARK, Notts, NG23 7NB. (hq)
  0845 026 0240   fax 01636 894909
  email info@uk-sda.org   http://www.uk-sda.org
  Sec: Terry Nash
- ▲ Company Limited by Guarantee
- ○ *T; to represent the sustainable development industry in the UK
- ● Conf - Mtgs - ET - Res - Exhib - SG - Inf
- M 20 f
  (Sub: £250)
- ¶ E-NL - 12; free.

United Kingdom Sweet Spreads Association
a sector of the **Food Processers Association**

United Kingdom Tea Association (UKTA) 1953
- NR 6 Catherine St, LONDON, WC2B 5JJ. (asa)
  http://www.tea.co.uk
- ▲ Un-incorporated Society
- ○ *T
- ● Mtgs - LG
- < Food & Drink Fedn (FDF)
- M 35 f

United Kingdom Textile Laboratory Forum (UKTLF) 2001
- ■ 8 Wentworth Way, LEEDS, W Yorks, LS17 7TG. (hsb)
  0113-225 0014
  email info@uktlf.com   http://www.uktlf.com
  Hon Sec: Alan Ross
- ▲ Un-incorporated Society
- ○ *N, *T; to provide a technical forum for UK based UKAS accredited textile laboratories; to provide a system of inter-laboratory correlations; to provide a professional interface with other relevant organisations
- Gp Fibre composition, Flammability, Uncertainty of measurement
- ● Mtgs - LG
- < Soc of Dyers & Colourists; ASBCI; UKAS
- M 27 f
  (Sub: £100)

United Kingdom Thalassaemia Society (UKTS) 1976
- ■ 19 The Broadway, Southgate Circus, LONDON, N14 6PH. (hq)
  020 8882 0011
  http://www.ukts.org
  Pres: M Michael,   Coordinator: Elaine Miller
- ▲ Registered Charity
- ○ *M,*W; to provide advice, information & counselling to sufferers & carriers of thalassaemia (a hereditary blood disorder)
- ● Conf - Mtgs - ET - Res - Inf
- < Thalassaemia Intl Fedn (TIF)
- M c 600 i, UK / c 130 i, o'seas
- ¶ News Review (NL) - 4.   AR.
  Various booklets & leaflets.

United Kingdom Timber Frame Association 2002
- NR The e-centre, Cooperage Way Business Village, ALLOA, Clackmannanshire, FK10 3LP. (chmn/b)
  01259 272140
  Chief Exec: Bryan Woodley
- ○ *T

United Kingdom Trades Confederation (UKTC) 1995
NR Unit 18, Holroyd Business Centre, Carr Bottom Rd, BRADFORD,
W Yorks, BD5 9BP. (hq)
01274 223188 fax 01274 223189
email membership@uktc.org http://www.uktc.com
Managing Dir: Derek Vaughan
▲ Company Limited by Guarantee
○ *N, *T; to protect business in the face of growing bureaucracy &
the legal minefield; to grow business in the ever-changing
business environment through recommendation & lead
generation; to save business money through specially
discounted services & products
< Allied Trs Confedn
M 3,500 f

**United Kingdom Transplant Co-ordinators Association
(UKTCA) 1983**
NR PO Box 47, KINGSBRIDGE, Devon, TQ7 4WG.
07071 223171
email info@uktca.org.uk http://www.uktca.co.uk
Sec: Philippa Stainton
▲ Un-incorporated Society
○ *N, *P; to promote organ donation & best practice in
transplantation; to support those working as transplant coordinators throughout the UK & Ireland transplant coordinators within the National Health Service

United Kingdom Travel Retail Forum (UKTRF) 1988
■ LGM House, Mill Green Rd, HAYWARDS HEATH, W Sussex,
RH16 1XL. (hq)
01444 474700 fax 01444 474701
email info@uktrf.co.uk http://www.uktrf.co.uk
Sec Gen: Barry Goddard
▲ Company Limited by Guarantee
○ *T; to improve trading conditions for companies involved in the
supply & sale of duty paid goods to international travellers
within the EU; to protect all duty & tax free sales where these
still exist
● Mtgs - Stat - Expt - LG
< Eur Travel Retail Coun
M 26 f

United Kingdom Ultimate Association (UKU) 1981
NR LONDON, WC1X 3XX. (mail/address)
0870 760 7189
http://www.ukultimate.com
▲ Un-incorporated Society
○ *S; for the seven-a-side team sport of ultimate - a game played
indoors & outdoors by men & women using a flying disc
M i

United Kingdom Vaccine Industry Group
NR 12 Whitehall, LONDON, SW1A 2DY.
http://www.uvig.org
○ *T; companies concerned with vaccine research, development &
manufacture
< is a group within the Association of the British Pharmaceutical
Industry
M 6 f

United Kingdom Vineyards Association (UKVA) 1996
■ PO Box 534, Frilford Heath, ABINGDON, Oxon, OX14 9BZ.
(hq)
01865 390188
email sian@ukva.org.uk http://www.ukva.org.uk
Gen Sec: Sian Liwiki
▲ Company Limited by Guarantee
○ *T; to promote viticulture & viniculture in the UK
● Conf - Comp - Inf - LG
< Nat Farmers U; Wine & Spirit Assn of GB
> Vineyard Assns: Thames & Chilterns, Wessex, South East, South
West, Mercia; East Anglia Winegrowers Assn
M 470 i, UK / 3 i, o'seas
(Sub: variable UK / £51 o'seas)
¶ The Grape Press - 2; ftm only.
Pesticides booklet - 1; ftm, £25 nm.

United Kingdom Warehousing Association (UKWA) 1944
■ Walter House, 418-422 Strand, LONDON, WC2R 0PT. (hq)
020 7836 5522 fax 020 7438 9379
email dg@ukwa.org.uk http://www.ukwa.org.uk
Chief Exec Officer: R J Williams
▲ Un-incorporated Society
○ *T; represents logistics companies in the UK
Gp Customs & tax warehousing; Operations & safety
● Conf - Mtgs - ET - Inf - VE - LG
< Intl Fedn of Warehousing Logistics Assns; Eur Warehousing &
Logistics Confedn
M 680 f
¶ NL - 10; ftm.
Directory of Members' Services - 2 yrly; ftm, £60 nm.
Fire Precautions Guide to Risk Assessment; £10 m, £20 nm.

United Kingdom Weighing Federation (UKWF) 1920
■ Brooke House, 4 The Lakes, Bedford Rd, NORTHAMPTON,
NN4 7YD. (asa)
01604 622023 fax 01604 631252
email ukwf@brookehouse.co.uk
http://www.ukwf.org.uk
▲ Company Limited by Guarantee
○ *T; acts on regulatory matters of legal metrology at UK, EEC &
international levels
● Conf - Mtgs - Inf - LG
< Eur Fedn Scale & Weighing Machine Mfrs & Repairers (CECIP)
M 100 f
¶ NL - 4; ftm. LM - 1; AR.

United Kingdom Windsurfing Association (UKWA) 1976
■ PO Box 703, HAYWARDS HEATH, W Sussex, RH16 9EE. (hq)
0845 410 3311 fax 01444 401567
http://www.ukwindsurfing.com
Admin: Arabella Andrup
Br 4 regions
○ *S; organisation of regional & national windsurfing, racing,
wave sailing, freestyle & speed sailing events
● Mtgs - PL - Regional & national windsurfing events
< Intl Windsurfing Assn (IWA); Royal Yachting Assn (RYA)
M 700+ i

© CBD Research Ltd · Beckenham · BR3 5JS · Tel 020 8650 7745 · Fax 020 8650 0768 · E-mail cbd@cbdresearch.com · www.cbdresearch.com

United Kingdom Youth   1911
NR   Avon Tyrell, BRANSGORE, Hants, BH23 8EE.   (hq)
         01425 672347   fax 01425 675108
         email info@ukyouth.org   http://www.ukyouth.org
         Chief Exec: John Bateman
▲   Registered Charity
Br   42
○   *Y; 'to support & develop high quality voluntary youth work &
         informal educational opportunities for & with young people
         through a range of projects, accredited learning
         programmes, events & publications'
●   Conf - ET - Inf - LG
<   Eur Confedn of Youth Clubs; Nat Coun of Voluntary Orgs; Nat
         Coun for Voluntary Youth Services
M   i in clubs
¶   Publications list available.
         Note: the correct name of this organisation is UK Youth;
         see also note under UK. . .

United Nations Association of Great Britain & Northern Ireland
(UNA-UK)   1945
NR   3 Whitehall Court, LONDON, SW1A 2EL.   (hq)
         020 7766 3444   fax 020 7930 5893
         http://www.una.org.uk
         Exec Dir: Sam Daws
▲   Company Limited by Guarantee
○   *X; to promote the principles of the UN charter & the role of the
         UN in international affairs

United Reformed Church History Society   (URCHS)   1972
■   c/o Westminster College, Madingley Rd, CAMBRIDGE,
         CB3 0AA.
         01223 741300   fax 01223 300765
         Hon Sec: Revd Elizabeth J Brown
▲   Registered Charity
○   *L, *Q, *R; research into the history of Congregational &
         Presbyterian churches
●   Annual lecture & meeting - Inf - Lib (Collection specialises in
         C17 - C19 Presbyterianism)
M   175 i, 5 churches, UK / 60 i, o'seas
¶   Jnl - 2; ftm.

United Road Transport Union   (URTU)   1890
NR   Almond House, Oak Green, Stanley Green Business Park,
         CHEADLE HULME, Cheshire, SK8 6QL.   (hq)
         0161-486 2100   fax 0161-485 3109
         email info@urtu.com   http://www.urtu.com
         Gen Sec: Robert F Monks
○   *U; to advance the interests of professional drivers in the road
         haulage, distribution & logistics industry
¶   Wheels (Jnl) - 6; ftm.

United Saddlebred Association   (USA UK)   1995
■   24 Coton Grove, Shirley, SOLIHULL, W Midlands, B90 1BS.
         (hsp)
         0121-439 2096
▲   Un-incorporated Society
○   *B; to promote interest in & care of American Saddlebreds; to
         show their versatility in all spheres of equestrianism
Gp   5-gaited; Saddle seat equitation
●   Conf - Mtgs - ET - Res - Exhib - Comp - Stat - Expt - Inf - Lib -
         PL - VE
<   Amer Saddle Horse Assn; Brit Morgan Horse Soc; Brit
         Skewbald, Piebald Assn; Coloured Horse & Pony Soc
M   c 100 i
¶   NL - 3;   Ybk - 1; both ftm only.   LM;   AR.

Unity   1825
NR   Hillcrest House, Garth St, Hanley, STOKE-on-TRENT, Staffs,
         ST1 2AB.   (hq)
         01782 272755   fax 01782 284902
         http://www.unitytheunion.org.uk
         Gen Sec: Geoff Bagnall
○   *U
M   i
×   2006 Ceramic & Allied Trades Union

Universities Association for Continuing Education
         since 2004 the **Universities Association for Lifelong Learning**

Universities Association for Lifelong Learning   (UALL)   1992
■   21 De Montfort St, LEICESTER, LE1 7GE.   (hq)
         0116-285 9702   fax 0116-204 6988
         email admin@uall.ac.uk   http://www.uall.ac.uk
         Admin: Lucy Bate
▲   Registered Charity
○   *P; to represent the continuing education community within
         higher education; to liaise with policy makers & policy
         making bodies
●   Conf - Mtgs - ET - Res - Inf - LG
M   8 i, 107 f, 1 org, UK / 15 f, o'seas
¶   Ybk & AR - 1; ftm.   LM - 3; free.
         Occasional Papers - 3/4; ftm, £3 nm.
         Working Papers - 1; ftm, £3 nm.
         Conference Proceedings - 1; ftm, £3 nm.
×   2004 Universities Association for Continuing Education

Universities & Colleges Employers' Association   (UCEA)   1994
■   Woburn House, 20 Tavistock Sq, LONDON, WC1H 9HU.   (hq)
         020 7383 2444   fax 020 7383 2666
         email enquiries@ucea.ac.uk   http://www.ucea.ac.uk
         Chief Exec Officer: Jocelyn Prudence
▲   Company Limited by Guarantee
○   *P; the employers association for universities & colleges in the
         UK; to provide a framework within which salaries, conditions
         of service employee relations can be discussed & advice &
         guidance sought
●   Conf - Mtgs - ET - Stat - Empl - Seminars
M   164 f

Universities & Colleges Information Systems Association
(UCISA)
NR   University of Oxford, 13 Banbury Rd, OXFORD, OX2 6NN.
         01865 283425   fax 01865 283426
         http://www.ucisa.ac.uk

Universities Federation for Animal Welfare   (UFAW)   1926
NR   The Old School, Brewhouse Hill, WHEATHAMPSTEAD, Herts,
         AL4 8AN.   (hq)
         01582 831818   fax 01582 831414
         email ufaw@ufaw.org.uk   http://www.ufaw.org.uk/
         Chief Exec: Dr James Kirkwood,
         Sec: Donald Davidson
▲   Company Limited by Guarantee; Registered Charity
○   *V; to develop & promote improvements in the welfare of all
         animals through scientific & educational activity worldwide
●   Conf - ET - Res - Inf - Lib - VE - LG
M   c 1,200 i & f
¶   Animal Welfare (Jnl) - 4.   NL - 1.   AR.
         Publications list available.

Universities Psychotherapy & Counselling Association (UPCA) 1993
- PO Box 142, St LEONARDS-on-SEA, E Sussex, TN38 1DN.
  01424 430431
  email upca@hotmail.co.uk
  Sec: Julia Croft
○ *Γ
● ET
M 1,300 i

Universities Scotland
NR 53 Hanover St, EDINBURGH, EH2 2PJ.
  0131-226 1111   fax 0131-226 1100
  http://www.universities-scotland.ac.uk
  Dir: David Caldwell
○ *N; to represent, promote & campaign for the Scottish higher education sector
M 21 org
¶ Books.

Universities UK (UUK) 2000
- Woburn House, 20 Tavistock Sq, LONDON, WC1H 9HQ.   (hq)
  020 7419 4111   fax 020 7388 8649
  email info@universitiesuk.ac.uk
  http://www.universitiesuk.ac.uk
  Chief Exec: Baroness Diana Warwick of Undercliffe
▲ Company Limited by Guarantee; Registered Charity
Br 2
○ *N; to be the essential voice for the UK universities; to promote & support their work & provide services to members; to speak out for a thriving & diverse higher education sector which creates benefits for all
Gp Higher education policy & research; Employability; Longer term strategy; Teacher education advisory group; Universities
  Policy c'ees: Business & industry, Funding & management, Health & social care, International & European, Research, Student experience
● Conf - Mtgs - Res - Stat - Inf - Lib - LG
> Higher Educ Wales; Universities Scotland; UK HE International Unit; UK Higher Educ Eur Unit; UK Res Integrity Office; Med Schools Voum
M 132 f
  (Sub: £4,050)
¶ [all publications are available as downloadable pdf files on website].

University Association for Contemporary European Studies (UACES) 1968
- School of Public Policy, University College London, 29-30 Tavistock Sq, LONDON, WC1H 9QU.   (hq)
  020 7679 4975
  http://www.uaces.org
  Exec Dir: Sue Davis
▲ Registered Charity
○ *L; exchanges ideas on Europe; to provide a forum for debate & act as a clearing house for information about European issues; it is directly involved in promoting research & establishing teaching & research networks.
  Members include academics (economists, political scientists, lawyers & historians) & practitioners & graduate students
Gp Graduate students of European studies
● Conf - Mtgs - Workshops
M 900 i, 105 universities, UK / 300 i, 20 universities, o'seas
¶ Jnl of Common Market Studies (JCMS) - 5.   NL - 4.
  Research interests of UACES Members; £28 m, £38 (or £123 nm).
  Listing of Courses in European Studies in UK Universities; online.
  Listing of Interests (at www.expertoneurope.com)

University & College Lecturers' Union
  in 2006 merged with the Association of University Teachers to form the **University & College Union**

University and College Union (UCU) 2006
NR 27 Britannia St, LONDON, WC1X 9JP.   (hq)
  020 7837 3636
  email hq@ucu.org.uk   http://www.ucu.org.uk
  Gen Sec: Sally Hunt
○ *E, *U
  2006 (Association of University Teachers (NATFHE (the University & College Lecturers Union)

Unlock Democracy (incorporating Charter 88) 1988
NR 6 Cynthia St, LONDON, N1 9JF.   (hq)
  020 7278 4443
  http://www.unlockdemocracy.org.uk
▲ Company Limited by Guarantee
○ *K; political pressure group campaigning for a modern & fair democracy through a democratic parliament, a freedom of information act, a bill of rights, decentralisation of power, a proportional voting system & a written constitution
M i
¶ Citizen (NL).

Unlock - National Association of Reformed Offenders (UNLOCK) 1999
- 35A High St, SNODLAND, Kent, ME6 5AG.   (hq)
  01634 247350   fax 01634 247351
  email enquiries@unlock.org.uk
  http://www.unlock.org.uk
  Chief Exec: Bobby Cummines
▲ Registered Charity
○ *K, *W; to improve facilities & opportunities for serving prisoners to prepare for release & to overcome social exclusion & discrimination hindering them from re-integration into society; to prevent offending & re-offending by young people especially at risk; to campaign for serving prisoner's right to vote
● ET - Inf - LG
M [not stated]
  Unlock - National Association of Ex-Offenders

Upkeep: the Trust for Training & Education in Building Maintenance (Upkeep) 1979
- The Building Centre (1st floor), 26 Store St, LONDON, WC1E 7BT.   (hq)
  020 7631 1677   fax 020 7631 1699
  email info@upkeep.org.uk   http://www.upkeep.org.uk
  Dir: Annette McGill
▲ Company Limited by Guarantee; Registered Charity
○ *E, *T; to promote good standards of repair, maintenance & improvement of buildings, particularly houses & flats
M org

Urdd Gobaith Cymru   (yr Urdd) 1922
NR Ffordd Llanbadarn, ABERYSTWYTH, Ceredigion, SY23 1EY.   (hq)
  01970 613102   fax 01970 626120
  email ywe@urdd.org   http://www.urdd.org
  Chief Exec: Efa Gruffudd Jones
▲ Company Limited by Guarantee; Registered Charity
Br 900
○ *Y; to give children & young people the chance to learn & socialise through the medium of Welsh speaking
M 50,000 i
¶ Cip, Bore Da, iaw! (Jnls) - each 10.

© CBD Research Ltd · Beckenham · BR3 5JS · Tel 020 8650 7745 · Fax 020 8650 0768 · E-mail cbd@cbdresearch.com · www.cbdresearch.com

Urostomy Association (UA) 1971

■   Central Office, 18 Foxglove Avenue, UTTOXETER, Staffs, ST14 8UN.   (hq)
    0845 241 2159 or 01889 563191
    email info.ua@classmail.co.uk   http://www.uagbi.org
    Nat Sec: Mrs Hazel Pixley
▲   Registered Charity
Br   16
○   *W; to assist those who are about to undergo (or have undergone) surgery resulting in diversion or removal of the bladder; to provide information, help & advice
●   Conf - Mtgs - ET - Res - Inf - LG
<   Intl Ostomy Assn
M   2,400 i, UK / 200 i, o'seas
¶   Magazine - 3; ftm.

Uveitis Information Group (UIG) 1998

■   South House, Sweening, VIDLIN, Shetland Isles, ZE2 9QE. (hsp)
    01806 577310
    email info@uveitis.net   http://www.uveitis.net
    Hon Sec: Phil Hibbert
▲   Registered Charity
○   *W; to provide inforamtion & support for sufferers of uveitis (inflammation of the eye); to further understanding of the condition amongst health professionals & other organisations involved in sight related matters
●   ET - Inf
M   350 i, UK / 100 i, o'seas
¶   NL - 3; ftm, £5 nm.

Vale of Glamorgan Agricultural Society 1772
- ■ Pancross Barn, Llancarfan, BARRY, Glamorgan, CF62 3AJ.
  (hsp)
  01446 710099
  email vale.show@btinternet.com
  http://www.valeglamorganshow.co.uk
  Hon Sec: Nicola Gibson
- ▲ Company Limited by Guarantee; Registered Charity
- ○ *F; to promote British agriculture & its related industries
- Gp Craft fair; Horticulture; Kennel Club dog show; Rural crafts;
  Livestock; Tradestands; Food Hall
  Competitions: Home produce, Livestock
- ● Exhib - Comp - Inf
- < R Horticl Soc; R Nat Rose Soc; Breed socs; Horse socs
- M 500 i, 10 f
- ¶ Schedule - 1.   AR.   Catalogue - 1.

Valpak 1997
- ■ Stratford Business Park, Banbury Rd, STRATFORD-upon-AVON,
  Warks, CV37 7GW.   (hsb)
  0845 068 2572   fax 0845 068 2532
  email info@valpak.co.uk   http://www.valpak.co.uk
  Chief Exec: Steve Gough
- ▲ Company Limited by Guarantee
- ○ *T; the nationwide compliance scheme for the packaging waste
  regulations
- ● LG
- < Pro Europe
- M c3,000 f
- ¶ Ybk; ftm only.

Vascular Surgical Society
  a group of the **Association of Surgeons of Great Britain &
  Ireland**

VAT Practitioners Group (VPG) 1982
- ■ 105 Oxhey Avenue, WATFORD, Herts, WD19 4HB.   (nat
  admin/p)
  01923 230788   fax 01923 240707
  email administrator@vpgweb.com
  http://www.vpgweb.com
  Nat Admin: Susan Holman
- ▲ Un-incorporated Society
- Br 28
- ○ *P; a discussion group on Value Added Tax which makes
  representation to HM Customs & Excise on VAT matters; also
  has interests in Insurance Premium Tax (IPT), Landfill Tax & Air
  Passenger Duty (APD)
- ● Conf - Mtgs
- M 520 i
- ¶ Bulletin - 10; ftm only.

Vegan Society Ltd 1944
- NR Donald Watson House, 21 Hylton St, Hockley, BIRMINGHAM,
  B18 6HJ.   .   (hq)
  0121-523 1730   fax 0121-523 1749
  email info@vegansociety.com
  http://www.vegansociety.com
  Media Officer: Amanda Baker
- ▲ Registered Charity
- ○ *K; 'to promote ways of living free from animal products, for
  the benefit of people, animals & the environment'
- ● ET - Res - Inf
- M c 5,000 i
- ¶ The Vegan Magazine - 4.
  The Animal-Free Shopper - 2 yrly.
  Vegan Passport.   Vegan Stories.
  Plant Based Nutrition & Health.

Vegetarian Society of Ireland 1978
- IRL PO Box 3010, DUBLIN 4, Republic of Ireland.
  353 (1) 873 0451
  email vegsoc@ireland.com   http://www.vegetarian.ie
  Hon Sec: Patricia Timoney
- ○ *K

Vegetarian Society (UK) Ltd (VegSoc) 1969
- ■ Parkdale, Dunham Rd, ALTRINCHAM, Cheshire, WA14 4QG.
  (hq)
  0161-925 2000   fax 0161-926 9182
  email info@vegsoc.org   http://www.vegsoc.org
  Chief Exec: Annette Pinner
- ▲ Company Limited by Guarantee; Registered Charity
- Br 150 local groups
- ○ *G, *K, *V; to promote knowledge of the vegetarian diet for the
  benefit of human health, animal welfare & the environment
- Gp Cordon Vert Cookery School for professional & amateur chefs
- ● Conf - ET - Exhib - Inf - Lib
- < Intl Vegetarian U
- M 14, 00 i, UK / 500 i, o'seas
  (Sub: £21 UK / £31 o'seas)
- ¶ The Vegetarian - 4; ftm.   AR - 1; ftm only.

Vehicle Builders' & Repairers' Association (VBRA) 1914
- ■ Belmont House, 102 Finkle Lane, Gildersome, LEEDS, W Yorks,
  LS27 7TW.   (hq)
  0113-253 8333   fax 0113-238 0496
  email vbra@vbra.co.uk   http://www.vbra.co.uk
  Chief Exec: Malcolm Tagg
- ▲ Company Limited by Guarantee
- ○ *T; to represent the motor repair & body building industry; to
  support members by providing advice, information & training
- Gp National Repairers Council; National Manufacturers Council
- ● Conf - Mtgs - ET - Exhib - Inf - VE - Empl - LG
- < Assn Intle des Réparateurs en Carrosserie (AIRC)(Brussels)
- M 1,100 f, 1,000 i (subscribers to Body)
- ¶ Body (Jnl) - 10; ftm, £4.50 each nm.   Ybk.   .

Vehicle Restraint Manufacturers Association (VRMA) 1997
- ■ Heathcote House, 136 Hagley Rd, Edgbaston, BIRMINGHAM,
  B16 9PN.   (hq)
  0121-454 4141   fax 0121-454 4949
  email sp@heathcote-coleman.co.uk
  http://www.heathcote-coleman.co.uk
  Sec: Mrs Sharon J Parker
- ▲ Un-incorporated Society
- ○ *T; to establish & maintain fundamental, technical &
  commercial principles within the industry
- Gp Product gps: Safety fence, Parapet, Anchorages
- ● Mtgs
- M 16 f
  2002-03 Parapet & Safety Fence Manufacturers Association

Vernacular Architecture Group (VAG) 1954
- ■ Ashley, Willows Green, Great Leighs, CHELMSFORD, Essex,
  CM3 1QD.   (hsp)
  01245 361408
  http://www.vag.org.uk
  Hon Sec: Mrs B A Watkin
- ▲ Registered Charity
- ○ *L; study of small traditional buildings in GB & abroad
- ● Conf - Res - Inf - Lib - VE
- M 619 i, 18 org, UK / 48 i, o'seas
- ¶ Vernacular Architecture - 1; ftm, £20 nm.
  NL - 2; ftm only.   Bibliography - 5 yrly; ftm, £9.50 nm.

Veteran-Cycle Club (V-CC) 1955
NR 8 Meadow Way, HITCHIN, Herts, SG5 2BN.   (mem/sp)
       http://www.v-cc.org.uk
       Hon Sec: Mike Sims
▲ Un-incorporated Society
Br 21 regional sections
○ *G; to promote the riding & restoration of old bicycles; to study
       & exchange information about the history of cycles & cycling
Gp Marque enthusiasts for 82 makes of machine
● Mtgs - Res - Exhib - Lib
< Intl Veteran Cycle Assn; Transport Trust
M 2,300 i
¶ News & Views - 6;   The 'Boneshaker' - 3;   Ybk - 1;
       all ftm only.

Veteran Horse Society (VHS) 2000
■ Hedre Fawr, St Dogmaels, CARDIGAN, N Pembrokeshire,
       SA43 3LZ.   (hq)
       0870 242 6653
       http://www.veteran-horse-society.co.uk
       Dir: Miss Julianne Aston
▲ Company Limited by Guarantee
○ *V; dedicated to the health, welfare & profile of the horse &
       pony over the age of 15
● Conf - Mtgs - ET - Res - Exhib - Comp - SG - Stat - Expt - Inf -
       PL - VE - Empl - LG
< Nat Equine Welfare Coun (NEWC); Brit Equestrian Tr Assn
       (BETA)
M 4,000 i, UK / 50 i, o'seas
¶ Voice of the Veteran - 4.

Veteran Speedway Riders Association
       since 2006 **World Speedway Riders Association**

Veterans' Lawn Tennis Association of Great Britain
       since 2004 **Vets Tennis GB**

**Veterinary Association for Arbitration & Jurisprudence
(VAAJ) 1992**
NR The Beeches, Rickerby, CARLISLE, Cumbria, CA3 9AA.   (hsp)
       01228 521450
       Hon Sec: Graham D Cawley
▲ Un-incorporated Society
○ *P; to promote the study of all aspects of jurisprudence,
       arbitration & Alternative Dispute Resolution (ADR) within the
       veterinary profession; to assist with training for members
Gp [all specialities]
● Conf - Mtgs - ET - Inf
< Forensic Science Soc; Inst of Biology
M 90 i, UK / 10 i, o'seas
¶ Proceedings - 2; ftm, £25 nm.   NL - irreg; free.

Veterinary Cardiovascular Society
       a group of the **British Small Animal Veterinary Association**

Veterinary Deer Society
       a group of the **British Veterinary Association**

Veterinary History Society 1962
■ 17 Anseres Place, WELLS, Somerset, BA5 2RT.   (hsp)
       01749 673558
       Hon Sec: Jean Mann
▲ Un-incorporated Society
○ *L, *V; promotion of interest in veterinary history in the UK
● Mtgs - Inf - VE
M 100 i, 15 libraries, UK / 20 i, 15 libraries, o'seas
¶ Bulletin of Veterinary History - 2; ftm, £15 nm.

Veterinary Ireland 1888
IRL 13 The Courtyard, Kilcarbery Park, Nangor Rd, DUBLIN 22,
       Republic of Ireland.
       353 (1) 457 7976   fax 353 (1) 457 7998
       email vetireland@eircom.net
       http://www.veterinary-ireland.org
○ *P, *V

Veterinary Orthopaedic Association
       a group of the **British Small Animal Veterinary Association**

Veterinary Public Health Association
       a group of the **British Veterinary Association**

Vets Tennis GB 1974
■ G01 Mandel House, Eastfields Avenue, LONDON,
       SW18 1JU.   (hsp)
       020 8875 1773
       email vw@vetstennisgb.org   http://www.vetstennisgb.org
       Sec: Valerie Willoughby
▲ Un-incorporated Society
○ *S; to provide opportunites for veteran tennis players to
       compete in individual & team events
● Conf - Comp - Inf
< Lawn Tennis Assn
M 20 clubs
¶ e NL - 3;   AR - 1; free.
× 2004 Veterans' Lawn Tennis Association of Great Britain

Victim Support 1979
■ Hallam House, 56-60 Hallam Street, LONDON, W1W 6JL.
       (hq)
       020 7268 0200   fax 020 7268 0210
       email contact@victimsupport.org.uk
       http://www.victimsupport.org
       Chief Exec: Gillian Guy
▲ Registered Charity
○ *N, *W; independent national charity which helps people cope
       with crime. Services are free & available to everyone, whether
       or not the crime has been reported & regardless of when it
       happened.
● Conf - ET - Res - Inf - Lib - LG
< Eur Forum for Victims Orgs; Nat Coun for Voluntary Orgs
       (NCVO)
M 374 schemes, 86 crown court witness services
¶ Publications list available.
       Registered name: National Association of Victim Support
       Schemes

Victim Support Scotland (VSS) 1985
■ 15-23 Hardwell Close, EDINBURGH, EH8 9RX.   (hq)
       0131-668 4486   fax 0131-662 5400
       email info@victimsupportsco.demon.co.uk
       http://www.victimsupport.org
       Chief Exec & Co Sec: David McKenna
▲ Company Limited by Guarantee
Br 32 affiliated services (Scotland)
○ *W; to offer practical help, emotional support & essential
       information to victims, witnesses & others affected by crime.
       The service is free & provided by trained volunteers through a
       network of community based victim & court based witness
       services
● Conf - Mtgs - ET - Res - Inf
       Helpline: 0845 603 9213 (Mon-Fri 0900-1630); outside these
       hours call UK Victim Support on 0845 303 0900
¶ Voice [NL] - 4.   AR.
       Generic Information Pack; free.

Victoria Cross & George Cross Association   (VC&GCAssn) 1956
- ■ Horse Guards, Whitehall, LONDON, SW1A 2AX.   (hq)
  020 7930 3506   fax 020 7930 4303
  Sec: Mrs D Grahame
- ○ *G; to establish a central focus for all Victoria Cross & George Cross holders
- ● Conf - Inf
- M 5 i (VC), 14 i (GC), UK / 6 i (VC), 7 i (GC), o'seas
- ¶ Rules.

Victorian Military Society   (VMS)   1975
- NR PO Box 5837, NEWBURY, Berks, RG14 7FJ.
  http://www.victorianmilitarysociety.org.uk
- ▲ Un-incorporated Society; Registered Charity
- ○ *L, *Q; to encourage & foster the study of military aspects of the Victorian era (nominally 1837-1901, the period has been extended to 1914 to include the campaigns of the earlier part of the 20th century); the principal interest is in the forces of the British Empire & its adversaries, but forces of other countries are not excluded
- Gp Anglo-Boer Wars; Sudan Wars; Wargames; 'The Diehard Company' - re-enactment based on the 57th Foot (Middlesex Regiment)
- ● Mtgs - Res - Exhib - Comp - SG - Stat - Inf - VE - Recording of all memorials of the Anglo-Boer War of 1899-1902
- M c 900 i
- ¶ Soldiers of the Queen (Jnl) - 4;
  Soldiers Small Book (NL) - 4; both ftm only.

Victorian Society   1958
- ■ 1 Priory Gardens, LONDON, W4 1TT.   (hq)
  020 8994 1019   fax 020 8747 5899
  email admin@victorian-society.org.uk
  http://www.victorian-society.org.uk
  Dir: Dr Ian Dungavell
- ○ *A, *L; to preserve & protect the best buildings of the 19th century; to study the arts & architecture of the period
- M c 3,500 i

Video Performance Ltd   (VPL)   1984
- NR 1 Upper James St, LONDON, W1F 9DE.   (hq)
  020 7534 1400
- ○ *T; licenses music videos for public performance, broadcast & new media use

**** VIEW**
  Organisation lost: see Introduction paragraph 3.

Viewing Facilities Association UK   (VFA)   1995
- ■ Davey House, 31 St Neots Rd, Eaton Ford, ST NEOTS, Cambs, PE19 7BA.
  01480 211288   fax 01480 211267
  email info@viewing.org.uk   http://www.viewing.org.uk
  Chmn: Liz Sykes
- ○ *T; for viewing facilities, market research, qualitative research
- ● Conf - Inf
- < Market Res Soc; Assn for Qualitative Res
- M 41 f
- ¶ [on website]

Viking Society for Northern Research   1892
- NR c/o Alison Finlay, Birkbeck College, University of London, Malet St, LONDON, WC1E 7HX.   (hsp)
  email a.finlay@bbk.ac.uk   http://www.le.ac.uk/ee/viking/
  Hon Sec: Alison Finlay
- ▲ Un-incorporated Society
- ○ *A, *Q; literature & antiquities of the Scandinavian north, including Iceland
- ● Conf - Mtgs - ET - Res - Lib
- M 296 i, 47 org, UK / 120 i, 152 org, o'seas
- ¶ The Saga Book; £20.   Text Series - irreg; prices vary.
  Dorothea Coke Memorial Lecture - irreg.

The Vikings   1972
- ■ 2 Wheatley Rd, ILKLEY, W Yorks, LS29 8TS.   (hq)
  01943 817924   fax 01943 817924
  http://www.vikingsonline.org.uk/
  Soc Leader: Tony Sayer
- ▲ Company Limited by Guarantee; Registered Charity
- Br c 30; Holland, USA
- ○ *G; dark age re-enactment (primarily that of the Vikings) incl battles, homelife, crafts & skills
- Gp Film extras
- ● Mtgs - Res - Exhib - Inf - Re-enactment shows - Banquets
- < Nat Assn Re-enactment Socs
- M 750 i, UK / 20 i, o'seas
- ¶ Runestaff (Jnl) - 6/8; ftm, £1 nm.
  Flyer (Broadsheet) - 6/8; free.   Ybk; £4.

Village Retail Services Association Educational Trust   (ViRSA) 1992
- NR The Quadrangle, WOODSTOCK, Oxon, OX20 1LH.   (hq)
  01993 814377   fax 01993 810849
  email virsa@plunkett.co.uk   http://www.virsa.org
  Dir: Donna Smith
- ▲ Registered Charity
- Br 12
- ○ *E, *K; assisting rural communities in England & Wales to maintain, improve or revive their retail services
- ● ET - Res - Stat - Inf - LG - Working with individuals, community groups & others on specific retailing problems in rural areas
- M c 200 subscribers
- ¶ Talking Shop (NL) - 4.   AR.
  Hbk (village shops & post offices - a guide to village investment).
  Information sheets (set of 19).

Vinegar Brewers' Federation   (VBF)   1929
- ■ Crescent House, 34 Eastbury Way, SWINDON, Wilts, SN25 2EN.   (hsb)
  01793 727387   fax 01793 726485
  email vinegarbrewers@aol.com
  Sec: Walter J Anzer
- ▲ Un-incorporated Society
- ○ *T
- ● Mtgs - LG
- < Permanent Intl Vinegar C'ee, Common Market (CPIV)
- M 5 f

**** Vintage Arms Association**

Vintage Carriages Trust   (VCT)   1964
- ■ The Railway Station, Haworth, KEIGHLEY, W Yorks, BD22 8NJ.   (mail add)
  01535 680425   fax 01535 610796
  email admin@vintagecarriagestrust.org
  http://www.vintagecarriagestrust.org
  Ingrow Railway Station Yard, Halifax Rd, Ingrow, KEIGHLEY, W Yorks, BD21 5AX.   (location)
  Hon Sec: David Carr
- ▲ Registered Charity
- ○ *G; the conservation & restoration of railway carriages & other railway artifacts, & the interpretation of these through museum display
- Gp Railway carriage restoration & preservation
- ● ET - Operating the Museum of Rail Travel at Ingrow
- < Fedn of Eur Rlys (FEDECRAIL); Heritage Rly Assn (HRA); Transport Trust (TT)
- M 580 i, UK / 4 i, o'seas
- ¶ NL - 4.   All Aboard; £3.00p.   AR - 1; free.
  All Aboard: your guide to the story of rail travel for the ordinary passenger.

© CBD Research Ltd · Beckenham · BR3 5JS · Tel 020 8650 7745 · Fax 020 8650 0768 · E-mail cbd@cbdresearch.com · www.cbdresearch.com

Vintage Glider Club of Great Britain   (VGC)   1973
NR   201 Bridge End Road, GRANTHAM, NG31 7HA.   (hsp)
      01476 564200
      email stephensen@talktalk.net
      http://www.vintagegliderclub.org.uk
      Hon Sec: Bruce Stephenson
Br   Australia, Austria, Belgium, Czech Republic, Denmark, France,
      Germany, Holland, Hungary, New Zealand, Norway, Poland,
      Sweden, Switzerland, USA
○   *S; 'to preserve old gliders in flying condition, & to prevent their
      mass destruction, as has happened in the past; there is no
      museum for them as yet in the UK'
●   Mtgs - Aeromodelling - Archive (plans, photographs, films/
      videos) - Holding national & international rallies
<   Oldtime Gliding Club Wasserkuppe
M   450 i, UK / 450 i, o'seas
¶   VGC News - 3.

**Vintage Horticultural & Garden Machinery Club   (VHGMC)
1993**
■   Glenview, Fosseway, Midsomer Norton, RADSTOCK, Somerset,
      BA3 4BB.   (sp)
      email vhgmc@btinternet.com
      http://www.tractorbox.co.uk
      Club Sec: C Moore
○   *G, *H; to collect, preserve, restore & use garden &
      horticultural machinery, including hand tools
●   Displays at vintage rallies & garden shows - Information service
      to members only
M   680 i
¶   The Cultivator (NL) - 5; ftm only.

Vintage Motor Cycle Club Ltd   (VMCC)   1946
■   Allen House, Wetmore Rd, BURTON upon TRENT, Staffs,
      DE14 1TR.   (hq)
      01283 540557   fax 01283 510547
      email hq@vmcc.net   http://www.vmcc.net
      Chief Exec: James Hewing
▲   Company Limited by Guarantee
Br   75
○   *G; to preserve, restore & use both for competition & pleasure,
      motorcycles, combinations & tricycles: veteran (pre 1914),
      vintage (1915-1930), post-vintage (1931-1944), post-war
      (1945-1960), & post-1960 (1961- & +25 yrs old)
Gp   Racing; Grasstrack; Sprint
●   Mtgs - Exhib - Inf - Lib - PL - Archives - Insurance scheme
<   Auto-Cycle U (ACU); Fedn of Brit Historic Vehicle
      Clubs (FBHVC); RAC
M   13,400 i, UK / 500 i, o'seas
¶   The Vintage Motor Cycle - 12; ftm only.

Vintage Sports Car Club Ltd   (VSCC)   1934
■   The Old Post Office, West St, CHIPPING NORTON, Oxon,
      OX7 5EL.   (hq)
      01608 644777   fax 01608 644888
      email info@vscc.co.uk   http://www.vscc.co.uk
      Sec: Mike Stripe
▲   Company Limited by Guarantee
○   *G, *S; for owners of historic racing cars: Edwardian (1905-
      1918), vintage (pre 1931), post-vintage thoroughbred (pre
      1941), & certain front engined cars (pre 1961)
Gp   Alfa Romeo; Delage; Frazer Nash; Light Car & Edwardian
●   Conf - Mtgs - Res - Comp - Inf - Lib - VE
<   RAC Motor Sports Assn; Fédn Intle des Automobiles Anciennes
M   c 7,500 i, 14 f, UK / 500 i, o'seas
¶   Bulletin - 4;   NL - 12;   Ybk; all ftm only.

Vintage Wooden Boat Association   (VWBA)
NR   14 West End Lane, POTTON, Beds, SG19 2RD.
      http://www.vwba.org
      Mem Sec: Sally Walsh
○   *G; to promote the use, maintenance & restoration of wooden
      boats
¶   The Log (Jnl)

Vintners' Federation of Ireland   (VFI)   1973
IRL   VFI House, Castleside Drive, Rathfarnham, DUBLIN 14,
      Republic of Ireland.
      353 (1) 492 3400   fax 353 (1) 492 3577
      email enquiries@vintners.ie   http://www.vfi.ie
      Chief Exec: Tadg O'Sullivan
○   *T
M   c 6,000 f

Viola da Gamba Society   (VdGS)   1948
NR   56 Hunters Way, Dringhouses, YORK, YO24 1JJ.   (hsp)
      01904 706959   fax 01904 706959
      email admin@vdgs.demon.co.uk
      http://www.vdgs.demon.co.uk
      Admin: Mrs Caroline Wood
▲   Registered Charity
○   *D; to advance the study of viols, their music, their playing &
      their making
●   Conf - Mtgs - Res - Exhib - Inf
<   Viola da Gamba Soc of America; Lute Soc (UK)
M   460 i, libraries & universities
¶   Music - 1; ftm.   Care of Viol (booklet).
      LM - 1; ftm.   AR.

Violet Needham Society   (VNS)   1985
■   19 Ashburnham Place, LONDON, SE10 8TZ.   (hsp)
      020 8692 4562
      email richardcheffins@aol.com
      http://www.violetneedhamsociety.org
      Hon Sec: Richard H A Cheffins
▲   Un-incorporated Society
○   *A; interest in the life & works of Violet Needham & other
      children's writers of the period (1940s & 50s) & in Ruritanian
      fiction in general
●   Mtgs - Res - Lib - VE
M   260 i, 3 org, UK / 27 i, 1 org, o'seas
¶   Souvenir (Jnl) - 3; ftm, £2.50 nm.   NL - 3; ftm only.

Virgil Society   1943
■   8 Purley Oaks Rd, SANDERSTEAD, Surrey, CR2 0NP.   (mem/sp)
      http://www.virgilsociety.org.uk
      Mem Sec: Jill Kilsby
▲   Registered Charity
○   *L; study & interpretation of Virgil as the symbol of the central
      educational tradition of Western Europe
●   Mtgs
M   c 120 i
¶   Proceedings - 3 yrly.   NL - 2.

Virginia Woolf Society of Great Britain   (VWSGB)   1998
■   106 Gloucester Rd, KINGSTON upon THAMES, Surrey,
      KT1 3QN.   (chmn/p)
      020 8546 5712
      email sbarkway@btinternet.com
      http://www.virginiawoolfsociety.co.uk
      Chmn: Stephen Barkway,   Sec: Lynne Newland
▲   Un-incorporated Society
○   *A; 'to present Virginia Woolf (1882-1941) in her true light as a
      great novelist, essayist, publisher & woman of letters'
●   Conf - Inf - VE
M   250 i, 6 org, UK / 150 i, 3 org, o'seas
¶   Virginia Woolf Bulletin - 3; ftm, £5 nm.
      Annual Birthday Lecture - 1; £4 (£5 o'seas).

Virus Tested Stem Cutting Growers Association
since 2007 **Pre Basic Growers Association**

Vision Homes Association   (VHA)   1985
- ■ TriGate, 210-222 Hagley Road West, Oldbury, BIRMINGHAM, B68 0NP.   (hq)
  0121-434 4644   fax 0121-434 5655
  email gayle@visionhomes.org
  http://www.visionhomes.org.uk
  Chief Exec: Ewa Stefanowska
- ▲ Company Limited by Guarantee; Registered Charity
- Br 8
- ○ *W; to provide residential & other services for people who have impaired vision & other (often profound) disabilities
- ● Mtgs - ET
- M 180 i
- ¶ Report; free.

Visual Arts & Galleries Association   (VAGA)   1978
- ■ The Old Village School, High St, Witcham, ELY, Cambs, CB6 2LQ.   (hq)
  01353 776356   fax 01353 775411
  email admin@vaga.co.uk   http://www.vaga.co.uk
  Dir: Hilary Gresty
- ○ *A, *P; to improve the status of the visual arts within contemporary culture
- ● Conf - Mtgs - Res - SG - Inf - LG
- M c 350 i, f & affiliates
- ¶ VAGA update - 6; free.

Visual Arts Scotland   (VAS)   1989
- NR 6/8 Newhaven Rd, Bonnington, EDINBURGH, EH6 5PU.   (admin/p)
  07796 990970
  email info@visualartsscotland.org
  http://www.visualartsscotland.org
  Admin: Rebecca Wilson
- ▲ Registered Charity
- ○ *A; to promote contemporary & applied arts
- M i

Vitiligo Society   1985
- NR 125 Kennington Rd, LONDON, SE11 6SF.   (hq)
  0800 018 2631
  http://www.vitiligosociety.org.uk
- ▲ Registered Charity
- Br 14
- ○ *W; to give support & advice to people with vitiligo (a skin condition in which patches of skin turn white, although neither painful nor infectious)
- ● Mtgs - Res - Inf
- M c 2,000 i
- ¶ Dispatches (NL) - 4.
  Vitiligo: understanding the loss of skin colour (Hbk).

Voice: the union for education professionals   2008
- ■ 2 St James' Court, Friar Gate, DERBY, DE1 1BT.   (hq)
  01332 372337   fax 01332 290310
  email enquiries@voicetheunion.org.uk
  http://www.voicetheunion.org.uk
  Gen Sec: Philip Parkin
- ○ *E, *U; for educational professionals working in education, early years & childcare settings
- ● Conf - Mtgs - ET - Res - Exhib - Stat - Inf - LG
- M 38,000 i
- ¶ Your Voice - 4; ftm, £2 nm.
  Hbk for Members - 1; ftm only.
- × 2008 (Professional Association of Nursery Nurses
  (Professional Association of Teachers
  (Professionals Allied to Teaching

Voice Care Network UK   (VCN)   1993
- ■ 25 The Square, KENILWORTH, Warks, CV8 1EF.   (hq)
  01926 864000   fax 01926 864000
  email info@voicecare.org.uk
  http://www.voicecare.org.uk
  Admin: Angela Brooks
- ▲ Registered Charity
- ○ *P; promotion & development of healthy & effective use of the voice for all professional voice users & in particular, for teachers
- ● Conf - ET - Res - SG - Stat - Inf - Practical workshops (group teaching & one-to-one teaching)
- < Assn Teachers Singing (AOTOS): Soc Teachers Speech & Drama
- > Brit Voice Assn
- M 250 i, UK / c 30 i, o'seas
- ¶ Voice Matters (NL) - 3; ftm.
  Keeping a Young Voice (leaflet).
  Booklets:
    More Care for Your Voice.
    Voice Warm-up Exercises.
    A Voice Care Guide for Call Centre Managers.

Voice of Chief Officers of Cultural, Community & Leisure Services   (VOCAL)   1975
- ■ c/o Lagoon Leisure Centre, 11 Christie St, PAISLEY, Renfrewshire, PA1 1NB.   (hsb)
  0141-887 2210
  Sec: Joyce McKellar
- ▲ Un-incorporated Society
- ○ *P; to promote recreation & leisure services in Scotland; to act as a support agency & forum for senior leisure professionals
- ● Conf - Mtgs - Res - LG
- M 50 i
- × 2007-08 Voice of Chief Officers of Culture, Community & Leisure Services in Scotland

Voice of the Listener & Viewer Ltd   (VLV)   1983
- ■ 101 King's Drive, GRAVESEND, Kent, DA12 5BQ.   (hq)
  01474 352835   fax 01474 351112
  email info@vlv.org.uk   http://www.vlv.org.uk
  Chmn: Mrs Jocelyn Hay
- ▲ Company Limited by Guarantee; Registered Charity
- ○ *K; an independent non-profit making body which represents the citizen & consumer interest in broadcasting & works to ensure high quality, diversity & independence in British broadcasting; to represent the interests of listeners & viewers on all broadcasting issues; to maintain the 'principle of public service in broadcasting'
- Gp Children's & educational broadcasting; Older people's broadcasting
- ● Conf - Mtgs - Conf - Inf - Lib - VE - LG
  Holds the archives of:
    British Action for Children's Television [ceased 1995]
    Broadcasting Research Unit [ceased 1991]
- < Eur Alliance of Listeners' & Viewers' Assns (EURALVA)
- M 2,000 i, 28 org, c 50 universities & colleges, UK / 30 i, o'seas
  (Sub: £25 i, £60 org (etc), UK / £35 i, £60 org o'seas)
- ¶ VLV Bulletin - 4; ftm; £30 (£35 o'seas) nm.
  Conference Proceedings Reports - 3/4; on application.
  Submissions to Official Consultations - irreg; free online, (hardcopy price on application).
  Other ad hoc publications.

Volleyball England
  the branded image of the **English Volleyball Association**

Voluntary Action History Society   (VAHS)   1991
- NR 16 Hillcrest Rd, NEWHAVEN, E Sussex, BN9 9EE.   (memsec/p)
  http://www.vahs.org.uk
  Mem Sec: Alison Penn
- ▲ Registered Charity
- ○ *G; to promote & study the history of philanthropy & voluntary organisations

© CBD Research Ltd · Beckenham · BR3 5JS · Tel 020 8650 7745 · Fax 020 8650 0768 · E-mail cbd@cbdresearch.com · www.cbdresearch.com

Voluntary Arts Network   (VAN)
- ■   121 Cathedral Road, Pontcanna, CARDIFF, CF11 9PH.   (hq)
  029 2039 5395
  email info@voluntaryarts.org
  http://www.voluntaryarts.org
  Chief Exec: Robin Simpson
- ▲   Company Limited by Guarantee; Registered Charity
- Br   5 centres
- ○   *A, *N; a development agency for amateur & voluntary arts & crafts; aims to promote participation across the UK & the Republic of Ireland
- ●   Conf - ET - Res - Inf - Help with starting a group - Support for umbrella bodies
- ¶   Update (NL) - 4, (with 4 Briefing sheets to each issue); £25-50.

Voluntary Euthanasia Society
  since 2006 **Dignity in Dying**

Voluntary Euthanasia Society of Scotland   (VESS)
- ■   17 Hart St, EDINBURGH, EH1 3RN.   (hq)
  0131-556 4404
  http://www.euthanasia.cc
  Dir: Chris Docker
- ▲   Un-incorporated Society
- ○   *K; to campaign for all nterested in euthanasia, living wills, & the connected medical ethics & bioethics
- ●   Conf - Res - Inf
- M   i
  (Sub: £20-£30)
- ¶   NL - 1; £20 m.   Five Last Acts (book); £10 m.
  Departing Drugs (booklet); £8 m.   all prices for UK.
  Note: is usually known as EXIT.

Voluntary Service Overseas   (VSO)   1958
- ■   317 Putney Bridge Rd, LONDON, SW15 2PN.   (hq)
  020 8780 7200   fax 020 8780 7300
  email enquiry@vso.org.uk   http://www.vso.org.uk
  Chief Exec: Mark Goldring
- ▲   Registered Charity
- Br   35 in Africa & Asia
- ○   *W; a voluntary charity dedicated to assisting development in the Third World by sending experienced, practical people on 2-year projects to share their skills in Africa, Asia, the Caribbean & the Pacific
- ●   ET - International development
- <   [too many to list]
- M   supporters
- ×   2005 (April) BESO (merged)

Volunteering England
- NR   Regent's Wharf, 8 All Saints Street, LONDON, N1 9RL.
  0845 305 6979
- ○   *K, *W; to promote volunteering as a force for change in the community

Von Hippel-Lindau Contact Group   (VHLCG)   2002
- ■   297 Holcombe Rd, Greenmount, BURY, Lancs, BL8 4BB.
  (coord/p)
  01204 886112
  email maryweetman@waitrose.com
  http://www.vhlcg.co.uk
  Coordinator: Mary Weetman
- ▲   Registered Charity
- ○   *W; to help families with Von Hippel-Lindau disease (an inherited genetic disease causing abnormal growth of tumours in various parts of the body)
- ●   Conf - ET - Fund raising
- M   50 i

Voucher Association   (TheVA)   1996
- ■   T-Wing, Crowthorne Business Estate, Old Wokingham Rd, CROWTHORNE, Berks, RG45 6AW.   (asa)
  0870 241 6445   fax 01344 751601
  email info@the-va.co.uk   http://www.the-va.co.uk
  Dir Gen: Andrew Johnson
- ▲   Un-incorporated Society
- ○   *T; an information & reference point for any company in the gift voucher, gift card, or prepaid cards market
- ●   Conf - Mtgs - ET - Res - Exhib - Stat - Inf - VE - LG
- <   Brit Promotional Merchandise Assn (BPMA); Direct Marketing Assn (DMA); Inst of Sales Promotion (ISP); Indep Print Inds Assn
- M   80 f
  (Sub: £2,200)

Vulval Pain Society   (VPS)   1996
- ■   PO Box 7804, NOTTINGHAM, NG3 5ZQ.   (mail/address)
  http://www.vulvalpainsociety.org
  Jt Secs: David Nunns,   Kay Thomas
- ▲   Un-incorporated Society
- ○   *W; to provide sufferers with an increase in understanding of their condition; to raise awareness of the condition as an important aspect of women's health
- ●   Inf
- M   c 200 i
- ¶   NL - 4; ftm only.   Factsheets; free.

W W Jacobs Appreciation Society (WWJ) 1988
■ 3 Roman Rd, SOUTHWICK, W Sussex, BN42 4TP   (hsp)
01273 596217
Hon Sec: A R James
Br 2
○ *A; develop interest in literary, dramatic & filmed works of the author W W Jacobs (1863-1943)
Gp Biographical; Bibliographical; Theatre & film
● Res - Inf - Lib - PL
< Assn of Literary Socs
M 40 i, UK / 15 i, o'seas
¶ Field Guide (bibliography); £6.
Biography; £12.   Films Directory; £2.
Bibliography (a specialist detailed work); £15.

Wagner Society 1953
■ 16 Doran Drive, REDHILL, Surrey, RH1 6AX.   (h/mem/p)
email mm@misterman.freeserve.co.uk
http://www.wagnersociety.org
Mem Sec: Mrs Margaret Murphy
▲ Registered Charity
○ *D; the appreciation & study of the life of Richard Wagner & his music
● Mtgs - Res - Lib
M i
¶ Wagner News - 6; ftm.

Wagon Building & Repairing Association (WBRA) 1991
NR Homelea, Westland Green, Little Hadham, WARE, Herts, SG11 2AG.   (hsp)
01279 843487
email geoffrey.pratt@btconnect.com
Sec Gen: Geoffrey Pratt
○ *T; all aspects of manufacture & repair of freight rolling stock
M 10 f

Wakeboard UK (WUK) 1996
■ Arden Croft, Forshaw Heath Lane, EARLSWOOD, Warks, B94 5LD.   (hsp)
01564 700309   fax 01564 700309
email graham@wakeboard.co.uk
http://www.wakeboard.co.uk
Chmn: Graham Creedy
▲ Un-incorporated Society
○ *S; to promote & monitor the sport of wakeboarding
Gp Competitions; Training for coaches to NVQ standard
● ET - Comp - Free 'come & try it days'
< Intl Waterski Fedn; Brit Waterski Fedn
M 150 i, UK / 10 i, o'seas
¶ NL - 4.

Wales-Argentine Society
English name of **Cymdeithas Cymru-Ariannin**

Wales Association of Community & Town Councils
in 2004 merged with the National Association of Local Councils in Wales to form **One Voice Wales**

Wales Council for Voluntary Action (Cyngor Gweithredu Gwirfoddol Cymru) (WCVA) 1934
■ Baltic House, Mount Stuart Square, CARDIFF BAY, Glamorgan, CF10 5FH.   (hq)
029 2043 1734   fax 029 2043 1701
email help@wcva.org.uk   http://www.wcva.org.uk
Chief Exec: Graham Benfield
▲ Company Limited by Guarantee; Registered Charity
Br 2
○ *W; the voice of the voluntary sector in Wales.   It represents the interests of, & campaigns for, all voluntary organisations
● Conf - Mtgs - ET - Res - Exhib - Stat - Inf - Lib - LG
< NCVO (sister org)
M 20 i, 80 f, 1,700 org
¶ NL - 12.   Directory - 2/3 yrly.
Wales Funding Handbook - 1.
publications list available.

Wales Craft Council (WCC) 1977
■ Henfaes Lane, WELSHPOOL, Powys, SY21 7BE.   (hq)
01938 555313   fax 01938 556237
email inf0@walescraftcouncil.co.uk
http://www.walescraftcouncil.co.uk
Chmn: Philomena Hearn
▲ Company Limited by Guarantee
○ *P, *T; for full-time professional craft, gift & textile producers in Wales
Gp Direct sales; Trade sales
● Exhib
M c 150 f
¶ Bulletin - 12; ftm.

Wales Pre-school Playgroups Association (Wales PPA) 1987
■ Unit 1 The Lofts, 9 Hunter St, Butetown, CARDIFF, CF10 5GX.   (hq)
029 2045 1242
email info@walesppa.org   http://www.walesppa.org
Dir: Thomas A Memery
▲ Company Limited by Guarantee; Registered Charity
Br 14
○ *E; to enhance the development, care & education of pre-school children in Wales by encouraging parents to understand & provide for their needs, through high quality pre-school groups
● Conf - Mtgs - ET - Res - Exhib - Comp - Stat - Inf - Lib - LG
M 1,200 org
¶ Small Talk - 6; £2.50 m, £3.50 nm.   AR; ftm, £5 nm.

Wales Trades Union Congress
NR Transport House, 1 Cathedral Rd, CARDIFF, Glamorgan, CF11 9SD.   (hq)
029 2034 7010
http://www.wtuc.org.uk
○ *U
No further information supplied

Wales Trekking & Riding Association
■ Sunny Bank, Velindre, BRECON, Powys, LD3 0ST.   (hsp)
01497 847464
http://www.ridingwales.com
○ *G
No further information supplied

© CBD Research Ltd · Beckenham · BR3 5JS · Tel 020 8650 7745 · Fax 020 8650 0768 · E-mail cbd@cbdresearch.com · www.cbdresearch.com

Wall Tie Installers Federation (WTIF) 1989
NR Heald House, Heald St, LIVERPOOL, L19 2LY.   (hq)
     0151-494 2503   fax 0151-494 2511
     email admin@wtif.org.uk   http://www.wtif.org.uk
     Gen Sec: Hugh Banks
▲ Company Limited by Guarantee
○ *T; installation of remedial & replacement wall ties & related
     services
● Conf - Mtgs - ET - Exhib - Inf - Lib - PL
M 80 f
¶ WTIF News - 12; ftm.

Wallcovering Distributors Association   (WDA)
■ c/o William Robinson, Daleside Rd, NOTTINGHAM, NG2 4DH.
     0115-979 9790
     Pres: Stuart Thorne,   Hon Sec: William Robinson
○ *T; for British distributors of wallcoverings, fabrics & decorating
     products
M f

Wallcovering Manufacturers' Association of Great Britain Ltd
▲ Company Limited by Guarantee
     since 2005 the Wallcoverings Sector Council, a section of the
     British Coatings Federation

Wallpaper History Society   1986
NR Lifford House, 199 Eade Rd, LONDON, N4 1DN.
     (mail address)
▲ Un-incorporated Society
○ *L; to encourage research & provide information on all aspects
     of wallpaper production, consumption & design.
     Encompasses not only the history of wallpaper, but also
     topics relating to other kinds of wallcoverings & interior
     design generally
● Conf - SG - VE
M c 225 i, f & org
¶ Jnl - 2 yrly; ftm.

Walmsley Society   1985
■ April Cottage, 1 Brand Rd, Hampden Park, EASTBOURNE,
     E Sussex, BN22 9PX.   (hsp)
     01323 506447
     email walmsley@mabarraclough.f9.co.uk
     http://www.walmsleysoc.org
     Hon Sec: Fred W Lane
▲ Un-incorporated Society
○ *A; to promote & encourage an appreciation of the literary &
     artistic heritage left to us by J Ulric Walmsley (1860-1954) &
     Leo Walmsley (1892-1966)
Gp Research/archives; Publicity; Biography planning
● Mtgs - Res - Inf - VE - Encouraging the reprinting of books by
     Leo Walmsley or concerning the Walmsleys
< Alliance Literary Socs
M 200 i, UK / 4 i, o'seas
¶ Jnl - 2; ftm, £3 nm.   NL - 4/5; ftm only.
     Books & booklets.

Walpole
■ 1 Southwark Bridge, LONDON, SE1 9HL.   (hq)
     020 7873 3803
     email charlotte.keesing@thewalpole.co.uk
     http://www.thewalpole.co.uk
     Contact: Charlotte Keesing
○ *T; an organisation of Britain's 100 famous luxury brands
M c 100 f
     no further information supplied

Walpole Society 1911
■ Dept of Prints & Drawings, The British Museum, LONDON,
     WC1B 3DG.   (mail/address)
     020 7323 8408
     email dkealey@supanet.com
     http://www.walpolesociety.org.uk
     Chmn: Simon Swyfen Jervis
▲ Registered Charity
○ *A; to collect & publish archival & other material relating to the
     history of the arts in Great Britain
● Res - Publications
M 280 i, 85 org, UK / 50 i, 130 org, o'seas
     (Sub: £45 i, £60 org]
¶ Walpole Society Volume - 1; ftm only.   AR.

Walter de la Mare Society   1997
■ 3 Hazelwood House, New River Crescent, LONDON,
     N13 5RE.   (hsp)
     020 8886 1771
     email fguthrie@talktalk.net   http://www.bluetree.co.uk/
     wdlmsociety
     Hon Sec & Treas: Frances Guthrie
○ *A; to honour the memory of novelist, poet & essayist Walter
     de la Mare (1873-1956); to promote the study & deepen the
     appreciation of his works
● Mtgs
M 65 i, UK / 10 i, o'seas
¶ Jnl - 1; ftm (£15 subn).

War Memorials Trust   (WMT)   1997
■ 4 Lower Belgrave St, LONDON, SW1W 0LA.   (hq)
     020 7259 0403   fax 020 7259 0862
     email info@warmemorials.org
     http://www.warmemorials.com
     Trust Mgr: Frances Moreton
▲ Registered Charity
○ *K; for the protection & conservation of war memorials in the
     UK
● Inf
M 1,500 i, UK / 100 i, o'seas
     (Sub: £20)
¶ Bulletin - 4.
× 2004 Friends of War Memorials

War Poets Association   (WPA)   2004
NR c/o Veale Wasbrough (DBMW), Orchard Court, Orchard Lane,
     BRISTOL, BS1 5WS.   (treas/b)
     01275 376916
     email treasurer@warpoets.org   http://www.warpoets.org
     Treas: Patrick Villa
▲ Registered Charity
○ *A; to promote interest in the work, life & historical context of
     poets whose subject is the experience of war
¶ War Poetry Review; NL.

War Research Society
§ 27 Courtway Ave, BIRMINGHAM, B14 4PP.   (hq)
     0121-430 5348   fax 0121-436 7401
     http://www.battlefieldtours.co.uk
     Office Mgr: Mike Heaven
     Organises guided tours of WW1 & WW2 sites; has taken
     thousands of pilgrims, veterans, widows & children to visit the
     battlefields, memorials & last resting places of the fallen.

War Widows Association of Great Britain (WWA) 1971
- ■ c/o British Legion, 48 Pall Mall, LONDON, SW1Y 5JY. (hq)
  0845 241 2189
  email info@warwidowsassociation.org.uk
  http://www.warwidowsassociation.org.uk
  The Hon Secretary
- ▲ Registered Charity
- ○ *W; to care for the welfare of War Widows; to speak on their behalf with government ministers
- ● Inf
- M 5,500 i
- ¶ Courage (NL) - 3; ftm, donations welcomed nm.

Warmblood Breeders' Studbook - UK (WBS-UK) 1977
- NR Lower Tredenham, Lanivet, BODMIN, Cornwall, PL30 5HL.
  (chmn/p)
  01208 832940
  http://www.bwbs.co.uk
  Chmn & Dir: Mrs S Wason
- ▲ Company Limited by Guarantee
- ○ *B; the controlled breeding of warm-blood horses, particularly Hanoverians, Holsteins & Dutch, Swedish & Danish Warm-Bloods, Trakehners & cross breeds
- ● 2-yearly show with mare & stallion gradings - Registering & passporting horses
- < Brit Horse Soc; Nat Stallion Approval Scheme
- M 400 i
- ¶ NL - 2.
- × 2008 (January) British Warm-Blood Society

Warrington Chamber of Commerce & Industry 1876
- NR International Business Centre, Delta Crescent, Westbrook, WARRINGTON, Cheshire, WA5 7WQ. (hq)
  01925 715150 fax 01925 715159
  email info@warrington-chamber.co.uk
  http://www.warrington-chamber.co.uk
  Chief Exec: Colin Daniels
- ▲ Company Limited by Guarantee
- ○ *C
- < Brit Chams Comm; Chams Comm NW

Waste Watch 1987
- NR 56-64 Leonard St, LONDON, EC2A 4JX. (hq)
  020 7549 0300 fax 020 7549 0301
  email info@wastewatch.org.uk
  http://www.wastewatch.org.uk
- ▲ Company Limited by Guarantee; Registered Charity
- ○ *K; to promote & support action for waste reduction & recycling by working with community groups, voluntary organisations, local authorities & businesses - providing practical support for local action; to encourage government & industry to support recycling; it is partly funded by DEFRA's Environmental Action Fund
- ● Inf - LG - Operates Wasteline: a telephone & postal information service on what can be re-cycled & where
- M i, f & org
- ¶ Practical guides & specialist reports; list available.

Water Colour Society of Ireland
- IRL c/o Hon Sec, 74 Grange Park, Raheny, DUBLIN 5, Republic of Ireland.
  353 (1) 848 0802
  http://www.watercoloursocietyofireland.ie
  Hon Sec: Pauline Doyle
- ○ *A

Water Feature 1981
- NR Kingsway House, Wrotham Road, MEOPHAM, Kent, DA13 0AV. (hsp)
- ▲ Un-incorporated Society
- ○ *T
- ● Conf - Mtgs - Inf - VE
- M 1 i, 11 f.
- × Ornamental Pool & Fountain Constructors Association

Water for Health Alliance
- ■ 1 Queen Anne's Gate, LONDON, SW1H 9BT.
  http://www.water.org.uk/home/water-for-health
  no further information supplied

Water Jetting Association 1980
- ■ 17 St Judith's Lane, Sawtry, HUNTINGDON, Cambs, PE28 5XE. (hq)
  01487 834034
  http://www.waterjetting.org.uk
  Dir: Norman Allen
- ○ *T; high pressure water jetting contractors, manufacturers & training providers
- M 120 f
- ¶ Pressure Points (Jnl) - 2.
  Codes of Practice for safe working.
  Medical notes.   Medical card.
  Training course manuals.

Water Management Society Ltd (WM Soc) 1970
- ■ 6 Sir Robert Peel Mill, Tolson's Enterprise Park, Fazeley, TAMWORTH, Staffs, B78 3QD. (hsb)
  01827 289558 fax 01827 250408
  email wmsoc@btconnect.com
  http://www.wmsoc.org.uk
  Gen Sec: Mrs Sue Pipe
- ▲ Company Limited by Guarantee
- ○ *P; the safe & efficient use of water in industry & commerce
- Gp Technical c'ee
- ● Conf - ET - LG
- M 594 i, UK / 20 i, o'seas
- ¶ Waterline - 4; ftm, £75 nm.
  Site Log Book for Water Services; £30 m, £50 nm.
  Guide to Risk Assessment for Water Services; £50 m, £75 nm.

Water UK 1998
- NR 1 Queen Anne's Gate, LONDON, SW1H 9BT. (hq)
  020 7344 1844
  http://www.water.org.uk
- ○ *N; for water services companies of England & Wales
- M f

Waterford Chamber of Commerce
- IRL 2 George's St, WATERFORD, Republic of Ireland.
  353 (51) 872639
  email info@waterfordchamber.ie
  http://www.waterfordchamber.ie
  Chief Exec: Monica Leech
- ○ *C

Waterheater Manufacturers Association
    in 2007 merged with Manufacturers of Domestic Unvented Systems to form the **Hot Water Association**

waterskiscotland 1974
- NR Scottish National Water Ski Centre, Townhill Country Park, DUNFERMLINE, Fife, KY12 0HT. (hq)
  01383 620123 fax 01383 620122
  email info@waterskiscotland.co.uk
  Nat Co-ordinator: Alan G Murray
- ▲ Company Limited by Guarantee
- ○ *S; to act as the national governing body promoting water skiing in Scotland
- Gp Tournament; Racing; Barefoot; Recreational; Kneeboard; Disabled; Wakeboarding; Schools; Youth; Corporate
- ● Conf - Mtgs - ET - Exam - Exhib - Comp - Inf - LG
- < Intl Water Ski Fedn; Brit Water Ski Fedn
- M c250 i
- ¶ NL - 4;   Rule Books;   Codes of Practice;   AR; all free.

© CBD Research Ltd · Beckenham · BR3 5JS · Tel 020 8650 7745 · Fax 020 8650 0768 · E-mail cbd@cbdresearch.com · www.cbdresearch.com

Waterway Recovery Group Ltd (WRG) 1970
NR   Island House, Moor Rd, CHESHAM, Bucks, HP5 1WA.   (hq)
     01494 783453
     http://www.wrg.org.uk
     Exec Dir: Neil Edwards
▲   Registered Charity
○   *G, *N; co-ordinating body for voluntary labour on the inland
     waterways of Britain; is a non-membership subsidiary
     company of the Inland Waterways Association interested in
     the conservation & restoration of the inland waterways of
     Britain
●   Mtgs - ET - Inf - LG
M   1,850 i, 20 f, 100 org, UK / 30 i, o'seas
¶   Navvies - 6.   Canal Camps Brochure - 1.
     Other occasional publications.

Watford & West Herts Chamber of Commerce & Industry   1895
NR   The Business Centre, Colne Way, WATFORD, Herts,
     WD24 7AA.   (hq)
     01923 442442
▲   Company Limited by Guarantee
○   *C

Way Foundation (WAY) 1997
NR   St Loyes House (suite 35), 10 St Loyes St, BEDFORD,
     MK40 1ZL.   (hq)
     0870 011 3450
     email info@wayfoundation.org.uk
     http://www.wayfoundation.org.uk
▲   Registered Charity
○   *W; a self-help group for men & women who are 50, or under,
     at the time of losing their partner; to help them, rebuild their
     lives by helping each other
●   Inf - Support network
M   1,500 i
¶   NL - 4.

Web-offset Newspaper Association (WONA) 1964
■   St Andrew's House, 18-20 St Andrew St, LONDON,
     EC4A 3AY.   (hq)
     020 7632 7400   fax 020 7632 7401
     email gary@cullumpublishing.org
     Sec: Gary Cullum
○   *T; to exchange technical information & experience of printing
     newspapers on web-offset presses
M   f

** Wedgwood Society of Great Britain
     Organisation lost; See Introduction paragraph 3

Welding Institute (TWI) 1968
■   Granta Park, Great Abington, CAMBRIDGE, CB21 6AL.   (hq)
     01223 899000
     email twi@twi.co.uk   http://www.twi.co.uk
     Chief Exec: Dr Bob John
▲   Company Limited by Guarantee
Br   3
○   *L, *P, *Q; to carry out confidential contract work on all aspects
     of welding& materials joining for industrial member
     companies; to teach good practice in welding, joining & non-
     destructive testing
Gp   10 technical gps on specific aspects of joining
●   Conf - ET - Exam - Res - Inf - Lib
<   Intl Inst Welding; Eur Welding Fedn; Assn Indep Res &
     Technology Orgs
M   7,000 i, 3,500 f
¶   Welding Abstracts (print) - 12; £656.
     Welding Abstracts (PDF) - 12; £578.
     (Both above) - 12; £788.
     Note: trades as TWI Ltd

Welding Manufacturers' Association
     association in the Power section of **BEAMA Ltd**

Well Drillers Association (WDA) 1985
NR   PO Box 4595, NUNEATON, Warks, CV11 9DX.
     07885 979583
     email david.s.duke@gmail.com
     http://www.welldrillers.org.uk
     Sec: Dave Duke
▲   Un-incorporated Society
○   *T; to promote the design & construction of water wells &
     boreholes
●   Mtgs - ET - Inf - LG
<   Brit Drilling Assn
M   29 f
¶   LM; free.

Well Services Contractors Association   (WSCA)
NR   PO Box 12089, ABERDEEN, AB16 9BB.
     01224 868118
     email chris_strang@wsca.co.uk   http://www.wsca.co.uk
     Dir: Chris Strang
○   *T

Welsh Agricultural Organisation Society Ltd   (WAOS) 1922
NR   Gorseland, North Rd, ABERYSTWYTH, Ceredigion,
     SY23 2HE.   (hq)
     01970 636688   fax 01970 624049
     email waos@wfsagri.net   http://www.wfsagri.net/
     waos.htm
     Chief Exec: Don Thomas
○   *F; agricultural marketing & consultancy (incl horticulture)

Welsh Amateur Boxing Association (WABA) 1910
NR   Marcross, LLANTWIT MAJOR, Glamorgan, CF61 1ZD.   (hsb/p)
     01446 794444
     Hon Gen Sec: D B Francis
▲   Registered Charity
○   *S; to promote amateur boxing in Wales
Gp   Training; Commissions
●   Conf - Mtgs - ET - Exam - Comp - Inf
M   i
¶   AR.

**Welsh Amateur Gymnastics Association   (Welsh Gymnastics)
1901**
NR   Cardiff Central Youth Club, Ocean Park, Ocean Way, CARDIFF,
     CF24 5HE.   (hq)
     029 2043 1240
     Gen Sec: Mrs Annette Brown
○   *S; governing body of gymnastics in Wales
Gp   Women's artistic, Men's artistic, Rhythmic, General recreational,
     Sports acrobatics, Sports aerobics, Preschool, People with
     disabilities
●   Mtgs - ET - Comp
<   C'wealth Confedn; Brit Gymnastics
M   i & clubs
¶   NL - 4.

Welsh Amateur Music Federation   (Ffederasiwn Cerddoriaeth Amatur Cymru)   (WAMF/FfCAC)   1968
- ■ Tŷ Cerdd, Wales Millennium Centre, Bute Place, CARDIFF, CF10 5AL.   (hq)
  029 2063 5640   fax 029 2063 5641
  email wamf@tycerdd.org   http://www.tycerdd.org
  Dir: Keith Griffin
- ▲ Registered Charity; Un-incorporated Society
- ○ *D, *N, Y; support for amateur music making organisations through advice, grants, workshops & courses
- Gp National Youth Brass Band of Wales; National Youth Choir of Wales;
  National Youth Jazz Orchestra of Wales; National Youth Wind Orchestra of Wales; National Youth Symphonic Brass Wales Bands; Choirs; Folk; Musical theatre societies
- ● Conf - Mtgs - ET - Res - Comp - Stat - Inf - Lib - VE - LG - Youth activities, grants & guarantees for performance - Music promotion & support
- M c 400 societies (representing 25,000 amateur performers)
- ¶ Annual Review of Activities; ftm, £1 nm.
  Various pamphlets etc.

Welsh Amateur Rowing Association   (WARA)
- NR 4 Garrick Drive, Thornhill, CARDIFF, CF14 9BG.   (hsp)
  029 2075 3910
  http://www.walesrowing.com
  Sec: Sally Haines
- ▲ Un-incorporated Society
- ○ *S; to regulate & promote the sport of rowing for men & women in Wales, for recreation as well as for national & international competition
- Gp Coastal rowing; Welsh Longboat Association
- ● Mtgs - ET - Exam - Comp - Liaison with Welsh Assembly & the Sports Council for Wales
- M 1,200 i (Wales)
- ¶ [website only]

Welsh Amateur Swimming Association   (WASA)   1897
- ■ Wales National Pool, Sketty Lane, SWANSEA, SA2 8QG.   (hq)
  01792 513636   fax 01792 513637
  email secretary@welshasa.co.uk
  http://www.welshasa.co.uk
  Head of Admin: Mrs Julie Tyler
- ○ *S; the governing body for swimming in Wales
- Gp Swimming; Diving; Water polo; Masters swimming
- ● ET (national team training) - Comp
- < Amat Swimming Fedn GB (ASFGB)
- M 10,000 i
- ¶ WASA Hbk - 1; £10 m.

Welsh Association of Sub Aqua Clubs   (WASAC)
- NR 3 Merrion Village, PEMBROKE, SA71 5HT.   (treas/p)
  01646 661357
  http://www.wasac.co.uk
  Treas: Colin Deller
- ○ *S; to promote the sport of underwater swimming & exploration

Welsh Athletics   1897
- NR Cardiff International Sport Stadium, CARDIFF, CF11 8AZ.   (hq)
  029 2064 4870   fax 029 2034 2687
  http://www.welshathletics.org
  Chief Exec: Matt Newman
  Dir of Devt: Steve Brace,
- ○ *S; to promote & develop athletics in Wales
- ● Mtgs - ET - Exam - Comp - Stat - Inf
- < Brit Athletics Fedn; Welsh Sports Assn
- M 100 clubs
- ¶ NL - 2.   Ybk.   AR.
- ✕ 2005 Athletics Association of Wales

Welsh Badminton Union   (Undeb Badminton Cymru)   (WBU)   1928
- NR Unit E4, South Point Industrial Estate, Foreshore Rd, CARDIFF, CF10 4SP.   (hq)
  029 2049 7225   fax 029 2049 7224
  http://www.welshbadminton.net
  Admin: Rob Short
- ○ *S; governing body of sport for badminton
- Gp Coaching & technical committee, Events committee, Disability working group
- < Intl Badminton Fedn (IBF); Eur Badminton U (EBU)
- M i & clubs

Welsh Beekeepers Association
- NR Tynewydd Cottage, Myddfai, LLANDOVERY, Carmarthenshire, SA20 0QD.   (sec/p)
  01550 720473
  http://www.wbka.com
  Sec: John Tayler
- ○ *G, *T

Welsh Black Cattle Society   (WBCS)   1904
- ■ 13 Bangor St, CAERNARFON, Gwynedd, LL55 1AP.   (hq)
  01286 672391   fax 01286 672022
  http://www.welshblackcattlesociety.org
  Chief Exec: Andrew James
- ▲ Registered Charity
- Br 2; Australia, Canada, Germany, N Zealand
- ○ *B
- ● Mtgs - Res - Exhib - Comp - Inf
- M 884 i, UK / 17 i, o'seas
- ¶ Jnl - 1; £7.50.   NL - irreg.   Herd Book - 1; £35.

Welsh Bowling Association   (WBA)   1904
- NR 6 Nordale Court, Fidlas Rd, CARDIFF, CF14 0NJ.   (hsp)
  029 2063 4995
  Hon Sec: Jim Ireland
- ▲ Un-incorporated Society
- ○ *S; to control & organise the men's flat green game of bowls in Wales
- Gp Welsh Bowls Umpires Assn; Welsh Bowls Coaching Assn
- ● Mtgs - Comp
- < Wld Bowls Bd; Brit Isles Bowling Coun
- M c 11,000 i
- ¶ WBA Official Ybk - 1.

Welsh Bowls Coaching Association
  a group of the **Welsh Bowling Association**

Welsh Bowls Umpires Association
  a group of the **Welsh Bowling Association**

Welsh Bridge Union   (WBU)   1933
- NR Meadow View, Llanddewi, LLANDRINDOD WELLS, Powys, LD1 6SE   (chiefexec/p)
  01597 850050
  email wbu@wbu.org.uk   http://www.wbu.org.uk
  Chief Exec: Neville Richards
- ▲ Un-incorporated Society
- ○ *G; for players of Contract Bridge
- ● Mtgs
- < Wld Bridge Fedn; Eur Bridge League
- > East, Mid, North & West Wales Bridge Assns
- M c 2,000 i
- ¶ Competition & Masterpoint Journal - 1; ftm, £5 nm.

Welsh Canoeing Association (WCA)

NR   Canolfan Tryweryn, Frongoch, BALA, Gwynedd, LL23 7NU. (hq)
    01678 521199   fax 01678 521158
    email welsh.canoeing@virgin.net
    http://www.welsh-canoeing.org.uk
    Admin: Pat Holmes
○   *S; to manage canoeing in Wales
M   1,800 i; 53 affil clubs (2,000 i)

Welsh Chess Union (WCU) 1960

■   3 Norfolk Close, CWMBRAN, Torfaen, NP44 5HI   (exec/dir)
    01633 483389
    Exec Director: W Arnold
▲   Un-incorporated Society
○   *S; to foster the game of chess in Wales
●   Exam
<   Fédn Intle des Echecs (FIDE)
M   900 i
¶   NL - 4.   Ybk - 1; ftm.
    Pawns (junior NL) - 12; free to juniors.

Welsh Culinary Association (WCA) 1994

■   c/o The Bungalow, Maes y Neuadd, TALSARNAU, Gwynedd, LL47 6YA.   (chmn/p)
    01766 780319   fax 01766 780211
    email info@welshculinaryassociation.com
    http://www.welshculinaryassociation.com
    Chmn: Peter Jackson,   Sec: Kevin Williams
▲   Company Limited by Guarantee
○   *P; to represent & promote the chefs of Wales
●   Conf - Mtgs - ET - Res - Exhib - Comp - Expt
<   Wld Assn of Cooks Socs
M   320 i, Wales / 2 i, o'seas

Welsh Cycling Union Ltd (WCU) 1972

■   Wales National Velodrome, Newport International Sports Village, NEWPORT, Monmouthshire, NP19 4PT.   (hq)
    01633 670540   fax 01633 670540
    email info@welshcycling.co.uk
    http://www.welshcyclingunion.com
    Admin: Edith Clark
    Events & Communications Officer: Michael Heaven
▲   Company Limited by Guarantee
○   *G, *S; the governing body for cycling in Wales & covers: road racing, track racing, mountain bike, BMX, cyclo cross & cycle speedway
●   Mtgs - ET - Comp - Inf - LG
<   Brit Cycling Fedn; Sports Coun Wales; U Cycliste Intle
M   950 i, 70 org

Welsh Federation of Housing Associations
    since 2006 **Community Housing Cymru**

Welsh Folk Dance Society
    English name of **Cymdeithas Ddawns Werin Cymru**

Welsh Folk Song Society (Cymdeithas Alawon Gwerin Cymru) (CAGC) 1906

■   Rhandir, Penrhyn-coch, ABERYSTWYTH, Ceredigion, SY23 3EQ.   (hsp)
    01766 522096
    email rri@aber.ac.uk   http://www.canugwerin.org
    Sec: Dr Rhiannon Ifans
▲   Registered Charity
○   *D; to collect, preserve, interpret & perform Welsh folk-songs; to foster an interest in folk literature & music in general
●   Conf - Res - Inf
M   250 i, 10 org, UK / 5 org, o'seas
¶   Canu Gwerin (Folk Song) (Jnl) - 1; £10 yr m.

Welsh Golfing Union
    in 2007 merged with the Welsh Ladies' Golf Union to form the **Golf Union of Wales**

Welsh Halfbred Sheep Breeders Association Ltd 1955

■   Brynteg, Pen-y-Garnedd, Llanrhaeadr Ym Mochnant, OSWESTRY, Powys, SY10 0AW.   (hsp)
    01691 860336
    http://www.welshhalfbredsheep.co.uk
    Sec: Mrs Gillian Napper
○   *B; marketing of the Welsh Halfbred sheep (the cross of a Welsh Mountain ewe & a Border Leicester ram)
●   Exhib - Shows & five annual sales
<   Nat Sheep Assn
M   400 i
¶   Welsh Halfbred News - 2; ftm only.

Welsh Highland Railways Association (WHR) 1964

■   Tremadog Rd, PORTHMADOG, Gwynedd, LL49 9DY. (hq/regd office)
    01766 513402   fax 01766 513402
    email info@whr.co.uk   http://www.whr.co.uk
    Chmn: James Hewett
▲   Company Limited by Guarantee; Registered Charity
○   *G; to recreate the Welsh Highland Railway of the 1920s & 1930s; to provide a quality education, interactive, visitor attraction; to preserve & increase the skills involved in running a railway
Gp   Locomotives - steam & diesel; Carriage & wagon; Civils; Commercial; Museum; Telecommunications
●   Mtgs - ET - Exhib - Inf - PL - VE
<   Heritage Rly Assn; N Wales Tourism; Great Little Trains of Wales
M   800 i, UK / 150 i, o'seas
    2006 (Welsh Highland Railway Ltd
       (Welsh Highland Railway Society
       (Welsh Highland Railway Heritage Group
¶   The Jnl - 3; ftm, £1.75 nm.   The Russell - irreg; free.

Welsh Hill Speckled Face Sheep Society 1968

NR   Nanty Farm, Pantmawr, LLANIDLOES, Powys, SY18 6SY.   (asa)
    01686 440279
    Sec: R Griffiths
▲   Un-incorporated Society
○   *B
●   Mtgs - Comp

Welsh Hockey Coaches Association
    a group of **Welsh Hockey Union Ltd**

Welsh Hockey Umpires Association
    a group of **Welsh Hockey Union Ltd**

Welsh Hockey Union Ltd (WHU) 1897

■   Severn House, Station Terrace, Ely, CARDIFF, Glamorgan, CF5 4AA.   (hq)
    029 2057 3940   fax 029 2057 3941
    email info@welsh-hockey.co.uk
    http://www.welsh-hockey.co.uk
    Chief Exec: Mike Leatt
▲   Company Limited by Guarantee
○   *S; governing body for hockey in Wales
Gp   Welsh Hockey Coaches Assn; Welsh Hockey Umpires Assn
●   Conf - ET - Exam - Comp - Inf - VE - LG
<   Fédn Intle de Hockey (FIH); Eur Hockey Fedn (EHF)
M   6,100 i, 115 clubs, 550 schools
¶   NL - 1;   Circulars - 4; both ftm.

Welsh Hospitals & Health Services Association   (WHA Healthcare)   1948
- 60 Newport Rd, CARDIFF, Glamorgan, CF24 1YG.   (hq)
  029 2048 5461   fax 029 2048 8859
  email mail@whahealthcare.co.uk
  http://www.whahealthcare.co.uk
  Chief Exec: Huw L Cooke
- ▲ Company Limited by Guarantee
- ○ *W; payment of cash benefits to members & their families in respect of incidental & statutory expenses incurred in obtaining NHS treatment as well as part refund of fees for specialist consultations & physiotherapy
- ● Conf - Mtgs
- < Brit Health Care Assn
- M 46,500 i, 600 f
- ¶ AR & Accounts; free.

Welsh Hound Association   (WHA)   1921
- Althrey Lodge Cottage, Overton Rd, Bangor-on-Dee, WREXHAM, LL13 0DA.   (hsp)
  01978 780598
  Hon Sec: Mike Medcalf
- ▲ Un-incorporated Society
- ○ *B; to promote, record & improve the breeding of the Welsh hound
- ● Annual hound show
- M 60 i, UK / 3 i, o'seas
  (Sub: £5)
- ¶ Welsh Hound Stud Book - 3 yrly, £5 m, £10 nm.

Welsh Indoor Bowls Association   (WIBA)   1934
- 50 Penyrheol Rd, Gorseinon, SWANSEA, Glam, SA4 4GA.   (hsp)
  01792 538061   fax 01792 548221
  Hon Sec: David Phillips
- ▲ Un-incorporated Society
- Br 25 clubs
- ○ *S; to promote indoor bowls throughout Wales
- < Wld Indoor Bowls Assn; Brit Isles Indoor Bowls Coun
- M 7,500 i, 25 clubs
- ¶ Hbk - 1; ftm, £1.50 nm.   AR; ftm only.

Welsh Jazz Society   1963
- 26 The Balcony, Castle Arcade, CARDIFF, Glamorgan, CF10 1BY.   (hq)
  029 2034 0591   fax 029 2066 5160
  email welshjazz@btconnect.com
  http://www.jazzwales.org.uk
  Chief Exec: B J Hennessey
- ▲ Company Limited by Guarantee; Registered Charity
- ○ *D; promotion, learning & presentation of jazz music
- ● Mtgs - ET - Inf - PL - Concert performances
- < Jazz Services Ltd
- M 800 i, 8 org
- ¶ Jazz UK - 6; free.

Welsh Judo Association   (WJA)   1964
- WIA Office - Welsh Institute of Sport, Sophia Gardens, CARDIFF, CF11 9SW.   (hsb)
  029 2033 8381
  email welshjudo@hotmail.co.uk
  http://www.welshjudo.com
  Gen Mgr: Niki Adams
- ▲ Company Limited by Guarantee
- ○ *S; promotion of judo
- ● Mtgs - ET - Exam - Comp
- < Brit Judo Assn; C'wealth Judo Assn
- M 2,200 i
- ¶ NL - 12; free.

Welsh Ladies' Golf Union
  in 2007 merged with the Welsh Golfing Union to form the **Golf Union of Wales**

Welsh Language Society
  English name of **Cymdeithas yr Iaith Gymraeg**

Welsh Library Association
  a division of **CILIP**

Welsh Local Government Association   1996
- NR Local Government House, Drake Walk, CARDIFF, Glamorgan, CF10 4LG.   (hq)
  029 2046 8600
  http://www.wlga.gov.uk
- ○ *N; to promote local democracy & represent the interests of local government in Wales

Welsh Mills Society   (Cymdeithas Melinau Cymru)   1984
- NR Y Felin, Tynygraig, YSTRAD MEURIG, Ceredigion, SY25 6AE.
  email hilary.milaws@btinternet.com
  http://www.welshmills.org.uk
  Sec: Hilary Malaws
- ○ *G, *L; to study, record, interpret & publicise the wind & water mills of Wales; to advise on their preservation & use; to encourage working millers
- ¶ Melin - 1.

Welsh Mines Society   (WMS)   1979
- 20 Lutterburn St, Ugborough, IVYBRIDGE, Devon, PL21 0NG.   (hsp)
  01752 896432
  http://www.welshmines.org
  Sec: Dr David Roe
- ○ *G; for those interested in all aspects of Welsh mines, especially the mineralogy, history & archaeology; preservation of sites
- M i

Welsh Mountain Sheep Society - Hill Flock Section   1950
- NR c/o WAOS, Gorseland, North Rd, ABERYSTWYTH, Ceredigion, SY23 2HE.   (hq)
  01970 636688
- ○ *B

Welsh Mountain Sheep Society - Registered Section   (WMSS)   1905
- Ty'n-y-Mynydd Farm, Boduan, PWLLHELI, Gwynedd, LL53 8PZ.   (hsp)
  01758 721898
  email info@welsh-sheep.org
  http://www.welsh-sheep.org
  Sec: Mrs D Tyne
- ▲ Registered Charity
- ○ *B
- ● Conf - Mtgs - Exhib - Comp - Inf - Production of a flock book
- < Nat Sheep Assn
- M 60 i
- ¶ NL - 2.   Ybk - 1.   Sale Catalogue - 1.
- × 18 May 2005 Welsh Mountain Sheep Society - Pedigree section

Welsh Mule Sheep Breeders Association   1978
- NR c/o WAOS, Gorseland, North Rd, ABERYSTWYTH, Ceredigion, SY23 2WB.   (hq)
  01970 636688
  http://www.welshmules.co.uk
- ○ *B

Welsh Music Guild   1954
- NR 9 Brown St, FERNDALE, Glamorgan, CF43 4SF.   (contact)
  Sec: John H Lewis
- ○ *D; to promote Welsh music in its composition, performance & the teaching of the same; emphasis on Welsh contemporary music & its composers
- M i
- × 2003 Guild for the Promotion of Welsh Music

© CBD Research Ltd · Beckenham · BR3 5JS · Tel 020 8650 7745 · Fax 020 8650 0768 · E-mail cbd@cbdresearch.com · www.cbdresearch.com

Welsh National Literature Promotion Agency
alternative name of **ACADEMI**

Welsh Netball Association   (WNA)   1945
- ■ 33-35 Cathedral Rd, CARDIFF, Glamorgan, CF11 9HB.   (hq)
  029 2023 7048   fax 029 2022 6430
  email welshnetball@welshnetball.com
  http://www.welshnetball.co.uk
  Chief Exec: Susan J Holvey
- ▲ Company Limited by Guarantee
- ○ *S; to promote & develop the game of netball within Wales
- ● Mtgs - ET - Comp
- < Intl Fedn Netball Assns (IFNA); Fedn Eur Netball Assns (FENA)
- M 2,500 i, 500 schools & colleges
- ¶ Netball News (Jnl) - 2; ftm, £1 nm.

Welsh Pony & Cob Society   (WPCS)   1901
- NR 6 Chalybeate St, ABERYSTWYTH, Ceredigion, SY23 1HP.   (hq)
  01970 617501
  http://www.wpcs.uk.com
  Sec: Mrs G Sazeykoven
- ▲ Company Limited by Guarantee; Registered Charity
- ○ *B; registration of Welsh Ponies & Cobs & their part-breeds
- ● Mtgs - ET - Exhib - Inf - Archive Museum
- < Brit Horse Soc; Nat Pony Soc
- M 8,000 i
- ¶ Jnl - 1.   NL - 2.   Welsh Ponies & Cobs (magazine) - 4.
  Stud Book - 1.

Welsh Rugby Union Ltd   (WRU)   1881
- ■ Westgate Terrace, Millennium Stadium, Westgate St, CARDIFF,
  CF10 1NS.   (hq)
  0870 013 8600
  http://www.wru.co.uk
  Chief Exec: Steven M Lewis
- ▲ Company Limited by Guarantee
- ○ *S; governing body of Rugby Union football in Wales
- ● Conf - Mtgs - ET - Comp - Inf - Lib - VE - Arranging
  international matches
- < Intl Rugby Football Bd (IRB)
- > Welsh Districts Rugby U; Welsh Schools Rugby U
- M 240+ clubs
- ¶ WRU Hbk - 1; ftm, £5 nm.

Welsh Surfing Federation   (WSF)
- NR 17 Southerndown Ave, Mayals, SWANSEA, SA3 5EL.
  01792 536032   fax 01792 413408
  email erylmason.wsf@ntlworld.com
  http://www.geocities.com/welshsurfing/
  Sec: Eryl Mason
- ○ *S; governing body for surfing in Wales
- < Brit Surfing Assn, Eur Surfing Fedn

Welsh Weight Training Association   (WWTA)   1985
- ■ 13 Barquentine Place, Atlantic Wharf, CARDIFF, Glamorgan,
  CF10 4NJ.   (hsp)
  029 2049 3919   fax 029 2049 3919
  Sec: Lorraine Gray
- ▲ Un-incorporated Society
- Br 5
- ○ *S; to promote weight training; to improve & standardise
  coaching & instruction throughout Wales
- ● Mtgs - ET - Exam (coaches)
- < Intl Coun for Health & Fitness
- M 2,000 i
- ¶ Basic Coaches Manual.

Welshpool & Llanfair Light Railway Preservation Co Ltd   1960
- NR The Station, Llanfair Caereinion, WELSHPOOL, Powys,
  SY21 0SF.   (hq)
  01938 810441
  http://www.wllr.org.uk
- ▲ Company Limited by Guarantee; Registered Charity
- ○ *G; preservation & operation of narrow-gauge railway, using
  British, African, Caribbean & Continental steam locomotives
  & rolling stock

Wensleydale Longwool Sheep Breeders' Association   1890
- ■ Coffin Walk, Sheep Dip Lane, Princethorpe, RUGBY, Warks,
  CV23 9SP.
  01926 633439
  http://www.wensleydale-sheep.com
  Sec: Dr D L Clouder
- ▲ Company Limited by Guarantee
- ○ *B
- ● Expt - Inf - Displays at agricultural shows & sheep events
- M 200 i, UK / 9 i, o'seas
- ¶ Jnl - Every 2-3 years; ftm, £2 nm.
  Flock Book - 1; ftm only.

Wesley Historical Society   (WHS)   1893
- ■ 7 Haugh Shaw Rd, HALIFAX, W Yorks, HX1 3AH.   (hsp)
  01422 250780
  email johnahargreaves@blueyonder.co.uk
  http://www.wesleyhistoricalsociety.org.uk
  Gen Sec: Dr John A Hargreaves
- ▲ Registered Charity
- Br 17; Irish (North & Eire), New Zealand (both automomous)
- ○ *R; to promote interest in and study of Methodism
- ● Conf - Mtgs - Res - Exhib - Lib - PL - VE
- M 388 i, 57 f, UK / 49 i, 78 f, o'seas
  (Sub: £12 i, £16 f UK / £21 i, £27 f o'seas)
- ¶ Proceedings - 3; ftm.

Wessex Association of Chambers of Commerce   (WACC)   1994
- ■ Pentagon House, 52 Castle St, TROWBRIDGE, Wilts,
  BA14 8AU.   (hq)
  01225 355553   fax 01225 355554
  email info@wessexchambers.org.uk
  http://www.wessexchambers.org.uk
  Chief Exec: Mike Williams
- ▲ Company Limited by Guarantee
- Br 17 towns in Wiltshire & Somerset
- ○ *C
- Gp Networks: Environmental, International, Training, Womans
- ● Conf - ET - Exhib - Comp - Expt - Inf - LG
- M 1,400 f
  (Sub: £65 - £3,500)
- ¶ Wessex in Business - 12; ftm.

West Africa Business Association   (WABA)   1956
- NR 2 Vincent St, LONDON, SW1P 4LD.   (hq)
  020 7828 5544
  http://www.waba.co.uk
- ▲ Un-incorporated Society
- Br Cote d'Ivoire, Ghana, Nigeria, Gambia, Senegal, Guinea,
  Sierra Leone, S Africa
- ○ *T; to represent & sustain overseas investment in the
  Anglophone & Francophone countries of West Africa
- ● Conf - Mtgs - Res - Expt - VE - LG
- < W African Enterprise Network; Business Coun Europe - Africa,
  Mediterranean; Brit African Business Assn
- M c 200 i & f
- ¶ London NL - 12;   Country Reports - 12; both ftm only.

West Kent Chamber of Commerce & Industry   1858
- NR Castle Lodge, Castle St, TONBRIDGE, Kent, TN9 1BH.   (hq)
  01732 366653
- ○ *C

West Lothian Chamber of Commerce
NR The Enterprise Centre, Almondvale Blvd, LIVINGSTON,
      W Lothian, EH54 6QP.
      01506 777937   fax 01506 777939
      email info.cumming@wlchamber.com
      http://www.wlchamber.com
      Chief Exec: Dab=ve McDougall
▲ Company Limited by Guarantee
○ *C

**West Wales Chamber of Commerce   (Siambr Fasnach Gorllewin
Cymru) (WWCC) 1846**
NR Ethos, Kings Rd, Swansea Waterfront, SWANSEA, SA1 8AS.
      (hq)
      01792 653297   fax 01792 648345
      email info@wwcc.co.uk   http://www.wwcc.co.uk
      Mgr: Lyn Harries
○ *C; covers the local authority areas of Carmarthenshire, Neath/
      Port Talbot, Pembrokeshire & Swansea
M c 300 f
      No further information supplied

Western Equestrian Society (WES) 1985
NR 24 Sandford Close, BOURNEMOUTH, Dorset, BH9 3PQ.   (sp)
      01202 779576
      email secretary@wes-uk.com   http://www.wes-uk.com
      Sec: Anne Batley
○ *S; to promote & stimulate interest & high standards in Western
      (American) style of horsemanship

Western Front Association (WFA) 1980
NR PO Box 1918, STOCKPORT, Cheshire, SK4 4WN.   (hq)
      0161-443 1918
      email westernfrontassociation.com
      Hon Sec: S Oram
▲ Registered Charity
○ *G; to educate the public in the history of the Great War with
      particular reference to the Western Front
● Conf - Mtgs - ET - Comp
M 6,500 i, UK / 1,000 i, o'seas
¶ Stand To - 3;   Bulletin - 3; both ftm only.

**Western Horsemen's Association of Great Britain   (WHA)
1968**
NR Brook Glen, 1 Brook Lane, Brookville, THETFORD, Norfolk,
      IP26 4RQ.   (mem/s/p)
      http://www.whagb.co.uk
      Mem Sec: Carol Judge
▲ Un-incorporated Society
○ *G; for all interested in the Western (American) way of riding
M i

Western Isles Chamber of Commerce 1995
NR 30 Francis St, STORNOWAY, Isle of Lewis, HS1 2ND.   (hq)
      Contact: Nicola Jarvie
▲ Un-incorporated Society
○ *C
● Mtgs - Inf - LG
< Aberdeen & Grampian Cham Comm
M c 100 i

Westminster Chamber of Commerce
      since 28 October 1994 a branch of the **London Chamber of
      Commerce & Industry**

Westminster Property Owners Association (WPOA) 1988
NR 1 Warwick Row (7th floor), LONDON, SW1E 5ER.   (hq)
      020 7630 1782
      http://www.wpoa.co.uk
▲ Un-incorporated Society
○ *T; interests of owners of property in the City of Westminster
M f

Westmorland County Agricultural Society (WCAS) 1799
■ Lane Farm, Crooklands, MILNTI IORPE, Cumbria, LA7 7NH.
      (hq)
      01539 567804   fax 01539 567011
      email manager@westmorland.org.uk
      http://www.westmorland-county-show.co.uk
      Chief Exec: Christine Knipe
▲ Company Limited by Guarantee; Registered Charity
○ *F, *H; to encourage & support agriculture, horticulture & rural
      crafts
● Conf - Mtgs - ET - Exhib - SG - Inf
< Assn Show & Agricl Orgs; Nat Farmers U; R Agricl Soc
      England; Nat Sheep Assn
M 1,019 i, 10 org
¶ Field & Fell NL - 4; ftm.   AR - 1; free.

Westmorland Damson Association
NR Lile Yaks, Cartmel Fell, WINDERMERE, Cumbria, LA23 3PD.
      Sec: Bill Clifford
○ *H

Wexford Chamber of Industry & Commerce
IRL The Ballast Office, Crescent Quay, WEXFORD, Republic of
      Ireland.
      353 (53) 912 2226   fax 353 (53) 912 4170
      email info@wexchamber.ie   http://www.wexchamber.ie
      Chief Exec: Emer Lovett
○ *C

Wey & Arun Canal Trust Ltd (W&ACT) 1970
■ The Granary, Flitchfold Farm, Vicarage Hill, Loxwood,
      BILLINGSHURST, W Sussex, RH14 0RH.   (hq/hsb)
      01403 752403   fax 01403 753991
      email office@weyandarun.co.uk
      http://www.weyandarun.co.uk
      Hon Sec: Julian Morgan
▲ Company Limited by Guarantee; Registered Charity
○ *G; to restore the derelict Wey & Arun canal in Surrey & W
      Sussex, linking the Thames with the English Channel
● Mtgs - Working parties - Exhib - Inf - Fund raising - Talks -
      Sales stalls - Public boat trips
< Inland Waterways Assn
M 2,500 i, 30 f
      (Subs: £10 i, £25 f)
¶ Wey-South - 4; ftm only.
      Wey-Arun Canal News - 2; free.

**Weymouth & Portland Chamber of Commerce, Industry &
Tourism (WPCCIT) 1928**
■ PO Box 3049, WEYMOUTH, Dorset, DT4 0YT.
      07790 892095
      email secretary@wpchamber.co.uk
      http://www.wpchamber.co.uk
      Sec: Michel Hooper-Immins
▲ Un-incorporated Society
○ *C
● Mtgs - LG
< Dorset Cham Comm & Ind (Poole)
M 128 f
¶ NL - 12 ftm only.

WHA Healthcare
      alternative name of the **Welsh Hospitals & Health Services
      Association**

Whale & Dolphin Conservation Society (WDCS) 1987
NR Brookfield House, 38 St Paul St, CHIPPENHAM, Wilts,
      SN15 1LJ.   (hq)
      01249 449500   fax 01249 449501
      email info@wdcs.org   http://www.wdcs.org
▲ Registered Charity
○ *K; to promote public awareness of the threats facing whales &
      dolphins throughout the world

© CBD Research Ltd · Beckenham · BR3 5JS · Tel 020 8650 7745 · Fax 020 8650 0768 · E-mail cbd@cbdresearch.com · www.cbdresearch.com

WheelPower - British Wheelchair Sport   1972
- ■ Stoke Mandeville Stadium, Guttmann Rd, STOKE MANDEVILLE, Bucks, HP21 9PP.   (hq)
  01296 395995   fax 01296 424171
  email info@wheelpower.org.uk
  http://www.wheelpower.org.uk
  Chief Exec: Martin McElhatton
- ▲ Company Limited by Guarantee; Registered Charity
- ○ *S, *W; the national organisation for wheelchair sport in the UK; to provide, promote & develop opportunities for men, women & children with disabilities to participate in recreational & competitive wheelchair sport
- Gp Sports associations throughout UK
- ● ET - Comp - Inf - Organises events at novice, junior, national & international level
- M c 3,000 i, 1 f, 20 org
- ¶ NL - 3/4; free.
- × 2004-05 British Wheelchair Sports Foundation

White Ensign Association Ltd   1958
- ■ HMS Belfast, Tooley St, LONDON, SE1 2JH.   (hq)
  020 7407 8658   fax 020 7357 6298
  email office@whiteensign.co.uk
  http://www.whiteensign.co.uk
  Sec: Mike Howell
- ▲ Company Limited by Guarantee; Registered Charity
- ○ *W; advisory service to serving & retired members of the Royal Navy & Royal Marines on employment, resettlement & financial matters
- ● ET - Inf
- M 115 i, 32 f
- ¶ LM;   AR; both free.

White Face Dartmoor Sheep Breeders Association   1950
- NR 13 West St, ASHBURTON, Devon, TQ13 7DT.   (hsb)
  01364 652304
  http://www.whitefacedartmoorsheep.co.uk
  Hon Sec: Gordon T Chambers
- ▲ Un-Incorporated Society
- ○ *B
- ● Mtgs - Comp
- < Nat Sheep Assn
- M 40 i

White Faced Woodland Sheep Breeders Group   1986
- NR 1 Tutta Bridge Cottages, Greta Bridge, BARNARD CASTLE, Durham, DL12 9SB.   (hsp)
  01833 627424
  Hon Sec: Rachel Godschalk
- ○ *B

White Goods Association   (WGA)
- IRL Confederation House, 84/86 Lower Baggot St, DUBLIN 2, Republic of Ireland.
  http://www.ibec.ie/wga
  Dir: Tommy McCabe
- ○ *T; companies involved in the sale & distribution of domestic appliances
- < IBEC
- M 11 f

White Park Cattle Society   (WPCS)   1972
- NR Wimpole Home Farm, Old Wimpole, ROYSTON, Herts, SG8 0BW.   (hsp)
  http://www.whiteparkcattle.org.uk
  Sec: Marie Handscombe
- ○ *B
- M i

Whitebred Shorthorn Association Ltd   1962
- ■ High Green Hill, Kirkcambeck, BRAMPTON, Cumbria, CA8 2BL.   (hsp)
  01697 748228
  email info@whitebredshorthorn.com
  http://www.whitebredshorthorn.com
  Hon Sec: Mrs Rosie Mitchinson
- ▲ Registered Charity
- ○ *B
- ● Mtgs - Sales - Shows
- < Nat Beef Assn
- M 51 i
- ¶ Herd Book - 2; ftm, £10 nm.   AR.

Wholesale Confectionery & Tobacco Alliance Ltd
Organisation dissolved

Wholesale Markets Brokers' Association   (WMBA)   1994
- ■ One Royal Exchange Ave, LONDON, EC3V 3LT.   (hq)
  020 7464 4141
  email wmba@wmba.org.uk   http://www.wmba.org.uk
  Chief Exec: Stewart Lloyd-Jones,
  Office Mgr: Michelle Caulfield
- ▲ Un-incorporated Society
- ○ *P; to represent broking companies listed by the Financial Services Authority whose primary purpose is to facilitate cooperation in areas of mutual interest & benefit to members
- ● Mtgs - ET - Exam - Comp - LG
- M 9 f

Wholesome Food Association   (WFA)   1999
- NR Ball Cottage, East Ball Hill, Hartland, BIDEFORD, Devon, EX39 6BU.
  01237 441118
  email sky@wholesome-food.org.uk
  http://www.wholesome-food.org.uk
  Sec: Marian Van Eyk McCain
- ○ *T; a network of growers, processors, suppliers & distributors of locally grown, wholesome food
- M 122 f

Wicklow & District Chamber of Commerce
- IRL Wicklow Enterprise Park, The Murrough, WICKLOW, Republic of Ireland.
  353 (404) 66610   fax 353 (404) 66607
  email info@wicklowchamber.ie
  http://www.wicklowchamber.ie
  Pres: Pascal Burke
- ○ *C

Wild Flower Society   (WFS)   1886
- ■ c/o Mike Hooper, 24 Muirfield Drive, Astley, MANCHESTER, M29 7QJ.   (asa)
  01942 886828
  email wfs@grantais.demon.co.uk
  http://www.thewildflowersociety.com
  Mem Sec: Mike Hooper,   Gen Sec: Stephen Parker
- ▲ Registered Charity
- ○ *G, *L; increasing the understanding of field botany in the UK
- ● Mtgs - Exhib - VE
- M 900 i
- ¶ Wild Flower Society Magazine - 4; ftm only.

Wild Trout Trust   (WTT)   1997
NR   PO Box 120, WATERLOOVILLE, Hants, PO8 0WZ.
    023 9257 0985
    http://www.wildtrout.org
    Admin: Christina Bryant (Mon-Thur 1000-1400)
▲   Registered Charity
○   *K, *V; conservation of wild trout habitat & populations in the
    UK & Ireland
●   Conf
M   1,650 i, 5 org, UK / 55 i, o'seas
¶   Jnl - 1;   NL - 4; both ftm only.
✕   2001 Wild Trout Society

Wildlife and Countryside Link
■   89 Albert Embankment, LONDON, SE1 7TP.
    020 7820 8600   fax 020 7820 8620
    http://www.wcl.org.uk
○   *N; for voluntary environmental organisations
M   org
    no further information supplied

Wildlife Sound Recording Society   (WSRS)   1968
■   c/o British Library, 96 Euston Rd, LONDON, NW1 2DB.
    (mail add)
    020 7412 7402
    http://www.wildlife-sound.org
▲   Un-incorporated Society
○   *L; to encourage the recording of wildlife sounds & further the
    appreciation of animal language
●   Mtgs - Comp
M   300 i, UK / 30 i, o'seas
¶   Wildlife Sound (Jnl) - 2;   NL - 3;   LM - 3 yrly;
    CD magazine of members' work - 4; all ftm.
    Introduction to Wildlife Sound Recording; £2.50.

**Wildlife Trust for Bedfordshire, Cambridgeshire,
Northamptonshire & Peterborough   1990**
■   The Manor House, Broad St, Great Cambourne, CAMBRIDGE,
    CB23 6DH.   (hq)
    01954 713500   fax 01954 710051
    email enquiries@wildlifebcnp.org
    http://www.wildlifebcnp.org
    Dir: Nicholas Hammond
▲   Registered Charity
Br 4
○   *G, *L; to improve habitats & biodiversity throughout the area &
    to enhance people's enjoyment & understanding of wildlife
●   ET - Res - VE - LG
M   21,000 i, c 40 f
¶   Wildlife Action - 4; ftm only.

Wildlife Trust of South & West Wales   2002
■   The Nature Centre, Fountain Rd, Tondu, BRIDGEND,
    Glamorgan, CF32 0EH.   (hq)
    01656 724100   fax 01656 726980
    email info@welshwildlife.org
    http://www.welshwildlife.org
    Chief Exec: Dr Madeleine Havard,   Chmn: Roger Turner
▲   Company Limited by Guarantee; Registered Charity
Br 2
○   *K; wildlife conservation across south & west Wales dealing with
    species & habitats
Gp Local wildlife; Species (birds, marine)
●   Conf - Mtgs - ET - Res - Inf - VE - LG - Surveys (habitat &
    species)
<   R Soc Wildlife Trusts (RSWT)
M   17,500 i, 29 org
¶   Welsh Wildlife - 3;   Local NL - 3;   AR; all ftm only.

Wildlife Trusts
    an umbrella group in the **Royal Society of Wildlife Trusts**

Wilfred Owen Association   1989
NR   29 Arthur Rd, LONDON, SW19 7DN.   (mem/sp)
    email vcedavis@hotmail.com
    http://www.1914-18.co.uk/owen
    Mem Sec: Vanessa Davis
▲   Registered Charity
○   *A; to commemorate & promote awareness of the life & work
    of Wilfred Owen, the First World War poet
●   Mtgs - Res - Exhib - Inf - VE
M   400 i
¶   Jnl - 1.   NL - 2.

Wilhelm Furtwängler Society UK   1967
■   6 Goodwin Court, Devonshire Rd, LONDON, SW19 2EQ.
    (chmn/p)
    Chmn: John Hunt
○   *D; liaison with record companies to obtain greater
    representation of Furtwängler's art on record; dissemination
    of news & matters relating to articles, books & records by &
    about Furtwängler as man & artist

Wilkie Collins Society   (WCS)   1981
■   3 Merton House, 36 Belsize Park, LONDON, NW3 4EA.
    (chmn/p)
    email apogee@apgee.co.uk
    http://www.wilkie-collins.info
    4 Ernest Gardens, LONDON, W4 3QU. (mem sec/p)
    email paul@paullewis.co.uk
    Chmn: Andrew Gasson,   Mem Sec: Paul Lewis
▲   Un-incorporated Society
Br USA
○   *A, *G; to promote research into the life & works of Wilkie
    Collins (1824-89); to foster original, critical studies of his
    novels, plays, stories & essays
●   Mtgs
<   Alliance of Literary Socs
¶   Jnl - 1.   NL - 2/3.   Occasional Reprints.

William Barnes Society   1983
■   58 Melstock Avenue, DORCHESTER, Dorset, DT1 2BQ.
    (chmn/p)
    01305 265358
    Chmn: Alfred W Barrett
○   *A; for those interested in the Rev William Barnes (1801-1886),
    the Dorset dialect poet
●   Mtgs - VE
M   200 i, UK / c 8 i, o'seas
¶   NL - 2/3; ftm only.

William Cobbett Society   1976
■   3 Park Terrace, Tillington, PETWORTH, W Sussex, GU28 9AE.
    (hsp)
    01798 342008
    http://www.williamcobbett.org.uk
    Chmn: Barbara Biddell
▲   Un-incorporated Society
○   *L; to make known the life & writings of William Cobbett
    (1763-1835)
●   Mtgs - Inf - Lib - VE
<   Alliance of Literary Socs; Historical Assn; Thomas Paine Soc
M   120 i, 6 libraries, UK / 6 i, i;seas
    (Sub: £8)
¶   Cobbett's New Register - 1.
    Anne Cobbett: account of the family; £4.50.
    William Cobbett in America by Molly Townsend; £15.50.

© CBD Research Ltd · Beckenham · BR3 5JS · Tel 020 8650 7745 · Fax 020 8650 0768 · E-mail cbd@cbdresearch.com · www.cbdresearch.com

William Herschel Society   1979
- ■ 19 New King St, BATH, BA1 2BL.   (hq)
  01225 446865
  email fredsch@tiscali.co.uk
  http://www.williamherschel.org.uk
  Chmn: Dr Peter Ford
- ▲ Registered Charity
- Br Germany, Japan
- ○ *L; for all interested in: the life & achievements of William Herschel, his family & immediate descendants; the history of science, astronomy & 18th century music; telescope making; links with modern space discovery
- ● Conf - Mtgs - Res - Public lectures on astronomy & space research
- < The Royal Soc; R Astronomical Soc
- > Herschel Soc of Japan
- M 178 i, 9 org UK / 18 i, 1 org, o'seas
  (Sub: £10 UK & Europe / £13 o'seas)
- ¶ The Speculum (Jnl) - 2; ftm, £13 nm.

William Morris Society   1955
- ■ Kelmscott House, 26 Upper Mall, LONDON, W6 9TA.   (hq)
  020 8741 3735   fax 020 8748 5207
  email william.morris@care4free.net
  http://www.morrissociety.org
  Hon Sec: Phillippa Bennett
- ▲ Registered Charity
- ○ *A, *L; to promote the study of the life, work & influence of William Morris (1834-96) designer & poet; to make his life, work & ideas better known
- ● Mtgs - ET - Res - Exhib - Inf - Lib - VE
- M 2,000 i
- ¶ Jnl - 2.   NL - 4; both ftm only.

Williams Syndrome Foundation Ltd   (WSF)   1980
- NR 161 High St, TONBRIDGE, Kent, TN9 1BX.   (hq)
  01732 365152
  http://www.williams-syndrome.org.uk
  Chief Exec: John Nelson
- ▲ Company Limited by Guarantee
- ○ *W; to help parents & carers of children & adults who have Williams Syndrome (infantile hypercalcaemia - a rare non-hereditary genetic syndrome occurring at random); to stimulate interest, particularly among the medical profession
- Gp Families with affected children; Medical profession; Students; Care workers
- ● Conf - Mtgs - Res - Inf - Lib
- < Mencap; Genetic Interest Gp; Contact-a-Family
- M 900 i, UK / 100 i, o'seas
- ¶ NL - 2.   Video.
  Various Guideline publications.

Willwriters' Association   (WA)   1987
- NR Harbro House, Crown Lane, DENBIGH, LL16 3SY.   (hq)
  0800 035 0604
  http://www.willwritersassociation.com
  Sec: Carol Baird
- ▲ Un-incorporated Society
- Br 2
- ○ *P; to advance quality of willwriting industry; members will visit homes to write wills
- Gp Legal helpline (24 hr); Will registration & storage; Marketing services; Willwriting software & system
- ● Conf - ET - Exam - Comp - Inf - LG
- < Assn Lawyers & Legal Advisers
- M 650 i, 600 f, 8 org
- ¶ Codicil - 1.   Briefing - 4.
  The Freephone Directory of Legal Services - 1.
  The British Directory of Legal Services - 2.

Wiltshire Archaeological & Natural History Society   (WANHS)   1853
- ■ Wiltshire Heritage Museum, 41 Long St, DEVIZES, Wilts, SN10 1NS.   (hq)
  01380 727369   fax 01380 722150
  email wanhs@wiltshireheritage.org.uk
  http://www.wiltshireheritage.org.uk
  Sec: Mrs W Lansdown
- ▲ Company Limited by Guarantee; Registered Charity
- ○ *L; to promote, research & publish on the archaeology, art, history & natural history of Wiltshire for the public benefit
- Gp Archaeology field gp
- ● Mtgs - ET - Res - Exhib - SG - Inf - Lib - PL - VE - Maintenance of a museum & library displaying designated collections
- M 1,041 i, 83 org
- ¶ Wiltshire Archaeological & Natural History Magazine (Jnl) - 1; ftm, £15 nm.
  NL - 2.   AR.

Wiltshire Horn Sheep Society   1923
- ■ Little Bache Farm House, Hurleston, NANTWICH, Cheshire, CW5 6BU.   (hsp)
  0844 800 1029
  http://www.wiltshirehorn.org.uk
  Sec: Mrs C Cormack
- ○ *B
- ● Mtgs - Exhib - Comp - Expt
- < Nat Sheep Assn
- M 125 i, UK / 5 i, o'seas
- ¶ Flock Book - 1.

Wiltshire Record Society   (WRS)   1937
- ■ Wiltshire & Swindon History Centre, Cocklebury Rd, CHIPPENHAM, Wilts, SN15 3QN.   (hsb)
  01249 705500
  Hon Sec: Dr James Lee
- ▲ Registered Charity
- ○ *L; to promote publication of documentary sources of Wiltshire history
- ● AGM & Lecture
- M 150 i, 63 universities & public libraries, UK / 10 i, 75 org, o'seas
- ¶ Volume of edited documents - 1; £15 m, £20 nm.
  AR; ftm only.

Wind Engineering Society   (WES)   1990
- ■ c/o Institution of Civil Engineers, 1 Great George St, LONDON, SW1P 3AA.   (hq)
  020 7665 2262   fax 020 7799 1325
  email adamKirkup@ice.org.uk
  http://www.ukwes.bham.ac.uk
  Sec: Adam Kirkup
- ○ *P; to promote cooperation in the advancement & application of knowledge in all aspects of wind engineering
- ● Conf - Mtgs
- < is an affiliated society of the Institution of Civil Engineers
- M i & f
  (Sub: £30 i, £90-£180 f)

Wine & Spirit Association of Ireland   1911
- IRL 14 Whitefriars, Peters Row, Aungier St, DUBLIN 2, Republic of Ireland.
  353 (1) 475 7580   fax 353 (1) 475 9274
  email info@wineboard.ie   http://www.wineboard.ie
  Mgr: Colleen Cook
- ○ *T

Wine & Spirit Trade Association (WSTA) 1824
- ■ International Wine & Spirit Centre, 39-45 Bermondsey St, LONDON, SE1 3XF.   (hq)
  020 7089 3877   fax 020 7089 3870
  email info@wsta.co.uk   http://www.wsta.co.uk
  Chief Exec: Jeremy Beadles
- ▲ Company Limited by Guarantee
- ○ *T; to represent the interests of shippers & distributors of wine & imported spirits in the UK
- Gp Distance seller; Importers; Logistics; UK wine growers
- ● Conf - Stat - Inf - LG
- < Fédn Intle de Vin et Spiritueux (FIVS); Eur Fedn of Wine & Spirit Importers & Distributors (EFWSID); Office Intle de de Vigne et du Vin (OIV); Comité Vins
- M 320 f, UK & o'seas
- ¶ Trade Voice - 12; ftm only   AR - 1.
  Checklists (the sole commercial guide to European wine & spirit legislation) - 1.
- ✕ 2005 Wine & Spirit Association

Wire Products Association (WPA) 1953
- ■ c/o F H Brundle, 24-36 Lamson Rd, RAINHAM, Essex, RM13 9YY.   (pres/b)
  01708 253545
  Pres: Richard Brundle
- ○ *T; wholesaling & marketing of agricultural wire products (incl chain-link fencing) & wire nails
- Gp Wire nails; Agricultural wire products
- ● Mtgs

Wireless for the Bedridden Society Inc (W4B) 1938
- § 159A High St, HORNCHURCH, Essex, RM11 3YB.   (hq)
  01708 621101   fax 01708 620816
  http://www.w4b.org.uk
  Chief Exec: Tim Leech
  National charity providing televisions &/or radios for people who are housebound & in financial need.

Wirral Chamber of Commerce & Industry 1911
- NR 16 Grange Road West, Birkenhead, WIRRAL, Merseyside, CH41 4DA.   (hq)
  0151-647 8899   fax 0151-650 0440
  email info@wirralchamber.org.uk
  http://www.wirralchamber.org.uk
  Chief Exec: Ken Davies
- ▲ Company Limited by Guarantee
- ○ *C
- Gp Education link; Environment; Central traders; Finance
- ● Conf - Mtgs - ET - Res - Exhib - Stat - Expt - Inf - VE - LG
- < Chams Comm NW
- M f
- ¶ Newsletter - 12.   LM - 1.   Diary - 1.

Wolf Society of Great Britain
    since September 2005 **Wolves & Humans Foundation**

Wolverton & District Archaeological & Historical Society 1955
- ■ 82 Clarence Rd, Stony Stratford, MILTON KEYNES, Bucks, MK11 1JD.   (hsp)
  01908 565481
  Hon Sec: Mrs Audrey Lambert
- ○ *L; archaeology & local history within the Milton Keynes area & adjoining villages of North Buckinghamshire & South Northamptonshire; preservation & recording of sites & buildings under threat of destruction
- ● Mtgs - Exhib - Inf - Lib
- < Coun Brit Archaeology; Bucks Archaeol Soc; Northants Archaeol Soc
- M 145 i
- ¶ NL - 6; ftm.

Wolves & Humans Foundation (WAH) 2005
- ■ 2 Blackrod Cottages, Compton Durville, SOUTH PETHERTON, Somerset, TA13 5EX.   (hsp)
  01460 242593
  email info@wolvesandhumans.org
  http://www.wolvesandhumans.org
  Sec: Richard Morley
- ▲ Registered Charity
- ○ *K; support & promotion of research & scientific study of wolves & other large carnivores; the education & training in methods of managing conflict between such animals & agriculture & other human interests
- ● Conf - ET - Res - Exhib - Inf
- M 200 i, UK / 20 i, o'seas
- ¶ Wolves & Humans NL - 4; ftm only (subscription £25).
- ✕ 2005 (September) Wolf Society of Great Britain

Women's Aid Federation (England) Ltd (WAFE) 1986
- ■ PO Box 391, BRISTOL, BS99 7WS.   (hq)
  0117-944 4411   fax 0117-924 1703
  email info@womensaid.org.uk
  http://www.womensaid.org.uk
  Chief Exec: Nicola Harwin
- ▲ Company Limited by Guarantee; Registered Charity
- Br 250
- ○ *N, *W; to coordinate & resource refuge groups for women & their children in need of temporary accommodation because of mental, physical or sexual abuse
- ● ET - Res - Inf - LG - Public information work on domestic violence - Seminars - Networking
  Helpline: 0800 200 0247 (freephone 24-hr) the national domestic violence helpline run in partnership between Women's Aid & Refuge
- < Fedn Indep Advice Centres (FIAC)
- ¶ NL - 12; ftm only.   Publications list available.

Women's Cycle Racing Association (WCRA) 1949
- NR 5 Coppsfield, Hurst Park, WEST MOLESEY, Surrey, KT8 1NN.
  020 8224 1269
  http://www.wcra.org.uk
  Gen Sec: Caroline Fantham
- ○ *S; to increase the opportunity for women in all forms of cycle sport
- < Brit Cycling Fedn

Women's Engineering Society (WES) 1919
- ■ Michael Faraday House, Six Hills Way, STEVENAGE, Herts, SG1 2AY.   (hq)
  01438 765506
  email info@wes.org.uk   http://www.wes.org.uk
  Contact: Hon Sec atfield
- ▲ Company Limited by Guarantee; Registered Charity
- Br Student groups
- ○ *P; to inspire women to achieve their potential as scientists, engineers & technologists; to assist educators, managers & employers in making this happen
- Gp Mentor set
- ● Conf - Mtgs - ET - Comp - Inf - PL - VE - LG - Student support - Dr Karen Burt Award - Young Woman Engineer Award
- M 700 i, 20 f, 12 student groups, UK / 40 i, 1 f, o'seas (Sub: £40 i, varies f)
- ¶ The Woman Engineer - 4; ftm, £25 yr (UK), £28 yr (o'seas) nm. LM; m only.   AR - 1.

Women's Environmental Network   (WEN)   1988
■ PO Box 30626, LONDON, E1 1TZ.   (hq)
020 7481 9004   fax 020 7481 9144
email info@wen.org.uk
Admin: Shirley Abranches
▲ Company Limited by Guarantee; Registered Charity
Br 55 local gps
○ *K; to inform, educate & empower women who care about the environment
● ET - Res - Exhib - Inf
M 3,500 i, 30 f, 160 org, UK / 50 i, 5 f, 10 org, o'seas
¶ NL - 4; ftm only.

Women's Farm & Garden Association   (WFGA)   1899
NR 175 Gloucester St, CIRENCESTER, Glos, GL7 2DP.   (hq)
01285 658339   fax 01285 642356
email admin@wfga.fsbusiness.co.uk
▲ Registered Charity
○ *F, *H; to unite all involved in agriculture & horticulture in the UK & overseas
M i

Women's Food & Farming Union   (WFU)   1979
NR WFU National Office, STONELEIGH PARK, Warks, CV8 2LZ. (hq)
024 7669 3171
Pres: Ionwen Lewis
Nat Sec: Sue Archer
▲ Un-incorporated Society
Br 26
○ *F; to link the producer & the consumer by promoting demand for British farm produce; to encourage farmers & growers to practise better marketing; to ensure British produce is available & well marketed; to lobby against unfair competition
Gp Crops; Dairy; Livestock
● Conf - Mtgs - ET - LG
< Nat Coun Women GB
M 800 i
¶ Update - 5; ftm only.   Annual Review - 1; free.

Women in Management
a group of the **Chartered Management Institute**

Women's Royal Voluntary Service   (WRVS)   1938
NR Garden House, Milton Hill, Steventon, ABINGDON, Oxon, OX13 6AD.   (hq)
01235 442900   fax 01235 861166
email info@wrvs.org.uk   http://www.wrvs.org.uk
Chief Exec: Mark Lever
▲ Company Limited by Guarantee; Registered Charity
Br 'hundreds'
○ *W; voluntary welfare service to local communities in Britain, working alongside local authorities & hospital trusts; 'to help people maintain independence & dignity in their local communities, particularly later in life'
● Hospital services; Emergency services; Services for older people
< NCVO
M 95,000 i
¶ AR.

Wood Panel Industries Federation   (WPIF)   1996
■ 28 Market Place, GRANTHAM, Lincs, NG31 6LR.   (hq)
01476 563707   fax 01476 579314
email enquiries@wpif.org.uk   http://www.wpif.org.uk
Dir Gen: Alastair F Kerr
▲ Company Limited by Guarantee
○ *T; technical standards & environmental data, developments & policy issues for industrial members only (does not include agents, distributors or merchants)
Gp Product application; Research evaluation; Ecology
● Mtgs - Res - Inf - LG
< Eur Confedn Woodworking Inds; Eur Fedn Assns Particleboard Mfrs; Nat Coun Bldg Material Producers
M 18 f, 3 org

Wood Protection Association   (WPA)   2006
NR 1 Gleneagles House, Vernongate, DERBY, DE1 1UP.   (hq)
01332 225104   fax 01332 225101
email info@wood-protection.org
http://www.wood-protection.org
Dir: Dr Chris Coggins
○ *T; treatment of new timber to protect against the risk of insect or fungal attack or fire in service; protective coatings against weathering and fire; DIY wood protection
✕ 2006 British Wood Preserving & Damp-proofing Association

Woodcraft Folk   1925
NR Units 9-10, 83 Crampton St, LONDON, SE17 3BF.
020 7730 4173   fax 020 7358 6370
email info@woodcraft.org
http://www.woodcraft.org.uk
Gen Sec: Kirsty Palmer
Br 500
○ *Y; an educational movement for children & young people which aims to develop self confidence & activity in society
Gp Woodchips (under 6 years); Elfins (6-9); Pioneers (10-12); Venturers (13-15); DFs (District Fellows - older teenagers & young adults)

Wooden Spoon Society
we do not wish to be included, thank you.

Woodworkers, Builders & Miscellaneous Tools Association
a group of the **Federation of British Hand Tool Manufacturers**

Woodworking Machinery Suppliers Association   (WMSA)   1983
■ The Counting House, Mill Rd, Cromford, MATLOCK, Derbys, DE4 3RQ.
01629 826998   fax 01629 826997
email info@wmsa.org.uk   http://www.wmsa.org.uk
Admin Coordinator: Claire Parkinson
Br Technical directorate (Bradford) 01535 273807
○ *T
● Conf - Mtgs - Exhib
M 90 f
¶ NL - 4; m only.
Directory of Members & Buyers' Guide - 2 yrly; free.

Woolhope Naturalists' Field Club   1851
■ Chy an Whyloryon, Wigmore, LEOMINSTER, Herefords, HR6 9UD.   (hsp)
01568 770356
http://www.woolhopeclub.org.uk
Hon Sec: J W Tonkin
▲ Registered Charity
○ *L; archaeology, natural history & allied subjects of Herefordshire & the area immediately adjacent
Gp Archaeology; Natural history
● Mtgs - SG - Lib - VE
M 550 i, 38 org, UK / 3 i, 6 org, o'seas
¶ Transactions - 1; m only.

Worcestershire Archaeological Society   (WAS)   1860
■ 26 Albert Park Rd, MALVERN, Worcs, WR14 1HN.   (hsp)
01684 565190
http://www.communigate.co.uk/worcs/worcestershirearchaeologicalsociety/index.phtml
Hon Sec: Janet Dunleavey
▲ Registered Charity
○ *L; to promote study of archaeology & local history in the County of Worcestershire & the diocese of Worcester
Gp Architectural study
● Mtgs - SG - Lib - VE
M 180 i, c 60 org, UK / c 30 org, o'seas
¶ The Worcestershire Recorder - 2; ftm.
Transactions - 2; ftm, £25 nm.

Worcestershire Chamber of Commerce
  sww **Herefordshire & Worcestershire Chamber of Commerce**

Work Experience UK
  a group of **English UK**

Work Foundation   1918
NR   21 Palmer St, LONDON, SW1H 0AD.   (hq)
       0870 165 6700
       http://www.theworkfoundation.com
       Chief Exec: Will Hutton
▲   Registered Charity
○   *K; 'to work with employees to improve the productivity &
       quality of working life in the UK'
●   Res - Inf - Lib - LG
M   400 i, 1,450 f, UK

Workers' Educational Association   (WEA)   1903
NR   Quick House, 65 Clifton St, LONDON, EC2A 4JE.   (hq)
       020 7426 3450   fax 020 7426 3451
       Gen Sec: Richard Bolsin
▲   Registered Charity
Br   650
○   *E; as the largest voluntary provider of adult education in the
       UK the WEA has particular concern for the socially,
       economically & educationally disadvantaged; the voluntary &
       democratic traditions have created an approach that is
       unique in adult education
M   5,000 i

Workers' Music Association   (WMA)   1936
■   12 St Andrew's Square, LONDON, W11 1RH.   (hsp)
       020 7243 0920
       email mavcook@talktalk.net
       http://www.wmamusic.org.uk
       Hon Sec: Mavis Cook
▲   Company Limited by Guarantee
○   *D; 'to print, publish & sell (including for export) music & the
       literature of music, & to deal in musical instruments
       (including instruments for the reproduction of music); to
       produce & sell (including for export) recorded music & films;
       to encourage the composition & performance of music, with
       special regard to music which 1) expresses the ideals & aims
       of mankind towards the improved organisation of society,
       2) exerts an influence against the social injustices of our
       present society, 3) encourages & reflects the activities &
       aspirations of the labour & peace movements for a new
       society, & to this latter end to provide whatever services of
       education & performance for the labour & peace movements
       as may be determined by the AGM of the Association; &
       generally, by all means which may be determined by the
       Executive Committee from time to time, including grants of
       financial aid to any persons, corporations or associations
       whether by loan, subscription or donation, to carry out these
       objects'
Gp   Summer school c'ee; WMA singers
●   Mtgs - ET - Lib - Annual summer school - Weekend musical
       events - Performances by WMA singers - Concerts
<   Birmingham Clarion Singers; Côr Cochion Caerdydd; Calumet
       Singers
M   119 i, 4 choirs, UK / 3 affiliates
       (Sub: £7 i, £25 affiliates)
¶   Bulletin - 4;   NL - irreg;   AR; all ftm.
       Peace Song Book.   Easter Rising in Song & Ballad.

Working Families   1985
■   1-3 Berry St, LONDON, EC1V 0AA.   (hq)
       020 7253 7243   fax 020 7253 6253
       email office@workingfamilies.org.uk
       http://www.workingfamilies.org.uk
       Chief Exec: Sarah Jackson
▲   Company Limited by Guarantee; Registered Charity
○   *W; to give advice to working parents & carers, whilst helping
       employers create workplaces which encourage work/life
       balance for everyone
●   Conf - ET - Comp - Inf
       Disability & careers issues: Janet Mearns 020 7253 7243
       Helpline: 0800 013 0313
M   [not stated]
¶   [see website]
×   2004 (New Ways to Work
       (Parents at Work

Working Men's Club & Institute Union Ltd   (CIU)   1862
■   253-254 Upper St, LONDON, N1 1RY.   (hq)
       020 7226 0221   fax 020 7354 1847
       email information@wmciu.org   http://www.wmciu.org
       Gen Sec: Kevin Smyth
Br   29
○   *W; 'an advisory & defensive organisation for non-profit
       making members' clubs'
●   Conf - Mtgs - ET - Exam - Res - Exhib - Comp - SG - Stat - Inf -
       VE - Empl - LG - Provision of convalescent homes, recreation
       & sporting facilities
<   C'ee of Registered Clubs Assns; Workers Educational Assn;
       Ruskin College
M   6,000,000 i, 2,903 clubs
¶   Club Jnl - 12; 60p each.   AR.

Working for Wellbeing
  alternative name of **Together**

World Orthopaedic Concern
  a specialist society of the **British Orthopaedic Association**

World Pheasant Association UK   (WPA)   1975
■   7-9 Shaftesbury St, FORDINGBRIDGE, Hants, SP6 1JF.   (hq)
       0845 241 0929   fax 01425 658053
       email office@pheasant.org.uk
       http://www.pheasant.org.uk
       Admin: Pat Savage
▲   Registered Charity
Br   Australia, Austria, Belelux, China, France, Germany, India,
       Nepal, Pakistan, Portugal, Taiwan
○   *K, *L; to ensure the survival of the individual species of
       pheasant & related gamebirds which are threatened with
       extinction; the maintenance of viable populations of these
       groups of birds in natural habitat in their countries of origin
Gp   Grouse; Megapose; Partridge, quail & francolin; Pheasants
●   Conf - Mtgs - ET - Res - Exhib - SG - Inf - Lib - LG
<   species survival commission of the Intl U for the Consvn of
       Nature (IUCN); Birdlife Intl
M   520 i, 5 f, UK / 107 i, 1 f, o'seas
       (Sub: £25 i, £100, UK / £30 i, £100 f o'seas)
¶   WPA News - 2; ftm only.
       WPA Annual Review - 1; ftm, £6 nm.
       Publications list available.

© CBD Research Ltd · Beckenham · BR3 5JS · Tel 020 8650 7745 · Fax 020 8650 0768 · E-mail cbd@cbdresearch.com · www.cbdresearch.com

World Speedway Riders Association   (WSRA)   1958

- ■ 90 Ruskin Ave, Long Eaton, NOTTINGHAM, NG10 3HX.   (hsp)
  0115-973 6041   fax 0115-946 5005
  email legend3333@btinternet.com
  Sec & Treas: Vic White
- Br Australia, New Zealand
- ○ *S; 'to help former colleagues to keep in touch, to stage frequent reunions & to enjoy the pleasures of reliving old times in convivial company'
- ● Exhib - Lunches - Dinners - Golf tournaments
- M c 550 i, UK & o'seas
- ¶ Opposite Lock (NL) - 4; ftm only.
- × 2006 Veteran Speedway Riders Association

World War Two Living History Association   (LHA)   1978

- NR 25 Olde Farm Drive, Darby Green, CAMBERLEY, Surrey, GU17 0DU.   (chmn/p)
  http://www.ww2lha.com
- ▲ Company Limited by Guarantee
- ○ *G; to mount public displays of battle re-enactment & private 'living history' re-enactments for members only
- M i

World War Two Railway Study Group   (WW2RSG)   1990

- NR 25 Woodcote Rd, LEAMINGTON SPA, Warks, CV32 6PZ.   (memsec/p)
  01926 429378
  http://www.saxoncourtbooks.co.uk/ww2rsg/
  Mem Sec: Mike Christensen
- ▲ Un-incorporated Society
- ○ *G, *Q; to collect, exchange & publish information on the operation of railways of the combatant nations during World War II

World-Wide Opportunities on Organic Farms   (WWOOF)   1971

- ■ PO Box 2154, Winslow, BUCKINGHAM, MK18 3WS.   (co-ordinator/p)
  http://www.wwoof.org.uk
  Coordinator: Fran Whittle
- ▲ Company Limited by Guarantee
- Br 24 countries o'seas
- ○ *F; in return for work on organic farms, gardens & smallholdings, volunteers are given meals & a place to sleep. Participants get first hand experience of organic farming & growing as well as the opportunity to get into the countryside. WWOOF operates on the Continent & there are similar organisations worldwide
- ● Conf - Practical work on farms
- M 2,000 i, 5,000 i (independents), UK / i, o'seas
- ¶ WWOOF UK News - 6; ftm.
  WWINDY News (NL) - 6; free, online only.
  List of branches overseas with host names.
- × 2003 Willing Workers on Organic Farms

Worldchoice   1978

- NR Worldchoice House, Minerva Business Park, Lynch Wood, PETERBOROUGH, Cambs, PE2 6FT.   (hq)
  01733 390900   fax 01733 396823
  email cheal@worldchoice.co.uk
  http://www.worldchoice.co.uk
  Chmn: Colin Heal,   Co Sec: Duncan Pickering
- ▲ Company Limited by Guarantee
- ○ *T; independent travel agent consortia
- ● Conf - ET
- M c 700 f

Worthing Chamber of Commerce & Industry   1938

- NR Shelley House, 23 Warwick St, WORTHING, W Sussex, BN11 3DG.   (hq)
  01903 203484   fax 01903 504697
  email info@worthingchamber.co.uk
  http://www.worthingchamber.co.uk
- ▲ Company Limited by Guarantee
- ○ *C
- ● Mtgs - Exhib - Inf - VE - LG - Corporate entertainment
- < Sussex Enterprise
- M c 300 f
- ¶ NL - 6.   Diary - 1.
- × 2003 Worthing Chamber of Trade & Commerce Ltd

Wound Care Society   (WCS)   1989

- ■ PO Box 170, Hartford, HUNTINGDON, Cambs, PE29 1PL.   (hq)
  01480 434401   fax 01480 434401
  email wound.care.society@talk21.com
  http://www.woundcaresociety.com
  Chmn: Louise Toner
- ▲ Registered Charity
- ○ *M, *P; to promote & further the best practice in the prevention, treatment & management of wounds through the provision of educational resources
- ● Conf - ET - Exhib - SG - Inf
- M 1,500 i, 37 f, 3 org, UK / 35 i, o'seas
- ¶ Wound Care Jnl - 4; ftm only.
  Educational booklets; all £2 m, £2.50 nm:
  Cavity Wounds.   Diabetic Foot.
  Eczema - Aetiology & Management.
  Equipment Selection.   Graduated Compression Hosiery.
  Management of Exuding Wounds.   Pain & Wound Care.
  Palliative Management of Fungating Malignant Wounds.
  Wounds & Infection.
  Educational booklets 4-hole punched:
  Anatomy & Physiology Wound Healing & Wound Assessment.
  Dressings Selection.
  Principles of Leg Ulcer Management & Prevention.
  Principles of Pressure Ulcer Management & Prevention.
  Standardised Assessment Tools & the Management of Complex Wounds.
  Silver in Wound Care & Management.
  Pressure Ulcer Prevention Manual; £5.

Woven Wire Association

- NR c/o Peter Mills, Soar Engineering Ltd, Beaumont Rd, BANBURY, Oxon, OX16 1SD.
  Sec: Peter Mills
- ○ *T
  no further information supplied

Writers' Copyright Association UK   (WCA)

- NR Ealing Studios, Ealing Green, LONDON, W5 5EP.
  0870 442 1513
  email admin@wcauk.com   http://www.wcauk.com
- ○ *G; to protect the copyright of scriptwriters
- < Musicians' Copyright Assn; Webmasters' Copyright Assn

Writers' Guild of Great Britain   (WGGB)   1959

- ■ 15 Britannia St, LONDON, WC1X 9JN.   (hq)
  020 7833 0777   fax 020 7833 4777
  email erik@writersguild.org.uk
  http://www.writersguild.org.uk
  Gen Sec: Bernie Corbett
- ○ *P, *U; for professional writers in the spheres of film, television, radio, theatre & books, children's writing & new media
- Gp Film & television; Radio; Theatre; Books; Children
- ● Mtgs - ET - Inf - Empl - LG - Legal & professional advice & representation of members over contracts, fees, rights & other issues connected with their work as writers
- < Writers' Guilds: Australia, Canada, Ireland, New Zealand, USA; European Writers' Congress; TUC
- M 2,000 i, 100 f, UK / 100 i, 10 f, o'seas
- ¶ UK Writer - 4; ftm, £25 yr nm.

Writers & Photographers unLimited   (WPU)   2003
- ■ PO Box 520, Bamber Bridge, PRESTON, Lancs, PR5 8LF.   (hsp)
  01772 321243   fax 0870 137 8888
  email info@wpu.org.uk   http://www.wpu.org.uk
  Mgr: Terry Marsh
- ▲ Un-incorporated Society
- ○ *P; to promote the work of members
- ● Inf - PL
- M   20 i

Writing Equipment Society   (WES)   1980
- ■ 33 Glanville Rd, HADLEIGH, Suffolk, IP7 5SQ.   (sp)
  Sec: John Daniels
- ○ *G; for all interested in the collection, conservation & study of writing instruments & accessories - including pens, pencils, inkpots, quills, letter scales & information & ephemera connected with the subject
- ● Mtgs - SG - VE
- M   400 i, 20 f, UK / 150 i, 10 f, 5 org, o'seas
- ¶ Jnl (incl LM) - 3;   LM; both ftm only.

Writing Instruments Association   (WIA)
- ■ Farringdon Point, 29-35 Farringdon Rd, LONDON, EC1M 3JF.   (hq)
  0845 450 1565   fax 020 7405 7784
  Chmn: Chris Reynolds
- ▲ Company Limited by Guarantee
- ○ *T
- ● Conf - Mtgs - SG - Stat
- < Eur Writing Instruments Assn; is an affiliate of the British Office Supplies & Services Federation
- M   f

WW2 HMSO Paperbacks Society   1994
- ■ 3 Roman Rd, SOUTHWICK, W Sussex, BN42 4TP.   (hsp)
  01273 596217
  Hon Sec: A R James
- ○ *G; interest & research in World War Two publications by the Ministry of Information &/or HM Stationery Office
- ● Res - SG - Inf - Lib - PL
- M   20 i, 1 f (HMSO), UK / 5 i, o'seas
- ¶ WW2 HMSO Paperbacks Collectors' Guide; £5.
  Informing the People (HMSO) 1996; £10.

Wyndham Lewis Society   1972
- ■ Library 304, University of Plymouth, Drake Circus, PLYMOUTH, Devon, PL4 8AA.
  01752 672567
  email amunton@plymouth.ac.uk   http://www.unirioja.es/wyndhamlewis/
  Contact: Dr Alan Munton
- ▲ Un-incorporated Society
- ○ *A; to promote interest in the works of Wyndham Lewis (1882–1957), novelist, painter & critic
- ● Conf - Res - Exhib - VE
- ¶ Wyndham Lewis Annual (jnl) - 1; £15.
  Lewisletter (NL) - 2; ftm only.

X

Xenophon   1989
- ■ 98 Cambridge Gardens, LONDON, W10 6HS.   (hsp)
  020 8968 1360
  email wolstan-dixie@hotmail.co.uk
  Hon Sec: Regor J Nagrom
- ▲ Un-incorporated Society
- ○ *G; the study, for recreational & historical purposes, of secret communication & its recovery
- ● Res - Comp - SG - Inf - Lib
- M   20 i
- ¶ Crypt - 1; ftm, £5 nm.

© CBD Research Ltd · Beckenham · BR3 5JS · Tel 020 8650 7745 · Fax 020 8650 0768 · E-mail cbd@cbdresearch.com · www.cbdresearch.com

Yacht Brokers, Designers & Surveyors Association
the management company for the **Association of Brokers & Yacht Agents** & the **Yacht Designers & Surveyors Association**

Yacht Charter Association
in September 2005 merged with the Association of Bonded Sailing Companies & the National Federation of Sea Schools to form the **Marine Leisure Association**

Yacht Designers & Surveyors Association   (YDSA)   1912
- ■ The Glass Works, Penns Rd, PETERSFIELD, Hants, GU32 2EW, (hq)
  01730 710425   fax 01730 710423
  email info@ybdsa.co.uk   http://www.ybdsa.co.uk
  Co Sec: Jane Gentry
- ▲ Company Limited by Guarantee
- ○ *P; for yacht surveyors & designers
- ● Conf - Mtgs - ET - Exam
- M 100 i, UK / 15 i, o'seas
- ¶ NL - 4; ftm only.
  Note: The Yacht Brokers, Designers & Surveyors Association is the management company for the YDSA & the Association of Brokers & Yacht Agents

Yacht Harbour Association Ltd   (TYHA)   1963
- ■ 12 Evegate Park Barn, Smeeth, ASHFORD, Kent, TN25 6SX. (hq)
  01303 814434
  http://www.yachtharbourassociation.com
  Sec: Sue Lambert,   Chief Exec: Sam J Bourne
- ▲ Company Limited by Guarantee
- ○ *T; for the development of international, coastal & inland boating facilities
- ● Conf - Mtgs - VE
- < Brit Marine Fedn
- M 290 f, UK / 20 f, o'seas
- ¶ Fore & Aft (NL) - 4.

Yachting Journalists' Association   (YJA)   1960
- NR 36 Church Lane, LYMINGTON, Hants, SO41 3RB.   (hsp)
  01590 673894
  email sec@yja.co.uk   http://www.yja.co.uk
  Hon Sec: Rachel Nuding
- ▲ Un-incorporated Society
- ○ *P; to promote greater awareness of a wide range of leisure boating activities through the professional services offered by members
- ● Mtgs - Inf - Organisation of annual awards - Yachtsman of the Year & Young Sailor of the Year
- M 270 i, UK / 28 i, o'seas
- ¶ Hbk (incl LM) - 1.

Yeovil Agricultural Society   (YAS)   1833
- NR Barwick Park Lodge, Barwick, YEOVIL, Somerset, BA22 9TA. (hsp)
  01935 424785
- ▲ Registered Charity
- ○ *F; interests of farming & assistance of students at colleges in Somerset & Dorset; applications in respect of education in farming methods
- ● Showground for use by local groups: horse shows, trials & events
- M 40 i

YMCA England   (YMCA)   1844
- NR 640 Forest Rd, LONDON, E17 3DZ.   (hq)
  020 8520 5599
- ▲ Registered Charity
- ○ *Y; to encourage the physical, mental & spiritual development of all young people (male & female) so that they make the most of their lives & play a worth-while role in their communities

YMCA Ireland
- NR 14 College Square North, BELFAST, BT1 6AR.
  028 9032 7757
  email admin@ymca-ireland.org
  http://www.ymca-ireland.org
  Chmn: Nichola Lynagh
- ○ *W, *Y; a cross denominational organisation committed to local youth need

Ymgyrch Diogelu Cymru Wledig
Welsh name of the **Campaign for the Protection of Rural Wales**

York & North Yorkshire Chamber of Commerce   1911
- NR Innovation Centre - York Science Park, Innovation Way, Heslington, YORK, YO10 5DG.   (hq)
  01904 567838
  Chief Exec: Len Cruddas
- ○ *C
- ● Stat - Expt - Inf
- M i, f & org
- ¶ Business Update - 6; Business North - 6; both free. Directory - 1; ftm.

Yorkshire Agricultural Society   1837
- ■ Great Yorkshire Showground, HARROGATE, N Yorks, HG2 8PW.   (hq)
  01423 541000   fax 01423 541414
  email info@yas.co.uk   http://www.yas.co.uk
  Chief Exec: Nigel Pulling
- ▲ Registered Charity
- ○ *F, *H; aims to improve agricultural practices & understanding within Yorkshire, incl forestry, pisciculture, the breeding of livestock & rural crafts; to hold the largest agricultural show in the North
- ● Conf - Mtgs - ET - Res - Exhib - Comp - SG - VE - Annual show
- M 9,500 i, 500 f
- ¶ NL - 3;   AR - 1; both ftm only. Great Yorkshire Show: Programme £3 / Catalogue £5.

Yorkshire Archaeological Society (YAS) 1863
■ Claremont, 23 Clarendon Rd, LEEDS, W Yorks, LS2 9NZ. (hq)
0113-245 7910 fax 0113-245 7992
email yas.secretary@googlemail.com
http://www.yas.org.uk
Hon Sec: M J Heron
▲ Company Limited by Guarantee, Registered Charity
○ *L; to promote research into all aspects of the history &
archaeology of the historic County of York
Gp Prehistory
Sections: Industrial history, Mediaeval, Roman history
Publishing sections: Parish registers, Record series, Wakefield
Court rolls
● Conf - Mtgs - ET - Res - Exhib - Inf - Lib - VE
< CBA; Archaeological & historical groups, university & similar
here & abroad
M i & org
(Sub: £40 i, £20 associates, £50 Insts, £45 affiliate orgs)
¶ Yorkshire Archaeological Jnl - 1; ftm, £25 nm.
Update (NL) - 3; free.
Yorkshire Parish Registers - 1; £18m.
Record Series - 1; £12 m.
Wakefield Court Rolls - 1; £12 m.
Yorkshire Archaeological Research; prices vary.
Yorkshire Occasional Papers; prices vary

Yorkshire Dialect Society (YDS) 1897
■ 51 Stepney Ave, SCARBOROUGH, N Yorks, YO12 5BW. (hsp)
01723 371296
Hon Sec: Michael Park
▲ Un-incorporated Society
○ *L; study of Yorkshire speech & traditional life
● Mtgs - Res - Inf
M 450 i, UK / 90 i, o'seas
¶ Transactions - 1; ftm, £4 nm.
Summer Bulletin - 1; LM - 5 yrly; both ftm only.

Yorkshire Geological Society (YGS) 1837
■ 19 Thorngate, BARNARD CASTLE, Co Durham, DL12 8QB.
(sp)
01833 638893
email tjm4@tutor.open.ac.uk
http://www.yorksgeolsoc.org.uk
Gen Sec: Dr Trevor J Morse
▲ Registered Charity
○ *L; to promote & record the results of research in geology & its
allied sciences, especially in Yorkshire & Northern England
● Conf - Mtgs - Exhib - Lib - VE
< Geologists' Assn
M 800 i, 80 f
¶ Proceedings - 2; £30 m. Circular - 8; ftm only.

Yorkshire Philosophical Society (YPS) 1822
■ The Lodge, Museum Gardens, YORK, YO1 7DR. (hq)
01904 656713 fax 01904 656713
email info@yorksphilsoc.org.uk
http://www.yorksphilsoc.org.uk
Clerk: Miss Frances Chambers, Hon Sec: William G Smith
▲ Registered Charity
○ *L; the study of natural science, archaeology & antiquities in the
county
Gp York excavation; Woodland history
● Conf - ET - VE
< is the local branch of the British Association for the
Advancement of Science
M 500 i, 10 org
¶ NL - 4; AR; both ftm.

Young Embroiderers
a group of the **Embroiderers' Guild**

Young Explorers' Trust (YET) 1970
NR at the Royal Geographical Society, 1 Kensington Gore,
LONDON, SW7 2AR. (regd/address)
email info@theyet.org http://www.theyet.org
Hon Gen Sec: Ted Grey
▲ Company Limited by Guarantee; Registered Charity
○ *E; to provide advice & support to schools, youth organisations,
commercial expedition providers & groups of friends who
intend to run their own youth expedition
M 29 i; 61 f/org

Young Women's Christian Association
full name of the **YWCA**

Youth Access 1975
■ 1-2 Taylor's Yard, 67 Alderbrook Rd, LONDON, SW12 8AD.
(hq)
020 8772 9900 fax 020 8772 9746
email admin@youthaccess.org.uk
Dir: Barbara Rayment
▲ Registered Charity
○ *W, *Y; provision of a referrals line for young people, parents &
carers, to obtain information of their most local advice,
counselling & information services
● ET - Inf - Consultancy
< Young Minds; Nat Children's Bureau
M i & agencies

Youth Action Network 1995
■ Crest House, 7 Highfield Rd, Edgbaston, BIRMINGHAM,
B15 3ED. (hq)
0121-455 9732 fax 0121-455 9697
email info@youthactionnetwork.org.uk
http://www.youthactionnetwork.org.uk
Chief Exec: Davina Goodchild
▲ Company Limited by Guarantee; Registered Charity
○ *Y; supports & develops a range of youth volunteering projects
across England; provides training, information & guidance
on recruiting, supporting & recognising the achievements of
young volunteers; develops youth action projects led by
young people & engages young people in decision making
● Conf - ET - Res - Inf - Lib - PL - VE - Development / start-up
support for orgs - Promotion of youth action in the media
M 95 org
¶ Activate - 4; ftm, £30 nm.
Reach Quality Assessment Framework; ftm (additional copies
£66.50 each), £95 nm.
VIP Kit; ftm (additional copies £28 each), £40 nm.
TREaD (Training & Education Programme); £63 m, £90 nm.
AR; free.

Youth Action Northern Ireland 1945
§ 14 College Square North, BELFAST, BT1 6AS. (hq)
028 9024 0551 fax 028 9024 8556
http://www.youthaction.org
Dir: June Trimble
Works to enable young people to achieve their full potential by
providing services, information, training & support to
community groups, youth groups, young people, their
trainers & workers.

Youth Hostel Association of Northern Ireland
former name of **Hostelling International Northern Ireland**

© CBD Research Ltd · Beckenham · BR3 5JS · Tel 020 8650 7745 · Fax 020 8650 0768 · E-mail cbd@cbdresearch.com · www.cbdresearch.com

Youth Hostels Association (England & Wales) Ltd   (YHA)   1930
NR   Trevelyan House, Dimple Rd, MATLOCK, Derbys, DE4 3YH.
        (hq)
        01629 592600   fax 01629 592702
        email customerservices@yha.org.uk
        http://www.yha.org.uk
        Chief Exec: Caroline White
▲   Company Limited by Guarantee; Registered Charity
Br   217
○   *Y; 'to help all, especially young people of limited means, to a
        greater knowledge, love & care of the countryside, &
        appreciation of the cultural values of towns & cities,
        particularly by providing youth hostels or other
        accommodation for them in their travels, & thus to improve
        their health, recreation & education'
●   Exhib - VE - Accommodation provision
<   Intl Youth Hostelling Fedn (IYHF)
M   230,000 i
¶   Triangle Magazine - 2;; ftm, £2 nm.   Escape To. . . - 1; free.
        Guidebook - 2 yrly; ftm, £3.99 nm.   AR; free.

Youth Scotland   1930
NR   Balfour House, 19 Bonnington Grove, EDINBURGH,
        EH6 4BL.   (hq)
        0131-554 2561
        Chief Exec: Carol Downie
▲   Company Limited by Guarantee; Registered Charity
Br   14 area assns
○   *N, *Y; 'to support, develop & improve the range & quality of
        informal educational, social & leisure opportunities available
        to young people in Scotland'
●   Conf - Mtgs - ET - Comp - Inf - Lib - LG
<   UK Youth; Youthlink; Scot Coun Voluntary Orgs (SCVO)
M   53,000 i, 670 clubs & area assns
¶   Magnet (Jnl) - 4; free. Area Association Newsletter - 6; ftm.
        Safe & Sound - Building a Safer Youth Work Environment; £5
        (first copy ftm).

Youth Work Ireland
        Is the trading name of **National Youth Federation**

YWCA of Ireland
IRL   64 Lower Baggot St, DUBLIN 2, Republic of Ireland.
        353 (1) 644 9536   fax 353 (1) 644 9537
        email ywca@indigo.ie   http://www.ywcaofirelend.ie
        Pres: Winnie Wilmot
○   *R; to share our faith in the Lord Jesus Christ with women and
        all young people; to serve the whole community by
        encouraging spiritual, physical and social development

YWCA (Young Women's Christian Association)   (YWCA)   1855
NR   Clarendon House, 52 Cornmarket St, OXFORD, OX1 3EJ.
        (hq)
        01865 304200   fax 01865 204805
        email info@ywca.org.uk   http://www.ywca.org.uk
        Chief Exec: Deborah Annetts
▲   Company Limited by Guarantee; Registered Charity
Br   18
○   *W, *Y; is a force for change for women who are facing
        discrimination & inequalities of all kinds; to enable young
        women who are experiencing disadvantage to identify &
        realise their full potential; to influence public policy in order
        to achieve equality & social justice for young women
¶   Members' NL - 2; ftm only.   Annual Review - 1; free.

Z

Zionist Federation of Great Britain & Ireland   (ZF)   1899
NR   741 High Rd, LONDON, N12 0BQ.   (hq)
        Exec Dir; Alan Iziz
○   *R; promotion of Zionism

Zipper Club
        alternative name of the **British Cardiac Patients Association**

Zoological Society of Ireland   1830
IRL   Phoenix Park, DUBLIN 8, Republic of Ireland.
        353 (1) 474 8900   fax 353 (1) 677 1660
        email info@dublinzoo.ie   http://www.dublinzoo.ie
○   *L, *V

Zoological Society of London   (ZSL)   1826
NR   Regent's Park, LONDON, NW1 4RY.   (hq)
        020 7722 3333
        http://www.zsl.org
▲   Company Limited by Guarantee; Registered Charity
○   *L, *Q, *V; to promote worldwide conservation of animal
        species & their habitats by stimulating public awareness &
        concern
M   i
¶   Journal of Zoology - 12.   Zoological Record - 1.

Zwartbles Sheep Association   (ZSA)   1995
■   Hillfields Lodge, Lighthorne, WARWICK, CV35 0BQ.   (hq)
        01926 651147
        email secretary@zwartbles.org   http://www.zwartbles.org
        Sec: Yvonne Froehlich
▲   Company Limited by Guarantee; Registered Charity
○   *B
●   Conf - Mtgs - ET - VE
<   Netherlands Zwartbles Soc (NZS); Nat Sheep Assn
M   270 i
¶   NL - 4;   Ybk; both free.

Directory of European Industrial & Trade Associations

Répertoire des Associations Européennes dans l'Industrie et le Commerce

Handbuch der Europäischen Verbände im Bereich der gewerblichen Wirtschaft

- *6,000 trade associations in Continental Europe, listed A-Z with:*

    addresses
    telephone & fax numbers
    contact names
    industrial sectors
    activities & services
    membership data
    publications
    official names in other languages

- **Index of 5,900 abbreviated names**

- *Subject index (in English, French & German) to more than 1,200 industries and trades represented*

We welcome your enquiries

CBD Research Ltd
15 Wickham Road, Beckenham, Kent, BR3 5JS
Tel: 020 8650 7745 **Fax:** 020 8650 0768
E-mail: cbd@cbdresearch.com
www.cbdresearch.com

A

A&A	Art & Architecture
A-A	Arrhythmia Alliance
A-DS	Anglo-Danish Soc
AA	Advertising Assn
	Alcoholics Anonymous
	Arboricultural Assn
	Arthritic Assn
	Automobile Assn
AAA	AAA - Action against Allergy
	Assn Authors' Agents
	Assn Average Adjusters
	Ayrshire Agricl Assn
AAA-NORCAP	Adults Affected Adoption NORCAP
AAAC	Assn Air Ambulance Charities
AAAofE	Amat Athletic Assn
AAB	Assn Applied Biologists
AABA	Assn Accountancy & Business Affairs
AAC	Assn ATOL Companies
AAD	Assn Amer Dancing
AAE	Assn Astronomy Educ
AAGB	Astrological Assn
AAGBI	Assn Anaesthetists
AAH	Assn Art Historians
AAI	Assn Advertisers Ireland
	Assn Alabaster Importers & Whlsrs
AAI&S	Assn Archaeol Illustrators & Surveyors
AAME	Assn Aviation Med Examiners
AAMRA	Aluminium Alloy Mfrg & Recycling Assn
AAPA	Assn Authorised Public Accountants
AAS	Anglesey Antiquarian Soc & Field Club
AASDN	Architectural & Archaeol Soc Durham & Northumberland
AAT	Assn Accounting Technicians
ABA	Antiquarian Booksellers Assn
	Assn Biomedical Andrologists
	Assn Burial Authorities
	Assn Business Administration
ABAC	Assn GB Athletics Clubs
ABAE	Amat Boxing Assn England
ABBA	Assn Business to Business Agencies
ABBC	Assn Brit Brewery Collectables
ABC	Assn Brickwork Contrs
	Assn Brit Climbing Walls
	Assn Brit Counties
	Austro-Brit Cham
ABCB	Assn Brit Certification Bodies
ABCC	Assn Brit Correspondence Colls
	Assn Brit Cycling Coaches
ABCD	Assn Bldg Cleaning Direct Service Providers
	Assn Brit Choral Dirs
ABCIFER	Assn Brit Civilian Internees Far East
ABCM	Assn Bldg Component Mfrs
ABCP	Assn Brit Concert Promoters
ABCUL	Assn Brit Credit Us
ABD	Assn Brit Drivers
	Assn Broadcasting Doctors
ABDO	Assn Brit Dispensing Opticians
ABDS	Assn Brit Designer Silversmiths
ABE	Assn Bldg Engrs
	Assn Business Executives
ABFA	Asset Based Finance Assn
ABFG	Assn Brit Fungus Gps
ABHI	Assn Brit Healthcare Inds
ABI	Assn Brit Insurers
	Assn Brit Investigators
ABIA	Assn Brit Introduction Agencies
ABIM	Assn Bakery Ingredient Mfrs
ABIS	Assn Brit & Ir Showcaves
ABJM	Assn Brit Jazz Musicians
ABKC	Assn Brit Kart Clubs
ABLS	Assn Brit Language Schools
ABM	Assn Breastfeeding Mothers
ABMA	Assn Business Mgrs & Administrators
ABMEC	Assn Brit Mining Eqpt Cos
ABN	Assn Brit Neurologists
ABO	Assn Brit Orchestras
ABOI	Assn Brit Offshore Inds
ABP	Assn Business Psychologists
ABPC	Assn Brit Pewter Craftsmen
ABPCO	Assn Brit Profl Conf Organisers
ABPI	Assn Brit Pharmaceutical Ind
ABPN	Assn Brit Paediatric Nurses
ABPS	Assn Brit Philatelic Socs
ABPT	Assn Blind Piano Tuners
ABRS	Assn Brit Riding Schools
ABS	Amat Boxing Scotland
	Anglo-Belgian Soc
	Assn Brit Sailmakers
	Assn Business Schools
ABSE	Assn Boat Safety Examiners
ABSP	Assn Brit Scrabble Players
ABSTD	Assn Basic Science Teachers Dentistry
ABSW	Assn Brit Science Writers
ABTA	Assn Brit Travel Agents
ABTAPL	Assn Brit Theological... Libraries
ABTEM	Assn Brit Transport & Engg Museums
ABTO	Assn Brit Tennis Officials
ABTOF	Assn Brit Tour Operators France
ABTT	Assn Brit Theatre Technicians
ABWAK	Assn Brit & Ir Wild Animal Keepers
ABYA	Assn Brokers & Yacht Agents
AC	Alpine Club
	Assn Coaching
ACA	Aircrew Assn
	Aircrewman's Assn
	Anglers Consvn Assn
	Assn Consultant Architects
	Assn Consulting Actuaries
	Assn Continence Advice
ACA (UK)	Assn Celebrity Assistants (UK)
ACADEMI	ACADEMI
ACAI	Assn Consultant Approved Inspectors
ACAL	Assn Child Abuse Lawyers
ACAMH	Assn Child & Adolescent Mental Health
ACAT	Assn Cognitive Analytic Therapy
ACAVA	Assn Cultural Advancement through Visual Art
ACB	Assn Clinical Biochemistry
ACBMC	Assn Community-based Maternity Care
ACCA	Assn Chart Certified Accountants
ACCC	Assn County & City Councils [IRL]
ACCD	Assn Certified Comml Diplomats
ACCE	Assn County Chief Executives
ACCEO	Assn Caravan & Camping Exempted Orgs
ACCI	Ayrshire Cham Comm & Ind
ACCM	Assn Computer Cable Mfrs
ACCS	Assn County Cricket Scorers
ACDM	Assn Clinical Data Mgt
ACE	Alliance Beverage Cartons & Environment
	Assn Catering Excellence
	Assn Circulation Executives
	Assn Confs & Events
	Assn Consultancy & Engg
	Assn Consvn Energy
	Assn Cruise Experts
ACEA	Assn Civil Enforcement Agencies
ACEG	Assn Careers Educ & Guidance
ACES	Assn Cannibals' Eqpt Suppliers
	Assn Chief Estates Surveyors... Public Sector
ACET	Assn Computer Engrs & Technicians
ACEVO	Assn Chief Executives Voluntary Orgs
ACF	Assn Charitable Foundations
ACFA	Army Cadet Force Assn
ACFM	Assn Cereal Food Mfrs
ACFO	ACFO Ltd

ACG	Anti Counterfeiting Gp		Assn Envtl Archaeology
	Arts Centre Gp		Assn Erotic Artists
ACH	Academy Curative Hypnotherapists	AECB	Assn Envt Conscious Bldg
ACID	Anti Copying Design	AECI	Assn Electrical Contrs, Ireland
ACIE	Assn Charity Indep Examiners	AEF	Aviation Envt Fedn
ACIFC	Assn Concrete Indl Flooring Contrs	AEGIS	Assn Educ & Guardianship Intl Students
ACIS	Assn Contemporary Iberian Studies	AEME	Assn Events Mgt Educ
ACJ	Assn Contemporary Jewellery	AEMES	Ancient Egypt & Middle East Soc
ACLM	Assn Contact Lens Mfrs	AEMT	Assn Electrical & Mechanical Trs
ACM	Assn Coll Mgt	AEO	Assn Event Organisers
ACMC	Assn Cost Mgt Consultants	AEP	Assn Educl Psychologists
ACML	Anti Common Market League		Assn Electricity Producers
ACO	ACOGB Autograph Club	AES	Agricl Economics Soc
ACoRP	Assn Community Rail Partnerships		Amat Entomologists' Soc
ACostE	Assn Cost Engrs		Audio Engg Soc
ACOSVO	Assn Chief Officers Scot Voluntary Orgs	AESS	Assn Engl Singers & Speakers
ACP	Assn Child Psychotherapists	AEV	Assn Event Venues
	Assn Circus Proprietors		Assn External Verifiers
	Assn Clinical Pathologists	AEWM	Assn Educ Welfare Mgt
	Assn Computer Profls	AF	Albinism Fellowship
ACPO	Assn Chief Police Officers [E&W&NI]		Audiovisual Fedn [IRL]
ACPOS	Assn Chief Police Officers Scotland	AFA	Advocates for Animals
ACRA	Assn Company Registration Agents		Aluminium Finishing Assn
ACRE	Action Communities Rural England		Amat Football Alliance
ACRIB	Air Conditioning & Refrigeration Ind Bd	AFAA	Assn Families Adopted Abroad
ACS	Additional Curates Soc	Afasic	Afasic
	Anglo Catalan Soc	AFB	Assn Foreign Banks
	Assn Charity Shops	AfC	Assn Charities
	Assn Consulting Scientists	AFC	Assn Fundraising Consultants
	Assn Convenience Stores	AFCA	Assn Financial Controllers & Administrators
	Assn Cricket Statisticians & Historians	AFCMA	Aberdeen Fish Curers'…Assn
ACSeS	Assn Coun Secretaries & Solicitors	AFDEC	Assn Franchised Distbrs Electronic Components
AcSS	Academy Social Sciences	AFHSW	Assn Family Hist Socs Wales
ACT	Aid Children with Tracheostomies	AFLS	Assn French Language Studies
	Assn Canoe Trades	AFMM	UK Assn Fish Meal Mfrs
	Assn Children's Palliative Care	AFO	Assn Festival Organisers
	Assn Christian Teachers	AfPE	Assn Physical Educ
	Assn Corporate Treasurers	AFS	Assn Football Statisticians
	Assn Cycle Traders		Assn Friendly Socs
ACTA	Animal Consultants & Trainers Assn	AFT	Assn Family Therapy
	Assn Cardiothoracic Anaesthetists	AGA	Asparagus Growers' Assn
ACTC	Assn Classic Trials Clubs	AGB	Assn Guernsey Banks
ACTCTC	Assn Charter Trustee Towns &… Couns	AGBIS	Assn Governing Bodies Indep Schools
ACTH	Assn Cushing's Treatment & Help	AGCAS	Assn Graduate Careers Advy Services
ACTO	Assn Community TV Operators	AGDS	Assn Garage Door Specialists
ACU	Assn C'wealth Universities	AGI	Assn Geographic Inf
	Auto-Cycle U	AGIF	Amusement & Gaming Ind Forum
ACVW	Assn Countryside Voluntary Wardens	AGIP	Assn Gp & Individual Psychotherapy
ACW	Gwartheg Hynafol Cymru	AGR	Assn Graduate Recruiters
ACWRT(UK)	American Civil War Round Table	AGRA	Assn Genealogists & Researchers in Archives
ADA	Antiquities Dealers Assn	AGS	Alpine Garden Soc
	Assn Dental Anaesthetists		Assn Geotechnical & Geoenvironmental Specialists
	Assn Drainage Authorities	AGSD(UK)	Assn Glycogen Storage Diseases
ADASS	Assn Directors Adult Social Services	AGT	Assn Gardens Trusts
ADCAS	Assn Ductwork Contrs & Allied Services	AGW	Assn Golf Writers
ADCCAT	Assn Distributors, Coaters… Adhesive Tapes	AHA	Alliance Healing Assns
ADCH	Assn Dogs & Cats Homes	AHC	Assn Healthcare Communicators
ADCS	Assn Directors Children's Services	AHC-UK	Assn Hist & Computing
ADES	Assn Directors Educ Scotland	AHCP	Assn Healthcare Cleaning Profls
ADF	Automotive Distribution Fedn	AHDA	Animal Health Distbrs Assn
ADFAM	ADFAM	AHDS	Assn Headteachers & Deputes Scotland
ADH	Assn Dental Hospitals	AHEM	Brit Fluid Power Assn
ADI	Assn Dental Implantology	AHG	Assn Hist Glass
ADINJC	Approved Driving Instructors Nat Jt Coun	AHGBI	Assn Hispanists
ADLS	Assn Dunkirk Little Ships	AHGTC	Ancient & Honourable Gld Town Criers
ADMG	Assn Deer Mgt Gps	AHI	Assn Heritage Interpretation
ADMT UK	Assn Dance Movement Therapy	AHIPP	Assn Home Information Pack Providers
ADP	Assn Disabled Profls	AHIS	Assn Heads Indep Schools
ADPH	Assn Directors Public Health	AHOEC	Assn Heads Outdoor Educ Centres
ADSA	Automatic Door Suppliers Assn	AHP(B)	Assn Humanistic Psychology
ADSET	ADSET	AHPMA	Absorbent Hygiene Products Mfrs Assn
ADSW	Assn Directors Social Work	AHS	Antiquarian Horological Soc
AEA	Academy Execs & Admins	AHSS	Architectural Heritage Soc Scotland
	Agricl Engrs Assn	AIA	Anglo-Israel Assn
	Aluminium Extruders Assn		Assn Indl Archaeology
	Assn Educ & Ageing		Assn Intl Accountants
	Assn Electoral Administrators	AIAC	Advice NI

© CBD Research Ltd · Beckenham · BR3 5JS · Tel 020 8650 7745 · Fax 020 8650 0768 · E-mail cbd@cbdresearch.com · www.cbdresearch.com

AIC	Agricl Inds Confedn	ALT	Assn Law Teachers
	Assn Investment Companies		Assn Learning Technology
AICA	Assn Indep Care Advisers	ALTO	ALTO [IRL]
	Assn Indep Construction Adjudicators	ALTT	Assn Light Touch Therapists
AICC	Assn Indep Crop Consultants	Alupro	UK Aluminium Packaging Recycling Org
AICES	Assn Intl Courier & Express Services	ALVA	Assn Leading Visitor Attractions
AICR	Assn Intl Cancer Res	AMA	Accident Mgt Assn
AICS	Assn Indep Computer Specialists		Amat Martial Assn
AIF	Assn Interchurch Families		Anthroposophical Med Assn
AIFA	Assn Indep Financial Advisers		Arts Marketing Assn
AIIC	Assn Indep Inventory Clerks		Assn Mining Analysts
AIL	Assn Indep Libraries		Assn Model Agents
AILU	Assn Laser Users	AMABO	Assn Med Advisers Brit Orchestras
AIM	Assn Indep Museums	AMCA	Amat Motor Cycle Assn
	Assn Indep Music	AMDEA	Assn Mfrs Domestic Appliances
AIMH UK	Assn Infant Mental Health UK	AMDIS	Assn Marketing & Devt Indep Schools
AIMS	A1 Motor Stores	AMEC	Assn Measurement & Evaluation Communication
	Assn Improvements Maternity Services	AMED	Assn Mgt Educ & Devt
	Assn Indep Meat Suppliers	AMEM	Assn Miniature Engine Mfrs
AIMUK	Assn Automatic Identification …Capture	AMHSA	Automated Material Handling Systems Assn
AINA	Assn Inland Navigation Authorities	AMI	Assn Meat Inspectors
AIOA	Assn Indep Organ Advisers		Assn Mortgage Intermediaries
AIPP	Assn Intl Property Profls	amii	Assn Med Insurance Intermediaries
AIRMIC	Assn Insurance & Risk Mgrs	AMIMB	Assn Members Indep Monitoring Bds
AIRSO	Assn Indl Road Safety Officers	AMLBO	River Assn Freight & Transport
AIRTO	AIRTO	AMM	Assn Med Microbiologists
AIS	Anglo-Indonesian Soc	AMMA	Art Metalware Mfrs' Assn
	Assn Insurance Surveyors	AMO	Assn Meter Operators
	Assn Interior Specialists	AMONO	Assn Mainframe Operators & Network Administrators
AISMA	Assn Indep Specialist Med Accountants		
AISSG	Androgen Insensitivity Syndrome Support Gp	AMPS	Assn Member-Directed Pension Schemes
AITA	Adult Ind Trade Assn		Assn Mfrs Power generating Systems
AITO	Assn Indep Tour Operators		Assn Mgt & Profl Staffs
AITS	Assn Indep Tobacco Specialists		Assn Motion Picture Sound
AITT	Assn Indl Truck Trainers	AMRA	Automotive Mfrs' Racing Assn
AIVC	Assn Inter-Varsity Clubs	AMRC	Assn Med Res Charities
AJA	Amat Jockeys Assn	AMRCO	Assn Motor Racing Circuit Owners
	Anglo-Jewish Assn	AMRSS	Assn Model Rly Socs Scotland
AJEX	Assn Jewish Ex-Servicemen & Women	AMS	Academy Medical Sciences
AJS	Anglo-Jordanian Soc		Academy Multi-Skills
Al-Anon	Al-Anon Family Gps		Agricl Manpower Soc
ALA	Agricl Law Assn		Ancient Monuments Soc
	Agricl Lime Assn		Antique Metalware Soc
	Auto Locksmiths Assn		Assurance Med Soc
ALACE	Assn Local Authority Chief Execs	AMSI	Assn Marine Scientific Ind
ALAE	Assn Licensed Aircraft Engrs	AMSPAR	Assn Med Secretaries, Practice Managers…
ALARM	ALARM	AMTRA	Animal Medicines Trg Regulatory Auth
ALBUM	Assn Local Bus Co Mgrs	AMUSF	Assn Master Upholsterers & Soft Furnishers
ALC	Assn Lawyers Children	An Taisce	Nat Trust Ireland
	Assn London Clubs	ANAIS	Assn New Age Inds
ALCD	Assn Law Costs Draftsmen	ANBG	Assn Natural Burial Grounds
ALCI	Assn Landscape Contrs Ireland (NI)	ANC	Assn Noise Consultants
ALCS	Assn Low Countries Studies	ANDISP	Assn Nat Driver Improvement Scheme Providers
	Authors' Licensing & Collecting Soc	ANEC	Assn N E Couns
ALD	Assn Lighting Designers	ANEW Ltd	Assd Nat Electrical Whlsrs
ALEM	Assn Loading & Elevating Eqpt Mfrs	ANH	Alliance Natural Health
ALEP	Assn Leasehold Enfranchisement Practitioners	ANHSO	Ashmolean Natural Hist Soc Oxfordshire
ALERT	ALERT	ANIC	Assn NI Colleges
ALFED	Aluminium Fedn	ANIELB	Assn NI Educ & Library Bds
ALG	London Councils	ANIFPO	Anglo North Irish Fish Producers Org
ALGAO	Assn Local Govt Archaeol Officers	ANLHS	Assn Northumberland Local Hist Socs
ALIP	Assn Leisure Ind Profls	ANLP	Assn Neuro-Linguistic Programming
ALK	Assn Lighthouse Keepers	ANM	Assn Natural Medicine
ALL	Assn Language Learning	ANMW	Assn Newspaper Magazine Whlsrs
	Assn Latin Liturgy	ANPA	Assn Nat Park Authorities
	Astrological Lodge Lond	ANR	Assn Nursing Religious
ALLEF UK	Assn Learning Languages en Famille	ANSA	Assn Nurses Substance Abuse
ALLMI	ALLMI Ltd	ANTC	Assn Nursery Training Colls
ALM	Assn Lloyd's Members	ANTOR	Assn Nat Tourist Office Representatives
ALMR	Assn Licensed Mult Retailers	ANTS	Anglo-Norman Text Soc
ALP	Assn Labour Providers	AOA	Airport Operators Assn
	Assn Learning Providers	AoC	Assn Colleges
	Horticultural Trs Assn	AoFA	Assn First Aiders
ALPSP	Assn Learned & Profl Soc Pubrs	AOHNP (UK)	Assn Occupational Health Nurse Practitioners
ALRC	Assn Land Rover Clubs	AoI	Assn Illustrators
ALS	Alliance Literary Socs	AOP	Assn Online Publishers
	Assn Lipspeakers		Assn Optometrists
		AOPA	Aircraft Owners & Pilots Assn

AOPA Ireland	Aircraft Owners & Pilots Assn [IRL]
AOR	Assn Organics Recycling
AoR	Assn Reflexologists
AoT	Assn Tutors
AOTI	Assn Occupational Therapists Ireland
AOTOS	Assn Teachers Singing
AOVC	Assn Old Vehicle Clubs NI
APA	Advertising Producers Assn
	Army Parachute Assn
	Assn Police Authorities
	Assn Practising Accountants
	Assn Profl Astrologers
	Assn Public Analysts
	Assn Publishing Agencies
	Audiobook Publishing Assn
APA(GBI)	Academic Paediatrics Assn
APACS	Assn Payment Clearing Services
APAGBI	Assn Paediatric Anaesthetists
APAP	Assn Profl Ambulance Personnel
APAS	Assn Public Analysts Scotland
APB	Assn Property Bankers
APBC	Assn Pet Behaviour Counsellors
APCC	Assn Private Crematoria & Cemeteries
APCI	Assn Police & Court Interpreters
APCIMS	Assn Private Client Investment Mgrs & Stockbrokers
APCMH	Assn Pastoral Care Mental Health
APCO	Assn Pleasure Craft Operators
APCT	Assn Painting Craft Teachers
APDT	Assn Pet Dog Trainers
APEA	Assn Petroleum & Explosives Admin
APEC	Action Pre-Eclampsia
APG	Account Planning Gp
APGI	Assn Profl Genealogists Ireland
APHA	Animal & Plant Health Assn [IRL]
	Assn Port Health Authorities
APHC	Assn Plumbing & Heating Contrs
API	Assn Play Inds
APIL	Assn Personal Injury Lawyers
APL	Assn Pension Lawyers
	Horticultural Trs Assn
APM	Assn Palliative Medicine
	Assn Project Mgt
APMC	Assn Pioneer Motor Cyclists
APMM	Assn Policy Market Makers
APMO	Assn Private Market Operators
APMT	Assn Profl Music Therapists
APNI	Assn Postnatal Illness
APNT	Assn Physical & Natural Therapists
APP	Assn Psychoanalytic Psychotherapy NHS
APPA	Aluminium Primary Producers Assn
APPC	Assn Profl Political Consultants
APPCC	Assn Private Pet Cemeteries & Crematoria
APPSS	Assn Police & Public Security Suppliers
APR	Assn Promoting Retreats
APRO	Assn Private Rly Wagon Owners
APRS	Assn Profl Recording Services
	Assn Protection Rural Scotland
APS	Assn Project Safety
APS (UK)	Assn Punjab Studies (UK)
APSA	Assn Profl Sales Agents (Sports & Leisure Inds)
	Assn Profls Services Adolescents
APSCEH	Assn Profl Staffs Colls Educ [IRL]
APSE	Assn Public Service Excellence
APSGB	Academy Pharmaceutical Sciences
APSI	Assn Profl Shooting Instructors
APT	Assn Psychological Therapies
	UK Assn Presvn Trusts
APTG	Assn Profl Tourist Guides
APV	Assn Profl Videomakers
AQHA-UK	American Quarter Horse Assn
AQR	Assn Qualitative Res
ARA	Aircraft Res Assn
	Amat Rowing Assn
	Assn Roman Archaeology
ARBA	Amat Rose Breeders Assn
ARC	Alliance Religions & Consvn
	Assn Real Change

	Assn Revenue & Customs
	Assn Running Clubs
ARCA	Adult Residential Colls Assn
	Asbestos Removal Contractors Asssn
ARCH	Action Rights Children
ARCISS	Assn Res Centres Social Sciences
ARCOS	Assn Rehabilitation Communication & Oral Skills
AREBT	Assn Rational Emotive Behaviour Therapy
AREF	Assn Real Estate Funds
ARH	Alliance Registered Homeopaths
ARHM	Assn Retirement Housing Mgrs
ARKS	Assn Racing Kart Schools
ARLA	Assn Residential Letting Agents
ARLIS	ARLIS/UK & Ireland
ARLT	Assn Latin Teaching
ARM	Assn Radical Midwives
ARMA	Arthritis & Musculoskeletal Alliance
	Assn Residential Managing Agents
ARMS	Assn Researchers in Medicine & Science
ARNO	Assn R Navy Officers
AROS	Assn Registrars Scotland
ARP	Assn Relocation Profls
ARPMA	Aluminium Rolled Products Mfrs Assn
ARR	Assn Radiation Res
ARS	Anaesthetic Res Soc
ARTP	Assn Respiratory Technology & Physiology
	Assn Rly Training Providers
ARTSM	Assn Road Traffic Safety & Mgt
ARVAC	Assn Res Voluntary & Community Sector
AS	Acupuncture Soc
	Alzheimer's Soc
	Avicultural Soc
ASA	Advice Services Alliance
	Aluminium Stockholders Assn
	Amat Swimming Assn
	Assn Sealant Applicators
	Assn Social Anthropologists
	Assn Subscription Agents & Intermediaries
ASAO	Assn Show & Agricl Orgs
ASAoGB	American Saddlebred Assn
ASAUK	African Studies Assn
ASBAH	Assn Spina Bifida & Hydrocephalus
ASBCI	ASBCI - Forum Clothing & Textiles
ASC	Assn Scotland's Colls
	Assn Security Consultants
	Assn Speakers Clubs
ASC/NAWCH	Action Sick Children
ASCC	Assn Scot Community Couns
ASCHB	Assn Studies Consvn Historic Bldgs
ASCII	Assn Copyright Infringement Investigators
ASCL	Assn School & College Leaders
ASDC	Assn Separated & Divorced Catholics
ASDMA	Architectural & Specialist Door Mfrs Assn
ASE	Assn Science Educ
	Astronomical Soc Edinburgh
ASEASUK	Assn South-East Asian Studies UK
ASEN	Assn Study Ethnicity & Nationalism
ASET	ASET
ASF	Assn Soft Furnishers
ASFB	Assn Salmon Fishery Bds
ASFCEW	Assn Sea Fisheries C'ees [E&W]
ASFI	Assn Suppliers Furniture Ind
ASFP	Assn Specialist Fire Protection
ASG	Air Safety Gp
	Anorchidism Support Gp
ASGBI	Anatomical Soc
	Assn Surgeons
ASGFM	Assn Stillwater Game Fishery Mgrs
ASGP	Assn Study German Politics
ASGRA	Assn Scot Genealogists & Researchers Archives
ASH	Action Smoking & Health
ASHTAV	Assn Small Historic Towns & Villages
ASI	Ambulance Service Inst
ASIIP	Adlerian Soc
ASIM	Assn Solicitors & Investment Mgrs
ASinGB	Anthroposophical Soc
ASiT	Assn Surgeons in Training
ASK	Assn Systematic Kinesiology

© CBD Research Ltd · Beckenham · BR3 5JS · Tel 020 8650 7745 · Fax 020 8650 0768 · E-mail cbd@cbdresearch.com · www.cbdresearch.com

ASLEC	Assn Signals, Lighting. . . Highway Electrical Connections
aslib	Aslib
ASLS	Assn Scot Literary Studies
ASLTIP	Assn Speech & Language Therapists. . .
ASM	Assn Supervisors Midwives
ASMCF	Assn Study Modern & Contemporary France
ASMD	Assn Sewing Machine Distbrs
ASME	Assn Study Med Educ
ASMI	Assn Study Modern Italy
ASN	Assn Solicitor Notaries Greater London
ASO	Assn Study Obesity
ASP	Assn Service Providers
ASPE	Assn Study Primary Educ
ASPEC	Assn Studio & Production Eqpt Companies
ASPECT	Assn Profls Educ & Children's Trusts
ASPIRE	Assn Spinal Injury Res. . .
ASPROM	Assn Study & Presvn Roman Mosaics
ASPS	Assn Scot Philatelic Socs
	Assn Scot Police Superintendents
ASRA	Assn Student Residential Accommodation
ASSA	Assn Scot Schools Architecture
ASSAP	Assn Scientific Study Anomalous Phenomena
ASSC	Assn Scotland's Self-Caterers
ASSG	Assn Scot Shellfish Growers
AssHFP	Assn Hot Foil Printers
AST	Assn Stress Therapists
ASTI	Assn Secondary Teachers, Ireland
ASTO	Assn Sea Training Orgs
ASTOS	Assn Specialist Techl Orgs Space
ASTRA	Assn Scotland Res Astronautics
ASUCplus	ASUCplus
ASVA	Assn Scot Visitor Attractions
ASYC	Assn Scot Yacht Charterers
ATA	Angling Trs Assn
ATA Assn	Air Transport Auxiliary Assn
ATAXIA	Ataxia UK
ATBA-UK	All Terrain Boarding Assn
ATC	Aromatherapy Tr Coun
	Assn Therapeutic Communities
	Assn Translation Companies
ATCM	Assn Tank & Cistern Mfrs
	Assn Town Centre Mgt
	Assn Traditional Chinese Medicine
ATCO	Assn Transport Co-ordinating Officers
ATCU	Assd Train Crew U
ATH	Assn Therapeutic Healers
ATL	Assn Teachers & Lecturers
	Assn Therapy Lecturers
ATLA	Assn Teachers Lipreading to Adults
ATLAS	Assn Technical Lighting & Access Specialists
ATM	Assn Teachers Mathematics
ATMA	Adhesive Tape Mfrs' Assn
ATOC	Assn Train Operating Companies
ATP	Assn Teaching Psychology
	Assn Therapeutic Philosophy
ATS	Ataxia-Telangiectasia Soc
ATSCO	Assn Technology Staffing Companies
ATSS	Assn Teaching Social Sciences
ATT	Assn Taxation Technicians
ATTP	Assn Thallophyte Treatment Plants
AUA	Assn University Administrators
AUKML	Assn UK Media Librarians
AUKOI	Assn UK Oil Indeps
AUKVA	Alliance UK Virtual Assistants
AUMPC	Assn Unpasteurised Milk Producers
AURA	Assn Users Res Agencies
AURIL	Assn University Res & Ind Links
AURPO	Assn University Radiation Protection Officers
AVA	Automatic Vending Assn
AVID	Assn Visitors Immigration Detainees
AVLP	Assn Valuers Licensed Property
AvMA	Action Med Accidents
AVRO	Assn Vehicle Recovery Operators
AWD	Assn Welding Distbrs
AWE	Assn Wine Educators
AWEBB	Assn Whls Electrical Bulk Buyers
AWFF	Animal Welfare Filming Fedn

AWG	Art Workers Gld
AWHEM	Assn Well Head Eqpt Mfrs
AXrEM	Assn X-ray Eqpt Mfrs
AYME	Assn Young People with ME
AYRS	Amat Yacht Res Soc

B

B MET A	Birmingham Metallurgical Assn
B&CCC	Brit & Colombian Cham Comm
B-AS	Britain-Australia Soc
BA	Basketmaker's Assn
	Booksellers Assn
BAA	Brit Academy Audiology
	Brit Accounting Assn
	Brit Aggregates Assn
	Brit Archaeol Assn
	Brit Astronomical Assn
BAAC	Brit Assn Aviation Consultants
BAAF	Brit Assn Adoption & Fostering
BAAL	Brit Assn Applied Linguistics
BAAM	Brit Assn Anger Mgt
BAAP	Brit Assn Academic Phoneticians
	Brit Assn Audiovestibular Physicians
BAAPS	Brit Assn Aesthetic Plastic Surgeons
BAAS	Brit Assn Amer Studies
BAASDC	Brit Assn Amer Square Dance Clubs
BAAT	Brit Assn Art Therapists
BABA	Brit African Business Assn
	Brit Artist Blacksmiths Assn
BABC	Brit Amer Business Coun
BABCP	Brit Assn Behavioural. . . Psychotherapies
BABi	Brit Amer Business Inc
BABO	Brit Assn Balloon Operators
BABS	Brit Assn Barbershop Singers
BABTAC	Brit Assn Beauty Therapy & Cosmetology
BAC	Business Archives Coun
BAC+S	Brit Academy Composers & Songwriters
BACA	Baltic Air Charter Assn
	Brit Assn Clinical Anatomists
BACB	Brit Assn Communicators in Business
BAcC	Brit Acupuncture Coun
BACC	Brit Argentine Cham Comm
BACDA	Brit Assn Community Doctors in Audiology
BACFI	Bar Assn Comm, Finance & Ind
BACG	Brit Assn Crystal Growth
BACM-TEAM	Brit Assn Colliery Mgt
BACP	Brit Assn Counselling & Psychotherapy
BACR	Brit Assn Cancer Res
BACS	Brit Assn Canadian Studies
	Brit Assn Chemical Specialities
	Brit Assn Chinese Studies
BACSA	Brit Assn Cemeteries S Asia
BACTA	Brit Amusement Catering Trs Assn
BAD	Brit Assn Dermatologists
BADA	Brit Antique Dealers Assn
	Brit Audio Dealers Assn
BADC	Brit Academy Dramatic Combat
BADCO	Ceretas
BADN	Brit Assn Dental Nurses
BADS	Brit Assn Day Surgery
BADT	Brit Assn Dental Therapists
BADth	Brit Assn Dramatherapists
BAeA	Brit Aerobatic Assn
BAEPD	Brit Assn Eur Pharmaceutical Distbrs
BAES	Brit Aviation Enthusiasts Soc
BAETS	Brit Assn Endocrine & Thyroid Surgeons
BAF	Brit Aerobiology Fedn
	Brit Armwrestling Fedn
BAFA	Brit Amer Football Assn
	Brit Arts Festivals Assn
BAFD	Brit Assn Fastener Distbrs
BAFE	Brit Approvals Fire Eqpt
BAFEP	Brit Assn Flower Essence Producers

BAFM	Brit Assn Forensic Medicine		BAS	Brit Alpaca Soc
	Brit Assn Friends Museums			Brit Ambulance Soc
BAFRA	Brit Antique Furniture Restorers Assn			Brit Andrology Soc
BAFS	Brit Academy Forensic Sciences			Brit Aphasiology Soc
BAFSA	Brit Automatic Fire Sprinkler Assn			Brit Arachnological Soc
BAFSAM	Brit Assn Feed Supplement & Additives Mfrs			Brit Assn Steelbands
BAFTA	Brit Academy Film & TV Arts			Brit Autogenic Soc
BAFTS	Brit Assn Fair Tr Shops		BASA	Black & Asian Studies Assn
BAFUNCS	Brit Assn Former UN Civil Servants			Brit Adhesives & Sealants Assn
BAGB	Bingo Association			Brit Airgun Shooters' Assn
BAGCC	Brit Assn Golf Course Constructors			Brit Assn Seed Analysts
BAGCD	Brit Assn Green Crop Driers		BASAS	Brit Assn S Asian Studies
BAGMA	Brit Agricl & Garden Machinery Assn		BASBWE	Brit Assn Symphonic Bands & Wind Ensembles
BAHA	Brit Activity Holiday Assn		BASC	Brit Assn Shooting & Consvn
	Brit Assn Hospitality Accountants			Brit Assn Skin Camouflage
BAHID	Brit Assn Human Identification		BASCD	Brit Assn Study Community Dentistry
BAHM	Brit Assn Homoeopathic Mfrs		BASDA	Business Application Software Developers Assn
BAHNO	Brit Assn Head & Neck Oncologists		BASE	Brit Assn Service Elderly
BAHREP	Brit Assn Hotel Representatives			Brit Assn Supported Employment
BAHS	Brit Agricl Hist Soc		BASEA	Brit Airport Services & Eqpt Assn
BAHSHE	Brit Assn Health Services in Higher Educ		BASEES	Brit Assn Slavonic & E Eur Studies
BAHVS	Brit Assn Homoeopathic Veterinary Surgeons		BASEM	Brit Assn Sport & Exercise Medicine
BAILER	Brit Assn Inf & Library Educ & Res		BASES	Brit Assn Seating Eqpt Suppliers
BAIS	Brit Assn Ir Studies			Brit Assn Sport & Exercise Sciences
BAJS	Brit Assn Japanese Studies		BASH	Brit Assn Study Headache
BAKS	Brit Assn Korean Studies		BASHH	Brit Assn Sexual Health & HIV
BALGPS	Bar Assn Local Govt & Public Service		BASI	Brit Assn Snowsport Instructors
BALH	Brit Assn Local Hist		BASICS	Brit Assn Immediate Care
BALI	Brit Assn Landscape Inds		BASMA	Boot & Shoe Mfrs Assn
BALID	Brit Assn Literacy in Devt		BASO-ACS	BASO
BALPA	Brit Air Line Pilots Assn		BASPCAN	Brit Assn Study & Prevention Child Abuse
BALPPA	Brit Assn Leisure Parks, Piers & Attractions		BASR	Brit Assn Study Religions
BALR	Brit Assn Lung Research			Brit Soc Study Religions
BAMA	Brit Aerosol Mfrs Assn		BASRT	Brit Assn Sexual & Relationship Therapy
BAMF	Brit Art Market Fedn		BASS	Brit Assn Ship Suppliers
BAMM	Brit Assn Med Mgrs		BASSAC	Brit Assn Settlements & Social Action Centres
BAMS	Brit Air Mail Soc		BASW	Brit Assn Social Workers
	Brit Art Medal Soc		BATA	Brit Air Transport Assn
BANA	Brit Acoustic Neuroma Assn		BATB	Brit Assn Tissue Banking
BANC	Brit Assn Nature Conservationists		BATC	Brit Apparel & Textile Confedn
BANS	Brit Assn Numismatic Socs		BATD	Brit Assn Teachers Dancing
BANT	Brit Assn Nutritional Therapy		BAThH	Brit Assn Therapeutical Hypnotists
BAO-HNS	Brit Assn Otorhinolaryngologists		BATOD	Brit Assn Teachers Deaf
BAOMS	Brit Assn Oral & Maxillofacial Surgeons		BAUS	Brit Assn Urological Surgeons
BAOT/COT	Brit Assn Occupational Therapists		BAVA	Brit Anti-Vivisection Assn[want??
BAP	Brit Assn Psychopharmacology		BAVE	Bates Assn Vision Educ
	Brit Assn Psychotherapists		BAW	Basketball Assn Wales
BAPAM	Brit Assn Performing Arts Medicine		BAWE	Brit Assn Women Entrepreneurs
BAPC	Brit Assn Print & Communication		BB	Boys' Brigade
	Brit Aviation Presvn Coun		BBA	Better Brickwork Alliance
BAPCA	Brit Assn Person-Centred Approach			Brit Bankers' Assn
BAPCO	Brit Assn Public Safety Communications Officers			Brit Biomagnetic Assn
BAPCR	Brit Assn Paintings Conservator-Restorers			Brit Bison Assn
BAPH	Brit Assn Paper Historians			Brit Bobsleigh Assn
BAPLA	Brit Assn Picture Libraries & Agencies			Brit Bridalwear Assn
BAPM	Brit Assn Perinatal Medicine			Brit Buddhist Assn
BAPO	Brit Assn Prosthetists & Orthotists			Brit Burn Assn
BAPRAS	Brit Assn Plastic, Reconstructive & Aesthetic Surgeons		BBAA	Brit Business Angels Assn
				Brit Business Awards Assn
BApS	Brit Appaloosa Soc		BBAC	Brit Balloon & Airship Club
BAPS	Brit Assn Paediatric Surgeons		BBC	Brit Bodyboard Club
	Brit Astrological & Psychic Soc		BBCC	Brit Bulgarian Cham Comm
BAPSH	Brit Assn Purebred Spanish Horse		BBCS	Brit Beermat Collectors' Soc
BAPT	Brit Assn Physical Training			Brit Big Cats Soc
	Brit Assn Play Therapists		BBCT	Bumblebee Conservation Trust
	Brit Assn Psychological Type		BBF	Brit Basketball Fedn
BAPTO	Brit Assn Pool Table Operators		BBFS	Brit Bulgarian Friendship Soc
BAPW	Brit Assn Pharmaceutical Whlsrs		BBG	Brit Brands Gp
BAR	Brit Assn Removers		BBGA	Brit Business & Gen Aviation Assn
BARA	Brit Automation & Robot Assn		BBI	Brit Bottlers' Inst
BARB	Brit Assn Rose Breeders		BBKA	Brit Bee-Keepers' Assn
BARC Ltd	Brit Automobile Racing Club		BBMA	Brit Barometer Makers Assn
BAREMA	Barema			Brit Battery Mfrs Assn [>lost(08)
BARG	Berkshire Archaeology Res Gp			Brit Bluegrass Music Assn
BARLA	Brit Amat Rugby League Assn			Brit Brush Mfrs Assn
BARMA	Boiler & Radiator Mfrs Assn		BBN	Blue Badge Network
BARQA	Brit Assn Res Quality Assurance		BBO	Brit Ballet Org
BARSC	Brit Assn Remote Sensing Companies		BBPA	Brit Body Piercing Assn

© CBD Research Ltd · Beckenham · BR3 5JS · Tel 020 8650 7745 · Fax 020 8650 0768 · E-mail cbd@cbdresearch.com · www.cbdresearch.com

BBRS	Blair Bell Res Soc
BBS	Brit Biophysical Soc
	Brit Boomerang Soc
	Brit Brick Soc
	Brit Bryological Soc
	Brit Button Soc
	Brittle Bone Soc
BBSA	Brit Blind & Shutter Assn
BBTS	Brit Blood Transfusion Soc
BCA	Brit Cables Assn
	Brit Camelids Assn
	Brit Casino Assn
	Brit Caving Assn
	Brit Cement Assn
	Brit Cheerleading Assn
	Brit Chiropractic Assn
	Brit Confectioners Assn
	Brit Costume Assn
	Brit Crystallographic Assn
bca	Business Centre Assn
BCAS	Brit Compressed Air Soc
BCBA	Brit Marine Fedn
BCBC	Brit Cattle Breeders' Club
BCC	Badge Collectors Circle
	Boston Cham Comm & Ind
	Brit Ceramic Confedn
	Brit Cham Comm Luxembourg
	Brit Chams Comm
	Brit Cleaning Coun
	Brit Cryogenics Coun
BCC CR	Brit Cham Comm Czech Republic
BCCA	Brit Cheque Cashers Assn
	Brit Correspondence Chess Assn
BCCB	Brit Cham Comm Belgium
BCCC	Brit Cham Comm China - Beijing
	Brit Chilean Cham Comm
BCCF	Brit Calcium Carbonates Fedn
BCCG	Brit Cham Comm Germany
BCCH	Brit Cham Comm Hungary
BCCI	Birmingham Cham Comm & Ind
	Brit Cham Comm Italy
BCCIB	Brit Cham Comm & Ind Brazil
BCCJ	Brit Cham Comm Japan
BCCL	Brit Cham Comm Latvia
BCCM	Brit Cham Comm Morocco
BCCMA	Brit Coun Chinese Martial Arts
BCCS	Brit Compact Collectors' Soc
BCCT	Brit Cham Comm Taipei
	Brit Cham Comm Thailand
	Brit Cham Comm Turkey
BCECA	Brit Chemical Engg Contrs Assn
BCF	Brit Coatings Fedn
	Brit Cycling Fedn
	English Chess Federation
BCFA	Brit Contract Furnishing Assn
BCG	Brit Chelonia Gp
BCGA	Brit Compressed Gases Assn
BCGBA	Brit Crown Green Bowling Assn
BCGTMA	Brit Ceramic Gift & Tableware Mfrs' Assn
BChA	Brit Chiropody & Podiatry Assn
BCHS	Brit Camargue Horse Soc
BCI	Business Continuity Inst
BCIA	Brit Clothing Ind Assn
	Building Controls Ind Assn
BCIS	Building Cost Infm Service
BCLA	Brit Comparative Literature Assn
	Brit Contact Lens Assn
BCMA	BEAMA
	Brit Colour Makers Assn
	Brit Complementary Medicine Assn
	Brit Country Music Assn
BCMPA	Brit Contract Mfrs & Packers Assn
BCO	Brit Coun Offices
	College Optometrists
BCofC	Bradford Cham Comm & Ind
BCPA	Brit Cardiac Patients Assn
BCPS	Brit Connemara Pony Soc
BCRA	Brit Cave Res Assn

BCRC	Brit Cave Rescue Coun
BCS	Biblical Creation Soc
	Black Country Soc
	Brit Cardiovascular Soc
	Brit Carillon Soc
	Brit Cartographic Soc
	Brit Classification Soc
	Brit Comedy Soc
	Brit Computer Soc
	Brit Conifer Soc
BCSA	Brit Constructional Steelwork Assn
	Brit Cutlery & Silverware Assn
BCSC	Brit Coun Shopping Centres
BCSS	Brit Cactus & Succulent Soc
	Brit Charollais Sheep Soc
BCT	Bat Consvn Trust
bctc	Bournemouth Cham Tr & Comm
BCTGA	Brit Christmas Tree Growers Assn
BCU	Brit Canoe U
BDA	Brick Devt Assn
	Brit Deaf Assn
	Brit Dental Assn
	Brit Dietetic Assn
	Brit Doula Assn
	Brit Dragon Boat Racing Assn
	Brit Drilling Assn
	Brit Dyslexia Assn
BDAA	Biodynamic Agricl Assn
BDF	Ballroom Dancers Fedn
BDFA	Batten Disease Family Assn
	Brit Deer Farmers Assn
	Brit Disabled Flying Assn
	Brit Dried Flowers Assn
BDFPA	Brit Drug Free Powerlifting Assn
BDGA	Brit Disc Golf Assn
BDMA	Brit Damage Mgt Assn
BDO	Brit Darts Org
BDOA	Brit Domesticated Ostrich Assn
BDPMA	Brit Dental Practice Mgrs Assn
BDRS	Brit Double Reed Soc
BDS	Brit Dam Soc
	Brit Deer Soc
	Brit Display Soc
	Brit Dragonfly Soc
	Brit Driving Soc
BDSC	Brit Deaf Sports Coun
BDTA	Brit Dental Tr Assn
BDWCA	Brit Decoy & Wildfowl Carvers Assn
BEA	Brit Egg Assn
	Brit Epilepsy Assn
BEAMA	BEAMA
beat	Eating Disorders Assn
BEAWec	Brit Energy Assn
BECA	Brit Electrostatic Control Assn
BECTU	Broadcasting, Entertainment Cinematograph...U
BEDA	Noctis
BEEF	Buildings Energy Efficiency Fedn
BEF	Brit Equestrian Fedn
BEHA	Baby Eqpt Hirers Assn
BELMAS	Brit Educl Leadership, Mgt & Admin Soc
BEMA	Brit Engg Mfrs Assn
	Brit Essence Mfrs' Assn
BEMCA	BEAMA
BENHS	Brit Entomological & Natural Hist Soc
BEOA	Brit Essential Oils Assn
BEPA	Brit Edible Pulse Assn
	Brit Egg Products Assn
BERA	Brit Educl Res Assn
BERSA	Brit Elastic Rope Sports Assn
BES	Brit Ecological Soc
	Brit Endodontic Soc
BESA	Brit Earth Sheltering Assn
	Brit Educl Suppliers Assn
BESCA	Heating & Ventilating Contrs Assn
BETA	Brit Educl Travel Assn
	Brit Equestrian Tr Assn
BExA	Brit Exporters Assn

BFA	Bee Farmers Assn
	Brit Fedn Audio
	Brit Florist Assn
	Brit Flyball Assn
	Brit Footwear Assn
	Brit Fragrance Assn
	Brit Franchise Assn
BFAWU	Bakers', Food & Allied Workers' U
BFBB	Brit Fedn Brass Bands
BFBi	Brewing, Food & Beverage Ind Suppliers Assn
BFC	Brit Falconers' Club
	Brit Fire Consortium
BFCMA	Brit Flue & Chimney Mfrs' Assn
BFFF	Brit Frozen Food Fedn
BFFS	Brit Fedn Film Socs
BFHS	Brit Fedn Histl Swordplay
BFI	Brit Film Inst
BFIDA	Brit Food Importers & Distrbrs Assn
BFJA	Brit Fruit Juice Assn
BFM	BFM Ltd
BFMC	Brit Friction Materials Coun
BFMS	Brit False Memory Soc
BFPA	Brit Fluid Power Assn
BFPDA	Brit Fluid Power Distbrs Assn
BFRC	Brit Flat Roofing Coun
BFREPA	Brit Free Range Egg Producers Assn
BFS	Brit Fantasy Soc
	Brit Fertility Soc
	Brit Flute Soc
	Brit Fuchsia Soc
BFSA	Brit Fire Services Assn
BFSTD	Brit Fedn Sexually Transmitted Diseases
BFTA	Brit Fur Tr Assn
BFVEA	Brit Flower &... Essences Assn
BFWG	Brit Fedn Women Graduates
BFWMSS	Badger Face Welsh Mountain Sheep Soc
BG	Brit Gymnastics
BGA	Brassica Growers Assn
	Brit Gear Assn
	Brit Geomembrane Assn
	Brit Geotechnical Assn
	Brit-German Assn
	Brit Gliding Assn
	Brit Glove Assn
	Brit Go Assn
	Brit Grooms Assn
BGAS	Bristol & Gloucestershire Archaeol Soc
BGIA	Brit Golf Ind Assn
BGJA	Brit-German Jurists' Assn
BGMA	Brit Generic Mfrs' Assn
BGS	Brit Geriatrics Soc
	Brit Gestalt Soc
	Brit Gladiolus Soc
	Brit Goat Soc
	Brit Grassland Soc
BGSS	Brit Gotland Sheep Soc
BGTW	Brit Gld Travel Writers
BH&HPA	Brit Holiday & Home Parks Assn
BHA	Brit Hamster Assn
	Brit Hawking Assn
	Brit Homoeopathic Assn
	Brit Horseball Assn
	Brit Hospitality Assn
	Brit Humanist Assn
	Brit Hydropower Assn
	Brit Hypnotherapy Assn
BHAB	Brit Helicopter Advy Bd
BHBF	Broads Hire Boat Fedn
BHBIA	Brit Healthcare Business Intelligence Assn
BHCA	Brit Health Care Assn
BHCC	Brit Hellenic Cham Comm
BHCF	Brit Hire Cruiser Fedn
BHDTA	Brit Horse Driving Trials Assn
BHECTA	Brit Hardmetal & Engineers' Cutting Tool Assn
BHETA	Brit Home Enhancement Tr Assn
BHF	Brit Hardware Fedn
	Brit Horological Fedn

BHG	Brit Hat Gld
	Horticultural Trs Assn
BHGS	Brit Histl Games Soc
BHHS	Brit Hanoverian Horse Soc
	Brit Hosta & Hemerocallis Soc
BHI	Brit Horological Inst
BHIVA	Brit HIV Assn
BHL	Brit Housewives League
BHMA	Brit Herbal Medicine Assn
	Brit Holistic Med Assn
BHPA	Brit Hang Gliding & Paragliding Assn
BHPR	Brit Health Profls in Rheumatology
BHPS	Brit Hedgehog Presvn Soc
BHRC	Brit Harness Racing Club
BHRS	Bedfordshire Histl Record Soc
BHS	Brit Haiku Soc
	Brit Herpetological Soc
	Brit Horn Soc
	Brit Horse Soc
	Brit Hydrological Soc
	Brit Hypertension Soc
BHSMA	Brit Hay & Straw Mchts' Assn
BHSS	Brit Banking History Soc
BHTA	Brit Healthcare Trs Assn
	Brit Herb Tr Assn
BIA	BioIndustry Assn
BIAC	Brit Inst Agricl Consultants
BIALL	Brit & Ir Assn Law Librarians
BIAS	Bristol Indl Archaeol Soc
BIAZA	Brit & Ir Assn Zoos & Aquariums
BIBA	Brit Insurance Brokers' Assn
	Brit Isles Backgammon Assn
BIBBA	Bee Improvement & Bee Breeders Assn
BIBC	Brit Isles Bowls Coun
BIBOA	Brit Inflatable Boat Owners Assn
BIBTA	Brit Isles Baton Twirling Assn
BICA	Brit Infertility Counselling Assn
	England Indoor Cricket Assn
BICSc	Brit Inst Cleaning Science
BIDA	Brit Interior Design Assn
BIDST	Brit Inst Dental & Surgical Technologists
BIE	Brit Inst Embalmers
BIEE	Brit Inst Energy Economics
BIFA	Brit Intl Freight Assn
BIFCA	Brit Indl Furnace Construction Assn
BIFD	Brit Inst Funeral Directors
BIFGA	Brit Indep Fruit Growers Assn
BIFM	Brit Inst Facilities Mgt
BIG	Brit Inst Graphologists
BIGGA	Brit & Intl Golf Greenkeepers' Assn
BII	Brit Inst Innkeeping
BIIBC	Brit Isles Indoor Bowls Coun
BIICL	Brit Inst Intl & Comparative Law
BIIS	Breast Implant Inf Soc
BILA	Brit Insurance Law Assn
BILD	Brit Inst Learning & Devt
	Brit Inst Learning Disabilities
BILETA	Brit & Ir Legal Educ Technology Assn
BIMA	Brit Interactive Media Assn
BIMM	Brit Inst Musculoskeletal Medicine
BIMTA	Brit Indep Motor Tr Assn
BInstNDT	Brit Inst Non-Destructive Testing
BIOA	Brit & Ir Ombudsman Assn
BIOG	Defence Mfrs Assn
BIOS	Brit Inst Organ Studies
	Brit & Ir Orthoptic Soc
BIPA	Brit Internet Publishers Alliance
BIPDT	Brit Inst Profl Dog Trainers
BIPHA	Brit Inline Puck Hockey Assn
BIPP	Brit Inst Profl Photography
BIPS	Brit Inst Persian Studies
BIR	Brit Inst Radiology
BIS	Brit Interplanetary Soc
	Brit Iris Soc
	Brit Italian Soc
BISA	Brit Intl Studies Assn
BISGBG	Brit Icelandic Sheep Breeders Gp
BiSHA	Brit Inline Skater Hockey Assn

© CBD Research Ltd · Beckenham · BR3 5JS · Tel 020 8650 7745 · Fax 020 8650 0768 · E-mail cbd@cbdresearch.com · www.cbdresearch.com

BISL	Business Sport & Leisure
BITA	Brit Indl Truck Assn
	Brit Interior Textiles Assn
BIVDA Ltd	Brit In Vitro Diagnostics Assn
BIVR	Brit Inst Verbatim Reporters
BJA	Boat Jumble Assn
	Brit Jewellers Assn
	Brit Judo Assn
BJGF	Brit Jewellery, Giftware & Finishing Fedn
BJPL	Brit Jigsaw Puzzle Library
BKA	Brit Kodály Academy
	Brit Korfball Assn
BKKPS	Brit Kune Kune Pig Soc
BKPA	Brit Kidney Patient Assn
BKSA	Brit Kite Surfing Assn
BKSTS	BKSTS
BLA	Brit Legal Assn
	Brit Lime Assn
BLC	BLC, Leather Technology Centre
BLCC	Belgian-Luxembourg Cham Comm GB
BLCS	Brit Limousin Cattle Soc
BLDSA	Brit Long Distance Swimming Assn
BLESMA	Brit Limbless Ex-Service Men's Assn
BLF	Brit Lace Fedn
BLISS	BLISS
BLKA	Brit Locksmiths & Keycutters Assn
BLMA	Brit Ladder Mfrs Assn
BLMRA	Brit Lawn Mower Racing Assn
BLOS	Brit Lingual Orthodontic Soc
BLPS	Brit Lop Pig Soc
BLS	Branch Line Soc
	Brit Lichen Soc
	Brit Longevity Soc
	Brit Lymphology Soc
BLSA	Brit Land Speedsail Assn
	Brit Leafy Salad Assn
BLSBA	Bluefaced Leicester Sheep Breeders Assn
BMA	Bathroom Mfrs' Assn
	Brit Med Assn
BMAA	Brit Microlight Aircraft Assn
BMAPA	Brit Marine Aggregate Producers' Assn
BMAS	Brit Med Acupuncture Soc
BMC	Brit Mountaineering Coun
BMCRC	Brit Motor Cycle Racing Club
BMEA	Brit Marine Electronics Assn
	Brit Marine Eqpt Assn
BMF	Brit Marine Fedn
	Brit Motorcyclists Fedn
	Builders Mchts Fedn
BMFA	Brit Marine Finfish Assn
	Brit Model Flying Assn
BMFMS	Brit Maternal & Fetal Medicine Soc
BMG	Brit Assn Mountain Guides
	Brit Menswear Gld
BMHA	Brit Malignant Hyperthermia Assn
BMHF	Brit Materials Handling Fedn
BMHS	Brit Morgan Horse Soc
	Brit Music Hall Soc
BMI	Birmingham & Mid Inst
BMIG	Brit Myriapod & Isopod Gp
BML&BS	Brit Matchbox, Label & Booklet Soc
BMLA	Brit Maritime Law Assn
	Brit Med Laser Assn
BMLDA	Brit Manual Lymph Drainage Assn
BMLSS	Brit Marine Life Study Soc
BMMC	Brit Motorsport Marshals Club
BMPA	Brit Meat Processors Assn
BMPCA	Brit Metallurgical Plant Constructors Assn
BMRA	Brit Metals Recycling Assn
BMS	Brit Magical Soc
	Brit Malaysian Soc
	Brit Menopause Soc
	Brit Mexican Soc
	Brit Microcirculation Soc
	Brit Moroccan Soc
	Brit Mule Soc
	Brit Museum Friends

	Brit Music Soc
	Brit Mycological Soc
BMSS	Brit Model Soldier Soc
BMTA	Brit Measurement & Testing Assn
BMUS	Brit Med Ultrasound Soc
BMVA	Brit Machine Vision Assn...
BNA	Brit Naturalists Assn
	Brit Naturopathic Assn
	Brit Neuroscience Assn
	Britain-Nigeria Educl Trust
BNARA	Brit N Amer Res Assn
BNBC	Britain Nigeria Business Coun
BNC	Berwickshire Naturalists Club
BNCC	Britain-Nepal Cham Comm
BNCS	Brit Nat Carnation Soc
BNE	Business New Europe
BNEA	Brit Naval Eqpt Assn
BNETS	Brit Educl Suppliers Assn
BNF	Brit Nutrition Foundation
BNFA	Brit Narrow Fabrics Assn
BNFMF	Brit Non-Ferrous Metals Fedn
BNHS	Birmingham Natural Hist Soc
	Brit Natural Hygiene Soc
BNMA	Brit Number Plate Mfrs Assn
BNMAA	Brit Nat Martial Arts Assns
BNMS	Brit Nuclear Medicine Soc
BNPA	Brit Neuropsychiatry Assn
BNS	Brit Neuropathological Soc
	Brit Neuropsychological Soc
	Brit Numismatic Soc
	Britain Nepal Soc
BNTA	Brit Numismatic Tr Assn
BNTL	Brit Nat Temperance League
BNZTC	Brit New Zealand Tr Coun
BOA	Brit Olympic Assn
	Brit Oncological Assn
	Brit Orthopaedic Assn
	Brit Osteopathic Assn
BOAS	Brit Ophthalmic Anaesthesia Soc
BOBMA	Brit Oat & Barley Millers Assn
BOC	Brit Orchid Coun
	Brit Ornithologists Club
BODY	Brit Organ Donor Soc
BOF	Brit Orienteering Fedn
	Brit Othello Fedn
BOGA	Brit Orchid Growers Assn
BOHS	Brit Occupational Hygiene Soc
BOOBA	Brit Olive Oil Buyer's Assn
BOPA	Brit Outdoor Profls Assn
BORDA	Brit Off Road Driving Assn
	Brit Oriental Rug Dealers Assn
BOS	Brit Origami Soc
	Brit Orthodontic Soc
BOSPA	Brit Obesity Surgery Patient Assn
BOSS	Brit Obesity Surgery Soc
BOU	Brit Ornithologists U
BP	BEAMA
BP&TUAA	Brit Pensioners & Tr U Action Assn
BPA	Baby Products Assn
	Brit Packaging Assn
	Brit Parachute Assn
	Brit Paralympic Assn
	Brit Parking Assn
	Brit Pig Assn
	Brit Porphyria Assn
	Brit Ports Assn
	Brit Psychodrama Assn
	Brit Pyrotechnists Assn
BPC	Backpackers Club
	Brit Peanut Coun
	Brit Polling Coun
	Brit Poultry Coun
	Brit Psychoanalytic Coun
BPCA	Brit Pest Control Assn
BPCC	Brit-Polish Cham Comm [Lond]
	Brit-Polish Cham Comm [Warsaw]
	Brit-Portuguese Cham Comm
BPCF	Brit Precast Concrete Fedn

BPF	Brit Plastics Fedn
	Brit Polio Fellowship
	Brit Property Fedn
BPG	Brit Photodermatology Gp
BPGS	Brit Plant Gall Soc
BPHS	Brit Percheron Horse Soc
BPI	DPI
BPIF	Brit Printing Inds Fedn
BPKA	Brit Power Kitesports Assn
BPMA	Brit Promotional Merchandise Assn
	Brit Pump Mfrs Assn
BPMTG	Brit Puppet & Model Theatre Gld
BPOA	Brit Protected Ornamentals Assn
BPPA	Brit Precision Pilots Assn
	Soc Wedding & Portrait Photographers
BPRS	Brit Polarological Res Soc
BPS	Brit Palomino Soc
	Brit Pharmacological Soc
	Brit Postmark Soc
	Brit Printing Soc
	Brit Psychological Soc
	Brit Pteridological Soc
BPTA	Brit Polyolefin Textiles Assn
BPW UK Ltd	Business & Profl Women
BQA	Brit Quadrathlon Assn
BQF	Brit Quality Foundation
BRA	Brit Records Assn
	Brit Reflexology Assn
	Brit Refrigeration Assn
BRADA	Brit Resorts & Destinations Assn
BrAPP	Brit Assn Pharmaceutical Physicians
BRBA	Brit Marine Fedn
BRBMA	Ball & Roller Bearing Mfrs Assn
BRC	Brit Rabbit Coun
	Brit Retail Consortium
BRCA	Brit Radio Car Assn
BRCS	Brit Red Cross Soc
BRE	BRE Trust
BRGA	Brit Reed Growers Assn
BRIC	Brit Refractories & Indl Ceramics
BRINDEX	Assn Brit Indep Oil Exploration Cos
BRISC	Biological Recording Scotland
BRISMES	Brit Soc Middle Eastn Studies
BritCham	Brit Cham Comm Singapore
British Onions	Brit Onion Producers' Assn
Britpave	Britpave
BRMCA	Brit Ready Mixed Concrete Assn
BROA	Brit Rig Owners Assn
BRPPA	Brit Rubber & Polyurethane Products Assn
BRPS	Bluebell Rly Presvn Soc
	Brit Retinitis Pigmentosa Soc
BRS	Bone Res Soc
BRSA	Brit Rope Skipping Assn
BRSCC	Brit Racing & Sports Car Club
BRTMA	Brit Rootzone & Top Dressing Mfrs Assn
BRUFMA	Brit Rigid Urethane Foam Mfrs Assn
BS	Beaumont Soc
	Brit Marine Fedn
	Budgerigar Soc
BSA	Beverage Service Assn
	Boarding Schools Assn
	Brit Sandwich Assn
	Brit Shakespeare Assn
	Brit Soc Aesthetics
	Brit Soc Audiology
	Brit Sociological Assn
	Brit Stammering Assn
	Brit Surfing Assn
	Building Socs Assn
	Business Services Assn
	Business Software Alliance
BSAC	Brit Soc Antimicrobial Chemotherapy
	Brit Sub-Aqua Club
BSACI	Brit Soc Allergy & Clinical Immunology
BSAS	Brit Sausage Appreciation Soc
	Brit Soc Animal Science
BSAVA	Brit Small Animal Veterinary Assn
BSBA	Brit Marine Fedn

BSBI	Botanical Soc Brit Isles
BSC	Brit Soc Cinematographers
	Brit Soc Criminology
BSCAH	BSCAH - Brit Soc Clinical... Hypnosis
BSCB	Brit Soc Cell Biology
BSCC	Brit Shell Collectors Club
	Brit Soc Clinical Cytology
	Brit Swedish Cham Comm Sweden
	Brit-Swiss Cham Comm [Zürich]
BSCDA	Brit Stock Car Drivers Assn
BSCH	Brit Soc Clinical Hypnosis
BSCN	Brit Soc Clinical Neurophysiology
BSCPIA	Brit Soluble Coffee Packers & Importers Assn
BSCRA	Brit Slot Car Racing Assn
BSCS	Brit Simmental Cattle Soc
BSCW	Brit Soc Comedy Writers
BSD	Brit Soc Dowsers
BSDA	Brit Sheep Dairying Assn
	Brit Soft Drinks Assn
BSDB	Brit Soc Developmental Biology
BSDH	Brit Soc Disability & Oral Health
BSDHT	Brit Soc Dental Hygiene & Therapy
BSDMFR	Brit Soc Dental & Maxillofacial Radiology
BSDR	Brit Soc Dental Res
BSE	Brit Soc Echocardiography
BSEM	Brit Soc Ecological Medicine
BSES	BSES Expeditions
BSF	Biosciences Fedn
	Brit Shogi Fedn
	Brit Soc Flavourists
BSFA	Brit Science Fiction Assn
BSG	Birthmark Support Gp
	Brit Soc Gastroenterology
	Brit Soc Gerontology
	Brit Stickmakers Gld
	Brit Sugarcraft Gld
BSGA	Brit Sign & Graphics Assn
BSGB	Bead Soc
BSGDS	Brit Soc Gen Dental Surgery
BSGE	Brit Soc Gynaecological Endoscopy
BSGT	Brit Soc Gene Therapy
BSH	Brit Soc Haematology
	Brit Soc Hypnotherapists
BSHA	Brit Show Horse Assn
BSHAA	Brit Soc Hearing Aid Audiologists
BSHG	Brit Soc Human Genetics
BSHM	Brit Soc Hist Mathematics
	Brit Soc Hist Medicine
BSHP	Brit Soc Hist Pharmacy
	Brit Soc Hist Philosophy
BSHS	Brit Soc Hist Science
BSI	Brit Soc Immunology
	Brit Suzuki Inst
BSIA	Brit Security Ind Assn
	Brit Starch Ind Assn
BSIF	Brit Safety Ind Fedn
BSKF	Brit Shorinji Kempo Fedn
BSMA	Building Socs Mems Assn
BSME	Brit Soc Magazine Editors
BSMFD	Brit Soc Mercury Free Dentistry
BSMGP	Brit Soc Master Glass Painters
BSMM	Brit Soc Med Mycology
BSMT	Brit Soc Microbial Technology
	Brit Soc Music Therapy
BSNG	Brit Educl Suppliers Assn
BSNR	Brit Soc Neuroradiologists
BSOE	Brit Soc Enamellers
BSOM	Brit Soc Oral Medicine
BSOP	Brit Soc Oral & Maxillofacial Pathology
BSoUP	Brit Soc Underwater Photographers
BSP	Brit Soc Parasitology
	Brit Soc Perfumers
	Brit Soc Periodontology
BSPA	Brit Skewbald & Piebald Assn
	Brit Speedway Promoters' Assn
BSPB Ltd	Brit Soc Plant Breeders
BSPFA	Brit Swimming Pool Fedn
BSPOGA	Brit Soc Psychosomatic Obstetrics...

© CBD Research Ltd · Beckenham · BR3 5JS · Tel 020 8650 7745 · Fax 020 8650 0768 · E-mail cbd@cbdresearch.com · www.cbdresearch.com

BSPP	Brit Soc Plant Pathology
BSpPS	Brit Spotted Pony Soc
BSPR	Brit Soc Proteome Res
BSPS	Brit Show Pony Soc
	Brit Soc Philosophy Science
	Brit Soc Population Studies
BSR	Brit Soc Rheology
	Brit Soc Rheumatology
BSRA	Brit Soc Res Ageing
	Brit Sound Recording Assn
BSRD	Brit Soc Restorative Dentistry
BSRIA	BSRIA
BSRM	Brit Soc Rehabilitation Medicine
BSS	Botanical Soc Scotland
	Brit Sleep Soc
	Brit Standards Soc
	Brit Sundial Soc
bssa	Brit Shops & Stores Assn
BSSA	Brit Sjogren's Syndrome Assn
	Brit Skeet Shooting Assn
	Brit Stainless Steel Assn
BSSAA	Brit Snoring & Sleep Apnoea Assn
BSSC	Brit Shooting Sports Coun
BSSG	Brit Soc Scientific Glassblowers
BSSH	Brit Soc Surgery Hand
BSSM	Brit Soc Sexual Medicine
	Brit Soc Strain Measurement
BSSO	Brit Scooter Sport Org
BSSPD	Brit Soc Study Prosthetic Dentistry
BSSS	Brit Soc Soil Science
BSSVD	Brit Soc Study Vulval Diseases
BSTP	Brit Soc Toxicological Pathologists
BSUK	BaseballSoftballUK
BSWA	Brit Structural Waterproofing Assn
BTA	Birth Trauma Assn
	Brit Thyroid Assn
	Brit Tinnitus Assn
	Brit Toilet Assn
	Brit Trout Assn
	Brit Tugowners Assn
BTAA	Brit Travelgoods & Accessories Assn
BTAF	Brit Tattoo Artists Fedn
BTBA	Brit Tenpin Bowling Assn
BTC	BTC Testing Advisory Gp
BTCA	Brit Tennis Coaches Assn
BTCV	Brit Trust Consvn Volunteers
BTDA	Brit Theatre Dance Assn
BTG	Brit Toymakers Gld
BTHA	Brit Toy & Hobby Assn
	Brit Travel Health Assn
BTHG	Birmingham Transport Histl Gp
BTLIA	Brit Turf & Landscape Irrigation Assn
BTMA	Brit Textile Machinery Assn
	Brit Turned-Parts Mfrs Assn
	Brit Tyre Mfrs Assn
BTO	Brit Trust Ornithology
BTOG	Brit Transport Officers Gld
BTRA	Brit Truck Racing Assn
BTRDA	Brit Trials & Rally Drivers Assn
BTS	Brit Tarantula Soc
	Brit Technion Soc
	Brit Titanic Soc
	Brit Toxicology Soc
	Brit Transplantation Soc
	Brit Trolleybus Soc
	Brit Trombone Soc
	Brit Tunnelling Soc
	Britain-Tanzania Soc
BTSA	Brit Tensional Strapping Assn
BTSS	Brit Texel Sheep Soc
BTTG	Brit Textile Technology Gp
BU	Baptist U
BUAV	Brit U Abolition Vivisection
BUFCA Ltd	Brit Urethane Foam Contrs Assn
BUFORA	Brit UFO Res Assn
BUFVC	Brit Universities Film & Video Coun
BUIRA	Brit Universities Indl Relations Assn
BUPMSA	Brit Used Printing Machinery Supplrs Assn

BURA	Brit Urban Regeneration Assn
BUSA	Brit Universities Sports Assn
BUUK	Bus Users UK
BVA	Brit Veterinary Assn
	Brit Video Assn
	Brit Voice Assn
BVAA	Brit Valve & Actuator Assn
BVC	Brit Vacuum Coun
BVCA	BVCA
BVCS	Brit Veterinary Camelid Soc
BVF	Brit Volleyball Fedn
BVHA	Brit Veterinary Hospitals Assn
BVMA	Brit Violin Making Assn
BVNA	Brit Veterinary Nursing Assn
BVRLA	Brit Vehicle Rental & Leasing Assn
BVS	Battery Vehicle Soc
BVSF	Brit Vehicle Salvage Fedn
BVWS	Brit Vintage Wireless Soc
BWA	Bonded Warehousekeepers' Assn
	Bridge Deck Waterproofing Assn
	Brit Waterbed Assn
	Brit Waterfowl Assn
	Brit Westerners Assn
	Brit Woodcarvers Assn
	Brit Wrestling Assn
BWAHDA	Brit Warm Air Hand Drier Assn
BWAS	Birmingham & Warwickshire Archaeol Soc
BWBA	Brit Wheelchair Bowls Assn
BWCA	Brit Water Cooler Assn
BWCMG	Brit Watch & Clock Makers Gld
BWCS	Brit White Cattle Soc
BWDA2000	Brit Western Dance Assn
BWEA	Brit Wind Energy Assn
BWF	Brit Walking Fedn
	Brit Woodworking Fedn
BWLA	Brit Weight Lifters Assn
BWMA	Brit Weights & Measures Assn
BWPA	Brit Women Pilots Assn
	Brit Wood Pulp Assn
BWRA	Brit Whippet Racing Assn
BWS	Brit Watercolour Soc
BWTA	Brit Wood Turners Assn
BWY	Brit Wheel Yoga
BYBA	Brit Youth Band Assn
BZA	Brit Zeolite Assn
BZS	Britain Zimbabwe Soc

C

C&I	Comm & Ind Gp
CA	Camanachd Assn
	Classical Assn
	Consumers' Assn
	Croquet Assn
	Cruising Assn
CAA	Cathedral Architects Assn
	Cement Admixtures Assn
	Cinema Advertising Assn
	Concert Artistes' Association
CAAA	County Antrim Agricl Assn
CAABU	Coun Advancement Arab-Brit Understanding
CAAT	Campaign Arms Trade
CAAV	Central Assn Agricl Valuers
CAB	Coun Aluminium Bldg
CAC	Campaign Censorship
CADAS	Coventry & District Archaeol Soc
CADD	Campaign Drinking & Driving
CAEF	Campaign Euro-federalism
CAGC	Welsh Folk Song Soc
CAH	Campaign Hysterectomy &...Operations on Women
CAI	Confedn Aerial Inds
CAJ	C'ee Admin Justice [NI]
CALH	Cambridgeshire Assn Local Hist
CAMILK	Campaign Real Milk

CAMRA	Campaign Real Ale	CDS	Conf Drama Schools
CANI	Canoe Assn NI	CDTA	Clinical Dental Technicians Assn
CAPEL	Capel	CE	Christian Educ
CAPPA	Compulsory Annuity Purchase Protest Alliance	CEA	Cinema Exhibitors Assn
CAPS	Captive Animals' Protection Soc		Combustion Engg Assn
CAS	Caithness Agricl Soc		Construction Eqpt Assn
	Cambridge Antiquarian Soc	CEDA	Catering Eqpt Distbrs Assn GB
	Catholic Archives Soc		Central Dredging Assn
	Cheshire Agricl Soc		Consumer Electronics Distbrs Assn [IRL]
	Chester Archaeol Soc	CEDIA	CEDIA
	Citizens Advice Scotland	CEF	Construction Emplrs Fedn
	Contemporary Art Soc	CEFF	Confedn Engl Fly Fishers
	Cornwall Archaeol Soc	CEGV	Church England Gld Vergers
CASE	Campaign Science & Engg UK	CEI	Cycle Engrs' Inst
	Campaign State Educ	CEM	College Emergency Medicine
CASH	Campaign Stage Hypnosis	CENTA	Combined Edible Nut Tr Assn
CASS GB	Clarinet & Saxophone Soc GB	CERAM	CERAM Res
CASW	Contemporary Art Soc Wales	CES	Christian Evidence Soc
CATRA	Cutlery & Allied Trs Res Assn	CESA	Catering Eqpt Suppliers' Assn
CAWS	County Armagh Wildlife Soc	CFA	CFA Soc
CBA	Canal Boatbuilders Assn		Chilled Food Assn
	Chemical Business Assn		Circus Friends Association of Great Britain
	Coun Brit Archaeology		Construction Fixings Assn
	Criminal Bar Assn		Contract Flooring Assn
CBBC	Caribbean-Brit Business Coun		Craft Gld Chefs
	China-Britain Business Coun	CFBA	Canine & Feline Behaviour Assn
CBC	Conservatoires UK	CFDG	Charity Finance Directors' Gp
CBDG	Concrete Bridge Devt Gp	CFDS	Campaign Dark Skies
CBHS	Children's Books Hist Soc	CFG	Comml Farmers Gp
	Cleveland Bay Horse Soc	CFHS	Catholic Family Hist Soc
CBI	Confedn Brit Ind	CFMA	Chair Frame Mfrs Assn
CBM	Confedn Brit Metalforming	CFOA	Chief Fire Officers Assn
CBS(UK)	Caspian Breed Soc	CFPF	Campaign Philosophical Freedom
CBSL	Carnival Band Secretaries League	CGA	Country Gentlemen's Assn
CBWT	Confedn Brit Wool Textiles	CGF	Child Growth Foundation
CC	Construction Confedn	CGGB	Cine Glds GB
CCA	Chilled Beam & Ceiling Assn		Colour Gp
	Company Chemists' Assn	CGS	Carnival Glass Soc
	Consumer Credit Assn		Contemporary Glass Soc
	Customer Contact Assn		Cottage Garden Soc
CCAA	Children's Chronic Arthritis Assn	CGTBF	Craft Gld Traditional Bowyers & Fletchers
CCAB	Cámara Comercio Argentino Britanica	CHA	Children's Heart Assn
CCBN	Central Coun Brit Naturism		Comml Horticl Assn
CCC	Cambridgeshire Chams Comm		Community Hospitals Assn
	Club Cricket Conf		Coun Hunting Assns
	Cumbria Cham Comm	CHAPS(UK)	Coloured Horse & Pony Soc
CCCB	Cámara Comercio Colombo Británica	CHCS	Chemical Hazards Communication Soc
CCCC	Canal Card Collectors Circle	CHE	Campaign Homosexual Equality
	Clarice Cliff Collectors Club	CHEM	Container Handling Eqpt Mfrs Assn
CCCI	Chichester Cham Comm & Ind	CHF	Crystal & Healing Fedn
	Cornwall Cham Comm & Ind	CHME	Coun Hospitality Mgt Educ
CCE	Conf Centres Excellence	CHO	Confedn Healing Orgs
CCFA	Combined Cadet Force Assn	CHPA	Combined Heat & Power Assn
CCFGB	Chambre Comm Française GB	CHS	Caernarvonshire Histl Soc
CCFRA	Campden & Chorleywood Food Res Assn		Caspian Horse Soc
CCG	Comics Creators Gld		Clarinet Heritage Soc
CCGB	Cartoonists' Club		Clydesdale Horse Soc
CCI	Chams Ireland	CHSA	Cleaning & Hygiene Suppliers' Assn
CCMAUK	Call Centre Mgt Assn	CIA	Chemical Inds Assn
CCMM	Cornish Cham Mines & Minerals	CIArb	Chart Inst Arbitrators
CCN	Community Composting Network	CIAT	Chart Inst Architectural Technologists
CCRA	Clinical Contract Res Assn	CIB	Campaign Indep Britain
CCS	Commemorative Collectors Soc	CIBSE	Chart Instn Bldg Services Engrs
	Computer Consvn Soc	CIC	Construction Ind Coun
	Confedn Construction Specialists	CICA	Chemical & Indl Consultants' Assn
CCSA	Carbon Capture & Storage Assn		Construction Ind Computing Assn
	Cathedral & Church Shops Assn	CICRA	Crohn's Disease Childhood Res Assn
CCT	Chesterfield Canal Trust	CIDDA	Cast Iron Drainage Devt Assn
CCTA	Consumer Credit Tr Assn	CIEH	Chart Inst Envtl Health
CCUA	Civil Court Users Assn	CIF	Cork Ind Fedn
CDA	Chemists' Defence Assn	CIFE	CIFE
	Copper Devt Assn	CIFMA	Corpn Insurance, Financial & Mortgage Advisers
	Country Doctors Assn	CiG	City Inf Gp
CDB	Coun Docked Breeds	CIG	Conf Interpreters Gp
CDdWC	Cymdeithas Ddawns Werin Cymru	CII	Chart Insurance Inst
CDET	Coun Dance Educ & Training	CIIG	Construction Ind Inf Gp
cdfa	Community Devt Finance Assn	CILA	Chart Inst Loss Adjusters
CDNA	Community & District Nursing Assn	CILIP	CILIP

© CBD Research Ltd · Beckenham · BR3 5JS · Tel 020 8650 7745 · Fax 020 8650 0768 · E-mail cbd@cbdresearch.com · www.cbdresearch.com

CILT(UK)	Chart Inst Logistics & Transport	CPA	Charities' Property Assn
CIM	Chart Inst Marketing		Chiropractic Patients' Assn
CIMA	Cereal Ingredients Mfrs' Assn		City Property Assn
	Chart Inst Mgt Accountants		Competing Pipers Assn
CIOB	Chart Inst Bldg		Concert Promoters Assn
CIoH	Chart Inst Housing		Construction Plant-hire Assn
CIOT	Chart Inst Taxation		Construction Products Assn
CIPA	Chart Inst Patent Attorneys		Consumer Protection Assn
CIPD	Chart Inst Personnel & Devt		Cornish Pasty Assn
CIPFA	CIPFA		Corrosion Prevention Assn
CIPR	Chart Inst Public Relations		Craft Potters Assn
CIPS	Chart Inst Purchasing & Supply		Credit Protection Assn
	Choice in Personal Safety		Crop Protection Assn
CIRIA	Construction Ind Res & Infm Assn		Inst Certified Public Accountants Ireland
CITA	Construction Ind Tr Alliance	CPAS	Car Park Appreciation Soc
CIU	Working Men's Club & Inst U	CPBF	Campaign Press & Broadcasting Freedom
CIWEM	Chart Instn Water & Envtl Management	CPCC	Caithness Paperweight Collectors Club
CIWM	Chart Instn Wastes Mgt	CPDA	Clay Pipe Devt Assn
CKS	Coble & Keelboat Soc	CPF	Crystal Palace Foundation
CL&CGB	Church Lads & Church Girls Brigade	CPI	Confedn Paper Inds
CLA	Care Leavers Assn	CPRE	Campaign Protect Rural England
	Country Land & Business Assn [E&W]	CPRW	Campaign Protection Rural Wales
CLAPA	Cleft Lip & Palate Assn	CPS	Cambridge Philosophical Soc
CLIMB	Children Living Inherited Metabolic Diseases		Carnivorous Plant Soc
CLING	Defence Mfrs Assn	CPSA	Clay Pigeon Shooting Assn
CLOA	Chief Cultural & Leisure Officers Assn	CPT	Confedn Passenger Transport
CLÉ	CLÉ	CQI	Chart Quality Inst
CMA	Cardiomyopathy Assn	CR/Ea/	Composting Assn Ireland
	Catering Mgrs Assn	CRA	Caledonian Rly Assn
	Communications Mgt Assn		Chemical Recycling Assn
	Community Media Assn		Concrete Repair Assn
	Complementary Med Assn		Creator's Rights Alliance
	Countryside Mgt Assn		Crime Reporters Assn
CMAS Ltd	Coal Mchts Assn Scotland	CRAE	Children's Rights Alliance England
CMBA	Classic Motor Boat Assn	CRC	Confedn Roofing Contrs
CMDA	Cornish Mining Devt Assn	CRCA	Comml Radio Companies Assn
CMF	Cast Metals Fedn	CRE	Campaign Real Educ
	Coal Mchts Fedn	CReSTeD	Coun Registration Schools Teaching Dyslexic Pupils
CMI	Chart Mgt Inst	CRM Soc	Charles Rennie Mackintosh Soc
CML	Coun Mortgage Lenders	CRN UK	Community Recycling Network
CMP	Coalition Medical Progress	CROP	Coalition Removal Pimping
CMPE	Contractors Mechanical Plant Engrs	CRS	Cambridgeshire Records Soc
CMS	Church Monuments Soc		Catholic Record Soc
	Cricket Memorabilia Soc		Conflict Res Soc
CMT	Commemoratives Museum Trust	CRSA	Cold Rolled Sections Assn
CMYF	Charlotte M Yonge Fellowship	CRT	Cambridge Refrigeration Technology
CND	Campaign Nuclear Disarmament	CRTC	Clay Roof Tile Coun
CNHSS	Croydon Natural Hist & Scientific Soc	CRUSE	Cruse Bereavement Care
CNITA	Chart & Nautical Instrument Tr Assn	CS	Café Soc
CNK	CNK Alliance		Chess Scotland
CNS	Cardiff Naturalists Soc	CSA	Channel Swimming Assn
COA	Cathedral Organists Assn		Choir Schools Assn
COA(UK)	Casino Operators' Assn		Commissioning Specialists Assn
COALPRO	Confedn UK Coal Producers		Credit Services Assn
COBSEO	Confedn Brit Service & Ex-Service Orgs	CSAR	Cambridge Soc Application Res
CODE	Confedn Dental Emplrs	CSAUK	Cued Speech Assn
CODP	College Operating Dept Practitioners	CSD	Chart Soc Designers
COF	Coach Operators Fedn	CSEU	Confedn Shipbuilding & Engg Us
CofCS	Coun Cricket Socs	CSGBI	Conchological Soc
COG	Component Obsolescence Gp	CSJ	Confraternity Saint James
COGDEM	Coun Gas Detection & Envtl Monitoring	CSMA	Cementitious Slag Makers Assn
Cognition	Cognition	CSNA	Convenience Stores & Newsagents Assn [IRL]
COMA	Coke Oven Mgrs Assn	CSO	Christian Social Order
COMBAR	Comml Bar Assn	CSP	Chart Soc Physiotherapy
COMPASS	Central Org Maritime Pastimes...	CSS	Costume Soc Scotland
CONDO	Defence Mfrs Assn		CSS
ConFor	Confedn Forest Inds	CSSA	Cleaning & Support Services Assn
Construct	Construct, Concrete Structures Gp	CSTA	Craniosacral Therapy Assn
CORCA	C'ee Registered Clubs Assns	CSV	Community Service Volunteers
CORDA	Coronary Artery Disease Res Assn	CTA	Cinema Theatre Assn
CORE	Comment Reproductive Ethics		Comml Trailer Assn
	Corporate Responsibility Coalition		Community Transport Assn
CORGI	Coun Registered Gas Installers	CTAUK	Chinese Takeaway Assn
COS	Cinema Organ Soc	CTC	Coach Tourism Coun
COSCA	COSCA	CTCC	Campaign Traditional Cathedral Choir
COSLA	Convention Scot Local Authorities	CTG	Charity Tax Gp
COTIS	Confedn Transcribed Inf Services	CTMA	Brit Civil Engg Test Eqpt Mfrs Assn
CP	Cats Protection	CTPA	Cosmetic, Toiletry & Perfumery Assn

CTS	Catholic Truth Soc
CTT	Cycling Time Trials
CU	Casualties Union
	Catholic U
CVBC	Cámara Venezolana Británica Comercio
CWA	Careers Writers' Assn
	Crime Writers Assn
CWAAS	Cumberland & Westmorland Antiquarian... Soc
CWAUK	Comedy Writers' Assn UK
CWU	Communication Workers U
CWW	Circle Wine Writers
CYP	Clubs Young People
	Clubs Young People (NI)
	Clubs Young People Scotland
	Clubs Young People Wales
CYWU	Community & Youth Workers U

D

D&AD	D&AD
D-UK	Depression UK
DA	Depression Alliance
	Design Assn
	Despatch Assn
DAAS	Dad's Army Appreciation Soc
DAAUK	Dwarf Athletic Assn
DACS	Design & Artists Copyright Soc
DAE	Discovery Award England
DAHS	Derbyshire Agricl & Horticl Soc
DAS	Derbyshire Archaeol Soc
	Devon Archaeol Soc
	Dorchester Agricl Soc
DASA	Domestic Appliance Service Assn
DATA	Design & Technology Assn
DATS	Dress & Textile Specialists
DAW	Drama Assn Wales
DBA	DBA - Barge Assn
	Design Business Assn
DBC	Deaf Broadcasting Coun
DBS	Donkey Breed Soc
DCAA	Devon County Agricl Assn
DCAS	Durham County Agricl Soc
DCBS	Devon Cattle Breeders' Soc
DCCE	Doncaster Cham
DCCI	Dorset Cham Comm & Ind
DCF	Digital Content Forum
DCLHS	Durham County Local Hist Soc
DCRS	Devon & Cornwall Record Soc
DCS	Diecasting Soc
DDA	Dispensing Doctors Assn
DDS	Dawn Duellists' Soc
DDSBA	Dorset Down Sheepbreeders Assn
DEA	Devt Educ Assn
DebRA	Dystrophic Epidermolysis Bullosa Res Assn
DELTA	Deaf Educ Listening & Talking
DEMSA	Debt Mgt Standards Assn
DES	Drake Exploration Soc
DFI	Disability Fedn Ireland
DFSG	Duchenne Family Support Gp
DGCC	Dumfries & Galloway Cham Comm
DGGB	Directors Gld
DGNHAS	Dumfriesshire & Galloway Natural Hist... Soc
DGSS	Derbyshire Gritstone Sheepbreeders Soc
DHAPS	Dun Horse & Pony Soc
DHDS	Dolmetsch Hist Dance Soc
DHF	Door & Hardware Fedn
DHS	Design Hist Soc
DHSBA	Dorset Horn & Poll Sheep Breeders Assn
DI	Dyslexia Inst
DIA	Design & Inds Assn
	Driving Instructors Assn
DIG Scotland	Disablement Income Gp Scotland
DISA	Defence Industry Security Assn
DLA	Dental Laboratories Assn
	Discrimination Law Assn

DMA	Defence Mfrs Assn
	Direct Marketing Assn (UK) Ltd
	Disabled Motorcyclists Assn
DMF	Disabled Motorists Fedn
DNCC	Derbyshire & Nottinghamshire Cham Comm
DNHAS	Dorset Natural Hist & Archaeol Soc
DPA	Dartmoor Presvn Assn
	Data Pubrs Assn
	Dental Practitioners Assn
DPAA	Draught Proofing Advy Assn
DPIS	Derby Porcelain Intl Soc
DPS	Dales Pony Soc
	Dartmoor Pony Soc
DRS	Derbyshire Record Soc
DSA	Devt Studies Assn
	Direct Selling Assn
	Down's Syndrome Assn
	Drilling & Sawing Assn
DSBA	Dartmoor Sheep Breeders Assn
DSFA	Diplomatic Service Families Assn
DSGB	Dozenal Soc
DSSA	Dental System Suppliers Assn
DSWA	Dry Stone Walling Assn
DTA	Dental Technologists Assn
	Devt Trusts Assn
DTIG	Defence Mfrs Assn
DUCC	Danish-UK Cham Comm
DWT	Durham Wildlife Trust
DWTA	BEAMA

E

E-AG	Eur-Atlantic Gp
EA	English Assn
EAA	Eastern Africa Assn
	Electricity Arbitration Assn
EAB	Esperanto Assn Britain
EADA	EADA [lost D18
EAGB	Executives Assn
EAHC	Essex Archaeol & Histl Congress
EAMA	Engg & Machinery Alliance
EAP	English Apples & Pears
EAS	Epilepsy Action Scotland
EASB	English Assn Snooker & Billiards
EASCO	English Assn Self Catering Operators
EAUK	Evangelical Alliance
EBA	Electric Boat Assn
	English Baseball Assn
	English Boccia Assn
EBBA	England Basketball
EBCC	Egyptian Brit Cham Comm
EBEA	Economics, Business & Enterprise Assn
EBF	Equine Behaviour Forum
EBS	Edinburgh Bibliographical Soc
EBU	English Bridge U
ECA	Educl Centres Assn
	Electrical Contrs Assn
	English Clergy Assn
	English Curling Assn
ECB ACO	England & Wales Cricket Bd Assn Cricket Officials
ECB CA	England & Wales Cricket Bd Coaches Assn
ECCA	English Community Care Assn
	English Cross Country Assn
ECCI	Essex Chams Comm
ECHO	English Carp Heritage Org
ECIA	Engg Construction Ind Assn
ECO	Environmental Communicators Org
ECSA	Estuarine & Coastal Sciences Assn
ECWS	English Civil War Soc
EDA	Electrical Distbrs Assn
	English Draughts Assn
EDC	Early Dance Circle
EDCC	Eastbourne & District Cham Comm
EDS	Ectodermal Dysplasia Soc
EEF	EEF

© CBD Research Ltd · Beckenham · BR3 5JS · Tel 020 8650 7745 · Fax 020 8650 0768 · E-mail cbd@cbdresearch.com · www.cbdresearch.com

EEMUA	Engg Eqpt & Materials Users Assn
EES	Egypt Exploration Soc
EESA	Electrical & Engg Staff Assn
EETS	Early English Text Soc
EEZING	Defence Mfrs Assn
EFA	Employers Forum on Age
	Eton Fives Assn
EFDS	English Fedn Disability Sport
EFDSS	English Folk Dance & Song Soc
EGAD	Defence Mfrs Assn
EGB	Endurance GB
EGBA	English Goat Breeders Assn
EGCS	English Guernsey Cattle Soc
EGS	English Goethe Soc
EGU	English Golf U
EHA	England Handball Assn
EHAS	E Herts Archaeol Soc
EHCCI	E Hampshire Cham Comm & Ind
EHRSS	Edinburgh Highland Reel & Strathspey Soc
EHS	Ecclesiastical Hist Soc
EHTF	English Historic Towns Forum
EI	Energy Inst
	Evaluation Intl
EIA	Electrical Insulation Assn
	Engg Inds Assn
	Environmental Investigation Agency
	Eur Inf Assn
	Events Ind Alliance
EIBA	English Indoor Bowling Assn
EIC	Energy Inds Coun
	Environmental Inds Commission
EIFI	Electrical Inds Fedn Ireland
EIG	Explosives Ind Gp
EIQA	Excellence Ireland Quality Assn
EIS	Educl Inst Scotland
	Engg Integrity Soc
EISA	EIS Assn
EJO Society	Elsie Jeanette Oxenham Appreciation Soc
ELA	Employment Lawyers Assn
	English Lacrosse Assn
ELAFNS	E Lothian Antiquarian... Naturalists Soc
ELAM	BEAMA
ELAS	Education Law Assn
ELCCI	E Lancs Cham Comm
eLN	eLearning Network
ELSPA	Entertainment & Leisure Software Pubrs Assn (UK)
ELWA	Eur Liquid Waterproofing Assn
EMCIA	EMC Ind Assn
EMDP	Exercise Movement & Dance Partnership
EMS	Edinburgh Mathematical Soc
ENABLE	ENABLE
ENCAMS	ENCAMS
ENT.UK	Brit Assn Otorhinolaryngologists
EO	Education Otherwise
EPA	English Pool Assn
EPCS	English Playing-Card Soc
Ephsoc	Ephemera Soc
EPNS	English Place-Name Soc
EPS	Emergency Planning Soc
	Experimental Psychology Soc
EPSG	Epiphytic Plant Study Gp
EPSS	English Poetry & Song Soc
EPTA	Electro-physiological Technologists Assn
Equity	Brit Actors' Equity Assn
ERA	Entertainment Retailers Assn
	Evacuees Reunion Assn
ERC	Economic Res Coun
ERoSH	ERoSH
ERRVA	Emergency Response & Rescue Vessels Assn
ERS	Electoral Reform Soc
	Electric Rly Soc
ES	Ergonomics Soc
ESA	Environmental Services Assn
ESAH	Essex Soc Archaeology & Hist
ESC	Snowsport England
ESG	Ekbom Support Gp
	Exhibition Study Gp
ESITO	Events Sector Ind Trg Org

ESMA	Equine Sports Massage Assn
ESMBA	English Short Mat Bowling Assn
ESMG	Electric Steel Makers Gld
ESRI	Economic & Social Res Inst [IRL]
ESSA	Emergency Social Services Assn
	Event Supplier & Services Assn
ESTA	Earth Science Teachers' Assn
	Energy Systems Tr Assn
ESU	English Speaking U C'wealth
ETA	ETA Services Ltd
ETAPS	Environmental & Technical Assn Paper Sack Ind
ETCI	Electro-Technical Coun Ireland
ETHIC	Electric Trace Heating Ind Coun
ETI	Ethical Trading Initiative
ETTA	English Table Tennis Assn
ETwA	English Tiddlywinks Assn
EURISOL-UK	EURISOL-UK
EVA	English Volleyball Assn
EVENTIA	Eventia
EWI	Expert Witness Inst
EWIBA	English Women's Indoor Bowling Assn
EWP	English Wine Producers
EWS	English Westerners Soc
EWT	Essex Wildlife Trust
EXIT	Voluntary Euthanasia Soc Scotland

F

F of M	Friends Mendelssohn
F&PA	Flowers & Plants Assn
FA	Families Anonymous
	Football Assn
FAA	Fife Agricl Assn
FAB	Futon Assn
FACE	Farming Countryside Education
FACE(UK)	Fedn Assns Country Sports Europe
FACT	Falsely Accused Carers & Teachers
	Fedn Artistic & Creative Therapy
	Fedn Copyright Theft
FACTA	Fabricated Access Covers Trade Association
FAEI	Fedn Aerospace Enterprises Ireland
FAGB	Fairground Assn
FAI	Football Assn Ireland
FAIA	Food Additives & Ingredients Assn
FARA	Fedn Active Retirement Assns [IRL]
	Formula Air Racing Assn
FARMA	Nat Farmers' Retail & Markets Assn
FAS	Fedn Astronomical Socs
FASET	Fall Arrest Safety Eqpt Training
FASNA	Foundation & Aided Schools Nat Assn
FASS	Fedn Aerospace Support Services
FAST	Farnborough Air Sciences Trust
	Fedn Software Theft
FATE	Fedn Automatic Transmission Engrs
FBA	Fedn Bloodstock Agents
	Fedn Brit Artists
	Freshwater Biological Assn
FBAF	Fédn Britannique Alliances Françaises
FBAS	Fedn Brit Aquatic Socs
FBCA	Fedn Burial & Cremation Authorities
FBCCI	Franco-British Chamber of Commerce & Industry
FBCMA	Fibre Bonded Carpet Mfrs' Assn
FBETM	Fedn Brit Engrs' Tool Mfrs
FBHTM	Fedn Brit Hand Tool Mfrs
FBHVC	Fedn Brit Hist Vehicle Clubs
FBS	Fire Brigade Soc
FBSC	Fedn Bldg Specialist Contrs
FBU	Fire Brigades' U
FBY Soc	Francis Brett Young Soc
FC&PMS	Fort Cumberland... Militaria Soc
FCA	FCA Membership Ltd
	Fedn Commodity Assns
	Fencing Contrs' Assn
FCBG	Fedn Children's Book Gps

FCC	Fedn Cocoa Commerce	FMD	Friends Medieval Dublin [IRL]
	Fedn Crafts & Comm	FMI	Family Matters Inst
FCDE	Fedn Clothing Designers & Executives	FMO	Fedn Mfrg Opticians
FCDL	Fedn Community Devt Learning	FMPS	Farm Machinery Presvn Soc
FCFCG	Fedn City Farms & Community Gardens	FNF	Families Need Fathers
FCM	Friends Cathedral Music	FNL	Friends Nat Libraries
FCMA	Fibre Cement Mfrs Assn	FOA	Fire Officers Assn
FCOT	Fellowship Cycling Old-Timers		Futures & Options Association
FCPPA	Frozen & Chilled Potato Processors' Assn	FOB	Fedn Bakers
FCS	Fedn Chefs Scotland		Friends Blue
	Fedn Clinical Scientists	FOBBS	Fedn Brit Bonsai Socs
	Fedn Communication Services	FOBFO	Fedn Brit Fire Orgs
FCSI (UK)	Foodservice Consultants Soc Intl (UK)	FoC	Friends Classics
FDA	Family Doctor Assn	FOCAL	Fedn Comml Audiovisual Libraries
	Film Distbrs' Assn	FODO	Fedn Ophthalmic & Dispensing Opticians
	First Division Assn	FOE	Friends Earth
FDAP	Fedn Drug & Alcohol Profls	FOM RCP	Fac Occupational Medicine
FDF	Food & Drink Fedn	FoMRHI	Fellowship Makers… Histl Instruments
FDP	Friends Dymock Poets	FoNSCA	Fedn Nat Self Catering Assns
FDW	Friends Dr Watson	FOPS	Fair Organ Presvn Soc
FDYW	Fedn Detached Youth Work	FOREST	Freedom Org Right Enjoy Smoking Tobacco
FedPAG	Fedn Profl Assns in Guidance	FoRL	Friends Real Lancashire
FEF	Forecourt Eqpt Fedn	FoRSTA	Fedn Road Surface Treatment Assns
FER	Fedn Engine Re-Mfrs	FOSC	Fedn Sidecar Clubs
FERA	Fastener & Engg Res Assn	FOSFA	Fedn Oils, Seeds & Fats Assns
	Further Educ Res Assn	FOSSUK	Fedn Swiss Socs UK
FeRFA	FeRFA	FPA	Family Planning Assn
FESA	Foundry Eqpt & Supplies Assn		Fire Protection Assn
FESH	Fedn Ethical Stage Hypnotists		Food Processors Assn
FETA	Fedn Envtl Tr Assns		Foodservice Packaging Assn
FEU	Fedn Entertainment Us		Foreign Press Assn Lond
FEW	Freemen England & Wales	FPB	Forum Private Business
FFA	Family Farmers' Assn	FPC	Fresh Produce Consortium
	Farmers Action	FPDC	Fedn Plastering & Drywall Contrs
	Flying Farmers Assn	FPFC	Fair Play for Children Assn
FfCAC	Welsh Amat Music Fedn	FPI	Friends Pianola Inst
FFHS	Fedn Family Hist Socs	FPM	Fellowship Postgraduate Medicine
FFLM	Fac Forensic & Legal Medicine	FPRA	Fedn Private Residents' Assns
FFMA	Funeral Furnishing Mfrs Assn	FPS	Fedn Petroleum Suppliers
FFS	Farms for Schools		Fedn Piling Specialists
FFVMA	Fire Fighting Vehicles Mfrs Assn		Fell Pony Soc
FGC	Flat Glass Coun	FRA	Fell Runners Assn
FGMA	Flat Glass Mfrs Assn		Flat Roofing Alliance
FHA	Family Holiday Assn	FRAME	Fund Replacement Animals Med Experiments
FHAGBI	Friesian Horse Assn	FRC	Pulp & Paper Fundamental Res Soc
FHBF Ltd	Freelance Hair & Beauty Fedn	FRG	Family Rights Gp
FHNSAofGB	Fjord Horse Nat Stud Book Assn	FRLTNI	Fedn Retail Licensed Tr NI
FHS	Flintshire Histl Soc	FRMS	Fedn Recorded Music Socs
	Friends Histl Soc	FRSL	Ffestiniog Railway Society Ltd
	Furniture Hist Soc	FSB	Fedn Small Businesses
FHSS	Fedn Heating Spares Stockists	FSBI	Fisheries Soc
FHT	Fedn Holistic Therapists	FSBL	Friends St Bride Library
FIA	Fibreoptic Ind Assn	FSC	Fedn Stadium Communities
	Fire Ind Assn		Field Studies Coun
	Fitness Ind Assn	FSDF	Food Storage & Distbn Fedn
FIBKA	Fedn Ir Beekeepers' Assns	FSF	Football Supporters' Fedn
FID	Fedn Indep Detectorists	FSG	Fortress Study Gp
FIEC	Fellowship Indep Evangelical Churches	FSI	Financial Services Ireland
FIM	Fedn Indep Mines	FSID	Foundation Study Infant Deaths
FIPO	Fedn Indep Practitioner Orgs	FSPA	Fedn Sports & Play Assns
FIRA	Furniture Ind Res Assn	FSPG	Fire Service Presvn Gp
FIRESA	Fire & Rescue Suppliers Assn	FSR	Fedn Specialist Restaurants
FIS	Fedn Ir Socs	FSS	Feng Shui Soc
FISS	Fedn Inline Speed Skating	FSSoc	Forensic Science Soc
FIT	Fedn Internet Traders	FSSS	Franco-Scottish Soc Scotland
FLA	Family Law Assn Scotland	FST	Fedn Scot Theatre
	Finance & Leasing Assn	FTA	Fedn Tax Advisers
FLBA	Family Law Bar Assn		Floatation Tank Assn
FLD	Friends Lake District		Freight Transport Assn
Fleet Data	Road Transport Fleet Data Society	FTI	Fedn Technological Inds
FLTA	Fork Lift Truck Assn	FTL	Free Trade League
FLVA	Fedn Licensed Victuallers Assns	FTMTA	Farm Tractor & Machinery Tr Assn [IRL]
FMA	Facilities Mgt Assn	FTO	Fedn Tour Operators
	Family Mediators' Assn	FULS	Fedn Ulster Local Studies
	Fan Mfrs' Assn	FUW	Farmers' U Wales
FMA UK	Fibromyalgia Assn	FWA	Family Welfare Assn
FMB	Fedn Master Builders		Fleece Washers & Dyers Assn
FMC	Fire Mark Circle	FWAG	Farming & Wildlife Advy Gp

© CBD Research Ltd · Beckenham · BR3 5JS · Tel 020 8650 7745 · Fax 020 8650 0768 · E-mail cbd@cbdresearch.com · www.cbdresearch.com

FWC	Fedn Window Cleaners
FWD	Fedn Whls Distbrs
FWWCP	Fedn Worker Writers & Community Pubrs

G

G&SS	Gilbert & Sullivan Soc
GA	Galvanizers Assn
	Geographical Assn
	Geologists' Assn
GADAR	Gld Antique Dealers & Restorers
GAFTA	Grain & Feed Tr Assn
GAG	Grandparents Action Gp
GAI	Gld Architectural Ironmongers
GAPAN	Gld Air Pilots & Air Navigators
GARDENEX	GARDENEX
GAS	Glasgow Agricl Soc
	Glasgow Archaeol Soc
	Group Analytic Soc
GATCO	Gld Air Traffic Control Officers
GAvA	Gld Aviation Artists
GBC	Gld Builders & Contrs
GBCT	Gld Brit Camera Technicians
GBD	Gld Brit Découpeurs
GBDF	Great Britain Diving Fedn
GBFE	Gld Brit Film & TV Editors
GBPCC	Great Britain Postcard Club
GBRF	Great Britain Racquetball Fedn
GBS	Guillain Barré Syndrome Support Gp
GCA	Garden Centre Assn
	Gasket Cutters' Assn
	Golf Consultants Assn
	Greeting Card Assn
GCCF	Governing Coun Cat Fancy
GCGB	Golf Club GB
GCI	Global Commons Inst
GCL	Gld Cleaners & Launderers
GCM	Gld Church Musicians
GCMA	Golf Club Mgrs' Assn
GCMT	Gen Coun Massage Therapy
GCRN	Gen Coun & Register Naturopaths
GCT / GCL	Game Conservancy Trust
GDBA	Guide Dogs for Blind Assn
GE	Gld Enamellers
GEA	Garage Eqpt Assn
GEM	Group Educ Museums
Gem-A	Gemmological Assn
GEO	Glosa Educ Org
GF	Ground Forum
GFA	Game Farmers Assn
GFFR	Gld Fine Food Retailers
GFS	George Formby Soc
GFTU	Gen Fedn Tr Us
GFW	Gld Food Writers
gGA	Good Gardeners' Assn
GGA	Guernsey Growers Assn
GGF	Glass & Glazing Fedn
GHC/ACW	Gwartheg Hynafol Cymru
GHS	Garden Hist Soc
GIG	Genetic Interest Gp
GIMA	GIMA
GKCSoc	Chesterton Soc
GLASS	Green Lane Assn
GLDA	Garden & Landscape Designers Assn
GLIAS	Greater Lond Indl Archaeology Soc
GLM Ltd	Gld Letting & Mgt
GLTA	Glued Laminated Timber Assn
GLULAM/GLTA	Glued Laminated Timber Assn
GMA	Glasgow Mathematical Assn
	Growing Media Assn
GMC	Gld Master Craftsmen
GMG	Garden Media Gld
GNAS	Grand Nat Archery Soc
GNR Society	Great Nthn Rly Soc
GNSRA	Great N Scotland Rly Assn

GoCB	Gld Church Braillists
GODA	Gld Drama Adjudicators
GOMW	Gld Motoring Writers
GOONS	Gld One-Name Studies
GOSPBC	Gloucestershire Old Spot Pig Breeders' Club
GP	Gld Photographers
GPBT	Gld Profl Beauty Therapists
GPDA	Gypsum Products Devt Assn
GPEA	Gld Profl Estate Agents
GPP	Gld Pastoral Psychology
GPTD	Gld Profl Teachers Dancing
GPV	Gld Profl Videographers
GRCA	Intl Glassfibre Reinforced Concrete Assn
GRS	German Rly Soc
GRTG	Gld Registered Tourist Guides
GSA	Girls' Schools Assn
GSIA	Gloucestershire Soc Indl Archaeology
GSPS	Goon Show Preservation Soc
GTA	Gun Tr Assn
GTMA	Gauge & Tool Makers Assn
GTMC	Gld Travel Mgt Cos
GTOA	Group Travel Organisers Assn
GVA	Gin & Vodka Assn
	Gulf Veterans Assn
GVCAC	Girls Venture Corps Air Cadets
GWS	Great Wstn Soc
GWT	Gwent Wildlife Trust

H

HA	Heritage Afloat
	Histl Assn
	Historic Artillery
	Honey Assn
HAA	Historic Aircraft Assn
HACSG	Hyperactive Children's Support Gp
HAS	Hawick Archaeol Soc
	History Anaesthesia Soc
HBA	Herring Buyers Assn
	Home Business Alliance
	Nat Assn Hospital Broadcasting Orgs
HBAA	Hotel Booking Agents Assn
HBEF	Health & Beauty Emplrs Fedn
HBF	Home Builders Fedn
HBS	Havergal Brian Soc
	Henry Bradshaw Soc
HBSA	Hairdressing & Beauty Suppliers Assn
	Histl Breechloading Smallarms Assn
HCA	History Curriculum Assn
	Holiday Centres Assn
	Hospital Caterers Assn
HCAUK	Handcycling Assn
HCC	Historic Caravan Club
HCCI	Hitchin Cham Comm & Ind
HCGB	Hovercraft Club
HCKA	Historic Canoe & Kayak Assn
HCS	Highland Cattle Soc
HCSA	Hospital Consultants & Specialists Assn
HCVS	Historic Comml Vehicle Soc
HDA	Huntington's Disease Assn
HDRA	Henry Doubleday Res Assn
HDS	Histl Diving Soc
HDSBA	Hampshire Down Sheep Breeders Assn
HEA	Horticultural Exhibitors Assn
HEADWAY	Headway
HEAS	Home Educ Advy Service
HEFF	Heart of England Fine Foods
HELOA	Higher Educ Liaison Officers' Assn
HEMSA	Highway Electrical Mfrs & Supprs Assn
HERO	Historic Endurance Rallying Org
HES(UK)	History Educ Soc
HEVAC	Heating, Ventilating & Air Conditioning Mfrs' Assn
HFC	Hampshire Field Club & Archaeol Soc
HFMA	Health Food Mfrs Assn
	Healthcare Financial Mgt Assn

HGA	Human Genetics Alert	IAPI	Inst Advertising Practitioners Ireland
HGS	Harness Goat Soc	IAPS	Inc Assn Preparatory Schools
	Hurdy-Gurdy Soc	IAS	Indl Agents Soc
HGWS	H G Wells Soc	IAT	Inst Animal Technology
HHA	Historic Houses Assn		Inst Asphalt Technology
HINI	Hostelling Intl NI	IATI	Inst Accounting Technicians Ireland
HIPPO	Help Intl Plant Protein Org	IAV	Inst Assessors & Internal Verifiers
HIPS (97)	HIPS (97)	IAVI	Ir Auctioneers & Valuers Inst
HISHA	Highlands & Islands Sheep Health Assn	IBA	Ir Bowling Assn
HLCC	Home Laundering Consultative Coun	IBAS	Indep Banking Advy Service
HLRA	Handbag Liners & Repairers Assn	IBAT	Inst Bookbinding & Allied Trs
HMA	Homeopathic Med Assn	IBC	Inst Barristers' Clerks
	Hop Mchts Assn		Inst Business Consulting
HMCA	Hospital & Med Care Assn	IBD	Inst Brewing & Distilling
HMES	Histl Med Eqpt Soc	IBDA	Indep Battery Distbrs Assn
HMRS	Histl Model Rly Soc	IBE	Inst Business Ethics
HMS	Histl Maritime Soc	IBEC	Ir Business & Emplrs Confedn
	Histl Metallurgy Soc	IBI	Indep Broadcasters Ireland [IRL]
HMSA	Hose Mfrs' & Suppliers Assn	IBIA	Ir BioIndustry Assn
	Hypermobility Syndrome Assn	IBIS	Imaginative Book Illustration Soc
HMT	Hovercraft Museum Trust	IBMS	Inst Biomedical Science
HOS	Hardy Orchid Soc	IBO	Inst Brit Organ Bldg
HOT	Hawk & Owl Trust	IBS	Inst Broadcast Sound
HPA	Handley Page Assn	IBSS	Intl Bond & Share Soc
	Heat Pump Assn	ICA	Ice Cream Alliance
	Hurlingham Polo Assn		Inst Consumer Affairs
HPMA	Healthcare People Mgt Assn		Inst Contemporary Arts
HPS	Hardy Plant Soc		Ir Countrywomen's Assn
	Highland Pony Soc	ICAEW	Inst Chart Accountants England & Wales
HRA	Heritage Rly Assn	ICAS	Inst Chart Accountants Scotland
	Horse Rangers Assn	ICATA	Ir Clothing & Textiles Alliance [IRL]
HRAS	Harry Roy Appreciation Soc	ICB	Inst Certified Book-Keepers
HRFBS	HRGB Handbell Ringers	ICBA	Instn Comml & Business Agents
HSA	Horseracing Sponsors Assn	ICCL	Ir Coun Civil Liberties
	Humane Slaughter Assn	ICCM	Inst Cemetery & Crematorium Mgt
HSBA	Herdwick Sheep Breeders Assn	ICCT	Islington Cham Comm & Tr
HSGB	Haflinger Soc	ICDA	Ir Cosmetics, Detergents... Products Assn
HSLC	Historic Soc Lancashire & Cheshire	ICE	Instn Civil Engrs
HSS	Humanist Soc Scotland	ICEA	Inst Cost & Executive Accountants
HSSA	Health & Safety Sign Assn		Intl Consulting Economists Assn
HTA	Heavy Transport Assn	ICES	Instn Civil Engg Surveyors
	Horticultural Trs Assn	ICF	Inst Chart Foresters
	Hound Trailing Assn	ICFM	Inst Car Fleet Mgt
HTFS	Heat Transfer & Fluid Flow Service	ICG	Inst Career Guidance
Hums	Humanities Assn	ICHA	Indep Children's Homes Assn
HVA	Herpes Viruses Assn	ICHAWI	Inst Consvn Historic &... Works Ireland
HVCA	Heating & Ventilating Contrs Assn	ICHCA	ICHCA Intl
HWA	Hot Water Assn	IChemE	Instn Chemical Engrs
HWPA	Horserace Writers & Photographers Assn	ICM	Inst Comml Mgt
HWS	Henry Williamson Soc		Inst Complementary & Natural Medicine
			Inst Conflict Mgt
			Inst Construction Mgt
			Inst Credit Mgt

I

		ICM-BRCP	Brit Register Complementary Practitioners
		ICMA	Ir Chemical Marketers Assn
		ICME	Inst Cast Metals Engrs
IA	IA	ICMMA	Indl Cleaning Machine Mfrs Assn
IAAS	Inst Auctioneers & Appraisers Scotland	ICMSA	Ir Creamery Milk Suppliers Assn
IAAT	Intl Assn Animal Therapists	ICOM	ICOM Energy Assn
IAATI UK	Intl Assn Auto Theft Investigators	ICON	Indep Consultants Consortium
IAB	Internet Advtg Bureau		Inst Consvn
IABA	Ir Amat Boxing Assn	ICorr	Inst Corrosion
IAC	Inst Amat Cinematographers	ICOS	Ir Co-op Org Soc
IACP	Ir Assn Counselling & Psychotherapy	ICPEM	Inst Civil Protection & Emergency Mgt
IAEA	Inst Automotive Engr Assessors	ICR	Inst Clinical Res
IAgrE	Instn Agricl Engrs	ICRA	ICRA
IAgSA	Inst Agricl Secretaries & Administrators	ICS	Inst Chart Shipbrokers
IAI	Inst Archaeologists Ireland		Inst Customer Service
	Inst Architectural Ironmongers		Intensive Care Soc
IAIEC	Ir Assn Intl Express Carriers	ICSA	ICSA [IRL]
IAL	Inst Art & Law		Inst Chart Secretaries & Administrators
IAM	Inst Administrative Mgt	ICSI	Inst Clay Shooting Instructors
	Inst Advanced Motorists	ICT	ICT Ireland
	Inst Assn Mgt		Inst Concrete Technology
	Inst Business Admin	ICTU	Ir Congress Tr Us
IAO	Inc Assn Organists	ICW	Inst Clayworkers
IAP	Instn Analysts & Programmers		Inst Clerks Works
IAPF	Ir Assn Pension Funds	IDA	Ir Dental Assn

© CBD Research Ltd · Beckenham · BR3 5JS · Tel 020 8650 7745 · Fax 020 8650 0768 · E-mail cbd@cbdresearch.com · www.cbdresearch.com

IDE	Inst Demolition Engrs	IIS	Ir Instn Surveyors
IDFA	Infant & Dietetic Foods Assn	IISP	Inst Inf Security Profls
IDGTE	Instn Diesel & Gas Turbine Engrs	IIT	Inst Indirect Taxation
IDHEE	Inst Domestic Heating... Engrs	IKA	Ir Kidney Assn
IDHS(GB)	Ir Draught Horse Soc	ILA	Insolvency Lawyers Assn
IDM	Inst Direct Marketing		Intl Law Assn
IDMA	Ir Direct Marketing Assn	ILAM	Inst Leisure & Amenity Mgt Ireland
IDS	Ir Deaf Soc	ILCA	Inst Legal Cashiers & Administrators
IDSc	Inst Decontamination Sciences	ILCU	Ir League Credit Us
IEA	Inst Economic Affairs	ILE	Instn Lighting Engrs
	Ir Exporters Assn	ILEX	Inst Legal Executives
IEAP	Inst Entertainment & Arts Profls	ILHS	Ir Legal Hist Soc
IED	Instn Economic Devt	ILI	Ir Landscape Inst
	Instn Engg Designers	ILM	Inst Leadership & Mgt
IEEF	Ir Engg Enterprises Fedn [IRL]	ILPA	Immigration Law Practitioners' Assn
IEEM	Inst Ecology & Envtl Mgt	ILS	Indl Locomotive Soc
IEMA	Inst Envtl Mgt & Assessment		Inst Legal Secretaries & PAs
IEnvSc	Instn Envtl Sciences	ILSGB	Intl Language [Ido] Soc
IER	Inst Employment Rights	ILT	Inst Paralegal Training
IESIS	Instn Engrs & Shipbuilders Scotland	ILTSA	Inst Licensed Tr Stock Auditors
IET	Instn Engg & Technology	IMA	Indep Midwives Assn
IExpE	Inst Explosives Engrs		Inst Mathematics & Applications
IFA	Indep Motor Tr Factors Assn		Intelligent Membrane Tr Assn
	Inst Field Archaeologists		Investment Mgt Assn
	Inst Financial Accountants	IManf	Inst Manufacturing
	Ir Football Assn	IMarEST	Inst Marine Engg, Science & Technology
IFB	Inst Family Business	IMCA	Inst Mgt Consultants & Advisers [IRL]
IFBB	Indep Family Brewers		Intl Marine Contrs Assn
iFE	Instn Fire Engrs	IMDA	Ir Med Devices Assn [IRL]
IFEDA	Indep Fire Engg & Distrbrs Assn	IMechE	Instn Mechanical Engrs
IFLSA	Brit Marine Fedn	IMEG	Ir Mining & Exploration Gp
IFM	Inst Fisheries Mgt	IMF	Inst Metal Finishing
IFMA	Inst Football Mgrs & Admin	IMHS	Indian Military Histl Soc
IFON	Indep Fedn Nursing Scotland	IMI	Inst Med Illustrators
IFP	Inst Financial Planning		Inst Motor Ind
IFPA	Ir Family Planning Assn		Ir Mgt Inst
IFRA	Indep Footwear Retailers Assn	IMIS	Inst Mgt Inf Systems
ifs	Inst Financial Services	IMIT	Inst Musical Instrument Technology
IFS	Inst Fiscal Studies	IMLA	Intermediary Mortgage Lenders Assn
IFSA	Instock Footwear Suppliers Assn		Ir Maritime Law Assn
	Intumescent Fire Seals Assn	IMO	Ir Med Org
IFST	Inst Food Science & Technology	IMPACT	Ir Municipal, Public & Civil TU
IFT	Inst Turnaround	IMPT	Inst Maxillofacial Prosthetists...
IFUT	Ir Fedn University Teachers	IMRG	Interactive Media Retail Group
IG	Defence Mfrs Assn	IMS	Inst Mgt Services
IGA	Inst Gp Analysis		Inst Mgt Specialists
IGAP	Indep Gp Analytical Psychologists	IMTD	Inst Master Tutors Driving
IGC	Inst Guidance Counsellors [IRL]	IMW	Inst Masters Wine
IGD	Inst Grocery Distbn	IMWoodT	Inst Machine Woodworking Technology
IGEM	Instn Gas Engrs & Mgrs	INA	Ir Naturist Assn
IGPA	Intl Gen Produce Assn	INCA	INCA [IRL]
IGRS	Ir Genealogical Res Soc		Insulated Render & Cladding Assn
IGS	Ir Georgian Soc	INCONTACT	Incontact
IHBC	Inst Historic Bldg Consvn	Incpen	Ind Coun Packaging & Envt
IHEEM	Inst Healthcare Engg & Estate Mgt	INFACT	Ir Nat Fedn Copyright Theft
IHFR	Health Food Inst	INO	Ir Nurses Org
IHGS	Inst Heraldic & Genealogical Studies	InstMC	Inst Measurement & Control
IHI	Inst Home Inspectors	InstP	Inst Piping
	Ir Hospitality Inst	INTO	Ir Nat Teachers Org
IHIE	Inst Highway Inc Engrs	IoA	Inst Acoustics
IHM	Inst Healthcare Mgt	IOB	Inst Biology
IHPE	Inst Health Promotion & Educ	IoBM	Inst Builders Mchts
IHRIM	Inst Health Record & Inf Mgt	IOC	Inst Carpenters
IHS	Inst Home Safety		Inst Copywriting
IHSGB	Icelandic Horse Soc	IOCS	Inst Construction Specialists
IHT	Instn Highways & Transportation	IoD	Inst Directors
IHU	Ir Homing U	IoE	Inst Export
IHUK	Ice Hockey UK	IOFGA	Ir Organic Farmers & Growers Assn
II	Inst Inventors	IOG	Inst Groundsmanship
IIA	Inst Internal Auditors UK & Ireland	IOH	Inst Horticulture
IIB	Inst Indep Business	IOJ	Chart Inst Journalists
	Inst Insurance Brokers	IoL	Chart Inst Linguists
IICM	Ir Inst Credit Mgt	IOL	Inst Outdoor Learning
IIE	Inst Indl Engrs [IRL]	IOM	Inst Operations Mgt
IIF	Ir Insurance Fedn	IOM3	Inst Materials, Minerals & Mining
IILP	Inst Intl Licensing Practitioners	IOMNHAS	Isle of Man Natural Hist...Soc
IIM	Inst Intl Marketing	ION	Inst Optimum Nutrition
IIPMM	Ir Inst Purchasing & Materials Mgt	IoP	Inst Physics

IoR	Inst Refrigeration
	Inst Roofing
IOS	Inst Shopfitting
	Inst Swimming
IOSF	Intl Otter Survival Fund
IOSH	Instn Occupational Safety & Health
IoTA	Inst Transport Administration
IOV	Inst Videography
IPA	Indep Pilots Assn
	Indl Packaging Assn
	Indl & Power Assn
	Insolvency Practitioners Assn
	Inst Practitioners Advertising
	Inst Public Administration [IRL]
	Involvement & Participation Assn
IPD	Inst Profl Designers
IPEM	Inst Physics & Engg in Medicine
IPF	Intl Pen Friends
	Investment Property Forum
	Ir Printing Fedn
IPG	Indep Pubrs Gld
	Inst Profl Goldsmiths
IPHA	Ir Pharmaceutical Healthcare Assn
IPHE	Inst Plumbing & Heating Engg
IPI	Inst Patentees & Inventors
	Inst Profl Investigators
IPIA	Indep Print Inds Assn
IPLA	Inst Public Loss Assessors
IPM	Inst Place Mgt
IPMA	Inflatable Play Mfrs Assn
IPP	Inst Payroll Profls
IPPA	IPPA Early Childhood Org [IRL]
IPROW	Inst Public Rights Way Mgt
IPS	Inc Phonographic Soc
	Infection Prevention Soc
	Instn Planning Supervisors
IPSA	Ir ProShare Assn
IPSM	Inst Public Sector Mgt
IPSS	Inst Profl Soil Scientists
IPW	Inst Profl Willwriters
IPWFI	Incorporation Plastic Window Fabricators & Installers
IQ	Inst Quarrying
IQPS	Inst Qualified Profl Secretaries
IR Society	Investor Relations Soc
IRATA	Indl Rope Access Tr Assn
IRC	Indep Retailers Confedn
IRCH	Intl Register Consultant Herbalists & Homoeopaths
IRE	Inst Refractories Engrs
IRFU	Ir Rugby Football U
IRM	Inst Risk Mgt
IRMA	Ir Recorded Music Assn
IRPM	Inst Residential Property Mgt
IRR	Inst Race Relations
IRRV	Inst Revenues, Rating & Valuation
IRS	Indl Rly Soc
IRSE	Instn Rly Signal Engrs
IRSO	Inst Road Safety Officers
IRTA	Ir Real Tennis Assn
IRTS	Ir Radio Transmitters Soc
ISA	Indep Schools Assn
	Indep Surveyors Assn
	Ir Soc Autism
	Ir Software Assn
ISAA	Ir Ship Agents' Assn
ISBA	Inc Soc Brit Advertisers
	Indep Schools Bursars Assn
ISBE	Inst Small Business & Entrepreneurship
ISC	Indep Schools Coun
ISCA	Indep Safety Consultants Assn
ISCE	Inst Sound & Communications Engrs
ISecM	Inst Security Mgt
ISIA	Ir Security Ind Assn
ISIDA	Ir Sudden Infant Death Assn
ISKB	Imperial Soc Knights Bachelor
ISM	Inc Soc Musicians
	Inst Spiritualist Mediums
ISMA UK	Intl Stress Management Assn UK

ISME	Inst Sheet Metal Engg
	Ir Small & Medium Enterprises Assn
ISMM	Inst Sales & Marketing Mgt
ISOB	Inc Soc Organ Builders
ISOM	Ir Soc Occupational Medicine
ISP	Inst Sales Promotion
ISPA UK	Internet Service Providers' Assn
ISPAL	Inst Sport, Parks & Leisure
ISPCA	Ir Soc Prevention Cruelty Animals
ISPCC	Ir Soc Prevention Cruelty Children
ISPE	Inst Swimming Pool Engrs
ISRM	Inst Sport & Recreation Mgt
ISRN	Inc Soc Registered Naturopaths
ISS	Inn Sign Soc
ISSE	Inst Specialist Surveyors & Engrs
IST	Inst Science & Technology
	Inst Spring Technology
ISTA	Intl Steel Tr Assn
ISTC	Inst Scientific & Technical Communicators
ISTD	Imperial Soc Teachers Dancing
	Intl Soc Typographic Designers
ISTR	Inst Safety Technology & Res
IStructE	Instn Structural Engrs
IT	Inst Trichologists
ITA	Indl Tyre Assn
	Inst Transactional Analysis
ITAI	Inst Traffic Accident Investigators
ITBA	Ir Thoroughbred Breeders Assn
ITC	Indep Theatre Coun
ITDN	Indep Tyre Distbrs Network
ITGA	Ir Timber Growers Assn
ITI	Inst Translation & Interpreting
ITIC	Ir Tourist Ind Confedn
ITM	Inst Transport Mgt
	Inst Travel Mgt
ITMA	Imported Tyre Mfrs Assn
	Inst Tr Mark Attorneys
ITOL	Inst Training & Occupational Learning
ITPAC	Imported Tobacco Products Advy Coun
ITSSAR	Indep Training Standards Scheme & Register
ITT	Inst Travel & Tourism
IUA	Ir Universities Assn
IVE	Inst Vitreous Enamellers
IVEA	Ir Vocational Educ Assn
IVM	Inst Value Mgt
IVR	Inst Vehicle Recovery
IWA	Indep Warranty Assn
	Inland Waterways Assn
	Inst Welsh Affairs
IWBA	Ir Women's Bowling Assn
IWMA	Ir Waste Mgt Assn
IWO	Inst Welfare
	IWO
IWPPA	Indep Waste Paper Processors Assn
IWPS	Inland Waterways Protection Soc
IWSc	Inst Wood Science
IYHA	Ir Youth Hostels Assn

J

JABS	Justice Awareness & Basic Support
JACT	Jt Assn Classical Teachers
JAPTA	Jazz Piano Teachers Assn
JBAS	Jussi Björling Appreciation Soc
JBS	Josephine Butler Soc
JCCI	Japanese Cham Comm & Ind UK
JCS	Jersey Cattle Soc
	Justices' Clerks' Soc
JDA	Jewellery Distributors' Association of the UK
JFU	Jersey Farmers' U
JHS	James Hilton Soc
	John Hampden Soc
JHSE	Jewish Histl Soc England
JIMA	John Innes Mfrs Assn
JKJ Society	Jerome K Jerome Soc

© CBD Research Ltd · Beckenham · BR3 5JS · Tel 020 8650 7745 · Fax 020 8650 0768 · E-mail cbd@cbdresearch.com · www.cbdresearch.com

JPR	Inst Jewish Policy Res
JSL	Johnson Soc Lond
JSS	Jacob Sheep Soc

K

K&ESR	Kent & E Sussex Rly Co
KaBCA	Kaolin & Ball Clay Assn
KAS	Kent Archaeol Soc
KBSA	Kitchen Bathroom Bedroom Specialists Assn
KC	Kennel Club
KCAS	Kent County Agricl Soc
KCCC	Kensington & Chelsea Cham Comm
KCoC	Kingston Cham Comm
KEBS	Kmoch Eur Bands Soc
KES	Karg-Elert Archive
KF	Kinesiology Fedn
KFA	Keep Fit Assn
KIF	Knitting Inds Fedn
KSA	Klinefelter's Syndrome Assn
KSGB	Kite Soc
KSMA	Keats-Shelley Memorial Assn
KWVRPS	Keighley & Worth Valley Rly Presvn Soc

L

LA	Lighting Assn
LAA	Lancashire Authors' Assn
	Light Aircraft Assn
	Livestock Auctioneers Assn
	London Anglers Assn
LABBS	Ladies' Assn Brit Barbershop Singers
LABC	LABC
LACA	Local Authority Caterers' Assn
LACEF	Local Authority Civil Enforcement Forum
LACS	League Cruel Sports
LAGB	Linguistics Assn
LAHS	Leicestershire Archaeol & Histl Soc
LAMAS	London & Middlesex Archaeol Soc
LANDInG	Defence Mfrs Assn
LANI	Landlords' Assn NI
LAPADA	Assn Art & Antique Dealers
LAPFAG	Local Authority PVC-u Frame Advy Gp
LARA	Motoring Orgs' Land Access & Recreation Assn
LARIA	Local Authorities Res & Intelligence Assn
LARSOA	Local Authority Road Safety Officers' Assn
LAS	London Appreciation Soc
LAS Ltd	Leicestershire Agricl Soc
LASA	Laboratory Animal Science Assn
LASMA	Ladder Systems Mfrs Assn
LASSA	Licensed Animal Slaughterers... Assn
LBBA	Brit Marine Fedn
	Brit Marine Fedn
LBES	Lifeboat Enthusiasts' Soc
LBL	Labour behind the Label
LBMA	London Bullion Mkt Assn
LBSG	Letter Box Study Gp
LBSGB	Lusitano Breed Soc
LC	Lutheran Coun
LCA	Lead Contrs Assn
	London Cornish Assn
LCAS	Lancashire & Cheshire Antiquarian Soc
LCC	London Cycling Campaign
LCCI	Liverpool Cham Comm & Ind
	London Cham Comm & Ind
LCF	Law Centres Fedn
	Librarians' Christian Fellowship
LCGB	Locomotive Club
LCRS	Record Soc Lancashire & Cheshire
LCTC	Loyal Company Town Criers
LDCA	Land Drainage Contrs Assn
LDS	Lakeland Dialect Soc
LDSA	London Dist Surveyors Assn

LDU	Legal Defence U
LDWA	Long Distance Walkers Assn
LEA	Leasehold Enfranchisement Assn
LECT	League Exchange C'wealth Teachers
LEEA	Lifting Eqpt Engrs Assn
LEIA	Lift & Escalator Ind Assn
LES	Licensing Executives Soc
LFI	Let's Face It
LFMA	London Fish Mchts (Billingsgate) Ltd
LGA	Local Govt Assn
LGU	Ladies' Golf U
LHA	Left-Handers Assn
	World War Two Living Hist Assn
LHC	Left Handers Club
LI	Landscape Inst
LIBA	London Investment Banking Assn
Liberty	Liberty
LIF	Lighting Ind Fedn
LIFE	LIFE
LIRMA	Intl Underwriting Assn Lond
LIS	List & Index Soc
LISE	Librarians of Insts & Schools of Educ
LIT & PHIL	Manchester Literary & Philosophical Soc
LITRG	Low Incomes Tax Reform Gp
LLSBA	Leicester Longwool Sheepbreeders Assn
LMA	League Mgrs Assn
	Lloyd's Market Assn
	Loan Market Assn
	London Mayors Assn
LMBBS	Laurence-Moon-Bardet-Biedl Soc
LMCA	Leisure Mgt Contractors Assn
LMCPA	London Motor Cab Proprietors' Assn
LMMA	London Money Market Assn
LMS	Latin Mass Soc
	London Mathematical Soc
	London Medieval Soc
LNHS	London Natural Hist Soc
LOFA	Leisure & Outdoor Furniture Assn
LOOK	LOOK
LPA	Leather Producers' Assn
LPGA	L P Gas Assn
LPOC	Listed Property Owners Club
LPRS	Lancashire Parish Register Soc
LRBA	London Rice Brokers Assn
LRCS	Lincoln Red Cattle Soc
LRG	Landscape Res Gp
LRS	Lincoln Record Soc
LRTA	Light Rail Transit Assn
LSA	Lead Sheet Assn
	Leisure Studies Assn
	Lowe Syndrome Assn
LSBA	Lonk Sheep Breeders Assn
LSDS	London Swing Dance Soc
LSGB	Lipizzaner Soc
LSN	Lymphoedema Support Network
LSRA	Lead Smelters & Refiners Assn
LSS	Leopold Stokowski Soc
LSSA	Legal Software Suppliers Assn
	London Subterranean Survey Assn
LTA	Lawn Tennis Assn
	Livestock Traders Assn
LTCA	Long-term Conditions Alliance
LTDA	Licensed Taxi Drivers' Assn
LTG	Little Theatre Gld
LTN	Lone Twin Network
LTS	London Topographical Soc
LTWA	Lawn Tennis Writers Assn
LURS	London Underground Rly Soc
LVTA	London Vintage Taxi Assn
LWA	London Welsh Assn
LYRPS	Lancashire & Yorkshire Rly Presvn Soc
LYRS	Lancashire & Yorkshire Rly Soc

M

M Her S	Military Heraldry Soc
M.A.R.S.	MARS
MA	Mathematical Assn
	Miscarriage Assn
	Museums Assn
MAA	Manufacturers' Agents' Assn
	Medical Artists Assn
MAARA	Midlands Asthma & Allergy Res Assn
MAC	Mastic Asphalt Coun
MACS	Micro & Anophthalmic Children's Soc
MADEC	Martial Arts Devt Commission
MAEA	Medical Ethics Alliance
MAFVA	Miniature Armoured Fighting Vehicle Assn
MAG(UK)	Motorcycle Action Gp
MAGB	Maltsters Assn
Malsoc	Malacological Soc Lond
MAMA	Meet-a-Mum Assn
MAMSA	Managing & Marketing Sales Assn
MARCH	Nat Assn Mental After-Care in... Homes
MARQUES	MARQUES
MAS	Merioneth Agricl Soc
MASS	Motor Accident Solicitors Soc
MATCH	Mothers Apart Children
MAUK	Mast Action UK
	Mining Assn
MBA	Marine Biological Assn
	Mountain Bothies Assn
MBF	Multiple Births Foundation
MBSGB	Musical Box Soc
MCA	Mail Consolidators Assn
	Management Consultancies Assn
	Master Carvers Assn
	Master Craftsmen's Assn
	McTimoney Chiropractic Assn
	Medical Coun Alcohol
MCCA	Minor Counties Cricket Assn
MCCC	Midlands Club Cricket Conf
MCCE	Macclesfield Cham Comm
MCGB	Master Chefs GB
MCI	Mountaineering Coun Ireland
MCIA	Motor Cycle Ind Assn
MCofS	Mountaineering Coun Scotland
MCRMA	Metal Cladding & Roofing Manufacturers Association Ltd
MCS	Marine Consvn Soc
MCU	Modern Churchpeople's U
MDA	Mobile Data Assn
MDAS	Malt Distillers Assn Scotland
MDDUS	Medical & Dental Defence U Scotland
MDF	MDF
MDHA	Masters Deerhounds Assn
MDS	Macular Disease Soc
MDSG	Myotonic Dystrophy Support Gp
MDU	Medical Defence U
MEA	Media Education Assn
	Medical Equestrian Assn
	Middle East Assn
	Myalgic Encephalopathy Assn
MEAA	Milking Eqpt Assn
MEC	Music Educ Coun
MeCCSA	Media, Communications & Cultural Studies Assn
MEDACT	Medical Action Global Security
MEDATS	Medieval Dress & Textile Soc
MEEMA	Marine Engine & Eqpt Mfrs Assn
MEG	Museum Ethnographers Gp
MELCC	Midlothian & E Lothian Cham Comm
MENCAP	Mencap
MERG	Model Electronic Rly Gp
MES	Minerals Engg Soc
MESF	Mobile Electronics & Security Fedn
METCOM	Mechanical & Metal Trs Confedn
MF	Morris Fedn
MFHA	Masters Foxhounds Assn

MGA	Maize Growers Assn
	Mushroom Growers Assn
	Myasthenia Gravis Assn
MGAGB	Mounted Games Assn
MGMA	Metal Gutter Mfrs Assn
MHA	Manila Hemp Assn
MHEA	Materials Handling Engrs Assn
MHNA	Mental Health Nurses Assn
MHRA	Modern Humanities Res Assn
MHS	Military Histl Soc
MIA	Maritime Inf Assn
	Meetings Ind Assn
	Mortar Ind Assn
	Motorsport Ind Assn
	Music Inds Assn
MICAF	Mobile Ind Crime Action Forum
MIG	Defence Mfrs Assn
MIHS	Merseyside Indl Heritage Soc
MILC	Shipbuilders & Shiprepairers Assn
MILMA	Miners' & Indl Lamp Mfrs' Assn
MIND	Mind (the mental health charity)
MINSOC	Mineralogical Soc
MIPAA	Motor Industry Public Affairs Assn Ltd
MIRA	MIRA Ltd
MIRAD	Inst Registration Agents & Dealers
MIRO	Mineral Ind Res Org
MJA	Medical Journalists Assn
MKKM	Assn Men Kent & Kentish Men
MLA	Marine Leisure Assn
	Master Locksmiths Assn
MLAGB	Muzzle Loaders Assn
MLSBG	Manx Loaghtan Sheep Breeders Gp
MLTA	Mountain Leader Training Assn
MMA	Microtome Mfrs Assn
	Music Masters' & Mistresses' Assn
MMDA	Miniature Mediterranean Donkey Assn
MMF	Music Managers Forum
MMMA	Metalforming Machinery Makers' Assn
MMS	Manchester Med Soc
MNFU	Manx Nat Farmers U
MNLPS	Merchant Navy Locomotive Presvn Soc
MOMENTUM	Momentum - Northern Ireland ICT Fedn
Mont Soc	Montessori Soc
MOOS	Mechanical Organ Owners Soc
MOS	Men Stones
MOSA	Medical Officers Schools Assn
MOTA	Mail Order Trs Assn
MPA	Major Projects Assn
	Master Photographers Assn
	Music Pubrs' Assn
MPAGB	Pentathlon GB
MPBA	Modular & Portable Bldg Assn
MPG	Museum Profls Gp
	Music Producers Gld
MPGA	Metropolitan Public Gardens Assn
MPMA	Metal Packaging Mfrs Assn
MPS	Medical Protection Soc
MPS Society	Soc Mucopolysaccharide Diseases
MRA	Machinery Ring Assn
MRC	Model Rly Club
MRG	Media Res Gp
MRI	Meuse Rhine Issel Cattle Soc
MRQSA	Market Res Quality Standards Assn
MRS	Market Res Soc
	Medical Res Soc
MS	Media Soc
MS Society	Multiple Sclerosis Soc
MSA	Malvern Spa Assn
	Margarine & Spreads Assn
	Modern Studies Assn
	Motor Schools Assn
	MultiService Assn
MSAG	Shipbuilders & Shiprepairers Assn
MSAUK	Motor Sports Assn
MSBA	Masham Sheep Breeders Assn
MSGB	Manorial Soc
MSHS	Medical Science Histl Soc
MSRG	Medieval Settlement Res Gp

© CBD Research Ltd · Beckenham · BR3 5JS · Tel 020 8650 7745 · Fax 020 8650 0768 · E-mail cbd@cbdresearch.com · www.cbdresearch.com

MSSC	Marine Soc & Sea Cadets
MTA	Manufacturing Technologies Assn
	Marine Trs Assn
	Microwave Technologies Assn
MTA-UK	Mac Technology Assn
MU	Mothers' U
	Musicians' U
MUA	Machinery Users Assn
	Mail Users' Assn
MVDA	Motor Vehicle Dismantlers Assn
MVRA Ltd	MVRA Ltd
MVT	Military Vehicle Trust
MVWGS	Multi Vintage Wine Growers Soc
MWF	Medical Women's Fedn
MWSA	Mixed Wood-chip Suppliers Assn
MYA	Model Yachting Assn
MYCCI	Mid Yorkshire Cham Comm & Ind

N

N.A.G.	Nat Assn Goldsmiths
N.A.P.P.	Nat Assn Patient Participation
NA	Napoleonic Assn
NAA	Nat Arenas Assn
NAAC	Nat Assn Agricl Contrs
Naace	Naace
NAAIDT	Nat Assn Advisers... Design & Technology
NAAONB	Nat Assn Areas Outstanding Natural Beauty
NAAOSEN	Nat Assn Advy Officers Special Educational Needs
NAAPS	Nat Assn Adult Placement Services
NAAS	Nerine & Amaryllid Soc
NAB	Nat Assn Bookmakers Ltd
NABAS	NABAS
NABBA	Nat Amat Bodybuilders Assn
NABBC	Nat Assn Brass Band Conductors
NABCO	Nat Assn Bldg Co-ops [IRL]
NABD	Nat Assn Bikers Disability
NABIC	Nat Assn Bank & Insurance Customers
NABIM	Inc Nat Assn Brit & Ir Millers
NABMA	Nat Assn Brit Market Authorities
NABO	Nat Assn Boat Owners
NAC	Nat Assn Choirs
	Nat Assn Councillors
NACAB	Citizens Advice Bureaux
NACB	Nat Assn Catering Butchers
NACC	Nat Assn Care Catering
	Nat Assn Colitis & Crohn's Disease
NACCC	Nat Assn Child Contact Centres
NACE	Nat Assn Able Children in Educ
	Nat Assn Chimney Engrs
NACFB	Nat Assn Comml Finance Brokers
NACHO	Nat Assn Credit Hire Operators
NACHP	Nat Assn Counsellors, Hypnotherapists...
NACM	Nat Assn Cider Makers
NACMO	Nat Assn Cigarette Machine Operators
NACO	Nat Assn Caravan Owners
	Nat Assn Co-operative Officials
NACOA	Nat Assn Children Alcoholics
NACS	Nat Assn Chimney Sweeps
NACSA	Nat Assn Child Support Action
NACT	Nat Assn Clinical Tutors
NADA	Nat Acupuncture Detoxification Assn
NADFAS	Nat Assn Decorative & Fine Arts Socs
NADP	Nat Assn Deafened People
NAEA	Nat Assn Estate Agents
NAEE	Nat Assn Envtl Educ
NAEGA	NAEGA
NAESC	Nat Assn Educ Sick Children
NAFAC	Nat Assn Fisheries & Angling Consultatives
NAFAE	Nat Assn Fine Art Education
NAFAS	Nat Assn Flower Arrangement Socs
NAFBAE	Nat Assn Farriers...
NAFD	Nat Assn Funeral Directors
NAFIS	Nat Assn Family Inf Services
NAFLIC	Nat Assn Leisure Ind Certification

NAFO	Nat Assn Fire Officers
NAFSO	Nat Assn Field Studies Officers
NAG	Nat Acquisitions Gp
NAGALRO	NAGALRO
NAGC	Nat Assn Gifted Children
NAGS	Nat Assn NFU Gp Secretaries
NAHEMI	Nat Assn Higher Educ Moving Image
NAHFO	Nat Assn Healthcare Fire Officers
NAHG	Nat Assn Homeopathic Gps
NAHPS	Nat Assn Hospital Play Staff
NAHS	Nat Assn Health Stores
NAHT	Nat Assn Head Teachers
NAIPS	Nat Assn Investigators & Process Servers
NAKMAS	Nat Assn Karate & Martial Art Schools
NALA	Nat Assn Language Advisers
NALC	Nat Assn Ladies Circles
	Nat Assn Laryngectomee Clubs
	Nat Assn Local Couns
NALD	Nat Assn Literature Devt
NALEO	Nat Assn Licensing & Enforcement Offrs
NALGAO	Nat Assn Local Govt Arts Officers
NALI	Nat Assn Launderette Ind
NALOO	Nat Assn Licensed Opencast Operators
NALP	Nat Assn Licensed Paralegals
NAMA	Nat Assn Mathematics Advisers
NAMB	Nat Assn Master Bakers
NAME	Nat Assn Microwave Engrs
	Nat Assn Music Educators
NAMEM	Nat Assn Med Educ Mgt
NAMHO	Nat Assn Mining Hist Orgs
NAMIR	Nat Assn Musical Instrument Repairers
NAMLC	Nat Assn Master Letter Carvers
NAMM	Nat Assn Memorial Masons
NAMSS	Nat Assn Mgrs Student Services Colleges
NANS	Nat Assn Nappy Services
NAO	Nat Accordion Org
NAOMI	Nat Assn Ovulation Method Instructors
NAOPV	Nat Assn Official Prison Visitors
NAPA	Nat Acrylic Painters' Assn
	Nat Alcohol Producers Assn
	Nat Approved Premises Assn
	Nat Assn Press Agencies
	Nat Assn Providers Activities Older People
NAPAC	Nat Assn People Abused Childhood
NAPAS	Nat Assn Private Ambulance Services
NAPC	Nat Assn Primary Care
NAPCE	Nat Assn Pastoral Care Educ
	Nat Assn Primary Care Educators
NAPE	Nat Assn Primary Educ
NAPF	Nat Assn Pension Funds
NAPFP	Nat Assn Pre-Paid Funeral Plans
NAPGC	Nat Assn Public Golf Courses
NAPHR	Nat Assn Park Home Residents
NAPIT	Nat Assn Profl Inspectors & Testers
NAPLIB	Nat Assn Aerial Photographic Libraries
NAPLIC	Nat Assn Profls... Language Impairment Children
NAPM	Nat Assn Paper Mchts
NAPO	Nat Assn Probation Officers
NAPS	Nat Assn Premenstrual Syndrome
	Nat Auricula & Primula Soc (Mid & West)
NAPT	Nat Assn Percussion Teachers
NARA	NARA
NARC	Nat Assn Rly Clubs
NARES	Nat Assn Re-enactment Socs
NARHI	Nat Assn Registered Home Inspectors
NARM	Nat Assn Rooflight Mfrs
NARPD	Nat Assn Relief Paget's Disease
NARPO	Nat Assn Retired Police Officers
NARTM	Nat Assn Road Transport Museums
NAS	Nat Arabidopsis Soc
	Nat Assn Shopfitters
	Nat Autistic Soc
	Nautical Archaeology Soc
	Noise Abatement Soc
NASAA	Nat Assn Supporting Artistes Agents
NASC	Nat Access & Scaffolding Confedn
NASCH	Nat Assn Swimming Clubs H'capped
NASCR	Nat Assn Specialist Computer Retailers

NASDU	Nat Assn Security Dog Users	NCMD	Nat Coun Metal Detecting
nasen	nasen	NCNE	Nat Campaign Nursery Educ
NASGP	Nat Assn Sessional GP's	NCP	Nat Coun Psychotherapists
NASH	Nat Assn Support Victims Stalking & Harassment	NCPTA	Nat Confedn Parent-Teacher Assns
NASL	Brit Assn Sport & Law	NCS	Nat Chinchilla Soc
NASMAH	Nat Assn Screen Make-up Artists & Hairdressers		Nat Chrysanthemum Soc
NASO	Nat Adult School Org	NCT	Nat Childbirth Trust
NASPCS	Nat Advy Service Parents Children with a Stoma	NCU	Northern Cricket U Ireland
NASPM	Brit Potato Tr Assn	NCWA	Nat Childrenswear Assn
NASS	Nat Ankylosing Spondylitis Soc	NCWJ	Nat Campaign Water Justice
	Nat Assn Small Schools	ND	Nat Drama
	Nat Assn Stable Staff	NDA	Nurse Directors Assn
	Nat Assn Steel Stockholders	NDCCI	N Devon Cham Comm & Ind
NaStA	Nat Stallion Assn	NDCS	Nat Deaf Children's Soc
NASUWT	Nat Assn Schoolmasters U Women Teachers	NDFA	Nat Drama Festivals Assn
NASWE	Nat Assn Social Workers Educ	NDFTA	Nat Dried Fruit Tr Assn
NAT	Nat Assn Toastmasters	NDNA	Nat Day Nurseries Assn
NATD	Nat Assn Teachers Dancing	NDS	Nat Dahlia Soc
	Nat Assn Teaching Drama	NDTA	Nat Dance Teachers Assn
	Nat Assn Tripe Dressers	NDWA	Nat Dog Wardens Assn
NATE	Nat Assn Teaching Engl	NEA	Nat Energy Action
	Nat Assn Therapeutic Educ		Nat Exhibitors Assn
NATECLA	Nat Assn Teaching Engl &...Community Languages	NEAC	Nat Entertainment Agents Coun
		NEHS	N England Horticl Soc
NATLL	Nat Assn Toy & Leisure Libraries	NEIMME	N England Inst Mining & Mechanical Engrs
NATN	Assn Perioperative Practice	NEMA	Nat Early Music Assn
NATO	Nat Assn Tenants Orgs	NEMAL	Nat Egg Marketing Assn
	Nat Assn Tree Officers	NEMSA	N England Mule Sheep Assn
NATRE	Nat Assn Teachers Religious Educ	NEODA	Nat Edible Oil Distbrs Assn
NatSCA	Natural Sciences Collections Assn	NES	Nat Eczema Soc
NATT	Nat Assn Teachers Travellers		Nat Endometriosis Soc
NATTA	Network Alternative Technology &... Assessment	NFA	Nat Fedn Anglers
NAVA	Nat Assn Valuers & Auctioneers		Nat Fillings Assn
NAVCA	Nat Assn Voluntary & Community Action		Nat Fireplace Assn
NAVS	Nat Anti-Vivisection Soc		Non-Ferrous Alliance
NAVSM	Nat Assn Voluntary Service Mgrs	NFAS	Nat Field Archery Soc
NAW	Nat Assn Widows	NFBA	Nat Fedn Bridleway Assns
NAWB(A)	Nat Assn Wine & Beer Makers	NFBR	Nat Fedn Biological Recording
NAWC	Nat Assn Women's Clubs	NFBUK	Nat Fedn Blind
NAWCH	Action Sick Children	NFCF	Nat Fedn Cemetery Friends
NAWDO	Nat Assn Waste Disposal Officers	NFDC	Nat Fedn Demolition Contrs
NAWE	Nat Assn Writers in Educ	NFEA	Nat Fedn Enterprise Agencies
NAWG	Nat Assn Writers' Gps	NFEC	Nat Forum Engg Centres
NAWO	Nat Alliance Women's Orgs	NFER	Nat Foundation Educl Res E&W
NAWP	Nat Assn Women Pharmacists	NFF	Nat Fedn Fishmongers
NAYCEO	Nat Assn Youth & Community Educ Officers	NFFF	Nat Fedn Fish Friers
NAYD	Nat Assn Youth Drama [IRL]	NFFO	Nat Fedn Fishermen's Orgs
NAYJ	Nat Assn Youth Justice	NFG	Nat Fedn Glaziers
NAYO	Nat Assn Youth Orchestras	NFIWFM	Nat Fedn Inland Whls Fish Mchts
NAYT	Nat Assn Youth Theatres	NFM	Nat Family Mediation
NBA	Nat Beef Assn	NFPB&CS	New Forest Pony... & Cattle Soc
	Nat Bursars Assn	NFRC	Nat Fedn Roofing Contrs
NBC UK	Defence Mfrs Assn	NFRS	Nat Fancy Rat Soc
NBF	Nat Bed Fedn	NFS	Nat Fedn Shopmobility
NBGA	Nat Bingo Game Assn	NFSA	Nat Fedn Sea Anglers
NBS	Nat Begonia Soc	NFSH	Nat Fedn Spiritual Healers
NBTA	Nat Baton Twirling Assn	NFSP	Nat Fedn Sub-Postmasters
NBTA Scotland	Nat Baton Twirling Assn Scotland	NFTMMS	Nat Fedn Terrazzo, Marble & Mosaic Specialists
NBTVA	Narrow Bandwidth TV Assn	NFU	Nat Farmers U
NCA	Nat Campaign Arts	NFUS	NFU Scotland
	Nat Cancer Alliance	NFWI	Nat Fedn Women's Insts
	Nat Care Assn	NFWS	Nat Ferret Welfare Soc
	Nat Coun Aviculture		Nat Fox Welfare Soc
	Nat Courier Assn	NFYFC	Nat Fedn Young Farmers Clubs (E&W)
NCASS	Nationwide Caterers Assn	ngb2b	Newport & Gwent Cham Comm, Enterprise & Ind
NCC	Nat Caravan Coun	NGCAA	Nat Golf Clubs Advy Assn
	Nat Cavy Club	NGDA	Nat Game Dealers Assn
NCCA	Nat Carpet Cleaners Assn	NGLIS	Network Govt Library & Inf Specialists
NCCPG	Nat Coun Consvn Plants & Gardens	NGO	Nat Gamekeepers Org
NCDS	Nat Coun Divorced & Separated	NGRC	Nat Greyhound Racing Club
NCF	Nat Consumer Fedn	NGRS	Narrow Gauge Rly Soc
	Nat Cooperage Fedn	NGS	Nat Gardens Scheme Charitable Trust
NCFGB	Nat Crossbow Fedn		Nat Gerbil Soc
NCFS	Nat Campaign Firework Safety	NGSA	Nat Grammar Schools Assn
NCH	Nat Coun Hypnotherapy	NGVA	Natural Gas Vehicle Assn
NCIUA	Nat Cochlear Implant Users Assn	NH	Nat Heritage
NCLS	New Canterbury Literary Soc	NHA	Nat Hop Assn
NCMA	Nat Childminding Assn		Nautical Heritage Assn

© CBD Research Ltd · Beckenham · BR3 5JS · Tel 020 8650 7745 · Fax 020 8650 0768 · E-mail cbd@cbdresearch.com · www.cbdresearch.com

NHBS	Nat Horse Brass Soc
NHCCI	N Hampshire Cham Comm & Ind
NHCRA	Naval Histl Collectors & Res Assn
NHF	Nat Hairdressers Fedn
NHI	Nursing Homes Ireland
NHIC	Nat Home Improvement Coun
NHL	Nat Harmonica League
NHLS	Nat Hedgelaying Soc
NHSC	Nat Historic Ships
NHSN	Natural Hist Soc Northumbria
NHSTA	NHS Trusts Assn
NI	Nautical Inst
NIA	Nat Insulation Assn
	Nuclear Ind Assn
NIAB	NIAB
NIACE	Nat Inst Adult Continuing Educ (E&W)
NIACRO	NI Assn Care & Resettlement Offenders
NIACT	NI Assn Christian Teachers
NIACTA	NI Amusement Caterer's Tr Assn
NIAF	NI Athletic Fedn
NIAPA	NI Agricl Producers' Assn
NIAS	NI Archery Soc
NIASP	NI Assn Study Psychoanalysis
NIBG	NI Bat Gp
NICCI	NI Cham Comm & Ind
NICF	Nat Inst Carpet & Floorlayers
	NI Cycling Fedn
NICSA	NI Countryside Staff Assn
NICVA	NI Coun Voluntary Action
NIDS	NI Deer Soc
NIF	Nat Inf Forum
NIFA	Network Indep Forensic Accountants
NIFDA	NI Food & Drink Assn
NIFGA	NI Fruit Growers Assn
NIFHA	NI Fedn Housing Assns
NIGTA	NI Grain Tr Assn
NILGA	NI Local Govt Assn
NIMBA	NI Master Butchers Assn
NIMEA	NI Meat Exporters Assn
NIMH	Nat Inst Med Herbalists
NIMMA	NI Mixed Marriage Assn
NIMPA	NI Master Plumbers Assn
NINA	Netball NI
NIPBA	NI Potato Breeders Assn
NIPSA	NI Public Service Alliance
NISA	Nat Ice Skating Assn
	NI Shows Assn
	NISA Today's Holdings Ltd
NISO	Nat Ir Safety Org
NITTA	NI Timber Tr Assn
NIVA	NI Volleyball Assn
NIWAF	NI Women's Aid Fedn
NJF	Nat Jumblers Fedn
NJUG	Nat Jt Utilities Gp
NKA	Nat Karting Assn
NLA	Nat Landlords' Assn
	Nat Literacy Assn
NLHA	Nottinghamshire Local Hist Assn
NMC	Nat Motorcycle Coun
	Nat Mouse Club
NMES	Northern Mill Engine Soc
NMI	Nat Microelectronics Inst
NMRS	Northern Mine Res Soc
NMTF	Nat Market Traders Fedn
NNAC	Nat Network Assessment Centres
NNAS	Norfolk & Norwich Archaeol Soc
NNI	Nat Newspapers Ireland
NNS	Neonatal Soc
NO PANIC	Nat Org Phobias, Anxiety. . .Inf & Care
NO2ID	NO2ID
NOA	Nat Outsourcing Assn
NOAH	Nat Office Animal Health
NOBs	Nat Org Beaters & Pickers Up
NODA	Nat Operatic & Dramatic Assn
NOEA	Nat Outdoor Events Assn
NOF	Nat Obesity Forum
NOF Energy	NOF Energy
NOS	Nat Osteoporosis Soc

NOTA	Nat Org Treatment of Abusers
NPA	Nat Pawnbrokers Assn
	Nat Pharmacy Assn
	Nat Pig Assn
	Nat Pigeon Assn
	Nat Portage Assn
	Nat Portraiture Assn
	New Producers Alliance
	Newspaper Pubrs Assn
NPC	Nat Packaging Coun
	Nat Pensioners' Convention
NPFA	Nat Playing Fields Assn
NPHA	Nat Private Hire Assn
NPS	Nat Philatelic Soc
	Nat Phobics Soc
	Nat Piers Soc
	Nat Pony Soc
	Northumbrian Pipers' Society
NPS UK	Nail Patella Syndrome UK
NPTA	Nat Pest Technicians Assn
NPWA	Nat Pure Water Assn
NQA	Nat Quoits Assn
NRA	Nat Rifle Assn
	Nat Rounders Assn
NRAC	Nat Register Access Consultants
NRAS	Nat Rheumatoid Arthritis Soc
NRHA	Nat Roller Hockey Assn
NRHP	Nat Register Hypnotherapists & Psychotherapists
NRPT	Nat Register Personal Trainers
NRS	Navy Records Soc
	Norfolk Record Soc
NS	Nat Soc Painters, Sculptors & Printmakers
NSA	Nat Sewerage Assn
	Nat Sheep Assn
	Nat Sprint Assn
	Nuclear Stock Assn
NSALG	Nat Soc Allotment & Leisure Gardeners
NSARDA	Nat Search & Rescue Dog Assn
NSBA	Nat School Band Assn
NSCA	Natural Sausage Casings Assn
NSCC	Nat Specialist Contrs Coun
NSCCI	N Staffs Cham Comm & Ind
NSE	Nat Soc Epilepsy
NSEAD	Nat Soc Educ in Art & Design
NSI	Nat Security Inspectorate
NSMT	Nat Soc Master Thatchers
NSPCC	Nat Soc Prevention Cruelty to Children
NSPH	Nat Soc Profl Hypnotherapists
NSPKU	Nat Soc Phenylketonuria
NSPP	Nat Soc Promotion Punctuality
NSPS	Nat Sweet Pea Soc
NSRA	Nat Small-Bore Rifle Assn
	Nat Soc Res Allergy
NSS	Nat Secular Soc
NSSF	Nat Small Schools Forum
NSVA	Nat Street Van Assn
NTA	Nat Taxi Assn
	Nat Trolleybus Assn
NTDA	Nat Tyre Distbrs Assn
NTF	Nat Trainers Fedn
NTS	Nat Trust Scotland
NTTA	Nat Trailer & Towing Assn
NUJ	Nat U Journalists
NUM	Nat U Mineworkers
NUMA	Needleloom Underlay Mfrs' Assn
NURA	Nat U Residents' Assns
NUS	Nat U Students UK
NUT	Nat U Teachers
NUTFA	New Under Ten Fishermen's Assn
NVS	Nat Vegetable Soc
NVTEC	Nat Vintage Tractor & Engine Club
NWA	NWA
NWLCC	N W Lond Cham Comm
	N & Wstn Lancs Cham Comm
NWMRCA	N Wstn Model Rly Clubs Assn
NWR	Nat Women's Register
NWT	Norfolk Wildlife Trust
NWTEC	Nat Wool Textile Expt Corpn

NWTTA	N W Timber Tr Assn
NYCGB	Nat Youth Choirs GB
NYCI	Nat Youth Coun Ireland
NYMR	N York Moors Hist Rly Trust

O

OA	Officers' Assn
	Overeaters Anonymous
OAA	Obstetric Anaesthetists Assn
	Outdoor Advertising Assn
OAHS	Oxfordshire Architectural & Hist Soc
OATA	Ornamental Aquatic Tr Assn
OBCofGB	Old Bottle Club
OCA	Offshore Contrs' Assn
	Open Canoe Assn
OCCA	Oil & Colour Chemists Assn
OCS	Oriental Ceramic Soc
OCSG	Open Canoe Sailing Gp
ODA	Offa's Dyke Assn
ODS	Owner Drivers Soc
ODSBA	Oxford Down Sheep Breeders Assn
OEDA	Occupational & Envtl Diseases Assn
OEMSA	Optical Eqpt Mfrs & Suppliers Assn
OES	Offshore Engg Soc
OEUK	Optra Exhibitions UK
OFF	Organic Food Fedn
OFIMA	Optical Frame Importers' & Mfrs' Assn
OFTEC	Oil Firing Technical Assn Petroleum Ind
OILC	Offshore Ind Liaison C'ee
OLMADA	Ophthalmic Lens Mfrs' & Distrbrs' Assn
OLS	Ocean Liner Soc
OMRS	Orders & Medals Res Soc
OPA	Occupational Pensioners Alliance
OPFS	One Parent Families Scotland
OPKA	Original Pearly Kings & Queens Assn
OPMA	Overseas Press & Media Assn
OPSCS	Observers Pocket Series Collectors' Soc
OPSIS	Nat Assn Educ, Training... Blind... People
OPT	Optimum Population Trust
OPTIC (UK)	Ophthalmological Prods Tr & Ind Conf
ORA	Oil Recycling Assn
ORS	Oxfordshire Record Soc
ORSoc	Operational Res Soc
OS	Omnibus Soc
	Ordnance Soc
OSB	Oxford Sandy & Black Pig Soc
OSCA	Onsite Communications Association
	Osteopathic Sports Care Assn
OSGB	Orchid Soc
OSMA	On Site Massage Assn
OSME	Ornithological Soc Middle East
OSS	Outdoor Swimming Soc
OTA	Offenders Tag Assn
	Orthodontic Technicians Assn
OUAS	Oxford University Archaeol Soc
OVW	One Voice Wales
OWC	Order Woodcraft Chivalry
OWG	Outdoor Writers' & Photographers' Gld
OWS	Oscar Wilde Soc

P

P&SEHCC&I	Portsmouth & S E Hampshire Cham Comm...
P&SS	Pike & Shot Soc
PA	Politics Assn
	Protestant Alliance
	Publishers Assn
PAA	Paper Agents Assn
	Profl Anglers Assn
PAAT	Profl Assn Alexander Teachers
PACE	PACE: Profl Assn Catering Educ

PACT	Prison Advice & Care Trust
	Producers Alliance Cinema & TV
PADS	People & Dogs Soc
PAGB	Photographic Alliance
	Proprietary Assn
PALS	Profl Assn Legal Services
PalSoc	Palaeontographical Soc
PAN UK	Pesticide Action Network
PAPA	Pizza, Pasta & Italian Food Assn
PAPAA	Psoriasis & Psoriatic Arthritis Alliance
PARN	Profl Assns Res Network
PAS	Pembrokeshire Agricl Soc
	Percussive Arts Soc
	Perthshire Agricl Soc
PASM	Proprietary Acoustic Systems Mfrs
PASMA	Prefabricated Access Suppliers' & Mfrs' Assn
Path Society	Pathological Soc
PBA	Profl Bodyguard Assn
PBFA	Provincial Booksellers Fairs Assn
PBGA	Pre Basic Growers Association
PBIF	Plastics & Board Inds Fedn
PBS	Prayer Book Soc
PBSA	Pony Breeders Shetland Assn
PBTM	Profl Business & Technical Mgt
PcA	Permaculture Assn
PCA	Profl Charter Assn
	Profl Computing Assn
	Profl Cricketers' Assn
	Property Care Assn
PCAM	Soc Producers & Composers Applied Music
PCC	Paperweight Collectors Circle
	Perthshire Cham Comm
PCCGB	Photographic Collectors' Club
PCCI	Plymouth Cham Comm & Ind
PCDS	Primary Care Dermatology Soc
PCFA	Profl Coarse Fisheries Assn
PCG	Profl Contrs Gp
PCGB	Poultry Club
PCL	Publicity Club Lond
PCS	Penguin Collectors' Soc
	Property Consultants Soc
	Public & Comml Services U
PDA	Pump Distbrs Assn
PDMHS	Peak District Mines Hist Soc
PDPA	Profl Darts Players Assn
PDS	Parkinson's Disease Soc
PDSG	Pick's Disease Support Gp
PEBA	Planning & Environment Bar Assn
PEC	Plain Engl Campaign
PELS	Locomotive 6201 Princess Elizabeth Soc
PESGB	Petroleum Exploration Soc
PETMA	Portable Electric Tool Mfrs Assn
PETS	Pre Eclampsia Soc
PF	Packaging Fedn
	Pagan Fedn
PFA	Power Fastenings Assn
	Profl Footballers Assn
PFA Scotland	Profl Footballers' Assn Scotland
PFAA	Paediatric First Aid Assn
PFEW	Police Fedn England & Wales
PFMA	Pet Food Mfrs Assn
PFNI	Police Fedn NI
PFPF	Passive Fire Protection Fedn
PFRA	Public Fundraising Regulatory Assn
PFS	Palmerston Forts Soc
	Personal Finance Soc
PFSS	Pet Fostering Service Scotland
PGA	Prison Governors Assn
PGDT	Pressure Gauge & Dial Thermometer Assn
PGG	Profl Gardeners' Gld
PGRO	Processors & Growers Res Org
PGS	Percy Grainger Society
PHA	Pullet Hatcheries Assn
	Pulmonary Hypertension Assn
PHC	Pet Health Coun
PHS	Pembrokeshire Histl Soc
PhS	Philosophical Soc England

© CBD Research Ltd · Beckenham · BR3 5JS · Tel 020 8650 7745 · Fax 020 8650 0768 · E-mail cbd@cbdresearch.com · www.cbdresearch.com

PHS	Plastics Histl Soc
	Police Hist Soc
	Postal Hist Soc
	Printing Histl Soc
PHSA	Provincial Hospital Services Assn
PHSI	Presbyterian Hist Soc Ireland
PHSS	Pharmaceutical & Healthcare Sciences Soc
PiA	Primary Immunodeficiency Assn
PIBA	Personal Injuries Bar Assn
PIC	Photo Imaging Coun
PICA GB	Police Insignia Collectors Assn
PICON	Picon Ltd
PiF	Patient Inf Forum
PIFA	Packaging & Indl Films Assn
PIG	Pipeline Inds Gld
PIPA	Pharmaceutical Inf & Pharmacovigilance Assn
PISUKI	Pacific Islands Soc
PITA	Paper Ind Technical Assn
PJA	Pipe Jacking Assn
	Profl Jockeys Assn
PLA	Pre-School Learning Alliance
	Private Libraries Assn
PLASA	Profl Lighting & Sound Assn
PLS	Philip Larkin Soc
	Publishers Licensing Soc
Plus	Nat Fedn Plus Areas
PMA	Personal Mgrs Assn
	Probation Mgrs Assn
PMATA	Paper Makers' Allied Trs Assn
PMC	Printmakers Coun
PMI	Pensions Mgt Inst
PMMDA	Polymer Machinery Mfrs & Distbrs Assn
PMMMA	Pattern, Model & Mould Manufacturers Association
PMMS	Plainsong & Mediæval Music Soc
PMNHS	Porcupine Marine Natural Hist Soc
PMPA	Public Mgt & Policy Assn
PMSA	Public Monuments & Sculpture Assn
PNFS	Peak & Nthn Footpaths Soc
POA	Pinball Owners Assn
	POA
Ponies(UK)	Ponies Assn
Pony Club	Pony Club
POVC	Post Office Vehicle Club
PPA	Periodical Pubrs Assn
	Play Providers Assn
	Pool Promoters Assn
	Potato Processors Assn
PPAi	Periodical Pubrs Assn - Interactive
PPF	Profl Players Fedn
PPG	Player Piano Gp
PPI	Phonographic Performance (Ireland)
PPL	Phonographic Performance
PPLA	Profl Photographic Laboratories Assn
PPMA	Processing & Packaging Machinery Assn
	Public Sector People Mgrs' Assn
PPORA	Point-to-Point Owners & Riders Assn
PPSA	Pigging Products & Services Assn
PPU	Peace Pledge U
PPUG	Profl Plant Users Gp
PRA	Paint Res Assn
	Picture Res Assn
	Pony Riders Assn
	Premium Rate Assn
	Profl Rugby Players Assn
	Psychiatric Rehabilitation Assn
	Pullet Rearers Assn
PRCA	Public Relations Consultants Assn
	Public Relations Consultants Assn [IRL]
Premsoc	Premenstrual Soc
PRESSBOF	Press Standards Bd Finance
PRFA	Pop & Rock Fans' Assn
PRFSS	Peterborough R Foxhound Show Soc
PRII	Public Relations Inst Ireland
PRS	Pre-Raphaelite Soc
	Protestant Reformation Soc
PS	Poetry Soc
PSA	Personal Safety Assn
	Political Studies Assn

	Production Services Assn
	Profl Speakers Assn
	Prostate Cancer Support Assn
PSANI	Superintendents' Assn NI
PSGB	Primate Soc
PSI	Statisticians Pharmaceutical Ind
PSnet	Public Services Network
PSNI	Pharmaceutical Soc NI
PSNS	Perthshire Soc Natural Science
PSOA	Permanent Show Organisers Assn
PSPA	Photoluminescent Safety Products Assn
PSPS	Paddle Steamer Presvn Soc
PSS	Partially Sighted Soc
PTA	Performance Textiles Assn
	Pianoforte Tuners' Assn
	Post Tensioning Assn
	Postcard Traders' Assn
PTF	Provision Tr Fedn
PTG	Ports & Terminals Gp
PTS	Pali Text Soc
	Philatelic Traders Soc
	Protestant Truth Soc
PUMPA	Purine Metabolic Patients Assn
PVGA	Processed Vegetable Growers Assn
PWF	Private Wagon Fedn
PWI	Permanent Way Instn
PWSA (UK)	Prader-Willi Syndrome Assn

Q

Q butchers	Gld Q Butchers
QBC	Quality Brit Celery Assn
QCA	Quoted Companies Alliance
QES	Queen's Engl Soc
QG	Quality Gld
QMC	Quekett Microscopical Club
QMS	Quality Meat Scotland
QNI	Queen's Nursing Inst
QPA	Quarry Products Assn
QRA UK	Quad Racing Assn
Quakers	Religious Society of Friends (Quakers)
QuiTE	Assn Promotion Quality TESOL Educ

R

R&A	R & Ancient Golf Club
R&CHS	Rly & Canal Histl Soc
R&D	Res & Devt Soc
R3	Assn Business Recovery Profls
RA	R Academy Arts
	Radionic Association Ltd
	Ramblers' Assn
	Retreat Assn
	Rice Assn
RABDF	R Assn Brit Dairy Farmers
RAD	R Academy Dance
	R Assn Deaf People
RADA	R Academy Dramatic Art
RADAR	R Assn Disability & Rehabilitation
Radius	Religious Drama Soc
RAEng	R Academy Engg
RAeS	R Aeronautical Soc
RAFA	R Air Forces Assn
RAFHS	R Air Force Histl Soc
RAFT	River Assn Freight & Transport
RAI	R Anthropological Inst
	R Archaeol Inst
RAM	R Academy Music
RAS	R Asiatic Soc
	R Astronomical Soc
RASC	R Agricl Soc C'wealth
RASE	R Agricl Soc England
RATD	Register Apparel & Textile Designers

RBA	Refined Bitumen Assn
	Retail Book, Stationery... Employees Assn
	Retail Bridalwear Assn
RBCC	Russo-Brit Cham Comm
RBLS	R Brit Legion Scotland
RBOA	Residential Boat Owners Assn
RBS	R Botanical & Horticl Soc Munich
	R Brit Soc Sculptors
RBSA	R Birmingham Soc Artists
RBST	Rare Breeds Survival Trust
RCA	R Cambrian Academy Art
	Racecourse Assn
	Rural Crafts Assn
RCAA	R Cornwall Agricl Assn
RCCC	R Caledonian Curling Club
RCCGB	Roller Coaster Club
RCGP	R Coll Gen Practitioners
RCHM	Register Chinese Herbal Medicine
RCHS	R Caledonian Horticl Soc
RCM	R Coll Midwives
RCN	R Coll Nursing
RCO	R Coll Organists
RCOG	R Coll Obstetricians & Gynaecologists
RCP	R Coll Physicians Lond
RCPath	R Coll Pathologists
RCPCH	R Coll Paediatrics & Child Health
RCPE	R Coll Physicians Edinburgh
RCPSGlasg	R Coll Physicians & Surgeons Glasgow
RCPsych	R Coll Psychiatrists
RCS	R Choral Soc
	R Coll Surgeons England
RCSEd	R Coll Surgeons Edinburgh
RCSI	R Coll Surgeons Ireland
RCSLT	R Coll Speech & Language Therapists
RCTA	Retail Confectioners & Tobacconists Assn
RCTS	Rly Correspondence & Travel Soc
RCVS	R Coll Veterinary Surgeons
RDS	R Dublin Soc
	Res Defence Soc
	Rly Devt Soc
RE	R Soc Painter-Printmakers
REA	Renewable Energy Assn
	Rhea & Emu Assn
REACH	REACH - Assn Children with Hand or Arm Deficiency
REAL	Road Emulsion Assn
REC	Recruitment & Employment Confedn
RedR	RedR UK
Regia	Regia Anglorum
REHIS	R Envtl Health Inst Scotland
REMA	BEAMA
	Retroreflective Eqpt Mfrs Assn
REntSoc	R Entomological Soc Lond
RES	R Economic Soc
RETRA	Radio, Electrical & TV Retailers' Assn
RFA	Rugby Fives Assn
RFBS	Ryeland Flock Book Soc
RFG	Rail Freight Gp
RFL	Rugby Football League
RFPG	R Fac Procurators in Glasgow
RFS	R Forestry Soc England, Wales & NI
	Robert Farnon Soc
RFSBA	Rough Fell Sheep Breeders Assn
RFU	Rugby Football U
RGA	Remote Gambling Assn
	Restricted Growth Assn
RGDATA	RGDATA [IRL]
RGI	Royal Glasgow Institute of the Fine Arts
RGS-IBG	R Geographical Soc
RHA	Road Haulage Assn
RHASS	R Highland & Agricl Soc Scotland
RHET	R Highland Educ Trust
RHistS	R Histl Soc
RHS	R Horticl Soc
	R Humane Soc
	Rider Haggard Soc
RHSI	R Horticl Soc Ireland
RI	R Instn GB

RIA	R Ir Academy
	Rly Ind Assn
	Roofing Ind Alliance
RIAC	R Ir Automobile Club
RIAI	R Inst Architects Ireland
RIAM	R Ir Academy Music
RIAS	R Incorporation Architects Scotland
RIBA	R Inst Brit Architects
RIC	R Instn Cornwall
RICA	Rail Ind Contrs Assn
RICS	R Instn Chart Surveyors
RIDBA	Rural & Indl Design & Bldg Assn
RIG	Remote Imaging Group
RIIA	R Inst Intl Affairs
RIN	R Inst Navigation
RINA	R Instn Naval Architects
RIPTA	Register Indep Profl Turfgrass Agronomists
RISW	R Instn S Wales
RIWAS	R Isle of Wight Agrl Soc
RJA&HS	R Jersey Agricl & Horticl Soc
RLAS	R Lancashire Agricl Soc
RLS	Road Locomotive Soc
RLS Club	Robert Louis Stevenson Club
RLSS UK	R Life Saving Soc
RLUK	RLUK
RMA	R Musical Assn
	Retread Mfrs Assn
RMCU	R Martyr Church U
RMetS	R Meteorological Soc
RMI	Retail Motor Ind Fedn
RMS	R Medical Soc
	R Microscopical Soc
	R Soc Miniature Painters ...
	Records Mgt Soc
RMT	Rail, Maritime & Transport U
RNA	R Naval Assn
	Romantic Novelists Assn
RNAA	R Norfolk Agricl Assn
RNAI	Regional Newspapers Assn Ireland
RNAS	R Nthn Agricl Soc
RNBWS	R Naval Bird Watching Soc
RNES	R Navy Enthusiasts' Soc
RNHA	Registered Nursing Home Assn
RNIB	R Nat Inst Blind
RNID	RNID
RNLI	R Nat Lifeboat Instn
RNRS	R Nat Rose Soc
RNS	R Numismatic Soc
ROA	Racehorse Owners Assn
ROOM	ROOM RTPI
ROSECARPE	N England Rosecarpe Horticl Soc
ROSL	R Over-Seas League
RoSPA	R Soc Prevention Accidents
ROW	Rights of Women
RPA	Rationalist Assn
RPAS	Restaurant Property Advisors Soc
RPRA	R Pigeon Racing Assn
RPS	R Philharmonic Soc
	R Photographic Soc
	Rare Poultry Soc
RPSG	R Philosophical Soc Glasgow
RPSGB	R Pharmaceutical Soc
RPSI	Rly Presvn Soc Ireland
RPSL	R Philatelic Soc Lond
RR	Railway Ramblers
RRA	Road Records Assn
	Road Roller Assn
RRC	Road Runners Club
RRRA	Road Rescue Recovery Assn
RRTHA	Roads & Road Transport Hist Assn
RSA	R Scot Academy
	R Soc ... Arts
	Refined Sugar Assn
	Regional Studies Assn
	Residential Sprinkler Associates
	Rett Syndrome Assn
	Rly Study Assn
	Rural Shops Alliance

© CBD Research Ltd · Beckenham · BR3 5JS · Tel 020 8650 7745 · Fax 020 8650 0768 · E-mail cbd@cbdresearch.com · www.cbdresearch.com

RSAI	R Soc Antiquaries Ireland	SACRO	SACRO
RSAMD	R Scot Academy Music & Drama	SACS	Scot Assn Country Sports
RSAS	R Surgical Aid Soc	SACU	Scot Auto Cycle U
RSAW	R Soc Architects Wales		Soc Anglo-Chinese Understanding
RSC	R Soc Chemistry	SADA	SAD Assn
RSCDS	R Scot Country Dance Soc	SAE-UK	Soc Automotive Engrs
RSCM	R School Church Music	SAEMA	Specialist Access Engg & Maintenance Assn
RSCTA	Rough & Smooth Collie Training Assn	SAFA	Scot Amat Football Assn
RSE	R Soc Edinburgh	SAFE	SAFE
RSFS	R Scot Forestry Soc	SAFEA	Sports & Fitness Eqpt Assn
RSGB	Radio Soc GB	SAFed	Safety Assessment Fedn
RSGS	R Scot Geographical Soc	SAFHS	Scot Assn Family Hist Socs
RSL	R Soc Literature	SAGB	Shellfish Assn
RSM	R Soc Medicine		Silk Assn
	R Soc Musicians		Skibob Assn
RSMA	Road Safety Markings Assn		Spiritualist Assn
RSMG	Rubber Stamp Mfrs' Gld	SAGBNI	Sportsman's Assn
RSPB	R Soc Protection Birds	SAGGA	Scout & Guide Graduate Assn
RSPBA	R Scot Pipe Band Assn	SAGSET	Soc Advancement Games & Simulations Educ &
RSPCA	R Soc Prevention Cruelty Animals		Training
RSPH	R Soc Public Health	SAGT	Scot Assn Geography Teachers
RSPSoc	Remote Sensing & Photogrammetry Soc	SAGTA	Soil & Groundwater Technology Assn
RSS	R Statistical Soc	SAH	Soc Automotive Historians
	Ronald Stevenson Soc	SAHAAS	Saint Albans & Hertfordshire Architectural. . . Soc
RSSA	R Scot Soc Arts (Science & Technology)	SAHGB	Soc Architectural Historians
RSSS	R S Surtees Soc	SAHR	Soc Army Histl Res
RSTA	Road Surface Treatments Assn	SAHS	Shropshire Archaeol & Histl Soc
RSTM&H	R Soc Tropical Medicine & Hygiene		Staffordshire Archaeol. . .Soc
RSUA	R Soc Ulster Architects	SAI	Soc Architectural Illustration
RSW	R Scot Soc Painters in Water Colours	SAIF	Nat Soc Allied & Indep Funeral Directors
RSWT	R Soc Wildlife Trusts	SALC	Scot Assn Law Centres
RTA	Rural Theology Assn	SALSC	Scot Assn Local Sports Couns
RTA Ltd	Racehorse Transporters Assn	SAM	Scot Assn Metals
RTBI	Nat Assn Round Tables	SAMA	Scot Amat Music Assn
RTCS	Round Tower Churches Soc	SAMB	Scot Assn Master Bakers
RTPI	R Town Planning Inst	SAME	Scot Assn Music Educ
RTS	R Television Soc	SAMH	Scot Assn Mental Health
	River Thames Soc	SAMS	Scot Assn Marine Science
RUA	R Ulster Academy Arts	SAMSA	Silica & Moulding Sands Assn
RUAS	R Ulster Agricl Soc	SAMW	Scot Assn Meat Whlsrs
RUF	Refractory Users Federation	SAN	Sonic Arts Network
RUI	Resource Use Inst	SANA	Scot Anglers Nat Assn
RUKBA	R UK Beneficent Assn	SANDS	Stillbirth & Neonatal Death Soc
RURAL	Soc Responsible Use Resources Agriculture & Land	SANE	SANE
RUSI	R Utd Services Inst Defence. . . Studies	SANHS	Somerset Archaeol & Natural Hist Soc
RVA	Residential Ventilation Assn	SANT	Soc Antiquaries Newcastle upon Tyne
	Returned Volunteer Action	SAOL	Sugar Assn Lond
RWA	Rabbit Welfare Assn	SAOS	Scot Agricl Org Soc
	Race Walking Assn	SAP	Soc Applied Philosophy
RWAS	R Welsh Agricl Soc	SAPCA	Sports & Play Construction Assn
RWS	R Watercolour Soc	SAPCT	Scot Assn Painting Craft Teachers
RYA	R Yachting Assn	SAPERE	SAPERE
RYAS	R Yachting Assn Scotland	SAPT	Scot Assn Public Transport
RZSS	Royal Zoological Society of Scotland	SARA	Scot Amat Rowing Assn
		SARS	Soc Academic & Res Surgery
		SAS	Surfers against Sewage

S

		SASA	Scot Swimming
		SASDA	Scot Assn Speech & Drama Adjudicators
		SASH	Scot Assn Spiritual Healers
		SASLI	Scot Assn Sign Language Interpreters
S&TA	Salmon & Trout Assn	SASO	Scot Assn Study Offending
S2C2	Scot Soc Contamination Control	SASS	Sir Arthur Sullivan Soc
SA	Salt Assn	SATA	Sleep Apnoea Trust Assn
	Schoolwear Assn	SATIPS	SATIPS
	Scot Athletics	SAUK	Scoliosis Assn
	Sexaholics Anonymous	SAVE	Save Britain's Heritage
SAA	Scot Aeromodellers Assn	SAYFC	Scot Assn Young Farmers Clubs
	Scot Archery Assn	SBA	Sailing Barge Assn
	Scot Assessors' Assn		Scot Beekeepers Assn
	Soc Archer-Antiquaries		Scot Bowling Assn
	Soc Artists' Agents		Soc Botanical Artists
	Specialist Anglers Alliance		Steam Boat Assn
	Sub-Aqua Assn	SBAC	Soc Brit Aerospace Cos
	Suffolk Agricl Assn	SBAS	Staffordshire & Birmingham Agricl Soc
SAAA	Scot Agricl Arbiters Assn	SBBA	Scot Brass Band Assn
SAAD	Soc Advancement Anaesthesia Dentistry	SBBA (WISE)	Straw Bale Bldg Assn
SABRITA	Brit Cham Business Sthn Africa	SBC	Scot Business Community
SACGB	Shark Angling Club	SBCA	Scot Bldg Contrs Assn

SBE	Soc Business Economists
SBGI	SBGI
SBHS	Strict Baptist Histl Soc
SBNS	Soc Brit Neurological Surgeons
SBP	Soc Business Practitioners
SBPA	Scot Beer & Pub Assn
SBS	Songbird Survival
SBTD	Soc Brit Theatre Designers
SBU	Scot Badminton U
SBWWI	Soc Brit Water & Wastewater Inds
SC	Scot Cycling
SCA	Scot Canoe Assn
	Scot Croquet Assn
	Smoke Control Assn
	Social Care Assn
	Specialist Cheesemakers' Assn
	Sprayed Concrete Assn
SCAG	Gld Stunt & Action Coordinators
SCALA	Scala
SCAS	Soc Companion Animal Studies
	Surrey County Agricl Soc
SCATA	Soc Computing & Technology Anaesthesia
SCB	Speedway Control Bd
SCBA	Shetland Cattle Breeders' Assn
SCC	Small Charities Coalition
	Soc Cheese Connoisseurs
SCCI	Sheffield Cham Comm & Ind
	Solihull Cham Comm & Ind
SCDA	Scot Community Drama Assn
SCDI	Scot Coun Devt & Ind
SCEME	Soc Electrical & Mechanical Engrs
SCF	Scot Crofting Foundation
SCGB	Satellite & Cable Broadcasters' Gp
SCHA	Scot Catholic Histl Assn
SCHC	Soc Coat Hook Collectors
SCHHA	Southern Counties Heavy Horse Assn
SCHVPT	Southern Counties Historic Vehicle Presvn Trust
SCI	Soc Chemical Ind
	Steel Construction Inst
SCL	Soc Chief Librarians
	Soc Computers & Law
	Soc Construction Law
SCLF	Scot Contaminated Land Forum
SCMA	Scot Childminding Assn
	Stilton Cheese Makers Assn
SCNP	Scot Coun Nat Parks
SCO	Scot C'ee Optometrists
SCOD	Scot Coun Deafness
SCoFF	Southern Counties Folk Fedn
Scolag	Scot Legal Action Gp
ScOPT	Scot Org Practice Teaching
ScotSAC	Scot Sub Aqua Club
SCOTSS	Soc Chief Officers Trading Standards Scotland
ScottishSPCA	Scot Soc Prevention Cruelty Animals
ScotWays	Scot Rights Way & Access Soc
SCP	Soc Chiropodists & Podiatrists
	Soc Clinical Psychiatrists
SCPA	Scot Cashmere Producers Assn
SCPC	Soc Crisp Packet Collectors
SCQS	Soc Construction & Quantity Surveyors
SCRA	Scot Countryside Rangers' Assn
SCREAMS	Soc Campaigning Removal Exasperating Automated Switchboards
SCRSS	Soc Cooperation Russian & Soviet Studies
SCS	Seal Consvn Soc
	Soc Chart Surveyors [IRL]
	Soc Cosmetic Scientists
	UK Soc Co-operative Studies
SCSH	Scot Coun Single Homeless
SCST	Soc Cardiological Science & Technology
SCT	Soc County Treasurers [E&W]
SCTA	Scot Clay Target Assn
	Scot Corn Tr Assn
SCTE	Soc Cable Telecommunication Engrs
SCTS	Soc Cardiothoracic Surgery
SCVO	Scot Coun Voluntary Orgs
SDA	Scot Darts Assn
	Scurry Driving Assn

SDC	Soc Designer Craftsmen
	Soc Dyers & Colourists
SDCC	S Devon Cham Comm
SDCCGB	Square Dance Callers Club
SDEA	Shop & Display Eqpt Assn
SDF	Scot Decorators Fedn
	Self Defence Fedn
SDHBS	S Devon Herd Book Soc
SDMA	Surgical Dressings Mfrs Assn
SDNS	Scot Daily Newspaper Soc
SDR	Soc Dance Res
SDS	S Downs Soc
	Scot Disability Sport
SDSA	Sudden Death Support Assn
SDT	Soc Dairy Technology
SDTA	Scot Dance Teachers Alliance
SEA	Scot Esperanto Assn
	Soc Equestrian Artists
	Surface Engg Assn
SEAMA	Small Electrical Appliance Marketing Assn
SEAS	S England Agricl Soc
SEB	Soc Experimental Biology
SEBDA	SEBDA
SEC	Soc Educ Consultants
SEC group	Specialist Engg Contrs Gp
SECCI	Scot Emplrs Coun Clay Inds
SECED	Soc Earthquake & Civil Engg Dynamics
SEDA	Scot Ecological Design Assn
	Staff & Educl Devt Assn
SEE	Soc Envtl Engrs
SEMA	Storage Eqpt Mfrs Assn
SEMPRE	Soc Educ Music & Psychology Res
SERA	Scot Educl Res Assn
	Socialist Envt & Resources Assn
SES	Scientific Exploration Soc
	Scot Economic Soc
SEW	Soc Expert Witnesses
SFA	Scot Football Assn
	Small Farms Assn
	Small Firms Assn [IRL]
	Solid Fuel Assn
SFAA	Scot Field Archery Assn
Sfam	Soc Applied Microbiology
SFC	Sexual Freedom Coalition
SFCCI	Southampton & Fareham Cham Comm & Ind
SFDF	Scot Food & Drink Fedn
SfEP	Soc Editors & Proofreaders
SFF	Scot Fishermen's Fedn
SFG	Scot Freshwater Gp
SFGB	Stone Fedn
SFHA	Scot Fedn Housing Assns
SFL	Scot Football League
SFMTA	Scot Fedn Meat Traders Assns
SFO	Scot Fishermen's Org
SfP	Sing for Pleasure
SFRMA	Synthetic Fibre Rug, Mat & Carpet Assn
SFS	Soc French Studies
SfS	Soc Storytelling
SFSA	Scot Fedn Sea Anglers
	Scot Field Studies Assn
SFTA	Scot Food Trs Assn
SFTAH	Autism Indep UK
SGA	Scot Gamekeepers Assn
	Scot Games Assn
	Scot Gymnastics Assn
SGD	Soc Garden Designers
SGF	Scot Grocers' Fedn
SGFA	Soc Graphic Fine Art
SGIA	Sporting Goods Ind Assn
SGM	Soc Gen Microbiology
SGPP	Soc Garlic Growers, Processors & Packers
SGR	Scientists Global Responsibility
SGT	Soc Glass Technology
SGTS	Scot Gaelic Texts Soc
SGU	Scot Gliding U
	Scot Golf U
SGVCC	Soc Greeting Card Collectors
SGWDA	Sliding Glass Window Distrbrs Assn

© CBD Research Ltd · Beckenham · BR3 5JS · Tel 020 8650 7745 · Fax 020 8650 0768 · E-mail cbd@cbdresearch.com · www.cbdresearch.com

SHA	Scot Handball Assn	SLTA	Scot Licensed Tr Assn
	Soc Heraldic Arts	SLTC	Soc Leather Technologists & Chemists
	Socialist Health Assn	SM&EE	Soc Model & Experimental Engrs
SHAC	Soc Hist Alchemy & Chemistry	SMA	Schools Music Assn
SHAPA	Solids Handling & Processing Assn		Soc Medieval Archaeology
SHAPS	Spotted Horse & Pony Soc		Soc Museum Archaeologists
SHB(GB)	Sport Horse Breeding		Soc Music Analysis
SHBA	Scotch Half Bred Assn		Sports Massage Assn
SHCG	Social Hist Curators Gp		Stage Mgt Assn
SHEDA	Storage & Handling Eqpt Distbrs Assn	SMAE	SMAE Fellowship
SHEPS	Soc Health Educ & … Specialists	SMDSA	Sanitary Med Disposal Services Assn
SHIP	Safe Home Income Plans	SMH&VTS	Scot Music Hall & Variety Theatre Soc
SHLSLM	Soc Hospital Linen Service & Laundry Mgrs	SMIRA	Selective Mutism Inf & Res Assn
SHMIS	Soc Headmasters & Headmistresses Indep Schools	SMMT	Soc Motor Mfrs & Traders
SHNH	Soc Hist Natural Hist	SMR	Soc Medicines Res
SHPF	Scot Hang Gliding & Paragliding Fedn	SMRC	Scot Motor Racing Club
SHS	Scot Hist Soc	SMS	Soc Model Shipwrights
	Shire Horse Soc	SMS/SPS	Stiff Man Syndrome Support Gp
	Social Hist Soc	SMSRTA	Scot Master Slaters & Roof Tilers Assn
SHU	Scot Hockey U	SMTA	Scot Motor Tr Assn
	Scot Homing U		Sewing Machine Tr Assn
SI	Soc Indexers	SMTO	Scot Massage Therapists Org
SIA	Solvents Ind Assn	SMWBA	Scot Master Wrights & Builders Assn
	Spinal Injuries Assn	SMWS	Scotch Malt Whisky Soc
	Stove Industry Alliance	SNACMA	Snack, Nut & Crisp Mfrs Assn
	Suffolk Inst Archaeology & Hist	SNAD	Soc Numismatic Artists & Designers
SIAA	Scot Indep Advocacy Alliance	SNFWB	Scot Nat Fedn Welfare Blind
SIAS	Sussex Indl Archaeol Soc	SNG	Scot Neuroscience Gp
SIBA	Scot Indoor Bowling Assn	SNIPEF	Scot & NI Plumbing Emplrs' Fedn
	Soc Indep Brewers	SNN	Soc Nursery Nursing Practitioners
SICS	Scot Intensive Care Soc	SNPA	Scot Newspaper Publishers Assn
SIESO	SIESO	SNR	Soc Nautical Res
SIF	Soc Individual Freedom	SNSBI	Soc Name Studies Britain & Ireland
SIFA	SIFA	SNSC	Snowsport Scotland
SIFD	Soc Intl Folk Dancing	SNU	Spiritualists Nat U
SIGB	Snowsport Inds	SOA	Scot Optoelectronics Assn
SIH	Soc Italic Handwriting		Scot Orienteering Assn
SIHS	Scot Indl Heritage Soc		Soc Ancients
SILA	Sarcoidosis & Interstitial Lung Assn	SoA	Soc Authors
SIMI	Soc Ir Motor Ind	SOAPA	Scot Pensions Assn
SIPA UK	UK Specialised Inf Publishers Assn	SOB	Soc Bookbinders
SIPTU	SIPTU [IRL]	SoBS	Save our Bldg Socs
SIRP	Soc Indep Roundabout Proprietors	SOC	Scot Ornithologists Club
SIS	Scientific Instrument Soc		Soc Olympic Collectors
	Spinal Injuries Scotland	SOCITM	Soc Inf Technology Mgt
SISA	Scot Ice Skating Assn	SODAC	Soc Decorative Art Curators
SITE	Soc Incentive & Travel Executives	SOE	Soc Operations Engrs
SIWA	Scot Inland Waterways Assn	SOEC	Scot Envtl & Outdoor Educ Centres Assn
SJA	School Journey Assn	SoF	Sea Faith Network (UK)
	Scot Justices Assn	SOF	Soc Floristry
	Sports Journalists' Assn GB	SOFAA	Soc Fine Art Auctioneers & Valuers
SJH	Soc Jewellery Historians	SOFHT	Soc Food Hygiene & Technology
SJJA	Scot Ju-Jitsu Assn	SofM	Soc Metaphysicians
SK	Sealed Knot	SoG	Soc Genealogists
SK-S	Sheila Kaye-Smith Soc	SOHDA	Scot Official Highland Dancing Assn
SKC	Scot Kennel Club	SOL	Soc Ley Hunters
SKCM	Soc King Charles Martyr	SOLACE	Soc Local Authority Chief Execs & Senior Mgrs
SKLR	Sittingbourne & Kemsley Light Rly	SOLAS	Soc Law Accountants Scotland
SLA	School Library Assn	SOLCAP	Soc Leisure Consultants & Pubrs
SLAD	Soc Lond Art Dealers	Solo NFSC	Nat Fedn Solo Clubs
SLANOPE	Scot Local Authority Network Physical Educ	SOM	Soc Occupational Medicine
SLAS	Scot Law Agents Soc	SOMW	Soc Medical Writers
SLCC	Soc Local Coun Clerks	SONE	Supporters Nuclear Energy
SLD	Scot Language Dictionaries	SOP	Save our Parsonages
SLEAT	Soc Laundry Engrs & Allied Trs	SOPA	Scot Organic Prodrs Assn
SLGA	Scot Ladies' Golfing Assn	SOPO	Soc Procurement Officers Local Govt
SLHA	Soc Lincolnshire Hist & Archaeology	SoR	Soc Radiographers
SLHS	Scot Labour Hist Soc	SOS	Scot Otolaryngological Soc
SLm	Soc Limners	SOSS	Soc Schoolmasters & Schoolmistresses
SLMA	Steel Lintel Mfrs Assn	SOTMAS	Stoke-on-Trent Museum Archaeol Soc
SLMG	Shetland Livestock Marketing Gp	SOTS	Soc Old Testament Study
SLS	School Leaders Scotland	SOVA	SOVA
	Scots Language Soc	SPA	Scot Pétanque Assn
	Soc Landscape Studies		Scot Pipers Assn
	Soc Legal Scholars		Scot Potters' Assn
	Stephenson Locomotive Soc		Sheet Plant Assn
SLSA	Socio-Legal Studies Assn		Soc Parliamentary Agents
SLSGB	Surf Life Saving Assn		Soc Popular Astronomy

	Soc Profl Accountants	SSAUK	Self Storage Assn
	Social Policy Assn	SSBA	Scot Spina Bifida Assn
	Soya Protein Assn		Shropshire Sheep Breeders Assn
SPAB	Soc Protection Ancient Bldgs		Swaledale Sheep Breeders Assn
SpaBA	Spa Business Assn	SSBR	Soc Sailing Barge Res
SPATA	Swimming Pool & Allied Trs Assn	SSC	Scot Ski Club
SPBS	Scot Prayer Book Soc		Silver Spoon Club
	Soc Promotion Byzantine Studies	SSCA	Scot Ship Chandlers Assn
SPBW	Soc Presvn Beers Wood	SSCC	Scot Sporting Car Club
SPC	Soc Pension Consultants	SSCCI	Sthn Staffordshire Cham Comm & Ind
	Steam Plough Club	SSCR	Scot Soc Crop Res
SPCA	Scot Parent Couns Assn	SSCSoc	Soc Solicitors Supreme Courts Scotland
SPCK	Soc Promoting Christian Knowledge	SSEG	Scot Solar Energy Gp
SPDS	Soc Personnel Dirs Scotland	SSF	Scot Schoolsport Fedn
SPE	Soc Profl Engrs		Scot Surfing Fedn
SPEF	Scot Print Emplrs Fedn	SSHA	Soc Sexual Health Advisers
SPES	S Place Ethical Soc	SSHB	Soc Study Human Biology
SPF	Scot Police Fedn	SSHM	Scot Soc Hist Medicine
SPFA	Scot Pelagic Fishermen's Assn		Soc Social Hist Medicine
SPG	Solicitor Sole Practitioners Gp	SSHoP	Scot Soc Hist Photography
SPHS	Soc Promotion Hellenic Studies	SSI	Sculptors' Soc Ireland
SPI	Soc Publishers Ireland		Soc Scribes & Illuminators
SPL	Scot Poetry Library	SSISI	Statistical & Social Inquiry Soc Ireland
SPM	Soc Pharmaceutical Medicine	SSLA	Scot Support Learning Assn
SPMA	Scot Modern Pentathlon Assn	SSLG	Scot Stone Liaison Gp
	Soc Post-Medieval Archaeology	SSLH	Soc Study Labour Hist
SPNM	Soc Promotion New Music	SSM	Soc Social Medicine
SPNS	Scot Place-Name Soc	SSNS	Scot Soc Nthn Studies
SPOA	Scot Plant Owners Assn	SSNTA	Scot Seed & Nursery Tr Assn
SPPA	Scot Pre-School Play Assn	SSP	Scot Soc Playwrights
SPR	Soc Property Researchers	SSPO	Scot Salmon Producers' Org
	Soc Psychical Res	SSPR	Scot Soc Psychical Res
SPRA	Single Ply Roofing Assn	SSS	Ship Stamp Soc
SPRS	Staffordshire Parish Registers Soc		Sunday Shakespeare Soc
SPS	Soc Portrait Sculptors	SSSG	Stickler Syndrome Support Gp
SPSBS	Shetland Pony Stud-Book Soc	SSSprint	Street Sled Sports Racers
SPSL	Scot Piping Soc Lond	SSSS	Soc Study Subterranean Survival
SPSS	Sports Pony Studbook Soc	SSTA	Scot Secondary Teachers' Assn
SPTW	Soc Promoting Training Women	STA	Soc Technical Analysts
SPUC	Soc Protection Unborn Children		Solar Tr Assn
SRA	Scot Rafting Assn		Source Testing Assn
	Scot Records Assn		Swimming Teachers Assn
	Scot Rifle Assn	STAGBI	Standardbred & Trotting Horse Assn
	Shooters' Rights Assn	STAR	Soc Ticket Agents & Retailers
	Social Res Assn	STAT	Soc Teachers Alexander Technique
	Strathspey Rly Assn	STAUK	Sugar Traders Assn
SRC	Scot Retail Consortium	STC	Soc Theatre Consultants
SRF	Scot Renewables Forum	STEMPRA	Science, Technology, Engg. . . Public Relations Assn
SRGC	Scot Rock Garden Club	STEP	Soc Trust & Estate Practitioners
SRHE	Soc Res Higher Educ	STEPS	STEPS
SRHSB	Soc Res Hydrocephalus & Spina Bifida	Stereo Society	Stereoscopic Soc
SRIA	Scot Record Ind Assn	STGA	Scot Tourist Guides Assn
SRIP	Soc Reproductive & Infant Psychology	STLD	Soc TV Lighting Directors
SRP	Soc Radiological Protection	STO	Scot Tenants Org
	Soc Recorder Players	STOWA	Scot Tug of War Assn
SRPBA	Scot Rural Property & Business Assn	STR	Soc Theatre Res
SRPS	Scot Rly Presvn Soc	STRI	Sports Turf Res Inst
SRS	Scot Reformation Soc	STS	Scot Text Soc
	Shakespeare Reading Soc	STSD	Soc Teachers Speech & Drama
	Soc Renaissance Studies	STSG	Scot Transport Studies Gp
	Suffolk Records Soc	STTA	Scot Table Tennis Assn
	Surrey Record Soc		Scot Timber Tr Assn
	Sussex Record Soc	STTS	Scot Tramway & Transport Soc
SRU	Scot Rugby U	STUC	Scot Trs U Congress
SS	Safe Speed	SUB.BRIT	Subterranea Britannica
	Surtees Soc (Northumbria)	SUKA	Singapore UK Assn
SSA	Sailing Smack Assn	SUSTAIN	Sustain
	Scot Security Assn	SUT	Soc Underwater Technology Ltd
	Scot Sports Assn	SVA	Scot Volleyball Assn
	Seasoning & Spice Assn	SVBWG	Scot Vernacular Bldgs Working Gp
	Shipbuilders & Shiprepairers Assn	SVVF	Scot Vintage Vehicle Fedn
	Side Saddle Assn	SWA	Scot Whls Assn
	Soc Scot Artists		Scotch Whisky Assn
	Soc Study Addiction Alcohol. . .		Small Woods Assn
SSAFA	Soldiers, Sailors & Airmen's Families Assn		Soc Women Artists
SSAISB	Soc Study Artificial Intelligence & Simulation Behaviour		Steel Window Assn
		SWCPA	S W Coast Path Assn
SSAM	Soc Sales & Marketing	SWE	Soc Wood Engravers

© CBD Research Ltd · Beckenham · BR3 5JS · Tel 020 8650 7745 · Fax 020 8650 0768 · E-mail cbd@cbdresearch.com · www.cbdresearch.com

SWF	Scot Women's Football
SWFPA	Scot White Fish Producers Assn
SWHIHR	Soc W Highland & Island Histl Res
SWHP	Soc Welfare Horses & Ponies
SWIBA	Scot Women's Indoor Bowling Assn
SWLG	Scot Wild Land Gp
SWMA	Scot Wirework Mfrs Assn
SWMAS	Shropshire & W Midlands Agricl Soc
SWPP/BPPA	Soc Wedding & Portrait Photographers
SWRI	Scot Women's Rural Insts
SWT	Scot Wildlife Trust
SWWAPS	Second Wld War Aircraft Presvn Soc
SyAS	Surrey Archaeol Soc
SYHA	Scot Youth Hostels Assn

T

T&CVA	Thames & Chiltern Vineyards Assn
TA	Telework Assn
	Translators Assn
	Transport Assn
	Tricycle Assn
TAA	Timber Arbitrators Assn
	Tropical Agriculture Assn
TABI	Tarot Assn
TAC	Aeroplane Collection
TACMA	BEAMA
TACS	Tiles & Architectural Ceramics Soc
TACT	Assn Corporate Trustees
TAF	Trade Assn Forum
TAG	Arthrogryposis Gp
	Local Govt Technical Advisers Gp
	Towpath Action Gp
TALES	Assn Library Eqpt Suppliers
TAMBA	Twins & Mult Births Assn
TandRA	Tennis & Rackets Assn
TAROE	Tenants & Residents Orgs England
TARS	Arthur Ransome Soc
TAS	Aviation Soc
TATHS	Tools & Trs Hist Soc
TBA	Thoroughbred Breeders' Assn
TBF	Trakehner Breeders Fraternity
TBPA	Tenpin Bowling Proprietors Assn
TBTA	Thames Boating Trs Assn
TC	Tandem Club
TCA	Timeshare Consumers Assn
TCAS	Three Counties Agricl Soc
TCF	Compassionate Friends
TCMA	Traffic Mgt Contrs Assn
TCPA	Town & Country Planning Assn
TCS	Token Corresponding Soc
	Traditional Cosmology Soc
	Train Collectors Soc
TCUGB	Tai Chi U
TDA	Timber Decking Assn
TDS	Dystonia Soc
TEAM	Eur Atlantic Movement
TEDct	Thyroid Eye Disease Charitable Trust
TEGAS	Electric Guitar Appreciation Soc
TEHVA	BEAMA
TELS	T E Lawrence Soc
TESA	Event Services Assn
TFA	Freedom Assn
	Tenant Farmers' Assn
	Textile Finishers Assn
TFIC	Fedn Image Consultants
TFMA	Tapestry Frame Mfrs Assn
TFSR	Tools Self Reliance
TFTA	Traditional Farmfresh Turkey Assn
TG	Townswomen's Glds
TGA	Brit Tomato Growers Assn
	Turfgrass Growers Assn
TGA Ltd	Tropical Growers' Assn
THA	Telephone Helplines Assn
THCA	Brit Marine Fedn

The BA	Brit Assn Advancement Science
The BAF	Brit Abrasives Fedn
The GA	Giftware Assn
The Hallé	Hallé Concerts Soc
The RA	Referees' Assn
TheCEP	Campaign English Parliament
TheVA	Voucher Assn
THG	Telecommunications Heritage Gp
THMAS	Ted Heath Musical Appreciation Soc
TI(UK)	Transparency Intl (UK)
TICA	Thermal Insulation Contrs Assn
TIEA	Tobacco Ind Emplrs Assn
TIF	Telecommunications & Internet Fedn [IRL]
TIGA	Tiga
TIMA	Tue Iron Mfrs Assn
TIMCON	Timber Packaging & Pallet Confedn
TIMSA	Thermal Insulation Mfrs & Suppliers Assn
TISA	Tax Incentivised Savings Assn
TLGA	Leek Growers' Assn
TLRS	Tramway & Light Rly Soc
TMA	Tobacco Mfrs' Assn
TMI	Movers Inst
	Tourism Mgt Inst
TMPDF	Trade Marks Patents & Designs Fedn
TMS	Tramway Museum Soc
	Transverse Myelitis Soc
TMS-GBI	Thomas Merton Soc
TMSA	Traditional Music & Song Assn Scotland
TMVA	BEAMA
TNA UK	Trigeminal Neuralgia Assn
TNAUK	Talking Newspaper Assn
TOFFS	Over Fifties Assn
TOFS	Tracheo-Oesophageal Fistula Support
TORRO	Tornado & Storm Res Org
TOW	Transport Water Assn
TOWA	Tug of War Assn
TPA	TaxPayers' Alliance
TPC	Tall Persons Club
TPG	Portman Gp
TRA	Reiki Assn
	Textile Recycling Assn
	Toy Retailers Assn
	Trussed Rafter Assn
	Tyre Recovery Assn
TRADA	TRADA Technology
Treoir	Nat Fedn Services Unmarried Parents...[IRL]
TRF	Trail Riders Fellowship
TRG	Tertiary Res Gp
	Tory Reform Gp
TRIC	TV & Radio Inds Club
TRPS	Talyllyn Rly Presvn Soc
TRSS	Trekking & Riding Soc Scotland
TS	Theosophical Soc England
	Tolkien Soc
TSA	Tank Storage Assn
	Telecare Services Assn
	Textile Services Assn
	Tuberous Sclerosis Assn
	UK Land & Hydrographic Survey Assn
TSA(UK)	Tourette Syndrome (UK) Assn
TSBA	Teeswater Sheep Breeders Assn
TSI	Trading Standards Inst
TSPA	Table Soccer Players Assn
TSS	Spelling Soc
TSSA	Transport Salaried Staffs Assn
TSSEA	Thermal Spraying & Surface Engg Assn
TSSS	Turner Syndrome Support Soc
TT	Transport Trust
TTA	Tile Assn
	Travel Trust Assn
TTAW	Table Tennis Assn Wales
TTF	Timber Tr Fedn
TTRA	TT Riders Assn
TTS	Transport Ticket Soc
TUBCS	Trade U Badge Collectors Soc
TUC	Trades U Congress
TUFF	Telecommunications UK Fraud Forum
TUK	Transfrigoroute UK

TVCCi	Thames Valley Cham Comm & Ind
TWI	Welding Inst
TYHA	Yacht Harbour Assn
TYMBA	Traditional Youth Marching Bands Assn

U

UA	Urostomy Assn
UAC	Ulster Automobile Club
UACES	University Assn Contemporary Eur Studies
UAF	Ulster Angling Fedn
UAHS	Ulster Architectural Heritage Soc
UALL	Universities Assn Lifelong Learning
UAS	Ulster Archaeol Soc
UCA	Ulster Chemists Assn
	Utd Chiropractic Assn
UCEA	Universities & Colls Emplrs' Assn
UCFF	Ulster Coarse Fishing Fedn
UCISA	Universities & Colls Inf Systems Assn
UCSW	U Country Sports Workers
UCU	University & College U
UDM	U Democratic Mineworkers
UFAW	Universities Fedn Animal Welfare
UFLS	Ulster Folk Life Soc
UFRC	Ulster Fedn Rambling Clubs
UFU	Ulster Farmers U
UHF	Ulster Histl Foundation
UHS	Unitarian Hist Soc
UIG	Uveitis Inf Gp
UK Skeptics	UK Skeptics
UK-ISES	Solar Energy Soc
UK-RHA	UK Rainwater Harvesting Assn
UK-SDA	UK Sustainable Development Assn
UKA	UK Alliance
	UK Alliance Dance Teachers
	UK Athletics
UKABIF	UK Acquired Brain Injury Forum
UKAFFP	UK Assn Frozen Food Producers
UKAFPO	UK Assn Fish Producer Orgs
UKALA	UK Assn Letting Agents
UKAMBY	UK Assn Mfrs Bakers Yeast
UKAN	Narcolepsy Assn
UKAPE	UK Assn Profl Engrs
UKAPMP	UK Assn Proposal Mgt Profls
UKAWP	UK Alliance Wedding Planners
UKBFF	UK Bodybuilding & Fitness Fedn
UKBG	UK Bartenders Gld
UKBS	UK Botswana Soc
UKCGA	UK Chrysanthemum Growers' Assn
UKCHO	UK Confedn Hypnotherapy Orgs
UKCMG	UK Computer Measurement Gp
UKCP	UK Coun Psychotherapy
UKCPA	UK Clinical Pharmacy Assn
UKCPI	UK Cleaning Products Ind Assn
UKCRA	UK Cartridge Remanufacturers Assn
	UK Catamaran Racing Assn
UKCSA	UK Cast Stone Assn
UKCTA	UK Competitive Telecommunications Assn
UKDDF	UK Dance Drama Fedn
UKEAPA	UK Employee Assistance Profls Assn
UKeHA	UK eHealth Assn
UKeiG	UK EInformation Gp
UKELA	UK Envtl Law Assn
UKEMS	UK Envtl Mutagen Soc
UKEP	UK Egg Producers Assn
UKFJB	UK Fedn Jazz Bands
UKFPA	UK Forest Products Assn
UKHA	UK Harp Assn
	UK Housekeepers Assn
UKHCA	UK Homecare Assn
UKHKA	UK Hand Knitting Assn
UKHSU	UK Horse Shoers U
UKIA	UK Irrigation Assn
UKISCRS	UK & I Soc Cataract & Refractive Surgeons
UKISUG	UK Indl Sugar Users Gp

UKIVA	UK Indl Vision Assn
UKLA	UK Literacy Assn
	UK Locksmiths Assn
	UK Lubricants Assn
UKMA	UK Metric Assn
UKMPA	UK Maritime Pilots' Assn
UKMTA	UK Money Transmitters Assn
UKNA	UK Noise Assn
UKNDA	UK Nat Defence Assn
UKOOG	UK Onshore Operators Gp
UKOPA	UK Onshore Pipeline Operators' Assn
UKOTA	UK O'seas Territories Assn
UKOWLA	UK One World Linking Assn
UKPA	UK Polocrosse Assn
UKPHA	UK Public Health Assn
UKPIA	UK Petroleum Ind Assn
UKPS	UK Pyrotechnics Soc
UKPSA	UK Practical Shooting Assn
UKPSF	UK Paintball Sports Fedn
UKPTA	UK Polarity Therapy Assn
UKQAA	UK Quality Ash Assn
UKRA	UK Renderers Assn
	UK Rocketry Assn
UKRAS	UK Roundabout Appreciation Soc
UKRFA	UK Resilient Flooring Assn
UKRIGS	Nat Assn UK Regionally Important Geological Sites
UKRPA	UK Revenue Protection Assn
UKSA	UK Shareholders' Assn
	UK Skateboarding Assn
	UK Sports Assn People Learning Disability
UKSCC	UK Spoon Collectors Club
UKSG	UK Serials Gp
UKSIF	UK Social Investment Forum
UKSMA	UK Software Metrics Assn
	UK Spring Mfrs Assn
UKSPA	UK Science Park Assn
UKSPILL	UK Spill Assn
UKSSA	UK Security Shredding Assn
UKSTAG	Defence Mfrs Assn
UKSTT	UK Soc Trenchless Technology
UKTA	UK Tea Assn
UKTC	UK Trs Confedn
UKTCA	UK Transplant Co-ordinators Assn
UKTLF	UK Textile Laboratory Forum
UKTRF	UK Travel Retail Forum
UKTS	UK Thalassaemia Soc
UKU	UK Ultimate Assn
UKVA	UK Vineyards Assn
UKWA	UK Warehousing Assn
	UK Windsurfing Assn
UKWF	UK Weighing Fedn
ULA	Ulster Launderers Assn
UNA-UK	Utd Nations Assn GB & NI
UNISON	Unison
UNLOCK	Unlock
UPCA	Universities Psychotherapy & Counselling Assn
Upkeep	Upkeep
UPNS	Ulster Place-Name Soc
URCHS	Utd Reformed Church Hist Soc
URTU	Utd Road Transport U
USA UK	Utd Saddlebred Assn
USDAW	U Shop, Distributive & Allied Workers
USLS	Ulster-Scots Language Soc
USPC	Ulster Soc Protection Countryside
USPCA	Ulster Soc Prevention Cruelty Animals
UTU	Ulster Teachers U
UUK	Universities UK
UUU	U UK Unicyclists
	U UK Unicyclists
UWHU	Ulster Women's Hockey U

V

V-CC	Veteran-Cycle Club
VAAJ	Veterinary Assn Arbitration & Jurisprudence

© CBD Research Ltd · Beckenham · BR3 5JS · Tel 020 8650 7745 · Fax 020 8650 0768 · E-mail cbd@cbdresearch.com · www.cbdresearch.com

VAG	Vernacular Architecture Gp
VAGA	Visual Arts & Galleries Assn
VAHS	Voluntary Action Hist Soc
VAN	Voluntary Arts Network
VAS	Visual Arts Scotland
VBF	Vinegar Brewers Fedn
VBRA	Vehicle Builders & Repairers Assn
VC&GCAssn	Victoria Cross & George Cross Assn
VCN	Voice Care Network
VCT	Vintage Carriages Trust
VdGS	Viola da Gamba Soc
VegSoc	Vegetarian Soc
VESS	Voluntary Euthanasia Soc Scotland
VFA	Viewing Facilities Assn UK
VFI	Vintners Fedn Ireland
VGC	Vintage Glider Club
VHA	Vision Homes Assn
VHGMC	Vintage Horticl & Garden Machinery Club
VHLCG	Von Hippel-Lindau Contact Gp
VHS	Veteran Horse Soc
ViRSA	Village Retail Services Assn...
VLV	Voice Listener & Viewer
VMCC	Vintage Motor Cycle Club
VMS	Victorian Military Soc
VNS	Violet Needham Soc
VOCAL	Voice Chief Offrs Cultural... Services
VPG	VAT Practitioners Gp
VPL	Video Performance Ltd
VPS	Vulval Pain Soc
VRMA	Vehicle Restraint Mfrs Assn
VSCC	Vintage Sports Car Club
VSO	Voluntary Service Overseas
VSS	Victim Support Scotland
VWBA	Vintage Wooden Boat Assn
VWSGB	Virginia Woolf Soc GB

W

W&ACT	Wey & Arun Canal Trust
W4B	Wireless Bedridden Soc
WA	Willwriters' Assn
WABA	W Africa Business Assn
	Welsh Amat Boxing Assn
WACC	Wessex Assn Chams Comm
WAFE	Women's Aid Fedn (England)
WAH	Wolves & Humans Foundation
Wales PPA	Wales Pre-school Playgroups Assn
WAMF/FfCAC	Welsh Amat Music Fedn
WANHS	Wiltshire Archaeol & Natural Hist Soc
WAOS	Welsh Agricultural Organisation Society Ltd
WARA	Welsh Amat Rowing Assn
WAS	Worcestershire Archaeol Soc
WASA	Welsh Amat Swimming Assn
WASAC	Welsh Assn Sub Aqua Clubs
WAY	Way Foundation
WBA	Welsh Bowling Assn
WBCS	Welsh Black Cattle Soc
WBRA	Wagon Bldg & Repairing Assn
WBS-UK	Warmblood Breeders' Studbook - UK
WBU	Welsh Badminton U
	Welsh Bridge U
WCA	Welsh Canoeing Assn
	Welsh Culinary Assn
	Writers' Copyright Assn
WCAS	Westmorland County Agricl Soc
WCC	Wales Craft Coun
WCRA	Women's Cycle Racing Assn
WCS	Wilkie Collins Soc
	Wound Care Soc
WCU	Welsh Chess U
	Welsh Cycling U
WCVA	Wales Coun Voluntary Action
WDA	Wallcovering Distbrs Assn
	Well Drillers Assn

WDCS	Whale & Dolphin Consvn Soc
WEA	Workers' Educl Assn
WEN	Women's Envtl Network
WES	Western Equestrian Soc
	Wind Engg Soc
	Women's Engg Soc
	Writing Eqpt Soc
WFA	Western Front Assn
	Wholesome Food Assn
WFDS	Cymdeithas Ddawns Werin Cymru
WFGA	Women's Farm & Garden Assn
WFS	Wild Flower Soc
WFU	Women's Food & Farming U
WGA	White Goods Assn [IRL]
WGGB	Writers' Gld
WGU	Golf U Wales
WHA	Welsh Hound Assn
	Western Horsemen's Assn
WHR	Welsh Highland Rlys Assn
WHS	Wesley Histl Soc
WHU	Welsh Hockey U
WI	Fedn Women's Insts NI
WIA	Writing Instruments Assn
WIBA	Welsh Indoor Bowls Assn
WJA	Welsh Judo Assn
WM Soc	Water Mgt Soc
WMA	BEAMA
	Workers' Music Assn
WMBA	Whls Markets Brokers' Assn
WMS	Welsh Mines Soc
WMSA	Woodworking Machinery Suppliers Assn
WMSS	Welsh Mountain Sheep Society - Registered Section
WMT	War Memorials Trust
WNA	Welsh Netball Assn
WONA	Web-offset Newspaper Assn
WPA	War Poets Assn
	Wire Products Assn
	Wood Protection Assn
	World Pheasant Assn UK
WPCCIT	Weymouth & Portland Cham Comm...
WPCS	Welsh Pony & Cob Soc
	White Park Cattle Soc
WPIF	Wood Panel Inds Fedn
WPOA	Westminster Property Owners Assn
WPU	Writers & Photographers unLimited
WRG	Waterway Recovery Gp
WRS	Wiltshire Record Soc
WRU	Welsh Rugby U
WRVS	Women's R Voluntary Service
WSCA	Well Services Contrs Assn
WSF	Welsh Surfing Fedn
	Williams Syndrome Foundation
WSRA	World Speedway Riders Assn
WSRS	Wildlife Sound Recording Soc
WSSociety	Soc Writers Her Majesty's Signet
WSTA	Wine & Spirit Trade Assn
WTIF	Wall Tie Installers Fedn
WTT	Wild Trout Trust
WUK	Wakeboard UK
WW2RSG	World War Two Rly Study Gp
WWA	War Widows Assn
WWCC	W Wales Cham Comm
WWJ	W W Jacobs Appreciation Soc
WWOOF	World-Wide Opportunities on Organic Farms
WWTA	Welsh Weight Training Assn

Y

YAS	Yeovil Agricl Soc
	Yorkshire Archaeol Soc
YDCW	Campaign Protection Rural Wales
YDS	Yorkshire Dialect Soc
YDSA	Yacht Designers & Surveyors Assn
YET	Young Explorers' Trust

YGS	Yorkshire Geological Soc
YHA	Youth Hostels Assn (E&W)
YJA	Yachting Journalists' Assn
YMCA	YMCA England
YPS	Yorkshire Philosophical Soc
YWCA	YWCA (Young Women's Christian Association)

Z

ZF	Zionist Fedn
ZSA	Zwartbles Sheep Assn
ZSL	Zoological Soc London

© CBD Research Ltd · Beckenham · BR3 5JS · Tel 020 8650 7745 · Fax 020 8650 0768 · E-mail cbd@cbdresearch.com · www.cbdresearch.com

PUBLICATIONS INDEX

Amputees Guide - Brit Limbless Ex-Service Men's Assn
AMSPAR Magazine - Assn of Medical Secretaries, Practice Managers, Administrators & Receptionists
The Analyst - R Soc of Chemistry
Analytical Abstracts - R Soc of Chemistry
Anastomosis - Anatomical Soc of GB & Ireland
Anatomy & Physiology Wound Healing & Wound Assessment - Wound Care Soc
Anglo Arab Stud Book - Arab Horse Soc
Anglo-Greek Review - Greek Inst
The Anglo-Hellenic Review - Anglo-Hellenic League
Anglo Norse Review - Anglo-Norse Soc
Anglo-Spanish Quarterly Review - Anglo-Spanish Soc
The Animal-Free Shopper - Vegan Soc
Animal Medicines Record Book - Animal Health Distributors Assn
Animal Science - Brit Soc of Animal Science
Animal Welfare - Universities Fedn for Animal Welfare
Annals of Actuarial Science - Inst of Actuaries
Annals of Applied Biology - Assn of Applied Biologists
Annals of Clinical Biochemistry - Assn for Clinical Biochemistry
Annals of Human Biology - Soc for the Study of Human Biology
Annals of Occupational Hygiene - Brit Occupational Hygiene Soc
Anne Cobbett: account of the family - William Cobbett Soc
Annotated Finance Act - Assn of Taxation Technicians
Annual Bulletin of Historical Literature - Historical Assn
Annual Competitions Review - Nat Assn of Public Golf Courses
Annual Local Authority Road Maintenance Survey - Asphalt Industry Alliance
Annual Reports on the Progress of Chemistry - R Soc of Chemistry
Annual Survey of Business Finance - Finance & Leasing Assn
Annual Survey of Scottish Export Sales - Scot Council for Development & Industry
Anomaly - Assn for the Scientific Study of Anomalous Phenomena
Anon Hen - Tolkien Soc
Anthropological Index Online - R Anthropological Inst of GB & Ireland
Anthropology Today - R Anthropological Inst of GB & Ireland
Anthroposophical Medical NL - Anthroposophical Medical Assn
Antiquarian Horology - Antiquarian Horological Soc
Antiquaries Jnl - Soc of Antiquaries of London
The Antiquary - Chester Archaeological Soc
Antisemitism in the World Today - Inst for Jewish Policy Research
Anxiety - SANE
Anxious Times - Nat Phobics Soc
Application & Measurement of Protective Coatings - Concrete Repair Assn
Applied Ergonomics - Ergonomics Soc
Applied Physics - Inst of Physics
Appointment of Consultants Document - Scala - Serving Construction & Architecture in Local Authorities
APSA Rapport - Assn for Professionals in Services for Adolescents
Arab Horse Soc News - Arab Horse Soc
Arabian Type & Standard - Arab Horse Soc
ARBA Annual - Amateur Rose Breeders Assn
Arbitration - Chartered Inst of Arbitrators
ARC News - Assn of Healthcare Communicators
ARCA News - Asbestos Removal Contractors Assn
ARCA Short breaks - Adult Residential Colleges Assn
Archaeologia Aeliana - Soc of Antiquaries of Newcastle upon Tyne
Archaeologia Cambrensis - Cambrian Archaeological Assn
Archaeologia Cantiana - Kent Archaeological Soc
Archaeological Jnl - R Archaeological Inst
The Archaeologist - Inst of Field Archaeologists
Archaeology Abroad - Archaeology Abroad
The Archbishop's town: the making of mediaeval Croydon - Croydon Natural History & Scientific Soc
Archery UK - Grand Nat Archery Soc
Architectural Heritage Jnl - Architectural Heritage Soc of Scotland
Architectural History - Soc of Architectural Historians of GB
Architectural Ironmongery Jnl - Guild of Architectural Ironmongers
Architectural Technology - Chartered Inst of Architectural Technologists
The Architectural Technology Careers Hbk - Chartered Inst of Architectural Technologists
Architecture Periodicals Index - R Inst of Brit Architects

Archive Zones - Fedn of Commercial Audiovisual Libraries
Archives - Brit Records Assn
Archives & User Series - Brit Records Assn
Archives of Disease in Childhood - R College of Paediatrics & Child Health
Archives of Natural History - Soc for the History of Natural History
Arena - Assn of Electoral Administrators
        Union of Shop, Distributive & Allied Workers
Argus - Nat Auricula & Primula Soc (Midland & West Section)
The Ark - Rare Breeds Survival Trust
The Arquebusier - Pike & Shot Soc
Art Antiquity & Law - Inst of Art & Law
The Art Book - Assn of Art Historians
Art Business Today - Fine Art Trade Guild
The Art Directors Book - D&AD
Art History - Assn of Art Historians
Art Libraries Jnl - ARLIS/UK & Ireland: the Art Libraries Soc
Art Quarterly - Nat Art Collections Fund (The Art Fund)
Art Treasures & War - Inst of Art & Law
Arthritis & Waterbeds - Brit Waterbed Assn
Arthritis News - Arthritis Care
Artisan - Scot Assn of Painting Craft Teachers
Artist Blacksmith - Brit Artist Blacksmiths Assn
The Artist's Guide to Selling Work - Fine Art Trade Guild
Arts Festivals Calendar & Directory - Brit Arts Festivals Assn
ARVAC Bulletin - Assn for Research in the Voluntary & Community Sector
AS News - Nat Ankylosing Spondylitis Soc
As We See It - Dyslexia Inst
Asbestos Facts - Occupational & Environmental Diseases Assn
Asepsis: preventing healthcare associated infection - Infection Prevention Soc
ASGARD - Assn in Scotland to Research into Astronautics
Asian Affairs - R Soc for Asian Affairs
Asides - Guild of Drama Adjudicators
Ask FIRA News - Furniture Industry Research Assn
Aspects of Applied Biology - Assn of Applied Biologists
Aspects of Motoring History - Soc of Automotive Historians in Britain
Asphalt Now - Asphalt Industry Alliance
Asphalt Professional - Inst of Asphalt Technology
Aspirations! - Assn for Spinal Injury Research, Rehabilitation & Reintegration
Assn Executive - Inst of Assn Management
Astrocalendar - Fedn of Astronomical Socs
Astrological Jnl - Astrological Assn of GB
Astrology - Astrological Lodge of London
Astrology & Medicine - Astrological Assn of GB
Astronomy & Geophysics - R Astronomical Soc
At the Sign of [...] - Inn Sign Soc
A-T: an overview - Ataxia-Telangiectasia Soc (A-T Soc)
The Ataxia - Ataxia UK
Ataxia-Telangiectasia guide for parents - Ataxia-Telangiectasia Soc (A-T Soc)
Ataxia-Telangiectasia guide for teachers - Ataxia-Telangiectasia Soc (A-T Soc)
Ataxia-Telangiectasia guide to therapies - Ataxia-Telangiectasia Soc (A-T Soc)
ATCO News - Assn of Transport Co-ordinating Officers
ATLA Jnl - Fund for the Replacement of Animals in Medical Experiments
Atlantic Daily Bulletin - Brit Titanic Soc
Atlas of Enamel Defects - Inst of Vitreous Enamellers & Vitreous Enamel Assn
Atomic, Molecular & Optical Physics - Inst of Physics
Audiens - Brit Assn of Community Doctors in Audiology
Audit of Political Engagement - Hansard Soc
The Author - Soc of Authors
          Translators Assn
Autism News - Autism Independent UK
Automobile Abstracts - MIRA
Automotive Business News - MIRA
Automotive Recycling & Disposal UK - Motor Vehicle Dismantlers Assn of GB
Autumn Bulletin - Delphinium Soc
The Avicultural Magazine - Avicultural Soc
Aware - Scot Motor Neurone Disease Assn

© CBD Research Ltd · Beckenham · BR3 5JS · Tel 020 8650 7745 · Fax 020 8650 0768 · E-mail cbd@cbdresearch.com · www.cbdresearch.com

Ayrshire Dairyman - Ayrshire Cattle Soc of GB & Ireland
Ayrshire Jnl - Ayrshire Cattle Soc of GB & Ireland

B

BABCP News - Brit Assn for Behavioural & Cognitive Psychotherapies
Baby Blues & Post Natal Depression - Assn for Postnatal Illness
Baby Watch - Meningitis Research Foundation
Back Chat - Chiropractic Patients' Assn
Backaches & Waterbeds - Brit Waterbed Assn
Backbone - Scoliosis Assn (UK)
Background - McTimoney Chiropractic Assn
Backpack - Backpackers Club
Baconiana - Francis Bacon Soc Inc
The Badge Mag - Brit Badge Collectors Assn
The Badger - Badge Collectors Circle
Badminton Magazine - Badminton England
The BAFRA Directory - Brit Antique Furniture Restorers' Assn
BAFRA Jnl - Brit Antique Furniture Restorers' Assn
BAGMA Bulletin - Brit Agricultural & Garden Machinery Assn
BAHA Times - Brit Assn of Hospitality Accountants
BAJ News - Brit Assn of Jnlists
Balance - Diabetes UK
A Balanced View: Practical Tips for a Healthy Diet - Arthritic Assn
Baling Out - Straw Bale Building Assn
Balloonies - NABAS (the Balloon Assn)
Bamboo Wireless - Assn of Brit Civilian Internees Far East Region
Bandersnatch - Lewis Carroll Soc
Bank of Scotland Learn to Swim Syllabus - Scot Swimming
Banking Matters to Me - Assn for Real Change
Bankruptcy Explained - Bankruptcy Assn
BAPOMAG - Brit Assn of Prosthetists & Orthotists
Baptist Quarterly - Baptist Historical Soc
Baptist Times - Baptist Union of GB
Baptist Union Directory - Baptist Union of GB
Barema Hbk - Barema
Barge Buyers' Hbk - DBA - The Barge Assn
BASDA News - Business Application Software Developers Assn
Base Thoughts - Antique Metalware Soc
Baseball & Softball Bulletins - BaseballSoftballUK
BASI Alpine Manual - Brit Assn of Snowsport Instructors
BASI Manual - Brit Assn of Snowsport Instructors
BASI News - Brit Assn of Snowsport Instructors
Basic Coaches Manual - Welsh Weight Training Assn
Basic Guides to Good Practice - Assn of Chief Executives of Voluntary Organisations
Basic Letterpress for Beginners (Jubilee issue) - Brit Printing Soc
Basic Principles - Confederation of Transcribed Information Services
Basic Steps - Assn for Real Change
Basking Shark & Whale Report - Basking Shark Soc
BASMA News - Boot & Shoe Mfrs' Assn
BASPCAN News - Brit Assn for the Study & Prevention of Child Abuse & Neglect
Bat Monitoring Post - Bat Conservation Trust
Bat News - Bat Conservation Trust
Battery Vehicle Review - Battery Vehicle Soc
Battle of Britain Remembered - Battle of Britain Historical Soc
BAWE Nat NL - Brit Assn of Women Entrepreneurs
BAWE West NL - Brit Assn of Women Entrepreneurs
BBGA Industry Directory - Brit Business & General Aviation Assn
BBKA News - Brit Bee-Keepers' Assn
BBS Information - Brit Brick Soc
bca News - Business Centre Assn
BCIS Bulletin - Building Cost Information Service
BDA News -
BDN Brit Deaf News - Brit Deaf Assn
Be My Parent Newspaper - Brit Assn for Adoption & Fostering
BEA Chronicle - Brit Energy Assn of the World Energy Council
BEAMA Bulletin - BEAMA
The Beat - Brit Cham Comm in China - Shanghai
Beat Magazine - Soc for the Promotion of New Music
Beating Anger - Brit Assn of Anger Management
Beating the Odds - Nat Assn of Steel Stockholders

Beaumont Magazine - Beaumont Soc
Beautyguild Bulletin - Guild of Professional Beauty Therapists
The Beckford Jnl - Beckford Soc
Becoming a Chartered Accountant - training with a medium sized firm - Assn of Practising Accountants
Beef Farmer - Nat Beef Assn
Beermat NL - Brit Beermat Collectors' Soc
BEHA News - Baby Equipment Hirers Assn
Behaviour & Information Technology - Ergonomics Soc
Behavioural & Cognitive Psychotherapy - - Brit Assn for Behavioural & Cognitive Psychotherapies
Behavioural Problems in Huntington's Disease. - Scot Huntington's Assn
Behind the Acanthus: the NADFAS story - Nat Assn of Decorative & Fine Arts Socs
Behind the Painted Smile: an insight into postnatal depression - Meet-a-Mum Assn
Being There - Tourism Concern
The Bells - a music jnl - Rachmaninoff Soc
BELUX - Belgian-Luxembourg Cham Comm in GB
Benefits of John Innes loam based compost - John Innes Mfrs Assn
Ben's Story: an introduction to child contact centres - Nat Assn of Child Contact Centres
Bereavement Care Jnl - Cruse Bereavement Care
Berkshire Archaeological Jnl - Berkshire Archaeological Soc
BESAbook - Brit Educational Suppliers Assn
Best Practice - Inst of Assessors & Internal Verifiers
Best Practice Guide to Timber Fire Doors - Architectural & Specialist Door Mfrs Assn
Best Practice Guidelines for the Production of Chilled Foods - Chilled Food Assn
Best Practice Guides - Construct: Concrete Structures Group
Best Practices Jnl - Nat Fedn of Enterprise Agencies
The Betjemanian - Betjeman Soc
Between a Rock & a Hard Place - Creator's Rights Alliance
Between the Flags - Point-to-Point Owners & Riders Assn
BH Magazine - Brit Hellenic Cham Comm
BHA News - Brit Humanist Assn
BHMA Post - Brit Herbal Medicine Assn
The BIAE Probe - Brit Inst & Assn of Electrolysis
Bibafax - Brit Isles Backgammon Assn
Bifalin - Brit InterNat Freight Assn
Bifocals without Tears - Assn of Brit Dispensing Opticians
The Big Youth Theatre Manual - Nat Assn of Youth Theatres
biiBUSINESS - Brit Inst of Innkeeping
BILA Jnl - Brit Insurance Law Assn
Biochemical Jnl - Biochemical Soc
Biographical Memoirs of Fellows - The R Soc
Biological Jnl - Linnean Soc of London
Biological Sciences - The R Soc
Biologist - Inst of Biology
Biomedical Scientist - Inst of Biomedical Science
The Bioneer - Brit Assn of Flower Essence Producers
Biotechnology & Applied Biochemistry - Biochemical Soc
Bird Study - Brit Trust for Ornithology
Bird Table - Brit Trust for Ornithology
Birds - R Soc for the Protection of Birds
Bison Hbk - Brit Bison Assn
BJOG: an interNat Jnl of Obstetrics & Gynaecology - R College of Obstetricians & Gynaecologists
Black & White Photography - Guild of Master Craftsmen
Black Powder - Muzzle Loaders Assn of GB
The Black Sheep - Hebridean Sheep Soc
The Blackcountryman - Black Country Soc
Blake Jnl - Blake Soc at St James's
Blasmusik Bulletin - Kmoch European Bands Soc
Blastpipe - Scot Railway Preservation Soc
BLESMAG - Brit Limbless Ex-Service Men's Assn
Blinds & Shutters - Brit Blind & Shutter Assn
Blink - Assn of Optometrists
Blithe Spirit - Brit Haiku Soc
Blonde - Brit Blonde Cattle Soc
Blonde News - Brit Blonde Cattle Soc
Blood R - Manorial Soc of GB
Blowout - Offshore Industry Liaison Committee
BLS News & Views - Brit Lymphology Soc
Blue Book - London Appreciation Soc

Blue Flag - DBA - The Barge Assn
Blue Print Magazine - Emergency Planning Soc
Bluebell News - Bluebell Railway Preservation Soc
BM News - Brit Marine Fedn
BMFA News - Brit Model Flying Assn
BMI Bulletin - Building Cost Information Service
BMI Insight - Birmingham & Midland Inst
BMI Price Book - Building Cost Information Service
BMS News - Brit Magical Soc
BMVA News - Brit Machine Vision Assn & Soc for Pattern Recognition
BNS Jnl - Britain Nepal Soc
BOA News - Brit Oncological Assn
Boat Jumble Fixtures List - Boat Jumble Assn
Boatyards, Marinas & Services around the River Thames - Thames Boating Trades Assn
Body - Vehicle Builders' & Repairers' Assn
The 'Boneshaker' - Veteran-Cycle Club
Book Collecting - Provincial Booksellers Fairs Assn
Book Fair Guide - Antiquarian Booksellers Assn (InterNat)
Book Trade Year Book - Publishers Assn
Bookbinder - Soc of Bookbinders
Bookmark - Bookmark Soc
The Bookplate Jnl - Bookplate Soc
Bookselling Essentials - Booksellers Assn of the UK & Ireland
Borate Glasses, Crystals & Melts - Soc of Glass Technology
Bore Da - Urdd Gobaith Cymru (yr Urdd)
Bosc d'Antic on Glassmaking - Soc of Glass Technology
The Boss - Home Business Alliance
Botanical Jnl - Linnean Soc of London
The Bottle Street Gazette - Margery Allingham Soc
The Bottom Line - Production Managers Assn
Bound to Fail - Anti Common Market League
The Bousfield Diaries - Bedfordshire Historical Record Soc
The Boutonneur - Buttonhook Soc
Bowls for the Beginner - Scot Bowling Assn
Bowls InterNat - Scot Indoor Bowling Assn
The Boys' Brigade Gazette - Boys' Brigade
BPI Statistical Hbk - BPI (Brit Recorded Music Industry)
B-Plus - Breast Implant Information Soc
bpma Directory: the authoritative guide for buyers of promotional merchandise - Brit Promotional Merchandise Assn
BPW News - Business & Professional Women UK
Bradleya - Brit Cactus & Succulent Soc
Branch Line News - Branch Line Soc
Brand Book - English Westerners Soc
Brazil Business Brief - Brazilian Cham Comm in GB
Breaking & Production - Brit Egg Products Assn
Breaking old Ground - a guide to contaminated land - Brit Urban Regeneration Assn
Breathe Easy - Fedn of Bakers
The Brewer & Distiller - Inst of Brewing & Distilling
Brewing & Distilling Directory - Inst of Brewing & Distilling
Brick Bulletin - Brick Development Assn
The Brief - Brit Cham Comm Thailand
Brit Oz Bulletin - Britain-Australia Soc
Britain - Anti Common Market League
Britain & Europe - Manorial Soc of GB
Britain & Overseas - Economic Research Council
Britain and the 're-opening ' of Japan: the Treaty of Yedo of 1858 & the Elgin Mission - Japan Soc
Britain Brasil - Brit Cham Comm & Industry in Brazil
Britaly Focus on Italy - Brit Cham Comm for Italy, Inc
Britannia - Soc for the Promotion of Roman Studies (Roman Soc)
Britannia Monographs - Soc for the Promotion of Roman Studies (Roman Soc)
Brit & Irish Archaeological Bibliography - Council of Brit Archaeology
Brit Actuarial Jnl - Inst of Actuaries
Brit American Business, the UK Hbk - Brit-American Business Inc
Brit Archaeology - Council of Brit Archaeology
Brit Bluegrass News - Brit Bluegrass Music Assn
The Brit Bobsleigh Annual - Brit Bobsleigh Assn
Brit Bottle Review - Old Bottle Club of GB
Brit Bulletin of Publications on Latin America, Spain & Portugal - Hispanic & Luso Brazilian Council
Brit Business in China - Brit Cham Comm in Hong Kong
Brit Business in China Directory - Brit Cham Comm in China - Shanghai

Brit Cinematographer Magazine - Brit Soc of Cinematographers
Brit Conference Destinations Directory - Brit Assn of Conference Destinations
Brit Crematoria in Public Profile - Cremation Soc of GB
Brit Dental Jnl - Brit Dental Assn
Brit Dental Nurses' Jnl - Brit Assn of Dental Nurses
The Brit Directory of Legal Services - Willwriters' Assn
Brit Educational Research Jnl - Brit Educational Research Assn
Brit Equestrian Directory - Brit Equestrian Trade Assn
Brit Farmer & Grower - Nat Farmers Union of England & Wales
Brit Go Jnl - Brit Go Assn
Brit Grooms - Brit Grooms Assn
Brit Herbal Compendium - Brit Herbal Medicine Assn
The Brit Herbal Pharmacopoeia - Brit Herbal Medicine Assn
Brit Homing World - R Pigeon Racing Assn
Brit Horse - Brit Horse Soc
Brit Hosta & Hemerocallis Soc Bulletin - Brit Hosta & Hemerocallis Soc
Brit Jnl for the Philosophy of Science - Brit Soc for the Philosophy of Science
Brit Jnl of Aesthetics - Brit Soc of Aesthetics
Brit Jnl of Biomedical Science - Inst of Biomedical Science
Brit Jnl of Canadian Studies - Brit Assn for Canadian Studies
Brit Jnl of Clinical Pharmacology - Brit Pharmacological Soc
Brit Jnl of Clinical Psychology - Brit Psychological Soc
Brit Jnl of Dermatology - Brit Assn of Dermatologists
Brit Jnl of Developmental Psychology - Brit Psychological Soc
Brit Jnl of Educational Psychology - Brit Psychological Soc
Brit Jnl of Haematology - Brit Soc for Haematology
Brit Jnl of Health Psychology - Brit Psychological Soc
Brit Jnl for the History of Philosophy - Brit Soc for the History of Philosophy
Brit Jnl for the History of Science - Brit Soc for the History of Science
Brit Jnl of Learning Disabilities - Brit Inst of Learning Disabilities
Brit Jnl of Mathematical & Statistical Psychology - Brit Psychological Soc
Brit Jnl of Middle Eastern Studies - Brit Soc for Middle Eastern Studies
Brit Jnl of Music Therapy - Brit Soc for Music Therapy
Brit Jnl of Orthodontics - Brit Orthodontic Soc
Brit Jnl of Pharmacology - Brit Pharmacological Soc
Brit Jnl of Psychology - Brit Psychological Soc
Brit Jnl of Social Work - Brit Assn of Social Workers
Brit Jnl of Sports Medicine - Brit Assn of Sport & Exercise Medicine
Brit Jnl for Special Education - nasen
Brit Jnl of Occupational Therapy - Brit Assn of Occupational Therapists
Brit Jnl of Oral & Maxillofacial Surgery - Brit Assn of Oral & Maxillofacial Surgeons
Brit Jnl of Podiatry - Soc of Chiropodists & Podiatrists
Brit Jnl of Psychiatry - R College of Psychiatrists
Brit Judo - Brit Judo Assn
Brit Latvian Trade - Brit Cham Comm in Latvia
Brit Medical Jnl - Brit Medical Assn
Brit Military Serials - Road Transport Fleet Data Soc
Brit Mining Memoirs - Northern Mine Research Soc
Brit Mining Monograph - Northern Mine Research Soc
Brit Museum Magazine - Brit Museum Friends
Brit Nat Formulary for Children - R College of Paediatrics & Child Health
Brit Naturopathic Jnl - Brit Naturopathic Assn
Brit Numismatic Jnl - Brit Numismatic Soc
Brit Origami - Brit Origami Soc
Brit Orthopaedic News - Brit Orthopaedic Assn
Brit Orthoptic Jnl - Brit & Irish Orthoptic Soc
Brit Paper Machinery News - Picon
Brit Pensioner Jnl - Brit Pensioners & Trade Union Action Assn
Brit Railway Brakevans & Ballast Ploughs - Historical Model Railway Soc
Brit Railway Track - Permanent Way Instn
Brit Railways Mark 1 Coaches - Historical Model Railway Soc
The Brit Sugarcraft News - Brit Sugarcraft Guild
Brit Tennis - Lawn Tennis Assn
Brit Water Ski & Wakeboard - Brit Water Ski
The Brit Weightlifter - Brit Weight Lifters Assn
Brit-German Review - Brit-German Assn

© CBD Research Ltd · Beckenham · BR3 5JS · Tel 020 8650 7745 · Fax 020 8650 0768 · E-mail cbd@cbdresearch.com · www.cbdresearch.com

The Britsoft Book - Entertainment & Leisure Software Publishers Assn
Broadband - Soc of Cable Telecommunication Engineers
Broadlines - Heritage Railway Assn
The Broker - Brit Insurance Brokers' Assn
Browning Soc Notes - Browning Soc
Brunel's Cornish Viaducts - Historical Model Railway Soc
BSBI News - Botanical Soc of the Brit Isles
BSGA News - Brit Sign & Graphics Assn
BSHAA News Therapists - Brit Soc of Hearing Aid Audiologists
BSIF Guide - Brit Safety Industry Fedn
BSNN News - Brit Soc for Medical Mycology
BSPS News - Brit Soc for Population Studies
BSS News - Botanical Soc of Scotland
BTMA Buyer's Guide - Brit Turned-Parts Mfrs Assn
BUAV Action - Brit Union for the Abolition of Vivisection
BUAV Update - Brit Union for the Abolition of Vivisection
The Buddhist Directory - Buddhist Soc
The Budgerigar - Budgerigar Soc
The Bugle - Soc for Producers & Composers of Applied Music
The Bugle Call Rag - Harry Roy Appreciation Soc
Building Engineer - Assn of Building Engineers
Building Maintenance Expenditure by Local Authorities - Scala - Serving Construction & Architecture in Local Authorities
Building & Repairing Dry Stone Walls - Dry Stone Walling Assn of GB
Building Services Engineering Research & Technology - Chartered Instn of Building Services Engineers
Building Services Jnl - Chartered Instn of Building Services Engineers
Building on Success - Biosciences Fedn
Bulletin Board - Sound Sense
Bulletin Subterranea Britannica - Subterranea Britannica
Bulletin of Veterinary History - Veterinary History Soc
The Bulwark - Scot Reformation Soc
Burney Jnl - Burney Soc
Burney Letter - Burney Soc
Burns Chronicle - Robert Burns World Fedn
The Bursar's Review - Independent Schools' Bursars Assn
Bus Fare - Brit Trolleybus Soc
Bus User - Bus Users UK
Busfare - Nat Playbus Assn
The Business - Dundee & Angus Cham Comm
    Nat Caravan Council
Business Chat - North Kent Cham Comm
Business Comment - Leith Cham Comm
Business Consultant - Inst of Business Consulting
The Business Economist - Soc of Business Economists
Business Edge - Sussex Cham Comm & Enterprise
Business Executives - Assn of Business Executives
Business Info Beyond the Lens - Assn of Photographers
Business Informer - Credit Protection Assn
Business Intelligence - Hull & Humber Cham Comm, Industry & Shipping
Business Jnl - Thames Valley Cham Comm & Industry
Business Link - Brit Cham Comm for Morocco
Business Magazine - Norfolk Cham Comm & Industry
Business Management Manual - Registered Nursing Home Assn
Business Matters - Lancaster District Cham Comm, Trade & Industry
Business News - Brit Assn of Landscape Industries
Business North - York & North Yorkshire Cham Comm
Business South - Croydon Cham Comm & Industry
Business Survey - Scot Chams Comm
Business Technology Outsourcer - Nat Outsourcing Assn
But - What do you do in the Winter? - Concert Artistes' Assn
Butterflies of Gower - Gower Soc
Button Lines - Brit Button Soc
Buyers Guide to Chillers - Polymer Machinery Mfrs' & Distributors' Assn
Buyers Guide to Dryers - Polymer Machinery Mfrs' & Distributors' Assn
Buyers Guide to Granulators - Polymer Machinery Mfrs' & Distributors' Assn
Buyers Guide to Robots - Polymer Machinery Mfrs' & Distributors' Assn
Buyers Guide to Temperature Control - Polymer Machinery Mfrs' & Distributors' Assn

Buying & Selling Reed - Brit Reed Growers' Assn
The Byron Jnl - Byron Soc

C

C & W In Business - Coventry & Warwickshire Cham Comm
CA Magazine - Inst of Chartered Accountants of Scotland
CAATnews - Campaign against Arms Trade
Cabletalk - SELECT
Cactus World - Brit Cactus & Succulent Soc
Café Culture Magazine - Café Soc
Cahiers - Assn for French Language Studies
Caledonian Gardener - R Caledonian Horticultural Soc
Calendar of Book Fairs - Provincial Booksellers Fairs Assn
The Call Boy - Brit Music Hall Soc
Cambrian Line Magazine - Cambrian Railways Soc
The Campaigner - Library Campaign: supporting friends & users of libraries
Campden & Chorleywood NL - Campden & Chorleywood Food Research Assn
Camping & Caravanning Magazine - Camping & Caravanning Club
Canal Camps Brochure - Waterway Recovery Group
Canoe Focus - Brit Canoe Union
Canoeing Hbk - Brit Canoe Union
Canu Gwerin - Welsh Folk Song Soc (Cymdeithas Alawon Gwerin Cymru)
Capel NL - Capel: the Chapels Heritage Soc
Car Parks of GB Calendar - Car Park Appreciation Soc
Caravan Club Magazine - Caravan Club
Caravanning Europe - Caravan Club
Care - Leukaemia CARE
Care Assistant Training Manual - Registered Nursing Home Assn
Care on the Road - R Soc for the Prevention of Accidents
The Care & Storage of Photographs: recommendations for good practice - Nat Assn of Aerial Photographic Libraries
Care of Viol - Viola da Gamba Soc
Careers Education & Guidance - Assn for Careers Education & Guidance
Careers Guidance Today - Inst of Career Guidance
Careers Software News - ADSET
Carefree Camping & Caravanning Guide to Europe - Camping & Caravanning Club
Cargo Companion - Cambridge Refrigeration Technology
Caribbean Airline News - Caribbean-Brit Business Council
Caribbean Briefing - Caribbean-Brit Business Council
Caring - Carers UK
Caring for the Nation's Health - Brit Health Care Assn
Carnation Ybk - Brit Nat Carnation Soc
Caroline Archer & Robert Harling - Friends of St Bride Library
The Carrollian - Lewis Carroll Soc
The Cartographic Jnl - Brit Cartographic Soc
Cartographiti - Brit Cartographic Soc
Cartophilic Notes & News - Cartophilic Soc of GB
Cascade - Action for Sick Children
The Case against Hysterectomy - Campaign against Hysterectomy & Unnecessary Operations on Women
The Case for Customer Magazines - Assn of Publishing Agencies
Case Notes for Professionals - Huntington's Disease Assn
The Case for Untreated Milk - Assn of Unpasteurised Milk Producers & Consumers
Casebook - Medical Protection Soc
Casemate - Fortress Study Group
CASEnotes - Campaign for State Education
The Caspian - Caspian Horse Soc
The Castles of Gower - Gower Soc
Casualty Simulation - Casualties Union
Catalogue of Brit Suppliers - Energy Industries Council
Catalysts & Catalysed Reactions - R Soc of Chemistry
Catchword - Assn of Teachers of Lipreading to Adults
Catena - Catenian Assn
Catering Manager - Catering Managers Assn of GB & the Channel Islands
Cathedral Music Singing in Cathedrals: a listing of choral services in the UK - Friends of Cathedral Music

Cathodic Protection of Reinforced Concrete: Status Report - Corrosion Prevention Assn

Catholic Ancestor - Catholic Family History Soc

Catholic Archives - Catholic Archives Soc

Catholic Medical Quarterly - Catholic Medical Assn

Catnap - Narcolepsy Assn UK

Cave & Karst Science - Brit Cave Research Assn

Cavies - Nat Cavy Club

Cavity Wounds - Wound Care Soc

CBS News - Caspian Breed Soc

CCA News - Consumer Credit Assn

CDH/DDH Plasters - STEPS

CDH/DDH Splints - STEPS

CDS Guide to Careers Back Stage - Conference of Drama Schools

CDS Guide to Professional Training in Drama & Technical Theatre - Conference of Drama Schools

Cecidology - Brit Plant Gall Soc

CEDA News - Catering Equipment Distributors Assn of GB

Celebration of New Forest Ponies - New Forest Pony Breeding & Cattle Soc

Cemetery & Churchyard Regulations - Assn of Burial Authorities

Centre Circle - Inst of Football Management & Administration

Centre Circle - League Managers Assn

A Century of Archaeology in East Herts - East Herts Archaeological Soc

Ceramic Review - Craft Potters' Assn of GB

Ceramics & Glass: a basic technology - Soc of Glass Technology

Cerebrospinal Fluid Research - Soc for Research into Hydrocephalus & Spina Bifida

Ceredigion - Cymdeithas Hanes Ceredigion - Ceredigion Historical Soc

Certificate of vesting - Confederation of Construction Specialists

Ceska Muzika - Kmoch European Bands Soc

CF Talk - Cystic Fibrosis Trust

CF Today - Cystic Fibrosis Trust

CFC Contract Furnishing Concepts - Assn of Master Upholsterers & Soft Furnishers

Chair Frame Mfrs' Assn

Challenger Wave - Challenger Soc for Marine Science

The Chamber - Surrey Chams Comm

Chance or Choice - Risk Management - Soc of Local Authority Chief Executives & Senior Managers

Changing the Future - Community Foundation Network

Changing with the Times - Scot Disability Sport

Chanter - Bagpipe Soc

Charity Finance Ybk - Charity Finance Directors' Group

Charles Williams Quarterly - Charles Williams Soc

Charolais News - Brit Charolais Cattle Soc

Chartered Architect - R Incorporation of Architects in Scotland

The Chartered Forester - Inst of Chartered Foresters

Chat - Children's Chronic Arthritis Assn
Deaf Education through Listening & Talking

Chat 2 - Children's Chronic Arthritis Assn

Chatham House NL - R Inst of InterNat Affairs

Checklists (the sole commercial guide to European wine & spirit legislation) - Wine & Spirit Trade Assn

Chemical Communications - R Soc of Chemistry

The Chemical Engineer - Instn of Chemical Engineers

Chemical Engineering Research & Design - Instn of Chemical Engineers

Chemical Hazards in Industry - R Soc of Chemistry

Chemical Soc Reviews - R Soc of Chemistry

Chemical World - R Soc of Chemistry

Cheque This Out - Brit Cheque Cashers Assn

Cherryburn Times - Bewick Soc

Cherub Bulletin - R College of Paediatrics & Child Health

Chess Moves - English Chess Fedn

Chester Zoo Life - North of England Zoological Soc (Chester Zoo)

Chew - Tracheo-Oesophageal Fistula Support

Child & Adolescent Mental Health - Assn for Child & Adolescent Mental Health

Child Abuse Review - Brit Assn for the Study & Prevention of Child Abuse & Neglect

Childminding - Scot Childminding Assn

Children & Pets - Soc for Companion Animal Studies

Children and the Media - mediawatch-uk: campaigning for decency & accountability in the media

Children in Prison - Howard League for Penal Reform

Chile News - Brit Chilean Cham Comm

Chilled Ceilings - Chilled Beam & Ceiling Assn

Chimney Jnl - Nat Assn of Chimney Sweeps

Chimney problems & how to cure them - Nat Fireplace Assn

China Eye - Soc for Anglo-Chinese Understanding

China-Britain Trade Review. - China-Britain Business Council

Chivalry - Imperial Soc of Knights Bachelor

Choice in Welfare - Inst of Economic Affairs

Choir Schools Today - Choir Schools Assn

Choosing a Boarding School: a guide for parents - Boarding Schools Assn

Choreography as Work - Dance UK

Chowkidar - Brit Assn for Cemeteries in South Asia

Christian Librarian - Librarians' Christian Fellowship

Chromatography Abstracts - R Soc of Chemistry

Chronicle - Regia Anglorum

Church & King - Soc of King Charles the Martyr

Church Monuments - Church Monuments Soc

Church Music Quarterly - R School of Church Music

The Churches & Chapels of Gower - Gower Soc

Churches Hbk - Fellowship of Independent Evangelical Churches

Cider - Nat Assn of Cider Makers

The Cigarette Packet - Cigarette Packet Collectors' Club of GB

CIGLET - City Information Group

Cip - Urdd Gobaith Cymru (yr Urdd)

CIPA - Chartered Inst of Patent Attorneys

CIPA Directory of Patent Agents - Chartered Inst of Patent Attorneys

Circle Update - Circle of Wine Writers

The Circler - Nat Assn of Ladies' Circles of GB & Ireland

Circuit - Girls Venture Corps Air Cadets

Circuit Chatter - Brit Radio Car Assn

Circular - Shipbuilders & Shiprepairers Assn

Circulation - Brit Hydrological Soc

Circus News - Circus Soc

Cirplan - Soc of Cirplanologists

Citizen - Unlock Democracy (incorporating Charter 88)

Civil Engineering Surveyor - Instn of Civil Engineering Surveyors

Clamavi - Regia Anglorum

Clarinet & Saxophone - Clarinet & Saxophone Soc of GB

Classical Quarterly - Classical Assn

Classical Review - Classical Assn

Classification of Adhesion of Vitreous Enamel to Steel - Inst of Vitreous Enamellers & Vitreous Enamel Assn

Clay Technology - Inst of Materials, Minerals & Mining

Cleaning Validation - Chartered Quality Inst

Clearing Blocked Crushers - Quarry Products Assn

The Clematis - Brit Clematis Soc

The Clerk - Soc of Local Council Clerks

Climb book 100 metabolic diseases - Children Living with Inherited Metabolic Diseases

Climb Update - Children Living with Inherited Metabolic Diseases

Clinical & Experimental Allergy - Brit Soc for Allergy & Clinical Immunology

Clinical & Experimental Dermatology - Brit Assn of Dermatologists

Clinical & Experimental Immunology - Brit Soc for Immunology

Clinical Anatomy - Brit Assn of Clinical Anatomists

Clinical Medicine - R College of Physicians of London

Clinical Oncology -

Clinical Radiology - R College of Radiologists

Clinical Research Focus - Inst of Clinical Research

Clinical Science - Biochemical Soc

Clinical Science - Medical Research Soc

Close Up - Mid Yorkshire Cham Comm & Industry

Clothes to Suit - Scoliosis Assn (UK)

Club Green News - Furniture Industry Research Assn

Coaching People with Learning Disability - UK Sports Assn for People with Learning Disability

Coachline - Brit Tennis Coaches Assn

Coal & log effect gas fires - Nat Fireplace Assn

Coal Trader - Coal Merchants Fedn (GB)

Coastal Racing Construction Regulations - Hovercraft Club of GB

Coat of Arms - Heraldry Soc

Coates Herd Book - Beef Shorthorn Cattle Soc

Coatings - Thermal Spraying & Surface Engineering Assn

© CBD Research Ltd · Beckenham · BR3 5JS · Tel 020 8650 7745 · Fax 020 8650 0768 · E-mail cbd@cbdresearch.com · www.cbdresearch.com

Cobbett's New Register - William Cobbett Soc
The Coble & Keelboat Soc - Coble & Keelboat Soc
Coblegram - Coble & Keelboat Soc
The Cobweb - Kentish Cobnuts Assn
Cochlear Implants: a collection of experiences of users of all ages - Nat Cochlear Implant Users Assn
Code of Practice for Mine exploration - Nat Assn of Mining History Organisations
Code of Practice for Mineral collecting - Nat Assn of Mining History Organisations
Code of Practice for Removal of artefacts - Nat Assn of Mining History Organisations
Code of Practice for Safe Use of Lifting Equipment - Lifting Equipment Engineers Assn
Code of Practice for Safeguarding Machinery - Quarry Products Assn
Code of Practice for Signing in at Surface Dressing Sites; both free to download - Road Surface Treatments Assn
Code of Practice for Surface Dressing - Road Surface Treatments Assn
Code of Practice for the better organisation of Traction Engine rallies, incorporating the Rally Authorisation Scheme - Nat Traction Engine Trust
Code of Practice for the Soluble Coffee Industry in the UK - Brit Soluble Coffee Packers & Importers Assn
Code of Practice for Traction Engines & Similar Vehicles - Nat Traction Engine Trust
Code of Practice: Window Installation Safety - Flat Glass Council
Codes of Practice on the design & Installation of Internal Flooring - Stone Fedn GB
Codes of Practice on the design & Installation of Kitchen Worktops - Stone Fedn GB
Codicil - Willwriters' Assn
The Coleridge Bulletin - Friends of Coleridge
Collateral Warranties - Assn of Geotechnical & Geoenvironmental Specialists
Collections for a history of Staffordshire - Staffordshire Record Soc
Collections News - Collections Trust
Colombian Correspondent - Brit & Colombian Cham Comm
Coloration Technology - Soc of Dyers & Colourists
Colour Index - Soc of Dyers & Colourists
Coloured Sheep News - Brit Coloured Sheep Breeders Assn
The Colourist - Soc of Dyers & Colourists
Come Gardening - THRIVE
Come Into Horticulture - Inst of Horticulture
Comfort Engineering - Inst of Domestic Heating & Environmental Engineers
Comment - CMT UK
          Saint Helens Cham
Comment Extra - Saint Helens Cham
Commentary on the Unidroit Convention - Inst of Art & Law
Commercial Update - Newspaper Soc
The Commercials Book - D&AD
The Commission Agent - Mfrs' Agents' Assn of GB & Ireland
Commissioning Engineers Compendium - Commissioning Specialists Assn
Commissioning Social Research: a good practice guide - Social Research Assn
Common Fisheries Policy - End or Mend? - Campaign for an Independent Britain
Communicate - Assn of Translation Companies
Communicating Quality - R College of Speech & Language Therapists
Communicator - Inst of Scientific & Technical Communicators
Communicators - Brit Assn of Communicators in Business
Communities - R Pharmaceutical Soc of GB
Community - Nat Fedn of Community Organisations
Community Audit Tool - Infection Prevention Soc
Community Extra - Nat Fedn of Community Organisations
Community Foundations & Community Needs Assessment - Community Foundation Network
Community Investment Relief Guide - Community Development Finance Assn
Community Transport - Community Transport Assn UK
Compact Scot Nat Dictionary -
Comparative Criticism - Brit Comparative Literature Assn

Compendium of Buttonhooks - Buttonhook Soc
Compendium of Data Sheets IOC Animal Medicines - Nat Office of Animal Health
Competition & Masterpoint Jnl - Welsh Bridge Union
Complete Corpus of Kempe Glass in the UK - Kempe Soc
The Complete Guide to Starting & Running a Bookshop - Booksellers Assn of the UK & Ireland
The Complete Guidebook to Avebury - Megalithic Soc
The Complete Music for Solo Piano - Havergal Brian Soc
Composites UK Bulletin - Composites UK
Composting News - Assn of Organics Recycling
Compressed Air Condensate - Brit Compressed Air Soc
Computer Resurrection - Computer Conservation Soc
Computers & Law - Soc for Computers & Law
Computers in Genealogy - Soc of Genealogists
Concise Scots Dictionary -
Concord - English Speaking Union of the Commonwealth
Concrete - Concrete Soc
Concrete Current Awareness - Brit Cement Assn
Concrete Cutter - Drilling & Sawing Assn
Concrete Engineers InterNat Jnl - Concrete Soc
Concrete Mix Design - Assn of Concrete Indl Flooring Contractors
Concrete Quarterly - Brit Cement Assn
Condensed Matter - Inst of Physics
The Conductor - Nat Assn of Brass Band Conductors
The Conduit - Cambridge Antiquarian Soc
Conference & Exhibition Fact Finder - Assn for Conferences & Events
Connect - Brit Inst for Learning & Development
          Homeless Link
          Long-term Conditions Alliance
The Conradian - Joseph Conrad Soc (UK)
Conservation Issues & the Maintenance of Cereal Varieties for Thatching - Nat Soc of Master Thatchers
Conserving Lakeland - Friends of the Lake District
Construction & Law Review - Instn of Civil Engineering Surveyors
Construction History Jnl - Construction History Soc
Construction Industry Forecasts - Construction Products Assn
Construction Information Quarterly - Chartered Inst of Building
Construction Manager - Chartered Inst of Building
Construction Markets Trends - Construction Products Assn
Construction Products Briefing - Construction Products Assn
Construction Products Trade Survey - Construction Products Assn
Construction Trends Survey - Construction Confederation
Consult - Assn for Consultancy & Engineering
Consultancy Resources Directory - Assn of Security Consultants
Consumer Credit - Consumer Credit Trade Assn
Consumer Policy Review - Consumers' Assn
Contact - Chartered Inst of Building
          Inst of Traffic Accident Investigators
Contact News - Contact the Elderly
Contact Point - Brit Assn of Dental Therapists
Contemporary Hypnosis - BSCAH - Brit Soc of Cinical & Academic Hypnosis
Context - Inst of Historic Building Conservation
Contract Catering Survey - Brit Hospitality Assn
The Contract Flooring Jnl - Contract Flooring Assn
Contracting Bulletin - Nat Assn of Agricultural Contractors
Contractors Directory - Nat Assn of Agricultural Contractors
Control - Inst of Operations Management
The Controversy of John Hampden's Death - John Hampden Soc
Convection - Tornado & Storm Research Organisation
Conway Memorial Lecture - South Place Ethical Soc
Co-operative Official - Nat Assn of Co-operative Officials
Co-operatives - Co-operatives UK
The Copy Book - D&AD
Cornish Archaeology - Cornwall Archaeological Soc
Corporate Plan - Quality Meat Scotland
Correlation - Astrological Assn of GB
Corrosion Management - Inst of Corrosion
Corrosion Science - Inst of Corrosion
Cosmic Voice - Aetherius Soc
Cosmos - Traditional Cosmology Soc
Cosmos & Culture - Astrological Assn of GB
Costings of Agricultural Operations -
Costs, Controls & Profit - Forum of Private Business
Costume - Costume Soc

Council Vehicle News - Road Transport Fleet Data Soc
The Councillor - Nat Assn of Councillors
The Councillors' Hbk - Northern Ireland Local Government Assn
Counselling & Psychotherapy Research - Brit Assn for Counselling & Psychotherapy
Counselling at Work - Brit Assn for Counselling & Psychotherapy
Counselling in Scotland - COSCA (Counselling & Psychotherapy in Scotland)
Counterfoil - Brit Banking History Soc
The Counties - Assn of Brit Counties
Country Sports - Countryside Alliance
Countryside Building - Rural & Indl Design & Building Assn
Courage - War Widows Assn of GB
Courier - Registered Nursing Home Assn
A Course for all Seasons: a guide to golf course management - R & Ancient Golf Club
The Court Historian - Soc for Court Studies
Courtesy Call - Campaign for Courtesy
CPA News - Craft Potters' Assn of GB
CPD Spotlight - Professional Assns Research Network
Creating a Fountain - Fountain Soc
The Creation Manifesto - Biblical Creation Soc
Creators Have Rights (Video) - Creator's Rights Alliance
Credit Management - Inst of Credit Management
Credit Union News - Assn of Brit Credit Unions
The Creel - Friends of Alan Rawsthorne
The Cricket Statistician - Assn of Cricket Statisticians & Historians
The Crier - Ancient & Honourable Guild of Town Criers
The Crofter - Scot Crofting Foundation
Cromford Venture Centre - Arkwright Soc
Cromwelliana - Cromwell Assn
The Croquet Gazette - Croquet Assn
Crossed Grain Magazine - Coeliac UK
Crossfire - American Civil War Round Table (UK)
Crossways - Assn for Low Countries Studies in GB & Ireland
Crossword - Crossword Club
Crossword Club Guide to Playfair - Crossword Club
The Crown - Monarchist League
Croydon Church Townscape - Croydon Natural History & Scientific Soc
Cruising Construction Regulations - Hovercraft Club of GB
Crypt - Xenophon
Crystallisation 2003 - Soc of Glass Technology
Crystallography News - Brit Crystallographic Assn
Crystals & Healing for Everyone - Crystal & Healing Fedn
Crystals Strong & Beautiful - Crystal & Healing Fedn
CrystEngComm - R Soc of Chemistry
CSDF Business Continuity Guide - Food Storage & Distribution Fedn
CSDF Fire Risk Minimisation Guidance - Food Storage & Distribution Fedn
CSDF Material Handling Safety Guide - Food Storage & Distribution Fedn
The Cuckoo - Chesterfield Canal Trust
Cue Line - Stage Management Assn
Cued Speech Explained by People who use it - Cued Speech Assn UK
Cued Speech Instructional Booklet - Cued Speech Assn UK
Cued Speech Instructional Video - Cued Speech Assn UK
The Cued Speech Research Book - Cued Speech Assn UK
The Cultivator - Vintage Horticultural & Garden Machinery Club
Cultural & Social History - Social History Soc
Current Awareness Service - Brit Inst of Learning Disabilities
Current Folklore - Folklore Soc
Curriculum Framework for Operating Department Practice - College of Operating Department Practitioners
Cushy - Assn for Cushing's Treatment & Help
The Custodian - Brit Assn for Shooting & Conservation
Customer First - Inst of Customer Service
Cutting Edge - Brit Olympic Assn
Cuttings - Brit Lawn Mower Racing Assn
Cyclamen Jnl - Cyclamen Soc
Cycle - CTC
Cymry Llundain - London Welshman - London Welsh Assn
Czech Music - Dvořák Soc for Czech & Slovak Music

D

D&AD Annual & DVD Showreel - D&AD
D&AD Student Annual - D&AD
Dad's Army Companion - Dad's Army Appreciation Soc
Dales Despatch - Dales Pony Soc
Dalton Transactions - R Soc of Chemistry
Dams & Reservoirs - Brit Dam Soc
Dance - Imperial Soc of Teachers of Dancing
Dance Gazette - R Academy of Dance
Dance Matters - Nat Dance Teachers Assn
Dance Research Jnl - Soc for Dance Research
Dance Teaching Essentials - Dance UK
Dance UK News - Dance UK
The Dancer - Brit Ballet Organization
Danceworld - Brit Theatre Dance Assn
Danny's Mum - Action for Prisoners' Families
Dark Horizons - Brit Fantasy Soc
Dartmoor Diary - Dartmoor Pony Soc
Dartmoor Matters - Dartmoor Preservation Assn
DATA Jnl - Design & Technology Assn
DATA News - Design & Technology Assn
Data Protection Act 1998: guidelines for social research - Social Research Assn
Database of Event & Conference Organisers - Brit Assn of Conference Destinations
Database of Long Distance Paths - Long Distance Walkers Assn
The David Jones Jnl - David Jones Soc
Davy's Devon Herd Book - Devon Cattle Breeders' Soc
Dawn - Drama Assn of Wales (Cymdeithas Ddrama Cymru)
Dawns - Cymdeithas Ddawns Werin Cymru (Welsh Folk Dance Soc (WFDS))
Deadline - Assn of UK Media Librarians
Deafness & Education
Assn Magazine - Brit Assn of Teachers of the Deaf
Decking - the essential guide for DIY - Timber Decking Assn
The Declaration - Assn of Independent Inventory Clerks
Dedicated - Inst of Legal Secretaries & PAs
Deer - Brit Deer Soc
Deer Farming - Brit Deer Farmers Assn
Deer News - Brit Deer Farmers Assn
The Delphinium Garden - Delphinium Soc
Delphiniums - Delphinium Soc
Dementia in Scotland - Alzheimer Scotland - Action on Dementia
The Democrat - Campaign against Euro-federalism
Democratic Broadsheet - Campaign against Euro-federalism
Demolition & Dismantling Jnl - Nat Fedn of Demolition Contractors
Demolition Engineer - Inst of Demolition Engineers
Dental Historian - Lindsay Soc for the History of Dentistry
Dental Implant Summaries - Assn of Dental Implantology UK
Dental Laboratory - Dental Laboratories Assn
Dental Therapy Update - Brit Assn of Dental Therapists
The Dental Trader - Brit Dental Trade Assn
Depression - SANE
Derby Awards brochure - Horserace Writers & Photographers Assn
Derbyshire Archaeological Jnl - Derbyshire Archaeological Soc
Derbyshire Miscellany - Derbyshire Archaeological Soc
Describing Illustrations - Confederation of Transcribed Information Services
Descriptions of Plant Viruses - Assn of Applied Biologists
Design Risk Management Guide - Assn for Project Safety
The Designer - Chartered Soc of Designers
The Designer Craftsman - Soc of Designer Craftsmen
Designing Magazine - Design & Technology Assn
Despatches Magazine - Despatch Assn
Deutsch: Lehren und Lernen - Assn for Language Learning
Development Education - Development Education Assn
Devon Archaeology - Devon Archaeological Soc
The Dexter Bulletin - Dexter Cattle Soc
Dhooraght - Yn Cheshaght Ghailckagh (the Manx Gaelic Soc)
Diabetes Update - Diabetes UK
Diabetic Foot - Wound Care Soc
Diabetic Medicine - Diabetes UK
Diagnostic Engineering - Instn of Diagnostic Engineers
Diagnostics in Healthcare - Brit In Vitro Diagnostics Assn

© CBD Research Ltd · Beckenham · BR3 5JS · Tel 020 8650 7745 · Fax 020 8650 0768 · E-mail cbd@cbdresearch.com · www.cbdresearch.com

Dialogue - Inst of Group Analysis
The Dickensian - Dickens Fellowship
Dictionary of Business Administration - Assn of Business
    Administration
Dictionary of Fire Technology - Instn of Fire Engineers
Dictionary of InterNat Marketing - Inst of InterNat Marketing
Dictionary of the Scots Language - Scot Language Dictionaries
Diecasting World - Inst of Cast Metals Engineers
Dietetics Today - Brit Dietetic Assn
Diffusion - Sonic Arts Network
The Digest - Brit Cham Comm Thailand
Digital Exchange - Telephone Helplines Assn
Direct - Directors Guild of GB
Direct News - Assn for Public Service Excellence
Direct Selling, Consumer Goods in the UK - Direct Selling Assn
Direct Selling: from door to door to network marketing -
    Direct Selling Assn
Directory of Accredited Behavioural / Cognitive & REBT
    Psychotherapists - Brit Assn for Behavioural & Cognitive
    Psychotherapies
Directory of Acquisitions Librarians - Nat Acquisitions Group
Directory of Antiquarian & Second Hand Booksellers -
    Provincial Booksellers Fairs Assn
Directory of Book Publishers - Booksellers Assn of the UK &
    Ireland
Directory of Booksellers - Booksellers Assn of the UK & Ireland
Directory of Brit Crematoria - Cremation Soc of GB
Directory of Brit Spring Manufacturers - UK Spring Mfrs Assn
Directory of Contracting Officers - Assn of Directors of Adult
    Social Services
Directory of Courses in Library & Information Studies in the
    UK - Brit Assn for Information & Library Education & Research
A Directory of Drama Adjudicators - Guild of Drama
    Adjudicators
Directory of Funded Organisations - London Councils
Directory of Guidance Provision for Adults in the
UK - ADSET
Directory of Insolvency Permit Holders - Inst of Chartered
    Accountants of Scotland
Directory of Irish Family History - Ulster Historical Foundation
Directory of Local Authority Building Control - LABC
Directory of Markets in England, Wales & Scotland - Livestock
    Auctioneers Assn
Directory of Pet Crematoria - Cremation Soc of GB
Directory of Police & Public Security Suppliers - Assn of Police &
    Public Security Suppliers
Directory of Postgraduate Medical Centres - Nat Assn of
    Clinical Tutors
Directory of Publishing in Scotland - Publishing Scotland
Directory of Pure Arabian Studs in GB & Ireland - Arab Horse
    Soc
Directory of Rehabilitation Services - UK Acquired Brain Injury
    Forum
Directory of Restoration: a compendium of examples - Quarry
    Products Assn
Directory of Storytellers - Soc for Storytelling
Directory of Veterinary Practices - R College of Veterinary
    Surgeons
Directory of Youth & Student Orchestras - Nat Assn of Youth
    Orchestras
Disability Now - Scope
Disability Rights Hbk - Disability Alliance
Discrimination Law Briefings - Discrimination Law Assn
DISKUS - Brit Soc for the Study of Religions
Dispatches - Vitiligo Soc
Dispensing Optics - Assn of Brit Dispensing Opticians
Distilleries to Visit Guide - Scotch Whisky Assn
Distillery Map - Scotch Whisky Assn
The Distributor - Jewellery Distributors' Assn of the UK
Distributors of PSI Report - Consumer Credit Assn
DLS Bulletin - Dorothy L Sayers Soc
DMA Annual Review - Defence Mfrs Assn
Dodo - E F Benson Soc
Dog Trainer - Assn of Pet Dog Trainers
Dog Warden News - Nat Dog Wardens Assn
Doing Business in Brazil - Brit Cham Comm & Industry in Brazil
The Dolls' House Magazine - Guild of Master Craftsmen
Domestic Sprinkler Systems - Brit Automatic Fire Sprinkler Assn

Doris Stockwell Memorial Papers - Brit Assn of Numismatic Socs
Double Reed News - Brit Double Reed Soc
The Double Tressure - Heraldry Soc of Scotland
Doula News - Brit Doula Assn
Dowsing Today - Brit Soc of Dowsers
The Dozenal Jnl - Dozenal Soc of GB
Dragon Line NL - Brit Dragon Boat Racing Assn
Dragonfly News - Brit Dragonfly Soc
The Drake Broadside - Drake Exploration Soc
The Drake NL - Drake Exploration Soc
Drama - Nat Drama
Drama NL - R Scot Academy of Music & Drama
The Dramatherapy Jnl - Brit Assn of Dramatherapists
Dressings Selection - Wound Care Soc
Driving after Amputation - Brit Limbless Ex-Service Men's Assn
Driving Instructor - Driving Instructors Assn
Driving Magazine - Driving Instructors Assn
Drummers Call - Corps of Drums Soc
Dry Shake Topping - Assn of Concrete Indl Flooring Contractors
Duchenne News - Duchenne Family Support Group
Due North - Fedn for Ulster Local Studies
The Dun Thing - Dun Horse & Pony Soc
Durbar - Indian Military Historical Soc
Durham Archaeological Jnl - Architectural & Archaeological Soc
    of Durham & Northumberland
Durham Biographies - Durham County Local History Soc
Durham City and its MPs - Durham County Local History Soc
The Durham Crown Lordships - Durham County Local History Soc
Durham Wildlife - Durham Wildlife Trust
Dutch Crossing - Assn for Low Countries Studies in GB & Ireland
DVC - UK Practical Shooting Assn
Dymock Poets & Friends - Friends of the Dymock Poets

E

E.U.News - Biosciences Fedn
Early 19th Century Glassmaking in Austria & Germany - Soc
    of Glass Technology
Early Education - Brit Assn for Early Childhood Education
Early Music Performer - Nat Early Music Assn
Early Settlement Rebate - Finance & Leasing Assn
Earth Matters - Friends of the Earth
Easter Rising in Song & Ballad - Workers' Music Assn
The Eastern Africa NL - Eastern Africa Assn
EBEA News - Economics, Business & Enterprise Assn
Ecclesiology Today - Ecclesiological Soc
The Eckhart Review - Eckhart Soc
Economic Affairs - Inst of Economic Affairs
Economic Development - Instn of Economic Development
Economic History Review - Economic History Soc
The Economic Jnl - R Economic Soc
Economic Trends UK - Japanese Cham Comm & Industry in the UK
Ecos: a review of conservation - Brit Assn of Nature
    Conservationists
Eczema - Aetiology & Management - Wound Care Soc
Edgar Evans of Gower - Gower Soc
EDS (English Dance & Song) - English Folk Dance & Song Soc
Education - Soc of Education Consultants
Education 3-13 - Assn for the Study of Primary Education
Education in Chemistry - R Soc of Chemistry
Education Libraries Jnl - Librarians of Insts & Schools of Education
Education Management & Administration - Brit Educational
    Leadership, Management & Administration Soc
Education Review - Nat Union of Teachers
Education in Science - Assn for Science Education
The Education Social Worker - Nat Assn of Social Workers in
    Education
Education Today - College of Teachers
Educational Gerontology - Assn for Education & Ageing
Educational Psychology in Practice - Assn of Educational
    Psychologists
Educational Therapy & Therapeutic Teaching - Caspari
    Foundation for Educational Therapy & Therapeutic Teaching
eDVC - UK Practical Shooting Assn
Effective Business in Taiwan - Brit Cham Comm in Taipei

EFNARC Specification for Sprayed Concrete - Sprayed Concrete Assn

The Egg Crafter - Egg Crafters Guild of GB

Egyptian Archaeology - Egypt Exploration Soc

Egyptian-Brit Trade - Egyptian Brit Cham Comm

El Hornero - Brit Uruguayan Soc

Electric Boat News - Electric Boat Assn

The Electric Railway - Electric Railway Soc

Electronic Letters - Instn of Engineering & Technology

Electronic Transfer of Geotechnical Data from Ground Investigations - Assn of Geotechnical & Geoenvironmental Specialists

Elements - R Instn of GB

Elements & Philosophy of Pharmaecutical QA - Chartered Quality Inst

The Elgar Jnl - Elgar Soc

The Elgar News - Elgar Soc

eLucidate - UK EInformation Group

The Embalmer - Brit Inst of Embalmers

Embroidery - Embroiderers' Guild

E-Motion - Assn for Dance Movement Therapy UK

Emotional & Behavioural Difficulties - SEBDA - the Social, Emotional & Behavioural Difficulties Assn

Employment & Support Alliance Guide 2008-09 - Disability Alliance

Endocrine Related Cancer - Soc for Endocrinology

The Endocrinologist - Soc for Endocrinology

Energy Action - Nat Energy Action

Energy World - Energy Inst

engage review - engage: Nat Assn of Gallery Education

engagements - engage: Nat Assn of Gallery Education

The Engineering Designer - Instn of Engineering Designers

Engineering in Emergencies: a practical guide - RedR UK

Engineering Integrity - Engineering Integrity Soc

Engineering & Technology - Instn of Engineering & Technology

Engineers' & Architects' Guide to Hot Dip Galvanising - Galvanizers Assn

England's Standard - R Soc of St George

English - English Assn

English 4-11 - English Assn

English Bridge - English Bridge Union

English Draughts Jnl - English Draughts Assn

English in the UK - English UK

English, Drama, Media - Nat Assn for the Teaching of English

Enjoy Sweet Peas - Nat Sweet Pea Soc

Enteral Feeding - Infection Prevention Soc

Enterprise Communities (wealth beyond welfare) - Community Development Finance Assn

Enthusing the Next Generation - Biosciences Fedn

Environmental Archaeology: Jnl of Human Palaeoecology - Assn for Environmental Archaeology

Environmental Education - Nat Assn for Environmental Education (UK)

Environmental Health Scotland - R Environmental Health Inst of Scotland

Environmental Law - UK Environmental Law Assn

Environmental Microbiology - Soc for Applied Microbiology

The Environmental Scientist - Instn of Environmental Sciences

Envirotech News EU - Environmental Industries Commission

Envirotech News UK - Environmental Industries Commission

The Ephemerist - Ephemera Soc

Epilepsy News - Epilepsy Action Scotland

Epilepsy Review - Nat Soc for Epilepsy

Epilepsy Today - Brit Epilepsy Assn

Epiphytes - Epiphytic Plant Study Group

Equal Opportunities - policy into practice - Independent Theatre Council

Equestrian Trade News - Brit Equestrian Trade Assn

Equine Behaviour - Equine Behaviour Forum

Equipment Selection - Wound Care Soc

Ergonomics - Ergonomics Soc

Ergonomics in design - Ergonomics Soc

The Ergonomist NL - Ergonomics Soc

ESBA Post - Badminton England

Escape To... - Youth Hostels Assn (England & Wales)

Escaping the Leasehold Trap - Leasehold Enfranchisement Assn

Escher Wyss & Co - Steam Boat Assn of GB

ESG 2004 - Soc of Glass Technology

Esperanto en Skotlando - Scot Esperanto Assn (Esperanto-Asocio de Skotlando)

ESSA News - Emergency Social Services Assn

Essays in Biochemistry - Biochemical Soc

Essence - Brit Flower & Vibrational Essences Assn

The Essential Guide to Aqueous Coating of Paper & Board - Paper Industry Technical Assn

Essex Archaeology & History - Essex Soc for Archaeology & History

Essex Archaeology & History News - Essex Soc for Archaeology & History

Essex Jnl - Essex Archaeological & Historical Congress

Essex Wildlife - Essex Wildlife Trust

The Estate Agent - Nat Assn of Estate Agents

Ethical Record - South Place Ethical Soc

Ethics & Wisdom in Medicine - Medical Ethics Alliance

Eureka - Kingston Cham Comm

EuroChoices - Agricultural Economics Soc

The European Advertising & Media Forecast - Advertising Assn

European Eating Disorders Review - Eating Disorders Assn

European Jnl for Dental Implantologists - Assn of Dental Implantology UK

European Jnl of Disorders of Communication - R College of Speech & Language Therapists

European Jnl of Information Systems - Operational Research Soc

European Jnl of Parenteral & Pharmaceutical Sciences - Pharmaceutical & Healthcare Sciences Soc

European Jnl of Phycology - Brit Phycological Soc

European Jnl of Prosthodontics & Restorative Dentistry - Brit Soc for Restorative Dentistry

European Jnl of Soil Science - Brit Soc of Soil Science

European Jnl of Surgical Oncology - BASO ~ the Assn for Cancer Surgery

European Morgan Horse Magazine - Brit Morgan Horse Soc

European Rail News - Railway Enthusiasts Soc (Rail Europe)

European-Atlantic Jnl - European-Atlantic Group

Europos Lietuvis - Lithuanian Assn in GB (Britanjos Lietuviai)

The Evacuee - Evacuees Reunion Assn

An Evaluation of the Grandparent & Toddler Group Initiative - Grandparents' Assn

Event Organiser - Event Services Assn

Event Organisers Update - Soc of Event Organisers

The Events Directory - Nationwide Caterers Assn

Evolution of Permanent Way - Permanent Way Instn

Excalibur - R Navy Enthusiasts' Soc

Excel - Assn of Healthcare Cleaning Professionals

Exchange - Nat Eczema Soc

Executive Accountant - Inst of Cost & Executive Accountants

Exhibition Standard - Assn of Event Organisers
Assn of Event Venues
Events Industry Alliance

Experimental Physiology - Physiological Soc

The Expert - Academy of Experts

Explaining Vending - Automatic Vending Assn

Explosives Engineering - Inst of Explosives Engineers

Export News - Brit Jewellery, Giftware & Finishing Fedn

The Exporter - UK Fashion Exports

Extra Cover - Club Cricket Conference

Eye - R College of Ophthalmologists

Eyes & Ears - Automotive Distribution Fedn

F

The FA NL - Families Anonymous

FAB - Fanderson: the official Gerry Anderson Appreciation Soc

Face Facts - Brit Compact Collectors' Soc

face2face - Confederation of Dental Employers

Fact & Fiction - Brit Waterbed Assn

FACTA Specification - Fabricated Access Covers Trade Assn

FACTion - Falsely Accused Carers & Teachers

Facts & Figures - Incorporated Nat Assn of Brit & Irish Millers

The Facts on the Performance of Timber Doors & Doorsets - Architectural & Specialist Door Mfrs Assn

Facts on Salt - Salt Assn

Fair Catalogues - Provincial Booksellers Fairs Assn

© CBD Research Ltd · Beckenham · BR3 5JS · Tel 020 8650 7745 · Fax 020 8650 0768 · E-mail cbd@cbdresearch.com · www.cbdresearch.com

Fairyworld News - Fairyworld
Faith & Worship - Prayer Book Soc
Falconer - Brit Falconers' Club
Familia: Ulster Genealogical Review - Ulster Historical Foundation
Family History - Inst of Heraldic & Genealogical Studies
Family Magazine - Fibromyalgia Assn UK
Family Matters - Family Rights Group
Faraday Discussions - R Soc of Chemistry
Farming News - Ulster Farmers Union
FASS Information - Fedn of Aerospace Support Services
Fast News - Farnborough Air Sciences Trust
Fasti of the General Assembly of the Presbyterian Church in Ireland 1840-1910 - Presbyterian Historical Soc of Ireland
FCA News - FCA Membership (Forestry Contracting Assn Membership)
FCEM News InterNat - Brit Assn of Women Entrepreneurs
Feathered World - Nat Pigeon Assn
Fedn Focus - Scot Fedn of Housing Assns
Fedn Jnl - General Fedn of Trade Unions
Federation News - General Fedn of Trade Unions
        Fedn for Community Development Learning
        Nat Market Traders Fedn
Feedback - Confederation of Aerial Industries
The Fell Runner - Fell Runners Assn
Fellows' Directory - Academy of Medical Sciences
Fellowship News - Fellowship of Cycling Old-Timers
Feng Shui News - Feng Shui Soc
Fern Gazette - Brit Pteridological Soc
FESI - European Insulation Standards - Thermal Insulation Contractors Assn
Festival of Hymns - Hymn Soc of GB & Ireland
Fidelity - Nat Council of Psychotherapists
Field & Fell NL - Westmorland County Agricultural Soc
Field Guide - W W Jacobs Appreciation Soc
Field Studies Magazine - Field Studies Council
The Fifth Fuel - Assn for the Conservation of Energy
Fight Back (physiotherapy video + DVD) - Nat Ankylosing Spondylitis Soc
Film & Video Maker - Inst of Amateur Cinematographers
Financial Controller - Assn of Financial Controllers & Administrators
Financial Planner - Inst of Financial Planning
Financial World - Inst of Financial Services
Finding Dad - Action for Prisoners' Families
Fine Food Digest - Guild of Fine Food Retailers
Fines & Charges in Public Libraries in England & Wales - Soc of Chief Librarians
Fingerprint Whorld - Fingerprint Soc
The Finial - Silver Spoon Club of GB
Fire & Thatch - Nat Soc of Master Thatchers
Fire Cover - Fire Brigade Soc
Fire Engineers Jnl - Instn of Fire Engineers
Fire Precautions Guide to Risk Assessment - UK Warehousing Assn
Fire Prevention - Fire Protection Assn
Fire Protection for Structural Steel in Buildings - Assn for Specialist Fire Protection
Fire Protection Ybk - Fire Protection Assn
Fire Technology - Calculations - Instn of Fire Engineers
Fire Technology - Chemistry Combustion - Instn of Fire Engineers
Fireplace safety, maintenance & chimney sweeping - Nat Fireplace Assn
Fireplace surrounds, their construction & installation - Nat Fireplace Assn
First - Local Government Assn
First Aid Manual - Saint Andrew's Ambulance Assn
First Five - Scot Pre-School Play Assn
First Voice - Fedn of Small Businesses
Fiscal Studies - Inst for Fiscal Studies
Fish - Inst of Fisheries Management
Fish Friers Review - Nat Fedn of Fish Friers
Fishing Boats - Forty Plus (40+) Fishing Boat Assn
Five Foot Three - Railway Preservation Soc of Ireland
Flagmaster - Flag Inst
Flareoff - Offshore Industry Liaison Committee
Fleet Operator - ACFO
Flipside - Instn of Engineering & Technology

The Flower Arranger - Nat Assn of Flower Arrangement Socs
FLS News - Folklore Soc
Flueways - Nat Assn of Chimney Engineers
Flyball Record - Brit Flyball Assn
The Flydresser - Flydressers Guild
The Flying Scot - Scot Hang Gliding & Paragliding Fedn
The Flywheel - Northern Mill Engine Soc
FM World - Brit Inst of Facilities Management
FMC News - Fire Mark Circle
Focal Point - Soc of Floristry
Focus - Assn of Lighting Designers
        Assn of Personal Injury Lawyers
        Brit Science Fiction Assn
        The Chamber - The Accredited Cham Comm for Bedfordshire & Luton
        Lancashire & Yorkshire Railway Soc
        Leukaemia CARE
        North Staffordshire Cham Comm & Industry
        Nystagmus Network
Focus Magazine - Brit Orienteering Fedn
        Inst of Videography
        Self Storage Assn
Focus NL - Brit Assn of Colliery Management, Technical Energy Administrative Management
Focus on Fives NL - Brit Assn for Adoption & Fostering
Focus on Haflingers - Haflinger Soc of GB
Focus on Swaziland - Swaziland Soc
Folk Arts England News - Assn of Festival Organisers
Folk Life: a jnl of ethnological studies - Soc for Folk Life Studies
Folk Music Jnl - English Folk Dance & Song Soc
Folklore - Folklore Soc
Follies - Folly Fellowship
FoMRHI Quarterly - Fellowship of Makers & Researchers of Historical Instruments
Food & Bioproducts Processing - Instn of Chemical Engineers
Food & Drinks Directory of the UK - Coeliac UK
Food Science & Technology - Inst of Food Science & Technology
Food Service Standards at Ward Level: good practice guide - Hospital Caterers Assn
Food Trader - Nat Fedn of Meat & Food Traders
Footprint - Brit Walking Fedn
Footprints - Brit Reflexology Assn
Fore & Aft - Yacht Harbour Assn
Forecourt - Retail Motor Industry Fedn
Forestry - Inst of Chartered Foresters
Forestry & Timber News - Confederation of Forest Industries
Forestry Jnl - Inst of Chartered Foresters
Forge - Nat Assn of Farriers, Blacksmiths & Agricultural Engineers
Forging Links - Tools for Self Reliance
Form of Appointment - Assn for Project Safety
The Formation Sign - Military Heraldry Soc (The Cloth Insignia Research & Collectors Soc)
The Formulary - Friends of Dr Watson
Fort - Fortress Study Group
Forty Years On - Assn of Past Rotarians
Forum - Brit Fedn of Brass Bands
Forward - Chartered Quality Inst
        Spinal Injuries Assn
Foster Care - Fostering Network
Foundry Trade Jnl - Inst of Cast Metals Engineers
Foundry Ybk & Castings Buyers Guide - Inst of Cast Metals Engineers
Four Four - Brit Academy of Composers + Songwriters
Four Seasons News - South of England Agricultural Soc
Framework - Leukaemia CARE
Framework - Construct: Concrete Structures Group
The Franco-Brit Trade Directory - Chambre de Commerce Française de Grande-Bretagne
Francophonie - Assn for Language Learning
Free Life - Libertarian Alliance
Free Press - Campaign for Press & Broadcasting Freedom
The Free Trader - Free Trade League
Freedom Today - Freedom Assn
The Freeman - Guild of Freemen of the City of London
Freemen of England & Wales - Freemen of England & Wales
The Freephone Directory of Legal Services - Willwriters' Assn
Freeway - Brit Nat Temperance League
Freight - Freight Transport Assn

Freight Services Directory - Brit InterNat Freight Assn
French Studies - Soc for French Studies
Freshwater Reviews - Freshwater Biological Assn
Friday Morning at BHTA - Brit Healthcare Trades Assn
Friends Connect - Attend
Friends for Life - Assn of Friendly Socs
Friends Magazine - Scot Soc for the Prevention of Cruelty to Animals
Fritillary - Ashmolean Natural History Soc of Oxfordshire
From Netley to Maiwand - Friends of Dr Watson
From Palace to Washhouse: a study of the Old Palace, Croydon, from 1780 to 1887 - Croydon Natural History & Scientific Soc
From Rome to Maastricht - a reappraisal of Britain's membership of the EC - Campaign for an Independent Britain
Frontline - Chartered Soc of Physiotherapy
Front-Line - Inst of Career Guidance
FSF News - Football Supporters' Fedn
Fuels for your fire - Nat Fireplace Assn
The Fulcrum - Craniosacral Therapy Assn of the UK
Full Orchestra - Nat Assn of Youth Orchestras
The Funeral Director Monthly - Nat Assn of Funeral Directors
Funerals without God - Brit Humanist Assn
The Funnel - Steam Boat Assn of GB
Fur & Feather (inc Rabbits) - Brit Rabbit Council
Furniture & Cabinetmaking - Guild of Master Craftsmen
Furniture History - Furniture History Soc
Future & the Inventor - Inst of Patentees & Inventors

G

G K Quarterly - Chesterton Soc
GA Magazine - Geographical Assn
The Gallipolian - Gallipoli Assn
Game Farming NL - Game Farmers Assn
The Garden - R Horticultural Soc
Garden Design Jnl - Soc of Garden Designers
Garden History - Garden History Soc
Gardens Open Directory - Alpine Garden Soc
The Gargoyle - Malcolm Muggeridge Soc
Gas Business - SBGI
Gas Installer Magazine - Council for Registered Gas Installers
Gatelodge - POA: the Professional Trades Union for Prison, Correctional & Secure Psychiatric Workers
Gauchers News - Gaucher's Assn
The Gavel - Nat Assn of Valuers & Auctioneers
Gazette - CILIP: Chartered Inst of Library & Information Professionals
Gazetteers of Industrial Archaeology - Derbyshire Archaeological Soc
GBCT TECHS Magazine - Guild of Brit Camera Technicians
Gender Trust Guide - Gender Trust
Genealogists' Magazine - Soc of Genealogists
General Dental Practitioner - Dental Practitioners Assn
General Requirements: for certification of personnel engaged in Indl rope access methods - Indl Rope Access Trade Assn
Generations Review - Brit Soc of Gerontology
Genes & Development - Genetics Soc
Geochemical Transactions - R Soc of Chemistry
Geoenvironmental Site Assessment: guide to the model report. - Assn of Geotechnical & Geoenvironmental Specialists
Geography - Geographical Assn
GeogScot - R Scot Geographical Soc
Geophysical Jnl InterNat - R Astronomical Soc
George Borrow Bulletin - George Borrow Soc
George Eliot Review - George Eliot Fellowship
German History - German History Soc
German Politics - Assn for the Study of German Politics
Get Carter Calendar - Car Park Appreciation Soc
Get Cruisewise - Assn of Cruise Experts
Get it Sussed - Meningitis Research Foundation
Getting Started: the common induction standards in adult social care - Assn for Real Change
Gifted & Talented - Nat Assn for Gifted Children
GIG Today - Genetic Interest Group

Gilbert & Sullivan News - Gilbert & Sullivan Soc
Giving Shares & Securities: information pack for financial advisers - Community Foundation Network
Glasgow Business Jnl - Glasgow Cham Comm
Glass Network - Contemporary Glass Soc
Glass News - Assn for the History of Glass (1977)
Glass Technology - Soc of Glass Technology
Glaucus - Brit Marine Life Study Soc
Glazed Expressions - Tiles & Architectural Ceramics Soc (Tile Soc)
Glazing Manual - Glass & Glazing Fedn
The Gleam - Sheila Kaye-Smith Soc
Global Youth Work - Development Education Assn
Globe Trotter - Brit Guild of Travel Writers
Glossary of Printing Terms - Brit Printing Soc
GN News - Great Northern Railway Soc
Gnomon - Assn for Astronomy Education
Going Green - ETA Services
Gold Top News - Quality Milk Producers
The Goldfish Club - Goldfish Club
Golf Club Management - Golf Club Managers' Assn
Gongoozler - Canal Card Collectors Circle
The Good Alternative Travel Guide - Tourism Concern
Good Beer Guide - Campaign for Real Ale
Good Beer Guide to Germany - Campaign for Real Ale
Good Bottled Beer Guide - Campaign for Real Ale
Good Cheese - Guild of Fine Food Retailers
Good Piers Guide - Nat Piers Soc
Good Practice in Boarding Schools: a resource handbook for all those working in boarding - Boarding Schools Assn
Good Quality Control Laboratory Practice - Chartered Quality Inst
Gower in Focus - Gower Soc
Gower Walks - Gower Soc
Gower Way - Gower Soc
Graduated Compression Hosiery - Wound Care Soc
The Grainger Soc Jnl - Percy Grainger Soc
Grandparent Times - Grandparents' Assn
The Grape Press - UK Vineyards Assn
The Grapevine - Care Leavers Assn
Grapevine NL - Nat Assn of Co-operative Officials
Graphic Archaeology - Assn of Archaeological Illustrators & Surveyors
The Graphics Book - D&AD
The Graphologist - Brit Inst of Graphologists
Grass & Forage Farmer - Brit Grassland Soc
Grass & Forage Science - Brit Grassland Soc
Grassbox - Old Lawn Mower Club
Great North Review - Great North of Scotland Railway Assn
Great Oxford Collection of Newsletter Essays - De Vere Soc
Great Western Echo - Great Western Soc
Greece & Rome - Classical Assn
Green Building Magazine - Assn for Environment Conscious Building
Green Chemistry - R Soc of Chemistry
Green Lanes - Green Lane Assn
Greensheet - Military Vehicle Trust
The Grieg Companion - Grieg Soc of GB
The Groundsman - Inst of Groundsmanship
Groundswell - Brit Surfing Assn
The Grower - Assn of Scot Shellfish Growers
Grower's & Buyer's Guide - Brit Orchid Council
　　　　　　　　　　　　　　　　Brit Orchid Growers Assn
The Growing Heap - Community Composting Network
Growing Places - Fedn of City Farms & Community Gardens
Growth Point - THRIVE
GSQ - GS1 UK
GTMA Directory of Gauging & Toolmaking Products & Services - Gauge & Tool Makers Assn
GTOA News - Group Travel Organisers Assn
Guernsey Breeders NL - English Guernsey Cattle Soc
Guidance for the Design, Construction & Maintenance of Petrol Filling Stations - Assn for Petroleum & Explosives Administration
Guidance Notes on the Correct Selection & Application of Fixings - Construction Fixings Assn
Guidance on Alcohol & Drug Misuse in the Workplace - Faculty of Occupational Medicine

© CBD Research Ltd · Beckenham · BR3 5JS · Tel 020 8650 7745 · Fax 020 8650 0768 · E-mail cbd@cbdresearch.com · www.cbdresearch.com

Guidance on Ethics for Occupational Physicians - Faculty of Occupational Medicine

A Guide to Anerobic Digestion + a Directory of Suppliers - Assn of Organics Recycling

Guide to Artificial Arms - REACH: the Assn for Children with Hand or Arm Deficiency

Guide to Best Practice for the Installation of Pipe Jacks & Microtunnels - Pipe Jacking Assn

Guide to Best Practice in Sport & Regeneration - Brit Urban Regeneration Assn

Guide to Brit Piers - Nat Piers Soc

Guide to Building a CDFI - Community Development Finance Assn

Guide to Careers in Outdoor Learning - Inst for Outdoor Learning

Guide to Community Composting - Community Composting Network

A Guide to Customer Publishing - Assn of Publishing Agencies

Guide to Daywork Rates - Building Cost Information Service

A guide to earnings opportunities in direct selling - Direct Selling Assn

A Guide to European Funding - Community Foundation Network

Guide to the Finest Cheeses of Britain & Ireland - Specialist Cheesemakers' Assn

Guide to Funerals & Bereavement - Assn of Burial Authorities

A Guide to Giving - Assn of Charitable Foundations

Guide to Good Practice for Scaffolding with Tubes & Fittings - Nat Access & Scaffolding Confederation

Guide to Gower - Gower Soc

Guide to History of Science Courses in Britain - Brit Soc for the History of Science

Guide to Homesearch - Assn of Relocation Professionals

A Guide to In-Vessel Composting + a Directory of Suppliers - Assn of Organics Recycling

Guide to Laboratory Testing - Assn of Geotechnical & Geoenvironmental Specialists

Guide List - Scot Tourist Guides Assn

The Guide to Literacy Resources - Nat Literacy Assn

Guide to Machine Vision - UK Indl Vision Assn

Guide to Making Model Hovercraft - Hovercraft Club of GB

A Guide to Marketing in Europe - Inst of InterNat Marketing

A Guide to Marketing in North America - Inst of InterNat Marketing

A Guide to Play Therapy - Brit Assn of Play Therapists

Guide Post - Guild of Registered Tourist Guides

A Guide to Private Equity - BVCA (Brit Private Equity & Venture Capital Assn)

Guide to Quality Chinchilla - Nat Chinchilla Soc

Guide to Reach - Brit Adhesives & Sealants Assn

Guide to Risk Assessment for Water Services - Water Management Soc

Guide to Safe Use of Mobile Access - Prefabricated Access Suppliers' & Mfrs' Assn

Guide to Scot Indl Heritage - Scot Indl Heritage Soc

Guide to the servicing of portable fire extinguishers - Fire Industry Assn

Guide to Shiatsu - Shiatsu Soc (UK)

Guide to Tortoises & Turtles - Tortoise Trust

A Guide to Traditional Herbal Medicines - Brit Herbal Medicine Assn

Guide to the UK - Assn of Relocation Professionals

Guidebook to Goddards - Lutyens Trust

Guidebook for Patients - Nat Ankylosing Spondylitis Soc

Guideline to Safe Operation of Cruising Hovercraft - Hovercraft Club of GB

Guidelines - Heritage Railway Assn
　　　　　　Scot Tourist Guides Assn

Guidelines for Combined Geoenvironmental & Geotechnical Investigation - Assn of Geotechnical & Geoenvironmental Specialists

Guidelines on Essence Production - Brit Assn of Flower Essence Producers

Guidelines for Preventing Intravascular Catheter related Infection - Infection Prevention Soc

Guidelines on the Regulation, Labelling, Advertising & Promotion of Aromatherapy Products - Aromatherapy Trade Council

Guidelines: on the use of rope access methods for Indl purposes - Indl Rope Access Trade Assn

Guiding - Girlguiding UK

Guild Gazette - Guild of Professional Beauty Therapists

Guild News - Guild of Air Pilots & Air Navigators of London
　　　　　　Guild of Architectural Ironmongers
　　　　　　Guild of Straw Craftsmen

Guildnews - Inst of Architectural Ironmongers

Gut - Brit Soc of Gastroenterology

Gut Reaction - Gut Trust

GWR Iron Minks - Historical Model Railway Soc

H

H+S File - Assn for Project Safety

Hackney Stud Book - Hackney Horse Soc

Haemophilia Quarterly - Haemophilia Soc UK

The Haggard Jnl - Rider Haggard Soc

Haggardiana - Rider Haggard Soc

Hampshire Studies - Hampshire Field Club & Archaeological Soc

Hand Chain Blocks & Lever Hoists in the Offshore Environment - Lifting Equipment Engineers Assn

Hand Decontamination Guidelines - Infection Prevention Soc

Handbook of School Health - Medical Officers of Schools Assn

Happy Talk - Brit Soc of Habromaniacs

Hardware Today - Brit Hardware Fedn

Harmonica World - Nat Harmonica League

Harmony Express - Brit Assn of Barbershop Singers

Harness Goat Soc - Harness Goat Soc

Havergal Brian on Music - Havergal Brian Soc

Havergal Brian's Gothic Symphony - Havergal Brian Soc

Hazard Analysis & Critical Control Point for Composting - Assn of Organics Recycling

Hazards in the Office - R Soc of Chemistry

Hbk for Fire Engineers - Instn of Fire Engineers

Hbk: a practical guide to thatch & thatching in the 21st century - Nat Soc of Master Thatchers

HBSA News - Hairdressing & Beauty Suppliers Assn

HCSA News - Hospital Consultants & Specialists Assn

Head to Head - Assn of Headteachers & Deputes in Scotland

Headlines - Newspaper Soc

Headway News - Headway - the Brain Injury Assn

Healing Today - Nat Fedn of Spiritual Healers

Health & Homeopathy - Brit Homoeopathic Assn

Health & Safety at Composting Sites - Assn of Organics Recycling

Health & Safety Matters - Brit Safety Industry Fedn

Health Club Management - Fitness Industry Assn

Health Estate Jnl - Inst of Healthcare Engineering & Estate Management

Health Management - Inst of Healthcare Management

Health Writer - Guild of Health Writers

Healthcare Counselling & Psychotherapy Jnl - Brit Assn for Counselling & Psychotherapy

Healthcare Finance - Healthcare Financial Management Assn

Health-Care Focus - Assn of Brit Healthcare Industries

Healthy & Organic Living - Guild of Master Craftsmen

Healthy Living Report - Soc of Local Authority Chief Executives & Senior Managers

Heart Beat - Children's Heart Assn

Heart Children: a practical handbook - Heart Line Assn

HEAS Bulletin - Home Education Advisory Service

HEAS Introductory Information Pack - Home Education Advisory Service

HEAS Resources Book - Home Education Advisory Service

Heavy Talk - Heavy Transport Assn

Hebe News - Hebe Soc

Hedgeline - Hedgeline

Help & Advice - Inst of Consumer Affairs

The Heraldic Craftsman - Soc of Heraldic Arts

The Heraldry Gazette - Heraldry Soc

Herbal Thymes - Nat Inst of Medical Herbalists

Herbnews - Brit Herb Trade Assn

Herbs - Herb Soc

Heredity - Genetics Soc

Herpes Simplex - A Guide - Herpes Viruses Assn

Hertfordshire Archaeology - Saint Albans & Hertfordshire Architectural & Archaeological Soc
Hertfordshire Archaeology - East Herts Archaeological Soc
Heyday Magazine - Heyday
The High Sheriff - High Sheriffs' Assn of England & Wales
Highland Railway Jnl - Highland Railway Soc
Highlights - Freelance Hair & Beauty Fedn
Highways - Inst of Highway Incorporated Engineers
Hints to Businessmen: Turkey - Brit Cham Comm Turkey
HIP Handling Guide - Assn of Home Information Pack Providers
Hippo News - Help InterNat Plant Protein Organisation
The Historian - Historical Assn
Historic Caravan Scene - Historic Caravan Club
Historic Commercial News - Historic Commercial Vehicle Soc
Historic House - Historic Houses Assn
Historical Dance - Dolmetsch Historical Dance Soc
Historical Diving Times - Historical Diving Soc
Historical Metallurgy - Historical Metallurgy Soc
History - Historical Assn
History of Education Jnl - History of Education Soc (UK)
History of Education Researcher - History of Education Soc (UK)
History of Printing Ink - Brit Printing Soc
HIV Medicine - Brit HIV Assn
HLM: Howard League Magazine - Howard League for Penal Reform
HMRS Jnl - Historical Model Railway Soc
HMRS News - Historical Model Railway Soc
Hobart Paperbacks - Inst of Economic Affairs
Hobart Papers - Inst of Economic Affairs
Hockey Scotland - Scot Hockey Union
Hodgkin Lymphoma - Lymphoma Assn
Hodgkin lymphoma & its treatments - Lymphoma Assn
Holidays with your Horse - UK Chasers & Riders
A Home Afloat - Residential Boat Owners Assn
Home Education Hbk - Home Education Advisory Service
Home Education Overseas - Home Education Advisory Service
The Homecarer - UK Homecare Assn
Homeopathy in Practice - Alliance of Registered Homeopaths
Homeopathy InterNat - Homeopathic Medical Assn
Homeopathy Jnl - Faculty of Homeopathy
Homeowners Manual - Nat Care Assn
Hoosta Ga'an On? - Lakeland Dialect Soc
Horizons Magazine - Inst for Outdoor Learning
Horological Jnl - Brit Horological Fedn
Horological Jnl - Brit Horological Inst
The Horticulturist - Inst of Horticulture
Hospital Caterer - Hospital Caterers Assn
Hospital Caterer Ybk - Hospital Caterers Assn
Hospital Pharmacist - R Pharmaceutical Soc of GB
Hospitality - Inst of Hospitality
Hospitality Matters - Brit Hospitality Assn
Hospitality Ybk - Inst of Hospitality
Hot & Cold - Assn of Plumbing & Heating Contractors
Hot Air - Tue Iron Mfrs Assn
Hot Dip Galvanizing - Galvanizers Assn
Hot Foil Printing: a guide to the whole business - Assn of Hot Foil Printers
Hot News - Raynaud's & Scleroderma Assn
Hot Rolled Asphalt Production Laying & Compaction - Inst of Asphalt Technology
House Builder Magazine - Home Builders Fedn
The House of Commons - Manorial Soc of GB
The House of Lords - Manorial Soc of GB
Householders Guide to Flat Roofing - Flat Roofing Alliance
Housing - Chartered Inst of Housing
Housing Today - Nat Housing Fedn
Housman Jnl - Housman Soc
Housman's Places - Housman Soc
Hover Humour - Hovercraft Club of GB
Hovercraft Construction Guide - Hovercraft Club of GB
Hovercraft Museum NL - Hovercraft Museum Trust
How Can I Keep from Singing - Brit Kodály Academy
How did it start? - Instn of Fire Engineers
How to be an Advanced Motorcyclist - Inst of Advanced Motorists
How to be an Advanced Motorist - Inst of Advanced Motorists
How to Buy a Boat - Canal Boatbuilders Assn
How to Grow Roses - R Nat Rose Soc

How to Profit from Contracting out - Cleaning & Support Services Assn
HQ too! - Haemophilia Soc UK
Hrafnes Wisprung (Raven's Whisper) - þa Engliscan Gesíþas (the English Companions)
HSR Monitor - R United Services Inst for Defence & Security Studies
IITA News - Horticultural Trades Assn
Human Fertility - Brit Fertility Soc
Human Genetics NL - Human Genetics Alert
Humanité - Humanist Soc of Scotland
Humanities Now - Humanities Assn
Humanities Too - Humanities Assn
Huntington's Disease: What's it all about? A guide for young people - Scot Huntington's Assn
HVCA Newslink - Heating & Ventilating Contractors' Assn
Hygiene Good Practice Guide - Hospital Caterers Assn
The Hygienist - Brit Natural Hygiene Soc

I

I Sang In My Chains, Essays & Poems in Tribute to Dylan Thomas - Dylan Thomas Soc of GB
ia Jnl - IA: the Ileostomy & Internal Pouch Support Group
iaw! - Urdd Gobaith Cymru (yr Urdd)
IBDA NL - Independent Battery Distributors Assn
Ibis - Brit Ornithologists' Union
IBIS Jnl - Imaginative Book Illustration Soc
IBIS Studies - Imaginative Book Illustration Soc
Ice Cream - Ice Cream Alliance
Ice Hockey Annual - Ice Hockey UK
Ice Link - Nat Ice Skating Assn of UK
Icenews & Ramblings - Brit Icelandic Sheep Breeders Group
ICNM Jnl - Inst for Complementary & Natural Medicine
idea - Evangelical Alliance UK
Idle Thoughts - Jerome K Jerome Soc
IFA Magazine - Irish Football Assn
IFRS White Paper - Business Application Software Developers Assn
Illustrated Guide to Fiction of Rider Haggard - Rider Haggard Soc
Illustrated Guide to Non-Fiction of Rider Haggard - Rider Haggard Soc
Illustrators Guide to Law & Business Practice - Assn of Illustrators
IMA Jnl of Applied Mathematics - Inst of Mathematics & its Applications
IMA Jnl of Management Mathematics - Inst of Mathematics & its Applications
IMA Jnl of Mathematical Control & Information - Inst of Mathematics & its Applications
IMA Jnl of Numerical Analysis - Inst of Mathematics & its Applications
Image - Assn of Photographers
Image Update - Fedn of Image Consultants
Imaging & Oncology - Soc of Radiographers
Imaging Science Jnl - R Photographic Soc of GB
IMBA Global Marine Environment - Marine Biological Assn of the UK
Immunology - Brit Soc for Immunology
Immunology News - Brit Soc for Immunology
Impact - Career Development Group
Impact - Inst of Traffic Accident Investigators
Impact Absorbing Surfaces for Children's Playgrounds - Nat Playing Fields Assn
Import & Export Statistics - Brit Egg Products Assn
In Brief - Assn for Qualitative Research
In Business - Derbyshire and Nottinghamshire Cham Comm
In Costume - Brit Costume Assn
In the Field - Berkshire Archaeology Research Group
In Flight Magazine - Brit Disc Golf Assn
In Focus - Assn of Brit Healthcare Industries
Brit Soc of Underwater Photographers
R Microscopical Soc
In the Frame - Telecommunications UK Fraud Forum
In the Know - Guillain Barré Syndrome Support Group

© CBD Research Ltd · Beckenham · BR3 5JS · Tel 020 8650 7745 · Fax 020 8650 0768 · E-mail cbd@cbdresearch.com · www.cbdresearch.com

In a Nutshell - Kentish Cobnuts Assn
　　Percy Grainger Soc
In Practice - Inst of Ecology & Environmental Management
　　UK Clinical Pharmacy Assn
In the Steps of the Patriot - John Hampden Soc
In There Somewhere - Dry Stone Walling Assn of GB
In Touch - Customer Contact Assn
　　Marfan Assn UK
　　Netherlands-Brit Cham Comm
　　On Site Massage Assn
　　Scot Soc for Autism
inbusiness - Inverness Cham Comm
Incontact - Incontact
Independence - Campaign for an Independent Britain
The Independent - Assn of Cycle Traders
Independent - Brit Textile Technology Group
Independent Adviser - AdviceUK
Independent Business Today - Inst for Independent Business
Independent Examiner - Assn of Charity Independent Examiners
The Independent Monitor - Assn of Members of Independent
　　Monitoring Boards
Independent Schools Ybk - Incorporated Assn of Preparatory
　　Schools
Independent Talking Pages - Assn of Speech & Language
　　Therapists in Independent Practice
Index - Commissioning Specialists Assn
Index to ISPA News & Small Printer - Brit Printing Soc
The Indexer - Soc of Indexers
Indexers Available - Soc of Indexers
Indicator - Scot Council for Development & Industry
Indirect Tax Voice - Inst of Indirect Taxation
The Individual - Soc for Individual Freedom
Indl Archaeology News - Assn for Indl Archaeology
Indl Archaeology Review - Assn for Indl Archaeology
Indl Railway Record - Indl Railway Soc
Industry Link - Nuclear Industry Assn
Infection Control Guidance for General Practice - Infection
　　Prevention Soc
Info - Chambre de Commerce Française de Grande-Bretagne
In-Focus - Fedn of Manufacturing Opticians
Infofact - Scot Motor Neurone Disease Assn
INFORM - Inst for Sport, Parks & Leisure
InfoRM - Inst of Risk Management
Informant - Assn of Registrars of Scotland
Information - Inst of Trade Mark Attorneys
Informed - Investor Relations Soc
The Informer - Gasket Cutters' Assn
Ingenia - R Academy of Engineering
Inland Racing Competition Regulation - Hovercraft Club of GB
Inland Waterways Guide - Inland Waterways Assn
Inner Wheel - Assn of Inner Wheel Clubs in GB & Ireland
Innes Review - Scot Catholic Historical Assn
Innovation in Print - Independent Print Industries Assn
Innovation into Success - UK Science Park Assn
Innovations in Primary Health Care Nursing - Community &
　　District Nursing Assn UK
InRoads - Inst of Road Safety Officers
Inscape - InterNat Jnl of Art Therapy - Brit Assn of Art Therapists
Inside Churches - Nat Assn of Decorative & Fine Arts Socs
Inside OR - Operational Research Soc
Inside Out - Community Development Finance Assn
Inside the Industry Report - Credit Services Assn
Inside Track - Green Alliance Trust
The Insider - Crohn's in Childhood Research Assn
Insight - Leukaemia CARE
　　Primary Immunodeficiency Assn
　　Theosophical Soc in England
In-Situ Concrete Frames: a report - Construct: Concrete
　　Structures Group
Insolvency Intelligence - Insolvency Lawyers' Assn
Inspire - Assn of Respiratory Technology & Physiology
The Installer - Nat Insulation Assn
Insulation - Thermal Insulation Mfrs & Suppliers Assn
Intentions - Oscar Wilde Soc
Interact - Soc for the Advancement of Games & Simulations in
　　Education & Training
Interaction - Action for ME
Intercom - Aircrew Assn

Interface - Inst of Measurement & Control
　　Professional Computing Assn
Interfaces - Forensic Science Soc
Interior Insight - Assn of Interior Specialists
Interiors Focus - Assn of Interior Specialists
Internal Auditing & Business Risk - Inst of Internal Auditors - UK
　　& Ireland
InterNat - Nat Acrylic Painters' Assn
InterNat Accountant - Assn of InterNat Accountants
InterNat Affairs - R Inst of InterNat Affairs
InterNat Endodontic Jnl - Brit Endodontic Soc
InterNat Exchange - Motor Neurone Disease Assn
InterNat Gas Engineering & Management - Instn of Gas
　　Engineers & Managers
**InterNat Guidelines: on the use of rope access methods for
　　Indl purposes -** Indl Rope Access Trade Assn
InterNat Jnl of Art & Design Education - Nat Soc for Education
　　in Art & Design
InterNat Jnl of Audiology - Brit Soc of Audiology
InterNat Jnl of Cosmetic Science - Soc of Cosmetic Scientists
InterNat Jnl of Dairy Technology - Soc of Dairy Technology
InterNat Jnl of Food Science & Technology - Inst of Food Science
　　& Technology
InterNat Jnl of Iberian Studies - Assn for Contemporary Iberian
　　Studies
InterNat Jnl of Injury Control & Safety Promotion - Ergonomics
　　Soc
InterNat Jnl of Market Research - Market Research Soc
InterNat Jnl of Meteorology - Tornado & Storm Research
　　Organisation
InterNat Jnl of Nautical Archaeology - Nautical Archaeology Soc
InterNat Jnl of Obstetric Anesthesia - Obstetric Anaesthetists
　　Assn
InterNat Jnl of Paediatric Dentistry - Brit Soc of Paediatric
　　Dentistry
InterNat Jnl of Pharmaceutical Medicine - Soc of
　　Pharmaceutical Medicine
InterNat Jnl of Pharmacy Practice - R Pharmaceutical Soc of GB
InterNat Jnl of Psychoanalysis - Brit Psychoanalytical Soc
InterNat Jnl of Remote Sensing - Remote Sensing &
　　Photogrammetry Soc
InterNat Jnl of Punjab Studies - Assn for Punjab Studies (UK)
InterNat Jnl of Systematic & Evolutionary Microbiology - Soc
　　for General Microbiology
InterNat Musculoskeletal Medicine Jnl - Soc of Orthopaedic
　　Medicine
InterNat Simulation & Gaming Research Ybk - Soc for the
　　Advancement of Games & Simulations in Education & Training
InterNat Therapist - Assn of Therapy Lecturers
InterNat Turfgrass Bulletin - Sports Turf Research Inst
The Interpreter - Assn of Police & Court Interpreters
The Intrepid Repairer - Nat Assn of Musical Instrument Repairers
Introducing Direct Democracy - Referenda Soc
Introducing LMBBS - Laurence-Moon-Bardet-Biedl Soc
An Introduction to Cochlear Implants - Nat Assn of Deafened
　　People
An Introduction to Creating Quality Decks - Timber Decking
　　Assn
An Introduction to Pipe Jacking & Microtunnelling Design -
　　Pipe Jacking Assn
An Introduction to Pipeline Pigging - Pigging Products & Services
　　Assn
Introduction to SAA - Sub-Aqua Assn
An Introduction to Tensional Strapping - Brit Tensional Strapping
　　Assn
Introduction to Volunteering Overseas - Returned Volunteer
　　Action
Introduction to Wildlife Sound Recording - Wildlife Sound
　　Recording Soc
Investigate - Assn of Brit Investigators
Investment Property Focus - Investment Property Forum
Invoice - Inst of Certified Book-Keepers
The Irish Genealogist - Irish Genealogical Research Soc
Irish Mountain Log - Mountaineering Council of Ireland
Irish Studies Review - Brit Assn for Irish Studies
Irrigation News - UK Irrigation Assn
Is it anything you ate? - Nat Soc for Research into Allergy
Island Business - Isle of Wight Cham Comm, Tourism & Industry

Isle of Wight Birds - Isle of Wight Natural History & Archaeological Soc

Issues in Environmental Science & Technology - R Soc of Chemistry

ISTC Hbk on Professional Communication & Information Design - Inst of Scientific & Technical Communicators

The ITC Practical Guide for Writers & Companies - Independent Theatre Council

ITI Bulletin - Inst of Translation & Interpreting

ITS Focus - ITS UK

J

Jacob Jnl - Jacob Sheep Soc

The Jacobite - Seventeen Fortyfive / 1745 Assn

Jade - Guild of Erotic Artists

James Hilton - James Hilton Soc

James Mosley - Friends of St Bride Library

Japan Experiences - Japan Soc

Japan Forum - Brit Assn of Japanese Studies

Jazz UK - Welsh Jazz Soc

JCCI Review - Japanese Cham Comm & Industry in the UK

Jem - English Goat Breeders Assn

Jersey at Home - R Jersey Agricultural & Horticultural Soc

The Jester - Cartoonists' Club of GB

The Jeweller - Nat Assn of Goldsmiths of GB & Ireland

Jewellery History Today - Soc of Jewellery Historians

Jewellery Studies - Soc of Jewellery Historians

JICS - Intensive Care Soc

Jigsaw - Scot Soc for Autism

The Jnl of Adolescence - Assn for Professionals in Services for Adolescents

Jnl of Adventure Education & Outdoor Learning - Inst for Outdoor Learning

Jnl of Agricultural Economics - Agricultural Economics Soc

Jnl of Agricultural Manpower - Agricultural Manpower Soc

Jnl of American Studies - Brit Assn for American Studies

Jnl of Analytical Atomic Spectrometry - R Soc of Chemistry

Jnl of Anatomy - Anatomical Soc of GB & Ireland

Jnl of Animal Technology & Welfare - Inst of Animal Technology

Jnl of Applied Microbiology - Soc for Applied Microbiology

Jnl of Applied Philosophy - Soc for Applied Philosophy

Jnl of Applied Research in Intellectual Disabilities - Brit Inst of Learning Disabilities

Jnl of Arts Marketing - Arts Marketing Assn

Jnl of Biological Education - Inst of Biology

Jnl of Bone & Joint Surgery - Brit Orthopaedic Assn

Jnl of Bryology - Brit Bryological Soc

Jnl Business - Salisbury & District Cham Comm & Industry

Jnl of Cataract & Refractive Surgery - UK & Ireland Soc of Cataract & Refractive Surgeons

Jnl of Child Health Care - Assn of Brit Paediatric Nurses

Jnl of Child Psychology & Psychiatry - Assn for Child & Adolescent Mental Health

Jnl of Classics Teaching - Joint Assn of Classical Teachers

The Jnl of Clinical Periodontology - Brit Soc of Periodontology

Jnl of Common Market Studies (JCMS) - University Assn for Contemporary European Studies

Jnl of Conchology - Conchological Soc of GB & Ireland

Jnl of Dental Research - Brit Soc for Dental Research

Jnl of Design History - Design History Soc

Jnl for Drama in Education - Nat Assn for the Teaching of Drama

Jnl of Egyptian Archaeology - Egypt Exploration Soc

Jnl of Electro-physiology & Technology - Electro-physiological Technologists' Assn

Jnl of Endocrinology - Soc for Endocrinology

Jnl of Environmental Monitoring - R Soc of Chemistry

Jnl of Experimental Botany - Soc for Experimental Biology

Jnl of Family Planning & Reproductive Healthcare - Faculty of Sexual & Reproductive Healthcare of the RCOG

Jnl of Family Therapy - Assn for Family Therapy

Jnl of French Language Studies - Assn for French Language Studies

Jnl of General Virology - Soc for General Microbiology

Jnl of Hand Surgery - Brit Soc for Surgery of the Hand

Jnl of Hellenic Studies - Soc for the Promotion of Hellenic Studies (Hellenic Soc)

Jnl of Human Nutrition & Dietetics - Brit Dietetic Assn

Jnl of Infection - Brit Infection Soc

Jnl of Infertility Counselling - Brit Infertility Counselling Assn

Jnl of Interactive Marketing - Inst of Direct Marketing

Jnl of InterNat Development - Development Studies Assn

Jnl of InterNat Marketing - Inst of InterNat Marketing

The Jnl of Latin Teaching - Assn for Latin Teaching

Jnl of Linguistics - Linguistics Assn of GB

Jnl of Materials Chemistry - R Soc of Chemistry

Jnl of Medical Microbiology - Soc for General Microbiology

Jnl into Melody - Robert Farnon Soc

Jnl of Microscopy - R Microscopical Soc

Jnl of Modern Italy - Assn for the Study of Modern Italy

Jnl of Molecular Endocrinology - Soc for Endocrinology

Jnl of Molluscan Studies - Malacological Soc of London

Jnl of Museum Ethnography - Museum Ethnographers Group

Jnl of Natural Medicine - InterNat Register of Consultant Herbalists & Homoeopaths

Jnl of Occupational & Organisational Psychology - Brit Psychological Soc

Jnl of Offshore Technology - Inst of Marine Engineering, Science & Technology

Jnl of One-Day Surgery - Brit Assn for Day Surgery

Jnl of One-Name Studies - Guild of One-Name Studies

Jnl of Orthopaedic Medicine - Brit Inst of Musculoskeletal Medicine

Jnl of Paediatric Surgery - Brit Assn of Paediatric Surgeons

Jnl of Pathology - Pathological Soc of GB & Ireland

Jnl of Perioperative Practice - Assn for Perioperative Practice

Jnl of Physics - Inst of Physics

Jnl of Physiology - Physiological Soc

Jnl Pioneers of Conservation - Selborne Soc

Jnl of Plastic, Reconstructive & Aesthetic Surgery - Brit Assn of Plastic, Reconstructive & Aesthetic Surgeons

Jnl for Play Therapy - Brit Assn of Play Therapists

Jnl of Psychopharmacology - Brit Assn for Psychopharmacology

Jnl of Reproductive & Infant Psychology - Soc for Reproductive & Infant Psychology

Jnl of Research in Reading - UK Literacy Assn

Jnl of Roman Studies - Soc for the Promotion of Roman Studies (Roman Soc)

Jnl of Roman Studies Monographs - Soc for the Promotion of Roman Studies (Roman Soc)

Jnl of Sexual Aggression - Nat Organisation for the Treatment of Abusers

Jnl of Simulation - Operational Research Soc

Jnl of Small Animal Practice - Brit Small Animal Veterinary Assn

Jnl of Sports Sciences - Ergonomics Soc

The Jnl of Stained Glass - Brit Soc of Master Glass Painters

Jnl of Stereo Imaging - Stereoscopic Soc

Jnl of Tissue Viability - Tissue Viability Soc

Jnl of Turfgrass & Sports Surface Science - Sports Turf Research Inst

Jnl of Ultrasound - Brit Medical Ultrasound Soc

Jnl of Visual Communication in Medicine (Vision) - Inst of Medical Illustrators

The Jnl for Weavers, Spinners & Dyers - Assn of Guilds of Weavers, Spinners & Dyers

Jnl of Zoology - Zoological Soc of London

The John Buchan Jnl - John Buchan Soc

John Hampden & His Times - John Hampden Soc

John Hampden of Buckinghamshire: the people's hero - John Hampden Soc

Joint Code of Practice for Sprinklers in Schools - Brit Automatic Fire Sprinkler Assn

Joint Report - Children's Chronic Arthritis Assn

Jordaniana - Anglo-Jordanian Soc

Joseph Bouet's Durham - Durham County Local History Soc

Journey of Discovery - Raynaud's & Scleroderma Assn

A Journey through Infertility - Infertility Network UK

Judo News - Judo Scotland

Justice Bulletin - Nat Campaign for Water Justice

The Justices' Clerk Jnl - Justices' Clerks' Soc

Justin Howes & Nigel Roche - Friends of St Bride Library

© CBD Research Ltd · Beckenham · BR3 5JS · Tel 020 8650 7745 · Fax 020 8650 0768 · E-mail cbd@cbdresearch.com · www.cbdresearch.com

K

Keeping a Young Voice - Voice Care Network UK
Kennel Gazette - Kennel Club
Kent - Assn of Men of Kent & Kentish Men
Kent Record Series & Monograph Series - Kent Archaeological Soc
Kent View - Kent County Agricultural Soc
Kerry Hill Flock Book - Kerry Hill Flock Book Soc
The Key - Prison Governors Assn
The Key Frame - Fair Organ Preservation Soc
Key Issues in District Nursing - Community & District Nursing Assn UK
Keynote - Inst of Food Science & Technology
The Keys of Peter - Christian Social Order
Keyways - Master Locksmiths' Assn
KF Today - Kinesiology Fedn
Kidney Life - Nat Kidney Fedn
King Pole - Circus Friends Assn of GB
The Kipling Jnl - Kipling Soc
The Kiteflier - Kite Soc
King's Army NL - English Civil War Soc
Knitstats - Knitting Industries' Fedn
Knitting - Guild of Master Craftsmen
Knotting Matters - InterNat Guild of Knot Tyers
Knowing the Score 2 - Assn of Brit Orchestras
Knowledge Management Research & Practice - Operational Research Soc
Korfball - Brit Korfball Assn

L

La Brita Esperantisto - Esperanto Assn of Britain (Esperanto-Asocio de Britio)
Lab on a Chip - R Soc of Chemistry
Lablink - Professional Photographic Laboratories Assn
Laboratory Animals - Laboratory Animal Science Assn
Laboratory Hazards Bulletin - R Soc of Chemistry
Labour & the House of Lords - Manorial Soc of GB
Labour History Review - Soc for the Study of Labour History
Lace - Lace Guild
Lacemaking - Lace Soc
Lakeland Gems - Lakeland Dialect Soc
Lakeland Treasury - Lakeland Dialect Soc
Lallans - Scots Language Soc
Lamp - Assn of Lighthouse Keepers
Lancashire Business View - East Lancashire Cham Comm & Industry
The Lancastrian - Friends of Real Lancashire
Land Business - Scot Rural Property & Business Assn
The Land Registration Act - Manorial Soc of GB
The Land Registration Bill - Manorial Soc of GB
Land Sailor - Brit Fedn of Sand & Land Yacht Clubs (Brit Landsailing)
Land Tenures & Customs of Manors - Manorial Soc of GB
Landlord Development Manual - Nat Landlords' Assn
Landscape History - Soc for Landscape Studies
Landscape News - Brit Assn of Landscape Industries
Landscape Research Jnl - Landscape Research Group
Landwards - Instn of Agricultural Engineers
Language & Literacy News - UK Literacy Assn
Language Issues - Nat Assn for Teaching English & other Community Languages to Adults
Language Learning Jnl - Assn for Language Learning
Language World - Assn for Language Learning
The Lantern - Brit Housewives League
LAPADA Views - Assn of Art & Antique Dealers
Laria News - Local Authorities Research & Intelligence Assn
The Laser User - Assn of Laser Users
Lasers in Medical Science - Brit Medical Laser Assn
The Last Straw - Straw Bale Building Assn
The Last Word - Assn of Brit Scrabble Players
Latin CD - Assn for Latin Liturgy
Laudate - Guild of Church Musicians

Launderette & Cleaning World - Nat Assn of the Launderette Industry
The Laurel & Hardy Magazine - Laurel & Hardy Appreciation Soc - Sons of the Desert
The Law Teacher - Assn of Law Teachers
Layman's Guide to Osteochondritis - Perthes Assn
Lead On - Seeing Dogs Alliance
Leaning Ladder & Stepladder User Guide - Brit Ladder Mfrs Assn
Learned Publishing - Assn of Learned & Professional Soc Publishers
Learning & Development: an introduction to childcare in an early years setting - Scot Pre-School Play Assn
Learning Blitz - Brit Inst for Learning & Development
Learning Disability Bulletin - Brit Inst of Learning Disabilities
Learning from Experience - Brit Urban Regeneration Assn
Learning to Live - Campaign for Learning
Leather Technician's Hbk - Leather Producers' Assn
The Left-Hander - Left-Handers Assn
Left Handers Club
Legal & Criminological Psychotherapy - Brit Psychological Soc
Legal Abacus - Inst of Legal Cashiers & Administrators
Legal Executive Jnl - Inst of Legal Executives
Legal Information Management - Brit & Irish Assn of Law Librarians
Legal Studies - Soc of Legal Scholars in the UK & Ireland
The Legion - R Brit Legion
Leisure Management - Fitness Industry Assn
Leisure Opportunities - Fitness Industry Assn
Les Nouvelles - Licensing Executives Soc
Lets Face It - Let's Face It
Let's Square Dance - Brit Assn of American Square Dance Clubs
Letters in Applied Microbiology - Soc for Applied Microbiology
Letting Update - UK Assn of Letting Agents
Lewis Carroll Review - Lewis Carroll Soc
Lewisletter - Wyndham Lewis Soc
Liberation - Liberation - incorporating the Movement for Colonial Freedom
Liberty - Liberty: Nat Council for Civil Liberties
The Library - Bibliographical Soc
Libyan Studies - Soc for Libyan Studies
The Licensed Conveyancer - Soc of Licensed Conveyancers
The Lichenologist - Brit Lichen Soc
Life Links - R Zoological Soc of Scotland
The Lifeboat - R Nat Lifeboat Instn
Lifeline - Brit Red Cross Soc
Overeaters Anonymous
Lifesavers Magazine - R Life Saving Soc UK
Lifting Engineers Hbk - Lifting Equipment Engineers Assn
Lifting Equipment - a user's pocket guide - Lifting Equipment Engineers Assn
Lifting the Veil of Silence on Emotional Problems after Childbirth - Meet-a-Mum Assn
LIFU Engineering - Steam Boat Assn of GB
Light Aviation - Aircraft Owners & Pilots Assn
Light Aircraft Assn
Light Hovercraft - Hovercraft Club of GB
Lightbox - Brit Assn of Picture Libraries & Agencies
Lighting & Sound America - Professional Lighting & Sound Assn
Lighting & Sound InterNat - Professional Lighting & Sound Assn
Lighting News - Lighting Assn
Lighting Research & Technology - Chartered Instn of Building Services Engineers
Lime Stabilisation Manual - Quarry Products Assn
Lincoln Record Soc - Lincoln Record Soc
Line Up - Inst of Broadcast Sound
The Linguist - Chartered Inst of Linguists
Lining old chimneys - Nat Fireplace Assn
Link - Assn for Spina Bifida & Hydrocephalus
Nat Fedn of Anglers
The Link - Scot Environment Link
Link Magazine - Nat Assn of Writers' Groups
The Linnean - Linnean Soc of London
The Lipizzaner - Lipizzaner Soc of GB
Lipservice - Assn of Leisure Industry Professionals
List of A1 Bulls - Longhorn Cattle Soc
List of Fellows 1660-2000 - The R Soc
The List of French Investments in the UK - Chambre de Commerce Française de Grande-Bretagne

Listed Heritage - Listed Property Owners Club
Listing of Dials in UK - Brit Sundial Soc
Lists of pre 1855 Monumental Inscriptions - Scot Genealogy Soc
Literacy - UK Literacy Assn
Literacy & ICT: cutting edge practice in the primary school - Nat Literacy Assn
Literature professional - Nat Assn for Literature Development
Little Bliss - BLISS
Little People - Miniature Mediterranean Donkey Assn
Liturgical Studies - Alcuin Club
Liverpool Chamber - Liverpool Cham Comm & Industry
Livin' Country - Union of Country Sports Workers
Living Afloat - Residential Boat Owners Assn
Living Earth - Soil Assn
Living Will + Forms - Assn of Natural Burial Grounds
Living Wills - Dignity in Dying
Living with Ankylosing Spondylitis - Nat Ankylosing Spondylitis Soc
LMBBS child at school - Laurence-Moon-Bardet-Biedl Soc
Local Area Analysis & Portfolio Construction - Soc of Property Researchers
Local Council Review - Nat Assn of Local Councils
The Local Historian - Brit Assn for Local History
Local News - Gwent Wildlife Trust
Locomotives of the Hull & Barnsley Railway - Historical Model Railway Soc
The Locomotives of the Stockton & Darlington Railway - Historical Model Railway Soc
The Log - Brit Air Line Pilots Assn
        Soc of Model Shipwrights
The Log Book - Ship Stamp Soc
Logopedics, Phoniatrics & Vocology - Brit Voice Assn
London Bird Report - London Natural History Soc
London Bulletin - London Councils
London Business Matters - London Cham Comm & Industry
London Cyclist - London Cycling Campaign
London Government Directory - London Councils
London Housing Magazine - London Councils
The London Naturalist - London Natural History Soc
London NL - West Africa Business Assn
The London Philatelist - R Philatelic Soc London
The London Practice - Friends of Dr Watson
London Topographical Record - London Topographical Soc
London's Indl Archaeology - Greater London Indl Archaeology Soc
Long Range Planning - Strategic Planning Soc
Long Term Advertising Expenditure Forecast - Advertising Assn
Look Before You Leap - Dance UK
Look North - Scot Committee of Optometrists
Looking Ahead - Bluefaced Leicester Sheep Breeders Assn
Loopholes - Pillbox Study Group & UK Fortifications Club
The Lost Hills - history of papermaking in County Durham - Durham County Local History Soc
Lottery Magazine - Lotteries Council
Low Grade Hodgkin Lymphomas - Lymphoma Assn
Lower Limb Deficiency - STEPS
Lube - UK Lubricants Assn
The Luing Jnl - Luing Cattle Soc
Luing News - Luing Cattle Soc
Lune Valley Engineering - Steam Boat Assn of GB
Luso News - Lusitano Breed Soc of GB
The Lute - Lute Soc
Lute News - Lute Soc
The Lutheran Link - Lutheran Council of GB
Lymphoma Fundraising News - Lymphoma Assn
Lymphoma NL - Lymphoma Assn
Lymphomas - Lymphoma Assn
Lynes - Lithuanian Assn in GB (Britanjos Lietuviai)

M

The Mace-Bearer - Guild of Mace-Bearers
Machinery Update - Processing & Packaging Machinery Assn
The Magic Circular - Magic Circle
The Magistrate - Magistrates' Assn

Magnet - Youth Scotland
Maize Grower - Maize Growers Assn
Make a Sundial - Brit Sundial Soc
Making Allowances Report - London Councils
Making Music News - Making Music
Making sense of Psychotherapy and Psychoanalysis - Brit Psychoanalytic Council
Making the Best of Amputation - Brit Limbless Ex-Service Men's Assn
Mallorn - Tolkien Soc
Mammal News - Mammal Soc
Mammal Review - Mammal Soc
Mammalaction News - Mammal Soc
Management of CDM Coordination - Assn for Project Safety
Management in Education - Brit Educational Leadership, Management & Administration Soc
Management of Exuding Wounds - Wound Care Soc
The Management Specialist - Inst of Management Specialists
Manager: the Brit Jnl of Administrative Management - Inst of Administrative Management
Managing Trade Assns - Trade Assn Forum
Manchester Memoirs - Manchester Literary & Philosophical Soc
Manic Depression - SANE
Man-made Mineral Fibre - Thermal Insulation Contractors Assn
Manorial Law - Manorial Soc of GB
Manpower News - HR Soc
The Manual of the Mace - Guild of Mace-Bearers
Manual of Sealant Practice - Brit Adhesives & Sealants Assn
Manufacturing - Inst of Manufacturing
Manufacturing Management - Inst of Manufacturing
MARCH Mental Health Circular - Nat Assn for Mental After-Care in Residential Care Homes
Marine Conservation - Marine Conservation Soc
Marine Engineers Review - Inst of Marine Engineering, Science & Technology
The Mariner's Mirror - Soc for Nautical Research
Maritime Information - Maritime Information Assn
Maritime IT & Electronics - Inst of Marine Engineering, Science & Technology
Market Leader - Marketing Soc
the marketer - Chartered Inst of Marketing
Marketing Newz - Sleep Council
The Marketing Pocket Book - Advertising Assn
Marques News Sheet - MARQUES the Assn of European Trade Mark Owners
The Marketing Pocket Book - Advertising Assn
Masonry chimneys, their design & construction - Nat Fireplace Assn
Masonry InterNat - InterNat Masonry Soc
Mass Spectrometry Bulletin - R Soc of Chemistry
Masterbuilder - Fedn of Master Builders
Masterchefs - Master Chefs of GB
Mastersinger - Assn of Brit Choral Directors
Match Label News - Brit Matchbox, Label & Booklet Soc
Materials World - Inst of Materials, Minerals & Mining
Mathematical & General Physics - Inst of Physics
Mathematical & Physical Sciences - The R Soc
Mathematical Medicine & Biology: a Jnl of the IMA - Inst of Mathematics & its Applications
Mathematical Proceedings - Cambridge Philosophical Soc
Mathematics Today - Inst of Mathematics & its Applications
Maths Pack - Home Education Advisory Service
Matrix - Brit Science Fiction Assn
May Catholics choose Cremation? - Cremation Soc of GB
Mayoral Directory - London Mayors' Assn
MCC Open Learning Manual - England & Wales Cricket Board Assn of Cricket Officials
McKenzie Magazine - Families Need Fathers
Me & My Face - Let's Face It
Measurement & Control - Inst of Measurement & Control
Meat Hygienist - Assn of Meat Inspectors GB
The Medal - Brit Art Medal Soc
Medau News - Medau Soc
Medical Companion - Myasthenia Gravis Assn
Medical Methods of Treatment - SANE
Medical Microbiologists - Assn of Medical Microbiologists
Medical Practitioners' Financial Hbk - Assn of Independent Specialist Medical Accountants

© CBD Research Ltd · Beckenham · BR3 5JS · Tel 020 8650 7745 · Fax 020 8650 0768 · E-mail cbd@cbdresearch.com · www.cbdresearch.com

Medical Woman - Medical Women's Fedn
Medication for Narcolepsy - Narcolepsy Assn UK
Medicine, Science & the Law - Brit Academy of Forensic Sciences
Medium sized firms of Chartered Accountants - the vital link between businesses & the City - Assn of Practising Accountants
Meeting Houses in Britain - Friends Historical Soc
Melin - Welsh Mills Soc (Cymdeithas Melinau Cymru)
Membership Executive - Tourism Soc
Memory Lane - Al Bowlly Circle
Mental Health Nursing - Mental Health Nurses Assn
The Mercia Bioscope - Mercia Cinema Soc
Mercury - Brit Astrological & Psychic Soc
Merkur - German Railway Soc
The Merton Jnl - Thomas Merton Soc of GB & Ireland
The Message - Nat Pensioners' Convention
Methods in Organic Synthesis - R Soc of Chemistry
MGA News - Myasthenia Gravis Assn
MGA Times - Maize Growers Assn
Microbiology - Soc for General Microbiology
Microbiology Today - Soc for General Microbiology
Microlight Flying - Brit Microlight Aircraft Assn
Microscope - Meningitis Research Foundation
The Middle Way - Buddhist Soc
Midwifery Matters - Assn of Radical Midwives
Milestones & Waymarkers On the Ground - Milestone Soc
Milk Digest - R Assn of Brit Dairy Farmers
Millennium Book - Manorial Soc of GB
The Miner - Nat Union of Mineworkers
Minerva: Jnl of Swansea History - R Instn of South Wales
Mining Heritage Guide - Nat Assn of Mining History Organisations
Mining History - Peak District Mines Historical Soc
Minor Counties Cricket Annual - Minor Counties Cricket Assn
Minutes of Meetings - Choice in Personal Safety
Miro News - Mineral Industry Research Organisation
Missing the Grade: Education for Children in Prison - Howard League for Penal Reform
The Missing Link - Brit Sausage Appreciation Soc
Mitteilungsblatt - Anglo-German Family History Soc
Mixed Marriage in Ireland: A companion to those involved, or about to be involved, in a mixed marriage - Northern Ireland Mixed Marriage Assn
Mixed Moss - Arthur Ransome Soc
MJA News - Medical Jnlists' Assn
Mobilise - Mobilise Organisation
The Mode of Future Existence - Campaign for Philosophical Freedom
Modelling Historic Architecture - Historical Model Railway Soc
Modern & Contemporary France - Assn for the Study of Modern & Contemporary France
Modern Believing - Modern Churchpeople's Union
Modern Language Review - Modern Humanities Research Assn
Modern Management - Inst of Leadership & Management
Modern Practical Masonry - Stone Fedn GB
MODUS - Design & Technology Assn
Mollusc World - Conchological Soc of GB & Ireland
The Monarchy - Manorial Soc of GB
Monarchy - Monarchist League
Money Laundering Guidelines - Brit Cheque Cashers Assn
Money Minder - Nat Assn of Bank & Insurance Customers
Money-go-Round: recycling finances, realising capital - Community Development Finance Assn
Monitoring & Evaluation; a practical guide for grant-making trusts - Assn of Charitable Foundations
Monitoring Report on Theatre Directors - Directors Guild of GB
Montage - Picture Research Assn
Montessori Direction - Montessori Soc (AMI) UK
Monthly Rice Circular - London Rice Brokers' Assn
Mood Food Magazine - Fedn of Specialist Restaurants
Moors Line - North Yorkshire Moors Historical Railway Trust
Moral Philosophy - Assn for Therapeutic Philosophy
More Care for Your Voice - Voice Care Network UK
More than meets the eye - Laurence-Moon-Bardet-Biedl Soc
Motor Caravanner - Motor Caravanners' Club
Motor Industry Magazine - Inst of the Motor Industry (Inc)
Motor Retailer - Retail Motor Industry Fedn
Motorcycle Rider - Brit Motorcyclists' Fedn
Motorcycling GB - Auto-Cycle Union
Movement & Dance - Laban Guild for Movement & Dance

Moving Forward: a guide to living with spinal cord injury -
Moving News - Movers Inst (TMI)
Moving on Up: a short guide for professionals - Assn for Real Change
Moving on Up: young people & families guide - Assn for Real Change
Moving Steel by Crane - Nat Assn of Steel Stockholders
MQR - Minerals Engineering Soc
MS Matters - Multiple Sclerosis Soc of GB & Northern Ireland
The Mule - Brit Mule Soc
Mule News - North of England Mule Sheep Assn
Multiples - Soc of Wood Engravers
The Museum Archaeologist - Soc of Museum Archaeologists
Museum News - Nat Heritage: the Museums Action Movement
Museum Practice - Museums Assn
Museums Jnl - Museums Assn
Mushroom Jnl - Mushroom Growers' Assn
Music - Viola da Gamba Soc
The Music Box - Musical Box Soc of GB
Music Copyright Matters - Music Publishers' Assn
Music Jnl - Incorporated Soc of Musicians
Musician - Musicians' Union
My Daughter & ME - Assn of Young People with ME

N

N.I. Master Butchers - Northern Ireland Master Butchers Assn
n:gauge - Nat Assn of Goldsmiths of GB & Ireland
NAC News & Views - Nat Assn of Choirs
NACSA News - Nat Assn for Child Support Action
NACVS Circulation - Nat Assn for Voluntary & Community Action
NADFAS Review - Nat Assn of Decorative & Fine Arts Socs
NAFIS Nat Quality Standards - Nat Assn Family Information Services
NAKMAS Review - Nat Assn of Karate & Martial Art Schools
Name magazine - Nat Assn of Music Educators
The Name & Nature of Poetry - Housman Soc
Napoleon - Napoleonic Soc
Narcolepsy: care & treatment - Narcolepsy Assn UK
Narcolepsy: a layman's guide - Narcolepsy Assn UK
Narrow Gauge - Narrow Gauge Railway Soc
Narrow Gauge News - Narrow Gauge Railway Soc
Nat & Specialists Soc Hbk - Assn of Brit Philatelic Socs
Nat B&W Premier League Fixture Book - Table Soccer Players Assn
Nat Hamster Council Jnl - Brit Hamster Assn
Nat Meeting Book of Abstracts - Brit Neuroscience Assn
The Nat Plant Collections Directory - Nat Council for the Conservation of Plants & Gardens
Nat Swimming Award Pack - Scot Swimming
Nat Tobacconists Trade Exhibition Catalogue - Assn of Independent Tobacco Specialists
Nations & Natism - Assn for the Study of Ethnicity & Natism
NatSCA News - Natural Sciences Collections Assn
Natterjack - Brit Herpetological Soc
Natterjack News - Landlife
The Natural Death Hbk - Assn of Natural Burial Grounds
Natural Medicine - Assn of Natural Medicine
Natural Products Reports - R Soc of Chemistry
Natural Products Updates - R Soc of Chemistry
Natural World - R Soc of Wildlife Trusts
Nature in Art - Nature in Art Trust
Nautical Archaeology NL - Nautical Archaeology Soc
The Naval Architect - R Instn of Naval Architects
Navvies - Waterway Recovery Group
NBTV - Narrow Bandwidth Television Assn
NBWS Bulletin - R Naval Bird Watching Soc
NCA News - Nat Campaign for the Arts
The Need for Property Data - Soc of Property Researchers
The Nelson Dispatch - Nelson Soc
Neometaphysical Digest - Soc of Metaphysicians
Netball News - Welsh Netball Assn
Network - Assn for Project Management
Brit Sociological Assn

Healthcare People Management Assn
Nat Assn of Deafened People

The Network - Network of Government Library & Information Specialists
Network London - Brit-American Business Inc
Network New York - Brit-American Business Inc
Network NL - Nat Security Inspectorate
Network for Regions - Motorcycle Action Group
Networker - Development Trusts Assn
Networking - Brit Dental Practice Managers Assn
Networks - Brit Manual Lymph Drainage Assn
Neuroblastoma - a booklet for parents - Neuroblastoma Soc
Neuroblastoma News - Neuroblastoma Soc
Neuropathology & Applied Neurobiology - Brit Neuropathological Soc
New Approach to Latin for the Mass - Assn for Latin Liturgy
New Arrivals - Brit Humanist Assn
New Books in Folklore - Folklore Soc
New Comparison - Brit Comparative Literature Assn
New Crystal Palace Matters - Crystal Palace Foundation
New Direction - Herefordshire & Worcestershire Cham Comm
New Generation - Nat Childbirth Trust
New Ground - Socialist Environment & Resources Assn
New Help for Charities - Assn for Charities
New Horizons - Brit Fantasy Soc
The New Humanist - Rationalist Assn
The New Idler - Johnson Soc of London
New Invention List - Inst of Inventors
New Jnl of Chemistry - R Soc of Chemistry
New Latin-English Sunday Missal - Assn for Latin Liturgy
New Notes - Soc for the Promotion of New Music
New Pesticide Outlook - R Soc of Chemistry
New Producer - New Producers Alliance
The New Rambler - Johnson Soc of London
New Sjogren's Hbk - Brit Sjogren's Syndrome Assn
New Specialist Angler - Specialist Anglers Alliance
New Steel Construction - Brit Constructional Steelwork Assn
New Steel Construction - Steel Construction Inst
The New Technical Guide - Mastic Asphalt Council
New Tracks to the Cities - Permanent Way Instn
New Vision - Assn of Separated & Divorced Catholics
New Welsh Review - ACADEMI - Welsh Nat Literature Promotion Agency
New Wetland Harvests - New Life for the Broads Fens - Brit Reed Growers' Assn
New Writing Scotland - Assn for Scot Literary Studies
The Newman - Newman Assn
The News - Motor Industry Public Affairs Assn
News 4 Energy - NOF Energy
Newsbrief - R United Services Inst for Defence & Security Studies
Nexus - Soc of Business Practitioners
Managing & Marketing Sales Assn
NFU Countryside - Nat Farmers Union of England & Wales
NFU Farming Wales - Nat Farmers Union of England & Wales
NFU Horticulture - Nat Farmers Union of England & Wales
NFU Professional - Nat Farmers Union of England & Wales
NI Pharmacy in Focus - Ulster Chemists' Assn
The Nibbler - Nat Gerbil Soc
Niche Commercial - Nat Assn of Commercial Finance Brokers
NIFA News - Network of Independent Forensic Accountants
Nigeria News Report - Britain Nigeria Business Council
Night - Noctis: the voice of the nighttime economy
NIPSA News - Northern Ireland Public Service Alliance
NMC News - Nat Mouse Club
No Overall Control? the impact of a 'hung parliament' on Brit Politics - Hansard Soc
No Pound: No Independence - Anti Common Market League
NODA Nat News - Nat Operatic & Dramatic Assn
NOMINA - Soc for Name Studies in Britain & Ireland
The Non-conformist experience in Croydon - Croydon Natural History & Scientific Soc
Non-metallic strapping - Brit Tensional Strapping Assn
Norfolk Archaeology - Norfolk & Norwich Archaeological Soc
Norfolk Reed Roofing Today - Brit Reed Growers' Assn
North Eastern Record Volume 1: Infrastructure - Historical Model Railway Soc
North Eastern Record Volume 2: Rolling Stock - Historical Model Railway Soc

North Eastern Record Volume 3: Locomotives - Historical Model Railway Soc
North West Notes - North Western Model Railway Clubs Assn
North Wind - George MacDonald Soc
Northamptonshire Archaeology - Northamptonshire Archaeological Soc
Northamptonshire Past & Present - Northamptonshire Record Soc
Northern Bulletin - Green Lane Assn
Northern Studies - Scot Soc for Northern Studies
North-West Geography - Manchester Geographical Soc
NOTA News - Nat Organisation for the Treatment of Abusers
Notes - Microtome Mfrs Assn
Notes for Company Managers - Stage Management Assn
Noticeboard - Headway - the Brain Injury Assn
NoticeBoard - Assn of Chief Executives of Voluntary Organisations
Nottinghamshire Historian - Nottinghamshire Local History Assn
November News - Bluefaced Leicester Sheep Breeders Assn
NPA Times - Nat Pawnbrokers Assn
NPS Magazine - Northumbrian Pipers' Soc
NSPH Members Jnl - Nat Soc of Professional Hypnotherapists
NSPS Annual - Nat Sweet Pea Soc
NTDA - Nat Tyre Distributors Assn
NTTA News - Nat Trailer & Towing Assn
Nuclear & Particle Physics - Inst of Physics
Nuclear Medicine Communications - Brit Nuclear Medicine Soc
The Numismatic Chronicle - R Numismatic Soc
Nurse Prescribing - Community & District Nursing Assn UK
Nursery News - Nat Day Nurseries Assn
Nursery Nursing Practitioner - Soc of Nursery Nursing Practitioners
Nursing Care - Community & District Nursing Assn UK
Nursing Home News - Registered Nursing Home Assn
Nursing Management Manual - Registered Nursing Home Assn
Nursing Scotland - Independent Fedn of Nursing in Scotland
Nursing Standard - R College of Nursing of the UK
Nutrition & Health - McCarrison Soc
The Nymph and the Grot - Friends of St Bride Library

O.R. Insight - Operational Research Soc
Obituaries of Fellows 1830-2000 - The R Soc
Observer - Russo-Brit Cham Comm
Obsessions - SANE
The Obstetrician & Gynaecologist - R College of Obstetricians & Gynaecologists
Occupational Medicine Jnl - Soc of Occupational Medicine
Occupational Safety & Health - R Soc for the Prevention of Accidents
Occupational Therapy News - Brit Assn of Occupational Therapists
Ocean Challenge - Challenger Soc for Marine Science
Oculus - Partially Sighted Soc
Off Air - Radio Academy
Off Road Rider - Amateur Motor Cycle Assn
Off the Run - Fire Service Preservation Group
Official List of Shows & Events - Assn of Show & Agricultural Organisations
Officiating News - Assn of Brit Tennis Officials
Offsets - Nat Auricula & Primula Soc (Southern)
Offshore Marine Technology - R Instn of Naval Architects
OH Today - Assn of Occupational Health Nurse Practitioners (UK)
Oil on the Rails - Historical Model Railway Soc
Old Fell Side - Lakeland Dialect Soc
Older People on Low Incomes: The case for a friendlier tax system - Low Incomes Tax Reform Group
Older People on Low Incomes: The taxman's response - Low Incomes Tax Reform Group
Omnibus Magazine - Joint Assn of Classical Teachers
The Omnibus Magazine - Omnibus Soc
On Air - Nat Assn of Hospital Broadcasting Organisations
On Display - Fair Organ Preservation Soc
On the Massage Scene - Scot Massage Therapists Organisation
On the Road - Assn of Brit Drivers

© CBD Research Ltd · Beckenham · BR3 5JS · Tel 020 8650 7745 · Fax 020 8650 0768 · E-mail cbd@cbdresearch.com · www.cbdresearch.com

On Track - Confederation of Transcribed Information Services
On Track Magazine - Fitness Industry Assn
On Trade Media Review - Assn of Licensed Multiple Retailers
One & All - Nat Adult School Organisation
One in Seven - RNID
Onze Taal - Assn for Language Learning
Open Book - Alliance of Literary Socs
Open fires for coal & wood - Nat Fireplace Assn
Open Hand Magazine - Deafblind UK
Open House - Nat Assn for Bikers with a Disability
Open Space - Commons, Open Spaces & Footpaths Preservation
Soc (Open Spaces Soc)
Operators Safety Code for Powered Indl Trucks - Brit Indl Truck
Assn
Opportunities - Brit-Peruvian Cham
Opportunity - Milton Keynes & North Bucks Cham Comm
**Opportunity: a directory of sources of careers & life-time
learning information -** ADSET
Opposite Lock - World Speedway Riders Assn
OPSCS Magazine - Observer's Pocket Series Collectors' Soc
Opticians in Business - Fedn of Ophthalmic & Dispensing
Opticians
Optics - Assn of Brit Dispensing Opticians
Optics at a Glance - Fedn of Ophthalmic & Dispensing Opticians
Optimum Nutrition - Inst for Optimum Nutrition
Oracle - Inst of Sheet Metal Engineering
Oral History - Oral History Soc
Orbit - Domestic Appliance Service Assn
Orchid Cultivation Booklet - Orchid Soc of GB
Orders & Medals - Orders & Medals Research Soc
Orders of the Day - Sealed Knot
Orff Times - Orff Soc UK
Organic & Biomolecular Chemistry - R Soc of Chemistry
Organic Farming - Soil Assn
Organisation & People Jnl - Assn for Management Education &
Development
Organists' Review - Incorporated Assn of Organists
Originals - Soc of Artists' Agents
Origins - Biblical Creation Soc
Ornithological Bulletin - London Natural History Soc
Orts - George MacDonald Soc
Osteopathy Today - Brit Osteopathic Assn
Osteoporosis News - Nat Osteoporosis Soc
Osteoporosis Review - Nat Osteoporosis Soc
The Ostomy Book - IA: the Ileostomy & Internal Pouch Support
Group
OT (Optometry Today/Optics Today) - Assn of Optometrists
Our Common Land - Commons, Open Spaces & Footpaths
Preservation Soc
Out on a Limb - Brit Limbless Ex-Service Men's Assn
Outdoor Focus - Outdoor Writers' & Photographers' Guild
Outdoor Photography - Guild of Master Craftsmen
Outdoor Sourcebook - Inst for Outdoor Learning
Outlaw - Arthur Ransome Soc
Outlook - Chemical Business Assn
Outlook - Fedn of Sidecar Clubs
The Outrigger - Pacific Islands Soc of the UK & Ireland
Overseas - R Over-Seas League
Overseas Press & Media Guide - Overseas Press & Media Assn
Owl - UK One World Linking Assn
The Oxford Down - One Hundred Years of Breeding - Oxford
Down Sheep Breeders Assn
Oxoniensia - Oxfordshire Architectural & Historical Soc

P

PA2 - Brit Pharmacological Soc
The Packaging Professional - Inst of Materials, Minerals & Mining
Paddle Wheels - Paddle Steamer Preservation Soc
Paddles Past - Historic Canoe & Kayak Assn
Pagan Dawn - Pagan Fedn
Pain & Wound Care - Wound Care Soc
Paint - SAA - the Soc for All Artists
Paintball Games in Woodlands - UK Paintball Sports Fedn
Paintball UK - UK Paintball Sports Fedn

Palaeontology - Palaeontological Assn
Palliative Management of Fungating Malignant Wounds -
Wound Care Soc
Pallidula - Brit Shell Collectors Club
Palomino - Brit Palomino Soc
Pan - Brit Flute Soc
Panpodium - Brit Assn of Steelbands
Paper Technology - Paper Industry Technical Assn
Paragraphs - Neil Munro Soc
The Paralegal - Nat Assn of Licensed Paralegals
Parallel Vision - Brit & Irish Orthoptic Soc
Paranormal Review Magazine - Soc for Psychical Research
Parapet Design - Timber Decking Assn
Parents' Guide to Maintained Boarding Schools - Boarding
Schools Assn
Parking News - Brit Parking Assn
Parson & Parish - English Clergy Assn
Partners in Progress - Brit Cham Comm Thailand
Pastoral Care in Education - Nat Assn for Pastoral Care in
Education
Pathfinder Business - Inst of Export
The Patriot - John Hampden Soc
Patternmaking News - Pattern, Model & Mould Mfrs Assn
Patterns of Prejudice - Inst for Jewish Policy Research
Pawnbrokers Guide - Nat Pawnbrokers Assn
Pawns - Welsh Chess Union
Pawprints - People & Dogs Soc
Payroll Professional - Inst of Payroll Professionals
PB - Scot Athletics
PCS View - Public & Commercial Services Union
Peace Song Book - Workers' Music Assn
Peewit! - Malcolm Saville Soc
Pelargonium News - Brit Pelargonium & Geranium Soc
Pelargonium News Ybk - Brit Pelargonium & Geranium Soc
Pencil Point - Obstetric Anaesthetists Assn
Pendulum - MDF - the BiPolar Organisation
The Penguin Collector - Penguin Collectors' Soc
Pension credit for beginners - Nat Pensioners' Convention
Pension Lawyer - Assn of Pension Lawyers
People & Places - InterNat Pen Friends
People Management - Chartered Inst of Personnel & Development
Per Annum - Assn of Chief Estates Surveyors & Property Managers in
the Public Sector
Pera Abstracts - PERA
Percussive Notes - Percussive Arts Soc
Peregrine - Hawk & Owl Trust
Performance Bond - Confederation of Construction Specialists
Performance Textiles - Performance Textiles Assn
Permaculture Works - Permaculture Assn (Britain)
The Permanent Way Instn - the first 100 years, 1884-1984 -
Permanent Way Instn
Permission to Speak Sir! - Dad's Army Appreciation Soc
Personal Experiences - Narcolepsy Assn UK
Personal Injuries Hbk - Personal Injuries Bar Assn
Perspective - R Soc of Ulster Architects
Perspectives - Assn of University Administrators
Brit-Swiss Cham Comm
Myalgic Encephalopathy Assn
Perspectives in Public Health - R Soc for Public Health
Petroleum Review - Energy Inst
Pharmaceutical Auditing - Chartered Quality Inst
Pharmaceutical Contract Manufacture - Chartered Quality Inst
Pharmaceutical Distribution - Chartered Quality Inst
Pharmaceutical Documentation - Chartered Quality Inst
The Pharmaceutical Historian - Brit Soc for the History of
Pharmacy
Pharmaceutical Jnl - R Pharmaceutical Soc of GB
Pharmaceutical Manufacturing - Chartered Quality Inst
Pharmaceutical Packaging Validation - Chartered Quality Inst
Pharmaceutical Premises & Environment - Chartered Quality
Inst
Pharmaceutical Statistics - Statisticians in the Pharmaceutical
Industry
Pharos InterNat - Cremation Soc of GB
The Philosopher - Philosophical Soc of England
Philosophic Counselling - Assn for Therapeutic Philosophy
Phobias - SANE
Photochemical & Photobiological Sciences - R Soc of Chemistry

The Photographer - Brit Inst of Professional Photography
The Photogrammetric Record - Remote Sensing & Photogrammetry Soc
Photographica World - Photographic Collectors' Club of GB
Phrysko - Friesian Horse Assn of GB & Ireland
PHS Jnl - Pembrokeshire Historical Soc
PhysChemComm - R Soc of Chemistry
Physical Chemistry Chemical Physics - R Soc of Chemistry
Physical Education & Sports Pedagogy - Assn for Physical Education
Physical Education Matters - Assn for Physical Education
Physicians Guide to the Management of Huntington's Disease - Huntington's Disease Assn
Physics & Chemistry of Glasses - Soc of Glass Technology
Physiotherapy - Chartered Soc of Physiotherapy
Physiotherapy (cassette tape) - Nat Ankylosing Spondylitis Soc
PICA Magazine - Police Insignia Collectors Assn of GB
Picture House - Cinema Theatre Assn
The Picture Restorer - Brit Assn of Paintings Conservator-Restorers
Piers - Nat Piers Soc
Pigging Industry News - Pigging Products & Services Assn
Pinball Player - Pinball Owners' Assn
Pine Cone - Order of Woodcraft Chivalry
Pint in Hand - Soc for the Preservation of Beers from the Wood
Pioneers & Pathfinders - Assn of Past Rotarians
The Pipe Band - R Scot Pipe Band Assn
Pipe Joint Guide - Brit Compressed Air Soc
Pipeline - Surfers against Sewage
Pipeline Industry Directory - Pipeline Industries Guild
The Piping Times - College of Piping
Pitkin Guide to George Eliot - George Eliot Fellowship
Plain English - Plain English Campaign 1979
Plainsong & Medieval Music - Plainsong & Mediæval Music Soc
Plangon - Doll Club of GB
Planning for Memorials - Assn of Burial Authorities
Planning for Memorials after Cremation - Assn of Burial Authorities
Plant Based Nutrition & Health - Vegan Soc
Plant Biotechnology - Soc for Experimental Biology
Plant Ecology & Diversity - Botanical Soc of Scotland
The Plant Engineer - Soc of Operations Engineers
Plant Finder - Construction Plant-hire Assn
Plant Heritage - Nat Council for the Conservation of Plants & Gardens
The Plant Jnl - Soc for Experimental Biology
Planting & Managing Amenity Woodlands - Arboricultural Assn
Plantlife - Plantlife InterNat: the wild plant conservation charity
Plastics & Board Jnl - Plastics & Board Industries Fedn
Plastiquarian - Plastics Historical Soc
The Platform - Fairground Soc
Play Matters - Nat Assn of Toy & Leisure Libraries (Play Matters)
Play Safety Guidelines - Nat Playing Fields Assn
Playaction - Fair Play for Children Assn
The Players Club - Professional Footballers Assn
The Players Jnl - Professional Footballers Assn
Playing a Part: a study of the impact of youth theatre on the personal, social & political development of young people - Nat Assn of Youth Theatres
Playwork - a guide for trainers - Nat Playing Fields Assn
PLS Plus - Publishers Licensing Soc
Plu Glosa Nota - Glosa Education Organisation
Plumb Heat - Scot & Northern Ireland Plumbing Employers' Fedn
Plumbheat - Northern Ireland Master Plumbers' Assn
Plus News - Nat Fedn of Plus Areas of GB
PMI News - Pensions Management Inst
The Pocket Guide to Hysterectomy - Hysterectomy Assn
Pocket Guide to Road Note 39 - Road Surface Treatments Assn
Podiatry Now - Soc of Chiropodists & Podiatrists
Podiatry Review - Inst of Chiropodists & Podiatrists
The Poetry News - Poetry Soc (Inc)
The Poetry Review - Poetry Soc (Inc)
Pointer - Scot Council for Development & Industry
Points per Second - Pentathlon GB
Poisoning in Veterinary Practice - Nat Office of Animal Health
Police - Police Fedn of England & Wales
Police Beat - Police Fedn for Northern Ireland
Political Digest - Assn of Licensed Multiple Retailers
Pollution Control Hbk - Environmental Protection UK

Pony Express - Mounted Games Assn of GB
Pop & Rock Fanzine - Pop & Rock Fans' Assn
Popular Astronomy - Soc for Popular Astronomy
Port Health Hbk - Assn of Port Health Authorities
Portfolio - Monumental Brass Soc
Post Horn - Post Office Vehicle Club
Post Natal Depression - Assn for Postnatal Illness
Postal History Jnl - Postal History Soc
Postal Auction - Photographic Collectors' Club of GB
Postbag - Nat Assn of Music Educators
Postcard World - GB Postcard Club
Postgraduate Medical Jnl - Fellowship of Postgraduate Medicine
Post-Medieval Archaeology - Soc for Post-Medieval Archaeology
Potters - Craft Potters' Assn of GB
The Power Engineer - Instn of Diesel & Gas Turbine Engineers
The Powys Jnl - Powys Soc
The Powys NL - Powys Soc
PPI News & Junk Mail - Brit Postmark Soc
Practical Greenkeeping - R & Ancient Golf Club
Practical Ophthalmic Lenses - Assn of Brit Dispensing Opticians
Practice - Brit Assn of Social Workers
Praxis Makes Perfect - Dyspraxia Foundation
Precedents for Consent Orders - Resolution
Precept Return - Soc of County Treasurers
Pre-construction Information - Assn for Project Safety
Pregnancy Loss & the Death of a Baby - Stillbirth & Neonatal Death Soc
Prep School - SATIPS - Support & Training in Prep Schools
Prep School Magazine - Incorporated Assn of Preparatory Schools
Pressure Points - Water Jetting Assn
Pressure Ulcer Prevention Manual - Wound Care Soc
Prevention of Infection in the Home (home hygiene booklet) - Infection Prevention Soc
Preview - R Caledonian Horticultural Soc
A Price not worth Paying - Campaign for an Independent Britain
Primary Geographer - Geographical Assn
Primary History - Historical Assn
Primary Science Review - Assn for Science Education
Primate Eye - Primate Soc of GB
Primed - Assn of Brit Healthcare Industries
Principles of Fire Investigation - Instn of Fire Engineers
Principles of Leg Ulcer Management & Prevention - Wound Care Soc
Principles of Ophthalmic Lenses - Assn of Brit Dispensing Opticians
Principles of Pressure Ulcer Management & Prevention - Wound Care Soc
Printed Parish Registers - Lancashire Parish Register Soc
Prism NL - Brit Fantasy Soc
Private Hire & Taxi Monthly - Nat Private Hire Assn
The Private Library - Private Libraries Assn
Private Owner Wagons from the Ince Waggon & Ironworks Co - Historical Model Railway Soc
Private Press Books - Private Libraries Assn
Proceedings - Assn of Dental Anaesthetists
　　　　　　Brit Academy
　　　　　　Cambridge Antiquarian Soc
　　　　　　Croydon Natural History & Scientific Soc
　　　　　　Devon Archaeological Soc
　　　　　　Huguenot Soc of GB & Ireland
　　　　　　Isle of Wight Natural History & Archaeological Soc
　　　　　　Japan Soc
Proceedings of the European Otter Conference - InterNat Otter Survival Fund
Process Safety & Environmental Protection - Instn of Chemical Engineers
Proclaim - Assn of Past Rotarians
ProContractor - Nat Assn of Agricultural Contractors
The Product Book - D&AD
Production Jnl - Newspaper Soc
Professional Business & Technical Management - Professional Business & Technical Management
The Professional Engineer - Soc of Professional Engineers
The Professional Gardener - Professional Gardeners' Guild
Professional Imagemaker - Soc of Wedding & Portrait Photographers
Professional Investor - CFA Soc of the UK
Professional Manager - Chartered Management Inst

© CBD Research Ltd · Beckenham · BR3 5JS · Tel 020 8650 7745 · Fax 020 8650 0768 · E-mail cbd@cbdresearch.com · www.cbdresearch.com

Professional Pest Controller - Brit Pest Control Assn
The Professional Remover - Nat Guild of Removers & Storers
Professional Social Work - Brit Assn of Social Workers
Profile - Chartered Inst of Public Relations
Professional Golfers' Assn
Profitable Mobile Catering - Nationwide Caterers Assn
Progress - Nat Home Improvement Council
Progressive Greetings - Greeting Card Assn
Project - Assn for Project Management
Pro-Life Times - Soc for the Protection of Unborn Children
Promota Bulletin - Promota (UK) (Promotional Merchandise Trade Assn)
Promotions Buyer - Brit Promotional Merchandise Assn
The Prompt - Brit Assn of Dramatherapists
Property Indices Report - Soc of Property Researchers
The Property Magazine - Guild of Professional Estate Agents
Pro-rat-a - Nat Fancy Rat Soc
Prospectus - Anglo-Norman Text Soc
Prosper - Black Country Cham Comm
Protestant Truth - Protestant Truth Soc (Inc)
Pruning Kentish Cobnuts - Kentish Cobnuts Assn
Psi Report - Scot Soc for Psychical Research
Psoriasis - Psoriasis Assn
Psoriatic Care Fact File - Psoriasis & Psoriatic Arthritis Alliance
Psychiatric Bulletin - R College of Psychiatrists
Psychoanalytic Psychotherapy - Assn for Psychoanalytic Psychotherapy in the NHS
The Psychologist - Brit Psychological Soc
Psychology & Psychotherapy - Brit Psychological Soc
Psychology of Music - Soc for Education, Music & Psychology Research
Psychology Teaching - Assn for Teaching Psychology
The Psychotherapist - UK Council for Psychotherapy
PTA - Nat Confederation of Parent-Teacher Assns
Pteridologist - Brit Pteridological Soc
PTS News - Philatelic Traders Soc
Public Address - Inst of Sound & Communications Engineers
Public Health - R Soc for Public Health
Public Relations Consultancy - Public Relations Consultants Assn
Public Sculpture of Britain - Public Monuments & Sculpture Assn
Public Security - Assn of Police & Public Security Suppliers
Public Service Magazine - First Division Assn
Public Utilities Bulletin - Road Transport Fleet Data Soc
Publicans Guide to the Health & Safety Act - Fedn of Licensed Victuallers Assns
Puerperal Psychosis - Assn for Postnatal Illness
Pugwash NL - Brit Pugwash Group
Pull! - Clay Pigeon Shooting Assn
Pumps from Britain - Brit Pump Mfrs' Assn
Puppet Master - Brit Puppet & Model Theatre Guild
Pura Raza Española - Brit Assn for the Purebred Spanish Horse
Pygmy Goat Hbk - Pygmy Goat Club
Pygmy Goat Notes - Pygmy Goat Club

Q

Q News - Guild of Q Butchers
Q Review - Assn of Private Client Investment Managers & Stockbrokers
QCA Voice - Quoted Companies Alliance
Quaker Monthly - Religious Soc of Friends (Quakers)
Quaker News - Religious Soc of Friends (Quakers)
Quaker Projects - Religious Soc of Friends (Quakers)
Quality in Agency - Brit Assn for Service to the Elderly
Quality Standards - Automatic Vending Assn
Quality World - Chartered Quality Inst
Quarry Management - Inst of Quarrying
Quarrying in Depth - recycling - Quarry Products Assn
Quarterly - Assn of Disabled Professionals
The Quarterly - Brit Assn of Paper Historians
Quarterly Account - Inst of Money Advisers
Quarterly Jnl of Experimental Psychology - Experimental Psychology Soc
Quarterly Jnl of Forestry - R Forestry Soc of England, Wales & Northern Ireland

Quarterly Magazine - Inst of Bookbinding & Allied Trades
Quarterly NL - Lead Contractors Assn
Quarterly Report - Brit Egg Assn
Quarterly Review - Scot Engineering
Quarterly Survey of Advertising Expenditure - Advertising Assn
Quartermation - Brit Automation & Robot Assn
Quasar Magazine - Brit Assn for Research Quality Assurance
The Quekett Jnl of Microscopy - Quekett Microscopical Club
Quest - Queen's English Soc
Quiet - Brit Tinnitus Assn
Quillers Today - Quilling Guild
The Quilter - Quilters' Guild of the Brit Isles
Quo Vadis? - Land's End - John O'Groats Assn

R

R A Magazine - R Academy of Arts
R&A News Bulletin - R & Ancient Golf Club
Rabbiting On - Rabbit Welfare Assn
Race against Time - Meningitis Research Foundation
Race Walking Record - Race Walking Assn
Racing Construction Regulation - Hovercraft Club of GB
Radcom - Radio Soc of GB
Radical Statistics - Radical Statistics Group
Radiography - Soc of Radiographers
The Radionic Jnl - Radionic Assn
Radius Performing - Religious Drama Soc
Rail Freight Group News - Rail Freight Group
Railwatch - Railway Development Soc
The Railway Observer - Railway Correspondence & Travel Soc
Railway Ramblings - Railway Ramblers
Random Round - Percy Grainger Soc
The Ranger - Brit Free Range Egg Producers Assn
Ranger - Countryside Management Assn
Rapport - Assn for Neuro-Linguistic Programming (UK)
Community & Youth Workers' Union
RATEL - Assn of Brit & Irish Wild Animal Keepers
The Ravilious Notebook - Friends of St Bride Library
Raw Power - Brit Drug Free Powerlifting Assn
A Ray of Hope - Assn of Young People with ME
Raynaud's: your questions answered - Raynaud's & Scleroderma Assn
RCCC Annual - R Caledonian Curling Club
RCHM Jnl - Register of Chinese Herbal Medicine
RCN Bulletin - R College of Nursing of the UK
RCO News - R College of Organists
RDA News - Riding for the Disabled Assn
Reach Quality Assessment Framework - Youth Action Network
Reaching Out - Guillain Barré Syndrome Support Group
Reaction - Nat Soc for Research into Allergy
Reading Masterclass - Confederation of Transcribed Information Services
Real Lives - Albinism Fellowship
Real Power - Brit Wind Energy Assn
A Reasonable Faith: introducing the Sea of Faith Network - Sea of Faith Network (UK)
Recommended Practice for Troughed Belt Conveyors - Materials Handling Engineers Assn
The Record - Lancashire Authors' Assn
Record Book for the Recording of Explosives kept in Quarries' Blasting Sites - Quarry Products Assn
Record Book for the Recording of Explosives kept in Quarries' Explosives Stores - Quarry Products Assn
Recorder News - Biological Recording in Scotland
Recording News - Brit Sound Recording Assn
Records of Buckinghamshire - Architectural & Archaeological Soc for the County of Buckinghamshire
Records of Huntingdon - Huntingdonshire Local History Soc
Recovery - Assn of Business Recovery Professionals
Brit Damage Management Assn
Recovery Operator - Retail Motor Industry Fedn
Recovery Operator Magazine - Assn of Vehicle Recovery Operators
Re-creating Communities: business, the arts & regeneration - Arts & Business

Recruitment Matters - Recruitment & Employment Confederation
Recusant History - Catholic Record Soc
Recycling Health & Safety Manual - Brit Metals Recycling Assn
Red Book - CEDIA UK
Red Herrings - Crime Writers Assn
Reedbed Management for Bitterns - Brit Reed Growers' Assn
Reedbed Management for Commercial & Wildlife Interests - Brit Reed Growers' Assn
Reference Manual for Construction Plant - Instn of Civil Engineering Surveyors
Reflexions - Assn of Reflexologists
Reformer - Tory Reform Group
Refractories Engineer - Inst of Refractories Engineers
Regional Studies - Regional Studies Assn
Register - Nat Women's Register
Register of Certificated Wallers/Dykers - Dry Stone Walling Assn of GB
Register of Homeopaths - Soc of Homeopaths
Register of Independent Midwives - Independent Midwives' Assn
Register of One-Name Studies - Guild of One-Name Studies
Register of Patent Agents - Chartered Inst of Patent Attorneys
Register of Practitioners Members - General Council & Register of Naturopaths
Register of Professional Private Music Teachers - Incorporated Soc of Musicians
Register of Psychotherapists - Brit Psychoanalytic Council
Register of Schools that help Dyslexic Children - Council for the Registration of Schools Teaching Dyslexic Pupils
Reiki Magazine InterNat - Reiki Assn
Reinforced Concrete: History, Properties & Durability - Corrosion Prevention Assn
Relative Values ... Missing out on Contact? - Grandparents' Assn
Relative Values ... The Best Interests of the Child? - Grandparents' Assn
Release - Captive Animals' Protection Soc
Religion 2 Liberty - Inst of Economic Affairs
The Remarkable James Livingstone - R Instn of South Wales
Removals & Storage - Brit Assn of Removers
Renaissance Studies - Soc for Renaissance Studies
Renew - Network for Alternative Technology & Technology Assessment
Renewables Ybk - Renewable Energy Assn
Renewables, Past, Present & Future: a review of government policy & the development of the UK Renewable Energy Programme 1994-97 - Network for Alternative Technology & Technology Assessment
Replacing the State? - Assn of Chief Executives of Voluntary Organisations
Reporter - Brit Inst of Organ Studies
The Reporter - Soc of Legal Scholars in the UK & Ireland
Representation: jnl of democracy & electoral systems - Electoral Reform Soc
Res Medica - R Medical Soc
Research Intelligence - Brit Educational Research Assn
Research MRS News - Market Research Soc
Resnews - Rescare
Resource - Nat Assn of Teachers of Religious Education
Resource Pack for Care Homes - Assn for Continence Advice
Restart - Assn of Classic Trials Clubs
Resurgam - Fedn of Burial & Cremation Authorities
Retail Alert - Brit Shops & Stores Assn
Retail Express - Nat Fedn of Retail Newsagents
Retail News - Scot Grocers' Fedn
Retail Newsagent - Nat Fedn of Retail Newsagents
Retail Outlook - Scot Grocers' Fedn
Retail Sales Garment Cleaning - Guild of Cleaners & Launderers
Retailers Guide to Service - Small Electrical Appliance Marketing Assn
The Retreader - Retread Mfrs Assn
Retreats - Assn for Promoting Retreats
Retreats - Retreat Assn
Retrospection - Nat Assn of Re-enactment Socs
Reverberations - Handbell Ringers of GB
Review - Aluminium Stockholders Assn
    Brit Interior Design Assn
    Brit Simmental Cattle Soc
    Cambridgeshire Assn for Local History

    Charlotte M Yonge Fellowship
    Nat Assn of Memorial Masons
    Nat Pony Soc
The Review - Naval Historical Collectors & Research Assn
Review of Building Prices - Building Cost Information Service
A Review of Hospitality Management Education in the UK - Council for Hospitality Management Education
Review of InterNat Studies - Brit InterNat Studies Assn
Revolutions - Motor Cycle Industry Assn
RFIC Fire Prevention Guide - Food Storage & Distribution Fedn
RFIC Guidance on the Assessment of Fire Risk - Food Storage & Distribution Fedn
RFIC Guide to the Storage & Handling of Frozen Foods - UK Assn of Frozen Food Producers
RFIC Storage & Handling of Frozen Foods - Food Storage & Distribution Fedn
Rheology Abstracts - Brit Soc of Rheology
Rheology Bulletin - Brit Soc of Rheology
Rheology Reviews - Brit Soc of Rheology
Rheumatic Review - Arthritic Assn
Rheumatology - Brit Soc for Rheumatology
RIBA Jnl - R Inst of Brit Architects
The Ricardian - Richard III Soc - Fellowship of the White Boar
The Ricardian Bulletin - Richard III Soc - Fellowship of the White Boar
The Rifleman - Nat Small-Bore Rifle Assn
Rights of Way: the authority of case law - Scot Rights of Way & Access Soc
Ring Directory - Morris Ring
Ringing Migration - Brit Trust for Ornithology
The Ringing World - Central Council of Church Bell Ringers
The River Wandle: Distribution of its flora - Croydon Natural History & Scientific Soc
Rivista - Brit Italian Soc
RLS Club News - Robert Louis Stevenson Club
RMA Research Chronicle - R Musical Assn
RNA News - Romantic Novelists Assn
The Road - Motorcycle Action Group
Road Haulage Manual - Road Haulage Assn
Roadway - Road Haulage Assn
The Rock Garden - Scot Rock Garden Club
Rolling - Road Roller Assn
Romany Magazine - Romany Soc
The Romney Flock Book - Romney Sheep Breeders' Soc
The Romney Hbk - Romney Sheep Breeders' Soc
Roofing Hbk - Flat Roofing Alliance
The Roofing Trades Jnl - Confederation of Roofing Contractors
Roomheaters & stoves - Nat Fireplace Assn
The Rose - R Nat Rose Soc
The Rotorhead - Brit Helicopter Advisory Board
Roundabouts from the Air - UK Roundabout Appreciation Soc
Roundabouts of Britain - UK Roundabout Appreciation Soc
Roundabouts of GB Calendar - UK Roundabout Appreciation Soc
Roundhead Assn NL - English Civil War Soc
Round-Up - Brit Westerners Assn
Route Notes N to S - Offa's Dyke Assn
Route Notes S to N - Offa's Dyke Assn
Route to a Successful Concrete Repair - Concrete Repair Assn
Routemaster Magazine - Routemaster Operators & Owners Assn
Rowing Action - Scot Amateur Rowing Assn
R Highland Review - R Highland & Agricultural Soc of Scotland
R Martyr Annual - R Martyr Church Union
R Stuart Papers - R Stuart Soc
R Stuart Review - R Stuart Soc
RPS Jnl - R Photographic Soc of GB
The RSA Jnl - R Soc for the encouragement of Arts, Manufactures & Commerce
RSE News - R Soc of Edinburgh
Runestaff - The Vikings
Running Elections - Soc of Local Authority Chief Executives & Senior Managers
Rupert Calendar - Followers of Rupert
RURAL Briefing - Soc for the Responsible Use of Resources in Agriculture & on the Land
Rural History Today - Brit Agricultural History Soc
Rural Matters - R Agricultural Soc of England
Rural Retailer - Rural Shops Alliance
Rural Review - R Lancashire Agricultural Soc

© CBD Research Ltd · Beckenham · BR3 5JS · Tel 020 8650 7745 · Fax 020 8650 0768 · E-mail cbd@cbdresearch.com · www.cbdresearch.com

Rural Theology - Rural Theology Assn
Rural Wales / Cymru Wledig - Campaign for the Protection of Rural Wales (Ymgyrch Diogelu Cymru Wledig) (YDCW)
RUSI Defence Systems - R United Services Inst for Defence & Security Studies
RUSI Jnl - R United Services Inst for Defence & Security Studies
The Ruskin Gazette - Ruskin Soc of Oxford
The Russell - Welsh Highland Railways Assn
Russian Chemical Reviews - R Soc of Chemistry
Russistika - Assn for Language Learning

S

SAAD Digest - Soc for the Advancement of Anaesthesia in Dentistry
SACS Jnl - Scot Assn for Country Sports
Safe & Sound - Building a Safer Youth Work Environment - Youth Scotland
Safe Use of & Operation of Marquees & Temporary Structures - Performance Textiles Assn
Safety & Health Practitioner - Instn of Occupational Safety & Health
Safety Education - R Soc for the Prevention of Accidents
Safety in Electrical Testing - Radio, Electrical & Television Retailers' Assn
Safety Express - R Soc for the Prevention of Accidents
Safety Guidelines for Steel Stockholders & Processors - Nat Assn of Steel Stockholders
Safety Training for Teachers - Nat Assn of Advisers & Inspectors in Design & Technology
The Saga Book - Viking Soc for Northern Research
SAIFinsight - Nat Soc of Allied & Independent Funeral Directors
Sail to Adventure - Assn of Sea Training Organisations
Salers Jnl - Salers Cattle Soc of the UK
Sales & Marketing Today - Soc of Sales & Marketing
Salon Focus - Nat Hairdressers' Fedn
Sampling Bituminous Materials - Inst of Asphalt Technology
Samuri NL - Scot Ju-Jitsu Assn
SANACAST - Scot Anglers Nat Assn
Sandgrouse - Ornithological Soc of the Middle East
Sandwich & Snack News - Brit Sandwich Assn
Sarbanes Oxley White Paper - Business Application Software Developers Assn
Saved from a Watery Grave - R Humane Soc
Saying Goodbye to Your Baby - Stillbirth & Neonatal Death Soc
SCALAnews - Scala - Serving Construction & Architecture in Local Authorities
Scan - Tuberous Sclerosis Assn
Scene Magazine - Scot Community Drama Assn
Schizophrenia - SANE
The School Librarian - School Library Assn
School is Not Compulsory - Education Otherwise
School Science Review - Assn for Science Education
Schumacher Briefings - Doctor E F Schumacher Soc
Schumacher NL - Doctor E F Schumacher Soc
Science & Justice - Forensic Science Soc
Science & Public Affairs - Brit Assn for the Advancement of Science
Science Policy Priorities - Biosciences Fedn
Science Policy Report - Biosciences Fedn
Science Technology - Inst of Science & Technology
Scleroderma - The Inside Story - Raynaud's & Scleroderma Assn
SCOLAG - Scot Legal Action Group
Scoliosis Hbk - Scoliosis Assn (UK)
Score - Scot Orienteering Assn
Scotch at a Glance - Scotch Whisky Assn
Scotch Whisky: matured to be enjoyed responsibly - Scotch Whisky Assn
Scotch Whisky: questions & answers - Scotch Whisky Assn
Scotland's Finest Visitor Attractions - Assn of Scot Visitor Attractions
ScotLit - Assn for Scot Literary Studies
Scotnotes - Assn for Scot Literary Studies
Scots Bowler - Scot Indoor Bowling Assn
Scots Thesaurus -
Scot Archaeological Jnl - Glasgow Archaeological Soc
Scot Archives - Scot Records Assn

Scot Badminton - Scot Badminton Union
The Scot Beekeeper - Scot Beekeepers Assn
Scot Bird News - Scot Ornithologists' Club
Scot Bird Report - Scot Ornithologists' Club
Scot Birds - Scot Ornithologists' Club
Scot Bylines - School Leaders Scotland
Scot Chess - Chess Scotland
Scot Country Dancer - R Scot Country Dance Soc
Scot Diver - Scot Sub Aqua Club
Scot Educational Jnl - Educational Inst of Scotland
Scot Esperanto Bulletin - Scot Esperanto Assn (Esperanto-Asocio de Skotlando)
Scot Farming Leader Update - NFU Scotland
Scot Forestry - R Scot Forestry Soc
Scot Gamekeeper - Scot Gamekeepers Assn
The Scot Genealogist - Scot Genealogy Soc
Scot Geographical Jnl - R Scot Geographical Soc
Scot Golfer - Scot Golf Union
Scot Hill Tracks - Scot Rights of Way & Access Soc
Scot Home & Country - Scot Women's Rural Insts
Scot Jnl of Political Economy - Scot Economic Soc
Scot Jujitsu - Scot Ju-Jitsu Assn
The Scot Justice - Scot Justices Assn
Scot Labour History - Scot Labour History Soc
Scot Language - Assn for Scot Literary Studies
The Scot Law Gazette - Scot Law Agents Soc
Scot Leader - School Leaders Scotland
Scot Legion News - R Brit Legion Scotland
Scot Licensee - Scot Licensed Trade Assn
The Scot Mountaineer - Mountaineering Council of Scotland
Scot Nat Directory - Aberdeen and Grampian Cham Comm (Inc)
Scot NL - Scot Prayer Book Soc
Scot Paddler - Scot Canoe Assn
Scot Philately - Assn of Scot Philatelic Socs
Scot Poetry Index - Scot Poetry Library
Scot Raptor Monitoring Scheme Report - Scot Ornithologists' Club
Scot Skate Update - Scot Ice Skating Assn
Scot Snowsport Hbk - Snowsport Scotland
Scot Studies Review - Assn for Scot Literary Studies
Scot Tennis - Tennis Scotland
Scot Transport - Scot Tramway & Transport Soc
Scot Transport Matters - Scot Assn for Public Transport
Scot Transport Review - Scot Transport Studies Group
Scot Wildlife - Scot Wildlife Trust
Scouting - Scout Assn
SCPA Bulletin - Scot Cashmere Producers Assn
Scrabble Club News - Scrabble Clubs (UK)
Scramble - Battle of Britain Historical Soc
The Scribe - Soc of Scribes & Illuminators
The Scrichowl - Seventeenth Century Life & Times
The Scroll - Loyal Company of Town Criers
SCRSS Information Digest - Soc for Cooperation in Russian & Soviet Studies
Scuba World - Sub-Aqua Assn
The Sculpture Jnl - Public Monuments & Sculpture Assn
Sea Lines - Ocean Liner Soc
SEA News - Surface Engineering Assn
Sea Swallow -
Seabird - Seabird Group
The Seafarer - Marine Soc & Sea Cadets
Secretary's Page - Scot Rock Garden Club
Securities & Investment Review - Securities & Investment Inst
Security Direct - Brit Security Industry Assn
Seen & Heard - NAGALRO
Sefton Business Directory - Sefton Cham Comm & Industry
Selecting a Business System & Selecting a Reseller - Business Application Software Developers Assn
Self & Soc - Assn for Humanistic Psychology in Britain
Serials - UK Serials Group
Serica - Silk Assn of GB
Service - Spiritualist Assn of GB
Sesame - Scientific Exploration Soc
The Sessional GP - Nat Assn of Sessional GPs
Sex Reassignment Surgery - Gender Trust
Sexual & Relationship Therapy - Brit Assn for Sexual & Relationship Therapy

SG4:05 - Preventing falls in scaffolding & falsework - Nat Access & Scaffolding Confederation

The Shadow NL - Fedn of Stadium Communities

Sharing the Future - Brit Humanist Assn

The Shavian - Shaw Soc

SHEDA News - Storage & Handling Equipment Distributors' Assn

Sheep Dairy News - Brit Sheep Dairying Assn

Sheetlines - Charles Close Soc for the Study of Ordnance Survey Maps

Sherborn Facsimiles - Soc for the History of Natural History

Sherlock Holmes Jnl - Sherlock Holmes Soc of London

The Shetland Breed - Shetland Sheep Soc

Shetland Pony Stud Book - Shetland Pony Stud-Book Soc

Shifting Ground - Quarry Products Assn

Ship & Boat Intl - R Instn of Naval Architects

Ship Repair & Conversion Technology - R Instn of Naval Architects

Shoe Service - MultiService Assn

Shona's Story - Scoliosis Assn (UK)

Shooting & Conservation - Brit Assn for Shooting & Conservation

Shopping at Home: consumer guide including the DSA Code of Practice - Direct Selling Assn

Shoptalk - Shop & Display Equipment Assn

Shorewatch - Brit Marine Life Study Soc

Shortcuts - Guild of Brit Découpeurs

Shorthorn Jnl - Beef Shorthorn Cattle Soc
  Shorthorn Soc of the UK of GB & I

The Shot - Brit Wheelchair Bowls Assn

Showground News - Staffordshire & Birmingham Agricultural Soc

Shropshire Business Matters - Shropshire Cham Comm & Enterprise

Shropshire History & Archaeology - Shropshire Archaeological & Historical Soc

Shroptalk - Shropshire Sheep Breeders Assn & Flock Book Soc

Shuttle Plus - Sewing Machine Trade Assn

SIBA Jnl - Soc of Independent Brewers

Side View - Macular Disease Soc

SIdelights - Soc of Indexers

Sidelights on Sayers - Dorothy L Sayers Soc

Sidelines - Heritage Railway Assn

SIFD News - Soc for InterNat Folk Dancing (Interfolk)

Sight & Sound - Brit Film Inst

Sign Matters - Brit Deaf Assn

Signals - Arthur Ransome Soc

Signet NL - Soc of Writers to Her Majesty's Signet

Significant Ship - R Instn of Naval Architects

Significant Small Craft - R Instn of Naval Architects

Signpost - Peak & Northern Footpaths Soc

Signs of the Times - Modern Churchpeople's Union

SIHS Review - Scot Indl Heritage Soc

Silver Boar - Soc of Friends of King Richard III

Silver in Wound Care & Management - Wound Care Soc

Silver Lining Appeal Brochure - Brit Kidney Patient Assn

Simple Guide to Planning Applications - Nat Union of Residents' Assns

Simpson Strickland - Steam Boat Assn of GB

Sing When You're Winning - E-Government - Soc of Local Authority Chief Executives & Senior Managers

Sisyphus - Assn of Circulation Executives

Site Recorder - Inst of Clerks of Works of GB Inc

Siteline - LABC

The Six Acre Standard - Nat Playing Fields Assn

Sizzle - Fedn of Chefs Scotland

Sjogren's Today - Brit Sjogren's Syndrome Assn

The Skeptic - UK Skeptics

Skin 'n' Bones Connection - Psoriasis & Psoriatic Arthritis Alliance

Skydive, the Brit Mag - Brit Parachute Assn

Skypointer - Independent Pilots Assn

Skywings - Brit Hang Gliding & Paragliding Assn

Sleep Matters - Sleep Apnoea Trust Assn

Sleipnir - Icelandic Horse Soc of GB

Slingshot - Soc of Ancients

Slip Knot - Knitting & Crochet Guild

Slot Car Racing News - Brit Slot Car Racing Assn

SLS Jnl - Stephenson Locomotive Soc

SMA Guide to Props & Propping - Stage Management Assn

Small Business Issues - Inst for Small Business & Entrepreneurship

Small Printer - Brit Printing Soc

Small Printing - Brit Printing Soc

Small Talk - Wales Pre-school Playgroups Assn

Small Voices - UK Fedn of Smaller Mental Health Agencies

Small Woods Information Pack - Small Woods Assn

Smallwoods - Small Woods Assn

SMR - Soc for Medicines Research

Snippets - Deafblind UK

Snowsport News - Snowsport Scotland

Snuff Bottle Review - Snuff Bottle Soc

So You Have Sarcoidosis! - Sarcoidosis & Interstitial Lung Assn

Social Caring - Social Care Assn

Social History in Museums - Social History Curators Group

Social History of Medicine - Soc for the Social History of Medicine

Social Inventions Annual Book - Inst for Social Inventions

Social Science Teacher - Assn for the Teaching of the Social Sciences

Socialism & Health - Socialist Health Assn

Soc Edition of Songs - Peter Warlock Soc

Soc Matters - Building Socs Assn

Socio-legal NL - Socio-Legal Studies Assn

Sociology - Brit Sociological Assn

SOFHT Focus - Soc of Food Hygiene & Technology

sofia - Sea of Faith Network (UK)

Soil Use & Management - Brit Soc of Soil Science

Soldier I Wish You Well - Housman Soc

Soldiers of the Queen - Victorian Military Soc

Soldiers Small Book - Victorian Military Soc

Solicitors of the Supreme Court of Northern Ireland: List - Law Soc of Northern Ireland

Solo Magazine - Solicitor Sole Practitioners Group

Songbird Survival - Songbird Survival

SORP Made Simple: a guidance for grant-making charities - Assn of Charitable Foundations

A Sound Ear - Assn of Brit Orchestras

Sound Track Audio Magazine - Brit Sound Recording Assn

Sounding Board - Sound Sense

Soundings - Hydrographic Soc UK
  Inst of Musical Instrument Technology
  Residential Boat Owners Assn

South Wales Business Directory - Newport & Gwent Cham Comm, Enterprise & Industry

The South West Coast Path Guide - South West Coast Path Assn

South Western Circular - South Western Circle

The Southdown Flock Book - Southdown Sheep Soc

The Southdown Sheep - Southdown Sheep Soc

The Southdown Year Book - Southdown Sheep Soc

Southern Bulletin - Green Lane Assn

Southern Express - Merchant Navy Locomotive Preservation Soc

Souvenir - Violet Needham Soc

SPAB News - Soc for the Protection of Ancient Buildings

Spacereport - Assn in Scotland to Research into Astronautics

Spark - UK Pyrotechnics Soc

SPC News - Soc of Pension Consultants

Speak to the World - Brit Cham Comm for Italy, Inc

The Speaker - Assn of Speakers Clubs

Speaking Out - Brit Stammering Assn

Special - nasen

Specialist Building Finisher - Fedn of Plastering & Drywall Contractors

Spectra - Management Consultancies Assn

Spectrum - Brit Security Industry Assn
  Brit Wheel of Yoga

The Speculum - William Herschel Soc

Speech & Drama - Soc of Teachers of Speech & Drama

Speleology - Brit Caving Assn

SPHERE - Herpes Viruses Assn

Spin - Statisticians in the Pharmaceutical Industry

Spode Soc Review - Spode Soc

Spohr Jnl - Spohr Soc of GB

The Sport & Exercise Scientist - Brit Assn of Sport & Exercise Sciences

Sport & the Law Jnl - Brit Assn for Sports & Law

Sports Therapy - Soc of Sports Therapists

Sportslife - Fedn of Sports & Play Assns

Spot Press - Gloucestershire Old Spot Pig Breeders' Club

Spotlight - HR Soc

Spouting - Nat Soc of Teapot & Kettle Collectors

SPR Property Review & Digest - Soc of Property Researchers

© CBD Research Ltd · Beckenham · BR3 5JS · Tel 020 8650 7745 · Fax 020 8650 0768 · E-mail cbd@cbdresearch.com · www.cbdresearch.com

Spring - Brit Fuchsia Soc
Sprinkler Facts - Brit Automatic Fire Sprinkler Assn
Sprinkler Systems: the facts - Brit Automatic Fire Sprinkler Assn
Sprinklers for Safety - Brit Automatic Fire Sprinkler Assn
Sprinklers in Heritage Buildings - Brit Automatic Fire Sprinkler Assn
Sprinklers in Retail Premises - Brit Automatic Fire Sprinkler Assn
Sprinklers in Schools - Brit Automatic Fire Sprinkler Assn
Sprinklers in Warehouses - Brit Automatic Fire Sprinkler Assn
Sprouts - R Highland Education Trust
SRA News - Social Research Assn
SRF Review - Scotland-Russia Forum
STA Communicator - Source Testing Assn
Stable Talk - Nat Assn of Stable Staff
Staffordshire Archaeological Studies - Stoke-on-Trent Museum Archaeological Soc
Stage Management Notes - Stage Management Assn
Stage Management: a career guide - Stage Management Assn
A Stage Manager's Guide to the Provincial Commercial Contract - Stage Management Assn
A Stage Manager's Guide to the Subsidised Repertory Agreement - Stage Management Assn
A Stage Manager's Guide to the West End Agreement - Stage Management Assn
Stage Screen & Radio - Broadcasting Entertainment Cinematograph & Theatre Union
Stagedoor - Scot Music Hall & Variety Theatre Soc
Stain Removal Guide - Guild of Cleaners & Launderers
Stained Glass - Brit Soc of Master Glass Painters
Stained Glass + Monograms - Nat Assn of Decorative & Fine Arts Socs
Stainless Steel Industry - Brit Stainless Steel Assn
The Stamp Lover - Nat Philatelic Soc
The Standard - Assn of Scotland's Self-Caterers
Stand To - Western Front Assn
Standard Issue - Road Safety Markings Assn
Standard Method of Measurement - Concrete Repair Assn
Standard Spending Indicators - Soc of County Treasurers
Standardised Assessment Tools & the Management of Complex Wounds - Wound Care Soc
Standardised Protocol for the Sampling & Enumeration of Airborne Microorganisms at Composting Facilities - Assn of Organics Recycling
Standards of Environmental Cleanliness in Hospitals - Assn of Healthcare Cleaning Professionals
Stanspec 2006 - Road Safety Markings Assn
Star & Furrow - Biodynamic Agricultural Assn
Start - Nat Soc for Education in Art & Design
Starting up a Gallery & Frame Shop - Fine Art Trade Guild
Startline - Brit Automobile Racing Club
State of the Region Fact Card - Assn of North East Councils
State of the Region Profile Report - Assn of North East Councils
The Statute Law Review - Statute Law Soc
Staying Alive - R Soc for the Prevention of Accidents
The Steam Car - Steam Car Club of GB
Steam Plough Times - Steam Plough Club
The Steamboat Register - Steam Boat Assn of GB
Steaming - Nat Traction Engine Trust
Steel & Its Distribution - Nat Assn of Steel Stockholders
Steel Construction News - Brit Constructional Steelwork Assn
Steel Fibre Reinforcement Admixtures - Assn of Concrete Indl Flooring Contractors
Steel specifications - UK Steel
Steel strapping - Brit Tensional Strapping Assn
Step Forward - Limbless Assn
STEP Jnl - Soc of Trust & Estate Practitioners
STEP USA Jnl - Soc of Trust & Estate Practitioners
The Stewarts - Stewart Soc
Stickler Syndrome: the elusive syndrome - Stickler Syndrome Support Group
The Stickmaker - Brit Stickmakers Guild
Still Improving Sport - Osteopathic Sports Care Assn
The Stock Auditor - Inst of Licensed Trade Stock Auditors
Stone Specifiers Guide - Stone Fedn GB
Stopwatch - Nat Soc for the Promotion of Punctuality
The Story of the Knights Bachelor - Imperial Soc of Knights Bachelor
Storylines Magazine - Soc for Storytelling

Straight Talk - Alcohol Concern
Strain - Brit Soc for Strain Measurement
Strands - Braid Soc
Strapping machines - Brit Tensional Strapping Assn
Strategy - Strategic Planning Soc
The Strathspey Express - Strathspey Railway Assn
Stress News - InterNat Stress Management Assn UK
STRI Green Pages Trade Directory - Sports Turf Research Inst
Strider - Long Distance Walkers Assn
The Structural Engineer - Instn of Structural Engineers
Studies in Anglesey History - Anglesey Antiquarian Soc & Field Club
Studies in Church History - Ecclesiastical History Soc
Studies in Ethnicity & Natism - Assn for the Study of Ethnicity & Natism
The Subpostmaster - Nat Fedn of Sub-Postmasters
Subterranea - Subterranea Britannica
Suffolk Horse Magazine - Suffolk Horse Soc
Suffolk Scene - Suffolk Agricultural Assn
Suicide & Self Harm Prevention - Howard League for Penal Reform
Summons - Medical & Dental Defence Union of Scotland
The Sun's Abundant Energy - Solar Trade Assn
Sundial Makers - Brit Sundial Soc
The Superintendent - Police Superintendents' Assn of England & Wales
Supply Management - Chartered Inst of Purchasing & Supply
Support for Learning - nasen
The Supporter - Cleaning & Support Services Assn
Surface Coatings InterNat - Oil & Colour Chemists' Assn
Surrey Archaeological Collections - Surrey Archaeological Soc
Survey of Londoners - London Councils
Survey of Salaries & Benefits - Soc of Property Researchers
Survival Underground - Soc for the Study of Subterranean Survival
Survive - Assn of Illustrators
Susannah Blamire - Lakeland Dialect Soc
Sussex Archaeological Collections - Sussex Archaeological Soc (The)
Sussex Indl History - Sussex Indl Archaeology Soc
Sussex Past & Present - Sussex Archaeological Soc (The)
SUT News - Soc for Underwater Technology
Swim & Save - Surf Life Saving Assn of GB
Swim & Save - Swimming Teachers' Assn
Swimming for People with Disabilities - Halliwick Assn of Swimming Therapy
Swimming Pool Industry Directory & Specifier (Spidas) - Inst of Swimming Pool Engineers
Swimming Times - Inst of Swimming
Swiss Chimes Jnl - Brown Swiss Cattle Soc (UK)
Synergy - Soc of Radiographers

T

T.G.M. a coherent dozenal metrology - Dozenal Soc of GB
Table Tennis News - English Table Tennis Assn
Tackling Multiple Disadvantage - Community Foundation Network
TACT Review - Assn of Corporate Trustees
Tag Talk - Arthrogryposis Group
Tai Chi Tuan & Oriental Arts - Tai Chi Union for GB
Tailboard - Photographic Collectors' Club of GB
Tak Tent - Heraldry Soc of Scotland
Takedown - Brit Wrestling Assn
Taking a Lead - Nat Playing Fields Assn
Taking Stock Book - Inst of Licensed Trade Stock Auditors
Tales of Northwick - Nystagmus Network
Tales of Uruguay - Brit Uruguayan Soc
Taliesin - ACADEMI - Welsh Nat Literature Promotion Agency
Talipes - STEPS
Talk - Nat Deaf Children's Soc
Talkback - Nat Backpain Assn (BackCare)
talkBACK - Scot Spina Bifida Assn
Talking About Turner Syndrome -

Talking Politics - Politics Assn
Talking Sense - Sense - Nat Deafblind & Rubella Assn
Talking Shop - Village Retail Services Assn Educational Trust
Talking Treatments - SANE
Talkshop Catalogue - Soc for Storytelling
Tall Suppliers Directory - Tall Persons Club GB & Ireland
Tally Sheet - English Westerners Soc
Talyllyn News - Talyllyn Railway Preservation Soc
Tandem Club Jnl - Tandem Club of the UK
Tankette - Miniature Armoured Fighting Vehicle Assn
Tanzanian Affairs - Britain-Tanzania Soc
Target MD - Muscular Dystrophy Campaign
Tattoo InterNat - Brit Tattoo Artists Fedn
Tattoo Club of GB
Tax Adviser - Assn of Taxation Technicians
Tax Advisers Practice Hbk - Assn of Taxation Technicians
TCS News - Train Collectors Soc
The Teacher - Nat Union of Teachers
Teaching Business & Education - Economics, Business & Enterprise Assn
Teaching Deaf People to Drive - Inst of Master Tutors of Driving
Teaching Earth Sciences - Earth Science Teachers' Assn
Teaching Geography - Geographical Assn
Teaching History - Historical Assn
Teaching Mathematics & its Applications - Inst of Mathematics & its Applications
Teaching Today - Nat Assn of Schoolmasters Union of Women Teachers
Technic - College of Operating Department Practitioners
Technical Specifications for Terrazzo & Marble - Nat Fedn Terrazzo, Marble & Mosaic Specialists
The Telegraph - Nautilus UK
Television Lighting - Soc of Television Lighting Directors
Teleworker - Telework Assn
Teleworking Handbook - Telework Assn
Template - Brit Zeolite Assn
Tempo - Guild of Professional Teachers of Dancing
Ten 26 - Nat Fedn of Young Farmers' Clubs (England & Wales)
Tenanted Farm Survey - Central Assn of Agricultural Valuers
Tennyson Research Bulletin - Tennyson Soc
Tenterden Terrier - Kent & East Sussex Railway Co
The Terrier - Assn of Chief Estates Surveyors & Property Managers in the Public Sector
Testament - Soc of Will Writers & Estate Planning Practitioners
Texel Bulletin - Brit Texel Sheep Soc
Text - Textile Soc: for the study of the history, art & design of textiles
Textile Progress - Textile Inst InterNat
Textiles for Launderers & Drycleaners - Guild of Cleaners & Launderers
Textiles Magazine - Textile Inst InterNat
TFIC News - Fedn of Image Consultants
Thames - Japanese Cham Comm & Industry in the UK
Thames Guardian - River Thames Soc
The Thatcher's Standard - Nat Soc of Master Thatchers
Theatre Notebook - Soc for Theatre Research
Theoretical Issues in Ergonomics - Ergonomics Soc
Therapeutic Communities - Assn of Therapeutic Communities
Therapeutic Philosophy - Assn for Therapeutic Philosophy
Therapy Today - Brit Assn for Counselling & Psychotherapy
There is an Alternative - Campaign for an Independent Britain
THG Jnl - Telecommunications Heritage Group
Third Force News & Inform - Scot Council for Voluntary Organisations
Thirst Choice - Can Makers
This Week - Proprietary Assn of GB
The Thomas Hardy Jnl - Thomas Hardy Soc
Thoroughbred Owner & Breeder - Thoroughbred Breeders' Assn
Thoroughbred Stallion Guide - Thoroughbred Breeders' Assn
Those of Us Who Loved Her: the men in George Eliot's life - George Eliot Fellowship
Three Bromsgrove Poets - Housman Soc
Thumbprint - Motor Neurone Disease Assn
Tile Bibliography - Tiles & Architectural Ceramics Soc (Tile Soc)
The Timber Decking Manual - Timber Decking Assn
Time and Tide: Sea of Faith beyond the Millennium - Sea of Faith Network (UK)
Time Haiku - Time Haiku
Tobacco Index - Assn of Independent Tobacco Specialists

Toccata - Leopold Stokowski Soc
Today's Technician - Nat Pest Technicians Assn
The TOF Child - Tracheo-Oesophageal Fistula Support
Together - Fellowship of Independent Evangelical Churches
Tommy's Dad - Action for Prisoners' Families
Tomorrow's Pharmacist - R Pharmaceutical Soc of GB
Tools & Trades - Tools & Trades History Soc
Top Marks - Road Safety Markings Assn
Topics - Inst of Public Sector Management
Topsail - Soc for Sailing Barge Research
Torch Bearer - Soc of Olympic Collectors
Torpedo - Brit Marine Life Study Soc
Tot Watch - Meningitis Research Foundation
Touch - Reiki Assn
Touchstone - R Soc of Architects in Wales
Tourism - Tourism Soc
Tourism in Focus - Tourism Concern
The Tourism Manager - Tourism Management Inst
Tourist Guides' Directory - Assn of Professional Tourist Guides
Towards Community Care - Assn of Directors of Adult Social Services
Towards Equality - Fawcett Soc
Townswoman - Townswomen's Guilds
The Toymaker - Brit Toymakers Guild
Trackside - Brit Motorsport Marshals Club
Traction Engine Register - Southern Counties Historic Vehicle Preservation Trust
Trade Fairs & Exhibitions in Turkey - Brit Cham Comm of Turkey (Assn)
Trade Talk - Assn of Suppliers to the Furniture Industry
Trade Voice - Wine & Spirit Trade Assn
Tradewinds - Portuguese Cham - the Portuguese UK Business Network
Trading Standards Appointments -
Trading Standards Today - Trading Standards Inst
Trail - Trail Riders Fellowship
Train Times - Assn of Community Rail Partnerships
Trainers Pack - Nat Assn of Security Dog Users
Training for the Caring Business - Assn of Directors of Adult Social Services
Training & Education Jnl - Brit Inst of Professional Dog Trainers
Training & Learning - Inst of Training & Occupational Learning
Training Your Harness Goat - Harness Goat Soc
Tramfare - Tramway & Light Railway Soc
Tramway Museum Guidebook - Tramway Museum Soc
Tramways & Urban Transit - Light Rail Transit Assn
Transactions - Anglesey Antiquarian Soc & Field Club
Inst of Measurement & Control
Inst of Transactional Analysis
Monumental Brass Soc
Transactions: Earth Sciences - R Soc of Edinburgh
Transfusion Medicine - Brit Blood Transfusion Soc
Transit Magazine - Astrological Assn of GB
Transition Care Pathway - Assn for Children's Palliative Care
Transmit - Guild of Air Traffic Control Officers
The Transport Digest - Transport Trust
Transport Engineer - Soc of Operations Engineers
Transport Management - Inst of Transport Administration
The Transport of Perishable Foodstuffs - Cambridge Refrigeration Technology
Transportation Professional - Instn of Highways & Transportation
The Travel Business - Guild of Travel & Tourism
Travelwise - Brit Travel Health Assn
TREaD - Youth Action Network
The Treasurer - Assn of Corporate Treasurers
Treating Arthritis Naturally - Arthritic Assn
Trees & Bats - Arboricultural Assn
Trends & Events - Trade Marks Patents & Designs Fedn
Triangle Magazine - Youth Hostels Assn (England & Wales)
The Trichologists - Inst of Trichologists (Inc)
Trolleybus - Brit Trolleybus Soc
Trolleybus Magazine - Nat Trolleybus Assn
Trollopiana Jnl - Trollope Soc
The Trombonist - Brit Trombone Soc
True Blue - Friends of Blue
The True Line - Caledonian Railway Assn
True Principles - Pugin Soc
Trust & Foundation News - Assn of Charitable Foundations

© CBD Research Ltd · Beckenham · BR3 5JS · Tel 020 8650 7745 · Fax 020 8650 0768 · E-mail cbd@cbdresearch.com · www.cbdresearch.com

TUK Talk - Transfrigoroute UK
Turner Soc News - Turner Soc
Turner Syndrome - lifelong guidance & support - Turner Syndrome Support Soc (UK)
Tuttitalia - Assn for Language Learning
Twins, Triplets & More - Twins & Multiple Births Assn
A Twist of Fate - Scoliosis Assn (UK)
Tyne & Tweed - Assn of Northumberland Local History Socs
Typefounders London A-Z - Friends of St Bride Library
Typographic - InterNat Soc of Typographic Designers

U

UK Allergy Clinic Database - Brit Soc for Allergy & Clinical Immunology
UK Chasers Handbook - UK Chasers & Riders
UK Conference Market Survey - Meetings Industry Assn
UK Contract Furnishing Directory - Brit Contract Furnishing Assn
UK Corrosion - Inst of Corrosion
UK Directory of Registered Dance Teachers - Council for Dance Education & Training (UK)
UK Excellence - Brit Quality Foundation
UK Landlord - Nat Landlords' Assn
UK Railway Suppliers Directory - Railway Industry Assn
UK Surface Coatings Hbk - Oil & Colour Chemists' Assn
UK Writer - Writers' Guild of GB
UKEP/LIB Hotwire - UK Egg Producers Assn
UKSA Update - UK Shareholders' Assn
UKSTT News - UK Soc for Trenchless Technology
Ullans - Ulster-Scots Language Soc
The Ulster Angler - Ulster Angling Fedn
Ulster Countrywoman - Fedn of Women's Insts of Northern Ireland
Ulster Folklife - Ulster Folk Life Soc
Ulster Jnl of Archaeology - Ulster Archaeological Soc
The Ultimate Cleavage: a complete practical guide to cosmetic breast enlargement surgery - Breast Implant Information Soc
Under Five - Pre-School Learning Alliance
Underground News - London Underground Railway Soc
Underpinning Knowledge Pack - Nat Assn of Security Dog Users
Understanding Medical Education - Assn for the Study of Medical Education
Understanding non-Hodgkin lymphoma - Lymphoma Assn
Understanding Nystagmus - Nystagmus Network
Understanding PMS - Nat Assn for Premenstrual Syndrome
Understanding Pregnancy Loss - Stillbirth & Neonatal Death Soc
Underwater Technology - Soc for Underwater Technology
University Chemistry Education - R Soc of Chemistry
Unkind to Unicorns - Housman Soc
Up & Under Updates - Australian Business
Upbeat - Eating Disorders Assn
Update - Brit Aviation Preservation Council
    CILIP: Chartered Inst of Library & Information Professionals
    Inst of Fundraising
    Voluntary Arts Network
    Women's Food & Farming Union
    Yorkshire Archaeological Soc
Update your Road Markings - Road Safety Markings Assn
Upholsterer & Soft Furnisher - Assn of Master Upholsterers & Soft Furnishers
Uplift - Fork Lift Truck Assn
Urban Regeneration - Brit Urban Regeneration Assn
The Uruguayan Short Story - Brit Uruguayan Soc
The Use of English - English Assn
Using a Pawnbroker - Nat Pawnbrokers Assn
Using Power Fastener Driving Tools Safely - Power Fastenings Assn
The USPC Countryside Recorder - Ulster Soc for the Protection of the Countryside
UTU News - Ulster Teachers' Union

V

Vacuum Technology, Applications & Ion Physics - Brit Vacuum Council
VAGA update - Visual Arts & Galleries Assn
Value Jnl - Inst of Value Management
Valve Users Manual - Brit Valve & Actuator Assn
Vaporising - Nat Vintage Tractor & Engine Club
Varoom - Assn of Illustrators
Vauxhall Motors & the Luton Economy 1900-2002 - Bedfordshire Historical Record Soc
Vector - Brit Science Fiction Assn
The Vegan Magazine - Vegan Soc
Vegan Passport - Vegan Soc
Vegan Stories - Vegan Soc
The Vegetarian - Vegetarian Soc (UK)
Vehicle Operator Lists - Road Transport Fleet Data Soc
Vehicle Salvage Professional - Brit Vehicle Salvage Fedn
Vehicle Technology - Soc of Automotive Engineers - UK
Vellum - George Formby Soc
VENDinform - Automatic Vending Assn
Vending - Automatic Vending Assn
Venesection record card - Haemochromatosis Soc
Vernacular Architecture - Vernacular Architecture Group
Vernacular Gower - Gower Soc
Veterinary Nursing Jnl - Brit Veterinary Nursing Assn
VGC News - Vintage Glider Club of GB
Vida Hispánica - Assn for Language Learning
Videoprofessional - Assn of Professional Videomakers
Vienna Music - Johann Strauss Soc of GB
The View - Girls' Brigade England & Wales
Viewpoint - Nat Fedn of the Blind of the UK
Viewpoint - Soc of Architectural Illustration
Viewpoint - Inst of Construction Management
The Vintage Motor Cycle - Vintage Motor Cycle Club
Virginia Woolf Bulletin - Virginia Woolf Soc of GB
Vitiligo: understanding the loss of skin colour - Vitiligo Soc
The Vitreous Enameller - Inst of Vitreous Enamellers & Vitreous Enamel Assn
VLV Bulletin - Voice of the Listener & Viewer
Voice - Assn of Teachers of Singing
The Voice - Brit Cleaning Council (BCC)
Voice - Communication Workers Union
The Voice - NWA
The Voice - One Voice Wales
The Voice - Ornamental Aquatic Trade Assn
Voice - Victim Support Scotland
A Voice Care Guide for Call Centre Managers - Voice Care Network UK
Voice for Change - Assn for Children's Palliative Care
Voice Matters - Voice Care Network UK
Voice of the Quarrying Industry - Quarry Products Assn
A Voice for all Time - Assn for Latin Liturgy
Voices from the Vaults - Dracula Soc
Voice of the Veteran - Veteran Horse Soc
Voice Warm-up Exercises - Voice Care Network UK
Volatile Substance Abuse - be aware - Brit Aerosol Mfrs Assn
Vouchers at a Glance - Fedn of Ophthalmic & Dispensing Opticians
Vox Humana - Mechanical Organ Owners Soc

W

Wagner News - Wagner Soc
Wakefield Court Rolls - Yorkshire Archaeological Soc
Wales Funding Handbook - Wales Council for Voluntary Action (Cyngor Gweithredu Gwirfoddol Cymru)
Walk - Living Streets
Waller & Dyker - Dry Stone Walling Assn of GB
Wallpaper - Max Wall Soc
Wanderer - Historic Caravan Club
The War Correspondent - Crimean War Research Soc
War Poetry Review - War Poets Assn
Warship Technology - R Instn of Naval Architects

Wastes Management - Chartered Instn of Wastes Management
Watchword - R Soc of Wildlife Trusts
 Surface Engineering Assn
Water & Environment Manager - Chartered Instn of Water & Environmental Management
Water Quality Management - Chilled Food Assn
Waterbed Owners Manual - Brit Waterbed Assn
Waterbeds - the facts - Brit Waterbed Assn
Waterfowl - Brit Waterfowl Assn
Waterline - Water Management Soc
The Waterloo Jnl - Assn of Friends of the Waterloo Committee
Waterways - Inland Waterways Assn
Watsonia - Botanical Soc of the Brit Isles
Watson's Wanderings - Friends of Dr Watson
Watson's Wanderings Again - Friends of Dr Watson
Watson's Weapons - Friends of Dr Watson
The Way Ahead - Disabled Motorists Fedn
Way of Life - Guild of Health
Waymark - Inst of Public Rights of Way Management
We Just Want Our Daughter to Live - Tracheo-Oesophageal Fistula Support
A Wee Ray of Hope - Cystitis & Overactive Bladder Foundation (COB Foundation)
The Week in Europe; Weekly - Caribbean-Brit Business Council
Welcome Aboard: good practice - Bus Users UK
Welding Abstracts - Welding Inst
Welfare World - Inst of Welfare
The Wellsian - H G Wells Soc
Welsh Ceramics In Context - R Instn of South Wales
Welsh Halfbred News - Welsh Halfbred Sheep Breeders Assn
Welsh Hound Stud Book - Welsh Hound Assn
Welsh Ponies & Cobs - Welsh Pony & Cob Soc
Welsh Wildlife - Wildlife Trust of South & West Wales
Wessex in Business - Wessex Assn of Chams Comm
West Highland Notes & Queries - Soc of West Highland & Island Historical Research
A Westerly Wanderer - Housman Soc
The Western Dancer Magazine - Brit Western Dance Assn
Wey-Arun Canal News - Wey & Arun Canal Trust
Wey-South - Wey & Arun Canal Trust
What is A-T? - Ataxia-Telangiectasia Soc (A-T Soc)
What is Play Therapy? - Brit Assn of Play Therapists
What is Psychoanalytic Psychotherapy? - Brit Psychoanalytic Council
What to Wear - Brit Equestrian Trade Assn
What's Bottling - Assn for Brit Brewery Collectables
What's Brewing - Campaign for Real Ale
What's in a Quarry - Quarry Products Assn
What's New in UK Aerospace - Soc of Brit Aerospace Companies
Wheatsheaf - Kempe Soc
Wheel & Palette - Guild of Railway Artists
Wheels - Brit Trolleybus Soc
 United Road Transport Union
Wheelspin - Ulster Automobile Club
When a Baby Dies - Stillbirth & Neonatal Death Soc
When a Pet Dies - Soc for Companion Animal Studies
Where to Find Harness & Carts - Harness Goat Soc
Which? - Consumers' Assn
Which? Gardening - Consumers' Assn
Which? Holiday - Consumers' Assn
Which? Money - Consumers' Assn
Whitehall Papers - R United Services Inst for Defence & Security Studies
Who Cares Wins: the Buildings at Risk Register - Save Britain's Heritage
Who Minds - Nat Childminding Assn
Who's Who in the Motor Industry - Guild of Motoring Writers
Whose Job is it Anyway? - Road Safety Markings Assn
Why Rich People Give - Assn of Charitable Foundations
WI Life - Nat Fedn of Women's Insts
Wiþowinde - þa Engliscan Gesíþas (the English Companions)
Wild Land News - Scot Wild Land Group
The Wildean - Oscar Wilde Soc
Wildflower Seed Catalogue - Landlife
Wildflower Seed & Plant Catalogue - Landlife
Wildfowling - Brit Assn for Shooting & Conservation
Wildlife Action - Wildlife Trust for Bedfordshire, Cambridgeshire, Northamptonshire & Peterborough

Wildlife in the Suburbs - Selborne Soc
Wildlife Sound - Wildlife Sound Recording Soc
William Bradshaw - a Leicestershire railway photographer - Historical Model Railway Soc
William Cobbett in America by Molly Townsend - William Cobbett Soc
Wiltshire Archaeological & Natural History Magazine - Wiltshire Archaeological & Natural History Soc
Wind & Watermill - Soc for the Protection of Ancient Buildings
Window Talk - Fedn of Window Cleaners
Winds - Brit Assn of Symphonic Bands & Wind Ensembles
Windscreen - Military Vehicle Trust
Winged Words - Aviation Soc
Winking World - English Tiddlywinks Assn
Winning Edge - Inst of Sales & Marketing Management
Wiring Matters - Instn of Engineering & Technology
With Our Complements - Complementary Medical Assn
Within Reach - REACH: the Assn for Children with Hand or Arm Deficiency
Wolves & Humans NL - Wolves & Humans Foundation
The Woman Engineer - Women's Engineering Soc
Women - 'Wise-up' on Pensions - Nat Pensioners' Convention
Woodcarver Gazette - Brit Woodcarvers Assn
Woodcarving - Guild of Master Craftsmen
Woodland Initiatives Register - Small Woods Assn
Woods & Jack - English Indoor Bowling Assn
Woodturning - Guild of Master Craftsmen
Woodworking plans & projects - Guild of Master Craftsmen
Woodworking Technology - Inst of Machine Woodworking Technology
Wooster Sauce - P G Wodehouse Soc (UK)
The Worcestershire Recorder - Worcestershire Archaeological Soc
Work, Employment & Soc - Brit Sociological Assn
Work & Stress - Ergonomics Soc
The Work of Subscription Agents - Assn of Subscription Agents & Intermediaries
Working in Schools - Independent Theatre Council
The Works - Brit Academy of Composers + Songwriters
World Bowls - Scot Indoor Bowling Assn
A World of Colour - Coloured Horse & Pony Soc
The World of Emissions - Garage Equipment Assn
The World Today - R Inst of InterNat Affairs
Worldlywise - Development Education Assn
Worldwide Directory on Defence & Security Prime Contractors - Defence Mfrs Assn
Wound Care Jnl - Wound Care Soc
Wounds & Infection - Wound Care Soc
WPA Annual Review - World Pheasant Assn UK
WPA News - World Pheasant Assn UK
The Writ - Law Soc of Northern Ireland
The Writer - Soc of Medical Writers
Writing in Education - Nat Assn of Writers in Education
WTIF News - Wall Tie Installers Fedn
WW2 HMSO Paperbacks Collectors' Guide - WW2 HMSO Paperbacks Soc
WWINDY News - World-Wide Opportunities on Organic Farms
WWOOF UK News - World-Wide Opportunities on Organic Farms
Wyndham Lewis Annual - Wyndham Lewis Soc

Y

Y Mag - Fedn of Museums & Art Galleries of Wales
Yarak Jnl - Brit Hawking Assn
Yarak NL - Brit Hawking Assn
The Yardstick - Brit Weights & Measures Assn
Year's Work in Critical & Cultural Theory - English Assn
Year's Work in English Studies - English Assn
The Yellow Book - Nat Gardens Scheme Charitable Trust
Yoga the World Over - Brit Wheel of Yoga
Yorkshire Archaeological Jnl - Yorkshire Archaeological Soc
Yorkshire Archaeological Research - Yorkshire Archaeological Soc
Yorkshire Parish Registers - Yorkshire Archaeological Soc
Young Batworker - Bat Conservation Trust

© CBD Research Ltd · Beckenham · BR3 5JS · Tel 020 8650 7745 · Fax 020 8650 0768 · E-mail cbd@cbdresearch.com · www.cbdresearch.com

Young Lacemaker - Lace Guild
Your Big Sites Book - Camping & Caravanning Club
Your Body Your Risk - Dance UK
Your Child in an Immobilising Plaster: a few hints - Perthes
Assn
Your Place in the Country - Camping & Caravanning Club
Your Retirement - Life Academy
Your Voice - Voice: the union for education professionals
Youth Justice - Nat Assn for Youth Justice
Youth Orchestra Tours Guide - Nat Assn of Youth Orchestras

Z

Zimbabwe Review - Britain Zimbabwe Soc
Zipper News - Brit Cardiac Patients Assn (Zipper Club)
Zone Press - England Basketball
Zoo Fedn News - Brit & Irish Assn of Zoos & Aquariums
Zoological Jnl - Linnean Soc of London
Zoological Record - Zoological Soc of London

Centres Bureaux & Research Institutes

directory of UK concentrations of effort, information and expertise

CBD

over 4,350 establishments giving:

- *abbreviation*
- *year formed*
- *address*
- *telephone*
- *fax*
- *web site*
- *key officials*
- *branches*

- *sources of finance*
- *sponsors*
- *objectives*
- *activities*
- *publications*

- *abbreviations index*
- *index of sponsors*
- *subject index*

We welcome your enquiries

CBD Research Ltd

15 Wickham Road, Beckenham, Kent, BR3 5JS

Tel: 020 8650 7745 **Fax:** 020 8650 0768

E-mail: cbd@cbdresearch.com

www.cbdresearch.com

SUBJECT INDEX

Chambers of commerce & industry are included under the heading 'Chambers of commerce' and subdivided into general, local and overseas trade.

County agricultural societies are brought together under the heading 'Agriculture: county societies' and are listed in county order.

County archaeological societies are brought together under the heading 'Archaeology: county societies' and are listed in county order.

County record societies are brought together under the heading 'Records: historical - county societies' and are listed in county order.

Associations concerned with the teaching, technology, equipment & supplies and similar aspects of an activity are generally listed under the activity heading.

In general, headings relate to substantive groups rather than qualifying factors; thus the Society for Experimental Biology is listed under 'Biology'.

Unverified and lost associations are not indexed.

A

Abaca > Hemp
Abattoirs
    Assn Indep Meat Suppliers
    Licensed Animal Slaughterers. . . Assn
    Nat Assn Brit Market Authorities
Abercrombie (Lascelles)
    Friends Dymock Poets
Abnormal loads
    Heavy Transport Assn
    > + Road: haulage
Abortion
    Abortion Rights
    Soc Protection Unborn Children
Abrasives
    Brit Abrasives Fedn
Abuse (sexual)
    Nat Org Treatment of Abusers
    > + Sex & sexual law reform

    Nat Register Access Consultants
Access covers
    Fabricated Access Covers Trade Association
Access floors
    Assn Interior Specialists
    > + Floors
Access engineering
    Prefabricated Access Suppliers' & Mfrs' Assn
Access scaffolding > Scaffolding
Accidents
    Accident Mgt Assn
    Inst Home Safety
    Inst Traffic Accident Investigators
    Medical Equestrian Assn
    R Soc Prevention Accidents
    > + Safety
Accidents: medical treatment > Medicine: accident & emergency
Accidents: victims
    Action Med Accidents
    Campaign Drinking & Driving
    Motor Accident Solicitors Soc
    Personal Injuries Bar Assn
    RoadPeace
Accommodation > Hotels & restaurants; Self catering; Students
Accordions & fiddles
    Nat Accordion Org
    Nat Assn Accordion & Fiddle Clubs
    Scot Fiddle Soc
Accountancy
    Assn Accountancy & Business Affairs
    Assn Accounting Technicians
    Assn Authorised Public Accountants
    Assn Chart Certified Accountants
    Assn Corporate Treasurers
    Assn Financial Controllers & Administrators
    Assn Indep Specialist Med Accountants
    Assn Intl Accountants
    Assn Practising Accountants
    Brit Accounting Assn
    Brit Assn Hospitality Accountants
    Chart Inst Mgt Accountants
    CIPFA
    District Auditors Soc

    Healthcare Financial Mgt Assn
    Insolvency Practitioners Assn
    Inst Accounting Technicians Ireland
    Inst Certified Public Accountants Ireland
    Inst Chart Accountants England & Wales
    Inst Chart Accountants Ireland
    Inst Chart Accountants Scotland
    Inst Cost & Executive Accountants
    Inst Financial Accountants
    Inst Inc Public Accountants [IRL]
    Inst Internal Auditors UK & Ireland
    Ir Assn Corporate Treasurers
    Network Indep Forensic Accountants
    Soc Law Accountants Scotland
    Soc Profl Accountants
    > + Bookkeeping; Cost management; Insolvency
Acoustic music
    Assn Festival Organisers
    FolkArts England
Acoustic neuromas
    Brit Acoustic Neuroma Assn
Acoustics
    Assn Noise Consultants
    Heating, Ventilating & Air Conditioning Mfrs' Assn
    Inst Acoustics
    Inst Sound & Communications Engrs
    Proprietary Acoustic Systems Mfrs
    > + Hearing
Acquired immune deficiency syndrome > Genito-urinary medicine
Acrylic (painting in)
    Brit Soc Painters (in Oil, Pastels & Acrylic)
    Nat Acrylic Painters' Assn
    > + Art & artists
Activity holidays > Holiday camps & centres
Actors & actresses
    Brit Actors' Equity Assn
    Nat Assn Supporting Artistes Agents
    R Academy Dramatic Art
    > + Theatre
Actuarial practice
    Assn Consulting Actuaries
    Fac Actuaries Scotland
    Inst Actuaries
    > + Insurance
Acupuncture
    Acupuncture Soc
    Brit Acupuncture Coun
    Brit Biomagnetic Assn
    Brit Med Acupuncture Soc
    Nat Acupuncture Detoxification Assn
    > + Complementary medicine
Addiction
    ADFAM
    Assn Nurses Substance Abuse
    Families Anonymous
    Fedn Drug & Alcohol Profls
    Nat Acupuncture Detoxification Assn
    R Coll Psychiatrists
    Salvation Army
    Sexaholics Anonymous
    Soc Study Addiction Alcohol. . .
    UK Alliance
    > + Alcoholism
Additives
    Food Additives & Ingredients Assn

Adhesive tape
      Adhesive Tape Mfrs' Assn
      Assn Distributors, Coaters... Adhesive Tapes
Adhesives
      Brit Adhesives & Sealants Assn
      Contract Flooring Assn
Adler (Alfred)
      Adlerian Soc
Admiralty chart agents
      Chart & Nautical Instrument Tr Assn
Adolescents > Youth headings
Adoption
      Adoption UK
      Adults Affected Adoption NORCAP
      Assn Families Adopted Abroad
      Brit Assn Adoption & Fostering
      Scot Adoption Assn
Adult education
      Adult Educ Officers' Assn [IRL]
      Adult Residential Colls Assn
      ASET
      Assn Colleges
      Assn Profl Staffs Colls Educ [IRL]
      Assn Scotland's Colls
      Brit Inst Learning & Devt
      Educl Centres Assn
      Inst Continuing Profl Devt
      NAEGA
      Nat Adult School Org
      Nat Inst Adult Continuing Educ (E&W)
      Principals' Profl Coun
      Universities Assn Lifelong Learning
      Workers' Educl Assn
Adult industry
      Adult Ind Trade Assn
Adventure playgrounds > Playgrounds & playgroups
Advertising
      Account Planning Gp
      Advertising Assn
      Assn Advertisers Ireland
      Assn Business to Business Agencies
      D&AD
      Inc Soc Brit Advertisers
      Inst Advertising Practitioners Ireland
      Inst Practitioners Advertising
      Internet Advtg Bureau
      Ir Direct Marketing Assn
      Overseas Press & Media Assn
      Publicity Club Lond
Advertising: gifts > Incentive marketing
Advertising: music
      Soc Producers & Composers Applied Music
Advertising: outdoor
      Outdoor Advertising Assn
      Outdoor Advertising Coun
      Outdoor Media Assn [IRL]
Advertising: television & screen
      Advertising Producers Assn
      Cinema Advertising Assn
Advice centres & bureaux
      Advice NI
      Advice Services Alliance
      AdviceUK
      Citizens Advice Bureaux
      Citizens Advice Scotland
Advocacy/advocates > Law: Scotland
Aerial navigation > Navigation
Aerial phenomena > Unidentified flying objects
Aerial survey & photography
      Brit Assn Remote Sensing Companies
      Gld Brit Camera Technicians
      Nat Assn Aerial Photographic Libraries
      > + Landscape; Photography
Aerials: radio, telephone & television
      Confedn Aerial Inds
      Mast Action UK
Aerobatics
      Brit Aerobatic Assn
Aerobiology
      Brit Aerobiology Fedn
      Midlands Asthma & Allergy Res Assn
Aerodromes > Aviation
Aerodynamics
      Aircraft Res Assn
      MIRA Ltd
      > + Aviation
Aeromodelling > Models: hobby

Aeronautical engineering > Aviation
Aerosols
      Aerosol Soc
      Brit Aerosol Mfrs Assn
Aerospace industry > Aviation
Aesthetic surgery > Plastic surgery
Aesthetics
      Brit Soc Aesthetics
Aethelflaed, Lady of Mercia (c870-918)
      Aethelflæd
Afghanistan
      Middle East Assn
Africa
      African Studies Assn
      Black & Asian Studies Assn
      Brit African Business Assn
      Brit Cham Business Sthn Africa
      R African Soc
      UK One World Linking Assn

After dinner speakers > + Speakers
Age discrimination > Employment
Ageing > Geriatrics & ageing
Agents > under specific headings
Aggregates
      Brit Aggregates Assn
      Brit Marine Aggregate Producers' Assn
      Quarry Products Assn
Agriculture
      Agricl Inds Confedn
      Agricl Manpower Soc
      Agricl Science Assn [IRL]
      Assn Show & Agricl Orgs
      Biodynamic Agricl Assn
      Brit Assn Seed Analysts
      Brit Inst Agricl Consultants
      Farming & Wildlife Advy Gp
      Help Intl Plant Protein Org
      Nat Assn Agricl Contrs
      NI Agricl Producers' Assn
      NI Shows Assn
      Permaculture Assn
      R Agricl Soc C'wealth
      R Agricl Soc England
      R Highland & Agricl Soc Scotland
      R Highland Educ Trust
      R Welsh Agricl Soc
      Scot Seed & Nursery Tr Assn
      Soc Applied Microbiology
      Soc Chemical Ind
      Soc Responsible Use Resources Agriculture & Land
      Soil Assn
      Sustain
      Tropical Agriculture Assn
      Women's Farm & Garden Assn
      Women's Food & Farming U
      > + Farmers' organisations; Horticulture; Organic growing &
      farming
Agriculture: buildings
      Rural & Indl Design & Bldg Assn
Agriculture: chemicals
      Animal & Plant Health Assn [IRL]
      Assn Applied Biologists
      Assn Public Analysts
      Assn Public Analysts Scotland
      Crop Protection Assn
      Instn Agricl Engrs
      Pesticide Action Network
      > + Fertilisers; Pest control
Agriculture: cooperatives
      Scot Agricl Org Soc
      Welsh Agricultural Organisation Society Ltd
Agriculture: county societies
      Aberdeenshire > R Nthn Agricl Soc
      Anglesey Agricl Soc
      Antrim > County Antrim Agricl Assn
      Ayrshire Agricl Assn
      Bedfordshire > E England Agricl Soc
      Berwickshire Agricl Assn
      Birmingham > Staffordshire & Birmingham Agricl Soc
      Border U Agricl Soc
      Brecknockshire Agricl Soc
      Bucks County Agricl Assn
      Caithness Agricl Soc
      Cambridgeshire > E England Agricl Soc
      Cardiganshire > Utd Counties Agricl Soc
      Carmarthenshire > Utd Counties Agricl Soc

© CBD Research Ltd · Beckenham · BR3 5JS · Tel 020 8650 7745 · Fax 020 8650 0768 · E-mail cbd@cbdresearch.com · www.cbdresearch.com

Cheshire Agricl Soc
Cleveland Agricl & Hortl Soc
Cornwall > R Cornwall Agricl Assn
County Antrim Agricl Assn
Cumberland Agricl Soc
Denbighshire & Flintshire Agricl Soc
Derbyshire Agricl & Horticl Soc
Devon County Agricl Assn
Dorchester Agricl Soc
Dorset > Dorchester Agricl Soc
Dorset > Yeovil Agricl Soc
Driffield Agricl Soc
Dublin > R Dublin Soc
Durham County Agricl Soc
E England Agricl Soc
Essex Agricl Soc
Fife Agricl Assn
Flintshire > Denbighshire & Flintshire Agricl Soc
Glamorgan > Vale Glamorgan Agricl Soc
Glasgow Agricl Soc
Gloucestershire > Three Counties Agricl Soc
Gwent > Monmouthshire Show Soc
Gwynedd > Merioneth Agricl Soc
Herefordshire > Three Counties Agricl Soc
Hertfordshire Agricl Soc
Isle of Man > R Manx Agricl Soc
Isle of Wight > R Isle of Wight Agricl Soc
Jersey > R Jersey Agricl & Horticl Soc
Kent County Agricl Soc
Lancashire > R Lancashire Agricl Soc
Leicestershire Agricl Soc
Lincolnshire Agricl Soc
Merioneth Agricl Soc
Monmouthshire Show Soc
N Somerset Agricl Soc
New Forest Agricl Show Soc
Newark & Nottinghamshire Agricl Soc
Newbury & District Agricl Soc
Norfolk > R Norfolk Agricl Assn
Northamptonshire > E England Agricl Soc
Nottinghamshire > Newark & Nottinghamshire Agricl Soc
Pembrokeshire Agricl Soc
Pembrokeshire > Utd Counties Agricl Soc
Perthshire Agricl Soc
R Bath & W England Soc
R Cornwall Agricl Assn
R Dublin Soc
R Guernsey Agricl & Horticl Soc
R Isle of Wight Agrl Soc
R Jersey Agricl & Horticl Soc
R Lancashire Agricl Soc
R Manx Agricl Soc
R Norfolk Agricl Assn
R Nthn Agricl Soc
R Ulster Agricl Soc
Rutland Agricl Soc
S England Agricl Soc
Shetland Livestock Marketing Gp
Shropshire & W Midlands Agricl Soc
Somerset > N Somerset Agricl Soc
Somerset > R Bath & W England Soc
Somerset > Yeovil Agricultural Soc
Staffordshire & Birmingham Agricl Soc
Suffolk Agricl Assn
Surrey County Agricl Soc
Sussex > S England Agricl Soc
Three Counties Agricl Soc
Ulster > R Ulster Agricl Soc
Utd Counties Agricl Soc
Vale Glamorgan Agricl Soc
W Midlands > Shropshire & W Midlands Agricl Soc
Westmorland County Agricl Soc
Worcestershire > Three Counties Agricl Soc
Yeovil Agricl Soc
Yorkshire Agricl Soc
Yorkshire > Driffield Agricultural Soc
Agriculture: economics
Agricl Economics Soc
Agriculture: education
Landex
Principals' Profl Coun
Agriculture: history
Brit Agricl Hist Soc
Agriculture: irrigation > Irrigation
Agriculture: journalism
Gld Agricl Journalists

Agriculture: law
Agricl Law Assn
Agriculture: machinery
Agricl Engrs Assn
Brit Agricl & Garden Machinery Assn
Brit Hardware Fedn
Farm Tractor & Machinery Tr Assn [IRL]
Instn Agricl Engrs
Soc Automotive Engrs
Agriculture: machinery - history
Farm Machinery Presvn Soc
Nat Vintage Tractor & Engine Club
Southern Counties Historic Vehicle Presvn Trust
Steam Plough Club
Agriculture: merchants
Grain & Feed Tr Assn
Ir Grain & Feed Assn
Agriculture: secretaries
Inst Agricl Secretaries & Administrators
Nat Assn NFU Gp Secretaries
Agriculture: valuation
Central Assn Agricl Valuers
Scot Agricl Arbiters Assn
Agrochemicals > Agriculture: chemicals
Agronomy
Assn Indep Crop Consultants
AIDS (disease) > Genito-urinary medicine
Aikido > Martial arts
Air: ambulances > Ambulance services
Air: cargo > Aviation: freight
Air: charter industry > Travel & tourism
Air: conditioning & ventilating
Air Conditioning & Refrigeration Ind Bd
Assn Ductwork Contrs & Allied Services
Brit Refrigeration Assn
BSRIA
Chart Instn Bldg Services Engrs
Chilled Beam & Ceiling Assn
Commissioning Specialists Assn
Fan Mfrs' Assn
Fedn Envtl Tr Assns
Heating, Ventilating & Air Conditioning Mfrs' Assn
Heating & Ventilating Contrs Assn
Hose Mfrs' & Suppliers Assn
Residential Ventilation Assn
Smoke Control Assn
> + Heating
Air: courier services
Assn Intl Courier & Express Services
Air: extraction > Dust control; Fans; Fumes & fume extraction
Air: guns & weapons > Arms & armour; Guns & ammunition; Shooting
Air: mail > Philately & postal history
Air: pilots, officers & crew > Aviation: pilots, officers & crew
Air: pollution
Environmental Protection UK
> + Air: conditioning & ventilating;   Pollution & pollution control
Air: sport
R Aero Club Records Racing & Rally Assn
R Aero Club UK
Air: surveying > Aerial survey & photography
Air: traffic control > Aviation: safety, control & training
Air: transport > Aviation
Aircraft > Aviation
Aircraft: historic > Aviation: history
Aircraft maintenance
Assn Licensed Aircraft Engrs
Fedn Aerospace Support Services
> + Aviation headings
Aircraft models > Models: hobby
Aircraft noise > Noise
Aircrete
Brit Precast Concrete Fedn
Aircrew
Aircrew Assn
> + Aviation: pilots & officers
Airfields noise > Noise
Airports > Aviation
Airports: services & equipment
Assn Port Health Authorities
Brit Airport Services & Eqpt Assn
Air-sea rescue
Goldfish Club
Airships > Balloons & airships
Alarms > Security
Albinism
Albinism Fellowship

Alchemy
Soc Hist Alchemy & Chemistry
Alcohol
Nat Alcohol Producers Assn
> + Drink & beverage industry
Alcoholism
ADFAM
Al-Anon Family Gps
Alcohol Concern
Alcoholics Anonymous
Fedn Drug & Alcohol Profls
Medical Coun Alcohol
Nat Assn Children Alcoholics
Portman Gp
Soc Study Addiction Alcohol. . .
UK Alliance
> + Addiction
Aldington (Richard)
New Canterbury Literary Soc
Ale > Brewing; Real ale
Alexander technique
Profl Assn Alexander Teachers
Soc Teachers Alexander Technique
Algae
Brit Phycological Soc
Alice in Wonderland
Daresbury Lewis Carroll Soc
Lewis Carroll Soc
Alkan (Charles Henri Valentin Morhange)
Alkan Soc
Allergy
AAA - Action against Allergy
Allergy UK
Anaphylaxis Campaign
Brit Aerobiology Fedn
Brit Inst Allergy & Envtl Therapy
Brit Soc Allergy & Clinical Immunology
Brit Soc Ecological Medicine
Brit Soc Immunology
Food & Chemical Allergy Assn
Hyperactive Children's Support Gp
Latex Allergy Support Gp
Midlands Asthma & Allergy Res Assn
Nat Soc Res Allergy
> + Immunology
Allingham (Margery)
Margery Allingham Soc
Allotments
Nat Soc Allotment & Leisure Gardeners
> + Gardens & gardening
Alloy(s) > Metal;   Steel: special & alloy
Almonds
Combined Edible Nut Tr Assn
Almshouses
Nat Assn Almshouses
Alopecia
Hairline Intl
Alpacas > Camelids
Alpine gardening
Alpine Garden Soc
> + Rock gardens
Alpine guiding
Brit Assn Mountain Guides
Alternative medicine > Complementary medicine; specific forms
Alternative technology > specific form of energy/technology
Altimeters
Challenger Soc Marine Science
Aluminium
Aluminium Alloy Mfrg & Recycling Assn
Aluminium Extruders Assn
Aluminium Fedn
Aluminium Finishing Assn
Aluminium Primary Producers Assn
Aluminium Rolled Products Mfrs Assn
Aluminium Stockholders Assn
Coun Aluminium Bldg
Inst Metal Finishing
UK Aluminium Packaging Recycling Org
Aluminium: foil
Assn Hot Foil Printers
Packaging & Indl Films Assn
> + Packaging
Aluminium: powder
Aluminium Powder & Paste Assn
Aluminium: towers
Prefabricated Access Suppliers' & Mfrs' Assn

Alzheimer's disease
Alzheimer Scotland
Alzheimer's Soc
Amaryllid
Nerine & Amaryllid Soc
Amateur activities > specific activity
Ambulance services
Ambulance Service Inst
Ambulance Service Network
Assn Air Ambulance Charities
Assn Profl Ambulance Personnel
Brit Ambulance Assn
Nat Assn Private Ambulance Services
> + First aid & immediate care
Ambulances: collection & restoration
Brit Ambulance Soc
> + Motor vehicles: historic
Amenity management > Leisure, recreation & amenity management
America > Latin America; USA
American Civil War
American Civil War Round Table
American football
Brit Amer Football Assn
American 'West'
Brit Western Dance Assn
Brit Westerners Assn
English Westerners Soc
Western Equestrian Soc
Western Horsemen's Assn
Ammunition > Guns & ammunition
Amnesia
Headway
Amphibians > Herpetology
Amputation > Limbless persons
Amusements & coin operated machines
Amusement & Gaming Ind Forum
Brit Amusement Catering Trs Assn
Brit Assn Leisure Parks, Piers & Attractions
> + Automatic vending
Amyotrophic lateral sclerosis > Motor neurone disease
Anaemia
Pernicious Anaemia Soc
Anaerobics
Renewable Energy Assn
Soc Anaerobic Microbiology
Anaesthesia
Anaesthetic Res Soc
Assn Anaesthetists
Assn Cardiothoracic Anaesthetists
Assn Dental Anaesthetists
Assn Paediatric Anaesthetists
Barema
Brit Malignant Hyperthermia Assn
Brit Ophthalmic Anaesthesia Soc
History Anaesthesia Soc
Obstetric Anaesthetists Assn
R Coll Anaesthetists
Soc Advancement Anaesthesia Dentistry
Soc Computing & Technology Anaesthesia
Analysts (computer) > Computers: professionals
Analysts (technical)
Soc Technical Analysts
> + Investment
Analytical chemistry
Assn Public Analysts
Assn Public Analysts Scotland
Chromatographic Soc
R Soc Chemistry
Anaphylaxsis > Allergy
Anatomy
Anatomical Soc
Brit Assn Clinical Anatomists
Anchorages (motor vehicle)
Vehicle Restraint Mfrs Assn
Ancient monuments > Historic buildings
Anderson (Gerry)
Fanderson. . .
Androgen insensitivity > Endocrinology
Andrology
Brit Andrology Soc
Brit Soc Psychosomatic Obstetrics. . .
Angels
Fairyworld
Anger management > Conflict & anger management
Angling > Fishing (sport);   Fishing tackle
Anglo-Saxon era
Engliscan Gesíþas

© CBD Research Ltd · Beckenham · BR3 5JS · Tel 020 8650 7745 · Fax 020 8650 0768 · E-mail cbd@cbdresearch.com · www.cbdresearch.com

Ranulf Higden Soc
Regia Anglorum
Angora wool
Brit Angora Goat Soc
Brit Goat Soc
Animal by-products
Brit Soc Animal Science
Natural Sausage Casings Assn
UK Renderers Assn
Animal feed
Brit Assn Feed Supplement & Additives Mfrs
Brit Assn Green Crop Driers
Brit Equestrian Tr Assn
Grain & Feed Tr Assn
Ir Grain & Feed Assn
N Scotland Grassland Soc
Nat Assn Agricl Contrs
> + Pets & pet trade
Animals
Brit Veterinary Assn
Primate Soc
R Inst Navigation
Rare Breeds Survival Trust
Soc Companion Animal Studies
> + Conservation; Nature conservation;   Veterinary headings;
Zoology & zoos; & specific animals
Animals: in entertainment
Animal Consultants & Trainers Assn
Animals: language
Wildlife Sound Recording Soc
Animals: slaughtering > Abattoirs
Animals: training
Assn Pet Behaviour Counsellors
Animals: transportation
Humane Slaughter Assn
Racehorse Transporters Assn
Animals: welfare
Advocates for Animals
Animal Concern
Animal Welfare Filming Fedn
Assn Dogs & Cats Homes
Cats Protection
Humane Slaughter Assn
Intl Assn Animal Therapists
Ir Soc Prevention Cruelty Animals
Nutrition Soc
R Soc Prevention Cruelty Animals
Scot Soc Prevention Cruelty Animals
Ulster Soc Prevention Cruelty Animals
Universities Fedn Animal Welfare
> + Pets & pet trade; Veterinary headings; Vivisection; specific
animal/trade
Ankylosing spondylitis
Nat Ankylosing Spondylitis Soc
Annuities (compulsory)
Compulsory Annuity Purchase Protest Alliance
Anodising
Aluminium Finishing Assn
Anophthalmia
Micro & Anophthalmic Children's Soc
Anorchidism
Anorchidism Support Gp
Anorexia & bulimia nervosa > Eating disorders
Antarctic > Polar research
Anthropology
Assn Social Anthropologists
Primate Soc
R Anthropological Inst
Anthroposophy
Anthroposophical Med Assn
Anthroposophical Soc
Anti > object opposed
Antiques
Assn Art & Antique Dealers
Brit Antique Dealers Assn
Brit Antique Furniture Restorers Assn
Gld Antique Dealers & Restorers
Meyrick Soc
R Instn Chart Surveyors
Antiques: shippers & packers
Assn Art & Antique Dealers
Antiquities
Antiquities Dealers Assn
Assn Study & Presvn Roman Mosaics
Soc Antiquaries Scotland
> + Archaeology; History
Anxiety attacks > Panic & anxiety attacks

Aphasia
Afasic
Brit Aphasiology Soc
Speakability
> + Speech
Apiculture > Bees & beekeeping
Apnoea > Snoring & apnoea
Apostrophe (the)
Apostrophe Protection Soc
Apparel > Clothing
Apparitions > Paranormal & psychical research
Appearance (personal)
Fedn Image Consultants
Appetite loss > Eating disorders
Apples
English Apples & Pears
Applied. . . > basic discipline
Appliqué
Quilters' Gld
Appraisers (property)
Inst Auctioneers & Appraisers Scotland
Aquaculture > Fish: farming
Aquaria
Brit & Ir Assn Zoos & Aquariums
Brit Marine Life Study Soc
> + Fish: tropical & ornamental
Aquatic science > Marine: biology & biochemistry
Aquatic trade > Fish: tropical & ornamental
Arab states & peoples
Coun Advancement Arab-Brit Understanding
Middle East Assn
Saudi-Brit Soc
Arachnology > Spiders
Arachnophobia > Phobias
Arbitration
Chart Inst Arbitrators
Electricity Arbitration Assn
Veterinary Assn Arbitration & Jurisprudence
Arboriculture > Forestry; Trees
Arc welding > Welding
Archaeology
Archaeology Abroad
Assn Archaeol Illustrators & Surveyors
Assn Envtl Archaeology
Assn Local Govt Archaeol Officers
Brit Academy
Brit Archaeol Assn
Brit Assn Local Hist
Brit Soc Dowsers
Coun Indep Archaeology
Egypt Exploration Soc
Histl Metallurgy Soc
Inst Field Archaeologists
Medieval Settlement Res Gp
Oriental Ceramic Soc
Prehistoric Soc
R Archaeol Inst
Remote Sensing & Photogrammetry Soc
Soc Landscape Studies
Soc Medieval Archaeology
Soc Museum Archaeologists
Soc Post-Medieval Archaeology
Archaeology: country societies
Archaeology Scotland
Cambrian Archaeol Assn
Coun Brit Archaeology
Inst Archaeologists Ireland
R Instn S Wales
R Ir Academy
R Soc Antiquaries Ireland
Soc Antiquaries Scotland
Wales > Cambrian Archaeol Assn
Archaeology: county societies
Abertay Histl Soc
Anglesey Antiquarian Soc & Field Club
Architectural & Archaeol Soc County Bucks
Ashmolean Natural Hist Soc Oxfordshire
Assn Northumberland Local Hist Socs
Berkshire Archaeol Soc
Berkshire Archaeology Res Gp
Berwickshire Naturalists Club
Birmingham & Warwickshire Archaeol Soc
Bristol & Gloucestershire Archaeol Soc
Buckinghamshire > Architectural & Archaeol Soc County Bucks
Buckinghamshire > Wolverton & Dist Archaeol & Histl Soc
Caernarvonshire Histl Soc
Cambridge Antiquarian Soc

Cambridgeshire Assn Local Hist
Cheshire > Historic Soc Lancashire & Cheshire
Cheshire > Lancashire & Cheshire Antiquarian Soc
Chester Archaeol Soc
Cornwall Archaeol Soc
Cornwall > R Instn Cornwall
Coventry & District Archaeol Soc
Croydon Natural Hist & Scientific Soc
Cumberland & Westmorland Antiquarian. . . Soc
Cymdeithas Hanes Ceredigion Histl Soc
Cymdeithas Hanes Sir Ddinbych
Denbighshire > Cymdeithas Hanes Sir Ddinbych
Derbyshire Archaeol Soc
Derbyshire > Hunter Archaeol Soc
Derbyshire Record Soc
Devon Archaeol Soc
Dorset Natural Hist & Archaeol Soc
Dublin > Friends Medieval Dublin [IRL]
Dumfriesshire & Galloway Natural Hist. . . Soc
Durham > Architectural & Archaeol Soc of Durham &
Northumberland
Durham County Local Hist Soc
Durham > Soc Antiquaries Newcastle upon Tyne
E Herts Archaeol Soc
E Lothian Antiquarian. . . Naturalists Soc
Essex Archaeol & Histl Congress
Essex Soc Archaeology & Hist
Flintshire Histl Soc
Friends Medieval Dublin [IRL]
Galloway > Dumfries & Galloway Natural Hist. . . Soc
Glamorgan Hist Soc
Glasgow Archaeol Soc
Gloucestershire > Bristol & Gloucestershire Archaeol Soc
Guernsey > Société Guernesiaise
Hampshire Field Club & Archaeol Soc
Hawick Archaeol Soc
Hertfordshire > E Herts Archaeol Soc
Hertfordshire > St Albans & Hertfordshire Architectural. . . Soc
Historic Soc Lancashire & Cheshire
Hunter Archaeol Soc
Huntingdonshire Local Hist Soc
Isle of Anglesey > Anglesey Antiquarian Soc
Isle of Man Natural Hist. . .Soc
Isle of Wight Natural Hist & Archaeol Soc
Jersey > Société Jersiaise
Kent Archaeol Soc
Kent > Croydon Natural Hist & Scientific Soc
Lancashire & Cheshire Antiquarian Soc
Lancashire > Cumberland & Westmorland Antiquarian & Archaeol
Soc
Lancashire > Historic Soc Lancashire & Cheshire
Leicestershire Archaeol & Histl Soc
Lincolnshire > Soc Lincolnshire Hist & Archaeol
London & Middlesex Archaeol Soc
London Topographical Soc
Lothian > E Lothian Antiquarian &. . .Naturalists Soc
Middlesex > London & Middlesex Archaeol Soc
Monmouthshire Antiquarian Assn
Norfolk & Norwich Archaeol Soc
Northamptonshire Archaeol Soc
Northamptonshire > Wolverton & Dist Archaeol & Histl Soc
Northumberland > Architectural & Archaeol Soc Durham &
Northumberland
Northumberland > Assn Northumberland Local Hist Socs
Northumberland > Berwickshire Naturalists' Club
Northumberland > Soc Antiquaries Newcastle upon Tyne
Nottinghamshire Local Hist Assn
Nottinghamshire > Thoroton Soc Nottinghamshire
Orkney Heritage Soc
Oxford University Archaeol Soc
Oxfordshire Architectural & Hist Soc
Oxfordshire > Ashmolean Natural Hist Soc
Pembrokeshire Histl Soc
Perthshire Soc Natural Science
Powys > Radnorshire Soc
R Instn Cornwall
Radnorshire Soc
Roxburghshire > Hawick Archaeol Soc
Rutland Local Hist & Record Soc
Saint Albans & Hertfordshire Architectural. . . Soc
Shropshire Archaeol & Histl Soc
Soc Antiquaries Lond
Soc Antiquaries Newcastle upon Tyne
Soc Lincolnshire Hist & Archaeology
Société Guernesiaise
Société Jersiaise
Somerset Archaeol & Natural Hist Soc

Staffordshire Archaeol. . .Soc
Staffordshire > Stoke on Trent Museum Archaeol Soc
Stoke-on-Trent Museum Archaeol Soc
Suffolk Inst Archaeology & Hist
Surrey Archaeol Soc
Surrey > Croydon Natural Hist Scientific Soc
Sussex Archaeol Soc
Tayside > Abertay Histl Soc
Thoresby Soc
Thoroton Soc Nottinghamshire
Ulster Archaeol Soc
W Midlands > Birmingham & Warwickshire Archaeol Soc
Warwickshire > Birmingham & Warwickshire Archaeol Soc
Warwickshire > Coventry & District Archaeol Soc
Westmorland > Cumberland & Westmorland Antiquarian & Archaeol
Soc
Wiltshire Archaeol & Natural Hist Soc
Wolverton & Dist Archaeol & Histl Soc
Worcestershire Archaeol Soc
Yorkshire Archaeol Soc
Yorkshire > Hunter Archaeol Soc
Yorkshire Philosophical Soc
Yorkshire > Thoresby Soc

Archaeology: industrial
Arkwright Soc
Assn Indl Archaeology
Brewery Hist Soc
Bristol Indl Archaeol Soc
Gloucestershire Soc Indl Archaeology
Greater Lond Indl Archaeology Soc
Indl Locomotive Soc
Merseyside Indl Heritage Soc
Peak District Mines Hist Soc
Scot Indl Heritage Soc
Subterranea Britannica
Sussex Indl Archaeol Soc
Tools & Trs Hist Soc
Trevithick Soc
> + specific field of interest

Archaeology: nautical
Nautical Archaeology Soc
Nautical Heritage Assn
Sub-Aqua Assn

Archery
Craft Gld Traditional Bowyers & Fletchers
Grand Nat Archery Soc
Nat Field Archery Soc
NI Archery Soc
Plantagenet Medieval Archery. . . Soc
Scot Archery Assn
Scot Assn Country Sports
Scot Field Archery Assn
Soc Archer-Antiquaries

Architecture
Architectural Assn
Art & Architecture
Arts Centre Gp
Assn Bldg Engrs
Assn Consultant Architects
Assn Scot Schools Architecture
Brit Earth Sheltering Assn
Chart Inst Architectural Technologists
Inst Profl Designers
Property Consultants Soc
Pugin Gld
R Incorporation Architects Scotland
R Inst Architects Ireland
R Inst Brit Architects
R Scot Academy
R Soc Architects Wales
R Soc Ulster Architects
Scala

Architecture: history & preservation
Alexander Thomson Soc
Architectural & Archaeol Soc County Bucks
Architectural & Archaeol Soc Durham & Northumberland
Architectural Heritage Soc Scotland
Assn Art Historians
Campaign Protection Rural Wales
Cathedral Architects Assn
Charles Rennie Mackintosh Soc
Georgian Gp
Ir Georgian Soc
Men Stones
Nat Trust
Nat Trust Ireland
Nat Trust Scotland

© CBD Research Ltd · Beckenham · BR3 5JS · Tel 020 8650 7745 · Fax 020 8650 0768 · E-mail cbd@cbdresearch.com · www.cbdresearch.com

Pugin Soc
R Archaeol Inst
Regency Soc Brighton & Hove
Saint Albans & Hertfordshire Architectural... Soc
Save Britain's Heritage
Soc Architectural Historians
Twentieth Century Soc
UK Assn Presvn Trusts
Ulster Architectural Heritage Soc
Vernacular Architecture Gp
Victorian Soc
> + Archaeology; Church: buildings

Architecture: illustration
Soc Architectural Illustration

Architecture: metalcraft
Gld Architectural Ironmongers
Inst Architectural Ironmongers

Architecture: naval > Shipbuilding & ship repairing
Architecture: religious > Church: buildings
Archives
Assn Genealogists & Researchers in Archives
Brit Assn Friends Museums
Business Archives Coun
Catholic Archives Soc
Ir Soc Archives
Soc Archivists
> + Records: historical

Arenas
Nat Arenas Assn

Argentina
Anglo-Argentine Soc
Cámara Comercio Argentino Britanica
Cymdeithas Cymru-Ariannin

Arithmetic
Dozenal Soc
> + Mathematics

Arkwright (Sir Richard)
Arkwright Soc

Armed forces & veterans: welfare
Gulf Veterans Assn
Soldiers, Sailors & Airmen's Families Assn
UK Nat Defence Assn
> + Ex-service organisations

Armorial bearings > Heraldry
Armoured fighting vehicles (miniature)
Miniature Armoured Fighting Vehicle Assn
> + Military vehicles

Arms & armour
Arms & Armour Soc
Histl Breechloading Smallarms Assn
Historic Artillery
Meyrick Soc
Muzzle Loaders Assn
Ordnance Soc
Palmerston Forts Soc
Pike & Shot Soc
Trebuchet Soc
> + Defence equipment; Shooting

Arms trade & control
Campaign Arms Trade

Arm wrestling
Brit Armwrestling Fedn

Army
Victorian Military Soc
> + Armed forces & veterans: welfare; Cadets; Military history

Aromatherapy
Aromatherapy & Allied Practitioners Assn
Aromatherapy Tr Coun
Scot Massage Therapists Org

Aromatic compounds > Fragrances & aromatic compounds
Arrhythmia
Arrhythmia Alliance
> + Cardiology

Arrows (for archery) > Archery
Art & artists
Art & Architecture
Art Workers Gld
Arts & Business
Arts Centre Gp
Arts Marketing Assn
Assn Cultural Advancement through Visual Art
Brit Soc Painters (in Oil, Pastels & Acrylic)
Contemporary Art Soc
Contemporary Art Soc Wales
Fedn Brit Artists
Fine Art Tr Gld
Gld Aviation Artists

Gld Rly Artists
Hilliard Soc Miniaturists
Inst Contemporary Arts
Medical Artists Assn
Nat Acrylic Painters' Assn
Nat Campaign Arts
Nat Portraiture Assn
Nat Soc Painters, Sculptors & Printmakers
Nature Art Trust
Pre-Raphaelite Soc
Public Monuments & Sculpture Assn
R Academy Arts
R Birmingham Soc Artists
R Cambrian Academy Art
R Philosophical Soc Glasgow
R Scot Academy
R Soc ... Arts
R Soc Miniature Painters ...
R Ulster Academy Arts
R Watercolour Soc
Royal Glasgow Institute of the Fine Arts
SAA
Soc Artists' Agents
Soc Botanical Artists
Soc Equestrian Artists
Soc Graphic Fine Art
Soc Heraldic Arts
Soc Scot Artists
Soc Women Artists
UK Coloured Pencil Soc
Visual Arts Scotland
Voluntary Arts Network
> + Artist by name; specific form of art

Art: appreciation
Brit Soc Aesthetics
engage
Oriental Ceramic Soc

Art: auctioneers > Art: trade
Art: conservation
ArtWatch UK
Brit Assn Paintings Conservator-Restorers
Fine Art Tr Gld
Inst Consvn
Inst Consvn Historic &... Works Ireland
Ir Profl Conservators' & Restorers' Assn
Nat Assn Decorative & Fine Arts Socs
Soc Decorative Art Curators
> + Historic buildings; Picture restoring

Art: education
Manchester Literary & Philosophical Soc
Nat Assn Local Govt Arts Officers
Nat Soc Educ in Art & Design

Art: festivals > Festivals: art, drama & music
Art: galleries
Assn Leading Visitor Attractions
Brit Assn Friends Museums
Contemporary Art Soc
Contemporary Art Soc Wales
Fedn Museums & Art Galleries Wales
Fine Art Tr Gld
Museums Assn
Nat Art Collections Fund
Nat Heritage
Visual Arts & Galleries Assn
> + Museums

Art: history
Assn Art Historians
Brit Academy
Walpole Soc

Art: law &
Inst Art & Law

Art: libraries
ARLIS/UK & Ireland

Art: management > Leisure, recreation & amenity management
Art: shippers & packers
Assn Art & Antique Dealers

Art: therapy
Brit Assn Art Therapists

Art: trade
Assn Art & Antique Dealers
Brit Art Market Fedn
Fine Art Tr Gld
Inst Auctioneers & Appraisers Scotland
Soc Fine Art Auctioneers & Valuers
Soc Lond Art Dealers

Arthritis & rheumatism
    Arthritic Assn
    Arthritis Care
    Arthritis & Musculoskeletal Alliance
    Behçet's Syndrome Soc
    Brit Coalition Heritable Disorders Connective Tissue
    Brit Health Profls in Rheumatology
    Brit Orthopaedic Assn
    Brit Soc Rheumatology
    Children's Chronic Arthritis Assn
    Fibromyalgia Assn
    Nat Ankylosing Spondylitis Soc
    Nat Rheumatoid Arthritis Soc
    Primary Care Rheumatology Soc
    Psoriasis Assn
    Psoriasis & Psoriatic Arthritis Alliance
Arthrogryposis
    Arthrogryposis Gp
Article numbering
    Assn Automatic Identification . . .Capture
    GS1 Ireland
    GS1 UK
Artificial intelligence
    Soc Study Artificial Intelligence & Simulation Behaviour
Artificial limbs > Prosthetics & orthoses
Artillery > Arms & armour
Artists > Art & artists
Asbestos
    Asbestos Removal Contractors Asssn
    Indep Safety Consultants Assn
    Occupational & Envtl Diseases Assn
    Thermal Insulation Contrs Assn
Ash
    UK Quality Ash Assn
Asia
    Assn Punjab Studies (UK)
    Assn South-East Asian Studies UK
    Black & Asian Studies Assn
    Oriental Ceramic Soc
    R Asiatic Soc
    R Soc Asian Affairs
    UK One World Linking Assn
Asia: languages
    Assn Language Learning
Asparagus
    Asparagus Growers' Assn
    > + Vegetables: growing
Asphalt & coated macadam
    Asphalt Ind Alliance
    Inst Asphalt Technology
    Mastic Asphalt Coun
    Quarry Products Assn
    > + Bitumen
Asphasia > + Speech
Asset sales services
    Nat Assn Valuers & Auctioneers
Assisted dying > Euthanasia
Association football > Football (Association)
Association management
    Inst Assn Mgt
    Profl Assns Res Network
Assurance > Insurance
Asthma
    Asthma Soc Ireland
    Asthma UK
    Brit Aerobiology Fedn
    Midlands Asthma & Allergy Res Assn
    > + Allergy
Astrology
    Assn Profl Astrologers
    Astrological Assn
    Astrological Lodge Lond
    Brit Assn Vedic Astrology
    Brit Astrological & Psychic Soc
    Fac Astrological Studies
    UK Skeptics
Astronautics > Space research & exploration
Astronomy
    Assn Astronomy Educ
    Assn Scotland Res Astronautics
    Astronomical Soc Edinburgh
    Brit Astronomical Assn
    Campaign Dark Skies
    Fedn Astronomical Socs
    Ir Astronomical Soc
    R Astronomical Soc
    R Inst Navigation

    Soc Popular Astronomy
    William Herschel Soc
Asylum seekers
    Assn Visitors Immigration Detainees
Ataxia
    Ataxia-Telangiectasia Soc
    Ataxia UK
Athletic clothing > Clothing
Athletics
    Amat Athletic Assn
    Assn GB Athletics Clubs
    Brit Quadrathlon Assn
    Brit Triathlon Fedn
    Dwarf Athletic Assn
    England Athletics
    NI Athletic Fedn
    Scot Athletics
    Scot Games Assn
    Triathlon England
    UK Athletics
    Welsh Athletics
    > + Sports
Atomic > Nuclear energy
Attention deficiency
    Nat Acupuncture Detoxification Assn
Au pairs > Nannies & au pairs
Auctioneering
    Inst Auctioneers & Appraisers Scotland
    Inst Profl Auctioneers & Valuers [IRL]
    Ir Auctioneers & Valuers Inst
    Nat Assn Valuers & Auctioneers
    Property Consultants Soc
    Soc Fine Art Auctioneers & Valuers
Audio engineering > Sound recording & reproduction
Audio tape > Sound recording & reproduction
Audio visual: aids & equipment
    Audiovisual Fedn [IRL]
    Brit Inst Profl Photography
    Brit Universities Film & Video Coun
    Deaf Broadcasting Coun
    > + Sound recording & reproduction
Audio visual: libraries
    Fedn Comml Audiovisual Libraries
Audiobooks
    Audiobook Publishing Assn
Audiology > Hearing
Auditing > Accountancy
Auriculas
    Nat Auricula & Primula Soc (Mid & West)
    Nat Auricula & Primula Soc (Nthn)
    Nat Auricula & Primula Soc (Sthn)
Austen (Jane)
    Jane Austen Soc
Australia
    Australian Business
    Britain-Australia Soc
Austria
    Anglo-Austrian Soc
    Austro-Brit Cham
    German Rly Soc
Authors > Writing & writers; individual by name
Authors' agents
    Assn Authors' Agents
    > + Writing & writers
Autism
    Autism Indep UK
    Hyperactive Children's Support Gp
    Ir Soc Autism
    Nat Autistic Soc
    Scot Soc Autism
    > + Children: handicapped
Auto-immune diseases
    Stiff Man Syndrome Support Gp
Auto theft > Motor vehicles: theft (of/from)
Autograph collecting
    Autograph Club
Autojumbles
    Nat Jumblers Fedn
Automata > Musical boxes
Automatic identification & data capture
    Assn Automatic Identification . . .Capture
    GS1 Ireland
    GS1 UK
    > + Article numbering
Automatic gates
    Fencing Contrs' Assn
Automatic metering > Meters & metering

© CBD Research Ltd · Beckenham · BR3 5JS · Tel 020 8650 7745 · Fax 020 8650 0768 · E-mail cbd@cbdresearch.com · www.cbdresearch.com

Automatic vending
>> Automatic Vending Assn
>> Nat Assn Cigarette Machine Operators
>> > + Amusements & coin operated machines
Automation
>> Assn Instrumentation, Control, Automation. . .
>> Brit Automation & Robot Assn
>> > + Computers; Control engineering; Production engineering
Automobile > Car headings; Motor headings
Automotive engineers > Motor industry
Auxiliary languages > Languages: auxiliary
Avebury
>> Megalithic Soc
Average adjusters
>> Assn Average Adjusters
Aviation
>> Air-Britain (Historians)
>> Air League
>> Air Transport Auxiliary Assn
>> Aircraft Res Assn
>> Airport Operators Assn
>> Assn ATOL Companies
>> Aviation Envt Fedn
>> Aviation Soc
>> Baltic Air Charter Assn
>> Brit Air Transport Assn
>> Brit Assn Aviation Consultants
>> Brit Business & Gen Aviation Assn
>> Britpave
>> Defence Mfrs Assn
>> Fedn Aerospace Enterprises Ireland
>> R Aero Club Trust
>> R Aeronautical Soc
>> Soc Automotive Engrs
>> Soc Brit Aerospace Cos
>> > + Air: sport; Gliding & soaring; Helicopters
Aviation: aircraft maintenance
Aviation: airships > Balloons & airships
Aviation: art
>> Gld Aviation Artists
Aviation: freight
>> Brit Intl Freight Assn
>> > + Freight Transport
Aviation: history
>> Aeroplane Collection
>> Air-Britain (Historians)
>> Brit Aviation Enthusiasts Soc
>> Brit Aviation Presvn Coun
>> Brooklands Soc
>> Farnborough Air Sciences Trust
>> Handley Page Assn
>> Historic Aircraft Assn
>> R Aeronautical Soc
>> Rly & Canal Histl Soc
>> Second Wld War Aircraft Presvn Soc
Aviation: medicine
>> Assn Aviation Med Examiners
>> R Aeronautical Soc
Aviation: pilots, officers & crew
>> Aircraft Owners & Pilots Assn
>> Aircraft Owners & Pilots Assn [IRL]
>> Aircrew Assn
>> Brit Air Line Pilots Assn
>> Brit Precision Pilots Assn
>> Brit Women Pilots Assn
>> Flying Farmers Assn
>> Gld Air Pilots & Air Navigators
>> Indep Pilots Assn
>> Ir Airline Pilots Assn
>> Nautilus UK
Aviation: safety, control & training
>> Air Safety Gp
>> Aircraft Owners & Pilots Assn
>> Gld Air Pilots & Air Navigators
>> Gld Air Traffic Control Officers
Aviation: sport
>> Brit Aerobatic Assn
>> Brit Microlight Aircraft Assn
>> Formula Air Racing Assn
>> Light Aircraft Assn
Aviculture > Birds
Ayurvedic medicine
>> Ayurvedic Med Assn

Babies > Cot deaths; Maternity; Obstetrics & gynaecology; Paediatrics
Baby goods > Nursery & baby products
Baby life-support systems
>> BLISS
Bach remedies
>> Brit Assn Flower Essence Producers
>> Crystal & Healing Fedn
Back pain > Chiropractic; Spine & spinal injury
Backgammon
>> Brit Isles Backgammon Assn
Backpacking
>> Backpackers Club
Bacon
>> Provision Tr Fedn
>> > + Pigs
Bacon (Francis) Baron Verulam
>> Francis Bacon Soc
Bacteriology > Microbiology
Badgers
>> Badger Trust
Badges & insignia
>> Badge Collectors Circle
>> Brit Badge Collectors Assn
>> Police Insignia Collectors Assn
>> Trade U Badge Collectors Soc
>> > + Numismatics
Badminton
>> Badminton England
>> Scot Badminton U
>> Welsh Badminton U
Bagpipes > Pipe bands & music
Bailiffs
>> Assn Brit Investigators
>> Assn Civil Enforcement Agencies
>> Enforcement Services Assn
Baking
>> Assn Bakery Ingredient Mfrs
>> Bakers', Food & Allied Workers' U
>> Brit Confectioners Assn
>> Fedn Bakers
>> Food & Drink Fedn
>> Nat Assn Master Bakers
>> Scot Assn Master Bakers
>> UK Assn Mfrs Bakers Yeast
Ball clay
>> Kaolin & Ball Clay Assn
>> > + Clay & clay products
Ball & roller bearings
>> Ball & Roller Bearing Mfrs Assn
Ball milling
>> Inst Vitreous Enamellers
Ballet
>> Brit Ballet Org
>> Imperial Soc Teachers Dancing
>> R Academy Dance
>> > + Dancing
Balloons & airships
>> Airship Assn
>> Brit Assn Balloon Operators
>> Brit Balloon & Airship Club
>> > + Inflatable toys & structures
Balloons (decorated/toy)
>> NABAS
Ballroom dancing > Dancing
Baltic countries > individual country
Bamboo
>> Bamboo Soc
Bands > Brass & silver bands; Dance bands; Pipe bands & music; Steel bands
Banjos > Ukuleles & banjos
Bank customers > Banking: customers & users
Banking
>> Assn Foreign Banks
>> Assn Guernsey Banks
>> Assn Payment Clearing Services
>> Brit Bankers' Assn
>> Chart Inst Bankers Scotland
>> Financial Services Ireland
>> Futures & Options Association
>> Indep Banking Advy Service
>> Inst Bankers Ireland
>> Ir Bankers Fedn
>> Loan Market Assn

London Investment Banking Assn
SAFE
Banking: customers & users
Campaign Community Banking Services
Nat Assn Bank & Insurance Customers
Banking: history
Brit Banking History Soc
Bankruptcy
Assn Business Recovery Profls
Bankruptcy Assn
Inst Money Advisers
Banks (Sir Joseph)
Sir Joseph Banks Soc
Banners > Flags, banners & bunting
Baptist church
Baptist Histl Soc
Baptist U
Strict Baptist Histl Soc
The Bar > Law
Bar dancers
Adult Ind Trade Assn
Barbecues
Leisure & Outdoor Furniture Assn
Barbershop singing
Brit Assn Barbershop Singers
Ladies' Assn Brit Barbershop Singers
Barbirolli (Sir John)
Barbirolli Soc
Barcodes & data synchronisation > Article numbering
Barges
DBA - Barge Assn
River Assn Freight & Transport
Sailing Barge Assn
Soc Sailing Barge Res
Barley
Brit Oat & Barley Millers Assn
Barn engines
Farm Machinery Presvn Soc
> + Agriculture: machinery & engineering
Barnes (William)
William Barnes Soc
Barometers
Brit Barometer Makers Assn
Barons > Manors
Barrels > Cooperage
Barriers (safety)
Retroreflective Eqpt Mfrs Assn
> + Stairs: gates & barriers
Barristers > Law
Bars (management & staff)
Noctis
UK Bartenders Gld
Baseball
BaseballSoftballUK
English Baseball Assn
Basements
ASUCplus
Basketball
Basketball Assn Wales
Basketball Ireland
Basketball Scotland
Brit Basketball Fedn
England Basketball
Baskets
Basketmaker's Assn
Scot Basketmakers' Circle
Bassoons (musical instruments)
Brit Double Reed Soc
Bathing water quality
Marine Consvn Soc
Baths & bathrooms
Bathroom Mfrs' Assn
Kitchen Bathroom Bedroom Specialists Assn
Baths: public > Swimming pools
Baton twirling
Brit Isles Baton Twirling Assn
Nat Baton Twirling Assn
Nat Baton Twirling Assn Scotland
Scot Fedn Baton Twirling
Bats
Bat Consvn Trust
NI Bat Gp
Batten disease
Batten Disease Family Assn
Battered wives > Domestic violence

Batteries
Indep Battery Distbrs Assn
Oil Recycling Assn
Battery vehicles > Electric: transport
Battle of Britain > World Wars II
Battlefields
Battlefields Trust
Battles (re-enactment) > Fights (historic/re-enactment); specific period of interest
Baxter (George)
New Baxter Soc
Beads
Bead Soc
Beagling
Ir Masters Beagles Assn
Beam engines
Trevithick Soc
Beams (concrete)
Brit Precast Concrete Fedn
> + Concrete & concrete products
Bearings
Ball & Roller Bearing Mfrs Assn
Bears ('teddies') > Rupert Bear
Beaters & pickers-up
Nat Org Beaters & Pickers Up
Beauty specialists/treatment
Assn Therapy Lecturers
Brit Assn Beauty Therapy & Cosmetology
Freelance Hair & Beauty Fedn
Gld Profl Beauty Therapists
Hairdressing & Beauty Suppliers Assn
Health & Beauty Emplrs Fedn
> + Cosmetology & cosmetic surgery; Electrolysis
Beckford (William)
Beckford Soc
Beddoes (Thomas Lovell)
Thomas Lovell Beddoes Soc
Bedrooms (fitted)
Kitchen Bathroom Bedroom Specialists Assn
Beds & bedding
Brit Waterbed Assn
Futon Assn
Nat Bed Fedn
Sleep Coun
Bedsores
Tissue Viability Soc
Beef > Cattle headings; Meat
Beekeeping > Bees & beekeeping
Beer > Brewing
Beer: bottles, cans, labels & mats
Assn Brit Brewery Collectables
Brit Beermat Collectors' Soc
Labologists Society
Bees & beekeeping
Assn Bee Appliance Mfrs
Bee Farmers Assn
Bee Improvement & Bee Breeders Assn
Brit Bee-Keepers' Assn
Buglife
Bumblebee Conservation Trust
Fedn Ir Beekeepers' Assns
Scot Beekeepers Assn
Welsh Beekeepers Assn
Beet sugar > Sugar headings
Begonias
Nat Begonia Soc
Behaviour simulation
Soc Study Artificial Intelligence & Simulation Behaviour
Behavioural studies
Assn Rational Emotive Behaviour Therapy
Brit Assn Behavioural... Psychotherapies
Behçet's syndrome
Behçet's Syndrome Soc
Belgium
Anglo-Belgian Soc
Assn Low Countries Studies
Belgian-Luxembourg Cham Comm GB
Brit Cham Comm Belgium
Bell (Adrian)
Adrian Bell Soc
Bellringing
Brit Carillon Soc
Central Coun Church Bell Ringers
Handbell Ringers
Bennett ([Enoch] Arnold)
Arnold Bennett Soc
Benson (Edward Frederic)
E F Benson Soc

© CBD Research Ltd · Beckenham · BR3 5JS · Tel 020 8650 7745 · Fax 020 8650 0768 · E-mail cbd@cbdresearch.com · www.cbdresearch.com

Bereavement
      Campaign Drinking & Driving
      Compassionate Friends
      Cruse Bereavement Care
      RoadPeace
      SAMM
      Sudden Death Support Assn
      Way Foundation
      > + specific cause of bereavement
Berlioz (Hector)
      Berlioz Soc
Bespoke tailoring > Tailoring
Betjeman (Sir John)
      Betjeman Soc
Betting > Bookmaking; Casinos; Gaming
Beverage industry > Drink & beverage industry; & specific beverages
Bewick (Thomas)
      Bewick Soc

Bible
      Biblical Creation Soc
      Soc Old Testament Study
Bibliography
      Bibliographical Soc
      Cambridge Bibliographical Soc
      Edinburgh Bibliographical Soc
      Soc Hist Natural Hist
      > + Book(s)
Bicross > Cycling
Bicycles > Cycles & motorcycles
Big cats
      Brit Big Cats Soc
Bill broking
      London Money Market Assn
Billiards > Cue sports
Bingo
      Bingo Association
      Nat Bingo Game Assn
Biochemistry & biotechnology
      Assn Clinical Biochemistry
      Biochemical Soc
      BioIndustry Assn
      Brit In Vitro Diagnostics Assn
      Brit Soc Proteome Res
      Brit Soc Toxicological Pathologists
      Genetics Soc
      Ir BioIndustry Assn
      Pharmaceutical & Healthcare Sciences Soc
Biocides
      Brit Assn Chemical Specialities
      Chemical Inds Assn
Biodegradable resources
      Assn Organics Recycling
      > + Composts & composting
Bioenergy
      Renewable Energy Assn
      Soc Metaphysicians
      > + Renewable energy
Biological engineering
      Soc Applied Microbiology
Biology
      Assn Applied Biologists
      Biological Recording Scotland
      Biosciences Fedn
      Brit Soc Developmental Biology
      Freshwater Biological Assn
      Inst Biology
      Inst Biology Ireland
      Natural Sciences Collections Assn
      Scot Freshwater Gp
      Soc Experimental Biology
      Soc Study Human Biology
      Systematics Assn
      > + Botany; Cell biology; Marine: biology & biochemistry; Plants
Biomagnetics
      Brit Biomagnetic Assn
Biomass > Bioenergy; Forestry
Biometrics
      Assn Automatic Identification . . .Capture
Biophysics
      Brit Biophysical Soc
Biotechnology > Biochemistry & biotechnology
Birds
      Avicultural Soc
      Birdcare Standards Assn
      Brit Assn Shooting & Consvn
      Brit Ornithologists Club

      Brit Ornithologists U
      Brit Trust Ornithology
      Foreign Bird Fedn
      Nat Coun Aviculture
      Ornithological Soc Middle East
      R Inst Navigation
      R Naval Bird Watching Soc
      R Soc Protection Birds
      Scot Ornithologists Club
      Scot Soc Protection Wild Birds
      Seabird Gp
      Songbird Survival
      > + Natural history
Birds of prey > Hawks & hawking
Birth & birth control > Family planning; Maternity; Obstetrics & gynaecology
Birthmarks & disfigurement
      Birthmark Support Gp
      Brit Assn Skin Camouflage
      Craniofacial Soc
      Headlines
      Let's Face It
      Treacher Collins Family Support Gp
      > + Children: handicapped
Births > Population registration
Biscuits
      Cereal Ingredients Mfrs' Assn
      Food & Drink Fedn
Bison
      Brit Bison Assn
Bitumen
      Refined Bitumen Assn
      Road Emulsion Assn
      > + Asphalt & coated macadam
Björling (Jussi)
      Jussi Björling Appreciation Soc
Blacksmiths
      Brit Artist Blacksmiths Assn
Bladder disease > Urology
Bladder problems > Incontinence
Blake (William)
      Blake Soc St James's
Blasting contractors
      Inst Explosives Engrs
Bleach
      Brit Assn Chemical Specialities
Bleeding disorders
      Haemophilia Soc
Blind & partially sighted
      Bates Assn Vision Educ
      Behçet's Syndrome Soc
      Brit Computer Assn Blind
      Brit Retinitis Pigmentosa Soc
      Community
      Confedn Transcribed Inf Services
      Deafblind UK
      Gld Church Braillists
      Guide Dogs for Blind Assn
      LOOK
      Macular Disease Soc
      Micro & Anophthalmic Children's Soc
      Nat Assn Educ, Training. . . Blind. . . People
      Nat Fedn Blind
      Nystagmus Network
      Partially Sighted Soc
      R Nat Inst Blind
      Saint Dunstan's
      Scot Nat Fedn Welfare Blind
      Seeing Dogs Alliance
      Talking Newspaper Assn
      Vision Homes Assn
Blinds > Windows: blinds & shutters
Blizzards > Snowfall & blizzards
Blokarting
      Brit Land Speedsail Assn
Blood > Haematology; Haemophilia
Blood pressure
      Blood Pressure Assn
Blood transfusion > Haematology
Bloodhounds
      Masters Draghounds & Bloodhounds Assn
Bloodstock > Horse(s) headings
Bloomfield (Robert)
      Robert Bloomfield Soc
Blues > Jazz & Blues
Blyton (Enid)
      Enid Blyton Soc
Board > Paper & paper products

Board: games > Wargaming; name of specific game
Board: sailing > Surfing, board & speed sailing
Boarding kennels
    Pet Care Trust
Boarding schools
    Assn Boarding School Survivors
    Boarding Schools Assn
    Girls' Schools Assn
    > + Independent & public schools
Boats & boating
    Assn Boat Safety Examiners
    Boat Jumble Assn
    Brit Dragon Boat Racing Assn
    Brit Hire Cruiser Fedn
    Brit Marine Fedn
    Brit Marine Fedn Scotland
    Broads Hire Boat Fedn
    Cruising Assn
    Electric Boat Assn
    Marine Leisure Assn
    Nat Assn Boat Owners
    Nat Community Boats Assn
    Profl Boatmans Assn
    Superyacht UK
    Thames Boating Trs Assn
    Vintage Wooden Boat Assn
    > + Sailing; Ship; Steam engines, boats & machinery; Yachts & yachting
Bob skeleton
    Brit Bob Skeleton Assn
Bobbins & bobbin-lace > Lace (handmade)
Bobsleighing > Toboggan & luge racing/riding
Boccia
    English Boccia Assn
Body piercing
    Adult Ind Trade Assn
    Brit Body Piercing Assn
Bodyboarding
    Brit Bodyboard Club
    > + Surfing, board & speed sailing
Bodybuilding
    Nat Amat Bodybuilders Assn
    UK Bodybuilding & Fitness Fedn
    > + Fitness
Bodyguards
    Profl Bodyguard Assn
Boilers & waterheaters
    Boiler & Radiator Mfrs Assn
    Hot Water Assn
    ICOM Energy Assn
    > + Heating
Boilers & boilersetting
    Refractory Users Federation
Bolts & nuts > Fasteners & turned parts
Bond collecting > Scripophily
Bondage
    Adult Ind Trade Assn
Bonded warehouses
    Bonded Warehousekeepers' Assn
Bone
    Bone Res Soc
    Brittle Bone Soc
    Nat Ankylosing Spondylitis Soc
    Nat Assn Relief Paget's Disease
    Nat Osteoporosis Soc
    > + Orthopaedics
Bonsai
    Fedn Brit Bonsai Socs
    Japan Soc

Book-keeping
    Inst Certified Book-Keepers
    Inst Financial Accountants
    Payroll Alliance
    > + Accountancy; Computers; Data processing
Bookmaking
    Assn Brit Bookmakers
    Nat Assn Bookmakers Ltd
    Rails Bookmakers Assn
Bookmatch cover collecting
    Bookmark Soc
    > Matchbox labels
Books
    Audiobook Publishing Assn
    Booktrust
    Brit Printing Inds Fedn
    > + Libraries/librarians; Printing; Publishing

Books: binding & print finishing
    Brit Printing Inds Fedn
    Soc Bookbinders
Books: bookplates
    Bookplate Soc
Books: collecting
    Observers Pocket Series Collectors' Soc
    Private Libraries Assn
    > + Paperback collecting
Books: illustrations
    Imaginative Book Illustration Soc
Books: secondhand
    Antiquarian Booksellers Assn
    Provincial Booksellers Fairs Assn
Bookselling
    Booksellers Assn
    Brit Educl Suppliers Assn
    Retail Book, Stationery. . . Employees Assn
Boomerangs
    Brit Boomerang Soc
Boots & shoes > Footwear headings
Boring > Drilling
Boroughs > Local government
Borrow (George Henry)
    George Borrow Soc
Botany
    Botanical Soc Brit Isles
    Botanical Soc Scotland
    Linnean Soc Lond
    Ray Soc
    Soc Botanical Artists
    Soc Experimental Biology
    Wild Flower Soc
    > + Horticulture; Nature conservation; Plants
Bothies > Mountain bothies
Botswana
    UK Botswana Soc
Bottle collecting
    Assn Brit Brewery Collectables
    Old Bottle Club
    Snuff Bottle Soc
Bottle feeding (babies)
    Baby Milk Action
Bottled water
    Brit Soft Drinks Assn
    Brit Water Cooler Assn
    > + Soft drinks; Water: treatment & supply
Bottling
    Brewing, Food & Beverage Ind Suppliers Assn
    Brit Bottlers' Inst
Boughton (Rutland)
    Rutland Boughton Music Trust
Bouncy castles > Inflatable toys & structures
Boundary hedges > Hedges & hedge-laying
Bowel disease > Colitis/colostomy
Bowel (problems with)
    Gut Trust
    Incontact

Bowling
    Bowls England
    Brit Crown Green Bowling Assn
    Brit Isles Bowls Coun
    Brit Isles Indoor Bowls Coun
    Brit Tenpin Bowling Assn
    Brit Wheelchair Bowls Assn
    English Indoor Bowling Assn
    English Short Mat Bowling Assn
    English Women's Indoor Bowling Assn
    Ir Bowling Assn
    Ir Women's Bowling Assn
    Scot Bowling Assn
    Scot Indoor Bowling Assn
    Scot Women's Bowling Assn
    Scot Women's Indoor Bowling Assn
    Sporting Goods Ind Assn
    Tenpin Bowling Proprietors Assn
    Welsh Bowling Assn
    Welsh Indoor Bowls Assn
Bowlly (Al)
    Al Bowlly Circle
Bows (for archery) > Archery
Bows (for string instruments)
    Brit Violin Making Assn
Bowyers
    Craft Gld Traditional Bowyers & Fletchers

© CBD Research Ltd · Beckenham · BR3 5JS · Tel 020 8650 7745 · Fax 020 8650 0768 · E-mail cbd@cbdresearch.com · www.cbdresearch.com

Boxes
> Brit Packaging Assn
> + Packaging
Boxing
> Amat Boxing Assn England
> Amat Boxing Scotland
> Ir Amat Boxing Assn
> Welsh Amat Boxing Assn
Boys clubs > Youth organisations
Braces > Prosthetics & orthoses
Bradburne (John)
> John Bradburne Memorial Soc
Bradshaw (Henry)
> Henry Bradshaw Soc
Braids
> Braid Soc
Braille
> Gld Church Braillists
> R Nat Inst Blind
Brain injury & research
> Brain Tumour UK
> Brit Neuropathological Soc
> Brit Neuroscience Assn
> Headway
> PSP Association
> UK Acquired Brain Injury Forum
> + Children: handicapped; Head & neck injury & disease
Brake linings
> Brit Friction Materials Coun
Branded products
> Anti Counterfeiting Gp
> Brit Brands Gp
> Walpole
Brass
> Cast Metals Fedn
> Copper Devt Assn
Brass & silver bands
> Brit Assn Symphonic Bands & Wind Ensembles
> Brit Fedn Brass Bands
> Brit Youth Band Assn
> Carnival Band Secretaries League
> Drum Corps UK
> Kmoch Eur Bands Soc
> Nat Assn Brass Band Conductors
> Nat School Band Assn
> Scot Brass Band Assn
> Traditional Youth Marching Bands Assn
> UK Fedn Jazz Bands
> Welsh Amat Music Fedn
> + individual instrument
Brasses & church monuments
> Church Monuments Soc
> Monumental Brass Soc
Brassicas
> Brassica Growers Assn
> + Vegetables: growing
Brazil
> Anglo-Brazilian Soc
> Brazilian Cham Comm GB
> Brit Cham Comm & Ind Brazil
> Hispanic & Luso Brazilian Coun
Brazil nuts
> Combined Edible Nut Tr Assn
Brazing & soldering
> Welding Inst
Breakfast cereals
> Assn Cereal Food Mfrs
Breast feeding
> Assn Breastfeeding Mothers
Breast implants
> Breast Implant Inf Soc
Breed societies > type of animal bred
Brewery collectables
> Assn Brit Brewery Collectables
Brewing
> Brewery Hist Soc
> Brewing, Food & Beverage Ind Suppliers Assn
> Brit Beer & Pub Assn
> Brit Gld Beer Writers
> Campaign Real Ale
> Craft Brewing Assn
> Indep Family Brewers
> Inst Brewing & Distilling
> Ir Brewers Assn
> Labologists Society
> Maltsters Assn
> Nat Assn Wine & Beer Makers

> Scot Beer & Pub Assn
> Soc Indep Brewers
> Soc Presvn Beers Wood
Brian (William Havergal)
> Havergal Brian Soc
Bribery > Corruption
Bricklaying
> Assn Brickwork Contrs
> Better Brickwork Alliance
> Gld Bricklayers
Bricks
> Brick Devt Assn
> Brit Brick Soc
> Brit Ceramic Confedn
> Brit Refractories & Indl Ceramics
> CERAM Res
> + Clay & clay products; Refractories
Brides & bridalwear > Weddings
Bridge (card game)
> English Bridge U
> Ir Bridge Union
> Welsh Bridge U
Bridges > Civil engineering; Road: construction
Bridges: concrete
> Concrete Bridge Devt Gp
Bridleways
> Nat Fedn Bridleway Assns
> + Footpaths & rights of way
Bright's disease
> Doctor Richard Bright Soc
British independence
> Anti Common Market League
> Brit Housewives League
> Campaign Indep Britain
British Telecom staff
> Communication Workers U
Broadband engineering > Cable & satellite communications
Broadcasting
> Assn Community TV Operators
> Assn Service Providers
> Assn UK Media Librarians
> Deaf Broadcasting Coun
> Indep Broadcasters Ireland [IRL]
> Inst Broadcast Sound
> Nat U Journalists
> Outdoor Writers' & Photographers' Gld
> Radio Academy
> Voice Listener & Viewer
> + Radio; Television
Brokers > specific subject
Brontë family
> Brontë Soc
Bronze
> Cast Metals Fedn
> Copper Devt Assn
Brooke (Rupert)
> Friends Dymock Poets
Browning (Robert & Elizabeth Barrett)
> Browning Soc
Brushes
> Brit Brush Mfrs Assn
> Coir Assn
Bryology
> Brit Bryological Soc

Buchan (John) Lord Tweedsmuir
> John Buchan Soc
Buddhism
> Brit Buddhist Assn
> Buddhist Soc
> Pali Text Soc
Budgerigars
> Budgerigar Soc
> Nat Coun Aviculture
Budo > Martial arts
Builders' materials & supplies > Building materials & supplies
Builders & plumbers merchants
> Builders Mchts Fedn
> Inst Builders Mchts
Building
> Assn Bldg Engrs
> Assn Envt Conscious Bldg
> BRE Trust
> BSRIA
> Building Controls Ind Assn
> Building Cost Infm Service
> Buildings Energy Efficiency Fedn

Chart Inst Architectural Technologists
Chart Inst Bldg
Chart Instn Bldg Services Engrs
Confedn Construction Specialists
Construction Confedn
Construction Emplrs Fedn
Cut the VAT Coalition
Fedn Bldg Specialist Contrs
Fedn Master Builders
Gld Builders & Contrs
Home Builders Fedn
Homes for Scotland
Inst Clerks Works
Intl Masonry Soc
LABC
London Dist Surveyors Assn
Nat Specialist Contrs Coun
Property Consultants Soc
Scot Bldg Contrs Assn
Scot Bldg Fedn
Scot Master Wrights & Builders Assn
> + Construction industries
Building board & timber > Insulation
Building materials & supplies
Assn Bldg Component Mfrs
Brit Hardware Fedn
Brit Precast Concrete Fedn
Building Materials Fedn [IRL]
Construction Products Assn
Coun Aluminium Bldg
Door & Hardware Fedn
Ir Hardware & Bldg Materials Assn
Straw Bale Bldg Assn
> + specific items
Building societies
Building Socs Assn
Building Socs Mems Assn
Ir Mortgage Coun
Save our Bldg Socs
Building: survey & inspection > Surveying
Buildings: cleaning & maintenance
Assn Bldg Engrs
Cleaning & Support Services Assn
Buildings: conservation
Folly Fellowship
Inst Historic Bldg Consvn
Nat Register Property Presvn Specialists
Scot Stone Liaison Gp
Stone Fedn
UK Assn Presvn Trusts
Upkeep
Vernacular Architecture Gp
Victorian Soc
> + Historic buildings
Buildings: earth sheltered
Brit Earth Sheltering Assn
Buildings: historic & listed > Historic buildings
Buildings: insulation > Insulation
Buildings: literary connections > Historic buildings
Buildings: open to the public > Historic buildings
Bulbs
Brit Flower Bulbs Assn
> + Flowers, flower arrangement & floristry
Bulgaria
Brit Bulgarian Friendship Soc
Bulimia nervosa > Eating disorders
Bulk solids > Materials: management/handling
Bulk storage
Solids Handling & Processing Assn
Tank Storage Assn
Bullion dealing
Brit Jewellers Assn
London Bullion Mkt Assn
Bungee jumping > Elastic rope sports
Bunting > Flags, banners & bunting
Burghs > Local government
Burglary
Assn Insurance Surveyors
> + Security
Burial & cremation
Assn Burial Authorities
Assn Natural Burial Grounds
Assn Private Crematoria & Cemeteries
Brit Inst Embalmers
Brit Inst Funeral Directors
Cremation Soc
Fedn Burial & Cremation Authorities

Funeral Furnishing Mfrs Assn
Inst Cemetery & Crematorium Mgt
Nat Assn Funeral Directors
Nat Assn Pre-Paid Funeral Plans
Nat Soc Allied & Indep Funeral Directors
Scot Cremation Soc
> + Cemeteries & churchyards
Burney (Fanny)
Burney Soc
Burns
Brit Burn Assn
Burns (Robert)
Robert Burns World Fedn
Bursars
Indep Schools Bursars Assn
Nat Bursars Assn
> + Independent & public schools
Bus & coach operators
Assn Local Bus Co Mgrs
Coach Operators Fedn
Coach Tourism Coun
Confedn Passenger Transport
Gld Brit Coach Operators
Routemaster Operators & Owners Assn
> + Passenger transport
Business
Alliance Business Consultants
Brit Business Angels Assn
Business Continuity Inst
Business Mgt Assn
Business Services Assn
EIS Assn
Executives Assn
Fedn Crafts & Comm
Fedn Small Businesses
Forum Private Business
Inst Business Admin
Inst Business Analysts & Consultants [IRL]
Inst Business Ethics
Inst Directors
Inst Family Business
Inst Indep Business
Inst Small Business & Entrepreneurship
Ir Small & Medium Enterprises Assn
Nat Fedn Enterprise Agencies
Quality Gld
Quoted Companies Alliance
R Soc ... Arts
Small Firms Assn [IRL]
Soc Business Practitioners
UK Trs Confedn
> + Employers
Business: administration > Management
Business: advisers > Management
Business: aircraft
Brit Business & Gen Aviation Assn
> + Aviation
Business: archives > Archives
Business: awards
Brit Business Awards Assn
Business: centres
Business Centre Assn
Business: communications systems > Radio: mobile;   Telecommunications
Business: counselling > Management
Business: economists
Soc Business Economists
Business: education
Assn Business Mgrs & Administrators
Assn Business Schools
Economics, Business & Enterprise Assn
> + Commerce
Business: equipment > Office equipment & systems
Business: graduates > Commerce
Business: law > Law: industrial
Business: property agents
Brit Coun Offices
Indl Agents Soc
Business: sponsorship
Arts & Business
Scot Business Community
Business: systems > Office equipment & systems
Business: travel > Travel & tourism
Business: valuation
Soc Share & Business Valuers
Butchers
Gld Q Butchers

© CBD Research Ltd · Beckenham · BR3 5JS · Tel 020 8650 7745 · Fax 020 8650 0768 · E-mail cbd@cbdresearch.com · www.cbdresearch.com

Nat Fedn Meat & Food Traders
> + Meat

Butlers
Gld Intl Butler Administrators...
Gld Intl Profl Toastmasters

Butter > Dairying

Buttercups (ranunculaceae)
Ranunculaceae Soc [IRL]

Butterflies & moths
Butterfly Consvn
> + Entomology

Buttonhook
Buttonhook Soc

Buttons
Assn Button Merchants
Brit Button Soc

Buy to Let
Nat Landlords' Assn

Buying > Purchasing & supply

Byron (George Gordon, Lord)
Byron Soc
Newstead Abbey Byron Soc

Byzantium
Soc Promotion Byzantine Studies

C

Cabbages > Brassicas

Cable & satellite communications
Confedn Aerial Inds
Nat Jt Utilities Gp
Satellite & Cable Broadcasters' Gp
Soc Cable Telecommunication Engrs
> + Telecommunications

Cables > Electric: cable & conduit

Cabs > Taxis & minicabs

Cacti & succulents
Brit Cactus & Succulent Soc
Mammillaria Soc

Cadets
Army Cadet Force Assn
Combined Cadet Force Assn

Cage birds > Birds; specific species

Cakes
Food & Drink Fedn
Food Processors Assn

Calcium carbonates
Brit Calcium Carbonates Fedn
> + Lime & limestone

Caldecott (Randolph)
Randolph Caldecott Soc

Calibration > Measurement

Call centres
Call Centre Mgt Assn
Customer Contact Assn

Calligraphy > Handwriting

Camelids
Brit Alpaca Soc
Brit Camelids Assn
Brit Llama Soc
Brit Veterinary Camelid Soc

Camera technicians & crews
Brit Soc Cinematographers
Gld Brit Camera Technicians
Gld TV Cameramen
> + Film

Cameras
UK Indl Vision Assn
> + Photograph headings

Campanology > Bellringing

Camping
Backpackers Club
Brit Holiday & Home Parks Assn
Camping & Caravanning Club
Order Woodcraft Chivalry
Phoenix Camping Club

Canada
Brit Assn Canadian Studies
Brit Canadian Cham Tr & Comm
Brit N Amer Res Assn
Canada-UK Cham Comm

Canals > Inland waterways

Canaries
Nat Coun Aviculture

Cancer
Assn Intl Cancer Res
Brain Tumour UK
Brit Assn Cancer Res
Brit Photodermatology Gp
Ir Cancer Soc
Nat Assn Relief Paget's Disease
Nat Cancer Alliance
Neuroblastoma Soc
Oesophageal Patients Assn
Ovacome: the ovarian cancer support network
Prostate Cancer Support Assn
UK Assn Cancer Registries
> + Oncology

Candida
Nat Candida Soc

Candles
Brit Candlemakers Fedn

Canes (walking)
Brit Stickmakers Gld

Canned foods > Cans & canning

Canoes & canoeing
Assn Canoe Trades
Backpackers Club
Brit Canoe U
Canoe Assn NI
Historic Canoe & Kayak Assn
Open Canoe Assn
Open Canoe Sailing Gp
Scot Canoe Assn
Welsh Canoeing Assn

Cans & canning
Brit Bottlers' Inst
Can Makers
Metal Packaging Mfrs Assn
Provision Tr Fedn
> + Food: packaging; specific commodity canned

Canvas & canvas goods > Tents & marquees; Sails & sailmaking

Capacitors
BEAMA

Car > entries below & Motor headings

Car hire > Motor vehicle hire; Taxis & minicabs

Car parks
Car Park Appreciation Soc
> + Parking

Car radios/audio systems > Radio: mobile

Car security
Auto Locksmiths Assn

Car transporters
Road Haulage Assn

Caravans & caravanning
Assn Caravan & Camping Exempted Orgs
Brit Holiday & Home Parks Assn
Camping & Caravanning Club
Caravan Club
Historic Caravan Club
Motor Caravanners Club
Nat Assn Caravan Owners
Nat Caravan Coun
Phoenix Camping Club
> + Motor vehicles: historic

Carbon capture
Carbon Capture & Storage Assn

Carbon monoxide
Brit Polarological Res Soc
Carbon Monoxide & Gas Safety Soc
Coun Gas Detection & Envtl Monitoring

Card collecting (cigarette & trade)
Cartophilic Soc

Cardiology
Arrhythmia Alliance
Assn Cardiothoracic Anaesthetists
Brit Cardiovascular Soc
Brit Polarological Res Soc
Cardiomyopathy Assn
Children's Heart Assn
Coronary Artery Disease Res Assn
Heart Line Assn
Heart UK
Marfan Assn
Soc Cardiothoracic Surgery

Cardiology: patients
Brit Cardiac Patients Assn

Care & carers
Assn Indep Care Advisers

Carers Assn [IRL]
Carers UK
Ceretas
Crossroads
Disablement Income Gp Scotland
Nat Assn Care Catering
Nat Care Assn
Relatives & Residents Assn
Shared Care Network
UK Homecare Assn
Youth Access
> + Geriatrics & ageing; Old peoples organisations;
Residential: homes
Care homes > Residential: homes
Care labelling
Home Laundering Consultative Coun
Careers
Assn Careers Educ & Guidance
Assn Graduate Careers Advy Services
Careers Writers' Assn
Fedn Profl Assns in Guidance
Inst Career Guidance
NAEGA
Carers > Care & carers
Cargo: handling > Freight transport; Transport
Cargo: health inspection
Assn Port Health Authorities
Caribbean > West Indies & the Caribbean
Carillons
Brit Carillon Soc
> + Bellringing
Carlyle (Thomas & Jane)
Carlyle Soc
Carnations
Brit Nat Carnation Soc
N England Rosecarpe Horticl Soc
Carnival bands > Brass & silver bands
Carnivals & carnival goods
Nat Carnival Gld
Carnivorous plants
Carnivorous Plant Soc
Carp fishing
Carp Soc
English Carp Heritage Org
Carpentry & joinery > Woodworking
Carpets
Brit Antique Furniture Restorers Assn
Brit Textile Technology Gp
Carpet Foundation
Contract Flooring Assn
Fibre Bonded Carpet Mfrs' Assn
Indl Cleaning Machine Mfrs Assn
Nat Carpet Cleaners Assn
Nat Inst Carpet & Floorlayers
> + Floors: floorcoverings
Carrier bags > Plastics: bags
Carroll (Lewis)
Daresbury Lewis Carroll Soc
Lewis Carroll Soc
Carrots
Brit Carrot Growers Assn
Cars > Car; Motor
Cartography
Brit Cartographic Soc
Charles Close Soc
R Inst Navigation
Cartonboard > Paper & paper products
Cartons
Alliance Beverage Cartons & Environment
Brit Printing Inds Fedn
> + Packaging; Paper & paper products
Cartoons
Brit Cartoonists' Assn
Cartoonists' Club
Political Cartoon Soc
Cartophily > Card collecting (cigarette & trade)
Cartridges (laser)
UK Cartridge Remanufacturers Assn
Carving
Brit Antique Furniture Restorers Assn
> + Stone masons & sculptors; Woodworking
Cases > Optical industry; Packaging; Travel goods & accessories
Cash & carry
Fedn Whls Distbrs
Scot Whls Assn
Cash: security handling
Brit Security Ind Assn

Cashew nuts
Combined Edible Nut Tr Assn
Cashmere
Brit Goat Soc
Scot Cashmere Producers Assn
Casings > Sausage & food casings
Casinos
Brit Casino Assn
Casino Operators' Assn
Cassettes > Sound recording & reproduction; Video
Cast stone
UK Cast Stone Assn
> + Stone
Casting (metal) > Metal: casting
Castles > Fortresses & forts; Historic buildings; Inflatable toys & structures
Casualty simulation
Casualties Union
Catalonia & Catalan language
Anglo Catalan Soc
Cataracts (eyes)
UK & I Soc Cataract & Refractive Surgeons
Catering
Assn Catering Excellence
Brit Hospitality Assn
Catering Mgrs Assn
Foodservice Consultants Soc Intl (UK)
Hospital Caterers Assn
Inst Hospitality
Ir Hospitality Inst
Local Authority Caterers' Assn
Nat Assn Care Catering
Nat Assn Catering Butchers
Nat Assn Master Bakers
NI Amusement Caterer's Tr Assn
PACE: Profl Assn Catering Educ
Catering: equipment
Catering Eqpt Distbrs Assn GB
Catering Eqpt Suppliers' Assn
Nat Assn Range Mfrs
Catering: outdoor
Nat Outdoor Events Assn
Nationwide Caterers Assn
Cathedral & church shops
Cathedral & Church Shops Assn
Cathedral & church music
Assn Indep Organ Advisers
Assn Latin Liturgy
Cathedral Organists Assn
Fac Church Music
Friends Cathedral Music
Gld Church Musicians
Hymn Soc
R School Church Music
Ulster Soc Organists & Choirmasters
> + Organs, organists & organ music
Cathodic protection
Corrosion Prevention Assn
Catholic > Roman Catholic
Cats
Assn Dogs & Cats Homes
Brit Big Cats Soc
Cats Protection
Governing Coun Cat Fancy
Catteries
Pet Care Trust
Cattle breed societies
Aberdeen-Angus Cattle Soc
Aubrac Cattle Soc
Ayrshire Cattle Soc
Beef Shorthorn Cattle Soc
Belted Galloway Cattle Soc
Black Simmental Soc
Blue Albion Cattle Soc
Brit Bazadais Cattle Soc
Brit Blonde Cattle Soc
Brit Blue Cattle Soc
Brit Charolais Cattle Soc
Brit Gelbvieh Cattle Soc
Brit Kerry Cattle Soc
Brit Limousin Cattle Soc
Brit Parthenais Cattle Soc
Brit Piemontese Cattle Soc
Brit Simmental Cattle Soc
Brit White Cattle Soc
Brown Swiss Cattle Soc
Chillingham Wild Cattle Assn
Devon Cattle Breeders' Soc

© CBD Research Ltd · Beckenham · BR3 5JS · Tel 020 8650 7745 · Fax 020 8650 0768 · E-mail cbd@cbdresearch.com · www.cbdresearch.com

Dexter Cattle Soc
English Guernsey Cattle Soc
Galloway Cattle Soc
Gascon Cattle Soc
Gloucester Cattle Soc
Gwartheg Hynafol Cymru
Hereford Cattle Soc
Highland Cattle Soc
Holstein UK
Ir Hereford Breed Soc
Ir Moiled Cattle Soc
Jersey Cattle Soc
Lincoln Red Cattle Soc
Longhorn Cattle Soc
Luing Cattle Soc
Meuse Rhine Issel Cattle Soc
Murray Grey Beef Cattle Soc
Red Poll Cattle Soc
Riggit Galloway Cattle Soc
S Devon Herd Book Soc
Salers Cattle Soc
Shetland Cattle Breeders' Assn
Shetland Cattle Herd Book Soc
Shorthorn Soc
Sussex Cattle Soc
Welsh Black Cattle Soc
White Park Cattle Soc
Whitebred Shorthorn Assn
Cattle food > Animal feed
Cattle & livestock
Assn Show & Agricl Orgs
Brit Cattle Breeders' Club
Brit Soc Animal Science
ICSA [IRL]
Livestock Auctioneers Assn
Livestock Traders Assn
Nat Assn Agricl Contrs
Nat Assn Cattle Foot Trimmers
Nat Beef Assn
Nat Cattle Assn - Dairy
New Forest Pony . . . & Cattle Soc
> + specific animals
Cattle markets > Markets: street, cattle & farmers'
Cattle troughs
Metropolitan Drinking Fountain &. . . Assn
Caves & caving
Assn Brit & Ir Showcaves
Brit Cave Res Assn
Brit Cave Rescue Coun
Brit Caving Assn
Cavies (guinea pigs)
Nat Cavy Club
Cavity insulation > Insulation
Cecidology
Brit Plant Gall Soc
Ceilings
Assn Interior Specialists
Chilled Beam & Ceiling Assn
Fedn Plastering & Drywall Contrs
Celebrity assistants
Assn Celebrity Assistants (UK)
Celery
Quality Brit Celery Assn
> + Vegetables: growing
Cell biology
Brit Soc Cell Biology
Brit Soc Clinical Cytology
Brit Soc Immunology
Comment Reproductive Ethics
R Microscopical Soc
Soc Gen Microbiology
Cement & cement products
Brit Cement Assn
Cement Admixtures Assn
Fibre Cement Mfrs Assn
Instn Civil Engrs
> + Concrete & concrete products
Cemeteries & churchyards
Assn Burial Authorities
Assn Private Pet Cemeteries & Crematoria
Brit Assn Cemeteries S Asia
Metropolitan Public Gardens Assn
Nat Fedn Cemetery Friends
> + Burial & cremation
Censorship
Campaign Censorship

mediawatch-uk
Nat Secular Soc
Census > Population: registration
Centipedes
Brit Myriapod & Isopod Gp
Central heating > Heating
Ceramic sanitaryware > Sanitaryware
Ceramics
Brit Ceramic Confedn
Brit Ceramic Gift & Tableware Mfrs' Assn
Brit Refractories & Indl Ceramics
CERAM Res
Clarice Cliff Collectors Club
Craft Potters Assn
Derby Porcelain Intl Soc
Oriental Ceramic Soc
R Birmingham Soc Artists
Scot Potters' Assn
Soc Women Artists
Tiles & Architectural Ceramics Soc
Unity
> + Clay & clay products; Pottery; Refractories; specific products
Ceramics & pottery collecting > specific type collected
Cereals
Campden & Chorleywood Food Res Assn
Scot Soc Crop Res
> + Grain
Cerebral palsy
Capability Scotland
Cedar Foundation
CP Sport England & Wales
Scope
Soc Stars
Certification bodies
Assn Brit Certification Bodies
> + Quality assurance & control
Chain-link fencing
Wire Products Assn
> + Fencing (enclosure)
Chains & chain testing
Lifting Eqpt Engrs Assn
> + Lifting & loading equipment
Chairmanship (meetings)
Assn Speakers Clubs
Chairs
Basketmaker's Assn
Chair Frame Mfrs Assn
> + Furniture
Chalet sites > Caravans & caravanning
Chalk > Lime & limestone
Chamber music > Music
Chambers of commerce: general
Brit Chams Comm
Chams Ireland
Harrogate Cham Tr & Comm
Intl Cham Comm UK
Lanarkshire Cham Comm
N E Cham Comm, Tr & Ind
NI Cham Comm & Ind
Scot Chams Comm
Chambers of commerce: local
Aberdeen & Grampian Cham Comm
Altrincham & Sale Cham Comm
Ayrshire Cham Comm & Ind
Ballymena Borough Cham Comm & Ind
Banbury & District Cham Comm
Barking & Dagenham Cham Comm
Barnsley > Cham Comm Barnsley & Rotherham
Bath Cham Comm
Bedfordshire > The Chamber. . . Bedfordshire & Luton
Bexley > S E London Cham Comm
Birmingham Cham Comm & Ind
Black Country Cham Comm
Boston Cham Comm & Ind
Bournemouth Cham Tr & Comm
Bradford Cham Comm & Ind
Bristol Cham Comm & Ind
Bromley > S E London Cham Comm
Buckinghamshire > Milton Keynes & N Bucks Cham Comm
Bury St Edmunds Cham Comm & Ind
Cairngorms Cham Comm
Caithness & Sutherland Cham Comm
Cambridgeshire Chams Comm
Cham Comm Barnsley & Rotherham
Cham Comm Pembrokeshire
Chamber - Accredited Cham Comm Bedfordshire & Luton
Chams Comm NW

Channel Cham Comm
Cheshire > S Cheshire Cham Comm & Ind
Chester, Ellesmere Port & N Wales Cham Comm
Chichester Cham Comm & Ind
Cork Cham Comm [IRL]
Cornwall Cham Comm & Ind
Coventry & Warwickshire Cham Comm
Croydon Cham Comm & Ind
Cumbria Cham Comm
Dagenham > Barking & Dagenham Cham Comm
Derbyshire & Nottinghamshire Cham Comm
Devon > N Devon Cham Comm & Ind
Devon > S Devon Cham Comm
District Wigtown Cham Comm
Doncaster Cham
Dorset Cham Comm & Ind
Dover Dist Cham Comm & Ind
Drogheda Cham Comm [IRL]
Dublin Cham Comm [IRL]
Dudley > Black Country Cham Comm
Dumfries & Galloway Cham Comm
Dundalk Cham Comm [IRL]
Dundee & Angus Cham Comm
E Hampshire Cham Comm & Ind
E Lancs Cham Comm
Ealing Cham Comm
Eastbourne & District Cham Comm
Edinburgh Cham Comm
Ellesmere Port > Chester, Ellesmere Port & N Wales Cham Comm
Essex Chams Comm
Exeter Cham Comm
Exmouth Cham Tr & Comm
Fareham > Southampton & Fareham Cham Comm...
Fife Cham Comm & Enterprise
Fort William & District Chamber of Commerce
Galloway > Dumfries & Galloway Cham Comm
Galway Cham Comm [IRL]
Glasgow Cham Comm
Gloucestershire Cham Comm & Ind
Grampian > Aberdeen & Grampian Cham Comm
Grantham Cham Comm
Greater Manchester Cham Comm
Greenock Cham Comm
Greenwich > S E London Cham Comm
Guernsey Cham Comm
Gwent > Newport & Gwent Cham Comm & Ind
Hampshire > E Hants Cham Comm & Ind
Hampshire > N Hampshire Cham Comm
Hampshire > Portsmouth & SE Hampshire Cham Comm...
Harrow > N W Lond Cham Comm
Hastings > Ten Sixty Six Enterprise
Helensburgh & Lomond Cham Comm
Herefordshire & Worcestershire Cham Comm
Hertfordshire Cham Comm & Ind
Hertfordshire > Watford & W Herts Cham Comm & Ind
Hitchin Cham Comm & Ind
Hull & Humber Cham Comm...
Inverness Cham Comm
Iona > Mull & Iona Cham Comm
Isle of Man Cham Comm
Isle of Wight Cham Commerce, Tourism & Ind
Islington Cham Comm & Tr
Jersey Cham Comm & Ind Inc
Kensington & Chelsea Cham Comm
Kent Invicta Cham Comm
Kent > Thanet & E Kent Cham
Kent > W Kent Cham Comm & Ind
Kingston Cham Comm
Knowsley Cham Ind & Comm
Lancashire > E Lancs Cham Comm
Lancashire > N & Wstn Lancashire Cham Comm
Lancaster Dist Cham Comm
Leeds Cham Comm
Leicestershire Cham Comm
Leith Cham Comm
Lewisham > S E London Cham Comm
Limerick Cham Comm [IRL]
Lincolnshire Cham Comm & Ind
Lisburn Cham Comm
Liverpool Cham Comm & Ind
London Cham Comm & Ind
London > N W Lond Cham Comm
Londonderry Cham Comm
Luton > The Chamber... Bedfordshire & Luton
Macclesfield Cham Comm
Maidenhead & Dist Cham Comm
Merton Cham Comm

Mid Yorkshire Cham Comm & Ind
Milton Keynes & N Bucks Cham Comm
Moray Cham Comm
Mull & Iona Cham Comm
N Devon Cham Comm & Ind
N Hampshire Cham Comm & Ind
N Kent Cham Comm
N London Cham Comm
N Staffs Cham Comm & Ind
N W Lond Cham Comm
N & Wstn Lancs Cham Comm
Newcastle > N E Cham Comm, Tr & Ind
Newport & Gwent Cham Comm, Enterprise & Ind
Norfolk Cham Comm & Ind
Northamptonshire Cham Comm...
Norwich > Norfolk Cham Comm
Nottinghamshire > Derbyshire & Nottinghamshire Cham Comm
Orkney Cham Comm
Pembrokeshire - Cham Comm Pembrokeshire
Penzance Chamb Comm
Perthshire Cham Comm
Peterborough > Cambridgeshire Chams Comm
Plymouth Cham Comm & Ind
Portsmouth & S E Hampshire Cham Comm...
Redbridge Cham Comm
Renfrewshire Cham Comm
Richmond Cham Comm
Rotherham > Cham Comm Barnsley & Rotherham
S Cheshire Cham Comm & Ind
S Devon Cham Comm
S E London Cham Comm
Saint Albans District Cham Comm
Saint Austell Dist Cham Comm & Ind
Saint Helens Cham
Saint Leonards > Ten Sixty Six Enterprise
Sale > Altrincham & Sale Cham Comm
Salisbury & Dist Cham Comm & Ind
Sandwell > Black Country Cham Comm
Scot Borders Cham Comm
Sefton Cham Comm & Ind
Sevenoaks & District Cham Comm
Sheffield Cham Comm & Ind
Shropshire Chamber of Commerce & Enterprise
Solihull Cham Comm & Ind
Somerset Cham Comm & Ind
Southampton & Fareham Cham Comm & Ind
Southport > Sefton Cham Comm & Ind
Southwark Cham Comm
Staffordshire > N Staffordshire Cham Comm & Ind
Staffordshire > Southern Staffordshire Cham Comm & Ind
Sthn Staffordshire Cham Comm & Ind
Suffolk Cham Comm & Ind
Surrey Chams Comm
Sussex Cham Comm & Enterprise
Sutton Cham
Swansea > W Wales Cham Comm
Taunton Cham Comm
Tayside > Dundee & Angus Cham Comm
Ten Sixty Six Enterprise
Thames Valley Cham Comm & Ind
Thanet & E Kent Cham
Torbay > S Devon Cham Comm
Tralee Cham Comm [IRL]
W Kent Cham Comm & Ind
W Lothian Cham Comm
W Wales Cham Comm
Wales > Chester, Ellesmere Port & N Wales Cham Comm
Walsall > Black Country Cham Comm
Warrington Cham Comm & Ind
Warwickshire > Coventry & Warwickshire Cham Comm & Ind
Waterford Cham Comm [IRL]
Watford & W Herts Cham Comm & Ind
Wessex Assn Chams Comm
Western Isles Cham Comm
Wexford Cham Comm [IRL]
Weymouth & Portland Cham Comm...
Wicklow & District Cham Comm [IRL]
Wirral Cham Comm & Ind
Wolverhampton > Black Country Cham Comm
Worcestershire > Herefordshire & Worcestershire Cham Comm
Worcestershire > Herefordshire & Worcestershire Cham Comm
Worthing Cham Comm & Ind
York & N Yorkshire Cham Comm
Yorkshire > Mid Yorkshire Cham Comm & Ind

Chambers of commerce: overseas trade
Africa > Brit Cham Business Sthn Africa
Arab Brit Cham Comm

© CBD Research Ltd · Beckenham · BR3 5JS · Tel 020 8650 7745 · Fax 020 8650 0768 · E-mail cbd@cbdresearch.com · www.cbdresearch.com

Argentina > Brit Argentine Cham Comm
Argentina > Cámara Comercio Argentino Britanica
Australian Business
Austro-Brit Cham
Belgian-Luxembourg Cham Comm GB
Belgium > Brit Cham Comm Belgium
Brazil > Brit Cham Comm & Ind Brazil
Brazilian Cham Comm GB
Brit Amer Business Coun
Brit Amer Business Inc
Brit Argentine Cham Comm
Brit Bulgarian Cham Comm
Brit Canadian Cham Tr & Comm
Brit Cham Business Sthn Africa
Brit Cham Comm Belgium
Brit Cham Comm China - Beijing
Brit Cham Comm China - Shanghai
Brit Cham Comm Czech Republic
Brit Cham Comm Germany
Brit Cham Comm Hong Kong
Brit Cham Comm Hungary
Brit Cham Comm & Ind Brazil
Brit Cham Comm Italy
Brit Cham Comm Japan
Brit Cham Comm Korea
Brit Cham Comm Latvia
Brit Cham Comm Luxembourg
Brit Cham Comm Morocco
Brit Cham Comm Singapore
Brit Cham Comm Slovak Republic
Brit Cham Comm Spain
Brit Cham Comm Taipei
Brit Cham Comm Thailand
Brit Cham Comm Turkey
Brit Chilean Cham Comm
Brit & Colombian Cham Comm
Brit Hellenic Cham Comm
Brit New Zealand Tr Coun
Brit-Peruvian Cham
Brit-Polish Cham Comm [Lond]
Brit-Polish Cham Comm [Warsaw]
Brit-Portuguese Cham Comm
Brit Swedish Cham Comm Sweden
Brit-Swiss Cham Comm [Zürich]
Britain-Nepal Cham Comm
Britain Nigeria Business Coun
Bulgaria > Brit Bulgarian Cham Comm
Cámara Chileno Británica Comercio
Cámara Comercio Argentino Britanica
Cámara Comercio Británica AC [Mexico]
Cámara Comercio Colombo Británica
Cámara Comercio Uruguayo Británica
Cámara Venezolana Británica Comercio
Canada > Brit Canadian Cham Tr & Comm
Canada-UK Cham Comm
Chambre Comm Française GB
Chile > Brit Chilean Cham Comm
Chile > Cámara Chileno-Britanica Comercio
China > Brit Cham Comm China - Beijing
China > Brit Cham Comm China - Shanghai
Colombia > Brit & Colombian Cham Comm
Colombia > Cámara Comercio Colombo-Británica
Czech Republic > Brit Cham Comm Czech Republic
Danish-UK Cham Comm
Egyptian Brit Cham Comm
Finnish-Brit Cham Comm
France > Chambre Comm Française GB
Franco-British Chamber of Commerce & Industry
German-Brit Cham Ind & Comm
Germany > Brit Cham Comm Germany
Greece > Brit Hellenic Cham Comm
Hong Kong > Brit Cham Comm Hong Kong
Hungary > Brit Cham Comm Hungary
Italian Cham Comm Ind UK
Italy > Brit Cham Comm Italy
Japan > Brit Cham Comm Japan
Japanese Cham Comm & Ind UK
Korea > Brit Cham Comm Korea
Latvia > Brit Cham Comm Latvia
Luxembourg > Belgian-Luxembourg Cham Comm in GB
Luxembourg > Brit Cham Comm Luxembourg
Mexico > Cámara Comercio Británica AC
Morocco > Brit Cham Comm Morocco
Nepal > Britain-Nepal Cham Comm
Netherlands-Brit Cham Comm
New Zealand > Australian Business
New Zealand > Brit New Zealand Tr Coun

Nigeria > Britain Nigeria Business Coun
Norwegian-Brit Cham Comm
Peru > Brit-Peruvian Cham
Poland > Brit-Polish Cham Comm [Lond]
Poland > Brit-Polish Cham Comm [Warsaw]
Portugal > Brit-Portuguese Cham Comm
Portuguese Cham
Russia > Russo-Brit Cham Comm
Russo-Brit Cham Comm
S Africa > Brit Cham Business Sthn Africa
Singapore > Brit Cham Comm Singapore
Slovakia > Brit Cham Comm Slovak Republic
Spain > Brit Cham Comm Spain
Spanish Cham Comm GB
Sweden > Brit Swedish Cham Comm Sweden
Swedish Cham Comm UK
Switzerland > Brit-Swiss Cham Comm [Lond]
Switzerland > Brit Swiss Cham Comm [Zürich]
Taiwan > Brit Cham Comm Taipei
Thailand > Brit Cham Comm Thailand
Turkey > Brit Cham Comm Turkey
Turkish-Brit Cham Comm & Ind
Uruguay > Cámara Comercio Uruguayo-Británica
USA > Brit Amer Business Coun
USA > Brit Amer Business Inc
Venezuela > Cámara Venezolana Británica Comercio
Champagne
    Champagne Agents' Assn
    > + Wines & spirits: trade
Chandlers > Ships: stores & supplies
Channel Islands > individual island
Channel swimming (& crossing)
    Channel Crossing Assn
    Channel Swimming Assn
Channels (concrete) > Culverts & channels
Chapels > Church headings
Charcoal
    FCA Membership Ltd
Charcot-Marie-Tooth disease
    CMT UK
Charcuterie
    UK Charcuterie Gld
Charities
    Assn Charitable Foundations
    Assn Charities
    Assn Charity Indep Examiners
    Assn Charity Shops
    Assn Med Res Charities
    Charities' Property Assn
    Charity Christmas Card Coun
    Charity Finance Directors' Gp
    Charity Law Assn
    Charity Tax Gp
    Inst Fundraising
    Public Fundraising Regulatory Assn
    Small Charities Coalition
Charities: guidance & lists > + Introduction paragraph 6
Charles I King of England
    R Martyr Church U
    Sealed Knot
    Soc King Charles Martyr
Charts (nautical)
    Chart & Nautical Instrument Tr Assn
Charter operators > Travel & tourism
Charter trustee towns
    Assn Charter Trustee Towns &... Couns
Chauffeurs
    Brit Chauffeurs Gld
    London Private Hire Car Assn
Cheerleading
    Brit Cheerleading Assn
Cheese
    Brit Goat Soc
    Brit Sheep Dairying Assn
    Provision Tr Fedn
    Specialist Cheesemakers' Assn
    Stilton Cheese Makers Assn
    UK Cheese Guild
Chefs
    Brit Culinary Fedn
    Fedn Chefs Scotland
    Master Chefs GB
    Welsh Culinary Assn
    > + Catering
Chelonia
    Brit Chelonia Gp
    Nat Tortoise Club

Tortoise Trust
> + Herpetology
Chemical allergy > Allergy
Chemical engineering
Brit Chemical Engg Contrs Assn
Instn Chemical Engrs
Chemical hazards
Brit Occupational Hygiene Soc
Chemical Hazards Communication Soc
Chemical industry & trade
BTC Testing Advisory Gp
Chemical Business Assn
Chemical & Indl Consultants' Assn
Chemical Inds Assn
Ir Chemical Marketers Assn
PharmaChemical Ireland
Soc Chemical Ind
Chemical specialities
Brit Assn Chemical Specialities
Chemical waste
Chemical Recycling Assn
> + Reclamation & recycling
Chemicals: packaging
Indl Packaging Assn
Chemistry
Inst Chemistry Ireland [IRL]
R Instn GB
R Soc Chemistry
Resource Use Inst
> + specific applications
Chemistry: history
Soc Hist Alchemy & Chemistry
Chemists & druggists > Pharmaceuticals; Pharmacy
Chemotherapy > Pharmacology & chemotherapy
Cheques
Brit Cheque Cashers Assn
> + Banking
Chess
Brit Correspondence Chess Assn
Chess Scotland
English Chess Federation
Welsh Chess U
Chest diseases > Thoracic diseases
Chesterton (Gilbert Keith)
Chesterton Soc
Chickens > Poultry
Child abuse
Assn Child Abuse Lawyers
Brit Assn Study & Prevention Child Abuse
Falsely Accused Carers & Teachers
Nat Assn People Abused Childhood
> + Children: welfare
Child contact centres
Nat Assn Child Contact Centres
Child Support Agency
Nat Assn Child Support Action
Childbirth > Maternity; Midwifery; Obstetrics & gynaecology
Childless > Fertility
Childminding (home/workplace)
Nat Childminding Assn
NI Childminding Assn
Scot Childminding Assn
> + Children: welfare;   Fostering & foster parents
Children: books
Children's Books Hist Soc
Fedn Children's Book Gps
George MacDonald Soc
Violet Needham Soc
> + Bookselling; individual authors
Children: clothing > Clothing
Children: cot deaths > Cot deaths
Children: death by accident/violence
Compassionate Friends
RoadPeace
Children: gifted
Nat Assn Able Children in Educ
Nat Assn Gifted Children
Children: handicapped
Afasic
Assn Spina Bifida & Hydrocephalus
Assn Wheelchair Children
Brit Assn Teachers Deaf
Capability Scotland
Cedar Foundation
Children's Heart Assn
Deaf Educ Listening & Talking
Foresight

Mencap
nasen
Nat Assn Toy & Leisure Libraries
Nat Portage Assn
REACH - Assn Children with Hand or Arm Deficiency
Rescare
Scope
SEBDA
Sense
Soc Stars
STEPS
> + specific types of handicap
Children: health > Paediatrics
Children: in hospital
Action Sick Children
Children Hospital Ireland
Nat Assn Educ Sick Children
Nat Assn Hospital Play Staff
Children: psychology
Assn Child & Adolescent Mental Health
Assn Child Psychotherapists
Assn Infant Mental Health UK
Soc Reproductive & Infant Psychology
Children: & the theatre > Theatre: young people
Children: welfare
4Children
Action Rights Children
Assn Children's Palliative Care
Assn Families Adopted Abroad
Assn Shared Parenting
Brit Assn Study & Prevention Child Abuse
Children 1st
Children Living Inherited Metabolic Diseases
Children's Rights Alliance England
Children Scotland
Families Need Fathers
Family Rights Gp
Foundation Study Infant Deaths
Heart Line Assn
Indep Children's Homes Assn
Ir Soc Prevention Cruelty Children
LOOK
Nat Assn Child Contact Centres
Nat Assn Child Support Action
Nat Assn Family Inf Services
Nat Care Assn
Nat Deaf Children's Soc
Nat Soc Prevention Cruelty to Children
One Parent Families Scotland
Rett Syndrome Assn
> + Fostering & foster parents; Social: service;   Welfare: administration
Chile
Anglo-Chilean Soc
Brit Chilean Cham Comm
Chilled beams & ceilings
Chilled Beam & Ceiling Assn
Chilled food > Food: frozen & chilled
Chimneys
Brit Flue & Chimney Mfrs' Assn
Nat Assn Chimney Engrs
Nat Assn Chimney Sweeps
Refractory Users Federation
Stove Industry Alliance
China (ceramic) > Ceramics; Pottery
China (country)
Brit Assn Chinese Studies
Brit Cham Comm China - Beijing
Brit Cham Comm China - Shanghai
China-Britain Business Coun
Soc Anglo-Chinese Understanding
China clay (Kaolin)
Cornish Cham Mines & Minerals
Kaolin & Ball Clay Assn
Trevithick Soc
Chinchillas
Nat Chinchilla Soc
Chinese food
Chinese Takeaway Assn
Chinese medicine
Acupuncture Soc
Assn Traditional Chinese Medicine
Register Chinese Herbal Medicine
> + Complementary medicine
Chippendale (Thomas)
Chippendale Soc
Chips & crisps > Potatoes: products

 © CBD Research Ltd · Beckenham · BR3 5JS · Tel 020 8650 7745 · Fax 020 8650 0768 · E-mail cbd@cbdresearch.com · www.cbdresearch.com

Chiropody & podiatry
    Alliance Private...Chiropody & Podiatry Practitioners
    Brit Chiropody & Podiatry Assn
    Inst Chiropodists & Podiatrists
    Ir Chiropodists/Podiatrists Org
    SMAE Fellowship
    Soc Chiropodists & Podiatrists
Chiropractic
    Brit Chiropractic Assn
    Chiropractic Patients' Assn
    McTimoney Chiropractic Assn
    Scot Chiropractic Assn
    Utd Chiropractic Assn
Chivalry
    Heraldry Soc
Chocolate > Cocoa & chocolate; Confectionery
Choirs & choral music
    Assn Brit Choral Dirs
    Assn Ir Choirs
    Campaign Traditional Cathedral Choir
    Choir Schools Assn
    Friends Cathedral Music
    Gregorian Assn
    Making Music
    Nat Assn Choirs
    Nat Youth Choirs GB
    R Choral Soc
    R Coll Organists
    R School Church Music
    Sing for Pleasure
    Ulster Soc Organists & Choirmasters
    Welsh Amat Music Fedn
    > + Cathedral & church music
Cholesterol
    Heart UK
    > + Cardiology
Chopin (Frédéric)
    Chopin Soc (Lond)
Choral music > Choirs & choral music
Choreography
    Dance UK
    Laban Gld Movement & Dance
    R Academy Dance
Christian activities
    Arts Centre Gp
    Assn Denominational Histl Socs Cognate Libs
    Christian Evidence Soc
    Christian Social Order
    Crusaders
    Librarians' Christian Fellowship
    Mothers' U
    > + Missionary organisations; Welfare organisations
Christian education
    Assn Christian Teachers
    Christian Educ
    Nat Assn Teachers Religious Educ
    Nat Soc (CofE) Promoting Religious Educ
Christmas cards
    Charity Christmas Card Coun
Christmas trees
    Brit Christmas Tree Growers Assn
    > + Trees
Chromatography
    Chromatographic Soc
Chrysanthemums
    Nat Chrysanthemum Soc
    UK Chrysanthemum Growers' Assn
    > + Flowers, flower arrangement & floristry
Church: bells > Bellringing
Church: brasses & monuments > Brasses & church monuments
Church: buildings
    Brit Assn Friends Museums
    Capel
    Cathedral Architects Assn
    Chapels Soc
    Ecclesiological Soc
    Friends Friendless Churches
    Nat Churchwatch
    Pugin Gld
    Round Tower Churches Soc
    Save our Parsonages
    Soc Friends St George's... [Windsor]
    > + Historic buildings
Church: editors
    Assn Church Editors
Church: of England
    English Clergy Assn

    Modern Churchpeople's U
    Protestant Reformation Soc
Church: of England liturgy > Liturgy
Church: history & records
    Canterbury & York Soc
    Catholic Record Soc
    Church England Record Soc
    Ecclesiastical Hist Soc
    Soc Archivists
    > + Parish registers; individual churches
Church: monuments > Brasses & church monuments
Church: music > Cathedral & church music; Choirs & choral music; Liturgy
Church: services > Liturgy
Church: shops > Cathedral & church shops
Churchyards > Cemeteries & churchyards
Cider & perry
    Craft Brewing Assn
    Nat Assn Cider Makers
    Three Counties Cider & Perry Assn
CIDP > Guillain-Barré Syndrome
Cigars & cigarettes
    Imported Tobacco Products Advy Coun
    Nat Assn Cigarette Machine Operators
    > + Tobacco
Cigars & cigarettes: accessories
    Cartophilic Soc
    Cigarette Packet Collectors Club
Ciné equipment > Audio visual aids & equipment; Photographic industry & trade
Cinema > Film
Cinema buildings
    Cinema Theatre Assn
    Mercia Cinema Soc
Cinema organs
    Cinema Organ Soc
    > + Organs, organists & organ music
Circles (in crops & corn) > Crop: circles
Circuit plans
    Soc Cirplanologists
Circuits > Printed circuits
Circuses & circus artistes
    Assn Circus Proprietors
    Captive Animals' Protection Soc
    Circus Friends Association of Great Britain
    Circus Soc
Cisterns, drums & tanks
    Assn Tank & Cistern Mfrs
    Indl Packaging Assn
Citizens' Advice Bureaux > Advice centres & bureaux
City farms
    Fedn City Farms & Community Gardens
Civil aviation > Aviation
Civil defence & industrial emergencies
    Emergency Planning Soc
    Inst Civil Protection & Emergency Mgt
    SIESO
Civil engineering
    Bridge Deck Waterproofing Assn
    Brit Civil Engg Test Eqpt Mfrs Assn
    Confedn Construction Specialists
    Construction Confedn
    Construction Emplrs Fedn
    Instn Civil Engg Surveyors
    Instn Civil Engrs
    Instn Structural Engrs
    Pipe Jacking Assn
    > + Construction industries
Civil liberties > Individual freedom
Civil Service
    Assn Higher Civil & Public Servants [IRL]
    Assn Revenue & Customs
    Bar Assn Local Govt & Public Service
    First Division Assn
    NI Public Service Alliance
    Prospect
    Public & Comml Services U
    > + Public administration
Civil War (English)
    Cromwell Assn
    English Civil War Soc
    John Hampden Soc
    Pike & Shot Soc
    Sealed Knot
Cladding
    Brit Precast Concrete Fedn
    Insulated Render & Cladding Assn

Metal Cladding & Roofing Manufacturers Association Ltd
> + Building materials & supplies
Clairvoyance
Brit Astrological & Psychic Soc
> + Paranormal & psychical research
Clare (John) 1793-1864
John Clare Soc
Clarinets & saxophones
Clarinet Heritage Soc
Clarinet & Saxophone Soc GB
Classic vehicles > Motor vehicles: historic
Classical studies
Assn Latin Teaching
Brit Academy
Brit Epigraphy Soc
Classical Assn
Friends Classics
Jt Assn Classical Teachers
Soc Promotion Hellenic Studies
Soc Promotion Roman Studies
Virgil Soc
Classification
Brit Classification Soc
Clay & clay products
Brit Ceramic Confedn
Clay Pipe Devt Assn
Clay Roof Tile Coun
Intl Masonry Soc
Kaolin & Ball Clay Assn
Mineralogical Soc
Resource Use Inst
Scot Emplrs Coun Clay Inds
> + Bricks; Pottery; Tiles (floor & wall)
Clay target (pigeon) shooting
Brit Skeet Shooting Assn
Clay Pigeon Shooting Assn
Scot Clay Target Assn
> + Shooting
Clean air > Air: pollution
Cleaning & cleaning science
Assn Bldg Cleaning Direct Service Providers
Assn Healthcare Cleaning Profls
Brit Cleaning Coun
Brit Inst Cleaning Science
Ir Contract Cleaning Assn
Cleaning equipment
Assn Healthcare Cleaning Profls
BEAMA
Cleaning & Hygiene Suppliers' Assn
Indl Cleaning Machine Mfrs Assn
UK Cleaning Products Ind Assn
> + Soap & detergents
Cleaning & dyeing
Gld Cleaners & Launderers
Nat Assn Launderette Ind
Soc Laundry Engrs & Allied Trs
Textile Services Assn
Ulster Launderers Assn
Cleanrooms
Scot Soc Contamination Control
Cleansing > Street cleaning
Clearing services (banking)
Assn Payment Clearing Services
Cleft lip & palate
Cleft Lip & Palate Assn
Clematis
Brit Clematis Soc
Clergy
English Clergy Assn
> + Church: of England; other individual churches
Clerks of local councils > Local government: officers
Clerks of works
Inst Clerks Works
Cliff (Clarice)
Clarice Cliff Collectors Club
Climate change
Campaign Climate Change
Global Commons Inst
Scientists Global Responsibility
Stop Climate Chaos Coalition
> + Environment; Meteorology
Climbing
Alpine Club
Assn Brit Climbing Walls
Assn Heads Outdoor Educ Centres
Brit Assn Mountain Guides
Brit Mountaineering Coun

Mountain Leader Training Assn
Mountaineering Coun Ireland
Mountaineering Coun Scotland
Clinical biochemistry
Assn Clinical Biochemistry
> + Biochemistry & biotechnology
Clinical data management
Assn Clinical Data Mgt
Brit In Vitro Diagnostics Assn
Clinical immunology > Allergy
Clinical pathology
Assn Clinical Pathologists
Clinical pharmacy > Pharmacy
Clinical trials
Brit Assn Res Quality Assurance
Clinical Contract Res Assn
Fac Pharmaceutical Med
Inst Clinical Res
Clocks > Horology
Close (Sir Charles Frederick Arden-)
Charles Close Soc
Closed-circuit television > Television: closed circuit
Closures (cork, metal, plastic)
Cork Ind Fedn
Metal Packaging Mfrs Assn
Clothing
ASBCI - Forum Clothing & Textiles
Brit Apparel & Textile Confedn
Brit Clothing Ind Assn
Fedn Clothing Designers & Executives
Ir Clothing & Textiles Alliance [IRL]
Labour behind the Label
Nat Childrenswear Assn
Register Apparel & Textile Designers
Schoolwear Assn
Textile Inst Intl
UK Fashion Exports
> + Fashion; Protective clothing/equipment; specific items of
clothing
Clowns > Circuses & circus artistes
Club foot > Talipes
Clubs
Assn Inter-Varsity Clubs
Assn London Clubs
C'ee Registered Clubs Assns
Nat Assn Rly Clubs
Noctis
Working Men's Club & Inst U
> + specific activities or interests
Clumsy child syndrome
Dyspraxia Foundation
Clutch facings
Brit Friction Materials Coun
CMV > Cytomegalovirus
Coaches > Bus & coach operators;   Passenger transport
Coaches: sports
Sports Coach UK
> + individual sports
Coaching
Assn Coaching
Coal: mining
Confedn UK Coal Producers
Fedn Indep Mines
Minerals Engg Soc
N England Inst Mining & Mechanical Engrs
Nat U Mineworkers
U Democratic Mineworkers
Coal: trade
Coal Mchts Assn Scotland
Coal Mchts Fedn
> + Solid fuel
Coarse fishing > Fishing (sport)
Coastal history
Nautical Heritage Assn
Coastal waters > Estuaries; Water
Coastal lookout stations
Nat Coastwatch Instn
Coated abrasives > Abrasives
Coated macadam > Asphalt & coated macadam
Coatings
Brit Coatings Fedn
Brit Textile Technology Gp
Brit Urethane Foam Contrs Assn
Eur Liquid Waterproofing Assn
Paint Res Assn
Performance Textiles Assn

© CBD Research Ltd · Beckenham · BR3 5JS · Tel 020 8650 7745 · Fax 020 8650 0768 · E-mail cbd@cbdresearch.com · www.cbdresearch.com

Sprayed Concrete Assn
Thermal Spraying & Surface Engg Assn
Cobbett (William)
William Cobbett Soc
Cobles & keelboats
Coble & Keelboat Soc
> + Ships: history & preservation
Cobnuts
Kentish Cobnuts Assn
Cobs > Horses & ponies
Cochlea implants
Brit Academy Audiology
Nat Cochlear Implant Users Assn
Cocktails
UK Bartenders Gld
Cocoa & chocolate
Chocolate Soc
Fedn Cocoa Commerce
Food & Drink Fedn
Coconut matting
Coir Assn
Codes of practice: standardisation
BSI
Coeliac disease
Coeliac Soc Ireland
Coeliac UK
Coffee
Brit Coffee Assn
Brit Soluble Coffee Packers & Importers Assn
Café Soc
Coffins
Funeral Furnishing Mfrs Assn
> + Burial & cremation
Coin operated machines > Amusements & coin operated machines; Automatic
vending
Coins & medals > Numismatics
Coir
Coir Assn
Coke
Coke Oven Mgrs Assn
> + Solid fuel
Cold rolled metal
Cold Rolled Sections Assn
> + Metal: working
Cold sores > Herpes
Cold storage > Refrigeration; Temperature controlled storage
Cold War
Subterranea Britannica
Coleridge (Samuel Taylor)
Friends Coleridge
Colitis/colostomy
Crohn's Disease Childhood Res Assn
IA
Nat Advy Service Parents Children with a Stoma
Nat Assn Colitis & Crohn's Disease
Collecting hobbies > Object(s) collected
Collection agencies > Credit: reporting
Colleges > Adult education; Education; Universities
Colleges: heads > Heads of schools & colleges
Collieries > Coal: mining
Collins ([William] Wilkie)
Wilkie Collins Soc
Coloboma
Micro & Anophthalmic Children's Soc
Colombia
Brit & Colombian Cham Comm
Cámara Comercio Colombo Británica
Colostomy > Colitis/colostomy
Colour
Brit Colour Makers Assn
Colour Gp
Oil & Colour Chemists Assn
Soc Dyers & Colourists
> + Paint
Colour: problem > Race relations
Colposcopy
Brit Assn Sexual Health & HIV
Combat (dramatic) > Fights (stage & film)
Combustion engineering
Combustion Engg Assn
ICOM Energy Assn
Comedy & comedy writers
Brit Comedy Soc
Brit Soc Comedy Writers
Comedy Writers' Assn UK
Comics
Comics Creators Gld

Commemorative items & souvenirs
Commemorative Collectors Soc
Commemoratives Museum Trust
Commerce
Assn Graduate Recruiters
Assn MBAs
Brit Chams Comm
Fedn Crafts & Comm
R Soc . . . Arts
R Soc Edinburgh
> + Chambers of commerce
Commercial management > Management
Commercial property agents
Indl Agents Soc
Instn Comml & Business Agents
> + Estate agents
Commercial travellers > Sales management & representation
Commercial vehicles
Historic Comml Vehicle Soc
Nat Assn Road Transport Museums
> + Motor headings
Commissioning (construction industry)
Commissioning Specialists Assn
Commodities
Fedn Commodity Assns
Futures & Options Association
> + names of specific commodities
Common Market > European Union
Common Prayer
Alcuin Club
Prayer Book Soc
Commons & open spaces > Open spaces; Parks & gardens
Commonwealth affairs
English Speaking U C'wealth
R Over-Seas League
Commonwealth (1649-1688)
Cromwell Assn
Communication services
ALTO [IRL]
Communications Mgt Assn
Fedn Communication Services
ICT Ireland
Momentum - Northern Ireland ICT Fedn
Onsite Communications Association
> + Cable & satellite communications
Communications
Brit Assn Communicators in Business
Inst Sound & Communications Engrs
Publicity Club Lond
> + form of communication
Communications: fraud
Telecommunications UK Fraud Forum
Community: care
Nat Care Assn
Community: development
Community Devt Finance Assn
Devt Trusts Assn
Devt Trusts Assn Scot
Scot Business Community
Community: drama > Theatre
Community: education
Fedn Community Devt Learning
Nat Assn Youth & Community Educ Officers
Community: medicine > Medical officers; Public health
Community: music
Sound Sense
Community: organisations
Assn Community Rail Partnerships
Assn Scot Community Couns
Campaign Community Banking Services
Community Foundation Network
Community Transport Assn
Fedn City Farms & Community Gardens
Nat Fedn Community Orgs
Community: resources (mobile) > Mobile community resources
Community: service (voluntary)
Assn Res Voluntary & Community Sector
Attend
Brit Red Cross Soc
Community Service Volunteers
Inst Volunteering Res
Nat Assn Round Tables
Returned Volunteer Action
Scot Coun Voluntary Orgs
Voluntary Service Overseas
Volunteering England

Women's R Voluntary Service
> + Welfare headings
Commuters > Passenger transport
Companies: independent > Business
Companies: quoted/London Stock Exchange
Quoted Companies Alliance
Company: directors
Inst Directors
Inst Directors Ireland
> + Management
Company: registration agents
Assn Company Registration Agents
Company: secretaries
Inst Business Admin
Inst Chart Secretaries & Administrators
> + Secretaries & administrators
Comparative law > Law: comparative
Compasses & compass adjusting
Chart & Nautical Instrument Tr Assn
Compères
Gld Profl Toastmasters
> + Toastmasters & masters of ceremonies
Complementary medicine
Assn Light Touch Therapists
Assn Physical & Natural Therapists
Assn Stress Therapists
Brit Complementary Medicine Assn
Brit Register Complementary Practitioners
Complementary Med Assn
Fedn Holistic Therapists
Inst Complementary & Natural Medicine
On Site Massage Assn
Register Chinese Herbal Medicine
SMAE Fellowship
UK Polarity Therapy Assn
> + specific forms eg Osteopathy
Composers: music > see individual by name
Composing > Music: composing
Composites
Composites UK
Electrical Insulation Assn
Composts & composting
Assn Organics Recycling
Community Composting Network
Composting Assn Ireland
Growing Media Assn
John Innes Mfrs Assn
Comprehensive education
Campaign State Educ
> + Education
Compressed air
Brit Compressed Air Soc
Compressed gases
Brit Compressed Gases Assn
Compulsive/obsessive disorders > Obsessive/compulsive disorders
Computer & video games
Brit Academy Film & TV Arts
Entertainment & Leisure Software Pubrs Assn (UK)
Entertainment Retailers Assn
Tiga
Computers
Brit Computer Assn Blind
Brit Computer Soc
Intellect
Ir Computer Soc
Nat Assn Specialist Computer Retailers
Profl Computing Assn
> + Software headings
Computers: application
Assn Hist & Computing
Assn Survey Computing
Construction Ind Computing Assn
Dental System Suppliers Assn
eLearning Network
INCA [IRL]
Instn Engg & Technology
Nat Outsourcing Assn
Computers: chips
Fedn Technological Inds
Computers: in education
Naace
Computers: historic
Computer Consvn Soc
Computers: professionals
Assn Certified IT Profls
Assn Computer Engrs & Technicians
Assn Computer Profls

Assn Indep Computer Specialists
Inst IT Training
Instn Analysts & Programmers
Mac Technology Assn
Soc Computers & Law
Computers: supplies for
Indep Print Inds Assn
Legal Software Suppliers Assn
UK Cartridge Remanufacturers Assn
Computers: vision Machine vision
Concentrates > Animal feed
Concerts
Assn Brit Concert Promoters
Concert Artistes' Association
Concert Promoters Assn
Hallé Concerts Soc
Nat Early Music Assn
> + Music; Orchestras
Conchology
Brit Shell Collectors Club
Conchological Soc
Malacological Soc Lond
Concrete & concrete products
Assn Concrete Indl Flooring Contrs
Brit Cement Assn
Brit Precast Concrete Fedn
Britpave
Concrete Bridge Devt Gp
Concrete Mfrs Assn Ireland
Concrete Repair Assn
Concrete Soc
Construct, Concrete Structures Gp
Corrosion Prevention Assn
Inst Concrete Technology
Instn Civil Engrs
Intl Glassfibre Reinforced Concrete Assn
Intl Masonry Soc
Ir Concrete Fedn
Ir Concrete Soc
Post Tensioning Assn
Sprayed Concrete Assn
UK Quality Ash Assn
Concrete cutting
Drilling & Sawing Assn
Concrete pumping
Construction Plant-hire Assn
Conductors: music > individual by name
Cones & cylinders (road)
Retroreflective Eqpt Mfrs Assn
> + Road: lighting, markings & traffic signs
Confectionery
Food & Drink Fedn
Nat Assn Master Bakers
Retail Confectioners & Tobacconists Assn
> + Baking
Conferences & conventions
Assn Brit Profl Conf Organisers
Assn Confs & Events
Eventia
Events Sector Ind Trg Org
Meetings Ind Assn
Soc Event Organisers
> + Exhibitions
Confinements (childbirth) > Maternity
Conflict & anger management
Brit Assn Anger Mgt
Conflict Res Soc
Inst Conflict Mgt
Personal Safety Assn
Congenital defects
Foresight
STEPS
> + Birthmarks & disfigurement;   Children: Handicapped
Congestion charging
Transport-Watch
Congregational Church
Utd Reformed Church Hist Soc
Conifers
Brit Christmas Tree Growers Assn
Brit Conifer Soc
Horticultural Trs Assn
> + Trees
Conjuring & magic
Brit Magical Soc
Magic Circle
Connective tissue disorders
Brit Coalition Heritable Disorders Connective Tissue

© CBD Research Ltd · Beckenham · BR3 5JS · Tel 020 8650 7745 · Fax 020 8650 0768 · E-mail cbd@cbdresearch.com · www.cbdresearch.com

Conrad (Joseph) 1857-1924
        Joseph Conrad Soc
Conservation
        Alliance Religions & Consvn
        Assn Envt Conscious Bldg
        Assn Protection Rural Scotland
        Brit Assn Shooting & Consvn
        Brit Trust Consvn Volunteers
        Campaign Protect Rural England
        Countryside Mgt Assn
        English Historic Towns Forum
        Environmental Investigation Agency
        Farming & Wildlife Advy Gp
        Friends Earth
        Inst Consvn
        Nat Assn UK Regionally Important Geological Sites
        Nat Trust
        Nat Trust Ireland
        Nat Trust Scotland
        Scot Wild Land Gp
        Selborne Soc
        Soc Envtl Exploration
        TimeWatch
        > + specific subjects eg Architecture; Natural history
Conservation: area organisations
        Black Country Soc
        Campaign Protection Rural Wales
        Dartmoor Presvn Assn
        Gower Soc
        NI Countryside Staff Assn
        Northumberland & Newcastle Soc
        S Downs Soc
        Ulster Soc Protection Countryside
        > + Nature conservation: local reserves
Conservative politics
        Tory Reform Gp
Conservatories > Glasshouses & conservatories
Conservators (art) > Art: conservation
Constitutional reform
        Unlock Democracy
Construction equipment
        Brit Compressed Air Soc
        Construction Eqpt Assn
        Construction Fixings Assn
        Construction Plant-hire Assn
        Construction Products Assn
        Construction Specialists Gp
        Contractors Mechanical Plant Engrs
        Scot Plant Owners Assn
        > + Materials: management/handling; specific items of equipment
Construction history
        Construction Hist Soc
Construction industries
        Assn Indep Construction Adjudicators
        Assn Project Safety
        Brit Civil Engg Test Eqpt Mfrs Assn
        Brit Constructional Steelwork Assn
        Builders' Conf
        Building Cost Infm Service
        Chart Inst Architectural Technologists
        Commissioning Specialists Assn
        Confedn Construction Specialists
        Construction Confedn
        Construction Ind Computing Assn
        Construction Ind Coun
        Construction Ind Fedn [IRL]
        Construction Ind Inf Gp
        Construction Ind Res & Infm Assn
        Construction Ind Tr Alliance
        Gld Builders & Contrs
        Inst Construction Mgt
        Inst Construction Specialists
        Instn Civil Engg Surveyors
        Instn Planning Supervisors
        Major Projects Assn
        Specialist Engg Contrs Gp
        Steel Construction Inst
        > + Building
Construction law & control > Law: construction
Construction materials > Building materials & supplies
Construction surveying
        Soc Construction & Quantity Surveyors
Constructional steelwork > Construction industries
Consultants > field of consultancy
Consumer affairs & protection
        Assn Public Analysts
        Assn Public Analysts Scotland

        Consumer Protection Assn
        Consumers' Assn
        Consumers Assn Ireland
        Inst Consumer Affairs
        Nat Consumer Fedn
        Trading Standards Inst
        > + Trading standards
Consumer credit > Credit: trade
Contact lens
        Assn Contact Lens Mfrs
        Brit Contact Lens Assn
        > + Optical industry
Containers > specific type of container
Containers: freight > Freight transport; Materials: management/handling
Contamination control > Cleanrooms; Land: contaminated
Contemporary art > Art & artists
Contemporary history > History
Continuing education > Adult education; Education
Continuing professional development
        Inst Continuing Profl Devt
Contraception > Family planning
Contract services
        Assn Catering Excellence
        Brit Contract Furnishing Assn
        Brit Vehicle Rental & Leasing Assn
        Cleaning & Support Services Assn
        Contract Flooring Assn
Contractors
        Profl Contrs Gp
        > + specific activity
Contractors plant > Construction equipment
Control engineering
        Assn Electrical & Mechanical Trs
        Assn Instrumentation, Control, Automation...
        BEAMA
        Brit Fluid Power Assn
        Electrical Contrs Assn
        Evaluation Intl
        ICOM Energy Assn
        Instn Engg & Technology
        Sira
        Solids Handling & Processing Assn
        > + Automation
Convent schools > Independent & public schools
Conventions > Conferences & conventions
Conveyancing
        Assn Lawyers & Legal Advisors
        Soc Licensed Conveyancers
        > + Property & land owners
Conveyors > Lifting & loading equipment
Cookery
        Academy Culinary Arts
        Craft Gld Chefs
        Master Chefs GB
        Welsh Culinary Assn
        > + Catering; Chefs
Cookware > Catering: equipment; Hardware & housewares
Cooling towers
        Water Mgt Soc
Cooperage
        Nat Cooperage Fedn
Co-operative movement
        Co-operatives UK Ltd
        Ir Co-op Org Soc
        Nat Assn Bldg Co-ops [IRL]
        Nat Assn Co-operative Officials
        UK Soc Co-operative Studies
        > + Agriculture: cooperatives
Co-partnership: industrial > Industrial involvement & participation
Copper
        Brit Non-Ferrous Metals Fedn
        Copper Devt Assn
Coppice crafts
        Brit Stickmakers Gld
        FCA Membership Ltd
Copyright
        Anti Copying Design
        Authors' Licensing & Collecting Soc
        Brit Assn Picture Libraries & Agencies
        Brit Soc Plant Breeders
        Chart Inst Patent Attorneys
        Creator's Rights Alliance
        Design & Artists Copyright Soc
        Fedn Copyright Theft
        Intellectual Property Lawyers Assn
        Ir Nat Fedn Copyright Theft
        Licensing Executives Soc

MCPS-PRS Alliance
Phonographic Performance
Phonographic Performance (Ireland)
Publishers Licensing Soc
Video Performance Ltd
Writers' Copyright Assn
> + Patents & trade marks
Copyshops > Quickprinters & copyshops
Copywriting
Inst Copywriting
Coracles
Coracle Soc
Cork
Contract Flooring Assn
Cork Ind Fedn
Corn > Agriculture: merchants; Flour; Grain
Corn circles > Crop: circles
Corn dollies
Gld Straw Craftsmen
Cornish pasties
Cornish Pasty Assn
Cornwall & Cornish language
Cornish Language Coun
Kesva an Taves Kernewek
London Cornish Assn
R Cornwall Agricl Assn
R Instn Cornwall
S W Coast Path Assn
Trevithick Soc
Coronary diseases > Cardiology
Coroners
Coroners Soc E&W
Corporate hospitality
Eventia
Soc Event Organisers
> + Catering; Shows & events
Corporate trustees > Trusts, trusteeship & estate planning
Correspondence colleges
Assn Brit Correspondence Colls
Corrosion
Corrosion Prevention Assn
Galvanizers Assn
Inst Corrosion
Inst Materials, Minerals & Mining
Thermal Spraying & Surface Engg Assn
Corrugated paper > Packaging
Corruption
Transparency Intl (UK)
Cosmetic items (collecting)
Brit Compact Collectors' Soc
Cosmetics
Brit Fragrance Assn
Cosmetic, Toiletry & Perfumery Assn
Ir Cosmetics, Detergents... Products Assn
Soc Cosmetic Scientists
Cosmetology & cosmetic surgery
Brit Assn Aesthetic Plastic Surgeons
Brit Assn Cosmetic Doctors
Brit Assn Plastic, Reconstructive & Aesthetic Surgeons
> + Beauty specialists/treatment
Cosmology
Traditional Cosmology Soc
Cost management
Assn Cost Engrs
Assn Cost Mgt Consultants
Costume history, design & conservation
Brit Costume Assn
Costume Soc
Costume Soc Scotland
Dolmetsch Hist Dance Soc
Dress & Textile Specialists
Medieval Dress & Textile Soc
Textile Soc
Cot deaths
Foundation Study Infant Deaths
Ir Sudden Infant Death Assn
Cottage gardens
Cottage Garden Soc
> + Gardens & gardening
Cotton > Textile headings
Council tax
IsItFair
Scot Assessors' Assn
Councillors > Local government
Counselling
Brit Assn Counselling & Psychotherapy
COSCA

Counselling
Inst Guidance Counsellors [IRL]
Ir Assn Counselling & Psychotherapy
Nat Assn Counsellors, Hypnotherapists...
Psychiatric Rehabilitation Assn
Universities Psychotherapy & Counselling Assn
> + field of counselling
Counterfeiting
Anti Counterfeiting Gp
Counties (British)
Assn Brit Counties
Country dancing & music > Folk dance & song
Countryside preservation > Conservation; Nature conservation
County agricultural societies > Agriculture: county societies
County archaeological societies > Archaeology: county societies
County councils > Local government
County history > Archaeology;   Records: historical
Courier services
Despatch Assn
Inst Couriers
Nat Courier Assn
Courtesy
Campaign Courtesy
Courts of law > Law headings; Magistrates & magistrates courts
Courts (royal)
Soc Court Studies
> + Monarchy
Covenanters (Scottish)
Scot Covenanter Memorials Assn
Cowboys > American 'West'
Cradles & suspended platforms
Construction Plant-hire Assn
Indl Rope Access Tr Assn
Nat Access & Scaffolding Confedn
Specialist Access Engg & Maintenance Assn
Crafts & craftsmanship
Art Workers Gld
Brit Toymakers Gld
Gld Master Craftsmen
Nat Assn Advisers... Design & Technology
Rural Crafts Assn
Soc Designer Craftsmen
Voluntary Arts Network
Wales Craft Coun
> + individual crafts
Cranes
Construction Plant-hire Assn
Heavy Transport Assn
> + Lifting & loading equipment
Cranio- > Head entries
Craniosacral therapy
Cranio Sacral Soc
Craniosacral Therapy Assn
Headlines
Cream > Dairying
Creationism
Biblical Creation Soc
Credit & magnetic strip(e) cards
Assn Automatic Identification ...Capture
> + Banking
Credit hire: vehicles
Nat Assn Credit Hire Operators
Credit: reporting
Civil Court Users Assn
Consumer Credit Tr Assn
Credit Services Assn
Credit: trade
Brit Cheque Cashers Assn
Consumer Credit Assn
Credit Protection Assn
Finance & Leasing Assn
Inst Credit Mgt
Ir Finance Houses Assn
Ir Inst Credit Mgt
Credit: unions
Ace Credit U Services
Assn Brit Credit Us
Ir League Credit Us
Cremation & crematoria > Burial & cremation
Creutzfeldt-Jakob disease > Alzheimers' disease
Cricket
Assn County Cricket Scorers
Assn Cricket Statisticians & Historians
Club Cricket Conf
Coun Cricket Socs
Cricket Memorabilia Soc
Cricket Scotland

© CBD Research Ltd · Beckenham · BR3 5JS · Tel 020 8650 7745 · Fax 020 8650 0768 · E-mail cbd@cbdresearch.com · www.cbdresearch.com

Cricket Soc
England Indoor Cricket Assn
England & Wales Cricket Bd Assn Cricket Officials
England & Wales Cricket Bd Coaches Assn
Midlands Club Cricket Conf
Minor Counties Cricket Assn
Northern Cricket U Ireland
Profl Cricketers' Assn
Cricket: pitches & equipment
Sporting Goods Ind Assn
Sports & Play Construction Assn
Criers > Town criers
Crime protection & prevention
Crime Concern
Intl Assn Auto Theft Investigators
Victim Support
Victim Support Scotland
Crime writers
Crime Writers Assn
Crimea War
Crimean War Res Soc
Criminal law
Criminal Bar Assn
Criminal Law Solicitors' Assn
> + Law
Criminology
Brit Soc Criminology
Howard League for Penal Reform
Scot Assn Study Offending
Crisis management > Civil defence & industrial emergencies
Crisps > Potatoes: products
Critical incident de-briefing
Nat Coun Psychotherapists
> + Counselling
Criticism
Critics' Circle
Crochet
Knitting & Crochet Gld
Crocuses
Brit Iris Soc
Crofters
Scot Crofting Foundation
Crohn's disease > Colitis/colostomy
Cromwell (Oliver)
Cromwell Assn
Crop: circles
Megalithic Soc
UK Skeptics
Crop: consultants
Assn Indep Crop Consultants
Crop: drying
Brit Assn Green Crop Driers
Instn Agricl Engrs
Crop: research
NIAB
> + Agriculture; Seeds
Crop: spraying & protection
Nat Assn Agricl Contrs
Croquet
Croquet Assn
Scot Croquet Assn
Cross country running > + Athletics; Running
Crossbow shooting
Grand Nat Archery Soc
Nat Crossbow Fedn
> + Archery
Crosswords
Crossword Club
Crown green bowling > Bowling
Cruise lines (shipping)
Assn Cruise Experts
Cruising > Boats & boating; Yachts & yachting
Crustacea > Shellfish
Cryogenics
Brit Cryogenics Coun
Heat Transfer & Fluid Flow Service
Cryptography
Xenophon
Crystal healing
Crystal & Healing Fedn
Crystal Palace
Crystal Palace Foundation
Crystallography
Brit Assn Crystal Growth
Brit Crystallographic Assn
Mineralogical Soc

Cue sports
Sporting Goods Ind Assn
Cued speech
Cued Speech Assn
> + Speech
Culverts & channels
Brit Precast Concrete Fedn
Curates (Church of England)
Additional Curates Soc
Curling
English Curling Assn
R Caledonian Curling Club
Curtains
Assn Soft Furnishers
Curtain track fitters
Assn Soft Furnishers
Curwen (John)
Curwen Inst
Cushing's Syndrome
Assn Cushing's Treatment & Help
Customer care
Inst Customer Service
Cutlery
Brit Cutlery & Silverware Assn
Cutlery & Allied Trs Res Assn
Cutters & reamers
Brit Hardmetal & Engineers' Cutting Tool Assn
Cutting tools > Tools
Cyclamen
Cyclamen Soc
Cycles & motorcycles
Assn Cycle Traders
Bicycle Assn
Cycle Engrs' Inst
Motor Cycle Ind Assn
Nat Motorcycle Coun
Retail Motor Ind Fedn
Veteran-Cycle Club
> + Motor cycling & scooter riding
Cyclical vomiting syndrome
Cyclical Vomiting Syndrome Assn
Cycling
Assn Brit Cycling Coaches
Brit Cycling Fedn
CTC
Cycling Time Trials
Fellowship Cycling Old-Timers
London Cycling Campaign
NI Cycling Fedn
Road Records Assn
Scot Cycling
Tandem Club
Tricycle Assn
Welsh Cycling U
Women's Cycle Racing Assn
Cyclo-Cross > Cycling
Cylinders (gas)
Brit Compressed Gases Assn
Cystic fibrosis
Cystic Fibrosis Trust
Cystitis
Cystitis & Overactive Bladder Foundation
Cytology > Cell biology
Cytomegalovirus
Congenital CMV Assn
Czech Republic
Brit Cham Comm Czech Republic
Dvořák Soc Czech & Slovak Music
Kmoch Eur Bands Soc

D

Dad's Army (TV programme)
Dad's Army Appreciation Soc
Daffodils
Daffodil Soc
Dahlias
Nat Dahlia Soc
Dairy cattle > Cattle headings
Dairying
Assn Unpasteurised Milk Producers
Brit Friesland Sheep Soc
Brit Goat Soc
Brit Sheep Dairying Assn

Campaign Real Milk
Dairy Executives Assn [IRL]
Dairy UK
Ir Creamery Milk Suppliers Assn
Milking Eqpt Assn
Quality Milk Producers
R Assn Brit Dairy Farmers
Soc Dairy Technology
Damage management
Brit Damage Mgt Assn
Dampcourses & dampproofing
Inst Specialist Surveyors & Engrs
Property Care Assn
Dams & reservoirs
Brit Dam Soc
> + Water: treatment & supply
Damsons
Westmorland Damson Assn
Dance bands
Harry Roy Appreciation Soc
Ted Heath Musical Appreciation Soc
Dance notation > Choreography
Dancing
Arts Centre Gp
Assn Amer Dancing
Assn Dance Movement Therapy
Ballroom Dancers Fedn
Brit Assn Teachers Dancing
Brit Ballet Org
Brit Theatre Dance Assn
Coun Dance Educ & Training
Dance UK
Dancesport Scotland
Dolmetsch Hist Dance Soc
EADA [lost D18
Early Dance Circle
Gld Profl Teachers Dancing
Imperial Soc Teachers Dancing
Inst Contemporary Arts
Laban Gld Movement & Dance
London Swing Dance Soc
Nat Assn Teachers Dancing
Nat Campaign Arts
Nat Dance Teachers Assn
Noctis
Old Time Dance Soc
R Academy Dance
Scot Dance Teachers Alliance
Soc Dance Res
UK Alliance Dance Teachers
UK Dance Drama Fedn
> + Ballet; Choreography; Folk dance & song
Dark skies
Campaign Dark Skies
Dartmoor
Dartmoor Presvn Assn
Darts
Brit Darts Org
Profl Darts Players Assn
Scot Darts Assn
Sporting Goods Ind Assn
Data capture/synchronisation > Automatic identification & data capture
Data processing
Assn Clinical Data Mgt
Inst Mgt Inf Systems
Records Mgt Soc
> + Computers; Information: services & technology
Data protection
Fedn Software Theft
> + Documents: confidential disposal
Day surgery
Brit Assn Day Surgery
> + Surgery
De-icing
Salt Assn
Deafness
Assn Lipspeakers
Assn Teachers Lipreading to Adults
Brit Assn Teachers Deaf
Brit Deaf Assn
Brit Deaf Sports Coun
Deaf Educ Listening & Talking
Deafblind UK
DeafHear
Hearing Concern
Ir Deaf Soc
Nat Assn Deafened People

Nat Cochlear Implant Users Assn
Nat Deaf Children's Soc
R Assn Deaf People
RNID
Scot Assn Sign Language Interpreters
Scot Coun Deafness
Sense
Treacher Collins Family Support Gp
> + Hearing; Speech
Death & bodily-death > Bereavement; Burial & cremation; Paranormal & psychical research; Population registration
Debt
Bankruptcy Assn
Civil Court Users Assn
Credit Services Assn
Debt Mgt Standards Assn
Inst Money Advisers
NARA
Debt collection > Credit: reporting
Decking (timber)
Timber Decking Assn
Decontamination
Inst Decontamination Sciences
Decorating > Painting & decorating
Decorations (medals) > Numismatics
Decorative arts
Nat Assn Decorative & Fine Arts Socs
> + Art headings
Decorative lighting > Lighting
Découpage
Gld Brit Découpeurs
Deer
Assn Deer Mgt Gps
Brit Deer Farmers Assn
Brit Deer Soc
Brit Veterinary Assn
Game Conservancy Trust
Ir Deer Farmers & Venison Assn
NI Deer Soc
Deerhounds
Masters Deerhounds Assn
> + Hunts & hunting
Defence
Brit Intl Studies Assn
Defence Industry Security Assn
R Utd Services Inst Defence... Studies
UK Nat Defence Assn
> + Civil defence & industrial emergencies; Fortresses & forts
Defence equipment
Defence Mfrs Assn
Intellect
Delinquency > Criminology
Delius (Frederick)
Delius Soc
Delphiniums
Delphinium Soc
Dementia
Alzheimer Scotland
Alzheimer's Soc
Pick's Disease Support Gp
> + Mental health
Demolition & dismantling
Brit Metals Recycling Assn
Inst Demolition Engrs
Inst Explosives Engrs
Nat Fedn Demolition Contrs
Denmark
Anglo-Danish Soc
Danish-UK Cham Comm
Dental hospitals
Assn Dental Hospitals
Dental hypnosis > Medical & dental hypnosis
Dental practice management
Brit Dental Practice Mgrs Assn
Dental radiology
Brit Soc Dental & Maxillofacial Radiology
Dentistry
Assn Dental Anaesthetists
Assn Dental Implantology
Assn Ir Dental Ind
Brit Assn Dental Nurses
Brit Assn Dental Therapists
Brit Assn Study Community Dentistry
Brit Assn Teachers Conservative Dentistry
Brit Dental Assn
Brit Dental Tr Assn
Brit Endodontic Soc

© CBD Research Ltd · Beckenham · BR3 5JS · Tel 020 8650 7745 · Fax 020 8650 0768 · E-mail cbd@cbdresearch.com · www.cbdresearch.com

Brit Homeopathic Dental Assn
Brit Inst Dental & Surgical Technologists
Brit Lingual Orthodontic Soc
Brit Orthodontic Soc
Brit Soc Dental Hygiene & Therapy
Brit Soc Dental Res
Brit Soc Disability & Oral Health
Brit Soc Gen Dental Surgery
Brit Soc Mercury Free Dentistry
Brit Soc Paediatric Dentistry
Brit Soc Periodontology
Brit Soc Restorative Dentistry
Brit Soc Study Prosthetic Dentistry
Clinical Dental Technicians Assn
Confedn Dental Emplrs
Craniofacial Soc
Dental Laboratories Assn
Dental Practitioners Assn
Dental System Suppliers Assn
Fac Dental Surgery
Fac Gen Dental Practice
Ir Dental Assn
Lindsay Soc Hist Dentistry
Nat Assn Med Educ Mgt
Orthodontic Technicians Assn
R Coll Physicians & Surgeons Glasgow
R Coll Surgeons Edinburgh
R Odonto-Chirurgical Soc Scot
Soc Advancement Anaesthesia Dentistry
Dentists: legal protection
Confedn Dental Emplrs
Medical & Dental Defence U Scotland
Medical Protection Soc
Department stores > Retail trade
Dependent territories (British) > Overseas territories (British)
Depression
Depression Alliance
Depression UK
MDF
SANE
Dermatitis herpetiformis
Coeliac UK
Dermatology
Brit Assn Dermatologists
Brit Photodermatology Gp
Primary Care Dermatology Soc
Design
Anti Copying Design
Art Workers Gld
Assn Art Historians
Chart Soc Designers
D&AD
Design Assn
Design Business Assn
Design Hist Soc
Design & Technology Assn
Inst Designers Ireland
Inst Profl Designers
Instn Engg Designers
Nat Assn Advisers... Design & Technology
Nat Soc Educ in Art & Design
R Soc ... Arts
Register Apparel & Textile Designers
Scot Ecological Design Assn
Design: industrial > Industrial design
Design registration > Patents & trade marks
Despatch industry > Courier services
Desserts
Food Processors Assn
Detection dogs
Nat Assn Security Dog Users
Detectives > Investigators
Detergents > Soap & detergents
Developing countries > Development education & studies; Overseas
development
Development education & studies
Devt Educ Assn
Devt Studies Assn
> + Education
Development trusts
Devt Trusts Assn
Devt Trusts Assn Scot
Developmental biology > Biology
de Vere (Edward) Earl of Oxford
De Vere Soc
Devon
S W Coast Path Assn

Diabetes
Diabetes Fedn Ireland
Diabetes UK
Diagnostic engineering
Instn Diagnostic Engrs
Dialects
Lakeland Dialect Soc
Lancashire Authors' Assn
Yorkshire Dialect Soc
> + English language & literature
Dialysis
Brit Kidney Patient Assn
Brit Transplantation Soc
Diamond drilling
Drilling & Sawing Assn
Diamonds > Industrial diamonds; Gemstones; Jewellery
Dianthus
Brit Nat Carnation Soc
Dickens (Charles John Huffam)
Dickens Fellowship
Diecasting
Diecasting Soc
Diesel engines & fuel
Instn Diesel & Gas Turbine Engrs
Dietetics
Brit Dietetic Assn
Infant & Dietetic Foods Assn
> + Nutrition
Digital print
Brit Printing Inds Fedn
Dinosaurs
Dinosaur Soc
Diplomatic Service
Assn Certified Comml Diplomats
Diplomatic Service Families Assn
Diptera
Dipterists Forum
Direct mail advertising > Advertising; Direct selling
Direct selling
Direct Marketing Assn (UK) Ltd
Direct Selling Assn
Ir Direct Marketing Assn
Publicity Club Lond
> + Mail order trade
Directors (company)
Inst Directors
Inst Directors Ireland
> + Management
Directory publishing
Data Pubrs Assn
> + Publishing
Disabled: road users
Blue Badge Network
Disabled Motorists Fedn
Mobilise Org
Nat Assn Bikers Disability
Disablement
Assn Disabled Profls
Brit Assn Supported Employment
Brit Inst Learning Disabilities
Brit Soc Rehabilitation Medicine
Capability Scotland
Cedar Foundation
Disability Alliance
Disability Fedn Ireland
Disablement Income Gp Scotland
Employers' Forum Disability
Fedn Artistic & Creative Therapy
Limbless Assn
Mencap
Nat Fedn Shopmobility
Nat Inf Forum
Nat Network Assessment Centres
R Assn Disability & Rehabilitation
Riding Disabled Assn
Scope
Support Dogs
Vision Homes Assn
> + Mobility aids; specific area of disability
Disarmament
Campaign Nuclear Disarmament
Medical Action Global Security
Scientists Global Responsibility
Disasters & disaster relief
RedR UK
Tornado & Storm Res Org

> + Civil defence & industrial emergencies;   Fire & flood damage
      restoration;   Welfare: organisations
Disc golf (flying discs)
      Brit Disc Golf Assn
      > + Ultimate
Discotheques & equipment
      Noctis
      Profl Lighting & Sound Assn
Discount market
      Asset Based Finance Assn
      London Money Market Assn
Discovery awards
      Discovery Award England
Discrimination
      Discrimination Law Assn
      > + Race relations
Discs (music) > Sound recording & reproduction
Disease > Infection control & study;   Occupational health & hygiene
Disfigurement > Birthmarks & disfigurement;   Skin camouflage
Disinfectants
      Brit Assn Chemical Specialities
      > + Sterilising
Dismantling (waste trades) > Demolition & dismantling
Dispensing doctors
      Country Doctors Assn
      Dispensing Doctors Assn
Dispensing opticians > Optical practice
Display
      Brit Display Soc
      Shop & Display Eqpt Assn
Disposables
      Absorbent Hygiene Products Mfrs Assn
      Foodservice Packaging Assn
Distilling
      Inst Brewing & Distilling
      Maltsters Assn
Distribution
      Chart Inst Logistics & Transport
      Food Storage & Distbn Fedn
      Freight Transport Assn
      Inst Grocery Distbn
      Ir Assn Distributive Trs
      U Shop, Distributive & Allied Workers
      UK Warehousing Assn
      Utd Road Transport U
      > + Materials: management/handling; Retail trade; specific trade
District councils > Local government
District heating
      Combined Heat & Power Assn
      > + Heating
District nursing > Nursing
Diving (professional & scientific)
      Histl Diving Soc
      Intl Marine Contrs Assn
      Nautical Archaeology Soc
      Soc Underwater Technology Ltd
      > + Ocean industries
Diving (sport) > Swimming & diving
Divining > Dowsing
Divorced & separated people > Singles, divorced & separated
DIY > Do-it-yourself
Docked breeds
      Coun Docked Breeds
      > + Dogs
Docks > Ports
Doctors > Medical practice
Documents: historical > Records: historical
Documents: confidential disposal
      Brit Security Ind Assn
      UK Security Shredding Assn
Dodgson (Charles Lutwidge)
      Daresbury Lewis Carroll Soc
      Lewis Carroll Soc
Dogs
      Assn Dogs & Cats Homes
      Assn Lurcher Clubs
      Brit Flyball Assn
      Brit Whippet Racing Assn
      Coun Docked Breeds
      Dogs Trust
      Kennel Club
      Nat Assn Regd Petsitters
      Nat Assn Security Dog Users
      Nat Dog Wardens Assn
      Nat Greyhound Racing Club
      Nat Search & Rescue Dog Assn

      Scot Kennel Club
      > + Hounds
Dogs: groomers
      Pet Care Trust
Dogs: training
      Assn Pet Behaviour Counsellors
      Assn Pet Dog Trainers
      Brit Inst Profl Dog Trainers
      Canine & Feline Behaviour Assn
      People & Dogs Soc
      Rough & Smooth Collie Training Assn
      Scot Working Trials Soc
      Support Dogs
      > + Pets & pet trade
Do-it-yourself
      Brit Hardware Fedn
Dolls & dolls' houses
      Doll Club GB
      > + Toys
Dolphins
      Whale & Dolphin Consvn Soc
Domestic appliances
      Assn Mfrs Domestic Appliances
      Community
      Domestic Appliance Service Assn
      White Goods Assn [IRL]
      > + Electrical industry & engineering
Domestic engineering > specific subjects, eg Heating
Domestic fowl > Poultry
Domestic heating > Heating
Domestic ventilation
      Residential Ventilation Assn
Domestic violence
      NI Women's Aid Fedn
      Women's Aid Fedn (England)
      > + Crime & crime prevention
Domiciliary care
      Nat Care Assn
      UK Homecare Assn
Donations (public)
      Donor Watch
Donizetti (Gaetano)
      Donizetti Soc
Donkeys
      Donkey Breed Soc
      Miniature Mediterranean Donkey Assn
Doors
      Architectural & Specialist Door Mfrs Assn
      Assn Garage Door Specialists
      Automatic Door Suppliers Assn
      Brit Woodworking Fedn
      Door & Hardware Fedn
      Local Authority PVC-u Frame Advy Gp
Double glazing
      Glass & Glazing Fedn
      Local Authority PVC-u Frame Advy Gp
      > + Insulation; Windows
Down's syndrome
      Down's Syndrome Assn
      Down's Syndrome Scotland
      > + Children: handicapped
Dowsing
      Assn Scientific Study Anomalous Phenomena
      Brit Soc Dowsers
      Scot Dowsing Assn
Draghounds
      Masters Draghounds & Bloodhounds Assn
Dragon boats
      Brit Dragon Boat Racing Assn
Dragonflies
      Brit Dragonfly Soc
Drainage
      Assn Drainage Authorities
      Cast Iron Drainage Devt Assn
      Clay Pipe Devt Assn
      Land Drainage Contrs Assn
      > + Concrete & concrete products; Pipes; Water
Drake (Sir Francis)
      Drake Exploration Soc
Drama > Theatre
Drama festivals > Festivals: art, drama & music
Dramatists
      Ir Playwrights & Screenwriters Gld
      Scot Soc Playwrights
      Soc Authors
      Soc Authors Scotland

© CBD Research Ltd · Beckenham · BR3 5JS · Tel 020 8650 7745 · Fax 020 8650 0768 · E-mail cbd@cbdresearch.com · www.cbdresearch.com

Writers' Gld
> + Writing & writers
Dramatherapy
Brit Assn Dramatherapists
Draught proofing > Insulation
Draughts (board game)
English Draughts Assn
Drawing > Art & artists
Dredging
Central Dredging Assn
Fedn Dredging Contrs
Dress > Costume history, design & conservation;   Fashion
Dressage > Horses & ponies
Dried flowers
Brit Dried Flowers Assn
> + Flowers, flower arrangement & floristry
Dried fruit
Nat Dried Fruit Tr Assn
Drilling
Brit Drilling Assn
Brit Rig Owners Assn
Drilling & Sawing Assn
Well Drillers Assn
Drink & beverage industry
Beverage Coun Ireland
Beverage Service Assn
Brewing, Food & Beverage Ind Suppliers Assn
Brit Soft Drinks Assn
Campden & Chorleywood Food Res Assn
Can Makers
Drinks Ind Gp Ireland
Food & Drink Fedn
Food & Drink Ind [IRL]
Nat Fruit Wine, Mead & Liqueur Producers Assn
NI Food & Drink Assn
Processing & Packaging Machinery Assn
Scot Food & Drink Fedn
> + Bottling
Drinking & driving
Campaign Drinking & Driving
Drinking (compulsive) > Alcoholism
Drinking fountains
Metropolitan Drinking Fountain &... Assn
Drinking straws & vessels
Foodservice Packaging Assn
Drinkwater (John)
Friends Dymock Poets
Drip mats > Beer: bottles, cans labels & mats
Driving (off-road)
Brit Off Road Driving Assn
Motoring Orgs' Land Access & Recreation Assn
Driving tuition
ADI Fedn
Approved Driving Instructors Nat Jt Coun
Assn Indl Road Safety Officers
Assn Nat Driver Improvement Scheme Providers
Driving Instructors Assn
Inst Advanced Motorists
Inst Master Tutors Driving
Motor Schools Assn
Dromedary camels > Camelids
Drug addiction > Addiction
Drugs > Pharmaceuticals; Pharmacology & chemotherapy
Drugs: detection
Nat Assn Security Dog Users
Druids
Pagan Fedn
Drums (containers) > Cisterns, drums & tanks
Drums (musical instruments)
Corps Drums Soc
> + Brass & silver bands
Dry cleaning > Cleaning & dyeing
Dry stone walling
Dry Stone Walling Assn
Dry waste
Container Handling Eqpt Mfrs Assn
> + Waste disposal
Drylining > Drywalling
Dryrot
Inst Specialist Surveyors & Engrs
> + Dampcourses & dampproofing
Drywalling
Fedn Plastering & Drywall Contrs
Dublin
Friends Medieval Dublin [IRL]
R Dublin Soc

Duchenne muscular dystrophy
Duchenne Family Support Gp
Ducks
Brit Poultry Coun
Brit Waterfowl Assn
> + Poultry
Ducks (decoy)
Brit Decoy & Wildfowl Carvers Assn
Ducting
Assn Ductwork Contrs & Allied Services
Heating & Ventilating Contrs Assn
Duelling
Dawn Duellists' Soc
Dumbness > Speech
Dunkirk
Assn Dunkirk Little Ships
Duodecimal system
Dozenal Soc
Dust control
Fan Mfrs' Assn
Solids Handling & Processing Assn
> + Air: conditioning & ventilating
Dutch > Netherlands: language & literature
Duty-free trade
Brit Assn Ship Suppliers
UK Travel Retail Forum
Dwarfism > Growth
Dyeing > Cleaning & dyeing
Dyeing & finishing
Assn Glds Weavers, Spinners & Dyers
Confedn Brit Wool Textiles
Soc Dyers & Colourists
Textile Finishers Assn
Dyestuffs
Chemical Business Assn
Dyking
Dry Stone Walling Assn
Dymock poets
Friends Dymock Poets
Dyslexia
Brit Dyslexia Assn
Coun Registration Schools Teaching Dyslexic Pupils
Dyslexia Assn Ireland
Dyslexia Inst
Dyslexia Scotland
nasen
Nat Network Assessment Centres
> + Children: handicapped
Dysmenorrhea
Nat Assn Premenstrual Syndrome
Premenstrual Soc
Dysphasia > Speech
Dysplasia (ectodermal)
Ectodermal Dysplasia Soc
Dyspraxia
Dyspraxia Foundation
Dystonia
Dystonia Soc
Dystrophy > Muscular dystrophy; Myotonic dystrophy

Dzhugashvili (Iosif Vissarionovich) > Stalin (Joseph)

E

Ear tags (animal)
Assn Automatic Identification ...Capture
Earth sciences, structure & resources
Earth Science Teachers' Assn
Geological Soc
Mineralogical Soc
Remote Sensing & Photogrammetry Soc
Soc Underwater Technology Ltd
UKspace
Yorkshire Geological Soc
> + Geology
Earth sheltered buildings
Brit Earth Sheltering Assn
Earthenware > Ceramics; Clay & clay products; Pottery
Earthquake engineering
Instn Civil Engrs
Soc Earthquake & Civil Engg Dynamics
East/Eastern Africa
Eastern Africa Assn
Eastern Europe > individual countries

Eating disorders
Eating Disorders Assn
Overeaters Anonymous
> + Obesity
EC > European Union
Ecclesiastical > Church headings; individual religions
Eckhart (Johannes)
Eckhart Soc
Ecology
Brit Ecological Soc
Inst Ecology & Envtl Mgt
> + Conservation; Environment
Economic development
Instn Economic Devt
Scot Coun Devt & Ind
Economic history
Economic Hist Soc
Economic & Social Hist Soc Ireland
Economics
Agricl Economics Soc
Brit Academy
David Hume Inst
Economic Res Coun
Economic & Social Res Inst [IRL]
Economics, Business & Enterprise Assn
Inst Economic Affairs
Inst Fiscal Studies
Intl Consulting Economists Assn
R Economic Soc
Resource Use Inst
Scot Economic Soc
Soc Business Economists
Statistical & Social Inquiry Soc Ireland
Ectodermal dysplasia
Ectodermal Dysplasia Soc
Ectopic pregnancy > Miscarriage
Ecuador
Anglo-Ecuadorian Soc
Eczema
Nat Eczema Soc
Edgings (concrete) > Concrete & concrete products
Edible nuts > Nuts (edible)
Edible oils & fats
Fedn Oils, Seeds & Fats Assns
Nat Edible Oil Distbrs Assn
Seed Crushers & Oil Processors Assn
UK Assn Fish Meal Mfrs
> + individual fats; Rendering
Edinburgh
Cockburn Assn
Editing & editors
Assn Church Editors
Assn Freelance Editors, Proofreaders & Indexers [IRL]
Brit Soc Magazine Editors
Picture Res Assn
Soc Editors
Soc Editors & Proofreaders
> + Publishing
Education
Assn Colleges
Assn Community & Comprehensive Schools [IRL]
Assn NI Colleges
Assn Study Primary Educ
Assn Tutors
Brit Assn Early Childhood Educ
Brit Educl Leadership, Mgt & Admin Soc
Brit Educl Res Assn
Campaign Learning
Campaign Real Educ
Campaign State Educ
Caspari Foundation for Educl Therapy. . .
CIFE
Further Educ Res Assn
Group Educ Museums
Honourable The Irish Soc
Ir Vocational Educ Assn
Modern Studies Assn
Montessori Soc
nasen
Nat Assn Envtl Educ
Nat Assn Primary Educ
Nat Assn Therapeutic Educ
Nat Forum Engg Centres
Nat Foundation Educl Res E&W
Nat Small Schools Forum
PSHE Assn
SAPERE

Scot Educl Res Assn
Scot Parent Couns Assn
Scot Support Learning Assn
Soc Res Higher Educ
Staff & Educl Devt Assn
> + Adult education; Independent & public schools; Teachers; specific subjects
Education: computers in
Naace
Education: equipment & supplies
ADSET
Brit Educl Suppliers Assn
Education: games & simulation
Soc Advancement Games & Simulations Educ & Training
Education: guardians
Assn Educ & Guardianship Intl Students
Education: guidance
NAEGA
Education: history
History Educ Soc
Education: home based
Education Otherwise
Home Educ Advy Service
Nat Assn Educ Sick Children
Nat Portage Assn
Schoolhouse Home Educ Assn
Education: occupational > Occupational training & education
Education: outdoor
Assn Heads Outdoor Educ Centres
Inst Outdoor Learning
Scot Envtl & Outdoor Educ Centres Assn
Education: specialists
Assn Coll Mgt
Assn Directors Children's Services
Assn Directors Educ Scotland
Assn Educ Welfare Mgt
Assn Educl Psychologists
Assn NI Educ & Library Bds
Assn Painting Craft Teachers
Assn Profls Educ & Children's Trusts
Assn University Administrators
College Teachers
Coun Hospitality Mgt Educ
Higher Educ Liaison Officers' Assn
History Curriculum Assn
Inst Educl Assessors
Inst Health Promotion & Educ
Librarians of Insts & Schools of Educ
Nat Assn Advy Officers Special Educational Needs
Nat Assn Mathematics Advisers
Nat Assn Youth & Community Educ Officers
Nat Governors' Assn
Nat Org Pupil Referral Units
Soc Educ Consultants
Education: technology
Assn Learning Technology
Brit Educl Suppliers Assn
Brit Inst Learning & Devt
EEC > European Union
Effluents > Sewers, sewage & effluents
Egg decoration
Egg Crafters Gld
Eggs & egg products
Brit Egg Assn
Brit Egg Products Assn
Brit Free Range Egg Producers Assn
Nat Egg Marketing Assn
UK Egg Producers Assn
Egypt
Ancient Egypt & Middle East Soc
Egypt Exploration Soc
Egyptian Brit Cham Comm
Ekbom syndrome
Ekbom Support Gp
Elastic materials > Narrow fabrics; Health care: equipment & supplies; Surgical equipment & supplies
Elastic rope sports
Brit Elastic Rope Sports Assn
UK Bungee Club
Electro-imaging
Elderly persons > Geriatrics & ageing; Old people's organisations
Elections & electoral legislation
Assn Electoral Administrators
Electoral Reform Soc
Scot Assessors' Assn
Unlock
Unlock Democracy

© CBD Research Ltd · Beckenham · BR3 5JS · Tel 020 8650 7745 · Fax 020 8650 0768 · E-mail cbd@cbdresearch.com · www.cbdresearch.com

Electoral reform > Elections & electoral legislation
Electric: cable & conduit
       Brit Cables Assn
Electric: fencing
       Fencing Contrs' Assn
Electric: heating > Heating
Electric: lighting > Lighting
Electric: motors
       BEAMA
Electric: tools
       Portable Electric Tool Mfrs Assn
Electric: transport
       Battery Vehicle Soc
       Electric Boat Assn
       Electric Rly Soc
Electrical goods trade
       Assd Nat Electrical Whlsrs
       Assn Electrical & Mechanical Trs
       Assn Whls Electrical Bulk Buyers
       Electrical Distbrs Assn
       Electrical & Electronic Retailers Assn Ireland
       Small Electrical Appliance Marketing Assn
Electrical industry & engineering
       Assn Electrical Contrs, Ireland
       Assn Mfrs Domestic Appliances
       BEAMA
       Chart Instn Bldg Services Engrs
       Electric Trace Heating Ind Coun
       Electrical Contrs Assn
       Electrical & Engg Staff Assn
       Electrical Inds Fedn Ireland
       EMC Ind Assn
       Select
Electricity
       Assn Electricity Producers
       Assn Mfrs Power generating Systems
       BEAMA
       Electricity Arbitration Assn
       Energy Inds Coun
       Energy Networks Assn
       Energy Retail Assn
       Indl & Power Assn
       Nat Jt Utilities Gp
       UK Revenue Protection Assn
Electricity meters > Meters & metering
Electro-ceramics
       Brit Refractories & Indl Ceramics
       > + Ceramics
Electrochemistry
       R Soc Chemistry
Electrodiagnostic medicine
       Brit Soc Clinical Neurophysiology
Electroencephalography
       Brit Soc Clinical Neurophysiology
       Electro-physiological Technologists Assn
Electroheat
       BEAMA
Electrohydraulic control
       Brit Fluid Power Assn
Electro-imaging
       Soc Metaphysicians
Electrolysis
       Brit Inst & Assn Electrolysis
       > + Beauty specialists/treatment
Electromagnetics
       EMC Ind Assn
Electronic: components (obsolescence)
       Component Obsolescence Gp
Electronic: industry & engineering
       Assn Franchised Distbrs Electronic Components
       Assn Instrumentation, Control, Automation...
       BEAMA
       Electro-Technical Coun Ireland
       EMC Ind Assn
       Instn Engg & Technology
       Intellect
       > + Computers; Data processing; Optoelectronics; Radio
Electronic: organs > Organs, organists & organ music
Electronic: surveillance > Security
Electronic: trade & commerce
       Brit Marine Electronics Assn
       CEDIA
       GS1 Ireland
       GS1 UK
       Radio, Electrical & TV Retailers' Assn

Electronic: traffic control
       ITS UK
       > + Road safety & control
Electro-optics > Optoelectronics
Electrophoresis
       Brit Soc Proteome Res
       > + Biochemistry & biotechnology
Electrophysiology
       Scot Neuroscience Gp
Electroplating
       Surface Engg Assn
Electro-static equipment
       Brit Electrostatic Control Assn
Elgar (Sir Edward)
       Elgar Soc
Elia
       Charles Lamb Soc
Eliot (George) [Mary Ann Evans]
       George Eliot Fellowship
Embalming
       Brit Inst Embalmers
Embroidery
       Embroiderers' Gld
Embryo research
       Brit Soc Developmental Biology
Emergency medicine > Medicine: accident & emergency
Emergency planning/management > Civil defence & industrial emergencies
Emigration > Immigration & emigration
Emission monitoring
       BTC Testing Advisory Gp
       Source Testing Assn
Employee assistance programmes
       UK Employee Assistance Profls Assn
Employee involvement > Industrial involvement & participation
Employers
       Confedn Brit Ind
       Employers' Forum Disability
       Ir Business & Emplrs Confedn
       > + specific industry
Employment
       Brit Assn Supported Employment
       Employers Forum on Age
       HR Soc
       Over Fifties Assn
       Recruitment Soc
       > + Careers
Employment agents & consultants
       Assn Graduate Recruiters
       Assn Technology Staffing Companies
       Recruitment & Employment Confedn
Emus
       Rhea & Emu Assn
       > + Ostrich farming
Enamel: vitreous > Vitreous enamel
Enamelling
       Brit Soc Enamellers
       Gld Enamellers
Encephalitis
       Encephalitis Soc
       > + Myalgic encephalitis/encephalopathy
Endocrinology
       Androgen Insensitivity Syndrome Support Gp
       Brit Assn Endocrine & Thyroid Surgeons
       Soc Endocrinology
Endodontics > Dentistry
Endometriosis
       Nat Endometriosis Soc
Endoscopy
       Brit Soc Gastroenterology
       Brit Soc Gynaecological Endoscopy
Endowment policies (secondhand)
       Assn Policy Market Makers
       > + Insurance
Energy
       Assn Consvn Energy
       Brit Assn Colliery Mgt
       Brit Energy Assn
       Brit Hydropower Assn
       Brit Inst Energy Economics
       Buildings Energy Efficiency Fedn
       Combined Heat & Power Assn
       Energy Inds Coun
       Energy Inst
       Energy Networks Assn
       Energy Systems Tr Assn
       Inst Domestic Heating... Engrs
       Instn Civil Engrs

Instn Engg & Technology
Ir Hydro Power Assn
Nat Energy Action
Renewable Energy Assn
Resource Use Inst
> + Renewable energy; specific form of energy

Enforcement agents
Assn Civil Enforcement Agencies
Enforcement Services Assn

Engineering
AIRTO
Assn Brit Transport & Engg Museums
Assn Consultancy & Engg
Assn Consulting Engrs Ireland
Brit Assn Advancement Science
Brit Engg Mfrs Assn
EEF
Engg Inds Assn
Engg Integrity Soc
Engrs Ireland
INCA [IRL]
Inst Indl Engrs [IRL]
Inst Materials, Minerals & Mining
Instn Civil Engrs
Instn Diagnostic Engrs
Instn Engg Designers
Instn Engg & Technology
Instn Engrs & Shipbuilders Scotland
Instn Mechanical Engrs
Intellect
Ir Engg Enterprises Fedn [IRL]
Prospect
R Academy Engg
Royal Soc (The)
Science, Engg & Mfrg Technologies Alliance
Science, Technology, Engg. . . Public Relations Assn
Scot Engg
Soc Operations Engrs
Soc Profl Engrs
UK Assn Profl Engrs
Women's Engg Soc
> + other branches of engineering

Engineering: bricks > Bricks
Engineering: education
Brit Educl Suppliers Assn
Nat Forum Engg Centres

Engineering: equipment & materials
Engg Eqpt & Materials Users Assn

Engineering: history
Newcomen Soc
Stephenson Locomotive Soc
Trevithick Soc

Engineering: plant > Plant: industrial
Engineers' tools
Fedn Brit Engrs' Tool Mfrs
> Tools

Engines > specific type of engine
England
Campaign English Parliament
Campaign Protect Rural England
R Soc St George

English language & literature
Aethelflæd
Anglo-Norman Text Soc
Assn Brit Language Schools
Assn Promotion Quality TESOL Educ
Early English Text Soc
Engliscan Gesíþas
English Assn
English Poetry & Song Soc
English UK
Modern Humanities Res Assn
Nat Assn Teaching Engl
Nat Assn Teaching Engl &. . .Community Languages
Plain Engl Campaign
Queen's Engl Soc
R Soc Literature
Ranulf Higden Soc
Spelling Soc
> + individual writers by name

Engravers
MultiService Assn
R Soc Painter-Printmakers
Soc Wood Engravers
> + Art & artists

Enterprise agencies
Nat Fedn Enterprise Agencies

Entertainment
Adult Ind Trade Assn
Agents Assn
Brit Magical Soc
Broadcasting, Entertainment Cinematograph. . .U
Concert Artistes' Association
Fedn Entertainment Us
Inst Entertainment & Arts Profls
Nat Entertainment Agents Coun
Personal Mgrs Assn
Production Services Assn
> + Leisure, recreation & amenity management;   specific forms of entertainment

Entertainment: equipment
Profl Lighting & Sound Assn

Entomology
Amat Entomologists' Soc
Assn Applied Biologists
Birmingham Natural Hist Soc
Brit Entomological & Natural Hist Soc
Buglife
R Entomological Soc Lond
> + Nature conservation

Environment
Assn Brit Certification Bodies
Assn Envtl Archaeology
Assn Heritage Interpretation
Aviation Envt Fedn
Brit Urban Regeneration Assn
Doctor E F Schumacher Soc
Environmental Communicators Org
Environmental Inds Commission
Environmental Investigation Agency
Environmental Protection UK
ETA Services Ltd
Friends Earth
Green Alliance Trust
Inst Ecology & Envtl Mgt
Inst Envtl Mgt & Assessment
Landscape Res Gp
Nat Assn Envtl Educ
Nat Register Access Consultants
Planning & Environment Bar Assn
Regional Studies Assn
Scot Envt Link
Soc Chemical Ind
Soc Envt
Soc Envtl Exploration
Soc Responsible Use Resources Agriculture & Land
Socialist Envt & Resources Assn
UK Envtl Law Assn
UK Forum Envtl Inds
Valpak
Wildlife & Countryside Link
Women's Envtl Network
> + Conservation; Pollution & pollution control

Environment: engineering/health
Assn Public Analysts
Assn Public Analysts Scotland
Brit Soc Ecological Medicine
Chart Inst Envtl Health
ENCAMS
Environmental Health Officers Assn [IRL]
Inst Domestic Heating. . . Engrs
Instn Envtl Sciences
R Envtl Health Inst Scotland
Scientists Global Responsibility
SIESO
Soc Envtl Engrs
UK Envtl Mutagen Soc

Environmental illness > Occupational health & hygiene
Environmental services
Environmental Services Assn

Enzootic abortion of ewes
Highlands & Islands Sheep Health Assn

Ephemera
Brit Matchbox, Label & Booklet Soc
English Playing-Card Soc
Ephemera Soc

Epidermolysis bullosa
Dystrophic Epidermolysis Bullosa Res Assn

Epigraphy
Brit Epigraphy Soc

Epilepsy
Brainwave
Brit Epilepsy Assn

© CBD Research Ltd · Beckenham · BR3 5JS · Tel 020 8650 7745 · Fax 020 8650 0768 · E-mail cbd@cbdresearch.com · www.cbdresearch.com

Epilepsy Action Scotland
Nat Soc Epilepsy
Epiphytes
Epiphytic Plant Study Gp
> + Plants
Equal opportunities
Nat Alliance Women's Orgs
Over Fifties Assn
Parity
> + Employment
Equestrian trade
Brit Equestrian Tr Assn
> + Horse headings
Equipment > Leasing; Mining: equipment; Office equipment & systems
Equity finance
BVCA
EIS Assn
Equity release plans
Safe Home Income Plans
Ergonomics
Ergonomics Soc
Eritrea
Middle East Assn
Erotic art
Assn Erotic Artists
Gld Erotic Artists
Escalators
Lift & Escalator Ind Assn
Esperanto
Esperanto Assn Britain
Scot Esperanto Assn
Essences
Brit Assn Flower Essence Producers
Brit Essence Mfrs' Assn
Essential oils
Aromatherapy Tr Coun
Brit Essential Oils Assn
Brit Soc Perfumers
Intl Gen Produce Assn
Estate agents
Assn Residential Letting Agents
Gld Letting & Mgt
Gld Profl Estate Agents
Inst Auctioneers & Appraisers Scotland
Nat Assn Estate Agents
Property Consultants Soc
UK Assn Letting Agents
> + Property & land owners
Estate management
Country Gentlemen's Assn
Country Land & Business Assn [E&W]
Inst Clerks Works
Inst Healthcare Engg & Estate Mgt
Manorial Soc
Estate & trust planning > Trusts, trusteeship & estate planning
Estuaries
Estuarine & Coastal Sciences Assn
Ethics
Comment Reproductive Ethics
S Place Ethical Soc
Ethiopia
Middle East Assn
Ethnic studies
Assn Study Ethnicity & Nationalism
Ethnography
Museum Ethnographers Gp
R Anthropological Inst
Eton Fives
Eton Fives Assn
Eugenics
Galton Inst
Eurhythmics
Dalcroze Soc
Laban Gld Movement & Dance
Europe
Brit Assn Slavonic & E Eur Studies
Eur-Atlantic Gp
Eur Atlantic Movement
Eur Inf Assn
Eur Movement
University Assn Contemporary Eur Studies
European Union
Anti Common Market League
Atlantic Coun
Brit Inst Intl & Comparative Law
Campaign Euro-federalism

Campaign Indep Britain
Democracy Movement
Euthanasia
ALERT
CNK Alliance
Dignity in Dying
Medical Ethics Alliance
Soc Protection Unborn Children
Voluntary Euthanasia Soc Scotland
Evacuees (WWII)
Evacuees Reunion Assn
Evangelism
Evangelical Alliance
Fellowship Indep Evangelical Churches
> + Christian activities
Evens (Rev G Bramwell)
Romany Soc
Events > Corporate hospitality; Exhibitions; Shows & events
Events management
Assn Events Mgt Educ
Excavation & land clearance
Inst Explosives Engrs
Exchanges: international
Assn Learning Languages en Famille
Exchequer records
Pipe Roll Soc
Exhibitions
Assn Brit Profl Conf Organisers
Assn Event Organisers
Assn Event Venues
Event Supplier & Services Assn
Events Ind Alliance
Events Sector Ind Trg Org
Exhibition Study Gp
Nat Exhibitors Assn
Soc Event Organisers
> + Conferences & conventions
Exhumation
Inst Cemetery & Crematorium Mgt
> + Burial & cremation
Experts & expert witness
Academy Experts
Assn Consulting Scientists
Assn Lawyers & Legal Advisors
Expert Witness Inst
Soc Expert Witnesses
Exploration
BSES Expeditions
Scientific Exploration Soc
Young Explorers' Trust
Exploration: history
Hakluyt Soc
Explosives
Assn Petroleum & Explosives Admin
Brit Cave Res Assn
Explosives Ind Gp
Inst Demolition Engrs
Inst Explosives Engrs
Nat Assn Security Dog Users
Explosives: detection
Nat Assn Security Dog Users
Export & import
Brit Exporters Assn
China-Britain Business Coun
Free Trade League
Inst Export
Inst Intl Tr [IRL]
Ir Exporters Assn
> + Chambers of commerce: overseas trade
Export packers
Brit Intl Freight Assn
> + specific trade
Express courier services
Assn Intl Courier & Express Services
Ex-service organisations
Assn Jewish Ex-Servicemen & Women
Brit Limbless Ex-Service Men's Assn
Confedn Brit Service & Ex-Service Orgs
Not Forgotten Assn
Officers' Assn
R Brit Legion
R Brit Legion Scotland
R Naval Assn
Saint Dunstan's
Extra sensory perception > Paranormal & psychical research
Eyes > Blind & partially sighted; Ophthalmology; specific diseases
Eyewear > Contact lens; Optical industry

F

Fabric care
 Home Laundering Consultative Coun
Fabrics > Textile: industry & trade
Fabry disease
 Soc Mucopolysaccharide Diseases
Facial disfigurement > Birthmarks & disfigurement
Facilities management
 Brit Inst Facilities Mgt
 Chart Inst Bldg
 Facilities Mgt Assn
 Ir Property & Facility Mgmt Assn
 R Instn Chart Surveyors
 > + Offices (serviced)
Factoring (banking & finance)
 Asset Based Finance Assn
 Nat Assn Comml Finance Brokers
Factors: motor > Motor factors
Fair trade
 Brit Assn Fair Tr Shops
Fairgrounds & equipment
 Fair Organ Presvn Soc
 Fairground Assn
 Fairground Soc
 Mechanical Organ Owners Soc
 Roller Coaster Club
 Showmen's Gld
 Soc Indep Roundabout Proprietors
Fairs
 Nat Assn Brit Market Authorities
Fairy rings & fairies
 Fairyworld
Faith healing > Spiritual healing
Falconry > Hawks & hawking
Falkland Islands
 Falkland Islands Assn
 Falklands Consvn
Falkner (John Meade)
 John Meade Falkner Soc
Fall arrest equipment
 Fall Arrest Safety Eqpt Training
False memory
 Brit False Memory Soc
Falsework
 Nat Access & Scaffolding Confedn
Familial hypercholesterolaemia
 Heart UK
 > + Cardiology
Family history > Genealogy
Family law
 Assn Family Therapy
 Family Law Assn Scotland
 Family Law Bar Assn
 Family Mediators' Assn
 Family Rights Gp
 NAGALRO
 Nat Family Mediation
 Resolution
Family planning
 Fac Sexual & Reproductive Healthcare
 Family Planning Assn
 Fertility Care Scotland
 Ir Family Planning Assn
 Nat Assn Nurses Contraception & Sexual Health
 Nat Assn Ovulation Method Instructors
Family therapy
 Assn Family Therapy
 Family Matters Inst
Family welfare > Welfare organisations
Fan clubs > subject of interest
Fancy dress
 Brit Costume Assn
 > + Costume history, design & conservation
Fancy goods > Giftware
Fans
 Fan Mfrs' Assn
 Heating, Ventilating & Air Conditioning Mfrs' Assn
 > + Air: conditioning & ventilating; Heating
Fantasy
 Brit Fantasy Soc
 Brit Science Fiction Assn
Fare collection
 Transport Ticket Soc
Farm animals > Animals; specific animals

Farm buildings
 Brit Constructional Steelwork Assn
 Instn Agricl Engrs
 Rural & Indl Design & Bldg Assn
Farm machinery > Agriculture: machinery
Farm shops & food
 Nat Farmers' Retail & Markets Assn
 Wholesome Food Assn
 Women's Food & Farming U
Farmers' markets > Markets: street, cattle & farmers'
Farmers' organisations
 Comml Farmers Gp
 Family Farmers' Assn
 Farmers Action
 Farmers Club
 Farmers' U Wales
 Farms for Schools
 Flying Farmers Assn
 Ir Farmers Assn
 Jersey Farmers' U
 Manx Nat Farmers U
 Nat Assn NFU Gp Secretaries
 Nat Farmers' Retail & Markets Assn
 Nat Farmers U
 Nat Fedn Young Farmers Clubs (E&W)
 NFU Scotland
 Scot Assn Young Farmers Clubs
 Small Farms Assn
 Tenant Farmers' Assn
 Ulster Farmers U
Farming > Agriculture; Dairying; Organic growing & farming
Farnon (Robert)
 Robert Farnon Soc
Farriers
 Nat Assn Farriers...
 UK Horse Shoers U
 > + Blacksmiths
Fashion
 Assn Model Agents
 Assn Photographers
 Brit Clothing Ind Assn
 Costume Soc
 > + Clothing; Costume history, design & conservation
Fasteners & turned parts
 Brit Assn Fastener Distbrs
 Brit Turned-Parts Mfrs Assn
 Confedn Brit Metalforming
 Power Fastenings Assn
Fat (obese) > Obesity
Fatigue (materials/metals) > Materials: technology & testing
Fatigue (physical)
 Action ME
 Assn Young People with ME
 Myalgic Encephalopathy Assn
Fats, edible & processing > Edible oils & fats; Rendering; individual fats
Fauna > Animals; Nature conservation; specific animals
Feed (animal) > Animal feed
Feet > Chiropody & podiatry; Footwear; Orthopaedics
Fell running
 Assn Running Clubs
 Fell Runners Assn
 > + Running
Felt
 Nat Fillings Assn
 Needleloom Underlay Mfrs' Assn
Felt & flat roofing > Roofing
Fencing (enclosure)
 Fencing Contrs' Assn
 Wire Products Assn
Fencing (sport)
 Brit Fedn Histl Swordplay
 Brit Fencing Assn
 Scot Fencing
Feng shui
 Feng Shui Soc
Ferns
 Brit Pteridological Soc
Ferrets
 Nat Ferret Welfare Soc
Ferries
 Assn Cruise Experts
 > + Shipping
Fertilisers
 Fertilizer Assn Ireland
 > + Agriculture: chemicals
Fertility
 Assn Biomedical Andrologists

© CBD Research Ltd · Beckenham · BR3 5JS · Tel 020 8650 7745 · Fax 020 8650 0768 · E-mail cbd@cbdresearch.com · www.cbdresearch.com

Brit Andrology Soc
Brit Fertility Soc
Brit Infertility Counselling Assn
Brit Soc Psychosomatic Obstetrics. . .
Daisy Network
Infertility Network UK
Soc Reproduction & Fertility
Festivals: art, drama & music
Assn Festival Organisers
Brit Arts Festivals Assn
Brit & Intl Fedn Festivals Music, Drama & Speech
Gld Drama Adjudicators
Nat Drama Festivals Assn
Fibre cement
Fibre Cement Mfrs Assn
Fibre optics
Fibreoptic Ind Assn
Fibreboard > Packaging
Fibromyalgia
Fibromyalgia Assn
Fiddles > Accordions & fiddles
Field archery
Nat Field Archery Soc
Scot Field Archery Assn
Field sports
Countryside Alliance
Countryside Ireland
Fedn Assns Country Sports Europe
Scot Assn Country Sports
U Country Sports Workers
> + individual sport
Field study > Natural history; other subjects of field study
Fights (historic/re-enactment)
English Civil War Soc
Historic Artillery
Knights R England
Medieval Siege Soc
Napoleonic Assn
Nat Assn Re-enactment Socs
Plantagenet Medieval Archery. . . Soc
Regia Anglorum
Sealed Knot
Victorian Military Soc
World War Two Living Hist Assn
> + Stunts & stunt coordination
Fights (stage/film)
Brit Academy Dramatic Combat
> + Stunts & stunt coordination
Filing systems > Office equipment & systems
Filling stations
Assn Petroleum & Explosives Admin
Fedn Petroleum Suppliers
Fillings (furniture)
Nat Fillings Assn
Film
access CINEMA [IRL]
Arts Centre Gp
Brit Academy Film & TV Arts
Brit Fedn Film Socs
Brit Film Inst
Fedn Comml Audiovisual Libraries
Inst Amat Cinematographers
Inst Contemporary Arts
Ir Film Inst
Mercia Cinema Soc
Nat Assn Higher Educ Moving Image
> + Photography
Film: advertising > Advertising: television & screen
Film: educational > Audio-visual aids & equipment
Film: festivals > Festivals: art, drama & music
Film: production & distribution
Advertising Producers Assn
Assn Studio & Production Eqpt Companies
BKSTS
Brit Soc Cinematographers
Broadcasting, Entertainment Cinematograph. . .U
Cine Glds GB
Cinema Exhibitors Assn
Directors Gld
Film Distbrs' Assn
Gld Brit Camera Technicians
Gld Brit Film & TV Editors
New Producers Alliance
Producers Alliance Cinema & TV
Production Mgrs Assn
Screen Producers Ireland
> + specialists concerned; Radio & TV; Video

Film: special effects
Inst Explosives Engrs
> + Stunts & stunt coordination
Film: stunts
Gld Stunt & Action Coordinators
> Stunts & stunt coordination
Filters
Heating, Ventilating & Air Conditioning Mfrs' Assn
Filtration
Filtration Soc
Finance/Financial services
Community Devt Finance Assn
Financial Services Ireland
Hundred Group of Finance Directors
Inst Financial Services
> + Accountancy; Banking; Investment; Management accountancy
Finance: brokers & agents
Corpn Insurance, Financial & Mortgage Advisers
Finance Ind Standards Assn
London Investment Banking Assn
Nat Assn Comml Finance Brokers
Whls Markets Brokers' Assn
Finance: hire purchase > Credit: trade;   Credit: unions
Finance: planning
Inst Financial Planning
Financial officers & controllers > Accountancy

Fine arts > Art headings
Fingerprinting
Fingerprint Soc
Finishes/finishing > Coatings; Metal: finishing; Paint
Finland
Finnish-Brit Cham Comm
Fire & flood damage restoration
Brit Damage Mgt Assn
Nat Carpet Cleaners Assn
Fire loss adjusters
Chart Inst Loss Adjusters
Fire marks
Fire Mark Circle
Fire protection & prevention
Architectural & Specialist Door Mfrs Assn
Assn Bldg Engrs
Assn Fire Consultants
Assn Specialist Fire Protection
Brit Approvals Fire Eqpt
Brit Fire Consortium
Brit Textile Technology Gp
Brit Urethane Foam Contrs Assn
Fedn Brit Fire Orgs
Fire Protection Assn
Glass & Glazing Fedn
Indep Fire Engg & Distrbrs Assn
Instn Fire Engrs
Intumescent Fire Seals Assn
Passive Fire Protection Fedn
Soc Protection Life Fire
Fire protection & prevention: equipment
Brit Automatic Fire Sprinkler Assn
Brit Fire Consortium
Fire Fighting Vehicles Mfrs Assn
Fire Ind Assn
Fire & Rescue Suppliers Assn
Nat Security Inspectorate
Residential Sprinkler Associates
Fire protection & prevention: history
Fire Brigade Soc
Fire Mark Circle
Fire Service Presvn Gp
Fire protection & prevention: personnel
Brit Fire Services Assn
Chief Fire Officers Assn
Chief Fire Officers Assn Ireland
Fire Brigades' U
Fire Officers Assn
Nat Assn Fire Officers
Nat Assn Healthcare Fire Officers
Firearms > Arms & armour; Guns & ammunition; Shooting
Firebricks > Refractories
Fires & fireplaces
Nat Fireplace Assn
Stove Industry Alliance
Fireworks
Brit Fireworks Assn
Brit Pyrotechnists Assn
Explosives Ind Gp
Inst Explosives Engrs

Nat Campaign Firework Safety
UK Pyrotechnics Soc
Firms > Business
First aid & immediate care
Assn First Aiders
Brit Assn Immediate Care
Brit Red Cross Soc
Cusoullies Union
Grand Priory... Hospital... St John
Ir Red Cross Soc
Medical Equestrian Assn
Order of Malta [IRL]
Saint Andrew's Ambulance Assn
Saint John Ambulance Assn
> + Medicine: accident & emergency
Fiscal studies
Inst Fiscal Studies
> + Taxation
Fish: biology > Ichthyology
Fish: curing
Aberdeen Fish Curers'...Assn
Fish: farming
Brit Marine Finfish Assn
Brit Trout Assn
Fedn Scot Aquaculture Producers
Scot Salmon Producers' Org
> + Salmon & trout
Fish: frying
Nat Assn Range Mfrs
Nat Fedn Fish Friers
Fish: meal & fish oil
UK Assn Fish Meal Mfrs
Fish: trade
Anglo North Irish Fish Producers Org
Fedn Brit Port Whls Fish Mchts Assns
Fedn Irish Fishermen
Herring Buyers Assn
Ir Fish Processors & Exporters Assn
Ir Fish Producers Org
London Fish Mchts (Billingsgate) Ltd
Nat Fedn Fishermen's Orgs
Nat Fedn Fishmongers
Nat Fedn Inland Whls Fish Mchts
Scot Seafood Processors Fedn
Seafood Scotland
UK Assn Fish Producer Orgs
Fish: tropical & ornamental
Fedn Brit Aquatic Socs
Ornamental Aquatic Tr Assn
Fishing
Anglo North Irish Fish Producers Org
Assn Salmon Fishery Bds
Assn Sea Fisheries C'ees [E&W]
Coracle Soc
Fedn Irish Fishermen
Fishermen's Assn
Inst Fisheries Mgt
Ir Fishermen's Org
New Under Ten Fishermen's Assn
Profl Coarse Fisheries Assn
Scot Fishermen's Fedn
Scot Fishermen's Org
Scot Pelagic Fishermen's Assn
Scot White Fish Producers Assn
Fishing (sport)
Anglers Consvn Assn
Angling Trs Assn
Assn Stillwater Game Fishery Mgrs
Carp Soc
Confedn Engl Fly Fishers
Countryside Alliance
Ir Fedn Sea Anglers
London Anglers Assn
Nat Assn Fisheries & Angling Consultatives
Nat Fedn Anglers
Nat Fedn Sea Anglers
Profl Anglers Assn
Salmon & Trout Assn
Scot Anglers Nat Assn
Scot Assn Country Sports
Scot Fedn Sea Anglers
Shark Angling Club
Specialist Anglers Alliance
U Country Sports Workers
Ulster Angling Fedn
Ulster Coarse Fishing Fedn

Fishing tackle
Angling Trs Assn
Fishing vessels > Ships: history & preservation
Fitness
Body Control Pilates Assn
Fitness Ind Assn
Fitness League
Fitness NI
Keep Fit Assn
Medau Soc
Nat Amat Bodybuilders Assn
Nat Register Personal Trainers
Profl Assn Alexander Teachers
Soc Teachers Alexander Technique
> + Health headings
Fitness equipment
Fitness Ind Assn
Sporting Goods Ind Assn
Sports & Fitness Eqpt Assn
Fives > Eton Fives; Rugby Fives
Fixing systems
Construction Fixings Assn
Flags, banners & bunting
Brit Sign & Graphics Assn
Flag Inst
Heraldry Soc
Pike & Shot Soc
Flat glass > Glass & glazing
Flat green bowling > Bowling
Flat roofing > Roofing
Flats: maintenance/management
Upkeep
Flavourings
Brit Essence Mfrs' Assn
Brit Soc Flavourists
Fleet Air Arm
Aircrewman's Assn
Fleet car operators & management
ACFO Ltd
Inst Car Fleet Mgt
Mobile Electronics & Security Fedn
> + Motor headings
Fletchers
Craft Gld Traditional Bowyers & Fletchers
Flexible hoses
Hose Mfrs' & Suppliers Assn
Flexible packaging > Packaging;   Plastics: film
Flies
Dipterists Forum
Flight safety > Aviation: safety, control & training
Flight simulation
R Aeronautical Soc
Floatation
Floatation Tank Assn
Flock & felt > Felt
Flood damage restoration > Fire & flood damage restoration
Flood protection
Assn Drainage Authorities
Flood Protection Assn
Flood research
Tornado & Storm Res Org
Floors
Assn Concrete Indl Flooring Contrs
Brit Precast Concrete Fedn
FeRFA
Nat Inst Carpet & Floorlayers
Floors: floorcoverings
Carpet Foundation
Contract Flooring Assn
Nat Inst Carpet & Floorlayers
UK Resilient Flooring Assn
> + Carpets
Floors: tiles & quarries > Tiles (floor & wall)
Floristry > Flowers, flower arrangement & floristry
Flour
Inc Nat Assn Brit & Ir Millers
Flowers, flower arrangement & floristry
Brit Dried Flowers Assn
Brit Florist Assn
Flower Import Tr Assn
Flowers & Plants Assn
Fresh Produce Consortium
Interflora
Nat Assn Flower Arrangement Socs
Pressed Flower Gld
Soc Floristry
> + Horticulture; specific varieties of flowers

© CBD Research Ltd · Beckenham · BR3 5JS · Tel 020 8650 7745 · Fax 020 8650 0768 · E-mail cbd@cbdresearch.com · www.cbdresearch.com

Flower remedies
        Brit Assn Flower Essence Producers
        Brit Flower &... Essences Assn
        Crystal & Healing Fedn
Flues > Chimneys
Fluid mechanics > Hydraulics & hydromechanics
Fluoridation
        Brit Fluoridation Soc
Flute playing
        Brit Flute Soc
Fly ash > Ash
Flyball
        Brit Flyball Assn
Fly-dressing
        Flydressers Gld
Flying > Air: sport; Aviation
Flying: discs (sport) > Disc golf (flying discs); Ultimate
Flying: training
        Brit Business & Gen Aviation Assn
        > + Aviation
Foam (plastic) > Plastics: foam
Foil: aluminium > Aluminium: foil
Folk dance & song
        Assn Festival Organisers
        Brit Bluegrass Music Assn
        Brit Country Music Assn
        Brit Western Dance Assn
        Cymdeithas Ddawns Werin Cymru
        Elsie Jeanette Oxenham Appreciation Soc
        English Folk Dance & Song Soc
        Folk Music Soc Ireland
        FolkArts England
        Musicians' U
        Order Woodcraft Chivalry
        R Scot Country Dance Soc
        Soc Intl Folk Dancing
        Southern Counties Folk Fedn
        Welsh Amat Music Fedn
        Welsh Folk Song Soc
        > + Highland dancing
Folk life & lore
        Cornish Language Coun
        Dracula Soc
        Folklore Ireland Soc
        Folklore Soc
        Lakeland Dialect Soc
        Soc Folk Life Studies
        Traditional Cosmology Soc
        Ulster Folk Life Soc
Follies
        Folly Fellowship
        > + Historic buildings
Food
        Assn Applied Biologists
        Bakers', Food & Allied Workers' U
        Brewing, Food & Beverage Ind Suppliers Assn
        Brit Nutrition Foundation
        Campden & Chorleywood Food Res Assn
        Food Devt Assn
        Food & Drink Fedn
        Gld Food Writers
        Inst Food Science & Technology
        Inst Food Science & Technology Ireland
        Instn Agricl Engrs
        Maltsters Assn
        McCarrison Soc
        NI Food & Drink Assn
        Soc Food Hygiene & Technology
        Sustain
        > + Health food; Organic growing & farming
Food: additives
        Assn Public Analysts
        Assn Public Analysts Scotland
        Food Additives & Ingredients Assn
        > + Animal feed
Food: allergy > Allergy
Food: casings > Sausage & food casings
Food: farm > Farm shops & food
Food: frozen & chilled
        Chilled Food Assn
        Food Storage & Distbn Fedn
        Provision Tr Fedn
        UK Assn Frozen Food Producers
Food: packaging
        Alliance Beverage Cartons & Environment
        Brit Bottlers' Inst
        Campden & Chorleywood Food Res Assn

        Foodservice Packaging Assn
        Indl Packaging Assn
        Metal Packaging Mfrs Assn
        Processing & Packaging Machinery Assn
Food: processing
        Food Processors Assn
        Instn Chemical Engrs
Food: safety
        Assn Port Health Authorities
        Brit Pest Control Assn
        R Envtl Health Inst Scotland
        Soc Applied Microbiology
Food: speciality & fine foods
        Cornish Pasty Assn
        Gld Fine Food Retailers
        Heart of England Fine Foods
        Infant & Dietetic Foods Assn
        Melton Mowbray Pork Pie Assn
        Provision Tr Fedn
        Rural Crafts Assn
Food: trade
        Brit Food Importers & Distrbrs Assn
        Brit Frozen Food Fedn
        Campden & Chorleywood Food Res Assn
        Food & Drink Ind [IRL]
        Ir Assn Distributive Trs
        Nat Fedn Meat & Food Traders
        Organic Food Fedn
        Scot Food & Drink Fedn
        Scot Food Trs Assn
        Wholesome Food Assn
        > + Grocery & provision trade; Health food; Takeaway & fast food
Food: transport > Road: haulage; Temperature controlled transport
Foodservice
        Foodservice Consultants Soc Intl (UK)
        Foodservice Packaging Assn
Foosball
        Brit Foosball Assn
Foot > Footwear; Orthopaedics
Football (American) > American football
Football (Association)
        Amat Football Alliance
        Assn Football Statisticians
        Football Assn
        Football Assn Ireland
        Football Assn Wales
        Football League
        Football Supporters' Fedn
        Football Writers Assn
        Inst Football Mgrs & Admin
        Ir Football Assn
        League Mgrs Assn
        Profl Footballers Assn
        Referees' Assn
        Scot Amat Football Assn
        Scot Football Assn
        Scot Football League
        Scot Women's Football
Football (Rugby)
        Brit Amat Rugby League Assn
        Ir Rugby Football U
        Profl Rugby Players Assn
        Rugby Football League
        Rugby Football U
        Rugby Memorabilia Soc
        Scot Rugby U
        Welsh Rugby U
Football (table)
        Brit Foosball Assn
        Table Soccer Players Assn
Football pools
        Pool Promoters Assn
Footpaths & rights of way
        Commons, Open Spaces... Presvn Soc
        Green Lane Assn
        Inst Public Rights Way Mgt
        Motoring Orgs' Land Access & Recreation Assn
        Offa's Dyke Assn
        Peak & Nthn Footpaths Soc
        Ramblers' Assn
        S Downs Soc
        S W Coast Path Assn
        Scot Rights Way & Access Soc
        Towpath Action Gp
        Trail Riders Fellowship
        > + Conservation; Open spaces

Footwear: industry
Boot & Shoe Mfrs Assn
Brit Equestrian Tr Assn
Brit Footwear Assn
Community
Master Craftsmen's Assn
Sporting Goods Ind Assn
Textile Inst Intl
Footwear: repairs
MultiService Assn
Footwear: trade
Indep Footwear Retailers Assn
Instock Footwear Suppliers Assn
Soc Shoe Fitters
Forage > Animal feed; Grass & grassland
Forces > Armed forces & veterans: welfare;   Army; Royal Navy
Forensic accountancy
Network Indep Forensic Accountants
> + Accountancy
Forensic science
Assn Consulting Scientists
Assn Lawyers & Legal Advisors
Brit Academy Forensic Sciences
Brit Assn Forensic Medicine
Brit Assn Human Identification
Fingerprint Soc
Forensic Science Soc
> + Medicine & the law
Forestry
Brit Inst Agricl Consultants
Confedn Forest Inds
FCA Membership Ltd
Horticultural Trs Assn
Inst Chart Foresters
Instn Agricl Engrs
Ir Timber Growers Assn
Permaculture Assn
R Forestry Soc England, Wales & NI
R Highland & Agricl Soc Scotland
R Scot Forestry Soc
R Welsh Agricl Soc
S England Agricl Soc
Soc Ir Foresters
Tropical Agriculture Assn
UK Forest Products Assn
> + Timber
Forestry: machinery
Agricl Engrs Assn
Forging > Metal: forming
Fork-lift trucks
Assn Indl Truck Trainers
Brit Indl Truck Assn
Fork Lift Truck Assn
Indep Training Standards Scheme & Register
> + Lifting & loading equipment
Formby (George)
George Formby Soc
Fortresses & forts
Fort Cumberland. . . Militaria Soc
Fortress Study Gp
Palmerston Forts Soc
Pike & Shot Soc
Pillbox Study Gp
Subterranea Britannica
Forwarding > Aviation; Shipping & forwarding
Fossils > Palaeontology
Fostering & foster parents
Brit Assn Adoption & Fostering
Fostering Network
Foundations (buildings)
ASUCplus
Fedn Piling Specialists
Ground Forum
Subsidence Forum
> + Building
Foundries
Foundry Eqpt & Supplies Assn
Inst Cast Metals Engrs
Fountains
Fountain Soc
Four by fours [4-wheel drive vehicles]
Alliance Urban 4x4s
Fowl > Poultry
Foxes
Nat Fox Welfare Soc
Foxhounds
Masters Foxhounds Assn

Peterborough R Foxhound Show Soc
> + Hunts & hunting
Fragile X syndrome
Fragile X Soc
Fragrances & aromatic compounds
Brit Fragrance Assn
Intl Gen Produce Assn
Frames > Concrete & concrete products; Picture framers
France
Assn Brit Tour Operators France
Assn Study Modern & Contemporary France
Fédn Britannique Alliances Françaises
Franco-British Chamber of Commerce & Industry
Franco-British Soc
Franco-Scottish Soc Scotland
Napoleonic Soc
France: language & literature
Anglo-Norman Text Soc
Assn French Language Studies
Assn Language Learning
Fédn Britannique Alliances Françaises
Soc French Studies
Franchising
Assn Franchised Distbrs Electronic Components
Brit Franchise Assn
Ir Franchise Assn
Free Churches > individual Churches
Free speech > Censorship
Free trade
Free Trade League
Freedom of the individual > Individual freedom
Freemasonry
Grand Lodge Antient. . . Masons Scotland
Utd Grand Lodge England
Freemen
Freemen England & Wales
Freemen & Glds City Chester
Gld Freemen City Lond
Freestyle dancing > Dancing
Freezing (& chilled) food > Food: frozen & chilled; Refrigeration
Freight transport
Brit Intl Freight Assn
Chart Inst Logistics & Transport
Freight Transport Assn
ICHCA Intl
Ir Intl Freight Assn
Rail Freight Gp
> + Road: haulage;   Transport
French > France: language & literature
Freshwater biology > Biology
Friction
Brit Friction Materials Coun
Friedreich's Ataxia
Ataxia UK
Friendly societies
Assn Friendly Socs
Friends (Quakers)
Friends Histl Soc
Religious Society of Friends (Quakers)
Frisbees > Disc golf (flying discs); Ultimate (sport)
Frost (Robert)
Friends Dymock Poets
Frozen food > Food: frozen & chilled; Refrigeration
Fruit: growing
Brit Indep Fruit Growers Assn
Brit Summer Fruits
English Apples & Pears
Ir Comml Horticl Assn
NI Fruit Growers Assn
Nuclear Stock Assn
Scot Soc Crop Res
Fruit: juice
Brit Fruit Juice Assn
Brit Soft Drinks Assn
Fruit: machines > Amusements & coin operated machines
Fruit: preserving
Food Processors Assn
Fruit: trade
Fresh Produce Consortium
Nat Dried Fruit Tr Assn
Frying media
Nat Edible Oil Distbrs Assn
Fuchsias
Brit Fuchsia Soc
Fuel
Chemical Recycling Assn
Natural Gas Vehicle Assn

© CBD Research Ltd · Beckenham · BR3 5JS · Tel 020 8650 7745 · Fax 020 8650 0768 · E-mail cbd@cbdresearch.com · www.cbdresearch.com

Renewable Energy Assn
> + specific fuels
Fuel ash > Ash
Fumes & fume extraction
Fan Mfrs' Assn
> + Air: pollution; Air: conditioning & ventilation
Fundraisers
Assn Fundraising Consultants
Inst Fundraising
Funerals > Burial & cremation
Fungi > Mycology
Fur
Brit Fur Tr Assn
Furnace technology & construction
Brit Glass Mfrs' Confedn
Brit Indl Furnace Construction Assn
Inst Refractories Engrs
Refractory Users Federation
Furnishing fabrics
Assn Soft Furnishers
Brit Interior Textiles Assn
Furniture
Assn Suppliers Furniture Ind
BFM Ltd
Brit Antique Furniture Restorers Assn
Brit Educl Suppliers Assn
Furniture Ind Res Assn
Leisure & Outdoor Furniture Assn
Furniture: contract > Contract services
Furniture: history
Chippendale Soc
Furniture Hist Soc
Furniture: warehousing & removal
Brit Assn Removers
Movers Inst
Nat Gld Removers & Storers
Further education > Adult education; Education; Technical education;
Universities
Furtwängler (Wilhelm)
Wilhelm Furtwängler Soc
Futons
Futon Assn
> + Beds & bedding
Futures & options
Futures & Options Association

G

Gaelic language & culture
Cheshaght Ghailckagh (Yn)
Comunn Clàrsaich
Comunn Gaidhealach
Fèisean Gàidheal
Gaelic Athletic Assn
R Celtic Soc
Scot Gaelic Texts Soc
> + Scotland: language & literature
Galliformes
World Pheasant Assn UK
> + Game & game birds
Gallipoli
Gallipoli Assn
Galls (plants)
Brit Plant Gall Soc
Galvanising
Galvanizers Assn
Game & game birds
Brit Assn Shooting & Consvn
Game Conservancy Trust
Game Farmers Assn
Nat Game Dealers Assn
Nat Gamekeepers Org
Nat Org Beaters & Pickers Up
Scot Gamekeepers Assn
World Pheasant Assn UK
Games > Athletics; Highland games; Sports; individual sports & games
Games: equipment > Sports: equipment
Gaming
Amusement & Gaming Ind Forum
Brit Casino Assn
Casino Operators' Assn
Remote Gambling Assn
> + Casinos

Garages (equipment & waste)
Assn Garage Door Specialists
Door & Hardware Fedn
Forecourt Eqpt Fedn
Garage Eqpt Assn
Oil Recycling Assn
Retail Motor Ind Fedn
> + Filling stations; Motor trade
Garden centres & shops
Garden Centre Assn
Garden furniture > Horticulture: machinery & supplies; Outdoor furniture
Garden machinery > Horticulture & garden: machinery
Gardens & gardening
Assn Gardens Trusts
Assn Leading Visitor Attractions
Brit Assn Landscape Inds
Cottage Garden Soc
E A Bowles of Myddleton House Soc
Fedn City Farms & Community Gardens
Garden Hist Soc
Garden & Landscape Designers Assn
Good Gardeners' Assn
Houses, Castles & Gardens Ireland
Japanese Garden Soc
Nat Coun Consvn Plants & Gardens
Nat Gardens Scheme Charitable Trust
Nat Soc Allotment & Leisure Gardeners
Profl Gardeners' Gld
Soc Garden Designers
> + Horticulture; Parks & gardens
Gardens & gardening: for disabled
Gardening Disabled Trust & Garden Club
THRIVE
Gardens & gardening: writers
Garden Media Gld
Gas
Brit Compressed Gases Assn
Carbon Monoxide & Gas Safety Soc
Coun Registered Gas Installers
Energy Inds Coun
Gas Forum
ICOM Energy Assn
Instn Gas Engrs & Mgrs
Nat Jt Utilities Gp
Offshore Contrs' Assn
Oil & Gas UK
SBGI
UK Onshore Operators Gp
UK Onshore Pipeline Operators' Assn
> + Ocean industries
Gas appliances > Domestic appliances; Gas detection
Gas chromatography
Chromatographic Soc
Gas detection
Coun Gas Detection & Envtl Monitoring
Gas engines & turbines
Instn Diesel & Gas Turbine Engrs
Natural Gas Vehicle Assn
Gaskell (Mrs Elizabeth Cleghorn)
Gaskell Soc
Gaskets
Gasket Cutters' Assn
Gastroenterology
Brit Soc Gastroenterology
GIST Support UK
Gates > Automatic gates; Stairs: gates & barriers
Guarantees (home improvements) > Warranty against work under guarantee
Gaucher's disease
Gaucher's Assn
Gauges
Gauge & Tool Makers Assn
Pressure Gauge & Dial Thermometer Assn
> + Control engineering
Gay organisations > Homosexuality
Gears
Brit Gear Assn
Geese
Brit Poultry Coun
Brit Waterfowl Assn
> + Poultry
Gemstones
Brit Jewellers Assn
Gemmological Assn
Gender dysphoria > Transsexuality & transvestism
Genealogy
Anglo-German Family Hist Soc
Assn Family Hist Socs Wales

Assn Genealogists & Researchers in Archives
Assn Profl Genealogists Ireland
Assn Scot Genealogists & Researchers Archives
Catholic Family Hist Soc
Fedn Family Hist Socs
Harleian Soc
Heraldry Soc
Inst Heraldic & Genealogical Studies
Ir Family Hist Soc
Ir Genealogical Res Soc
Scot Assn Family Hist Socs
Scot Genealogy Soc
Soc Genealogists
Ulster Histl Foundation
> + Heraldry
General practitioners > Hospitals; Medical practice
Generators (electrical power)
Assn Mfrs Power generating Systems
> + Electricity
Generic medicines
Brit Generic Mfrs' Assn
> + Pharmaceuticals
Genetics
BioIndustry Assn
Brit Livestock Genetics Consortium Ltd
Brit Soc Human Genetics
Genetic Interest Gp
Genetics Soc
GeneWatch
Human Genetics Alert
Scientists Global Responsibility
Soc Gen Microbiology
Genito-urinary medicine
Brit Assn Sexual Health & HIV
Brit Fedn Sexually Transmitted Diseases
Brit HIV Assn
Soc Sexual Health Advisers
Genomics > Genetics
Geography
Assn Geographic Inf
Geographical Assn
Geographical Soc Ireland
Manchester Geographical Soc
R Geographical Soc
R Scot Geographical Soc
Scot Assn Geography Teachers
Systematics Assn
Geology
Earth Science Teachers' Assn
Edinburgh Geological Soc
Geological Soc
Geologists' Assn
Inst Geologists Ireland
Ir Assn Economic Geology
Ir Geological Assn
Mineral Ind Res Org
Nat Assn UK Regionally Important Geological Sites
Remote Sensing & Photogrammetry Soc
Tertiary Res Gp
Yorkshire Geological Soc
> + Earth sciences, structure & resources; Palaeontology
Geomembranes
Brit Geomembrane Assn
Geomorphology
Geological Soc
Nat Assn UK Regionally Important Geological Sites
> + Geography
Geophysics
R Astronomical Soc
George Cross
Victoria Cross & George Cross Assn
Geospatial engineering
Instn Civil Engg Surveyors
Geotechnics
Assn Geotechnical & Geoenvironmental Specialists
Brit Geotechnical Assn
Ground Forum
Soc Underwater Technology Ltd
Geraniums & pelargoniums
Hardy Plant Soc
Pelargonium & Geranium Soc
Gerbils
Nat Gerbil Soc
Geriatrics & ageing
Assn Educ & Ageing
Brit Assn Service Elderly
Brit Geriatrics Soc

Brit Longevity Soc
Brit Soc Gerontology
Brit Soc Res Ageing
Relatives & Residents Assn
> + Old people's organisations
German > Germany: language & literature
German measles (Rubella)
Sense
Germany
Anglo-German Family Hist Soc
Assn Study German Politics
Brit Cham Comm Germany
Brit-German Assn
German-Brit Cham Ind & Comm
German Hist Soc
German Rly Soc
Germany: language & literature
Assn Language Learning
Germany: law
Brit-German Jurists' Assn
Gestalt Therapy
Brit Gestalt Soc
Ghosts
Assn Scientific Study Anomalous Phenomena
> + Paranormal & psychical research
Gibson (Wilfred)
Friends Dymock Poets
Gift vouchers & cards
Voucher Assn
Gifted children > Children: gifted
Gifts (public) > Donations (public)
Giftware
Brit Ceramic Confedn
Brit Ceramic Gift & Tableware Mfrs' Assn
Brit Jewellery, Giftware & Finishing Fedn
Giftware Assn
Wales Craft Coun
Gilbert (Sir William Schwenk)
Gilbert & Sullivan Soc
Gilding
Brit Antique Furniture Restorers Assn
Gin & vodka
Gin & Vodka Assn
> + Wines & spirits trade
Gipsies > Gypsies & travelling people
Girls organisations > Youth organisation headings
Gladiolus
Brit Gladiolus Soc
Glamour items > Cosmetic items (collecting)
Glass & glazing
Brit Glass Mfrs' Confedn
Flat Glass Coun
Flat Glass Mfrs Assn
Glass & Glazing Fedn
Nat Fedn Glaziers
Soc Glass Technology
Glass blowing/making
Brit Soc Scientific Glassblowers
Carnival Glass Soc
Contemporary Glass Soc
Scot Glass Soc
Glass engraving
Contemporary Glass Soc
Gld Glass Engravers
Glass painting
Brit Soc Master Glass Painters
Glass & Glazing Fedn
Kempe Soc
Glassfibre
Intl Glassfibre Reinforced Concrete Assn
Glasshouse crops > Horticulture
Glasshouses & conservatories
Glass & Glazing Fedn
Glassware
Assn Hist Glass
Contemporary Glass Soc
Glass Circle
Glassware: scientific
Brit Soc Scientific Glassblowers
> + Laboratory equipment & technology
Glazing > Glass & glazing
Gliding & soaring
Brit Gliding Assn
Scot Gliding U
Vintage Glider Club
> + Hang gliding
Global warming > Climate change

© CBD Research Ltd · Beckenham · BR3 5JS · Tel 020 8650 7745 · Fax 020 8650 0768 · E-mail cbd@cbdresearch.com · www.cbdresearch.com

Glosa
        Glosa Educ Org
Gloves
        Brit Glove Assn
Glucose
        Brit Starch Ind Assn
Glue sniffing > Solvent abuse
Glulam (glued laminated timber)
        Glued Laminated Timber Assn
Glycogen storage disease
        Assn Glycogen Storage Diseases
Gnomonics > Sundials
Go
        Brit Go Assn
Goats
        Anglo-Nubian Breed Soc
        Bagot Goat Soc
        Brit Angora Goat Soc
        Brit Goat Soc
        Brit Veterinary Assn
        English Goat Breeders Assn
        Golden Guernsey Goat Soc
        Harness Goat Soc
        Pygmy Goat Club
        Scot Cashmere Producers Assn
Goethe (Johann Wolfgang von)
        English Goethe Soc
Gold (dealing in) > Bullion dealing
Gold panning
        Brit Goldpanning Assn
Goldsmiths & silversmiths
        Assn Brit Designer Silversmiths
        Brit Cutlery & Silverware Assn
        Brit Jewellery, Giftware & Finishing Fedn
        Company Goldsmiths Dublin
        Inst Profl Goldsmiths
        Nat Assn Goldsmiths
Golf
        Assn Golf Writers
        English Golf U
        Golf Club GB
        Golf Club Mgrs' Assn
        Golf Consultants Assn
        Golf U Wales
        Golfing U Ireland
        Ir Ladies Golf U
        Ladies' Golf U
        Nat Golf Clubs Advy Assn
        Profl Golfers Assn
        R & Ancient Golf Club
        Scot Golf U
        Scot Ladies' Golfing Assn
Golf courses
        Brit Assn Golf Course Constructors
        Brit & Intl Golf Greenkeepers' Assn
        Nat Assn Public Golf Courses
        Sports Turf Res Inst
        > + Sportsgrounds & synthetic surfaces
Golf equipment
        Brit Golf Ind Assn
Goon Show
        Goon Show Preservation Soc
Gothic literature > Horror literature
Gout
        Purine Metabolic Patients Assn
Government > Parliamentary government
Government: accountability
        Transparency Intl (UK)
Graduates in business > Commerce
Graffiti
        Anti-Graffiti Assn
Grain
        Grain & Feed Tr Assn
        Ir Grain & Feed Assn
        NI Grain Tr Assn
        Scot Corn Tr Assn
        > + Agriculture: merchants;   Flour
Grainger (Percy Aldridge)
        Percy Grainger Society
Grammar schools
        Nat Grammar Schools Assn
        > + Education;   Independent & public schools
Gramophones > Sound recording & reproduction
Grandparents
        Grandparents Action Gp
        Grandparents Assn
        > + Parents

Grapes > Wines & viticulture
Graphic arts & design
        Brit Assn Print & Communication
        Chart Soc Designers
        > + Industrial graphics; Printing headings
Graphology & graphoanalysis
        Brit Astrological & Psychic Soc
        Brit Inst Graphologists
Grass & grassland
        Brit Grassland Soc
        Ir Grassland Assn
        N Scotland Grassland Soc
        > + Seeds; Sportsgrounds & synthetic surfaces; Turf
Grasses (dried)
        Brit Dried Flowers Assn
Gravel > Sand & gravel
Gravy
        Food Processors Assn
Grease > Lubricants
Greece
        Anglo-Hellenic League
        Brit Hellenic Cham Comm
        Greek Inst
        Soc Promotion Hellenic Studies
        > + Classical studies
Green lanes/roads > Footpaths & rights of way
Greenhouses > Glasshouses & conservatories
Greeting cards
        Greeting Card Assn
Greyhounds
        Brit Veterinary Assn
        Nat Greyhound Racing Club
Grief > Bereavement
Grieg (Edvard Hagerup)
        Grieg Soc
Grills & security shutters
        Brit Blind & Shutter Assn
        > + Doors; Windows: blinds & shutters
Grinding & milling machinery
        Solids Handling & Processing Assn
Grit > Aggregates
Grocery & provision trade
        Assn Convenience Stores
        Convenience Stores & Newsagents Assn [IRL]
        Fedn Whls Distbrs
        Inst Grocery Distbn
        NISA Today's Holdings Ltd
        Provision Tr Fedn
        RGDATA [IRL]
        Scot Food Trs Assn
        Scot Grocers' Fedn
        Scot Whls Assn
        > + Food
Grooms & grooming (pets)
        Brit Grooms Assn
        Pet Care Trust
Grottoes
        Folly Fellowship
Groundnuts
        Fedn Oils, Seeds & Fats Assns
Groundsmen
        Inst Groundsmanship
        > + Sportsgrounds & synthetic surfaces
Group analysis
        Group Analytic Soc
        Inst Gp Analysis
Grouse > Game & game birds
Grouts & grouting
        UK Quality Ash Assn
Growth
        Child Growth Foundation
        Prader-Willi Syndrome Assn
        Restricted Growth Assn
        Tall Persons Club
        Turner Syndrome Support Soc
Guanacos > Camelids
Guard & patrol services
        Brit Security Ind Assn
Guardians (educational) > Education: guardians
Guernsey (Channel Islands)
        Guernsey Cham Comm
        Guernsey Growers Assn
        Société Guernesiaise
Guide dogs
        Guide Dogs for Blind Assn
        Seeing Dogs Alliance
Guide lecturers > Travel & tourism: guides

Guides (girls) > Youth organisation headings
Guillain Barré syndrome
        Guillain Barré Syndrome Support Gp
Guinea pigs > Cavies
Gulf War veterans
        Gulf Veterans Assn
Gums > Resins & gums
Gunite > Concrete & concrete products
Guns & ammunition
        Gun Tr Assn
        Histl Breechloading Smallarms Assn
        Ordnance Soc
        > + Shooting
Guttering
        Metal Gutter Mfrs Assn
Gwenllian (Princess) of Wales
        Princess Gwenllian Soc
Gymnasium: equipment
        Fitness Ind Assn
        Sports & Fitness Eqpt Assn
Gymnastics
        Brit Gymnastics
        Scot Gymnastics Assn
        Welsh Amat Gymnastic Assn
        > + Physical education
Gynaecology > Maternity; Obstetrics & gynaecology
Gypsies & travelling people
        Nat Assn Teachers Travellers
Gypsum
        Gypsum Products Devt Assn

H

Hacks > Horse(s) headings
Haematology
        Brit Blood Transfusion Soc
        Brit Hypertension Soc
        Brit Microcirculation Soc
        Brit Soc Haematology
        Haemochromatosis Soc
Haemophilia
        Haemophilia Soc
Haggard (Sir (Henry) Rider
        Rider Haggard Soc
Haiku
        Brit Haiku Soc
        Time Haiku
Hailstorms
        Tornado & Storm Res Org
Hair (curled)
        Nat Fillings Assn
Hair & scalp treatment
        Hairline Intl
        Inst Trichologists
Hairdressing
        Freelance Hair & Beauty Fedn
        Hairdressing & Beauty Suppliers Assn
        Inc Gld Hairdressers
        Nat Assn Screen Make-up Artists & Hairdressers
        Nat Hairdressers Fedn
Halibut
        Brit Marine Finfish Assn
        > + Fish headings
Ham > Bacon
Hammer-throwing
        Hammer Circle
Hampden (John) 1594-1693
        John Hampden Soc
Hamsters
        Brit Hamster Assn
Hand driers (warm air)
        Brit Warm Air Hand Drier Assn
Hand knitting > Knitting & knitting wool/yarns
Hand tools > Tools
Handbags
        Brit Travelgoods & Accessories Assn
        > + Leathergoods
Handball
        England Handball Assn
        Gaelic Athletic Assn
        Scot Handball Assn
Handbell ringing
        Handbell Ringers
        > + Bellringing

Handcycling
        Handcycling Assn
Handicapped persons > Children: handicapped;   Disablement
Handicraft > Crafts & craftsmanship
Handley Page (Sir Frederick)
        Handley Page Assn
Handling > Materials: management/handling
Hands
        Brit Soc Surgery Hand
Handwriting
        Calligraphy & Lettering Arts Soc
        Soc Italic Handwriting
        Soc Limners
        Soc Scribes & Illuminators
        > + Graphology & graphoanalysis
Hang gliding
        Brit Hang Gliding & Paragliding Assn
        Scot Hang Gliding & Paragliding Fedn
        > + Gliding & soaring
Harassment
        Nat Assn Support Victims Stalking & Harassment
Harbours > Ports; Yachts & yachting
Hardmetal > Metal
Hardware & housewares
        Brit Hardware Fedn
        Brit Home Enhancement Tr Assn
        Cutlery & Allied Trs Res Assn
        Door & Hardware Fedn
        Ir Hardware & Bldg Materials Assn
        > + Building materials & supplies
Hardwoods
        Timber Tr Fedn
        > + Timber
Hardy (Thomas)
        Dorset Natural Hist & Archaeol Soc
        Thomas Hardy Soc
Hares
        Assn Masters Harriers & Beagles
        Game Conservancy Trust
Harmonicas
        Nat Harmonica League
Harness racing
        Brit Harness Racing Club
Harps & harp playing
        Comunn Clàrsaich
        UK Harp Assn
Hat pins
        Hat Pin Soc
Hatcheries
        Pullet Hatcheries Assn
Hats
        Brit Hat Gld
Haulage > Freight transport; Road: haulage
Hauntings > Paranormal & psychical research
Hawks & hawking
        Brit Falconers' Club
        Brit Hawking Assn
        Hawk & Owl Trust
        Scot Assn Country Sports
        > + Birds
Hay & straw
        Brit Hay & Straw Mchts' Assn
        Straw Bale Bldg Assn
Haydn (Franz Joseph)
        Haydn Soc
Hayfever > Allergy
Hazards > Home: safety; Road: safety & control; Safety
Hazel nuts
        Combined Edible Nut Tr Assn
Head & neck injury & disease
        Brit Assn Head & Neck Oncologists
        Brit Assn Otorhinolaryngologists
        Cranio Sacral Soc
        Craniofacial Soc
        Craniosacral Therapy Assn
        Headlines
Headaches > Migraine & headaches
Heads of schools & colleges
        Assn Heads Indep Schools
        Assn Headteachers & Deputes Scotland
        Assn School & College Leaders
        Foundation & Aided Schools Nat Assn
        Girls' Schools Assn
        Headmasters & Headmistresses Conf
        Nat Assn Head Teachers

© CBD Research Ltd · Beckenham · BR3 5JS · Tel 020 8650 7745 · Fax 020 8650 0768 · E-mail cbd@cbdresearch.com · www.cbdresearch.com

School Leaders Scotland
Soc Headmasters & Headmistresses Indep Schools
> + Teachers

Headwear
Brit Hat Gld
> + Protective clothing/equipment

Healing
Assn Therapeutic Healers
Brit Soc Dowsers
Confedn Healing Orgs
> + Complementary medicine; Medicine headings

Health
Alliance Health Profls
Alliance Natural Health
Brit Assn Sport & Exercise Sciences
Gld Health Writers
Health & Beauty Emplrs Fedn
Inst Health Promotion & Educ
Ir Health Services Mgt Inst
McCarrison Soc
Soc Health Educ & . . . Specialists
UK Public Health Assn
> + other aspects of health

Health administration
Assn Healthcare Communicators
Inst Healthcare Mgt
> + National Health Service

Health care
Brit Healthcare Business Intelligence Assn
CNK Alliance
Fedn Healthcare Science
HL7 UK Ltd
Ir Pharmaceutical Healthcare Assn
Nat Assn Primary Care
UK eHealth Assn

Health care: equipment & supplies
Assn Brit Healthcare Inds
Brit Assn Pharmaceutical Whlsrs
Brit Healthcare Trs Assn
Health Care Supply Assn
Ir Med Devices Assn [IRL]
Performance Textiles Assn
Pharmaceutical & Healthcare Sciences Soc

Health & fitness > Fitness

Health food
Consumers Health Choice
Health Food Inst
Health Food Mfrs Assn
Nat Assn Health Stores
> + Food

Health records
Inst Health Record & Inf Mgt

Health resorts > Spas

Health & safety
Health & Safety Sign Assn
Indep Safety Consultants Assn
> + subject concerned eg Health

Hearing
Brit Academy Audiology
Brit Assn Audiovestibular Physicians
Brit Assn Community Doctors in Audiology
Brit Soc Audiology
Brit Soc Hearing Aid Audiologists
Brit Tinnitus Assn
> + Deafness

Heart disease > Cardiology

Heat treatment
Inst Materials, Minerals & Mining
Surface Engg Assn

Heat pumps
Heat Pump Assn

Heath (Edward) [Ted]
Ted Heath Musical Appreciation Soc

Heaths & heathers
Heather Soc
Horticultural Trs Assn

Heating
Assn Plumbing & Heating Contrs
BEAMA
BSRIA
Chart Instn Bldg Services Engrs
Combined Heat & Power Assn
Commissioning Specialists Assn
Fedn Heating Spares Stockists
Heat Pump Assn
Heat Transfer & Fluid Flow Service
Heating, Ventilating & Air Conditioning Mfrs' Assn

Heating & Ventilating Contrs Assn
Hose Mfrs' & Suppliers Assn
ICOM Energy Assn
Inst Domestic Heating. . . Engrs
Inst Plumbing & Heating Engg
Oil Firing Technical Assn Petroleum Ind
SBGI
Scot & NI Plumbing Emplrs' Fedn
Stove Industry Alliance
> + Air: conditioning & ventilating

Hebe
Hebe Soc

Hedgehogs
Brit Hedgehog Presvn Soc

Hedges & hedge-laying
Hedge Laying Assn Ireland
Hedgeline
Horticultural Trs Assn
Nat Hedgelaying Soc

Helicopters
Brit Helicopter Advy Bd
R Aeronautical Soc
> + Aerial photography; Aviation

Hellenic studies > Classical studies

Helplines
Telephone Helplines Assn
> + specific area of interest

Hemerocallis > Hostas & Hemerocallis

Hemp
Manila Hemp Assn

Hens > Poultry

Henty (George Alfred)
Henty Soc

Heraldry
Harleian Soc
Heraldry Soc
Heraldry Soc Scotland
Inst Heraldic & Genealogical Studies
Pike & Shot Soc
Soc Heraldic Arts
> + Genealogy

Herbicides > Agriculture: chemicals

Herbs & herbal medicine
Brit Herb Tr Assn
Brit Herbal Medicine Assn
Consumers Health Choice
Herb Soc
Intl Gen Produce Assn
Intl Register Consultant Herbalists & Homoeopaths
Nat Inst Med Herbalists
Register Chinese Herbal Medicine

Herpes
Congenital CMV Assn
Herpes Viruses Assn

Herpetology
Brit Herpetological Soc

Herring
Herring Buyers Assn
Scot Pelagic Fishermen's Assn
> + Fish headings; Fishing

Herschel (Sir [Frederick] William)
William Herschel Soc

Hides & skins > Leather

Hi-fi > Radio & TV trade; Sound recording & reproduction

Higden (Ranulf/Ralph)
Ranulf Higden Soc

High frequency welding
Plastics & Board Inds Fedn

Higher education > Education; Technical education; Universities

Highland dancing
Brit Assn Teachers Dancing
Edinburgh Highland Reel & Strathspey Soc
R Scot Country Dance Soc
Scot Dance Teachers Alliance
Scot Official Highland Dancing Assn
UK Alliance Dance Teachers
> + Dancing

Highland games
Scot Games Assn

Highway > Road headings

Hill farming
Blackface Sheep Breeders Assn
> + Agriculture

Hill running > Running

Hill walking > Walking

Hillclimbs (motorcycling)
    Nat Hillclimb Assn
    > + Motor cycling & scooter riding
Hilton (James) 1900-1954
    James Hilton Soc
Hip (diseases of)
    Brit Orthopaedic Assn
    Perthes Assn
    STEPS
HIPs
    Assn Home Information Pack Providers
Hire purchase > Credit trade
Hispanists > Portugal; Spain
Historic aircraft > Aviation: history
Historic buildings
    Ancient Monuments Soc
    Assn Local Govt Archaeol Officers
    Assn Studies Consvn Historic Bldgs
    Brit Assn Friends Museums
    Campaign Protection Rural Wales
    Charles Rennie Mackintosh Soc
    English Historic Towns Forum
    Historic Houses Assn
    Houses, Castles & Gardens Ireland
    Inst Consvn Historic &... Works Ireland
    Inst Historic Bldg Consvn
    Listed Property Owners Club
    Medieval Settlement Res Gp
    Nat Assn Field Studies Officers
    Nat Trust
    Nat Trust Ireland
    Nat Trust Scotland
    Save Britain's Heritage
    Scot Vernacular Bldgs Working Gp
    Soc Antiquaries Lond
    Soc Protection Ancient Bldgs
    TimeWatch
    UK Assn Presvn Trusts
    Vernacular Architecture Gp
    > + Archaeology: county societies;   Architecture;   Church:
    buildings;   Conservation: area organisations
Historic vehicles > Motor vehicles: historic
Historical documents & records > Archives; Record agents;   Records: historical
History
    Assn Hist & Computing
    Brit Academy
    Fedn Local History Socs [RoI]
    Histl Assn
    History Curriculum Assn
    London Medieval Soc
    Oral Hist Soc
    R Histl Soc
    Soc Genealogists
    Social Hist Curators Gp
    Social Hist Soc
    > + Archaeology; other headings with 'history' as a sub-heading
HIV positive > Genito-urinary medicine
Hobbies
    Brit Toy & Hobby Assn
    > + object of interest
Hockey
    England Hockey
    Ir Hockey Assn
    Scot Hockey U
    Sporting Goods Ind Assn
    Ulster Women's Hockey U
    Welsh Hockey U
    > + Skating: board, inline & roller
Hodgkin's disease
    Lymphoma Assn
Hoists
    Construction Plant-hire Assn
    Materials Handling Engrs Assn
Holiday camps & centres
    Assn Heads Outdoor Educ Centres
    Brit Activity Holiday Assn
    Holiday Centres Assn
Holiday property owners > Self catering
Holiday resorts
    Brit Resorts & Destinations Assn
    Tourism Mgt Inst
Holiday timesharing > Timeshare industry
Holidays > Travel & tourism
Holistic medicine & therapy
    Assn Reflexologists
    Assn Therapy Lecturers
    Brit Holistic Med Assn

    Fedn Holistic Therapists
    Holistic Healers Assn
    Inst Holistic Therapies
    > + Complementary medicine
Holland > Netherlands
Holmes (Sherlock)
    Friends Dr Watson
    Sherlock Holmes Soc Lond
Holography
    R Photographic Soc
Home: care > Domiciliary care
Home: confinements > Maternity
Home: decoration
    Nat Home Improvement Coun
    > + Paint; Wallcoverings & wallpaper
Home: equity release schemes
    HIPS (97)
    Safe Home Income Plans
Home: information packs
    Assn Home Information Pack Providers
    SPLINTA
Home: laundering
    Home Laundering Consultative Coun
    > + Laundering
Home: safety
    Inst Home Safety
Home: shopping
    Mail Order Trs Assn
    > + Mail order trade
Home: working from
    Home Business Alliance
    Telework Assn
Homeless
    Homeless Link
    Salvation Army
    Scot Coun Single Homeless
    Shelter
Homes > Housing; Nursing homes; Social service
Homeworkers > Home: working from
Homing pigeons > Pigeons
Homoeopathy
    Alliance Registered Homeopaths
    Brit Assn Homoeopathic Mfrs
    Brit Assn Homoeopathic Veterinary Surgeons
    Brit Homeopathic Dental Assn
    Brit Homoeopathic Assn
    Fac Homeopathy
    Homeopathic Med Assn
    Intl Register Consultant Herbalists & Homoeopaths
    Nat Assn Homeopathic Gps
    Soc Homeopaths
Homosexuality
    Campaign Homosexual Equality
Honey
    Honey Assn
Hong Kong
    Brit Cham Comm Hong Kong
    Hong Kong Assn
Hopkins (Gerard Manley)
    Hopkins Soc
Hoppers > Silos & hoppers
Hops
    Brewery Hist Soc
    Hop Mchts Assn
    Nat Hop Assn
Horace [Quintus Horatius Flaccus]
    Horatian Soc
Hormone study & related diseases > Endocrinology
Hormone replacement therapy (HRT)
    Brit Menopause Soc
Horns (musical instruments)
    Brit Horn Soc
Horology
    Antiquarian Horological Soc
    Brit Horological Fedn
    Brit Horological Inst
    Brit Jewellers Assn
    Brit Jewellery, Giftware & Finishing Fedn
    Brit Sundial Soc
    Brit Watch & Clock Makers Gld
    MultiService Assn
    Nat Assn Goldsmiths
Horror literature
    Brit Fantasy Soc
    Dracula Soc
Horse: brasses
    Nat Horse Brass Soc

© CBD Research Ltd · Beckenham · BR3 5JS · Tel 020 8650 7745 · Fax 020 8650 0768 · E-mail cbd@cbdresearch.com · www.cbdresearch.com

Horse: loggers
　　FCA Membership Ltd
Horse: racing
　　Amat Jockeys Assn
　　Brit Harness Racing Club
　　Fedn Bloodstock Agents
　　Horserace Writers & Photographers Assn
　　Horseracing Sponsors Assn
　　Ir Thoroughbred Breeders Assn
　　Nat Assn Stable Staff
　　Nat Trainers Fedn
　　Permit Trainers Assn
　　Point-to-Point Owners & Riders Assn
　　Profl Jockeys Assn
　　Racecourse Assn
　　Racehorse Owners Assn
　　Racehorse Transporters Assn
Horse: riding & driving
　　Assn Brit Riding Schools
　　Brit Driving Soc
　　Brit Equestrian Fedn
　　Brit Horse Driving Trials Assn
　　Brit Horse Soc
　　Brit Show Horse Assn
　　Brit Show Pony Soc
　　Horse Rangers Assn
　　London Harness Horse Parade Soc
　　Medical Equestrian Assn
　　Mounted Games Assn
　　Nat Fedn Bridleway Assns
　　Pleasure Horse Soc
　　Point-to-Point Owners & Riders Assn
　　Riding Disabled Assn
　　Scot Assn Country Sports
　　Scot Carriage Driving Assn
　　Scot Sports Horse
　　Scurry Driving Assn
　　Side Saddle Assn
　　Standardbred & Trotting Horse Assn
　　Trekking & Riding Soc Scotland
　　UK Chasers & Riders Ltd
　　Welsh Trekking & Riding Assn
　　Western Equestrian Soc
　　Western Horsemen's Assn
　　> + American 'West'
Horseball
　　Brit Horseball Assn
Horseboxes & trailers
　　Org Horsebox & Trailer Owners
Horses & ponies
　　Brit Equestrian Fedn
　　Brit Equestrian Tr Assn
　　Brit Horse Soc
　　Endurance GB
　　Equine Behaviour Forum
　　Equine Shiatsu Assn
　　Equine Sports Massage Assn
　　HorseSport Ireland
　　Nat Pony Soc
　　Ponies Assn
　　Pony Club
　　Pony Riders Assn
　　Soc Welfare Horses & Ponies
　　Thoroughbred Breeders' Assn
　　Veteran Horse Soc
　　> + Cattle & livestock; Pony trekking
Horses & ponies: breed societies
　　American Quarter Horse Assn
　　American Saddlebred Assn
　　Arab Horse Soc
　　Brit Appaloosa Soc
　　Brit Assn Purebred Spanish Horse
　　Brit Camargue Horse Soc
　　Brit Connemara Pony Soc
　　Brit Hanoverian Horse Soc
　　Brit Morgan Horse Soc
　　Brit Palomino Soc
　　Brit Percheron Horse Soc
　　Brit Skewbald & Piebald Assn
　　Brit Spotted Pony Soc
　　Caspian Breed Soc
　　Caspian Horse Soc
　　Cleveland Bay Horse Soc
　　Clydesdale Horse Soc
　　Coloured Horse & Pony Soc
　　Connemara Pony Breeders Soc [IRL]
　　Dales Pony Soc

Dartmoor Pony Soc
Donkey Breed Soc
Dun Horse & Pony Soc
Eriskay Pony Soc
Exmoor Pony Soc
Fell Pony Soc
Fjord Horse Nat Stud Book Assn
Friesian Horse Assn
Glasgow Agricl Soc
Gypsy Cob Soc
Hackney Horse Soc
Haflinger Soc
Highland Pony Soc
Icelandic Horse Soc
Ir Draught Horse Soc
Lipizzaner Nat Stud Book Assn GB
Lipizzaner Soc
Lusitano Breed Soc
Nat Stallion Assn
New Forest Pony . . . & Cattle Soc
Scot Icelandic Horse Assn
Shetland Pony Stud-Book Soc
Shire Horse Soc
Southern Counties Heavy Horse Assn
Sport Horse Breeding
Spotted Horse & Pony Soc
Suffolk Horse Soc
Trakehner Breeders Fraternity
UK Paint Horse Assn
Utd Saddlebred Assn
Warmblood Breeders' Studbook - UK
Welsh Pony & Cob Soc
Horses & ponies: grooms
　　Brit Grooms Assn
Horticulture
　　Brit Dried Flowers Assn
　　Brit Inst Agricl Consultants
　　Brit Protected Ornamentals Assn
　　Comml Horticl Assn
　　Flowers & Plants Assn
　　Garden Centre Assn
　　Guernsey Growers Assn
　　Horticultural Exhibitors Assn
　　Horticultural Trs Assn
　　Inst Horticulture
　　Ir Comml Horticl Assn
　　N England Horticl Soc
　　N England Rosecarpe Horticl Soc
　　Nat Coun Consvn Plants & Gardens
　　Nat Farmers U
　　Nuclear Stock Assn
　　R Botanical & Horticl Soc Manch
　　R Caledonian Horticl Soc
　　R Guernsey Agricl & Horticl Soc
　　R Horticl Soc
　　R Horticl Soc Ireland
　　R Welsh Agricl Soc
　　S England Agricl Soc
　　Scot Seed & Nursery Tr Assn
　　Shropshire & W Midlands Agricl Soc
　　Soc Botanical Artists
　　UK Irrigation Assn
　　Westmorland County Agricl Soc
　　Women's Farm & Garden Assn
　　> + Agriculture: county societies; Gardens & gardening; Landscape
Horticulture: disabled > Gardens & gardening: for disabled
Horticulture: education
　　Landex
　　Principals' Profl Coun
Horticulture & garden: machinery
　　Agricl Engrs Assn
　　Brit Agricl & Garden Machinery Assn
　　Brit Hardware Fedn
　　Farm Machinery Presvn Soc
　　Farm Tractor & Machinery Tr Assn [IRL]
　　Fedn Brit Hand Tool Mfrs
　　GARDENEX
　　GIMA
　　Vintage Horticl & Garden Machinery Club
　　> + Agriculture: machinery
Hoses (flexible)
　　Hose Mfrs' & Suppliers Assn
Hosiery
　　Knitting Inds Fedn
Hospices
　　Assn Children's Hospices

Hospitality
    Assn Events Mgt Educ
    Brit Hospitality Assn
    Coun Hospitality Mgt Educ
    Foodservice Consultants Soc Intl (UK)
    Inst Hospitality
    PACE: Profl Assn Catering Educ
    > + Catering, Corporate hospitality; Hotels & restaurants; Shows & events
Hospitals
    Assn Dental Hospitals
    Community Hospitals Assn
Hospitals: administrative staff
    Brit Assn Med Mgrs
    Hospital Caterers Assn
    Nat Assn Healthcare Fire Officers
    Soc Hospital Linen Service & Laundry Mgrs
    UK Housekeepers Assn
    > + National Health Service
Hospitals: broadcasting
    Nat Assn Hospital Broadcasting Orgs
Hospitals: contributory schemes
    Brit Health Care Assn
    Hospital & Med Care Assn
    Welsh Hospitals & Health Services Assn
Hospitals: decontamination & cleaning
    Assn Healthcare Cleaning Profls
    Inst Decontamination Sciences
Hospitals: engineering & equipment
    Inst Healthcare Engg & Estate Mgt
Hospitals: medical staff
    College Emergency Medicine
    College Operating Dept Practitioners
    Hospital Consultants & Specialists Assn
    Ir Hospital Consultants Assn
Hospitals: nursing staff > Nursing
Hospitals: patients > Patients
Hospitals: veterinary
    Brit Veterinary Hospitals Assn
Hostas & hemerocallis
    Brit Hosta & Hemerocallis Soc
    Hardy Plant Soc
Hostels (bail) > Probation service
Hot air balloons > Balloons & airships
Hot air engines
    Stirling Engine Soc
Hot water storage & supply > Heating
Hotel accountants
    Brit Assn Hospitality Accountants
Hotels & restaurants
    Brit Assn Hotel Representatives
    Brit Hospitality Assn
    Fedn Specialist Restaurants
    Hotel Booking Agents Assn
    Inst Hospitality
    Ir Hospitality Inst
    Ir Hotels Fedn
    NI Hotels Fedn
    Restaurant Property Advisors Soc
    Restaurants Assn Ireland
Hound trailing
    Hound Trailing Assn
Hounds
    Masters Deerhounds Assn
    Masters Draghounds & Bloodhounds Assn
    Masters Foxhounds Assn
    Peterborough R Foxhound Show Soc
    Welsh Hound Assn
    > + Hunts & hunting
House alarm systems > Intruder alarms; Security
House building > Building
House maintenance
    Upkeep
House plants > Indoor & houseplants; Horticulture; individual plant
Household distribution
    Direct Marketing Assn (UK) Ltd
Household textiles > Textile headings
Housekeepers
    UK Housekeepers Assn
Houses open to the public > Historic buildings
Housewares > Hardware & housewares
Housewives
    Nat Women's Register
    > + Women's organisations
Housing
    Chart Inst Housing
    Community Housing Cymru

    Confedn Co-operative Housing
    Housing Inst Ireland
    Nat Assn Bldg Co-ops [IRL]
    Nat Housing Fedn
    NI Fedn Housing Assns
    R Envtl Health Inst Scotland
    ROOM RTPI
    Scot Fedn Housing Assns
    > + Building societies; Tenants & residents
Housman (A E) & family
    Housman Soc
Hovercraft
    Hovercraft Club
    Hovercraft Museum Trust
Howells (Herbert) 1892-1983
    Herbert Howells Soc
Huguenots
    Huguenot Soc
Human identification
    Brit Assn Human Identification
Human relationships
    Soc Companion Animal Studies
Human rights > Individual freedom
Humanism
    Brit Humanist Assn
    Humanist Assn Ireland
    Humanist Soc Scotland
    Nat Secular Soc
    Rationalist Assn
    S Place Ethical Soc
Humanities
    Humanities Assn
Humidity control
    Heating, Ventilating & Air Conditioning Mfrs' Assn
    > + Air: conditioning & ventilating
Hungary
    Brit Cham Comm Hungary
Huntington's disease
    Huntington's Disease Assn
    Scot Huntington's Assn
Hunts & hunting
    Assn Masters Harriers & Beagles
    Countryside Alliance
    Hunting Assn Ireland
    Ir Coun against Blood Sports
    Masters Draghounds & Bloodhounds Assn
    U Country Sports Workers
    > + Hounds
Hurdy-gurdy
    Hurdy-Gurdy Soc
Hurling (sport)
    Gaelic Athletic Assn
Hydraulics & hydromechanics
    Brit Fluid Power Assn
    Brit Fluid Power Distbrs Assn
    Shipbuilders & Shiprepairers Assn
Hydrocephalus > Spina bifida & hydrocephalus
Hydrogen fluoride
    Chemical Inds Assn
Hydrology > Water
Hydromechanics > Hydraulics & hydromechanics
Hydropower > Water: power; Renewable energy
Hydrotherapy > Spas
Hygiene > Cleaning; Health; Natural health & therapeutics; Occupational health & hygiene; Public health
Hymns
    Hymn Soc
Hyper active children
    Fragile X Soc
    Hyperactive Children's Support Gp
    > + Children: welfare
Hypercalcaemia
    Williams Syndrome Foundation
Hypermobility Syndrome
    Hypermobility Syndrome Assn
Hypertension
    Brit Hypertension Soc
Hyperthermia
    Brit Malignant Hyperthermia Assn
Hypertrophic cardiomyopathy
    Cardiomyopathy Assn
Hypnosis & hypnotherapy
    Academy Curative Hypnotherapists
    Assn Therapeutic Philosophy
    Brit Hypnotherapy Assn
    Brit Soc Clinical Hypnosis
    Brit Soc Hypnotherapists

© CBD Research Ltd · Beckenham · BR3 5JS · Tel 020 8650 7745 · Fax 020 8650 0768 · E-mail cbd@cbdresearch.com · www.cbdresearch.com

BSCAH - Brit Soc Clinical... Hypnosis
Campaign Stage Hypnosis
Fedn Ethical Stage Hypnotists
Nat Assn Counsellors, Hypnotherapists...
Nat Coun Hypnotherapy
Nat Coun Psychotherapists
Nat Register Hypnotherapists & Psychotherapists
Nat Soc Profl Hypnotherapists
Soc Stress Mgrs
UK Confedn Hypnotherapy Orgs
Hypnotic regression
Assn Scientific Study Anomalous Phenomena
UK Skeptics
Hysterectomy
Campaign Hysterectomy &...Operations on Women
Hysterectomy Assn

I

Iberia > Portugal; Spain
IBS > Irritable bowel syndrome (disease)
Ice climbing > Climbing
Ice cream
Ice Cream Alliance
Ice hockey
Ice Hockey UK
Ice skating
Nat Ice Skating Assn
Scot Ice Skating Assn
Icehouses
Sussex Indl Archaeol Soc
Ichthyology
Marine Biological Assn
Identity cards
NO2ID
Ido
Intl Language [Ido] Soc
Ileostomy
Assn Coloproctology
IA
Nat Advy Service Parents Children with a Stoma
Illiteracy > Reading
Illuminated signs > Road lighting, markings & traffic signs;   Signs
Illumination > Lighting
Illuminators
Soc Scribes & Illuminators
Illustration
Assn Illustrators
Brit Cartoonists' Assn
Comics Creators Gld
Imaginative Book Illustration Soc
Inst Med Illustrators
Outdoor Writers' & Photographers' Gld
Picture Res Assn
Randolph Caldecott Soc
Soc Architectural Illustration
Soc Artists' Agents
> + Art & artists
Image development (personal)
Fedn Image Consultants
Image processing
Brit Assn Picture Libraries & Agencies
Brit Machine Vision Assn...
Photo Imaging Coun
Profl Photographic Laboratories Assn
R Photographic Soc
Sira
UK Indl Vision Assn
Immediate care > First aid & immediate care
Immigration & emigration
Assn Visitors Immigration Detainees
Immigration Law Practitioners' Assn
Immunology
Brit Soc Allergy & Clinical Immunology
Brit Soc Immunology
Brit Transplantation Soc
Primary Immunodeficiency Assn
> + Allergy
Impact absorbing surfaces
Assn Play Inds
Imperial weights & measures
Brit Weights & Measures Assn
Metric Martyrs
> + Measurement

Implants (medical)
Breast Implant Inf Soc
Pharmaceutical & Healthcare Sciences Soc
UK & I Soc Cataract & Refractive Surgeons
Import > Export & import
Impotence > Sexual dysfunction
Incentive marketing
Brit Promotional Merchandise Assn
Promota UK Ltd
Soc Incentive & Travel Executives
Income tax > Taxation
Incontinence
Absorbent Hygiene Products Mfrs Assn
Assn Continence Advice
Cystitis & Overactive Bladder Foundation
Incontact
Nat Advy Service Parents Children with a Stoma
Independent companies > Business
Independent further education > Education
Independent & public schools
Assn Governing Bodies Indep Schools
Assn Heads Indep Schools
Assn Marketing & Devt Indep Schools
Girls' Schools Assn
Headmasters & Headmistresses Conf
Inc Assn Preparatory Schools
Indep Schools Assn
Indep Schools Bursars Assn
Indep Schools Coun
Soc Headmasters & Headmistresses Indep Schools
Indexing
Assn Freelance Editors, Proofreaders & Indexers [IRL]
Soc Indexers
India & Indian people
Brit Assn S Asian Studies
India: armed forces history
Indian Military Histl Soc
Indirect taxation > Taxation
Individual freedom
C'ee Admin Justice [NI]
Campaign Philosophical Freedom
Choice in Personal Safety
Freedom Assn
Freedom Org Right Enjoy Smoking Tobacco
Ir Coun Civil Liberties
Libertarian Alliance
Liberty
Nat Secular Soc
NO2ID
Soc Individual Freedom
Statewatch
Indonesia
Anglo-Indonesian Soc
Indoor bowling > Bowling
Indoor & houseplants
Brit Protected Ornamentals Assn
Flowers & Plants Assn
Garden Centre Assn
Saintpaulia & Houseplant Soc
> + Horticulture; individual plants
Industrial agents
Indl Agents Soc
Industrial archaeology > Archaeology: industrial
Industrial biology > Biology
Industrial catering > Catering
Industrial cleaning > Cleaning equipment
Industrial containers > specific type of container, or material used in their
manufacture
Industrial copyright > Copyright;   Patents & trade marks
Industrial design
Chart Soc Designers
Design & Inds Assn
Fac R Designers Ind
Intellectual Property Lawyers Assn
> + Design
Industrial development > Industry
Industrial diamonds
Brit Abrasives Fedn
Industrial editors
Brit Assn Communicators in Business
> + Technical writing & publishing
Industrial education > Occupational training & education
Industrial emergencies > Civil defence & industrial emergencies
Industrial fasteners > Fasteners & turned parts
Industrial finishing > Coatings; Metal: finishing

Industrial involvement & participation
        Involvement & Participation Assn
        Ir ProShare Assn
Industrial law > Law: industrial
Industrial leather > Leather
Industrial management > Management
Industrial marketing > Marketing
Industrial participation > Industrial involvement & participation
Industrial plant > Plant: industrial
Industrial pollution > Pollution & pollution control
Industrial property > Copyright; Patents & trade marks
Industrial relations
        Brit Universities Indl Relations Assn
        Ethical Trading Initiative
        Inst Employment Rights
        Ir Assn Indl Relations
Industrial research
        AIRTO
        Cambridge Soc Application Res
        Major Projects Assn
        Res & Devt Soc
        > + specific industries
Industrial safety > Safety
Industrial security > Security
Industrial trucks
        Assn Indl Truck Trainers
Industrial training & education > Occupational training & education
Industrial vision
        UK Indl Vision Assn
Industrialised building components
        Assn Bldg Component Mfrs
        > + Building materials & supplies
Industry
        Assn University Res & Ind Links
        Chemical & Indl Consultants' Assn
        Confedn Brit Ind
        Ir Business & Emplrs Confedn
        R Soc Edinburgh
        Scot Coun Devt & Ind
Infant food
        Cereal Ingredients Mfrs' Assn
        Infant & Dietetic Foods Assn
Infants > Children: welfare;   Cot deaths
Infection control & study
        Brit Infection Soc
        Infection Prevention Soc
        John Snow Soc
        Soc Applied Microbiology
Infertility > Fertility
Inflatable toys & structures
        Assn Play Inds
        Brit Toy & Hobby Assn
        Inflatable Play Mfrs Assn
        Performance Textiles Assn
        Plastics & Board Inds Fedn
        > + Air: boats & inflatables
Information: destruction > Documents: confidential disposal
Information: freedom of
        Campaign Freedom Infm
        Campaign Press & Broadcasting Freedom
Information: management > Data processing; Information services & technology
Information: services & technology
        ADSET
        Aslib
        Assn Geographic Inf
        Brit Assn Inf & Library Educ & Res
        Business Services Assn
        CILIP
        City Inf Gp
        Communications Mgt Assn
        Construction Ind Inf Gp
        Eur Inf Assn
        ICT Ireland
        Inst Mgt Inf Systems
        Inst Scientific & Technical Communicators
        Instn Engg & Technology
        Intellect
        Momentum - Northern Ireland ICT Fedn
        Network Govt Library & Inf Specialists
        Select
        Soc Inf Technology Mgt
        UK Computer Measurement Gp
        UK EInformation Gp
        Universities & Colls Inf Systems Assn
        > + Data processing
Infra-red heating > Electroheat

Injections
        Pharmaceutical & Healthcare Sciences Soc
Inkpots > Writing equipment & accessories
Inland waterways
        Assn Inland Navigation Authorities
        Assn Pleasure Craft Operators
        Campaign Better Transport
        Canal Boatbuilders Assn
        Canal Card Collectors Circle
        Chesterfield Canal Trust
        Inland Waterways Assn
        Inland Waterways Assn Ireland
        Inland Waterways Protection Soc
        Nat Assn Boat Owners
        Rly & Canal Histl Soc
        Scot Inland Waterways Assn
        Thames & Medway Canal Assn
        Towpath Action Gp
        Transport Water Assn
        Waterway Recovery Gp
        Wey & Arun Canal Trust
        > + Rivers
Inline skating & rollerblading
        Brit Inline Skater Hockey Assn
Innes (John)
        John Innes Mfrs Assn
        > + Composts & composting
Innovation > Invention & innovation
Inns of Court > Law
Inns & innkeeping
        Brit Inst Innkeeping
        Inn Sign Soc
        > + Wines & spirits: trade
Insects > Entomology
Insignia > Badges & insignia; Numismatics
Insolvency
        Assn Business Recovery Profls
        Insolvency Lawyers Assn
        Insolvency Practitioners Assn
        > + Accountancy
Instrumentation & control > Control engineering; Measurement
Instruments: musical > Musical instruments
Insulation
        Brit Rigid Urethane Foam Mfrs Assn
        Brit Urethane Foam Contrs Assn
        Chart Instn Bldg Services Engrs
        Draught Proofing Advy Assn
        EURISOL-UK
        Insulated Render & Cladding Assn
        Nat Insulation Assn
        Proprietary Acoustic Systems Mfrs
        Thermal Insulation Contrs Assn
        Thermal Insulation Mfrs & Suppliers Assn
        > + Building; Heating
Insulation: electrical
        Electrical Insulation Assn
Insurance
        Assn Average Adjusters
        Assn Brit Insurers
        Assn Consulting Actuaries
        Assn Lloyd's Members
        Assn Policy Market Makers
        Brit Insurance Law Assn
        Chart Insurance Inst
        Fac Actuaries Scotland
        Financial Services Ireland
        Inst Risk Mgt
        Insurance Inst Ireland
        Intl Underwriting Assn Lond
        Ir Insurance Fedn
        Lloyd's Market Assn
        Personal Finance Soc
        > + Warranty protection
Insurance: brokers
        Brit Insurance Brokers' Assn
        Corpn Insurance, Financial & Mortgage Advisers
        Inst Insurance Brokers
Insurance: companies staff
        Assn Insurance & Risk Mgrs
Insurance: customers
        HIPS (97)
        Nat Assn Bank & Insurance Customers
Insurance: history
        Fire Mark Circle
Insurance: medicine
        Assn Med Insurance Intermediaries

© CBD Research Ltd · Beckenham · BR3 5JS · Tel 020 8650 7745 · Fax 020 8650 0768 · E-mail cbd@cbdresearch.com · www.cbdresearch.com

Assurance Med Soc
Provincial Hospital Services Assn
Insurance: private health > Hospitals: contributory schemes
Intellectual property rights
Alliance Intellectual Property Theft
Authors' Licensing & Collecting Soc
Licensing Executives Soc
MARQUES
Intelligence
Nat Assn Gifted Children
Intensive care
Intensive Care Soc
Scot Intensive Care Soc
Interactive publishing
Assn Online Publishers
Periodical Pubrs Assn - Interactive
Interchurch families
Assn Interchurch Families
NI Mixed Marriage Assn
> + Welfare: organisations
Interior decoration & design
Assn Interior Specialists
Brit Assn Landscape Inds
Brit Interior Design Assn
Chart Soc Designers
Inst Profl Designers
Kitchen Bathroom Bedroom Specialists Assn
Wallpaper Hist Soc
Intermediate bulk containers
Indl Packaging Assn
Internal auditors
Inst Internal Auditors UK & Ireland
> + Accountancy
Internal combustion engines > Motor industry
International affairs
Brit Pugwash Gp
R Inst Intl Affairs
International friendship > individual countries
International law > Law: international
International mail consolidators > Postal services
International studies
Brit Intl Studies Assn
Internet
Brit Internet Publishers Alliance
Fedn Internet Traders
ICRA
Internet Advtg Bureau
Internet Service Providers' Assn
Ir Internet Assn
Online Content UK
ScotlandIS
Telecommunications & Internet Fedn [IRL]
> + Website design
Internment
Assn Brit Civilian Internees Far East
Interplanetary travel > Space research & exploration
Interpreters > Translation & interpretation
Intestinal disorders > specific illness
Introduction agencies & marriage bureaux
Assn Brit Introduction Agencies
Intruder alarms
Nat Security Inspectorate
> + Security
Invention & innovation
Ideas UK
Inst Intl Licensing Practitioners
Inst Inventors
Inst Patentees & Inventors
R Scot Soc Arts (Science & Technology)
Inventories
Assn Indep Inventory Clerks
> + Production control; Stocktaking/auditing
Investigators
Assn Brit Investigators
Inst Profl Investigators
Nat Assn Investigators & Process Servers
Investment
Assn Consulting Actuaries
Assn Corporate Trustees
Assn Indep Financial Advisers
Assn Investment Companies
Assn Mining Analysts
Assn Private Client Investment Mgrs & Stockbrokers
Assn Real Estate Funds
Assn Solicitors & Investment Mgrs
Brit Insurance Brokers' Assn
BVCA

CFA Soc
Financial Services Ireland
Futures & Options Association
Gld Shareholders
Indep Valuers Assn
Investment Mgt Assn
Investment Property Forum
Investor Relations Soc
Ir Assn Investment Mgrs
London Investment Banking Assn
London Money Market Assn
Securities & Investment Inst
SIFA
Soc Technical Analysts
Tax Incentivised Savings Assn
UK Social Investment Forum
> + Trusts, trusteeship & estate planning
Investment casting > Metal: casting
In Vitro diagnostics
Brit In Vitro Diagnostics Assn
Invoice factors > Factoring (banking & finance)
Iran
Brit Inst Persian Studies
Iran Soc
Middle East Assn
Ireland
Fedn Ir Socs
Inst Public Administration [IRL]
Ir Assn Cultural, Economic & Social Relations
Ireland: history, language & literature
Brit Assn Ir Studies
Economic & Social Hist Soc Ireland
Fedn Ulster Local Studies
Friends Nat Collections Ireland
Ir Texts Soc
R Ir Academy
R Soc Antiquaries Ireland
Irises
Brit Iris Soc
Irish > Ireland
Iron
Cast Metals Fedn
Community
Inst Materials, Minerals & Mining
> + Steel
Iron & steel scrap > Metal: scrap
Iron & steel stockholders
Nat Assn Steel Stockholders
Ironfoundries > Foundries
Ironmongery
Brit Hardware Fedn
Gld Architectural Ironmongers
Inst Architectural Ironmongers
> + Hardware & housewares
Irrigation
Brit Turf & Landscape Irrigation Assn
UK Irrigation Assn
> + Water
Irritable bowel syndrome (disease)
Gut Trust
Isopods
Brit Myriapod & Isopod Gp
Israel
Anglo-Israel Assn
Brit Technion Soc
> + Jewish organisations
Italian > Italy: language & literature
Italic hand > Handwriting
Italy
Assn Study Modern Italy
Brit Cham Comm Italy
Brit Italian Soc
Italian Cham Comm Ind UK
Pizza, Pasta & Italian Food Assn
Italy: language & literature
Assn Language Learning

J

Jacobites
R Stuart Soc
Seventeen Fortyfive Assn
Jacobs (W[illiam] W[ymark]
W W Jacobs Appreciation Soc

Jams
    Food Processors Assn
Japan
    Brit Assn Japanese Studies
    Brit Cham Comm Japan
    Japan Soc
    Japan Soc Scotland
    Japanese Cham Comm & Ind UK
Japan: literature
    Brit Haiku Soc
    Time Haiku
Japanning > Lacquer & japanning
Jazz & Blues
    Assn Brit Jazz Musicians
    Jazz Piano Teachers Assn
    Musicians' U
    Welsh Amat Music Fedn
    Welsh Jazz Soc
Jefferies (Richard)
    Richard Jefferies Soc
Jellies
    Food Processors Assn
Jerome (Jerome K)
    Jerome K Jerome Soc
Jersey (Channel Islands)
    R Jersey Agricl & Horticl Soc
    Société Jersiaise
Jetting (water)
    Water Jetting Assn
Jewellery
    Assn Contemporary Jewellery
    Bead Soc
    Brit Jewellers Assn
    Brit Jewellery, Giftware & Finishing Fedn
    Fedn Jewellery Mfrs Ireland
    Gld Enamellers
    Inst Profl Goldsmiths
    Jewellery Distributors' Association of the UK
    Nat Assn Goldsmiths
    Soc Jewellery Historians
Jewish history & lore
    Chapels Soc
    Jewish Histl Soc England
Jewish organisations
    Anglo-Jewish Assn
    Assn Jewish Ex-Servicemen & Women
    Fedn Synagogues
    Inst Jewish Policy Res
    Zionist Fedn
Jigsaws
    Brit Jigsaw Puzzle Library
Jirds
    Nat Gerbil Soc
Jiu jitsu > Martial arts
Jockeys > Horse: racing
John O'Groats
    Land's End - John O'Groats Assn
Johnson (Dr Samuel)
    Johnson Soc
    Johnson Soc Lond
Joinery > Woodworking
Joints
    Arthrogryposis Gp
Jones (David Michael)
    David Jones Soc
Jordan
    Anglo-Jordanian Soc
Journalism
    Assn Brit Science Writers
    Assn Regional City Editors
    Brit Assn Journalists
    Chart Inst Journalists
    Crime Reporters Assn
    Foreign Press Assn Lond
    Gld Food Writers
    Gld Motoring Writers
    Media Soc
    Medical Journalists Assn
    Nat Assn Press Agencies
    Nat U Journalists
    Sports Journalists' Assn GB
    Yachting Journalists' Assn
    > + Media; Newspapers; Writing & writers
Jousting
    Knights R England
Ju jitsu > Martial arts
Judo > Martial arts

Jurisprudence > Law
Justices clerks > Magistrates & magistrates courts

Juvenile > Children headings; Family Law

K

Kaolin > China clay
Karate > Martial arts
Karg-Elert (Sigfrid)
    Karg-Elert Archive
Karting
    Assn Brit Kart Clubs
    Assn Racing Kart Schools
    Brit Superkart Assn
    Motor Sports Assn
    Nat Karting Assn
Kayaks
    Assn Canoe Trades
    Historic Canoe & Kayak Assn
    Open Canoe Sailing Gp
Kaye-Smith (Sheila)
    Sheila Kaye-Smith Soc
Keats (John)
    Keats-Shelley Memorial Assn
Keelboats > Cobles & keelboats
Keep fit > Fitness
Kegs > Cisterns, drums & tanks
Kempe (Charles)
    Kempe Soc
Kempe (Margery)
    Margery Kempe Soc
Kempe (Rudolf)
    Rudolf Kempe Soc
Kendo > Martial arts
Kennels
    Pet Care Trust
Kent
    Assn Men Kent & Kentish Men
Kerbs > Paving & kerbs
Keys
    Brit Locksmiths & Keycutters Assn
    MultiService Assn
    > + Locks & latches
Kick boxing > Martial arts
Kidney structure & disease > Nephrology
Kilvert (Francis)
    Kilvert Soc
Kinesiology
    Assn Light Touch Therapists
    Assn Systematic Kinesiology
    Kinesiology Fedn
    > + Complementary medicine
Kings > under individual's name
Kipling ([Joseph] Rudyard)
    Kipling Soc
Kippers > Herring
Kitchen furniture & equipment
    Brit Woodworking Fedn
    Catering Eqpt Distbrs Assn GB
    Cutlery & Allied Trs Res Assn
    Kitchen Bathroom Bedroom Specialists Assn
Kite buggying
    Brit Fedn Sand & Land Yacht Clubs
    Brit Power Kitesports Assn
Kite flying
    Kite Soc
Kite surfing > Surfing, board & speed sailing
Klinefelter's syndrome
    Klinefelter's Syndrome Assn
Knacker industry
    Licensed Animal Slaughterers. . . Assn
Knights bachelor
    Imperial Soc Knights Bachelor
Knitting & knitting wool/yarns
    Community
    Knitting & Crochet Gld
    UK Hand Knitting Assn
    > + Wool & wool products
Knitwear
    Knitting Inds Fedn
    UK Fashion Exports
Knots (tying)
    Intl Gld Knot Tyers

© CBD Research Ltd · Beckenham · BR3 5JS · Tel 020 8650 7745 · Fax 020 8650 0768 · E-mail cbd@cbdresearch.com · www.cbdresearch.com

Kodály (Zoltán)
  Brit Kodály Academy
Korea
  Brit Assn Korean Studies
  Brit Cham Comm Korea
Korfball
  Brit Korfball Assn
Kung fu > Martial arts

L

Labels: collecting
  Brit Matchbox, Label & Booklet Soc
  Labologists Society
Labels: self adhesive & roll
  Brit Printing Inds Fedn
Laboratory animals
  Fund Replacement Animals Med Experiments
  Inst Animal Technology
  Laboratory Animal Science Assn
  Res Defence Soc
  > + Animals: welfare
Laboratory equipment & technology
  Assn Instrumentation, Control, Automation...
  Brit Assn Res Quality Assurance
  Inst Biomedical Science
  Inst Science & Technology
  UK Textile Laboratory Forum
Labour politics
  Inst Employment Rights
  Scot Labour Hist Soc
  Soc Study Labour Hist
Labour (provision of)
  Assn Labour Providers
Labour relations > Industrial relations
Lace (handmade)
  Lace Gld
  Lace Soc
Lace & net
  Brit Lace Fedn
Lacquer & japanning
  Brit Antique Furniture Restorers Assn
Lacrosse
  English Lacrosse Assn
Ladders
  Brit Ladder Mfrs Assn
  Ladder Systems Mfrs Assn
Ladies circles
  Nat Assn Ladies Circles
  > + also Women's organisations
Legacies (public) > Donations (public)
Lake District
  Friends Lake District
Lamas > Camelids
Lamb (Charles)
  Charles Lamb Soc
Lamb(s) > Meat; Sheep
Laminates
  Brit Laminate Fabricators Assn
Lancashire
  Friends Real Lancashire
Land: access & rights of way > Footpaths & rights of way
Land-based education
  Landex
Land: contaminated
  Assn Geotechnical & Geoenvironmental Specialists
  Brit Urban Regeneration Assn
  Soil & Groundwater Technology Assn
Land: drainage
  Assn Drainage Authorities
  Land Drainage Contrs Assn
  > + Plastics: pipes; Pipes; Water
Land: owners > Estate management; Property & land owners
Land: survey > Earth sciences, structure & resources;   Surveying
Land: usage > Conservation; Town & country planning
Land: valuation > Valuation
Land: yachting
  Brit Fedn Sand & Land Yacht Clubs
Landlords > Property & land owners
Land's End
  Land's End - John O'Groats Assn
Landscape
  Assn Landscape Contrs Ireland (NI)
  Brit Assn Landscape Inds

Brit Turf & Landscape Irrigation Assn
  Garden & Landscape Designers Assn
  Horticultural Trs Assn
  Inst Profl Designers
  Ir Landscape Inst
  Landscape Inst
  Landscape Res Gp
  Permaculture Assn
  Profl Plant Users Gp
  Scot Seed & Nursery Tr Assn
  Soc Landscape Studies
  Soc Ley Hunters
  > + Earth sciences, structure & resources
Languages
  Assn Brit Language Schools
  Assn Language Learning
  Assn Learning Languages en Famille
  Brit Academy
  Brit Assn Academic Phoneticians
  Brit Assn Applied Linguistics
  Chart Inst Linguists
  Cheshaght Ghailckagh (Yn)
  Linguistics Assn
  Modern Humanities Res Assn
  Nat Assn Language Advisers
  Philological Soc
  R Coll Speech & Language Therapists
  UK Literacy Assn
  Ulster-Scots Language Soc
  > + Dialects; individual country
Languages: auxiliary
  Esperanto Assn Britain
  Glosa Educ Org
  Intl Language [Ido] Soc
  Scot Esperanto Assn
Larkin (Philip)
  Philip Larkin Soc
Laryngology/Laryngectomy
  Nat Assn Laryngectomee Clubs
  > Otolaryngology
Laser printer cartridges
  UK Cartridge Remanufacturers Assn
  > + Printing machinery & supplies
Lasers
  Assn Laser Users
  Brit Med Laser Assn
  Ophthalmological Prods Tr & Ind Conf
Latex allergy
  Latex Allergy Support Gp
  > + Allergy
Latin > Classical studies
Latin America
  Hispanic & Luso Brazilian Coun
  Latin Amer Assn
  UK One World Linking Assn
Latin American dancing > Dancing
Latin Mass > Liturgy
Latvia
  Brit Cham Comm Latvia
Lauder (Sir Harry)
  Scot Music Hall & Variety Theatre Soc
Laundering
  Gld Cleaners & Launderers
  Nat Assn Launderette Ind
  Nat Assn Nappy Services
  Soc Laundry Engrs & Allied Trs
  Textile Services Assn
  Ulster Launderers Assn
Laurel & Hardy
  Laurel & Hardy Appreciation Soc
Laurence-Moon-Bardet-Biedl disease
  Laurence-Moon-Bardet-Biedl Soc
Law
  Assn Lawyers & Legal Advisors
  Assn Personal Injury Lawyers
  Bar Assn Comm, Finance & Ind
  Bar Assn Local Govt & Public Service
  Brit Legal Assn
  Comml Bar Assn
  Criminal Bar Assn
  Family Law Bar Assn
  Law Soc
  Legal Aid Practitioners Gp
  Magistrates Assn
  Medico-Legal Soc
  Soc Advanced Legal Studies
  Socio-Legal Studies Assn

Solicitor Sole Practitioners Gp
> + headings below; Forensic science
Law: Ireland
Brit & Ir Assn Law Librarians
Honorable Soc King's Inns [IRL]]
Law Soc Ireland
Law: Northern Ireland
C'ee Admin Justice [NI]
Law Soc NI
Law: Scotland
Fac Advocates
Law Soc Scotland
Procurators Fiscal Soc
R Fac Procurators in Glasgow
Scot Indep Advocacy Alliance
Scot Law Agents Soc
Scot Legal Action Gp
Soc Solicitors Supreme Courts Scotland
Soc Writers Her Majesty's Signet
Law: art
Inst Art & Law
Law: centres
Law Centres Fedn
Scot Assn Law Centres
Law: charity
Charity Law Assn
Law: children
Assn Lawyers Children
Nat Assn Youth Justice
Law: clerks
Inst Barristers' Clerks
Justices' Clerks' Soc
Law: comparative
Brit Inst Intl & Comparative Law
Law: construction
Assn Consultant Approved Inspectors
Instn Planning Supervisors
Soc Construction Law
Law: costs
Assn Law Costs Draftsmen
Assn Lawyers & Legal Advisors
Law: court officers
Scot Justices Assn
Law: education
Assn Law Teachers
Brit & Ir Legal Educ Technology Assn
Education Law Assn
Soc Legal Scholars
Law: employment
Employment Lawyers Assn
Law: environment
UK Envtl Law Assn
Law: European
Brit-German Jurists' Assn
UK Assn Eur Law
> + Law: international
Law: expert witness > Experts & expert witness
Law: family > Family law
Law: history
Ir Legal Hist Soc
Selden Soc
Stair Soc
Law: immigration
Immigration Law Practitioners' Assn
Law: industrial
Bar Assn Comm, Finance & Ind
Comm & Ind Gp
Indl Law Soc
Law: insolvency
Insolvency Lawyers Assn
Law: insurance
Brit Insurance Law Assn
Law: international
Brit Inst Intl & Comparative Law
Intl Law Assn
Law: libraries
Brit & Ir Assn Law Librarians
Law: maritime
Brit Maritime Law Assn
Ir Maritime Law Assn
Law: motor accidents
Motor Accident Solicitors Soc
Law: paralegal
Inst Legal Executives
Inst Paralegal Training
Nat Assn Licensed Paralegals

Law: pension
Assn Pension Lawyers
Law: reform
Abortion Rights
> + specific aspects
Law: secretaries
Inst Legal Secretaries & PAs
Inst Paralegal Training
> + Law: paralegal
Law: Statute
Statute Law Soc
Lawn bowling > Bowling
Lawn mowers
Brit Lawn Mower Racing Assn
Old Lawn Mower Club
> + Horticulture & garden: machinery
Lawn tennis > Tennis
Lawrence (David Herbert)
D H Lawrence Soc
Lawrence (Thomas Edward)['of Arabia']
T E Lawrence Soc
Lawyers > Law; Legal advisers
Laying on of hands > Spiritual healing
Lead
Lead Contrs Assn
Lead Sheet Assn
Lead Smelters & Refiners Assn
Learned society publishing
Assn Learned & Profl Soc Pubrs
Learning disability
Assn Real Change
Brit Dyslexia Assn
Brit Inst Learning Disabilities
Caspari Foundation for Educl Therapy. . .
Nat Assn Toy & Leisure Libraries
Scot Consortium Learning Disability
Scot Support Learning Assn
> + Children: handicapped
Learning resources > Education: technology
Leasing
Assn Leasehold Enfranchisement Practitioners
Finance & Leasing Assn
Leasehold Enfranchisement Assn
Leather
BLC, Leather Technology Centre
Brit Antique Furniture Restorers Assn
Leather Producers' Assn
Soc Leather Technologists & Chemists
Leathergoods
Brit Menswear Gld
Brit Travelgoods & Accessories Assn
Soc Master Saddlers
Lebanon
Brit Lebanese Assn
Lecturers
Assn Teachers & Lecturers
University & College U
> + Adult education; Teachers
Leeks
Leek Growers' Assn
> + Vegetable: growing
Left-handed people
Left-Handers Assn
Left Handers Club
Legacies (public) > Donations (public)
Legal > Law; & headings below
Legal advisers/services
Assn Lawyers & Legal Advisors
Profl Assn Legal Services
Legal cashiers
Inst Legal Cashiers & Administrators
Legal secretaries > Law: secretaries
Legal studies > Law
Legionnaire's disease
Inst Plumbing & Heating Engg
Leisure parks
Assn Leading Visitor Attractions
Brit Assn Leisure Parks, Piers & Attractions
> + Amusements
Leisure, recreation & amenity management
Assn Heritage Interpretation
Assn Profl Sales Agents (Sports & Leisure Inds)
Chief Cultural & Leisure Officers Assn
Fitness Ind Assn
Inst Entertainment & Arts Profls
Inst Leisure & Amenity Mgt Ireland
Inst Sport, Parks & Leisure

© CBD Research Ltd · Beckenham · BR3 5JS · Tel 020 8650 7745 · Fax 020 8650 0768 · E-mail cbd@cbdresearch.com · www.cbdresearch.com

Leisure Mgt Contractors Assn
Leisure Studies Assn
Nat Assn Agricl Contrs
Nat Assn Leisure Ind Certification
Scot Countryside Rangers' Assn
Soc Leisure Consultants & Pubrs
Voice Chief Offrs Cultural. . . Services
Leisure software > Software: leisure
Lending rights > Copyright
Lenses > Optical industry
Lepidoptera > Entomology
Lesch-Nyhan syndrome
Purine Metabolic Patients Assn
Letter boxes
Letter Box Study Gp
Letter carving > Stone masons & sculptors;   Wood carving
Letter files
Brit Office Supplies & Services Fedn
> + Office equipment & systems
Letter scales > Scales & weighing machines;   Writing equipment & accessories
Letting agents
Assn Residential Letting Agents
UK Assn Letting Agents
Lettuces
Brit Leafy Salad Assn
> + Vegetables: growing
Leukaemia
Leukaemia CARE
Lewis (Wyndham)
Wyndham Lewis Soc
Leylandii hedges
Hedgeline
Leylines
Assn Scientific Study Anomalous Phenomena
Soc Ley Hunters
Liberty > Individual freedom
Libraries/librarians
ARLIS/UK & Ireland
Aslib
Assn Brit Theological. . . Libraries
Assn Denominational Histl Socs Cognate Libs
Assn Indep Libraries
Assn NI Educ & Library Bds
Assn UK Media Librarians
Brit Assn Friends Museums
Brit & Ir Assn Law Librarians
Career Devt Gp
CILIP
Friends Nat Libraries
Librarians of Insts & Schools of Educ
Library Assn Ireland
Library Campaign
London Library
Nat Acquisitions Gp
Nat Assn Aerial Photographic Libraries
Network Govt Library & Inf Specialists
Private Libraries Assn
RLUK
School Library Assn
Soc Chief Librarians
Voice Chief Offrs Cultural. . . Services
> + Picture libraries
Library schools
Brit Assn Inf & Library Educ & Res
Library suppliers
Assn Library Eqpt Suppliers
Libya
Soc Libyan Studies
Licensed property (valuation)
Assn Valuers Licensed Property
Restaurant Property Advisors Soc
Licensed trade > Bars (management & staff); Wines & spirits: trade
Licensing laws
Campaign Real Ale
Licensing (product) > Product licensing
Lichen
Brit Lichen Soc
Life assurance > Insurance
Life saving
Brit Canoe U
Brit Long Distance Swimming Assn
R Humane Soc
R Life Saving Soc
R Nat Lifeboat Instn
Surf Life Saving Assn
Swimming Teachers Assn
> + Safety

Lifeboats
Lifeboat Enthusiasts' Soc
R Nat Lifeboat Instn
Lifting & loading equipment
ALLMI Ltd
Assn Loading & Elevating Eqpt Mfrs
Automated Material Handling Systems Assn
Lifting Eqpt Engrs Assn
Solids Handling & Processing Assn
> + Construction equipment; Fork-lift trucks; Materials: management/handling
Lifts
Chart Instn Bldg Services Engrs
Lift & Escalator Ind Assn
Light alloys & metals > Metal headings
Light music > Music
Light railways > Railways: light;   Tramways & trams
Lighter-than-air craft > Balloons & airships
Lighterage
River Assn Freight & Transport
Lighthouses & lightships
Assn Lighthouse Keepers
Lighting
Assn Interior Specialists
Chart Instn Bldg Services Engrs
Instn Lighting Engrs
Lighting Assn
Lighting Ind Fedn
> + Road: lighting, markings & traffic signs
Lightning
Tornado & Storm Res Org
Lightning conductors
Assn Technical Lighting & Access Specialists
Limbless persons
Limbless Assn
> + Disablement
Lime & limestone
Agricl Lime Assn
Brit Calcium Carbonates Fedn
Brit Lime Assn
Fertilizer Assn Ireland
Ground Limestone Producers Assn [IRL]
Quarry Products Assn
Limekilns
Sussex Indl Archaeol Soc
Limousines
Nat Limousine & Chauffeur Assn
Line dancing
Brit Western Dance Assn
> + Dancing
Linen
Ir Linen Gld
> + Textile headings
Liners (ships) > Ships: history & preservation
Linesmen > Referees
Linguistics > Languages
Linguists > Translation & interpretation
Linoleum
Contract Flooring Assn
UK Resilient Flooring Assn
Lintels
Steel Lintel Mfrs Assn
> + Doors; Windows
Lipreading & lipspeaking
Assn Lipspeakers
Assn Teachers Lipreading to Adults
Cued Speech Assn
> + Deafness
Liquefied petroleum gas
L P Gas Assn
Liqueurs > Wines & spirits: trade
Liquid roofing > Roofing
Liquidators
Insolvency Practitioners Assn
> + Insolvency
Liquids: packaging
Alliance Beverage Cartons & Environment
Liquids: storage/warehousing
Tank Storage Assn
> + Cisterns, drums & tanks
List broking
Direct Marketing Assn (UK) Ltd
> + Advertising
Listed property
Listed Property Owners Club
> + Historic buildings

Literacy
>		Brit Assn Literacy in Devt
		Nat Literacy Assn
		UK Literacy Assn
		> + Reading
Literary agents > Authors' agents
Literary rights > Copyright
Literary societies > individual writer; [Country]: language & literature
Literature
		Alliance Literary Socs
		Brit Academy
		Brit Comparative Literature Assn
		Manchester Literary & Philosophical Soc
		Nat Assn Literature Devt
		> + English language & literature; & individual countries
Lithuania
		Lithuanian Assn
Litigation > Law
Litigation: support
		Network Indep Forensic Accountants
Liturgy
		Alcuin Club
		Ecclesiological Soc
		Henry Bradshaw Soc
		Latin Mass Soc
		Prayer Book Soc
		Scot Prayer Book Soc
Liver disease
		Brit Soc Gastroenterology
Liverworts
		Brit Bryological Soc
Livestock > Cattle & livestock; Poultry; Sheep
Living history
		Engliscan Gesíþas
		Regia Anglorum
		Seventeenth Century Life & Times
		Vikings (The)
		> + Fights (historic/re-enactment)
Living wills
		ALERT
		Dignity in Dying
		Voluntary Euthanasia Soc Scotland
		> + Euthanasia
Llamas > Camelids
Load conveyors > Lifting & loading equipment
Load restraint
		Performance Textiles Assn
Loading equipment > Lifting & loading equipment
Lobbyists
		Assn Profl Political Consultants
Local government
		Action Communities Rural England
		Assn Charter Trustee Towns &. . . Couns
		Assn County & City Councils [IRL]
		Assn Municipal Authorities Ireland
		Assn N E Couns
		Convention Scot Local Authorities
		Local Authorities Res & Intelligence Assn
		Local Govt Assn
		London Councils
		Nat Assn Councillors
		Nat Assn Local Couns
		NI Local Govt Assn
		One Voice Wales
		Welsh Local Govt Assn
Local government: officers
		Assn Chief Estates Surveyors. . . Public Sector
		Assn Coun Secretaries & Solicitors
		Assn County Chief Executives
		Assn Local Authority Chief Execs
		Assn Local Govt Archaeol Officers
		Assn Local Govt Communications
		Assn Town Clerks Ireland
		Assn Transport Co-ordinating Officers
		Bar Assn Local Govt & Public Service
		Chief Cultural & Leisure Officers Assn
		CIPFA
		County Educ Officers Two Tier Authorities
		Inst Public Sector Mgt
		Instn Economic Devt
		LABC
		Local Authority Caterers' Assn
		Local Authority Road Safety Officers' Assn
		Local Govt Technical Advisers Gp
		Planning Officers Soc
		Public Mgt & Policy Assn
		Public Sector People Mgrs' Assn

		Public Services Network
		Soc Construction & Quantity Surveyors
		Soc County Treasurers [E&W]
		Soc District Coun Treasurers
		Soc Electrical & Mechanical Engrs
		Soc Local Authority Chief Execs & Senior Mgrs
		Soc Local Coun Clerks
		Soc Procurement Officers Local Govt
Local government: services
		ALARM
		Assn Public Service Excellence
		Inst Sport, Parks & Leisure
Local government: vehicles
		Road Transport Fleet Data Society
Local history & topography
		Brit Assn Local Hist
		Fedn Ulster Local Studies
		Orkney Heritage Soc
		Scot Local History Forum
		> + Archaeology: county societies; Records: historical
Locks
		Assn Insurance Surveyors
		Auto Locksmiths Assn
		Brit Locksmiths & Keycutters Assn
		Master Locksmiths Assn
		UK Locksmiths Assn
		> + Security
Locomotives > Railway headings
Locomotives: road
		Road Locomotive Soc
Logistics > Materials: management/handling
London
		London Appreciation Soc
		London & Middlesex Archaeol Soc
		London Natural Hist Soc
		London Soc
		London Subterranean Survey Assn
		London Topographical Soc
London boroughs > Local government
Long-bow archery > Archery
Long range planning > Strategic planning
Longevity > Geriatrics & ageing
Lords-of-the-Manor > Manors
Lorry loaders
		ALLMI Ltd
		> + Lifting & loading equipment
Loss assessment
		Chart Inst Loss Adjusters
		Inst Public Loss Assessors
Lost wax casting > Metal: casting
Lotteries
		Lotteries Coun
Lovespoon carving
		Brit Woodcarvers Assn
Low Countries
		Assn Low Countries Studies
		> + Belgium; Netherlands
Low frequency noise
		UK Noise Assn
		> + Noise
Low temperatures > Cryogenics
Lowe syndrome
		Lowe Syndrome Assn
Lower limb deficiency
		STEPS
		> + Disablement
Lubricants
		Oil Recycling Assn
		UK Lubricants Assn
Luge racing > Toboggan & luge racing/riding
Luggage & travel goods > Travel goods & accessories
Lumber > Timber
Lung(s), disease & research > Thoracic diseases
Lupus
		Lupus UK
Lutes & lute playing
		Lute Soc
Lutheran Church
		Lutheran Coun
Lutyens (Sir Edwin)
		Lutyens Trust
Luxembourg
		Belgian-Luxembourg Cham Comm GB
		Brit Cham Comm Luxembourg
Lymphoedema & lymphology
		Brit Lymphology Soc
		Brit Manual Lymph Drainage Assn

© CBD Research Ltd · Beckenham · BR3 5JS · Tel 020 8650 7745 · Fax 020 8650 0768 · E-mail cbd@cbdresearch.com · www.cbdresearch.com

Lymphoedema Support Network
Lymphoma Assn

M

Macadam > Asphalt & coated macadam
MacDonald (George)
     George MacDonald Soc
Macebearers
     Gld Mace-Bearers
Macedonia
     Macedonian Soc GB
Machen (Arthur)
     Friends Arthur Machen
Machine tools
     Brit Hardmetal & Engineers' Cutting Tool Assn
     Engg & Machinery Alliance
     Gauge & Tool Makers Assn
     Manufacturing Technologies Assn
Machine vision
     Brit Machine Vision Assn...
     UK Indl Vision Assn
Machinery
     Machinery Users Assn
     Woodworking Machinery Suppliers Assn
     > + specific types of machinery
Machinery: safety
     Safety Assessment Fedn
Mackerel
     Herring Buyers Assn
     Scot Pelagic Fishermen's Assn
     > + Fish headings; Fishing
Mackintosh (Charles Rennie)
     Charles Rennie Mackintosh Soc
Macular disease
     Macular Disease Soc
     > + Blind & partially sighted
Madagascar
     Anglo-Malagasy Soc
Magazines > Newspapers & periodicals: distribution; Periodicals
Magic > Conjuring & magic
Magic lanterns
     Magic Lantern Soc
Magistrates & magistrates courts
     Justices' Clerks' Soc
     Magistrates Assn
Magnetic compasses > Compasses & compass adjusting
Magnetic strip(e) cards > Credit & magnetic strip(e) cards
Magnetism
     UK Magnetics Soc
Mail > Postal services
Mail order trade
     Mail Order Trs Assn
     > + Advertising; Direct selling
Maintenance > Buildings: cleaning & maintenance;   Plant: industrial
Maintenance products
     Brit Assn Chemical Specialities
Maize & maize starch
     Brit Starch Ind Assn
     Maize Growers Assn
     UK Maize Millers' Assn
Majorettes
     Brit Isles Baton Twirling Assn
     Nat Baton Twirling Assn
Make-up (stage & screen)
     Nat Assn Screen Make-up Artists & Hairdressers
     > + Beauty specialists/treatment
Malacology > Conchology
Maladjusted children > Children: handicapped
Malaysia
     Brit Malaysian Soc
Malt & malt products
     Malt Distillers Assn Scotland
     Maltsters Assn
     > + Whisky
Mammals
     Mammal Soc
     Marine Consvn Soc
     > + Nature conservation
Mammography
     Brit Machine Vision Assn...
Management
     Academy Execs & Admins
     Assn Business Administration

     Assn Business Executives
     Assn Business Schools
     Assn Mgt Educ & Devt
     Brit Educl Leadership, Mgt & Admin Soc
     Business Mgt Assn
     Chart Mgt Inst
     Corporate Responsibility Coalition
     Ergonomics Soc
     Inst Administrative Mgt
     Inst Business Admin
     Inst Comml Mgt
     Inst Leadership & Mgt
     Inst Mgt Services
     Inst Mgt Specialists
     Inst Value Mgt
     Ir Mgt Inst
     Profl Business & Technical Mgt
     Strategic Planning Soc
     UK Assn Proposal Mgt Profls
     > + Project management
Management accountancy
     Chart Inst Mgt Accountants
Management consultancy
     Indep Consultants Consortium
     Inst Business Consulting
     Inst Mgt Consultants & Advisers [IRL]
     Management Consultancies Assn
     > + Employment agents & consultants
Mangold hurling
     Mangold Hurling Assn
Manhole covers
     Fabricated Access Covers Trade Association
Manic depression > Depression
Manila hemp > Hemp
Manipulative medicine > specific type eg Osteopathy
Manors
     Manorial Soc
Manpower > Employment
Manslaughter > Murder & manslaughter
Manufacturers/manufacturing
     Brit Assn Res Quality Assurance
     Brit Contract Mfrs & Packers Assn
     Confedn Brit Ind
     Ind Res & Devt Gp [IRL]
     Inst Manufacturing
     PERA
     Rapid Prototyping & Mfrg Assn
     Science, Engg & Mfrg Technologies Alliance
     > + specific industries
Manufacturers' agents
     Manufacturers' Agents' Assn
Manx language
     Cheshaght Ghailckagh (Yn)
Maps > Cartography
Marble
     Brit Antique Furniture Restorers Assn
     Nat Fedn Terrazzo, Marble & Mosaic Specialists
Mare, de la (Walter)
     Walter de la Mare Soc
Marfan syndrome
     Marfan Assn
Margarine
     Margarine & Spreads Assn
Marinas
     Yacht Harbour Assn
     > + Yachts & yachting
Marine: aggregates
     Brit Marine Aggregate Producers' Assn
     > + Aggregates
Marine: biology & biochemistry
     Brit Marine Life Study Soc
     Challenger Soc Marine Science
     Linnean Soc Lond
     Marine Biological Assn
     Marine Consvn Soc
     Porcupine Marine Natural Hist Soc
     Scot Assn Marine Science
     Scot Sub Aqua Club
     Sub-Aqua Assn
     > + Oceanography
Marine: catering > Catering
Marine: contractors
     Intl Marine Contrs Assn
     > + Ocean industries
Marine: education
     Central Org Maritime Pastimes...

Marine Inst [IRL]
> Marine Soc & Sea Cadets
Marine: energy > Renewable energy
Marine: engineering & equipment
> Assn Marine Scientific Ind
> Brit Marine Eqpt Assn
> Brit Naval Eqpt Assn
> Inst Marine Engg, Science & Technology
> Instn Civil Engrs
> Marine Engine & Eqpt Mfrs Assn
> R Instn Naval Architects
> Soc Automotive Engrs
> Soc Consulting Marine Engrs & Ship Surveyors
> Soc Maritime Inds
> > + Shipbuilding & ship repairing; Underwater engineering & research
Marine: information
> Maritime Inf Assn
> > + Nautical history
Marine: trading > Ships stores & supplies
Mariners
> Nautical Inst
> > + Merchant Navy
Marital studies > Family headings
Maritime law > Law: maritime
Marker posts
> Retroreflective Eqpt Mfrs Assn
> > + Road markings, lighting & traffic signs
Market gardening > Fruit: trade;   Horticulture
Marketing
> Arts Marketing Assn
> Assn Users Res Agencies
> Chart Inst Marketing
> Direct Marketing Assn (UK) Ltd
> Inst Direct Marketing
> Inst Intl Marketing
> Inst Sales Promotion
> Ir Direct Marketing Assn
> Market Res Soc
> Marketing Communication Consultants Assn
> Marketing Inst [IRL]
> Marketing Soc
> Marketing Soc [IRL]
> Profl Services Marketing Gp
> Publicity Club Lond
> Soc Sales & Marketing
> > + Incentive marketing; Sales management & representation
Marketing: researchers & interviewers
> Assn Qualitative Res
> Brit Polling Coun
> Market Res Quality Standards Assn
> Viewing Facilities Assn UK
Markets: street, cattle & farmers'
> Assn Private Market Operators
> Fedn Street Traders Us
> Humane Slaughter Assn
> Livestock Auctioneers Assn
> Nat Assn Brit Market Authorities
> Nat Farmers' Retail & Markets Assn
> Nat Market Traders Fedn
> Retail Markets Alliance
Marlowe (Christopher)
> Marlowe Soc
Marmalades
> Food Processors Assn
Marquees > Tents & marquees
Marquetry
> Marquetry Soc
Marriage bureaux > Introduction agencies & marriage bureaux
Marriage guidance
> Family Matters Inst
Marriages > Population registration
Martial arts
> Amat Martial Assn
> Brit Coun Chinese Martial Arts
> Brit Fedn Histl Swordplay
> Brit Judo Assn
> Brit Nat Martial Arts Assns
> Brit Shorinji Kempo Fedn
> Judo Scotland
> Martial Arts Devt Commission
> Nat Assn Karate & Martial Art Schools
> Scot Ju-Jitsu Assn
> Soc Martial Arts
> Tai Chi U
> Welsh Judo Assn

Mary, Queen of Scots
> Marie Stuart Soc
Mary Rose (the)
> Mary Rose Soc
Masefield (John)
> John Masefield Soc
Masonry > Stone
Massage
> Gen Coun Massage Therapy
> On Site Massage Assn
> Scot Massage Therapists Org
> Sports Massage Assn
Massenet (Jules)
> Massenet Soc
Masters of ceremonies > Toastmasters & masters of ceremonies
Mastic asphalt > Asphalt & coated macadam
Masts (radio/telephone) > Aerials: radio, telephone & television
Matchbox labels
> Brit Matchbox, Label & Booklet Soc
Materials (fabrics) > type of material
Materials: control > Stock & materials control
Materials: management/handling
> Automated Material Handling Systems Assn
> Brit Intl Freight Assn
> Brit Materials Handling Fedn
> Chart Inst Logistics & Transport
> Chart Inst Logistics & Transport Ireland
> Container Handling Eqpt Mfrs Assn
> Materials Handling Engrs Assn
> Solids Handling & Processing Assn
> Storage & Handling Eqpt Distbrs Assn
> UK Warehousing Assn
> > + Freight transport
Materials: recycling > Reclamation & recycling
Materials: technology & testing
> Brit Civil Engg Test Eqpt Mfrs Assn
> Brit Inst Non-Destructive Testing
> Brit Measurement & Testing Assn
> Brit Soc Strain Measurement
> BTC Testing Advisory Gp
> Engg Integrity Soc
> Inst Materials, Minerals & Mining
> Lifting Eqpt Engrs Assn
> R Microscopical Soc
> Soc Dyers & Colourists
> Welding Inst
Maternity
> Action Pre-Eclampsia
> Assn Community-based Maternity Care
> Assn Improvements Maternity Services
> Assn Postnatal Illness
> Assn Radical Midwives
> Assn Supervisors Midwives
> Birth Trauma Assn
> Brit Doula Assn
> LIFE
> Meet-a-Mum Assn
> Nat Childbirth Trust
> Neonatal Soc
> Stillbirth & Neonatal Death Soc
> > + Midwifery; Obstetrics & gynaecology
Mathematics
> Assn Teachers Mathematics
> Brit Soc Hist Mathematics
> Dozenal Soc
> Edinburgh Mathematical Soc
> Glasgow Mathematical Assn
> Inst Mathematics & Applications
> London Mathematical Soc
> MatheMagic
> Mathematical Assn
> Nat Assn Mathematics Advisers
Mats & matting
> Coir Assn
Maxillofacial disease
> Craniofacial Soc
> > + Oral medicine
Mayors
> London Mayors Assn
ME (disease) > Myalgic encephalomyelitis
Mead
> Nat Fruit Wine, Mead & Liqueur Producers Assn
Meals on wheels
> Ceretas
Measurement
> Assn Instrumentation, Control, Automation...
> Brit Measurement & Testing Assn

© CBD Research Ltd · Beckenham · BR3 5JS · Tel 020 8650 7745 · Fax 020 8650 0768 · E-mail cbd@cbdresearch.com · www.cbdresearch.com

Brit Weights & Measures Assn
Evaluation Intl
Inst Measurement & Control
Scot Optoelectronics Assn
Trading Standards Inst
UK Metric Assn
> + Scales & weighing machines
Meat
Assn Indep Meat Suppliers
Assn Meat Inspectors
Brit Meat Processors Assn
Gld Q Butchers
Ir Deer Farmers & Venison Assn
Mutton Renaissance Campaign
Nat Assn Catering Butchers
Nat Fedn Meat & Food Traders
NI Master Butchers Assn
NI Meat Exporters Assn
Provision Tr Fedn
Quality Meat Scotland
Scot Assn Meat Whlsrs
Scot Fedn Meat Traders Assns
UK Charcuterie Gld
> + Bacon; Poultry
Meat substitutes
Soya Protein Assn
Mechanical components: obsolescence
Component Obsolescence Gp
Mechanical engineering
Instn Engg & Technology
Instn Mechanical Engrs
Mechanical & Metal Trs Confedn
N England Inst Mining & Mechanical Engrs
> + Engineering
Mechanical handling > Materials: management/handling
Medals > Numismatics
Media
Arts Centre Gp
Assn Measurement & Evaluation Communication
Assn UK Media Librarians
Brit Assn Communicators in Business
Brit Interactive Media Assn
Community Media Assn
Creator's Rights Alliance
Directors Gld
Fedn Entertainment Us
Media, Communications & Cultural Studies Assn
Media Res Gp
Media Soc
Online Content UK
Publicity Club Lond
> + Newspapers & periodicals;   Radio; Television; Multimedia
Mediæval history
London Medieval Soc
Medieval Settlement Res Gp
Medieval Siege Soc
Ranulf Higden Soc
Scot Medievalists
Soc Ancients
> + Records: historical
Mediation
Mediators Inst Ireland
Medical accidents
Action Med Accidents
Medical accountants
Assn Indep Specialist Med Accountants
Medical apparatus & appliances > Health care: equipment & supplies;
Sterilising; Surgical equipment & supplies
Medical broadcasts
Assn Broadcasting Doctors
Medical conditions: long-term
Long-term Conditions Alliance
Medical & dental hypnosis
Brit Assn Med Hypnosis
BSCAH - Brit Soc Clinical... Hypnosis
> + Hypnosis & hypnotherapy
Medical education
Assn Study Med Educ
Nat Assn Clinical Tutors
Nat Assn Primary Care Educators
Medical herbalists > Herbs & herbal medicine
Medical illustration
Inst Med Illustrators
Medical Artists Assn
R Photographic Soc
Medical insurance > Hospitals: contributory schemes;   Medical practitioners'
legal defence

Medical journalism > Medical writing/journalism
Medical laboratory technology > Medical technology
Medical officers
Assn Directors Public Health
Medical Officers Schools Assn
Soc Occupational Medicine
Medical physics
Inst Physics & Engg in Medicine
Medical practice
Balint Soc
Brit Assn Med Mgrs
Catholic Med Assn
Country Doctors Assn
Family Doctor Assn
Fedn Indep Practitioner Orgs
Medical Ethics Alliance
Medical Women's Fedn
Nat Assn Med Educ Mgt
Nat Assn Patient Participation
Nat Assn Sessional GP's
Nat Health Service Consultants' Assn
R Coll Gen Practitioners
> + Medicine
Medical practice: administration
Assn Med Secretaries, Practice Managers...
NHS Alliance
Medical practitioners' legal defence
Medical Defence U
Medical & Dental Defence U Scotland
Medical Protection Soc
Medical records
Inst Health Record & Inf Mgt
Medical research
Academy Medical Sciences
Anaesthetic Res Soc
Assn Researchers in Medicine & Science
Coalition Medical Progress
Inst Clinical Res
Medical Res Soc
Patients' Voice Med Advance
Pharmaceutical & Healthcare Sciences Soc
> + Medicine
Medical secretaries
Assn Med Secretaries, Practice Managers...
Medical technology
Assn Brit Healthcare Inds
Brit Med Laser Assn
Inst Biomedical Science
Inst Physics & Engg in Medicine
Medical Science Histl Soc
Pharmaceutical & Healthcare Sciences Soc
> + individual science
Medical waste
Sanitary Med Disposal Services Assn
Medical writing/journalism
Assn Brit Science Writers
Medical Journalists Assn
Soc Medical Writers
Medicinal preparations > Pharmaceuticals
Medicine
Anthroposophical Med Assn
Assn Med Res Charities
Assn Palliative Medicine
Brit Holistic Med Assn
Brit Med Assn
Brit Med Ultrasound Soc
Brit Nuclear Medicine Soc
Brit Soc Rehabilitation Medicine
Fac Pharmaceutical Med
Fellowship Postgraduate Medicine
Harveian Soc Lond
Hunterian Soc
Intensive Care Soc
Ir Coll Gen Practitioners
Ir Med Org
Manchester Med Soc
Medical Soc Lond
Medical Women's Fedn
R Academy Medicine Ireland
R Coll Physicians Edinburgh
R Coll Physicians Ireland
R Coll Physicians Lond
R Coll Physicians & Surgeons Glasgow
R Medical Soc
R Soc Medicine
R Soc Tropical Medicine & Hygiene

Royal Soc (The)
Soc Social Medicine
Medicine: accident & emergency
Brit Assn Immediate Care
College Emergency Medicine
Medicine: alternative > Complementary medicine; & specific forms
Medicine: herbal > Herbs & herbal medicine
Medicine: history
Brit Soc Hist Medicine
Histl Med Eqpt Soc
Medical Science Histl Soc
Scot Soc Hist Medicine
Soc Social Hist Medicine
Medicine & the law
Medico-Legal Soc
> + Forensic science
Medicine & religion
Assn Nursing Religious
Catholic Med Assn
Gld Health
Gld Pastoral Psychology
Medical Ethics Alliance
Medicine: sports > Sports: medicine & therapy
Medicine: travel > Travel & tourism: health
Meetings (conduct of)
Assn Speakers Clubs
Megaliths
Megalithic Soc
Megapodes > Game & game birds
Membranes (intelligent)
Intelligent Membrane Tr Assn
Memorials
Brit Epigraphy Soc
Church Monuments Soc
Nat Assn Memorial Masons
Public Monuments & Sculpture Assn
> + Stone masons & sculptors
Memory
Brit False Memory Soc
Mendelssohn-Bartholdy (Felix)
Friends Mendelssohn
Ménière's disease
Ménière's Soc
Meningitis
Meningitis Assn Scotland
Meningitis Res Foundation
Menopause (the)
Brit Menopause Soc
Brit Soc Psychosomatic Obstetrics...
Daisy Network
Menswear
Brit Menswear Gld
> + Clothing; Tailoring
Mental health
Assn Child & Adolescent Mental Health
Assn Infant Mental Health UK
Assn Pastoral Care Mental Health
Assn Therapeutic Communities
Eating Disorders Assn
ENABLE
Fragile X Soc
Inclusion Ireland
Mencap
Mental Health Ireland
Mental Health Nurses Assn
Mind (the mental health charity)
Nat Assn Mental After-Care in... Homes
Nat Network Assessment Centres
Nat Phobics Soc
NI Assn Mental Health
Psychiatric Rehabilitation Assn
Rethink
Scot Assn Mental Health
Together
UK Fedn Smaller Mental Health Agencies
> + Psychiatry; specific forms of mental illness
Mental stress > Stress (physical & mental)
Merchant Navy
Nautilus UK
Rail, Maritime & Transport U
> + Shipping
Mercury in dentistry
Brit Soc Mercury Free Dentistry
Merry-go-rounds > Fairgrounds & equipment
Merton (Thomas)
Thomas Merton Soc
Messaging > Mobile phones

Messengers-at-Arms
Soc Messengers-at-Arms & Sheriff Officers
Metabolic disorders
Children Living Inherited Metabolic Diseases
Metal
Aluminium Alloy Mfrg & Recycling Assn
Brit Hardmetal & Engineers' Cutting Tool Assn
Community
Inst Materials, Minerals & Mining
Mechanical & Metal Trs Confedn
Minor Metals Tr Assn
Non-Ferrous Alliance
Scot Assn Metals
Metal: abrasives > Abrasives
Metal: boxes
Metal Packaging Mfrs Assn
Metal: casting
Cast Metals Fedn
Inst Cast Metals Engrs
Metal: detecting
Fedn Indep Detectorists
Nat Coun Metal Detecting
Metal: finishing
Aluminium Finishing Assn
Brit Jewellery, Giftware & Finishing Fedn
Inst Metal Finishing
Inst Vitreous Enamellers
Surface Engg Assn
Metal: forming
Confedn Brit Metalforming
Metalforming Machinery Makers' Assn
Metal: mining > Mining
Metal: non-ferrous
Aluminium Stockholders Assn
Brit Non-Ferrous Metals Fedn
Metal: powder > Powder metallurgy
Metal: scrap
Aluminium Alloy Mfrg & Recycling Assn
Brit Metals Recycling Assn
> + Reclamation & recycling
Metal: sheet
Inst Sheet Metal Engg
Metal: sintering > Powder metallurgy
Metal: spraying
Thermal Spraying & Surface Engg Assn
Metal: working
Art Metalware Mfrs' Assn
Brit Antique Furniture Restorers Assn
Brit Artist Blacksmiths Assn
Brit Metallurgical Plant Constructors Assn
Cold Rolled Sections Assn
Metalforming Machinery Makers' Assn
UK Lubricants Assn
Metallurgy
Birmingham Metallurgical Assn
Histl Metallurgy Soc
Inst Materials, Minerals & Mining
Mineral Ind Res Org
Minerals Engg Soc
Metals: precious > Gemstones; Goldsmiths & Silversmiths; Jewellery
Metalware (antique)
Antique Metalware Soc
Metamorphic technique
Metamorphic Assn
Metaphysics
Aetherius Soc
Soc Metaphysicians
Meteorology
R Meteorological Soc
Remote Imaging Group
Tornado & Storm Res Org
Meters & metering
Assn Meter Operators
BEAMA
Nat Campaign Water Justice
SBGI
Soc Brit Water & Wastewater Inds
UK Metering Forum
UK Revenue Protection Assn
Methane
UK Onshore Operators Gp
Methodist Church
Soc Cirplanologists
Wesley Histl Soc
Metrology
Dozenal Soc
Gauge & Tool Makers Assn

© CBD Research Ltd · Beckenham · BR3 5JS · Tel 020 8650 7745 · Fax 020 8650 0768 · E-mail cbd@cbdresearch.com · www.cbdresearch.com

Metric Martyrs
Trading Standards Inst
UK Metric Assn
UK Weighing Fedn
> + Measurement

Mexico
Brit Mexican Soc
Cámara Comercio Británica AC [Mexico]

Mice
Nat Mouse Club

Microbiology
Assn Applied Biologists
Assn Med Microbiologists
Brit Occupational Hygiene Soc
Brit Soc Antimicrobial Chemotherapy
Pathological Soc
Scot Microbiology Soc
Soc Anaerobic Microbiology
Soc Applied Microbiology
Soc Gen Microbiology

Microcirculation > Haematology

Microelectronics
Nat Microelectronics Inst

Microlight aircraft
Brit Microlight Aircraft Assn

Microphthalmia
Micro & Anophthalmic Children's Soc

Microscopy
Quekett Microscopical Club
R Microscopical Soc

Microwave ovens
Microwave Technologies Assn
Nat Assn Microwave Engrs

Middle East
Ancient Egypt & Middle East Soc
Brit Soc Middle Eastn Studies
Middle East Assn

Midwifery
Assn Radical Midwives
Assn Supervisors Midwives
Indep Midwives Assn
R Coll Midwives
> + Maternity; Obstetrics & gynaecology

Migraine & headaches
Brit Assn Study Headache
Migraine Action Assn

Milestones
Milestone Soc

Military bands > Brass & silver bands

Military history
Army Records Soc
Brit Cartographic Soc
Brit Model Soldier Soc
Corps Drums Soc
Military Heraldry Soc
Military Histl Soc
Patton Histl Soc
Pike & Shot Soc
R Air Force Histl Soc
Soc Ancients
Soc Army Histl Res
Victorian Military Soc
Western Front Assn
> + Fortresses & forts

Military vehicles
Military Vehicle Trust
Miniature Armoured Fighting Vehicle Assn
> + Defence equipment

Milk (incl milk products) > Dairying; Unpasteurised milk

Milk cartons
Alliance Beverage Cartons & Environment
> + Packaging

Milking equipment
Milking Eqpt Assn

Millinery > Headwear

Milling > Grinding & milling machinery; & product milled

Millipedes
Brit Myriapod & Isopod Gp

Mills & mill engines
Northern Mill Engine Soc
Soc Protection Ancient Bldgs
> + Steam engines, boats & machinery

Mineral insulating fibres > Insulation
Mineral water > Bottled water; Water treatment & supply

Minerals
Brit Aggregates Assn
Mineral Ind Res Org
Mineralogical Soc
Russell Soc
> + Geology

Miniature painting
Hilliard Soc Miniaturists
R Soc Miniature Painters . . .
Soc Limners
> + Art & artists

Minicabs > Taxis & minicabs

Mining
Assn Mining Analysts
Brit Aggregates Assn
Brit Assn Colliery Mgt
Cornish Cham Mines & Minerals
Cornish Mining Devt Assn
Ir Assn Economic Geology
Ir Mining & Exploration Gp
Ir Mining & Quarrying Soc
Mineral Ind Res Org
Minerals Engg Soc
Mining Assn
N England Inst Mining & Mechanical Engrs
Nat Assn Licensed Opencast Operators
> + Coal mining

Mining: equipment
Assn Brit Mining Eqpt Cos
Miners' & Indl Lamp Mfrs' Assn

Mining: history
Nat Assn Mining Hist Orgs
Northern Mine Res Soc
Peak District Mines Hist Soc
Subterranea Britannica
Trevithick Soc
Welsh Mines Soc

Mire research
Brit Ecological Soc

Mirrors
Glass & Glazing Fedn

Miscarriage
Foresight
Miscarriage Assn
> + Maternity

Missionary organisations
Soc Promoting Christian Knowledge

Mnemonics

Mobile catering > Catering: outdoor

Mobile communications > Communication services; Mobile phones; Paging (radio); Radio: mobile

Mobile community resources
Nat Playbus Assn

Mobile data
Assn Automatic Identification . . .Capture
Mobile Data Assn

Mobile homes
Nat Assn Park Home Residents
> + Caravans & caravanning

Mobile phones
Fedn Technological Inds
Ir Cellular Industry Assn
Mast Action UK
Mobile Electronics & Security Fedn
Mobile Indl Crime Action Forum
Mobile Operators Assn
One Hundred & Sixty (160) Characters Assn

Mobile radio > Radio: mobile

Mobility aids
Brit Healthcare Trs Assn
Ir Wheelchair Assn
> + Blind & partially sighted; Disabled: road users; Health care: equipment & supplies

Model making
Soc Architectural Illustration
Soc Model & Experimental Engrs
> + Models: hobby

Model theatre > Theatre: model
Models: fashion > Fashion
Models: hobby
Brit Model Flying Assn
Brit Model Soldier Soc
Brit Radio Car Assn
Brit Slot Car Racing Assn
Histl Model Rly Soc
Miniature Armoured Fighting Vehicle Assn
Model Electronic Rly Gp

Model Rly Club
Model Yachting Assn
N Wstn Model Rly Clubs Assn
Scot Aeromodellers Assn
Soc Model Shipwrights
Train Collectors Soc
Modern dancing > Dancing
Modern languages > Languages; & specific countries
Modular & portable buildings
Modular & Portable Bldg Assn
Molluscs > Conchology; Shellfish
Monarchy
Monarchist League
R Stuart Soc
> + Courts (royal)
Money transmission
Assn Payment Clearing Services
UK Money Transmitters Assn
Monumental masonry > Stone masons & sculptors
Monuments > Brasses; Historic buildings; Memorials
Moon type
R Nat Inst Blind
Moore (John) conservationist
John Moore Soc
Moorland
Moorland Assn
Scot Assn Country Sports
Morocco
Brit Cham Comm Morocco
Brit Moroccan Soc
Morris dancing
Morris Fedn
Morris Ring
> + Folk dance & song
Morris (William)
William Morris Soc
Mortar
Brit Lime Assn
Intl Masonry Soc
Mortar Ind Assn
Mortgages
Assn Mortgage Intermediaries
Corpn Insurance, Financial & Mortgage Advisers
Coun Mortgage Lenders
Indep Banking Advy Service
Intermediary Mortgage Lenders Assn
Ir Mortgage Coun
Nat Assn Comml Finance Brokers
Nat Assn Mortgage Victims
Safe Home Income Plans
Mosaics
Assn Study & Presvn Roman Mosaics
Nat Fedn Terrazzo, Marble & Mosaic Specialists
Mosses > Bryology
Mothers > Maternity; Obstetrics & gynaecology; Women's organisations
Moths > Butterflies & moths; Entomology
Motor > entries below & Car headings
Motor boats > Boats & boating
Motor cycles > Cycles & motorcycles
Motor cycles: historic > Motor vehicles: historic
Motor cycling & scooter riding
Amat Motor Cycle Assn
Assn Pioneer Motor Cyclists
Auto-Cycle U
Brit Motor Cycle Racing Club
Brit Motorcyclists Fedn
Brit Scooter Sport Org
Brit Speedway Promoters' Assn
Fedn Sidecar Clubs
Inst Advanced Motorists
Motorcycle Action Gp
Nat Assn Bikers Disability
Nat Hillclimb Assn
Nat Sprint Assn
Scot Auto Cycle U
Speedway Control Bd
Trail Riders Fellowship
TT Riders Assn
Vintage Motor Cycle Club
World Speedway Riders Assn
Motor(s): electric > Electric motors
Motor engines: reconditioning
Fedn Engine Re-Mfrs
Motor factors
Automotive Distribution Fedn
Group Auto U
Indep Motor Tr Factors Assn

Motor industry
Automotive Mfrs' Racing Assn
BTC Testing Advisory Gp
Fedn Automatic Transmission Engrs
Fire Fighting Vehicles Mfrs Assn
Inst Automotive Engr Assessors
Inst Motor Ind
MIRA Ltd
Motor Industry Public Affairs Assn Ltd
Motor Vehicle Dismantlers Assn
MVRA Ltd
Soc Automotive Engrs
Soc Ir Motor Ind
Soc Motor Mfrs & Traders
Vehicle Builders & Repairers Assn
> + Electric: transport
Motor insurance > Insurance
Motor neurone disease
Motor Neurone Disease Assn
Scot Motor Neurone Disease Assn
Motor sport
Assn Motor Racing Circuit Owners
Automotive Mfrs' Racing Assn
Brit Automobile Racing Club
Brit Motorsport Marshals Club
Brit Off Road Driving Assn
Brit Racing & Sports Car Club
Brit Stock Car Drivers Assn
Brit Truck Racing Assn
Brooklands Soc
Motor Sports Assn
Motoring Orgs' Land Access & Recreation Assn
Motorsport Ind Assn
RSAC Motorsport
Scot Motor Racing Club
Scot Sporting Car Club
Ulster Automobile Club
Motor trade
A1 Motor Stores
Automotive Distribution Fedn
Brit Indep Motor Tr Assn
Nat Jumblers Fedn
Retail Motor Ind Fedn
Scot Motor Tr Assn
> + Garages & garage equipment
Motor vehicles: customised
Nat Street Rod Assn
Nat Street Van Assn
Motor vehicles: electronic equipment
Mobile Electronics & Security Fedn
Motor vehicles: fleet management
Inst Car Fleet Mgt
Motor vehicles: hire
Accident Mgt Assn
Brit Vehicle Rental & Leasing Assn
Car Rental Coun Ireland
London Private Hire Car Assn
Nat Assn Licensing & Enforcement Offrs
Nat Limousine & Chauffeur Assn
Nat Private Hire Assn
Motor vehicles: historic
Assn Classic Trials Clubs
Assn Land Rover Clubs
Assn Old Vehicle Clubs NI
Brit Ambulance Soc
Brooklands Soc
Classic Rally Assn
Farm Machinery Presvn Soc
Fedn Brit Hist Vehicle Clubs
Fire Service Presvn Gp
Historic Comml Vehicle Soc
Military Vehicle Trust
Nat Assn Road Transport Museums
Nat Jumblers Fedn
Nat Traction Engine Trust
Nat Trolleybus Assn
Nat Vintage Tractor & Engine Club
Post Office Vehicle Club
Road Locomotive Soc
Road Roller Assn
Road Transport Fleet Data Society
Roads & Road Transport Hist Assn
Scot Vintage Vehicle Fedn
Soc Automotive Historians
Southern Counties Historic Vehicle Presvn Trust
Steam Car Club
Steam Plough Club

© CBD Research Ltd · Beckenham · BR3 5JS · Tel 020 8650 7745 · Fax 020 8650 0768 · E-mail cbd@cbdresearch.com · www.cbdresearch.com

Transport Trust
Vintage Motor Cycle Club
Vintage Sports Car Club
Motor vehicles: lining & racking
Mobile Electronics & Security Fedn
Motor vehicles: number plates
Brit Number Plate Mfrs Assn
Motor vehicles: recovery
Assn Vehicle Recovery Operators
Inst Vehicle Recovery
Retail Motor Ind Fedn
Road Rescue Recovery Assn
Motor vehicles: salvage
Brit Vehicle Salvage Fedn
Motor vehicles: taxation
Alliance Urban 4x4s
Motor vehicles: theft (of/from)
Intl Assn Auto Theft Investigators
Motoring journalism
Gld Motoring Writers
Motoring organisations
Assn Brit Drivers
Automobile Assn
Blue Badge Network
Disabled Motorists Fedn
Drivers' Alliance
Inst Advanced Motorists
Mobilise Org
R Ir Automobile Club
Motoring schools > Driving tuition
Moulding sand
Silica & Moulding Sands Assn
Moulds > Patternmaking
Mountain bothies
Mountain Bothies Assn
Mountaineering > Climbing
Mounted games/activities > Horse: riding & driving
Movable walls
Assn Interior Specialists
Mowers > Lawn mowers
Mucopolysaccharidosis
Soc Mucopolysaccharide Diseases
Muggeridge (Malcolm)
Malcolm Muggeridge Soc
Mules
Brit Mule Soc
Multiple births > Twins & multiple births
Multiple sclerosis
Multiple Sclerosis Nat Therapy Centres
Multiple Sclerosis Soc
Multiple Sclerosis Soc Ireland
Multiple shops > Retail trade
Mumming > Folk dance & song
Municipal > Local government
Munro (Neil)
Neil Munro Soc
Murder & manslaughter
SAMM
> + Children: death by accident/violence
Murray (Keith)
Keith Murray Collectors Club
Muscular Dystrophy
Duchenne Family Support Gp
Muscular Dystrophy Campaign
Muscular Dystrophy Ireland
Musculoskeletal medicine
Arthritis & Musculoskeletal Alliance
Brit Inst Musculoskeletal Medicine
Soc Orthopaedic Medicine
> + Arthritis & rheumatism
Museums
Assn Brit Transport & Engg Museums
Assn Indep Museums
Assn Leading Visitor Attractions
Brit Assn Friends Museums
Brit Museum Friends
Collections Trust
Fedn Museums & Art Galleries Wales
Group Educ Museums
Heritage Rly Assn
Ir Museums Assn
Museum Profls Gp
Museums Assn
Nat Art Collections Fund
Nat Assn Road Transport Museums
Nat Heritage
Scot Museums Fedn

Soc Museum Archaeologists
Social Hist Curators Gp
Mushroom growing
Mushroom Growers Assn
> + Mycology
Music
Assn Indep Music
Brit Fedn Brass Bands
Brit Music Soc
Campaign Freedom Piped Music
Dvořák Soc Czech & Slovak Music
Entertainment Retailers Assn
Fedn Recorded Music Socs
Inst Contemporary Arts
Ir Recorded Music Assn
Light Music Soc
Making Music
Music Inds Assn
Music Managers Forum
Nat Assn Brass Band Conductors
Nat Early Music Assn
Plainsong & Mediæval Music Soc
Pop & Rock Fans' Assn
Production Services Assn
R Musical Assn
R Philharmonic Soc
R Scot Academy Music & Drama
Robert Farnon Soc
Scot Amat Music Assn
Scot Record Ind Assn
Soc Music Analysis
Soc Producers & Composers Applied Music
Soc Promotion New Music
Sonic Arts Network
Sound Sense
Viola da Gamba Soc
Welsh Amat Music Fedn
Welsh Music Gld
Workers' Music Assn
> + Choirs & choral music; Church music; Orchestras
Music: composers & conductors
Brit Music Rights
> individual by name
Music: composing
Brit Academy Composers & Songwriters
Music: copyright > Copyright
Music: festivals > Festivals: art, drama & music
Music: hall
Brit Music Hall Soc
Scot Music Hall & Variety Theatre Soc
Music: psychology
Soc Educ Music & Psychology Res
Music: recording > Sound recording & reproduction
Music: sheet
Music Pubrs' Assn
Music: teaching
Brit Kodály Academy
Brit Suzuki Inst
Conservatoires UK
Curwen Inst
Fedn Music Services
Inc Soc Musicians
Jazz Piano Teachers Assn
Music Educ Coun
Music Masters' & Mistresses' Assn
Nat Assn Music Educators
Nat Assn Percussion Teachers
Percussive Arts Soc
R Academy Music
R Ir Academy Music
Schools Music Assn
Scot Assn Music Educ
UK Fedn Jazz Bands
Music: therapy
Assn Profl Music Therapists
Brit Soc Music Therapy
Musical boxes
Musical Box Soc
Musical instruments
Brit Assn Symphonic Bands & Wind Ensembles
Electric Guitar Appreciation Soc
Fair Organ Presvn Soc
Fellowship Makers. . . Histl Instruments
Galpin Soc
Hurdy-Gurdy Soc
Inst Musical Instrument Technology
Music Inds Assn

Nat Assn Musical Instrument Repairers
Nat Early Music Assn
> + specific instruments
Musicians
Brit Music Rights
Gld Musicians & Singers
Inc Soc Musicians
Musicians' U
R Soc Musicians
Mussels > Shellfish
Mutism
Selective Mutism Inf & Res Assn
> + Speech
Mutton
Mutton Renaissance Campaign
Muzak
Campaign Freedom Piped Music
Myalgic encephalitis/encephalopathy
Action ME
Assn Young People with ME
Myalgic Encephalopathy Assn
Myasthenia
Myasthenia Gravis Assn
Mycology
Assn Brit Fungus Gps
Birmingham Natural Hist Soc
Brit Mycological Soc
Brit Soc Antimicrobial Chemotherapy
Brit Soc Med Mycology
Myelitis
Transverse Myelitis Soc
Myositis
Myositis Support Gp
Myotonic dystrophy
Myotonic Dystrophy Support Gp
Myriapods
Brit Myriapod & Isopod Gp
Myths & legends
Traditional Cosmology Soc

> + Folk life & lore

N

Naevus > Birthmarks & disfigurement
Nails
Wire Products Assn
> + Wire & wire products
Names
English Place-Name Soc
Gld One-Name Studies
Soc Name Studies Britain & Ireland
Nannies & au pairs
Voice
Napoleon I, II & III
Assn Friends Waterloo C'ee
Napoleonic Assn
Napoleonic Soc
Nappies
Absorbent Hygiene Products Mfrs Assn
Nat Assn Nappy Services
Narcissus
Daffodil Soc
Narcolepsy
Narcolepsy Assn
Narrow fabrics
Braid Soc
Brit Narrow Fabrics Assn
National Health Service
Ambulance Service Network
Health Care Supply Assn
Healthcare Financial Mgt Assn
Healthcare People Mgt Assn
Inst Healthcare Mgt
Nat Assn Healthcare Security
Nat Assn Primary Care
Nat Assn Voluntary Service Mgrs
NHS Support Fedn
NHS Trusts Assn
Socialist Health Assn
National Parks
Assn Nat Park Authorities
Scot Coun Nat Parks
> + Parks & gardens

National vocational qualifications
Inst Assessors & Internal Verifiers
Nationalism
Assn Study Ethnicity & Nationalism
Natural energy > Renewable energy; Solar energy
Natural gas
Natural Gas Vehicle Assn
Natural health & therapeutics
Alliance Natural Health
Assn Natural Medicine
Assn Physical & Natural Therapists
Assn Systematic Kinesiology
Brit Natural Hygiene Soc
College Vibrational Medicine Practitioner Assn
Consumers Health Choice
Radionic Association Ltd
> + Complementary medicine
Natural history
Brit Entomological & Natural Hist Soc
Brit Naturalists Assn
Field Studies Coun
Linnean Soc Lond
Nat Assn Field Studies Officers
Northamptonshire Natural History Soc
Ray Soc
Scot Field Studies Assn
Soc Hist Natural Hist
Somerset Archaeol & Natural Hist Soc
Wiltshire Archaeol & Natural Hist Soc
> + Archaeology: county societies;   Conservation: area
organisations
Nature conservation
Assn Natural Burial Grounds
Brit Assn Nature Conservationists
Butterfly Consvn
Countryside Alliance
Farming & Wildlife Advy Gp
Landlife
Marine Consvn Soc
Nat Assn Areas Outstanding Natural Beauty
Nat Coun Consvn Plants & Gardens
Nat Fedn Biological Recording
R Soc Wildlife Trusts
Scot Envt Link
Scot Wildlife Trust
Small Farms Assn
> + Conservation
Nature conservation: local reserves
Armagh > County Armagh Wildlife Soc
Ashmolean Natural Hist Soc Oxfordshire
Bedfordshire > Wildlife Trust Bedfordshire, Cambridgeshir. . .
Birmingham Natural Hist Soc
Cambridgeshire > Wildlife Trust Bedfordshire, Cambridgeshir. . .
County Armagh Wildlife Soc
Croydon Natural Hist & Scientific Soc
Durham Wildlife Trust
Essex Wildlife Trust
Falklands Consvn
Glasgow Natural Hist Soc
Gwent Wildlife Trust
Herefordshire > Woolhope Naturalists' Field Club
Isle of Wight Natural Hist & Archaeol Soc
London Natural Hist Soc
Natural Hist Soc Northumbria
Norfolk Wildlife Trust
Northamptonshire > Wildlife Trust Bedfordshire, Cambridgeshir. . .
Northumbria > Natural Hist Soc Northumbria
Peterborough > Wildlife Trust Bedfordshire, Cambridgeshir. . .
Wildlife Trust Bedfordshire, Cambridgeshire. . .
Wildlife Trust (S & W Wales)
Woolhope Naturalists' Field Club
Naturism
Central Coun Brit Naturism
Ir Naturist Assn
Naturopathy
Brit Naturopathic Assn
Gen Coun & Register Naturopaths
Inc Soc Registered Naturopaths
> + Natural health & therapeutics
Nautical archaeology > Archaeology: nautical
Nautical history
Hakluyt Soc
Mary Rose Soc
Naval Histl Collectors & Res Assn
Navy Records Soc
Soc Nautical Res

© CBD Research Ltd · Beckenham · BR3 5JS · Tel 020 8650 7745 · Fax 020 8650 0768 · E-mail cbd@cbdresearch.com · www.cbdresearch.com

Nautical instruments
    Chart & Nautical Instrument Tr Assn
Nautical training > Marine: education; Sailing
Naval archaeology > Archaeology: nautical
Naval architecture & equipment > Marine: engineering & equipment;
    Shipbuilding & ship repairing
Naval history > Nautical history
Navigation
    Assn Lighthouse Keepers
    Gld Air Pilots & Air Navigators
    Nautical Inst
    R Inst Navigation
    Sub-Aqua Assn
    UKspace
Navy > Royal Navy
Neck injury & disease > Head, neck & brain injury & disease
Needham (Violet)
    Violet Needham Soc
Nelson (Admiral, Lord Horatio)
    Nelson Soc
    R Navy Enthusiasts' Soc
Nematology
    Assn Applied Biologists
Neonatal death > Maternity
Nepal
    Britain-Nepal Cham Comm
    Britain Nepal Soc
Nephrology
    Brit Kidney Patient Assn
    Doctor Richard Bright Soc
    Ir Kidney Assn
    Nat Kidney Fedn
    Purine Metabolic Patients Assn
    Renal Assn
Nerine
    Nerine & Amaryllid Soc
Nesbit (Edith)
    Edith Nesbit Soc
Netball
    All England Netball Assn
    Netball NI
    Netball Scotland
    Welsh Netball Assn
Netherlands
    Anglo-Netherlands Soc
    Assn Low Countries Studies
    Netherlands-Brit Cham Comm
Netherlands: language & literature
    Assn Language Learning
Netsuke carving
    Brit Woodcarvers Assn
Netting > Lace & net; Wire & wire products
Networking
    Intellect
    Nat Outsourcing Assn
Neuralgia
    Trigeminal Neuralgia Assn
Neuroblastoma
    Neuroblastoma Soc
    > + Cancer
Neurofibromatosis
    Neurofibromatosis Assn
Neurology
    Assn Brit Neurologists
    Assn Neuro-Linguistic Programming
    Batten Disease Family Assn
    Brit Neuropsychiatry Assn
    Brit Neuropsychological Soc
    Brit Soc Neuroradiologists
    CMT UK
    Guillain Barré Syndrome Support Gp
    Neurological Alliance
    Stiff Man Syndrome Support Gp
Neuropathology
    Brit Neuropathological Soc
Neurophysiology
    Brit Soc Clinical Neurophysiology
    Electro-physiological Technologists Assn
Neuroscience
    Brit Neuropsychiatry Assn
    Brit Neuroscience Assn
    Physiological Soc
    Scot Neuroscience Gp
Neurosurgery
    Soc Brit Neurological Surgeons
Neutral alcohol
    Nat Alcohol Producers Assn

New Zealand
    Australian Business
    Brit New Zealand Tr Coun
    Hebe Soc
Newsagents > Newspapers & periodicals: distribution
Newsletters
    UK Specialised Inf Publishers Assn
    > + Periodicals
Newspapers
    Assn Circulation Executives
    Assn Regional City Editors
    Assn UK Media Librarians
    Foreign Press Assn Lond
    Nat Newspapers Ireland
    Newspaper Conf
    Newspaper Pubrs Assn
    Newspaper Soc
    Press Standards Bd Finance
    Regional Newspapers Assn Ireland
    Scot Daily Newspaper Soc
    Scot Newspaper Publishers Assn
    Soc Editors
    Talking Newspaper Assn
    Web-offset Newspaper Assn
Newspapers & periodicals: distribution
    Assn Newspaper Magazine Whlsrs
    Assn Subscription Agents & Intermediaries
    Convenience Stores & Newsagents Assn [IRL]
    Nat Fedn Retail Newsagents
Nickel
    Surface Engg Assn
Nigeria
    Britain Nigeria Business Coun
    Britain-Nigeria Educl Trust
Noise
    Assn Noise Consultants
    Aviation Envt Fedn
    Campaign Freedom Piped Music
    Engg Integrity Soc
    Environmental Protection UK
    Fencing Contrs' Assn
    Heating, Ventilating & Air Conditioning Mfrs' Assn
    Inst Acoustics
    MIRA Ltd
    Noise Abatement Soc
    Proprietary Acoustic Systems Mfrs
    UK Envtl Law Assn
    UK Noise Assn
    > + Insulation
Non-destructive testing > Materials: technology & testing
Non-ferrous metal > Metal
Non-wovens
    Brit Textile Technology Gp
    > + Textile headings
Norman-French texts
    Anglo-Norman Text Soc
    > + English language & literature
North America > USA; Canada
Norway
    Anglo-Norse Soc
    Norwegian-Brit Cham Comm
Notaries public
    Assn Solicitor Notaries Greater London
    Notaries Soc [E&W]
Novelists > under individual name
Nuclear disarmament > Disarmament
Nuclear energy
    Instn Civil Engrs
    Nuclear Ind Assn
    Nuclear Inst
    Supporters Nuclear Energy
Nudism > Naturism
Number plates
    Brit Number Plate Mfrs Assn
    Inst Registration Agents & Dealers
Numeracy > Literacy & numeracy
Numerical analysis
    Inst Mathematics & Applications
Numismatics
    Brit Art Medal Soc
    Brit Assn Numismatic Socs
    Brit Numismatic Soc
    Brit Numismatic Tr Assn
    Orders & Medals Res Soc
    R Numismatic Soc
    Soc Numismatic Artists & Designers
    Token Corresponding Soc

Nurseries & nursery schools
     Brit Assn Early Childhood Educ
     Nat Campaign Nursery Educ
     Nat Children's Nurseries Assn [IRL]
     Nat Day Nurseries Assn
     Pre-School Learning Alliance
     Voice
Nursery & baby products
     Baby Eqpt Hirers Assn
     Baby Products Assn
     Plastics & Board Inds Fedn
Nursery stock > Horticulture
Nursing
     Assn Brit Paediatric Nurses
     Assn Nursery Training Colls
     Assn Nurses Substance Abuse
     Assn Nursing Religious
     Assn Occupational Health Nurse Practitioners
     Assn Perioperative Practice
     Brit Assn Dental Nurses
     Brit Red Cross Soc
     Community & District Nursing Assn
     Indep Fedn Nursing Scotland
     Ir Nurses Org
     Mental Health Nurses Assn
     Nat Care Assn
     Nurse Directors Assn
     Pharmaceutical & Healthcare Sciences Soc
     Queen's Nursing Inst
     R Coll Nursing
     Soc Nursery Nursing Practitioners
     > + Veterinary medicine
Nursing homes
     English Community Care Assn
     Nursing Homes Ireland
     Registered Nursing Home Assn
Nutrition
     Brit Assn Nutritional Therapy
     Brit Dietetic Assn
     Brit Housewives League
     Brit Nutrition Foundation
     Brit Soc Ecological Medicine
     Health Food Inst
     Inst Optimum Nutrition
     McCarrison Soc
     Nutrition Soc
     > + Food
Nuts & bolts > Fasteners & turned parts
Nuts (allergy to)
     Anaphylaxis Campaign
     > + Allergy
Nuts (edible)
     Brit Peanut Coun
     Combined Edible Nut Tr Assn
     Fedn Oils, Seeds & Fats Assns
     Kentish Cobnuts Assn
     Snack, Nut & Crisp Mfrs Assn
     > + Peanuts
NVQs > National vocational qualifications
Nystagmus
     Nystagmus Network

O

Oatmeal
     Brit Oat & Barley Millers Assn
Obesity
     Assn Study Obesity
     Brit Obesity Surgery Patient Assn
     Brit Obesity Surgery Soc
     Nat Obesity Forum
     Prader-Willi Syndrome Assn
     > + Eating disorders
Oboes (musical instruments)
     Brit Double Reed Soc
Observer's Pocket Series
     Observers Pocket Series Collectors' Soc
Obsessive/compulsive disorders
     Nat Acupuncture Detoxification Assn
     Nat Phobics Soc
     OCD Action
     Tourette Syndrome (UK) Assn
     > + Mental health

Obsolescence (electronic & mechanical)
     Component Obsolescence Gp
Obstetrics & gynaecology
     Blair Bell Res Soc
     Brit Assn Perinatal Medicine
     Brit Soc Gynaecological Endoscopy
     Brit Soc Psychosomatic Obstetrics. . .
     Fac Sexual & Reproductive Healthcare
     Obstetric Anaesthetists Assn
     Ovacome: the ovarian cancer support network
     R Coll Obstetricians & Gynaecologists
     > + Maternity; Midwifery
Occultism
     Aetherius Soc
Occupational health & hygiene
     Assn Med Advisers Brit Orchestras
     Assn Occupational Health Nurse Practitioners
     Brit Occupational Hygiene Soc
     Fac Occupational Medicine
     Inst Safety Technology & Res
     Instn Occupational Safety & Health
     Ir Soc Occupational Medicine
     Occupational & Envtl Diseases Assn
     Soc Chemical Ind
     Soc Occupational Medicine
Occupational safety > Safety
Occupational therapy
     Assn Occupational Therapists Ireland
     Brit Assn Occupational Therapists
Occupational training & education
     Assn Learning Providers
     Inst Training & Occupational Learning
     Ir Inst Trg & Devt
     > + Education
Ocean energy > Renewable energy
Ocean industries
     Assn Brit Indep Oil Exploration Cos
     Assn Brit Offshore Inds
     Assn Well Head Eqpt Mfrs
     Brit Rig Owners Assn
     Emergency Response & Rescue Vessels Assn
     Energy Inds Coun
     Inst Marine Engg, Science & Technology
     Intl Marine Contrs Assn
     Ir Offshore Operators Assn
     NOF Energy
     Offshore Contrs' Assn
     Offshore Engg Soc
     Offshore Ind Liaison C'ee
     Oil & Gas UK
     Well Services Contrs Assn
Oceanography
     Challenger Soc Marine Science
     Hydrographic Soc UK
     R Meteorological Soc
     Remote Sensing & Photogrammetry Soc
     Scot Assn Marine Science
     > + Earth sciences, structure & resources
Odontology > Dentistry; Teeth
Oesophageal conditions > Tracheostomy
Offa's Dyke
     Offa's Dyke Assn
Offenders > Prisoners: welfare & rehabilitation
Office equipment & systems
     Brit Assn Removers
     Brit Inst Facilities Mgt
     Brit Office Supplies & Services Fedn
     Indep Print Inds Assn
     Intellect
     Records Mgt Soc
     Storage Eqpt Mfrs Assn
     > + Computers
Office management
     Brit Inst Facilities Mgt
     Facilities Mgt Assn
     Inst Administrative Mgt
Offices (serviced)
     Brit Coun Offices
     Business Centre Assn
Off-licences > Wines & spirits: trade
Off-road driving > Driving (off-road); Four by fours
Offshore engineering > Ocean industries
Off-street parking > Parking
Oil > Petroleum; & entries below
Oil burners & appliances
     ICOM Energy Assn

© CBD Research Ltd · Beckenham · BR3 5JS · Tel 020 8650 7745 · Fax 020 8650 0768 · E-mail cbd@cbdresearch.com · www.cbdresearch.com

Oil Firing Technical Assn Petroleum Ind
> + Boilers & waterheaters
Oil painting
Brit Soc Painters (in Oil, Pastels & Acrylic)
> + Art & artists
Oil spills > Spill control
Oils: edible > Edible oils & fats
Oils: essential > Essential oils
Oils: hydrocarbon > Petroleum
Oils: lubricating
UK Lubricants Assn
Oils: packaging
Indl Packaging Assn
Oils: recovery/waste
Oil Recycling Assn
Oilseed
Fedn Oils, Seeds & Fats Assns
Seed Crushers & Oil Processors Assn
Soc Chemical Ind
Old people's organisations
Abbeyfield Soc
Contact the Elderly
Discovery Award England
Heyday
Nat Assn Almshouses
Nat Assn Providers Activities Older People
Nat Inf Forum
Nat Pensioners' Convention
R Surgical Aid Soc
R UK Beneficent Assn
Relatives & Residents Assn
> + Retirement
Old Testament > Bible
Olympic games
Brit Olympic Assn
Pentathlon GB
Soc Olympic Collectors
Oman
Anglo-Omani Soc
Ombudsman
Brit & Ir Ombudsman Assn
Oncology
BASO
Brain Tumour UK
Brit Acoustic Neuroma Assn
Brit Assn Head & Neck Oncologists
Brit Oncological Assn
Von Hippel-Lindau Contact Gp
> + Cancer
One parent families > Singles, divorced & separated
Onions
Brit Onion Producers' Assn
Online retailers
Interactive Media Retail Group
Online users & publishers
Assn Online Publishers
Periodical Pubrs Assn - Interactive
UK EInformation Gp
Onshore engineering
UK Onshore Operators Gp
UK Onshore Pipeline Operators' Assn
Open learning
Brit Inst Learning & Devt
> + Education
Open spaces
Commons, Open Spaces. . . Presvn Soc
GreenSpace
> + Conservation; Footpaths & rights of way; Parks & gardens
Opencast mining > Mining; Coal mining
Opera
Nat Operatic & Dramatic Assn
> + name of composer or singer
Operational research
Inst Operations Mgt
Operational Res Soc
Ophthalmic opticians > Optical practice
Ophthalmology
Brit Ophthalmic Anaesthesia Soc
Ophthalmological Prods Tr & Ind Conf
R Coll Ophthalmologists
UK & I Soc Cataract & Refractive Surgeons
Opinion polls
Brit Polling Coun
Market Res Soc
Optical character recognition
Assn Automatic Identification . . .Capture

Optical industry
Assn Contact Lens Mfrs
Brit Contact Lens Assn
Fedn Mfrg Opticians
Ophthalmic Lens Mfrs' & Distrbrs' Assn
Optical Eqpt Mfrs & Suppliers Assn
Optical Frame Importers' & Mfrs' Assn
Optra Exhibitions UK
Optical practice
Assn Brit Dispensing Opticians
Assn Optometrists
Assn Optometrists Ireland
College Optometrists
Fedn Ophthalmic & Dispensing Opticians
Scot C'ee Optometrists
Options > Futures & options
Optoelectronics
Photonics Cluster
Scot Optoelectronics Assn
Oral medicine
Brit Assn Oral & Maxillofacial Surgeons
Brit Soc Dental Hygiene & Therapy
Brit Soc Dental Res
Brit Soc Disability & Oral Health
Brit Soc Oral & Maxillofacial Pathology
Brit Soc Oral Medicine
Inst Maxillofacial Prosthetists. . .
> + Dentistry
Orchestras
Assn Brit Orchestras
Assn Med Advisers Brit Orchestras
Hallé Concerts Soc
Making Music
Nat Assn Youth Orchestras
R Philharmonic Soc
Welsh Amat Music Fedn
> + Music
Orchids
Brit Orchid Coun
Brit Orchid Growers Assn
Orchid Soc
Orders (insignia) > Badges & insignia;   Numismatics
Ordnance > Arms & armour
Ordnance Survey
Charles Close Soc
Orff (Carl)
Orff Soc
Organ donors
Brit Organ Donor Soc
NI Transplant Assn
> + Transplants & transplant surgery
Organic chemicals > Chemical industry & trade
Organic growing & farming
Assn Organics Recycling
Biodynamic Agricl Assn
Henry Doubleday Res Assn
Ir Organic Farmers & Growers Assn
Organic Food Fedn
Organic Living Assn
Scot Organic Prodrs Assn
Soil Assn
World-Wide Opportunities on Organic Farms
Organisation & methods > Management
Organs, organists & organ music
Assn Indep Organ Advisers
Brit Inst Organ Studies
Cathedral Organists Assn
Cinema Organ Soc
Fair Organ Presvn Soc
Inc Assn Organists
Inc Soc Organ Builders
Inst Brit Organ Bldg
Karg-Elert Archive
Mechanical Organ Owners Soc
Organ Club
R Coll Organists
Ulster Soc Organists & Choirmasters
> + Musical instruments
Oriental carpets & rugs
Brit Oriental Rug Dealers Assn
> + Carpets
Orienteering
Brit Orienteering Fedn
NI Orienteering Assn
Scot Orienteering Assn
Origami
Brit Origami Soc

Ornamental fish > Fish: tropical & ornamental
Ornithology > Birds; Nature conservation
Orthodontics > Dentistry
Orthopaedics
       Brit Coalition Heritable Disorders Connective Tissue
       Brit Orthopaedic Assn
       Soc Orthopaedic Medicine
Orthoptics
       Brit & Ir Orthoptic Soc
       > + Ophthalmology
Orthoses > Prosthetics & orthoses
Osteopathy
       Brit Osteopathic Assn
       Cranio Sacral Soc
       Osteopathic Sports Care Assn
       Sutherland Soc
Osteoporosis > Bone
Ostrich farming
       Brit Domesticated Ostrich Assn
       > + Emus; Rheas
Othello (board game)
       Brit Othello Fedn
Otolaryngology
       Brit Assn Otorhinolaryngologists
       Brit Voice Assn
       Nat Assn Laryngectomee Clubs
       Scot Otolaryngological Soc
Otters
       Intl Otter Survival Fund
Outdoor advertising > Advertising: outdoor
Outdoor catering > Catering: outdoor
Outdoor centres > Holiday camps & centres
Outdoor education > Education: outdoor
Outdoor events > specific type of event
Outdoor furniture
       Leisure & Outdoor Furniture Assn
       > + Furniture
Outdoor professionals
       Brit Outdoor Profls Assn
Outsourcing (business technology)
       Nat Outsourcing Assn
Ovens
       Microwave Technologies Assn
       > + Domestic appliances
Overalls & workwear > Protective clothing/equipment
Overeating > Eating disorders;   Obesity
Overseas development
       Devt Studies Assn
       Voluntary Service Overseas
Overseas property
       Assn Intl Property Profls
       Nat Assn Estate Agents
       > + Property & land owners
Overseas territories (British)
       UK O'seas Territories Assn
Ovulation
       Nat Assn Ovulation Method Instructors
Owen (Wilfred) 1893-1918
       Wilfred Owen Assn
Owls
       Hawk & Owl Trust
Oxenham (Elsie Jeanette)
       Elsie Jeanette Oxenham Appreciation Soc
Oysters
       Assn Scot Shellfish Growers
       Shellfish Assn

P

Pacific Islands
       Pacific Islands Soc
Packaging
       Alliance Beverage Cartons & Environment
       Brit Aerosol Mfrs Assn
       Brit Bottlers' Inst
       Brit Brands Gp
       Brit Packaging Assn
       Brit Plastics Fedn
       Brit Printing Inds Fedn
       Ind Coun Packaging & Envt
       Indl Packaging Assn
       Ir Corrugated Packaging Assn
       Metal Packaging Mfrs Assn

       Nat Packaging Coun
       Packaging Fedn
       Packaging & Indl Films Assn
       Paper Agents Assn
       Pira Intl
       Processing & Packaging Machinery Assn
       Sheet Plant Assn
       Timber Packaging & Pallet Confedn
       Valpak
Packers & shippers for various trades
       Brit Contract Mfrs & Packers Assn
       > + trade concerned
Packing & packing cases > Packaging
Paddle steamers
       Paddle Steamer Presvn Soc
Paediatrics
       Academic Paediatrics Assn
       Assn Brit Paediatric Nurses
       Assn Paediatric Anaesthetists
       Brit Assn Paediatric Surgeons
       Brit Soc Gastroenterology
       Children's Chronic Arthritis Assn
       Neonatal Soc
       Paediatric First Aid Assn
       R Coll Paediatrics & Child Health
       > + Children headings
Paeonies
       Hardy Plant Soc
Paganism
       Pagan Fedn
Paget Gorman Signed Speech
       Paget Gorman Soc
       > + Sign language
Pagets disease
       Nat Assn Relief Paget's Disease
Paging (radio)
       Fedn Communication Services
       Onsite Communications Association
Pain
       Brit Pain Soc
       Brit Soc Hypnotherapists
       > + Anaesthesia
Paint
       Brit Coatings Fedn
       Oil & Colour Chemists Assn
       Paint Res Assn
       Surface Engg Assn
Paintball
       UK Paintball Sports Fedn
Painters > Art & artists
Painting & decorating
       Assn Painting Craft Teachers
       Painting & Decorating Assn
       Scot Assn Painting Craft Teachers
       Scot Decorators Fedn
Pakistan
       Brit Assn S Asian Studies
Palaeontology
       Dinosaur Soc
       Palaeontographical Soc
       Palaeontological Assn
       Systematics Assn
       Tertiary Res Gp
Palate > Cleft lip & palate
Pallets
       Timber Packaging & Pallet Confedn
       > + Materials: management/handling; Packaging
Palliative care
       Assn Palliative Medicine
       CNK Alliance
       > + Medicine & related headings
Palmistry
       Brit Astrological & Psychic Soc
Palm oil
       Tropical Growers' Assn
Palsy > Head & neck injury & disease
Pancreas
       Pancreatic Soc
Panels (wood)
       Timber Tr Fedn
Panic & anxiety attacks
       Nat Org Phobias, Anxiety...Inf & Care
       Nat Phobics Soc
Paper & paper products
       Brit Assn Paper Historians
       Brit Packaging Assn
       Confedn Paper Inds

© CBD Research Ltd · Beckenham · BR3 5JS · Tel 020 8650 7745 · Fax 020 8650 0768 · E-mail cbd@cbdresearch.com · www.cbdresearch.com

Environmental & Technical Assn Paper Sack Ind
Foodservice Packaging Assn
Indep Print Inds Assn
Inst Paper, Printing & Publishing Intl
Nat Assn Paper Mchts
Paper Agents Assn
Paper Ind Technical Assn
Pira Intl
Pulp & Paper Fundamental Res Soc
Paper: conservation
Inst Consvn
Paper: folding > Origami
Paper: making equipment
Paper Makers' Allied Trs Assn
Picon Ltd
Paper: recovered & waste
Confedn Paper Inds
Indep Waste Paper Processors Assn
Pulp & Paper Fundamental Res Soc
Paperback collecting
Penguin Collectors' Soc
WW2 HMSO Paperbacks Soc
> + Book: collecting
Paperweights
Caithness Paperweight Collectors Club
Paperweight Collectors Circle
Parachuting
Army Parachute Assn
Brit Hang Gliding & Paragliding Assn
Brit Parachute Assn
Scot Hang Gliding & Paragliding Fedn
Parakarting
Brit Fedn Sand & Land Yacht Clubs
Brit Land Speedsail Assn
Parallel trading
Parallel Traders Assn
Paramedics > First aid & immediate care
Paranormal & psychical research
Assn Scientific Study Anomalous Phenomena
Brit Astrological & Psychic Soc
Scot Soc Psychical Res
Soc Metaphysicians
Soc Psychical Res
UK Skeptics
Parapet fences
Vehicle Restraint Mfrs Assn
Paraplegia > Disablement; Spine & spinal injury;   Sports: disabled &
handicapped
Parasitology
Brit Soc Parasitology
Parent-teacher associations
Nat Confedn Parent-Teacher Assns
Parents
Assn Shared Parenting
Brit False Memory Soc
Compassionate Friends
Families Need Fathers
Galton Inst
Grandparents Assn
Mothers Apart Children
Nat Assn Child Contact Centres
Nat Fedn Services Unmarried Parents. . .[IRL]
One Parent Families / Gingerbread
Working Families
> + Adoption;   Fostering & foster parents;   Singles, divorced &
separated
Parish registers
Harleian Soc
Lancashire Parish Register Soc
Staffordshire Parish Registers Soc
Yorkshire Archaeol Soc
> + Records: historical;   Church: history & records
Park homes
Nat Assn Park Home Residents
Nat Caravan Coun
Parking
Brit Parking Assn
Parkinson's disease
Brit Geriatrics Soc
Parkinson's Disease Soc
Parks & gardens
GreenSpace
Inst Sport, Parks & Leisure
Metropolitan Public Gardens Assn
> + National Parks; Sportsgrounds & synthetic surfaces
Parliamentary agents
Soc Parliamentary Agents

Parliamentary government
Campaign English Parliament
Hansard Soc
Unlock Democracy
> + Government: accountability
Parrots
Parrot Soc
> + Birds
Parsnips
Brit Carrot Growers Assn
Parsonages
Save our Parsonages
> + Church: buildings
Partially sighted > Blind & partially sighted
Partitioning
Assn Interior Specialists
Partridges > Game & game birds
Passenger conveyors
Lift & Escalator Ind Assn
Passenger transport
ACT TravelWise
Assn Transport Co-ordinating Officers
Bus Users UK
Coach Tourism Coun
Confedn Passenger Transport
Gld Brit Coach Operators
Ocean Liner Soc
Omnibus Soc
River Assn Freight & Transport
Routemaster Operators & Owners Assn
Scot Assn Public Transport
> + specific types of transport
Pasta
Pizza, Pasta & Italian Food Assn
Pastels (art)
Brit Soc Painters (in Oil, Pastels & Acrylic)
> + Art & artists
Pastoral care
Assn Pastoral Care Mental Health
Patchwork & quilting
Quilters' Gld
Patent glazing > Glass & glazing
Patents & trade marks
Chart Inst Patent Attorneys
Inst Intl Licensing Practitioners
Inst Patentees & Inventors
Inst Tr Mark Attorneys
Intellectual Property Lawyers Assn
Licensing Executives Soc
MARQUES
Trade Marks Patents & Designs Fedn
> + Copyright
Pathology
Assn Clinical Pathologists
Brit In Vitro Diagnostics Assn
Brit Soc Toxicological Pathologists
Pathological Soc
R Coll Pathologists
Pathology (of plants)
Brit Soc Plant Pathology
> + Plants
Patients
Action Sick Children
Nat Assn Patient Participation
Nat Cancer Alliance
Patient Inf Forum
Patients Assn
> + Medicine
Patio doors > Glass & glazing; Windows
Pattern recognition
Brit Machine Vision Assn. . .
> + Article numbering
Pattern sensing
Remote Sensing & Photogrammetry Soc
Patternmaking
Gauge & Tool Makers Assn
Pattern, Model & Mould Manufacturers Association
Patton (General George S)
Patton Histl Soc
Paving & kerbs
Brit Precast Concrete Fedn
Pawnbroking
Nat Pawnbrokers Assn
Pay-to-play > Amusements & coin operated machines
Payroll staff
Inst Payroll Profls
Payroll Alliance

Peace
> Brit Pugwash Gp
> Medical Action Global Security
> Peace Pledge U

Peal ringing
> Central Coun Church Bell Ringers

Peanuts
> Anaphylaxis Campaign
> Brit Peanut Coun
> > + Nuts (edible)

Pearls
> Brit Jewellers Assn

Pearly kings & queens
> Original Pearly Kings & Queens Assn

Pears
> English Apples & Pears
> > + Fruit: growing

Peas
> Processors & Growers Res Org

Peat
> Growing Media Assn
> Ir Peatland Consvn Coun

Pedestrians' safety
> Living Streets
> > + Road: safety & control

Peel (Sir Robert)
> Peel Soc

Pelagic fish > Fish headings; Fishing

Pelargoniums > Geraniums & pelargoniums

Pen friends
> Intl Pen Friends

Penal reform
> Howard League for Penal Reform
> Offenders Tag Assn
> Unlock

Penguin books (collecting)
> Penguin Collectors' Soc

Penine Way
> Pennine Way Assn

Pens & pencils > Writing equipment & accessories

Pensions
> Assn Consulting Actuaries
> Assn Member-Directed Pension Schemes
> Assn Pension Lawyers
> Brit Pensioners & Tr U Action Assn
> Compulsory Annuity Purchase Protest Alliance
> Inst Payroll Profls
> Ir Assn Pension Funds
> Ir Inst Pensions Mgrs
> Nat Assn Pension Funds
> Nat Pensioners' Convention
> Occupational Pensioners Alliance
> Parity
> Pensions Action Gp
> Pensions Mgt Inst
> Scot Pensions Assn
> Soc Pension Consultants
> Unite: the National Federation of Royal Mail & BT Pensioners

Pentathlon
> Pentathlon GB
> Scot Modern Pentathlon Assn

Percussion (playing)
> Nat Assn Percussion Teachers
> Percussive Arts Soc

Performing animals > Animals: welfare;   Circuses & circus artistes

Performing arts medicine
> Brit Assn Performing Arts Medicine

Performing right > Copyright

Perfumery
> Brit Fragrance Assn
> Brit Soc Perfumers
> Cosmetic, Toiletry & Perfumery Assn
> Inc Gld Hairdressers

Perfusion
> Soc Clinical Perfusion Scientists

Perinatal medicine
> Brit Assn Perinatal Medicine

Periodicals
> Assn Circulation Executives
> Assn Online Publishers
> Assn Publishing Agencies
> Brit Soc Magazine Editors
> Periodical Publishers Assn Ireland
> Periodical Pubrs Assn
> Periodical Pubrs Assn - Interactive
> Press Standards Bd Finance
> UK Serials Gp

UK Specialised Inf Publishers Assn
> > + Newspapers & periodicals: distribution

Periodontology > Dentistry

Permaculture
> Permaculture Assn

Perry > Cider & perry

Persia > Iran

Personal: assistants & secretaries > Secretaries & administrators

Personal: injury
> Assn Personal Injury Lawyers
> Personal Injuries Bar Assn

Personal: rights > Individual freedom

Personal: safety > Guard & patrol services; Protective equipment (personal); Safety

Personal: trainers
> Nat Register Personal Trainers

Personnel management
> Chart Inst Personnel & Devt
> Work Foundation
> > + Management

Personnel services > Employment agents & consultants

Perthes disease
> Perthes Assn

Peru
> Anglo-Peruvian Soc
> Brit-Peruvian Cham

Pest control & pesticides
> Assn Applied Biologists
> Brit Pest Control Assn
> Nat Pest Technicians Assn
> Pesticide Action Network
> > + Agriculture: chemicals

Pet > Pets & pet trade

Pétanque
> Scot Pétanque Assn

Petrochemicals > Petroleum

Petrol pumps
> Forecourt Eqpt Fedn

Petroleum
> Assn Brit Indep Oil Exploration Cos
> Assn Petroleum & Explosives Admin
> Assn UK Oil Indeps
> BTC Testing Advisory Gp
> Energy Inds Coun
> Energy Inst
> Fedn Petroleum Suppliers
> Geological Soc
> Hydrographic Soc UK
> NI Oil Fedn
> Offshore Contrs' Assn
> Oil & Gas UK
> Petroleum Exploration Soc
> Retail Motor Ind Fedn
> UK Onshore Operators Gp
> UK Onshore Pipeline Operators' Assn
> UK Petroleum Ind Assn

Petroleum gas
> L P Gas Assn

Petrology
> Ir Assn Economic Geology
> Mineralogical Soc

Pets & pet trade
> Assn Pet Behaviour Counsellors
> Brit Hardware Fedn
> Nat Assn Regd Petsitters
> Pet Care Trust
> Pet Food Mfrs Assn
> Pet Fostering Service Scotland
> Pet Health Coun
> Soc Companion Animal Studies
> > + Animal headings; individual animal

Pets: burial & cremation
> Assn Private Pet Cemeteries & Crematoria
> Cremation Soc

Pewter
> Assn Brit Pewter Craftsmen
> Pewter Soc

Pharmaceuticals
> Academy Pharmaceutical Sciences
> Assn Brit Pharmaceutical Ind
> Assn Clinical Data Mgt
> BioIndustry Assn
> Brit Assn Eur Pharmaceutical Distbrs
> Brit Assn Pharmaceutical Physicians
> Brit Assn Pharmaceutical Whlsrs
> Brit Generic Mfrs' Assn
> Clinical Contract Res Assn

© CBD Research Ltd · Beckenham · BR3 5JS · Tel 020 8650 7745 · Fax 020 8650 0768 · E-mail cbd@cbdresearch.com · www.cbdresearch.com

Fac Pharmaceutical Med
Inst Clinical Res
Ir Pharmaceutical Healthcare Assn
Ir Pharmaceutical U
Pharmaceutical & Healthcare Sciences Soc
Pharmaceutical Inf & Pharmacovigilance Assn
Pharmaceutical Soc Ireland
Pharmaceutical Soc NI
PharmaChemical Ireland
Proprietary Assn
Soc Chemical Ind
Soc Medicines Res
Soc Pharmaceutical Medicine
Statisticians Pharmaceutical Ind
> + Pharmacy
Pharmacology & chemotherapy
Brit Assn Psychopharmacology
Brit Pharmacological Soc
Brit Soc Antimicrobial Chemotherapy
Scot Neuroscience Gp
Soc Medicines Res
Pharmacy
Assn Pharmacy Technicians
Chemists' Defence Assn
Community Pharmacy Scotland
Company Chemists' Assn
Nat Assn Women Pharmacists
Nat Pharmacy Assn
R Pharmaceutical Soc
UK Clinical Pharmacy Assn
Ulster Chemists Assn
Pharmacy: history
Brit Soc Hist Pharmacy
Pharology > Lighthouses & lightships
Pheasants
World Pheasant Assn UK
> + Game & gamebirds
Phenolic composites
Composites UK
Phenomena > Paranormal & psychical research;   specific type of phenomena
Phenylketonuria
Nat Soc Phenylketonuria
Philanthropy: history
Voluntary Action Hist Soc
Philately & postal history
Assn Brit Philatelic Socs
Assn Scot Philatelic Socs
Brit Air Mail Soc
Brit Postmark Soc
Letter Box Study Gp
Nat Philatelic Soc
Philatelic Traders Soc
Postal Hist Soc
R Philatelic Soc Lond
Ship Stamp Soc
Soc Olympic Collectors
Phillumeny > Matchbox labels
Philology
Philological Soc
> + Dialects; Languages
Philosophy
Aristotelian Soc
Assn Brit Theological. . . Libraries
Assn Therapeutic Philosophy
Brit Soc Hist Philosophy
Brit Soc Philosophy Science
Philosophical Soc England
R Inst Philosophy
R Philosophical Soc Glasgow
Soc Applied Philosophy
Soc Existential Analysis
Phobias
Brit Soc Hypnotherapists
Nat Org Phobias, Anxiety. . .Inf & Care
Nat Phobics Soc
Phonetics
Brit Assn Academic Phoneticians
Brit Voice Assn
> + Speech
Phonography > Shorthand writing;   Sound recording & reproduction
Photogrammetry
Instn Civil Engg Surveyors
Remote Sensing & Photogrammetry Soc
Photographic agencies
Brit Assn Picture Libraries & Agencies
Nat Assn Press Agencies

Photographic industry & trade
Photo Imaging Coun
Profl Photographic Laboratories Assn
Photographic waste
Photo Imaging Coun
Photography
Assn Photographers
Brit Cave Res Assn
Brit Inst Profl Photography
Brit Soc Underwater Photographers
Camera Club
Gld Photographers
Inst Consvn
Inst Med Illustrators
Ir Profl Photographers Assn
Master Photographers Assn
Nat Assn Aerial Photographic Libraries
Outdoor Writers' & Photographers' Gld
Photographic Alliance
Photographic Collectors' Club
R Photographic Soc
Scot Sub Aqua Club
Soc Wedding & Portrait Photographers
Stereoscopic Soc
Writers & Photographers unLimited
> + Film
Photoluminescent products
Photoluminescent Safety Products Assn
Photonics
Photonics Cluster
Scot Optoelectronics Assn
UK Consortium Photonics & Optics
Phycology
Brit Phycological Soc
Physical disability > Disablement
Physical education
Assn Physical Educ
Brit Assn Physical Training
Scot Local Authority Network Physical Educ
Sports & Fitness Eqpt Assn
Physical fitness > Fitness
Physical fitness: Equipment
Physically handicapped > Children: handicapped; Disablement
Physicians > Medical practice; Medicine
Physics
Inst Physics
Inst Physics & Engg in Medicine
Physiology
Physiological Soc
Soc Orthopaedic Medicine
Physiotherapy
Chart Soc Physiotherapy
Ir Soc Chart Physiotherapists
Physio First
SMAE Fellowship
Pianolas & pianola rolls
Friends Pianola Inst
Player Piano Gp
Pianos & piano playing
Assn Blind Piano Tuners
Jazz Piano Teachers Assn
Pianoforte Tuners' Assn
Pick-your-own > Farm shops & food
Pickles & sauces
Food Processors Assn
Pick's disease
Pick's Disease Support Gp
Picts
Pictish Arts Soc
Picture dealers > Art: trade
Picture framers
Fine Art Tr Gld
Picture libraries
Brit Assn Picture Libraries & Agencies
Nat Assn Aerial Photographic Libraries
Picture researching
Picture Res Assn
Picture restoring
Brit Assn Paintings Conservator-Restorers
Fine Art Tr Gld
> + Art: conservation
Piercing > Body piercing
Piers
Brit Assn Leisure Parks, Piers & Attractions
Nat Piers Soc
Pigeons
Confedn Long Distance Racing Pigeon Us

Ir Homing U
Nat Pigeon Assn
R Pigeon Racing Assn
Scot Homing U
Pigging (pipeline)
Pigging Products & Services Assn
Pigment
Brit Colour Makers Assn
Pigs
Brit Kune Kune Pig Soc
Brit Lop Pig Soc
Brit Pig Assn
Brit Saddleback Breeders Club
Brit Veterinary Assn
Gloucestershire Old Spot Pig Breeders' Club
Livestock Auctioneers Assn
Middle White Pig Breeders CLub
Nat Pig Assn
Oxford Sandy & Black Pig Soc
Tamworth Breeders Group
> + Bacon; Cattle & livestock; Pigging (pipelines)
Pilates
Body Control Pilates Assn
Pilates Inst
Pilchard
Herring Buyers Assn
> + Fish; Fishing
Pilgrims
Confraternity Saint James
Piling
Fedn Piling Specialists

Pillow-lace > Lace (handmade)
Pilots > Aviation: pilots, officers & crew;   Sea pilots
Pinball
Pinball Owners Assn
> + Amusements & coin operated machines
Pinks (flowers) > Dianthus
Pinnipeds
Seal Consvn Soc
Pipe bands & music
Bagpipe Soc
College Piping
Edinburgh Highland Reel & Strathspey Soc
Inst Piping
Northumbrian Pipers' Society
Piobaireachd Soc
Pipers' Gld
R Scot Pipe Band Assn
Scot Pipers Assn
Scot Piping Soc Lond
Traditional Music & Song Assn Scotland
Pipe organs > Organs, organists & organ music
Pipejacking
Pipe Jacking Assn
Pipelines
Land Drainage Contrs Assn
Pigging Products & Services Assn
Pipeline Inds Gld
Soc Brit Water & Wastewater Inds
UK Onshore Pipeline Operators' Assn
Pipes
Brit Ceramic Confedn
Brit Precast Concrete Fedn
Clay Pipe Devt Assn
Soc Brit Water & Wastewater Inds
> + Plastics: pipes;   Steel: tubes
Piracy (copyrighted goods) > Copyright
Pistachios
Combined Edible Nut Tr Assn
Pistol shooting
Nat Rifle Assn
> + Shooting
Pizzas
Pizza, Pasta & Italian Food Assn
Place-names
English Place-Name Soc
Scot Place-Name Soc
Ulster Place-Name Soc
> + Names
Placement services (adult)
Nat Assn Adult Placement Services
> + Social: service
Plainsong
Plainsong & Mediæval Music Soc

Planetary sciences
R Astronomical Soc
> + Astronomy
Planning > Town & country planning
Plant: construction > Construction equipment
Plant: industrial
Brit Ceramic Confedn
Brit Metallurgical Plant Constructors Assn
Engg Construction Ind Assn
Instn Diagnostic Engrs
Safety Assessment Fedn
Soc Operations Engrs
Plants
Assn Applied Biologists
Assn Indep Crop Consultants
Brit Assn Rose Breeders
Brit Mycological Soc
Brit Protected Ornamentals Assn
Brit Soc Plant Breeders
Brit Soc Plant Pathology
Epiphytic Plant Study Gp
Hardy Plant Soc
Linnean Soc Lond
Nat Coun Consvn Plants & Gardens
Plantlife Intl
Profl Plant Users Gp
Scot Soc Crop Res
> + Flowers, flower arrangement & floristry; specific plants
Plants: galls
Brit Plant Gall Soc
Plaques
Brit Sign & Graphics Assn
> + Signs
Plaster & plastering
Fedn Plastering & Drywall Contrs
Gypsum Products Devt Assn
Plastic surgery
Brit Assn Aesthetic Plastic Surgeons
Brit Assn Plastic, Reconstructive & Aesthetic Surgeons
> + Surgery
Plastics
Brit Laminate Fabricators Assn
Brit Plastics Fedn
Composites UK
NI Polymers Assn
Plastics & Board Inds Fedn
Plastics Histl Soc
Plastics Ireland
Rapra Technology Ltd
Plastics: bags
Carrier Bag Consortium
Plastics: cladding > Cladding
Plastics: drums > Cisterns, drums & tanks
Plastics: film
Packaging & Indl Films Assn
Picon Ltd
Plastics: foam
Brit Rigid Urethane Foam Mfrs Assn
Brit Urethane Foam Contrs Assn
Plastics: machinery
Polymer Machinery Mfrs & Distbrs Assn
Plastics: pipes
Brit Plastics Fedn
Soc Brit Water & Wastewater Inds
Plastics: recycling
RECOUP
> + Reclamation & recycling
Platforms > Cradles & suspended platforms
Play centres
Play Providers Assn
Play equipment
Assn Play Inds
Sporting Goods Ind Assn
> + Sports headings
Play therapy
Brit Assn Play Therapists
Playbuses
Nat Playbus Assn
Playgrounds & playgroups
Fair Play for Children Assn
IPPA Early Childhood Org [IRL]
Nat Assn Hospital Play Staff
Nat Playing Fields Assn
Scot Pre-School Play Assn
Wales Pre-school Playgroups Assn
Playing cards & games
English Playing-Card Soc

© CBD Research Ltd · Beckenham · BR3 5JS · Tel 020 8650 7745 · Fax 020 8650 0768 · E-mail cbd@cbdresearch.com · www.cbdresearch.com

Playing fields > Sportsgrounds & synthetic surfaces
Playrights & plays > Dramatists; Theatre; Writing & writers
Pleasurecraft
  Assn Pleasure Craft Operators
  > + Boats & boating; Yachts & yachting
Ploughing
  Soc Ploughmen
  Southern Counties Heavy Horse Assn
Plumbers' merchants > Builders' & plumbers' merchants
Plumbing
  Assn Plumbing & Heating Contrs
  Inst Plumbing & Heating Engg
  NI Master Plumbers Assn
  Scot & NI Plumbing Emplrs' Fedn
Pneumatics
  Brit Compressed Air Soc
  Brit Fluid Power Assn
  Brit Fluid Power Distbrs Assn
  Solids Handling & Processing Assn
  > + Hydraulics & hydromechanics
Podiatry > Chiropody & podiatry
Poetry
  English Poetry & Song Soc
  Friends Dymock Poets
  Poetry Soc
  Scot Poetry Library
  War Poets Assn
  > + individual by name
Poisons > Toxicology
Poland
  Anglo-Polish Soc
  Brit-Polish Cham Comm [Lond]
  Brit-Polish Cham Comm [Warsaw]
  Polish Soc
Polar research
  Trans-Antarctic Assn
Polarity therapy
  UK Polarity Therapy Assn
Polarography & polarology
  Brit Polarological Res Soc
  R Soc Chemistry
Police
  Assn Chief Police Officers [E&W&NI]
  Assn Chief Police Officers Scotland
  Assn Police Authorities
  Assn Police & Public Security Suppliers
  Assn Scot Police Superintendents
  Nat Assn Retired Police Officers
  Police Fedn England & Wales
  Police Fedn NI
  Police Superintendents' Assn England & Wales
  Scot Police Fedn
  Superintendents' Assn NI
  > + Security
Police: history
  Peel Soc
  Police Hist Soc
  Police Insignia Collectors Assn
Policy research
  David Hume Inst
Polidori (John William)
Poliomyelitis
  Brit Polio Fellowship
Polishes
  Brit Assn Chemical Specialities
Politeness
  Campaign Courtesy
Political correctness
  Campaign Political Correctness
Political consultants
  Assn Profl Political Consultants
Political economy > Economics
Political parties > [Party] politics
Political studies & reform
  Political Studies Assn
  Politics Assn
  Unlock Democracy
Pollen
  Brit Aerobiology Fedn
  > + Allergy
Pollution & pollution control
  ACT TravelWise
  Anglers Consvn Assn
  Environmental Inds Commission
  Marine Biological Assn
  Marine Consvn Soc
  Source Testing Assn

  Surfers against Sewage
  UK Spill Assn
  > + Air: pollution
Polo
  Hurlingham Polo Assn
Polocrosse
  UK Polocrosse Assn
Polyester fibre
  Nat Fillings Assn
Polyethylene foam > Plastics: foam
Polymers
  Inst Materials, Minerals & Mining
  NI Polymers Assn
  Plastics Histl Soc
  Polymer Machinery Mfrs & Distbrs Assn
  Rapra Technology Ltd
Polyolefin & polypropylene textiles
  Brit Polyolefin Textiles Assn
  > + Textile: industry & trade
Polytechnics > Adult education; Technical education; Universities
Ponies > Horse headings
Pony trekking
  Trekking & Riding Soc Scotland
  Welsh Trekking & Riding Assn
Pool
  Brit Assn Pool Table Operators
  Brit Profl Pool Players Assn
  English Pool Assn
  > + Cue sports
Pools > Football pools; Swimming pools
Pop & rock music
  Pop & Rock Fans' Assn
Population: registration
  Assn Registrars Scotland
Population: study of
  Brit Soc Population Studies
  Optimum Population Trust
Porcelain > Ceramics; Pottery
Pork butchery > Meat
Pork pies
  Melton Mowbray Pork Pie Assn
Porphyria
  Brit Porphyria Assn
Portable buildings > Modular & portable buildings
Portable engines
  Road Locomotive Soc
Portable lamps (industrial)
  Miners' & Indl Lamp Mfrs' Assn
Portage
  Nat Portage Assn
Portland Cement
  Brit Cement Assn
  > + Cement & cement products
Portraits > Art & artists; Weddings: photography
Ports
  Brit Ports Assn
  Naval Dockyards Soc
  Ports & Terminals Gp
  Soc Sailing Barge Res
Ports: health
  Assn Port Health Authorities
Portugal
  Anglo-Portuguese Soc
  Assn Contemporary Iberian Studies
  Brit-Portuguese Cham Comm
  Hispanic & Luso Brazilian Coun
  Portuguese Cham
Portugal: language & literature
  Assn Language Learning
Post Office staff
  Communication Workers U
  > + Sub-postmasters
Post Office (GPO & BT) vehicles
  Post Office Vehicle Club
Postal history > Philately & postal history
Postal services
  Mail Consolidators Assn
  Mail Users' Assn
Postcards
  Canal Card Collectors Circle
  Great Britain Postcard Club
  Postcard Traders' Assn
Poster advertising > Advertising: outdoor
Postgraduate medical education
  Nat Assn Clinical Tutors
Postmarks > Philately & postal history

Post-natal depression
        Assn Postnatal Illness
        Meet-a-Mum Assn
Post-tensioning
        Concrete Bridge Devt Gp
        Post Tensioning Assn
Post-viral infection
        Action ME
        Assn Young People with ME
        Myalgic Encephalopathy Assn
Pot holing > Caves & caving
Pot plants > Horticulture; Indoor & houseplants; individual plants
Potatoes
        Brit Potato Tr Assn
        Fresh Produce Consortium
        NI Potato Breeders Assn
        NI Potato Marketing Assn
        Pre Basic Growers Association
        Scot Soc Crop Res
        > + Vegetables: trade
Potatoes: products
        Frozen & Chilled Potato Processors' Assn
        Potato Processors Assn
        Snack, Nut & Crisp Mfrs Assn
Potter (Beatrix)
        Beatrix Potter Soc
Pottery
        Brit Ceramic Gift & Tableware Mfrs' Assn
        CERAM Res
        Scot Potters' Assn
        > + Ceramics
Pottery & ceramics collecting
        Clarice Cliff Collectors Club
        Friends Blue
        Old Bottle Club
        Spode Soc
        > + specific type collected
Pottery: sanitary > Sanitaryware
Potting composts > Composts & composting
Poultry
        Assn Meat Inspectors
        Brit Poultry Coun
        Brit Veterinary Assn
        Domestic Fowl Trust
        Henkeepers' Assn
        NI Poultry Fedn
        Poultry Club
        Pullet Hatcheries Assn
        Pullet Rearers Assn
        Rare Poultry Soc
        Traditional Farmfresh Turkey Assn
        > + Game & game birds; Meat
The Pound
        Democracy Movement
Powder coatings
        Brit Coatings Fedn
        Surface Engg Assn
Powder compacts (collecting)
        Brit Compact Collectors' Soc
Powder handling
        Solids Handling & Processing Assn
Powder metallurgy
        Inst Materials, Minerals & Mining
Power > specific type of power
Power boating & powercraft
        R Yachting Assn
Power generation > Electricity
Power presses
        Metalforming Machinery Makers' Assn
Power tools > Tools
Power track systems
        BEAMA
Powered access
        Assn Loading & Elevating Eqpt Mfrs
        Construction Plant-hire Assn
        Specialist Access Engg & Maintenance Assn
Powerlifting
        Brit Drug Free Powerlifting Assn
Powys (John Cooper) & family
        Powys Soc
Prader-Willi syndrome
        Prader-Willi Syndrome Assn
Prams & pushchairs > Nursery & baby products
Prayer book(s) > Common Prayer; Liturgy
Precast concrete > Concrete & concrete products
Precious metals & stones > Gemstones; Goldsmiths & silversmiths; Jewellery
Precision casting > Metal: casting

Pre-conceptual care > Family planning; Maternity
Pre-eclampsia
        Action Pre-Eclampsia
        Pre Eclampsia Soc
Prefabricated buildings > Modular & portable buildings
Pregnancy > Family planning; Maternity; Obstetrics & gynaecology
Prehistory
        Megalithic Soc
        Prehistoric Soc
        R Anthropological Inst
Premature ageing > Geriatrics & ageing
Premenstrual syndrome
        Nat Assn Premenstrual Syndrome
        Premenstrual Soc
Premium promotions > Incentive marketing
Preparatory schools
        Inc Assn Preparatory Schools
        SATIPS
        > + Independent & public schools
Pre-Raphaelites
        Pre-Raphaelite Soc
Presbyterian church: history
        Presbyterian Hist Soc Ireland
        Scot Covenanter Memorials Assn
        Utd Reformed Church Hist Soc
Pre-school playgroups > Playgrounds & playgroups
Preservation > Conservation; object preserved
Preserves
        Food Processors Assn
Press > Information: freedom of; Journalism; Media; Newspapers; Periodicals
Press agencies
        Nat Assn Press Agencies
Pressure gauges > Gauges
Pressure sores
        Tissue Viability Soc
Pressure washers
        Indl Cleaning Machine Mfrs Assn
Priestley (John Boynton)
        J B Priestley Soc
Primary care > Health care
Primary education > Education
Primulas
        Nat Auricula & Primula Soc (Mid & West)
        Nat Auricula & Primula Soc (Nthn)
        Nat Auricula & Primula Soc (Sthn)
Print finishing > Books: binding & print finishing
Printed circuits & wiring boards
        Inst Metal Finishing
Printing
        Assn Hot Foil Printers
        Brit Printing Inds Fedn
        Brit Printing Soc
        D&AD
        Friends St Bride Library
        Indep Print Inds Assn
        Inst Paper, Printing & Publishing Intl
        Ir Master Printers Assn
        Ir Printing Fedn
        New Baxter Soc
        Pira Intl
        Printing Histl Soc
        Printmakers Coun
        R Birmingham Soc Artists
        Scot Print Emplrs Fedn
Printing machinery & supplies
        Brit Coatings Fedn
        Brit Used Printing Machinery Supplrs Assn
        Oil & Colour Chemists Assn
        Picon Ltd
Prints
        R Scot Academy
        R Soc Painter-Printmakers
        Soc Graphic Fine Art
Prison service
        POA
        Prison Governors Assn
Prisoners: of war
        Assn Brit Civilian Internees Far East
Prisoners: welfare & rehabilitation
        Assn Members Indep Monitoring Bds
        Assn Visitors Immigration Detainees
        Howard League for Penal Reform
        NACRO
        Nat Approved Premises Assn
        Nat Assn Official Prison Visitors
        NI Assn Care & Resettlement Offenders
        Prisoners Abroad

© CBD Research Ltd · Beckenham · BR3 5JS · Tel 020 8650 7745 · Fax 020 8650 0768 · E-mail cbd@cbdresearch.com · www.cbdresearch.com

SACRO
SOVA
Unlock
> + Penal reform
Prisoners: wives & families
Action Prisoners' Families
Prison Advice & Care Trust
Private business > Business
Private hire
Nat Private Hire Assn
> + Motor vehicles: hire; Taxis & minicabs
Private medicine > Hospitals: contributory schemes
Private schools > Independent & public schools
Private secretaries > Secretaries & administrators
Probation service
Nat Approved Premises Assn
Nat Assn Probation Officers
Probation Assn
Probation Mgrs Assn
SOVA
Process control > Control engineering
Process engineering
Energy Inds Coun
Instn Chemical Engrs
Processing & Packaging Machinery Assn
Solids Handling & Processing Assn
Process servers
Assn Brit Investigators
Nat Assn Investigators & Process Servers
Proctology
Assn Coloproctology
Procurators-Fiscal
Procurators Fiscal Soc
R Fac Procurators in Glasgow
> + Law: Scotland
Produce packaging & processing
Fresh Produce Consortium
Product licensing
Inst Intl Licensing Practitioners
Licensing Executives Soc
Production control
Inst Operations Mgt
Production engineering
Engg & Machinery Alliance
PERA
> + Automation
Products: counterfeiting
Anti Counterfeiting Gp
Programme producers > Film: production & distribution; Television: production
Project management
Assn Project Mgt
Major Projects Assn
Promotion merchandise > Incentive marketing
Proofreading
Assn Freelance Editors, Proofreaders & Indexers [IRL]
Soc Editors & Proofreaders
Property & land owners
Brit Property Fedn
City Property Assn
Country Land & Business Assn [E&W]
Nat Assn Estate Agents
Nat Landlords' Assn
Residential Landlords Assn
Scot Assn Landlords
Scot Rural Property & Business Assn
Westminster Property Owners Assn
> + Estate management
Property: investment
Investment Property Forum
Property: maintenance/management
Assn Residential Letting Agents
Assn Residential Managing Agents
Inst Residential Property Mgt
UK Assn Letting Agents
> + Buildings: cleaning & maintenance
Property: market research
Soc Property Researchers
Property: marking (security)
Brit Security Ind Assn
Property: theft
Alliance Intellectual Property Theft
Property: unit trusts
Assn Real Estate Funds
Proportional representation > Elections & electoral administration
Proposal management
UK Assn Proposal Mgt Profls

Proprietary medicines
Proprietary Assn
> + Pharmaceuticals
Prostate disease
Prostate Cancer Support Assn
Prosthetics & orthoses
Brit Assn Prosthetists & Orthotists
Brit Orthopaedic Assn
Brit Soc Study Prosthetic Dentistry
Inst Maxillofacial Prosthetists...
Let's Face It
REACH - Assn Children with Hand or Arm Deficiency
Prostitution
Josephine Butler Soc
Protective clothing/equipment
Brit Clothing Ind Assn
Brit Footwear Assn
Brit Safety Ind Fedn
Defence Mfrs Assn
Photoluminescent Safety Products Assn
Retroreflective Eqpt Mfrs Assn
Protectorate (1649-1688) > Commonwealth (1649-1688);   Fights (historic/re-enactment)
Protein (vegetable) > Vegetables: protein
Proteomics
Brit Soc Proteome Res
Protestants
Protestant Alliance
Protestant Reformation Soc
Protestant Truth Soc
Scot Reformation Soc
Prototype design & manufacture
Rapid Prototyping & Mfrg Assn
Provision trade > Grocery & provision trade
Psoriasis
Psoriasis Assn
Psoriasis & Psoriatic Arthritis Alliance
Psychiatry
Assn Therapeutic Communities
Brit Neuropsychiatry Assn
College Psychiatry Ireland
Mental Health Nurses Assn
R Coll Psychiatrists
Soc Clinical Psychiatrists
Psychical research > Paranormal & psychical research
Psychoanalysis
Assn Jungian Analysts
Balint Soc
Brit Psychoanalytical Soc
Inst Psychoanalysis
NI Assn Study Psychoanalysis
Soc Existential Analysis
> + Group analysis
Psychology
Adlerian Soc
Assn Business Psychologists
Assn Educl Psychologists
Assn Humanistic Psychology
Assn Profls Services Adolescents
Assn Teaching Psychology
Brit Assn Psychological Type
Brit Inst Graphologists
Brit Neuropsychological Soc
Brit Psychological Soc
Brit Soc Psychosomatic Obstetrics...
Experimental Psychology Soc
Gld Pastoral Psychology
Indep Gp Analytical Psychologists
Nat Assn Therapeutic Educ
Psychological Soc Ireland
Soc Existential Analysis
Soc Reproductive & Infant Psychology
Psychopharmacology
Brit Assn Psychopharmacology
Psychotherapy
Assn Child Psychotherapists
Assn Cognitive Analytic Therapy
Assn Gp & Individual Psychotherapy
Assn Psychoanalytic Psychotherapy NHS
Assn Psychological Therapies
Assn Therapeutic Philosophy
Brit Assn Behavioural... Psychotherapies
Brit Assn Counselling & Psychotherapy
Brit Assn Psychotherapists
Brit Autogenic Soc
Brit Gestalt Soc
Brit Hypnotherapy Assn

Brit Psychoanalytic Coun
Brit Psychodrama Assn
Brit Psychological Soc
Gld Psychotherapists
Group Analytic Soc
Inst Gp Analysis
Inst Transactional Analysis
Nat Assn Counsellors, Hypnotherapists. . .
Nat Coun Psychotherapists
Nat Register Hypnotherapists & Psychotherapists
R Coll Psychiatrists
Scot Assn Psychoanalytical Psychotherapists
UK Coun Psychotherapy
Universities Psychotherapy & Counselling Assn
Pteridology > Ferns
Public access > Footpaths & rights of way; Open spaces
Public administration
Inst Public Administration [IRL]
> + Civil Service; Local government
Public analysts
Assn Public Analysts
Assn Public Analysts Scotland
Public auditing > Accountancy
Public conveniences
Brit Toilet Assn
Public gardens > Parks & gardens
Public health
Assn Directors Public Health
Assn Port Health Authorities
Chart Inst Envtl Health
Chart Instn Water & Envtl Management
Community & District Nursing Assn
Fac Public Health
HealthWatch
Ir Soc Public Health Medicine
R Soc Public Health
Scot Soc Contamination Control
> + Health
Public houses
Brit Beer & Pub Assn
Campaign Real Ale
Scot Beer & Pub Assn
Public lighting > Lighting
Public relations
Assn Local Govt Communications
Chart Inst Marketing
Chart Inst Public Relations
Public Relations Consultants Assn
Public Relations Consultants Assn [IRL]
Public Relations Inst Ireland
Science, Technology, Engg. . . Public Relations Assn
Public safety
Brit Assn Public Safety Communications Officers
Public schools > Independent & public schools
Public sector officials > Local government headings
Public speaking > Speakers
Public transport > Passenger transport
Public utilities > individual utility
Publicity > Advertising
Publishing
Assn Learned & Profl Soc Pubrs
Assn Publishing Agencies
Brit Business Awards Assn
Chart & Nautical Instrument Tr Assn
CLÉ
Data Pubrs Assn
Digital Content Forum
Folio Soc
Indep Pubrs Gld
Inst Paper, Printing & Publishing Intl
Ir Educl Pubrs Assn
Periodical Pubrs Assn
Personal Mgrs Assn
Pira Intl
Publishers Assn
Publishers Licensing Soc
Publishing Scotland
Soc Leisure Consultants & Pubrs
Soc Publishers Ireland
Trade & Profl Pubrs Assn [IRL]
> + Books; & other aspects of publishing
Pubs > Public houses
Pugin (Augustus Welby)
Pugin Soc
Pullets > Poultry
Pulmonaria
Hardy Plant Soc

Pulmonary hypertension
Pulmonary Hypertension Assn
> + Thoracic diseases
Pulp > Paper headings; Wood pulp
Pulses: edible
Brit Edible Pulse Assn
Grain & Feed Tr Assn
Pumps & pumping
Assn Electrical & Mechanical Trs
Brit Pump Mfrs Assn
Fire Fighting Vehicles Mfrs Assn
Pump Distbrs Assn
Punch & Judy
Punch & Judy Coll Professors
Punctuation
Apostrophe Protection Soc
Punjab studies
Assn Punjab Studies (UK)
Puppetry
Brit Puppet & Model Theatre Gld
Purchasing & supply
Chart Inst Purchasing & Supply
Ir Inst Purchasing & Materials Mgt
Soc Procurement Officers Local Govt
Purine metabolic disorders
Purine Metabolic Patients Assn
Push chairs > Nursery & baby products
PVC
Brit Plastics Fedn
Plastics & Board Inds Fedn
> + Plastics headings
Pyrotechnics > Fireworks

Q

Quad bike racing
Quad Racing Assn
Quadrathlon
Brit Quadrathlon Assn
Quadricycling
Assn Pioneer Motor Cyclists
> + Cycles & motorcycles
Quail > Game & game birds
Quakers > Friends (Quakers)
Quality assurance & control
Assn Brit Certification Bodies
Assn External Verifiers
Brit Approvals Fire Eqpt
Brit Assn Res Quality Assurance
Brit Civil Engg Test Eqpt Mfrs Assn
Brit Quality Foundation
BSI
Chart Quality Inst
Excellence Ireland Quality Assn
Market Res Quality Standards Assn
Mechanical & Metal Trs Confedn
> + Materials: technology & testing
Quantity surveying
Instn Civil Engg Surveyors
Soc Construction & Quantity Surveyors
Quarries & quarrying
Brit Aggregates Assn
Inst Explosives Engrs
Inst Quarrying
Ir Mining & Quarrying Soc
Minerals Engg Soc
Quarry Products Assn
Subterranea Britannica
> + specific stone quarried
Quarry tiles > Tiles (floor & wall)
Quickprinters & copyshops
Brit Assn Print & Communication
Quilling
Quilling Gld
Quills (pens) > Writing equipment & accessories
Quilting
Assn Soft Furnishers
Quilt Assn
Quilters' Gld
Quoits (game)
Nat Quoits Assn

© CBD Research Ltd · Beckenham · BR3 5JS · Tel 020 8650 7745 · Fax 020 8650 0768 · E-mail cbd@cbdresearch.com · www.cbdresearch.com

R

Rabbits
    Brit Rabbit Coun
    Rabbit Welfare Assn
Race relations
    Assn Jewish Ex-Servicemen & Women
    Discrimination Law Assn
    Inst Race Relations
Racecourses
    Assn Ir Racecourses
    Racecourse Assn
Rachmaninov (Sergei)
    Rachmaninoff Soc
Racing > Horse racing; Motor sport
Rackets (equipment)
    Sporting Goods Ind Assn
Rackets (squash)
    English Racketball
    Great Britain Racquetball Fedn
    Scot Squash
    Squash Rackets Assn
    Squash Wales
    > + Tennis
Racking
    Storage Eqpt Mfrs Assn
    > + Storage equipment
Radiation > Radiology/radiation
Radiators
    Boiler & Radiator Mfrs Assn
Radiesthesia > Radionics & radiesthesia
Radio
    Assn Service Providers
    Comml Radio Companies Assn
    Community Media Assn
    Intellect
    Radio Academy
    TV & Radio Inds Club
    > + Aerials: radio & television;   Telecommunications
Radio: amateur
    Ir Radio Transmitters Soc
    Radio Soc GB
Radio: for blind & bedridden
    Wireless Bedridden Soc
Radio: control
    Brit Radio Car Assn
    > + Models: hobby
Radio: community
    Community Media Assn
Radio: engineering & industry > Electronic: industry & engineering
Radio: mobile
    Fedn Communication Services
    Mobile Electronics & Security Fedn
    > + Radio: amateur
Radio: officers
    Nautilus UK
Radio: paging > Paging (radio)
Radio & TV: actors & actresses > Actors & actresses; Theatre
Radio & TV: censorship
    mediawatch-uk
    Voice Listener & Viewer
Radio & TV: medical broadcasts
    Assn Broadcasting Doctors
Radio & TV: history
    Brit Vintage Wireless Soc
    Narrow Bandwidth TV Assn
Radio & TV: rental
    Radio, Electrical & TV Retailers' Assn
Radio & TV: script writing
    Soc Authors
    Soc Authors Scotland
    Writers' Gld
Radio & TV: trade
    Brit Audio Dealers Assn
    Confedn Aerial Inds
    Consumer Electronics Distbrs Assn [IRL]
    Radio, Electrical & TV Retailers' Assn
Radiography > Radiology/radiation
Radiology/radiation
    Assn Radiation Res
    Assn University Radiation Protection Officers
    Brit Inst Radiology
    Brit Occupational Hygiene Soc
    Brit Soc Dental & Maxillofacial Radiology
    Brit Soc Neuroradiologists

    R Coll Radiologists
    Soc Radiographers
    Soc Radiological Protection
Radionics & radiesthesia
    Radionic Association Ltd
    Soc Metaphysicians
Radiotherapy > Radiology/radiation
Rafters
    Trussed Rafter Assn
    > + Roofing
Rafting
    Brit Canoe U
    Scot Rafting Assn
    > + Canoes & Canoeing
Railways: development > Railways: promotion & development
Railways: engineering
    Britpave
    Rail Ind Contrs Assn
Railways: equipment & rolling stock
    Assn Private Rly Wagon Owners
    Private Wagon Fedn
    Rly Ind Assn
    Wagon Bldg & Repairing Assn
Railways: history & preservation
    Branch Line Soc
    Campaign Better Transport
    Colonel Stephens Soc
    German Rly Soc
    Gld Rly Artists
    Heritage Rly Assn
    Histl Model Rly Soc
    Indl Locomotive Soc
    Indl Rly Soc
    Locomotive Club
    Merchant Navy Locomotive Presvn Soc
    Narrow Gauge Rly Soc
    Nat Assn Rly Clubs
    Railway Ramblers
    Rly & Canal Histl Soc
    Rly Correspondence & Travel Soc
    Rly Enthusiasts Soc
    Rly Presvn Soc Ireland
    Scot Rly Presvn Soc
    Swiss Rlys Soc
    Transport Trust
    Vintage Carriages Trust
    World War Two Rly Study Gp
    > + Models: hobby
Railways: history & preservation - local
    Bluebell Rly Presvn Soc
    Caledonian Rly Assn
    Cambrian Railways Soc
    Ffestiniog Railway Society Ltd
    Great N Scotland Rly Assn
    Great Nthn Rly Soc
    Great Wstn Soc
    Highland Rly Soc
    Keighley & Worth Valley Rly Presvn Soc
    Kent & E Sussex Rly Co
    Lancashire & Yorkshire Rly Presvn Soc
    Lancashire & Yorkshire Rly Soc
    Locomotive 6201 Princess Elizabeth Soc
    London Underground Rly Soc
    N York Moors Hist Rly Trust
    S Wstn Circle
    Sittingbourne & Kemsley Light Rly
    Stephenson Locomotive Soc
    Strathspey Rly Assn
    Sussex Indl Archaeol Soc
    Talyllyn Rly Presvn Soc
    Welsh Highland Rlys Assn
    Welshpool & Llanfair Light Rly Presvn Co
Railways: light
    Colonel Stephens Soc
    Heritage Rly Assn
    Light Rail Transit Assn
    Tramway & Light Rly Soc
    > + Tramways & trams
Railways: model
    Assn Model Rly Socs Scotland
    Model Electronic Rly Gp
    N Wstn Model Rly Clubs Assn
    Train Collectors Soc
Railways: operating
    Assn Rly Training Providers
    Assn Train Operating Companies
    Instn Rly Operators

Rly Forum
Rly Study Assn
Railways: promotion & development
    Assn Community Rail Partnerships
    Electric Rly Soc
    Locomotive & Carriage Instn
    Permanent Way Instn
    Rail Freight Gp
    Rly Devt Soc
    Transport-Watch
Railways: signalling
    Instn Rly Signal Engrs
Railways: workers
    Assd Train Crew U
    Rail, Maritime & Transport U
    Transport Salaried Staffs Assn
Rainwater
    UK Rainwater Harvesting Assn
    > + Water: treatment & supply
Rambling
    Long Distance Walkers Assn
    Mountaineering Coun Ireland
    Ramblers' Assn
    Ulster Fedn Rambling Clubs
Rangers & wardens
    Assn Countryside Voluntary Wardens
    Countryside Mgt Assn
    Scot Countryside Rangers' Assn
Ranges (cooking) > Catering: equipment
Ransome (Arthur Mitchell)
    Arthur Ransome Soc
Rare breeds
    Rare Breeds Survival Trust
    > + Cattle; Sheep etc
Rating
    Assn Chief Estates Surveyors. . . Public Sector
    Inst Revenues, Rating & Valuation
    Rating Surveyors Assn
    Scot Assessors' Assn
Rats
    Nat Fancy Rat Soc
Raw sugar > Sugar
Rawsthorne (Alan)
    Friends Alan Rawsthorne
Raynaud's disease
    Raynaud's & Scleroderma Assn
Razors > Shaving equipment & razors
Reading
    Brit Dyslexia Assn
    Dyslexia Inst
    Nat Literacy Assn
    Reading Assn Ireland
    UK Literacy Assn
Ready-mixed concrete
    Brit Ready Mixed Concrete Assn
    Quarry Products Assn
    > + Concrete & concrete products
Real ale
    Campaign Real Ale
    Soc Presvn Beers Wood
    > + Brewing
Real estate > Estate headings; Property headings
Real tennis > Tennis
Real time locating systems
    Assn Automatic Identification . . .Capture
Receivers
    Insolvency Practitioners Assn
    NARA
Receptionists (medical)
    Assn Med Secretaries, Practice Managers. . .
Reclamation & recycling
    Aluminium Alloy Mfrg & Recycling Assn
    Brit Metals Recycling Assn
    Brit Vehicle Salvage Fedn
    Can Makers
    Chart Instn Wastes Mgt
    Confedn Paper Inds
    Environmental Services Assn
    Indl Packaging Assn
    Inst Demolition Engrs
    Ir Waste Mgt Assn
    Oil Recycling Assn
    Textile Recycling Assn
    UK Aluminium Packaging Recycling Org
    UK Cartridge Remanufacturers Assn
    Waste Watch
    > + Metal: scrap; & other waste trades

Reconstructive surgery > Plastic surgery
Record agents
    Assn Genealogists & Researchers in Archives
Recorders (musical instruments)
    Soc Recorder Players
Recording studios
    Assn Profl Recording Services
Records: historical
    Brit Record Soc
    Brit Records Assn
    Business Archives Coun
    Catholic Record Soc
    Ephemera Soc
    Friends Nat Libraries
    Hakluyt Soc
    Harleian Soc
    List & Index Soc
    Manorial Soc
    Navy Records Soc
    Pipe Roll Soc
    Scot Records Assn
    > + Archives; Parish registers
Records: historical - county societies
    Bedfordshire Histl Record Soc
    Caernarvonshire Histl Soc
    Cambridgeshire Records Soc
    Cheshire > Chetham Soc
    Cheshire > Record Soc Lancashire & Cheshire
    Chetham Soc
    Cornwall > Devon & Cornwall Record Soc
    Derbyshire Record Soc
    Devon & Cornwall Record Soc
    Dugdale Soc
    Durham > Soc Antiquaries Newcastle upon Tyne
    Hertfordshire > St Albans & Hertfordshire Architectural. . . Soc
    Lancashire > Chetham Soc
    Lancashire > Record Soc Lancashire & Cheshire
    Lincoln Record Soc
    London Record Soc
    Norfolk Record Soc
    Northamptonshire Record Soc
    Northumberland > Soc Antiquaries Newcastle upon Tyne
    Northumbria > Surtees Soc
    Oxfordshire Record Soc
    Record Soc Lancashire & Cheshire
    Rutland Local Hist & Record Soc
    Saint Albans & Hertfordshire Architectural. . . Soc
    Soc Antiquaries Newcastle upon Tyne
    Somerset Record Soc
    Staffordshire Record Soc
    Surrey Record Soc
    Surtees Soc (Northumbria)
    Sussex Record Soc
    Warwickshire > Dugdale Soc
    Wiltshire Record Soc
Records: historical (conservation)
    Assn Local Govt Archaeol Officers
    > Archives: conservation
Records management
    Records Mgt Soc
Records: musical > Copyright;   Sound recording & reproduction
Recovery & recycling > Reclamation & recycling
Recreation > Leisure, recreation & amenity management
Recruitment services > Employment agents & consultants
Recycling trades > Reclamation & recycling
Reeds & sedges
    Brit Reed Growers Assn
Reef fishing
    Shark Angling Club
Re-enactment of battles, fights etc > Fights (historic/re-enactment)
Referees
    Referees' Assn
Referenda
    Referenda Soc
Reflexology
    Assn Light Touch Therapists
    Assn Reflexologists
    Assn Therapy Lecturers
    Brit Reflexology Assn
    Scot Massage Therapists Org
Reformed Church (Scottish)
    Scot Reformation Soc
Refractive surgery
    UK & I Soc Cataract & Refractive Surgeons
Refractories
    Brit Ceramic Confedn
    Brit Refractories & Indl Ceramics

© CBD Research Ltd · Beckenham · BR3 5JS · Tel 020 8650 7745 · Fax 020 8650 0768 · E-mail cbd@cbdresearch.com · www.cbdresearch.com

CERAM Res
Inst Refractories Engrs
Refractory Users Federation
Refreshment vending
Automatic Vending Assn
Refrigerated transport > Temperature controlled transport
Refrigeration
Air Conditioning & Refrigeration Ind Bd
Brit Refrigeration Assn
Heat Transfer & Fluid Flow Service
Inst Refrigeration
Ir Cold Storage Fedn
> + Cryogenics; Temperature controlled storage
Refugees
Assn Visitors Immigration Detainees
Immigration Law Practitioners' Assn
Nat Inf Forum
Refuse disposal > Waste disposal
Refuse incineration
Combined Heat & Power Assn
Registered designs > Copyright; Industrial design; Patents & trade marks
Registration of births etc > Population: registration
Regression > Hypnotic regression
Rehabilitation
Brit Soc Rehabilitation Medicine
English Community Care Assn
R Assn Disability & Rehabilitation
> + Disablement
Reiki healing
Assn Light Touch Therapists
Confedn Healing Orgs
Reiki Assn
Re-incarnation
UK Skeptics
Reinforcement
Intl Glassfibre Reinforced Concrete Assn
UK Steel
Reinsurance > Insurance
Relaxation
Brit Autogenic Soc
Floatation Tank Assn
Religion
Assn Brit Theological... Libraries
Assn Denominational Histl Socs Cognate Libs
Brit Assn Study Religions
Brit Soc Study Religions
Eckhart Soc
Pagan Fedn
Rural Theology Assn
Sea Faith Network (UK)
Traditional Cosmology Soc
Religion & medicine > Medicine & religion
Religious drama
Religious Drama Soc
Religious education > Christian education; & individual religions
Relocation agents & consultants
Assn Relocation Profls
Remedial education > Education
Remote imaging/sensing
Brit Assn Remote Sensing Companies
Mineralogical Soc
R Meteorological Soc
Remote Imaging Group
Remote Sensing & Photogrammetry Soc
Sira
UKspace
Removers > Furniture: warehousing & removal
Renaissance
Pike & Shot Soc
Scot Medievalists
Soc Renaissance Studies
Renal structure & disease > Nephrology
Rendering
UK Renderers Assn
> + Animal by-products
Renewable energy
Brit Wind Energy Assn
Network Alternative Technology &... Assessment
Renewable Energy Assn
Scot Renewables Forum
Solar Energy Soc
Wind Engg Soc
> + specific types of energy
Rented accommodation
Nat Landlords' Assn
Rents > Property & land owners; Tenants & residents
Repertory theatres > Theatre

Repetitive strain injury > Occupational health & hygiene; Performing arts
medicine
Reporters > Journalism
Reproductive ethics
Comment Reproductive Ethics
Reptiles > Herpetology
Rescue dogs
Nat Search & Rescue Dog Assn
Rescue equipment
Fire & Rescue Suppliers Assn
Rescue organisations > First aid & immediate care;   Welfare organisations; &
field of rescue
Research > subject of research
Reservoirs > Dams & reservoirs
Residential: boats
Residential Boat Owners Assn
Residential: colleges
Adult Residential Colls Assn
> + Adult education
Residential: homes
Assn Indep Care Advisers
English Community Care Assn
Inst Home Inspectors
Relatives & Residents Assn
> + Nursing homes
Residential: property > Property: maintenance/management
Residential: settlements
Brit Assn Settlements & Social Action Centres
Residential: social work > Social: service
Residents > Tenants & residents
Resins & gums
FeRFA
Resorts > Holiday resorts
Respiratory equipment
Assn Respiratory Technology & Physiology
Barema
Rest homes > Residential homes
Restaurants > Hotels & restaurants
Restaurants: engineering > Catering: equipment
Restless legs
Ekbom Support Gp
Restorative dentistry > Dentistry
Restorers/restoration > object(s) restored
Restricted growth > Growth
Resuscitation techniques > Life saving
Retail trade
Assn Private Market Operators
Brit Assn Fair Tr Shops
Brit Retail Consortium
Brit Shops & Stores Assn
Consumer Credit Assn
Indep Retailers Confedn
Inst Grocery Distbn
Retail Ireland
RGDATA [IRL]
Rural Shops Alliance
Scot Retail Consortium
U Shop, Distributive & Allied Workers
UK Travel Retail Forum
Village Retail Services Assn...
> + specific trades
Retina (diseases of)
Brit Retinitis Pigmentosa Soc
Retirement
Brit Pensioners & Tr U Action Assn
Fedn Active Retirement Assns [IRL]
Heyday
Life Academy
Retirement homes & sheltered housing
Assn Retirement Housing Mgrs
ERoSH
NWA
> + Nursing homes
Retreats (religious)
Assn Promoting Retreats
Retreat Assn
Retroreflective equipment
Retroreflective Eqpt Mfrs Assn
Rett syndrome
Rett Syndrome Assn
Revenue protection (electricity)
UK Revenue Protection Assn
Rheas
Rhea & Emu Assn
> + Ostrich farming
Rheology
Brit Soc Rheology

Rheumatism > Arthritis & rheumatism
Rhinology > Otolaryngology
Ribbon
   Brit Narrow Fabrics Assn
Rice
   Grain & Feed Tr Assn
   London Rice Brokers Assn
   Rice Assn
Richard III King of England
   Richard III Soc
   Soc Friends King Richard III
Riding > Horse: riding & driving
Rifle shooting
   Nat Rifle Assn
   Nat Small-Bore Rifle Assn
   Scot Rifle Assn
   Scot Target Shooting Fedn
   > + Shooting
Rights of the individual > Individual freedom
Rights of way > Footpaths & rights of way
Rigs (drilling)
   Brit Rig Owners Assn
Risk assessment
   SIESO
   > Civil defence & industrial emergencies
Risk management
   ALARM
   Inst Risk Mgt
   > + Insurance
Rivers
   Anglers Consvn Assn
   Assn Rivers Trusts
   Estuarine & Coastal Sciences Assn
   > + Inland waterways; Water
Rivets > Fasteners & turned parts
Road: accidents > Accidents; Road: safety & control
Road: construction
   Britpave
   CSS
   Inst Highway Inc Engrs
   Instn Civil Engrs
   Instn Highways & Transportation
Road: construction materials
   Asphalt Ind Alliance
   Brit Precast Concrete Fedn
   Refined Bitumen Assn
   Road Emulsion Assn
   Road Surface Treatments Assn
   UK Quality Ash Assn
Road: control > Road: safety & control

   Heavy Transport Assn
   Ir Road Haulage Assn
   Road Haulage Assn
   Soc Operations Engrs
   Transport Assn
   Utd Road Transport U
Road: lighting, markings & traffic signs
   Assn Road Traffic Safety & Mgt
   Assn Signals, Lighting... Highway Electrical Connections
   Highway Electrical Mfrs & Supprs Assn
   Photoluminescent Safety Products Assn
   Retroreflective Eqpt Mfrs Assn
   Road Safety Markings Assn
   > + Signs
Road: locomotives
   Road Locomotive Soc
   > + Steam engines, boats & machinery
Road: rollers > Steam engines, boats & machinery
Road: safety & control
   Assn Indl Road Safety Officers
   Campaign Drinking & Driving
   Inst Road Safety Officers
   Inst Traffic Accident Investigators
   ITS UK
   Local Authority Road Safety Officers' Assn
   R Soc Prevention Accidents
   RoadPeace
   Safe Speed
   Traffic Mgt Contrs Assn
   Vehicle Restraint Mfrs Assn
   > + Motoring organisations; Safety
Road: signs > Road: lighting, markings & traffic signs; Signs
Road: sweeping > Street cleaning
Road: transport > Road: haulage
Robotics
   Brit Automation & Robot Assn

Materials Handling Engrs Assn
Soc Underwater Technology Ltd
Rock climbing > Climbing
Rock gardens
   Alpine Garden Soc
   Hardy Plant Soc
   Scot Rock Garden Club
Rock mechanics > Soil & rock mechanics
Rock > Pop & rock music
Rocketry
   Assn Scotland Res Astronautics
   MARS
   UK Rocketry Assn
Roller bearings > Ball & roller bearings
Roller coasters
   Roller Coaster Club
   > + Fairgrounds & equipment
Roller hockey
   Nat Roller Hockey Assn
Roller skating
   Fedn Artistic Roller Skating
Rollerblading > Skating: board, inline & roller
Roman archaeology & antiquities
   Assn Roman Archaeology
   Assn Study & Presvn Roman Mosaics
   Roman Finds Gp
   Soc Promotion Roman Studies
   > + Archaeology
Roman Catholic Church
   Assn Separated & Divorced Catholics
   Catenian Assn
   Catholic Archives Soc
   Catholic Family Hist Soc
   Catholic Med Assn
   Catholic Record Soc
   Catholic Truth Soc
   Catholic U
   Chapels Soc
   Latin Mass Soc
   Newman Assn
   Scot Catholic Histl Assn
   > + Liturgy
Roman Empire
   Soc Promotion Roman Studies
   > + Classical studies
Romanies > Gypsies & travelling people
Romantic novelists
   Romantic Novelists Assn
Romany of the BBC
   Romany Soc
Roofing
   Brit Precast Concrete Fedn
   Clay Roof Tile Coun
   Confedn Roofing Contrs
   Copper Devt Assn
   Eur Liquid Waterproofing Assn
   Flat Roofing Alliance
   Inst Roofing
   Intelligent Membrane Tr Assn
   Metal Cladding & Roofing Manufacturers Association Ltd
   Nat Fedn Roofing Contrs
   Roofing Ind Alliance
   Scot Master Slaters & Roof Tilers Assn
   Single Ply Roofing Assn
   Stone Roofing Assn
   Trussed Rafter Assn
Rooflights
   Nat Assn Rooflight Mfrs
   > + Windows
Rootzone materials
   Brit Rootzone & Top Dressing Mfrs Assn
   > + Composts & composting
Rope access (safety & usage)
   Indl Rope Access Tr Assn
Ropes
   Performance Textiles Assn
Ropework
   Intl Gld Knot Tyers
Roses
   Amat Rose Breeders Assn
   Brit Assn Rose Breeders
   Horticultural Trs Assn
   N England Rosecarpe Horticl Soc
   R Nat Rose Soc
Rotary
   Assn Inner Wheel Clubs
   Assn Past Rotarians

© CBD Research Ltd · Beckenham · BR3 5JS · Tel 020 8650 7745 · Fax 020 8650 0768 · E-mail cbd@cbdresearch.com · www.cbdresearch.com

Rotating electrical machines
        Assn Electrical & Mechanical Trs
        BEAMA
Rotorcraft > Helicopters
Round tables
        Nat Assn Round Tables
Roundabouts (fairground) > Fairgrounds & equipment
Roundabouts (traffic)
        UK Roundabout Appreciation Soc
        > + Road markings, lighting & traffic signs
Rounders
        Gaelic Athletic Assn
        Nat Rounders Assn
Roundheads > Cromwell (Oliver);   Fights (historic/re-enactment)
Route guidance
        ITS UK
        > + Road: safety & control
Routemaster buses
        Routemaster Operators & Owners Assn
Rowing
        Amat Rowing Assn
        Scot Amat Rowing Assn
        Welsh Amat Rowing Assn
Roy (Harry)
        Harry Roy Appreciation Soc
Royal Air Force
        R Air Force Histl Soc
        R Air Forces Assn
        Soldiers, Sailors & Airmen's Families Assn
        > + Armed forces & veterans: welfare
Royal Marines
        White Ensign Assn
Royal Navy
        Aircrewman's Assn
        Assn R Navy Officers
        Naval Dockyards Soc
        Navy Records Soc
        R Naval Assn
        R Navy Enthusiasts' Soc
        White Ensign Assn
        > + Armed forces & veterans: welfare
Royal warrant holders
        R Warrant Holders Assn
Rubber
        Brit Plastics Fedn
        Brit Tyre Mfrs Assn
        Rapra Technology Ltd
        Tropical Growers' Assn
Rubber stamps
        Brit Office Supplies & Services Fedn
        Rubber Stamp Mfrs' Gld
Rubella > German measles
Rugby Fives
        Rugby Fives Assn
Rugby football > Football: Rugby
Rugs > Carpets; Oriental carpets & rugs
Running
        Assn Running Clubs
        English Cross Country Assn
        Fell Runners Assn
        Road Runners Club
        > + Athletics
Rupert Bear
        Followers Rupert
Rural interests
        Country Land & Business Assn [E&W]
        Scot Rural Property & Business Assn
        Westmorland County Agricl Soc
        > + Conservation; Environment;   Local government
Rural life: history > Agriculture: history
Ruritanian fiction
        Violet Needham Soc
Ruskin (John)
        Ruskin Soc
        Ruskin Soc Oxford
Rusks
        Cereal Ingredients Mfrs' Assn
Russia & associated states
        Brit Assn Slavonic & E Eur Studies
        Russo-Brit Cham Comm
        Scotland-Russia Forum
        Soc Cooperation Russian & Soviet Studies
Russia: language & literature
        Assn Language Learning
        Brit Assn Slavonic & E Eur Studies
        Pushkin Club

S

Sacks
        Environmental & Technical Assn Paper Sack Ind
SAD (seasonal affective disorder)
        SAD Assn
Saddlery
        Brit Equestrian Tr Assn
        Soc Master Saddlers
        > + Leathergoods
Safes
        Brit Security Ind Assn
Safety
        Brit Assn Public Safety Communications Officers
        Brit Safety Ind Fedn
        Crime Concern
        Health & Safety Sign Assn
        Indep Safety Consultants Assn
        Inst Safety Technology & Res
        Instn Occupational Safety & Health
        Nat Ir Safety Org
        Photoluminescent Safety Products Assn
        Retroreflective Eqpt Mfrs Assn
        Safety & Reliability Soc
        Scot Hazards Campaign Gp
        Select
        Soc Chemical Ind
        > + Home: safety;   Road safety & control
Safety: assessment
        Assn Boat Safety Examiners
        Safety Assessment Fedn
Safety: barriers & fences
        Fencing Contrs' Assn
        Vehicle Restraint Mfrs Assn
Safety: lamps
        Miners' & Indl Lamp Mfrs' Assn
        > + Mining: equipment
Safety: personal
        Brit Safety Ind Fedn
        Choice in Personal Safety
        Fall Arrest Safety Eqpt Training
        Personal Safety Assn
Safety: rigging/nets
        Fall Arrest Safety Eqpt Training
Sailing
        Assn Sea Training Orgs
        Ir Sailing Assn
        Old Gaffers Assn
        Sailing Smack Assn
        > + Boats & boating;   Ships: history & preservation;   Yachts & yachting
Sailors > Merchant Navy; Royal Navy
Sailors' welfare
        Soldiers, Sailors & Airmen's Families Assn
        > + Ex-service organisations
Sailplanes > Gliding & soaring
Sails & sailmaking
        Assn Brit Sailmakers
        Brit Marine Fedn
        Performance Textiles Assn
St James of Compostela
        Confraternity Saint James
Saintpaulia
        Saintpaulia & Houseplant Soc
Salads
        Brit Leafy Salad Assn
        > + Vegetable(s) headings
Sales agents (general)
        Brit Intl Freight Assn
Sales management & representation
        Inst Sales & Marketing Mgt
        Inst Sales Promotion
        Managing & Marketing Sales Assn
        Sales Inst Ireland
        Soc Sales & Marketing
        > + Marketing
Salmon & trout
        Assn Salmon Fishery Bds
        Brit Trout Assn
        Fedn Scot Aquaculture Producers
        Salmon & Trout Assn
        Scot Anglers Nat Assn
        Scot Salmon Producers' Org
        Wild Trout Trust
        > + Fish: farming

Salt
  Salt Assn
Salvage > Reclamation & recycling; Towage & salvage
Salvage (underwater) > Underwater engineering & research
Salvage corps
  Brit Fire Services Assn
Sand & gravel
  Quarry Products Assn
Sand yachting
  Brit Fedn Sand & Land Yacht Clubs
Sandwiches & sandwich bars
  Brit Sandwich Assn
  Nationwide Caterers Assn
Sanitary protection
  Absorbent Hygiene Products Mfrs Assn
Sanitaryware
  Brit Ceramic Confedn
Sarcoidosis
  Sarcoidosis & Interstitial Lung Assn
  > + Thoracic diseases
Sassoon (Siegfried Louvain)
  Siegfried Sassoon Fellowship
Satellite communications > Cable & satellite communications
Satellite navigation
  UKspace
Sauces > Pickles & sauces
Saunas
  Health & Beauty Emplrs Fedn
Sausage & food casings
  Natural Sausage Casings Assn
Sausages
  Brit Sausage Appreciation Soc
  Gld Q Butchers
  > + Meat
Saville (Malcolm)
  Malcolm Saville Soc
Savoy Operas
  Gilbert & Sullivan Soc
Sawmilling > Timber
Saxifrages (Saxifraga)
  Saxifrage Soc
Saxophones > Clarinets & saxophones
Sayers (Dorothy L[eigh])
  Dorothy L Sayers Soc
Scaffolding
  Nat Access & Scaffolding Confedn
  Prefabricated Access Suppliers' & Mfrs' Assn
Scales & weighing machines
  Solids Handling & Processing Assn
  UK Weighing Fedn
  > + Measurement
Scallops > Shellfish
Scandinavia: literature & antiquities
  Regia Anglorum
  Scot Soc Nthn Studies
  Viking Soc Nthn Res
Scanning
  UK Indl Vision Assn
Scepticism
  UK Skeptics
Schizophrenia
  SANE
  Schizophrenia Ireland
School bands
  Nat School Band Assn
School governors
  Foundation & Aided Schools Nat Assn
School heads > Heads of schools & colleges
School secretaries & administrators
  Nat Bursars Assn
  > + Secretaries & personal assistants
School teachers > Teachers
School uniform
  Schoolwear Assn
Schools
  Nat Assn Small Schools
  Nat Small Schools Forum
  > + Education; Teachers; & individual type of school
Schools: hygiene
  Medical Officers Schools Assn
Schools: independent
  Indep Schools Coun
Schools: inspection
  Assn Profls Educ & Children's Trusts
Schools: meals service
  Local Authority Caterers' Assn

Schubert (Franz Peter)
  Schubert Soc
Schumacher (Dr E F)
  Doctor E F Schumacher Soc
Science
  Assn Basic Science Teachers Dentistry
  Assn Brit Science Writers
  Assn Mgt & Profl Staffs
  Assn Researchers in Medicine & Science
  Assn Science Educ
  Brit Assn Advancement Science
  Brit Soc Philosophy Science
  Cambridge Philosophical Soc
  Campaign Science & Engg UK
  Manchester Literary & Philosophical Soc
  R Instn GB
  R Ir Academy
  R Scot Soc Arts (Science & Technology)
  R Soc Chemistry
  R Soc Edinburgh
  Royal Soc (The)
  Science, Engg & Mfrg Technologies Alliance
  Science, Technology, Engg. . . Public Relations Assn
  Scientists Global Responsibility
  UK Skeptics
  > + specific disciplines
Science fiction
  Brit Fantasy Soc
  Brit Science Fiction Assn
Science: history
  Brit Soc Hist Science
  Natural Sciences Collections Assn
Science parks
  UK Science Park Assn
Science: technology > Laboratory equipment & technology
Scientific film > Film
Scientific instruments
  Scientific Instrument Soc
  > + Glassware: scientific
Scientists > Science; specific disciplines
Scleroderma
  Raynaud's & Scleroderma Assn
  Scleroderma Soc
Sclerosis
  Multiple Sclerosis Nat Therapy Centres
  Multiple Sclerosis Soc
  Multiple Sclerosis Soc Ireland
  Tuberous Sclerosis Assn
Scoliosis
  Brit Orthopaedic Assn
  Scoliosis Assn
Scooter riding > Motor cycling & scooter riding
Scorpions
  Brit Arachnological Soc
  Brit Tarantula Soc
Scotland
  Assn Protection Rural Scotland
  Assn Scot Visitor Attractions
  Saint Andrew Soc
  Saltire Soc
  Scot Envt Link
  Scot Stone Liaison Gp
  Scot Wild Land Gp
  Scotland-Russia Forum
Scotland: archaeology
  Soc Antiquaries Scotland
  > + Archaeology: county societies
Scotland: history
  Pictish Arts Soc
  R Celtic Soc
  Scot Catholic Histl Assn
  Scot Hist Soc
  Seventeen Fortyfive Assn
  Soc W Highland & Island Histl Res
Scotland: language & literature
  Assn Scot Literary Studies
  Robert Burns World Fedn
  Scot Language Dictionaries
  Scot Poetry Library
  Scot Text Soc
  Scots Language Soc
  Ulster-Scots Language Soc
  > + Gaelic language & culture
Scotland: law history
  Stair Soc
Scotland: music
  R Celtic Soc

© CBD Research Ltd · Beckenham · BR3 5JS · Tel 020 8650 7745 · Fax 020 8650 0768 · E-mail cbd@cbdresearch.com · www.cbdresearch.com

Robert Burns World Fedn
Traditional Music & Song Assn Scotland
> + Pipe bands & music
Scott (Sir Walter)
Edinburgh Sir Walter Scott Club
Scouts > Youth organisations
Scrabble
Assn Brit Scrabble Players
Scrabble Clubs (UK)
Scrap > Materials: management/handling; Reclamation & recycling
Screen (film & television) > Film; Television headings
Screen printing
Prism
Screens > Sieves & screens
Screws & rivets > Fasteners & turned parts
Scribes
Soc Scribes & Illuminators
Scripophily
Intl Bond & Share Soc
Scriptwriting
Brit Soc Comedy Writers
> + Writing & writers
Scrubber driers
Indl Cleaning Machine Mfrs Assn
Scuba diving
Scot Sub Aqua Club
> + Water: sports
Sculpture
Brit Art Medal Soc
Nat Soc Painters, Sculptors & Printmakers
Public Monuments & Sculpture Assn
R Birmingham Soc Artists
R Brit Soc Sculptors
R Cambrian Academy Art
R Scot Academy
Sculptors' Soc Ireland
Soc Portrait Sculptors
Soc Women Artists
> + Stone masons & sculptors
Sea > Marine; Nautical; Sailing etc
Sea angling
Assn Sea Fisheries C'ees [E&W]
Nat Fedn Sea Anglers
Scot Fedn Sea Anglers
> + Fishing (sport)
Sea pilots
Europilots
Nautical Inst
UK Maritime Pilots' Assn
> + Navigation
Sea pollution > Pollution & pollution control
Sea-bed exploration > Ocean industries
Seabirds > Birds
Seafood > Fish headings; individual type of fish
Sealants & sealing
Assn Sealant Applicators
Brit Adhesives & Sealants Assn
Brit Fluid Power Assn
Brit Textile Technology Gp
Extruded Sealants Assn
Gasket Cutters' Assn
Seals
Seal Consvn Soc
Seamanship > Marine training; Sailing
Seamen > Merchant Navy; Royal Navy
Seaside piers > Piers
Seasonal affective disorder
SAD Assn
Seasonings > Spices & seasonings
Seat belts
Baby Products Assn
Choice in Personal Safety
> + Personal safety
Seating (audience/sports)
Brit Assn Seating Eqpt Suppliers
Seaweed > Algae
Secondary metal > Metal: scrap
Secondary schools
School Leaders Scotland
Secondary teachers > Teachers
Secret passages
Subterranea Britannica
Secret writing
Xenophon
Secretaries & administrators
Alliance UK Virtual Assistants
Assn Celebrity Assistants (UK)

Assn Coun Secretaries & Solicitors
Assn Med Secretaries, Practice Managers...
Gld Intl Butler Administrators...
Inst Agricl Secretaries & Administrators
Inst Assn Mgt
Inst Legal Secretaries & PAs
Inst Paralegal Training
Inst Qualified Profl Secretaries
Nat Assn NFU Gp Secretaries
Nat Bursars Assn
Secularism
Campaign Philosophical Freedom
Nat Secular Soc
> + Humanism
Securities > Investment; Stock & share dealing
Security
Assn Automatic Identification ...Capture
Assn Insurance Surveyors
Assn Police & Public Security Suppliers
Assn Security Consultants
Brit Blind & Shutter Assn
Brit Machine Vision Assn...
Brit Security Ind Assn
Defence Industry Security Assn
Electrical Contrs Assn
Fencing Contrs' Assn
Fibreoptic Ind Assn
Inst Security Mgt
Ir Security Ind Assn
Mobile Electronics & Security Fedn
Nat Assn Healthcare Security
Nat Assn Security Dog Users
Nat Security Inspectorate
Scot Security Assn
Security Inst Ireland
Telecare Services Assn
UK Indl Vision Assn
> + Defence; Police
Security: shredding > Documents: confidential disposal
Sedges > Reeds & sedges
Sedimentology
Geological Soc
Sedums (Crassulaceae)
Sedum Soc
Seed crushing > Oilseed; Seeds
Seed potatoes > Potatoes
Seeds
Biodynamic Agricl Assn
Brit Assn Seed Analysts
Brit Assn Seed Producers
Ir Seed Tr Assn
Nat Assn Agricl Contrs
NIAB
Scot Seed & Nursery Tr Assn
Self adhesive labels > Labels: self adhesive & roll
Self catering
Assn Scotland's Self-Caterers
Brit Holiday & Home Parks Assn
English Assn Self Catering Operators
Fedn Nat Self Catering Assns
> + Caravans & caravanning; Travel & tourism etc
Self defence
Self Defence Fedn
Self employment
Fedn Small Businesses
> + Business
Self harm
Purine Metabolic Patients Assn
Self healing
Metamorphic Assn
Selling > Direct selling; Sales management & representation
Semi conductors > Electronics: industry & engineering
Sensing > Remote imaging/sensing
Separated & divorced people > Singles, divorced & separated
Separation techniques
Chromatographic Soc
Sequence dancing > Dancing
Serials > Periodicals
Servicemen's welfare > Armed forces & veterans: welfare;   Ex-service
organisations
Services (local government)
Assn Public Service Excellence
Settlements > Archaeology; Residential: settlements; Welfare: organisations
Sewers, sewage & effluents
Chart Instn Water & Envtl Management
Nat Sewerage Assn
Soc Brit Water & Wastewater Inds

Sewing articles (collecting) > Thimbles
Sewing machines
        Assn Sewing Machine Distbrs
        Sewing Machine Tr Assn
        Tools Self Reliance
Sex equality > Women: equal rights
Sex & sexual law reform
        Brit Assn Sexual & Relationship Therapy
        Campaign Homosexual Equality
        Josephine Butler Soc
        Sexaholics Anonymous
        Sexual Freedom Coalition
Sexual dysfunction
        Androgen Insensitivity Syndrome Support Gp
        Brit Soc Sexual Medicine
        Sexual Dysfunction Assn
Sexually transmitted disease > Genito-urinary medicine
Shaft sinking > Tunnelling & shaft sinking
Shakespeare (William)
        De Vere Soc
        Shakespeare Reading Soc
        Sunday Shakespeare Soc
Share certificates (collecting) > Scripophily
Shareholders
        English Assn Amer Bond & Shareholders
        UK Shareholders' Assn
        > + Investment; Stock & share dealing
Sharks
        Basking Shark Soc
        Shark Angling Club
Shaving equipment & razors
        Cutlery & Allied Trs Res Assn
Shaw (George Bernard)
        Shaw Soc
Shaw (Thomas Edward) > Lawrence (Thomas Edward)['of Arabia']
Sheep
        Brit Veterinary Assn
        Highlands & Islands Sheep Health Assn
        ICSA [IRL]
        Livestock Auctioneers Assn
        Mutton Renaissance Campaign
        Nat Sheep Assn
Sheep: breed societies
        Badger Face Welsh Mountain Sheep Soc
        Balwen Welsh Mountain Sheep Soc
        Beltex Sheep Soc
        Black Welsh Mountain Sheep Breeders Assn
        Blackface Sheep Breeders Assn
        Bluefaced Leicester Sheep Breeders Assn
        Brecknock Hill Cheviot Sheep Soc
        Brit Berrichon du Cher Sheep Soc
        Brit Bleu du Maine Sheep Soc
        Brit Charollais Sheep Soc
        Brit Coloured Sheep Breeders Assn
        Brit Friesland Sheep Soc
        Brit Gotland Sheep Soc
        Brit Icelandic Sheep Breeders Gp
        Brit Île de France Sheep Soc
        Brit Rouge de l'Ouest Sheep Soc
        Brit Texel Sheep Soc
        Brit Vendeen Sheep Soc
        Cambridge Sheep Soc
        Castlemilk Moorit Sheep Soc
        Charmoise Hill Sheep Soc
        Cheviot Sheep Soc
        Clun Forest Sheep Breeders Soc
        Cotswold Sheep Soc
        Cymdieithas Defaid Llanwenog
        Dalesbred Sheep Breeders' Assn
        Dartmoor Sheep Breeders Assn
        Derbyshire Gritstone Sheepbreeders Soc
        Devon Closewool Sheep Breeders Soc
        Devon & Cornwall Longwool Flock Book Assn
        Dorset Down Sheepbreeders Assn
        Dorset Horn & Poll Sheep Breeders Assn
        Eppynt Hill & Beulah Speckled Face Sheep Soc
        Exmoor Horn Sheep Breeders' Soc
        Hampshire Down Sheep Breeders Assn
        Hebridean Sheep Soc
        Herdwick Sheep Breeders Assn
        Jacob Sheep Soc
        Kerry Hill Flock Book Soc
        Leicester Longwool Sheepbreeders Assn
        Lincoln Longwool Sheep Breeders Assn
        Lleyn Sheep Soc
        Lonk Sheep Breeders Assn
        Manx Loaghtan Sheep Breeders Gp

Masham Sheep Breeders Assn
N Country Cheviot Sheep Soc
N England Mule Sheep Assn
N Ronaldsay Sheep Fellowship
Norfolk Horn Breeders Gp
Oxford Down Sheep Breeders Assn
Portland Sheep Breeders Gp
Romney Sheep Breeders' Soc
Rough Fell Sheep Breeders Assn
Roussin Sheep Soc
Ryeland Flock Book Soc
Scotch Half Bred Assn
Scotch Mule Assn
Shetland Cheviot Marketing Soc
Shetland Flock Book Soc
Shetland Sheep Soc
Shropshire Sheep Breeders Assn
Soc Border Leicester Sheep Breeders
Southdown Sheep Soc
Suffolk Sheep Soc
Swaledale Sheep Breeders Assn
Talybont Welsh Sheep Soc
Teeswater Sheep Breeders Assn
Welsh Halfbred Sheep Breeders Assn
Welsh Hill Speckled Face Sheep Soc
Welsh Mountain Sheep Soc - Hill Flock
Welsh Mountain Sheep Society - Registered Section
Welsh Mule Sheep Breeders Assn
Wensleydale Longwool Sheep Breeders' Assn
White Face Dartmoor Sheep Breeders Assn
White Faced Woodland Sheep Breeders Gp
Wiltshire Horn Sheep Soc
Zwartbles Sheep Assn
> + Cattle & livestock
Sheep: dairying
        Brit Milksheep Soc
        Brit Sheep Dairying Assn
Sheet metal > Metal: sheet
Sheet music > Music
Shelley (Percy Bysshe)
        Keats-Shelley Memorial Assn
Shellfish
        Assn Scot Shellfish Growers
        Shellfish Assn
Shells > Conchology
Sheltered housing > Retirement homes & sheltered housing
Shelving & racking > Storage equipment
Shepherds' crooks
        Brit Stickmakers Gld
Sheriffs & sheriff officers
        High Sheriffs' Assn
        Soc Messengers-at-Arms & Sheriff Officers
Shiatsu
        Equine Shiatsu Assn
        Shiatsu Soc
        > + Complementary medicine
Shingles
        Herpes Viruses Assn
Shinty (sport)
        Camanachd Assn
Shipbroking
        Inst Chart Shipbrokers
        Ir Ship Agents' Assn
Shipbuilding & ship repairing
        Amat Yacht Res Soc
        Brit Marine Fedn
        Confedn Shipbuilding & Engg Us
        Instn Engrs & Shipbuilders Scotland
        R Instn Naval Architects
        Shipbuilders & Shiprepairers Assn
        Steam Boat Assn
        Thames Boating Trs Assn
        > + Marine: engineering
Shippers & packers for specific trades > trade concerned
Shipping
        Assn Cruise Experts
        Assn Port Health Authorities
        Cambridge Refrigeration Technology
        Cham Shipping
        Freight Transport Assn
        Grain & Feed Tr Assn
        Ir Cham Shipping
        Ir Marine Fedn
        London Shipowners' & River Users' Soc
Shipping & forwarding
        Brit Intl Freight Assn

© CBD Research Ltd · Beckenham · BR3 5JS · Tel 020 8650 7745 · Fax 020 8650 0768 · E-mail cbd@cbdresearch.com · www.cbdresearch.com

Ir Intl Freight Assn
> + Freight transport
Ships: history & preservation
Brit Titanic Soc
Coble & Keelboat Soc
Cutty Sark Trust
Forty Plus (40+) Fishing Boat Assn
Heritage Afloat
Mary Rose Soc
Nat Historic Ships
Ocean Liner Soc
Soc Sailing Barge Res
Ships: stores & supplies
Brit Assn Ship Suppliers
Marine Trs Assn
Scot Ship Chandlers Assn
Ships: survey
Soc Consulting Marine Engrs & Ship Surveyors
Shipwrecks > Ships: history & preservation
Shirts
Brit Clothing Ind Assn
Master Craftsmen's Assn
Shoehorns
Buttonhook Soc
Shoes > Footwear

Shooting
Brit Airgun Shooters' Assn
Brit Assn Shooting & Consvn
Brit Shooting
Brit Shooting Sports Coun
Countryside Alliance
Scot Assn Country Sports
Shooters' Rights Assn
Sportsman's Assn
U Country Sports Workers
UK Practical Shooting Assn
> + Arms & armour; Rifle shooting
Shopfitting
Glass & Glazing Fedn
Inst Shopfitting
Nat Assn Shopfitters
Shop & Display Eqpt Assn
Shopmobility
Nat Fedn Shopmobility
Shopping centres
Brit Coun Shopping Centres
Shopping from home > Home: shopping
Shops & stores > Retail trade
Shoring technology
Construction Plant-hire Assn
Shorinji kempo > Martial arts
Shorthand writing
Brit Inst Verbatim Reporters
Inc Phonographic Soc
Show jumping
Brit Equestrian Fedn
> + Horse headings
Showmen (fairground)
Showmen's Gld
Soc Indep Roundabout Proprietors
> + Fairgrounds & equipment
Shows & events
Assn Event Venues
Assn Profl Videomakers
Event Services Assn
Events Sector Ind Trg Org
Horticultural Exhibitors Assn
Nat Outdoor Events Assn
Soc Event Organisers
> + Corporate hospitality; Agriculture: county societies
Shredders (scrap)
Brit Metals Recycling Assn
Shredding (security) > Documents: confidential disposal
Shutters > Windows: blinds & shutters
Sibelius (Jean)
UK Sibelius Soc
Sickle cell anaemia
Sickle Cell Soc
Side saddle riding
Side Saddle Assn
Sidecars
Fedn Sidecar Clubs
> + Motor cycling & scooter riding
Sieves & screens
Solids Handling & Processing Assn
Sight > Blind & partially sighted;   specific disease

Sigillology > Badges & insignia
Sign language
Brit Deaf Assn
Ir Deaf Soc
Paget Gorman Soc
R Assn Deaf People
Scot Assn Sign Language Interpreters
> + Deafness
Signals (highway/road)
Assn Signals, Lighting… Highway Electrical Connections
Signs
Brit Sign & Graphics Assn
Health & Safety Sign Assn
> + Road: lighting, markings & traffic signs
Silhouettes
Silhouette Collectors Club
Soc Limners
Silica
Quarry Products Assn
Silica & Moulding Sands Assn
Silk
Brit Throwsters Assn
Silk Assn
Silos & hoppers
Solids Handling & Processing Assn
Silver
Silver Soc
Silver bands > Brass & silver bands
Silver (dealing in) > Bullion dealing
Silversmiths > Goldsmiths & silversmiths
Simultaneous translation
Conf Interpreters Gp
Singapore
Brit Cham Comm Singapore
Singapore UK Assn
Singing
Assn Engl Singers & Speakers
Assn Teachers Singing
Brit Voice Assn
Gld Musicians & Singers
Sing for Pleasure
> + Choirs & choral music
Single transferable vote > Elections & electoral legislation
Singles, divorced & separated
Assn Separated & Divorced Catholics
Assn Shared Parenting
Families Need Fathers
Nat Coun Divorced & Separated
Nat Fedn Solo Clubs
One Parent Families / Gingerbread
One Parent Families Scotland
Phoenix Camping Club
Relationships Scotland
> + Widows & widowers
Site investigation > Surveying
Sixth form colleges
Assn Colleges
CIFE
Sjogren's syndrome
Brit Sjogren's Syndrome Assn
Skateboarding > Skating: board, inline & roller
Skater hockey > Skating: board, inline & roller
Skating: ice > Ice skating
Skating: board, inline & roller
All Terrain Boarding Assn
Brit Inline Skater Hockey Assn
Fedn Artistic Roller Skating
UK Skateboarding Assn
Skeet shooting > Clay target (pigeon) shooting
Skibob
Skibob Assn
Skiing > Snowsports; Water sports
Skin camouflage
Brit Assn Skin Camouflage
> + Birthmarks & disfigurement
Skin disease > Dermatology; individual diseases
Skin diving > Water: sports
Skins > Leather
Skipping
Brit Rope Skipping Assn
Sky (visibility of)
Campaign Dark Skies
Skylights > Rooflights
Slag: cementitious
Cementitious Slag Makers Assn
Slate(s)
Scot Master Slaters & Roof Tilers Assn

Stone Fedn
Stone Roofing Assn
Slaughtering > Abattoirs
Slavonic languages & culture
Brit Assn Slavonic & E Eur Studies
Sleep
Brit Sleep Soc
Brit Snoring & Sleep Apnoea Assn
Brit Waterbed Assn
Narcolepsy Assn
Sleep Apnoea Trust Assn
Sleep Coun
Sleepers (concrete)
Brit Precast Concrete Fedn
> + Railways: engineering
Sliding doors
Assn Interior Specialists
> + Doors
Slimming > Dietetics; Eating disorders; Obesity
Slot cars
Brit Slot Car Racing Assn
Slot machines (vintage)
Soc Indep Roundabout Proprietors
Slovak Republic
Brit Cham Comm Slovak Republic
Slovakia: music
Dvořák Soc Czech & Slovak Music
Small arms > Arms & armour; Shooting
Small business > Business; Self employment
Small claims
Chart Inst Arbitrators
Small woods > Woodlands
Smart cards > Credit & magnetic strip(e) cards
Smoke & smoke control
Intumescent Fire Seals Assn
Smoke Control Assn
> + Air: conditioning & ventilating;   Air: pollution
Smoking
Action Smoking & Health
Freedom Org Right Enjoy Smoking Tobacco
Smoking: of food > type of food smoked
Snacks
Snack, Nut & Crisp Mfrs Assn
Snakes > Herpetology
Snooker > Cue sports
Snoring & apnoea
Brit Snoring & Sleep Apnoea Assn
Snow (John)
John Snow Soc
Snowboarding > Snowsports
Snowfall & blizzards
Tornado & Storm Res Org
Snowsports
Alpine Club
Backpackers Club
BASP UK Ltd
Brit Assn Mountain Guides
Brit Assn Snowsport Instructors
Mountaineering Coun Scotland
Scot Ski Club
Ski Club
Skibob Assn
Snowsport Cymru/Wales
Snowsport England
Snowsport GB
Snowsport Inds
Snowsport Scotland
Soap & detergents
Ir Cosmetics, Detergents... Products Assn
UK Cleaning Products Ind Assn
Soaring > Gliding & soaring
Social: history > History
Social: inventions
Inst Social Inventions
Social: sciences/research
Academy Social Sciences
Assn Res Centres Social Sciences
Assn Teaching Social Sciences
Brit Sociological Assn
Inst Social Inventions
Market Res Soc
Modern Studies Assn
Social Policy Assn
Social Res Assn
Socio-Legal Studies Assn
Sociological Assn Ireland
Statistical & Social Inquiry Soc Ireland

Social: service
Assn Directors Adult Social Services
Assn Directors Social Work
Assn Educ Welfare Mgt
Brit Assn Social Workers
Ceretas
Community
Emergency Social Services Assn
Inst Welfare
Ir Assn Social Workers
NAGALRO
Nat Assn Adult Placement Services
Nat Assn Social Workers Educ
Nat Fedn Community Orgs
Scot Org Practice Teaching
Social Care Assn
> + Community service: voluntary;   Welfare: administration
Social service: area organisations
NI Coun Voluntary Action
Wales Coun Voluntary Action
Socialism
Fabian Soc
Socialist Health Assn
Sociology > Social: sciences/research
Soft drinks
Beverage Coun Ireland
Brit Soft Drinks Assn
Soft furnishings
Assn Master Upholsterers & Soft Furnishers
Assn Soft Furnishers
Nat Carpet Cleaners Assn
> + Carpets; Upholstery
Soft tissue > Tissue paper
Softball
BaseballSoftballUK
Software
Component Obsolescence Gp
Intellect
Ir Software Assn
ScotlandIS
> + Computers
Software: development
Business Application Software Developers Assn
HL7 UK Ltd
UK Software Metrics Assn
Software: leisure
Entertainment & Leisure Software Pubrs Assn (UK)
Software: protection
Business Software Alliance
Fedn Software Theft
Softwoods
Timber Tr Fedn
> + Timber
Soil
Brit Soc Soil Science
Growing Media Assn
Instn Agricl Engrs
Soil Assn
Soil & rock mechanics
Brit Geotechnical Assn
Instn Civil Engrs
Solar technology
R Astronomical Soc
Renewable Energy Assn
Scot Solar Energy Gp
Solar Energy Soc
Solar Tr Assn
> + Renewable energy
Soldering > Brazing & soldering
Soldiers' welfare > Armed forces & veterans: welfare
Sol-fa > Tonic Sol-fa
Solicitors > Law
Solicitors: matrimonial law > Family law
Solid fuel
ICOM Energy Assn
Solid Fuel Assn
Stove Industry Alliance
> + Coal headings
Solid waste
Chart Instn Wastes Mgt
Solids in bulk > Materials: management/handling
Solo musicians
Inc Soc Musicians
> + performer by name
Soluble coffee > Coffee
Solvent abuse
Re-Solv - Soc Prevention Solvent... Abuse

© CBD Research Ltd · Beckenham · BR3 5JS · Tel 020 8650 7745 · Fax 020 8650 0768 · E-mail cbd@cbdresearch.com · www.cbdresearch.com

Solvents
  Brit Coatings Fedn
  Chemical Recycling Assn
  Solvents Ind Assn
  > + Cleaning equipment
Songbirds > Birds
Songs & songwriting
  Brit Academy Composers & Songwriters
  Brit Music Rights
  English Poetry & Song Soc
Sound > Acoustics; Insulation; Noise
Sound recording & reproduction
  Assn Motion Picture Sound
  Assn Profl Recording Services
  Audio Engg Soc
  BPI
  Brit Fedn Audio
  Brit Sound Recording Assn
  Confedn Transcribed Inf Services
  Fedn Recorded Music Socs
  Friends Pianola Inst
  Inst Broadcast Sound
  Inst Sound & Communications Engrs
  Ir Recorded Music Assn
  Music Producers Gld
  Profl Lighting & Sound Assn
  > + Video
Soups
  Food Processors Assn
South Downs
  S Downs Soc
Southern Africa
  Brit Cham Business Sthn Africa
Souvenirs > Commemorative items & souvenirs
Soviet Union > Russia & associated states
Soya
  Soya Protein Assn
Space: research & exploration
  Assn Scotland Res Astronautics
  Assn Specialist Techl Orgs Space
  Brit Interplanetary Soc
  R Aeronautical Soc
  Soc Brit Aerospace Cos
  UKspace
Space: visitors from > Unidentified flying objects
Spain
  Anglo-Spanish Soc
  Assn Contemporary Iberian Studies
  Brit Cham Comm Spain
  Hispanic & Luso Brazilian Coun
Spain: language & literature
  Assn Language Learning
Spas
  Inst Swimming Pool Engrs
  Malvern Spa Assn
  Spa Business Assn
  Swimming Pool & Allied Trs Assn
Spastics > Cerebral palsy
Speakers
  Assn Engl Singers & Speakers
  Assn Speakers Clubs
  Profl Gld After Dinner Speakers
  Profl Speakers Assn
Special education > Education
Spectacles > Optical industry
Spectator seating
  Brit Assn Seating Eqpt Suppliers
Speech
  Afasic
  Assn Engl Singers & Speakers
  Assn Lipspeakers
  Assn Rehabilitation Communication & Oral Skills
  Assn Speech & Language Therapists. . .
  Brit Aphasiology Soc
  Brit Assn Academic Phoneticians
  Brit Stammering Assn
  Brit Voice Assn
  Craniofacial Soc
  Cued Speech Assn
  R Coll Speech & Language Therapists
  Scot Assn Speech & Drama Adjudicators
  Selective Mutism Inf & Res Assn
  Soc Teachers Speech & Drama
  Speakability
  Voice Care Network
  > + Deafness
Speedsailing > Surfing, board & speed sailing

Speedway > Motor cycling & scooter riding
Speleology > Caves & caving
Spelling reform
  Spelling Soc
Spices & seasoning
  Intl Gen Produce Assn
  Seasoning & Spice Assn
  > + Flavourings
Spiders
  Brit Arachnological Soc
  Brit Tarantula Soc
  Buglife
Spill control
  UK Spill Assn
Spina bifida & hydrocephalus
  Assn Spina Bifida & Hydrocephalus
  Ir Assn Spina Bifida & Hydrocephalus
  Scot Spina Bifida Assn
  Soc Res Hydrocephalus & Spina Bifida
Spine & spinal injury
  Assn Light Touch Therapists
  Assn Spinal Injury Res. . .
  Brit Orthopaedic Assn
  Nat Ankylosing Spondylitis Soc
  Nat Backpain Assn
  Scoliosis Assn
  Spinal Injuries Assn
  Spinal Injuries Scotland
Spinning: hand
  Assn Glds Weavers, Spinners & Dyers
Spirits > Wines & spirits trade; Individual spirits
Spiritual healing
  Aetherius Soc
  Alliance Healing Assns
  Assn Therapeutic Healers
  Confedn Healing Orgs
  Crystal & Healing Fedn
  Nat Fedn Spiritual Healers
  Scot Assn Spiritual Healers
  > + Healing
Spiritualism
  Inst Spiritualist Mediums
  Spiritualist Assn
  Spiritualists Nat U
Splints > Prosthetics & orthoses
Spode china
  Spode Soc
Spohr (Louis)
  Spohr Soc
Spoken word > Audiobooks
Spondylitis > Ankylosing spondylitis
Spoonbending
  UK Skeptics
Spoons > Cutlery
Spoons: collecting
  Silver Spoon Club
  UK Spoon Collectors Club
Sporting guns & rifles > Shooting
Sports
  Brit Assn Sport & Exercise Sciences
  Brit Olympic Assn
  Brit Outdoor Profls Assn
  Brit Universities Sports Assn
  Inst Sport, Parks & Leisure
  Inst Sport & Recreation Mgt
  Profl Players Fedn
  Scot Assn Local Sports Couns
  Scot Schoolsport Fedn
  Scot Sports Assn
  Sports Journalists' Assn GB
  > + individual sports
Sports: country
  Countryside Alliance
  U Country Sports Workers
  > + individual sport
Sports: disabled & handicapped
  Brit Deaf Sports Coun
  Brit Paralympic Assn
  CP Sport England & Wales
  English Boccia Assn
  English Fedn Disability Sport
  Nat Assn Swimming Clubs H'capped
  Scot Disability Sport
  UK Sports Assn People Learning Disability
  WheelPower

Sports: equipment
>Sporting Goods Ind Assn
>Sports & Fitness Eqpt Assn
Sports: history
>Brit Soc Sports Hist
Sports: law
>Brit Assn Sport & Law
Sports: medicine & therapy
>Assn Therapy Lecturers
>Brit Assn Sport & Exercise Medicine
>Brit Orthopaedic Assn
>Osteopathic Sports Care Assn
>Scot Massage Therapists Org
>SMAE Fellowship
>Soc Sports Therapists
>Sports Massage Assn
Sports: stadia
>Fedn Stadium Communities
Sports: trade
>Assn Play Inds
>Assn Profl Sales Agents (Sports & Leisure Inds)
>Fedn Sports & Play Assns
Sportsgrounds & synthetic surfaces
>Brit Rootzone & Top Dressing Mfrs Assn
>Land Drainage Contrs Assn
>Nat Assn Agricl Contrs
>Nat Playing Fields Assn
>Sports & Play Construction Assn
>Sports Turf Res Inst
>UK Irrigation Assn
>> + Playgrounds & playgroups
Sportshall equipment
>Sports & Fitness Eqpt Assn
Sportswear
>Fedn Sports & Play Assns
>Sporting Goods Ind Assn
>> + Clothing
Sprats
>Herring Buyers Assn
>> + Fish; Fishing
Sprayed concrete > Concrete & concrete products
Spreads & spreadable products
>Food Processors Assn
>Margarine & Spreads Assn
Springs
>Inst Spring Technology
>UK Spring Mfrs Assn
Sprinklers: fire
>Brit Automatic Fire Sprinkler Assn
>Residential Sprinkler Associates
>> + Fire protection & prevention
Sprouts > Brassicas
Square dancing
>Brit Assn Amer Square Dance Clubs
>Square Dance Callers Club
Squash rackets > Rackets (squash)
Squirrels (red)
>Friends Red Squirrel
Stable staff
>Nat Assn Stable Staff
>> + Horse: racing
Stadia (sports)
>Fedn Stadium Communities
Staff recruitment > Employment agents & consultants
Staffordshire blue & white ware
>Friends Blue
>Spode Soc
Stage > Theatre
Staged fights > Fights (stage & film)
Staging / gantries
>Nat Access & Scaffolding Confedn
>> + Construction equipment
Stained glass > Glass painting
Stainless steel > Steel: special & alloy
Stairs
Stairs: gates & barriers
>Baby Products Assn
Stalin (Joseph)
>Stalin Soc
Stalking & harassment
>Nat Assn Support Victims Stalking & Harassment
Stammering
>Brit Stammering Assn
>> + Speech
Stamp collecting > Philately & postal history
Standardisation
>Brit Standards Soc

BSI
>Chart Quality Inst
Standby ships
>Emergency Response & Rescue Vessels Assn
>> + Ocean industries
Starch
>Brit Starch Ind Assn
Static electricity > Electro-static equipment
Stationery
>Brit Office Supplies & Services Fedn
>Brit Printing Inds Fedn
>Plastics & Board Inds Fedn
Statistics
>R Statistical Soc
>Radical Statistics Gp
>Statistical & Social Inquiry Soc Ireland
>Statisticians Pharmaceutical Ind
Statute law
>Statute Law Soc
>> + Law headings
Statutory auditors
>Assn Authorised Public Accountants
Steam engines, boats & machinery
>Nat Traction Engine Trust
>Northern Mill Engine Soc
>Paddle Steamer Presvn Soc
>Road Locomotive Soc
>Road Roller Assn
>Soc Indep Roundabout Proprietors
>Southern Counties Historic Vehicle Presvn Trust
>Steam Boat Assn
>Steam Car Club
>Steam Plough Club
>Transport Trust
>Trevithick Soc
>> + Archaeology: industrial;   Fairgrounds & equipment; Railways;
>Shipbuilding & ship repairing
Steel
>Brit Stainless Steel Assn
>Cast Metals Fedn
>Community
>Electric Steel Makers Gld
>Intl Steel Tr Assn
>Nat Assn Steel Stockholders
>UK Steel
>> + Iron
Steel: bands
>Brit Assn Steelbands
Steel: construction > Construction industries
Steel: drums > Cisterns, drums & tanks
Steel: foundries > Foundries
Steel: special & alloy
>Aluminium Stockholders Assn
>Brit Stainless Steel Assn
>Nat Assn Steel Stockholders
Steel: stockholders > Iron & steel stockholders
Steel: tubes
>Nat Assn Steel Stockholders
Steel: wire > Wire & wire products
Steeplejacks
>Assn Technical Lighting & Access Specialists
Steiner (Rudolf)
>Anthroposophical Soc
>Biodynamic Agricl Assn
Stereoscopy
>Stereoscopic Soc
Sterilisation > Family planning
Sterilising
>Inst Decontamination Sciences
>Pharmaceutical & Healthcare Sciences Soc
Stevenson (Robert Louis)
>Robert Louis Stevenson Club
Stevenson (Ronald)
>Ronald Stevenson Soc
Stickler syndrome
>Stickler Syndrome Support Gp
Stickmaking
>Brit Stickmakers Gld
>Brit Woodcarvers Assn
Stiff man syndrome
>Stiff Man Syndrome Support Gp
Stillbirth > Maternity; Obstetrics & gynaecology
Stock (animals) > Cattle & livestock
Stock & materials control
>Chart Inst Logistics & Transport
>Ir Inst Purchasing & Materials Mgt
>> + Materials management/handling

© CBD Research Ltd · Beckenham · BR3 5JS · Tel 020 8650 7745 · Fax 020 8650 0768 · E-mail cbd@cbdresearch.com · www.cbdresearch.com

Stock & share dealing
    Assn Foreign Banks
    Assn Private Client Investment Mgrs & Stockbrokers
    Fac Actuaries Scotland
    London Investment Banking Assn
    London Stock Exchange
    Securities & Investment Inst
    > + Investment
Stockings > Hosiery
Stocktaking/auditing
    Inst Licensed Tr Stock Auditors
Stokowski (Leopold)
    Leopold Stokowski Soc
Stoma > Colitis/colostomy; Ileostomy; Urology
Stone
    Brit Antique Furniture Restorers Assn
    Cornish Cham Mines & Minerals
    Men Stones
    Scot Stone Liaison Gp
    Stone Fedn
    Stone Roofing Assn
    UK Cast Stone Assn
    > + Quarries & quarrying; specific types of stone
Stone masons & sculptors
    Intl Masonry Soc
    Master Carvers Assn
    Nat Assn Master Letter Carvers
    Nat Assn Memorial Masons
Stonehenge
    Megalithic Soc
Stones (precious) > Gemstones
Stoolball
    Stoolball England
Storage
    Movers Inst
    Nat Gld Removers & Storers
    Self Storage Assn
Storage equipment
    Storage Eqpt Mfrs Assn
    Storage & Handling Eqpt Distbrs Assn
    > + Materials: management/handling
Store cards
    Finance & Leasing Assn
Stores: control > Stock & materials control
Stores: department/general > Retail trade
Storm research > Tornado & storm research
Storytelling
    Soc Storytelling
Stoves > Catering equipment;   Domestic appliances;   Fires & fireplaces
Strain injury > Repetitive strain injury;   Sports: medicine & therapy
Strain measurement
    Brit Soc Strain Measurement
    > + Materials: technology & testing
Strapping
    Brit Tensional Strapping Assn
Strategic planning
    CSS
    Strategic Planning Soc
Strauss (Johann) & family
    Johann Strauss Soc
Strauss (Richard)
    Richard Strauss Soc
Straw > Hay & straw
Straw: crafts
    Gld Straw Craftsmen
Street cleaning
    Chart Instn Wastes Mgt
Street furniture > Road: lighting, markings & traffic signs
Street lighting > Road: lighting, markings & traffic signs
Street luge
    Street Sled Sports Racers
Street markets > Markets: street, cattle & farmers'
Street organs > Organs & organists
Stress (physical & mental)
    Assn Stress Therapists
    Brit Assn Anger Mgt
    Brit Autogenic Soc
    Floatation Tank Assn
    Intl Stress Management Assn UK
    Nat Acupuncture Detoxification Assn
    Nat Coun Hypnotherapy
    Soc Stress Mgrs
String instruments > Musical instruments; & individual instruments
Strokes
    Stroke Assn

Structural engineering
    Instn Structural Engrs
    > + Construction industries
Structural steel > Construction industries
Structural waterproofing
    Brit Structural Waterproofing Assn
Stuart, House of
    R Stuart Soc
    Stewart Soc
Students
    Assn Educ & Guardianship Intl Students
    Assn Student Residential Accommodation
    Brit Assn Health Services in Higher Educ
    Brit Educl Travel Assn
    Nat Assn Mgrs Student Services Colleges
    Nat Network Assessment Centres
    Nat U Students UK
    > + Youth organisations
Stunts & stunt coordination
    Gld Stunt & Action Coordinators
    UK Bungee Club
Stuttering > Stammering
Sub-aqua > Underwater; Water: sports
Sub-contractors > Building
Sub-postmasters
    Nat Fedn Sub-Postmasters
Sub-sea > Underwater headings
Subbuteo
    Table Soccer Players Assn
Submersibles
    Soc Underwater Technology Ltd
Subsidence > Foundations (buildings)
Substance abuse > Addiction
Succulents > Cacti & succulents
Sudden infant death syndrome > Cot deaths
Sugar
    Refined Sugar Assn
    Sugar Assn Lond
    Sugar Traders Assn
    UK Indl Sugar Users Gp
Sugar beet seed
    Brit Soc Plant Breeders
Sugarcraft
    Brit Sugarcraft Gld
    Nat Sugar Art Assn
Suggestion schemes
    Ideas UK
Suicide
    ALERT
    CNK Alliance
    Compassionate Friends
    Samaritans
Suitcases > Travel goods & accessories
Sullivan (Sir Arthur Seymour)
    Gilbert & Sullivan Soc
    Sir Arthur Sullivan Soc
Sunbeds
    Sunbed Assn
Sunblinds > Windows: blinds & shutters
Sundials
    Brit Sundial Soc
Supermarkets > Grocery & provision trade
Supervisory management
    Inst Leadership & Mgt
Supply > Purchasing & supply
Supply chain management
    Brit Intl Freight Assn
Surface coatings > Coatings
Surfactants
    Brit Assn Chemical Specialities
    Soc Chemical Ind
Surfing, board & speed sailing
    Brit Bodyboard Club
    Brit Kite Surfing Assn
    Brit Land Speedsail Assn
    Brit Power Kitesports Assn
    Brit Surfing Assn
    R Yachting Assn
    Scot Surfing Fedn
    UK Windsurfing Assn
    Welsh Surfing Fedn
Surgery
    Assn Surgeons
    Assn Surgeons in Training
    Brit Assn Day Surgery
    Brit Assn Endocrine & Thyroid Surgeons
    Brit Assn Plastic, Reconstructive & Aesthetic Surgeons

Brit Soc Surgery Hand
College Emergency Medicine
Medical Soc Lond
R Coll Physicians & Surgeons Glasgow
R Coll Surgeons Edinburgh
R Coll Surgeons England
R Coll Surgeons Ireland
Soc Academic & Res Surgery
> + specific branches
Surgical apppliances
Assn Brit Healthcare Inds
Brit Assn Prosthetists & Orthotists
Brit Healthcare Trs Assn
Brit Inst Dental & Surgical Technologists
Surgical equipment & supplies
Cutlery & Allied Trs Res Assn
Surgical Dressings Mfrs Assn
Surtees (Robert Smith)
R S Surtees Soc
Surveying
Assn Bldg Engrs
Assn Consultant Approved Inspectors
Assn Geotechnical & Geoenvironmental Specialists
Brit Cartographic Soc
Chart Inst Bldg
Chief Bldg Surveyors Soc
Ground Forum
Hydrographic Soc UK
Instn Civil Engg Surveyors
Ir Instn Surveyors
LABC
London Dist Surveyors Assn
Property Consultants Soc
R Instn Chart Surveyors
Rating Surveyors Assn
Soc Chart Surveyors [IRL]
UK Land & Hydrographic Survey Assn
Suspended access equipment & cradles > Cradles & suspended platforms
Suspended ceilings > Ceilings
Sussex Downs
S Downs Soc
Sustainable development
UK Sustainable Development Assn
Sutures > Surgical equipment & supplies
Suzuki (Dr Shinichi)
Brit Suzuki Inst
Swaziland
Swaziland Soc
Sweden
Anglo-Swedish Soc
Brit Swedish Cham Comm Sweden
Swedish Cham Comm UK
Swedenborg (Emanuel)
Swedenborg Soc
Sweeping machines
Indl Cleaning Machine Mfrs Assn
Sweet peas
N England Rosecarpe Horticl Soc
Nat Sweet Pea Soc
Sweets > Confectionery
Swimming & diving
Amat Swimming Assn
Brit Long Distance Swimming Assn
Brit Swimming
Great Britain Diving Fedn
Halliwick Assn Swimming Therapy
Inst Swimming
Nat Assn Swimming Clubs H'capped
Nat Fedn SwimSchools
Outdoor Swimming Soc
Scot Swimming
Swimming Teachers Assn
Welsh Amat Swimming Assn
> + Water: sports
Swimming pools
Brit Swimming Pool Fedn
Inst Sport & Recreation Mgt
Inst Swimming Pool Engrs
Swimming Pool & Allied Trs Assn
Swing dance
London Swing Dance Soc
> + Dancing
Switchgear (electrical)
BEAMA
Switzerland
Brit-Swiss Cham Comm [Zürich]
Fedn Swiss Socs UK

Swordplay > Fencing (sport)
Synagogues
Fedn Synagogues
> + Jewish organisations
Synchronised swimming
Amat Swimming Assn
Brit Swimming
> + Swimming & diving
Synthetic surfaces > Sportsgrounds & synthetic surfaces
Systematics
Systematics Assn

T

Table football
Brit Foosball Assn
Table Soccer Players Assn
Table tennis
English Table Tennis Assn
Scot Table Tennis Assn
Table Tennis Assn Wales
Table wines > Wines
Tableware > Cutlery; Glass; Pottery
Taekwondo > Martial arts
Tai Chi > Martial arts
Tailoring
Brit Clothing Ind Assn
Master Craftsmen's Assn
Taiwan
Brit Cham Comm Taipei
Takeaway & fast food
Chinese Takeaway Assn
Nationwide Caterers Assn
Talipes (club foot)
STEPS
Tall people
Tall Persons Club
> + Growth
Tangsoodo > Martial arts
Tank storage
Tank Storage Assn
> + Cisterns, drums & tanks
Tankers > + Shipping
Tankers (road)
Road Haulage Assn
Tanning > Leather headings; Sunbeds
Tanzania
Britain-Tanzania Soc
Tape recording > Sound recording & reproduction
Tapes
Brit Narrow Fabrics Assn
Tarantulas
Brit Tarantula Soc
Target archery > Archery
Target shooting > Pistol shooting; Rifle shooting
Tarot
Brit Astrological & Psychic Soc
Tarot Assn
Tarpaulins
Performance Textiles Assn
Tatting
Ring of Tatters
Tatting
Lace Soc
Tattooing
Adult Ind Trade Assn
Brit Tattoo Artists Fedn
Tattoo Club
Taxation
Assn Corporate Trustees
Assn Revenue & Customs
Assn Taxation Technicians
Charity Tax Gp
Chart Inst Taxation
EIS Assn
Fedn Tax Advisers
Inst Fiscal Studies
Inst Indirect Taxation
Ir Taxation Inst
IsItFair
Low Incomes Tax Reform Gp
Profl Contrs Gp
Soc Trust & Estate Practitioners

© CBD Research Ltd · Beckenham · BR3 5JS · Tel 020 8650 7745 · Fax 020 8650 0768 · E-mail cbd@cbdresearch.com · www.cbdresearch.com

TaxPayers' Alliance
VAT Practitioners Gp
Taxidermy
Gld Taxidermists
Taxis & minicabs
Ir Taxi Drivers' Fedn
Licensed Taxi Drivers' Assn
London Motor Cab Proprietors' Assn
London Private Hire Car Assn
London Vintage Taxi Assn
Nat Private Hire Assn
Nat Taxi Assn
Owner Drivers Soc
> + Motor vehicles: hire
Tea
UK Tea Assn
Teachers
Assn Christian Teachers
Assn Promotion Quality TESOL Educ
Assn Secondary Teachers, Ireland
Assn Teachers & Lecturers
Brit Assn Local Hist
Educl Inst Scotland
Ir Fedn University Teachers
Ir Nat Teachers Org
League Exchange C'wealth Teachers
Nat Assn Schoolmasters U Women Teachers
Nat Assn Teachers Travellers
Nat U Teachers
NI Assn Christian Teachers
SATIPS
Scot Secondary Teachers' Assn
Soc Schoolmasters & Schoolmistresses
Teachers' U Ireland
Ulster Teachers U
University & College U
Voice
> + Education; for teachers of specific subjects see subject taught
Technical drawing
Assn Illustrators
Technical education
Design & Technology Assn
Inst Scientific & Technical Communicators
Nat Assn Advisers. . . Design & Technology
Technical information > Information: services & technology
Technical terminology
BSI
Technical writing & publishing
Assn Brit Science Writers
Inst Scientific & Technical Communicators
The Technion (Israel Inst of Technology)
Brit Technion Soc
Technology parks > Science parks
Technology transfer
AIRTO
Inst Intl Licensing Practitioners
Licensing Executives Soc
PERA
UK Science Park Assn
Tectonics
Geological Soc
Teeth
Bone Res Soc
> + Dentistry
Tegestology
Brit Beermat Collectors' Soc
Telecommunications
ALTO [IRL]
Communication Workers U
Communications Mgt Assn
CONNECT
Customer Contact Assn
Fedn Communication Services
ICT Ireland
Intellect
Nat Jt Utilities Gp
One Hundred & Sixty (160) Characters Assn
Premium Rate Assn
Select
Soc Cable Telecommunication Engrs
Telecommunications & Internet Fedn [IRL]
UK eHealth Assn
UK Competitive Telecommunications Assn
UKspace
> + Electronic: industry & engineering
Telecommunications: history
Telecommunications Heritage Gp

Telecottages
Telework Assn
Telepathy > Paranormal & psychical research
Telephone cables > Electric: cable & conduit
Telephones > Mobile phones; Telecommunications
Telescopes
William Herschel Soc
Television
Animal Welfare Filming Fedn
Assn Community TV Operators
Assn Studio & Production Eqpt Companies
BKSTS
Brit Academy Film & TV Arts
Brit Film Inst
Broadcasting, Entertainment Cinematograph. . .U
Directors Gld
Gld TV Cameramen
R Television Soc
Soc TV Lighting Directors
TV & Radio Inds Club
Voice Listener & Viewer
> + Audio visual aids & equipment
Television: advertising > Advertising: television & screen
Television: cable > Cable & satellite communications
Television: closed circuit
Brit Security Ind Assn
Nat Security Inspectorate
Television: engineering
Fibreoptic Ind Assn
Narrow Bandwidth TV Assn
> + Electronic: industry & engineering
Television: history > Radio & TV: history
Television: manufacturing > Electronic: industry & engineering
Television: production
Gld Brit Film & TV Editors
Producers Alliance Cinema & TV
Production Mgrs Assn
Satellite & Cable Broadcasters' Gp
Television: rental > Radio & TV: rental
Television: trade > Radio & TV: trade
Teleworkers
Telework Assn
Temperance
Brit Nat Temperance League
UK Alliance
Temperature controlled storage
Assn Meat Inspectors
Brit Refrigeration Assn
Cambridge Refrigeration Technology
Food Storage & Distbn Fedn
Nat Assn Brit Market Authorities
UK Warehousing Assn
Temperature controlled transport
Cambridge Refrigeration Technology
Food Storage & Distbn Fedn
Transfrigoroute UK
Tenants & residents
Fedn Private Residents' Assns
Nat Assn Tenants Orgs
Nat U Residents' Assns
Scot Tenants Org
Tenant Farmers' Assn
Tenants & Residents Orgs England
> + Property & land owners
Tennis
Assn Brit Tennis Officials
Brit Tennis Coaches Assn
Ir Real Tennis Assn
Lawn Tennis Assn
Lawn Tennis Writers Assn
Tennis & Rackets Assn
Tennis Scotland
Tennis Wales
Vets Tennis GB
Tennis courts & equipment
Sports & Play Construction Assn
Tennyson (Alfred, Lord)
Tennyson Soc
Tenpin bowling > Bowling
Tensional strapping > Strapping
Tents & marquees
Performance Textiles Assn
Plastics & Board Inds Fedn
Terminals (ports) > Ports
Terrapins > Chelonia
Terrazzo-mosaic
Nat Fedn Terrazzo, Marble & Mosaic Specialists

Tertiary colleges > Adult education
Tertiary era geology
        Tertiary Res Gp
        > + Geology
Test pilots
        R Aeronautical Soc
        > + Aviation: pilots, officers & crew
Testing laboratories
        Assn Consulting Scientists
        > + Materials: technology & testing
Testing methods
        AIRTO
Testing (non-destructive) > Materials: technology & testing
Textile: conservation
        Brit Antique Furniture Restorers Assn
        > + Costume history, design & conservation
Textile: design
        Chart Soc Designers
        Register Apparel & Textile Designers
        Textile Inst Intl
        Textile Soc
Textile: industry & trade
        Arts Centre Gp
        ASBCI - Forum Clothing & Textiles
        Brit Apparel & Textile Confedn
        Brit Interior Textiles Assn
        Brit Narrow Fabrics Assn
        Brit Polyolefin Textiles Assn
        Brit Textile Machinery Assn
        Brit Textile Technology Gp
        Brit Throwsters Assn
        Confedn Brit Wool Textiles
        Ir Clothing & Textiles Alliance [IRL]
        Performance Textiles Assn
        Textile Finishers Assn
        Textile Inst Intl
        UK Textile Laboratory Forum
        Wales Craft Coun
        Wallcovering Distbrs Assn
        > + specific textiles
Textile: rental
        Textile Services Assn
Thai boxing > Martial arts
Thailand
        Anglo-Thai Soc
        Brit Cham Comm Thailand
Thalassaemia
        UK Thalassaemia Soc
Thalidomide
        Thalidomide Soc
Thames
        River Assn Freight & Transport
        River Thames Alliance
        River Thames Soc
        Thames Boating Trs Assn
Thatching & thatched roofs
        Nat Soc Master Thatchers
Theatre
        Assn Brit Theatre Technicians
        Broadcasting, Entertainment Cinematograph. . .U
        Conf Drama Schools
        Directors Gld
        Drama Assn Wales
        Drama League Ireland
        Fedn Ethical Stage Hypnotists
        Fedn Scot Theatre
        Gld Drama Adjudicators
        Gld Profl Teachers Dancing
        Indep Theatre Coun
        Inst Contemporary Arts
        Little Theatre Gld
        Nat Assn Teaching Drama
        Nat Drama
        Nat Operatic & Dramatic Assn
        Player-Playwrights
        R Academy Dramatic Art
        R Scot Academy Music & Drama
        Religious Drama Soc
        Scot Assn Speech & Drama Adjudicators
        Scot Community Drama Assn
        Soc Brit Theatre Designers
        Soc Teachers Speech & Drama
        Soc Theatre Consultants
        Stage Mgt Assn
        UK Dance Drama Fedn
        Writers' Gld
        > + Entertainment;   Music: hall

Theatre: history
        Cinema Theatre Assn
        Malone Soc
        Soc Theatre Res
Theatre: lighting
        Assn Lighting Designers
        Profl Lighting & Sound Assn
Theatre: model
Theatre: young people
        Nat Assn Youth Drama [IRL]
        Nat Assn Youth Theatres
        Nat Drama
        Scot Community Drama Assn
Theology > Religion
Theosophy
        Theosophical Soc England
Therapeutic communities
        Assn Therapeutic Communities
        > + Mental health
Therapeutic education
        Nat Assn Therapeutic Educ
        > + Education headings
Therapy
        Assn Physical & Natural Therapists
        Assn Rational Emotive Behaviour Therapy
        Assn Therapy Lecturers
        > + individual forms of therapy
Thermal insulation > Insulation
Thermal spraying
        Thermal Spraying & Surface Engg Assn
        > + Coatings
Thermal waters > Spas
Thermoplastics > Plastics
Thermometers
        Pressure Gauge & Dial Thermometer Assn
Thimbles
        Thimble Soc Lond
Thirkell (Angela)
        Angela Thirkell Soc
Thomas (Dylan Marlais)
        Dylan Thomas Soc
Thomas ([Philip] Edward)
        Edward Thomas Fellowship
        Friends Dymock Poets
Thomson (Alexander)
        Alexander Thomson Soc
Thoracic diseases
        Brit Assn Lung Research
        Pulmonary Hypertension Assn
        Sarcoidosis & Interstitial Lung Assn
        Soc Cardiothoracic Surgery
Throwsters
        Brit Throwsters Assn
Throwsticks
        Brit Boomerang Soc
Thunderstorms
        Tornado & Storm Res Org
Thyroid disease
        Brit Assn Endocrine & Thyroid Surgeons
        Brit Thyroid Assn
        Thyroid Eye Disease Charitable Trust
Tickets
        Omnibus Soc
        Soc Ticket Agents & Retailers
        Token Corresponding Soc
        Transport Ticket Soc
Tidal energy > Renewable energy
Tiddlywinks
        English Tiddlywinks Assn
Ties
        Brit Menswear Gld
        Master Craftsmen's Assn
        > + Menswear
Tights > Hosiery
Tiles (floor & wall)
        Cork Ind Fedn
        Nat Fedn Terrazzo, Marble & Mosaic Specialists
        Tile Assn
        Tiles & Architectural Ceramics Soc
Tiles & tiling (roof) > Roofing
Timber
        Confedn Forest Inds
        Glued Laminated Timber Assn
        N W Timber Tr Assn
        NI Timber Tr Assn
        Scot Timber Tr Assn
        Timber Arbitrators Assn

© CBD Research Ltd · Beckenham · BR3 5JS · Tel 020 8650 7745 · Fax 020 8650 0768 · E-mail cbd@cbdresearch.com · www.cbdresearch.com

Timber Decking Assn
Timber Tr Fedn
TRADA Technology
UK Forest Products Assn
> + Forestry; Wood
Timber buildings
Modular & Portable Bldg Assn
TRADA Technology
UK Timber Frame Assn
Timber containers > Packaging
Timber decking
Timber Decking Assn
Timber preserving
Property Care Assn
Timber roofing > Roofing
Time recording
Antiquarian Horological Soc
> Horology
Timeshare industry
Timeshare Consumers Assn
> + Property & landowners
Tin boxes > Metal: boxes
Tin cans > Cans & canning
Tin mining > Mining
Tinnitus
Brit Tinnitus Assn
Tinplate
Metal Packaging Mfrs Assn
Tipping vehicles
Road Haulage Assn
Tissue banking
Brit Assn Tissue Banking
Tissue paper
Confedn Paper Inds
> + Paper & paper products
Tissue viability
Tissue Viability Soc
Titanic (the RMS)
Brit Titanic Soc
Toadstools > Mycology
Toastmasters & masters of ceremonies
Brit Profl Toastmasters Authority
Gld Intl Profl Toastmasters
Gld Profl Toastmasters
Nat Assn Toastmasters
Toastmasters England
Toastmasters GB
Toastmasters Royal Occasions
Tobacco
Assn Indep Tobacco Specialists
Cigarette Packet Collectors Club
Imported Tobacco Products Advy Coun
Nat Assn Cigarette Machine Operators
Retail Confectioners & Tobacconists Assn
Tobacco Ind Emplrs Assn
Tobacco Mfrs' Assn
Tobacco Retailers Alliance
> + Cigars & cigarettes; Smoking
Toboggan & luge racing/riding
Brit Bob Skeleton Assn
Brit Bobsleigh Assn
Great Britain Luge Assn
Street Sled Sports Racers
Toiletries
Cosmetic, Toiletry & Perfumery Assn
Ir Cosmetics, Detergents… Products Assn
Toilets (public)
Brit Toilet Assn
Tokens
Token Corresponding Soc
Tolkien (J R R)
Tolkien Soc
Tomatoes
Brit Tomato Growers Assn
> + Vegetable: growing
Tonic Sol-fa
Brit Kodály Academy
Curwen Inst
> + Music: teaching
Tools
Brit Compressed Air Soc
Brit Hardmetal & Engineers' Cutting Tool Assn
Brit Hardware Fedn
Cutlery & Allied Trs Res Assn
Fedn Brit Engrs' Tool Mfrs
Fedn Brit Hand Tool Mfrs
Gauge & Tool Makers Assn

Portable Electric Tool Mfrs Assn
Power Fastenings Assn
Tools Self Reliance
> + specific tool
Tools: historic
Tools & Trs Hist Soc
Vintage Horticl & Garden Machinery Club
Top dressing materials
Brit Rootzone & Top Dressing Mfrs Assn
Tornado & storm research
Tornado & Storm Res Org
Tortoises > Chelonia
Tourette syndrome
Tourette Syndrome (UK) Assn
Tourism > Travel & tourism
Tourist guides
Assn Profl Tourist Guides
Towage & salvage
Brit Tugowners Assn
Towbars
Nat Trailer & Towing Assn
Tower cranes > Cranes
Tower fabricators
Brit Constructional Steelwork Assn
Prefabricated Access Suppliers' & Mfrs' Assn
Towing equipment (motor)
Mobile Electronics & Security Fedn
Town & country planning
Assn Project Safety
Assn Small Historic Towns & Villages
Assn Town Centre Mgt
English Historic Towns Forum
Ir Planning Inst
London Soc
Planning & Environment Bar Assn
Planning Officers Soc
R Town Planning Inst
Regional Studies Assn
ROOM RTPI
Town & Country Planning Assn
Town criers
Ancient & Honourable Gld Town Criers
Brit Town Criers Authority
Loyal Company Town Criers
Townswomen
Townswomen's Glds
Towpaths > Footpaths & rights of way
Toxicology
Brit Soc Toxicological Pathologists
Brit Toxicology Soc
Fund Replacement Animals Med Experiments
Soc Medicines Res
Soc Pharmaceutical Medicine
UK Envtl Mutagen Soc
Toxophily > Archery
Toys
Baby Products Assn
Brit Toy & Hobby Assn
Brit Toymakers Gld
Doll Club GB
Equitoy
Nat Assn Toy & Leisure Libraries
Toy Retailers Assn
Trace heating
Electric Trace Heating Ind Coun
Tracheostomy
Aid Children with Tracheostomies
Tracheo-Oesophageal Fistula Support
Track events > Athletics
Tracking (cars)
Mobile Electronics & Security Fedn
Tracks (sport) > Sportsgrounds & synthetic surfaces
Traction engines > Steam engines, boats & machinery;　Fairgrounds &
equipment
Tractors > Agriculture: machinery
Trade > Commerce; Export & import; individual trades
Trade associations
Inst Assn Mgt
Trade Assn Forum
Trade marks & names > Patents & trade marks
Trade unions
Communication Workers U
Fedn Entertainment Us
Gen Fedn Tr Us
Ir Conf Profl & Service Assns
Ir Congress Tr Us
Ir Municipal, Public & Civil TU

Rail, Maritime & Transport U
Scot Trs U Congress
SIPTU [IRL]
Trades U Congress
Unison
Unite U (Amicus section)
Unite U (T&G section)
Wales Tr U Congress
Trading standards
    Soc Chief Officers Trading Standards Scotland
    Trading Standards Inst
    > + Consumer affairs & protection
Traffic: accidents > Accidents; Road safety & control
Traffic: control
    Traffic Mgt Contrs Assn
    > Road safety & control; Transport
Traffic: gyratory systems
    UK Roundabout Appreciation Soc
    > + Road: markings, lighting & traffic signs
Traffic: signs > Road: lighting, markings & traffic signs; Signs
Trail riding
    Trail Riders Fellowship
Trailers: motor vehicle
    Comml Trailer Assn
    Nat Trailer & Towing Assn
    Org Horsebox & Trailer Owners
Training (industrial) > Occupational training & education
Trains > Railways
Tramways & trams
    Heritage Rly Assn
    Light Rail Transit Assn
    Omnibus Soc
    Rly & Canal Histl Soc
    Scot Tramway & Transport Soc
    Tramway & Light Rly Soc
    Tramway Museum Soc
    > + Railways: light
Tranquiliser withdrawal
    Nat Org Phobias, Anxiety...Inf & Care
Transactional analysis
    Inst Transactional Analysis
Transformers > Electrical industry & engineering
Transfusion science > Haematology
Transit shed operators
    Brit Intl Freight Assn
Translation & interpretation
    Assn Police & Court Interpreters
    Assn Translation Companies
    Chart Inst Linguists
    Conf Interpreters Gp
    Inst Translation & Interpreting
    Ir Translators & Interpreters Assn
    Translators Assn
    > + Languages
Transmission towers > Tower fabricators
Transplants & transplant surgery
    Brit Assn Tissue Banking
    Brit Transplantation Soc
    Transplant Support Network
    UK Transplant Co-ordinators Assn
    > + Organ donors
Transport
    Assn Brit Transport & Engg Museums
    Brit Intl Freight Assn
    Brit Transport Officers Gld
    Campaign Better Transport
    Chart Inst Logistics & Transport
    Chart Inst Logistics & Transport Ireland
    Community Transport Assn
    ETA Services Ltd
    Freight Transport Assn
    Hovercraft Museum Trust
    Inst Highway Inc Engrs
    Inst Transport Administration
    Inst Transport Mgt
    Instn Civil Engrs
    Instn Engg & Technology
    Instn Highways & Transportation
    Ir Assn Intl Express Carriers
    Rail, Maritime & Transport U
    Road Transport Fleet Data Society
    Scot Transport Studies Gp
    Transform Scotland
    Transport Salaried Staffs Assn
    Transport Ticket Soc
    Transport-Watch
    > + individual forms of transport

Transport: (of animals) > Animals: transportation
Transport: history
    Birmingham Transport Histl Gp
    Rly & Canal Histl Soc
    Roads & Road Transport Hist Assn
    Scot Tramway & Transport Soc
    Transport Trust
    > + specific forms of transport
Transport: security
    Brit Security Ind Assn
    > + Security
Transsexuality & transvestism
    Beaumont Soc
    Gender Trust
Travel & tourism
    Advantage
    Assn Brit Tour Operators France
    Assn Brit Travel Agents
    Assn Indep Tour Operators
    Assn Leading Visitor Attractions
    Assn Leisure Ind Profls
    Assn Nat Tourist Office Representatives
    Assn Scot Visitor Attractions
    Baltic Air Charter Assn
    Brit Gld Travel Writers
    Brit Resorts & Destinations Assn
    Eventia
    Family Holiday Assn
    Fedn Tour Operators
    Gld Travel Mgt Cos
    Gld Travel & Tourism
    Group Travel Organisers Assn
    Inst Travel Mgt
    Inst Travel & Tourism
    Ir Tourist Ind Confedn
    Ir Travel Agents Assn
    Outdoor Writers' & Photographers' Gld
    Scot Tourism Forum
    Tourism for All
    Tourism Alliance
    Tourism Concern
    Tourism Mgt Inst
    Tourism Soc
    Travel Trust Assn
    UKinbound
    Worldchoice
    > + individual modes of travel
Travel & tourism: educational
    Brit Educl Travel Assn
    School Journey Assn
Travel & tourism: guides
    Gld Registered Tourist Guides
    Scot Tourist Guides Assn
Travel & tourism: health
    Brit Travel Health Assn
Travel goods & accessories
    Brit Menswear Gld
    Brit Travelgoods & Accessories Assn
Travelling people > Gypsies & travelling people
Treacher Collins
    Treacher Collins Family Support Gp
Treasurers > Accountancy;   Local government: officers
Trees
    Ancient Tree Forum
    Arboricultural Assn
    Brit Christmas Tree Growers Assn
    Horticultural Trs Assn
    Nat Assn Tree Officers
    Tree Coun Ireland
    > + Forestry
Trenchless technology
    Soc Brit Water & Wastewater Inds
    UK Soc Trenchless Technology
Triathlon
    Brit Triathlon Fedn
    Triathlon England
Tribology > Friction
Trichology
    Inst Trichologists
    > + Hair & scalp treatment
Trichotillomania
    Hairline Intl
Tricycling
    Assn Pioneer Motor Cyclists
    Tricycle Assn
    > + Cycles & motorcycles

© CBD Research Ltd · Beckenham · BR3 5JS · Tel 020 8650 7745 · Fax 020 8650 0768 · E-mail cbd@cbdresearch.com · www.cbdresearch.com

Tridentine Mass
        Latin Mass Soc
Trigeminal neuralgia > Neuralgia
Tripedressing
        Nat Assn Tripe Dressers
Trolleybuses
        Brit Trolleybus Soc
        Nat Trolleybus Assn
        Omnibus Soc
Trollope (Anthony)
        Trollope Soc
Trombones
        Brit Trombone Soc

Tropical crops
        Tropical Growers' Assn
Tropical environment
        Soc Envtl Exploration
Tropical fish > Fish: tropical & ornamental
Tropical medicine
        R Soc Tropical Medicine & Hygiene
        > + Medicine
Troughed belt conveyors
        Materials Handling Engrs Assn
Trout > Salmon & trout
Trucks > Fork-lift trucks; Lifting & loading equipment
Trucks: racing
        Brit Truck Racing Assn
Trusts, trusteeship & estate planning
        Assn Corporate Trustees
        Assn Member-Directed Pension Schemes
        Insolvency Practitioners Assn
        Soc Trust & Estate Practitioners
        Soc Will Writers & Estate Planning Practitioners
        > + Investment; Pensions
TT racing
        TT Riders Assn
        > + Motor cycling & scooter riding
Tuberculosis > Thoracic diseases
Tuberous sclerosis
        Tuberous Sclerosis Assn
Tubes > Pipes
Tug of war
        Scot Tug of War Assn
        Tug of War Assn
Tugs
        Brit Tugowners Assn
Tumours & tumorous diseases > Oncology
Tunnel lining
        Brit Precast Concrete Fedn
Tunnelling & shaft sinking
        Brit Tunnelling Soc
        Ground Forum
        Inst Explosives Engrs
        Joseph Williamson Soc
        Pipe Jacking Assn
        Subterranea Britannica

Turbines > Gas engines & turbines
Turf
        Agricl Engrs Assn
        Brit Turf & Landscape Irrigation Assn
        Land Drainage Contrs Assn
        Register Indep Profl Turfgrass Agronomists
        Turfgrass Growers Assn
        > + Grass & grassland; Sportsgrounds & synthetic surfaces
Turkey
        Anglo-Turkish Soc
        Brit Cham Comm Turkey
        Middle East Assn
Turkeys (birds)
        Brit Poultry Coun
        Traditional Farmfresh Turkey Assn
        Turkey Club
        > + Poultry
Turnaround specialists
        Assn Business Recovery Profls
        Inst Turnaround
Turned parts > Fasteners & turned parts
Turner (Joseph Mallord William)
        Indep Turner SocIndep   Turner Soc
        Turner Soc
Turner syndrome
        Turner Syndrome Support Soc
Turning > Woodworking
Turtles > Chelonia

Tutors
        Assn Tutors
Tweed > Wool & wool products
Twins & multiple births
        Lone Twin Network
        Multiple Births Foundation
        Twins & Mult Births Assn

Tyres
        Brit Tyre Mfrs Assn
        Imported Tyre Mfrs Assn
        Indep Tyre Distbrs Network
        Indl Tyre Assn
        Ir Tyre Ind Assn
        Nat Tyre Distbrs Assn
        Retread Mfrs Assn
        Tyre Recovery Assn
        TyreSafe

U

UFOs > Unidentified flying objects
Ukuleles & banjos
        Ukulele Soc
Ulcers
        Tissue Viability Soc
Ulster-Scots language
        Ulster-Scots Language Soc
Ultimate (sport)
        UK Ultimate Assn
Ultrasound
        Brit Med Ultrasound Soc
Umbrellas
        Brit Menswear Gld
Umpires > Cricket
Underfelt
        Needleloom Underlay Mfrs' Assn
Underfloor heating > Heating
Underground (the London)
        London Underground Rly Soc
        > + Railways: history & preservation
Underground machinery > Mining: equipment
Underground structures
        Subterranea Britannica
Underlay (carpet)
        Needleloom Underlay Mfrs' Assn
Underpinning > Foundations (buildings)
Underwater engineering & research
        Histl Diving Soc
        Inst Explosives Engrs
        Inst Marine Engg, Science & Technology
        Nautical Archaeology Soc
        Soc Underwater Technology Ltd
        Subsea UK
        > + Marine: biology & biochemistry; Ocean industries
Underwater photography
        Gld Brit Camera Technicians
Underwater sports > Water: sports; individual sport
Underwriting > Insurance

        U UK Unicyclists
Unidentified flying objects
        Assn Scientific Study Anomalous Phenomena
        Brit UFO Res Assn
Uniforms & protective clothing > Protective clothing/equipment
Unions > Trade unions
Unit trusts > Investment
Unitarian Church
        Unitarian Hist Soc
United Nations
        Brit Assn Former UN Civil Servants
        Utd Nations Assn GB & NI
United Reformed Church
        Utd Reformed Church Hist Soc
United States > USA
Universities
        Assn C'wealth Universities
        Assn University Administrators
        Assn University Res & Ind Links
        Brit Universities Sports Assn
        Ir Universities Assn
        Universities & Colls Emplrs' Assn
        Universities Scotland

Universities UK
University & College U
University students > Students
Unpasteurised milk
Assn Unpasteurised Milk Producers
Campaign Real Milk
> + Dairying
Unvented heating systems
Hot Water Assn
Upholstery
Assn Master Upholsterers & Soft Furnishers
Nat Carpet Cleaners Assn
Nat Fillings Assn
Urban studies > Environment
Urethane foam > Plastics: foam
Urology
Assn Continence Advice
Brit Assn Urological Surgeons
Cystitis & Overactive Bladder Foundation
Nat Advy Service Parents Children with a Stoma
Urostomy Assn
> + Genito-urinary medicine
Uruguay
Brit Uruguayan Soc
Cámara Comercio Uruguayo Británica
USA
Brit Assn Amer Studies
Brit N Amer Res Assn
English Speaking U C'wealth
Pilgrims (The)
USSR
Stalin Soc
> + Russia & associated states; Slavonic languages & culture
Uveitis
Uveitis Inf Gp

V

Vaccination
Justice Awareness & Basic Support
UK Vaccine Ind Gp
Vacuum technology
Brit Compressed Air Soc
Brit Vacuum Coun
Solids Handling & Processing Assn
Valuation
Assn Art & Antique Dealers
Assn Chief Estates Surveyors… Public Sector
Assn Valuers Licensed Property
Central Assn Agricl Valuers
Indep Valuers Assn
Inst Profl Auctioneers & Valuers [IRL]
Inst Revenues, Rating & Valuation
Ir Auctioneers & Valuers Inst
Nat Assn Valuers & Auctioneers
Property Consultants Soc
Scot Assessors' Assn
Soc Fine Art Auctioneers & Valuers
Soc Share & Business Valuers
> + Rating
Value management
Inst Value Mgt
Valves & actuators
BEAMA
Brit Valve & Actuator Assn
Solids Handling & Processing Assn
> + Electronic: industry & engineering
Vampires > Horror literature
Vans: lining & racking
Mobile Electronics & Security Fedn
Variety theatre > Music: hall
VAT (value added tax)
VAT Practitioners Gp
> + Taxation
Veganism > Vegetarianism & veganism
Vegetables: growing
Ir Comml Horticl Assn
Nat Vegetable Soc
Processed Vegetable Growers Assn
Processors & Growers Res Org
> + individual vegetable
Vegetables: oils > Edible oils & fats
Vegetables: preserving
UK Assn Frozen Food Producers

Vegetables: protein
Help Intl Plant Protein Org
Soya Protein Assn
Vegetables: trade
Fresh Produce Consortium
Vegetarianism & veganism
Vegan Soc
Vegetarian Soc
Vegetarian Soc Ireland
Vehicles > Electric transport; Military vehicles; Motor headings
Vehicle number plates > Number plates
Vending machines > Automatic vending
Venereal disease > Genito-urinary medicine
Venezuela
Anglo-Venezuelan Soc
Cámara Venezolana Británica Comercio
Venison
Assn Deer Mgt Gps
Brit Deer Farmers Assn
Ir Deer Farmers & Venison Assn
> + Deer; Meat
Ventilating > Air: conditioning & ventilating
Venture capital
BVCA
Venues > Arenas; Corporate hospitality
Verbatim reporting
Brit Inst Verbatim Reporters
> + Shorthand writing
Verse > Poetry
Veteran cars > Motor vehicles: historic
Veteran horses & ponies
Veteran Horse Soc
Veterans > Ex-service organisations
Veterinary medicine
Animal Health Distbrs Assn
Animal Medicines Trg Regulatory Auth
Animal & Plant Health Assn [IRL]
Brit Veterinary Hospitals Assn
Equine Shiatsu Assn
Equine Sports Massage Assn
Intl Assn Animal Therapists
> + specific animal
Veterinary science
Brit Assn Homoeopathic Veterinary Surgeons
Brit Small Animal Veterinary Assn
Brit Soc Immunology
Brit Veterinary Assn
Brit Veterinary Nursing Assn
R Coll Veterinary Surgeons
Veterinary Assn Arbitration & Jurisprudence
Veterinary Hist Soc
Veterinary Ireland
Veterinary tranquiliser dart recovery
Fedn Indep Detectorists
Vexillology > Flags, banners & bunting
Vibration
Assn Noise Consultants
Engg Integrity Soc
Heating, Ventilating & Air Conditioning Mfrs' Assn
Vibration healing
Brit Flower &… Essences Assn
College Vibrational Medicine Practitioner Assn
Crystal & Healing Fedn
Victims of accidents > Accidents: victims
Victims of crime > Crime protection & prevention; Domestic violence
Victoria Cross
Victoria Cross & George Cross Assn
Victuallers > Meat;   Wines & spirits: trade
Vicuñas > Camelids
Video
Adult Ind Trade Assn
Advertising Producers Assn
Assn Motion Picture Sound
Assn Profl Videomakers
Audiovisual Fedn [IRL]
Brit Interactive Media Assn
Brit Soc Underwater Photographers
Brit Universities Film & Video Coun
Brit Video Assn
Deaf Broadcasting Coun
Gld Profl Videographers
Inst Videography
Nat Assn Higher Educ Moving Image
Production Mgrs Assn
Video Performance Ltd
> + Film;   Sound recording & reproduction;   Television
Video games > Computer & video games

© CBD Research Ltd · Beckenham · BR3 5JS · Tel 020 8650 7745 · Fax 020 8650 0768 · E-mail cbd@cbdresearch.com · www.cbdresearch.com

Viewing facilities
  Viewing Facilities Assn UK
Vikings > Scandinavia: literature & antiquities
Villages: deserted
  Medieval Settlement Res Gp
Villages: shops
  Rural Shops Alliance
  Village Retail Services Assn. . .
Vinegar
  Vinegar Brewers Fedn
Vintage vehicles > Motor vehicles: historic
Vintners > Wines & spirits: trade
Vinyl flooring
  Contract Flooring Assn
  UK Resilient Flooring Assn
Violins & violas
  Brit Violin Making Assn
  Viola da Gamba Soc
  > + Musical instruments
Violence (work-related)
  Inst Conflict Mgt
Virgil
  Virgil Soc
Virology > Microbiology
Virus tested stock
  Nuclear Stock Assn
  Pre Basic Growers Association
Vision > [Blind & partially sighted; Ophthalmology; Orthoptics
Vision technology > Machine vision
Visual aids > Audio visual aids & equipment
Visually impaired > Blind & partially sighted
Viticulture > Wines & viticulture
Vitiligo
  Vitiligo Soc
Vitreous enamel
  Inst Vitreous Enamellers
Vivisection
  Advocates for Animals
  Animal Concern
  Brit U Abolition Vivisection
  Fund Replacement Animals Med Experiments
  Ir Anti-Vivisection Soc
  Nat Anti-Vivisection Soc
  Res Defence Soc
Vocational guidance > Careers
Vodka
  Gin & Vodka Assn
  > + Wines & spirits trade
Voice
  Voice Care Network
  > + Speech
Voice recognition
  Assn Automatic Identification . . .Capture
Volcanoes
  Geological Soc
  > + Earth sciences, structure & resources; Geology
Volleyball
  Brit Volleyball Fedn
  English Volleyball Assn
  NI Volleyball Assn
  Scot Volleyball Assn
Voluntary organisations/service
  Assn Chief Officers Scot Voluntary Orgs
  Inst Volunteering Res
  > + Charities; Community service: voluntary; Social: service;
  Welfare headings
Voluntary service: history
  Voluntary Action Hist Soc
Vomiting
  Cyclical Vomiting Syndrome Assn
Voucher system
  Voucher Assn
Vulval disease & pain
  Brit Soc Study Vulval Diseases
  Vulval Pain Soc

W

Wagner ([Wilhelm] Richard)
  Wagner Soc
Wakeboarding
  Wakeboard UK
Wales
  Campaign Protection Rural Wales

Inst Welsh Affairs
Welsh Local Govt Assn
Wales: archaeology, language & culture
  ACADEMI
  Cambrian Archaeol Assn
  Capel
  Cardiff Naturalists Soc
  Cymdeithas Ddawns Werin Cymru
  Cymdeithas Iaith Gymraeg
  Honourable Soc Cymmrodorion
  London Welsh Assn
  R Instn S Wales
  Urdd Gobaith Cymru
  Welsh Folk Song Soc
  Welsh Music Gld
  > + Archaeology: county societies
Walking
  Brit Mountaineering Coun
  Brit Walking Fedn
  Long Distance Walkers Assn
  Mountaineering Coun Ireland
  Mountaineering Coun Scotland
  Pennine Way Assn
  Race Walking Assn
Walking sticks
  Brit Stickmakers Gld
  Brit Woodcarvers Assn
Wall (Max[well George Lorimer])
  Max Wall Soc
Wall(s): insulation
  Insulated Render & Cladding Assn
  > + Insulation
Wall(s): movable > Partitioning
Wall(s): ties
  Wall Tie Installers Fedn
Wall(s): tiles > Tiles (floor & wall)
Wallcoverings & wallpaper
  Brit Coatings Fedn
  Brit Hardware Fedn
  Wallcovering Distbrs Assn
  Wallpaper Hist Soc
Walling
  Dry Stone Walling Assn
Walmsley (Ulric & Leo)
  Walmsley Soc
Walnuts
  Combined Edible Nut Tr Assn
War(s) > under name of War
War memorials
  War Memorials Trust
Wardens > Rangers & wardens
Warehousing
  Bonded Warehousekeepers' Assn
  Chart Inst Logistics & Transport
  Chart Inst Logistics & Transport Ireland
  UK Warehousing Assn
  > + Materials: management/handling
Wargaming
  Brit Histl Games Soc
  Pike & Shot Soc
  Soc Ancients
  Victorian Military Soc
  > + Fights (historic/re-enactment);   Models: hobby
Warlock (Peter)
  Peter Warlock Soc
Warm air hand driers
  Brit Warm Air Hand Drier Assn
Warne (Frederick) publishers
  Observers Pocket Series Collectors' Soc
Warranty against work under guarantee
  Indep Warranty Assn
Wars of the Roses
  Soc Friends King Richard III
Warships > Marine: engineering & equipment
Washing instruction & labelling
  Home Laundering Consultative Coun
Waste disposal
  Chart Instn Wastes Mgt
  Chemical Recycling Assn
  Combined Heat & Power Assn
  Container Handling Eqpt Mfrs Assn
  CSS
  Environmental Inds Commission
  Environmental Services Assn
  Ir Waste Mgt Assn
  Nat Assn Waste Disposal Officers
  Oil Recycling Assn

R Envtl Health Inst Scotland
Valpak
> + Water: treatment & supply
Waste disposal: medical
Sanitary Med Disposal Services Assn
Waste disposal: photographic
Photo Imaging Coun
Waste trades > Reclamation & recycling; specific type of waste
Watches > Horology
Water
Assn Drainage Authorities
Brit Cave Res Assn
Brit Hydrological Soc
Estuarine & Coastal Sciences Assn
Hydrographic Soc UK
Land Drainage Contrs Assn
R Meteorological Soc
UK Land & Hydrographic Survey Assn
UK Rainwater Harvesting Assn
Water Health Alliance
> + Hydraulics & hydromechanics; Water treatment & supply

Water: divining
Brit Soc Dowsers
Water: jetting
Water Jetting Assn
Water: mills > Wind & water mills
Water: power
Brit Hydropower Assn
> + Renewable energy
Water: softening
Salt Assn
Water: sports
Amat Swimming Assn
Brit Sub-Aqua Club
Brit Swimming
Brit Water Ski
Scot Sub Aqua Club
Scot Swimming
Sub-Aqua Assn
waterskiscotland
Welsh Amat Swimming Assn
Welsh Assn Sub Aqua Clubs
Water: treatment & supply
Assn Public Analysts
Assn Public Analysts Scotland
Brit Assn Chemical Specialities
Brit Polarological Res Soc
Brit Water
Brit Water Cooler Assn
Chart Instn Water & Envtl Management
Instn Civil Engrs
IWO
Nat Campaign Water Justice
Nat Jt Utilities Gp
Nat Pure Water Assn
Soc Brit Water & Wastewater Inds
Soil & Groundwater Technology Assn
UK Irrigation Assn
Water Mgt Soc
Water UK
Well Drillers Assn
> + Bottled water
Waterbeds
Brit Waterbed Assn
> + Beds & bedding
Watercolour painting
Brit Watercolour Soc
R Scot Soc Painters in Water Colours
R Watercolour Soc
Water Colour Soc Ireland
> + Art & artists
Watercoolers
Brit Water Cooler Assn
Waterfowl
Brit Waterfowl Assn
Waterheaters > Boilers & waterheaters
Waterloo (Battle of)
Assn Friends Waterloo C'ee
Waterproofing
Brit Structural Waterproofing Assn
Eur Liquid Waterproofing Assn
Intelligent Membrane Tr Assn
Property Care Assn
Waterways: inland > Inland waterways

Watson (Dr John)
Friends Dr Watson
Sherlock Holmes Soc Lond
Wave energy
Brit Wind Energy Assn
> + Renewable energy
Wealth management > Investment
Weapons
Brit Pugwash Gp
Defence Mfrs Assn
> + Arms & armour; Defence equipment; Guns & ammunition
Weather > Meteorology
Weaving
Assn Glds Weavers, Spinners & Dyers
Confedn Brit Wool Textiles
Webb (Mary Gladys)
Mary Webb Soc
Webbing
Brit Narrow Fabrics Assn
Website design
Inst Profl Designers
Weddings
Brit Bridalwear Assn
Retail Bridalwear Assn
UK Alliance Wedding Planners
Weddings: photography
Assn Profl Videomakers
Brit Inst Profl Photography
Gld Photographers
Master Photographers Assn
Soc Wedding & Portrait Photographers
Weighing machines > Scales & weighing machines
Weight control (personal) > Obesity
Weight lifting & training
Brit Weight Lifters Assn
Welsh Weight Training Assn
Weights & measures > Consumer affairs & protection; Measurement; Trading standards
Welding
Assn Welding Distbrs
BEAMA
Plastics & Board Inds Fedn
Welding Inst
Welfare: administration
Assn Chief Executives Voluntary Orgs
Inst Welfare
Nat Assn Voluntary & Community Action
Nat Assn Voluntary Service Mgrs
> + Social: services
Welfare: organisations
Brit Assn Settlements & Social Action Centres
Brit Red Cross Soc
Care Leavers Assn
Family Welfare Assn
Friedreichs Ataxia Soc Ireland
Grand Priory... Hospital... St John
Ir Red Cross Soc
Nat Assn Pastoral Care Educ
Nat Family Mediation
Relationships Scotland
Saint John Ambulance Assn
Shared Care Network
SOVA
Women's R Voluntary Service
Youth Access
> + Community service; objects of welfare
Well drilling & equipment
Assn Well Head Eqpt Mfrs
UK Onshore Operators Gp
Well Drillers Assn
Well Services Contrs Assn
Wellington (Arthur Wellesley) Duke of
Assn Friends Waterloo C'ee
Wells (Herbert George ['HG'])
H G Wells Soc
Welsh > Wales: archaeology, language & culture
Wesley (John & Charles)
Wesley Histl Soc
West Africa
W Africa Business Assn
West Indies & the Caribbean
Black & Asian Studies Assn
Caribbean-Brit Business Coun
UK One World Linking Assn
Western Front
Western Front Assn
> + World Wars I & II

© CBD Research Ltd · Beckenham · BR3 5JS · Tel 020 8650 7745 · Fax 020 8650 0768 · E-mail cbd@cbdresearch.com · www.cbdresearch.com

Wet garden plants
    Brit Hosta & Hemerocallis Soc
Whales
    Whale & Dolphin Consvn Soc
Wharves
    River Assn Freight & Transport
Wheelchairs
    Ir Wheelchair Assn
    > + Health care: equipment & supplies
Whippets
    Brit Whippet Racing Assn
Whisky
    Malt Distillers Assn Scotland
    Scotch Malt Whisky Soc
    Scotch Whisky Assn
    > + Wines & spirits trade
White goods > Domestic appliances
White Star Line
    Brit Titanic Soc
Whole milk > Unpasteurised milk
Wholesale markets > Finance: brokers & agents
Wholesale trade > Cash & Carry; specific trade
Widows & widowers
    Cruse Bereavement Care
    Nat Assn Widows
    Nat Coun Divorced & Separated
    Nat Fedn Solo Clubs
    War Widows Assn
    Way Foundation
    > + Singles, divorced & separated; Women's organisations
Wigs
    Hairdressing & Beauty Suppliers Assn
    Inc Gld Hairdressers
    > + Hairdressing
Wild animals
    Assn Brit & Ir Wild Animal Keepers
    Brit Big Cats Soc
    Captive Animals' Protection Soc
    Universities Fedn Animal Welfare
    > + Zoology & zoos; specific animal
Wild flowers
    Landlife
Wilde (Oscar Fingall O'Flahertie Wills)
    Oscar Wilde Soc
Wildfowl
    Brit Assn Shooting & Consvn
    Brit Decoy & Wildfowl Carvers Assn
    Brit Waterfowl Assn
    > + Birds
Wildlife: art
    Nature Art Trust
Wildlife: recording
    Nat Fedn Biological Recording
    Wildlife Sound Recording Soc
    > + Nature conservation
Williams (Charles)
    Charles Williams Soc
Williams syndrome
    Williams Syndrome Foundation
Williamson (Henry)
    Henry Williamson Soc
Wills
    ALERT
    Assn Lawyers & Legal Advisors
    Inst Profl Willwriters
    Soc Trust & Estate Practitioners
    Soc Will Writers & Estate Planning Practitioners
    Willwriters' Assn
Wind instruments > Brass & silver bands; Musical instruments
Wind energy/engineering
    Brit Wind Energy Assn
    Wind Engg Soc
    > + Renewable energy
Wind tunnel testing
    Aircraft Res Assn
Wind & water mills
    Soc Protection Ancient Bldgs
    Sussex Indl Archaeol Soc
    Welsh Mills Soc
Windows
    Brit Plastics Fedn
    Brit Woodworking Fedn
    Incorporation Plastic Window Fabricators & Installers
    Local Authority PVC-u Frame Advy Gp
    Nat Assn Rooflight Mfrs
    Plastics Window Fedn

Steel Window Assn
    > + Glass & glazing
Windows: blinds & shutters
    Brit Blind & Shutter Assn
    Door & Hardware Fedn
Windows: cleaning
    Fedn Window Cleaners
Windsurfing > Surfing, board & speed sailing
Windsurfing > Surfing, board & speed sailing

Wines & spirits: trade
    Assn Convenience Stores
    Assn Licensed Mult Retailers
    Bonded Warehousekeepers' Assn
    Fedn Licensed Victuallers Assns
    Fedn Retail Licensed Tr NI
    Gin & Vodka Assn
    Inst Masters Wine
    Licensed Vintners' Assn [IRL]
    Nat Fruit Wine, Mead & Liqueur Producers Assn
    Nat Off-Licence Assn [IRL]
    Scot Grocers' Fedn
    Scot Licensed Tr Assn
    Scotch Whisky Assn
    Vintners Fedn Ireland
    Wine & Spirit Assn Ireland
    Wine & Spirit Trade Assn
Wines & viticulture
    Assn Wine Educators
    Circle Wine Writers
    English Wine Producers
    Thames & Chiltern Vineyards Assn
    UK Vineyards Assn
Wire & wire products
    Scot Wirework Mfrs Assn
    Wire Products Assn
    Woven Wire Assn
Wireless: for blind & bedridden > Radio: for blind & bedridden
Wireless: history
    Brit Vintage Wireless Soc
Witchcraft
    Pagan Fedn
Witness (expert) > Experts & expert witness
Wodehouse (Sir P[elham] G[renville])
    P G Wodehouse Soc
Wolves
    Wolves & Humans Foundation
Women: employment
    Brit Assn Women Entrepreneurs
    Business & Profl Women
    Soc Promoting Training Women
    Working Families
    > + special occupations
Women: equal rights
    Fawcett Soc
    Nat Alliance Women's Orgs
    Rights of Women
Women's organisations
    Brit Fedn Women Graduates
    Brit Housewives League
    Brit Women Pilots Assn
    Fedn Women's Insts NI
    Ir Countrywomen's Assn
    Mothers Apart Children
    Nat Alliance Women's Orgs
    Nat Assn Ladies Circles
    Nat Assn Women's Clubs
    Nat Fedn Women's Insts
    Nat Women's Register
    NI Women's Aid Fedn
    Scot Women's Rural Insts
    Townswomen's Glds
    Women's Aid Fedn (England)
    YWCA (Young Women's Christian Association)
Women's wear > Clothing; Fashion
Wood
    Inst Wood Science
    UK Forest Products Assn
    > + Timber
Wood burning stoves
    Nat Fireplace Assn
    Stove Industry Alliance
Wood carving
    Brit Decoy & Wildfowl Carvers Assn
    Brit Woodcarvers Assn
    Chippendale Soc
    Master Carvers Assn

Wood floors > Floors
Wood panels
      Wood Panel Inds Fedn
Wood preservation & care
      Property Care Assn
      Timber Decking Assn
      Wood Protection Assn
Wood pulp
      Brit Wood Pulp Assn
Woodforde (James)
      Parson Woodforde Soc
Woodlands
      Confedn Forest Inds
      Small Woods Assn
      > + Forestry
Woodlice
      Brit Myriapod & Isopod Gp
Woodworking
      Brit Wood Turners Assn
      Brit Woodworking Fedn
      Inst Carpenters
      Inst Machine Woodworking Technology
      Register Profl Turners
      Soc Wood Engravers
      Woodworking Machinery Suppliers Assn
Woodworm
      Inst Specialist Surveyors & Engrs
Wool & wool products
      Brit Textile Technology Gp
      Cloth Merchants Assn
      Confedn Brit Wool Textiles
      Nat Wool Textile Expt Corpn
      UK Hand Knitting Assn
      Welsh Mills Soc
      > + Sheep: breed societies
Woolf (Virginia)
      Virginia Woolf Soc GB
Word blindness > Dyslexia
Work-related violence
      Inst Conflict Mgt
Work sciences & study > Management
Worker participation > Industrial involvement & participation
Working dogs
      Brit Inst Profl Dog Trainers
      > + Dogs
Works management > Management
Workspaces (managed)
      Business Centre Assn
Workwear > Protective clothing/equipment
World War I
      War Research Soc
      Western Front Assn
World War II
      Battle Britain Histl Soc
      War Research Soc
      World War Two Living Hist Assn
      World War Two Rly Study Gp
      WW2 HMSO Paperbacks Soc
Wound care & equipment
      Surgical Dressings Mfrs Assn
      Tissue Viability Soc
      Wound Care Soc
Woven labels
      Brit Narrow Fabrics Assn
Wrestling
      Brit Wrestling Assn
Writers' agents > Authors' agents
Writers to the Signet > Law: Scotland
Writing equipment & accessories
      Brit Office Supplies & Services Fedn
      Writing Eqpt Soc
      Writing Instruments Assn
Writing & writers
      Alliance Literary Socs
      Assn Golf Writers
      Brit Soc Comedy Writers
      Fedn Worker Writers & Community Pubrs
      Gld Health Writers
      Ir Writers' U
      Keats-Shelley Memorial Assn
      Lancashire Authors' Assn
      Nat Assn Writers in Educ
      Nat Assn Writers' Gps
      Outdoor Writers' & Photographers' Gld
      Romantic Novelists Assn
      Soc Authors
      Soc Authors Scotland

Writers' Gld
Writers & Photographers unLimited
      > + Journalism; & individual subjects
Writing & writers: authors > under individual author's name

Wurlitzers > Cinema organs

X

X-ray equipment
      Assn X-ray Eqpt Mfrs

Y

Yachts & yachting
      Assn Brokers & Yacht Agents
      Brit Fedn Sand & Land Yacht Clubs
      Cruising Assn
      R Yachting Assn
      R Yachting Assn Scotland
      UK Catamaran Racing Assn
      Yacht Harbour Assn
      Yachting Journalists' Assn
Yachts: building & designing
      Amat Yacht Res Soc
      Brit Marine Fedn
      Model Yachting Assn
      Yacht Designers & Surveyors Assn
Yachts: chartering
      Assn Scot Yacht Charterers
      Marine Leisure Assn
      Profl Charter Assn
Yarns
      Brit Throwsters Assn
      Coir Assn
      > + Textile headings;   Wool & wool products
Yeast
      UK Assn Mfrs Bakers Yeast

Yoga
      Brit Wheel Yoga
Yoghurt
      Provision Tr Fedn
      > + Dairying
Yonge (Charlotte Mary)
      Charlotte M Yonge Fellowship
Young farmers clubs > Farmers organisations
Young (Francis Brett)
      Francis Brett Young Soc
Youth employment > Careers
Youth hostels
      Hostelling Intl NI
      Ir Youth Hostels Assn
      Scot Youth Hostels Assn
      Youth Hostels Assn (E&W)
Youth organisations
      Brit Nat Temperance League
      Central Org Maritime Pastimes. . .
      Church Lads & Church Girls Brigade
      Clubs Young People
      Clubs Young People (NI)
      Clubs Young People Scotland
      Clubs Young People Wales
      Horse Rangers Assn
      Marine Soc & Sea Cadets
      Nat Assn Youth Orchestras
      Nat Fedn Plus Areas
      Nat Youth Coun Ireland
      Scot Assn Young Farmers Clubs
      Scout Assn
      Scout & Guide Graduate Assn
      UK Youth
      Urdd Gobaith Cymru
      Woodcraft Folk
      YMCA England
      Young Explorers' Trust
      Youth Access
      Youth Action Network
      Youth Action NI
      Youth Scotland

© CBD Research Ltd · Beckenham · BR3 5JS · Tel 020 8650 7745 · Fax 020 8650 0768 · E-mail cbd@cbdresearch.com · www.cbdresearch.com

Youth organisations: boys & young men
    Boys' Brigade
    Scouting Ireland
    YMCA Ireland
Youth organisations: girls & young women
    Girlguiding UK
    Girls' Brigade
    Girls Venture Corps Air Cadets
    Ir Girl Guides
    YWCA Ireland
Youth psychiatry
    Assn Profls Services Adolescents
Youth work
    Community & Youth Workers U
    Nat Assn Youth & Community Educ Officers
    Nat Assn Youth Justice
    Nat Youth Fedn [IRL]

Z

Zen Buddhism > Buddhism
Zeolites
    Brit Zeolite Assn
Zimbabwe
    Britain Zimbabwe Soc
Zinc
    Cast Metals Fedn
Zinc coatings
    Galvanizers Assn
Zionism > Jewish organisations
Zoology & zoos
    Assn Brit & Ir Wild Animal Keepers
    Brit Herpetological Soc
    Brit & Ir Assn Zoos & Aquariums
    Captive Animals' Protection Soc
    Linnean Soc Lond
    N England Zoological Soc
    Natural Sciences Collections Assn
    Ray Soc
    Royal Zoological Society of Scotland
    Zoological Soc Ireland
    Zoological Soc London

Directory of BRITISH ASSOCIATIONS

*All entries in this Directory are **FREE** - you incur no financial obligation by completing & returning this form*

1. **Name of organisation** (as stated in Articles, Constitution or Rules):

2. **Abbreviation** by which the organisation is generally known:

3. **Year of formation:**

4. **Telephone:**

5. **Postal address**, including postcode:

6. **Fax:**

7. **Email:**

8. **Website:**

9. Is the above address that of:

   Permanent headquarters with its own staff ☐   Honorary secretary's private house ☐

   A firm of secretaries, accountants or solicitors ☐   Honorary secretary's business office ☐

   Other:

10. **Name** of Secretary / Honorary Secretary / Chief Executive – please state office held:

11. **Branches** in the UK – give number only: Branches overseas – give countries only:

12. **Objects / Sphere of interest** – please state concisely the purpose of your organisation & its field of interest – this information is required for the subject index, therefore please explain any technical terms used:

13. **Specialist groups** or sections – please list fully:

14. **Subject index** – please suggest any specific subjects under which your organisation should be indexed:

15. **Affiliations:** to international & other organisations – please give names in **FULL**:

    Affiliations: bodies affiliated to yours:

16. **Membership** – give present number in each category and relevant subscription:

	Individual persons	Companies / Firms	Other organisations (clubs, societies etc.)
UK	£	£	£
Overseas	£	£	£

Please complete overleaf ➤

17. **Activities:**

- ☐ Conferences
- ☐ Regular Meetings
- ☐ Education & / or training
- ☐ Examinations
- ☐ Research
- ☐ Exhibitions

Other activities

- ☐ Competitions
- ☐ Study Groups
- ☐ Statistics
- ☐ Export promotion
- ☐ Information service
- ☐ Library

- ☐ Picture Library
- ☐ Visits & / or excursions
- ☐ Negotiations of pay / employment
- ☐ Liaison with government

18. **Publications:** Please give details (Journal, Newsletter, List of Members, Yearbook, Annual Report etc).
Please supply specimen copies and, if possible put us on your mailing list, thank you.
Please give member's price if not included in subscription

Title	Frequency	Price (members)	Price (non-members)

19. Changes of name, or amalgamations, during the last 5 years – please give names and dates:

20. **Moving or changing name?** if likely in the next 2 years please tick here ☐ and send new details when known.
We answer 100's of enquiries a year about associations that have moved. **PLEASE** tell us when you do.

21. Are you also secretary of any other international / national organisation? Please give full title(s):

22. Is your organisation:

a Company limited by guarantee ☐   a Registered Charity ☐   an Un-incorporated Society ☐

23. Your name and office held (in CAPITALS please):

If you wish to receive details of the Directory of British Associations when it is published please tick ☐

The editors' decision over the content, or exclusion, of any entry is final.		19

CBD Research Ltd   15 Wickham Road, Beckenham, Kent BR3 5JS, UK.   Tel: 020 8650 7745   Fax: 020 8650 0768
Established 1961   cbd@cbdresearch.com   www.cbdresearch.com

MEMBERS OF: Data Publishers Association   Independent Publishers Guild